THE EVERYMAN ENGLISH DICTIONARY

THE EVERYMAN ENGLISH DICTIONARY

BY

D. C. BROWNING
MA (Glasgow), BA, B. Litt. (Oxon)

BLITZ EDITIONS

This edition published 1990 by
The Promotional Reprint Company Limited
for Blitz Editions, an imprint
of Bookmart Limited. (Registered No 2372865)
60, Charles Street, Leicester, LE1 1FB

ISBN 185 605 0068

Printed and bound in Great Britain by
Mackays of Chatham PLC, Chatham, Kent

A

A, (*math.*) known number; (*mus.*) note and scale. **A1,** (of ships) first-class in Lloyd's register; (*colloq.*) first-rate.

a, an, *a.* (termed the indefinite article) one, some, any. (O.E. *án*, one)

a, *dial.* for **he** or **she.**

a, *prep.* on, towards, into. us. written as prefix, as in **afoot, ashore, nowadays,** or with verbal nouns, as in **a-doing, a-going.** (O.E. *an*, on)

a, prep. from. *a fortiori*, with stronger reason, more conclusively. *a posteriori*, inductively, from effect to cause. *a priori*, deductively, from cause to effect. (L.)

à, prep. to, for. *à deux*, for two. *à discrction* at discretion, without restriction. *à fond*, thoroughly. *à la*, in the manner of, as *á l'anglaise*, in the English manner. *à la carte*, by the bill of fare. *à la mode*, in the fashion. *à merveille*, wonderfully. *à outrance*, to the death. *à propos de bottes*, apropos of boots, i.e. irrelevantly. (F.)

a-, an-, *pref.* not, without, as in **anarchy, amoral.** (Gk.)

a', *Scot.* form of **all.**

aam, *n.* Dutch liquid measure, about 40 gallons. (Gk. *amē*, bucket)

aardvark, *n.* ant-bear, a S. African quadruped. (Du. *aarde*, earth; *vark*, pig)

aardwolf, *n.* earth-wolf, S. African carnivore like hyena. (Du. *aarde*, earth)

Aaron's beard, *n.* large-flowered St John's wort. **Aaron's rod,** *n.* goldenrod; mullein; (*archit.*) rod with one serpent twined round it.

aasvogel, *n.* S. African vulture. (S. Afr. Du. *aas*, carrion; *vogel*, bird)

ab, prep. from. *ab extra*, from outside. *ab initio, ab origine, ab ovo*, from the beginning. *ab urbe condita*, (*abbr.* A.U.C.) from the foundation of Rome (753 B.C.). (L.)

ab- (a-, abs-, au-), *pref.* away, from, apart, as in **abrupt,** etc. (L.)

aba, *n.* Syrian woollen stuff; outer garment made of it. (Arab.)

abaca, *n.* Manila hemp. (native)

abacay, *n.* kind of white parrot. (native)

aback, *adv.* backwards, esp. of sails pressed against mast by head wind. **taken a.,** disconcerted, surprised.

abacus, *n.* calculating-frame, us. with balls sliding on wires; (*archit.*) flat tablet at top of column. (Gk. *abax*, tablet)

Abaddon, *n.* destroying angel, devil; hell. (Heb. = destruction)

abaft, *adv.* on ship's aft or stern part.—*prep.* behind, aft of. (O.E. *be*, by; *æftan*, behind)

abalone, *n.* sea-ear, Californian mollusc yielding mother-of-pearl. (Sp.)

abandon, *v.t.* give up, yield, forsake.—*n.* careless freedom. **abandoned,** *a.* very wicked. **abandonee,** *n.* insurer to whom a wreck has been abandoned. **abandonment,** *n.* (O.F. *à*, to; *bandon*, jurisdiction)

abase, *v.t.* lower, humble. **abasement,** *n.* (L.L. *ad*, to; *bassus*, short)

abash, *v.t.* confuse with shame. **abashment,** *n.* (O.F. *bahir*, cry bah!)

abask, *a.* and *adv.* in pleasant warmth.

abate, *v.t.* and *i.* diminish, lessen; deduct; (*law*) put an end to; make void; (*Shake.*) blunt; humble. **abatement,** *n.* (L. *ad*, to; *batuere*, beat)

abatis, abattis, *n.* defence-work of felled trees with branches towards the enemy. (F.)

abattoir, *n.* slaughter-house. (F.)

abaya, same as **aba.**

abb, *n.* woof-yarn. (*web*)

abbacy, *n.* office, rights, of an abbot. **abbatial,** *a.* of an abbey or abbot. (*abbot*)

abbate, *n.* Italian ecclesiastic. **abbé,** *n.* French ecclesiastic. (*abbot*)

abbess, *n.* lady superior of a nunnery.

abbey, *n.* monastery under an abbot; church attached to it. (*abbot*)

abbot, *n.* head of an abbey. **abbotcy,** *n.* abbacy. (Aram. *abba*, father)

abbreviate, *v.t.* shorten; abridge.—also *a.* **abbreviation,** *n.* part of word put for the whole. (L. *brevis*, short)

A B C, *n.* alphabet; first rudiments; alphabetical guide.

abdicate, *v.t.* and *i.* renounce; give up throne or office. **abdication,** *n.* (L. *ab*, from; *dicare*, proclaim)

abdomen, *n.* belly. **abdominal,** *a.* **abdominous,** *a.* corpulent. (L.)

abduct, *v.t.* carry off by fraud or force; (*anat.*) draw (limb etc.) from natural position. **abducent,** *a.* (*anat.*). **abduction, abductor,** *nn.* (L. *ab*, from; *ducere*, lead)

abeam, *adv.* (*naut.*) at right angles to a ship's length, abreast. (*beam*)

abear, *v.t.* (*prov.*) endure; (*Spens.*) bear, behave.

abecedarian, *a.* of the A B C, elementary; arranged alphabetically.—*n.* (*Amer.*) pupil learning A B C, beginner. (*A B C D*)

abed, *adv.* in bed.

abeigh, *adv.* (*Scot.*) aloof.

abele, *n.* white poplar. (L. *albus*, white)

abelmosk, *n.* N. African mallow yielding musk seeds. (Arab. *abu'l misk,* father of musk)
Aberdeen, *n.* **A. (terrier),** rough-haired Scotch terrier. **Aberdonian,** *a.* and *n.* (native) of Aberdeen.
aberdevine, *n.* siskin, kind of finch.
aberglaube, *n.* excessive belief, superstition. (G.)
Abernethy, *a.* and *n.* kind of hard (biscuit).
aberration, *n.* deviation from right or normal; (*astron.*) apparent alteration of star's position, due to earth's motion in its orbit. **aberrant,** *a.* **aberrance, aberrancy,** *nn.* (L. *errare,* wander)
abet, *v.t.* incite by encouragement or aid (us. in bad sense). **abetment, abetter, abettor,** *nn.* (O.F. *beter,* bait)
abeyance, *n.* state of suspension, temporary disuse. (L.L. *badare,* gape)
abhominable, old spelling of **abominable,** due to mistaken derivation from *homo.*
abhor, *v.t.* shrink with horror from, loathe. **abhorrence,** *n.* **abhorrent,** *a.* hateful; inconsistent; intolerant. (L. *horrēre,* shudder)
abide, *v.i.* and *t.* (*past* and *p.p.* **abode** or **abided**) dwell, stay; wait for; endure. **a. by,** adhere to. **abidance,** *n.* **abiding,** *a.* permanent. (O.E. *bīdan,* wait)
abigail, *n.* lady's - maid. (Biblical character)
ability, *n.* capacity, power; mental skill, cleverness. (L. *habilis,* deft)
abiogenesis, *n.* spontaneous generation. **abiogenetic,** *a.* **abiogenist,** *n.* one who believes in this. (Gk. *a-,* not; *bios,* life; *genesis,* birth)
abject, *a.* miserable; craven, base.—*n.* outcast. **abjection, abjectness,** *nn.* (L. *ab,* away; *jacere,* throw)
abjure, *v.t.* renounce on oath; swear perpetual absence from. **abjuration,** *n.* (L. *ab,* from; *jurare,* swear)
abkari, abkary, *n.* manufacture or sale of spirits; excise duty on it. (Pers.)
ablactation, *n.* weaning. (L. *lac,* milk)
ablation, *n.* removal; (*geol.*) attrition, wasting, of glacier or rock. (L. *ablatio*)
ablative, *a.* and *n.* (case in Latin nouns) expressing source or instrumentality. (L. *ablativus*)
ablaut, *n.* vowel permutation, change of root vowel in derivation, as in *sing, sang, sung, song.* (G.)
ablaze, *a.* and *adv.* on fire; glittering; excited. (*blaze*)
able, *a.* having the power; clever, talented.—*v.t.* (*Shake.*) warrant, vouch for. **a.-bodied,** *a.* robust; (of seaman, *abbr.* **A.B.**) first-class. (L. *habilis,* deft)
-able, *adj.suf.* capable of, as in **suitable, get-at-able.** (L.)
ablegate, *n.* papal envoy, esp. one carrying insignia to a newly appointed cardinal. (*legate*)
ablet, ablen, *n.* small river fish, bleak. (L. *albus.* white)
ablings, ablins, same as **aiblins.**
abloom, *a.* and *adv.* blooming.
ablush, *a.* and *adv.* blushing.
ablution, *n.* (us. *pl.*) washing; (*sing.*) liquid used for it. **ablutionary,** *a.* (L. *abluere,* wash away)
ably, *adv.* in an able manner.
abnegate, *v.t.* renounce; deny. **abnegation,** *n.* rejection, self-sacrifice. (L. *negare,* deny)
abnormal, *a.* exceptional, not according to type. **abnormality, abnormity,** *nn.* (L. *norma,* rule)
aboard, *adv.* and *prep.* on board; (*Amer.*) on a train. **lay a ship a.,** place one's own alongside her to fight. (*board*)
abode, *n.* dwelling-place; stay. (*abide*)
abode, *v.t.* (*Shake.*) forebode. **abodement,** *n.*
aboil, *a.* and *adv.* boiling.
abolish, *v.t.* do away with. **abolishment, abolition,** *nn.* **abolitionist,** *n.* supporter of the movement against slavery. **abolitionism,** *n.* (L. *abolēre,* destroy)
abomasum, *n.* fourth stomach of ruminant animal. (*ab-+omasum*)
abominable, *a.* detestable, revolting. **abominate,** *v.t.* loathe, detest. **abomination,** *n.* loathing; loathsome act or thing. (L. *abominari,* deprecate as of bad omen)
aboon, *adv.* (*Scot.*) above.
aboriginal, *a.* indigenous, earliest.—*n.* original inhabitant of country. so **aborigines,** *n.pl.* (*ab origine*)
abort, *v.i.* miscarry; become sterile, shrink away. **aborted,** *a.* undeveloped. **abortifacient,** *a.* and *n.* (drug etc.) causing abortion. **abortion,** *n.* premature delivery; procuring of this; mis-shapen being; failure (of plan). **abortionist,** *n.* one who procures abortion. **abortive,** *a.* born untimely; rudimentary; unsuccessful. (L. *aboriri*)
aboulia, *n.* (*med.*) loss of will-power. (Gk. *a-,* not; *boulesthai,* will)
abound, *v.i.* overflow; be or possess in plenty. (L. *abundare,* overflow)
about, *prep.* around; near; concerning; occupied with.—*adv.* around; approximately; up and down; facing round. **put a.,** disturb; (of ship) turn. **turn a.,** alternately. (O.E. *būtan,* outside)
above, *prep.* over, higher than.—*adv.* overhead, higher up; in addition. **a.-board,** *a.* fair, straightforward. (O.E. *ābufan*)
abracadabra, *n.* cabbalistic word used as charm; spell; gibberish.
abrade, *v.t.* scrape off; injure by rubbing. (L. *radere,* scrape)
Abraham-man, *n.* lunatic beggar of 16th century. (Luke xvi)
abranchiate, abranchial, *a.* having no gills. (Gk. *a-,* not; *brangchia,* gills)

abrasion, *n.* scraping off; wound made by rubbing. **abrasive,** *a.* and *n.* (substance) that scrapes. (*abrade*)
abray, abrayd, *v.t.* and *i.* (*Spens.*) arouse: startle; awake.
abreact, *v.t.* (*psycho-anal.*) remove (complex) by acting it out or talking it out. **abreaction,** *n.*
abreast, *adv.* side by side.
abreed, *adv.* (*Scot.*) abroad; in breadth.
abridge, *v.t.* shorten; epitomize; curtail. **abridgment, abridgement,** *n.* shortening; abstract; (*Shake.*) pastime. (L. *brevis*, short)
abroach, *a.* and *adv.* broached, pierced so as to let the liquor run.
abroad, *adv.* out of doors; in a foreign country; widely. (*broad*)
abrogate, *v.t.* repeal, annul. **abrogation,** *n.* (L. *ab*, from; *rogare*, propose)
abrook, *v.t.* (*Shake.*) brook, endure.
abrupt, *a.* sudden, hasty; steep. **abruption,** *n.* (*Shake.*) breaking off. (L. *rumpere*, break)
abscess, *n.* gathering of pus in some part of the body. (L. *abscessus*)
abscind, *v.t.* cut off. **abscission,** *n.* **abscissa** (*pl.* **abscissae, (absciss, abscisse** (*pl.* **abscisses**), *n.* (*geom.*) one of the two co-ordinates fixing position of a point. (L. *scindere*, cut)
abscond, *v.i.* go away secretly, fly from the law. (L. *condere*, stow)
absence, *n.* being away; lack; mental abstraction. **absent,** *a.* not present; abstracted. — *v.refl.* keep (oneself) away. **absent-minded,** *a.* forgetful, preoccupied. **absentee,** *n.* one who is absent, esp. landlord who lives away from his estate, hence **absenteeism,** *n.* (L. *abesse*, be away)
absinth, absinthe, *n.* wormwood; liqueur made with it. (Gk. *apsinthion*)
absit omen, may the foreboding caused by some unlucky word or event not come to pass. (L.=let there be no omen)
absolute, *a.* free from limits; complete, perfect, pure; without constitutional checks, despotic; (*gram.*) not dependent; (*philos.*) self-existent; (*Shake.*) positive, certain. **absolutely,** *adv.* positively, quite; (*colloq.*) yes, quite so. **absolution,** *n.* formal declaration of pardon for sins; acquittal. **absolutism,** *n.* principle of despotic government. **absolutist,** *n.* adherent of this. (L. *solvere*, free)
absolve, *v.t.* set, pronounce, free from; pardon, acquit. (L. *absolvere*)
absorb, *v.t.* swallow up, suck in; engage wholly. **absorbefacient,** *a.* and *n.* (thing) that causes absorption. **absorbent,** *a.* and *n.* (substance) tending to suck in. **absorbing,** *a.* engrossing.
absorption, *n.* sucking in; incorporation; engrossment. **absorptive,** *a.* tending to absorb. (L. *absorbēre*)
absquatulate, *v.i.* make off, decamp. (Amer. jocular coinage)
abstain, *v.i.* refrain. **abstainer,** *n.* esp. one who refrains from alcohol. (L. *tenēre*, hold)
abstemious, *a.* sparing in food, drink etc., temperate. (L. *abstemius*)
abstergent, *a.* and *n.* cleansing (substance). **abstersion,** *n.* cleansing. **abstersive,** *a.* (L. *tergere*, wipe)
abstinence, *n.* refraining, esp. from alcohol. **abstinent,** *a.* (*abstain*)
abstract, *v.t.* deduct, take away; summarize.—*n.* summary, essence.—*a.* not concrete, theoretical, ideal. **abstracted,** *a.* inattentive. **abstraction,** *n.* withdrawal; absence of mind; abstract conception. (L. *trahere*, draw)
abstruse, *a.* difficult to understand, profound. (L. *trudere*, push)
absurd, *a.* unreasonable, silly. **absurdity,** *n.* absurd thing; folly. (L. *surdus*, deaf)
abulia, same as **aboulia.**
abundance, *n.* great plenty, affluence; overflowing emotion. **abundant,** *a.* plentiful; rich. (L. *abundare*, overflow)
abuse, *v.t.* misuse, make bad use of; deceive; revile.—*n.* misuse, perversion; corrupt practice; vituperation. **abusive,** *a.* insulting. (L. *uti*, use)
abut, *v.i.* adjoin, border upon; lean against. **abutment,** *n.* support for end of arch. **abutter,** *n.* (*law*) owner of adjoining property. (O.F. *à*, to; *but*, *bout*, end)
aby, abye, *v.t.* (*arch.*) suffer for, pay penalty of. (O.E. *bycgan*, buy)
abyss (earlier **abysm**), *n.* primal chaos; bottomless or deep chasm; immeasurable depth. **abysmal,** *a.* bottomless, profound. **abyssal,** *a.* pertaining to oceanic depths. (Gk. *a-*, without; *bussos*, bottom)
ac-, form of **ad-** before *c*, *k*, *q*.
acacia, *n.* kinds of tree yielding gum arabic. **false a.,** locust-tree. (Gk. *akakia*)
academy, *n.* school of Plato; place of study or training, higher school; society for promoting art or science. **academic,** *a.* of Platonic school; scholarly; abstract, unpractical.—*n.* Platonist; member of a university; (*pl.*) academic arguments; academicals. **academical,** *a.* of an academy. —*n.pl.* college dress. **academically,** *adv.* theoretically, unpractically. **academician, academist,** *nn.* member of an academy. (*Akadēmos*, after whom the original Academy was named)
Acadian, *n.* Nova-Scotian. (F. *Acadi* orig. name of Nova Scotia)
acaleph, acalepha, *n.* jelly-fish, medusa, sea-nettle. (Gk. *akalēphē*, nettle)
acanthus, *n.* prickly plant, bear's-breech or brank-ursine; (*archit.*) ornament resembling its leaf. (Gk. *akanthos*)
acapsular, *a.* without capsule.

acardiac, *a.* without a heart. (Gk. *a-*, not; *kardia*, heart)
acarid, *n.* mite. (Gk. *akari*)
acarpellous, *a.* without carpels.
acarpous, *a.* not producing fruit. (Gk. *a-*, not; *karpos*, fruit)
acatalectic, *a.* and *n.* (verse) with complete number of syllables, not catalectic.
acatalepsy, *n.* (*philos.*) incomprehensibility. **acataleptic,** *a.* (Gk. *a-*, not; *kata*, down; *lambanein*, grasp)
acaulescent, acauline, acaulose, acaulous, *aa.* stemless, with very short stem. (*a-*+L. *caulis*, stalk)
Accadian, *a.* of Accad.—*n.* language preserved in cuneiform inscriptions.
accede, *v.i.* agree, consent; come to, enter, office. (L. *cedere*, go)
accelerando, *a.* and *n.* (*mus.*) (passage played) gradually quicker. (It.)
accelerate, *v.t.* and *i.* make or become quicker, hasten. **acceleration,** *n.* **accelerative,** *a.* **accelerator,** *n.* attachment in motor-car for increasing speed. (L. *celer*, swift)
accent, *n.* differentiation of syllables by stress or pitch; mark indicating this; local or national mode of pronunciation; modulation of voice; (*pl.*) speech.—*v.t.* pronounce or mark with accent; emphasize. **accentual,** *a.* **accentuate,** *v.t.* accent; emphasize. **accentuation,** *n.* (L. *cantus*, singing)
accentor, *n.* hedge-sparrow. (L. *canere*, sing)
accept, *v.t.* receive; agree to, believe; undertake to meet (bill). **acceptable,** *a.* pleasing, welcome. **acceptance,** *n.* act of accepting; agreement; accepted bill. **acceptation,** *n.* favourable reception; usual meaning of a word. **accepted,** *a.* generally recognized. **acceptor,** *n.* one who accepts a bill. (L. *capere*, take)
access, *n.* approach; means of approach; attack (of illness). **accessible,** *a.* able to be reached. **accessibility,** *n.* **accession,** *n.* coming to; acceding to throne or office; addition. **accessory, accessary,** *a.* additional, contributing to, aiding.—*n.* accomplice, adjunct. (L. *cedere*, go)
accidence, *n.* the part of grammar dealing with inflexions (which are accidents, not essentials).
accident, *n.* event without apparent cause; unexpected event; unintentional act; non-essential. **accidental,** *a.* and *n.* (L. *cadere*, fall)
accidie, *n.* sloth, torpor. (Gk. *a-*, not; *kēdos*, care)
accipitral, *a.* hawklike, rapacious. (L. *accipiter*, hawk)
accite, *v.t.* (*Shake.*) summon.
acclaim, *v.t.* welcome loudly; hail as.—*n.* shout of applause. **acclamation,** *n.* shout of applause; loud united assent. **acclamatory,** *a.* (L. *clamare*, shout)
acclimatize, acclimate, *vv.t.* accustom to new climate. **acclimatization, acclimatation, acclimation,** *nn.* (*climate*)
acclivity, *n.* upward slope. (L. *clivus*, slope)
accloy, *v.t.* (*Spens.*) clog up, encumber.
accoast, (*Spens.*) same as **accost.**
accoil, *v.i.* (*Spens.*) gather together. (L. *colligere*, collect)
accolade, *n.* ceremony of bestowing knighthood, by embrace, kiss, or tap on shoulder with a sword; (*mus.*) line or brace coupling staves. (L. *collum*, neck)
accommodate, *v.t.* adapt; reconcile; provide lodging for. **accommodating,** *a.* obliging. **accommodation,** *n.* fitness, adjustment; settlement; lodging. (L. *commodus*, fitting)
accompany, *v.t.* go with, attend; supplement; (*mus.*) support (singer, player, piece) by playing additional part. **accompaniment,** *n.* appendage; (*mus.*) subsidiary part. **accompanist, accompanyist,** *nn.* (F. *compagne*, companion)
accomplice, *n.* associate in crime. (L. *complex*, interwoven)
accomplish, *v.t.* perform; complete. **accomplished,** *a.* perfected in polite acquirements. **accomplishment,** *n.* completion; cultured attainment in art or manners. (L. *complēre*, complete)
accompt, accomptant, *arch.* for **account, accountant.**
accord, *v.t.* grant.—*v.i.* agree, be in harmony.—*n.* agreement; treaty; harmony. **accordance,** *n.* agreement, conformity. **accordant,** *a.* **accordingly,** *adv.* consequently. **according as,** in proportion as. **according to,** on the authority of. (L. *cor*, heart)
accordion, *n.* portable musical instrument with keyboard and bellows. **a. pleating,** pleating like folds in an accordion.
accost, *v.t.* speak first to, address; (of prostitute) solicit; (*Spens.*) adjoin, fly near ground. (L. *costa*, side)
accouchement, *n.* delivery in childbed. **accoucheur,** *n.* obstetrician. **accoucheuse,** *n.* midwife. (F.)
account, *v.t.* reckon, regard as.—*v.i.* give reckoning or reason.—*n.* counting, reckoning; financial statement; estimation; ground, reason; report. **accountable,** *a.* responsible; explicable. **accountancy,** *n.* profession of accountant. **accountant,** *n.* keeper or inspector of accounts. (L. *computare*, reckon)
accoutre, *v.t.* dress, equip (esp. for battle). **accoutrement,** *n.* (us. *pl.*) equipment; soldier's outfit. (F.)
accredit, *v.t.* give credit or authority to; furnish with credentials; ascribe. (L. *credere*, believe)
accrete, *v.t.* and *i.* grow together; form round; attract.—*a.* (*bot.*) grown into one. **accretion,** *n.*

growth; growing of things into one; addition from outside. (L. *crescere*, grow)
accrue, *v.i.* come as natural increase (esp. interest on money), be added. (L. *crescere*, grow)
accubation, *n.* Roman style of reclining on couch at meals. **accumbent**, *a.* (L. *cubare*, lie)
accumulate, *v.t.* heap up; amass.—*v.i.* increase, grow numerous. **accumulation**, *n.* heaping up; mass. **accumulative**, *a.* cumulative; acquisitive. **accumulator**, *n.* one who collects; device for storing electricity. (L. *cumulus*, heap)
accurate, *a.* correct, exact. **accuracy**, *n.* (L. *cura*, care)
accursed, accurst, *a.* under a curse, ill-fated; detestable. (*curse*)
accuse, *v.t.* bring charge against; blame. **accusation**, *n.* **accusative**, *a.* and *n.* (*gram.*) objective (case). **accusatorial**, *a.* (of procedure) in which prosecutor and judge are not the same (opp. to inquisitorial). **accusatory**, *a.* conveying accusation. **accuser**, *n.* (L. *accusare*)
accustom, *v.t.* habituate. **accustomed**, *a.* usual. (*custom*)
ace, *n.* one on dice, dominoes, or cards; (*rackets*) one point; (*tennis*) service that beats opponent; smallest possible amount; airman who has brought down ten enemy aeroplanes; (*sl.*) good performer. (L. *as*, unit)
-acea, *suf.* forming pl. names for orders of animals, e.g. **Crustacea. -aceae**, *suf.* forming pl. names for orders of plants, e.g. **Rosaceae. -acean, -aceous**, *suff.* forming adjectives from above, e.g. **crustacean, rosaceous.**
acephalous, without a head. (Gk. *a-*, not; *kephalē*, head)
acerbity, *n.* sourness; bitterness, severity. (L. *acerbus*, sour)
aceric, *a.* of the maple. (L. *acer*, maple)
acerose, *a.* full of chaff; like a needle. (L. *acus*, chaff+confusion with L. *acus*, needle)
acervate, *a.* growing in compact clusters. (L. *acervus*, heap)
acescent, *a.* turning sour; rather sour. (L. *acēre*, be sour)
acet- from L. *acetum*, vinegar, used in **acetabulum**, *n.* (*pl.* **acetabula**) cup to hold vinegar, socket of thigh-bone; **acetarious**, *a.* used in salads; **acetated**, *a.* treated with acetic acid; **acetic**, *a.* of vinegar, sour (**acetic acid**, sour principle of vinegar); **acetify**, *v.t.* and *i.* turn into vinegar; **acetone**, *n*, colourless liquid used as solvent of organic compounds; **acetous**, *a.* like vinegar, sour; **acetylene**, *n.* a gas used for lighting.
achar, *n.* (*Anglo-Ind.*) pickles.
acharnement, *n.* fury; gusto. (F.)
Achátēs, *n.* faithful friend. (Aeneas's friend in Vergil)
ache, *n.* continuous pain.—*v.i.* suffer such pain. (O.E. *acan*)
ache, same as **aitch.**
achieve, *v.t.* accomplish; acquire; reach. **achievement**, *n.* completion; feat achieved; escutcheon in memory of distinguished feat. (O.F. *à chef venir*, come to a head)
achromatic, *a.* colourless; transmitting light without decomposing it. **achromaticity, achromatism**, *nn.* **achromatize**, *v.t.* (Gk. *a-*, not; *chrōma*, colour)
achtung, *n.* attention. (G.)
acicular, aciculate, *aa.* needle-shaped. (L. *acus*, needle)
acid, *a.* sour.—*n.* sour substance; compound of hydrogen with other elements which neutralizes alkalis. **acidify**, *v.t.* and *i.* make, become, sour; turn into acid. **acidity**, *n.* sourness, acid quality. **acidimeter**, *n.* instrument for measuring strength of acids. **acidosis**, *n.* acid condition of blood. **acidulated, acidulous**, *aa.* somewhat acid. (L. *acēre*, be sour)
-acious, *suf.* forming adjectives meaning full of, inclined to, as **mendacious. -acity**, *suf.* forming corresponding nouns of quality, as **mendacity.** (L.)
ack emma, *adv.* and *n.* (*sl.*) a.m. (before noon); air mechanic. (signallers' names for letters A, M)
acknowledge, *v.t.* admit truth of; recognize, own; intimate receipt of; reward (service). **acknowledgment, acknowledgement**, *n.* (*knowledge*)
aclinic, *a.* **a. line**, magnetic equator, on which the needle does not dip. (Gk. *a-*, not; *klinein*, bend)
acme, *n.* highest point, culmination. (Gk. *akmē*, point)
acne, *n.* pimple; skin disease.
acnestis, *n.* part of animal's back between shoulder-blade and loins. (Gk. *aknēstis*, spine)
acold, *a.* (*arch.*) cold.
acolyte, *n.* priest's attendant; assistant, novice. (Gk. *akolouthos*, follower)
aconite, *n.* monk's-hood, wolf's-bane; poison extracted from it. (Gk. *akoniton*)
acorn, *n.* fruit of the oak. (O.E. *æcern*)
acotyledon, *n.* plant without seed-lobes. (*cotyledon*)
acouchy, *n.* rodent resembling guinea-pig. (F. *acouchi*)
acoustic, *a.* of the sense of hearing.—*n.pl.* science of sound; properties of audibility of a building. **acoustician**, *n.* **acousticon**, *n.* instrument for enabling deaf to hear. (Gk. *akouein*, hear)
acquaint, *v.t.* make aware, inform. **acquaintance**, *n.* moderate knowledge of; person one knows. (L. *cognoscere*, know)
acquest, *n.* thing acquired; (*law*) property gained otherwise than by inheritance. (*acquire*)
acquiesce, *v.i.* agree tacitly, comply.

acquiescent, *a.* **acquiescence,** *n.* (L. *quiescere,* keep quiet)
acquire, *v.t.* gain; win; come to have. **acquirement,** *n.* mental attainment. **acquisition,** *n.* act of acquiring; useful addition. **acquisitive,** *a.* eager to acquire, grasping. (L. *quaerere,* seek)
acquit, *v.t.* declare not guilty; release, clear; pay (debt); conduct (oneself). **acquittal,** *n.* judicial discharge from accusation; performance (of duty). **acquittance,** *n.* discharge from debt or obligation; receipt in full. (L. *quies,* rest)
acre, *n.* measure of land, 4,840 square yards; (*pl.*) lands, fields. **acreage,** *n.* extent in acres. **acred,** *a.* possessing acres. (O.E. *æcer,* field)
acrid, *a.* bitter, pungent. **acridity,** *n.* (L. *acer,* sharp)
acrimony, *n.* bitterness of feeling or language. **acrimonious,** *a.* (L. *acer,* sharp)
Acrita, *n.pl.* (*zool.*) plant-like animals such as sponges. (Gk. *akritos,* indistinguishable)
acro-, from Gk. *akros,* topmost, extreme, used in **acrogen,** *n.* non-flowering plant with growing part at extremity, as ferns and mosses; **acrolith,** *n.* statue with only the extremities of stone; **acromegaly,** *n.* over-development of the extremities. **acronychal,** *a.* (*astron.*) (of stars) that rise at sunset and set at sunrise (opp. to cosmical); **acrophobia,** *n.* dread of heights.
acrobat, *n.* rope-dancer, gymnast. **acrobatic,** *a.* (Gk. *akrobatos,* walking on tiptoe)
acropolis, *n.* citadel, esp. that of Athens. (Gk. *akros,* topmost; *polis,* city)
across, *prep.* and *adv.* on, to, the other side (of); crosswise, from side to side. **put it a.,** (*sl.*) get the better of.
acrostic, *n.* poem etc. in which the first or first and last letters of the lines form words. (Gk. *akros,* extreme; *stichos,* line)
act, *n.* deed, thing done; doing, operation; law; part of play.—*v.t.* perform action; behave, serve.—*v.t.* play (part), represent (character). **acting,** *a.* doing duty as. (L. *agere,* do)
actinism, *n.* property of light by which chemical changes are caused, as in photography. **actinic,** *a.* **actinometer,** *n.* instrument for measuring actinic effects. **actinotherapy,** *n.* treatment of disease by light rays, usually ultra-violet. (Gk. *aktis,* ray)
actinium, *n.* radioactive element found in pitchblende. (Gk. *aktis,* ray)
action, *n.* deed; operation; mode of acting; mechanism; battle; lawsuit. **actionable,** *a.* giving grounds for a lawsuit. (*act*)
active, *a.* acting, working; busy, energetic; nimble; (*gram.*) (of verb) indicating action by the subject. **activism,** *n.* policy of energetic action. **activist,** *n.* **activistic,** *a.* **activity,** *n.* being active; (*pl.*) spheres of energy. (*act*)
acton, *n.* quilted jacket worn under mail. (Arab. *al,* the; *qutun,* cotton)
actor, *n.* (*fem.* **actress**) dramatic performer; (rare) doer. (*act*)
actual, *a.* real; existing at present. **actuality,** *n.* reality; (*pl.*) present conditions. **actualize,** *v.t.* realize in action; describe realistically. **actually,** *adv.* really; strange though it seems. (*act*)
actuary, *n.* expert on insurance. **actuarial,** *a.* (L. *actuarius,* bookkeeper)
actuate, *v.t.* put in motion; impel, influence. **actuation,** *n.* (*act*)
acture, *n.* (*Shake.*) performance.
acuity, *n.* sharpness; acuteness. (L. *acus,* needle)
aculeate, aculeated, *aa.* (*zool.*) having sting; (*bot.*) having prickles. (L. *aculeus,* sting)
acumen, *n.* quickness of perception, penetration. **acuminate,** *v.t.* sharpen. —*a.* pointed. (L. *acuere,* sharpen)
acushla, *n.* darling. (Ir. *ā cuisle,* O my heart)
acute, *a.* sharp; keen, penetrating; shrill; shrewd; (of disease) coming quickly to a crisis (opp. to chronic); (of angle) less than 90°. (L. *acutus*)
-acy, *suf.* forming nouns of state or quality, e.g. **piracy.** (L. and Gk.)
ad, *colloq. abbr.* of **advertisement.**
ad, prep. to. *ad absurdum,* to absurdity. *ad eundem* (*gradum*), to the same (degree at another university). *ad extremum,* to the extreme. *ad finem,* to the end. *ad gustum,* to taste. *ad hoc,* for this purpose. *ad hominem,* to the man, personal. *ad infinitum,* to infinity. *ad interim,* for the meantime. *ad Kalendas Graecas,* at the Greek Calends, i.e. never, as the Greeks had no calends. *ad libitum,* as much as desired. *ad literam,* to the letter. *ad majorem Dei gloriam,* for the greater glory of God. *ad misericordiam,* (appealing) to pity. *ad nauseam,* till causing disgust. *ad rem,* to the point or purpose. *ad summam,* to sum up. *ad summum,* to the highest. *ad unguem* (*factus*), highly finished. *ad valorem,* in proportion to value. *ad verbum,* word for word. *ad vitam aut culpam,* during good behaviour. (L.)
ad-, *pref.* to, as in **adhere.** It appears as **a-, ab-, ac-, ad-, af-, ag-, al-, an-, ap-, ar-, as-, at-,** according to following letter. (L.)
adage, *n.* proverb, saw. (L. *adagium*)
adagio, a. and *n.* (*mus.*) slow (passage). (It.)
adalin, *n.* a sedative. (G.)
Adam, *n.* first man. **A.'s ale,** water. **A.'s apple,** projection in front of

throat. **Adamite,** *n.* child of Adam; member of sect who went naked.

adamant, *n.* very hard substance; diamond. **adamantine, adamantean,** *aa.* (Gk. *a-*, not; *damaein*, tame)

adapt, *v.t.* fit, make suitable; modify. **adaptability, adaptation,** *nn.* **adaptable, adaptive,** *aa.* (L. *aptus*, fit)

add, *v.t.* put together; increase by; sum up. **addendum,** *n.* (*pl.* **addenda**) thing to be added; appendix. (L. *addere*)

addax, *n.* large N. African antelope with twisted horns. (L.)

adder, *n.* small venomous snake, viper. **a.'s-tongue,** *n.* kind of fern. (O.E. *nædre*, *n* being lost by mistaken division of M.E. *a naddre* into *an addre*)

addict, *v.t.* give (oneself) up to, habituate (us. in bad sense.)—*n.* person addicted to specified drug etc. **addiction,** *n.* (L. *addicere*, assign)

addition, *n.* act of adding; thing added; (*Shake.*) title, style of address. **additional,** *a.* added, extra. (*add*)

addled, addle, *aa.* (of egg) rotten, yielding no chicken; empty; muddled. **addle,** *v.t.* and *i.* make or grow addled. —*n.* (*Scot.*) foul and putrid water. **addle - headed,** *a.* muddle - headed. (O.E. *adela*, mud)

address, *v.t.* direct to; prepare (oneself) for; speak or write to.—*n.* speech, formal application; manners, bearing; dexterity; direction of a letter; place of residence; (*pl.*) courtship. **addressee,** *n.* person to whom letter is addressed. (L. *directum*, straight)

addressograph, *n.* addressing-machine. (*address*+Gk. *graphein*, write)

adduce, *v.t.* cite, bring forward as proof. **adduct,** *v.t.* (of muscles) draw to a common centre. **adduction,** *n.* adducing; adducting. (L. *ducere*, lead)

aden(o)-, from Gk. *adēn*, gland, used in **adenitis,** *n.* inflammation of a gland; **adenodynia,** *n.* pain in a gland; **adenology,** *n.* science of glands; **adenoma,** *n.* gland-like benign tumour.

adenoids, *n.pl.* swollen tissue at back of the nose. (Gk. *adēn*, gland)

adept, *a.* and *n.* proficient, expert; skilled alchemist. (L. *adipisci*, attain)

adequate, *a.* proportionate; sufficient. **adequacy,** *n.* (L. *aequus*, equal)

adespota, *n.pl.* literary works not attributed to any author. (Gk. *a-*, not; *despotēs*, master)

adhere, *v.i.* stick; be attached. **adherence,** *n.* **adherent,** *a.* sticking; incident (to).—*n.* partisan. **adhesion,** *n.* adhering. **adhesive,** *a.* sticky. (L. *haerēre*, stick)

adiabatic, *a.* not gaining or losing heat. (Gk. *adiabatos*, impassable)

adhibit, *v.t.* apply; attach. **adhibition,** *n.* (L. *adhibēre*, employ)

adiantum, *n.* maidenhair fern. (Gk. *adiantos*, dry, from its habitat)

adiaphorism, *n.* toleration in non-essential points of religion. (Gk. *a-*, not; *diaphoros*, different)

adieu, *int.* and *n.* (*pl.* **adieus, adieux**) good-bye, farewell. (F. *à*, to; *Dieu*, God)

adipocere, *n.* fatty substance resulting from decomposition of animal bodies in moist places. (L. *adeps*, fat; *cera*, wax)

adipose, *a.* of fat, fatty.—*n.* animal fat. **adiposity,** *n.* (L. *adeps*, fat)

adit, *n.* approach; (horizontal) entrance to mine. (L. *aditus*)

adjacent, *a.* lying near, contiguous. **adjacency,** *n.* (L. *jacēre*, lie)

adjective, *a.* dependent.—*n.* (*gram.*) word which qualifies or limits a noun. **adjectival,** *a.* (L. *jacere*, throw)

adjoin, *v.t.* lie next to. (*join*)

adjourn, *v.t.* put off till another time, postpone.—*v.i.* break up. **adjournment,** *n.* (L. *diurnus*, daily)

adjudge, *v.t.* decide or award judicially; sentence. **adjudgment,adjudgement,***n.*

adjudicate, *v.t.* adjudge.—*v.i.* sit in judgment. **adjudication,** *n.* act of adjudging; court's decision. **adjudicator,** *n.* (L. *judex*, judge)

adjunct, *n.* thing added as a subordinate part; (*logic*) non-essential attribute; (*Shake.*) attendant.—*a.* (*Shake.*) consequent. **adjunctive,** *a.* (L. *jungere*, join)

adjure, *v.t.* charge on oath; request earnestly. **adjuration,** *n.* adjuring; oath used in it. (L. *jurare*, swear)

adjust, *v.t.* put in order; adapt; settle. **adjustment,** *n.* adjusting; arrangement. (L. *juxta*, near)

adjutage, ajutage, *n.* mouthpiece of fountain. (F. *ajoutage*)

adjutant, *n.* army officer who assists superiors in details of duty, correspondence etc.; large Indian stork. **adjutancy,** *n.* office of adjutant. (L. *adjutare*, assist)

adjuvant, *a.* and *n.* helpful, auxiliary; helper. (L. *juvare*, help)

admeasure, *v.t.* apportion; measure. **admeasurement,** *n.* admeasuring; adjustment of proportions; dimensions. (*measure*)

adminicle, *n.* aid; (*law*) corroboratory evidence. **adminicular,** *a.* (L. *adminiculum*, prop)

administer, *v.t.* manage; dispense; supply, give; apply.—*v.i.* contribute. **administration,** *n.* act of administering; government, ministry. **administrative,** *a.* of management; executive. **administrator,** *n.* (*fem.* **administratrix**) one who administers; person authorized to manage estate for minor or for one who dies intestate. (L. *minister*, servant)

admirable, *a.* excellent. **A. Crichton,** James Crichton (1560–82) taken as type of all-round excellence.

admiral, *n.* commander of navy, fleet, or squadron; admiral's ship, flagship; kinds of butterfly. **admiralty**, *n.* board of commissioners administering naval affairs; office of admiral; sea-power. (Arab. *amir*, chief)
admire, *v.t.* wonder at; look with pleasure at; esteem highly. **admiration**, *n.* **admirer**, *n.* one who admires; lover. (L. *mirari*, wonder at)
admissible, *a.* capable of being admitted; allowable. **admission**, *n.* admitting, leave to enter; fee paid for this; acknowledgment. **admissive**, *a.* tending to admit. (*admit*)
admit, *v.t.* let in; concede as true, acknowledge. **admittable**, *a.* **admittance**, *n.* **admittedly**, *adv.* confessedly. (L. *mittere*, send)
admix, mix (with), add as ingredient. **admixture**, *n.* (*mix*)
admonish, *v.t.* warn, advise; reprove mildly; exhort. **admonition**, *n.* reproof; warning. **admonitory**, *a.* (L. *monēre*, warn)
adnoun, *n.* adjective, word added to a noun. **adnominal**, *a.* (*noun*)
ado, *n.* fuss; trouble. (*do*)
adobe, *n.* and *a.* (made of) unburnt sun-dried brick. (Sp.)
adolescent, *n.* and *a.* (person) between child and man (14–25) or child and woman (12–21). **adolescence, adolescency**, *nn.* (L. *adolescere*, grow)
Adonis, *n.* dandy. **adonize**, *v.refl.* and *i.* adorn (oneself). (name in myth)
adopt, *v.t.* take as one's own (another's child, idea etc.); choose. **adoption**, *n.* **adoptive**, *a.* that adopts or is adopted. (L. *optare*, choose)
adorable, *a.* worthy of adoration; (*colloq.*) lovely, charming. (*adore*)
adore, *v.t.* worship, reverence as divine; love intensely. **adorer**, *n.* lover. **adoration**, *n.* worship, homage. (L. *orare*, pray)
adorn, *v.t.* ornament, deck; give beauty to. **adornment**, *n.* (L. *ornare*, furnish)
adown *adv.* and *prep.* (*arch.* and *poet.*) down. (O.E. *of*, from; *dun*, hill)
adrad, adred, *a.* (*Spens.*) afraid.
adrenal, *a.* near the kidney. **a. glands**, two small ductless glands over the kidneys. **adrenalin**, *n.* secretion of these glands; this extracted from animals for medicinal use. (L. *rēn*, kidney)
adrift, *adv.* and *a.* floating at random; loose. (*drift*)
adroit, *a.* dexterous, skilful. (F. *droit*, right)
adry, *adv.* and *a.* dry, thirsty. (*dry*)
adscititious, *a.* added from without; supplementary. (L. *adsciscere*, adopt)
adscriptus glebae, (man) attached to the soil. (L.)
adsorb, *v.t.* collect by adsorption. **adsorbent**, *n.* adsorbing substance. **adsorption**, *n.* action of a solid in condensing and holding a gas upon it. (L. *sorbēre*, suck in)
adsum, I am here. (L.)
adulate, *v.t.* flatter excessively or basely. **adulation, adulator**, *nn.* **adulatory**, *a.* (L. *adulari*, fawn on)
adult, *a.* and *n.* grown-up, mature (person). (L. *adultus*, full-grown)
adulterate, *v.t.* make impure by adding inferior ingredients, debase.—*a.* corrupted, counterfeit; adulterous; born of adultery. **adulterant**, *a.* and *n.* (thing) used in adulterating. **adulteration, adulterator**, *nn.* (L. *adulterare*, corrupt)
adultery, *n.* unchastity of married person. **adulterer**, *n.* (*fem.* **adulteress**). **adulterine**, *a.* of adultery; adulterated. **adulterous**, *a.* guilty of adultery. (L. *adulter*, adulterer)
adumbral, *a.* overshadowing; shady.
adumbrate, *v.t.* indicate faintly, outline; foreshadow; overshadow. **adumbrant, adumbrative**, *aa.* **adumbration**, *n.* (L. *umbra*, shade)
adust, *a.* scorched, dried up; sunburnt; gloomy. (L. *urere*, burn)
advance, *v.t.* put or bring forward; promote; hasten; raise (price); pay beforehand; lend.—*v.i.* move forward, progress; rise in price.—*n.* going forward; improvement; rise in price; paying beforehand. **advanced**, *a.* (of studies) not elementary; (of ideas) ahead of times. **advancement**, *n.* (L. *ab*, from; *ante*, before)
advantage, *n.* superiority, benefit; favouring circumstance; (*tennis*) next point won after deuce.—*v.t.* be beneficial to; promote. **advantageous**, *a.* (F. *avant*, before)
advent, *n.* coming of Christ, Incarnation; second coming of Christ; season before Christmas; any (important) arrival. **Adventist**, *n.* one who believes in Christ's second coming to set up a kingdom on earth. **advental**, *a.* of Advent. (L. *venire*, come)
adventitious, *a.* accidental, casual.
adventure, *n.* risk; daring enterprise; unexpected happening; business speculation.—*v.t.* and *i.* risk; dare, venture. **adventurer**, *n.* (*fem.* **adventuress**) one who seeks adventures; speculator; one who lives by his wits. **adventuresome**, *a.* given to adventures. **adventurous**, *a.* rash, enterprising. (L. *adventurus*, about to happen)
adverb, *n.* word that qualifies verb, adjective, or other adverb. **adverbial**, *a.* (L. *verbum*, word)
adverse, *a.* opposed, unfavourable; placed opposite. **adversary**, *n.* opponent, enemy. **adversative**, *a.* (of words) denoting opposition or contrariety. **adversity**, *n.* trouble, misfortune. (L. *vertere*, turn)
advert, *v.i.* turn attention, refer.

advertent, *a.* heedful. **advertence,** *n.* (L. *vertere,* turn)
advertise, *v.t.* and *i.* give public notice of; announce for sale; notify; (*Shake.*) inform, instruct; admonish. **advertisement,** *n.* public announcement. (*advert*)
advice, *n.* counsel; intelligence; formal notice. **advise,** *v.t.* and *i.* give advice to, counsel; deliberate; inform. **advisable,** *a.* expedient. **advised,** *a.* deliberate; judicious. **advisedly,** *adv.* deliberately. **adviser,** *n.* **advisory,** *a.* (L. *vidēre,* see)
advocate, *n.* one who pleads the cause of another; one who recommends (policy etc.); barrister.—*v.t.* plead for, support. **Lord A.,** principal law-officer of the Crown in Scotland. **devil's a.,** person appointed to oppose claims to canonization. **advocacy,** *n.* support; recommendation. (L. *advocatus*)
advowson, *n.* right of presentation to a benefice. **advowee,** *n.* one who has this right. (L. *vocare,* call)
adynamia, *n.* want of vital power, prostration. (Gk. *dunamis,* power)
adytum, *n.* (*pl.* **adyta**) inner part of temple; sanctum. (Gk. *a-,* not; *duein,* enter)
adze, *n.* tool like axe with blade at right angles to handle.—*v.t.* cut with adze. (O.E. *adesa*)
ae, *a.* (*Scot.*) one. (O.E. *án*)
-ae, *suf.* forming plural of L. and Gk. 1st declension nouns in *-a,* ordinary *-s* termination being used for more familiar or less technical ones, e.g. **larvae,** mathematical **formulae,** but hyenas, religious formulas.
aedile, *n.* Roman magistrate in charge of public works. (L. *aedilis*)
aeger, *n.* note certifying that student is ill. (L.=sick)
aegis, *n.* impregnable shield; protection. (Gk. *aigis,* shield of Zeus)
aegrotat, *n.* certificate that student is too ill to attend examination etc. (L.=he is ill)
Aeolian, *a.* of Aeolis in Asia Minor; of Aeolus, god of winds. **A. harp,** stringed instrument sounded by the wind. **Aeolic,** *a.* of Aeolis.—*n.* Aeolic dialect.
aeolipyle, aeolipile, *n.* instrument showing the force of steam escaping through a narrow orifice. (Gk. *Aiolou pulai,* gates of Aeolus, god of winds)
aeon, eon, *n.* immense period; age. (Gk. *aiōn*)
aerate, *v.t.* expose to action of the air; charge with carbonic acid gas. **aeration,** *n.* (Gk. *aēr,* air)
aerial, *a.* of or like air, gaseous; existing in the air; immaterial.—*n.* overhead wire of radio set. **a. railway,** cars running suspended from overhead cables. **a. torpedo,** torpedo launched from aircraft. (*air*)
aerie, aery, eyrie, eyry, *n.* nest of bird of prey, esp. eagle; high-perched dwelling. (L.L. *aeria*)
aeriform, *a.* like air; unsubstantial.
aero, *n.* and *a.* (*colloq.*) (of) air-vessel or aviation.
aerobatics, *n.* stunting in the air. (Gk. *aēr,* air; *bainein,* go)
aerobe, *n.* microbe that cannot live without air. **aerobian, aerobic,** *aa.* (Gk. *aēr,* air; *bios,* life)
aerobomb, aerodart, *nn.* bomb, dart dropped from fighting aircraft.
aerobus, *n.* (*sl.*) aeroplane. (*bus*)
aerodrome, *n.* landing-ground for aircraft. (Gk. *dromos,* course)
aerodynamics, *n.* science of gases in motion. (*dynamics*)
aerofoil, *n.* wing, lifting surface of aeroplane. (*foil*)
aerogram, *n.* wireless message. (Gk. *graphein,* write)
aerohydroplane, *n.* flying boat.
aerolite, aerolith, *n.* meteorite. (Gk. *lithos,* stone)
aeronaut, *n.* aviator. **aeronautic,** *a.* —*n.pl.* science of air-navigation. (Gk. *aēr,* air; *naus,* ship)
aeroplane, *n.* flying-machine heavier than air. (*plane*)
aerostat, *n.* balloon; balloonist. **aerostatics,** *n.* science of gases in equilibrium; science of air-navigation. **aerostation,** *n.* ballooning. (Gk. *aēr,* air; *statos,* standing)
aeruginous, *a.* of or like verdigris or copper-rust. (L. *aes,* copper)
aery, see **aerie.**
Aesculapius, *n.* Roman god of medicine; doctor. **Aesculapian,** *a.* (L.)
aesthetics, *n.* theory of the beautiful; principles of taste or art. **aesthetic,** *a.* **aesthete,** *n.* follower of aestheticism. **aestheticism,** *n.* cult of the beautiful, esp. fantastic art movement at end of 19th cent. (Gk. *aisthanesthai,* perceive)
aestival, estival, *a.* of summer. **aestivation,** *n.* (*bot.*) arrangement of petals in flower-bud; (*zool.*) spending dry season in dormant state. (L. *aestas,* summer)
aetatis, *a.* (*abbr.* **aet., aetat.**) of, at, the age of. (L.)
aetiology, *n.* study of causation, esp. causes of disease. (Gk. *aitia,* cause)
af-, form of **ad-** before *f.*
afar, *adv.* at, to, a long distance.
afeard, *a.* (*Shake.*) afraid. (*fear*)
aff, *Scot.* form of **off.**
affable, *a.* of easy manners, courteous. **affability,** *n.* (L. *fari,* speak)
affair, *n.* business, matter; intrigue; (*colloq.*) thing; (*pl.*) public concerns. (O.F. *à faire,* to do)
affaire de cœur, love affair. (F.)
affect, *v.t.* produce effect upon; move feelings of; assume, pretend. **affectation,** *n.* studied display, posing. **affected,** *a.* disposed; full of affectation. **affecting,** *a.* moving, pathetic.

affection, *n.* love; disease. **affectionate,** *a.* loving. **affective,** *a.* emotional. (L. *afficere*)
affeer, *v.t.* (*Shake.*) confirm. (O.F. *afeurer*, fix price of)
afferent, *a.* bringing to. (L. *ferre*, carry)
affettuoso, *adv.* (*mus.*) feelingly. (It.)
affiance, *v.t.* promise in marriage.—*n.* faith; marriage contract. (L. *fides*, faith)
affiche, *n.* placard, bill. (F.)
affidavit, *n.* written declaration on oath. (L. *fides*, faith)
affiliate, *v.t.* adopt (into family, society etc.); connect attach; (*law*) fix paternity of illegitimate child. **affiliation,** *n.* (L. *filius*, son)
affinity, *n.* relationship by marriage; connection; attraction; (*chem.*) tendency of certain elements to unite. affined, *a.* (L. *affinis*, related)
affirm, *v.t.* and *i.* assert strongly, declare; (*law*) make affirmation; ratify. **affirmation,** *n.* affirming; (*law*) solemn declaration by one who objects to taking oath. **affirmative,** *a.* and *n.* affirming; saying yes. (L. *firmus*, strong)
affix, *v.t.* fix to, attach.—*n.* appendage; (*gram.*) prefix, suffix. (*fix*)
afflatus, *n.* poetic or divine inspiration. (L. *flare*, blow)
afflict, *v.t.* distress; pain, trouble. **affliction,** *n.* distress; pain; calamity. **afflictive,** *a.* (L. *affligere*, dash down)
affluent, *a.* abundant; wealthy.—*n.* tributary stream. **affluence,** *n.* abundance; wealth. **afflux, affluxion,** *nn.* flowing towards. (L. *fluere*, flow)
afford, *v.t.* be able to buy, spare; furnish; yield. (O.E. *geforthian*, further)
afforest, *v.t.* convert into forest, plant with trees. **afforestation,** *n.*
affranchise, *v.t.* free from slavery or obligation. (O.F. *franc*, free)
affrap, *v.t.* (*Spens.*) strike, strike down. (It. *frappare*, strike)
affray, *n.* brawl, riot; (*Spens.*) fear.—*v.t.* (*obs.*) frighten. (L.L. *exfridare*, break the king's peace)
affreightment, *n.* chartering of ship to carry cargo. (F. *affréter*, charter)
affright, *v.t.* and *n.* (*arch.*) alarm.
affront, *v.t.* insult openly, abash; face boldly.—*n.* open insult. (L. *frons*, forehead)
affusion, *n.* pouring upon, esp. in baptism. (L. *fundere*, pour)
affy, *v.t.* (*Shake.*) betroth; entrust. (L. *fides*, faith)
afield, *adv.* on, in, to, the field; away from home.
afire, *adv.* and *a.* on fire.
aflame, *adv.* and *a.* flaming, in a glow.
afloat, *adv.* and *a.* floating; at sea; adrift; in circulation.
afoot, *adv.* and *a.* on foot; on the move; in operation.
afore, *adv.* and *prep.* in front, before (*naut.*); previously. so **aforementioned, aforenamed, aforesaid, aforethought,** *aa.* **aforetime,** *adv.* in past times. (O.E. *on foran*, in front)
afraid, *a.* frightened. (*affray*)
afreet, afrit, afrite, *n.* evil demon in Arabian mythology. (Arab. *'ifrīt*)
afresh, *adv.* anew, with fresh start.
Afrikaans, *n.* S. African Dutch, the Taal. **Afrikander, Afrikaner,** *n.* S. African native white, esp.of Dutch descent.
aft, *adv.* in, towards, stern of ship. (O.E. *afta*, behind)
after, *a.* later; nearer stern of ship.—*adv.* behind; later.—*prep.* behind; in search of; about; for; according to, in imitation of.—*conj.* after the time that. (O.E. *æfter*, compar. of *af*, off)
afterbirth, *n.* membrane round foetus, which is expelled after childbirth.
aftercrop, *n.* second crop.
afterdamp, *n.* choke-damp, gas in mine after explosion of fire-damp.
afterglow, *n.* glow in the sky after sunset.
afterguard, *n.* men stationed aft to work the after sails.
after-image, *n.* image that remains momentarily after the eye has been withdrawn from an object.
aftermath, *n.* grass that grows after first crop has been mown; consequences, results. (O.E. *máwan*, mow)
aftermost, *a.* farthest aft.
afternoon, *n.* time between noon and evening.
afterpains, *n.* pains after childbirth.
aftertaste, *n.* taste that remains after eating or drinking.
afterthought, *n.* reflection after an act; idea that occurs to one later.
afterwards, *adv.* later, subsequently.
ag-, form of **ad-** before *g*.
aga, *n.* Turkish commander. (Turk. *agha*)
again, *adv.* another time, once more; further; in response. (O.E. *ongeán*)
against, *prep.* in opposition to; in contact with; in provision for.—*conj.* (*arch.*) by the time that. (*again*)
agama, *n.* short-tongued lizard found in India and Africa. (Carib)
agami, *n.* the trumpeter, a bird of tropical America. (native name)
agamic, *a.* asexual. **agamogenesis,** *n.* asexual reproduction. **agamous,** *a.* without visible sexual organs. (Gk. *a-*, not; *gamos*, marriage)
agapanthus, *n.* ornamental plant with bright blue flowers. (Gk. *agapē*, love; *anthos*, flower)
agape, *a.* and *adv.* open-mouthed.
ágapē, *n.* love-feast of early Christians at communion time. **agapémonē,** *n.* love-abode, hence **Agapemonite,** *n.* member of 19th-century sect believed to practise free love. (Gk. =love)
agar-agar, *n.* preparation of seaweed used for jelly, glue, and bacteria culture. (Malay)

agaric, *n.* mushroom; kinds of fungi. (Gk.)

agastric, *a.* having no stomach.

agate, *n.* precious stone of semi-transparent tinted quartz; (*Amer.*) 5½-point or ruby type. (Gk. *achatēs*)

agave, *n.* American aloe, century plant. (Gk. *Agauē*, name in myth)

agazed, *a.* (*Shake.*) astounded.

age, *n.* length of life; generation; great period; old age.—*v.t.* and *i.* grow or cause to grow old. **of a.**, 21 years old. **a. of discretion**, 14. **aged**, *a.* of the age of; old. **ageless**, *a.* never growing old. (L. *aevum*)

agee, see **ajee.**

agency, *n.* action; instrumentality; agent's office. (L. *agere*, do)

agenda, *n.pl.* items for meeting's consideration etc. (L.=things to be done)

agent, *n.* person or thing causing effect; business representative. (*act*)

agent provocateur, spy professing sympathy, who encourages suspects to incriminate themselves by overt acts. (F.)

agglomerate, *v.t.* and *i.* collect into mass.—*n.* rock consisting of volcanic fragments. **agglomeration**, *n.* (L. *glomus*, ball)

agglutinate, *v.t.* and *i.* stick together; turn into glue; form words into compounds. **agglutination**, *n.* (esp.) formation of words by combination, not inflexion. (L. *gluten*, glue)

aggrandize, *v.t.* increase power of, exalt; exaggerate. **aggrandizement**, *n.* (L. *grandis*, large)

aggrate, *v.t.* (*Spens.*) please, charm. (L. *gratus*, pleasing)

aggravate, *v.t.* make worse; (*colloq.*) exasperate. **aggravating**, *a.* **aggravation**, *n.* (L. *gravis*, heavy)

aggregate, *a.* collected; total.—*n.* whole assemblage, sum total.—*v.t.* and *i.* gather together; amount to. **aggregation**, *n.* (L. *grex*, flock)

aggression, *n.* unprovoked attack. **aggressive**, *a.* quarrelsome. **aggressor**, *n.* one who begins quarrel. (L. *aggredi*, attack)

aggrieve, *v.t.* pain; injure; (*pass.*) have grievance. (L. *gravis*, heavy)

aghast, *a.* stupefied with horror or terror. (O.E. *gǽstan*, terrify)

agile, *a.* nimble, quick-moving; active. **agility**, *n.* (L. *agilis*)

agin, *dial.* for **against.**

agio, *n.* charge for changing paper money into cash, or one currency into another. **agiotage**, *n.* exchange business; stock-jobbing. (It. =ease)

agist, *v.t.* pasture others' cattle; charge (lands etc.) with public burden. **agistment**, *n.* (O.F. *agister*)

agitate, *v.t.* shake, stir; disturb; discuss.—*v.i.* arouse public attention. **agitation, agitator**, *nn.* (L. *agitare*, move to and fro)

agitato, *adv.* (*mus.*) in an agitated manner. (It.)

aglet, aiglet, *n.* tag (of lace etc.); spangle, metallic ornament; catkin. (L. *acus*, needle)

agley, *adv.* (*Scot.*) wrong, astray.

aglow, *adv.* and *a.* in a glow.

agnail, *n.* soreness round nail; whitlow. (O.E. *angnægl*, hard lump, corn)

agnate, *a.* and *n.* (one) related by the father's side or with same male ancestor; (*fig.*) akin. (L. *agnatus*)

agnize, *v.t.* (*Shake.*) acknowledge. (L. *noscere*, know)

agnostic, *n.* one who holds that the existence of God or anything outside the visible world is unproved.—*a.* of this theory. **agnosticism**, *n.* (Gk. *a-*, not; *gnōstikos*, good at knowing)

ago, *adv.* and *a.* past; since. (*go*)

agog, *a.* and *adv.* eager, on the look-out.

agonic, *a.* making no angle. (Gk. *a-*, not; *gōnia*, angle)

agonistic, *a.* of athletic contests; polemic. (Gk. *agōnistēs*, combatant)

agony, *n.* violent pain or struggle. **agonize**, *v.t.* cause agony to, torture. —*v.i.* writhe in agony; wrestle. (Gk. *agōn*, contest)

agood, *adv.* (*Shake.*) in good earnest.

agoraphobia, *n.* morbid fear of crowds or open places. (Gk. *agora*, market-place; *phobia*, fear)

agouti, *n.* S. American rodent like guinea-pig. (native word)

agraphia, *n.* inability to write, due to mental illness. (Gk. *a-*, not; *graphein*, write)

agrarian, *a.* of agriculture or landed property.—*n.* advocate of redistribution of landed property. **agrarianism**, *n.* (L. *ager*, field)

agree, *v.i.* be of one mind, consent. **agreeable**, *a.* pleasant; well disposed; conformable. **agreement**, *n.* mutual understanding; contract. (L. *gratus*, pleasing)

agrestic, *a.* rustic; uncouth. (L. *agrestis*)

agriculture, *n.* cultivation of land, farming. **agricultural**, *a.* **agriculturist, agriculturalist**, *nn.* (L. *ager*, field; *cultura*, culture)

agrimony, *n.* yellow-flowered plant.

agrimotor, *n.* motor vehicle or tractor used for agriculture.

agrise, *v.t.* (*Spens.*) terrify; make frightful. (O.E. *agrisan*, dread)

agronomy, *n.* rural economy, husbandry. **agronomic, agronomical**, *aa.* **agronomics, agronomist**, *nn.* (Gk. *agros*, field; *nemein*, deal out)

aground, *adv.* and *a.* (of ship) stranded.

aguardiente, *n.* coarse Spanish brandy; any coarse spirits. (Sp.)

ague, *n.* malaria, periodic fever; quaking. **agued**, *a.* having ague. **aguish**, *a.* of, like, subject to ague. (L. *acutus*, sharp)

aguise, *v.t.* (*Spens.*) deck, fashion.

ah, *int.* of joy, sorrow, pity etc.

aha, *int.* of triumph or mockery.

ahead, *adv.* and *a.* in front; forward.

aheap, *adv.* and *a.* in a heap, prostrate.
ahem, *int.* to attract notice. (*hem*)
a-hold, *adv.* (*Shake.*) close to the wind.
ahoy, *int.* used in hailing at sea.
ahull, *a.* (*naut.*) with sails furled and helm lashed on the lee side. (*hull*)
ai, *n.* S. American three-toed sloth. (imitation of its cry)
aiblins, *adv.* (*Scot.*) perhaps. (*able*)
aid, *v.t* help, assist.—*n.* help; helper, helpful thing. **aidance,** *n.* (*Shake.*) assistance. **aidant,** *a.* (*Shake.*). (L. *adjuvare*)
aide-de-camp, *n.* (*pl.* **aides-de-camp**) officer attending general to carry orders etc. **aide-mémoire,** *n.* document serving as aid to memory. (F.)
aigrette, *n.* egret; plume of feathers or gems, like heron's crest. (F.)
aiguille, *n.* sharp peak of rock. **aiguillette,** *n.* ornamental tag on military dress. (L. *acus,* needle)
aik, *Scot.* form of **oak.**
ail, *v.t.* and *i.* trouble, afflict; be ill. **ailment,** *n.* illness. (O.E. *eglan*)
aileron, *n.* control flap on aeroplane's wing-tip. (L. *ala,* wing)
aim, *v.t.* and *i.* point, direct; endeavour after.—*n.* direction; object, design. **aimless,** *a.* purposeless. (L. *aestimare,* reckon)
ain, *Scot.* form of **own.**
air, *n.* atmosphere; breeze; melody; manner; (*pl.*) affectation.—*v.t.* expose to air, heat; parade, display. **a.-bed,** *n.* inflated mattress; so **a.-cushion, a.-jacket, a.-pillow** etc., *nn.* **a.-brake,** *n.* brake worked by compressed air; so **a.-engine, a.-gun** etc., *nn.* **give person the a.,** dismiss him. **on the a.,** broadcasting by wireless. (Gk. *aēr*)
air-brick, *n.* brick perforated for ventilation.
aircraft, *n.* flying machine; flying machines collectively. **a. carrier,** ship acting as base for aircraft. **aircraftman, aircraftsman,** *n.* a rank in the Royal Air Force.
Airedale, *n.* large rough-coated terrier. (district in Yorkshire)
airless, *a.* stuffy; still, windless
air-line, *n.* service of aeroplanes; (*Amer.*) direct line. **air-liner,** *n.* large passenger aeroplane.
airman, *n.* aviator.
air-mast, *n.* mooring-mast for airships.
air-minded, *a.* interested in aviation.
airn, *n.* (*Scot.*) iron.
airplane, *n.* aeroplane.
air-pocket, *n.* patch of rarefied air causing aeroplane to drop abruptly.
air-port, *n.* fully equipped aerodrome, us. with custom-house etc.
air-pump, *n.* machine for pumping out air.
air-raid, *n.* attack by aircraft.
airship, *n.* dirigible balloon.
airt, *n.* (*Scot.*) direction, point of the compass. (Gael. *aird*)
air-tight, *a.* impermeable to air.
air-truck, *n.* aeroplane with truck body for freight.
airway, *n.* ventilating passage in mine; route used by aircraft.
airworthy, *a.* fit to fly.
airy *a.* of or in air; lofty; immaterial; light, sprightly.
aisle, *n.* wing of church; passage between pews; (*Amer.*) passage-way in train. (L. *ala,* wing)
ait, *n.* small island in river or lake.
aitch, *n.* letter H.
aitch-bone, *n.* rump-bone; cut of beef lying over it. (L. *natis,* rump. *n* lost by M.E. *a nage* becoming *an age*)
aith, *Scot.* form of **oath.**
aits, *Scot.* form of **oats.**
aiver, *n.* (*Scot.*) old horse.
aizle, *n.* (*Scot.*) live coal.
ajar, *adv.* partly open. (O.E. *cyrr,* turn)
ajee, agee, *adv.* (*Scot.*) aside, askew; ajar. (Scot. *gee,* move aside)
ajutage, see **adjutage.**
akimbo, *adv.* (of arms) with hands on hips and elbows turned outwards.
akin, *a.* of kin; related. (*kin*)
al-, form of **ad-** before *l.*
-al, *adj.suf.* of, of the nature of, as in mortal, **colossal.**—*n.suf.,* esp. of verbal action, as in **approval.** (L.)
alabaster, *n.* white semi-transparent stone.—*a.* of, like, alabaster. so **alabastrine,** *a.* (Gk. *alabastros*)
alack, *int.* (*arch.*) of sorrow.
alacrity, *n.* briskness, cheerful readiness. (L. *alacer,* brisk)
alalonga, *n.* long-finned tunny. (It.)
alar, *a.* of wings; winged; winglike. (L. *ala,* wing)
alarm, *n.* cry or notice of danger; sudden surprise with fear.—*v.t.* give notice of danger; excite fear in. **alarmist,** *n.* one who keeps prophesying danger, panic-monger. (It. *all' arme !* to arms!)
alarum, *n.* alarm signal; mechanical device for arousing from sleep, hence **a.-clock,** *n.* **aa. and excursions,** noise and bustle. (*alarm*)
alary, *a.* alar.
alas, *int.* of grief. (L. *lassus,* weary)
alb, *n.* priest's white vestment reaching to feet. (L. *albus,* white)
albacore, *n.* large kind of tunny. (Arab. *al,* the; *bukr,* young camel)
albatross, *n.* largest of sea-birds, allied to petrel.
albeit, *conj.* although.
albert, *n.* kind of watch - chain. (*Albert,* consort of Queen Victoria)
albescent, *a.* growing white. (*alb*)
albino, *n.* person or animal with white hair and skin and pink eyes. **albiness, albinism,** *nn.* (L. *albus,* white)
Albion, *n.* old name for Britain.
album, *n.* blank book for autographs, photographs, stamps etc. (L.=tablet)
albumen, *n.* viscid substance found nearly pure in white of egg. **albu-**

minoid, *a.* like albumen.—*n.* class of compounds forming main part of animal and vegetable tissues. **albuminous,** *a.* **albuminuria,** *n.* presence of albumen in the urine. (L.= white of egg)

alburnum, *n.* soft wood between bark and hard wood, sap-wood. (L.)

alcaid, *n.* N. African judge or governor. **alcalde,** *n.* Spanish magistrate. (Arab. *al,* the; *qadi,* judge)

alchemy, alchymy, *n.* medieval chemistry, esp. attempts to change baser metals into gold. **alchemic, alchemical,** *aa.* **alchemist,** *n.* **alchemize,** *v.t.* transmute. (Arab. *al,* the; *kimia,* from Gk. *chēmia,* transmutation—form 'alchymy' apparently due to confusion with Gk. *chumeia,* pouring)

alcohol, *n.* pure spirit of wine; liquor containing it. **alcoholic,** *a.* **alcoholism,** *n.* effects of alcohol on the system. **alcoholize,** *v.t.* convert into alcohol; treat with it. (Arab. *al,* the; *koh'l,* staining powder)

Alcoran, *n.* Koran, Mohammedan sacred book. (Arab. *al,* the; *qoran,* reading)

alcove, *n.* recess; arbour; summerhouse. (Arab. *al,* the; *qobbah,* vault)

aldehyde, *n.* volatile fluid of suffocating smell, obtained from alcohol. (L. *alcohol dehydrogenatum,* alcohol deprived of hydrogen)

alder, *n.* kind of tree. (O.E. *alor*)

alderman, *n.* town magistrate next below mayor. **aldermanic,** *a.* **aldermanry,** *n.* ward of alderman. **aldermanship,** *n.* (O.E. *aldor,* old man)

ale, *n,* malt liquor; merrymaking. **aleconner,** *n.* ale-taster. **alehouse,** *n.* where ale is sold. (O.E. *alu*)

aleatory, *a.* depending on dice or chance. (L. *alea,* die)

alee, *adv.* and *a.* on the lee, to leeward.

alegar, *n.* sour ale. (F. *aigre,* sour)

alembic, *n.* old-time chemists' distilling apparatus. (Arab. *al,* the; *ambig,* still)

alert, *a.* watchful; active.—*n.* alarm; air-raid warning, period it lasts. (It. *all' erta,* to the watch-tower)

Alexandrine, *a.* and *n.* (verse) of six iambic feet. (F.)

alexia, *n.* inability to read, due to mental illness. (Gk. *a-,* not; *legein,* speak, confused with L. *legere,* read)

alexin, *n.* disease-resisting proteid in blood serum. **alexipharmic,** *a.* and *n.* (acting as) antidote. (Gk. *alexein,* ward off; *pharmakon,* poison)

alfa, *n.* esparto grass. (Arab. *halfā*)

alfalfa, *n.* lucerne. (Sp.)

alfresco, *adv.* and *a.* in the open air; open-air. (It. *al fresco,* in the fresh)

alga, *n.* (*pl.* algae) sea-weed. **algal,** *a.* **algologist, algology,** *nn.* (L.)

algate, *adv.* (*Spens.*) wholly; in all ways.

algebra, *n.* method of calculating by symbols, generalized arithmetic. **algebraic, algebraical,** *aa.* **algebraist, algebrist,** *nn.* (Arab. *al-jebr,* the reuniting of broken parts)

algid, *a.* cold. (L. *algēre,* be cold)

algorism, *n.* arabic (decimal) numeration; arithmetic. (Arab. *al-Khowarazmi,* the man of Khiva, a 9th-century mathematician)

alguazil, *n.* Spanish warrant-officer.

alias, *adv.* at another time.—*n.* assumed name. (L.)

alibi, *adv.* elsewhere.—*n.* plea of absence (during crime etc.); (*sl.*) excuse for failure. (L.)

alien, *a.* of another; foreign; of a different nature; repugnant.—*n.* stranger, foreigner. **alienable,** *a.* that may be alienated. **alienate,** *v.t.* estrange; transfer to another's ownership. **alienation,** *n.* alienating; insanity. **alienism,** *n.* study of mental disease. **alienist,** *n.* mad-doctor. (L. *alienus,* of another)

alight, *v.i.* dismount; descend; come to earth. (O.E. *lihtan,* light)

alight, *a.* burning; lighted up.

align, aline, *v.t.* place, bring into line. —*v.i.* form in line. **alignment, alinement,** *n.* (L. *linea,* line)

alike, *a.* similar, like.—*adv.* in similar manner. (O.E. *gelic*)

aliment, *n.* food. **alimental,** *a.* **alimentary,** *a.* nourishing; providing maintenance. **alimentary canal,** passage along which food passes in body. **alimentation,** *n.* **alimony,** *n.* allowance made to wife legally separated from husband. (L. *alere,* feed)

aline, alinement, see **align, alignment.**

aliphatic, *a.* (*chem.*) of fat. (Gk. *aleiphar,* unguent)

aliquot, *a.* and *n.* (part) contained an exact number of times by the whole, as 3 is by 12. (L.= some)

alive, *adv.* and *a.* living; susceptible (to); active; swarming. (*live*)

alizarin, *n.* red colouring-matter of madder. (Arab. *al,* the; *'açarah,* extract)

alkahest, *n.* supposed universal solvent of alchemists. (sham Arab.)

alkali, *n.* (*pl.* **alkalis, alkalies**), caustic base, such as soda and ammonia, that neutralizes acids. **alkalescent,** *a.* slightly alkaline. **alkalify,** *v.t.* and *i.* make or become an alkali. **alkaline,** *a.* **alkaloid,** *n.* nitrogenous base with alkaline reaction. (Arab. *al,* the; *qaliy,* calcined ashes)

alkanet, *n.* red dye or plant that yields it. (Sp. *alcaneta*)

all, *a.* the whole; every one of.—*pron.* the whole number.—*n.* the whole world.—*adv.* wholly, entirely. **a. but,** nearly. **a. in,** (*Amer.*) exhausted; (of wrestling) unrestricted style. **a. out,** at top speed. **a-overish,** *a.* (*sl.*) generally indisposed. **a. there,** (*sl.*) not mentally wanting. **at a.,** in the least degree. (O.E.)

Allah, *n.* Mohammedan name of God.

allamanda, *n.* tropical American tree with large yellow flowers. (J. N. S. *Allamand*)
all-amort, *a.* (*Shake.*) utterly dejected. (F. *à la morte*, to the death)
allay, *v.t.* quiet, repress; alleviate.—*n.* (*Shake.*) alleviation. **allayment,** *n.* (*lay*)
allege, *v.t.* produce as argument, assert. **allegation,** *n.* (L. *allegare*)
allegiance, *n.* subject's duty to sovereign or state; loyalty. (*liege*)
allegory, *n.* narrative describing one thing under the image of another. **allegoric, allegorical,** *aa.* **allegorist,** *n.* **allegorize,** *v.t.* and *i.* turn into, use, allegory. (Gk. *allos*, other; *agoreuein*, speak)
allegro, a. and *n.* (*mus.*) gay, brisk (passage). *allegretto, a.* and *n.* somewhat brisk (passage). (It.)
allelomorph, *n.* either of a pair of contrasting characteristics, one or the other of which is found unmixed in descendants of a cross between parental forms respectively possessing them. (Gk. *allēlōn*, of one another; *morphē*, form)
alleluia, *n.* song of praise to God. (Heb. *halleluyah*, praise Jehovah)
alleviate, *v.t.* mitigate, lessen. **alleviation,** *n.* (L. *levis*, light)
allergy, *n.* abnormal sensitivity to some food or substance which is innocuous to most people; anaphylaxis. **allergic,** *a.* (Gk. *allos*, other+*energy*)
alley, *n.* narrow street; garden walk; enclosure for skittles etc.; (*Amer.*) back-lane. (F. *aller*, go)
alliaceous, *a.* of, like, onions or garlic. (L. *allium*, garlic)
alliance, *n.* union by marriage or treaty; confederation. (*ally*)
alligator, *n.* American reptile like crocodile. **a. pear,** avocado. (Sp. *el lagarto*, the lizard)
alliteration, *n.* repetition of the same consonantal sound in successive words, e.g. 'welling water's winsome word.' **alliterate,** *v.i.* **alliterative,** *a.* (L. *litera*, letter)
allocate, *v.t.* assign (share to). **allocation,** *n.* (L. *locus*, place)
allocution, *n.* formal address, esp. one by the pope. (L. *loqui*, speak)
allodium, *n.* freehold estate; land which is the absolute property of the owner. **allodial,** *a.* (L.L.)
allogamy, *n.* cross-fertilization. (Gk. *allos*, other; *gamos*, marriage)
allopathy, *n.* orthodox medical practice, treatment of disease by inducing a different tendency, opp. to homoeopathy. **allopathic,** *a.* **allopathist,** *n.* (Gk. *allos*, other; *pathos*, feeling)
allophylian, *a.* and *n.* (one) of another race; neither Aryan nor Semitic. (Gk. *allos*, other; *phulē*, tribe)
allot, *v.t.* distribute by lot; assign. **allotment,** *n.* allotting; share; small plot of land let out for cultivation.
allottee, *n.* one to whom allotment is made; plot-holder. (*lot*)
allottery, *n.* (*Shake.*) portion.
allotheism, *n.* worship of strange gods. (Gk. *allos*, other; *theos*, god)
allotropy, *n.* substance's property of existing in more than one form, e.g. carbon as coal and diamond. **allotropic,** *a.* **allotropism,** *n.* (Gk. *allos*, other; *tropos*, turn)
allow, *v.t.* permit; admit; grant.—*v.i.* provide. **allowance,** *n.* fixed sum allowed; rebate.—*v.t.* put upon allowance. **allowedly,** *adv.* admittedly. (L. *locare*, place, and *laudare*, praise)
alloy, *v.t.* mix with baser metal; mix, debase.—*n.* baser metal mixed with finer; mixture of metals; quality (of gold or silver). (L. *alligare*, bind)
allspice, *n.* pimenta, Jamaica pepper. (supposed to combine flavours of cinnamon, nutmeg, and cloves)
allude, *v.i.* refer indirectly (to), hint at. (L. *ludere*, play)
allure, *v.t.* tempt by lure, entice; fascinate.—*n.* charm, fascination. **alluring,** *a.* **allurement,** *n.* (*lure*)
allusion, *n.* indirect or incidental reference. **allusive,** *a.* (*allude*)
alluvion, *n.* wash of sea or river against shore; deposit left by this. **alluvium,** *n.* (*pl.* **alluvia, alluviums**) deposit of river or flood. **alluvial,** *a.* (L. *luere*, wash)
ally, *v.t.* join, esp. by marriage or treaty; connect.—*n.* allied person or state. (L. *alligare*, bind)
ally, *n.* playing-marble of alabaster or real marble. (*alabaster*)
allycholy, *n.* (*Shake.*) melancholy.
alma, almah, *n.* Egyptian dancing-girl. (Arab. *'almah*, learned)
almagest, *n.* great astronomical treatise of Ptolemy; other similar treatises. (Gk. *megistos*, greatest)
Alma Mater, one's university or school. (L.= fostering mother)
almanac, almanack, *n.* calendar for the year, with astronomical and other data. (L.L.)
almandine, *n.* violet-tinted garnet. (*Alabanda*, town in Caria)
almighty, *a.* omnipotent, all-powerful; (*sl.*) very great. **the A.,** God.
almira, *n.* (*Anglo-Ind.*) cupboard, chest of drawers etc. (Hind.)
almond, *n.* kernel of fruit allied to plum; tree that bears it; tonsil. (Gk. *amugdalē*)
almoner, *n.* distributor of alms. **almonry, almry,** *n.* place where alms are distributed. (*alms*)
almost, *adv.* very nearly, all but.
alms, *n.* voluntary relief given to the poor. **almshouse,** *n.* house endowed by charity for lodging the poor. (Gk. *eleēmosunē*, pity)
aloe, *n.* plant with erect spikes of flowers and bitter juice; (*pl.*) purgative drug made from this juice.

aloetic, *a.* and *n.* (medicine) containing aloes. (Gk. *aloē*)
aloft, *adv.* on high, overhead.
alogical, *a.* non-logical.
alone, *a.* solitary, by oneself.—*adv.* only, exclusively. (*all*; *one*)
along, *prep.* within the length of.—*adv.* lengthwise, throughout; in company; forward. **alongside,** *adv.* and *prep.* beside; side by side. (O.E. *andlang*)
aloof, *adv.* and *a.* apart, withdrawn; (*naut.*) to windward. **aloofness,** *n.* lack of sympathy. (*luff*)
alopecia, *n.* baldness; scurf. (Gk. *alōpēkia*, fox-mange)
aloud, *adv.* loudly; audibly.
alow, *adv.* to, in, lower part; below.
alp, *n.* mountain-peak.
alpaca, *n.* Peruvian llama; its wool, or cloth made from it. (Sp.)
alpeen, *n.* (*Anglo-Ir.*) cudgel. (Ir. *ailpin*)
alpenstock, *n.* climber's iron-shod staff. (G. = stick of the Alps)
alpha, *n.* Greek letter A. **A. and Omega,** beginning and end. **a. rays,** streams of **a. particles,** or particles of helium, given off by radium. (Gk.)
alphabet, *n.* letters used in a language; first principles. **alphabetic,** *a.* **alphabetical,** *a.* of, in the order of, the alphabet. (Gk. *alpha*, *beta*, first two letters)
Alpine, *a.* of the Alps; very high.—*n.* plant that grows on high ground. **Alpinist,** *n.* Alpine climber. (*Alps*)
already, *adv.* by this time; previously. (*all*; *ready*)
alright, a frequent spelling of **all right.**
Alsatia, *n.* haunt or sanctuary of criminals. (nickname of once notorious Whitefriars district in London)
Alsatian, *n.* large German wolf-hound. (*Alsatia*, Alsace)
also, *adv.* besides, too. (*all*; *so*)
alt, *n.* (*mus.*) high tone. **in a.,** in octave above treble stave beginning with G. (L. *altus*, high)
altar, *n.* block of stone etc. for offering sacrifice; communion table. **a.-piece,** *n.* painting or sculpture behind altar. (L. *altare*)
altazimuth, *n.* instrument for determining altitude and azimuth of stars.
alter, *v.t.* and *i.* change. **alterable,** *a.* **alteration,** *n.* **alterative,** *a.* tending to alter.—*n.* medicine that alters nutritive processes. (L. = other)
altercate, *v.i.* dispute, wrangle. **altercation,** *n.* controversy. (L.)
alter ego, other self, close friend. (L. = other I)
alternate, *a.* by turns, one after the other.—*v.t.* and *i.* arrange, occur, by turns. **alternation,** *n.* **alternative,** *a.* offering choice of two things.—*n.* choice of two or more things: one of such things. **alternator,** *n.* dynamo for producing **alternating current,** i.e. current which flows in alternate directions in a circuit. (L. *alter*, other)
although, *conj.* though.
altimeter, *n.* instrument for showing or measuring height above sea-level.
altitude, *n.* height: height above sea-level; (us. *pl.*) high place. (L. *altus*, high)
alto, *a.* (*mus.*) higher than tenor but lower than treble.—*n.* alto voice, part, or singer. (It. = high)
alto-relievo, *n.* high relief, figures projecting half or more from background. (It. *alto-rilievo*)
altogether, *adv.* entirely, without exception; on the whole. **the a.,** (*colloq.*) the nude.
altruism, *n.* the principle of acting for the interests of others, opp. to egoism. **altruist,** *n.* **altruistic,** *a.* (It. *altrui*, of others)
alum, *n.* a mineral salt, double sulphate of aluminium and potassium. **alumina,** *n.* an earth, oxide of aluminium. **aluminous,** *a.* of, containing, alum or alumina. **aluminium,** *n.* light white unrustable metal. (L. *alumen*)
alumnus, *n.* (*pl.* **alumni**; *fem.* **alumna.** *pl.* **alumnae**) graduate, pupil, of school or university. (L. = foster-son)
alveolus, *n.* tooth-socket; small cavity, cell of honeycomb. **alveolar,** *a.* of tooth-sockets. **alveolate,** *a.* honeycombed, pitted. (L.)
always, alway, *adv.* at all times; for ever. (*all*; *way*)
amadavat, avadavat, *n.* small Indian song-bird. (native name)
amadou, *n.* German tinder, made from fungi. (F.)
amah, *n.* wet-nurse; nurse. (Port. *ama*)
amain, *adv.* vehemently; in haste. (O.E. *mægn*, force)
amalgam, *n.* alloy of mercury; plastic mixture. (F. *amalgame*)
amalgamate, *v.t.* and *i.* mix; unite, combine; (of metal) mix mercury with. **amalgamation,** *n.* mixing; merger, uniting of two or more business concerns into one. (*amalgam*)
amanuensis, *n.* one who writes from dictation; secretary. (L.)
amaracus, *n.* dittany. (Gk. *amarakos*)
amaranth, *n.* legendary unfading flower; love-lies-bleeding; purple colour. **amaranthine,** *a.* (Gk. *a-*, not; *marainein*, fade)
amaryllis, *n.* kinds of bulbous flowers, incl. narcissus. (Gk. name)
amass, *v.t.* heap together, accumulate. (*mass*)
amate, *v.t.* (*Spens.*) daunt, terrify. (O.F. *amater*)
amateur, *n.* one who follows study or art for love and not for gain, non-professional sportsman. **amateurish,**

a. inexpert, untrained. **amateurism,** *n.* (L. *amare,* love)
amative, *a.* amorous. **amatory,** *a.* of love or lovers. (L. *amare,* love)
amatol, *n.* a high explosive. (*ammonia*)
amaurosis, *n.* blindness from disease of optic nerve. **amaurotic,** *a.* (Gk. *amauros,* dark)
amaze, *v.t.* overwhelm with wonder.—*n.* (*poet.*) astonishment, perplexity. **amazing,** *a.* **amazement,** *n.* (*maze*)
Amazon, *n.* female warrior of legend; masculine woman. **Amazonian,** *a.* (Gk.)
amban, *n.* Chinese resident official in Tibet. (Manchu)
ambassador, *n.* (*fem.* **ambassadress**) diplomatic minister representing one state in another, either permanently or on special mission. **ambassadorial,** *a.* (Celt. *ambactus,* servant)
ambatch, *n.* an African shrub, pith-tree. (native)
amber, *n.* yellow translucent fossil resin.—*a.* of amber; brownish-yellow. **amberite,** *n.* a smokeless explosive. **ambroid,** *n.* pressed amber. (Arab. *'anbar,* ambergris)
ambergris, *n.* wax-like secretion of sperm-whale, used in perfumery. (F. *ambre gris,* grey amber)
ambidexter, *a.* and *n.* (person) using both hands equally well; double-dealer. **ambidexterity,** *n.* **ambidextrous,** *a.* ambidexter. (L. *ambo,* both; *dexter,* right-handed)
ambient, *a.* surrounding. (*ambit*)
ambiguous, *a.* of double or doubtful meaning; obscure. **ambiguity,** *n.* (L. *ambigere,* waver)
ambit, *n.* compass; sphere of action. (L. *ambire,* go round)
ambition, *n.* desire for superiority or distinction; aspiration, aim. **ambitious,** *a.* full of ambition, aspiring. (*ambit,* with idea of canvassing)
ambivalent, *a.* (*psycho-anal.*) having either or both of two contrary values or qualities. **ambivalency,** *n.* (L. *ambo,* both; *valēre,* be strong)
amble, *v.i.* (of horse) move by lifting two feet on one side together; move at easy pace.—*n.* horse's pace between walk and trot; easy pace. (L. *ambulare,* walk)
amblyopia, *n.* defective sight. **amblyopic,** *a.* (Gk. *amblus,* dull; *ōps,* eye)
ambo, *n.* (*pl.* **ambos, ambones**) pulpit, reading-desk. (Gk. *ambōn,* rising)
amboyna, *n.* variegated wood. (place of origin)
ambrosia, *n.* food of the gods; anything delightful to taste or smell. **ambrosial,** *a.* divine; fragrant; delicious. (Gk. *a-,* not; *brotos,* mortal)
ambry, *n.* recess in church wall for sacred vessels; cupboard; chest; pantry. (L. *armarium,* chest)
ambs-ace, ames-ace, *n.* two ones, lowest throw at dice; bad luck. (O.F.)
ambulance, *n.* conveyance for sick or wounded; mobile field hospital. **ambulant,** *a.* walking, moving about. **ambulatory,** *a.* of walking; movable. —*n.* arcade, cloister. (L. *ambulare,* walk)
ambury, see **anbury.**
ambuscade, *n.* ambush.—*v.t.* and *i.* lie, conceal, in ambush. (*ambush*)
ambush, *n.* hiding for surprise attack; hidden force.—*v.t.* and *i.* attack from hiding, waylay; lie in wait (for). (*in*; *bush*)
âme damnée, tool, blindly, devoted adherent. (F.= damned soul)
ameer, amir, *n.* prince, ruler in Mohammedan countries. (Arab.)
ameliorate, *v.t.* and *i.* improve, make or grow better. **amelioration,** *n.* (L. *melior,* better)
amen, *int.* so let it be. **say a. to,** assent to. (Heb.= certainty)
amenable, *a.* tractable; liable, responsible. **amenability,** *n.* (L. *minari,* threaten)
amend, *v.t.* and *i.* correct; improve; reform. **amendment,** *n.* amending; proposed change in bill, motion etc. **amends,** *n.* reparation, compensation. (L. *menda,* fault)
amende honorable, public apology. (F.)
amenity, *n.* pleasantness; (*pl.*) pleasant features. (L. *amoenus,* lovely)
ament, amentum, *n.* catkin. **amentaceous,** *a.* (L. *amentum,* thong)
amentia, *n.* mental imbecility. (L.)
amerce, *v.t.* fine; punish. **amerciable,** *a.* **amercement,** *n.* penalty at court's discretion. (*mercy*)
American, *a.* and *n.* (native) of America or the United States. **A. organ,** kind of harmonium. **Americanism,** *n.* U.S. idiom or word; sympathy with American institutions. **Americanize,** *v.t.* and *i.* make, become, American.
americani, *n.* kind of cotton cloth. (Swahili)
Amerind, Amerindian, *nn.* and *aa.* American Indian. (contr.)
ames-ace, see **ambs-ace.**
amethyst, *n.* violet-blue precious stone. **amethystine,** *a.* (Gk. *a-,* not; *methu,* wine, because it was supposed to prevent drunkenness)
amiable, *a.* lovable; friendly. **amiability,** *n.* (L. *amare,* love)
amiantus, amianthus, *n.* fine fibrous asbestos. (Gk. *amiantos,* stainless, because cleansed by fire)
amic, *a.* of ammonia. (*ammonia*)
amicable, *a.* friendly. **amicability,** *n.* (L. *amicus,* friend)
amice, *n.* pilgrim's cloak; strip of white linen worn by R.C. priest when serving mass; cap, hood, or badge of religious orders. (L. *amictus,* dress, and O.F. *aumusse,* cap)
amicus curiae, disinterested adviser. (L.= friend of the court)
amid, amidst, *prepp.* in the middle of;

among. **amidships,** *adv.* in middle of the ship. (*mid*)

amildar, *n.* native revenue-collector, factor, in India. (Arab. *'amal,* work. Pers. *dar,* holder)

amir, see **ameer.**

amiss, *a.* wrong.—*adv.* in faulty manner; badly. **amissing,** *a.* wanting, lost.

amity, *n.* friendship, goodwill. (L. *amicus,* friend)

ammeter, *n.* instrument for measuring force of electric currents. (*ampere*)

ammonal, *n.* a high explosive. (*ammonia*)

ammonia, *n.* a pungent volatile alkali. **ammoniac,** *a.*—*n.* (also **gum ammoniac**) a gum resin. **sal ammoniac,** ammonium chloride. **ammoniated,** *a.* combined with ammonia. **ammonium,** *n.* hypothetical base of ammonia. (temple of Jupiter *Ammon*)

ammonite, *n.* whorled fossil shell. (Jupiter *Ammon's* horned statues)

ammunition, *n.* military projectiles; (formerly) military stores of all kinds, hence *a.* of regulation type, as in **a. boots** etc. (*munition*)

amnesia, *n.* loss of memory. (Gk.)

amnesty, *n.* general pardon of political offenders.—*v.t.* grant amnesty to. (Gk. *amnēstos,* not remembered)

amnion, *n.* (*pl.* **amnia**) innermost membrane enclosing foetus in womb. (Gk.)

amoeba, *n.* (*pl.* **amoebae, amoebas**) microscopic protozoon continually changing shape, simplest form of animal life. **amoeboid,** *a.* (Gk. *amoibē,* change)

amoebean, *a.* alternately answering. (Gk. *amoibē,* change)

amok, same as **amuck.**

among, amongst, *prep.* in the midst of; of the number of; between. (O.E. *on,* in; *gemang,* assemblage)

Amontillado, *n.* a pale dry sherry, (Sp.)

amoral, *a.* not concerned with morals, non-moral. **amoralism, amoralist, amorality,** *nn.*

amorce, *n.* priming-charge; cap for toy pistol. (F. *mordre,* bite)

amoret, *n.* (*obs.*) sweetheart; love-poem. **amorist,** *n.* amateur in love, philanderer. (L. *amor,* love)

amorous, *a.* of love; in love; inclined to love. (L. *amor,* love)

amorphous, *a.* shapeless; uncrystallized. **amorphism,** *n.* (Gk. *a-,* not; *morphē,* form)

amortize, *v.t.* pay off (debt) through a sinking fund. **amortization,** *n.* (L. *ad mortem,* to death)

amount, *v.i.* come, be equivalent (to). —*n.* whole sum; quantity. (*mount*)

amour, *n.* love-affair; intrigue. **amourette,** *n.* petty love-affair. (F.)

amour-propre, *n.* self-love, vanity. (F.)

ampelopsis, *n.* kinds of vine-creeper, incl. Virginia creeper. (Gk.)

ampere, *n.* unit of electric current. (*Ampère,* physicist)

ampersand, *n.* (also **ampassy, ampassy-and, ampussyand** etc.) the sign & (*and per se,* and by itself)

amphi-, *pref.* of both kinds; on both sides; around. (Gk.)

Amphibia, *n.pl.* class of vertebrates between reptiles and fishes, such as frogs. **amphibian,** *n.* and *a.* (animal) capable of living both on land and in water; (aeroplane) that can alight on either land or water. **amphibious,** *a.* **amphibiology,** *n.* (Gk. *bios,* life)

amphibology, *n.* ambiguous phrase, quibble. (Gk. *ballein,* throw)

amphibrach, *n.* three-syllabled foot, short - long - short. (Gk. *brachus,* short)

amphigamous, *a.* without distinct sexual organs. (Gk. *gamos,* marriage)

amphimacer, *n.* three-syllabled foot, long-short-long. (Gk. *makros,* long)

amphimixis, *n.* mingling of male and female germs in sexual reproduction.

amphioxus, *n.* lancelet, a fish. (Gk. *oxus,* sharp)

amphipod, *n.* kinds of crustacean, incl. sand-hopper. (Gk. *pous,* foot)

amphiprostyle, *a.* with portico at both ends.

amphisbaena, *n.* fabled serpent with head at each end; kinds of lizard. (Gk. *bainein,* go)

amphitheatre, *n.* round building with rows of seats rising from a central arena; lower gallery of theatre. (*theatre*)

amphora, *n.* ancient two-handled vessel. **amphoric,** *a.* (Gk. *amphi,* on both sides; *pherein,* bear)

ample, *a.* large, spacious; quite sufficient. **amplify,** *v.t.* and *i.* add to, enlarge; expatiate. **amplification,** *n.* **amplifier,** *n.* instrument for increasing volume of sound in radio receiver. **amplitude,** *n.* largeness, abundance. (L. *amplus*)

ampulla, *n.* Roman two-handled flask; sacred vessel. **ampullaceous,** *a.* **ampoule,** *n.* small glass container for hypodermic dose. (L.)

amputate, *v.t.* cut off (limb etc.). **amputation,** *n.* (L. *putare,* prune)

amuck, *adv.* **run a.,** rush about in murderous frenzy. (Malay *amoq*)

amulet, *n.* thing carried or worn as charm against evil. (L. *amuletum*)

amuse, *v.t.* entertain; cause laughter. **amusement,** *n.* pastime; entertainment. (O.F. *amuser,* cause to muse)

amygdalic, *a.* of almonds. **amygdaloid,** *a.* almond-shaped. (Gk. *amugdalē,* almond)

amyl, *n.* radical of various alcohols. **a. nitrite,** drug inhaled to relieve spasms. **amylic,** *a.* **amylaceous,** *a.* of starch, starchy. **amyloid,** *a.* and *n.* starchy (food). **amylopsin,** *n.* pancreatic ferment converting starch into sugar. (Gk. *amulon,* starch)

an, *conj.* (*arch.*) if. (*and*)
an, form of **a** used before vowel.
an-, form of **ad-** before *n*.
-an, -ain, -ane, *adj.suf.* of, of the nature of, as in **suburban, certain, humane.** (L.)
ana, *n.* (*pl.* **anas, ana**) collection of person's sayings or anecdotes about him. **-ana**, *n.suf.* sayings of, publications about, e.g. **Shakespeariana.** (L.)
ana-, *pref.* up, anew, again. (Gk.)
anabaptist, *n.* one who believes in the re-baptizing of adults on their profession of faith. **anabaptism**, *n.*
anabas, *n.* Indian perch, fish that climbs trees. (Gk. *bainein*, go)
anabasis, *n.* inland march, esp. that of Xenophon. **anabatic**, *a.* (of wind) caused by upward current of air. (Gk.)
anabiosis, *n.* coming to life again, resuscitation. (Gk. *bios*, life)
anabolism, *n.* constructive metabolism. (Gk. *anabolē*, rising up)
anabranch, *n.* stream that leaves river and re-enters it lower down.
anachronism, *n.* assigning of thing to wrong period; out-of-date thing. **anachronistic**, *a.* (Gk. *chronos*, time)
anaclastic, *a.* of refraction. (Gk. *klaein*, bend)
anacoluthon, *n.* break in grammatical sequence. (Gk. *a-*, not; *akolouthos*, following)
anaconda, *n.* huge python allied to boa-constrictor.
Anacreontic, *a.* and *n.* convivial, amatory (poem) in manner of Anacreon.
anacrusis, *n.* unstressed syllable at beginning of verse. (Gk. *anakrousis*)
anadiplosis, *n.* repetition of last word of line or clause at beginning of next. (Gk. = doubling back)
anadromous, *a.* (of fish) ascending rivers to spawn. (Gk. *dromos*, run)
anaemia, *n.* bloodlessness; paleness. **anaemic**, *a.* (Gk. *a-*, not; *haima*, blood)
anaerobe, *n.* microbe that can live without air. **anaerobian, anaerobic, anaerobious**, *aa.* **anaerobiosis**, *n.* life devoid of oxygen. (*a-*; *aerobe*)
anaesthesia, *n.* insensibility. **anaesthetic**, *a.* and *n.* (substance) that causes insensibility. **anaesthetize**, *v.t.* render insensible. **anaesthetist**, *n.* (Gk. *a-*, not; *aisthanesthai*, perceive)
anaglyph, *n.* ornament carved in low relief. (Gk. *gluphein*, carve)
anagnorisis, *n.* *dénouement* in a drama. (Gk. = recognition)
anagógē, anagogy, *n.* mystical interpretation, hidden sense. **anagogic**, *a.* (Gk. *anagein*, lead up)
anagram, *n.* word or sentence made by transposing the letters of another, e.g. 'astronomer' = 'moonstarer.' **anagrammatic**, *a.* **anagrammatist**, *n.* (Gk. *graphein*, write)
anal, *a.* of, near, the anus.
analects, analecta, *n.pl.* literary extracts. (Gk. *legein*, gather)
analeptic, *a.* and *n.* restorative. (Gk. *lambanein*, take)
analgesia, *n.* absence of pain. **analgesic, analgetic**, *aa.* removing pain.—*nn.* pain-removing drug, anodyne. (Gk. *a-*, not; *algein*, feel pain)
analogous, *a.* similar, parallel. **analogue**, *n.* analogous word or thing.
analogy, *n.* parallelism, likeness in certain respects; construction of words by imitation; (*logic*) reasoning from parallel cases; (*math.*) proportion. **analogic, analogical**, *aa.* **analogism**, *n.* (esp.) reasoning from cause to effect. **analogist**, *n.* **analogize**, *v.t.* and *i.* explain by, show, analogy. (Gk. *analogia*)
analyse, *v.t.* resolve into simple elements; examine minutely. **analysis**, *n.* analysing; tracing underlying principles. **analyst**, *n.* **analytic**, *a.* of analysis. **analytical**, *a.* using analysis: (of language) using separate words, not inflexions. (Gk. *luein*, loose)
anamnesis, *n.* recollection. (Gk.)
anamorphosis, *n.* image appearing distorted from one viewpoint, regular from another; (*bot.*) abnormal development. (Gk. *morphē*, form)
ananas, anana, *n.* pine-apple.
anandrous, *a.* without stamens. (Gk. *a-*, not; *anēr*, man)
anapaest, *n.* three-syllabled foot, short-short-long. (Gk. *anapaistos*)
anaphora, *n.* repetition of same word in successive clauses. (Gk.)
anaphylaxis, *n.* excessive sensitivity to a substance or germ due to prior inoculation with it, allergy. (Gk. *phulassein*, guard)
anarchy, *n.* absence of government; disorder. **anarchic, anarchical**, *aa.* lawless. **anarchist**, *n.* one who promotes anarchy. (Gk. *a-*, not; *archē*, rule)
anasarca, *n.* dropsy. (Gk. *sarx*, flesh)
anastatic, *a.* (*print.*) with letters in relief. (Gk. *anastatos*, raised up)
anastigmat, *n.* lens corrected for astigmatism. **anastigmatic**, *a.*
anastomosis, *n.* cross-connection of arteries, rivers etc. (Gk. *stoma*, mouth)
anathema, *n.* curse, ban of the Church; accursed thing. **anathematize**, *v.t.* curse. (Gk.)
anatine, *a.* and *n.* (bird) of duck family. (L. *anas*, duck)
anatomy, *n.* science of body's structure; dissection; skeleton; analysis. **anatomical**, *a.* **anatomize**, *v.t.* dissect; analyse. **anatomist**, *n.* (Gk. *temnein*, cut)
anatta, *n.* orange-red dye.
anbury, ambury, *n.* disease of turnips; tumour on horses etc.
ance, *Scot.* form of **once.**
-ance, *n.suf.* denoting quality or action, as in **arrogance, penance.**
ancestor, *n.* (*fem.* **ancestress**) one from

whom a person is descended, forefather. **ancestral,** *a.* **ancestry,** *n.* lineage, ancient descent. (L. *ante,* before; *cedere,* go)

anchithere, *n.* fossil ancestor of the horse. (Gk. *angchi,* near; *thērion,* wild beast)

anchor, *n.* heavy hooked instrument to secure ship to bottom; (*fig.*) what gives safety.—*v.t.* fix with anchor.—*v.i.* cast anchor; stop. **anchorage,** *n.* place, or dues paid, for anchoring. (Gk. *angkura*)

anchor, (*Shake.*) same as **anchorite.**

anchoret, anchorite, *n.* (*fem.* **anchoress, ancress, anchoritess**) hermit, recluse. (Gk. *ana-,* apart; *chōrein,* go)

anchovy, *n.* small fish like herring. **a. pear,** W. Indian fruit like mango.

anchylosis, ankylosis, *n.* stiffening of joint by fibrous bands or union of bones. (Gk. *angkulos,* crooked)

ancien régime, the old order, esp. France before Revolution. (F.)

ancient, *a.* of long ago; old.—*n.pl.* nations of antiquity. **A. of Days,** God. **ancientry,** *n.* (L. *ante,* before)

ancient, *n.* (*arch.*) ensign. (corrupt.)

ancillary, *a.* subservient, auxiliary. (L. *ancilla,* maid-servant)

ancle, see **ankle.**

ancress, see **anchoret.**

and, *conj.* connecting words etc. (O.E.)

andante, *a.* and *n.* (*mus.*) moderately slow (passage). *andantino,* *a.* and *n.* rather quicker than *andante.* (It.)

Anderson shelter, small air-raid shelter of trench with iron roofing covered with earth. (Sir J. *Anderson*)

andiron, *n.* iron supporting logs or on which spit turns. (O.F. *andier*)

androgynous, *a.* partaking of both sexes, hermaphrodite. **androgyny,** *n.* (Gk. *anēr,* man; *gunē,* woman)

ane, *a.* (*Scot.*) one; **a.** (O.E. *án*)

anecdote, *n.* account of incident, short story. **anecdotal,** *a.* **anecdotist,** *n.* **anecdotage,** *n.* anecdotes; garrulous old age. (Gk. *anekdotos,* unpublished)

anele, aneal, *v.t.* anoint; give extreme unction to. (O.E. *ele,* oil)

anemograph, *n.* instrument recording force of wind. **anemometer,** *n.* wind-gauge. **anemophilous,** *a.* wind-fertilized. (Gk. *anemos,* wind)

anemone, *n.* wind-flower. **sea a.,** plant-like sea animal.

anent, *prep.* (*arch.*) concerning.

aneroid, *a.* and *n.* (barometer) measuring air-pressure by vacuum box, not column of liquid. (Gk. *a-,* not; *nēros,* wet)

aneurysm, aneurism, *n.* dilatation of artery. (Gk. *eurus,* wide)

anew, *adv.* in a new way; again.

anfractuous, *a.* winding, intricate. **anfractuosity,** *n.* (L. *anfractus,* bending)

angareb, *n.* Arabian stretcher or light bedstead. (native)

angary, angaria, *n.* belligerent's right to seize and use neutral property, for which it pays indemnity. (Gk. *anggaros,* courier)

angekok, *n.* Eskimo medicine-man. (Eskimo)

angel, *n.* divine messenger, spirit; lovely or innocent being; old English coin=10*s.* **a.-fish,** *n.* kind of shark. **angelic, angelical,** *aa.* **angelolatry,** *n.* angel-worship. (Gk. *anggelos,* messenger)

angelica, *n.* aromatic plant.

angelus, *n.* devotional service in R.C. Church, commemorating the Incarnation, and said at morning, noon, and sunset; (also **a.-bell**) bell rung for this. (opening word)

anger, *n.* rage, violent displeasure.—*v.t.* enrage. (O.N. *angr,* trouble)

angina, *n.* quinsy. **a. pectoris,** painful spasm due to heart disease. (L.)

angle, *n.* corner; meeting-point, inclination, of two lines; point of view. (L. *angulus*)

angle, *n.* fish-hook; fishing-rod with line and hook.—*v.i.* fish with angle. **angler,** *n.* one who angles; kind of sea-fish. (O.E. *angel,* hook)

Anglic, *n.* form of English with simplified spelling proposed as universal language. **Anglican,** *a.* and *n.* (member) of Church of England, esp. High Church. *anglicè,* *adv.* in English. **anglicism,** *n.* English idiom. **anglicize,** *v.t.* make English. (L. *Angli,* English)

Anglo-, from L. *Anglus,* English, used in **Anglo-Catholic,** *n.* Anglican who repudiates the term 'Protestant'; **Anglo-Indian,** *n.* Englishman born or living in India; **Anglomania, Anglophobia,** *nn.* excessive admiration, excessive fear, of English institutions; **Anglo-Saxon,** *n.* and *a.* English (person, language) before Norman Conquest, English-speaking (person). hence **Anglo-Saxondom,** *n.*

angola, *n.* mohair, cloth made from wool of Angora goat. (*angora*)

angora, *n.* angola. **a. goat, cat, rabbit,** long-haired kinds. (town)

angostura, angustura, *n.* bark used as febrifuge and tonic. (town)

angry, *a.* enraged; inflamed. (*anger*)

ångström, *n.* a unit in spectroscopy, one hundred-millionth of a centimetre. (name of Swedish physicist)

anguine, *a.* snake-like. (L. *anguis,* snake)

anguish, *n.* great pain of body or mind. (L. *angustia,* tightness)

angular, *a.* having angles; sharp-cornered; bony; unaccommodating. **angularity,** *n.* (*angle*)

angusti-, from L. *angustus,* narrow, used in **angustifoliate,** *a.* narrow-leaved, etc.

anhydrous, *a.* without water. (Gk. *a-,* not; *hudōr,* water)

ani, *n.* tropical American bird of cuckoo family. (Brazilian)

aniconic, *a.* (of idols) not of human or animal form. (Gk. *eikon*, image)
anicut, annicut, *n.* dam for irrigation in India. (Tamil)
anigh, *adv.* and *prep.* near.
anil, *n.* indigo shrub or dye. (Arab. *al*, the; *nil*, indigo)
anile, *a.* old-womanish; imbecile. **anility,** *n.* dotage. (L. *anus*, old woman)
aniline, *n.* product of indigo or coal-tar, basis of many dyes. (*anil*)
animadvert, *v.i.* pass censure, criticize. **animadversion,** *n.* (L. *animus*, mind; *vertere*, turn)
animal, *n.* being with sentient life and motion; beast.—*a.* of animals; sensual. **a. spirits,** exuberance. **animalcule,** *n.* (*pl.* **animalcules, animalcula**) microscopic animal. **animalism,** *n.* animal activity; sensuality. **animality,** *n.* animal nature. **animalize,** *v.t.* make animal, brutify. (L.)
animate, *v.t.* give life to; enliven; inspire.—*a.* living. **animated,** *a.* lively, full of spirit. **animation,** *n.* life; vigour. **animatograph,** *n.* old name for cinematograph. (L. *anima*, life)
animé, *n.* a W. Indian resin. (F.)
animism, *n.* primitive religion, belief that natural effects are due to spirits, and that inanimate objects have spirits. **animist,** *n.* **animistic,** *a.* (L. *anima*, soul)
animus, *n.* actuating spirit; bitter feeling (against). **animosity,** *n.* hatred; enmity. (L.=mind)
anion, *n.* electro-negative ion.
anise, *n.* plant with aromatic seeds. **aniseed,** *n.* its seed, used as carminative; liqueur made from it, also called **anisette.** (Gk. *anison*)
anker, *n.* liquid measure used in N. Europe, formerly in England, = 8⅓ gallons. (Du.)
ankh, *n.* Egyptian key-like cross, symbol of life. (Egyptian=life)
ankle, ancle, *n.* joint between foot and leg. **anklet,** *n.* ankle-ornament. (O.E. *ancléow*)
ankus, *n.* elephant-goad. (Hind.)
ankylosis, see **anchylosis.**
anna, *n.* Indian coin worth one-sixteenth part of rupee. (Hind. *ana*)
annals, *n.pl.* historical records. **annalist,** *n.* writer of annals. **annates,** *n.pl.* first year's revenue of R.C. living, paid to the pope. (L. *annus*, year)
anneal, *v.t.* temper. (O.E. *ǽlan*, bake)
annelid, *n.* red-blooded worm, such as earth-worm. (L. *anulus*, ring)
annex, *v.t.* append, attach; take possession of. **annexation,** *n.* **annexe,** *n.* addition to document; supplementary building. **annexion, annexment,** *nn.* (*Shake.*) adjunct. (L. *nectere*, bind)
annicut, see **anicut.**
annihilate, *v.t.* wipe out, destroy utterly. **annihilation,** *n.* (L. *nihil*, nothing)
anniversary, *n.* yearly recurrence of a date; celebration of this. (L. *annus*, year; *vertere*, turn)
Anno Domini, (*abbr.* A.D.) in the year of our Lord, dating from the birth of Christ; (*colloq.*) advancing age. (L.)
annotate, *v.t.* and *i.* add notes to; make notes, comment. **annotation, annotator,** *nn.* (L. *nota*, mark)
announce, *v.t.* proclaim; make known. **announcement,** *n.* **announcer,** *n.* (esp.) broadcasting official who announces items of programme. (L. *nuntius*, messenger)
annoy, *v.t.* trouble, vex.—*n.* (*arch.*) annoyance. **annoyance,** *n.* vexation or its cause. (L. *in odio*, hateful)
annual, *a.* yearly; of a year.—*n.* yearly publication; plant that lives a year. **annuity,** *n.* investment securing yearly payments for a given period (e.g. term of investor's life), the capital sum not being returnable; yearly grant. **annuitant,** *n.* holder of an annuity. (L. *annus*, year)
annul, *v.t.* make null, cancel; abolish. **annulment,** *n.* (L. *nullus*, none)
annular, *a.* ring-like. **annulated,** *a.* furnished, marked, with rings. **annulet,** *n.* small ring; (*arch.*) fillet. (L. *anulus*, ring)
annunciate, *v.t.* proclaim. **annunciation,** *n.* announcement, esp. of the Incarnation, made to the Virgin Mary; festival of this, Lady Day, 25 March. **annunciator,** *n.* indicator showing in which room bell has been rung etc. (*announce*)
anoa, *n.* small wild ox of Celebes.
anode, *n.* (*electr.*) positive pole. (Gk. *anodos*, way up)
anodyne, *n.* pain-relieving drug.—*a.* soothing. (Gk. *a-*, not; *odunē*, pain)
anoesis, *n.* consciousness with sensation but without thought. (Gk. *a-*, not; *noein*, perceive)
anoint, *v.t.* smear; pour oil on, consecrate with oil. (L. *in*, upon; *ungere*, anoint)
anomalure, *n.* African squirrel with scaly tail. (Gk. *anomalos*, abnormal; *oura*, tail)
anomaly, *n.* irregularity, deviation from rule; (*astron.*) angular distance of planet from its last perihelion, hence **anomalistic,** *a.*, **anomalistic year,** from perihelion to perihelion. **anomalous,** *a.* irregular, abnormal. (Gk. *a-*, not; *homalos*, even)
anon, *adv.* (*arch.*) soon; at once. (O.E. *on*, in; *an*, one)
anonymous, *a.* without name; of unknown name or authorship. **anonymity,** *n.* **anonym,** *n.* unnamed person; assumed name. (Gk. *a-*, not; *onoma*, name)
anópheles, *n.* malarial mosquito. (Gk. *a-*, not; *ōphelein*, benefit)
another, *a.* and *pron.* additional (one); not the same (one). (*other*)

anourous, *a.* tailless. (Gk. *a-*, not; *oura*, tail)
Anschluss, *n.* union of Germany with Austria. (G.=annexation)
anserine, *a.* of or like a goose; silly. (L. *anser*, goose)
answer, *v.t.* and *i.* reply (to); be responsible (for); correspond (to); satisfy; succeed.—*n.* reply; solution. **answerable,** *a.* able to be answered; responsible. (O.E. *and*, against; *swerian*, swear)
ant, *n.* emmet, small insect noted for its industry. **white a.,** termite, destructive insect. **a.-bear,** *n.* aardvark. **a.-eater,** *n.* ant-eating animal, e.g. pangolin. **a.-hill,** *n.* hillock above ants' nest. **a.-thrush,** *n.* ant-eating bird. (O.E. *ǣmete*)
-ant, *adj.suf.* as in **repentant.**—*n.suf.* denoting agent, as in **celebrant.**
antacid, *a.* and *n.* preventive of acidity.
antagonist, *n.* opponent, adversary. **antagonistic,** *a.* **antagonism,** *n.* **antagonize,** *v.t.* provoke to opposition; counteract; oppose. (Gk. *anti*, against; *agōn*, contest)
antaphrodisiac, *n.* preventive of sexual desire. (*anti-*)
antarctic, *a.* south polar. **A. circle,** parallel of 66° 32′ S.
ante, *n.* stake put down by poker-player before drawing new cards.—*v.t.* stake, bet; pay (up). (L.=before)
ante-, *adj.pref.* before, as in **ante-nuptial, ante-reformation.** (L.)
antecedent, *a.* before in time, prior.—*n.* preceding thing or event; (*gram.*) noun etc. to which relative refers; (*pl.*) previous record. **antecedence,** *n.* priority. (L. *antecedere*, go before)
antechamber, *n.* room leading to chief apartment.
antedate, *v.t.* and *n.* date before true time; anticipate.
antediluvian, *a.* before the flood; primitive.—*n.* old-fashioned person. (L. *diluvium*, deluge)
antelope, *n.* swift, graceful, deer-like animal. (Gk. *antholops*)
ante meridiem, (*abbr.* **a.m.**) between midnight and noon. **antemeridian,** *a.* (L.)
antemundane, *a.* before the world's creation. (L. *mundus*, world)
antenatal, *a.* before birth. (*natal*)
antenna, *n.* (*pl.* **antennae**) one of the feelers or horns of insect or crustacean; (*wireless*) aerial. **antennal, antennary, antenniform, antenniferous,** *aa.* (L.=sail-yard)
antenuptial, *a.* before marriage.
antependium, *n.* covering for front of altar. (L. *pendēre*, hang)
antepenult, antepenultimate, *a.* and *n.* last but two (us. of syllables). (L. *paene*, almost; *ultimus*, last)
ante-post, *a.* (*betting*) before the numbers of the runners go up on the board.
anteprandial, *a.* before-dinner. (L. *prandium*, dinner)
ante-reformation, *a.* before the Reformation.
anterior, *a.* before, in front; prior **anteriority,** *n.* (L.=former)
ante-room, *n.* antechamber.
anthelion, *n.* luminous ring thrown on cloud or fog-bank opposite to the sun. (Gk. *anti*, opposite; *helios*, sun)
anthem, *n.* hymn sung in alternate parts; Scripture passage set to music; song of praise. (*antiphon*)
anther, *n.* part of flower's stamen containing pollen. **antheral, antheroid,** *aa.* (Gk. *anthos*, flower)
anthology, *n.* collection of poems or literary extracts. **anthologist,** *n.* (Gk. *anthos*, flower; *legein*, gather)
Anthony, *n.* smallest pig in a litter. **(St.) A.'s fire,** erysipelas. (saint)
anthracene, *n.* a hydro-carbon got from coal-tar, source of a red dye. **anthracite,** *n.* non-bituminous coal that burns almost without smoke or flame. (Gk. *anthrax*, coal)
anthrax, *n.* disease of sheep or cattle; carbuncle. (Gk.)
anthropo-, from Gk. *anthropos*, man, used in **anthropocentric,** *a.* centring in man; **anthropography,** *n.* science of the geographical distribution of races; **anthropolite, anthropolith,** *n.* fossil human remains.
anthropoid, *a.* resembling man.—*n.* anthropoid ape.
anthropology, *n.* science, natural history, of the human race. **anthropological,** *a.* **anthropologist,** *n.*
anthropomorphous, *a.* formed like man. **anthropomorphize,** *v.t.* **anthropomorphism,** *n.* conception of God with human attributes. **anthropomorphic,** *a.* **anthropomorphist,** *n.* (Gk. *morphē*, form)
anthropophagi, *n.pl.* man-eaters. **anthropophagy,** *n.* cannibalism. **anthropophagous,** *a.* (Gk. *phagein*, eat)
anti-, ant-, anth-, *pref.* opposite, against, as in **anti-vaccination, anti-constitutional.** (Gk.)
anti-aircraft, *a.* for use against aircraft.
antiar, *n.* upas-tree; poison got from it. (Javanese *antjar*)
antibody, *n.* substance in the blood counteracting toxins etc.
antic, *a.* (*arch.*) fantastic.—*n.* (*Shake.*) buffoon; (us. *pl.*) buffoonery, capers. —*v.t.* (*Shake.*) make grotesque. (L. *antiquus*, old)
antichrist, *n.* great enemy of Christ, variously identified. **antichristian,** *a.* of antichrist; opposed to Christianity.
anticipate, *v.t.* forestall; expect; use, discuss, beforehand. **anticipation, anticipator,** *nn.* **anticipative, anticipatory,** *aa.* (L. *ante*, beforehand; *capere*, take)
anticlimax, *n.* opposite of climax, descent from great to trivial.
anticlinal, *a.* inclined in opposite directions. (Gk. *klinein*, lean)

anticyclone, *n.* system of winds moving round centre of high barometric pressure.

antidote, *n.* remedy to counteract poison or disease. **antidotal**, *a.* (Gk. *didonai*, give)

antigen, *n.* substance introduced into the blood to stimulate production of antibodies. (Gk. *gignesthai*, become)

antigropelos, *n.pl.* waterproof leggings. (Gk. *hugros*, wet; *pēlos*, mud)

antilogarithm, *n.* number which a logarithm represents.

antilogy, *n.* contradiction. (Gk. *antilogia*)

antimacassar *n.* covering for chair-back etc. (*macassar* hair-oil)

antimasque, antimask, *n.* grotesque interlude between parts of a masque.

antimony, *n.* brittle bluish-white metal. **antimonial**, *a.* (L.L. *antimonium*)

antinomianism, *n.* belief that moral law is not binding on Christians. **antinomian**, *a.* and *n.* (Gk. *nomos*, law)

antinomy, *n.* contradiction in law or authorities or conclusions.

antipathy, *n.* natural dislike; settled aversion. **antipathetic**, *a.* **antipathic**, *a.* of contrary character. (Gk. *pathos*, feeling)

antiphlogistic, *a.* and *n.* (medicine) allaying inflammation.

antiphon, *n.* verse or sentence sung by one choir in response to another; anthem. **antiphonal**, *a.* sung alternately.—*n.* collection of antiphons. **antiphonary**, *n.* book of antiphons. **antiphony**, *n.* antiphon; alternate singing; echo. (Gk. *phōnē*, voice)

antiphrasis, *n.* use of words in a sense opposite to the proper one. **antiphrastic**, *a.* ironical. (Gk.)

antipodes, *n.pl.* countries, peoples, on opposite side of the globe. **antipodal, antipodean**, *aa.* (Gk. *pous*, foot)

antipope, *n.* rival pope.

antipyretic, *a.* and *n.* fever-allaying (drug). **antipyrin**, *n.* a particular one. (Gk. *puretos*, fever)

antique, *a.* ancient; old-fashioned.—*n.* relic of ancient art or times. **antiquary**, *n.* student or collector of antiquities. **antiquarian**, *a.* and *n.* **antiquated**, *a.* out of date; grown old. **antiquity**, *n.* great age; ancient times; (*pl.*) relics, customs, of the ancients. (L. *antiquus*, old)

antirabic, *a.* of use against rabies.

antirrhinum, *n.* snapdragon. (Gk. *anti*, opposite; *rhis*, nose)

antisabbatarian, *a.* and *n.* (person) opposed to Sabbath observance.

anti-saloon, *a.* (*Amer.*) opposed to drinking-saloons.

antiscorbutic, *a.* and *n.* (remedy) against scurvy.

anti-Semite, *n.* opponent of Jews. **anti-Semitic**, *a.* **anti-Semitism**, *n.*

antiseptic, *a.* and *n.* (treatment etc.) preventing putrefaction.

antisocial, *a.* opposed to the principles and usages of society.

antispast, *n.* four-syllabled foot, short-long-long-short. (Gk. *antispastos*, drawn in contrary directions)

antistrophē, *n.* stanza or movement of Greek chorus alternating with strophe. **antistrophic**, *a.* (*strophe*)

antithesis, *n.* (*pl.* **antitheses**) contrast of thoughts or words; direct opposite. **antithetic, antithetical**, *aa.* (Gk.)

antitoxin, *n.* serum used to neutralize poisons of disease. **antitoxic**, *a.*

anti-trade, *a.* and *n.* (wind) blowing in opposite direction to trade wind.

antitype, *n.* that which a type or symbol stands for. **antitypical**, *a.*

antivenene *n.* antidote to snake-poison. (L. *venenum*, poison)

antler, *n.* branch of deer's horn. **antlered**, *a.* (L. *ante*, before; *oculus*, eye)

antonomasia, *n.* use of a common noun for a proper, e.g. 'the Great Lexicographer'; or of a proper for a common, e.g. 'some mute inglorious Milton.' (Gk. *anti*, instead; *onoma*, name)

antonym, *n.* word of opposite meaning to another. (Gk. *onoma*, name)

antre, *n.* (*Shake.*) cave. (*antrum*)

antrum, *n.* cavity, esp. in upper jawbone. (Gk. *antron*, cave)

Antwerp, *n.* **A.** (pigeon), kind of carrier-pigeon. (town)

anus, *n.* lower orifice of bowels. (L.)

anvil, *n.* iron block on which smiths hammer work into shape. (O.E. *anfilte*)

anxious, *a.* troubled, concerned; very desirous. **anxiety**, *n.* (L. *anxius*)

any, *a.* and *pron.* one, some; every.—*adv.* at all. **a. one**, a single; anybody. **anybody**, *n.* any person. **anyhow**, *adv.* in any way; at any rate; at haphazard. **anyone**, *n.* any person. **anything**, *n.* any thing.—*adv.* in any measure. **anywhere**, *adv.* in any place. **anywise**, *adv.* in any manner. (O.E. *ǽnig*)

Anzac, *n.* and *a.* (one of) Australian and New Zealand Army Corps in the Great War. (initial letters)

aorist, *n.* (*Gk. gram.*) simple past tense. (Gk. *a-*, not; *horizein*, limit)

aorta, *n.* great artery rising from left ventricle of heart. **aortal, aortic**, *aa.* (Gk. *aeirein*, raise)

aoudad, *n.* wild sheep of N. Africa. (F.)

ap-, form of ad- before *p.*

apace, *adv.* swiftly, fast.

apache, *n.* Parisian street ruffian, hooligan; tribe of N. American Indians. (native=enemy)

apanage, appanage, *n.* provision for younger sons of kings etc.; perquisite; dependency; attribute. (L. *ad*, to; *panis*, bread)

apart, *adv.* separately, aside.

apartment, *n.* room; (*Amer.*) set of rooms; (*pl.*) lodgings.

apathy, *n.* want of feeling, indifference. **apathetic,** *a.* (Gk. *a-*, not; *pathos*, feeling)

ape, *n.* tailless monkey; imitator.—*v.t.* imitate, mimic. (O.E. *apa*)

apeak, *adv.* and *a.* (*naut.*) vertical.

apepsy, *n.* weakness of digestion. (Gk. *a-*, not; *peptein*, digest)

aperçu, *n.* brief outline, survey. (F.)

aperient, aperitive, *aa.* and *nn.* laxative (medicine). **aperitif,** *n.* liquid appetizer. (L. *aperire*, open)

aperture, *n.* opening, gap. (*aperient*)

apery, *n.* mimicry; ape-house. (*ape*)

apetalous, *a.* without petals.

apex, *n.* (*pl.* **apices, apexes**) top point; vertex. L.)

aphasia, *n.* loss of speech through brain affection. (Gk.)

aphelion, *n.* point of planet's orbit farthest from sun. **apheliotropic,** *a.* (*bot.*) turning from the sun. (Gk. *apo*, from; *hēlios*, sun)

aphesis, *n.* gradual loss of unaccented vowel at beginning of word, as in 'squire' for 'esquire.' **aphetic,** *a.* (Gk.=letting go)

aphis, *n.* (*pl.* **aphides**) plant-louse, green fly, tended by ants for the honeydew it secretes. **aphidian,** *a.*

aphonia, aphony, *n.* dumbness, loss of voice. (Gk.)

aphorism, *n.* short pithy saying, esp. a definition. **aphorismic, aphoristic,** *aa.* (Gk. *apo*, from; *horos*, limit)

aphrodisiac, *a.* and *n.* (drug) exciting sexual desire. (*Aphroditē*, Greek goddess of love)

aphyllous, *a.* (*bot.*) without leaves. (Gk. *a-*, without; *phullon*, leaf)

apiary, *n.* place where bees are kept. **apiarian,** *a.* of bee-keeping. **apiarist,** *n.* (L. *apis*, bee)

apical, *a.* of, at, apex. (*apex*)

apiculture, *n.* bee-keeping. (*apiary*)

apiece, *adv.* to each, severally.

apish, *a.* like an ape; silly.

aplanat, *n.* (*phot.*) symmetrical achromatic doublet lens. (Gk. *a-*, not; *planaein*, wander)

aplomb, *n.* self-possession, assurance. (F.=perpendicularity)

apnoea, *n.* suspension of breathing. (Gk. *a-*, not; *pnoē*, breath)

apo-, *pref.* off, from, away; un-; quite. (Gk.)

apocalypse, *n.* revelation, esp. that of St John. **apocalyptic,** *a.* (Gk. *apo-*, un-; *kaluptein*, cover)

apocentre, *n.* point in eccentric orbit most distant from centre.

apochromat, *n.* highly achromatic lens. **apochromatic,** *a.* (Gk. *apo*, from; *chroma*, colour)

apocope, *n.* cutting off of end of word. (Gk. *koptein*, cut)

apocrypha, *n.* Old Testament books accepted as authentic by R.C. Church but not by Protestants. **apocryphal,** *a.* of the apocrypha; false, spurious. (Gk. *kruptein*, hide)

apod, *a.* and *n.* footless (bird etc.). (Gk. *a-*, not; *pous*, foot)

apodeictic, apodictic, *a.* clearly established. (Gk. *deiknunai*, show)

apodosis, *n.* (*pl.* **apodoses**) consequent clause in conditional sentence. (Gk. =giving back)

apogamy, *n.* absence of sexual reproduction; asexual reproduction. (Gk. *gamos*, marriage)

apogee, *n.* point in moon's orbit farthest from earth; greatest distance of sun from earth in aphelion; climax. (Gk. *apo*, away from; *gē*, earth)

apolaustic, *a.* self-indulgent. (Gk. *apolauein*, enjoy)

Apollinaris, *n.* a mineral water. (place)

Apollo, *n.* Greek sun-god and god of music; handsome man. (Gk. *Apollōn*)

apologetic, *a.* regretfully acknowledging or excusing; said in defence.—*n.pl.* reasoned defence. (*apology*)

apologia, *n.* written defence of writer's principles or conduct. (*apology*)

apologue, *n.* moral story, fable. (Gk. *apologos*)

apology, *n.* regretful acknowledgment; excuse: defence. **apologize,** *v.i.* make apology. **apologist,** *n.* one who defends by argument. (Gk. *apologia*)

apophthegm, apothegm, *n.* terse saying, maxim. **apophthegmatic,** *a.* pithy, sententious. (Gk. *phthengesthai*, utter)

apoplexy, *n.* loss, by sudden stroke, of sense and motion, usually through haemorrhage in brain. **apoplectic,** *a.* (Gk. *plēssein*, strike)

aposiopesis, *n.* sudden breaking off in speech, for effect, e.g. 'Bertrand is—what I dare not name.' (Gk.)

apostasy, *n.* desertion of religion, principles, or party. **apostate,** *n.* and *a.* **apostatize,** *v.i.* (Gk. *apo*, away from: *stasis*, standing)

apostil, *n.* marginal note. (F. *apostille*)

apostle, *n.* one of the twelve disciples; founder of Christian Church in a country; leader of reform. **apostleship, apostolate,** *nn.* **apostolic, apostolical,** *aa.* (Gk. *stellein*, send)

apostrophe, *n.* digression to appeal to someone dead or absent; sign (') of omitted letter or possessive case. **apostrophic,** *a.* **apostrophize,** *v.t.* and *i.* address in, use, apostrophe. (Gk. *apo*, from; *strephein*, turn)

apothecary, *n.* (*arch.*) druggist. (Gk. *apothēkē*, storehouse)

apothegm, see **apophthegm.**

apotheosis, *n.* (*pl.* apotheoses) deification; canonization. **apotheosize,** *v.t.* (Gk. *theos*, god)

appal, *v.t.* terrify, dismay. —*v.i.* (*Spens.*) fail, decay.

appanage, see **apanage.**

apparatus, *n.* (*pl.* **apparatuses**) appliance, set of instruments for work. *a. criticus*, materials for critical study of document. (L. *parare*, prepare)

apparel, *n.* dress, clothing.—*v.t.* dress, adorn. (L. *par*, equal)

apparent, *a.* visible; evident. **apparition**, *n.* appearance; spectre. (L. *parēre*, appear)

apparitor, *n.* beadle; usher; herald.

appay, *v.t.* (*Spens.*) please, satisfy; pay.

appeach, *v.t.* (*Shake.*) inform against.

appeal, *v.i.* and *t.* call upon, make request; refer; be attractive; apply, remove (case), to higher tribunal.—*n.* act or right of appealing. **appealable**, *a.* (L. *appellare*, address)

appear, *v.i.* become visible or present; seem. **appearance**, *n.* act of appearing; look, semblance; (*pl.*) outward show. (L. *parēre*)

appease, *v.t.* pacify, quiet; satisfy. **appeasement**, *n.* (L. *pax*, peace)

appellant, *n.* one who appeals to a higher court. **appellate**, *a.* dealing with appeals. **appellation**, *n.* name. **appellative**, *a.* and *n.* general (word); common, not proper (noun). (*appeal*)

append, *v.t.* hang on, attach; add. **appendage**, *n.* **appendant**, *a.* and *n.* (person, thing) attached in subordinate capacity to another. **appendix**, *n.* (*pl.* **appendices, appendixes**) subsidiary addition (to book etc.). **vermiform appendix**, narrow tube leading out of intestine. **appendicitis**, *n.* inflammation of this. (L. *pendere*, hang)

apperception, *n.* perception with consciousness of self.

apperil, *n.* (*Shake.*) peril.

appertain, *v.i.* belong, relate (to).

appetence, appetency, *n.* desire, craving; affinity. **appetent**, *a.* (L. *petere*, seek)

appetite, *n.* natural desire; hunger. **appetitive**, *a.* **appetizing**, *a.* inviting. **appetizer**, *n.* thing that gives appetite. (L. *petere*, seek)

applaud, *v.i.* and *t.* express loud approval, esp. by clapping hands; commend, praise. **applause**, *n.* (L. *plaudere*, clap)

apple, *n.* round firm fruit; tree that bears it. **a. brandy**, liquor distilled from cider. **a.-cart**, *n.* **upset one's a.-c.**, spoil one's plans. **a.-dumpling**, *n.* apple cooked in paste. **a.-jack**, *n.* (*Amer.*) apple brandy. **a. of discord**, cause of dissension. **a. of Sodom**, fruit turning to ashes; fair but disappointing thing. **a. of the eye**, pupil; cherished object. **a.-pie bed**, with sheets folded so that one's legs cannot get down. **a.-pie order**, perfect order. **a.-sauce**, *n.* (*Amer.*) flattery; nonsense. (O.E. *æppel*)

appleringie, *n.* (*Scot.*) southernwood.

appliqué, *n.* work cut from one material and laid on another.—*v.t.* ornament with this. (F.=applied)

apply, *v.t.* place close (to); put to use; devote.—*v.i.* make request; have reference (to). **appliance**, *n.* thing applied; instrument. **applicable**, *a.* that may be applied; appropriate. **applicant**, *n.* one who applies. **application**, *n.* act of applying, request; close study; bearing of a thing. (L. *applicare*)

appoggiatura, *n.* (*mus.*) grace-note. (It.)

appoint, *v.t.* fix, prescribe; assign to post; equip. **appointee**, *n.* one who is appointed. **appointment**, *n.* appointing; engagement; decree; (*pl.*) outfit. (L. *ad*, to; *punctum*, point)

apport, *n.* moving of material object without material agency at spiritualistic séance; object so moved. (L. *portare*, carry)

apportion, *v.t.* divide in just shares; assign share (to). **apportionment**, *n.*

apposite, *a.* to the point, appropriate. **appositeness**, *n.* **apposition**, *n.* juxtaposition; (*gram.*) use of noun in same case as another which it defines. (L. *ponere*, place)

appraise, *v.t.* estimate worth of, value. **appraisal, appraisement, appraiser**, *nn.* (*praise*)

appreciate, *v.t.* and *i.* value highly; estimate justly, estimate; raise or rise in value. **appreciable**, *a.* perceptible. **appreciation, appreciator**, *nn.* **appreciative, appreciatory**, *aa.* (L. *pretium*, price)

apprehend, *v.t.* arrest; grasp by senses or intellect, understand; fear. **apprehensible**, *a.* **apprehension**, *n.* arrest; conception; fear. **apprehensive**, *a.* afraid, suspicious. (L. *prehendere*, take hold of)

apprentice, *n.* one bound to another to learn a craft; novice.—*v.t.* bind as apprentice. **apprenticeship**, *n.* (F. *apprendre*, learn)

apprise, *v.t.* inform. (*apprehend*)

apprize, *v.t.* appraise, set value on.

appro, commercial *abbr.* for **approval**.

approach, *v.t.* and *i.* draw near (to); resemble; make overtures to.—*n.* drawing near; access, path; (*golf*) shot that should reach green. (L. *prope*, near)

approbation, *n.* sanction, approval. **approbatory**, *a.* **approbate**, *v.t.* (*Amer.*) approve formally, sanction. (L. *probare*, approve)

approof, *n.* (*Shake.*) proof; approval.

appropriate, *a.* suitable; belonging, peculiar (to).—*v.t.* take for oneself; set apart for special purpose. **appropriation, appropriator**, *nn.* **appropriative**, *a.* (L. *proprius*, one's own)

approve, *v.t.* pronounce, consider, good; confirm, accept; give evidence of. **approval**, *n.* commendation; sanction. **approver**, *n.* (esp.) one who turns king's evidence. (*prove*)

approximate, *a.* very near; nearly correct.—*v.t.* and *i.* bring or come near. **approximately** *adv.* nearly, about. **approximation,** *n.* close approach. (L. *proximus,* very near)

appui, *n.* defensive support. **point of a.,** *point d'a.,* fixed object on which troops form into line. (F.)

appurtenance, *n.* belonging, accessory. **appurtenant,** *a.* (*appertain*)

apricot (earlier **apricock**), *n.* orange-coloured stone-fruit like plum. (L. *praecox,* early-ripe)

April, *n.* fourth month of year. (L. *aprilis*)

apron, *n.* piece of cloth etc. worn in front of dress to protect it or as official distinction; covering for legs in open carriage; strip of stage for playing scenes before curtain. (L. *mappa,* napkin, with loss of *n,* a *napron* becoming *an apron*)

apropos, *adv.* and *a.* to the purpose; timely. **a. of,** in reference to. (F. *à propos*)

apse, *n.* semicircular or polygonal recess in building. **apsis,** *n.* (*pl.* **apsides**) point at which planet is nearest or farthest from sun, or satellite from primary. **apsidal,** *a.* of apse or apsis. (Gk. *haptein,* join)

apt, *a.* suitable; inclined; quick. **aptness,** *n.* (L. *aptus,* fitted)

apterous, *a.* without wings. **apteryx,** *n.* kiwi, New Zealand bird with rudimentary wings and no tail. (Gk. *a-,* not; *pterux,* wing)

aptitude, *n.* fitness; ability. (*apt*)

aqua-fortis, *n.* nitric acid. **aquamarine,** *n.* sea-green beryl or colour. **aquaplane,** *n.* plank towed at high speed.—*v.i.* ride on one. **aquarelle,** *n.* painting with Chinese ink and thin water-colours. **aquarium,** *n.* pond or tank for water plants and animals; place containing such tanks. **Aquarius,** *n.* water-carrier, 11th sign of zodiac, which sun enters on 21 Jan. **aquatic,** *a.* living in or near water; done in or on water.—*n.pl.* water sports. **aquatint,** *n.* kind of etching imitating drawings etc. **aqua-vitae,** *n.* alcohol, spirits. **aqueduct,** *n.* artificial channel for water, esp. raised structure of stone; conduit. **aqueous,** *a.* of water; watery. (L. *aqua,* water)

aquilegia, *n.* columbine.

aquiline, *a.* of, like, eagle; hooked like eagle's beak. (L. *aquila,* eagle)

ar-, form of ad- before *r.*

-ar, *adj.suf.* of, belonging to, as in angular, popular.

Arab, *n.* and *a.* Arabian (native, horse). **street a.,** homeless child. **arabesque,** *n.* and *a.* fanciful carved or painted decoration of Arabian design. **Arabian,** *a.* of Arabia. **Arabian bird,** phoenix. **Arabic,** *a.* and *n.* Arabian (language). **arabic numerals,** 1, 2 etc. **Arabist,** *n.* student of Arabic. (Gk. *Araps*)

arabis, *n.* kinds of low-growing plant with white or purple flowers. (*Arab*)

arable, *a.* and *n.* (land) fit for ploughing or tillage. (L. *arare,* plough)

arachnid, *n.* one of class containing spiders, scorpions, and mites. (Gk. *arachnē,* spider)

araise, *v.t.* (*Shake.*) raise.

Aramaic, *n.* language of Palestine at the time of Christ.—*a.* Syrian.

araneidan, *a.* and *n.* (member) of spider family. (L. *aranea,* spider)

arapunga, *n.* campanero or bell-bird. (Tupi *araponga*)

araucaria, *n.* kinds of pine including monkey-puzzle. (province of *Arauco*)

arbalest, arblast, *n.* crossbow with drawing mechanism. (L. *arcus,* bow; *ballista,* military engine)

arbiter, *n.* (*fem.* **arbitress**) person chosen by parties to settle dispute between them, umpire; one who has entire control (of). **arbitrage,** *n.* traffic in stocks etc. to profit by varying prices in different markets. **arbitrament, arbitrement,** *n.* arbiter's judgment; authoritative decision. **arbitrary,** *a.* depending on one's own will; despotic; capricious. **arbitrate,** *v.t.* and *i.* act as arbiter; decide by arbitration. **arbitration,** *n.* judgment by arbiter. **arbitrator,** *n.* arbiter. (L.=judge)

arbor, *n.* main support of machine; axis, spindle. **A. Day,** special day of the year set apart in U.S. for tree-planting. (L.=tree)

arboraceous, *a.* tree-like. **arboreal,** *a.* of, living in, trees. **arboreous,** *a.* wooded. **arborescent,** *a.* growing or formed like a tree. **arboret,** *n.* (*Spens.*) little tree. **arboretum,** *n.* (*pl.* **arboreta**) botanical tree-garden. **arboriculture,** *n.* cultivation of trees and shrubs, forestry. **arboricultural,** *a.* **arboriculturist,** *n.* (L. *arbor,* tree)

arbour, *n.* seat shaded by trees or plants, bower. (L. *herba,* plant)

arbutus, *n.* strawberry-tree. (L.)

arc, *n.* part of circle or other curve; (*electr.*) luminous discharge between two terminals, hence **a.-lamp, a.-light,** *nn.* (L. *arcus,* bow)

arcade, *n.* passage arched over; covered walk lined with shops; row of arches. **arcaded,** *a.* (*arc*)

Arcades ambo, rascals both. (L.= both Arcadians)

Arcadia, Arcady, *n.* (*poet.*) ideal countryside. **Arcadian,** *a.* and *n.* poetically rustic. (place)

arcanum, *n.* (*pl.* **arcana**) mystery, secret. (L.)

arch, *n.* curved structure supporting weight; curve; vault.—*v.t.* and *i.* cover with arch; form (into) arch. **archway,** *n.* arched entrance; vaulted passage. **archwise,** *adv.* (L. *arca,* chest, later confused with *arcus,* bow)

arch, *a.* roguish, waggish, cunning; (as *pref.,* as in **archangel, arch-knave**) chief, worst. (Gk. *archos,* chief)

archaean, *a.* of earliest geological

period. **archaeology,** *n.* science of antiquities, esp. prehistoric remains. **archaeological,** *a.* **archaeologist,** *n.* (Gk. *archaios*, ancient)

archaeopteryx, *n.* oldest fossil bird. (Gk. *archaios*, ancient; *pterux*, wing)

archaic, *a.* ancient; obsolete. **archaism,** *n.* archaic word or phrase. **archaist,** *n.* **archaistic,** *a.* **archaize,** *v.t.* and *i.* affect the archaic; make archaistic. (Gk. *archaios*)

archangel, *n.* angel of highest order.

archbishop, *n.* chief bishop; metropolitan. **archbishopric,** *n.* see, office, of archbishop.

archdeacon, *n.* church dignitary next to bishop, superintendent of rural deans. **archdeaconry,** *n.* his office, jurisdiction, or residence.

archdiocese, *n.* archbishop's province.

archduke, *n.* (*fem.* **archduchess**) son of Emperor of Austria. **archducal,** *a.* **archduchy, archdukedom,** *nn.*

archer, *n.* one who shoots arrows from a bow; 9th sign of zodiac. **archery,** *n.* archer's art. (*arc*)

archetype, *n.* original model, prototype. **archetypal,** *a.* (*type*)

arch-fiend, *n.* Satan.

archidiaconal, *a.* of an archdeacon.

archie, *n.* (*army sl.*) anti-aircraft gun. (name in popular song)

archiepiscopal, *a.* of an archbishop.

archil, *n.* kinds of lichen; violet dye made from them. (O.F. *orchel*)

archimandrite, *n.* head of monastery in Greek Church. (Gk. *mandra*, monastery)

archipelago, *n.* sea with many islands, esp. the Aegean; group of islands. (Gk. *pelagos*, sea)

architect, *n.* master-builder; one who designs buildings and superintends their erection; contriver. **architectonic,** *a.* of architecture; constructive; of the systematizing of knowledge. **architectonics,** *n.* **architecture,** *n.* art, science, of building; structure; workmanship. **architectural,** *a.* (Gk. *tektōn*, builder)

architrave, *n.* epistyle, main part of entablature resting immediately on column; parts round door or window. (L. *trabs*, beam)

archives, *n.pl.* public records or the place where they are kept. **archivist,** *n.* keeper of archives. (Gk. *archē*, government)

archivolt, *n.* under-curve of arch or moulding upon it. (*arch*; *vault*)

archon, *n.* one of nine chief magistrates in ancient Athens. (Gk.)

arctic, *a.* of the north pole; very cold. **A. circle,** parallel of 66° 32′ N. (Gk. *arktos*, Great Bear)

ardent, *a.* passionate, eager; burning. **a. spirits,** alcoholic spirits. **ardency, ardour,** *nn.* warmth of feeling, eagerness; heat. (L. *ardēre*, burn)

arduous, *a.* hard, laborious; strenuous. (L. *arduus*, steep)

are, see **be.**

are, *n.* French unit of land measure, 100 sq. metres, =119·6 sq. yds. (F.)

area, *n.* superficial extent; region, tract; scope; sunk court in front of basement of house. (L.=open space)

aread, areed, *v.t.* (*Spens.*) declare; explain; counsel. (O.E. *arédan*)

areca, *n.* kinds of palm. **a.-nut,** *n.* betel-nut. (Port.)

arena, *n.* sand-strewn centre of amphitheatre, where combats were held; place of contest. **arenaceous,** *a.* sand-like, sandy. (L.=sand)

areola, *n.* (*pl.* **areolae**) very small area; interstice in tissue. (*area*)

areometer, *n.* instrument for measuring specific gravity of liquids. (Gk. *araios*, thin; *metron*, measure)

Areopagus, *n.* supreme court of ancient Athens. **Areopagite,** *n.* member of it. (hill where it sat)

arête, *n.* sharp mountain ridge. (F.)

argal, *adv.* (*Shake.*) therefore. (L. *ergo*)

argala, *n.* adjutant-bird, great Indian stork. (Hind. *hargila*)

argali, *n.* great wild sheep of Siberia and Central Asia. (Mongol)

argand, *a.* (of lamp-wick, gas-burner) with circular flame. (inventor)

argent, *n.* and *a.* (*heraldry*) silver. **argentiferous,** *a.* silver-bearing. **argentine,** *a.* and *n.* of silver, silvery; imitation silver. (L. *argentum*)

argil, *n.* clay, esp. potter's. **argillaceous,** *a.* (Gk. *argēs*, white)

argle-bargle, *n.* tedious discussion.—*v.i.* argue at length. (*argue*)

argol, *n.* deposit of crude tartar on sides of wine-vessels.

argon, *n.* a gas, inert constituent of air. (Gk. *a-*, not; *ergon*, work)

argosy, *n.* large richly laden merchant ship. (*Ragusa* in Italy)

argot, *n.* slang, esp. of thieves. (F.)

argue, *v.t.* and *i.* maintain by reasoning; reason, discuss; prove. **argufy,** *v.i.* (*sl.*) argue tediously, wrangle. **argument,** *n.* reason offered; reasoning, discussion; summary of book. **argumentation,** *n.* **argumentative,** *a.* fond of arguing. (L. *arguere*, make clear)

argumentum, *n.* *a. ad hominem*, appeal to a man's particular nature; *a. ad ignorantiam*, one based on his ignorance; *a. baculinum*, appeal to force. (L.)

Argus, *n.* fabulous being with a hundred eyes. **a.-eyed,** *a.* watchful. (Gk. *Argos*)

argute, *a.* shrewd; shrill. (*argue*)

Arian, *a.* and *n.* (person) denying divinity of Christ. **Arianism,** *n.* (*Arius* of Alexandria, 4th cent.)

arid, *a.* dry, parched; dull. **aridity,** *n.* (L. *aridus*)

Ariel, *n.* angel; air-spirit. (Heb.)

ariel, *n.* kind of gazelle. (Arab. *aryil*)

Aries, *n.* the Ram, 1st sign of zodiac, which sun enters on 21 March. (L.)

aright, *adv.* rightly.
aril, *n.* outer seed-covering. (L. *arillus*)
arise, *v.i.* (*past* **arose,** *p.p.* **arisen**) rise up, appear; result; occur.
arista, *n.* awn, beard, of grasses. **aristate,** *a.* bearded. (L.)
aristocracy, *n.* government by the best citizens, oligarchy; nobility, upper class. **aristocrat,** *n.* member of aristocracy. **aristocratic,** *a.* of the aristocracy, grand, stylish. (Gk. *aristos,* best; *kratos,* power)
arithmetic, *n.* science of numbers, reckoning by figures. **arithmetical,** *a.* **arithmetician,** *n.* **arithmometer,** *n.* calculating-machine. (Gk. *arithmos,* number)
ark, *n.* large floating vessel; chest; coffer containing Jewish tables of law. (O.E. *arc*)
arles, *n.* (*Scot.*) earnest-money given on making bargain or engaging servant.
arm, *n.* limb from shoulder to hand; sleeve; branch; projecting part of sea, machine etc. **armchair,** *n.* with rests for arms. **armpit,** *n.* hollow under shoulder. **with open aa.,** cordially. **armful,** *n.* (O.E.)
arm, *n.* weapon; branch of service; (*pl.*) military profession; heraldic device.—*v.t.* and *i.* furnish with arms, furnish; take up arms. **fire-a.,** *n.* using explosive. **small aa.,** not requiring carriage. **lay down aa.,** surrender. **up in aa.,** in rebellion. (L. *arma,* arms)
armada, *n.* fleet of warships. (Sp.)
armadillo, *n.* S. American animal with body encased in bony plates. (Sp.)
armament, *n.* war force, military equipment, esp. of navy. (*arm*)
armature, *n.* arms, armour; piece of iron connecting poles of magnet; revolving part of dynamo. (*arm*)
arme blanche, cavalry sword or lance; cavalry. (F.)
armiger, *n.* one entitled to a coat of arms, esquire. (L.=armour-bearer)
armillary, *a.* of bracelet; made of rings. **a. sphere,** skeleton celestial globe showing movements of stars etc.
Arminian, *a.* and *n.* (person) denying Calvin's doctrine of predestination. **Arminianism,** *n.* (*Arminius,* Du. divine)
armipotent, *a.* (*Shake.*) mighty in arms.
armistice, *n.* cessation of hostilities, short truce. **A. Day, 11 Nov.,** commemorating end of the Great War. (L. *arma,* arms; *sistere,* stop)
armlet, *n.* band worn round arm.
armory, *n.* heraldry. **armorial,** *a.* of heraldic arms. (*arm*)
armour, *n.* protective dress or covering; steel plates sheathing warship. —*v.t.* furnish with armour. **armourer,** *n.* one who makes or has charge of arms. **armoury,** *n.* place where arms are kept; (*Amer.*) armourer's workshop.
army, *n.* land forces of a state; vast number; organized body, such as Salvation Army. **a. corps,** main division of army. **A. List,** official list of commissioned officers. (*arm*)
arnica, *n.* kinds of plant; tincture one yields, used for bruises.
aroint, *int.* (*Shake.*) **a. thee!** begone!
aroma, *n.* sweet smell, fragrance; subtle charm. **aromatic,** *a.* spicy, fragrant. **aromatize,** *v.t.* (Gk.)
arose, see **arise.**
around, *adv.* and *prep.* on all sides (of); all round; (*sl.*) somewhere round.
arpeggio, *n.* (*mus.*) playing notes of chord in rapid succession, not together; chord so played. (It.)
arquebus, harquebus, *n.* old-fashioned hand-gun fired from forked rest. (O.H.G. *haken,* hook; *bühse,* gun)
arrack, *n.* eastern native spirits, esp. that made from coco-palm. (Arab. *'araq,* juice)
arrah, *int.* (*Ir.*) of amazement etc.
arraign, *v.t.* put on trial; indict, accuse. **arraignment,** *n.* (L. *ratio,* reason)
arrange, *v.t.* set in order; prepare; (*mus.*) adapt.—*v.i.* take steps; agree. **arrangement,** *n.* settlement; classification; (*pl.*) plans. (*range*)
arrant, *a.* downright, unmitigated. (*errant,* orig. of roving thieves)
arras, *n.* tapestry; hanging screen of it. **arrased,** *a.* (town in Artois)
array, *v.t.* draw up (forces); dress, adorn.—*n.* order; imposing show; dress. (O.F. *areyer*)
arrear, *n.* hinder part; (*pl.*) overdue debts; work in which one is behindhand. **in a.** or **aa.,** behindhand. **arrearage,** *n.* being in arrears; (*pl.*) debts. (L. *ad,* to; *retro,* backwards)
arrect, *a.* (of ears) pricked up; alert. (L. *regere,* straighten)
arrest, *v.t.* stop; seize by authority; catch attention of.—*n.* stoppage; legal apprehension. **arrestive,** *a.* **arrestment,** *n.* (L. *restare,* remain)
arride, *v.t.* (*arch.*) please, gratify. (L. *arridēre,* smile upon)
arrière-pensée, *n.* mental reservation. (F.)
arriero, *n.* Spanish muleteer. (Sp.)
arris, *n.* (*archit.*) sharp ridge or edge. (*arista*)
arrive, *v.i.* reach place; attain object. **arrival,** *n.* arriving; person, thing, that arrives. **arrivance,** *n.* (*Shake.*) company arriving. *arriviste,* *n.* self-seeker. (L. *ripa,* shore)
arrogant, *a.* overbearing, proud, haughty. **arrogance, arrogancy,** *nn.*
arrogate, *v.t.* claim unduly; assume. **arrogation,** *n.* (L. *rogare,* ask)
arrondissement, *n.* subdivision of French department; municipal subdivision of Paris etc. (F.)
arrow, *n.* pointed missile shot from bow. **arrowy,** *a.* (O.E. *arwe*)

arrowroot, *n.* nutritious starch obtained from West Indian plants. (used to cure wounds from poisoned arrows)
arse, *n.* rump. (O.E. *ears*)
arsenal, *n.* public store or manufactory of war munitions. (Arab. *dar*, house; *al*, the; *çinā'ah*, art)
arsenic, *n.* soft, grey, metallic element; its oxide, a poison.—*a.* of, containing, arsenic.—so **arsenical, arsenious,** *aa.* (Arab. *al*, the; *zernikh*, orpiment)
arsis, *n.* stressed syllable of poetical foot. (Gk.=raising)
arson, *n.* felonious burning of houses, haystacks, ships, forests, or similar property. (L. *ardēre*, burn)
art, see **be.**
art, *n.* acquired skill; skill applied to design; craft, profession; principles of good execution; dexterity, cunning; (*pl.*) certain branches of learning. **black a.,** magic. **fine a.,** painting, sculpture, music, poetry etc., opp. to **useful a.,** in which hands are used more than mind. (L. *ars*)
artel, *n.* Russian workers' guild. (Russ.)
artery, *n.* one of tubes conveying blood from heart; main channel of communication. **arterial,** *a.* **arterial road,** main road with many branches. **arterialize,** *v.t.* **arteriosclerosis,** *n.* hardening of arteries. **arteriotomy,** *n.* opening of artery. (Gk. *arteria*)
artesian, *a.* **a. well,** well made by boring deeply till water rises spontaneously. (*Artois* in France)
artful, *a.* sly, cunning.
arthritis, *n.* inflammation of joint, gout. **arthritic,** *a.* of joints; of gout. **arthropod,** *n.* animal with jointed legs, such as spider or crustacean. **arthrosis,** *n.* articulation. (Gk. *arthron*, joint)
artichoke, *n.* edible plant like thistle. **Jerusalem a.,** sunflower with edible roots. (Arab. *alkharshuf*; 'Jerusalem' corrupt. of It. *girasole*, sunflower)
article, *n.* thing, object, item; rule, clause of agreement; short literary composition; (*gram.*) 'a' or 'the.'—*v.t.* bind by articles; indict. (L. *artus*, limb)
articular, *a.* of joints. **articulate,** *a.* jointed; distinct, clear.—*v.t.* and *i.* connect by joints; speak distinctly. **articulation,** *n.* jointing; distinct utterance; consonant. (L. *artus*, limb)
artifice, *n.* contrivance; trick, cunning. **artificer,** *n.* craftsman; inventor. (L. *ars*, art; *facere*, make)
artificial, *a.* made by art, not natural; not real, synthetic; feigned, affected. **artificiality,** *n.*
artillery, *n.* cannon; troops managing them; gunnery. **artillerist, artilleryman,** *nn.* (*art*)
artisan, *n.* skilled workman, mechanic.
artist, *n.* one who practises one of the fine arts, esp. painting; one who makes a fine art of his craft. **artistic,** *a.* of, according to, art. **artistry,** *n.*
artiste, *n.* public performer, singer, actor etc. (F.)
artless, *a.* unskilful, crude; simple guileless.
arty, *a.* (*colloq.*) ostentatiously, affectedly, artistic.
arum, *n.* kinds of plant including wake-robin. **a. lily,** white arum. (Gk. *aron*)
-ary, *adj.* and *n.suf.* connected with, as in dictionary.
Aryan, *a.* and *n.* (member) of Indo-European race. (Sanskr. *arya*, noble)
as, *adv.* in the degree, manner, form; for example.—*conj.* since; when; that.—*rel. pron.* that. **as for, as to,** in respect of. **as it were,** so to speak. **as well,** advisable; in addition. **as yet,** hitherto. (O.E. *allswá*, wholly so)
as, *n.* Roman copper coin. (L.)
as-, form of **ad-** before *s.*
asafoetida, *n.* gum-resin with offensive smell used in medicine. (Pers. *aza*, mastic. L. *foetidus*, stinking)
asbestos, *n.* fibrous mineral; incombustible fabric woven from it. **asbestic, asbestine,** *aa.* of asbestos; incombustible. (Gk.=unquenchable)
ascend, *v.t.* and *i.* climb, go up; rise, mount. **ascendancy, ascendency,** *n.* influence, power. **ascendant,** *a.* rising; (*astrol.*) just above horizon; predominant.—*n.* superiority; ancestor; (*astrol.*) sign of zodiac rising above horizon at person's birth; horoscope. **in the ascendant,** supreme, dominating. **ascension,** *n.* ascending; rising (of star). **Ascension Day,** Holy Thursday, commemorating ascent of Christ after the Resurrection. **right ascension,** celestial longitude. **ascensive,** *a.* rising, progressive. **ascent,** *n.* ascending, rise; slope, way up. (L. *scandere*, climb)
ascertain, *v.t.* find out, determine. **ascertainable,** *a.* **ascertainment,** *n.* (*certain*)
ascetic, *a.* rigidly abstinent, austere.—*n.* one who practises severe self-discipline; hermit. **asceticism,** *n.* (Gk. *askein*, exercise)
ascidian, *n.* sea-squirt, kind of mollusc. (Gk. *askos*, wine-skin)
ascititious, same as **adscititious.**
Asclepiad, *n.* verse made up of a spondee, two (or three) choriambi, and an iambus. (*Asklepiadēs*, Gk. poet)
ascribe, *v.t.* attribute, impute; assign. **ascribable,** *a.* **ascription,** *n.* (L. *scribere*, write)
asdic, *n.* apparatus for locating submarines. (*A*llied *S*ubmarine *D*etection *I*nvestigation *C*ommittee)
ase, *n.* (*Scot.*) ashes.
aseity, *n.* (*metaphys.*) self-origination, esp. of God. (L. *a se*, from self)
asepsis, *n.* absence of putrefactive matter; surgical method aiming at this. **aseptic,** *a.* not liable to putrefy, sterilized. (Gk. *sēpein*, rot)

asexual, *a.* without sex. **asexuality,** *n.*

ash, *n.* a forest tree; its wood. **a.-key,** *n.* its winged seed. **mountain a.,** rowan. **ashen,** *a.* (O.E. *æsc*)

ash, *n.* (us. *pl.*) residue of anything burned; remains of cremated body, dead body. **a.-bin, a.-pit,** *nn.* receptacle for ashes and refuse. **a.-tray,** *n.* tray for tobacco-ash. **A. Wednesday,** first day of Lent. **ashen,** *a.* of ashes; pale. (O.E. *asce*)

ashamed, *a.* affected with shame.

ashet, *n.* (*Scot.*) large flat oval dish for joint, etc. (F. *assiette*)

ashlar, *n.* squared stone used in building; masonry of this. **ashlaring,** *n.* low wall of garret, built close to where rafters reach floor. (L. *axis,* board)

ashore, *adv.* to, on, shore; aground.

ashy, *a.* of ashes; ash-coloured, pale.

aside, *adv.* on, to, one side; away, apart.—*n.* remark in undertone.

asinine, *a.* of, like, ass; silly. **asininity,** *n.* **asinico,** *n.* (*Shake.*) ass. (L. *asinus,* ass)

ask, *v.t.* and *i.* inquire, question; request; invite. (O.E. *ácsian*)

askance, askant, *adv.* sideways; with indirect glance or meaning. **look a. at,** view with suspicion.

askari, *n.* European-trained African native soldier. (Arab. *'askar,* army)

askew, *adv.* and *a.* obliquely; awry.

asklent, *Scot.* form of **aslant.**

aslant, *adv.* obliquely.—*prep.* slantingly across, athwart. (*slant*)

asleep, *a.* and *adv.* sleeping, in sleep; (of limb) benumbed.

aslope, *a.* and *adv.* on a slope, sloping; crosswise. (O.E. *aslupan,* slip away)

asp, (*poet.*) **aspic,** *n.* small venomous serpent. (Gk. *aspis*)

asp, see **aspen.**

asparagus, *n.* plant whose young shoots are a table delicacy. (Gk. *asparagos*)

aspect, *n.* appearance. expression; view, direction a thing faces. (L. *aspicere,* look at)

aspen, asp, *n.* trembling poplar. **aspen,** *a.* of aspen; tremulous. (O.E. *æspe*)

aspergillum, *n.* brush for sprinkling holy water. (L. *spargere,* sprinkle)

asperity, *n.* harshness; roughness.

asperse, *v.t.* besprinkle; bespatter, slander. **aspersion,** *n.* calumny; (*Shake.*) sprinkling. **aspersorium,** *n.* vessel for holy water. (L. *spargere,* sprinkle)

asphalt, *n.* hard bituminous substance used for paving. —*v.t.* lay with asphalt. **asphaltic,** *a.* (Gk. *asphaltos*)

asphodel, *n.* kind of lily; (*poet.*) immortal flower blooming in Elysium. (Gk. *asphodelos*)

asphyxia, asphyxy, *n.* suspended animation; suffocation. **asphyxial,** *a.* **asphyxiate,** *v.t.* **asphyxiation,** *n.* (Gk. *a,* not; *sphuxis,* pulse)

aspic, *n.* savoury meat jelly containing fish, game, boiled eggs etc. (F.)

aspic, see **asp.**

aspidistra, *n.* plant with large broad leaves. (Gk. *aspis,* shield)

aspire, *v.i.* feel earnest desire; be ambitious; (*Shake.*) rise, ascend; mount (to). **aspirant,** *n.* one who aspires, candidate. **aspirate,** *v.t.* pronounce with sound of *h*; draw out (gas etc.) from vessel.—*n.* sound of *h* or consonant blended with it. **aspiration,** *n.* aspirating; eager pursuit, ambition. **aspirator,** *n.* apparatus to draw out gas or liquid by suction; winnowing-machine. (L. *spirare,* breathe)

aspirin, *n.* acetylsalicylic acid, used to allay pain and fever. (trade name)

asquint, *adv.* and *a.* squinting, out of the corner of the eye; obliquely.

ass, *n.* long-eared quadruped; stupid person. (O.E. *assa*)

assagai, assegai, *n.* S. African throwing-spear. (Berber *zaghayah*)

assai, adv. (*mus.*) very. (It.)

assail, *v.t.* attack, assault. **assailable,** *a.* **assailant,** *n.* (L. *salire,* leap)

assassin, *n.* one who kills by treacherous violence; murderer. **assassinate,** *v.t.* **assassination,** *n.* (Arab. *hashashin,* hashish-eaters, a sect of murderous fanatics)

assault, *n.* sudden attack; storming; (*law*) unlawful attack on person.—*v.t.* make assault upon. **a. at arms,** display of fencing. (L. *saltare,* leap)

assay, *v.t.* examine, analyse; test fineness of (metal).—*v.i.* (*arch.*) attempt. —*n.* act of assaying; metal to be assayed. (L. *exagium,* weighing)

assegai, see **assagai.**

assemblance, *n.* (*Shake.*) semblance.

assemble, *v.t.* and *i.* bring, meet, together; (*mechanics*) fit (parts of machine) together. **assemblage,** *n.* assembling, collection. **assembly,** *n.* gathering of people; deliberative body. **General Assembly,** highest court of Presbyterian Church. **Legislative Assembly,** lower house of legislature in British colonies etc. (L.L. *assimulare*)

assent, *v.i.* agree, concur.—*n.* acquiescence, compliance; sanction. **assentation,** *n.* obsequiousness. **assentient,** *a.* and *n.* (one) that assents. **assentor,** *n.* (L. *sentire;* think)

assert, *v.t.* declare positively; maintain claim to. **assertion,** *n.* statement; insistence on rights. **assertive.** *a.* positive, pushing. **assertor,** *n.* champion. (L. *asserere,* lay hand on slave's head to free him)

assess, *v.t.* fix amount of tax; tax, fine; value property for taxation. **assessment,** *n.* **assessor,** *n.* one who assesses; expert who assists judge or magistrate. (L. *sedēre,* sit)

assets, *n.pl.* property available to discharge liabilities; entire property of company etc.; (*sing.*) possession, useful quality. (L. *ad satis,* to sufficiency)

asseverate, *v.t.* declare solemnly. **asseveration,** *n.* (L. *severus,* serious)
assibilate, *v.t.* make sibilant. **assibilation.** *n.* (L. *sibilare,* hiss)
assiduous, *a.* diligent, persevering. **assiduity,** *n.* close application; (*pl.*) constant attentions. (L. *assiduus*)
assign, *v.t.* allot; make over; appoint; ascribe.—*n.* one to whom property is legally transferred. **assignat,** *n.* paper currency secured on state lands, esp. in French Revolution. **assignation,** *n.* assigning, transference; appointment to meet, esp. by lovers. **assignee,** *n.* assign; one appointed to act for another. **assignment,** *n.* act of assigning; thing assigned. **assignor,** *n.* one who assigns. (L. *signum,* sign)
assimilate, *v.t.* make similar, compare; absorb, digest.—*v.i.* become like; be absorbed. **assimilation, assimilator,** *nn.* **assimilative, assimilatory,** *aa.* (L. *similis,* like)
assist, *v.t.* and *i.* help; support; take part. **assistance,** *n.* **assistant,** *a.* helping.—*n.* helper, subordinate. (L. *assistere,* stand by)
assize, *n.* statutory price (of bread etc.); (*Scot.*) trial by jury, jury; (us. *pl.*) court held periodically in each county by judges on circuit. (L. *sedēre,* sit)
associate, *v.t.* join, unite; connect in idea.—*v.i.* combine, keep company (with). — *a.* associated. — *n.* companion, partner, ally; subordinate member of association. **association,** *n.* act of associating, connection; organized body of people. **association football,** played with round ball which is not handled. **associative, associatory,** *aa.* (L. *socius,* allied)
assoil, *v.t.* (*arch.*) absolve from sin; acquit, release. **assoilment,** *n.* **assoilzie,** *v.t.* (*Scots law*) acquit. (L. *absolvere*)
assonance, *n.* resemblance of sound; rhyming of vowels only. **assonant,** *a.* (L. *assonare,* respond)
assort, *v.t.* arrange, classify.—*v.i.* suit, harmonize. **assorted,** *a.* of various sorts. **assortment,** *n.* assorting; selection of goods. (*sort*)
assuage, *v.t.* soften, allay; appease.—*v.i.* abate. **assuagement,** *n.* (L. *suavis,* sweet)
assubjugate, *v.t.* (*Shake.*) subjugate.
assume, *v.t.* take upon oneself, simulate; take for granted; undertake. **assuming,** *a.* arrogant. **assumption,** *n.* assuming, thing assumed; arrogance. **Assumption of Virgin Mary,** her ascent into heaven, celebrated 15 August. **assumptive,** *a.* taken for granted; arrogant. (L. *sumere,* take)
assure, *v.t.* make sure or secure; tell positively; insure (life). **assurance,** *n.* positive assertion; guarantee; certainty; self-confidence, impudence; insurance (of life). **assured,** *a.* certain; self-confident. **assuredly,** *adv.* certainly. **assurer,** *n.* insurer, underwriter. (*sure*)
assurgent, *a.* rising; (*bot.*) rising in a curve. (L. *surgere,* rise)
astatic, *a.* having tendency not to stand still. (Gk. *astatos,* unstable)
aster, *n.* kinds of plant with round composite flowers; (*Amer.*) Michaelmas daisy. (Gk.=star)
-aster, *n.suf.* petty, imitation, as in **poetaster.**
asterisk, *n.* star (*) used as mark of reference. — *v.t.* mark with one. **asterism,** *n.* star-cluster; group of asterisks (⁂) calling attention to passage. (Gk. *astēr,* star)
astern, *adv.* in, at, stern; behind; backwards.
asteroid, *n.* any of small planets revolving between the orbits of Mars and Jupiter.—*a.* star-shaped. (*aster*)
asthma, *n.* disease causing difficulty in breathing. **asthmatic,** *a.* of, suffering from, good for, asthma.—*n.* asthmatic person. (Gk.)
asthore, *n.* (*Ir.*) darling. (Ir. *stōr,* treasure.
astigmatism, *n.* defect of focus in eye or lens. **astigmatic,** *a.* (Gk. *a-,* not; *stigma,* point)
astir, *adv.* and *a.* in motion; excited; out of bed.
astonish, *v.t.* amaze, surprise. **astonishment,** *n.* **astonied,** *p.p.* (*arch.*) stunned, dismayed. (L. *ex,* out; *tonare,* thunder)
astound, *v.t.* astonish greatly, shock with amazement. (*astonish*)
astraddle, *adv.* astride, straddling.
astragal, *n.* ring of moulding round top or bottom of column; ring round cannon near mouth. (Gk. *astragalos,* ankle-bone)
astrakhan, *n.* lambskin with curled wool. (*Astrakhan* in Russia)
astral, *a.* of the stars or spirit world. (L. *astrum,* star)
astray, *adv.* out of the right way. (L. *extra,* outside; *vagari,* wander)
astrict, *v.t.* bind. **astriction,** *n.* binding, contraction. (L. *stringere,* bind)
astride, *adv.* and *prep.* with one leg on each side (of), straddling.
astringe, *v.t.* bind together; contract; constipate. **astringent,** *a.* binding, styptic; austere.—*n.* astringent substance. (*astrict*)
astro-, from Gk. *astron,* star, used in **astrogony,** *n.* stellar cosmogony; **astrography,** *n.* mapping the stars; **astrolabe,** *n.* instrument formerly used for taking altitudes of sun and stars; **astrolatry,** *n.* star-worship; **astrolithology,** *n.* study of meteoric stones; **astro-physics,** *n.* study of physical conditions of the stars.
astrology, *n.* science of foretelling events by the stars; (formerly) astronomy. **astrologer,** *n.* professor of astrology. **astrologic, astrological,** *aa.* (Gk. *astron,* star; *legein,* speak)

astronomy, *n.* science of the heavenly bodies. **astronomer,** *n.* one versed in astronomy. **astronomic, astronomical,** *aa.* (Gk. *astron,* star; *nomos,* law)
astute, *a.* shrewd; crafty. (L. *astutus*)
asunder, *adv.* apart; in pieces.
asylum, *n.* institution for the care of insane, dumb, blind, or destitute; sanctuary, refuge. (Gk. *asulos,* inviolate)
asymmetry, *n.* lack of symmetry. **asymmetrical,** *a.*
asymptote, *n.* (*math.*) line that continually approaches nearer to a given curve without ever meeting it. (Gk. *a-,* not; *sun,* with; *piptein,* fall)
asyndeton, *n.* figure of speech in which conjunctions are omitted. (Gk. *a-,* not; *sun,* with; *dein,* bind)
At, *n.* (sl.) member of Auxiliary Territorial Service. (initials)
at, *prep.* in, on, to, by, near. **at all,** in any degree. **at all events,** in any case. **at first,** to begin with. **at least, most,** using lowest, highest, estimate. **at one,** in harmony. **at that,** moreover. (O.E. *æt*)
at-, form of **ad-** before *t.*
ataraxy, ataraxia, *n.* impassivity. (Gk. *a-,* not; *tarassein,* disturb)
ataunto, *adv.* (*naut.*) with all sails set. **all a.,** shipshape. (F. *autant,* as much)
atavism, *n.* reversion to earlier type; recurrence of ancestral peculiarity or weakness. **atavistic,** *a.* (L. *atavus,* great-great-great-grandfather)
ataxy, ataxia, *n.* irregularity of bodily functions. **locomotor a.,** loss of control of voluntary movements. **ataxic,** *a.* (Gk. *a-,* not; *tassein,* arrange)
ate, see **eat.**
-ate, *adj.suf.* having, furnished with, as in **foliate;** forming equivalent of *p.p.* as in **associate.**
atelier, *n.* workshop, studio. (F.)
atheism, *n.* disbelief in the existence of God. **atheist,** *n.* **atheistic, atheistical,** (*obs.*) **atheous,** *aa.* (Gk. *a-,* not; *theos,* god)
athenaeum, *n.* public institution for lectures, reading etc.; literary club. (Gk. *Athēnaion,* temple of Athēnē)
athetize, *v.t.* set aside (passage) as spurious. (Gk. *athetein,* set aside)
athirst, *a.* thirsty; eager (for).
athlete, *n.* competitor in physical sport; vigorous person. **athletic,** *a.* of athletes, strong; (*pl.*) sports; physical exercises. **athleticism,** *n.* devotion to athletics. (Gk. *athlētēs*)
athwart, *adv.* and *prep.* across, from side to side (of); adversely (to).
-ation, *n.suf.* denoting action or its result, as in **flirtation, vacation.**
atlas, *n.* book of maps. **atlantes,** *n.pl.* (*archit.*) figures of men acting as columns. **atlantosaurus,** *n.* huge fossil reptile. (*Atlas,* Titan who bore the world on his shoulders)
atmo-, from Gk. *atmos,* vapour, used in **atmology,** *n.* science of vaporization; **atmolysis,** *n.* separation of gases; **atmometer,** *n.* instrument for measuring evaporation.
atmosphere, *n.* air round earth, air; surrounding influence; normal air pressure of 15 lb. on square inch. **atmospheric,** *a.*—*n.pl.* interference with wireless reception, due to electrical disturbances in ether. **atmospherical,** *a.* (Gk. *sphaira,* ball)
atoll, *n.* ring-shaped coral-island with central lagoon. (native)
atom, *n.* smallest portion into which matter can be divided; very small part or thing. **atomic,** *a.* of atoms. **atomic philosophy,** doctrine that all things come from atoms. **atomic theory,** that all chemical combinations result from the atoms of bodies uniting in fixed proportions. **atomical,** *a.* **atomicity,** *n.* number of atoms in molecule of an element. **atomism,** *n.* atomic philosophy or theory. **atomist,** *n.* **atomize,** *v.t.* reduce to atoms. **atomizer,** *n.* instrument for spraying liquids. **atomy,** *n.* tiny being. (Gk. *a-,* not; *temnein,* cut)
atomy, *n.* skeleton. (*anatomy,* taken as *an atomy*)
atonal, *a.* (*mus.*) characterized by **atonality,** *n.* absence of key.
atone, *v.i.* and *t.* make amends, expiate; (*arch.*) reconcile. **atonement,** *n.* (*at; one*)
atonic, *a.* unaccented. (*tone*)
atop, *adv.* on, at, the top.
atrabiliar, atrabilious, *aa.* melancholy, gloomy; bad-tempered. (L. *ater,* black; *bilis,* bile)
atramental, *a.* inky, black. (L. *atramentum,* ink)
atrip, *adv.* (of anchor) just out of the ground. (*trip*)
atrium, *n.* entrance-hall of Roman house; forecourt. (L.)
atrocious, *a.* extremely wicked; execrable. **atrocity,** *n.* wickedness; wicked deed. (L. *atrox,* cruel)
atrophy, *n.* wasting away, emaciation. —*v.t.* and *i.* (cause to) waste away. (Gk. *a-,* not; *trephein,* nourish)
atropine, *n.* poison got from deadly nightshade. (Gk. *Atropos,* a Fate)
atta, *n.* (*Anglo-Ind.*) wheaten flour or meal. (Punjabi)
attaboy, *int.* (*Amer.*) go it! (corrupt. of *that's the boy!*)
attach, *v.t.* fasten, cause to adhere; attribute; win over; seize.—*v.i.* adhere. **attaché,** *n.* one attached to ambassador's suite. **attaché case,** small rectangular case for papers etc. **attachment,** *n.* fastening; affection. (O.F. *atachier*)
attack, *v.t.* and *i.* fall upon, assail; take offensive.—*n.* assault; onset; hostile criticism. (*attach*)
attain, *v.t.* and *i.* reach, arrive; obtain, accomplish. **attainment,** *n.* attaining; acquisition; (*pl.*) acquirements in learning. (L. *tangere,* touch

attainder, *n.* loss of estate and civil rights following conviction for high treason. **attaint,** *v.t.* subject to attainder; infect; stain, disgrace. **attaintment, attainture,** *nn.* (*attain,* +confusion with *taint*)

attar, *n.* fragrant oil made from rose petals. (Pers. *atar*)

attask, *v.t.* (*Shake.*) take to task.

attemper, *v.t.* mix in due proportion; modify; adapt (to); temper (metal). **attemperment,** *n.* (*temper*)

attempt, *v.t.* try, endeavour; attack.—*n.* trial, effort; attack (*tempt*)

attend, *v.t.* and *i.* wait upon, accompany; be present at; pay attention. **attendance,** *n.* attending; people present. **attendant,** *a.* waiting upon.—*n.* servant. **attent,** *a.* and *n.* (*Spens.*) attentive; attention. **attention,** *n.* act of attending; application; heed, care; (*pl.*) acts of special regard, courtship. **attentive,** *a.* heedful; polite. (L. *ad,* to; *tendere,* stretch)

attenuate, *v.t.* make thin; reduce, weaken.—*a.* slender; dilute. **attenuation,** *n.* (L. *tenuis,* thin)

attest, *v.t.* and *i.* testify, bear witness (to); call to witness; enrol for military service. **attestation,** *n.* attesting; formal confirmation by signature, oath etc. (L. *testis,* witness)

attic, *n.* room in roof of house, garret; dialect of ancient Athens.—*a.* of Athens. **A. order,** square column of any of the five orders. **A. salt, wit,** delicate wit. **Atticism,** *n.* Athenian idiom; elegant expression. (*Attica,* in which Athens lies)

attire, *v.t.* dress, array.—*n.* dress. (O.F. *à,* to; *tire,* order)

attitude, *n.* posture; behaviour showing opinion. **attitudinal,** *a.* **attitudinize,** *v.i.* assume affected postures. (L. *aptus,* fit)

attorn, *v.t.* and *i.* transfer; make legal acknowledgment of new landlord. **attorney,** *n.* one legally appointed to act for another; solicitor. **letter, power, of attorney,** formal instrument by one person authorizing another to act for him. **Attorney-General,** *n.* chief law officer of Crown in England. (O.F. *à,* to; *tourner,* turn)

attract, *v.t.* draw towards; allure. **attraction,** *n.* act of attracting; drawing force; thing that attracts. **attractive,** *a.* attracting; pleasing. **attractor,** *n.* (L. *ad,* to; *trahere,* draw)

attribute, *v.t.* ascribe as belonging, impute, assign.—*n.* quality, property, characteristic. **attribution,** *n.* attributing; function. **attributive,** *a.* expressing attribute; (*gram.*) qualifying.—*n.* qualifying word. (L. *tribuere,* assign)

attrited, *a.* worn by friction. **attrition,** *n.* rubbing, friction; wearing out. (L. *terere,* rub)

attune, *v.t.* adjust one sound to another; make accordant; tune. (*tune*)

atween, *prep.* (*Scot.*) between.

atypical, *a.* not according to type.

au, to the. *au contraire,* on the contrary. *au courant,* well-informed. *au fait,* conversant. *au fond,* at bottom. *au grand sérieux,* quite seriously. *au naturel,* in the natural state, cooked plainly. *au pair,* (of arrangement between two people) paid for by mutual service, without money passing. *au pied de la lettre,* literally. *au revoir,* till we meet again. (F.)

aubade, *n.* musical announcement of dawn; sunrise song. (F.)

auberge, *n.* inn. (F.)

aubrietia, *n.* small purple-flowered perennial. (Claude *Aubriet,* artist)

auburn, *a.* reddish-brown. (L. *alburnus,* whitish)

auction, *n.* public sale to highest bidder. **Dutch a.,** in which price starts high, and is reduced till a purchaser is found. **auctioneer,** *n.* one licensed to sell by auction.—*v.i.* conduct auction. (L. *augēre,* increase)

audacious, *a.* daring, bold; impudent. **audacity,** *n.* (L. *audax*)

audible, *a.* able to be heard. **audibility,** *n.* **audience,** *n.* hearing; formal interview; assembly of hearers. **audile,** *a.* received through hearing. **audiometer,** *n.* instrument for testing hearing. **audiphone,** *n.* instrument assisting hearing. (L. *audire,* hear)

audit, *n.* official examination of accounts.—*v.t.* and *i.* verify (accounts) by audit. **audition,** *n.* hearing; trial performance of singer etc. **auditive,** *a.* of hearing. **auditor,** *n.* one who audits; hearer. **auditorial,** *a.* of an audit. **auditorium,** *n.* part of building occupied by audience. **auditory,** *a.* of hearing.—*n.* audience; auditorium. (L. *audire,* hear)

auf wiedersehen, till we meet again. (G.)

Augean, *a.* filthy. (stables of *Augeas,* which Hercules cleansed)

auger, *n.* boring-tool, large gimlet. (O.E. *nafu,* nave; *gár,* piercer; with loss of *n* as in *adder, apron*)

aught, *n.* anything.—*adv.* (*arch.*) in any degree. (O.E. *á,* ever; *wiht,* whit)

augment, *v.t.* and *i.* make or grow larger, increase.—*n.* increase; (*philol.*) prefixed vowel indicating past tense. **augmentation,** *n.* enlargement, addition. **augmentative,** *a.* and *n.* (affix etc.) increasing in force the idea of a word. (L. *augēre,* increase)

augur, *n.* diviner, soothsayer.—*v.t.* and *i.* foretell from signs; forebode, bode. **augural,** *a.* **augury,** *n.* divination; omen; prediction. (L.)

august, *a.* majestic, imposing. (L. *augustus,* venerable)

August, *n.* eighth month of the year,

Augustan, *a.* of the time of Augustus; classical. (*Augustus* Caesar)
auk, *n.* northern sea-bird with short wings used as paddles. **great a.,** garefowl, now extinct. (O.N. *álka*)
auld, *a.* (*Scot.*) old. **a.-farrant,** *a.* old-fashioned; prudent. **a.-warld,** *a.* old-world. **a. lang syne,** days of old, long ago.
aulic, *a.* of a royal court. (Gk. *aulē*. court)
aumbry, same as **ambry.**
aumous, *Scot.* form of **alms.**
aunt, *n.* parent's sister or uncle's wife. **A. Sally,** game of throwing sticks at dummy head. (L. *amita*)
aura, *n.* subtle emanation from anything; atmosphere surrounding person; symptoms preceding epileptic fit. **aural,** *a.* (Gk.=breeze)
aural, *a.* of the ear. (L. *auris,* ear)
aureate, *a.* golden, gilded. **aurelia,** *n.* chrysalis. **aurelian,** *a.*—*n.* insect-collector. **aureola, aureole,** *nn.* gold disk round heads in sacred pictures; halo. **auric,** *a.* of gold. (L. *aurum,* gold)
auricle, *n.* external ear; either of two upper cavities of heart. **auricula,** *n.* bear's-ear, kind of primula. **auricular,** *a.* of the ear; secret; of, shaped like, auricle of heart. **auriculate,** *a.* with ear-like projections. **auriform,** *a.* ear-shaped. **aurilave,** *n.* instrument for cleansing ears. **aurist,** *n.* ear specialist. (L. *auris,* ear)
auriferous, *a.* gold-bearing. (L. *aurum,* gold; *ferre,* bear)
aurochs, *n.* extinct wild ox (G.)
aurora, *n.* dawn, morning light. **a. borealis,** northern lights, luminous radiation seen towards north magnetic pole. **a. australis,** same in south hemisphere. (L.=goddess of dawn)
auscultation, *n.* (*med.*) act of listening to heart, lungs etc. by ear or stethoscope. **auscultator,** *n.* **auscultatory,** *a.* (L. *auscultare,* listen)
auspice, *n.* augury, omen; (*pl.*) patronage. **auspicate,** *v.t.* inaugurate, initiate.—*v.i.* augur. **auspicious,** *a.* of good omen, propitious. (L. *auspex,* bird-seer, soothsayer)
Aussie, *n.* (*sl.*) Australian. (abbr.)
austere, *a.* harsh, severe; rigidly moral; severely simple. **austerity,** *n.* (Gk. *auein,* dry)
austral, *a.* southern. (L. *Auster,* south wind)
Australasian, *a.* and *n.* (native) of Australasia (Australia, New Zealand, and adjacent islands). **Australian,** *a.* and *n.* (native) of Australia.
autarky, autarchy, *n.* self-sufficiency, esp. in economic sphere. (Gk. *autos,* self; *arkein,* suffice)
aut Caesar aut nullus or *nihil,* the highest place or nothing. (L.= either Caesar or no one)
authentic, *a.* genuine; true, trustworthy. **authenticate,** *v.t.* prove true or genuine; certify authorship of. **authentication,** *n.* authenticating. **authenticity,** *n.* genuineness. (Gk. *authentēs,* one who does thing with his own hand)
authigenic, *a.* originating where found. (Gk. *autos,* self; *gignesthai,* become)
author, *n.* (*fem.* **authoress**) writer of book; originator, constructor. **authorial,** *a.* **authorship,** *n.* writing profession; origin (of book). (L. *augēre,* promote)
authority, *n.* power, weight, influence; permission; person, body, in control; expert. **authoritative,** *a.* having authority; dictatorial. **authorize,** *v.t.* empower, sanction. **authorization,** *n.* (L. *auctoritas*)
autism, *n.* (*psycho-anal.*) absorption in fantasy, constant day-dreaming. (Gk. *autos,* self)
auto-, *pref.* self-, by oneself, independent. (Gk. *autos,* self)
auto, *n.* (*sl.*) motor-car. (abbr. of *automobile*)
autobahn, *n.* (*pl. autobahnen*) German arterial road. (G.)
autobiography, *n.* life of a person written by himself. **autobiographer,** *n.* **autobiographic, autobiographical** *aa.* (Gk. *autos,* self; *bios,* life; *graphein,* write)
autobus, autocar, *nn.* motor-bus, motor-car.
autocephalous, *a.* having its own head; independent. (Gk. *kephalē,* head)
autochrome, *n.* photographic plate giving natural colours. (Gk. *autos,* self; *chrōma,* colour)
autochthon, *n.* (*pl.* **autochthones, autochthons**) aboriginal inhabitant. **autochthonic, autochthonous,** *aa.* indigenous, native to the soil. **autochthonism, autochthony,** *nn.* (Gk. *autos,* self; *chthōn,* land)
autocrat, *n.* (*fem.* **autocratrix**) absolute ruler. **autocracy,** *n.* absolute rule, despotism. **autocratic,** *a.* (Gk. *autos,* self; *kratos,* power)
auto-da-fé, *n.* (*pl. autos-da-fé*) judgment of Spanish Inquisition; burning of heretic. (Port.=act of faith)
auto-erotism, *n.* self-produced sexual emotion. (Gk. *erōs,* love)
autogamy, *n.* self-fertilization. (Gk. *gamos,* marriage)
autogeny, *n.* spontaneous generation. **autogenous,** *a.* (Gk. *genos,* offspring)
autograph, *n.* one's own handwriting; signature; original manuscript; reproduction by autography.—*v.t.* sign; copy by autography. **autographic,** *a.* **autography,** *n.* one's own handwriting; lithographic process giving facsimile of writing etc. (Gk. *autos,* self; *graphein,* write)
autogiro, autogyro, *n.* kind of aeroplane with horizontal lifting vanes. (Gk. *autos,* self; *guros,* ring)
autoharp, *n.* musical instrument like zither.

auto-intoxicant, *n.* poison produced within the body. **auto-intoxication,** *n.*

autoist, *n.* (*Amer.*) motorist.

autolysis, *n.* destruction of cells of a body by action of its own serum. (Gk. *autos*, self; *lusis*, destruction)

automatic, *a.* self-acting; mechanical, unconscious.—*n.* automatic pistol. **automatism,** *n.* involuntary action; mechanical routine. **automaton,** *n.* self-moving mechanism; person acting mechanically. (Gk. *automatos*)

automobile, *n.* motor-car.—*v.i.* (*Amer.*) ride in one. **automobilist,** *n.* motorist. **automobilism, automobility,** *nn.* use of motor-cars. **automobilize,** *v.i.* and *t.* ride in, traverse by, motor-car. (F.)

autonomy, *n.* self-government; independence, freedom. **autonomous,** *a.* (Gk. *autos*, self; *nomos*, law)

autonym, *n.* real name, esp. of author (opp. to pseudonym). (Gk. *autos*, self; *onoma*, name)

autopsy, *n.* post-mortem examination; personal observation. **autoptic, autoptical,** *aa.* (Gk. *autopsia*)

auto-suggestion, *n.* (*psycho-anal.*) self-applied suggestion.

autotoxin, *n.* poisonous substance produced by changes within an organism. **autotoxic,** *a.* **autotoxication,** *n.* (Gk. *toxicon*, poison)

autotype, *n.* photographic reproduction process; facsimile.—*v.t.* reproduce by this process.

autumn, *n.* third season of year, September-November; (*astron.*) 22 Sept.-21 Dec.; season of decay. **autumnal,** *a.* (L. *autumnus*)

auxanometer, *n.* instrument for measuring growth in plants. (Gk. *auxanein*, increase; *metron*, measure)

auxiliary, *a.* helping, subsidiary.—*n.* helper; (*gram.*) verb used to form tenses etc. of others; (*pl.*) foreign troops serving with army. (L. *auxilium*, help)

ava', (*Scot.*) at all.

avadavat, see **amadavat.**

avail, *v.t.* and *i.* be of use or service (to); aid, benefit.—*n.* use, profit. **a. oneself of,** make use of. **available,** *a.* capable of being used; at hand. (L. *valēre*, be strong)

avail, same as **avale.**

aval, *a.* of a grandparent. (L. *avus*, grandfather)

avalanche, *n.* mass of snow, ice etc. sliding down mountain. (F. *avaler*, descend)

avale, *v.t.* and *i.* (*Spens.*) sink, lower. (L. *ad vallem*, to the valley)

avant-courier, *n.* one who runs before; (*pl.*) skirmishers. (F. *avant*, before)

avarice, *n.* greed for wealth, cupidity. **avaricious,** *a.* greedy, miserly. (L. *avarus*, greedy)

avast, *int.* (*naut.*) stop. (Du. *houd vast*, hold fast)

avatar, *n.* descent to earth of Hindu deity; incarnation, manifestation. (Sanskr.=descent)

avaunt, *int.* begone.—*v.i.* (*Spens.*) advance. (L. *ab*, from; *ante*, before)

ave, *int.* hail. **A. Maria,** prayer said to Virgin Mary. (L.)

avenge, *v.t.* take vengeance on behalf of (person) or on account of (thing). **avenger,** *n.* (L. *vindicare*)

avens, *n.* kinds of plant incl. herb bennet. (O.F. *avence*)

aventurine, *n.* brown, spangled kind of Venetian glass. (It. *avventura*, chance, from its accidental discovery)

avenue, *n.* drive lined by trees; double row of trees; wide street; means of approach. (L. *ad*, to; *venire*, come)

aver, *v.t.* assert, affirm; (*law*) justify (plea). (L. *verus*, true)

average, *n.* mean of several quantities; ordinary standard.—*a.* medium, ordinary.—*v.t.* find average; usually amount to.

averment, *n.* statement; (*law*) offer to prove, proof of, plea. (*aver*)

averruncator, *n.* instrument for pruning trees. (L. *averruncare*, avert)

averse, *a.* opposed; unwilling. **aversion,** *n.* dislike, hatred; object of dislike. (*avert*)

avert, *v.t.* turn away; ward off. (L. *avertere*)

avertin, *n.* an anaesthetic drug. (trade name)

avian, *a.* of birds. **aviary,** *n.* place for keeping birds. (L. *avis*, bird)

aviate, *v.i.* pilot, travel in, aircraft. **aviation, aviator,** *nn.* **aviatress, aviatrix,** *nn.* female aviator. **avion,** *n.* warplane. (L. *avis*, bird)

avid, *a.* eager, greedy. **avidity,** *n.* (L. *avidus*)

aviette, *n.* aeroplane worked by man-power, kind of glider. (*avion*)

avifauna, *n.* birds of a region.

aviso, *n.* dispatch-boat. (Sp.)

avizandum, *n.* (*Scots law*) private consideration by judge, before passing judgment. (L.L. *avizare*, consider)

avocado, *n.* alligator pear. (Sp.)

avocation, *n.* vocation, calling; minor occupation; calling of a case to a higher tribunal; (*arch.*) diversion. (L. *a*, from; *vocare*, call)

avocet, avoset, wading bird like snipe. (It. *avosetta*)

avoid, *v.t.* shun; evade; (*law*) annul; (*Shake.*) leave. **avoidance,** *n.* avoiding; vacancy. (*void*)

avoirdupois, *n.* ordinary system of weights, in which 1 lb.=16 oz.; (*Amer.*) weight. (F.=to have weight)

avouch, *v.t.* guarantee; maintain; own.—*n.* (*Shake.*) evidence. **avouchment,** *n.* (L. *advocare*, call to aid)

avow, *v.t.* declare openly, confess. **avowal,** *n.* **avowedly,** *adv.* (*vow*)

avulsion, *n.* tearing away. (L. *a*, from; *vellere*, pluck)

avuncular, *a.* of, like, an uncle. (L. *avunculus*, maternal uncle)
awa, *Scot.* form of **away.**
await, *v.t.* wait for, expect; be in store for. (*wait*)
awake, *v.t.* (*past* **awoke,** *p.p.* **awoke, awaked**) wake, rouse from sleep.—*v.i.* stop sleeping; become active.—*a.* not asleep; vigilant. **awaken,** *v.t.* and *i.* awake, rouse to sense of. (*wake*)
award, *v.t.* adjudge; assign.—*n.* judgment, arbitrator's decision; thing awarded. (*ward*)
aware, *a.* conscious, cognizant. **awareness,** *n.* (O.E. *gewær*)
awash, *a.* level with water's surface; washed by the waves.
away, *adv.* out of the way, to a distance, absent. **cannot a. with,** cannot endure. **do, make, a. with,** abolish, destroy. **fire a.,** go ahead. **out and a.,** beyond comparison. **work etc. a.,** keep on working. (O.E. *onweg*)
awe, *n.* reverential fear.—*v.t.* inspire with awe. **awesome,** *a.* **awestruck,** *a.* struck with awe. (O.E. *ege*)
awful, *a.* dreadful; solemnly impressive; (*sl.*) ugly; extreme. **awfully,** *adv.* (*sl.*) very. (*awe*)
awhile, *adv.* for a time.
awkward, *a.* clumsy, ungainly; ill-adapted for use; difficult.
awl, *n.* small pointed boring-tool used by shoemakers etc. (O.E. *æl*)
awn, *n.* spine, beard, on ear of corn or grass-head. **awned, awny,** *aa.*
awning, *n.* canvas roof or shelter.
awoke, see **awake.**
awry, *adv.* askew, crookedly; amiss.—*a.* crooked. (*wry*)
axe, ax, *n.* tool for chopping or hewing.—*v.t.* cut down (costs etc.). **a. to grind,** ulterior motive. (O.E. *æx*)
axial, *a.* of, forming, round, an axis.
axil, *n.* (*bot.*) upper angle between leaf and stem, or branch and trunk. (L. *axilla*, armpit)
axile, *a.* of, in, axis. (*axis*)
axillary, *a.* of armpit; (*bot.*) in axil.
axiom, *n.* self-evident truth; accepted principle. **axiomatic, axiomatical,** *aa.* (Gk. *axioein*, think worthy)
axis, *n.* (*pl.* **axes**) line round which body rotates; centre line of symmetrical figure; central core (of organ), central column (of plant). **Rome-Berlin A.,** alliance between Italy and Germany. (L.)
axle, *n.* spindle on which wheel turns; axle-tree. **a.-box,** *n.* inner part of hub. **a.-tree,** *n.* cross-bar connecting wheels. (*axis*)
axolotl, *n.* Mexican reptile like salamander. (Aztec=servant of water)
ay, aye, *adv.* yes.—*n.* affirmative answer or vote.
ayah, *n.* native Indian nurse or lady's maid. (Port. *aia*)
aye, ay, *adv.* ever, always. (O.N. *ei*)
aye-aye, *n.* small Madagascar lemur like squirrel. (Malagasy *aiay*)
ayont, *prep.* (*Scot.*) beyond.
azalea, *n.* kinds of shrubby plants, with white, yellow, or crimson flowers. (Gk. *azaleos*, dry)
azan, *n.* Mohammedan call to prayer, (Arab. *adān*, invitation)
Azilian, *a.* between Palaeolithic and Neolithic. (Mas d'*Azil* in France)
azimuth, *n.* vertical arc from zenith to horizon; angular distance of this from meridian. **azimuthal,** *a.* (Arab. *al*, the; *samt*, way)
azoic, *a.* without life; (of rocks) without fossils, formed before animal life. (Gk. *a-*, not; *zoē*, life)
azote, *n.* old name for nitrogen. **azotic,** *a.* (Gk. *a-*, not; *zaein*, live)
Aztec, *a.* and *n.* (member) of tribe ruling Mexico before Spanish conquest.
azure, *a.* and *n.* sky-blue (colour); sky. (Pers. *lazhward*, lapis lazuli)
azygous, *a.* not yoked; (*anat.*) not one of a pair. (Gk. *a-*, not; *zugon*, yoke)

B

B, (*math.*) second known quantity; (*mus.*) note and scale.
ba', *Scot.* form of **ball.**
baa, *n.* sheep's cry.—*v.i.* bleat. (imit.)
Baalam, *n.* misleading prophet; padding for newspaper. (Bible name)
baas, *n.* (*S.Afr.*) master, sir. (Du.)
baba, *n.* finger-shaped cake, soaked in wine.
babacoote, *n.* large lemur. (Malagasy *babakoto*)
babbitry, *n.* (*Amer.*) U.S. business man's standards or outlook. (*Babbitt*, novel)
babbitt-metal, *n.* soft anti-friction alloy used for bearings. (inventor)
babble, *v.t.* and *i.* talk childishly or incoherently; tell (secrets); (of stream) murmur.—*n.* foolish talk. **babblement, babbler,** *nn.* (imit.)
babe, *n.* (*poet.*) baby; inexperienced person. (imit. of child's talk)
babel, *n.* confused noise or scene. (place in Bible)
baboo, babu, *n.* Hindu gentleman: (as title) Mr.; native clerk. **b. English,** weird English used by some. (Hind.)
baboon, *n.* large short-tailed monkey found in Africa and S. Asia.
babouche, *n.* oriental slipper. (Pers. *pa*, foot; *posh*, covering)
baby, *n.* infant; childish person; (*sl.*)

girl, sweetheart. **b. car**, small car. **b.-farmer**, *n.* one who keeps babies for payment. **b. grand**, small grand piano. **babyhood**, **babyism**, *nn.* **babyish**, *a.* (*babe*)

Babylonian, *a.* of Babylon, vicious; popish. (ancient *Babylon*)

baccalaureate, *n.* university degree of bachelor. (*bachelor*)

baccarat, **baccara**, *n.* gambling card-game. (F.)

baccate, *a.* having berries; berry-shaped. (L. *bacca*, berry)

Bacchanal, *n.* priest of Bacchus; drunken reveller.—*a.* riotous. **Bacchanalia**, *n.pl.* drunken revels. **Bacchanalian**, *a.* **Bacchant**, *n.* (*fem.* **Bacchante**) priest, votary, of Bacchus; drunkard. **Bacchic**, *a.* of Bacchus; drunken. (Gk. *Bakchos*, wine-god)

bacciferous *a.* berry-bearing. **bacciform**, *a.* berry-shaped. **baccivorous**, *a.* berry-eating. (L. *bacca*, berry)

baccy, *n.* (*colloq.*) tobacco. (abbr.)

bach, *v.i.* (*Amer. sl.*) keep house as bachelor. (*bachelor*)

bachelor, *n.* unmarried man; holder of lowest university degree; (formerly) young knight following another's banner. **knight b.**, one not belonging to a special order. **b.'s buttons**, double-flowered buttercup. **bachelorhood**, **bachelorship**, **bachelorism**, *nn.* (L. *baccalarius*, farm-servant)

bachle, *n.* (*Scot.*) old or worn shoe; clumsy person, butt.

bacillus, *n.* (*pl.* **bacilli**) rod-like vegetable micro-organism, microbe. **bacillary**, *a.* **bacilliform**, *a.* rod-shaped. (L. *baculus*, stick)

back, *n.* hinder part of man or thing; upper part of animal; rear; (*football*) player at rear.—*a.* hinder; former; reversed.—*adv.* to rear; to former position, state, or time; in return.—*v.t.* and *i.* put or be back to: help; bet on; endorse; ride (horse); move, go, backwards; (of wind) change round against the sun; (*Amer.*) address (letter). **b. number**, former issue; out-of-date person. **b. talk**, impudence. **b. up**, support. **put one's b. up**, antagonize. **b. water**, reverse action of oars. (O.E. *bæc*)

back, *n.* shallow vat. (Du. *bak*)

backbite, *v.t.* slander. **backbiter**, *n.*

back-blocks, *n.pl.* (*Austral.*) interior parts of settlement. **back-blocker**, *n.*

backboard, *n.* board at back of cart; board worn at back to correct stoop.

backbone, *n.* spine; main support; firmness.

backdoor, *n.* rear door.—*a.* underhand.

back-end, *n.* late autumn.

backer, *n.* supporter; one who bets.

backfire, *n.* ignition of gas in engine's cylinder at wrong time.

backfisch, *n.* (*sl.*) girl, flapper. (G.)

backgammon, *n.* game on double board with draughts and dice. (*game*)

background, *n.* remoter part of scene or picture, setting; obscurity.

backhand, *n.* writing sloping backward.—*a.* (also **backhanded**) given with back of hand; indirect, reversed.

backing, *n.* support; lining for back.

backlash, *n.* irregular recoil of machine's wheels.

backmarker, *n.* scratch man in race.

backsheesh, same as **baksheesh**.

backside, *n.* rump.

back-slang, *n.* slang formed by pronouncing words backwards, as 'ynnep.'

backslide, *v.i.* relapse into sin or disbelief. **backslider**, *n.*

backstairs, *n.pl.* stairs at back.—*a.* secret, underhand.

backstays, *n.pl.* ropes supporting mast at back.

backstitch, *n.* and *v.t.* (sew with) overlapping stitches.

backsword, *n.* one-edged sword; singlestick.

backveld, *n.* (*S. Afr.*) remote country parts.—*a.* primitive. **backvelder**, *n.*

backward, **backwards**, *adv.* to rear, past, or starting-point; back foremost. **backward**, *a.* shy, dull. **backwardation**, *n.* payment by seller of stock for right to delay delivery.

backwash, *n.* motion of receding wave.

backwater, *n.* still pool or channel fed by river; water thrown back from paddles; stagnant condition.

backwoods, *n.pl.* uncleared forest land in new country. **backwoodsman**, *n.*

bacon, *n.* back and sides of pig cured for eating. **bacony**, *a.* (O.F.)

bacterium, *n.* (*pl.* **bacteria**) microscopic rod-shaped fungus found in decomposing matter, microbe. **bacterial**, *a.* **bacteriology**, **bacteriologist**, *nn.* **bacteriolysis**, *n.* destruction of bacteria by a serum. **bacteriolytic**, *a.* (Gk. *baktron*, stick)

baculine, *a.* of the stick or cane. (L. *baculus*, stick)

bad, *a.* (*compar.* worse, *superl.* worst) evil, wicked; faulty, worthless; ill. —*n.* misfortune; ruin. **b. blood**, ill feeling. **b. coin**, false coin. **b. debt**, not recoverable. **b. egg**, **hat**, (*sl.*) rascal. **b. form**, ill manners; vulgar. **b. shot**, wrong guess. **go b.**, rot. **in a b. sense**, unfavourably. **to the b.**, to ruin: in deficit. **with b. grace**, unwillingly. **baddish**, *a.* (M.E. *badde*)

bad, **bade**, see **bid**.

badge, *n.* distinguishing mark, symbol. (M.E.)

badger, *n.* burrowing night animal, between weasel and bear; paintbrush made of its hair.—*v.t.* pester, worry. (*badge*, from mark on forehead)

badger, *n.* (*dial.*) hawker, pedlar.

badinage, *n.* banter, chaff. (F.)

badly, *adv.* faultily; unsuccessfully; cruelly; very much. (*bad*)
badmash, *n.* (*Anglo-Ind.*) rascal. (Pers.)
badminton, *n.* game played with rackets and shuttlecocks; cooling drink of claret and soda. (village)
baff, *n.* (*Scot.*) blow.
baffle, *v.t.* check, frustrate; (*obs.*) disgrace publicly. **b.-plate,** *n.* plate regulating outlet.
baffy, *n.* golf-club like brassy, but with more loft.
baft, *n.* coarse cheap cotton fabric. (Pers.=woven)
bag, *n.* sack, pouch; what sportsman has shot; (*pl., sl.*) trousers.—*v.t.* put in bag, secure; (*colloq.*) take, steal.—*v.i.* bulge. **b. fox,** one brought, not found.
bag, *v.t.* cut (wheat etc.) with hook.
bagasse, *n.* sugar-cane refuse. (F).
bagatelle, *n.* trifle; game with balls and cue, like billiards. (F.)
baggage, *n.* portable equipment of army; luggage; worthless woman; cheeky girl, minx. (O.F. *bagage*)
baggie, *n.* (*Scot.*) stomach. (*bag*)
baggy, *a.* bulging, hanging in folds.
bagman, *n.* commercial traveller.
bagnio, *n.* baths; oriental prison; brothel. (L. *balneum,* bath)
bagpipe, bagpipes, *n.* musical wind-instrument. **bagpiper,** *n.*
bah, *int.* of disgust or scorn. (F.)
Bahadur, *n.* Indian title of respect; (*Anglo-Ind. sl.*) consequential official. (Hind.=brave)
bahar, *n.* Eastern measure of weight, 223–625 lb.
baikie, *n.* (*Scot.*) square wooden box or trough for firewood etc.
bail, *n.* security for person's reappearance in court; person providing this. —*v.t.* give bail for, free on bail; deliver (goods) in trust. **b. out,** bail (prisoner). **b. up,** (*Austral.*) hold up, as bushrangers. **go b. for,** bail, guarantee. **give leg b.,** make off. (L. *bajalus,* porter)
bail, *n.* bar separating horses in open stable; (*cricket*) cross-piece over stumps; (formerly) outer line of fortification. (L. *baculum,* stick)
bail, *n.* hoop-handle of kettle or pail; hoop supporting wagon-tilt. (O.E. *bēgan,* bend)
bail, bale, *v.t.* empty out water (from boat etc.). (L. *baca,* tub)
bailable, *a.* admitting of bail.
bailee, *n.* one to whom goods are delivered in trust. (*bail*)
bailer, *n.* (*cricket*) ball that hits bails.
bailey, *n.* outer wall of castle; castle yard or court.
bailie, *n.* Scottish municipal officer corresponding to English alderman.
bailiff, *n.* (formerly) king's deputy; sheriff's officer; agent, steward.
bailiwick, *n.* jurisdiction of bailie or bailiff. (L. *bajulus,* porter)
bailment, *n.* bailing (of goods or prisoner). **bailor,** *n.* one who delivers goods in trust. **bailsman,** *n.* one who gives bail for another.
bairn, *n.* (*Scot.*) child. (O.E. *bearn*)
bait, *n.* food to entice fish; lure, enticement; halt for refreshment.—*v.t.* and *i.* worry (animal) by setting dogs at it; torment with jeers; give, take, food on journey; furnish with bait. (O.N. *beita,* food, and *beita,* cause to bite)
bait, see **bate.**
baith, *Scot.* form of **both.**
baize, *n.* coarse woollen stuff. (L. *badius,* bay-coloured)
bajri, *n.* kinds of Indian grain. (native)
bake, *v.t.* and *i.* cook or harden by dry heat; scorch, be scorched. **baker,** *n.* one who bakes bread. **baker's dozen,** thirteen. **bakery, bakehouse,** *nn.* (O.E. *bacan*)
bakelite, *n.* hard synthetic resin used for dishes etc. (trade name)
baksheesh, *n.* gratuity, tip. (Pers.)
balalaika, *n.* Russian three-stringed guitar. (Russ.)
balance, *n.* pair of scales, instrument for weighing; counterpoise; equilibrium; surplus, remainder.—*v.t.* and *i.* weigh; bring, come, to equilibrium; match; make up (accounts); hesitate. **b.-sheet,** *n.* statement of assets and liabilities. **b.-wheel,** *n.* escapement of clock. (L. *bi-,* double; *lanx,* dish)
balas, *n.* kind of spinel ruby. (*Badakhshan,* near Samarcand)
balata, *n.* dried gum of a S. American tree, used as substitute for gutta-percha. (Sp.)
balcony, *n.* railed platform outside window; gallery. (*balk*)
bald, *a.* without hair on head, bare; (of style) dull, unadorned. **b.-coot,** *n.* coot. **b.-faced,** *a.* (of horse) having white on face. **baldhead, baldpate,** *nn.* (Gael. *bal,* spot)
baldachin, baldaquin, *n.* canopy, esp. over throne or altar. (*Baghdad*)
balderdash, *n.* words jumbled senselessly together, nonsense.
baldicoot, *n.* coot; bald person.
baldmoney, *n.* kinds of gentian.
baldric, *n.* shoulder-belt for sword etc. (L. *balteus,* belt)
bale, *n.* evil, destruction, woe. **baleful,** *a.* (O.E. *bealu*)
bale, *n.* compact package of goods. —*v.t.* make up in bale. **b. out,** leave aircraft by parachute. (O.H.G. *balla,* ball)
bale, *n.* (arch.) balefire. (O.E. *bǣl*)
bale, see **bail.**
baleen, *n.* whalebone. (L. *balaena,* whale)
balefire, *n.* beacon-fire; funeral pyre; bonfire. (*bale*)
balk, baulk, *n.* unploughed ridge between furrows; squared timber beam; hindrance; part of billiard table.—*v.t.* thwart, frustrate; shirk. —*v.i.* jib, shy. (O.E. *balca,* ridge)

ball, *n.* sphere; bullet, missile for firearm; (*cricket*) single delivery of bowler.—*v.i.* and *t.* form into ball. **keep the b. rolling**, keep (talk) from flagging. **balled up**, (*Amer. sl.*) mixed up. **b. bearings**, with small balls to avoid friction. **b.-cock**, *n.* automatic cistern tap.

ball, *n.* assembly for dancing. **ball-room**, *n.* **open the b.**, begin operations. (L.L. *ballare*, dance)

ballad, *n.* short narrative poem; simple song. **b.-monger**, *n.* **ballade**, *n.* poem of (us.) three eight-line stanzas and envoy, all with same rhymes and refrain. (L.L. *ballare*, dance)

ballast, *n.* heavy material used to give ship stability; slag used for railroad bed etc.—*v.t.* load with ballast; make steady. **in b.** (of ship) without cargo.

ballerina, *n.* (*pl.* **ballerinas** or **ballerínē**) ballet-girl, dancer. (It.)

ballet, *n.* theatrical scene acted in dancing. (*ball*)

ballistic, *a.* of projectiles. — *n.pl.* science of projectiles. (L. *ballista*, military engine)

ballon d'essai, experiment to see how policy will be received, feeler. (F. =trial balloon)

balloon, *n.* hollow sphere; gas-filled envelope or aircraft it supports.—*v.i.* ascend in balloon; puff out. **balloonist**, *n.* **ballonet**, *n.* small balloon; subdivision of airship's gas-bag. (It. *ballone*, large ball)

ballot, *n.* secret voting by putting ball or ticket in box; ball or ticket used; lot.—*v.i.* vote by ballot; draw lots. **ballotage**, *n.* second ballot between two highest candidates with less than legal majority. (It. *ballotta*, little ball)

bally, *a.* and *adv.* (*sl.*) used intensively. (pronunciation of *bl——y*)

ballyhoo, *n.* vulgar, noisy, publicity or advertisement.

ballyrag, *v.t.* hustle, jeer at.—*v.i.* indulge in horse-play.

balm, *n.* aromatic substance or tree yielding it; healing ointment; soothing influence. (*balsam*)

balm-cricket, *n.* cicada. (G. *baumgrille*, tree-cricket)

balmoral, *n.* kinds of Scotch bonnet, laced boot, petticoat. (place)

balmy, *a.* of or like balm, fragrant; mild, soothing; (*sl.*) cracked.

balneology, *n.* science of baths and their effect. (L. *balneum*, bath)

balsam, *n.* fragrant resinous substance or tree yielding it; kinds of ointment; a plant. **balsamic**, **balsamous**, *aa.* (L. *balsamum*)

baltimore, *n.* orange and black American starling. (Lord *Baltimore's* livery)

baluster, *n.* short pillar; (*pl.*) banisters. **balustrade**, *n.* ornamental parapet with pillared coping. (Gk. *balaustion*, wild pomegranate)

bam, *v.t.* and *n.* (*arch. sl.*) hoax.

bamboo, *n.* tropical giant grass with hollow woody stem. (Malay *bambu*)

bamboozle, *v.t.* (*sl.*) mystify, cheat. **bamboozlement**, *n.*

ban, *v.t.* prohibit, forbid use of; (*Shake.*) curse.—*n.* curse, proscription; prohibition. (O.E. *bannan*, summon)

ban, *n.* governor of a **banat**, military division of Hungary. (Pers.=lord)

banal, *a.* commonplace, vulgar, trite. **banality**, *n.* (F.)

banana, *n.* tropical tree; its finger-shaped yellow fruit. (native)

banausic, *a.* of, suited to, a mere mechanic; mean, illiberal. (Gk. *baunos*, forge)

band, *n.* bond, hoop; strip, stripe; company, troop; body of musicians. —*v.t.* and *i.* bind together, associate; stripe. **b. of hope**, total abstinence society. **bandbox**, *n.* light box for millinery. **bandmaster**, **bandsman**, **bandstand**, *nn.* conductor, member, platform, of cal musiband. (*bind*)

bandage, *n.* strip of cloth for binding wound etc.—*v.t.* bind with one.

bandanna, **bandana**, *n.* richly coloured spotted handkerchief. (Hind. *bandhnu*, mode of spot-dyeing)

bandar, *n.* (*Anglo-Ind.*) monkey. **b.-log**, *n.* the monkey race. (Hind.)

bandeau, *n.* band for hair; fitting-band inside hat. (F.)

banderilla, *n.* bull-fighter's barbed dart, used by **banderillero**. (Sp.)

banderol, **banderole**, *n.* long narrow flag with cleft end; small flag on lance, streamer; scroll, band, with inscription. (F.)

bandicoot, *n.* huge Indian rat; Australian insect-eating marsupial. (Telugu *pandikokku*, pig rat)

bandit, *n.* (*pl.* **bandits**, **banditti**) outlaw; robber, brigand. (*ban*)

bandobast, *n.* (*Anglo-Ind.*) organization, arrangement of details. (Pers. =tying and binding)

bandog, *n.* watch-dog on chain. (*band*)

bandolero, *n.* highwayman. (Sp.)

bandolier, **bandoleer**, *n.* shoulder-belt for holding cartridges. (It. *bandola*, little band)

bandoline, *n.* gummy dressing for hair.

bandy, *n.* kind of hockey; stick used in it.—*v.t.* and *i.* throw, strike, to and fro; exchange; contend.—*a.* (also **b.-legged**) with legs bent outward.

bandy, *n.* Indian cart. (Telugu *bandi*)

bane, *n.* ruin, destruction; poison. **baneful**, *a.* (O.E. *bana*, death)

bang, *n.* loud noise, explosion; blow; fringe of hair cut straight across forehead.—*v.t.* beat, strike, slam; cut in bang.—*v.i.* make loud noise.—*adv.* with a bang, abruptly. **b.-up**, *a.* (*sl.*) stylish. (O.N. *banga*, hammer)

bangle, *n.* bracelet, anklet. (Hind. *bangri,* glass bracelet)
banian, banyan, *n.* Indian fig-tree with vast rooting branches; Hindu trading caste; morning-gown. **b. day,** (*naut.*) on which no meat is served. **b. hospital,** for animals. (Hind. *banya,* trader)
banish, *v.t.* condemn to exile, expel. **banishment,** *n.* (*ban*)
banister, *n.* (us. *pl.*) staircase rail and supports. (corrupt. of *baluster*)
banjo, *n.* (*pl.* **banjos, banjoes**) stringed instrument with parchment body and neck like guitar, played with fingers. **banjoist,** *n.* (Gk. *pandoura*)
bank, *n.* ridge of ground, slope; mass of cloud; margin of river or lake; shoal.—*v.t.* and *i.* confine with banks; pile up; pack (fire) close for slow burning; (of aeroplane) tilt. (*bench*)
bank, *n.* bench (in galley); tier (of oars); row (of organ keys).
bank, *n.* establishment for keeping and trading in money; pool at gaming-table.—*v.t.* and *i.* deposit in bank; keep bank. **b. on,** count on. **b.-bill,** *n.* (*Amer.*) bank-note. **b. holiday,** general statutory holiday. **b.-note,** *n.* promissory note of bank, passing as money. **b.-rate,** *n.* rate at which Bank of England will discount bills. **bankable,** *a.* (*bench*)
banker, *n.* director etc. of bank; keeper of gaming-table; a card-game; mason's bench.
banket, *n.* gold-bearing conglomerate rock found in S. Africa. (Du.)
bankrupt, *n.* insolvent debtor, esp. one subjected to legal process; one who fails in business. — *a.* insolvent; bereft.—*v.t.* make bankrupt. **bankruptcy,** *n.* (L. *rumpere,* break)
banksia, *n.* a flowering shrub. (Sir J. *Banks*)
banner, *n.* flag of country etc.; military standard, ensign. **banneret,** *n.* higher class of knight; one dubbed in field for valour. **bannerol,** *n.* small banner, banderole. (*band*)
bannock, *n.* thick flat home-made cake of oatmeal or barley. (Gael. *bannach*)
banns, *n.pl.* proclamation of intended marriage, made in church. (*ban*)
banquet, *n.* feast; formal dinner with speeches.—*v.t.* and *i.* have, give, banquet. **banqueter,** *n.* (F.)
banquette, *n.* firing-step behind parapet; footway of bridge. (F.)
banshee, *n.* female fairy whose wail portends death in family. (Ir. *bean sidhe,* woman of the fairies)
bantam, *n.* small kind of fowl; small but pugnacious person.—also *a.* **b.-weight,** *a.* and *n.* (boxer) not over 8 st. 4 lb. (place in Java)
banter, *n.* good-humoured ridicule.—*v.t.* and *i.* make fun of, rally.
banting, *n.* a slimming dietary. **bant,** *v.i.* follow it. (inventor)
bantling, *n.* young child, brat.
Bantu, *n.* large group of S. African races and languages, incl. Kaffir and Zulu. (native=people)
banxring, *n.* insect-eating Javanese animal like squirrel. (Javanese)
banyan, see **banian.**
banzai, int. Japanese cheer or salute. (Jap.=live for ever)
baobab, *n.* monkey-bread, African tree with enormously thick trunk. (native)
bap, *n.* (*Scot.*) large breakfast roll.
baptize, *v.t.* immerse in, sprinkle with, water, esp. as religious rite; christen, name. **baptism,** *n.* **baptismal,** *a.* **baptist,** *n.* one who baptizes; one who believes in adult baptism by immersion. **baptistery, baptistry,** *nn.* place where baptism is administered. (Gk. *baptein,* dip)
bar, *n.* rod of rigid substance; bolt, obstacle; sandbank at river mouth; counter in tavern; rail in lawcourt; tribunal; profession of barrister; stripe; short division of music or line marking it. — *v.t.* fasten, secure; hinder, exclude; stripe; (*sl.*) dislike. **b. sinister,** (error for bend sinister) badge of illegitimacy. **called to the b.,** admitted as barrister. **b.-bell,** *n.* gymnast's bar weighted at ends.
bar, *n.* unit of atmospheric pressure, =1,000,000 dynes per square centimetre. (Gk. *baros,* weight)
bar, *n.* a large sea-fish. (F.)
barb, *n.* back-turned point in arrow-head, fish-hook etc.; lateral filament of feather.—*v.t.* furnish with barbs. (L. *barba,* beard)
barb, *n.* Barbary horse or pigeon. (*Barbary*)
barbarian, *a.* wild, uncultured; foreign, esp. non-Greek or non-Christian.—*n.* uncivilized or uncultured person; savage. **barbaric,** *a.* of barbarians or suited to their taste. **barbarism,** *n.* foreign or vulgar expression or its use; uncultured state. **barbarity,** *n.* savage cruelty. **barbarize,** *v.t.* and *i.* make or become barbarous. **barbarous,** *a.* uncivilized, cruel, coarse; barbarian; (of language) not pure, illiterate. (Gk. *barbaros,* foreign)
barbate, *a.* tufted, bearded. (L. *barba,* beard)
barbecue, *n.* framework for smoking or drying meat; ox, hog etc., roasted whole; (*Amer.*) social entertainment with lavish hospitality; floor for drying coffee-beans.—*v.t.* roast whole. (Haitian *barbacòa*)
barbel, *n.* a fresh-water fish with beard-like filaments at its mouth; such filament, hence **barbelled,** *a.*
barber, *n.* one who shaves beards and cuts hair. (L. *barba,* beard)
barberry, berberry, *n.* thorny shrub with yellow flowers; its red berry.
barbet, *n.* tropical bird with tufts at base of bill.

barbette, *n.* raised platform for guns to fire over parapet; type of armoured turret in warship. (F.)
barbican, *n.* tower over gate or bridge to defend town or castle. (F. *barbacane*)
barbitone, *n.* veronal. **barbituric acid,** a product of uric acid. (L. usnea *barbata,* bearded lichen+*uric*)
barbule, *n.* small barb; filament fringing barb of feather. (*barb*)
barcarole, barcarolle, *n.* gondolier's boat-song. (It. *barca,* boat)
bard, *n.* Celtic minstrel; poet. **bardic,** *a.* **bardling, bardlet,** *nn.* poetaster. (Gael. *bàrd*)
bard, *n.* protective armour for war-horse. **barded,** *a.* (F. *barde*)
bare, *a.* naked, exposed; unadorned; scanty; mere.—*v.t.* make bare, expose. **bareback,** *a.* and *adv.* without a saddle. **barefaced,** *a.* shameless, undisguised. (O.E. *bær*)
bare, see **bear.**
barège, *n.* silky dress-stuff like gauze. (F.)
barely, *adv.* openly; merely, scarcely.
baresark, same as **berserk.**
bargain, *n.* contract, agreement; purchase, esp. favourable one.—*v.t.* make bargain, haggle. **b. for,** be prepared for. **into the b.,** over and above. (O.F. *bargaine*)
barge, *n.* flat-bottomed freight boat; warship's second boat; ornamental boat for state occasions.—*v.i.* (*sl.*) lurch. **bargee,** *n.* man who works on barge. (O.F.)
barge-, from L.L. *bargus,* gallows, used in **b.-board,** *n.* board at gable screening rafters; **b.-couple,** *n.* two beams bounding gable; **b.-course,** *n.* roof projecting beyond them.
baric, *a.* of, containing, barium.
barilla, *n.* alkali made from kinds of marine plant or seaweed. (Sp.)
baritone, *n.* and *a.* (singer, voice) between tenor and bass. (Gk. *barus,* heavy; *tonos,* tone)
barium, *n.* a white metallic element. (*baryta*)
bark, *n.* outer covering, rind, of tree; tan; quinine.—*v.t.* strip of bark; graze (shins etc.). (Scand.)
bark, *n.* (*poet.*) ship; barque.
bark, *n.* sharp cry of dog.—*v.i.* utter bark; speak sharply. **b. up wrong tree,** accuse wrong person. **barker,** *n.* tout; (*sl.*) pistol. (O.E. *beorcan*)
barley, *n.* grain used for food and making malt. **b.-bree,** *n.* strong ale. **b.-meal,** *n.* barley flour. **b.-mow,** *n.* stack of barley. **b.-sugar,** *n.* kind of twisted sweetmeat. **b.-water,** *n.* decoction of pearl **b.,** grain ground small. (O.E. *bærlic*)
barley, *n.* (*Scot.*) parley, truce. **b.-break,** *n.* chasing game like tag.
barleycorn, *n.* grain of barley; measure of length, ⅓ in. **John B.,** personification of malt liquor.
barm, *n.* froth on fermenting liquor, yeast. (O.E. *beorma*)
barmaid, barman, *nn.* attendant in public-house.
Barmecide, *n.* one giving make-believe feast.—*a.* unreal, imaginary. **barmecidal,** *a.* (prince in 'Arabian Nights')
barmy, *a.* frothy; (*sl.*) crazy. (*barm*)
barn, *n.* (*Shake.*) child. (*bairn*)
barn, *n.* storehouse for grain. **b.-stormer,** *n.* strolling player. **barn-yard,** *n.* farmyard. (O.E. *bere,* barley; *ærn,* place)
barnacle, *n.* shell-fish that adheres to rocks and ships' bottoms; kind of wild goose. (O.F. *bernaque*)
barnacle, *n.* (us. *pl.*) pincers put on horse's nose to keep him still; (*sl.*) spectacles. (O.F. *bernac,* muzzle)
barney, *n.* (*sl.*) humbug; prize-fight.
barograph, *n.* self-recording aneroid barometer. **barology,** *n.* science of weight. (Gk. *baros,* weight)
barometer, *n.* instrument for measuring atmospheric pressure and so forecasting weather. **barometric, barometrical,** *aa.* **barometry,** *n.* (Gk. *baros,* weight; *metron,* measure)
baron, *n.* (*fem.* **baroness**) peer of lowest rank; (formerly) great lord. **b. of beef,** double sirloin. **baronage,** *n.* body or list of barons. **baronial,** *a.* **barony,** *n.* rank, domain, of baron; (*Scot.*) large manor; (*Ir.*) division of county. **baronet,** *n.* lowest British hereditary title. **baronetage, baronetcy,** *nn.* (L.L. *baro,* man)
baroque, *a.* grotesque, whimsical.—*n.* such style or ornamentation. (F.)
barouche, *n.* four-wheeled carriage for four with collapsible roof over rear seat. (L. *bi-,* double; *rota,* wheel)
barque, *n.* three-masted vessel square-rigged on fore and main masts only; bark. **barquentine,** *n.* vessel with foremast square-rigged, main and mizzen fore-and-aft rigged. (L. *barca,* boat)
barrack, *n.* building for lodging soldiers; huge bare building.—*v.t.* and *i.* jeer at, hoot. **barracoon,** *n.* depot for slaves. (Sp. *barraca,* tent)
barracoota, barracouta, barracuda, *n.* voracious W. Indian sea-fish.
barrage, *n.* dam; curtain of artillery fire making line impassable. (F.)
barranca, *n.* deep steep gorge. (Sp.)
barratry, *n.* defrauding of ship's owner by master or crew; stirring-up of lawsuits. **barrater, barrator,** *nn.* **barratrous,** *a.* (O.F. *barat,* fraud)
barrel, *n.* round wooden vessel, cask; its capacity; cylinder; tube of gun. —*v.t.* put in barrels. **b.-organ,** *n.* mechanical piano or organ played by revolving cylinder. (F. *baril*)
barren, *a.* unfruitful, sterile; unproductive; dull. (O.F. *baraine*)
barret, *n.* flat cap, biretta. (F. *barrette,* biretta)

barricade, *n.* barrier; improvised fortification.—*v.t.* block, defend, with one. **barricado,** *n.* barricade. (F.)

barrier, *n.* bar, fence; obstacle; gate where customs are collected; lists in tournament.—*v.t.* close, shut in, with barrier. (*bar*)

barrister, *n.* lawyer qualified to practise in higher courts. (*bar*)

barrow, *n.* box with shafts and one wheel, wheel-barrow; frame with handles, hand-barrow; two-wheeled handcart; barrowful. (*bear*)

barrow, *n.* mound raised over grave, tumulus. (O.E. *beorg*)

barrow, *n.* infant's long sleeveless flannel garment. (O.E. *beorgan*, protect)

barter, *v.t.* and *i.* exchange.—*n.* trade by exchange of things.

bartizan, *n.* overhanging corner turret. (coined by Sir W. Scott from misspelling of *bratticing*, parapet)

barton, *n.* farmyard. (O.E. *bere*, barley; *tún*, enclosure)

baryta, *n.* a heavy alkaline earth. **barýtēs,** *n.* barium sulphate, heavy spar. **barytic,** *a.* (Gk. *barus*, heavy)

barytone, same as **baritone.**

bas, *adv.* (*Anglo-Ind.*) enough.

basal, *a.* of, at, base; fundamental.

basalt, *n.* dark-coloured igneous rock. **basaltic,** *a.* (L. *basaltes*)

basan, basil, *n.* tanned sheepskin.

bas bleu, bluestocking. (F.)

bascule, *n.* lever apparatus, counterpoise. **b.-bridge,** *n.* kind of drawbridge. (F.=see-saw)

base, *n.* bottom, foundation; support; chief ingredient, principle; starting-point; place from which army operates; station at baseball; (*chem.*) compound forming a salt when united with an acid (term including, but wider than, alkali).—*v.t.* found, establish. **basic,** *a.* (Gk. *basis*)

base, *a.* low, mean, vile; worthless. **b. coin,** counterfeit. **b. metal,** not precious. **b.-born,** *a.* of low birth; illegitimate. (L. *bassus*, short)

baseball, *n.* U.S. national game, with bat, ball, and nine men a side.

baseless, *a.* groundless, unfounded.

basement, *n.* storey below ground level.

bases, *n.pl.* (*Shake.*) plaited skirt appended to doublet and reaching to knee.

bash, *v.t.* smash in.

bashaw, early form of **pasha.**

bashful *a.* shy, diffident. (*abash*)

bashi-bazouk, *n.* Turkish irregular trooper. **bashi-bazoukery,** *n.* atrocities such as they committed. (Turk.)

basil, *n.* kinds of aromatic herb. (Gk. *basilikos*, royal)

basil, see basan.

basilica, *n.* (orig.) palace; oblong hall, church, with double colonnade and apse. **basilican,** *a.* **basilicon, basilicum,** *n.* kinds of ointment. (Gk. *basilikos*, royal)

basilisk, *n.* fabulous monster hatched from cock's egg by serpent, dealing death by its gaze; cockatrice; (*zool.*) crested lizard. (Gk. *basiliskos*)

basin, *n.* wide open vessel, bowl; dock; area drained by river. (L.L. *bachinus*)

basinet, basnet, *n.* light steel headpiece. (*basin*)

basis, *n.* (*pl.* **bases**) base, foundation, main principle. (*base*)

bask, *v.i.* sun oneself, lie in warmth or light.

basket, *n.* vessel made of plaited twigs, rushes etc. **b.-ball,** *n.* game played with large ball, goals being baskets 10 ft. above ground. **b. hilt,** hilt shaped like basket. **b.-work, basketry,** *nn.*

basnet, see **basinet.**

bason, *n.* hatter's bench; basin.

basque, *n.* short-skirted bodice; native of W. Pyrenees. (L.L. *Vasco*)

bas-relief, bass-relief, *n.* low relief; sculpture standing out less than half true depth from background. (*base*)

bass, *a.* and *n.* deep; (of) lowest part in music; bass voice or singer. **b. horn,** obsolete wind instrument, improved form of serpent. **b. viol,** violoncello. (It. *basso*)

bass, *n.* perch, sea-perch. (O.E. *bærs*)

bass, *n.* bast; mat made of it. (*bast*)

basset, *n.* short-legged hound like badger-dog. (F. *bas*, low)

basset, *n.* old card game. **b. horn,** tenor clarinet. (It. *basso*, low)

basset, *n.* and *v.i.* (*geol.*) outcrop.

bassinet, bassinette, *n.* hooded wicker cradle; hooded perambulator. (F.)

bassoon, *n.* wood-wind instrument of low tone. **bassoonist,** *n.* (F. *bas*, low)

basso-rilievo, *n.* bas-relief. (It.)

bast, *n.* inner bark of lime; other similar fibre. (O.E. *bæst*)

basta, *int.* enough. (It.)

bastaard, *n.* (*S. Afr.*) person of mixed white and coloured parentage. (Du.)

bastard, *n.* child whose parents are not married to each other; (*Shake.*) a sweet Spanish wine.—*a.* illegitimate, spurious; hybrid. **b. title,** short title on page before title-page. **b. trenching,** shallow digging without bringing subsoil to top. **bastardize,** *v.t.* declare illegitimate. **bastardy,** *n.* (O.F. *fils de bast*, son of the pack-saddle)

baste, *v.t.* sew together loosely, tack. (O.F. *bastir*)

baste, *v.t.* moisten (roasting meat) with fat; thrash, beat.

bastille, *n.* fortress; prison. (F.)

bastinado, *v.t.* beat with stick on soles of feet.—*n.* (also **bastinade**) this punishment. (Sp. *bastón*, stick)

bastion, *n.* tower, projection, at angle of fortification. (F.)

basyl, basyle, *n.* (*chem.*) body uniting with oxygen to form a base. (*base*)

bat, *n.* heavy stick; club used in cricket or baseball.—*v.i.* use bat.

off one's own b., unaided. **batsman, batter,** *nn.* (L. *batuere,* beat)
bat, *n.* nocturnal mouse-like quadruped with wings. **have bb. in the belfry** (*sl.*) be crazy. (M.E. *bakke*)
bat, *n.* (*Anglo-Ind.*) native language. **sling the b.,** (*sl.*) speak the lingo. (Hind.)
bat, *n.* (*sl.*) pace; (*Amer.*) spree, good time. **b. round** (*Amer.*) have good time.
bat, *v.t.* (*Amer.*) wink. (*bate*)
batata, *n.* sweet potato. (Sp.)
batch, *n.* quantity of loaves baked at one time; group of things dealt with together, set. (*bake*)
bate, *v.t.* and *i.* restrain; deduct; lessen. (=*abate*)
bate, *n.* (*obs.*) strife, contention; (*sl.*) rage. (=*debate*)
bate, *v.i.* (*Shake.*) flutter, beat wings.
bateless, *a.* (*Shake.*) not to be blunted, keen.
batfowling, *n.* hunting roosting birds at night. (*bat,* club)
bath, *n.* washing, immersion; water, vessel, place, for washing.—*v.t.* give bath to. **bathroom,** *n.* (O.E. *bæth*)
Bath, *n.* **b.-brick,** *n.* preparation of earths for cleaning metal. **b.-bun,** *n.* made with candied peel and currants. **b.-chair,** *n.* wheeled chair for invalids. **B. Oliver,** kind of biscuit. (town)
bathe, *v.t.* and *i.* immerse, lie, in water; moisten; envelope.—*n.* act of bathing. **bather,** *n.* **bathing-machine,** *n.* wheeled dressing-box for sea-bathing. (O.E. *bathian*)
bathometer, *n.* instrument for measuring depth of water. (*bathos*)
bathos, *n.* descent from elevated to mean in writing or speech, anticlimax. **bathetic,** *a.* (Gk.=depth)
bathrobe, *n.* (*Amer.*) dressing-gown.
bathygraphical, *a.* (of map) showing sea-depths. **bathyorographical,** *a.* showing this and also land altitudes. (Gk. *bathus,* deep; *oros,* mountain; *graphein,* write)
bathysphere, *n.* hollow sphere for descending to great depths in the sea. (Gk. *bathus,* deep; *sphaira,* sphere)
batik, *n.* fabric with coloured designs printed by Javan process; the process or designs used. (Javanese *'mbatik,* drawing)
batiste, *n.* kind of cambric; fabric like cambric. (*Baptiste,* maker)
batlet, *n.* (*Shake.*) small club for beating linen at wash. (*bat*+dim.)
batman, *n.* officer's servant. (O.F. *bast,* pack-saddle)
baton, *n.* staff of marshal or conductor; policeman's truncheon.—*v.t.* strike with one. **b. sinister,** heraldic badge of bastardy. (F.)
batrachian, *a.* of frogs.—*n.* animal of frog order. (Gk. *batrachos,* frog)
batta, *n.* (*Anglo-Ind.*) extra allowance to officers or men, esp. in the field. (Port. *bata*)
battailous, *a.* (*Spens.*) ready for battle, warlike. (*battle*)
battalion, *n.* unit of infantry, us. about 1,000 men; body of troops in battle array. (F. *battaglia,* battle)
batteilant, *a.* (*Spens.*) combatant.
battels, *n.pl.* Oxford college bill.
batten, *v.i.* feed greedily, grow fat.
batten, *n.* long narrow board; strip of wood, esp. to secure ship's hatches.—*v.t.* secure with battens. (*baton*)
batter, *n.* (*sl.*) spree.
batter, *v.t.* and *i.* strike repeatedly; wear by hard use; attack with artillery.—*n.* (*print.*) defect in type; (*cookery*) ingredients beaten up with liquid into paste. **battering-ram,** *n.* ancient war-engine for breaching walls. **battery,** *n.* unit of artillery; platform for guns; (*electr.*) set of cells; (*law*) unlawful striking. (L. *battuere,* beat)
battil, *v.i.* (*Spens.*) become fat.
battle, *n.* fight between armies; combat.—*v.i.* struggle. **line of b.,** troops arrayed for battle. **line-of-b. ship,** (*obs.*) of 74 or more guns. **pitched b.,** fought by common consent. **b.-axe,** *n.* two-headed axe. **b.-bowler,** *n.* (*sl.*) soldier's steel hat. **b.-cruiser,** *n.* heavy-gunned ship, with higher speed and lighter armour than battleship. **battlefield,** *n.* scene of battle. **b.-plane,** *n.* large fighting aeroplane. **b. royal,** *mêlée,* free fight. **battleship,** *n.* large fighting warship. (*batter*)
battledore, *n.* wooden bat used in washing, baking etc.; bat in game **b. and shuttlecock,** resembling badminton.
battlement, *n.* indented parapet, wall with embrasures. **battlemented,** *a.*
battue, *n.* driving up of game by beaters; wholesale slaughter. (F.)
batty, *a.* (*sl.*) off one's head, dotty.
bauble, *n.* toy, trifle, showy trinket; jester's baton. (O.F. *babel*)
bauchle, same as **bachle.**
baudrons, *n.* (*Scot.*) cat, puss.
bauld, *Scot.* form of **bold.**
baulk, see **balk.**
bauxite, *n.* clay yielding aluminium. (*Baux* in France)
bawbee, *n.* (*Scot.*) halfpenny.
bawbling, *a.* (*Shake.*) trifling. (*bauble*)
bawcock, *n.* (*Shake.*) fine fellow. (F. *beau coq*)
bawd, *n.* procuress. **bawdy,** *a.* lewd, obscene.—*n.* obscene talk. **bawdy house,** brothel. **bawdry,** *n.* lewdness.
bawl, *v.t.* and *i.* speak noisily, shout. **b. out,** (*Amer.*) reprove noisily. (L.L. *baulare,* bark)
bawley, *n.* (*dial.*) fishing-smack.
bawn, *n.* court of castle; enclosure for cattle. (Ir. *bábhun,* bailey)
bawsint, *a.* (*Scot.*) having white streak on the face.
bay, *n.* laurel; (*pl.*) laurel wreath. **b. rum,** perfumed cosmetic got from

leaves of the **bayberry,** a W. Indian tree. (L. *baca,* berry)
bay, *n.* wide inlet of sea, inward bend of shore. (L.L. *baia*)
bay, *n.* division of wall between buttresses etc.; recess. **b. window,** projecting window. **sick b.,** ship's hospital. (L. *badata*)
bay, *v.i.* and *t.* bark (at).—*n.* cry of hound or pursuing pack. **hold at b.,** keep off (assailant). **stand at b.,** await onset. (O.F. *bayer*)
bay, *a.* and *n.* reddish-brown (horse). (L. *badius*)
bayadère, *n.* Hindu dancing-girl. (F.)
Bayard, *n.* chivalrous man. (name)
bayonet, *n.* blade for fixing to rifle-muzzle.—*v.t.* stab with it. (*Bayonne* in France)
bayou, *n.* (*Amer.*) marshy inlet of lake or river. (L. *botulus,* sausage)
bay-salt, *n.* salt in large crystals, orig. made from sea-water.
bazaar, bazar, *n.* Eastern market; indoors fair, esp. for charity. (Pers.)
bazan, same as **basan.**
bdellium, *n.* a fragrant gum; the tree yielding it. (Gk. *bdellion*)
be, *v.i.* (*pres.indic.* **am, art, is,** *pl.* **are ;** *past indic.* **was, wast** or **wert, was,** *pl.* **were ;** *pres.part.* **being ;** *p.p.* **been**) exist; remain; have a certain state or quality. (O.E. *béon*)
be-, *pref.* all over, thoroughly, as in **bespatter ;** make, as in **bedim ;** call, as in **bedevil;** forming transitive verbs from intransitive, as **bewail.** (O.E. =about)
beach, *n.* shore, esp. pebbly or sandy one.—*v.t.* run, haul, (ship) on shore. **beachcomber,** *n.* long rolling wave; loafing longshoreman, esp. on Pacific island. **b.-master,** *n.* officer in charge of disembarking troops.
beach-la-mar, *n.* pidgin English used in South Seas. (*bêche-de-mer*)
beacon, *n.* signal fire on height; sea-mark, lighthouse.—*v.i.* guide, act as beacon. (O.E. *béacn*)
bead, *n.* small ball pierced for threading on string of necklace, rosary etc.; bubble; knob of gun-sight; flange of tyre; narrow moulding.—*v.t.* and *i.* furnish with, form, beads; string together. **draw a b. upon,** take aim at. **tell one's bb.,** be at prayer. **beading,** *n.* bead-moulding. **b.-roll,** *n.* list of names. (O.E. *biddan,* pray)
beadle, *n.* officer of lawcourt, parish, or church; mace-bearer. **beadledom,** *n.* stupid officiousness. (O.E. *bydel*)
beadsman, *n.* pensioner who prays for benefactor; (*Scot.*) licensed beggar.
beady, *a.* like, covered with, beads; (of eyes) small and bright. (*bead*)
beagle, *n.* small hound used for hunting hares on foot; spy.—*v.i.* hunt with beagles.
beak, *n.* bird's bill; thing resembling it, such as nose, prow, spout. **beaked,** *a.* (F. *bec*)
beak, *n.* (*sl.*) magistrate; schoolmaster.
beaker, *n.* large drinking-cup; glass vessel with beak used by chemists.
beam, *n.* long straight piece of timber; ship's cross-timber, side, or width; bar of balance; shaft of light.—*v.i.* emit light, shine; look radiantly. **b. ends,** side of ship. **b. wireless,** with controlled direction. **beamy,** *a.* massive; shining; (of ship) broad. (O.E. *béam,* tree)
bean, *n.* flat kidney-shaped seed in pod; plant yielding it; seed of coffee etc.; (*sl.*) coin; (*Amer. sl.*) head. **full of bb.,** vigorous. **give one bb.,** (*sl.*) punish, scold. **old b.,** (*sl.*) old chap. **beanfeast, beano,** *nn.* employees' annual treat; outing, celebration. (O.E. *béan*)
bear, *v.t.* and *i.* (*past* **bore,** *arch.* **bare ;** *p.p.* **borne, born**) carry; endure, suffer; lean, incline; give birth to, yield. **b. arms,** be a soldier; have heraldic bearings. **b. down,** overwhelm; swoop. **b. hard,** be hard (on). **b. in hand,** (*Shake.*) lead on, delude. **b. out,** corroborate. **b. up,** keep up heart. **b. with,** make allowance for. **b. witness,** give testimony. **bearable,** *a.* endurable. (O.E. *beran*)
bear, *n.* heavy furred quadruped; rough person; one who speculates for fall in stocks.—*v.i.* speculate in this way. **Great, Little, B.,** groups of stars. **b.-garden,** *n.* rowdy assembly. **b.-leader,** *n.* travelling tutor. **b.'s-breech,** *n.* acanthus. **b.'s-grease,** *n.* pomade. **bearskin,** *n.* guardsman's high fur cap. **bearish,** *a.* surly. (O.E. *bera*)
bear, bere, *n.* (*Scot.*) barley. (O.E.)
beard, *n.* hair on chin; barbel of fish, gills of oyster, awn of grass.—*v.t.* defy, oppose openly. **bearded,** *a.* **beardless,** *a.* youthful. (O.E.)
bearer, *n.* carrier, esp. of letter or coffin; presenter of cheque; (*Anglo-Ind.*) palanquin-carrier; body-servant.
bearing, *n.* behaviour; relation; direction, relative position; heraldic device; (*pl., mech.*) surfaces bearing friction. **b.-rein,** *n.* fixed rein forcing horse to arch its neck. (*bear*)
beast, *n.* animal; quadruped; brutal man. **the b.,** animal nature; antichrist. **beastly,** *a.* like a beast, brutal; nasty, dirty; (*colloq.*) disagreeable. **beastlihead,** *n.* (*Spens.*) beast's nature. (L. *bestia*)
beat, *v.t.* (*past* **beat,** *p.p.* **beaten**) strike repeatedly; thrash, hammer; defeat, overcome; (*Amer.*) defraud.—*v.i.* give strokes; throb; sail against wind.—*n.* recurring stroke; pulsation; appointed round; (*Amer.*) something that surpasses, newspaper scoop; (*Amer.*) sponger. **b. about the bush,** approach subject indirectly. **b. it,** (*Amer. sl.*) go away. **b. out,** forge (metal). **b. retreat,** retire. **b.**

the air, waste effort. **b. the bounds,** trace parish boundaries ceremonially. **b. up,** make froth of (eggs); collect (recruits). **dead b.,** completely exhausted. (O.E. *béatan*)

beater, *n.* one who rouses game for shooters.

beatify, *v.t.* make happy; pronounce in eternal blessedness (first step in canonization). **beatific,** *a.* making blessed. **beatification,** *n.* **beatitude,** *n.* blessedness; heavenly happiness; (*pl.*) Christ's sayings in Matthew v. (L. *beare,* bless)

beau, *n.* (*pl.* **beaux**) fop; suitor. ***b. geste,*** display of magnanimity. **b. ideal,** ideal excellence, standard of perfection. ***b. monde,*** fashionable world. **for one's *beaux yeux,*** just to gratify one. (F.)

Beaune, *n.* a red wine of Burgundy. (town)

beauty, *n.* pleasing qualities, loveliness; beautiful person or thing. **b. parlour,** cosmetic expert's establishment. **b.-sleep,** *n.* sleep before midnight. **b.-spot,** *n.* patch on face as foil to complexion; beautiful scene. **beaut,** *n.* (*Amer. sl.*) beauty. **beauteous,** *a.* (*poet.*) beautiful. **beautician,** *n.* (*Amer.*) expert in cosmetics. **beautiful,** *a.* delighting senses, charming. **beautify,** *v.t.* make beautiful, adorn. **beautifier,** *n.* (*beau*)

beaver, *n.* amphibious rodent with flat tail; its fur; hat made of this; (*sl.*) bearded man. **beaverteen,** *n.* twilled cloth with pile of loops. (O.E. *beofor*)

beaver, *n.* lower or movable part of helmet's face-guard. (O.F. *bavière,* bib)

beaver, *n.* snack. (L. *bibere,* drink)

beblubbered, *a.* tear-stained.

becall, *v.t.* miscall, call names.

becalm, *v.t.* make calm; keep (ship) motionless from want of wind.

became, see become.

because, *conj.* for the reason that, since.—*adv.* by reason. (*by; cause*)

beccafico, *n.* small bird of warbler family eaten in Italy. (It. *beccare,* peck; *fico,* fig)

bechamel, *n.* a white sauce. (inventor)

bêche-de-mer, *n.* sea-slug, eaten by Chinese; beach-la-mar. (F.)

beck, *n.* sign, gesture; (*Scot.*) gesture of salutation.—*v.t.* and *i.* signal (to), beckon. **at one's b.,** subject to one's will. (*beckon*)

beck, *n.* brook, mountain stream. (O.N. *bekkr*)

becket, *n.* rope-loop, hook, or bracket for securing sails, tackle etc.

beckon, *v.t.* and *i.* call by gesture, make sign (to). (O.E. *biecnan*)

becloud, *v.t.* obscure by clouds, dim.

become, *v.i.* (*past* **became,** *p.p.* **become**) come to be.—*v.t.* suit, befit. **becoming,** *a.* proper, suitable. **becomingly,** *adv.* (O.E. *becuman,* arrive)

bed, *n.* couch, place to sleep on; place on which thing rests; bottom of sea or river; stratum; garden plot.—*v.t.* put in bed or layer, plant. **brought to b.,** in childbirth. **take to one's b.,** become ill. **bedclothes,** *n.pl.* sheets, blankets etc. **b.-pan,** *n.* chamber utensil for use in bed. **b.-plate,** *n.* base plate of machine. **b.-rock,** *n.* solid rock under superficial formations; ultimate facts. **bedspread,** *n.* coverlet. **bedchamber,** (*sl.*) **bedder,** *nn.* bedroom. **bedding,** *n.* mattress and bed-clothes. **bedfellow,** *n.* sharer of bed. **bedridden,** *a.* confined to bed by infirmity. **bedroom,** *n.* room for sleeping in. **bedsore,** *n.* ulcer caused by lying in bed. **bedstead,** *n.* frame of bed. **bedstraw,** *n.* kinds of plant. **bedtick,** *n.* cloth case holding feathers, hair etc. for bed. (O.E.)

bedabble, *v.t.* splash, wet. (*dabble*)

bedad, *Ir.* corrupt. of begad.

bedaub, *v.t.* daub over, smear.

bedeck, *v.t.* adorn.

bedeguar, *n.* spongy gall on rose-bush, caused by insect. (Pers. *badawar,* wind-brought)

bedel, bedell, *n.* university officer at Oxford and Cambridge. (*beadle*)

bedevil, *v.t.* torment, abuse, diabolically; bewitch, confound: call devil. **bedevilment,** *n.*

bedew, *v.t.* moisten, sprinkle.

bedight, *a.* (*poet.*) adorned, arrayed.

bedim, *v.t.* make dim.

bedizen, *v.t.* dress gaudily.

bedlam, *n.* madhouse; scene of uproar **bedlamite,** *n.* lunatic. (Hospital of St Mary of *Bethlehem,* in London)

bedouin, *n.* (*pl.* same) Arab desert nomad; gipsy. (Arab. *badawin*)

bedrabbled, *a.* dirty with rain and mud.

bedraggle, *v.t.* soil by trailing in wet or dirt.

bee, *n.* four-winged insect that makes honey; busy worker; meeting for combined work, esp. **spelling-b.,** *n.* contest in spelling. **have a b. in one's bonnet,** be unbalanced on some point. **beehive,** *n.* dome-shaped house for bees. **b.-line,** *n.* direct line. **b.-master,** *n.* one who keeps bees. **beeswax,** *n.* wax secreted by bees.—*v.t.* polish with this. **beeswing,** *n.* gauze-like crust in old port. (O.E. *béo*)

beebee, same as bibi.

beech, *n.* smooth-barked forest tree; its wood. **beechen,** *a.* **beechmast,** *n.* nut of beech. (O.E. *béce*)

beef, *n.* (*pl.* **beeves**) flesh of ox or cow; (*pl.*) oxen.—*v.i.* (*Amer. sl.*) complain fussily. **b.-tea,** *n.* stewed beef-juice. **beefeater,** *n.* yeoman of the guard. **beefy,** *a.* like beef; muscular, fleshy; stolid. (L. *bos,* ox)

Beelzebub, *n.* Satan; a devil. (Heb. *ba'alz'būb,* ruler of flies)

been, see be.

beer, *n.* alcoholic drink made from malt flavoured with hops. **small b.,** light beer; trifling matter. **b. and**

skittles, round of pleasure. **b.-engine**, *n.* for drawing beer. **beerhouse**, *n.* selling beer but not spirits. **b.-money**, *n.* allowance in place of beer. **beery**, *a.* of, affected by, beer. (O.E. *béor*)

beer, *n.* one of the groups into which threads of warp are divided. (=*bier*)

beestings, *n.pl.* first milk given by cow after calving. (O.E. *béost*)

beet, *v.t.* (*Scot.*) add fuel to, incite.

beet, *n.* plant with edible root. **red b.**, used for salads. **white b.**, for making sugar. **beetroot**, *n.* its root. (L. *beta*)

beetle, *n.* insect with four wings, two of which form hard sheaths; black-beetle, cockroach; short-sighted person.—*v.i.* (*sl.*) hurry (off). (O.E. *bitan*, bite)

beetle, *n.* heavy wooden mallet.—*v.t.* beat, ram, with one. (*beat*)

beetle, *a.* projecting, shaggy.—*v.i.* overhang, jut out.

beeves, see **beef.**

beezer, *n.* (*sl.*) nose.

befall, *v.t.* and *i.* (*past* **befell**, *p.p.* **befallen**) occur, happen to. (*fall*)

befit, *v.t.* suit, become, be right for. **befitting**, *a.*

befog, *v.t.* involve in fog, confuse.

befool, *v.t.* make a fool of.

before, *prep.* in front of; previous to; in presence of; in preference to.—*adv.* in front; earlier.—*conj.* sooner than. **beforehand**, *adv.* previously, in anticipation. (*fore*)

befoul, *v.t.* make foul, soil.

befriend, *v.t.* act as friend to, help.

beg, *v.t.* and *i.* entreat, ask for favour; ask, live by, charity. **b. off**, get (person) excused. **b. to**, take leave to. **b. the question**, assume the fact that has to be proved.

begad, *int.* by God.

began, see **begin.**

beget, *v.t.* (*past* **begot**, *arch.* **begat**; *p.p.* **begotten**) generate; give rise to. (*get*)

beggar, *n.* one who begs or lives by begging, poor person; (*colloq.*) fellow.—*v.t.* reduce to poverty; outdo. **b.-my-neighbour**, *n.* a card game. **beggarly**, *a.* poor; mean, contemptible. **beggary**, *n.* extreme poverty.

begin, *v.t.* and *i.* (*past* **began**, *p.p.* **begun**) commence, originate, take rise. **beginner**, *n.* starter, novice. **beginning**, *n.* origin, commencement. (O.E. *beginnan*)

begird, *v.t.* gird round, encompass.

begone, *int.* go away! be off! (*go*)

begonia, *n.* plant with petal-less flowers and lopsided leaves. (Michel *Begon*, botanist)

begorra, *int.* (*Ir.*) by God. (corrupt.)

begot, begotten, see **beget.**

begrime, *v.t.* make grimy, soil deeply.

begrudge, *v.t.* grudge, envy (one) the possession of.

beguile, *v.t.* cheat, impose upon; amuse; while away. **beguiler, beguilement**, *nn.* (*guile*)

begum, *n.* Mohammedan queen or lady of high rank. (fem. of *bey*)

begun, see **begin.**

begunk, *v.t.* and *n.* (*Scot.*) trick.

behalf, *n.* account, interest (in phrase on b. of etc.). (*by*; *half*)

behave, *v.i.* and *refl.* conduct oneself, act; show good manners. **behaviour**, *n.* conduct, manners. **behaviourism**, *n.* doctrine that human action is governed by external stimuli. (*have*)

behead, *v.t.* cut head off.

beheld, see **behold.**

behemoth, *n.* enormous animal.

behest, *n.* (*poet.*) command; charge. (*hest*)

behight, *v.t.* (*Spens.*) call, name; pronounce; promise; command; grant, entrust. (*hight*)

behind, *prep.* and *adv.* at back, in rear (of), after; late.—*n.* rump. **b. time**, late. **b. the times**, out of date. **behindhand**, *a.* and *adv.* late, in arrears.

behold, *v.t.* (*past*, *p.p.* **beheld**) see, look upon. **beholder**, *n.* **beholden**, (*Shake.*) **beholding**, *aa.* obliged, indebted. (*hold*)

behoof, *n.* benefit, use. **behove, behoove**, *v.t.* befit, be incumbent. **behoveful**, *a.* (*Shake.*) necessary. (O.E. *behóf*, advantage)

behowl, *v.t.* (*Shake.*) howl at.

beige, *n.* undyed woollen cloth; its colour.—*a.* beige-coloured, grey. (F.)

bein, *a.* (*Scot.*) comfortable; well off; good. **beinness**, *n.*

being, *n.* existence; substance; person, creature. (*be*)

bejan, bejant, *n.* freshman at Aberdeen or St Andrews University. (F. *bec jaune*, yellow beak, nestling)

bejewel, *v.t.* deck with jewels.

belabour, *v.t.* beat soundly, thump.

belaccoyle, *n.* (*Spens.*) kind greeting. (O.F. *bel acoil*)

belamour, *n.* (*Spens.*) gallant; fair lady; a flower. (F.=fair love)

belamy, *n.* (*Spens.*) good friend. (F. *bel ami*)

belated, *a.* late, made late; benighted.

belaud, *v.t.* praise highly.

belay, *v.t.* (*naut.*) secure (rope) by coiling it round cleat or belaying-pin; (*Spens.*) beset, encompass; adorn. **b.!** (*sl.*) stop! **belaying-pin**, *n.* (*lay*)

belch, *v.i.* and *t.* emit wind from stomach through mouth; utter violently; emit.—*n.* eructation. (O.E. *bealcian*)

belcher, *n.* kind of spotted neckerchief. (Jim *Belcher*, boxer)

beld, *Scot.* form of **bald.**

beldam, beldame, *n.* old woman, hag. (F. *belle*, fine; *dame*, lady)

beleaguer, *v.t.* besiege. (Du. *leger*, camp)

belemnite, *n.* pointed fossil bone of cuttle-fish. (Gk. *belemnon*, dart)

bel esprit, (*pl. beaux esprits*) person of wit or genius. (F.)

belfry, *n.* bell-tower, bell-chamber; siege-tower. **belfried,** *a.* (O.F. *berfrei,* watch-tower)
belgard, *n.* (*Spens.*) kind looks. (It. *bel guardo,* fair look)
Belgian, *a.* and *n.* (native) of Belgium. **Belgic,** *a.* of Belgians or Belgae.
Belgravia, *n.* a fashionable part of London, containing Belgrave Square. **Belgravian,** *a.* aristocratic.
Belial, *n.* devil. **son of B.,** wicked man. (Heb. *b'li,* not; *yaal,* use)
belie, *v.t.* falsify, speak falsely of, fail to confirm. (*lie*)
believe, *v.t.* and *i.* regard as true; have faith (in); suppose. **make b.,** pretend. **belief,** *n.* believing; what one believes, religious creed. **believer,** *n.* one who believes; adherent of religion. (O.E. *gelēfan*)
belike, *adv.* (*arch.*) probably; perhaps. (*by*; *like*)
Belisha beacon, yellow globe on post marking pedestrian crossing. (L. Hore-*Belisha*)
belittle, *v.t.* make small; disparage.
bell, *n.* cup-shaped metal vessel giving musical sound; thing shaped like it.—*v.t.* furnish with bell. **bear the b.,** be first. **sound as a b.,** perfectly sound. **b.-boy,** *n.* (*Amer.*) hotel page. **b.-buoy,** *n.* one with warning bell. **b.-founder,** *n.* one who casts bells. **b.-glass,** *n.* of bell shape. **b.-hanger,** *n.* one who fits up bells. **b.-hop,** *n.* (*Amer. sl.*) bell-boy. **bellman,** *n.* town crier. **b.-metal,** *n.* alloy of copper and tin. **b.-pull,** *n.* rope, handle, for bell. **b.-punch,** *n.* ticket-punch with bell. **b.-wether,** *n.* leading sheep of flock, with bell on neck. (O.E. *belle*)
bell, *n.* stag's cry.—*v.i.* make this cry, roar. (O.E. *bellan,* bark)
belladonna, *n.* deadly nightshade or drug made from it. (It.=fair lady)
belle, *n.* beautiful woman; reigning beauty. (F.)
belles-lettres, *n.* artistic literature, incl. poetry, essays etc. **belletrist,** *n.* **belletristic,** *a.* (F.=fine letters)
bellibone, *n.* (*Spens.*) fair maid.
bellicose, *a.* warlike, pugnacious. **bellicosity,** *n.* (L. *bellum,* war)
belligerent, *a.* and *n.* (state, person) engaged in war; contending party. **belligerence, belligerency,** *nn.* (L. *bellum,* war; *gerere,* wage)
Bellona, *n.* goddess of war. (L.)
bellow, *v.i.* and *t.,* and *n.* roar, cry, shout.
bellows, *n.pl.* instrument for creating blast of air; lungs. (*belly*)
belly, *n.* lower part of trunk; stomach; bulging part.—*v.t.* and *i.* swell out. **b.-ache,** *n.* colic.—*v.i.* (*Amer. sl.*) complain. **b.-band,** *n.* girth. **bellyful,** *n.* sufficiency. **b.-god,** *n.* glutton. **b.-timber,** *n.* provisions. (O.E. *bælg,* bag)
belong, *v.i.* be property of; pertain (to); reside. **belongings,** *n.pl.* possessions; relatives; accessories. (O.E. *gelang,* dependent on)
beloved, *a.* much loved.—*n.* dear one.
below, *prep.* beneath in place, rank, or quality; not worthy of.—*adv.* in, to, a lower place; (*naut.*) downstairs.
belt, *n.* girdle; zone, strip; driving-band of machine.—*v.t.* surround, mark, with belt; thrash. **below the b.,** unfair. (O.E.)
Beltane, *n.* ancient Celtic festival, celebrated with bonfires on 1 May. (Gael. *bealltainn*)
beluga, *n.* white whale. (Russ.)
belvedere, *n.* raised turret or summer-house for viewing scenery. (It.)
belyve, *adv.* (*Scot.*) quickly; soon.
bema, *n.* inner part of chancel in Greek church. (Gk.=platform)
bemire, *v.t.* soil with mire; (*pass.*) be stuck in mud.
bemoan, *v.t.* lament, bewail.
bemoil, *v.t.* (*Shake.*) bemire.
bemonster, *v.t.* (*Shake.*) make monstrous.
bemuse, *v.t.* stupefy; (*pass.*) be lost in thought.
ben, *n.* (*Scot.*) mountain. (Gael. *beann*)
ben, *prep.* and *adv.* (*Scot.*) to inner part of (house), within.—*n.* inner room. (O.E. *binnan,* within)
bename, *v.t.* (*obs.*) name.
bench, *n.* long seat, form; thwart; judge's seat, body of judges; working-table.—*v.t.* exhibit (dog) at show. **b.-mark,** *n.* surveyor's mark. **bencher,** *n.* senior member of Inns of Court. (O.E. *benc*)
bend, *v.t.* (*past, p.p.* **bent,** except in phr. **bended knees**) curve, arch; turn; subdue; (*naut.*) attach.—*v.i.* curve, incline; yield.—*n.* bending, curve; (*naut.*) knot; (*heraldry*) diagonal band from left top to right base on escutcheon, a **b. sinister,** from right to left, being sign of illegitimacy. **the bb.,** caisson-disease of divers. **bent on,** determined on. (O.E. *bendan*)
bender, *n.* (*sl.*) sixpenny bit; (*Amer.*) drinking-bout, spree. (*bend*)
beneaped, *a.* left aground by neap-tide.
beneath, *prep.* under, below; unworthy of.—*adv.* below. (O.E. *beneothan*)
benĕdícitĕ, *n.* blessing; grace; a canticle. (L.=bless ye)
benedick, benedict, *n.* newly married man, esp. if previously confirmed bachelor. (name in Shakespeare)
Benedictine, *n.* and *a.* (monk) of the order of St Benedict, black monk; kind of liqueur.
benediction, *n.* invocation of blessing; blessing. **benedictory,** *a.* **Benedictus,** *n.* a canticle. **benedight,** *a.* blessed. (L. *bene,* well; *dicere,* speak)
benefaction, *n.* doing food; grant, gift. **benefactor,** *n.* (*fem.* **benefactress**) helper, donor. (L. *bene,* well; *facere,* do)

benefice, *n.* Church living. **beneficence,** *n.* active kindness, doing good. **beneficent,** *a.* useful, helpful. **beneficiary,** *n.* receiver of benefits; holder of benefice.—*a.* (*law*) holding, held, by feudal tenure. (*benefit*)

benefit, *n.* advantage, profit; allowance under insurance scheme; performance, match, of which proceeds go to a particular person; (*sl.*) hard time, job.—*v.t.* and *i.* do good to; receive benefit. **b. of clergy,** exemption from trial by secular court. **b.-society,** *n.* friendly society. (L. *bene,* well; *facere,* do)

benevolent, *a.* kindly, wishing well to others; charitable. **benevolence,** *n.* (L. *bene,* well; *velle,* wish)

Bengal, *a.* **B. light,** firework used for signals. **B. tiger,** tiger proper. **Bengali,** *n.* and *a.* (native, language) of Bengal. (Indian province)

benighted, *a.* overtaken by night; in moral darkness or ignorance. (*night*)

benign, *a.* kindly, favourable; (of disease) mild, not malignant. **benignant,** *a.* kindly, gracious. **benignancy, benignity,** *nn.* kindliness. (L. *benignus*)

benison, *n.* (*arch.*) benediction.

Benjamin, *n.* youngest son; favourite. (name in Bible)

benjamin, *n.* benzoin. **b. tree,** tree yielding this; a N. American aromatic shrub. (corrupt. of *benzoin*)

bennet, *n.* herb bennet, common avens. (L. *herba benedicta,* blessed herb)

bent, *n.* bias, tendency, inclination. **to the top of one's b.,** to heart's content. (*bend*)

bent, *n.* kinds of coarse grass; withered grass-stalk; heath. (O.E. *beonet*)

bent, see **bend.**

Benthamism, *n.* doctrine of greatest happiness for the greatest number. **Benthamite,** *n.* (*Bentham,* jurist)

benthos, *n.* flora and fauna at bottom of sea. (Gk.=depth of the sea)

ben trovato, cleverly invented, plausible. (It.)

benumb, *v.t.* make numb, deaden; stupefy. (*numb*)

benzene, benzol, benzole, *n.* a hydrocarbon got from coal-tar.

benzine, *n.* a distillate of American petroleum, used for cleaning.

benzoin, *n.* resin of a Javanese tree. **benzoic,** *a.* (Arab. *luban jawi,* frankincense of Java)

benzol, benzole, see **benzene.**

benzoline, *n.* benzine; impure benzene.

bequeath, *v.t.* leave by will; commit. **bequest,** *n.* bequeathing; legacy. (O.E. *cwethan,* say)

ber, *n.* Chinese date. (Hind.)

berate, *v.t.* scold.

berattle, *v.t.* (*Shake.*) fill with din.

berberry, see **barberry.**

bere, see **bear.**

bereave, *v.t.* (*past, p.p.* **bereaved** or **bereft**) rob, deprive; leave desolate. **bereavement,** *n.* loss, esp. by death. (O.E. *berēafian*)

beret, *n.* round flat cap. (F.)

berg, *n.* iceberg; (*S. Afr.*) mountain. (Du.=hill)

bergamot, *n.* kind of citron; perfume made from it. (*Bergamo* in Italy)

bergamot, *n.* kind of pear. (Turk. *beg-armudi,* prince's pear)

bergschrund, *n.* crevasse between glacier and the side of its valley. (G.)

berhyme, *v.t.* write verses on; lampoon.

beriberi, *n.* tropical disease like dropsy. (Cingalese)

Berlin, *n.* (also **Berline**) four-wheeled carriage with hood behind. **B. blue,** Prussian blue. **B. warehouse,** dealing in **B. wool,** fine dyed knitting wool. (town)

berm, *n.* ledge between ditch and rampart. (F. *berme*)

Bermudian, *a.* **B.-rigged,** *a.* with high tapering sail. (*Bermuda*)

Bernardine, *a.* and *n.* Cistercian. (St. *Bernard* of Clairvaux, founder)

berry, *n.* small juicy stoneless fruit; egg in fish-roe.—*v.i.* go berry-picking. **berried,** *a.* (O.E. *berie*)

bersaglieri, ***n.pl.*** Italian sharpshooters. (It.)

berserk, berserker, *n.* wild Norse warrior fighting with irresistible fury. —*a.* frenzied in this way. (Icel. *berserkr,* lit. bear-shirt)

berth, *n.* sea-room; ship's mooring-place; sleeping-place; post, appointment.—*v.t.* moor (ship). **give a wide b. to,** keep clear of. (*bear*)

bertha, *n.* wide lace collar. **Big B.,** German long-range gun used to bombard Paris. (name)

Berthon boat, a collapsible boat for liners etc. (*Berthon,* inventor)

Bertillon system, method of identifying criminals by measurements. (inventor)

beryl, *n.* gem like emerald, us. pale-green; aquamarine. **beryllium,** *n.* glucinum. (Gk. *bērullos*)

beseech, *v.t.* (*past, p.p.* **besought**) implore, entreat; ask earnestly for. **beseechingly,** *adv.* (M.E. *besechen*)

beseem, *v.i.* suit, be fitting (to). **beseemingly,** *adv.* (*seem*)

beset, *v.t.* (*past, p.p.* **beset**) surround, invest; assail. **besetting sin,** habitual sin. **besetment,** *n.* (*set*)

beshrew, *v.t.* (*arch.*) curse. (*shrew*)

beside, *prep.* near, by the side of; wide of. **b. oneself,** out of one's mind. **besides,** *prep.* over and above; except. —*adv.* moreover; else. (*by; side*)

besiege, *v.t.* lay siege to; throng round, press upon. **besieger,** *n.*

beslaver, *v.t.* slobber over; flatter fulsomely.

beslobber, *v.t.* beslaver; kiss effusively.

beslubber, *v.t.* bedaub, besmear.

besmear, *v.t.* smear with sticky stuff; soil.

besmirch, *v.t.* soil, sully.

besom, *n.* broom made of twigs; (*Scot.*) hussy. (O.E. *besema*)
besort, *v.t.* (*Shake.*) befit.—*n.* (*Shake.*) what is becoming.
besot, *v.t.* make sottish, stupefy. **besottedly,** *adv.*
besought, see **beseech.**
bespangle, *v.t.* cover with spangles.
bespeak, *v.t.* (*past* **bespoke,** *p.p.* **bespoke bespoken**) order or engage beforehand; betoken, be evidence of; (*Shake.*) address.
besprent, *p.p.* (*poet.*) sprinkled; scattered. (O.E. *besprengan*, besprinkle)
besprinkle, *v.t.* sprinkle over.
best, *a.* (*superl.* of **good**) most excellent, good in the highest degree.—*adv.* (*superl.* of **well**) in the best way.—*v.t.* get the better of, worst. **at b.,** on the most hopeful view. **for the b.,** with good intentions or results. **get the b. of it,** be victorious. **had b.,** would find it wisest to. **b. girl,** (*sl.*) sweetheart. **b. man, b. maid,** groomsman, bridesmaid, at wedding. **b. seller,** (*sl.*) popular book etc. **Sunday b.,** best clothes. (O.E. *betst*)
bestead, *v.t.* and *i.* avail, help.
bested, *a.* beset; situated. (O.N. *staddr*, placed)
bestial, *a.* of, like, a beast, brutish; lustful, obscene. **bestiality,** *n.* **bestialize,** *v.t.* **bestiary,** *n.* medieval treatise on beasts. (L. *bestia*, beast)
bestir, *v.refl.* rouse, exert (oneself).
bestow, *v.t.* confer (gift); deposit; accommodate. **bestowal,** *n.* (*stow*)
bestraught, *a.* (*Shake.*) distracted.
bestrew, *v.t.* (*p.p.* **bestrewed or bestrewn**) strew; lie scattered over.
bestride, *v.t.* (*past* **bestrode,** *p.p.* **bestridden**) sit, stand, astride of.
bet, *v.t.* risk (money etc.) on result of event.—*n.* wager; stake. **you b.,** (*sl.*) you may be sure. (*abet*)
beta, *n.* second letter of Greek alphabet. **b.-rays,** penetrating rays emitted by radio-active substances.
betake, *v.refl.* (*past* **betook,** *p.p.* **betaken**) have recourse (to); go.
beteem, *v.t.* (*Shake.*) grant, allow.
betel, *n.* kind of pepper, of which Indians chew the leaf. **b.-nut,** *n.* areca nut. (Malay *vettila*)
bête noire, bugbear, pet aversion. (F.= black beast)
bethankit, *n.* (*Scot.*) grace after meat.
bethel, *n.* hallowed spot; nonconformist chapel; seamen's church. (Heb. *beth-el*, house of God)
bethink, *v.refl.* (*past, p.p.* **bethought**) reflect, stop to think; recall.
betide, *v.i.* and *t.* befall, happen (to). (*tide*)
betimes, *adv.* early, in good time.
bêtise, *n.* stupidity, ill-chosen remark. (F.)
betoken, *v.t.* augur, signify.
betony, *n.* purple-flowered plant. (L. *vettonica*)
betook, see **betake.**
betray, *v.t.* give up, reveal, treacherously; be disloyal to; seduce; disclose inadvertently; show. **betrayal, betrayer,** *nn.* (L. *tradere*, give up)
betroth, *v.t.* bind to marry, affiance. **betrothal,** *n.* engagement. (*troth*)
better, *a.* (*compar.* of **good**) more excellent; improved in health.—*adv.* (*compar.* of **well**) in a better way.—*n.* (us. *pl.*) superior.—*v.t.* and *i.* improve; improve upon, surpass. **b. half,** wife. **b. off,** richer. **b. part,** majority. **get the b. of,** defeat. **had b.,** would find it wiser to. **know b.,** be more sensible. **quite b.,** (*Scot. colloq.*) recovered from illness. **think b. of it,** change one's mind. **betterment,** *n.* improvement. (O.E. *betera*)
better, bettor, *n.* one who bets.
betty, *n.* man who does women's work; burglar's jemmy. (name)
between, *prep.* in, into, the middle of two or any interval; to and from; shared by two.—*adv.* midway, intermediately. **b. whiles,** at intervals. **b. you and me,** in confidence. **b.-maid,** *n.* servant assisting two others, tweeny. (O.E. *betwéonum*)
betwixt, *prep.* and *adv.* between. **b. and between,** in a middling position. (O.E. *betwix*)
bevel, *n.* sloping edge or surface, slant; tool for setting off angles.—*a.* slanted. —*v.t.* cut on slant. **b.-gear, b.-wheels,** *nn.* wheels with bevelled cogs, working on each other at an angle. (F. *biveau*)
beverage, *n.* liquor for drinking. (L. *bibere*, drink)
bevy, *n.* company, esp. of ladies; flock of quails, larks etc.
bewail, *v.t.* and *i.* lament, wail (over)
beware, *v.i.* and *t.* be on one's guard (against), take care. (*ware*)
bewilder, *v.t.* perplex, lead astray. **bewilderingly,** *adv.* **bewilderment,** *n.* (*wilderness*)
bewitch, *v.t.* put magic spell upon; charm. **bewitching,** *a.* **bewitchment,** *n.* fascination. (*witch*)
bewray, *v.t.* reveal unintentionally, divulge. (O.E. *wregan*, accuse)
bey, *n.* Turkish governor. **beylic,** *n.* his district. (Turk.)
beyond, *prep.* farther on, later, than; more than; out of reach of.—*adv.* farther away; besides. **back of b.,** very remote place. **the b.,** the future life. (O.E. *geond*, across)
bezant, *n.* gold or silver coin; (*heraldry*) small gold circle. (*Byzantium*, where it was first struck)
bezel, *n.* groove holding watch-glass or gem; facet of gem; sloping edge of chisel. (F. *biseau*)
bezique, *n.* a card game. (F. *bésigue*)
Bezonian, *n.* (*Shake.*) beggar, base fellow; recruit. (It. *bisogno*)
bhang, *n.* Indian hemp, chewed or smoked as intoxicant or narcotic. (Hind.)

bheesty, bheestie, bhistee, bhisti, *n.* (*Anglo-Ind.*) water-carrier. (Pers. *bihisht*, paradise)
bi-, *pref.* having two, as in **bilingual**; doubly, as in **biconcave**; twice a —, as in **biannual**; every two, as in **biennial**; (*chem.*) having twice the amount of acid or base, as in **bicarbonate.** (L.)
biannual, *a.* twice a year.
bias, *n.* bulge, loading, or lopsided course of bowl; inclination, prejudice; slant.—*v.t.* (*past, p.p.* **biased, biassed**) influence, prejudice. (F. *biais*, oblique)
biaxial, *a.* having two (optic) axes.
bib, *n.* cloth put under child's chin; apron-top.—*v.i.* drink much, tipple. **best b. and tucker,** best clothes.
bib, *n.* kind of fish, whiting-pout.
bibasic, *a.* (*chem.*) having two bases.
bibble-babble, *n.* (*Shake.*) idle talk.
bibelot, *n.* trinket, knick-knack. (F.)
bibi, *n.* (*Anglo-Ind.*) Indian lady; (formerly) mem-sahib. (Pers.=wife)
Bible, *n.* sacred writings of Christian Church, Old and New Testaments; authoritative textbook. **B. oath,** one taken on the Bible. **biblical,** *a.* of, contained in, the Bible. **biblicist,** *n.* biblical scholar; fundamentalist. (Gk. *biblos*, book)
biblio-, from Gk. *biblion*, book, used in **bibliography,** *n.* history of books and their editions, list of books of one author or subject, hence **bibliographer,** *n.*, **bibliographic bibliographical,** *aa.*; **bibliolatry,** *n.* superstitious reverence for the Bible, book-worship; **bibliology,** *n.* biblical literature; **bibliomania,** *n.* mania for possessing rare books, hence **bibliomaniac,** *n.*; **bibliopegy,** *n.* fine art of bookbinding, **bibliopegist,** *n.* bookbinder; **bibliophile, bibliophil,** *n.* booklover; **bibliopole,** *n.* bookseller, **bibliopoly,** *n.* bookselling.
bibulous, *a.* absorbent; given to drinking. (L. *bibere*, drink)
bicameral, *a.* (of legislature) having two chambers. (L. *camera*, room)
bicarbonate, *n.* (*chem.*) carbonate having two equivalents of carbonic acid to one of a base.
bice, *n.* dull blue or green pigment. (It. *bigio*)
bicentenary, *n.* and *a.* (of) the two hundredth anniversary.
bicentennial, *a.* lasting, occurring every, two hundred years.—*n.* bicentenary.
bicephalous, *a.* two-headed. (Gk. *kephalē*, head)
biceps, *n.* large muscle in upper arm. (L.=two-headed)
bichloride, *n.* (*chem.*) compound with double proportion of chlorine.
bichromate, *n.* (*chem.*) salt with double proportion of chromic acid.
bicker, *v.i.* contend in petty way; ripple, quiver.—*n.* quarrel. **bickering,** *n.* skirmish. (M.E. *bikeren*)
bicker, *n.* bowl, esp. of wood. (*beaker*)
bicoloured, *a.* having two colours.
bicuspid, *a.* and *n.* (tooth) with two fangs. (L. *cuspis*, point)
bicycle, *n.* vehicle with two wheels, one in front of the other.—*v.i.* ride bicycle. **bicyclist,** *n.* (*cycle*)
bid, *v.t.* and *i.* (*past* **bade, bad,** bid; *p.p.* **bidden, bid**) command, tell; invite; express (greeting); offer (price).—*n.* offer of price, attempt, proposal. **b. fair,** appear likely (to). **biddable,** *a.* obedient. **bidder,** *n.* **bidding,** *n.* command. **bidding-prayer,** *n.* one in which congregation are invited to join. (O.E. *béodan*, offer, and *biddan*, beg)
bidarka, *n.* skin-covered Eskimo canoe. (native)
biddy, *n.* (*colloq.*) maidservant. (*Bridget*)
biddy, *n.* (*Shake.*) chicken.
bide, *v.t.* and *i.* (*arch.*) abide, dwell. **b. one's time,** await an opportunity. **biding,** *n.* (*Shake.*) abode. (O.E. *bīdan*)
bield, *n.* (*Scot.*) shelter.
bien, same as **bein.**
biennial, *a.* occurring every two years; lasting two years.—*n.* plant that lives two years. (L. *annus*, year)
bienséance, *n.* decorum. (F.)
bier, *n.* wooden frame for carrying dead to grave. (O.E. *bær*)
biestings, same as **beestings.**
biff, *n.* (*sl.*) blow.—*v.t.* strike.
biffin, *n.* red baking-apple. (*beef*)
bifid, bifidate, *aa.* divided by a deep cleft. (L. *findere*, cleave)
bifocal, *a.* with two foci (of spectacles divided for near and distant vision).
bifold, *a.* double; of two kinds.
bifoliate, *a.* (*bot.*) having two leaves. (L. *folium*, leaf)
bifurcate, *v.t.* and *i.* divide into two branches, fork.—*a.* forked. **bifurcation,** *n.* division into two branches; branch, fork. (L. *furca*, fork)
big, *a.* large, great; boastful; pregnant. **too b. for one's boots,** conceited. **talk b.,** boast. **b. bug,** (*Amer. sl.*) important person. **b. four** etc., (*sl.*) chiefs of concern. **b. noise,** (*Amer. sl.*) local celebrity. **b.-horn,** *n.* (*Amer.*) Rocky Mountain sheep.
big, *v.t.* (*Scot.*) build. (O.N. *byggja*)
big, same as **bigg.**
bigamy, *n.* having two wives or husbands at once. **bigamist,** *n.* person guilty of this. **bigamous,** *a.* (Gk. *gamos*, marriage)
bigaroo, bigaroon, *n.* large whiteheart cherry. (F. *bigarré*, variegated)
bigeminal, *a.* arranged in two pairs. (L. *geminus*, twin)
bigg, *n.* kind of barley. (O.N. *bygg*)
biggin, biggen, *n.* child's cap; (*Shake.*) nightcap. (F. *béguin*)
biggin, *n.* (*Scot.*) building, house. (*big*)
bight, *n.* loop of rope; inward bend of coast, open bay. (O.E. *byht*)
bigot, *n.* one blindly and obstinately

devoted to opinion or creed. **bigoted,** *a.* **bigotry,** *n.* blind zeal. (F.)

bigwig, *n.* (*colloq.*) important person.

bijou, *n.* (*pl.* **bijoux**) trinket, jewel.—*a.* small and elegant. **bijouterie,** *n.* bijoux collectively, small articles of virtu. (F.)

bike, *n.* (*colloq.*) bicycle. (abbr.)

bike, *n.* (*Scot.*) nest of wasps etc.; swarm, crowd.

bikh, *n.* (*Anglo-Ind.*) aconite. (Hind.)

bilateral, *a.* two-sided; of, on, two sides or parties.

bilberry, *n.* whortleberry, a small moorland shrub; its dark-blue fruit.

bilbo, *n.* sword, rapier. (*Bilbao* in Spain)

bilboes, *n.pl.* iron bar with shackles to confine prisoner's feet.

bile, *n.* yellow digestive fluid secreted by liver; disorder of this; ill humour. (L. *bilis*)

bilge, *n.* ship's bottom; foulness inside it; bulging part of cask; (*sl.*) nonsense, rot.—*v.t.* and *i.* stave in, spring leak in, bilge; swell out. **b.-keel,** *n.* keel on bilge to prevent rolling. **b.-water,** *n.* foul water in bilge. (*bulge*)

biliary, *a.* of the bile.

bilingual, *a.* speaking, written in, two languages, (L. *lingua*, tongue)

bilious, *a.* suffering from, caused by, disorder of the bile; peevish. **biliousness,** *n.* (*bile*)

-bility, see **-ble.**

bilk, *v.t.* evade payment by disappearing, cheat, swindle; (*cribbage*) spoil opponent's score.

bill, *n.* account of charges; draft of Act of Parliament; bill of exchange; poster, programme; (*law*) written statement of case; (*Amer.*) bank-note. —*v.t.* announce on poster; cover with placards. **b. of exchange,** written order to pay sum by given date. **b. of fare,** menu. **b. of health,** ship's certificate of health. **b. of lading,** ship-master's receipt for goods shipped. **b. of sale,** document transferring personal property. **true b.,** case sent by grand jury for trial. **b.-broker,** *n.* dealer in bills of exchange. **b.-poster, b.-sticker,** *nn.* man who pastes up bills. (L. *bulla*, seal)

bill, *n.* bird's beak; thing like it, narrow headland.—*v.i.* stroke bills together; caress. (O.E. *bile*)

bill, *n.* halberd; (also **billhook**) pruning tool. (O.E.)

billabong, *n.* (*Austral.*) backwater. (native *billa*, river; *bung*, dead)

billet, *n.* note; soldier's lodging or requisition for it; situation, post.—*v.t.* quarter (troops on). *b.-doux*, *n.* love-letter. (dim. of *bill*)

billet, *n.* small log of firewood; bar of metal; (*archit.*) moulding ornament like billet. (F. *bille*, log)

billiards, *n.pl.* game played with cue and balls on table with pockets at sides and corners. **billiard-marker,** n. attendant keeping score. (F. *billard*, cue)

Billingsgate, *n.* coarse abuse, foul language. (name of fish-market)

billion, *n.* a million millions; (in U.S. and France) a thousand millions. (*bi-*, doubly; *million*)

billow, *n.* great wave; (*poet.*) sea.—*v.i.* roll in waves, surge. **billowy,** *a.* (O.N. *bylgja*)

billy, *n.* (*Austral.*) tin can used as kettle by campers. (name)

billyboy, *n.* one-masted barge.

billycock, *n.* low round felt hat, wide-awake; bowler. (*bully-cocked*, in the style of the bullies)

billy-goat, *n.* male goat. (name)

billyo, billy-ho, *n.* **like b.,** (*colloq.*) vigorously, fiercely.

bilobate, *a.* with two lobes.

biltong, *n.* (*S. Afr.*) strips of meat dried in the sun. (S. Afr. Du.)

Bim. *n.* (*colloq.*) inhabitant of Barbados.

bimanal, bimanous, *aa.* (*zool.*) two-handed. (L. *manus*, hand)

bimbashi, *n.* captain, commander. (Turk.=head of a thousand)

bimensal, *a.* happening once in two months. (L. *mensis*, month)

bimetallism, *n.* monetary system using both gold and silver as standard currency at fixed relative value. **bimetallic,** *a.* **bimetallist,** *n.* advocate of bimetallism.

bimonthly, *a.* once in two months; twice a month, fortnightly.

bin, *n.* chest, receptacle, for corn, bottles, refuse etc. (O.E. *binn*)

binary, *a.* composed of two, dual. **b. measure,** (*mus.*) of two beats to bar. **b. scale,** (*math.*) notation based on 2 instead of 10. **b. star,** (*astron.*) double star, two revolving round common centre of gravity. **binate,** *a.* in pairs. (L. *bini*, two together)

binaural, *a.* of, used with, both ears.

bind, *v.t.* and *i.* (*past, p.p.* **bound**) tie, fasten together; tie round, wreathe; protect with border or cover; confine; oblige; indenture; constipate, cohere; (*R.A.F. sl.*) bore.—*n.* bine; (*mus.*) tie, slur; (*R.A.F. sl.*) bore. **b. over,** put under legal obligation. **b. up,** bandage; bind in one volume. **I 'll be bound,** I 'll guarantee. **bounden duty,** moral obligation. **binder,** *n.* book-binder; sheaf-binding machine; tie-beam; through-stone in wall; loose cover. **bindery,** *n.* book-binder's workshop. **binding,** *a.* obligatory; constipating.—*n.* book-cover; edging. (O.E. *bindan*)

bindweed, *n.* kinds of climbing plant; convolvulus.

bine, *n.* stem of climbing plant, esp. hop. (=*bind*)

bing, *n.* heap, pile.

binge, *n.* (*sl.*) spree, carouse; gay party. (dial.=soak)

bingle, *n.* style of hairdressing between bob and shingle.—*v.t.* cut hair thus. (bob; sh*ingle*)
bink, *n.* (*Scot.*) bench, shelf, rack; wasps' nest.
binnacle, *n.* case, stand, holding ship's compass. (L. *habitaculum*, dwelling-place)
binocular, *a.* for two eyes.—*n.pl.* field-glasses. (L. *bini*, pair)
binomial, *a.* and *n.* (*algebra*) (expression) consisting of two terms. **b. theorem,** formula for finding any power of a binomial. **binominal,** *a.* using two names, esp. of classification by genus and species. (L. *binominis*, having two names)
binturong, *n.* prehensile-tailed civet of India. (Malay)
bio-, from Gk. *bios*, life, used in **bioblast,** *n.* formative cell, biophore; **biochemistry,** *n.* chemistry of living substances; **biodynamics,** *n.pl.* science of vital force; **biogenesis,** *n.* theory that only living matter can produce living matter; **biomagnetism,** *n.* animal magnetism; **biometrics, biometry,** *nn.* statistics of biology or probable duration of life; **bionomics,** *n.pl.* oecology; **biophore,** *n.* vital unit, smallest body capable of life; **biophysics,** *n.pl.* physics of living things; **bioplasm,** *n.* germinal matter, living protoplasm; **biotaxy,** *n.* classification of living things by structure. **biotic,** *a.* of life.
biócellate, *a.* marked with two eyelike spots. (L. *oculus*, eye)
biograph, *n.* primitive cinematograph. (Gk. *bios*, life; *graphein*, describe)
biography, *n.* life-story of individual; this branch of literature. **biographee, biographer,** *nn.* subject, writer, of biography. **biographic, biographical,** *aa.* (Gk. *bios*, life; *graphein*, write)
biology, *n.* science of physical life. **biologic, biological,** *aa.* **biologist,** *n.* (Gk. *bios*, life; *legein*, speak)
bioscope, *n.* primitive cinematograph. (Gk. *bios*, life; *skopein*, view)
biparous, *a.* bringing forth two at a birth. (L. *parere*, bring forth)
bipartite, *a.* divided into two parts; affecting two parties. **bipartition,** *n.* (*part*)
biped, *n.* two-footed animal. **bipedal,** *a.* (L. *pes*, foot)
bipennate, *a.* having two wings. (L. *penna*, wing)
bipinnate, *a.* (*bot.*) having lobes that are lobed themselves. (*pinna*)
biplane, *n.* aeroplane with two pairs of wings, one above the other.
bipod, *n.* two-legged stand. (Gk. *pous*, foot)
bipolar, *a.* having two poles or extremities.
Bipontine, *a.* printed at Zweibrücken. (L. *Bipontium*, Zweibrücken)
biquadratic, *a.* of the fourth power.—*n.* quantity twice squared.
birch, *n.* slender forest tree with white smooth bark; bundle of its twigs used for flogging.—*v.t.* flog with birch. **birchen,** *a.* (O.E. *berc*)
bird, *n.* feathered animal; (*sl.*) girl; (*Amer. sl.*) first-rate person or thing. **b. of paradise,** bright-coloured bird of New Guinea. **b. of passage,** migratory bird; sojourner. **bb. of a feather,** people of similar type. **get the b.,** (*sl.*) be hissed. **little b.,** unnamed informant. **old b.,** wary person. **b.-fancier,** *n.* dealer in birds. **b.-lime,** *n.* sticky stuff used to catch birds. **b.-seed,** *n.* for pet birds. **b.'s-eye,** *n.* kinds of flower and cut tobacco.—*a.* seen from above. **b.'s-nesting,** *n.* hunting for nests. **birdie,** *n.* (*golf sl.*) hole done in one under par. **birding,** *n.* (*Shake.*) hawking. (O.E. *brid*)
bireme, *n.* ancient galley with two banks of oars. (L. *remus*, oar)
biretta, *n.* square cap worn by clergy. (L.L. *birretum*)
birk, *n.* (*Scot.*) birch. **birken,** *a.*
birkie, *n.* (*Scot.*) swaggering fellow; fellow.—*a.* active.
birl, *v.t.* and *i.* (*Scot.*) spin, whirl round.
birl, birle, *v.t.* and *i.* (*Scot.*) pour, ply with, drink; carouse. **birling,** *n.* (O.E. *byrele*, cup-bearer)
birlinn, *n.* chief's barge, galley, in Hebrides. (Gael. *biorlinn*)
birr, *n.* (*Scot.*) accent, twang; whirr; push.
birse, *n.* (*Scot.*) bristle; temper. **set up one's b.,** enrage. **birsy,** *a.* (O.E. *byrst*)
birsle, *v.t.* (*Scot.*) toast, scorch.
birth, *n.* bearing of offspring, being born; origin, parentage; noble descent. **birthday,** *n.* anniversary of birth. **birthmark,** *n.* discoloured patch, blemish, on body, dating from birth. **birthright,** *n.* right acquired by birth. (M.E. *byrthe*)
bis, *adv.* twice; (*mus.*) repeat. *b. dat qui cito dat*, he gives twice who gives quickly. (L.)
biscuit, *n.* thin cake of unraised bread; unglazed porcelain; (*Amer.*) small scone.—*a.* pale brown. (L. *bis*, twice; *coquere*, cook)
bisect, *v.t.* cut in halves. **bisection,** *n.* **bisector,** *n.* bisecting line. (L. *secare*, cut)
bisexual, *a.* having organs or characteristics of both sexes.
bishop, *n.* clergyman governing diocese; diagonally moving chessman; kind of spiced wine. **bishopric,** *n.* office of bishop, diocese. (Gk. *episkopos*, overseer)
bisk, *n.* rich soup made from birds, shellfish etc. (F. *bisque*)
Bismillah, *int.* in the name of Allah. (Arab.)
bismuth, *n.* a reddish-white metal, used in medicine etc. (G.)

bison, *n.* shaggy wild ox of Europe; American buffalo. (L.)
bisque, *n.* (*croquet, tennis, golf*) odds to be taken when desired. (F.)
bisque, *n.* unglazed porcelain. (*biscuit*)
bissextile, *n.* (also **b. year**) leap-year. (L. *bissextus*, intercalary day)
bisson, *a.* (*Shake.*) purblind; blinding. (O.E. *bisen*, blind)
bistort, *n.* herb with twisted roots, snakeweed. (L. *torquēre*, twist)
bistoury, *n.* surgeon's knife, scalpel. (F. *bistouri*)
bistre, *n.* warm-brown pigment made from soot.—*a.* of this colour. (F.)
bit, *n.* small piece, morsel; small coin, (*Amer.*) 12½ cents. **do one's b.**, do one's share. **not a b.**, not at all. **long, short, b.**, (*Amer.*) 15, 10, cents. (O.E. *bītan*, bite)
bit, *n.* boring or cutting part of tool; mouthpiece of bridle.—*v.t.* put bit on; curb. **take b. between teeth**, throw off restraint. (O.E. *bītan*, bite)
bit, see **bite**.
bitch, *n.* female dog; abusive term for woman. (O.E. *bicce*)
bite, *v.t.* and *i.* (*past* **bit**, *p.p.* **bitten, bit**) cut into or off, seize, with teeth; sting, pain; corrode.—*n.* biting; wound made by it; mouthful. **b. the dust**, be slain. **biting**, *a.* severe, sarcastic. **biter**, *n.* **bitten**, *p.p.* swindled; infected (with). (O.E. *bītan*)
bitt, *v.t.* (*naut.*) fasten round bitts.—*n.pl.* posts on ship's deck to which cables are made fast.
bitter, *a.* harsh-tasting, acrid; painful, showing grief; relentless; stinging.—*n.* bitterness; bitter beer; (*pl.*) extracts of bitter herbs as appetizer. **b. end**, final extremity. **b.-sweet**, *n.* woody nightshade. (O.E. *biter*)
bittern, *n.* marsh bird like heron, with booming cry. (O.F. *butor*)
bittock, *n.* (*Scot.*) little bit.
bittor, bittour, same as **bittern**.
bitumen, *n.* mineral pitch, asphalt; naphtha, petroleum etc. **bituminous**, *a.* **bituminize**, *v.t.* make into, mix with, bitumen. (L.)
bivalent, *a.* (*chem.*) having a valency of two.
bivalve, *n.* and *a.* (shell-fish) with hinged double shell, oyster. **bivalved, bivalvular**, *aa.* (*valve*)
bivouac, *n.* encampment without cover.—*v.i.* (*past, p.p.* **bivouacked**) pass night in open. (F.)
bi-weekly, *a.* every two weeks, fortnightly; twice a week, semi-weekly.
biz, *n.* (*colloq.*) business. (abbr.)
bizarre, *a.* fantastic, grotesque, extravagant. **bizarrerie**, *n.* (F.)
blaa, same as **blah**.
blab, *v.t.* and *i.* talk, tell, indiscreetly; let out (secrets).—*n.* gossip. **blabber**, *n.* tale-teller, sneak.
black, *a.* of darkest colour; dark, without light; dusky; wicked; sullen.—*n.* dark colour, cloth, fleck etc.; negro; (*pl.*) black clothes.—*v.t.* make black; polish with blacking. **b. and blue**, livid with bruise. **b. and white**, writing, print; line-drawing. **b. art**, magic, necromancy. **b. belt**, negro area of U.S. **b. books**, record of offenders; disfavour. **b. bottom**, a dance. **b. bread**, rye bread. **B. Country**, smoky district round Birmingham. **b. death**, plague of 14th century. **b. dog**, sulks. **b. draught**, an aperient. **b. eye**, discoloration round eye caused by blow. **b. flag**, pirate's flag. **B. Friar**, Dominican. **b. frost** without rime. **B. Maria**, prison van. **b. market**, illegal traffic in rationed goods. **b. mass**, travesty of mass used by Satanists. **b. monk**, Benedictine. **b. out**, obliterate. **b. pudding**, sausage of blood, suet etc. **B. Rod**, usher of the Garter and House of Lords. **b. sheep**, disreputable member of community. **B. Watch**, 42nd Highlanders. (O.E. *blac*)
blackamoor, *n.* black man, negro. (*Moor*)
blackavised, *a.* (*arch.*) dark-complexioned, swart. (F. *vis*, face)
blackball, *v.t.* reject by adverse vote. (*ball* used in ballot)
blackbeetle, *n.* cockroach.
blackberry, *n.* fruit of bramble.
blackbird, *n.* black kind of thrush; (*Amer.*) redwing; kidnapped negro. **blackbirder**, *n.* slave ship. **blackbirding**, *n.* slave trade.
blackboard, *n.* class-room board, written on with chalk.
blackcap, *n.* kinds of bird.
black-cock, *n.* male of black grouse, heath-cock.
black-currant, *n.* a garden shrub; its fruit.
blacken, *v.t.* and *i.* make, grow, black; vilify.
blackfellow, *n.* Australian native.
blackguard, *n.* scoundrel; foul-mouthed person.—*v.t.* abuse scurrilously, revile. **blackguardism**, *n.* **blackguardly**, *a.* (formerly=scullion)
blackhead, *n.* small kind of pimple with black top.
blacking, *n.* black boot-polish.
black-jack, *n.* leathern drinking-vessel.
black-lead, *n.* plumbago, graphite.—*v.t.* polish with this.
blackleg, *n.* workman who takes striker's place, scab; turf-swindler.—*v.i.* and *t.* act, injure, as blackleg.
black-letter, *n.* old English or Gothic type (black-letter) used in earliest printed books.
blackmail, *n.* extortion of money by threat of exposure; hush-money; (formerly) tribute paid to robbers for protection.—*v.t.* levy blackmail on. **blackmailer**, *n.* (O.E. *mál*, tribute)

black-out, *n.* obscuring of lights at night as air-raid precaution; temporary loss of vision or memory.—*v.t.* obscure lights in.
blackshirt, *n.* fascist. (uniform)
blacksmith, *n.* smith who works in iron.
blackthorn, *n.* kind of thorn, sloe; cudgel of its wood.
blad, *n.* (*Scot.*) large piece; blow.—*v.t.* strike, slap.
bladder, *n.* membranous bag in body, esp. that holding urine; inflated bag; windbag. **bladderwort,** *n.* a water plant. **bladdery,** *a.* (O.E. *blǣdre*)
blade, *n.* leaf of grass; flat part of oar, bat etc.; cutting part of knife, sword etc.; sword; gay, dashing fellow. (O.E. *blæd*)
blae, *a.* (*Scot.*) dark-blue, livid. **blaeberry,** *n.* bilberry. **blaes,** *n.* shale, red when burnt, used for surfacing tennis courts. (*blue*)
blague, *n.* bounce; humbug. (F.)
blah, *n.* (*Amer. sl.*) foolish talk, exaggeration; blunder.
blain, *n.* inflamed sore, pimple, blister. (O.E. *blegen*)
blame, *v.t.* find fault with, reproach.—*n.* censure; culpability. **to b.,** at fault. **blamable, blameful, blameworthy,** *aa.* deserving blame. **blameless,** *a.* innocent. (Gk. *blasphēmein,* speak ill of)
blanch, *v.t.* and *i.* take colour out of, make or grow white. (F. *blanc,* white)
blancmange, *n.* white jelly of gelatine, cornflour etc., and milk. (F. *blanc,* white; *manger,* eat)
bland, *a.* polite, suave; balmy; mild. **blandish,** *v.t.* flatter, wheedle; fondle. **blandishment,** *n.* flattering attention, cajolery. (L. *blandus*)
blank, *a.* without writing or marks; void of interest or result; vacant, nonplussed; sheer.—*n.* blank paper or space; lottery ticket that wins no prize; dash put for oath. **b. (cartridge),** without bullet. **b. verse,** unrhymed, esp. five-foot iambic. (F. *blanc,* white)
blanket, *n.* woollen cloth used for bed-covering; horse-cloth. — *a.* (*Amer.*) covering, inclusive. — *v.t.* cover with, toss in, blanket; stifle, hush up; take wind from sails of (vessel) by passing to windward. **B. Indian,** (*Amer.*) wild Indian. **born on wrong side of the b.,** illegitimate. **wet b.,** depressing person. (F. *blanc,* white, +dim.)
blankly, *adv.* helplessly; flatly.
blare, *v.i.* and *t.* and *n.* sound like trumpet; trumpet forth.
blarney, *n.* wheedling talk, flattery.—*v.i.* and *t.* use this; cajole. (supposed magic stone of *Blarney* Castle)
blasé, *a.* cloyed, sated, with pleasure; bored. (F.)
blaspheme, *v.i.* and *t.* speak impiously of God, swear; profane in words. **blasphemous,** *a.* **blasphemy,** *n.* profane speaking. (Gk. *blasphēmein,* speak ill of)
blast, *n.* strong gust; sound of wind-instrument; explosion.—*v.t.* blight, shrivel, ruin; blow up.—*int.* confound. **b.-furnace,** *n.* smelting furnace using compressed air. (O.E. *blǣst*)
blasto-, from Gk. *blastos,* bud, used in **blastoderm,** *n.* layer of embryonic cells in egg from which organism is formed; **blastogenesis,** *n.* reproduction by budding.
blatant, *a.* noisy, loudly obtrusive. **blatancy,** *n.*
blate, *a.* (*Scot.*) bashful.
blather, blatherskite, see **blether.**
blaud, same as **blad.**
blauwbok, *n.* (*S.Afr.*) large antelope with bluish hair. (Du.=blue buck)
blaze, *n.* bright flame or fire; outburst, display; (*pl., sl.*) hell.—*v.i.* flame, emit bright light; burn with anger etc.; be conspicuous. **b. away,** fire continuously. **blazing,** *a.* (of scent) strong. (O.E. *blæse,* torch)
blaze, *n.* white mark on animal's face; white notch cut on tree.—*v.t.* mark (tree, path) by chipping bark. (O.N. *blesi,* star on horse's forehead)
blaze, *v.t.* proclaim, publish widely.
blazer, *n.* coloured flannel sports jacket; (*sl.*) great lie. (*blaze*)
blazon, *n.* coat of arms; heraldic description; record.—*v.t.* describe heraldically; inscribe with arms; set forth, proclaim. **blazonment,** *n.* **blazonry,** *n.* blazons; art of blazoning; bright display. (F. *blason,* shield)
bleach, *v.t.* and *i.* whiten, be whitened, by sunlight or chemical process. **bleaching-powder,** *n.* chloride of lime. **bleacher,** *n.*; (*pl., Amer.*) unroofed seats at baseball field. **bleachery,** *n.* place for bleaching. (O.E. *blǣcan*)
bleak, *n.* kinds of small fish.
bleak, *a.* desolate, dismal; cold, unsheltered; colourless.
blear, *a.* (of eyes) sore, dim with inflammation.—*v.t.* make (eyes) sore; dim, blur. **b.-eyed,** *a.* (M.E. *blere*)
bleat, *n.* cry of sheep, goat etc.—*v.i.* and *t.* utter this cry; talk, say, feebly. (O.E. *blǣtan*)
bleb, *n.* small blister; bubble in water or glass. (imit.)
bleed, *v.i.* and *t.* (*past, p.p.* **bled**) emit blood; die by slaughter; draw blood from surgically; extort money from, suffer extortion. **bleeding,** *a.* (*vulg.*) bloody. **bleeder,** *n.* person subject to haemophilia. (O.E. *blēdan*)
blellum, *n.* (*Scot.*) idle talking fellow.
blemish, *n.* defect, stain, flaw.—*v.t.* mar, sully. (O.F. *blesme,* pale)
blench, *v.i.* and *t.* flinch, quail; shrink from, blink. (O.E. *blencan,* cheat)
blend, *v.t.* and *i.* (*past, p.p.* blended or **blent**) mix together, mingle intimately; shade imperceptibly into each other; (*Spens.*) confound; defile; dazzle.—*n.* mixture. (O.N. *blanda*)

blende, *n.* native sulphide of zinc. (G. *blenden*, deceive, because it looks like sulphide of lead)

Blenheim, *n.* kind of spaniel. **B. orange**, kind of apple. (place)

blenn(o)-, from Gk. *blennos*, mucus, used in **blennogenous**, *a.* producing mucus; **blennorrhoea**, *n.* discharge of mucus.

blenny, *n.* small spiny-finned fish. (Gk. *blennos*, mucus)

blent, see **blend.**

blepharitis, *n.* inflammation of the eyelids. (Gk. *blepharon*, eyelid)

blesbok, *n.* (*S. Afr.*) white-faced antelope. (Du. *bles*, blaze; *bok*, buck)

bless, *v.t.* (*Spens.*) wave, brandish.

bless, *v.t.* (*past, p.p.* **blessed** and **blest**) consecrate; invoke blessing on; praise, glorify; make happy; (*Spens.*) preserve, protect, deliver. **blessed, blest**, *a.* consecrated; in heaven, beatified; happy, fortunate. **blessedness**, *n.* **single blessedness**, unmarried state. **blessing**, *n.* divine favour, benediction; grace at meals; source of happiness, benefit. (O.E. *blētsian*, consecrate with blood)

blether, blather, *v.i.* chatter foolishly.—*n.* garrulous nonsense or one who talks it. **blatherskite, bletherskate**, *nn.* blethering or blustering person. (O.N. *blathr*, nonsense)

blew, see **blow.**

blewit, *n.* an edible mushroom. (*blue*)

blight, *n.* disease causing plants to wither, mildew; malignant influence; close, hazy weather.—*v.t.* affect with blight, wither, spoil. **blighter**, *n.* (*sl.*) annoying person.

Blighty, *n.* (*army sl.*) Britain, home; wound that ensures return home. (Hind. *bilāti*, foreign parts, England)

blimey, *int.* (*vulg.*) of surprise. (=*God blind me*)

blimp, *n.* small non-rigid airship. (*limp*)

blin, *v.t.* (*Spens.*) cease from, stop.—*n.* stoppage. (O.E. *blinnan*)

blind, *a.* lacking sight; ignorant, heedless; unaimed, mechanical; invisible, concealed; (*sl.*) drunk.—*v.t.* make blind.—*v.i.* go, drive, recklessly.—*n.* screen for window; blinder; pretext, something to mislead; (*sl.*) spree. **b. alley**, street closed at one end; occupation, inquiry, that leads to nothing. **b. coal**, anthracite. **b. flying**, by instruments only. **b. hazard, hookey**, card games. **b. man's holiday**, time before lighting candles. **b. pig, tiger** (*Amer.*) illicit liquor-shop. **b. side**, unguarded side, weak point. **Venetian b.**, screen of laths running on webbing. (O.E.)

blindage, *n.* screen for troops in siege, mantlet. (*blind*)

blinder, *n.* horse's blinker.

blindfold, *v.t.* cover eyes of, prevent from seeing.—*a.* and *adv.* with eyes bandaged; unwarily. (corrupt. of M.E. *blindfellen*, strike blind)

blindly, *adv.* without seeing; recklessly.

blind-man's-buff, *n.* game in which blindfold person tries to catch and identify others. (O.F. *buffe*, blow)

blind-story, *n.* (*archit.*) triforium below clerestory admitting no light.

blind-worm, *n.* slow-worm, a legless lizard with very small eyes.

blink, *v.i.* and *t.* close and open eyes rapidly, wink; shine unsteadily, twinkle; ignore, evade (fact).—*n.* gleam, glimpse. **blinker**, *n.* (*us. pl.*) screen for horse's eye, preventing it from seeing sideways. **blinking**, *a.* (*vulg.*) confounded. (M.E. *blenken*)

bliss, *n.* perfect happiness; blessedness. **blissful**, *a.* (O.E. *blīthe*, blithe+confusion with *bless*)

blister, *n.* swelling on skin full of watery matter; similar swelling on painted wood etc.; (*med.*) application to raise blister; (*sl.*) bore.—*v.t.* and *i.* raise, rise in, blister; (*sl.*) weary. (M.E. *blester*)

blithe, *a.* happy, gay. **blithesome**, *a.* blithe. (O.E.)

blithering, *a.* (*colloq.*) talking nonsense; contemptible. (*blether*)

blitzkrieg, *n.* warfare in which blitz is employed. **blitz**, *n.* (*colloq.*) intense sudden overwhelming onslaught, esp. by air.—*v.t.* attack with blitz. (G. *blitz*, lightning; *krieg*, war)

blizzard, *n.* blinding, intensely cold, storm of wind and snow. (imit.)

bloat, *v.t.* and *i.* inflate, puff out; swell.—**bloated**, (*Shake.*) **bloat**, *aa.* stuffed with food, overgrown, pampered. (M.E. *blout*, soft)

bloat, *v.t.* cure, dry by smoke. **bloater**, *n.* smoked herring.

blob, *n.* drop of liquid, round spot; a nought. (imit.)

blobber-lipped, *a.* with thick protruding lips. (imit.)

bloc, *n.* combination of political parties, nations etc. (F.=block)

block, *n.* solid piece of wood, squared stone etc.; such piece used for chopping on or mounting horse from; piece engraved for printing from; mould for shaping hat or wig; pulley with its frame; group of houses bounded by streets; traffic jam; stolid person.—*v.t.* obstruct, stop; shape (hat). **the b.**, execution by beheading. **b. in, out**, sketch roughly, plan. **b. letters**, like printed capitals. **b. system**, for safety on railway, allowing only one train on a section at a time. **b.-buster**, *n.* (*sl.*) very heavy bomb of great penetrative power.

blockade, *n.* enclosing of a place by ships or troops to cut off supplies, siege.—*v.t.* enclose thus. **run b.**, evade blockading force. **b.-runner, blockader**, *nn.* (*block*)

blockhead, *n.* dolt, stupid person.

blockhouse, *n.* small fort, orig. of timber; log house.

blockish, *a.* stolid; insensate.
bloke, *n.* (*sl.*) fellow, chap.
bloncket, *a.* (*Spens.*) grey. (F. *blanc*, white+dim.)
blond, *a.* (*fem.* **blonde**) fair; (of hair) golden, light brown.—*n.* person with blond complexion and hair and blue eyes; kind of silk lace. (F.)
blood, *n.* red liquid in veins; sap of plant; descent; kinship; temperament; dandy, swell.—*v.t.* give first taste of blood to; (*med.*) bleed. **bad b.,** ill feeling. **blue b.** ,high birth. **his b. is up,** he is enraged. **in cold b.,** deliberately. **b.-ally,** *n.* red-veined playing-marble. **b.-and-thunder,** *a.* melodramatic. **b.-heat,** *n.* 98° F. **b.-money,** *n.* reward paid for capture of murderer; compensation for murder. **b. orange.** one with red juice. **b.-red,** *a.* red as blood. **b.-relation,** *n.* one related by descent, not marriage. **b.-stained,** *a.* stained with blood. **b.-vessel,** *n.* artery, vein. (O.F. *blód*)
blooded, *a.* (*Amer.*) of good stock.
bloodhound, *n.* large dog with acute scent, used for tracking.
bloodless, *a.* without blood or slaughter; unfeeling.
bloodshed, *n.* slaughter.
bloodshot, *a.* suffused with blood.
bloodstock, *n.* thoroughbred horses collectively.
bloodstone, *n.* a precious stone streaked with red; heliotrope.
bloodsucker, *n.* leech; extortioner.
bloodthirsty, *a.* eager for blood.
bloody, *a.* of, like, blood; blood-stained; attended with bloodshed; murderous; (*vulg.*) damned.—*adv.* (*vulg.*) excessively.—*v.t.* stain with blood.
bloom, *n.* flower of plant; blossoming; prime, perfection; glow; powdery dust on fruit.—*v.i.* flower; flourish. (O.N. *blóm*)
bloom, *n.* mass of incandescent iron for hammering.—*v.t.* make (iron) into bloom. **bloomery, bloomary,** *n.* first forge through which iron passes when melted from ore. (O.E. *blóma*)
bloomer, *n.* (*sl.*) ludicrous blunder.
bloomers, *n.pl.* women's knickerbockers. (name of inventor)
blooming, *a.* (*sl.*) confounded, bloody.
blore, *n.* violent gust of wind.
blossom, *n.* flower; mass of flowers on tree.—*v.i.* open into flower. **blossomy,** *a.* (O.E. *blóstm*)
blot, *n.* spot of ink etc.; blemish.—*v.t.* smudge; mar; efface; dry up (ink). **blotting-paper,** *n.* absorbent paper for drying ink writing.
blotch, *n.* large irregular spot; pustule. **blotchy,** *a.*
blotter, *n.* pad of blotting-paper.
blottesque, *a.* coarsely delineated.
blotto, *a.* (*sl.*) fuddled with drink.
blouse, *n.* light loose upper garment; women's bodice tucked in at waist; (*Amer.*) undress uniform jacket. (F.)
blow *v.i.* and *t.* (*past* **blew,** *p.p.* **blown**) make current of air; puff, pant; drive by wind; shape (glass); sound (blast); (of fly) deposit eggs on; (of whale) spout; (*sl.*) squander; (*sl.*) confound; (*Amer.*) treat (to); (*Austral.*) brag.—*n.* blowing, gust. **b. in,** (*sl.*) drop in. **b. up,** scatter by explosive, explode; inflate; (*sl.*) scold. **b. upon,** discredit. **b.-out,** *n.* large meal. **blower,** *n.* sheet of iron for increasing fire's draught. **blowhole,** *n.* nostril of whale; air-vent in tunnel etc. **blowpipe,** *n.* tube for blowing glass: dart-tube. **blowy,** *a.* windy. (O.E. *blawan*)
blow, *v.i.* (*past* **blew,** *p.p.* blown) blossom.—*n.* bloom. (O.E. *blowan*)
blow, *n.* stroke, knock; disaster. **at a b.,** at one operation.
blowse, *n.* (*Shake.*) fat, red-cheeked wench. **blowzed, blowzy,** *aa.* fat and ruddy, slatternly.
blubber, *n.* whale-fat; weeping.—*v.i.* and *t.* weep noisily, sob; disfigure (face) with weeping. **b.-lipped,** *a.* with thick lips. (M.E. *blober*)
blucher, *n.* strong half-boot or high shoe. (Marshal *Blücher*)
bludgeon, *n.* short heavy stick.—*v.t.* strike with one.
blue, *a.* coloured like sky; gloomy; indecent.—*n.* blue colour, paint etc.; sky, sea; athlete representing university; (*pl.*) dumps; dance like foxtrot; Royal Horse Guards.—*v.t.* make blue; dip in blue liquid; (*sl.*) squander. **b. blood,** noble birth. **b. bonnet,** Scottish trooper. **b. funk,** abject fear. **b. gum,** kind of eucalyptus. **once in a b. moon,** very rarely. **B. Peter,** blue flag with white centre, hoisted when ship is about to sail. **b. pill,** purgative mercury pill. **b. ribbon,** ribbon of Garter; highest honour; badge of teetotalism. **b. rock,** kind of pigeon. **b. ruin,** bad gin. **b. water,** open sea. **true b.,** faithful. (O.F. *bleu*)
bluebell, *n.* wild hyacinth; (*Scot.*) harebell.
blue-book, *n.* parliamentary report.
bluebottle, *n.* a large blue fly; blue cornflower; (*sl.*) policeman.
bluejacket, *n.* seaman in navy.
Blue-nose, *n.* (*colloq.*) Nova-Scotian.
blueprint, *n.* photo-print with white lines on blue ground, or vice versa.
bluestocking, *n.* woman having or affecting learning.
blue-stone, *n.* sulphate of copper.
bluey, *n.* (*Austral.*) bushman's bundle. **hump b.,** go on tramp. (*blue* wrap)
bluff, *a.* with broad steep front; brusque, frank, hearty.—*n.* bluff bank or headland.
bluff, *v.i.* and *t.* make, deceive by, fictitious show of strength.—*n* bluffing, empty threat.
blunder, *v.i.* and *t.* make stupid error, bungle.—*n.* gross mistake. **blunderer,** *n.* (M.E. *blondren*)
blunderbuss, *n.* short hand-gun with

wide bore firing many balls. (Du. *donderbus*, thunder gun)

blunge, *v.t.* (*pottery*) mix clay with water. (*bl*end; pl*unge*)

blunt, *a.* with dull edge or point, not sharp; outspoken, abrupt.—*n.* thick kind of needle; (*sl.*) ready cash.—*v.t.* dull, make blunt.

blur, *v.t.* and *i.* smear, sully; make indistinct.—*n.* smudge; dim confused appearance.

blurb, *n.* publisher's introductory puff of book.

blurt, *v.t.* utter suddenly or tactlessly. (imit.)

blush, *v.i.* redden, esp. in the face with shame; feel shame.—*n.* blushing, rosy glow. **at first b.,** at first sight. **blushful,** *a.* (O.E. *ablisian*)

bluster, *v.i.* and *t.* blow boisterously, storm; utter overbearingly, swagger. —*n.* blustering, noisy threats. **blusterous, blustery,** *aa.*

bo, *int.* used to startle.

bo, *n.* (*Amer.*) mate, old chap.

boa, *n.* large snake that crushes its prey, python; long fur scarf. **b.-constrictor,** *n.* largest boa.

Boanerges, *n.* loud-voiced preacher. (Heb. *b'ney regesh,* sons of thunder)

boar, *n.* male pig, wild hog. (O.E. *bár*)

board, *n.* thin plank; wooden slab; stiff paper; table, meals; council, committee; (*naut.*) tack; (*pl.*) the stage.—*v.t.* and *i.* cover with planks; supply, receive, meals; embark on, attack, ship; tack; (*Shake.*) accost. **above b.,** openly. **by the b.,** overboard. **on b.,** aboard. **sweep the b.,** take all the stakes. **b.-school,** *n.* public elementary school. **b.-walk,** *n.* (*Amer.*) footway of boards. **boarder,** *n.* lodger supplied with meals; one who boards ship. **boarding,** *n.* covering of planks. **boarding-house,** *n.* where boarders are received. **boarding-school,** *n.* where pupils live in. (O.E. *bord*)

boast, *n.* expression of pride, brag; thing one is proud of; (*tennis*) stroke hitting side-wall before crossing net. —*v.i.* and *t.* brag, vaunt; be proud possessor of. **boastful,** *a.* given to boasting. (M.E. *bost*)

boat, *n.* small open vessel; ship; boat-shaped dish.—*v.i.* and *t.* sail about, carry, in boat. **in the same b.,** in the same circumstances. **b. train,** for steamer passengers. **b.-bill,** *n.* S. American heron. **b.-hook,** *n.* hooked pole for drawing boat to land. **b.-house,** *n.* shed for boats. **boater,** *n.* flat straw hat. **boatman,** *n.* boat-hirer; waterman. **boatswain,** *n.* officer in charge of ship's boats, sails etc. (O.E. *bát*)

bob, *n.* pendant, weight on pendulum; jerk, curtsy; bobbed hair, docked tail; knot of hair, curl; knot of worms as bait; short line ending stanza; (*Shake.*) taunt.—*v.i.* and *t.* (*past, p.p.* **bobbed**) move, jerk, up and down; dangle; curtsy; angle with bob; cut (hair) to hang short of shoulders. **b. minor, triple, major, royal, maximus,** (*bell-ringing*) changes on 6, 7, 8, 10, 12 bells. **b.-wig,** *n.* with short curls.

bob, *n.* (*sl.; pl.* same) shilling.

bob, *v.t.* (*Shake.*) cheat; filch.

bob, *n.* (*sl.*). **dry-b., wet-b.,** *nn.* cricketing, boating, Etonian.

bobachee, *n.* (*Anglo-Ind.*) male cook. (Hind. *bawarchi*)

Bobadil, *n.* boastful swaggerer. (name in play)

bobbery, *n.* (*Anglo-Ind.*) rumpus, row. —*a.* noisy; skittish; of all sorts and kinds. (Hind. *bap re,* O father!)

bobbin, *n.* cylinder on which thread etc. is wound, reel; small bar and string for raising door-latch. **bobbinet,** *n.* machine-made cotton netting. (F. *bobine*)

bobbish, *a.* (*sl.*) spry, well. (*bob*)

bobby, *n.* (*sl.*) policeman. (Sir *Robert* Peel)

bobcat, *n.* American lynx. (*bob*)

bobolink, *n.* an American song-bird, rice-bird. (imit.)

bobsled, bobsleigh, *nn.* sledge made of two short ones coupled together.

bobstay, *n.* rope holding bowsprit down to stem.

bobtail, *n.* (animal with) docked tail; rabble.—*a.* with docked tail. (*bob*)

Boche, *n.* and *a.* (*sl.*) German. (F.)

bock, *n.* kind of lager beer; glass of beer. (*Einbeck* in Hanover)

bock, *v.i.* (*Scot.*) vomit.

boddle, *n.* (*Scot.*) small copper coin worth $\frac{1}{6}$*d.*

bode, *n.* (*Spens.*) abode.

bode, *v.t.* and *i.* portend, augur; foresee, foretell. **bodeful,** *a.* ominous. **bodement,** *n.* (O.E. *boda,* messenger)

bodega, *n.* wine-shop. (Sp.)

bodice, *n.* part of woman's dress above waist; inner vest over stays. (orig. pair of *bodies*)

bodied, *a.* having body; embodied. **bodiless,** *a.* without body; incorporeal. **bodily,** *a.* of the body, physical.—*adv.* entirely, as a whole; in person. (*body*)

bodkin, *n.* large blunt needle; tool for piercing holes; pin for fastening hair; small dagger. **sit, ride, b.,** squeezed between two others.

bodrag, *n.* (*Spens.*) raid.

body, *n.* whole frame of man or animal; trunk without head or limbs; main part; corpse; bodice; person; collection, society; piece of matter; solidity, substance.—*v.t.* give form to; typify. **b. politic,** state. **b.-colour,** *n.* opaque colour. **b.-line bowling,** fast bowling designed to hurt or intimidate batsman. **b.-servant,** *n.* valet. **b.-snatcher,** *n.* one who steals corpses from graves.

bodyguard, *n.* escort, personal guard. (O.E. *bodig*)
Boeotian, *a.* and *n.* dull, stupid (person). (*Boeotia* in Greece)
Boer, *n.* and *a.* Dutch-descended S. African. (Du.=peasant)
bog, *n.* morass, quagmire; wet spongy ground.—*v.t.* engulf in bog. **b.-trotter,** *n.* Irishman. **boggy,** *a.* (Gael. *bog,* soft)
bog, *n.* (*vulg.*) latrine.
bogey, *n.* (*golf*) score of imaginary good player (higher than 'par').
bogey, see **bogie, bogy.**
boggard, boggart, *n.* (*dial.*) bogy, spectre; bugbear.
boggle, *v.i.* hesitate, demur; equivocate; fumble, start with fright. **boggler** *n.* (*Shake.*) waverer. (*bogle*)
bogie, bogey, *n.* low four-wheeled truck, trolly; pivoted undercarriage of railway engine etc.
bogle, *n.* goblin, spectre; scarecrow; bugbear.
bogus, *a.* sham, false.
bogy, bogey, *n.* goblin, spectre; bugbear; the devil.
boh, *n.* (*Anglo-Ind.*) dacoit chief. (Burmese *bo*)
boh, same as **bo.**
bohea, *n.* black tea of lowest quality. (*Wu-i* in China)
Bohemian, *a.* and *n.* unconventional (person). **Bohemianism,** *n.* free and easy habits. (F. *bohémien,* gipsy)
bohunk, *n.* (*Amer. sl.*) low-class S. European labourer, rough. (*Bohemia; Hungary*)
boil, *n.* inflamed suppurating swelling, small tumour. (O.E. *býl*)
boil, *v.i.* bubble up from action of heat; seethe, be agitated.—*v.t.* heat to boiling-point; cook by boiling.—*n.* state of boiling. **b. away,** evaporate by boiling. **b. down,** reduce by boiling; abridge. **b. over,** overflow from boiling. **boiled,** *a.* (*sl.*) drunk. **boiled shirt,** (*Amer. sl.*) starched shirt. **boiling hot,** (*colloq.*) very hot. **whole boiling,** (*sl.*) entire lot. **boiling-point,** *n.* heat at which liquid vaporizes (212° F. for water). **boiler,** *n.* vessel for boiling, making steam, or heating water. (L. *bulla,* bubble)
boisterous, *a.* rough, turbulent; noisily cheerful.
boko, *n.* (*sl.*) nose.
bolas, *n.* S. American missile of balls connected by thong, used to entangle legs of animal. (Sp. *bola,* ball)
bold, *a.* audacious, daring; forward, impudent; vigorous, striking; prominent. make b., presume. (O.E. *bald*)
bole, *n.* tree-trunk. (O.N. *bolr*)
bolection, *n.* (*archit.*) raised moulding.
bolero, *n.* a Spanish dance; woman's short loose jacket. (Sp.)
bolide, *n.* large meteor, fire-ball. (Gk. *ballein,* throw)
boll, *n.* round seed-vessel, pod. **b.-weevil, b.-worm,** *nn.* (*Amer.*) infesting cotton bolls. **bolled,** *a.* **bollen,** *a.* (*Shake.*) swollen. (=*bowl*)
bollard, *n.* post on quay or ship for securing ropes to.
bolometer, *n.* instrument for measuring radiation. (Gk. *bolē,* ray)
boloney, *n.* (*Amer. sl.*) nonsense, humbug, rubbish.
Bolshevik, *n.* Russian communist; revolutionary. **bolshevism,** *n.* **Bolshevist,** (*sl.*) **Bolshy,** *n.* and *a.* (Russ. *bolsheviki,* majority party)
bolster, *n.* long pillow; pad.—*v.t.* support, prop. **b. up,** preserve from deserved overthrow. (O.E.)
bolt, *n.* short arrow, quarrel; discharge of lightning; strong pin for fastening; bar, catch, for securing; length of cloth; sudden flight.—*v.t.* fasten, secure, with bolt; swallow hastily; start, dislodge (quarry); (*Amer.*) run away from.—*v.i.* rush away, break from control; (*Amer.*) be political turncoat. **b. upright,** straight upright. (O.E.)
bolt, boult, *v.t.* sift; investigate. **bolter, boulter,** *n.* sieve, sifting-machine. (O.F. *bulter*)
bolus, *n.* large pill. (Gk. *bōlos,* lump)
boma, *n.* fenced enclosure, native village; boa. (native)
bomb, *n.* explosive missile thrown by hand or dropped from aircraft.—*v.t.* attack with bombs. **b.-proof,** *a.* able to withstand bombs. **bombshell,** *n.* shell. **bombard,** *n.* old form of cannon; (*Shake.*) leather jug.—*v.t.* attack with artillery, shell; assail (with abuse etc.). **bombardier,** *n.* an artillery N.C.O. **bombardment,** *n.* shelling. **bomber,** *n.* soldier, aeroplane, using bombs. (Gk. *bombos,* hum)
bombardon, bombardone, *n.* deep-toned brass instrument; bass reed-stop on organ. (It.)
bombasine, *n.* twilled fabric of silk and worsted. (Gk. *bombux,* silk)
bombast, *n.* high-sounding language, fustian. **bombastic,** *a.* **bombastically,** *adv.* (L.L. *bombax,* cotton)
bombazine, same as **bombasine.**
bombe, *n.* (*cookery*) cone-shaped dish. (F.)
bon, *a.* good. *b. mot,* witty saying (lit. good word). *b. ton.* (*arch.*) good breeding; high society. *b. vivant,* gourmet. (F.)
bona fidēs, good faith. **bona fide,** genuine; sincerely. (L.)
bonanza, *n.* rich vein, windfall.—*a.* very prosperous. (Sp.=fair weather)
bona-roba, *n.* (*Shake.*) showy wanton. (It. *buona roba,* fine gown)
bonbon, *n.* sweet. *bonbonnière,* *n.* fancy box for sweets. (F.)
bonce, *n.* large playing-marble.
bond, *n.* thing that binds, link; duty; written agreement to pay sum or perform contract; scrip of public

loan, debenture; (*pl.*) fetters; captivity.—*v.t.* put in bond; guarantee payment by issue of bonds. **in b.,** stored in **bonded warehouse,** where imported goods are kept by customs till duty is paid. **b.-stone, bonder,** *nn.* stone running through wall and so binding it. (=*band*)

bond, *a.* in slavery. **bondage,** *n.* slavery; captivity; restraint. **bondmaid, bondman, bondservant, bondsman, bondswoman, bondwoman,** *nn.* slave, serf. (O.E. *bonda*, farmer)

bone, *n.* substance, piece, of animal skeleton; (*pl.*) corpse; castanets; dice.—*v.t.* remove bones from; (*sl.*) steal. **b. of contention,** source of strife. **b. to pick,** grievance. **make no bb. of,** not scruple to. **to the b.,** right through. **b.-dry,** *a.* quite dry. **b.-setter,** *n.* one who treats fractures, osteopath. **b.-shaker,** *n.* (*colloq.*) bicycle without rubber tyres. **bonehead,** *n.* (*Amer.*) dolt. (O.E. *bán*)

bonfire, *n.* large open-air fire, for celebration or burning rubbish. (*bone*, material formerly used)

bongo, *n.* large striped African antelope. (native)

bonhomie, *n.* good nature. (F.)

bonne, *n.* French nursemaid. *b. bouche,* titbit (lit. good mouth). (F.)

bonnet, *n.* brimless headgear, us. tied on with strings; Scotch cap; cover of motor-car engine; gambler's decoy.—*v.t.* knock hat down over eyes of. **blue b.,** Scottish trooper. **b. laird,** (*Scot.*) petty landowner. *b. rouge,* red cap, revolutionary. (L.L. *bonetus*, kind of material)

bonny, *a.* nice-looking, pretty; considerable; cheerful. **bonnily,** *adv.*

bonspiel, *n.* great curling match.

bontebok, *n.* pied antelope of S. Africa. (Du.=spotted buck)

bonus, *n.* extra dividend or gratuity, premium. (L. *bonus*, good)

bonze, *n.* Buddhist priest. (Port. *bonzo*)

bonzer, *a.* (*Austral. sl.*) first-rate.

boo, *int.* of disapproval.—*v.i.* and *t.* and *n.* hoot. (imit.)

booby, *n.* stupid fellow, dunce; kinds of gannet. **b.-trap,** *n.* things balanced on door so as to fall on person entering. **boob,** *n.* (*Amer. sl.*) simpleton, booby. **boobyish,** *a.*

boodle, *n.* (*Amer.*) money for political bribery, graft; lot, caboodle.

boohoo, *v.i.* weep noisily. (imit.)

book, *n.* collection of paper leaves bound together; literary work; main division of this; libretto; bets on a race; (*pl.*) accounts.—*v.t.* enter in book; issue, take, ticket (for). **bring to b.,** call to account. **b. ends,** props for row of books. **bookcase,** *n.* case with shelves for books. **b.-keeper, b.-keeping,** *nn.* keeper, keeping, of accounts. **b.-learning,** *n.* theoretical knowledge. **bookmark, bookmarker,** *nn.* thing to mark place in book. **b.-mate,** *n.* (*Shake.*) fellow student. **b.-plate,** *n.* label in book with owner's name. **b.-slide,** *n.* small expanding stand for books. **booking-clerk, booking-hall, booking-office,** *nn.* official, office, issuing tickets. (O.E. *bóc*)

bookie, *n.* (*sl.*) bookmaker.

bookish, *a.* fond of reading; pedantic.

booklet, *n.* small book, pamphlet.

bookmaker, *n.* professional betting man; compiler of books.

bookman, *n.* literary man, scholar.

bookseller, *n.* one who sells books.

bookstall, *n.* stall for sale of books.

bookwork, *n.* study of theory, opp. to practice.

bookworm, *n.* maggot that eats holes in books; great reader.

boom, *n.* deep resonant sound; sudden commercial activity or popularity.—*v.i.* and *t.* emit boom, hum; be in great demand, launch with éclat. (imit.)

boom, *n.* spar extending bottom of sail; floating barrier across harbour. (Du.=beam)

boomer, *n.* large male kangaroo.

boomerang, *n.* Australian curved wooden missile, returning to thrower. (native)

boon, *n.* request; favour, blessing. (O.N. *bón*, prayer)

boon, *a.* bountiful; convivial, jolly. (*bon*)

boor, *n.* peasant; coarse person, lout. **boorish,** *a.* (*Boer*)

boost, *v.t.* and *n.* (*sl.*) lift up, hoist; puff, boom, advertise; (*electr.*) supplement voltage of (battery). **booster,** *n.*

boot, *n.* (*arch.*) advantage, use.—*v.i.* (*arch.*) avail. **to b.,** as well. (O.E. *bót*)

boot, *n.* foot-covering coming above ankle; kind of rack for leg; luggage receptacle in coach; leather apron for driver's seat; (*Shake.*) plunder; (*pl.*) hotel attendant who carries luggage etc.—*v.t.* (*sl.*) kick. **the b.,** (*sl.*) dismissal. **like old bb.,** (*sl.*) tremendously. **b. and saddle,** cavalry signal to mount. **booted,** *a.* wearing boots. **b.-tree,** *n.* last for keeping boot in shape. **bootee,** *n.* infant's wool boot; kind of woman's boot. (O.F. *bote*)

booth, *n.* temporary erection, stall, hut. **polling-b.,** *n.* place for voting. (M.E. *bothe*)

bootjack, *n.* appliance for drawing off boots.

bootlegger, *n.* liquor-smuggler. **bootlegging,** *n.*

bootless, *a.* useless, unavailing.

bootlicker, *n.* toady.

booty, *n.* spoil taken by force, plunder; any rich gain.

booze, *v.i.* drink to excess.—*n.* drinking-bout; strong drink. **boozy,** *a.* given to drink, tipsy. (M.E. *bousen*)

bo-peep, *n.* game of hiding and then suddenly showing face. (*bo*; *peep*)
bora, *n.* cold dry NE. wind of Adriatic. (*Boreas*)
bora, *n.* Mohammedan hawker. (Hind. *bohra*)
boracic, *a.* of borax. **b. acid, boric acid.**
borage, *n.* blue-flowered herb, used in salad etc. (L.L. *borrago*)
borax, *n.* a crystalline salt, used as antiseptic and in soldering. (Arab. *bauraq*)
Bordeaux, *n.* kinds of wine, claret. (place)
bordel, *n.* brothel. (L.L. *borda*, hut)
border, *n.* edge, margin; frontier; edging, narrow flower-bed.—*v.t.* and *i.* put border to; adjoin; verge. **borderer**, *n.* dweller on frontier. **borderland**, *n.* land on border; intermediate state. **bordure**, *n.* (*heraldry*) border round shield. (O.F. *bordure*)
bordereau, *n.* memorandum of contents, docket. (F.)
bore, *v.t.* and *i.* pierce, make hole (in); make way by effort; (*racing*) push (another) aside.—*n.* hole bored; calibre of gun. (O.E. *borian*)
bore, *n.* nuisance; tedious person.—*v.i.* and *t.* weary by prolixity or dullness.
bore, *n.* tidal wave with high front rushing up estuary.
bore, see **bear.**
Bóréās, *n.* north wind personified. **boreal**, *a.* (Gk.)
borecole, *n.* kail. (Du. *boerenkool*, peasant's cabbage)
boredom, *n.* being bored, tedium. **boresome**, *a.* tedious.
boric, *a.* of boron.
born, borne, see **bear.**
borné, *a.* limited, narrow-minded. (F.)
boron, *n.* a non-metallic element found in borax. (*bor*ax+carb*on*)
borough, *n.* town with corporation; town sending member to parliament. **close, pocket, rotten, b.**, whose representative was nominated by some person (abolished in 1832). **b.-English**, *n.* tenure by which youngest son inherits. (O.E. *burg*)
borrel, *a.* (*arch.*) unlearned, rude. (O.F. *burel*, coarse cloth)
borrow, *v.t.* and *i.* obtain on loan; adopt; derive (from); (*golf*) allow for slope. **borrower**, *n.* (O.E. *borg*, pledge)
Borstal, *n.* **B. system**, reformatory system by which sentence depends on prisoner's conduct. (place)
bort, *n.* diamond fragments made in cutting.
borzoi, *n.* Russian wolf-hound. (Russ.)
bos, *n.* (*sl.*) bad shot, miss.—*v.t.* and *i.* miss, bungle. **b.-eyed**, *a.* (*sl.*) blind in one eye; crooked.
boscage, *n.* growth of trees, leafy mass. (L.L. *boscum*, wood)
bosh, *n.* (*sl.*) nonsense, foolish talk.—*v.t.* (*sl.*) tease. (Turk.=empty)
bosk, bosket, *nn.* thicket. **boskage**, same as **boscage. bosky**, *a.* wooded, bushy. (M.E.=bush)
bosom, *n.* breast; heart; embrace; expanse; inmost recess; (*Amer.*) shirt-front.—*a.* intimate, dear.—*v.t.* enclose in bosom. (O.E. *bósm*)
boss, *n.* protuberance; knob, raised ornament. **bossed, bossy**, *aa.* (O.F. *boce*)
boss, *n.* master, foreman; (*Amer.*) wirepuller.—*v.t.* be manager of. **bossy**, *a.* managing. (*baas*)
boss, same as **bos.**
Boston, *n.* kind of waltz. (place)
Boswell, *n.* intimate biographer. **Boswellian**, *a.* (name)
bot, *n.* parasitic worm; (*pl.*) horse disease it causes.
botany, *n.* science of plants. **botanic, botanical**, *aa.* **botanist**, *n.* student of botany. **botanize**, *v.i.* study plants. (Gk. *botanē*, plant)
botargo, *n.* relish made of mullet or tunny roe. (Coptic *ou*, a. Gk. *tarichion*, pickle)
botch, *n.* clumsy patch; ill-finished work.—*v.t.* and *i.* mend clumsily.
both, *a.* and *pron.* the pair (of), the two.—*adv.* equally. (O.E. *bá*)
bother, *v.t.* and *i.* annoy, worry, give or take trouble.—*n.* worry, fuss. **botheration**, *n.* bothering.—*int.* confound it! **bothersome**, *a.*
bothy, bothie, *n.* (*Scot.*) hut, cottage; farm servants' quarters.
bo-tree, *n.* peepul, sacred tree of Buddhists. (Sanskr. *bodhi*, enlightenment)
bott, same as **bot.**
bottine, *n.* half-boot; small or lady's boot. (F.)
bottle, *n.* narrow-necked vessel for liquid; its contents.—*v.t.* put into bottles; (*sl.*) nab. **b.-glass**, *n.* coarse green glass. **b.-green**, *a.* dark green. **b.-holder**, *n.* second at prize-fight, supporter. **b.-neck**, *n.* narrow outlet. **b.-nose**, *n.* swollen nose; kind of whale. **b.-washer**, *n.* underling, factotum. (L.L. *butis*, vessel)
bottle, *n.* bundle (of hay etc.). (O.F. *botel*)
bottom, *n.* lowest part, base, foot; seat, rump; ground beneath water; valley; ship; stamina; origin, essential facts.—*a.* lowest, last.—*v.t.* and *i.* furnish with, reach, bottom; base; fathom. **at b.**, in reality. **bottomless**, *a.* unfathomable. **bottomry**, *n.* borrowing of money by owner on security of ship.—*v.t.* pledge (ship) thus. (O.E. *botm*)
botulism, *n.* kind of food-poisoning. (L. *botulus*, sausage)
boudoir, *n.* lady's private room. (F. *bouder*, sulk)
bouffant, *a.* puffed out (of skirt etc.). (F.)

bougainvillaea, bougainvilia, *n.* tropical plant with large rosy or purple bracts. (*Bougainville*, explorer)
bough, *n.* branch of tree. (O.E. *bóg*)
bought, see **buy.**
bougie, *n.* (*med.*) thin flexible instrument for inserting into gullet etc. (F.=wax candle)
bouillabaisse, *n.* French fish-stew.
bouilli, *n.* boiled or stewed meat.
bouillon, *n.* clear meat-broth. (F.)
boulder, *n.* large rounded stone; (*geol.*) stone detached from native bed. (M.E. *bulderston*)
Boúlē, *n.* ancient Greek senate; modern Greek legislature. (Gk.)
boulevard, *n.* broad tree-lined street. **boulevardier,** *n.* man about town. (G. *bollwerk*, rampart)
bouleversement, *n.* overturning, overthrow. (F.)
boulter, *n.* long fishing-line with many hooks.
bounce, *v.i.* and *t.* rebound, cause to bound; leap suddenly; brag; bluff (into); (*Amer.*) eject.—*n.* rebound; sudden spring; boastfulness, swagger; (*Shake.*) bang. — *adv.* startlingly. **bouncer,** *n.* one who bounces; barefaced lie; (*sl.*) whopper; (*Amer. sl.*) chucker-out. **bouncing,** *a.* big and hearty. (M.E. *bunsen*, thump)
bound, *v.i.* spring, leap; rebound.—*n.* jump; bounce. (F. *bondir*)
bound, *n.* (us. *pl.*) limit, boundary, restriction.—*v.t.* limit, set bounds to. (L.L. *butina*)
bound, *a.* ready to go, going; destined; obliged. (O.N. *búa*, prepare)
bound, see **bind.**
boundary, *n.* dividing line. (*bound*)
bounden, see **bind.**
bounder, *n.* (*colloq.*) noisy vulgar person. (*bound*)
boundless, *a.* unlimited, vast.
bounty, *n.* generous giving; charitable gifts; state premium to foster production; (*arch.*) gratuity. **king's b.,** grant to mother of triplets. **bounteous, bountiful,** *aa.* liberal, generous; plentiful. (L. *bonus*, good)
bouquet, *n.* bunch of flowers; perfume of wine. (F.)
bouquetin, *n.* Alpine ibex. (F.)
bourbon, *n.* (*Amer.*) political die-hard; Kentucky whisky. (name)
bourd, *n.* (*obs.*) jest, sport. **bourder,** *n.* jester. (O.F. *bourde*)
bourdon, *n.* dull-toned bass stop in organ. (F.=humming tone)
bourgeois, *n.* and *a.* middle-class (person), between aristocracy and workers; humdrum, conventional. **bourgeoisie,** *n.* middle class. (F.)
bourgeois, *n.* (*print.*) 9-point type, between long primer and brevier.
bourgeon, same as **burgeon.**
bourn, *n.* small stream. (*burn*)
bourn, bourne, *n.* bound, goal; realm. (F. *borne*)
bourse, *n.* foreign stock exchange. (F.)
bourtree, *n.* (*Scot.*) elder.
bouse, same as **booze.**
boustrophēdon, *n.* ancient mode of writing lines alternately from left to right and from right to left. (Gk. =as ox turns in ploughing)
bout, *n.* spell, turn, round; trial.
boutade, *n.* whim, caprice. (F.)
boutonnière, *n.* buttonhole; spray of flowers worn in it. (F.)
bouts rimés, given rhymes; verses made to fit them. (F.=rhymed ends)
bovine, *a.* of, like, a cow; stolid, dull. (L. *bos*, ox)
bovrilize, *v.t.* concentrate, boil down. (*Bovril*, a meat extract)
bow, *n.* weapon for shooting arrows; curved thing, rainbow; implement for playing violin; slip-knot with loop; (*Shake.*) yoke.—*v.t.* and *i.* use bow on (violin). **draw the long b.,** exaggerate. **b. compasses,** with jointed legs. **b. window,** curved bay window. **b.-head,** *n.* Greenland whale. **b.-legged,** *a.* bandy. **saddle-b.,** *n.* arched front of saddle. (O.E. *boga*)
bow, *v.i.* and *t.* bend, incline; submit, subdue; incline head or body in respect or assent.—*n.* act of bowing. (O.E. *bugan*)
bow, *n.* forepart of ship, prow; rower nearest bow. **on the b.,** within 45° of a point right ahead.
bowdlerize, *v.t.* expurgate, remove indelicate words from. **bowdlerization, bowdlerism,** *nn.* (T. *Bowdler*, expurgator of Shakespeare)
bowel, *n.* intestine; (*pl.*) entrails, inside; pity. (L.L. *botellus*, small sausage)
bower, *n.* arbour, shady recess; inner room, boudoir; (*poet.*) dwelling. **b.-bird,** *n.* Australian bird like starling. **bowery,** *a.* shady. (O.E. *búr*, dwelling)
bower, *n.* (also **b.-anchor**) anchor at ship's bow. (*bow*)
bower, *n.* one of two knaves in euchre. (G. *bauer*, peasant)
bowie, *n.* (also **b.-knife**) long American hunting-knife. (inventor)
bowl, *n.* basin; hollow part of thing. **the b.,** conviviality; poison. (O.E. *bolla*)
bowl, *n.* wooden ball with bias; (*pl.*) game with these; skittles.—*v.i.* and *t.* play bowls; trundle, roll; (*cricket*) deliver ball, put out (batsman) thus. **b. along,** move smoothly and rapidly. **b. over,** knock down, overwhelm. **bowling-alley,** *n.* enclosure for skittles. **bowling-crease,** *n.* (*cricket*) from which bowler delivers ball. **bowling-green,** *n.* lawn for playing bowls. (L. *bulla*, bubble)
bowlder, same as **boulder.**
bowler, *n.* (*bowls*) player; (*cricket*) player who delivers ball.
bowler, *n.* hard felt hat. (*bowl*)
bowline, *n.* rope from weather side of square sail to bow; knot used in making fixed end loop.

bowman, *n.* archer.
bowman, *n.* oarsman nearest bow.
bowsprit, *n.* spar projecting from ship's bow. (*bow*; *sprit*)
bow-wow, *n.* dog's bark; dog. (imit.)
bowyer, *n.* maker, seller, of bows.
box, *n.* an evergreen shrub; its hard wood. (L. *buxus*)
box, *n.* rigid case; its contents; driver's seat; compartment; hut, small house.—*v.t.* enclose in box; deposit in law-court. **b. the compass,** name all its points in order; make complete turn. **b. up,** confine. **in the wrong b.,** in a false position. **b.-bed,** *n.* one enclosed with sliding panels. **b.-car,** *n.* (*Amer.*) enclosed freight car. **b.-office,** *n.* theatre ticket-office. **b.-pleat,** *n.* double fold in cloth. **b.-wallah,** *n.* (*Anglo-Ind.*) pedlar; commercial traveller. **Boxing Day,** first week-day after Christmas.
box, *n.* slap, buffet.—*v.t.* and *i.* slap (ears); fight with fists, us. in padded **boxing-gloves. boxer,** *n.* pugilist; (*Austral.*) bowler hat.
boxhaul, *v.t.* (*naut.*) veer (ship) round on her heel. (*box*)
boxiana, *n.pl.* literature of boxing.
boy, *n.* male child, lad under 20; man; native servant or labourer. **the b.,** (*sl.*) champagne. **B. Scouts, Boys' Brigade,** organizations for boys. **b.'s-love,** *n.* southernwood.
boyar, *n.* Russian of old aristocratic order. (Russ. *boyarin*)
boycott, *v.t.* refuse to have dealings with, ostracize.—*n.* concerted isolation of this kind. (name)
boyhood, *n.* state of being a boy. **boyish** *a.* like a boy; puerile.
bozo, *n.* (*Amer. sl.*) fellow, chap
brabble, *v.i.* and *n.* (*arch.*) brawl, quarrel. (Du. *brabbelen,* jabber)
brace, *n.* clasp, clamp; strut; pair; (*naut.*) rope to work ship's yard; (*print.*) coupling-mark ({); (*pl.*) trouser-suspenders.—*v.t.* bind, hold, closely; strengthen, tighten; invigorate. **b. and bit,** revolving tool for boring. **splice the main b.,** (*naut.*) have drink. **bracing,** *a.* tonic, invigorating. (L. *brachium,* arm)
bracelet, *n.* ornament for wrist; (*sl.*) handcuff. **braceleted,** *a.* (*brace*)
bracer, *n.* wrist-guard in archery etc.; (*Amer. sl.*) pick-me-up. (*brace*)
brach, *n.* bitch hound. (O.F. *brachet*)
brachial, *a.* of, like, arm. **brachiate,** *a.* having branches in pairs, each at right angles to the next. **brachiopod,** *n.* animal like mollusc with arm-like appendages at side of mouth. (L. *brachium,* arm)
brachy-, from Gk. *brachus,* short, used in **brachycephalic,** *a.* short-headed; **brachygraphy,** *n.* old kinds of shorthand; **brachylogy,** *n.* conciseness, condensed expression. **brachypterous,** *a.* short-winged.
bracken, *n.* large fern; mass of this.
bracket, *n.* support, shelf, gas-pipe, projecting from wall; (*print.*) marks for enclosing words, ( ), [ ], { }.—*v.t.* enclose in brackets; couple; range by dropping shells over and short of mark. (L. *bracae,* breeches)
brackish, *a.* saltish (of water). (Du. *brak*)
bract, *n.* small leaf on stem below calyx. **bracteal, bracteate,** *aa.* (L. *bractea,* gold-leaf)
brad, *n.* thin small nail.
bradawl, *n.* small boring-tool.
bradbury, *n.* (*sl.*) Treasury note for £1 or 10*s.* (name)
Bradshaw, *n.* a railway guide. (compiler)
brady-, from Gk. *bradus,* slow, used in **bradypeptic,** *a.* slow of digestion; **bradypod,** *n.* sloth.
brae, *n.* (*Scot.*) hill-slope. (O.N. *brá*)
brag, *v.i.* and *t.* boast (of).—*n.* boast, boastful talk; card game like poker. **braggadocio,** *n.* bragging talk; boaster. **braggart,** *n.* and *a.* boastful (person).
Brahma, *n.* supreme Hindu god; divine essence. **brahmin, brahman,** *n.* Hindu of priestly caste. **brahminic, brahminical, brahmanic, brahmanical,** *aa.* **brahminism, brahmanism,** *nn.* **brahminee,** *n.* female brahmin.—*a.* of brahmin caste.
brahmapootra, brahma, *n.* breed of fowl. (name of river)
braid, *v.t.* plait, interweave; bind with braid.—*n.* plait (of hair); woven band, plaited cord. (O.E. *bregdan,* move to and fro)
braid, *v.t.* (*Shake.*) upbraid, reproach.
braid, *Scot.* **form of broad.**
Braidism, *n.* hypnotism. (Dr. *Braid*)
braik, *n.* (*Scot.*) kind of harrow.
brail, *n.* rope to truss sail before furling.—*v.t.* haul (up) with this. (L. *bracale,* waist-belt)
braille, *n.* type of raised dots, for blind readers. (inventor)
brain, *n.* nervous organ in skull; (often *pl.*) intellect, understanding.—*v.t.* dash out brains of; (*Shake.*) conceive. **bear a b.,** (*Shake.*) have remembrance. **have thing on the b.,** be crazy about it. **pick one's bb.,** use one's ideas. **b.-fag,** *n.* nervous exhaustion. **b. fever,** meningitis. **b.-fever bird,** Indian cuckoo. **b.-pan,** *n.* cranium. **b.-storm,** *n.* sudden violent disturbance of brain. **b.-wave,** *n.* bright idea. **brainish,** *a.* (*Shake.*) headstrong. **brainless,** *a.* silly. **brainy,** *a.* clever. (O.E. *brægen*)
braird, *n.* first shoots (of corn etc.).—*v.i.* sprout. (O.E. *brerd,* brim)
braise, *v.t.* stew in covered pan. (F. *braise,* hot charcoal)
brake, see **break.**
brake, *n.* bracken.
brake, *n.* thicket, brushwood.
brake, *v.t.* crush (flax, hemp) by

beating.—*n.* toothed instrument for this; heavy harrow. (M.L.G.)
brake, *n.* device for checking motion of wheel or vehicle; large wagonette. —*v.t.* and *i.* check with, apply, brake. **b.-van**, *n.* carriage containing brake. **brakesman**, *n.* man in charge of brake.
bramble, *n.* blackberry-bush; blackberry; any prickly shrub. — *v.i.* gather brambles. **brambly**, *a.* **brambling**, *n.* mountain finch.
brame, *n.* (*Spens.*) longing. (It *brama*)
bran, *n.* husks separated from flour. **b. pie**, kind of lucky dip. (O.F. *bren*)
brancard, *n.* horse-drawn litter. (F.)
branch, *n.* limb of tree, bough; offshoot, member, section.—*v.i.* put forth branches, diverge, spread. **root and b.**, thoroughly. (L.L. *branca*, paw)
branchial, *a.* of gills. **branchiate**, *a.* having gills. **branchiopod**, *n.* crustacean with gills on feet. (L. *branchiae*, gills)
branchlet, *n.* twig.
branchy, *a.* with many branches.
brand, *n.* burning or charred stick, torch; red-hot iron stamp; mark made by this, trade mark; grade, make; stigma; (*arch.*) sword.—*v.t.* burn with hot iron, mark; stigmatize. **b.-new**, **bran-new**, *a.* quite new. **brandish**, *v.t.* wave, flourish (weapon). **brandling**, *n.* small striped worm used as bait. (O.E.)
brandreth, *n.* wooden stand for cask etc.; fence round well. (O.N. *brandreith*, grate)
brandy, *n.* spirits made from wine. **b.-ball**, *n.* kind of sweet. **b.-pawnee**, *n.* brandy-and-water. **b.-snap**, *n.* ginger wafer. (Du. *brandewijn*, burnt wine)
brank, *n.* buckwheat.
brank, *v.i.* prance, strut. **branky**, *a.*
branks, *n.pl.* bridle to gag scolds.
branks, *n.pl.* mumps.
brank-ursine, *n.* bear's-breech, acanthus. (L. *branca ursina*, bear's paw)
bran-new, see brand.
brant, **brant-goose**, same as **brent** etc.
brash, *n.* fragments of rock or ice; hedge-clippings.—*a.* brittle.
brash, *a.* (*Amer. sl.*) hasty; cheeky.
brash, *n.* acid eructation, fit of sickness; rash; burst of rain.
brass, *n.* alloy of copper and zinc; tablet, ornament, of brass; impudence; (*sl.*) cash.—*a.* of brass. **the b.**, (*mus.*) brass instruments. **b. band**, using these. **b. farthing**, smallest amount. **b. hat**, staff officer. **b. plate**, name-plate on door. **b. tacks**, (*sl.*) details. **b. up**, (*sl.*) pay up. **part b. rags**, dissolve friendship. **brassage**, *n.* sum levied for coinage. **brassed off** (*R.A.F. sl.*) fed up, depressed. (O.E. *bræs*)
brassard, *n.* armlet. (F. *bras*, arm)
brasserie, *n.* beer-saloon, us. supplying eatables also. (F-=brewery)
brassière, *n.* under-bodice supporting breasts. (F.)
brassy, *a.* like brass.—*n.* (*golf*) wooden club with brass sole.
brat, *n.* child (us. contemptuous). **bratling**, *n.* little brat.
brattice, **bratticing**, *nn.* (*min.*) wooden partition, lining, in pit-shaft. (O.F. *breteske*, parapet)
brattle, *n.* (*Scot.*) clatter; short race.
brava, **bravissima**, used sometimes for **bravo** etc. when applauding actress.
bravado, *n.* show of courage, boastful threat. (Sp. *bravada*)
brave, *a.* courageous, daring; (*arch.*) fine, handsome, excellent.—*n.* Red Indian warrior.—*v.t.* meet boldly, defy. **bravery**, *n.* courage; finery. (It. *bravo*)
bravo, *n.* (*pl.* **bravoes**, **braves**) hired assassin, desperado. (It.)
bravo, *int.* well done!—*n.* cry of applause. **bravissimo**, *int.* very well done! (It.)
bravura, *n.* (*mus.*) brilliant execution; (passage of) florid style. (It.)
brawl, *v.i.* quarrel noisily; (of stream) gurgle.—*n.* row, squabble.
brawl, *n.* (*Shake.*) a French dance. (F. *branle*)
brawn, *n.* muscle, muscular strength; pickled pork. **brawny**, *a.* muscular. (O.F. *braon*, flesh)
braxy, *n.* (*Scot.*) a disease of sheep; diseased mutton.—*a.* so diseased.
bray, *v.t.* pound small. (O.F. *breier*)
bray, *n.* cry of ass, harsh cry.—*v.i.* and *t.* utter this; blare. (imit.)
braze, *v.t.* solder with alloy of brass and zinc.
braze, *v.t.* colour like brass; cover, ornament, with brass. (*brass*)
brazen, *a.* of, like, brass; harsh-sounding; shameless.—*v.t.* make bold. **b. age**, fabled age of violence, succeeding silver age. **b. out**, face brazenly. **b.-faced**, *a.* (*brass*)
brazier, *n.* worker in brass. **braziery**, *n.* his workshop. (*braze*)
brazier, *n.* pan for burning coals. (F. *braise*, hot coal)
brazil, *n.* a heavy red wood. **b.-nut**, *n.* large three-cornered nut. (place)
breach, *n.* breaking, infringement (of rule etc.); quarrel; gap, fissure.—*v.t.* make breach in. **b. of the peace**, public disturbance, riot. **b. of promise**, us. of marriage. (*break*)
bread, *n.* flour baked in loaves; food. **b. and butter**, livelihood; (of girl) prim; (of letter) thanking for hospitality. **b. and scrape**, thinly buttered bread. **b.-basket**, *n.* (*sl.*) stomach. **breadwinner**, *n.* supporter of family. **b.-line**, *n.* (*Amer.*) queue for bread ration. (O.E. *bréad*)
breadth, *n.* broadness, extent from side to side; freedom from prejudice, toleration; bold effect. **breadthways**, **breadthwise**, *advv.* (O.E. *bráedu*)
break, *v.t.* and *i.* (*past* **broke**, *arch.*

brake; *p.p.* **broken, broke**) separate forcibly; destroy, shatter, dissolve; burst asunder or forth; subdue, give way; bankrupt, cashier, fail; transgress; disclose, become known; interrupt; fall out; (*cricket*, of ball) change direction on pitching.—*n.* breaking, rupture, gap; pause, interruption; (*billiards*) scoring sequence; (*Amer. sl.*) chance; breach of good manners. **b. bread,** have meal. **b. bulk,** begin unloading. **b. cover,** come into open. **b. down,** overcome; collapse, fail. **b. ground,** begin operations. **b. in,** force way in, intervene; train. **b. of day,** dawn. **b. off,** cease. **b. on wheel,** torture. **b. out,** appear, begin; throw off restraint. **b. the ice,** overcome shyness. **b. up,** dissolve, disperse, decay. **b. wind,** vent wind. **bad b.,** (*colloq.*) gaffe. (O.E. *brecan*)

breakage, *n.* breaking, fracture.

breakdown, *n.* collapse, failure of health or power; (*Amer.*) negro dance.

breaker, *n.* trainer; breaking wave.

breaker, *n.* (*naut.*) small cask. (Sp. *barrica*, cask)

breakfast, *n.* first meal of day.—*v.i.* and *t.* take, furnish with, this.

breakneck, *a.* dangerously steep or fast.

breakwater, *n.* harbour-wall to break force of waves.

bream, *n.* broad fish like carp. (O.F. *bresme*)

bream, *v.t.* (*naut.*) clean (ship's bottom) by fire.

breast, *n.* milk-secreting organ; chest; heart, affections.—*v.t.* face, oppose; mount (hill). **make clean b. of,** confess. **b.-bone,** *n.* connecting ribs in front. **breastplate,** *n.* armour for breast; coffin-plate. **breastsummer,** *n.* supporting beam, lintel. **breastwork,** *n.* parapet. (O.E. *bréost*)

breath, *n.* air used by lungs, respiration; life; breeze, whisper, fragrance. **below one's b.,** in whisper. **take b.,** rest. **take one's b. away,** astound. **breathless,** *a.* out of breath, panting. **breathy,** *a.* (of voice) not clear-sounding. (O.E. *brǣth*, smell of burning)

breathe, *v.i.* and *t.* inhale and exhale (air); live; pause; utter softly; (*Shake.*) exercise. **b. again,** be relieved. **b. one's last,** die. **b. upon,** tarnish. **breather,** *n.* short spell of exercise or rest; (*Shake.*) creature. **breathing,** *n.* respiration; (*Gk. gram.*) mark showing whether initial vowel is aspirated or not.—*a.* lifelike. (*breath*)

breccia, *n.* rock of angular fragments cemented by lime etc. (It.)

bred, see **breed.**

brede, *arch.* form of **braid.**

bree, *n.* (*Scot.*) broth. (O.E. *briw*)

breech, *n.* buttocks; hinder part, esp. of gun-barrel; (*pl.*) trousers.—*v.t.* furnish with breeches; flog. **wear the bb.,** be master of house. **b.-loader,** *n.* gun loaded at breach. **bb.-buoy,** *n.* lifebuoy on hawser to take people off wreck. **breeching,** *n.* harness round horse's hindquarters.—*a.* (*Shake.*) subject to whipping. (O.E. *bréc*, breeches—a double plural)

breed, *v.t.* and **i.** (*past, p.p.* **bred**) bear, propagate (young); produce; arise.—*n.* race, strain. **b. in and in,** always marry near relations. **breeder,** *n.* **breeding,** *n.* rearing; manners, courtesy. (O.E. *brédan*)

breeks, *n.pl.* (*Scot.*) breeches.

breer, *v.i.* (*Scot.*) sprout.

breeze, *n.* coke-dust, cinders; refuse.

breeze, *n.* gadfly. (O.E. *briosa*)

breeze, *n.* gentle wind; (*sl.*) quarrel. **breezy,** *a.* windy; cheerful, jovial. (O.Sp. *briza*, NE. wind)

Brehon, *n.* ancient Irish judge. **B. law,** native Irish code. (O.Ir. *brithem*, judge)

brekker, *n.* (*sl.*) breakfast.

breme, *a.* (*Spens.*) fierce, rough.

bren, *v.t.* (*obs.*; *p.p.* **brent**) burn. (O.E. *brinnan*)

Bren gun, kind of light machine-gun. (*Br*no in Czechoslovakia; *En*field in England)

brent, *a.* (*Scot.*) lofty; smooth, unwrinkled. (O.E. *brant*)

brent, brent-goose, *n.* smallest kind of wild goose.

brer, *n.* (*Amer. negro dial.*) brother.

bressummer, same as **breastsummer.**

brethren, see **brother.**

breve, *n.* (*mus.*) longest note now used, ‖O‖, equal to four minims; mark (˘) of short vowel. (L. *brevis*, short)

brevet, *n.* commission conferring rank without corresponding pay; warrant.—*a.* nominal, honorary.—*v.t.* confer brevet rank on. **brevetcy,** *n.* (F.)

brevi-, from L. *brevis*, short, used in **breviped,** *a.* short-legged; **brevirostrate,** *a.* short-billed.

breviary, *n.* book of daily services in R.C. Church. (L. *brevis*, short)

brevier, *n.* (*print.*) 8-point type, between bourgeois and minion. (used in *breviaries*)

brevity, *n.* shortness, conciseness. (L. *brevis*, short)

brew, *v.t.* and *i.* make (beer) by fermentation; infuse (tea); concoct; be forming.—*n.* liquor brewed; its quality. **brewage,** *n.* drink brewed; concoction. **brewer,** *n.* **brewery,** *n.* place for brewing beer. (O.E. *bréowan*)

brewis, *n.* (*arch.*) pottage, broth. (O.F. *brouetz*)

brewster, *n.* (*obs.*) female brewer. **b. sessions,** licensing sessions.

briar, *n.* (also **b.-pipe**) tobacco-pipe of heather root; brier.

Briarean, *a.* many-handed. (*Briareus*, mythical giant)

bribe, *n.* gift to corrupt or influence unduly. — *v.t.* pervert by bribe.

bribee, *n.* one who is bribed. **briber, bribery,** *nn.*

bric-à-brac, *n.* curious, antique, or artistic articles. (F.)

brick, *n.* building-block of baked clay; oblong block; (*sl.*) good chap.—*a.* of brick.—*v.t.* lay, build, with bricks. **b. up,** block with bricks. **drop a b.,** commit social blunder. **brickbat,** *n.* piece of brick. **b.-kiln,** *n.* for baking bricks. **b.-red,** *a.* greyish red. **bricken,** *a.* **bricklayer,** *n.* builder with bricks. **bricky,** *a.* full of, like, bricks.

bricole, *n.* (*billiards, tennis*) stroke in which ball is hit first against cushion, wall. (F.)

bride, *n.* woman on wedding-day or honeymoon. **bridal,** *n.* wedding.—*a.* of bride or wedding. **bridegroom,** *n.* man on wedding-day. **bridesmaid,** *n.* girl attendant of bride. (O.E. *brýd*)

bride, *n.* the network of lace; bonnet-string. (F.=bridle)

bridewell, *n.* house of correction, jail. (London prison)

bridge, *n.* structure for crossing river etc.; upper part of nose; prop under violin strings; (*naut.*) raised platform for captain; (*billiards*) support for cue.—*v.t.* make bridge over, span. **b.-head,** *n.* defensive work covering end of bridge nearest enemy. (O.E. *brycg*)

bridge, *n.* card-game founded on whist. **auction, contract, b.,** kinds of it.

bridle, *n.* harness for horse's head; restraint; (*naut.*) mooring-cable.—*v.t.* put bridle on; restrain, curb.—*v.i.* draw head up and chin in. **b.-path,** *n.* one open to riders but not vehicles. (O.E. *bregdan,* twitch)

bridoon, *n.* snaffle and rein of military bridle. (F. *bridon*)

Brie, *n.* a cream cheese. (place)

brief, *a.* short, concise.—*n.* papal letter; (*law*) abstract of case for use of barrister.—*v.t.* (*law*) make abstract of; instruct, employ (barrister) in case. **hold b. for,** be counsel, plead, for. **briefly,** *adv.* in short. (L. *brevis*)

brier, briar, *n.* white heath. (F. *bruyère,* heath)

brier, briar, *n.* thorny shrub. **b.-rose,** *n.* dog-rose. **sweet-b.,** *n.* wild rose. **briery, briary,** *a.* (O.E. *brér*)

brig, *n.* vessel with two masts, both square-rigged. (*brigantine*)

brig, *Scot.* form of **bridge.**

brigade, *n.* subdivision of army; organized band.—*v.t.* form into, unite in, brigade. **Boys' B.,** an organization for boys. **brigadier, brigadier-general,** *nn.* commander of brigade. (L.L. *briga,* strife)

brigand, *n.* bandit, freebooter. **brigandage, brigandism,** *nn.* (O.F.)

brigantine, *n.* two-masted vessel, square-rigged on foremast only. (It. *brigantino*)

bright, *a.* shining, full of light; vivid; illustrious; cheerful, vivacious; clever.—*adv.* brightly. **brighten,** *v.t.* and *i.* make, become, bright. (O.E. *beorht*)

Bright's disease, a kidney disease. (Dr. R. *Bright*)

brill, *n.* flat-fish like turbot.

brilliant, *a.* sparkling, lustrous; distinguished; talented.—*n.* diamond of finest cut; (*print.*) smallest type, 3-point. **brilliance, brilliancy,** *nn.* **brilliantine,** *n.* cosmetic to make hair glossy. (F. *briller,* shine)

brim, *n.* edge, lip, of vessel or hollow; rim of hat.—*v.t.* and *i.* fill, be full, to brim. **b. over,** overflow. **brimful,** *a.* completely full. **brimmer,** *n.* bumper. (M.E. *brimme*)

brimstone, *n.* sulphur.—*a.* sulphur-coloured. **brimstony,** *a.* (M.E. *brinnen,* burn+*stone*)

brindled, brindle, (*Shake.*) **brinded,** *a.* tawny with streaks, streaked.

brine, *n.* salt water; pickle; the sea; (*poet.*) tears.—*v.t.* steep in brine. **briny,** *a.* very salt.—*n.* (*sl.*) sea. (O.E. *brýne*)

bring, *v.t.* (*past, p.p.* **brought**) fetch; carry with one; cause to come, conduct; cause; prefer (charge). **b. about,** effect. **b. back,** recall. **b. down,** humble; kill, wound. **b. down the house,** get great applause. **b. forth,** give birth to, produce. **b. forward,** adduce; carry (sum) to next page. **b. home to,** convict, convince, of. **b. in,** introduce; yield. **b. off,** accomplish successfully. **b. on,** lead to. **b. out,** express; publish; introduce (girl) to society. **b. over,** convert. **b. round, to,** restore to consciousness. **b. to bear,** apply. **b. up,** educate, rear; sue; vomit; anchor (ship). **b. up the rear,** come last. (O.E. *bringan*)

brinjal, *n.* (*Anglo-Ind.*) fruit of egg-plant. (Sanskr. *vātin-gana*)

brinjarry, *n.* (*Anglo-Ind.*) pedlar of grain and salt. (Hind. *bānjāra*)

brink, *n.* edge of steep place; margin, verge. (M.E.)

brio, *n.* vivacity. (It.)

brioche, *n.* sponge cake or roll. (F.)

briquette, briquet, *n.* block of compressed coal-dust. (F.)

brise-bise, *n.* curtain across lower part of window. (F.)

brisk, *a.* active, lively; keen; stimulating.—*v.t.* and *i.* enliven, cheer up.

brisket, *n.* breast of animal as joint.

bristle, *n.* short, stiff hair, esp. of hog.—*v.i.* and *t.* stand up, erect, like bristles; show temper; be thickly set (with). **bristly,** *a.* set with bristles; rough. (O.E. *byrst*)

bristling, brisling, *n.* small fish like sardine.

Bristol, *n.* **B. fashion,** in good order. **B. board,** a smooth pasteboard.

brit, *n.* whitebait, fry of herring.

Britain, *n.* (also **Great B.**) England, Wales, and Scotland; (also **Greater B.**) British Empire. **North B.,** Scotland. **Britannia,** *n.* Britain personified. **Britannia metal,** white alloy of tin etc. **Britannic,** *a.* of Britain. (L. *Brittania*)

briticism, *n.* anglicism. **British,** *a.* of Britain; of ancient Britons. **British warm,** military overcoat. **Britisher,** *n.* (*Amer.*) British subject. **britishism,** *n.* anglicism. **Briton,** *n.* native of Britain, esp. before Anglo-Saxon conquest. **North Briton,** Scotsman. (O.E. *Bret,* Briton)

brittle, *a.* apt to break, fragile. (O.E. *breotan,* break)

britzka, britzska, *n.* carriage with hooded top and space for reclining. (Pol. *bryka,* wagon)

brize, *n.* gadfly. (=*breeze*)

broach, *n.* roasting spit; boring-tool; kind of church spire.—*v.t.* and *i.* tap (cask), draw (liquor); bring up for discussion. **b. to,** turn (ship) to windward, presenting side to waves. (L. *broccus,* projecting)

broad, *a.* wide, extensive; of stated breadth; manifest; bold; indelicate; tolerant; (of accent) marked.—*n.* expansion of stream.—*adv.* broadly. **b. arrow,** Government mark, used on convicts. **B. Church,** favouring comprehension. **b.-minded,** *a.* tolerant. (O.E. *brád*)

broadcast, *a.* scattered freely.—*adv.* in this manner.—*v.t.* and *i.* (*past* **broadcasted,** *p.p.* **broadcast**) scatter, disseminate widely; (*wireless*) transmit (message).—*n.* wireless message.

broadcloth, *n.* a fine woollen cloth.

broaden, *v.t.* and *i.* grow, make, broader.

broadness, *n.* coarseness, indelicacy.

broadsheet, *n.* sheet printed on one side only; short pamphlet, squib.

broadside, *n.* ship's side; (discharge of) all guns on this; broadsheet.

broadsword, *n.* sword with broad straight blade.

Brobdingnag, *n.* land of giants. **brobdingnagian,** *a.* colossal. (name in book)

brocade, *n.* fabric woven with raised patterns.—*v.t.* work in this way. (Sp. *brocado*)

broccoli, brocoli, *n.* kind of cauliflower. (It.=cabbage-tops)

broch, *n.* (*Scot.*) ancient dry-built circular tower. (O.N. *borg,* fort)

brochure, *n.* booklet, pamphlet. (F.)

brock, *n.* badger. (O.E. *broc*)

brocket, *n.* stag in its second year. (F. *brocart*)

brog, *n.* boring-tool, awl.

brogue, brogan, *nn.* stout coarse shoe. (Gael. *brog,* shoe)

brogue, *n.* dialect, accent, esp. Irish.

broider, *arch.* for **embroider.**

broil, *n.* noisy quarrel, tumult. (F. *brouiller,* quarrel)

broil, *v.t.* and *i.* cook on gridiron, grill; make, be, very hot.

broke, *n.* short wool on parts of fleece. (O.E. *brecan,* break)

broke, *a.* penniless; dismissed the service. (*break*)

broken, *a.* in pieces, incomplete; uneven, rough (ground); interrupted. **b. English,** imperfect. **b. meat,** scraps. **b.-hearted,** *a.* grief-stricken. **b.-winded,** *a.* having heaves. (*break*)

broker, *n.* middleman, agent; go-between; seller of second-hand or distrained goods. **brokerage,** *n.* business, commission, of broker. **broking,** *n.* acting as broker. (*broach*)

brolga, *n.* Australian crane. (native)

brolly, *n.* (*sl.*) umbrella. (abbr.)

bromine, *n.* evil-smelling element like chlorine. **bromal, bromate,** *nn.* compounds of bromine. **bromic,** *a.* **bromide,** *n.* compound of bromine; sedative; (*sl.*) bore, trite remark. **bromide paper,** (*phot.*) used for enlarging. (Gk. *brōmos,* stench)

bronchi, bronchia, *nn.pl.* branches, ramifications, of windpipe. **bronchial,** *a.* **bronchitis,** *n.* inflammation of bronchi. **bronchocele,** *n.* goitre. **broncho-pneumonia,** *n.* diffuse inflammation of lungs. (L.)

bronco, *n.* (*Amer.*) unbroken horse. (Sp.=rough)

brontosaurus, *n.* huge fossil lizard. (Gk. *brontē,* thunder; *sauros,* lizard)

bronze, *n.* alloy of copper and tin; statue in this.—*a.* of, like, bronze.—*v.t.* make bronze-coloured, tan. **b. age,** between stone and iron. **bronzy,** *a.* (L. *Brundusium,* Brindisi)

broo, *n.* (*Scot.*) broth.

brooch, *n.* ornamental clasp or safety-pin. (M.E. *broche*)

brood, *n.* young of bird, hatch; offspring; swarm, crew.—*v.i.* sit on eggs; meditate, fret (over). **broody,** *a.* (of hen) wishing to sit. (O.E. *bród*)

brook, *n.* small stream. **brooklet,** *n.* little brook. **brooklime,** *n.* kind of speedwell. (O.E. *bróc*)

brook, *v.t.* bear, endure. (O.E. *brucan*)

broom, *n.* yellow-flowered shrub; brush for sweeping. **b.-rape,** *n.* a parasitic plant. **broomstick,** *n.* handle of broom. (O.E. *bróm*)

brose, *n.* oatmeal with boiling water or milk poured on it. (*brewis*)

broth, *n.* liquid in which anything has been boiled; meat soup. **b. of a boy,** (*Ir.*) good fellow. (*brew*)

brothel, *n.* house of prostitution. (O.E. *bréothan,* go to ruin)

brother, *n.* (*pl.* **brothers, brethren**) son of same parents; fellow-member, associate, equal; member of religious order. **b.-german,** *n.* full brother. **b.-in-law,** *n.* brother of husband or wife; husband of sister. **b.-uterine,** *n.* of same mother but different father. **half-b.,** having one parent only in common. **brotherhood,** *n.* brotherliness; association. **brotherly,** *a.* fraternal. (O.E. *bróthor*)

brougham, *n.* light closed carriage. (Lord *Brougham*)

brought, see **bring.**
brow, *n.* (*naut.*) gangway.
brow, *n.* ridge over eyes, forehead; mien; edge of hill. **browbeat,** *v.t.* bully with looks or words. (O.E. *brú*)
brown, *a.* between black and orange; tanned.—*n.* brown colour; (*sl.*) copper.—*v.t.* and *i.* make, become, brown. **B. Bess,** old flint-lock musket. **b. bread,** of unbolted flour. **b. coal,** lignite. **b. paper,** coarse wrapping-paper. **b. study,** reverie. **b. sugar,** half-refined sugar. **do b.,** (*sl.*) cheat. **fire into the b.,** let fly at mass indiscriminately. **browned off,** (*sl.*) fed up, depressed. **brownie,** *n.* benevolent domestic sprite; junior girl guide (8–11 years); kind of camera. **browning,** *n.* colouring for gravy. **brownshirt,** *n.* member of Nazi Party. **brownstone,** *n.* (*Amer.*) kind of sandstone. (O.E. *brún*)
Browning, *n.* type of automatic pistol. (person)
browse, *v.i.* and *t.* graze, pasture (on); read desultorily.—*n.* young shoots as fodder; browsing. (O.F. *broust,* sooth)
browst, *n.* (*Scot.*) amount brewed at one time.
Bruin, *n.* bear personified. (Du.= brown)
bruise, *n.* discoloration caused by blow, contusion; dint.—*v.t.* and *i.* crush, break small; batter; deal bruise; show effects of blow. **bruiser,** *n.* prize-fighter. (O.E. *brysan,* crush, and O.F. *bruser,* break)
bruit, *n.* (*arch.*) report, rumour.—*v.t.* report, noise abroad. (F.)
brulyie, brulzie, *n.* (*Scot.*) broil.
brumby, *n.* (*Austral.*) wild horse.
brume, *n.* fog. **brumal, brumous,** *aa.* wintry; foggy. (L. *bruma,* winter)
Brummagem, *n.* Birmingham.—*a.* sham, cheap and showy. (dial.)
brunch, *n.* (*sl.*) breakfast and lunch run into one. (words combined)
brunette, *n.* and *a.* brown-complexioned, dark-haired (woman). (F.)
brunt, *n.* chief stress or shock.
brush, *n.* small shrubs, undergrowth; implement with hair, bristles etc. set in handle; fox's tail; skirmish; (*electr.*) brush-like metal piece assisting conduction.—*v.t.* and *i.* clean, rub, smooth, with brush; touch, move, lightly. **b. aside,** ignore. **b. up,** furbish, renew memory of. **b.-work,** *n.* style of painting. **brushwood,** *n.* undergrowth. **brushy,** *a.* shaggy. (O.F. *brosse*)
brusque, *a.* abrupt in manner, blunt. **brusquerie,** *n.* (It. *brusco,* sour)
Brussels, *n.* **B.** carpet, lace, made there. **B. sprouts,** buds of kind of cabbage.
brut, *a.* (of wines) unsweetened. (F.)
brute, *a.* unreasoning, soulless; brutal. —*n.* beast; brutal person; man's lower nature. **brutal,** *a.* savage, cruel; grossly sensual. **brutality,** *n.* **brutalize, brutify,** *v.t.* and *i.* make, grow, brutal. **brutish,** *a.* bestial, gross. (L. *brutus,* dull)
brutum fulmen, empty threat. (L.)
bryology, *n.* science of mosses. **bryologist,** *n.* (Gk. *bruon,* mossy kind of seaweed; *legein,* speak)
bryony, *n.* kinds of climbing hedge plant. (Gk. *bruein,* swell)
bub, *n.* (*sl.*) strong drink.
bub, *n.* (*Amer. sl.*) brother. (abbr.)
bubal, *n.* an African antelope. (Gk. *boubalos*)
bubble, *n.* globe of liquid, cavity, filled with air; anything empty; fraudulent scheme.—*a.* unsubstantial.—*v.i.* and *t.* rise in bubbles; gurgle, boil; (*arch.*) delude. **b.-and-squeak,** *n.* meat and vegetables fried together. **bubbly,** *a.* full of bubbles.—*n.* (*sl.*) champagne. **bubbly-jock,** *n.* turkey-cock. (imit.)
bubo, *n.* inflamed swelling in groin or armpit. **bubonic,** *a.* **bubonocele,** *n.* hernia of groin. (Gk. *boubōn,* groin)
buccaneer, *n.* sea-rover, pirate.—*v.i.* be pirate. (F. *boucanier,* hunter)
buccinator, *n.* flat muscle of cheek. (L. *buccinare,* blow trumpet)
Bucephalus, *n.* riding-horse. (name of Alexander the Great's charger)
Buchmanism, *n.* undenominational evangelical movement emanating from America in the 1930's. **Buchmanite,** *n.* adherent of this. (F. *Buchman*)
buck, *n.* male of deer, rabbit etc.; dandy; (*Amer.*) male negro.—*a.* male.—*v.i.* and *t.* (of horse) leap with back arched and legs stiff, throw (rider) thus. **b.-horn,** *n.* horn of deer. **b.-hound,** *n.* small kind of staghound. **b.-jump,** *v.i.* buck. **b.-shot,** *n.* coarse shot. **b.-tooth,** *n.* one that projects. (O.E. *buc*)
buck, *v.i.* and *t.* (*sl.*). **b. up,** make haste; cheer up.
buck, *v.i.* butt (against etc.).
buck, *n.* wickerwork eel-trap.
buck, *n.* lye for bleaching clothes.—*v.t.* steep in this.
buck, *n.* (*Amer. sl.*) dollar.
buck, *n.* (*cards*; *Amer. sl.*) object to mark dealer's place. **pass the b.,** shift responsibility (to).
buck, *n.* (*Anglo-Ind.*) conversation; brag.—*v.i.* chat; swagger. (Hind. *bak*)
buck-bean, *n.* water-plant with pinkish flowers. (Du. *bocks boonen,* goats' beans)
buckboard, *n.* light carriage with elastic board bearing seats.
bucket, *n.* vessel for water, pail; piston of pump; holder for carbine, whip etc.—*v.t.* and *i.* ride (horse) hard; (*rowing*) hurry stroke. **kick the b.,** (*sl.*) die. **b.-shop,** *n.* office for gambling in stocks.
buckie, *n.* (*Scot.*) shellfish; refractory person.
buckish, *a.* dandified. (*buck*)
buckle, *n.* metal clasp for strap etc.—

v.t. and *i.* fasten with this; bend, crumple up. **b. to,** set to work. **buckler,** *n.* small shield; protection.—*v.t.* defend. (L. *buccula,* cheek-strap)
bucko, *a.* and *n.* (*naut.*) swaggering (fellow). (*buck*)
buckra, *n.* (*negro dial.*) white man.
buckram, *n.* coarse stiffened cloth.—*a.* of this; stiff, precise. (O.F. *boquerant*)
buckshee, *n.* (*sl.*) extra allowance, windfall.—*a.* and *adv.* free, for nothing. (*baksheesh*)
buckskin, *n.* soft leather of deerskin etc.; (*pl.*) breeches of this.
buckstick, *n.* braggart. (*buck*)
buckthorn, *n.* a thorny shrub.
buckwheat, *n.* cereal with triangular seeds. (O.E. *bóc,* beech-tree)
bucolic, *a.* rustic; (*pl.*) pastoral poems. (Gk. *boukolos,* herdsman)
bud, *n.* first shoot of stem or leaf; unopened flower.—*v.i.* and *t.* put forth buds; begin to develop; graft. **nip in the b.,** destroy at early stage. (M.E. *budde*)
bud, *n.* (*Amer. sl.*) brother. (abbr.)
Buddha, *n.* Gautama, Indian teacher of 6th century B.C. **Buddhism,** *n.* his religion. **Buddhist,** *n.* and *a.* (devotee) of Buddhism.
buddleia, *n.* shrub with lilac or yellow flowers. (A. *Buddle*)
buddy, *n.* (*Scot.*) person. (*body*)
buddy, *n.* (*Amer. sl.*) chum. (*bud*)
budge, *v.i.* and *t.* give way; move slightly. (F. *bouger,* stir)
budge, *n.* lambskin fur.—*a.* pompous, pedantic.
budgerigar, *n.* green parakeet, Australian love-bird. (native)
budgery, *a.* (*Austral.*) good. (native)
budget, *n.* bag with its contents; stock, store; annual financial estimate, esp. of nation. **b. for,** allow for in this. **budgetary,** *a.* (L. *bulga,* knapsack)
budlet, *n.* small bud.
budmash, same as **badmash.**
buff, *n.* stout velvety yellow leather; bare skin; polishing wheel.—*a.* light yellow.—*v.t.* polish with buff; make (leather) velvety. **the Bb.,** East Kent regiment. (F. *buffle,* buffalo)
buff, *n.* (*obs.*) blow.—*v.t.* strike.
buffalo, *n.* kinds of ox; (*incorrectly*) bison. (Gk. *boubalos,* antelope)
buffer, *n.* shield to deaden shock. **b. state,** neutral country between two others. (*buff*)
buffer, *n.* (*sl.*) fellow, elderly man.
buffet, *n.* blow with hand; misfortune.—*v.t.* and *i.* beat, knock about; struggle (with). (*buff*)
buffet, *n.* cupboard; refreshment bar; low stool. (F.)
buffo, *n.* comic actor. (It.)
buffoon, *n.* one who makes himself ridiculous to raise laughter, clown. **buffoonery,** *n.* (It. *buffa,* jest)
bug, *n.* flat red insect infesting beds; (*sl.* or *Amer.*) any insect. **b.-hunter,** *n.* (*sl.*) entomologist.
bug, *n.* (*Shake.*) hobgoblin, spectre. **big b.,** important person. **bugaboo, bugbear,** *nn.* object of needless terror, mental bogy. (M.E. *bugge*)
bugger, *n.* sodomite; (*vulg.*) chap. **buggery,** *n.* (L. *Bulgarus,* heretic from Bulgaria)
buggy, *n.* light vehicle, gig.
bughouse, buggy, *aa.* (*Amer. sl.*) crazy. (*bug*)
bught, *n.* (*Scot.*) sheep-pen.
bugle, *n.* long glass bead, us. black.—*a.* (*Shake.*) black.
bugle, *n.* kinds of plant. (L.L. *bugula*)
bugle, *n.* brass instrument like small trumpet.—*v.i.* and *t.* sound (on) this. **bugler,** *n.* **buglet,** *n.* small bugle. (L. *buculus,* young ox)
bugloss, *n.* a rough-leaved plant. (Gk. *bous,* ox; *glōssa,* tongue)
buhl, *n.* inlaid work of tortoise-shell, metal etc. (A. C. *Boule*)
build, *v.t.* and *i.* (*past, p.p.* built, builded) construct, erect, establish; base hopes on.—*n.* shape, make. **b. up,** make by degrees; close, cover, by building. **builder,** *n.* **building,** *n.* edifice. **building society,** company issuing loans to enable people to buy their own houses. (O.E. *bold,* dwelling)
buirdly, *a.* (*Scot.*) stalwart, well-built. (*burly*)
bulb, *n.* plant-bud like onion yielding leaves and roots; round swelling; electric globe.—*v.i.* swell into bulb. **bulbiform, bulbous,** *aa.* (Gk. *bolbos,* onion)
bulbul, *n.* an Eastern song-bird; poet. (Arab.)
bulge, *n.* swelling, protuberance; bilge.—*v.i.* and *t.* swell out, stuff out. **have the b. on,** (*sl.*) have advantage over. **bulger,** *n.* (*golf*) wooden club with convex face. **bulgy,** *a.* (L. *bulga,* knapsack)
bulimy, bulimia, *n.* morbid hunger, voracity. (Gk. *boulimia*)
bulk, *n.* size, volume; large body or size; greater part; cargo.—*v.i.* and *t.* appear in size; pile (fish) in heaps. **in b.,** loose; in large quantities. **bulky,** *a.* large, unwieldy.
bulk, *n.* framework in front of shop. **bulkhead,** *n.* partition in ship's hull.
bull, *n.* male of cattle etc.; centre of target; speculator for rise in stocks; (*astron.*) Taurus, 3rd sign of zodiac.—*a.* male; like bull's.—*v.i.* and *t.* speculate (in) as bull. **take the b. by the horns,** face difficulty. **b.-calf,** *n.* male calf; simpleton. **b.-of-the-bog,** *n.* bittern. **b.-puncher,** *n.* (*Austral.*) bullock-driver. **b.'s-eye,** *n.* centre of target; circular window, lantern with this; kind of sweet; boss in centre of blown glass sheet. **b.-terrier,** *n.* cross between bulldog and terrier. **b.-whack,** *n.* (*Amer.*) ox-whip. (M.E. *bole*)

bull, *n.* papal edict. (*bulla*)
bull, *n.* (or **Irish b.**) ludicrous contradiction in speech, e.g. ' childlessness is hereditary in our family.'
bull, *n.* water flavoured in empty liquor cask.
bulla, *n.* seal on papal document; vesicle, bleb. (L.=bubble)
bullace, *n.* wild plum. (O.F. *beloce*)
bullate, *a.* blistered; puffy. (*bulla*)
bulldog, *n.* a short-haired dog of great courage; university proctor's attendant; kind of pistol.—*a.* tenacious, brave.
bulldoze, *v.t.* (*Amer. sl.*) coerce, bully.
bullet, *n.* lead missile; small ball. **b.-headed**, *a.* round-headed. (*bulla*)
bulletin, *n.* short official report. (It. *bulletino*)
bullfight, *n.* Spanish sport of baiting bull.
bullfinch, *n.* a bright-coloured songbird; hedge with ditch.
bullfrog, *n.* large American frog.
bullion, *n.* gold or silver in lump or by weight; fringe of gold or silver thread. **bullionist**, *n.* opponent of paper currency. (L. *bullire*, boil)
bullock, *n.* castrated bull, ox. (O.E. *bulluc*)
bullring, *n.* arena for bullfight.
bullroarer, *n.* kind of noisy toy.
bully, *n.* noisy overbearing person, tyrant; bravo; (*Shake.*) gallant, darling.—*v.t.* and *i.* persecute, tease; bluster.—*int.* and *a.* (*Amer. sl.*) well done, first rate. **b. off**, (*hockey*) crossing of sticks to begin match.
bully, *n.* (also **b.-beef**) tinned beef.
bullyrag, same as **ballyrag.**
bulrush, *n.* tall water-rush; papyrus.
bulwark, *n.* side of ship above deck; breakwater, earthwork; defence.—*v.t.* protect.
bum, *n.* buttocks; (*Amer. sl.*) tramp, sponger; spree.—*a.* (*Amer. sl.*) good-for-nothing, rotten. — *v.i.* and *t.* (*Amer. sl.*) drink to excess; sponge; live as vagabond. **b.-bailiff**, *n.* sheriff's officer for arrests. **b.-boat**, *n.* carrying provisions to ships.
bum, *v.i.* and *t.* hum. (imit.)
bumble-bee, *n.* a large bee. (*bum*)
bumbledom, *n.* fussy parochial officialism. (*Bumble*, beadle in Dickens)
bumble-puppy, *n.* game with captive tennis - ball ; badly played whist, etc.
bumbo, *n.* a kind of punch.
bumf, *n.* (*sl.*) toilet-paper; paper-chase; papers. (*bum-f*odder)
bummalo, *n.* a small Asiatic fish. (Mahratti *bombil*)
bummaree, *n.* middleman in fish-trade.
bummer, *n.* (*Amer. sl.*) worthless loafer.
bummle, *v.i.* (*Scot.*) bungle.
bump, *n.* collision, knock; protuberance; (*aviation*) air-current, gust.—*v.t.* and *i.* push (against); jolt, collide (with); (*cricket*, of ball) rise abruptly. —*adv.* violently, suddenly. **b. off**, (*Amer. sl.*) murder. (imit.)
bump, *n.* cry of bittern.—*v.i.* utter this. (imit.)
bumper, *n.* brimming glass; anything large; fender of motor-car.—*a.* very large, record. (*bump*)
bumpkin, *n.* country lout, yokel.
bumptious, *a.* self-assertive. (*bump*)
bumpy, *a.* full of bumps, rough.
bun, *n.* small soft round cake; round mass of hair. **have b. on**, (*Amer. sl.*) be drunk.
bun, *n.* squirrel, rabbit.
bunch, *n.* number of things tied or growing together, lot; (*sl.*) gang.—*v.t.* and *i.* form into bunch, gather together. **b. of fives**, fist.
bunco, *n.* and *v.t.* (*Amer. sl.*) swindle, esp. at cards. **b.-steerer**, *n.* decoy, confidence-man.
buncombe, same as **bunkum.**
bund, *n.* league, confederacy. (G.)
bund, *n.* (*Anglo-Ind.*) embankment; quay. (Hind. *band*)
bunder, *n.* (*Anglo-Ind.*) landing-place, harbour. (Hind.)
Bundesrat, *Bundesrath*, *n.* federal council of German Empire. (G.)
bundle, *n.* number of things bound together, package.—*v.t.* and *i.* tie in bundle; throw (into); go, send, away unceremoniously.
bundobust, same as **bandobast.**
bundook, *n.* (*Anglo-Ind.*) musket; (*sl.*) rifle. (Pers. *bunduq*)
bung, *n.* stopper for hole in cask; (*sl.*) lie.—*v.t.* stop up; close, seal; (*sl.*) hurl. (L. *pungere*, prick)
bung, *n.* (*Shake.*) pickpocket.
bungalow, *n.* single-storeyed house. **bungaloid**, *a.* (*joc.*). (Hind. *bangla*, of Bengal)
bungle, *v.i.* and *t.* act clumsily; mismanage, botch.—*n.* piece of bungling, muddle. **bungler**, *n.*
bungy, *n.* (*Anglo-Ind.*) sweeper, scavenger. (Hind. *bhangī*)
bunion, *n.* inflamed swelling on toe.
bunk, *n.* sleeping-berth.
bunk, *v.i.* (*sl.*) make off. **do a b.**, (*sl.*) vanish.
bunk, *n.* (*Amer. sl.*) humbug, rot. (*bunkum*)
bunker, *n.* large bin for coals; bench; obstacle; (*golf*) sandpit.—*v.t.* trap in bunker, place in difficulty.
bunkum, *n.* nonsense; big talk, claptrap. (member for *Buncombe*)
bunnia, *n.* (*Anglo-Ind.*) Hindu trader or shopkeeper. (Hind. *banya*)
bunny, *n.* pet name for rabbit. **b.-hug**, *n.* kind of dance. (*bun*)
Bunsen burner, one using mixture of gas and air to produce great heat. (inventor)
bunt, *v.i.* and *t.* (*aviation*) do half outside loop and then half roll; (*baseball*) tap (ball) within infield.—*n.* this stroke.

bunt, *n.* disease of wheat; fungus causing this.

bunt, *n.* bulge of sail, net etc. **b.-line,** *n.* rope used in furling.

bunting, *n.* worsted stuff used for flags; flags collectively.

bunting, *n.* kinds of bird of finch family; grey shrimp.

bunyip, *n.* mythical swamp-monster of Australia. (native)

buoy, *n.* anchored float marking channel, rock etc.; lifebuoy.—*v.t.* mark with buoy. **b. up,** keep afloat; sustain. **buoyage,** *n.* placing of buoys. **buoyant,** *a.* able to float; light, elastic; cheerful. **buoyancy,** *n.* (L. *boia,* chain)

bur, *n.* prickly clinging seed-case; plant with this; person hard to shake off. (Da. *borre*)

burble, *v.i.* bubble, gurgle. (imit.)

burbot, *n.* freshwater fish like eel. (Gk. *borboros,* mud)

burden, *n.* load, weight; thing hard to bear; ship's capacity; refrain of song; gist.—*v.t.* load; encumber. **burdensome,** *a.* onerous. (O.E. *byrthen*)

burdock, *n.* weed with prickly flowers and broad leaves. (*bur; dock*)

bureau, *n.* (*pl.* **bureaux, bureaus**) writing-desk with drawers; chest of drawers; office, government department. **bureaucracy,** *n.* centralized government; officials; officialism. **bureaucrat,** *n.* advocate of bureaucracy; self-important official. **bureaucratic,** *a.* (F.)

burette, *n.* graduated glass tube for measuring liquids. (F.)

burg, *n.* (*Amer.*) town. (*borough*)

burgage, *n.* (*law*) ancient form of tenure. (L.L. *burgus,* fort)

burgee, *n.* swallow-tailed pennant of yacht-club.

burgeon, *n.* and *v.i.* sprout, bud; begin to grow. (O.F. *burjon*)

burgess, *n.* inhabitant, freeman, of borough; M.P. for borough. (O.F. *burgeis*)

burgh, *n.* (*Scot.*) borough. **burgher,** *n.* (*arch.*) citizen. (*borough*)

burglar, *n.* thief who breaks into a house by night. **burglary,** *n.* **burglarious,** *a.* **burgle,** *v.i.* and *t.* (*colloq.*) commit burglary, rob. (L.L. *burglator*)

burgomaster, *n.* chief magistrate of Dutch town. (borough)

burgonet, *n.* kind of steel cap or helmet. (*Bourgogne,* Burgundy)

burgoo, *n.* (*naut.*) thick oatmeal gruel.

burgrave, *n.* governor of town or castle. (G. *burggraf*)

burgundy, *n.* red wine of W. France. (place)

burhel, *n.* Himalayan wild sheep. (Hind. *bharal*)

burial, *n.* interment, funeral. **b.-ground,** cemetery. (*bury*)

burin, *n.* engraving-tool. (F.)

burke, *v.t.* smother; **hush up;** avoid. (name of murderer)

burl, *n.* knot in thread or wood.—*v.t.* pick knots from. (O.F. *bourle*)

burlap, *n.* coarse canvas.

burlesque, *n.* travesty, comic imitation.—*a.* mocking.—*v.t.* caricature, parody. (It. *burla,* jest)

burly, *a.* of stout sturdy build. (M.E. *borlich*)

burn, *v.t.* and *i.* (*past, p.p.* **burnt, burned**) consume, injure, by fire; be on fire, blaze; give light; feel hot, be inflamed with passion; brand.—*n.* injury, mark, caused by fire. **b. one's boats,** commit oneself irrevocably. **b. one's fingers,** suffer for rashness. **b. up,** consume totally. **burner,** *n.* part of lamp shaping flame. **burning,** *a.* flagrant; hotly debated. **burning-glass,** *n.* lens focusing sun's rays. **burnt offering,** sacrifice by fire. **burnt sienna,** reddish-brown pigment. (O.E. *bærnan*)

burn, *n.* (*Scot.*) small stream.

burnet, *n.* brown-flowered plant. (F. *brun,* brown)

burnish, *v.t.* and *i.* polish by friction; take polish.—*n.* gloss, lustre. **burnisher,** *n.* (O.F. *burnir*)

burnous, burnouse, *n.* hooded cloak worn by Arabs. (Arab. *burnus*)

burp, *v.i.* (*Amer. sl.*) belch. (imit.)

burr, *n.* trilled pronunciation of *r*; whirr.—*v.t.* and *i.* pronounce with burr, speak indistinctly.

burr, *n.* lunar halo; ridge on cut metal; bur.

burro, *n.* (*Amer.*) donkey. (Sp.)

burrow, *n.* rabbit's hole etc.—*v.i.* and *t.* make, live in, burrow; excavate; hide oneself; search deeply.

bursar, *n.* treasurer of college; (*Scot.*) holder of bursary. **bursary,** *n.* bursar's office; (*Scot.*) scholarship. **bursarial,** *a.* (L.L. *bursa,* purse)

burst, *v.t.* and *i.* (*past, p.p.* same) break open, fly asunder; rend, split; make way violently.—*n.* bursting; explosion, outbreak; spurt; (*sl.*) spree. **b. into,** give way to, emit, suddenly. **b. up,** collapse. **bursting,** *a.* crammed. (O.E. *berstan*)

burthen, same as **burden.**

burton, *n.* light two-block tackle.

bury, *v.t.* (*past, p.p.* **buried**) put in grave, inter; hide, conceal; forget. **b. the hatchet,** cease strife. (O.E. *byrgan*)

bus, 'bus, *n.* public road vehicle on fixed route; (*sl.*) motor-car, aeroplane.—*v.i.* go by bus. **miss the b.,** (*sl.*) lose opportunity. **busman,** *n.* bus driver. **busman's holiday,** spent at one's regular work. (*omnibus*)

busby, *n.* hussar's tall fur cap.

bush, *n.* metal lining of hole in which axle turns.

bush, *n.* thick shrub; (formerly) ivy-bunch as tavern sign; (*Austral., S. Afr.*) backwoods, uncleared wild country. **b.-bean,** *n.* (*Amer.*) kidney bean. **b.-harrow,** *n.* frame with branches interwoven. **b.-hook,** *n.* (*Amer.*) bill-hook. **bushed,** *a.* (*Austral.*) lost in the bush. (O.N. *buskr*)

bushel, *n.* measure of capacity, 8 gallons. (L.L. *buxis*, box)

Bushido, *n.* code of Samurai, chivalry of Japan. (Jap. *bu*, military; *shi*, knight; *do*, principle)

bushman, *n.* S. African aboriginal; dweller in Australian bush.

bushmaster, *n.* a deadly S. American snake.

bushranger, *n.* Australian brigand.

bushwhack, *v.i.* (*Amer.*) work one's way through bush. **bushwhacker,** *n.* (*Amer.*) backwoodsman; guerrilla fighter; tool for cutting brushwood.

bushy, *a.* overgrown; thick.

business, *n.* employment, trade; firm; task, concern; affair, matter; action of actor, dumb show. **do his b.,** kill him. **good b!** well done! **man of b.,** agent. **mean b.,** be in earnest. **b.-like,** *a.* systematic, practical. (*busy*)

busk, *n.* stiff rib in stays. (F. *busc*)

busk, *v.t.* and *i.* get oneself ready, dress. (O.N. *buask*)

busker, *n.* (*sl.*) wandering musician or actor.

buskin, *n.* half-boot; high boot once worn by tragic actors; tragic drama. **buskined,** *a.*

buss, *n.* (*arch.*) smacking kiss.—*v.t.* kiss. (L. *basium*)

buss, *n.* small fishing-vessel. (L.L. *bussa*)

bust, *n.* sculpture of upper part of body; breast, woman's bosom. (It. *busto*)

bust, *sl.* form of **burst. buster,** *n.* (*sl.*) something large; spree.

bustard, *n.* large swift-running bird. (L. *avis tarda*, slow bird)

bustle, *v.i.* and *t.* be noisily busy, hurry about, hustle.—*n.* fuss, stir.

bustle, *n.* pad to hold skirt out behind.

busy, *a.* actively employed, occupied; industrious; fussy, prying.—*n.* (*sl.*) detective.—*v.t.* occupy, keep busy. **busyness,** *n.* **busybody,** *n.* meddlesome person. (O.E. *bisig*)

but, *conj.* yet; that not; unless.—*prep.* without; except.—*adv.* only.—*a.* (*Scot.*) outside. **all b.,** nearly. **b. and ben,** (*Scot.*) house with outer and inner room. **b. me no bb.,** raise no objections. (O.E. *butan*, outside)

butcher, *n.* one who kills animals for food, dealer in meat; bloodthirsty person.—*v.t.* slaughter savagely or wantonly; ruin. **b.-bird,** *n.* kind of shrike. **b.'s-broom,** *n.* an evergreen shrub. **butcherly,** *a.* like a butcher. **butchery,** *n.* massacre, carnage; shambles. (O.F. *bochier*, killer of goats)

butler, *n.* head manservant, servant in charge of wine-cellar. (O.F. *bouteillier*, bottle-bearer)

butt, *n.* target; mound behind this; grouse-shooter's stand; aim; object of ridicule; (*pl.*) shooting-range. (F. *but*, goal)

butt, *v.i* and *t.* and *n.* push with head. **b. in,** meddle. (O.F. *boter*, thrust)

butt, *n.* thick end, base; remnant; flat-fish. **b.-end,** *n.*

butt, *n.* large cask holding 108–140 gallons, barrel. (L.L. *buttis*)

butte, *n.* (*Amer.*) abrupt isolated hill. (F.=knoll)

butter, *n.* oily substance got from cream by churning; gross flattery.—*v.t.* spread with butter. **b. up,** (*colloq.*) flatter. **as if b. would not melt in mouth,** demure. **b.-fingers,** *n.* one who lets things slip. **b.-muslin,** *n.* thin loosely woven cloth. (Gk. *bouturon*)

butterbump, *n.* bittern. (*bump*)

buttercup, *n.* golden-flowered plant.

butterfly, *n.* daylight insect with large coloured wings; gay trifler. **b.-nut,** *n.* one with finger-grips.

butterine, *n.* old name for margarine.

butteris, *n.* tool for paring horse's hoof.

buttermilk, *n.* milk that remains after churning.

butternut, *n.* kind of sweet; (*Amer.*) white walnut-tree; its nut.

butterscotch, *n.* kind of toffee.

butterwort, *n.* violet-flowered bog-plant which traps insects.

buttery, *a.* like, smeared with, butter.

buttery, *n.* store-room for provisions. (O.F. *boterie*, place for bottles)

buttock, *n.* either half of rump; wrestling-throw. (*butt*)

button, *n.* disk fastening dress or for ornament; bud; knob, catch; (*pl.*) page-boy.—*v.t.* and *i.* furnish, fasten, with buttons. **a b. short,** of weak intellect. **buttonhole,** *n.* slit to receive button; flower worn in this.—*v.t.* hold by button, accost. **button-hook,** *n.* tool for fastening buttons. **buttony,** *a.* with many buttons. (O.F. *boton*, bud)

buttress, *n.* support built against wall; prop.—*v.t.* support.

butty, *n.* (*colloq.*) mate, chum.

butyr(o)-, from L. *butyrum*, butter, used in **butyraceous,** *a.* like butter; **butyric,** *a.* derived from butter.

buxom, *a.* plump, healthy; cheerful, jolly; (*arch.*) obedient. (O.E. *búgan*, bend)

buy, *v.t.* (*past, p.p.* **bought**) get by payment, purchase; bribe.—*n.* (*Amer.*) bargain. **b. in,** buy a stock of; buy back for owner at auction. **b. off, out,** pay price of release or non-opposition. **b. over,** bribe. **b. up,** buy all one can of. **I'll b. it,** (*sl.*) I give it up. **buyer,** *n.* (O.E. *bycgan*)

buzz, *v.i.* and *t.* hum; whisper; spread (news) secretly; (*sl.*) throw hard; (*sl.*) send by buzzer.—*n.* hum, stir, sound of talk.—*int.* (*Shake.*) stale news! **b. off,** (*sl.*) clear off. **b.-saw,** *n.* circular saw. (imit.)

buzz, *v.t.* empty to last drop.

buzzard, *n.* kinds of falcon; (*Amer.*) kinds of vulture. (O.F. *busart*)

buzzer, *n.* whistle, electric sounder; (*sl.*) signaller; (*Shake.*) tattler.

bwana, *n.* master, sir. (Swahili)

by, *prep.* near, beside; along, past; through agency of; according to; as soon as.—*adv.* near; aside; past. **by and by,** before long, presently. **by and large,** on the whole. **by oneself,** alone. **by the by, by the bye, by the way,** incidentally, parenthetically. (O.E. *bi*)

by, bye, *a.* (often hyphened) subordinate, side, secret. **by-blow,** *n.* side-blow; bastard. **by-election,** *n.* one held apart from general election. **by-end,** *n.* private or subordinate aim. **by-lane, by-road, by-street,** *nn.* unfrequented or side lane etc. **by-name,** *n.* nickname. **by-pass,** *n.* subsidiary gas-jet kept alight to save relighting; road to divert traffic from crowded centre. **by-product,** *n.* one incidental to main process. **by-work,** *n.* work for leisure hours. (*by*)

bye, *n.* something subordinate; odd man in knock-out competition; (*cricket*) run scored without ball being hit by batsman; (*golf*) holes after match is decided; (*lacrosse*) goal. (*by*)

bye-bye, *n.* sleep; bed.

bye-bye, *int.* good-bye.

bygone, *a.* past.—*n.pl.* past offences.

byke, same as **bike.**

by-law, bye-law, *n.* regulation of local authority. (O.E. *bý*, town)

bynempt, (*Spens.*) form of **benamed.**

bypath, *n.* secluded path.

byplay, *n.* action, dumb show, aside from main action.

byre, *n.* cow-house. (O.E.)

byssus, *n.* fine cloth; tuft of filaments of shell-fish. **byssal, byssine, byssoid,** *aa.* (Gk. *bussos*)

bystander, *n.* looker-on.

byway, *n.* side road; short cut; less-known side of subject.

byword, *n.* familiar saying; object of derision.

Byzantine, *a.* and *n.* (inhabitant) of Byzantium or Constantinople; (*archit.*) in style of the Eastern Empire.

C

C, (*math.*) third known quantity; (*mus.*) note and scale; (*roman numerals*) 100.

ca', *Scot.* form of **call.**

ca', *v.t.* (*Scot.*) drive.

Caaba, *n.* Moslem shrine at Mecca, containing sacred black stone. (Arab. *ka'bah*)

cab, *n.* carriage plying for public hire; driver's shelter on railway engine.—*v.i.* go by cab. (abbr. of *cabriolet*)

cab, *n.* (*sl.*) translation, crib.—*v.i.* use cab. (arch. *cabbage*, pilfer)

cabal, *n.* secret intrigue; political coterie.—*v.i.* form cabal, plot. **caballer,** *n.* (*cabbala*)

cabala, same as **cabbala.**

caballero, *n.* Spanish gentleman. (Sp.)

cabaret, *n.* restaurant with variety turns; French tavern. (F.)

cabbage, *n.* green vegetable with round head. **c. butterfly,** white kinds. **c. rose,** large coarse pink rose. (L. *caput*, head)

cabbala, *n.* mystic interpretation of Scripture by Jewish rabbis; occult lore. **cabbalism, cabbalist,** *nn.* **cabbalistic,** *a.* (Heb. *qabbalah*, tradition)

cabby, *n.* (*colloq.*) cabman.

caber, *n.* rough pole tossed as trial of strength at highland sports. (Gael. *cabar*)

cabin, *n.* small house, hut; room on ship; (*Shake.*) beast's den.—*v.t.* and *i.* confine, cramp; (*Shake.*) lodge. **c.-boy,** *n.* junior servant on ship. (L.L. *capanna*)

cabinet, *n.* case with drawers or shelves, cupboard; small private room; committee of ministers forming government; (*Shake.*) nest. **C. council,** meeting of Cabinet. **c. edition,** of medium cost and size. **c. photograph,** size $5\frac{1}{2}\times 4$ in. **c. pudding,** of sponge, peel, raisins, etc. **c.-maker,** *n.* maker of fine furniture. **c.-making,** *n.* (dim. of *cabin*)

cable, *n.* strong thick rope; anchor-chain; bundle of insulated wires for submarine telegraphy; measure of length, 100 fathoms; rope-shaped ornament; cablegram.—*v.t.* and *i.* furnish, fasten, with cable; send (message) by cable. **c.-laid,** *a.* of three triple strands. **cablegram,** *n.* cabled message. (L.L. *capulum*, halter)

cabman, *n.* driver of cab.

cabobs, *n.pl.* meat roasted in small pieces on skewers. (Arab. *kabab*)

cabochon, *n.* precious stone polished but not faceted. (F.)

caboodle, *n.* (*Amer. sl.*) lot, set.

caboose, *n.* ship's galley; (*Amer.*) guard's van of goods train.

cabriolet, *n.* motor-car body with folding hood and fixed sides; early type of hansom cab. (F.)

cacao, *n.* tropical American plant; its

seeds, from which cocoa and chocolate are made. (Sp.)
cachalot, *n.* kind of whale with teeth in lower jaw. (F.=toothed)
cache, *n.* secret hiding-place; store of food left for use of explorers etc.—*v.t.* place in cache. (F.)
cachet, *n.* mark of authenticity; distinguishing mark, stamp; (*med.*) flat capsule for taking nauseous medicine in. (F.)
cachexy, cachexia, *n.* (*med.*) bad state of general health. **cachectic,** *a.* (Gk. *kakos,* bad; *hexis,* condition)
cachinnate, *v.i.* laugh loudly. **cachinnation,** *n.* **cachinnatory,** *a.* (L. *cachinnare*)
cacholong, *n.* kind of opal. (Kalmuck *kaschtschilon,* beautiful stone)
cachou, *n.* lozenge used to sweeten breath. (F.=cashew)
cachucha, *n.* quick Spanish dance. (Sp.)
cacique, *n.* W. Indian or Red Indian chief; political boss. (Sp.)
cackle, *n.* clucking of hen; shrill silly talk or laughter.—*v.i.* and *t.* emit, utter with, cackle. (imit.)
caco-, from Gk. *kakos,* bad, used in **cacodemon, cacodaemon,** *n.* evil spirit; **cacodyl,** *n.* evil-smelling compound of arsenic and methyl; **cacoepy,** *n.* bad pronunciation; **cacŏēthēs,** *n.* bad habit of body or mind; *cacoethes scribendi,* mania for scribbling; **cacography,** *n.* bad handwriting (opp. to calligraphy); **cacology,** *n.* bad choice of words or pronunciation; **cacophonous,** *a.* harsh, ill-sounding; **cacophony,** *n.* ugly sound, discord.
cacoon, *n.* large polished bean of tropical African shrub.
cactus, *n.* (*pl.* **cacti, cactuses**) kinds of plant with thick fleshy stem studded with prickles. **cactaceous, cactal,** *aa.* (Gk. *kaktos,* cardoon)
cad, *n.* ill-bred, vulgar, or unchivalrous person; low fellow. (*cadet*)
cadastre, *n.* register of lands for taxation purposes. **cadastral,** *a.* (L. *caput,* head)
cadaverous, *a.* corpse-like; deadly pale; gaunt. **cadaveric,** *a.* (*med.*) characteristic of a corpse. (L. *cadaver,* corpse)
caddie, *n.* one who carries golfer's clubs for him. (*cadet*)
caddis, caddice, *n.* (also **c.-worm**) larva of mayfly, used as bait.
caddis, *n.* (*Shake.*) worsted ribbon.
caddish, *a.* like a cad, ill-bred.
caddy, *n.* small box or tin for holding tea. (Malay *kati,* weight of $1\frac{1}{3}$ lb.)
caddy, same as **caddie.**
cade, *n.* barrel. (L. *cadus*)
cade, *a.* and *n.* (lamb etc.) bred by hand.
cadence, *n.* rhythm; intonation; fall of voice at end of sentence; (*mus.*) close of phrase. **cadency,** *n.* (*heraldry*) descent of younger branch of family; cadetship. **cadent,** *a.* (*Shake.*) falling. *cadenza,* *n.* (*mus.*) ornamental flourish at close of movement. (L. *cadere,* fall)
cadet, *n.* younger son; student at naval or military college in training for commission. **c. corps,** school organization training boys on military lines. (L. *caput,* head+dim.)
cadge, *v.i.* and *t.* beg, get by begging; sponge on others. **cadger,** *n.* beggar, loafer; hawker, carrier.
cadi, *n.* minor Mohammedan judge. (Arab.)
cadmium, *n.* white metallic element. **cadmic,** *a.* (Gk. *kadmeia,* calamine)
cadre, *n.* permanent nucleus, skeleton, of military unit; framework. (F.)
caduceus, *n.* winged wand of Hermes, entwined with two serpents; ancient herald's wand. (Gk. *kērux,* herald)
caducous, *a.* fleeting; perishable; (*bot.*) falling early. **caducity,** *n.* (L. *cadere,* fall)
caecum, *n.* (*pl.* **caeca**) blind gut, containing vermiform appendix. **caecal,** *a.* (L. *caecus,* blind)
Caesar, *n.* title of ancient Roman emperors; emperor, autocrat. **Caesarean, Caesarian,** *aa.* **Caesarean, Caesarian, operation,** for delivering child by cutting abdomen and womb. **Caesarism,** *n.* autocracy. **Caesarist,** *n.* adherent of this. (L.)
caesious, *a.* (*bot.*) bluish grey. **caesium,** *n.* rare silvery alkaline metal. (L. *caesius*)
caesura, *n.* natural pause in rhythm of verse-line; (in Latin and Greek verse) break between words within foot. **caesural,** *a.* (L.)
café, *n.* restaurant, us. unlicensed, providing light refreshments; foreign restaurant. **c.** *au lait, noir,* coffee with, without, milk. **cafeteria,** *n.* restaurant in which customers serve themselves with food. **caffeic,** *a.* (*chem.*) of coffee. **caffeine,** *n.* alkaloid got from coffee and tea plants. (F.=coffee)
caftan, *n.* long wide-sleeved oriental gown with girdle. (Turk. *qaftan*)
cage, *n.* box, enclosure, with bars for confining animal; prison; open framework; car for raising and lowering men in mine-shaft.—*v.t.* shut in cage, confine. (L. *cavea*)
cahoot, *n.* (*Amer. sl.*). **in cc. or c.,** in league or partnership.
caiman, same as **cayman.**
Cainozoic, *a.* of third geological period, Tertiary. (Gk. *kainos,* new; *zōon,* animal)
caique, *n.* light Turkish rowing-boat. (Turk. *kaik*)
caird, *n.* (*Scot.*) wandering tinker, vagrant. (Gael. *ceard*)
cairn, *n.* pile of rough stones; (also **c. terrier**) small shaggy-haired terrier. (Gael. *carn*)
cairngorm, *n.* yellow or wine-coloured gem. (mountain in Scotland)

caisson, *n.* large watertight chamber for men to work in under water; camel for floating sunk vessel; ammunition wagon. (F.)

caitiff, *n.* (*arch.*) coward; rascal; (*Shake.*) wretch.—*a.* (*arch.*) base, despicable. (L. *captivus*, captive)

cajole, *v.t.* persuade, soothe, by flattery or deceit; wheedle. **cajolement, cajolery**, *nn.* (F. *cajoler*)

cake, *n.* kinds of sweet fancy bread; oatcake; compact mass, slab; (*arch.*) small flattish loaf.—*v.t.* and *i.* form into hard mass; coagulate. **land of cc.**, Scotland. **my c. is dough**, (*Shake.*) my plans are frustrated. **piece of c.**, (*R.A.F. sl.*) easy thing, cinch. **take the c.**, (*sl.*) carry off honours, rank first. **cakewalk**, *n.* grotesque negro step-dance. **caky**, *a.* lumpy, cohesive. (O.N. *kaka*)

calabar bean, poisonous bean of a W. African plant. (place)

calabash, *n.* kinds of gourd; shell of these as drinking or cooking vessel. (Sp. *calabaça*)

calaboose, *n.* (*Amer. sl.*) prison. (Sp. *calabozo*, dungeon)

calamanco, *n.* a glossy woollen stuff.

calamander, *n.* hard Indian wood used for cabinet-making.

calamary, *n.* cuttlefish with pen-shaped inner shell. (L. *calamus*, pen)

calamine, *n.* kind of zinc ore. (Gk. *kadmeia*)

calamint, *n.* aromatic herb of mint family. (Gk. *kalaminthē*)

calamite, *n.* fossil plant found in coal measures. (L. *calamus*, reed)

calamity, *n.* disastrous event, great misfortune; adversity. **calamitous**, *a.* disastrous. (L. *calamitas*)

calash, *n.* hooded carriage; carriage hood; woman's hooped hood; (*Canada*) two-wheeled single-seater carriage. (F. *calèche*)

calcareous, calcarious, *a.* of, containing, lime. (L. *calx*, lime)

calcedony, same as **chalcedony**.

calceolaria, *n.* kinds of plant with slipper-shaped flower. **calceolate**, *a.* (*bot.*) slipper-shaped. (L. *calceus*, shoe+dim.)

calcium, *n.* a metallic element, the basis of lime. **calcic** *a.* of calcium. **calciferous**, *a.* yielding carbonate of lime. **calcify**, *v.i.* and *t.* harden by deposit of lime; petrify; turn into, replace by, lime. **calcimine**, *n.* white or tinted wash for walls. **calcine, calcinate**, *vv.t.* and *i.* reduce, be reduced, to chalky powder by action of heat; burn to ashes. **calcination**, *n.* **calcite**, *n.* native carbonate of lime. **calcsinter**, *n.* crystalline deposit from lime-springs. (L. *calx*, lime)

calculate, *v.t.* and *i.* reckon, compute by mathematics; (*Amer. colloq.*) suppose, believe. **calculated**, *a.* deliberate, cold-blooded; adapted, suited (to). **calculating**, *a.* shrewd; scheming. **calculation**, *n.* calculating; result got from this. (*calculus*)

calculus, *n.* (*pl.* **calculi**) stone-like concretion in kidneys etc.; mode of calculation. (L.=small stone)

caldron, same as **cauldron**.

Caledonian, *a.* and *n.* (native) of Scotland. (L. *Caledonia*, N. Britain)

calefacient, *a.* and *n.* (*med.*) heat-producing (agent). **calefaction**, *n.* **calefactive, calefactory**, *aa.* (L. *calēre*, be warm; *facere*, make)

calendar, *n.* table of months and days in year; system of reckoning dates; register, list, esp. of saints.—*v.t.* enter in list; arrange and index (documents). (*calends*)

calender, *n.* machine with rollers for smoothing cloth etc., steam mangle; (*arch.*) one who calenders.—*v.t.* smooth with calender. (Gk. *kulindros*, roller)

calender, *n.* mendicant dervish. (Pers. *qalandar*)

calends, *n.pl.* first day of Roman month. **Greek C.**, time that never comes. (L. *kalendae*)

calenture, *n.* tropical fever with delirium. (L. *calēre*, be hot)

calescent, *a.* growing warm. **calescence**, *n.* (L. *calēre*, be hot)

calf, *n.* (*pl.* **calves**) fleshy part of leg behind shank. (O.N. *kálfi*)

calf, *n.* (*pl.* **calves**) young of cow; young of elephant, whale, seal etc.; callow loutish youth; calfskin. **c. love**, immature love. **golden c.**, wealth as object of worship. **calfhood**, *n.* **calfskin**, *n.* calf leather. (O.E. *cealf*)

calibre, caliber, *n.* internal diameter of gun or tube; capacity, standing, moral weight. **calibrate**, *v.t.* find internal diameter of: determine or verify scale of measuring-instrument. **calibration**, *n.* (It. *calibro*)

calicle, *n.* small cup-like cavity. **calicular**, *a.* (*calix*+dim.)

calico, *n.* cotton cloth.—*a.* made of this. (*Calicut* in E. Indies)

calipash, calipee, *nn.* dull green, light yellow, part of turtle flesh.

caliper, same as **calliper**.

caliph, calif, *n.* successor of Mohammed, official head of Islam. **caliphate**, *n.* office, dignity, of caliph. (Arab. *khalifah*, successor)

caliver, *n.* (*Shake.*) light musket.

calix, *n.* (*pl.* **calices**) cup-like cavity or organ. (L.=cup)

calk, same as **caulk**.

calk, *v.t.* copy (drawing) by covering back with chalk etc. and tracing with point along outlines. (L. *calcare*, tread)

calk, *n.* calkin.—*v.t.* provide with calkin. **calkin**, *n.* turned-down heel of horseshoe, preventing slipping. (L. *calx*, heel)

call, *v.i.* and *t.* shout, cry out; summon, convoke; name, designate rouse from sleep; **pay short visit.**—*n.* cry, shout; summons; note of bird; signal on bugle; use of telephone; religious vocation; occasion, need; short visit by person or ship; (*auction bridge*) player's turn to make bid; (*stock exchange*) option of claiming stock at given date. **c. down,** (*Amer. colloq.*) reprove, abuse. **c. for,** demand, require. **c. off,** call away; renounce. **c. on,** appeal to. **c. out,** exclaim; elicit; challenge to duel. **c. over,** read over (list of names). **c. up,** summon to serve in army; ring up on telephone; imagine, picture. **c.-boy,** *n.* prompter's attendant telling actors when to go on. **c.-loan,** *n.* loan subject to recall without notice. (O.N. *kalla*)

calla, *n.* (also **c.-lily**) bog **arum.**

callant, *n.* (*Scot.*) lad.

callat, same as **callet.**

caller, *n.* one who pays visit.

caller, *a.* (*Scot.*) fresh; cool.

callet, *n.* (*Shake.*) lewd woman, trull.

calligraphy, *n.* handwriting; beautiful writing. **calligrapher, calligraphist,** *nn.* **calligraphic,** *a.* (Gk. *kallos,* beauty; *graphein,* write)

calling, *n.* occupation, trade, profession; (*Shake.*) name.

Calliopē, *n.* muse of epic poetry; steam-organ.

calliper, *n.* (us. *pl.*) two-legged instrument for measuring diameters etc.—*v.t.* measure with callipers.

callisthenics, *n.pl.* light gymnastic exercises. **callisthenic,** *a.* (Gk. *kallos,* beauty; *sthenos,* strength)

callithumpian, *a.* (*Amer., joc.*) serenading with noisy and discordant music.—*n.* member of callithumpian band. (Gk. *kallos,* beauty+*thump*)

callous, *a.* (of skin) hardened, hard; (of person) unfeeling, insensible. **callosity,** *n.* hardness of skin; hardened lump. (*callus*)

callow, *a.* unfledged; raw, undeveloped. (O.E. *calu*)

callus, *n.* (*med.*) hardened skin or tissue. (L.)

calm, *a.* windless; still, unruffled; quiet, peaceful.—*n.* calmness, stillness; tranquillity.—*v.t.* and *i.* make, become, calm. **calmative,** *a.* and *n.* (*med.*) sedative. (Gk. *kauma,* heat)

calomel, *n.* preparation of mercury used as purgative. (Gk. *kalos,* fair; *melas,* black)

calorescence, *n.* change of heat rays to light rays. (L. *calor,* heat)

calorie, calory, *n.* unit of heat, amount used in raising 1 gramme of water from 0° to 1° centigrade. **great c.,** 1,000 calories. **calorifacient, calorific,** *aa.* heat-producing. **calorifically,** *adv.* **calorification,** *n.* **calorimeter,** *n.* instrument for measuring quantities of heat. (L. *calor,* heat)

calotte, *n.* small skull-cap. (F.)

caltrop, *n.* four-spiked iron ball placed on ground to lame horses. (L. *calx,* heel+*trap*)

calumet, *n.* long-stemmed Red Indian tobacco-pipe, symbol of peace. (L. *calamus,* reed+dim.)

calumny, *n.* slander; false accusation. **calumnious,** *a.* **calumniate,** *v.t.* slander. **calumniation,** *n.* (L. *calumnia*)

calvary, *n.* place, representation, of the Crucifixion. (L. *calvaria,* skull =Golgotha)

calve, *v.i.* and *t.* give birth to (calf); (of glacier) shed (mass of ice)

Calvinist, *n.* adherent of John Calvin and his religious doctrine of predestination. **Calvinistic, Calvinistical,** *aa.* **Calvinism,** *n.* **Calvinize,** *v.i.* and *t.* turn to Calvinism.

calvitiēs, *n.* (*med.*) baldness. (L.)

calx, *n.* (*pl.* **calces**) powder left when metal or mineral has been subjected to great heat. (L.=lime)

calyx, *n.* (*pl.* **calyxes, calyces**) outer series of leaves forming cup from which petals of flower spring; calix. **calycifloral, calyciflorate, calyciflorous,** *aa.* with stamens and petals inserted in calyx. **calycine, calycinal,** *aa.* having a calyx; of, on, the calyx. **calycle,** *n.* secondary calyx below true calyx. (Gk. *kalux*)

cam, *n.* projecting part of wheel or other device to change rotary into reciprocating motion. (*comb*)

camaraderie, *n.* comradeship. (F.)

camarilla, *n.* political clique. (Sp.)

camaron, *n.* large freshwater prawn. (Sp.=shrimp)

camber, *n.* slight convexity in surface of road etc.—*v.t.* construct with camber, arch slightly. (*camera*)

cambist, *n.* expert in exchanges; dealer in bills of exchange. (*cambium*)

cambium, *n.* soft formative layer of stem between wood and bark. (L.= exchange)

cambrel, *n.* bent piece of wood on which butcher hangs carcases.

Cambrian, *a.* of Wales; (*geol.*) of earliest Palaeozoic period, before Silurian. (W. *Cymru,* Wales)

cambric, *n.* and *a.* (of) fine white linen. (*Cambrai* in France)

came, see **come.**

camel, *n.* large four-footed long-necked humped animal; watertight structure for raising sunk ships. **Arabian, Bactrian, c.,** kind with one, two, humps. **cameleer,** *n.* camel-driver. (Gk. *kamēlos*)

camellia, *n.* evergreen oriental shrub with flower like rose. (G. J. *Kamel*)

camelopard, *n.* giraffe. (*camel*; *pard*)

camelry, *n.* troops mounted on camels.

Camembert, *n.* soft rich delicately flavoured French cheese. (place)

cameo, *n.* onyx or other gem carved in relief, often with colour-layers used for background. (L.L. *cammaeus*)

camera, *n.* apparatus with lens for

taking photographs. **c. obscura,** darkened chamber in which views of surrounding country are shown on sheet by means of lenses. ***in c.,*** (*law*) in judge's private room, not open court. (L.=vault)

Cameronian, *n.* member of Reformed Presbyterian Church; (*pl.*) first battalion, the Scottish Rifles. (Richard *Cameron*, founder)

camion, *n.* heavy lorry, wagon. (F.)

camis, *n.* (*Spens.*) light loose robe; chemise.

camisole, *n.* under-bodice. **cami-knickers,** *n.pl.* combined camisole and knickers. (F.)

camlet, *n.* kinds of light cloth. (F. *camelot*)

cammock, *n.* rest-harrow. (O.E. *cammoc*)

camomile, *n.* an aromatic plant. **c. tea,** infusion of its flowers. (Gk. *chamaimēlon*, earth-apple)

Camorra, *n.* secret terrorist organization in Italy. (It.)

camouflage, *n.* paint, screen, used to disguise gun, ship etc. from enemy observers; means of putting people off the scent.—*v.t.* conceal, disguise, with camouflage. (F.)

camp, *n.* assemblage of tents or huts for housing soldiers; temporary open-air quarters; soldier's life.—*v.i.* and *t.* lodge in camp, encamp. **c. out,** sleep in the open. **in the same c.,** on the same side. **c.-bed, c.-chair, c.-stool,** *nn.* folding or portable kinds. **c.-follower,** *n.* non-military hanger-on of army on march. **c.-meeting,** *n.* (*Amer.*) religious open-air meeting. (L. *campus*, plain)

campaign, *n.* series of military operations, time during which an army keeps the field; organized course of action.—*v.i.* serve on campaign. (F. *campagne*)

campanile, *n.* high detached tower with bells. **campanology,** *n.* bell-lore. **campanologer, campanologist,** *nn.* **campanological,** *a.* **campanula,** *n.* kinds of plant incl. harebell. **campanulate,** *a.* bell-shaped. (It. *campana*, bell)

camphor, *n.* white transparent volatile aromatic substance. **camphorated,** *a.* impregnated with camphor. **camphoric,** *a.* of, containing, camphor. (Malay *kapur*, chalk)

campion, *n.* kinds of wild plant of the pink family, the commonest having red or white flowers.

campshed, *v.t.* face with **campshot,** *n.* facing of piles and boarding along river-bank.

campus, *n.* (*Amer.*) grounds of school or college. (L.=plain)

camstairy, camsteerie, *a.* (*Scot.*) wild, unmanageable, unruly.

camwood, *n.* hard red W. African wood.

can, *n.* vessel for holding liquids or preserving solids.—*v.t.* preserve in can, tin; (*Amer.* ***sl.***) cease, stop. (O.E. *canne*)

can, *v.i.* and *t.* (*2nd pers. sing.* **canst,** *3rd sing.* **can;** *past* **could,** *2nd sing.* **couldst** or **couldest**) be able to; have right to; be allowed to; (*Shake.*) be skilled in. (O.E. *cunnan*)

can, (*Shake.*) form of **gan.**

Canadian, *a.* and *n.* (native) of Canada. **C. canoe,** (***sl.***) **Canader,** *n.* kind with single-bladed paddle or paddles.

canaille, *n.* rabble, vulgar herd. (F.)

canakin, (*Shake.*) form of **cannikin.**

canal, *n.* artificial waterway cut across land; duct in body.—*v.t.* provide with canals. **canaliculate, canaliculated,** *aa.* with longitudinal grooves. **canalize,** *v.t.* make canal through; make into canal. **canalization,** *n.* (L. *canalis*)

canard, *n.* false report, baseless rumour. (F.)

canary, *n.* bright yellow song-bird; a light sweet wine; (*Shake.*) lively Spanish dance.—*v.i.* (*Shake.*) dance canary. **c.-coloured,** *a.* bright yellow. **c.-creeper, canariensis,** *nn.* yellow-flowered trailing plant. (*Canary* Islands)

canaster, *n.* kind of coarse tobacco. (Gk. *kanastron*, basket)

can-can, *n.* indecent dance with sinuous body movements. (F.)

cancel, *v.t.* cross out; obliterate; countermand; (*math.*) strike out (factor) on each side of equation.—*n.* (*print.*) suppression of sheet set up, the suppressed or substituted sheet. **c. out,** cancel each other. **cancellate, cancellated,** *aa.* marked with cross-lines or ridges. **cancellation,** *n.* cancelling; annulment. (L. *cancelli*, cross-bars)

cancer, *n.* malignant disease which destroys tissues of body, malignant tumour; corroding evil, canker; the Crab, 4th sign of zodiac, which sun enters about 21 June. **cancerous,** *a.* **cancroid,** *a.* like crab or cancer. (L.=crab)

candelabrum, candelabra, *n.* (*pl.* **candelabra, candelabras**) large branched candlestick. (L.)

candescent, *a.* glowing; white-hot. **candescence,** *n.* (L. *candēre*, glow)

candid, *a.* frank, outspoken; unprejudiced. (L. *candidus*, white)

candidate, *n.* one who offers himself for election or appointment; aspirant. **candidature,** (*Amer.*) **candidacy,** *nn.* state of being candidate. **candidatus,** *n.* (*Shake.*) candidate. (L. *candidatus*, white-robed)

candied, *a.* sugared, honeyed.

candle, *n.* stick of wax with wick for giving light; candle-power. **burn the c. at both ends,** waste energy in two directions. **not fit to hold a c. to,** not comparable with. **c.-end,** *n.* stump of candle. **c.-holder,** *n.* (*Shake.*) onlooker. **c.-mine,** *n.*

(*Shake.*) magazine of tallow. **c.-waster,** *n.* (*Shake.*) bookworm. **Candlemas,** *n.* feast of the purification of the Virgin, 2 Feb. **candlestick,** *n.* holder for candle. (L. *candela*)

candour, *n.* candidness, frankness.

candy, *n.* crystallized sugar; (*Amer.*) sweets of any kind.—*a.* (*Shake.*) sugared.—*v.t.* preserve by coating with candy. (Arab. *qand*, sugar)

candy, *n.* Indian measure of weight, about 500 lb. (Tamil)

candytuft, *n.* plant with pink, white, or purple flowers. (L. *Candia*, Crete)

cane, *n.* stem of small palm or large grass; rod for punishment; walking-stick.—*v.t.* thrash with cane; weave cane into. **c.-sugar,** *n.* made from sugarcane. (Gk. *kanna*, reed)

cangue, cang, *n.* heavy board worn round neck by Chinese criminals as punishment. (Port. *cango*)

canine, *a.* of, like, a dog.—*n.* (also **c. tooth**) pointed tooth between incisors and molars. **canicide,** *n.* dog-killing; dog-killer. (L. *canis*, dog)

canister, *n.* box or case, us. of tin. **c.-shot,** *n.* old kind of shrapnel. (Gk. *kanastron*, wicker basket)

canker, *n.* ulcerous sore; diseases of fruit-trees, horses' feet etc.; corrupting influence; canker-worm; (*Shake.*) dog-rose.—*v.t.* consume with canker; corrupt. **c.-bloom,** *n.* (*Shake.*) dog-rose. **c.-blossom,** *n.* (*Shake.*) canker-worm. **c.-worm,** *n.* a destructive caterpillar. **cankered,** *a.* soured, malignant. (*cancer*)

canna, *n.* showy American tropical plant. (L.=reed)

cannabis, *n.* kinds of plant incl. hemp. (L.)

canned, *a.* (*sl.*) drunk. (*can*)

cannel, *n.* (also **c.-coal**) kinds of fine brightly burning coal.

cannibal, *n.* one who eats human flesh; animal that feeds on its own species. **cannibalism,** *n.* **cannibalistic,** *a.* (=*Carib*)

cannikin, *n.* small can. (dim.)

cannon, *n.* large mounted gun; machine-gun firing small shells. **c.-ball,** *n.* round projectile. **c.-bit,** *n.* smooth round bit. **c.-bone,** *n.* tube-shaped bone between hock and fetlock. **cannonade,** *n.* bombardment.—*v.i.* and *t.* bombard. (L. *canna*, reed)

cannon, *n.* (*billiards*) stroke in which one's own ball hits both others in succession.—*v.i.* make cannon; strike and rebound, collide. (*carom*)

cannot, same as **can not.**

canny, *a.* (*Scot.*) knowing, shrewd; cautious, careful; thrifty; not uncanny. **ca' c.,** be careful; restriction of output by workers. (*can*)

canoe, *n.* very light boat propelled with paddle or paddles.—*v.i.* travel by canoe. **canoeist,** *n.* (Sp. *canoa*)

canon, *n.* decree of Church; general rule; standard, criterion; list of Bible books, or of author's writings, accepted as genuine; part of mass containing words of consecration; part of bell by which it is hung; member of cathedral chapter; (*mus.*) composition with different parts taking up same theme successively; (*print.*) 48-point type. **c. law,** ecclesiastical law. **canonical,** *a.* of, according to, canon; appointed by canon law; regular, accepted.—*n.pl.* official dress of clergy. **canonic,** *a.* (*arch.*). **canonicity,** *n.* **canonist,** *n.* expert in canon law. **canonistic,** *a.* **canonize,** *v.t.* enrol in list of saints, regard as saint. **canonization,** *n.* **canonry,** *n.* office of cathedral canon. (Gk. *kanōn*, rule)

cañon, see **canyon.**

canoodle, *v.i.* and *t.* (*sl.*) cuddle, fondle.

canopy, *n.* roof-like covering over throne, bed etc.; overhanging shelter. —*v.t.* cover with or as with canopy. (Gk. *kōnōpeion*, mosquito-net)

canorous, *a.* melodious, sonorous. (L. *canere*, sing)

canstick, *n.* (*Shake.*) candlestick.

cant, *n.* inclination, tilt; slanting surface, bevel.—*v.t.* and *i.* give cant to, slant; (*naut.*) swing round.

cant, *n.* insincere use of pious phrases, hypocritical talk; jargon; secret slang of thieves.—*v.i.* use cant. **canting,** *a.* (*heraldry*) punning on name.

can't, *contr.* of **cannot.**

Cantabrigian, *n.* and *a.* (member) of Cambridge University. **Cantab,** *n.* (L. *Cantabrigia*, Cambridge)

cantaloup, *n.* kind of melon. (*Cantalupo* in Italy)

cantankerous, *a.* ill-natured, quarrelsome.

cantata, *n.* choral work like oratorio but us. shorter. (It.)

canteen, *n.* shop for liquor and provisions in camp or barracks; soldier's mess-tin or water-bottle; case of cutlery. (It. *cantina*, cellar)

canter, *n.* easy gallop.—*v.i.* ride at canter. (*Canter*bury pilgrims)

canterbury, *n.* stand with divisions for music or papers. **C. bell,** large kind of campanula. (place)

cantharides, *n.* dried Spanish fly. (Gk. *kantharis*, blister fly)

canticle, *n.* short hymn; one of the Prayer Book hymns; (*pl.*) Song of Solomon. (L. *canere*, sing)

cantilever, *n.* projecting beam supporting balcony etc. **c. bridge,** with cantilevers springing from piers.

cantle, *n.* piece, slice; rising rear part of saddle. (*cant*+dim.)

canto, *n.* (*pl.* **cantos**) division of long poem. **canton,** *n.* (*Shake.*) song. (It.=song)

canton, *n.* division of country; any of Swiss federal states; (*heraldry*) small square bearing device in upper corner of shield or flag.—*v.t.* place (device) in canton; quarter (soldiers). **cantonal,**

a. **cantonment,** *n.* troops' quarters; military station in India. (O.F.= corner)
cantorial, *a.* of precentor's or north side of choir (opp. to decanal). (L. *cantor*, singer)
cantrip, *n.* (*Scot.*) prank, piece of mischief; magic spell.
canty, *a.* (*Scot.*) cheerful, lively.
Canuck, *n.* (*sl.*) Canadian, esp. French-Canadian.
canvas, *n.* strong coarse cloth of hemp or flax; sails; painting on canvas. **under c.,** in tents; with sails spread. **c.-back,** *n.* American kind of duck.
canvass, *v.t.* and *i.* discuss, examine thoroughly; solicit votes or custom (of); (*Shake.*) toss in sheet, take to task.—*n.* canvassing. (Gk. *kannabis*, hemp)
canyon, cañon, *n.* deep gorge. (Sp.)
canzonet, *n.* short light song. (It. *canzonetta*)
caoutchouc, *n.* and *a.* rubber. (Carib *cahuchu*)
cap, *n.* soft brimless headgear; cap-like part, lid, top; distinctive cap, member, of team.—*v.t.* put cap on; lie on top of, crown; match, surpass; lift cap to; (*Scot.*) confer university degree on. **c. and bells,** jester's insignia. **c. and gown,** academic costume. **c. in hand,** as humble suppliant. **percussion c.,** small metal cap containing detonating charge. **set one's c. at,** (of woman) try to attract as suitor. (L.L. *cappa*, cape)
capable, *a.* efficient, competent; susceptible (of); (*Shake.*) comprehensive; impressible. **c. of,** wicked enough for; (*Shake.*) qualified to hold. **capability,** *n.* being capable; undeveloped faculty. (L. *capere*, hold)
capacious, *a.* able to hold a great deal, roomy. **capacitate,** *v.t.* render capable for. **capacity,** *n.* power of holding or grasping; cubic content; ability, power of mind; character, function. (L. *capere*, hold)
cap-à-pie, *adv.* from head to foot. (F.)
caparison, *n.* harness, equipment, esp. of horse.—*v.t.* put caparison on. (L.L. *cappa*, cape)
cape, *n.* short sleeveless cloak, either separate or forming part of coat. (L.L. *cappa*)
cape, *n.* headland, promontory. **the C.,** Cape of Good Hope. **C. boy,** S. African of mixed black and white descent. **C. cart,** two-wheeled cart with hood and pole. **C. smoke,** S. African brandy. (L. *caput*, head)
capelin, *n.* small sea-fish allied to smelt. (F. *capelan*)
caper, *v.i.* skip about, frisk.—*n.* frisky movement or leap; frolic, escapade. (*capriole*)
caper, *n.* a prickly shrub; (*pl.*) its buds pickled, used in **c. sauce.** (Gk. *kapparis*)
capercailzie, capercailye, *n.* largest kind of grouse. (Gael. *capull coille*, horse of the wood)
capias, *n.* writ for arrest. (L.=take thou)
capillary, *a.* of hair; hair-like.—*n.* thin hair-like blood-vessel. **c. attraction,** by which liquid is drawn up tube of hair-like calibre. **capillarity,** *n.* capillary attraction, power of exercising it. (L. *capillus*, hair)
capital, *n.* head, uppermost part, of pillar. (L. *caput*, head+dim.)
capital, *a.* chief, principal; leading, first-class; excellent; (of offence) punishable by death; (of error) fatal. —*n.* chief city of country, seat of government; capital letter; stock or money for carrying on business; accumulated wealth used to produce more, owners of this as a class. **c. letter,** large letter used for initials etc. **c. punishment,** death penalty. **make c. out of,** turn to advantage. **capitalism,** *n.* system of individual ownership of wealth; dominance of private capitalists. **capitalist,** *n.* person controlling production by ownership of capital. **capitalistic,** *a.* **capitalize,** *v.t.* convert into capital or money; convert (periodical payments) into lump sum; write in capitals. **capitalization,** *n.* **capitally,** *adv.* in a capital manner; excellently. (L. *caput*, head)
capitate, capitated, *aa.* (*bot.*) growing in a head. **capitation,** *n.* tax per head. (L. *caput*, head)
Capitol, *n.* U.S. Congress House; a U.S. state legislature building; temple of Jupiter in Rome. (L. *Capitolium*)
capitular, *a.* of a chapter.—*n.* member of cathedral chapter. **capitulary,** *n.* collection of decrees. (L. *capitulum*, chapter)
capitulate, *v.i.* surrender on terms; give in; (*Shake.*) propose terms. **capitulation,** *n.* capitulating; (*pl.*) conventions by which foreign powers were given extra-territorial rights in Turkey. (L. *capitulum*, chapter)
caplin, same as **capelin.**
capnomancy, *n.* divination by smoke. (Gk. *kapnos*, smoke; *manteia*, divination)
capon, *n.* castrated cock, esp. one fattened for table; (*Shake.*) love-letter. (L. *capo*)
caporal, *n.* a French tobacco. (F.)
capot, *n.* winning of all tricks at piquet. —*v.t.* defeat thus. (F.)
capriccio, *n.* (*mus.*) light irregular composition. *capriccioso*, *a.* (It.)
caprice, *n.* passing fancy, whim; fanciful artistic work. **capricious,** *a.* unstable, inconstant; unreliable; (*Shake.*) fantastic. (L. *caper*, goat)
Capricorn, *n.* the Goat, tenth sign of zodiac, which sun enters about 21 Dec. (L. *caper*, goat; *cornu*, horn)
caprifole, *n.* (*Spens.*) woodbine. (L. *caper*, goat; *folium*, leaf)

caprine, *a.* of, like, a goat. (L. *caper,* goat)

capriole, *v.i.* caper, kick up heels.—*n.* caper. (L. *caper,* goat+dim.)

capsicum, *n.* kinds of plant from which cayenne pepper is made.

capsize, *v.t.* and *i.* upset, overturn (vessel). **capsizal,** *n.*

capstan, *n.* upright revolving cylinder for winding cable. (L. *capere,* hold)

capsule, *n.* small gelatine case enclosing drug to be swallowed; metallic top for bottle; (*anat.*) membranous envelope; (*bot.*) seed-case. **capsular,** *a.* (L. *capsa,* case+dim.)

captain, *n.* officer commanding ship; naval officer between commander and rear-admiral; army officer between lieutenant and major; great soldier; leader of team or enterprise. —*v.t.* act as captain of. **captaincy, captainship,** *nn.* (L. *caput,* head)

captation, *n.* reaching out, appeal for, applause or favour. (L. *captare,* catch at)

caption, *n.* heading, title; (*law*) arrest; certificate attached to document. (L. *capere,* take)

captious, *a.* apt to find fault, given to carping; sophistical; (*Shake.*) capacious. (L. *capere,* take)

captive, *n.* prisoner.—*a.* held prisoner, in confinement; of captivity.—*v.t.* (*Shake.*) capture. **c. balloon,** fastened by rope to ground. **captivity,** *n.* state of being prisoner. **captivate,** *v.t.* fascinate, charm; (*Shake.*) take captive. **captivation,** *n.* **captivating,** *a.* delightful, alluring. **captor,** *n.* (*fem.* **captress**) one who takes prisoner. **capture,** *v.t.* make prisoner of; take (fortress).—*n.* capturing; person or thing captured. (L. *capere,* take)

Capuchin, *n.* Franciscan friar of new rule of 1528; woman's hooded cloak. **C. monkey, pigeon,** with hair, feathers, like cowl. (It. *capuccio,* hood)

caput mortuum, worthless residue. (L.=dead head)

capybara, *n.* large S. American rodent allied to guinea-pig. (Brazilian)

car, *n.* wheeled vehicle; motor-car; tram; basket of balloon; (*poet.*) chariot; (*Amer.*) railway carriage. (L. *carrus,* wagon)

carabineer, *n.* mounted soldier armed with carbine; (*pl.*) 6th Dragoon Guards. **carabine,** same as **carbine.**

caracal, *n.* kind of lynx; its fur. (Turk. *qarah-qulaq,* black-ear)

carack, same as **carrack.**

caracole, caracol, *n.* and *v.i.* (of horse) half-turn to right or left. (Sp. *caracol,* spiral shell)

carafe, *n.* glass water-bottle for table. (Sp. *garrafa*)

caramel, *n.* kind of sweet; burnt sugar for cooking or colouring. (Sp. *caramelo*)

carapace, *n.* upper shell of turtle, crab etc. (Sp. *carapacho*)

carat, *n.* measure of weight for gems, about 3⅓ grains; measure of gold's purity, 24 carat being completely pure. (Arab. *qirat*)

caravan, *n.* covered wagon used as travelling house; company of merchants travelling together for safety in the East. **caravanserai, caravansery,** *n.* eastern inn with courtyard where caravans spend night. (Pers. *karwan*)

caravel, *n.* ancient small light fast Spanish ship. (It. *caravella*)

caraway, *n.* plant with pungent aromatic seeds. (L.L. *carui*)

carbide, *n.* compound of carbon with another element; (also **calcium c.**) product of carbon and lime used for making acetylene gas.

carbine, *n.* short rifle carried by mounted troops. **carbineer,** same as **carabineer.** (F. *carabin,* musketeer)

carbohydrate, *n.* kinds of compound of carbon, hydrogen, and oxygen, esp. as heat-giving foodstuff, e.g. sugar.

carbolic acid, disinfectant made from coal-tar. **carbolize,** *v.t.* sterilize with carbolic acid. (L. *carbo,* coal; *oleum,* oil)

carbon, *n.* a non-metallic element, the substance of pure charcoal; charcoal pencil of electric lamp; duplicate made with carbon-paper. **c. dioxide,** gas breathed out by humans and absorbed by plants. **c. monoxide,** a poisonous odourless gas. **c.-paper,** *n.* paper covered with lamp-black etc. for copying. **carbonaceous,** *a.* containing carbon. **carbonate,** *n.* salt of carbonic acid. **carbonic,** *a.* of, got from, carbon. **carbonic acid gas,** carbon dioxide. **carboniferous,** *a.* coal-bearing. **carbonize,** *v.t.* convert into carbon; reduce to charcoal. (L. *carbo,* coal)

carbonado, *n.* (*Shake.*) piece of meat cut crossways for broiling.—*v.t.* slash; broil. (Sp. *carbonada*)

carborundum, *n.* compound of carbon and silicon, used for grinding. (*carbon+corundum*)

carboy, *n.* large glass jar enclosed in basket-work for holding corrosive chemicals. (Pers. *qarabah*)

carbuncle, *n.* large inflamed boil; pimple on nose or face; garnet cut in boss shape. **carbuncular,** *a.* (L. *carbo,* coal+dim.)

carburet, *v.t.* combine with carbon. **carburettor, carburetter,** *n.* device in motor engine for making explosive mixture of air and petrol vapour.

carcajou, *n.* wolverine; cougar.

carcanet, *n.* (*arch.*) collar of jewels. (L.L. *carcannum*)

carcass, carcase, *n.* dead body of animal; mere body; decaying remains; framework. (It. *carcassa*)

carcinoma, *n.* (*pl.* **carcinomata**) kind of cancer. (Gk. *karkinos*, crab)
card, *n.* toothed instrument, wire brush.—*v.t.* comb (wool) with card; torture with card. (L. *carduus*, thistle)
card, *n.* pasteboard; small piece of this marked with figure or picture for playing games; visiting-card; ticket, notice; dial of compass; (*sl.*) droll original fellow. **c. vote,** of delegates each counting for number of his constituents. **house of cc.,** flimsy thing. **on the cc.,** likely. **safe c.,** sound plan. **speak by the c.,** be exact. **c.-case,** *n.* for carrying visiting-cards. **c.-sharper,** *n.* swindler at cards. (Gk. *chartēs*, leaf of papyrus)
cardamon, cardamom, *n.* an E. Indian spice. (Gk. *kardamōmon*)
cardboard, *n.* thick stiff paper.
cardecu, *n.* (*Shake.*) old French silver coin worth about 1*s.* 6*d.* (F. *quart d'écu*, quarter of crown)
cardiac, *a.* of the heart.—*n.* heart stimulant. (Gk. *kardia*, heart)
cardigan, *n.* woollen waistcoat with or without sleeves. (person)
cardinal, *a.* of chief importance, fundamental; deep scarlet.—*n.* prince of Roman Catholic Church; woman's short hooded cloak; cardinal number or colour; (*Amer.*) scarlet grosbeak. **c. numbers,** 1, 2, 3 etc. **c. points,** north, south, east, west. **cardinalate,** *n.* rank, dignity, of cardinal; body of cardinals. (L. *cardo*, hinge)
cardio-, from Gk. *kardia*, heart, used in cardiology, *n.* study of the heart; **cardiometer,** *n.* apparatus for measuring heart-beats.
carditis, *n.* inflammation of heart.
cardoon, *n.* vegetable allied to artichoke. (L. *carduus*, thistle)
care, *n.* anxiety, concern; cause of this; serious attention, heed; thing to be seen to; protection, charge.—*v.i.* be anxious or concerned; have affection (for); look after, provide (for); be inclined. (O.E. *caru*)
careen, *v.t.* and *i.* tilt (ship) and expose bottom for cleaning and repair; heel over. **careenage,** *n.* act of, place for, careening. (L. *carina*, keel)
career, *n.* rapid course, onward movement; mode of living, progress through life; (*Shake.*) frisk, gambol.—*v.i.* rush rapidly and wildly. **careerist,** *n.* one who aims mainly at personal advancement. (L. *carrus*, wagon)
careful, *a.* painstaking; attentive; cautious; thrifty; done with care; (*Shake.*) anxious.
careless, *a.* light-hearted; thoughtless, negligent; heedless (of).
caress, *n.* fondling touch or pat; kiss.—*v.t.* bestow caress on, fondle. (L. *carus*, dear)
caret, *n.* mark (‸) showing where to insert something omitted. (L.= there is wanting)
caretaker, *n.* person left in charge of house in owner's absence etc.
carex, *n.* kinds of plant incl. sedge. (L.)
cargo, *n.* (*pl.* **cargoes**) what ship carries, its freight. (Sp.)
Carib, *n.* aboriginal native of W. Indies.
caribou, cariboo, *n.* N. American reindeer. (Canadian F.)
caricature, *n.* likeness made ludicrous by exaggeration or distortion of characteristic features; burlesque, parody.—*v.t.* make caricature of. **caricaturist,** *n.* (It. *caricare*, load)
cárĭēs, *n.* decay of tooth or bone. (L.)
carillon, *n.* peal, set, of bells; tune played on this. (F.)
carinate, *a.* keel-shaped. (L. *carina*, keel)
carious, *a.* decayed. (*caries*)
carking, *a.* burdensome. (L.L. *carricare*, load)
carl, carle, *n.* (*arch.*) rustic; (*Scot.*) fellow. **carline,** *n.* (*Scot.*) old woman. (O.N. *karl*)
carline, *n.* kinds of plant like thistle. (*Charlemagne*)
carlot, *n.* (*Shake.*) peasant. (*carl*)
Carmagnole, *n.* song and dance of French revolutionists. (F.)
carman, *n.* carter.
Carmelite, *n.* and *a.* (member) of mendicant order founded on Mount Carmel, White Friar; fine woollen stuff.
carminative, *a.* and *n.* (drug) expelling flatulence. (L. *carminare*, card)
carmine, *n.* and *a.* (of) vivid crimson colour. (Arab. *qirmazi*, crimson)
carnage, *n.* great slaughter. (L. *caro*, flesh)
carnal, *a.* of the flesh, sensual; sexual; worldly; (*Shake.*) flesh-eating, cruel. **c. knowledge of,** sexual intercourse with. **carnalism, carnality,** *nn.* **carnalist,** *n.* sensualist. (L. *caro*, flesh)
carnation, *n.* and *a.* (of) rosy pink colour. (L. *caro*, flesh)
carnation, *n.* kinds of clove pink.
carnelian, same as cornelian.
carney, same as carny.
carnival, *n.* week preceding Lent, festivities held during it; riotous revelry. (L. *carnem levare*, take away meat)
carnivorous, *a.* flesh-eating. **carnivore,** *n.* one of the **Carnivora,** *n.pl.* order of flesh-eating mammals. (L. *caro*, flesh; *vorare*, devour)
carny, *v.t.* (*colloq.*) coax, wheedle.
carob, *n.* locust-tree; its horn-like pod. (Arab. *kharrubah*, bean-pod)
carol, *n.* joyful song; Christmas hymn; (*poet.*) song of birds.—*v.i.* and *t.* sing carol (to). (O.F. *carole*)
Caroline, *a.* of time of Charles I or Charles II. (L. *Carolus*, Charles)

carom, *n.* (*Amer.*) cannon at billiards. (Sp. *carambola*)

carotid, *n.* (also **c. artery**) either of two great arteries of neck. (Gk. *karōtides*, carotids)

carouse, *v.i.* drink deeply and jovially.—*n.* drinking-bout; drunken revelry. **carousal,** *n.* carouse; jovial feast. (G. *gar aus*, right out)

carp, *n.* brown-and-yellow freshwater fish. (L.L. *carpa*)

carp, *v.i.* take exception, find fault.

carpal, *a.* of carpus.

carpe diem, seize opportunity. (L.)

carpel, *n.* pistil or pistil-cell. **carpellary,** *a.* **carpellate,** *a.* having carpel. (Gk. *karpos*, fruit)

carpenter, *n.* one who works in wood, esp. for building.—*v.i.* and *t.* do, make by, carpentry. **c.-ant, c.-bee,** *nn.* kinds that make nests in wood. **carpentry,** *n.* art, work, of carpenter. (L.L. *carpentum*, wagon)

carpet, *n.* thick woven fabric for covering floor.—*v.t.* cover with carpet; strew; (*colloq.*) summon for reprimand. **on the c.,** under consideration; (*colloq.*) being reprimanded. **c.-bag,** *n.* old-fashioned bag made of carpet. **c.-bagger,** *n.* itinerant politician, adventurer. **c.-knight,** *n.* knight who has never seen war, ladies' man. **c.-monger,** *n.* (*Shake.*) effeminate person. **c.-snake,** *n.* variegated Australian kind. (L. *carpere*, pluck)

carpology, *n.* section of botany dealing with fruit. (Gk. *karpos*, fruit; *legein*, speak)

carpus, *n.* (*pl.* **carpi**) wrist; horse's knee. (Gk. *karpos*)

carrack, *n.* ancient armed merchantship of Spain. (L.L. *carraca*)

carrageen, *n.* an edible seaweed. (*Carragheen* in Ireland)

carriage, *n.* act of carrying, transport; charge for this; deportment, bearing; behaviour; kinds of vehicle, esp. with four wheels; railway coach or compartment; (*Shake.*) burden. **c. forward,** cost of transport to be paid by receiver. **c.-dog,** *n.* spotted Dalmatian. **c.-drive,** *n.* road through private grounds. **carriageable,** *a.* (of road) fit for carriages. (*carry*)

carrier, *n.* one who conveys goods; luggage-bracket; person transmitting infectious disease without catching it. **c.-pigeon,** *n.* kind used to carry written messages.

carriole, *n.* small open carriage for one. (L. *carrus*, wagon+dim.)

carrion, *n.* dead putrefying flesh; anything vile. **c.-beetle, c.-crow,** *nn.* kinds feeding on carrion. (L. *caro*, flesh)

carritch, *n.* (*Scot.*) catechism.

carronade, *n.* a short naval gun. (*Carron* in Scotland)

carron oil, mixture of linseed oil and lime-water. (*Carron* in Scotland)

carrot, *n.* orange-red tapering edible root; plant with it; (*pl., sl.*) red-haired person. **carroty,** *a.* reddish. (Gk. *karōton*)

carry, *v.t.* and *i.* (*past, p.p.* **carried**) convey, transport; support, bear; have about one; hold (oneself); extend, prolong; gain by attack, win over; obtain approval for; (*golf*) hit over; (*Shake.*) conduct.—*n.* range; portage between rivers; (*golf*) distance ball flies before landing. **c. forward,** transfer (figures) to next column or page. **c. off,** gain, win; cause to pass muster. **c. on,** keep up, continue; misbehave; flirt (with). **c. one's bat,** (*cricket*) be not out at end of innings. **c. out,** put into practice. **c. over,** (*stock exchange*) keep over till next settling-day. **be carried away,** be greatly excited, have head turned. (L. *carrus*, wagon)

carse, *n.* (*Scot.*) low fertile land skirting river.

cart, *n.* vehicle for carrying loads; light two-wheeled horse-carriage.—*v.t.* and *i.* convey in cart; (*sl.*) defeat easily in game. **c. about,** take about with one. **in the c.,** (*sl.*) in a fix. **c.-horse,** *n.* large heavy breed of horse. **c.-load,** *n.* amount a cart will hold. **c.-track,** *n.* rough road. **c.-wheel,** *n.* sideways somersault; (*sl.*) large coin. **cartage,** *n.* conveyance in cart; cost of this.

carte, *n.* a guard in fencing. (F.)

carte, *n.* card. *c. blanche*, full power of action. *c.-de-visite*, *n.* photograph $3\frac{1}{2}\times2\frac{1}{4}$ in. (F.)

cartel, *n.* written challenge to duel; agreement for exchange of prisoners; combination of manufacturers or political parties. (F.)

Cartesian, *a.* and *n.* (follower) of Descartes or his philosophy.

Carthusian, *a.* and *n.* (monk) of St. Bruno's order; (pupil) of Charterhouse School. (*Chatrousse* in France)

cartilage, *n.* strong elastic animal tissue, gristle. **cartilaginous,** *a.* like, made of, cartilage; with skeleton of cartilage. (L. *cartilago*)

cartography, *n.* map-making. **cartographic, cartographical,** *aa.* **cartographer,** *n.* (F. *carte*, chart. Gk. *graphein*, write)

cartomancy, *n.* telling fortunes by playing-cards. (It. *carta*, card. Gk. *manteia*, divination)

carton, *n.* pasteboard box. (F.)

cartoon, *n.* humorous picture, caricature, dealing with current events; full-size preparatory sketch for reproduction on fresco etc.—*v.i.* and *t.* draw cartoon (of). **cartoonist,** *n.* (*carton*)

cartouche, *n.* scroll-shaped architectural ornamentation; oval containing ancient Egyptian king's name and titles; canvas cartridge-case. (F.)

cartridge, *n.* charge of explosive for gun made up in case. **ball c.**, containing bullet. **blank c.**, with explosive only. **c.-belt**, *n.* for holding cartridges. **c.-paper**, *n.* strong rough kind. (corrupt. of *cartouche*)

cartulary, *n.* collection, register, of charters. (*charter*)

caruncle, *n.* fleshy excrescence. (L. *caro*, flesh+dim.)

carve, *v.t.* and *i.* (*p.p.* **carved, carven**) shape by cutting; adorn with designs; cut up (meat) at table; (*Shake.*) show great courtesy. **c. up**, subdivide. **carver**, *n.* one who carves; carving-knife. **carving**, *n.* carved work. (O.E. *ceorfan*)

carvel, same as **caravel**. **c.-built**, *a.* with outer boards or plates meeting flush, not overlapping.

caryatid, *n.* sculptured female figure acting as pillar. (Gk. *karuatis*)

cascade, *n.* small waterfall; loose wavy fall of lace.—*v.i.* fall in cascade. (L. *cadere*, fall)

cascara sagrada, a laxative drug. (Sp.=sacred bark)

case, *n.* instance; state of affairs; condition, circumstances; lawsuit; argument for one side; (*sl.*) character; (*gram.*) relation of noun to other words, form indicating this; (*med.*) patient under treatment. **c. of conscience**, in which conscience must decide between opposing principles. **in any c.**, at all events. **in c.**, if, lest. **c.-ending**, *n.* inflexional suffix indicating case. **c.-law**, *n.* law as settled by precedent. (L. *cadere*, fall)

case, *n.* receptacle, box, covering; box and its contents, set; enclosing framework.—*v.t.* cover, enclose in case; (*Shake.*) skin. **lower, upper, c.**, (*print.*) small letters, capitals. **c.-hardened**, *a.* with hard steel surface; made callous. **c.-knife**, *n.* sheath-knife. **c.-shot**, *n.* canister-shot. (L. *capsa*)

casein, *n.* a protein in cheese. (L. *caseus*, cheese)

casemate, *n.* bomb-proof vault in fortification; armoured enclosure for gun in warship. (F.)

casement, *n.* window opening on hinges.

caseous, *a.* like cheese. (L. *caseus*, cheese)

cash, *n.* money in coin or notes; ready money.—*v.t.* give or get cash for (cheque). **c. down**, paid on the spot. **c. in**, (*Amer.*) settle accounts; die. **c. on delivery**, (*abbr.* **C.O.D.**) to be paid for to postman or carrier. **c.-register**, *n.* self-registering till. (L. *capsa*, case)

cash, *n.* (*pl.* same), small Chinese coin, $\frac{1}{1000}$ of tael. (Tamil *kasu*)

cashew, *n.* Brazilian tree with kidney-shaped nuts. (Brazilian *acajoba*)

cashier, *n.* person in charge of payments and receipts. (*cash*)

cashier, *v.t.* dismiss (officer) from military service. (L. *quatere*, shake, and *cassare*, annul)

cashmere, *n.* soft material made from wool of Cashmere goat; shawl of this.

casino, *n.* building with public dance-halls, gaming tables etc. (It.)

cask, *n.* large round wooden vessel, barrel; this and its contents.

casket, *n.* small case for jewels etc.; (*Amer.*) coffin.

casque, *n.* (*poet.*) helmet. (F.)

cassation, *n.* annulment. **Court of C.**, highest French court of appeal. (L. *cassus*, void)

cassava, *n.* a W. Indian tree; starchy flour made from its root. (Haytian *casavi*)

casserole, *n.* fireproof dish in which meat is cooked and served. (F.)

cassia, *n.* tropical plant yielding senna. (Gk. *kasia*)

cassock, *n.* long close-fitting black garment worn by clergy; (*Shake.*) soldier's cloak. (F. *casaque*)

cassowary, *n.* large running bird related to ostrich. (Malay *casuari*)

cast, *v.t.* and *i.* (*past, p.p.* same) throw, fling; set, place; throw off, shed; discard, reject; project (shadow); let down (anchor); give (vote); direct (glance); reckon up (accounts); compute (horoscope); shape (molten metal) in mould; choose (actor) for part, assign (part) to actor; (of dam) drop prematurely; (*law*) give or get decision against; (*Shake.*) dismiss; vomit.—*n.* throw; excrement of earthworm; reckoning; mould for casting, thing cast in it; form, type, quality; tinge; slight squint; set of actors in play. **c. about**, contrive; search. **c. down**, depress. **c. off**, abandon; unmoor; (*knitting*) close loops and make selvedge; (*print.*) estimate space taken in print by MS. copy. **c. up**, cast ashore; reckon. **c.-iron**, *a.* made of cast iron; untiring; rigid, unadaptable. (O.N. *kasta*)

Castalian, *a.* poetic. (*Castalia*, fountain of the muses)

castanet, *n.* one of a pair of small wooden or ivory shells clicked together in time with dancing or music. (L. *castanea*, chestnut+dim.)

castaway, *n.* shipwrecked person.

caste, *n.* any of India's mutually exclusive hereditary classes; this system; exclusive social group. **lose c.**, forfeit right to social privileges. (Sp. *casta*, lineage)

castellan, *n.* governor of castle. **castellated**, *a.* having battlements and turrets, like a castle.

caster, see **castor**.

castigate, *v.t.* chastise, punish; correct. **castigation, castigator**, *nn.* **castigatory**, *a.* (L. *castigare*)

casting, *n.* piece of metal cast in

mould. **c.-net,** *n.* hand-net. **c.-vote,** *n.* deciding vote of chairman when sides are equal.

castle, *n.* large fortified house, stronghold; country mansion like this; (*chess*) rook. **c. in the air, c. in Spain,** pleasant day-dream. (L. *castellum*)

castor, caster, *n.* bottle with perforated top for sprinkling pepper, sugar etc.; (*pl.*) cruet. (*cast*)

castor, caster, *n.* small swivelled wheel on table-leg etc. (*cast*)

castor, *n.* oily substance got from beaver. (Gk. *kastōr*, beaver)

castor, *n.* small callosity on inner side of horse's leg.

castor oil, vegetable oil used as purgative and lubricant.

castrametation, *n.* laying out of camps. (L. *castra*, camp; *metari*, measure)

castrate, *v.t.* remove testicles of, geld; expurgate. **castration,** *n.* (L. *castrare*)

casual, *a.* chance, accidental; undesigned; careless, unmethodical; occasional.—*n.* vagrant. **c. labourer,** one who has no permanent work. **c. ward,** ward in workhouse for tramps etc. (L. *casus*, chance)

casualty, *n.* case of bodily injury through accident or battle; mishap; (*pl.*) number of killed and wounded.

casuist, *n.* one who studies and resolves cases of conscience; one skilled in casuistry; quibbler. **casuistic, casuistical,** *aa.* **casuistry,** *n.* study or application of rules of right and wrong; sophistical or false reasoning, esp. on moral matters. (L. *casus*, case)

casus belli, act, occurrence, justifying war. (L.)

cat, *n.* small furry domesticated quadruped; feline animal; spiteful woman; tapered piece of wood used in tipcat; cat-o'-nine-tails.—*v.i.* and *t.* (*colloq.*) vomit; (*naut.*) raise (anchor) to cathead. **c. burglar,** one who enters by climbing. **let the c. out of the bag,** give secret away. **c.-and-dog life,** of constant quarrels. **c.-and-mouse Act,** (*sl.*) permitting release and rearrest of hunger-strikers. **c.-eyed,** *a.* able to see in the dark. **c.-ice,** *n.* unsound brittle ice. **c.-nap,** *n.* very short nap. **c.-o'-mountain,** same as **catamountain. c.-o'-nine-tails,** *n.* whip with nine lashes. **c.'s-cradle,** *n.* game of making designs with string looped over fingers. **c.'s-eye,** *n.* an opalescent gem. **c.'s-meat,** *n.* horseflesh on skewers as food for cat. **c.'s-paw,** *n.* person used as tool by another; (*naut.*) light breeze. **c.'s-tail,** *n.* kinds of grass. **c.'s-whisker,** *n.* (*wireless*) fine contact wire in crystal set. (O.E.)

cata-, cath-, *pref.* down, as in **catadromous**; wrongly, as in **catachresis**; thoroughly, as in **cataphract.** (Gk. *kata*)

catabolism, same as katabolism.

catachresis, *n.* misapplication of words; formation of words on false analogy. **catachrestic, catachrestical** *aa.* (Gk. *kata-*, wrongly; *chrēsthai*, use)

cataclasm, *n.* disruption. (Gk. *kata*, down; *klaein*, break)

cataclysm, *n.* deluge; violent change, upheaval. **cataclysmal, cataclysmic,** *aa.* (Gk. *kata*, down; *kluzein*, wash)

catacomb, *n.* underground gallery with recesses for tombs. (L.L. *catacumbas*)

catadioptric, *a.* of, due to, both refraction and reflection of light. (*catoptric*; *dioptric*)

catadromous, *a.* going down to the sea to spawn. (Gk. *kata*, down; *dromos*, run)

catafalque, *n.* stand for coffin during lying in state. (It. *catafalco*)

catalectic, *a.* lacking a syllable in last foot. (Gk. *kata*, down; *lēgein*, cease)

catalepsy, *n.* disease causing trance-like condition; (*philos.*) grasping by the mind. **cataleptic,** *a.* and *n.* (person) having catalepsy. (Gk. *kata*, down; *lambanein*, seize)

catalogue, *n.* list or register, us. alphabetical.—*v.t.* make catalogue of. (Gk. *kata*, down; *legein*, choose)

catalpa, *n.* American tree with trumpet-shaped flowers. (W. Indian)

catalysis, *n.* acceleration or retardation of chemical reaction owing to presence of catalyst. **catalyst,** *n.* substance changing speed of chemical reaction in other substance without itself undergoing chemical change. **catalytic,** *a.* **catalyse,** *v.t.* cause catalysis in. (Gk. *kata*, down; *luein*, loose)

catamaran, *n.* raft of logs; boat formed of two hulls side by side; cross-grained woman. (Tamil *kattu*, binding; *maram*, wood)

catamenia, *n.* menstruation. (Gk. *kata*, during; *mēn*, month)

catamite, *n.* sodomite's minion. (corrupt. of *Ganymede*)

catamountain, *n.* leopard; wild cat.

cataphract, *n.* coat of mail, soldier clad in one. (Gk. *kata-*, thoroughly; *phrassein*, protect)

cataplasm, *n.* poultice. (Gk. *kataplassein*, smear over)

catapult, *n.* ancient military engine for throwing stones or darts; boy's forked stick with elastic for shooting stones; device for propelling aircraft from deck of ship etc.—*v.t.* and *i.* shoot with catapult. (Gk. *katapeltēs*)

cataract, *n.* waterfall, esp. large sheer one; downpour; disease of eye causing dimming of lens and loss of vision. (Gk. *katarrhaktēs*)

catarrh, *n.* inflammation of mucous membrane; a cold. **catarrhal,** *a.* (Gk. *kata*, down; *rheein*, flow)

catarrhine, catarhine, *a.* and *n.* (kinds of monkey) with nostrils directed downwards and opposable thumbs. (Gk. *kata*, down; *rhis*, nostril)

catastrophe, *n.* great disaster, calamity; sudden violent change; final event in drama, *dénouement*; (*Shake.*, *joc.*) backside. **catastrophic, catastrophical,** *aa.* **catastrophism,** *n.* old theory that geological changes were due to sudden upheavals. (Gk. *kata*, down; *strephein*, turn)

Catawba, *n.* an American grape; wine made from it. (river)

catbird, *n.* (*Amer.*) kind of thrush.

catboat, *n.* small sailing-boat with single mast set well forward.

catcall, *n.* shrill whistle or cry.—*v.i.* and *t.* emit, assail with, this.

catch, *v.t.* and *i.* (*past*, *p.p.* caught, *Shake.* **catched**) capture, take; lay hold of, grasp; ensnare, trap, become entangled; hit; overtake; detect, apprehend; contract (disease).—*n.* act of catching; thing caught or worth catching; sudden check; device for fastening; artful trick; song of which the parts are caught up in succession by different voices. **c. it,** (*sl.*) be punished. **c. me!** (*sl.*) no fear of my doing that. **c. on,** become popular; understand. **c. out,** detect in mistake. **c. up,** overtake. (L. *capere*, take)

catcher, *n.* (*baseball*) player who stands behind batter to catch ball.

catching, *a.* infectious; attractive.

catchment-basin, *n.* area from which river or reservoir draws water.

catchpenny, *a.* made to sell quickly, cheap and showy.

catchpole, catchpoll, *n.* sheriff's officer. (L.L. *chassipullus*, lit. chase-chicken)

catchup, see **ketchup.**

catchword, *n.* temporarily popular phrase; first word of page printed at foot of previous page; word given at head of column of book of reference, as **catarrhine** on this page.

catchy, *a.* (of tune) easy to remember.

cate, *n.* (*arch.*, us. *pl.*) dainty. (*cater*)

catechize, *v.t.* instruct by question and answer; cross-examine. **catechism,** *n.* catechizing; church doctrine given in form of question and answer. **catechist,** *n.* **catechetic, catechetical,** *aa.* instructing orally; proceeding by question and answer; of catechism. (Gk. *katēcheein*, din into the ears)

catechu, *n.* astringent substance got from tropical plants. (Malay *kachu*)

catechumen, *n.* convert under instruction before baptism. (*catechize*)

category, *n.* class, order; (*logic*) class that comes under no higher class, ultimate conception. **categorical,** *a.* of category; unconditional, absolute; positive, explicit. **categorical imperative,** (*philos.*) absolute and unconditional command of moral law. (Gk. *katēgoria*, statement)

catena, *n.* chain; series. **catenary,** *n.* curve formed by hanging chain. **catenarian,** *a.* **catenate,** *v.t.* link together. **catenation,** *n.* (L.)

cater, *n.* four at cards or dice. (L. *quattuor*, four)

cater, *v.i.* purvey food; provide amusement (for). **caterer,** *n.* (O.F. *acateor*, buyer)

cateran, *n.* (*Scot.*) highland robber or freebooter. (Gael. *ceathairne*, peasantry)

cater-cousin, *n.* intimate friend.

caterpillar, *n.* worm-like larva of butterfly or moth; ribbed band in place of wheels, enabling tank etc. to move over rough ground.

caterwaul, *n.* discordant scream of cat. —*v.i.* utter this; quarrel like cats. (*cat*; *waul*)

catfish, *n.* fish with long barbels.

catgut, *n.* material for strings of fiddle, racket etc., made from intestines of sheep or horse (not cat).

cath-, see **cata-.**

catharsis, *n.* (*pl.* **catharses**) emotional relief given by art, esp. tragedy; (*med.*) purgation. **cathartic,** *a.* and *n.* purgative. (Gk. *katharos*, clean)

cathead, *n.* projection from each side of bow for carrying anchor.

cathedral, *n.* chief church of diocese, containing bishop's throne.—*a.* ranking as, containing, belonging to, a cathedral. (L. *cathedra*, chair)

Catherine-wheel, *n.* spinning firework; sideways somersault; (*archit.*) circular spoked window. (*saint*)

catheter, *n.* tube introduced into bladder through urethra. (Gk. *kata*, down; *hienai*, send)

cathode, *n.* (*electr.*) negative terminal; electrode by which current leaves. **c. ray,** ray consisting of electrons. **cathodic,** *a.* (Gk. *kata*, down; *hodos*, way)

catholic, *a.* universal, all-embracing; broad-minded, liberal; of all Christians; of the Western Church; of the Roman Catholic Church; of the Anglican Church.—*n.* member of Catholic Church; Roman Catholic. **C. Epistles,** those of James, Peter, Jude, and John, which are addressed to believers generally. **catholically, catholicly,** *advv.* **catholicism,** *n.* adherence to Catholic, esp. Roman Catholic, Church. **catholicity,** *n.* universality, comprehensiveness; accordance with Catholic, esp. Roman Catholic, Church doctrine. **catholicize,** *v.t.* convert to catholicism. **catholicon,** *n.* panacea. (Gk. *kata*, throughout; *holos*, whole)

cation, *n.* electro-positive ion. (*cata-*)

catkin, *n.* downy hanging flower-cluster of willow etc. (*cat*+dim.)

catlike, *a.* like a cat; stealthy, noiseless.

catling, *n.* small cat; fine catgut; amputating knife. (*cat*+dim.)

catmint, catnip, *nn.* blue-flowered aromatic plant attractive to cats.

catoptric, *a.* of, produced by, reflection of light.—*n.pl.* branch of optics dealing with reflection. (Gk. *katoptron,* mirror)
catsup, see **ketchup.**
cattish, catty, *aa.* sly and spiteful.
cattle, *n.* live stock, esp. bulls and cows. **c.-lifter, c.-lifting,** *nn.* stealer, stealing, of cattle. **c.-plague,** *n.* rinderpest. **c.-rustler,** *n.* (*Amer.*) cattle-thief. (L. *caput,* head)
Caucasian, *a.* and *n.* (member) of white race, Indo-European. (*Caucasus*)
caucus, *n.* small powerful committee, esp. in political party.
caudal, *a.* of tail. **caudate,** *a.* having tail. (L. *cauda,* tail)
caudle, *n.* warm drink of spiced gruel for invalids. (L. *calidus,* warm)
caught, see **catch.**
caul, *n.* membrane sometimes covering head of new-born infant. (O.F. *cale,* small cap)
cauld, *a.* (*Scot.*) cold. **cauldrife,** *a.* cold, chilly.
cauldron, *n.* large vessel for boiling, us. basin-shaped. (L. *calidus,* warm)
caulescent, *a.* with visible stem. **caulicle,** *n.* rudimentary stem. **caulicolous,** *a.* living on stem. **cauliflower,** *n.* kind of cabbage with white fleshy flower-head. **cauline,** *a.* of, on, stem. (L. *caulis,* stalk)
caulk, *v.t.* stop up (seams) with oakum and pitch; make (ship) watertight thus.—*n.* (*naut.*) snooze. (L. *calcare,* tread)
cause, *n.* that which produces an effect; reason, motive; justification; principle for which people strive; lawsuit, case of party in it; (*Shake.*) accusation; affair; disease.—*v.t.* bring about, effect; make (to do something). *c. célèbre,* lawsuit making public stir. **First C.,** the Creator. **make common c.,** unite for common object. **c.-list,** *n.* list of cases coming on for trial. **causal,** *a.* relating to, expressing, cause. **causality,** *n.* state of being a cause; relation, universal operation, of cause and effect. **causation,** *n.* causing. **causative,** *a.* acting as, expressing, cause. **causeless,** *a.* without cause; groundless. (L. *causa*)
causerie, *n.* discursive conversational article. (F.)
causeway, causey, *n.* raised road across low ground or marsh; raised footpath at side of road. (L. *calcare,* tread)
caustic, *a.* burning, corrosive; biting, sarcastic.—*n.* corrosive substance. **caustically,** *adv.* **causticity,** *n.* (Gk. *kaiein,* burn)
cautel, *n.* (*Shake.*) deceit, stratagem. **cautelous,** *a.* (*arch.*) crafty; cautious. (L. *cavēre,* beware)
cauterize, *v.t.* burn, sear, so as to destroy infection or dead tissue. **cautery,** *n.* cauterizing; hot iron etc. for this. (Gk. *kaiein,* burn)
caution, *n.* carefulness, care for safety; warning; (*sl.*) strange or droll person; (*Scot.*) bail; (*Shake.*) precaution.—*v.t.* warn (against); admonish. **c. money,** deposit paid by member of college etc. as security against debts. **cautionary,** *a.* of a warning nature. **cautious,** *a.* careful, circumspect. (L. *cavēre,* beware)
cavalcade, *n.* company, procession, of riders. (L. *caballus,* horse)
cavalier, *n.* horseman; escort in attendance on lady, gallant; royalist in 17th-century civil war.—*a.* careless, free and easy; brusque, discourteous. **cavaleiro,** *n.* (*Shake.*) gallant. *cavaliere servente,* one who waits upon a lady with fantastic devotion. (L. *caballus,* horse)
cavally, *n.* **horse - mackerel.** (Sp. *cavalla,* mackerel)
cavalry, *n.* **horse-soldiers.** (L. *caballus,* horse)
cavatina, *n.* short simple song. (It.)
cave, *n.* hollow place extending horizontally underground; small group of seceders from political party.—*v.t.* and *i.* hollow out. **c. in,** fall in, subside; bash in; give in. **c.-man,** *n.* prehistoric cave-dweller; man of primitive instincts. (L. *cavus,* hollow)
cávě, *int.* (*school sl.*) look out! **keep c.,** act as sentry. **caveat,** *n.* (*law*) process to suspend proceedings. (L. *cavēre,* beware)
cavendish, *n.* tobacco sweetened and pressed into cake, negro-head.
cavern, *n.* cave. **cavernous,** *a.* huge and deep; like a cavern; full of caverns. (L. *caverna*)
caviare, caviar, *n.* pickled sturgeon-roe. **c. to the general,** appealing only to cultivated taste.
cavie, *n.* (*Scot.*) hen-coop.
cavil, *v.i.* find fault, make trifling objections.—*n.* unnecessary objection. **caviller,** *n.* (L. *cavillari*)
cavity, *n.* hollow place. (L. *cavus,* hollow)
cavort, *v.i.* (*colloq.*) prance.
cavy, *n.* kinds of small rodent incl. guinea-pig. (Carib *cabiai*)
caw, *n.* cry of rook.—*v.i.* utter this. (imit.)
cay, *n.* small low island. (=*quay*)
cayenne, *n.* (also **c. pepper**) hot red pepper made from capsicum. (Brazilian *kyynha*)
cayman, *n.* alligator of South and Central America.
cayuse, *n.* (*Amer.*) Indian pony.
cease, *v.i.* and *t.* stop, come to an end; desist (from), discontinue.—*n.* cessation. **ceaseless,** *a.* continuous. (L. *cedere,* yield)
cecity, *n.* blindness. (L. *caecus,* blind)
cedar, *n.* large evergreen tree; its strong fragrant wood. **cedarn,** *a.* of cedar-wood. (Gk. *kedros*)
cede, *v.t.* yield to another, give up; transfer (territory). (L. *cedere*)
cedilla, *n.* comma-like mark below **c**

(ç) indicating that it is pronounced like *s*. (Gk. *zēta*, Z+dim.)
ceiling, *n.* inner roof of room; lining of this; limit of height to which aircraft can climb. **ceil,** *v.t.* line roof of (room). (L. *caelum*, sky)
celadon, *n.* and *a.* willow-green. (F.)
celandine, *n.* kinds of wild plant with star-shaped yellow flowers. (Gk. *chelidōn*, swallow)
celanese, *n.* kind of artificial silk. (proprietary name)
celebrate, *v.t.* and *i.* make famous; praise, extol; perform with proper rites, mark with ceremony; keep (festival). **celebration, celebrator,** *nn.* **celebrant,** *n.* priest celebrating mass or eucharist. **celebrated,** *a.* distinguished, famous. **celebrity,** *n.* fame; famous or well-known person. (L. *celebrare*)
celeriac, *n.* turnip-rooted celery.
celerity, *n.* swiftness, dispatch. (L. *celer*, swift)
celery, *n.* kitchen vegetable with long juicy stalks. (Gk. *selinon*, parsley)
celeste, *n.* and *a.* sky-blue; (also **voix c.**) an organ stop. **celesta,** *n.* kind of glockenspiel with keyboard. (F.)
celestial, *a.* of the sky; heavenly, divine.—*n.* Chinaman. **C. Empire,** China. (L. *caelum*, sky)
celibate, *a.* unmarried; vowed to single life.—*n.* celibate person. **celibacy,** *n.* unmarried state. **celibatarian,** *a.* and *n.* (person) advocating celibacy. (L. *caelebs*)
cell, *n.* small room for one in prison or monastery; small cavity or compartment; unit of living tissue, mass of protoplasm containing nucleus; persons forming centre of revolutionary propaganda; (*electr.*) unit of battery. (L. *cella*, small room)
cellar, *n.* underground room or vault; place for storing wine or coal; stock of wine.—*v.t.* store in cellar. **cellarage,** *n.* capacity of cellar; storage in cellar, charge for this. **cellarer,** *n.* keeper of monastery's wine and food. **cellaret,** *n.* wine-cabinet. (*cell*)
cello, 'cello, *n.* violoncello. **cellist, 'cellist,** *n.* (abbr.)
cellophane, *n.* transparent wrapping material made from wood-pulp. (proprietary name)
cellule, *n.* small cell. **cellular,** *a.* containing cells; of open texture. **cellulate, cellulated,** *aa.* composed of cells. **cellulation,** *n.* **celluloid,** *n.* substance like ivory made from gun-cotton and camphor. **cellulose,** *n.* starch-like carbohydrate forming cell walls of plants. **cellulous,** *a.* (*cell*+dim.)
celt, *n.* prehistoric edged implement of stone or bronze.
Celt, *n.* member of any of peoples comprising Irish, Welsh, Scottish Gaels, Bretons etc. **Celtic,** *a.* and *n.* (language) of Celts. **celticism,** *n.* Celtic custom or idiom. **celtomania,** *n.* mania for Celtic ways. **celtophobia,** *n.* fear of Celts. (L. *Celta*)
cement, *n.* mixture of lime and water applied as paste and drying hard like stone, mortar; substance used to stick things; bony covering of tooth-fang; bond of union.—*v.t.* join with cement; unite firmly. (L. *caementum*, stone chippings)
cemetery, *n.* burial-ground other than churchyard. (Gk. *koimaein*, put to sleep)
cenobite, same as coenobite.
cenotaph, *n.* monument to one who is buried elsewhere. (Gk. *kenos*, empty; *taphos*, tomb)
censer, *n.* pan in which incense is burned. **cense,** *v.t.* burn incense before. (*incense*)
censor, *n.* official who examines plays and books in order to suppress what is immoral or offensive; one who examines news reports and letters in war-time to prevent leakage of vital information; one who censures, critic; ancient Roman magistrate with charge of public morals; (*psycho-anal.*) power preventing elements in unconscious from entering into consciousness.—*v.t.* examine as censor. **censorship,** *n.* **censorial,** *a.* of censor. **censorious,** *a.* fault-finding, given to judging others. **censure,** *n.* expression of disapproval or blame; (*Shake.*) opinion, judgment.—*v.t.* and *i.* condemn as wrong; reprimand; (*Shake.*) give opinion (of). (L.)
census, *n.* official counting of inhabitants of country. (L.)
cent, *n.* American coin worth hundredth part of dollar, about ½*d.* **per c.,** in every hundred. **c. per c.,** interest as great as principal. **cental,** *n.* weight of 100 lb. (L. *centum*, hundred)
centaur, *n.* (*fem.* **centauress**) fabulous monster, half man, half horse; expert horseman; a southern constellation. **centaury,** *n.* a medicinal herb. (Gk. *kentauros*)
centavo, *n.* small S. American coin, $\frac{1}{100}$ peso. (Sp.)
centenary, *a.* of a hundred years.—*n.* hundredth anniversary; a hundred years. **centenarian,** *a.* and *n.* (person) a hundred years old. **centennial,** *a.* having lived or lasted a hundred years; happening every hundred years.—*n.* hundredth anniversary. (L. *centum*, hundred)
center, see **centre.**
centesimal, *a.* counting or counted by hundredths.
centiare, *n.* square metre. (*are*)
centigrade, *a.* using thermometer scale with freezing-point 0°, boiling-point 100°. (L. *centum*, hundred; *gradus*, step)
centigram, centigramme, *n.* hundredth part of gramme. **centilitre,** *n.* hundredth part of litre. (L. *centum*, hundred)

centillion, *n.* hundredth power of million, 1 with 600 ciphers; (in U.S. and France) hundredth power of thousand, 1 with 300 ciphers.
centime, *n.* French coin, $\frac{1}{100}$ franc. (F.)
centimetre, *n.* hundredth part of metre.
centipede, *n.* small segmented animal with many legs. (L. *centum*, hundred: *pes*, foot)
centner, *n.* German measure of weight, about 1 cwt. (G.)
cento, *n.* poem composed of lines from other authors, composition made up of quotations. (L.=patchwork)
central, *a.* of, at, in, the centre; important, cardinal. **c. heating**, by pipes filled with steam from central boiler. **centrality**, *n.* **centralism**, *n.* policy of centralizing. **centralist**, *n.* **centralize**, *v.t.* bring to centre; concentrate (administration, organization) at single centre. **centralization**, *n.*
centre, center, *n.* middle point; middle part, interior; pivot; pin on which work turns on lathe; point of concentration, source; political moderates.—*a.* of, at, centre.—*v.t.* and *i.* place in centre; concentrate; be fixed. **c. of gravity**, point in body about which all parts balance one another. **c.-bit**, *n.* kind of boring tool. **c.-board**, *n.* keel that can be raised within hull, yacht with this. **c.-forward**, *n.* (*football*) middle forward. **c.-piece**, *n.* central ornament. **centric**, *a.* at, near, from, centre. **centricity**, *n.* relation to centre. **centring, centreing, centering**, *n.* framework to support arch etc. while under construction. (Gk. *kentron*, spike)
centrifugal, *a.* tending to move away from centre. **c. force**, tending to make body moving in curve fly off at tangent. **c. machine, centrifuge**, *n.* machine which by whirling separates cream from milk etc. (L. *centrum*, centre; *fugere*, flee)
centripetal, *a.* tending to move towards centre. (L. *centrum*, centre; *petere*, seek)
centuple, centuplicate, *aa.* and *nn.* hundredfold (amount).—*vv.t.* multiply by a hundred. (L. *centum*, hundred; *plicare*, fold)
century, *n.* period of a hundred years; set of a hundred; a hundred runs at cricket; company of Roman legion. **c. plant**, American aloe. **sixth, nineteenth, century etc.**, A.D. 501–600, 1801–1900 etc., inclusive. **centurion**, *n.* officer commanding Roman century. (L. *centum*, hundred)
cephalic, *a.* of the head. **c. index**, proportion of length of head to its breadth. **cephalalgia**, *n.* headache. **cephalopod**, *n.* mollusc with tentacles attached to head. **cephalothorax**, *n.* coalesced head and thorax of spider etc. (Gk. *kephalē*, head)
ceramics, *n.pl.* art of pottery. **ceramic**, *a.* **ceramist**, *n.* (Gk. *keramos*, pottery)
cerastes, *n.* the horned viper. (Gk. *keras*, horn)
cere, *n.* wax-like membrane at base of bird's beak. (L. *cera*, wax)
cereal, *a.* and *n.* (of) corn or edible grain. (L. *Ceres*, goddess of corn)
cerebrum, *n.* brain proper, front part of brain. **cerebral**, *a.* **cerebration**, *n.* action of brain. **cerebellum**, *n.* hinder part of brain. **cerebellar**, *a.* **cerebro-spinal**, *a.* of brain and spinal cord. **cerebro-spinal meningitis**, spotted fever. (L.)
cerecloth, *n.* waxed cloth for wrapping dead body. **cerement**, *n.* cerecloth; (*pl.*) grave-clothes. (L. *cera*, wax)
ceremony, *n.* sacred rite; formal observance or procedure; usage of courtesy; (*Shake.*) symbol of state; omen. **stand on c.**, insist on conventions. **ceremonial**, *a.* of or with ceremony, formal.—*n.* set of rites or ceremonies. **ceremonialism**, *n.* regard for forms and ceremonies. **ceremonialist**, *n.* **ceremonious**, *a.* observant of ceremony, punctilious; marked by formality. (L. *caerimonia*)
ceriph, same as **serif.**
cerise, *a.* and *n.* cherry colour. (F.)
cerium, *n.* a metallic element. (discovered just after planet *Ceres*)
cero-, from Gk. *kēros*, wax, used in **cerography**, *n.* art of writing on wax, painting with wax colours; **ceroplastics**, *n.pl.* wax-modelling, **ceroplastic**, *a.*
certain, *a.* sure, positive; unerring, reliable; sure to happen, inevitable; definite, fixed; some, one. **for c.**, assuredly. **of a c. age**, no longer young. **cert**, *n.* (*sl.*) thing certain to happen. **certainly**, *adv.* undoubtedly; infallibly; yes. **certainty**, *n.* being certain; undoubted fact; absolute conviction. (L. *certus*)
certes, *adv.* (*arch.*) assuredly. (O.F.)
certie, *adv.* (*Scot.*) certainly.
certify, *v.t.* declare in writing, attest formally; assure; officially declare insane. **certifiable**, *a.* **certificate**, *n.* document formally attesting fact; testimonial of character or qualifications.—*v.t.* furnish with certificate. **certification**, *n.* (L. *certus*, certain; *facere*, make)
certiorari, *n.* writ for transference of hearing to higher court. (L.)
certitude, *n.* feeling certain.
cerulean, *a.* deep blue; sky-blue. (L. *caeruleus*)
cerumen, *n.* wax of ear. **ceruminous**, *a.* (L. *cera*, wax)
ceruse, *n.* white lead. (L. *cerussa*)
cervical, *a.* of neck. (L. *cervix*, neck)
cervine, *a.* of, like, deer. (L. *cervus*, deer)
cesarevitch, cesarewitch, *n.* czar's eldest son. (Russ.)

cess, *n.* tax, rate. **bad c. to you**, (*Ir.*) bad luck to you. **out of all c.**, (*Shake.*) excessively. (*assess*)
cessation, *n.* stoppage, pause. **cesser**, *n.* (*law*) discontinuance. (*cease*)
cession, *n.* ceding, giving up. **cessionary**, *n.* assign. (*cede*)
cesspit, *n.* midden. **cesspool**, *n.* pit to receive house drainage.
cestoid, *n.* flat intestinal worm. (Gk. *kestos*, girdle; *eidos*, form)
cestus, *n.* ancient loaded boxing-glove. (L.)
cetacean, *a.* and *n.* (animal) of whale family. **cetaceous**, *a.* **ceteosaur**, **ceteosaurus**, *n.* huge extinct lizard. (Gk. *kētos*, whale)
ceteris paribus, other things being equal. (L.)
Chablis, *n.* a French white wine. (place)
chabuk, **chabouk**, *n.* Persian horse-whip. **c. sowar**, rough-rider. (Hind.)
Chadband, *n.* unctuous hypocrite. (name in Dickens)
chafe, *v.t.* and *i.* rub (limb) to restore warmth; make or become sore by rubbing, gall; irritate, feel irritation, fret.—*n.* sore; irritated state. **chafing-dish**, *n.* vessel for heating or cooking food on table. (L. *calēre*, be hot; *facere*, make)
chafer, *n.* kinds of beetle, cockchafer. (O.E. *cefer*)
chaff, *n.* husks of grain; chopped hay or straw; worthless stuff.—*v.t.* chop (straw). (O.E. *ceaf*)
chaff, *n.* good-natured teasing, banter. —*v.t.* banter.
chaffer, *v.i.* bargain, haggle. (O.E. *céap*, price; *faru*, way)
chaffinch, *n.* a small song-bird. (*chaff*; *finch*)
chagrin, *n.* mortification, vexation.—*v.t.* disappoint deeply. (*shagreen*)
chai, *n.* woman. (Gipsy)
chain, *n.* series of connected links; fetters, bond; measuring-line; its length, 66 ft.; sequence, series; (*pl.*, *naut.*) plates on ship's side to which shrouds are fastened.—*v.t.* fasten, secure, with chain; unite closely; (*Shake.*) embrace. **c.-armour**, **c.-mail**, *nn.* armour of interlaced steel rings. **c.-bridge**, *n.* suspension bridge. **c.-shot**, *n.* shot joined by chain for cutting rigging. **c.-store**, *n.* one of series of shops owned by one firm. (L. *catena*)
chair, *n.* separate seat for one; seat of authority, professorship; steel block holding rail on sleeper; chairman.—*v.t.* install, carry aloft, in chair. **c.-days**, *n.pl.* (*Shake.*) time of repose. **chairman**, *n.* (*pl.* **chairmen**, *fem.* **chairwoman**) person who presides over meeting; president of board or committee; man who draws bath-chair. **chairmanship**. *n.* (Gk. *kathedra*)
chaise, *n.* light pleasure or travelling carriage. **c. *longue***, long chair with support for legs, couch. (F.)
chal, *n.* man, fellow. (Gipsy)
chalcedony, *n.* precious stone of quartz kind. (Gk. *chalkēdōn*)
chalco-, from Gk. *chalkos*, copper, used in **chalcography**, *n.* art of engraving on copper; **chalcopyrite**, *n.* a copper ore.
chaldron, *n.* measure of coals, 36 bushels. (*cauldron*)
chalet, *n.* Swiss wooden cottage; villa in this style; urinal. (F.)
chalice, *n.* cup; communion cup. **chaliced**, *a.* cup-shaped. (*calix*)
chalk, *n.* white substance, carbonate of lime; crayon.—*v.t.* mark, rub, with chalk. **by a long c.**, (*colloq.*) by far. **c.-stone**, *n.* gouty concretion in joints. (L. *calx*, lime)
challenge, *v.t.* summon to fight or contest; claim (attention); call in question, take exception to; (of sentry) hail and interrogate; (*Shake.*) accuse.—*n.* act of challenging; summons to contest; defiance. (L. *calumnia*, false accusation)
challis, *n.* soft dress-fabric.
chalybeate, *a.* (of water) impregnated with iron. (Gk. *chalups*, steel)
Cham, *n.* (*Shake.*) Khan. **Great C.**, autocrat (used of Dr. Johnson).
chamber, *n.* room; deliberative body, division of legislature; debating-room of this; cavity, compartment; part of gun-bore containing charge; chamber-pot; (*Shake.*) metropolis; small cannon. **c. concert, music**, suitable for room but not for hall. **c.-pot**, *n.* vessel for urine. **chamberer**, *n.* (*Shake.*) gallant. **chambering**, *n.* (*arch.*) lewd behaviour. **chamberlain**, *n.* officer in charge of household of sovereign or noble; treasurer of city or corporation. **chambermaid**, *n.* hotel maid attending bedrooms. (L. *camera*)
chameleon, *n.* small lizard changing its colour to that of its surroundings; inconstant person. (Gk. *chamai*, on ground; *leōn*, lion)
chamfer, *n.* flat surface made by paring off angle, bevel.—*v.t.* make chamfer on; channel, flute. (O.F. *chanfraindre*)
chamois, *n.* wild mountain antelope. (also **c.-leather**) soft pliable leather; (F.)
chamomile, same as **camomile**.
champ, *v.t.* and *i.* munch noisily; mouth with, make, chewing action.
champagne, *n.* kinds of sparkling white wine. *fine c.*, liqueur brandy. (French district)
champaign, *n.* open country, level expanse. (L. *campania*)
champerty *n.* offence of aiding another's lawsuit in order to share in gains from it. **champertous**, *a.* (L. *campus*, field; *pars*, part)
champion, *n.* one who fights for

another; one who upholds a cause; hero; competitor successful against all others.—*v.t.* defend; uphold cause of; (*Shake.*) challenge.—*a.* (*vulg.*) first-class. **championship,** *n.* (L. *campus*, field)

champlevé, *n.* and *a.* (enamel) bearing indentations filled with colour. (F.)

chance, *n.* course of events; fortune, luck, accident; opportunity, possibility; risk; (*arch.*) event.—*a.* accidental.—*v.i.* and *t.* happen; risk. **c. upon,** light upon unexpectedly. **stand a c.,** have a prospect. **the main c.,** money-making. (L. *cadere*, fall)

chancel, *n.* eastern part of church, where altar is placed. (L. *cancelli*, lattice-bars)

chancellor, *n.* kinds of high state or law official; head of university; chief minister of state in Germany; (*Scot.*) foreman of jury; (*Shake.*) secretary. **bishop's c.,** law officer of diocese. **C. of the Exchequer,** British minister of finance. **Lord (High) C.,** chief English judge and chairman of House of Lords. **chancellorship,** *n.* **chancellery, chancellory,** *n.* chancellor's department or office; office attached to an embassy. (L.L. *cancellarius*)

chance-medley, *n.* (*law*) justifiable homicide; inadvertency. (O.F. *chance medlée*, mingled chance)

Chancery, *n.* a division of the High Court of Justice; office for public records; (*Amer.*) court of equity. **in C.,** under control of Lord Chancellor; (*boxing*) with head held under opponent's arm. (*chancellery*)

chancre, *n.* syphilitic ulcer. **chancrous,** *a.* (F.)

chancy, *a.* hazardous, risky.

chandelier, *n.* branched hanging support for lights. **chandler,** *n.* dealer in candles, oil, soap etc. **chandlery,** *n.* chandler's shop or wares. (L. *candela*, candle)

change, *v.t.* and *i.* make or become different, alter; interchange, exchange; put on different clothes; give or get money change for; (*Shake.*) change colour. — *n.* alteration; variety; substitution; fresh clothing; money in small coins, balance returned after payment; (*Shake.*) exchange; fickleness; (*pl.*) different orders in which peal of bells can be rung. **Change, 'Change,** *n.* place where merchants meet. **c. colour,** blush or turn pale. **c. of life,** menopause. **get no c. out of,** (*sl.*) fail to score off. **c.-house,** *n.* (*Scot.*) tavern. **changeable,** *a.* prone to change, inconstant; (*Shake.*) varying in colour, shot. **changeful,** *a.* often changing. **changeless,** *a.* constant, immutable. **changeling,** *n.* child, esp. elf-child, substituted for another; (*Shake.*) fickle person. (L. *cambire*, barter)

channel, *n.* bed of stream; broad strait; deeper part of waterway; groove, furrow; means of passing or conveying; (*Shake.*) gutter.—*v.t.* form channel in; groove. **the C.,** the English Channel. (*canal*)

channel, *n.* projection from ship's side to spread shrouds and keep them clear of bulwarks. (*chain-wale*)

chanson, *n.* song. (F.)

chant, *n.* song; sacred music to which prose is sung; sing-song intonation. —*v.i.* and *t.* sing; recite in singing manner; sell (horses) fraudulently. (L. *canere*, sing)

chantage, *n.* blackmail. (F.)

chanter, *n.* one who chants; bagpipe's melody-pipe with finger-holes.

chanterelle, *n.* yellow mushroom. (F.)

chantey, see **chanty.**

chanticleer, *n.* name for domestic cock. (*chant*; *clear*)

chantress, *n.* female singer.

chantry, *n.* endowment for singing of masses; priest, chapel, so endowed.

chanty, chantey, shanty, *n.* rhythmical song to which sailors haul on ropes.

chaos, *n.* formless void preceding creation; utter confusion, muddle. **chaotic,** *a.* utterly without order or arrangement. **chaotically,** *adv.* (Gk.)

chap, *n.* crack, soreness, in skin, caused by cold; (*Scot.*) knock.—*v.t.* and *i.* affect with, develop, chaps; (*Scot.*) knock. (M.E. *chappen*)

chap, chop, *n.* (us. *pl.*) jaw, cheek. **c.-fallen,** *a.* with jaw hanging down, dispirited.

chap, *n.* (*colloq.*) fellow. (*chapman*)

chaparajos, chaparejos, chaps, *nn. pl.* cowboys' leather leg-coverings. (*chaparral*)

chaparral, *n.* dense thorny bush or scrub. (Sp. *chaparra*, evergreen oak)

chap-book, *n.* small book of ballads etc., formerly hawked by chapman.

chape, *n.* metal tip of scabbard; part attaching scabbard to belt. (*cap*)

chapel, *n.* place of worship attached to institution or house; division of church with its own altar; place of worship of dissenters; printing-office, association of journeyman printers. **c. of ease,** for worshippers far from parish church. *chapelle ardente*, chamber for lying in state, lit with candles. **chapelry,** *n.* district served by chapel. (L.L. *cappa*, cloak+dim., first chapel having St. Martin's cloak as relic)

chaperon, *n.* lady accompanying girl on social occasions for propriety.—*v.t.* attend as chaperon. **chaperonage,** *n.* (F.)

chapiter, *n.* (*arch.*) capital of column. (*chapter*)

chaplain, *n.* clergyman attached to regiment, warship, institution, family etc. **chaplaincy,** *n.* office of chaplain. (*chapel*)

chaplet, *n.* wreath or circlet for head; string of beads, minor rosary. (O.F. *chape*, head-dress+dim.)

chapman, *n.* (*arch.*) hawker, pedlar; trader; (*Shake.*) customer. (O.E. *céap*, barter)
chaprasi, same as **chuprassi.**
chapter, *n.* main division of book; assembly of canons of cathedral; organized branch of society or fraternity. **c. of accidents,** unforeseen course of events. **c.-house,** *n.* room for meetings of cathedral chapter. (L. *caput*, head+dim.)
char, *n.* fish of trout kind.
char, *v.t.* and *i.* blacken by burning, scorch; burn to charcoal.
char, *v.i.* and *t.* act as charwoman, scrub and clean.—*n.* job of work, task; (*colloq.*) charwoman. (O.E. *cerran*, turn)
charabanc, char-à-banc, *n.* long open coach with seats facing forward. (F. *char à bancs*, carriage with benches)
character, *n.* symbol, letter; script; nature, sort; moral qualities, disposition; moral strength, backbone; reputation; statement of person's qualities, testimonial; person in play or novel; role, guise; person of marked individuality or eccentricity; (*Shake.*) writing.—*v.t.* inscribe; describe. **in c.,** in keeping with part played. **charact,** *n.* (*Shake.*) distinctive mark. **characteristic,** *a.* typical.—*n.* distinguishing quality or trait. **characteristically,** *adv.* **characterize,** *v.t.* describe, designate; be characteristic of, mark. **characterization,** *n.* **characterless,** *a.* ordinary, undistinguished. **charactery,** *n.* writing. (Gk. *charassein*, engrave)
charade, *n.* game of guessing word from acted representation of syllables and whole. (F.)
charcoal, *n.* form of carbon got by partially burning wood.
chare, same as **char.**
charge, *v.t.* and *i.* attack at run, make onset (on); load, fill, saturate; fill with electricity; lay task on, enjoin; accuse; ask as price, enter cost to; (*heraldry*) place device on.—*n.* impetuous attack or rush; load, filling; task, commission; trust, custody; thing or person entrusted; accusation; price, expense; (*heraldry*) device; (*Shake.*) weight, importance. **c. one with, lay to one's c.,** accuse him of. **give one in c.,** hand him over to police. **c.-house,** *n.* (*Shake.*) boarding-school. **chargeable,** *a.* *chargé d'affaires,* (*pl.* *chargés d'affaires*) ambassador at minor court, deputy ambassador. **charger,** *n.* officer's horse; large flat dish. (L. *carrus*, wagon)
charily, *adv.* reluctantly; cautiously. **chariness,** *n.* being chary.
chariot, *n.* triumphal car; two-wheeled car used in ancient fighting; 18th-century four-wheeled carriage. **charioteer,** *n.* driver of chariot. (O.F.)
charity, *n.* love of one's fellow men; disposition to think well of others; liberality to the poor, almsgiving; alms. **charitable,** *a.* of, for, charity; benevolent; lenient in judging others. **charitably,** *adv.* (L. *carus*, dear)
charivari, *n.* medley of sounds, rough discordant music; hurly-burly. (F.)
charlady, *n.* charwoman.
charlatan, *n.* impostor; quack. **charlatanism, charlatanry,** *nn.* (It. *ciarlare*, patter)
Charleston, *n.* American dance with side-kicks from knee. (town)
charlock, *n.* wild mustard. (O.E. *cerlic*)
charlotte, *n.* pudding of stewed fruit covered with bread-crumbs. **c. russe,** custard enclosed in sponge-cake. (F.)
charm, *n.* magic verse or formula; object bringing luck, amulet; alluring quality, fascination.—*v.t.* influence by spell, enchant; protect by magic; tame (snake); delight, captivate. **charming,** *a.* delightful, attractive. (L. *carmen*, song)
charneco, *n.* (*Shake.*) kind of wine.
charnel-house, *n.* vault containing corpses or bones. (L. *caro*, flesh)
charpoy, *n.* (*Anglo-Ind.*) light Indian bedstead. (Hind. *charpai*)
chart, *n.* navigator's sea-map, showing depth of water etc.; diagram, tabulated statement.—*v.t.* make chart of. (L. *charta*, a paper)
charter, *n.* document granting rights, privileges, ownership of land etc.—*v.t.* grant charter or privilege to; hire. **c.-party,** *n.* contract for temporary hire of ship. (*chart*)
chartism, *n.* movement for extension of political power to working class, embodied in People's Charter of 1838. **chartist,** *n.* (*charter*)
chartography, same as **cartography.**
chartreuse, *n.* kinds of liqueur; Carthusian monastery. (place)
chartulary, same as **cartulary.**
charwoman, *n.* woman who works by the day at house-cleaning. (*char*)
chary, *a.* cautious; sparing; (*Shake.*) careful and scrupulous.—*adv.* (*Shake.*) carefully. (O.E. *cearu*, care)
chase, *v.t.* engrave, emboss. (*enchase*)
chase, *n.* frame for holding page of type; groove. (L. *capsa*, case)
chase, *v.t.* pursue, run after; drive (away), dispel.—*n.* chasing, hunting; unenclosed game-preserve. **c. yourself,** (*Amer. sl.*) clear out. **chaser,** *n.* pursuer; drink of water etc. taken after neat spirits; (formerly) gun at bow or stern. (L. *capere*, take)
chasm, *n.* deep cleft, fissure; abyss; wide difference in opinions etc.; hiatus. (Gk. *chasma*)
chassé, *n.* rapid gliding step in dancing.—*v.i.* perform chassé. (F.)
chassepot, *n.* obsolete type of French rifle. (inventor)

chassis, *n.* (*pl.* same) base framework of carriage or motor-car; aeroplane's under-carriage. (F.)
chaste, *a.* pure, abstaining from unlawful sexual intercourse; virgin; modest; (*art*) restrained, unadorned; (*Shake.*) unmarried. (L. *castus*)
chasten, *v.t.* correct by suffering, discipline; purify, refine; restrain, subdue. (*chaste*)
chastise, *v.t.* punish; beat. **chastisement,** *n.* (L. *castigare*)
chastity, *n.* chasteness.
chasuble, *n.* sleeveless vestment worn over alb by priest celebrating mass. (L. *casa*, cottage+dim.)
chat, *v.i.* talk in easy familiar manner, —*n.* light talk, gossip; kinds of bird. (*chatter*)
château, *n.* (*pl.* **châteaux**) French country house. **chatelaine,** *n.* lady of house, hostess; chain hanging from woman's belt for keys etc. (F.)
chatta, *n.* (*Anglo-Ind.*) umbrella. (Hind.)
chattel, *n.* (us. *pl.*) goods, possessions; (*law*) movable property. (*cattle*)
chatter, *v.i.* talk aimlessly and rapidly; (of animal) utter rapid cries; (of teeth etc.) rattle together.—*n.* idle rapid talk; sound of chattering. **chatterbox,** *n.* incessant talker. (imit.)
chatty, *n.* (*Anglo-Ind.*) common earthenware water-pot. (Hind. *chāti*)
chatty, *a.* talkative.
chaudron, *n.* (*Shake.*) entrails. (O.F. *chaudun*)
chauff, chaufe, (*Spens.*) forms of **chafe.**
chauffer, *n.* metal basket holding fire; portable furnace. (L. *calēre*, be hot; *facere*, make)
chauffeur, *n.* (*fem.* **chauffeuse**) motor-car driver. (F.)
chaumontel, *n.* large kind of pear. (place)
chaunt, same as **chant.**
chaussure, *n.* footgear. (F.)
chauvinism, *n.* aggressive patriotism, jingoism. **chauvinist,** *n.* and *a.* **chauvinistic,** *a.* **chauvinistically,** *adv.* (*Chauvin*, name in play)
chavender, *n.* chub.
chaw, *v.t.* (*vulg.*) chew, munch.—*n.* quid of tobacco. **c. up,** (*Amer.*) defeat utterly; injure badly. **c.-bacon,** *n.* yokel. (*chew*)
cheap, *a.* inexpensive, low-priced; of little worth or account; (*colloq.*) out of sorts.—*adv.* cheaply. **c.-jack,** *n.* travelling hawker. **cheapen,** *v.t.* and *i.* make or become cheap, depreciate; (*arch.*) haggle. (O.E. *céap*, barter)
cheat, *n.* fraud, deception; cheater.—*v.t.* and *i.* swindle, deceive; play unfairly. **cheater,** *n.* one who cheats; (*Shake.*) officer who collected fines due to Exchequer. (*escheat*)
check, *n.* cross-lined pattern.
check, *n.* sudden stoppage; reverse, set-back; control, supervision; ticket, token, bill; cheque; (*chess*) threatening of king; (*Shake.*) reproof.—*v.t.* and *i.* bring, come, to a stand; restrain, retard; test accuracy of; admonish, reprove; (*chess*) threaten (king); (*Amer.*) register (luggage); (*Shake.*, of hawk) leave quarry for chance bird. **hand in one's cc.,** (*sl.*) die. (Pers. *shah*, king)
checker, see **chequer. checkers,** *n.pl.* (*Amer.*) game of draughts.
checklaton, *n.* rich kind of cloth. (O.E. *ciclaton*)
checkmate, *n.* winning move at chess; complete frustration.—*v.t.* defeat at chess; discomfit, thwart. (Arab. *shah mata*, king is dead)
cheddar, *n.* kind of cheese. (place)
chee-chee, *n.* (*Anglo-Ind.*) minced English spoken by Eurasians. Hind. *chhī-chhī*, fie!)
cheek, *n.* side of face below eye; (*colloq.*) impudence.—*v.t.* (*colloq.*) address impudently. **c. by jowl,** side by side. **cheeky,** *a.* (*colloq.*) impudent. (O.E. *céce*)
cheep, *n.* faint shrill sound of young bird etc.—*v.i.* utter cheep. (imit.)
cheer, *n.* frame of mind, spirits; food, fare; encouragement; shout of applause, hurrah; (*Shake.*) face, aspect. —*v.t.* and *i.* gladden; encourage; applaud, shout hurrah. **c. up,** hearten; recover spirits. **cheerful,** *a.* in good spirits. **cheerio,** *int.* (*sl.*) goodbye. **cheerless,** *a.* dismal, depressing. **cheerly,** *adv.* (*naut.*) heartily. **cheery,** *a.* lively, genial. **cheerily,** *adv.* (L.L. *cara*, face)
cheese, *v.t.* **c. it,** (*sl.*) stop it.
cheese, *n.* **the c.,** (*sl.*) the correct thing. **cheesy,** *a.* (*sl.*) stylish. (Hind. *chīz*, thing)
cheese, *n.* curds of milk pressed into hard mass. **green c.,** cheese not yet dried. **c.-paring,** *n.* rind of cheese. —*a.* stingy. **cheesecake,** *n.* kind of small sweet cake. **cheesecloth,** *n.* loosely woven cotton cloth. **cheesy,** *a.* like cheese. (L. *caseus*)
cheetah, *n.* kind of leopard used for hunting in India. (Hind. *chita*)
chef, *n.* male head-cook. *c.-d'œuvre*, *n.* masterpiece. (F.)
cheiro-, same as **chiro-.**
cheiropteran, *n.* bat. **cheiropterous,** *a.* (Gk. *cheir*, hand; *pteron*, wing)
Cheka, *n.* Russian secret police, superseded by Ogpu. (Russ.)
chela, *n.* Buddhist novice or disciple. (Hind.)
chela, *n.* claw-like pincer of crab etc. (Gk. *chēlē*)
chelonian, *a.* and *n.* (of the order of) tortoise or turtle. (Gk. *chelōnē*)
chemical, *a.* of, made by, chemistry.—*n.* substance used in chemistry or got by chemical process.
chemin de fer, (*colloq.*) **chemmy,** *n.* kind of baccarat. (F.)

chemise, *n.* woman's undergarment, shift. **chemisette**, *n.* kind of bodice; lace etc. filling neck opening of dress. (L.L. *camisia*, shirt)
chemist, *n.* expert in chemistry; one who sells drugs, apothecary. **chemistry**, *n.* science which treats of the properties of substances and their combinations and reactions. (*alchemist*)
chenille, *n.* velvety cord used for trimming. (F.=caterpillar)
cheque, *n.* money order on bank. **c.-book**, *n.* book of forms for this.
chequer, **checker**, *n.* pattern like chess-board, with alternate light and dark squares.—*v.t.* mark with this pattern, variegate; diversify. (*check*)
cherish, *v.t.* tend lovingly, foster; keep in mind. (L. *carus*, dear)
cheroot, *n.* cigar with both ends open. (Tamil *shuruttu*, roll)
cherry, *n.* small stone-fruit; tree bearing it.—*a.* bright red. **c. brandy**, liqueur made by steeping cherries in brandy. **c.-pie**, *n.* garden heliotrope. **c.-pit**, *n.* (*Shake.*) game of throwing stones into small hole. (Gk. *kerasos*)
chersonese, *n.* peninsula. (Gk. *chersos*, dry; *nēsos*, island)
chert, *n.* flint-like quartz.
cherub, *n.* (*pl.* **cherubim**) angel of second order, angelic being; (*pl.* **cherubs**) winged child or child's head; beautiful child. **cherubic**, *a.* **cherubically**, *adv.* **cherubin**, *n.* (*Shake.*) cherub. (Heb. *k'rub*)
chervil, *n.* garden herb used in salads. (Gk. *chairephullon*)
chess, *n.* one of the flooring planks of a pontoon bridge.
chess, *n.* game with 32 pieces on chequered board of 64 squares. **c.-board**, **c.-man**, *nn.* (*check*)
chessel, *n.* cheese-making mould.
chest, *n.* large strong box; treasury; part of body enclosed by ribs. **c. of drawers**, frame with several drawers. **c.-note**, *n.* lowest sound of voice. (Gk. *kistē*)
chesterfield, *n.* kinds of overcoat and couch. (person)
chestnut, *n.* glossy brown nut; tree bearing it; chestnut colour or horse; stale story or joke.—*a.* deep reddish-brown. (Gk. *kastanea*)
cheval-glass, *n.* full-length mirror in swinging frame. (F. *cheval*, horse)
chevalier, *n.* knight; gallant. *c. d'industrie*, adventurer, swindler. (L. *caballus*, horse)
chevaux-de-frise, *n.pl.* line of iron spikes. (F.)
chevelure, *n.* head of hair. (F.)
cheveril, *n.* (*Shake.*) kid-leather. (L. *caper*, goat+dim.)
chevet, *n.* apse; group of apses. (F.)
cheviot, *n.* cloth made from wool of sheep of Cheviot Hills.
chevron, *n.* V-shaped stripe on N.C.O.'s arm indicating rank; (*heraldry*) bent bar like inverted V. (F.)
chevrotain, **chevrotin**, *n.* small musk-deer. (L. *caper*, goat+double dim.)
chevy, same as **chivy**.
chew, *v.t.* and *i.* grind between teeth, masticate; ponder, think over.—*n.* act of chewing; quid of tobacco. **c. the rag**, (*sl.*) grouse. **chewing-gum**, *n.* flavoured gum for chewing. (O.E. *cēowan*)
chewet, *n.* (*Shake.*) chough. (F. *chouette*, owl)
Chianti, *n.* a red Italian wine. (place)
chiaroscuro, *n.* effects of light and shade; treatment of this in art; use of contrast and relief in literature. (It.)
chiasmus, *n.* figure of speech by which order of words in first of two parallel clauses is reversed in second, e.g. 'To stop too fearful and too faint to go.' (Gk. *chiasmos*, cross arrangement)
chibouk, **chibouque**, *n.* long Turkish tobacco-pipe. (Turk. *chibuk*, tube)
chic, *a.* stylish.—*n.* elegance, style; effectiveness. (F.)
chicane, *n.* chicanery; (*bridge*) hand with no trumps.—*v.i.* and *t.* use chicanery, trick. **chicanery**, *n.* underhand dealing, verbal subterfuge; legal trickery. (F.)
chick, *n.* (*Anglo-Ind.*) bamboo screen-blind. (Hind. *chik*)
chick, *n.* newly hatched bird; young child. **chickabiddy**, *n.* term of endearment to child. (*chicken*)
chickadee, *n.* (*Amer.*) titmouse. (imit.)
chickaree, *n.* American red squirrel. (imit.)
chicken, *n.* (*Anglo-Ind.*) embroidery. (Pers. *chikin*, needlework)
chicken, *n.* young domestic fowl; youthful person; (*Amer.*) fowl of any age. **Mother Carey's c.**, stormy petrel. **c.-hearted**, *a.* cowardly. **c.-pox**, *n.* mild eruptive disease of children. (O.E. *cicen*)
chickling, *n.* kind of vetch. **chick-pea**, *n.* dwarf pea. (L. *cicer*, vetch)
chickweed, *n.* small white-flowered plant of pink family. (*chick*)
chicle, *n.* juice of sapodilla, main ingredient of chewing-gum. (Mex. *tzictli*)
chicory, *n.* blue-flowered plant; its powdered root, used to mix with coffee. (Gk. *kichōrion*)
chide, *v.t.* and *i.* (*past* **chid**, *p.p.* **chidden** or **chid**) find fault (with), rebuke, scold; (*Shake.*) resound, cry out. (O.E. *cīdan*)
chief, *n.* leader, commander; head of tribe or clan; (*heraldry*) upper part of shield.—*a.* principal, most important. **chiefly**, *adv.* mainly. **chieftain**, *n.* (*fem.* **chieftainess**) highland chief; robber captain. **chieftaincy**, **chieftainship**, *nn.* (L. *caput*, head)
chield, **chiel**, *n.* (*Scot.*) person.

chiff-chaff, *n.* bird of warbler family. (imit.)

chiffon, *n.* thin gauzy material; (*pl.*) frills. (F.)

chiffonier, *n.* cupboard with sideboard top. (F.)

chignon, *n.* mass of hair in pad at back of head, bun. (F.)

chigoe, *n.* W. Indian flea that burrows under skin, jigger. (W. Ind.)

chilblain, *n.* inflamed swelling on hands etc. due to cold. (*chill*; *blain*)

child, *n.* (*pl.* **children**) young human being; offspring; descendant; product; (also **childe,** *arch.*) youth of noble birth. **this c.,** (*sl.*) me. **with c.,** pregnant. **c.'s-play,** *n.* easy task. **childbed, childbirth,** *nn.* parturition, labour. **Childermas,** *n.* Holy Innocents' Day, 28 Dec. **childhood,** *n.* period between birth and puberty. **second childhood,** dotage. **childing,** *a.* (*Shake.*) fruitful. **childish,** *a.* of, suited to, a child; silly, trifling. **childless,** *a.* **childlike,** *a.* innocent, simple, candid, like a child. **childness,** *n.* (*Shake.*) childish ways. **childly,** *a.* and *adv.* (*poet.*) like a child. (O.E. *cild*)

chiliad, *n.* a thousand; a thousand years. **chiliasm,** *n.* doctrine of millennium. **chiliast,** *n.* **chiliastic,** *a.* (Gk. *chilioi*, a thousand)

chill, *n.* sensation of cold; illness caused by exposure to cold.—*a.* feeling cold; unemotional, formal.—*v.t.* and *i.* make, become, cold; harden (metal) by sudden cooling; depress. (O.E. *cele*)

chilli, chilly, *n.* dried pod of capsicum. (Mex.)

chillum, *n.* (*Anglo-Ind.*) bowl of hookah; hookah; smoking. **chillumchee,** *n.* wash-basin. (Hind. *chilam*)

chilly, *a.* feeling rather cold; sensitive to cold; unfriendly, frigid.—*adv.* in chill manner.

chime, chimb, *n.* rim formed by ends of staves of cask. (M.E. *chimbe*)

chime, *n.* harmonious sound of bell; harmony; correspondence; (*pl.*) set of bells.—*v.t.* and *i.* sound harmoniously; harmonize. **c. in,** join in, in agreement. (Gk. *kumbalon*, cymbal)

chimera, chimaera, *n.* fabled monster with lion's head, goat's body, and serpent's tail; wild impossible scheme or fancy; bogy. **chimerical,** *a.* fantastic, visionary. (Gk. *chimaira*)

chimere, *n.* bishop's long black robe. (O.F. *chamarre*)

chimney, *n.* passage for smoke, funnel; narrow vertical cleft in rock; (*Shake.*) fire-place. **c.-corner,** *n.* recess in fire-place. **c.-piece,** *n.* mantelpiece. **c.-pot,** *n.* pipe extending chimney at top. **c.-pot hat,** top hat. **c.-stack,** *n.* group of chimneys. **c.-sweep,** *n.* person who removes soot from chimney. (Gk. *kaminos*, furnace)

chimpanzee, *n.* African ape resembling man. (native)

chin, *n.* part of face below mouth.—*v.i.* (*sl.*) talk. (O.E. *cin*)

china, *n.* fine earthenware, porcelain.—*a.* made of this. **c.-clay,** *n.* kaolin. (country)

Chinaman, *n.* Chinese. **Chinatown,** *n.* Chinese quarter.

chinch, *n.* (*Amer.*) bed-bug. (L. *cimex*)

chinchilla, *n.* small S. American rodent; its soft grey fur. (*chinch*)

chin-chin, *int.* of farewell. (Chin. *ts'ing ts'ing*)

chincough, *n.* whooping-cough. (*chink*)

chine, *n.* backbone; cut of meat including this; ridge. (O.F. *eschine*)

chine, *n.* small ravine. (O.E. *cinu*)

Chinese, *a.* and *n.* (*pl.* same) (native, language) of China. **C. lantern,** collapsible paper kind. **C. white,** a white pigment. **Chinee, Chink,** *nn.* (*sl.*) Chinaman.

chink, *n.* narrow opening, crack, slit.

chink, *n.* clinking sound; (*sl.*) cash.—*v.i.* and *t.* clink. (imit.)

chinkapin, chinquapin, *n.* American dwarf chestnut. (Amer. Ind.)

chintz, *n.* cotton cloth printed in coloured designs. (pl. of Hind. *chint*, spotted cotton cloth)

chip, *n.* wrestling-trick.—*v.t.* trip.

chip, *n.* piece cut or broken off, splinter; chipped place; (*sl.*) counter; piece of money; (*pl.*) fried strips of potato; (*naut. sl.*) ship's carpenter.—*v.t.* and *i.* knock chip off; shape, make, by chipping; (*colloq.*) tease. **c. in,** (*sl.*) interrupt. **c. of the old block,** son like father. **c.-shot,** *n.* (*golf*) short lofted approach. (*chop*)

chipmunk, chipmuck, *n.* small striped American squirrel.

Chippendale, *n.* light style of drawing-room furniture. (maker)

chipper, *a.* (*Amer. sl.*) lively, cheerful.

chippy, *a.* (*sl.*) dry; seedy.

chiro-, from Gk. *cheir*, hand, used in **chirograph,** *n.* legal document formally signed; **chiromancer,** *n.* palmist, **chiromancy,** *n.* palmistry, hence **chiromantic,** *a.*; **chiropodist,** *n.* person skilled in **chiropody,** *n.* care and treatment of hands, feet, nails, corns etc.; **chiropractic,** *n.* manipulation of spine as method of curing disease, hence **chiropractor,** *n.*

chirp, *n.* sharp shrill note of bird.—*v.i.* utter this; talk cheerfully. **chirpy,** *a.* lively, cheerful. (imit.)

chirr, *n.* shrill rasping sound of grasshopper.—*v.i.* make this. (imit.)

chirrup, *v.i.* twitter; make clicking sound to horse.—*n.* chirruping sound. (*chirp*)

chirurgeon, chirurgery, chirurgical, *arch.* for **surgeon, surgery, surgical.**

chisel, *n.* tool with square cutting end.—*v.t.* cut, carve, with chisel; (*sl.*) cheat, swindle. **chiselled,** *a.* clear-cut. (L. *caedere*, cut)

chit, *n.* young child; little woman. (*kit*)
chit, *n.* (*Anglo-Ind.*) note, report; testimonial; voucher given for payment. (Sanskr. *chitra*, mark)
chit, *n.* (*prov.*) sprout. (O.E. *cíth*)
chital, *n.* Indian spotted deer. (Hind.)
chit-chat, *n.* trivial talk. (*chat*)
chitin, *n.* substance forming horny cover of beetles and crustaceans. **chitinous,** *a.* (Gk. *chitōn*, tunic)
chitter, *v.i.* (*Scot.*) shiver.
chitterling, *n.* (us. *pl.*) smaller intestines of pig etc. as food.
chitty, same as **chit.**
chivalry, *n.* medieval system of knighthood; body of knights; knightly qualities, bravery and courtesy, respect for women. **chivalrous,** *a.* of chivalry; brave, gallant; generous to the weak. (L. *caballus*, horse)
chive, *n.* herb of onion kind. (L. *cepa*, onion)
chivy, *n.* hunt; boys' chasing game.—*v.t.* and *i.* chase; scamper.
chlorine, *n.* non-metallic element, yellowish-green poison gas. **chloral,** *n.* a hypnotic and anaesthetic. **chlorate,** *n.* salt of chloric acid. **chloric, chlorous,** *aa.* of chlorine. **chloride,** *n.* compound of chlorine. **chlorinate,** *v.t.* bleach or disinfect with chlorine. **chlorination,** *n.* **chloroform,** *n.* colourless volatile liquid used as anaesthetic.—*v.t.* render insensible with chloroform. **chloroformist,** *n.* (Gk. *chlōros*, green)
chloro-, from Gk. *chlōros*, green, used in **chlorophyll,** *n.* green colouring-matter in plants; **chlorosis,** *n.* anaemia in young women.
chock, *n.* wooden block to keep cask etc. from rolling.—*v.t.* secure with chocks. **c.-a-block, c.-full,** *aa.* packed tight.
chocolate, *n.* paste of ground cacao seeds; sweetmeat, drink, made from this.—*a.* dark brown. (Mex. *chocolatl*)
choice, *n.* choosing, selection; alternative; thing chosen; choice part.—*a.* of picked quality, specially good; fastidious. (*choose*)
choir, *n.* organized band of singers, esp. belonging to church; part of church used by them, chancel.—*v.t.* and *i.* sing in chorus. (Gk. *choros*)
choke, *n.* centre part of artichoke.
choke, *v.t.* and *i.* stop breath of, stifle; block (up).—*n.* fit of choking; narrow part of choke-bore etc. **c. off,** discourage. **c.-bore,** *n.* shot-gun with bore narrowing towards muzzle. **c.-damp,** *n.* carbonic acid gas in mines. **choker,** *n.* cravat; high collar. (M.E. *choken*)
chokidar, *n.* (*Anglo-Ind.*) watchman. (Urdu *chaukidar*)
choky, *a.* tending to choke, esp. from emotion.
choky, *n.* (*sl.*) prison. (Hind. *chauki*, shed)
cholagogue, *n.* purgative expelling bile. (Gk. *cholē*, bile; *agein*, lead)
choler, *n.* bile; anger, irascibility; (*Shake.*) biliousness. (*cholera*)
cholera, *n.* (also **Asiatic** or **malignant c.**) infectious and deadly disease attacking bowels; (also **European** or **summer c.**) acute biliousness with diarrhoea, due to heat. (Gk.)
choleric, *a.* irascible; (*Shake.*) causing bile. (*choler*)
choliamb, *n.* iambic verse with last foot spondee, scazon. **choliambic,** *a.* (Gk. *chōlos*, lame)
chondri-, chondro-, from Gk. *chondros*, cartilage, used in **chondrify,** *v.t.* and *i.* change into cartilage; **chondrogenesis,** *n.* formation of cartilage; **chondroid,** *a.* like cartilage.
choose, *v.t.* and *i.* (*past* **chose,** *p.p.* **chosen**) pick out, select; decide, think fit; (*Shake.*) do as one likes. **cannot c. but,** (*arch.*) must. (O.E. *céosan*)
chop, *v.t.* and *i.* cut by striking, hack; (of waves) have jerky motion.—*n.* chopping stroke or motion; thick slice of meat containing rib. **c.-house,** *n.* cheap restaurant. (*chap*)
chop, *v.t.* and *i.* and *n.* change. **c. and change,** be inconstant. **c. logic,** bandy arguments.
chop, *n.* (*Anglo-Ind.*) seal, official stamp; licence; trade mark, brand. **first c.,** first-rate. (Hind. *chhāp*)
chop, *v.t.* (*Shake.*) clap, pop.
chop, see **chap.**
chop-chop, *adv.* (*pidgin English*) quickly. (Chin. *k'wai-k'wai*)
chopine, *n.* woman's thick-soled shoe of 17th century. (Sp. *chapin*)
chopper, *n.* short axe, cleaver.
choppy, *a.* (of sea) chopping, jerky.
chopstick, *n.* one of a pair of small sticks used in China instead of fork. (*chop-chop*; *stick*)
chop-suey, *n.* kind of Chinese stew. (Chin.=mixed bits)
choral, *a.* of, for, sung by, choir.—*n.* (also **chorale**) hymn tune.
chord, *n.* string of harp etc.; (*anat.*) string-like structure; (*geom.*) straight line joining ends of arc. **chordal,** *a.* (Gk. *chordē*)
chord, *n.* harmonious combination of simultaneous notes. **chordal,** *a.* (*accord*)
chore, *n.* (*Amer.*) piece of housework, odd job.—*v.i.* do chores. (*char*)
chorea, *n.* St. Vitus's dance. (L.)
choree, *n.* trochee. **choreic,** *a.* (Gk. *choreios*, for dance)
choreograph, choreographer, *nn.* designer of ballet. **choreography,** *n.* **choreographical,** *a.* (Gk. *choros*, dance; *graphein*, write)
choriambus, choriamb, *n.* four-syllabled foot, long-short-short-long. **choriambic,** *a.* (*choree*; *iambus*)
choric, *a.* of, for, a Greek chorus.
chorion, *n.* membrane enclosing foetus. (Gk.)

choripetalous, chorisepalous, *aa.* with petals, sepals, separated. (Gk. *chōris,* apart)
chorister, *n.* member of choir; choirboy; (*Amer.*) leader of choir.
choro-, from Gk. *chōra,* land, used in **chorography,** *n.* geographical description of a region; **chorology,** *n.* study of geographical distribution of plants and animals.
chortle, *v.i.* (*sl.*) chuckle exultantly.—*n.* chortling. (*chuckle; snort*)
chorus, *n.* company of singers and dancers forming background to play; band of singers, choir; thing sung or said by many at once; refrain.—*v.t.* and *i.* sing, speak, in chorus. **in c.,** all singing etc. together. (Gk. *choros*)
chose, chosen, see **choose.**
chose jugée, settled matter. (F.)
chota hazri, (*Anglo-Ind.*) light early breakfast. (Hind.)
chough, *n.* red-legged crow; (*Shake.*) jackdaw.
choultry, *n.* (*Anglo-Ind.*) caravanserai; colonnade. (Malayalam)
chouse, *v.t.* and *n.* (*colloq.*) swindle. (Turk. *chiaus,* envoy)
chow, *n.* (*Amer. army sl.*) food.
chow, *n.* Chinese breed of dog; (*Austral. sl.*) Chinese.
chow-chow, *n.* Chinese pickles. (Chin.)
chowder, *n.* (*Amer.*) stew of fish or clams with pork, onions, biscuits etc. (L. *calidus,* hot)
chowry, *n.* (*Anglo-Ind.*) fly-whisk. (Hind. *chaunri*)
chrematistic, *a.* of money-making.—*n.pl.* science of wealth. (Gk. *chrēmata,* money)
chrestomathy, *n.* collection of extracts for learning foreign language; phrase-book; anthology. (Gk. *chrēstos,* useful; *manthanein,* learn)
chrism, *n.* consecrated oil. **chrismal,** *a.* **chrisom,** *n.* infant's baptismal robe. (Gk. *chriein,* anoint)
Christ, *n.* Jesus; Messiah. **Christhood,** *n.* (Gk. *christos,* anointed)
christen, *v.t.* baptize into Christian religion; give name to. **Christendom,** *n.* the Christian world; (*Shake.*) Christian name.
Christian, *n.* follower of Christ, adherent of Christianity; (*colloq.*) human being, decent person.—*a.* of or like Christ; based on His teaching; (*sl.*) civilized, decent. **C. burial,** with church ceremonial. **C. era,** reckoned from supposed year of Christ's birth. **C. name,** given at baptism. **C. Science,** religious system in which sin and disease are regarded as mental errors, to be overcome by faith. **C. Scientist,** *n.* adherent of this. **Christianity,** *n.* Christian faith; Christian quality or character. **christianize,** *v.t.* convert to Christianity. **christianization,** *n.* **christianlike, christianly,** *aa.* like, befitting, a Christian.
Christlike, *a.* resembling Christ. **Christly,** *a.* of or like Christ.
Christmas, *n.* (also **C. Day**) festival of Christ's birth, held on 25 Dec. **C. Eve,** 24 Dec., evening of this. **C. rose,** winter-blossoming hellebore. **C. card,** card of greeting sent at Christmas. **C.-box,** *n.* tip given at Christmas. **C.-tree,** *n.* small fir hung with candles and presents at Christmas. **Christmassy,** *a.* suited to Christmas. **Christmastide,** *n.* Christmas season. (*Christ; mass*)
Christology, *n.* branch of theology which treats of Christ's nature. **Christologist,** *n.* (Gk. *legein,* speak)
christom, (*Shake.*) form of **chrisom.**
Christophany, *n.* appearance of Christ after the Resurrection. (Gk. *phainein,* appear)
Christy minstrels, troup of singers imitating negroes, with blackened faces, banjos etc. (person)
chromatic, *a.* of, in, colour; (*mus.*) using tones outside key in which passage is written.—*n.pl.* science of colour. **c. scale,** proceeding by semitones. **chromatically,** *adv.* **chromatin,** *n.* protoplasmic substance in cell nucleus forming chromosomes. **chromatism,** *n.* abnormal coloration. **chromatography,** *n.* treatise on colours. (Gk. *chrōma,* colour)
chrome, *n.* chromium; chrome yellow. **c. yellow, green, red,** pigments made from compounds of chromium. **chromic,** *a.* of chromium. **chromium,** *n.* greyish-white metallic element. (Gk. *chrōma,* colour)
chromo-, from Gk. *chrōma,* colour, used in **chromograph,** *n.* gelatine copying-apparatus using aniline dye; **chromo-lithograph, chromo,** *nn.* coloured lithograph, hence **chromolithographer, chromolithography,** *nn.*, **chromolithographic,** *a.*; **chromophotography,** *n.* colour photography; **chromosome,** *n.* one of small gene-carrying bodies present in cell-nucleus before cell-division; **chromosphere,** *n.* gaseous envelope round sun above photosphere.
chronic, *a.* (of disease) lasting a long time, constantly recurring; (of invalid) confirmed; (*vulg.*) bad, severe. **chronically,** *adv.* **chronicity,** *n.* (Gk. *chronos,* time)
chronicle, *n.* record of events in order of time; account.—*v.t.* record in chronicle. *chronique scandaleuse,* current body of scandalous gossip. (Gk. *chronos,* time)
chrono-, from Gk. *chronos,* time, used in **chronogram,** *n.* inscription in which certain letters give date in roman numerals, hence **chronogrammatic,** *a.*; **chronograph,** *n.* stop-watch; **chronology,** *n.* science or system of reckoning dates, table of events with dates; **chronological,** *a.* in order of time; **chronologer, chrono-**

logist, *nn.* student of chronology; **chronometer,** *n.* very accurate watch used in navigation; **chronometry,** *n.* scientific measurement of time; **chronopher,** *n.* apparatus for distributing electric time-signals; **chronoscope,** *n.* instrument for measuring velocity of projectiles.

chrysalis, *n.* (*pl.* **chrysalises, chrysalides**) form taken by caterpillar in torpid stage before it becomes butterfly, pupa; case then enclosing it. **chrysalid,** *a.* and *n.* (of) chrysalis. (Gk. *chrusos*, gold)

chrysanthemum, *n.* garden plant with large mop-headed flower. (Gk. *chrusos*, gold; *anthemon*, flower)

chryselephantine, *a.* overlaid with gold and ivory. (Gk. *chrusos*, gold; *elephas*, ivory)

chryso-, from Gk. *chrusos*, gold, used in **chrysoberyl,** *n.* yellowish-green gem; **chrysocracy,** *n.* plutocracy; **chrysography,** *n.* writing in gold letters; **chrysolite,** *n.* olive-green gem; **chrysoprase,** *n.* apple-green kind of chalcedony.

chthonian, *a.* (of Greek gods) of the underworld (opp. to Olympian.) (Gk. *chthōn*, earth)

chub, *n.* river fish of carp family.

chubby, *a.* plump, round-faced.

chuck, *v.t.* (*colloq.*) throw; stop, give up.—*n.* act of chucking. **c. out,** eject, expel. **c. under the chin,** give playful upward tap there. **c. up,** abandon. **c.-farthing,** *n.* quoit game with coins.

chuck, *n.* part of lathe holding work.—*v.t.* fix in chuck. (*chock*)

chuck, *int.* calling fowls or urging on horse.—*v.i.* utter this. (imit.)

chuck, *n.* darling.

chuck, *n.* (*sl.*) food. **c.-wagon,** *n.* (*Amer.*) provision-cart.

chucker, see **chukker.**

chuckie, *n.* (*Scot.*) pebble.

chuckle, *n.* quiet laugh.—*v.i.* laugh softly; gloat. (imit.)

chuckle-head, *n.* dolt. **chuckle-headed,** *a.*

chuddar, *n.* (*Anglo-Ind.*) large sheet worn as shawl. (Hind. *chadar*)

chuff, *n.* surly fellow, boor; (*Shake.*) avaricious person.

chug, *n.* explosive sound of car exhaust etc.—*v.i.* make chug. (imit.)

chukker, chucker, chukka, *n.* each period of play in game of polo. (Hind. *chakar*)

chum, *n.* close friend; room-mate.—*v.i.* be friendly (with); room together. **new c.,** (*Austral.*) recent immigrant. **chummy,** *a.* friendly.

chump, *n.* thick block of wood; thick end of loin of mutton; (*sl.*) head; fool.

chunk, *n.* thick piece, lump.

chupatty, *n.* (*Anglo-Ind.*) small cake of coarse unleavened bread. (Hind. *chapāti*)

chuprassi, *n.* (*Anglo-Ind.*) office messenger. (Hind. *chaprāsi*)

church, *n.* building for Christian worship; Christians collectively; sect of Christian religion; clerical profession; public worship; body professing common creed.—*v.t.* perform thanksgiving service over (woman) after childbirth. **C. Army,** Anglican organization like Salvation Army. **C. militant,** Christians as warring against evil. **c. service,** public worship; book containing Common Prayer and lessons. **Established C.,** that recognized by State. **c.-rate,** *n.* levied by vestry for upkeep of parish church. **c.-text,** *n.* kind of black-letter. (Gk. *kurios*, lord)

churchman, *n.* (*fem.* **churchwoman**) member of established Church; (*Shake.*) clergyman.

churchwarden, *n.* elected lay representative of parish; long clay pipe.

churchyard, *n.* enclosed ground round church, often used for burial.

churl, *n.* surly rude person; niggard; (*arch.*) peasant. **churlish,** *a.* ill-bred, surly; (*Shake.*) rough; miserly. (O.E. *ceorl*)

churn, *n.* butter-making contrivance; large milk-can.—*v.t.* agitate (cream) in churn, make (butter) thus; stir violently. (O.E. *cyrin*)

churr, *n.* whirring noise, deep trill.—*v.i.* make this. (imit.)

chut, *int.* of impatience.

chute, *n.* inclined plane or channel for sliding things down; smooth fall of water over slope. (F.=fall)

chutney, chutnee, *n.* hot Indian pickle or relish. (Hind. *chatni*)

chyle, *n.* milky fluid made from chyme and passing fatty substance into blood. **chyme,** *n.* semi-liquid pulp into which stomach converts food. (Gk. *cheein*, pour)

chymist, *arch.* form of **chemist.**

chypre, *n.* mixture of resins used as perfume. (F.=Cyprus)

ciborium, *n.* (*pl.* **ciboria**) covered chalice for reserving the sacrament; canopy over altar. (Gk. *kibōrion*, seed-vessel of Egyptian bean)

cicada, cicala, cigala, *n.* winged chirping insect. (L.=cricket)

cicatrice, cicatrix, *n.* scar; scarlike mark. **cicatricial, cicatricose,** *aa.* **cicatricule, cicatricle,** *n.* germinating point in egg. **cicatrize,** *v.t.* and *i.* make new skin over, heal; mark with scars. **cicatrization,** *n.* (L.)

cicely, *n.* kinds of plant allied to chervil. (Gk. *seselis*)

ciceróně, *n.* (*pl.* **ciceroni**) guide who explains antiquities etc. (*Cicero*)

Ciceronian, *a.* eloquent, pure, as Cicero's style.—*n.* expert on Cicero.

cicisbeo, *n.* (*pl. cicisbei*) professed lover of married woman. (It.)

-cide, *n.suf.* killing or killer of, as in regicide. (L. *caedere*, kill)

cider, *n.* fermented apple-juice as drink. (Heb. *shekar*, strong drink)

ci-devant, *a.* former, ex-. (F.)

cigala, see **cicada.**

cigar, *n.* small roll of tobacco-leaf for smoking. **c.-shaped,** *a.* cylindrical with tapering ends. **cigarette,** *n.* shredded tobacco rolled in paper for smoking. (Sp. *cigarro*)

cilia, *n.pl.* eyelashes; fringe of hairs on leaf etc.; hairlike outgrowths used by microscopic organisms for propulsion. **ciliary,** *a.* **ciliate,** *a.* having cilia. (L.)

cilice, *n.* hair-cloth. (*Cilicia*)

Cimmerian, *a.* very dark, gloomy. (people in Homer)

cinch, *n.* girth of saddle; (*Amer. sl.*) firm hold, easy job; certainty. (L. *cingere*, gird)

cinchona, *n.* a S. American tree; its bark, yielding quinine and other drugs. **cinchonaceous, cinchonic,** *aa.* **cinchonism,** *n.* condition due to overuse of quinine. **cinchonize,** *v.t.* treat with cinchona. (Countess of *Chinchon*)

cincture, *n.* girdle, belt, border.—*v.t.* enclose with cincture. (L. *cingere*, gird)

cinder, *n.* residue of burnt coals, ember; (*pl.*) ashes. **c.-path,** *n.* running-track. **Cinderella,** *n.* beauty in humble guise. (O.E. *sinder*)

cinema, *n.* moving pictures, theatre showing them. **cinematograph,** *n.* apparatus for projecting moving pictures on screen.—*v.t.* film. **cinematographic,** *a.* **cinematographically,** *adv.* **cinematography,** *n.* **cine-camera,** *n.* camera for taking motion films. (Gk. *kineein*, move)

cinerary, *a.* of ashes. **c. urn,** for ashes of cremated dead. **cineraria,** *n.* kinds of plant of aster family. **cinereous,** *a.* ash-grey. (L. *cinis*, ashes)

Cingalese, *a.* and *n.* (native, language) of Ceylon. (Sanskr. *sinhalas*)

cingulum, *n.* belt. (L.)

cinnabar, *n.* sulphide of mercury.—*a.* vermilion. (Gk. *kinnabari*)

cinnamon, *n.* a Ceylon laurel; spice made from its bark.—*a.* yellowish-brown. (Gk. *kinnamōmon*)

cinque, cinq, *n.* five at dice or cards. **cinquefoil, cinqfoil,** *n.* plant with leaves divided into five lobes; (*archit.*) decoration of this shape. **cinquepace,** *n.* (*Shake.*) a lively dance. (L. *quinque*, five)

cinquecento, *n.* and *a.* (Italian art) of 16th century. (It.)

cipher, cypher, *n.* zero, 0; any single figure; thing, person, of no importance; method of secret writing; monogram.—*v.t.* and *i.* write in cipher; work with figures; (*Shake.*) decipher. (Arab. *çifr*, empty)

circa, circiter, *prepp.* (*abbr. circ., c.,*) about. (L.)

circinate, *a.* (of leaf) rolled up with tip inwards. (Gk. *kirkinos*, circle)

circle, *n.* perfectly round figure, line enclosing it; round enclosure; ring; group of tiers of seats in theatre; set, class, sphere; period, cycle; (*Shake.*) crown.—*v.t.* and *i.* encompass; move in circle; revolve (round). **reason in a c.,** take what is to be proved as basis of argument. **circlet,** *n.* small circle; circular band, hoop. (L. *circus*, ring+dim.)

circuit, *n.* distance round; circular course; detour; round of visitation, esp. of judge; path of electric current; (*Shake.*) diadem. **circuitous,** *a.* roundabout, indirect. (L. *circum*, round; *ire*, go)

circular, *a.* shaped like a circle, round; sent to a number of persons.—*n.* advertisement, notice, sent out in quantities. **circularity,** *n.* **circularize,** *v.t.* send circulars to.

circulate, *v.i.* and *t.* move round, finishing at starting-point; pass from hand to hand or place to place. **circulating decimal,** recurring decimal. **circulating library,** lending library. **circulation,** *n.* circulating; movement to and fro; extent of sale of newspaper; currency. **circulator,** *n.* **circulative, circulatory,** *aa.*

circum-, *pref.* round, about, as in **circumnavigate.**

circumambient, *a.* (of air etc.) surrounding. **circumambiency,** *n.*

circumambulate, *v.t.* and *i.* walk round; walk about. **circumambulation,** *n.* (L. *ambulare*, walk)

circumbendibus, *n.* (*joc.*) roundabout way; circumlocution. (*bend*)

circumcise, *v.t.* cut off foreskin of, esp. as religious rite of Jews; purify. **circumcision,** *n.* (L. *caedere*, cut)

circumference, *n.* line bounding circle; distance round. **circumferential,** *a.* (L. *ferre*, bear)

circumflex, *n.* (also **c. accent**) mark (^ or ⌒) placed over vowel to indicate contraction, length etc.—*a.* (*anat.*) bent round. **circumflexion,** *n.*

circumfluent, *a.* flowing round. **circumfluence,** *n.* (L. *fluere*, flow)

circumfuse, *v.t.* pour round; bathe (with). **circumfusion,** *n.* (L. *fundere*, pour)

circumgyrate, *v.i.* turn, revolve; go round in circle. **circumgyration,** *n.*

circumjacent, *a.* situated around. (L. *jacēre*, lie)

circumlocution, *n.* use of more words than are necessary, roundabout expression. **circumlocutional, circumlocutionary, circumlocutory,** *aa.* (L. *loqui*, speak)

circummured, *a.* (*Shake.*) walled round. (L. *murus*, wall)

circumnavigate, *v.t.* sail round. **circumnavigation, circumnavigator,** *nn.*

circumnutate, *v.i.* (*bot.*) turn successively to all points of compass. **circumnutation,** *n.*

circumpolar, *a.* near north or south pole; (*astron.*) always above horizon.

circumscribe, *v.t.* draw line round, enclose; limit, restrict; (*geom.*) describe (figure) round another. **circumscription,** *n.* (L. *scribere,* write)

circumsolar, *a.* revolving round sun.

circumspect, *a.* prudent, cautious; heedful of conduct. **circumspection,** *n.* **circumspective,** *a.* (L. *specere,* look)

circumstance, *n.* occurrence, incident; detail; ceremony; (*Amer. colloq.*) comparable thing; (*pl.*) state of affairs; condition in life. **in, under, the cc.,** considering the position. **circumstanced,** *a.* situated. **circumstantial,** *a.* detailed; (of evidence) indirect, inferential. **circumstantiality,** *n.* **circumstantiate,** *v.t.* describe, verify, in detail. (L. *stare,* stand)

circumvallate, *v.t.* surround with rampart. **circumvallation,** *n.* (*vallum*)

circumvent, *v.t.* frustrate by stratagem, outwit. **circumvention,** *n.* (L. *venire,* come)

circumvolution, *n.* rolling round, winding; coil. (L. *volvere,* roll)

circus, *n.* travelling show of performing animals, acrobats, clowns etc.; rounded arena with tiers of seats, amphitheatre; open space with streets converging on it; circular row of houses. **cirque,** *n.* natural amphitheatre, ring. (L.)

cirrhosis, *n.* hardened condition, esp. of liver. (Gk. *kirrhos,* tawny)

cirrus, *n.* (*pl.* **cirri**) highest form of cloud; (*bot.*) tendril; (*zool.*) thread-like appendage. **cirro-cumulus,** *n.* mackerel sky. **cirrose, cirrous,** *aa.* (L.=curl)

cis-, *pref.* on this side of, used in **cisalpine,** *a.* on the Roman side of the Alps; **cisatlantic,** *a.* on the European side of the Atlantic; **cispontine,** *a.* (in London) north of the Thames. (L.)

cissy, same as **sissy.**

cist, *n.* prehistoric stone coffin. (Gk. *kistē,* box)

Cistercian, *a.* and *n.* (monk) of branch of Benedictines founded in 1098 at Cîteaux. (L.L. *Cistercium,* Cîteaux)

cistern, *n.* water-tank. (*cist*)

cistus, *n.* rock-rose. (Gk. *kistos*)

cit, *obs. contr.* of **citizen.**

citadel, *n.* fortress in or near city. (L. *civitas,* city+dim.)

cite, *v.t.* summon officially to appear in court; quote, give as example or authority; (*Shake.*) excite. **cital,** *n.* (*Shake.*) accusation. **citation,** *n.* citing; quotation. (L. *ciēre,* stir)

cithern, cither, cittern, *n.* (*arch.*) wire-stringed instrument shaped like lute but with flat back. (Gk. *kithara*)

citizen, *n.* inhabitant of city or state; freeman of city; civilian.—*a.* (*Shake.*) town-bred. **citizenship,** *n.*

citole, *n.* kind of cithern. (O.F.)

citron, *n.* large fruit like lemon; tree bearing it. **citric,** *a.* **citrate,** *n.* salt of citric acid. **citrine,** *a.* lemon-coloured. (L. *citrus*)

cittern, see **cithern.**

city, *n.* (*pl.* **cities**) important or cathedral town; business circles; (in strict sense) town created city by charter. **c. company,** corporation representing medieval guild. (L. *civis,* citizen)

cive, same as **chive.**

civet, *n.* strong musky perfume; (also **c.-cat**) catlike animal yielding this. (Arab. *zabad*)

civic, *a.* of city, citizen, or citizenship. —*n.pl.* principles of good citizenship. (L. *civis,* citizen)

civil, *a.* polite, obliging; of citizens or the state; not military or ecclesiastical; (*law*) relating to private rights; (*Shake.*) orderly. **c. disobedience,** refusal to pay taxes etc. as part of political campaign. **c. engineer,** one who constructs roads, bridges etc. **C. List,** expenses of sovereign's household. **c. service,** paid service of state, apart from fighting services. **c. servant,** member of this. **c. war,** between citizens of same state. **civilian,** *a.* and *n.* non-military (person); (*arch.*) expert in civil law. **civility,** *n.* politeness. (L. *civis,* citizen)

civilize, *v.t.* reclaim from barbarism, instruct in arts and refinements. **civilization,** *n.* civilizing; advanced stage of social culture.

civvies, *n.pl.* (*sl.*) civilian clothes.

clabber, *n.* (*Scot.*) mud.

clachan, *n.* (*Scot.*) small village. (Gael.)

clack, *n.* sharp sound as of wood striking wood; clatter of tongue.—*v.i.* emit clack; chatter. **c.-dish,** *n.* (*Shake.*) beggar's wooden dish.

clad, see **clothe.**

claes, *Scot.* form of **clothes.**

clag, *v.i.* (*Scot.*) clog, stick. **claggy,** *a.* sticky.

claim, *v.t.* demand as right; call for, require; profess (to have); assert.—*n.* act of claiming; title, right; (*mining*) piece of ground marked out or allotted. **claimant,** *n.* (L. *clamare,* call out)

clairaudience, *n.* power of hearing things not present to senses. **clairaudient,** *a.* and *n.* (person) with this. (L. *clarus,* clear; *audire,* hear)

clairschach, *n.* old Celtic wire-strung harp. (Gael. *clairseach,* harp)

clairvoyance, *n.* power of seeing things not present to senses, second sight. **clairvoyant,** *a.* and *n.* (person) with this. (L. *clarus,* clear; *vidēre,* see)

clam, *n.* edible bivalve shell-fish; (*Amer.*) taciturn person. (*clamp*)

clamant, *a.* insistent, crying; clamorous. (L. *clamare,* call out)

clamber, *v.i.* climb with difficulty.—*n.* laborious climb.

clamjamfry, *n.* (*Scot.*) company, mob; odds and ends.

clammy, *a.* moist and sticky.

clamour, *n.* loud confused cry; loud noise; insistent demand.—*v.i.* make clamour. **clamorous,** *a.* (L. *clamor*)

clamp, *n.* rigid band or brace; gripping-tool worked by screw.—*v.t.* fasten, strengthen, with clamp.

clamp, *n.* heavy tread.—*v.i.* tread heavily, clump. (imit.)

clamp, *n.* and *v.t.* pile.

clan, *n.* Scottish highlanders with common ancestor, under single chief; people with same surname; party, clique. (Gael. *clann*)

clandestine, *a.* done secretly, surreptitious. (L. *clam*, secretly)

clang, *n.* loud metallic sound of bell etc.—*v.i.* and *t.* make, cause to make, clang. **clangour,** *n.* repeated clanging. **clangorous,** *a.* (L. *clangere*, make clang)

clank, *n.* sharp metallic sound of chain etc.—*v.i.* and *t.* make, cause to make, clank.

clannish, *a.* closely united to exclusion of others. **clanship,** *n.* clan system; clannishness. **clansman,** *n.* member of clan.

clap, *n.* (*vulg.*) gonorrhoea.

clap, *v.t.* and *i.* strike (hands) together sharply, applaud thus; slap; put, place, suddenly or vigorously.—*n.* sudden sharp noise; spell of handclapping. **c. eyes on,** see. **c. hands,** (*Shake.*) make bargain. **c. up,** make hastily. **clapnet,** *n.* fowler's net, closed by pulling string. **clapper,** *n.* one who claps; tongue of bell; rattle for scaring birds. **clapper-claw,** *v.t.* scratch and hit; abuse. **claptrap,** *n.* trick to gain applause; empty words.—*a.* showy.

claque, *n.* band of paid applauders. *claqueur*, *n.* member of this. (F.)

clarabella, *n.* fluty organ-stop. (L. *clarus*, clear; *bellus*, pretty)

clarence, *n.* closed four-wheeled carriage like brougham. (person)

clarendon, *a.* and *n.* thick-faced (type), **as in this.**

claret, *n.* red wine of Bordeaux; (*sl.*) blood.—*a.* purplish-red. (L. *clarus*, clear+dim.)

clarify, *v.t.* and *i.* make, become, clear or intelligible; free, become free, from impurities. **clarification,** *n.* (L. *clarus*, clear; *facere*, make)

clarion, *n.* shrill trumpet formerly used in war; rousing sound.—*a.* ringing. **clarinet, clarionet,** *n.* straight woodwind instrument with single reed. **clarinettist,** *n.* (L. *clarus*, clear)

clàrsach, same as **clairschach.**

clarity, *n.* clearness. (*clear*)

clarkia, *n.* bright-flowered garden plant. (W. *Clarke*)

clart, *n.* (*Scot.*) dirt, mud. **clarty,** *a.*

clash, *n.* loud noise of striking weapons etc.; encounter, conflict; (*Scot.*) chatter.—*v.t.* and *i.* make, dash together with, clash; conflict; be at variance (with).

clasp, *v.t.* and *i.* grasp firmly, embrace; fasten with clasp.—*n.* hold, embrace; catch, buckle; bar on medal-ribbon. **c.-knife,** *n.* with blade that shuts into handle. (M.E. *claspen*)

class, *n.* division, group; kind, sort; set of pupils taught together; grade of merit, quality; rank, standing, in society; all conscripted recruits of a year; (*natural history*) highest division of kingdom; (*Amer.*) set of students graduating together.—*v.t.* put into class. **no c.,** (*sl.*) very inferior. **the cc.,** the upper classes (opp. to the masses). **c.-conscious,** *a.* aware of and taking part in the conflict between labouring and other classes. **c.-fellow, c.-mate,** *nn.* pupil in same class. (L. *classis*)

classic, *a.* of recognized excellence, referred to as standard; associated with great writers; classical.—*n.* classic writer, artist, or production; ancient Greek or Latin author or book. **classical,** *a.* of Greek or Latin authors, based on these; classic; (*art, literature*) preferring proportion and finish to passion and imagination, subordinating content to form (opp. to romantic). **classicality,** *n.* being classical. **classicism,** *n.* use of classical style; belief in classical education; Greek or Latin idiom in modern language. **classicist,** *n.* (*class*)

classify, *v.t.* arrange in classes. **classification,** *n.* **classificatory,** *a.* (L. *facere*, make)

classman, *n.* one taking honours degree.

classy, *a.* (*sl.*) superior.

clastic, *a.* (*geol.*) composed of fragments. (Gk. *klaein*, break)

clatter, *n.* rattling noise; noisy talk.—*v.i.* and *t.* make, cause to make, clatter; fall or go with clatter. (O.E. *clatrian*, make clatter)

clause, *n.* single article or stipulation in treaty, law, contract etc.; (*gram.*) short sentence, division of sentence. (L. *claudere*, shut)

claustral, *a.* of cloister. **claustrophobia,** *n.* morbid dread of closed places. (L. *claudere*, shut)

claut, *v.t.* (*Scot.*) scratch, claw.—*n.* clutch; handful.

clavate, *a.* club-shaped. (L. *clava*, club)

claver, *v.i.* and *n.* (*Scot.*) gossip.

clavichord, *n.* old keyboard instrument, predecessor of piano. (L. *clavis*, key; *chorda*, string)

clavicle, *n.* collar-bone. **clavicular,** *a.* (L. *clavis*, key+dim.)

claviform, *a.* club-shaped. (*clavate*)

claw, *n.* sharp hooked nail of beast or

bird; bird's foot; claw-like thing, grappling-iron.—*v.t.* and *i.* seize or scrape with claws; clutch (at); (*naut.*) beat to windward; (*Shake.*) flatter. **c.-hammer,** *n.* hammer with claw for drawing out nails; (*joc.*) swallow-tail coat. (O.E. *clawu*)

clay, *n.* a tenacious ductile earth; earth, mud; human flesh or body; (also **c. pipe**) tobacco-pipe of baked clay. **c.-brained,** *a.* (*Shake.*) stupid. **clayey,** *a.* (O.E. *clæg*)

claymore, *n.* ancient Scottish highlander's two-edged broadsword. (Gael. *claidheamh,* sword; *mor,* great)

clean, *a.* free from dirt, unsoiled; cleanly; morally or ceremonially pure; shapely; complete, decisive. —*adv.* entirely, outright.—*v.t.* remove dirt from.—*n.* cleaning. **c. out,** empty; leave without money. **c. up,** clear away. **come c.,** (*Amer. sl.*) confess. **c.-cut,** *a.* sharply defined. **c.-handed,** *a.* upright. **c.-limbed,** (*Shake.*) **c.-timbered,** *aa.* well built. **cleanly,** *a.* of clean habits.—*adv.* in a clean manner; (*Shake.*) cleverly. **cleanness,** *n.* (O.E. *clǽne*)

cleanse, *v.t.* make clean or pure. (*clean*)

clear, *a.* bright, not dim; easily seen or heard; unimpeded, open; free from clouds; transparent; quit (of); plain, distinct, lucid; keen, discerning; positive, sure; (*Shake.*) innocent. —*v.t.* and *i.* make, become, clear; rid (of), remove; free from suspicion, vindicate; disentangle; pass by or over without touching; make as profit; (of ship) leave port; (*sl.*) make off. **c. out,** empty; decamp. **c. up,** tidy up; solve (mystery); (of weather) become clear. **c.-sighted,** *a.* discerning. (L. *clarus*)

clearance, *n.* removal, riddance; space for parts of machinery to pass; certificate that ship's dues have been paid, and permit to sail.

clearing, *n.* piece of land cleared of wood. **c.-house,** *n.* where cheques are exchanged.

clearly, *adv.* in a clear manner; evidently.

clearstory, same as clerestory.

cleat, *n.* wedge; strip of wood nailed crosswise to give footing etc.; projection for making ropes fast to.

cleave, *v.i.* (*past* cleaved, clave) be faithful (to); (*arch.*) stick. (O.E. *clifian*)

cleave, *v.t.* and *i.* (*past* **clove, cleft,** *p.p.* **cloven, cleft**) cut in two, split asunder; make (way) through. **in a cleft stick,** in a fix. **cloven hoof,** evil nature. **cleavage,** *n.* way thing splits; divergence. **cleaver,** *n.* short-handled chopper. (O.E. *cléofan*)

cleavers, *n.* goose-grass.

cleck, *v.t.* (*Scot.*) hatch. (O.N. *klekja*)

cleek, *n.* large hook or crook; (*golf*) iron with narrow straight face.—*v.t.* (*Scot.*) seize.

clef, *n.* sign indicating pitch of stave in music. (F.)

cleft, *n.* fissure, chasm. (*cleave*)

cleg, *n.* horse-fly. (O.N. *kleggi*)

cleistogamy, *n.* (*bot.*) self-fertilization without opening of flower. **cleistogamic,** *a.* (Gk. *kleistos,* closed; *gamos,* marriage)

clem, *v.t.* and *i.* starve.

clematis, *n.* bright-flowered climbing plant. (Gk. *klēmatis*)

clement, *a.* gentle, merciful; (of weather) mild. **clemency,** *n.* (L. *clemens*)

clench, *v.t.* and *i.* close (fist etc.) tightly; secure (nail) by hammering point sideways; clinch.—*n.* act of clenching. (O.E. *clencan*)

clepe, *v.t.* (*Shake.*) call. (O.E. *clipian*)

clepsydra, *n.* clock showing time by passage of water through hole. (Gk. *kleptein,* steal; *hudōr,* water)

clerestory, *n.* windowed part of wall of cathedral etc. above aisle roofs.

clergy, *n.* body of ordained ministers, persons in holy orders. **clergyman,** *n.* member of clergy. (*cleric*)

cleric, *n.* clergyman.—*a.* (*arch.*) of clergy. **clerical,** *a.* of clergy or clergyman; of clerk or copyist.—*n.* member of clergy party in parliament. **clericalism,** *n.* undue influence of clergy. (Gk. *klēros,* lot, clergy)

clerihew, *n.* short nonsensical or satirical poem, us. in four lines of varying length, e.g.:

Sir Christopher Wren
Said, 'I 'm going to dine with some
men.
If any one calls,
Say I 'm designing St Paul's.'

(E. *Clerihew* Bentley)

clerk, *n.* employee who keeps books, conducts correspondence etc.; secretary of town or corporation; lay officer who leads responses in English Church service; clergyman; (*arch.*) scholar, penman; (*Amer.*) salesman. —*v.i.* act as clerk. **clerkess,** *n.* female clerk. **clerkly,** *a.* scholarly. **clerkship,** *n.* (*cleric*)

clever, *a.* intelligent, able, ingenious; skilful, adroit.

clew, *n.* ball of thread; sail-corner to which sheet is attached; clue.—*v.t.* draw (sail) up to yard for furling. (O.E. *cliwen*)

cliché, *n.* trite or hackneyed phrase, literary tag. (F.)

click, *n.* slight sharp sound; catch, latch.—*v.i.* make click. (imit.)

click, *v.i.* (*sl.*) have luck, attain one's aim; strike up friendship.

client, *n.* one who employs another professionally; patron, customer; (*arch.*) dependant. **cliental,** *a.* **clientele, clientèle,** *n.* body of clients, connection, following. **clientship,** *n.* (L. *cliens*)

cliff, *n.* high steep rock-face. (O.E. *clif*)

climacteric, *n.* critical period, turning-point, esp. **in** life of individual; menopause.—*a.* of climacteric, forming crisis. **grand c.,** 63rd year. (*climax*)

climactic, *a.* of climax.

climate, *n.* weather characteristics of a region; (*Shake.*) region. — *v.i.* (*Shake.*) dwell. **climatic,** *a.* **climatology,** *n.* science of climates. (Gk. *klinein*, slope)

climax, *n.* sequence of words or ideas increasing in forcefulness; last of these, culmination; most exciting point of story. (Gk.=ladder)

climb, *v.t.* and *i.* (*past* **climbed,** *arch.* **clomb**) mount with effort, ascend; (of plant) grow up (wall); rise in social scale.—*n.* piece of climbing. **c. down,** descend; give up one's point.

clime, *n.* (*poet.*) region. (*climate*)

clinch, *v.t.* and *i.* confirm (bargain), drive home (argument); clench; (*boxing*) seize one another.—*n.* (*boxing*) clinching. **clincher,** *n.* decisive argument. **clincher-built,** same as **clinker-built.** (*clench*)

cling, *v.i.* and *t.* (*past, p.p.* **clung**) adhere, be attached (to); keep hold by embracing or entwining; (*Shake.*) pinch with hunger. **clingstone,** *a.* with pulp adhering to stone. (O.E. *clingan*)

clinic, *n.* demonstration of medicine or surgery given at bed-side in hospital. **clinical,** *a.* of sick-bed. **clinical thermometer,** for taking person's temperature. (Gk. *klinē*, bed)

clink, *n.* (*sl.*) prison.

clink, *n.* slight metallic sound.—*v.i.* and *t.* make, cause to make, this. **clinker,** *n.* very hard-burnt brick; mass of slag or cinder; fine specimen. **clinking,** *a.* (*colloq.*) first-rate. (imit.)

clinker-built, *a.* with outer boards or plates overlapping. (*clinch*)

clinometer, *n.* instrument for measuring angles of slopes. **clinometric,** *a.* **clinometry,** *n.* (Gk. *klinein*, slope; *metron*, measure)

clinquant, *a.* glittering.—*n.* tinsel. (F.)

Clio, *n.* muse of history. (L.)

clip, *v.t.* hold firmly; (*arch.*) embrace. —*n.* device for holding papers etc. together. (O.E. *clyppan*)

clip, *v.t.* cut, trim, with scissors; pare (edge of coin); shorten or slur (words). —*n.* haircutting, shearing; yield of wool; smart blow. **clipper,** *n.* sharp-built fast-sailing vessel; (*sl.*) fine specimen; (*pl.*) two-bladed clipping instrument. **clipping,** *n.* piece clipped off.

clique, *n.* small exclusive set. **cliquish, cliquy, cliquey,** *aa.* (F.)

clitoris, *n.* small penis-like female organ near mouth of vagina. (Gk. *kleitoris*)

clivers, same as **cleavers.**

cloaca, *n.* (*pl.* **cloacae**) sewer, privy; (*zool.*) cavity receiving all bodily excretions. **cloacal,** *a.* (L.)

cloak, *n.* loose sleeveless outdoor garment; covering, pretext.—*v.t.* cover with cloak; hide. **c.-bag,** *n.* (*Shake.*) portmanteau. **cloakroom,** *n.* room for leaving overcoats; left-luggage office; lavatory. (L.L. *cloca*, bell-shaped cape)

clobber, *n.* (*sl.*) clothes.

cloche, *n.* bell-glass. **c. (hat),** woman's close-fitting bell-shaped hat. (F.= bell)

clock, *n.* ornamental pattern on sides of stocking.

clock, *v.i.* (*Scot.*) cluck; **hatch, sit.** (O.E. *cloccian*)

clock, *n.* (*Scot.*) beetle.

clock, *n.* device for measuring time; dandelion head in seed.—*v.i.* and *t.* register by clock. **clockwise,** *adv.* in the direction of clock's hands. **clockwork,** *n.* machinery of clock; mechanism like this.—*a.* mechanically regular. (L.L. *cloca*, bell)

clod, *n.* lump of earth or clay; cloddish person. **cloddish,** *a.* stupid; phlegmatic. **clodhopper,** *n.* yokel, lout. **clodpole,** *n.* blockhead. (*clot*)

clog, *n.* wooden-soled shoe; block fastened to animal's leg to prevent straying; impediment.—*v.t.* and *i.* impede, hamper; choke (up); adhere. **cloggy,** *a.* lumpy; sticky.

cloisonné, *a.* and *n.* (enamel decoration) with colours of pattern set in spaces partitioned off by wires. (F.)

cloister, *n.* roofed pillared walk, us. with one side open, of convent, college etc.; place of religious retirement. —*v.t.* confine in convent. **cloistral,** *a.* **cloistress,** *n.* (*Shake.*) nun. (L. *claudere*, shut)

cloke, *arch.* form of **cloak.**

clonus, *n.* (*med.*) series of convulsive spasms. **clonic,** *a.* (Gk. *klonos*)

cloop, *n.* sound of drawing cork.— *v.i.* make this. (imit.)

cloot, *n.* (*Scot.*) hoof of cow or sheep. **Clootie,** *n.* (*Scot.*) the devil.

close, *v.t.* and *i.* shut; stop up; conclude, finish; draw near; (*electr.*) complete (circuit).—*n.* completion, end; grapple; (*Shake.*) cadence. **c. in,** enclose; come nearer. **c. up,** block up; draw together. **c. with,** grapple with; strike bargain with, accept (offer). (L. *claudere*)

close, *a.* shut; tight; sultry, airless; reticent, secret; restricted; stingy; near; dense, compact; evenly balanced.—*adv.* closely.—*n.* precinct of cathedral; (*Scot.*) entry-passage of tenement. **c. call, shave,** narrow escape. **c. on,** nearly. **c. season,** when certain game may not be killed. **c. vowel,** pronounced with mouth nearly closed. **c.-fisted,** *a.* stingy. **c.-hauled,** *a.* with sails trimmed for sailing near wind. **c.-stool,** *n.* commode. **c.-up,** *n.* part of film, photograph, taken near at hand. (L. *claudere*, shut)

closet, *n.* small or private room; cupboard; water-closet. **c. play,** to be read, not acted. **closeted,** *a.* having private interview (with). (O.F. *clos*, enclosure+dim.)

closure, *n.* closing of debate by vote of majority; (*Shake.*) enclosure.—*v.t.* apply closure to.

clot, *n.* coagulated mass, esp. of blood. —*v.i.* and *t.* form into clots; curdle.

clotpole, same as **clodpole.**

cloth, *n.* woven fabric; woollen material; clerical dress, clergy; duster; table-cloth. **c. binding,** of linen over cardboard. **c. of gold, silver,** fabric with interwoven gold, silver, threads. **painted c.** (*Shake.*) tapestry. **c.-yard shaft,** arrow a yard long. (O.E. *cláth*)

clothe, *v.t.* and *i.* (*past, p.p.* **clothed** or **clad**) cover with garments, dress; surround, endow (with); embody (in). (*cloth*)

clothes, *n.pl.* garments, apparel. **c.-basket,** *n.* laundry-basket. **c.-horse,** *n.* wooden frame for airing linen etc. **c.-line,** *n.* rope on which washing is hung to dry. **c.-peg,** *n.* for securing to clothes-line. **clothier,** *n.* dealer in clothes; cloth-maker. **clothing,** *n.* clothes.

clou, *n.* centre of attraction. (F.)

cloud, *n.* visible mass of water-vapour floating in sky; mass of steam, smoke etc.; multitude; threatening thing, gloomy look.—*v.t.* and *i.* overspread with clouds; obscure; mar; mark with dark patches; become overcast. **in the cc.,** dreamy, absent-minded. **under a c.,** out of favour. **c.-burst,** *n.* violent downpour over limited area. **cloudberry,** *n.* kind of wild raspberry. **cloudless,** *a.* **cloudlet,** *n.* small cloud. **cloudy,** *a.* of, full of, clouds; not clear.

clough, *n.* ravine, gully.

clout, *n.* cloth; garment; bull's-eye of archery target; (*colloq.*) blow.—*v.t.* patch roughly; (*colloq.*) strike roughly. (O.E. *clút*)

clove, *n.* one of small bulbs making up compound bulb. (O.E. *clufu*)

clove, *n.* a tropical tree; its dried bud, used as spice; (also **c. gillyflower, c. pink**) pink with scent of cloves. (L. *clavus*, nail)

clove, cloven, see **cleave.**

clove hitch, kind of knot. (*cleave*)

clover, *n.* low-growing plant used as fodder, trefoil. **in c.,** in luxury. (O.E. *cláfre*)

clown, *n.* buffoon in circus; rustic; lout.—*v.i.* play the fool.

cloy, *v.t.* (*Shake.*) stroke with claw.

cloy, *v.t.* fill to loathing, satiate; (*Spens.*) gore. **cloyless,** *a.* (*Shake.*) that does not cloy. **cloyment,** *n.* (*Shake.*) satiety. (L. *clavus*, nail)

club, *n.* heavy stick as weapon; stick with head for playing golf; association of persons for social purpose etc., its premises; playing-card with black trefoil markings.—*v.t.* and *i.* beat with, use as, club; combine together; share in common expense. **c. law,** rule of force. **clubbable,** *a.* suitable for a club, sociable. **club-foot,** *n.* malformation of foot. **club-man,** *n.* member of club. (M.E. *clubbe*)

club-haul, *v.t.* tack by anchoring and cutting cable when there is no room to wear.

cluck, *n.* call of hen.—*v.i.* emit cluck. (imit.)

clue, *n.* guide to solution of puzzle or mystery; clew. (*clew*)

clumber, *n.* breed of spaniel. (place)

clump, *n.* cluster of trees; lump; thick extra sole.—*v.t.* and *i.* mass together; tread heavily.

clumsy, *a.* awkward, without skill or grace; ill-made; tactless, gauche. **clumsiness,** *n.* (M.E. *clumsen*, be benumbed)

clung, see **cling.**

cluster, *n.* bunch of fruits or flowers; swarm; group.—*v.i.* and *t.* form, arrange in, cluster. (O.E. *clyster*)

clutch, *n.* set of eggs hatched at once; brood of chickens. (*cleck*)

clutch, *v.t.* and *i.* seize, grasp tightly; snatch (at); (*Shake.*) clench.—*n.* tight grip; snatch, grab; device for throwing parts of machine into or out of action. (O.E. *clyccean*)

clutter, *n.* confusion, disorder.—*v.t.* and *i.* litter; bustle about. (*clot*)

cly, *v.t.* (*sl.*) steal.

Clydesdale, *n.* **heavy breed of cart-horse.** (place)

clypeus, *n.* shield-like part of insect's head. **clypeal, clypeate,** *aa.* shield-shaped. (L.=shield)

clyster, *n.* liquid injected into rectum, enema. (Gk. *kluzein*, wash)

co-, *pref.* together, joint, alike, as in **co-operate, coeval.** (L. *cum*, with)

coach, *n.* large covered four-wheeled carriage; railway carriage; instructor, trainer, of competitors for examination or athletic contest.—*v.t.* and *i.* drive in coach; instruct as coach; prime with facts. **c.-box,** *n.* raised seat for driver. **c.-house,** *n.* for keeping carriages in. **coachman,** *n.* driver of horse carriage. (*Kocs* in Hungary)

coact, *v.t.* compel. (L. *cogere*)

coact, *v.i.* (*Shake.*) act together. **coactive,** *a.* (*Shake.*). (*co-*)

coadjutor, *n.* (*fem.* **coadjutrix**) helper; assistant to infirm bishop. (L. *adjuvare*, help)

co-administrator, *n.* joint administrator.

coadunate, *a.* (*bot.*) united, growing together. (L. *adunare*, unite)

coagulate, *v.i.* and *t.* change from liquid to partially solid state, clot, curdle. **coagulation,** *n.* **coagulant,** *n.* coagulating agent. (L. *agere*, drive)

coaita, *n.* spider-monkey of S. America (Brazilian *coatá*)

coal, *n.* black mineral used for fuel; piece of this.—*v.i.* and *t.* take in, supply with, coal. **carry cc.,** (*Shake.*) submit to indignity. **carry cc. to Newcastle,** take thing where there is plenty already. **haul over the cc.,** reprimand. **heap cc. of fire on one's head,** cause remorse by returning good for evil. **c.-bed, c.-measure,** *nn.* stratum of coal. **c.-black,** *a.* black as coal. **c.-box, c.-scuttle,** *nn.* for room's supply of coal. **c.-cellar, c.-hole,** *nn.* for storing coal. **coal-field,** *n.* region yielding coal. **c.-gas,** *n.* gas got from coal and used for lighting and heating. **c.-master, c.-owner,** *nn.* owner of colliery. **c.-mine, c.-pit,** *nn.* excavation from which coal is dug. **c.-tar,** *n.* tar got from bituminous coal. **coalheaver,** *n.* man who loads coal. **coalmouse, c.-tit,** *nn.* dark kind of titmouse. (O.E. *col*)

coalesce, *v.i.* come together and form one, merge, unite. **coalescent,** *a.* **coalescence,** *n.* **coalition,** *n.* temporary union of parties or states. **coalitionist,** *n.* member, advocate, of coalition. (L. *alere*, nourish)

coaming, *n.* raised edge round outside of ship's hatch etc.

coarse, *a.* common, inferior; large in texture; rough, harsh; gross; vulgar; obscene. **coarsen,** *v.t.* and *i.* make, become, coarse. (*course*)

coast, *n.* seashore; act of coasting.—*v.i.* sail along coast; sledge, cycle without pedalling, down slope; (*Shake.*) go roundabout way. **coastal,** *a.* **coaster,** *n.* coasting vessel. **coastguard,** *n.* (member of) service keeping watch on coast for vessels or aircraft in distress or danger, wrecks etc. **coastwise,** *adv.* along the coast. (L. *costa*, rib)

coat, *n.* sleeved outer garment, jacket; outdoor garment, overcoat; animal's covering of fur or feathers; layer, rind; covering of paint etc.—*v.t.* cover with coating. **c. of arms,** heraldic bearings; tabard. **trail one's c.,** invite quarrel. **turn one's c.,** change party or principles. **c.-armour,** *n.* escutcheon; armorial devices. **c.-card,** *n.* court-card. **coatee,** *n.* short close-fitting coat. **coating,** *n.* coat of paint etc. (L.L. *cotta*, tunic)

coati, *n.* raccoon-like S. American animal. (Brazilian)

coax, *v.t.* and *i.* persuade by entreaty or flattery, wheedle; force gently. (obs. *cokes*, fool)

coaxal, coaxial, *aa.* having common axis.

cob, *n.* composition of clay and straw used for building.

cob, *n.* small stocky riding-horse; round lump of coal; corn-cob; (also **c. swan**) male swan; (also **c.-loaf**) round-headed loaf; (also **c.-nut**) large kind of hazel nut.

cobalt, *n.* metallic element; deep-blue pigment made from it.—*a.* deep-blue. **cobaltic, cobaltous,** *aa.* (G.)

cobber, *n.* (*Austral.*) chum, pal.

cobble, *n.* rounded stone used for paving.—*v.t.* pave with cobbles.

cobble, *v.t.* mend, patch, roughly. **cobbler,** *n.* mender of boots and shoes; clumsy workman; kinds of iced drink. **cobbler's wax,** resinous substance for waxing thread.

cobby, *a.* thickset, stocky.

cobelligerent, *n.* power co-operating with another in carrying on war.

coble, *n.* small flat-bottomed fishing-boat.

cobra, *n.* (also **c. de capello**) venomous hooded snake. (L. *colubra*, snake)

cobweb, *n.* spider's web; flimsy thing; entanglement. **cobwebby,** *a.*

coca, *n.* a Bolivian shrub; its leaves, chewed as stimulant. **cocaine,** *n.* drug got from coca and used as local anaesthetic. **cocainism,** *n.* morbid state resulting from excess of cocaine. **cocainize,** *v.t.* treat with cocaine. (Peruvian *cuca*)

coccus, *n.* (*pl.* **cocci**) spherical bacterium. (Gk. *kokkos*, seed)

coccyx, *n.* triangular bone ending spinal column. **coccygeal,** *a.* (Gk. *kokkux*, cuckoo)

cochin-china, *n.* breed of fowl. (place)

cochineal, *n.* scarlet dye made from dried insects. (Gk. *kokkos*, seed)

cochlea, *n.* (*pl.* **cochleae**) spiral cavity of inner ear. (L. = snail)

cochleare, *n.* (*med.*, *abbr.* **cochl.**) spoonful. (L. *cochlear*, spoon)

cock, *n.* male fowl; male bird; tap; hammer of gun; cocked position; (*vulg.*) penis.—*v.t.* and *i.* set erect, stick up; set (hat) at angle; bring hammer of (gun) to firing position. **c. of the walk,** dominant person. **c. one's eye,** glance knowingly. **full, half, c.,** with hammer drawn back, half-way back, to firing position. **old c.,** (*sl.*) old chap. **that c. won't fight,** that argument won't work. **c.-and-bull story,** incredible story. **cocked hat,** brimless hat pointed in front and behind. (O.E. *cocc*)

cock, *n.* small pile of hay.

cock, *n.* (*Shake.*) cockboat.

Cock, (*Shake.*) corrupt. of God.

cockade, *n.* badge worn in hat.

cock-a-doodle-doo, *n.* cry of cock. (imit.)

cock-a-hoop, *a.* elated, exultant.

Cockaigne, *n.* imaginary land of plenty; cockneyland, London. (O.F. *coquaigne*)

cock-a-leekie, *n.* Scotch dish of broth with leeks.

cockalorum, *n.* young cock; perky little man.

cockatoo, *n.* crested parrot. (Malay *kakatúa*)

cockatrice, *n.* fabulous reptile with death-dealing glance, basilisk. (L. *calcare*, tread)

Cockayne, same as **Cockaigne.**
cockboat, *n.* small ship's boat.
cockchafer, *n.* large winged beetle. (*chafer*)
cock-crow, *n.* time of dawn.
cocker, *v.t.* pamper, coddle.
cocker, *n.* breed of spaniel.
Cocker, *n.* according to C., correct, orthodox. (teacher of arithmetic)
cockerel, *n.* young cock; pugnacious youth. (dim. of *cock*)
cock-eyed, *a.* squinting; crooked.
cock-fight, *n.* organized fight between gamecocks.
cock-horse, *n.* stick child rides astride of.
cockle, *n.* an edible shell-fish. **c. hat,** (*Shake.*) hat with scallop-shell, badge of pilgrim. **warm the cc. of one's heart,** hearten one. **c.-shell,** *n.* shell of cockle; frail boat. (Gk. *kongchē*, cockle+dim.)
cockle, *n.* purple-flowered weed; disease of wheat. (O.E. *coccel*)
cockle, *v.t.* and *i.* curl up, pucker.—*n.* wrinkle, bulge.
cockle, *n.* kinds of stove.
cock-loft, *n.* small upper loft; garret.
cockney, *n.* native Londoner; London dialect; (*Shake.*) effeminate person. **cockneyfy,** *v.t.* vulgarize on cockney model. **cockneyism,** *n.* cockney idiom or pronunciation. (M.E. *cokeney*, cock's egg)
cockpit, *n.* enclosure for cock-fighting; part of lower deck of old man-of-war used for wounded in action; scene of many battles; place for pilot in fuselage of aeroplane.
cockroach, *n.* kinds of insect incl. blackbeetle. (Sp. *cucaracha*)
cockscomb, *n.* cock's crest; kinds of plant.
cock-shy, *n.* thing set up to be thrown at; throw at this. (*cock; shy*)
cock-sure, *a.* quite certain; over-confident.
cocktail, *n.* drink of spirit with bitters and flavourings; horse nearly but not quite thoroughbred; bounder.
cocky, cocksy, *a.* bumptious, conceited.
cocky-leeky, same as **cock-a-leekie.**
coco, cocoa, *n.* tropical palm. **coconut,** *n.* its large brown nut; (*sl.*) head. (Port.=grimace)
cocoa, *n.* powder of ground cocoa beans; drink made from this. **c. bean,** seed of cacao plant. (corrupt. of *cacao*)
cocoon, *n.* silky case spun by larva of silkworm to protect it in chrysalis stage. (F. *coque*, shell+dim.)
cocotte, *n.* fashionable prostitute. (F.)
cod, *n.* (also **c.-fish**) large sea-fish. **c.-liver oil,** used as tonic.
cod, *v.t.* and *n.* (*sl.*) hoax, swindle.
cod, *n.* (*Scot.*) pillow.
cod, *n.* (*obs.*) pod. **c.-piece,** *n.* (*Shake.*) baggy appendage worn in front of hose. **codding,** *a.* (*Shake.*) wanton. (O.E. *codd*, small bag)
coda, *n.* (*mus.*) passage added at end of composition or section to give greater sense of finality. (It.)
coddle, *v.t.* treat as invalid, pamper.
code, *n.* systematic body of laws; set of rules or conventions; system of signals; system of words or symbols arbitrarily used for brevity or secrecy; cipher.—*v.t.* put (message) into code. (*codex*)
codex, *n.* (*pl.* codices) volume of manuscripts of Bible or classical texts. (L.=book)
codger, *n.* (*colloq.*) queer fellow, buffer.
codicil, *n.* addition to will modifying its provisions. **codicillary,** *a.* (*codex* +dim.)
codify, *v.t.* reduce (laws) to code. **codification,** *n.* (L. *facere*, make)
codling, codlin, *n.* kind of apple.
codling, *n.* small cod. (dim.)
co-education, *n.* teaching of boys and girls in same school or college. **co-ed,** *n.* (*Amer. sl.*) girl student at co-educational institution.
coefficient, *n.* thing that acts together with another; (*math.*) symbol placed before another as multiplier.
coeliac, *a.* of belly. (Gk. *koilos*, hollow)
coenobite, *n.* member of religious community. **coenobitic, coenobitical,** *aa.* (Gk. *koinos*, common; *bios*, life)
coequal, *a.* having complete equality.
coerce, *v.t.* compel, constrain, force. **coercible, coercive,** *aa.* **coercion,** *n.* forcible compulsion; government by force. **coercionary,** *a.* **coercionist,** *n.* (L. *arcēre*, shut up)
coessential, *a.* of the same substance.
coeternal, *a.* equally eternal.
coeval, *a.* and *n.* (person) of same age, contemporary. (L. *aevum*, age)
coexist, *v.i.* exist at the same time. **coexistence,** *n.* **coexistent,** *a.*
coextensive, *a.* extending over same space or time.
coffee, *n.* drink made from roasted and ground seeds of an Arabian shrub; the seeds or shrub. **c.-bean, c.-berry,** *nn.* coffee seed. **c.-house,** *n.* refreshment house. **c.-mill,** *n.* for grinding seeds. **c.-pot,** *n.* for making coffee in. **c.-room,** *n.* hotel dining-room. (Arab. *qahweh*)
coffer, *n.* box for valuables; (*pl.*) treasury, funds. **c.-dam,** *n.* enclosure for excluding water during bridge-building. (Gk. *kophinos*, basket)
coffin, *n.* chest in which corpse is buried.—*v.t.* put in coffin. **c.-bone,** *n.* bone inside horse's hoof. (Gk. *kophinos*, basket)
cog, *n.* tooth-like projection on rim of wheel. **c.-wheel,** *n.*
cog, *v.t.* and *i.* fraudulently control fall of (dice); cheat. **cogged dice,** loaded dice.
cog, *n.* small fishing-boat.
cog, *n.* (*Scot.*) wooden dish.

cogent, *a.* persuasive, convincing. **cogency,** *n.* (L. *cogere*, compel)
cogitate, *v.i.* and *t.* think deeply, ponder; devise. **cogitable, cogitative,** *aa.* **cogitation, cogitator,** *nn.* (L. *cogitare*)
cognac, *n.* French brandy. (place)
cognate, *a.* sprung from common stock; having common source or origin; kindred, related.—*n.* relative; cognate word. (L. *gnatus*, born)
cognition, *n.* mental act of perceiving; knowledge. **cognitional, cognitive,** *aa.* **cognizable,** *a.* within cognizance of court; knowable. **cognizance,** *n.* extent of knowledge; awareness; judicial notice; (*heraldry*) distinctive badge. **cognizant,** *a.* aware, informed (of). **cognize,** *v.t.* have cognition of. (L. *gnoscere*, get to know)
cognomen, *n.* surname; nickname. (L.)
cognoscente, n. (*pl. cognoscenti*) connoisseur. (It.)
cognoscible, *a.* capable of being known.
cognovit, n. (*law*) defendant's acknowledgment that plaintiff's cause is just. (L.=he has acknowledged)
cohabit, *v.i.* live together as husband and wife. **cohabitation,** *n.* (L. *habitare*, dwell)
coheir, *n.* (*fem.* **coheiress**) joint heir.
cohere, *v.i.* stick together, remain united; be consistent. **coherent,** *a.* cohering; consistent, not rambling; properly articulated; intelligible. **coherence, coherency,** *nn.* **coherer,** *n.* device used in wireless reception. **cohesion,** *n.* cohering, sticking together; force causing this; interdependence. **cohesive,** *a.* (L. *haerēre*, stick)
cohort, *n.* tenth part of Roman legion; (*pl.*) troops; band. (L. *cohors*)
coif, *n.* close-fitting cap. *coiffeur, n.* (*fem. coiffeuse*) hairdresser. **coiffure,** *n.* style of hairdressing. (O.F. *coife*)
coign, *n.* quoin. **c. of vantage,** place for viewing something. (*coin*)
coil, *v.t.* and *i.* wind in rings or folds; twist into spiral or circular shape.—*n.* coiled length of rope; single ring of this; (*electr.*) spiral wire for passage of current.
coil, *n.* (*arch.*) tumult, disturbance.
coin, *n.* piece of stamped metal as money; (*colloq.*) money.—*v.t.* and *i.* make into money, mint; invent (word). **coinage,** *n.* coining; issue of coins, currency; coined word. (L. *cuneus*, wedge)
coincide, *v.i.* occupy same portion of space; happen at same point of time; agree exactly. **coincidence,** *n.* coinciding; occurrence of an event at same time as another without apparent connection. **coincident,** *a.* coinciding. **coincidental,** *a.* of coincidence. (L. *in*, in; *cadere*, fall)
coiner, *n.* maker of counterfeit coins.
coinstantaneous, *a.* exactly at same moment.
coir, *n.* fibre made from husk of coconut. (Malayalam *kayar*, cord)
coistrel, coistril, *n.* (*Shake.*) knave.
coition, coitus, *nn.* sexual intercourse. (L. *ire* go)
coke, *n.* coal from which gas has been expelled.—*v.t.* convert (coal) into coke.
coker-nut, *vulg.* form of coco-nut.
col, *n.* pass between mountain peaks. (F.=neck)
col-, form of **com-** before *l.*
cola, same as **kola.**
colander, cullender, *n.* vessel with holes in bottom, used as strainer in cookery.—*v.t.* strain with colander. (L. *colare*, strain)
colcannon, *n.* stew of pounded cabbage and potatoes.
colchicum, *n.* autumn crocus; narcotic made from its seeds. (*Colchis*)
colcothar, *n.* red peroxide of iron. (Arab. *qolqotar*)
cold, *a.* lacking heat or warmth; unemotional; unmoved; undemonstrative, unfriendly; (of scent) faint.—*n.* low temperature; cold weather; catarrh of nose or throat. **catch c.,** contract catarrh. **c. colours,** blues and greys. **c. cream,** cooling ointment. **c. feet,** (*army sl.*) fear. **get person c.,** (*sl.*) have him at one's mercy. **give one the c. shoulder, c.-shoulder,** *v.t.* treat as unwelcome. **throw c. water on,** discourage (plan). **c.-blooded,** *a.* having cold blood; sensitive to cold; callous. **c.-chisel,** *n.* tempered chisel for cutting cold iron. (O.E. *cald*)
cole, *n.* kinds of cabbage. **c.-slaw,** *n.* (*Amer.*) salad of sliced cabbage. (L. *caulis*)
colemouse, same as **coalmouse.**
coleopterous, *a.* with outer pair of wings formed into hard sheathes for inner. (Gk. *koleon*, sheath; *pteron*, wing)
colibri, *n.* humming-bird. (Sp.)
colic, *n.* acute spasmodic pain in abdomen. **colicky,** *a.* of, causing, colic. **colitis,** *n.* inflammation of colon. (*colon*)
coll, *v.t.* (*Spens.*) embrace round neck. (L. *collum*, neck)
collaborate, *v.i.* work jointly or together, esp. in literature. **collaboration, collaborator,** *nn.* (*labour*)
collapse, *v.i.* fall down; come to ruin, fail; break down physically or mentally.—*n.* collapsing; breakdown, prostration. **collapsible, collapsable,** *a.* folding. (L. *labi*, slip)
collar, *n.* band worn round neck as part of dress; band round dog's neck, part of horse's harness; neck-chain; ring, flange.—*v.t.* seize by collar, capture; (*sl.*) get, get control of; (*Rugby football*) lay hold of and stop (man with ball). **c.-bone,** *n.* bone

joining breastbone and shoulder-blade. **collarette,** *n.* woman's collar of lace, fur etc. (L. *collum,* neck)

collate, *v.t.* examine and compare (manuscripts etc.); (of bishop) appoint to benefice. (L. *latus,* brought)

collateral, *a.* side by side; accompanying but secondary; descended from same ancestor but not directly.—*n.* collateral relation or security. **c. security,** property pledged as guarantee for repayment of loan.

collation, *n.* collating; light repast. **collator,** *n.* one who collates.

colleague, *n.* associate in same office or profession, fellow worker. (L. *legere,* choose)

colleague, *v.i.* join in league, ally.

collect, *v.t.* and *i.* bring together, gather, assemble; regain command over, concentrate (thoughts etc.).—*n.* short prayer for particular occasion. **collectable, collectible,** *aa.* **collectanea,** *n.pl.* miscellany. **collected,** *a.* self-possessed, cool. **collection,** *n.* act of collecting; accumulation; money collected at meeting; group of things collected for beauty, rarity, or value; (*Shake.*) inference; (*pl.*) informal college examination. **collective,** *a.* viewed as a whole, taken as one; combined, common; (*gram.*) used in singular to express multitude. **collectivism,** *n.* theory that the state should own all means of production. **collectivist,** *n.* and *a.* (adherent) of collectivism. **collector,** *n.* one who collects; chief administrative official of district in India. **collectorate, collectorship,** *nn.* district, office, of collector. (L. *legere,* gather)

colleen, *n.* (*Anglo-Ir.*) girl. (Ir. *cailin*)

college, *n.* self-governing educational institution; its buildings; body of colleagues, association (of cardinals etc.); (*Scot.*) university. **colleger, collegian,** *nn.* member of college. **collegiate,** *a.* of, containing, connected with, having status of, a college. (L. *legere,* gather)

collet, *n.* part of ring that holds the stone; small band. (F.)

collide, *v.i.* come into violent contact (with), dash together. (L. *laedere,* strike)

collie, *n.* Scotch sheep-dog.

collied, *a.* (*Shake.*) blackened. (*coal*)

collier, *n.* coal-miner; vessel carrying coal; member of its crew. **colliery,** *n.* coal-mine. (*coal*)

collieshangie, *n.* (*Scot.*) noisy wrangling.

colligate, *v.t.* bind together; bring (isolated facts) under general principle. **colligation,** *n.* (L. *ligare,* bind)

collimate, *v.t.* make parallel; adjust line of sight of. **collimation, collimator,** *nn.* (*collimare,* misreading of L. *collineare,* from *linea,* line)

collinear, *a.* in same straight line.

collision, *n.* colliding; violent impact of moving bodies; clash of interests etc. **c.-mat,** *n.* to put over hole in ship's side.

collocate, *v.t.* place together; arrange. **collocation,** *n.* collocating; relative situation.

collocutor, *n.* one who takes part in colloquy.

collodion, *n.* solution of gun-cotton in ether, used in photography. (Gk. *kolla,* glue; *eidos,* form)

collogue, *v.i.* talk confidentially. (*colloquy*)

colloid, *a.* gluey; (*chem.*) of gummy non-crystalline kind.—*n.* colloid substance. **colloidal,** *a.* (Gk. *kolla,* glue; *eidos,* form)

collop, *n.* slice of meat.

colloquy, *n.* conversation, dialogue. **colloquial,** *a.* of conversation; used in familiar but not formal talk, not literary. **colloquialism,** *n.* colloquial word or phrase; use of these. **colloquist,** *n.* one who takes part in colloquy. (L. *loqui,* speak)

collotype, *n.* gelatine photographic plate used for printing from in ink. (Gk. *kolla,* glue)

collusion, *n.* fraudulent secret understanding, esp. when ostensible opponents play into each other's hands. **collusive,** *a.* **collude,** *v.i.* (*arch.*) act in collusion. (L. *ludere,* play)

collyrium, *n.* (*pl.* collyria) eye-salve; suppository. (Gk. *kollurion*)

collywobbles, *n.pl.* (*joc.*) abdominal pain or discomfort.

colocynth, *n.* kind of cucumber; purgative it yields. (Gk. *kolokunthis*)

colon, *n.* part of large intestine from caecum to rectum. (Gk. *kolon*)

colon, *n.* punctuation-mark (:) between semicolon and full stop. (Gk. *kōlon,* limb)

colonel, *n.* officer in command of regiment or battalion. **c. commandant,** commander of brigade. **colonelcy,** *n.* status of colonel. (It. *colonna,* column)

colonial, *a.* of colony or colonies.—*n.* inhabitant of colony. **colonist,** *n.* one who takes part in founding colony, settler; colonial. **colonize,** *v.t.* and *i.* establish colony in; settle in colony. **colonization,** *n.*

colonitis, *n.* colitis.

colonnade, *n.* series of columns placed at regular intervals; avenue of trees. (It. *colonna,* column)

colony, *n.* body of people who settle in new country, continuing subject to parent state; country they settle in; group of aliens occupying district in city or country; group of related organisms. **Roman c.,** settlement in conquered territory acting as garrison. (L. *colere,* cultivate)

colophon, *n.* tail-piece at end of old books, with date, publisher etc. (Gk. *kolophōn,* finishing stroke)

colophony, *n.* rosin. (*Colophon* in Asia Minor)
coloquintida, same as colocynth.
Colorado beetle, kind of beetle destructive to potatoes. (place)
coloration, colouration, *n.* colouring, disposition of colours. **colorific,** *a.* producing colour. **colorimeter,** *n.* instrument measuring intensity of colour.
coloratura, *n.* and *a.* highly ornamented or florid (vocal passage). (It.)
colossus, *n.* (*pl.* **colossi, colossuses**) gigantic statue; person, thing, of overawing size or greatness. **colossal,** *a.* gigantic; (*colloq.*) remarkable, splendid. (Gk. *kolossos*)
colotomy, *n.* incision in colon. (Gk. *temnein,* cut)
colour, *n.* hue, tint; paint, pigment; complexion; show of reason; pretext; use of imagery, vividness, in literature; (us. *pl.*) flag of regiment; coloured badge or dress worn as symbol.—*v.t.* and *i.* give colour to; paint; blush; misrepresent; palliate; influence. **change c.,** grow red or pale. **come off with flying cc.,** be very successful. **high c.,** bright complexion. **in one's true cc.,** in one's real character. **join the cc.,** enlist. **off c.,** in poor form, out of sorts. **person of c.,** one who is not a white. **sail under false cc.,** be impostor. **c.-blind,** *a.* unable to distinguish colours. **c.-sergeant,** *n.* old name for company sergeant-major. **colourable,** *a.* capable of being coloured; specious, plausible. **colouration,** see **coloration. coloured man,** negro. **colourful,** *a.* full of colour, vivid. **colouring,** *n.* disposition or use of colours. **colourless,** *a.* clear like water; pale; insipid; characterless, non-committal. **colourman,** *n.* dealer in paints. (L. *color*)
colporteur, *n.* one who hawks books, esp. Bibles. (F.)
Colt, *n.* kind of revolver. (inventor)
colt, *n.* young horse; inexperienced youth, tiro; (*naut.*) rope's-end.—*v.t.* (*naut.*) flog; (*Shake.*) cheat. **coltish,** *a.* like a colt, frisky. **coltsfoot,** *n.* yellow-flowered weed.
colubrine, *a.* snake-like. (L. *coluber,* snake)
columbine, *a.* like a dove.—*n.* a garden plant, aquilegia. **columbarium,** *n.* dove-cot; place with niches for cinerary urns. (L. *columba,* dove)
Columbine, *n.* female character in pantomime.
columbium, *n.* metallic element now called niobium. (*Columbia,* America)
column, *n.* round pillar; thing shaped like this; support; vertical division of page; narrow-fronted deep formation of troops. **columnar,** *a.* (L. *columna*)
colure, *n.* celestial circle passing through poles and equinoctial or solstitial points. (Gk. *kolos,* docked; *oura,* tail)
colza, *n.* rape-seed. **c.-oil,** *n.* made from this. (*cole*)
com-, *pref.* with, as in combat; wholly, as in compel. (L. *cum*)
coma, *n.* state of deep insensibility, stupor. **comatose,** *a.* of, in, coma. (Gk. *kōma*)
coma, *n.* (*pl.* **comae**) nebulous envelope round nucleus of comet; (*bot.*) silky hairs at end of seed. **comate,** *a.* hairy. (L.=hair)
comate, *n.* (*Shake.*) companion. (*co-*)
comb, *n.* toothed instrument for arranging or confining hair; part of machine like this; crest of cock; honeycomb.—*v.t.* and *i.* arrange (hair), dress (wool), with comb; (of wave) curl over. (O.E. *camb*)
combat, *v.t.* and *i.* strive against, oppose; do battle.—*n.* contest, fight; strife. **combatant,** *a.* and *n.* (person) engaged in fighting. **combative,** *a.* pugnacious, quarrelsome. (L. *batuere,* beat)
combe, see **coomb.**
comber, *n.* wool-combing machine; long curling wave, breaker.
combine, *v.t.* and *i.* join together, unite intimately; possess together; co-operate; (*chem.*) form compound (with); (*Shake.*) bind.—*n.* commercial combination, syndicate. **combinate,** *a.* (*Shake.*) betrothed. **combination,** *n.* combining; union; set of things or persons combined; motor-cycle and side-car; (*pl.*) undergarment for body and legs; (*math.*) different collections possible of given number of things in groups of given smaller number. **combinative,** *a.* (L. *bini,* two at a time)
combustion, *n.* process of burning. **spontaneous c.,** from heat generated within substance. **combustible,** *a.* capable of burning; easily set alight. —*n.* combustible thing. **combustibility,** *n.* **combustious,** *a.* (*Shake.*) combustible. (L. *comburere,* burn up)
come, *v.i.* (*past* **came,** *p.p.* **come**) approach; arrive; reach; happen (to); originate; turn out (to be); (*sl.*) play the part of; (*Shake.*) become.—*int.* now then! **c. about,** happen; (of ship) wear. **c. across,** meet with; (*Amer. sl.*) pay up. **c. away,** get detached. **c. by,** pass; acquire. **c. down,** descend; fall. **c. forward,** present oneself. **c. in,** enter; find place. **c. of,** result from. **c. off,** fare; succeed; (*Shake.*) escape; pay. **c. on,** advance; arise. **c. out,** be revealed or published; go on strike; make début. **c. over,** befall; (*Shake.*) surpass. **c. round,** recover normal state; look in as visitor. **c. to,** attain; amount to; revive. **c. under,** be subjected to; be classed among. **c. up,** approach; grow. **c. up to,** equal. **c. up with,** overtake.

c.-at-able, *a.* accessible. **c.-back,** *n.* return from retirement; (*Amer.*) retort. **c.-down,** *n.* downfall. **coming-on,** *a.* (*Shake.*) compliant. (O.E. *cuman*)

comeddle, *v.t.* (*Shake.*) mix.

comedy, *n.* play dealing with lighter side of life and having happy ending; humorous play, story, or incident. **comedian,** *n.* player of comic parts; writer of comedies. **comedienne,** *n.* comedy actress. **comedietta,** *n.* short comedy. **comedist,** *n.* writer of comedies. (Gk. *kōmos,* revel; *aeidein,* sing)

comely, *a.* pleasing to the eye, good-looking; decent, seemly. **comeliness,** *n.* (O.E. *cyme,* fine; *lic,* like)

comestible, *n.* (us. *pl.*) thing to eat. (L. *edere,* eat)

comet, *n.* heavenly body like star with tail. **cometary, cometic,** *aa.* (Gk. *komē,* hair)

comfit, *n.* sweetmeat. (*confection*)

comfort, *n.* consolation in sorrow, relief in trouble; bodily ease; (*pl.*) things between necessaries and luxuries.—*v.t.* and *i.* bring consolation to; soothe; cheer; (*arch.*) aid; (*Shake.*) be consoled. **comfortable,** *a.* promoting comfort; at ease; adequate; (*Shake.*) helpful. **comfortably,** *adv.* in a comfortable manner; easily. **comforter,** *n.* one who comforts; woollen scarf; baby's dummy teat. **the Comforter,** the Holy Spirit. **comfortless,** *a.* having or giving no comfort. (L. *fortis,* strong)

comfrey, *n.* tall bell-flowered ditch-plant. (O.F. *confirie*)

comfy, *a.* (*colloq.*) comfortable.

comic, *a.* of comedy; funny, facetious; meant to amuse.—*n.* (*colloq.*) comic person or paper. **comical,** *a.* funny, laughable; droll, ludicrous. **comicality,** *n.* (Gk. *kōmos,* revel)

Comintern, *n.* Russian Communist International. (abbr.)

comitadji, *n.* Balkan guerrilla band. (Serbian)

comity, *n.* courtesy, friendliness. (L. *cōmis,* courteous)

comma, *n.* punctuation-mark (,) used to mark shortest pause. **inverted cc.,** (' ' or " ") used to mark quotations. (Gk. *komma,* clause)

command, *v.t.* and *i.* order, bid; be in authority (over); control; have at disposal; evoke, compel; look down over.—*n.* order; control; disposal; position of authority; troops, district, under commander. **at c.,** available. **commandant,** *n.* commanding officer, esp. governor of fortress. **commandeer,** *v.t.* seize for military purposes; conscript; appropriate. **commander,** *n.* one who commands, leader; naval officer ranking next below captain. **commander-in-chief,** *n.* commander of a state's entire forces. **commanding,** *a.* in command; dominating; impressive. **commandment,** *n.* divine command; mandate. order. **commando,** *n.* special unit of picked men trained for raiding; (*S. Afr.*) military party. (L. *mandare,* entrust)

comme il faut, well-bred. (F.)

commemorate, *v.t.* keep in memory by ceremony or writing; be memorial of. **commemoration,** *n.* commemorating; annual Oxford festival in memory of founders. **commemorative,** *a.* **commemorator,** *n.* (L. *memor,* mindful)

commence, *v.t.* and *i.* begin; (*arch.*) set up as. **commencement,** *n.* start; day, ceremony, of conferring degrees at Cambridge. (L. *in,* into; *ire,* go)

commend, *v.t.* speak favourably of, praise; recommend; entrust; (*arch.*) remember (one to).—*n.* (*Shake.*) praise. **commendable,** *a.* praiseworthy. **commendation,** *n.* **commendatory,** *a.* (L. *mandare,* entrust)

commensal, *a.* and *n.* (person, organism) living and feeding with another. **commensalism, commensality,** *nn.* (L. *mensa,* table)

commensurable, *a.* measurable by same standard; divisible without remainder by same quantity; proportionate (to). **commensurability,** *n.* **commensurate,** *a.* coextensive; proportionate (to).

comment, *n.* remark, observation, criticism; explanatory note.—*v.i.* make comment (upon); annotate. **commentary,** *n.* series of explanatory notes; running criticism. **commentator,** *n.* writer of commentary. (L. *mens,* mind)

commerce, *n.* buying and selling, trade; intercourse, dealings; (*arch.*) sexual relations. **c.-destroyer,** *n.* warship harrying enemy's merchant ships. **commercial,** *a.* of commerce, mercantile.—*n.* (*colloq.*) commercial traveller. **commercial traveller,** agent who goes about to obtain orders for his firm. **commercialism,** *n.* commercial methods or standpoint. **commercialize,** *v.t.* make an affair of business. (L. *merx,* merchandise)

commination, threatening of divine vengeance, denunciation, cursing. **comminatory,** *a.* threatening, denunciatory. (L. *minari,* threaten)

commingle, *v.t.* and *i.* mingle together.

comminute, *v.t.* reduce to minute particles or powder. **comminution,** *n.*

commiserate, *v.i.* and *t.* sympathize (with) in distress; feel pity for. **commiseration,** *n.* **commiserative,** *a.* (L. *miser,* wretched)

commissar, *n.* head of government department in Soviet Russia. **commissariat,** *n.* army department of food and stores; food supply. **commissary,** *n.* head of army commissariat; deputy. **commissarial,** *a.* (*commit*)

commission, *n.* committing; business committed to someone; authority to act; document appointing army or navy officer of rank of lieutenant or above; body of persons appointed for specified duties; percentage on sales paid to agent; brokerage.—*v.t.* empower, appoint, by commission; employ service of, authorize; put in commission. **put in c.,** man and equip (warship). **commissionaire,** *n.* uniformed porter or door-keeper. **commissioner,** *n.* member of commission. **commissioner for oaths,** person authorized to receive sworn declarations. **High Commissioner,** chief representative of British dominion in Britain.

commissure, *n.* (*anat.*) line of junction, seam. **commissural,** *a.* (*commit*)

commit, *v.t.* and *i.* (*past, p.p.* **committed**) entrust; consign (to prison etc.); do, perpetrate; pledge, involve; (*Shake.*) sin, commit adultery. **c. to memory,** learn by heart. **commitment,** *n.* engagement that restricts freedom; committal. **committal,** *n.* act of committing. **committee,** *n.* body of persons appointed from larger body to consider or manage some matter; (*law*) person entrusted with charge of lunatic. (L. *mittere,* send)

commix, *v.t.* and *i.* mix together. **commixture,** *n.* commixing; blend.

commode, *n.* chamber-pot enclosed in stool; chest of drawers. (*commodious*)

commodious, *a.* roomy; (*arch.*) handy; (*Shake.*) accommodating. **commodity,** *n.* article of commerce; useful thing; (*arch.*) convenience; (*Shake.*) consignment; profit. (L. *modus,* measure)

commodore, *n.* naval rank between captain and rear-admiral; commander of naval squadron; senior captain, leading vessel, of shipping line. (L.L. *commandator,* commander)

common, *a.* belonging equally to more than one; public; usual, ordinary; frequent; easily got, not rare; low, vulgar; (of noun) applying to any of a class; (of gender) indifferently masculine or feminine.—*n.* tract of open public land; (*Shake.*) vulgar tongue; (*pl.*) the common people; House of Commons; provisions, rations. **c. law,** unwritten English law based on usage. **c. or garden,** (*sl.*) of usual kind. **c. people,** the general body of people. **C. Prayer,** liturgy of Church of England. **c. sense,** sound practical sense. **c. time,** (*mus.*) two or four beats in a bar. **c. weal,** public good. **in c.,** in joint use; equally. **out of the c.,** unusual. **junior, senior, c.-room,** *n.* room used in common by undergraduates, fellows, of Oxford college. (L. *communis*)

commonage, *n.* right of pasturing on common land; commonalty.

commonalty, *n.* the common people.

commoner, *n.* one not a peer; member of House of Commons; (*Shake.*) harlot.

commonplace, *a.* undistinguished, ordinary, trite.—*n.* commonplace thing or remark. **c.-book,** *n.* book of notable passages.

commonwealth, *n.* state, body politic; republic; (formerly) common weal.

commove, *v.t.* move violently; excite. **commotion,** *n.* disturbance; tumult.

commune, *v.i.* converse intimately, have intercourse (with); partake of communion.—*n.* small territorial administrative division. **the C.,** Paris revolutionary government of 1789–94 and 1871. **communal,** *a.* of commune; for common use; on communalistic principles; (*India*) relating to religious sects. **communalism,** *n.* political system based on local self-government. **communalist,** *n.* supporter of this. **communalistic,** *a.* **communalize,** *v.t.* make over to community. (L. *communis,* common)

communicate, *v.t.* and *i.* impart, share; connect (with); partake of communion. **communicable,** *a.* **communicability,** *n.* **communicant,** *n.* one who receives communion; one who imparts news. **communication,** *n.* communicating; information; intercourse; connecting passage or channel; (*pl.*) connection between army's base and front. **communication-cord,** *n.* by which passenger can stop train. **communicative,** *a.* ready to give information. **communicator,** *n.* (L. *communis,* common)

communion, *n.* common possession, sharing; intercourse, fellowship; religious body; (also **holy c.**) celebration of the Lord's Supper. **c. cup, c. table,** *nn.* used for holy communion. **communionist,** *n.* (*commune*)

communiqué, *n.* official announcement. (F.)

communism, *n.* the having property in common; extreme form of socialism based on this. **communist,** *n.* supporter of communism. **communistic,** *a.* (L. *communis,* common)

community, *n.* organized political or social body; body of people in same locality; the public, society; joint ownership; common character; (*Shake.*) commonness. **c. singing,** in which all join. (L. *communis,* common)

commute, *v.t.* and *i.* exchange (for), change (to); reduce (punishment) to one less severe; (*Amer.*) travel daily from suburban home to city office. **commutation,** *n.* **commutative,** *a.* **commutator,** *n.* device for reversing direction of electric current. **commuter,** *n.* (*Amer.*) season-ticket holder. (L. *mutare,* change)

comose, *a.* hairy; tufted. (*coma*)

compact, *n.* agreement, contract; treaty. (*pact*)

compact, *a.* closely packed; condensed, terse; (*Shake.*) made up (of).—*v.t.* press or pack closely; compose (of); (*Shake.*) confirm.—*n.* small vanity-case. (L. *pangere*, fix)

compages, *n.* structure, framework. (L.)

companion, *n.* wooden shelter over companion-way; (also **c.-ladder, c.-way**) ladder, staircase, from deck to cabin. (L. *panis*, bread)

companion, *n.* comrade; partner, associate; one of a pair of matched things; member of lowest grade of order of knighthood; (*Shake.*) fellow. *v.t.* and *i.* accompany; associate. **companionable,** *a.* sociable. **companionate marriage,** regulated cohabitation. **companionship,** *n.* fellowship; (*print.*) company of compositors working together. (L. *panis*, bread)

company, *n.* assemblage of people; association of persons for carrying on a business; ship's crew; companionship, society; division of battalion (about 250 men); (*Shake.*) companion. —*v.t.* (*arch.*) accompany. **keep c. with,** associate with; court. (*companion*)

compare, *v.t.* and *i.* make one thing measure of another; observe similarity between, liken; bear comparison; (*gram.*) give comparative and superlative forms of (adjective).—*n.* comparison. **comparable,** *a.* **comparability,** *n.* **comparative,** *a.* estimated by comparison; relative, not absolute; (*gram.*) expressing more; (*Shake.*) fertile in comparisons.—*n.* comparative degree; (*Shake.*) rival. **comparison,** *n.* act of comparing; illustration; (*Shake.*) satirical simile. (L. *par*, equal)

compart, *v.t.* partition. **compartment,** *n.* space partitioned off; division of railway carriage.

compass, *n.* circuit, circumference; extent, area; range of voice; instrument with magnetic needle indicating points of compass; (*pl.*) two-legged instrument for drawing circles.—*v.t.* bring about, contrive; encircle, go round, hem in. **fetch a c.,** (*arch.*) make detour. **points of the c.,** north, south, east, west etc. **compassed,** *a.* (*Shake.*) arched, round. (L. *passus*, step)

compassion, *n.* sorrow for others' suffering, pity. **compassionate,** *a.* showing compassion; merciful.—*v.t.* have compassion for. (L. *pati*, suffer)

compatible, *a.* agreeing or fitting in (with), consistent. **compatibility,** *n.* (L. *pati*, suffer)

compatriot, *n.* fellow-countryman.

compear, *v.i.* (*Scots law*) appear at court. (L. *parēre*, appear)

compeer, *n.* equal; companion.—*v.i.* (*Shake.*) equal.

compel, *v.t.* force, constrain; bring about by force; (*poet.*) drive forcibly. **compellable,** *a.* (L. *pellere*, drive)

compendium, *n.* (*pl.* **compendiums, compendia**) abridgement, summary. **compendious,** *a.* containing much in small space, succinct. (L. *pendere*, weigh)

compensate, *v.t.* counterbalance, make up for; recompense; indemnify. **compensation,** *n.* compensating; set-off; sum given to compensate. **compensational, compensative, compensatory,** *aa.* **compensator,** *n.* (L. *pendere*, weigh)

compete, *v.i.* strive in rivalry (with), vie; contend for prize. (L. *petere*, seek)

competent, *a.* fit, capable; legally qualified; open, permissible. **competence, competency,** *nn.* being competent; sufficiency, adequate fortune. (L. *petere*, seek)

competition, *n.* competing, rivalry; contest in skill or knowledge. **competitive,** *a.* of, by, competition. **competitor,** *n.* one who competes; (*Shake.*) confederate.

compile, *v.t.* collect, make up, from various sources; amass. **compilation,** *n.* compiling; book composed of material from others. (L. *compilare*, plunder)

complacent, *a.* self-satisfied. **complacence, complacency,** *nn.* self-satisfaction; gratification. (L. *placēre* please)

complain, *v.i.* find fault, grumble; be ill; (*poet.*) express grief, make mournful sound. **complainant,** *n.* (*law*) plaintiff. **complaint,** *n.* act of complaining; formal protest; grievance; ailment, disease. (L. *plangere*, lament)

complaisant, *a.* disposed to please, obliging; compliant. **complaisance,** *n.* (L. *placēre*, please)

complement, *n.* something making up a whole; full allowance, equipment, or number); (*Shake.*) outward demeanour.—*v.t.* form complement to. **c. of an angle,** angle that with it makes up right angle. **complemental, complementary,** *aa.* (L. *plēre*, fill)

complete, *a.* entire, free from deficiency; finished; unqualified.—*v.t.* make complete; finish. **completely,** *adv.* entirely, utterly. **completion,** *n.* **completive,** *a.* (L. *plēre*, fill)

complex, *a.* intricate, not simple; consisting of interconnected parts.—*n.* complex whole; (*psycho-anal.*) kinds of mental abnormality caused by repression of primitive instincts. **c. sentence,** with one principal and one or more subordinate clauses. (L. *plectere*, plait)

complexion, *n.* colour and texture of skin of face; aspect, character; (*Shake.*) constitution, disposition. (L. *plectere*, plait)

complexity, *n.* complexness.

compliant, *a.* yielding, submissive. **compliance,** *n.* complying; compliantness.

complicate, *v.t.* make intricate or involved; mix up. **complicacy,** *n.* complexity. **complicated,** *a.* complex; tangled. **complication,** *n.* complicated state, entanglement; complicating circumstance. **complicative,** *a.* (L. *plicare,* fold)

complicity, *n.* state of being an accomplice. **complice,** *n.* (*Shake.*) confederate.

compliment, *n.* polite expression of praise, flattering tribute; (*pl.*) formal greeting or expression of regard.—*v.t.* pay compliment to, flatter; congratulate (on). **complimentary,** *a.* (*complement*)

compline, complin, *n.* last service of day in Roman Catholic ritual. (L. *plēre,* fill)

complot, *n.* (*arch.*) conspiracy.

comply, *v.i.* act in accordance (with); yield, agree; (*Shake.*) use ceremony. (L. *plēre,* fill)

compo, *n.* kinds of plaster or stucco. (*composition*)

component, *a.* going to the making of a whole, constituent.—*n.* component part. (L. *ponere,* put)

comport, *v.t.* and *i.* conduct (oneself); be compatible, accord (with). (L. *portare,* carry)

compose, *v.t.* and *i.* make up, form; construct in one's mind, write; arrange, put in order; settle, adjust; tranquillize; (*print.*) set up. **composed,** *a.* calm, self-possessed. **composer,** *n.* one who composes, esp. music. (L. *pausare,* halt+confusion with *ponere,* place)

composite, *a.* made up of distinct parts or elements; (*archit.*) blending Ionic and Corinthian orders; (*bot.*) having many flowers in guise of one, as daisy.—*n.* composite thing or flower. (L. *ponere,* place)

composition, *n.* composing; sentence-construction, art of writing; musical or literary work; arrangement, grouping; constitution, make-up; mixture, compound artificial substance; compromise; agreement whereby payment of part of debt is taken for whole; (*Shake.*) compact; consistency. **compositive,** *a.* combining. **compositor,** *n.* type-setter. (L. *ponere,* place)

compos mentis, sane. (L.)

compossible, *a.* able to coexist.

compost, (*Shake.*) **composture,** *nn.* fertilizing mixture. (*composite*)

composure, *n.* calmness, self-possession; (*Shake.*) disposition. (*compose*)

compotation, *n.* tippling together.

compote, *n.* fruit preserved in syrup. (F.)

compound, *v.t.* and *i.* combine (parts, ingredients) into whole, mix; make up; settle (debt) by partial payment; commute (subscription) for lump sum; condone (offence) for money.—*a.* compounded, made up of several parts; not simple.—*n.* mixture; compound word. **c. addition,** dealing with different denominations. **c. fracture,** with skin wound in addition. **c. sentence,** with more than one principal clause. (L. *ponere,* place)

compound, *n.* (*India, China*) enclosure in which house or factory stands.

comprador, *n.* native agent or manager in European business office in China. (Port.=buyer)

comprehend, *v.t.* understand; include, embrace; comprise. **comprehensible,** *a.* intelligible. **comprehension,** *n.* understanding; inclusion. **comprehensive,** *a.* wide in scope, including a great deal. (L. *prehendere,* grasp)

compress, *v.t.* press or squeeze together; bring into smaller bulk, condense.—*n.* soft pad for compressing artery etc.; wet bandage to relieve inflammation. **compressible,** *a.* **compression, compressor,** *nn.*

comprise, *v.t.* consist of; include. **comprisable,** *a.* (*comprehend*)

compromise, *n.* settlement of dispute by mutual concession; middle course or view between two opposed ones.—*v.t.* and *i.* settle by mutual concession, effect compromise; imperil or injure (person's reputation) by indiscreet action. (*promise*)

compt, *n.* (*Shake.*) account, reckoning. **compter,** *n.* counter. **comptible,** *a.* susceptible. **comptroller,** form of controller in some titles. (*count*)

compulsion, *n.* compelling, constraint. **compulsive,** *a.* tending to compel. **compulsory,** *a.* enforced, obligatory; compelling (opp. to permissive). **compulsorily,** *adv.* (L. *pellere,* drive)

compunction, *n.* pricking of conscience; scruple. **compunctious,** *a.* (L. *pungere,* prick)

compurgation, *n.* vindication; (*obs. law*) clearing of person by others swearing that he was innocent. **compurgator,** *n.* **compurgatory,** *a.*

compute, *v.t.* and *i.* calculate, reckon. **computable, computative,** *aa.* **computation,** *n.* reckoning; estimate. (L. *putare,* reckon)

comrade, *n.* companion; mate, fellow. **comradeship,** *n.* (L. *camera,* chamber)

Comtism, *n.* positivism. **Comtist,** *n.* (A. *Comte,* French philosopher)

con, *v.t.* study; learn by heart. (O.E. *cunnan,* know)

con, *v.t.* direct course of (ship). **conning-tower,** *n.* warship's armoured pilot-house.

con, *v.t.* (*Amer. sl.*) swindle. **c. man,** confidence man. (*confidence*)

con, prep. with. *c. amore,* with enthusiasm. *c. brio*, with spirit. *c. espressione*, with expression. *c. fuoco*, with fire. (It.)

con, *abbr.* of **contra.**

con-, same as **com-.**

conation, *n.* (*philos.*) faculty or power which directs to effort. **conative,** *a.* of, expressing, endeavour. (L. *conari*, try)

concatenate, *v.t.* link together. **concatenation,** *n.* concatenating; string of connected ideas or events. (L. *catena*, chain)

concave, *a.* curving inwards, hollow. **concavity,** *n.* (L. *cavus*, hollow)

conceal, *v.t.* hide, keep from sight; keep secret. **concealment,** *n.* concealing; hiding-place; (*Shake.*) mystery. (L. *celare*, hide)

concede, *v.t.* grant; admit to be true, allow. (L. *cedere*, yield)

conceit, *n.* over-high opinion of oneself, vanity; personal judgment; farfetched comparison, quaint fancy; (*Shake.*) understanding, imagination. —*v.t.* (*arch.*) imagine. **out of c. with,** no longer pleased with. **conceited,** *a.* full of conceit, vain; (*Shake.*) fanciful. **conceitless,** *a.* (*Shake.*) witless. (*conceive*)

conceive, *v.t.* and *i.* become pregnant (with); form in the mind, think out, imagine; understand; express. **conceivable,** *a.* **conceivability,** *n.* (L. *capere*, take)

concentrate, *v.t.* and *i.* bring or converge together to one point; direct to single object or purpose; collect one's thoughts or efforts; (*chem.*) increase strength of by diminishing bulk, condense. **concentrated,** *a.* intense. **concentration,** *n.* concentrating. **concentration camp,** for housing prisoners or internees. **concentrative,** *a.* **concentrator,** *n.* (*centre*)

concentre, *v.t.* and *i.* bring, come, to common centre. **concentric,** *a.* having a common centre. **concentrically,** *adv.* **concentricity,** *n.*

concept, *n.* (*philos.*) idea, general notion. **conception,** *n.* conceiving; thing conceived, idea, notion. **conceptional, conceptive,** *aa.* **conceptious,** *a.* (*Shake.*) fruitful. **conceptual,** *a.* of mental conceptions. **conceptualism,** *n.* (*philos.*) doctrine that universal truths exist in the mind apart from any concrete embodiment. (*conceive*)

concern, *v.t.* relate or apply to; fill with anxiety; interest (oneself) in; (*pass.*) take part, be mixed up (in).—*n.* thing that concerns one; anxiety, misgiving; business, firm; (*colloq.*) thing; (*pl.*) affairs. **concernancy,** *n.* (*Shake.*) meaning. **concerned,** *a.* troubled, worried. **concerning,** *prep.* about.—*n.* (*Shake.*) affair. **concernment,** *n.* (L. *cernere*, regard)

concert, *n.* union, agreement; harmony; musical entertainment.—*v.t.* plan together, prearrange with others; devise. **c. pitch,** pitch slightly above normal; state of exceptional efficiency. **concerted,** *a.* (*mus.*) arranged in parts. **concertina,** *n.* portable wind instrument with bellows and keys worked by hands. **concerto,** *n.* musical composition for solo instrument and orchestra. (It. *concertare*, accord together)

concession, *n.* conceding; thing conceded; privilege granted by government, monopoly. **concessionary,** *a.* **concessionaire, concessionnaire,** *n.* holder of concession. **concessive,** *a.* of, expressing, concession.

concettism, *n.* use of conceits or fanciful turns in literary style. (It. *concetto*, conceit)

conch, *n.* large spiral marine shell; this used as trumpet; concha; (*archit.*) dome of semicircular apse. **concha,** *n.* (*pl.* **conchae**) external ear or its cavity. **conchiferous,** *a.* shell-bearing. **conchoid,** *a.* shell-like. **conchology,** *n.* study of shells and shell-fish. **conchological,** *a.* **conchologist,** *n.* student of conchology. (Gk. *kongchē*, cockle)

conchy, *n.* (*sl.*) conscientious objector to military service. (abbr.)

concierge, *n.* French house-porter or caretaker. (F.)

conciliar, *a.* of ecclesiastical councils. (L. *concilium*, council)

conciliate, *v.t.* win over from hostility, make friendly; propitiate; reconcile; gain (goodwill). **conciliation, conciliator,** *nn.* **conciliative, conciliatory,** *aa.* (L. *concilium*, council)

concinnity, *n.* neatness, elegance. (L. *concinnus*, well adjusted)

concise, *a.* brief, condensed, terse. **concision,** *n.* mutilation; conciseness. (L. *caedere*, cut)

conclave, *n.* private assembly; meeting-place of cardinals for election of pope. (L. *clavis*, key)

conclude, *v.t.* and *i.* bring or come to an end, finish; effect, settle; infer; resolve. **conclusion,** *n.* concluding; end, close; inference; final opinion; (*logic*) proposition deduced from premises; (*Shake.*) riddle; experiment. **try cc.,** engage in contest (with). **conclusive,** *a.* decisive, convincing. (L. *claudere*, shut)

concoct, *v.t.* prepare by mixing ingredients; invent, make up. **concoction, concoctor,** *nn.* **concoctive,** *a.* (L. *coquere*, cook)

concolorous, *a.* of uniform colour.

concomitant, *a.* and *n.* accompanying (thing or circumstance). **concomitance, concomitancy,** *nn.* coexistence. (L. *comes*, companion)

concord, *n.* agreement; harmony; treaty; (*gram.*) agreement in person etc. between words; (*mus.*) pleasing combination of notes. **concordance,**

n. agreement; index or dictionary of leading words in Bible or of any author. **concordant,** *a.* agreeing, harmonious. **concordat,** *n.* agreement between pope and secular government; compact, treaty. (L. *cor,* heart)

concourse, *n.* flocking together, confluence; crowd, throng.

concrescence, *n.* growing together, coalescence. (L. *crescere,* grow)

concrete, *a.* existing in material form, real; made of concrete; (*gram.*) denoting a thing, not a quality (opp. to abstract).—*n.* concrete thing; mixture of sand, cement etc., used in building.—*v.t.* and *i.* form into mass, solidify; face or line with concrete. **concretion,** *n.* coalescence; mass of coalesced particles; stone-like formation in the body. **concretionary, concretive,** *aa.* (L. *crescere,* grow)

concubine, *n.* woman living with man as his wife but not married to him, mistress; (in polygamy) secondary wife. **concubinage,** *n.* (L. *cubare,* lie)

concupiscence, *n.* sexual desire, lust. **concupiscent,** (*Shake.*) **concupiscible,** *aa.* lustful. (L. *cupere,* desire)

concur, *v.i.* happen together, coincide; co-operate; be of same opinion, agree. **concurrent,** *a.* concurring; running or existing together. (L. *currere,* run)

concuss, *v.t.* shake violently, agitate; cause concussion of brain to. **concussion,** *n.* concussing; violent shock of impact or explosion; brain injury due to blow on head. (L. *quatere,* shake)

condemn, *v.t.* blame, censure; find guilty; inflict legal penalty on; declare unfit for use. **condemnation,** *n.* **condemnatory,** *a.* (L. *damnare,* condemn)

condense, *v.t.* and *i.* reduce to smaller compass, compress; pack into few words; concentrate; turn from vapour or gas into liquid. **condensable,** *a.* **condensation,** *n.* **condenser,** *n.* apparatus for converting steam into water; lens for concentrating light.

condescend, *v.i.* deign, stoop; waive one's superiority. **condescending,** *a.* kindly to inferiors; patronizing. **condescension,** *n.* condescending act or manner. (*descend*)

condign, *a.* adequate, merited. (L. *dignus,* worthy)

condiment, *n.* seasoning, relish. (L. *condire,* pickle)

condition, *n.* state, mode of being; social rank; health, fitness; thing on which fulfilment of something depends; stipulation, provision; (*Shake.*) disposition; (*pl.*) circumstances.—*v.t.* be essential to happening or existence of; stipulate, agree upon; make fit. **on c. that,** provided that. **conditional,** *a.* depending on conditions; not absolute; (*gram.*) expressing condition.—*n.* conditional clause or conjunction. **conditionality,** *n.* **conditioned,** *a.* circumstanced; conditional. (L. *dicere,* say)

condole, *v.i.* express sympathy (with) in sorrow; (*Shake.*) grieve. **condolatory,** *a.* **condolement,** *n.* (*Shake.*) sorrowing. **condolence,** *n.* expression of sympathy. (L. *dolēre,* grieve)

condom, *n* contraceptive sheath. (inventor)

condominium, *n.* joint rule by two or more states. (L. *dominus,* lord)

condone, *v.t.* overlook, treat as non-existent (esp. wife's infidelity). **condonation,** *n.* (L. *donare,* give)

condor, *n.* large S. American vulture. (Peruvian *cuntur*)

condottiere, **n.** (*pl. condottieri*) captain of mercenaries, military adventurer. (It.)

conduce, *v.i.* tend to bring about, contribute (to). **conducive,** *a.* (L. *ducere,* lead)

conduct, *v.t.* and *i.* lead, escort; manage, carry on; transmit (heat, electricity); (*mus.*) direct (orchestra) by indicating time and expression.—*n.* direction, management; behaviour; (*Shake.*) guide, escort. **c. oneself,** behave. **conductible,** *a.* capable of conducting or being conducted. **conductibility,** *n.* **conduction,** *n.* conducting; transmission by conductor. **conductive,** *a.* capable of transmitting heat etc. **conductivity,** *n.* **conductor,** *n.* (*fem.* **conductress**) leader, guide; one who conducts orchestra; official who takes fares on bus or tram; conductive substance. (L. *ducere,* lead)

conduit, *n.* channel, pipe; aqueduct. (L. *ducere,* lead)

conduplicate, *a.* (*bot.*) folded lengthwise along the middle.

condyle, *n.* knuckle-like process at end of bone fitting into another bone. **condyloid,** *a.* shaped like condyle. (Gk. *kondulos,* knuckle)

cone, *n.* solid pointed figure with circular base; cone-shaped thing; fruit of pine or fir. (Gk. *kōnos*)

coney, see **cony.**

confabulate, *v.i.* talk familiarly together. **confabulation,** (*colloq.*) **confab,** *nn.* familiar discussion, chat. **confabulatory,** *a.* (L. *fabula,* tale)

confection, *n.* anything made with sugar, sweetstuff; woman's elegant garment; (*rare*) compounding.—*v.t.* make (confection). **confectionary,** *a.* **confectioner,** *n.* one who makes or sells confectionery. **confectionery,** *n.* sweets, chocolate etc. (L. *facere,* make)

confederate, *a.* banded together by treaty; united in confederation.—*n.* partner in design, accomplice; ally. —*v.t.* and *i.* bring, come, into alliance or confederacy. **C. States of America,** those that seceded from U.S. 1860–5.

confederacy, *n.* body of confederates; conspiracy; league of states formed for temporary object. **confederation,** *n.* body of independent states permanently united for joint action. (L. *foedus*, league)

confer, *v.i.* (*abbr.* **cf.**) compare (passage). (L.)

confer, *v.t.* and *i.* grant, bestow; consult, take counsel (with). **conferee, conferrer,** *nn.* person on, by, whom something is conferred. **conference,** *n.* meeting for discussion, consultation. **conferential,** *a.* **conferment,** *n.* bestowal. **conferrable,** *a.* (L. *ferre*, bear)

confess, *v.t.* and *i.* acknowledge, admit; disclose (sins) to confessor; (of priest) hear confession of. **confessant,** *n.* one making confession. **confessedly,** *adv.* avowedly. **confession,** *n.* confessing; admission; acknowledgment of fault or sin, esp. to confessor; statement of one's religious beliefs, creed; religious body, communion. **confessional,** *a.* of confession.—*n.* confessor's stall or box. **confessionist,** *n.* adherent of creed. **confessor,** *n.* priest who hears confession and grants absolution; one who confesses; person who suffers persecution for his religion. (L. *fatēri*, admit)

confetti, *n.pl.* small pieces of coloured paper strewn at carnivals or weddings. (It.=sweets)

confide, *v.i.* and *t.* put confidence (in); impart, entrust. **confiding,** *a.* unsuspicious. **confidant,** *n.* (*fem.* **confidante**) person trusted with one's secrets. (L. *fidere*, trust)

confidence, *n.* firm trust, faith; self-reliance; assurance; act of confiding, secret confided. **c. man,** who practises **c. trick,** persuading victim to hand over valuables as proof of confidence. **in c.,** as a secret. **in one's c.,** allowed to know his private affairs. **confident,** *a.* full of confidence, positive, bold; cocksure. **confidential,** *a.* told in confidence, secret; entrusted with secrets.

configure, *v.t.* give shape to. **configuration,** *n.* general outline, conformation; (*astrol.*) relative position of planets.

confine, *v.t.* keep within limits, restrict; imprison; (*pass.*) be brought to bed of a child.—*n.* boundary; (*Shake.*) prison; (*pl.*) borderland, edge. **c. with,** border on. **confinement,** *n.* being confined; imprisonment; childbed. **confiner,** *n.* (*Shake.*) inhabitant. (L. *finis*, end)

confirm, *v.t.* make stronger; establish firmly; make valid, ratify; corroborate; administer rite of confirmation to. **confirmand,** *n.* candidate for confirmation. **confirmation,** *n.* confirming; convincing proof; rite by which persons are admitted to full communion in Anglican and other churches. **confirmative, confirmatory,** *aa.* confirming; corroboratory. **confirmed,** *a.* permanent, chronic. **confirmee,** *n.* person to whom confirmation is administered.

confiscate, *v.t.* seize by authority; appropriate to the state as penalty. **confiscable, confiscatory,** *aa.* **confiscation, confiscator,** *nn.* (L. *fiscus*, treasury)

confixed, *a.* (*Shake.*) firmly fixed.

conflagration, *n.* great destructive fire. (L. *flagrare*, blaze)

conflation, *n.* fusing together; combining of two variant readings of text into one. (L. *flare*, blow)

conflict, *n.* fight, contest; strife, quarrel; conflicting state.—*v.i.* be at variance, clash (with); struggle. **conflicting,** *a.* incompatible, contradictory. **confliction,** *n.* (L. *fligere*, strike)

confluent, *a.* flowing together, uniting. —*n.* confluent stream. **confluence, conflux,** *nn.* union, meeting-place, of confluents; concourse. (L. *fluere*, flow)

conform, *v.t.* and *i.* adapt, make like; be of same form; comply, be obedient (to); be conformist. **conformable,** *a.* corresponding, adapted (to); compliant. **conformation,** *n.* arrangement of parts, structure; adaptation. **conformist,** *n.* one who conforms to usages of English Church. **conformity,** *n.* correspondence, likeness; compliance; conforming to Anglican usage.

confound, *v.t.* mix up, obscure; perplex, astound; overthrow; mistake one thing for another; (*Shake.*) destroy, waste. **c. it!** a mild imprecation. **confounded,** *a.* annoying; consummate. (L. *fundere*, pour)

confraternity, *n.* brotherhood; gang.

confrère, *n.* colleague. (F.)

confront, *v.t.* stand in front of, face; bring face to face (with); compare. **confrontation,** *n.*

Confucian, *n.* follower of Chinese philosopher Confucius. **Confucianism,** *n.*

confuse, *v.t.* throw into disorder, mix up; perplex, disconcert; obscure; mistake one thing for another. **confusion,** *n.* confusing; confused state, disorder; embarrassment; discomfiture; (*Shake.*) ruin. (*confound*)

confute, *v.t.* prove wrong, convict of error; overcome in argument. **confutation,** *n.* (L. *confutare*)

congé, *n.* dismissal; (*arch.*) formal bow, esp. at parting. (F.)

congeal, *v.t.* and *i.* change from liquid to solid by cooling; coagulate. **congealment,** *n.* (L. *gelu*, frost)

congee, same as *congé* or **conjee.**

congelation, *n.* congealing; congealed state or substance.

congener, *n.* person or thing of same

kind as another.—*a.* akin, allied.
congeneric, congenerous, *aa.* (L. *genus*, kind)
congenial, *a.* of similar disposition or tastes, kindred; suited, agreeable (to). **congeniality,** *n.* (*genial*)
congenital, *a.* existing at, dating from, birth. (L. *gignere*, beget)
conger, *n.* (also **c.-eel**) large sea eel. (Gk. *gonggros*)
congériēs, *n.* (*pl.* same) gathered mass, heap; conglomeration. (L.)
congest, *v.t.* overcrowd; (*med.*) affect with congestion. **congestion,** *n.* overcrowding; (*med.*) excessive accumulation of blood in any organ. (L. *gerere*, bring)
conglobate, *a.* conglobated.—*v.t.* and *i.* (also **conglobe**) form into a ball. **conglobation,** *n.* (*globe*)
conglomerate, *a.* stuck together in a mass.—*v.t.* and *i.* gather into a ball. —*n.* rock of pebbles cemented together. **conglomeration,** *n.* conglomerating; mass stuck together; collection. (L. *glomus*, ball of yarn)
conglutinate, *v.t.* and *i.* stick together, unite by adhesion. **conglutination,** *n.* (L. *gluten*, glue)
congou, *n.* kind of black China tea. (Chin. *kung-fu*, labour)
congratulate, *v.t.* express sympathetic pleasure at success or good fortune of. **congratulation,** *n.* congratulating; (*pl.*) congratulatory expressions. **congratulant, congratulative, congratulatory,** *aa.* **congratulator,** *n.* (L. *gratus*, pleasing)
congree, *v.i.* (*Shake.*) agree. (L. *gratus*, pleasing)
congreet, *v.t.* (*Shake.*) greet mutually.
congregate, *v.i.* and *t.* flock together, assemble; gather into crowd or mass. **congregation,** *n.* gathering, assembly; body of people assembled for worship; assembly of Masters and Doctors resident and engaged in teaching work at Oxford. **congregational,** *a.* of congregation or Congregationalism. **Congregationalism,** *n.* form of church government in which each congregation has management of its own affairs. **Congregationalist,** *n.* adherent of Congregationalism. (L. *grex*, flock)
congress, *n.* formal meeting of delegates for discussion; Senate and House of Representatives of U.S. or other American republic; coming together; coition. **congressional,** *a.* **Congressman,** *n.* member of Congress, esp. of House of Representatives. (L. *gradi*, walk)
congruent, congruous, *aa.* in agreement or correspondence; suitable, fitting; (*geom.*) exactly coincident. **congruence, congruency, congruity,** *nn.* **congrue,** *v.i.* (*Shake.*) agree. (L. *congruere*, run together)
conic, *a.* of cones.—*n.pl.* study of conic sections. **c. sections,** curves formed from cone—ellipse, parabola, hyperbola. **conical,** *a.* cone-shaped.
conifer, *n.* coniferous tree. **coniferous,** *a.* bearing fruit-cones.
conine, coniine, *n.* poisonous alkaloid got from hemlock. (Gk. *kōneion*, hemlock)
conjecture, *n.* guess, guess-work; proposed emendation of text.—*v.t.* and *i.* make conjecture, guess, surmise. **conjectural,** *a.* depending on conjecture. (L. *jacere*, throw)
conjee, *n.* (*Anglo-Ind.*) water in which rice has been boiled. **c.-house,** *n.* military prison. (Tamil *kañji*)
conjoin, *v.t.* and *i.* make into, become, a single whole. **conjoint,** *a.* united, combined.
conjugal, *a.* of marriage, connubial. **conjugality,** *n.* **conjugate,** *v.t.* and *i.* give parts of (verb); unite sexually, enter into conjugation.—*a.* conjoint; (*bot.*) growing in pairs. **conjugation,** *n.* conjoining; group of verbs with same inflexions; union of cells in reproduction. (L. *jugum*, yoke)
conjunct, *a.* joined together; associated. **conjunction,** *n.* union; simultaneous occurrence; (*astron.*) apparent proximity of two heavenly bodies; (*gram.*) word connecting words or clauses. **conjunctional,** *a.* **conjunctive,** *a.* connective; (*gram.*) copulative; introduced by a conjunction; (*Shake.*) united. **conjuncture,** *n.* combination of circumstances; crisis. (L. *jungere*, join)
conjunctiva, *n.* membrane lining eyelid and joining it with eyeball. **conjunctivitis,** *n.* inflammation of this. (L. *jungere*, join)
conjure, *v.t.* and *i.* entreat solemnly, implore; call up (spirits) by invocation; produce magical effects; do sleight-of-hand tricks, juggle. **a name to c. with,** one of great influence. **c. up,** bring before imagination. **conjuration,** *n.* solemn entreaty; incantation. **conjurer, conjuror,** *nn.* one who conjures; adept at sleight-of-hand. (L. *jurare*, swear)
conk, *v.i.* (*colloq.*) break down.
conk, *n.* (*sl.*) nose.
connate, *a.* inborn, congenital; (of leaves) united at base. **connation,** *n*, **connatural,** *a.* congenital; having same nature. (L. *nasci*, be born)
connect, *v.t.* and *i.* fasten together, join; relate together, link up. **connected,** *a.* coherent. **well connected,** of good family. **connection, connexion,** *n.* act of connecting; state of being connected; thing that connects; relation, association; relative; religious body; clientele; sexual union. **connective,** *a.* serving to connect. (L. *nectere*, bind)
conniption, *n.* (*Amer. sl.*) fit of hysteria or rage.
connive, *v.i.* permit tacitly, wink (at). **connivance,** *n.* conniving; pretence of ignorance. (L. *connivēre*)

connivent, *a.* converging. (*connive*)
connoisseur, *n.* trained discriminating judge, esp. of fine arts. (F.)
connote, *v.t.* imply; indicate; mean. **connotation,** *n.* **connotative,** *a.*
connubial, *a.* of marriage; of husband or wife. **connubiality,** *n.* (L. *nubere,* marry)
conoid, *n.* solid formed by revolution of conic section about its axis.—*a.* somewhat conical. **conoidal,** *a.* (Gk. *kōnos,* cone; *eidos,* form)
conquer, *v.t.* and *i.* gain victory (over), defeat; acquire by conquest; overcome, master. **conqueror,** *n.* **conquest,** *n.* conquering; winning of person's affection, person so won. (L. *quaerere,* seek)
conquistador, *n.* (*pl.* **conquistadors, conquistadores**) one of the Spanish conquerors of Central and S. America. (Sp.)
consanguineous, consanguine, *aa.* related by birth, akin. **consanguinity,** *n.* blood-relationship. (L. *sanguis,* blood)
conscience, *n.* sense of right and wrong; self passing moral judgments; (*Shake.*) consciousness; inmost thought. **bad, good, c.,** sense of guilt, virtue. **c. money,** sent to Treasury by repentant evader of tax. **have on one's c.,** feel guilty about. **in all c.,** certainly. **my c.!** (*vulg.*) exclamation of astonishment. **conscienceless,** *a.* unprincipled. **conscientious,** *a.* following dictates of conscience, scrupulous. **conscientious objector,** man who refuses to serve in war because he thinks it wrong. **conscionable,** *a.* governed by conscience, just. (L. *scire,* know)
conscious, *a.* aware (of); awake to one's surroundings; (of action) realized by the doer. **consciousness,** *n.* being conscious; perception; whole body of man's thoughts and feelings. (L. *scire,* know)
conscribe, *v.t.* conscript. **conscript,** *a.* and *n.* conscripted (man).—*v.t.* enlist by compulsion for naval or military service. **conscription,** *n.* (L. *scribere,* write)
consecrate, *v.t.* dedicate (church) to the service of God; set apart as sacred, sanctify; ordain (bishop); devote (to).—*a.* consecrated. **consecration, consecrator,** *nn.* **consecratory,** *a.* (L. *sacer,* sacred)
consectary, *n.* deduction, corollary. (L. *sequi,* follow)
consecution, *n.* following on; logical sequence. **consecutive,** *a.* following in regular order without break, successive; (*gram.*) expressing consequence. (L. *sequi,* follow)
consenescence, *n.* general decay from old age. (L. *senex,* old man)
consensus, *n.* agreement, unanimity; general trend. **consensual,** *a.* caused by sympathetic action. (*consent*)
consent, *v.i.* agree (to), comply; acquiesce.—*n.* permission; agreement, concurrence. **consentaneous,** *a.* agreeable, suited; unanimous. **consentaneity,** *n.* **consentient,** *a.* agreeing, concurring. (L. *sentire,* feel)
consequence, *n.* result, outcome; importance, moment; (*pl.*) round game in which each player writes part of a story without knowing what has gone before. **consequent,** *a.* following as result or deduction.—*n.* event that follows another; natural effect. **consequential,** *a.* resultant; self-important, pompous. **consequently,** *adv.* as a result; therefore; (*Shake.*) afterwards. (L. *sequi,* follow)
conserve, *v.t.* keep from loss or injury.—*n.* (*arch.*) preserved fruit; jam. **conservancy,** *n.* board controlling river or port; (*rare*) conservation. **conservation,** *n.* conserving, preservation. **conservation of energy,** fact that amount of energy in universe remains same though its form changes. **conservative,** *a.* tending to preserve; opposed to innovation; (of estimate) moderate.—*n.* member of Conservative Party; conservative person. **Conservative Party,** political party favouring maintenance of existing institutions. **conservatism,** *n.* conservative principles. **conservatoire,** *n.* school of music and elocution on Continent. **conservator,** *n.* member of conservancy; custodian, keeper; preserver. **conservatory,** *n.* greenhouse for exotic plants; conservatoire. (L. *servare,* keep)
consider, *v.t.* and *i.* reflect (upon), contemplate; examine, weigh merits of; take into account; regard as; be of opinion; (*Shake.*) recompense. **considerable,** *a.* of some importance; more than a little.—*n.* (*Amer. colloq.*) considerable amount. **considerably,** *adv.* **considerance,** *n.* (*Shake.*) reflection. **considerate,** *a.* thoughtful, careful of others' feelings; (*arch.*) deliberate. **consideration,** *n.* considering, deliberation; point of importance; inducement, bribe; thoughtfulness; deference. **considered,** *a.* well thought out. **considering,** *prep.* in view of. (L. *considerare*)
consign, *v.t.* hand over, commit; send goods addressed (to); (*Shake.*) agree. **consignation,** *n.* **consignee, consignor,** *nn.* person to, by, whom goods are consigned. **consignment,** *n.* consigning; collection of goods consigned.
consilient, *a.* (of inferences drawn from different phenomena) agreeing. **consilience,** *n.* (L. *salire,* leap)
consist, *v.i.* be made up (of); be comprised (in); be compatible (with); (*Shake.*) insist (on). **consistence,** *n.* degree of density, esp. of thick

liquids. **consistency,** *n.* consistence; state of being consistent. **consistent,** *a.* compatible, not contradictory; uniform in thought or action. (L. *sistere,* stand)

consistory, *n.* ecclesiastical court of pope and cardinals, Anglican bishop, or Presbyterian presbyters. **consistorial,** *a.* (*consist*)

consociate, *v.t.* and *i.* and *n.* associate. **consociation,** *n.* (L. *socius,* companion)

console, *v.t.* bring consolation to, cheer in distress. **consolation,** *n.* alleviation of grief or disappointment. **consolation event, race,** open only to those unsuccessful in former event. **consolatory,** *a.* (L. *solari,* comfort)

console, *n.* bracket supporting shelf. **c.-table,** *n.* supported by bracket against wall. (F.)

consolidate, *v.t.* and *i.* solidify; establish firmly, strengthen; combine into single whole. **consolidated annuities, consols,** *n.pl.* British Government securities consolidated into single stock. **consolidated fund,** national account into which proceeds of taxation are paid. **consolidation, consolidator,** *nn.* **consolidatory,** *a.*

consommé, *n.* kind of meat soup. (F.)

consonant, *a.* consistent, in keeping (with).—*n.* sound that forms syllable only in combination with a vowel; letter other than vowel. **consonance, consonancy,** *nn.* agreement, accord; (*mus.*) concord. **consonantal,** *a.* of consonant. (L. *sonare,* sound)

consort, *n.* husband or wife; ship sailing with another; (*Shake.*) company.—*v.i.* and *t.* associate, keep company; be in keeping (with). **king** or **prince, queen, c.,** husband, wife, of reigning sovereign. **consortium,** *n.* temporary association of several powers or interests. (L. *sors,* lot)

conspectus, *n.* general view; summary, synopsis. **conspectuity,** *n.* (*Shake.*) sight. (L. *specere,* look)

conspicuous, *a.* easily seen, prominent; outstanding, eminent. **conspicuity,** *n.* (L. *specere,* look)

conspire, *v.i.* and *t.* combine secretly for an evil purpose; plot, devise. **conspiracy,** *n.* plot. **conspirator,** *n.* (*fem.* **conspiratress**) one who conspires. (L. *spirare,* breathe)

conspue, *v.t.* express detestation of, spurn. (L. *spuere,* spit)

constable, *n.* policeman; (formerly) high official of royal household. **chief c.,** head of police force in city or county. **constabulary,** *a.* of constables.—*n.* police force. (L.L. *comes stabuli,* count of the stable)

constant, *a.* continuous, unceasing; unchanging, unvarying; firm, steadfast; faithful.—*n.* quantity that does not vary. **constancy,** *n.* firmness, steadfastness; fidelity. **constantly,** *adv.* continually, continuously, often. (L. *stare,* stand)

constellate, *v.t.* and *i.* form into constellation. **constellation,** *n.* group of stars. (L. *stella,* star)

consternate, *v.t.* dismay. **consternation,** *n.* surprise and alarm, dismay. (L. *sternere,* strew)

constipate, *v.t.* affect with constipation. **constipation,** *n.* sluggishness of bowels, costiveness. (L. *stipare,* press)

constituent, *a.* forming part of whole, component; essential; appointing, electing; having power to revise constitution.—*n.* component part; member of elective body, voter. **constituency,** *n.* body of electors; parliamentary division. (*constitute*)

constitute, *v.t.* set up by authority, establish; frame, form; appoint; compose, make up. **constitution,** *n.* constituting; structure, composition; fundamental physical condition; disposition, temperament; principles of government of a state; system of laws and customs; (formerly) ordinance. **constitutional,** *a.* of, due to, bodily constitution; having, limited by, in harmony with, political constitution. —*n.* walk taken for health. **constitutionalism,** *n.* constitutional government; adherence to constitutional principles. **constitutionalist,** *n.* **constitutionalize,** *v.t.* and *i.* make constitutional; take walk for health. **constitutive,** *a.* having power to enact, constituent. **constitutor,** *n.* (L. *statuere,* set up)

constrain, *v.t.* compel, force; hinder by force; confine, imprison. **constrained,** *a.* enforced; embarrassed. **constraint,** *n.* compulsion; forcible confinement; repression of feeling; embarrassment. (*constrict*)

constrict, *v.t.* draw together, squeeze, compress. **constricted,** *a.* narrowed; cramped. **constriction,** *n.* compression; tightness. **constrictive,** *a.* **constrictor,** *n.* constrictive muscle; serpent that crushes its prey. (L. *stringere,* draw tight)

constringe, *v.t.* compress; cause to contract. **constringency,** *n.* **constringent,** *a.* (*constrict*)

construct, *v.t.* make, build, fit together; compose. **construction,** *n.* constructing; structure; interpretation; (*gram.*) arrangement of words in sentence. **constructional,** *a.* **constructive,** *a.* tending to construct, creative; inferred, virtual. **constructor,** *n.* (L. *struere,* build)

construe, *v.t.* and *i.* translate word for word; analyse grammatically; take in particular sense, interpret. (*construct*)

consubstantial, *a.* formed from same substance. **consubstantiality,** *n.* **consubstantiate,** *v.t.* and *i.* unite in one substance. **consubstantiation,** *n.*

presence of body and blood of Christ in the eucharistic elements.

consuetude, *n.* established custom. **consuetudinary,** *a.* customary.—*n.* manual of customs, esp. of monastic house. (L. *suescere*, be wont)

consul, *n.* state's agent protecting its subjects in foreign town; either of two chief magistrates of ancient Rome; (*Shake.*) senator. **consular,** *a.* **consulate,** *n.* official residence of modern consul; office of Roman consul. **consulship,** *n.* (L.)

consult, *v.t.* and *i.* seek advice from; deliberate, confer. **consultant,** *n.* one who consults; physician who gives advice in special cases. **consultation,** *n.* consulting; conference. **consultative,** *a.* advisory; deliberative. (L. *consulere*)

consume, *v.t.* and *i.* destroy; use up; eat or drink up; waste away. **consumedly,** *adv.* (*arch.*) excessively. **consumer,** *n.* user of an article (opp. to producer). (L. *sumere*, take)

consummate, *a.* complete, perfect.—*v.t.* bring to perfection, be the crown of; complete (marriage) by sexual intercourse. **consummation, consummator,** *nn.* **consummative,** *a.* (L. *summus*, highest)

consumption, *n.* consuming, using up; wasting disease, tuberculosis. **consumptive,** *a.* tending to consume; tending to, affected with, consumption.—*n.* consumptive person.

contact, *n.* touch, touching; connection; (*med.*) person who has been in contact with infection.—*v.t.* (*Amer.*) establish contact with. **come into c. with,** meet. **make, break, c.,** complete, interrupt, electric circuit. (L. *tangere*, touch)

contadino, n. (*pl. contadini; fem. contadina, pl. contadine*) peasant. (It.)

contagion, *n.* communicating of disease by contact; contagious disease; moral corruption; catching influence. **contagious,** *a.* (of disease) spread by contact; (of influence) catching, infectious. (L. *tangere*, touch)

contain, *v.t.* hold, enclose; comprise, include; hem in; (*math.*) be multiple of; (*Shake.*) keep. **c. oneself,** keep one's feelings under control. **container,** *n.* holder. **containing,** *n.* (*Shake.*) contents. (L. *tenēre*, hold)

contaminate, *v.t.* render impure, pollute. **contamination,** *n.* pollution; blending of two plays etc. into one. (L. *contamen*, pollution)

contango, *n.* (*stock exchange*) charge paid by buyer for postponing payment from one settling-day to next. **c. day,** second before settling-day.

conte, n. short story. (F.)

conteck, *n.* (*Spens.*) dispute, contest. (O.F. *contek*)

contemn, *v.t.* despise; scornfully disregard. (L. *temnere*, slight)

contemplate, *v.t.* and *i.* look at steadily; reflect upon, meditate; have in view, intend. **contemplation,** *n.* **contemplative,** *a.* of, given to, contemplation. **contemplator,** *n.* (L. *templum*, temple)

contemporaneous, *a.* existing, occurring, at the same time; of the same period. **contemporaneity,** *n.* (L. *tempus*, time)

contemporary, *a.* of these times, present-day; living, happening, at the same time.—*n.* living or contemporary person; person of one's own age; rival newspaper. (L. *tempus*, time)

contempt, *n.* act of despising, scorn; disgrace. **c. of court,** disregard of its ruling, offence against its dignity. **contemptible,** *a.* despicable, base; (*Shake.*) contemptuous; (*pl.*) British Expeditionary Force of 1914. **contemptuous,** *a.* scornful; (*Shake.*) contemptible. (*contemn*)

contend, *v.i.* and *t.* take part in contest, strive (for); quarrel; maintain (that). (L. *tendere*, stretch)

content, *n.* capacity, volume; (*pl.*) what is contained; list of matters treated in book. (*contain*)

content, *a.* satisfied (with), not desiring more; willing (to).—*n.* state of being content, satisfaction; (*Shake.*) desire. —*v.t.* make content, satisfy. **contented,** *a.* content. **contentless,** *a.* (*Shake.*). (*contain*)

contention, *n.* strife, controversy; point maintained in argument. **contentious,** *a.* quarrelsome; controversial. (*contend*)

conterminal, conterminous, *aa.* having common boundary (with). (L. *terminus*, boundary)

contest, *v.t.* and *i.* call in question, dispute; fight to gain, compete for; strive.—*n.* struggle, encounter; competition; dispute. **contestant,** *n.* party in contest. **contestation,** *n.* disputation; contention. (L. *testis*, witness)

context, *n.* what comes before and after word or passage, esp. as fixing meaning. **contextual,** *a.* **contexture,** *n.* structure; fabric; style of composition. (L. *texere*, weave)

contiguous, *a.* touching, adjoining; near. **contiguity,** *n.* (L. *tangere*, touch)

continent, *a.* practising self-restraint; chaste; (*Shake.*) restrictive. **continence,** *n.* (L. *tenēre*, hold)

continent, *n.* one of the main divisions of land; (*Shake.*) thing that contains; abstract, sum. **the C.,** mainland of Europe. **continental,** *a.* of a continent; foreign as opp. to English. **continentalism, continentalist,** *nn.* (L. *tenēre*, hold)

contingent, *a.* possible, that may happen; chance; dependent (on); incidental (to).—*n.* draft of troops. **contingency,** *n.* being contingent; event that may take place, possibility. (L. *tangere*, touch)

continue, *v.t.* and *i.* go on (with), not cease; prolong, extend; remain, stay; last; resume, carry further; retain (in office etc.). **continuable,** *a.* **continual,** *a.* frequently repeated; going on all the time. **continuance,** *n.* continuing in existence, duration. **continuant,** *a.* and *n.* (consonant) of which sound can be prolonged, as *f, v.* **continuate,** *a.* (*Shake.*) uninterrupted. **continuation,** *n.* continuing; prolongation; resumption; thing that continues something else, sequel; (*pl., sl.*) trousers. **continuative,** *a.* **continuity,** *n.* continuousness; unbroken sequence or extent. **continuous,** *a.* connected throughout in space or time; without break or interruption. **continuum,** *n.* (*pl.* continua) continuous and homogeneous thing. (L. *tenēre,* hold)

cont-line, *n.* space between casks stowed side by side.

contorniate, *a.* and *n.* (medallion) with groove round edge. (It. *contorno,* contour)

contort, *v.t.* twist out of normal shape, pull awry. **contortion,** *n.* **contortionist,** *n.* acrobat who twists his body into unnatural postures. (L. *torquēre,* twist)

contour, *n.* line bounding figure, outline.—*v.t.* mark with contour lines. **c. line,** line on map passing through places of same altitude. **c. map,** showing contour lines. (F.)

contra, *n.* thing that may be urged against. (L.=against)

contra-, *pref.* against, in opposition, as in **contradict.**

contraband, *n.* smuggled goods; smuggling.—*a.* prohibited from importation. **c. of war,** goods supplied to one belligerent and seizable by another. **contrabandist,** *n.* smuggler. (L.L. *bandum,* ban)

contrabass, *n.* double-bass.

contraception, *n.* birth-control. **contraceptive,** *a.* and *n.* (appliance, drug) for preventing conception. (*contra-+conception*)

contract, *n.* compact, bargain; agreement to supply goods or perform work at stated price; agreement enforceable by law.—*v.t.* and *i.* make, undertake by, contract; bargain (for); betroth; enter into (alliance); form (habit); catch (cold); make, become, smaller or narrower; draw together; confine; shorten (word) by omission of letters. **c. bridge,** form of auction bridge. **contracted,** *a.* narrow; illiberal. **contractile,** *a.* able or causing to grow smaller. **contractility,** *n.* **contraction,** *n.* contracting; shrinkage; contracted word, as 'can't.' **contractive,** *a.* serving to contract. **contractor,** *n.* one who makes business contract, esp. builder; contracting muscle. **contractual,** *a.* of legal contract. (L. *trahere,* draw)

contradict, *v.t.* and *i.* deny, assert opposite of; be at variance (with). **contradiction,** *n.* contradicting; inconsistency. **contradictious,** *a.* fond of contradicting. **contradictor,** *n.* **contradictory,** *a.* involving contradiction, inconsistent, mutually destructive. (L. *dicere,* say)

contradistinguish, *v.t.* mark difference between two things by contrasting their opposite qualities. **contradistinction,** *n.* **contradistinctive,** *a.*

contralto, *n.* lowest female voice; part for, singer with, this. (It.)

contraposition, *n.* opposition, antithesis.

contraption, *n.* (*sl.*) contrivance, queer appliance.

contrapuntal, *a.* of, according to, counterpoint. **contrapuntist,** *n.* expert in counterpoint. (It. *contrappunto,* counterpoint)

contrary, *a.* opposed, opposite; unfavourable; contradictory; (*colloq.*) perverse, self-willed.—*n.* exact opposite.—*adv.* in opposition (to).—*v.t.* (*Shake.*) thwart, oppose. **on the c.,** so far from that being so. **to the c.,** to the opposite effect. **contrariant,** *a.* opposed (to). **contrariety,** *n.* opposition; discrepancy. **contrariness,** *n.* (*colloq.*) perversity. **contrarious,** *a.* (*arch.*) opposed; perverse; adverse. **contrariwise,** *adv.* on the other hand; conversely. (*contra*)

contrast, *v.t.* and *i.* bring out differences between, set in opposition for comparison; show marked difference. —*n.* exhibition of differences; marked difference, thing showing this. (L. *contra,* against; *stare,* stand)

contrate, *a.* (of wheel) with teeth at right angles to its plane. (*contra*)

contravallation, *n.* fortification built by besiegers about place invested. (L. *vallum,* rampart)

contravene, *v.t.* infringe, transgress; conflict with, contradict. **contravention,** *n.* (L. *venire,* come)

contretemps, *n.* unexpected mishap, hitch. (F.)

contribute, *v.t.* and *i.* give to common stock or fund; write (article) for paper. **c. to,** help to bring about. **contribution,** *n.* contributing; thing, literary article, contributed; payment into collection. **contributor,** *n.* **contributory,** *a.* (L. *tribuere,* bestow)

contrite, *a.* deeply sorrowful for sin, humbly penitent; showing contrition. **contrition,** *n.* (L. *terere,* rub)

contrive, *v.t.* and *i.* devise, design; bring about, manage. **contrivance,** *n.* contriving; artifice; invention; mechanical device. (O.F. *trover,* find)

contrive, *v.t.* (*Shake.*) wear out, spend. (L. *terere,* rub)

control, *n.* check, restrain; govern; regulate.—*n.* restraint; command; means of controlling, check; standard of comparison for checking experiment; station at which motor-cars etc. in race are allowed to stop for overhaul; (*spiritualism*) spirit directing medium; (*pl.*) gear-lever, clutch etc., of motor-car. **controllable,** *a.* **controller,** *n.* one who controls; official controlling expenditure. (L. *contra*, against; *rotulus*, roll)

controvert, *v.t.* argue against; disprove, refute. **controvertible,** *a.* **controversy,** *n.* disputation; argument conducted in the press. **controversial,** *a.* of controversy; disputable. **controversialist,** *n.* (L. *contra*, against; *vertere*, turn)

contumacious, *a.* resisting authority, insubordinate; obstinate. **contumacy,** *n.* (L. *contumax*)

contumely, *n.* scornful insolence or abuse; reproach, disgrace. **contumelious,** *a.* insolent and abusive. (L. *contumelia*)

contuse, *v.t.* wound without breaking skin, bruise. **contusion,** *n.* (L. *tundere*, pound)

conundrum, *n.* riddle involving pun; puzzling question.

convalesce, *v.i.* recover health after illness. **convalescence,** *n.* convalescing; period of this. **convalescent,** *a.* and *n.* (person) convalescing. (L. *valēre*, be strong)

convection, *n.* transmission of heat through liquid by currents. (L. *vehere*, carry)

convenances, *n.pl.* proprieties, conventions. (F.)

convene, *v.t.* and *i.* call together, convoke; summon before tribunal; assemble. **convenable,** *a.* **convener,** *n.* (L. *venire*, come)

convenient, *a.* handy, suitable; commodious; (*Shake.*) proper, becoming. **convenience, conveniency,** *nn.* what suits one; useful appliance; water-closet; (*arch.*) vehicle; (*Shake.*) propriety; (*pl.*) material comforts. **at your convenience,** at a time that suits you. (L. *venire*, come)

convent, *n.* religious community, esp. of women; building occupied by this. —*v.t.* (*Shake.*) summon. (L. *venire*, come)

conventicle, *n.* meeting-house; secret meeting; (formerly) prohibited meeting of Nonconformists or Covenanters. (L. *conventus*, meeting+dim.)

convention, *n.* convening; political or ecclesiastical assembly; agreement, treaty; social custom, established usage. **conventional,** *a.* of, based on, social custom; not spontaneous; (*art*) following accepted rules. **conventionalism,** *n.* adherence to established usage. **conventionalist,** *n.* **conventionality,** *n.* being conventional. **conventionalize,** *v.t.* make conventional.

conventual, *a.* and *n.* (member, inmate) of convent.

converge, *v.i.* and *t.* tend to one point, incline together. **convergence, convergency,** *nn.* **convergent,** *a.*

converse, *v.i.* have conversation, talk; associate (with).—*n.* (*arch.*) discourse; intercourse. **conversable,** *a.* disposed to converse, sociable. **conversant,** *a.* well acquainted, familiar (with). **conversance,** *n.* **conversation,** *n.* familiar discourse, talk; (*arch.*) intercourse; (*Shake.*) conduct. **conversational,** *a.* of, fond of, conversation; colloquial. **conversationalist,** *n.* one who converses well. **conversazionĕ,** *n.* (*pl.* **conversaziones, conversazioni**) social gathering, esp. of literary or art society. (L. *vertere*, turn)

converse, *a.* opposite; reversed in order or relation.—*n.* converse thing or statement, contrary. (L. *vertere*, turn)

convert, *v.t.* change from one thing, condition, or religion to another; produce spiritual conversion in; apply to different use, appropriate; (*Rugby football*) complete (try) by kicking goal.—*n.* one who has become religious or has changed his religion. **convertible,** *a.* **convertibility,** *n.* **convertite,** *n.* (*Shake.*) convert. **conversion,** *n.* converting, change; change of heart impelling to religious life. (L. *vertere*, turn)

convex, *a.* curving outwards. **convexity,** *n.* (L. *vehere*, carry)

convey, *v.t.* transport; conduct, transmit; make known, communicate; (*law*) make over (property); (*Shake.*) manage secretly; pass (oneself) off (as). **conveyance,** *n.* carrying; vehicle, carriage; (*law*) act, document, by which title to property is transferred; (*Shake.*) cunning management. **conveyancer,** *n.* lawyer dealing with conveyances. **conveyancing,** *n.* his work. (L. *via*, way)

convict, *v.t.* prove or pronounce guilty.—*n.* convicted criminal, esp. one sentenced to penal servitude. **convicted,** *a.* (*Shake.*) defeated. **conviction,** *n.* convicting, being found guilty; convincing; settled opinion, firm belief. **carry conviction,** be convincing. **convince,** *v.t.* firmly persuade, satisfy by proof; (*Shake.*) overcome; convict. **convincing,** *a.* compelling belief. (L. *vincere*, conquer)

convivial, *a.* of feast or merrymaking; festive. **conviviality,** *n.* **convive,** *v.i.* (*Shake.*) feast together. (L. *vivere*, live)

convoke, *v.t.* call together, summon to assemble. **convocation,** *n.* convoking; assembly; ecclesiastical conference; assembly of all Oxford Masters and Doctors. **convocational,** *a.* (L. *vocare*, call)

convolve, *v.t.* and *i.* roll together. **convolute, convoluted,** *aa.* rolled up, coiled. **convolution,** *n.* fold, twist; coiling. **convolvulus,** *n.* kinds of twining plant, bindweed. (L. *volvere*, roll)

convoy, *v.t.* accompany for protection, escort.—*n.* act of convoying; escorting force; ships, lorries etc., convoyed. (*convey*)

convulse, *v.t.* agitate violently, cause upheaval in; throw into convulsions. **convulsion,** *n.* violent agitation; (*pl.*) bodily seizure with muscular spasms; violent fit of laughter. **convulsive,** *a.* (L. *vellere*, pluck)

cony, coney, *n.* rabbit; rock-badger. **c.-catch,** *v.t.* (*Shake.*) cheat. (L. *cuniculus*)

coo, *n.* note of pigeon; soft murmuring sound.—*v.i.* utter coo; speak caressingly. (imit.)

cooee, *n.* cry used as long-distance signal by Australians.—*v.i.* utter this.

coof, *n.* (*Scot.*) stupid fellow.

cook, *n.* one who does cooking.—*v.t.* and *i.* prepare (food) by heat; subject to great heat; (*colloq.*) fake, falsify (accounts etc.). **c. one's goose,** (*sl.*) finish him off. **c.-book,** *n.* (Amer.) cookery book. **cookhouse,** *n.* outdoor kitchen. **c.-shop,** *n.* eating-house. **cooker,** *n.* stove for cooking; fruit suitable for cooking. **cookery,** art of cooking. **cookery book,** *n.* book of recipes. **cookie, cooky,** *n.* (*Scot.*) plain bun; (*Amer.*) small flat cake. (L. *coquus*)

cool, *a.* slightly cold; calm, unruffled; lacking enthusiasm; casual, impudent.—*n.* coolness.—*v.t.* and *i.* make, become, cool. **c. one's heels,** be kept waiting. **c.-headed,** *a.* not easily excited. **cooler,** *n.* vessel for cooling. **coolly,** *adv.* **coolness,** *n.* being cool; disagreement. **coolth,** *n.* coolness. (O.E. *cól*)

coolie, cooly, *n.* Indian or Chinese hired labourer. (Hind. *quli*)

coom, *n.* (*Scot.*) coal-dust, soot.

coomb, combe, *n.* hollow on side of hill; steep valley. (O.E. *cumb*)

coon, *n.* racoon; (*Amer.*) negro; fellow. (abbr.)

coon-can, *n.* card game for two. (Sp. *con quien?* with whom?)

coop, *n.* cage or pen for fowls.—*v.t.* keep in coop; confine narrowly. **cooper,** *n.* one who makes and mends casks.—*v.t.* repair (cask). **cooperage,** *n.* work, workshop, of cooper. (M.E. *cupe*, basket)

cooper, see **coper.**

co-operate, *v.i.* work together. **co-operant,** *a.* and *n.* **co-operation,** *n.* co-operating, joint effort. **co-operative,** *a.* **co-operative society, stores,** for cheaper purchase of goods, profits being shared as dividend among customers.

co-opt, *v.t.* elect into body by votes of existing members. **co-optation,** *n.* **co-optative,** *a.* (L. *optare*, choose)

co-ordinate, *a.* equal in degree or status.—*n.* co-ordinate thing; (*math.*) any of a system of magnitudes used to fix position of point, line etc.—*v.t.* make co-ordinate; adjust, harmonize. **co-ordination,** *n.* **co-ordinative,** *a.* (L. *ordo*, order)

coot, *n.* kinds of water-bird. (M.E. *cote*)

cootie, *n.* (*army sl.*) louse. (Maori *kutu*)

cop, *n.* conical ball of thread on spindle; (*obs.*) top. (O.E.)

cop, *v.t.* (*sl.*) catch; arrest.—*n.* (*sl.*) capture; policeman.

copaiba, copaiva, *n.* an aromatic balsam. (Brazilian *cupauba*)

copal, *n.* a resin used in varnishes. (Mex. *copalli*, resin)

coparcener, same as **parcener.**

copartner, *n.* joint partner. **copartnership, copartnery,** *nn.*

copatain, *a.* (*Shake.*) high-crowned.

cope, *n.* ecclesiastical vestment like long cloak; canopy (of heaven); coping.—*v.t.* provide with cope or coping. (L.L. *capa*, cap)

cope, *v.t.* and *i.* deal successfully, contend on even terms (with); (*Shake.*) meet (with). (F. *couper*, strike)

copeck, *n.* Russian copper coin worth about $\frac{1}{4}d.$ (Russ. *kopeika*)

coper, *n.* horse-dealer; (also **cooper**) vessel selling liquor to North Sea fishermen. (Du. *koopen*, buy)

Copernican, *a.* of Copernicus and his teaching that earth and planets revolve round sun.

copesmate, *n.* (*Shake.*) companion.

cophosis, *n.* deafness. (Gk. *kōphos*, deaf)

coping, *n.* top course of wall. **c.-stone,** *n.* top stone of structure; crowning touch. (*cope*)

copious, *a.* plentiful, abundant; (of style) exuberant, wordy. (L. *copia*, plenty)

copper, *n.* (*sl.*) policeman.

copper, *n.* reddish ductile metallic element; bronze coin, penny etc.; washing cauldron.—*a.* made of copper.—*v.t.* cover with copper. **c.-bottom,** *v.t.* sheathe bottom of (ship) with copper. **copperas,** *n.* green vitriol. **copperhead,** *n.* venomous American snake. **copperplate,** *n.* plate of copper for engraving or etching; print from this; copy-book writing. **coppersmith,** *n.* worker in copper. (*Cyprus*)

coppice, copse, *nn.* wood of small growth for periodical cutting; thicket. (Gk. *kolaphos*, blow with fist)

copra, *n.* dried coco-nut kernels. (Port.)

copro-, from Gk. *kopros*, dung, used in **coprolite,** *n.* fossil dung, hence **coprolitic,** *a.*; **coprology,** *n.* study of dung, treatment of filthy subjects in literature and art; **coprophagous,** *a.* dung-eating; **coprophilia,** *n.* love of obscenity.

copse, see **coppice.**
Copt, *n.* native Egyptian Christian. **Coptic**, *a.* (Gk. *Aiguptios*, Egyptian)
copula, *n.* link, connecting part; (*gram.*) word joining subject and predicate. **copulate**, *v.i.* have sexual intercourse. **copulation**, *n.* copulating; grammatical connection. **copulative**, *a.* of sexual union; (*gram.*) serving as copula; uniting ideas as well as words.—*n.* copulative conjunction. **copulatory**, *a.* of copulation. (L.)
copy, *n.* reproduction; transcript; single specimen of book; model to be copied; manuscript for printing; subject-matter for writer; (*Shake.*) copyhold; theme.—*v.t.* and *i.* make copy of, reproduce; take as model, imitate; crib from neighbour at school. **c.-book**, *n.* book of handwriting exercises. **copyhold**, *n.* tenure, land held, according to custom of a manor. **copyholder**, *n.* tenant by copyhold; (*print.*) reader's assistant. **copyist**, *n.* one who copies. **copyright**, *n.* exclusive right to print or sell a book or work of art.—*a.* protected by copyright.—*v.t.* secure copyright for. (L. *copia*, abundance)
coquette, *n.* woman who trifles with men's affections.—*v.i.* (also **coquet**) play the coquette, flirt; dally, trifle. **coquetry**, *n.* coquetting; coquettish behaviour. **coquettish**, *a.* artfully enticing. (F.)
coquito, *n.* Chilian palm. (Sp.)
cor-, form of **com-** before *r.*
coracle, *n.* boat of wicker covered with skin. (W. *cwrwg*, boat+dim.)
coral, *n.* hard substance composed of skeletons of sea-polyps; coral ornament or toy; lobster roe.—*a.* made of, red like, coral. **coralliferous**, *a.* producing coral. **coralline**, *n.* coral-like seaweed or animal.—*a* coral. **corallite**, *n.* fossil coral; coral skeleton of single polyp. **coralloid**, *a.* and *n.* (organism) like coral. (Gk. *korallion*)
coram, *prep.* in the presence of. *c. judice*, in judge's presence. *c. populo*, in public. (L.)
cor anglais, tenor oboe. (F.=English horn)
coranto, *n.* a lively dance. (Sp.)
corbel, *n.* stone or timber projection from wall to support something.—*v.t.* furnish with, support by, corbel. (L. *corvus*, raven+dim.)
corbie, *n.* (*Scot.*) raven. (L. *corvus*)
cord, *n.* thick string or thin rope; ribbed fabric; measure of wood, 128 cubic ft.; (*pl.*) corduroy breeches.—*v.t.* fasten with cord. **cordage**, *n.* ropes or rigging collectively. (Gk. *chordē*)
cordate, *a.* heart-shaped. (L. *cor*, heart)
cordelier, *n.* Franciscan friar of strict rule. (F.)
cordial, *a.* hearty, warm; friendly; invigorating, stimulating.—*n.* stimulating medicine or drink; liqueur; heartening influence. **cordiality**, *n.* (L. *cor*, heart)
cordillera, *n.* mountain ridge, esp. of Andes. (Sp.)
cordite, *n.* a smokeless explosive. (like *cord* in appearance)
cordon, *n.* chain of police or military posts preventing passage; string-course; ornamental cord; ribbon of order; fruit-tree pruned to single stem. *c. bleu*, (*joc.*) first-class cook. (F.)
cordovan, *n.* leather of Cordova.
corduroy, *n.* strong cotton stuff with velvety ribbed surface; (*pl.*) trousers of this. **c. road**, (*Amer.*) of tree-trunks laid crosswise.
cordwainer, *n.* (*arch.*) shoemaker. (*cordovan*)
core, *n.* innermost part, heart; inner part of apple etc. containing seeds.—*v.t.* remove core from.
co-relation, same as **correlation.**
co-religionist, *n.* person of same religion.
coreopsis, *n.* kinds of plant with rayed flowers. (Gk. *koris*, bug; *opsis*, sight)
co-respondent, *n.* man charged in divorce suit with committing adultery.
corf, *n.* basket for keeping fish alive in water; basket for hauling coal.
corgi, corgy, *n.* small Welsh breed of dog. (W.)
coriaceous, *a.* of leather; leathery. (L. *corium*, hide)
coriander, *n.* a plant. **c. seed**, its fruit, used for flavouring. (Gk. *koriannon*)
Corinthian, *a.* of Corinth.—*n.* (*arch.*) man about town, patron of sport. **C. order**, (*archit.*) lightest and most ornate of classic orders.
co-rival, same as **corrival.**
cork, *n.* bark of a kind of oak; cork stopper for bottle.—*a.* made of cork.—*v.t.* stop up with cork; bottle (up); give taste of cork to (wine); blacken with burnt cork. **c. jacket**, lifebelt of cork. **corkage**, *n.* corking, uncorking, of bottles; charge made in hotel for serving liquor got from outside. **corker**, *n.* (*sl.*) something conclusive or superlatively good; flagrant lie. **corkscrew**, *n.* screw for drawing corks.—*a.* twisted spirally.—*v.t.* and *i.* move spirally. **corky**, *a.* like cork; (*colloq.*) vivacious, skittish; (*Shake.*) withered. (L. *cortex*, bark)
corm, *n.* bulb-like subterraneous stem of crocus etc., solid bulb. (Gk. *kormos*, lopped trunk of tree)
cormorant, *n.* a voracious sea-bird; glutton. (L. *corvus marinus*, sea-raven)
corn, *n.* small hard painful growth on foot. **tread on one's cc.**, hurt his feelings. (L. *cornu*, horn)
corn, *n.* grain or seed of cereal plant,

(in England) wheat, (in Scotland) oats, (in U.S.) maize.—*v.t.* preserve (meat) by sprinkling it with salt. **c.-chandler,** *n.* corn retailer. **c.-cob,** *n.* centre of ear of maize, used for tobacco-pipe bowls. **c.-dodger,** *n.* (*Amer.*) fried cake of corn-flour. **c. exchange,** corn market. **c.-factor,** *n.* corn merchant. **c.-flag,** *n.* gladiolus. **cornflour,** *n.* meal of finely ground maize or of rice etc. **c.-juice,** *n.* (*Amer. sl.*) whisky. **c.-pone,** *n.* (*Amer.*) maize bread. (O.E.)

corncrake, *n.* bird with harsh cry, landrail. (*corn*; *crake*)

cornea, *n.* transparent membrane in front of eyeball. (L. *cornu,* horn)

cornel, *n.* cornelian cherry, dogwood. (L. *cornus*)

cornelian, *n.* dull-red chalcedony. (F. *corneline*)

corneous, *a.* horny. (L. *cornu,* horn)

corner, *n.* point where sides meet, angle; secret or confined place; difficulty, fix; buying up of whole stock of a commodity; (*football*) free kick from corner flag given to opponents when player sends ball over his own goal-line.—*v.t.* drive into corner; make corner in (commodity). **turn the c.,** pass crisis safely. **c.-boy,** *n.* street loafer. **c.-man,** *n.* end man of nigger-minstrel troupe. **c.-stone,** *n.* principal stone; indispensable part. (L. *cornu,* horn)

cornet, *n.* instrument of trumpet kind with valves; performer on this; cone-shaped holder for ice-cream etc.; (*obs.*) second lieutenant of cavalry. **c.-à-piston,** *n.* cornet (instrument). **cornetcy,** *n.* (*obs.*) rank of cornet. (L. *cornu,* horn)

cornflower, *n.* a blue-flowered weed.

cornice, *n.* moulding of room-wall just below ceiling; carved moulding round top of building. (It.)

cornopean, *n.* cornet.

cornucopia, *n.* (*pl.* **cornucopias**) horn filled with fruit and flowers, symbol of plenty; abundance. (L. *cornu copiae,* horn of plenty)

cornuted, *a.* horned. **cornuto,** *n.* (*Shake.*) cuckold. (L. *cornu,* horn)

corolla, *n.* whorl of flower's petals. (L. *corona,* crown+dim.)

corollary, *n.* additional inference from proposition already proved; result; (*Shake.*) surplus. (*corolla*)

corona, *n.* (*pl.* **coronae**) top, crown; luminous halo or envelope round sun; (*archit.*) flat projecting member of cornice. (L.)

coronach, *n.* (*Scot.*) dirge, lament. (Gael. *corranach*)

coronal, *n.* circlet for head; garland. —*a.* of corona. **coronate, coronated,** *aa.* having corona. **coronation,** *n.* ceremony of crowning.

coroner, *n.* crown officer who holds inquest into causes of accidental or suspicious deaths. (*corona*)

coronet, *n.* small crown; lowest part of horse's pastern. (*corona*+dim.)

coronoid, *a.* beak-shaped. (Gk. *korōnē,* crow; *eidos,* form)

corozo, *n.* S. American palm with nuts yielding vegetable ivory. (native)

corporal, *n.* non-commissioned officer below sergeant. (It. *caporale*)

corporal, *a.* of the body; (*Shake.*) material.—*n.* communion cloth. **c. punishment,** whipping. **corporality,** *n.* state of having a body. (*corpus*)

corporate, *a.* legally united into a body; of, having, a corporation. **corporation,** *n.* body of persons authorized by law to act as one individual; city council; (*colloq.*) protuberant stomach. **corporative,** *a.* of corporation. **corporator,** *n.* member of corporation. (*corpus*)

corporeal, *a.* of, having, body; material; tangible. **corporeality, corporeity,** *nn.* (*corpus*)

corposant, *n.* flame-like electric discharge from ship's mast etc. in thundery weather, St. Elmo's fire. (L. *corpus sanctum,* holy body)

corps, *n.* (*pl.* same) military force; organized body. **army c.,** two divisions. *c. de ballet,* dancers of ballet. *c. diplomatique,* all ambassadors at particular capital. (F.)

corpse, *n.* dead body. (*corpus*)

corpulent, *a.* fleshy, fat. **corpulence,** *n.* (*corpus*)

corpus, *n.* (*pl.* **corpora**) body of written works. **C. Christi,** festival in honour of the host, held on Thursday after Trinity Sunday. *c. delicti,* essence of crime charged. *c. vile,* worthless thing. (L.=body)

corpuscle, corpuscule, *n.* particle; blood-cell; electron. **corpuscular,** *a.* (*corpus*+dim.)

corral, *n.* pen for cattle; laager.—*v.t.* put, keep, in corral. (Sp.)

correct, *a.* right, true, accurate; conforming to etiquette, proper.—*v.t.* set right, remove errors from; reprove, punish; counteract, neutralize. **correction,** *n.* correcting; emendation; punishment. **correctional,** *a.* **correctioner,** *n.* (*Shake.*). **correctitude,** *n.* correctness, esp. of conduct. **corrective,** *a.* and *n.* (thing) serving to correct or counteract. **corrector,** *n.* (L. *regere,* rule)

correlate, *v.i.* and *t.* have, bring into, mutual relation.—*n.* either of two things so related that one implies the other. **correlation,** *n.* **correlative,** *a.* and *n.* (word, thing) having or expressing mutual relation.

correspond, *v.i.* answer, agree, be similar (to); exchange letters (with). **correspondence,** *n.* corresponding; agreement, analogy; letters. **correspondent,** *n.* letter-writer; person employed to send news to paper; agent.—*a.* corresponding; (*Shake.*) obedient.

corridor, *n.* long passage connecting several rooms or compartments. **c. train,** with passage running through it. (L. *currere*, run)
corrie, *n.* (*Scot.*) round hollow on hillside. (Gael. *coire*, cauldron)
corrigenda, *n.pl.* (*sing.* **corrigendum**) things to be corrected, esp. in book.
corrigible, *a.* capable of being corrected; (*Shake.*) submissive; correcting. (L.)
corrival, *n.* and *v.t.* rival.
corroborate, *v.t.* confirm, make more certain. **corroborant,** *a.* and *n.* corroborating (fact); (*med.*) tonic. **corroboration, corroborator,** *nn.* **corroborative, corroboratory,** *aa.* (L. *robur*, strength)
corroboree, *n.* Australian native festivity and dance. (native)
corrode, *v.t.* and *i.* eat away by degrees, rust; wear away, decay. **corrosion,** *n.* **corrosive,** *a.* and *n.* (agent) producing corrosion. **corrosive sublimate,** a poisonous compound of mercury. (L. *rodere*, gnaw)
corrugate, *v.t.* and *i.* form into wrinkles; bend into wavy ridges. **corrugation,** *n.* **corrugator,** *n.* muscle contracting brow. (L. *ruga*, wrinkle)
corrupt, *v.t.* and *i.* make or become putrid, decompose; deprave; seduce, bribe; destroy purity of (language). —*a.* rotten; tainted; depraved, vicious; venal; (of text or manuscript) defective through errors or alterations. **corruptible,** *a.* **corruptibility,** *n.* **corruption,** *n.* corrupting; rottenness; putrid matter. (L. *rumpere*, break)
corsac, corsak, *n.* a small Asiatic fox. (Turki)
corsage, *n.* part of woman's dress covering bust. (O.F.)
corsair, *n.* pirate; pirate ship. (L. *currere*, run)
corse, *poet.* form of corpse.
corset, *n.* stiffened close-fitting inner bodice; pair of stays. (F.)
corslet, corselet, *n.* armour for body, leather cuirass. (F.)
cortège, *n.* train; procession; funeral procession. (F.)
Cortes, *n.pl.* two chambers making up legislative assembly of Spain. (Sp.)
cortex, *n.* (*pl.* **cortices**) bark; grey matter of brain. **cortical,** *a.* of bark or rind. **corticate, corticated,** *aa.* having bark. (L.)
corundum, *n.* a very hard mineral, native alumina. (Tamil *kurundam*)
coruscate, *v.i.* sparkle, flash. **coruscation,** *n.* (L. *coruscare*)
corvée, *n.* system of exacting unpaid labour. (F.)
corvette, *n.* small escort ship with anti-submarine devices; (formerly) warship smaller than frigate, with one tier of guns. (F.)
corvine, *a.* of raven or crow kind. (L. *corvus*, raven)
Corybant, *n.* priest of goddess Cybele, worshipped with frenzied dancing. **corybantic,** *a.* (Gk. *Korubas*)
corymb, *n.* flower-cluster like flat-topped raceme. **corymbose,** *a.* (Gk. *korumbos*, cluster)
coryphaeus, *n.* leader of chorus. (Gk. *koruphē*, head)
coryza, *n.* catarrh. (Gk. *koruza*)
cos, *n.* kind of lettuce. (place)
cos, same as coss.
cosecant, *n.* (*trigonometry, abbr.* **cosec**) secant of complement of angle.
coseismal, coseismic, *aa.* showing simultaneous shocks of earthquake.
cosh, *v.t.* and *n.* (*sl.*) bludgeon.
cosher, *v.t.* pamper, coddle.
co-signatory, *n.* person signing along with another.
cosily, *adv.* in a cosy manner.
cosine, *n.* (*trigonometry, abbr.* **cos**) sine of complement of angle.
cosmetic, *a.* beautifying.—*n.* preparation for beautifying skin or hair. (Gk. *kosmein*, arrange, adorn)
cosmic, cosmical, *aa.* of the universe or cosmos. **cosmism,** *n.* conception of cosmos as self-acting whole.
cosmo-, from Gk. *kosmos*, universe, used in **cosmogony,** *n.* origin of the universe, theory of this, hence **cosmogonic, cosmogonical,** *aa.*, **cosmogonist,** *n.*; **cosmography,** *n.* description, mapping, of universe or earth as a whole, hence **cosmographic, cosmographical,** *aa.*, **cosmographer,** *n.*; **cosmology,** *n.* science of the universe as an orderly system, hence **cosmological,** *a.*, **cosmologist,** *n.*; **cosmoplastic,** *a.* moulding the universe; **cosmorama,** *n.* peep-show illustrating all parts of the world, hence **cosmoramic,** *a.*
cosmopolitan, *a.* of all parts of the world; free from national prejudices. —*n.* cosmopolitan person. **cosmopolitanism,** *n.* **cosmopolitanize,** *v.t.* make cosmopolitan. **cosmopolite,** *n.* citizen of the world, person without patriotism. **cosmopolitism,** *n.* **cosmopolitical,** *a.* of world politics. (Gk. *kosmos*, world; *politēs*, citizen)
cosmos, *n.* universe as an ordered whole; orderly system. (Gk. *kosmos*)
coss, *n.* Indian measure of length, averaging 1¼ miles. (Hind. *kōs*)
Cossack, *n.* member of Russian people famous as horsemen; (*pl.*) trousers. (Turki *quzzaq*, adventurer)
cosset, *n.* lamb reared by hand, pet lamb.—*v.t.* fondle, pamper.
cost, *v.t.* (*past* same) involve the payment, loss, or sacrifice of; have as price; fix price of.—*n.* price; expenditure of time, labour etc.; (*pl.*) expenses of lawsuit. **c. price,** wholesale price. **to one's c.,** by unhappy experience. (L. *con-*, with; *stare*, stand)
costal, *a.* of ribs. **costate,** *a.* ribbed; ridged. (L. *costa*, rib)
costard, *n.* large kind of apple;

(*arch.*) head. **costermonger, coster,** *nn.* one who sells fruit, fish, etc. from barrow in street.
costive, *a.* constipated. (*constipate*)
costly, *a.* expensive; valuable.
costume, *n.* style of dress; dress; theatrical clothes; woman's coat and skirt of same material.—*v.t.* provide with costume. **c. piece, play,** in which actors wear dress of former period. **costumier,** *n.* dealer in costumes. (L. *consuetudo,* custom)
cosy, *a.* comfortable, snug.—*n.* quilted cover to keep teapot warm.
cot, *n.* small shelter; (*poet.*) cottage.—*v.t.* put (sheep) in cot. **c.-quean,** *n.* (*Shake.*) man who busies himself with women's affairs. (O.E.)
cot, *n.* small bed, crib; swinging bed on ship. (Hind. *khat*)
cot, cote, *n.* (*Spens.*) small boat. dug-out. (Ir.)
cotangent, *n.* (*trigonometry, abbr.* **cot**) tangent of complement of angle.
cote, *n.* shed, shelter, for animals or birds. (O.E.)
co-temporary, same as **contemporary.**
co-tenant, *n.* joint tenant.
coterie, *n.* circle of persons with common interests; social clique. (F.)
cothurnus, *n.* thick-soled boot of Greek tragic actor. (Gk. *kothornos*)
co-tidal, *a.* (of lines) showing places that have high tide at same time.
cotillion, cotillon, *n.* kinds of lively dance. (F. = petticoat)
cotta, *n.* short surplice. (L.L. =tunic)
cottage, *n.* small house, esp. in the country; (*Amer.*) house at pleasure-resort. **cottager,** *n.* one who lives in cottage. (*cot*)
cottar, *n.* (*Scot.*) peasant living in cottage for which he gives labour.
cotter, *n.* kinds of wedge or bolt; split pin.
cotton, *n.* plant of mallow family; soft hairs covering its seeds; thread, fabric, made from this.—*a.* made of cotton.—*v.i.* become attached, take (to); harmonize. **c. waste,** refuse yarn. **c. wool,** raw cotton; wadding made from this. **c.-cake,** *n.* compressed cotton seeds used as fodder. **c.-grass,** *n.* plant with long silky hairs. **c.-tail,** *n.* American rabbit. **cottonocracy,** *n.* cotton magnates. **Cottonopolis,** *n.* nickname for Manchester. **cottony,** *a.* like cotton, downy. (Arab. *qutun*)
cotyledon, *n.* rudimentary leaf in embryo of plant; kinds of plant incl. pennywort. **cotyledonous,** *a.* having cotyledons. **cotyloid,** *a.* cup-shaped. (Gk. *kotulē,* cup)
couch, *n.* piece of furniture for lying on by day; (*poet.*) bed.—*v.i.* and *t.* lie down; have one's bed or lair; crouch ready for springing; word, express, in specified manner; bring (spear) to attacking position; depress, remove (cataract in eye); (*Shake.*) cause to crouch. **couchant,** *a.* (*heraldry*) lying down with head up. (L. *collocare,* place)
couch, *n.* (also **c.-grass**) kind of coarse grass. (*quitch*)
Couéism, *n.* system of treatment by auto-suggestion. (E. *Coué*)
cougar, *n.* large tawny animal of cat family, puma. (F. *couguar*)
cough, *v.i.* and *t.* expel air from lungs with sudden effort and noise.—*n.* act of coughing; disease causing cough. **c. up,** eject by cough; (*sl.*) pay over. **c.-drop, c.-lozenge,** *nn.* sweetmeat to relieve cough. (imit.)
could, see **can.**
couleur de rose, rose colour. (F.)
coulisse, *n.* groove for thing to slide in; side-scene of theatre. (F.)
couloir, *n.* deep gully in mountain-side. (F.)
coulomb, *n.* quantity of electricity conveyed by current of one ampere in one second. (C. A. de *Coulomb*)
coulter, *n.* vertical blade in front of ploughshare. (L. *culter,* knife)
coumarin, *n.* crystalline substance got from tonka bean. (F.)
council, *n.* deliberative or administrative assembly; meeting of this. **c. of war,** meeting of officers for consultation in emergency. **c-.board, c.-chamber,** *nn.* where council sits. **councillor,** *n.* member of council. (L. *concilium*)
counsel, *n.* advice; consultation; barrister. — *v.t.* advise; recommend. **keep one's own c.,** keep secret. **take c. with,** consult. **counsellor,** *n.* adviser. (L. *consilium*)
count, *n.* foreign title corresponding to earl. (L. *comes,* companion)
count, *v.t.* and *i.* reckon, number; include, be included; consider to be; depend (on); be of importance.—*n.* counting; reckoning; total; (*law*) item in list of charges. **c. out,** adjourn (House of Commons) because fewer than 40 members are present; declare (boxer) loser on his failing to rise within ten seconds after being knocked down. **c. up,** find sum of. **counting-house,** *n.* book-keeping department or office. (*compute*)
countenance, *n.* face; expression of face; composure; favour, support.—*v.t.* sanction; approve. (L. *continēre,* contain)
counter, *n.* one who counts; disk used for scoring, token; table in bank or shop across which money or goods are passed. **c.-jumper,** *n.* shop assistant.
counter, *a.* opposed, opposite.—*adv.* in opposite direction.—*v.t.* and *i.* oppose; retort; give return blow.—*n.* return blow or parry; answering move. (L. *contra,* against)
counter, *n.* horse's breast; part of ship's stern from water-line to overhang; back part of shoe round heel.

counter-, *pref.* rival, as in **counter-attraction**; opposed, as in **counteract**; reversed, as in **counter-clockwise**; matched, as in **counterpart.** (L. *contra*, against)
counteract, *v.t.* act in opposition to; neutralize. **counteraction,** *n.* **counteractive,** *a.*
counter-attack, *n.* and *v.i.* and *t.* attack after close of enemy's attack.
counter-attraction, *n.* rival attraction; attraction in opposite direction.
counterbalance, *n.* weight balancing another.—*v.t.* act as counterbalance to; act against with equal power.
counterblast, *n.* vigorous declaration in answer to something.
counterchange, *v.t.* and *i.* interchange; chequer.—*n.* (*Shake.*) exchange.
countercharge, *n.* and *v.t.* charge in opposition to another.
countercheck, *n.* check on a check; opposing check; (*arch.*) retort.
counter-claim, *n.* claim set up against another, esp. by defendant in suit.
counter-clockwise, *adv.* in opposite direction to hands of a clock.
counterfeit, *a.* made in imitation, forged; feigned, sham.—*n.* counterfeit thing; impostor; (*Shake.*) likeness.—*v.t.* imitate; forge; feign, simulate. (L. *facere*, make)
counterfoil, *n.* part of cheque, receipt etc., retained as record.
counter-irritant, *n.* application or action irritating body surface to relieve internal inflammation. **counter-irritation,** *n.*
countermand, *v.t.* cancel (order); recall by countermand; (*Shake.*) keep in check, prohibit.—*n.* order cancelling previous one. (L. *mandare*, order)
countermarch, *v.i.* and *t.* and *n.* march in reverse direction.
countermark, *n.* additional mark on goods.
countermine, *n.* mine made to intercept that of enemy.—*v.i.* make countermine; counterplot.
counterpane, *n.* outer covering of bedclothes, coverlet. (L. *culcita*, quilt; *puncta*, stitched)
counterpart, *n.* thing exactly like another, duplicate; corresponding or complementary part or thing.
counterplot, *n.* and *v.i.* plot to defeat another plot.
counterpoint, *n.* art, mode, of combining melodies; melody added as accompaniment to another.
counterpoise, *n.* weight, force, influence, that balances another; equilibrium.—*v.t.* counterbalance.
counter-reformation, *n.* reforming movement in Roman Catholic Church following on Protestant Reformation.
counter-revolution, *n.* revolution undoing work of previous one.
counterscarp, *n.* outer slope of ditch, nearest besiegers.
countersign, *n.* word to be given in answer to sentry's challenge; countermark.—*v.t.* add confirming signature to. **countersignature,** *n.*
countersink, *v.t.* bevel edge of (screw-hole); sink (screw-head) by this means below surface of wood.
counter-tenor, *n.* high tenor, alto
countervail, *v.t.* and *i.* counterbalance; avail against. (L. *valēre*, be strong)
counterwork, *n.* opposing work.—*v.t.* work against, try to frustrate.
countess, *n.* wife or widow of earl or count; lady ranking with earl or count in her own right.
countless, *a.* too many to count.
country, *n.* region, district; territory of a nation; state; land of birth or residence; rural parts.—*a.* rural, rustic. **c. dance,** with couples face to face in two lines. **c. house, seat,** gentleman's country residence. **go to the c.,** have general election. **in the c.,** (*cricket sl.*) far from wickets. **countrified,** *a.* rural in appearance or manners. **countryman,** *n.* (*fem.* **countrywoman**) peasant; compatriot. **countryside,** *n.* rural district. (L. *contra*, opposite)
county, *n.* division of country, shire; county families; (*arch.*) count. **c. borough,** one of over 50,000 inhabitants, reckoned as administrative county. **c. council,** elected governing body of county. **c. court,** court for civil actions. **c. family,** with ancestral seat in county. **c. town,** (*Amer.*) **c. seat,** capital of county. (*count*)
coup, *v.t.* (*Scot.*) overturn; empty out.
coup, *n.* successful stroke or move. *c. de grâce*, finishing or fatal blow. *c. de main*, sudden violent onslaught. *c. d'état*, sudden overthrow of government by unconstitutional methods. *c. d'œil*, glance; rapid general survey. *c. de théâtre*, sudden dramatic or sensational action. (F.)
coupé, *n.* closed car or carriage for two; half-compartment at end of railway carriage. (F.)
couple, *n.* two of same kind; married or engaged pair; leash for two hounds.—*v.t.* and *i.* link, join; associate; (of animals) copulate. **couplement,** *n.* (*Shake.*) union; pair. **couplet,** *n.* two lines of verse that rhyme with each other; (*Shake.*) pair. **coupling,** *n.* chain connecting railway coaches or parts of machine. (*copula*)
coupon, *n.* detachable ticket entitling to payment of interest, food ration etc. (F.)
courage, *n.* bravery, fortitude; (*Shake.*) disposition; lust. **courageous,** *a.* brave. (L. *cor*, heart)
courier, *n.* express messenger; attendant who looks after convenience of travellers. (L. *currere*, run)
course, *n.* movement in space or time; career; line of conduct; series (of lectures etc.); distinct part of meal;

continuous layer of stone in wall; (*naut.*) sail.—*v.t.* and *i.* hunt, chase; run about, run. **of c.**, naturally. **courser**, *n.* (*poet.*) swift horse. **coursing**, *n.* chasing of hares with greyhounds. (L. *currere*, run)

court, *n.* space enclosed by buildings; area marked off for various games; residence, retinue, establishment, of sovereign; body with judicial powers, place where it sits.—*v.t.* seek friendship of; woo in marriage; invite. **out of c.**, not entitled to hearing or consideration. **pay c. to**, court. **c.-cupboard**, *n.* (*Shake.*) sideboard. **c. hand**, style of handwriting formerly used in records. **c. martial**, judicial court of naval or military officers; trial by this. **c.-martial**, *v.t.* try by court martial. **c. plaster**, sticking-plaster. (L. *cohors*, enclosure)

court-card, *n.* king, queen, or knave. (*coat-card*)

courteous, *a.* polite; considerate. (*court*)

courtesan, **courtezan**, *n.* high-class prostitute. (*court*)

courtesy, *n.* courteous manner or action; curtsy. **c. title**, given by custom, not legal right.

courtier, *n.* one who frequents a royal court; (*Shake.*) wooer.

courtly, *a.* ceremoniously polite, of imposing manner; flattering.

courtship, *n.* courting, wooing; (*Shake.*) courtly manners.

courtyard, *n.* paved space adjoining house.

couscous, *n.* African dish like gruel. (Arab. *kuskus*)

cousin, *n.* son or daughter of uncle or aunt; remote kinsman; title used by one sovereign to another. **first c.**, **c. german**, cousin. **first c. once removed**, son or daughter of cousin. **second c.**, son or daughter of parent's cousin. **cousinhood**, **cousinship**, *nn.* **cousinly**, *a.* like a cousin. (L. *con-*, with; *soror*, sister)

coûte que coûte, at all costs. (F.)

couthie, *a.* (*Scot.*) friendly, kindly.

couturier. *n*, (*fem. couturière*) dressmaker. (F.)

couvade, *n.* primitive custom by which when a child is born the father takes to his bed. (L. *cubare*, lie)

cove, *n.* small bay; sheltered nook; (*archit.*) concave arch.—*v.t.* arch over. (O.E. *cofa*, room)

cove, *n.* (*sl.*) fellow, chap.

coven, *n.* muster of witches. (*convent*)

covenant, *n.* mutual agreement; (*law*) sealed contract; clause of this.—*v.i.* and *t.* make, promise by, covenant. **covenanter**, *n.* one who covenants; adherent of Scottish National Covenant of 1638, made to preserve religious liberty. (L. **con-**, with; *venire*, come)

covent, (*Shake.*) form of **convent**.

Coventry, *n.* **send one to C.**, refuse to speak to him. (place)

cover, *v.t.* extend over, overlie; strew thoroughly; shield, conceal; aim at with gun; include; be enough for (expenses); (of stallion) copulate with; (*journalism*) report; (*Shake.*) lay (table); put hat on.—*n.* thing that covers, lid, wrapper; binding of book; outer tyre; shelter; screen, pretence; requisites for each person at table; funds to meet liability. **c.-point**, *n.* (*cricket*) fielder, position, behind point. (L. *con-*, wholly; *operire*, cover)

coverlet, **coverlid**, *nn.* outer covering of bedclothes, counterpane.

covert, *a.* secret; not open.—*n.* wood, thicket, affording cover for game. **c. coat**, short light overcoat.

coverture, *n.* cover; (*law*) status of married woman.

covet, *v.t.* desire eagerly, long to possess (what is another's). **covetous**, *a.* avaricious, grasping, acquisitive. (L. *cupere*, desire)

covey, *n.* brood of partridges; company, set. (L. *cubare*, lie)

covin, *n.* (*law*) collusion. (*convene*)

cow, *n.* (*pl.* **cows**, *arch.* **kine**) female ox; female of elephant, whale etc. **c.-catcher**, *n.* (*Amer.*) fender in front of railway engine. **c.-parsley**, *n.* wild chervil. **c.-parsnip**, *n.* wild parsnip. **c.-puncher**, *n.* (*Amer.*) cowboy. (O.E. *cú*)

cow, *v.t.* take spirit out of, intimidate.

coward, *n.* person lacking courage.—*a.* cowardly.—*v.t.* (*Shake.*) make cowardly. **cowardice**, *n.* cowardliness. **cowardly**, *a.* faint-hearted. (L. *cauda*, tail)

cowbane, *n.* water hemlock.

cowboy, *n.* boy who tends cows; (*Amer.*) man in charge of cattle on ranch.

cower, *v.i.* crouch, be huddled up; shrink with fear, quail.

cowherd, *n.* one who tends cattle.

cowhide, *n.* leather of cow's skin; whip of this.

cowish, *a.* (*Shake.*) cowardly.

cowl, *n.* monk's hood. (L. *cucullus*)

cowl, *n.* elaborate kind of chimney-pot. (O.E. *cufle*)

cowl, *n.* water-tub carried by two on **c.-staff**, *n.*

cowlick, *n.* tuft of hair brushed over forehead.

cowpox, *n.* pustular disease of cow, from which vaccine is made.

cowrie, **cowry**, *n.* a small sea-shell. (Hind. *kauri*)

cowslip, *n.* yellow-flowered wild plant. (O.E. *cú*, cow; *slyppe*, slime)

cox, *n.* coxswain, esp. of racing boat. —*v.t.* act as cox, steer.

coxa, *n.* (*pl.* **coxae**) hip-joint. **coxal**, *a.* (L.)

coxcomb, *n.* conceited affected person, fop; medieval jester's red cap. **coxcombical**, *a.* **coxcombry**, *n.* (*cock's comb*)

coxswain, *n.* petty officer in charge of ship's boat; steersman of boat. (*cock*; *swain*)
coxy, same as **cocky.**
coy, *a.* shy, bashful; (*Shake.*) disdainful.—*v.t.* and *i.* (*Shake.*) fondle; disdain. (L. *quietus*, quiet)
coyote, *n.* N. American prairie-wolf. (Mex. *coyotl*)
coypu, *n.* a S. American water-rodent; its fur, nutria. (native)
coystril, same as **coistrel.**
coz, *arch. abbr.* of **cousin.**
coze, *v.i.* and *n.* chat.
cozen, *v.t.* and *i.* cheat, beguile; act deceitfully. **cozenage,** *n.*
cozier, *n.* (*Shake.*) cobbler. (L. *con-*, together; *suere*, sew)
cozy, same as **cosy.**
crab, *n.* ten-legged crustacean; Cancer, fourth sign of zodiac; pubic louse; (*colloq.*) drawback; (*pl.*) lowest throw at dice, two aces.—*v.t.* and *i.* (of hawks) scratch, claw (each other); (*colloq.*) find fault with, carp at. **catch a c.,** get oar stuck in water through faulty stroke. **c.-pot,** *n.* wicker trap for crabs. (O.E. *crabba*)
crab, *n.* (also **c.-apple**) wild apple.
crabbed, *a.* cross-grained, ill-natured; (of handwriting) cramped, hard to read; (of style) awkward, harsh, obscure. (*crab*)
crack, *n.* split, fissure; partial break, flaw; sudden sharp sound; sharp blow; good player, expert; (*Scot.*) chat; (*Amer.*) witticism; (*Shake.*) urchin.—*v.t.* and *i.* break partially, split; make sharp noise (with); make (joke); open (bottle); (of voice) become dissonant; (*Shake.*) boast.—*a.* (*colloq.*) first-rate. **c. of doom,** end of the world. **c. up,** (*colloq.*) collapse; praise. **in a c.,** in a moment. **c.-brained,** *a.* flighty, crazy. **cracked,** *a.* (*colloq.*) rather mad. (O.E. *cracian*)
cracker, *n.* small firework; paper toy exploding when pulled; small dry biscuit. **crackerjack,** *n.* (*Amer, sl.*) fine specimen. **crackers,** *a.* (*sl.*) mad.
crackle, *n.* series of slight cracking sounds.—*v.i.* emit crackle. **crackling,** *n.* rind of roast pork.
cracknel, *n.* thick puffy dry biscuit.
cracksman, *n.* burglar.
-cracy, *suf.* government by, as in democracy. (Gk. *kratos*, power)
cradle, *n.* infant's bed on rockers; infancy; place of origin; thing like cradle, frame under ship for launching it, gold-washing basket. —*v.t.* place in or as in cradle. (O.E. *cradol*)
craft, *n.* cunning, guile; skill; skilled trade; members of this; (*pl.* **craft**) boat, vessel.—*v.i.* (*Shake.*) exercise one's craft. **craftsman,** *n.* one who practises a craft. **craftsmanship,** *n.* skilled workmanship. **crafty,** *a.* cunning, wily; dexterous. (O.E. *cræft*)
crag, *n.* steep rugged rock. **craggy,** *a.* full of crags; rugged. **cragsman,** *n.* rock-climber.
craig, *n.* (*Scot.*) neck.
craik, *v.i.* (*Scot.*) whine, grumble.
crake, *n.* bird of rail kind. (imit.)
crake, *v.i.* and *n.* (*Spens.*) boast. (*crack*)
cram, *v.t.* and *i.* pack tightly, stuff; feed to excess; prepare quickly for examination.—*n.* cramming; crowd. crush; (*sl.*) lie. **c.-full,** *a.* as full as it can be crammed. (O.E. *crammian*)
crambo, *n.* game in which rhymes have to be found for given word. **dumb c.,** in which word has to be guessed from rhyming words acted in dumb show.
crammer, *n.* special tutor or coach.
cramoisy, cramesy, *a.* and *n.* (*arch.*) crimson. (Arab. *qirmiz*, kermes)
cramp, *n.* painful spasmodic contraction of muscle; kinds of clamp for holding masonry etc. together.—*v.t.* affect with cramp; confine narrowly, hamper; fasten with cramp.—*a.* cramped. **cramped,** *a.* narrow, restricted; (of writing) too small or close. (O.F. *crampe*)
crampon, *n.* grappling-iron; spiked iron plate worn on shoe for climbing on ice. (F.)
cran, *n.* (*Scot.*) measure of herrings, 37½ gallons. **coup the c.,** be upset.
cranage, *n.* use of crane, dues paid for this.
cranberry, *n.* small red sour berry; shrub it grows on. (*crane*)
crane, *n.* tall wading-bird; machine for raising heavy weights.—*v.t.* and *i.* move with crane; stretch out (neck). **c.-fly,** *n.* daddy-long-legs. **c.'s-bill,** *n.* kinds of wild geranium. (O.E. *cran*)
cranium, *n.* (*pl.* **crania**) skull, esp. part enclosing brain. **cranial,** *a.* **craniology,** *n.* study of cranium. **craniological,** *a.* **craniologist,** *n.* **craniometer,** *n.* instrument for measuring cranium. (Gk. *kranion*)
crank, *n.* arm attached to shaft for turning it; fanciful turn of speech; fad; eccentric person, faddist; (*Shake.*) winding path.—*v.t.* and *i.* furnish with crank; turn, wind.—*a.* weak, shaky. **c. up,** start (motor-car engine) with crank. **crankle,** *v.i.* and *n.* bend, twist. **cranky,** *a.* sickly; full of whims, eccentric; cantankerous. (O.E. *cranc*)
crank, *a.* (of ship) liable to capsize.
crank, *a.* (*obs.*) brisk; merry.
crannog, *n.* prehistoric dwelling on piles in lake. (Ir. *crann*, tree)
cranny, *n.* crevice, chink. **crannied,** *a.*
cranreuch, *n.* (*Scot.*) hoar-frost. (Gael.)
crants, *n.* (*Shake.*) garland. (G. *kranz*)
crape, *n.* black gauze-like crimped silk material, used for mourning.—*v.t.* clothe with crape. (*crêpe*)

craps, *n.pl.* (*Amer.*) gambling game played with two dice.
crapulence, *n.* sickness from drinking to excess. **crapulent, crapulous,** *aa.* (Gk. *kraipalē*, drunken headache)
crare, *n.* (*Shake.*) small trading vessel. (O.F. *craier*)
crash, *n.* burst of mixed loud sound; violent fall or impact; sudden collapse; faulty landing damaging aircraft.—*v.i.* and *t.* emit, fall or strike with, crash; collapse, ruin; (of aircraft) land with crash; (*sl.*) intrude into (party). (imit.)
crash, *n.* coarse linen cloth.
crasis, *n.* contraction of two vowels into one long vowel or diphthong. (Gk.=mixture)
crass, *a.* gross; very stupid. **crassitude,** *n.* (L. *crassus*, thick)
cratch, *n.* rack for fodder. (O.F. *creche*)
crate, *n.* openwork case of light boarding or wicker for fragile goods. (L. *cratis*, hurdle)
crater, *n.* mouth of volcano; cavity of shell-explosion. (Gk. *kratēr*, mixing-bowl)
cravat, *n.* man's neckcloth; necktie. (G. *Krabate*, Croatian)
crave, *v.t.* and *i.* ask humbly, beg; have strong desire (for). **craving,** *n.* intense desire. (O.E. *crafian*)
craven, *a.* cowardly, spiritless.—*n.* craven person, poltroon. —*v.t.* (*Shake.*) make cowardly.
craw, *n.* bird's crop. (M.E. *crawe*)
crawl, *v.i.* move on belly or hands and knees, creep; move slowly; abase oneself; swarm (with).—*n.* crawling motion; a racing stroke in swimming. **crawler,** *n.* one who crawls; louse; (*pl.*) baby's overalls.
crayfish, crawfish, *n.* freshwater crustacean like small lobster. (O.F. *crevice*+confusion with *fish*)
crayon, *n.* stick, pencil, of coloured chalk; drawing done with crayons. (L. *creta*, chalk)
craze, *v.t.* render insane, derange; (*Shake.*) impair.—*n.* excessive enthusiasm, mania. **crazy,** *a.* insane, mad; shaky, rickety. **crazily,** *adv.* **craziness,** *n.* (Swed. *krasa*)
creak, *n.* shrill grating noise of unoiled hinge etc.—*v.i.* emit creak.
cream, *n.* rich oily part of milk; preparation like this; best part, pick.—*a.* yellowish-white.—*v.t.* and *i.* remove cream from; form cream or scum. **c. of tartar,** potassium bitartrate. **c.-laid, c.-wove,** paper, laid, wove, paper of cream colour. **c.-separator, creamer,** *nn.* machine, dish, separating cream from milk. **creamery,** *n.* butter factory; shop for milk and cream. **creamy,** *a.* like cream. (Gk. *chrisma*, unguent)
crease, *n.* line made by folding; wrinkle; (*cricket*) line defining position of batsman or bowler.—*v.t.* and *i.* make creases in; form creases. **creasy,** *a.*
create, *v.t.* and *i.* bring into being; give rise to; make, produce; (*sl.*) make a fuss. **creation,** *n.* creating; thing created; the whole world or universe; production of human mind. **creationism,** *n.* belief in special creation, not evolution; belief that God creates a soul for every human being at birth. **creationist,** *n.* **creative,** *a.* of creation; having power to create. **creator,** *n.* (*fem.* **creatress**) one who creates. **the Creator,** God. **creature,** *n.* living being; created thing; contemptible person; mere tool. **the creature,** (*sl.*) whisky. (L. *creare*)
creatin, *n.* organic base found in juice of flesh. (Gk. *kreas*, flesh)
crèche, *n.* public nursery. (F.)
credence, *n.* belief; (also **c. table**) small side table for eucharistic elements before consecration. **credentials,** *n.pl.* letters of introduction; documents proving identity or honesty. **credent,** *a.* (*Shake.*) believing; credible. **credible,** *a.* believable; trustworthy. **credibility,** *n.* **credibly,** *adv.* (L. *credere*, believe)
credit, *n.* belief, trust; good reputation; source of honour; trust in a person's ability to pay, time allowed for payment; sum at person's disposal in bank, entry in account of sum received.—*v.t.* believe; put on credit side of account. **c. one with,** believe he has. **creditable,** *a.* bringing honour, praiseworthy. **creditor,** *n.* one to whom debt is owing. **credo,** *n.* (*pl.* **credos**) creed. **credulous,** *a.* over-ready to believe, easily imposed on. **credulity,** *n.* (L. *credere*, believe)
creed, *n.* system of religious belief, faith; summary of Christian doctrine; set of opinions or principles. (L. *credere*, believe)
creek, *n.* narrow inlet; (*Austral.*) small river.
creel, *n.* angler's fishing-basket.
creep, *v.i.* (*past, p.p.* **crept**) move on belly or hands and knees, crawl; move stealthily or slowly; cringe, fawn; (of plant) grow along ground or wall; (of flesh) feel as if things were creeping over it; (*naut.*) drag with creeper.—*n.* spell of creeping. **the cc.,** (*colloq.*) shrinking horror. **creeper,** *n.* creeping or climbing plant; grapnel. **creepy, creepy-crawly,** *aa.* **creepie,** *n.* (*Scot.*) low stool. (O.E. *crēopan*)
creese, same as **kris.**
creesh, *v.t.* and *n.* (*Scot.*) grease. (L. *crassus*, fat)
cremate, *v.t.* consume (corpse) by fire. **cremation, cremator,** *nn.* **crematorium,** *n.* (*pl.* **crematoriums, crematoria**) establishment for cremation. (L. *cremare*, burn)

crème, **n.** cream. *c. de la c.*, very best. **c. de menthe**, greenish liqueur flavoured with peppermint. (F.)

Cremona, **n.** superior kind of violin. (town in Italy)

cremona, *n.* an organ reed-stop. (G. *krummhorn*, crooked horn)

crenate, crenated, *aa.* notched, indented. **crenation, crenature**, *nn.* **crenel, crenelle**, *n.* gap between raised parts in battlement. **crenellate, crenelate**, *v.t.* furnish with battlements or loopholes. **crenellation**, *n.* (It. *crena*, notch)

creole, *n.* native of W. Indies or Spanish America with European ancestors; (*Amer.*) descendant of French or Spanish settlers in Louisiana. (Sp. *criollo*)

creosote, *n.* oily liquid distilled from wood tar. (Gk. *kreas*, meat; *sōzein*, save)

crêpe, *n.* gauze-like crimped material. *c. de Chine*, silk *crêpe*. (F.)

crepitate, *v.i.* make crackling sound. **crepitation**, *n.* (L. *crepare*, creak)

crept, see **creep**.

crepuscular, *a.* of, appearing at, twilight. (L. *crepusculum*, twilight)

crescendo, *a.* gradually increasing in loudness or intensity, moving to climax.—*n.* crescendo passage or effect. (It.)

crescent, *n.* figure of moon in first or last quarter; this as Mohammedan badge; curved row of houses.—*a.* crescent-shaped; increasing. **crescive**, *a.* (*Shake.*) growing. (L. *crescere*, grow)

cress, *n.* kinds of plant with pungent edible leaves. (O.E. *cresse*)

cresset, *n.* light-giving brazier on pole. (O.F. *graisse*, grease)

crest, *n.* tuft of hair or feathers on animal's head; plume or central ridge of helmet; top of hill; curl of foam on wave; distinctive device above shield on coat of arms, often used separately on seal etc.—*v.t.* and *i.* furnish with crest, crown; mount to top of. **crestfallen**, *a.* mortified by failure; dejected. (L. *crista*)

cretaceous, *a.* chalky; (*geol.*) of last mesozoic period. **cretify**, *v.t.* impregnate with salts of lime. **cretification**, *n.* (L. *creta*, chalk)

cretic, *n.* three-syllabled foot, long-short-long. (*Crete*)

cretin, *n.* mentally and physically deficient person, deformed idiot. **cretinism**, *n.* cretinous state, due to thyroid deficiency. **cretinous**, *a.* (*Christian*, because just human)

cretonne, *n.* unglazed cotton cloth printed with coloured patterns. (F.)

crevasse, *n.* deep cleft in glacier. (F.)

crevice, *n.* crack, chink. (L. *crepare*, creak)

crew, *n.* those who man a ship or boat; set, company; gang, mob. (L. *crescere*, grow)

crew, see **crow**.

crewel, *n.* thin worsted yarn. **c.-work**, *n.* embroidery with crewels.

crib, *n.* rack for fodder, manger; stall for oxen; hovel, hut; child's cot with high sides; piece of plagiarism; literal translation; dealer's cards at cribbage, laid aside from other hands; (*sl.*) situation, post; (*Amer.*) bin.—*v.t.* and *i.* confine, cramp; copy (from) unfairly, plagiarize; pilfer. **crack a c.**, (*sl.*) break into house. **cribbage**, *n.* a card game. (O.E.)

cribriform, *a.* with small holes like a sieve. (L. *cribrum*, sieve)

crick, *n.* sudden painful stiffness of muscles.—*v.t.* produce crick in.

cricket, *n.* a chirping insect. (O.F. *criquet*)

cricket, *n.* open-air game played with wickets, bat, and ball, by eleven players a side. **not c.**, (*colloq.*) unsporting. **cricketer**, *n.*

cried, see **cry**.

crier, *n.* one who cries; officer who makes public proclamations.

crikey, *int.* (*sl.*) of astonishment.

crime, *n.* violation of law, grave offence; wicked act, sin; ill-judged action.—*v.t.* (*army*) charge with military offence. **criminal**, *a.* of the nature of, guilty of, crime.—*n.* one who has committed crime. **criminal connection, conversation,** (*abbr.* **crim. con.**) illegal sexual intercourse. **criminality**, *n.* **criminate**, *v.t.* accuse; incriminate; censure strongly. **crimination**, *n.* **criminative, criminatory**, *aa.* **criminology**, *n.* scientific study of crime. **criminologist**, *n.* **criminous clerk**, clergyman guilty of crime. (L. *crimen*)

criminy, *int.* (*arch.*) of surprise.

crimp, *v.t.* press into small folds, frill, corrugate; curl (hair) artificially; gash flesh of (fish) to give it firmness. (*cramp*)

crimp, *n.* person luring or shanghaiing sailors aboard vessel.—*v.t.* decoy thus.

crimson, *a.* and *n.* deep red.—*v.t.* and *i.* dye crimson; blush. (*cramoisy*)

cringe, *v.i.* shrink in fear, cower; behave with servility, fawn.—*n.* cringing. (O.E. *cringan*, sink down)

cringle, *n.* loop of rope containing metal ring for another rope to pass through.

crinite, *a.* hairy. (L. *crinis*, hair)

crinkle, *n.* wrinkle, corrugation.—*v.i.* and *t.* form crinkles (in). **crinkly**, *a.* **crinkum-crankum**, *n.* thing of twists and turns. (*crank*)

crinoid, *a.* lily-shaped.—*n.* kind of sea-urchin. **crinoidal**, *a.* (Gk. *krinon*, lily; *eidos*, form)

crinoline, *n.* hooped skirt made to project all round; warship's torpedo-netting. **crinolette**, *n.* kind of bustle. (L. *crinis*, hair; *linum*, thread)

cripple, *n.* lame person; one who is

disabled or deformed.—*v.t.* lame; disable; impair. (O.E. *crypel*)

crisis, *n.* (*pl.* **crises**) turning-point; moment of danger, emergency. (Gk. *krinein*, separate)

crisp, *a.* dry and brittle; bracing; brisk, decided; (of hair) curly; (of style) sharp, incisive.—*n.* (*sl.*) bank-notes.—*v.t.* and *i.* make, become, crisp; form into curls, crimp. **crispate,** *a.* crisped; (*bot.*) with wavy margin. **crispy,** *a.* (L. *crispus*)

criss-cross, *a.* crossing; in cross lines. —*adv.* crosswise.—*v.i.* and *t.* intersect; mark with cross lines.—*n.* intersecting; mark of cross; game of noughts and crosses. **c. row,** (*arch.*) alphabet. (*Christ's cross*)

cristate, *a.* crested. (*crest*)

criterion, *n.* (*pl.* **criteria**) standard by which anything is judged, principle of criticism. (Gk. *kritēs*, judge)

crith, *n.* unit of weight for gases, ·0899 gramme. (Gk. *krithē*, barley)

critic, *n.* one who passes judgment; fault-finder; one skilled in judging merits of literary or artistic works.—*a.* (*Shake.*) censorious. **critical,** *a.* exercising, skilled in, criticism; captious; of the nature of a crisis, crucial. **criticaster,** *n.* inferior critic. **criticism,** *n.* criticizing, judging of merit. **higher criticism,** dealing with composition and authenticity of books of the Bible. **criticize,** *v.t.* estimate, discuss, as critic; find fault with. **critique,** *n.* critical essay or review. (Gk. *kritēs*, judge)

croak, *n.* deep hoarse discordant cry. —*v.i.* and *t.* utter croak; speak hoarsely or gloomily; (*sl.*) die, kill.

croceate, *a.* saffron-coloured. (*crocus*)

crochet, *n.* kind of knitting done with hooked needle.—*v.i.* and *t.* do, make with, crochet. (F.)

crocidolite, *n.* blue asbestos. (Gk. *krokis*, nap on cloth; *lithos*, stone)

crock, *n.* earthenware pot; broken piece of earthenware. **crockery,** *n.* earthenware vessels. (O.E. *croc*)

crock, *n.* broken-down horse; (*sl.*) worn-out or unfit person, cripple.—*v.i.* and *t.* become, make, unfit.

crocket, *n.* small curved ornament on side of gable, spire etc. (*crochet*)

crocodile, *n.* large amphibious lizard-like reptile; line of schoolgirls walking two and two. **c. bird,** African bird like plover. **c. tears,** sham tears. **crocodilian,** *a.* (Gk. *krokodeilos*)

crocus, *n.* (*pl.* **crocuses**) bulbous plant with yellow, purple, or white flowers. (Gk. *krokos*, crocus, saffron)

Croesus, *n.* very rich man. (person)

croft, *n.* small piece of arable land adjoining house; small farm. **crofter,** *n.* one who works a croft.

cromlech, *n.* prehistoric monument of flat stone resting on others, dolmen. (W. *crom*, bent; *llech*, flat stone)

crone, *n.* withered old woman. (O.F. *carogne*, carrion)

crony, *n.* intimate friend.

crood, croodle, *vv.i.* (*Scot.*) coo.

crook, *n.* shepherd's hooked staff; bend, curve; (*sl.*) swindler, criminal. —*a.* crooked.—*v.t.* bend into shape of hook. **crooked,** *a.* bent, twisted; dishonest. (M.E. *crok*)

croon, *v.t.* and *i.* hum, sing, in undertone.—*n.* crooning. **crooner,** *n.* wireless entertainer who sings sentimental songs in low voice.

crop, *n.* year's or season's produce of any cultivated plant; harvest; pouch in bird's gullet; stock of whip; hunting-whip; cropping of hair, cropped hair.—*v.t.* and *i.* clip short; poll; bite off or eat down (grass); sow, plant; (of land) yield. **c. out,** (*geol.*) come to surface. **c. up,** arise unexpectedly. **c.-eared,** *a.* with clipped ears; short-haired. **cropper,** *n.* thing that crops; (*sl.*) heavy fall. (O.E.)

croquet, *n.* game in which wooden balls are hit with mallets through series of hoops fixed in lawn; croqueting. —*v.t.* and *i.* drive away (player's ball) by striking one's own placed in contact with it.

croquette, *n.* rissole. (F.)

crore, *n.* a hundred lakhs, ten million (rupees). (Hind, *kror*)

crosier, crozier, *n.* pastoral staff of bishop. (L.L. *crocia*, crook)

cross, *n.* structure of upright and crosspiece, used for crucifixion; thing of this shape; mark formed by intersection of two lines; affliction, misfortune, trial; intermixture of breeds, hybrid; (*Shake.*) coin.—*v.t.* and *i.* pass across; intersect; meet and pass; place crosswise; make sign of the cross over; thwart, oppose; modify (breed) by intermixture (with), interbreed.—*a.* transverse; reaching from side to side; intersecting; (*colloq.*) out of temper, peevish. **the C.,** that on which Christ suffered; symbol of Christianity. **c. benches,** (in House of Commons) for those who support neither Government nor Opposition. **c. fire,** directed from different sides. **c. off, out,** cancel. **c. one's mind,** occur to one. **fiery c.,** charred cross as signal for Scottish clans to rally. **Greek c.,** like plus (+). **Latin c.,** with long upright (†). **Maltese c.,** with indented ends (✠). **St Andrew's c.,** like X. **St Anthony's, tau, c.,** like T. (L. *crux*)

crossbar, *n.* transverse bar.

crossbill, *n.* bird whose mandibles cross when bill is closed.

crossbow, *n.* bow set crosswise on stock, shooting bolts along groove.

cross-breed, *n.* hybrid animal. **cross-bred,** *a.*

cross-buttock, *n.* wrestling throw over hip.—*v.t.* throw with this.

cross-country, *a.* across fields.

crosse, *n.* long-handled racket in which ball is caught and carried in lacrosse. (F.)

cross-examine, *v.t.* question closely; (*law*) question (witness) who has been already questioned by counsel on other side. **cross-examination,** *n.*

cross-eyed, *a.* squinting.

cross-fertilize, *v.t.* fertilize (plant) with pollen from another.

cross-grained, *a.* with grain running across; cantankerous.

cross-hatch, *v.t.* shade with crossed lines.

crossing, *n.* intersection of roads or railway lines; place for crossing street. **c.-sweeper,** *n.*

crosspatch, *n.* (*colloq.*) bad-tempered person.

cross-piece, *n.* transverse piece.

cross-purpose, *n.* contrary purpose. **be at cc.,** talk without either party realizing that the other is talking about a different thing.

cross-question, *v.t.* and *n.* question to elicit details or test accuracy of account already given.

cross-reference, *n.* reference from one part of book to another.

crossroad, *n.* road crossing another.

cross-row, *n.* (*Shake.*) alphabet.

cross-section, *n.* cutting at right angles to length; surface then shown.

crosstie, *n.* (*Amer.*) railway sleeper.

cross-trees, *n.pl.* timbers placed across head of lower mast to support mast above.

crosswise, *adv.* in the manner of a cross.

crossword, *n.* (also **c. puzzle**) puzzle in which interlocking words to be inserted vertically and horizontally in squared diagram are indicated by clues.

crotch, *n.* angle between legs or branches, fork.

crotchet, *n.* fad, whim; small hook; (*mus.*) note equal to half a minim. **crotcheteer,** *n.* faddist. **crotchety,** *a.* (F. *croc,* hook+dim.)

croton, *n.* kinds of tropical plant. **c. oil,** strong purgative made from seeds of croton. (Gk. *krotōn,* tick)

crouch, *v.i.* stoop low, take huddled-up attitude; bend servilely.—*n.* crouching posture.

croup, *n.* children's disease of throat with hard cough. (obs. *croup,* croak)

croup, croupe, *n.* hindquarters of horse. (F.)

croupier, *n.* one who presides at gaming-table and rakes in money; assistant-chairman at public dinner. (F.)

crouse, *a.* (*Scot.*) lively, pert.—*adv.* pertly.

crow, *n.* cry of cock; joyful cry of infant; kinds of black bird incl. raven and rook.—*v.i.* (*past* **crew** or **crowed**) express triumph, exult. **as the c. flies,** in direct line. **eat c.,** (*Amer.*) submit to humiliation. **have a c. to pick with,** have matter to settle with. **c.-keeper,** *n.* (*Shake.*) scarecrow. **c.'s foot,** *n.* wrinkle at corner of eye; caltrop. **c.'s nest,** *n.* shelter at masthead for look-out man. **crowbar,** *n.* iron bar for use as lever. **crowberry,** *n.* black edible berry; shrub bearing it; (*Amer.*) cranberry. (imit.)

crowd, *n.* (*arch.*) obsolete instrument like fiddle. (W. *crwth,* fiddle)

crowd, *n.* dense multitude, throng; large number; (*colloq.*) set, lot.—*v.i.* and *t.* flock together, throng; fill, occupy, cram; push, thrust; (*Amer.*) importune. **c. (on) sail,** hoist unusual spread of sail. (O.E. *crúdan,* press)

crowdie, *n.* (*Scot.*) brose.

crowfoot, *n.* buttercup.

crown, *n.* diadem of monarch; regal power; the sovereign; wreath for head; five-shilling piece; any of various foreign coins; size of paper, 20×15 in.; top of head; summit; reward; completion, consummation. —*v.t.* place crown on; top, cap; be reward of; put finishing touch to. **c. colony,** one subject to control of home government. **c. glass,** fine thick kind. **c. prince,** heir apparent to throne. **c. princess,** his wife. **c. wheel,** wheel with cogs at right angles to its plane. (L. *corona*)

crowner, *n.* (*arch.*) coroner. **c.'s quest,** inquest.

crozier, see **crosier.**

crucial, *a.* decisive, critical; (*anat.*) cross-shaped. **cruciate,** *a.* (*bot.*) cross-shaped. (L. *crux,* cross)

crucible, *n.* melting-pot. (L.L. *crucibulum*)

crucifix, *n.* image of Christ on cross. **crucifixion,** *n.* crucifying. **crucify,** *v.t.* nail to cross, execute thus; chasten, mortify (passions etc.). (L. *crux,* cross; *figere,* fix)

cruciform, *a.* cross-shaped. (*crux*)

crude, *a.* in natural state, raw; unripe; rough, unfinished, lacking polish; blunt. **crudity,** *n.* (L. *crudus*)

cruel, *a.* delighting in or callous to others' pain, hard-hearted, merciless; painful, distressing.—*adv.* (*vulg.*) extremely. **cruelty,** *n.* (L. *crudelis*)

cruet, *n.* small bottle for sauce or condiment; (also **c.-stand**) stand with cruets, esp. salt, pepper, and mustard. (O.F. *cruie,* pot+dim.)

cruise, *v.i.* sail about without definite destination, sail for pleasure.—*n.* wandering voyage. **cruiser,** *n.* warship lighter and faster than battleship. **cruiser weight** (*boxing*) light heavy, 11 st. 6 lb. to 12 st. 7 lb. (L. *crux,* cross)

crumb, *n.* small fragment of bread; soft part of bread; small piece, morsel.—*v.t.* break into, cover with, crumbs. **crumble,** *v.t.* and *i.* break, fall, into crumbs or fragments; disintegrate, decay. **crumbly,** *a.* apt to crumble. **crumby, crummy,** *aa.* in crumbs; soft. (O.E. *cruma*)

crummock, *n.* (*Scot.*) staff with crooked head.

crump, *v.t.* (*colloq.*) hit (ball) hard.—*n.* (*colloq.*) hard hit; heavy fall; (*army sl.*) bursting shell. (imit.)

crumpet, *n.* flat soft round cake; (*sl.*) head.

crumple, *v.t.* and *i.* crush into folds, crease, rumple. **c. up,** overwhelm; collapse. (obs. *crump,* crooked)

crunch, *v.t.* and *i.* crush with teeth, tread underfoot, with force and noise; make sound like this.—*n.* act, sound, of crunching. (imit.)

crupper, *n.* strap attached to back of saddle and passing under horse's tail; horse's hind quarters. (*croup*)

crural, *a.* of leg. (L. *crus,* leg)

crusade, *n.* medieval Christian expedition to recover Holy Land from Mohammedans; holy war; campaign against evil.—*v.i.* go on crusade. **crusader,** *n.* (L. *crux,* cross)

crusado, *n.* a Portuguese coin worth about 2*s.* 4*d.* (Port. *cruzado*)

cruse, *n.* (*arch.*) earthenware jar. **widow's c.,** never-failing supply.

crush, *v.t.* and *i.* compress so as to break, bruise, or crumple; squash; pulverize; subdue, overwhelm; disconcert.—*n.* dense crowd; (*colloq.*) large party. **have a c. on,** (*sl.*) be in love with. **c.-hat,** *n.* opera hat.

crust, *n.* hard outer part of bread, pastry covering pie; hard covering, shell; hard exterior of earth; incrustation on wine-bottle.—*v.t.* and *i.* cover or be covered with, form into, crust. (L. *crusta*)

crustacean, *n.* one of the **Crustacea,** *n.pl.* order of hard-shelled animals, e.g. crab, lobster. **crustaceous,** *a.* having hard shell; crust-like. **crustaceology,** *n.* study of crustaceans. (*crust*)

crusty, *a.* like crust; having hard thick crust; irritable, surly.

crutch, *n.* staff with cross-piece to go under arm of lame person; prop, support; fork. (O.E. *crycc*)

crux, *n.* hard question, knotty point. (L.=cross)

cry, *v.i.* and *t.* (*past, p.p.* **cried**) call out; proclaim; shed tears, weep.—*n.* (*pl.* **cries**) inarticulate sound; urgent appeal; common report; battle-cry, party catchword; spell of weeping; (*Shake.*) pack of hounds. **a far c.,** a great distance. **c. down,** disparage. **c. off,** withdraw from bargain. **c. up,** praise. **in full c.,** (of hounds) in full pursuit. **c.-baby,** *n.* child who weeps easily. **crying,** *a.* clamant, flagrant. (L. *quiritare*)

cryo-, from Gk. *kruos,* frost, used in **cryogen,** *n.* freezing-mixture; **cryolite,** *n.* mineral yielding aluminium; **cryometer,** *n.* instrument for measuring very low temperatures.

crypt, *n.* underground chamber, vault, esp. of church. **cryptic,** *a.* secret, mysterious; (*zool.*) concealing. **cryptically,** *adv.* (Gk. *kruptein,* conceal)

crypt(o)-, from Gk. *kruptos,* hidden, used in **cryptaesthesia,** *n.* clairvoyance; **cryptogam,** *n.* plant without stamens or pistil, non-flowering plant, hence **cryptogamic, cryptogamous,** *aa.*; **cryptogram, cryptograph,** *nn.* piece of writing in cipher, hence **cryptographer,** *n.* writer of, expert on, cryptograms. **cryptography,** *n.*, **cryptographic,** *a.*

crystal, *n.* clear transparent quartz; piece of this; superior kind of glass; cut-glass ware; (*chem.*) piece of matter which has taken a definite geometrical form with plane faces.—*a.* of, like, clear as, crystal. **c. set,** wireless set in which block of crystal rectifies current. **c.-gazing,** *n.* fortune-telling by peering into a ball of crystal. **crystalline,** *a.* crystal; (*chem.*) having structure of crystal. **crystallize,** *v.t.* and *i.* form into crystals; take definite shape. **crystallization,** *n.* **crystallogeny,** *n.* formation of crystals. **crystallogenic,** *a.* **crystallography,** *n.* science of crystal structure. **crystallographic,** *a.* **crystallographer,** *n.* **crystalloid,** *a.* crystal-like; of crystalline structure (opp. to colloid).—*n.* crystalloid substance. (Gk. *kruos,* frost)

ctenoid, *a.* with comb-like edge. (Gk. *kteis,* comb)

cub, *n.* young of fox, bear, wolf etc.; ill-mannered boy.—*v.i.* bring forth cubs. **cubbing,** *n.* hunting of fox-cubs. **cubbish,** *a.* ill-mannered.

cubage, cubature, *nn.* cubic content; finding of this.

cubby-hole, *n.* snug place. (obs. *cub,* pen)

cube, *n.* regular solid with six equal square sides; cube-shaped block; product of a number multiplied by itself twice.—*v.t.* raise (number) to third power. **c. root,** number that gives stated number when cubed. (Gk. *kubos*)

cubeb, *n.* dried fruit of a pepper plant. (Arab. *kababah*)

cubic, *a.* of three dimensions; involving third power; cubical. **c. foot, inch,** etc., volume of cube whose side is foot, inch etc. **cubical,** *a.* cube-shaped.

cubicle, *n.* small separate sleeping-compartment in dormitory. (L. *cubare,* lie)

cubiform, *a.* cube-shaped.

cubism, *n.* style of painting in which things are depicted as assemblage of geometrical forms. **cubist,** *n.*

cubit, *n.* ancient measure of length,

about 18 in. **cubital,** *a.* of the fore-arm. (L. *cubitum*, elbow)
cuboid, *a.* like a cube.—*n.* rectangular parallelepiped. **cuboidal,** *a.* (Gk. *eidos*, form)
cucking-stool, *n.* ancient chair for ducking female scolds etc.
cuckold, *n.* husband of unfaithful wife.—*v.t.* make cuckold of. **cuck-oldly,** *a.* (*Shake.*). **cuckoldry,** *n.* adultery. (O.F. *cucu*, cuckoo)
cuckoo, *n.* bird which lays its eggs in other birds' nests; its call.—*a.* (*sl.*) crazy. **c.-clock,** *n.* clock striking hours with cuckoo-call. **c.-flower,** *n.* ladysmock. **c.-pint,** *n.* wild arum. **c.-spit,** *n.* frothy substance deposited on leaves by insects to protect larvae. (imit.)
cucullate, cucullated, *aa.* hooded; hood-shaped. (L. *cucullus*, hood)
cucumber, *n.* long juicy fruit used in salad; creeping plant yielding it. **cool as a c.,** imperturbable. (L. *cucumis*)
cucurbit, *n.* gourd. **cucurbitaceous,** *a.* (L. *cucurbita*)
cud, *n.* food which ruminant animal brings back into its mouth to chew. **chew the c.,** reflect. (O.E. *cwidu*)
cudbear, *n.* purple dye made from lichens. (*Cuthbert* Gordon, patentee)
cuddle, *v.t.* and *i.* and *n.* hug, embrace. **c. up,** nestle together; curl up. **cuddlesome, cuddly,** *aa.* given to cuddling; tempting to cuddle.
cuddy, *n.* (*naut.*) cabin of half-decked boat; small cabin, galley.
cuddy, *n.* (*Scot.*) donkey; fool.
cudgel, *n.* short thick stick.—*v.t.* be-labour. **c. one's brains,** think hard. **take up the cc. for,** defend vigorously. (O.E. *cycgel*)
cue, *n.* last words of speech in play, serving as signal for next actor to enter or begin to speak; hint on what to do, lead.
cue, *n.* long tapering rod for striking in billiards; pigtail, queue. **cueist,** *n.* billiard-player. (L. *cauda*, tail)
cuff, *v.t.* strike with fist or open hand. —*n.* such blow.
cuff, *n.* end of sleeve; stiff detached linen band worn round wrist.
cui bono? who benefits? (L.)
cuirass, *n.* defensive armour for breast and back. **cuirassier,** *n.* cavalryman with cuirass. (L. *corium*, leather)
cuisine, *n.* kitchen arrangements; style of cooking. (F.=kitchen)
cuisse, cuish, *n.* defensive armour for thighs. (L. *coxa*, hip)
cul-de-sac, *n.* street or tube open at one end only, blind alley. (F.)
-cule, *n.suf.* with diminutive force, as in **animalcule.** (L. *-culus*)
culinary, *a.* of, suitable for, cooking. (L. *culina*, kitchen)
cull, *v.t.* pick (flowers); select; pick out and discard as inferior. (L. *colligere*, collect)
cullender, see **colander.**
cullet, *n.* refuse glass.
cullion, *n.* base fellow. (L. *coleus*, scrotum)
cully, *n.* (*sl.*) dupe, simpleton; pal.
culm, *n.* stem of grasses. (L. *culmus*)
culm, *n.* coal dust.
culminate, *v.i.* reach its highest point; come to climax (in); (*astron.*) reach meridian. **culminant,** *a.* **culmination,** *n.* (L. *culmen*, summit)
culpable, *a.* blameworthy; criminal. **culpability,** *n.* (L. *culpa*, fault)
culprit, *n.* offender; (*law*) prisoner at the bar. (O.F. *culpable*, guilty; *prest*, ready, i.e. to prove it, formerly said by clerk of crown)
cult, *n.* system of religious belief; devotion, homage. (L. *colere*, till, worship)
cultivate, *v.t.* till (land); raise (crops); improve by care and study, civilize, refine; cherish; seek society of. **cultivable,** *a.* **cultivation, cultivator,** *nn.* (*cult*)
cultrate, cultriform, *aa.* (*bot.*) knife-edged. (L. *culter*, knife)
culture, *n.* tillage; artificial rearing; set of bacteria so reared; education, training; refinement of taste and manners; stage of this attained at place or time. **cultural,** *a.* **cultured,** *a.* showing culture.
culver, *n.* (*dial.*) wood-pigeon. (O.E. *culfre*)
culverin, *n.* ancient type of long cannon. (L. *colubra*, snake)
culvert, *n.* channel, pipe, carrying water under roadway; channel for electric cable.
cum, prep. with. *c. grano salis*, with reserve (lit. with a grain of salt). **c. dividend,** (*abbr.* **cum div.**) including dividend. (L.)
cumber, *v.t.* hamper; burden.—*n.* hindrance; embarrassments. **cumbersome, cumbrous,** *aa.* inconveniently heavy or large, unwieldy. (L.L. *cumbrus*, heap)
cumin, cummin, *n.* an eastern plant; its aromatic seeds. (Gk. *kuminon*)
cummer, *n.* (*Scot.*) woman companion, gossip; godmother; woman. (L. *con-*, with; *mater*, mother)
cummerbund, *n.* waist sash. (Pers. *kamarband*, loin band)
cumquat, *n.* small kind of orange. (Chin. *kin ku*, golden orange)
cumshaw, *n.* (in China) tip, baksheesh. (Chin. *kan hsieh*, grateful thanks)
cumulate, *v.t.* and *i.* accumulate.—*a.* heaped up. **cumulation,** *n.* **cumulative,** *a.* growing by successive additions; gathering strength as it grows. **cumulative voting,** in which each voter has as many votes as there are candidates, and may give all to one candidate. (*cumulus*)
cumulus, *n.* (*pl.* **cumuli**) heap; cloud in heaped-up woolly masses. (L.)
cuneate, *a.* wedge-shaped. **cuneiform,** *a.* wedge-shaped.—*n.* cunei-

form writing of ancient Persia and Assyria. (L. *cuneus*, wedge)

cunning, *a.* artful, wily; skilful; (*Amer.*) prettily or piquantly interesting.—*n.* artfulness, guile; skill. (*can*)

cup, *n.* drinking-vessel, esp. small one with handle; ornamental cup as trophy; hollow, socket; iced drink of claret etc. sweetened and flavoured; fated portion.—*v.t.* (*med.*) bleed with cupping-glass; (*Shake.*) ply with drink. **in one's cc.,** under influence of liquor. **c.-bearer,** *n.* one who serves wine at banquet, esp. officer of great household. **cupping-glass,** *n.* for applying suction in surgical bleeding. **cupboard,** *n.* set of shelves with door. **cupboard love,** directed to material gain. **cupful,** *n.* as much as cup will hold. (L. *cupa*, tub)

cupel, *n.* small flat vessel used in assaying precious metals.—*v.t.* assay in cupel. **cupellation,** *n.* (L. *cupa*, tub+dim.)

Cupid, *n.* god of love. **cupidity,** *n.* greed of gain. (L. *cupere*, desire)

cupola, *n.* dome, esp. of pointed or bulbous shape; furnace for melting metals. (L. *cupa*, tub+dim.)

cupreous, *a.* of, like, copper. **cupric, cuprous,** *aa.* containing copper. (L. *cuprum*, copper)

cupule, *n.* (*bot., zool.*) cup-shaped part of organ. (*cupola*)

cur, *n.* worthless or snappish dog; base or cowardly fellow.

curable, *a.* able to be cured.

curaçao, curaçoa, *n.* Dutch liqueur flavoured with orange peel. (place)

curacy, *n.* office of curate.

curare, curari, *n.* vegetable extract used as arrow poison by S. American Indians. **curarize,** *v.t.* poison with curare. (native *wurali*)

curassow, *n.* turkey-like bird of S. America. (island of *Curaçao*)

curate, *n.* assistant of vicar or rector; (*colloq.*) small poker. (L. *cura*, care)

curative, *a.* tending to cure.—*n.* curative agent or drug.

curator, *n.* superintendent, custodian; (*Scots law*) guardian of minor etc. **curatorial,** *a.* **curatorship,** *n.* (L.)

curb, *n.* part of bridle passing under horse's lower jaw; check, restraint; hard swelling on horse's leg; kerb.—*v.t.* hold in with curb; restrain, check. **c. roof,** with double slope, lower being steeper. (L. *curvus*, bent)

curcuma, *n.* kinds of plant incl. turmeric. (Arab. *kurkum*, turmeric)

curd, *n.* coagulated part of milk, used to make cheese; (*pl.*) broken-up curd as food. **curdle,** *v.t.* and *i.* turn into curd; congeal.

cure, *n.* remedy; remedial treatment; restoration to health; spiritual charge.—*v.t.* and *i.* restore to health, heal; remedy; preserve by salting or pickling; vulcanize (rubber). (L. *cura*, care)

cure, *n.* (*sl.*) odd or eccentric person.

curé, *n.* French parish priest. (F.)

curette, *n.* surgical instrument for scraping body cavity.—*v.t.* scrape with this. (F.)

curfew, *n.* ringing of bell at fixed evening hour as sign that every one must be indoors; the bell or hour. (O.F. *covrir*, cover; *feu*, fire; orig. sign for extinguishing fires)

curia, *n.* (*pl.* **curiae**) papal court; senate-house of ancient Rome. **curial,** *a.* (L.)

curie, *n.* standard unit of radium emanation, being quantity in equilibrium with one gramme of radium. (Mme. *Curie*)

curio, *n.* (*pl.* **curios**) curiosity of kind sought by collectors. **curiosity,** *n.* being curious, inquisitiveness; interesting object, curio. **curious,** *a.* anxious to know; prying, inquisitive; strange, remarkable, odd; minutely careful, skilfully wrought. (L. *cura*, care)

curl, *v.t.* and *i.* form into curved shape, coil; twist into ringlets; proceed in curve, bend; play at curling.—*n.* spiral form, twist; bend; ringlet of hair. **c. up,** roll up; cockle; (*sl.*) collapse. **c.-papers, curling-tongs,** *nn.pl.* for keeping or making hair curled. **curlicue,** *n.* fantastic curl. **curliewurlie,** *n.* (*Scot.*) fantastic round ornament. **curling,** *n.* game like bowls, played on ice. **curling-stone,** *n.* heavy flat stone for this. **curly,** *a.* having curls; curling. **curliness,** *n.* (M.E. *crull*, curly)

curlew, *n.* large wading-bird with long bill. (O.F. *courlieus*)

curmudgeon, *n.* ill-natured churlish fellow; mean person, miser. **curmudgeonly,** *a.*

currach, *n.* coracle. (Ir. *curach*)

currance, *n.* (*Shake.*) current.

currant, *n.* kind of small dried grape; kinds of fruit or plant allied to gooseberry. (*Corinth*)

current, *a.* in circulation, generally accepted; of present time, now going on; (of style) fluent, running.—*n.* body of water or air in motion, flow; transmission of electricity through conductor; tendency, course. **currency,** *n.* time during which a thing is current; state of being in use; money current in a country. **currency note,** Treasury note for £1 or 10*s.* (L. *currere*, run)

curricle, *n.* obsolete two-horse two-wheeled open carriage. (*curriculum*)

curriculum, *n.* (*pl.* **curricula**) prescribed course of study. (L.=racecourse)

currier, *n.* leather-dresser. (L. *corium*, hide)

curry, *n.* dish of curried meat etc., us. served with rice.—*v.t.* cook, flavour, with curry-powder. **c.-powder,** *n.* seasoning of turmeric and spices. (Tamil *kari,* sauce)

curry, *v.t.* and *i.* (*past, p.p.* **curried**) rub down and groom (horse); dress (leather); (*Shake.*) use flattery. **c. favour,** seek favour by flattery etc. **c.-comb,** *n.* metal comb for currying horses. (O.F. *correier*)

curse, *n.* invocation of destruction or evil, malediction; profane oath, swear; bane, scourge.—*v.t.* and *i.* invoke curse on; swear, blaspheme; afflict, torment. **c. of Scotland,** nine of diamonds at cards. **not care a c.,** be indifferent. **cursed,** *a.* damnable, hateful.

cursive, *a.* and *n.* running (script) with letters joined, as in modern handwriting. **cursor,** *n.* slide of slide-rule. **cursorial,** *a.* (of bird) with limbs adapted for running. **cursory,** *a.* hasty, passing; superficial, careless. **cursorary,** *a.* (*Shake.*) cursory. (L. *currere,* run)

curst, *a.* (*arch.*) ill-tempered, shrewish; cursed.

curt, *a.* rudely brief, abrupt; concise; short. **curtail,** *v.t.* cut short; deprive of part (of). **curtailment,** *n.* (L. *curtus*)

curtain, *n.* cloth hung as screen; screen separating audience from stage in theatre; end to act or scene of play; part of rampart between two bastions—*v.t.* provide, cover, with curtain. **c.-fire,** *n.* barrage. **c.-raiser,** *n.* short play preceding main one. (L.L. *cortina*)

curtal, *a.* with docked tail. (*curt*)

curtilage, *n.* (*law*) land attached to house. (O.F. *cortil,* courtyard)

curtle-axe, *arch.* for **cutlass.**

curtsy, curtsey, *n.* woman's gesture of respect made by bending knees.—*v.i.* make curtsy. **drop c.,** curtsy. (*courtesy*)

curule, *a.* **c. chair,** ornate chair used by **c. magistrate,** ancient Roman magistrate of highest rank. (L. *curulis*)

curve, *n.* bent form or thing; graph; (*geom.*) line of which no part is straight.—*v.t.* and *i.* form into curve, bend. **curvature,** *n.* state of being curved. **curvet,** *n.* bounding action of horse.—*v.i.* make curvet. **curvicaudate, curvidentate,** *aa.* with curved tail, teeth. **curvifoliate,** *a.* with leaves bent back. **curvilinear,** *a.* of, bounded by, curved lines. (L. *curvus,* bent)

cuscus, *n.* fibrous root of Indian grass. (Hind. *khas khas*)

cuscus, same as **couscous.**

cusec, *n.* (flow of) one cubic foot of water per second. (*cu*bic; *sec*ond)

cushat, *n.* ringdove, wood-pigeon.

cushion, *n.* case stuffed with soft material for resting on; pad for woman's hair; elastic lining of billiard-table's sides.—*v.t.* furnish with cushions; protect by padding; (*billiards*) leave (ball) close to cushion. **c. tyre,** with rubber stuffing. **cushiony,** *a.* (L. *coxa,* hip)

cushy, *a.* (*sl.,* of job) easy, comfortable. (Hind. *khush,* pleasant)

cusp, *n.* sharp point, peak; crown of tooth; (*astron.*) either point of crescent moon. **cuspid,** *n.* canine tooth. **cuspidal,** *a.* of, like, a cusp. **cuspidate, cuspidated,** *aa.* having cusps. (L. *cuspis*)

cuspidor, cuspidore, *n.* (*Amer.*) spittoon. (L. *conspuere,* spit upon)

cussedness, *n.* (*sl.*) contrariness. **cuss,** *n.* (*Amer. sl.*) fellow, creature; curse.

custard, *n.* mixture of eggs, milk etc., sweetened and flavoured.

custody, *n.* keeping; guardianship; imprisonment. **custodial,** *a.* **custodian,** *n.* keeper; caretaker. (L. *custos,* guardian)

custom, *n.* habitual practice, established usage; business patronage; (*pl.*) duties paid on foreign imports; department levying these. **c.-house,** *n.* office where customs are collected. **customary,** *a.* usual, habitual. **customer,** *n.* one who buys in shop, esp. regularly; (*colloq.*) fellow; (*Shake.*) harlot. (L. *consuescere,* grow accustomed)

cut, *v.t.* and *i.* (*past, p.p.* same) penetrate, wound, divide, sever, with edged instrument; shape by cutting; reduce, abridge; cross, intersect; hit (ball) with chopping action; strike sharply (at); ignore socially; hurt sensibilities of; divide (pack of cards) at random; (*cinema*) change to other scene; (*sl.*) go quickly.—*n.* act of cutting; gash, slash; stroke with sword or whip; excision; slight; joint of meat; style, fashion; (*Shake.*) bobtailed horse. **a c. above, a** stage above. **c. and dried,** ready-made; unadaptable. **c. and run,** be off quickly. **c. down,** reduce. **c. in,** interpose. **c. losses,** abandon losing speculation. **c. off,** destroy; intercept. **c. out,** shape; design; supplant. **c. short,** abridge. **c. tooth,** have it appear from gum. **c. up,** carve; criticize severely; deeply grieved. **c. up rough,** become angry. **draw cc.,** draw lots with straws of uneven length. **short c.,** near way. **c.-throat,** *n.* murderer.—*a.* merciless; (*cards*) three-handed.

cutaneous, *a.* of skin. (*cutis*)

cutaway, *n.* (also **c. coat**) tailcoat with skirt cut back from waist.

cutcha, *a.* (*Anglo-Ind.*) slight, makeshift. (Hind. *kachcha,* raw)

cutcherry, cutchery, *n.* (*Anglo-Ind.*) court-house; business office. (Hind. *kachahri*)

cute, *a.* (*colloq.*) shrewd, sharp; ingenious; (*Amer. colloq.*) pretty, attractive. (*acute*)

Cuthbert, *n.* (*sl.*) evader of military service. (name)
cuticle, *n.* outer skin, epidermis. **cuticular,** *a.* (*cutis*+dim.)
cutie, *n.* (*Amer. sl.*) bright smart girl. (*cute*)
cutis, *n.* inner skin. (L.=skin)
cutlass, *n.* sailor's short heavy sword. (L. *culter*, knife)
cutler, *n.* maker of, dealer in, knives. **cutlery,** *n.* knives, edged instruments, collectively. (L. *culter*, knife)
cutlet, *n.* small slice of veal etc. for cooking; small chop. (L. *costa*, rib+double dim.)
cutpurse, *n.* pickpocket.
cutter, *n.* one who cuts, esp. clothes; single-masted type of sailing vessel; warship's rowing and sailing boat.
cutting, *n.* open excavation through hill for railway etc.; newspaper clipping; slip from plant.—*a.* piercing; stinging.
cuttle, *n.* (us. **c.-fish**) tentacled sea mollusc ejecting inky fluid when attacked. **c.-bone,** *n.* its internal bone. (O.E. *cudele*)
cutty, *n.* short clay pipe; (*Scot.*) bad or roguish girl.—*a.* (*Scot.*) short. **c. stool,** stool of repentance in old Scottish church discipline. (*cut*)
cutwater, *n.* fore part of ship's prow.
cyanic, *a.* blue; of, containing, cyanogen. **cyanide,** *n.* compound of cyanogen. **cyanogen,** *n.* a colourless poisonous gas. **cyanometer,** *n.* instrument for measuring blueness of sky. **cyanosis,** *n.* blue jaundice. (Gk. *kuanos*, a dark-blue mineral)
cycad, *n.* sago palm.
cyclamen, *n.* bulbous plant of primrose family. (Gk. *kuklaminos*)
cycle, *n.* recurring series of events or phenomena, period of this; body of epics or romances with common theme; bicycle, tricycle.—*v.i.* go in cycles; ride cycle. **c.-car,** *n.* small light motor-car. **cyclic, cyclical,** *aa.* of a cycle; recurring in cycles. **cyclist,** *n.* rider of cycle. **cycloid,** *n.* curve traced by point on circle as it rolls along straight line. **cycloidal,** *a.* **cyclometer,** *n.* instrument for measuring circular areas; instrument recording distance run by bicycle. (Gk. *kuklos*, circle)
cyclone, *n.* violent circular storm, tornado; system of winds moving round centre of low barometric pressure. **cyclonic,** *a.* (Gk. *kuklos*, circle)
cyclopaedia, cyclopedia, *n.* encyclopaedia. **cyclopaedic,** *a.* (abbr.)
Cyclops, *n.* (*pl.* **Cyclopses, Cyclopes**) legendary one-eyed giant; one-eyed person. **Cyclopean, Cyclopian,** *aa.* of Cyclops; huge; (*archit.*) built of huge stones without mortar. (Gk. *kuklos*, circle; *ōps*, eye)
cyclorama, *n.* circular panorama. (Gk. *kuklos*, circle; *horama*, sight)
cyclostomous, *a.* round-mouthed. (Gk. *kuklos*, circle; *stoma*, mouth)
cyclostyle, *n.* duplicating apparatus with stencil paper written on by pen with toothed wheel. (Gk. *kuklos*, circle+*style*)
cyder, same as **cider.**
cygnet, *n.* young swan. (L. *cygnus*, swan+dim.)
cylinder, *n.* roller-shaped body with straight sides and parallel circular ends; piston-chamber of engine. **cylindrical,** *a.* **cylindroid,** *a.* and *n.* (figure) like cylinder. (Gk. *kulindein*, roll)
cyma, *n.* ogee moulding of cornice; cyme. (Gk. *kuma*, wave)
cymar, *n.* woman's loose light garment. (O.F. *chimarre*)
cymbal, *n.* (*mus.*) one of a pair of brass plates clashed together. **cymbalist,** *n.* **cymbalon,** *n.* kind of dulcimer. (Gk. *kumbē*, hollow vessel)
cymbiform, *a.* boat-shaped. (L. *cymba*, boat)
cyme, *n.* flower-cluster in which main stem ends in flower, while from each side of main stem secondary stems branch off to end in flower, and tertiary stems from those etc. **cymose,** *a.* (*cyma*)
cymo-, from Gk. *kuma*, wave, used in **cymometer,** *n.* instrument measuring frequency of electric waves; **cymoscope,** *n.* (*wireless*) wave-detector.
Cymric, *a.* and *n.* Welsh (language). (W. *Cymru*, Wales)
cynic, *n.* cynical person; member of Greek philosophical sect professing contempt for pleasure. **cynical,** *a.* sceptical of or sneering at goodness; shameless in admitting unworthy motives. **cynicism,** *n.* being cynical. (Gk. *kuōn*, dog)
cynocephalous, *a.* dog-headed. (Gk. *kuōn*, dog; *kephalē*, head)
cynosure, *n.* centre of attraction; guiding star; (constellation containing) pole-star. (Gk. *kuōn*, dog; *oura*, tail)
cypher, see **cipher.**
cypress, *n.* evergreen tree with dark foliage; branch of this as symbol of mourning. (Gk. *kuparissos*)
cypress, *n.* crape-like fabric. (*Cyprus*)
Cyprian, *a.* and *n.* (native) of Cyprus; licentious (person); prostitute.
cyst, *n.* hollow organ containing liquid secretion; sac containing pus. **cystic,** *a.* of the bladder; of the nature of a cyst. **cystiform,** *a.* bladder-shaped. **cystitis,** *n.* inflammation of bladder. **cystoid,** *a.* cystlike. **cystolith,** *n.* stone in bladder. **cystology,** *n.* study of cysts. **cystoscope,** *n.* instrument for examining bladder. **cystotomy,** *n.* operation of cutting open bladder. (Gk. *kustis*, bladder)

cyto-, from Gk. *kutos*, vessel, used in **cytoblast**, *n.* cell nucleus; **cytogenesis**, *n.* cell formation; **cytology**, *n.* study of cells; **cytoplasm**, **cytosome**, *nn.* substance, body, of cell as opp. to nucleus.

czar, **tsar**, **tzar**, *n.* emperor (used of Russian ruler before 1917). **czarevitch**, **tsarevitch**, *n.* eldest son of czar, cesarevitch. **czaritsa**, **tsaritsa**, **czarina**, **tsarina**, *nn.* czar's wife. (*Caesar*)

D

D, (*mus.*) note and scale; (*roman numerals*) 500

da, same as dad.

dab, *v.t.* touch lightly with something soft or moist; tap; smear.—*n.* quick light tap; peck. **dabber**, *n.*

dab, *n.* a small flat-fish.

dab, *n.* (*colloq.*) expert, adept.

dabble, *v.t.* and *i.* dip in and out of (water), splash about; engage superficially (in). **dabbler**, *n.* dilettante. (*dab*)

dabchick, *n.* a water-bird, little grebe.

dabster, *n.* expert; daubster.

da capo, (*mus.*, *abbr.* **D.C.**) repeat from the beginning. (It.)

dace, *n.* small river-fish like carp. (O.F. *darz*, dart)

dachshund, *n.* dog with long body and short legs. (G.=badger-dog)

dacoit, *n.* Indian bandit. **dacoity**, *n.* brigandage. (Hind. *dakait*)

dacry(o)-, from Gk. *dakru*, tear, used in **dacryoma**, *n.* stoppage of tear-duct; **dacryops**, *n.* wateriness of eye.

dactyl, *n.* three-syllabled foot, long-short-short. **dactylic**, *a.* and *n.* (verse) of dactyls. **dactylioglyph**, *n.* engraver of gems. **dactylogram**, *n.* fingerprint. **dactylography**, *n.* science of fingerprints. **dactylology**, *n.* sign language, deaf-and-dumb alphabet. (Gk. *daktulos*, finger)

dad, **daddy**, *nn.* (*colloq.*) father. **daddy-long-legs**, *n.* crane-fly.

Dada, *n.* school of art and literature which aims at suppressing all relations between thought and expression. **Dadaism**, **Dadaist**, *nn.*

daddle, *v.i.* walk unsteadily, totter.

dado, *n.* lower part of room wall when distinguished by decoration or panelling; solid block forming body of pedestal. **dadoed**, *a.* (It).

daedal, *a.* skilfully wrought, ingenious; complex, mysterious. (Gk. *daidalos*)

Daedalian, **Daedalean**, *a.* intricate, labyrinthine. (*Daedalus* of Greece)

daemon, *n.* inward spirit, genius; inferior deity. **daemonic**, *a.* supernatural. (Gk. *daimōn*)

daff, *v.t.* (*arch.*) put off or aside. (=*doff*)

daff, *v.i.* (*Scot.*) sport, play.

daffodil, *n.* a spring flower, narcissus; its colour, pale yellow. **daffodilly**, **daffadowndilly**, *nn.* (*poet.*) daffodil. (Gk. *asphodelos*)

daft, *a.* (*Scot.*) silly, weak-minded; mad. (O.E. *gedæfte*, mild)

dag, *n.* old kind of long pistol.

dagger, *n.* short weapon for stabbing; (*print.*) obelus. **at dd. drawn**, in bitter enmity. **look dd.**, glare.

daggle, *v.t.* and *i.* trail in mud or wet.

dago, *n.* contemptuous term for Spaniard or Italian. (Sp. *Diego*, James)

dagoba, *n.* Buddhist relic temple in Ceylon. (Cingalese *dagaba*)

daguerreotype, *n.* an early photographic process; picture taken by it. (*Daguerre*, inventor)

dah, *n.* Burmese sword-knife. (Burmese)

dahabeeyah, **dahabiah**, **dahabieh**, *n.* Nile sailing-boat. (Arab.)

dahlia, *n.* garden plant with compound flowers of many colours. (A. *Dahl*)

dai, *n.* (*Anglo-Ind.*) wet-nurse. (Hind.)

daidle, *Scot.* form of **daddle**.

Dail Eireann, Chamber of Deputies of Eire. (Ir.=assembly of Eire)

daily, *a.* and *adv.* (happening, done) every day.—*n.* daily newspaper; non-resident servant. (*day*)

daimen, *a.* (*Scot.*) occasional, rare.

daimio, *n.* hereditary noble of Japan under old regime. (Jap.)

dainty, *a.* choice; elegant, prettily neat; nice, fastidious.—*n.* delicacy, titbit. (L. *dignus*, worthy)

dairy, *n.* place for keeping milk and making butter; milk-shop. **d.-farm**, *n.* for producing milk. **dairymaid**, **dairyman**, *nn.* (O.E. *dǽge*, maid)

dais, *n.* low platform at end of hall for throne etc. (L. *discus*, disk)

daisy, *n.* flower with yellow centre and white petals; (*sl.*) fine specimen. **ox-eye d.**, kind of chrysanthemum. **d.-cutter**, *n.* horse lifting feet very little; (*cricket*) ball that skims ground. (*day's eye*)

dak, **dâk**, *n.* (*Anglo-Ind.*) transport by relays of men or horses; mail. **d.-bungalow**, *n.* travellers' rest-house. (Hind.)

dal, same as **dhal**.

dale, *n.* valley. **dalesman**, *n.* esp. of Lake District. (O.E. *dæl*)

dali, same as dolly.

dally, *v.i.* trifle, delay; toy amorously, coquet (with). **dalliance**, *n.* lovemaking; delay. (O.F. *dalier*, chat)

Dalmatian, *n.* spotted carriage-dog. (*Dalmatia*)
dalmatic, *n.* loose vestment with open sides worn by bishop, king at coronation etc. (*Dalmatia*)
dal segno, (*mus., abbr.* **D.S.**) repeat from point indicated. (It.)
dalt, *n.* (*Scot.*) foster-child. (Gael. *dalta*)
dalton, *n.* measure of mass, equivalent to $\frac{1}{16}$ that of oxygen atom. (person)
daltonism, *n.* colour-blindness. (J. *Dalton*)
dam, *n.* embankment to restrain water; water so checked.—*v.t* confine by dam; block (up). (M.E.)
dam, *n.* mother, us. of animal. (=*dame*)
dam, *n.* small Indian coin, one-fortieth of rupee. (Hind.)
damage, *n.* hurt, injury; (*colloq.*) price, cost; (*pl., law*) payment in compensation.—*v.t.* do harm to, injure. (L. *damnum,* loss)
damascene, *n.* kind of small plum. (*Damascus*)
damask, *n.* linen with design shown by reflection of light; figured cloth; steel with wavy pattern; rose colour.—*a.* of damask cloth or colour.—*v.t.* weave with figured design; suffuse with blush. **damascene, damaskeen,** *v.t.* ornament (steel) with pattern of inlaid gold etc. (*Damascus*)
dambrod, *n.* (*Scot.*) draught-board.
dame, *n.* lady; matron; title of baronet's or knight's wife. **d.-school,** *n.* children's school kept by old woman. (L. *domina,* mistress)
dammar, *n.* a resin used for varnish. (Malay *damar*)
damn, *v.t.* and *i.* consign to eternal punishment; condemn. censure; ruin; curse.—*n.* curse; negligible amount. **damnable,** *a.* deserving damnation; (*colloq.*) annoying. **damnation,** *n.* damning, being damned; ruin, destruction. **damnatory,** *a.* conveying censure. **damned,** *a.* doomed to hell; detestable; (*colloq.*) confounded.—*adv.* (*colloq.*) very. **damnify,** *v.t.* (*law*) cause loss to. **damnification,** *n.* **damning,** *a.* causing condemnation. (L. *damnum,* loss)
damnosa hereditas, inheritance that brings more burden than profit. (L.)
Damocles, *n.* **sword of D.,** constant threatening danger. (person)
damosel, damozel, same as **damsel.**
damp, *n.* moisture, humidity; firedamp; dejection.—*a.* moist, slightly wet.—*v.t.* make damp; depress. **d. down,** heap (fire) with ashes to slow burning. **d.-course,** *n.* damp-proof layer in wall. **dampen,** *v.t.* and *i.* make, become, damp; blight. **damper,** *n.* thing that damps; sliding plate for opening or closing flue; pad for checking vibration of piano wire; (*Austral.*) thin cake of flour and water baked in ashes.
damsel, *n.* (*arch.*) girl. (*dame*)
damson, *n.* small purple sour plum; tree bearing it. (*damascene*)
dan, *n.* (*arch.*) master, sir. (L. *dominus*)
dance, *v.i.* and *t.* move, leap, rhythmically; caper about; execute (steps); dandle.—*n.* dancing; special form of it; dancing party. **lead one a d.,** entangle him in useless pursuit. **St. Vitus's d.,** nervous disease with jerky movements. **dancer,** *n.* (O.F. *danser*)
dancette, *a.* (*heraldry*) indented. (L. *dens,* tooth)
dandelion, *n.* yellow-flowered wild plant. (F. *dent de lion,* lion's tooth)
dander, *n.* temper, fighting spirit.
dander, *v.i.* and *n.* (*Scot.*) saunter.
Dandie Dinmont, breed of terrier. (name in Scott)
dandle, *v.t.* jig (baby) on knee, fondle. (cf. It. *dandola,* doll)
dandruff, dandriff, *n.* scales on skin under hair, scurf.
dandy, dandi, *n.* (*Anglo-Ind.*) boatman on Ganges; litter of cloth hammock slung from pole. (Hind.)
dandy, *n.* man of fashion, fop, exquisite; yawl.—*a.* finely dressed, smart; (*Amer. colloq.*) excellent. **d.-brush,** *n.* whalebone brush for cleaning horse. **d.-horse,** *n.* velocipede. **dandiacal,** *a.* **dandyism,** *n.*
dandy, same as **dengue.**
dandyprat, *n.* urchin, pygmy.
Dane, *n.* native of Denmark. **Great D.,** large short-haired breed of dog.
dane-hole, same as **dene-hole.**
dang, minced form of **damn.**
danger, *n.* exposure to harm; risk; menace; (*Shake.*) range (of weapon); mischief. **d.-signal,** *n.* sign of danger. **dangerous,** *a.* unsafe, perilous; menacing. (L. *dominium,* power)
dangle, *v.i.* and *t.* hang and swing loosely; hold suspended; tempt with. **d. after,** hang about.
Danish, *a.* and *n.* (language) of Denmark.
dank, *a.* disagreeably damp; oozy.
danseuse, *n.* female dancer. (F.)
dap, *v.i.* and *t.* drop bait gently into water; dip lightly; bounce (ball).—*n.* bounce.
daphne, *n.* kinds of flowering shrub. (Gk.=laurel)
dapper, *a.* neat and smart, spruce; little and active.
dapple, *v.t.* and *i.* mark with, show, spots or patches of different colour; variegate.—*n.* this effect. **d.-grey,** *a.* and *n.* (horse) of grey with darker spots.
darbies, *n.pl.* (*sl.*) handcuffs.
Darby and Joan, old devoted married couple.
dare, *v.i.* and *t.* (*3rd sing. pres.* **dares, dare**; *past* **dared, durst**) be bold enough, venture; defy, challenge. —*n.* challenge; (*Shake.*) defiance.

d. say, suppose. **d.-devil,** *a.* and *n.* reckless (person). (O.E. *durran*)

dare, *v.t.* (*Shake.*) dazzle and fascinate; daunt. (O.E. *darian*, lurk)

darg, *n.* (*Scot.*) task, day's work.

dari, same as **durrah.**

daring, *a.* bold, audacious.—*n.* adventurous courage.

dark, *a.* without light; sombre, gloomy; brown-complexioned; mysterious, obscure; evil; sullen; unenlightened.—*n.* dark state or colour. **D. Ages,** 600–1100. **D. Continent,** Africa. **d. horse,** of unknown powers. **keep d.,** be silent (about). **d.-lantern,** *n.* with shutter for concealing light. **d.-room,** *n.* (*phot.*) us. with red light only. **darken,** *v.t.* and *i.* make, become, dark; perplex. **darkle,** *v.i.* become overcast; lie hid. **darkling,** *adv.* in the dark.—*a.* dusky. **darkness,** *n.* **Prince of Darkness,** devil. **darksome,** *a.* (*poet.*). **darky, darkey,** *n.* (*colloq.*) negro. (O.E. *deorc*)

darling, *a.* and *n.* dearly loved or lovable (person); favourite. (*dear*+ dim.)

darn, *v.t.* mend (hole), imitating texture of fabric.—*n.* place darned. **darning-needle,** *n.* large-eyed needle for this; (*Amer.*) dragon-fly.

darn, minced form of damn.

darnel, *n.* kind of rye-grass, tares.

darraign, darrayne, *v.t.* and *i.* (*Shake.*) prepare for battle, array. (O.F. *deraisnier*, render account of)

dart, *n.* pointed throwing-weapon; sudden movement; (*pl.*) indoor game with darts and target.—*v.i.* and *t.* start, shoot forth, suddenly; hurl. **darter,** *n.* kinds of bird and fish. **dartle,** *v.i.* dart about. (O.F.)

dartre, *n.* kinds of skin eruption. **dartrous,** *a.* (F.)

Darwinian, *a.* and *n.* (adherent) of Charles Darwin and his doctrine of evolution by natural selection. **Darwinism, Darwinist, Darwinite,** *nn.*

dash, *v.t.* and *i.* fling violently, shatter; go hastily, rush; flavour, dilute (with); (*sl.*) confound.—*n.* rush, onset; impetuous vigour; tinge; (*print.*) short line (—) to denote pause etc. **cut a d.,** make showy impression. **d. off,** sketch hastily. **dashboard,** *n.* mud-shield in front of carriage; instrument-board in front of motor-driver. **dasher,** *n.* part of churn which agitates cream. **dashing,** *a.* bold, spirited; showy.

dastard, *n.* malicious coward, poltroon. **dastardly,** *a.*

dastur, dasturi, dastoor, *n.* (*Anglo-Ind.*) custom; usual fee. (Pers.)

dasy-, from Gk. *dasus*, thick, hairy, used in **dasymeter,** *n.* instrument for measuring density of gases; **dasyphyllous,** *a.* with downy leaves; **dasypod,** *n.* kinds of armadillo; **dasyure,** *n.* a small Australian marsupial.

data, see **datum.**

dataller, *n.* workman paid by the day. (*day*; *tale*)

date, *n.* day or time of occurrence, period; statement of this in letter etc.; (*arch.*) age, duration; (*sl.*) appointment.—*v.t.* and *i.* affix date to, note date of; reckon time; (*art*) be recognizable as of particular period. **out of d.,** obsolete. **up to d.,** modern, in the fashion. **d.-line,** *n.* where day begins and ends, at longitude 180°. **dateless,** *a.* undated; immemorial. (L. *dare*, give)

date, *n.* sweet sticky single-stoned fruit; (also **d.-palm**) tree bearing it. (Gk. *daktulos*, finger)

dative, *a.* and *n.* (case) denoting indirect object. **datival,** *a.* (L. *dare*, give)

datum, *n.* (*pl.* **data**) fact given or admitted; basis of assumption; fixed starting-point of scale. (L.= given)

datura, *n.* kinds of narcotic plant, incl. stramonium. (Hind. *dhatura*)

daub, *v.t.* and *i.* smear, overlay (with clay etc.); paint incompetently.—*n.* smear; coarse painting. **dauber, daubster,** *nn.* bad artist. **daubery,** *n.* (*Shake.*) false show. (L. *dealbare*, whitewash)

daud, *v.t.* (*Scot.*) knock.—*n.* lump.

daughter, *n.* female child; female descendant. **d.-in-law,** *n.* son's wife. **daughterhood,** *n.* **daughterly** *a.* of, proper to, a daughter. (O.E. *dohtor*)

daunder, dauner, same as **dander.**

daunt, *v.t.* intimidate, discourage, cow. **dauntless,** *a.* intrepid. (L. *domare*, tame)

dauphin, *n.* eldest son of king of France. **dauphiness,** *n.* his wife. (*Dauphiné*, place)

daur, *Scot.* form of **dare.**

davenport, *n.* kind of small writing-desk; (*Amer.*) kind of settee.

davit, *n.* upright with tackle for lowering ship's boat or anchor.

Davy, *n.* (also **D. lamp**) miner's safety lamp. (Sir Humphry *Davy*)

davy, *vulg. sl.* for **affidavit.**

Davy Jones's locker, bottom of sea, watery grave.

daw, *n.* kind of crow, jackdaw.

dawdle, *v.i.* and *t.* loiter, waste time; idle (away).—*n.* dawdler.

dawk, same as **dak.**

dawn, *v.i.* (of day) begin to grow light; begin to appear.—*n.* daybreak; first sign. **d. upon,** be realized by.

dawt, *v.t.* (*Scot.*) caress, pet.

day, *n.* time when sun is above horizon; 24 hours from midnight to midnight; daylight; (us. *pl.*) period, epoch. **better dd.,** more prosperous times. **d. by d.,** daily. **D. of Judgment,** end of world. **dd. of grace,** three days allowed for payment of bill of exchange after it becomes due. **end one's dd.,** die. **have one's d.,**

have time of success. **name the d.**, fix day of marriage. **one, some, d.**, at a time in the past, future. **the d.**, (*Scot.*) to-day. **win, lose, the d.**, be victorious, defeated. **d.-bed**, *n.* (*Shake.*) couch. **d.-boarder**, *n.* fed but not lodged at school. **d.-boy**, *n.* attending but not boarding at school. **daydream**, *n.* reverie. **d.-labourer**, **d.-taler**, *nn.* workman paid by the day. **d.-school**, *n.* one for day-pupils only. **d.-woman**, *n.* (*Shake.*) dairywoman. (O.E. *dæg*)

daybook, *n.* account-book for day's transactions.

daybreak, *n.* first appearance of daylight, dawn.

daylight, *n.* light of sun; dawn; publicity; visible gap. **see d.**, reach solution. **d.-saving**, *n.* use of summer time, for which clock is advanced one hour in spring and put back one in autumn.

dayspring, *n.* (*poet.*) dawn.

daze, *v.t.* stupefy, bewilder.—*n.* stupefaction, bewilderment.

dazzle, *v.t.* and *i.* confuse sight of, be partially blinded, by strong light; overwhelm with brilliance.—*n.* glitter. **d. paint**, *n.* kind of camouflage. **dazzlement**, *n.* (*daze*)

de, *prep.* from, concerning. *de facto*, actual, in virtue of things as they are. *de fide*, required to be held as an article of faith. *de integro*, afresh. *de jure*, by law, rightful. *de minimis non curat lex*, the law does not concern itself with trifles. *de mortuis nil nisi bonum*, nothing but good about the dead. *de novo*, anew. *de profundis*, from the depths (of sorrow). (L.)

de, *prep.* from, of. *de haut en bas*, in a condescending way, contemptuously. *de luxe*, luxurious, sumptuous. *de nouveau*, afresh, once more. *de rigueur*, obligatory. *de trop*, not wanted, in the way. (F.)

de-, *pref.* down, as in **descend**; off, as in **defend**; completely, as in **declare**; un-, as in **denaturalize**. (L.)

deacon, *n.* lowest order in Episcopal Church, below priest; secular officer of Presbyterian congregation. **deaconess**, *n.* churchwoman appointed to dispense charity. **deaconhood**, **deaconship**, *nn.* **deaconry**, *n.* deacons collectively; office of deacon. (Gk. *diakonos*, servant)

dead, *a.* without life; inanimate, inert; numb, insensible; obsolete, extinct; spiritless, dull; complete, exact; (of ball) out of play; (*golf*) within certain holing distance.—*adv.* completely; (*golf*) without run.—*n.* dead person; quietest time. **d. centre, point**, position at which crank exerts no power. **d. end**, cul-de-sac. **d. heat**, race in which two or more finish equal, tie. **d. letter**, law no longer enforced; unclaimed letter. **d. lift, pull**, without leverage. **d. loss**, with no compensation. **d. march**, funeral music. **d. men**, (*sl.*) empty bottles. **d. reckoning**, taking ship's position by log and compass, not astronomical observations. **d. set**, determined attempt. (O.E. *déad*)

dead-alive, *a.* monotonous, depressing.

dead-beat, *a.* utterly exhausted.—*n.* (*Amer. sl.*) sponging loafer.

deaden, *v.t.* render numb or insensible; blunt, muffle.

deadeye, *n.* kind of pulley.

deadfall, *n.* trap with falling weight that kills or disables.

deadhead, *n.* non-paying theatre-goer, passenger etc.

dead-house, *n.* mortuary.

deadlight, *n.* storm-shutter for cabin window.

deadlock, *n.* clash of interests making progress impossible; standstill.

deadly, *a.* fatal; implacable; insupportable. **d. nightshade**, belladonna. **d. sin**, meriting damnation.

deadnettle, *n.* non-stinging weed like nettle.

deaf, *a.* unable to hear; hearing badly; heedless. **d.-and-dumb alphabet**, signs with fingers for spelling words. **d.-mute**, *n.* deaf-and-dumb person. **deafen**, *v.t.* deprive of hearing. **deafening**, *a.* very loud. (O.E. *déaf*)

deal, *v.t.* and *i.* (*past*, *p.p.* **dealt**) deliver, inflict; distribute, (cards etc.); do business.—*n.* transaction; dealing of cards; quantity. **d. by**, treat. **d. in**, sell. **d. with**, settle, arrange; behave towards. **good d.**, large amount. **New D.**, economic reforms in U.S. by President F. D. Roosevelt. **raw d.**, unfair treatment. **dealer**, *n.* trader. **dealing**, *n.* conduct; (*pl.*) intercourse. (O.E. *dǽlan*)

deal, *n.* fir or pine timber; plank of this.

deambulation, *n.* walking. **deambulatory**, *a.* (L. *ambulare*, walk)

dean, *n.* head of cathedral chapter; college fellow in charge of discipline; head of university faculty. **D. of Faculty**, president of the Faculty of Advocates in Scotland. **rural d.**, head clergyman of group of parishes. **deanery**, *n.* office, residence, of dean. (L.L. *decanus*, chief of ten)

dean, see **dene**.

dear, *a.* loved, precious; charming; expensive; (*Shake.*) earnest, important.—*adv.* at a high price.—*n.* dear person, sweetheart.—*int.* of distress etc. (O.E. *déore*)

dear, *a.* (*Shake.*) hard, grievous. (O.E. *déor*)

dearth, *n.* scarcity, lack. (*dear*)

deary, dearie, *n.* dear one.

death, *n.* end of life, dying; being dead; destruction. **be in at the d.**, see quarry killed or enterprise completed. **do, put, to d.** kill. **sure as**

d., certainly. to d., utterly. d.-adder, *n.* venomous Australian snake. d.-agony, *n.* struggle before death. d.-blow, *n.* blow causing death. d.-duties, *n.pl.* taxes paid on inheritance after death. d.-mask, *n.* plaster cast of face taken immediately after death. d.-rate, *n.* yearly proportion of deaths to population. d.'s-head, *n.* skull; kind of moth. d.-trap, *n.* unsafe place. d.-warrant, *n.* order for execution. d.-watch, *n.* small beetle that makes ticking sound. **deathbed,** *n.* bed one dies on. **deathless,** *a.* immortal. **deathly,** *a.* like death, pale, still. (O.E. *déath*)

deave, *v.t.* (*Scot.*) deafen.

deb, *n.* (*colloq.*) débutante.

debacle, *débâcle, n.* break-up of ice in river; utter collapse, overwhelming disaster. (F.)

debag. *v.t.* (*sl.*) remove trousers from.

debar, *v.t.* bar out from, exclude.

debark, *v.i.* and *t.* land from ship. **debarkation, debarkment,** *nn.* (*bark*)

debase, *v.t.* lower character or worth of, degrade; adulterate (coinage). **debasement** *n.*

debate, *v.t.* and *i.* discuss thoroughly, argue; consider; contest.—*n.* discussion, esp. in Parliament. **debatable,** *a.* open to question, disputed. (L. *batuere,* beat)

debauch, *v.t.* lead astray, seduce; corrupt, dissipate.—*n.* drinking-bout. orgy. **debauchee,** *n.* dissolute person, libertine. **debauchery,** *n.* sensual vice; drunkenness. (F. *débaucher,* entice from master)

debenture, *n.* bond of corporation or company with guaranteed interest and forming first charge on assets; custom-house certificate entitling to drawback. (L. *debentur.* are due)

debilitate, *v.t.* weaken, enervate. **debilitation,** *n.* **debility,** *n.* weakness of health. (L. *debilis,* weak)

debit, *n.* entry of sum owed, opp. to credit; left side of account-book, used for this.—*v.t.* charge. (*debt*)

debonair, *a.* (*arch.*) genial, affable; (*Shake.*) gentle. (O.F. *de bonne aire,* of good disposition)

deboshed, *arch.* for debauched.

debouch, *v.i.* march, flow, out from narrow space to open ground. **debouchment,** *n.* (F. *bouche,* mouth)

Debrett, *n.* peerage list. (compiler)

debris, *débris, n.* broken fragments, wreckage. (F.)

debt, *n.* sum owed; state of owing; obligation. **bad d.,** given up as irrecoverable. **d. of honour,** gambling debt. **d. of nature,** death. **national d.,** owed by state. **floating d.,** part of this repayable on demand or at stated time. **funded d.,** part converted into permanent form. **debtor,** *n.* one who owes debt. (L. *debēre,* owe)

debunk, *v.t.* remove false sentiment from.

debus, *v.t.* and *i.* set down, alight from, motor vehicles. (*bus*)

début, *n.* first appearance in society or as public performer. **débutante,** *n.* girl coming out or being presented at court; (*masc.* **débutant**) performer making début. (F.)

decachord, *a.* and *n.* (harp) with ten strings. (Gk. *deka,* ten)

decade, decad, *n.* period of ten years; group of ten. **decadal, decadic,** *aa.* (Gk. *deka,* ten)

decadent, *a.* declining, deteriorating. —*n.* decadent person; writer or artist with morbid sensuous style. **decadence,** *n.* (L. *cadere,* fall)

decagon, *n.* ten-sided plane figure. **decagonal,** *a.* (Gk. *deka,* ten; *gōnia,* angle)

decagram, decagramme, dekagram, dekagramme, *n.* weight of ten grammes, ·353 oz. (Gk. *deka,* ten)

decahedron, *n.* solid with ten faces. **decahedral,** *a.* (Gk. *deka,* ten; *hedra,* base)

decalcify, *v.t.* deprive (bone etc.) of its lime. **decalcification,** *n.*

decalitre, dekalitre, *n.* measure of ten litres, about 2¼ gallons. (Gk. *deka,* ten)

decalogue, *n.* the ten commandments. (Gk. *deka,* ten; *logos,* word)

decametre, dekametre, *n.* length of ten metres, about 32 ft 9 in. (Gk. *deka,* ten)

decamp, *v.i.* break camp; make off, abscond. **decampment,** *n.*

decanal, *a.* of dean or his office; of south side of choir. (*dean*)

decandrous, *a.* with ten stamens. (Gk. *deka,* ten; *anēr,* man)

decant, *v.t.* pour (wine etc.) from one vessel to another, leaving sediment behind. **decantation,** *n.* **decanter,** *n.* ornamental bottle for decanted liquor. (*cant*)

decapitate, *v.t.* behead. **decapitation, decapitator,** *nn.* (L. *caput,* head)

decapod, *n.* ten-footed crustacean, e.g. lobster. **decapodal, decapodous,** *aa.* (Gk. *deka,* ten; *pous,* foot)

decarbonize, *v.t.* take carbon or carbon deposit from. **decarbonization,** *n.*

decastich, *n.* poem of ten lines. (Gk. *deka,* ten; *stichos,* line)

decastyle, *n.* ten-pillared portico. (Gk. *deka,* ten; *stulos,* column)

decasualize, *v.t.* do away with casual labour in. **decasualization,** *n.*

decasyllable, decasyllabic, *nn.* and *aa.* ten-syllabled (line). (Gk. *deka,* ten)

decathlon, *n.* composite Olympic contest of 100-metre, 400-metre, and 1,500-metre run, 100-metre hurdle, broad and high jumps, pole vault, throwing javelin and discus, putting shot. (Gk. *deka,* ten; *athlon,* contest)

decay, *v.i.* and *t.* rot, decompose; deteriorate.—*n.* decaying, decline; dissolution. (L. *cadere,* fall)

decease. *n.* death.—*v.i.* die. **deceased,** *n.* (*law*) dead person. (L. *cedere*, go)
deceive, *v.t.* and *i.* mislead, delude, impose upon; (*arch.*) disappoint. **deceit,** *n.* deceiving; trick; deceitfulness. **deceitful,** *a.* treacherous, insincere; misleading. (L. *capere*, take)
decelerate, *v.t.* and *i.* reduce speed (of). **deceleration,** *n.* (*accelerate*)
December, *n.* last month of year. **Decembrists,** *n.pl.* Russian revolutionaries of 1825. (L. *decem*, ten, because tenth month of Roman year)
decemvir, *n.* one of board of ten, esp. early Roman lawgivers. **decemviral,** *a.* **decemvirate,** *n.* (L.)
decency, *n.* decentness, propriety, decorum.
decennary, *a.* and *n.* (of) period of ten years. **decenniad, decennium,** *n.* ten-year period. **decennial,** *a.* of, happening every, ten years. (L. *decem*, ten; *annus*, year)
decent, *a.* seemly; modest, not obscene; respectable; adequate; (*colloq.*) kind, generous; pleasant. (L. *decēre*, befit)
decentralize, *v.t.* divide (government, organization) among local centres. **decentralization,** *n.*
deception, *n.* deceiving; illusion, fraud. **deceptious,** *a.* (*Shake.*) illusive. **deceptive,** *a.* apt to mislead (*deceive*).
decern, *v.t.* and *i.* (*Scots law*) pass judgment, decree. (*decree*)
dechristianize, *v.t.* deprive of Christianity. **dechristianization,** *n.*
decibel, *n.* unit of loudness of sound.
decide, *v.t.* and *i.* determine; settle, give judgment (on). **decided,** *a.* unhesitating; clearly marked. **decidedly,** *adv.* definitely, certainly. **decider,** *n.* deciding round, final heat. (L. *caedere*, cut)
deciduous, *a.* shed periodically; (of trees) shedding leaves, not evergreen. (L. *cadere*, fall)
decigram, decigramme, *n.* $\frac{1}{10}$ gramme, 1·5432 grains. **decilitre,** *n.* $\frac{1}{10}$ litre, ·176 pint. (L. *decem*, ten)
decillion, *n.* tenth power of million, 1 with 60 ciphers; (in U.S. and France) eleventh power of thousand, 1 with 33 ciphers. (L. *decem*, ten+ *million*)
decimal, *a.* reckoning by multiples of ten.—*n.* (also **d. fraction**) fraction whose denominator (not expressed) is power of ten. **d. notation, numeration,** ordinary system of counting, with arabic figures. **d. point,** dot preceding decimal. **d. system, coinage,** with each denomination ten times the one below it. **decimalize,** *v.t.* **decimate,** *v.t.* kill every tenth man or large number of. **decimation,** *n.* (L. *decimus*, tenth)
decimetre, *n.* $\frac{1}{10}$ metre, 3·937 in. (L. *decem*, ten)
decimo-sexto, same as **sextodecimo.**
decipher, *v.t.* make out (indistinct or secret writing); decode; unravel. **decipherment,** *n.*
decision, *n.* settlement, ruling; determination, firmness. **decisive,** *a.* determining the issue, conclusive; decided. (*decide*)
decivilize, *v.t.* barbarize.
deck, *v.t.* adorn, array; cover with deck.—*n.* plank flooring of ship; pack of cards. **d.-chair** *n.* portable folding chair with canvas seat. **d.-hand,** *n.* common sailor.
deckle, *n.* gauge on paper-making machine. **d.-edge,** *n.* rough edge of hand-made paper. (G. *deckel*)
declaim, *v.i.* and *t.* speak loudly and dramatically; inveigh. **declamation,** *n.* **declamatory,** *a.* noisy and rhetorical. (L. *clamare*, shout)
declare, *v.t.* and *i.* affirm, proclaim; admit possession of (dutiable goods); (*bridge*) name trump suit; (*cricket*) announce innings closed. **d. for, against,** side with, against. **d. oneself,** show oneself in true colours. **declared,** *a.* avowed. **declarant,** *n.* maker of legal declaration. **declaration,** *n.* affirmation; emphatic or formal statement; (*law*) pleading. **declaratory,** *a.* (L. *clarus*, clear)
declassé, *a.* (*fem.* *déclassée*) fallen in the social scale. (F.)
declension, *n.* declining; falling off, lapse; (*gram.*) case-inflexion of noun. **declensional,** *a.* (*decline*)
decline, *v.i.* and *t.* slope, bend down; deteriorate, fall away; diminish; refuse, reject; (*army.*) give cases of.—*n.* declining; wasting disease, consumption. **declinable,** *a.* (*gram.*) **declination,** *n.* downward bend; deviation of compass from true north; (*astron.*) angular distance from equator, celestial latitude. **declinational,** *a.* **declinometer,** *n.* instrument for measuring declination of compass. (L. *clinare*, bend)
declivity, *n.* downward slope. **declivitous, declivous,** *aa.* (L. *clivus*, slope)
declutch, *v.i.* disengage clutch.
decoct, *v.t.* boil down; (*Shake.*) warm up. **decoction,** *n.* decocting; essence extracted by boiling. (L. *coquere*, cook)
decode, *v.t.* translate from code to ordinary language.
decollate, *v.t.* behead, truncate. **decollation,** *n.* (L. *collum*, neck)
décolleté, *a.* (*fem.* *décolletée*) low-necked, wearing low-necked dress. *décolletage,* *n.* low-cut dress; exposure of shoulders by it. (F.)
decolour, decolorize, decolourize, *vv.t.* remove colour from, bleach. **decolorant, decolourant,** *a.* and *n.* bleaching (agent). **decolouration, decolorization, decolourization,** *nn.*
decomplex, *a.* doubly complex; with complex parts.
decompose, *v.t.* and *i.* resolve into its elements; rot; analyse (motive etc.).

decomposition, *n.* decay. **decomposite, decompound,** *a.* and *n.* (substance, word) compounded of compounds.

decompress, *v.t.* relieve pressure on (diver) by means of air-lock. **decompression, decompressor,** *nn.*

deconsecrate, *v.t.* secularize.

decontaminate, *v.t.* clear of poison gas. **decontamination,** *n.*

decontrol, *v.t.* and *n.* release from control.

décor, *n.* decoration, get-up, of theatre stage or room. (F.)

decorate, *v.t.* adorn, beautify; invest with order or medal. **Decorated style,** (*archit.*) with elaborate ornamentation, between Early English and Perpendicular. **decoration,** *n.* decorating; ornament; medal, badge of honour. **decorative,** *a.* **decorator,** *n.* one who paints and papers houses. (L. *decus,* beauty)

decorous, *a.* well-behaved; in good taste, sober. (*decorum*)

decorticate, *v.t.* strip bark from. **decortication,** *n.* (L. *cortex,* bark)

decorum, *n.* decency, propriety, etiquette. (L.)

decoy, *n.* lure, enticement; tame or imitation bird used to allure others; netted pond for trapping wild duck; swindler's confederate.—*v.t.* entice by decoy, lure into trap. **d.-duck,** *n.* (L. *cavea,* cage)

decrease, *v.i.* and *t.* diminish, lessen.—*n.* diminution. (L. *crescere,* grow)

decree, *n.* authoritative order, edict; law of God or nature.—*v.t.* ordain, enjoin. **d. nisi,** order for divorce unless cause to the contrary is shown within period. (L. *cernere,* sift)

decrement, *n.* decrease, amount of it (opp. to increment). (*decrease*)

decrepit, *a.* old and feeble, infirm; worn out, ramshackle. (L. *crepare,* creak)

decrepitate, *v.t.* and *i.* calcine (salt, mineral) till it crackles; crackle under extreme heat. **decrepitation,** *n.* (L. *crepare,* creak)

decrepitude, *n.* being decrepit.

decrescendo, *a.* and *n.* (passage) with gradual reduction of loudness. (It.)

decrescent, *a.* waning. (*decrease*)

decretal, *n.* papal decree; (*pl.*) part of canon law made up of these. **decretive, decretory,** *aa.* (*decree*)

decrial, *n.* decrying.

decrustation, *n.* removing of crust (opp. to incrustation).

decry, *v.t.* disparage, run down.

decuman, *a.* (of wave) extra large and powerful. (L. *decumanus,* of tenth)

decumbent, *a.* (*bot.*) resting on ground, trailing. (L. *cumbere,* lie)

decuple, *a.* and *n.* tenfold (amount).—*v.t.* multiply by ten. (L. *decem,* ten)

decurrent, decursive, *aa.* running, extending, downward.

decussate, *v.t.* and *i.* intersect in form of X.—*a.* X-shaped; (of leaves) in pairs, at right angles to those above and below. **decussation,** *n.* (L. *decussis,* number ten, X)

dedans, *n.* (*tennis*) open gallery at end of court; spectators in it. (F.)

dedicate, *v.t.* set apart by solemn ritual; devote wholly; inscribe (book) as compliment. **dedication,** *n.* dedicating; dedicatory inscription. **dedicator, dedicatee,** *nn.* **dedicative, dedicatory,** *aa.* (L. *dicare,* devote)

deduce, *v.t.* infer, draw as conclusion; trace down ancestry of. **deducible,** *a.* **deduct,** *v.t.* take away, subtract (part of wages etc.). **deduction,** *n.* deducting; sum deducted; deducing, reasoning from general to particular; inference. **deductive,** *a.* deducing. (L. *ducere,* lead)

dee, *n.* D-shaped harness-ring.

dee, *Scot.* form of die.

deed, *n.* action; exploit; fact, performance; legal document. — *v.t.* (*Amer.*) transfer by deed. **d.-poll,** *n.* deed executed by one party only. (O.E. *dǣd*)

deem, *v.t.* judge, consider, believe. —*n.* (*Shake.*) thought, judgment. **deemster,** *n.* Manx judge. (O.E. *déman*)

deep, *a.* extending far down or in; in depth; profound; intense, extreme; cunning; engrossed; (of colour) dark, rich; (of sound) low-pitched.—*adv.* far down, deeply.—*n.* sea; abyss, mysterious depth; (*cricket*) field behind bowler near boundary; (*naut.*) fathom-point on lead-line which is not one of the marks. **go off the d. end,** be furious. **in d. water,** in great difficulty. **d.-laid,** *a.* secret and elaborate. **d.-mouthed,** *a.* sonorous. **deepen,** *v.t.* and *i.* make, become, deep or deeper. (O.E. *déop*)

deer, *n.* (*pl.* same) four-footed animal with deciduous horns; (*obs.*) any animal. **d.-forest,** *n.* wild tract, not necessarily wooded, reserved for deer. **d.-hound,** *n.* large rough-haired greyhound. **d.-neck,** *n.* thin neck (of horse). **d.-stalker,** *n.* one who hunts deer by stalking; cloth cap with peaks. (O.E. *déor*)

deface, *v.t.* mar, disfigure; obliterate (inscription). **defacement,** *n.*

defalcate, *v.i.* embezzle money held in trust. **defalcation,** *n.* misappropriation of funds; deficiency due to this. **defalcator,** *n.* (L. *falx,* scythe)

defame, *v.t.* take away good name of, slander, vilify. **defamation,** *n.* **defamatory,** *a.*

default, *n.* want, absence; neglect to do what duty or law requires.—*v.i.* and *t.* neglect obligation; fail to attend court etc.; give judgment against defaulting party. **defaulter,** *n.* one who defaults; soldier guilty of military offence. (*fault*)

defeasance, *n.* (*law*) annulment; condition annexed to deed, which being performed renders the deed void. **defeasible,** *a.* able to be annulled. (O.F. *desfaire,* undo)
defeat, *v.t.* vanquish, worst; frustrate, ruin; (*Shake.*) disfigure, deface.—*n.* defeating; lost contest, overthrow. **defeatism,** *n.* advocacy of surrender. **defeatist,** *a.* and *n.* **defeature,** *v.t.* make unrecognizable.—*n.* (*Spens.*) defeat; (*Shake.*) disfigurement. (L. *facere,* do)
defecate, *v.t.* and *i.* clear of dregs, purify; void excrement. **defecation,** *n.* (L. *faex,* dregs)
defect, *n.* fault, shortcoming, want. **defection,** *n.* failure in duty, deserting. **defective,** *a.* incomplete, faulty; deficient; (*gram.*) not having all inflexions. — *n.* imbecile. (L. *facere,* do)
defence, *n.* defending, protection; vindication; (*law*) defendant's plea or proceedings; (*pl.*) fortifications. **D. of the Realm Act,** (*abbr.* **D.O.R.A.**) giving government wide powers during war of 1914-18. **defenceless,** *a.*
defend, *v.t.* protect, shield; argue in favour of; conduct legal defence; (*arch.*) avert. **defendant,** *n.* (*law*) person accused or prosecuted. **defender,** *n.* **defensible,** *a.* easily defended; justifiable. **defensive,** *a.* serving for defence, not aggressive. (L. *defendere*)
defer, *v.i.* yield to another's opinion. **deference,** *n.* deferring; respect, regard. **deferent,** *a.* deferential; (*anat.*) conveying away. **deferential,** *a.* respectful. (L. *de,* down; *ferre,* bear)
defer, *v.t.* and *i.* put off, postpone; procrastinate. **deferment,** *n.* (L. *dis-,* apart; *ferre,* carry)
defiance, *n.* challenge to contest; open disobedience. **defiant,** *a.*
deficient, *a.* lacking, inadequate. **deficiency,** *n.* shortage, lack; amount by which thing falls short. **deficit,** *n.* deficiency; excess of expenditure over receipts. (*defect*)
defilade, *v.t.* protect against enfilading fire.—*n.* this protection.
defile, *v.i.* march in file.—*n.* narrow valley, pass. (*file*)
defile, *v.t.* render unclean, pollute; desecrate. **defilement,** *n.* (O.F. *defouler,* trample + confusion with O.E. *fýlan,* foul)
define, *v.t.* mark limits of, show clearly; describe in exact terms. **definite,** *a.* clearly defined; precise, distinct, not vague. **definite article,** the. **definition,** *n.* defining; statement of precise meaning; distinctness, esp. of image given by lens. **definitive,** *a.* final, not subject to revision; limiting. (L. *finis,* end)
deflagrate, *v.i.* and *t.* burn with rapid flame. **deflagration,** *n.* (L. *flagrare,* blaze)
deflate, *v.t.* let air out of; reduce inflation of (currency). **deflation,** *n.* deflating; reduction of issue of paper money, causing fall in prices. (L. *flare,* blow)
deflect, *v.t.* and *i.* turn aside, deviate. **deflection, deflexion,** *nn.* (L. *flectere,* bend)
defloration, *n.* deflowering. (L. *flos,* flower)
deflower, *v.t.* strip of flowers; ravish; ravage.
defluent, *a.* and *n.* down-flowing (part). (L. *fluere,* flow)
deforce, *v.t.* (*law*) keep out of possession by force; (*Scots law*) resist (officer of law in execution of his duty). **deforcement,** *n.*
deforest, *v.t.* clear of trees, disforest.
deform, *v.t.* spoil shape or appearance of, disfigure. **deformed,** *a.* misshapen. **deformation,** *n.* change for the worse; perverted form of word, **e.g.** 'sparrow-grass.' **deformity,** *n.* physical or moral disfigurement, ugliness; malformation.
defraud, *v.t.* cheat, swindle.
defray, *v.t.* pay, bear cost of; (*Spens.*) appease. **defrayal, defrayment,** *nn.* (F. *frais,* expenses)
defrock, *v.t.* unfrock.
deft, *a.* adroit, neat, skilful. (O.E. *gedæfte,* mild)
defunct, *a.* and *n.* dead; obsolete. **defunction,** *n.* (*Shake.*) death. (L. *fungi,* perform)
defy, *v.t.* challenge; disobey openly, resist successfully. (L. *fidus,* faithful)
dégagé, *a.* unconstrained, at ease. (F.)
de-gauss, *v.t.* equip (ship) with apparatus which prevents it from detonating magnetic mines. (*gauss*)
degenerate, *a.* having reverted to lower type; fallen from excellence to baseness.—*n.* degenerate person. —*v.i.* deteriorate. **degeneracy,** *n.* **degeneration,** *n.* degenerating; (*med.*) morbid change in tissue. (*genus*)
deglutinate, *v.t.* unglue. (L. *gluten,* glue)
deglutition, *n.* swallowing. (L. *glutire,* swallow)
degrade, *v.t.* and *i.* lower self-respect or moral tone of, debase; reduce rank of; degenerate; (*geol.*) disintegrate. **degraded,** *a.* mean, base. **degrading,** *a.* humiliating. **degradation,** *n.*
degree, *n.* grade, relative position; status; academical rank; nearness of relationship; unit of temperature; (*gram.*) grade in comparison of adjective; (*math.*) $\frac{1}{360}$ of circle, unit of angular measurement. **by dd.,** little by little. **forbidden dd.,** relations one may not marry. **third d.** (*Amer.*), long severe cross-examination. **to a d.,** exceedingly. (L. *gradus,* step)
degression, *n.* going down; decrease in taxation rate. (L. *gradi,* walk)

degust, *v.t.* taste, sample, relish. **degustation,** *n.* (L. *gustus,* taste)

dehisce, *v.i.* gape; (of seed-vessel) burst open. **dehiscence,** *n.* **dehiscent,** *a.* (L. *hiscere,* yawn)

dehortative, *a.* and *n.* (thing) meant to dissuade. (L. *hortari,* exhort)

dehumanize, *v.t.* divest of human qualities, brutalize.

dehydrate, *v.t.* (*chem.*) remove water from. (Gk. *hudōr,* water)

dehypnotize, *v.t.* rouse from hypnotic state.

de-ice, *v.t.* free (aircraft) from ice which has formed on it. **de-icer,** *n.*

deicide, *n.* killing, killer, of a god. (L. *deus,* god; *caedere,* kill)

deictic, *a.* (*gram.*) demonstrative; (*logic*) proving directly. (Gk. *deiknunai,* show)

deify, *v.t.* make god of, worship as a god. **deification,** *n.* **deiform,** *a.* godlike in form. (L. *deus,* god; *facere,* make)

deign, *v.i.* and *t.* condescend, stoop; vouchsafe. (L. *dignari,* think worthy)

dei gratia, by the grace of God. (L.)

deil, *Scot.* form of **devil.**

deipnosophist, *n.* adept in table-talk. (Gk. *deipnon,* dinner; *sophos,* wise)

deism, *n.* belief in the existence of God on rational grounds, without accepting revealed religion. **deist,** *n.* adherent of deism. **deistic, deistical,** *aa.* **deity,** *n.* godhead, divinity; god. (L. *deus,* god)

deject, *v.t.* dispirit, dishearten. **dejected,** *a.* cast down, gloomy. **dejection,** *n.* depression, low spirits, (*med.*) excretion, excrement. **dejecta,** *n.pl.* excrements, droppings. (L. *jacere,* throw)

déjeuner, n. breakfast; luncheon. (F.)

dekagram, dekagramme, dekalitre, dekametre, same as **decagram** etc.

dekko, *n.* (*sl.*) look. (Hind. *dekhna,* look)

delaine, *n.* light fabric of wool and cotton. (F. *de laine,* of wool)

delate, *v.t.* inform against (person); report (offence). **delation, delator,** *nn.* (L. *delator,* informer)

delay, *v.t.* and *i.* put off, defer; cause to wait, hinder; linger, dawdle.—*n.* postponement, tardiness. (O.F. *delaier*)

del credere, guarantee of commission-agent that buyer is solvent. (It.)

dēlē, *v.t.* (*print., abbr.* d) delete. (L.)

delectable, *a.* delightful, pleasant. **delectation,** *n.* pleasure, enjoyment. (L. *delectare,* delight)

delectus, *n.* school-book of selected passages. (L. *legere,* choose)

delegate, *v.t.* send as representative to conference etc.; commit (duties to). —*n.* deputy, representative. **delegation,** *n.* delegating; body of delegates; (*Amer.*) representatives of single state in Congress. (L. *lēgare,* send on public mission)

delete, *v.t.* erase, strike out. **deletion,** *n.* (L. *delēre,* destroy)

deleterious, *a.* harmful, noxious. (Gk. *dēleisthai,* injure)

delf, delft, *n.* kind of glazed earthenware. (town in Holland)

deliberate, *v.i.* and *t.* take counsel, debate; consider, reflect upon.—*a.* intentional; slow and careful. **deliberation,** *n.* deliberating; mature reflection; deliberateness, slowness. **deliberative,** *a.* of, appointed for, deliberation. (L. *libra,* balance)

delicate, *a.* sensitive, fastidious; refined, modest; considerate; frail, not robust; needing careful handling; exquisite, fine; (*Shake.*) delightful, voluptuous. **delicacy,** *n.* delicateness, refinement; tact; dainty. (L. *delicatus*)

delicatessen, *n.* cooked meats, preserves etc.; shop selling these. (G.)

delicious, *a.* very delightful to senses, giving exquisite pleasure. (L. *deliciae,* delight)

delict, *n.* legal offence. (L. *delictum*)

delight, *v.t.* and *i.* please highly; find pleasure (in).—*n.* great pleasure; source of this. **delightful,** *a.* very pleasing; charming. **delightsome,** *a.* (*arch.*). (L. *delectare*)

delimit, delimitate, *v.t.* fix boundaries of. **delimitation,** *n.*

delineate, *v.t.* trace in outline, depict; describe. **delineation, delineator,** *nn.* (L. *linea,* line)

delinquent, *a.* neglecting duty.—*n.* offender. **delinquency,** *n.* sin of omission; misdeed. (L. *linquere,* leave)

deliquesce, *v.i.* become liquid; melt. **deliquescent,** *a.* **deliquescence,** *n.* (L. *liquēre,* be fluid)

delirious, *a.* wandering in mind, light-headed; wildly excited. **delirium,** *n.* mental disorder due to fever etc.; ecstasy. **delirium tremens** (*colloq. abbr.* **D.T.**) violent delirium with hallucinations, caused by excessive drinking. (L. *delirare,* rave)

delitescent, *a.* (*med.*) latent. **delitescence,** *n.* (L. *latēre,* lie hid)

deliver, *v.t.* set free, save; hand over; deal (blow); utter (speech); disburden (woman of child). **d. oneself of,** solemnly announce. **d. the goods,** carry out bargain. **d. up,** surrender. **deliverance,** *n.* rescue; authoritative utterance. **deliverer,** *n.* preserver. **delivery,** *n.* delivering; childbirth; distribution of letters; style of making speech; (*cricket*) style of bowling; (*law*) formal transfer. (L. *liber,* free)

dell, *n.* small wooded hollow.

Delphian, Delphic, *aa.* of Apollo's oracle at Delphi; obscure, ambiguous.

delta, *n.* a Greek letter (Δ); triangular alluvial tract at mouth of river. **deltaic,** *a.* **deltoid,** *a.* triangular.—*n.* muscle that lifts upper arm. (Gk.)

delude, *v.t.* impose upon, deceive. (L. *ludere,* play)

deluge, *n.* great flood; downpour.—*v.t.* flood; overwhelm. (L. *diluvium*)
delusion, *n.* deluding; mistaken belief; hallucination. **delusive,** *a.* deceptive, disappointing, unreal.
delve, *v.t.* and *i.* dig with spade; make researches (into).—*n.* cavity; wrinkle. (O.E. *delfan*)
demagnetize, *v.t.* deprive of magnetic power.
demagogue, *n.* mob leader, political agitator. **demagogic,** *a.* **demagogism, demagoguery, demagogy,** *nn.* (Gk. *dēmos*, people; *agein*, lead)
demand, *v.t.* ask (for) as right, require peremptorily; call for.—*n.* urgent or authoritative claim or inquiry; (*economics*) requirements of consumers. **in d.,** sought after. **demandant,** *n.* plaintiff. (L. *mandare*, order)
demarcate, *v.t.* delimit. **demarcation,** *n.* division between adjacent areas. (*mark*)
démarche, *n.* diplomatic announcement of policy or plan. (F.)
dematerialize, *v.t.* and *i.* deprive of, give up, material form.
deme, *n.* township of ancient Greece. (Gk. *dēmos*)
demean, *v.refl.* conduct (oneself). **demeanour,** *n.* bearing, behaviour. (L. *minari*, threaten)
demean, *v.refl.* degrade (oneself), condescend. (*mean*)
dement, *v.t.* drive mad. **demented,** *a.* crazy. (L. *mens*, mind)
démenti, *n.* official denial. (F.)
dementia, *n.* insanity showing feebleness of mind. **d. praecox,** schizophrenia. (L.)
demerara, *n.* kind of brown sugar. (division of British Guiana)
demerit, *n.* fault, bad quality; (*pl. Shake.*) deserts. **demeritorious,** *a.* deserving ill.
demersal, *a.* (*zool.*) found in deep water or on sea bottom. (L. *mergere*, dip)
demesne, *n.* estate, territory; sphere of action. **hold in d.,** have unrestricted possession of. (L. *dominus*, lord)
demi-, *pref.* half. (L. *dimidium*)
demigod, *n.* being half divine and half human; inferior deity.
demijohn, *n.* large bottle with wicker case. (F. *dame-jeanne*, Lady Jane)
demilune, *n.* crescent-shaped fortification. (F.=half-moon)
demi-monde, *n.* upper class of courtesans. *demi-mondaine,* *n.* member of this. (F.=half world)
demi-rep, *n.* woman of doubtful virtue. (abbr. of *demi-reputable*)
demise, *v.t.* convey (estate) by will or lease.—*n.* demising; death, esp. of sovereign. **d. of the Crown,** its transfer by death or abdication. **demisable,** *a.* (*demit*)
demisemiquaver, *n.* (*mus.*) half a semiquaver.
demit, *v.t.* and *i.* resign (office), abdicate. **demission,** *n.* (L. *dis-*, apart; *mittere*, send)
demi-tasse, *n.* small cup (of black coffee). (F.)
demiurge, *n.* creator of world (in Platonic philosophy etc.). **demiurgic,** *a.* (Gk. *dēmos*, people; *ergon*, work)
demobilize, (*sl.*) **demob,** *v.t.* disband (forces); discharge (soldier). **demobilization,** *n.*
democracy, *n.* government by the people; state having this; principle that all have equal rights. **democrat,** *n.* supporter of democracy; member of U.S. Democratic Party. **democratic, democratical,** *aa.* **Democratic Party,** one of two chief parties in U.S., opp. to Republican. **democratize,** *v.t.* **democratization,** *n.* (Gk. *dēmos*, people; *kratos*, power)
démodé, *a.* out of fashion. (F.)
demography, *n.* statistics of births, deaths, and diseases of community. **demographer,** *n.* **demographic,** *a.* (Gk. *dēmos*, people; *graphein*, write)
demoiselle, *n.* damsel; Numidian crane. (F.)
demolish, *v.t.* pull down; overthrow; (*colloq.*) eat up. **demolition,** *n.* (L. *moles*, mass)
demon, *n.* evil spirit, devil; personified vice; wicked, malignant person; daemon. (Gk. *daimōn*)
demonetize, *v.t.* withdraw (coin) from circulation; abandon (gold etc.) as currency. **demonetization,** *n.*
demoniac, *a.* of, like, influenced by, demons; fiendish; frenzied.—*n.* person possessed by evil spirit. **demoniacal,** *a.* demoniac. **demonic,** *a.* abnormal in insight, inspired. **demonism,** *n.* belief in power of demons. **demonize,** *v.t.* make into, represent as, a demon. **demonolater,** *n.* demon-worshipper. **demonolatry,** *n.* **demonology,** *n.* study of demons and superstitions about them.
demonstrate, *v.t.* and *i.* show by reasoning, prove; describe by example; make, take part in, demonstration. **demonstrable,** *a.* **demonstration,** *n.* proof, proving; practical illustration; organized expression of opinion by procession etc.; display of armed force. **demonstrational,** *a.* **demonstrationist,** *n.* **demonstrative,** *a.* conclusive; showing feelings openly, unreserved; (*gram.*) pointing out.—*n.* demonstrative word. **demonstrator,** *n.* professor's assistant in laboratory etc. (L. *monstrare*, show)
demoralize, *v.t.* injure morally, pervert; injure morale, destroy discipline, of. **demoralization,** *n.*
Demos, *n.* populace personified. (Gk.)
demote, *v.t.* (*Amer. colloq.*) reduce (student etc.) to lower grade (opp. to promote). (L. *movēre*, move)
demotic, *a.* popular; in the simplified style of ancient Egyptian writing. (Gk. *dēmos*, people)

demulcent, *a.* and *n.* soothing (substance). (L. *mulcēre*, soothe)
demur, *v.i.* object, take exception; (*law*) put in demurrer.—*n.* objecting, hesitation. (L. *mora*, delay)
demure, *a.* sedate, quiet, modest; roguishly grave. (L. *maturus*, ripe)
demurrable, *a.* open to legal objection.
demurrage, *n.* charge for keeping ship, truck etc. beyond the time agreed for unloading. (*demur*)
demurrer, *n.* (*law*) plea that opponent's facts are irrelevant; exception taken.
demy, *n.* (*pl.* **demies**) size of paper, $22\frac{1}{2} \times 17\frac{1}{2}$ in. for printing, $20 \times 15\frac{1}{2}$ in. for writing; holder of demyship. **demyship,** *n.* special scholarship at Magdalen College, Oxford. (=*demi-*)
den, *n.* lair of beast; haunt of vice or misery; private study or workshop. —*v.i.* live in den. **d. up,** (*Amer. colloq.*) retire for hibernation. (O.E. *denn*)
denary, *a.* of ten, decimal. **denarius,** *n.* ancient Roman silver coin, worth about 9*d.* (L. *decem*, ten)
denationalize, *v.t.* deprive of national rights or character. **denationalization,** *n.*
denaturalize, *v.t.* make unnatural; deprive of acquired citizenship. **denaturalization,** *n.*
denature, *v.t.* change nature of by adulteration; make (alcohol) too nasty to drink. **denaturant,** *n.* substance used for this.
denay, *n.* (*Shake.*) denial.
dendr(o)-, from Gk. *dendron*, tree, used in **dendral,** *a.* arboreal; **dendrite,** *n.* mineral with branched tree-like markings, hence **dendritic,** *a.*; **dendroid,** *a.* like a tree; **dendrolite,** *n.* fossil tree; **dendrology,** *n.* study of trees, hence **dendrologist,** *n.*; **dendrometer,** *n.* instrument for measuring trees.
dene, *n.* low sandy tract near sea, dune.
dene, dean, *n.* small valley. (O.E. *denu*)
denegation, *n.* (*arch.*) denial.
dene-hole, *n.* ancient excavation in chalk with deep vertical shaft.
dengue, *n.* infectious tropical fever with pain in joints.
denial, *n.* refusal; contradiction; disavowal. **deniable,** *a.* **denier,** *n.* (*deny*)
denier, *n.* old French coin of small value; small sum. (O.F.)
denigrate, *v.t.* blacken; defame. **denigration, denigrator,** *nn.* (L. *niger*, black)
denizen, *n.* inhabitant; naturalized person, animal, plant, or word.—*v.t.* naturalize; people. (L. *de intus*, from within)
denominate, *v.t.* name, designate, describe as. **denomination,** *n.* designation, name; religious sect, Church; class of units. **denominational,** *a.* of, by, religious sects. **denominationalize,** *v.t.* **denominative,** *a.* giving name. **denominator,** *n.* divisor in vulgar fraction.
denote, *v.t.* mark, distinguish; express, mean. **denotation,** *n.* designation; symbol; primary meaning; (*logic*) aggregate of objects included under a word (opp. to connotation). **denotative,** *a.* indicative; (*logic*) merely designating.
denouement, *dénouement*, *n.* issue, final situation; unravelling of plot. (F.)
denounce, *v.t.* accuse publicly; inform against; invoke; terminate, repudiate (treaty). **denouncement,** *n.* (L. *nuntius*, messenger)
dense, *a.* tightly packed, thick; crass, stupid. **density,** *n.* denseness; mass per unit of volume. (L. *densus*)
dent, *n.* depression in surface.—*v.t.* mark with dent, dint. (=*dint*)
dental, *a.* of teeth or dentistry; (of letter) made with tongue-tip against front teeth.—*n.* dental letter, e.g. *d, t.* **dentate,** *a.* toothed, notched. **dentation,** *n.* **denticle,** *n.* small tooth or tooth-like projection; dentil. **denticular, denticulate,** *aa.* having denticles. **dentiform,** *a.* tooth-shaped. **dentifrice,** *n.* tooth powder or paste. **dentil,** *n.* (*archit.*) small square projecting block on moulding. **dentilingual,** *a.* and *n.* (consonant) formed between teeth and tongue, e.g. *th.* **dentine,** *n.* hard tissue of teeth. **dentist,** *n.* dental surgeon. **dentistry,** *n.* **dentition,** *n.* arrangement, development, of teeth. **dentoid,** *a.* tooth-like. **denture,** *n.* set of false teeth. (L. *dens*, tooth)
denude, *v.t.* make bare, strip. **denudation,** *n.* denuding; (*geol.*) disappearance of surface soil, baring by erosion. **denudative,** *a.* (*nude*)
denunciation, *n.* denouncing, public accusation. **denunciative, denunciatory,** *aa.*
deny, *v.t.* contradict, declare untrue; refuse; repudiate; forbid access to. **d. oneself,** be abstinent. (L. *negare*, say no)
deodand, *n.* (*law*) chattel which having caused death was forfeited to Crown for pious uses. (L. *deo dandum*, thing to be given to God)
deodar, *n.* Himalayan cedar. (Sanskr. *deva-dara*, divine tree)
deodorize, *v.t.* remove smell from, disinfect. **deodorant, deodorizer,** *nn.* substance for this. **deodorization,** *n.* (L. *odor*, smell)
deontology, *n.* science of duty. **deontological,** *a.* **deontologist,** *n.* (Gk. *dei*, it is right)
Deo volente, (*abbr.* **D.V.**) God willing, if nothing prevents. (L.)
deoxidize, *v.t.* deprive of oxygen.
depart, *v.i.* and *t.* go away, leave; die; (*obs.*) part, divide. **d. from,** deviate from, alter. **departed,** *a.* past, bygone.—*n.* dead. **department,** *n.*

branch of administration or business; sphere, province; administrative district. **department store,** (*Amer.*) with great variety of goods. **departmental,** *a.* **departmentalism,** *n.* red-tape. **departure,** *n.* leaving; divergence, change; (*naut.*) distance due east or west made by ship.

depasture, *v.t.* and *i.* graze upon; graze, feed (cattle). **depasturage,** *n.*

depauperate, *v.t.* impoverish, weaken; stunt. **depauperation,** *n.* **depauperize,** *v.t.* free from paupers or poverty.

depend, *v.i.* rely; be contingent; be pending; (*arch.*) hang. **dependable,** *a.* trustworthy. **dependant,** *n.* one supported by another; retainer. **dependence,** *n.* depending, being dependent; reliance. **dependency,** *n.* subject territory. **dependent,** *a.* depending; contingent; subject; living at another's cost; (*bot.*) hanging down; (*gram.*) subordinate. —*n.* dependant. (L. *pendere*, hang)

dephosphorize, *v.t.* rid of phosphorus.

depict, *v.t.* draw, paint; portray in words. **depicter, depictor, depiction,** *nn.* **depictive,** *a.* **depicture,** *v.t.* picture. (L. *pingere*, paint)

depilate, *v.t.* remove hairs from. **depilation,** *n.* **depilatory,** *a.* and *n.* depilating (agent). (L. *pilus*, hair)

deplane, *v.i.* and *t.* alight, unload, from aircraft.

deplenish, *v.t.* empty, deprive of stock. (L. *plenus*, full)

deplete, *v.t.* empty out, exhaust; reduce; (*med.*) relieve of congestion. **depletion,** *n.* **depletive, depletory,** *aa.* (L. *plēre*, fill)

deplore, *v.t.* lament, grieve over; be scandalized by. **deplorable,** *a.* lamentable, disastrous. (L. *plorare*, weep)

deploy, *v.i.* and *t.* extend (troops) from column into line; spread out. **deployment,** *n.* (L. *plicare*, fold)

deplume, *v.t.* strip of feathers, pluck.

depolarize, *v.t.* deprive of polarity; dissolve (prejudices). **depolarization,** *n.*

depone, *v.t.* and *i.* (*Scot.*) testify upon oath, depose. **deponent,** *a.* (*gram.*) passive in form but active in meaning. —*n.* one who makes deposition; deponent verb. (L. *ponere*, place)

depopulate, *v.t.* reduce population of. **depopulation, depopulator,** *nn.*

deport, *v.t.* send out of country, banish.—*v.refl.* conduct (oneself), behave. **deportation,** *n.* banishment. **deportee,** *n.* person deported. **deportment,** *n.* carriage, bearing, manners; way a thing behaves. (L. *portare*, carry)

depose, *v.t.* and *i.* dethrone, remove from office; give evidence on oath. (L. *pausare*, halt+confusion with *ponere*, place)

deposit, *v.t.* lay down; leave lying; entrust for safe keeping.—*n.* thing stored; sediment, precipitated matter; money in bank, us. at interest; sum paid in advance, earnest money. **depositary,** *n.* person to whom thing is committed. (L. *ponere*, place)

deposition, *n.* deposing; sworn testimony; the taking down of Christ from the Cross. (L. *ponere*, place, but with senses mainly from *depose*)

depositor, *n.* one who makes deposit. **depository,** *n.* storehouse.

depot, *n.* storehouse; emporium; headquarters of regiment; (*Amer.*) railway station. (F. *dépôt*)

deprave, *v.t.* pervert, corrupt morals of. **depraved,** *a.* wicked. **depravation,** *n.* deterioration. **depravity,** *n.* wickedness, viciousness. (L. *pravus*, crooked)

deprecate, *v.t.* express disapproval of; argue against; seek to avert by prayer. **deprecation,** *n.* **deprecative, deprecatory,** *aa.* (L. *precari*, pray)

depreciate, *v.t.* and *i.* diminish in value; disparage, belittle. **depreciation,** *n.* depreciating; allowance made for wear and tear. **depreciatory,** *a.* (L. *pretium*, price)

depredation, *n.* (us. *pl.*) plundering; encroachment. **depredator,** *n.* despoiler. (L. *praeda*, booty)

depress, *v.t.* press down, lower; reduce activity of; discourage, sadden. **depressed area,** where unemployment is rife. **depressed classes** (*India*) untouchables. **depressant,** *a.* and *n.* lowering, sedative (drug). **depressing,** *a.* **depression,** *n.* hollow, dip; gloom, dejection; torpid state of trade; lowering of atmospheric pressure, cyclone; (*astron.*) angular distance below horizon.

deprive, *v.t.* take away from, dispossess, strip. **deprival,** *n.* **deprivation,** *n.* being deprived; felt loss. (L. *privare*, deprive)

depth, *n.* deepness; profundity, intensity; breadth of border, shelf etc.; (*pl.*) abyss. **out of one's d.,** unable to touch bottom; finding subject too hard. **d.-charge,** *n.* bomb for use against submarines. (*deep*)

depurate, *v.t.* and *i.* free, become free, from impurities. **depuration, depurator,** *nn.* **depurative,** *a.*

depute, *v.t.* appoint as substitute; delegate (task) to another. **deputation,** *n.* body of persons sent to speak for others, delegation. **deputize,** *v.i.* act as deputy or understudy. **deputy,** *n.* one who acts for another, substitute; member of foreign parliament. (L. *putare*, think)

deracinate, *v.t.* tear up by roots. (L. *radix*, root)

derail, *v.t.* cause (train) to leave rails. **derailment,** *n.*

derange, *v.t.* disorganize, confuse; upset action of; render insane. **derangement,** *n.* disorder; insanity.

derate, *v.t.* relieve from burden of local rates.

Derby, *n.* a famous horse-race; (*Amer.*) bowler hat. **D. scheme,** of voluntary conscription, 1915. (Lord *Derby*)

Derbyshire neck, goitre. **Derbyshire spar,** fluorspar. (place)

derelict, *a.* abandoned, ownerless; (*Amer.*) neglectful of duty.—*n.* derelict ship or article. **dereliction,** *n.* abandoning; neglect, sin of omission; withdrawal of sea exposing land. (L. *relinquere,* leave)

deride, *v.t.* laugh to scorn, scoff at. **derision,** *n.* ridicule; laughing-stock. **derisive,** *a.* scornful; ironical. **derisory,** *a.* futile, not to be taken seriously; derisive. (L. *ridēre,* laugh)

derive, *v.t.* and *i.* obtain, spring, from source; trace origin (from). **derivation,** *n.* source, descent; origin, etymology, of word. **derivative,** *a.* and *n.* (word, substance) derived, not original. (L. *rivus,* stream)

derm, *n.* skin, esp. true skin under cuticle. **dermal, dermic,** *aa.* of skin. **dermatitis,** *n.* inflammation of skin. **dermatoid, dermoid,** *aa.* skin-like. **dermatology,** *n.* science of the skin. **dermatologist,** *n.* (Gk. *derma,* skin)

dern, *a.* (*Shake.*) dark, drear. (O.E. *derne,* secret)

dernier, *a.* last. *d. cri,* last word, latest fashion. *d. ressort,* last shift. (F.)

derogate, *v.i.* detract, take part (from); degenerate. **derogation,** *n.* impairment, debasement. **derogatory,** *a.* involving injury or discredit, degrading. (L. *rogare,* ask)

derrick, *n.* hoisting-machine, kind of crane; framework over oil-well; (*obs.*) gallows. (name of hangman)

derring-do, *n.* bravery, reckless valour. (M.E. *dorryng don,* daring to do, misinterpreted by Spenser)

derringer, *n.* small pistol with large bore. (inventor)

dervish, *n.* Mohammedan friar vowed to poverty and austerity. (Pers. *darvesh,* poor)

descant, *n.* song, melody; (*mus.*) sung accompaniment to plainsong; counterpoint.—*v.i.* hold forth; dwell freely. (L. *dis-,* apart; *cantus,* song)

descend, *v.i.* and *t.* go, come, down; slope downwards; derive, be sprung; pass by inheritance. **d. to,** stoop to. **d. upon,** attack suddenly; visit unexpectedly. **descendant,** *n.* person descended from another. **descent,** *n.* descending; incline, way down; sudden attack; ancestry. (L. *scandere,* climb)

describe, *v.t.* set forth in words; (*geom.*) trace out. **description,** *n.* account in words; sort, kind. **descriptive,** *a.* describing. (L. *scribere,* write)

descry, *v.t.* catch sight of, espy.

desecrate, *v.t.* divert from sacred purpose, profane. **desecration, desecrator,** *nn.* (L. *sacer,* sacred)

desert, *n.* merit, virtue; (*us. pl.*) what one deserves, due. (O.F.)

desert, *v.t.* and *i.* abandon, forsake, withdraw from; run away from army etc.—*a.* uninhabited; barren.—*n.* barren waterless region, wilderness; solitude. **deserter,** *n.* one who deserts from service. **desertion,** *n.* deserting; being forsaken. (L. *serere,* join)

deserve, *v.t.* and *i.* be worthy (of), merit. **d. well, ill, of,** serve so as to deserve reward, punishment. **deservedly,** *adv.* justly. **deserving,** *a.* meritorious; worthy (of). (L. *servire,* serve)

déshabillé, same as **dishabille.**

desiccate, *v.t.* and *i.* dry, dry up; reduce to powder form. **desiccation, desiccator,** *nn.* **desiccative,** *a.* (L. *siccus,* dry)

desiderate, *v.t.* feel lack of, desire earnestly. **desiderative,** *a.* and *n.* (verb) expressing desire. **desideratum,** *n.* (*pl.* **desiderata**) felt want. (L. *desiderare,* long for)

design, *v.t.* and *i.* intend, purpose; plan out, make working drawings for; select (for).—*n.* scheme, project; deliberate purpose; sketch, plan; arrangement of details; decorative pattern. (L. *signum,* mark)

designate, *v.t.* distinguish, mark out; describe as; appoint.—*a.* appointed but not yet installed. **designation,** *n.* designating; name, title. **designator,** *n.* (*design*)

designedly, *adv.* on purpose.

designer, *n.* one who draws designs.

designing, *a.* artful, scheming.

designment, *n.* (*Shake.*) undertaking.

desilverize, *v.t.* extract the silver from.

desipience, *n.* trifling, silliness. (L. *sapere,* be wise)

desire, *v.t.* and *i.* wish, have desire for; request.—*n.* wish, longing; lust; thing wished for. **desirable,** *a.* to be wished; pleasing. **desirability,** *n.* **desirous,** *a.* wishful, eager. (L. *desiderare*)

desist, *v.i.* cease (from), stop. (L. *sistere,* stop)

desk, *n.* table, often with sloping top, for writing or reading; writing-box; pulpit. (L. *discus,* disk)

desman, *n.* small water-animal like mole. (Swedish=musk)

desmology, *n.* anatomy of ligaments. (Gk. *desmos,* bond; *legein,* speak)

desolate, *a.* uninhabited; left alone; neglected, wretched; disconsolate.—*v.t.* lay waste; leave forlorn. **desolation, desolator,** *nn.* (L. *solus,* alone)

despair, *v.i.* lose hope (of), despond.—*n.* hopelessness; cause of this. (L. *sperare,* hope)

despatch, see **dispatch.**

desperado, *n.* (*pl.* **desperadoes**) wild ruffian, reckless criminal. (Sp.)

desperate, *a.* almost beyond hope; extremely serious or difficult; used in last extremity; reckless from despair. **desperation,** *n.* desperateness; recklessness. (*despair*)

despicable, *a.* mean, contemptible. (*despise*)

despise, *v.t.* look down upon, contemn. (L. *despicere*)

despite, *n.* malice, spite; (*arch.*) outrage, injury.—*prep.* in spite of. **despiteful,** *a.* malicious. (*despise*)

despoil, *v.t.* plunder, rob, spoil. **despoiler, despoilment, despoliation,** *nn.*

despond, *v.i.* lose heart, be depressed. —*n.* (*arch.*) dejection. **despondent,** *a.* dejected, gloomy. **despondency,** *n.* (L. *spondēre,* promise)

despot, *n.* tyrant, oppressor; absolute ruler. **despotic,** *a.* arbitrary, with no constitutional checks; tyrannous. **despotism,** *n.* autocratic government; state with this; tyranny. **despotist,** *n.* supporter of despotism. (Gk. *despotēs*)

desquamate, *v.i.* and *t.* peel or scale off. **desquamation,** *n.* **desquamative, desquamatory,** *aa.* (L. *squama,* scale)

dessert, *n.* final dinner-course of fruit, sweets etc. **d.-spoon,** *n.* twice size of tea-spoon. (F. *desservir,* clear table)

destine, *v.t.* determine future of, foreordain; design. **destination,** *n.* place one is bound for, goal. **destiny,** *n.* fate, providence; appointed lot. (L. *destinare*)

destitute, *a.* in extreme want, penniless; devoid, bereft (of). **destitution,** *n.* (L. *statuere,* place)

destrier, *n.* war-horse, charger. (O.F.)

destroy, *v.t.* make away with, demolish; ruin, kill. **destroyer,** *n.* small fast warship with torpedoes. (L. *struere,* build)

destruction, *n.* destroying, being destroyed. **destructible,** *a.* destroyable. **destructive,** *a.* destroying, deadly; (of criticism) negative, pulling down without building up. **destructor,** *n.* incinerator. (*destroy*)

desuetude, *n.* disuse, discontinuance. (L. *suescere,* be wont)

desulphurize, *v.t.* free from sulphur.

desultory, *a.* flitting from one thing to another, rambling, unmethodical. (L. *desultor,* circus rider)

desynonymize, *v.t.* cause (synonyms) to became different in meaning.

detach, *v.t.* unfasten, take off, separate; send (part of force) on special service. **detached,** *a.* standing alone; impartial, impersonal. **detachment,** *n.* detaching; troops detached; aloofness. (F. *détacher*)

detail, *n.* item, particular; single or unimportant part; small detachment; (*art*) treatment of single parts. —*v.t.* relate in full; select (men) for duty. **in d.,** minutely. (F. *tailler,* cut)

detain, *v.t.* hinder, keep waiting; withhold, retain possession of; (*law*) hold in custody. **detainer,** *n.* (*law*) detaining of person or goods; writ for holding on another charge person already arrested. (L. *tenēre,* hold)

detect, *v.t.* discover, find out; discern, perceive. **detection,** *n.* **detective,** *a.* engaged in detection.—*n.* police or private agent investigating crime. **detector,** *n.* thing for detecting. **detectaphone,** *n.* telephonic apparatus for eavesdropping. (L. *tegere,* cover)

detent, *n.* catch for locking machinery or regulating striking of clock. (L. *tendere,* stretch)

détente, *n.* lessening of diplomatic tension between states. (F.)

détenu, *n.* person detained in custody. (F.)

detention, *n.* detaining; arrest, confinement. (*detain*)

deter, *v.t.* discourage, hinder. (L. *terrēre,* frighten)

detergent, *a.* and *n.* surface-cleansing (substance). (L. *tergere,* wipe)

deteriorate, *v.t.* and *i.* make, become, worse. **deterioration,** *n.* **deteriorative,** *a.* (L. *deterior,* worse)

determent, *n.* deterring.

determine, *v.t.* and *i.* decide; fix, define; ascertain; (*law*) terminate. **determinant,** *a.* and *n.* determining (factor). **determinate,** *a.* definite. limited. —*v.t.* (*Shake.*) fix limits of, end. **determination,** *n.* resolve; fixity of purpose; judicial decision; (*med.*) flow (of blood) to one part. **determinative,** *a.* tending to decide; defining **determined,** *a.* resolute, firm. **determinism,** *n.* doctrine that human action is determined by forces independent of the will (opp. to free will). **determinist,** *n.* and *a.* (adherent) of determinism. **deterministic.** *a.* (L. *terminus,* end)

deterrent, *a.* and *n.* (thing) that deters. **deterrence,** *n.*

detersive, *a.* and *n.* detergent.

detest, *v.t.* dislike intensely, loathe. **detestable,** *a.* abominable. **detestation,** *n.* abhorrence. (L. *testari,* call to witness)

dethrone, *v.t.* remove from throne, depose. **dethronement,** *n.*

detinue, *n.* (*law*) writ for recovery of property wrongfully detained. (O.F. *detenir,* detain)

detonate, *v.i.* and *t.* explode with loud report. **detonation,** *n.* **detonative,** *a.* **detonator,** *n.* device for exploding; fog-signal. (L. *tonare,* thunder)

detour, *n.* circuitous route, roundabout. (F. *détour*)

detract, *v.t.* and *i.* take away (from), depreciate. **detraction,** *n.* disparagement. **detractor,** *n.* slanderer. **detractive,** *a.* (L. *trahere,* draw)

detrain, *v.t.* and *i.* set down, alight, from train.

detriment, *n.* injury. loss. **detrimental,** *a.* harmful.—*n.* (*colloq.*) undesirable suitor. (L. *terere,* rub)

detritus, *n.* (*geol.*) worn-down matter, gravel, silt; debris. **detrital,** *a.* **detrited,** *a.* (*geol.*) disintegrated. **detrition,** *n.* wearing down by rubbing. (L. *terere,* rub)

deuce, *n.* card, die, with two spots; *lawn tennis*) forty all. **d.-ace** *n.* (*Shake.*) throw of two and one at dice. (L. *duo,* two)

deuce, *n.* mischief; devil. **deuced,** *a.* (*colloq.*) confounded.—*adv.* very.

deuch-an-doris, same as doch-an-doris.

deus ex machina, divine interposition, artificial solution of difficulties, esp. in play. (L.=god from crane)

deuter(o)-, from Gk. *deuteros,* second, used in **deuteragonist,** *n.* second principal actor; **deuterium,** *n.* heavy hydrogen; **deuterogamy,** *n.* second marriage; **Deuteronomy,** *n.* fifth book of Old Testament (second giving laws), hence **Deuteronomist,** *n.* its author, **Deuteronomic, Deuteronomical.** *aa.*; **deuteron, deuton,** *nn.* nucleus of deuterium atom; **deutoplasm,** *n.* food-matter of egg, yolk.

deutzia, *n.* a white-flowered shrub. (J. *Deutz*)

deux-temps, *n.* quick-time waltz. **(F.)**

devall, *v.i.* and *n.* (*Scot.*) stop.

devaluate, *v.t.* reduce value of; stabilize (currency) at level to which it has fallen.

devastate, *v.t.* lay waste, ravage. **devastation, devastator,** *nn.* (L. *vastare,* lay waste)

develop, *v.t.* and *i.* unfold, reveal; bring, come, to maturity; promote, progress; (*phot.*) bring out latent image on. **developer,** *n.* **development,** *n.* developing; growth, expansion; evolution. **developmental,** *a.* (F. *développer*)

deviate, *v.i.* turn aside, swerve; digress. **deviation,** *n.* deviating; deflection of compass-needle by iron in ship etc. (L. *via,* way)

device, *n.* scheme, plan; apparatus, contrivance; design, emblem; motto; (*arch.*) make. (*devise*)

devil, *n.* spirit of evil, Satan; wicked person, fiend; spirit, fierceness; (*sl.*) fellow; (*S. Afr.*) dust-storm.—*v.i.* and *t.* do another man's drudgery; season highly and grill. **d.'s advocate,** person appointed to oppose claims to canonization; one who sees weaknesses only. **d.'s bedpost,** four of clubs. **d.'s books,** playing-cards. **d.'s coach-horse,** a large dark beetle. **D.'s Own,** 88th Foot; Inns of Court Volunteers. **d.'s tattoo,** drumming with fingers or feet. **d. to pay,** bad trouble ahead. **give the d. his due,** be fair to enemies. **have a d.,** (*arch.*) be possessed. **play the d. with,** ruin. **printer's d.,** printer's errand-boy. **Tasmanian d.,** fierce nocturnal pouched animal. (Gk. *diabolos,* slanderer)

devil-fish, *n.* kind of ray; octopus.

devil-may-care, *a.* reckless, rollicking.

devildom, *n.* rank, domain, of devils.

devilish, *a.* fiendish, malignant.— *adv.* (*colloq.*) very.

devilism, *n.* devilishness; devil-worship.

devilment, *n.* mischievous prank; wild spirits; wizardry.

devilry, deviltry, *n.* black magic, powers of evil; wickedness, mischief; reckless daring.

devious, *a.* out-of-the-way, rambling, roundabout; erring. (L. *via,* way)

devise, *v.t.* contrive, invent; (*law*) leave (real estate) by will.—*n.* (*law*) devising. **deviser,** *n.* contriver. **devisor, devisee,** *nn.* one by, to, whom estate is left. (L. *dividere,* divide)

devitalize, *v.t.* deprive of vitality or vigour. **devitalization,** *n.*

devitrify, *v.t.* deprive of glassy quality, make opaque. **devitrification,** *n.*

devoid, *a.* destitute, empty (of).

devoir, *n.* duty, one's best; (*pl.*) civilities. (L. *debēre,* owe)

devolute, *v.t.* delegate (work). **devolution,** *n.* devolving; deputing of power from Parliament to subsidiary bodies, decentralization; retrograde development (opp. to evolution); descent of property. **devolve,** *v.t.* and *i.* transfer, hand down; pass in succession. (L. *volvere,* roll)

Devonian, *a.* of Devon; (*geol.*) between Silurian and Carboniferous.

devote, *v.t* dedicate, set apart; give (oneself) to. **devoted,** *a.* attached, fond; doomed to destruction. **devotee,** *n.* zealous follower, votary. **devotion,** *n.* strong affection; attachment, loyalty; religious worship; (*pl.*) prayers. **devotional,** *a.* of devotions. (L. *vovēre,* vow)

devour, *v.t.* eat up, eat greedily; consume utterly, overwhelm; read, gaze at, eagerly. (L. *vorare,* swallow)

devout, *a.* deeply religious, pious; earnest. (*devote*)

dew, *n.* moisture from air deposited in drops at night; freshness; tears.—*v.i.* and *t.* form dew; bedew. **mountain d.,** illicitly distilled whisky. **d.-claw,** *n.* rudimentary inner toe of dog. **d.-point,** *n.* temperature at which dew condenses. **d.-pond,** *n.* ancient artificial pond on downs. (O.E. *déaw*)

dewan, *n.* native prime minister or minister of finance in India; native business manager or major-domo. **dewani,** *n.* his office. (Arab. *diwan*)

dewberry, *n.* kind of blackberry.

dewlap, *n.* thick fold of skin hanging from throat of cattle.

dewy, *a.* wet with dew; fresh.

dexter, *a.* right; (*heraldry*) to viewer's left. **dexterity,** *n.* deftness, skill; right-handedness. **dexterous,** *a.* neat-handed, deft; clever; right-handed. **dextral,** *a.* (of shell) with whorls going to right. **dextrin, dextrine,** *n.* gum made from starch.

dextrorotation, *n.* right-handed or clockwise rotation. **dextrorotatory,** *a.* **dextrose,** *n.* starch-sugar. **dextrorse,** *a.* (*bot.*) twining spirally from left to right. **dextrous,** *a.* dexterous. (L.)

dey, *n.* governor of Algiers before French conquest. (Turk. *dāī*, uncle)

dhak, dhawk, *n.* E. Indian tree with brilliant flowers. (Hind.)

dhal, *n.* (*Anglo-Ind.*) split pulse; porridge of this. (Hind.)

dharma, *n.* law of Buddha; virtue, righteousness. **dharmsala,** *n.* traveller's rest-house. (Sanskr.)

dhobi, *n.* (*Anglo-Ind.*) native washerman. (Hind.)

dhole, *n.* Indian wild dog. (Hind.)

dhoti, dhooti, *n.* Hindu loin-cloth. (Hind.)

dhow, *n.* Arab ship with single mast and lateen sail, commonly slaver.

dhurra, same as **durra.**

dhurrie, dhurry, *n.* Indian cotton carpet with fringed ends. (Hind. *dari*)

di-, *pref.* two, double, as in **diarchy.** (Gk. *dis*, twice)

di-, same as **dis-.**

dia-, di-, *pref.* through, as in **diameter**; apart, as in **diaeresis**; across, as in **diaphragm.** (Gk.)

diabetes, *n.* emaciating disease, us. marked by sugar in urine. **diabetic,** *a.* and *n.* (victim) of diabetes. (Gk. *dia*, through; *bainein*, go)

diablerie, *n.* devil's work, sorcery; devil-lore; mischief. (F.)

diabolic, diabolical, *aa.* devilish, fiendish. **diabolism,** *n.* devil-worship, sorcery; devilish conduct. **diabolize,** *v.t.* make into, represent as, devil. (Gk. *diabolos*, devil)

diabolo, *n.* game of whirling reel on string between two sticks. (coined)

diachylon, diachylum, *n.* kind of sticking-plaster. (Gk. *dia chulōn*, by juices)

diaconal, *a.* of a deacon. **diaconate,** *n.* office of deacon; deacons collectively. (*deacon*)

diacritical, *a.* distinguishing, distinctive (esp. of accents etc. attached to letters). (*critic*)

diactinic, *a.* transparent to actinic rays. (Gk. *dia*, through)

diaculum, same as **diachylon.**

diadelphous, *a.* with stamens in two bundles. (Gk. *dis*, twice; *adelphos*, brother)

diadem, *n.* crown, headband, as badge of royalty; sovereignty. (Gk. *dia*, across; *dein*, bind)

diaeresis, *n.* mark over second of two vowels, showing they are not one sound, as in 'coöperate.' (Gk. *dia*, apart; *hairein*, take)

diagnose, *v.t.* make diagnosis of. **diagnosis,** *n.* (*pl.* **diagnoses**) identification of disease by symptoms; critical scrutiny, judgment based on it. **diagnostic,** *a.* of, aiding, diagnosis.—*n.* symptom. **diagnostician,** *n.* (Gk. *dia*, between; *gignōskein*, know)

diagonal, *a.* crossing from corner to corner, oblique.—*n.* diagonal line. (Gk. *dia*, through; *gōnia*, angle)

diagram, *n.* plan or figure illustrating statement, proof etc. **diagrammatic,** *a.* **diagrammatize,** *v.t.* put in form of diagram. (Gk. *dia*, through; *graphein*, write)

diagraph, *n.* instrument for enlarging maps etc. mechanically. (*diagram*)

dial, *n.* face of clock; indicating plate of gauge or meter; sun-dial; (*sl.*) human face.—*v.t.* measure, indicate, with dial; call on automatic telephone. (L. *dies*, day)

dialect, *n.* subordinate variety of a language. **class, regional, d.,** peculiar to particular class, district. **dialectal,** *a.* (Gk. *dia*, between; *legein*, speak)

dialectic, *n.* (often *pl.*) art of logical discussion, debating method.—*a.* (also **dialectical**) of dialectics; dialectal. **dialectician,** *n.* logician. (*dialect*)

dialectology, *n.* study of dialects.

dialogue, *n.* conversation; literary representation of this. **dialogic,** *a.* **dialogist,** *n.* (Gk. *dialogos*)

dialyse, *v.t.* separate crystalline from colloid parts of mixture by filtration. **dialysis** *n.* (*pl.* **dialyses**) this process. **dialytic,** *a.* (Gk. *dia*, apart; *luein*, loose)

diamagnetic, *a.* cross-magnetic, tending to point east and west. **diamagnetism,** *n.*

diamanté, *a.* and *n.* (material) glittering with powdered crystal. (F.)

diamantiferous, *a.* diamond-bearing.

diameter, *n.* straight line from side to side through centre of circle etc.; transverse measurement, thickness; unit of magnifying-power. **diametral,** *a.* **diametrical,** *a.* of diameter; exactly opposite. **diametrically,** *adv.* (Gk. *dia*, through; *metron*, measure)

diamond, *n.* a precious stone, hardest substance known; lozenge-shaped figure, rhombus; a suit at cards; (*print.*) 4½-point type, smaller than pearl.—*a.* set with, shaped like, diamond. **black dd.,** coals. **d. cut d.,** astuteness meets its match. **d. jubilee, wedding,** 60th anniversary. **rough d.,** worthy but unpolished person. **d.-drill, d.-point,** *nn.* tools tipped with diamond. (Gk. *adamas*)

Diana, *n.* moon-goddess; huntress, horsewoman. (L.)

diapason, *n.* loud burst of harmony; gamut, entire compass; organ-stop extending through whole scale. (Gk. *dia pasōn*, through all)

diaper, *n.* geometric pattern; fine linen marked with this; small towel, napkin.—*v.t.* decorate with diaper. (Gk. *dia*, through; *aspros*, white)

diaphanous, *a.* transparent. (Gk. *dia,* through; *phainein,* show)
diaphoretic, *a.* and *n.* (drug) causing profuse perspiration. (Gk. *dia,* through; *pherein,* carry)
diaphragm, *n.* muscular partition between abdomen and chest; vibrating disk in telephone or radio. **diaphragmatic,** *a.* (Gk. *dia,* across; *phrassein,* fence)
diarchy, dyarchy, *n.* government by two independent authorities. (Gk. *dis,* doubly; *archē,* rule)
diarist, *n.* one who keeps a diary. **diaristic,** *a.* **diarize,** *v.i.* and *t.*
diarrhoea, *n.* excessive looseness of bowels. **diarrhoeal,** *a.* (Gk. *dia,* through; *rhein,* flow)
diary, *n.* daily record, journal; book for this. **diarial,** *a.* (L. *dies,* day)
diastase, *n.* digestive ferment turning starch into sugar. **diastatic,** *a.* (Gk. *dia,* through: *histanai,* place)
diástolĕ, *n.* dilatation of heart and arteries, alternating with systole. **diastolic,** *a.* (Gk.)
diatessaron, *n.* combination of the four Gospels into single narrative. (Gk. *dia tessarōn,* by four)
diathermancy, *n.* property of transmitting radiant heat. **diathermanous, diathermic,** *aa.* having this. (Gk. *dia,* through; *thermos,* warm)
diathesis, *n.* constitutional tendency, predisposing factor. (Gk.)
diatom, *n.* minute one-celled water-plant. **diatomaceous,** *a.* (Gk. *dia,* through; *temnein,* cut)
diatomic, *a.* (*chem.*) of two atoms. (Gk. *dis,* doubly)
diatonic, *a.* (of scale) regular major or minor; (of melody) composed in such a scale. (Gk *diatonikos,* with intervals of a tone)
diatribe, *n.* violently critical speech, invective, denunciation. (Gk. *dia,* through; *tribein,* rub)
dib, *n.* knuckle-bone; (*pl.*) child's game with these; money.
dib, same as **dap.**
dibasic, *a.* (*chem.*) with two bases or two atoms of a base. (Gk. *dis,* twice)
dibber, *n.* dibble. (*dib*)
dibble, *n.* tool for making holes for seeds etc.—*v.t.* plant with dibble.
dicast, *n.* Athenian juryman. (Gk. *dikē,* right)
dice, see **die.**
dicephalous, *a.* two-headed. (Gk. *dis,* twice; *kephalē,* head)
dichlamydeous, *a.* having calyx and corolla. (Gk. *dis,* twice; *chlamus,* cloak)
dichogamous, *a.* with stamens and pistils maturing at different times, preventing self-fertilization. **dichogamy,** *n.* (Gk. *dicha,* apart; *gamos,* marriage)
dichotomy, *n.* division into two; (*bot.*) repeated forking. **dichotomic, dichotomous,** *aa.* (Gk. *dicha,* apart; *temnein,* cut)
dichroic, *a.* (of crystal) showing two colours. **dichroism,** *n.* (Gk. *dis,* twice; *chrōs,* colour)
dichromatic, *a.* two-coloured. **dichromic,** *a.* seeing only two of the three primary colours. **dichromism,** *n.* (Gk. *dis,* twice; *chrōma,* colour)
dicht, *v.t.* and *n.* (*Scot.*) wipe.
dick, *n.* (*sl.*) **take one's d.,** swear.
dick, *n.* (*sl.*) detective.
dickens, *n.* (*colloq.*) deuce.
dicker, *v.i.* (*Amer.*) haggle, chaffer.
dicky, dickey, *n.* false shirt-front; seat at back of carriage or car; (*sl.*) donkey. **d.-bird,** *n.* small bird.
dicky, *a.* shaky, unsound.
dicotyledon, *n.* plant with two seed-leaves. **dicotyledonous,** *a.* (*di-*)
dicrotic, *a.* double-beating. **dicrotism,** *n.* (Gk. *dis,* twice; *krotos,* beat)
dicta, see **dictum.**
dictaphone, *n.* machine recording dictation and later reproducing it for typist. (*dictate*)
dictate, *v.t.* and *i.* say or read (matter to be written down; prescribe, give peremptory orders (to).—*n.* (us. *pl.*) commands. **dictation,** *n.* dictating, passage dictated. **dictator,** *n.* (*fem.* **dictatress**) absolute ruler, us. temporary. **dictatorial,** *a.* of dictator; imperious, overbearing. **dictatorship,** *n.* (L. *dicere,* say)
diction, *n.* wording, phraseology, verbal style. (L. *dicere,* say)
dictionary, *n.* book with list of words and their meanings, lexicon; informative work, similarly arranged, on special subject. **d. English,** pedantic. (*diction*)
dictograph, *n.* sound-recording instrument much used for eavesdropping. (L. *dicere,* say. Gk. *graphein,* write)
dictum, *n.* (*pl.* **dicta, dictums**) saying, maxim, formal pronouncement. (L.)
did, see **do.**
didactic, *a.* meant to teach, instructive; having manner of schoolmaster. **didactically,** *adv.* **didacticism,** *n.* (Gk. *didaskein,* teach)
didapper, *n.* dabchick. (*dive; dap*)
diddle, *v.t.* (*sl.*) cheat, swindle.
diddle, *v.i.* (*Scot.*) jog, sway.
dido, *n.* (*Amer. sl.*) prank, caper.
didymium, *n.* a rare metal. (Gk. *didumos,* twin, as found with lanthanum)
die, *v.i.* (*pres. part.* **dying**) cease to live, perish; wither. **d. away,** fade gradually. **d. game,** keep up spirit to last. **d. off,** die in large numbers. **d. out,** become extinct. **d.-hard,** *n.* rabid Tory. **dying to,** wildly eager to. (M.E. *deyen*)
die, *n.* (*pl.* **dice**) small cube numbered one to six on faces; (*pl.*) gambling with dice; (*pl.* **dies**) stamp for coining, embossing etc.; screw-cutting tool; (*archit.*) main block of pedestal

the d. is cast, great decision is made. **dice,** *v.i.* gamble with dice. **dice-box,** *n.* for throwing dice. **dicer,** *n.* (L. *dare,* give)

dielectric, *a.* non-conducting.—*n.* insulator. (Gk. *dia,* through)

dies, **n.** day. *d. faustus, infaustus,* lucky, unlucky, day. *d. irae,* Day of Judgment; a hymn. *d. non,* day that does not count, or on which no legal business is transacted. (L.)

Diesel engine, internal combustion engine using crude oil. (inventor)

diet, *n.* assembly; foreign parliament; (*Scot.*) religious service. (L.L. *dieta,* day's work)

diet, *n.* what one eats; prescribed course of food.—*v.t.* and *i.* keep to diet. **dietary,** *a.* of diet.—*n.* allowance of food in workhouse etc. **dietetic,** *a.* of diet.—*n.pl.* science of diet. (Gk. *diaita,* way of life)

dif-, for **dis-** before *f.*

differ, *v.i.* be different; disagree. **difference,** (*Shake.*) **differency,** *n.* unlikeness; amount of this; distinguishing mark; disagreement. **different,** *a.* unlike, dissimilar; various. (L. *dis-,* apart; *ferre,* bear)

differentia, *n.* (*pl.* **differentiae**) what distinguishes a thing from others.

differential, *a.* distinctive, special; varying with circumstances.—*n.* (also **d. gear**) mechanism permitting hind wheels of motor-car to revolve at different speeds when rounding corner. **d. calculus,** method of calculating rate of change for continuously varying quantities.

differentiate, *v.t.* and *i.* distinguish, discriminate; develop into unlikeness. **differentiation,** *n.*

difficile, **a.** hard to get on with, exacting, unaccommodating. (F.)

difficult, *a.* hard to do or understand; troublesome, not easy; touchy, exacting. **difficulty,** *n.* being difficult; hindrance; obscurity; embarrassment; demur (L. *facultas,* means)

diffident, *a.* lacking self-confidence, modest, shy. **diffidence,** *n.* shyness; (*Shake.*) suspicion. (L. *fides,* faith)

diffluent, *a.* flowing apart; becoming fluid. **diffluence,** *n.* (*dif-*)

diffract, *v.t.* break up (beam of light) into series of dark and light bands or coloured spectra. **diffraction,** *n.* this process, caused by slit or edge of opaque body. **diffrangible,** *a.* able to be diffracted. (L. *frangere,* break)

diffuse, *v.t.* and *i.* shed, give forth; mix by diffusion.—*a.* spread out, not concentrated; wordy, not concise. **diffusible, diffusive,** *aa.* **diffusion,** *n.* (L. *fundere,* pour)

dig, *v.t.* (*past, p.p.* **dug,** *obs.* **digged**) break up (ground), excavate; make research; thrust into, poke; (*Amer. sl.*) study hard.—*n.* piece of digging; poke, nudge; taunt. **d. in,** mix with soil; entrench. **d. out, up,** reveal, remove, by digging.

digamist, *n.* one who marries for second time. **digamous** *a.* **digamy,** *n.* (Gk. *dis,* twice; *gamos,* marriage)

digastric, *a.* with two swollen ends. (Gk. *dis,* twice; *gastēr,* belly)

digest, *v.t.* and *i.* change (food) into absorbable form; take in, reflect on; arrange methodically, classify; stomach (insult).—*n.* methodical summary, compendium, esp. of laws. **digestible,** *a.* wholesome. **digestion,** *n.* digesting; capacity for this. **digestive,** *a.* of, aiding, digestion. (L. *dis-,* apart; *gerere,* bear)

digger, *n.* one who digs, esp. for gold; (*sl.*) Australian. **diggings,** *n.pl.* goldfield; (*colloq.*) lodgings; (*Amer. colloq.*) place.

dight, *v.t.* (*past, p.p.* same) deck, array. (L. *dictare,* dictate)

dight, same as **dicht.**

digit, *n.* finger or toe; finger's breadth, $\frac{3}{4}$ in.; any of the figures 0–9; (*astron.*) $\frac{1}{12}$ of sun's or moon's diameter. **digital,** *a.* (L. *digitus*)

digitalis, *n.* heart-stimulant got from foxglove. (Mod. L.=foxglove)

digitate, digitated, *aa.* having separate fingers or toes. **digitigrade,** *a.* (*zool.*) walking on toes. (*digit*)

dignify, *v.t.* do honour to, exalt. **dignified,** *a.* stately. **dignitary,** *n.* holder of high office, esp. in church. **dignity,** *n.* grave stateliness; high office, rank, or repute; worthiness. (L. *dignus,* worthy; *facere,* make)

digraph, *n.* group of two letters expressing one sound, e.g. *ph.* (Gk. *dis,* twice; *graphein,* write)

digress, *v.i.* turn aside, stray; depart temporarily from main theme. **digression,** *n.* **digressive,** *a.* (L. *dis-,* apart; *gradi,* walk)

dihedral, *a.* with two plane faces. (Gk. *dis,* twice; *hedra,* base)

dik-dik, *n.* small African antelope.

dike, dyke, *n.* ditch; low wall; embankment against flood; causeway. —*v.t.* supply with dikes. (O.E. *dic*)

dilapidate, *v.t.* and *i.* bring, fall, into disrepair. **dilapidated,** *a.* decayed, in ruins; shabby, down-at-heel. **dilapidation,** *n.* being dilapidated; wear and tear of church property during incumbency. (L. *dis-,* apart; *lapis,* stone)

dilate, *v.t.* and *i.* make, grow, larger; expand, widen; expatiate, speak at length. **dilatation, dilation,** *nn.* **dilator,** *n.* (*anat.*) dilating muscle. (L. *dis-,* apart; *latus,* wide)

dilatory, *a.* tending to delay; tardy, belated. (L. *differre,* defer)

dilemma, *n.* position giving choice of evils, awkward predicament. **dilemmatic,** *a.* (Gk. *dis,* twice; *lēmma,* assumption)

dilettante, *n.* (*pl.* **dilettanti**) amateur of art or letters, dabbler.—*a.* amateurish, desultory. **dilettantish,** *a.* **dilettantism,** *n.* (It.)

diligence, *n.* steady application, industry; foreign stage-coach or motor-coach. **diligent,** *a.* industrious, hard-working. (L. *diligere,* love)

dill, *n.* yellow-flowered herb. (O.E. *dili*)

dilly-dally, *v.i.* (*colloq.*) hesitate, vacillate. (*dally*)

dilute, *v.t.* thin, make weaker, by adding water; weaken.—*a.* diluted; washed-out. **d. labour,** substitute proportion of women or unskilled men for skilled workers. **diluent,** *a.* and *n.* diluting (agent). **dilution,** *n.* (L. *dis-*, apart; *luere,* wash)

diluvium, *n.* flood; (*geol.*) deposit due to catastrophic water-action. **diluvial,** *a.* of flood; (*geol.*) of the glacial drift. (L.)

dim, *a.* faint, not bright; indistinct, obscure; not seeing clearly.—*v.t.* and *i.* make, grow, dim; outshine. (O.E.)

dime, *n.* American ten-cent piece. **d. novel,** cheap shocker. (L. *decem,* ten)

dimension, *n.* measurement; (*pl.*) size, extent, scope. **dimensional,** *a.* (L. *dis-*, apart; *metiri,* measure)

dimerous, *a.* (*bot.*) consisting of two parts. (Gk. *dis,* twice; *meros,* part)

dimeter, *n.* verse of two measures, a measure being one or two feet, according to the metre. **dimetric,** *a.* (Gk. *dis,* twice; *metron,* measure)

dimidiate, *a.* halved, split in two. (L. *dimidium,* half)

diminish, *v.t.* and *i.* make, become, smaller; lessen; (*archit.*) taper. **diminished,** *a.* humbled. *diminuendo,* *a.* and *n.* (*mus., abbr. dim.*) (passage) getting gradually softer. **diminution,** *n.* lessening. **diminutive,** *a.* very small, tiny; (*gram.*) expressing smallness or youngness.—*n.* diminutive word. (L. *dis-*, apart; *minuere,* lessen)

dimissory, *a.* giving leave to depart. (*dismiss*)

dimity, *n.* strong striped or figured cotton cloth used for curtains etc. (Gk. *dis,* twice; *mitos,* warp-thread)

dimorphism, *n.* difference of form or colour between members of same species. **dimorphic, dimorphous,** *aa.* (Gk. *dis,* twice; *morphē,* form)

dimple, *n.* small hollow in cheek etc.; ripple, indentation.—*v.t.* and *i.* form dimples in; show dimples.

din, *n.* loud continued noise.—*v.t.* and *i.* assail with, make, din; obtrude noisily. (O.E. *dyne*)

dinar, *n.* Serbian monetary unit or franc; old oriental coin. (*denarius*)

dine, *v.i.* and *t.* take dinner; give dinner to. **d. with Duke Humphrey,** go without meal. **dining-room,** *n.* used for meals. **diner,** *n.* one who dines; railway restaurant-car. (F. *dîner*)

ding, *v.t.* and *i.* hurl, dash, beat; fall; (*Scot.*) defeat, be defeated.

ding, *v.i.* and *t.* ring, keep sounding; nag. **d.-dong,** *n.* sound of bells.—*a.* closely contested. (imit.)

dinges, *n.* (*S. Afr.*) thingummy. (Du. *ding,* thing)

dinghy, dingey, *n.* small boat carried by ship. (Hind. *dengi,* boat)

dingle, *n.* wooded hollow, deep dell.

dingo, *n.* Australian wild dog. (native)

dingy, *a.* dull, grimy, dirty-looking.

dinic, *a.* of dizziness. (Gk. *dinos,* whirling)

dink, *a.* (*Scot.*) braw, trim.

dinkum, *a.* (*Austral.*) genuine, honest. —*n.* work. **d. oil,** honest truth.

dinky, *a.* (*colloq.*) neat, smart, attractive.

dinna, *Scot.* form of **do not.**

dinner, *n.* chief meal of day, taken at midday or evening; banquet. **d.-jacket,** *n.* less formal dress-coat, without tails. **d.-wagon,** *n.* movable sideboard. (*dine*)

dino-, from Gk. *deinos,* terrible, used in **dinoceras,** *n.* huge extinct horned animal; **dinornis,** *n.* large extinct bird like ostrich; **dinosaur,** *n.* gigantic extinct reptile; **dinothere, dinotherium,** *n.* huge extinct animal like elephant.

dint, *n.* mark left by blow, dent; (*arch.*) stroke.—*v.t.* make dint in. by **d. of,** by force of. (O.E. *dynt*)

diocese, *n.* bishop's district. **diocesan,** *a.* of diocese.—*n.* bishop; member of diocese. (Gk. *dia,* through; *oikos,* house)

dioecious, *a.* (*bot., zool.*) having male and female organs respectively in separate individuals. (Gk. *dis,* twice; *oikos,* house)

diopter, dioptre, *n.* unit of refractive power, equal to that of lens with focal length of one metre. **dioptric,** *a.* aiding sight by refraction; refractive.—*n.pl.* science of refraction of light. (Gk. *dia,* through; *opsis,* sight)

diorama, *n.* scenic picture with effects given by special lighting; exhibition of these. **dioramic,** *a.* (Gk. *dia,* through; *horaein,* see)

dioxide, *n.* compound of two parts of oxygen with one of metal. (Gk. *dis,* twice)

dip, *v.t.* and *i.* plunge for a moment into liquid, immerse; dye, wash; scoop (up); lower and raise (flag); sink, slope down.—*n.* immersion; inclination; short bathe; tallow candle. **d. into,** glance at, study cursorily. (O.E. *dyppan*)

diphtheria, *n.* acute infectious disease in which throat becomes coated with membrane. **diphtherial, diphtheric, diphtheritic,** *aa.* (Gk. *diphthera,* hide)

diphthong, *n.* two vowels forming compound sound, e.g. *oi* in 'oil'; digraph, ligature. **diphthongal,** *a.*

diphthongize, *v.t.* (Gk. *dis,* twice; *phthonggos,* sound)
diplo-, from Gk. *diplos,* double, used in **diploblastic,** *a.* with two germ layers; **diplodocus,** *n.* extinct reptile with enormous tail and small head; **diplogen,** *n.* deuterium.
diploma, *n.* certificate of proficiency; document conferring privilege. **diplomacy,** *n.* management of international relations; skill in this; tact. **diplomaed, diploma'd,** *a.* holding a diploma. **diplomat, diplomatist,** *nn.* member of diplomatic service; adroit negotiator. **diplomatic,** *a.* of diplomacy or foreign legations; tactful, uncandid.—*n.pl.* science of deciphering ancient documents, palaeography. **diplomatically,** *adv.* **diplomatize,** *v.i.* act as diplomatist. (Gk. = folded paper)
diplon, *n.* deuteron.
dipnoad, *a.* and *n.* (fish) with both gills and lungs. (Gk. *dis,* twice; *pnoē* breath)
dipper, *n.* ladle; water-ouzel; Baptist; (*Amer.*) Great Bear. **dippy,** *a.* (*sl.*) crazy.
dipsomania, *n.* uncontrollable craving for alcohol. **dipsomaniac,** *n.* victim of this. **dipsomaniacal,** *a.* **dipsosis,** *n.* morbid thirst. (Gk. *dipsa,* thirst)
dipteral, *a.* with double peristyle. **dipterous,** *a.* two-winged. (Gk. *dis,* twice; *pteron,* wing)
diptych, *n.* ancient folding writing-tablet; painting, esp. altar-piece, on two leaves hinged together. (Gk. *dis,* twice; *ptussein,* fold)
dirdum, *n.* (*Scot.*) uproar, scolding.
dire, *a.* dreadful; disastrous. (L. *dirus*)
direct, *v.t.* and *i.* manage, control; order; turn, aim (towards); address (letter); inform of the way (to).—*a.* straight, not turned aside; immediate; straightforward, plain.—*adv.* in a straight line. **d. action,** social pressure by strikes or revolts. **d. speech,** (*gram.*) actual words, in first person. **direction,** *n.* directing, control; order, instruction; course, quarter. **direction-finder,** *n.* (*wireless*) apparatus for finding bearings of transmitting stations. **directional,** *a.* **directive,** *a.* giving guidance. **directly,** *adv.* straight; immediately, without delay.—*conj.* (*colloq.*) as soon as. (L. *dis-,* apart; *regere,* put straight)
directoire, *a.* imitating low-necked high-waisted dress or curving oriental furniture of Directory period. (F.)
director, *n.* (*fem.*) **directress, directrix**) supervisor; member of company's board of management; stage-manager of cinema film. **directorate,** *n.* board of directors. **directorship,** *n.* **directory,** *n.* book with names, addresses, telephone numbers etc. in district; book of directions; French revolutionary government 1795–9.
direful, *a.* dreadful, dire.
dirge, *n.* funeral song, lament. (L. *dirige,* lead thou, opening word of anthem in Latin office for dead)
dirigible, *a.* steerable (of balloon)—*n.* airship. (*direct*)
diriment, *a.* nullifying. (L. *dirimere,* interrupt)
dirk, *n.* kind of dagger or poniard.—*v.t.* stab with dirk.
dirl, *v.i.* (*Scot.*) thrill, vibrate.—*n.* vibration; tingling.
dirt, *n.* filth, dust; earth, soil: worthless things; foul talk, obscenity. **eat d.,** swallow insult. **d.-cheap,** *a.* very cheap. **d.-track,** *n.* of rolled earth earth for motor-cycle racing. **dirty,** *a.* covered with dirt; soiled, foul; base, mean; obscene; (of weather) stormy, wet.—*v.t.* and *i.* make, become, dirty. **do the dirty,** play shabby trick. (M.E. *drit*)
dirzi, *n.* (*Anglo-Ind.*) native tailor. (Pers. *darz,* sewing)
Dis, *n.* Pluto, god of underworld. (L.)
dis-, *pref.* apart, as in **dismiss**; not, the reverse of, as in **disapprove, disconnect**; deprive of, as in **disburden**; wholly, as in **disannul.** (L.)
disable, *v.t.* make unfit, incapacitate; cripple; (*law*) disqualify. **disablement,** *n.* **disability,** *n.* thing that disables; drawback.
disabuse, *v.t.* undeceive, disillusion.
disaccord, *v.i.* disagree, be at variance. —*n.* disagreement, incongruity.
disadvantage, *n.* unfavourable condition, drawback; loss, detriment. **disadvantageous,** *a.* unfavourable.
disaffected, *a.* estranged; disloyal, inclined to sedition. **disaffection,** *n.* political discontent.
disaffirm, *v.t.* (*law*) set aside, reverse. **disaffirmation,** *n.*
disafforest, *v.t.* reduce from legal state of forest to that of ordinary land. **disafforestation,** *n.*
disagree, *v.i.* differ, be unlike; dissent, quarrel. **d. with,** be unsuited to health of. **disagreeable,** *a.* unpleasant; bad-tempered. **disagreement,** *n.* difference; dispute.
disallow, *v.t.* refuse to sanction, reject, prohibit; (*Shake.*) disapprove.
disanimate, *v.t.* (*Shake.*) discourage.
disannul, *v.t.* annul completely.
disappear, *v.i.* pass from view, vanish; be lost. **disappearance,** *n.*
disappoint, *v.t.* fail to fulfil hopes of; vex thus; frustrate, belie; break appointment with. **disappointed,** *a.* (*Shake.*) unprepared. **disappointing,** *a.* not up to expectations. **disappointment,** *n.* event that disappoints, distress resulting.
disapprobation, *n.* disapproval. **disapprobative, disapprobatory,** *aa.*
disapprove, *v.t.* and *i.* form, express, unfavourable opinion (of). **disapproval,** *n.*
disarm, *v.t.* and *i.* deprive of weapons;

dismantle; reduce armaments (of); conciliate, render harmless. **disarmament,** *n.* abandonment or reduction of warlike establishment.

disarrange, *v.t.* make untidy; disorganize. **disarrangement,** *n.*

disarray, *v.t.* throw into confusion; undress.—*n.* disorder.

disarticulate, *v.t.* separate, take to pieces. **disarticulation,** *n.*

disassociation, same as **dissociation.**

disaster, *n.* great and sudden misfortune, calamity; ill luck. **disastrous,** *a.* calamitous. (L. *dis-*, apart; *astrum*, star)

disaventrous, *a.* (*Spens.*) unfortunate, unhappy. **disaventure,** *n.* (*Spens.*) mishap, misfortune. (*adventure*)

disavow, *v.t.* disown, deny knowledge of, repudiate. **disavowal,** *n.*

disband, *v.t.* and *i.* break up, disperse (troops). **disbandment,** *n.*

disbar, *v.t.* deprive of status of barrister. **disbarment,** *n.*

disbelieve, *v.t.* and *i.* refuse to believe; be a sceptic. **disbelief,** *n.*

disbench, *v.t.* deprive of membership of an Inn of Court.

disbranch, *v.t.* remove branches from.

disburden, *v.t.* and *i.* relieve of load; ease mind (of).

disburse, *v.t.* and *i.* pay out (money). **disbursement,** *n.* (*bourse*)

disc, see **disk.**

discalceate, discalceated, discalced, *aa.* barefoot, wearing sandals. (L. *dis-*, apart; *calceus*, shoe)

discandy, *v.t.* (*Shake.*) thaw.

discard, *v.t.* and *i.* throw out (card) from hand; cast aside, give up; dismiss.—*n.* discarding, card thrown out.

discarnate, *a.* having no body. (L. *dis-*, apart; *caro*, flesh)

discern, *v.t.* perceive, make out; distinguish. **discernible,** *a.* **discerning,** *a.* shrewd; discriminating. **discernment,** *n.* insight, penetration. (L. *dis-*, apart; *cernere*, sift)

discerp, *v.t.* pluck apart; tear off, sever. **discerptible,** *a.* **discerption,** *n.* (L. *dis-*, apart; *carpere*, pluck)

discharge, *v.t.* and *i.* emit, eject; dismiss, release from service; unload (cargo); fire (gun); perform (duty); pay (debt); suppurate.—*n.* discharging, being discharged; matter from abscess; discharge certificate.

disciple, *n.* follower, adherent; one of the twelve apostles. **discipleship,** *n.* **discipular,** *a.* (L. *discere*, learn)

discipline, *n.* subjection to rule; obedience, self-control, order; training through correction or suffering; system of religious rules; (*arch.*) branch of instruction.—*v.t.* train to obedience; chastise. **disciplinary,** *a.* **disciplinarian,** *n.* maintainer of discipline. (*disciple*)

disclaim, *v.t.* and *i.* renounce right (in); repudiate, disown. **disclaimer,** *n.* renunciation, disavowal.

disclose, *v.t.* reveal, expose to view. **disclosure,** *n.* disclosing; revelation.

discobolus, *n.* discus-thrower. (L.)

discoid, *a.* round and flat like disk.

discolour, *v.t.* impair colour of, stain. —*v.i.* become discoloured. **discoloration, discolouration, discolourment,** *nn.*

discomfit, *v.t.* defeat, rout; disconcert, baffle. **discomfiture,** *n.* (L. *dis-*, not; *conficere*, prepare)

discomfort, *n.* want of comfort, uneasiness; (*Shake.*) sorrow.—*v.t.* make uneasy; (*Shake.*) discourage; grieve.

discommode, *v.t.* put to inconvenience.

discommon, *v.t.* enclose (common land).

discompose, *v.t.* disturb the calmness of; ruffle. **discomposure,** *n.*

disconcert, *v.t.* put out of countenance, embarrass; throw into confusion, upset. **disconcertment,** *n.*

disconnect, *v.t.* sever connection of, disjoin. **disconnected,** *a.* incoherent; unrelated. **disconnection, disconnexion,** *n.*

disconsolate, *a.* forlorn, inconsolable, deeply dejected. (*console*)

discontent, *n.* dissatisfaction, aggrieved state.—*a.* discontented. **discontented,** *a.* dissatisfied, not pleased. **discontentment,** *n.*

discontiguous, *a.* not in contact.

discontinue, *v.t.* and *i.* leave off, intermit, cease. **discontinuance, discontinuation,** *nn.* **discontinuous,** *a.* not continuous, intermittent, interrupted. **discontinuity,** *n.*

discord, *n.* disagreement, strife; harsh noise; (*mus.*) combination of notes which do not harmonize.—*v.i.* disagree; jar, clash. **discordant,** *a.* conflicting; unmusical. **discordance,** *n.* (L. *dis-*, not; *cor*, heart)

discount, *n.* deduction from price for prompt payment etc.; deduction made for interest when discounting bill.—*v.t.* advance, receive, money for (bill of exchange not yet due); lessen, depreciate; use up effect of beforehand; allow for exaggeration in. **at a d.,** below par; out of favour.

discountenance, *v.t.* refuse moral support to, discourage, frown upon.

discourage, *v.t.* dishearten, depress; deter; discountenance. **discouragement,** *n.*

discourse, *n.* lecture, sermon; treatise; conversation.—*v.i.* and *t.* hold forth, lecture; (*Shake.*) tell, utter.

discourteous, *a.* ill-mannered, rude. **discourtesy,** *n.* incivility.

discover, *v.t.* find out, realize; (*arch.*) reveal, disclose.

discovert, *a.* (*law*) without a husband. (O.F. *descovert*, uncovered)

discovery, *n.* discovering, disclosure; find.

discredit, *v.t.* refuse to believe; damage credibility or reputation of.—*n.* loss of repute, reproach; doubt. **discreditable,** *a.* damaging; shameful.

discreet, *a.* prudent, circumspect; avoiding even appearance of evil. (=*discrete*)

discrepant, *a.* inconsistent, not tallying. **discrepancy,** *n.* (L. *dis-*, apart; *crepare*, sound)

discrete, *a.* separate, disunited, discontinuous. (L. *dis-*, apart; *cernere*, sift)

discretion, *n.* discreetness, prudence; freedom to act as one thinks fit. **at the d. of,** depending on decision made by. **surrender at d.,** unconditionally. **years of d.,** time at which one becomes responsible person (14 in English law). **discretionary,** *a.* left to discretion; unrestricted.

discriminate, *v.t.* and *i.* observe or mark differences (between), distinguish; treat differently. **discriminating,** *a.* discerning, acute. **discrimination,** *n.* penetration, discernment. **discriminative,** *a.* making distinctions. (L. *discrimen*, distinction)

discrown, *v.t.* depose, dethrone.

discursive, *a.* rambling, not sticking to main subject; (*philos.*) proceeding by reasoning, not intuitive. (L. *dis-*, apart; *currere*, run)

discus, *n.* large quoit thrown in athletic contest at Olympic Games. (L.)

discuss, *v.t.* debate, examine by argument; consume (food). **discussible,** *a.* **discussion,** *n.* discussing; argument. (L. *dis-*, apart; *quatere*, shake)

disdain, *v.t.* scorn, think beneath one. —*n.* contempt; lofty aloofness. **disdainful,** *a.* (L. *de-*, un-; *dignus*, worthy)

disease, *n.* illness, disorder; malady. **diseased,** *a.* ill, unhealthy.

disedge, *v.t.* (*Shake.*) take the edge off appetite of.

disembark, *v.t.* and *i.* put, go, ashore from ship. **disembarkation,** *n.*

disembarrass, *v.t.* free from embarrassment; relieve (of); disentangle. **disembarrassment,** *n.*

disembody, *v.t.* divest of body; free from concrete; disband. **disembodiment,** *n.*

disembogue, *v.i.* and *t.* (of river etc.) discharge, pour forth. (Sp. *des-*, apart; *en*, in; *boca*, mouth)

disembosom, *v.t.* reveal; unburden (oneself).

disembowel, *v.t.* remove bowels from, gut; wound so as to show entrails. **disembowelment,** *n.*

disembroil, *v.t.* extricate from confusion or entanglement.

disenchant, *v.t.* free from spell, disillusion; dispel glamour of. **disenchantment,** *n.*

disencumber, *v.t.* free from burden or hindrance.

disendow, *v.t.* deprive (esp. Church) of endowments. **disendowment,** *n.*

disengage, *v.t.* and *i.* unfasten, come apart; release. **disengaged,** *a.* at liberty; vacant. **disengagement,** *n.*

disentail, *v.t.* free from entail.

disentangle, *v.t.* and *i.* unravel, untwist; free from confusion, straighten out. **disentanglement,** *n.*

disenthral, disenthrall, *v.t.* free from bondage, emancipate. **disenthralment,** *n.*

disentomb, *v.t.* remove from tomb; unearth; find out by research.

disentrail, *v.t.* (*Spens.*) draw forth, cause to flow.

disestablish, *v.t.* displace from settled position; sever (Church) from connection with State. **disestablishment,** *n.*

disesteem, *n.* and *v.t.* disfavour, dislike.

diseur, *n.* (*fem. diseuse*) reciter. (F.)

disfavour, *n.* disapproval, distaste; being out of favour.—*v.t.* regard with disfavour, discountenance.

disfeature, *v.t.* disfigure.

disfigure, *v.t.* impair appearance of; mar, deface. **disfiguration,** *n.* disfiguring. **disfigurement,** *n.* blemish, defect.

disforest, *v.t.* clear of trees; disafforest.

disfranchise, *v.t.* deprive of vote; deprive (place) of right to return M.P. **disfranchisement,** *n.*

disfrock, *v.t.* expel from clergy.

disgorge, *v.t.* and *i.* eject, pour forth; make restitution (of), give up.

disgrace, *n.* shame, dishonour; loss of favour; cause of shame, reproach.—*v.t.* bring shame upon; degrade. **disgraceful,** *a.* shameful. **disgracious,** *a.* (*Shake.*) out of favour.

disgruntled, *a.* discontented, sulky. (*grunt*)

disguise, *v.t.* change appearance of; make unrecognizable; conceal, cloak. —*n.* false appearance or dress; assumed manner.

disgust, *n.* strong distaste, loathing, nausea; keen disappointment.—*v.t.* cause disgust in. **disgustful,** *a.* (L. *dis-*, apart; *gustare*, taste)

dish, *n.* flat shallow vessel; food in this; kind of food.—*v.t.* put into dish, serve; frustrate, outmanœuvre. **d. of tea,** (*arch.*) cup of tea. **d. up,** present. **made d.,** of many ingredients. **d.-clout, d.-water,** *nn.* used for washing dishes. (L. *discus*, disk)

dishabille, *n.* partly clad state, undress, *négligé.* (F. *déshabillé*)

dishabituate, *v.t.* make unaccustomed.

dishallucination, *n.* disillusionment.

disharmony, *n.* discord. **disharmonize,** *v.t.* put out of harmony; set at variance.

dishearten, *v.t.* discourage, make despondent. **disheartenment,** *n.*

disherison, *n.* disinheritance. (L. *dis-*, apart; *heres*, heir)

dishevelled, *a.* with hair in disorder; unkempt, untidy, tousled. **dishevelment,** *n.* (L. *dis-*, apart; *capillus*, hair)

dishonest, *a.* not honest, fraudulent;

disposed to cheat or steal; insincere; (*Shake.*) unchaste. **dishonesty,** *n.*

dishonour, *n.* disgrace, shame; reproach; indignity.—*v.t.* bring shame upon; insult; seduce; refuse to pay (cheque), repudiate. **dishonourable,** *a.* disgraceful, shameful; unprincipled, blackguardly.

dishorn, *v.t.* remove horns from.

dishouse, *v.t.* deprive of house.

disillusion, *v.t.* open eyes of, wake to unpleasant realities.—*n.* disenchantment. **disillusionize,** *v.t.* **disillusionment,** *n.*

disincline, *v.t.* make indisposed (to). **disinclination,** *n.* unwillingness, reluctance.

disincorporate, *v.t.* deprive of corporate rights.

disinfect, *v.t.* purge of infection or harmful germs. **disinfectant,** *a.* and *n.* disinfecting (agent). **disinfection,** *n.*

disingenuous, *a.* insincere, not candid or straightforward.

disinherit, *v.t.* deprive of inheritance; disown as heir. **disinheritance,** *n.*

disintegrate, *v.t.* and *i.* break up into component parts; lose cohesion. **disintegration, disintegrator,** *nn.*

disinter, *v.t.* take out of grave; bring out from obscurity, unearth. **disinterment,** *n.*

disinterest, *v.refl.* cease to concern (oneself). **disinterested,** *a.* free from self-seeking, impartial.

disjecta membra, scattered fragments. (L.)

disjoin, *v.t.* sunder, disunite.

disjoint, *v.t.* dislocate; take to pieces. **disjointed,** *a.* (of thought etc.) incoherent; disconnected.

disjunction, *n.* severance, disconnection. **disjunctive,** *a.* disjoining; alternative; (*gram.*) marking adverse sense.—*n.* disjunctive conjunction.

disk, disc, *n.* thin flat circular object. (Gk. *diskos,* quoit)

dislike, *v.t.* not like.—*n.* aversion.

disliken, *v.t.* (*Shake.*) disguise.

dislimn, *v.t.* (*Shake.*) efface, obliterate.

dislocate, *v.t.* put out of joint, displace; upset working of. **dislocation,** *n.*

dislodge, *v.t.* force, drive, out of position. **dislodgment, dislodgement,** *nn.*

disloyal, *a.* unfaithful; false to allegiance, disaffected. **disloyalist, disloyalty,** *nn.*

dismal, *a.* depressing, cheerless; gloomy, miserable.—*n.pl.* dumps. (L. *dies mali,* unlucky days)

dismantle, *v.t.* remove furnishings, equipment, or defences from. **dismantlement,** *n.*

dismast, *v.t.* deprive (ship) of mast or masts.

dismay, *n.* consternation, apprehension.—*v.t.* discourage; reduce to temporary despair; (*Spens.*) defeat, rout.

disme, *n.* (*Shake.*) tenth man sacrificed. (*dime*)

dismember, *v.t.* tear or cut limb from limb; partition (country). **dismemberment,** *n.*

dismiss, *v.t.* send away, disperse; expel from service, discharge; banish from mind; (*law*) refuse to hear (case) further. **dismissal, dismission,** *nn.* **dismissible,** *a.* (L. *dis-,* apart; *mittere,* send)

dismount, *v.i.* and *t.* alight from horseback; unhorse; remove from mounting.

disnatured, *a.* (*Shake.*) unnatural.

disobey, *v.t.* and *i.* not obey; disregard orders (of). **disobedience,** *n.* **disobedient,** *a.*

disoblige, *v.t.* ignore wishes of. **disobliging,** *a.* unaccommodating, inconsiderate.

disorder, *n.* confusion, untidiness; breach of laws, tumult; ailment, disease.—*v.t.* disarrange; upset. **disorderly,** *a.* untidy; unruly, riotous. **disorderly house,** brothel.

disorganize, *v.t.* upset system of, throw into disorder. **disorganization,** *n.*

disorientate, *v.t.* build (church) out of usual east and west alignment; cause to lose bearings, perplex. **disorientation,** *n.*

disown, *v.t.* deny ownership or authorship of, repudiate, disclaim.

disparage, *v.t.* speak slightingly of, belittle; (*arch.*) lower dignity of. **disparagement,** *n.* (*disparity*)

disparate, *a.* fundamentally different, with no basis for comparison.—*n.pl.* things of different kinds. (L. *dis-,* apart; *parare,* prepare+association with *dispar,* unequal)

disparity, *n.* inequality, incongruity. (L. *dis-,* not; *par,* equal)

dispark, *v.t.* throw open (enclosed land).

dispart, *v.t.* and *i.* separate, divide up.

dispart, *n.* difference between width of gun-barrel at breech and at muzzle; sight allowing for this.

dispassionate, *a.* unemotional, cool; unbiased.

dispatch, despatch, *v.t.* send off; transact promptly, settle; eat up; kill.—*n.* dispatching; official message, report; promptitude. **happy d.,** hara-kiri. **d.-box,** *n.* for carrying papers. **d.-rider,** *n.* mounted military messenger. (L. *dis-,* apart; *pangere,* fasten)

dispel, *v.t.* drive away. (L. *dis-,* apart; *pellere,* drive)

dispence, *v.t.* (*Spens.*) pay for.—*n.* (*Spens.*) expense.

dispense, *v.t.* and *i.* distribute, deal out; make up and issue (medicines); exempt. **d. with,** do without; render unnecessary. **dispensable,** *a.* able to be dispensed (with). **dispensary,** *n.* place where medicines are dispensed.

dispensation, *n.* dispensing; provision (of fate etc.); religious system; exemption from penalty or duty (esp. in R. C. Church). **dispenser,** *n.* maker-up of medicines. (L. *dis-*, apart: *pendere*, weigh)

dispeople, *v.t.* depopulate.

disperse, *v.t.* and *i.* scatter, dispel; drive asunder, spread abroad; divide (light) into its coloured rays. **dispersedly,** *adv.* at intervals, here and there. **dispersal, dispersion,** *nn.* (L. *dis-*, apart; *spargere*, scatter)

dispirit, *v.t.* make downcast, dishearten.

dispiteous, *a.* pitiless, ruthless. (*despite*+association with *pity*)

displace, *v.t.* move from its place; take place of; remove from office. **displacement,** *n.* displacing; amount of shift; weight of liquid displaced by a solid in it.

displant, *v.t.* (*Shake.*) uproot; depose.

display, *v.t.* show, exhibit; allow to appear.—*n.* displaying; things displayed; parade, ostentation.

displease, *v.t.* offend, annoy; arouse disapproval (of). **displeasing,** *a.* disagreeable; annoying. **displeasure,** *n.* resentment; anger, vexation; (*Shake.*) unpopularity; offence.

displume, *v.t.* strip of feathers.

disponge, *v.t.* (*Shake.*) squeeze out as if from sponge.

disport, *v.i.* and *refl.* frolic; amuse (oneself).—*n.* (*arch.*) pastime. (L. *dis-*, apart; *portare*, carry)

dispose, *v.t.* and *i.* arrange, settle; incline, make willing; bestow. **d. of,** get rid of, sell; finish off. **disposable,** *a.* **disposal,** *n.* disposing (of); control; arrangement; bestowal. (O.F. *dis-*, apart; *poser*, place)

disposition, *n.* arrangement; dispensation; tendency; nature, temperament; (*pl.*) plans. (L. *dis-*, apart; *ponere*, place)

dispossess, *v.t.* deprive, rid (of); eject. **dispossession, dispossessor,** *nn.*

dispraise, *v.t.* disparage; censure.—*n.* depreciation; reproach.

disproof, *n.* refutation.

disproperty, *v.t.* (*Shake.*) alienate (possession).

disproportion, *n.* want of proportion. **disproportionate,** *a.* relatively too large or too small.

disprove, *v.t.* show to be false, refute.

dispurse, (*Shake.*) form of **disburse.**

dispute, *v.t.* and *i.* discuss, argue; quarrel; call in question; oppose, contend for.—*n.* argument, difference of opinion; quarrel. **beyond d.,** certainly; undoubted. **in d.,** not yet decided. **disputable,** *a.* open to question, uncertain. **disputant,** *n.* person disputing. **disputation,** *n.* argumentative discourse or treatise. **disputatious,** *a.* fond of argument. (L. *dis-*, apart; *putare*, think)

disqualify, *v.t.* incapacitate, disable; rule out. **disqualification,** *n.* disqualifying; thing that disqualifies.

disquantity, *v.t.* (*Shake.*) diminish.

disquiet, *n.* uneasiness, anxiety.—*v.t.* fill with misgiving.—*a.* worried, perturbed. **disquietude,** *n.*

disquisition, *n.* systematic exposition; elaborate essay. (L. *dis-*, wholly; *quaerere*, seek)

disrate, *v.t.* (*naut.*) reduce to lower rank.

disregard, *v.t.* ignore, pay no heed to.—*n.* inattention, neglect.

disrelish, *n.* and *v.t.* dislike.

disremember, *v.t.* (*vulg.*) fail to remember.

disrepair, *n.* bad condition for want of repair.

disrepute, *n.* ill repute, discredit; disfavour. **disreputable,** *a.* not respectable; disgraceful.

disrespect, *n.* want of deference, incivility. **disrespectful,** *a.*

disrobe, *v.t.* and *i.* undress; uncover.

disroot, *v.t.* uproot; dislodge.

disrupt, *v.t.* break asunder, shatter. **disruption,** *n.* violent dissolution; severance; schism in Scottish Church in 1843. **disruptive,** *a.* (L. *dis-*, apart; *rumpere*, break)

dissatisfy, *v.t.* fail to please, make discontented. **dissatisfaction,** *n.* disapproval, discontent.

dissect, *v.t.* cut up (dead body etc.) to show its structure; examine in detail, analyse. **dissection, dissector,** *nn.* (L. *dis-*, apart; *secare*, cut)

dissemble, *v.t.* and *i.* conceal or disguise (feelings); act the hypocrite. **dissembler,** *n.* (L. *dis-*, apart; *simulare*, feign)

disseminate, *v.t.* sow, scatter abroad; propagate. **dissemination, disseminator,** *nn.* (L. *dis-* apart; *semen*, seed)

dissent, *v.i.* disagree, differ in opinion.—*n.* disagreement; refusal to accept doctrines of established church. **dissenter,** *n.* nonconformist. **dissentient,** *a.* and *n.* (person) disagreeing with majority. **dissension,** *n.* disunion; strife. (L. *dis-*, apart; *sentire*, feel)

dissepiment, *n.* (*bot., zool.*) partition, septum. (L. *dis-*, apart; *saepes*, hedge)

dissert, dissertate, *v.i.* hold forth. **dissertation,** *n.* formal discourse, treatise. (L. *dis-*, apart; *serere*, join)

disserve, *v.t.* serve badly. **disservice,** *n.* ill turn.

dissever, *v.t.* and *i.* cut apart, disunite. **disseverance,** *n.*

dissident, *a.* disagreeing, conflicting.—*n.* dissentient. **dissidence,** *n.* (L. *dis-*, apart; *sedēre*, sit)

dissight, *n.* eyesore.

dissilient, *a.* (*bot.*) bursting open violently. (L. *dis-*, apart; *salire*, leap)

dissimilar, *a.* unlike. **dissimilarity.**

dissimilitude, *nn.* **dissimilate,** *v.t.* develop difference in (sounds). **dissimilation,** *n.*

dissimulate, *v.t.* and *i.* pretend not to have (feeling etc.); dissemble, practise deceit. **dissimulation, dissimulator,** *nn.*

dissipate, *v.t.* and *i.* scatter, disperse; waste, squander; engage in dissipation. **dissipated,** *a.* dissolute, debauched. **dissipation,** *n.* dispersion, waste; frivolous pleasure; intemperance. **dissipative,** *a.* (L. *dissipare*)

dissociate, *v.t.* separate, think of as distinct; (*chem.*) decompose. **d. oneself,** disclaim connection (with). **dissociated personality,** existence of two distinct personalities in one person. **dissociation,** *n.* dissociating; (*psychoanal.*) separation of one element of consciousness from main stream. **dissociative,** *a.* (L. *dis-*, apart; *socius*, companion)

dissoluble, *a.* dissolvable. **dissolubility,** *n.* **dissolute,** *a.* vicious, profligate. **dissolution,** *n.* dissolving; annulment (of marriage etc.); dismissal of Parliament with view to fresh election; death. (*dissolve*)

dissolve, *v.t.* and *i.* break up, disintegrate, vanish; make, become, liquid; annul, terminate; dismiss (Parliament). **dissolvable,** *a.* **dissolvent,** *a.* and *n.* solvent. (L. *dis-*, apart; *solvere*, loosen)

dissonant, *a.* discordant, harsh, jarring. **dissonance,** *n.* (L. *dis-*, apart; *sonare*, sound)

dissuade, *v.t.* advise to refrain, persuade not to. **dissuasion,** *n.* **dissuasive,** *a.* (L. *dis-*, apart; *suadēre*, advise)

dissyllable, see **disyllable.**

dissymmetrical, *a.* symmetrical in opposite directions, like right and left hands. **dissymmetry,** *n.*

distaff, *n.* stick on which wool or flax is wound for spinning. **d. side,** female line. (O.E. *distæf*)

distain, *v.t.* (*Shake.*) defile.

distal, *a.* (*anat.*) at end remote from body. (*distant*)

distance, *n.* remoteness, interval of space; reserve.—*v.t.* leave far behind. **keep one's d.,** avoid familiarity. **middle d.,** between foreground and background. **distant,** *a.* far off, remote; at distance of; (of manner) cold, stand-offish. (L. *dis-*, apart; *stare*, stand)

distaste, *n.* dislike, repugnance.—*v.t.* (*Shake.*) dislike, disgust; make distasteful. **distasteful,** *a.*

distemper, *n.* derangement, ailment; a catarrhal disease of dogs; political disorder; (*Shake.*) ill humour.—*v.t.* disorder, derange. **distemperance, distemperature,** *nn.* (*Shake.*) illness, discomposure. (*temper*)

distemper, *n.* watery kind of paint for indoor walls; mode of painting with this, tempera.—*v.t.* coat with distemper. (*temper*)

distend, *v.t.* and *i.* inflate, swell out, dilate. **distensible,** *a.* **distension,** *n.* (L. *dis-*, apart; *tendere*, stretch)

distich, *n.* couplet. **distichous,** *a.* (*bot.*) arranged in two rows. (Gk. *dis*, twice; *stichos*, line)

distil, *v.t.* and *i.* give out in drops, trickle down; extract essence (of), make (spirit), by evaporation and condensation; reduce to pure state. **distillate,** *n.* product of distillation. **distillation,** *n.* distilling. **distillatory,** *a.* **distiller,** *n.* **distillery,** *n.* place for distilling spirit. (L. *dis-*, apart; *stilla*, drop)

distinct, *a.* separate, different; clear, easily seen; definite, positive; (*arch.*) adorned. **distinction,** *n.* distinguishing; point of difference; mark of honour; eminence, repute; (of style) individuality, high quality. **distinctive,** *a.* characteristic. (*distinguish*)

distingué, *a.* of superior manner, distinguished, striking. (F.)

distinguish, *v.t.* and *i.* make out, discern; perceive, mark, difference; characterize; make (oneself) prominent. **distinguishable,** *a.* **distinguished,** *a.* celebrated, famous; of superior manner. (L. *dis-*, apart; *stinguere*, extinguish)

distort, *v.t.* twist out of shape; garble, falsify. **distortion,** *n.* distorting; (*wireless*) lack of correctness in sound transmitted. **distortional,** *a.* **distortionist,** *n.* caricaturist; contortionist. (L. *dis-*, apart; *torquēre*, twist)

distract, *v.t.* divert, draw away; perplex, bewilder; madden. **distracted,** *a.* frantic. **distraction,** *n.* distracting; amusement, recreation: anger, bewilderment; frenzy; (*Shake.*) division, detachment. (L. *dis-*, apart; *trahere*, draw)

distrain, *v.i.* seize goods in payment for debt. **distrainer, distrainor,** *nn.* person who distrains upon **distrainee,** *n.* **distrainment, distraint,** *nn.* distraining. (L. *dis-*, apart; *stringere*, squeeze)

distrait, *a.* (*fem.* *distraite*) absent-minded, preoccupied. (F.)

distraught, *a.* (*arch.*) beside oneself with grief etc.; crazed, distracted. (*distract*)

distress, *n.* sorrow, grief; exhaustion, breathlessness; poverty, misery, straits; (*law*) distraint.—*v.t.* make unhappy; afflict, exhaust. **d. oneself,** feel anxious. **d.-gun,** *n.* fired by ship in distress. **d.-warrant,** *n.* authorizing distraint. **distressful,** *a.* suffering or causing distress. (L. *dis-*, apart; *stringere*, squeeze)

distribute, *v.t.* dispense, hand out; dispose at intervals, spread; classify; (*print.*) break up (type). **distributable,** *a.* **distributary,** *n.* river-branch that does not return to main stream.

distribution, *n.* distributing, allotment. **distributional,** *a.* **distributism,** *n.* principle of individual ownership and trade. **distributist,** *n.* **distributive,** *a.* of distribution; (*gram.*) referring to each of a number.—*n.* distributive word. **distributor,** *n.* (L. *dis-*, apart; *tribuere*, assign)

district, *n.* administrative division of country, county etc.; region. **D. Railway,** a London suburban line. **d. visitor,** church worker under clergyman. (L. *dis-*, apart; *stringere*, squeeze)

distrust, *n.* want of confidence; doubt, suspicion.—*v.t.* doubt, not rely on. **distrustful,** *a.*

disturb, *v.t.* break rest of; trouble, perplex; interrupt, disorganize. **disturbance,** *n.* disturbing; tumult, uproar; (*law*) interference with property or rights. (L. *dis-*, apart; *turba*, crowd)

disunion, *n.* separation, want of union, dissension. **disunite,** *v.t.* and *i.* sever connection with, separate.

disuse, *v.t.* cease to use.—*n.* disused state, desuetude.

disvalue, *v.t.* (*Shake.*) disparage.

disvouch, *v.t.* (*Shake.*) contradict.

disyllable, dissyllable, *n.* word, foot, of two syllables. **disyllabic, dissyllabic,** *a.* (Gk. *dis*, twice)

ditch, *n.* trench for drainage; moat.—*v.t.* and *i.* make, mend (ditches); throw (car) off road; ruin. **d.-water,** *n.* stagnant water. **ditcher,** *n.* (O.E. *dic*)

ditheism, *n.* belief in two equal gods, esp. one good and one evil. (Gk. *dis*, twice; *theos*, god)

dither, *v.i.* tremble, quiver; talk nonsense.—*n.* flutter.

dithyramb, *n.* hymn to Bacchus; ecstatic poem or speech, rhapsody. **dithyrambic,** *a.* wild and impassioned. (Gk. *dithurambos*)

dittany, *n.* small herb once used as tonic. (Gk. *diktamnon*)

dittay, *n.* (*Scots law*) indictment. (L. *dictare*, dictate)

ditto, *n.* (*abbr.* **do.**) the aforesaid, the same; (*pl. sl.*) clothes all of one material. (L. *dicere*, say)

dittography, *n.* writing same letter or word twice by mistake. **dittographic,** *a.* (Gk. *dittos*, double; *graphein*, write)

ditty, *n.* short simple song. (L. *dictare*, dictate)

ditty-bag, ditty-box, *nn.* sailor's housewife or bag for odds and ends.

diuretic, *a.* and *n.* (substance) promoting flow of urine. (Gk. *dia*, through; *ouron*, urine)

diurnal, *a.* of the daytime; daily; (*astron.*) occupying one day. (L. *dies*, day)

div, *n.* Persian evil spirit. (Pers.)

diva, *n.* great woman singer, prima donna. (It.)

divagate *v.i.* ramble; digress. **divagation,** *n.* (L. *dis-*, apart; *vagari*, wander)

divalent, *a.* having a valency of two, bivalent. (Gk. *dis*, twice. L. *valēre*, be worth)

divan, *n.* oriental council of state or council chamber; long cushioned seat against wall; smoking-room, cigar-shop; collection of poems. (Pers. *devan*)

divaricate, *v.i.* diverge, branch.—*a.* forked. **divarication,** *n.* (L. *dis-*, apart; *varus*, crooked)

dive, *v.i.* plunge into, go under, water; go headlong, dart (into); make search, plunge hand (into).—*n.* diving, plunge; (*sl.*) cheap restaurant, low resort. **diving-bell,** *n.* open-bottomed chamber for working under water. **diver,** *n.* one who descends into deep water; kinds of diving-bird. (O.E. *dúfan*, sink, and *dýfan*, immerse)

diverge, *v.i.* and *t.* go in different directions, turn aside; differ, deviate. **divergence, divergency,** *nn.* diverging; difference. **divergent,** *a.* (L. *dis-*, apart; *vergere*, incline)

divers, *a.* (*arch.*) several, various. (=*diverse*)

diverse, *a.* of different kinds; differing (from). **diversiform,** *a.* of several shapes. **diversify,** *v.t.* produce variety in, variegate. **diversion,** *n.* diverting; distraction of attention, feint; recreation, amusement. **diversity,** *n.* variety, difference. **divert,** *v.t.* turn aside, ward off; distract; entertain, amuse. **diverting,** *a.* amusing. (L. *dis-*, apart; *vertere*, turn)

divertissement, *n.* light entertainment, ballet, interlude. (F.)

Dives, *n.* rich man. (L.=rich)

divest, *v.t.* strip; deprive, rid. **divestiture, divestment,** *nn.* (L. *dis-*, apart; *vestis*, dress)

divide, *v.t.* and *i.* separate; distribute; classify; sunder, cut off; set at variance; part into two sets for voting; (*math.*) find how many times one number contains another.—*n.* watershed. **Great D.,** death. **dividend,** *n.* sum payable as profit of company or interest on loan; payment to creditors from bankrupt's estate; (*math.*) number to be divided. **divider,** *n.* that which divides; (*pl.*) measuring-compasses. **dividual,** *a.* separate, separable. (L. *dividere*)

divi-divi, *n.* a W. Indian plant; its astringent pods, used for tanning. (Carib)

divine, *a.* of, like, granted by, God; sacred; superhumanly excellent; (*sl.*) delightful.—*n.* student of theology; clergyman.—*v.t.* find by intuition, magic, or inspiration; foresee, guess. **divining-rod,** *n.* forked twig used by dowser to detect underground water. **divination,** *n.* divining, esp. by magic. **diviner,** *n.* one who divines; water-

diviner, dowser. **divinity,** *n.* divineness, godhead; God; a god; theology; adored person. **divinize,** *v.t.* deify. (L. *divus*, god)
division, *n.* dividing, being divided; section, department; barrier; disunion, antagonism; voting on motion in Parliament; military unit of two or more brigades, with cavalry (or tanks) and artillery. **long, short, d.,** methods of dividing by numbers above, up to, twelve. **divisional,** *a.* **divisible,** *a.* able to be divided, esp. (*math.*) by another number an exact number of times. **divisibility,** *n.* **divisor,** *n.* number by which another is to be divided. (*divide*)
divorce, *n.* legal dissolution of marriage; severance.—*v.t.* separate, get rid of, by divorce; sunder. **divorceable,** *a.* **divorcee,** *n.* person divorced. **divorcement,** *n.* divorcing. (L. *dis-*, apart; *vortere*, turn)
divot, *n.* (*Scot.*) turf, sod; (*golf*) piece of turf cut out by stroke.
divulge, *v.t.* let out (secret), make known. **divulgation, divulgement, divulgence,** *nn.* (L. *dis-*, apart; *vulgus*, people)
divulsion, *n.* rending apart. **divulsive,** *a.* (L. *dis-*, apart; *vellere*, pluck)
diwan, same as **dewan.**
Dixie, *n.* southern states of U.S.; a song. (*Dixon*, surveyor)
dixie, dixy, *n.* camp cooking-pot. (Pers. *degcha*, little iron pot)
dizen, *v.t.* deck out, bedizen.
dizzy, *a.* giddy, dazed; causing giddiness, very high.—*v.t.* make dizzy, confuse. (O.E. *dysig*, foolish)
djibba, djibbah, same as **jibba.**
djinn, same as **jinn.**
do, same as **doh.**
do, *v.t.* and *i.* (*2nd sing.* **dost, doest;** *3rd sing.* **does,** *arch.* **doth, doeth;** *past* **did,** *2nd sing.* **didst;** *p.p.* **done**) perform, act; deal with, complete; bestow, impart; arrange (hair); solve (problem); suit, be good enough; fare, prosper; (*colloq.*) cheat, swindle; entertain.—*v.aux.* used in negative and interrogative sentences etc.—*n.* (*colloq.*) swindle, fraud; party. **do away with,** abolish; kill. **do brown,** (*sl.*) make fool of. **do by,** treat. **do for,** finish off, kill; look after house of. **do in,** (*colloq.*) murder. **do in the eye,** (*sl.*) cheat. **do into,** translate into. **do one's best, damnedest,** make every effort. **do out,** clean out. **do to,** inflict on. **do to death,** (*arch.*) kill. **do up,** renovate; arrange; button up, wrap. **do with** endure; be satisfied with; be glad of. **do without,** dispense with. (O.E. *dón*)
doat, same as **dote.**
Dobbin, *n.* draught horse. (*Robert*)
doch-an-doris, *n.* (*Scot.*) parting drink, stirrup-cup. (Gael. *deoch*, drink; *an*, the; *dorus*, door)
dochmius, *n.* (*pl.* **dochmii**) five-syllabled foot, short-long-long-short-long. **dochmiac,** *a.* and *n.* (line) of dochmii. (L.)
docile, *a.* easy to teach or manage; tractable. **docility,** *n.* (L. *docēre*, teach)
dock, *n.* basin with floodgates where ships are loaded or repaired.—*v.t.* and *i.* put (ship) into dock. **dry, graving, d.,** for repairing, water being pumped out. **floating d.,** dry dock of floating caissons. **wet d.,** with water kept at high-tide level.
dock, *n.* enclosure for prisoner in court. **d. brief,** undertaken free for poor prisoner.
dock, *n.* solid part of animal's tail.—*v.t.* cut short (tail); cut down (supplies), curtail; (*law*) cut off (entail). (O.N. *dokkr*, tail)
dock, *n.* a coarse weed with large leaves. (O.E. *docce*)
dockage, *n.* charge for use of dock.
docker, *n.* labourer who works in dock.
docket, *n.* label on document with note of contents, on goods with destination etc.; (*law*) abstract of proceedings in case; register of such entries.—*v.t.* enter on, endorse with, docket.
dockize, *v.t.* make into range of docks.
dockyard, *n.* enclosure with docks and equipment for repairing ships.
doctor, *n.* medical practitioner, physician; learned man; holder of highest university degree; (*naut. sl.*) cook.—*v.t.* treat medically; repair, tinker; adulterate, falsify. **doctoral, doctorial,** *aa.* **doctorate,** *n.* doctor's degree, persons holding it. **doctress,** *n.* lady doctor. (L. *docēre*, teach)
doctrine, *n.* what s taught, instruction; belief, body of principles. **doctrinal,** *a.* **doctrinaire, doctrinarian,** *aa.* theoretic and unpractical; dogmatic.—*n.* person who seeks to apply theory without regard for circumstances. **doctrinairism,** *n.* (L. *doctrina*)
document, *n.* piece of writing; thing that furnishes evidence.—*v.t.* furnish, prove, with documents. **documentary,** *a.* **documentation,** *n.* (L. *documentum*)
dodder, *v.i.* shake with frailty; totter, potter. **dodderer,** *n.* infirm or futile person.
dodder, *n.* a slender leafless parasitic plant. (M.E. *doder*)
doddered, *a.* pollarded, with top lopped.
dodec(a)-, from Gk. *dōdeka*, twelve, used in **dodecagon,** *n.* twelve-sided plane figure; **dodecahedron,** *n.* solid with twelve faces; **dodecasyllable,** *n.* verse of twelve syllables; **dodecuple scale,** (*mus.*) with twelve notes considered of equal importance.
dodgasted, *a.* (*Amer. sl.*) confounded.
dodge, *v.i.* and *t.* move to and fro; swerve, turn aside; shuffle, quibble; elude, evade.—*n.* trick, artifice; plan,

device. **dodger,** *n.* trickster; (*naut.*) canvas wind-screen; (*Amer.*) small handbill.

dodo, *n.* large extinct bird of Mauritius. (Port. *doudo,* silly)

doe, *n.* female deer; female rabbit, hare etc. (O.E. *dá*)

doer, *n.* man of action. **does,** see **do.**

doff, *v.t.* take off (hat etc.); lay aside, discard. (*do off*)

dog, *n.* four-footed animal of wolf kind; male of this; scoundrel; fellow; (*Amer. sl.*) style, swank; (*pl.*) kind of tongs; support for burning logs or fire-irons.—*v.t.* follow closely; pursue, track. **d. in the manger,** one who prevents others from enjoying what he cannot use. **d.'s chance,** slightest chance. **d.'s life,** worried life. **go to the dd.,** be ruined. **Greater, Lesser, D.,** two constellations. **hair of the d. that bit you,** small drink to cure after-effects of too much. **hot d.,** (*Amer.*) hot sausage sandwich. **the dd.,** greyhound racing. (O.E. *docga*)

dog-box, *n.* railway van for dogs.

dogcart, *n.* light two-wheeled carriage with cross seats back to back.

dog-cheap, *a.* very cheap.

dog-collar, *n.* collar for dog; clergyman's collar, fastening behind.

dog-days, *n.pl.* sultry part of summer.

doge, *n.* chief magistrate of republic of Venice. (L. *dux,* leader)

dog-ear, dog's-ear, *v.t.* crumple, turn down, corner of (leaf of book).

dogfish, *n.* kind of shark.

dogged, *a.* stubborn, persistent; (*Shake.*) cruel.

dogger, *n.* two-masted Dutch fishing-boat.

doggerel, *n.* worthless verse; burlesque poetry.—*a.* halting, unpoetic.

doggish, *a.* like a dog, surly.

doggo, *adv.* (*sl.*). **lie d.,** wait silent and still. (*dog*)

doggone, *a.* (*Amer. sl.*) cursed, confounded. (*go to the dogs*)

doggy, *n.* pet name for dog.—*a.* like, fond of, dogs; (*Amer. sl.*) stylish.

dog-latin, *n.* incorrect, barbarous, Latin.

doglike, *a.* like a dog, faithful.

dogma, *n.* (*pl.* **dogmas,** rarely **dogmata**) article of faith, tenet; body of principles or beliefs, esp. as laid down by authority of Church. **dogmatic,** *a.* of dogma; asserting positively, overbearing.—*n.pl.* doctrinal theology. **dogmatism, dogmatist,** *nn.* **dogmatize,** *v.t.* and *i.* assert positively; lay down the law. (Gk.)

dog-rose, *n.* wild rose.

dog-star, *n.* Sirius.

dog-tired, *a.* tired out, dead-beat.

dogtooth, *n.* small conical ornament in Early English architecture.

dog-watch, *n.* one of the two-hour watches, from 4–6 or 6–8 p.m.

dogwood, *n.* kind of shrub, cornel.

doh, *n.* first note in sol-fa notation.

doilt, *a.* (*Scot.*) crazy, foolish.

doily, *n.* small ornamental cloth laid on or under dishes. (inventor)

doing, *n.* happening, event; (*pl. joc.*) thingummy.

doit, *n.* very small sum, trifle. (Du. *duit*)

doited, *a.* (*Scot.*) crazy, esp. with age.

dolce, a. (*mus.*) sweet. *d. far niente,* pleasant idleness. (It.)

doldrums, *n.pl.* low spirits, dumps; (*naut.*) region of calms and light winds near equator.

dole, *n.* measured share; charitable gift; unemployment relief; (*arch.*) lot, fate.—*v.t.* deal (out) sparingly. (O.E. *dál*)

dole, *n.* grief, woe. **doleful,** *a.* sad, mournful. (L. *dolor*)

dolicho-, from Gk. *dolichos,* long, used in **dolichocephalic, dolichocephalous,** *aa.* with skull long in proportion to its breadth, long-headed; **dolichopodous,** *a.* having long feet.

doll, *n.* toy baby, puppet; silly pretty girl. **d. up,** (*Amer. sl.*) dress up smartly.

dollar, *n.* U.S. coin worth about 7*s.*; various other coins; (*colloq.*) five-shilling piece. (G. *thaler,* from mines of Joachims*thal*)

dollop, *n.* (*colloq.*) shapeless lump, esp. of food.

dolly, *n.* pet name for doll; stick for stirring clothes in wash; block used in pile-driving.—*a.* babyish. **d.-shop,** *n.* marine store; pawnshop.

dolly, *n.* (*Anglo-Ind.*) complimentary present of fruit, flowers etc. (Hind. *dāli*)

Dolly Varden, flower-trimmed hat with one side bent down; flowered muslin dress with tucked-up skirt. (name in Dickens)

dolman, *n.* loose Turkish robe; hussar's short cape. (Turk, *dolaman*)

dolmen, *n.* prehistoric monument of large stone resting on others, cromlech. (F.)

dolomite, *n.* magnesian limestone; (*pl.*) range of mountains in Tyrol. **dolomitic,** *a.* (*Dolomieu,* geologist)

dolorous, *a.* mournful, doleful. (*dolour*)

dolose, *a.* (*law*) with criminal intent. (L. *dolus,* guile)

dolour, *n.* grief, sorrow, distress. (L. *dolor*)

dolphin, *n.* sea animal like porpoise; dorado. (Gk. *delphis*)

dolt, *n.* stupid slow-witted person. **doltish,** *a.*

Dom, *n.* title of certain Roman Catholic dignitaries; Portuguese form of Don. (L. *dominus,* lord)

-dom, *n.suf.* domain of, as in **kingdom.** (O.E.)

domain, *n.* estate, lands; realm, dominions; sphere, scope. **domanial,** *a.* (L. *dominus,* lord)

Domdaniel, *n.* magician's hall under sea; infernal cave. (Gk. *dōma Daniel,* house of Daniel)

dome, *n.* round globe-shaped roof; vault of sky; (*poet.*) stately building; (*Amer. sl.*) head. **domed,** *a.* (L. *domus,* house)
Domesday Book, record of William I's survey of England, 1086. (*doomsday*)
domestic, *a.* of family or household; home, not foreign; tame, not wild; home-keeping.—*n.* household servant. **domesticate,** *v.t.* make fond of home life; tame (animal); naturalize (plant). **domesticable,** *a.* **domestication,** *n.* **domesticity,** *n.* home life or privacy; homeliness. (L. *domus,* home)
domett, *n.* fabric of wool and cotton.
domicile, *n.* person's regular place of abode.—*v.t.* (also **domiciliate**) establish, settle permanently. **domiciliary,** *a.* **domiciliation,** *n.* (L. *domus,* home)
dominate, *v.t.* and *i.* sway, control; be most powerful among; tower above. **dominant,** *a.* ruling, chief; established in power.—*n.* (*mus.*) fifth note in scale. **dominance,** *n.* **domination,** *n.* ascendancy; (*pl.*) fourth rank of angels. (L. *dominus,* lord)
domineer, *v.i.* tyrannize (over), act imperiously. **domineering,** *a.* overbearing. (*dominate*)
dominical, *a.* of the Lord; of Sunday. **d. letter,** denoting Sunday in church calendar (A if 1 Jan. is Sunday, B if 2 Jan. etc.). **d. year,** of Christian era. (L. *dominus,* lord)
Dominican, *a.* and *n.* (monk) or order founded by St. Dominic, Black Friar.
dominie, *n.* (*Scot.*) schoolmaster; (*Amer.*) minister. (L. *domine,* sir)
dominion, *n.* authority; rule, sovereignty; territory of a government; self-governing country of British Commonwealth. (L. *dominus,* lord)
domino, *n.* (*pl.* **dominoes**) long robe with hood and mask; wearer of this; brick-shaped piece marked with pips; (*pl.*) game with these.
don, *n.* Spanish title, Sir; Spaniard; fellow or tutor of college; (*colloq.*) adept. **D. Juan,** profligate. (Sp.)
don, *v.t.* put on (garment). (*do on*)
donah, dona, *n.* (*sl.*) woman; sweetheart. (L. *domina,* lady)
donate, *v.t.* make donation of, present. **donation,** *n.* gift to fund or institution, benefaction. **donative,** *n.* largess, gratuity; benefice given by patron without reference to bishop. **donatory,** *n.* receiver of donation. (L. *donum,* gift)
done, *a.* tired out. **d. to a turn,** cooked just right. (*do*)
donee, *n.* receiver of gift. (*donor*)
donga, *n.* (*S. Afr.*) gully, ravine.
donjon, *n.* central tower of castle, keep. (arch. form of *dungeon*)
donkey, *n.* ass; foolish person. **d.'s years,** (*joc.*) very long time. **d.-engine,** *n.* small auxiliary engine on ship.
donna, *n.* Italian or Spanish lady. (It.)
donnered, *a.* (*Scot.*) stupefied, stunned.
donnish, *a.* pedantic, old-maidish, like a university don.
donor, *n.* giver. (L. *donum,* gift)
donsie, *a.* (*Scot.*) neat, trim.
donsie, *a.* (*Scot.*) unlucky.
don't, *abbr.* of **do not.**
doo, *Scot.* form of dove.
doob, *n.* an Indian grass used for fodder. (Hind.)
dood, *n.* riding-camel. (Bengali)
doodle, *v.i.* (*sl.*) scrawl aimlessly.
doodle, *v.t.* (*Scot.*) dandle.
dook, *v.i.* and *t.* and *n.* (*Scot.*) dip, bathe. (*duck*)
dool, same as **dule.**
doolie, dooly, *n.* simple Indian litter, used as ambulance. (Hind. *doli*)
doom, *n.* fate, destiny; ruin; (*arch.*) judgment, sentence.—*v.t.* sentence, destine. **doomsday,** *n.* Judgment Day. **Doomsday Book,** Domesday Book. (O.E. *dóm*)
door, *n.* barrier for closing entrance; means of approach. **next d. to,** in next house to; almost. **out of dd.,** in open air. **show one the d.,** turn him out. **d.-keeper,** *n.* janitor. **door-mat,** *n.* for wiping boots before entering. **d.-nail,** *n.* with which doors used to be studded. **d.-plate,** *n.* with name of occupant. **d.-post,** *n.* jamb. **doorway,** *n.* entrance. (O.E. *duru*)
doosuti, *n.* (*Anglo-Ind.*) coarse cotton fabric. (Hind. *do,* two; *sūt,* thread)
dop, *n.* (*S. Afr.*) coarse brandy; cup for holding diamond during cutting.
dope, *n.* thick liquid; kinds of varnish; (*sl.*) drug, narcotic; (*Amer. sl.*) inside information; senseless person.—*v.t.* apply dope to; (*Amer. sl.*) predict, work (out). (Du. *doop,* sauce)
doppel-gänger, *n.* wraith of living person. (G.)
dor, *n.* kinds of beetle. (O.E. *dora*)
Dora, *n.* (*joc.*) Defence of the Realm Act; its provisions. (initials)
dorado, *n.* a brilliantly coloured sea-fish. (L. *deaurare,* gild)
Dorcas society, of ladies to make clothes for poor. (name in Bible)
Dorian, *a.* and *n.* (member) of an early Greek race. **Doric,** *a.* and *n.* (dialect) of Dorians; any broad dialect; of oldest and simplest style of Greek architecture. (Gk. *Dōrios*)
Dorking, *n.* breed of fowl. (place)
dormant, *a.* inactive as in sleep, latent; in abeyance. **dormancy,** *n.*
dormer, *n.* (also **d.-window**) upright window in sloping roof. **dormeuse,** *n.* carriage fitted for sleeping in; kind of couch. **dormitory,** *n.* sleeping-room with several beds; suburban district housing city workers. (L. *dormire,* sleep)
dormouse, *n.* (*pl.* **dormice**) small hibernating mouse-like animal.
dormy, dormie, *a.* (*golf*) leading by as many holes as remain to be played.
dorothy bag, lady's wrist-bag. (name)

dorp, *n.* (*S. Afr.*) small town. (Du.)
dorsal, *a.* of, on, back. **dorsabdominal,** *a.* of back and belly. **dorsiventral,** *a.* having differentiated back and front. (L. *dorsum*, back)
dortour, dorter, *n.* dormitory in monastery. (O.F.)
dorty, *a.* (*Scot.*) pettish; delicate.
dory, *n.* (also **John D.**) edible yellow sea-fish. (F. *dorer*, gild)
dory, *n.* light flat-bottomed boat of Newfoundland fishing-vessel.
dose, *n.* amount to be taken at one time.—*v.t.* give medicine to; adulterate. **dosage,** *n.* method of dosing; size of dose. (Gk. *didonai*, give)
doss, *n.* (*sl.*) bed; sleep.—*v.i.* sleep. **d.-house,** *n.* low lodging-house.
dossal, *n.* hanging behind altar. (L. *dorsum*, back)
dossier, *n.* set of documents forming record of person, event etc. (F.)
dossy, *a.* (*sl.*) smart-looking.
dost, see **do.**
dot, *n.* small round mark, point; tiny object.—*v.t.* mark with dot; place here and there, sprinkle; (*sl.*) hit. **off one's d.,** crazy. **d.-and-go-one,** *a.* lame. (O.E. *dott*, head of boil)
dot, *n.* dowry. **dotal,** *a.* (F.)
dote, *v.i.* be silly, esp. from age. **d. on,** be foolishly fond of. **dotage,** *n.* senility. **dotard,** *n.* **doting,** *a.* fondly solicitous.
doth, see **do.**
dotterel, dottrel, *n.* kind of plover. (*dote*)
dottle, dottel, *n.* remnant of tobacco left in smoked pipe. (*dot*)
dotty, *a.* marked with dots; (*colloq.*) half-witted, cracked; shaky.
douane, *n.* foreign custom-house. (F.)
double, *a.* twofold; of twice the amount; having two parts; serving for two; deceitful.—*adv.* twice; in a pair.—*n.* double amount; person mistakable for another, duplicate; military running pace; game between two pairs.—*v.t.* and *i.* multiply by two; fold over; clench (fist); make sudden turn; go at double; play two parts in same play; (*naut.*) sail round. **d. axe, eagle,** two-headed kind. **d. Dutch,** gibberish. *d. entendre*, phrase with two meanings, one indelicate. **d. entry,** book-keeping system in which each item is entered twice. **d. first,** first-class honours in two subjects; person taking this. **d. star,** two stars so close together as to seem one. **d. up,** (cause to) curl up. **mixed d.,** game with man and woman on each side. (L. *duplus*)
double-barrelled, *a.* with two barrels; ambiguous; (of name) hyphened.
double-bass, *n.* largest instrument of violin kind.
double-breasted, *a.* able to button down either side.
double-cross, *v.t.* (*Amer.*) betray; sell to both sides.
double-dealer, *n.* cheat, dissembler.
double-dyed, *a.* thorough-paced, utter.
double-faced, *a.* hypocritical.
doublet, *n.* man's close-fitting garment; one of two words of same derivation but different sense, e.g. 'fragile' and 'frail'; (*pl.*) throw in which both dice show same number.
doubleton, *n.* two cards only of a suit (in player's hand).
doubloon, *n.* old Spanish coin worth about a guinea. (*double*)
doublure, *n.* ornamental lining inside book-cover. (F.)
doubt, *v.i.* and *t.* hesitate to believe; be uncertain (of); suspect; (*arch.*) fear; (*Scot.*) think.—*n.* uncertainty, indecision; suspicion. **doubtful,** *a.* feeling or causing doubt, uncertain. **doubtless,** *adv.* certainly, presumably. (L. *dubitare*)
douce, *a.* (*Scot.*) sober, gentle, sedate. (L. *dulcis*, sweet)
douceur, *n.* tip; bribe. (F.)
douche, *n.* jet of water; bath, injection, by means of this.—*v.t.* apply douche to. (L. *ducere*, lead)
dough, *n.* moist kneaded flour; (*sl.*) money. **doughboy,** *n.* boiled dumpling; (*Amer. sl.*) U.S. soldier. **doughnut,** *n.* cake of dough sweetened and fried, with hole in middle. (O.E. *dáh*)
dought, see **dow.**
doughty, *a.* (*arch.*) bold, valiant. (O.E. *dohtig*)
doum, *n.* Egyptian palm-tree. (Arab. *dum*)
doup, *n.* (*Scot.*) bottom, buttocks.
dour, *a.* (*Scot.*) severe, grim, obstinate.
douse, *v.t.* dip in water, drench; extinguish (light); (*naut.*) lower (sail).
dout, *v.t.* (*Shake.*) extinguish.
dove, *Amer. colloq. past* of **dive.**
dove, *n.* pigeon; symbol of peace or innocence. **d.-colour,** *a.* pinkish grey. **dovecote, dovecot,** *n.* pigeon-house. **dovetail,** *n.* interlocking joint with fan-shaped tenon.—*v.t.* and *i.* join with this; fit together closely.
dover, *v.i.* (*Scot.*) doze, drowse.
dow, *v.i.* (*Scot.*; *past* **dought**) be able.
dow, same as **dhow.**
dowager, *n.* widow with title or dower derived from husband. (O.F. *douage*, dower)
dowdy, *a.* not smart or stylish; ill-dressed.—*n.* dowdy woman.
dowel, *n.* headless peg.—*v.t.* fasten with one.
dower, *n.* widow's share for life of husband's estate; dowry; natural gift.—*v.t.* provide with dowry; endow (with). (L. *dos*, dowry)
dowf, *a.* (*Scot.*) dull, spiritless.
dowie, *a.* (*Scot.*) melancholy, sad.
dowlas, *n.* kind of coarse calico. (*Doulas* in France)
dowle, *n.* (*Shake.*) soft fine feather.
down, *n.* soft under-feathers; soft hair or fibre; fluff. (O.N. *dún*)

down, *n.* open high land, esp. in S. England. **the Dd.,** roadstead for shipping near Deal. (O.E. *dún,* hill)

down, *adv.* to, in, towards, lower position; to later time; on ground; with current; from main centre; (of payment) on the spot; (*naut.*) to leeward.—*prep.* to, at, lower part of; along; with.—*a.* going down.—*v.t.* knock, lay, down. **be d. on,** treat severely. **d. and out,** ruined. **d. on one's luck,** in ill-luck. **d. to the ground,** thoroughly. **d. under,** in the Antipodes. **have a d. on,** bear grudge against. **ups and dd.,** changes of fortune. **d.-at-heel,** *a.* shabby, slovenly. **d.-easter,** *n.* (*Amer.*) New Englander. **d.-hearted,** *a.* depressed. (*adown*)

downcast, *a.* sad dejected; (of eyes) looking down.

downfall, *n.* fall from power, ruin.

downpour, *n.* heavy shower.

downright, *a.* blunt, straightforward; sheer.—*adv.* positively, quite.

downstairs, *adv.* and *a.* and *n.* (to, in) lower part of house.

downtrodden, *a.* oppressed, kept under.

downward, *a.* and *adv.* (moving etc.) to a lower place. **downwards,** *adv.*

downy, *a.* like, covered with, down; (*sl.*) knowing, astute.

downy, *a.* like downs, undulating.

dowry, *n.* property wife brings to husband at marriage; natural gift, talent. (*dower*)

dowse, *v.i.* search for water etc. by means of **dowsing-rod** or divining-rod. **dowser,** *n.* water-diviner.

dowse, same as **douse.**

doxology, *n.* hymn of praise to God. (Gk. *doxa,* glory; *legein,* speak)

doxy, *n.* beggar's wench, sweetheart.

doxy, *n.* (*joc.*) opinion. (ortho*doxy*)

doyen, *n.* senior member of body, esp. of diplomatic corps. (F.)

doyley, same as **doily.**

doze, *v.i.* sleep lightly or fitfully.—*n.* nap. **dozy,** *a.* drowsy.

dozen, *n.* twelve; set of twelve. **baker's, printer's d.,** thirteen. **talk nineteen to the d.,** incessantly. (L. *duodecim*)

drab, *a.* dull brown; dingy, colourless. —*n.* mud colour; monotony. **drabbet,** *n.* coarse drab linen fabric.

drab, *n.* slut; prostitute.—*v.i.* whore.

drabble, *v.i.* and *t.* splash about in, soil with, mud and water.

drachm, *n.* $\frac{1}{16}$ oz. avoirdupois; $\frac{1}{8}$ oz. apothecaries' weight; drachma. **drachma,** *n.* (*pl.* **drachmas, drachmae**) Greek silver coin, monetary unit; ancient Greek weight. (Gk. *drachmē*)

Draconian, Draconic, *a.* (of laws) severe, harsh. (*Draco* of Athens)

draff, *n.* dregs, lees; refuse from malt after brewing.

draft, *n.* rough outline or scheme; drawing of money from bank; bill or cheque drawn; contingent of troops.—*v.t.* rough out, draw up, esp. Parliamentary bill; detach (troops). **draftsman,** *n.* one who drafts documents. (variant of *draught*)

drag, *v.t.* and *i.* draw along with force or friction; dredge with grapnel; harrow; trail, go heavily.—*n.* check on progress; iron shoe to retard wheel; high open coach; heavy harrow; rough sledge; grapnel; artificial lure drawn before hounds, hunt using this. **d. in,** bring in irrelevantly. **d. on,** be tedious. **d. out,** protract. **d. up,** rear roughly. **d.-net,** *n.* net drawn along bottom of river.

dragée, *n.* chocolate drop, sweet. (F.)

draggle, *v.t.* and *i.* trail in mud; soil and crumple thus. **d.-tail,** *n.* slattern.—*a.* (also **d.-tailed**) with muddy skirts, slovenly.

dragoman, *n.* (*pl.* **dragomans, dragomen**) interpreter, guide, in Near East. (Arab. *targuman*)

dragon, *n.* fabulous monster like winged reptile; kinds of lizard and pigeon; grim female, chaperon. **d.'s-blood,** *n.* red juice of a tree. **dragon-fly,** *n.* long slender insect with gauzy wings. (Gk. *drakōn*)

dragoon, *n.* cavalryman of certain regiments.—*v.t.* force by harsh measures; persecute. **dragonnade,** *n.* persecution by troops. (F. *dragon,* carbine)

drail, *n.* weighted fish-hook for dragging through water.

drain, *v.t.* and *i.* draw, carry, flow, off (of liquid); make, become, dry thus; drink up, empty to dregs; deprive of resources, exhaust.—*n.* channel, pipe, carrying off liquid; sewer; strain, demand; (*colloq.*) small drink. **drainage,** *n.* draining; system of drains. (O.E. *dréahnian*)

drake, *n.* male duck.

drake, *n.* kind of may-fly; beaked galley. (O.E. *draca,* dragon)

dram, *n.* drachm; drink of spirits etc. (*drachm*)

drama, *n.* composition for stage, play; art of plays; set of events with unity and vividness of play. **dramatic,** *a.* of drama; striking and impressive; theatrical. *dramatis personae,* characters in play. **dramatist,** *n.* playwright. **dramatize,** *v.t.* put into form of play. **dramaturge,** *n.* playwright. **dramaturgic,** *a.* **dramaturgy,** *n.* (Gk.)

drank, see **drink.**

drap, *Scot.* form of **drop.**

drape, *v.t.* cover, hang, with cloth; arrange in folds. **draper,** *n.* dealer in cloth. **drapery,** *n.* clothing, hangings; arrangement of these, esp. in painting; draper's trade, shop, or goods. (F. *drap,* cloth)

drappie, *n.* (*Scot.*) little drop, esp. of spirits.

drastic, *a.* acting strongly, vigorous, violent. (Gk. *draein*, do)
drat, *v.t.* (*vulg.*) confound. (*God rot*)
draught, *n.* drawing, traction; amount of liquid drunk at a time; dose of medicine; depth of ship in water; current of air; artist's sketch for picture; draft; (*pl.*) game on chess-board with twelve men a side; (*Shake.*) cesspool, privy, sewer. **black d.,** a purgative. **d.-horse,** *n.* cart-horse. **draught-board,** *n.* chess-board. **draughtsman,** *n.* (*fem.* **draughtswoman**) one who draws plans; piece in draughts. **draughtsmanship,** *n.* **draughty,** *a.* full of air-currents. (*draw*)
draw, *v.t.* and *i.* (*past* **drew,** *p.p.* **drawn**) pull, haul; extract, elicit; attract, bring; derive, deduce; delineate, sketch; stretch; get by lot; inhale; disembowel; write (cheque); search (covert); make (wire); infuse (tea); finish (contest) even; come, go; shrink; cause draught; (of ship) require (depth of water).—*n.* act of drawing; lottery; tie; attraction; act of pulling out revolver. **d. blank,** find nothing. **d. in,** grow shorter. **d. it mild,** (*colloq.*) do not exaggerate. **d. out,** protract, lengthen; induce to talk. **d. rein,** check horse. **d. stumps,** (*cricket*) cease play. **d. the long bow,** exaggerate. **d. up,** compose (document); form up (troops); stop. (O.E. *dragan*)
drawback, *n.* disadvantage; refund of duty on goods which are re-exported.
drawbridge, *n.* bridge that can be raised and lowered.
Drawcansir, *n.* swashbuckler, braggart. (name in play)
drawee, *n.* one on whom bill is drawn.
drawer, *n.* one who draws; sliding receptacle in chest etc.; (*Shake.*) tapster; (*pl.*) undergarment for legs.
drawing, *n.* delineation with pen or pencil, sketch. **d.-board,** *n.* flat board on which paper is fixed with **d.-pins.**
drawing-room, *n.* reception-room; levee, court reception. (*withdrawing*)
drawl, *v.i.* and *t.* speak, say, with affected slowness.—*n.* slow utterance. **drawlingly,** *adv.*
dray, *n.* low sideless cart for heavy loads. **drayman,** *n.* driver of dray. (O.E. *dragan*, draw)
dread, *v.t.* and *i.* fear greatly, be in terror (of).—*n.* terror, shrinking fear. —*a.* dreaded, awesome. **dreadful,** *a.* terrible; (*colloq.*) horrid. **penny dreadful,** cheap sensational novel.
dreadnought, *n.* a heavy cloth; overcoat of this; battleship with main armament entirely of big guns. (O.E. *ondrǣdan*, fear)
dream, *n.* vision during sleep; fancy, reverie; aspiration.—*v.i.* and *t.* (*past, p.p.* **dreamt, dreamed**) have, see in, dream; think of as possible. **dreamer,** *n.* one who dreams; unpractical person. **dreamland,** *n.* unreal world; sleep. **dreamy,** *a.* given to reverie; languid; vague, misty.
dream-hole, *n.* hole in wall of tower for light and air.
dreary, (*poet.*) **drear,** *a.* gloomy, dismal, tedious. **dreariment, drearihead,** *nn.* (*Spens.*) dreariness, affliction. (O.E. *dréor*, gore)
dredge, *v.t.* and *i.* bring up from under water; deepen (channel) by dredge; use dredge.—*n.* kind of scoop or grab. **dredger,** *n.* ship for dredging.
dredge, *v.t.* sprinkle with flour etc. **dredger,** *n.* box with perforated lid for sprinkling. (Gk. *tragēma*, sweet-meat)
dree, *v.t.* (*arch.*) endure. **d. one's weird,** abide one's fate. (O.E. *dréogan*)
dreg, *n.* (us. *pl.*) sediment, grounds; worthless refuse. **dreggy,** *a.*
dreich, *a.* (*Scot.*) long, tedious. (*dree*)
drench, *v.t.* soak thoroughly, steep; physic.—*n.* potion, purgative; down-pour. (O.E. *drencan*, give to drink)
dress, *v.t.* and *i.* put clothes on; arrange, adorn, prepare; align (troops); wash and bandage (wound). —*n.* clothing; frock. **d. down,** rub down (horse); scold. **d. rehearsal,** final one, in costume. **d. up,** put on elaborate clothes. **evening d.,** that worn at dinners. **full d.,** most elaborate uniform. **morning d.,** ordinary clothes. **d.-circle,** *n.* lowest gallery in theatre. **d.-coat,** *n.* black swallow-tailed coat. (L. *dirigere*, direct)
dresser, *n.* one who dresses wounds or shop-windows; actress's attendant; kitchen sideboard.
dressing, *n.* sauce; bandage, ointment etc. for wound; manure. **d.-gown, d.-jacket, d.-room, d.-table,** *nn.* for making toilet in or at.
dressmaker, *n.* woman who makes frocks.
dressy, *a.* smart, stylish.
drew, see **draw.**
drey, *n.* squirrel's nest.
dribble, *v.i.* and *t.* trickle, let fall in drops; run at mouth; (*football*) work (ball) forward with short kicks. **driblet, dribblet,** *n.* small portion. (*drip*)
dried, see **dry.**
drift, *n.* being driven by current; deviation due to current or rotation; current, tendency; trend of thought; heap formed by wind or water; (*S. Afr.*) ford.—*v.i.* and *t.* float along, go passively; drive, be driven, into heaps. **d.-net,** *n.* large net for sea-fishing. **d.-wood,** *n.* wood cast ashore by tide. **drifter,** *n.* boat with drift-net. (*drive*)
drill, *v.t.* and *i.* pierce, bore hole in; train by systematic movements and exercises.—*n.* drilling; discipline, rou-

tine; boring tool or machine. **d.-sergeant,** *n.* instructor in drill. (Du. *drillen*)

drill, *n.* narrow trench for seeds; row of plants.—*v.t.* sow in drills.

drill, *n.* coarsely woven material. (L. *tres,* three; *licium,* thread)

drill, *n.* kind of baboon.

drily, see **dryly.**

drink, *v.t.* and *i.* (*past* **drank,** *p.p.* **drunk**) swallow (liquid); drain (glass); absorb (moisture); take intoxicants, esp. to excess.—*n.* beverage or portion of it; strong liquor: intemperance. **d. hard,** be drunkard. **d. health of,** toast. **d. in,** absorb; listen to, view, with delight. **d. to,** pledge, wish in drinking. **d.-offering,** *n.* wine poured out as sacrificial rite. (O.E. *drincan*)

drip, *v.i.* and *t.* fall, let fall, drop by drop.—*n.* act of dripping. **dripping,** *a.* very wet.—*n.* grease from roasted meat. **dripstone,** *n.* projecting moulding over door or window to prevent rain from running down. (O.E. *dryppan*)

drive, *v.t.* and *i.* (*past* **drove,** *p.p.* **driven**) impel, propel; urge on; force (into); overwork; control (engine); go, convey, in vehicle; (*golf*) make stroke from tee.—*n.* driving; journey in vehicle; carriage-road; energy; organized effort to collect money. **d. at,** mean. **d. mad,** madden. **driving-wheel,** *n.* one communicating motion to others. (O.E. *drifan*)

drivel, *v.i.* slaver, dribble; talk nonsense.—*n.* nonsense, twaddle. **driveller,** *n.* (O.E. *dreflian*)

driver, *n.* coachman; man who controls engine; (*golf*) wooden club used from tee.

drizzle, *v.i.* rain in small drops.—*n.* fine rain. (O.E. *dreosan,* fall)

droddum, *n.* (*Scot.*) buttocks.

drogher, *n.* slow heavy W. Indian coasting-vessel. (Du.)

drogue, *n.* buoy at end of harpoon line; canvas cylinder flown from aerodrome mast to show direction of wind.

droil, *v.i.* (*Spens.*) drudge.

droit, *n.* legal right. (F.)

droll, *a.* comical, funny, queer.—*n.* wag.—*v.i.* play the buffoon. **drollery,** *n.* quaint humour; (*Shake.*) puppet-show. (F. *drôle*)

dromedary, *n.* swift one-humped riding camel. (Gk. *dromas,* running)

dromond, *n.* large medieval ship. (Gk. *dromos,* race)

drone, *n.* male bee, which does no work; idler; deep hum; bass-pipe of bagpipe, its note.—*v.i.* and *t.* sing, speak, in dull monotonous tone; buzz. (O.E. *drán*)

drook, *v.t.* (*Scot.*) drench.

drool, *v.i.* slaver, drivel. (*drivel*)

droop, *v.i.* and *t.* hang down, incline; flag, wilt.—*n.* drooping state. (O.N. *drúpa*)

drop, *n.* liquid globule; minute quantity; fall, descent; trap-door; ear-ring; round sweet; (*pl.*) medicine measured in drops.—*v.i.* and *t.* fall, let fall; shed in drops, drip; utter, be uttered, casually; lose, cease; discard, omit; (of animal) bear (young); (*football*) make drop-kick, score thus. **d. in,** pay casual visit. **d.-curtain, d.-scene,** *nn.* theatre curtain lowered between acts. **d.-kick,** *n.* kicking football as it bounds when dropped from hands. **d.-shot,** *n.* (*lawn tennis*) one dropping just over net. **droplet,** *n.* little drop. **droppings,** *n.pl.* dung. (O.E. *dropa*)

dropsy, *n.* disease causing collection of watery fluid in body; overswollen state. **dropsical,** *a.* (Gk. *hudōr,* water)

dropwort, *n.* plant like meadowsweet.

droshky, drosky, *n.* light four-wheeled open Russian carriage; German cab. (Russ. *drozhki*)

drosometer, *n.* instrument for measuring dewfall. (Gk. *drosos,* dew; *metron,* measure)

dross, *n.* scum of molten metal; impurities; refuse. (O.E. *drós*)

drought, (*poet.*) **drouth,** *n.* long spell of dry weather, want of rain; thirst; (*arch.*) dryness. **droughty, drouthy,** *aa.* (O.E. *drúgian,* dry)

drove, *n.* herd, flock, crowd, esp. on move. **drover,** *n.* cattle-driver; cattle-dealer; (*Spens.*) kind of fishing-boat. (*drive*)

drown, *v.i.* and *t.* die, kill, by suffocation in liquid; drench, flood; make (sound) inaudible; deaden (grief etc.) with drink.

drowse, *v.i.* and *t.* be half asleep; be, make, sleepy. **drowsy,** *a.* sleepy; lulling, soporific. **drowsihead,** *n.* (*arch.*) drowsiness.

drub, *v.t.* thrash, beat. **drubbing,** *n.*

drudge, *v.i.* toil hard at distasteful task; slave.—*n.* servile worker, hack. **drudgery,** *n.*

drug, *n.* medicinal substance, medicine; narcotic.—*v.t.* and *i.* mix drug with (food etc.); administer drug to; take drugs to excess. **d. in the market,** unsaleable thing. (F. *drogue*)

drugget, *n.* coarse woollen stuff; over-carpet of this. (F. *droguet*)

druggist, *n.* apothecary.

Druid, *n.* (*fem.* **Druidess**) ancient Celtic priest; (*pl.*) a benefit society. **Druidic, Druidical,** *aa.* **Druidism,** *n.* (Celt.)

drum, *n.* percussion instrument of skin stretched on frame; cylindrical box or attachment; section of pillar; tympanum of ear; (*arch.*) large evening party.—*v.i.* and *t.* play on drum; rap continuously; drive (lesson into person). **bass, big, d.,** one beaten on both sides. **d. out,** expel formally from army. **d.-major,** *n.* regimental band-leader. **drumfire,** *n.*

rapid concentrated gunfire. **drumhead,** *n.* skin of drum. **drumhead court martial,** summary one at front. **drummer,** *n.* player of drum; (*Amer.*) commercial traveller. **drumstick,** *n.* stick for beating drum; lower part of cooked fowl's leg; (*Amer.*) stilt-sandpiper.

drum, drumlin, *nn.* (*geol.*) narrow hill formed by glacial drift. (Gael. *druim,* ridge)

drumble, *v.i.* (*Shake.*) be sluggish.

drumly, *a.* (*Scot.*) muddy; gloomy.

drummock, *n.* (*Scot.*) meal and water mixed.

drunk, *a.* intoxicated.—*n.* drunk man; case of drunkenness; (*sl.*) drinking-bout. **drunkard,** *n.* person often drunk. **drunken,** *a.* drunk; given to, caused by, intoxication. (*drink*)

drupe, *n.* fleshy fruit with stone, e.g. plum. **drupaceous,** *a.* **drupel, drupelet,** *nn.* small drupe in compound fruit, e.g. raspberry. (Gk. *druppa,* over-ripe olive)

druse, *n.* crust of crystals; rock-cavity lined with this. (G.)

dry, *a.* without, lacking in, moisture; not rainy; thirsty; teetotal, prohibiting sale of intoxicants; unemotional, matter-of-fact; (of book) dull, uninteresting; (of wine) free from sweetness.—*v.t.* and *i.* make, become, dry. **d. battery,** electric battery without liquid. **d. fly fishing,** without letting fly touch water. **d. goods,** non-liquid wares; (*Amer.*) textiles. **d. measure,** measure of bulk, used for grain. **d. point,** engraving without acid; needle for this. **d. rot,** a fungoid decay in wood. **d. up,** evaporate; stop talking; (of actor) forget lines. **d.-clean,** *v.t.* clean with petrol etc. **d.-nurse,** *n.* one who tends but does not suckle child. **d.-stone,** *a.* built without mortar. (O.E. *drȳge*)

dryad, *n.* wood-nymph. (Gk. *drus,* tree)

dryasdust, *n.* dull historian.—*a.* uninteresting. (name in Scott)

dryly, drily, *adv.* in a dry manner; coldly, sarcastically.

drysalter, *n.* dealer in dyes, oils etc. **drysaltery,** *n.* (*dry*; *salt*)

dryshod, *a.* without wetting feet.

dual, *a.* of, denoting, two; double, forming pair.—*n.* (*gram.*) dual number. **D. Monarchy,** Austria-Hungary. **dualin,** *n.* kind of dynamite. **dualism,** *n.* duality; (*philos.*) doctrine that universe is based on two principles, e.g. good and evil, mind and matter. **dualist,** *n.* believer in this. **dualistic,** *a.* **duality,** *n.* dualness. **dualize,** *v.t.* (L. *duo,* two)

dub, *v.t.* confer knighthood on by touching with sword; nickname; rub with grease.

dub, *v.i.* (*sl.*). **d. up,** pay up.

dub, *n.* (*Scot.*) deep pool; puddle.

dub, *n.* (*Anglo-Ind.*) small copper coin; money, cash.

dub, *n.* (*Amer. sl.*) fool.

dubber, *n.* (*Anglo-Ind.*) large leather vessel for oil etc.

dubbin, dubbing, *n.* grease for softening and waterproofing leather. (*dub*)

dubious, *a.* feeling or causing doubt; uncertain, unreliable; of suspected character. **dubiety,** *n.* **dubitation,** *n.* hesitation. **dubitative,** *a.* expressing, inclined to, doubt. (L. *dubius*)

ducal, *a.* of, like, a duke. (*duke*)

ducat, *n.* old gold coin worth about 9*s.* (L.L. *ducatus,* duchy)

Dúcē, *n.* chief, Italian Fascist dictator. (It.)

duchess, *n.* duke's wife or widow; female holder of duchy; (*sl.*) coster's wife. **duchy,** *n.* duke's domain, dukedom. (L. *dux,* leader)

duchesse, *n.* kind of satin. (F.)

duck, *n.* kind of coarse cloth; (*pl.*) trousers of this.

duck, *n.* short-legged water-bird; its flesh; nice person, pet; (*cricket*) no score. **break one's d.,** (*cricket*) get first run. **lame d.,** disabled person. **play dd. and drakes,** make flat stone ricochet on water; squander money. **d.-billed platypus, duckbill,** *nn.* Australian egg-laying furred mammal with webbed feet and bill. **d.-board,** *n.* path of wooden slats over mud. **d.-hawk,** *n.* marsh harrier; (*Amer.*) peregrine falcon. **d.'s-egg,** *n.* (*cricket*) duck. **duckling,** *n.* young duck. **duckweed,** *n.* kind of water-plant. **ducky,** *n.* darling. (O.E. *duce*)

duck, *v.i.* and *t.* bob down, lower (head); dip, thrust, quickly under water; (*colloq.*) drop curtsy.—*n.* ducking; bob. **d. out,** (*Amer.*) leave. **ducking-stool,** *n.* for ducking scold. (M.E. *duken*)

duct, *n.* conduit; (*anat.*) tube conveying secretion. (L. *ducere,* lead)

ductile, *a.* malleable; capable of being drawn into wire; plastic, pliable; docile. (L. *ducere,* lead)

dud, *n.* (*sl.*) useless person or thing; bad coin; shell that does not go off; (*pl.*) clothes, rags.—*a.* worthless. **duddy,** *a.* (*Scot.*) ragged.

dude, *n.* (*Amer. sl.*) fop, exquisite, swell.

dudeen, dudheen, *n.* (*Ir.*) short clay tobacco-pipe.

dudgeon, *n.* resentment, ill-humour.

dudgeon, *n.* (*arch.*) hilt of dagger.

due, *a.* owing; merited; fitting, proper; appointed, timed, for.—*adv.* directly. *n.* person's right, desert; (us. *pl.*) legal charge, toll; (*Shake.*) debt. **d. to,** because of. **d.-bill,** *n.* (*Amer.*) written acknowledgment of debt. (L. *debēre,* owe)

duel, *n.* formally arranged single combat with deadly weapons; two-sided contest. **duellist,** *n.* **duello,** *n,* (*Shake.*) duellists' code. (L. *duellum.* old form of *bellum,* war)

duenna, *n.* elderly guardian and governess of girls; chaperon. (Sp. *dueña*)
duet, *n.* musical composition for two voices or instruments; dialogue; couple. **duettist**, *n.* (L. *duo*, two)
duff, *n.* pudding boiled in bag. (form of *dough*)
duff, *v.t.* fake up, give new appearance to; (*golf*) mishit; (*Austral.*) steal and re-brand (cattle).
duffel, duffle, *n.* coarse woollen cloth with thick nap; camper's change of clothes. (town in Belgium)
duffer, *n.* (*colloq.*) awkward or stupid person, bungler; pedlar: sham article, faker of these; unproductive mine.
dug, *n.* teat, udder, of animal.
dug, see **dig**. **d.-out**, *n.* canoe made of hollowed tree-trunk; underground shelter; (*sl.*) retired officer recalled to service.
dugong, *n.* seal-like water-animal, sea-cow. (Malay *duyong*)
duiker, *n.* small S. African antelope. (Du.)
duke, *n.* peer of highest rank; (in Europe) sovereign prince; (*obs.*) leader; (*pl. sl.*) fists. **dukedom**, *n.* **Dukeries**, *n.pl.* a district in Notts. (L. *dux*, leader)
dulcet, *a.* sweet, melodious. **dulcify**, *v.t.* sweeten, make gentle. **dulcification**, *n.* **dulcimer**, *n.* stringed instrument played with hammers, prototype of piano. (L. *dulcis*, sweet)
dulcitone, *n.* keyboard instrument with hammers striking tuning-forks.
dule, *n.* (*Scot.*) woe. (*dole*)
dull, *a.* stupid, obtuse; slow in perception, not keen; sluggish, listless; tedious, uninteresting; dim, overcast, not bright.—*v.t.* and *i.* make, become, dull; blunt, mitigate. **dullard**, *n.* slow-witted person.
dulse, *n.* an edible seaweed. (Gael. *duileasg*)
duly, *adv.* fitly, properly. (*due*)
Duma, *n.* Russian parliament, 1906–1917. (Russ.)
dumb, *a.* unable to speak; silent, taciturn; (*Amer. colloq.*) dull, stupid.—*v.t.* silence. **d. piano**, silent keyboard for exercising fingers. **d. show**, expressive actions without words. **d.-bell**, *n.* weight swung in hand for exercise; (*Amer. sl.*) stupid person. **d.-waiter**, *n.* stand with revolving shelves; dinner-wagon; (*Amer.*) food-lift. **dumbfound**, *v.t.* astound, nonplus. (O.E.)
dumdum bullet, soft-nosed expanding bullet. (*Dumdum* in India)
dummy, *n.* lay figure, sham object; figurehead, mere tool; dolt; child's comforter; (*cards*) hand exposed on table and played by partner.—*a.* sham. (*dumb*)
dump, *v.t.* and *i.* set down, drop, heavily; deposit (rubbish); export (surplus goods) for sale at low price so as to maintain home price and capture new market.—*n.* thud; refuse-heap; temporary munition depot.
dump, *n.* small thick kinds of coin, bolt, skittle, sweet; rope quoit.
dumpling, *n.* cooked ball of dough, often enclosing fruit.
dumps, *n.pl.* depression, low spirits.
dumpy, *a.* short and stout, squat.—*n.* a breed of fowls.
dun, *v.t.* press persistently for payment of debt. — *n.* importunate creditor; debt-collector.
dun, *a.* dull greyish brown; (*poet.*) dark.—*n.* dun colour or horse. (O.E.)
dun, *n.* fortified hill. (Celtic)
dunce, *n.* slow learner, dullard. (*Duns* Scotus, schoolman)
dunch, *v.t.* and *n.* (*Scot.*) push with elbow, jolt.
dunderhead, *n.* blockhead. **dunderheaded**, *a.* crassly stupid.
Dundreary **whiskers**, long side-whiskers without beard. (name in play)
dune, *n.* sandhill on coast. (F.)
dung, *n.* animal's excrement.—*v.i.* and *t.* void dung; manure (ground). **d.-beetle, d.-fly**, *nn.* kinds feeding on dung. **d.-cart, d.-fork**, *nn.* for loading and spreading manure. (O.E.)
dungaree, *n.* coarse cotton stuff; (*pl.*) overalls of this. (Hind. *dungrī*)
dungeon, *n.* underground vault or cell; donjon.—*v.t.* confine in dungeon. (L. *dominus*, lord)
dunghill, *n.* manure-heap.
duniwassal, dunniewassal, *n.* (*Scot.*) highland gentleman of inferior rank. (Gael. *duine*, man; *uasal*, noble)
dunlin, *n.* red-backed sandpiper. (*dun* + dim.)
dunnage, *n.* loose wood etc. to pack cargo or keep it out of bilge-water.
dunnock, *n.* hedge-sparrow. (*dun*)
dunt, *n.* blow given to aircraft by vertical current of air suddenly met; (*Scot.*) blow.—*v.t.* strike.
duo, *n.* duet; pair of artistes. **duodecimal**, *a.* of twelve; proceeding by twelves. **duodecimo**, *n.* (*abbr.* 12mo) book of sheets folded into twelve leaves; this size, about 8 × 5 in. **duodenary**, *a.* in twelves; proceeding by twelves. (L.=two)
duodenum, *n.* upper part of small intestine. **duodenal**, *a.* (L. *duodecim*, twelve, because 12 in. long)
duologue, *n.* conversation between two people; play with two actors. (Gk. *duo*, two; *legein*, speak)
duomo, *n.* Italian cathedral. (It.)
dup, *v.t.* (*Shake.*) open. (*do up*)
dupe, *n.* deceived or credulous person, gull.—*v.t.* deceive, impose upon. **dupable**, *a.* **dupery**, *n.* (F.)
duple, *a.* double; (*mus.*) of two beats to bar. **duplet**, *n.* (*mus.*) two notes played in time of three (L. *duplus*)
duplex, *a.* double. **d. lamp**, with two wicks. **d. telegraphy**, transmitting both ways at once on one wire. (L.

duplicate, *a.* double; exactly like or reproducing.—*n.* replica.—*v.t.* make double; copy exactly. **duplication,** *n.* **duplicator,** *n.* copying-machine. **duplicity,** *n.* deceitfulness; bad faith. (*duplex*)

durable, *a.* lasting; able to resist wear. **durability,** *n.* **duralumin,** *n.* a strong aluminium alloy. *dura mater,* outer membrane of brain. **durance,** *n.* imprisonment. **duration,** *n.* time thing lasts, continuance. (L. *durus,* hard)

durbar, *n.* state levee or reception in India. (Hind. *darbar,* court)

dure, *v.i.* (*poet.*) endure, last. **duress, duresse,** *n.* imprisonment; unlawful compulsion by threats etc. (L. *durus,* hard)

durgah, *n.* shrine of Mohammedan saint in India. (Hind.)

durian, *n.* oval fruit with fetid smell and pleasant taste; tree bearing it. (Malay)

during, *prep.* all through; in course of. (*dure*)

durmast, *n.* kind of oak.

durn, same as darn.

durra, *n.* Indian millet. (Arab. *durah*)

durrie, same as **dhurrie.**

durst, see **dare.**

durwan, *n.* (*Anglo-Ind.*) door-keeper. (Hind. *darwān*)

dusk, *n.* late twilight; gloom.—*a.* dusky.—*v.i.* and *t.* become, make, dusky. **dusky,** *a.* shadowy, dark; swarthy, black. (O.E. *dox,* dark)

dust, *n.* fine particles of matter; remains of dead.—*v.t.* and *i.* remove dust (from); sprinkle with powder. **bite the d.,** fall, be killed. **lick the d.,** grovel. **raise a d.,** make a fuss. **throw d. in one's eyes,** mislead. **d.-cloth, d.-coat,** *nn.* to keep off dust. **d.-cover,** *n.* book's jacket. **d.-up,** *n.* row. **dustbin,** *n.* receptacle for refuse. **duster,** *n.* cloth for dusting. **dusting,** *n.* (*sl.*) tossing in storm. **dustman,** *n.* scavenger; sandman. (O.E.)

dustoor, dustoory, same as **dastur.**

dustuck, dustuk, *n.* (*Anglo-Ind.*) passport.

dusty, *a.* like, coated with, dust. **d. miller,** auricula. **not so d.,** (*sl.*) not so bad.

dutch, *n.* (*sl.*) wife. (*duchess*)

Dutch, *a.* and *n.* (people, language) of Holland. **double D.,** gibberish. **D. auction,** at which price is lowered till buyer is found. **D. courage,** got from drink. **D. oven,** box for cooking before open fire. **D. treat,** where each pays for himself. **like a D. uncle,** with stern kindness. **Dutchman,** *n.* native of Holland; (*Amer. colloq.*) German. (Du. *dutsch*)

duty, *n.* what one ought to do, obligation; respect, deference; office, function; tax, impost, on goods. **do d. for,** serve as. **on, off, d.,** engaged in one's business, disengaged. **d.-free,** *a.* free from customs duty. **duteous,** *a.* (*poet.*) dutiful. **dutiable,** *a.* liable to duties. **dutiful,** *a.* attentive to duty; obedient to parents and superiors. (*due*)

duumvir, *n.* (*pl.* **duumvirs, duumviri**) member of **duumvirate,** *n.* governing body of two. (L.)

duvet, *n.* eiderdown quilt. (F.)

dux, *n.* head boy in school or class. (L. =leader)

duyker, same as **duiker.**

dwale, *n.* deadly nightshade.

dwalm, *n.* (*Scot.*) swoon, sudden sickness. (O.E. *dwolma,* confusion)

dwarf, *n.* undersized person, animal, or plant; gnome.—*a.* of small kind; stunted.—*v.t.* stunt growth of; cause to look small. **dwarfish,** *a.* (O.E. *dweorh*)

dwell, *v.i.* (*past, p.p.* **dwelt**) live, reside. **d. upon,** linger, brood, over; expatiate upon. **dwelling,** *n.* abode. **dwelling-house,** *n.* residence, not shop etc. (O.E. *dwellan,* delay)

dwindle, *v.i.* grow smaller, shrink; decline. **dwine,** *v.i.* (*Scot.*) pine, waste away. (O.E. *dwinan,* fade)

dyad, *n.* pair; (*chem.*) bivalent atom, element, or radical. **dyadic,** *a.* (Gk. *duo,* two)

Dyak, *n.* Borneo aboriginal. (Malay)

dyarchy, see **diarchy.**

dye, *n.* colouring liquid; colour produced by it; hue.—*v.t.* and *i.* (*pres. part.* **dyeing**) colour, take colour, by immersion in dye; stain, tinge. **d.-stuff,** *n.* material yielding dye. **d.-works,** *n.pl.* where dyeing is done. **dyer,** *n.* (O.E. *déag*)

dying, see **die.**

dyke, see **dike.**

dynamic, *a.* of force or dynamics; forceful, energetic; (*med.*) functional. —*n.* motive force; (*pl.*) science of action of force in producing motion or equilibrium. **dynamical,** *a.* of dynamics or dynamism. **dynamism,** *n.* (*philos.*) theory that the universe is constituted by forces. **dynamist,** *n.* expert in dynamics; believer in dynamism. (Gk. *dunamis,* force)

dynamite, *n.* high explosive made with nitro-glycerine.—*v.t.* blow with this. **dynamiter, dynamitard,** *nn.* user of dynamite, esp. for revolutionary purposes. (Gk. *dunamis,* force)

dynamo, *n.* machine that transforms mechanical into electrical energy, generator of electricity. **d.-electric,** *a.* of current electricity. (Gk. *dunamis,* force)

dynamometer, *n.* instrument measuring energy expended. (Gk. *dunamis,* force; *metron,* measure)

dynast, *n.* hereditary ruler. **dynasty,** *n.* succession of rulers of same family. **dynastic,** *a.* (Gk. *dunastēs*)

dyne, *n.* unit of force, causing in one gramme an acceleration per second of one centimetre per second. (Gk. *dunamis,* force)

dys-, *pref.* bad, used in **dysaesthesia**, *n.* loss of sense of touch; **dyschroa**, *n.* skin discoloration; **dyscrasia**, *n.* constitutional weakness; **dysentery**, *n.* bowel disease with ulceration and diarrhoea, hence **dysenteric**, *a.*; **dysgenic**, *a.* having a bad effect on the race (opp. to eugenic); **dyslogistic**, *a.* unfavourable (opp. to eulogistic); **dysmenorrhoea**, *n.* painful menstruation; **dyspepsia, dyspepsy**, *n.* indigestion, esp. chronic, hence **dyspeptic**. *a.* of, afflicted with, indigestion.—*n.* dyspeptic sufferer; **dysphagia**, *n.* difficulty in swallowing; **dysphoria**, *n.* morbid restlessness, fidgets; **dyspnoea**, *n.* shortness of breath; **dysprosium**, *n.* highly magnetic metallic element; **dystomic**, *a.* having an imperfect fracture; **dysuria**, *n.* difficulty in passing urine. (Gk. *dus-*)

dyvour, *n.* (*Scot.*) bankrupt.

dziggetai, *n.* Asiatic wild ass. (Mongolian *tchikhitei*, long-eared)

E

E, (of ship) second-class in Lloyd's register; (*mus.*) note and scale. **E-boat**, *n.* small fast motor-boat armed with torpedoes.

e-, see **ex-**.

ea, *n.* (*dial.*) river, ditch, inlet. (O.E. *éa*)

each, *a.* and *pron.* every (one) taken separately. (O.E. *ǽlc*)

eager, *a.* keenly desirous; ardent; impatient; (*Shake.*) pungent, bitter. (L. *acer*)

eagle, *n.* large keen-eyed bird of prey; Roman military standard; U.S. gold coin worth 10 dollars; (*golf*) hole done in two under par. **e.-eyed**, *a.* sharp-sighted. **e.-owl**, *n.* great horned owl. **eaglet**, *n.* young eagle. (L. *aquila*)

eagre, *n.* great tidal wave in estuary, bore.

ean, eanling, *obs.* for **yean, yeanling.**

ear, *n.* spike of corn. (O.E. *éar*)

ear, *v.t.* (*Shake.*) plough. (O.E. *erian*)

ear, *n.* hearing organ; (discriminating) sense of hearing; ear-shaped thing, handle; attention, audience. **about one's ee.**, all around one. **head over ee.**, very deeply. **set by the ee.**, set at strife. **walls have ee.**, there may be listeners. **earphone**, *n.* headphone. **e.-trumpet**, *n.* tube to aid in hearing. (O.E. *éare*)

earache, *n.* pain in the ear.

eardrum, *n.* tympanum.

earing, *n.* (*naut.*) rope attaching upper corner of sail to yard.

earl, *n.* nobleman ranking between marquis and viscount. **E. Marshal**, president of Heralds' College. **earldom**, *n.* earl's domain or title. (O.N. *jarl*)

early, *adv.* and *a.* near, nearer, the beginning; soon. **e. bird**, early riser. **earlier on**, at an earlier stage. (O.E. *árlice*)

earmark, *n.* owner's mark on ear of sheep.—*v.t.* mark thus; assign, reserve (for special purpose).

earn, *v.t.* gain by labour; merit. **earnings**, *n.pl.* money earned. (O.E. *earnian*)

earn, *obs.* for **yearn.**

earnest, *a.* serious, not trifling, zealous. **in e.**, seriously, not in jest. (O.E. *eorneste*)

earnest, *n.* pledge, foretaste; (also **e.-money**) money given in token of bargain.

earring, *n.* ornamental ring hanging from ear-lobe.

earshot, *n.* hearing distance.

earth, *n.* this planet, the world; dry land, ground; soil, mould; hole of fox; (*chem.*) any of several metallic oxides; (*electr.*) communication with earth.—*v.t.* and *i.* cover, connect, with earth; run to earth. **e.-born**, *a.* mortal. **e.-closet**, *n.* dry privy. **e.-house**, *n.* prehistoric underground dwelling, Pictish house. **e.-nut**, *n.* pignut; ground-nut. (O.E. *eorthe*)

earthen, *a.* made of earth or baked clay; earthly. **earthenware**, *n.* baked clay (vessels), crockery.

earthly, *a.* of the earth, terrestrial; worldly. **no e. use**, no use whatever. **not an e.**, (*sl.*) no chance at all.

earthquake, *n.* shaking, convulsion, of the earth's surface.

earthwork, *n.* bank of earth in fortification.

earthworm, *n.* common worm; mean person.

earthy, *a.* of, like, earth; grossly material, unrefined.

earwig, *n.* insect like beetle; (*Amer. colloq.*) small centipede.—*v.t.* bias by whispered suggestions. (once believed to creep into the *ear*)

ease, *n.* freedom from pain or trouble, relief; freedom from constraint, naturalness; facility; leisure.—*v.t.* and *i.* relieve; alleviate; facilitate; slacken, relax. **e. her**, (*naut.*) reduce speed. **easeful**, *a.* restful; slothful. (O.F. *aise*)

easel, *n.* frame to support picture etc. (Du. *ezel*, ass)

easement, *n.* relief; (*law*) right of way etc. over another's land.

east, *n.* quarter where sun rises; eastern lands, orient.—*a.* and *adv.* on, to, the east; (of wind) from the east. **Far E.**, China, Japan etc. **Middle E.**, Irak, Iran etc. **Near E.**, Turkey, Palestine etc. (O.E. *éast*)

Easter, *n.* movable festival of the Resurrection. **E. Day,** Easter Sunday. **E. egg,** egg, egg-shaped box with sweets etc., as Easter present. (O.E. *éastre*)

easterly, *a.* and *adv.* towards the east; (of wind) from the east. **eastern,** *a.* of, dwelling in, the east; oriental. **Eastern Church,** Greek Church. **Eastern Empire,** part of later Roman Empire with capital at Byzantium. **easterner,** *n.* native of the east. **easting,** *n.* distance sailed eastwards from a given meridian. **eastward,** *a.* and *adv.* towards the east. **eastwards,** *adv.*

easy, *a.* not difficult; free from pain; at ease, unconstrained; compliant; not oppressive; (of market) not showing eager demand.—*adv.* easily. **e. all!** stop rowing. **easy chair,** *n.* armchair designed for comfort. **e. circumstances,** affluence. **e. mark,** (*Amer.*) gullible person. **e.-going,** (*Scot.*) **easy-osy,** *aa.* not hard to please; indolent. (*ease*)

eat, *v.t.* and *i.* (*past* **ate, eat;** *p.p.* **eaten,** *obs.* **eat**) chew and swallow; consume; corrode.—*n.pl.* (*Amer. sl.*) food. **e. away,** destroy gradually. **e. one's heart out,** pine away with brooding. **e. one's terms,** study for the Bar. **e. one's words,** retract, recant. **e. the air,** (*Shake.*) be fed on promises. **e. up,** finish; absorb. **eating-house,** *n.* restaurant. **eatable,** *a.* fit to eat.—*n.* solid food. **eatage,** *n.* grazing. **eater,** *n.* (O.E. *etan*)

eath, *a.* (*Spens.*) easy. (O.E. *éathe,* easily)

eau, **n.** water. **e.-de-Cologne,** *n.* a perfume. *e. de Nil,* a greenish colour. *e.-de-vie,* *n.* brandy. (F.)

eaves, *n.pl.* projecting edge of roof. **eavesdrop,** *v.i.* listen secretly. **eavesdropper,** *n.* (O.E. *efes*)

ebb, *n.* flowing back of tide; decline. —*v.i.* recede, decline. **e.-tide,** *n.* ebbing tide. (O.E. *ebba*)

Eblis, *n.* Mohammedan Satan. (Arab. *iblis*)

ebon, *a.* (*poet.*) ebony. **ebonite,** *n.* vulcanite. **ebony,** *n.* hard black wood.—*a.* made of, black as, ebony. **ebonize,** *v.t.* (Gk. *ebenos*)

ebrious, *a.* of drunkenness; drunk. **ebriety,** *n.* (L. *ebrius*)

ebullient, *a.* boiling; exuberant. **ebullience, ebulliency,** *nn.* **ebullition,** *n.* boiling, bubbling; outburst. (L. *bullire,* boil)

eburnean, eburnine, *aa.* of, like, ivory. (L. *ebur,* ivory)

écarté, *n.* a card game for two. (F.)

ecbasis, *n.* figure of speech in which things are treated according to their consequences. (Gk. *ekbasis*)

ècbolē, *n.* digression. (Gk. *ekbolē*)

eccentric, *a.* placed, having axis, away from centre; (of circle) not having same centre as another; (of orbit) not circular; irregular; odd, peculiar. —*n.* eccentric circle or person; (*mech.*) device for changing rotatory into to-and-fro movement. **eccentrically,** *adv.* **eccentricity,** *n.* (Gk. *ek,* out of; *kentron,* centre)

ecchymosis, *n.* discoloured spot due to effusion of blood into tissue. (Gk. *ek,* out; *chumos,* juice)

ecclesia, *n.* popular assembly of ancient Athens. **ecclesiast,** *n.* member of this. **Ecclesiastes,** *n.* a book of the Old Testament. **ecclesiastic,** *n.* clergyman, priest.—*a.* ecclesiastical. **ecclesiastical,** *a.* of church or clergy. **ecclesiasticism,** *n.* **ecclesiology,** *n.* science of church-building. **ecclesiological,** *a.* **ecclesiologist,** *n.* (Gk. *ekklēsia*)

eccysis, *n.* sloughing, moulting; slough (Gk. *ekduein,* put off)

echelon, *n.* formation (of troops etc.) like flight of steps.—*v.t.* arrange thus. **in e.,** *en é.,* so drawn up. (F. *échelon*)

echidna, *n.* spiny ant-eater, animal like hedgehog. (Gk.=viper)

echinus, *n.* sea-urchin; (*archit.*) rounded egg-shaped moulding. **echinate,** *a.* prickly. **echinite,** *n.* fossil sea-urchin. **echinoderm,** *n.* animal of sea-urchin or starfish class. (Gk. *echinos,* hedgehog)

echo, *n.* (*pl.* **echoes**) repetition of sound by reflection; close imitation or imitator.—*v.i.* and *t.* emit echo, resound; reflect, repeat (sound); copy. **to the e.,** loudly. **echoic,** *a.* **echoism,** *n.* onomatopoeia. (Gk.)

éclair, *n.* finger-shaped cake filled with cream and iced. (F.)

éclaircissement, **n.** clearing up, explanation. (F.)

eclampsia, *n.* convulsive seizure. (Gk. *eklampein,* shine forth)

éclat, **n.** striking effect, applause; splendour, social distinction. (F.)

eclectic, *a.* selecting; choosing (best) from different systems etc.; broad, not exclusive.—*n.* eclectic philosopher. **eclecticism,** *n.* (Gk. *ek,* out; *legein,* choose)

eclipse, *n.* obscuring of heavenly body by intervention of another; obscuration, temporary failure.—*v.t.* intercept light of; outshine, surpass. **ecliptic,** *a.* of eclipse.—*n.* sun's apparent path among stars; great circle on globe corresponding to this. (Gk. *ek,* out; *leipein,* leave)

eclogue, *n.* pastoral poem. (Gk. *eklogē,* selection)

ecology, *n.* science of plants and animals in relation to their surroundings. (Gk. *oikos,* house; *legein,* speak)

economy, *n.* management of community's concerns and resources, organization; system of operation; frugality, economizing act. **political e.,** science of production and distribution of wealth. **economic,** *a.* of (political) economy; on business lines, paying costs.—*n.pl.* political economy; material condition (of state). **economical,** *a.* saving, thrifty; inexpensive; of economics. **economist,** *n.* manager; thrifty person; writer on economics. **economize,** *v.t.* and *i.* use sparingly; reduce expenditure. **economization,** *n.* (Gk. *oikos,* house; *nemein,* manage)

écru, *n.* pale yellow-brown, colour of unbleached linen. (F.=unbleached)

ecstasy, *n.* overwhelming delight, rapture; mystic trance or frenzy. **ecstasize,** *v.t.* and *i.* throw, go, into ecstasy. **ecstatic,** *a.* of, in, ecstasy; rapturous. **ecstatically,** *adv.* (Gk. *existanai,* derange)

ecto-, from Gk. *ektos,* outside, used in **ectoblast,** *n.* outer wall of cell; **ectoderm,** *n.* outer layer of embryo or skin; **ectogenetic,** *a.* born without gestation; **ectoplasm,** *n.* exterior protoplasm of cell, (*spiritualism*) emanation from medium; **ectozoon,** *n.* external parasite.

écu, *n.* old French crown; five-franc piece. (F.)

ecumenical, same as **oecumenical.**

eczema, *n.* an inflammatory skin disease. (Gk. *ek,* out; *zein,* boil)

-ed, *suf.* forming past tense and past participle of regular or weak verbs, as in formed.—*adj.suf.* having, as in **wooded.** (O.E. *ed, ede*)

edacious, *a.* of eating; devouring, greedy. **edacity,** *n.* (L. *edere,* eat)

Edam, *n.* Dutch yellow pressed cheese. (place)

Edda, *n.* **Younger** or **Prose E.,** 13th-century commentary on old Norse mythological poetry, of which **Elder** or **Poetic E.** is an anthology.

eddy, *n.* small whirl, counter-current, in water, smoke etc.—*v.i.* and *t.* move round and round.

edelweiss, *n.* white-flowered Alpine plant. (G. *edel,* noble; *weiss,* white)

Eden, *n.* garden of Adam and Eve; paradise, delightful place. (Heb.)

edentate, *a.* toothless; without front teeth.—*n.* edentate animal. (L. *e,* out; *dens,* tooth)

edge, *n.* cutting side of blade; sharpness, keenness; verge, brink, boundary.—*v.t.* and *i.* give edge to, sharpen; move sideways or gradually. **be on e.,** be irritable. **e. on,** egg on. **set teeth on e.,** jar on nerves. **e.-bone,** *n.* aitch-bone. **e.-tool,** *n.* cutting tool. **edgeways, edgewise,** *advv.* edge foremost, sideways. **edging,** *n.* border, fringe. **edgy,** *a.* sharp; irritable; (of painting) hard in outline. (O.E. *ecg*)

edible, *a.* fit for eating.—*n.* eatable. **edibility,** *n.* (L. *edere,* eat)

edict, *n.* order proclaimed by authority, decree. **edictal,** *a.* (L. *edicere,* proclaim)

edifice, *n.* building, esp. a large one. (*edify*)

edify, *v.t.* improve morally, instruct. **edification,** *n.* (L. *aedis,* temple; *facere,* make)

edit, *v.t.* prepare, revise, for publication; conduct (periodical). **edition.** *n.* form in which book etc. is published; number of copies printed at one time, issue. **edition de luxe,** handsome edition. *editio princeps,* first printed edition. **editor,** *n.* (*fem.* **editress**) one who conducts a newspaper or edits work. **editorial,** *a.* of an editor.—*n.* leading article. **editorship,** *n.* (L. *e,* out; *dare,* give)

educate, *v.t.* bring up, develop mentally; instruct, train, teach. **educable,** *a.* able to be educated. **education,** *n.* upbringing, training; (course of) instruction. **educational,** *a.* **educationist, educationalist,** *nn.* person versed in theory, advocate, of education. **educative,** *a.* educating. **educator,** *n.* (L. *e,* out; *ducere,* lead)

educe, *v.t.* bring out, elicit; deduce; (*chem.*) extract from compound. **educible,** *a.* **educt,** *n.* inference; (*chem.*) substance educed. **eduction,** *n.* (L. *e,* out; *ducere,* lead)

edulcorate, *v.t.* free from acids etc. by washing; purify, sweeten. **edulcoration,** *n.* (L. *dulcis,* sweet)

ee, *n.* (*Scot.*; *pl.* **een**) eye.

-ee, *n. suf.* indicating indirect or direct object of action, as in **trustee,** employee. (L. *-atus*)

eel, *n.* snake-like slippery fish. **e.-basket, e.-buck,** *nn.* wicker trap for eels. (O.E. *ǣl*)

een, see **ee.**

e'en, e'er, *contr.* **for even, ever.**

eerie, eery, *a.* causing or feeling superstitious fear; uncanny.

efface, *v.t.* rub out, wear away; render indistinguishable. **effaceable,** *a.* **effacement,** *n.* (*face*)

effect, *n.* result, consequence; purport; impression; (*pl.*) property.—*v.t.* bring about, accomplish; (*Shake.*) produce. **give e. to, take e.,** make, become, operative. **in e.,** for practical purposes. **effective,** *a.* having effect, operative; striking; serviceable.—*n.* soldier ready for service. **effectual,** *a.* answering its purpose; valid; (*Shake.*) pertinent. **effectually,** *adv.* efficaciously. **effectuate,** *v.t.* effect, fulfil. **effectuation,** *n.* (L. *effectus*)

effeminate, *a.* womanish, unmanly; voluptuous. **effeminacy,** *n.* (L. *femina,* woman)

effendi, *n.* Turkish title of respect, sir. (Gk. *authentēs,* autocrat)

efferent, *a.* (*anat.*) conveying out, discharging. (L. *ex,* out; *ferre,* bear)

effervesce, *v.i.* give off bubbles, froth up. **effervescent,** *a.* **effervescence,** *n.* (L. *fervere,* boil)

effete, *a.* worn out, spent; feeble. (L. *effetus*, worn out by breeding)
efficacious, *a.* producing, able to produce, desired result. **efficacy,** *n.* efficaciousness, potency. (*effect*)
efficient, *a.* producing effect; capable, competent. **efficiency,** *n.* (*effect*)
effigy, *n.* image, likeness. **burn in e.,** burn image of. (L. *fingere*, form)
effloresce, *v.i.* blossom forth; (*chem.*) form surface of white dust or minute crystals. **efflorescence,** *n.* **efflorescent,** *a.* (L. *flos*, flower)
effluent, *a.* flowing out.—*n.* stream that flows out of lake or larger stream. **effluence,** *n.* flowing out; what flows out. **effluvium,** *n.* (*pl.* **effluvia**) exhalation; noxious vapours from decaying matter. **efflux, effluxion,** *nn.* outflow, effluence. (L. *ex*, out; *fluere*, flow)
effort, *n.* exertion of power; attempt, endeavour. **effortless,** *a.* without effort, easy; making no effort. (L. *fortis*, strong)
effrontery, *n.* shamelessness, impudence. (L. *frons*, forehead)
effulgent, *a.* shining forth, radiant. **effulgence,** *n.* (L. *ex*, out; *fulgēre*, shine)
effuse, *v.t.* pour out, shed.—*a.* (*bot.*) spreading loosely. **effusion,** *n.* outpouring, issue; poem. **effusive,** *a.* demonstrative, gushing. (L. *ex*, out; *fundere*, pour)
eft, *n.* newt. (O.E. *efeta*)
eft, *adv.* (*Spens.*) afterwards; again; also. **eftsoons, eftsoon,** *adv.* (*arch.*) soon after. (O.E.)
egad, *int.* a minced oath. (*God*)
egal, *a.* (*Shake.*) equal. (F.)
egest, *v.t.* void, excrete. **egestion,** *n.* **egesta,** *n.pl.* excrements. (L. *e*, out; *gerere*, bear)
egg, *n.* oval body containing germ from which young of bird is developed; ovum; (*army sl.*) bomb. **bad e.,** (*sl.*) ne'er-do-well. **good e.!** (*sl.*) well done! **e.-cup, e.-spoon,** *nn.* used in eating boiled egg. **e.-flip, e.-nog,** *nn.* drink of egg beaten up with wine etc. **e.-shell,** *n.* egg's brittle shell; fragile thing. (O.E. *ǽg*)
egg, *v.t.* urge (on). (O.N. *eggja*)
egger, *n.* a large moth.
eglantine, *n.* sweetbrier. (O.F. *aiglent*)
ego, *n.* the self. **egocentric,** *a.* centred in the ego, self-centred. **egoism,** *n.* systematic selfishness, opp. to altruism; (*ethics*) theory that bases morality on self-interest; (*philos.*) doctrine that we can prove nothing but our own existence. **egoist,** *n.* **egoistic, egoistical,** *aa.* **egotism,** *n.* habit of talking about oneself, self-praise. **egotist,** *n.* **egotistic, egotistical,** *aa.* (L.=I)
egregious, *a.* outstanding, flagrant; (*arch.*) distinguished. (L. *e*, out of; *grex*, flock)
egress, *n.* going, way, out; right of departure; (*astron.*) emergence from eclipse etc. **egression,** *n.* going forth. (L. *e*, out; *gradi*, step)
egret, *n.* small white heron; down of dandelion etc. (=*aigrette*)
Egyptian, *a.* and *n.* (native) of Egypt. **Egyptology,** *n.* study of Egyptian antiquities. **Egyptologist,** *n.*
eh, *int.* of inquiry or surprise.
eident, *a.* (*Scot.*) diligent.
eider, *n.* (also **e.-duck**) an Arctic duck. **eiderdown,** *n.* its breast-feathers; quilt stuffed with these.
eidograph, *n.* instrument for enlarging or reducing drawings. (Gk. *eidos*, form; *graphein*, write)
eidolon, *n.* (*pl.* **eidolons, eidola**) apparition, phantom. (Gk.=image)
eight, *a.* and *n.* one more than seven; eight-oared racing-boat; its crew. **have one over the e.,** (*sl.*) be drunk. **eighth,** *a.* next after seventh.—*n.* one of eight equal parts. **eighteen,** *a.* and *n.* eight and ten. **eighteenth,** *a.* and *n.* **eighteenmo,** *n.* octodecimo. **eightfold,** *a.* eight times. **eightsome,** *n.* Scotch reel for eight persons. **eighty,** *a.* and *n.* eight times ten. **eightieth,** *a.* and *n.* (O.E. *ahta*)
eild, *n.* (*Scot.*) old age.
eirenicon, *n.* peace proposal. (Gk. *eirēnē*, peace)
eisel, *n.* (*Shake.*) vinegar. (L. *acetum*)
eistedfodd, *n.* annual congress of Welsh bards, with competitions in poetry and music. (W.)
either, *a.* and *pron.* one or other of two; each (one).—*conj.* introducing first of two alternatives. (O.E. *ǽghwædher*)
ejaculate, *v.t.* and *i.* utter suddenly, exclaim; eject swiftly. **ejaculation, ejaculator,** *nn.* **ejaculatory,** *a.* (L. *jaculum*, javelin)
eject, *v.t.* throw out, expel; emit. **ejection, ejectment, ejector,** *nn.* (L. *e*, out; *jacere*, throw)
ek dum, (*Anglo-Ind.*) at once.
eke, *v.t.* **e. out,** supplement; (*incorrectly*) barely make (living). (O.E. *ēcan*)
eke, *adv.* (*arch.*) also. (O.E. *éac*)
ekka, *n.* (*Anglo-Ind.*) small horse-carriage or bullock-cart. (Hind.)
elaborate, *v.t.* produce with labour; work out in detail.—*a.* highly finished; complicated. **elaboration, elaborator,** *nn.* **elaborative,** *a.* **elaboratory,** *n.* laboratory. (L. *labor*, work)
elaeo-, from Gk. *elaion*, olive oil, used in **elaeometer,** *n.* instrument for testing purity of oils; **elaeoptene,** *n.* liquid part of vegetable oil.
élan, *n.* dash, impetuosity. (F.)
eland, *n.* largest S. African antelope. (Du.=elk)
elapse, *v.i.* (of time) pass. (*lapse*)
elastic, *a.* resuming original shape

after distortion, springy; buoyant; flexible.—*n.* fabric made elastic with indiarubber; (*Amer.*) elastic band, garter etc. **elasticity,** *n.* (Gk. *elaunein*, drive)

elate, *v.t.* raise spirits of; make proud. —*a.* exultant, flushed with success. **elation,** *n.* high spirits; pride. (L. *elatus*, elevated)

elbow, *n.* joint, bend, of arm; angle, sharp turn.—*v.t.* and *i.* thrust, jostle. **at one's e.,** close at hand. **out at ee.,** ragged, worn. **up to the ee.,** busily engaged. **e.-grease,** *n.* vigorous rubbing. **e.-room,** *n.* space to move, scope. (O.E. *elnboga*)

elchee, *n.* ambassador. (Turk. *ilchi*)

eld, *n.* old age; olden time. (O.E. *ald*, old)

elder, *n.* small white-flowered tree. **e. wine,** *n.* made from its berries. **e.-gun,** *n.* (*Shake.*) pop-gun. (O.E. *ellærn*)

elder, *a.* older, senior.—*n.* aged person; senior; office-bearer of certain churches: senator. **elderly,** *a.* getting old. **eldest,** *a.* oldest; first-born. (*eld*)

El Dorado, fabled land rich in gold. (Sp.=the gilded)

eldritch, *a.* (*Scot.*) weird, hideous.

elecampane, *n.* pungent composite plant; sweetmeat flavoured with it. (L.L. *enula campana*)

elect, *v.t.* choose; choose by vote.—*a.* chosen; choice; chosen for office but not yet in it. **the e.,** those divinely chosen for salvation. **election,** *n.* choosing, esp. by voting. **general election,** of whole House of Commons. **by-election,** *n.* of single M.P. to fill vacancy. **electioneer,** *v.i.* work, canvass, at political election. **elective,** *a.* appointed, filled, by election; entitled to elect; (*Amer.*) optional. **elector,** *n.* (*fem.* **electress**) one who elects; German prince with right of electing the emperor. **electoral,** *a.* **electorate,** *n.* body of electors. **electorship,** *n.* (L. *e*, out; *legere*, choose)

electric, *a.* of, charged with, worked by, producing, electricity.—*n.* substance in which electricity can be excited by friction. **e. battery,** cells producing electricity by chemical action. **e. blue,** steely blue. **e. chair,** for electrocuting criminals. **e. charge, circuit, current,** accumulation, path, flow, of electricity. **e. eel,** freshwater fish giving electric shock. **e. shock,** effect of discharge of electricity. **e. storm,** violent disturbance of earth's electrical condition. (Gk. *ēlektron*, amber)

electrical, *a.* concerned with electricity; electric. **electrically,** *adv.* by means of electricity.

electrician, *n.* electrical mechanic.

electricity, *n.* natural agency or force developed by friction, chemical action, heat, or magnetism; science of this. **positive, negative, e.,** kind produced by friction on glass, on resin. (*electric*)

electrify, *v.t.* charge with electricity; convert to electric working; excite, startle. **electrification,** *n.*

electrize, *v.t.* electrify. **electrization,** *n.*

electro, *n.* and *v.t.* (*colloq.*) electroplate; electrotype. (abbr.)

electro-, *pref.* of, by, electricity.

electro-biology, *n.* science of electrical phenomena of living beings.

electro-chemistry, *n.* science of chemical changes caused by electricity.

electrocute, *v.t.* execute, kill, by electricity. **electrocution,** *n.* (*electro-*+ exe*cute*)

electrode, *n.* terminal of electric circuit. (Gk. *hodos*, way)

electrodynamics, *n.* dynamics of electricity.

electrokinetics, *n.* science of electricity in motion. (*kinetic*)

electrolier, *n.* cluster of electric lights. (*electro-*+chandel*ier*)

electrology, *n.* science of applied electricity. (Gk. *legein*, speak)

electrolyse, *v.t.* decompose by electricity. **electrolysis,** *n.* **electrolyte,** *n.* body that is or can be electrolysed. (Gk. *luein*, loose)

electro-magnet, *n.* iron core magnetized inductively by passing electric current through wire coiled round it. **electro-magnetic,** *a.* **electro-magnetism,** *n.* magnetism produced by electric current; science of relations between electricity and magnetism.

electrometer, *n.* instrument for measuring electricity. **electrometric,** *a.*

electro-motion, *n.* motion of galvanic current; mechanical motion produced by electricity. **electro-motive,** *a.* **electro-motor,** *n.* machine driven by electricity.

electron, *n.* one of the fundamental particles of matter, a constituent of the atom, identified with unit charge of negative electricity; electrum. **electronic,** *a.*

electro-negative, *a.* of negative electricity.

electropathy, *n.* electrical treatment of disease. (Gk. *pathos*, feeling)

electrophore, electrophorus, *n.* instrument for induction of electric charge. (Gk. *pherein*, bear)

electroplate, *v.t.* coat with silver by electrolysis.—*n.* ware so coated.

electro-positive, *a.* of positive electricity.

electroscope, *n.* instrument showing presence or quality of electricity.

electrostatics, *n.* science of electricity at rest. (*static*)

electrotherapeutics, electrotherapy, *nn.* use, science, of electricity as curative agent. **electrotherapist,** *n.*

electrotype, *n.* facsimile made by deposit of copper on mould by galvanic action.—*v.t.* copy in this way. **electrotypy**, *n.* this process.

electrum, *n.* ancient alloy of gold and silver. (Gk. *ēlektron*, amber)

electuary, *n.* medicinal powder mixed with honey etc. (L.L. *electuarium*)

eleemosynary, *a.* of alms; given in, dependent on, charity. (Gk. *eleēmosunē*, pity)

elegant, *a.* graceful; refined, tasteful; (*vulg.*) excellent.—*n.* person of fashion. **elegance**, *n.* (L. *elegans*)

elegy, *n.* lament for dead; mournful poem; poem in elegiacs. **elegiac**, *a.* suited to elegies; in metre of alternate hexameter and pentameter.—*n.pl.* elegiac verse. **elegist**, *n.* writer of elegy. **elegize**, *v.t.* write elegy (upon) (Gk. *elegos*)

element, *n.* component part, ingredient; earth, air, fire, or water; proper abode or sphere; (*chem.*) substance not separable into others; (*pl.*) atmospheric agencies; first principles, rudiments; bread and wine of eucharist. **elemental**, *a.* of, like, powers of nature; tremendous, primal; uncompounded.—*n.* spirit of earth, air, fire, or water. **elementary**, *a.* rudimentary; (*chem.*) not decomposable. (L. *elementum*)

elemi, *n.* a resin used in medicines and varnish.

elenchus, *n.* refutation by argument. **elenctic**, *a.* (Gk. *elengchos*)

elephant, *n.* huge four-footed thick-skinned animal with tusks and trunk; size of paper, 28 by 23 in. **white e.**, gift causing more trouble than it is worth. **elephantiasis**, *n.* disease making skin like elephant's hide. **elephantine**, *a.* of, like, an elephant; huge, ungainly. **elephantoid**, *a.* elephant-like. (Gk. *elephas*)

eleuthero-, from Gk. *eleutheros*, free, used in **eleutheromania**, *n.* mad zeal for freedom, hence **eleutheromaniac**, *n.* **eleutherophyllous**, *a.* with distinct leaves.

elevate, *v.t.* raise, lift up; exalt; animate; edify. **elevated**, *a.* (*colloq.*) tipsy. **elevation**, *n.* elevating, exaltation; elevated place, eminence; altitude; angle (of gun) with horizontal; (*archit.*) vertical plan of side of building. **elevator**, *n.* that which elevates; lift; (*anat.*) muscle that raises limb etc.; (*Amer.*) warehouse for storing grain. **elevatory**, *a.* (L. *levis*, light)

eleven, *a.* and *n.* one more than ten; side at cricket, association football, or hockey; (*pl.*) forenoon snack. **the E.**, the disciples (without Judas). **eleventh**, *a.* next after tenth.—*n.* one of eleven equal parts. **eleventh hour**, last available moment. (O.E. *endleofon*)

elf *n.* (*pl.* **elves**) sprite, fairy, small mischievous creature.—*v.t.* (*Shake.*) tangle (hair). **e.-child**, *n.* changeling. **e.-lock**, *n.* matted mass of hair. **e.-struck**, *a.* bewitched. **elfin**, *a.* of elves.—*n.* sportive child. **elfish** *a.* like an elf, mischievous. (O.E. *ælf*)

elicit, *v.t.* draw out, evoke; educe. (L. *elicere*)

elide, *v.t.* cut off, slur (final vowel etc.). (L. *e*, out; *laedere*, dash)

eligible, *a.* fit to be chosen, qualified. **eligibility**, *n.* (*elect*)

eliminate, *v.t.* remove, get rid of; excrete, expel; ignore. **eliminable**, *a.* **elimination, eliminator**, *nn.* (L. *e*, out; *limen*, threshold)

elision, *n.* eliding; suppression of vowel, passage etc. (*elide*)

élite, *n.* choice part, best, flower (of). (F.)

elixir, *n.* alchemist's preparation for transmuting metals into gold or (also **e. vitae**) prolonging life indefinitely; quintessence; (*med.*) compound tincture. (Arab. *al*, the; *iksir*, philosophers' stone)

elk, *n.* largest kind of deer, moose; wapiti. (O.E. *elch*)

ell, *n.* old measure of length, 1¼ yd. (O.E. *eln*)

ellagic, *a.* of gall-nuts.

ellipse, *n.* regular oval; ellipsis. **ellipsis**, *n.* (*pl.* **ellipses**) omission of words obviously implied, e.g. 'St. Paul's' (cathedral). **ellipsoid**, *n.* regular solid oval. **ellipsoidal**, *a.* egg-shaped. **elliptic, elliptical**, *aa.* of, like, ellipse; having part understood. **ellipticity**, *n.* deviation of oval from circle or sphere. (Gk. *elleipein*, fall short)

elm, *n.* forest tree with serrated leaves. **elmy**, *a.* (O.E.)

elocution, *n.* art, manner, of public speaking; delivery. **elocutionary**, *a.* **elocutionist**, *n.* teacher of elocution. (L. *e*, out; *loqui*, speak)

éloge, **elogium, elogy**, *nn.* funeral oration, panegyric. (L. *elogium*, inscription on tomb)

elongate, *v.t.* and *i.* make longer, extend, draw out.—*a.* (*bot.*) tapering. **elongation**, *n.* lengthening; part added; (*astron.*) apparent distance of planet from sun.

elope, *v.i.* run away from husband or home with lover; abscond. **elopement**, *n.* (*leap*)

eloquence, *n.* fluent, forceful, and persuasive speaking; rhetoric. **eloquent**, *a.* (L. *e*, out; *loqui*, speak)

else, *adv.* besides, instead, otherwise. **elsewhere**, *adv.* in, to, another place. (O.E. *elles*)

elucidate, *v.t.* make clear, explain; illustrate. **elucidation, elucidator**, *nn.* **elucidative, elucidatory**, *aa.* (L. *lux*, light)

elucubration, *n.* lucubration.

elude, *v.t.* escape by stratagem, dodge; evade; baffle. **elusion**, *n.* **elusive, elusory**, *aa.* (L. *eludere*)

elvan, *n.* a hard igneous rock.

elvan, elvish, *aa.* elfish. **elves,** see **elf.**
elver, *n.* young eel. (*eel-fare,* brood of eels)
Élysée, *n.* official residence of French President. (F.)
Elysium, *n.* ancient Greek paradise; place, condition, of perfect happiness. **Elysian,** *a.*
elytron, elytrum, *nn.* (*pl.* **elytra**) hard wing-case of beetle; vagina. (Gk. *elutron,* sheath)
Elzevir, *a.* and *n.* (book) printed by Elzevirs at Amsterdam, Leyden etc. in 16th–17th centuries.
em, *n.* letter M; (*print.*) unit of width, $\frac{1}{6}$ in.
'em, *colloq.* for **them.** (obs. *hem,* taken as contraction)
em-, see **en-.**
emaciate, *v.t.* make thin; waste. **emaciation,** *n.* (L. *macies,* leanness)
emanate, *v.i.* issue, proceed, spring (from). **emanation,** *n.* issuing; what issues, efflux. **emanative,** *a.* (L. *e,* out; *manare,* flow)
emancipate, *v.t.* set free (slave); free from moral or intellectual restraint. **emancipation, emancipator,** *nn.* **emancipatory,** *a.* **emancipationist,** *n.* one who advocates freeing slaves. **emancipist,** *n.* (*Austral.*) ex-convict. (L. *e,* out; *manus,* hand; *capere,* take)
emasculate, *v.t.* castrate; make effeminate; weaken by expurgation.—*a.* deprived of virility. **emasculation,** *n.* **emasculative, emasculatory,** *aa.* (L. *e,* out; *masculus,* male)
embalm, *v.t.* preserve (corpse) from decay by aromatic drugs; keep in remembrance; make fragrant. **embalmment,** *n.* (*balm*)
embank, *v.t.* enclose, protect, with bank. **embankment,** *n.* artificial mound carrying road, railway etc.
embargo, *n.* (*pl.* **embargoes**) order stopping movement of ships; suspension of trade; ban.—*v.t.* lay embargo on; requisition. (L.L. *barra,* bar)
embark, *v.t.* and *i.* put, go, on board ship; engage (in). **embarkation,** *n.* (L. *barca,* boat)
embarrass, *v.t.* perplex, disconcert; impede; involve in debt. **embarrassment,** *n.* *embarras de choix, de richesse,* perplexing variety or abundance. (F. *embarrasser*)
embase, *v.t.* (*Spens.*) cast down, humiliate.
embassy, *n.* function, mission, official residence, of ambassador; deputation; (*Shake.*) message. **embassador,** *n.* (*obs.*) ambassador. **embassage,** *n.* (*arch.*) embassy. (Celt. *ambactus,* servant)
embattle, *v.t.* draw up in order of battle. (*battle*)
embattle, *v.t.* furnish with battlements. (*battlement*)
embay, *v.t.* bring, drive (ship) into bay; shut in.
embay, *v.t.* (*Spens.*) bathe.
embed, imbed, *v.t.* fix fast (in something solid). (*bed*)
embellish, *v.t.* make beautiful, adorn; enrich (story) with fanciful additions. **embellishment,** *n.* (L. *bellus,* handsome)
ember, *n.* live coal; (*pl.*) red-hot ashes. (O.E. *æmerge*)
Ember Days, three fast days in each quarter, Wednesday, Friday, and Saturday of first week in Lent and Whit week, and following 14 Sept. and 13 Dec. (O.E. *ymbren*)
ember-goose, *n.* an Orkney sea-bird, loon. (Norwegian *emmer*)
embezzle, *v.t.* divert fraudulently, misappropriate (money etc). **embezzlement,** *n.* (O.F. *besillier,* maltreat)
embitter, *v.t.* make bitter or more bitter; exasperate. **embitterment,** *n.*
emblazon, *v.t.* adorn with heraldic figures; deck in bright colours; celebrate, extol. **emblazonment,** *n.* **emblazonry,** *n.* blazonry.
emblem, *n.* symbol, symbolic figure; heraldic device; type.—*v.t.* symbolize. **emblematic, emblematical,** *aa.* **emblematist,** *n.* maker of emblems. (Gk. *en,* in; *ballein,* throw)
emblements, *n.pl.* growing crop; profits from it. (L.L. *in,* in; *bladum,* wheat)
embody, *v.t.* give body to; make concrete; incorporate, include; represent, be expression of. **embodiment,** *n.*
embolden, *v.t.* encourage. (*bold*)
embolism, *n.* intercalation; (*med.*) obstruction of blood-vessel by blood-clot. (Gk. *en,* in; *ballein,* throw)
embonpoint, *n.* plumpness. (F.)
embosom, *v.t.* embrace, foster; enclose.
emboss, *v.t.* stamp, mould, carve, in relief; adorn with raised work. **embossment,** *n.* (*boss*)
emboss, *v.t.* (*Shake.*) hunt down, exhaust, cause to foam at mouth.
emboss, *v.t.* (*Spens.*) enclose; plunge.
embouchure, *n.* mouth of river, cannon etc.; mouthpiece of wind-instrument, mode of applying it. (F.)
embowel, *v.t.* disembowel; embed, bury.
embower, *v.t.* enclose as in bower.
embrace, *v.t.* and *i.* clasp in arms, enclose; seize, accept; comprise.—*n.* embracing, hug. **embraceable,** *a.* **embracement,** *n.* (L. *brachium,* arm)
embracer, *n.* (*law*) one who attempts to influence jury corruptly. **embracery,** *n.* (O.F. *embraser,* set fire to)
embranchment, *n.* branching out.
embrangle, imbrangle, *v.t.* entangle, confuse. **embranglement,** *n.*
embrasure, *n.* opening in wall for cannon; inward splaying of door or window. (O.F. *embraser,* splay)

embrasure, *n.* (*Shake.*) embrace.
embrocate, *v.t.* bathe and rub (limb etc.). **embrocation,** *n.* lotion for this. (Gk. *en,* in; *brechein,* wet)
embroider, *v.t.* ornament with needlework; embellish (story). **embroidery,** *n.* embroidering; embroidered work. (O.F. *embroder*)
embroil, *v.t.* involve in strife; confuse, distract. **embroilment,** *n.*
embrown, *v.t.* make brown.
embrute, see **imbrute.**
embryo, *n.* (*pl.* **embryos**) unborn or undeveloped offspring, germ; beginning, first state, of thing.—*a.* (also **in e.**) undeveloped, incipient. **embryoctony,** *n.* destruction of foetus. **embryogenesis, embryogeny,** *nn.* formation and development of embryo. **embryology,** *n.* science of embryo, hence **embryologist,** *n.* **embryonic,** *a.* of embryo; rudimentary. **embryotomy,** *n.* cutting up of foetus in womb. (Gk. *embruon*)
embus, *v.t.* and *i.* put, get, into motor lorries. (*bus*)
embusqué, *n.* evader of war service on plea of indispensability. (F.)
emend, *v.t.* remove errors from (text), correct. **emendation, emendator,** *nn.* **emendatory,** *a.* (L. *e.* out; *menda,* fault)
emerald, *n.* green precious stone; 6½-point type, between nonpareil and minion.—*a.* bright green. **E. Isle,** Ireland. **emeraldine,** *a.* (Gk. *smaragdos*)
emerge, *v.i.* rise up, come out; come to notice, crop up. **emergence,** *n.* emerging. **emergency,** *n.* sudden or unexpected juncture; urgent need. **emergent,** *a.* (L. *e,* out; *mergere,* plunge)
emeritus, *a.* (of professor etc.) retired after long service. (L.)
emerods, *arch.* for **haemorrhoids.**
emersion, *n.* emerging; (*astron.*) reappearance after eclipse or occultation. (*emerge*)
emery, *n.* hard mineral used for polishing. **e.-cloth, e.-paper,** *nn.* coated with powdered emery. (Gk. *smēris*)
emetic, *a.* and *n.* (medicine) causing vomiting. (Gk. *emein,* vomit)
emeu, same as **emu.**
émeute, *n.* popular rising, riot. (F.)
emiction, *n.* urination. (L. *e,* out; *mingere,* make water)
emigrate, *v.i.* and *t.* go and settle in another country; assist to do this; (*colloq.*) remove. **emigration,** *n.* **emigrant,** *a.* emigrating.—*n.* one who emigrates. **emigratory,** *a.* *émigré,* *n.* French refugee during Revolution. (*migrate*)
eminence, *n.* distinction; rising ground; title of cardinal; (*Shake.*) homage. **eminent,** *a.* distinguished, notable. **eminently,** *adv.* notably, decidedly. (L. *eminēre,* jut)
emir, *n.* Arab chief or governor; descendant of Mohammed. (=*ameer*)
emissary, *n.* one sent on mission; secret agent. (*emit*)
emit, *v.t.* give out, put forth. **emission,** *n.* giving out or off; thing emitted. **emissive,** *a.* (L. *e,* out; *mittere,* send)
emmesh, see **enmesh.**
emmet, *n.* ant. (O.E. *æmete*)
emollient, *a.* softening, making supple. —*n.* emollient application. (L. *mollis,* soft)
emolument, *n.* salary; profit from work. (L. *emolumentum*)
emong, (*Spens.*) form of **among.**
emotion, *n.* feeling; agitation of mind. **emotional,** *a.* of, appealing to, emotion; easily moved. **emotionalism,** *n.* **emotive,** *a.* of, causing, emotion. (*motion*)
empanel, impanel, *v.t.* enrol (jury); enter on jury-list. (*panel*)
emparadise, same as **imparadise.**
empathy, *n.* (*philos.*) power of putting oneself in another's place or in imaginary situation and understanding it. (Gk. *en,* in; *pathos,* suffering)
empeach, *v.t.* (*Spens.*) hinder, prevent. —*n.* hindrance. (=impeach)
emperor, *n.* ruler of empire. **purple e.,** kind of butterfly. **emperorship,** *n.* **empery,** *n.* power, empire. (L. *imperare,* command)
emphasis, *n.* stress on words; special force of language, intensity; boldness of outline. **emphasize,** *v.t.* lay stress on. **emphatic,** *a.* forcible, strong; stressed; using emphasis. **emphatically,** *adv.* (Gk.)
emphysema, *n.* (*med.*) unnatural distension of part with air. **emphysematous,** *a.* (Gk. *en,* in; *phusaein,* blow)
empierce, *v.t.* (*Spens.*) pierce through.
empight, *p.p.* (*Spens.*) fixed.
empire, *n.* supreme dominion or control; large territory, esp. aggregate of states under supreme ruler.—*a.* in style of first French Empire. **the E.,** Holy Roman Empire. **E. City,** New York. **E. Day,** 24 May, birthday of Queen Victoria. (L. *imperium*)
empiric, *a.* based, relying, on trial and experience, not scientific theory.—*n.* empiric worker; quack. **empirical,** *a.* **empiricism, empiricist,** *nn.* (Gk. *peira,* experiment)
emplacement, *n.* putting in position; gun-platform. (*place*)
emplane, *v.i.* and *t.* go, put, on board aeroplane.
employ, *v.t.* use; use services of; busy, keep occupied. **employable,** *a.* **employer,** *n.* **employee,** *employé,* *nn.* person employed for wages. **employment,** *n.* employing; work; occupation, trade. (L. *implicare,* enfold)
empoison, *v.t.* taint, corrupt; embitter; (*Shake.*) poison.
emporium, *n.* (*pl.* **emporiums, emporia**) centre of commerce, mart; large store,

shop. **emporeutic, emporetic,** *aa.* of trade. (Gk. *emporion*)
empower, *v.t.* authorize; enable.
empress, *n.* woman ruling empire; consort of emperor. (O.F. *emperesse*)
empressement, n. cordiality. (F.)
emprise, *n.* (*arch.*) enterprise, hazardous undertaking. (O.F.)
emption, *n.* buying, purchase. (L. *emere*, buy)
empty, *a.* containing nothing; vacant; senseless, vain, futile; (*colloq.*) hungry. —*n.* empty box etc.—*v.t.* and *i.* remove contents of; become empty; discharge. **e.-handed,** *a.* without a gift. (O.E. *æmetig*, at leisure)
empurple, *v.t.* make purple.
empyema, *n.* collection of pus in pleura etc. (Gk. *en*, in; *puon*, pus)
empyrean, *n.* highest heaven; sky.—*a.* ethereal, celestial. **empyreal,** *a.* (Gk. *en*, in; *pur*, fire)
emu, *n.* Australian bird like ostrich.
emulate, *v.t.* try to equal or excel, vie with; imitate. **emulation, emulator,** *nn.* **emulous,** *a.* ambitiously imitative, rivalling; desirous (of). (L. *aemulus*, emulous)
emulsion, *n.* milky liquid with particles of oil suspended in it. **emulsify,** *v.t.* make into emulsion. **emulsive,** *a.* (L. *e*, out; *mulgēre*, milk)
emunctory, *a.* and *n.* excretory (organ). (L. *emungere*, blow nose)
en, *n.* (*print.*) measure of width, half an em. (letter)
en, prep. in. *en avant*, forward. *en bloc*, in a lump, as a whole. *en déshabillé*, in undress. *en effet*, in effect. *en famille*, at home, among one's family. *en fête*, making holiday, in gala dress. *en garçon*, in bachelor style. *en masse*, in a body. *en passant*, by the way. *en prince*, in princely style. *en prise*, (*chess*) in position to be taken. *en rapport*, in touch or sympathy. *en règle*, in due form, according to rule. *en route*, on the way. *en suite*, in succession or set. *en tout cas*, in any case or emergency. (F.)
en-, *verbal pref.* (**em-** before *b, m, p*) put into, as in **engulf**; make (into) as in **enslave.** (L. *in-*)
enable, *v.t.* make able; empower, authorize.
enact, *v.t.* decree, make law; act part of, perform. **enactive, enactory,** *aa.* **enactment,** *n.* enacting; decree.
enallagē, *n.* (*gram.*) substitution of one case, mood etc. for another. (Gk.)
enamel, *n.* glassy substance for coating metal, pottery etc.; varnish, cosmetic, like this; hard outer layer of teeth; enamelled ware. — *v.t.* coat, inlay, portray, with enamel; adorn with varied colours. (L.L. *smaltum*)
enamour, *v.t.* inspire with love, captivate. (L. *amor*, love)
enantio-, from Gk. *enantios*, opposite, used in **enantiopathy,** *n.* system of treating one disease by inducing another of opposite kind; **enantiosis,** *n.* figure of speech in which the opposite is meant to what is said, irony.
enarthrosis, *n.* (*anat.*) ball-and-socket joint. (Gk.)
enaunter, *conj.* (*Spens.*) lest. (*in adventure*)
encage, incage, *v.t.* put in cage; shut up.
encamp, *v.t.* settle in camp; lodge in tents. **encampment,** *n.* encamping; camp.
encase, incase, *v.t.* put in case; cover, enclose. **encasement,** *n.*
encash, *v.t.* convert into cash, realize. **encashment,** *n.*
encaustic, *a.* with colours burned in. —*n.* painting in melted wax; art of this. (Gk. *en*, in; *kaiein*, burn)
-ence, *n.suf.* denoting quality, as in **affluence.**
enceinte, a. pregnant.—*n.* enclosure of fortress. (F.)
encephalic, *a.* of the brain. **encephalitis,** *n.* inflammation of brain. **encephalitis lethargica,** sleepy sickness. (Gk. *en*, in; *kephalē*, head)
enchain, *v.t.* chain up, fetter; hold fast. **enchainment,** *n.*
enchant, *v.t.* bewitch; charm, delight. **enchanter,** *n.* (*fem.* **enchantress**) magician; charmer. **enchantment,** *n.* (L. *incantare*, chant spell over)
encharge, *v.t.* entrust, charge.
enchase, *v.t.* give setting to; engrave, emboss. (L. *capsa*, box)
encheason, *n.* (*Spens.*) reason, occasion. (O.F. *encheoir*, fall in)
enchiridion, *n.* handbook, manual. (Gk. *en*, in; *cheir*, hand)
enchorial, *a.* native, domestic; demotic. (Gk. *en*, in; *chora*, land)
encircle, *v.t.* surround; enfold; go round. **encirclement,** *n.*
enclasp, *v.t.* enfold, clasp.
enclave, *n.* piece of territory enclosed within foreign land. (F.)
enclitic, *a.* and *n.* (word) attached for pronunciation to previous word, e.g. 'thee' in 'prithee.' **enclitically,** *adv.* (Gk. *en*, in; *klinein*, bend)
enclose, inclose, *v.t.* surround; fence, hem, in; put in envelope, case etc. **enclosure, inclosure,** *n.* enclosing; space, thing, enclosed; barrier; enclosing of common as private land.
encomium, *n.* formal commendation, eulogy. **encomiast,** *n.* composer of encomium; flatterer. **encomiastic,** *a.* (Gk. *engkōmion*)
encompass, *v.t.* surround; contain; (*Shake.*) outwit. **encompassment,** *n.*
encore, *int.* again, once more.—*v.t.* call for repetition.—*n.* repetition; further item given in response. (F.)
encounter, *v.t.* meet with; meet in hostility; (*Shake.*) befall.—*n.* casual meeting; fight; (*Shake.*) behaviour. (L. *contra*, against)

encourage, *v.t.* hearten, embolden; urge; promote, further. **encouragement,** *n.* **encouragingly,** *adv.*
encrimson, *v.t.* make crimson.
encrinite, *n.* stone-lily, a fossil marine animal. (Gk. *krinon*, lily)
encroach, *v.i.* intrude (on another's rights etc.); trespass. **encroachment,** *n.* (O.F. *encrochier*)
encrust, incrust, *v.t.* and *i.* cover with, form, crust. **encrustment,** *n.*
encumber, *v.t.* impede, hamper; burden (with debt). **encumbrance,** *n.* burden, impediment; dependant, child; (*law*) lien, claim, on estate. **encumbrancer,** *n.* one who has legal claim on estate.
encyclical, encyclic, *aa.* for general circulation.—*nn.* pope's circular letter on church questions. (*cycle*)
encyclopaedia, encyclopedia, *n.* reference work of information on all subjects or all branches of a subject; general course of instruction. **encyclopaedic, encyclopedic,** *a.* of, like, an encyclopaedia; all-embracing. **encyclopaedist,** *n.* compiler of, collaborator in, encyclopaedia, esp. great 18th-century French one. (Gk. *en*, in; *kuklos*, circle; *paideia*, instruction)
encyst, *v.t.* and *i.* enclose, become enclosed, in cyst. **encystation, encystment,** *nn.*
end, *v.t.* (*Shake.*) get in, garner (crop).
end, *n.* limit, extremity; latter part, conclusion; death; event, issue; aim, purpose; (*pl.*) remnants.—*v.t.* and *i.* bring, come, to an end; be at end of; destroy, die. **at a loose e.,** disengaged. **e. for e.,** reversed. **e. up,** conclude. **in the e.,** at last. **keep one's e. up,** acquit oneself well. **latter e.,** death. **make ee. meet,** live within income. **no e. of,** much, great. **on e.,** erect; continuously. **to the e. that,** in order that. (O.E. *ende*)
endamage, *v.t.* damage.
endanger, *v.t.* imperil; hazard.
endear, *v.t.* render dear. **endearment,** *n.* loving word, caress.
endeavour, *v.t.* try, attempt; strive (after).—*n.* effort, attempt. (F. *devoir*, duty)
endecagon, same as **hendecagon.**
endemic, *a.* and *n.* (disease) peculiar to special locality or people. **endemically,** *adv.* **endemicity,** *n.* (Gk. *en*, in; *dēmos*, people)
ending, *n.* conclusion; termination.
endiron, *n.* movable plate changing size of grate in range. (*end*)
endive, *n.* curly-leaved herb used as salad. (L. *intibus*)
endless, *a.* infinite; incessant.
endlong, *adv.* lengthwise; on end.
endo-, from Gk. *endon*, within, used in **endocardium,** *n.* membrane lining heart, **endocarditis,** *n.* inflammation of this; **endocarp,** *n.* inner coat of fruit; **endocrine,** *a.* secreting internally, **endocrinology,** *n.* science of ductless glands; **endoderm,** *n.* inner layer of blastoderm; **endogamy,** *n.* marriage within tribe only, hence **endogamous,** *a.*; **endogen,** *n.* plant that grows from within, hence **endogenous,** *a.*; **endomorph,** *n.* mineral enclosed within another; **endoparasite,** *n.* internal parasite; **endophagy,** *n.* cannibalism within tribe only; **endoplasm, endosarc,** *nn.* inner layer of protoplasm; **endoscope,** *n.* instrument for examining internal organs; **endosmosis,** *n.* osmosis inward; **endosperm,** *n.* albumen of seeds; **endospore,** *n.* inner coat of spore, spore formed in case; **endothelium,** *n.* lining of blood-vessels.
endorse, indorse, *v.t.* write, sign, on back of; assign (bill) thus; confirm, sanction; register conviction on (licence). **endorsement,** *n.* (L. *dorsum*, back)
endow, *v.t.* bestow fund or income on; furnish, invest (with). **endowment,** *n.* **endowment assurance,** providing fixed sum at agreed age or on death. (L. *dos*, dowry)
endue, indue, *v.t.* put on; clothe, furnish (with). (L. *inducere*, draw+association with *induere*, put on)
endure, *v.t.* and *i.* undergo; tolerate, bear; remain firm, last. **endurable,** *a.* **endurance,** *n.* act, power, of enduring. **enduring,** *a.* lasting. (L. *durus*, hard)
endways, endwise, *advv.* end foremost; on end.
enema, *n.* injection, medicine injected, into rectum; syringe for this. (Gk.)
enemy, *n.* hostile person, opponent; hostile force, foe.—*a.* of enemy. **the e.** (*colloq.*) devil; time. (L. *in*, not; *amicus*, friend)
energumen, *n.* fanatic, one possessed. (Gk. *energoumenos*, wrought upon)
energy, *n.* vigour, force, activity; (*mech.*) power of doing work. **energetic,** *a.* strenuously active, vigorous. —*n.pl.* science of energy. **energetically,** *adv.* **energic,** *a.* energetic. **energize,** *v.t.* and *i.* give energy to; act with force. (Gk. *en*, in; *ergon*, work)
enervate, *v.t.* weaken, deprive of vigour.—*a.* spiritless, weak. **enervation,** *n.* (L. *e*, out; *nervus*, nerve)
enface, *v.t.* write, stamp, on face of document. **enfacement,** *n.*
enfant terrible, child who makes awkward remarks. (F.)
enfeeble, *v.t.* weaken, debilitate. **enfeeblement,** *n.*
enfeoff, *v.t.* invest with fief, give freehold property to; convey. **enfeoffment,** *n.* (*feoff*)
enfilade, *n.* raking fire.—*v.t.* rake (troops) lengthwise with fire. (F.)
enfold, infold, *v.t.* enwrap, envelop; embrace.

enforce, *v.t.* put into force; impose; urge, drive home; (*Shake.*) drive, get, by force; violate. **enforceable,** *a.* **enforcement,** *n.*

enframe, *v.t.* set in frame.

enfranchise, *v.t.* give vote or political privileges to; set free. **enfranchisement,** *n.* (*franchise*)

engage, *v.t.* and *i.* bind by contract; promise, pledge; betroth; hire, book; occupy; involve, embark (in); begin to fight; interlock (with). **engagement,** *n.* betrothal; battle; appointment. **engaging,** *a.* attractive, winning. (*gage*)

engender, *v.t.* beget, give rise to.

engine, *n.* mechanical contrivance; propelling mechanism; locomotive; instrument, means.—*v.t.* fit with engine. **e.-driver,** *n.* driver of locomotive. **engineer,** *n.* engine-maker, mechanic; man in charge of engine; designer, constructor, of military works (**Royal Engineers**) or public works, roads, bridges etc. (**civil engineer**); (*Amer.*) engine-driver.—*v.t.* construct, manage, as engineer; contrive. **engineering,** *n.* art of making and using machinery. **enginery,** *n.* engines collectively. (L. *ingenium,* skill)

engird, engirdle, *vv.t.* gird, encompass.

Englander, *n.* (*Amer.*) Englishman. **Little E.,** opponent of imperialism.

English, *a.* and *n.* (native, citizen, language) of England; 14-point type, larger than pica; (*Amer. billiards*) side.—*v.t.* translate into English. **Old E.,** language to 1150. **Middle E.,** 1150–1500. **Basic E.,** simplified form with vocabulary of 850 words. **plain E.,** plain words. **Englishman, Englishwoman,** *nn.* (O.E. *Engle,* Angle)

englut, *v.t.* (*Shake.*) swallow up.

engorge, *v.t.* devour greedily; glut, cram; (*med.*) congest with blood. **engorgement,** *n.*

engraft, ingraft, *v.t.* graft in; implant; incorporate; add.

engrail, *v.t.* ornament with serrated edge. (O.F. *engresler*)

engrain, ingrain, *v.t.* dye, infuse, deeply. **engrained,** *a.* inveterate.

engrave, *v.t.* cut in lines on metal plate for printing; carve, incise; impress deeply. **engraver,** *n.* **engraving,** *n.* engraved plate; print, copy of picture, from this. (*grave*)

engrave, *v.t.* inter. (*grave*)

engross, *v.t.* occupy wholly, absorb; monopolize, corner; write, copy, in large hand; put in legal form; (*Shake.*) collect. **engrossment,** *n.* (*gross*)

engulf, ingulf, *v.t.* swallow up (in gulf). **engulfment,** *n.*

enhance, *v.t.* raise, intensify; add to; exaggerate. **enhancement,** *n.* (L. *altus,* high)

enharmonic, *a.* (*mus.*) of, having, intervals smaller than a semitone.

enigma, *n.* riddle; obscure thing, puzzle. **enigmatic, enigmatical,** *aa.* obscure, puzzling. **enigmatize,** *v.t.* utter in riddles. (Gk. *ainos,* fable)

enisle, inisle, *v.t.* make into, place on, island; isolate. (*isle*)

enjambment, *n.* running on of sense from one verse to next, so that grammatical pause does not coincide with metrical pause. (F. *enjambement*)

enjoin, *v.t.* command; impose, prescribe; (*law*) prohibit by injunction.

enjoy, *v.t.* delight in; have use of. **e. oneself,** have good time. **enjoyable,** *a.* delightful. **enjoyment,** *n.*

enkindle, *v.t.* set on fire; inflame.

enlace, *v.t.* entwine; enfold. **enlacement,** *n.*

enlarge, *v.t.* and *i.* make, grow, larger; expand; expatiate; (*phot.*) reproduce on larger scale; (*arch.*) set free. **enlargement,** *n.*

enlighten, *v.t.* shed light on; instruct; free from superstition etc. **enlightenment,** *n.*

enlist, *v.t.* and *i.* enrol for military service; secure support of, gain over. **enlistment,** *n.* (*list*)

enliven, *v.t.* animate; make active or gay.

enmesh, emmesh, immesh, *v.t.* catch in net; entangle. **enmeshment,** *n.*

enmity, *n.* hostility, hatred. (*enemy*)

ennea-, nine, used in **ennead,** *n.* set of nine; **enneagon,** *n.* nine-sided plane figure; **enneandrous,** *a.* with nine stamens; **enneaphyllous,** *a.* nine-leaved. (Gk.)

ennoble, *v.t.* make noble, elevate; raise to peerage. **ennoblement,** *n.*

ennui, *n.* boredom, weariness from satiety. **ennuied,** *ennuyé, aa.* (F.)

enormous, *a.* immense, huge; monstrous. **enormity,** *n.* great wickedness, atrocity. (L. *e,* out of; *norma,* rule)

enough, *a.* and *n.* sufficient (quantity), as much or many as necessary.—*adv.* sufficiently. (O.E. *genóg*)

enounce, *v.t.* set forth, proclaim; pronounce. **enouncement,** *n.* (L. *e,* out; *nuntiare,* announce)

enow, *arch.* for **enough.**

enquire, enquiry, see **inquire.**

enrage, *v.t.* infuriate, anger.

enrank, *v.t.* (*Shake.*) put in battle array.

enrapture, *v.t.* delight intensely.

enregiment, *v.t.* form into regiment; make orderly.

enrich, *v.t.* make rich; add to; adorn; fertilize. **enrichment,** *n.*

enrol, enroll, *v.t.* put (name of) on roll; enlist, receive as member; enter, record. **enrolment,** *n.*

ens, *n.* (*pl.* **entia**) entity, being. (L.L. pres. part. of *esse,* be)

Ensa, *n.* organization for entertaining troops and war-workers. (*E*ntertainment *N*ational *S*ervice *A*ssociation)

ensample, *arch.* for **example.**

ensanguined, *a.* blood-stained, bloody. (L. *sanguis,* blood)
ensconce, *v.t.* settle comfortably; establish in safety, hide. (*sconce*)
ensemble, *n.* general effect, whole; (*mus.*) concerted passage. (F.)
enshrine, *v.t.* enclose as in shrine; cherish with sacred affection.
enshroud, *v.t.* cover up, hide from view.
ensiform, *a.* sword-shaped. (L. *ensis,* sword)
ensign, *n.* flag of nation or regiment; emblem, badge; standard-bearer; sub-lieutenant of U.S. Navy or (*obs.*) of British Army. **blue, red, white, e.,** flag of Royal Naval Reserve, merchant service, Royal Navy. **ensigncy,** *n.* rank of ensign. (*insignia*)
ensilage, *n.* storage in pit or silo; green fodder preserved by this. **ensile,** *v.t.* store in silo. (*silo*)
enslave, *v.t.* make slave of. **enslavement, enslaver,** *nn.*
ensnare, *v.t.* entrap.
ensoul, *v.t.* animate with soul.
ensphere, *v.t.* enclose, encircle.
ensue, *v.i.* and *t.* follow as consequence, happen later; strive after. (L. *sequi,* follow)
ensure, *v.t.* make safe or certain; secure; insure. (*sure*)
enswathe, *v.t.* wrap in bandage. **enswathement,** *n.*
entablature, *n.* (*archit.*) part surmounting columns, including architrave, frieze, and cornice. (*table*)
entablement, *n.* (*archit.*) platform of statue, above dado and base. (*table*)
entail, *v.t.* settle (estate) on persons in succession, none of whom can then dispose of it; involve, necessitate.—*n.* entailing, entailed estate. **entailment,** *n.* (*tail*)
entail, *v.t.* (*Spens.*) carve, inlay. (L.L. *in,* into; *taleare,* cut)
entangle, *v.t.* make tangled, intertwist; ensnare; perplex. **entanglement,** *n.* entangling; wire barrier.
entasis, *n.* slight convexity of shaft of column (to correct illusion of concavity). (Gk.)
entelechy, *n.* (*philos.*) realization, perfect fulfilment of function; informing spirit. (Gk. *en telei echein,* be complete)
entente, *n.* friendly understanding, less definite than alliance. *E. cordiale,* between Britain and France. **Little E.,** Czechoslovakia, Yugoslavia, and Rumania. **Triple E.,** Britain, France, and Russia. (F.)
enter, *v.i.* and *t.* go, come, in or into; be admitted, join; write in, register; begin, engage; break in, train. **e. an appearance,** show oneself. **e. into,** engage in; be part of. **e. on, upon,** begin; take possession of. **e. protest,** record, make, protest. (L. *intrare*)
enteron, *n.* alimentary canal. **enteric,** *a.* of the intestines.—*n.* typhoid (fever). **enteritis,** *n.* bowel inflammation. **enterocele,** *n.* hernia of bowel. **enterology,** *n.* science of viscera. **enterotomy,** *n.* dissection, incision, of bowels. (Gk.)
enterprise, *n.* bold or hazardous undertaking; readiness for this. **enterprising,** *a.* adventurous. (O.F. *entreprise*)
entertain, *v.t.* amuse, divert; receive as guest; admit, cherish; consider favourably; maintain; (*Shake.*) treat. **entertainer,** *n.* **entertainment,** *n.* accommodation; amusement, public performance. (L. *inter,* among; *tenēre,* hold)
enthral, enthrall, *v.t.* enslave, hold spellbound. **enthralment,** *n.*
enthrone, *v.t.* place on throne; induct (bishop). **enthronement, enthronization,** *nn.*
enthuse, *v.i.* (*colloq.*) show enthusiasm, gush. (*enthusiasm*)
enthusiasm, *n.* fervent zeal, intense interest, keenness. **enthusiast,** *n.* one full of enthusiasm; visionary. **enthusiastic,** *a.* **enthusiastically,** *adv.* (Gk. *entheos,* possessed by a god)
enthymeme, *n.* (*logic*) syllogism in which one premiss is suppressed. (Gk. *enthumēma*)
entice, *v.t.* allure, inveigle, tempt. **enticement,** *n.* (O.F. *enticier*)
entire, *a.* whole, complete; continuous; unqualified, pure; not castrated. —*n.* kind of ale. **entirely,** *adv.* wholly; solely. **entirety,** *n.* sum total. (L. *integer*)
entitle, *v.t.* give title to, style; give claim to.
entity, *n.* being, reality; existing thing. (*ens*)
entomb, *v.t.* place in tomb, bury; serve as tomb for. **entombment,** *n.*
entom(o)-, from Gk. *entoma,* insects, used in **entomic,** *a.* of insects; **entomolite,** *n.* fossil insect; **entomology,** *n.* science of insects, hence **entomological,** *a.*, **entomologist,** *n.* student of entomology, **entomologize,** *v.i.*; **entomophagous,** *a.* insect-eating; **entomophilous,** *a.* fertilized by insects; **entomotomy,** *n.* insect anatomy.
entourage, *n.* surroundings; retinue, associates. (F.)
en-tout-cas, *n.* umbrella-sunshade. (F.)
entozoon, *n.* internal parasite. **entozoic,** *a.* (Gk. *entos,* within; *zōon,* animal)
entr'acte, *n.* interval between acts of play; music etc. during this. (F.)
entrail, *v.t.* (*Spens.*) twist, entwine.—*n.* (*Spens.*) entanglement.
entrails, *n.pl.* intestines; inner parts. (L.L. *intralia*)
entrain, *v.t.* and *i.* put, get, into train.
entrance, *v.t.* throw into trance; ravish with delight. **entrancement,** *n.*
entrance, *n.* entering; right of admis-

sion; door, gateway. **entrant,** *n.* one who enters; competitor. (*enter*)
entrap, *v.t.* catch as in trap, ensnare.
entreat, *v.t.* and *i.* ask earnestly, implore; plead; (*Shake.*) treat. **entreaty,** *n.* earnest request. (*treat*)
entrée, *n.* right of admission; dish between fish and joint. (F.)
entremets, *n.* dainty between chief courses, small side-dish. (F.)
entrench, intrench, *v.t.* and *i.* surround with trench, dig (oneself) in; encroach. **entrenchment,** *n.*
entre nous, between ourselves, in confidence. (F.)
entrepôt, *n.* warehouse, mart; centre for import and export. (F.)
entrepreneur, *n.* organizer of entertainment, musical director. (F.)
entresol, *n.* low storey between first and ground floor, mezzanine. (F.)
entrust, intrust, *v.t.* confide, commit (to); charge (with).
entry, *n.* entering; entrance (passage); registration; item entered. (*enter*)
entwine, intwine, *v.t.* twine round, interlace.
entwist, intwist, *v.t.* twist round.
enucleate, *v.t.* lay bare, explain; (*med.*) extract (tumour) from covering. **enucleation,** *n.* (*nucleus*)
enumerate, *v.t.* count; name singly. **enumeration, enumerator,** *nn.* **enumerative,** *a.* (L. *numerus,* number)
enunciate, *v.t.* state formally, proclaim; pronounce. **enunciation, enunciator,** *nn.* **enunciative,** *a.* (L. *e,* out; *nuntiare,* announce)
enure, see **inure.**
enuresis, *n.* incontinence of urine. (Gk. *en,* in; *ouron,* urine)
envelop, *v.t.* wrap up, cover wholly; encircle. **envelopment,** *n.* **envelope,** *n.* wrapper, covering, esp. of letter. (O.F. *enveloper*)
envenom, *v.t.* put poison or venom into; embitter.
enviable, *a.* fitted to excite envy.
envious, *a.* full of envy.
environ, *v.t.* surround, encircle.—*n.pl.* outskirts. **environment,** *n.* environing; surroundings. (F.=about)
envisage, *v.t.* face; see mentally, visualize.
envoy, envoi, *n.* concluding part of poem; author's final words. (O.F.)
envoy, *n.* messenger; diplomatic agent, plenipotentiary. **envoyship,** *n.*
envy, *n.* pain felt at another's success or superiority; object of this; (*Shake.*) malice.—*v.t.* feel envy of, grudge. (L. *invidia*)
enweave, see **inweave.**
enwheel, *v.t.* (*Shake.*) encircle.
enwrap, inwrap, *v.t.* wrap up; engross.
enwreathe, *v.t.* wreathe round, intertwine.
enzootic, *a.* and *n.* endemic among animals. (Gk. *en,* in; *zōon,* animal)
enzyme, *n.* catalyst elaborated by living organism, digestive ferment. (Gk. *en,* in; *zume,* leaven)
eo-, from Gk. *ēōs,* dawn, used in **eoan,** *a.* of dawn; *Eoanthropus,* *n.* ape-like man deduced from skull found at Piltdown; **Eocene,** *a.* (*geol.*) of earliest Tertiary period; **eolithic,** *a.* of earliest part of Stone Age; **eosin,** *n.* red fluorescent dye-stuff; **eozoic,** *a.* (*geol.*) showing first traces of animal life.
eonism, *n.* (*psycho-anal.*) tendency to adopt opposite sex's manners, clothes, and mentality. (Chevalier d'*Éon*)
epact, *n.* moon's age on 1st Jan.; excess of solar over lunar year. (Gk. *epagein,* intercalate)
epana-, from Gk. *epi,* in addition, *ana,* again, used in **epanadiplosis,** *n.* repetition at end of sentence of word used at beginning; **epanalepsis,** *n.* repetition of word or clause after intervening matter; **epanástrophē,** *n.* figure by which the end word of one sentence becomes first word of the next; **epanorthosis,** *n.* figure in which a word is recalled to substitute a stronger or more correct term.
eparch, *n.* governor of **eparchy** or Greek province. (Gk. *eparchos*)
epaulement, *n.* breastwork protecting flank. (F.)
epaulet, epaulette, *n.* shoulder-ornament of uniform. (F.)
épée, *n.* duelling-sword; fencing-foil. (F.)
epenthesis, *n.* insertion of letter or syllable in body of word, e.g. *b* in 'nimble.' **epenthetic,** *a.* (Gk.)
epergne, *n.* branched centre-piece, ornamental stand, for dinner-table.
epexegesis, *n.* additional words to make meaning clear. **epexegetic, epexegetical,** *aa.* (*epi-*+*exegesis*)
ephah, *n.* Hebrew dry measure of about a bushel. (Heb.)
ephebe, *n.* young citizen (18–20) of ancient Greece. (Gk. *ephēbos*)
ephemera, *n.* (*pl.* **ephemeras**) may-fly; short-lived insect or thing. **ephemeral,** *a.* lasting only a day; short-lived, transient. **ephemerality,** *n.* **ephemeris,** *n.* (*pl.* **ephemerides**) astronomical almanac or tables; diary. **ephemeron,** *n.* (*pl.* **ephemerons, ephemera**) ephemera. (Gk. *ephēmeros,* lasting only a day)
ephod, *n.* vestment of Jewish priest. (Heb.)
ephor, *n.* ancient Spartan magistrate; overseer. (Gk. *ephoros*)
epi-, *pref.* upon, at, in addition. (Gk.)
epiblast, *n.* outermost layer of blastoderm. (Gk. *epi,* upon; *blastos,* germ)
epic, *a.* relating great events in heroic style.—*n.* epic poem or story. **epical,** *a.* **epically,** *adv.* (*epos*)
epicarp, *n.* outer skin of fruit. (Gk. *epi,* upon; *karpos,* fruit)
epicedium, *n.* funeral ode. (Gk. *epi,* upon; *kēdos,* care)
epicene, *a.* common to both sexes;

(*gram.*) of either gender. (Gk. *epikoinos*, promiscuous)

epicentre, epicentrum, *nn.* focus of earthquake.

epicure, *n.* one with refined taste in food and drink, gourmet. **epicurean,** *a.* and *n.* (person) given to refined sensuous enjoyment; (follower) of Epicurus, who taught that pleasure was the chief good. **epicureanism, epicurism,** *nn.*

epicycle, *n.* circle whose centre moves on circumference of greater circle. **epicyclic,** *a.* **epicycloid,** *n.* curve traced by point on circle rolling round circumference of another. **epicycloidal.** *a.* (Gk. *epi*, upon; *kuklos*, circle)

epideictic, *a.* done for effect, rhetorical. (Gk. *epideiknunai*, display)

epidemic, *a.* and *n.* (disease) temporarily prevalent among community. **epidemical,** *a.* **epidemiology,** *n.* science of epidemics. (Gk. *epi*, among; *dēmos*, people)

epidermis, *n.* outer layer of animal's skin, cuticle; plant's true skin below cuticle. **epidermal, epidermic,** *aa.* (Gk. *epi*, upon; *derma*, skin)

epidiascope, *n.* magic lantern for use with opaque as well as translucent pictures. (Gk. *epi*, upon; *dia*, through; *skopein*, view)

epigastrium, *n.* middle of abdomen above stomach. **epigastric,** *a.* (Gk. *epi*, upon; *gastēr*, belly)

epigenesis, *n.* theory that germ does not pre-exist in the parent, but is brought into being during conception. (*epi-+genesis*)

epiglottis, *n.* cartilage that covers opening of windpipe in swallowing. **epiglottic,** *a.* (*epi-+glottis*)

epigram, *n.* short poem with witty ending; pointed saying. **epigrammatic,** *a.* **epigrammatically,** *adv.* **epigrammatist,** *n.* writer of epigrams. **epigrammatize,** *v.t.* and *i.* make epigram (on). (Gk. *epigramma*)

epigraph, *n.* inscription; motto at beginning of book, chapter-heading. **epigraphic,** *a.* **epigraphy,** *n.* study of inscriptions. **epigraphist,** *n.* (Gk. *epi*, upon; *graphein*, write)

epilepsy, *n.* disease of brain causing fits and convulsions, falling sickness. **epileptic,** *a.* of, subject to, epilepsy. —*n.* epileptic patient. (Gk. *epilēpsia*, seizure)

epilogue, *n.* speech, short poem, addressed to audience at end of play; conclusion of book. **epilogist,** *n.* (Gk. *epi*, in addition; *legein*, say)

epiphany, *n.* bodily manifestation of a deity, esp. that of Christ to Magi, celebrated 6 Jan., Twelfth Day. (Gk. *epiphainein*, show forth)

epiphenomenon, *n.* attendant symptom, mere concomitant, by-product. (*epi-+phenomenon*)

epiphyte, *n.* plant growing on another but not fed by it. **epiphytic,** *a.* (Gk. *epi*, upon; *phuton*, plant)

episcopacy, *n.* government by, body of, bishops. **episcopal,** *a.* of, ruled by, bishops. **episcopalism,** *n.* **episcopalian,** *a.* and *n.* (adherent) of episcopal church or system. **episcopalianism,** *n.* **episcopate,** *n.* bishop's office, see, or term of office; body of bishops. (Gk. *episkopos*, overseer)

episode, *n.* incident; incidental narrative, digression. **episodic, episodical,** *aa.* (Gk. *epi*, in addition; *eis*, into; *hodos*, way)

epispastic, *a.* and *n.* (*med.*) blistering (agent), plaster. (Gk. *epi*, upon; *spaein*, draw)

epistasis, *n.* act of suppressing secretion. (Gk.=stoppage)

epistaxis, *n.* bleeding at the nose. (Gk.)

epistemology, *n.* science of processes and grounds of knowledge. (Gk. *epistēmē*, knowledge; *legein*, speak)

epistle, *n.* letter, esp. of apostle; lesson in communion service. **epistolary,** *a.* **epistoler,** *n.* reader of liturgical epistle. (Gk. *epistolē*)

epistrophĕ, *n.* ending of several successive clauses or sentences with same word. (Gk.=turning about)

epistyle, *n.* architrave. (Gk. *epistulion*)

epitaph, *n.* memorial inscription on tomb. (Gk. *epi*, upon; *taphos*, tomb)

epithalamium, *n.* (*pl.* **epithalamiums, epithalamia**) nuptial song or poem. **epithalamial, epithalamic,** *aa.* (Gk. *epi*, upon; *thalamos*, bridal chamber)

epithelium, *n.* outer layer of mucous membrane. **epithelial,** *a.* (Gk. *epi*, upon; *thēlē*, nipple)

epithet, *n.* adjective denoting quality or attribute; appellation; (*Shake.*) term, phrase. **epithetic, epithetical,** *aa.* (Gk. *epithetos*, added)

epitomĕ, *n.* summary, abridgment; miniature representation. **in e.,** on a small scale. **epitomist,** *n.* **epitomize,** *v.t.* condense. (Gk.=incision)

epitrite, *n.* foot of three long syllables and one short, in any order. (Gk. *epi*, in addition; *tritos*, third)

epizootic, *a.* and *n.* epidemic among animals. (Gk. *epi*, among; *zōon*, animal)

epoch, *n.* period of great events; beginning of era. **epochal,** *a.* (Gk. *epochē*, pause)

epode, *n.* kind of lyric poem; last part of lyric ode. (Gk. *epōdos*)

eponym, *n.* one from whom place etc. takes its name, mythical founder; name so derived. **eponymous,** *a.* (Gk. *epi*, upon; *onoma*, name)

epos, *n.* early unwritten epic poetry; epic. **epopee,** *n.* epic poem or poetry. (Gk. *epos*, word; *poiein*, make)

Epsom salts, sulphate of magnesium, used as purgative. (town)

equable, *a.* uniform, even; tranquil **equability,** *n.* (*equate*)

equal, *a.* the same in number, size, quality etc.; adequate, fit; evenly balanced; (*Shake.*) fair.—*n.* person equal in rank.—*v.t.* be equal to. **equality,** *n.* **equalize,** *v.t.* and *i.* make equal; even score. **equalization,** *n.* (L. *aequus,* even)

equanimity, *n.* composure, calmness. (L. *aequus,* even; *animus,* mind)

equate, *v.t.* state, assume, equality of. **equation,** *n.* making equal; allowance for inaccuracy; (*math.*) equating of two expressions. **equational,** *a.* (L. *aequus,* even)

equator, *n.* great circle of earth or heavens, equidistant from poles. **equatorial,** *a.* of, near, equator.—*n.* telescope mounted so that it can follow motion of stars. (*equate*)

equerry, *n.* officer attending sovereign in public; officer in charge of nobleman's horses. (L.L. *scuria,* stable)

equestrian, *a.* of horse-riding; on horseback.—*n.* (*fem.* **equestrienne**) rider, performer, on horse. **equestrianism,** *n.* (L. *equus,* horse)

equi-, from L. *aequus,* equal, used in **equiangular,** *a.* having equal angles; **equidistant,** *a.* at equal distances; **equilateral,** *a.* and *n.* (figure) with all sides equal.

equilibrate, *v.t.* and *i.* balance; counterpoise. **equilibration,** *n.* **equilibrist,** *n.* rope-walker, acrobat. **equilibrium,** *n.* state of balance. (L. *aequus,* even; *libra,* balance)

equimultiple, *a.* and *n.* (number) having common factor with another.

equine, *a.* of, like, horse. (L. *equus,* horse)

equinox, *n.* time when sun crosses equator and day and night are equal. **autumnal, vernal, e.,** about 23 Sept. and 21 March. **equinoctial,** *a.* of, during, equinoxes.—*n.* (also **equinoctial line**) celestial equator; (*pl.*) equinoctial storms. (L. *aequus,* equal; *nox,* night)

equip, *v.t.* furnish, fit out. **equipage,** *n.* accoutrements, requisites; carriage, horses, and attendants. **equipment,** *n.* equipping; outfit. (F. *équiper*)

equipoise, *n.* state of balance; counterpoise.—*v.t.* counterbalance.

equipollent, *a.* equal in power.—*n.* equivalent. **equipollence,** *n.* (L. *aequus,* equal; *pollēre,* be strong)

equiponderate, *v.t.* and *i.* make, be, equal in weight (to). **equiponderant,** *a.* and *n.* (L. *aequus,* equal; *pondus,* weight)

equitable, *a.* fair, just. (*equity*)

equitation, *n.* horsemanship. (L. *equus,* horse)

equity, *n.* impartiality; natural justice; use, system, of this to supplement law. (L. *aequus,* even)

equivalent, *a.* equal in value; having same meaning or result; corresponding.—*n.* equivalent thing, word etc.

equivalence, equivalency, *nn.* (L. *aequus,* equal; *valēre,* be worth)

equivocal, *a.* of double or doubtful meaning, ambiguous; questionable. **equivocate,** *v.i.* use ambiguous words to mislead; prevaricate. **equivocation, equivocator,** *nn.* **equivoque, equivoke,** *nn.* pun, ambiguity. (L. *aequus,* equal; *vocare,* call)

-er, *n.suf.* denoting person, thing, that does something, as in **stoker, poker;** dealer in, as in **hatter;** inhabitant of, as in **Londoner.** (O.E.)

-er, *adj.suf.* forming comparative, as in **older.** (O.E. *-ra*)

era, *n.* period of time, reckoned from some great event; the event itself; period. (L. *aera,* counters)

eradiation, *n.* emission of rays. (L. *e,* out; *radius,* ray)

eradicate, *v.t.* pull up by roots, extirpate. **eradicable,** *a.* **eradication, eradicator,** *nn.* (L. *e,* out; *radix,* root)

erase, *v.t.* rub, scrape, out; efface. **eraser,** *n.* (L. *e,* out; *radere,* scrape)

Erastian, *a.* and *n.* (follower) of doctrine of Erastus, subordinating Church to State. **Erastianism,** *n.*

erasure, *n.* obliteration; trace of erasing. (*erase*)

ere, *prep.* and *conj.* before, sooner than. (O.E. *ǣr*)

erect, *v.t.* set upright, raise; build, form; distend.—*a.* upright, vertical. **erectile,** *a.* able to be erected. **erection,** *n.* erecting; structure. **erector,** *n.* (L. *erigere*)

eremite, *n.* hermit. **eremitic, eremitical,** *aa.* (Gk. *erēmos,* desert)

erethism, *n.* (*med.*) abnormal excitement. (Gk. *erethizein,* irritate)

erg, ergon, *nn.* unit of work in C.G.S. system, work done by force acting for one second on mass of one gramme, producing velocity of one centimetre per second. **ergatocracy,** *n.* government by workers. (Gk. *ergon,* work)

ergo, adv. therefore. (L.)

ergot, *n.* fungoid disease of grain. **ergotism,** *n.* poisoning from ergot-infected flour. (O.F. *argot,* spur)

ericaceous, *a.* of the heath family. (Gk. *ereikē,* heath)

Erin, *n.* (*poet.*) Ireland.

eringo, *n.* sea-holly; its candied root. (Gk. *erunggos*)

eristic, *a.* seeking to win argument rather than find truth.—*n.* art of controversy. (Gk. *eris,* strife)

erk, *n.* (*R.A.F. sl.*) ordinary aircraftman

ermine, *n.* animal of weasel kind; its winter fur, white with black tufts, used for judges' robes; office of judge. **ermined,** *a.* (O.F.)

erne, *n.* golden eagle, sea-eagle. (O.E. *earn*)

erode, *v.t.* eat into, wear away. **erosion,** *n.* **erosive,** *a.* (L. *e,* out; *rodere,* gnaw)

erotic, *a.* of sexual love. **eroticism,** *n.* **erotomania,** *n.* melancholy, madness, caused by love. (Gk. *erōs,* love)

err, *v.i.* make mistakes; be wrong, sin. (L. *errare,* wander)

errand, *n.* short journey, mission, of messenger; purpose. **e-boy,** *n.* for running errands. (O.E. *ærende*)

errant, *a.* itinerant; erring. **knight e.,** one roving in quest of adventure. **errancy,** *n.* erring. **errantry,** *n.* state, conduct, of knight errant.

erratic, *a.* having no certain course; irregular, eccentric; (*geol.*) not belonging to surrounding strata.

erratum, *n.* (*pl.* **errata**) mistake noted for correction. (L.)

error, *n.* mistake, inaccuracy; wrong belief; sin. **erroneous,** *a.* incorrect, wrong. (L.)

ersatz, n. and *a.* substitute. (G.)

Erse, *a.* and *n.* (Irish) Gaelic. (*Irish*)

erst, erstwhile, *advv.* formerly, of old. (superl. of *ere*)

erubescent, *a.* reddish, blushing. **erubescence,** *n.* (L. *ruber,* red)

eruciform, *a.* caterpillar-like. **erucivorous,** *a.* feeding on caterpillars. (L. *eruca,* caterpillar)

eructation, *n.* belching. (L. *e,* out; *ructare,* belch)

erudite, *a.* learned, scholarly. **erudition,** *n.* learning. (L. *e,* from; *rudis,* rude)

erupt, *v.i.* break out or through. **eruption,** *n.* ejection of lava from volcano; outbreak; rash, pimples. **eruptional, eruptive,** *aa.* (L. *e,* out; *rumpere,* break)

-ery, *n.suf.* characteristic qualities of, as in **knavery**; art, trade, of, as in **archery, pottery**; workshop, breeding-place of, as in **bakery, piggery.** (F. *-erie*)

erysipelas, *n.* local febrile disease causing deep redness of skin, St Anthony's fire. (Gk. *erusipelas*)

erythema, *n.* patchy redness of skin. (Gk. *eruthros,* red)

erythro-, from Gk. *eruthros,* red, used in **erythrocyte,** *n.* red blood-corpuscle; **erythroid,** *a.* reddish; **erythrophobia,** *n.* aversion to red light, fear of blushing; **erythropsia,** *n.* seeing all objects red.

escalade, *n.* scaling of walls by ladders. **escalator,** *n.* moving staircase. (L. *scala,* ladder)

escallop, same as **scallop.**

escapade, *n.* flighty exploit, prank. (Sp. *escapada*)

escape, *v.i.* and *t.* get away or free; issue (from); go unpunished or safe; avoid, elude.—*n.* escaping; leakage; fire-escape. **escapement,** *n.* outlet; mechanism connecting motive power and regulator of clock. **escapism,** *n.* tendency to shirk unpleasant realities by withdrawing into world of fantasy. **escapist,** *n.* **escapologist,** *n.* performer who escapes from handcuffs, locked boxes etc. (L.L. *ex cappa,* out of one's cloak)

escarp, *n.* steep bank in front of rampart.—*v.t.* make into steep slope. **escarpment,** *n.* precipitous side of hill; escarp. (*scarp*)

-escent, *adj.suf.* beginning to be, as in **obsolescent.** (L. *-escens*)

eschalot, same as **shallot.**

eschatology, *n.* study of death and future life. **eschatological,** *a.* (Gk. *eschatos,* last; *legein,* speak)

escheat, *n.* lapsing of property to state from lack of heir or by forfeiture; property so lapsing.—*v.t.* and *i.* confiscate; revert by escheat. (L. *ex,* out; *cadere,* fall)

eschew, *v.t.* abstain from, shun. (O.F. *eschiver*)

eschscholtzia, *n.* garden plant of poppy family. (J. F. von *Eschscholtz*)

esclandre, n. scandal. (F.)

escort, *n.* armed guard, guard of honour, on journey; attendant, guide; protection.—*v.t.* act as escort to. (L. *ex-,* entirely; *corrigere,* correct)

escot, *v.t.* (*Shake.*) pay reckoning for. (*scot*)

escritoire, *n.* writing-desk with drawers. (L.L. *scriptorium*)

escrow, *n.* (*law*) contract kept in third person's custody till fulfilment of a condition. (O.F. *escroe,* scroll)

escudo, *n.* a silver coin, monetary unit of Portugal. (L. *scutum,* shield)

esculent, *a.* and *n.* eatable. (L. *esca,* food)

escutcheon, *n.* shield with coat of arms; part of ship's stern bearing name; keyhole-cover. **blot on the e.,** stain on one's good name. (L. *scutum,* shield)

eskar, *n.* (*geol.*) ridge of gravel glacially deposited. (Ir. *eiscir*)

Eskimo, *n.* (*pl.* **Eskimoes**) native of Arctic America.

esophagus, same as **oesophagus.**

esoteric, *a.* meant only for initiates; secret, private; initiated. **esoterically,** *adv.* **esotericism, esoterism,** *nn.* (Gk. *esō,* within)

espagnolette, *n.* fastening of french window. (F.)

espalier, *n.* lattice-work for training trees; tree, row of trees, so trained. (It. *spalla,* shoulder)

esparto, *n.* (also **e. grass**) Spanish grass used in paper-making. (Sp.)

especial, *a.* chief, more than ordinary, particular. **especially,** *adv.*

esperance, *n.* (*Shake.*) hope. (F.)

Esperanto, *n.* artificial language designed for universal use. **Esperantist,** *n.*

espial, *n.* espying, observation.

espièglerie, n. roguishness. (F.)

espionage, *n.* profession, use, of spies; spying. (It. *spione,* spy)

esplanade, *n.* level space or walk; seaside promenade. (F.)

espouse, *v.t.* marry; give in marriage; adopt, embrace (cause) **espousal,** *n.* espousing; (us. *pl.*) marriage; betrothal. (L. *spondēre,* promise)
espressivo, adv. (*mus.*) with expression. (It.)
esprit, *n.* wit; sprightliness. *e. de corps,* loyalty, attachment, to body one belongs to. (F.)
espy, *v.t.* catch sight of, descry; detect. (*spy*)
-esque, *adj.suf.* after the manner of, as in **statuesque.** (It. *-esco*)
Esquimau, *n.* (*pl.* **Esquimaux**) Eskimo.
esquire, *n.* gentleman's courtesy title, used on letters; (*arch.*) squire. (L. *scutarius,* shield-bearer)
ess, *n.* letter S; S-shaped thing.
-ess, *n.suf.* forming feminine, as in **poetess.** (Gk. *-issa*)
essay, *n.* effort, trial; prose composition, short treatise.—*v.t.* and *i.* test, make trial of; attempt. **essayist,** *n.* essay-writer. (L. *exagium,* weighing)
ėssė, *n.* essential being. *in e.,* in existence, (L.=to be)
essence, *n.* entity; absolute being; that which makes a thing what it is, intrinsic nature; concentrated extract; perfume. **essential,** *a.* of, constituting, a thing's essence; indispensable, vital; highly rectified, pure.—*n.* essential element; chief point. **essential oils,** volatile fragrant oils got from plants. **essentiality,** *n.* **essentially,** *adv.* in the highest degree. (*esse*)
essoin, *n.* and *v.t.* (*Spens.*) excuse. (O.F. *essoine*)
-est, *adj.suf.* denoting superlative, as in **oldest.** (O.E.)
establish, *v.t.* set up, fix firmly, settle; prove, make generally accepted; make (Church) state institution. **establishment,** *n.* establishing; organization; household, business, public institution; established church system. **establishmentarian,** *a.* and *n.* (person) supporting church establishment. (*stable*)
estaminet, *n.* café. (F.)
estancia, *n.* cattle ranch in Latin America. (Sp.)
estate, *n.* condition of life; rank, order, class; property in land (real **e.**) or movables (**personal e.**); (*arch.*) state. **fourth e.,** (*joc.*) the press. **Three Ee.,** Lords Spiritual, Lords Temporal, and Commons. (*state*)
esteem, *v.t.* think highly of; appraise; deem.—*n.* favourable opinion, respect; estimation. (*estimate*)
ester, *n.* compound of an acid and an alcohol residuum. (coined)
esthetics, same as **aesthetics.**
estimable, *a.* worthy of esteem.
estimate, *v.t.* compute, judge; calculate roughly.—*n.* computed cost or value of thing; appraisement. **estimation,** *n.* judgment, opinion; esteem. **estimative,** *a.* **estimator,** *n.* (L. *aestimare*)
estop, *v.t.* (*law*) bar, preclude. **estoppage,** *n.* **estoppel,** *n.* (*law*) being precluded from course by one's own previous action. (L. *stuppa,* tow)
estovers, *n.pl.* (*law*) necessary supplies (of firewood etc.) allowed to tenant from estate on which he lives. (O.F. *estovoir,* be necessary)
estrade, *n.* platform, dais. (F.)
estrange, *v.t.* alienate, make unfriendly. **estrangement,** *n.* (*strange*)
estreat, *n.* (*law*) copy of court records, esp. of fines etc.—*v.t.* extract such copy; levy under estreat. (O.F. *estraire,* extract)
estridge, *n.* (*obs.*) ostrich; (*Shake.*) goshawk. (*ostrich*)
estuary, *n.* expanded tidal mouth of river, firth. **estuarine,** *a.* (L. *aestus,* tide)
esurient, *a.* hungry; ill-fed. **esurience, esuriency,** *nn.* (L. *edere,* eat)
état-major, *n.* staff, staff-office. (F.)
et cetera, etcetera, *n.* (*abbr.* **etc., &c.**) and the like, and so on; (*pl.*) extras, sundries. (L.=and the rest)
etch, *v.t.* and *i.* engrave design on metal plate by eating out lines with acid; portray thus. **etching,** *n.* this art; print from etched plate. (G. *ätzen,* corrode)
eternal, *a.* without beginning or end, everlasting; (*colloq.*) too frequent. **the E.,** God. **E. City,** Rome. **eternalize, eternize,** *vv.t.* make eternal; perpetuate. **eterne,** *a.* (*Shake.*). **eternity,** *n.* infinite time or duration; immortality. (L. *aeternus*)
Etesian winds, blowing from NW. in Mediterranean for about forty days every summer. (Gk. *etos,* year)
-eth, *suf.* (*arch.*) forming 3rd pers. sing. of verb. (O.E.)
ethane, *n.* an odourless gas, burning with pale flame. (*ether*)
ether, *n.* clear upper air; supposed intangible fluid carrying waves of light and electricity; (*chem.*) volatile liquid got by action of sulphuric acid etc. on alcohol, used as anaesthetic. **ethereal, etherial,** *aa.* heavenly; spiritlike; light, airy; (*chem.*) of, like, ether. **ethereality,** *n.* **etherealize,** *v.t.* **etherealization,** *n.* **etheric,** *a.* of the ether of space. **etherify,** *v.t.* (*chem.*) make into ether. **etherize,** *v.t.* put (patient) under ether. **etherization,** *n.* (Gk. *aithēr*)
ethics, *n.pl.* science, rules, of morality. **ethical, ethic,** *aa.* relating to moral principles; moral. **ethic dative,** of person indirectly concerned. **ethicize,** *v.t.* make ethical; treat from ethical standpoint. (*ethos*)
Ethiopian, (*arch.*) **Ethiop,** *a.* and *n.* (native) of Ethiopia; blackamoor.
ethmoid, *a.* sieve-like. **e. bone,** at root of nose. (Gk. *ēthmos,* sieve)
ethnic, ethnical *aa.* of races or nations;

heathen. **ethnicism,** *n.* heathenism.
ethnography, *n.* scientific description of races of men. **ethnographer,** *n.* **ethnographic, ethnographical,** *aa.*
ethnology, *n.* science of races. **ethnologic, ethnological,** *aa.* **ethnologist,** *n.* (Gk. *ethnos,* nation)
ethos, *n.* characteristic spirit, genius, of community, age etc. **ethology,** *n.* science of character-formation. **ethological,** *a.* (Gk.=character)
ethyl, *n.* a radical of alcohol and ether; kind of petrol. (*ether*)
etiolate, *v.t.* and *i.* make pale, blanch, by depriving of light etc. **etiolation,** *n.* (F. *étioler*)
etiology, same as **aetiology.**
etiquette, *n.* conventional rules of behaviour; ceremonial. (F.)
etna, *n.* small combined spirit-lamp and boiler. (volcano)
Eton, *n.* **E. collar,** starched collar worn outside jacket. **E. crop,** woman's hair cut short like man's. **E. jacket,** very short tailless jacket. **Etonian,** *n.* one educated at Eton College. (place)
et sequentes, et sequentia, (*abbr. et seq.*) and the following (passage). (L.)
ettle, *v.t.* and *i.* (*Scot.*) purpose, intend; guess.—*n.* purpose.
étude, *n.* short musical composition. (F.)
etui, etwee, *n.* pocket case for small articles. (F. *étui*)
etymology, *n.* origin, derivation, and development of words; science of this; part of grammar dealing with inflexions. **etymologic, etymological,** *aa.* **etymologist,** *n.* student of etymology. **etymologize,** *v.t.* and *i.* trace etymology of; study etymology. (Gk. *etumos,* true; *legein,* speak)
etymon, *n.* primary word, root. (Gk. *etumos,* true)
eucalyptus, *n.* Australian gum-tree etc. **e. oil, a** disinfectant. (Gk. *eu,* well; *kaluptos,* covered)
eucharist, *n.* sacrament of the Lord's Supper; consecrated elements, esp. bread. **eucharistic, eucharistical,** *aa.* (Gk. *eu,* well; *charis,* thanks)
euchlorine, *n.* greenish explosive gas. (Gk. *eu,* well; *chlōros,* green)
euchre, *n.* American card game.—*v.t.* win hand at this; outwit.
Euclid, *n.* a Greek geometer; his works, ordinary geometry. **Euclidean,** *a.*
eudemonism, eudaemonism, *n.* (*philos.*) doctrine that happiness is aim and measure of virtue. **eudemonist, eudaemonist,** *n.* (Gk. *eudaimōn,* happy)
eudiometer, *n.* instrument showing amount of oxygen in air. (Gk. *eudios,* clear; *metron,* measure)
eugenic, *a.* of race improvement by judicious mating.—*n.pl.* science of this. **eugenist,** *n.* (Gk. *eugenēs,* well-born)
euhemerism, *n.* interpretation of myths on historical basis. **euhemerist,** *n.* **euhemeristic,** *a.* **euhemerize,** *v.t.* (*Euhemerus* of Sicily)
eulogy, eulogium, *nn.* laudatory speech or writing; praise. **eulogize,** *v.t.* extol in speech, commend. **eulogist,** *n.* **eulogistic,** *a.* **eulogistically,** *adv.* (Gk. *eu,* well; *legein,* speak)
eunuch, *n.* castrated man, often harem attendant or chamberlain. (Gk. *eunē,* bed; *echein,* hold)
euonymous, *a.* appropriately named. (*euonymus*)
euonymus, *n.* spindle-tree and allied shrubs. (Gk. *eu,* well; *onoma,* name)
eupepsia, *n.* good digestion. **eupeptic,** *a.* (Gk.)
euphemism, *n.* mild term used for less pleasant one, e.g. 'passed away' for 'died'; this figure. **euphemistic,** *a.* **euphemistically,** *adv.* **euphemize,** *v.t.* and *i.* (Gk. *eu,* well; *phēmē,* talk)
euphonium, *n.* bass saxhorn. (*euphony*)
euphony, *n.* pleasing sound; smoothness of pronunciation. **euphonic, euphonious,** *aa.* **euphonize,** *v.t.* (Gk. *eu,* well; *phōnē,* sound)
euphorbia, *n.* plant of spurge family. (*Euphorbus,* Greek doctor)
euphrasy, *n.* small meadow plant, eyebright. (Gk. *euphrasia,* delight)
euphuism, *n.* affected style using elaborate antithesis, alliteration, and conceits; high-flown diction. **euphuist,** *n.* **euphuistic,** *a.* **euphuistically,** *adv.* (*Euphues,* book)
Eurasian, *a.* and *n.* (person) of mixed European and Asiatic (esp. Indian) parentage; of Europe and Asia.
eureka, *int.* I have found it. (Gk.)
eurhythmic, *a.* symmetrical.—*n.pl.* art of rhythmic movement. (Gk. *eu,* well; *rhuthmos,* rhythm)
European, *a.* and *n.* (native) of Europe. **Europeanism,** *n.* **Europeanize,** *v.t.*
eusol, *n.* an antiseptic. (*E*dinburgh *u*niversity *sol*ution of *l*ime)
Eustachian tube, tube from pharynx to middle ear. (*Eustachus,* doctor)
Euterpe, *n.* muse of music. (Gk.)
euthanasia, euthanasy, *nn.* easy death or mode of dying. (Gk.)
euthycomic, *a.* having straight hair. (Gk. *euthus,* straight; *komē,* hair)
evacuate, *v.t.* empty, discharge (of bowels); withdraw from (of troops); transfer (people) from danger zone. **evacuant,** *a.* and *n.* purgative; emetic. **evacuation,** *n.* **evacuee,** *n.* person evacuated. (L. *e,* out; *vacuus,* empty)
evade, *v.t.* elude, avoid; baffle. (L. *e,* out; *vadere,* go)
evaginate, *v.t.* turn inside out. (L. *e,* out; *vagina,* sheath)
evaluate, *v.t.* determine value of.
evanesce, *v.i.* fade away. **evanescent,** *a.* fleeting, transient; imperceptible. **evanescence,** *n.* (L. *e,* out; *vanus,* empty)

evangel, *n.* Gospel. **evangelic, evangelical,** *aa.* of, according to, Gospel teaching; of Protestant school that maintains salvation by faith, not works. **evangelicalism, evangelism,** *nn.* this doctrine. **evangelist,** *n.* writer of one of the four Gospels; preacher of the Gospel; mission-worker; (*Amer.*) revivalist. **evangelistic,** *a.* **evangelize,** *v.t.* and *i.* preach Gospel (to); convert to Christianity. **evangelization,** *n.* (Gk. *eu,* well; *angellein,* bear news)

evanish, *v.i.* vanish. **evanishment,** *n.*

evaporate, *v.t.* and *i.* turn into, pass off in, vapour; be dissipated. **evaporable, evaporative,** *aa.* **evaporation, evaporator,** *nn.* (*vapour*)

evasion, *n.* act of evading; subterfuge, excuse. **evasive,** *a.* shuffling, not straightforward. (*evade*)

eve, *n.* day or evening before; time just before; evening. (=*even*)

evection, *n.* periodical irregularity of moon's motion. (L. *e,* out; *vehere,* carry)

even, *n.* (*poet.*) evening. (O.E. *æfen*)

even, *a.* level, smooth; uniform, equable; equal, balanced; divisible by two.—*v.t.* make even or equal.—*adv.* giving emphasis; just, simply. **be e. with,** be revenged on. **e. up,** balance. **of e. date,** of to-day. **e.-handed,** *a.* impartial, fair. **e.-tempered,** *a.* calm. (O.E. *efen*)

evening, *n.* close of day; decline, end. **e. dress,** formal dress for evening. **e. star,** planet prominent after sunset, often Venus. **evensong,** *n.* evening prayer. (*even*)

event, *n.* occurrence; (important) happening; item in sports; result, issue. **at all ee.,** in any e., in any case. **eventful,** *a.* full of incidents; momentous. (L. *eventus*)

eventide, *n.* evening.

eventual, *a.* ultimate; happening as a result. **eventuality,** *n.* contingency. **eventuate,** *v.i.* turn out; (*Amer.*) happen. (*event*)

ever, *adv.* always, at all times; at any time. **e. and anon,** sometimes. **e. so,** (*colloq.*) very. **for e.,** eternally. **everglade,** *n.* (*Amer.*) tract of swampy land. **evergreen,** *a.* always fresh or green.—*n.* plant that keeps its leaves all year round. **everlasting,** *a.* eternal, perpetual; too long.—*n.* eternity. **evermore,** *adv.* eternally. (O.E. *æfre*)

evert, *v.t.* turn inside out. **eversion,** *n.* (L. *e,* out; *vertere,* turn)

every, *a.* each of all. **e. one,** each; everybody. **e. other,** every second. **everybody, everyone,** *pronn.* every person. **everyday,** *a.* daily; commonplace. **Everyman,** *n.* ordinary, typical, man. **everything,** *pron.* all things. **everywhere,** *adv.* in all places. (O. E. *æfre,* ever; *ælc,* each)

evict, *v.t.* expel, dispossess, by law. **eviction, evictor,** *nn.* (L. *e-,* entirely; *vincere,* conquer)

evidence, *n.* sign, indication, proof; information in law case, testimony; (*Shake.*) witness.—*v.t.* show, prove. **in e.,** conspicuous. **turn king's e.,** give evidence against accomplices. **evident,** *a.* obvious, plain. **evidential, evidentiary,** *aa.* of evidence. (L. *e,* out; *vidēre,* see)

evil, *a.* bad, wicked; harmful.—*n.* sin; harm, affliction.—*adv.* evilly. **e. eye,** supposed baleful influence through glance. **the E. One,** Satan. **king's e.,** scrofula. **evildoer,** *n.* sinner. (O.E. *yfel*)

evince, *v.t.* show, indicate. **evincive,** *a.* (*evict*)

evirate, *v.t.* castrate; emasculate. **eviration,** *n.* (L. *e,* out; *vir,* man)

eviscerate, *v.t.* disembowel. **evisceration,** *n.* (*e-*+*viscera*)

evitate, *v.t.* (*Shake.*) avoid. (L. *e,* out; *vitare,* avoid)

evoke, *v.t.* call up; (*law*) summon to higher court. **evocation,** *n.* **evocative, evocatory,** *aa.* (L. *e,* out; *vocare,* call)

evolute, *n.* original curve from which involute is described. (*evolve*)

evolution, *n.* unfolding, development, evolving; planned movement, manœuvre, of troops etc.; origination of species by development from earlier forms; theory of this; (*math.*) extraction of roots. **evolutional, evolutionary,** *aa.* **evolutionism,** *n.* theory of evolution. **evolutionist,** *n.* **evolutive,** *a.* tending to evolution. (*evolve*)

evolve, *v.t.* and *i.* unfold, unroll; work out, develop by natural process. (L. *e,* out; *volvere,* roll)

evulsion, *n.* plucking out by force. (L. *e,* out; *vellere,* pluck)

ewe, *n.* female sheep. **e.-lamb,** *n.* dearest possession. (O.E. *eowu*)

ewer, *n.* pitcher; jug for wash-stand. (L. *aqua,* water)

ewigkeit, *n.* eternity. (G.)

ex, *prep.* out of, from. *ex animo,* heartily, sincerely. *ex cathedra,* authoritatively (lit. from the chair). **ex dividend,** (*abbr.* **ex div.** or **x.d.**) not including next dividend. *ex libris,* from the library (of). *ex nihilo nihil fit,* out of nothing nothing comes. *ex officio,* in virtue of one's office. *ex parte,* on behalf of one side only, partisan. *ex pede Herculem,* (we recognize) Hercules by his foot. *ex post facto,* retrospective. **ex ship,** store, sold from the ship, store. *ex ungue leonem,* (judge) the lion by his claw. *ex voto,* votive (offering). (L.)

ex-, e-, *pref.* out, forth, as in exit, exact; quite, entirely, as in exalt; formerly, as in **ex-convict.** (L.)

exacerbate, *v.t.* aggravate, make worse; irritate. **exacerbation,** *n.* (L. *ex-,* entirely; *acerbus,* bitter)

exact, *a.* accurate, precise; rigorous.—*v.t.* enforce payment of, extort; demand, call for. **exacting,** *a.* severe or excessive in demands. **exaction,** *n.* exacting, sum exacted; exorbitant demand. **exactitude,** *n.* exactness. **exactly,** *adv.* precisely; just so. **exactor,** *n.* (L. *ex,* out; *agere,* drive)

exaggerate, *v.t.* magnify beyond truth, overstate; aggravate. **exaggeration, exaggerator,** *nn.* **exaggerative,** *a.* (L. *ex-,* quite; *agger,* heap)

exalt, *v.t.* raise up; make noble; praise, extol; elate. **exaltation,** *n.* elevation; rapture. (L. *ex-,* quite; *altus,* high)

examine, *v.t.* and *i.* scrutinize, inquire into; test by examination. **examinant, examiner,** *nn.* one who examines. **examination,** *n.* inspection; (*abbr.* **exam**) test of knowledge by questions. **examinational, examinatorial,** *aa.* **examinee,** *n.* one who is examined. (L. *examen,* tongue of balance)

example, *n.* illustration of rule, specimen; pattern; precedent, instance; warning case.—*v.t.* exemplify. **make e. of,** punish severely. (L. *exemplum*)

exanimate, *a.* lifeless, spiritless. (L. *ex,* out; *anima,* life)

exarch, *n.* Byzantine viceroy. **exarchate,** *n.* his province. (Gk. *exarchos*)

exasperate, *v.t.* irritate, provoke; make worse. **exasperation,** *n.* (L. *ex-,* quite; *asper,* rough)

excavate, *v.t.* hollow out; make by digging; unearth. **excavation, excavator,** *nn.* (L. *ex,* out; *cavus,* hollow)

exceed, *v.t.* and *i.* be greater than, surpass; go beyond limit of. **exceeding,** *a.* very great.—*adv.* (*arch.*) extremely. **exceedingly,** *adv.* (L. *ex,* out; *cedere,* go)

excel, *v.t.* and *i.* surpass, outdo; be distinguished (in). **excellence,** *n.* great merit. **excellency,** *n.* title of ambassador or governor. **excellent,** *a.* very good. (L. *excellere*)

excelsior, *int.* higher.—*n.* (*Amer.*) soft wood-shavings for stuffing. (L.)

except, *v.t.* and *i.* leave out, omit; raise objection.—*prep.* omitting, but.—*conj.* (*arch.*) unless. **excepting,** *prep.* except. **exception,** *n.* excepting, thing excepted; objection. **exceptionable,** *a.* open to objection. **exceptional,** *a.* rare; superior. **exceptive,** *a.* including, making, an exception; captious. (L. *ex,* out; *capere,* take)

excerpt, *v.t.* select, quote (passage from book).—*n.* extract. **excerption,** *n.* (L. *ex,* out; *carpere,* pluck)

excess, *n.* act, amount, of exceeding; extreme degree; outrage, intemperance.—*v.t.* surcharge (on railway). **excessive,** *a.* extreme, unreasonable. (*exceed*)

exchange, *v.t.* and *i.* give, receive, one thing for another; pass from one regiment etc. to another.—*n.* exchanging, barter; thing exchanged; system of settling debts by bills without money passing; changing of money into other currency, charge for this; value of one currency in terms of another; building where merchants meet for business; central telephone office. **exchangeable,** *a.*

exchequer, *n.* government department in charge of revenue, treasury; finances. (L.L. *scaccarium,* chequered cloth for reckoning on)

excise, *n.* duty on certain home goods and trade licences.—*v.t.* levy excise on. **excisable,** *a.* **exciseman,** *n.* officer collecting and enforcing excise.

excise, *v.t.* cut out or away. **excision,** *n.* (L. *ex,* out; *caedere,* cut)

excite, *v.t.* stir up, rouse; move to strong emotion; stimulate. **excitable,** *a.* easily excited. **excitant,** *a.* and *n.* stimulant. **excitation,** *n.* stimulation. **excitative, excitatory,** *aa.* **excitement,** *n.* agitation, excited state. **exciting,** *a.* thrilling. (L. *ex,* out; *ciēre,* stir up)

exclaim, *v.t.* cry out. **exclamation,** *n.* sharp utterance. interjection; mark (!) of this. **exclamatory,** *a.* (L. *ex,* out; *clamare,* shout)

exclave, *n.* separate part of country surrounded by foreign territory. (L. *ex,* out; *clavis,* key)

exclude, *v.t.* shut out; debar (from); preclude. **exclusion,** *n.* **exclusive,** *a.* excluding; inclined to exclude outsiders, select; (of right) sole; (of terms) not inclusive. **exclusively,** *adv.* **exclusivism,** *n.* systematic exclusiveness. (L. *ex,* out; *claudere,* shut)

excogitate, *v.t.* think out, devise. **excogitation,** *n.* **excogitative,** *a.*

excommunicate, *v.t.* cut off from rites and sacraments of the Church. **excommunication, excommunicator,** *nn.* **excommunicative, excommunicatory,** *aa.* (L. *ex,* out; *communis,* common)

excoriate, *v.t.* abrade skin of, flay; peel off (skin). **excoriation,** *n.* (L. *ex,* off; *corium,* hide)

excrement, *n.* waste matter from bowels, dung; (*Shake.*) outgrowth of hair, beard. **excremental, excrementitious,** *aa.* (*excrete*)

excrescence, *n.* unnatural outgrowth, wart; superfluous part. **excrescent,** *a.* growing out; redundant. (L. *ex,* out; *crescere,* grow)

excrete, *v.t.* separate and expel (waste matter) from system. **excretion,** *n.* **excretive, excretory,** *aa.* **excreta,** *n.pl.* faeces and urine. (L. *ex,* out; *cernere,* sift)

excruciate, *v.t.* torture, rack. **excruciating,** *a.* agonizing. **excruciation,** *n.* (L. *ex,* out; *crux,* cross)

exculpate, *v.t.* free from blame, exonerate; acquit. **exculpation,** *n.* **exculpatory,** *a.* (L. *ex,* out; *culpa,* fault)

excurse, *v.i.* digress; make excursion. **excurrent,** *a.* running out; (*bot.*) projecting. **excursion,** *n.* journey, trip, for pleasure; pleasure party; (*arch.*) sortie. **excursionist,** *n.* tripper. **excursive,** *a.* digressive, rambling. **excursus,** *n.* appended dissertation on special point. (L. *ex,* out; *currere,* run)

excuse, *v.t.* pardon, forgive; apologize for, extenuate; gain exemption for; free, remit.—*n.* apology, plea in extenuation. **excusable, excusatory,** *aa.* (L. *excusare*)

éxĕăt, *n.* leave of absence from school. (L.=let him go out)

execrate, *v.t.* and *i.* feel, express, detestation of; curse. **execrable,** *a.* abominable. **execration,** *n.* **execrative, execratory,** *aa.* (L. *ex,* from; *sacer,* sacred)

execute, *v.t.* carry out; perform; put to death by law; (*law*) make valid by signing, sealing etc.; convey (estate). **executant,** *n.* performer. **execution,** *n.* executing; skill in performance; capital punishment; deadly work; (*law*) seizure of goods for debt. **executioner,** *n.* person who executes criminal. **executive,** *a.* carrying into effect, administrative.—*n.* administrative branch of government; person with executive post. **executor,** *n.* (*fem.* **executrix**) person appointed to carry out provisions of will. **executorial,** *a.* **executorship,** *n.* (L. *ex,* out; *sequi,* follow)

exegesis, *n.* exposition, interpretation, esp. of the Bible. **exegetic, exegetical,** *aa.* (Gk.)

exemplar, *n.* model, pattern, ideal; type. **exemplary,** *a.* serving as example or warning; commendable; typical. **exemplify,** *v.t.* give, be, example of; make attested copy of. **exemplification,** *n.* (L.)

exempt, *a.* free (from), not liable.—*v.t.* grant immunity (from). **exemption,** *n.* (L. *ex,* out; *emere,* buy)

exenterate, *v.t.* disembowel. (Gk. *ex,* out; *enteron,* intestine)

exequatur, *n.* government permit to foreign consul to fulfil his duties. (L.=let him perform)

exequies, *n.pl.* funeral rites. (L. *exequiae*)

exercise, *v.t.* and *i.* employ; practise; train by use, drill; worry, harass.—*n.* exercising; practice; exertion of body; lesson, task, for training; (*Amer.*) formal programme of events; (*Shake.*) act of worship; skill. **exercitation,** *n.* practice, training; discourse. (L. *exercēre*)

exergue, *n.* space below main design on reverse of coin for date etc. **exergual,** *a.* (F.)

exert, *v.t.* bring into active operation. **e. oneself,** strive. **exertion,** *n.* (L. *ex* out; *serere,* connect)

exeunt, see *exit.*

exfoliate, *v.i.* flake off; (of tree) shed bark. **exfoliation,** *n.* (L. *ex,* off; *folium,* leaf)

exhale, *v.t.* and *i.* breathe out, emit; evaporate; be given off. **exhalant,** *a.* **exhalation,** *n.* puff of breath; evaporation; effluvium; (*Shake.*) meteor. (L. *ex,* out; *halare,* breathe)

exhaust, *v.t.* draw off; use up, empty completely; treat, discuss, thoroughly; tire out.—*n.* used steam, waste gases, from engine; (also **e.-pipe**) passage for this. **exhaustion,** *n.* exhausting; extreme fatigue. **exhaustive,** *a.* tending to exhaust; comprehensive. **exhaustible,** *a.* (L. *ex,* out; *haurire,* draw)

exhibit, *v.t.* show, display; show publicly or formally; (*Shake.*) submit (petition).—*n.* thing shown publicly; (*law*) document produced in court as evidence. **exhibition,** *n.* exhibiting, display; public show of art, manufactures etc.; allowance made to student. **exhibitioner,** *n.* student holding exhibition. **exhibitionism,** *n.* tendency towards excessive display; (*psycho-anal.*) desire to expose oneself indecently. **exhibitionist,** *n.* **exhibitor,** *n.* one who exhibits in show. **exhibitory,** *a.* (L. *ex,* out; *habēre,* hold)

exhilarate, *v.t.* enliven, gladden. **exhilarant,** *a.* and *n.* **exhilaration,** *n.* enlivenment, high spirits. (L. *ex-,* quite; *hilaris,* merry)

exhort, *v.t.* urge strongly; admonish earnestly. **exhortation,** *n.* exhorting; religious discourse, counsel. **exhortative, exhortatory,** *aa.* (L. *ex-,* entirely; *hortari,* urge)

exhume, *v.t.* dig up, disinter. **exhumation,** *n.* (L. *ex,* out; *humus,* ground)

exigent, *a.* exacting; urgent, pressing. **exigence, exigency,** *nn.* pressing need, emergency. **exigible,** *a.* that may be exacted. (*exact*)

exiguous, *a.* scanty, small. **exiguity,** *n.* (L. *exiguus*)

exile, *n.* expulsion, absence from one's country; banishment; exiled person.—*v.t.* banish, expel from native land. (L. *exilium*)

exility, *n.* thinness, subtlety. (L. *exilis,* slender)

exist, *v.i.* be, have being; live. **existence,** *n.* life, mode of living; what exists. **existent,** *a.* existing; current. (L. *existere*)

exit, *n.* way out; going out; departure from stage; death. *exit, v.i.* (*pl. exeunt*) goes off stage. (L. *ex,* out; *ire,* go)

ex-libris, *n.* book-plate. (L.)

exo-, from Gk. *exo,* outside, used in **exoderm,** *n.* outer layer of blastoderm; **exogamy,** *n.* marriage outside of tribe only, hence **exogamous,** *a.*;

exogen, *n.* dicotyledon, hence **exogenous,** *a.*; **exopathic,** *a.* (of disease) originating outside the body; **exophagy,** *n.* cannibalism outside of tribe only; **exoplasm,** *n.* outer layer of protoplasm; **exosmosis,** *n.* osmosis outward.

exodus, *n.* departure of crowd, esp. of emigrants; a book of the Bible. (Gk. *ex,* out: *hodos,* way)

exonerate, *v.t.* free from (blame), exculpate; relieve (from duty etc.). **exoneration,** *n.* **exonerative,** *a.* (L. *ex,* out; *onus,* burden)

exophthalmus, *n.* protrusion of eyeball. **exophthalmic,** *a.* marked by this. (Gk. *ex,* out; *ophthalmos,* eye)

exorbitant, *a.* grossly excessive, inordinate. **exorbitance,** *n.* (L. *ex,* out of; *orbita,* wheel-track)

exorcize, *v.t.* cast out (evil spirit) by prayer or use of holy name; free of spirits thus. **exorcism, exorcist,** *nn.* (Gk. *ex,* out; *horkos,* oath)

exordium, *n.* (*pl.* **exordiums, exordia**) beginning, introduction, of discourse etc. **exordial,** *a.* (L.)

exoteric, exoterical, *aa.* meant for ordinary people, popular; uninitiated. **exotericism,** *n.* (Gk. *exō,* outside)

exotic, *a.* introduced from abroad, foreign.—*n.* exotic plant etc. **exoticism,** *n.* (Gk. *exō,* outside)

expand, *v.t.* and *i.* spread out; distend, dilate; develop; write out in full; become genial. **expanse,** *n.* wide area or extent. **expansible, expansile,** *aa.* able to be expanded. **expansion,** *n.* expanding. **expansive,** *a.* able, tending, to expand; wide, comprehensive; effusive. (L. *ex,* out; *pandere,* spread)

expatiate, *v.i.* speak, write, at length; enlarge. **expatiation,** *n.* **expatiatory,** *a.* (L. *ex,* out; *spatium,* space)

expatriate, *v.t.* banish, exile. **e. oneself,** emigrate; renounce citizenship. **expatriation,** *n.* (L. *ex,* out; *patria,* native land)

expect, *v.t.* look forward to, anticipate; look for as one's due; (*colloq.*) suppose. **expectant,** *a.* expecting; waiting; prospective.—*n.* candidate for office etc. **expectant mother,** pregnant woman. **expectancy,** *n.* **expectation,** *n.* anticipation; ground for this, promise; thing expected; probability; (*pl.*) prospects of gain. **expectation of life,** probable duration after specified age. **expectative,** *a.* reversionary. (L. *ex,* out; *spectare,* look)

expectorate, *v.t.* and *i.* cough up, spit out; spit. **expectorant,** *a.* and *n.* (medicine) promoting expectoration. **expectoration,** *n.* (L. *ex,* out; *pectus,* breast)

expedient, *a.* advantageous, fitting; more politic than just; (*Shake.*) expeditious.—*n.* device, shift. **expedience, expediency,** *nn.* **expediential,** *a.* (*expedite*)

expedite, *v.t.* help on, hasten; dispatch. **expedition,** *n.* promptness; journey for war, exploration etc.; party sent on this. **expeditionary,** *a.* **expeditionist,** *n.* member of expedition. **expeditious,** *a.* speedy, prompt. (L. *ex,* out; *pes,* foot)

expel, *v.t.* drive out, eject; send away. **expellent,** *a.* (L. *ex,* out; *pellere,* drive)

expend, *v.t.* spend; consume, use up. **expenditure,** *n.* expending, amount spent. **expense,** *n.* expenditure; cost; (*pl.*) charges incurred, outlay; (*Scots law*) costs of case. **expensive,** *a.* dear. (L. *ex,* out; *pendere,* weigh)

experience, *n.* what happens to one; observation of, contact with, facts or events; knowledge gained from life or by trial and practice.—*v.t.* undergo, pass through; feel. **experienced,** *a.* having had much experience; knowing. (L. *experientia*)

experiment, *n.* trial; operation to test theory or make discovery.—*v.i.* make experiment. **experimental,** *a.* based on experiment or experience; tentative. **experimentalism, experimentalist,** *nn.* **experimentalize,** *v.i.* try experiments. **experimentation,** *n.* experimenting. (*expert*)

expert, *a.* skilful from practice, proficient; (*Shake.*) proved.—*n.* expert person, specialist. *experto crede,* trust one who has tried it. (L. *experiri,* try)

expiate, *v.t.* atone for; pay penalty of. **expiable, expiatory,** *aa.* **expiation, expiator,** *nn.* (L. *expiare*)

expire, *v.t.* and *i.* breathe out; die, come to an end; become void. **expiration,** *n.* **expiratory,** *a.* **expiry,** *n.* termination. (L. *ex,* out; *spirare,* breathe)

expiscate, *v.t.* fish out, search out artfully. (L. *ex,* out; *piscis,* fish)

explain, *v.t.* make plain or intelligible; account for. **e. away,** soften down. **explainable, explanatory,** *aa.* **explanation,** *n.* (L. *ex-,* quite; *planus,* plain)

expletive, *a.* filling up; added for emphasis or ornament.—*n.* expletive word etc.; oath. (L. *ex-,* entirely; *plēre,* fill)

explicate, *v.t.* unfold, develop; (*arch.*) explain. **explicable,** *a.* explainable. **explication,** *n.* explicating. **explicative, explicatory,** *aa.* explanatory. **explicit,** *a.* distinctly stated, not merely implied; plain, definite; outspoken. (L. *ex,* out; *plicare,* fold)

explode, *v.i.* and *t.* burst, cause to burst, with loud noise; detonate; demolish, refute. (L. *explodere,* hiss off stage)

exploit, *n.* achievement, heroic deed; feat.—*v.t.* develop, turn to advantage; use for selfish ends. **exploitage, exploitation, exploiter,** *nn.* (*explicate*)

explore, *v.t.* travel over and examine (country); examine by touch; investigate. **explorer, exploration,** *nn.* **exploratory,** *a.* (L. *explorare*)

explosion, *n.* exploding; report; outburst. **explosive,** *a.* tending to explode.—*n.* explosive agent; mute consonant, *p, t, g* etc. (*explode*)

exponent, *n.* interpreter, performer; type, representative; (*math.*) index of power. **exponential,** *a.* (L. *ex*, out; *ponere*, place)

export, *v.t.* send (goods) abroad in way of commerce.—*n.* exporting, article exported. **exportable,** *a.* **exportation, exporter,** *nn.* (L. *ex*, out; *portare*, carry)

expose, *v.t.* leave unprotected; lay open (to); lay out, exhibit; unmask, disclose; abandon (child); (*phot.*) subject to light. ***exposé,*** *n.* explanatory statement; showing up. (L. *ex*, out; *pausare*, cease+confusion with *ponere*, place)

exposition, *n.* explanation, description; exhibition; exposure. **expositive, expository,** *aa.* explanatory. **expositor,** *n.* (*expound*)

expostulate, *v.i.* reason earnestly(with), remonstrate; (*Shake.*) discuss. **expostulation,** *n.* **expostulatory,** *a.* (*postulate*)

exposture, (*Shake.*) form of exposure.

exposure, *n.* act of exposing or being exposed; aspect. (*expose*)

expound, *v.t.* explain, interpret, set forth. **expounder,** *n.* (L. *ex*, out; *ponere*, place)

express, *v.t.* put into words; make known, represent; squeeze out; (*Amer.*) send by express.—*a.* explicit, definitely stated; specially designed, exact.—*n.* express train, company etc.—*adv.* with speed. **e. company,** (*Amer.*) for transport of goods. **e. delivery,** by special postal messenger. **e. rifle,** sporting rifle with heavy charge and light bullet. **e. train,** *n.* fast, non-stop. (L. *ex*, out; *premere*, press)

expressible, *a.* able to be expressed.

expression, *n.* expressing; phrase, wording; (*art, mus.*) mode of expressing feeling or character; (*math.*) combination of symbols. **expressional,** *a.* **expressionism,** *n.* theory that artist should aim chiefly at expressing his own personality rather than reproducing the world about him. **expressionist,** *a.* and *n.* **expressionist play,** in which all characters but chief one are depicted as he would see them. (*express*)

expressive, *a.* serving to express; significant, forcible.

expressly, *adv.* explicitly.

expressure, *n.* (*Shake.*) expression; image, picture.

exprobration, *n.* upbraiding, reproof. (L. *ex-*, quite; *probrum*, abuse)

expropriate, *v.t.* dispossess; take away. **expropriation,** *n.* (L. *ex*, out; *proprius*, one's own)

expulsion, *n.* expelling, ejection. **expulsive,** *a.* (*expel*)

expunge, *v.t.* wipe out, erase; omit. **expunction,** *n.* (L. *expungere*)

expurgate, *v.t.* purge; remove offensive or erroneous parts from (book etc.). **expurgation, expurgator,** *nn.* **expurgatorial, expurgatory,** *aa.* (L. *ex*, out; *purgare*, cleanse)

exquisite, *a.* of extreme beauty or delicacy; keen, intense; fastidious; (*Shake.*) far-fetched.—*n.* fop, dandy. (L. *ex*, out; *quaerere*, seek)

exsanguinate, *v.t.* drain of blood. **exsanguine,** *a.* bloodless. (L. *ex*, out; *sanguis*, blood)

exscind, *v.t.* cut off or out, excise. (L. *ex*, out; *scindere*, cleave)

exsert, *v.t.* protrude. (=*exert*)

exsiccate, *v.t.* dry up; drain dry. **exsiccation,** *n.* (L. *ex*, out; *siccus*, dry)

extant, *a.* still existing. (L. *ex*, out; *stare*, stand)

extasy, same as **ecstasy.**

extempore, *adv.* and *a.* without preparation, off-hand, impromptu. **extemporaneous, extemporary,** (*Shake.*) **extemporal,** *aa.* **extemporize,** *v.t.* and *i.* compose, speak, extempore. **extemporization,** *n.* (L. *ex tempore*, from the time)

extend, *v.t.* and *i.* stretch out; enlarge, prolong; reach, cause to reach; accord, grant; write out (shorthand) at length; tax powers of (athlete); (*law*) value; seize for debt. **extendible, extensible, extensile,** *aa.* capable of extension. **extension,** *n.* extending; extent; additional part. **extensive,** *a.* large, wide; comprehensive. **extensor,** *n.* straightening muscle. **extent,** *n.* space covered; degree, scope; large tract; (*law*) valuation; seizure. (L. *ex*, out; *tendere*, stretch)

extenuate, *v.t.* make less blameworthy, palliate; make thin; (*Shake.*) disparage. **extenuation,** *n.* **extenuatory,** *a.* (L. *ex-*, quite; *tenuis*, thin)

exterior, *a.* outer, external.—*n.* outside, outward appearance. **exteriority,** *n.* **exteriorize,** *v.t.* give outward form to, externalize. (L.)

exterminate, *v.t.* destroy utterly, annihilate. **extermination, exterminator,** *nn.* **exterminatory,** *a.* (L. *ex*, out; *terminus*, limit)

external, *a.* outside, outward; objective.—*n.pl.* outward parts or forms; non-essentials. **externality,** *n.* **externalize,** *v.t.* give, attribute, external existence to. **externalization,** *n.* (L. *externus*)

exterritorial, *a.* (of embassy etc.) outside the jurisdiction of the country in which it is. **exterritoriality,** *n.* (*ex-*+*territory*)

extinct, *a.* no longer living or active; quenched; lapsed, obsolete. **extinction,** *n.* extinguishing; being, becoming, extinct; destruction. (*extinguish*)

extinguish, *v.t.* quench, put out; eclipse, outshine; abolish, destroy. **extinguisher,** *n.* metal cap to put out candle; apparatus to put out fire. **extinguishment,** *n.* (L. *ex,* out; *stinguere,* quench)

extirpate, *v.t.* root out, destroy utterly. **extirpation, extirpator,** *nn.* (L. *ex,* out; *stirps,* root)

extol, *v.t.* praise highly, magnify. (L. *ex,* out; *tollere,* raise)

extort, *v.t.* gain by violence, threats, or injustice; wring. **extortion,** *n.* unjust exaction. **extortionate,** *a.* using extortion; exorbitant. **extortioner,** *n.* **extortive,** *a.* (L. *ex,* out; *torquēre,* twist)

extra, *a.* and *adv.* in addition; better, more, than usual.—*n.* extra thing; extra edition of paper; (*cricket*) run not scored off bat.

extra-, *pref.* outside, beyond scope of, as in **extra-cosmical,** *a.* outside the universe, **extra-cranial,** *a.* outside the skull. (L.)

extract, *v.t.* draw out, esp. by force; elicit; get by pressure, distillation etc.; derive; select, quote.—*n.* essence, concentrated preparation; passage from book. **extractable,** *a.* **extraction,** *n.* extracting; descent, lineage. **extractive,** *a.* **extractor,** *n.* (L. *ex,* out; *trahere,* draw)

extradition, *n.* surrender of criminal by one state to another. **extradite,** *v.t.* make, obtain, extradition of. **extraditable,** *a.* liable to, warranting, extradition. (L. *ex,* out; *tradere,* hand over)

extrados, *n.* upper or outer curve of arch. (F.)

extragalactic, *a.* outside of the Milky Way.

extrajudicial, *a.* out of the ordinary course of legal procedure; not made in court, not belonging to the case before it. (*judicial*)

extrality, *n.* exterritoriality. (contr. of *extraterritoriality*)

extramundane, *a.* beyond the material world. (*mundane*)

extramural, *a.* outside the city boundaries; (of lecturer) from outside a university. (*mural*)

extraneous, *a.* added from without; not belonging, foreign (to). (*extra*)

extraordinary, *a.* exceptional, remarkable; additional, special. **extraordinarily,** *adv.* (*extra-+ordinary*)

extraparochial, *a.* outside the parish.

extrapolate, *v.t.* and *i.* calculate (unknown terms of a series etc.) from those already known, e.g. compute birth-rate of 1950 from figures for 1900–25. **extrapolation,** *n.* (*extra-* + *interpolate*)

extraterritorial, same as **exterritorial.**

extravagant, *a.* wasteful, prodigal; excessive, unrestrained; exorbitant. **extravagance,** *n.* **extravaganza,** *n.* fantastic composition or language. **extravagate,** *v.i.* rove; be extravagant. (L. *extra,* outside; *vagari,* wander)

extravasate, *v.t.* and *i.* force out (blood etc.) from its proper vessel; flow out. **extravasation,** *n.* (L. *extra,* outside; *vas,* vessel)

extravert, same as **extrovert.**

extreme, *a.* at the end, outermost, final; of highest degree; severe; excessive, uncompromising.—*n.* end thing, first or last of series; utmost degree. **go to ee.,** use extreme measures. **in the e.,** extremely. **extremely,** *adv.* exceedingly. **extremist,** *n.* supporter of extreme views or policy. **extremism,** *n.* **extremity,** *n.* end; utmost distress; (*pl.*) hands and feet; extreme measures. (L. *extremus*)

extricate, *v.t.* set free, disentangle; disembarrass. **extricable,** *a.* **extrication,** *n.* (L. *ex,* out; *tricae,* perplexities)

extrinsic, *a.* extraneous, not belonging (to); not inherent or intrinsic. **extrinsically,** *adv.* (L. *extrinsecus*)

extrorse, *a.* (*bot.*) turned outwards. (L. *extrorsus*)

extrospection, *n.* habitual interest in or examination of matters outside oneself (opp. to introspection).

extrovert, *n.* sociable person not given to introspection. **extroversion,** *n.* (*med.*) turning of inward part outward; (*psycho-anal.*) state of having thoughts and activities directed to things outside oneself. (L. *extra,* outside; *vertere,* turn)

extrude, *v.t.* thrust out. **extrusion,** *n.* (L. *ex,* out; *trudere,* thrust)

exuberant, *a.* luxuriant; overflowing, abundant; vivacious. **exuberance,** *n.* **exuberate,** *v.i.* abound; indulge freely. (L. *ex-,* quite; *uber,* fertile)

exude, *v.i.* and *t.* ooze out; give off (moisture). **exudation,** *n.* **exudative,** *a.* (L. *ex,* out; *sudare,* sweat)

exult, *v.i.* rejoice openly, triumph. **exultant,** *a.* **exultancy, exultation,** *nn.* (L. *exultare*)

exuviae, *n.pl.* cast-off skin or shell of animal. **exuvial,** *a.* **exuviate,** *v.t.* shed, slough. **exuviation,** *n.* (L.)

eyas, *n.* young untrained hawk. (L. *nidus,* nest, *a nyas* becoming misdivided as *an eyas*)

eye, *n.* organ of sight; iris; eyesight; glance, observation; hole of needle, ring for hook; seed-bud of potato; spot on peacock's tail.—*v.t.* look at, view.—*v.i.* (*Shake.*) appear. **all my e.** (**and Betty Martin**), (*sl.*) humbug. **clap, set, ee. on,** see. **have an e. for,** be a judge of. **in the ee. of,** from the point of view of. **keep an e. on,** look after. **make (sheep's) ee. at,** ogle. **mind your e.,** (*sl.*) take care. **my e! my word! see e. to e.,** think

alike. **with half an e.**, at a glance. **e.-beam,** *n.* (*Shake.*) glance. **e.-opener,** *n.* startling thing. **e.-service,** *n.* working only while watched. **e.-string,** *n.* muscle of eye. **e.-tooth,** *n.* canine tooth under eye. **e.-witness,** *n.* one who sees thing done. (O.E. *éage*)
eyeball, *n.* globe of eye; pupil.
eyebright, *n.* a small plant, euphrasy.
eyebrow, *n.* arch of hair over eye.
eyeglass, *n.* lens to aid sight, monocle; pair of such lenses, held on nose by spring or in hand.
eyelash, *n.* hair, row of hairs, fringing eyelid.
eyeless, *a.* without eyes; blind.
eyelet, *n.* small hole for lace, rope etc.; loophole; small eye.
eyelid, *n.* movable cover of eye.
eyepiece, *n.* lens at viewing end of telescope or microscope.
eyeshot, *n.* seeing-distance.
eyesight, *n.* power of seeing, vision.
eyesore, *n.* thing offensive to sight.
eyewash, *n.* (*sl.*) pretence, humbug.
eyewater, *n.* eye-lotion; tears.
eyne, *arch. pl.* of **eye.**
eyot, *n.* small island in river. (=*ait*)
eyre, *n.* circuit, court, of itinerant justices or **justices in e.** (*errant*)
eyrie, eyry, see **aerie.**

F

F, (*mus.*) note and scale.
fa, same as fah.
fa', *Scot.* for fall.
fabaceous, *a.* bean-like. (L. *faba*, bean)
Fabian, *a.* wearing down by delay, cautiously persistent. **F. Society,** seeking socialism by moral suasion. (Q. *Fabius*, Roman general)
fable, *n.* short story, often with animal characters, teaching moral; legend, fiction; plot of play.—*v.i.* and *t.* romance (about). **fabled.** *a.* legendary. **fabler,** *n.* (L. *fabula*)
fabliau, *n.* (*pl.* **fabliaux**) medieval French metrical tale. (F.)
fabric, *n.* structure, frame, building; texture, workmanship; woven material. **fabricate,** *v.t.* construct; invent (lie); forge (document) **fabrication, fabricator,** *nn.* (L. *faber*, smith)
fabulist, *n.* writer of fables; liar. **fabulous,** *a.* famed in fable, legendary; incredible. **fabulosity,** *n.*
façade, *n.* front of building. (F.)
face, *n.* front of head; front, chief side, surface; dial; outward appearance; grimace; effrontery.—*v.t.* and *i.* front, turn (towards); be opposite (to); meet firmly; give surface to. **f. down,** abash. **f. off,** (*lacrosse*) place ball between sticks to start game. **f. out,** brazen out. **f. to f.,** confronted. **f. value,** value marked on coin etc.; apparent worth. **in f. of,** despite. **lose f.,** be humiliated. **on the f. of it,** judging by appearances. **save one's f.,** spare from humiliation. **set one's f. against,** oppose. **to one's f.,** in one's presence. **f.-ache,** *n.* neuralgia. **f.-card,** *n.* court-card. (L. *facies*)
facer, *n.* blow in face; staggering or unexpected set-back.
facet, *n.* one side of cut gem, crystal etc. **faceted,** *a.* (*face*+dim.)
facetious, *a.* humorous, jocular. **facetiae,** *n.pl.* pleasantries; humorous or indecent books. (L. *facetus*)
facia, *n.* name-board over shop-front. (=*fascia*)
facial, *a.* of the face.—*n.* (*Amer.*) facial massage.
facile, *a.* easily done or mastered; working easily, fluent; easy-going, pliant. *fácilĕ princeps*, easily first. **facilitate,** *v.t.* make easy, help forward. **facilitation, facilitator,** *nn.* **facility,** *n.* easiness; dexterity, fluency; pliancy; (*pl.*) opportunities, good conditions. (L. *facilis*)
facinerious, *a.* (*Shake.*) infamous, wicked. (L. *facinus*, crime)
facing, *n.* front covering; (*pl.*) collar, cuffs etc. of soldier's coat.
façon de parler, way of speaking, conventional formula. (F.)
facsímilĕ, *n.* exact reproduction.—*v.t.* copy exactly. (L.=make like)
fact, *n.* happening, deed; thing known to be true; reality. (L. *facere*, do)
faction, *n.* self-interested or contentious party, sect; dissension, cliquishness. **factional,** *a.* **factious,** *a.* given to faction, seditious. (L. *facere*, do)
factitious, *a.* artificial, got-up. **factitive,** *a.* (*gram.*) causative, with sense 'make to be.' (*fact*)
factor, *n.* agent, dealer; commission-agent; thing contributing to result; (*math.*) any of numbers whose product is a given number; (*Scot.*) steward of estate. **factorage,** *n.* factor's commission. **factorial,** *n.* (*math.*) integer multiplied by all lower integers, e.g. factorial 4 = 4×3×2×1. **factory,** *n.* building where things are manufactured; foreign trading-station. **factotum,** *n.* man employed to do all kinds of work. (L.)
factual, *a.* relating or containing facts. (on analogy of *actual*)
facula, *n.* (*pl.* **faculae**) bright spot or

streak on sun. **facular, faculous,** *aa.* (L. *fax,* torch)

faculty, *n.* ability, aptitude, knack; power of mind or body; department, governing body, of university; members of a profession; authorization. **the F.,** medical men. **facultative,** *a.* optional, contingent. (L. *facultas*)

fad, *n.* pet idea, craze, hobby. **faddish, faddy,** *aa.* **faddism, faddist,** *nn.* **faddle,** *v.i.* trifle.

fade, *v.i.* decay, wither; lose colour, grow dim; vanish gradually.—*v.t.* cause to fade. **f. in, out,** (*wireless*) bring on, cut off, gradually. **fadeless,** *a.* unfading. (O.F.=dull)

fadge, *v.i.* (*Shake.*) fit, be suitable.

faeces, *n.pl.* sediment; excrement. **faecal,** *a.* (L. *faex,* dregs)

faerie, faery, *n.* the fairy world; enchantment.—*a.* visionary. (=*fairy*)

fag, *n.* toil; exhaustion; junior schoolboy who does services for senior; (*sl.*) cigarette.—*v.i.* and *t.* drudge; tire out; act, employ, as fag. **f.-end,** *n.* last part; inferior remnant.

fagaceous, *a.* of beech family. (L. *fagus,* beech)

faggot, fagot, *n.* bundle of sticks for fuel etc.; stick; bundle of steel rods. —*v.t.* and *i.* form into faggots. **f. vote,** created by sham property qualification. **f.-voter,** *n.* (F.)

fah, *n.* fourth note in sol-fa notation.

Fahrenheit, *a.* (*abbr.* **F.**) using thermometer-scale with freezing-point 32°, boiling-point 212°. (inventor)

faience, *n.* glazed earthenware or porcelain. (F. *faïence*)

faik, *v.t.* (*Scot.*) abate; excuse.

fail, *v.i.* and *t.* be insufficient or wanting (to); lose power, die away; be unsuccessful, miscarry; go bankrupt; disappoint; omit (to); reject, be rejected, at examination. **without f.,** for certain. **failing,** *n.* weakness, shortcoming.—*prep.* in default of. **failure,** *n.* act of failing; unsuccess; unsuccessful person or thing. (L. *fallere,* deceive)

faille, *n.* a soft untwilled silk. (F.)

fain, *a.* willing; content, constrained (to).—*adv.* gladly. (O.E. *fægen*)

fain, fains, (*school sl.*) bar, don't want (opp. to bag).

fainéant, *a.* inactive, do-nothing.—*n.* idler. (F.)

faint, *a.* weak, feeble; pale, indistinct; inclined to swoon; (of air) sickly.—*v.i.* swoon; lose courage.—*n.* swoon; (*pl.*) impure spirit coming first and last in distillation. **f.-hearted,** *a.* timid. (O.F. *faindre,* feign)

fair, *n.* great periodical market; festival with shows and amusements. **a day after the f.,** too late. (L. *feria,* holiday.)

fair, *a.* beautiful; ample; specious; blond, light-coloured; clear, clean; just, honest; pretty good; (of weather) favourable.—*adv.* in fair manner; according to rules.—*n.* (*arch.*) woman. **bid f.,** seem likely. **f. and softly,** not so fast. **f. copy,** final draft after corrections. **f. play,** equal opportunities, honest dealing. **f. trade,** reciprocity in customs duties. **speak f.,** address courteously. **the f.** (sex), women. **f.-spoken,** *a.* civil; plausible. (O.E. *fæger*)

fairing, *n.* present from fair.

fairing, *n.* (*aviation*) stream-lining.—*n.* casing, shape, to effect this.

fairly, *adv.* in a fair manner; utterly, completely; rather, tolerably.

fairway, *n.* navigable channel; (*golf*) smooth turf between rough.

fairy, *n.* small graceful being with magic powers; enchantress.—*a.* of, like, fairies; imaginary; exquisite. **f. lamp,** small coloured lamp for decorations. **f. ring,** dark or bare circle in grass, due to fungi. **f.-tale,** *n.* tale of fairies; marvellous account. **fairydom, fairyhood, fairyism,** *nn.* **fairyland,** *n.* home of fairies; enchanted place. (O.F. *fae,* fay)

fait accompli, thing done and past arguing about. (F.)

faith, *n.* trust, reliance; belief without proof; acceptance of divine truth; religion, creed; promise; loyalty, fidelity. **bad f.,** intent to deceive. **good f.,** honesty. **Punic f.,** treachery. **f.-cure,** *n.* healing by suggestion. **faithful,** *a.* loyal, constant; true, accurate. **the faithful,** Mohammedans. **faithless,** *a.* unbelieving; false, unreliable. (L. *fides*)

faitor, faitour, *n.* impostor, cheat, scoundrel. (O.F.=doer)

faix, *int.* (*Ir.*) by my faith.

fake, *v.t.* (*naut.*) coil (rope).—*n.* one round of coil.

fake, *v.t.* counterfeit, doctor, make up.—*n.* sham, swindle. **fakement,** *n.* **faker,** *n.* swindler; pickpocket.

fakir, *n.* religious beggar, naked ascetic, of India. (Arab. *faquir,* poor man)

Falangist, *n.* Spanish fascist.

falbala, *n.* trimming; flounce.

falcate, falcated, falciform, *aa.* sickle-shaped. (L. *falx,* sickle)

falchion, *n.* broad curved sword. (L. *falx,* sickle)

falcon, *n.* a bird of prey; female of this. **falconer,** *n.* one who trains or hunts with hawks. **falconet,** *n.* kind of shrike; small cannon. **falconry,** *n.* hawking; breeding of hawks. (L.L. *falco*)

falderal, *n.* trifling ornament, gewgaw.

faldstool, *n.* kneeling stool; desk from which litany is said; bishop's armless chair. (*fold*; *stool*)

Falernian, *n.* an old Roman wine.

fall, *v.i.* (*past* **fell,** *p.p.* **fallen**) drop; hang down; become lower, decline; come to the ground, collapse; perish, be captured; sin; become, pass; happen, light; (of river) discharge.—*n.* descent; thing, distance, amount, fallen; yielding to temptation; wrestling bout or throw; rope of hoisting tackle; kind of veil; (*Amer.*) autumn; (us. *pl.*) cascade. **f. back,** retreat. **f. behind,** lag; be in arrears. **f. flat,** fail of effect. **f. for,** (*Amer. sl.*) be taken in by; fall in love with. **f. foul of,** collide, quarrel, with. **f. in,** sink inward; take place in rank; become due; (of lease) run out. **f. off,** decrease; degenerate. **f. out,** quarrel; happen; leave ranks. **f. short,** be deficient. **f. through,** miscarry. **f. to,** begin. **f. upon,** attack; chance upon. **the F.,** Adam's sin. **falling sickness,** epilepsy. **falling star,** meteor.

fallacy, *n.* misleading argument, false reasoning; illusion. **pathetic f.,** artistic convention making nature share in human emotions. **fallacious,** *a.* containing fallacy; delusive, deceptive. (L. *fallere,* deceive)

fal-lal, *n.* piece of finery.

fallible, *a.* liable to error. **fallibility,** *n.* (*fallacy*)

Fallopian tubes, human oviducts. (*Fallopius,* doctor)

fallow, *a.* left unsown after being ploughed; untilled; neglected.—*n.* fallow land.—*v.t.* break up (land). (M.E. *falwe,* ploughed land)

fallow, *a.* brownish or reddish yellow. **f.-deer,** *n.* small deer so coloured. (O.E. *falu*)

false, *a.* wrong, erroneous; deceptive; faithless, untrue; sham, artificial. **f. bottom,** partition above real bottom. **f. colours,** flag one has no right to. **f. quantity,** incorrect length of vowel in verse etc. **play one f.,** cheat. **falsehood,** *n.* lie, lying; falseness. (L. *falsus*)

falsetto, *n.* shrill voice above natural range. (It.)

falsify, *v.t.* alter fraudulently, forge; misrepresent; disappoint (hopes). **falsification,** *n.* **falsity,** *n.* falseness.

Falstaffian, *a.* fat, convivial, swaggering, like *Falstaff* in Shakespeare.

falter, *v.i.* and *t.* speak hesitatingly, stammer; waver, flinch; stumble. **falteringly,** *adv.*

fame, *n.* report, rumour; reputation; renown, celebrity. **house of ill f.,** brothel. **famed,** *a.* famous; reported. (Gk. *phēmē*)

familiar, *a.* intimate, closely acquainted; well-known, common; informal, unconstrained; (*arch.*) of one's family.—*n.* intimate; household servant of R.C. bishop; (also **f. spirit**) attendant demon. **familiarity,** *n.* intimacy, close knowledge; informality; (*pl.*) liberties. **familiarize,** *v.t.* make familiar (with), accustom. **familiarization,** *n.* (*family*)

family, *n.* household; person's children; set of parents and children or relatives; genealogy, noble lineage; race; group of related things; group between order and genus. **f. Bible,** large one with page for recording births etc. **f. butcher,** supplying families. **f. man,** husband and father. **f. tree,** genealogical chart. **in the f. way,** pregnant. (L. *familia*)

famine, *n.* general scarcity of food; dearth; starvation. **famish,** *v.t.* and *i.* starve; feel extreme hunger. (L. *fames,* hunger)

famous, *a.* renowned; noted; (*colloq.*) first-rate. (*fame*)

famulus, *n.* attendant on magician. (L.=servant)

fan, *n.* winnowing-implement; sector-shaped instrument for agitating air to cool face; revolving vane for ventilation; small sail keeping windmill's head to wind; (*naut.*) blade of screw.—*v.t.* and *i.* winnow (away); move (air) with fan, blow gently on; kindle (flame); spread out fanwise. (L. *vannus*)

fan, *n.* (*sl.*) enthusiast, devotee, admirer. (abbr. of *fanatic*)

fanatic, *n.* extreme enthusiast, visionary zealot.—*a.* (also **fanatical**) extravagantly zealous, esp. in religion. **fanaticism,** *n.* **fanaticize,** *v.i.* and *t.* (L. *fanum,* temple)

fancy, *n.* imagination; mental image; notion, inclination, whim; followers of a hobby; (*Shake.*) love.—*a.* ornamental, not plain; whimsical, irregular, bred for particular points.—*v.t.* imagine; like; suppose; breed (animals); (*colloq.*) think a lot of. **f. dress,** masquerade costume. **f. fair,** bazaar for **f. goods,** ribbons, laces, ornamental articles. **f. man,** sweetheart; (*sl.*) man living on prostitute's earnings. **f. price,** exorbitant price. **the F.,** followers of boxing. **f.-free,** *a.* not in love. **f.-work,** *n.* ornamental needlework. **fancier,** *n.* connoisseur. **fanciful,** *a.* whimsical, fantastic; imaginary. (contr. of *fantasy*)

fandangle, *n.* fantastic ornament; tomfoolery.

fandango, *n.* lively Spanish dance with castanets; tune for it. (Sp.)

fane, *n.* (*poet.*) temple. (L. *fanum*)

fanfare, *n.* flourish of trumpets. **fanfaronade,** *n.* brag, bluster; fanfare. (F.)

fang, *n.* tooth of beast of prey; serpent's poison-tooth; root, prong, of tooth; spike of tool.—*v.t.* (*Shake.*) seize. (O.E.)

fanion, *n.* small marking-flag. (L.L. *fano*)

fanlight, *n.* fan-shaped window; window over door.

fanner, *n.* winnowing-machine. (*fan*)

fantail, *n.* kind of pigeon. (*fan*)

fan-tan, *n.* Chinese gambling game of guessing hidden counters. (Chin.)

fantasy, phantasy, *n.* imagination, extravagant fancy; mental image; fanciful design, caprice. **fantasia,** *n.* fanciful musical composition. **fantast,** *n.* visionary, dreamer. **fantastic,** (*obs.*) **fantastical,** *aa.* grotesque, quaint; whimsical, wild. **fantasticality, fantasticism,** *nn.* (Gk. *phainein,* show)

Fantee, *n.* member of Gold Coast negro tribe. **go f.,** go native.

fantoccini, n.pl. marionettes. (It.)

fap, *a.* (*Shake.*) drunk.

faquir, same as **fakir.**

far, *a.* (*compar.* **farther, further;** *superl.* **farthest, furthest**) remote; more distant of two.—*adv.* at, to, a great distance; by very much.—*n.* great distance or amount. **a f. cry,** a great distance. **f. and away,** by a great deal. **go f.,** do well; last long. **f.-away,** *a.* distant; abstracted. **f.-between,** *a.* infrequent. **f.-fetched,** *a.* unnatural, forced. **f.-flung,** *a.* widely extended. **f.-seeing, f.-sighted,** *aa.* prudent. (O.E. *feor*)

farad, *n.* unit of electrical capacity. **faradaic,** *a.* inductive. (Michael *Faraday*)

farandole, *n.* Provençal street-dance in 6–8 time. (F.)

farce, *n.* grotesque and exaggerated comedy; absurd or futile affair, mockery; force-meat.—*v.t.* (*arch.*) cram; season. *farceur, n.* joker, wag. **farcical,** *a.* ludicrous. **farcicality,** *n.* (L. *farcire,* stuff)

farcy, *n.* horse-disease like glanders. **f.-bud,** *n.* small tumour in this. (L. *farciminum*)

fardel, *n.* (*arch.*) bundle, burden. (O.F.)

fare, *v.i.* go, travel; happen; get on, be treated or fed.—*n.* charge for transport of passenger; passenger; food. (O.E. *faran*)

farewell, *int.* good-bye.—*n.* leave-taking.—*a.* parting.

farina, *n.* ground corn, meal; (*bot.*) pollen; (*chem.*) starch. **farinaceous,** *a.* mealy. **farinose,** *a.* yielding farina; powdery. (L.)

farl, farle, *n.* (*Scot.*) quarter-round, piece, of oatmeal cake. (*fourth*; *deal*)

farm, *n.* tract of land used by tenant for cultivation or pasture; buildings attached to this; place where children are farmed.—*v.t.* and *i.* cultivate, till the soil; let out, collect (tax etc.) for fixed sum; contract for maintenance of (child etc.). **home f.,** worked by owner of estate. **farmer, farming,** *nn.* **farmhouse,** *n.* dwelling-house on farm. **farmstead,** *n.* farm with buildings. **farmyard,** *n.* yard of farmhouse. (L.L. *firma,* fixed payment)

faro, *n.* gambling card-game. (*Pharaoh*)

farouche, a. sullen, unsociable. (F.)

farrago, *n.* confused mass, hotchpotch. **farraginous,** *a.* (L.)

farrier, *n.* shoeing-smith; veterinary surgeon. **farriery,** *n.* his art. (L. *ferrarius,* blacksmith)

farrow, *n.* litter of pigs.—*v.t.* and *i.* bear (pigs). (O.E. *fearh,* pig)

fart, *v.i.* (*vulg.*) break wind.—*n.* emission of wind.

farther, *a.* and *adv.* more far, distant, or advanced; further. **farthermost,** *a.* farthest. **farthest,** *a.* and *adv.* to, at, greatest distance. (compar., superl., of *far*)

farthing, *n.* copper coin value ¼*d.* (O.E. *féortha,* fourth)

farthingale, *n.* hooped petticoat. (Sp. *verdugo,* rod)

fasces, *n.pl.* bundle of rods with axe forming Roman badge of authority. (L.)

fascia, *n.* stripe, band; (*anat.*) thin sheath of tissue; (*archit.*) long flat surface between mouldings; facia. **fasciated,** *a.* (*bot.*) fascicled; striped. **fascicle, fascicule, fasciculus,** *nn.* one part of book published by instalments; (*bot.*) bunch, close cluster. **fascicled, fascicular, fasciculate,** *aa.* (*bot.*) arranged in fascicles. **fasciculation,** *n.* (L.)

fascinate, *v.t.* and *i.* make powerless by look or presence; charm, captivate. **fascination,** *n.* **fascinator,** *n.* one who fascinates; opera-hood. (L. *fascinum,* spell)

fascine, *n.* long faggot for lining trenches etc. (L. *fascina*)

fascism, *fascismo, nn.* dictatorial political system or doctrine opposed to socialism, originating in Italy. **fascist,** *n.* (also *fascista, pl. fascisti*) supporter of this. (*fasces*)

fash, *v.t.* and *i.* and *n.* (*Scot.*) bother, trouble. **fashery,** *n.* **fashious,** *a.* vexatious. (L. *fastidium,* loathing)

fashion, *n.* style, make, cut; manner; custom, current usage, esp. in dress; upper society.—*v.t.* shape, make. **after a f.,** in a way. **set the f.,** give lead in changing it. **f.-plate,** *n.* picture showing style of dress. **fashionable,** *a.* in the prevailing mode; of, used by, polite society. **fashioner,** *n.* (L. *facere,* make)

fashions, (*Shake.*) form of farcy.

fast, *a.* firm, fixed; immovable, permanent.—*adv.* firmly, tightly. **make f.,** lock, secure. **play f. and loose,** act irresponsibly. **fasten,** *v.t.* and *i.* attach, fix, secure; be secured; seize (upon). **fastener, fastening,** *nn.* clasp etc. to fasten with. (O.E. *fæst*)

fast, *a.* quick, rapid; dissipated; (of clock) ahead of true time.—*adv.* swiftly; in quick succession. (a special use of *fast,* firm)

fast, *v.i.* abstain wholly or partially from food, esp. as religious duty.—*n.* fasting; season or day appointed for it. **break one's f.,** breakfast. **f.-day,** *n.* (O.E. *fæstan*)

fasti, *n.pl.* records, annals. (L.=calendar)

fastidious, *a.* hard to please, particular. (L. *fastidium,* loathing)
fastigiate, *a.* narrowing at apex. (L. *fastigium,* gable)
fastness, *n.* stronghold, fortress; being fast.
fat, *a.* (*compar.* **fatter,** *superl.* **fattest**) stout, plump, fleshy; containing much fat, greasy; fertile, lucrative; fed up for slaughter; (*Amer.*) resinous.—*n.* solid oily animal substance; best part.—*v.t.* fatten. **a f. lot,** (*sl., ironical*) very little. **the f. is in the fire,** there will be a row. **fathead,** *n.* dolt. (O.E. *fætt*)
fatal, *a.* deadly, causing death; destructive; ill-advised, disastrous; inevitable, fated. **fatalism,** *n.* belief that everything is predetermined; submission to fate. **fatalist,** *n.* believer in fatalism. **fatalistic,** *a.* **fatality,** *n.* law of fate, destiny; calamity; death by accident. **fatalize,** *v.i.* and *t.* incline, subject, to fatalism. (*fate*)
fata morgana, a kind of mirage. (It.)
fate, *n.* power preordaining events, destiny; final issue; appointed lot; death, destruction; (*pl.*) three goddesses of destiny, Atropos, Clotho, Lachesis. **fated,** *a.* decreed by fate; doomed. **fateful,** *a.* charged with fate, momentous; prophetic; controlled by fate. (L. *fatum*)
father, *n.* male parent; ancestor; early leader, originator; priest, confessor; oldest member, doyen; (*pl.*) leading men, elders.—*v.t.* beget, originate; adopt; claim to be father or author of. **be gathered to one's ff.,** die and be buried. **f. of lies,** the devil. **Ff. of the Church,** earliest Christian writers. **f. superior,** head of monastery. **(Heavenly) F.,** God, First Person of the Trinity. **Holy F.,** pope. **f.-in-law,** *n.* father of one's husband or wife. **fatherhood, fathership,** *nn.* **fatherland,** *n.* native land, esp. Germany. **fatherless,** *a.* **fatherlike, fatherly,** *aa.* like a father; tender. (O.E. *fæder*)
fathom, *n.* (*naut.*) measure of length, 6 ft.—*v.t.* sound; get to bottom of, understand. **fathomless,** *a.* too deep to fathom. (O.E. *fæthm,* outstretched arms)
fatidical, *a.* having gift of prophecy. (L. *fatum,* fate; *dicere,* tell)
fatigue, *n.* weariness from exertion; wearying toil; soldier's non-military duty; (*mech.*) weakness in metals after long strain.—*v.t.* tire, exhaust. **fatiguing,** *a.* (L. *fatigare,* weary)
fatling, *n.* young fattened animal.
fatten, *v.t.* and *i.* make, become, fat, esp. for market; enrich (soil).
fatter, fattest, see **fat.**
fatty, *a.* of, like, fat.—*n.* fat person. **f. degeneration,** partial transformation of tissues into fat.
fatuous, *a.* complacently stupid; silly, idiotic; illusory. **fatuity,** *n.* (L. *fatuus*)
faubourg, **n.** suburb, esp. of Paris. (F.)
fauces, *n.pl.* (*anat.*) upper part of throat. **faucal,** *a.* and *n.* deeply guttural (sound). (L.)
faucet, *n.* tap, cock. (F. *fausset*)
faugh, *int.* of disgust.
fault, *n.* defect, blemish; misdeed, slight offence; blame; (*electr.*) leak in circuit; (*geol.*) break in strata; (*hunting*) failure of scent, check; (*tennis*) ball wrongly served.—*v.t.* (*geol.*) cause fault in. **at f.,** blameworthy; puzzled. **find f. (with),** complain; blame. **f.-finding,** *a.* censorious, captious. **faultless,** *a.* perfect; blameless. **faulty,** *a.* defective, wrong. (L. *fallere,* deceive)
faun, *n.* woodland deity, half man, half beast. (L. *Faunus*)
fauna, *n.* (*pl.* **faunae, faunas**) animals of region or epoch collectively; treatise on these. **faunal,** *a.* **faunist,** *n.* writer on fauna. **faunistic, faunistical,** *aa.* (*faun*)
faute de mieux, for want of better. (F.)
fauteuil, **n.** arm-chair; stall in theatre. (F.)
faux pas, false step, offence against convention. (F.)
faveolate, *a.* honeycombed. (L. *favus,* honeycomb)
favonian, *a.* of the west wind, favourable. (L. *Favonius,* west wind)
favour, *n.* goodwill, approval; kindness; partiality; support; badge, love-token; letter; (*arch.*) pardon; looks.—*v.t.* regard, use, with favour; oblige (with); treat with partiality; aid; resemble in features. **favourable,** *a.* propitious, approving; helpful. **favourite,** *a.* habitually preferred.—*n.* favourite person etc.; horse etc. expected to win. **favouritism,** *n.* habitual partiality. (L. *favor*)
fawn, *n* young deer.—*a.* light yellowish-brown.—*v.i.* and *t.* (of deer) bear (young). (*foetus*)
fawn, *v.i.* cringe, behave servilely; (of dog) grovel, lick hand etc. (O.E. *fahnian*)
fawsont, *a.* (*Scot.*) decent, seemly.
fay, *n.* fairy. (O.F. *fae*)
fay, *n.* (*arch.*) faith. (O.F. *fei*)
faze, *v.t.* (*Amer. sl.*) discompose, disconcert; daunt.
fealty, *n.* vassal's oath of fidelity to feudal lord; fidelity, loyalty. (L. *fides,* faith)
fear, *n.* dread, alarm; anxiety; reverence.—*v.i.* and *t.* be afraid (of); be in awe of; hesitate; (*Shake.*) frighten; doubt. **no f.,** it is not likely. **fearful,** *a.* terrible, awful; timid, apprehensive; (*colloq.*) annoying. **fearless,** *a.* brave, intrepid. **fearnought,** *n.* kind of stout woollen cloth. **fearsome,** *a.* appalling. (O.E. *fær*)
feasible, *a.* practicable, possible; (*colloq.*) convenient, plausible. **feasibility,** *n.* (L. *facere,* do)

feast, *n.* banquet, lavish meal; religious anniversary, festival; rich enjoyment.—*v.i.* and *t.* fare sumptuously; regale. **feaster,** *n.* (L. *festus,* festal)

feat, *n.* notable deed; striking act of skill, strength etc.—*a.* (*arch.*) adroit, deft. (L. *facere,* do)

feather, *n.* plume of bird; plumage; game-birds.—*v.t.* and *i.* provide, line, coat, with feathers; turn (oar) edgeways. **birds of a f.,** people of one kind. **f. in one's cap,** thing to be proud of. **f. one's nest,** enrich oneself. **in high f.,** in good spirits. **white f.,** cowardice. **f.-bed,** *n.* mattress stuffed with feathers. **f.-brain, f.-head,** *nn.* giddy or flighty person. **f.-edge,** *n.* thin edge of wedge-shaped board. **feathery,** *a.* like, covered with, feathers. **featherweight,** *n.* very light person; (*boxing*) between 8 st. 4 lb. and 9 st. (O.E. *fether*)

feature, *n.* part of face, lineament; distinctive or characteristic part.—*v.t.* be feature of; portray, outline; give prominence to; (*Amer.*) show on cinema screen. **featureless,** *a.* uneventful. (L. *facere,* make)

febrile, *a.* of fever; feverish. **febrifuge,** *n.* drug to allay fever. **febrifugal,** *a.* (L. *febris,* fever)

February, *n.* second month of year. (L. *februa,* feast of expiation)

fecit, *v.t.* (*pl. fecerunt*) made (used with artist's signature). (L.)

feck, *n.* (*Scot.*) force; amount. **feckless,** *a.* feeble, unpractical, spiritless. **feckly,** *adv.* mostly.

fecket, *n.* (*Scot.*) under-waistcoat.

feculent, *a.* full of sediment, turbid; fetid. **feculence,** *n.* (*faeces*)

fecund, *a.* fruitful, fertile; fertilizing. **fecundate,** *v.t.* make fruitful; impregnate. **fecundation, fecundity,** *nn.* (L. *fecundus*)

fed, see **feed.**

federal, *a.* based on treaty or covenant; of, consisting in, several states united under central government but retaining internal independence; of, favouring, this central government; of Northern party in U.S. civil war. **federalism, federalist,** *nn.* **federalize,** *v.t.* **federalization,** *n.* **federate,** *v.t.* and *i.* unite in league or on federal basis. **federation,** *n.* federating; federal empire or union. **federationist,** *n.* (L. *foedus,* treaty)

fedora, *n.* (*Amer.*) soft felt hat with curled brim and crown creased lengthwise. (name of play)

fee, *n.* payment for professional services, charge; tip; heritable estate; fief, feud.—*v.t.* (*past, p.p.* **fee'd**) pay fee to, hire. **f. simple,** unrestricted ownership, freehold. **f. tail,** estate entailed to owner's heirs. **hold in f.,** own absolutely. **f.-grief,** *n.* (*Shake.*) private grief. **feeing-market,** *n.* (*Scot.*) fair at which farm-servants are hired for season. (O.E. *fiu*)

feeble, *a.* weak, infirm; lacking vigour, insipid; dim. **f.-minded,** *a.* mentally deficient. (L. *flēre,* weep)

feed, *v.t.* and *i.* (*past, p.p.* **fed**) give food (to), take food, graze; supply; support.—*n.* feeding; allowance of fodder; pasturage, fodder; material supplied to machine; (*colloq.*) meal. **f. on,** consume. **f. up,** fatten; satiate, bore. **off one's f.,** with no appetite. **f.-pipe,** *n.* carrying water to boiler etc. **feeding-bottle,** *n.* for child's milk. **feeder,** *n.* eater; feeding-apparatus; child's feeding-bottle or bib; tributary; (*rounders*) player who tosses ball to striker. (O.E. *fēdan*)

fee-faw-fum, *int.* and *n.* shout of ogre etc.; fearsome thing.

feel, *v.t.* and *i,* (*past, p.p.* **felt**) examine, perceive, by touch; grope, reconnoitre; be conscious of, experience; be affected by (sentiment); be consciously, seem; sympathize; have emotional conviction.—*n.* sense of touch; sensation. **feeler,** *n.* organ of touch of insect etc.; proposal made to test opinion. **feeling,** *n.* sense of touch; sensation; emotion; tenderness; sentiment. (*pl.*) susceptibilities.—*a.* sensitive; sympathetic; heartfelt. (O.E. *fēlan*)

feer, same as **fere.**

feet, see **foot.**

feign, *v.t.* and *i.* pretend; sham, simulate; (*arch.*) invent, forge. (L. *fingere,* form)

feil, *a.* (*Scot.*) soft, smooth.

feint, *n.* sham attack, deceptive movement to divert attention; pretence.—*v.i.* make feint.—*a.* (of lines) faint. (F. *feinte*)

feist, *n.* (*Amer.*) small dog, cur.

feldspar, felspar, *n.* a crystalline mineral found in granite etc. **feldspathic, felspathic,** *a.* (G. *feld,* field; *spath,* spar)

felicide, *n.* cat-killing. (L. *feles,* cat; *caedere,* kill)

felicity, *n.* great happiness, bliss; blessing; aptness, apt phrase. **felicific,** *a.* making happy. **felicitate,** *v.t.* wish happiness to, congratulate. **felicitation, felicitator,** *nn.* **felicitous,** *a.* well-chosen, apt, happy. (L. *felix,* happy)

feline, *a.* of cats; catlike.—*n.* felid. **felinity,** *n.* **felid,** *n.* animal of cat tribe. (L. *feles,* cat)

fell, *v.t.* knock down; cut down (tree). **feller,** *n.* (O.E. *fellan*)

fell, *a.* (*poet.*) fierce, cruel; dire, deadly; (*Scot.*) huge; keen. (*felon*)

fell, *n.* hide, pelt, skin. (O.E.)

fell, *n.* barren hill; moorland. (O.N. *fiall*)

fell, see **fall.**

fellah, *n.* (*pl.* **fellaheen, fellahin, fellahs**) Egyptian peasant. (Arab.)

felloe, felly, *n.* circumference, outer part, of wheel; section of this. (O.E. *felg*)

fellow, *n.* companion, associate; counterpart, match, other of pair; senior member (of college, society etc.); (*colloq.*) man.—*a.* of same kind. **f. citizen, f. countryman,** one belonging to same city, country. **f. feeling,** sympathy. **fellowship,** *n.* association, fraternity; intercourse, friendship; sharing, joint interest; status, income, of college fellow. (O.E. *féolaga,* one who lays down money in partnership)

felly, see **felloe.**

felo-de-se, *n.* self-murder; self-murderer. (L.=felon about himself)

felon, *n.* kind of whitlow.

felon, *n.* one guilty of felony; convict, criminal.—*a.* wicked, cruel. **felonious,** *a.* criminal; (*law*) of, involving, felony. **felony,** *n.* felons collectively. **felony,** *n.* grave crime, such as is punishable by penal servitude or death. (L.L. *fello*)

felspar, felspathic, see feldspar.

felstone, felsite, *nn.* compact form of feldspar. (G. *fels,* rock: *stein,* stone)

felt, *n.* unwoven fabric of wool etc. matted by beating and pressure; felt hat.—*a.* made of felt.—*v.t.* make into, cover with, **felt; become matted.** (O.E.)

felt, see **feel.**

felteric, *n.* a horse disease.

felucca, *n.* two-masted Mediterranean vessel with lateen sails. (It.)

female, *a.* of the sex that bears young; of women; (*bot.*) fruit-bearing; (*mech.*) made for corresponding male part to fit into.—*n.* female person or animal. (L. *femina,* woman)

feme covert, (*law*) **married woman. feme sole,** spinster, widow. (O.F.)

feminality, *n.* female nature or trait.

feminine, *a.* of women; womanly; (*gram.*) of gender denoting female. **f. ending,** with accent on second-last syllable of verse. **f. rhyme,** of two syllables, second unstressed, e.g. 'flatter,' 'matter.' **femineity, femininity, feminity,** *nn.* womanliness. **feminism,** *n.* influence of women; advocacy of women's rights. **feminist,** *n.* **feminize,** *v.t.* and *i.* make, become, feminine. **feminization,** *n.* (L. *femina,* woman)

femme de chambre, chambermaid. (F.)

femur, *n.* (*pl.* **femurs, femora**) thighbone. **femoral,** *a.* of the thigh. (L.)

fen, *n.* low marshy land, swamp. **f.-berry,** *n.* cranberry. **f.-fire,** *n.* will-o'-the-wisp. **f.-pole,** *n.* for use in jumping ditches. (O.E.)

fen, fens, same as **fain.**

fence, *n.* swordsmanship; skill in debate; railing, hedge; guard in machine; receiver, receiving-house, of stolen goods.—*v.i.* and *t.* practise sword-play; talk evasively; enclose with railing, fortify; deal in stolen goods. **ring f.,** enclosing whole estate. **sit on the f.,** be neutral. **sunk f.,** along bottom of ditch. **f.-season, f.-time,** *nn.* close time. **fenceless,** *a.* unenclosed; defenceless. **fencer,** *n.* **fencible,** *n.* soldier for home defence. **fencing,** *n.* fences, material for them. (abbr. of *defence*)

fend, *v.t.* and *i.* ward off, repel; provide (for). **fender,** *n.* frame round hearth; bundle of rope etc. to protect ship's side. (abbr. of *defend*)

fenestella, *n.* niche in wall on south side of altar for piscina etc. **fenestrate,** *a.* (*bot.*) with small window-like holes. **fenestration,** *n.* being fenestrate; (*archit.*) arrangement of windows of building. (L. *fenestra,* window)

Fenian, *a.* and *n.* (member) of Irish-American league for overthrow of English rule in Ireland. **Fenianism,** *n.* (O.Ir. *féne,* the Irish+confusion with *fíann,* king's bodyguard)

fenks, *n.pl.* refuse of whale blubber.

fennec, *n.* small African fox with large ears. (Moorish)

fennel, *n.* yellow-flowered fragrant plant. **f.-flower,** *n.* love-in-a-mist. (L. *faeniculum*)

feoff, *n.* feud, fief.—*v.t.* enfeoff, grant possession of. **feoffer** or **feoffor, feoffee,** *nn.* person by, to, whom fief is granted. **feoffment,** *n.* (*fee*)

ferae naturae, wild, not domesticated. (L.=of wild nature)

feral, *a.* wild, untamed; brutal. (L. *fera,* wild beast)

fer-de-lance, *n.* yellow viper of tropical America, very venomous. (F.)

fere, *n.* companion, mate. (O.E. *geféra*)

fere, *a.* (*Scot.*) sound, healthy.

feretory, *n.* shrine, bier, for saint's relics; chapel for keeping this. (Gk. *pherein,* bear)

ferial, *a.* (of day) ordinary, not festival or fast. (L. *feria,* holiday)

ferine, *a.* wild, feral. (L. *fera,* wild beast)

Feringhee, *n.* Hindu name for European, esp. Indian-born Portuguese. (corrupt. of *Frank*)

ferly, *a.* (*Scot.*) strange, wonderful.—*n.* wonder, spectacle.

ferment, *n.* fermenting-agent, leaven; fermentation; tumult, excitement.—*v.i.* and *t.* undergo, subject to, fermentation; stir up. **fermentation,** *n.* chemical change, decomposition, which produces alcohol etc.; agitation, restless action. **fermentative,** *a.* (L. *fervēre,* boil)

fermeture, *n.* breech-closing mechanism of gun. (F.)

fern, *n.* plant with feathery fronds. **f.-owl,** *n.* nightjar. **fernery,** *n.* place for growing ferns. **ferny,** *a.* full of ferns. (O.E. *fearn*)

ferocious, *a.* savage, fierce; cruel. **ferocity,** *n.* (L. *ferox*)

-ferous, *adj. suf.* bearing, as in **auriferous.** (L. *ferre,* bear)

ferrate, *n.* a salt of ferric acid.
ferreous, *a.* of, containing, iron. (L. *ferrum,* iron)
ferrel, see **ferrule.**
ferret, *n.* kind of narrow tape. (L. *flos,* flower)
ferret, *n.* animal like weasel, bred for hunting rabbits.—*v.i.* and *t.* hunt, drive out, with ferret; search (out) cunningly. **ferrety,** *a.* (L. *fur,* thief)
ferriage, *n.* conveyance by, fare for, ferry.
ferric, ferrous, *aa.* of iron; (*chem.*) containing iron in higher, lower, proportion. **ferriferous,** *a.* yielding iron. **ferro-concrete,** *n.* reinforced concrete. **ferrotype,** *n.* positive photograph on thin iron plate; this process. **ferruginous,** *a.* of iron rust; rust-coloured, reddish-brown. (L. *ferrum,* iron)
ferrule, ferrel, *n.* metal cap or ring to strengthen end of stick etc. (L. *viriae,* bracelets)
ferry, *v.t.* and *i.* carry, pass, across river, strait etc. by boat.—*n.* ferry-boat, place where it plies. **f.-bridge,** *n.* train-carrying ferry. **ferryman,** *n.* (O.E. *ferian,* convey)
fertile, *a.* bearing abundantly; reproductive; inventive. **fertility,** *n.* **fertilize,** *v.t.* make fertile; fecundate. **fertilization, fertilizer,** *nn.* (L. *ferre,* bear)
ferula, *n.* giant fennel; ferule. **ferule,** *n.* flat ruler, cane.—*v.t.* punish with this. (L.)
fervent, *a.* ardent, vehement; glowing, hot. **fervid,** *a.* impassioned, fervent. **fervency, fervour,** *nn.* (L. *fervēre,* boil)
Fescennine, *a.* (of verses) scurrilous. (*Fescennia* in Italy)
fescue, *n.* teacher's small pointer; kinds of grass. (L. *festuca,* straw)
fesse, fess, *n.* (*heraldry*) broad horizontal band across middle of escutcheon. (*fascia*)
festal, *a.* of a feast or holiday; gay. (L. *festus*)
fester, *v.i.* and *t.* suppurate, produce matter; putrefy; cause festering in. —*n.* suppurating condition, sore. (*fistula*)
festina lente, hasten slowly. (L.)
festive, *a.* of a feast; joyous, jovial. **festival,** *n.* joyful celebration, merry-making; periodical season of entertainment.—*a.* of a feast. **festivity,** *n.* social gaiety; rejoicing. (*festal*)
festoon, *n.* wreath, garland, hung between two points.—*v.t.* and *i.* adorn with, form, festoon. **festoonery,** *n.* (It. *festone*)
fet, (*Shake.*) form of **fetched.**
fetal, see **foetal.**
fetch, *v.t.* and *i.* go and get, bring; draw forth; be sold for; delight, rouse; deal (blow).—*n.* trick, dodge. **f. a compass,** take roundabout way. **f. and carry,** run errands. **f. up,** come to a stand. **fetching,** *a.* attractive. (O.E. *feccan*)
fetch, *n.* apparition of living person, wraith; person's double.
fête, *n.* festival, holiday; outdoor entertainment; day of saint whose name one bears.—*v.t.* entertain, make much of. (F.)
feticide, see **foeticide.**
fetid, foetid, *a.* stinking. (L. *fetēre,* stink)
fetish, fetich, fetiche, *n.* inanimate object worshipped as abode of spirit or credited with magic powers; object of unreasoning devotion. **f.-man,** *a.* medicine-man. **fetishism,** *n.* fetish-worship, belief in charms. **fetishist,** *n.* **fetishistic,** *a.* (Port. *feitiço,* magic)
fetlock, *n.* tuft of hair, part where it grows, above and behind horse's hoof. (M.E. *fytlok*)
fetor, *n.* stench. (L.)
fetter, *n.* chain for feet, shackle; restraint, hindrance.—*v.t.* chain up; restrain. **fetterlock,** *n.* shackle for horse's leg. (O.E. *feter*)
fettle, *n.* condition, trim.—*v.t.* put in order.
fetus, see **foetus.**
fetwa, *n.* decision by mufti or Mohammedan judge. (Arab.)
feu, *n.* (*Scot.*) tenure of land in perpetuity at fixed rent; land so held.—*v.t.* lease in feu. **f.-duty,** *n.* rent for feu. **feuar,** *n.* leaseholder. (=*fee*)
feud, *n.* deadly quarrel between two families, tribes etc.; vendetta; mutual hatred. (O.F. *fede*)
feud, *n.* fief. **feudal,** *a.* of fief or feudalism. **feudal system,** medieval polity in which land was held by vassal from superior on condition of military service. **feudalism,** *n.* feudal system or its principles. **feudalist,** *n.* **feudalistic,** *a.* **feudality,** *n.* feudalism; fief. **feudalize,** *v.t.* **feudalization,** *n.* **feudatory,** *a.* and *n.* (person) feudally subject, vassal. (L.L. *feudum*)
feu de joie, firing of guns in token of joy; bonfire. (F.)
feuilleton, *n.* French newspaper's lower half-page devoted to light literature; article in this; newspaper serial. (F.)
fever, *n.* condition, disease, marked by high temperature and pulse; extreme excitement, agitation.—*v.t.* throw into fever. **feverfew,** *n.* white-flowered herb once used as febrifuge. **feverish,** *a.* having symptoms of, causing, fever; restless, morbidly eager. **feverous,** *a.* infested with fever. (L. *febris*)
few, *a.* not many.—*n.* small number. **a f.,** (*colloq.*) very much. **a good f.,** a fair number. **in f.,** (*arch.*) briefly. **not a f.,** many. (O.E. *féawe*)
fewter, *v.t.* (*Spens.*) place (spear) in rest. (O.F. *feutre,* socket for spear)
fey, *a.* (*Scot.*) fated to die, under

shadow of death; unnaturally gay, over-confident, at death's approach. (O.E. *fǽge*)

fez, *n.* red brimless tasselled close-fitting Turkish cap. (Turk. *fes*)

fiacre, *n.* French four-wheeled cab. (F.)

fiancé, *n.* (*fem.* **fiancée**) betrothed person. (F.)

fiar, *n.* (*Scot*). freeholder. (*fee*)

fiars, *n.pl.* (*Scot.*) prices of grain fixed for current year by Fiars Court. (L. *forum,* market)

fiasco, *n.* failure of actor; total failure, breakdown. (It. = bottle)

fiat, *n.* formal command; warrant. (L.=let it be done)

fib, *n.* harmless or trivial lie; falsehood.—*v.i.* tell fib. **fibber,** *n.*

fib, *n.* blow.—*v.t.* strike.

fibre, *n.* filament forming part of animal or plant tissue; raw material of textiles; fibrous substance or structure; character, grain. **fibril,** *n.* small fibre. **fibrillar, fibrillate, fibrillose,** *aa.* **fibrin,** *n.* fibrous proteid in blood causing coagulation. **fibrinous,** *a.* **fibroid,** *a.* like fibre.—*n.* fibroid uterine tumour. **fibroin,** *n.* main constituent of silk and cobweb. **fibroline,** *n.* yarn from waste in spinning. **fibroma,** *n.* fibrous tumour. **fibrous,** *a.* made of fibres. (L. *fibra*)

fibster, *n.* fibber.

fibula, *n.* (*pl.* **fibulae, fibulas**) slender outer bone of lower leg; brooch, buckle. **fibular,** *a.* (L.)

-fic, *adj.suf.* making, doing, as in **pacific, terrific. -fication,** *suf.* forming nouns from verbs in *-fy,* as in **solidification.** (L. *facere,* make)

ficelle, *a.* string-coloured. (F.=string)

fichu, *n.* woman's three-cornered lace cape for neck and shoulders. (F.)

fickle, *a.* capricious, inconstant. (O.E. *ficol*)

fico, *n.* (*Sh.ake*) fig, snap of fingers. (It.)

fictile, *a.* moulded; plastic; of pottery. (L. *fingere,* fashion)

fiction, *n.* invention; invented or false story; novels collectively, story-telling; legal assumption, pretence. **fictional,** *a.* **fictionist,** *n.* story-teller. **fictitious,** *a.* false, forged; imaginary, not real. **fictive,** *a.* creating, created, by imagination. (L. *fingere,* fashion)

fid, *n.* (*naut.*) bar to support topmast; pin for opening strands of rope.

fiddle, *n.* violin; (*naut.*) frame to keep dishes from sliding off table.—*v.i.* and *t.* play on fiddle; potter, trifle. **fit as a f.,** very fit. **play first, second, f.,** take leading, subordinate, part. **f.-faddle,** *n.* trifles, idle talk; idler.—*a.* petty; fussy.—*v.i.* fuss; fiddle. **f.-head,** *n.* ornament at ship's prow. **fiddlededee,** *int.* nonsense. **fiddler,** *n.* violinist; kind of small crab. **fiddlestick,** *n.* violin-bow; (*pl.*) nonsense.

fiddling, *a.* petty, trifling. (O.E. *fithele*)

fiddley, *n.* (*naut.*) iron framework round hatchway opening.

fidelity, *n.* faithfulness, loyalty; accuracy. (L. *fides,* faith)

fidget, *v.i.* and *t.* move uneasily, be restless; make nervous, worry.—*n.* nervous restlessness; fussy person. **fidgety,** *a.*

fidibus, *n.* paper spill for lighting.

fiducial, *a.* (*astron.*) taken as standard of reference. **fiduciary,** *a.* of, held or given in, trust; (of paper currency) depending on public confidence for value.—*n.* trustee. (L. *fiducia,* trust)

fidus Achātēs, faithful friend. (name in Vergil)

fie, *int.* for shame. **f.-f.,** *a.* scandalous. (L. *fi*)

fief, *n.* land held on condition of service, feudal estate. (F.)

field, *n.* enclosed piece of farming land; mining area; battle-field, battle; playing-ground; expanse, area; sphere, range of activity; competitors exclusive of favourite; (*heraldry*) surface of escutcheon; (*Shake.*) open country, land.—*a.* (of artillery, hospital etc.) movable, for use in the field.—*v.t.* and *i.* put (team) in field; (*cricket*) stop and return (ball). **F. Marshal,** highest rank in Army. **hold the f.,** not be superseded. **take the f.,** begin operations. (O.E. *feld*)

field-allowance, *n.* extra pay for officer on active service.

field-day, *n.* military manœuvres; day of unusual activity; (*Amer.*) athletic meeting.

fielder, *n.* (*cricket*) man who fields.

fieldfare, *n.* kind of thrush wintering in Britain. (M.E. *feldefare*)

field-glass, *n.* portable double telescope.

field-mouse, *n.* mouse that lives in fields.

field-officer, *n.* officer of rank between captain and general.

field-sports, *n.pl.* outdoor sports, esp. hunting, shooting, and fishing.

fieldwork, *n.* temporary fortification.

fiend, *n.* devil; diabolically wicked person; enthusiast, addict. **fiendish,** *a.* (O.E. *féond*)

fierce, *a.* ferocious, savage; vehement, violent; ardent. (L. *ferus*)

fieri facias, (*abbr. fi. fa.*) writ for sheriff to distrain defendant's goods. (L.=see that it is done)

fiery, *a.* of, like, fire; flaming; pugnacious, passionate; inflamed; inflammable. (*fire*)

fiesta, *n.* festivity, holiday. (Sp.)

fife, *n.* shrill flute used in martial music with drum.—*v.i.* and *t.* play on fife. **fifer,** *n.* (O.H.G. *pfifan,* pipe)

fife-rail, *n.* (*naut.*) rail round mast holding belaying-pins.

fifteen, *a.* and *n.* five and ten; Rugby football team. **the F.,** Jacobite rising of 1715. **fifteenth,** *a.* and *n.* **fifth,** *a.* next after fourth.—*n.* one of five equal parts; (*mus.*) interval of three tones and semitone. **fifth column,** individuals and organizations within a country which are ready to give help to an enemy. **fifth-columnist,** *n.* **fifthly,** *adv.* in the fifth place. **fifty,** *a.* and *n.* five times ten. **fiftieth,** *a.* and *n.* (*five*)

fig, *n.* pulpy pear-shaped fruit; tree bearing it; worthless thing. **f.-leaf,** *n.* covering for nakedness. (L. *ficus*)

fig, *n.* dress; form, trim. **f. out,** get up, adorn.

fight, *v.i.* and *t.* (*past, p.p.* **fought**) contend (with) in war or single combat; strive (against); contest (case). —*n.* combat, battle; contest. **f. off,** repel with effort. **f. out,** settle by fighting. **f. shy of,** hold aloof from. **show f.,** resist. **fighter,** *n.* combatant; combative person; fighting aeroplane. **fighting,** *a.* fitted, trained, to fight. **fighting-cock,** *n.* game-cock. **fighting-top,** *n.* gun - platform on mast. (O.E. *feohtan*)

figment, *n.* invention, fabrication. (L. *fingere,* fashion)

figurant, *n.* (*fem.* *figurante*) ballet-dancer. (F.)

figuration, *n.* giving of form, representation; figure, shape; (*mus.*) use of florid counterpoint. **figurative,** *a.* metaphorical, not literal; using, full of, figures of speech; emblematic; pictorial. (*figure*)

figure, *n.* form; bodily shape; appearance; personage, character; diagram, illustration; statue, likeness; decorative pattern; evolution in dancing etc.; (*astrol.*) horoscope; (*geom.*) space enclosed by lines or surfaces; (*gram.*) figure of speech; (*Shake.*) phantasm. —*v.t.* and *i.* calculate, estimate; represent; imagine; appear (as). **f. of speech,** abnormal mode of expression used for effect, e.g. metaphor. **f. out, up,** reckon up. (L. *figura*)

figured, *a.* adorned with figures.

figurehead, *n.* carved bust at ship's prow; nominal head; (*joc.*) face.

figurine, *n.* statuette. (*figure*)

fike, *n.* (*Scot.*) vexatious requirement, fad; exacting person.—*v.i.* fidget. **fikery,** *n.* fuss. **fiky,** *a.* pernickety.

filagree, see **filigree.**

filament, *n.* threadlike body, fibre; wire in electric bulb, made incandescent by current; (*bot.*) anther-bearing stalk of stamen. **filamentary, filamentous,** *aa.* **filature,** *n.* reeling of silk from cocoons; place for this. (L. *filum,* thread)

filbert, *n.* kinds of hazel; hazel-nut. (ripe on St. *Philibert's* day)

filch, *v.t.* pilfer, steal.

file, *n.* row of men, etc., one behind another.—*v.i.* and *t.* march, move, in file. **a f. of men,** two men told off. **in f.,** in column two broad. **Indian, single, f.,** column one broad. (L. *filum,* thread)

file, *n.* stiff wire, clip, drawer etc. holding papers for reference; papers so kept.—*v.t.* place in file, put in records. (L. *filum,* thread)

file, *n.* roughened tool for smoothing or rubbing down; (*sl.*) dodger.—*v.t.* smooth, reduce, with file; polish, elaborate. (O.E. *féol*)

file, *v.t.* (*Shake.*) defile, sully.

filemot, *a.* and *n.* russet-yellow. (F. *feuille morte,* dead leaf)

filet, *n.* kind of net with square mesh. (F.=thread)

filial, *a.* of, befitting, a son or daughter. **filiate,** *v.t.* affiliate. **filiation,** *n.* relation of child to father; formation of branches, branch; descent. (L. *filius,* son)

filibeg, philabeg, philibeg, *n.* kilt. (Gael. *feileadhbeag,* little fold)

filibuster, *n.* one who makes unauthorized war; (*Amer.*) one who delays legislation.—*v.i.* act as filibuster. (Du. *vrijbuiter,* freebooter)

filigree, filagree, *n.* fine tracery or openwork of metal, us. gold or silver wire; showy but frail thing. (L. *filum,* thread; *granum,* grain)

filing, *n.* particle filed off.

fill, *v.t.* and *i.* make, become, full; occupy wholly, pervade; satisfy, glut; stop (tooth); hold, discharge duties of, appoint man to (post); execute (order).—*n.* full supply; single charge. **f. in,** insert, supply omissions in. **f. out,** extend to proper limit. **f. the bill,** be only important item. **f. up,** fill completely. (O.E. *fyllan*)

fille, *n.* daughter. *f. de chambre,* chambermaid. *f. de joie,* prostitute. (F.)

filler, *n.* funnel for filling bottle.

fillet, *n.* ribbon, band, encircling hair; thin strip; piece of meat or fish boned, rolled, and tied; undercut of sirloin; (*archit.*) narrow flat band between mouldings.—*v.t.* bind with fillet; remove bones from. (L. *filum,* thread)

filling, *a.* satisfying.—*n.* tooth stopping. **f. station,** roadside depot for petrol.

fillip, *n.* sharp jerk of finger from bent position against thumb; stimulus, incentive; mere trifle.—*v.t.* give fillip to, flip.

fillister, *n.* plane for grooving.

filly, *n.* female foal; young lively girl.

film, *n.* thin skin or layer; dimness over eyes, slight haze; (*phot.*) sensitized coating; celluloid sheet or roll bearing this; cinema picture.—*v.t.* and *i.* cover, become covered, with film; take moving-picture of. **f.-star,** *n.* leading cinema actor or actress. **filmy,** *a.* like, made of, film. (O.E. *filmen,* membrane)

filoselle, *n.* floss silk. (F.)

fils, **n.** son, junior. (F.)
filter, *n.* device for cleansing liquid by passing it through porous material; strainer.—*v.t.* and *i.* pass through filter; percolate, leak out; pass into another lane of traffic. (L.L. *filtrum*)
filth, *n.* foul matter, dirt; vileness; obscenity. **filthy,** *a.* foul, unclean, impure. (O.E. *fȳlth*)
filtrate, *v.t.* and *i.* filter.—*n.* filtered liquor. **filtration,** *n.*
fimbriate, fimbriated, *aa.* (*bot.*) fringed. (L. *fimbria*, fringe)
fimetic, *a.* of dung. (L. *fimus*, dung)
fin, *n.* propelling organ of fish; (*sl.*) hand. **f.-back,** *n.* kinds of whale, rorqual. (O.E. *finn*)
finable, *a.* liable to a fine.
final, *a.* at the end, last; decisive; respecting an end in view.—*n.* deciding match or heat; (*pl.*) concluding examination. **finálĕ,** *n.* last movement in musical composition, piece of music closing act in opera; last act of play; wind-up. **finalist,** *n.* competitor in final. **finality,** *n.* completeness, conclusiveness; teleology. (L. *finis*, end)
finance, *n.* management of money; (*pl.*) money resources.—*v.t.* supply capital for. **financial,** *a.* **financier,** *n.* one skilled in finance, capitalist.—*v.i.* and *t.* deal with money; (*Amer.*) swindle. (O.F.)
finch, *n.* kinds of small bird. (O.E. *finc*)
find, *v.t.* (*past, p.p.* **found**) discover; come upon; obtain, ascertain; provide, supply; determine.—*n.* important discovery. **f. oneself,** discover one's vocation; supply one's own needs. **f. out,** discover; solve; detect in offence. **all found,** with all necessaries provided. **finder,** *n.* discoverer; aiming-device for camera, telescope etc. **finding,** *n.* verdict of jury. (O.E. *findan*)
fin de siècle, typical of the nineties, decadent; up to date. (F.)
fine, *a.* excellent, of high quality; refined, pure; thin, minute; subtle, sensitive; handsome, smart, ornate; (of weather) fair.—*adv.* finely, well. —*n.* fine weather.—*v.t.* and *i.* refine, clarify; become clear. **f. art,** one appealing to sense of beauty, esp. painting, sculpture, and architecture. **f. away, down, off,** make, become, finer or thinner. *f. champagne*, liqueur brandy. **f.-draw,** *v.t.* sew up with imperceptible join. **f.-spun,** *a.* delicate, flimsy; oversubtle. (F. *fin*)
fine, *n.* sum paid as penalty for offence; (*Shake.*) end.—*v.t.* impose fine on. **in f.,** to sum up. (L. *finis*, end)
finery, *n.* showy clothes or decoration; furnace for making iron malleable.
finesse, *n.* subtlety, artifice; delicate manipulation.—*v.i.* and *t.* use finesse; wheedle, trick; (*cards*) try to take trick with lower card while holding higher one. (F.)
finger, *n.* digit of hand, esp. other than thumb; thing like this, pointer, index; finger's breadth; part of glove holding finger.—*v.t.* and *i.* handle with fingers; take (bribe etc.); (*mus.*) play with fingers in particular way; mark this way on (music). **have a f. in,** be concerned in. **have at one's f.-ends,** know thoroughly. **his ff. are all thumbs,** he is awkward. **stir a f.,** make least effort. **f.-alphabet,** *n.* deaf-and-dumb alphabet. **f.-bowl, f.-glass,** *nn.* for rinsing fingers at table. **f.-fish,** *n.* starfish. **f.-plate,** *n.* beside door-handle to prevent finger-marks. (O.E.)
fingering, *n.* yarn for knitting stockings. (obs. *fingram*)
fingerpost, *n.* direction post.
fingerprint, *n.* impression of finger-markings as means of identification.
fingerstall, *n.* protective sheath for finger.
finial, *n.* (*archit.*) ornament at top of pinnacle, canopy etc. (=*final*)
finical, *a.* fastidious, over-particular, fussy; affectedly fine. **finicality,** *n.* **finicking, finicky, finikin,** *aa.* finical.
finis, *n.* end, esp. of book. (L.)
finish, *v.t.* and *i.* bring, come, to an end; complete, perfect; kill; complete education (of).—*n.* last stage, end of race etc.; decisive result; what gives completeness, last touches, polish. **finisher,** *n.* man, machine, doing last operation; crushing blow. (*finis*)
finite, *a.* having limits, not infinite; (*gram.*) limited by number and person. (L. *finire*, finish)
finnan, *n.* (also **f.-haddock**) kind of smoked haddock.
finner, *n.* fin-back. **finny,** *a.* like, having, fins; of, full of, fish.
fiord, fjord, *n.* long narrow rock-bound inlet in Norway. (Norwegian)
fiorin, *n.* white bent-grass. (Ir. *fiorthán*)
fir, *n.* kinds of cone-bearing resinous tree; its wood. **f.-needle,** *n.* its pointed leaf.
fire, *n.* burning, conflagration; flame, glow; burning fuel; great heat, inflammation; ardour, fervour; gunfire.—*v.t.* and *i.* set on fire, kindle, inflame; catch fire, become heated; discharge, explode; shoot; bake (bricks); (*sl.*) dismiss. **catch, take, f.,** be ignited. **f. away,** (*colloq.*) go ahead. **f. off,** discharge (gun); ejaculate. **f. up,** show sudden anger. **Greek f.,** semi-liquid substance for setting fire to enemy's ships etc. **on f.,** burning; excited. **St. Anthony's f.,** erysipelas. **set f. to,** set on f., ignite. **under f.,** exposed to shot. (O.E. *fȳr*)
fire-alarm, *n.* device giving warning of fire.

fire-arm, *n.* gun, rifle, pistol etc.
fireball, *n.* globe lightning; meteor; kind of grenade.
fire-blast, *n.* a disease of plants.
firebox, *n.* furnace of railway engine.
firebrand, *n.* piece of burning wood; kindler of strife.
firebrick, *n.* brick made to resist action of fire.
fire-brigade, *n.* company of firemen.
fire-bug, *n.* (*Amer.*) incendiary.
fire-clay, *n.* fire-resisting clay.
fire-control, *n.* system of directing warship's guns from single centre.
firedamp, *n.* carburetted hydrogen, inflammable gas found in coal-mines.
firedog, *n.* andiron.
fire-eater, *n.* juggler who pretends to eat fire; swaggering bully.
fire-engine, *n.* machine for throwing water to extinguish fire.
fire-escape, *n.* device for escape from burning building.
fire-extinguisher, *n.* container with chemicals for smothering fire.
fire-flair, *n.* sting-ray.
firefly, *n.* a phosphorescent insect.
fireguard, *n.* protective grating or rail in front of fire.
fire-insurance, *n.* insurance against loss of fire.
fire-irons, *n.pl.* poker, tongs, and shovel.
firelighter, *n.* prepared kindling-fuel.
firelock, *n.* old type of musket fired by spark from lock.
fireman, *n.* man trained to extinguish fires; man who tends furnace.
fire-office, *n.* fire-insurance office.
fireplace, *n.* grate, hearth, in room.
fire-plug, *n.* (*abbr.* **F.P.**) connection in water-main for hose.
fireproof, *a.* incombustible.
fire-raising, *n.* arson.
fire-screen, *n.* movable screen to keep off heat of fire.
fire-ship, *n.* ship filled with combustibles to set enemy's ships on fire.
fireside, *n.* hearth; home life.
firestep, *n.* ledge on which soldiers stand to fire over trench parapet.
fire-warden, *n.* (*Amer.*) officer protecting forests against fire.
fire-water, *n.* whisky, spirits.
firewood, *n.* wood for fuel.
firework, *n.* device to give spectacular effects by explosions and coloured flames; (*pl.*) display of wit.
firing, *n.* fuel; discharge of guns. **f.-step,** *n.* firestep.
firk, *v.t.* (*Shake.*) beat, trounce.
firkin, *n.* small cask for butter etc.; measure of capacity, ¼ barrel or 9 gallons.
firm, *a.* fixed, solid, unyielding; steady, unwavering; settled.—*adv.* firmly.—*v.t.* and *i.* solidify; fix firmly. (L. *firmus*)
firm, *n.* business house, partnership. (L. *firmare*, confirm)
firmament, *n.* vault of heaven, orig. regarded as solid; sky. **firmamental,** *a.* (L. *firmamentum*)
firman, *n.* decree, licence, passport, issued by oriental ruler. (Pers. *ferman*)
first, *a.* earliest; foremost; most important.—*adv.* before all others; rather.—*n.* first-class honours, student taking this. **at f.,** at the beginning. **at f. blush,** on first consideration. **f. aid,** help given before doctor comes. **f. and last,** on the whole. **F. Commoner,** Speaker. **f. day,** Sunday. **f. floor,** next above ground-floor; (*Amer.*) ground-floor. **f. offender,** *n.* one not previously convicted. **the F.,** 1 September, when partridge-shooting begins. **f.-born,** *a.* and *n.* eldest (child). **f.-class,** *a.* excellent.—*n.* best accommodation on train; highest class in examination. **f.-foot,** *n.* first visitor of new year. **f.-fruits,** *n.pl.* first produce of season; first profits. **f.-hand,** *a.* direct from source. **f.-rate,** *a.* excellent, of highest quality.—*adv.* very well.—*n.* line-of-battle ship. **firstling,** *n.* first offspring; first-fruits. **firstly,** *adv.* in the first place, first. (O.E. *fyrst*)
firth, frith, *n.* arm of the sea, estuary.
fisc, *n.* state treasury. **fiscal,** *a.* of public revenue; financial.—*n.* (*Scot.*) public prosecutor. (L. *fiscus*)
fish, *n.* (*pl.* **fishes, fish**) vertebrate living in water and breathing through gills; twelfth sign of zodiac; (*colloq.*) person.—*v.i.* and *t.* try to catch fish; search in water, seek by indirect means (for); draw (out). **drink like a f.,** to excess. **feed the ff.,** be drowned; be seasick. **have other f. to fry,** be busy with something else. **f.-ball,** *n.* cake of chopped fish. **f.-carver, f.-knife, f.-slice,** *nn.* for serving or eating fish. **f.-glue,** *n.* isinglass. **f.-hook,** *n.* for catching fish. **f.-sound,** *n.* fish's swimming-bladder. **f.-story,** *n.* (*Amer.*) tall story. (O.E. *fisc*)
fish, *n.* rigid strip to strengthen mast, joint etc.,—*v.t.* strengthen, join, with fish. **f.-plate,** *n.* plate joining lengths of railway rails.
fish, *n.* counter used at cards. (F. *fiche*)
fisher, *n.* fisherman; fishing animal. **fisherman,** *n.* one who lives by fishing; angler. **fishery,** *n.* business of fishing; fishing-ground.
fishing, *n.* catching fish. **f.-line, f.-net, f.-rod,** *nn.* used in this.
fishmonger, *n.* dealer in fish.
fishpond, *n.* pond in which fish are kept.
fishwife, fishwoman, *nn.* woman who hawks fish.
fishy, *a.* like, full of, fish; (of eye) lustreless; (*sl.*) questionable.
fisk, same as fisc.
fissile, *a.* capable of being split, cleavable. **fissility,** *n.* **fission,** *n.*

splitting; reproduction by division of body into two parts, each of which becomes complete organism. **fissiparous,** *a.* propagating by fission. **fissirostral,** *a.* with deeply cleft beak.

fissure, *n.* cleft, chasm, slit; furrow; cleavage.—*v.t.* and *i.* split. (L. *findere,* cleave)

fist, *n.* clenched hand; (*colloq.*) handwriting.—*v.t.* punch. **fistiana,** *n.pl.* boxing anecdotes. **fistic, fistical,** *aa.* (*joc.*) of boxing. **fisticuffs,** *n.pl.* fighting with fists. (O.E. *fýst*)

fistula, *n.* narrow duct; deep pipe-like ulcer. **fistular, fistulous,** *aa.* (L.=pipe)

fit, *a.* (*compar.* **fitter,** *superl.* **fittest**) suitable, qualified, worthy; proper, befitting; prepared; in good condition, well.—*v.t.* and *i.* be or make suited (to); be of right size or shape (for); adjust; supply.—*n.* adjustment; way garment fits. **f. on,** try on. **f. out, up,** equip, furnish. **see f.,** decide.

fit, *n.* sudden passing attack of illness; convulsion, seizure; sudden outburst, passing mood. **by ff. and starts,** spasmodically. **give one ff.,** defeat easily. (O.E. *fitt*)

fit, fytte, *n.* (*arch.*) division of poem. (O.E. *fitt*)

fitch, *n.* polecat's hair; brush made of it. **fitchew,** *n.* polecat. (Du. *fisse,* polecat)

fitment, *n.* piece of furniture.

fitter, *n.* man who adjusts machine.

fitting, *a.* suitable, right.—*n.* fixture, apparatus. **f.-shop,** *n.* where parts of machine are assembled.

fitful, *a.* spasmodic, capricious.

five, *a.* and *n.* one more than four. **f.-a-side,** *n.* football with teams of five. **fivefold,** *a.* and *adv.* repeated five times. **fiver,** *n.* (*sl.*) five-pound note; (*Amer.*) five-dollar bill. **fives,** *n.* ball-game played in walled court. (O.E. *fif*)

fives, *n.* (*Shake.*) a disease of horses. (F. *avives*)

fix, *v.t.* and *i.* make firm, secure, fasten; settle, appoint, determine; make or become rigid; stiffen, congeal; set, hold (attention); make (colour etc.) fast; (*Amer. colloq.*) set in order, repair; do for, square.—*n.* predicament. **f. up,** arrange. **f. upon,** choose. **fixed idea,** obsession. **fixed star,** star, not planet. **fixation,** *n.* fixing, being fixed; (*psycho-anal.*) arrest of development. **fixative,** *a.* and *n.* (substance) that fixes (colours etc.). **fixature,** *n.* dressing for fixing hair. **fixedly,** *adv.* intently. **fixings,** *n.pl.* trimmings. **fixity,** *n.* fixedness. **fixture,** *n.* immovable fitting; sporting event; engagement. **fixure,** *n.* (*Shake.*) stability. (L. *figere*)

fizgig, *n.* giddy girl; firework of damp powder, cracker.—*a.* flighty.

fizz, *v.i.* hiss, splutter.—*n.* fizzing; champagne, soda-water etc. **fizzle,** *v.i.* fizz feebly.—*n.* fizzling; fiasco. **fizzle out,** come to nothing. **fizzy,** *a.* (imit.)

fjord, see **fiord.**

flabbergast, *v.t.* overwhelm with astonishment, dumbfound.

flabby, *a.* hanging loose, limp; soft, feeble. (*flap*)

flabellate, flabelliform, *aa.* (*bot.*) fan-shaped. (L. *flabellum,* fan)

flaccid, *a.* lacking firmness, yielding, flabby. **flaccidity,** *n.* (L. *flaccus,* flabby)

flag, *n.* piece of bunting as standard or signal; tail of setter etc.—*v.t.* deck, mark, signal, with flags. **black f.,** of pirate. **red f.,** danger signal; flag of revolution; a socialist song. **yellow f.,** of ship in quarantine. **white f.,** flag of truce, asking for parley. **fly, hoist, one's f. in,** have, take, command of (ship). **strike one's f.,** surrender. **f.-captain,** *n.* captain of flagship. **f.-day,** *n.* street-collection by sale of small flags worn as sign of having given; (*Amer.*) 14 June, anniversary of adoption of stars and stripes. **f.-lieutenant,** *n.* admiral's A.D.C. **f.-officer,** *n.* admiral. **f.-waver,** *n.* jingoist. **flagship,** *n.* admiral's ship. **flagstaff,** *n.* pole for flag.

flag, *n.* (also **flagstone**) flat slab of stone; (*pl.*) pavement of these.—*v.t.* pave with flags.

flag, *n.* plant with sword-shaped leaf, iris; long thin plant-blade.

flag, *v.i.* hang down, droop; lose vigour, languish.

flagellum, *n.* (*pl.* **flagella**) whiplike appendage; (*bot.*) runner. **flagellant,** *n.* one who scourges himself as religious exercise.—*a.* flagellating. **flagellate,** *v.t.* scourge, whip.—*a.* having flagella. **flagellation, flagellator,** *nn.* (L.=whip)

flageolet, *n.* instrument like flute with mouthpiece at end and six holes. (F.)

flageolet, *n.* kind of kidney-bean. (F.)

flagitate, *v.t.* importune. (L. *flagitare*)

flagitious, *a.* abominably wicked, atrocious. (L. *flagitium,* crime)

flagon, *n.* drinking-vessel with handle, spout, and lid; large squat bottle. (O.F. *flacon*)

flagrant, *a.* glaring, scandalous. **flagrancy,** *n.* (L. *flagrare,* blaze)

flail, *n.* threshing-implement of wooden bar hinged to handle. (O.E. *fligel*)

flair, *n.* instinctive discernment, nose. (F. = scent)

flak, *n.* anti-aircraft fire. (G. *Flugabwehrkanone,* anti-aircraft gun)

flake, *n.* small layer, chip, scale; loose filmy mass.—*v.t.* and *i.* form into flakes; scale off; sprinkle. **f. white,** pigment of white lead. **flaky,** *a.*

flam, *n.* hoax, pretence; blarney.

flambeau, *n.* (*pl.* **flambeaus, flambeaux**) flaming torch. (F.)
flamboyant, *a.* highly coloured, gorgeous, showy; (*archit.*) marked by flame-like tracery. (F.)
flame, *n.* burning vapour, blaze; bright light; passion, ardour; (*joc.*) sweetheart.—*v.i.* emit flames, blaze; burst out; shine. **f. up,** blush deeply. **flaming,** *a.* very hot; gaudy; exaggerated. (L. *flamma*)
flamen, *n.* ancient Roman priest. (L.)
flamingo, *n.* bright-red tropical bird with long legs and neck. (Port. *flamengo*)
flammable, *a.* inflammable.
flammenwerfer, **n.** flame-thrower. (G.)
flan, *n.* open fruit tart. (F.)
flâneur, **n.** lounger. *flânerie,* **n.** idling. (F.)
flange, *n.* raised edge on wheel-rim to keep it on rail; projecting rib.—*v.t.* provide with flange.
flank, *n.* side of animal between ribs and hip; side of army or fortification.—*v.t.* adjoin, guard, strengthen, attack, on flank. (F. *flanc*)
flannel, *n.* soft woollen cloth of loose texture; piece of this; (*pl.*) sports clothes, underwear, of this.—*a.* made of flannel. **flannelette,** *n.* cotton imitation of flannel. **flannelly,** *a.* like flannel.
flap, *n.* broad thin hanging piece; table-leaf etc.; slap.—*v.t.* and *i.* move to and fro, flutter; strike, drive off, with flat thing. **flapdoodle,** *n.* twaddle. **flapjack,** *n.* griddle-cake; flat case for face-powder. **flapper,** *n.* fly-switch, clapper, flap; young wild duck; (*sl.*) girl in her teens. **flapper-bracket,** *n.* pillion-seat of motor-cycle. (imit.)
flare, *v.i.* and *t.* blaze with unsteady flame; bulge, spread, outward.—*n.* unsteady flame; signal-light; outward spread. **f. up,** show sudden rage.
flash, *v.i.* and *t.* break into sudden flame; gleam, cause to gleam; appear suddenly, move swiftly; telegraph; coat (glass) with tinted film; (of water) rise, flood.—*n.* sudden blaze of light; sudden outburst; instant; badge, ribbon; rush of water.—*a.* showy; sham; cant; connected with thieves. **f. in the pan,** misfire; showy start not followed up. **f.-board,** *n.* board on mill-dam to increase depth of water. **f.-point,** *n.* temperature at which oil-vapour ignites. **flashing,** *n.* metal strip to make roof-joint watertight. **flash-light,** *n.* used for signals, snapshots etc.; electric torch. **flashy,** *a.* gaudy, tawdry.
flask, *n.* pocket-bottle; case for gunpowder; wicker-covered glass vessel. **flasket,** *n.* small flask; long shallow basket.
flat, *a.* (*compar.* **flatter,** *superl.* **flattest**) level; prostrate; smooth, even; dull, insipid; downright; (*mus.*) below true pitch.—*n.* level plain; broad part; (*mus.*) note a semitone below natural pitch, sign (♭) of this; (*sl.*) duffer, dupe. **f. rate,** the same for all cases. **f.-car,** *n.* (*Amer.*) open sideless truck. **f.-fish,** *n.* sole, plaice etc. **f.-footed,** *a.* with feet not normally arched; (*Amer.*) determined, blunt. **f.-iron,** *n.* for smoothing linen. **flatten,** *v.t.* and *i.* make, become, flat. **flatways, flatwise,** *advv.* flat side downwards. (O.N. *flatr*)
flat, *n.* storey; suite of rooms on one floor. (O.E. *flet,* floor)
flatter, *v.t.* and *i.* court with compliments; praise insincerely; represent too favourably; raise (false) hopes in. **flatterer, flattery,** *nn.*
flattie, *n.* (*sl.*) policeman.
flatulence, flatulency, *nn.* wind in stomach; windiness, verbosity. **flatulent,** *a.* troubled with, caused by, causing, flatulence; pretentious. *flatus,* *n.* wind in stomach. (L. *flare,* blow)
flaunt, *v.i.* and *t.* wave proudly, show off.—*n.* flaunting, parade. **flaunty,** *a.*
flautist, *n.* flute-player. (It. *flauto,* flute)
flavescent, *a.* yellowish, turning yellow. **flavin,** *n.* a yellow dye and antiseptic. (L. *flavus,* yellow)
flavour, *n.* distinctive taste, savour; vague characteristic. — *v.t.* give flavour to. **flavouring,** *n.* seasoning. **flavorous, flavoursome,** *aa.*
flaw, *n.* blemish, defect; crack; (*Shake.*) fragment, flake.—*v.t.* and *i.* crack, mar. **flawless,** *a.* perfect.
flaw, *n.* gust of wind, squall.
flawn, *n.* (*arch.*) custard, pancake. (O.H.G. *flado*)
flax, *n.* a blue-flowered plant; its fibre, spun into linen. **f.-seed,** *n.* linseed. **flaxen,** *a.* of flax; (of hair) pale yellow. (O.E. *fleax*)
flay, *v.t.* skin; strip off; criticize savagely. (O.E. *fléan*)
flea, *n.* small blood-sucking jumping insect. **f. in the ear,** irritating rebuff. **f.-bane, f.-wort,** *nn.* kinds of plant. **fleabite,** *n.* bite of flea; spot like this; mere trifle. **flea-bitten,** *a.* flecked with red spots on light ground. (O.E. *fléah*)
fleam, *n.* lancet for bleeding cattle. (Gk. *phleps,* vein; *temnein,* cut)
flèche, *n.* slender spire, esp. at intersection of nave and transept. (F.)
fleck, *n.* spot, speck, freckle; patch of colour. — *v.t.* variegate, dapple. **flecker,** *v.t.* fleck; scatter in patches. **fleckless,** *a.* unspotted. (O.N. *flekkr*)
fled, see **flee.**
fledge, *v.t.* furnish with feathers; wing for flight. **fledgling, fledgeling,** *n.* young bird; inexperienced person. (O.E. *flycge*)
flee, *v.i.* and *t.* (*past,* *p.p.* **fled**) run

away (from), take to flight; avoid. (O.E. *fléon*)

fleece, *n.* sheep's coat of wool.—*v.t.* shear (sheep); strip of money, rob by fraud; overspread. **Golden F.,** an order of knighthood. **fleecy,** *a.* woolly. (O.E. *fléos*)

fleech, *v.i.* (*Scot.*) flatter, beseech.

fleer, *v.i.* laugh mockingly, sneer.—*n.* derisive look, jeer.

fleet, *n.* division of navy, sea-force; number of ships, aircraft, cars etc. under one owner. (O.E. *fléot,* ship)

fleet, *v.i.* glide away, pass swiftly, flit. —*a.* swift, rapid; shallow. **fleeting,** *a.* transient. (O.E. *fleotan*)

fleet, *n.* creek. **F. Street,** centre of London journalism. (O.E. *fléot*)

fleg, *n.* (*Scot.*) kick, random blow.

Fleming, *n.* inhabitant of Flanders. **Flemish,** *a.* (Du. *Vlâming*)

flemish, *v.i.* (of hound) make quivering movement while on scent.

flench, flense, cut up and strip blubber from (whale). (Da.)

flesh, *n.* soft parts of animal; meat; pulp of plant; body, carnal appetites; living things.—*v.t.* incite by taste of blood; initiate in bloodshed. **f. and blood,** human nature; kindred; living, real. **in the f.,** in bodily form. **f.-brush,** *n.* to stimulate circulation. **f.-coloured,** *a.* yellowish-pink. **f.-pots,** *n.pl.* high living. **f.-wound,** *n.* superficial wound. **flesher,** *n.* (*Scot.*) butcher. **fleshings,** *n.pl.* flesh-coloured tights. **fleshly,** *a.* material, worldly; carnal, sensual. **fleshy,** *a.* of, like, flesh; plump; pulpy. (O.E. *flǽsc*)

flether, *v.i.* (*Scot.*) flatter, fawn.

fleur-de-lis, fleur-de-lys, *n.* heraldic lily, arms of France; iris. **fleuret,** *n.* ornament like small flower. **fleury,** *a.* (*heraldry*) decorated with fleurs-de-lis. (F.=lily flower)

flew, see **fly.**

flews, *n.pl.* pendulous lips, chops.

flex, *v.t.* (*anat.*) bend (limb).—*n.* flexible insulated wire. **flexible,** *a.* easily bent, pliable; adaptable, elastic. **flexibility,** *n.* **flexile,** *a.* supple; docile. **flexility,** *n.* **flexion,** *n.* bending; curve; (*gram.*) inflexion. **flexor,** *n.* muscle that bends limb. **flexuose, flexuous,** *aa.* winding, sinuous; zigzag. **flexuosity,** *n.* **flexure,** *n.* flexion; joint; (*math.*) curving of line or surface. (L. *flectere*)

fley, *v.t.* (*Scot.*) scare.

flibbertigibbet, *n.* impish, flighty, or gossipy person. (imit.)

flick, *n.* light quick stroke of whip etc. —*v.t.* strike with, deal, flick; jerk. (imit.)

flick, *n.* (*sl.*) moving picture, film. (*flicker*)

flicker, *v.i.* waver, flutter; shine fitfully.—*n.* unsteady light or motion. (O.E. *flicorian*)

flier, flies, see **fly.**

flight, *n.* fleeing, hasty departure. **put to f.,** rout. **take to f.,** run away. (*flee*)

flight, *n.* act, manner, of flying; aviation; distance flown; flock (of birds), shower (of arrows), series (of steps); excursion (of fancy); unit of air force.—*v.t.* shoot on wing. **f.-lieutenant,** *n.* R.A.F. rank below squadron-leader. (*fly*)

flighty, *a.* capricious, giddy; fanciful. (*fly*)

flim-flam, *n.* nonsense; trick.

flimsy, *a.* weak, thin, unsubstantial; paltry, frivolous.—*n.* thin paper; reporter's copy; (*sl.*) paper money.

flinch, *v.i.* shrink, draw back; wince. (O.F. *flenchir*)

flinch, same as **flench.**

flinders, *n.pl.* fragments.

fling, *v.i.* and *t.* (*past, p.p.* **flung**) rush violently, flounce; throw, hurl, toss; (of horse) kick, plunge.—*n.* cast; gibe; unrestrained pleasure; a lively dance. **f. out,** break into abuse.

flint, *n.* a hard steel-grey stone; piece of this, used with steel to strike spark; flint implement of stone age. **f.-glass,** *n.* lustrous kind. **flintlock,** *n.* gun fired by spark from flint. **flinty,** *a.* (O.E.)

flip, *n.* warmed and sweetened drink of beer and spirit etc.

flip, *v.t.* and *i.* strike, move, with flick; fillip.—*n.* flick, fillip; short trip in aeroplane. **f.-flap,** *n.* huge mechanical swing; kind of somersault; a firework. (imit.)

flipe, *v.t.* (*Scot.*) turn (stocking) inside out; fold back (cuff).

flippant, *a.* treating serious things lightly, pert. **flippancy,** *n.*

flipper, *n.* limb (of seal etc.) used for swimming; (*sl.*) hand. (*flip*)

flipperty-flopperty, *a.* loose, dangling.

flirt, *v.t.* and *i.* move jerkily, wave briskly; play at making love.—*n.* flick, jerk; coquette, philanderer. **flirtatious, flirtish, flirty,** *aa.* coquettish. **flirtation,** *n.* (imit.)

flisk, *v.i.* (*Scot.*) skip, caper.—*n.* whim.

flit, *v.i.* pass lightly, dart; depart; (*Scot.*) move house.—*n.* removal, flitting. (O.N. *flytja*)

flit, *a.* (*Spens.*) swift; changing; light. (*fleet*)

flitch, *n.* side of bacon salted and cured; steak of halibut; plank cut from tree.—*v.t.* cut into flitches. (O.E. *flicce*)

flitter, *v.i.* flit about. **f.-mouse,** *n.* bat. (*flit*)

flivver, *n.* (*Amer. sl.*) cheap motor-car.

flix, *n.* beaver-down; soft fur.

float, *v.i.* and *t.* swim on liquid, be buoyed up; hover, glide; (of liquid) support, bear along; circulate (rumour); launch (company); be current.—*n.* cork of fishing-line; ball-cock; raft; board of paddle-wheel; light flat cart; footlights. **floatage**

n. floating; **craft afloat, flotsam.** (O.E. *flotian*)

floatation, see **flotation.**

floating, *a.* that floats. **f. bridge,** bridge of rafts; steam-ferry. **f. capital,** goods or money. **f. debt,** repayable on demand or at stated time. **f. dock,** floating structure usable as graving dock. **f. kidney,** one that has become disconnected. **f. light,** lightship; lifebuoy with lantern. **f. rib,** not joined to breastbone.

floccose, *a.* tufted. **floccule,** *n.* small tuft, flake. **flocculent, flocculose, flocculous,** *aa.* like, showing, tufts. (L. *floccus,* flock)

flock, *n.* company of sheep, birds etc.; crowd; congregation.—*v.i.* gather in crowd, troop. (O.E. *flocc*)

flock, *n.* lock, tuft, of wool; wool-refuse for stuffing. **flocky,** *a.*

floe, *n.* sheet of floating ice.

flog, *v.t.* beat, thrash, whip. **f. dead horse,** waste energy.

flong, *n.* stereotyping paper. (*flan*)

flood, *n.* flow of water; outpouring, inundation; high tide; (*poet.*) sea, river.—*v.t.* and *i.* deluge, overflow; irrigate. **f.-tide,** *n.* rising tide. **floodgate,** *n.* sluice controlling body of water. **flooding,** *n.* discharge of blood from womb. **floodlighting,** *n.* artificial lighting of building exterior. **floodlit,** *a.* (O.E. *flód*)

floor, *n.* lower surface of room; bottom of sea etc.; rooms on one level, storey; flat space.—*v.t.* supply with floor; knock down; nonplus; overcome. **first f.,** next above (*Amer.* same as) **ground f.,** on street level. **take the f.,** speak in debate. **f.-cloth,** *n.* linoleum, oilcloth etc. **floorer,** *n.* knock-down blow; unanswerable question. **flooring,** *n.* boards of floor. **floorwalker,** *n.* overseer in retail store. (O.E. *flór*)

flop, *v.i.* and *t.* move limply, slouch; plump (down) suddenly.—*n.* thump, thud; (*sl.*) failure. **floppy,** *a.* limp, flaccid. (=*flap*)

flora, *n.* flowers of region or epoch collectively; treatise on these. **floral,** *a.* of flowers or floras. **florescence,** *n.* state or time of flowering. **floret,** *n.* small flower forming part of composite flower; floweret. **floriate,** *v.t.* decorate with floral ornament. **floriculture,** *n.* cultivation of flowers. **floricultural,** *a.* **floriculturist,** *n.* (L. *flos,* flower)

florid, *a.* ruddy, high-coloured; ornate, containing flowers of rhetoric. **floridity,** *n.* (L. *flos,* flower)

floriferous, *a.* bearing flowers. (L. *flos,* flower; *ferre,* bear)

florilegium, *n.* anthology. (L.)

florin, *n.* silver two-shilling piece; Dutch gulden; (*obs.*) gold coin value 6*s.* 8*d.* (stamped with lily)

florist, *n.* dealer in flowers; nurseryman (L. *flos.* flower)

floruit, *n.* (*abbr.* **fl.**) period of person's life or eminence. (L.=he flourished)

flory, same as **fleury.**

floscule, *n.* floret. **floscular, flosculous,** *aa.* having florets, composite-flowered. (L. *flos.* flower)

floss, *n.* rough silk enveloping cocoon; (also **f.-silk**) lustrous untwisted silk. **flossy,** *a.* downy.

flotation, floatation, *n.* launching, financing, of company etc. (*float*)

flote, *n.* (*Shake.*) sea. (=*float*)

flotilla, *n.* fleet of small vessels; small fleet. (Sp.)

flotsam, *n.* wreckage or cargo found floating in sea. (*float*)

flounce, *n.* ornamental plaited strip sewn to skirt of dress.—*v.t.* trim with flounces. (O.F. *fronce,* wrinkle)

flounce, *v.i.* rush abruptly or impatiently, fling.—*n.* flouncing, plunge.

flounder, *v.i.* struggle awkwardly, plunge about; make mistakes, bungle. —*n.* blundering attempt.

flounder, *n.* small flat fish.

flour, *n.* sifted finer part of meal, esp. wheat-meal; fine powder. —*v.t.* sprinkle flour on. (=*flower*)

flourish, *v.i.* and *t.* grow vigorously, prosper; be in one's prime; use florid language; brandish, wave about; give flourishes (to).—*n.* ornamental curve; flowery expression; waving of weapon etc.; musical prelude, fanfare. (L. *flos,* flower)

flout, *v.t.* treat with contempt, mock. —*n.* scoff, insult.

flow, *v.i.* glide along, move in stream; gush out; circulate; hang loosely; (of talk) move easily; (of tide) rise; (*arch.*) abound.—*n.* flowing, quantity that flows; plentiful supply; rise of tide. **f. of soul,** genial intercourse. (O.E. *flowan*)

flower, *n.* coloured part of plant, blossom; choicest part, pick; prime; ornament of style.—*v.i.* and *t.* bloom; ornament with floral work. **f.-de-luce,** *n.* fleur-de-lis. **floweret,** *n.* small flower. **flowerpot,** *n.* earthenware pot for plant. **flowery,** *a.* full of flowers; full of fine words or figures of speech. (L. *flos*)

flown, *a.* (*arch.*) puffed up, flushed. (*flow*)

flown, see **fly.**

flu, *n.* (*sl.*) influenza. (abbr.)

fluctuate, *v.i.* rise and fall, vary; waver; undulate. **fluctuation,** *n.* (L. *fluctus,* wave)

flue, *n.* pipe or passage for smoke or hot air, chimney.

flue, *n.* soft downy matter, fluff.

flue, *v.i.* and *t.* splay, widen inwards or outwards.

flue, *n.* kind of fishing-net.

flue, same as **flu.**

fluent, *a.* copious and ready (of speech); easy, flowing. **fluency,** *n.* (L. *fluere* flow)

fluff *n.* down, nap, soft fur.—*v.t.*

make into fluff; dress (hair) loosely; (*theatre sl.*) forget, bungle (part). **fluffy,** *a.* soft and downy.

fluid, *a.* flowing easily, liquid; not solid or rigid.—*n.* liquid, gas. **fluidify,** *v.t.* make fluid. **fluidity,** *n.* (L. *fluere*, flow)

fluke, *n.* part of anchor that fastens in ground; (*pl.*) whale's tail.

fluke, *n.* parasitic worm found in sheep's liver; kind of potato; flounder. (O.E. *flóc*)

fluke, *n.* lucky stroke.—*v.i.* and *t.* make, score by, fluke. **fluky,** *a.* got by luck; uncertain.

flume, *n.* (*Amer.*) artificial water-channel; ravine with stream.—*v.t.* transport, divert, by flume. (L. *flumen*, river)

flummery, *n.* kind of custard or blancmange; sowens; empty compliment, humbug. (W. *llymru*)

flummox, *v.t.* (*sl.*) perplex, bewilder.

flump, *v.i.* and *t.* throw (oneself) down heavily, plump.—*n.* action, sound, of this. (imit.)

flung, see **fling.**

flunk, *n.* (*Amer.*) failure in examination etc.—*v.i.* and *t.* fail, shirk.

flunkey, *n.* footman, liveried servant; toady. **flunkeydom, flunkeyism,** *nn.*

fluor, fluorspar, *nn.* calcium fluoride. **fluorescence,** *n.* coloured luminosity produced in transparent body by direct action of light; power of rendering ultra-violet rays visible. **fluorescent,** *a.* **fluoresce,** *v.i.* exhibit fluorescence. **fluorine,** *n.* a non-metallic element. **fluoroscope,** *n.* instrument with fluorescent screen used to study X-ray effects. (L.=flow)

flurry, *n.* sudden blast, gust; bustle, agitation; death-agony of whale.—*v.t.* agitate, confuse. (imit.)

flush, *v.i.* and *t.* rush out, spurt; cleanse by rush of water; redden, glow, blush; inflame, elate.—*n.* rush of water; abundance; elation, excitement; glow, reddening; freshness, vigour. — *a.* full, in flood; having plenty, abundant; level, even (with); (*Shake.*) lusty. **f. deck,** level from stem to stern.

flush, *v.i.* and *t.* take wing and fly off; put up (birds).

flush, *n.* set of cards all of one suit.

fluster, *v.t.* and *i.* confuse, make hot and bothered; fuddle.—*n.* flurry, bustle.

flustra, *n.* (*pl.* **flustrae, flustras**) sea-mat, kind of polyzoa. (coined)

flute, *n.* wind instrument with holes stopped by fingers or keys and blow-hole in side; vertical groove in pillar etc.—*v.i.* and *t.* play on, speak etc. like, flute; make grooves in. **fluter, flutist,** *nn.* flute-player. (O.F. *fleüte*)

flutter, *v.i.* and *t.* flap (wings) rapidly; flit, hover; quiver; agitate, be excited.—*n.* fluttering; nervous excitement, stir; (*sl.*) gamble, speculation. (O.E. *flotorian*)

fluty, *a.* soft and clear like flute.

fluvial, fluviatile, *aa.* of, found in, rivers. **fluviograph,** *n.* instrument recording river's rise and fall. (L. *fluvius*, river)

flux, *n.* flowing; morbid discharge (of blood etc.); succession of changes; substance mixed with metal to help fusion.—*v.i.* and *t.* flow copiously; melt, fuse. **fluxion,** *n.* flowing; (*math.*) differential; (*med.*) excessive flow. **fluxional, fluxionary,** *aa.* **fluxive,** *a.* (*Shake.*) flowing. (L. *fluere*, flow)

fly, *n.* a two-winged insect; plant-disease caused by it; imitation fly as bait. **f. in the ointment,** slight unpleasant element. **no ff. on him,** (*sl.*) he is efficient. **f.-blow,** *n.* egg of fly.—*v.t.* lay this in. **f.-blown,** *a.* tainted. **f.-paper,** *n.* sticky, for catching flies. **f.-weight,** *n.* (*boxing*) not over 8 st. (O.E. *flýge*)

fly, *v.i.* and *t.* (*past* **flew,** *p.p.* **flown**) move through, float in, air; cause to do this; travel, convey, by aircraft; rush, be driven; clear (fence); flee, avoid.—*n.* flying; one-horse hackney carriage; flap of tent or garment; part of flag farthest from staff; speed-regulator; (*pl.*) part of theatre above stage. **f. at,** rush at, attack. **f. high,** be ambitious. **f. in the face of,** defy. **f. kite,** raise money by accommodation bill; put out feeler. **f. off,** become detached. **f. out,** burst into rage. **let f.,** shoot, hit (at). **f.-away,** *a.* loose; flighty. **f.-leaf,** *n.* blank leaf at beginning or end of book. (O.E. *fléogan*)

fly, *a.* (*sl.*) knowing, artful.

flyboat, *n.* kinds of fast vessel.

flycatcher, *n.* a small bird.

flyer, flier, *n.* aviator; swift runner, vehicle etc.

flying, *a.* that flies; brief, hurried. **f. buttress,** arch-shaped prop from pier to wall with space below. **F. Dutchman,** a spectral ship. **f. jump,** with run. **f. squad,** special mobile detachment of police. **f. start,** having got up speed. **with f. colours,** triumphantly. **f.-boat,** *n.* seaplane in which boat forms fuselage and float. **f.-fish,** *n.* kind that can rise in air by its fins; (*sl.*) native of Barbados. **f.-fox,** *n.* a fruit-eating bat. **f.-machine,** *n.* aeroplane. **f.-officer,** *n.* rank in R.A.F. below flight-lieutenant. **f.-squirrel,** *n.* with folds of skin joining legs.

flyte, *v.i.* (*Scot.*) scold, wrangle. **flyting,** *n.* scolding-match. (O.E. *flitan*, strive)

flywheel, *n.* heavy wheel regulating motive power.

foal, *n.* young of horse.—*v.t.* and *i.* bear (foal). (O.E. *fola*)

foam, *n.* froth, bubbles on surface of liquid; (*poet.*) sea.—*v.i.* emit, gather, foam. **foamy**, *a.* (O.E. *fám*)
fob, *n.* small pocket in waistband of breeches; short watch-chain.
fob, *v.t.* cheat; put (off with); palm (off upon).
focus, *n.* (*pl.* **foci, focuses**) point at which rays meet after being refracted or reflected; adjustment of eye or lens giving clear image; central point.—*v.t.* and *i.* (*past, p.p.* **focused, focussed**) adjust focus of; bring, come, to focus; concentrate. **focal**, *a.* of, at, focus. **focalize**, *v.t.* focus. (L.=hearth)
fo'c's'le, contr. form of **forecastle.**
fodder, *n.* food for cattle.—*v.t.* give fodder to. (O.E. *fódor*)
fodgel, *a.* (*Scot.*) squat, plump.
foe, *n.* enemy, opponent. **foeman**, *n.* (*arch.*) adversary in war. (O.E. *fáh*, hostile)
foetid, see **fetid.**
foetus, fetus, *n.* fully developed young in womb or egg. **foetal, fetal**, *a.* **foeticide, feticide**, *n.* abortion. (L. *fetus*, offspring)
fog, *n.* thick mist, watery vapour.—*v.t.* overcast; cloud; perplex. **f.-bank**, *n.* dense mass of fog. **f.-horn**, *n.* siren. **f.-signal**, *n.* detonator on railway etc.
fog, *n.* aftermath; rank grass; (*Scot.*) moss.—*v.t.* feed on fog.
fogey, same as **fogy.**
foggage, *n.* rank grass.
foggy, *a.* full of fog, murky; indistinct; confused.
fogle, *n.* (*sl.*) handkerchief.
fogy, *n.* old-fashioned fellow. **fogydom, fogyism**, *nn.* **fogyish**, *a.*
foh, *int.* of disgust.
föhn, *n.* warm dry Alpine wind. (G.)
foible, *n.* failing, weakness; point half of sword or foil. (O.F.=feeble)
foil, *n.* leaf, thin sheet, of metal; backing for mirror or gem; thing that sets off another by contrast; (*archit.*) small arc or space in tracery of window.—*v.t.* cover, back, adorn, with foil; set off. (L. *folium*, leaf)
foil, *v.t.* and *i.* baffle, frustrate; defeat; trample and spoil (scent).—*n.* trail of hunted game; (*arch.*) check. (O.F. *fouler*, trample)
foil, *n.* fencing rapier with button on point.
foin, *v.i.* and *n.* (*Shake.*) thrust with weapon. (L. *fuscina*, trident)
foison, *n.* (*arch.*) abundance; strength. (L. *fundere*, pour)
foist, *v.t.* insert secretly or unwarrantably; palm off (on). **foister**, *n.*
fold, *v.t.* and *i.* double over on itself; clasp, wind; wrap.—*n.* folding; doubled part; crease, pleat, hollow; coil. **f. up**, fold into compact form. (O.E. *fealdan*)
fold, *n.* enclosure for sheep; church, body of believers.—*v.t.* shut up in fold. (O.E. *fald*)
-fold, *suf.* times repeated, as in **tenfold.**
folder, *n.* cover for loose papers; leaflet; (*pl.*) folding eye-glasses.
folderol, same as **falderal.**
foliage, *n.* leaves; leafage. **foliaceous**, *a.* of, like, leaves; laminated. **foliar**, *a.* of leaves. **foliate**, *a.* leaf-shaped; leaved.—*v.i.* and *t.* divide into laminae; number leaves of (book); (*archit.*) ornament with foils. **foliation**, *n.* (L. *folium*, leaf)
folio, *n.* leaf of book or manuscript; page number; sheet of paper folded once; largest size of book, made of these; double page in account-book; unit of length, 72 or 90 words. **in f.**, made of folios. (L. *folium*, leaf)
foliole, *n.* division of compound leaf. (L. *foliolum*, little leaf)
folk, *n.* nation; (*pl.*) people; relatives. **f.-dance, f.-song, f.-speech**, *nn.* those traditional among common people. **f.-etymology**, *n.* perversion of word to try to explain it, as in 'sparrow-grass' for 'asparagus.' **folklore**, *n.* traditional customs, superstitions etc.; study of these. **folklorist**, *n.* (O.E. *folc*)
follicle, *n.* small sac or gland; seed vessel. **follicular, folliculated**, *aa.* (L. *follis*, bellows)
follow, *v.t.* and *i.* go, come, after; go along (road); obey, conform to; accompany; engage in; result (from); understand. **f. on**, (*cricket*) take second innings immediately after first. **f. suit**, play card of same suit; do same thing. **f. through**, (*golf etc.*) continue swing after hitting ball. **f. up**, pursue steadily; supplement. **follower**, *n.* disciple; maidservant's admirer. **following**, *a.* succeeding.—*n.* body of adherents. (O.E. *folgian*)
folly, *n.* foolishness; foolish act; costly and useless structure. (*fool*)
foment, *v.t.* bathe with warm water or lotions; stir up, instigate. **fomenter, fomentation**, *nn.* (L. *fovēre*, cherish)
fómēs, *n.* (*pl.* **fómitēs**) substance carrying infection. (L.=touchwood)
fon, *n.* (*Spens.*) fool.
fond, *a.* loving, devoted; weakly indulgent; over-credulous, simple. **f. of**, having liking for. (M.E. *fon*, fool)
fondant, *n.* kind of sweetmeat. (F.)
fondle, *v.t.* and *i.* caress; dally. (*fond*)
fons et origo, source and origin. (L.)
font, (*print.*) same as **fount.**
font, *n.* bowl for baptismal or holy water; oil-container of lamp. **fontal**, *a.* of baptism; primary. (L. *fons*, fountain)
fontanel, fontanelle, *n.* gap between bones of skull in infant. (F.)
food, *n.* what one feeds on; solid nourishment; material. **foodstuff**, *n.* substance used as food. (O.E. *fóda*)
fool, *n.* dish of fruit stewed and crushed, with cream.
fool, *n.* silly or unwise person; jester,

clown; butt, dupe.—*a.* (*Amer.*) foolish.—*v.t.* and *i.* play tricks (on), cheat; trifle, joke. **April f.,** person fooled on All Fools' Day, 1 April. **f. about,** idle, dally. **f. away,** waste foolishly. **f.'s errand,** futile quest. **f.'s paradise,** illusory happiness. **make a f. of,** ridicule; disappoint. **play the f.,** act the buffoon; trifle. **foolery, fooling,** *nn.* foolish behaviour; buffoonery. **foolhardy,** *a.* foolishly bold, rash. **foolish,** *a.* silly, stupid; indiscreet. **foolocracy,** *n.* government by fools. **foolproof,** *a.* so easy that no mistake is possible. **foolscap,** *n.* size of paper, about 17×13½ in.; jester's or dunce's cap. (L. *follis,* windbag)

foot, *n.* (*pl.* **feet**) leg below ankle; step, tread; lower part, base; infantry; measure of length, 12 in.; metrical unit; (*pl.* **foots**) dregs, residue.—*v.t.* and *i.* put foot on (stocking); add (up); pay (bill). **f. it,** dance. **carry person off his ff.,** rouse his enthusiasm. **keep one's ff.,** not fall. **on f.,** walking; in progress. **put one's f. down,** be firm. **put one's f. in it,** blunder, be tactless. (O.E. *fót*)

foot-and-mouth disease, a contagious fever of cattle.

football, *n.* large inflated ball. **association f.,** game played by teams of 11, kicking a round ball. **Rugby f.,** by teams of 15, with elliptical ball, using feet and hands. **American f.,** like Rugby. **footballer,** *n.* football player.

foot-bath, *n.* bath for washing feet.

footboard, *n.* step for entering, footman's platform behind, carriage.

footbridge, *n.* narrow bridge for foot-passengers.

footer, *n.* (*sl.*) football game.

footfall, *n.* sound of footstep.

foot-fault, *n.* (*lawn tennis*) overstepping base-line when serving.

footgear, *n.* boots, shoes, socks etc.

footguards, *n.pl.* the five infantry regiments of household troops.

foothill, *n.* low hill at base of mountain-range.

foothold, *n.* support for feet.

footing, *n.* foothold; secure position; standing, relation to others; admittance to trade etc.; (*archit.*) projecting course at base of wall.

footle, *v.i.* (*sl.*) be incompetent, bungle. —*n.* folly; piffle. **footling,** *a.* trifling.

footlights, *n.pl.* row of lights along front of stage.

footloose, *a.* free, untrammelled.

footman, *n.* (*pl.* **footmen**) liveried servant who attends door, waits at table etc.; trivet; foot-soldier.

footmark, *n.* footprint.

foot-muff, *n.* muff for warming feet.

footnote, *n.* note at foot of page.

footpad, *n.* highwayman on foot.

footpath, *n.* path for pedestrians.

footplate, *n.* driver's platform on railway engine.

foot-pound, *n.* unit of energy, work required to raise 1 lb. through 1 ft.

footprint, *n.* impression left by foot.

foot-rot, *n.* a disease of sheep.

footrule, *n.* measure a foot long.

footslog, *v.i.* (*sl.*) march, tramp.

footsore, *a.* with feet sore from travel.

footstalk, *n.* stem of leaf or flower; attachment of barnacle.

foot-stall, *n.* woman's stirrup.

footstool, *n.* stool for seated person.

footwarmer, *n.* flat hot-water tin in railway carriage.

foozle, *v.t.* and *i.* and *n.* (*sl.*) bungle.

fop, *n.* dandy; (*Shake.*) fool. **fopling,** *n.* petty fop. **foppery,** *n.* **foppish,** *a.* affectedly fine.

for, *prep.* in place of; in favour of; on account of; with respect to; in the character of, as; in spite of; to the extent of; concerning.—*conj.* because. **be f. it,** (*sl.*) be marked for punishment. **f. all that,** nevertheless. **f. all the world,** exactly. **f. ever,** eternally; continually. **f. good,** permanently. (O.E.)

for-, *pref.* expressing prohibition, as in **forbid**; neglect, as in **forsake**; bad effect, as in **fordo**; intensity, as in **forlorn.** (O.E.)

forage, *n.* food for cattle and horses, esp. of army; foraging.—*v.t.* and *i.* collect forage from, plunder; supply forage; search about, rummage. **f.-cap,** *n.* infantry undress cap. **forager,** *n.* (O.F. *feurre,* fodder)

foramen, *n.* (*pl.* foramina) hole, small opening. **foraminated,** *a.* (L.)

forasmuch as, seeing that, since.

foray, *n.* raid, inroad.—*v.i.* make foray. **forayer,** *n.* (*forage*)

forbad, forbade, see **forbid.**

forbear, forebear, *n.* ancestor. (*fore-* + *be*)

forbear, *v.i.* and *t.* (*past* forbore, *p.p.* forborne) refrain (from); withhold; be patient. **forbearance,** *n.*

forbid, *v.t.* (*past* **forbade, forbad**; *p.p.* **forbidden**) prohibit, order not to; refuse. **forbidding,** *a.* repellent, disagreeable.

forbore, forborne, see **forbear.**

forbye, forby, *adv.* and *prep.* (*Scot.*) besides, in addition.

force, *n.* strength, power; armament; compulsion, violence; validity, influence; point, meaning; (*mech.*) what causes motion; (*pl.*) troops.—*v.t.* compel, constrain; break open, ravish; strain, urge; drive; extort; artificially hasten maturity of. **by f. of,** by means of. **f. the pace,** hasten unduly. **in f.,** in operation; in great numbers. **of f.,** of necessity. **the f.,** police. **f.-pump,** *n.* pump forcing water beyond range of atmospheric pressure. **forced,** *a.* compulsory; strained. (L. *fortis,* strong)

force, *n.* waterfall.

force, *v.t.* (*Shake.*) stuff. (=*farce*)

forceful, *a.* full of force, forcible.
force majeure, compelling force, unavoidable circumstances. (F.)
force-meat, *n.* meat chopped and seasoned for stuffing. (*farce*)
forceps, *n.* surgical pincers; (*zool.*) organ like this. **forcipate,** *a.* (L.)
forcible, *a.* done by force; vigorous, telling, impressive. **f.-feeble,** *a.* trying to look strong while really weak.
forcite, *n.* kind of dynamite.
ford, *n.* shallow place in river which can be crossed by wading.—*v.t.* and *i.* wade across. **fordable,** *a.*
fordo, *v.t.* (*arch.*) ruin; kill. **fordone,** *p.p.* exhausted, spent.
fore, *a.* and *adv.* at the front.—*n.* fore part, bow.—*prep.* in presence of, by. **f. and aft,** at bow and stern; lengthwise in ship. **to the f.,** at hand; conspicuous. (O.E.)
fore, *int.* (*golf*) warning person in way of shot.
fore-, *pref.* in front, as in **forerunner;** beforehand, as in **foretell.**
forearm, *n.* part from elbow to wrist.
forearm, *v.t.* arm beforehand.
forebear, see **forbear.**
forebode, *v.t.* have presentiment of (us. evil); presage, portend; foretell. **foreboding,** *n.* presentiment; omen. (*bode*)
forecast, *v.t.* (*past, p.p.* **forecast** or **forecasted**) estimate beforehand, predict.—*n.* prediction, esp. of weather; foresight.
forecastle, *n.* crew's quarters below deck forward of foremast; (formerly) raised deck at bow.
foreclose, *v.t.* and *i.* prevent, stop; take away right of redeeming (mortgage) on non-payment of money due. **foreclosure,** *n.*
forecourt, *n.* front or outer court.
forefather, *n.* ancestor.
forefinger, *n.* finger next thumb.
forefoot, *n.* front foot of animal; (*naut.*) foremost piece of keel.
forefront, *n.* extreme front, van.
foregather, see **forgather.**
forego, *v.t.* and *i.* (*past* **forewent,** *p.p.* **foregone**) go before, precede. **foregone conclusion,** one formed before knowing facts; result that was inevitable. **foregoer,** *n.*
forego, less correct form of **forgo.**
foreground, *n.* part of view nearest spectator.
forehand, *n.* part of horse in front of rider.—*a.* (*lawn tennis*) made with palm leading. **forehanded,** *a.* (*Amer.*) thrifty.
forehead, *n.* face above eyes, brow.
foreign, *a.* of another nation or country; remote, irrelevant; brought from outside. **F. Office,** department for foreign affairs; its building. **foreigner,** *n.* alien; stranger. **foreignism,** *n.* **foreignize,** *v.t.* and *i.* (L. *foris,* abroad)
forejudge, *v.t.* judge before hearing evidence.
foreknow, *v.t.* (*past* **foreknew,** *p.p.* **foreknown**) know beforehand. **foreknowledge,** *n.*
forel, *n.* thin kind of parchment. (O.F. *forre,* sheathe)
foreland, *n.* cape; land in front.
foreleg, *n.* front leg of animal.
forelock, *n.* lock of hair over brow.
foreman, *n.* overseer of workmen; leader and spokesman of jury.
foremast, *n.* mast nearest bow.
foremost, *a.* first in place or dignity; most advanced.—*adv.* in the first place. (O.E. *formest,* superl. of *forma,* first, superl. of *fore;* wrongly taken as fore+most)
forenoon, *n.* time before midday, morning.
forensic, *a.* of, used in, lawcourts or debate. **f. medicine,** medical jurisprudence. (*forum*)
foreordain, *v.t.* decree beforehand, predestinate. **foreordination,** *n.*
forepeak, *n.* end of ship's hold in angle of bows.
fore-reach, *v.t.* and *i.* gain upon; forge ahead.
forerun, *v.t.* precede, foreshadow. **forerunner,** *n.* precursor; harbinger.
foresail, *n.* largest sail on foremast.
foresee, *v.t.* (*past* **foresaw,** *p.p.* **foreseen**) see beforehand, anticipate.
foreshadow, *v.t.* typify beforehand, prefigure; forebode.
fore-sheets, *n.pl.* inner part of boat's bows.
foreshore, *n.* part between high and low water marks; strip of land next shore.
foreshorten, *v.t.* (of perspective) cause apparent shortening of (object); represent this in drawing.
foreshow, *v.t.* (*p.p.* **foreshown**) predict; foreshadow, portend.
foresight, *n.* foreseeing; prudence, forethought; front sight of gun.
foreskin, *n.* fold of skin ensheathing end of penis, prepuce.
forest, *n.* large wood or wooded tract; trees in this; tract kept waste for hunting.—*a.* of forest, silvan.—*v.t.* plant with trees; make into forest. (L. *foris,* out of doors)
forestall, *v.t.* be beforehand with, anticipate; buy up in advance.
forestay, *n.* stay from top of foremast to bowsprit.
forester, *n.* man in charge of forest; forest-dweller. **forestry,** *n.* art of cultivating timber; wooded country.
foretaste, *n.* partial experience in advance, anticipation.—*v.t.* taste before possession; have foretaste of.
foretell, *v.t.* and *i.* (*past, p.p.* **foretold**) predict, prophesy; presage.
forethought, *n.* thought for the future, provident care.
foretime, *n.* the past, old times.
foretoken, *n.* sign of thing to come, omen.—*v.t.* portend.

foretop, *n.* platform at head of foremast. **fore-topmast,** *n.* mast above foremast, carrying **fore-topsail. fore-topgallant-mast,** *n.* mast above this, carrying **fore-topgallant-sail.**

foretype, *n.* type of coming thing.

forever, *adv.* eternally; continually.

foreward, *n.* (*Shake.*) vanguard.

forewarn, *v.t.* warn beforehand.

forewoman, *n.* woman overseer; spokeswoman of jury of matrons.

foreword, *n.* preface; introductory note, esp. by another than the author.

forfairn, *a.* (*Scot.*) worn out, spent.

forfeit, *v.t.* lose, pay, as penalty for fault, crime, or breach of condition. —*a.* forfeited.—*n.* thing forfeited; penalty, fine; (*Shake.*) violation; (*pl.*) game in which player redeems forfeit by performing ludicrous task. **forfeiture,** *n.* (L. *foris,* outside; *facere,* do)

forfend, *v.t.* ward off, avert.

forficate, *a.* (*zool.*) scissor-shaped. (L. *forfex,* scissors)

forfoughten, *a.* (*Scot.*) exhausted.

forgather, foregather, *v.i.* assemble, meet, fraternize.

forgave, see **forgive.**

forge, *v.i.* move steadily, advance.

forge, *n.* blacksmith's open fire; smithy; workshop for melting or refining metal.—*v.t.* shape (metal) by heating and hammering; invent, fabricate; counterfeit (signature etc.). **forger,** *n.* **forgery,** *n.* forging of signature, document etc.; spurious thing. (L. *faber,* smith)

forget, *v.t.* and *i.* (*past* **forgot,** *p.p.* **forgotten** or **forgot**) lose remembrance of, not recall; cease to think of; neglect. **f. oneself,** lose self-control, act unbecomingly; lose consciousness. **f.-me-not,** *n.* plant with small blue flower, myosotis; keepsake. **forgetful,** *a.* apt to forget.

forgive, *v.t.* (*past* **forgave,** *p.p.* **forgiven**) pardon; remit. **forgiveness,** *n.* **forgiving,** *a.* merciful, mild.

forgo, *v.t.* (*past* **forwent,** *p.p.* **forgone**) go without, give up, renounce.

forjeskit, *a.* (*Scot.*) jaded, tired out.

fork, *n.* pronged farm tool for digging or lifting; pronged table implement; branch, branching-point.—*v.i.* and *t.* divide into branches; dig, pitch, with fork. **f. out, up,** (*sl.*) pay up. **forked,** *a.* branching, cleft. (L. *furca*)

forlorn, *a.* forsaken; wretched; desperate. **f. hope,** desperate enterprise; men chosen for this.

form, *n.* shape, figure; visible aspect; variety, kind; style as opp. to matter; set order, arrangement; physical condition, spirits; formality; blank schedule to be filled in; bench; school class; hare's bed; (*philos.*) inherent nature, essence; (*print.*) type secured in chase for printing, forme. —*v.t.* and *i.* shape, take shape; mould, train; frame, organize; conceive; make up; draw up in order. **good, bad, f.,** conforming, contrary, to current etiquette. **in, out of, f.,** in good, bad, condition or training. (L. *forma*)

formal, *a.* according to rule, ceremonious, stiff; explicit; perfunctory; concerned with form, not matter. **formalism,** *n.* strict conformity to set forms, esp. in religion. **formalist,** *n.* **formality,** *n.* formal business, ceremony; propriety, ceremoniousness. **formalize,** *v.t.* make formal; clothe with legal formality. **formalization,** *n.*

formaldehyde, *n.* gas got from methyl alcohol. **formalin,** *n.* solution of this, used as preservative and disinfectant. (*formic*; *aldehyde*)

format, *n.* size and shape, get-up, of book. (F.)

formate, *n.* a salt of formic acid.

formation, *n.* forming, thing formed, production; structure, shape, arrangement; (*geol.*) group of strata with common characteristics. **formative,** *a.* serving to form; (*gram.*) used in forming words. (*form*)

forme, *n.* (*print.*) form.

former, *a.* earlier, previous; first of two.—*pron.* former person or thing. **formerly,** *adv.* previously; heretofore. (compar. on analogy of *foremost*)

formic, *a.* of ants. **f. acid,** a colourless corrosive acid. **formicary,** *n.* ant-hill. **formication,** *n.* feeling as of ants crawling over skin. (L. *formica,* ant)

formidable, *a.* to be feared; hard to overcome, redoubtable, serious. **formidability,** *n.* (L. *formidare,* fear)

formless, *a.* without distinct form, shapeless.

formula, *n.* (*pl.* **formulae, formulas**) set form of words for use in ceremony, expressing principle etc.; prescription, recipe; (*chem., math.*) rule, fact, expressed in symbols. **formularize, formulize,** *vv.t.* formulate. **formulary,** *a.* of formulas, ritual.—*n.* book of prescribed forms. **formulate,** *v.t.* express in formula; state systematically. **formulation, formulator,** *nn.* **formulism,** *n.* blind adherence to formula. **formulist,** *n.* (L. *forma,* form + dim.)

fornent, *adv.* and *prep.* (*Scot.*) right opposite (to).

fornicate, *v.i.* have sexual intercourse without marriage. — *a.* (*archit.*) vaulted, arched. **fornication, fornicator,** *nn.* (L. *fornix,* arch, brothel)

forpined, *a.* (*arch.*) wasted away.

forrader, *colloq.* for **forwarder.**

forrit, *adv.* (*Scot.*) forward.

forrel, same as forel.

forsake, *v.t.* (*past* **forsook,** *p.p.* **forsaken**) desert, abandon; give up; (*Shake.*) refuse. (O.E. *for-,* intensive; *sacan,* contend)

forslow, *v.i.* (*Shake.*) delay.—*v.t.* (*Spens.*) waste in sloth, neglect.
forsooth, *adv.* in truth, no doubt.
forspent, *a.* exhausted.
forswear, *v.t.* and *refl.* (*past* **forswore,** *p.p.* **forsworn**) abjure, renounce; swear falsely, perjure (oneself).
forsythia, *n.* a yellow-flowered shrub. (W. *Forsyth*)
fort, *n.* fortified place, castle; trading station. **fortalice,** *n.* small fort, outwork; (*arch.*) fortress. (L. *fortis,* strong)
forte, *n.* thing one excels at; hilt half of sword or foil. (F. *fort*)
fórtě, *adv.* (*mus.*) loudly. (It.)
forth, *adv.* forward, onwards; into view, out.—*prep.* (*arch.*) forth from. **and so f.,** and the like. **forthcoming,** *a.* about to appear; ready when wanted. **forthright,** *a.* going straight; outspoken; decisive.—*adv.* (*arch.*) straight forward; at once.—*n.* straight course. **forthwith,** *adv.* at once, without delay. (O.E.)
forthink, *v.t.* (*Spens.*) repent, be sorry for.
forthy, *adv.* (*Spens.*) therefore.
fortify, *v.t.* strengthen against attack; strengthen, confirm. **fortification,** *n.* defensive work; making, science, of this. (L. *fortis,* strong; *facere,* make)
fortissimo, *adv.* (*mus.*) very loud. (It.)
fortitude, *n.* passive courage, patient endurance, firmness. (L. *fortis,* strong)
fortnight, *n.* two weeks. **fortnightly,** *a.* and *adv.* (done etc.) once a fortnight. (*fourteen nights*)
fortress, *n.* stronghold, castle, fortified town.—*v.t.* (*Shake.*) guard. (O.F. *forteresse*)
fortuitous, *a.* accidental, chance. **fortuitism,** *n.* belief that evolutionary adaptations are due to chance, not design. **fortuitist,** *n.* **fortuity,** *n.* fortuitousness; accident. (L. *fors,* chance)
fortune, *n.* luck, chance; lot in life; good luck, prosperity; wealth; vast sum.—*v.i.* occur, chance (upon). **make a f.,** become rich. **f.-hunter,** *n.* man seeking rich wife. **f.-teller,** *n.* one who predicts person's fortune. **fortunate,** *a.* lucky, prosperous; favourable. (L. *fortuna*)
forty, *a.* and *n.* four times ten. **f. winks, nap. roaring ff.,** stormy latitudes from 40° to 50°. **the F.-five,** Jacobite rebellion of 1745. (*four*)
forum, *n.* public place in Rome where cases were tried and orations delivered; law court, tribunal. (L.)
forward, *adv.* ahead, onward; to, in, forepart of ship.—*a.* in, towards, the front; well-advanced, early; officious, presumptuous, pert.—*n.* (*football*) front-line player.—*v.t.* promote; dispatch, send on. **carriage f.,** not prepaid. **come f.,** present oneself. **put f.,** allege. **forwardly,** *adv.* pertly. **forwards,** *adv.* forward. (*fore; -ward*)
forwearied, forworn, *aa.* (*arch.*) tired out.
forwent, see **forgo.**
fosse, foss, *n.* ditch, trench, esp. of fortification; (*anat.*) depression. (L. *fossa*)
fossick, *v.i.* (*sl.*) search by picking over, rummage. **fossicker,** *n.*
fossil, *n.* petrified remains of animal or plant found in earth's strata; out-of-date person.—*a.* in condition of fossil; antiquated; dug up. **fossilate, fossilize,** *vv.t.* and *i.* turn into fossil. **fossilation, fossilization,** *nn.* **fossiliferous,** *a.* containing fossils. (L. *fodere,* dig)
fossorial, *a.* for digging. **fossor,** *n.* gravedigger. (L. *fodere,* dig)
foster, *v.t.* encourage, be favourable to; (*arch.*) tend, nourish; cherish. **f.-brother, f.-child, f.-daughter, f.-father, f.-parent, f.-sister, f.-son,** *nn.* brother etc. by nursing or bringing up, not by birth. **f.-mother,** *n.* woman who suckles a child not her own; incubator. **fosterage,** *n.* fostering. **fosterling,** *n.* foster-child. (O.E. *fóstor,* nourishment)
fother, *v.t.* stop (leak in ship) while afloat, by letting down sail to be sucked into it.
fou, *a.* (*Scot.*) full; drunk.
foudroyant, *a.* quick, dazzling, like lightning. (F.)
fougasse, *n.* small mine shaped like well and filled with explosives. (F.)
fought, see **fight.**
foul, *a.* loathsome, offensive; dirty, soiled; clogged, encrusted; scurrilous, obscene, profane; vile; ugly; unfair, against rules; entangled; (of weather) wet, stormy.—*n.* collision; unfair play.—*adv.* unfairly.—*v.t.* and *i.* make, become, foul; entangle, jam; become entangled, collide (with). **f. play,** unfair play; murder. **f.-mouthed,** *a.* using foul language. (O.E. *fúl*)
foulard, *n.* light fabric of silk and cotton; neckerchief of this. (F.)
foulder, *v.i.* (*Spens.*) thunder. (L. *fulgur,* lightning)
foulé, *n.* light woollen fabric with glossy surface. (F.)
foully, *adv.* abominably, vilely.
foumart, *n.* polecat. (O.E. *fúl,* foul; *mearth,* marten)
found, *v.t.* establish, base, build; originate; endow; rely. **foundation,** *n.* founding; institution founded, endowment for its support; base of building, groundwork; basis. **foundationer,** *n.* person supplied out of endowment funds. **founder,** *n.* (L. *fundus,* bottom)
found, *v.t.* melt and pour into mould, cast. **founder,** *n.* one who casts metal. **foundry,** *n.* workshop for this. (L. *fundere,* pour)
found, see **find.**
founder, *v.i.* (of ship) fill with water

and sink; (of building) fall down or in; (of horse) collapse, go lame.—*v.t.* cause to founder.—*n.* inflammation of horse's feet from overwork. (L. *fundus*, bottom)
foundling, *n.* deserted child of unknown parents. (*find*)
foundress, *n.* female founder.
fount, *n.* (*poet.*) fountain, source. (L. *fons*)
fount, *n.* (*print.*) set of type of one size and style. (*found*)
fountain, *n.* spring, source; artificial jet of water; structure for this or supplying drinking-water; oil-reservoir of lamp. **f.-head,** *n.* source. **f.-pen,** *n.* with reservoir of ink. (*fount*)
four, *a.* and *n.* one more than three; four-oared boat or its crew. **on all ff.,** on hands and knees; analogous. **f.-flusher,** *n.* (*Amer.*) bluffer. **f.-foot way,** between railway rails (4 ft. 8½ in.). **f.-handed,** *a.* for four players; (*mus.*) for two at piano. **f.-in-hand,** *n.* coach with four horses; kind of necktie. **f.-poster,** *n.* bed with four posts and canopy. **f.-square,** *a.* square; firm, steadfast. **f.-wheeler,** *n.* four-wheeled horse-cab. **fourfold,** *a.* and *adv.* four times repeated. (O.E. *féower*)
fourgon, *n.* luggage-van. (F.)
foursome, *n.* (*golf*) game between two pairs, each pair with one ball.
fourteen, *a.* and *n.* four and ten. **fourteenth,** *a.* and *n.*
fourth, *a.* next after third.—*n.* quarter. **f. estate,** the press. **F. of July,** U.S. Independence Day. (*four*)
fouth, *n.* (*Scot.*) abundance.
fow, *n.* (*Scot.*) pitchfork.
fowl, *n.* domestic cock or hen; bird, its flesh.—*v.i.* shoot, hunt, wild-fowl. **fowler,** *n.* **fowling-piece,** *n.* light gun. (O.E. *fugel*)
fox, *n.* red-furred bushy-tailed animal, preserved for hunting; sly person.—*v.i.* act cunningly, sham.—*v.t.* discolour (page) with brown spots. **f.-brush,** *n.* tail of fox. **f.-terrier,** *n.* small white short-haired dog. **foxglove,** *n.* tall plant with purple or white flowers. **foxhound,** *n.* dog bred for foxhunting. **foxtail,** *n.* kinds of grass. **foxtrot,** *n.* a ballroom dance. **foxy,** *a.* fox-like; red-dish-brown; sly, sly-looking. (O.E.)
foy, *n.* (*Spens.*) allegiance, faith. (F. *foi*)
foyer, *n.* hall in theatre for audience to promenade in between acts. (F.)
fozy, *a.* (*Scot.*) spongy.
fra, *n.* friar (as title). (It.)
fracas, *n.* noisy quarrel; uproar. (F).
fraction, *n.* numerical quantity not whole number; fragment, scrap; (*Shake.*) discord. **proper, improper, f.,** less, greater, than 1. **vulgar f.,** expressed by numerator and denominator. **fractional, fractionary,** *aa.* of fractions; inconsiderable. **fractionate,** *v.t.* separate elements of (mixture) by distillation. **fractionize,** *v.t.* break up into fractions. (L. *frangere*, break)
fractious, *a.* cross, peevish. (*fraction*)
fracture, *n.* breakage, esp. of bone.—*v.t.* and *i.* break, crack (bone). (L. *frangere*, break)
frae, (*Scot.*) form of from.
fragile, *a.* easily broken; delicate, weak. **fragility,** *n.* (L. *fragilis*)
fragment, *n.* part broken off; imperfect or unfinished portion. **fragmentary,** *a.* (L. *frangere*, break)
fragrant, *a.* sweet-smelling. **fragrance,** *n.* scent. (L. *fragrare*, smell)
frail, *n.* rush basket. (O.F. *frayel*)
frail, *a.* fragile; infirm; morally weak, unchaste. **frailty,** *n.* frailness; failing. (*fragile*)
fraise, *n* palisade of pointed stakes in rampart; tool for enlarging drill-hole. (F.=ruff)
framboesia, frambesia, *n.* yaws. (F. *framboise*, raspberry)
frame, *v.t.* and *i.* put together; direct, dispose, adapt; encase in frame; promise, shape; (*Amer.*) put in false position, concoct charge against.—*n.* structure; established order, plan; constitution, build; mood, humour; case for picture, setting; glass case for plants. **f. aerial,** (*wireless*) of wire wound round wooden frame. **f.-up,** *n.* (*Amer.*) conspiracy, manufactured evidence. **framework,** *n.* supporting work, skeleton. (O.E. *framian*, avail)
frampold, *a.* (*Shake.*) disagreeable.
franc, *n.* French monetary unit, former value 9½*d.*, now about ½d. (F.)
franchise, *n.* right to vote; citizenship; (formerly) exceptional right or privilege. (O.F. *franc*, free)
Franciscan, *a.* and *n.* (friar) of the order of St. Francis.
Franco-, from *France*, used in **Francophile, Francophobe,** *nn.* one who admires, fears, France.
francolin, *n.* kind of partridge. (F.)
franc-tireur, *n.* armed peasant, man of light irregular troops. (F.)
frangible, *a.* brittle, fragile. **frangibility,** *n.* (L. *frangere*, break)
frangipane, frangipani, *n.* perfume of red jasmine; paste, cake, of almonds and cream. (F.)
franion, *n.* (*Spens.*) paramour.
frank, *a.* candid, open; sincere; (*Shake.*) liberal.—*n.* signature on letter of person entitled to send it free of postage; such letter.—*v.t.* mark with frank; give free passage to; exempt. (*Frank*)
frank, *n.* (*Shake.*) pigsty.—*v.t.* shut up in one. (O.F. *franc*)
Frank, *n.* member of Germanic tribe that conquered Gaul and founded France; Levantine term for European. (O.H.G. *Franko*)
Frankenstein, *n.* **F.'s monster,** creation

that brings disaster to its **author.** (book by Mrs. Shelley)

frankfurter, frankfurt, *nn.* a highly seasoned sausage. (German town)

frankincense, *n.* aromatic vegetable resin used for incense. (*frank*; *incense*)

franklin, *n.* middle-class landowner of 14th and 15th centuries. (*frank*)

frantic, *a.* frenzied, distracted, beside oneself. **frantically, franticly,** *advv.* (Gk. *phrēn*, brain)

frap, *v.t.* (*naut.*) bind tightly, undergird. (O.F. *fraper*, bind)

frappé, *a.* iced; cooled. (F.)

frass, *n.* excrement of larvae. (G.)

fratch, *v.i.* and *n.* (*prov.*) quarrel.

fratě, *n.* (*pl. frati*) friar. (It.)

frater, *n.* refectory. (O.F. *fraitur*)

fraternal, *a.* of brothers, brotherly. **fraternity,** *n.* brotherliness; religious brotherhood, guild; (*Amer.*) college society. **fraternize,** *v.i.* associate, make friends. **fraternization,** *n.* (L. *frater*, brother)

fratricide, *n.* killing, killer, of brother or sister. **fratricidal,** *a.* (L. *frater*, brother; *caedere*, kill)

frau, *n.* (*pl. frauen*) German married woman, Mrs. (G.)

fraud, *n.* imposture, swindle; criminal deception; cheat, disappointing person. **pious f.,** well-meant deception; religious humbug. **fraudulent,** *a.* using, showing, obtained by, fraud. **fraudulence,** *n.* (L. *fraus*)

fraught, *a.* laden, stored.—*v.t.* (*Shake.*) load. **f. with,** full of, involving. **fraughtage,** *n.* (*Shake.*) cargo.

fräulein, *n.* German unmarried woman, Miss. (G.)

fraxinella, *n.* garden dittany. (L. *fraxinus*, ash)

fray, *v.t.* and *i.* chafe; make, become, ragged at edge. (L. *fricare*, rub)

fray, *n.* fight, brawl.—*v.t.* (*Shake.*) frighten. (*affray*)

frazil, *n.* (*Amer.*) ice at bottom of stream, anchor-ice.

frazzle, *v.t.* (*Amer.*) fray, tatter.—*n.* exhausted state.

freak, *n.* whim, vagary; monstrosity, oddity; eccentric person. **freaked,** *a.* streaked. **freakish,** *a.* queer.

freckle, *n.* brownish spot on skin.—*v.t.* and *i.* mark, become marked, with these. (O.N. *freknur*, freckles).

free, *a.* at liberty, not bound; not under arbitrary government; independent; not attached; disengaged; exempt; gratuitous; frank, familiar; lavish; having privileges (of); (of translation) not literal; (*chem.*) not combined; (*Shake.*) innocent.—*v.t.* make free; deliver, rid; clear. **f. and easy,** unceremonious; smoking concert. **F. Church,** not subject to state control. **f. companion,** medieval mercenary. **f. fight,** indiscriminate contest, mêlée. **f. hand,** right of acting at discretion. **f. labour,** of men not members of trade union. **f. list,** of duty-free articles, people admitted free etc. **f. love,** indiscriminate sexual relations. **f. trade,** unrestricted by tariffs. **f. verse,** without rhyme or regular metre. **f. wheel,** bicycle driving wheel that can revolve while pedals are at rest. **f. will,** liberty of choice, power of self-determination. **make f.,** take liberties. (O.E. *fréo*)

freeboard, *n.* side of ship above water-line.

freebooter, *n.* roving robber, pirate.

free-born, *a.* born of free parents.

freedman, *n.* emancipated slave.

freedom, *n.* liberty; independence; immunity, exemption; frankness, undue familiarity; facility; share of privileges; citizenship.

free-hand, *a.* drawn without guiding instruments.

free-handed, *a.* open-handed, generous.

freehold, *n.* tenure without rent or service, absolute ownership; estate so held. **freeholder,** *n.*

freelance, *n.* medieval mercenary; unattached journalist or politician.

freeman, *n.* one who is not slave; person with civic rights.

freemartin, *n.* hermaphrodite calf.

freemason, *n.* member of secret society for mutual help, having elaborate ritual. **freemasonry,** *n.* their system; instinctive sympathy.

freesia, *n.* fragrant flowering plant of iris kind.

free-spoken, *a.* outspoken, blunt.

freestone, *n.* easily sawn sandstone or limestone; peach with loose stone.

freethinker, *n.* one who rejects authority in religion, sceptic.

freewill, *a.* voluntary, spontaneous.

freeze, *v.t.* and *i.* (*past* **froze,** *p.p.* **frozen**) turn solid by frost, become ice; stiffen, kill, preserve, by cold; chill, be chilled, by fear. **f. on to,** keep close hold of. **f. out,** exclude from business by competition etc. **freezing,** *a.* very cold; unfriendly, distant. **freezing-point,** *n.* at which liquid freezes (32° F. for water). (O.E. *fréosan*)

freight, *n.* cargo, load; transport of goods by sea or (*Amer.*) rail; charge, hire of ship, for this.—*v.t.* load, charter (ship). **f.-car, f.-train,** *nn.* (*Amer.*) goods truck, train. **freightage,** *n.* charge for freight; cargo. **freighter,** *n.* one who freights; cargo-boat.

freit, *n.* (*Scot.*) belief in omens. **freity,** *a.* superstitious.

fremit, fremd, *a.* (*Scot.*) strange, foreign.—*n.* stranger. (O.E. *fremde*)

French, *a.* and *n.* (people, language) of France. **F. bean,** kidney or haricot bean. **F. bread,** kind of fancy bread. **F. chalk,** a soapstone used as dry lubricant etc. **F. horn,** brass wind-instrument with long coiled tube and wide bell. **F. leave,** hasty or secret departure. **F. letter** condom. **f. polish**, shellac varnish for furniture. **F. roof,** mansard roof. **F. toast,** with one side buttered and other toasted. **f. window,** long window opening like door. **frenchify,** *v.t.* make French in form, manner etc. **frenchification,** *n.* **Frenchman,** *n.* (*fem.* **Frenchwoman**). **Frenchy,** *a.* in French style.—*n.* (*colloq.*) Frenchman. (O.E. *frencisc*)

frenetic, same as **phrenetic.**

frenne, *n.* (*Spens.*) stranger. (*fremd*)

frenzy, *n.* violent excitement, fury; temporary madness.—*v.t.* infuriate, madden. (Gk. *phrēn,* brain)

frequent, *a.* happening often, common; numerous.—*v.t.* visit often, haunt. **frequency,** *n.* frequentness; (*electr.*) number of cycles per second of alternating current. **frequentative,** *a.* and *n.* (verb) expressing repetition or intensity. (L. *frequens,* crowded)

fresco, *n.* (*pl.* **frescoes, frescos**) painting in water-colour on plaster of wall before it dries; this method.—*v.t.* paint in fresco. (It.)

fresh, *a.* new, recent; additional; pure, sweet; not salt or salted; strong, vigorous; not stale or faded or exhausted; inexperienced; tipsy; (*Amer. sl.*) cheeky, quarrelsome.—*adv.* newly.—*n.* freshet. **f.-coloured,** *a.* ruddy. **freshen,** *v.t.* and *i.* make, become, fresh; strengthen; revive. **freshet,** *n.* stream of fresh water; flood in river from rain etc. **freshman,** (*sl.*) **fresher,** *nn.* first-year student. **freshwater,** *a.* of river; not sea-going. (O.E. *fersc*)

fret, *n.* pattern of straight lines intersecting.—*v.t.* ornament with carved work; variegate. **f.-saw,** *n.* narrow saw for cutting patterns in wood. **fretwork,** *n.* wood so cut; open or carved ornamental work.

fret, *v.t.* and *i.* wear away, chafe; vex, worry; flow in ripples.—*n.* irritation. **fretful,** *a.* peevish, querulous. (O.E. *fretan*)

fret, *n.* wire or bar on fingerboard of guitar etc. to aid fingering.

Freudian, *a.* and *n.* (disciple) of S. Freud or his doctrines of psychoanalysis.

friable, *a.* easily crumbled. **friability,** *n.* (L. *friare,* crumble)

friar, *n.* member of a mendicant religious order. **Austin Ff.,** Augustines. **Black Ff.,** or **Ff. Major,** Dominicans. **Grey Ff.** or **Ff. Minor,** Franciscans. **White Ff.,** Carmelites. **f.'s balsam,** tincture of benzoin. **f.'s lantern,** will-o'-the-wisp. **friary,** *n.* monastery. (L. *frater,* brother)

fribble, *v.i.* trifle, frivol.—*n.* trifler. (imit.)

fricandeau, *n.* (*pl.* **fricandeaux**) veal stewed and spiced. (F.)

fricassee, *n.* meat, birds etc. cut small, stewed, and served with sauce.—*v.t.* cook thus. (F. *fricassée*)

fricative, *a.* and *n.* (consonant) made by friction of breath in narrow opening, e.g. *f, th.* (L. *fricare,* rub)

friction, *n.* rubbing; medical chafing; disagreement; (*mech.*) resistance to body from surface on which it moves. **f.-balls,** *n.pl.* to lessen friction. **f.-clutch,** *n.* transmitting motion by friction. **frictional,** *a.* (L. *fricare,* rub)

Friday, *n.* sixth day of week. **Good F.,** that before Easter, commemorating Crucifixion. (O.E. *Frig,* a goddess)

friend, *n.* one attached to another by affection, intimate; supporter; (*Scot.*) relation.—*v.t.* (*poet.*) befriend. **make ff. with,** get to know. **Society of Ff.,** Quakers. **friendly,** *a.* as, like, a friend; amicable, not hostile; favourable. **friendly society,** for mutual insurance against sickness etc. **friendship,** *n.* friendly relation or feeling. (O.E. *fréond*)

frier, same as **fryer.**

frieze, *n.* (*archit.*) part of entablature between architrave and cornice, often filled with sculpture; band of decoration. (F. *frise*)

frieze, *n.* kind of coarse woollen cloth. (F. *friser,* curl)

frig, *sl. abbr.* for **refrigerator.**

frigate, *n.* large type of corvette; old sailing warship corresponding to modern cruiser. **f.-bird,** *n.* tropical sea-bird. (It. *fregata*)

fright, *n.* sudden fear, alarm; grotesque figure.—*v.t.* (*poet.*) frighten. **frighten,** *v.t.* make afraid, terrify; compel by fright. **frightful,** *a.* dreadful, shocking; hideous; (*sl.*) very great. **frightfulness,** *n.* being frightful; organized terrorism. (O.E. *fyrhto*)

frigid, *a.* cold; unfeeling, apathetic; formal; dull. **f. zones,** within polar circles. **frigidity,** *n.* **frigorific,** *a.* causing cold. (L. *frigus,* cold)

frill, *n.* pleated or crimped edging of cloth or paper, ruffle; fringe of hair or feathers; (*phot.*) puckering of film; (*pl. colloq.*) airs, useless adornment. **frillery,** *n.* **frillies,** *n.pl.* (*colloq.*) frilled petticoats etc.

fringe, *n.* ornamental bordering of threads or tassels; edging, outskirts; front hair cut to hang over brow.—*v.t.* adorn with fringe, border. (L. *fimbria*)

frippery, *n.* tawdry finery, trumpery; affected elegance; (*Shake.*) old-clothes shop. (O.F. *frepe,* rag)

frisette, *n.* fringe of false curls. ***friseur,*** *n.* hairdresser. (F.)

frisk, *v.i.* and *t.* gambol, leap playfully; (*Amer. sl.*) feel over, search (person) for weapons etc.—*n.* frolic. (O.F. *frisque,* lively)

frisket, *n.* (*print.*) light frame holding sheet in position while printing. (F. *frisquette*)

frisky, *a.* lively, frolicsome.
frit, *n.* mixture of sand and fluxes from which glass is made.—*v.t.* make into frit. (It. *friggere,* fry)
frit-fly, *n.* small fly destructive to grain.
frith, see **firth.**
fritillary, *n.* plant of lily kind; kinds of spotted butterfly. (L. *fritillus,* dice-box)
fritter, *n.* small fried batter-cake, us. with fruit etc. inside; (*pl.*) fenks. (L. *frigere,* fry)
fritter, *v.t.* break into fragments. **f. away,** dissipate.
Fritz, *n.* (*sl.*) German. (name)
frivol, *v.i.* trifle. **frivolous,** *a.* silly, light-minded; futile, not serious. **frivolity,** *n.* levity; trifling. (L. *frivolus,* paltry)
frizz, *v.i.* and *n.* sizzle. **frizzle,** *v.t.* and *i.* cook with sizzling noise. (*fry*+ imit.)
frizz, friz, *v.t.* curl, crisp.—*n.* frizzed hair, curls. **frizzle,** *v.t.* and *i.* form into small curls.—*n.* frizz. **frizzly, frizzy,** *aa.* (F. *friser*)
fro, *prep.* (*Shake.*) from. **to and f.,** back and forward. (O.N. *frá*)
frock, *n.* woman's or child's dress; loose wide-sleeved gown of monk.—*v.t.* invest with office of priest. **f.-coat,** *n.* full-skirted man's coat. (L.L. *froccus*)
Froebelism, *n.* kindergarten system. (F. W. A. *Froebel*)
frog, *n.* horny growth in sole of horse's hoof.
frog, *n.* section of rail where two lines cross.
frog, *n.* ornamental loop or fastening for frock or cloak; attachment on belt to carry sword. **frogged,** *a.*
frog, *n.* a tailless amphibian. **f.'s march,** being carried face downwards by four men, each holding limb. **f.-eater,** *n.* Frenchman. **f.-fish,** *n.* angler. **f.-in-the-throat,** *n.* hoarseness. **froggy,** *a.* cold as, full of, frogs.—*n.* (*sl.*) Frenchman. (O.E. *frogga*)
frolic, *v.i.* gambol; play tricks.—*n.* gaiety, revelry; prank.—*a.* (*poet.*) sportive. **frolicsome,** *a.* (Du. *vrolijk*)
from, *prep.* out of, away; since; because of. **f. a child,** from childhood. **f. day to day,** daily. **f. time to time,** occasionally. (O.E.)
frond, *n.* combined leaf and stem. **frondage,** *n.* fronds collectively. **frondescence,** *n.* opening of leaves; foliage. **frondose,** *a.* like, having, fronds. (L. *frons,* leaf)
front, *n.* forepart, face; forehead; battle line or area; false hair for forehead; shirt-front; boldness.—*a.* of, in, front.—*v.i.* and *t.* face; oppose; furnish with front. **come to the f.,** come into prominence. **f. door,** main entrance. **in f.,** ahead. (L. *frons*)
frontage, *n.* land abutting on street or water; front of building; extent of front; outlook.
frontal, *a.* of front or forehead.—*n.* covering for front of altar.
frontier, *n.* boundary of country, border; (*Shake.*) outwork.
frontispiece, *n.* illustration facing title-page of book; (*archit.*) main face of building; (*sl.*) face. (L. *frons,* forehead; *specere,* view)
frontless, *a.* shameless.
frontlet, *n.* band for forehead, fillet; animal's forehead.
fronton, *n.* pediment. (*front*)
frontward, *a.* and *adv.* towards front.
frore, *a.* (*poet.*) frozen, frosty. (O.E. *froren*)
frost, *n.* act, state, of freezing: freezing weather; frozen dew, hoar-frost; (*sl.*) fiasco.—*v.t.* cover, damage, with frost; powder with sugar; give roughened surface to; silver (hair). **white, black, f.,** with, without, frozen dew. **f.-bite,** *n.* freezing of part of body. **f.-bitten,** *a.* **frosty,** *a.* cold with frost; chilly, distant; hoary. (O.E.)
froth, *n.* bubbles on liquid, foam; scum; empty talk.—*v.t.* emit, gather, foam. **frothy,** *a.*
frou-frou, *n.* rustle of dress. (F.)
frounce, *v.t.* and *n.* plait, curl. (O.F. *froncier*)
frow, *n.* Dutchwoman. (Du. *vrouw*)
froward, *a.* (*arch.*) perverse, wayward. (*fro*; *-ward*)
frown, *v.i.* and *t.* knit brows, scowl; look with disfavour; lour.—*n.* wrinkled brow; stern look. **f. down,** quell with frown. (O.F. *froignier*)
frowst, *n.* (*colloq.*) close, stuffy atmosphere.—*v.i.* stay in this. **frowsty,** *a.* stuffy.
frowzy, *a.* fusty, musty, ill-smelling; unkempt, slatternly.
frozen, *a.* (of credits) unrealizable. **the f. limit,** (*sl.*) utterly intolerable. (*freeze*)
fructify, *v.i.* and *t.* bear fruit; make fruitful. **fructification,** *n.* fructifying; plant's reproductive parts. **fructiferous,** *a.* bearing fruit. **fructose,** *n.* fruit sugar. **fructuous,** *a.* fruitful. (L. *fructus,* fruit; *facere,* make)
frugal, *a.* thrifty, economical, esp. in food. **frugality,** *n.* (L. *frux,* fruit)
frugivorous, *a.* fruit-eating. (L. *frux,* fruit; *vorare,* eat)
fruit, *n.* vegetable products; seed and its envelope; offspring; result, benefit.—*v.i.* and *t.* bear, cause to bear, fruit. **f. cake,** with currants etc. **f. salad,** of various fruits sliced and mixed. **f.-knife,** *n.* with stainless blade. **fruitage,** *n.* fruit-bearing; fruits collectively. **fruitarian,** *n.* one who lives on fruit. **fruiter,** *n.* fruit grower, ship, or tree. **fruiterer,** *n.* dealer in fruit. **fruitful,** *a.* yielding fruit; prolific; beneficial. (L. *fructus*)

fruition, *n.* enjoyment; fulfilment. (L. *frui*, enjoy)
fruitless, *a.* barren; vain, useless, profitless.
fruity, *a.* full-flavoured, rich; (of wine) tasting of grape.
frumenty, *n.* hulled wheat boiled in milk. (L. *frumentum*, corn)
frump, *n.* dowdy old-fashioned woman. **frumpish, frumpy,** *aa.*
frush, *v.t.* (*Shake.*) bruise, batter. (L. *frustum*, fragment)
frustrate, *v.t.* baffle, thwart; bring to nothing, disappoint.—*a.* frustrated. **frustration,** *n.* (L. *frustra*, in vain).
frustum, *n.* (*pl.* **frusta, frustums**) part of cone, pyramid etc. left when top is cut off; slice of solid. **frustule,** *n.* shell of diatom. (L.=bit)
frutex, *n.* shrub. **frutescent, fruticose,** *aa.* like a shrub; shrubby. **fruticetum,** *n.* shrub-garden. (L.)
fry, *n.* young fishes just spawned; young of frog etc. **small f.,** persons, things, of little account. (O.N. *frió*, seed)
fry, *v.t.* and *i.* cook with fat in shallow pan.—*n.* fried meat; parts for frying. **frying-pan, fryer,** *nn.* (L. *frigere*)
fub, (*Shake.*) form of **fob.**
fubsy, *a.* squat, dumpy.
fuchsia, *n.* shrub with pendulous purplish-red flowers. **fuchsine,** *n.* a dark red dye-stuff. (*Fuchs*, botanist)
fucus, *n.* (*pl.* **fuci**) kind of flat seaweed. **fucoid,** *a.* like seaweed. (L.)
fud, *n.* (*Scot.*) tail of rabbit.
fuddle, *v.t.* and *i.* make stupid with drink; confuse; tipple.—*n.* drinking-bout.
fudge, *v.t.* and *i.* patch up, botch; fake.—*n.* makeshift; kind of soft toffee; (*print.*) piece of late matter inserted in stop-press of paper.
fudge, *n.* and *int.* nonsense, stuff.
fuel, *n.* material for fire, firing; thing that feeds passion etc.—*v.t.* and *i.* supply with, get, fuel. (L. *focus*, hearth)
fuff, *n.* (*Scot.*) puff, light gust; spitting of cat.—*v.i.* and *t.* puff.
fug, *n.* (*sl.*) fustiness, close atmosphere; fluff, dust.—*v.i.* frowst.
fugacious, *a.* elusive; fleeting. **fugacity,** *n.* (L. *fugere*, flee)
fugal, *a.* of the nature of a fugue.
fuggy, *a.* hot and stuffy. (*fug*)
fugitive, *a.* fleeing; transient; liable to fade; (of verse) occasional.—*n.* one who flees, runaway; refugee. (L. *fugere*, flee)
fugleman, *n.* soldier standing in front of others to demonstrate drill; ringleader, spokesman. **fugle,** *v.i.* act as fugleman. (G. *flügel*, wing)
fugue, *n.* (*mus.*) contrapuntal composition in which theme or themes are repeated in different parts.—*v.t.* compose, play, fugue. **fuguist,** *n.* (L. *fuga*, flight)
Führer, *n.* title of Nazi dictator. (G.=leader)
-ful, *adj.suf.* full of, as in **doleful.**—*n.suf.* amount needed to fill, as in **cupful.** (*full*)
fulcrum, *n.* (*pl.* **fulcra**) support on which lever works; (*bot.*) accessory organ. (L. *fulcire*, prop)
fulfil, *v.t.* accomplish, carry out; satisfy (desire etc.) **fulfilment,** *n.* (*full*; *fill*)
fulgent, *a.* shining, radiant. **fulgency,** *n.* (L. *fulgēre*, shine)
fulgurant, *a.* like lightning. **fulgurate,** *v.i.* flash. **fulgurite,** *n.* rock, sand, vitrified by lightning; an explosive. (L. *fulgur*, lightning)
fulham, *n.* loaded die.
fuliginous, *a.* sooty, smoky. (L. *fuligo*, soot)
full, *a.* filled, replete; abundantly supplied; copious; complete, entire; swelling; (of colour) deep.—*n.* complete measure, whole.—*adv.* quite, utterly; exactly; (*colloq.*) more than necessary.—*v.t.* and *i.* bunch; become full. **f. dress,** ceremonial dress. **f. face** seen from in front. **f. hand,** (*poker*) with three of a kind and pair. **f. moon,** with whole disk illuminated. **f. pitch,** (*cricket*) without touching ground. **f. stop,** period. **f. up,** with no room for more. **in f.,** without reduction. **of f. age,** having reached majority. **f.-back,** *n.* football player at rear. **f.-blooded,** *a.* of pure descent; lusty, vigorous. **f.-blown,** *a.* (of flower) fully open. **f.-bottomed,** *a.* (of wig) long behind. **f.-grown,** *a.* mature. (O.E. *ful*)
full, *v.t.* clean and thicken (cloth) by beating. **fuller,** *n.* **fuller's earth,** kind of clay used in fulling. (L. *fullo*, fuller)
fullam, same as **fulham.**
fuller, *n.* tool for grooving and shaping iron; groove made by it. (*full*)
fullness, *n.* being full; richness. **f. of time,** destined time.
fully, *adv.* completely; quite.
fulmar, *n.* sea-bird, kind of petrel.
fulminate, *v.i.* and *t.* detonate, flash; thunder forth; issue official censure.—*n.* explosive compound. **fulminant,** *a.* fulminating; (*med.*) developing suddenly. **fulmination, fulminator,** *nn.* **fulminatory,** *a.* **fulmine,** *v.i.* and *t.* fulminate. (L. *fulmen*, lightning)
fulness, same as **fullness.**
fulsome, *a.* offensive from excess, cloying.
fulvous, *a.* tawny. (L. *fulvus*)
fumade, *n.* smoked pilchard. **fumarole,** *n.* volcano's smoke-vent. **fumatory,** *n.* fumigating chamber. (L. *fumus*, smoke)
fumble, *v.i.* and *t.* feel about; handle awkwardly.—*n.* awkward attempt.
fume, *n.* exhalation, reek; aromatic smoke; fit of anger.—*v.i.* and *t.* emit, subject to, fumes; show anger, chafe;

darken (oak) by fumes of ammonia. (L. *fumus*, smoke)
fumigate, *v.t.* disinfect by vapour; perfume. **fumigation, fumigator,** *nn.* (L. *fumigare*)
fumitory, (*Shake.*) **fumiter,** *n.* a medicinal herb. (L. *fumus*, smoke; *terra*, earth)
fun, *n.* sport, amusement, jest.—*v.i.* joke. **for, in, f.,** not seriously. **like f.,** vigorously; quickly. **make f. of, poke f. at,** ridicule, tease.
funambulist, *n.* rope-walker. (L. *funis*, rope; *ambulare*, walk)
function, *n.* work a thing is designed to do; office, duty; calling, profession; public gathering or ceremony; (*math.*) quantity whose value depends on varying value of another.—*v.i.* discharge duty; operate, work. **functional,** *a.* of function; (*med.*) of, affecting, functions only, not organic; having function, not rudimentary. **functionary,** *n.* holder of office, official. **functionate,** *v.i.* function. (L. *fungi*, perform)
fund, *n.* sum of money for special object; capital; stock, supply; (*pl.*) money resources.—*v.t.* convert (floating debt) into stock; place in fund. **in ff.,** having money. **sinking f.,** set aside for reduction of public debt. **the ff.,** stock of national debt. **f.-holder,** *n.* investor in this. (L. *fundus*, bottom)
fundament, *n.* buttocks, anus. (L. *fundamentum*, foundation)
fundamental, *a.* essential, primary; of, serving as, base.—*n.* basic principle; essential part. **fundamentalism,** *n.* belief in literal truth of the Bible, esp. its account of creation. **fundamentalist,** *n.* (L. *fundamentum*, foundation)
funebrial, *a.* of funeral. (L. *funebris*)
funeral, *n.* burial; ceremony connected with it, obsequies.—*a.* funerary. **funerary,** *a.* of funeral. **funereal,** *a.* suited to a funeral; gloomy, dismal. (L. *funus*)
fungal, *a.* of fungus.
fungible, *a.* (*law*) replaceable by another similar specimen.—*n.* fungible thing, e.g. a shilling. (L. *fungi*, perform)
fungus, *n.* (*pl.* **fungi, funguses**) mushroom, toadstool, mildew, and allied plants; (*med.*) morbid spongy growth. **fungicide,** *n.* fungus-killer. **fungoid,** *a.* like a fungus. (L.)
funicular, *a.* of rope or its tension. **f. railway,** cable mountain railway. (L. *funis*, cord)
funk, *n.* (*sl.*) fear, panic; coward.—*v.i.* and *t.* show cowardice, be afraid (of), flinch (from). **blue f.,** terror. **f.-hole,** *n.* dug-out. **funky,** *a.*
funnel, *n.* chimney of ship or locomotive; cone-shaped tube for pouring liquid into bottle. (M.E. *fonel*)
funny, *n.* narrow clinker-built sculling-boat, lighter than whiff.
funny, *a.* comical, amusing; queer, peculiar. **f.-bone,** *n.* point of elbow. **f.-man,** *n.* jester. **funniment,** *n.* drollery; joke.
fur, *n.* soft short hair of animal, skin with it; garment, necklet etc. of this; furred animals collectively; coating on tongue, crust on wine, scurf on inside of boiler.—*v.t.* clothe, line, coat, with fur; clean scurf from. **make f. fly,** make row. (O.F. *forre*, sheath)
furbelow, *n.* flounce; trimming; kind of wrinkled seaweed. (=*falbala*)
furbish, *v.t.* scour till bright, polish up; renovate, revive. (O.H.G. *forban*)
furcate, *a.* forked, branching.—*v.i.* fork, divide. **furcation,** *n.* (L. *furca*, fork)
furfur, *n.* scurf, dandruff. **furfuraceous, furfurous,** *aa.* (L.)
furious, *a.* full of fury, enraged; violent, impetuous. **fast and f.,** uproarious. (*fury*)
furl, *v.t.* and *i.* roll up (sail) round yard; fold up, close.
furlong, *n.* eighth of mile. (O.E. *furlang*, length of furrow)
furlough, *n.* leave of absence.—*v.t.* grant leave to. (Du. *verlof*)
furmenty, furmety, same as **frumenty.**
furnace, *n.* oven, enclosed fire-place, for melting ores, central heating etc.; severe trial.—*v.t.* heat in furnace. (L. *fornax*)
furnish, *v.t.* provide, fit up (with); supply, afford. **furniture,** *n.* household articles, tables, chairs etc.; contents; equipment, harness. (O.H.G. *frummen*, further)
furore, *n.* burst of enthusiasm; craze. (L. *furor*, frenzy)
furrier, *n.* dealer in furs. **furriery,** *n.* fur-trade.
furrow, *n.* trench made by plough; track, groove, wrinkle.—*v.t.* and *i.* make furrow (in), plough; groove. (O.E. *furh*)
further, *adv.* to, at, greater distance; in addition, more.—*a.* more remote; additional.—*v.t.* promote, help forward. **furtherance,** *n.* furthering. **furthermore,** *adv.* besides, moreover. **furthermost,** *a.* most remote. **furthest,** *a.* and *adv.* at, to, greatest distance. (O.E. *furthor*)
furtive, *a.* stealthy, clandestine; sly, secret. (L. *fur*, thief)
furuncle, *n.* boil. **furuncular, furunculous,** *aa.* (L. *furunculus*)
fury, *n.* fierce passion, rage; frenzy; violence; virago; (*pl.*) three goddesses of vengeance, Alecto, Megaera, Tisiphone. (L. *furia*)
furze, *n.* yellow-flowered prickly bush, gorse, whin. (O.E. *fyrs*)
fuscous, *a.* dark-coloured, sombre; brownish-black. (L. *fuscus*)

fuse, *v.t.* and *i.* liquefy by heat, melt; unite by melting, blend.—*n.* (*electr.*) wire with low melting-point used as safety device. (L. *fundere*, pour)
fuse, *n.* cord, tube, casing, soaked or filled with combustible matter for igniting charge, bomb etc.—*v.t.* fit fuse to. (L. *fusus*, spindle)
fusee, *n.* large-headed match; conical spindle in clock. (*fuse*)
fuselage, *n.* body, framework, of aeroplane. (F.)
fusel-oil, *n.* nauseous liquid mixture of various alcohols formed in distillation. (G. *fusel*, bad spirit)
fushionless, *a.* (*Scot.*) pithless.
fusible, *a.* that may be fused. **fusibility,** *n.*
fusiform, *a.* spindle-shaped. (L. *fusis*, spindle)
fusil, *n.* light flintlock musket. **fusilier,** *n.* soldier with this; (*pl.*) name of various regiments. **fusillade,** *n.* continuous shooting.—*v.t.* attack, shoot down, by this. (L. *focus*, hearth)
fusion, *n.* fusing, blending; fused mass; coalition. (*fuse*)
fuss, *n.* bustle, stir; needless concern, flurry.—*v.i.* and *t.* make fuss, worry. **make a f. of,** pet. **fussed up,** (*Amer.*) embarrassed; dressed up. **fussy,** *a.* fidgety; particular.
fust, *v.i.* (*Shake.*) grow or smell mouldy. (O.F. *fust*, cask)
fustanella, *n.* white kilt worn by modern Greeks. (It.)
fustian, *n.* coarse twilled cotton cloth, corduroy etc.; ranting language, bombast.—*a.* of fustian; turgid; sorry, worthless. (L.L. *fustaneus*)
fustic, *n.* a yellow dye; kinds of wood yielding it. (Arab. *fustuq*)
fustigate, *v.t.* (*joc.*) cudgel. **fustigation,** *n.* (L. *fustis*, stick)
fustilarian, *n.* (*Shake.*) fat frowzy woman.
fusty, *a.* mouldy, musty; stuffy; old-fashioned. (*fust*)
futhorc, *n.* runic alphabet. (its first six letters, *th* counting as one)
futile, *a.* useless, vain; trifling. **futility,** *n.* (L. *futilis*)
futtock, *n.* curved timber of ship's lower framework. **f. shrouds,** short shrouds connecting topmast rigging to lower mast.
future, *a.* that will be hereafter; (*gram.*) expressing futurity.—*n.* time to come; future state; (*gram.*) future tense; (*pl.*) things bought and sold for future delivery. **futurism,** *n.* a twentieth-century revolt against tradition in art, using arbitrary symbols for expression. **futurist,** *n.* **futuristic,** *a.* **futurity,** *n.* future time or events. (L. *futurus*, about to be)
fuze, fuzee, same as **fuse, fusee.**
fuzz, *n.* fluff, dust; nap, frizzed hair. **f.-ball,** *n.* puff-ball. **fuzzy,** *a.* fluffy; frayed, blurred; fuddled.
fy, fye, same as **fie.**
-fy, *verb.suf,* make, as in **pacify,** solidify. (L. *facere*, make)
fylfot, *n.* swastika.
fyrd, *n.* military force of entire nation in Anglo-Saxon times. (O.E.)
fytte, see **fit.**

G

G, (*mus.*) note and scale. **g,** symbol for acceleration of gravity, about 32 ft. per second per second. **G-man,** *n.* U.S. federal detective.
gab, *n.* (*colloq.*) idle talk; (*Scot.*) mouth.—*v.i.* chatter, talk. **gift of the g.,** talent for talking, loquacity.
gabardine, *n.* a fine cloth like serge; gaberdine.
gabble, *v.i.* and *t.* talk volubly or fast, jabber; cackle.—*n.* rapid talk. **gabbler,** *n.* (imit.)
gabbro, *n.* igneous rock like granite. (It.)
gabby, *a.* (*Amer.*) talkative. (*gab*)
gabelle, *n.* tax, esp. old French salt-tax. (F.)
gaberdine, *n.* long loose upper garment formerly worn by pilgrims, Jews etc. (O.F. *gauvardine*)
gaberlunzie, *n.* (*Scot.*) wallet; wandering beggar.
gabion, *n.* wicker cylinder filled with earth. **gabionade,** *n.* defensive work, line, of gabions. (It. *gabbia*, cage)
gable, *n.* triangular part of end-wall from eaves to ridge of roof; canopy of same shape. **g.-end,** *n.* wall with gable. **gablet,** *n.* small gable. (O.N. *gafl*)
gaby, *n.* simpleton.
gad, *v.i.* (*past, p.p.* **gadded**) go about idly, rove; straggle. **gadabout, gadder,** *nn.*
gad, *n.* metal spike or wedge; graver; goad. **upon the g.,** (*Shake.*) suddenly. (O.N. *gaddr*)
gad, *int.* of surprise etc. (=*God*)
gadfly, *n.* cattle-biting fly, breeze; worrying person; frenzy. (*gad*)
gadget, *n.* (*colloq.*) fitment, device.
Gadhelic, *a.* of Scottish, Irish, or Manx branch of Celts. (Ir. *Gaedheal*, Gael)
gadoid, *a.* and *n.* (fish) of cod kind. (Gk. *gados*, cod)
gadolinium, *n.* a rare metallic element. (J. *Gadolin*, chemist)
gadroon, *n.* ornamental edge of inverted fluting. (F. *godron*)

gadsman, *n.* (*Scot.*) ploughboy.
gadzooks, *int.* (*arch.*) an oath.
gae, *Scot.* form of go.
Gael, *n.* Scottish Celt. **Gaelic,** *a.* of Gaels: Gadhelic.—*n.* dialect of Scottish highlands. (Gael. *Gaidheal*)
gaff, *n.* stick with hook for landing large fish; upper spar of fore-and-aft sail.—*v.t.* seize, land, with gaff. (F. *gaffe,* boat-hook)
gaff, *n.* (us. **penny g.**) low theatre.
gaff, *n.* (*sl.*). **blow the g.,** reveal plot.
gaffe, *n.* indiscreet act or remark, *faux pas.* (F.)
gaffer, *n.* elderly rustic, old man; foreman. (=*grandfather*)
gag, *n.* thing thrust into mouth to prevent speech or distend jaws; closure.—*v.t.* (*past, p.p.* **gagged**) apply gag to, silence. **g.-bit,** *n.* strong one for horse-breaking.
gag, *n.* impromptu interpolation by actor; comic effect; joke, imposture. —*v.i.* and *t.* (*past, p.p.* **gagged**) make gags (in); hoax.
gaga, *a.* (*sl.*) gibbering with fright or agitation; crazy. (F.)
gage, *n.* pledge, security; glove etc. thrown down as challenge.—*v.t.* pledge. stake. (O.F. *guage*)
gage, *n.* kinds of plum; greengage.
gage, same as **gauge.**
gaiety, *n.* gayness, mirth; finery; (*pl.*) amusements. **gaily,** *adv.* in a gay manner, merrily; showily. (*gay*)
gain, *v.t.* and *i.* obtain as profit; win, earn; reach; improve, increase; gain ground.—*n.* profit, increase; money-making. **g. ground,** advance. **g. on, upon,** overtake by degrees; encroach upon. **g. time,** effect delay. **gainful,** *a.* profitable; bent on gain. **gainings,** *n.pl.* sums gained. (O.F. *gaaignier*)
gainsay, *v.t.* (*past, p.p.* **gainsaid**) deny, contradict. **gainsayer,** *n.* (O.N. *gegn,* against+*say*)
gainst, 'gainst, *poet.* for **against.**
gait, *n.* manner of walking, step. (=*gate*)
gaiter, *n.* covering for ankle or leg below knee; (*Amer.*) elastic-sided shoe. **gaitered,** *a.* (F. *guêtre*)
gal, *vulg.* form of **girl.**
gala, *n.* festive show or occasion, fête. (It.=finery)
galact(o)-, from Gk. *gala,* milk, used in **galactagogue,** *a.* and *n.* (drug) promoting flow of milk; **galactic,** *a.* of the Milky Way; **galactometer,** *n.* instrument for testing milk.
Galahad, *n.* chivalrous and pure man. (a knight of the Round Table)
galantine, *n.* veal, chicken etc. freed from bones, spiced, tied up, boiled, and served cold. (F.)
galanty show, shadow pantomime made with puppets.
galatea, *n.* a striped cotton fabric. (name on children's sailor suits)
galaxy, *n.* band of faint stars encircling heavens, Milky Way; brilliant assemblage. (Gk. *gala,* milk)
galbanum *n.* kinds of gum resin. (Gk. *chalbanē*)
gale, *n.* strong wind; (*naut.*) storm; (*poet.*) soft breeze.
gale, *n.* bog-myrtle, sweet gale. (O.E. *gagel*)
gale, *n.* payment of rent at stated intervals.
galea, *n.* (*bot., zool.*) helmet-like structure. **galeate,** *a.* (L.=helmet)
galeeny, *n.* guinea-fowl. (Sp. *gallina,* hen)
galena, *n.* sulphide of lead. (L.=lead ore)
Galenic, Galenical, *aa.* of ancient physician Galen or his methods.
Galilean, *a.* of Galilee; of Galileo the astronomer.—*n.* Christian.
galilee, *n.* porch, chapel, at western end of church. (place)
galimatias, *n.* gibberish, rigmarole. (F.)
galingale, *n.* aromatic root of an E. Indian plant; kind of sedge. (Arab. *khalanjan*)
galiot, same as **galliot.**
galipot, *n.* white resinous juice of pine-tree. (F.)
gall, *n.* bile of animals; gall-bladder; bitterness, rancour; (*Amer.*) cheek, assurance. **g.-stone,** *n.* concretion formed in **g.-bladder,** reservoir for bile. (O.E. *gealla*)
gall, *n.* painful swelling, esp. on horse; sore, blister; (*Amer.*) patch of barren soil.—*v.t.* and *i.* break skin by rubbing, chafe; irritate. (O.E. *gealla*)
gall, *n.* (also **g.-nut**) growth caused on trees, esp. oak, by insect called **g.-fly.** (L. *galla,* oak-apple)
gallant, *a.* brave; dashing, showy; chivalrous, attentive to women.—*n.* man of fashion, ladies' man; suitor; seducer.—*v.t.* and *i.* flirt (with), escort. **gallantry,** *n.* bravery, dashing courage; courtliness, polite act; intrigue. (O.F. *galer,* make merry)
galleass, *n.* heavy low-built war-vessel, large galley. (*galley*)
galleon, *n.* large high-built Spanish sailing-ship. (Sp. *galeon*)
gallery, *n.* upper floor of seats in church, theatre etc., balcony; colonnade, portico, veranda; passage, corridor, tunnel; room for showing works of art; theatre gallery audience, crowd of onlookers. **play to the g.,** appeal to vulgar taste. (F. *galerie*)
galley, *n.* low flat one-decked vessel, us. propelled by oars; warship's large row-boat; ship's kitchen; (*print.*) tray which receives type from composing-stick. **g.-proof,** *n.* in slip form, not page. **g.-slave,** *n.* one condemned to row in galley; drudge. (L.L. *galea*)
galliambic, *a.* and *n.* (verse) of four Ionic *a minore* feet (short-short-long-long). (L. *Galli,* priests of Cybele)

galliard, *n.* lively dance in triple time. (O.F. *gaillard*)

galliass, same as **galleass.**

Gallic, *a.* of ancient Gaul; French. *gallicè, adv.* in French. **gallicism,** *n.* French word or idiom. **gallicize,** *v.t.* make French in manners etc. (L. *Gallia,* Gaul)

gallic, *a.* of, made of, gall-nuts.

galligaskins, *n.pl.* trousers; leggings. (It. *Grechesco,* Greekish)

gallimaufry, *n.* medley, hotch-potch. (F. *galimafrée*)

gallinaceous, *a.* of the order including domestic fowls, pheasants etc. **gallinacean,** *a.* and *n.* **gallinazo,** *n.* American vulture, turkey-buzzard. (L. *gallina,* hen)

galliot, *n.* kind of Dutch cargo-boat; small light galley. (*galley*)

gallipot, *n.* small glazed earthenware jar for ointment etc.

gallium, *n.* soft greyish-white metallic element. (L. *gallus=Lecoq* de Boisbaudran, discoverer)

gallivant, *v.i.* gad about; flirt.

galliwasp, *n.* a W. Indian lizard.

Gallo-, from L. *Gallus,* French, used in **Gallomania,** *n.* mania for French ways, hence **Gallomaniac,** *n.*; **Gallophil,** *n.* lover of France; **Gallophobia,** *n.* fear of France, hence **Gallophobe,** *n.*

gallon, *n.* measure of capacity, four quarts. (O.F. *galon*)

galloon, *n.* narrow braid or trimming of silk, gold lace etc. (F. *galon*)

gallop, *n.* horse's fastest pace, with forefeet lifted together and hind feet together.—*v.i.* and *t.* go, ride, at gallop; read, talk, fast. **gallopade,** *n.* a lively dance. **galloper,** *n.* dispatch-rider; cavalry field-gun. (F. *galop*)

gallow, *v.t.* (*Shake.*) frighten. (O.E. *gælwan*)

galloway, *n.* small strong horse; breed of cattle. (place)

gallowglass, *n.* ancient Irish heavy-armed foot-soldier. (Ir. *gall,* foreign; *óglách,* youth)

gallows, *n.* upright with cross-bar on which criminals are hanged; support like this; hanging; (*pl., Scot.*) braces.—*a.* (*Scot.*) villainous, wild.—*adv.* (*Scot.*) very. **g.-bird,** *n.* one who deserves the gallows. **g.-tree,** *n.* gallows. (O.E. *galga*)

galoot, *n.* (*colloq.*) clumsy lout; raw recruit.

galop, *n.* lively dance in 2-4 time.—*v.i.* dance this. (F.)

galore, *adv.* in plenty.—*n.* abundance. (Ir. *go leór,* to sufficiency)

galosh, *n.* rubber overshoe for wet weather. (F. *galoche*)

galumph, *v.i.* prance triumphantly. (*gal*lop; tri*umph*)

galvanism, *n.* electricity produced by chemical action; medical use of this. **galvanic,** *a.* of, produced by, galvanism; spasmodic. **galvanist,** *n.* student of galvanism. **galvanize,** *v.t.* apply galvanism to; coat with metal by galvanism; stimulate, rouse. **galvanized iron,** coated with zinc. **galvanization, galvanizer,** *nn.* **galvanometer, galvanoscope,** *nn.* instruments for measuring, detecting, galvanic currents. (*Galvani,* inventor)

gam, *v.t.* and *i.* (us. of whaler) make call on; gather together.—*n.* school of whales.

gambade, gambado, *n.* horse's bound, curvet; flourish, caper. (F.)

gambier, *n.* astringent extract of a Malayan plant. (Malay *gambir*)

gambit, *n.* chess-opening with sacrifice of pawn or piece. (It. *gambetto,* tripping up)

gamble, *v.i.* play game of chance for money stake; speculate wildly; take great risks.—*n.* risky undertaking. **g. away,** lose by gambling. **gambler,** *n.* **gamblesome,** *a.*

gamboge, *n.* gum resin used as yellow pigment and purgative. (*Cambodia*)

gambol, *n.* caper, playful leap.—*v.i.* frisk. (It. *gamba,* leg)

gambrel, *n.* hock of horse. **g. roof,** one with double slope, curb roof. (O.F. *gamberel*)

game, *n.* sport, diversion, pastime; match or subdivision of it; winning score; jest; scheme, trick; animals or birds hunted, their flesh; (*pl.*) athletic meeting.—*a.* spirited; having spirit (for).—*v.i.* gamble. **big g.,** larger animals hunted. **fair g.,** legitimate quarry. **make g. of,** ridicule; hoax. **on, off, one's g.,** in good, bad, form. **play the g.,** be sportsmanlike. **round g.,** without fixed number of players. **the g. is up,** the plan has failed. **g.-bag,** *n.* for holding killed game. **g.-ball,** *n.* state of game with one point needed to win. **g.-cock,** *n.* one bred for fighting. **g.-laws,** *n.pl.* laws of killing and preserving game. (O.E. *gamen*)

game, *a.* (of limb) lame, disabled.

gamekeeper, *n.* man employed to watch game and prevent poaching.

gamely, *adv.* pluckily.

gamesome, *a.* sportive.

gamester, *n.* gambler; (*Shake.*) frolicsome or lewd person.

gamete, *n.* sexual reproductive cell. (Gk. *gamos,* marriage)

gamgee, *n.* (also **g. tissue**) an absorbent wool for dressings. (inventor)

gamic, *a.* (*zool.*) having a sexual character. (Gk. *gamos,* marriage)

gamin, *n.* street arab, mischievous urchin. (F.)

gamma, *n.* third letter, G, of Greek alphabet. **g.-rays,** *n.pl.* penetrative rays given off by radium. **gammadion,** *n.* fylfot, swastika. (Gk.)

gammer, *n.* old (rustic) woman. (=*grandmother*)

gammon, *n.* lower end of side of bacon; smoked ham.—*v.t.* cure (bacon). (O.F. *gambon*)

gammon, *n.* bosh; humbug.—*v.i.* and *t.* talk plausibly; bamboozle, hoax.
gammon, *n.* (*backgammon*) victory before opponent has withdrawn a man.—*v.t.* defeat thus.
gamo-, from Gk. *gamos,* marriage, used in **gamogenesis,** *n.* (*bot.*) sexual reproduction; **gamopetalous, gamosepalous,** *aa.* with petals, sepals, united.
gamp, *n.* (*sl.*) umbrella, esp. if clumsy or dilapidated. (name in Dickens)
gamut, *n.* whole series of musical notes, major scale; compass of voice etc.; range. (*gamma. ut,* words used for names of notes)
gamy, *a.* full of game; high-flavoured.
ganch, *v.t.* (*obs.*) impale on hooks. (It. *gancio,* hook)
gander, *n.* male goose; simpleton; (*sl.*) look. (O.E. *gandra*)
gan, see **gin.**
gang, *n.* company, squad (of workmen, convicts, etc.); band of criminals; set (of tools). **ganger,** *n.* foreman of gang. (O.E.)
gang, *v.i.* (*Scot.*) go. **g. your ain gait,** take your own course. **g.-board, g.-plank,** *nn.* gangway to ship. (O.E. *gangan*)
gangling, *a.* (*Amer. colloq.*) loosely built, lanky.
ganglion, *n.* (*pl.* **ganglia, ganglions**) nerve centre; tumour in sheath of tendon. **gangliated, ganglionated, ganglionic,** *aa.* (Gk. *ganglion*)
gangrel, *n.* vagrant. (*gang*)
gangrene,*n.* first stage of mortification, necrosis.—*v.i.* and *t.* mortify, affect with gangrene. **gangrenous,** *a.* (Gk. *ganggraina*)
gangster, *n.* member of criminal gang.
gangue, *n.* earth or matrix in which ore is found. (G. *gang,* lode)
gangway, *n.* bridge from ship to shore; opening in side for this; passage along ship's side; passage between rows of seats; way. (*gang*; *way*)
gannet, *n.* a large sea-bird, solan goose. (O.E. *ganot*)
ganoid, *a.* and *n.* (fish) with enamelled bony scales, e.g. sturgeon. (Gk. *ganos,* brightness)
gant, *v.i.* and *n.* (*Scot.*) yawn.
gantlet, gantlope, same as **gauntlet.**
gantry, *n.* structure to support crane, railway signals etc.; stand for casks.
Ganymede, *n.* waiter; pathic; one of Jupiter's moons. (Gk. *Ganumēdēs,* cup-bearer of Zeus)
gaol, gaoler, gaoleress, see **jail.**
gap, *n.* opening, breach; cleft, gorge; interval, blank.—*v.t.* (*past, p.p.* **gapped**) make gap in. (O.N.)
gape, *v.i.* open (mouth) wide, yawn; stare.—*n.* gaping. **the gg.,** fit of yawning; a disease of poultry. **gaper,** *n.* kinds of bird and shellfish. (O.N. *gapa*)
gar, garfish, *n.* long slender fish with pointed head. (O.E. =dart)
gar, *v.t.* (*Scot.*) cause, compel.
garage, *n.* place for housing motorcars.—*v.t.* put in garage. (F.)
garb, *n.* dress; fashion of dress.—*v.t.* clothe. (It. *garbo,* elegance)
garbage, *n.* refuse; offal.
garble, *v.t.* make unfair selection from; mutilate, falsify; sift. **garbler,** *n.* (Arab. *gharbala,* sift)
garboard, *n.* (also **g. strake**) plank, plate, on ship's bottom next keel. (Du. *gaarboord*)
garboil, *n.* (*Shake.*) tumult, broil.
garçon, *n.* waiter. (F.)
gardant, *a.* (*heraldry*) full-face towards spectator. (F. *garder,* look)
garden, *n.* ground for growing flowers, fruit, or vegetables; (*pl.*) pleasure grounds.—*v.i.* cultivate, work in, garden. **common or g.,** (*sl.*) ordinary. **g. city,** one systematically planned in country surroundings. **g.-stuff,** *n.* vegetables and fruit. **gardener,** *n.* one who tends gardens. (O.F. *gardin*)
gardenia, *n.* shrub with fragrant white or yellow flowers. (Dr. *Garden*)
gardyloo, *int.* (*Scot.*) warning cry of housewife emptying slops from window. (F. *gare l'eau,* beware of the water)
garefowl, *n.* great auk. (O.N. *geir-fugl*)
garfish, see **gar.**
gargantuan, *a.* gigantic, huge. (*Gargantua,* giant in Rabelais)
gargle, *v.t.* and *i.* wash (throat) keeping liquid from going down by gentle expiration.—*n.* liquid so used. (F. *gargouiller*)
gargoyle, *n.* spout of roof-gutter in form of grotesque figure. (O.F. *gargouille*)
garibaldi, *n.* kind of blouse, orig. red; currant biscuit. (person)
garish, *a.* gaudy, showy; flighty.
garland, *n.* wreath of flowers or leaves; anthology.—*v.t.* crown, deck, with garland. (O.F. *garlande*)
garlic, *n.* plant with bulbous root of pungent taste, used for seasoning. **g.-mustard,** *n.* weed with smell like garlic .**garlicky,** *a.* smelling of garlic. (O.E. *gár,* spear; *léac,* leek)
garment, *n.* article of dress; (*pl.*) clothing.—*v.t.* (*poet.*) attire. (O.F. *garniment*)
garner, *n.* granary, storehouse for corn etc.—*v.t.* store, collect. (L. *granarium*)
garnet, *n.* a hard mineral, esp. red kind used as gem. (L.L. *granatum,* pomegranate)
garnish, *v.t.* adorn; embellish (dish); (*law*) warn by garnishment.—*n.* materials for garnishing, relish. **garnishee,** *n.* (*law*) person garnished. **garnisher,** *n.* **garnishment,** *n.* embellishment; (*law*) notice to third party to appear in suit; notice to holder of another's attached property not to give it to him but to account for it in court. **garniture,**

n. accessories, trimmings, esp. of dish; dress. (O.F. *garnir*, fortify)

garotte, same as **garrotte.**

garret, *n.* room next roof, attic; (*sl.*) head. **garreteer,** *n.* garret-dweller; poor author. (O.F. *garite*, watch-tower)

garrison, *n.* troops in fortress or town to guard it.—*v.t.* man (fortress). (O.F. *garison*, defence)

garron, *n.* small breed of horse. (Gael. *gearran*)

garrot, *n.* kind of sea-duck. (F.)

garrotte, *n.* method of execution by strangling; instrument for this, with metal collar and spike which pierces spine.—*v.t.* execute by garrotte; half-throttle and rob. **garrotter,** *n.* (Sp. *garrote*)

garrulous, *a.* talkative; babbling. **garrulity,** *n.* loquacity. (L. *garrire*, chatter)

garter, *n.* band holding up stocking. —*v.t.* bind with garter. **the G.,** Order of the Garter, highest order of British knighthood. **g.-snake,** *n.* a harmless American striped snake. (O.F. *gartier*)

garth, *n.* (*arch.*) yard, garden, paddock. (O.N. *garthr*)

gas, *n.* elastic fluid such as air; coal-gas used for heating and lighting; laughing-gas; empty talk; (*Amer. sl.*) petrol. — *v.t.* and *i.* supply, poison, with gas; talk vaguely, brag. **blister, mustard, tear, g.,** kinds of poison gas. **step on the g.,** (*sl.*) accelerate, hurry. **g.-attack,** *n.* with poison gas. **gasbag,** *n.* balloon's gas container; empty talker. **g.-bracket,** *n.* pipe with burner projecting from wall. **g.-engine,** *n.* worked by explosions of gas. **g.-helmet, g.-mask,** *nn.* with respirator to protect from poison gas. **g.-meter,** *n.* for recording amount of gas consumed. **g.-oven, g.-ring,** *nn.* for cooking with gas. **g.-shell,** *n.* filled with poison gas. **g.-works,** *n.* for making gas. (coined word)

gasalier, same as **gaselier.**

Gascon, *n.* native of Gascony; braggart. **gasconade,** *n.* boasting.—*v.i.* brag.

gaselier, *n.* branched hanging support for gas lights. (imit. of *chandelier*)

gaseous, *a.* of, like, gas. **gaseity,** *n.*

gasfitter, *n.* mechanic who fits and repairs gas-pipes.

gash, *n.* gaping wound, slash; cleft. —*v.t.* cut deep. (O.F. *garser*)

gash, *a.* (*Scot.*) talkative; witty, shrewd.—*v.i.* tattle.

gash, *a.* (*Scot.*) ghastly, hideous.

gasify, *v.t.* and *i.* turn into gas **gasification,** *n.* (L. *facere*, make)

gasket, *n.* cord to tie sail to yard when furled; hemp, tow, for packing piston etc.

gaskins, same as **galligaskins.**

gasogene, same as **gazogene.**

gasoline, gasolene, *n.* a liquid got from petroleum; (*Amer.*) petrol.

gasometer, *n.* tank, vessel, for storing gas.

gasp, *v.i.* and *t.* catch breath convulsively; pant.—*n.* act of gasping. **at one's last g.,** dying; at the end of one's resources. **g. out,** utter with gasp. **gasper,** *n.* (*sl.*) cheap cigarette. (O.N. *geispa*, yawn)

gassy, *a.* full of, like, gas; windy, verbose.

gast, *v.t.* (*Shake.*) terrify. (O.E. *gæstan*)

gasteropod, *n.* shell-fish with disk-like foot under belly. **gasteropodous,** *a.* (Gk. *gastēr*, belly; *pous*, foot)

gastness, *n.* (*Shake.*) terror. (*gast*)

gastric, *a.* of stomach. **g. fever,** typhoid. **g. juice,** digestive fluid in stomach. (Gk. *gastēr*, belly)

gastr(o)-, from Gk. *gastēr*, belly. used in **gastralgia,** *n.* stomach-ache; **gastritis,** *n.* inflammation of stomach; **gastro-enteric,** *a.* of stomach and bowels; **gastrology,** *n.* science of cookery, hence **gastrologer, gastrologist,** *nn.*; **gastronome,** *n.* epicure; **gastronomy,** *n.* art of good eating, hence **gastronomer, gastronomist,** *nn.*, **gastronomic, gastronomical,** *aa.*; **gastropod,** same as **gasteropod.**

gat, *n.* channel, strait.

gat, *n.* (*sl.*) pistol, revolver.

gat, see **get.**

gata, *n.* kind of shark of tropical Atlantic.

gate, *n.* opening in wall, entrance; barrier closing this; sluice; gate-money.—*v.t.* confine (undergraduate) to college. **g.-crasher,** *n.* uninvited intruder. **g.-money,** *n.* sum taken for admission to sports-ground etc. **g.-post,** *n.* on which gate hangs. **gatehouse,** *n.* lodge; house over gate. **gateway,** *n.* frame of gate; passage-way. (O.E. *geat*)

gate, *n.* (*Scot.*) way, path; manner. (O.N. *gata*)

gâteau, *n.* (*pl.* *gâteaux*) cake. (F.)

gather, *v.t.* and *i.* bring, come, together; collect, cull; draw together, pucker; deduce; summon (up); form swelling full of pus.—*n.pl.* gathered-in part of dress. **g. breath,** have respite. **g. head,** gain strength. **g. way,** begin to move. **gatherer,** *n.* **gathering,** *n.* assemblage; abscess. (O.E. *gaderian*)

Gatling, *n.* (also **G. gun**) machine-gun with clustered barrels. (inventor)

gauche, *a.* awkward, uncouth; tactless. *gaucherie*, *n.* (F.)

gaucho, *n.* Spanish-Indian cowboy of S. American pampas. (Sp.)

gaucie, gaucy, *a.* (*Scot.*) jolly; large, stately.

gaud, *n.* piece of finery, trinket, toy; (*pl.*) gaieties.—*v.i.* (*Shake.*) adorn. **gaudery,** *n.* **gaudy,** *a.* vulgarly showy, tawdry.—*n.* feast; college reunion dinner. (L. *gaudēre*, rejoice)

gauffer, same as **goffer.**
gauge, *n.* standard measure; measuring instrument; criterion, test; capacity, extent; distance between rails of railway; (*naut.*) position with respect to wind.—*v.t.* take measure of, estimate; test. **have weather, lee, g. of,** be to windward, leeward, of. **gauger,** *n.* exciseman. (O.F.)
Gaul, *n.* old name for France; Frenchman. **Gaulish,** *a.* (L. *Gallia*)
gault, *n.* (*geol.*) clay beds between upper and lower greensand.
gaum, *v.t.* smear, daub.
gaun, *Scot.* form of going.
gaunt, *a.* lean; haggard.
gauntlet, *n.* steel glove; glove with long loose wrist. **throw down, take up, the g.,** offer, accept, challenge. **gauntleted,** *a.* (F. *gant*, glove)
gauntlet, *n.* **run the g.,** run between two lines of men who strike as one passes; undergo ordeal. (Swed. *gata*, lane; *lopp*, course)
gauntry, gauntree, same as **gantry.**
gaur, *n.* Indian wild ox. (Hind.)
gauss, *n.* (*electr.*) unit of density of magnetic field. (person)
gauze, *n.* thin transparent fabric of silk, wire etc. **gauzy,** *a.* (F. *gaze*)
gavage, *n.* forced feeding of poultry etc. (F.)
gave, see **give.**
gavel, *n.* small hammer of chairman or auctioneer.
gavel, *Scot.* form of gable.
gavelkind, *n.* (*law*) Kentish land-tenure by which all sons inherit equally. (O.E. *gafol*, tribute)
gavotte, *n.* old dance like minuet but livelier; music for it. (F.)
gawcie, gawcy, same as **gaucie.**
gawk, *n.* booby. **gawky,** *a.* awkward, clumsy; bashful.
gay, *a.* light-hearted, merry; showy, bright; wanton; (*Amer. sl.*) cheeky, fresh.—*adv.* (*Scot.*) gey. (F. *gai*)
gazabo, gazebo, *n.* (*Amer. sl.*) gawky person; guy, fellow. (Sp. *gazapo*, blunder)
gaze, *v.i.* look fixedly, stare.—*n.* intent look. **at g.,** in gazing attitude.
gazebo, see **gazabo.**
gazebo, *n.* balcony, summer-house etc., with wide view; belvedere.
gazelle, *n.* small graceful antelope with beautiful dark eyes. (Arab. *ghazal*)
gazette, *n.* newspaper, esp. official journal.—*v.t.* publish in this. **gazetteer,** *n.* geographical dictionary; (*obs.*) news-writer. (It. *gazetta*)
gazogene, *n.* apparatus for making soda-water. (*gas*)
geal, *a.* of the earth. (Gk. *gē*, earth)
gear, *n.* tackle, tools; dress, harness; connection by cogged wheels; (*Scot.*) goods, riches; (*Shake.*) stuff, thing, matter.—*v.t.* provide with, put in, gear. **high, low, g.,** by which driven part moves faster, slower, relatively to engine. **in, out of, g.,** with driving mechanism connected, disconnected. **g.-box, g.-case,** *nn.* enclosing gear of machine. **gearing,** *n.*
geason, *a.* (*Spens.*) rare, uncommon. (O.E. *gǽsne*, barren)
geck, *n.* fool; dupe.
geck, *v.i.* and *t.* (*Scot.*) toss head in scorn, deride.
gecko, *n.* wall-lizard. (Malay *gekoq*)
ged, *n.* (*Scot.*) pike.
gee, *int.* commanding horse to go on, go faster, or turn to off side.—*n.* (*colloq.*; also **g.-g.**) horse. **g.-ho, g.-up, g.-wo,** *intt.* commands to horse.
gee, *int.* (*Amer.*) a mild oath. (*Jesus*)
geese, see **goose.**
gee-whizz, geewhillikins, *intt.* (*Amer.*) of surprise or delight.
geezer, *n.* (*sl.*) old person, codger. (*guiser*)
gegg, *n.* (*Scot.*) trick.—*v.t.* hoax.
Gehenna, *n.* hell. (valley of *Hinnom*, where children were sacrificed)
geisha, *n.* Japanese dancing-girl. (Jap.)
geist, *n.* dominating principle (of age etc.); sensibility. (G.=spirit)
gel, *n.* a semi-solid colloidal solution. (*gelatine*)
gelatine, gelatin, *n.* animal jelly got by stewing skin, tendons etc. **g. paper,** (*phot.*) coated with sensitized gelatine. **gelatinate, gelatinize,** *vv.t.* and *i.* make, become, gelatine or jelly. **gelatinous,** *a.* of gelatine like jelly. (It. *gelata*, jelly)
gelation, *n.* solidification by cold. (L. *gelare*, freeze)
geld, *v.t.* castrate, emasculate; deprive (of). **gelding,** *n.* castrated horse. (O.N. *gelda*)
geld, *n.* tribute, tax. (O.E.)
gelid, *a.* ice-cold, icy; chilly. **gelidity** *n.* (L. *gelu*, frost)
gelignite, *n.* a nitro-glycerine explosive. (*gelatine*+L. *ignis*, fire)
gelotometer, *n.* gauge for measuring laughter. (Gk. *gelōs*, laughter)
gem, *n.* precious stone, jewel; treasure.—*v.t.* adorn with gems. (*gemma*)
Gemini, *n.* the Twins, 3rd sign of zodiac, which sun enters about 21 May; (*Shake.*) pair.—*int.* of surprise. **geminate,** *v.t.* double, repeat. —*a.* (*bot.*) set in pairs. **gemination,** *n.* (L.)
gemma, *n.* (*pl.* **gemmae**) leaf-bud; growth on animal or plant budding off as separate individual. **gemmate,** *v.i.* have buds; propagate by gemmae. —*a.* gemmiparous. **gemmation,** *n.* **gemmative,** *a.* **gemmiferous,** *a.* producing gemmae or gems. **gemmiparous,** *a.* propagating by gemmae. **gemmule,** *n.* point of growth of embryo; small gemma. (L.)
gemmy, *a.* covered with, like, gems.
gemot, gemote, *n.* assembly. (O.E.)
gemsbok, *n.* large straight-horned S. African antelope. (Du.)

gen, *n.* (*R.A.F. sl.*) information. (*genuine*)

genappe, *n.* smooth kind of worsted. (town)

gendarme, *n.* French armed policeman. *gendarmerie*, *n.* force of these. (F.)

gender, *n.* (*gram.*) classification by sex; (*joc.*) sex; (*Shake.*) kind, class.—*v.t.* (*poet.*) beget. (*genus*)

gene, *n.* hereditary factor, one from each parent, in germ-cell. (*genesis*)

genealogy, *n.* pedigree, lineage; study of family descent. **genealogical**, *a.* **genealogize**, *v.t.* and *i.* trace out descent (of). **genealogist**, *n.* (Gk. *genea*, race; *legein*, speak)

genera, see **genus**.

general, *a.* of whole, affecting all, not partial or particular or detailed; common, usual; miscellaneous.—*n.* commander of army, rank below Field Marshal; tactician; (*colloq.*) general servant; (*arch.*) general public. **g. election**, over whole country. **g. practitioner**, doctor treating cases of all kinds. **g. servant**, maid-of-all-work. **in g.**, for the most part; (*Shake.*) universally. (L. *generalis*)

generalissimo, *n.* commander of combined forces. (It.)

generality, *n.* generalness; general statement; majority (of).

generalize, *v.t.* and *i.* reduce to general laws; draw general conclusion; speak vaguely. **generalization**, *n.* general inference; induction.

generally, *adv.* on the whole, usually; (*Shake.*) as a whole, universally.

generalship, *n.* office of general; military skill; management.

generate, *v.t.* bring into being, produce; (*math.*) trace out. **generation**, *n.* procreation, production; people of same period, contemporaries; average gap between parents and children, about 30 years or ⅓ century; (*Shake.*) breed, offspring. **generative**, *a.* of procreation; productive. **generator**, *n.* begetter; apparatus making gas etc., dynamo. (L. *generare*, beget)

generic, *a.* of a genus or class; comprehensive. (*genus*)

generous, *a.* liberal, not mean; magnanimous, noble; ample, abundant, rich. **generosity**, *n.* (L. *generosus*)

genesis, *n.* origin, generation; first book of the Bible. (Gk.)

genet, *n.* animal like civet-cat; its fur. (Arab. *jarnait*)

genethliac, *a.* of birthday or nativity.—*n.* birthday poem; (*pl.*) art of casting horoscopes. (Gk. *genethlē*, birth)

genetic, *a.* of, concerning, origin.—*n.pl.* science of heredity, art of breeding. (*genesis*)

geneva, *n.* spirit flavoured with juniper berries, Hollands. (L. *juniperus*, juniper)

genial, *a.* kindly, cordial, sociable; (of climate) healthful, mild; nuptial. **geniality**, *n.* (L. *genialis*)

genial, *a.* (*anat.*) of the chin. (Gk. *geneion*, chin)

geniculate, **geniculated**, *aa.* having knee-like joints. (L. *genu*, knee)

genie, *n.* (*pl.* genii) Arabian sprite, jinnee. (*genius*)

genii, see **genius**.

genista, *n.* kinds of yellow-flowered shrub. (L.)

genital, *a.* of generation.—*n.pl.* external sexual organs. (L. *gignere*, beget)

genitive, *a.* and *n.* (*gram.*) possessive (case). **genitival**, *a.* (L. *genitivus*, of generation, mistranslation of Gk. *genikos*, of class)

genius, *n.* (*pl.* geniuses) natural bent, animating spirit; exceptional inborn power or aptitude; person so gifted; (*pl.* genii) spirit watching over destinies of man or place. (L.)

gennet, (*Shake.*) form of jennet.

genre, *n.* kind, style; realistic (painting) of everyday scenes. (F.)

Genro, *n.pl.* Elder Statesmen of Japan. (Jap.=old men)

gens, *n.* (*pl.* ***gentes***) ancient Roman clan. (L.)

gent, *vulg.* for gentleman.

gent, *a.* (*Spens.*) noble. (*gentle*)

genteel, *a.* well-bred, refined; elegant, stylish. (F. *gentil*)

gentian, *n.* a bitter herb used as tonic. (*Gentius*, king of Illyria)

gentile, *a.* and *n.* non-Jewish (person); heathen: gentilitial. **gentiledom**, *n.* **gentilitial**, *a.* of a family, clan, or country. (*gens*)

gentility, *n.* gentle birth; genteelness, social superiority. (*genteel*)

gentle, *a.* mild, amiable, kind; moderate, gradual; (*arch.*) noble, well-born.—*n.* larva of bluebottle; (*pl.*) gentlefolk.—*v.t.* tame (horse). **g. craft**, angling or shoemaking. **g. passion**, love. **gentlefolk**, *n.* people of good family. **gentlehood**, *n.* position or character attaching to gentle birth. (O.F. *gentil*)

gentleman, *n.* (*pl.* gentlemen) well-bred man; man of good social position; (*arch.*) man who has coat of arms but no title; (*pl.*) public urinal. **g.'s agreement**, binding in honour, not legal. **g.'s g.**, valet. **old g.**, the devil. **g.-at-arms**, *n.* one of sovereign's bodyguard. **gentlemanlike**, **gentlemanly**, *aa.* like, befitting, a gentleman.

gentlewoman, *n.* well-bred woman, lady. **gentlewomanhood**, *n.* **gentlewomanlike**, **gentlewomanly**, *aa.*

gently, *adv.* mildly, kindly; softly, slowly. **g. born**, well-born.

gentoo, *n.* Hindu as opp. to Mohammedan. (Port. *gentio*, gentile)

gentry, *n.* class next below nobility; persons; (*Shake.*) nobility, courtesy.

genual, *a.* of the knee. **genuflect,** *v.i.* bend knee in worship. **genuflexion,** *n.* **genuflectory,** *a.* (L. *genu*, knee; *flectere*, bend)

genuine, *a.* authentic, real, true, sincere; pure-bred. (L. *genuinus*)

genus, *n.* (*pl.* **genera**) group (of animals etc.) with common characteristics, us. comprising several species; class, order, kind. (L.)

geocentric, *a.* (*astron.*) seen, measured, from the earth; having the earth as centre. (Gk. *gē*, earth)

geode, *n.* cavity lined with crystals; stone containing this. **geodic,** *a.* (Gk. *geōdēs*, earthlike)

geodesy, *n.* science of measuring the earth or large part of it. **geodesic, geodetic, geodetical,** *aa.* **geodesist,** *n.* (Gk. *gē*, earth; *daiein*, divide)

geognosy, *n.* geology, esp. of a district or particular rocks. **geognostic, geognostical,** *aa.* (Gk. *gē*, earth; *gnōsis*, knowledge)

geogony, *n.* science of the earth's formation. **geogonic,** *a.* (Gk. *gē*, earth; *gonē*, generation)

geography, *n.* science of the earth's surface, climate, peoples etc.; book on this. **geographer,** *n.* one versed in, writer on, geography. **geographic, geographical,** *aa.* (Gk. *gē*, earth; *graphein*, write)

geology, *n.* science of earth's crust, rocks, strata etc. **geologist,** *n.* **geologic, geological,** *aa.* **geologize,** *v.i.* and *t.* study geology (of). (Gk. *gē*, earth; *legein*, speak)

geomancy, *n.* divination by random casting of loose earth or blindfold marking of lines. **geomancer,** *n.* **geomantic,** *a.* (Gk. *gē*, earth; *manteia*, divination)

geometry, *n.* science of the properties and relations of lines, surfaces, and solids; book on this. **geometer, geometrician,** *nn.* one versed in geometry. **geometric, geometrical,** *aa.* **geometrize,** *v.i.* and *t.* work, make, by geometrical methods. (Gk. *gē*, earth; *metron*, measure)

geophagy, *n.* eating earth. **geophagist,** *n.* earth-eater. **geophagous,** *a.* (Gk. *gē*, earth; *phagein*, eat)

geophysics, *n.* the physics of the earth. **geophysical,** *a.* **geophysicist,** *n.*

geopolitics, *n.pl.* study of relationship between geographical situation of a nation and its politics.

geoponic, *a.* agricultural.—*n.pl.* husbandry. (Gk. *gē*, earth; *ponos*, toil)

Geordie, *n.* collier, coal-boat.

George, *n.* figure of St. George. **St. G.'s day,** 23 April. **St. G.'s cross,** of upright and horizontal red bars.

georgette, *n.* a silk fabric. (name)

Georgian, *a.* of the times of the four Georges (1714–1830) or of George V (1910–36).—*n.* inhabitant of Georgia in U.S.A. or Georgia in Caucasus.

Georgic, *n.* poem in husbandry, esp. one of Virgil's. (Gk. *gē*, earth; *ergon*, work)

geoselenic, *a.* concerning the earth and moon in their relations. (Gk. *gē*, earth; *selēnē*, moon)

geotropism, *n.* (*bot.*) tendency of roots etc. to grow downward. **negative g.,** opposite tendency of stems. **geotropic,** *a.* (Gk. *gē*, earth; *trepein*, turn)

geranium, *n.* plant with seed-vessel like crane's bill; pelargonium. (Gk. *geranos*, crane)

gerent, *n.* ruler, manager. (L. *gerere*, administer)

gerfalcon, *n.* large northern falcon. (O.F. *gerfaucon*)

germ, *n.* rudimentary form of organism, seed; origin, source; microbe. (*germen*)

German, *a.* and *n.* (inhabitant, language) of Germany. **G. measles,** disease like mild measles. **G. Ocean,** North Sea. **G. silver,** white alloy of nickel etc. **G. text,** black letter. **High G.,** dialect of S. Germany, now in general literary use. **Low G.,** other German dialects. (L. *Germanus*)

german, *a.* of same parents; germane. **cousin g.,** first cousin. (L. *germanus*)

germander, *n.* kinds of wild plant. (Gk. *chamai*, on ground; *drus*, oak)

germane, *a.* relevant, pertinent. (= *german*)

Germanic, *a.* of Germans; Teutonic. **germanism,** *n.* German word or idiom. **Germanity,** *n.* German characteristics. **germanize,** *v.t.* and *i.* make, become, German in manners etc. **Germanomania,** *n.* mania for German ways. **Germanophil, Germanophilist,** *n.* lover of Germany. **Germanophobia,** *n.* fear of Germany. **Germanophobe,** *n.*

germen, *n.* ovary; germ. (L.)

germicide, *n.* substance for killing microbes. **germicidal,** *a.* (L. *caedere*, kill)

germinal, *a.* of germs; incipient.

germinate, *v.i.* and *t.* begin to grow, sprout; produce. **germinant,** *a.* developing. **germination, germinator,** *nn.* **germinative,** *a.* (*germen*)

germon, *n.* long-finned tunny.

gerontocracy, *n.* government by old men. (Gk. *gerōn*, old man; *kratos*, power)

gerrymander, *v.t.* manipulate unfairly; divide (electoral district) so as to favour one party. **gerrymanderer,** *n.* (Governor *Gerry* of Massachusetts)

gerund, *n.* kind of verbal noun. **gerundial,** *a.* **gerundive,** *a.* of, like, gerund.—*n.* verbal adjective expressing necessity. (L. *gerundium*)

gesso, *n.* gypsum, plaster of Paris. (It.)

gest, *n.* (*arch.*) gesture, bearing. (L. *gerere*, bear)

gest, *n.* (*arch.*) deed, exploit; medieval romance. (L. *gerere*, bear)

gest, *n.* (*Shake.*) time for halt on journey. (O.F. *giste*) *gestalt*, **n.** (*psychol.*) integral pattern or system of phenomena forming functional unit. (G.)

Gestapo, n. Nazi secret police. (G. *geheime Staatspolizei*, secret state police)

gestation, n. act, period, of carrying young in womb. (L. *gerere*, bear)

geste, same as gest.

gesticulate, v.i. and *t.* make gestures or expressive motions; express thus. **gesticulation, gesticulator, nn. gesticulatory, a.** (*gesture*)

gesture, n. movement of hands etc. expressing feeling; significant move, friendly advance.—*v.i.* gesticulate. (L. *gerere*, bear)

get, *v.t.* (*past* **got,** *arch.* **gat;** *p.p.* **got, gotten**) obtain, gain, win; learn; suffer, experience; catch, corner; cause to be; induce; beget; receive sentence of; (*sl.*) understand.—*v.i.* become; go, reach, attain; (in *perfect* **have got**) have, be bound (to). —*n.* begetting, offspring. **g. across,** (*sl.*) be effective. **g. along,** succeed; fare. **g. at,** reach; (*sl.*) mean; (*sl.*) attack, banter. **g. away with,** do with impunity. **g. back,** recover; return. **g. down,** descend, dismount. **g. in,** enter; collect. **g. it,** (*sl.*) be punished. **g. off,** alight; escape; doff; procure acquittal of; (*sl.*) make acquaintance. **g. on,** mount; don; prosper; agree. **g. on to,** (*Amer.*) understand. **g. out,** disengage; elicit; go away, escape. **g. over,** surmount; recover from. **g. round,** circumvent, cajole. **g. the best, worst, of it,** be victorious, vanquished. **g. there,** be successful. **g. together,** collect. **g. up,** organize; dress, prepare; rise. **g. with child,** impregnate. **g.-at-able,** *a.* accessible. **g.-up,** *n.* style; format. **getable,** *a.* **getaway,** *n.* (*Amer. sl.*) escape. **getter,** *n.* (O.N. *geta*)

geum, n. kinds of plant, avens. (L.)

gewgaw, n. showy trifle, bauble, toy.

gey, *adv.* (*Scot.*) very, considerably. (=*gay*)

geyser, n. intermittent hot spring; bathroom water-heater. (*Geysir*, hot spring in Iceland)

gharry, n. (*Anglo-Ind.*) horse-vehicle like bathing-machine. (Hind. *gāṛī*)

ghastly, a. deathlike, pale; hideous, frightful; (*sl.*) unpleasant. (O.E. *gæstan*, terrify)

ghat, ghaut, n. mountain pass or chain; landing-place with steps. **burning-g., n.** place near river ghat where Hindus burn their dead. (Hind.)

Ghazi, n. warrior champion, title of Turkish ruler; Mohammedan fanatic slayer of infidels. (Arab.)

ghee, n. buffalo-milk butter clarified by boiling. (Hind. *ghi*)

gherkin, n. small cucumber used for pickling. (Du. *agurkje*)

ghetto, n. (*pl.* **ghettos, ghetti**) Jewish quarter of town. (It.)

ghost, n. apparition of dead person, spectre; spirit, soul; shadow, faint image; one who does literary or artistic work for another person who takes the credit; (*Shake.*) corpse. **give up the g.,** die. **Holy G.,** the Divine Spirit. **the g. walks,** (*theatre sl.*) salaries are paid. **g.-word, n.** one based on misreading or misprint, e.g. 'helpmeet.' **ghosthood, n. ghostly, a.** of a ghost, spectral; spiritual, religious. (O.E. *gást*)

ghoul, n. fabled demon feeding on corpses; fiend. **ghoulish, a.** (Arab. *ghul*)

ghyll, same as **gill.**

giallo antico, golden-yellow marble of Italian ruins. (It.)

giant, n. (*fem.* **giantess**) huge being of human shape; person, animal etc. of great size or powers.—*a.* gigantic. **g.'s-stride, n.** pole with ropes by which holder can take huge strides round it. (Gk. *gigas*)

giaour, n. infidel, Turkish term for Christian. (Pers. *gaur*)

gib, n. pin, wedge.

gib, n. (*Shake.*) tom cat. (*Gilbert*)

gibber, v.i. speak fast and inarticulately.—*n.* chatter. **gibberish, n.** meaningless words. (imit.)

gibber, n. (*Austral.*) stone, boulder. (native)

gibbet, n. gallows; post on which bodies of executed criminals were hung.—*v.t.* hang on gibbet; hold up to public scorn. (O.F. *gibe*, club)

gibbon, n. a long-armed ape. (F.)

gibbous, a. protuberant, humped; (of moon) between full and half-full. **gibbosity, n.** (L. *gibbus*, hump)

gibe, jibe, v.i. and *t.* jeer, scoff (at).—*n.* taunt, sneer. **giber, jiber, n.**

giblets, n.pl. edible entrails of fowl. (O.F. *gibelet*)

gibus. n. opera hat. (maker)

gid, n. staggers in sheep, sturdy.

giddy, a. dizzy, inclined to fall; causing dizziness; flighty, frivolous. —*v.t.* and *i.* make, become, giddy. **giddiness, n.** (O.E. *gydig*, mad)

gie, *Scot.* form of **give.**

gif, *obs.* form of **if.**

gift, n. thing given, present; natural talent; giving.—*v.t.* bestow; endow (with). **look g.-horse in the mouth,** criticize present. **gifted, a.** talented. (*give*)

gig, n. kind of fish-spear. (Sp. *fisga*, harpoon)

gig, n. light two-wheeled carriage; long light boat; (*Shake.*) whipping-top. **g.-lamps, n.pl.** (*sl.*) spectacles. **g.-mill, n.** machine for raising nap on cloth.

gigantic, a. giant-like, immense, huge; **gigantesque, a.** as if by a giant. **gigantomachy, n.** war of giants. (Gk. *gigas*, giant)

giggle, *n.* half-suppressed laugh, titter. —*v.i.* utter this. **giggler,** *n.* (imit.)
giglet, giglot, *n.* giddy girl; (*Shake.*) wanton woman.
gigman, *n.* narrow middle-class Philistine. **gigmanity,** *n.* (keeps a *gig*)
gigolo, *n.* professional male dancing-partner. (F.)
gigot, *n.* leg of mutton. (F.)
gigue, *n.* a lively tune, jig. (F.)
gila monster, orange-and-black venomous American lizard. (*Gila* river)
Gilbertian, *a.* grotesquely farcical, topsyturvy. (like play of W. S. *Gilbert*)
gild, see **guild.**
gild, *v.t.* overlay thinly with gold; tinge with gold colour; gloss over. **gilded spurs,** knighthood. **gilded youth,** young men of fashion. **gilder,** *n.* **gilding,** *n.* gilt surface. (*gold*)
gill, *n.* breathing-organ of fish; fowl's wattle; flesh about chin or jaws.—*v.t.* gut (fish).
gill, *n.* quarter-pint liquid measure. (L.L. *gillo*)
gill, *n.* glen, ravine; torrent in this. (O.N. *gil*)
gill, *n.* girl, wench; ground-ivy. (*Gillian,* name)
gillaroo, *n.* Irish trout. (Ir. *giolla,* fellow; *ruadh,* red)
gillie, gilly, *n.* attendant on highland chief or sportsman. (Gael. *gille*)
gillyflower, (*Shake.*) **gillyvor,** *n.* stock, clove-scented pink etc. (Gk. *karuon,* nut; *phullon,* leaf)
gilpy, gilpey, *n.* (*Scot.*) lively, boisterous, boy or girl.
gilt, *a.* covered with, yellow like, gold.—*n.* gilding. **g.-edged,** *a.* (of stocks etc.) offering best security. (*gild*)
gimbals, *n.pl.* pivoted rings to keep compass etc. level at sea. (L. *gemelli,* twins)
gimcrack, *a.* showy but worthless, trumpery.—*n.* toy, gewgaw. **gimcrackery,** *n.* **gimcracky,** *a.*
gimlet, *n.* small tool with pointed screw for boring. (O.F. *guimbelet*)
gimmal, gimmer, *nn.* (*Shake.*) connecting part in clockwork, contrivance. (L. *gemellus,* twin)
gimmer, *n.* two-year-old ewe. (O.N. *gymbr,* ewe lamb one year old)
gimp, *n.* trimming of silk or cotton woven round cord.
gin, *n.* spirit flavoured with juniper berries. **g.-palace, g.-shop,** *nn.* low public-house. **g.-sling,** *n.* cold drink of sweetened gin. (*geneva*)
gin, *n.* trap, snare; windlass; machine to separate seeds from cotton.—*v.t.* clear (cotton) thus. (*engine*)
gin, *n.* Australian native woman. (native)
gin, *conj.* (*Scot.*) if.
gin, *v.i.* (*Shake.*; *past* **gan**) begin. (O.E. *ginnan*)
ging, same as **gang.**
gingall, same as **jingall.**
ginger, *n.* a tropical plant; its hot spicy root; (*sl.*) spirit, mettle.—*a.* light red.—*v.t.* flavour with ginger; rouse (up), stimulate. **g. wine,** alcoholic drink, **g.-ale, g.-beer, g.-pop,** aerated drinks, **g.-nut, g.-snap,** kinds of biscuit, **gingerbread,** dark-coloured cake, flavoured with ginger. **take gilt off gingerbread,** destroy illusion. (Sanskr. *crnga,* horn; *vera,* body)
gingerly, *adv.* cautiously, avoiding noise or injury.—*a.* wary, dainty.
gingham, *n.* kind of cotton cloth, us. with check pattern.—*n.* (*colloq.*) umbrella. (Malay *ginggang,* striped)
gingival, *a.* of the gums. **gingivitis,** *n.* inflammation of the gums. (L. *gingiva,* gum)
ginglymus, *n.* (*anat.*) joint like hinge. (Gk. *gingglumos,* hinge)
gink, *n.* (*Amer. sl.*) chap, fellow.
ginkgo, *n.* Japanese tree with fan-shaped leaves. (Chin. *yin,* silver; *hing,* apricot)
ginnery, *n.* (*S. Afr.*) cotton factory. (*gin*)
ginseng, *n.* a Chinese plant; its root, used as medicine. (Chin. *jên shên*)
gippo, *n.* (*army sl.*) soup, stew.
gipsy, gypsy, *n.* one of a wandering race of Hindu origin; Romany; dark-complexioned person; sly woman. **g. bonnet,** with large side flaps. **g. rose,** scabious. **g. wagon,** caravan. **gipsydom, gypsydom,** *n.* gipsy world. **gipsyfy, gypsyfy,** *v.t.* make like gipsy. **gipsyhood, gypsyhood,** *n.* (*Egyptian*)
giraffe, *n.* long-necked spotted African quadruped, camelopard. (Arab. *zarifah*)
girandole, *n.* branched chandelier; revolving firework or water-jet; pendant with small stones round large one. (Gk. *guros,* circle)
girasol, girasole, *n.* fire-opal. (L. *gyrare,* turn round; *sol,* sun)
gird, *v.t.* (*past, p.p.* **girded, girt**) put belt round; clothe (with); put (sword on); encircle. **g.** (**up**) **one's loins,** prepare for action. (O.E. *gyrdan*)
gird, *v.i.* and *n.* gibe, taunt.
girder, *n.* beam supporting joists; beam, latticed structure, forming span. (*gird*)
girdle, *n.* belt, waistband; thing that surrounds; (*anat.*) bony support of limb.—*v.t.* surround with girdle; remove ring of bark from (tree). (O.E. *gyrdel*)
girdle, *Scot.* form of **griddle.**
girl, *n.* female child; young woman; maidservant. (**best**) **g.,** sweetheart. **G. Guides,** organization like Boy Scouts. **girlhood,** *n.* **girlie,** *n.* little girl. **girlish,** *a.* of, like, a girl.
girn, *v.i.* (*Scot.*) snarl, grumble. **girny,** *a.* bad-tempered. (*grin*)
girr, *n.* (*Scot.*) iron hoop.

girt, see **gird**.
girth, *n.* belly-band of saddle; measurement round thing.—*v.t.* surround, secure, with girth. (O.N. *georth*)
gist, *n.* main point, substance, pith. (O.F. *gésir*, lie)
gitana, *n.* Spanish gipsy woman. (Sp.)
gittern, same as **cithern**.
giust, *obs.* form of **joust**.
give, *v.t.* (*past* **gave**, *p.p.* **given**) bestow, deliver, present, grant, impart; utter; pledge; devote.—*v.i.* make gifts; yield; open (upon).—*n.* elasticity. **g. and take**, mutual concession. **g. away**, betray; give in marriage. **g. birth to**, bring forth. **g. chase**, pursue. **g. ear**, listen. **g. forth**, emit, publish. **g. ground**, fall back. **g. him best**, admit defeat. **g. in**, yield. **g. it him**, (*sl.*) punish him. **g. off**, emit. **g. out**, report; emit; fail, be used up. **g. over**, surrender; desist. **g. place**, retire. **g. rise to**, result in. **g. tongue**, bay. **g. up**, abandon; devote; cease from; pronounce insoluble. **g. way**, withdraw; yield, break down; begin to row. **giveaway**, *n.* (*Amer.*) unwitting disclosure. **given**, *a.* addicted; stated. **giver**, *n.* donor. (O.E. *giefan*)
gizz, *n.* (*Scot.*) wig.
gizzard, *n.* muscular grinding stomach of bird etc. **fret one's g.**, worry. (O.F. *gezier*)
glabrous, *a.* without hair, smooth-skinned. (L. *glaber*, smooth)
glacé, *a.* smooth and glossy; (of cake) iced.
glacial, *a.* of, caused by, ice; icy; (*chem.*) crystallized. **g. epoch**, when Europe was covered with ice-sheet. **glaciate**, *v.t.* cover, abrade, polish, with ice. **glaciation**, *n.* (L. *glacies*, ice)
glacier, *n.* slowly moving river or mass of ice. **glaciered**, *a.* (F.)
glacis, *n.* sloping bank in front of fort. (F.)
glad, *a.* pleased, happy; joyful; gay. —*v.t.* gladden. **g. eye**, (*sl.*) flirtatious look. **g. hand**, welcome. **g. rags**, (*Amer. sl.*) dress clothes. **gladden**, *v.t.* make glad. (O.E. *glæd*)
glade, *n.* grassy open space or passage in wood.
gladiate, *a.* sword-shaped. (L. *gladius*, sword)
gladiator, *n.* professional fighter in Roman arena. **gladiatorial**, *a.* (L.)
gladiolus, *n.* (*pl.* **gladioluses, gladioli**) kind of iris, sword-lily. (L.)
gladsome, *a.* glad, joyful, gay.
Gladstone, *n.* (also **G. bag**) kind of light travelling-bag. (statesman)
glaikit, *a.* (*Scot.*) giddy, foolish.
glair, *n.* white of egg; size made from it; sticky substance.—*v.t.* smear with glair. **glaireous, glairy**, *aa.* (F. *glaire*)
glaive, *n.* broadsword; kind of halberd. (O.F.)
glamour, *n.* enchantment; delusive charm, witchery. — *v.t.* fascinate. **glamorous**, *a.* (corrupt. of *grammar*)
glance, *v.i.* and *t.* glide off obliquely; give brief look (at); allude in passing; dart ray.—*n.* glimpse, quick look; flash, gleam; glancing movement. **glancingly**, *adv.*
glance, *n.* lustrous ore. (G. *glanz*, brightness)
gland, *n.* secreting organ of body; secreting cell of plant. **glanders**, *n.pl.* contagious disease of mucous membrane in horses. **glandered, glanderous**, *aa.* (L. *glans*, acorn)
glandiferous, *a.* bearing acorns. **glandiform**, *a.* shaped like an acorn or gland. (*gland*)
glandular, glandulous, *aa.* of, having, glands. **glandule**, *n.* small gland.
glare, *v.i.* and *t.* shine dazzlingly; be over-conspicuous; stare fiercely; express (hate etc.) by look.—*n.* strong oppressive light; showiness. **glaring**, *a.* gaudy; grossly evident. **glary**, *a.* (M.E.)
glass, *n.* transparent brittle substance; articles of this; tumbler or its contents, drink; hour-glass, mirror, telescope, microscope, barometer; (*pl.*) spectacles.—*v.t.* mirror; make glassy. **g. eye**, false eye of glass. **g.-blower**, *n.* one who blows and shapes glass. **g.-house**, *n.* greenhouse. **g.-paper**, *n.* coated with powdered glass for polishing. **g.-snake**, *n.* American lizard with brittle tail. **glassy**, *a.* like glass, smooth; (of eye) dull. (O.E. *glæs*)
Glaswegian, *a.* and *n.* (inhabitant) of Glasgow.
Glauber's salt or salts, sulphate of sodium, used as aperient. (chemist)
glaucoma, *n.* an eye disease. **glaucomatous**, *a.* (Gk. *glaukōma*)
glaucous, *a.* sea-green; (*bot.*) covered with bloom. (Gk. *glaukos*)
glaum, *v.i.* and *t.* and *n.* (*Scot.*) grasp clutch (at).
glaur, *n.* (*Scot.*) soft mud, mire. (*glair*)
glaze, *v.i.* (*Shake.*) glare, stare.
glaze, *v.t.* and *i.* fit with glass or windows; overlay with glassy film or transparent colour; make, become, glossy.—*n.* glassy coating; glossy surface. **glazed frost**, silver thaw. **glazer**, *n.* **glazier**, *n.* one who glazes windows. **glaziery**, *n.* (*glass*)
gleam, *n.* faint or fitful light; slight or passing show.—*v.i.* emit gleam, glow. **gleamy**, *a.* (O.E. *glǽm*)
glean, *v.i.* and *t.* gather corn left by reapers; pick up, scrape together. **gleaner**, *n.* (O.F. *glener*)
glebe, *n.* earth, soil, field; land going with benefice. (L. *gleba*)
glede, *n.* kite. (O.E. *glida*)
glee, *n.* lively delight, mirth; (*mus.*) unaccompanied song for three or more voices. **gleeful**, *a.* (O.E. *gléo*)

gleed, *n.* hot coal. (O.E. *glēd*)
gleek, *n.* and *v.i.* (*Shake.*) gibe, jest.
gleeman, *n.* minstrel. **gleesome,** *a.* gleeful. (*glee*)
gleet, *n.* thin morbid discharge, esp. from urethra. (O.F. *glette,* slime)
gleg, *a.* (*Scot.*) sharp, quick, clever.
glen, *n.* narrow valley. (Gael. *gleann*)
glengarry, *n.* boat-shaped highland cap.
Glenlivet, *n.* a Scotch whisky. (places)
gley, *v.i.* (*Scot.*) squint. **gleyed,** *a.* squint-eyed.
glib, *a.* fluent, voluble, plausible; smooth.—*adv.* glibly.
glib, *v.t.* (*Shake.*) geld.
glide, *v.i.* pass smoothly and continuously; go gently or stealthily; volplane.—*n.* gliding movement; (*mus.*) slur. **glider,** *n.* engineless aeroplane. (O.E. *glīdan*)
gliff, *n.* (*Scot.*) moment; scare.
glim, *n.* (*sl.*) light, candle.
glimmer, *v.i.* shine feebly, blink.—*n.* glimmering. **glimmering,** *n.* faint gleam; glimpse, inkling.
glimpse, *n.* brief view; faint light; slight trace.—*v.t.* and *i.* catch glimpse of; see, appear, faintly. (M.E. *glymsen*)
glint, *v.i.* and *t.* glance, glitter; reflect; (*Scot.*) pass quickly.—*n.* gleam, shine.
glisk, *n.* (*Scot.*) glimpse. (O.E. *glisian,* glance)
glissade, *n.* and *v.i.* slide down steep snow-slope; (*dancing*) sliding step. (F. *glisser,* slip)
glisten, *v.i.* and *n.* gleam, glitter, sparkle. (O.E. *glisnian*)
glister, *v.i.* and *n.* (*arch.*) sparkle, glitter. (O.E. *glisian*)
glitter, *v.i.* sparkle, glisten; shine, be showy.—*n.* lustre, brilliance.
gloaming, *n.* (*Scot.*) evening twilight. (O.E. *glóm*)
gloat, *v.i.* gaze on with triumph, lust, or avarice. **gloatingly,** *adv.*
globe, *n.* sphere, ball; earth; sphere with map of earth or heavens; round vessel; eyeball.—*v.t.* and *i.* make, become, globular. **g.-fish,** *n.* one that can swell out into globular form. **g.-flower,** *n.* plant with round yellow flowers. **g.-lightning,** *n.* fireball. **g.-trotter,** *n.* hasty sightseeing traveller. **global,** *a.* taking in whole group of classes etc. **globoid,** *a.* and *n.* nearly globular (figure). **globose,** *a.* **globosity,** *n.* **globular,** *a.* spherical; made of globules. **globule,** *n.* small globe; drop, pellet; blood corpuscle. **globulin,** *n.* a proteid found in blood. (L. *globus*)
glochidiate, *a.* (*bot.*) bearing barbs. (Gk. *glōchis,* arrowhead)
glockenspiel, *n.* instrument of flat metal bars played with mallet; carillon. (G.=bell-play)
glode, *Spens.* form of glided.
glomerate, *a.* (*bot.*) compactly clustered. **glomerule,** *n.* clustered flower-head. (L. *glomus,* ball)
gloom, *n.* partial darkness, obscurity; melancholy, depression.—*v.i.* and *t.* be sullen; frown, lour; darken, make dismal. **gloomy,** *a.* dark, dismal; depressing; morose, sad.
gloria, *n.* aureole. *G. in excelsis,* Glory be to God on high, 'greater doxology.' *G. Patri,* Glory be to the Father, 'lesser doxology.' (L.)
glory, *n.* renown, fame; source of pride; splendour, magnificence; adoring praise; heavenly bliss; halo.—*v.i.* take pride (in). **go to g.,** die. **g.-hole,** *n.* lumber-room. **glorify,** *v.t.* make glorious; shed radiance on; exalt, extol. **glorification,** *n.* **gloriole,** *n.* aureole. **glorious,** *a.* illustrious; conferring renown; resplendent; very delightful; (*colloq.*) tipsily happy. (L. *gloria*)
gloss, *n.* lustre, polish; fair outside.—*v.t.* glaze; make plausible, palliate.
gloss, *n.* marginal explanation, comment; glossary.—*v.t.* and *i.* write glosses (on), annotate. (Gk. *glōssa,* tongue)
glossal, *a.* (*anat.*) of the tongue. (Gk. *glōssa,* tongue)
glossary, *n.* vocabulary of special or technical words. **glossarial,** *a.* **glossarist,** *n.* **glossator,** *n.* commentator. (*gloss*)
gloss(o)-, from Gk. *glōssa,* tongue, used in **glossitis,** *n.* inflammation of the tongue; **glossographer,** *n.* scholiast; **glossography,** *n.* making of glossaries, description of the tongue. **glossology,** *n.* terminology, science of language.
glossy, *a.* shiny, polished.
glottis, *n.* opening at top of windpipe. **glottal, glottic,** *aa.* **glottology,** *n.* glossology. (Gk.)
glove, *n.* hand-covering with sheath for each finger; (also **boxing-g.**) padded glove for boxing.—*v.t.* provide with gloves. **fit like a g.,** fit exactly. **throw down, take up, the g.,** make, accept, challenge. **g.-fight,** *n.* with gloves, opp. to prize-fight with bare fists. **glover,** *n.* glove-maker. (O.E. *glóf*)
glow, *v.i.* give out light and heat without flame, shine; feel, look, hot; be animated.—*n.* incandescence; warmth of colour, redness; ardour. **g.-worm,** *n.* female insect giving out green light. (O.E. *glowan*)
glower, *v.i.* and *n.* scowl, glare.
gloxinia, *n.* tropical plant with bell-shaped flowers. (B. P. *Gloxin*)
gloze, *v.i.* and *t.* use fair words, flatter; extenuate; comment (upon). (F. *glose,* gloss)
glucinum, *n.* white metallic element, beryllium. (Gk. *glukus,* sweet)
glucose, *n.* grape-sugar, dextrose. **glucosic,** *a.* (Gk. *glukus,* sweet)
glue, *n.* coarse gelatine used as adhesive.—*v.t.* stick with glue; attach tightly. **gluey,** *a.* (L.L. *glus*)

glum, *a.* moody, sullen. (*gloom*)
glume, *n.* bract of grasses, husk. **glumaceous, glumose,** *aa.* (L. *gluma*)
glunch, *v.i.* and *n.* (*Scot.*) frown.
glut, *v.t.* feed to the full, gorge; overstock.—*n.* surfeit; over-supply.
gluten, *n.* sticky substance; viscid part of dough. **glutinous,** *a.* sticky, gluey. **glutinosity,** *n.* (L=glue)
glutton, *n.* one who overeats; person greedy (for work etc.); wolverine. **gluttonize,** *v.i.* gormandize. **gluttony,** *n.* (L. *glutire,* swallow)
glycerine, glycerin, *n.* sweet colourless liquid got from oils. **glyceric,** *a.* **glyceride** *n.* an ester of glycerol. **glycerinate,** *v.t.* treat with glycerine. **glycerol,** *n.* (*chem.*) glycerine. (Gk. *glukeros,* sweet)
glycogen, *n.* animal starch. **glycogenic,** *a.* (Gk. *glukus,* sweet)
glyconic, *a.* and *n.* (verse) of three trochees and a dactyl. (*Glycon,* poet)
glycosuria, *n.* disease with sugar in urine. **glycosuric,** *a.* (F. *glycose,* glucose. Gk. *ouron,* urine)
glyph, *n.* (*arch.*) fluting. **glyphograph,** *n.* an engraving in relief for printing, made by electrotype. **glyphographer, glyphography,** *nn.* **glyphographic,** *a.* (Gk. *gluphein,* carve; *graphein,* write)
glyptic, *a.* of carving.—*n.pl.* art of gem-engraving. **glyptodon,** *n.* giant extinct armadillo with fluted teeth. **glyptography,** *n.* glyptics. (Gk. *gluphein,* carve)
gnar, gnarr, gnarl, *v.i.* snarl. (imit.)
gnarled, gnarly, *aa.* knobby, twisted, rugged. (*knurl*)
gnash, *v.i.* and *t.* grind (teeth) together.
gnat, *n.* small winged insect, mosquito. **gnatty,** *a.* (O.E. *gnæt*)
gnathic, *a.* of jaws. (Gk. *gnathos,* jaw)
gnaw, *v.t.* and *i.* (*p.p.* **gnawed, gnawn**) bite persistently; wear away by this; corrode, pain. (O.E. *gnagan*)
gneiss, *n.* stratified rock of quartz, feldspar, and mica. **gneissic, gneissoid, gneissy,** *aa.* (G.)
gnome, *n.* aphorism, maxim. **gnomic,** *a.* didactic, sententious. (Gk.)
gnome, *n.* small earth-spirit guarding mines; goblin, dwarf. **gnomish,** *a.*
gnomon, *n.* pin of sun-dial, style; (*geom.*) part of parallelogram left when similar one is taken from its corner. **gnomonic,** *a.*—*n.pl.* art of dialling. (Gk.)
gnosis, *n.* higher knowledge; mysticism. **gnostic,** *a.* of, having, gnosis. —*n.* one of early Christian sect seeking salvation by knowledge, not faith. **gnosticism,** *n.* doctrine of the Gnostics. (Gk.=knowledge)
gnu, *n.* S. African antelope like ox. (Hottentot)
go, *v.i.* (*past* **went,** *p.p.* **gone**) proceed, journey; depart; die, fail; be spent; pass; be habitually; extend, reach; turn out; become; work; (*arch.*) walk.—*n.* energy; turn, helping; affair; fashion. **go about,** attend to; (*naut.*) tack. **go at,** attack. **go bad,** putrefy. **go down,** decline; be believed. **go dry,** adopt Prohibition. **go for,** pass for; attack. **go for nothing,** be ineffective. **go halves,** share equally. **go in for,** take as object or profession. **go it,** act vigorously. **go native,** adopt native ways. **go off,** leave; explode; fade; fare. **go on,** proceed; behave; (*colloq.*) nag. **go one better,** excel. **go out,** leave; be extinguished; strike. **go over,** examine; change side. **go phut,** (*sl.*) collapse. **go round,** suffice for all. **go through,** perform; undergo. **go to!** come now! **go to pieces,** break up. **go under,** succumb. **go west,** (*army sl.*) be killed. **go with,** accompany; match. **go without,** not have. **going on for,** getting near. **going to,** about to. (O.E. *gán*)
goa, *n.* Tibetan gazelle. (Tibetan *dgoba*)
goad, *n.* spiked stick for driving cattle; thing that incites or torments.—*v.t.* urge on with goad; torment. (O.E. *gád*)
go-ahead, *a.* energetic.
goal, *n.* winning-post at race; aim, object; destination; turning-post; (*football, hockey* etc.) space, point won by driving ball, between **g.-posts. goalkeeper,** (*colloq.*) **goalie,** *nn.* player guarding goal.
go-as-you-please, *a.* without rules.
goat, *n.* long-haired rank-smelling horned quadruped; Capricorn, 10th sign of zodiac, which sun enters about 22 Dec.—*v.t.* (*Amer. sl.*) butt. **get one's g.,** (*sl.*) irritate one. **g.-god,** *n.* Pan. **g.'s-beard,** *n.* kind of spiraea; salsify. **goatee,** *n.* chin tuft like goat's beard. **goatherd,** *n.* **goatish,** *a.* lustful; of rank smell. **goatling,** *n.* young goat. **goatskin,** *n.* bottle, garment, of goat's skin. **goatsucker,** *n.* nightjar. (O.E. *gát*)
gob, *n.* clot of mucus or spittle.—*v.i.* spit. (O.F. *gobe,* mouthful)
gob, *n.* (*Amer. sl.*) sailor.
gobang, *n.* game with counters on board of 256 squares. (Chin. *k'i pan,* chess-board)
gobbet, *n.* lump, esp. of flesh; short extract set for comment in examination. (*gob*)
gobble, *v.t.* and *i.* eat greedily or hastily, gulp.—*n.* (*golf*) putt hit strongly into hole. **gobbler,** *n.*
gobble, *n.* gurgling cry of turkey.—*v.i.* utter this. **gobbler,** *n.* turkey-cock. (imit.)
Gobelin, *a.* **G. tapestry,** rich French kind. (*Gobelins,* famous dyers)
go-between, *n.* intermediary.
gobemouche, *n.* silly gossipy person. (F. *gober,* swallow; *mouches,* flies)
goblet, *n.* glass with foot and stem;

(*arch.*) large drinking-cup without handle. (O.F. *gobel*, cup)
goblin, *n.* mischievous ugly demon; sprite. (F. *gobelin*)
goby, *n.* small sea-fish. (Gk. *kōbios*, gudgeon)
go-by, *n.* evasion. **give the go-by**, set aside; slight, cut.
God, *n.* the Supreme Being, Creator and Ruler of the universe. **god**, *n.* (*fem.* **goddess**) deity, object of worship, idol; adored person; (*pl.*) theatre gallery audience.—*v.t.* deify. **with G.**, dead. **G.-a-mercy**, *int.* (*Shake.*) God have mercy. **G.'s-acre**, *n.* churchyard. **g.-forsaken**, *a.* hopeless, dismal. **g.-speed**, *n.* wish for success. **godfather, godmother, g.-parent**, *nn.* sponsor for child at baptism. **g.-child, g.-daughter, godson**, *nn.* child so sponsored. (O.E.)
godet, *n.* triangular insertion at foot of skirt to make flare.
godetia, *n.* hardy annual with cup-shaped leaves. (*Godet*, botanist)
godfearing, *a.* reverencing God.
godhead, *n.* divine nature, deity.
godless, *a.* impious, wicked; atheistical.
godlike, *a.* like a god, divine.
godling, *n.* minor deity.
godly, *a.* devout, righteous.
Godman, *n.* Jesus Christ.
godown, *n.* (*Anglo-Ind.*) warehouse. (Malay *godong*)
godsend, *n.* unexpected piece of luck.
godship, *n.* rank of god, divinity.
godward, *a.* and *adv.* towards God.
godwit, *n.* wading bird like curlew.
goer, *n.* one that goes.
goety, *n.* black magic. **goetic**, *a.* (Gk. *goēs*, sorcerer)
goffer, gofer, *v.t.* make wavy, crimp, with hot irons.—*n.* goffering iron; plaiting. (F. *gaufrer*, figure)
go-getter, *n.* (*Amer. colloq.*) enterprising person, thruster.
goggle, *v.i.* and *t.* roll (eyes) about; squint; (of eyes) project.—*a.* bulging, staring.—*n.pl.* protective spectacles. **g.-eyed**, *a.*
goglet, *n.* (*Anglo-Ind.*) long-necked water-vessel. (Port. *gorgoleta*)
going, *n.* surface, state of ground. **goings-on**, *n.pl.* strange or questionable conduct.
goitre, *n.* swelling of neck due to enlargement of thyroid gland. **goitrous**, *a.* (L. *guttur*, throat)
gold, *n.* yellow precious metal; gold coins, money; precious thing; bright yellow; (*archery*) bull's-eye.—*a.* of, like, gold. **g. standard**, gold as standard of monetary value. **g. stick**, gilt rod for state occasions, officer who carries it. **old g.**, dull brownish-yellow. **g.-beater**, *n.* one who beats out gold-leaf. **g.-beater's skin**, membrane used to separate the leaves or to cover slight wounds. **g.-digger**, *n.* gold-miner; (*Amer. sl.*) mercenary flirt. **g.-field**, *n.* district yielding gold. **g.-filled**, *a.* coated with gold. **g.-foil, g.-leaf**, *nn.* thin, very thin, layer of gold. **g.-mine**, *n.* source of wealth. **g.-plate**, *n.* vessels of gold. **g.-rush**, *n.* to new gold-field. (O.E.)
golden, *a.* of, like, gold; valuable; excellent. **g. age**, fabled early age of innocence; flowering of nation's civilization or art. **g. calf**, wealth as god. **g. eagle**, a large eagle. **G. Fleece**, an order of knighthood. **g. mean**, neither too much nor too little. **g. number**, of year in lunar cycle of 19 years, used in fixing Easter. **g. opinions**, high respect. **g. rain**, kind of firework. **g. rule**, to do as you would be done by. **g. wedding**, 50th anniversary. (*gold*)
golden-rod, *n.* a yellow-flowered plant.
goldfinch, *n.* song-bird with yellow patch on wings.
goldfish, *n.* small orange-coloured Chinese carp.
goldilocks, *n.* kind of buttercup.
goldsmith, *n.* worker in gold.
golf, *n.* game in which ball is struck with clubs over grass etc. into hole. —*v.i.* play golf. **g.-club**, *n.* golf implement or society. **g.-course, g.-links**, *nn.* series of holes, us. 18.
goliard, *n.* medieval wandering jester. **goliardic**, *a.* (L.L. *goliardus*)
Goliath, *n.* giant. (name in Bible)
golliwog, gollywog, *n.* grotesque doll with black face and bristling hair.
golly, *int.* of dismay etc. (*God*)
golosh, same as **galosh**.
goluptious, goloptious, *a.* (*joc.*) luscious, delicious, scrumptious.
gombeen, *n.* (*Ir.*) usury. **g.-man**, *n.* money-lender. (Ir. *gaimbin*)
gombroon, gomroon, *n.* kind of pottery, orig. Persian. (town)
gomeril, *n.* (*Scot.*) stupid fellow.
gonad, *n.* germ-gland. (Gk. *gonos*, seed)
gondola, *n.* Venetian canal-boat with raised bow and stern; car of airship. **gondolier**, *n.* rower of gondola. (It.)
gone, *a.* lost, departed. **g. on**, (*sl.*) in love with. **g. coon, goner**, *n.* person in hopeless plight.
gonfalon, *n.* banner, us. with streamers, hung from cross-bar. **gonfalonier**, *n.* its bearer. (It. *gonfalone*)
gong, *n.* metal disk with rim, giving deep note when struck with mallet; saucer-shaped bell; (*army sl.*) medal. —*v.t.* (of police) signal (motorist) to pull up for exceeding speed limit. (imit.)
gongorism, *n.* florid pedantic Spanish style resembling euphuism. (*Góngora* y Argote, Spanish poet)
goniometer, *n.* instrument for measuring solid angles. **goniometry**, *n.* (Gk. *gōnia*, angle; *metron*, measure)
gonorrhoea, *n.* venereal disease with

discharge from urethra or vagina. (Gk. *gonos*, seed; *rhoia*, flux)

goo, *n.* (*Amer. sl.*) any sticky substance; sickly sentiment.

good, *a.* (*compar.* **better**, *superl.* **best**) right, adequate; proper, suitable; beneficial, wholesome; virtuous, well-behaved, kind; pleasant; clever, skilful; valid, genuine, sound; considerable.—*n.* well-being; use, benefit; virtue; (*pl.*) personal property; merchandise; (*Amer. sl.*) resources.—*int.* right! **a g. deal**, a fair amount. **as g. as**, the same as. **do g.**, benefit. **for g.**, finally. **g. breeding**, politeness. **g. day, evening**, salutations. **g. fellow**, sociable person. **g. for**, able to perform or pay. **G. Friday**, commemorating Christ's crucifixion, Friday before Easter. **g. graces**, favour. **g. lady**, wife. **g. looks**, beauty. **g. money**, (*vulg.*) high wages. **g. morning**, (*arch.*) **morrow, night**, salutations. **g. people**, fairies. **g. sense**, sound judgment. **g. turn**, friendly action. **g. word**, recommendation. **have a g. mind**, be inclined. **in g. spirits**, cheerful. **make g.**, fulfil (expectations); compensate for. **stand g.**, be valid. **the gg.**, (*sl.*) ideal. **to the g.**, as profit; beneficial. **up to no g.**, bent on mischief. (O.E. *gód*)

goodbye, *int.* and *n.* farewell. (=*God be with you*)

good-for-nothing, *a.* and *n.* worthless (person).

good-humoured, *a.* genial, cheerful.

goodish, *a.* pretty good, fair.

good-looking, *a.* handsome.

goodly, *a.* handsome, noble; considerable, large. **goodlihead**, *n.* (*Spens.*) goodness.

goodman, *n.* master of house, husband.

good-natured, *a.* amiable, easy-going.

goodness, *n.* virtue, kindness, excellence.—*int.* of impatience, etc.

good-tempered, *a.* not easily angered.

goodwife, *n.* mistress of house.

goodwill, *n.* kindly feeling; zeal; value of business apart from stock.

goody, *n.* sweet; (*arch.*) goodwife.—*a.* (also **g.-g.**) primly, obtrusively, or weakly virtuous.

gooey, *a.* (*Amer. sl.*) sticky, gummy; sentimental, sloppy. (*goo*)

goof, *n.* (*sl.*) daft person. **goofy**, *a.* silly, sloppy, infatuated.

googly, *n.* (*cricket*) off-break ball bowled with leg-break action.

goo-goo eyes, (*sl.*) ogling.

gooroo, same as **guru**.

goosander, *n.* a web-footed bird.

goose, *n.* (*pl.* **geese**) bird between swan and duck; its flesh; simpleton; (*pl.* **gooses**) tailor's smoothing-iron. **g.-club**, *n.* through which Christmas goose is paid for by instalments. **g.-flesh, g.-skin**, *nn.* roughness of skin caused by cold or fear. **g.-grass**, *n.* plant eaten by geese, cleavers. **g.-neck**, *n.* iron swivel fastening boom to mast. **g.-step**, *n.* formal parade step; balancing-drill. (O.E. *gós*)

gooseberry, *n.* a thorny shrub; its hairy berry; chaperon to lovers. **goosegog**, *n.* (*sl.*) gooseberry.

gooseherd, *n.* one who tends geese.

goosey, goosie, *n.* little silly.

gopher, *n.* (*Amer.*) pouched rat; ground squirrel; burrowing tortoise.

gopher, *n.* tree from wood of which Noah's ark was made. (Heb.)

gopher, same as **goffer**.

goral, *n.* Himalayan antelope. (native)

gorbellied, *a.* (*Shake.*) fat-paunched.

gorcock, *n.* male red grouse.

Gordian, *a.* **cut the G. knot**, solve hard problem by bold measures or evasion. (King *Gordius*, whose knot was cut by Alexander the Great)

gore, *n.* clotted blood; blood. (O.E. *gor*, dung)

gore, *v.t.* pierce with horn or tusk.

gore, *n.* triangular piece let in to adjust width of garment; triangular piece in umbrella, dome, etc.—*v.t.* shape with gore. (I.E. *gár*, spear)

gorge, *n.* gullet; contents of stomach; surfeit; narrow pass between hills; entrance to outwork of fort. *v.i.* and *t.* feed, swallow, greedily; stuff (oneself) with food. (O.F.)

gorgeous, *a.* richly coloured, splendid, sumptuous. (O.F. *gorgias*)

gorget, *n.* armour for throat; wimple; necklace; (*zool.*) patch of colour on throat. (*gorge*)

Gorgio, *n.* gipsy name for non-gipsy. (Romany)

gorgon, *n.* fabled woman whose awful aspect turned beholder to stone; repellent woman. **gorgonian**, *a.* **gorgonia**, *n.* sea-fan. **gorgonize**, *v.t.* petrify. (Gk. *Gorgō*)

gorgonzola, *n.* a rich cheese. (town)

gorilla, *n.* ferocious African ape, largest anthropoid. (native)

gory, *a.* covered with gore, bloody.

gormandize, *v.i.* and *t.* eat greedily.—*n.* gluttony. **gormandizer**, *n.* (*gourmand*)

gorse, *n.* prickly yellow-flowered shrub, furze, whin. **gorsy**, *a.* (O.E. *gorst*)

gosh, *int.* of surprise etc. (*God*)

goshawk, *n.* large short-winged hawk. (*goose*; *hawk*)

gosling, *n.* young goose. (*goose*)

gospel, *n.* Christian revelation, teachings of Christ; record of His life; guiding principle; truth. **g.-pusher**, *n.* (*Amer.*) parson. **gospeller**, *n.* reader of gospel in communion service. **hot gospeller**, zealous evangelist. (O.E. *gód spel*, good tidings)

gossamer, *n.* film of cobweb which floats in air; flimsy thing; thin gauze; (*Amer.*) thin waterproof.—*a.* very fine or flimsy. **gossamery**, *a.* (M.E. *gossomer*)

gossip, *n.* chat, tittle-tattle; baseless rumour; tattler, scandalmonger;

(*arch.*) friend; god-parent.—*v.i.* chat; tell idle tales about others. **gossiper, gossipry,** *nn.* **gossipy,** *a.* (*God*; *sib*)

gossoon, *n.* (*Ir.*) boy. (F. *garçon*)

got, see **get.**

Goth, *n.* one of an ancient Germanic nation; barbarian. (Gk. *Gothoi*)

Gothic, *a.* and *n.* (language) of the Goths; (*archit.*) in the pointed arch style, including Early English, Decorated, and Perpendicular; (*print.*) black-letter. **G. revival,** renewal of interest in medieval art in late 18th century.

go-to-meeting, *a.* Sunday best (suit).

gotten, see **get.**

gouache, *n.* method of water-colour painting with opaque colours mixed with gum and honey. (F.)

gouge, *n.* rounded chisel for cutting grooves; (*Amer.*) groove; (*Amer. sl.*) cheat.—*v.t.* scoop out; force out eye of. (L.L. *gubia*)

goulash, *n.* seasoned stew of steak and vegetables. (Magyar *gulyás,* herdsman; *hús,* meat)

gourd, *n.* a trailing plant; its large juicy fruit; rind of this as vessel. (L. *cucurbita*)

gourd, *n.* (*Shake.*) kind of false dice.

gourmand, *n.* glutton.—*a.* greedy. *gourmandise,* *n.* gluttony. (F.)

gourmet, *n.* connoisseur of wines and meats, epicure. (F.)

gout, *n.* inflammatory disease of joints; disease of wheat; (*Shake.*) drop. **gouty,** *a.* subject to gout. (L. *gutta,* drop)

goût, *n.* taste; relish. (F.)

govern, *v.t.* and *i.* rule with authority, administer; have command (of); direct, guide; control; (*gram.*) be followed by (case etc.). **governance,** *n.* act of governing, sway. (Gk. *kubernaein,* steer)

governess, *n.* woman teacher of children in private household; (*Shake.*) ruler, mistress. **g.-car, g.-cart,** *nn.* light two-wheeled carriage with side-seats face to face.

government, *n.* governing, control; administration of public affairs; ruling power of state, ministry; (*Shake.*) conduct, behaviour. **governmental,** *a.*

governor, *n.* ruler; official governing province, town etc.; Crown's representative in colony; regulator for speed of engine; (*sl.*) father, boss, sir. **g.-general,** *n.* supreme governor; viceroy. **governorship,** *n.*

gowan, *n.* (*Scot.*) daisy.

gowd, gowf, *Scot.* forms of gold, golf.

gowk, *n.* (*dial.*) cuckoo; simpleton, fool. (O.N. *gaukr*)

gowl, *v.i.* (*Scot.*) howl.

gown, *n.* loose flowing garment; woman's dress; official robe.—*v.t.* attire in gown. **town and g.,** tradesmen and university men. **gownsman,** *n.* civilian, member of university. (L.L. *gunna,* fur)

gowpen, *n.* (*Scot.*) two hands cupped together, double handful.

Graafian follicle, vesicle, small sac enclosing eggs in ovary of mammal. (R. de *Graaf*)

graal, same as **grail.**

grab, *n.* Eastern two-masted coasting-vessel. (Arab. *ghurab,* crow)

grab, *v.t.* and *i.* seize suddenly; clutch (at); arrest.—*n.* snatch, attempt to seize; greedy proceedings; clutching mechanism; a card game. **grabber,** *n.* **grabble,** *v.i.* feel about, grope.

grabby, *n.* (*naut. sl.*) soldier.

grace, *n.* elegance, ease of form or movement; accomplishment, adornment; goodwill, favour; divine influence or mercy; prayer at meal; delay granted; (*pl.*) three goddesses of grace, Euphrosyne, Aglaia, Thalia. —*v.t.* adorn, favour, honour. **fall from g.,** lapse. **good gg.,** favour. **his, your, g.,** address to duke or archbishop. **with good, bad, g.,** willingly, reluctantly. **year of g.,** A.D. **g.-cup,** *n.* loving-cup for final health. **g.-note,** *n.* extra note as ornamental flourish. (L. *gratus,* pleasing)

graceful, *a.* elegant, showing grace.

graceless, *a.* shameless; depraved.

gracile, *a.* slender. (L. *gracilis*)

gracious, *a.* kindly, affable; indulgent, merciful; (*Shake.*) popular, attractive, pious, happy.—*int.* of surprise.

grackle, *n.* bird like starling. (L. *graculus,* jackdaw)

grad, *n.* (*Amer. sl.*) graduate.

gradate, *v.i.* and *t.* (of colours) shade, cause to shade, into one another. *gradatim,* *adv.* by degrees. **gradation,** *n.* stage in transition, degree, step; series of these; arrangement in grades; gradating; ablaut. **gradational,** *a.* (*grade*)

grade, *n.* degree in rank, merit etc.; class; gradient; hybrid got by grading native cattle; (*math.*) $\frac{1}{100}$ of a right angle.—*v.t.* and *i.* classify, sort, take rank; gradate; adjust slope of (road); cross (stock) with better breed. **make the g.,** (*Amer.*) succeed in task. **on the up, down, g.,** rising, falling. **g.-crossing,** *n.* (*Amer.*) level crossing. (L. *gradus,* step)

gradely, *a.* (*dial.*) excellent, fine; handsome; real, true.—*adv.* properly; very. (*graith*)

Gradgrind, *n.* unfeeling person who goes by rules. (name in Dickens)

gradient, *n.* degree of slope; incline. (*grade*)

gradin, gradine, *n.* one of tier of seats; ledge at back of altar. (F.)

gradual, *a.* happening by degrees, slow and regular, not steep.—*n.* response sung after epistle. (*grade*)

graduate, *n.* holder of university

degree; (*Amer.*) one who has completed course of study at school.—*v.t.* and *i.* take, admit to, academical degree; mark out scale on; grade. **graduand,** *n.* one about to receive degree. **graduation,** *n.* graduating; degree ceremony. (*grade*)

gradus, *n.* dictionary of Greek and Latin prosody. (*gradus ad Parnassum,* stair to abode of muses)

graecism, *n.* Greek idiom, spirit, or style. **graecize,** *v.t.* and *i.* give Greek form to, imitate Greek. **Graecomania,** *n.* mania for Greek ways. **Graecomaniac,** *n.* **Graecophil,** *n.* lover of Greece. (L. *Graecus,* Greek)

graf, *n.* German count. (G.)

graff, *obs.* for **graft.**

graffito, *n.* ancient scribblings on walls of Pompeii etc. (It.)

graft, *n.* shoot of plant set in stock of another; transplanted living tissue. —*v.t.* insert, transplant (graft). (Gk. *graphion,* style, pencil)

graft, *n.* spadeful. (*grave*)

graft, *n.* (*Amer. colloq.*) bribery, political manipulation; spoils gained by this.—*v.i.* get, use, graft. **grafter,** *n.*

grail, *n.* (us. **holy g.**) cup, dish, used by Christ at the Last Supper. (L.L. *gradalis*)

grail, *n.* comb-maker's file. (L. *gracilis,* slender)

grail, same as **gradual.**

grain, *n.* seed or fruit of cereal; wheat corn etc.; small particle; $\frac{1}{5760}$ lb. troy, $\frac{1}{7000}$ lb. avoirdupois; rough surface; texture, lines of fibre; dye, colour; nature, temper; (*pl.*) refuse malt after brewing.—*v.t.* and *i.* form into grains; paint in imitation of wood-grain; remove hair from (hide). **against the g.,** against natural inclination. **gg. of paradise, Guinea gg.,** pungent seeds of African plant. **in g.,** in the raw state; by nature, thorough. **grainer,** *n.* (L. *granum*)

grains, *n.* barbed fish-spear, harpoon. (O.N. *grein,* division)

graip, *n.* (*Scot.*) dung-fork. (*grope*)

graith, *a.* (*Scot.*) ready.—*n.* dress; gear, harness.—*v.t.* make ready, equip. (O.N. *greidhr*)

grallatorial, *a.* of family of long-legged wading birds. (L. *grallae,* stilts)

gralloch, *v.t.* disembowel (deer).—*n.* deer's entrails. (Gael. *grealach*)

gram, *n.* chick-pea; pulse. **g.-fed,** *a.* getting best of everything. (L. *granum,* grain)

gram, see **gramme.**

-gram, *n.suf.* thing written, as in **epigram.** (Gk. *graphein,* write)

grama, *n.* (also **g. grass**) a low pasture grass in western U.S.A. (Sp.)

gramarye, *n.* (*arch.*) magic, necromancy. (O.F. *gramaire,* learning)

grame, *n.* misery. (O.E. *grama,* anger)

gramercy, *int.* (*arch.*) thank you. (O.F. *grant merci,* great reward)

graminaceous, gramineous, *aa.* of, like, grass; grassy. **graminivorous,** *a.* grass-eating. (L. *gramen,* grass)

grammalogue, *n.* (*shorthand*) single symbol for word. (Gk. *gramma,* letter; *logos,* word)

grammar, *n.* science of structure and usages of a language; book on this; correct use of words. **g. school,** *n.* secondary school; (formerly) one for teaching Latin; (*Amer.*) school between primary and secondary. **grammarian,** *n.* one versed in grammar. **grammatical,** *a.* of, according to, grammar. **grammatize,** *v.t.* render grammatical. (Gk. *gramma,* letter)

gramme, gram, *n.* unit of weight in metric system, 15·432 grains troy. (Gk. *gramma,* small weight)

gramophone, *n.* instrument for reproducing sounds recorded on revolving disk. (inversion of *phonogram*)

grampus, *n.* small kind of whale; one who breathes hard.

granadilla, *n.* passion-flower; its fruit. (Sp.)

granary, *n.* storehouse for grain; region fertile in grain. (*grain*)

grand, *a.* chief; of high dignity or importance; main, final; full; lofty, imposing, distinguished; (*colloq.*) excellent.—*n.* grand piano; (*Amer. sl.*) a thousand dollars. **do the g.,** put on airs. **G. Duke,** (*fem.* **G. Duchess**) sovereign prince; son of czar. **g. finale,** impressive closing scene. **G. Monarch,** Louis XIV. **G. National,** annual steeplechase at Liverpool. **g. piano,** with horizontal frame. **g. tour,** (*arch.*) tour of Europe completing education. **G. Turk,** (*arch.*) Sultan of Turkey. (L. *grandis,* tall)

grandad, grand-dad, *n.* (*colloq.*) grandfather.

grandam, grandame, *n.* (*arch.*) grandmother; old woman.

grand-aunt, *n.* father's or mother's aunt, great-aunt.

grandchild, *n.* son's or daughter's child.

grand-daughter, *n.* son's or daughter's daughter.

grandee, *n.* Spanish nobleman of first rank; great personage. (Sp. *grande*)

grandeur, *n.* grandness, magnificence, splendour, distinction. (*grand*)

grandfather, *n.* father's or mother's father. **g., g.'s, clock,** worked by weights in tall wooden case.

grandiloquent, *a.* pompous or inflated in speech. **grandiloquence,** *n.* bombast. (L. *loqui,* speak)

grandiose, *a.* imposing, affectedly grand. **grandiosity,** *n.* (*grand*)

grandmamma, grandma, *nn.* grandmother.

grandmother, *n.* father's or mother's mother.—*v.t.* coddle. **grandmotherly,** *a.* fussy, interfering.

grand-nephew, *n.* nephew's or niece's son, great-nephew.

grand-niece, *n.* nephew's or niece's daughter, great-niece.

grandpapa, grandpa, *n.* grandfather.
grandsire, *n.* grandfather; ancestor.
grandson, *n.* son's or daughter's son.
grand-stand, *n.* raised seats for spectators.
grand-uncle, *n.* father's or mother's uncle, great-uncle.
grange, *n.* country house with farm-buildings; (*arch.*) granary; (*Amer.*) farmer's union. (L. *granum*, grain)
grangerize, *v.t.* interleave (book) with illustrations cut from others. **grangerization, grangerism,** *nn.* (J. *Granger*)
graniferous, *a.* bearing grain-like seeds. (L. *ferre*, bear)
granite, *n.* hard crystalline rock of quartz, feldspar, and mica. **granitic, granitoid,** *aa.* (L. *granum*, grain)
granivorous, *a.* feeding on grain or seeds. (L. *vorare*, swallow)
granny, *n.* grandmother; old woman; (also **g. knot**) reef-knot crossed the wrong way and thus insecure.
grant, *v.t.* and *i.* bestow, transfer legally; concede, allow; admit; (*Shake.*) assent.—*n.* granting, bestowal; sum granted. **grantee, grantor,** *nn.* (*law*) person to, by, whom property is transferred. (L. *credere*, entrust)
granular, *a.* of, like, grain. **granularity,** *n.* **granulate,** *v.t.* and *i.* form into grains; roughen surface of; (of wound) begin to heal by granular formations. **granulation,** *n.* **granule,** *n.* little grain. **granulous,** *a.* granular. (*grain*)
grape, *n.* berry of vine; grape-shot; tumour on horse's leg. **sour gg.,** things disparaged because unattainable. **g.-fruit,** *n.* like large orange. **g.-shot,** *n.* shot packed in layers, scattering when fired. **g.-stone,** *n.* seed of grape. **g.-sugar,** *n.* glucose. **grapery,** *n.* vinery. (O.F.=cluster of grapes)
graph, *n.* symbolic diagram of mathematical relation or statistics. (abbr. of *graphic formula*)
graph, *n.* gelatine copying-apparatus. —*v.t.* copy with this. (abbr. of *hectograph* etc.)
-graph, *n.suf.* thing written, as in **autograph**; recording instrument, as in **seismograph. -grapher,** *n.suf.* one versed in the science of, as in **bibliographer.** (Gk. *graphein*, write)
graphic, graphical, *aa.* of writing, drawing, painting, or graphs; picturesquely described, vivid. **graphically,** *adv.* (Gk. *graphein*, write)
graphite, *n.* carbon forming 'lead' of pencils, plumbago. **graphitic, graphitoid,** *aa.* (Gk. *graphein*, write)
grapho-, from Gk. *graphein*, write, used in **graphology,** *n.* art of reading character from handwriting; **graphophone,** *n.* kind of phonograph; **graphospasm,** *n.* writer's cramp; **graphotype,** *n.* process for making blocks for surface-printing; block so made.
-graphy, *n.suf.* descriptive science of, as in **bibliography**; style of writing, drawing etc. as in **lithography.** (Gk. *graphein*, write)
grapnel, *n.* small anchor with several flukes; grappling-iron. (O.F. *grapin*)
grapple, *v.t.* and *i.* seize, grip, bind; contend hand to hand, tussle.—*n.* close fight or hold; grapnel. **g. with,** tackle. **grappling-iron,** *n.* hooked instrument for taking hold of ship etc. (O.F. *grape*, hook)
grasp, *v.t.* and *i.* seize, grip; catch (at); understand.—*n.* fast hold, clasp; reach; comprehension. **grasping,** *a.* greedy. (M.E. *grapsen*)
grass, *n.* herbage; kinds of cereal, reed etc.; pasture; (*sl.*) asparagus. —*v.t.* turf; (*sl.*) bring down, fell, land. **at g.,** grazing, out of work. **g. widow,** wife whose husband is absent. **g.-snake,** *n.* a common harmless kind. **grasshopper,** *n.* hopping chirping insect. **grassy,** *a.* like, covered with, grass. (O.E. *græs*)
grat, (*Scot.*) *past* of **greet.**
grate, *n.* fireplace; its frame of bars; grating. (L. *cratis*, hurdle)
grate, *v.t.* and *i.* rub to small bits on rough surface; grind with harsh noise; creak; have irritating effect, rasp. (O.F. *grater*)
grateful, *a.* thankful; pleasing, refreshing. (L. *gratus*)
grater, *n.* utensil for grating.
graticulation, *n.* division of design into squares, for purpose of reproduction. (*grate*)
gratify, *v.t.* please, delight; indulge, oblige; reward, bribe, fee; (*Shake.*) grace. **gratification,** *n.* (L. *gratus*, pleasing; *facere*, make)
gratin, *n.* dish cooked with bread-crumbs, forming light crust. *au g.* so cooked. (F.)
grating, *n.* frame of bars. (*grate*)
grating, *a.* harsh, discordant. (*grate*)
gratis, *adv.* free, for nothing. (L.)
gratitude, *n.* thankfulness, warm appreciation of favour. (L. *gratus*, thankful)
gratuitous, *a.* given free, done for nothing; uncalled-for, motiveless. **gratuity,** *n.* tip, present; bounty to soldier. (L. *gratuitus*)
gratulate, *v.t.* (*arch.*) congratulate; (*Shake.*) greet. **gratulatory,** *a.* congratulatory. (L. *gratulari*)
gravamen, *n.* weightiest part, chief ground (of charge); grievance. (L. *gravis*, heavy)
grave, *n.* hole dug for corpse, tomb; death, destruction. **with one foot in the g.,** near death. **g.-clothes,** *n.pl.* wrappings of corpse. (O.E. *græf*)
grave, *v.t.* (*p.p.* **graved, graven**) carve, engrave; fix indelibly; bury. **graven image,** idol. (O.E. *grafan*)
grave, *a.* important, weighty; serious,

sober; solemn; sombre; (of accent) low-pitched.—*n.* grave accent (\`). (L. *gravis*)

grave, *v.t.* clean (ship's bottom) by scraping. **graving dock,** dry dock.

gravel, *n.* small stones, pebbles; (*med.*) urinary crystals, disease with these. —*v.t.* lay with gravel; embarrass, nonplus. **g.-blind,** *a.* almost blind. **gravelly,** *a.* (O.F. *grave,* shore)

graver, *n.* carver in stone; his cutting tool, burin.

gravestone, *n.* stone marking grave.

graveyard, *n.* burial-ground.

gravid, *a.* pregnant. (L. *gravidus*)

gravigrade, *a.* (*zool.*) heavy-footed. (L. *gravis,* heavy; *gradus,* step)

gravity, *n.* importance, seriousness; solemnity, staidness; force causing things to fall to earth, similar attraction between all bodies of matter. **specific g.,** weight of substance relative to water. **gravitate,** *v.i.* and *t.* move by gravity; sink, settle; be drawn. **gravitation,** *n.* gravitating; force of gravity. **gravitational, gravitative,** *aa.* (*grave*)

gravy, *n.* juices from meat in cooking; dressing for food. **g.-boat,** *n.* boat-shaped dish for gravy.

gray, graybeard, see grey.

grayling, *n.* silver-grey freshwater fish like salmon. (*gray*; *-ling*)

graze, *v.t.* and *i.* touch lightly in passing; abrade, scratch, scrape.—*n.* grazing, abrasion.

graze, *v.i.* and *t.* feed (cattle) on grass, browse; pasture, tend (cattle). **grazier,** *n.* one who pastures cattle or breeds them for market. **grazing,** *n.* pasture. (*grass*)

grease, *n.* soft animal fat; thick oil or lubricant; uncleansed wool; disease in horses' heels.—*v.t.* lubricate, coat, soil, with grease. **g. palm of,** bribe. **in g.,** (of game) fat. **wool in the g.,** in fleeces. **g.-gun,** *n.* for injecting grease into machinery. **g.-paint,** *n.* for actors' make-up. **greaser,** *n.* head fireman on steamer; (*Amer. sl.*) Mexican or Spanish American. (L. *crassus,* fat)

great, *a.* large, big; long; important; eminent, highly gifted; in fullest sense; (*sl.*) very satisfactory.—*n.pl.* Oxford final classical school. **the g.,** great persons. **g. at,** skilful in. **g. circle,** dividing sphere's surface in halves. **G. Dane,** a large dog, boarhound. **g. gross,** twelve gross. **G. Powers,** Britain, U.S.A., France, Germany, Italy, Russia, and Japan. **g. unwashed,** (*joc.*) working classes. **g. with child,** (*Shake.*) **g.-bellied,** *a.* pregnant. **g.-hearted,** *a.* high-spirited, generous. **g.-aunt, g.-uncle,** *nn.* parent's aunt, uncle. **g.-nephew, g.-niece,** *nn.* son, daughter, of nephew or niece. **g.-grandfather, g.-grandmother,** *nn.* father, mother, of grandparent. **g.-g.-grandfather,** *n.* father of great-grandparent. so **g.-g.-g.-grandfather** etc. (O.E.)

greatcoat, *n.* overcoat.

greaten, *v.t.* and *i.* make, become, greater.

greatly, *adv.* much, by much.

greaves, *n.pl.* armour for legs. (O.F. *greve,* shin)

greaves, *n.pl.* sediment of melted tallow. (G. *greven*)

grebe, *n.* tailless diving bird. (F. *grèbe*)

Grecian, *a.* Greek.—*n.* Greek scholar. **G. bend,** affected posture in vogue about 1870. **G. nose,** straight and continuing forehead line. **grecism** etc., same as **graecism** etc. (*Greece*)

gree, *n.* (*Scot.*) rank; mastery; prize. (L. *gradus,* step)

gree, *v.i.* (*Shake.*) agree.—*n.* goodwill, satisfaction. (*agree*)

greedy, *a.* eagerly desirous; voracious, gluttonous. **greed,** *n.* eager longing, greediness. (O.E. *grǣdig*)

gree-gree, same as **gri-gri.**

Greek, *a.* and *n.* (native, language) of Greece; trickster. **G. Church,** Eastern or Orthodox Christian Church, chiefly in Balkans and Russia. **G. cross,** upright with equal arms. **G. fire,** burning liquid used in ancient sea-fights. **G. gift,** treacherous gift. **G. meets G.,** champions are matched. **G. to me,** unintelligible. (Gk. *Graikos*)

green, *a.* grass-coloured; vegetable, leafy; unripe, young; inexperienced, gullible; not dried or seasoned; pale.—*n.* green colour; grass plot, common; (*golf*) putting-green; links; (*pl.*) green vegetables.—*v.i.* and *t.* become, make, green; (*sl.*) hoax. **g. cloth,** billiard or gaming table. **g. eye,** jealousy. **g. fly,** aphis. **g. yule,** without snow. **g.-sickness,** *n.* chlorosis. **greenback,** *n.* American bank-note. **greenbrier,** *n.* smilax. **greenery,** *n.* vegetation. **greenfinch,** *n.* bird with gold and green plumage. **greengage,** *n.* kind of plum. **greengrocer,** *n.* dealer in vegetables or **greengrocery. greenhorn,** *n.* novice, simpleton. **greenhouse,** *n.* glass-house for rearing plants. **greening,** *n.* kind of apple green when ripe. **greenkeeper,** *n.* man in charge of golf-course. **greenroom,** *n.* actors' retiring-room at theatre. **greensand,** *n.* green sandstone. **greensome,** *n.* (*golf*) foursome in which both partners drive from tee and then proceed with either ball. **greenstone,** *n.* New Zealand jade. **greensward,** *n.* turf. **greenth,** *n.* verdure. **greenwood,** *n.* leafy woodland. (O.E. *grēne*)

Greenwich time, British standard time, reckoned from Greenwich meridian.

greet, *v.i.* (*Scot.*) weep. (O.E. *grētan*)

greet, *v.t.* and *i.* salute, accost, hail; address kind wishes to. **greeting,** *n.* salutation. (O.E. *grētan*)

greeve, same as **grieve.**

greffier, *n.* registrar. (F.)

gregarious, *a.* living in flocks or communities; fond of company, sociable. (L. *grex*, flock)
grege, *a.* and *n.* (colour) between grey and beige. (*grey*+*beige*)
Gregorian, *a.* of Pope Gregory. **G. calendar,** established by Gregory XIII in 1582 and now in use. **G. chant,** named after Gregory I.
gregory-powder, *n.* aperient of ginger, magnesia, and rhubarb. (name)
gremial, *a.* of bosom or lap.—*n.* bishop's apron. (L. *gremium*, bosom)
gremlin, *n.* (*R.A.F. sl.*) imaginary trouble-making sprite.
grenade, *n.* explosive bomb, thrown by hand or shot from rifle-barrel; glass projectile with chemicals for extinguishing fire. **grenadier,** *n.* soldier of Grenadier Guards, formerly grenade-thrower. (Sp. *granada*, pomegranate)
grenadilla, same as **granadilla.**
grenadine, *n.* gauze-like dress fabric. (F.)
grenadine, *n.* dish of veal etc. larded and glazed. (F. *grenadin*)
grenadine, *n.* syrup made from pomegranates. (Sp. *granada*, pomegranate)
Gresham's law, principle that debased money tends to drive good money out of circulation. (name)
gressorial, *a.* adapted for walking. (L. *gradi*, walk)
grew, see **grow.**
grey, gray, *a.* between black and white; hoary, aged; dull, dismal.—*n.* grey colour, horse, or clothes.—*v.i.* and *t.* become, make, grey; give soft effect to (photograph). **the Gg.,** Scots Greys, 2nd Dragoons. **g. crow,** hooded crow. **G. Friar,** Franciscan. **g. matter,** active part of brain. **g. monk,** Cistercian. **greybeard, graybeard,** *n.* old man; earthenware jug. (O.E. *græg*)
greyhound, *n.* swift slender keen-sighted dog. **ocean g.,** fast liner. **g.-racing,** (*colloq.*) **greycing,** *nn.* after electric hare. (O.E. *grighund*—not connected with *grey*)
greylag, graylag, *n.* common wild goose.
greywacke, *n.* conglomerate rock of pebbles and sand. (G. *grauwacke*)
grid, *n.* grating; gridiron; car's luggage-bracket; (*electr.*) part of amplifying valve; system of main transmission lines. (*gridiron*)
griddle, *n.* flat iron plate for baking **g.-cakes;** large sieve.—*v.t.* screen with griddle.
gride, *v.t.* cut, pierce, harshly; grate. —*n.* grating sound.
gridiron, *n.* frame of iron bars for broiling; frame to support ship in dock; (*Amer.*) football-field. (M.E. *gredire*+confusion with *iron*)
grief, *n.* deep sorrow or trouble. **come to g.,** be destroyed. **grievance,** *n.* real or imaginary ground of complaint; (*Shake.*) oppression, trouble. **grieve,** *v.t.* and *i.* give, feel, grief; vex; sorrow. **grievous,** *a.* painful; oppressive, severe; heinous. (O.F.)
grieve, *n.* (*Scot.*) overseer, steward.
griffin, griff, *n.* (*Anglo-Ind.*) white person new to the East, greenhorn. **griffinage,** *n.* one's first year in India. **griffinhood,** *n.*
griffin, griffe, *n.* (*Amer.*) mulatto; offspring of negro and mulatto woman. (F.)
griffin, griffon, *n.* fabulous animal, half lion, half eagle; watchful chaperon. (Gk. *grups*)
griffon, *n.* rough-haired liver-coloured dog like terrier. (F.)
grig, *n.* sand-eel; grasshopper, cricket.
gri-gri, *n.* African charm or fetish.
grill, *n.* gridiron; broiled meat; grille. —*v.t.* and *i.* broil; torment; (*Amer.*) cross-question. **g.-room,** *n.* where steaks etc. are broiled and served. (F. *gril*)
grille, *n.* latticed screen; grating in door; (*tennis*) square opening in wall. **grillage,** *n.* framework of cross-beams supporting erection on marshy ground. (F.)
grilse, *n.* young salmon that has only once been to sea.
grim, *a.* of forbidding aspect; ghastly, dismal; stern, relentless.
grimace, *n.* distortion of face; affected look.—*v.i.* make grimace. (F.)
grimalkin, *n.* old she-cat; spiteful hag.
grime, *n.* ingrained dirt.—*v.t.* soil deeply, blacken. **grimy,** *a.*
grin, *v.i.* show teeth; smile broadly or wryly.—*n.* act of grinning. **g. through horse-collar,** at rustic grimacing-match. (O.E. *grennian*)
grin, *n.* snare, trap. (O.E.)
grind, *v.t.* and *i.* (*past, p.p.* **ground**) powder, pulverize; oppress; sharpen, smooth; grate, rub together; study hard; turn handle of (hurdy-gurdy). —*n.* grinding; drudgery; walk for exercise. **g. out,** produce laboriously. **ground glass,** made non-transparent. **grinder,** *n.* one that grinds; molar tooth; crammer. **grindery,** *n.* cobbler's materials. **grindstone,** *n.* round revolving stone for grinding tools. (O.E. *grindan*)
gringo, *n.* Spanish-American name for Englishman or American. (Sp.)
grip, *v.t.* and *i.* grasp tightly; impress deeply.—*n.* firm hold, clasp; mode of grasping; control, mastery; handle, device for holding; (*Amer.*) *colloq.*) gripsack. **come to gg.,** grapple. (*gripe*)
grip, *n.* small ditch, trench. (O.E. *grype*)
gripe, *v.t.* and *i.* clutch, squeeze; oppress; give pain to bowels of.—*n.* griping; hold, handle; (*pl.*) colic. (O.E. *gripan*)
gripe, *n.* (*Shake.*) griffin. (Gk. *grups*)

grippe, **n.** influenza. (F.)

gripsack, *n.* (*Amer.*) hand-bag, suit-case.

Griqua, *n.* (*S. Afr.*) offspring of Boer and Hottentot woman.

grisaille, *n.* decorative painting in grey monochrome, esp. on glass. **griseous,** *a.* bluish-grey. *grisette*, *n.* gay young French working-girl. (F. *gris*, grey)

griskin, *n.* lean of loin of pork.

grisly, *a.* grim and ghastly, causing horror. (O.E. *grislic*)

grist, *n.* corn to grind; malt crushed for brewing; supply. (O.E.)

grist, *n.* size or thickness of rope.

gristle, *n.* tough elastic animal tissue, cartilage. (O.E.)

grit, *n.* rough hard particles, sand; coarse sandstone; (*colloq.*) courage, determination.—*v.i.* and *t.* grate; grind (teeth). (O.E. *gréot*)

Grit, *n.* (*Canadian politics*) Liberal.

grits, *n.pl.* oats husked but unground; coarse oatmeal. (O.E. *grytte*)

grivet, *n.* green and white Abyssinian monkey.

grize, *n.* (*Shake.*) step. (*gree*)

grizzle, *v.i.* (*colloq.*) whimper.

grizzly, *a.* grey, greyish; grey-haired. —*n.* (also **g. bear**) large American bear. **grizzled,** *a.* grizzly. (F. *gris*, grey)

groan, *v.i.* and *t.* make deep sound of pain or disapproval, moan; be afflicted or loaded.—*n.* groaning sound. **groaningly,** *adv.* (O.E. *gránian*)

groat, *n.* obsolete silver fourpenny-piece. (O.Du. *groot*, thick coin)

groats, *n.pl.* hulled and crushed oats; grits.

Grobian, *n.* clumsy lout. (G.)

grocer, *n.* dealer in tea, spices, and domestic stores. **grocery,** *n.* his goods, shop, or trade. (orig. one who dealt in *gross*)

grog, *n.* spirit, esp. rum, and water. —*v.i.* drink grog. **groggy,** *a.* tipsy; unsteady, shaky, weak.

grogram, *n.* coarse cloth of silk and mohair. (F. *gros grain*, large grain)

groin, *n.* hollow where thigh joins trunk; (*archit.*) angular curve formed by arches intersecting.—*v.t.* build with groins. **groining,** *n.*

grommet, same as **grummet.**

gromwell, *n.* herb of borage family. (O.F. *gromil*)

groom, *n.* servant in charge of horses; officer of royal household; bridegroom.—*v.t.* tend, curry (horse); make neat. **groomsman,** *n.* friend attending bridegroom, best man.

groove, *n.* channel, long hollow; rut, routine.—*v.t.* cut groove in. **groovy,** *a.* (Du. *groeve*, furrow)

grope, *v.i.* feel about, search blindly. **gropingly,** *adv.* (O.E. *grápian*)

grosbeak, *n.* small bird with thick strong beak. (F. *grosbec*)

groschen, *n.* obsolete silver German coin, worth about 1½*d.* (G.)

gross, *a.* fat, bloated; rank, dense; coarse, indecent; obvious, flagrant; total, not net; (*Shake.*) dull, stupid. —*n.* bulk, mass; twelve dozen. (L. *grossus*, thick)

grot, *n.* (*poet.*) grotto. (F. *grotte*)

grotesque, *a.* fantastic, extravagant, distorted; absurd.—*n.* comically distorted figure etc.; (*art*) decorative painting of fanciful figures, plants etc. **grotesquerie,** *n.* (It. *grottesca*, antique work)

grotto, *n.* (*pl.* **grottoes, grottos**) picturesque or artificial cave. (Gk. *kruptē*, vault)

grouch, *n.* (*Amer. colloq.*) fit of ill temper, sulks; peevish person.—*v.i.* grumble. (*grudge*)

ground, see **grind.**

ground, *n.* surface of earth, soil; portion of this, land; sea-bottom, floor; field, place of action; foundation, basis; reason, motive; (*art*) surface worked upon; (*pl.*) enclosed land round house; dregs.—*v.t.* and *i.* place on ground; establish, base; instruct in elements; run ashore; prevent flying of (aircraft); (*electr.*) earth. **break g.,** make start. **down to the g.,** (*colloq.*) thoroughly. **fall to the g.,** come to nothing. **gain, give, g.,** advance, retire. **g. floor,** on level with street. **g. stroke,** (*lawn tennis*) made after ball bounds. **g. swell,** heavy sea after storm. **shift, stand, one's g.,** change, maintain, one's argument. **g.-bait,** *n.* thrown into water to attract fish. **g.-game,** *n.* hares, rabbits etc. **g.-ice,** *n.* formed at bottom of water. **g.-ivy,** *n.* a creeping plant, ale-hoof. **groundnut,** *n.* earth-nut; peanut. **g.-plan,** *n.* plan of ground floor; general design. **g.-rent,** *n.* rent for land leased for building. (O.E. *grund*)

groundage, *n.* dues paid for space ship occupies in port.

groundless, *a.* without reason, baseless.

groundling, *n.* fish living at bottom; spectator, reader, of vulgar taste.

groundsel, *n.* a yellow-flowered weed. (O.E. *gundæswelgiæ* — not from *ground*)

groundsel, *n.* timber serving as foundation; threshold. (*ground*; *sill*)

groundsman, groundman, *n.* man who looks after cricket pitch etc.

groundwork, *n.* foundation; chief ingredient.

group, *n.* number of persons or things placed or classed together; cluster; (*art*) figures forming artistic whole. —*v.t.* and *i.* form, fall, into groups; arrange. **g.-captain,** *n.* rank in R.A.F. corresponding to colonel in Army. **groupage,** *n.* (It. *gruppo*)

grouper, *n.* an edible sea-fish. (Port. *garupa*)

grouse, *n.* (*pl.* same) kinds of game-bird, esp. red grouse; their flesh. **black g.,** black-cock. **red g.,** moorcock.

white g., ptarmigan. **wood or great g.,** capercailzie.
grouse, *v.i.* and *n.* (*sl.*) grumble.
grout, *n.* fluid mortar; fine plaster.—*v.t.* fill in, finish, with grout.
grout, *v.i.* and *t.* (of pigs) turn up (earth) with snout.
grouty, *a.* (*Amer. colloq.*) sulky, sullen.
grove, *n.* small wood, group of trees. **grovy,** *a.* (O.E. *gráf*)
grovel, *v.i.* lie prone, crawl; be mean or debased. **groveller,** *n.* (M.E. *groveling,* on the face, mistaken for participle)
grow, *v.i.* (*past* **grew,** *p.p.* **grown**) develop naturally, sprout; increase in size; (of plant) live; become; (*Shake.*) accrue.—*v.t.* cause to grow, cultivate; (*passive*) be covered with growth. **g. on,** become (more) admired by. **g. together,** unite. **g. up,** reach maturity; (of custom) arise. **grown-up,** *a.* and *n.* adult. **grower,** *n.* (O.E. *grówan*)
growl, *n.* deep angry murmur; rumble; grumble.—*v.i.* and *t.* make growl, snarl. **growler,** *n.* one who growls; four-wheeled cab; small iceberg; (*Amer. sl.*) beer-jug. **growlery,** *n.* growling; private room, den.
grown, see **grow.**
growth, *n.* growing; increase; what has grown; morbid formation.
groyne, *n.* timber structure to stop shifting of sand on beach.—*v.t.* supply with groynes.
grozet, *n.* (*Scot.*) gooseberry.
grub, *v.i.* and *t.* root in earth, rummage; clear (ground), root out; plod; (*sl.*) feed.—*n.* larva of insect, maggot; drudge, hack; (*sl.*) food. **g.-stake,** *n.* (*Amer. sl.*) miner's outfit supplied in return for share of finds.—*v.t.* supply this. **grubby,** *a.* infested with grubs; dirty, grimy.
Grub-street, *n.* (home of) literary hacks.—*a.* of these. (street in London, now Milton St.)
grudge, *v.t.* and *i.* be unwilling to give, give with reluctance; envy.—*n.* ill will, resentment. **grudging,** *a.* reluctant. (O.F. *groucier*)
grue, *n.* shudder; feeling of horror.—*v.i.* (*obs.*) shudder.
gruel, *n.* thin porridge; (*sl.*) punishment.—*v.t.* (*sl.*) thrash. **gruelling,** *a.* exhausting. (L.L. *grutum,* meal)
gruesome, *a.* horrible, grisly. (*grue*)
gruff, *a.* surly, rough-mannered; hoarse.
gruine, *a.* of the crane kind. (L. *grus,* crane)
grum, *a.* surly, gruff. (O.E. *grom*)
grumble, *v.i.* and *t.* murmur with discontent, growl; rumble.—*n.* complaint; grumbling sound. **grumbler,** *n.*
grume, *n.* (*med.*) clot of blood; viscid fluid. **grumous,** *a.* (L.L. *grumus,* small heap)
grummet, *n.* (*naut.*) ring of rope; metal ring as rowlock. (F. *gourmer,* curb)
grumph, *v.i* and *n.* (*Scot.*) grunt. **grumphy,** *n.* sow.
grumpy, grumpish, *a.* surly, ill-tempered; low-spirited.
Grundyism, *n.* conventionality, prudery. (Mrs. *Grundy* in play)
grunt, *n.* low gruff sound of pig.—*v.i.* and *t.* utter (like) this. **grunter,** *n.* pig. (O.E. *grunian*)
grunzie, *n.* (*Scot.*) snout, mouth.
grushie, *a.* (*Scot.*) of thriving growth.
grutch, *obs.* for **grudge.**
gruyère, *n.* Swiss milk cheese, full of holes. (town)
gryphon, same as **griffin.**
grysbok, *n.* small S. African antelope. (Du. *grijs,* grey; *bok,* buck)
guacharo, *n.* a nocturnal S. American bird, oil-bird. (Sp.)
guaiacum, *n.* a tree, lignum vitae; gum from it. (Sp. *guayaco*)
guan, *n.* S. American bird like turkey.
guana, *n.* (*Austral.*) any large lizard. (*iguana*)
guanaco, *n.* wild llama of S. America. (native *huanaco*)
guano, *n.* dung of sea-fowl.—*v.t.* manure with it. (native *huanu*)
guarantee, *n.* guaranty; guarantor; person to whom guaranty is given.—*v.t.* be guarantee, answer, for; engage, warrant; secure. **guarantor,** *n.* one who gives a guaranty. **guaranty,** *n.* promise to perform what another has undertaken, should he make default; thing given as security.—*v.t.* guarantee. (F. *garant,* warrant)
guard, *n.* protection, defence; posture of defence; watch, sentry duty; soldiers protecting anything; protector, device to prevent injury, loss etc.; conductor of train; (*Shake.*) trimming; (*pl.*) household troops.—*v.t.* and *i.* protect, defend; be careful (of). **mount g.,** take sentry duty. **on, off, one's g.,** prepared, unprepared, for attack etc. **g.-house, g.-room,** *nn.* for military guard or prisoners. **g.-rail,** *n.* to prevent falling. **g.-ring,** *n.* to keep other ring on finger. **guardage,** *n.* (*Shake.*) safe-keeping. **guardant,** *n.* (*Shake.*) sentinel. **guarded,** *a.* cautious, circumspect. (F. *garde*)
guardian, *n.* protector, keeper; (*law*) person having custody of infant etc.—*a.* protecting. **guardianship,** *n.*
guardsman, *n.* soldier of the Guards.
guava, *n.* a tropical tree; its pear-shaped fruit, used for jelly. (Sp. *guayaba*)
gubernatorial, *a.* of government or governor. (L. *gubernare,* govern)
guddle, *v.t.* (*Scot.*) catch (fish) by groping with hands.
gude, same as **guid.**
gudgeon, *n.* small freshwater fish; gullible person. (Gk. *kōbios*)
gudgeon, *n.* pivot, bearing; socket for rudder. (O.F. *gojon*)

guelder rose, tree with white ball-like flowers. (*Guelders* in Prussia)
guerdon, *n.* and *v.t.* (*poet.*) reward, recompense. (O.H.G. *wider*, again; *lón*, reward, confused with L. *donum*, gift)
guernsey, *n.* thick jersey; breed of dairy cattle. (island)
guerrilla, guerilla, *n.* (also **g. war**) irregular warfare by small marauding bands; member of these. (Sp.=little war)
guess, *v.t* and *i.* surmise; estimate without full knowledge; hit upon at random; (*Amer.*) think, suppose.—*n.* rough estimate, conjecture. **guess-work,** *n.* guessing. (M.E. *gessen*)
guest, *n.* visitor received and entertained; person lodging at hotel; parasite. **paying g.,** boarder. **g.-chamber,** *n.* one kept for guests. **g.-house,** *n.* superior boarding-house. **guestship,** *n.* (O.E. *giest*)
guff, *n.* (*Amer. sl.*) empty talk.
guffaw, *n.* coarse laugh.—*v.i.* laugh boisterously. (imit.)
guggle, same as **gurgle.**
gugglet, same as **goglet.**
guichet, *n.* hatch, ticket-office window. (F.)
guid, *a.* (*Scot.*) good. **g.-brother, g.-daughter, g.-father, g.-mother, g.-sister, g.-son,** *nn.* brother-in-law, daughter-in-law etc. **g.-willie,** *a.* hearty.
guide, *n.* one who shows way, conductor; adviser, directing principle; manual, guide-book; (*mech.*) rod etc. directing motion.—*v.t.* lead, direct, act as guide to. **the Gg.,** an Indian frontier corps. **Girl Gg.,** organization parallel to Boy Scouts. **g.-book,** *n.* handbook for tourists. **g.-post,** *n.* direction post. **g.-rope,** *n.* guy. **guidance,** *n.* direction, leading. (F. *guider*)
guidon, *n.* forked or pointed military pennon. (It. *guidone*)
guild, gild, *n.* society for common object or mutual aid. **guildhall,** *n.* meeting-place of guild or corporation. **guildry,** *n.* (*Scot.*) guild or its members. (O.E.)
guilder, *n.* Dutch florin. (*gulden*)
guile, *n.* cunning, treachery; stratagem, wile. **guileful,** *a.* crafty, deceitful. **guileless,** *a.* artless. (O.F.)
guillemot, *n.* kinds of sea-bird. (F.)
guilloche, *n.* (*archit.*) ornament like braided ribbons. (F. *guillochis*)
guillotine, *n.* machine for beheading; paper-cutting machine; time-limit imposed on parliamentary debate.—*v.t.* use guillotine upon, behead with it. (*Guillotin*, inventor)
guilt, *n.* guiltiness, culpability; sin. **guiltless,** *a.* innocent; without knowledge (of). **guilty,** *a.* having broken law or committed sin; wicked; **conscious of guilt.** (O.E. *gylt*)
guimp, same as **gimp.**
guinea, *n.* old coin, now money of account, worth 21*s.* **g.-fowl,** *n.* grey bird with white spots. **G. grains,** grains of paradise. **g.-pig,** *n.* small rodent from S. America; (*sl.*) company director who does no work for his fee. **g.-worm,** *n.* tropical skin parasite. (place)
Guinness, *n.* kind of stout. (maker)
guipure, *n.* a coarse lace; kind of gimp. (F.)
guise, *n.* external appearance; semblance, pretence; (*arch.*) garb, fashion. **guiser,** (*Scot.*) **guisard,** *n.* Christmas mummer. (F.)
guitar, *n.* six-stringed instrument of lute kind. **guitarist,** *n.* (Gk. *kithara*)
gulch, *n.* ravine, gully.
gulden, *n.* Austrian florin; guilder. (Du.=golden)
gules, *a.* and *n.* (*heraldry*) red. (O.F.)
gulf, *n.* large arm of sea; chasm, abyss; whirlpool.—*v.t.* swallow up. (Gk. *kolpos*)
gull, *n.* long-winged web-footed sea-bird.
gull, *n.* dupe.—*v.t.* cheat, impose upon.
gullet, *n.* food-passage from mouth to stomach; throat; strait. (L. *gula*)
gullible, *a.* easily gulled or deceived. **gullibility,** *n.* (*gull*)
gully, *n.* large knife.
gully, *n.* narrow ravine, gorge; gutter, drain.—*v.t.* wear channel in.
gulosity, *n.* gluttony. (L. *gula*, gullet)
gulp, *v.t.* and *i.* swallow eagerly or in large draughts; gasp, choke.—*n.* act of gulping; swallow, mouthful. **g. down,** gulp; suppress. (imit.)
gum, *int.* a mild oath. (*God*)
gum, *n.* sticky juice of certain trees, soluble in water; secretion of eyelid; adhesive; jujube; (*pl.*, *sl.*) rubber boots.—*v.t.* stick, smear, stiffen, with gum. **g. arabic,** got from acacia. **g.-boots,** *n.pl.* rubber boots. **g.-resin,** *n.* secretion of mixed gum and resin. **g.-tree,** *n.* eucalyptus. **up a g.-tree,** (*sl.*) in a fix. (Gk. *kommi*)
gum, *n.* (us. *pl.*) flesh round teeth. **gumboil,** *n.* abscess in this. (O.E. *goma*)
gumbo, *n.* (*Amer.*) okra plant or pods; soup made with these. (negro)
gumdragon, *n.* tragacanth. (*gum*)
gumgum, *n.* (*Anglo-Ind.*) gong made of hollow iron bowl.
gumlie, *a.* (*Scot.*) muddy, discoloured.
gumma, *n.* (*pl.* **gummas, gummata**) syphilitic tumour. **gummatous,** *a.* (*gum.*)
gummy, *a.* sticky; exuding gum; puffy.
gump, *n.* (*Amer. sl.*), fool, noodle.
gumption, *n.* (*colloq.*) common sense, shrewdness; resource.
gun, *n.* firearm, cannon; member of shooting-party; (*sl.*) revolver.—*v.i.* hunt with gun. **blow great gg.,** very violently. **great g.,** eminent person. **son of a g.,** rascal. **stick to one's gg.,** maintain position. **sure as a g.,**

beyond question. **g.-barrel,** *n.* tube of gun. **g.-bus,** *n.* (*sl.*) armed aeroplane. **g.-carriage,** *n.* support of cannon. **g.-cotton,** *n.* explosive of cotton steeped in nitric and sulphuric acids. **g.-metal,** *n.* alloy of copper and tin. **g.-runner, g.-running,** *nn.* smuggler, smuggling, of firearms into country. **g.-shy,** *a.* (of dog) frightened at report of gun. **g.-stock,** *n.* wooden mounting of gun-barrel.

gunboat, *n.* small warship.

gunman, *n.* (*Amer. sl.*) armed gangster.

gunnel, *n.* small eel-shaped sea-fish, butter-fish.

gunnel, same as **gunwale.**

gunner, *n.* private of artillery; (*naut.*) warrant-officer in charge of battery etc. **gunnery,** *n.* science of artillery; firing of guns.

gunnera, *n.* a large-leafed plant, prickly rhubarb. (J. E. *Gunnerus*)

gunpowder, *n.* explosive of nitre, sulphur, and charcoal; fine kind of green tea.

gunroom, *n.* mess-room of warship's junior officers.

gunshot, *n.* range of gun.

gunsmith, *n.* one who make or repairs small-arms.

gunter, *n.* (also **G.'s scale**) rule with scales for navigator's calculations. **G.'s chain,** surveying-chain. (name)

gunwale, *n.* upper edge of boat's side.

gunyah, *n.* (*Austral.*) native hut. (native)

gup, *n.* (*Anglo-Ind.*) gossip. (Hind.)

gurgitation, *n.* whirling motion, surging. (L. *gurges,* whirlpool)

gurgle, *n.* bubbling sound.—*v.i.* and *t.* utter (with) gurgle; flow in broken noisy current. (imit.)

gurgoyle, same as **gargoyle.**

gurly, *a.* (*obs.*) fierce, stormy.

gurnard, gurnet, *n.* spiny sea-fish with armoured head.

gurry, *n.* fish offal.

gurry, *n.* small Indian fort. (Hind. *garhi*)

guru, *n.* Hindu spiritual teacher. (Sanskr.=grave)

gush, *v.i.* and *t.* flow out, emit, copiously and violently; spurt; talk effusively. — *n.* gushing (stream); effusiveness. **gusher,** *n.* oil-well with large natural flow. **gushy,** *a.*

gusset, *n.* tapering piece let into garment to give width or strength; iron bracket to strengthen angles. **gusseted,** *a.* (O.F. *gousse,* pod)

gust, *n.* sudden blast of wind; outburst of passion, sound etc.

gust, *n.* (*arch.*) sense of taste, relish, savour. **gustation,** *n.* tasting. **gustative, gustatory,** *aa.* **gusto,** *n.* zest, enjoyment. (L. *gustus*)

gusty, *a.* windy; irritable. (*gust*)

gut, *n.* intestine; catgut; strait, bend of river; narrow lane; (*pl.*) bowels; courage; force.—*v.t.* remove guts of (fish); destroy, remove, contents of. (O.E.)

gutcher, *n.* (*Scot.*) grandfather.

gutta, *n.* (*pl.* **guttae**) (*archit.*) drop-shaped ornament. (L.=drop)

gutta-percha, *n.* flexible hardened juice of a Malayan tree. (Malay *gatah,* gum; *percha,* the tree)

guttate, *a.* speckled. (*gutta*)

gutter, *n.* channel at side of street, trough under eaves, for carrying away water; channel, groove.—*v.t.* and *i.* furrow; flow in streams; (of candle) run down in drops. **g.-man,** *n.* street vendor. **g. press,** sensational newspapers. **g.-snipe,** *n.* street arab, slum child. (*gutta*)

guttural, *a.* of, formed in, the throat. —*n.* guttural letter, *k, g* etc. **gutturalize,** *v.t.* form (sound) in throat. **gutturalism,** *n.* (L. *guttur,* throat)

gutty, *n.* (*golf*) solid gutta-percha ball. (abbr.)

guy, *n.* effigy of Guy Fawkes, burned on 5 Nov.; odd figure, fright; (*Amer. sl.*) fellow.—*v.t.* and *i.* treat as guy, poke fun at; (*sl.*) run away. **do a g.,** (*sl.*) bolt. (name)

guy, *n.* (also **g.-rope**) rope used to steady load of crane, balloon, tent etc.—*v.t.* keep in position with guy. (O.F. *guis*)

guzzle, *v.i.* and *t.* eat or drink greedily. —*n.* gorge. **guzzler,** *n.*

gwyniad, *n.* white-fleshed fish like salmon. (Welsh *gwyn,* white)

gybe, *v.i.* and *t.* (of sail or boom) swing over from one side to the other; (of ship) alter course in this way.

gyle, *n.* a single brewing of beer. (Du. *gijlen,* ferment)

gym, *n.* (*sl.*) gymnasium, gymnastics.

gymkhana, *n.* (*Anglo-Ind.*) display of athletic sports, esp. races; place for this. (*gym*nastics+Hind. *khana,* house)

gymnasium, *n.* (*pl.* **gymnasiums, gymnasia**) place with facilities for gymnastics; German school of highest grade. **gymnasial,** *a.* **gymnast,** *n.* expert in gymnastics. **gymnastic,** *a.* of bodily exercise.—*n.pl.* muscular exercises; art of performing these, physical culture. **gymnastically,** *adv.* (Gk. *gumnazein,* exercise)

gymno-, from Gk. *gumnos,* naked, used in **gymnosophist,** *n.* one of contemplative ascetic Hindu sect who wore little clothing, hence **gymnosophy,** *n.* their doctrine; **gymnorhinal,** *a.* with unfeathered nostrils; **gymnosperm,** *n.* plant whose seeds are not enclosed in covering, hence **gymnospermous,** *a.*; **gymnotus,** *n.* electric eel.

gymp, same as **gimp.**

gynaec(o)-, gyn(o)-, from Gk. *gunē,* woman, used in **gynaeceum,** *n.* women's apartments in ancient Greek house, (*bot.*) female organs of flower; **gynaecocracy,** *n.* government by woman or women; **gynaecology,** *n.*

branch of medicine dealing with diseases of women, hence **gynaecological,** *a.*, **gynaecologist,** *n.*; **gynaecolatry,** *n.* worship of women; **gynaecomania,** *n.* satyriasis; **gynaecomorphous,** *a.* having female form; **gynandroid,** *a.* female with masculine physique, hence **gynandrism,** *n.*; **gynandrous,** *a.* with stamens and pistil united; **gynarchy, gynocracy,** *nn.* gynaecocracy; **gynoecium,** incorrect form of **gynaeceum. gynophore,** *n.* (*bot.*) stalk supporting carpels.

gyp, *n.* (*sl.*) toko. **give one g.,** (*sl.*) scold, punish etc. severely.

gyp, *n.* Cambridge college servant.

gypsum, *n.* sulphate of lime, burned to make plaster of Paris.—*v.t.* manure with gypsum. **gypseous, gypsous,** *aa.* **gypsophila,** *n.* plant with threadlike stalks. (Gk. *gupsos*)

gypsy, see **gipsy.**

gyrate, *v.i.* revolve, spin; move spirally.—*a.* (*bot.*) arranged in rings. **gyration,** *n.* whirling, circular motion. **gyratory,** *a.* **gyre,** *v.i.* and *n.* (*poet.*) gyrate, gyration. (Gk. *guros*, ring)

gyre-carlin, *n.* (*Scot.*) witch.

gyrfalcon, same as **gerfalcon.**

gyr(o)-, from Gk. *guros*, ring, used in **gyro-compass,** *n.* compass using gyroscope; **gyrograph,** *n.* instrument for recording revolutions; **gyroidal,** *a.* arranged spirally; **gyromancy,** *n.* divination by walking in a circle till dizziness causes fall; **gyropter,** *n.* aeroplane with revolving wings; **gyroscope,** *n.* wheel spinning at high speed, used to maintain equilibrium of torpedo etc., hence **gyroscopic,** *a.*; **gyrose,** *a.* (*bot.*) turned round like a crook; **gyro-stabilizer,** *n.* device of two or more gyroscopes to prevent rolling of ship or aircraft; **gyrostat,** *n.* kind of gyroscope used in studying **gyrostatics,** *n.pl.* dynamics of rotating bodies; **gyrus,** *n.* convolution (of brain).

gyte, *a.* (*Scot.*) crazy, mad.

gyve, *v.t.* fetter.—*n.* (us. *pl.*) shackle. (M.E. *give*)

H

ha, *int.* expressing surprise, joy etc.

ha', *Scot.* form of hall.

haaf, *n.* deep-sea fishing ground off Shetland coast. (O.N. *haf*, sea)

haar, *n.* (*Scot.*) cold sea-mist. (*hoar*)

habble, *v.t.* (*Scot.*) perplex. —*v.i.* stammer.—*n.* perplexity. (*hobble*)

habeas corpus, writ directing the production of a prisoner in court. (L. =have the body)

haberdasher, *n.* dealer in small drapery, such as ribbons, tape etc., termed **haberdashery.**

habergeon, *n.* sleeveless coat of chain-armour. (F. *haubergeon*)

habile, *a.* adroit, skilful. (=*able*)

habiliment, *n.* (us. *pl.*) dress, attire. **habilable,** *a.* capable of being clothed. (O.F. *habiller*, dress)

habilitate, *v.t.* provide capital to work (mine).—*v.i.* qualify for post. **habilitation,** *n.* qualification.

habit, *n.* settled practice or tendency, custom; constitution; dress, esp. of religious order or lady rider.—*v.t.* dress. (L. *habēre*, have)

habitable, *a.* fit to live in. **habitant,** *n.* inhabitant; a French Canadian. **habitat,** *n.* natural home of plant or animal; dwelling-place. **habitation,** *n.* inhabiting; abode.

habitual, *a.* customary; constant. **habituate,** *v.t.* accustom. **habituation,** *n.* **habitude,** *n.* usual mode of action, tendency. *habitué*, *n.* constant visitor, frequenter. (*habit*)

bachel, *n.* (*Scot.*) sloven.

hachure, *n.* shading on a map to show hills. (F.)

hacienda, *n.* farm, estate, ranch, in Spain or Latin America. (Sp.)

hack, *v.t.* and *i.* cut, chop, mangle; kick (shin); give short dry cough.—*n.* gash, bruise; kick. (O.E. *haccian*)

hack *n.* hired horse; horse for ordinary riding; drudge.—*v.t.* and *i.* hire out; ride hack. (*hackney*)

hack, *n.* frame, rack. **at h.** (of hawk) not allowed to prey for itself. (*hatch*)

hackbut, *n.* arquebus. (Du. *haakbus*)

hackee, *n.* chipmunk. (imit.)

hackery, *n.* (*Anglo-Ind.*) bullock-cart.

hackle, *n.* comb for sorting flax; neck feather of cock; artificial fly dressed with this.—*v.t.* dress with hackle.

hackle, *v.t.* mangle, tear asunder. **hackly,** *a.* rough, jagged. (*hack*)

hackmatack, *n.* American larch. (native)

hackney, *n.* horse for general use or hire; hireling.—*v.t.* make commonplace. **h. carriage,** coach, carriage plying for hire. **hackneyed,** *a.* trite. (O.F. *haquenée*, ambling horse)

had, see **have.**

haddock, *n.* sea-fish of the cod family. **haddie,** *Scot.* form.

hade, *n.* and *v.i.* (*min.*) dip, incline (of lode or fault)

Hades, *n.* underworld, abode of dead; hell. (Gk.=Pluto)

hadji, hajji, *n.* Mohammedan who has made pilgrimage to Mecca. (Arab. *haji*)

hae, *Scot.* form of **have.**

haecceity, *n.* (*philos.*) thisness; individuality. (L. *hic*, this)

haemacyte, *n.* blood-corpuscle. **haemal**, *a.* of the blood. **haematic**, *a.* of, containing, blood.—*n.* medicine acting on blood. **haematin**, *n.* a constituent of haemoglobin. **haematite**, *n.* an iron ore. **haematoma**, *n.* (*pl.* **haematomata**) collection of blood in tissues forming swelling. **haematuria**, *n.* discharge of blood in urine. (Gk. *haima*, blood)

haemoglobin, *n.* colouring matter of red corpuscles of the blood. **haemophilia**, *n.* constitutional tendency to excessive bleeding. **haemorrhage, hemorrhage**, *n.* escape of blood. **haemorrhoids, hemorrhoids**, *n.pl.* piles. (Gk. *haima*, blood)

haet, hait, hate, *n.* (*Scot.*) whit.

haffet, *n.* (*Scot.*) side of head, temple.

hafflin, *a.* (*Scot.*) half-grown.—*n.* fool.

hafiz, *n.* Mohammedan who knows the Koran by heart. (Arab.)

hafnium, *n.* a rare metal. (Da. Kjöben*havn*, Copenhagen)

haft, *n.* handle (of knife etc.).—*v.t.* fit in, with, handle. (O.E. *hæft*)

hag, *n.* ugly old woman; witch; fish like lamprey. **h.-ridden**, *a.* afflicted by nightmare. **haggish**, *a.*

hag, *n.* firm patch in bog.

hagbut, same as **hackbut.**

haggard, *a.* lean, hollow-eyed, from age, want, or suffering; (of hawk) wild. —*n.* untamed hawk. (O.F. *hagard*)

haggard, *n.* stackyard. (*hay*; *yard*)

haggis, *n.* sheep's heart, lungs, and liver, chopped up, seasoned, and boiled in stomach-bag.

haggle, *v.t.* mangle, hack.—*v.i.* dispute over terms, chaffer; cavil.—*n.* chaffering. **haggler**, *n.* (*hack*)

hagi(o)-, from Gk. *hagios*, holy, used in **hagiarchy**, *n.* rule, order, of saints; **hagiography**, *n.* a Jewish division of the Old Testament, lives of saints, hence **hagiographer**, *n.*; **hagiolatry**, *n.* worship of saints; **hagiology**, *n.* literature about saints; **hagioscope**, *n.* oblique opening in chancel wall giving view of altar, squint.

hah, same as **ha.**

ha ha, *int.* imitating laughter.

ha-ha, haw-haw, *n.* sunk fence. (F.)

haik, haick, *n.* oblong Arab wrap for head and body. (Arab. *hak*, weave)

hail, *v.i.* and *t.* call (to), greet.—*n.* call.—*int.* greeting! **h. fellow well met**, on familiar terms. **h. from**, come from. (O.N. *heill*, hale)

hail, *n.* shower of frozen vapour; shower.—*v.i.* and *t.* rain hail; pour down. **hailstone**, *n.* pellet of hail. **haily**, *a.* (O.E. *hagol*)

hain, *v.t.* (*Scot.*) preserve; spare. (O.N. *hegna*, protect)

hain't, haint, for **have not, has not.**

hair, *n.* filament growing from skin; such filaments collectively; hairlike thing, jot. **keep h. on**, keep cool. **not turn a h.**, be unruffled. **to a h.**, exactly. **h. of the dog that bit him**, morning glass after night's debauch. **hairbrush, h.-net, h.-oil, hairpin, h.-powder**, *nn.* brush etc. used for hair. **haircloth, h.-line, h. shirt**, *nn.* cloth etc. made of hair. **hairbreadth, h.'s breadth**, *n.* minute distance. **hairdresser**, *n.* barber. **h.-splitting**, *a.* and *n.* making fine distinctions. **h.-spring**, *n.* fine spring of watch. **h.-stroke**, *n.* upstroke in writing. **h.-trigger**, *n.* secondary trigger releasing main one on slight pressure. **hairy**, *a.* covered with hair, hirsute. (O.E. *hǽr*)

hairst, *Scot.* form of **harvest.**

hait, see **haet.**

haith, *int.* (*Scot.*) by my faith.

hajj, see **hadj.**

hake, *n.* sea-fish of cod family.

hakeem, hakim, *n.* physician, doctor, in Mohammedan countries. (Arab. *hakim*)

hakim, *n.* judge, governor, in Mohammedan countries. (Arab. *hākim*)

halation, *n.* (*phot.*) halo-like appearance, caused by reflection of light.

halberd, halbert, *n.* combined spear and battle-axe. **halberdier**, *n.* man armed with one. (O.F. *halebarde*)

halcyon, *n.* kingfisher, fabled to have floating nest and calm sea.—*a.* calm, happy, esp. **h. days.** (Gk. *alkuōn*)

hald, *Scot.* form of **hold.**

hale, *a.* healthy, sound of body.—*n.* (*Spens.*) welfare. **haleness**, *n.* (O.E. *hal*)

hale, *v.t.* (*arch.*) drag forcibly, haul. (O.H.G. *halôn*)

half, *n.* (*pl.* **halves**) one of two equal parts; (*colloq.*) school term.—*a.* forming a half.—*adv.* to the extent of half; equally.—*v.t.* divide into halves. **cry, go, hh.**, claim, grant, equal share. **not h.**, (*sl.*) very much. (O.E. *healf*)

half-back, *n.* (*football*) man behind forwards.

half-baked, *a.* underdone, half-witted.

half-binding, *n.* with sides of cloth, corners and back of leather etc.

half-blood, *n.* relationship, person, with one parent in common; half-breed.

half-bound, *a.* in half-binding.

half-breed, *n.* one whose parents are of different races. **half-bred**, *a.* of mixed breed, mongrel.

half-brother, *n.* brother by one parent only.

half-caste, *n.* half-breed, esp. of European and Asiatic parents.

half-cheek, *n.* (*Shake.*) profile.

half-cock, *n.* middle position of gun's cock.

half-crown, *n.* silver coin worth 2*s.* 6*d.*

halfen, halfendeal, *nn.* (*Spens.*) half.

half-hearted, *a.* lukewarm.

halfling, *n.* half-grown person, between boy and man.

half-moon, *n.* moon when half illuminated; half-circle.
half-nelson, *n.* a wrestling hold.
halfpenny, *n.* (*pl.* **halfpence**) bronze coin worth ½*d.*
half-seas-over, *a.* (*sl.*) tipsy.
half-sister, *n.* sister by one parent only.
half-sovereign, *n.* gold coin worth 10*s.*
half-tone, *n.* process block made by photographing through ruled screen.
half-volley, *n.* striking of ball the instant it bounces.
half-witted, *a.* imbecile.
halibut, holibut, *n.* largest kind of flat-fish. (M.E. *hali,* holy; *butte,* plaice)
halicore, *n.* dugong, sea-cow. (Gk. *hals,* sea; *korē,* maid)
halidom, *n.* (*Spens.*) holiness; (*arch.*) holy thing, relic. **by my h.!** an oath. (O.E. *halig,* holy)
halieutic, *a.* of fishing.—*n.pl.* art of fishing. (Gk. *hals,* sea)
halitosis, *n.* offensive breath. (L. *halitus,* breath)
hall, *n.* large public room; entrance-passage of house; house of landed proprietor; college. **Liberty H.,** place where one may do as one likes. **hallmark,** *n.* mark indicating standard of gold and silver.—*v.t.* stamp with this. (O.E. *heall*)
hallan, *n.* (*Scot.*) partition between cottage door and fireplace.
hallelujah, halleluiah, *n.* and *int.* song, shout, of praise to God. (Heb. *halelu,* praise ye; *Jāh,* Jehovah)
halliard, see **halyard.**
hallion, hallyon, *n.* lazy rascal.
hallo, halloa, *int.* to call attention, greet, express surprise etc.
halloo, *int.* and *n.* hunting cry or cry to draw attention.—*v.i.* and *t.* utter, urge on with, this cry.
hallow, *v.t.* make, honour as, holy. **All Hallows, Hallowmass,** *n.* All Saints' Day, 1 Nov. **Hallowe'en,** *n.* (*Scot.* and *Amer.*) eve of this. (O.E. *halgian*)
hallow, *v.t.* chase, incite, with shouts. (O.F. *halloer*)
hallucination, *n.* illusion; seeing, hearing etc., something that is not there. **hallucinate,** *v.t.* delude mind. **hallucinatory,** *a.* (L.L. *hallucinatio*)
halm, see **haulm.**
halma, *n.* game played on chequered board of 256 squares. (Gk.=leap)
halo, *n.* luminous circle round sun, moon etc.; disk of light round saint's head in picture; ideal glory attaching to someone.—*v.t.* surround with halo. (Gk. *halōs,* threshing-floor)
halogen, *n.* any element which forms with a metal a saline compound. **halogenous,** *a.* **haloid,** *a.* like common salt. (Gk. *hals,* salt)
halse, *n.* (*obs.*) neck; pass.—*v.t.* (*Spens.*) clasp round neck. (O.E. *heals*)
halt, *n.* stoppage on march or journey; minor stopping-place on railway.—*v.i.* and *t.* come, bring, to stand. (G.)
halt, *a.* (*arch.*) lame.—*v.i.* go hesitatingly; limp, be defective.—*n.* limp; (*Scot.*) impediment in speech. (O.E.)
halter, *n.* head-rope to lead or hold horse; noose for hanging person.—*v.t.* fasten, hang, with one. (O.E. *hælftre*)
halve, *v.t.* divide into halves; reduce to half; (*golf*) do (hole) in same number of strokes as opponent. (*half*)
halyard, halliard, haulyard, *n.* (*naut.*) rope, tackle, for raising or lowering sail, yard, or flag. (*hale*)
ham, *n.* back of thigh; hog's thigh salted and dried; (*Amer. sl.*) inexperienced actor; amateur, tyro. (O.E. *hamm*)
hamadryad, *n.* wood-nymph; giant cobra; kind of baboon. (Gk. *hama,* together; *drus,* tree)
hamate, *a.* hooked; hook-like. (L. *hamus,* hook)
hame, *n.* (*Scot.*) home. **hamesucken,** *n.* (*Scots law*) assaulting of a man in his own house.
hames, *n.pl.* curved bars for traces on collar of draught horse. (M.E.)
hamlet, *n.* small village, esp. one without a church. (O.E. *hám,* home)
hammam, *n.* Turkish bath. (Arab.)
hammer, *n.* tool, machine, for beating, breaking, etc.; auctioneer's mallet.—*v.t.* and *i.* beat with hammer, beat heavily; declare (person) a defaulter on stock exchange. **come under the h.,** be sold by auction. **h. and tongs,** with might and main. **h.-cloth,** *n.* cloth covering coach-box. **h.-head,** *n.* kind of shark. **hammerman,** *n.* smith who works with hammer. (O.E. *hamor*)
hammock, *n.* bed of cloth or netting, hung by cords. (Sp. *hamaca*)
hamose, hamous, *aa.* hooked. (L. *hamus,* hook)
hamper, *v.t.* obstruct movement of, impede.—*n.* (*naut.*) cumbrous gear.
hamper, *n.* large covered basket. (O.F. *hanapier,* case)
hamshackle, *v.t.* shackle (animal) by tying head to foreleg. (*hamper*)
hamster, *n.* large rat-like animal. (G.)
hamstring, *n.* tendon at back of knee. —*v.t.* (*past, p.p.,* **hamstringed** or **hamstrung**) cripple by cutting this.
hamulus, *n.* small hook. **hamular,** *a.* hook-like. **hamulate,** *a.* tipped with a small hook. (L.)
hand, *n.* arm below wrist; forefoot; pointer of clock etc.; side, quarter; workman, performer; style of writing; cards held by player; measure of horse's height, 4 in.; (*sl.*) applause; (*pl.*) control, agency.—*v.t.* give, conduct, with hand. **at h.,** near. **at first h.,** direct from source. **at second h.,** with one intermediary. **bear a h.,** help. **bear in h.,** (*Shake.*) lead on, delude. **cap in h., humbly. from h.**

to mouth, without provision beforehand. **h. and** or **in glove,** very intimate. **h. of glory,** charm made from mandrake root or hand of executed criminal. **h. to h.,** at close quarters. **hh. down,** with ease. **hh. up!** surrender! **off h.,** without preparation. **out of h.,** out of control; extempore. **take in h.,** deal with. **to h.,** in readiness. **with a high h.,** arrogantly. **handbag, h.-barrow, h.-bell, h.-glass, h.-grenade, h.-loom,** *nn.* bag etc. for use by hand. **h.-canter, h.-gallop,** *nn.* gentle, easy, canter etc. **h.-made, h.-finished, h.-sewn,** *aa.* made etc. by hand, not machinery' (O.E.)

handbill, *n.* loose sheet with notice.

handbook, *n.* manual, short treatise.

handcuff, *n.* (us. *pl.*) fetter for wrists.—*v.t.* put handcuffs on.

handfast, *n.* hold; contract, betrothal.—*v.t.* pledge, betroth.

handful, *n.* as much as fills hand; small quantity; (*colloq.*) troublesome person or task.

handicap, *n.* race, contest, in which chances are equalized by weights carried, starts etc.; condition so imposed; disadvantage.—*v.t.* impose handicap; hinder. **handicapper,** *n.*

handicraft, *n.* manual trade, art, or skill. **handicraftsman,** *n.*

handiwork, *n.* work done by the hands or by any one in person.

handkerchief, *n.* square of linen etc. for wiping face; neckerchief.

handle, *n.* part of thing to hold it by; opportunity, pretext.—*v.t.* touch, feel with hands; deal with, deal in. **h. to one's name,** title. (*hand*)

handless, *a.* awkward, clumsy.

handmaid, handmaiden, *n.* maidservant.

handrail, *n.* rail of staircase, footbridge etc.

handsaw, (*Shake.*) corrupt. of **hernshaw.**

handsel, hansel, *n.* gift on beginning something, New Year gift; earnest-money.—*v.t.* give handsel to; be first to use, inaugurate. (O.E. *handselen,* give into person's hands)

handsome, *a.* fine-looking, graceful with dignity; generous; ample.

handspike, *n.* iron-shod wooden lever.

handwriting, *n.* writing; person's style of writing.

handy, *a.* clever with the hands; convenient, ready to hand. **h.-dandy,** *n.* (*Shake.*) game in which one player has to guess in which of the other's hands an object is. **h.-man,** *n.* man good at odd jobs. (*hand*)

hang, *v.t.* and *i.* (*past, p.p.* **hung**) suspend, be suspended; droop, hover; attach (wall-paper), fit up (doors etc.); decorate (wall); (*past, p.p.* **hanged**) execute by suspension.—*int.* a mild imprecation.—*n.* way a thing hangs. **h. back,** hesitate. **h. fire,** (of weapon) be slow in going off. **h. on,** depend on, cling to. **h. out,** display; (*sl.*) reside. **h. up,** defer, shelve. **h.-bird,** *n.* Baltimore oriole. **h.-dog,** *a.* sneaking, shamefaced. **h.-over,** *n.* after-effects of drinking-bout. (O.E. *hangian*)

hangar, *n.* shed for aircraft. (F.)

hanger, *n.* that which hangs or on which thing is hung; short sword; writing stroke with double curve; wood on hill-slope. **h.-on,** *n.* dependant.

hanging, *n.* execution by halter; (us. *pl.*) drapery for walls. **h. gardens,** rising in terraces. **h. matter,** crime deserving capital punishment.

hangman, *n.* public executioner.

hangnail, corrupt. of **agnail.**

hank, *n.* coil, skein; length (840 yds. cotton or 560 yds. worsted); (*naut.*) ring for fixing sails to stays. (O.N. *hönk*)

hanker, *v.i.* crave, long (for). **hankering,** *n.*

hanky, *n.* (*sl.*) handkerchief.

hanky-panky, *n.* jugglery, trickery.

Hanse, *n.* guild of merchants; entrance-fee to guild; political and commercial league of Germanic towns, hence **Hanseatic,** *a.* (O.H.G. *hansa,* company)

hansom, *n.* light two-wheeled cab with driver's seat raised behind. (inventor)

hant, *n.* (*Amer., joc.*) ghost. (*haunt*)

hantle, *n.* (*Scot.*) good many.

hap, *n.* chance, luck, accident.—*v.i.* happen, befall. (O.N. *happ*)

hap, *v.t.* (*Scot.*) wrap up.—*n.* cloak.

hapax legomenon, (*pl. hapax legomena*) word, phrase, occurring only once. (Gk. = once said)

haphazard, *n.* and *a.* chance.—*adv.* at random, casually. so **at, by, h.**

hapless, *a.* unlucky, unhappy.

haplography, *n.* writing (letter, word etc.) once when it should be written twice. (Gk. *haplous,* single)

haply, *adv.* by chance, perhaps, maybe.

ha'p'orth, for **halfpennyworth.**

happen, *v.i.* take place, occur; chance (to). **h. upon,** find by chance **happening,** *n.*

happy, *a.* glad, content; lucky, fortunate; apt, felicitous. **h. dispatch,** *n.* hara-kiri. **h.-go-lucky,** *a.* casual, light-hearted. **happily,** *adv.* **happiness,** *n.*

haptic, *a.* of sense of touch.—*n.pl.* study of sensations. **haptometer,** *n.* instrument measuring acuteness of sense of touch. (Gk. *haptein,* fasten)

hara-kiri, *n.* ceremonious suicide by disembowelment. (Jap. *hara,* belly; *kiri,* cut)

harangue, *n.* declamatory speech. address to assembly.—*v.i.* and *t.* make harangue, address vehemently. (O.F.)

haras, *n.* stud-farm. (O.F. *haraz*)

harass, *v.t.* worry, torment, weary; attack repeatedly. **harassment,** *n.* (F. *harasser*)

harbinger, *n.* forerunner. — *v.t.* announce approach of another. (*harbour*)
harborough, *obs.* form of harbour.
harbour, *n.* port, haven, for ships; shelter.—*v.t.* give shelter to, entertain.—*v.i.* come to harbour. **h.-master,** *n.* officer in charge of port. **harbourage,** *n.* shelter. (O.H.G. *hari*, army; *bergen*, protect)
hard, *a.* firm, solid; difficult to understand, do, or bear; unfeeling; unjust; strenuous; distressing; (of water) not making lather well with soap; (*Amer.* of drink) alcoholic.—*adv.* strenuously; with difficulty.—*n.* landing-beach; (*sl.*) hard labour. **die h.,** with a struggle or impenitent. **h. and fast,** strict. **h. by,** close by. **h. drinker,** drunkard. **h. lines,** undeserved ill luck. **h. of hearing,** rather deaf. **h. on,** severe on. **h. set,** rigid; hungry. **h. swearing,** persistent perjury. **h. tack,** ship's biscuit. **h. up,** short of money; (*naut.* of tiller) as far as possible to windward. **h. upon,** close to. **h.-boiled,** *a.* (*sl.*) callous, tough. **h.-favoured, h.-featured,** *aa.* with coarse or ugly features. **h.-fisted,** *a.* stingy. **h.-headed,** *a.* shrewd, practical. **h.-hearted,** *a.* merciless. **h.-mouthed,** *a.* (of horse) not easily controlled by bit. (O.E. *heard*)
hardbake, *n.* almond toffee.
hardbitten, *a.* tough in a fight.
harden, *v.t.* and *i.* make or become hard, callous, or robust.
hardihood, *n.* audacity, boldness.
hardiment, *n.* (*Spens.*).
hardly, *adv.* scarcely, with difficulty; severely, harshly.
hardock, *n.* burdock.
hardshell, *a.* with hard shell; uncompromising, strictly orthodox.
hardship, *n.* privation, suffering; injustice; hard lot.
hardware, *n.* ironmongery.
hardwood, *n.* close-grained wood of deciduous trees, as opposed to pines.
hardy, *a.* robust, vigorous, able to bear cold; bold, audacious, impudent. **hardily,** *adv.* **hardiness,** *n.* (*hard*)
hare, *n.* timid swift rodent with divided upper lip.—*v.i.* (*sl.*) run very fast, hurry. **h. and hounds,** paper-chase. **run with the h. and hunt with the hounds,** keep in with both sides. **h.-brained,** *a.* giddy; rash. **h.-lip,** *n.* fissure of upper lip. (O.E. *hara*)
harebell, *n.* bluebell; wild hyacinth.
harem *n.* women's part of Mohammedan dwelling; one man's collection of wives. (Arab. *haram*, forbidden)
haricot, *n.* ragout (us. of mutton; (also **h. bean**) kidney bean. (F.)
hari-kari, incorrect form of **hara-kiri.**
hark, *v.i.* listen.—*v.t.* recall (hounds). **h. back,** retrace course to find scent; revert (to). (O.E. *hercnian*)
harka, *n.* body of Moroccan irregular troops. (Arab.)
harken, see **hearken.**
harl, harle, *n.* barb, fibre, of flax, feather etc.
harl, *v.t.* and *i.* (*Scot.*) drag along, drag oneself; rough-cast (wall) with lime. —*n.* small quantity, scraping.
harlequin, *n.* in old pantomime, mute character, supposed invisible, who plays tricks, buffoon; kind of sea-duck. **harlequinade,** *n.* part of pantomime where harlequin appears; buffoonery. (F.)
harlot, *n.* whore, prostitute.—*a.* lewd. **harlotry,** *n.* (O.F. *herlot*, vagabond)
harm, *n.* injury, damage.—*v.t.* hurt, injure. **harmful,** *a.* hurtful. **harmless,** *a.* doing no harm. (O.E. *hearm*)
harmala, *n.* wild rue. **harmaline,** *n.* alkaloid made from its seeds. (Gk.)
harmattan, *n.* parching wind blowing from interior of Africa to Atlantic.
harmony, *n.* agreement, concord; combination of notes to form chords; melodious sound. **harmonic,** *a.* of or in harmony; (of tones) produced by vibration of aliquot parts of strings; (of quantities) whose reciprocals are in arithmetical progression, as $\frac{1}{2}$, $\frac{1}{3}$, $\frac{1}{4}$. —*n.* (*pl.*) science of musical sounds. **harmonica,** *n.* musical glasses; instrument of metal plates, struck with mallet; mouth-organ. **harmonicon,** *n.* mouth-organ; orchestrion. **harmonious,** *a.* in agreement; tuneful. **harmonize,** *v.t.* and *i.* bring into, be in, harmony. **harmonist, harmonization,** *nn.* **harmonium,** *n.* keyboard instrument with metal reeds. (Gk. *harmonia*)
harn, *n.* (*Scot.*) coarse linen.
harness, *n.* gear of draught-horse; working equipment; armour.—*v.t.* put harness on; use (river etc.) for power. **die in h.,** die at work. (O.F. *harneis*, armour)
harns, *n.pl.* (*Scot.*) brains. (O.E. *hærnes*)
harp, *n.* triangular stringed instrument played by fingers.—*v.i.* play harp; dwell tediously (on). **harper, harpist,** *nn.* (O.E. *hearpe*)
harpoon, *n.* barbed spear for catching whales.—*v.t.* strike with harpoon. **h.-gun,** *n.* gun for firing it. **harpooner, harponeer,** *n.* man who throws harpoon. (Gk. *harpē*, sickle)
harpsichord, *n.* old instrument like piano with strings plucked by quill points. (O.F. *harpechorde*)
harpy, *n.* fabulous monster with body and face of woman, wings and claws of bird; S. American eagle; rapacious person. (Gk. *harpuiai*, pl.)
harquebus, see **arquebus.**
harridan, *n.* quarrelsome old woman, hag.
harrier, *n.* hound for hunting hares; kind of falcon; (*pl.*) club of cross-country runners.

Harrovian, *n.* member of Harrow School.

harrow, *n.* toothed frame for smoothing ploughed land and covering seed. —*v.t.* draw harrow over; distress greatly. **harrowing,** *a.* (M.E. *harwe*)

harry, *v.t.* ravage, plunder; worry. **harrying, harrowing, of hell,** Christ's descent into hell to free souls in bondage. (O.E. *hergian*)

harsh, *a.* rough, discordant; severe, unkind.

hart, *n.* male deer, stag, esp. after fifth year. **h.'s-tongue,** *n.* kind of fern. (O.E. *heort*)

hartal, *n.* closing of shops in mourning or as political gesture. (Hind.)

hartebeest, hartbeest, *n.* a S. African antelope. (S. Afr. Du.)

hartshorn, *n.* solution of ammonia. so **spirit of h. salt of h.,** smelling-salts. (source)

harum-scarum, *a.* reckless, flighty.—*n.* giddy, rash person.

harvest, *n.* season of gathering grain; the gathering; fruit, crop; product.—*v.t.* reap and gather in. **h.-bug,** *n.* kind of mite. **h. festival,** thanksgiving service for harvest. **h. home,** festival at completion of harvest. **h. moon,** full moon nearest 22 Sept. **h. mouse,** smallest mouse. **harvester,** *n.* reaper; reaping-machine; harvest-bug. (O.E. *hærfest*)

has, see **have.**

has-been, *n.* (*colloq.*) person, thing, that has lost efficiency.

hash, *v.t.* chop small.—*n.* dish of chopped meat; medley; (*Scot.*) lout. **make a h. of,** bungle. **settle one's h.,** make an end of one. (F. *hacher*)

hashish, hasheesh, *n.* Indian hemp, dried for smoking or chewing. (Arab.)

haslet, harslet, *n.* edible entrails, esp. of pig. (O.F. *haste,* spit)

hasp, *n.* flap passing over staple and secured by pin; skein of yarn.—*v.t.* fasten with hasp. (O.E. *hæpse*)

hassock, *n.* cushion for kneeling; stuffed footstool; tuft of grass. (O.E. *hassuc*)

hast, see **have.**

hastate, *a.* spear-shaped. (L. *hasta,* spear)

haste, *n.* quickness, hurry; vehemence. —*v.i.* make haste. **hasten,** *v.t.* and *i.* hurry, accelerate. **hasty,** *a.* hurried, speedy; rash; quick-tempered. **hasty pudding,** kind of porridge. (O.F.)

hat, *n.* head-covering, us. with brim.—*v.t.* cover with hat. **bad h.,** (*sl.*) rogue. **h.-peg, h.-rack, h.-stand,** *nn.* place for hanging hat. **h.-trick,** *n.* (*cricket*) taking three wickets with successive balls. **opera h.,** compressible hat. **pass round h.,** make collection. **red h.,** office of cardinal. **talk through one's h.,** (*sl.*) talk nonsense; boast. **top h.,** silk hat. (O.E. *hæt*)

hatch, *v.t.* and *i.* bring, come, forth from egg, incubate; form (plot).—*n.* hatching; brood hatched. **hatchery,** *n.* place for hatching fish. (M.E. *hacchen*)

hatch, *n.* lower half of divided door; opening in door or wall; (*naut.*) covering over hatchway. **under hh.,** below deck; under arrest. (O.E. *hæc*)

hatch, *v.t.* (*drawing*) shade by short parallel lines. **hatching,** *n.* (F. *hacher*)

hatchet, *n.* small axe. **bury the h.,** make peace. **h.-faced,** *a.* sharp-featured. (F. *hache,* axe)

hatchment, *n.* tablet with dead person's armorial bearings placed on house or tomb. (corrupt. of *achievement*)

hatchway, *n.* opening in ship's deck into hold or lower deck. (*hatch*)

hate, *v.t.* dislike intensely, bear malice to.—*n.* hatred. **hateful,** *a.* exciting hatred, detestable. **hater,** *n.* **hatred,** *n.* intense dislike, ill will. (O.E. *hatian*)

hate, see **haet.**

hath, see **have.**

hatter, *n.* maker of, dealer in, hats.

hatti, hatti-sherif, *n.* irrevocable Turkish edict signed by sultan. (Turk.)

hauberk, *n.* coat of ringed mail. (O.F. *hauberc*)

haud, *Scot.* form of **hold.**

haugh, *n.* level land near river.

haughty, *a.* proud, arrogant, disdainful; (*Spens.*) high. (L. *altus,* high)

haul, *v.t.* and *i.* drag, pull forcibly; alter ship's course; (of wind) veer.—*n.* hauling; catch. **haulage,** *n.* conveyance of loads; charge for it. **haulier,** *n.* hauler; carter. (*hale*)

hauld, *n.* (*Scot.*) hold. **out of house and h.,** homeless and destitute.

haulm, halm, *n.* stalk, stalks, of beans, peas etc.; thatch of this. (O.E. *healm*)

haun, *Scot.* form of **hand.**

haunch, *n.* fleshy part of hip; leg and loin of venison; (*Shake.*) rear; (*archit.*) side of arch between crown and piers. (O.F. *hanche*)

haunt, *v.t.* and *i.* frequent, visit frequently; (*p.p.*) infested by ghosts.—*n.* place much resorted to. (F. *hanter*)

hausfrau, *n.* housewife. (G.)

haustellum, *n.* (*pl.* **haustella**) sucking organ of insect or crustacean. **haustellate,** *a.* **haustorium,** *n.* (*pl.* **haustoria**) sucker of parasitic plant. (L. *haurire,* draw off)

hautboy, *n.* wood-wind instrument, oboe; reed-stop on organ; kind of strawberry. (F. *haut,* high; *bois,* wood)

hauteur, *n.* haughtiness. *haut-goût,* *n.* taint; high flavour. *haut ton,* (people of) high fashion. *haute école,* the more difficult feats of horsemanship. (F.)

Havana, *n.* fine brand of cigar. (town)
have, *v.t.* and *i.* (*2nd sing.* **hast**; *3rd sing.* **has**: *past, p.p.* **had**) own, possess, hold; enjoy, suffer; obtain; be obliged (to do); (*sl.*) cheat; as *auxiliary*, forms perfect tense.—*n.* (*sl.*) swindle. **h. at,** assail. **h. done,** make an end. **h. it out,** settle dispute by discussion. **h. up,** call to account before lawcourt. (O.E. *habban*)
haven, *n.* harbour; refuge. (O.E. *hæfen*)
haver, *v.i.* (*Scot.*) talk nonsense. **haverel,** *n.* foolish person. **havers,** *n.pl.* foolish talk.
haversack, *n.* soldier's or hiker's provision-bag. (G. *haber*, oats)
havildar, *n.* (*Anglo-Ind.*) native N.C.O. equal to sergeant. (Pers.)
having, *n.* property, belongings.
haviour, *n.* (*obs.*) behaviour.
havoc *n.* devastation, destruction.—*int.* hunting-cry or war-cry.—*v.t.* (*past, p.p.* **havocked**) lay waste. (O.F. *havot*)
haw, *n.* hawthorn berry; hedge, enclosure. **hawfinch,** *n.* small bird with large beak. (O.E. *haga*, hedge)
haw, *n.* third eyelid of horse etc.; disease of this membrane.
haw, *n.* hesitation in speech.—*v.i.* drawl, speak with haw. **h.-h.,** *a.* affected. (imit.)
haw-haw, *n.* and *v.i.* guffaw. (imit.)
haw-haw, see **ha-ha.**
hawk, *n.* bird of prey like falcon; rapacious person.—*v.i.* and *t.* hunt with hawk; attach like hawk. **h.-eyed,** *a.* keen-eyed. (O.E. *habuc*)
hawk, *v.t.* carry about for sale. **hawker,** *n.* itinerant dealer, pedlar.
hawk, *v.i.* clear throat noisily.
hawk, *n.* plasterer's board.
hawked, *a.* (*Scot.*) spotted, streaked.
hawkweed, *n.* kinds of composite plants, us. yellow-flowered.
hawse, *n.* (*naut.*) part of bows containing **h.-holes,** *n. pl.* through which cables pass. (O.N. *hals*, neck)
hawse, *n.* (*Scot.*) neck, throat. (*halse*)
hawser, *n.* large rope, small cable. (L.L. *altiare*, hoist)
hawthorn, *n.* thorny shrub much used for hedges; its white flower. (*haw*)
hay, *n.* (*Shake.*) country dance with winding movement.
hay, *n.* (*Shake.*) home-thrust. (It. *hai*, you have it)
hay, *n.* grass mown and dried. **hit the h.,** (*Amer. sl.*) go to bed. **make h. of,** throw into confusion. **h.-box,** *n.* box packed with hay in which food can be kept hot and cooked. **haycock,** *n.* small heap of hay. **h.-fever,** *n.* summer catarrh. **haymaker.** *n.* one who lifts and spreads hay; (*sl.*) swinging blow. **hayrick, haystack,** *nn.* large mound of hay. **hayseed,** *n.* (*Amer. sl.*) rustic. **haywire,** *a.* (*Amer. sl.*) crazy. (O.E. *hieg*)
hayward, *n.* official in charge of commons and enclosures. (*haw*)
hazard, *n.* a game at dice; chance; risk; (*billiards*) pocketing stroke; (*golf*) bunker; (*tennis*) winning opening.—*v.t.* expose to chance or danger, risk. **hazardous,** *a.* risky, dependent on chance. (O.F. *hasard*)
haze, *n.* mist, obscurity.—*v.t.* make hazy.
haze, *v.t.* (*naut.*) overwork, persecute; (*Amer.*) bully. **hazing,** *n.* horse-play.
hazel, *n.* bush bearing **h.-nut.**—*a.* light brown. (O.E. *hæsel*)
he, *pron.* (*objective* **him,** *possessive* **his**) the male person named before.—*n.* and *a.* male. **he-man,** *n.* (*Amer.*) virile man. (O.E.)
head, *n.* upper part of body; upper or chief part; brain; chief, leader; individual; section of discourse; source; culmination; pressure; front; (*naut.*) bows.—*a.* chief; (of wind) contrary.—*v.t.* act, put, as head to; govern; outstrip; lop off.—*v.i.* face, make for. **h. back, off,** turn back, aside. **h. over ears,** deeply. **h. over heels,** topsyturvy, sprawling. **give** (horse etc.) **his h.,** let him go freely. **keep one's h.,** keep calm. **lose one's h.,** be beheaded; become confused. **make h.,** gain ground. **off one's h.,** crazy. **over one's h.,** beyond one's comprehension. (O.E. *héafod*)
headache, *n.* continuous pain in the head. **headachy,** *a.*
headband, *n.* band worn round head.
headborough, *n.* petty constable.
head-dress, *n.* ornamental covering for head.
header, *n.* plunge head first; brick laid at right angle to face of wall.
headfast, *n.* mooring rope at bow.
headgear, *n.* covering for head, hat.
heading, *n.* title at head of page etc.
headland, *n.* promontory.
headless, *a.* without a head.
headlight, *n.* strong front light of car or locomotive.
headline, *n.* line at top of page; newspaper heading.
headlong, *adv.* head first; precipitately; rashly.—*a.* impetuous, rash; steep.
headman, *n.* chief man (of tribe etc.)
headmaster, headmistress, *nn.* chief master, mistress, of a school.
headmost, *a.* foremost.
headphones, *n.pl.* telephone receivers which fit over the head, for radio listening etc.
headpiece, *n.* helmet; head, intellect; engraving at head of chapter in book.
headquarters, *n.pl.* commander-in-chief's quarters; central office.
head-rhyme, *n.* alliteration.
headsman, *n.* one who beheads, executioner.
headstall, *n.* part of bridle that fits round head.
headstone, *n.* tombstone.
headstrong, *a.* self-willed, obstinate.
head-voice, *n.* one of higher registers of voice, falsetto.

headway, *n.* motion ahead, progress.
head-work, *n.* mental work.
heady, *a.* affecting the head, intoxicating; impetuous, violent.
heal, *v.t.* and *i.* make well, cure; become sound. **healer,** *n.* **health,** *n.* soundness of body or mind; bodily condition; toast drunk in person's honour. **healthful,** *a.* health-giving. **healthy,** *a.* having good health, vigorous; wholesome. (O.E. *hǽlan*)
heap, *n.* pile of things lying one on another; great number.—*v.t.* pile in heap; load (with). **struck all of a h.,** utterly confounded. **heapy,** *a.* full of heaps. (O.E. *héap*)
hear, *v.t.* and *i.* (*past, p.p.* **heard**) perceive by ear; listen to; try judicially; grant; be informed. **h.! h.!** exclamation of approval. **h. tell of,** (*arch.*) be told of. **hearer,** *n.* **hearing,** *n.* perception by ear; audience; earshot. (O.E. *híeran*)
hearken, harken, *v.i.* listen. (*hark*)
hearsay, *n.* gossip, rumour.—*a.* not based on personal knowledge.
hearse, *n.* funeral carriage conveying coffin. (L. *hirpex,* harrow)
heart, *n.* organ which makes the blood circulate; seat of emotions or affections; mind, soul; courage; central part; playing-card marked with heart. **at h.,** at bottom. **break one's h.,** overwhelm with grief. **by h.,** by memory. **give, lose, one's h. to,** fall in love with. **have one's h. in one's mouth,** be violently startled. **have the h.,** be unfeeling enough (to). **h. to h.,** with candour. **lay to h.,** think over seriously. **out of h.,** in poor spirits. **searchings of h.,** misgivings. **take h.,** be encouraged. **take to h.,** be much affected by. **wear one's h. upon one's sleeve,** show feelings openly. **with all one's h.,** sincerely. (O.E. *heorte*)
heartache, *n.* sorrow, anguish.
heartbeat, *n.* pulsation of heart.
heartbreak, *n.* overwhelming sorrow. **heartbreaking, heartbroken,** *aa.* crushing, crushed, with grief.
heartburn, *n.* burning sensation in the chest, cardialgia. **heartburning,** *n.* discontent; enmity.
hearten, *v.t.* encourage, cheer.
heartfelt, *a.* deeply felt, sincere.
hearth, *n.* floor of fireplace; fireside. **hearthrug,** *n.* rug in front of fireplace. **hearthstone,** *n.* slab forming hearth; soft stone used for whitening hearths etc. (O.E. *heordh*)
heartily, *adv.* with goodwill, in a hearty manner; very.
heartless, *a.* unfeeling, cruel.
heart-rending, *a.* distressing, agonizing.
heartsease, *n.* pansy.
heartsick, *a.* depressed, despondent.
heart-strings, *n.pl.* affections.
heart-whole, *a.* not in love; sincere.
hearty, *a.* cordial; genuine; vigorous, healthy; (of meal) satisfying.
heat, *n.* hotness; sensation of warmth; hot weather; excitement, anger; sexual excitement in animals; single course in a race.—*v.t.* and *i.* make or become hot, inflame. **h.-wave,** *n.* spell of hot weather. **prickly h.,** skin disease common in hot climates. **heater,** *n.* **heatedly,** *adv.* (O.E. *hǽtu*)
heath, *n.* tract of waste land, moor; kinds of shrub. **h.-bell,** *n.* flower of heath. **h.-cock,** *n.* blackcock. **heathy,** *a.* (O.E. *hædh*)
heathen, *n.* and *a.* pagan, infidel; irreligious (person). **heathendom,** *n.* lands inhabited by heathens. **heathenish,** *a.* **heathenism,** *n.* **heathenize,** *v.t.* and *i.* (O.E. *hædhen*)
heather, *n.* ling, small shrub with bell-like flower called **h.-bell. h. mixture,** cloth of mixed hues like heather. **heathery,** *a.*
heave *v.t.* (*past, p.p.* **heaved** or **hove**) lift, throw, with effort; (of stratum) displace; utter (sigh etc.); pant, retch; (*naut.*) haul.—*v.i.* swell, rise. —*n.* heaving; displacement (of stratum); (*pl.*) disease of horses, broken wind. **h. in sight,** come into view. **h. to,** bring ship to stop. (O.E. *hebban*)
heaven, *n.* sky; abode of God and the blessed; God, Providence; supreme happiness. **seventh h.,** state of exalted happiness. **heavenly,** *a.* of heaven, divine; of the sky; supremely excellent. **heavenly-minded,** *a.* devout; pure. (O.E. *hefen*)
Heaviside layer, layer of the atmosphere that reflects wireless waves back. (name of physicist)
heavy, *a.* of great weight; abundant; difficult, oppressive; dull, slow; sad; drowsy; (of food) indigestible; (of soil) miry. **h.-handed,** *a.* clumsy; oppressive. **h.-laden,** *a.* heavily burdened. **h. metal,** big guns; formidable opponent. **h. spar,** barytes. **h. water,** water in which the hydrogen content is replaced by heavy hydrogen. **h.-weight,** *n.* and *a.* (person) over normal weight; (*boxing*) over 12 st. 7 lb. (O.E. *hefig*)
hebdomad, *n.* group of seven; week. **hebdomadal,** *a.* weekly. **Hebdomadal Council,** board meeting weekly at Oxford University. (Gk. *hepta,* seven)
Hebe, *n.* goddess of youth; (*joc.*) barmaid. (Gk.)
hebetate, *v.t.* and *i.* make or become dull. **hebetation, hebetude,** *nn.* (L. *hebes,* blunt)
hebetic, *a.* (*med.*) of, occurring at, puberty. (Gk. *hēbē,* youth)
Hebrew, *n.* Jew, Israelite; ancient Jewish language.—*a.* Jewish. **Hebraic,** *a* **hebraism,** *n.* Hebrew idiom. **hebraist,** *n.* student of Hebrew. (Heb. *'ibri,* one from the other side)
hecatomb, *n.* sacrifice of a large

number of victims. (Gk. *hekaton*, hundred; *bous*, ox)
hecatontome, *n.* vast number of books. (Gk. *hekaton*, hundred; *tomos*, book)
hech, *int.* (*Scot.*) of surprise.
heck, *n.* rack for fodder; frame for catching fish. (O.E. *hec*)
heck, *Amer.* euphemism for hell.
heckle, *v.t.* comb (flax etc.); ask awkward questions of. **heckler,** *n.*
hectare, *n.* area of 100 ares=10,000 sq. metres=2·471 acres. (Gk. *hekaton*, hundred)
hectic, *a.* consumptive, flushed; (*sl.*) exciting, wild.—*n.* hectic fever or patient. (Gk. *hexis*, habit of body)
hecto-, from Gk. *hekaton*, hundred, used in metric system, **hectogramme, hectogram,** *n.* weight of 100 grammes (3·527 oz.); **hectolitre, hectoliter,** *n.* capacity of 100 litres (22·01 imperial gallons); **hectometre, hectometer,** *n.* length of 100 metres (328·089 ft.).
hectograph, *n.* kind of duplicator.—*v.t.* reproduce with this. (Gk. *hekaton*, hundred; *graphein*, write)
hector, *n.* blusterer.—*v.t.* and *i.* bully. (Homeric hero)
hederaceous, *a.* of, like, ivy. (L. *hedera*, ivy)
hedge, *n.* fence of bushes; turf or stone barrier.—*v.t.* surround with hedge; hem in.—*v.i.* make, trim, hedge; guard against loss by betting on both sides; shift, shuffle. **h.-bill,** *n.* bill-hook for dressing hedge. **h.-sparrow,** *n.* small singing bird. **hedgehog,** *n.* small prickly quadruped. **hedgehoggy,** *a.* **hedgepig,** *n.* (*Shake.*) young hedgehog. **hedger,** *n.* one who makes hedges. **hedgerow,** *n.* row of bushes forming hedge. (O.E. *hecg*)
hedonism, *n.* doctrine that pleasure is the chief good. **hedonic, hedonistic,** *aa.* **hedonist,** *n.* votary of hedonism. (Gk. *hēdonē*, pleasure)
heeby-jeebies, *n.pl.* a dance; (*sl.*) fit of nerves, jumpiness.
heed, *v.t.* attend to, take notice of.—*n.* attention, caution. **heedful,** (*Spens.*) **heedy,** *aa.* **heedless,** *a.* inattentive, careless. (O.E. *hédan*)
hee-haw, *n.* ass's bray; guffaw. (imit.)
heel, *n.* hinder part of foot; corresponding part of sock, shoe etc.; hind foot of animal; (*Amer. sl.*) worthless or contemptible person.—*v.t.* furnish, touch, with heel; kick backwards. **heeled,** *a.* shod; (*Amer. sl.*) supplied with money; (*Amer. sl.*) armed with revolver. **at h.,** upon **one's hh.,** close behind. **cool, kick, one's hh.,** be kept waiting. **down at hh.,** having heels worn down; slovenly. **head over hh.,** in a somersault. **h. of Achilles,** vulnerable part. **lay by the hh.,** imprison. **show a clean pair of hh.,** escape. **to h.,** (of dog) under control. **turn on one's h.,** turn sharply round. (O.E. *héla*)
heel *v.i.* (of ship) lean over.—*n.* list. (O.E. *hieldan*)
heelball, *n.* polishing-wax for shoes.
heeler, *n.* (*Amer.*) political hanger-on.
heel-tap, *n.* piece of leather in heel; drink left in bottom of glass.
heeze, *v.t.* (*Scot.*) hoist, heave.
heft, *n.* heaving; (*Shake.*) retching; (*Amer.*) weight.—*v.t.* lift, try the weight of. **hefty,** *a.* sturdy, stalwart. (*heave*)
hegemony, *n.* leadership. **hegemonic,** *a.* (Gk. *hēgemōn*, leader)
hegira, hejira, *n.* Mohammed's flight from Mecca, 16 July, A.D. 622, from which is dated the Mohammedan era. (Arab. *hijrah*, departure)
heifer, *n.* young cow. (O.E. *heahfore*)
heigh, *int.* of encouragement. **h.-ho,** *int.* of boredom or weariness. (imit.)
height, *n.* measure from base to top; quality of being high; high position, eminence; highest degree; hill-top. **heighten,** *v.t.* make higher; intensify. (O.E. *hiehtho*)
heinous, *a.* very wicked, atrocious. (F. *haïr*, hate)
heir, *n.* (*fem.* **heiress**) person entitled to inherit property or rank. **h. apparent,** acknowledged heir. **h. presumptive,** heir whose right may be defeated by the birth of a nearer relative. **heirdom, heirship,** *nn.* rights, state, of an heir. **heirloom,** *n.* thing that has been in a family for generations. (L. *heres*)
hejira, see **hegira.**
helco-, from Gk. *helkos*, ulcer, used in **helcoid,** *a.* like an ulcer; **helcology,** *n.* science of ulcers; **helcosis,** *n.* ulceration, hence **helcotic,** *a.*
held, see **hold.**
heliacal, *a.* (*astron.*) emerging from light of the sun or passing into it. (Gk. *hēlios*, sun)
helianthus, *n.* sunflower. (Gk. *hēlios*, sun; *anthos*, flower)
helical, *a.* spiral. **helicoid, helicoidal,** *aa.* screw-shaped. (*helix*)
helicopter, *n.* aircraft made to rise vertically by horizontally revolving airscrews. (*helix*; Gk. *pterux*, wing)
helio-, from Gk. *helios*, sun, used in **heliocentric, heliocentrical,** *aa.* taking the sun as centre; **heliochromy,** *n.* photography in natural colours; **heliogravure,** *n.* photogravure; **heliolatry,** *n.* sun-worship; **heliometer,** *n.* instrument for measuring diameters of sun and planets; **helioscope,** *n.* telescope for viewing the sun without injury to the eyes; **heliosis,** *n.* sunstroke; **heliotherapy,** *n.* curative use of sun-baths; **heliotropic,** *a.* moving towards the sun; **heliotypy,** *n.* method of printing photographs from a gelatine surface.
heliogram, *n.* message by heliograph.
heliograph, *n.* signalling instrument

reflecting sun's rays from mirror; apparatus for photographing sun; engraving made by exposure to light. —*v.t.* send message, take photograph, by heliograph. **heliographic,** *a.* **heliography,** *n.* (Gk. *hēlios,* sun; *graphein,* write)
heliotrope, *n.* plant with fragrant purple flowers; their colour or scent; bloodstone, a kind of chalcedony. (Gk. *hēlios,* sun; *trepein,* turn)
helium, *n.* a light, non-inflammable gas, used in airships. (Gk. *hēlios,* sun, where it was discovered)
helix, *n.* (*pl.* **helices**) spiral; (*zool.*) snail or its shell; (*anat.*) rim of the ear; (*archit.*) small volute. (Gk.)
hell, *v.t.* (*Spens.*) cover, hide. (O.E. *helan*)
hell, *n.* place of punishment for wicked after death; abode of dead; place, state, of vice or misery; infernal powers; gambling resort; (*Amer. sl.*) drunken frolic. **h. for leather,** at top speed. **h.-cat,** *n.* malignant hag. **hellhound,** *n.* fiend. **hellish,** *a.* (O.E. *hel*)
hellebore, *n.* plant anciently used to cure madness; Christmas rose. (Gk. *helleboros*)
Hellene, *n.* Greek. **Hellenic,** *a.* **Hellenism,** *n.* Greek idiom or culture. **hellenize,** *v.t.* and *i.* **Hellenist,** *n.* Greek-speaking foreigner. **Hellenistic,** *a.* (Gk. *Hellēn*)
hellicat, *a.* flighty.—*n.* (*Scot.*) wicked creature.
hello, same as **hallo.**
helm, *n.* tiller, wheel, controlling rudder; guidance.—*v.t.* steer, control. **put down h.,** bring rudder to windward. **put up h.,** bring rudder to leeward. **helmsman,** *n.* steersman. (O.E. *helma*)
helm, *n.* (*arch.*) helmet. (O.E.)
helmet, *n.* defensive head-covering; upper part of retort; (*bot.*) hooded upper lip of some flowers. **helmeted,** *a.* (*helm*)
helminth, *n.* worm. **helminthic,** *a.* and *n.* of worms, (medicine) for worms. **helminthoid,** *a.* worm-shaped. **helminthology,** *n.* natural history of worms. **helminthological,** *a.* (Gk. *helmins*)
heloma, *n.* (*med.*) corn. **helotomy,** *n.* cutting of corns. (Gk. *hēlos,* nail)
helot, *n.* serf in ancient Sparta; any serf. **helotism, helotry,** *nn.* (Gk. *Heilōs*)
help, *v.t.* (*arch. past* **holp,** *p.p.* **holpen**) assist, aid; serve with, serve (food); prevent, remedy.—*n.* aid, support; remedy; helper, (*Amer.*) servant. **helper,** *n.* **helpful,** *a.* useful. **helping,** *n.* portion of food. **helpless,** *a.* unable to help oneself. **helpmate,** *n.* wife, husband; helpful partner. (O.E. *helpan*)
helpmeet, *n.* helpmate. (misunderstanding of Genesis ii. 18, 20)
helter-skelter, *adv.* and *a.* in confused hurry. (imit.)
helve, *n.* handle of tool, esp. axe. (O.E. *helfe*)
Helvetian, *a.* and *n.* Swiss. (L. *Helvetius*)
hem, *n.* edge of cloth, esp. when doubled down and sewed.—*v.t.* sew hem on. **h. in, round,** enclose, confine. **hemstitch,** *n.* an ornamental stitch. (O.E.)
hem, *int.* and *n.* half-cough to draw attention.—*v.i.* clear throat; hesitate in speech. (imit.)
hematite, see **haematite.**
hemi-, *pref.* half, used in **hemianopsia,** *n.* blindness as to half the field of vision; **hemicycle,** *n.* half-circle; **hemidemisemiquaver,** *n.* half a demisemiquaver; **hemihedral,** *a.* (of crystal) having half normal number of faces; **hemiplegia,** *n.* paralysis of one side. (Gk.)
hemisphere, *n.* half sphere; half the earth. **eastern h.,** Europe, Asia, and Africa. **western h.,** America. **northern, southern h.,** earth north, south, of equator. **hemispherical,** *a.*
hemistich, *n.* half of a line of verse. (Gk. *hemi-,* half; *stichos,* verse)
hemlock, *n.* a poisonous plant; the poison it yields. (O.E. *hemlic*)
hemorrhage, hemorrhoids, see **haemorrhage, haemorrhoids.**
hemp, *n.* an Indian plant; its fibre, used for rope, coarse cloth etc.; hangman's rope; hashish. **hempen,** *a.* (O.E. *henep*)
hen, *n.* female bird, esp. domestic fowl. **h.-coop,** *n.* cage for poultry. **h.-harrier,** *n.* kind of hawk. **h.-party,** *n.* party for women only. **henpeck,** *v.t.* (of wife) domineer over husband. **h.-roost,** *n.* roosting-place for fowls. (O.E. *henn*)
hence, *adv.* from here; from now; by reason of this.—*int.* begone! **henceforth, henceforward,** *advv.* from this time forward. (M.E. *hennes*)
henchman, *n.* trusty follower; chief attendant of highland chief; squire, page. (O.E. *hengest,* horse; *man*)
hendeca-, eleven, used in **hendecagon,** *n.* eleven-sided plane figure; **hendecasyllable,** *n.* verse of eleven syllables; **hendecasyllabic,** *a.* (Gk.)
hendiadys, *n.* use of two connected words to express one idea, as 'with might and main.' (Gk. *hen dia duoin,* one thing by two)
henism, *n.* doctrine that there is only one kind of substance, whether mind or matter; monism. (Gk. *heis,* one)
henna, *n.* Egyptian privet; dye made from it. (Arab.)
hennery, *n.* poultry farm. **henny,** *a.* hen-like.—*n.* hen-like cock.
henotheism, *n.* belief in one god without holding that he is the only one. (Gk. *heis,* one; *theos,* god)
henry, *n.* (*pl.* **henries**) unit of induc-

tance; inductance of a circuit in which 1 volt is induced by current varying at rate of 1 ampere per second. (person)

hent, *v.t.* (*obs.*; *past, p.p.* same) seize, take.—*n.* (*obs.*) clutch; intention. (O.E. *hentan*)

hep, *a.* (*Amer. sl.*) informed.

hep, see **hip.**

hepatic, *a.* of, good for, the liver; liver-coloured. **hepatitis,** *n.* inflammation of the liver. **hepatize,** *v.t.* convert (lungs) into liver substance. **hepatology,** *n.* science of the liver. **hepatoscopy,** *n.* divination from the livers of animals. (Gk. *hēpar*, liver)

hepta-, seven, used in **heptachord,** *n.* seven-stringed instrument; **heptad,** *n.* group of seven; **heptaglot,** *a.* and *n.* (book) in seven languages; **heptagon,** *n.* seven-sided plane figure; **heptahedron,** *n.* solid with seven faces; **heptameron,** *n.* book containing the doings of seven days, esp. that written by Queen Margaret of Navarre; **heptameter,** *n.* verse of seven feet; **heptarchy,** *n.* government by seven, esp. seven kingdoms of early England; **heptasyllabic,** *a.* of seven syllables; **heptateuch,** *n.* first seven books of the Bible; **heptavalent,** *a.* having a valency of seven. (Gk.)

her, see **she.**

herald, *n.* officer who makes royal proclamations, arranges ceremonies, and regulates armorial bearings; messenger, envoy.—*v.t.* proclaim approach of, usher in. **heraldic,** *a.* of heraldry. **heraldry,** *n.* science of armorial bearings. (O.F. *heralt*)

herb, *n.* plant with soft stem that dies to the root every year; plant yielding medicine, food, or scent. **h. bennet,** common avens. **h.-of-grace,** *n.* rue. **herbaceous,** *a.* of, like, herbs. **herbage,** *n.* herbs, grass, pasture. **herbal,** *a.* of herbs.—*n.* treatise on herbs. **herbalist,** *n.* writer on, dealer in, herbs. **herbarium,** *n.* (*pl.* **herbariums, herbaria**) collection of dried plants. **herbiferous,** *a.* bearing herbs. **herbivorous,** *a.* herb-eating. **herborize,** *v.i.* gather herbs, botanize. **herborist,** *n.* **herby,** *a.* herb-like; rich in herbs. (L. *herba*, grass)

Herculean, *a.* of Hercules; strong; extremely difficult. (*Hercules*, Gk. hero)

herd, *n.* company of animals of one kind; crowd, rabble; herdsman.—*v.t.* tend (herd); drive together.—*v.i.* go in herd. **herdsman,** *n.* one who tends a herd. (O.E. *heord*)

here, *adv.* in this place, life, or state; to this place; at this point. **h. and there,** in various places. **neither h. nor there,** not to the point, of no consequence. **hereabout, hereabouts,** *adv.* near here. **hereafter,** *adv* after this; in future, in the world to come.—*n.* next world. **hereat,** *adv.* (*arch.*) at this. **hereaway,** *adv.* (*colloq.*) hereabout. **hereby,** *adv.* by this means; near. (O.E. *hér*)

heredity, *n.* transmission of qualities from parents to their offspring. **hereditable,** *a.* that can be inherited. **hereditament,** *n.* hereditable property; inheritance. **hereditary,** *a.* descending, holding office, by inheritance; transmitted from one generation to another. (L. *heres*, heir)

herein, *adv.* in this. **hereinafter,** *adv.* afterwards in this. **hereof,** *adv.* (*arch.*) of this.

heresy, *n.* opinion contrary to usual belief, esp. in religion; heterodoxy. **heresiarch,** *n.* leader, founder, of a heresy. **heresiology,** *n.* study of heresies. **heretic,** *n.* holder of a heresy. **heretical,** *a.* (Gk. *hairesis*, choice, sect)

hereto, *adv.* (*arch.*) to this. **heretofore,** *adv.* before this, formerly. **hereunder,** *adv.* below. **hereupon,** *adv.* after this, in consequence of this. **herewith,** *adv.* with this.

heriot, *n.* (*law*) tribute paid to lord of manor on decease of tenant. (O.E. *here*, army; *geatwe*, apparel)

heritable, *a.* that can be inherited or inherit. **h. property,** (*Scots law*) real property. **heritage,** *n.* what is or may be inherited; portion, lot. **heritor,** *n.* one who inherits; proprietor. (L. *heres*, heir)

hermaphrodite, *n.* and *a.* (animal, plant) having characteristics of both sexes. **hermaphroditical,** *a.* **hermaphroditism,** *n.* (*Hermaphroditos* in Gk. myth)

hermeneutic, *a.* of interpretation; explanatory. **hermeneutics,** *n.pl.* science of interpretation, esp. of the Bible. (Gk. *hermeneuein*, interpret)

hermetic, *a.* of alchemy, magical; perfectly close. **hermetically,** *adv.* **hermetically sealed,** closed completely, so as to be air-tight. (*Hermes* Trismegistos, god of alchemy)

hermit, *n.* person living in solitude, esp. from religious motives; recluse. **h.-crab,** *n.* crab that lives in cast-off shell of whelk etc. **hermitage,** *n.* hermit's cell, solitary dwelling. (Gk. *erēmos*, solitary)

hern, see **heron.**

hernia, *n.* rupture. **hernial, herniary,** *aa.* **herniotomy,** *n.* operation of cutting for hernia. (L.)

hernshaw, see **heron.**

hero, *n.* (*fem.* **heroine**) specially valiant or great man; chief figure in story; demigod. **heroic,** *a.* of, worthy of, a hero; having qualities of a hero, brave, daring; (of poetry) dealing with heroes, epic; (of language) grand, high-flown.—*n.* heroic verse; (*pl.*) high-flown language. **heroic verse,** that used in heroic poetry, i.e. the hexameter in Greek and Latin, the iambic pentameter (heroic couplet) in English, and the Alexandrine in French. **heroi-comic,** *a.* combining heroic with comic. **heroify,** *v.t.* make a hero of. **heroism,** *n.* heroic conduct or qualities, bravery. **heroize,** *v.t.* and *i.* make a hero of; play the hero. (Gk. *hērōs*)

heroin, *n.* sedative made from morphia.

heron, hern, *n.* wading-bird with long legs and neck. **heronry,** *n.* herons' breeding-place. **heronshaw, hernshaw,** *n.* young heron. (O.H.G. *heigir*)

herpes, *n.* skin disease. **herpetic,** *a.* (Gk.=shingles)

herpetology, *n.* science of reptiles. **herpetologist,** *n.* (Gk. *herpein,* creep)

Herr, *n.* (*pl. Herren*) German for Mr., gentleman.

herring, *n.* small edible sea-fish. **kippered h.,** kipper. **red h.,** smoked herring; subject introduced to divert attention. **h.-bone,** *n.* kind of cross-stitch; (*archit.*) zigzag arrangement of stones.—*v.t.* stitch, mark, with this pattern. **h.-pond,** *n.* (*joc.*) N. Atlantic. (O.E. *hǣring*)

herry, *v.t.* (*Scot.*) harry. **herriment,** *n.*

hers, see **she.**

herself, *pron.* emphatic and refl. form of **she**; in her real character, sane.

hertz, *n.* (*wireless*) unit of frequency, 1 cycle per second. **Hertzian waves,** waves caused by electricity, used in wireless telegraphy. (person)

hery, *v.t.* (*Spens.*) praise. (O.E. *herian*)

hesitate, *v.i.* hold back; feel, show, indecision; be reluctant. **hesitant,** *a.* **hesitation, hesitancy,** *nn.* (L. *haerēre,* stick)

Hesperus, *n.* evening star. **Hesperian,** *a.* (*poet.*) western. **hesperornis,** *n.* American fossil bird. (Gk. *hesperos,* evening)

Hessian, *a.* of Hesse in Germany.—*n.* coarse cloth of jute. **H. (boot),** kind of high boot. **H. fly,** fly whose larva destroys wheat.

hest, *n.* (*arch.*) behest. (O.E. *hǣs*)

het, *a.* (*Scot.*) hot. **h. up,** (*Amer. sl.*) agitated, annoyed.

hetaera, hetaira, *n.* (*pl.* **hetaerae, hetairae**) courtesan, harlot. **hetaerism, hetairism,** *n.* open concubinage. (Gk.)

hetero-, from Gk. *heteros,* other, used in **heterochromous,** *a.* of different colours; **heteroclite,** *a.* irregularly inflected; **heterogamous,** *a.* (*bot.*) bearing two kinds of flowers which differ sexually; **heteromorphic,** *a.* of dissimilar forms; **heteronomous,** *a.* subject to the rule of another; **heteronym,** *n.* word of same spelling as another but different sound and meaning, e.g. 'sow,' female pig, and 'sow,' scatter seed; **heteropathic,** *a.* allopathic; **heterophyllous,** *a.* bearing leaves of different forms on same stem; **heterosexual,** *a.* directed towards opposite sex; **heterosuggestion,** *n.* (*psycho-anal.*) suggestion imposed by another, opp. to autosuggestion.

heterodox, *a.* contrary to accepted opinion, not orthodox; heretical. **heterodoxy,** *n.* (Gk. *doxa,* opinion)

heterodyne, heterodyning, *nn.* (*wireless*) method by which a wave of different length is imposed on a transmitted wave to produce pulsations of audible frequency. (Gk. *dunamis,* power)

heterogeneous, *a.* of another kind, diverse; composed of diverse elements. **heterogeneity, heterogeneousness,** *nn.* (Gk. *genos,* kind)

heterogenesis, *n.* spontaneous generation; birth other than from parent of same kind. (Gk. *genesis,* generation)

hetman, *n.* Cossack commander-in-chief or head. (Polish)

heugh, *n.* (*Scot.*) pit, ravine; crag.

hew, *v.t.* and *i.* (*p.p.* **hewed** or **hewn**) chop, hack, with axe or sword; shape. **hewer,** *n.* (O.E. *hēawan*)

hexa-, from Gk. *hex,* six, used in **hexachord,** *n.* diatonic series of six notes, with semitone between third and fourth; **hexad,** *n.* group of six; **hexagon,** *n.* six-sided plane figure, hence **hexagonal,** *a.*; **hexagram,** *n.* figure formed by two intersecting equilateral triangles; **hexahedron,** *n.* solid with six faces, esp. cube, hence **hexahedral,** *a.*; **hexameter,** *n.* verse of six feet, hence **hexametric,** *a.*, **hexametrist,** *n.*; **hexapla,** *n.* edition, esp. of the Bible, in six versions; **hexapod,** *n.* and *a.* (animal) with six feet; **hexapody,** *n.* verse with six feet; **hexastich,** *n.* stanza of six lines; **hexastyle,** *a.* and *n.* (portico) with six pillars; **hexasyllable,** *n.* word of six syllables, hence **hexasyllabic,** *a.*; **hexateuch,** *n.* first six books of the Old Testament; **hexavalent,** *a.* having a valency of six.

hey, *int.* calling attention, or of joy or interrogation. **h.-day,** *int.* of frolic, exultation, or wonder. (imit.)

heyday, *n.* full bloom, flush (of youth etc.).

hi, *int.* calling attention. (imit.)

hiatus, *n.* gap, break in series, lacuna; break between two successive vowels, esp. in consecutive words. (L.)

hibernate, *v.i.* winter, spend winter in torpid state. **hibernal,** *a.* of winter. **hibernant,** *a.* hibernating. **hibernation,** *n.* (L. *hibernare*)

Hibernian, *a.* and *n.* Irish (person). **hibernicism,** *n.* Irish idiom or bull. (L. *Hibernia,* Ireland)

hibiscus, *n.* kinds of mallow. (Gk. *hibiskos*)

hiccough, erroneous for **hiccup.** (fancied connection with *cough*)

hiccup, *n.* abrupt kind of cough caused by spasm of breathing organs.—*v.i.* and *t.* utter, say with, hiccup. (imit.)

hic jacet, epitaph. (L.=here lies)

hick, *n.* (*Amer. sl.*) farmer, provincial.

hickory, *n.* N. American nut-bearing tree; its heavy tenacious wood. (native *pohickery*)
hickwall, *n.* green woodpecker.
hid, hidden, see **hide.**
hidalgo, *n.* Spanish gentleman, don. (Sp. *hijo de algo*, son of something)
hide, *v.t.* (*past* **hid,** *p.p.* **hidden, hid**) put, keep, out of sight, conceal; keep secret.—*v.i.* conceal oneself. **h. and seek,** children's game. **h. one's head,** keep out of sight. (O.E. *hýdan*)
hide, *n.* skin of animal; (in contempt) human skin.—*v.t.* (*colloq.*) flog. **hidebound,** *a.* having tight hide or bark, impeding movement or growth: confined by rules, bigoted. (O.E. *hýd*)
hide, *n.* ancient measure of land. (O.E. *hid*)
hideous, *a.* frightful, repulsive, horrible. (O.F. *hisde*, fear)
hiding, *n.* place of concealment. so **h.-place,** *n.* (*hide*)
hiding, *n.* thrashing. (*hide*)
hidrosis, *n.* perspiration. **hidrotic,** *a.* and *n.* sudorific. (Gk. *hidrōs*)
hie, *v.i.* and *refl.* (*poet.*) hasten, go quickly. (O.E. *higian*, strive)
hiems, *n.* (*Shake.*) winter. **hiemal,** *a.* of winter. (L.)
hierarch, *n.* chief priest. **hierarchy,** *n* government by priests; priesthood organized by grades; any graded organization. **hieratic,** *a.* of the priests (esp. of ancient Egyptian writing or art); priestly. (Gk. *hieros*, sacred; *archein*, rule)
hiero-, from Gk. *hieros*, sacred, used in **hierocracy,** *n.* government by priests; **hieroglyph,** *n.* sacred character or symbol, picture-writing, hence **hieroglyphic,** *a.*—*n.pl.* hieroglyphs; **hierogram, hierograph,** *nn.* sacred inscription; **hierolatry,** *n.* worship of saints; **hierophant,** *n.* initiating priest, expounder of sacred mysteries; **hierurgy,** *n.* sacred performance, hence **hierurgical,** *a.*
higgle, *v.i.* dispute in bargaining; chaffer. **higgler,** *n.* pedlar.
higgledy-piggledy, *adv.* and *a.* in confusion, jumbled up.
high, *a.* tall, lofty; far above ground, elevated; of great rank or quality; great, intense; luxurious; (of altar, priest etc.) chief; (of meat) tainted; (of road) main; (of sea) stormy; (of season) advanced; (of sound) shrill; (of words) angry.—*adv.* far up; to a great extent, strongly; at a high pitch or rate. **h. and dry** (of ship) out of the water. **h. and low,** rich and poor. **h. and mighty,** arrogant. **h. command,** commander-in-chief and his staff. **h. day,** festal day, holiday. **h. farming,** extensive use of fertilizers. **h. life,** the upper class; their mode of life. **h. lights,** brightest parts of picture. **h. seas,** part of the ocean not under jurisdiction of any power. **h. table,** table on dais for fellows of college etc. **h. tea,** meat tea. **h. time,** specially good time; fully time. **h. water,** high tide. **h.-water-mark,** *n.* point then reached; any maximum. **on h.,** aloft; in, to, heaven. **with a h. hand,** arrogantly. (O.E. *héah*)
high-angle, *a.* (of gunfire) **at** high elevation, us. over 30°.
highball, *n.* (*Amer.*) whisky and soda.
high-blower, *n.* horse that flaps nostrils noisily.
high-born, *a.* of noble birth.
high-boy, *n.* (*Amer.*) chest of drawers on legs, tallboy.
high-bred, *a.* bred to high life; thoroughbred.
highbrow, *a.* and *n.* (*sl.*) (person, book) of intellectual type.
High-Church, *a.* giving great importance to ecclesiastical dignities and ceremonies. **High-Churchman,** *n.*
high-coloured, *a.* florid, of strong colour.
high-explosive, *n.* (*abbr.* **H.E.**) explosive of great power and rapid action, such as dynamite, T.N.T.
high-falutin, high-faluting, *a.* pretentious.—*n.* bombast.
high-flown, *a.* extravagant, turgid.
high-flyer, high-flier, *n.* ambitious person. **high-flying,** *a.*
high-hat, *v.i.* and *t.* (*Amer. sl.*) affect superiority; treat patronizingly.—*n.* one who behaves in this way.
high-handed, *a.* overbearing, arbitrary.
highland, *a.* of, in, mountains.—*n.pl.* mountainous country, esp. north part of Scotland. **h. fling,** lively Scottish dance by one person. **highlander, highlandman,** *nn.* inhabitant of the highlands.
highly, *adv.* in a high degree; favourably.
high-minded, *a.* of high moral character; proud.
highness, *n.* state of being high; title of prince or princess.
high-pitched, *a.* (of sound) shrill; (of roof) steep.
high-proof, *a.* containing a high percentage of alcohol, highly rectified.
high-roller, *n.* (*Amer. sl.*) leader of fashion, swell.
high-sounding, *a.* imposing, pompous.
high-spirited, *a.* of lofty or courageous spirit.
high-stepper, *n.* horse that lifts feet high; supercilious person; social climber.
high-strung, *a.* very sensitive.
hight, *v.t.* and *i.* (*past* **hot, hote;** *p.p.* **hight, hot, hote**) (*Spens.*) name, be called. (O.E. *hatan*)
hight, highth, *obs.* forms of **height.**
highty-tighty, same as **hoity-toity.**
highway, *n.* public road; main route. **highwayman,** *n.* man, us. mounted, who robs on the highway.
hijacker, *n.* (*Amer. sl.*) bandit who preys on smugglers or bootleggers.

hijra, hijrah, same as **hegira.**

hike, *n.* ramble, walking-tour.—*v.i.* go for tramp.—*v.t.* hoist, shoulder. **hiker,** *n.*

hilarious, *a.* cheerful, very merry. **hilarity,** *n.* gaiety. (L. *hilaris*)

Hilary, *a.* **H. term** law or university term beginning in January. (St. *Hilary*)

hilch, *v.i.* (*Scot.*) hobble.—*n.* limp.

hilding, *a.* mean, cowardly.—*n.* dastard.

hill, *n.* high mass of land, small mountain; mound.—*v.t.* bank up. **hilly,** *a.* full of hills. (O.E. *hyll*)

hillo, hilloa, *int.* calling distant person or expressing surprise.

hillock, *n.* small hill. **hillocky,** *a.*

hilt, *n.* handle of sword or dagger. **up to the h.,** completely. **hilted,** *a.* (O.E.)

him, see **he.**

himself, *pron.* emphatic and refl. form of **he**; in his real character, sane.

hind, *n.* female of red deer. (O.E.)

hind, *n.* farm worker; peasant, rustic. (O.E. *hiwan*, domestics)

hind, hinder, *aa.* at the back, posterior. **hindmost, hindermost,** *aa.* farthest behind. **hind-foremost,** *adv.* back foremost. **hind quarters,** rear parts of animal. (*hinder*)

hinder, *v.t.* obstruct, impede, delay. **hindrance,** *n.* obstruction; obstacle. (O.E. *hinder*, behind)

Hindi, *a.* and *n.* (vernacular language) of N. India. **Hindu, Hindoo,** *n.* and *a.* Indian, one who professes Hinduism. **Hinduism, Hindooism,** *n.* polytheistic Hindu religion. **hinduize, hindooize,** *v.t.* render Hindu. **Hindustani, Hindoostanee,** *a.* of Hindustan. —*n.* Hindu, Mohammedan, of N. India; language of Mohammedan conquerors of India, Urdu. (Hind. *Hind*, India)

hinge, *n.* joint on which door etc. turns; central principle.—*v.t.* attach with or as with hinge.—*v.i.* turn, depend, (on). **hinged,** *a.* (*hang*)

hinny, hinnie, *n.* (*Scot.*) honey; sweetheart.

hinny, *n.* offspring of stallion and she-ass. (L. *hinnus*)

hinny, *v.i.* whinny.

hint, *n.* slight allusion, indirect suggestion; (*Shake.*) occasion, opportunity.—*v.t.* and *i.* suggest slightly, give hint (of).

hinterland, *n.* region behind coast. (G.)

hip, *n.* projection of thigh-bone, haunch. **have on the h.,** get advantage over. **smite h. and thigh,** smite unsparingly. **h.-bath,** *n.* in which one is immersed to the hips. (O.E. *hype*)

hip, hep, *n.* fruit of rose, esp. the wild rose. (O.E. *hiope*)

hip, hyp, *n.* morbid depression, the blues.—*v.t.* depress. (*hypochondria*)

hip, *int.* introducing cheer.

hippo-, from Gk. *hippos*, horse, used in **hippo,** *n.* (*colloq.*) hippopotamus; **hippocampus,** *n.* kinds of small fish, sea-horse; **hippocentaur,** *n.* centaur; **Hippocrene,** *n.* fountain on Mount Helicon, sacred to the muses; **hippocrepian,** *a.* horse-shoe shaped; **hippodame,** *n.* (*Spens.*) sea-horse; **hippodrome,** *n.* course for chariot races; circus; **hippogriff, hippogryph,** *n.* fabulous monster, half horse, half griffin; **hippology,** *n.* study of horses; **hippopathology,** *n.* veterinary medicine; **hippophagous,** *a.* eating horse-flesh, hence **hippophagy,** *n.*; **hippopotamus,** *n.* (*pl.* **hippopotamuses, hippopotami**) large thick-skinned African river quadruped.

hippocras, *n.* spiced wine. (*Hippocrates*, a Gk. doctor)

hircine, *a.* goat-like. (L. *hircus*, goat)

hire, *n.* payment for use of thing, wages.—*v.t.* employ, let out, on hire. **h.-purchase, h.-system,** *n.* system by which thing becomes hirer's after certain number of payments. **hireling,** *n.* one who works for hire, mercenary (us. in contempt). **hirer,** *n.* (O.E. *hýr*)

hirple, *v.i.* (*Scot.*) walk as if crippled.—*n.* limping gait.

hirsel, *n.* (*Scot.*) crowd; flock of sheep.

hirsle, *v.i.* (*Scot.*) slide, move, in sitting position.

hirsute, *a.* hairy. (L. *hirsutus*)

hirudinean, *a.* and *n.* (animal) of leech family. (L. *hirudo*, leech)

hirundine, *a.* of the swallow. (L. *hirundo*, swallow)

his, see **he, it.**

Hispanic, *a.* Spanish. **hispanicism,** *n.* Spanish idiom or phrase. **Hispanophile,** *a.* and *n.* (person) fond of Spain. (L. *Hispania*, Spain)

hispid, *a.* (*bot., zool.*) shaggy, bristly. (L. *hispidus*)

hiss, *n.* sound of *s*, sibilant.—*v.i.* make this sound; express disapproval by it.—*v.t.* pronounce, deride, with hiss. (imit.)

hist, *int.* calling attention, imposing silence, or inciting dog.

histie, *a.* (*Scot.*) dry, barren.

histo-, from Gk. *histos*, web, tissue, used in **histogenesis, histogeny,** *nn.* formation of organic tissues, hence **histogenetic,** *a.*; **histology,** *n.* science of organic tissues, hence **histological,** *a.*, **histologist,** *n.*

history, *n.* methodical record of events; past events or their study; career, esp. an eventful one. **natural h.,** science of living things. **historian,** *n.* writer of history. **historic,** *a.* noted in history; (*gram.*) past. **historical,** *a.* of history or the past; based on history. **historicity,** *n.* historical character, genuineness. **historiographer,** *n.* official historian. **historiography,** *n.* writing of history. **historiographic,** *a.* (Gk. *historia*, inquiry)

histrion, *n.* stage-player. **histrionic**, *a.* of acting or actors; stagy, affected. —*n.pl.* theatrical art, play-acting. **histrionism, histrionicism**, *nn.* (L. *histrio*)

hit, *v.t.* strike; affect injuriously; find; suit; (*Amer. sl.*) arrive at.—*v.i.* aim blow; light (upon).—*n.* blow; stroke of satire; success. **h. it**, find solution. **h. it off with**, agree with. **h. up** (*cricket*) score. (O.E. *hyttan*)

hitch, *v.t.* and *i.* raise, move, with jerk; fasten, be fastened, with loop. —*n.* jerk; (*naut.*) kinds of knot; difficulty, obstruction. **h. up**, harness (horse). **h.-hike**, *v.i.* travel by getting lifts from motorists.

hither, *adv.* to this place.—*a.* nearer, on this side. **h. and thither**, to and fro. **hitherto**, *adv.* up to this time. **hitherward**, *adv.* towards this place. (O.E. *hider*)

Hitlerite, *n.* follower of Hitler; supporter of German National-Socialist regime. **Hitlerism**, *n.* (name)

hive, *n.* bees' nest, natural or artificial; community of bees; busy company. —*v.t.* and *i.* collect, place, live, in hive. (O.E. *hýf*)

hives, *n.pl.* skin eruption; laryngitis.

hizzy, *Scot.* form of **hussy**.

hoar, *a.* grey with age; greyish-white. —*n.* hoariness, hoar-frost. **h.-frost**, *n.* frozen dew. (O.E. *hár*)

hoard, *n.* stock, hidden store, esp. of money.—*v.t.* amass and hide away, store up. (O.E. *hord*)

hoarding, *n.* temporary fence round building operations etc.; boarding on which bills are posted. (O.H.G. *hurt*, hurdle)

hoarhound, same as **horehound**.

hoarse, *a.* (of voice) harsh-sounding, husky; with hoarse voice. **hoarsen**, *v.t.* and *i.* (O.E. *hás*)

hoary, *a.* (of hair) grey with age; venerable; mouldy; (*bot.*) covered with short whitish hairs. (*hoar*)

hoast, *n.* and *v.i.* (*Scot.*) cough.

hoax, *n.* deceptive trick, practical joke.—*v.t.* deceive, take in, as a joke. **hoaxer**, *n.*

hob, *n.* flat part at side of grate; peg, mark, in quoits etc.; shoe of sledge; nave of wheel; hobnail.

hob, *n.* clownish fellow; fairy. **hobbinoll**, *n.* rustic. (*Robin*)

hobbadehoy, hobbedehoy, same as **hobbledehoy**.

hobble, *v.i.* limp; walk, move, awkwardly.—*v.t.* tie legs of (horse etc.).—*n.* limping gait; rope for hobbling; awkward situation. **h. skirt**, very narrow round foot.

hobbledehoy, *n.* awkward youth, between boy and man. **hobbledehoyhood, hobbledehoyism**, *nn.*

hobby, *n.* favourite pursuit, pastime; (*arch.*) small horse. **h.-horse**, *n.* wicker horse used in morris-dance; toy horse, rocking-horse; horse on roundabout; hobby; (*Shake.*) disreputable person. (O.F. *hobin*)

hobby, *n.* kind of falcon. (O.F. *hobé*)

hobgoblin, *n.* mischievous elf, bogy.

hobnail, *n.* large-headed nail for boot-soles; yokel. **hobnailed**, *a.*

hobnob, *v.i.* drink together, be familiar (with). (lit. give and take, from O.E. *habban*, have; *nabban*, not have)

hobo, *n.* wandering workman, tramp.

hoch, *int.* and *n.* hurrah. (G.)

hock, see **hough**.

hock, *n.* white Rhenish wine. (*Hochheim* in Germany)

hock, *v.t.* (*Amer. sl.*) pawn, pledge. **in h.**, in pawn or prison.

hockey, *n.* game with ball and curved sticks between goals, 11 men a side.

hocus, *v.t.* hoax; drug.

hocus-pocus, *n.* jugglery, conjuring formula; humbug.—*v.t.* and *i.* play tricks (on). (sham Latin)

hod, *n.* builder's trough on staff for carrying mortar.

hodden, *n.* (*Scot.*) coarse woollen cloth. **h. grey**, typical rustic dress.

Hodge, *n.* typical country labourer.

hodge-podge, same as **hotch-potch**.

hodiernal, *a.* of the present day. (L. *hodie*, to-day)

hodman, *n.* mason's labourer; hack.

hodograph, *n.* graph showing velocities.

hodometer, *n.* instrument attached to axle showing distance travelled by vehicle. (Gk. *hodos*, road)

hoe, *n.* tool for loosening earth or weeding.—*v.t.* and *i.* use hoe (on), weed with hoe. (O.H.G. *houwa*)

hoe, *n.* promontory. (O.E. *hoh*)

hog, *n.* swine, pig; castrated boar; coarse or greedy person.—*v.t.* cut (mane) short.—*v.i.* raise back, rise in middle archwise. **go the whole h.**, do the thing thoroughly. **hog-back, h.'s back**, *n.* crested hill-ridge. **h.-fish**, *n.* fish with bristles on head. **h.-mane**, *n.* horse's mane cut short. **h.-wash**, *n.* kitchen swill given to hogs. **hoggish, hoglike**, *aa.* **hogweed**, *n.* cow-parsnip. (M.E.)

hog, hogg, hoggerel, hogget, *nn.* yearling sheep, not yet shorn.

Hogmanay, *n.* (*Scot.*) New Year's Eve.

hogshead, *n.* large cask; liquid measure, 52½ imperial gallons.

hoick, hoik, *v.t.* and *i.* turn (aeroplane) abruptly upwards.

hoick, hoicks, *int.* to incite hounds.

hoi polloi, the majority, rabble. (Gk.)

hoist, *v.t.* raise aloft, raise with tackle. —*n.* hoisting, heave; lift, elevator. **h. with one's own petard**, ruined by one's own device.

hoity-toity, *int.* of contemptuous surprise.—*a.* full of airs; frolicsome.

hokey-pokey, hoky-poky, *n.* cheap ice-cream; hocus-pocus. (*hocus-pocus*)

hokum, *n.* (*Amer. sl.*) trashy plot, stage business, or scenario; bunkum.

hold, *v.t.* (*past* **held**, *p.p.* **held, holden**)

grasp; keep, possess; contain; celebrate; restrain; consider, believe.—*v.i.* remain fixed, continue; apply, be valid.—*n.* grasp; influence; fortress. **h.!** stop! **h. back,** restrain; refrain. **h. forth,** make speech. **h. good,** be valid. **h. hard,** stop. **h. on,** retain grasp. **h. one's own,** not give way. **h. out,** offer; endure. **h. over,** postpone. **h. to,** adhere to. **h. up,** support; display; (*Amer.*) stop and rob. **h. water,** be sound. **h. with,** approve of. (O.E. *haldan*)

hold-all, *n.* portable case, wrapper, for carrying clothes etc.

holder, *n.* tenant possessor; device for holding.

holdfast, *n.* staple, clamp.

holding, *n.* land, stocks etc. held; (*Scots law*) tenure.

hold, *n.* space below ship's deck for cargo. (*hole*)

hole, *n.* hollow place, cavity, perforation; mean place; (*golf*) cavity into which ball is played, extent from tee to this; (*sl.*) scrape.—*v.t.* make hole in, pierce; drive into hole. **h. out,** (*golf*) play ball into hole. **pick hh. in,** find fault with. **h.-and-corner,** *a.* secret, underhand. **holey,** *a.* full of holes. (O.E. *hol*)

holi, same as **hoolee.**

holibut, see **halibut.**

holiday, *n.* day of recreation or cessation from work; (us. *pl.*) vacation; religious festival. (*holy*; *day*)

holiness, *n.* sanctity. **his H.,** the pope.

holism, *n.* (*philos.*) the creation by creative evolution of wholes that are greater than the sum of the parts. (Gk. *holos,* whole)

holla, see **hollo.**

holland, *n.* a linen fabric. (origin)

hollands, *n.* gin from Holland, schnapps.

hollo, hollow, holla, holloa, *n.* and *v.i.* shout; call to hounds.—*int.* calling attention. (F. *holà*)

hollow, *a.* not solid; sunken; empty; unsound, insincere.—*n.* hole, depression, valley.—*v.t.* make hole in, excavate.—*adv.* completely, clean. **h.-eyed,** *a.* with sunken eyes. **h.-hearted,** *a.* faithless. (O.E. *holh*)

holly, *n.* evergreen shrub with prickly leaves and scarlet berries. (O.E. *holegn*)

hollyhock, *n.* tall large-flowered garden plant. (*holy*+O.E. *hoc,* mallow)

holm, *n.* islet in river; rich flat land near river. (O.N. *holmr*)

holm, *n.* (*Spens.*) holly. **h.** or **h.-oak,** *n.* evergreen oak, ilex. (*holly*)

holo-, from Gk. *holos,* whole, used in **holocaust,** *n.* sacrifice in which entire victim was consumed, wholesale destruction; **holograph,** *a.* and *n.* (document) written wholly by the person in whose name it appears. **holohedral,** *a.* (of crystal) having full number of planes for perfect symmetry; **holometabolic,** *a.* (of insect) undergoing complete metamorphosis; **holophote,** *n.* apparatus in lighthouses for throwing all light in required direction; **holophrastic,** *a.* having the force of a whole phrase; **holothurian,** *n.* sea-cucumber, sea-slug.

holp, holpen, see **help.**

holster, *n.* leather case for pistol, fixed to saddle or belt.

holt, *n.* (*poet.*) wood, wooded hill. (O.E.)

holt, *n.* lair, otter's den. (*hold*)

holus-bolus, *adv.* at a gulp, all at once. —*n.* whole. (*whole*)

holy, *a.* belonging, devoted, to God; religious, sacred; free from sin, pure. —*n.* innermost shrine. **H. City,** Jerusalem; heaven. **H. Cross Day,** festival of the Exaltation of the Cross, 14 Sept. **h. day,** religious festival. **H. Ghost, Spirit,** third person of the Trinity. **H. Land,** Palestine. **H. Office,** Inquisition. **h. of holies,** innermost sanctuary. **h. orders,** ordination to priesthood. **H. Rood,** cross of Christ. **h. terror,** (*sl.*) formidable person; mischievous child. **H. Thursday,** Ascension Day. **h. water,** consecrated by priest. **H. Week,** week before Easter. **H. Writ,** the Bible. (O.E. *hálig*)

holystone, *n.* sandstone for scouring decks.—*v.t.* scour with it.

homage, *n.* submission of tenant to feudal superior; respect, reverence. (L.L. *homaticum*)

hombre, *n.* (*Amer. sl.*) man, fellow. (Sp.)

homburg, *n.* man's soft felt hat with dented crown, trilby. (town)

home, *n.* dwelling-place, residence; native place; institution.—*a.* of, pertaining to, home; not foreign.—*adv.* to, at, one's home; to the mark.—*v.i.* go home. **at h.,** at one's ease, familiar (with); accessible to visitors. **bring h. to,** impress upon. **H. Counties,** those near London, Middlesex, Surrey, Kent, Essex, and sometimes Hertfordshire and Sussex. **h.-farm,** *n.* the farm near the mansion-house. **h.-felt,** *a.* felt intimately. **H. Guard,** (man of) British citizen army first established in 1940 under name of Local Defence Volunteers. **H. Office,** department, office, of Home Secretary. **H. Rule,** self-government. **homesick,** *a.* depressed through absence from home. **last h.,** grave. (O.E. *ham*)

homely, *a.* domestic; unpretending, familiar; (of face) plain.

homeopathy, see **homoeopathy.**

homer, *n.* homing pigeon.

Homeric, *a.* of, like, Homer or his poems.

homespun, *a.* spun at home; plain, homely.—*n.* cloth made from homespun yarn; unpolished rustic.

homestead, *n.* house, esp. farmhouse, with its surroundings. (*stead*)

homeward, homewards, *adv.* towards home. **homeward,** *a.* leading home. **homeward bound,** (of ship) on the way home.

homicide, *n* killing, killer, of a human being. **homicidal,** *a.* (L. *homo,* man; *caedere,* kill)

homily, *n.* sermon; moralizing discourse. **homiletic,** *a.* of homilies.—*n.pl.* art of preaching. (Gk. *homilos,* crowd)

homing, *a.* (of pigeon) trained to fly home.

hominy, *n.* kind of Indian-corn porridge, boiled maize. (Amer. Indian)

homo, *n.* (*zool.*) man. **h. sapiens,** man regarded as species. (L.)

homo, *a.* and *n.* (*sl.*) homosexual (person). (abbr.)

homo-, from Gk. *homos,* same, used in **homocentric,** *a.* having the same centre; **homocercal,** *a.* with both tail-lobes equal; **homodont,** *a.* having the teeth all alike; **homodromous,** *a.* (*bot.*) taking the same direction.

homoeopathy, *n.* treatment of disease by minute quantities of those drugs which excite symptoms similar to those of the disease. **homoeopath, homoeopathist,** *n.* one who practises homoeopathy. **homoeopathic,** *a.* **homoeopathically,** *adv.* (Gk. *homoios,* like; *pathos,* suffering)

homoeoteleuton, *n.* rhetorical figure in which successive words or clauses end with the same sounds. (Gk. *homoios,* like; *teleutē,* end)

homogeneal, *a.* homogeneous.

homogeneous, *a.* of the same kind; consisting of parts all of the same kind, uniform. **homogeneity, homogeneousness,** *nn.* (Gk. *homos,* same; *genos,* kind)

homogenetic, *a.* having common descent. **homogeny,** *n.* similarity due to common descent. (Gk. *homos,* same; *genesis,* birth)

homograph, *n.* word spelt like another but differing in meaning, homonym. (Gk. *homos,* same; *graphein,* write)

homoiousian, *a.* of like substance.—*n.* one who maintained that Christ was of similar but not same nature with God. (Gk. *homoios,* like; *ousia,* essence)

homologate, *v.t.* (*Scot.*) approve, confirm. **homologation,** *n.* (*homologous*)

homologous, *a.* corresponding in position, proportion, or value; agreeing. **homologue,** *n.* homologous thing. **homology,** *n.* correspondence, sameness of relation. **homological,** *a.* **homologize,** *v.i.* and *t.* (Gk. *homos,* same; *legein,* say)

homomorphic, homomorphous, *aa.* of same or similar form. (Gk. *homos,* same; *morphē,* form)

homonym, *n.* word of same form as another but different in sense, e.g. 'bear' (carry), 'bear' (animal); namesake. **homonymic, homonymous,** *aa.* (Gk. *homos,* same; *onoma,* name)

homoousian, homousian, *a.* of same substance.—*n.* one who maintained that Christ was of same, not merely similar, nature with God. (Gk. *homos,* same; *ousia,* essence)

homophone, *n.* word having same sound as another, but of different meaning, e.g. 'beer,' 'bier'; letter having same sound as another. **homophonous,** *a.* **homophony,** *n.* (Gk. *homos,* same; *phonē,* sound)

homoplastic, *a.* similar in structure. **homoplasmy, homoplasy,** *nn.* (Gk. *homos,* same; *plassein,* form)

homosexual, *a.* and *n.* (person) attracted sexually to members of same sex. **homosexuality,** *n.* (Gk. *homos,* same)

homotaxis, *n.* (*geol.*) similarity of order, contemporaneity. **homotaxial, homotaxic,** *aa.* (Gk. *tassein,* arrange)

homotonous, *a.* of same tenour or tone.

homotype, *n.* part, organ, like another in structure. **homotypy,** *n.* (*type*)

homuncule, homuncle, *n.* little man, manikin. (L. *homunculus*)

homy, *a.* homelike.

hone, *n.* whetstone.—*v.t.* sharpen on one. (O.E. *hān*)

honest, *a.* upright; fair, dealing fairly; unadulterated; chaste. **honesty,** *n.* uprightness; a plant with semi-transparent seed-pods. **h. injun,** (*sl.*) truthfully. **make h. woman of,** marry (seduced woman). (L. *honestas,* honour)

honey, *n.* sweet thick fluid collected by bees from flowers; sweetness, sweetheart. **h.-bee,** *n.* hive bee. **h.-buzzard,** *n.* falcon that feeds on bees. **honeycomb,** *n.* structure of hexagonal wax cells in which bees store honey; large flaw in metal; hexagonal decoration.—*v.t.* fill with holes, undermine; decorate hexagonally. **h.-dew,** *n.* insect secretion on leaves of plants; nectar; tobacco sweetened with molasses. **honeyed, honied,** *a.* sweet. **honeymoon,** *n.* holiday of newly married couple. **honeysuckle,** *n.* fragrant yellow-flowered climbing shrub, woodbine. **h.-sweet,** *a.* sweet as honey. (O.E. *hunig*)

hong, *n.* warehouse, foreign trading factory, in Far East. (Chin.)

honied, see **honeyed.**

honk, *n.* and *v.i.* (of goose) cry; (of motor-horn) sound. (imit.)

honorarium, *n.* (*pl.* **honorariums, honoraria**) voluntary fee for professional services. (*honour*)

honorary, *a.* conferred as honour only, without usual requirements; unpaid.

honorific, *a.* and *n.* (expression) implying respect. **honorificabilitudinity,** *n.* honourableness.

honour, *n.* high respect, renown;

reputation; chastity; high rank; moral excellence; mark of respect; (*pl.*) distinction in examination.—*v.t.* respect highly; confer honour on; pay (bill etc.). **affair of h.,** duel. **bound in h.,** morally obliged. **maid of h.,** lady attending queen. **word of h., h. bright!** minor asseveration. (L. *honor*)

honourable, *a.* illustrious; worthy of, conferring, honour; upright; title (*abbr.* **Hon.**) of children of peers below marquess, maids of honour etc. **Most H.,** used of marquess. **Right H.,** of peer below marquess, Privy Councillor etc.

hooch, hootch, *n.* (*Amer. sl.*) intoxicating drink. (Amer. Indian *hoochinoo*)

hood, *n.* covering for head and neck, cowl; hood-like thing, roof of car, badge of academic gown.—*v.t.* cover with hood. **hoodie, hoodie-crow,** *n.* hooded crow. (O.E. *hód*)

-hood, *n.suf.* status of a, as in **sainthood**; time of being a, as in **girlhood**; quality of being, as in **hardihood.** (O.E. *-hád*, quality)

hoodlum, *n.* (*Amer.*) street rowdy.

hoodman-blind, *n.* (*Shake.*) blindman's-buff.

hoodoo, *n.* bad luck; cause of it, Jonah.—*v.t.* bring ill luck to. (*voodoo*)

hoodwink, *v.t.* deceive, humbug; blindfold. (*hood*; *wink*)

hooey, *n.* (*Amer. sl.*) nonsense, humbug.

hoof, *n.* (*pl.* **hoofs, hooves**) horny shield of foot of horse, cow etc.—*v.t.* strike with hoof; (*sl.*) kick. **h. it, pad the h.,** go on foot. (O.E. *hóf*)

hook, *n.* bent piece of metal for catching or hanging; snare; curved tool for cutting grain.—*v.t.* and *i.* catch, attach, with hook; ensnare; steal; (*boxing*) strike with elbow bent; (*cricket, golf*) play (ball) to left. **by h. or by crook,** by any means whatever. **h. it, take one's h.,** make off. **on one's own h.,** on one's own responsibility. (O.E. *hóc*)

hookah, *n.* tobacco-pipe in which smoke is passed through water. (Arab. *huqqa*)

hooked, *a.* hook-like; provided with hook.

hooker, *n.* kinds of fishing vessel. **the old h.,** (*sl.*) any ship. (Du. *hoeker*)

hookey, *n.* **blind h.,** gambling card-game. **play h.,** (*Amer. sl.*) play truant.

hookworm, *n.* parasite which lodges in human intestines, causing **h. disease.**

hool, *n.* (*Scot.*) outer skin, husk.

hoolee, *n.* Hindu festival in honour of Krishna and the milkmaids. (Hind.)

hooligan, *n.* street rough, ruffian. **hooliganism,** *n.* (name)

hooly, *adv.* (*Scot.*) softly, carefully.

hoondi, *n.* bill of exchange of native Indian banker. (Hind. *hundī*)

hoop, *n.* circular wood or metal strip for binding cask etc.; paper-covered ring through which circus riders jump; circle trundled as toy; material to expand skirt; ring; (*croquet*) arch.—*v.t.* bind with hoops; encircle. **go through the h.,** undergo ordeal. **h.-la,** *n.* game played at fairs, in which rings are thrown over objects. (O.E. *hóp*)

hoop, hooping-cough, see **whoop.**

hoopoe, hoopoo, *n.* bird with gay plumage and large crest. (L. *upupa*)

hoosegow, *n.* (*Amer. sl.*) prison. (L. *judicare*, judge)

hoosh *n.* (*sl.*) stew, hotchpotch.

hoot, *n.* cry of owl; scornful cry; sound of motor-horn, siren etc.—*v.t.* and *i.* utter hoot; sound horn; deride with hoots. **not worth a h.,** not worth anything. **hooter,** *n.* siren, horn. (imit.)

hoot, hoots, *int.* (*Scot.*) of impatience.

hootch, see **hooch.**

hoove, *n.* cattle disease, with distension of stomach. (*heave*)

hooves, see **hoof.**

hop, *v.i.* leap on one leg; leap, spring.—*n.* hopping; (of aeroplane) single flight; (*sl.*) dance. **h.-o'-my-thumb,** *n.* dwarf. **h. the twig,** (*sl.*) die. (O.E. *hoppian*)

hop, *n.* climbing plant; (*pl.*) its bitter cones, used to flavour beer.—*v.t.* flavour with hops.—*v.i.* gather hops. **h.-bind, h.-bine,** *n.* stalk of hop. **h.-fly,** *n.* aphis destructive to hop. **h.-pillow,** *n.* pillow stuffed with hops to induce sleep. **h.-pole,** *n.* pole on which plant is trained. (Du.)

hope, *n.* expectation with desire; trust, anticipation; person, thing, that hope centres in.—*v.i.* and *t.* expect with desire; feel hope. **h. against h.,** cling to faint possibility. **hopeful,** *a.* feeling or inspiring hope. **young hopeful,** promising boy or girl. **hopeless,** *a.* without hope, desperate. (O.E. *hopa*)

hoplite, *n.* heavy-armed foot-soldier of ancient Greece. (Gk. *hoplitēs*)

hopper, *n.* one who hops; flea; trough feeding grain into mill etc.; barge carrying away mud from dredger. (*hop*)

hopper, *n.* hop-picker. (*hop*)

hopple, *v.t.* tie legs (of horse) together.—*n* fetter for grazing horses.

hopscotch, *n.* child's game of hopping while pushing flat stone over lines or scotches.

horal, *a.* of an hour. **horary,** *a.* of an hour; noting the hours; lasting an hour; hourly. (L. *hora*, hour)

horde, *n.* troop of nomads; rabble, gang. (Pers. *ordu*, camp)

hordeaceous, *a.* of, like, barley. (L. *hordeum*, barley)

horehound, *n.* bitter herb used as

tonic and for coughs. (O.E. *hár*, hoar; *húne*, plant)

horizon, *n.* line at which earth and sky appear to meet; limit of mental vision etc. **horizontal,** *a.* of, at, horizon; at right angles to vertical; level, flat.—*n.* horizontal line, bar etc. **horizontality,** *n.* (Gk. *horizein*, bound)

hormone, *n.* glandular secretion that passes into blood and stimulates organs. (Gk. *hormaein*, impel)

horn, *n.* hard pointed projection on heads of cattle, deer etc.; thing like or made of horn; substance of which horns consist; wind instrument.—*v.t.* furnish with horns; gore. **draw in one's hh.,** restrain oneself. **h. in,** (*Amer.*) intrude. **h.-mad,** *a.* stark mad. **put to the h.,** (*old Scots law*) proclaim outlaw. **wear hh.,** be a cuckold. (O.E.)

hornbeam, *n.* tree like beech, often grown for hedges.

hornbill, *n.* bird with a horny projection on its bill.

hornblende, *n.* mineral found in granite. (*horn.* G. *blenden*, deceive)

hornbook, *n.* ancient primer with alphabet etc. mounted in frame covered with transparent plate of horn.

horner, *n.* one who works in horn or blows a horn.

hornet, *n.* large kind of wasp. **bring h.'s nest about one's ears,** stir up crowd of enemies. (O.E. *hyrnet*)

Hornie, *n.* (*Scot.*) the devil.

hornpipe, *n.* lively air or dance popular among sailors.

hornstone, *n.* flint-like quartz, chert.

hornswoggle, *v.t.* (*Amer.*) deceive, swindle.

horny, *a.* like horn, hard, callous.

horo-, from Gk. *hora*, time, used in **horography,** *n.* art of making clocks or dials; **horologe,** *n.* any instrument for telling the hours, timepiece, clock; **horologer, horologist,** *nn.* one versed in horology, clock-maker; **horologiography, horology,** *nn.* art of measuring time or of making timepieces; **horometry,** *n.* art, practice, of measuring time.

horoscope, *n.* observation of the heavens at time of person's birth, from which astrologer predicted events of his life; chart of this. **horoscopic, horoscopical,** *aa.* **horoscopy,** *n.* art of casting horoscopes. (Gk. *hōra*, time; *skopein*, observe)

horrent, *a.* (of bristles) standing erect; bristling. (L. *horrēre*, shudder)

horrible, *a.* causing horror; dreadful, hideous; (*colloq.*) excessive, disagreeable. **horrid,** *a.* terrible; (*arch.*) rough, bristling; (*colloq.*) excessive, disagreeable. **horrific,** *a.* horrifying.

horrify, *v.t.* strike with horror; shock. (*horror*)

horripilation, *n.* goose-flesh, bristling of skin caused by chill or fright. (L. *horrēre*, bristle; *pilus*, hair)

horrisonous, *a.* sounding dreadfully.

horror, *n.* shuddering; terror and loathing; cause of this. **the hh.,** violent depression; delirium tremens. (L.)

hors, adv. and *prep.* outside. *h. concours*, (of exhibit) not competing. *h. de combat*, unfit to fight, disabled. *h. de loi*, outlawed. *h.-d'œuvre, n.* extra dish as relish. (F.)

horse, *n.* solid-hoofed quadruped used for drawing and carrying; cavalry; vaulting block; supporting frame.—*v.t.* and *i.* mount, provide with horse. **flog dead h.,** deal with outworn theme. **h. artillery,** mounted gunners with light guns, to work with cavalry. **H. Guards,** cavalry brigade of English Household troops, esp. Royal Horse Guards or Blues; their headquarters opposite Whitehall; military authorities. **h. marine,** person out of his element. **tell that to the h. marines,** said of incredible or absurd story. **look gift h. in the mouth,** criticize gift. **mount the high h.,** put on airs. **take h.,** get on horseback. **work like a h.,** work very hard. (O.E. *hors*)

horse-block, *n.* platform for mounting horse from.

horse-box, *n.* railway van for horses.

horse-breaker, *n.* one who breaks in horses.

horse-chestnut, *n.* a large tree; its brown bitter nut.

horse-cloth, *n.* covering for horse.

horse-coper, *n.* horse-dealer.

horse-faced, *a.* with long coarse face.

horse-fly, *n.* large fly that stings horses.

horsehair, *n.* hair from mane or tail of horse; haircloth.

horse-laugh, *n.* loud boisterous laugh.

horse-leech, *n.* large kind of leech; insatiable person.

horseman, *n.* man on horseback, skilled rider. **horsemanship,** *n.* art of riding.

horseplay, *n.* rough play.

horse-power, *n.* (*abbr.* **h.p.**) unit of rate of doing work, 33,000 foot-pounds per minute.

horse-radish, *n.* plant with pungent root used as condiment.

horse-sense, *n.* (*colloq.*) common sense.

horseshoe, *n.* curved iron shoe for horse.—*a.* shaped like a horseshoe.

horsewhip, *n.* whip for horse.—*v.t.* thrash with one.

horsewoman, *n.* woman rider.

horsy, *a.* concerned with horses or racing; like groom in dress, language, etc.

hortative, hortatory, *aa.* serving to exhort, urging. (L. *hortari*, exhort)

horticulture, *n.* gardening. **horticultural,** *a.* **horticulturist,** *n.* (L. *hortus*, garden)

hortus siccus, classified collection of dried plants. (L.=dry garden)

hosanna, *n.* cry of praise to God. (Heb. *hoshi'-ahnna,* save, we pray)

hose, *n.pl.* stockings, socks; (*arch.*) breeches.—*n.sing.* flexible tube for conveying water.—*v.t.* water with hose. **h.-tops,** *n.pl.* stockings without feet. **hosier,** *n.* dealer in stockings, underclothing etc., known as **hosiery.** (O.E. *hosa*)

hospice, *n.* travellers' rest-house kept by religious order; home for destitute or sick. (L. *hospes,* guest)

hospitable, *a.* showing hospitality.

hospital, *n.* building for care of the sick, infirmary; charitable institution; establishment of Knights Hospitallers. **cottage h.,** hospital on a small scale. **H. Saturday, Sunday,** days for collecting money for local hospitals. **h.-ship,** *n.* ship fitted out as hospital. **lock h.,** one for treatment of venereal disease. **hospitalism,** *n.* the hospital system or its hygienic faults. (L. *hospes,* guest)

hospitality, *n.* friendly and generous reception of guests or strangers.

hospitaller, hospitaler, *n.* member of charitable religious order; hospital chaplain. **Knights Hh.,** ancient order of military monks.

hospodar, *n.* governor of Wallachia or Moldavia; lord. (Slav.)

host, *n.* (*fem.* **hostess**) one who entertains another; innkeeper. —*v.i.* (*Shake.*) lodge, put up. **reckon without one's h.,** overlook difficulty. (L. *hospes*)

host, *n.* large number; (*arch.*) army. (L. *hostis,* enemy)

host, *n.* in Roman Catholic Church, the consecrated bread of the eucharist. (L. *hostia,* sacrificial victim)

hostage, *n.* person left with enemy as pledge for fulfilment of treaty etc.; pledge, security. (L. *obses*)

hostel, *n.* (*arch.*) inn; lodging-house for students etc. **hostelry,** *n.* (*arch.*) inn. (*host*)

hostile, *a.* of an enemy; opposed, unfriendly. **hostility,** *n.* enmity; (*pl.*) acts of warfare. (L. *hostis,* enemy)

hostler, see **ostler.**

hot, *a.* very warm; giving, feeling, heat; pungent; angry, passionate; (of news) fresh; (of team, stroke etc.) skilful, formidable; (of dance music) highly elaborated.—*v.t.* (*vulg.*) heat. **make place too h. to hold person,** make it impossible for him to stay there. **h. air,** excited or boastful talk. **h. and h.,** fresh from oven. **h. and strong,** vehemently. **h. cockles,** old game in which blindfold person guesses who strikes him. **h. dog.** (*Amer. colloq.*) hot sausage-roll. **h. stuff,** (*sl.*) skilful, high-spirited, or passionate person. **h. water,** trouble, disgrace. (O.E. *hát*)

hot, hote, see **hight.**

hot-bed, *n.* bed of earth heated by fermenting manure for growing plants quickly; any place fostering growth (of vice etc.).

hot-blooded, *a.* high-spirited, ardent.

Hotchkiss, *n.* kind of machine-gun. (inventor)

hotchpotch, hotchpot, *n.* dish of many mixed ingredients; mixed mass, medley; (*law*) mingling of properties to secure equal division. (F. *hocher,* shake+*pot*)

hotel, *n.* house for travellers, large inn. (F.)

hotfoot, *adv.* in hot haste, swiftly.

hot-gospeller, *n.* (*Amer. sl.*) revivalist preacher.

hothead, *n.* hasty person. **hot-headed,** *a.* impetuous, rash.

hothouse, *n.* heated house for growing plants out of season; any heated chamber; (*Shake.*) bagnio, brothel.

hot-pot, *n.* meat cooked with potatoes in tight-lidded pot.

hot-press, *n.* press with hot plates for giving paper etc. a glossy surface.—*v.t.* press in one.

Hottentot, *n.* member of pale-brown S. African native race; barbarian.

houff, see **howff.**

hough, hock, *n.* joint of quadruped's hind leg between knee and fetlock.—*v.t.* hamstring. **hougher,** *n.* one who hamstrings. (O.E. *hóh,* heel)

houghmagandie, *n.* (*Scot.*) fornication.

hound, *n.* hunting dog; despicable person.—*v.t.* chase, urge. **h. on,** incite. **h.'s-tongue,** *n.* plant like borage. (O.E. *hund*)

hour, *n.* twenty-fourth part of a day; the time o'clock; time, occasion; (*pl.*) times of work or going to bed; (in R.C. Church) prayers at stated hours. **eleventh h.,** last moment possible. **in an evil h.,** unluckily. **h.-circle,** *n.* meridian. **hourglass,** *n.* sand-glass measuring an hour. (Gk *hōra*)

houri, *n.* nymph of Mohammedan paradise; voluptuously beautiful girl. (Arab. *haura*)

hourly, *a.* and *adv.* (done) every hour.

house, *n.* dwelling-place; building for specified purpose; assembly; family, dynasty; business firm; theatre, audience; (*astrol.*) twelfth part of heavens.—*v.t.* receive, store.—*v.i.* dwell (in). **the H.,** House of Lords or Commons; London Stock Exchange; Christ Church at Oxford; workhouse. **bring down the h.,** provoke loud applause. **h. of ill fame,** brothel. **keep h.,** look after household. **keep the h.,** stay indoors. **like a h. on fire,** very quickly or vigorously. (O.E. *hús*)

house-agent, *n.* one who sells or lets houses.

houseboat, *n.* barge fitted up for living in on river etc.

housebreaker, *n.* thief who breaks into

house by day; one who demolishes old houses.
house-factor, *n.* (*Scot.*) house-agent.
house-flag, *n.* flag of shipping firm.
household, *n.* inmates of house.—*a.* domestic. **h. gods,** most valued domestic things. **h. stuff,** furniture of house. **H. troops,** the Guards. **h. word,** familiar name. **householder,** *n.* one who owns the house he occupies.
housekeeper, *n.* woman managing affairs of house. **housekeeping,** *n.* domestic economy.
housel, *n.* the eucharist.
houseleek, *n.* plant with red star-like flowers growing on walls and roofs.
housemaid, *n.* maid who cleans rooms. **h.'s knee,** inflammation of knee-cap.
housemaster, *n.* head of school boarding-house.
house-physician, house-surgeon, *nn.* resident doctor of hospital.
house-warming, *n.* party to celebrate moving into new house.
housewife, *n.* mistress of house; domestic manager; small hold-all for sewing materials. **housewifely,** *a.* **housewifery,** *n.* housekeeping.
housing, *n.* saddle-cloth; (*pl.*) horse-trappings. (O.F. *huche*)
hove, see **heave.**
hovel, *n.* mean dwelling; open shed.
hoveller, *n.* unlicensed pilot, longshoreman.
hover, *v.i.* (of bird) hang in air; loiter about.—*n.* state of suspense.
how, *adv.* in what way, by what means, in what state, to what degree.—*n.* the way a thing is done. **and h.!** (*Amer. sl.*) and a great deal more. (O.E. *hū*)
how, howe, *n.* (*Scot.*) hollow, dell, narrow plain.
how, *n.* (*prov.*) low hill, hillock.
howbeit, *adv.* (*arch.*) nevertheless.
howdah, *n.* seat, us. with canopy, on elephant's back. (Arab. *hawdaj*)
howdie, howdy, *n.* (*Scot.*) midwife.
however, *adv.* in whatever way or degree; all the same; (*arch.*) in any case.
howff, houff, *n.* and *v.i.* (*Scot.*) resort, haunt. (O.E. *hof.* house)
howitzer, *n.* short gun for shelling at steep angle. (Bohemian *haufnice,* sling)
howk, *v.i.* and *t.* (*Scot.*) dig, dig up.
howl, *n.* long doleful cry of dog etc.; long cry of pain or derision; (*wireless*) continuous oscillations in receiving-set.—*v.i.* and *t.* utter howl, shriek out. **howler,** *n.* one that howls; a S. American monkey; (*sl.*) ludicrous blunder. (imit.)
howlet, same as **owlet.**
howling, *a.* that howls; (*sl.*) glaring.
howso, howsoever, *advv.* in what way soever; although; however.
hox, *v.t.* (*Shake.*) hough, hamstring.
hoy, *n.* type of coasting vessel.
hoy, *int.* calling attention.
hoya, *n.* climbing plant with pink, yellow, or white flowers. (*Hoy.* gardener)
hoyden, *n.* romping, boisterous girl, tomboy. **hoydenhood, hoydenism,** *nn.* **hoydenish,** *a.*
hoyte, *v.i.* (*Scot.*) move clumsily.
hub, *n.* central point of wheel, from which spokes radiate, nave; central point of any system; mark in quoits.
hub, *n.* (*sl.*) husband. (abbr.)
hubble-bubble, *n.* water-pipe, hookah; bubbling noise, confused talk. (imit.)
hubbub, *n.* confused shouting; uproar, riot. (imit.)
hubby, *n.* (*sl.*) husband. (abbr.)
hubris, *n.* insolent pride. **hubristic,** *a.* (Gk.)
huckaback, *n.* coarse linen with raised figures on it, used for towels.
huckle, *n.* hip; hump. **h.-backed,** *a.* round-shouldered. **h.-bone,** *n.* hip-bone.
huckleberry, *n.* a N. American shrub; its blue berry.
huckster, *n.* (*fem.* **huckstress**) hawker, pedlar; mean tricky fellow.—*v.i.* and *t.* hawk; bargain, haggle; adulterate. **hucksterage, huckstery,** *nn.*
huddle, *v.t.* and *i.* heap, crowd, or nestle together confusedly; botch.—*n.* confused heap; bustle.
hue, *n.* colour, tint. **hued,** *a.* (O.E. *hīw*)
hue, *n.* **h. and cry,** proclamation for capture of criminal; clamour of pursuit; outcry. (O.F. *huer,* shout)
huff, *v.t.* and *i.* blow, bluster; offend, take offence; (*draughts*) remove (man) from board as forfeit.—*n.* fit of petulance or anger. **huffish, huffy,** *aa.* (imit.)
hug, *v.t.* hold closely in one's arms, embrace, squeeze; cling, keep close, to; congratulate (oneself).—*n.* close embrace; wrestling grip. **h.-me-tight,** *n.* woollen wrap.
huge, *a.* very big, enormous. **hugely,** *adv.* very much. **hugeous,** *a.* (us. *joc.*) huge.
hugger-mugger, *n.*, *a.*, and *adv.* (in) secrecy; (in) confusion.—*v.t.* conceal, hush up.—*v.i.* muddle.
hula, *n.* Hawaiian woman's dance. (native)
hulk, *n.* dismantled ship; unwieldy thing, big clumsy person; (*pl.*) old ships used as prisons. **hulking,** *a.* unwieldy, bulky. (O.E. *hulc*)
hull, *n.* pod (of peas etc.), outer covering.—*v.t.* remove hull of. (O.E. *hulu*)
hull, *n.* body or frame of ship.—*v.t.* send shot into hull of.—*v.i.* (*Shake.*) drift with sails furled.
hullabaloo, *n.* uproar.
hullo, hulloa, same as **hallo, halloa.**
hum, *v.i.* and *t.* make continuous buzzing noise like bee; sing with closed lips; (*sl.*) smell unpleasantly.—*n.* low dull noise, buzz; (*sl.*) bad smell.—*int.* of doubt, hesitation etc. **h. and ha,** hesitate in answering.

make things h., set things going briskly. (imit.)

hum, *n.* and *v.t.* (*sl.*) hoax. (*humbug*)

human, *a.* of man or mankind; having qualities of a man.—*n.* (*colloq.*) human being. **humane**, *a.* having feelings proper to a man; kind, merciful. **humane killer**, instrument for painless slaughter of cattle. **Humane Society**, for rescue of drowning persons. **humanism**, *n.* devotion to human interests; philosophy rejecting supernatural and concerned only with man's welfare; literary culture. **humanist**, *n.* student of human affairs; classical scholar. **humanitarian**, *n.* believer in humanism; visionary philanthropist.—*a.* having such views. **humanitarianism**, *n.* **humanity**, *n.* man's proper nature; kindness, benevolence; (*Scot.*) Latin; (*pl.*) polite learning. **humanize**, *v.t.* and *i.* make, become, human or humane. **humanization**, *n.* **humankind**, *n.* mankind. (L. *homo*, human being)

humble, *a.* modest, unassuming; of lowly condition.—*v.t.* bring low, abase, humiliate. **humbleness**, (*Spens.*) **humbless**, *nn.* **eat h. pie**, submit to humiliation. **h. plant**, sensitive plant. (L. *humus*, ground)

humble-bee, *n.* bumble-bee.

humbug, *n.* sham, fraud; nonsense; impostor; kind of sweetmeat.—*v.t.* delude, cheat. **humbuggery**, *n.*

humdinger, *n.* (*Amer. sl.*) something superlatively good.

humdrum, *a.* dull, commonplace.—*n.* dullness, monotony. (*hum*; *drum*)

humdudgeon, *n.* (*Scot.*) needless outcry.

humefy, *v.t.* moisten. (*humid*)

humerus, *n.* (*anat.*) bone of upper arm. **humeral**, *a.* of the shoulder. (L. =shoulder)

humid, *a.* moist, damp. **humidity**, *n.* **humidify**, *v.t.* (L. *humēre*, be moist)

humidor, *n.* cabinet, room, in which cigars etc. are kept moist. (*humid*)

humiliate, *v.t.* lower dignity of, mortify, humble. **humiliating**, *a.* **humiliation**, *n.* **humility**, *n.* humbleness, modesty. (L. *humilis*, low)

hummel, *a.* (*Scot.*) hornless.

humming, *a.* that hums; (*colloq.*) vigorous. **h.-bird**, *n.* small bright-coloured tropical bird whose wings hum. **h.-top**, *n.* top that hums when it spins.

hummock, *n.* hillock, knoll; (in ice-field) ridge. **hummocky**, *a.*

humoral, *a.* of the bodily humours. **humoralism**, *n.* doctrine that diseases have their seat in the humours. **humoralist**, *n.* believer in this. **humoralistic**, *a.* (*humour*)

humoresque, *n.* musical caprice.

humorist, *n.* humorous talker or writer. **humorous**, *a.* full of humour; facetious, funny; capricious.

humour, *n.* state of mind, mood; comicality; faculty of saying or perceiving what excites amusement; (*med.*) fluid of the body.—*v.t.* gratify, indulge; comply with. **cardinal hh.**, four bodily fluids (blood, phlegm, choler, melancholy) once thought to determine a person's nature. **out of h.**, displeased. **humourless**, *a.* without humour. **humoursome**, *a.* capricious, peevish. (L. *humor*, moisture)

hump, *n.* lump, hunch, on back; hillock; (*sl.*) fit of depression or annoyance.—*v.t.* make hump-shaped; (*Austral.*) shoulder (pack); (*Amer. sl.*) exert (oneself), hurry. **humpback**, *n.* person, back, with hump, hence **humpbacked**, *a.* **humped**, **humpy**, *aa.*

humph, *int.* of doubt or dissatisfaction.—*v.i.* utter this.

humpy, *n.* Australian hut. (native *oompi*)

humus, *n.* vegetable mould. (L.= ground)

Hun, *n.* one of fierce Asiatic nomad race that ravaged Europe in fourth and fifth centuries; barbarian; (*war sl.*) German.

hunch, *n.* hump; thick piece; (*Amer. sl.*) intuition, suspicion.—*v.t.* thrust out into hump, arch. **hunchback**, *n.* person with hump on back. **hunchbacked**, *a.*

hundred, *n.* ten times ten; old division of a county. **hh. and thousands**, tiny sweets used for decorating cakes. **hundredfold**, *a.* multiplied by a hundred. **hundredth**, *a.* coming last of a hundred.—*n.* one of a hundred equal parts. **Old Hundredth**, **Hundred**, a setting of the 100th psalm. **hundredweight**, *n.* (*abbr.* cwt.) 112 lb. avoirdupois; (*Amer.*) 100 lb.

hung, see **hang**.

hunger, *n.* weakness from lack of food; craving for food; strong desire (for).—*v.i.* feel hunger; have craving (for).—*v.t.* starve. **h.-march**, *n.* march of protest by unemployed. **h.-strike**, *n.* prisoner's refusing of food as protest. **hungry**, *a.* feeling, showing, inducing, hunger. (O.E. *hungor*)

hunk, *n.* large piece, lump. hunch.

hunker, *v.i.* (*Scot.*) squat down. **hunkers**, *n.pl.* hams.

hunks, *n.* miser.

hunky-dory, *a.* (*Amer. sl.*) first-rate.

hunt, *v.t.* and *i.* chase, prey on; chase animals for sport; seek (for), search; drive (away).—*n.* hunting; hunting party or district. **h. down**, destroy by persecution. **h. out**, **h. up**, search out. **h.-the-slipper**, *n.* a parlour game. **hunter**, *n.* (*fem.* huntress) one who hunts; horse for hunting; watch with cover protecting glass. **hunter's moon**, full moon following harvest moon. **hunting-box**, **hunting-lodge**, *nn.* small house for hunting season. **hunting-crop**, *n.* short whip with looped thong. **huntsman**, *n.* man in charge of pack of hounds. **hunts-up**,

n. (*Shake.*) early morning song to rouse hunters. (O.E. *hunta*, hunter)
hurdies, *n.pl.* (*Scot.*) buttocks.
hurdle, *n.* movable frame of twigs or timber for fences; similar obstacle in **h.-race.**—*v.t.* fence off with hurdles; leap over. **hurdler,** *n.* one who makes hurdles or runs in hurdle-races. (O.E. *hyrdel*)
hurdy-gurdy, *n.* stringed instrument with droning sound played by turning handle; barrel-organ. (imit.)
hurl, *v.t.* throw violently; (*Scot.*) convey in car.—*n.* violent throw; (*Scot.*) ride in car. **hurley, hurling,** *nn.* (*Ir.*) kind of hockey. **hurly,** *n.* (*Scot.*) trolly. **hurly-burly,** (*Shake.*) hurly, *nn.* commotion, tumult.
hurrah, hurray, *int.* of joy or applause. —*v.i.* shout this.
hurricane, *n.* storm with violent wind; cyclone. **h.-bird,** *n.* frigate bird. **h.-deck,** *n.* light upper deck. **h.-lamp,** *n.* lamp designed to defy strong wind. (Sp. *huracan*)
hurry, *v.i.* move, act, with haste.—*v.t.* urge forward, hasten.—*n.* undue haste; eagerness; urgency. **h.-scurry,** *n.* and *a.* (in) confused haste. **hurriedly,** *adv.* (imit.)
hurst, *n.* wood; wooded eminence; hillock; sandbank. (O.E. *hyrst*)
hurt, *v.t.* injure, damage, wound; distress, pain.—*v.i.* (*colloq.*) suffer injury.—*n.* wound, injury, harm. **hurtful,** *a.* causing hurt, mischievous. **hurtless,** *a.* without injury; harmless. (O.F. *hurter*, knock)
hurtle, *v.i.* move quickly with whirring sound; dash (against); hurl swiftly.
husband, *n.* married man.—*v.t.* furnish with husband; manage thriftily. **husbandhood, husbandship,** *nn.* **husbandman,** *n.* working farmer. **husbandry,** *n.* farming; economy, management. (O.N. *hús*, house; *búa*, dwell)
hush, *v.t.* and *i.* silence, be silent.—*n.* quiet, stillness. **h.-h.,** *a.* (*sl.*) secret. **h.-money,** *n.* money paid to **h. up** or suppress matter. (imit.)
hushion, *n.* (*Scot.*) footless stocking.
husk, *n.* dry covering of some fruits or seeds; worthless outer shell; a cattle-disease.—*v.t.* strip husk from. **husky,** *a.* full of, dry as, husks; hoarse; (*Amer. sl.*) strong, powerful. (M.E. *huske*)
husky, *n.* Canadian sledge-dog; Eskimo person or language. (*Eskimo*)
hussar, *n.* light-armed cavalry soldier. (It. *corsaro*, freebooter)
hussy, huzzy, *n.* worthless woman; impudent girl. (*housewife*)
hustings, *n.* election proceedings; platform from which parliamentary candidates used to be nominated; court held in Guildhall of London. (O.N. *hús*, house; *thing*, assembly)
hustle, *v.t.* and *i.* push roughly, jostle; hurry, bustle.—*n.* hustling, speed, energetic activity. **hustler,** *n.* quick worker. (Du. *husselen*, shake)
hut, *n.* small house, cabin; temporary wooden house for troops.—*v.t.* and *i.* lodge in huts. **hutment,** *n.* camp of huts. (F. *hutte*)
hutch, *n.* box-like pen for rabbits; chest, hut; low wagon used in mines. (L.L. *hutica*, box)
huzoor, *n.* Indian title of respect. (Arab. *huzur*, the presence)
huzza, *int.* of joy or applause, hurrah. —*v.i.* utter this. (imit.)
huzzy, see **hussy.**
hyacinth, *n.* bulbous plant with bell-shaped flowers of many colours; purplish-blue colour; jacinth. **hyacinthine,** *a.* (Gk. *huakinthos*)
hyaena, see **hyena.**
hyaline, *a.* glassy, vitreous.—*n.* (*poet.*) glassy sea; clear sky. **hyalite,** *n.* a colourless opal. **hyalography,** *n.* art of engraving on glass. **hyaloid,** *a.* glassy. (Gk. *hualos*, glass)
hybrid, *n.* product of two different species of animal or plant; word formed of elements from different languages.—*a.* cross-bred, heterogeneous. **hybridism, hybridity,** *nn.* **hybridize,** *v.t.* and *i.* produce hybrids; interbreed. **hybridization,** *n.* (L. *hybrida*)
hybris, same as *hubris*.
hydatid, *n.* (*med.*) watery cyst in animal tissue. (Gk. *hudatis*)
hydra, *n.* fabulous many-headed water-serpent; water-snake; fresh-water polyp; any manifold evil. **h.-headed,** *a.* hard to root out. (Gk. *hudra*)
hydrangea, *n.* kinds of showy-flowered shrub. (Gk. *hudōr*, water; *anggeion*, vessel)
hydrant, *n.* fire-plug in water-main.
hydrate, *n.* (*chem.*) compound of water with another compound or an element.—*v.t.* combine with water.
hydraulic, *a.* conveying water; worked by water-pressure; relating to hydraulics. **h. cement,** cement that hardens under water. **hydraulics,** *n.pl.* science of water conveyed in pipes. **hydraulician,** *n.* (Gk. *hudōr*, water; *aulos*, pipe)
hydric, *a.* (*chem.*) of, containing, hydrogen. **hydride,** *n.*
hydriotaphia, *n.* urn-burial. (Gk. *hudria*, urn; *taphē*, burial)
hydro, *n.* (*colloq.*) hydropathic. (abbr.)
hydro-aeroplane, *n.* seaplane.
hydrocarbon, *n.* compound of hydrogen and carbon.
hydrocephalus, *n.* water on the brain. **hydrocephalic, hydrocephalous,** *aa.* (Gk. *hudōr*, water; *kephalē*, head)
hydrochloric, *a.* containing hydrogen and chlorine.
hydrocyanic, *a.* containing hydrogen and cyanogen. **h. acid,** prussic acid.
hydrodynamics, *n.pl.* science of fluid pressures. **hydrodynamic,** *a.*

hydro-electric, *a.* of electricity got from water power or steam.

hydrogen, *n.* inflammable odourless gas, an element which combines with oxygen to form water. **hydrogenate, hydrogenize,** *vv.t.* combine with hydrogen. **hydrogenous,** *a.* (Gk. *hudōr*, water; *genesis*, origin)

hydrography, *n.* scientific description of seas, lakes, and rivers. **hydrographer,** *n.* chart-maker. **hydrographic, hydrographical,** *aa.*

hydroid, *a.* hydra-like.

hydrokinetics, *n.pl.* science of fluids in motion.

hydrology, *n.* science of water. **hydrologic,** *a.* **hydrologist,** *n.*

hydrolysis, *n.* chemical decomposition by which elements of water are fixed in distinct compounds. **hydrolytic,** *a.*

hydromancy, *n.* divination by water.

hydromania, *n.* craving for water.

hydromechanics, *n.pl.* science of use of fluids as motive-power.

hydromel, *n.* mixture of honey and water. (Gk. *hudōr*, water; *meli*, honey)

hydrometeorology, *n.* branch of meteorology dealing with rain, snow etc.

hydrometer, *n.* instrument for finding specific gravity of liquids. **hydrometric, hydrometrical,** *aa.* **hydrometry,** *n.*

hydropathy, *n.* medical treatment by internal and external use of water. **hydropathic,** *a.*—*n.* hotel providing this treatment. (Gk. *pathein*, suffer)

hydrophane, *n.* opal that becomes translucent in water. (Gk. *phainein*, shine)

hydrophobia, *n.* morbid aversion to water, a symptom of rabies, disease caused by bite of mad dog; rabies. **hydrophobic,** *a.* (Gk. *phobos*, fear)

hydrophone, *n.* instrument for detecting sound through water.

hydrophyte, *n.* water-plant. (Gk. *hudōr*, water; *phuton*, plant)

hydropic, see **hydropsy.**

hydroplane, *n.* light motor-boat that skims water at high speed; fin directing vertical movement of submarine.

hydropneumatic, *a.* involving combined action of water and air.

hydroponics, *n.pl.* cultivation of plants without soil. (Gk. *hudōr*, water; *ponos*, work)

hydropsy, *n.* dropsy. **hydropic, hydroptic,** *aa.* dropsical; thirsty.

hydroscope, *n.* kind of water-clock.

hydrosphere, *n.* water-envelope of the earth.

hydrostat, *n.* device for detecting presence of water.

hydrostatic, *a.* of hydrostatics. **h. press,** hydraulic press. **hydrostatics,** *n.pl.* science of fluids at rest.

hydrotherapeutics, hydrotherapy, *nn.* water-cure, hydropathy. **hydrotherapeutic,** *a.* (Gk. *therapeuein*, cure)

hydrothermal, *a.* of hot springs.

hydrotimeter, *n.* instrument for measuring hardness of water. (Gk. *hudrotēs*, moisture; *metron*, measure)

hydrotropism, *n.* tendency to turn towards or away from moisture. (Gk. *hudōr*, water; *tropos*, turn)

hydrous, *a.* containing water.

hyena, hyaena, (*Shake.*) **hyen,** *n.* wild carnivorous animal like dog. **striped, laughing, h.,** kind with howl like hysterical laughter. (Gk. *huaina*)

hyet(o)-, from Gk. *huetos*, rain, used in **hyetal,** *a.* of rainfall; **hyetograph,** *n.* chart of rainfall; **hyetometer,** *n.* rain-gauge.

Hygeia, *n.* goddess of health, health personified. **hygeian,** *a.* (Gk. *Hugeia*)

hygiene, *n.* principles of health, sanitary science. **hygienic, hygienical,** *aa.* **hygienist,** *n.* (Gk. *hugiēs*, healthy)

hygro-, from Gk. *hugros*, wet, used in **hygrodeik, hygrometer,** *nn.* instruments for measuring humidity of air, hence **hygrometric,** *a.*, **hygrometry,** *n.*; **hygrology,** *n.* study of humidity of the atmosphere; **hygroscope,** *n.* instrument for detecting humidity in air; **hygroscopic,** *a.* of hygroscope, sensitive to moisture.

hyl(o)-, from Gk. *hulē*, matter, wood, used in **hylic,** *a.* of matter, material; **hylomorphism,** *n.* doctrine that matter is first cause of universe; **hylopathism,** *n.* doctrine that matter has feeling; **hylophagous,** *a.* wood-eating; **hylotheism,** *n.* identification of God with matter; **hylotomous,** *a.* boring in wood; **hylozoism,** *n.* doctrine that matter has life, materialism.

Hymen, *n.* god of marriage; (*anat.*) virginal membrane of vagina. **hymeneal,** *a.* **hymenopterous,** *a.* (of insects) with four membranous wings. (Gk. *Humēn*)

hymn, *n.* song of praise, esp. to God. —*v.t.* and *i.* praise in, sing, hymn. **hymnal, hymnic,** *aa.* of hymns. **hymnal, hymnary,** *nn.* hymn-book. **hymnody,** *n.* singing, composition, of hymns; hymns collectively. **hymnodist,** *n.* **hymnographer,** *n.* writer about hymns. **hymnology,** *n.* study, a collection, of hymns. **hymnologic,** *a.* **hymnologist,** *n.* (Gk. *humnos*)

hyoid, *a.* U-shaped. **h. bone,** bone at base of tongue. (Gk. *huoeidēs*)

hyoscamine, hyoscine, *nn.* poisonous alkaloids contained in henbane. (Gk. *hus*, pig; *kuamos*, bean)

hyp, see **hip.**

hypaethral, hypethral, *a.* open to the sky, roofless. (Gk. *aithēr*, air)

hypallagē, *n.* a figure in which the relations of things in a sentence are mutually interchanged, e.g. 'Apply the wound to water.' (Gk. *hupallagē*)

hyper-, *pref.* above, too, exceeding. (Gk. *huper*)

hyperacute, *a.* excessively acute.

hyperaesthesia, *n.* excessive sensitiveness. **hyperaesthetic**, *a.* over-aesthetic; morbidly sensitive. (Gk. *aisthanesthai*, perceive)

hyperbaton, *n.* change in the normal order of words for emphasis. (Gk. *huper*, beyond; *bainein*, go)

hyperbola, *n.* (*geom.*) curve produced when cone is cut by plane making greater angle with base than the side of the cone makes. **hyperbolic**, *a.* (Gk. *huper*, beyond; *ballein*, throw)

hypérbolĕ, *n.* rhetorical exaggeration, e.g. 'All the perfumes of Arabia will not sweeten this little hand.' **hyperbolical**, *a.* **hyperbolism**, *n.* use of hyperbole; hyperbolical expression. **hyperbolist**, *n.* (*hyperbola*)

hyperborean, *a.* and *n.* (inhabitant) of extreme north. (Gk. *Boreas*, north wind)

hypercatalectic, *a.* (of verse) having a final syllable beyond regular measure. **hypercatalexis**, *n.* (*catalectic*)

hypercritical, *a.* over-critical. **hypercriticism**, *n.* **hypercriticize**, *v.t.*

hypermetric, hypermetrical, *aa.* beyond the normal metre of a line; having a syllable too much.

hypermetropia, *n.* morbidly long sight, opp. of myopia. **hypermetropic**, *a.* (Gk. *huper*, beyond; *metron*, measure; *ōps*, eye)

hyperphysical, *a.* supernatural.

hyperpiesis, *n.* abnormally high blood pressure. (Gk. *piezein*, press)

hypersensitive, *a.* unduly sensitive.

hypersthene, *n.* greenish mineral like hornblende. (Gk. *sthenos*, strength)

hyperthyroidism, *n.* excessive activity of thyroid glands, causing exophthalmic goitre.

hypertrophy, *n.* over-nourishment; abnormal enlargement of part of the body due to this. **hypertrophic, hypertrophied**, *aa.* (Gk. *trephein*, nourish)

hypervitaminosis, *n.* state caused by excess of vitamines in diet.

hypethral, see **hypaethral**.

hyphen, *n.* short stroke (-) connecting words or syllables.—*v.t.* join, write, with hyphen. **hyphenate**, *v.t.* hyphen. (Gk. *hupo*, under; *hen*, one)

hypno-, from Gk. *hupnos*, sleep, used in **hypnogenesis**, *n.* induction of hypnosis; **hypnology**, *n.* science of sleep; **hypnopompic**, *a.* preventing sleep.

hypnosis, *n.* state like deep sleep in which the subject acts on external suggestion; artificial sleep. **hypnotic**, *a.* of hypnosis; causing sleep.—*n.* person under, thing producing, hypnosis; opiate. **hypnotism**, *n.* production of hypnosis; hypnosis. **hypnotist**, *n.* **hypnotize**, *v.t.* (Gk. *hupnos*, sleep)

hypo, *n.* (*phot.*) hyposulphite of soda, used for fixing. (abbr.)

hyp(o)-, *pref.* below; slightly. (Gk. *hupo*)

hypóbolĕ, *n.* rhetorical device of anticipating objections in order to refute them. (Gk. *hupo*, under; *ballein*, throw)

hypocaust, *n.* hot-air chamber under Roman bath. (Gk. *hupo*, under; *kaiein*, burn)

hypochondria, hypochondriasis, *nn.* morbid depression; groundless fears about health. **hypochondriac**, *a.* of hypochondria.—*n.* victim of it. **hypochondriacal**, *a.* (Gk. *hupo*, under; *chondros*, cartilage)

hypocorism, *n.* pet name. **hypocoristic**, *a.* (*hypo-*, slightly + Gk. *koros*, child)

hypocrisy, *n.* feigning to be what one is not; insincerity. **hypocrite**, *n.* person given to this, dissembler. **hypocritical**, *a.* (Gk. *hupokritēs*, actor)

hypocycloid, *n.* curve traced by point on circumference of a circle which rolls on the inside of another circle.

hypodermic, *a.* (of injection) introduced beneath the skin; subcutaneous. **hypodermically**, *adv.* (Gk. *hupo*, under; *derma*, skin)

hypogeal, hypogean, *aa.* underground. **hypogeum**, *n.* (*pl.* **hypogea**) underground chamber. (Gk. *hupo*, under; *gē*, earth)

hypogene, *a.* (of rocks) formed under surface. (Gk. *hupo*, under; *genesis*, origin)

hypophysis, *n.* pituitary body. (Gk. *hupophusis*, outgrowth)

hypostasis, *n.* (*pl.* **hypostases**) underlying substance; essence, personality, of the three persons of the Godhead; (*med.*) excess of blood in organs. **hypostatic, hypostatical**, *aa.* **hypostasize, hypostatize**, *vv.t.* (Gk. *hupo*, under; *stasis*, state)

hypóstrophĕ, *n.* return to main theme after digression; (*med.*) relapse, falling back. (Gk. *hupostrophē*, turning back)

hypostyle, *n.* pillared hall or court, colonnade. (Gk. *hupo*, under; *stulos*, pillar)

hypotenuse, *n.* side opposite right angle in right-angled triangle. (Gk. *hupo*, under; *teinein*, stretch)

hypothec, *n.* (*Scots law*) lien or security over goods in respect of debt due by their owner. **hypothecary**, *a.* **hypothecate**, *v.t.* pledge, mortgage. **hypothecation**, *n.* (Gk. *hupothēkē*, pledge)

hypothesis, *n.* supposition used as basis of reasoning, assumption. **hypothesize**, *v.i.* and *t.* form hypothesis, assume. **hypothetic, hypothetical**, *aa.* (Gk. *hupothesis*, foundation)

hypothyroidism, *n.* deficient activity of thyroid glands, causing cretinism.

hypso-, from Gk. *hupsos*, height, used in **hypsography**, *n.* part of geography dealing with altitudes; **hypsometer**, *n.* instrument for measuring altitudes; **hypsometry**, *n.* science of measuring altitudes.

hyrax, *n.* kinds of small rabbit-like animal. (Gk. *hurax*, shrew-mouse)

hyson, *n.* fine Chinese green tea. (Chin. *hsi-ch'un*, bright spring)

hy-spy, **I spy**, *n.* kind of hide-and-seek.

hyssop, *n.* small aromatic plant. (Gk. *hussōpos*)

hysteresis, *n.* magnetic inertia. (Gk. *husteros*, later)

hysteria, *n.* disturbance of nervous system; morbid excitement. **hysteric, hysterical**, *aa.* of, affected by, hysteria; violently emotional. **hysterics**, *n.pl.* hysterical fit or paroxysm. (Gk. *hustera*, womb)

hystero-, from Gk. *hustera*, womb, used in **hysterology**, *n.* treatise on the uterus; **hysterotomy**, *n.* operation of cutting into the uterus, Caesarean operation.

hysteron proteron, figure of speech in which what should follow comes first; inversion, e.g. 'I die, I faint, I fail.' (Gk. *husteros*, latter; *proteros*, former)

hyte, *a.* (*Scot.*) mad.

I

I, *pron.* (*objective* **me**, *possessive* **my, mine**; *pl.* **we**, *objective* **us**, *possessive* **our, ours**) 1st personal pronoun, the speaker or writer.—*n.* object of self-consciousness, ego. (O.E. *ic*)

-i, *suf.* forming plural of Latin nouns in -us, as in **foci**; or of Italian nouns, as in **dilettanti.**

iambus (*pl.* **iambuses, iambi**), **iamb**, *nn.* two-syllabled foot, short-long. **iambic**, *a.* of, containing iambuses.—*n.* iambic line. (Gk. *iambos*, lampoon)

-ian, *suf.* of, inhabitant of, as in **Addisonian, Arabian.**

iatric, iatrical, *aa.* of doctors or medicine. (Gk. *iatros*, doctor)

ibex, *n.* a wild mountain goat with large recurved horns. (L.)

ibidem, *adv.* (*abbr.* **ib., ibid.**) in the same place, passage etc. (L.)

ibis, *n.* stork-like wading-bird venerated by ancient Egyptians. (Gk.)

-ible, *adj.suf.* capable of, as in **flexible, terrible.** (L. *-ibilis*)

-ic, *suf.* of the nature of, containing, as in **sulphuric**; forming nouns, esp. in plural, as in **critic, dynamics.** (Gk.)

ice, *n.* frozen water; frozen confection, ice-cream.—*v.t.* freeze; cool in, cover with, ice; cover (cake) with concreted sugar. **break the i.**, make start, break through reserve. **cut no i.**, (*sl.*) count for nothing. **dry i.**, solid carbon dioxide. (O.E. *is*)

ice-axe, *n.* mountaineer's axe for cutting steps in ice.

iceberg, *n.* large mass of floating ice.

iceblink, *n.* reflection of ice from below horizon.

ice-boat, *n.* boat mounted on runners for travelling on ice; ice-breaker.

ice-bound, *a.* surrounded, fixed in, with ice.

ice-breaker, *n.* steamer used for clearing channel of ice.

ice-cream, *n.* flavoured cream artificially frozen.

ice-fall, *n.* steep part of glacier like frozen waterfall.

ice-field, *n.* wide expanse of ice.

ice-floe, *n.* sheet of floating ice.

ice-foot, *n.* belt of ice along shore in Arctic regions.

ice-house, *n.* storehouse for ice.

iceman, *n.* man skilled in travelling over ice; dealer in ice.

ice-pack, *n.* drifting ice-floes packed together.

ice-pail, *n.* pail filled with ice for cooling wine.

ice-pudding, *n.* a frozen confection.

ice-run, *n.* ice-track for tobogganing.

ice-wool, *n.* glossy wool used in crochet.

ichneumon, *n.* small animal like mongoose, which eats crocodiles' eggs. **i. fly**, a parasitic insect. (Gk. *ichneuein*, hunt after)

ichno-, from Gk. *ichnos*, track, used in **ichnography**, *n.* drawing of ground-plans; **ichnolite, ichnite**, *nn.* fossil footprint; **ichnology**, *n.* study of fossil footprints.

ichor, *n.* fabled juice in veins of Greek gods; (*med.*) watery discharge from ulcer etc. **ichorous**, *a.* (Gk.)

ichthyo-, from Gk. *ichthus*, fish, used in **ichthyography**, *n.* treatise on fishes; **ichthyoid**, *a.* fish-like; **ichthyolatry**, *n.* worship of a fish-god; **ichthyolite**, *n.* fossil fish or its impression; **ichthyology**, *n.* natural history of fishes, hence **ichthyological**, *a.*, **ichthyologist**, *n.*; **ichthyophagous**, *a.* fish-eating; **ichthyornis**, *n.* extinct toothed bird; **ichthyosaurus**, *n.* gigantic extinct marine reptile; **ichthyosis**, *n.* disease in which skin becomes dry and scaly.

-ician, *n.suf.* person skilled in, as in **geometrician.**

icicle, *n.* tapering spike of ice, caused by freezing of dripping water. (O.E. *is*, ice; *gicel*, icicle)

icing, *n.* concreted sugar.
icker, *n.* (*Scot.*) ear of corn.
ickle, child's corruption of **little.**
icon, *n.* image, statue; (*Greek Church*) sacred painting, mosaic etc. **iconic,** *a.* conventional. **iconoclasm,** *n.* breaking of images. **iconoclast,** *n.* image-breaker; one who assails accepted usages. **iconoclastic,** *a.* **iconography,** *n.* treatise on pictures or statuary; art of illustration. **iconolatry,** *n.* image-worship **iconology,** *n.* study of icons. **iconomachy,** *n.* war against religious use of images. **iconometer,** *n.* (*phot.*) direct-vision view-finder. **iconostasis,** *n.* screen between sanctuary and main part of Byzantine church. (Gk. *eikōn*)
icosahedron, *n.* solid with twenty plane faces. **icosahedral,** *a.* (Gk. *eikosi,* twenty; *hedra,* base)
icterus, *n.* jaundice. **icteric,** *a.* **icterine,** *a.* yellow. (Gk. *ikteros*)
ictus, *n.* stress in verse. **ictic,** *a.* (L.=stroke)
icy, *a.* of, like, ice; very cold.
id, *n.* (*psycho-anal.*) instinctive impulses of the individual. (L.=it)
id, ide, *n.* fish like carp. (Swedish)
-ide, *suf.* (*chem.*) forming names of simple compounds of an element with another element or a radical, as in **sulphide.**
idea, *n.* mental image, notion; vague belief, fancy; plan, aim; (*Platonic philos.*) eternally existing pattern of which individual thing is imperfect copy. **idea'd, ideaed,** *aa.* **ideal,** *a.* perfect; existing only in idea, visionary; consisting of ideas.—*n.* perfect type. **idealism,** *n.* imaginative treatment; representation of things in ideal form; doctrine that ideas are the only realities. **ideality,** *n.* ideal state; imaginative faculty. **idealize,** *v.t.* represent, look upon, as ideal. **idealization,** *n.* **ideate,** *v.t.* and *i.* imagine; form ideas. (Gk. *idein,* see)
identical, *a.* exactly the same. **identic,** *a.* (of diplomatic note) couched in same terms. **identify,** *v.t.* establish identity of; associate (oneself with); treat as identical. **identification,** *n.* **identity,** *n.* absolute sameness; individuality, personality. (L. *idem,* same)
idée fixe, obsession, monomania. (F. =fixed idea)
idem, *n.* (*abbr.* id.) the same (author, word etc.). *i. quod,* the same as. (L.)
ideo-, from *idea,* used in **ideogram, ideograph,** *nn.* character representing an idea, not a word; **ideologue, ideologist,** *nn.* theorist, visionary; **ideology,** *n.* science, system, of ideas, abstract speculation.
ides, *n.pl.* in ancient Rome, the 15th of March, May, July, October, and the 13th of the other months. (L. *Idūs*)
id est, (*abbr.* **i.e.**) that is to say. (L.)
idiocrasy, *n.* constitutional peculiarity, idiosyncrasy. (Gk. *idios,* own; *krasis,* mixing)
idiocy, *n.* imbecility; folly. (*idiot*)
idiom, *n.* language, dialect; mode of expression peculiar to one, phraseology. **idiomatic,** *a.* characteristic of a language; using idioms, colloquial. **idiomatically,** *adv.* (Gk. *idiōma*)
idiopathy, *n.* primary disease, one not occasioned by another. **idiopathic,** *a.* **idiopathically,** *adv.* (Gk. *idios,* own)
idioplasm, *n.* portion of plasm that determines an organism's nature.
idiosyncrasy, *n.* peculiarity of person's temperament or constitution, characteristic. **idiosyncratic,** *a.* (Gk. *idios,* own; *sun,* together; *krasis,* mixing)
idiot, *n.* person of extreme mental deficiency; utter fool. **i.-stitch,** *n.* tricot-stitch. **idiotic, idiotical,** *aa.* (Gk. *idiōtēs,* layman)
idioticon, *n.* dialect dictionary. (Gk. *idios,* peculiar)
idle, *a.* unoccupied, unemployed; lazy; useless, ineffective, groundless.—*v.i.* do nothing. **i. away,** spend in idleness. **idler, idleness, idlesse,** *nn.* **idly,** *adv.* (O.E. *idel*)
Ido, *n.* auxiliary international language based on Esperanto. **Idist,** *n.*
idol, *n.* image that is worshipped; object of excessive devotion; (*logic*) fallacy. **idolater,** *n.* (*fem.* **idolatress**) worshipper of idols; devoted admirer, adorer. **idolatry,** *n.* **idolatrous,** *a.* **idolize,** *v.t.* make idol of; love, admire, to excess. **idolization,** *n.* **idolum,** *n.* mental image; (*logic*) fallacy. (Gk. *eidōlon,* phantom)
idyll, idyl, *n.* short pastoral poem; picturesque rustic scene, incident, or story. **idyllic,** *a.* **idyllically,** *adv.* **idyllist,** *n.* **idyllize,** *v.t.* (Gk. *eidullion*)
-ie, see **-y.**
ieroe, *n.* (*Scot.*) great-grandchild.
if, *conj.* in case, supposing, that; whether. — *n.* supposition. (O.E. *gif*)
igloo, *n.* Eskimo dome-shaped hut. (Eskimo)
igneous, *a.* of or like fire; (*geol.*) produced by volcanic action. **ignipotent,** *a.* (*poet.*) presiding over fire. (L. *ignis,* fire)
ignis fatuus, (*pl.* **ignes fatui**) will-o'-the-wisp, phosphorescent light seen in marshy places at night; delusive hope. (L.=foolish fire)
ignite, *v.t.* set fire to, take fire, kindle; make luminous with heat. **ignitable,** *a.* **ignition,** *n.* igniting; mechanism for igniting explosive mixture in internal-combustion engine. (L. *ignis,* fire)
ignoble, *a.* mean, base, dishonourable; of low birth. (L. *in-,* not; *noble*)

ignominy, *n.* disgrace, infamy; infamous conduct. **ignominious,** *a.* humiliating. (L. *ignominia*)
ignomy, (*Shake.*) form of **ignominy.**
ignore, *v.t.* disregard; set aside. **ignoramus,** *n.* (*pl.* **ignoramuses**) ignorant person. **ignorant,** *a.* without knowledge; uninformed. **ignorance,** *n.* (L. *ignorare*)
ignotum per ignotius, (explaining) the unknown by the more unknown. (L.)
iguana, *n.* large S. American tree-lizard. **iguanodon,** *n.* gigantic extinct herbivorous reptile. (Carib *iwana*)
il-, form of **in-** before *l.*
ileum, *n.* (*anat.*) last part of small intestine. **ileac,** *a.* (L.L.)
ilex, *n.* holm-oak. (L.)
iliac, *a.* of the flank or hip-bone. **i. passion,** kind of colic. (L. *ilia,* flanks)
Iliad, *n.* Homer's epic describing the siege of Troy. (Gk. *Ilias*)
ilk, *a.* (*Scot.*) same. **of that i.,** of the same (used when person's name is the same as that of his estate). **that i.,** (*vulg.*) that family. (O.E. *ilca*)
ilka, *a.* (*Scot.*) each. (O.E. *ǽlc*)
ill, *a.* (*compar.* **worse,** *superl.* **worst**) in bad health, sick; evil, harmful; faulty.—*n.* evil, harm; (*pl.*) misfortunes.—*adv.* badly; unfavourably; scarcely. **i. at ease,** embarrassed. **i. blood,** resentment, enmity. **i. breeding,** bad manners. **i. will,** unkind feeling, hostility. **i.-advised,** *a.* injudicious. **i.-bred,** *a.* badly brought up; rude. **i.-favoured,** *a.* ugly. **i.-gotten,** *a.* got by evil means. **i.-natured,** *a.* peevish, churlish. **i.-starred,** *a.* unlucky. **i.-timed,** *a.* unseasonable. **i.-treat, i.-use,** *vv.t.* treat badly. (O.N. *illr*)
illation, *n.* inference, deduction; thing deduced. **illative,** *a.* (of words) stating an inference; inferential. (L. *in,* into; *ferre,* bear)
illegal, *a.* not legal; contrary to law. **illegality,** *n.*
illegible, *a.* unreadable, indistinct. **illegibility,** *n.*
illegitimate, *a.* not born in wedlock, bastard; not according to law, improper; wrongly inferred. — *n.* bastard.—*v.t.* declare illegitimate. **illegitimacy, illegitimation,** *nn.*
illiberal, *a.* not befitting a free man; mean, stingy; narrow-minded; uncultured. **illiberality,** *n.*
illicit, *a.* unlawful, forbidden. (L. *in-,* not; *licēre,* be allowed)
illimitable, *a.* boundless, infinite. **illimitability, illimitableness,** *nn.*
illiterate, *a.* unlearned; unable to read or write.—*n.* illiterate person. **illiteracy, illiterateness,** *nn.*
illness, *n.* sickness; disease.
illogical, *a.* contrary to logic. **illogicality,** *n.*
illth, *n.* evil state. (*ill*)
illude, *v.t.* play upon by artifice, deceive. (L. *in,* upon; *ludere,* play)
illume, *v.t.* (*poet.*) light up, make bright.
illuminate, *v.t.* light up; enlighten. throw light upon; decorate with lights; decorate (manuscript) with gold and colours. **illuminant,** *a.* giving light.—*n.* source of light. **illumination, illuminator,** *nn.* **illuminative,** *a.* **illuminati,** *n.pl.* persons, society, claiming to possess special enlightenment; hence **illuminism, illuminist,** *nn.* **illumine,** *v.t.* light up; enlighten. (L. *lumen,* light)
illusion, *n.* deceptive appearance or belief; deception; conjuring-trick. **illusionism,** *n.* disbelief in objective existence. **illusionist,** *n.* follower of illusionism; conjurer. **illusive, illusory,** *aa.* deceptive, false. (*illude*)
illustrate, *v.t.* make clear by examples, elucidate; explain, adorn, with pictures. **illustration,** *n.* illustrating; example; picture in book etc. **illustrative,** *a.* serving as an example. **illustrator,** *n.* (L. *illustrare,* light up)
illustrious, *a.* distinguished, famous, glorious. (L. *illustris*)
im-, form of **in-** before *b, m, p.*
image, *n.* likeness, representation; statue; counterpart; reflection; simile or metaphor.—*v.t.* make image of; picture; reflect. **imagery,** *n.* imaginative or figurative description; images. (L. *imago*)
imagine, *v.t.* picture mentally; conjecture; suppose, think. **imaginable,** *a.* that can be imagined. **imaginal,** *a.* of an insect imago. **imaginary,** *a.* existing only in imagination, not real. **imagination,** *n.* faculty of making mental pictures, fancy; creative faculty of the mind. **imaginative,** *a.* of, showing, full of, imagination.
imagist, *n.* member of modern poetical group who seek clarity of expression through use of precise images.
imago, *n.* (*pl.* **imagines, imagos**) final or perfect state of insect life, e.g. butterfly. (L.=image)
imam, imaum, *n.* priest of Mohammedan mosque; Mohammedan potentate. **imamate,** *n.* (Arab. *amma,* go before)
imbecile, *a.* mentally or physically weak, feeble-minded.—*n.* idiot, defective. **imbecility,** *n.* (L. *imbecillus*)
imbed, see **embed.**
imbibe, *v.t.* drink in, drink, absorb; receive in the mind. **imbibition,** *n.* (L. *bibere,* drink)
imbrangle, see **embrangle.**
imbricate, *v.t.* and *i.* arrange, be arranged, so as to overlap like tiles. **imbricative,** *a.* **imbrication,** *n.* (L. *imbrex,* tile)
imbroglio, *n.* complicated situation or plot; misunderstanding; confused heap. (It.=confusion)

imbrue, *v.t.* drench; stain. **imbruement,** *n.* (L. *bibere,* drink)
imbrute, embrute, *v.t.* brutalize.
imbue, *v.t.* saturate, dye; inspire; imbrue. (L. *bibere,* drink)
imitate, *v.t.* strive to be the same as; mimic, be like; copy. **imitable,** *a.* capable, worthy, of imitation. **imitability,** *n.* **imitation,** *n.* imitating; copy, likeness.—*a.* counterfeit. **imitative,** *a.* **imitator,** *n.* (L. *imitari*)
immaculate, *a.* spotless, pure; faultless. **I. Conception,** dogma that the Virgin Mary was born free from taint of original sin. **immaculacy, immaculateness,** *nn.* (L. *macula,* spot)
immanent, *a.* indwelling; inherent; (of God) pervading all things. **immanence, immanency,** *nn.* (L. *manēre,* remain)
immanity, *n.* (*Shake.*) cruelty, barbarity. (L. *immanis,* monstrous)
immask, *v.t.* (*Shake.*) cover, hide.
immaterial, *a.* not consisting of matter; incorporeal; unimportant. **immateriality,** *n.* **immaterialize,** *v.t.* **immaterialism,** *n.* doctrine that matter has no existence apart from mind, idealism. **immaterialist,** *n.* believer in this.
immature, *a.* not mature or ripe; premature. **immaturity,** *n.*
immeasurable, *a.* that cannot be measured; immense. **immeasurability,** *n.*
immediate, *a.* without delay; direct, with nothing intervening; proximate, nearest. **immediacy,** *n.* immediateness; (*Shake.*) direct holding of office. **immediately,** *adv.* at once, instantly. (*mediate*)
immemorial, *a.* beyond the reach of memory; very old.
immense, *a.* huge, vast; (*sl.*) first-rate. **immensity,** *n.* vastness; infinity. (L. *in,* not; *metiri,* measure)
immensurable, *a.* that cannot be measured.
immerse, *v.t.* dip, plunge (in); baptize by dipping whole body; absorb, involve. **immersion,** *n.* immersing; (*astron.*) disappearance of celestial body behind or in shadow of another. (L. *in,* into; *mergere,* plunge)
immesh, see **enmesh.**
immethodical, *a.* without method or order.
immigrate, *v.i.* and *t.* come, bring, as settler to a country. **immigrant,** *a.* immigrating.—*n.* one who immigrates. **immigration,** *n.* (*migrate*)
imminent, *a.* impending, near at hand. **imminence,** *n.* (L. *in,* upon; *minēre,* project)
immiscible, *a.* incapable of being mixed. **immiscibility,** *n.* (L. *in-,* not; *miscēre,* mix)
immit, *v.t.* send into; inject. **immission,** *n.* (L. *in,* into; *mittere,* send)
immitigable, *a.* incapable of being softened or toned down.
immix, *v.t.* (*poet.*) mix. **immixture,** *n.* mixing up; being involved (in).
immobile, *a.* immovable; motionless. **immobility,** *n.* **immobilize,** *v.t.* fix immovably; make (troops) incapable of being shifted; withdraw (specie) from circulation. (*mobile*)
immoderate, *a.* excessive, extravagant.
immodest, *a.* indecent, indelicate; impudent. **immodesty,** *n.*
immolate, *v.t.* kill, offer, in sacrifice; sacrifice. **immolation, immolator,** *nn.* (L. *immolare*)
immoment, *a.* (*Shake.*) of no moment.
immoral, *a.* morally wrong, wicked; vicious, licentious. **immorality,** *n.*
immortal, *a.* exempt from death; imperishable; famous for all time.—*n.* immortal being; god of antiquity; author etc. of lasting fame; (*pl.*) royal bodyguard of ancient Persia. **immortality,** *n.* **immortalize,** *v.t.* endow with endless life or lasting fame. **immortalization,** *n.* (*mortal*)
immortelle, *n.* kinds of composite flower retaining colour when dried. (F.)
immovable, *a.* not movable; unalterable; steadfast, unyielding; emotionless.—*n.pl.* (*law*) property consisting of land, houses etc. **immovability,** *n.*
immune, *a.* secure, exempt; proof against (disease). **immunity,** *n.* **immunize,** *v.t.* **immunization,** *n.* (L. *immunis,* exempt from public burden)
immure, *v.t.* wall in, shut up, imprison. **immurement,** *n.* (L. *murus,* wall)
immutable, *a.* unchangeable; unalterable. **immutability,** *n.*
imp, *n.* little devil, wicked spirit; mischievous child; (*arch.*) shoot, child.—*v.t.* graft; strengthen (bird's damaged wing) by inserting feather. (O.E. *impa,* young shoot)
impact, *n.* striking against, collision. —*v.t.* press firmly, drive forcibly (into). **impaction,** *n.* (*impinge*)
impaint, *v.t.* (*Shake.*) depict.
impair, *v.t.* diminish; injure; weaken. **impairment,** *n.* (L. *pejor,* worse)
impair, *a.* (*Shake.*) unsuitable. (*par*)
impale, *v.t.* transfix (on stake), execute thus; fence in with stakes; (*heraldry*) combine (two escutcheons) by placing them side by side on one shield. **impalement,** *n.* (L. *palus,* stake)
impalpable, *a.* imperceptible to the touch, intangible; not easily understood. **impalpability,** *n.*
impanate, *a.* (of the body of Christ) contained in the consecrated bread in the eucharist. **impanation,** *n.* (L. *panis,* bread)
impanel, see **empanel.**
imparadise, *v.t.* put in a paradise or state of supreme happiness; make a paradise of.
imparity, *n.* inequality.
impark, *v.t.* enclose (land) for park; enclose (animals) in park.

impart, *v.t.* give share of, give; communicate. **impartation,** *n.*
impartial, *a.* not taking sides, unprejudiced, fair. **impartiality,** *n.*
impartible, *a.* that can be imparted.
impartible, *a.* (of estate) not divisible.
impartment, *n.* communication.
impassable, *a.* incapable of being traversed or passed. **impassability,** *n.* **impasse,** *n.* blind alley; deadlock, fix.
impassible, *a.* incapable of feeling; immune from suffering or injury. **impassibility,** *n.* (L. *in-*, not; *pati*, suffer)
impassioned, *a.* deeply moved, ardent.
impassive, *a.* without feeling or emotion; not showing feeling, calm; impassible. **impassivity,** *n.* (*passive*)
impaste, *v.t.* make into paste, knead; paint in impasto. **impasto,** *n.* laying on of pigment thickly; thickness of paint on canvas. (*paste*)
impatient, *a.* not patient; intolerant (of); desirous (for). **impatience,** *n.*
impawn, *v.t.* deposit as security, pledge.
impayable, *a.* invaluable; (*colloq.*) going beyond ordinary limits. (F.)
impeach, *v.t.* accuse; cite before a court for official misconduct; call in question, disparage. **impeacher, impeachment,** *nn.* (L. *pedica*, fetter)
impearl, *v.t.* adorn with or as with pearls; make like pearls.
impeccable, *a.* not liable to sin; faultless. **impeccability,** *n.* **impeccant,** *a.* sinless. (L. *peccare*, sin)
impecunious, *a.* having no money, poor. **impecuniosity,** *n.* (L. *pecunia*, money)
impede, *v.t.* hinder, obstruct. **impedance,** *n.* (*electr.*) virtual resistance due to self-induction in electrified body. **impediment,** *n.* obstacle, hindrance; stammer. **impedimenta,** *n.pl.* baggage. **impedimental,** *a.* (L. *impedīre*)
impel, *v.t.* drive forward, propel; force, instigate. **impellent,** *a.* and *n.* (L. *in*, on; *pellere*, drive)
impend, *v.i.* hang over; threaten, be imminent. **impendence, impendency,** *nn.* **impendent,** *a.* (L. *impendere*)
impenetrable, *a.* incapable of being penetrated or pierced; impervious, unimpressible; inscrutable, unfathomable. **impenetrability,** *n.*
impenetrate, *v.t.* penetrate deeply.
impenitent, *a.* not penitent. **impenitence, impenitency,** *nn.*
impennate, *a.* wingless; having short wings useless for flight. (L. *in-*, not; *penna*, wing)
imperative, *a.* expressive of command; peremptory; necessary.—*n.* (*gram.*) imperative mood. **imperatival,** *a.* (*gram.*). (L. *imperare*, command)
imperator, *n.* commander-in-chief in ancient Rome; emperor. **imperatorial,** *a.* (L.)
imperceptible, *a.* not perceptible; very minute, gradual, or subtle. **imperceptibility,** *n.*
impercipient, *a.* lacking perception.
imperfect, *a.* not perfect; incomplete; defective, faulty; (*gram.*) denoting continuous action.—*n.* (*gram.*) imperfect tense. **imperfection,** *n.* incompleteness; blemish.
imperforate, *a.* (of stamp) not perforated; (*anat.*) without normal opening.
imperial, *a.* of an empire or emperor; supreme, majestic; (of weights and measures) used by statute in Britain; (of paper) size 30×22 in.—*n.* tuft of hair on lower lip; kinds of dome and trunk. **imperialism,** *n.* government by an emperor; belief in value of colonies; wish to found or extend empire. **imperialist,** *n.* **imperialistic,** *a.* (L. *imperium*, command)
imperil, *v.t.* endanger.
imperious, *a.* commanding, dictatorial; urgent, imperative.
imperishable, *a.* indestructible, everlasting. **imperishability,** *n.*
imperium, *n.* supreme power; empire. *i. in imperio*, a government within another. (L.)
impermanent, *a.* not permanent. **impermanence, impermanency,** *nn.*
impermeable, *a.* not permitting passage, impervious. **impermeability,** *n.*
impermissible, *a.* not permissible.
imperscriptible, *a.* without written authority. (L. *perscribere*, register)
impersonal, *a.* without personality; having no personal reference; (*gram.* of verb) without personal subject. **impersonality,** *n.*
impersonate, *v.t.* pretend to be (someone else), act (character); invest with personality, personify. **impersonator, impersonation,** *nn.*
impertinent, *a.* rude, impudent; not to the point, irrelevant. **impertinence,** *n.*
imperturbable, *a.* not excitable, calm, cool. **imperturbability,** *n.* (*perturb*)
impervious, *a.* not affording passage, impenetrable; deaf (to argument).
impetigo, *n.* contagious pustular disease of skin. **impetiginous,** *a.* (L.)
impetrate, *v.t.* obtain by entreaty or petition. **impetration,** *n.* **impetratory,** *a.* (L. *patrare*, bring to pass)
impetus, *n.* force with which a body moves, momentum; impulse. **impetuous,** *a.* moving violently or rapidly; acting rashly, vehement, precipitate. **impetuosity,** *n.* (L.=attack)
impeyan, *n.* bright-hued Himalayan pheasant. (Sir Elijah *Impey*)
impi, *n.* Zulu regiment. (Zulu)
impiety, *n.* ungodliness, irreverence; impious act.
impinge, *v.i.* and *t.* strike, dash (against); touch upon. **impingement,** *n.* (L. *impingere*)
impious, *a.* irreverent, rreligious; profane; wicked.
impish, *a.* of, like, an imp; mischievous.

impiteous, *a.* (*poet.*) pitiless.
implacable, *a.* not appeasable, inexorable. **implacability,** *n.* (*placate*)
implacental, *a.* with no placenta.
implant, *v.t.* insert, fix (in); instil; plant. **implantation,** *n.*
impledge, *v.t.* pledge, pawn.
implement, *n.* tool, instrument, utensil. —*v.t.* fulfil (contract); supplement. (L. *implēre*, fill)
impletion, *n.* filling; fullness.
implicate, *v.t.* entangle; involve; imply.—*n.* thing implied. **implication,** *n.* implicating; thing implied. **implicative,** *a.* **implicit,** *a.* implied though not plainly expressed; unquestioning. (L. *implicare*)
implore, *v.t.* ask earnestly for, entreat. **imploringly,** *adv.* (L. *plorare*, weep)
impluvium, *n.* rain-water cistern in hall of ancient Roman house. (L.)
imply, *v.t.* involve the truth of; signify; insinuate; (*Spens.*) enfold. **impliedly,** *adv.* (L. *implicare*, enfold)
impolder, *v.t.* reclaim from sea. (*polder*)
impolicy, *n.* bad policy.
impolite, *a.* uncivil, rude.
impolitic, *a.* injudicious, inexpedient.
imponderable, *a.* without perceptible weight, very light; (of electricity, mind etc.) not to be estimated by weight.—*n.* imponderable thing.
impone, *v.t.* (*Shake.*) stake, wager. **imponent,** *a.* and *n.* (person) that imposes duty etc. (L. *in*, on; *ponere*, place)
import, *v.t.* introduce, bring from abroad; convey, signify; be of consequence to.—*n.* goods imported; meaning, significance; importance. **importation, importer,** *nn.* bringing, bringer, of goods from abroad. (L. *in*, in; *portare*, carry)
important, *a.* of great consequence, momentous; consequential. **importance,** *n.* (*import*)
importune, *v.t.* urge with requests, solicit repeatedly. **importunate,** *a.* persistent in soliciting. **importunity,** *n.* (L. *importunus*, inconvenient)
impose, *v.t.* and *i.* place upon; lay (tax, obligation) upon; palm off. **i. upon,** overawe, impress, deceive. **imposing,** *a.* impressive. **imposition,** *n.* imposing; laying on of hands in ordination; tax, duty; deception, overcharge; punishment task given at school. (L. *in*, on; *pausare*, halt, and *ponere*, place)
impossible, *a.* not possible; (*colloq.*) intolerable, absurd. **impossibility,** *n.*
impost, *n.* tax, duty; (*archit.*) moulding on top of pillar, bearing arch; (*sl.*) weight racehorse carries in handicap.—*v.t.* (*Amer.*) classify (imports) for fixing duty. (*impose*)
impostor, *n.* one who assumes a false character; cheat, swindler. (*impose*)
impostume, imposthume, *n.* abscess; purulent swelling. **impostumate, imposthumate,** *v.i.* and *t.* form, affect with, impostume. **impostumation, imposthumation,** *n.* (Gk. *apostēma*, separation)
imposture, *n.* deception, sham, fraud.
impotent, *a.* powerless; helpless; (of male) without sexual power. **impotence, impotency,** *nn.* (*potent*)
impound, *v.t.* shut up in pound; confine; confiscate. (*pound*)
impoverish, *v.t.* make poor; exhaust resources of. **impoverishment,** *n.* (L. *pauper*, poor)
impracticable, *a.* not able to be done; unmanageable; (of road) impassable. **impracticability,** *n.* **impractical,** *a.* unpractical; impracticable. (*practice*)
imprecate, *v.t.* invoke, call down (evil upon). **imprecation,** *n.* curse. **imprecatory,** *a.* (L. *in*, upon; *precari*, pray)
impregnable, *a.* that cannot be taken by arms; proof against attack. **impregnability,** *n.* (L. *in-*, not; *prehendere*, take)
impregnate, *v.t.* make pregnant; fecundate; fill, saturate.—*a.* pregnant; permeated. **impregnation,** *n.* (L. *in*, in; *praegnans*, pregnant)
impresario, *n.* organizer of public entertainment, operatic manager. (It.)
imprescriptible, *a.* not subject to prescription or loss through disuse.
impress, *v.t.* mark by pressure, stamp; imprint, fix deeply (in mind); affect deeply.—*n.* stamping; mark impressed; device, motto. **impressible,** *a.* **impression,** *n.* impress; print from type or engraving; issue, edition, of book; effect produced (on mind); vague belief, idea. **impressionable,** *a.* easily influenced. **impressionism,** *n.* painting, writing etc. to give general effect without detail. **impressionist,** *n.* and *a.* **impressionary, impressionistic,** *aa.* **impressive,** *a.* solemn; affecting. (*press*)
impress, *v.t.* force (men) to serve in army or navy; seize for, press into, service. **impressment,** *n.* (*press*)
imprest, *n.* money advanced; earnest-money. (L. *praestare*, be surety for)
imprimatur, *n.* licence to print book; sanction. (L.=let it be printed)
imprimis, *adv.* in the first place. (L.)
imprint, *v.t.* impress, stamp; fix (in mind).—*n.* impression; name of publisher, printer etc. on title-page or at end of book. (*print*)
imprison, *v.t.* put in prison; confine **imprisonment,** *n.*
improbable, *a.* unlikely; incredible. **improbability,** *n.* **improbably,** *adv.*
improbity, *n.* wickedness, dishonesty.
impromptu, *a.* and *adv.* without preparation, off-hand, extempore.—*n.* improvisation. (L. *in promptu*, in readiness)
improper, *a.* unfit, incorrect; unbecoming, indecent. **i. fraction,** with numerator greater than denominator.
impropriate, *v.t.* place (ecclesiastical

property) in hands of layman.—*a.* vested in a layman. **impropriation,** *n.* **impropriator,** *n.* layman who holds benefice. (L. *proprius,* own)

impropriety, *n.* wrongness, unfitness, indecency; improper act. (*improper*)

improve, *v.t.* and *i.* make or become better, progress; make good use of. **i. upon,** make something better than. **improver,** *n.* one who improves; one who works at low wages or none to improve his skill; pad for woman's dress, bustle. **improvement,** *n.* (L. *pro,* forward)

improvident, *a.* without foresight; thriftless. **improvidence,** *n.*

improvise, *v.t.* and *i.* compose, recite, extempore; bring about, act, without preparation. **improvisation,** *n.* **improvisator,** *improvisatore, improvvisatore* (*fem. improvisatrice, improvvisatrice*) *n.* one who improvises. **improvisatorial, improvisatory,** *aa.* (L. *in-,* not; *provisus,* foreseen)

imprudent, *a.* rash, incautious; indiscreet. **imprudence,** *n.*

impudent, *a.* shameless, bold; disrespectful, insolent, rude. **impudence,** *n.* **impudicity,** *n.* shamelessness, immodesty. (L. *in-,* not; *pudēre,* be ashamed)

impugn, *v.t.* attack by arguments; call in question, challenge. **impugnment,** *n.* (L. *in,* against; *pugnare,* fight)

impuissant, *a.* powerless, weak. **impuissance,** *n.* (*in-*; *puissant*)

impulse, *n.* force suddenly applied, push; impetus; sudden inclination to act; mental incitement. **impulsion,** *n.* **impulsive,** *a.* tending to impel; given to acting without reflection. (L. *impellere,* drive on)

impunity, *n.* exemption from punishment; freedom from injurious consequences. (L. *in-,* not; *poena,* punishment)

impure, *a.* unclean, dirty; unchaste; adulterated, mixed. **impurity,** *n.*

impute, *v.t.* attribute, ascribe (to). **imputation,** *n.* imputing; censure, reproach. **imputative,** *a.* imputed. (L. *in,* in; *putare,* reckon)

in, *prep.* within, during; by, through; into.—*adv.* within.—*n.pl.* political party in office. **in for,** committed to; competing in. **in order that,** to the end that. **in order to,** for the purpose of. **in so far as,** to the extent that. **in that,** in virtue of the fact that. **in with,** (*colloq.*) intimate, friendly, with. **breed in-and-in,** breed repeatedly within the same stock. **in-patient,** *n.* patient lodged as well as treated in hospital. (O.E.)

in, prep. in, into. *in absentia,* in absence. *in aeternum,* for ever. *in articulo mortis,* in the instant of death. *in camera,* in private room, not public court. *in esse,* in being, actual. *in extenso,* at length, unabridged. *in extremis,* at the point of death. *in flagrante* (or *flagranti*) *delicto,* in the very act of committing the crime, red-handed. *in forma pauperis,* as a poor person. *in loco parentis,* in the place of a parent. *in malam partem,* in an unfavourable manner. *in medias res,* into the thick of things. *in memoriam,* in memory (of). *in nomine,* in the name (of). *in nubibus,* in the clouds, speculative. *in pace,* in peace. *in partibus* (*infidelium*), in a heretical country. *in perpetuum,* perpetually, for ever. *in posse,* potential, potentially. *in propria persona,* in one's own person. *in puris naturalibus,* stark naked. *in re,* in the matter of. *in saecula saeculorum,* for ever and ever (lit. to the ages of the ages). *in situ,* in its (original) place. *in statu pupillari,* under guardianship. *in statu quo* (*ante*), in the position in which it was before. *in terrorem,* as a warning. *in toto,* completely. (L.)

in-, *pref.* on, into, towards, against. (L.)

in-, *pref.* not. (L.)

inability, *n.* being unable; incapacity, want of power. (*able*)

inaccessible, *a.* that cannot be reached; unapproachable. **inaccessibility,** *n.*

inaccurate, *a.* erroneous, not exact. **inaccuracy,** *n.*

inaction, *n.* idleness, rest; inertness. **inactive,** *a.* **inactivity,** *n.*

inadequate, *a.* not equal to the purpose, insufficient. **inadequacy,** *n.*

inadhesive, *a.* not adhesive.

inadmissible, *a.* not allowable. **inadmissibility,** *n.*

inadvertent, *a.* not attentive, negligent; (of actions) unintentional. **inadvertence, inadvertency,** *nn.* negligence, oversight. (*advert*)

inalienable, *a.* that cannot be transferred or taken away. **inalienability,** *n.*

inalterable, *a.* unalterable. **inalterability,** *n.*

inamorato, n. (*fem. inamorata*) person with whom one is in love; lover. (It.)

inane, *a.* empty, void; senseless, silly. —*n.* empty space. (L. *inanis*)

inanimate, *a.* without life, dead; without animation, dull. **inanimation,** *n.*

inanition, *n.* emptiness; exhaustion from want of food. **inanity,** *n.* emptiness; silliness. (*inane*)

inappeasable, *a.* not appeasable.

inappellable, *a.* that may not be appealed against. (L. *in-,* not; *appellare,* appeal)

inappetence, *n.* want of appetence.

inapplicable, *a.* not applicable; unsuitable. **inapplicability,** *n.*

inapposite, *a.* not pertinent, out of place, unsuitable.

inappreciable, *a.* imperceptible, not worth reckoning. **inappreciation,** *n.* failure to appreciate. **inappreciative,** *a.* not appreciating or valuing.

inapprehensible, *a.* that cannot be grasped or understood.
inapproachable, *a.* not approachable, inaccessible.
inappropriate, *a.* unsuitable.
inapt, *a.* inappropriate; unfit, unskilful. **inaptitude,** *n.*
inarch, *v.t.* graft by connecting growing branch without separating it from original stem. (*arch*)
inarm, *v.t.* (*poet.*) encircle, embrace.
inarticulate, *a.* not speaking or spoken distinctly; dumb; (*zool.*) not jointed. **inarticulation,** *n.*
inartificial, *a.* artless, natural; inartistic.
inartistic, *a.* lacking artistic taste, crude; unskilled in art.
inasmuch, *adv.* i. as, since, seeing that; (*arch.*) in so far as.
inattentive, *a.* heedless, negligent. **inattention,** *n.*
inaudible, *a.* not able to be heard. **inaudibility,** *n.*
inaugurate, *v.t.* formally install in office; begin (undertaking); initiate, open, ceremonially. **inaugural,** *a.* **inauguration,** *n.* (L. *augurare*, take omens)
inauspicious, *a.* ill-omened, unlucky.
inboard, *a.* and *adv.* within hull, towards centre, of ship.
inborn, *a.* innate, implanted by nature.
inbreathe, *v.t.* breathe (thing) in.
inbred, *a.* inherent, innate, natural.
inbreed, *v.t.* breed in-and-in, breed from animals closely related.
inby, inbye, *adv.* (*Scot.*) towards the interior (of house etc.); inside.
Inca, *n.* king or prince of ancient Peru. (Peruvian)
incage, see **encage.**
incalculable, *a.* beyond calculation; not calculable, uncertain.
incandesce, *v.i.* and *t.* glow, cause to glow, with heat. **incandescent,** *a.* white or glowing with heat; (of light) produced by glowing of filament or mantle. **incandescence,** *n.* (L. *candēre*, be white)
incantation, *n.* magic formula, spell, charm. (L. *incantare*, enchant)
incapable, *a.* not capable; not able to comprehend; lacking normal powers. **incapability,** *n.* **incapacitate,** *v.t.* render incapable or unfit. **incapacitation,** *n.* **incapacity,** *n.* inability; legal disqualification.
incarcerate, *v.t.* imprison; confine. **incarceration, incarcerator,** *nn.* (L. *carcer*, prison)
incarnadine, *a.* crimson.—*v.t.* dye crimson. (*incarnate*)
incarnate, *v.t.* embody in flesh; put into concrete form; be living embodiment of.—*a.* embodied in flesh, in human form. **incarnation,** *n.* embodiment; living type. (L. *caro*, flesh)
incase, see **encase.**
incautious, *a.* rash.
incendiary, *n.* one who maliciously sets fire to property; one who stirs up strife; incendiary bomb.—*a.* of incendiarism; causing fire; inflammatory. **incendiarism,** *n.* (L. *incendere*, set on fire)
incense, *v.t.* enrage. **incensement,** *n.* (*Shake.*). (L. *incendere*, set on fire)
incense, *n.* gum, spice, burned in religious rites; its perfume; flattery. —*v.t.* perfume with incense; burn incense to. **incensation,** *n.* **incensory** *n.* censer.
incentive, *a.* inciting, encouraging.—*n.* incitement, motive. (L. *incentivus*, setting the tune)
incept, *v.i.* (at Cambridge University) commence the taking of Master's or Doctor's degree. **inceptor,** *n.*
inception, *n.* beginning; incepting. **inceptive,** *a.* beginning, initial; (of verb) denoting beginning of action. (L. *incipere*, begin)
incertitude, *n.* uncertainty, doubt.
incessant, *a.* unceasing, continual; repeated. **incessancy,** *n.* (L. *in-*, not; *cessare*, cease)
incest, *n.* sexual intercourse within forbidden degrees of kindred. **incestuous,** *a.* (L. *in-*, not; *castus*, chaste)
inch, *n.* island. (Gael. *innis*)
inch, *n.* twelfth part of foot; small distance; (*pl.*) height.—*v.t.* and *i.* move by inches, edge forward. **by ii.,** bit by bit. **every i.,** entirely. **inchmeal,** *adv.* by inches, gradually, (L. *uncia*, twelfth part)
inchoate, *a.* just begun; undeveloped. —*v.t.* begin, originate. **inchoation,** *n.* **inchoative,** *a.* (L. *inchoare*, begin)
incidence, *n.* falling upon, meeting with (a thing); range of influence. **incident,** *a.* falling upon; apt to occur, attaching, (to).—*n.* occurrence; subordinate event; episode. **incidental,** *a.* casual, accidental; incident (to). (L. *incidere*)
incinerate, *v.t.* reduce to ashes, burn up. **incineration,** *n.* **incinerator,** *n.* furnace for refuse. (L. *cinis*, ashes)
incipient, *a.* beginning, in early stage. **incipience, incipiency,** *nn.* (L. *incipere*, begin)
incise, *v.t.* cut into; engrave. **incision,** *n.* cutting into; gash, notch. **incisive,** *a.* cutting, penetrating; acute; sarcastic. **incisor,** *n.* front tooth between canines. (L. *incidere*)
incite, *v.t.* urge on, rouse to action. **incitation, incitement,** *nn.* (L. *incitare*)
incivility, *n.* rudeness, disrespect.
inclearing, *n.* total of cheques and bills received through clearing-house for settlement by a bank.
inclement, *a.* (of weather) severe, cold, stormy; harsh. **inclemency,** *n.*
incline, *v.t.* and *i.* bend, turn from vertical; lean; dispose, be disposed. —*n.* slope, ascent. **inclinable,** *a.* tending, disposed (to), **inclination,** *n.* inclining; slope, angle; tendency;

liking, affection. **inclinometer,** *n.* instrument for measuring slopes or vertical intensity of magnetic force. (L. *in*, towards; *clinare*, bend)

inclose, see **enclose.**

include, *v.t.* reckon in, embrace as part of whole; comprise, contain; shut in. **inclusion,** *n.* **inclusive,** *a.* including, comprising; including stated limits. (L. *claudere*, shut)

incognito, *a.* (*pl.* **incogniti**: *fem.* **incognita,** *pl.* **incógnitē**; *colloq.* **incog.**) not revealing identity; under false name. —*n.* such concealment or person using it. (It.=unknown)

incognizable, *a.* that cannot be perceived, known, or distinguished. **incognizant,** *a.* unaware, unconscious (of). **incognizance,** *n.* (*cognizance*)

incoherent, *a.* not coherent; inconsistent, rambling. **incoherence,** *n.* want of cohesion; incongruity.

incombustible, *a.* incapable of being consumed by fire. **incombustibility,** *n.*

income, *n.* gain, profit, from business etc.; annual receipts, revenue; (*Shake.*) arrival; (*Scot.*) disease coming without known cause. **i.-tax,** *n.* tax levied on income. **incomer,** *n.* immigrant, intruder; successor. **incoming,** *n.* arrival; (*pl.*) income.—*a.* accruing; ensuing. (*in*; *come*)

incommensurable, *a.* (*math.*) having no common measure; irrational, surd; not worthy to be measured with. **incommensurability.** *n.* **incommensurate,** *a.* out of proportion, inadequate; incommensurable.

incommode, *v.t.* inconvenience, annoy; hinder. **incommodious,** *a.* not having good accommodation, uncomfortable.

incommunicable, *a.* that cannot be imparted or told. **incommunicability,** *n.* **incommunicative,** *a.* not disposed to give information, reserved; unsociable.

incommunicado, *a.* (*Amer.*) without means of communication; in solitary confinement. (Sp. *incomunicado*)

incommutable, *a.* that cannot be exchanged or commuted.

incompact, *a.* not compact.

incomparable, *a.* matchless.

incompatible, *a.* inconsistent, contradictory; incapable of existing together in harmony. **incompatibility,** *n.*

incompetent, *a.* not qualified or able (to), not competent. **incompetence, incompetency,** *nn.*

incomplete, *a.* not finished or perfect.

incomprehensible, *a.* incapable of being understood; boundless. **incomprehensibility,** *n.* **incomprehension,** *n.* failure to understand.

incompressible, *a.* that cannot be compressed, unsqueezable. **incompressibility,** *n.*

incomputable, *a.* incalculable, that cannot be reckoned.

inconceivable, *a.* that cannot be imagined; impossible. **inconceivability,** *n.*

inconclusive, *a.* not decisive or convincing, not settling point in debate.

incondensable, *a.* not able to be condensed or compressed.

incondite, *a.* ill-composed; crude, unfinished. (L. *inconditus*)

inconformity, *n.* lack of conformity, dissimilarity; nonconformity.

incongruous, *a.* disagreeing, unsuitable; out of place, absurd. **incongruity,** *n.* inconsistency; absurdity.

inconsecutive, *a.* not succeeding in regular order.

inconsequent, *a.* not following naturally or logically; irrelevant, disconnected. **inconsequence,** *n.* **inconsequential,** *a.* inconsequent; of no consequence.

inconsiderable, *a.* not worth considering; small, unimportant. **inconsiderate,** *a.* thoughtless, lacking in regard for others' feelings; rash. **inconsiderateness, inconsideration,** *nn.*

inconsistent, *a.* not agreeing, incompatible; not uniform, self-contradictory. **inconsistency,** *n*

inconsolable, *a.* that cannot be comforted.

inconsonant, *a.* not harmonizing or accordant (with). **inconsonance,** *n.*

inconspicuous, *a.* not noticeable or eminent; hardly discernible.

inconstant, *a.* changeable, fickle; variable. **inconstancy,** *n.*

inconsumable, *a.* that cannot be consumed or wasted; not intended for consumption.

incontestable, *a.* indisputable, undeniable.

incontinent, *a.* not restraining the passions, unchaste; unable to hold in. **incontinence,** *n.* **incontinently,** *adv.* (*arch.* **incontinent**) at once, immediately; recklessly.

incontrollable, *a.* not controllable.

incontrovertible, *a.* indisputable, incontestable.

inconvenient, *a.* awkward, unsuitable, troublesome; uncomfortable. **inconvenience,** *n.* trouble, discomfort; what causes this. —*v.t.* trouble, incommode, put to inconvenience.

inconvertible, *a.* unable to be changed or exchanged (esp. of paper money). **inconvertibility,** *n.*

inconvincible, *a.* not able to be convinced.

incony, *a.* (*Shake.*) fine, dainty, rare.

inco-ordination, *n.* want of co-ordination.

incorporate, *v.t.* and *i.* unite, combine into one body or mass; form into a corporation; become incorporated.—*a.* united; formed into a corporation. **incorporation, incorporator,** *nn.*

incorporeal, *a.* not material; spiritual; intangible. **incorporeity,** *n.*

incorpsed, *a.* (*Shake.*) made into one body.

incorrect, *a.* untrue, inaccurate; faulty; improper.

incorrigible, *a.* incurably bad, depraved beyond hope of reform. **incorrigibility,** *n.*

incorruptible, *a.* that cannot decay; eternal; that cannot be bribed, inflexibly just. **incorruptibility,** *n.* **incorruption,** *n.* (*arch.*) freedom from decay.

incrassate, *v.t.* and *i.* make, become, thick.—*a.* of thick or swollen form. **incrassation,** *n.* (L. *crassus,* thick)

increase, *v.i.* and *t.* grow; make or become greater or more numerous; advance, extend.—*n.* growth, enlargement; increment, profit; progeny. (L. *crescere,* grow)

incredible, *a.* that cannot be believed; (*colloq.*) surprising. **incredibility,** *n.* **incredulous,** *a.* unbelieving. **incredulity,** *n.* scepticism.

increment, *n.* increase; amount of increase; profit; (*math.*) finite increase of a variable quantity. **unearned i.,** increased value of land due to external causes, not owner's labour or outlay. (L. *crescere,* grow)

incriminate, *v.t.* charge with crime; involve in accusation. **incriminatory,** *a.* (L. *crimen,* charge)

incrust, *v.t.* encrust. **incrustation,** *n.* encrusting; crust, hard coating; facing, inlaying, of marble. (*crust*)

incubate, *v.t.* and *i.* hatch (eggs); sit on eggs, brood. **incubation,** *n.* hatching; (*med.*) period between implanting and development of disease. **incubator,** *n.* apparatus for artificially hatching eggs, rearing prematurely born children, or developing bacteria. (L. *in,* upon; *cubare,* lie)

incubus, *n.* nightmare; oppressive spirit or thing; encumbrance.

inculcate, *v.t.* impress (on mind) by frequent repetition. **inculcation, inculcator,** *nn.* (L. *in,* upon; *calcare,* tread)

inculpate, *v.t.* blame, censure; involve in charge. **inculpation,** *n.* **inculpatory,** *a.* (L. *culpa,* fault)

incult, *a.* uncultivated; unpolished, coarse. (L. *in-,* not; *colere,* till)

incumbent, *a.* lying, resting, on.—*n.* holder of ecclesiastical benefice or any office. **it is i. on,** it is the duty of. **incumbency,** *n.* tenure, sphere, of incumbent, benefice. (L. *in,* upon; *cumbere,* lie)

incunabula, *n.pl.* very early printed books, esp. before 1500; early stages, origin. (L.=swaddling-clothes)

incur, *v.t.* become liable to, bring on oneself. (L. *in,* into; *currere,* run)

incurable, *a.* that cannot be cured.—*n.* one past cure. **incurability,** *n.*

incurious, *a.* indifferent, heedless; uninteresting. **incuriosity,** *n.*

incursion, *n.* hostile inroad, sudden attack. **incursive,** *a.* (*incur*)

incurve, *v.t.* and *i.* bend into curve, curve inwards. **incurvation,** *n.*

incus, *n.* bone of middle ear. (L.= anvil)

incuse, *v.t.* (of coin) impress by stamping; mark.—*a.* hammered, stamped in.—*n.* impression. (L. *cudere,* forge)

Ind, *n.* (*poet.*) India. (F. *Inde*)

indaba, *n.* (*S. Afr.*) native council; conference with natives. (Zulu=news)

indagate, *v.t.* search out. **indagation,** *n.* (L. *indagare,* trace)

indebted, *a.* owing money (to); obliged (to), beholden. (*debt*)

indecent, *a.* unbecoming; indelicate, obscene. **indecency,** *n.*

indeciduous, *a.* not deciduous; evergreen.

indecipherable, *a.* that cannot be deciphered; illegible.

indecision, *n.* want of decision; hesitation. **indecisive,** *a.* inconclusive; undecided; irresolute.

indeclinable, *a.* (*gram.*) having no inflexions.

indecomposable, *a.* that cannot be resolved into elements or decay.

indecorous, *a.* unbecoming, in bad taste. **indecorum,** *n.* want of decorum, breach of good manners.

indeed, *adv.* in fact, in truth, really. (*in; deed*)

indefatigable, *a.* tireless, unremitting, persevering. **indefatigability,** *n.* (*fatigue*)

indefeasible, *a.* that cannot be forfeited or annulled. **indefeasibility,** *n.*

indefectible, *a.* unfailing; faultless.

indefensible, *a.* that cannot be defended or justified, untenable. **indefensibility,** *n.*

indefinable, *a.* that cannot be defined. **indefinite,** *a.* unlimited, undefined; vague, uncertain. **i. article,** a, an. **indefinitude,** *n.*

indehiscent, *a.* not bursting open.

indelible, *a.* that cannot be effaced or erased. **indelibility,** *n.* (L. *in-,* not; *delēre,* wipe out)

indelicate, *a.* immodest, coarse; tactless. **indelicacy,** *n.*

indemnify, *v.t.* secure against harm, loss, or legal responsibility; compensate for loss etc. **indemnification,** *n.* **indemnity,** *n.* security against loss; compensation, damages; sum paid by defeated country as condition of peace. (L. *damnum,* loss)

indemonstrable, *a.* incapable of proof.

indent, *v.t.* cut into points like teeth, notch; make dent in, impress; draw up (document) in duplicate; (*print.*) set back farther from margin than rest of paragraph; order (goods).—*v.i.* make requisition; make terms. —*n.* notch, recess, dent; order. **indentation,** *n.* hollow, depression; notch, recess. **indention,** *n.* (*print.*) indenting of line. **indenture,** *n.* indenting; written agreement, contract; (*law*) deed under seal.—*v.t.*

bind by indenture, apprentice. (L. *dens*, tooth, and *dent*)

independent, *a.* not dependent or relying on others; free, autonomous; self-supporting; unwilling to be under obligation.—*n.* non-party politician; Congregationalist. **independence, independency,** *nn.* **Independence Day,** 4 July, anniversary of the American Declaration of Independence.

indescribable, *a.* vague; beyond description. **indescribability,** *n.*

indestructible, *a.* that cannot be destroyed. **indestructibility,** *n.*

indeterminable, *a.* that cannot be ascertained, settled, or classified. **indeterminate,** *a.* unfixed in extent or character; vague; undecided. **indeterminate vowel,** sound of *a* in ago, *u* in support etc. **indetermination,** *n.* indecision, wavering. **indeterminism,** *n.* theory that motives do not entirely determine human action.

index, *n.* (*pl.* **indexes,** in *math.* **indices**) pointer, indicator; list of references in book; (*anat.*) forefinger; (*math.*) exponent of a power.—*v.t.* provide with, place in, index. **I.** (*librorum prohibitorum*) list of books forbidden to Roman Catholics. *i. expurgatorius*, list of passages to be expunged in books otherwise permitted. (L.= forefinger)

India, *n.* **Indiaman,** *n.* large ship used in India trade. **I. paper,** soft absorbent paper from China; **Oxford I. paper,** very thin tough printing-paper. **indiarubber,** *n.* rubber, eraser.

Indian, *a.* and *n.* (native) of India. **Red I.,** N. American aboriginal. **I. civilian,** member of I.C.S. **I. club,** gymnast's bottle-shaped club. **I. corn,** maize. **I. cress,** nasturtium. **I. fig,** banyan tree. **I. file,** single file. **I. ink,** black pigment made in China. **I. summer,** period of calm dry hazy weather in late autumn in N. America. **I. weed,** tobacco.

indicate, *v.t.* point out, show; be a sign of; (*med.*) call for (treatment). **indication,** *n.* indicating; mark; symptom. **indicative,** *a.* giving sign, suggestive; (*gram.*) stating a fact. **indicator,** *n.* recording instrument. **indicatory,** *a.* (L. *indicare*)

indicium, *n.* (*pl.* **indicia**) sign. (L.)

indict, *v.t.* formally charge with a crime, esp. before grand jury. **indictable,** *a.* liable to, giving ground for, indictment. **indictee,** *n.* one who is indicted. **indiction,** *n.* proclamation; cycle of fifteen years, instituted by Constantine the Great and adopted by the popes. **indictment,** *n.* formal or written accusation; (*Scots law*) form under which a criminal is put to trial at instance of Lord Advocate. (L. *dictare*, dictate)

indifferent, *a.* impartial, unconcerned; mediocre; unimportant. **indifference,** *n.* unconcern, neutrality; unimportance. **indifferentism,** *n.* attitude of indifference, esp. in religion. (*different*)

indigene, *n.* native. **indigenous,** *a.* native, belonging naturally (to soil etc.) (L. *indigena*)

indigent, *a.* poor, destitute. **indigence,** *n.* poverty, need. (L. *indigens*)

indigested, *a.* not digested; shapeless, disordered. **indigestible,** *a.* hard to digest, unwholesome. **indigestibility,** *n.* **indigestion,** *n.* difficulty in digesting, dyspepsia. **indigestive,** *a.* having, tending to, indigestion.

indign, *a.* (*arch.*) unworthy, disgraceful. **indignant,** *a.* moved by anger and disdain or resentment. **indignation,** (*Spens.*) **indignance,** *nn.* anger excited by baseness, injustice etc. **indignify,** *v.t.* (*Spens.*) dishonour. **indignity,** *n.* unworthy treatment, slight; contumely. (L. *indignus*)

indigo, *n.* a plant; blue dye made from it.—*a.* deep blue. **indigotic,** *a.* (L. *Indicus*, Indian)

indirect, *a.* not straight, oblique; not straightforward, crooked; not directly aimed at. **i. object,** (*gram.*) person, thing, affected by verb but less directly than the object. **i. speech,** (*gram.*) reported speech. **indirection,** *n.* roundabout means; trickery.

indiscernible, *a.* imperceptible.

indiscerptible, *a.* incapable of dissolution by separation of parts. **indiscerptibility,** *n.*

indiscipline, *n.* want of discipline.

indiscreet, *a.* injudicious, imprudent.

indiscrete, *a.* not separated into distinct parts.

indiscretion, *n.* rashness; imprudent act; *faux pas.*

indiscriminate, *a.* not discriminating; confused, promiscuous. **indiscrimination,** *n.* **indiscriminative,** *a.*

indispensable, *a.* necessary, that cannot be done without; (of law etc.) not to be set aside. **indispensability,** *n.*

indispose, *v.t.* render unfit or unable; make averse. **indisposed,** *a.* unwell. **indisposition,** *n.* ill-health, slight illness; disinclination.

indisputable, *a.* certain, too evident to admit dispute. **indisputability,** *n.*

indissoluble, *a.* that cannot be dissolved or broken; binding for ever, lasting. **indissolubility,** *n.*

indistinct, *a.* not clear; confused, obscure, dim. **indistinctive,** *a.* not capable of making distinctions. **indistinguishable,** *a.* that cannot be distinguished.

indite, *v.t.* compose; write; (*Shake.*) invite. **inditement,** *n.* (*indict*)

indivertible, *a.* that cannot be turned aside.

individual, *a.* single; particular, taken by itself; characteristic of particular person.—*n.* single person, animal, or thing; person. **individualism,** *n.* being self-centred, egoism; system opposing interference of State in affairs of individuals. **individualist,** *n.* believer in individualism. **individualistic,** *a.* **individuality,** *n.* separate existence; distinctive character. **individualize, individuate,** *vv.t.* distinguish individually; particularize. **individualization, individuation,** *nn.* **individually,** *adv.* one by one, separately; personally; in a distinctive manner. (L. *in-*, not; *dividere,* divide)

indivisible, *a.* not divisible.—*n.* (*math.*) infinitely small quantity. **indivisibility,** *n.*

Indo-, from *India,* used in **Indo-European,** *a.* Aryan; **Indonesian,** *a.* of the East Indian islands.

indocile, *a.* intractable; not disposed to be taught. **indocility,** *n.*

indoctrinate, *v.t.* instruct in doctrine, imbue with principles. **indoctrination,** *n.* (*doctrine*)

indolent, *a.* habitually lazy, slothful; (*med.*) causing no pain. **indolence,** *n.* (L. *in-*, not; *dolēre,* grieve)

indomitable, *a.* that cannot be tamed, unyielding, stubborn. (L. *domitare,* tame)

indoor, *a.* done within house or under cover; domestic. **indoors,** *adv.*

indorse, *v.t.* endorse. **indorsation,** *n.* endorsement. **indorsee,** *n.* one in whose favour bill is endorsed.

indraught, indraft, *n.* inlet, inward current; air drawn in.

indri, *n.* babacoote, lemur of Madagascar. (Malagasy *indry,* behold)

indubitable, *a.* beyond doubt, certain. (L. *dubitare,* doubt)

induce, *v.t.* persuade; bring about; infer; (*electr.*) produce (current) by induction. **inducement,** *n.* attraction, incentive. (L. *ducere,* lead)

induct, *v.t.* install; introduce, esp. to possession of benefice. (*induce*)

inductance, *n.* the capacity of a conductor for induction.

inductile, *a.* not ductile, that cannot be drawn into wire or threads.

induction, *n.* introduction; reasoning from particular to general; (*electr.*) electrification of an uncharged body by the proximity of a charged one. **inductive,** *a.* inferential; of electric induction. **inductor,** *n.* one who inducts clergyman; any part of electric induction apparatus. (*induce*)

indue, see **endue.**

indulge, *v.t.* and *i.* gratify; give free course to. **indulgence,** *n.* habitual indulging of desire; granting of religious freedom; (in R.C. Church) remission of temporal punishment due after absolution. **indulgenced,** *a.* (in R.C. Church) procuring indulgence to the user. **indulgent,** *a.* gratifying, favouring; compliant.

indult, *n.* pope's licence authorizing something not sanctioned by church law. (L. *indulgēre*)

induna, *n.* (*S. Afr.*) Zulu councillor or leader. (Zulu)

indurate, *v.t.* and *i.* make or grow hard; make callous. **induration,** *n.* **indurative,** *a.* (L. *durus,* hard)

industry, *n.* diligence, steady application; trade, manufacture. **industrial,** *a.* of trade or industry.—*n.pl.* shares in industrial concern. **Industrial Revolution,** changes brought about by introduction of machinery round 1800. **industrial school,** where children are taught a trade. **industrialism,** *n.* system involving, prevalence of, industries. **industrialist,** *n.* manufacturer. **industrialize,** *v.t.* **industrious,** *a.* hard-working, busy. (L. *industria*)

indwell, *v.t.* and *i.* occupy, dwell in. **indweller,** *n.*

-ine, *adj.suf.* belonging to, of the nature of, as in **marine, asinine.**

inebriate, *v.t.* make drunk, intoxicate; exhilarate.—*a.* drunk.—*n.* habitual drunkard. **inebriation, inebriety,** *nn.* drunkenness. (L. *ebrius,* drunk)

inedible, *a.* not fit to be eaten.

inedited, *a.* unpublished; not edited.

ineffable, *a.* inexpressible, beyond description.

ineffaceable, *a.* that cannot be wiped or rubbed out. **ineffaceability,** *n.*

ineffective, *a.* not producing effect wanted; inefficient, useless. **ineffectual,** *a.* without result, fruitless. **inefficacious,** *a.* not having power to produce effect wanted. **inefficient,** *a.* not fully capable or qualified, incompetent. **inefficiency,** *n.*

inelastic, *a.* not elastic, incompressible; unadaptable. **inelasticity,** *n.*

inelegant, *a.* ungraceful; lacking refinement or polish. **inelegance,** *n.*

ineligible, *a.* incapable of being chosen or elected; unqualified (for military service etc.). **ineligibility,** *n.*

ineluctable, *a.* against which it is vain to struggle, inevitable. (L. *eluctari,* struggle out)

inenarrable, *a.* that cannot be told, indescribable. (L. *enarrare,* tell)

inept, *a.* unsuitable, out of place; absurd, silly. **ineptitude,** *n.* (*apt*)

inequable, *a.* not uniform; of unequal incidence.

inequality, *n.* want of equality, disparity; unevenness; variability.

inequitable, *a.* unfair, unjust. **inequity,** *n.* unfairness.

ineradicable, *a.* that cannot be rooted out. (*eradicate*)

inerrable, *a.* not liable to err. **inerrability,** *n.* **inerrant,** *a.* unerring. **inerrancy,** *n.* (*err*)

inert, *a.* without power of moving itself or of active resistance; slow, sluggish; without active chemical properties. **inertia,** *n.* inertness;

property of matter by which it tends to remain at rest when still and in uniform motion when moving. (L. *iners*)

inescapable, *a.* that cannot be escaped, inevitable.

inescutcheon, *n.* (*heraldry*) a small shield within a shield.

inessential, *a.* not indispensable; immaterial.

inestimable, *a.* too great to be estimated, priceless. (*estimate*)

inevitable, *a.* unavoidable, sure to happen or appear; (*sl.*, of book's plot etc.) convincing. **inevitability,** *n.* (L. *in-*, not; *e*, out of; *vitare*, avoid)

inexact, *a.* not precisely correct or true. **inexactitude,** *n.* **inexactitudinarian,** *n.* (*joc.*) liar.

inexcusable, *a.* that cannot be justified, unpardonable.

inexecutable, *a.* that cannot be carried out.

inexhaustible, *a.* unfailing.

inexorable, *a.* not to be moved by entreaty, relentless; unalterable. **inexorability,** *n.* (L. *in-*, not; *ex*, out of; *orare*, pray)

inexpectant, *a.* not expectant.

inexpedient, *a.* inadvisable; unfitting. **inexpediency,** *n.*

inexpensive, *a.* cheap.

inexperience, *n.* want of experience. **inexperienced,** *a.*

inexpert, *a.* unskilled.

inexpiable, *a.* that cannot be atoned for; implacable. (*expiate*)

inexplicable, *a.* that cannot be explained. **inexplicability,** *n.* **inexplicit,** *a.* not clear. (L. *in-*, not; *explicare*, unfold)

inexplosive, *a.* not explosive.

inexpressible, *a.* beyond words, unutterable.—*n.pl.* (*joc.*) trousers. **inexpressive,** *a.* not expressive or significant; (*arch.*) inexpressible.

inexpugnable, *a.* impregnable; invincible. (L. *in-*, not; *expugnare*, storm)

inextensible, *a.* that cannot be extended.

inextinguishable, *a.* unquenchable.

inextricable, *a.* that cannot be disentangled, solved, or escaped from.

infallible, *a.* incapable of error; unfailing, certain. **infallibility,** *n.* **infallibilism,** *n.* principle of the pope's infallibility.

infamous, *a.* notoriously evil; vile, abominable. **infamize,** *v.t.* render infamous. **infamy,** *n.* ill fame, vileness; (*law*) loss of status incurred by convict. (L. *in-*, not; *fama*, fame)

infant, *n.* baby, child under 7; (*law*) minor, person under 21.—*a.* of, for, infants. **infancy,** *n.* early childhood; early stage of development; (*law*) minority. **infántě,** *n.* (*fem.* **infanta**) any son of Spanish or Portuguese king except the heir apparent. **infanticide,** *n.* murder or murderer of an infant; custom of killing new-born infants. **infanticidal,** *a.* **infantile, infantine,** *aa.* of, in, infancy; babyish. (L. *in-*, not; *fari*, speak)

infantry, *n.* foot-soldiers. **mounted i.,** mounted for transit but fighting on foot. (It. *infante*, foot-soldier)

infatuate, *v.t.* affect with folly; infect with foolish passion. **infatuation,** *n.* (L. *fatuus*, foolish)

infaust, *a.* unlucky. (L. *in*, not; *faustus*, propitious)

infeasible, *a.* impracticable.

infect, *v.t.* affect with disease; imbue (with opinion); taint. **infection,** *n.* communication of disease by air or distant means; contamination; diffusive influence. **infectious,** *a.* transmissible by infection; catching; pestilential. (L. *inficere*, taint)

infeft, *v.t.* (*Scots law*) invest with heritable property. **infeftment,** *n.* (*enfeoff*)

infelicific, *a.* causing unhappiness. **infelicitous,** *a.* unhappy; inappropriate. **infelicity,** *n.* misery; inaptness.

infer, *v.t.* deduce, conclude; imply. **inferable,** *a.* **inference,** *n.* inferring; thing inferred, deduction. **inferential,** *a.* deduced, deducible. (L. *in*, in; *ferre*, bring)

inferior, *a.* lower in rank, quality, or position; of poor quality; (of planet) nearer sun than earth is; (*print.*) set below the line.—*n.* person lower in rank or station. **inferiority,** *n.* **inferiority complex,** (*psycho-anal.*) suppressed feeling of inferiority, causing assertiveness etc. as compensation. (L.)

infernal, *a.* of hell; hellish, devilish; (*colloq.*) confounded. **i. machine,** disguised bomb. **infernality,** *n.* **inferno,** *n.* hell; scene of horror. (L. *infernus*, below)

inferrable, same as inferable.

infertile, *a.* unfruitful.

infest, *v.t.* swarm in, overrun, plague. —*a.* (*Spens.*) hostile. **infestation,** *n.* (L. *infestus*, hostile)

infeudation, *n.* granting possession of freehold estate; granting (of tithes) to laymen. (L. *feudum*, fee)

infibulation, *n.* fastening of sexual organs with clasp to prevent copulation. (L. *fibula*, clasp)

infidel, *n.* unbeliever; disbeliever in religion, non-Christian.—*a.* unbelieving; of infidels. **infidelity,** *n.* unfaithfulness in marriage; treachery; disbelief in Christianity. (L. *fides*, faith)

infield, *n.* farm land near farm; land under tillage; (*baseball*) space within baselines; (*cricket*) part of ground near wicket.

infighting, *n.* boxing at closer quarters than arm's length.

infiltrate, *v.t.* and *i.* percolate, trickle through; cause to pass through pores. **infiltration,** *n.*

infinite, *a.* boundless, endless; vast, innumerable. **the I.,** God. **infinitesimal,** *a.* extremely or infinitely small. **infinitive,** *a* (*gram.*) expressing verbal notion without person or number.—*n.* infinitive mood or verb in it. *infinito, a.* (*mus.*) perpetual. **infinitude, infinity,** *nn.* boundlessness, immensity; infinite number or extent. (L. *finis*, end)

infirm, *a.* feeble, weak through age; mentally weak, irresolute. **infirmary,** *n.* hospital, sick-quarters. **infirmity,** *n.* weakness, failing; disease. (*firm*)

infix, *v.t.* fix, insert, impress, in.—*n.* (*gram.*) modifying element in body of a word.

inflame, *v.t.* and *i.* set alight, catch fire; excite, become excited; (*med.*) affect, be affected, with inflammation. **inflammable,** *a.* easily set on fire; excitable. **inflammability,** *n.* **inflammation,** *n.* inflaming; (*med.*) disease of part of body with heat, pain, redness and swelling. **inflammatory,** *a.* tending to inflame.

inflate, *v.t.* blow up with air or gas; puff up; raise (price) artificially. **inflated,** *a.* bombastic. **inflation,** *n.* inflating; excessive issue of fiduciary money. **inflator,** *n.* (L. *in*, into; *flare*, blow)

inflect, *v.t.* bend inwards; modulate (voice); (*gram.*) vary in terminations. **inflective,** *a.* (*gram.*) of inflexion. **inflexible,** *a.* that cannot be bent; unyielding, stern. **inflexion, inflection,** *n.* bending; modulation; (*gram.*) suffix showing case, number, tense etc. **inflexional,** *a.* (L. *in*, in; *flectere*, bend)

inflict, *v.t.* lay on, deal (stroke etc.); impose as punishment. **infliction,** *n.* inflicting; punishment, burden. **inflictor,** *n.* (L. *in*, against; *fligere*, dash)

inflorescence, *n.* arrangement or aggregate of flowers on stem; flowering. (L. *inflorescere*, begin to blossom)

inflow, inflowing, *nn.* flowing in.

influence, *n.* power invisibly exercised; moral power, ascendancy; thing, person, exercising this.—*v.t.* exert influence upon, sway. (L. *in*, into; *fluere*, flow)

influent, *a.* flowing in.—*n.* tributary.

influential, *a.* having great influence.

influenza, *n.* epidemic feverish illness with severe catarrh. (*influence*)

influx, *n.* flowing or crowding in.

infold, see **enfold.**

inforce, *obs.* for **enforce.**

inform, *v.t.* tell; inspire, imbue; shape. —*v.i.* bring charge (against); (*Shake.*) take shape. (*form*)

informal, *a.* without formality, irregular. **informality,** *n.*

informant, *n.* one who tells. **information,** *n.* what is told, knowledge; charge, complaint. **informative, informatory,** *aa.* giving information, instructive. **informed,** *a.* instructed, enlightened. **informer,** *n.* one who lays charge. (*inform*)

infra, adv. (*abbr. inf.*) below; further on (in book). *i. dig.*, beneath one's dignity. **i.-red,** *a.* (of rays) beyond the red end of the visible spectrum. **i.-renal,** *a.* beneath the kidneys. **i.-scapular,** *a.* beneath the shoulder-blade. (L.)

infraction, *n.* infringement, violation, breach. (*infringe*)

infralapsarian, *n.* Calvinist who held that God's decree of election and reprobation was consequent to His foreknowledge of man's fall. **infralapsarianism,** *n.* (L. *lapsus*, fall)

infrangible, *a.* that cannot be broken; not to be violated. **infrangibility,** *n.*

infrequent, *a.* rare. **infrequency,** *n.*

infringe, *v.t.* transgress, violate. **infringement,** *n.* (L. *frangere*, break)

infructuous, *a.* unfruitful; fruitless.

infundibular, *a.* funnel-shaped. (L. *infundibulum*, funnel)

infuriate, *v.t.* enrage, madden.

infuse, *v.t.* and *i.* pour in, instil; steep, be steeped, in liquid to extract soluble properties. **infuser,** *n.* (L. *infundere*)

infusible, *a.* that cannot be fused or melted. (*fuse*)

infusion, *n.* infusing; liquid extract obtained by steeping; admixture. **infusoria,** *n.pl.* microscopic organisms inhabiting liquids. **infusorial, infusorian, infusory,** *aa.*

ingathering, *n.* gathering in, harvest.

ingeminate, *v.t.* repeat, reiterate. (L. *geminus*, twin)

ingenious, *a.* skilful at inventing or contriving; skilfully contrived. (L. *ingenium*, natural ability)

ingénue, n. artless girl, esp. as stage type. (F.)

ingenuity, *n.* ingeniousness, skill in contriving. (*ingenuous*, which was confused with ingenious)

ingenuous, *a.* frank, honourable; artless, naïve. (L. *ingenuus*, free-born)

ingest, *v.t.* take (food) into stomach. **ingestion,** *n.* (L. *in*, in; *gerere*, bear)

ingine, *n.* (*Scot.*) genius; ingenuity.

ingle, *n.* (*Scot.*) fire; fireplace. **i.-cheek, i.-nook, i.-side,** *nn.* fireside.

inglobe, *v.t.* encircle; involve.

inglorious, *a.* ignominious, disgraceful; obscure.

ingoing, *a.* and *n.* going in.

ingot, *n.* mass of unwrought gold, silver, or other metal, cast in mould.

ingraft, see **engraft.**

ingrain, *v.t.* engrain.—*a.* dyed in yarn before manufacture; inherent, inveterate. **ingrained,** *a.* deep-rooted, inveterate.

ingrate, *a.* and *n.* (*arch.*) ungrateful (person). (L. *in-*, not; *gratus*, grateful)

ingratiate, *v.refl.* get oneself into favour. **ingratiatingly,** *adv.* (L. *in*, into; *gratia*, favour)

ingratitude, *n.* want of gratitude.

ingravescent, *a.* (*med.*) growing worse. **ingravescence,** *n.* (L. *gravis*, heavy)
ingredient, *n.* element in mixture; component part. (L. *ingredi*, enter)
ingress, *n.* going in; right, means, of entrance. (L. *ingredi*, enter)
ingrowing, *a.* growing inwards or into flesh. **ingrowth,** *n.*
inguinal, *a.* of the groin. (L. *inguen*, groin)
ingulf, see **engulf.**
ingurgitate, *v.t.* swallow up greedily; engulf. **ingurgitation,** *n.* (L. *gurges*, whirlpool)
inhabit, *v.t.* dwell in, occupy. **inhabitant, inhabitation,** *nn.* **inhabitancy,** *n.* residence, esp. to qualify for rights. (L. *habitare*, dwell)
inhabitable, *a.* that may be inhabited. (*inhabit*)
inhabitable, *a.* (*Shake.*) not habitable, uninhabitable. (*in-*, not)
inhale, *v.t.* breathe in, draw into lungs. **inhalation,** *n.* **inhaler,** *n.* respirator. (L. *halare*, breathe)
inharmonic, *a.* wanting harmony. **inharmonious,** *a.* discordant, unmusical.
inhere, *v.i.* exist in, belong to; be vested in. **inherence, inherency,** *nn.* **inherent,** *a.* forming inseparable property, innate. (L. *haerēre*, stick)
inherit, *v.t.* receive as heir; derive from parents.—*v.i.* succeed as heir. **inheritable,** *a.* capable of inheriting or being inherited. **inheritance,** *n.* inheriting; what is inherited. **inheritor,** *n.* (*fem.* **inheritress, inheritrix**) heir. (L. *heres*, heir)
inhesion, *n.* inherence.
inhibit, *v.t.* restrain; forbid, prohibit, esp. priest from exercise of his office. **inhibition,** *n.* inhibiting; (*psycho-anal.*) habitual shrinking from some action. **inhibitory,** *a.* (L. *inhibēre*)
inhospitable, *a.* giving no welcome or shelter. **inhospitality,** *n.*
inhuman, *a.* cruel, unfeeling, barbarous. **inhumanity,** *n.*
inhume, *v.t.* bury. **inhumation,** *n.* (L. *in*, in; *humus*, ground)
inimical, *a.* not friendly, hostile; harmful. (L. *in-*, not; *amicus*, friend)
inimitable, *a.* defying imitation; supremely excellent. (*imitate*)
iniquity, *n.* wickedness, sin; injustice. **iniquitous,** *a.* wicked; grossly unfair. (L. *in-*, not; *aequus*, just)
initial, *a.* of, placed at, beginning; commencing.—*n.* first letter of word, esp. of name.—*v.t.* sign with initials. (L. *initium*, beginning)
initiate, *v.t.* begin, set going; introduce (to society etc.); instruct (in principles).—*n.* one who has been initiated. **initiation,** *n.* initiating. **initiative,** *a.* originating.—*n.* first step; power to initiate, esp. legislation. **initiator,** *n.* (*fem.* **initiatrix**) one who initiates. *initio*, *adv.* (*abbr.* *init.*) at the beginning.
inject, *v.t.* drive, force (fluid into) as by syringe; fill by this means. **injection,** *n.* injecting; liquid injected. **injector,** *n.* (L. *injicere*)
injoint, *v.i.* (*Shake.*) join.
injudicious, *a.* unwise, ill-advised.
injunction, *n.* enjoining; command, precept; writ of prohibition granted by a court. (L. *injungere*, lay on)
injure, *v.t.* damage, hurt, impair; do wrong to. **injured,** *a.* wronged; offended, hurt. **injurious,** *a.* mischievous, wrongful; damaging, insulting. **injury,** *n.* harm, hurt; wrong. (L. *injuria*, injury)
injustice, *n.* want of justice, unfairness; unjust act, wrong.
ink, *n.* black or other coloured fluid used in writing, printing etc.—*v.t.* mark, daub, with ink. **i.-bottle, i.-horn, i.-pot, i.-well,** *nn.* vessels for holding ink. **inker,** *n.* inking roller. **inkstand,** *n.* stand for ink-bottle. **inky,** *a.* like, blackened with, ink; black. (L.L. *encaustum*)
inkle, *n.* (*Shake.*) kind of broad linen tape.
inkling, *n.* hint, slight knowledge or suspicion (of).
inkosi, *n.* Zulu chief. (Zulu)
inlaid, see **inlay.**
inland, *n.* interior of a country.—*a.* within a country, domestic; remote from the sea.—*adv.* in, towards, interior. **inlander,** *n.* **inlandish,** *a.*
inlay, *v.t.* (*past, p.p.* **inlaid**) embed, insert; ornament with inserted pieces of fine wood, ivory etc.—*n.* inlaid work.
inlet, *n.* small bay, creek; place of ingress; piece inserted.
inly, *adv.* (*poet.*) inwardly, in the heart; intimately.
inlying, *a.* lying inside.
inmate, *n.* occupant (of house etc.), lodger.
inmost, *a.* (*superl.* of in) farthest in; deepest, most intimate.
inn, *n.* public house for lodging or refreshment of travellers, tavern, hotel. **Ii. of Court,** four legal societies admitting to English bar; their buildings. (*in*)
innate, *a.* inborn, natural, inherent. (L. *in*, in; *nasci*, be born)
innavigable, *a.* impassable by ships.
inner, *a.* (*comp.* of in) farther in; interior, internal.—*n.* division of target next bull's-eye; shot striking this. **i. man,** soul; (*joc.*) stomach. **innermost,** *a.* farthest in.
innings, *n.* (*pl.* same, *colloq.* **inningses**) (*cricket, baseball*) team's or player's turn of batting; period of dominance; spell, turn. (*in*)
innkeeper, *n.* host, landlord, of inn.
innocent, *a.* sinless, pure; not guilty; guileless, harmless.—*n.* innocent person, young child; idiot. **i. of,** (*colloq.*) without. **innocence, innocency,** *nn.* (L. *in-*, not; *nocēre*, hurt)

innocuous, *a.* not hurtful, harmless. **innocuity,** *n.* (L. *innocuus*)
innominate, *a.* unnamed. **i. bone,** (*anat.*) hip-bone.
innovate, *v.i.* introduce novelties; make changes. **innovation, innovator,** *nn.* (L. *novus,* new)
innoxious, *a.* harmless.
innuendo, *n.* oblique hint, allusive remark, insinuation (us. disparaging). —*v.i.* make innuendoes. (L. *innuere,* nod)
innumerable, *a.* countless.
innutrition, *n.* want of nourishment. **innutritious,** *a.* not nourishing.
inobservance, *n.* inattention; failure to observe (law etc.). **inobservant,** *a.*
inoccupation, *n.* want of occupation.
inoculate, *v.t.* engraft; implant (disease germs in); infect with mild form of disease as protective measure. **inoculation, inoculator,** *nn.* **inoculative,** *a.* (L. *oculus,* bud)
inodorous, *a.* without smell.
inoffensive, *a.* giving no offence; harmless.
inofficious, *a.* without office or function; (*law*) regardless of moral duty.
inoperable, *a.* that cannot be operated upon. **inoperative,** *a.* not working; producing no effect.
inopportune, *a.* unseasonable, untimely.
inordinate, *a.* excessive, immoderate; irregular. (L. *ordo,* order)
inorganic, *a.* without life or organized structure, as rocks. **i. chemistry,** chemistry of minerals. **inorganization,** *n.* lack of organization.
inosculate, *v.i.* and *t.* (of blood-vessels, fibres etc.) join, unite closely. **inosculation,** *n.* (L. *os,* mouth)
inpouring, *n.* pouring in.
input, *n.* amount of energy received by a machine; (*Scot.*) contribution.
inquest, *n.* judicial inquiry; coroner's investigation into cause of a death; coroner's jury. (*inquire*)
inquietude, *n.* uneasiness, disquiet.
inquiline, *a.* and *n.* (animal) living in abode of another, as hermit-crab. **inquilinous,** *a.* (L. *incola,* inhabitant)
inquire, enquire, *v.i.* and *t.* make investigation; seek information; ask to be told. **inquirer, enquirer,** *n.* **inquiring,** *a.* given to inquiry. **inquiringly,** *adv.* **inquiry, enquiry,** *n.* asking, question; search, investigation. (L. *in,* in; *quaerere,* seek)
inquisition, *n.* investigation; official inquiry; Roman Catholic tribunal for examining and punishing heretics. **inquisitional,** *a.* of the Inquisition. **inquisitive,** *a.* curious, prying. **inquisitor,** *n.* official investigator; officer of the Inquisition. **inquisitorial,** *a.* of, like, an inquisitor; offensively prying. (*inquire*)
inroad, *n.* raid, invasion; encroachment.
inrush, *n.* rushing in, irruption.
insalivate, *v.t.* mix (food) with saliva. **insalivation,** *n.* (*saliva*)
insalubrious, *a.* (of climate) unhealthy. **insalubrity,** *n.*
insane, *a.* mad; crazy, senseless. **insanity,** (*Shake.*) **insanie,** *n.* madness.
insanitary, *a.* not sanitary. **insanitation,** *n.* defective sanitation.
insatiable, *a.* that cannot be sated or satisfied; very greedy. **insatiability,** *n.* **insatiate,** *a.* never satisfied. (*satiate*)
insconce, same as **ensconce.**
inscribe, *v.t.* write upon; mark, engrave; address, dedicate; issue (stock) in form of shares with registered holders; (*geom.*) draw (figure) inside another. **inscription,** *n.* inscribing; words inscribed. **inscriptional, inscriptive,** *aa.* (L. *in,* upon; *scribere,* write)
inscrutable, *a.* incomprehensible, mysterious. **inscrutability,** *n.* (L. *in-,* not; *scrutari,* search out)
insculp, *v.t.* (*Shake.*) carve, engrave. **insculpture,** *n.* (*Shake.*) inscription.
insect, *n.* small invertebrate animal with six legs and usually two or four wings; insignificant creature. **insectarium,** *n.* place for keeping insects. **insecticide,** *n.* preparation for killing insects. **insecticidal,** *a.* **insectivore,** *n.* insect-eater. **insectivorous,** *a.* **insectology,** *n.* science of insects, economic entomology. (L. *insectus,* cut into)
insecure, *a.* unsafe; (of footing etc.) liable to give way. **insecurity,** *n.*
inseminate, *v.t.* sow; implant. **insemination,** *n.* (L. *semen,* seed)
insensate, *a.* without sensibility, unfeeling; without sense, stupid. **insensible,** *a.* unconscious; unaware; unfeeling, callous; imperceptible. **insensibility,** *n.* **insensibly,** *adv.* imperceptibly. **insensitive,** *a.* not sensitive. **insentient,** *a.* inanimate.
inseparable, *a.* that cannot be separated. **inseparability,** *n.*
insert, *v.t.* put, thrust, in; introduce. **insertion,** *n.* inserting; thing inserted; lace, embroidery, inserted in dress. (L. *in,* into; *serere,* join)
insessorial, *a.* perching. (L. *in,* on; *sedēre,* sit)
inset, *v.t.* insert.—*n.* extra piece added in book, dress etc.; small photograph inside larger one.
inshore, *adv.* and *a.* near shore (on sea). **i. of,** nearer shore than.
inside, *n.* inner side, interior; inside passenger; (*colloq.*) stomach.—*a.* and *adv.* of, in, on, into, the inside.—*prep.* within, on inner side of. **insider,** *n.* one in the secret.
insidious, *a.* treacherous; (of disease) proceeding secretly or subtly. (L. *insidiae,* ambush)
insight, *n.* mental penetration, discernment.
insignia, *n.pl.* badges, emblems, of office or honour. (L. *signum,* sign)

insignificant, *a.* unimportant, trifling; contemptible; meaningless. **insignificance,** *n.*
insincere, *a.* false, hypocritical, deceitful. **insincerity,** *n.*
insinuate, *v.t.* introduce gently or gradually; work into favour; hint, convey indirectly. **insinuatingly,** *adv.* in a wheedling manner. **insinuation,** *n.* insinuating; hint. **insinuative,** *a.* **insinuator,** *n.* (L. *in,* into; *sinus,* bend)
insipid, *a.* tasteless, flavourless; spiritless, dull. **insipidity,** *n.* (L. *in-,* not; *sapere,* taste)
insist, *v.i.* and *t.* dwell (on), emphasize; maintain; persist in demanding. **insistence, insistency,** *nn.* **insistent,** *a.* (L. *in,* upon; *sistere,* stand)
insobriety, *n.* intemperance.
insolent, *a.* overbearing; insulting, rude. **insolence,** *n.* (L. *insolens*)
insoluble, *a.* that cannot be dissolved or solved. **insolubility,** *n.* **insolvent,** *a.* not able to pay one's debts; relating to bankrupts.—*n.* bankrupt. **insolvency,** *n.*
insomnia, *n.* sleeplessness. (L.)
insomuch, *adv.* to such a degree, so.
insouciant, *a.* careless, unconcerned. **insouciance,** *n.* (F.)
inspan, *v.t.* (*S. Afr.*) yoke (oxen) to wagon; harness wagon. (Du. *inspannen*)
inspect, *v.t.* examine closely or officially. **inspection,** *n.* **inspector,** *n.* official examiner; police officer above sergeant. **inspectoral, inspectorial,** *aa.* **inspectorate,** *n.* office, district, of inspector; body of inspectors. **inspectorship,** *n.* office of inspector. (L. *inspicere*)
inspire, *v.t.* and *i.* breathe in, inhale; breathe into, infuse; arouse feeling, create thought; instruct by divine agency; animate (with feeling). **inspiration,** *n.* inspiring, inhalation; divine influence inspiring Bible; elevating influence; happy idea. **inspirational,** *a.* **inspirationism,** *n.* belief in direct inspiration of the Bible. **inspirationist,** *n.* **inspirator,** *n.* device for drawing in air or vapour. **inspiratory,** *a.* of inhalation. **inspired,** *a.* directed by divine influence or elevated feeling; (of newspaper article) prompted by influential person. (L. *inspirare*)
inspirit, *v.t.* put life into, invigorate; encourage. **inspiriting,** *a.*
inspissate, *v.t.* thicken (fluid), condense. **inspissation,** *n.* (L. *spissus,* thick)
instability, *n.* lack of stability; inconstancy, fickleness.
install, *v.t.* place (person in office); establish with ceremony; have (apparatus) put in. **installant,** *a.* and *n.* **installation,** *n.* installing; fitting, apparatus. **instalment,** *n.* part of sum payable at intervals; part of consignment etc. (*stall*)
instance, *n.* illustrative example; particular case; solicitation; (*Shake.*) motive; evidence, proof.—*v.t.* cite as example; exemplify. **for i.,** for example. **in the first i.,** in the first place. **instancy,** *n.* urgency.
instant, *a.* pressing, urgent; immediate; (*abbr.* inst.) of current month. —*n.* moment, point of time. *instantané,* *n.* snap-shot, lightning sketch. **instantaneous,** *a.* occurring, done, in a moment. **instantly, instanter,** *advv.* immediately, at once. (L. *in,* upon; *stare,* stand)
instate, *v.t.* put in possession, install.
instauration, *n.* restoration, renewal. **instaurator,** *n.* (L. *instaurare,* renew)
instead, *adv.* in place (of); as a substitute.
instep, *n.* top of foot between toes and ankle; horse's hind leg between ham and pastern-joint.
instigate, *v.t.* urge on, incite; foment. **instigation, instigator,** *nn.* (L. *instigare*)
instil, instill, *v.t.* pour in by drops; infuse slowly (into mind). **instillation, instilment,** *nn.* (L. *stilla,* drop)
instinct, *n.* natural propensity which in animals takes the place of reason; natural impulse, involuntary prompting; intuition, unconscious skill.—*a.* charged, imbued (with). **instinctive,** *a.* prompted by instinct, involuntary. (L. *instinguere,* incite)
institorial, *a.* (*law*) of an agent or factor. (L. *institor,* agent)
institute, *v.t.* set up, establish; set on foot; appoint.—*n.* society, organization; building used by this; (*pl.*) book of principles, esp. in jurisprudence. **institution,** *n.* instituting; established law, order, or custom; (*colloq.*) familiar object. **institutional,** *a.* of institutions; authoritative; (of religion) finding expression through churches, ritual etc. (L. *in,* in; *statuere,* set up)
instruct, *v.t.* teach; inform; order, direct. **instruction,** *n.* teaching; (*pl.*) directions. **instructional,** *a.* **instructive,** *a.* informative. **instructor,** *n.* (*fem.* instructress) teacher. (L. *instruere*)
instrument, *n.* tool, implement; means, agent; contrivance for producing music; legal document.—*v.t.* arrange (music) for instruments. **instrumental,** *a.* serving as means; of, performed on, instrument. **instrumentalist,** *n.* performer on a musical instrument. **instrumentality,** *n.* agency, means. **instrumentation,** *n.* (*mus.*) arrangement of composition for playing by different instruments; instrumentality. (L. *instruere,* instruct)
insubordinate, *a.* disobedient, rebellious. **insubordination,** *n.*
insubstantial, *a.* unreal, lacking solidity. **insubstantiality,** *n.*

insufferable, *a.* intolerable; unbearably conceited.
insufficient, *a.* not enough, inadequate. **insufficiency,** *n.*
insufflate, *v.t.* blow (air, powder) into or on. **insufflation,** *n.* insufflating; breathing on, as rite in exorcism. **insufflator,** *n.* injector for insufflating. (L. *sufflare,* blow)
insular, *a.* of, like, an island or islanders; narrow-minded. **insularism, insularity,** *nn.* (L. *insula,* island)
insulate, *v.t.* make into an island; keep apart, isolate, esp. (*electr.*) by non-conductor. **insulation,** *n.* **insulator,** *n.* (*electr.*) non-conductor.
insulin, *n.* extract made from pancreas of animals, used in treating diabetes. (L. *insula,* island, because got from islets of cells)
insulse, *a.* stupid. **insulsity,** *n.* (L. *insulsus,* insipid)
insult, *v.t.* treat with contempt, abuse; affront.—*n.* scornful abuse; affront. **insultingly,** *adv.* **insultment,** *n.* (*Shake.*). (L. *insultare*)
insuperable, *a.* that cannot be got over, insurmountable. **insuperability,** *n.* (L. *in-,* not; *superare,* overcome)
insupportable, *a.* unbearable.
insure, *v.t.* make safe, secure; ensure, make certain; issue, take out, insurance policy for. **insurance,** *n.* insuring; contract to make good loss by fire, pay agreed amount on death etc. in return for periodical payments called premiums; the premium paid. **insurance policy,** written contract of insurance. **insurant,** *n.* holder of insurance policy. **insurer,** *n.* one who insures, underwriter.
insurgent, *a.* rushing in or upon; rising in revolt, rebellious.—*n.* rebel. **insurgency,** *n.* (L. *surgere,* rise)
insurmountable, *a.* that cannot be overcome, insuperable.
insurrection, *n.* rising, revolt. **insurrectional, insurrectionary,** *aa.* **insurrectionist,** *n.* (*insurgent*)
insusceptible, *a.* not susceptible.
intact, *a.* untouched, unharmed; entire.
intaglio, *n.* engraved design; stone with design cut into it (opp. to cameo).—*v.t.* engrave thus. **intagliated,** *a.* incised, engraved. (It.)
intake, *n.* what is taken in; inlet of channel or pipe; point where tube or stocking narrows; air-shaft in mine; land reclaimed from moor.
intangible, *a.* not perceptible to touch, impalpable. **intangibility,** *n.* (L. *in-,* not; *tangere,* touch)
integer, *n.* whole, thing complete in itself; (*math.*) whole number. **integral,** *a.* of, essential to, a whole; complete, not fractional.—*n.* (*math.*) quantity of which a given function is the differential. **integral calculus,** branch of mathematics dealing with integrals. **integrant,** *a.* component, making up a whole. **integrate,** *v.t.* make entire; combine (parts) into whole; give total of; (*math.*) find integral of.—*a.* made up of parts; complete. **integration, integrator,** *nn.* **integrative,** *a.* **integrity,** *n.* wholeness; soundness; uprightness, honesty. (L.=untouched)
integument, *n.* natural covering, skin, husk. **integumentary,** *a.* (L. *tegere,* cover)
intellect, *n.* mind, understanding; faculty of thinking. **intellection,** *n.* act of understanding. **intellective,** *a.* **intellectual,** *a.* of, appealing to, the intellect; having a good understanding.—*n.* enlightened person. **intellectualism,** *n.* theory that all knowledge is derived from pure reason. **intellectualist,** *n.* **intellectuality,** *n.* state of being intellectual; intelligence. **intellectualize,** *v.t.* and *i.* endow with intellect; employ intellect (on). **intellectualization,** *n.* (L. *intelligere,* understand)
intelligent, *a.* endowed with reason; mentally acute, sensible. **intelligence,** *n.* intellect; quickness of understanding, wisdom; rational being; information, news. **intelligencer,** *n.* informant, spy. **intelligential,** *a.* of the intelligence. **intelligentsia, intelligentzia,** *n.* the educated and cultured classes. **intelligible,** *a.* that can be understood, comprehensible, clear. **intelligibility,** *n.* (*intellect*)
intemperate, *a.* immoderate, unrestrained, violent; indulging an appetite to excess; given to excessive drinking. **intemperance,** *n.*
intend, *v.t.* purpose, design; mean; (*Shake.*) pretend; (*Spens.*) extend. **intendant,** *n.* superintendent, manager. **intendancy,** *n.* his office. **intended,** *n.* (*colloq.*) affianced lover. **intendment,** *n.* true meaning as fixed by law; (*Shake.*) intention. (L. *in,* towards; *tendere,* stretch)
intenible, *a.* (*Shake.*) incapable of holding.
intense, *a.* extreme in degree, strong, vehement; ardent; emotional. **intensify,** *v.t.* and *i.* make, become, intense; (*phot.*) increase contrast in. **intension,** *n.* intensity, making intense; straining. **intensity,** *n.* intenseness, degree. **intensive,** *a.* of, producing, intensity; concentrated, unremitted; serving to increase production; (*gram.*) giving emphasis.
intent, *a.* resolved, bent (on); absorbed; earnest, eager.—*n.* intention, aim, purpose. **to all ii. and purposes,** virtually. **intention,** *n.* intending; purposes, design; (*pl.*) purposes in respect of marriage. **intentional,** *a.* done on purpose, deliberate. **well-intentioned,** *a.* well-meant. (*intend*)
inter, *v.t.* bury. (L. *in,* in; *terra,* earth)
inter, prep. between, among. *i. alia,*

among other things. *i. nos*, between ourselves. *i. pocula*, over one's cups. *i. se*, among themselves. *i. vivos*, (of gift) between the living. (L.)

inter-, *pref.* between, among, as in **intercostal**; mutually, as in **interconvertible.**

interact, *n.* interval between acts of play; interlude.—*v.i.* act reciprocally or on each other. **interaction**, *n.* **interactive**, *a.*

interarticular, *a.* (*anat.*) between surfaces of a joint.

interbed, *v.t.* embed between others.

interblend, *v.t.* and *i.* blend, mix, with each other.

interbreed, *v.t.* and *i.* breed by crossing one species with another.

intercalary, *a.* (of day or month) inserted in calendar to harmonize it with solar year; (of year) having such addition; interpolated. **intercalate**, *v.t.* insert (intercalary day); interpose. **intercalation**, *n.* (L. *calare*, proclaim)

intercede, *v.t.* interpose, plead, for another; mediate, act as peacemaker. **interceder**, *n.* (L. *inter*, between; *cedere*, go)

intercellular, *a.* lying between cells.

intercensal, *a.* between two censuses.

intercept, *v.t.* catch, seize, in transit; cut off; (*math.*) comprehend between. **interception**, **interceptor**, *nn.* **interceptive**, *a.* (L. *capere*, take)

intercession, *n.* interceding, esp. by prayer. **intercessor**, *n.* one who intercedes; bishop administering vacant see. **intercessorial**, **intercessory**, *aa.*

interchange, *v.t.* and *i.* make exchange of; put (each of two things) in other's place; succeed by turns, alternate.—*n.* mutual exchange; alternation. **interchangeable**, *a.*

intercipient, *a.* intercepting.—*n.* person or thing that intercepts.

intercollegiate, *a.* existing, shared, between different colleges.

intercolonial, *a.* existing, carried on, between colonies.

intercolumnar, *a.* placed between columns. **intercolumniation**, *n.* spacing of, interval between, pillars.

intercommunicate, *v.i.* have mutual intercourse; have passage to each other. **intercommunication**, *n.* **intercommunicable**, *a.* that may be mutually communicated. **intercommunion**, *n.* intimate intercourse; mutual relation. **intercommunity**, *n.* possession or being possessed in common.

interconnect, *v.t.* and *i.* connect by reciprocal links. **interconnection**, *n.*

interconvertible, *a.* interchangeable.

intercostal, *a.* (*anat.*) lying between the ribs. (L. *costa*, rib)

intercourse, *n.* social communication; mutual dealings, commerce; coition.

intercross, *v.t.* and *i.* lay, lie, across each other; interbreed.

intercurrent, *a.* intervening; (of disease) occurring during course of another; recurring. **intercurrence**, *n.*

interdepend, *v.i.* depend on each other. **interdependence**, *n.* **interdependent**, *a.*

interdict, *v.t.* prohibit, forbid; forbid use of.—*n.* prohibition; decree of pope restraining clergy from performing divine service; (*Scots law*) injunction. **interdiction**, *n.* **interdictory**, *a.* (L. *interdicere*)

interdigital, *a.* between fingers or toes. **interdigitate**, *v.t.* and *i.* interlock like fingers of clasped hands. **interdigitation**, *n.* (*digit*)

interest, *v.t.* engage attention of, arouse curiosity or concern in; cause to take share (in).—*n.* attention, curiosity, concern; advantage; personal influence; share, right; cause, or party upholding it; payment for use of money. **vested i.**, right inalienable except for public use and upon compensation. **interested**, *a.* having, taking, interest; biased, selfish. **interesting**, *a.* arousing interest, engrossing. **in an interesting condition**, pregnant. (L.=it concerns)

interfacial, *a.* (*geom.*) included between two faces or surfaces.

interfemoral, *a.* between the thighs.

interfere, *v.i.* meddle, intervene; be obstacle, collide; (of light waves) strike each other. **interference**, *n.* interfering; (*wireless*) interruption of reception by atmospherics or unwanted signals. **interfering**, *a.* meddlesome. **interferometer**, *n.* instrument for measuring length of light waves by interference phenomena. (L. *inter*, between; *ferire*, strike)

interfluent, *a.* flowing into each other. (L. *fluere*, flow)

interfoliaceous, *a.* (*bot.*) placed alternately between opposite leaves.

interfuse, *v.t.* and *i.* mix, intersperse; blend. **interfusion**, *n.*

interglacial, *a.* occurring between two glacial periods.

intergrade, *v.i.* change form gradually. —*n.* intervening grade. **intergradation**, *n.* gradual approximation.

intergrowth, *n.* growing together.

interim, *n.* intervening time, meantime.—*a.* temporary, provisional.—*adv.* (*arch.*) meanwhile. (L.)

interior, *a.* inner, internal; inland.—*n.* inside; inland region; room or picture of one; home affairs of a country. **interiorly**, *adv.* (L.)

interjacent, *a.* lying between, intervening. (L. *jacēre*, lie)

interjaculate, *v.i.* interrupt remarks with ejaculation. **interjaculatory**, *a.* (L. *jaculari*, throw)

interject, *v.t.* throw between, interpose; remark parenthetically. **interjection**, *n.* interjecting; exclamation, ejaculation. **interjectural**, **interjectory**, *aa.* (L. *jacere*, throw)

interknit, *v.t.* unite closely.
interlace, *v.t.* and *i.* bind intricately together, interweave; intersect. **interlacement,** *n.*
interlap, *v.t.* and *i.* overlap.
interlard, *v.t.* diversify by mixture.
interleaf, *n.* extra leaf (us. blank) inserted in book. **interleave,** *v.t.* insert interleaves in.
interline, *v.t.* write between lines. **interlinear,** *a.* **interlineation,** *n.*
interlink, *v.t.* link together.
interlobular, *a.* between lobes.
interlock, *v.i.* and *t.* be locked together, engage; lock, clasp, together.
interlocution, *n.* dialogue; conference. **interlocutor,** *n.* (*fem.* **interlocutress, interlocutrix**) one who takes part in conversation; (*Scots law*) intermediate decree before final decision. **interlocutory,** *a.* (L. *loqui,* talk)
interlope, *v.i.* intrude into matter in which one has no fair concern. **interloper,** *n.* intruder. (*lope*)
interlude, *n.* interval during play; performance filling this; incident, event, interposed; any interval. (L. *ludus,* play)
interlunar, interlunary, *a.* between old and new moon.
intermarry, *v.i.* (of races, families etc.) become connected by marriage. **intermarriage,** *n.*
intermeddle, *v.i.* meddle officiously, interfere improperly.
intermediary, *a.* acting between, mediatory; intermediate.—*n.* go-between, mediator. **intermediate,** *a.* coming between, intervening.—*n.* intermediate thing.—*v.i.* act between others, mediate. **intermediation,** *n.*
intermedium, *n.* (*pl.* **intermedia, intermediums**) intervening medium or instrument. (L. *medius,* middle)
interment, *n.* burial. (*inter*)
intermezzo, *n.* short light dramatic or musical interlude.
intermigration, *n.* reciprocal migration.
interminable, *a.* endless; of tedious length. (*terminate*)
intermingle, *v.t.* and *i.* mingle or mix together.
intermit, *v.t.* and *i.* cease, cause to cease, for a time; suspend, interrupt. **intermission,** *n.* intermitting; interval, pause. **intermittent,** *a.* ceasing at intervals. **intermittence,** *n.* (L. *inter,* between; *mittere,* send)
intermix, *v.t.* and *i.* mix together. **intermixture,** *n.*
intermobility, *n.* capacity of things to move among themselves.
intermundane, *a.* between worlds.
intermural, *a.* between walls.
intermutation, *n.* interchange.
intern, *v.t.* confine within prescribed limits.—*n.* (also **interne**; *Amer.*) advanced student or graduate, resident in hospital, and acting as assistant surgeon. **internee,** *n.* person interned. **internment,** *n.* **internment camp,** for prisoners of war and aliens. (*internal*)
internal, *a.* interior, inward; of inner nature, intrinsic; of home affairs.—*n.pl.* intrinsic qualities. **i. combustion engine,** driven by explosions of gas, as in motor-car. **i. evidence,** that derived from contents of the thing itself. **internality,** *n.* **internally,** *adv.* (L. *internus*)
international, *a.* between different nations.—*n.* association for uniting the working classes of all countries; member of this; player representing his country in any sport. **First, Second, Third I.,** associations organized respectively by Marxists, French socialists, and Russian communists. **Internationale,** *n.* French socialist hymn; international association. **internationalism,** *n.* promotion of goodwill between nations. **internationalist,** *n.* supporter of this; international. **internationalize,** *v.t.* make international; bring under joint control of different nations.
internecine, *a.* mutually destructive; deadly. (L. *necare,* kill)
internode, *n.* (*bot.*) space between two nodes or leaf-joints; (*anat.*) part between two joints. **internodal,** *a.*
internuncio, *n.* pope's representative at minor courts; messenger. **internuncial,** *a.* of an internuncio; (*anat.*) transmitting nervous impressions. (L. *nuntius,* messenger)
interoceanic, *a.* between, connecting, two oceans.
interosculate, *v.i.* intermingle; form connecting link. **interosculation,** *n.*
interosseous, *a.* between bones.
interpage, *v.t.* print, insert, on intermediate pages.
interpellate, *v.t.* question; (in French Chamber) interrupt debate by demanding explanation of (minister). **interpellation, interpellator,** *nn.* (L. *inter,* between; *pellere,* drive)
interpenetrate, *v.t.* and *i.* penetrate thoroughly, pervade; penetrate each other. **interpenetration,** *n.* **interpenetrative,** *a.*
interplait, *v.t.* plait together.
interplanetary, *a.* between planets.
interplay, *n.* action of two things on each other, interaction.
interplead, *v.i.* (*law*) discuss point incidentally arising or concerning third party.
interpolate, *v.t.* insert new (esp. misleading) matter in book etc., foist in; interject (remark). **interpolation, interpolator,** *nn.* (L. *interpolare,* furbish up)
interpose, *v.t.* insert, thrust in; put in the way; interject (remark).—*v.i.* intervene. **interposal, interposition,** *nn.* (L. *ponere,* place)
interpret, *v.t.* and *i.* explain meaning of, make clear; translate into language of hearer; understand; represent

artistically, render. **interpretation,** *n.* interpreting, explanation, rendering. **interpretative,** *a.* **interpreter,** *n.* (*fem.* **interpretess**) one who translates between two parties; one who interprets. **interpretership,** *n.* (L. *interpres,* interpreter)

interpunction, interpunctuation, *nn.* punctuation within a sentence.

interracial, *a.* between races.

interregnum, *n.* (*pl.* **interregna, interregnums**) period between successive reigns or governments; interval. **interrex,** *n.* regent. (L. *regnum,* reign)

interrelation, *n.* mutual relation, interconnection. **interrelationship,** *n.*

interrogate, *v.t.* and *i.* ask questions (of); examine by questioning. **interrogation,** *n.* questioning; question. **point, mark, of interrogation,** (?). **interrogative,** *a.* denoting, expressed as, a question; (*gram.*) used in questions. **interrogatory,** *a.* of inquiry.—*n.* examination by questions. (L. *rogare,* ask)

interrupt, *v.t.* and *i.* break in upon; break continuity of; obstruct. **interruptedly,** *adv.* intermittently. **interrupter,** *n.* **interruption,** *n.* interrupting; hindrance; remark interposed. **interruptory,** *a.* (L. *rumpere,* break)

interscapular, *a.* (*anat.*) between the shoulder-blades.

intersect, *v.t.* and *i.* cut into, divide; cut, cross, each other. **intersection,** *n.* intersecting; point. line, of crossing. **intersectional,** *a.* (L. *inter,* between; *secare,* cut)

interseptal, *a.* (*anat.*) between septa or partitions.

intershoot, *v.t.* and *i.* shoot, glance, at intervals. **intershot,** *a.* variegated with different colours.

interspace, *n.* space between, interval.

intersperse, *v.t.* scatter (among), set here and there; diversify thus. **interspersion,** *n.* (L. *spargere,* scatter)

interspinal, interspinous, *aa.* between spines.

interstate, *a.* between different states of a federation.

interstellar, interstellary, *a.* between, among, the stars; beyond the solar system.

interstice, *n.* small intervening space, chink, crevice. **interstitial,** *a.* (L. *inter,* between; *sistere,* stand)

interstratified, *a.* interspersed with strata; (of strata) set between other strata. **interstratification,** *n.*

intertangle, *v.t.* tangle together. **intertanglement,** *n.*

intertexture, *n.* interweaving.

intertribal, *a.* between tribes.

intertwine, *v.t.* and *i.* twine, twist, closely together. **intertwinement,** *n.*

intertwist, *v.t.* twist together.

interval, *n.* time or distance between; pause, break; (*mus.*) difference of pitch between two sounds. **intervallic,** *a.* (L. *inter,* between; *vallum,* rampart)

interveined, *a.* intersected as with veins.

intervene, *v.i.* come, be, between others; happen in interval, occur; interfere, interpose. **intervener, intervention,** *nn.* **intervenient,** *a.* (L. *inter,* between; *venire,* come)

interview, *n.* meeting face to face for conference; reporter's visit to get person's views etc.—*v.t.* have interview with. **interviewer,** *n.*

intervolve, *v.t.* wind, roll up, within each other.

interweave, *v.t.* weave together, interlace; intermingle.

interwind, *v.t.* wind together.

interwork, *v.t.* interweave.—*v.i.* work upon each other.

intestate, *a.* not having made a will; not disposed of by will.—*n.* person dying intestate. **intestacy,** *n.* (L. *in-,* not; *testari,* make will)

intestine, *a.* internal; (of wars etc.) domestic, civil.—*n.* (us. *pl.*) bowel, gut. **intestinal,** *a.* of the bowels. (L. *intestinus*)

intil, *prep.* (*Scot.*) in, into, unto.

intimate, *a.* inmost, private; close, familiar.—*n.* close friend.—*v.t.* announce, state; hint, imply. **intimacy,** *n.* close familiarity; sexual relations. **intimation,** *n.* intimating; notice, announcement. (L. *intimus*)

intimidate, *v.t.* frighten, cow; influence by threats. **intimidation, intimidator,** *nn.* (*timid*)

intimity, *n.* inwardness; privacy.

intinction, *n.* Eastern mode of administering both elements of communion at once by dipping bread into wine. (L. *intingere,* dip in)

intitule, same as entitle.

into, *prep.* expressing motion or direction inwards, or change from one state to another. (*in*; *to*)

in-toed, *a.* having toes turned inwards.

intolerable, *a.* that cannot be endured. **intolerant,** *a.* not able to endure; not enduring difference of opinion; persecuting. **intolerance,** *n.*

intone, intonate, *vv.t.* recite in singing voice, chant; utter with particular tone. **intonation,** *n.* intoning; modulation of voice, accent; (*mus.*) act, manner, of sounding notes; opening phrase of plain-song melody.

intort, *v.t.* twist, wind. **intorsion,** *n.* (L. *torquēre*)

intoxicate, *v.t.* make drunk; excite, exhilarate, to excess. **intoxicant,** *a.* and *n.* intoxicating (drink). **intoxication,** *n.* intoxicating; drunkenness. (Gk. *toxikon,* poison)

intra-, *pref.* within, used in **intracranial,** *a.* within the skull; **intranational,** *a.* within a country, not international; **intra-territorial,** *a.* within a territory; **intra-tropical,** *a.* within the tropics. (L.)

intractable, *a.* refractory, unmanageable; (of things) hard to deal with. **intractability,** *n.* (L. *tractare,* handle)
intrados, *n.* (*archit.*) interior curve of arch. (F.)
intramural, *a.* within the walls.
intransigent, *a.* uncompromising in politics.—*n.* irreconcilable. **intransigence,** *n.* (Sp. *intransigente,* extreme republican)
intransitive, *a.* (*gram.*) (verb) that does not take a direct object.
intrant, *n.* one who enters on some office; entrant into college etc. (L. *intrare,* enter)
intreat, *v.t.* (*Spens.*) induce; treat; treat of. **intreatful,** *a.*
intrench, see **entrench.**
intrenchant, *a.* (*Shake.*) incapable of being cut.
intrepid, *a.* fearless, brave, undaunted. **intrepidity,** *n.* (L. *intrepidus*)
intricate, *a.* complicated, involved; puzzlingly entangled; obscure. **intricacy,** *n.* (L. *tricae,* hindrances)
intrigue, *n.* complex plot, secret scheme; illicit love affair, liaison.—*v.t.* plot secretly, carry on intrigue; use underhand influence.—*v.t.* puzzle, fascinate. **intriguant, intrigant** (*fem.* **intriguante, intrigante**), **intriguer,** *nn.* (F. *intriguer*)
intrince, *a.* (*Shake.*) entangled.
intrinsic, *a.* inherent, essential, real. **intrinsically,** *adv.* (L. *intrinsecus*)
intrinsicate, *a.* (*Shake.*) intricate.
intro-, *pref.* inwards, used in **introflexion,** *n.* inward bending; **introgression,** *n.* entrance. (L.)
introduce, *v.t.* bring in or forward; put into, insert; bring into notice or practice; make (person) known (to another). **introduction,** *n.* introducing; preliminary matter of book etc.; formal presentation of person to another. **introductory,** *a.* (L. *intro,* within; *ducere,* lead)
introit, *n.* psalm, antiphon, sung at beginning of the mass, as priest approaches altar. (L.=he goes within)
intromit, *v.t.* send within, admit; insert. **intromission,** *n.* intromitting; (*Scots law*) assumption of authority to deal with another's property. **intromittent,** *a.* (L. *mittere,* send)
introspect, *v.i.* examine one's own thoughts and feelings. **introspection,** *n.* self-examination. **introspective,** *a.* (L. *spicere,* look)
introvert, *v.t.* turn (mind) inwards; turn (organ) back within itself, like fingers of tight glove when hand is withdrawn.—*n.* introspective, unsociable, person. **introversion,** *n.* **introversive, introvertive,** *aa.* (L. *vertere,* turn)
intrude, *v.i.* enter uninvited, thrust oneself (upon).—*v.t.* force into or upon. **intruder,** *n.* **intrusion,** *n.* intruding, encroachment; (*geol.*) irruption of rock among other strata. **intrusive,** *a.* (L. *trudere,* thrust)
intrust, see **entrust.**
intubate, *v.t.* (*med.*) insert tube into (larynx etc.). **intubation,** *n.*
intuit, *v.t.* know by intuition. **intuition,** *n.* instinctive knowledge; act, power, of immediate mental perception without reasoning; truth so perceived. **intuitional,** *a.* **intuitionalism, intuitionism,** *nn.* doctrine that the perception of truth is by intuition. **intuitionalist, intuitionist,** *nn.* **intuitive,** *a.* perceiving, perceived, by intuition. **intuitivism,** *n.* doctrine that ethical principles are matters of intuition. **intuitivist,** *n.* (L. *intuēri,* look upon)
intumescence, *n.* swelling; tumid state. **intumescent,** *a.* (L. *tumēre,* swell)
intussusception, *n.* withdrawal, introversion, of one portion of intestine within another; taking in (of food, ideas etc.). (L. *intus,* within; *suscipere,* take up)
intwine, intwist, see **entwine, entwist.**
inunction, *n.* anointing, smearing with oil. (*unction*)
inundate, *v.t.* overflow, flood; overwhelm. **inundation,** *n.* (L. *unda,* wave)
inurbane, *a.* discourteous. **inurbanity,** *n.*
inure, enure, *v.t.* accustom; harden (to toil etc.); (*law*) pass into use, take effect. **inurement,** *n.* (L. *opera,* work)
inurn, *v.t.* put (ashes) in urn.
inutile, *a.* useless. **inutility,** *n.* (L. *in-,* not; *utilis,* useful)
invade, *v.t.* make hostile inroad into; attack, assail; encroach upon. **invader,** *n.* (L. *in,* into; *vadere,* go)
invaginate, *v.t.* put in sheath; introvert. **invagination,** *n.* intussusception. (L. *vagina,* sheath)
invalid, *a.* ill, disabled.—*n.* sick person.—*v.t.* and *i.* send away as invalid; put, go, on sick-list. **invalidity,** *n.* infirmity. (*valid*)
invalid, *a.* not valid; of no legal force, void. **invalidate,** *v.t.* render invalid; weaken, destroy, force of. **invalidation,** *n.* **invalidity,** *n.* want of validity. (*valid*)
invaluable, *a.* priceless; extremely useful.
invar, *n.* alloy of nickel and steel, used in scientific instruments because of its invariability. (abbr.)
invariable, *a.* unchanging; always the same; (*math.*) constant. **invariability,** *n.* **invariably,** *adv.* constantly.
invasion, *n.* hostile inroad, attack; encroachment. **invasive,** *a.*
invective, *n.* abusive speech, vituperation. (*inveigh*)
inveigh, *v.i.* attack with words, rail (against), revile. (L. *invehere*)
inveigle, *v.t.* entice, seduce (into); wheedle. **inveiglement,** *n.* (F. *aveugler,* blind)
invenit, invenerunt, *vv.t.* (*abbr.* ***inv.***)

(used with signature) designed (this work). (L.)

invent, *v.t.* contrive, originate; make up. **invention,** *n.* inventing; contrivance; fabrication; inventiveness. **Invention of the Cross,** festival on 3 May commemorating alleged finding of the Cross in 326. **inventive,** *a.* ready in contrivance, resourceful. **inventor,** *n.* (*fem.* **inventress**) one who devises something new. **inventory,** *n.* detailed list of goods etc.—*v.t.* enter on list, catalogue. (L. *invenire,* find)

inveracity, *n.* untruthfulness.

Inverness, *n.* (also **I. coat**) sleeveless overcoat with cape. (town)

inverse, *a.* inverted, in reverse order. —*n.* inverted state, opposite. **inversion,** *n.* inverting, turning upside down; (*gram.*) reversal of usual order of words. (*invert*)

invert, *v.t.* turn upside down; reverse order or relation of.—*n.* inverted arch; (*psycho-anal.*) person whose sexual instincts are inverted. (L. *invertere*)

invertebrate, *a.* without backbone, spineless; weak-willed.—*n.* invertebrate animal.

invest, *v.t.* and *i.* dress, clothe; endue with (power etc.); establish in office; lay siege to; lay out money (in stocks etc.). (L. *vestire,* clothe)

investigate, *v.t.* examine, inquire into. **investigation,** *n.* study, inquiry. **investigative,** *a.* inquiring, curious. **investigator,** *n.* **investigatory,** *a.* (L. *vestigare,* track)

investiture, *n.* formal installation in office; enduing. **investment,** *n.* investing; money invested; stock etc. invested in; blockade, besieging. **investor,** *n.* one who invests.

inveterate, *a.* long-established; deep-rooted, confirmed. **inveteracy,** *n.* (L. *vetus,* old)

invidious, *a.* giving offence; likely to provoke ill will or envy. (L. *invidia,* envy)

invigilate, *v.i.* maintain surveillance over students at examination. **invigilation, invigilator,** *nn.* (L. *vigilare,* watch)

invigorate, *v.t.* give vigour or energy to, strengthen. **invigorative,** *a.* **invigorator,** *n.* (*vigour*)

invincible, *a.* unconquerable. **invincibility,** *n.* (L. *vincere,* conquer)

inviolable, *a.* not to be profaned, broken, or harmed. **inviolacy,** *n.* state of being inviolate. **inviolate,** *a.* not violated, unbroken, unprofaned. (*violate*)

invisible, *a.* incapable of being seen. **invisibility,** *n.*

invite, *v.t.* request the company of; ask, solicit; call forth; (of thing) be attractive. **invitation,** *n.* **invitatory,** *a.* **invitingly,** *adv.* in a tempting manner. (L. *invitare*)

invocation, *n.* invoking, calling upon in prayer. **invocatory,** *a.* (*invoke*)

invoice, *n.* detailed list of goods sent, with prices.—*v.t.* make an invoice of. (O.F. *envoiier,* send)

invoke, *v.t.* call on in prayer; appeal to, summon; ask earnestly for (vengeance etc.). (L. *vocare,* call)

involucre, *n.* (*anat.*) envelope; (*bot.*) whorl of leaves round base of flower. (*involve*)

involuntary, *a.* unintentional, not done on purpose.

involute, *a.* intricate; curled spirally, turned inwards.—*n.* (*math.*) curve traced by the end of a string unwinding itself from another curve. **involution,** *n.* involving; entanglement, complication; curling inwards; part so curled; (*math.*) raising of quantity to any power. (*involve*)

involve, *v.t.* enwrap; entangle, implicate; entail, imply; wind spirally. **involvement,** *n.* involving; financial embarrassment. (L. *volvere,* roll)

invulnerable, *a.* that cannot be wounded or hurt. **invulnerability,** *n.*

invultuation, *n.* making of wax image of person to injure him by witchcraft. (L. *vultus,* face)

inward, *a.* placed within, internal; mental, spiritual.—*adv.* inwards.—*n.pl.* entrails. **inwardly,** *adv.* on the inside; privately. **inwardness,** *n.* essence, inner nature. **inwards,** *adv.* towards the inside; into the mind or soul. (*in+-ward*)

inweave, enweave, *v.t.* weave in.

inwick, *n.* (*curling*) a cannon off another stone resulting in a close approach to the tee.

inwit, *n.* (*obs.*) inner knowledge, conscience.

inwith, *prep.* (*Scot.*) within, inside of.

inwrap, see **enwrap.**

inwrought, *a.* wrought in or on (fabric etc.); adorned (with). (*work*)

inyala, *n.* a S. African antelope. (native)

iodine, *n.* greyish soft non-metallic element. **iodic,** *a.* **iodide,** *n.* a compound of iodine. **iodism,** *n.* morbid condition caused by iodine. **iodize,** *v.t.* treat, impregnate, with iodine. **iodoform,** *n.* compound of iodine used as antiseptic. (Gk. *ion,* violet, from the colour of its vapour)

ion, *n.* electrified particle due to alteration in number of electrons in atom. (Gk. *ienai,* go)

-ion, *n.suf.* (appearing as **-sion, -tion, -xion,** and esp. **-ation**) denoting verbal action, as in **collision**; the resulting state, as in **confusion**; or the resulting product, as in **coalition.** (L.)

Ionic, *a.* of Ionia in Greece. **I. order,** (*archit.*) distinguished by the ram's-horn volute of its capital. **I. school,** group of ancient Greek philosophers beginning with Thales. **i.** *a majore,* four-syllable foot, long-long-short-

short. i. *a minore*, four-syllable foot, short-short-long-long. **Ionian,** *a.* and *n.*

ionium, *n.* radioactive element of uranium series. (*ion*)

ionosphere, *n.* ionized region high up in stratosphere, from which wireless waves are reflected.

iota, *n.* Greek letter I; very small quantity, jot. (Gk.)

I O U, *n.* memorandum of debt signed by borrower. (=I owe you)

ipecacuanha, *n.* Brazilian plant; medicine made from its root, used as emetic etc. (native *ipekaaguene*)

ipse dixit, dogmatic statement; dictum (lit. he himself said it). ***ipsissima verba,*** the very or precise words used. ***ipso facto,*** by that very fact. (L.)

irade, *n.* written decree of Sultan of Turkey. (Arab. *iradah,* will)

Irak, Iraq, *n.* Arab kingdom including Mesopotamia. **Iraki, Iraqi,** *a.*

Iran, *n.* Persia. **Iranian,** *a.* and *n.* Persian. (Pers.)

irascible, *a.* hot-tempered, irritable, testy. **irascibility,** *n.* **irate,** *a.* angry. (*ire*)

ire, *n.* anger. **ireful,** *a.* (L. *ira*)

irenic, irenical, *aa.* aiming at peace, pacific. **irenicon,** *n.* peace proposal, eirenicon. (Gk. *eirēnē,* peace)

iridaceous, *a.* of the flag-flower kind. (*iris*)

iridescent, *a.* rainbow-coloured; glittering with changing colours. **iridescence,** *n.* (*iris*)

iridium, *n.* heavy white metal of platinum group. **iridosmine,** *n.* native alloy of osmium and iridium, used in pointing gold pens. (*iris*)

iris, *n.* rainbow; broad coloured ring round pupil of eye; plant with sword-shaped leaves and showy flowers, flag-flower. **i. diaphragm,** device of overlapping plates regulating admission of light to lens. **irised,** *a.* showing colours like rainbow. (Gk.)

Irish, *a.* of Ireland. **I. bull,** ludicrous contradiction in speech, e.g. 'Thank God I am an atheist.' **I. stew,** of mutton, potatoes, and onions. **Irishism,** *n.* Irish idiom; bull. **Irishize,** *v.t.* make Irish. **Irishman, Irishwoman,** *nn.* **Irishry,** *n.* people of Ireland.

iritis, *n.* inflammation of the iris;

irk, *v.t.* weary, bore; give pain to. **irksome,** *a.* tedious, tiresome. (M.E. *irken*)

iron, *n.* a common metal; tool made of it; flat-iron; (*golf*) iron-headed club; (*pl.*) fetters; stirrups; leg-supports.—*a.* of, like, iron; strong, unyielding; merciless.—*v.t.* furnish, shackle, with iron; smooth with flat-iron. **have too many ii. in the fire,** try to do too many things at once. **I. Age,** era of iron implements; age of cruelty. **I. Cross,** German war decoration. **I. Duke,** Duke of Wellington. **i. horse,** railway engine; bicycle. **i. man,** (*Amer. sl.*) silver dollar. **i. ration,** emergency ration for one day, carried by soldier. (O.E. *iren*)

ironbark, *n.* kind of eucalyptus.

iron-bound, *a.* bound with iron; (of coast) rock-bound; rigorous.

ironclad, *a.* protected with iron.—*n.* armoured warship.

iron-founder, *n.* maker of iron castings. **iron-foundry,** *n.* his workshop.

iron-grey, *a.* and *n.* grey like freshly-broken iron.

ironic, ironical, *aa.* of, using, given to, irony. **ironist,** *n.*

ironmaster, *n.* owner of ironworks.

ironmonger, *n.* dealer in iron goods. **ironmongery,** *n.* hardware.

ironmould, *n.* spot caused by rust or ink-stain.

ironside, *n.* brave, resolute man; (*pl.*) Cromwell's troopers.

ironstone, *n.* kind of iron ore.

ironwood, *n.* kinds of tree with very hard wood.

ironwork, *n.* things made of iron; (*pl.*) place where iron is smelted.

irony, *a.* of, like, iron.

irony, *n.* saying the opposite of what is meant, as in conveying reproof by mocking praise; mock adoption of another's views. **i. of fate,** fulfilment of wishes when useless or too late. **Socratic i.,** feigned ignorance used to entrap opponent in argument. **tragic, dramatic, i.,** use of phrase with prophetic meaning unknown to speaker. (Gk. *eirōneia,* feigned ignorance)

irradiant, *a.* shining brightly. **irradiance,** *n.* **irradiate,** *v.t.* shine upon; throw light on; light up (face etc.). **irradiation,** *n.* illumination; apparent extension of edges of illuminated object seen against dark background. **irradiative,** *a.* **irradiator,** *n.*

irrational, *a.* unreasonable, illogical, absurd; not endowed with reason; (*math.*) not accurately expressible in natural figures, e.g. $\sqrt{2}$.—*n.* surd. **irrationality,** *n.* **irrationalize,** *v.t.*

irreclaimable, *a.* that cannot be reclaimed or reformed; incorrigible.

irrecognizable, *a.* unrecognizable.

irreconcilable, *a.* implacably hostile, hopelessly estranged; incompatible.—*n.* uncompromising political opponent. **irreconcilability,** *n.*

irrecoverable, *a.* that cannot be recovered or remedied, irretrievable.

irrecusable, *a.* that must be accepted. (L. *in-,* not; *recusare,* refuse)

irredeemable, *a.* irreclaimable, hopeless; (of government loan etc.) not subject to repayment at nominal value; (of paper currency) not convertible into cash.

irredentist, *n.* advocate of the return to a country of neighbouring regions claimed on language and other grounds. **irredentism,** *n.* (It. Italia *irredenta,* unredeemed Italy)

irreducible, *a.* that cannot be reduced or simplified. **irreducibility**, *n.*
irreflective, *a.* not reflective.
irrefragable, *a.* irrefutable, unanswerable. (L.L. *in-*, not; *refragari*, oppose)
irrefrangible, *a.* inviolable; incapable of being refracted.
irrefutable, *a.* that cannot be refuted, incontrovertible. **irrefutability**, *n.*
irregular, *a.* not according to rule, abnormal; unsystematic, varying; uneven, crooked; (*gram.*) not normally inflected.—*n.* soldier not in regular service. **irregularity**, *n.* departure from rule, order, or method; crookedness. **irregulous**, *a.* (*Shake.*) lawless.
irrelative, *a.* unconnected, unrelated (to); absolute.
irrelevant, *a.* not pertinent or to the point. **irrelevance**, **irrelevancy**, *nn.*
irreligious, *a.* not religious, ungodly. **irreligion**, *n.* disregard of, hostility to, religion. **irreligionist**, *n.*
irremeable, *a.* not admitting of return. (L. *in-*, not; *remeare*, go back)
irremediable, *a.* that cannot be remedied or redressed.
irremissible, *a.* unpardonable; unalterably binding. (*remit*)
irremovable, *a.* not removable, steadfast. **irremovability**, *n.*
irreparable, *a.* that cannot be repaired, rectified, or made good.
irrepealable, *a.* that cannot be repealed or annulled.
irreplaceable, *a.* that cannot be replaced in case of loss.
irreprehensible, *a.* free from blame.
irrepressible, *a.* not able to be repressed or restrained.
irreproachable, *a.* blameless, faultless; upright. **irreproachability**, *n.*
irresistible, *a.* too strong, convincing, charming etc., to be resisted. **irresistibility**, *n.*
irresolute, *a.* not firm in purpose, undecided, wavering. **irresolution**, *n.*
irresolvable, *a.* that cannot be resolved or solved.
irrespective, *a.* and *adv.* without taking account (of), without reference to. **irrespectively**, *adv.*
irresponsible, *a.* not responsible, not accountable (for); acting, done, without proper sense of responsibility. **irresponsibility**, *n.*
irresponsive, *a.* not responsive (to).
irretention, *n.* failure to retain. **irretentive**, *a.* not retentive.
irretrievable, *a.* that cannot be recovered; irreparable. **irretrievability**, *n.* (*retrieve*)
irreverent, *a.* wanting in reverence. **irreverence**, *n.*
irreversible, *a.* that cannot be reversed, recalled, or annulled. **irreversibility**, *n.*
irrevocable, *a.* unalterable; gone beyond recall. **irrevocability**, *n.* (L. *in-*, not; *revocare*, recall)
irrigate, *v.t.* water; supply (land) with water; refresh as with moisture. **irrigable**, **irrigative**, *aa.* **irrigation**, *n.* watering of land, esp. by artificial channels. **irrigator**, *n.* (L. *irrigare*, moisten)
irrision, *n.* laughing, jeering, at another. (L. *irridēre*)
irritate, *v.t.* make angry, provoke, vex; inflame, stimulate. **irritable**, *a.* easily annoyed, touchy; sensitive to contact. **irritability**, *n.* **irritancy**, *n.* irritation, annoyance. **irritant**, *a.* and *n.* (thing) causing irritation or stimulation. **irritation**, *n.* irritating; annoyance, vexation; excitement. **irritative**, *a.* (L. *irritare*)
irritate, *v.t.* (*Scots law*) render null and void. **irritancy**, *n.* (L. *in-*, not; *ratus*, established)
irruption, *n.* bursting in; incursion, invasion. (L. *in*, into; *rumpere*, break)
is, see **be**.
Isabella, **Isabel**, *a.* and *n.* yellowish grey. **isabelline**, *a.* (name)
isagogic, *a.* introductory.—*n.pl.* study of literary and external history of the Bible. (Gk. *eis*, into; *agein*, lead)
isatin, *n.* (*chem.*) crystalline reddish substance got from indigo. (Gk. *isatis*, woad)
ischiatic, **ischiadic**, *a.* of the hip, sciatic. **ischiagra**, *n.* gout in the hip. **ischialgia**, *n.* sciatica. (Gk. *ischion*, hip-joint)
ish, *n.* (*Scot.*) issue, liberty of going out.
-ish, *adj.suf.* somewhat, as in thickish; of the nature of (often disparaging) as in feverish, childish; indicating nationality, as in Danish. (O.E. *-isc*)
Ishmael, *n.* outcast, one at war with society. **Ishmaelite**, *n.* (name in Bible)
isinglass, *n.* kind of gelatine got from fish, esp. sturgeon. (Du. *huizen*, sturgeon; *blas*, bladder)
Islam, *n.* Mohammedan faith or world. **Islamic**, **Islamitic**, *aa.* **Islamism**, **Islamite**, *nn.* (Arab.=surrender)
island, *n.* piece of land surrounded by water; isolated mass; street refuge.—*v.t.* isolate; dot as with islands. **islander**, *n.* inhabitant of island. **isle**, *n.* (*poet.*) island. **islesman**, *n.* islander, esp. Hebridean. **islet**, *n.* small island; isolated spot. (O.E. *igland*)
ism, *n.* any distinctive doctrine or practice. **ismatic**, **ismatical**, *aa.* given to faddish theories. (*-ism*)
-ism, *n.suf.* indicating system, doctrine, as in Protestantism; state, condition, as in barbarism; action, as in criticism; peculiarity, idiom, as in archaism, gallicism; morbid condition caused by abuse of drugs, as in alcoholism. (Gk. *-ismos*)
iso-, *pref.* equal, as in isobar. (Gk. *isos*)
isobar, *n.* chart-line of places with same mean barometric pressure. **isobaric**, *a.* (Gk. *baros*, weight)

isocheim, *n.* chart-line of places with same mean winter temperature. **isocheimal, isochimenal,** *aa.* (Gk. *cheima,* winter)
isochromatic, *a.* of the same colour; (*phot.*) giving equal intensity to different colours. (Gk. *chrōma,* colour)
isochronous, *a.* of equal time; (of pendulums) of uniform beat. (Gk. *chronos,* time)
isoclinal, *a.* and *n.* (chart-line of places) where dip of magnetic needle is the same. **isoclinic,** *a.* (Gk. *klinein,* bend)
isocracy, *n.* form of government in which all have equal power. **isocratic,** *a.* (Gk. *kratos,* power)
isogeotherm, *n.* chart-line of points in earth's interior having same temperature. **isogeothermal,** *a.* (Gk. *gē,* earth; *thermē,* heat)
isogon, *n.* figure with equal angles. (Gk. *gonia,* angle)
isohel, isohyet, isokeraunic, *nn.* line on map passing through places with same hours of sunshine, same rainfall, equal occurrence of thunderstorms. (Gk. *hēlios,* sun; *huein,* rain; *keraunos,* thunderbolt)
isolate, *v.t.* place apart or alone; quarantine; (*chem.*) obtain in uncombined form; (*electr.*) insulate. **isolation,** *n.* (L. *insula,* island)
isomer, *n.* substance composed of same elements as another and in same proportions, but having different chemical properties. **isomeric, isomerous,** *aa.* (Gk. *meros,* part)
isomorphous, *a.* crystallizing in same geometrical forms. **isomorphism,** *n.* property of doing so. (Gk. *morphē,* form)
isonomy, *n.* equality of political rights. (Gk. *nomos,* law)
isoperimetrical, *a.* having equal perimeters.
isopod, *n.* crustacean with seven pairs of equal legs. (Gk. *pous,* foot)
isósceles, *a.* (of triangle) having two sides equal. (Gk. *skelos,* leg)
isoseismal, *a.* and *n.* (chart-line) of points at which earthquake-shock is of same intensity. (Gk. *seismos,* shaking)
isothere, *n.* chart-line of places with same mean summer temperature. **isotheral,** *a.* (Gk. *theros,* summer)
isotherm, *n.* chart-line of places with same mean annual temperature. **isothermal,** *a.* (Gk. *thermē,* heat)
isotope, *n.* element chemically identical with another but of different atomic weight. **isotopic,** *a.* (Gk. *topos,* place)
I-spy, *n.* hide-and-seek. (call)
Israel, *n.* the Jewish people. **Israelite,** *n.* Jew. **Israelitish,** *a.*
issue, *n.* going out; outflow, discharge; outlet; outcome, result; dispute, question; copies of journal etc. issued at one time; children.—*v.i.* go, come, out, emerge; be derived, result; come out, be published.—*v.t.* send forth; publish, put in circulation; supply (soldier) with equipment. **at i.,** at variance. **join i.,** debate. **issuable,** *a.* **issuance,** *n.* **issueless,** *a.* without issue, childless. (L. *exitus*)
-ist, *n.suf.* one who believes in doctrine in -ism, as in **atheist**; agent or user, as in **parodist, motorist.** (Gk. *-istēs*)
isthmus, *n.* (*pl.* **isthmuses**) neck of land uniting two larger portions; narrow connecting part. **isthmian,** *a.* (Gk. *isthmos*)
ístlē, *n.* kind of fibre made from Mexican agave. (Mex. *ixtli*)
it, *pron.* (*poss.* **its,** *arch.* his, it) the thing referred to.—*n.* player in children's game chosen to oppose the others; (*sl.*) *ne plus ultra,* very thing; (*sl.*) sex-appeal. (O.E. *hit*)
Italian, *a.* and *n.* (language, native) of Italy. **I. warehouseman,** dealer in Italian groceries. **Italianate, Italianize,** *v.t.* and *i.* make, become, Italian. **Italic,** *a.* of ancient Italy; (of type) sloping as *thus,* used for emphasis etc.—*n.pl.* italic letters. **italicize,** *v.t.* print in italics. **Italiot, Italiote,** *n.* and *a.* (inhabitant) of Greek colonies in S. Italy. (L. *Italia,* Italy)
itch, *n.* irritation in the skin; contagious disease accompanied by this and caused by **i.-mite**; restless craving or desire.—*v.i.* feel itch; hanker uneasily. **itchy,** *a.* (O.E. *gicce*)
-ite, *n.suf.* belonging to or connected with, as in **Pre-Raphaelite, ebonite.** (Gk. *-itēs*)
item, *n.* one of a list of things, unit; entry in account etc.; detail, particular. — *adv.* also. **itemize,** *v.t.* (*Amer.*) state in items. (L.=likewise)
iterate, *v.t.* repeat; utter, do, repeatedly. **iteration,** *n.* **iterative,** *a.* (L. *iterum,* again)
ither, *Scot.* form of other.
Ithuriel, *n.* **I.'s spear,** infallible test of genuineness. (name in Milton)
ithyphallic, *a.* in the manner of rites or hymns of Bacchus; obscene.—*n.* poem of this type. (Gk. *ithus,* straight; *phallos,* phallus)
itinerant, *a.* travelling from place to place; travelling, preaching, on circuit. **itineracy, itinerancy,** *nn.* **itinerary,** *n.* route, line of travel; guide-book; record of travel—*a.* of travelling or roads. **itinerate,** *v.t.* travel from place to place; preach on circuit. **itineration,** *n.* (L. *iter,* journey)
-itis, *n.suf.* inflammation of, as in **appendicitis.**
its, see **it.**
itself, *pron.* emphatic and refl. form of it. **by i.,** apart; automatically. **in i.,** considered separately.
-ium, *n.suf.* forming names of metals, as in **iridium.**

-ive, *adj.suf.* tending to, as in **formative.**

ivory, *n.* hard white substance forming tusks of elephant, walrus etc.; colour of this; (*pl., sl.*) billiard-balls, dice, piano-keys, teeth.—*a.* of, like, ivory. **black i.**, African negro slaves. **i. black**, black pigment from calcined ivory. (L. *ebur*)

ivy, *n.* evergreen climbing plant, with dark shining leaves. **ivied**, *a.* overgrown with ivy. (O.E. *ifig*)

iwis, ywis, *adv.* (*arch.*) certainly, assuredly. (O.E. *gewis*, certain)

ixia, *n.* iris-like S. African plant. (Gk.)

Ixion, *n.* **I.'s wheel**, on which he revolved for ever in Hades. (Gk. myth)

ixtle, same as **istle.**

izard, *n.* Pyrenean chamois. (F. *isard*)

-ize, *verb.suf.* make, become, as in **Americanize, pulverize.** (words properly spelt with -ise, as advertise, are of different origin). (Gk. *-izein*)

izzard, *n.* (*arch.*) letter Z.

izzat, *n.* (*Anglo-Ind.*) honour, self-respect. (Arab.)

J

J, J pen, broad-pointed pen.

jaal-goat, *n.* Egyptian wild goat. (Heb. *ya'el*)

jab, *v.t.* poke roughly, stab; thrust abruptly (into).—*n.* sharp poke, stab.

jabber, *v.i.* and *t.* talk, utter, rapidly and indistinctly; chatter.—*n.* gabble, chatter. (imit.)

jabble, *n.* (*Scot.*) agitation on surface of water.—*v.t.* splash.

jabiru, *n.* stork-like bird of tropical America. (native)

jaborandi, *n.* Brazilian plant used as sudorific and diuretic. (native)

jabot, *n.* ornamental frill on bodice or (formerly) shirt. (F.)

jacamar, *n.* S. American bird like kingfisher. (F.)

jacana, *n.* small tropical wading bird. (native)

jacaranda, *n.* S. American tree with hard, heavy, wood. (Brazilian)

jacchus, *n.* kind of marmoset.

jacinth, *n.* reddish-orange gem, kind of zircon or garnet. (*hyacinth*)

Jack, *n.* familiar form of John; sailor; odd-job man; screw for raising weight or wheel; machine for turning spit; young pike; small spar; small flag at bow of ship; (*bowls*) small ball aimed at; (*cards*) knave; (*Amer. sl.*) money.—*v.t.* lift with jack. **before you could say J. Robinson**, very suddenly. **every man j.**, every single person. **J. Johnson**, (*sl.*) very large German shell. **J. Ketch**, hangman. **j. of all trades**, one who can turn his hand to anything. **j. pudding**, buffoon. **j. tar**, common sailor. **j. up**, (*sl.*) abandon, chuck. **yellow j.**, (*sl.*) yellow fever. (L. *Jacobus*)

jack, *n.* (*arch.*) soldier's sleeveless tunic; coat of mail. **black j.**, leather pitcher or bottle. (F. *jaque*)

jack, *n.* E. Indian fruit like bread-fruit. (Malay *chakka*)

jack-a-dandy, *n.* little fop, dandy.

jackal, *n.* wild animal like dog; one who does dirty work for another, parasite.—*v.i.* drudge. (Pers. *shagal*)

jackanapes, *n.* pert fellow or child; (*arch.*) monkey. (=Jack of apes)

jackaroo, *n.* (*Austral. sl.*) new chum, novice. (*Jack*; *kangaroo*)

jackass, *n.* he-ass; blockhead. **laughing j.**, great Australian kingfisher.

jack-boot, *n.* long boot coming above knee.

jackdaw, *n.* small kind of crow, daw.

jacket, *n.* short coat; outer covering, skin; wrapper of book.—*v.t.* cover with jacket. (F. *jaque*)

Jack-in-office, *n.* fussy official.

jack-in-the-box, *n.* toy that springs out of a box when it is opened.

jack-knife, *n.* large clasp-knife.

jack-o'-lantern, *n.* will-o'-the-wisp; (*Amer.*) pumpkin lantern.

jack-plane, *n.* plane for coarse work.

jack-pot, *n.* pool at game of poker.

jack-snipe, *n.* kind of small snipe.

jack-staff, *n.* small flagstaff at ship's bow or above masthead.

jack-towel, *n.* roller towel.

Jacob, *n.* **J.'s ladder**, blue-flowered garden-plant; shaft of sunrays through cloud-rift; (*naut.*) rope-ladder with wooden rungs. **J.'s staff**, surveyor's stand or measuring-rod.

Jacobean, *a.* of the period of James I of England; of St. James the Less.

Jacobin, *n.* Dominican friar; member of extreme democratic faction in the French Revolution; extreme radical; hooded pigeon. **Jacobinic, Jacobinical**, *aa.* **Jacobinism**, *n.* **Jacobinize**, *v.t.*

Jacobite, *n.* supporter of Stuart cause after James II's abdication. **Jacobitical**, *a.* **Jacobitism**, *n.*

jacobus, *n.* English gold coin of James I's reign, worth 20*s.*

jaconet, *n.* thin cotton fabric, esp. waterproofed for poulticing. (*Jagannathi* in India)

jacquerie, *n.* peasant revolt, esp. that of 1357–8 in France. (F.)

jactitation, *n.* (*law*) false pretence of marriage; (*med.*) restless tossing, twitching. (L. *jactitare*, toss)

jade, *n.* poor or worn-out horse; mean woman.—*v.t.* tire out, weary.
jade, *n.* hard, ornamental stone, us. dark green. **jadeite, jadite**, *n.* a stone resembling it. (L. *ilia*, flanks, because said to cure colic)
jag, *n.* sharp or ragged projection; (*Scot.*) stab.—*v.t.* make notches in; stab. **jagged**, *a.* notched, rough-edged.
jag, *n.* small load; (*Amer. sl.*) drinking-bout.
jaggery, *n.* a coarse brown sugar. (Sanskr. *çarkara*)
jaggy, *a.* jagged, uneven.
jäger, same as **yager**.
jaghir, jaghire, *n.* (*India*) assignment of land and its revenue as annuity; land, revenue, so assigned. **jaghirdar**, *n.* holder of jaghir. (Hind.)
jaguar, *n.* large spotted American animal like leopard. (native *yaguara*)
Jah, *n.* Jehovah. (Heb. *Yah*)
jail, gaol, *n.* prison; imprisonment.—*v.t.* imprison. **j.-bird, g.-bird**, *n.* one who is often in jail. **j., g , fever**, typhus. **jailer, jailor, gaoler**, *n.* (*fem.* **jaileress, jailoress, gaoleress**) warder, turnkey. (L. *cavea*, cage)
Jain, *n.* adherent of Hindu religion like Buddhism. **Jainism**, *n.* (Hind.)
jakes, *n.* (*arch.*) privy.
jalap, *n.* purgative got from root of Mexican plant. (*Jalapa* in Mexico)
jalouse, *v.t.* (*Scot.*) suspect. (*jealous*)
jalousie, *n.* external shutter with slats like Venetian blind. (F.=jealousy)
jam, *v.t.* and *i.* press, squeeze tight; block, make unworkable; become wedged; (*wireless*) make (message) unintelligible by transmitting on similar wavelength. — *n.* crush, squeeze; stoppage; (*sl.*) awkward position, fix. (imit.)
jam, *n.* conserve of fruit boiled with sugar.
Jam, *n.* title of certain Indian rulers.
Jamaica, *n.* **J. pepper**, allspice.
jama, jamah, *n.* long cotton gown worn by Hindus.
jamb, *n.* door-post; sidepiece of doorway, fireplace etc. (L.L. *gamba*, hoof)
jambe, *n.* leg armour. (F.=leg)
jambee, *n.* light walking-stick.
jambok, same as **sjambok**.
jamboree, *n.* (*sl.*) celebration, spree; great rally of Boy Scouts.
jamewar, *n.* goat's-hair cloth of Cashmere; shawl made of it. (native)
jammy, *a.* smeared with jam.
jampan, *n.* sedan chair with four bearers or **jampanees**.
jamrach, *n.* place where wild animals are kept for sale. (dealer's name)
jane, *n.* (*Amer. sl.*) woman. (name)
jane, *n.* (*Spens.*) silver Genoese coin. (L. *Genua*, Genoa)
jangle, *v.i.* and *t.* sound, cause to sound, discordantly; speak noisily; (*arch.*) wrangle.—*n.* harsh metallic sound; (*arch.*) quarrel. (O.F. *jangler*)
janissary, same as **janizary**.
janitor, *n.* (*fem.* **janitress, janitrix**) doorkeeper; (*Amer.*) caretaker.
janizary, *n.* Turkish infantryman, esp. of sultan's bodyguard; personal instrument of tyranny. (Turk. *yeni*, new: *tsheri*, soldiery)
jankers, *n. pl.* (*army sl.*) detention, punishment.
jannock, *a.* (*dial.*) straightforward, genuine.—*n.* fair play.
jannock, *n.* oaten cake or bread.
January, *n.* first month of year, dedicated by Romans to **Janus**, two-faced god of gates. (L. *Januarius*)
Japan, *n.* **Japanese**, (*colloq.*) **Jap**, *n.* and *a.* (inhabitant) of Japan.
japan, *n.* kind of hard varnish.—*v.t.* lacquer with this; make black and glossy. (orig. from *Japan*)
jape, *v.i.* and *n.* jest.
Japonic, *a.* Japanese. **japonica**, *n.* Japanese quince, pear etc.
jar, *v.i.* and *t.* sound, vibrate, harshly; strike, cause to strike, gratingly; be inconsistent, wrangle.—*n.* grating sound or shock; discord, quarrel. **jarringly**, *adv.* (imit.)
jar, *n.* round wide-mouthed vessel of earthenware etc. (Arab. *jarrah*)
jar, *n.* **on the j.**, (*colloq.*) ajar.
jararaka, *n.* fer-de-lance. (Brazilian)
jardinière, *n.* flower-stand. (F.)
jargon, *n.* unintelligible talk, gibberish; excessively technical language. **jargonize**, *v.t.* and *i.* (O.F.)
jargon, jargoon, *n.* translucent colourless, yellowish, or smoky kind of zircon.
jargonelle, *n.* kind of pear. (F.)
jarl, *n.* Old Norse chief, noble. (O.N.)
jarrah, *n.* mahogany gum-tree of Australia. (native)
jarvey, *n.* driver of Irish car; (*sl.*) cab-driver. (*Jarvis*, name)
jasey, *n.* (*sl.*) wig, esp. of worsted.
jasmine, jasmin, *n.* kinds of shrub with fragrant white or yellow flowers. (Pers. *yasmin*)
jasper, *n.* a precious stone, opaque quartz of various colours. (Gk. *iaspis*)
jauk, *v.i.* (*Scot.*) dally, trifle.
jaunce, *v.t.* and *i.* (*Shake.*) ride hard, fatigue; run to and fro.—*n.* jaunt.
jaunder, *v.i.* (*Scot.*) talk idly.—*n.* foolish talk, gossip.
jaundice, *n.* disease marked by yellowness of skin. **jaundiced**, *a.* affected with jaundice; prejudiced, jealous. (L. *galbus*, yellow)
jaunt, *n.* excursion, ramble.—*v.i.* take jaunt. **jaunting-car**, *n.* two-wheeled Irish car with side-seats back to back.
jaunty, *a.* having a self-satisfied air, sprightly.—*n.* (*naut.*) head of ship's police. (F. *gentil*)
jaup, *v.t.* (*Scot.*) spatter.—*n.* water, mud, splashed up.
javel, *n.* (*Spens.*) rascal.
javelin, *n.* light spear for hrowing, dart. (F. *javeline*)
jaw, *n.* bone in which teeth . . set; (*sl.*) loquacity; lecture; (*pl.*) n. h

or thing like it.—*v.i.* and *t.* talk lengthily, lecture. **jawbone,** *n.* bone of jaw. **j.-breaker,** *n.* word hard to pronounce. **jawed,** *a.* having jaws.

jaw, *v.t.* (*Scot.*) pour out; splash. **j.-box, j.-hole,** *nn.* sink.

jay, *n.* noisy bright-coloured bird of crow family; chatterer, simpleton; flashy or light woman. **j.-walker,** *n.* heedless pedestrian. (O.F.)

jazz, *n.* syncopated music or dancing, rag-time; noisy proceedings.—*a.* (*sl.*) discordant, bizarre in colour etc.—*v.i.* play, dance, indulge in, jazz. **j. up,** (*Amer.*) excite, stir up.

jealous, *a.* suspicious of, incensed at, rivalry; envious; watchfully tenacious (of rights etc.). **jealousy,** *n.* (Gk. *zelos,* rivalry)

Jeames, *n.* flunkey, lackey. (name in Thackeray)

jean, *n.* twilled cotton cloth, kind of fustian; (*pl.*) overalls; trousers.

Jeddart, *n.* (*arch.*) Jedburgh. **J. axe,** steel-headed pole. **J. justice,** hanging first and trying afterwards.

jedge, *n.* (*Scot.*) gauge, standard.

jeep, *n.* light utility van used by army. (*G.P.*, general purposes)

jeer, *v.i.* and *t.* scoff; deride, mock.—*n.* gibe, taunt.

jehad, same as **jihad.**

Jehovah, *n.* Hebrew name of God. (Heb. *yahaveh*)

Jehu, *n.* driver. (name in Bible)

jejune, *a.* meagre; poor, barren; uninteresting. (L. *jejunus,* hungry)

jelly, *n.* transparent gelatinous substance; juice of fruit boiled with sugar.—*v.t.* and *i.* turn into jelly, congeal. **j.-bag,** *n.* bag for straining jelly. **jellyfish,** *n.* medusa, sea-nettle. **jellygraph,** *n.* copying apparatus using sheet of jelly. (L. *gelare,* freeze)

jemadar, *n.* native lieutenant in Indian army; native police-officer; head servant; (*Anglo-Ind. colloq.*) sweeper. (Urdu)

jemimas, *n.pl.* (*colloq.*) elastic-sided boots; galoshed cloth over-boots.

jemmy, *n.* burglar's crowbar; (*sl.*) baked sheep's head. (*James*)

jemmy, *a.* neat, smart, spruce.

je ne sais quoi, an indescribable something. (F.=I know not what)

jennet, *n.* small Spanish horse. (Sp. *jinete,* light horseman)

jenneting, *n.* kind of early apple.

jenny, *n.* early spinning-machine; travelling crane. **j. wren,** wren. (*Janet*)

jeofail, *n.* (*law*) error in pleadings or procedure. (O.F. *je faille,* I fail)

jeopardy, *n.* danger, peril. **jeopardize,** *v.t.* endanger. **jeopardous,** *a.* exposed to danger. (O.F. *iu parti,* divided game, even chance)

jequirity, *n.* Indian shrub with parti-coloured seeds. (native *jekiriti*)

jerboa, *n.* small African jumping rodent with long hind legs. (Arab *yarbu'*).

Jeremiah, *n.* dismal prophet. **jeremiad,** *n.* doleful complaint. (name in Bible)

jerid, *n.* Arab horseman's javelin or game played with it. (Arab. *jarid*)

jerk, *n.* sharp, abruptly stopped movement; sharp pull; twitch.—*v.t.* and *i.* move, throw, with jerk. **physical jj.,** (*sl.*) gymnastics. **jerky,** *a.* (imit.)

jerk, *v.t.* preserve (beef) by cutting in strips and drying in the sun. (Peruvian *ccharqui,* dried flesh)

jerk, same as **jerque.**

jerkin, *n.* man's close-fitting jacket or coat, often of leather.

Jeroboam, *n.* huge bottle, eight times ordinary size. (name in Bible)

jerque, *v.t.* search (vessel) for contraband. **jerquer,** *n.* customs searcher. (F. *chercher,* seek)

jerran, *a.* (*Austral.*) afraid.

Jerry, *n.* (*sl.*) German soldier; the Germans. (corrupt. of *German*)

jerry, *n.* (*sl.*) chamber-pot.

jerry-built, *a.* flimsily built with bad materials. **jerry-builder, jerry-building,** *nn.* **jerry-shop,** *n.* low beer-shop. (name)

jerrymander, same as **gerrymander.**

jersey, *n.* close-fitting knitted jacket or vest, pullover. (name)

Jerusalem, *n.* **J. pony,** donkey. **J. artichoke,** see **artichoke.**

jess, *n.* short strap round leg of falcon by which it is held.—*v.t.* fit with jesses. (O.F. *ges*)

jessamine, jessamin, *n.* jasmine. **jessamy,** *a.* like jasmine.—*n.* dandy.

Jesse, *n.* large branched candlestick. **J. window,** stained-glass window showing Christ's genealogy.

jest, *n.* joke; fun; banter; object of derision.—*v.i.* joke, make jests. **in j.,** not seriously. **jestingly,** *adv.* **jester,** *n.* court fool, buffoon. (O.F. *geste,* exploit)

Jesuit, *n.* member of Society of Jesus, a religious order; (*colloq.*) prevaricator, intriguer. **J.'s bark,** cinchona. **Jesuitical,** *a.* of Jesuits; (*colloq.*) crafty. **Jesuitism, Jesuitry,** *nn,* principles of Jesuits; (*colloq.*) deceit, craft. **Jesuitize,** *v.t.* and *i.* (*Jesus*)

jet, *n.* thin stream of liquid or gas; spout, nozzle, emitting this.—*v.t.* and *i.* spurt forth in jets; strut; encroach (upon). (L. *jacere,* throw)

jet, *n.* hard black lignite, used for ornaments.—*a.* deep, glossy, black. **j.-black,** *a.* (*Gagas* in Lycia)

jettison, *n.* throwing overboard of goods to lighten ship in distress.—*v.t.* throw overboard thus. **jetsam,** *n.* goods jettisoned and washed ashore. (L. *jacere,* throw)

jetton, *n.* stamped counter. (F. *jeton*)

jetty, *n.* small pier, wharf; mole, breakwater. (O.F. *jetee,* thrown out)

jetty, *a.* like jet, jet-black.

jeu, *n.* play. *j. de mots,* play on words, pun. *j. d'esprit,* witticism, humorous trifle. (F.)

jeune premier, juvenile lead. (F.)
jeunesse dorée. gilded youth. (F.)
Jew, *n.* (*fem.* **Jewess**) member of Hebrew race; (*colloq.*) driver of hard bargains. **J.'s harp,** small musical instrument held between teeth and played by finger. (Heb. *y'hudah,* Judah)
jewel, *n.* precious stone, gem; jewelled dress ornament; precious thing.—*v.t.* adorn, furnish, with jewels. **jeweller,** *n.* dealer in jewels. **jewellery, jewelry,** *nn.* jewels in general. **jewelly,** *a.* (O.F. *joel*)
Jewish, *a.* of the Jews. **Jewry,** *n.* the Jews; Judaea; Jewish quarter in town.
jezail, *n.* long Afghan musket. (Pers. *jaza'il*)
Jezebel, *n.* abandoned woman; woman who paints her face. (Scripture name)
jheel, *n.* (*Anglo-Ind.*) lake, pond. (Hind. *jhil*)
jib, *n.* triangular sail at ship's bow; arm of crane.—*v.t.* and *i.* pull (sail) round to other side of ship; (of sail) swing round. **cut of one's j.,** personal appearance. **j.-boom,** *n.* extension of bowsprit on which jib is set. **j. door,** door flush with wall and disguised by painting etc.
jib, *v.i.* (of horse) balk, refuse to go on; show objection, demur. **jibber,** *n.*
jibba, jibbah, jubba, jubbah, *n.* Mohammedan's long loose coat. (Arab.)
jibe, *v.i.* (*Amer.*) agree.
jibe, see **gibe.**
jiff, jiffy, *n.* very short time, moment.
jig, *n.* lively dance; music for it; (*Amer. sl.*) day's work.—*v.i.* and *t.* dance jig; jerk up and down quickly; (*mining*) separate ores with jigger. **jigsaw,** *n.* (*Amer.*) machine fretsaw. **jigsaw puzzle,** picture cut up into irregular pieces.
jigamaree, jiggumbob, *nn.* thingummy.
jigger, *n.* small tackle, sail, or smack; any small mechanical device; miner's sieve for separating ores; (*billiards*) rest for cue; (*golf*) kind of iron. **j.-mast,** *n.* aftermost mast in four-master.
jigger, *n.* chigoe, W. Indian flea that burrows under skin. (corrupt.)
jiggered, *a.* confounded.
jiggery-pokery, *n.* (*colloq.*) underhand work; humbug.
jiggle, *v.t.* jerk lightly. (*jig*)
jigot, same as **gigot.**
jihad, *n.* Mohammedan holy war against unbelievers; crusade. (Arab.)
jilt, *v.t.* cast off (lover) after encouraging.—*n.* one who does this.
Jim Crow, (*Amer.*) negro.
jiminy, *int.* Gemini! (corrupt.)
jim-jams, *n.pl.* (*sl.*) nervous fluster, jumpiness; delirium tremens.
jimp, *a.* (*Scot.*) slender, graceful; scanty. **jimply,** *adv.* neatly; hardly.
jingal, *n.* Chinese swivel-musket.
jingle, *n.* clinking sound, as of small bells; correspondence of sound; doggerel, covered two-wheeled car.—*v.i.* and *t.* make, cause to make, jingle. (imit.)
jingo, *n.* (*pl.* **jingoes**) blustering patriot, warmonger. **jingoism, jingoist,** *nn.* **jingoistic,** *a.* **by j.,** a mild oath.
jink, *v.i.* and *t.* (*Scot.*) move nimbly; dodge.—*n.* quick turn. **high jj.,** boisterous sport, merrymaking.
jinnee, jinn, *n.* (*pl.* **jinn,** *fem.* **jinneeyeh**) demon that can assume different shapes, genie. (Arab. *jinni*)
jinricksha, jinrikisha, *n.* light two-wheeled man-drawn vehicle. (Jap. *jin,* man; *riki,* power; *sha,* vehicle)
jinx, *n.* (*Amer.*) person or thing that brings bad luck, hoodoo.
jirga, *n.* assembly of Afghan headmen. (Pushtu)
jitney, *n.* (*Amer. sl.*) five cents; motor-bus with low rates.—*a.* cheap.
jitters, *n.pl.* (*sl.*) nervous fluster. **jitterbug,** *n.* (*sl.*) excitable alarmist; (*Amer.*) jazz dancer.
jiu-jitsu, *n.* Japanese method of wrestling. (Jap. *ju-jutsu*)
jo, *n.* (*Scot.*) sweetheart; joy.
job, *n.* piece of work; post; unscrupulous transaction.—*v.i.* and *t.* do odd jobs; hire (horse) for definite time; buy and sell as broker; handle corruptly. **bad j.,** unfortunate affair. **do person's j.,** kill, ruin, him. **j. lot,** goods bought as speculation. **on the j.,** in action. **jobber,** *n.* **jobbery,** *n.* intriguing for private profit. **jobmaster,** *n.* one who jobs (horses etc.).
job, *v.t.* and *i.* prod, thrust; hurt (horse) with bit.—*n.* prod; jerk at bit.
Job, *n.* **J.'s comforter,** one whose consolations aggravate distress. **jobation,** *n.* scolding, tedious reproof. (Scripture name)
jobbernowl, *n.* blockhead. (*noll*)
Jock, *n.* (*sl.*) Highland soldier; Scot.
jock, *n.* (*sl.*) jockey.
jocko, *n.* (*pl.* **jockos**) chimpanzee. (F.)
jockey, *n.* professional rider in horse-races.—*v.t.* and *i.* cheat; manœuvre. **jockeydom, jockeyship,** *nn.* (*Jock*)
jocose, *a.* playful, waggish. **jocosity,** *n.* **jocular,** *a.* given to joking, humorous. **jocularity,** *n.* (L. *jocus,* jest)
jocteleg, *n.* (*Scot.*) clasp-knife. (*Jacques de Liége*)
jocund, *a.* merry, cheerful. **jocundity** *n.* (L. *jucundus*)
jodhpurs, *n.pl.* long riding-breeches, tight from knee to ankle. (place)
Joe, *n.* **not for J.!** (*sl.*) not for me!
Joe Miller, stale joke. (comedian)
joey, *n.* (*sl.*) fourpenny-piece. (*Joseph* Hume, M.P.)
joey, *n.* (*Austral.*) young kangaroo; day labourer. (native)
jog, *v.t.* and *i.* shake with push; nudge; stimulate (memory); walk, trot, at slow pace.—*n.* push, nudge; slow walk; (*Amer.*) irregularity of line or surface. **j.-trot,** *n.* slow regular trot. —*a.* monotonous.

joggle, *v.t.* and *i.* shake, move to and fro in jerks.—*n.* slight shake. (*jog*)
joggle, *n.* key or notch in stones to prevent them sliding on one another; joint so designed. — *v.t.* join by joggle.
Johannine, *a.* of the Apostle John.
John, *n.* **J.-a-dreams,** *n.* (*Shake.*) dreamy fellow. **J. Bull,** typical Englishman. **J. Company,** (*colloq.*) E. India Company. **J. Dory,** an edible sea-fish. **j.-go-to-bed-at-noon,** *n.* goat's-beard.
johnny, *n.* (*colloq.*) fellow; fashionable idler. **j.-cake,** *n.* meal-cake. **J. Raw,** novice, greenhorn.
joie de vivre, joy of living. (F.)
join, *v.t.* and *i.* put together, fasten, unite; be united or connected (with); come into the company of.—*n.* place, line, of joining. **j. battle,** begin fighting. **j. hands,** clasp hands. **j. up,** enlist. **joinder,** *n.* (*law*) joining. **joiner,** *n.* one who joins; carpenter. **joinery,** *n.* (L. *jungere*)
joint, *n.* point where two things join; structure by which two bones etc. fit together; section; (*cookery*) bone with meat; (*geol.*) fissure in mass of rock; (*Amer. sl.*) low public - house, gambling-den.—*a.* common, shared by two or more.—*v.t.* connect by, divide into, joints; point (wall). **out of j.,** dislocated; out of order. **universal j.,** allowing movement in all directions. **j. stock,** common fund, share capital. **j.-stool,** *n.* (*Shake.*) well-finished stool. **jointer,** *n.* tool for pointing; kind of plane. **jointress,** *n.* widow holding jointure. **jointure,** *n.* property settled on wife for her use after husband's death.—*v.t.* provide with jointure. (*join*)
joist, *n.* one of the beams from wall to wall on which floor or ceiling is fixed. **joisted,** *a.* (L. *jacēre,* lie)
joke, *n.* thing said or done to cause laughter, jest; something not in earnest.—*v.i.* and *t.* make jokes; poke fun at. **no j.,** a serious matter. **practical j.,** trick played on person. **joker,** *n.* one who jokes; (*sl.*) fellow; extra card in pack, used in poker etc. **jokingly,** *adv.* (L. *jocus*)
jokul, *jökull,* *n.* snow-mountain in Iceland. (Icel.)
joky, *a.* full, fond, of jokes.
jole, joll, same as **jowl.**
jolly, *a.* merry, festive; (*colloq.*) delightful.—*n.* (*naut. sl.*) marine.—*v.t.* (*Amer. sl.*) chaff, talk into good humour, flatter.—*adv.* (*colloq.*) very. **j. along,** (*sl.*) wheedle. **jollify,** *v.i.* and *t.* make merry, esp. with drink; make jolly. **jollification,** *n.* **jollity,** *n.* festivity. (O.F. *joli,* gay)
jolly-boat, *n.* small boat carried by ship.
jolt, *n.* jerk throwing upwards, from seat etc.—*v.t.* and *i.* move, shake, with jolts. **jolty,** *a.*
jolterhead, *n.* blockhead, dunce.
Jonah, *n.* bringer of bad luck. (Scripture name)
Jonathan, *n.* kind of apple. **Brother J.,** typical U.S. citizen.
jongleur, *n.* wandering minstrel. (F.)
jonquil, *n.* rush-leaved daffodil; pale yellow. (L. *juncus,* rush)
jook, jookery, same as **jouk, joukery.**
jordan, *n.* (*Shake.*) chamber-pot.
jorum, *n.* large drinking-vessel; its contents, esp. punch.
Joseph, *n.* chaste man; woman's caped riding-cloak. (Scripture name)
josh, *v.t.* and *i.* (*Amer. sl.*) make fun, ridicule.—*n.* good-natured joke, hoax. **josher,** *n.* joker.
joskin, *n.* yokel, dolt.
joss, *n.* Chinese idol; luck, fate. **j.-house,** *n.* Chinese temple. **j.-stick,** *n.* stick of Chinese incense.
joss-block, *n.* (*prov.*) horse-block.
josser, *n.* (*sl.*) fool; chap.
jostle, *v.i.* and *t.* push (against), elbow; struggle with.—*n.* jostling. (*joust*)
jot, *n.* small amount, whit.—*v.t.* write (down) briefly. **jotter,** *n.* note-book. **jotting,** *n,* memorandum. (*iota*)
jougs, *n.* iron neck-ring, Scottish pillory. (L. *jugum,* yoke)
jouk, *v.i.* and *t.* (*Scot.*) duck, dodge; bow. **joukery,** *n.* trickery.
joule, *n.* (*electr.*) unit of energy, work done in 1 second by 1 ampere flowing through 1 ohm, =about 10 million ergs. (name of physicist)
jounce, *v.t.* and *i.* bump, jolt.
journal, *n.* daily record; log-book; newspaper, periodical; part of axle or shaft resting on bearings.—*a.* (*Shake.*) daily. **journalist,** *n.* one who writes for or conducts a periodical. **journalese,** *n.* his jargon. **journalism,** *n.* his profession. **journalistic,** *a.* **journalize,** *v.t.* enter in, keep, journal. (L. *diurnalis,* daily)
journey, *n.* travel, us. by land, excursion; distance travelled.—*v.i.* travel. **journeyman,** *n.* qualified artisan; hired workman. (L. *diurnus,* daily)
joust, *n.* combat with lances etc. between mounted knights. — *v.i.* engage in joust, run at tilt. (L. *juxta,* near)
Jove, *n.* Jupiter. **by J.,** a mild oath. (L. *Jovis,* of Jupiter)
jovial, *a.* merry, convivial. **joviality,** *n.* good-fellowship. (*Jove*)
Jovian, *a.* of, like, Jove or Jupiter.
jow, *v.t.* and *i.* (*Scot.*) ring, toll.—*n.* stroke of bell.
jowl, *n.* jaw; cheek; dewlap of cattle; crop of bird; head part of fish. **cheek by j.,** tête-à-tête. (O.E. *ceafl,* jaw, and *ceolur,* throat)
jowl, *v.t.* (*Shake.*) dash, knock.
jowter, *n.* fish-hawker.
joy, *n.* gladness, happiness; cause of this.—*v.i.* and *t.* rejoice; gladden. **j.-ride,** *n.* (*sl.*) pleasure-ride, stolen ride, in car. **joystick,** *n.* control lever of aeroplane. **joyance,** *n.* (*Spens.*)

mirth. **joyful, joyous,** *aa.* very glad, happy. (L. *gaudium*)
juba, *n.* kind of negro breakdown or dance. (word *juba* sung in refrain)
jubate, *a.* maned. (L. *juba,* mane)
jubba, jubbah, see **jibba.**
jubilate, *v.i.*, exult, show joy. **jubilātĕ,** *n.* shout of triumph; 100th Psalm as canticle. **jubilance, jubilation,** *nn.* **jubilant,** *a.* exultant. (L. *jubilare*)
jubilee, *n.* fiftieth anniversary; season of rejoicing, exultation; Jewish festival of emancipation, held every fifty years. **silver, diamond, j.,** twenty-fifth, sixtieth, anniversary. (Heb. *yobel,* trumpet)
Judaic, *n.* Jewish. **judaize,** *v.t.* and *i.* make, become, Jewish. **judaism, judaist,** *nn.* (Gk. *Ioudaios,* Jew)
Judas, *n.* traitor; peep-hole in jail door. **J.-coloured,** *a.* (of hair) red. **J.-tree,** *n.* a tree with purple flowers appearing before leaves. (disciple)
Judenhetze, **n.** persecution of Jews. (G.)
judge, *n.* officer who decides cases in lawcourts; arbiter, umpire; qualified critic; (in Jewish history) ruler.—*v.t.* and *i.* act as judge; pronounce sentence on; try (case); decide authoritatively; estimate, suppose; censure. **judgmatic, judgmatical,** *aa.* (*colloq.*) judicious, discerning. **judgment, judgement,** *n.* sentence of court; divine punishment; criticism, taste; opinion; good sense. **Judgment Day,** day of God's final judgment. **judgment-seat,** *n.* judge's seat, tribunal. **judgeship,** *n.* office of judge. (L. *judex*)
judicable, *a.* that may be judged. **judicative,** *a.* having power to judge. **judicatory,** *a.* dispensing justice.—*n.* court; distribution of justice. **judicature,** *n.* power, system, of dispensing justice; jurisdiction; body of judges; tribunal. **judicial,** *a.* of, by, lawcourt or judge; having power to judge; critical; impartial. **judicial murder,** legal but unjust execution. **judiciary,** *n.* judges of a state collectively.—*a.* of lawcourts; passing judgment. **judicious,** *a.* sensible, sound, discreet.
judo, *n.* advanced form of **jiu-jitsu.**
jug, *n.* deep vessel for liquids, us. with handle and spout; (*sl.*) jail.—*v.t.* stew, boil, in jug; (*sl.*) imprison. **jugful,** *n.*
jug, *v.i.* (of nightingale etc.) utter **jug-jug,** its song. (imit.)
jugate, *a.* (*bot.*) having leaflets in pairs. (L. *jugum,* yoke)
Juggernaut, *n.* Krishna, Hindu god; his idol, dragged yearly in processional car, under whose wheels devotees formerly threw themselves; belief to which people sacrifice themselves. (Sanskr. *Jagannatha,* lord of world)
juggins, *n.* (*sl.*) silly fellow.
juggle, *v.i.* and *t.* manipulate objects dexterously; play conjuring tricks; cheat, get by trickery.—*n.* sleight of hand; fraud. **juggler,** *n.* one who juggles, conjurer; trickster, cheat. **jugglery,** *n.* (L. *jocus,* jest)
jugular, *a.* of neck or throat.—*n.* jugular vein. **j. veins,** great veins of neck. **jugulate,** *v.t.* arrest (disease by strong measures). (L. *jugulum,* collar-bone)
juice, *n.* liquid part of vegetable, fruit, or meat; essence; (*sl.*) petrol, electricity. **juicy,** *a.* succulent; (of weather) wet; (*colloq.*) interesting. (L. *jus,* broth)
ju-ju, **n.** (*W. Afr.*) fetish, charm; ban effected by it.
jujube, *n.* lozenge of sugar and gum; kinds of shrub or their fruit. (Gk. *zizuphon*)
ju-jutsu, same as **jiu-jitsu.**
julep, *n.* sweet drink in which nauseous medicines are taken; medicated drink; (*Amer.*) iced and spiced spirit and water. (Pers. *gul,* rose; *ab,* water)
Julian, *a.* of Julius Caesar. **J. calendar,** introduced by him and used in Britain till 1752. (L. *Julianus*)
julienne, **n.** clear soup with shredded vegetables. (F.)
July, *n.* seventh month. (*Julius* Caesar)
jumart, *n.* offspring of bull and mare, or horse and cow. (F.)
jumbal, jumble, *n.* kinds of crisp thin sweet cake.
jumble, *v.t.* and *i.* mix up, move about in confusion.—*n.* muddle, confused heap. **j.-sale,** *n.* charity bazaar of miscellaneous articles. **jumbly,** *a.*
jumbo, *n.* big clumsy person, animal, or thing; colossus.
jump, *v.i.* and *t.* leap, spring; start up, cause to start; leap over, skip; agree, coincide; (*Shake.*) hazard, risk; (*Amer.*) take possession of claim which owner is not working.—*n.* leap, bound; (*Shake.*) venture. —*adv.* (*Shake.*) exactly. **j. at,** accept eagerly. **j. down one's throat,** (*colloq.*) answer violently. **j. on, upon,** reprimand. **jumper,** *n.* one who jumps; flea; (*pl.*) sect of Welsh Methodists.
jumper, *n.* sailor's loose jacket; woman's jersey, slipped over head.
jumping-bean, *n.* seed of Mexican plant which enclosed larva causes to jump. **jumping-deer,** *n.* black-tailed American deer. **jumping-jack,** *n.* toy whose limbs are worked by string.
jumpy, *a.* nervous, panicky.
juncaceous, juncous, *aa.* of, like, rushes. (L. *juncus,* rush)
junction, *n.* joining; union, point of union; station where railway lines meet. **juncture,** *n.* point of union; critical point, state of affairs. (L. *jungere,* join)
jundie, *v.t.* (*Scot.*) jostle, jog.

June, *n.* sixth month. (L. *Junius*)
jungle, *n.* tangled vegetation or land covered with it; tangled mass. **j.-hen,** *n.* mound-bird of Australia. **j.-rice,** *n.* millet. **jungled, jungly,** *aa.* **jungli,** *n.* and *a.* (person) inhabiting jungle; (*Anglo-Ind. colloq.*) uncouth, boorish. (Hind. *jangal,* desert)
junior, *a.* younger; of lower position.—*n.* junior person. **juniority,** *n.* (L.)
juniper, *n.* an evergreen shrub. **oil of j.,** made from its berries, used in making gin. (L. *juniperus*)
junk, *n.* flat-bottomed Chinese sailing-vessel, high at bow and stern.
junk, *n.* lump, chunk; old cordage; odds and ends, rubbish; (*naut.*) salt meat.—*v.t.* divide into chunks. **j.-shop,** *n.* marine store.
junker, *n.* young German noble; member of reactionary Prussian aristocracy. (G.)
junket, *n.* sweetened curds and cream; feast; sweetmeat.—*v.i.* feast, picnic. **junketing,** *n.* merry feast. (O.F. *jonquette,* rush-basket)
Juno, *n.* queen of gods, wife of Jupiter; queenly woman; an asteroid. (L.)
junta, *n.* state council in Spain or Italy; junto. **junto,** *n.* political faction, cabal. (Sp.)
jupe, *n.* woman's skirt. (F.)
Jupiter, *n.* king of gods; largest planet. **J. Pluvius,** god of rain. (L.)
jupon, *n.* sleeveless jacket or coat; petticoat; coat worn over armour. (F.)
jural, *a.* of law; of moral rights and obligations. (L. *jus,* law)
Jurassic, *a.* (*geol.*) of the middle system of Mesozoic rocks, including the Lias and Oolites. (*Jura* Mountains)
jurat, *n.* municipal officer; magistrate; record of time, place etc. of affidavit. (L. *jurare,* swear)
juridical, *a.* of judicial proceedings, legal. (L. *jus,* law; *dicere,* say)
jurisconsult, *n.* one learned in law, jurist. (L. *jurisconsultus*)
jurisdiction, *n.* administration of justice; authority; limits of this, territory it extends over. **jurisdictional,** *a.* (L. *jus,* law; *dicere,* say)
jurisprudence, *n.* science of, skill in, law. **medical j.,** forensic medicine. **jurisprudential,** *a.* of jurisprudence. **jurisprudent,** *a.* and *n.* (one) skilled in law. (L. *jus,* law)
jurist, *n.* one versed in law; legal writer; law student. **juristic, juristical,** *aa.* (L. *jus,* law)
juror, *n.* member of jury; one who takes an oath. (L. *jurare,* swear)
jury, *n.* body of persons sworn to return verdict in court of law; judging committee in competition. **grand j.,** inquiring into indictments before they go to trial jury. **trial, common, petty, j.,** body of 12 persons to determine issue of fact in civil or criminal cases. **j. of matrons,** for cases where pregnancy is pleaded in stay of execution. **j.-box,** *n.* enclosure where jury sit. **juryman,** *n.* member of jury. (L. *jurare,* swear)
jury-mast, *n.* temporary mast. **jury-rigged,** *a.* rigged in makeshift way.
jussive, *a.* (*gram.*) expressing command. (L. *jubēre,* order)
just, *a.* upright, righteous; fair; true, exact; right, proper.—*adv.* exactly; barely; not long before; (*colloq.*) positively. **j. now,** at this moment; a little ago. (L. *justus*)
just, same as **joust.**
justice, *n.* fairness, justness; desert; judicial proceedings; judge, magistrate. **do j. to,** treat fairly. **do oneself j.,** show one's full abilities. **j. of the peace,** (*abbr.* **J.P.**) a minor magistrate. **justiceship,** *n.* **justiciable,** *a.* and *n.* (person) subject to jurisdiction. **justiciar, justiciary,** *nn.* administrator of justice; chief justice. **High Court of Justiciary,** supreme criminal court in Scotland. (L. *justitia*)
justify, *v.t.* show to be just or right; vindicate; warrant; absolve from sin; (*print.*) space evenly, adjust. **justifiable,** *a.* defensible, excusable. **justification,** *n.* justifying; adequate reason; absolution. **justificative, justificatory,** *aa.* (*just*)
justle, same as **jostle.**
jut, *v.i.* stick out, protrude.—*n.* projection. (*jet*)
jute, *n.* fibre of Indian plant, used for making canvas, rope etc. (Sanskr. *jata,* braid of hair)
jutty, *n.* projection; jetty.—*v.t.* (*Shake.*) project over. (*jut*)
juvenal, *n.* (*Shake.*) youth. **juvenescence,** *n.* transition from childhood to youth; youth. **juvenescent,** *a.* (L.)
juvenile, *a.* young; of, for, the youthful.—*n.* young person, child; (*pl.*) books for children. **j. offender,** person under sixteen who commits crime. **juvenilia,** *n.pl.* works produced in author's youth. **juvenility,** *n.* youthfulness. (L. *juvenis,* young)
juxtapose, *v.t.* place side by side. **juxtaposition,** *n.* contiguity. (L. *juxta,* next; *ponere,* place)
jynx, *n.* (*pl.* **jynges**) wryneck. (Gk. *iungx*)

K

Kaaba, same as Caaba.
kaama, *n.* (*S. Afr.*) hartebeest.
kabbalah, same as cabbala.
kaddish, *n.* Jewish mourner's prayer. (Aram. *qaddish*, holy)
kadi, same as cadi.
kae, *n.* (*Scot.*) jackdaw.
Kaffir, Kafir, *n.* S. African native of Bantu stock, incl. Zulus; native of Kafiristan in Asia; (*pl.*) S. African mine shares. (Arab.=infidel)
kafila, *n.* caravan, camel-train.
kago, *n.* Japanese basketwork palanquin slung on pole. (Jap. *kango*)
kai, *n.* (*New Zealand*) food. **kaikai,** *n.* (*New Zealand*) feast. (Maori)
kail, *n.* ninepin.
kail, see kale.
kain, *n.* (*old Scots law*) rent in kind.
kainga, *n.* (*New Zealand*) village. (Maori)
kainite, *n.* a mineral fertilizer. (Gk. *kainos*, new)
kaiser, *n.* emperor, esp. German emperor. **kaisership,** *n.* (L. *Caesar*)
kaka, *n.* New Zealand parrot. **kakapo,** *n.* owl parrot, flightless nocturnal bird nesting in burrows. (Maori)
kakemono, *n.* Japanese wall-picture, unrolling vertically. (Jap.)
kakistocracy, *n.* government by the worst men. (Gk. *kakistos*, worst)
kala, *n.* time, destiny. (Sanskr.)
kalamdan, *n.* Persian writing-case.
kale, kail, *n.* cole, cabbage, esp. borecole, with wrinkled leaves; broth of this. **Scotch k.,** kind with purplish leaves. **k.-yard,** *n.* kitchen garden. **k.-yard school,** novelists describing humbler Scottish life. (*cole*)
kaleidoscope, *n.* optical toy which by arrangement of reflecting surfaces shows endless variety of beautiful patterns; changing group of bright objects. **kaleidoscopic,** *a.* (Gk. *kalos*, beautiful; *eidos*, form; *skopein*, see)
kalendar, kalends, same as **calendar, calends.**
kali, *n.* prickly saltwort. (Arab. *qali*)
kali, *n.* Persian carpet with long pile.
Kali, *n.* Hindu goddess of destruction, wife of Siva. (Sanskr.=black)
kalian, kalioun, *n.* Persian hookah. (Arab. *qalyan*)
kalmia, *n.* American laurel. (Peter *Kalm*, botanist)
kalology, *n.* science of beauty in itself. (Gk. *kalos*, beautiful)
kalong, *n.* Malay fox-bat, largest known bat. (Malay)
kalpa, *n.* day of Brahma, Hindu great age of 4,320 million years. (Sanskr.)
kam, *a.* (*Shake.*) wrong, awry. (Celt.)
Kama, *n.* Hindu god of love. (Hind.)
kame, *n.* (*Scot.*) comb; ridge, eskar.
kamerad, *n.* comrade; German word of surrender in Great War. (G.)
kami, *n.* lord, Japanese title for divinity, demigod, mikado etc. (Jap.)
kamichi, *n.* a bird, horned screamer. (F.)
kamptulicon, *n.* floor-cloth of rubber and cork on canvas. (Gk. *kamptos*, flexible; *oulos*, thick)
kanaka, *n.* South Sea Islander, esp. one brought as labourer to Australia. (Hawaiian=man)
kang, *n.* Chinese water-jar or brick sleeping-place with fire inside.
kangaroo, *n.* Australian pouched quadruped, with hind legs strongly developed for jumping; (*pl., sl.*) W. Australian mine shares. **k.-mouse, k.-rat,** *nn.* small Australian marsupials.
kanoon, *n.* kind of harp with fifty to sixty strings. (Arab. *qanun*)
Kanuck, same as **Canuck.**
kaolin, *n.* fine white clay, used for porcelain. **kaolinize,** *v.t.* (F.)
kapellmeister, *n.* conductor of orchestra, leader of choir. (G.)
kapje, *n.* (*S. Afr.*) woman's cape.
kapok, *n.* fibre of silk-cotton tree used to stuff cushions. (Malay)
kaput, *a.* (*sl.*) done for, smashed. (G.)
karma, *n.* Buddhist conception of person's actions in one of his successive states of existence deciding his fate in the next; destiny. (Sanskr.)
karoo, karroo, *n.* S. African table-land, barren in dry season. (Hottentot)
kaross, *n.* S. African skin cloak.
karri, *n.* giant gum-tree of W. Australia. (native)
kartel, *n.* wooden bed in S. African ox-wagon. (S. Afr. Du.)
kartell, *n.* manufacturer's union. (G.)
kasha, *n.* ladies' dress-fabric.
katabolism, *n.* process by which protoplasm is broken down; destructive metabolism. (Gk. *kataballein*, throw down)
kation, same as **cation.**
katipo, *n.* venomous black spider of Australia. (Maori)
katydid, *n.* large green American insect like grasshopper. (imit. of note)
kauri, *n.* New Zealand pine. (Maori)
kava, *n.* Polynesian shrub; intoxicating drink made from it. (native)
kavass, *n.* Turkish armed constable or servant. (Turk. *qaws*, bow)
kayak, *n.* Eskimo canoe of sealskins stretched on frame. (Eskimo)
kea, *n.* New Zealand parrot that kills sheep. (Maori)
kebar, *n.* (*Scot.*) rafter.
kebbie, *n.* (*Scot.*) cudgel.
kebbock, kebbuck, *n.* (*Scot.*) cheese. (Gael. *cabag*)

keck, *v.i.* make sound as if about to vomit; feel loathing. (imit.)
keddah, same as **kheda.**
kedge, *n.* small anchor.—*v.i.* and *t.* move, warp (ship) by means of kedge.
kedgeree, kedjeree, *n.* fish cooked with rice and eggs; Indian dish of rice, butter, onions etc. (Hind. *khichri*)
keech, *n.* (*Shake.*) lump of fat.
keek, *v.i.* and *n.* (*Scot.*) peep.
keel, *n.* lowest longitudinal support of ship's framework; (*poet.*) ship.—*v.t.* turn keel up. **k. over,** upset, capsize. **k.-haul,** *v.t.* haul under keel as punishment. (O.N. *kjolr*)
keel, *n.* flat-bottomed boat, Tyne coal-barge. (Du. *kiel*)
keel, *v.t.* (*Shake.*) cool, keep (pot) from boiling over. (O.E. *célan*)
keel, *n.* and *v.t.* (*Scot.*) ruddle.
keelie, *n.* (*Scot.*) kestrel; hooligan, rough. (imit.)
keeling, *n.* (*Scot.*) codfish.
keelivine, *n.* (*Scot.*) lead pencil.
keelman, *n.* one who works on a keel.
keelson, see **kelson.**
keen, *a.* sharp; strong, penetrating; acute, severe; eager, enthusiastic. **k.-set,** *a.* hungry, eager. (O.E. *céne*)
keen, *n.* Irish wailing dirge.—*v.i.* and *t.* lament over dead; bewail. (Ir. *caoine*)
keep, *v.t.* (*past, p.p.* **kept**) observe, carry out; protect; retain possession of; maintain; detain; cause to continue; reserve.—*v.i.* continue, endure; remain good; (*Shake.* etc.) lodge.—*n.* maintenance, food; tower, stronghold. **k. at it,** persist. **k. back,** hold back, withhold. **k. company,** associate (with). **k. down,** repress. **k. goal, wicket,** be goalkeeper, wicket-keeper. **k. in with,** maintain friendship with. **k. under,** hold down. **k. up,** support, continue. **k. your hair on,** (*sl.*) do not lose your temper. **for keeps,** (*sl.*) for good, permanently. (O.E. *cépan*)
keeper, *n.* owner; gamekeeper; lunatic's attendant; ring to guard wedding-ring.
keeping, *n.* care, custody; harmony.
keepsake, *n.* token of remembrance.
kef, keif, *n.* drowsy state produced by bhang; bhang. (Arab. = well-being)
keffiyeh, *n.* kerchief head-dress of Bedouin Arab. (Arab. *kaffiyah*)
keg, *n.* small cask. (Icel. *kaggi*)
kelp, *n.* large seaweed; its ashes, yielding iodine.
kelpie, kelpy, *n.* (*Scot.*) malevolent water-spirit, us. in form of horse.
kelson, keelson, *n.* inner keel, to which floor-timbers are bolted. (*keel*)
kelt, *n.* salmon that has just spawned.
Kelt, same as **Celt.**
kelter, same as **kilter.**
ken, *v.t.* (*Scot.*) know; recognize at sight.—*n.* range of sight or knowledge. (O.E. *cennan*)
ken, *n.* (*sl.*) house.
kennel, *n.* shelter for house-dog or hounds; pack of hounds.—*v.i.* and *t.* keep, live, in kennel. (L. *canis,* dog)
kennel, *n.* gutter. (F. *canel*)
kenning, *n.* ken; (*Scot.*) little bit.
kenosis, *n.* laying aside by Christ of His divinity on His incarnation. **kenotic,** *a.* **kenoticism,** *n.* (Gk. = emptying)
kenspeckle, *a.* (*Scot.*) conspicuous. (*ken*)
kentledge, *n.* (*naut.*) pig-iron ballast.
kep, *v.t.* (*Scot.*) catch. (*keep*)
kepi, *n.* French flat-topped military cap with straight peak. (F. *képi*)
kept, see **keep.**
keramics, same as **ceramics.**
keratin, *n.* chief constituent of horn, nails etc. **keratitis,** *n.* inflammation of the cornea. **keratose,** *a.* and *n.* horny (substance). (Gk. *keras,* horn)
keraunograph, *n.* instrument detecting distant thunderstorm; pattern made by lightning on struck object. (Gk. *keraunos,* thunderbolt; *graphein,* write)
kerb, *n.* stone edging to pavement or path. **kerbstone,** *n.* stone of kerb. (*curb*)
kerchief, *n.* cloth worn as head-covering etc.; (*poet.*) handkerchief. (O.F. *covrir,* cover; *chief,* head)
kerf, *n.* slit made by saw etc.; cut end of felled tree. (O.E. *cyrf*)
kérmĕs, *n.* a female insect; crimson dye made from it. **k. oak,** evergreen oak on which it feeds. (Arab. *qirmiz*)
kermess, *kermis,* *n.* fair in Holland. (Du.)
kern, kerne, *n.* light-armed Irish foot-soldier; boor. (Ir. *ceithern*)
kern, *v.i.* granulate, harden.
kern, same as **quern.**
kernel, *n.* soft inner part of nut or fruit-stone; body of seed within husk; centre, essential part. (O.E. *cyrnel*)
kerosine, *n.* lamp-oil distilled from petroleum etc. (Gk. *kēros,* wax)
Kerry blue, kind of terrier. (place)
kersey, *n.* a coarse woollen cloth.
kerseymere, *n.* twilled cloth of fine wool; (*pl.*) trousers of this. (*Cashmere*)
kesar, *arch.* form of **kaiser.**
kestrel, *n.* kind of small hawk.
ket, *n.* (*Scot.*) carrion.
ket, *n.* (*Scot.*) fleece.—*a.* hairy.
ketch, *n,* small two-masted coasting vessel, us. rigged like yawl.
ketchup, catchup, catsup, *n.* sauce made from mushrooms etc.
ketone, *n.* kinds of compound of carbon incl. acetone. (*acetone*)
kettle, *n.* metal vessel, with spout, for boiling water; (*Shake.*) kettledrum. **k. of fish,** awkward mess. **kettledrum,** *n.* drum of parchment spread over metal hemisphere; large tea-party. **kettledrummer,** *n.* (O.E. *cetel*)
kevel, *n.* (*naut.*) cleat for belaying ropes. (L. *clavis,* key)
kex, *n.* dry stalk of hemlock etc.

key, *n.* instrument for moving bolt of lock, winding clock etc.; solution, code, crib; piece of wood let into another crossways to prevent warping; lever for finger in piano, typewriter etc.; tone, mode, of thought; (*mus.*) set of related notes.—*v.t.* fasten with wedge, bolt; regulate pitch of strings of. **have k. of the street,** be homeless. **House of Kk.,** elective branch of Manx legislature. **k. up,** brace up; raise. (O.E. *cǽg*)
key, *n.* low island, reef, cay. (*cay*)
key, *n.* winged fruit, as of ash.
keyboard, *n.* set of keys on piano etc.
keyhole, *n.* hole for inserting key.
keynote, *n.* basic note of musical key; dominant idea. **keynoter,** *n.* (*Amer. sl.*) one who outlines policy of campaign.
keystone, *n.* (*archit.*) central stone of arch; central principle.
khabar, *n.* (*Anglo-Ind.*) news. (Hind.)
khaddar, *n.* Indian homespun cloth. (Hind.)
khaki, *a.* dull yellow, drab.—*n.* khaki cloth or uniform. (Hind. = dusty)
khalifa, khalifat, same as **caliph, caliphate.**
khamsin, *n.* hot southerly wind in Egypt for about 50 days in spring. (Arab.)
khan, *n.* title of ruler, prince or official in Asia. **khanate,** *n.* his rule or district. (Turk.)
khan, *n.* caravanserai. (Arab. = inn)
khansamah, *n.* (*Anglo-Ind.*) house-steward; head cook. (Urdu)
kheda, *n.* enclosure for catching wild elephants. (Hind.)
khedive, *n.* title of viceroy of Egypt. **khedival,** *a.* (Turk.)
khidmutgar, khitmutgar, *n.* male table servant in India. (*Hind.*)
khud, *n.* (*Anglo-Ind.*) ravine. (Hind. *khad*)
kiang, *n.* wild ass of Tibet. (Tibetan *kyang*)
kia ora, *int.* (*New Zealand*) your health.
kiaugh, *n.* (*Scot.*) care, trouble.
kibble, *n.* bucket of well or mine-shaft.
kibble, *v.t.* grind coarsely.
kibe, *n.* ulcerated chilblain.
kibitka, *n.* Tartar circular tent; Russian hooded sledge. (Russ.)
kiblah, *n.* point to which Mohammedans turn at prayer, Mecca. (Arab. *qiblah*)
kibosh, *n.* (*sl.*) nonsense.—*v.t.* dispose of. **put the k. on,** do for. (Ir. *caidhp báis,* cap of death)
kick, *v.t.* and *i.* strike, strike out, with foot; recoil; show opposition, rebel; (*football*) score (goal).—*n.* blow with foot; recoil (of gun); resilience; (*sl.*) thrill; (*Amer. sl.*) protest, complaint. **k. the bucket,** (*sl.*) die. **k.-off,** *n.* (*football*) start of game. (M.E. *kiken*)
kick, *n.* indentation at bottom of glass bottle.
kickshaw, *n.* toy, trifle; light, fancy dish. (F. *quelque chose,* something)
kicksy-wicksy, *a.* flickering, uncertain. —*n.* (*Shake.*) wife.
kid, *n.* young goat; leather of its skin; (*sl.*) child; (*sl.*) humbug.—*v.t.* and *i.* give birth to (kid); (*sl.*) hoax, deceive. **kidder,** *n.* (*sl.*) joker. **kiddy,** *n.* little child. (M.E. *kide*)
kiddle, *n.* stake-fence in river for catching fish. (O.F. *quidel*)
kidnap, *v.t.* steal (child), abduct (person). **kidnapper,** *n.* (*kid; nab*)
kidney, *n.* either of pair of glandular organs which secrete urine; nature, temperament. **k. bean,** dwarf French bean; scarlet-runner.
kie-kie, *n.* New Zealand climbing plant with leaves used for baskets. (Maori)
kier, *n.* vat in which cloth is boiled for bleaching. (cf. O.N. *ker*)
kieselguhr, *n.* mineral remains of algae, used in dynamite and for polishing. (G. *kiesel,* gravel; *guhr,* sediment)
kike, *n.* (*Amer. sl.*) Jew.
kilderkin, *n.* small cask; liquid measure of 18 gallons. (Du. *kindeken*)
kill, *v.t.* put to death, slay; destroy, make useless; overwhelm.—*n.* killing; animal killed in sport. **got up to k.,** fascinatingly dressed. **k.-joy,** *n.* depressing person. **killer,** *n.* **killing,** *a.* fascinating; uproariously funny. **killingly,** *adv.*
killadar, *n.* (*Anglo-Ind.*) governor of fort or castle. (Hind.)
killick, killock, *n.* heavy stone used as anchor; small anchor.
kiln, *n.* large oven for baking or drying (lime, bricks, hops etc.). **k.-dry,** *v.t.* (L. *culina,* kitchen)
kilo-, from Gk. *chilioi,* 1,000, used in metric system, as **kilocycle,** *n.* frequency of 1,000 alternations per second; **kilogram, kilogramme,** *n.* weight of 1,000 grammes (2·205 lb.); **kilogrammetre,** *n.* energy that will raise one kilogramme to the height of one metre; **kilolitre, kiloliter,** *n.* measure of 1,000 litres (220 gallons); **kilometre, kilometer,** *n.* length of 1,000 metres (1·093·6 yards). **kilowatt,** *n.* electric power of 1,000 watts.
kilt, *n.* Scottish highlander's pleated skirt.—*v.t.* tuck up (skirts); pleat vertically. **kilted,** *a.* dressed in kilt.
kilter, *n.* (*Amer.*) good working order; good condition
kiltie, *n.* soldier of kilted regiment.
kimmer, *Scot.* form of **cummer.**
kimono, *n.* loose wide-sleeved Japanese robe; wrap like it. (Jap.)
kin, *n.* stock, family; relatives; relationship.—*a.* related. (O.E. *cynn*)
-kin, *n.suf.* forming diminutive, as in **lambkin, napkin.** (G. *-chen*)
kinchin, *n.* (*sl.*) child. **k. lay,** stealing money from children sent on errands.
kincob, *n.* rich embroidered Indian silk stuff. (Hind. *kimkhab*)
kind, *n.* race; sort, class; (*arch.*) nature,

natural way.—*a.* considerate, benevolent, sympathetic; (*arch.*) affectionate. **in k.** (of payment) in goods, not money; of same sort as is received. **k. of,** (*colloq.*) somewhat. **k.-hearted,** *a.* (O.E. *gecynde*)

kindergarten, *n.* infant school using object lessons and games. (G.)

kindle, *v.t.* set fire to, light; inspire, excite.—*v.i.* catch fire; glow; be excited. **kindling,** *n.* setting on fire; small wood for lighting fires.

kindly, *a.* kind; (of climate) genial; (*arch.*) native-born.—*adv.* in a kind manner. **kindlily,** *adv.* (*kind*)

kindred, *n.* blood-relationship; relations.—*a.* related; allied, similar. (*kin*+O.E. *ræden,* condition)

kine, see **cow.**

kinema, kinematograph, same as **cinema, cinematograph.**

kinematic, *a.* of pure motion, without reference to force.—*n.pl.* science of this. **kinematical,** *a.* **kinetic,** *a.* of motion in relation to force.—*n.pl.* science of this. (Gk. *kinein,* move)

king, *n.* male ruler of nation, monarch; card with picture of king; (*chess*) chief piece; (*draughts*) piece that is crowned.—*v.i.* act the king. **K.-at-arms, K.-of-arms,** *n.* chief officer of Heralds' College. **k.-pin,** *n.* central pin in ninepins; (*colloq.*) chief person. **K.'s Bench,** a division of the High Court of Justice. **K.'s Counsel,** (*abbr.* **K.C.**) barrister appointed as counsel to the Crown. **k.'s evil,** scrofula, once supposed curable by king's touch. **k.'s peg,** champagne and brandy. (O.E. *cyning*)

kingcraft, *n.* art of governing.

kingcup, *n.* marsh marigold; buttercup.

kingdom, *n.* state, territory, ruled by king; domain; (of God) spiritual reign. **k.-come,** *n.* (*sl.*) next world.

kingfisher, *n.* brightly coloured bird that dives for fish, halcyon.

kinglet, *n.* petty king; golden-crested wren. **kingling,** *n.* little king.

kingly, *a.* of, like, a king.

kingpost, *n.* upright from tie-beam to ridge of roof.

kingship, *n.* state or dignity of king.

kink, *n.* short twist in rope, chain etc.; mental twist, crotchet.—*v.i.* and *t.* form kink (in). (Du.)

kinkajou, *n.* nocturnal quadruped like racoon. (native)

kinky, *a.* full of kinks; crotchety.

kinnikinic, *n.* mixture of leaves and bark smoked by Red Indians. (Amer. Ind.)

kino, *n.* astringent vegetable gum.

kinsfolk, *n.* blood relations. **kinship,** *n.* relationship; affinity. **kinsman, kinswoman,** *nn.* (*kin*)

kintal, early form of **quintal.**

kintra, *Scot.* form of **country.**

kiosk, *n.* open pavilion; small roofed stall or booth. (Turk. *kiushk*)

kip, *n.* hide of young animal.

kip, *n.* (*sl.*) doss-house, lodging; bed.

kip, *v.i.* (*Scot.*) play truant.

kipper, *v.t.* cure (herring etc.) by splitting open, salting, drying, and smoking.—*n.* kippered fish, esp. herring; male salmon in spawning time.

kirk, *n.* (*Scot.*) church. **k. session,** governing body of Scottish congregation. **kirkin,** *n.* first church attendance of couple after marriage.

kirkyard, *n.* graveyard. (*church*)

kirn, *n.* (*Scot.*) churn; last sheaf of harvest, harvest home.

kirschwasser, kirsch, *n.* spirit made from wild cherries. (G.)

kirsen, *v.t.* (*Scot.*) christen.

kirtle, *n.* (*arch.*) gown or outer petticoat; man's tunic. **kirtled,** *a.* wearing a kirtle. (O.E. *cyrtel*)

kismet, *n.* fate, destiny. (Turk.)

kiss, *v.t.* and *i.* touch, caress, with lips; (of billiard balls) make contact when both are in motion or both at rest.—*n.* caress, salute, with lips. **k. the book,** kiss Bible in taking oath. **k. the rod,** accept punishment submissively. **k.-curl,** *n.* curl worn on forehead. **k.-in-the-ring,** *n.* children's kissing game. **k.-me-quick,** *n.* small bonnet. **kissable,** *a.* **kissing-comfit,** *n.* perfumed sweet to sweeten breath. **kissing-crust,** *n.* soft crust where loaf has touched another in baking. **kissing-gate,** *n.* gate hung in U- or V-shaped enclosure. (O.E. *cyssan*)

kist, *n.* (*Scot.*) chest.

kit, *n.* wooden tub; outfit, equipment, of soldier, sailor, or workman. **k.-bag,** *n.* strong bag for holding kit.

kit, *n.* small fiddle.

kit, *n.* shortened form of **kitten.**

kit-cat, *n.* portrait less than half-length but including hands. **K. Club,** Whig literary club, founded about 1700. (*Kit Catling,* keeper of pie-house)

kitchen, *n.* room where food is cooked; thing eaten as relish with bread etc. **k. garden,** vegetable garden. **k.-maid,** *n.* servant under cook. **k. midden,** prehistoric refuse-heap. **k. physic,** (*joc.*) substantial fare. **kitchener,** *n.* cooking-range. **kitchenette,** *n.* small room, alcove, used as miniature kitchen. (L. *coquere,* cook)

kite, *n.* bird of prey like falcon; rapacious person; paper-covered frame flown in wind; (*sl.*) accommodation bill.—*v.i.* and *t.* soar, fly, like kite. **fly a k.,** make experiment to gauge public opinion. **k. balloon,** military captive balloon. (O.E. *cȳta*)

kite, *n.* (*Scot.*) belly. (O.E. *cwith,* womb)

kith, *n.* **k. and kin,** friends and relations. (O.E. *cunnan,* know)

kitling, *n.* (*Scot.*) kitten.

kitten, *n.* young cat; playful girl.—*v.t.* bring forth kittens. **kittenish,** *a.* (M.E. *kitoun*)

kittiwake, *n*. kind of sea-gull. (imit.)

kittle, *a*. (*Scot.*) ticklish, difficult to deal with.—*v.t.* (*Scot.*) tickle. **kittly**, *a*. ticklish, sensitive.

kittul, *n*. kind of palm; fibre made from it. (Cingalese *kitul*)

kitty, *n*. pet name for cat; pool in some games; (*bowls*) jack. (*kit*)

kiutle, *v.t.* (*Scot.*) cuddle, fondle.

kiwi, *n*. apteryx, New Zealand bird with rudimentary wings; (*sl.*) non-flying member of Air Force. (Maori)

klang, *n*. (*mus.*) complex tone. (G.)

klaxon, *n*. powerful electric motor-horn. (trade name)

kleptomania, *n*. mania for stealing. **kleptomaniac**, *n*. (Gk. *kleptein*, steal)

klip, *n*. (*S. Afr.*) rock; (*sl.*) diamond. **klipspringer**, *n*. small antelope. (Du.)

kloof, *n*. (*S. Afr.*) ravine, deep narrow valley. (Du.=cleft)

knack, *n*. acquired dexterity; adroit trick; habit, mannerism.

knacker, *n*. one who buys worn-out horses or old houses, ships etc. for destruction. **knackery**, *n*.

knacky, *a*. having a knack; cunning.

knag, *n*. knot in wood; peg. **knaggy**, *a*. knotty, rugged. (cf. G. *knagge*)

knap, *n*. hill-crest, knoll. (O.E. *cnæp*)

knap, *v.t.* snap; break (flints) with hammer. **knapper**, *n*. (imit.)

knapsack, *n*. soldier's or traveller's bag to strap on the back, rucksack. (Du. *knappen*, bite)

knapweed, *n*. purple-flowered weed. (*knop*)

knar, *n*. knot on tree. (M.E. *knarre*)

knave, *n*. deceitful person, rogue; lowest court-card, jack; (*Shake.*) boy, servant. **knavery**, *n*. dishonesty, villainy. **knavish**, *a*. (O.E. *cnafa*)

knead, *v.t.* work up (flour) into dough; make (bread) thus; work, massage; blend. **kneader**, *n*. (O.E. *cnedan*)

knee, *n*. joint between thigh and lower leg; part of garment covering this; angular piece of iron or timber.—*v.t.* touch with knee; (*colloq.*) cause (trousers) to bulge at knees. **give a k.**, act as second in fight. **on the kk. of the gods**, undetermined. **k.-breeches**, *n.pl.* breeches reaching to just below knees. **k.-cap**, **k.-pan**, *nn*. small flat bone in front of knee-joint, patella. (O.E. *cnéow*)

kneel, *v.i.* (*past*, *p.p.* **kneeled** or **knelt**) fall, rest, on knees. (*knee*)

knell, *n*. sound of bell, esp. at death or funeral; portent of doom.—*v.i.* and *t.* (*arch.*) sound knell. (O.E. *cnyll*)

knelt, see **kneel**.

knew, see **know**.

knickerbockers, *n.pl.* loose breeches gathered in at knee; (*sing.*) New Yorker. **knickers**, *n.pl.* woman's drawers; (*colloq.*) knickerbockers. (*Knickerbocker*, pseudonym of Washington Irving)

knick-knack, *n*. trifle, trinket. **knick-knackery**, *n*. knick-knacks collectively. **knick-knackish**, *a*. (*knack*)

knife, *n*. (*pl.* **knives**) tool for cutting; blade.—*v.t.* stab with knife. **get one's k. into**, (*colloq.*) cherish spite against. **the k.**, surgical operation. **war to the k.**, relentless war. **k.-board**, *n*. board for cleaning knives; back-to-back bench on old buses. **k.-rest**, *n*. support for carving knife and fork. (O.E. *cnif*)

knight, *n*. man of rank below baronet, designated 'Sir'; (formerly) one of honourable military rank, champion; a piece at chess.—*v.t.* make (man) a knight. **k. errant**, medieval knight wandering in quest of adventure; quixotic person. **k.-errantry**, *n*. **k. of the rainbow, road, spigot, stick, flunkey, highwayman, tapster, compositor. knightage**, *n*. body, list, of the knights. **knighthood**, *n*. character, order, of knights. **knightly**, *a*. and *adv*. (O.E. *cniht*)

knit, *v.t.* and *i.* (*past*. *p.p.* **knitted** or **knit**) form (fabric, garment) by looping together yarn or thread; unite closely; make, become, compact; wrinkle (brow). **knitter**, *n*. **knitting**, *n*. knitted work. **knitting-needle**, *n*. eyeless needle used for knitting. **knittle**, *n*. (*naut.*) small line made of yarn. (O.E. *cnyttan*)

knives, see **knife**.

knob, *n*. rounded protuberance; round handle; small lump (of coal etc.). **with kk. on**, (*sl.*) that, and more. **knobbed**, *a*. having knobs. **knobble**, *n*. small knob. **knobbly**, **knobby**, *aa*. **knobkerrie**, *n*. round-headed stick used as weapon by Kaffirs. **knob-stick**, *n*. knobbed stick; (*sl.*) blackleg, scab. (M.E.)

knock, *v.t.* and *i.* strike; drive, be driven (against); rap; (of engine) make thumping noise; (*sl.*) amaze; (*Amer. sl.*) disparage.—*n*. blow, rap; (*cricket sl.*) innings. **k. down**, fell to ground; sell at auction. **k. off**, stop (work); perform quickly. **k. on the head**, stun, kill. **k. out**, render (boxer) unconscious with blow. **k. under**, submit. **k. up**, make hastily; arouse; exhaust, collapse; (*cricket*) score runs. (O.E. *cnocian*)

knockabout, *a*. and *n*. noisily boisterous (comedian, show).

knock-down, *a*. overwhelming (blow); minimum (auction price).

knocker, *n*. kind of hammer hinged to a door for knocking. **up to the k.**, (*sl.*) thoroughly well.

knock-kneed, *a*. having **knock-knees**, or inward-curving legs.

knock-out, *n*. and *a*. finishing (blow); (auction) where bids are arranged in advance by confederates; (*sl.*) wonder.

knock-up, *n*. casual game, practice.

knoll, *n*. small rounded hill, mound. (O.E. *cnoll*)

knoll, *v.t.* and *i.* (*arch.*) ring, toll; summon by bell. (*knell*)
knop, *n.* (*arch.*) knob; bud. (M.E.)
knosp, *n.* unopened bud of flower; (*archit.*) ornament like this. (G. *knospe*)
knot, *n.* fastening of ropes etc. by intertwining; ribbon etc. tied as ornament; bond, union; group, cluster; lump, esp. of wood at junction of branch; tangle, difficulty; (*naut.*) speed of 1 nautical mile an hour.—*v.t.* and *i.* tie knot in; make knots; entangle. **porter's k.,** pad for carrying load on head. **knotgrass,** *n.* weed with jointed stem and pink flowers. **knotwork,** *n.* kind of fancy needlework. **knotty,** *a.* full of knots; puzzling, intricate. (O.E. *cnotta*)
knot, *n.* kind of sandpiper.
knout, *n.* whip formerly used in Russia. —*v.t.* flog with it. (Russ. *knut*)
know, *v.t.* and *i.* (*past* **knew,** *p.p.* **known**) be aware (of); perceive clearly; be acquainted with; recognize; have information.—*n.* (*Shake.*) knowledge. **k. the ropes,** understand procedure. **k.-nothing,** *n.* ignoramus; agnostic. **knowable,** *a.* **knowing,** *a.* cunning, sly; (*colloq.*) stylish, smart. **knowingly,** *adv.* cunningly; consciously, deliberately. **knowledge,** *n.* knowing; information; understanding; learning. **knowledgeable,** *a.* intelligent, well-informed. (O.E. *cnáwan*)
knowe, *n.* (*Scot.*) knoll.
knuckle, *n.* projecting part of finger-joint; joint of animal's knee or hock. —*v.t.* strike, rub, with knuckles.—*v.i.* (*marbles*) place knuckles on ground. **k. down, under,** submit. **near the k.,** all but indecent. **k.-duster,** *n.* knobbed bar worn on knuckles to make blow more formidable. (M.E. *knokel*)
knur, knurr, *n.* knot in tree-trunk; hard lump; ball used in **k. and spell,** game like trap-ball. (M.E. *knorre*)
knurl, *n.* knot, bead; knob for turning typewriter platen; (*Scot.*) dwarf.—*v.t.* furnish with knurls; mill (edge of coin).
knut, *joc.* spelling of **nut** (dandy).
koa, *n.* Hawaiian acacia. (native)
koala, *n.* Australian native bear. (native)
kob, *n.* S. African water-antelope.
kobold, *n.* household goblin, brownie; spirit of the mines. (G.)
kodak, *n.* hand-camera using films.—*v.t.* take snapshot of. (trade name)
koel, *n.* Indian and Australian kinds of cuckoo. (Sanskr. *kokila*)
koftgar, *n.* one who inlays gold on steel. **koftgari,** *n.* such work. (Hind.)
koh-i-noor, *n.* famous Indian diamond; superb specimen. (Pers. *koh,* mountain; *nur,* light)
kohl, *n.* powdered antimony, used for darkening eyelids. (Arab. *koh'l*)
kohlrabi, *n.* cabbage with turnip-shaped stem. (G.)
kola, *n.* a W. African tree; its nuts or seeds, used as tonic and condiment; an aerated water. (native)
kolinsky, *n.* Siberian mink; its fur. (*Kola* in Russia)
kolkhos, *n.* collective farm in Soviet Russia. (Russ.)
komitaji, komitadji, same as **comitadji.**
koodoo, *n.* S. African striped antelope with long spiral horns. (native)
kookaburra, *n.* laughing jackass, great kingfisher of Australia. (native)
koolah, same as **koala**
koorbash, same as **kourbash.**
kop, *n.* (*S. Afr.*) hill. (Du.=head)
kopec, kopeck, kopek, same as **copeck.**
kopje, *n.* (*S. Afr.*) small hill. (*kop*)
Koran, *n.* Mohammedan scriptures. **koranic,** *a.* (Arab. *qoran,* recitation)
kosher, *a.* pure, clean, according to requirements of Jewish law.—*n.* such food or shop. (Heb. *kasher,* right)
kotow, same as **kowtow.**
koumiss, *n.* spirit made from fermented mare's milk. (Tartar *kumiz*)
kourbash, *n.* hide whip used in Egypt and Turkey. (Arab. *qurbash*)
kowhai, *n.* a leguminous tree of New Zealand. (Maori)
kowtow, *n.* Chinese obeisance by touching ground with forehead.—*v.i.* prostrate oneself thus; act obsequiously. (Chin. *k'o,* knock; *t'ou,* head)
kraal, *n.* S. African native village; cattle enclosure. (*corral*)
krait, *n.* deadly Indian rock snake. (Hind. *karait*)
kraken, *n.* fabled sea-monster. (Scand.)
krang, *n.* carcass of whale after blubber has been removed. (Du.)
krantz, kranz, *n.* (*S. Afr.*) overhanging wall of rock, precipice. (S. Afr. Du.)
kremlin, *n.* citadel of Russian town, esp. Moscow. (Russ. *kreml*)
kreutzer, *n.* small obsolete Austrian copper coin. (G. *kreuz,* cross)
kriegspiel, *n.* war-game with blocks on maps, to train officers. (G.)
kris, *n.* Malay dagger with wavy blade. (Malay)
Krishna, *n.* great deity of later Hinduism. **Krishnaism,** *n.*
kromesky, *n.* small fried roll of minced chicken etc. (Russ.)
krone, *n.* silver coin of Austria or Denmark, Norway, and Sweden; German 10-mark gold piece. (G. = crown)
Kroo, Krou, Kru, *n.* and *a.* W. African negro. **K.-boy,** *n.* Kroo seaman. (native)
krypton, *n.* a gaseous constituent of the atmosphere. (Gk. *kruptein,* hide)
kshatriya, *n.* member of second or military Hindu caste. (Sanskr.)
kudos, *n.* (*sl.*) credit, glory. (Gk.)
kuou, same as **koodoo.**
Kufic, same as **Cufic.**
Ku-Klux, Ku-Klux-Klan, *n.* (*Amer.*) secret society hostile to negroes.

kukri, *n.* broad curved knife used by Gurkhas. (Hind.)
kulak, *n.* independent well-to-do peasant in Russia. (Russ.=fist)
kultur, *n.* German ideals of civilisation. (G.)
kumara, *n.* (*New Zealand*) sweet potato.
kümmel, *n.* cumin-flavoured liqueur. (G.)
kunkur, *n.* coarse Indian limestone.
Kurd, *n.* native of Kurdistan.
kursaal, *n.* reception-room of German spa. (G.=cure-saloon)
kvass, *n.* Russian rye-beer. (Russ. *kvas*)
kyang, same as **kiang.**
kyanize, *v.t.* preserve wood from dry rot by injecting corrosive sublimate. (J. H. *Kyan,* inventor)
kybosh, same as **kibosh.**
kye, ky, *n.pl.* (*Scot.*) cows.
kyle, *n.* strait, sound. (Gael. *caol*)
kyloe, *n.* one of breed of small long-horned highland cattle.
kymograph, *n.* instrument recording pressure, oscillations, sound-waves etc. (Gk. *kuma,* wave; *graphein,* write)
Kyrie, Kyrie eleison, *n.* prayer, part of mass; musical setting of this; response in Anglican communion service. (Gk.=Lord have mercy)
kyte, same as **kite** (*Scot.*).
kythe, *v.t.* and *i.* (*Scot.*) make known, discover; appear. (O.E. *cythan*)

L

L, (*roman numerals*) 50; **L-iron,** *n.* angle-iron.
la, same as **lah.**
la, *int.* (*arch.*) of surprise; look!
laager, *n.* (*S. Afr.*) camp in circle of wagons, encampment.—*v.t.* and *i.* encamp thus. (S. Afr. Du.)
lab, *n.* (*sl.*) laboratory.
labarum, *n.* symbolic banner, esp. Constantine's with Christ's monogram. (L.)
labdacism, same as **lambdacism.**
labefaction, *n.* weakening, overthrow. (L. *labare,* totter; *facere,* make)
label, *n.* slip of paper, metal etc. fixed to thing to give information about it; classifying phrase; stamp; (*archit.*) dripstone.—*v.t.* affix label to; set down as. (O.F.=ribbon)
labial, *a.* of, like, serving as, lips.—*n.* sound, letter, formed by lips, as *b, p.* **labialize,** *v.t.* **labialization,** *n.* **labiate,** *a.* and *n.* lip-like; (plant) with corolla or calyx divided into two parts like lips. (*labium*)
labile, *a.* (*chem.*) unstable. (*lapse*)
labium, *n.* (*pl.* **labia**) (*anat.*) lip. **labiodental,** *a.* and *n.* (sound, letter) formed by lips and teeth, as *f, v.* (L.)
laboratory, *n.* chemist's workroom; place for scientific experiments; manufactory. **laboratorial,** *a.* (*labour*)
laborious, *a.* hard-working; toilsome; laboured, not fluent. (*labour*)
labour, *n.* exertion, toil; task; pains of childbirth; the working classes.—*v.i.* work hard, strive; be troubled; (of ship) toss heavily.—*v.t.* elaborate, stress excessively. **hard l.,** work imposed on convicts. **L. Bureau, Exchange,** registry office for those seeking work. **L. Party,** that representing working classes. **laboured,** *a.* elaborate, not spontaneous. **labourer,** *n.* (esp. unskilled) workman. **Labourite,** *n.* adherent of Labour Party. (L. *labor*)
Labrador, *n.* small black variety of Newfoundland dog. (place)
labret, *n.* shell etc. worn in lip as ornament by savages. (L. *labrum,* lip)
laburnum, *n.* small tree with golden hanging flowers. (L.)
labyrinth, *n.* network of winding passages, maze; tangle, perplexity; (*anat.*) cavity of inner ear. **labyrinthiform, labyrinthine,** *aa.* **labyrinthodon, labyrinthodont,** *n.* large extinct amphibian with mazy pattern of teeth. (Gk. *laburinthos*)
lac, *n.* dark-red resin used in the East as dye. (Sanskr. *laksha*)
lac, lakh, *n.* (*Anglo-Ind.*) 100,000 (rupees). (Sanskr. *laksha*)
lace, *n.* cord to draw together edges of boots, stays etc.; ornamental braid; openwork patterned fabric.—*v.t.* and *i.* fasten, tighten, be compressed, with laces; embroider with lace; flavour with spirit. **l. into,** flog hard. (L. *laqueus,* noose)
lacerate, *v.t.* mangle, tear; distress. —*a.* rent. **lacerable, lacerative,** *aa.* **laceration,** *n.* (L. *lacer,* torn)
lacertian, lacertine, *aa.* of, like, lizards. (L. *lacerta,* lizard)
lacet, *n.* lace with inserted braid.
laches, *n.* (*law*) undue delay in claiming right etc.; negligence. (*lax*)
lachrymal, *a.* of, for, tears.—*n.* lachrymatory. **lachrymation,** *n.* flow of tears. **lachrymatory,** *n.* tear-phial found in ancient Roman tombs.—*a.* of, causing, tears. **lachrymose,** *a.* tearful. (L. *lacrima,* tear)
lachryma Christi, sweet red S. Italian wine. (L.=tear of Christ)
laciniate, laciniated, *aa.* (*bot., zool.*) cut into narrow lobes, fringed. (L. *lacinia,* flap)
lack, *n.* want, deficiency.—*v.t.* and *i.* want, be without.
lackadaisical, *a.* languidly superior; listless; affectedly pensive. **lackaday,**

lackadaisy, *intt.* (*arch.*) alas. (*alack-a-day*)
lacker, see **lacquer**.
lackey, **lacquey**, *n.* footman; obsequious person.—*v.t.* and *i.* wait upon; behave servilely (to). (F. *laquais*)
laconic, *a.* using few words, concise, brief. **laconicism**, **laconism**, *nn.* concise style; pithy phrase. (Gk. *Lakōn*, Spartan)
lacquer, **lacker**, *n.* hard varnish, us. of shellac and alcohol.—*v.t.* coat with this. (F. *lacre*)
lacrimal, **lacrymal**, same as **lachrymal**.
lacrosse, *n.* national ball-game of Canada, played by teams of 12 with long-handled racket or crosse. (F.)
lactate, *n.* a salt of lactic acid.
lactation, *n.* suckling; secreting of milk. **lacteal**, *a.* of milk; conveying chyle.—*n.pl.* (*anat.*) chyle-conveying vessels. **lactescence**, *n.* milky appearance or juice. **lactescent**, *a.* turning to milk, milky; yielding milky juice. **lactic**, *a.* of milk. **lactic acid**, made from sour milk. **lactiferous**, *a.* yielding milk or milky juice. **lactometer**, **lactoscope**, *nn.* instruments for testing quality of milk. **lactose**, *n.* sugar got from milk. (L. *lac*, milk)
lacuna, *n.* (*pl.* **lacunae**, **lacunas**) hiatus, gap; missing part; cavity. **lacunal**, **lacunar**, **lacunose**, *aa.* (L. *lacus*, lake)
lacustrine, *a.* of lakes. **l. age**, age of lake dwellings. (L. *lacus*, lake)
lacy, *a.* of, like, lace.
lad, *n.* boy, youth; (*Scot.*) lover. (M.E. *ladde*)
ladder, *n.* portable frame of bars between uprights used for ascending; means of rising; flaw in stocking etc. caused by thread parting.—*v.i.* form such flaw. **ladderproof**, *a.* proof against laddering. (O.E. *hlǣder*)
laddie, *n.* little lad, boy. (*lad*)
lade, *v.t.* (*p.p.* **laden**) load (ship); ship (goods); burden, weigh down; dip up (liquid). (O.E. *hladan*)
la-di-da, *a.* and *n.* languidly affected or foppish (person). (imit.)
ladify, same as **ladyfy**.
lading, *n.* loading, cargo. (*lade*)
ladle, *n.* large spoon for transferring liquids.—*v.t.* dip out with ladle. **ladleful**, *n.* (*lade*)
lady, *n.* gentlewoman; title of wives of knights, daughters of earls, and all higher ranks; mistress of household, wife, love. **our L.**, the Virgin Mary. **L.-chapel**, *n.* chapel dedicated to her. **L. Day**, the Annunciation, 25 March. **l. help**, gentlewoman servant. **l. in waiting**, lady attending sovereign. **l.-killer**, *n.* male flirt. **l.-love**, *n.* sweetheart. **l.'s-maid**, *n.* personal maid who attends to lady's toilet. **l's bedstraw**, yellow-flowered plant. **l.'s slipper**, kind of native orchid; calceolaria. **ladies' man**, one fond of female society. (O.E. *hlǣfdige*)
ladybird, (*Amer.*) **ladybug**, **ladycow**, *nn.* small spotted reddish-brown beetle.
ladyfy, *v.t.* make lady of, treat as lady. **ladyfied**, *a.* having the airs of a fine lady. (L. *facere*, make)
ladyhood, *n.* condition, character, of a lady.
ladylike, *a.* behaving as, befitting, a lady; (of man) effeminate.
ladyship, *n.* title of a Lady, esp. in phrases **her**, **your**, **l.**
ladysmock, *n.* cuckoo-flower.
laevo-rotation, *n.* left-handed or counter-clockwise rotation. **laevo-rotatory**, *a.* **laevulose**, *n.* fruit-sugar. (L. *laevus*, left)
lag, *v.i.* move slowly, fall behind.—*n.* retardation (in current etc.); one who is last, fag-end.
lag, *v.t.* (*sl.*) send to penal servitude; arrest.—*n.* convict.
lagan, *n.* (*law*) goods, wreckage, lying on bed of sea.
lager, **lager beer**, *n.* light kind of German beer. (G. *lager*, store)
laggard, *n.* and *a.* sluggish, backward (person); one who lags behind. **lagger**, *n.* laggard. **lagging**, *a.* (*lag*)
lagoon, **lagune**, *n.* salt-water lake separated from sea by sandbank or enclosed by atoll. (*lacuna*)
lah, *n.* sixth note in sol-fa notation.
laic, *a.* non-clerical, secular, lay.—*n.* layman. **laical**, *a.* **laicize**, *v.t.* render lay; throw open to laymen. **laicization**, *n.* (*lay*)
laich, *a.* (*Scot.*) low.
laid, see **lay**.
lain, see **lie**.
lair, *n.* beast's den or lying-place; (*Scot.*) ground for one grave in burying-place.—*v.i.* and *t.* place, rest, in lair. (O.E. *leger*, bed)
lair, *v.i.* (*Scot.*) sink in mud.—*n.* mire, bog. (O.N. *leir*)
lair, *Scot.* form of **lore**.
laird, *n.* (*Scot.*) landowner, squire. **lairdship**, *n.* estate. (*lord*)
laissez-aller, *n.* unconstraint, ease of manner. *laissez-faire*, *n.* letting alone; doctrine of non-interference by government in commercial affairs. (F.=let go, let act)
laith, *Scot.* form of **loath**.
laity, *n.* the people as distinct from the clergy, laymen. (*lay*)
lake, *n.* large body of inland water. **l.-dweller**, *n.* prehistoric inhabitant of **l. dwelling**, built on piles in lake. **L. Poets**, Wordsworth, Coleridge, and Southey, who lived in the **L. District** in N. England. **lakelet**, *n.* little lake. **laky**, *a.* (L. *lacus*)
lake, *n.* crimson pigment. (*lac*)
lakh, see **lac**.
lakin, *n.* (*Shake.*) lady. (*lady*; *-kin*)
Lallan, *a.* and *n.* (*Scot.*) Scottish Lowland.
lallation, *n.* pronouncing *r* like *l*, lambdacism. (L. *lallare*, sing lullaby)
lam, *v.t.* and *i.* (*sl.*) thrash, hit.

lama, *n.* Buddhist priest of Tibet or Mongolia. **lamaism**, *n.* his religion. **lamaist**, *n.* **lamasery**, *n.* monastery of lamas. (Tibetan *blama*)
lama, old spelling of llama.
lamb, *n.* young sheep; its meat; innocent or gentle creature.—*v.i.* and *t.* bring forth (lamb). **L. of God**, Christ. **l.'s-tails**, *n.pl.* hazel catkins. (O.E.)
lambaste, lambast, *v.t.* thrash, beat.
lambda, *n.* Greek letter L. **lambdacism**, *n.* pronunciation of *r* like *l*. **lambdoid, lambdoidal**, *aa.* shaped like lambda (Λ). (Gk.)
lambent, *a.* (of flame) playing about a surface, flickering; softly radiant, gently brilliant. **lambency**, *n.* (L. *lambere*, lick)
lambert, *n.* measure of brightness, brightness of surface radiating 1 lumen per square centimetre. (person)
lambkin, *n.* little lamb. (*-kin*, dim.)
lambrequin, *n.* short hanging over door, mantelpiece etc. (F.)
lame, *a.* disabled in limb, crippled; limping; (of excuse) unconvincing; (of metre) halting.—*v.t.* cripple. **l. duck**, disabled person; defaulter on stock exchange; (*Amer.*) official not re-elected. (O.E. *lama*)
lamé, *a.* and *n.* (material) with gold or silver thread inwoven. (F.)
lamella, *n.* (*pl.* lamellae) thin plate, scale, or film. **lamellar, lamellate, lamellose**, *aa.* (L.)
lament, *n.* sorrow expressed in cries; elegy, dirge. — *v.i.* and *t.* wail; express, feel, grief (for); mourn (for). **lamentable**, *a.* deplorable, mournful. **lamentation**, *n.* (L. *lamentum*)
lamia, *n.* monster, half serpent, half woman; sorceress, vampire. (Gk.)
lamiaceous, *a.* of the mint family. (L. *lamium*, deadnettle)
lamina, *n.* (*pl.* laminae) thin plate, flake, or layer. **laminar, laminose**, *aa.* **laminate**, *v.t.* and *i.* beat into, overlay with, thin plates; split into layers.—*a.* plated; in layers. **lamination**, *n.* (L.)
lamish, *a.* a little lame. (*lame*)
Lammas, *n.* 1 August, Scottish quarter-day, formerly kept as harvest festival. (O.E. *hláf*, loaf; *mæsse*, mass)
lammergeyer, *n.* the bearded vulture. (G. *lämmer*, lambs; *geier*, vulture)
lamming, *n.* (*sl.*) beating. (*lam*)
lamp, *n.* vessel with oil and wick for giving light; a light of any kind. **smell of the l.**, show signs of laborious effort. **l.-black**, *n.* pigment made from soot. **l.-lighter**, *n.* man who lights street lamps. **l.-post**, *n.* support of street lamp. (Gk. *lampas*)
lamp, *v.i.* (*Scot.*) scamper, go jauntily.
lampas, *n.* kind of flowered silk. (F.)
lampas, lampass, *n.* horse-disease with swelling in roof of mouth. (F.)
lampion, *n.* small coloured lamp used in illuminations, fairy lamp. (*lamp*)
lampoon, *n.* scurrilous or personal satire.—*v.t.* satirize thus. **lampooner, lampoonist**, *nn.* (F. *lampon*)
lamprey, *n.* eel-like fish with sucker mouth. (L.L. *lampreda*)
lanary, *n.* wool-store. **lanate, lanated**, *aa.* woolly. (L. *lana*, wool)
lance, *n.* spear, esp. horseman's.—*v.t.* pierce with lance; open with lancet; (*poet.*) launch, fling. **l.-corporal**, (*sl.*) **l.-jack**, *nn.* N.C.O. below corporal. **l.-fish**, *n.* launce. **l.-snake**, *n*, fer-de-lance. (L. *lancea*)
lancelet, *n.* a small fish. (*lance*)
lanceolate, *a.* (*bot.*) tapering to each end. (L. *lanceola*, little lance)
lancer, *n.* cavalry soldier armed with lance; (*pl.*) kind of quadrilles.
lancet, *n.* pointed two-edged surgical knife; high narrow window or arch, pointed like lance. **lanceted**, *a.*
lancewood, *n.* a tough elastic wood.
land, *n.* solid part of earth's surface; soil, ground; country, nation; real estate; (*Scot.*) block of dwellings under one roof; (*pl.*) estates.—*v.t.* and *i.* come, set, on land; alight, arrive; catch, win. **l. of cakes**, Scotland. **l. of the leal**, heaven. **l.-breeze**, *n.* off-shore breeze. **l.-fish**, *n.* (*Shake.*) unnatural creature. **l.-jobber**, *n.* speculator in land. **l.-mine**, *n.* mine set to explode under advancing troops etc.; heavy bomb dropped by parachute. **l.-rail**, *n.* corncrake. **l.-steward**, *n.* manager of estate. (O.E.)
landau, *n.* four-wheeled carriage with roof that folds down. **landaulet, landaulette**, *n.* small landau. (place)
lande, *n.* flat sandy coastal tract, heathy plain, in SW. France. (F.)
landed, *a.* possessing, consisting of, land.
landfall, *n.* (*naut.*) first land sighted after voyage; making land.
landgrave, *n.* (*fem.* landgravine) German count. (G. *graf*, count)
landholder, *n.* tenant, owner, of land.
landing, *n.* disembarkation; level part of staircase between flights. **l.-stage**, *n.* platform for disembarking.
landlocked, *a.* almost or quite enclosed by land.
landlord, *n.* (*fem.* landlady) owner of land or house occupied by tenant; keeper of inn or lodging-house.
landlubber, *n.* (*naut.*) landsman.
landmark, *n.* boundary-mark; object as guide to direction.
landocracy, *n.* (*joc.*) the landed class. **landocrat**, *n.* (Gk. *kratein*, rule)
landowner, *n.* one who owns land.
landscape, *n.* piece, picture, of country scenery. **l. gardening**, laying out of grounds to imitate natural scenery. **landscapist**, *n.* landscape painter. (Du. *landschap*)
landskip, *arch.* form of landscape.
landslide, *n.* landslip; (*Amer.*) collapse of political party. **landslip**, *n.* fall of earth from cliff etc.

landsman, *n.* one who lives on land.

landsturm, *n.* general levy in war, final reserve of German army. (G.)

Landtag, *n.* diet of a German state. (G.)

landwehr, *n.* second reserve of German army, fully trained civilians. (G.)

landward, landwards, *adv.* towards land.

lane, *n.* narrow road or street; passage; ocean route for ships. (O.E.)

lane, (*Scot.*) lone, alone.

langrage, langridge, *n.* iron fragments as shot used to damage rigging.

lang, *a.* (*Scot.*) long. **l. syne,** time long past; long ago.

language, *n.* human speech; tongue of a people; method, style, of expression. **bad l.,** oaths and abuse. **dead l.,** obsolete one. (L. *lingua,* tongue)

langue d'oc, langue d'oïl, *nn.* medieval French spoken S., N., of the Loire, latter being staple of modern French. (*oc, oïl,* words for 'yes' in the respective dialects)

languor, *n.* faintness; want of vigour or interest; soft mood or influence. **languorous,** *a.* full of, causing, languor; lazy. **languid,** *a.* weak, inert; spiritless, listless; dull. **languish,** *v.i.* be, become, languid; lose vitality; droop, pine (for); look tenderly. **languishment,** *n.* (L.)

langur, *n.* Indian long-tailed monkey. (Hind.)

laniard, same as **lanyard.**

laniary, *a.* fitted for tearing.—*n.* canine tooth. (L. *laniare,* tear)

laniferous, lanigerous, *aa.* wool-bearing. (L. *lana,* wool)

lank, *a.* tall and lean; spare, shrunken; (of hair, grass etc.) long and limp. **lanky,** *a.* ungracefully lean and long; lank. (O.E. *hlanc*)

lanner, *n.* kind of female falcon. **lanneret,** *n.* male of it. (F. *lanier*)

lanolin, *n.* grease from wool, used in ointments. (L. *lana,* wool)

lansquenet, *n.* a card-game. (G. *landsknecht,* soldier of fortune)

lantern, *n.* transparent case for light; glazed erection on dome or roof; magic lantern. **Chinese l.,** collapsible with paper sides. **dark l.,** with opaque slide. **magic l.,** optical instrument throwing enlarged image of glass picture on darkened screen. **l. jaws,** long, thin jaws giving hollow look. **l.-jawed,** *a.* (L. *lanterna*)

lanthanum, *n.* a rare metallic element. (Gk. *lanthanein,* lie hid)

lanthorn, *arch.* spelling of **lantern,** from use of *horn* for sides.

lanuginous, *a.* downy. (L. *lanugo,* down)

lanyard, *n.* cord for firing gun, securing whistle etc.; (*naut.*) short rope securing anything. (F. *lanière*)

Laodicean, *a.* and *n.* (person) lukewarm in religion. (Revelation iii. 14–16)

lap, *n.* overhanging flap, fold; knees of seated person, dress covering them; single turn of wound thread; one circuit of course in race.—*v.t.* and *i.* enfold, wrap round; overlap, cause to overlap; outstrip (runner) by lap. **lapful,** *n.* (O.E. *lappa*)

lap, *v.t.* and *i.* drink by scooping up with tongue; take in greedily; (of waves) beat softly.—*n.* liquid food; sound of wavelets. (O.E. *lapian*)

lapar(o)-, from Gk. *lapara,* flank, used in **laparocele,** *n.* lumbar hernia; **laparotomy,** *n.* cutting of abdominal walls.

lapdog, *n.* small pet dog. (*lap*)

lapel, *n.* part of breast of coat folded back. **lapelled,** *a.* (*lap*)

lapidary, *a.* of stones; engraved on stone; of inscriptions, monumental. —*n.* cutter, engraver, of gems. **lapidate,** *v.t.* stone, stone to death. **lapidation,** *n.* **lapidify,** *v.t.* and *i.* turn into stone. **lapidification,** *n.* (L. *lapis,* stone)

lapis lazuli, a bright blue stone; its colour. (L.=stone of azure)

lappet, *n.* flap, fold (of garment, flesh etc.). **lappeted,** *a.* (*lap*)

lapse, *n.* slip, slight mistake; fall from virtue; termination of right through disuse; gliding, flow; passing (of time).—*v.i.* fall back or away; become void; elapse. (L. *labi,* glide)

lapsus calami, slip of the pen. *lapsus linguae,* slip of the tongue. (L.)

lapwing, *n.* pewit. (O.E. *hleapewince*)

larboard, *n.* and *a.* (*obs., naut.*) port (side of ship). (M.E. *ladeborde*)

larceny, *n.* (*law*) theft. **grand, petty, l.,** of property valued at more, less, than a shilling. **larcener, larcenist,** *nn.* **larcenous,** *a.* (L. *latro,* robber)

larch, *n.* bright-leaved tree of pine kind; its tough timber. (L. *larix*)

lard, *n.* melted fat of pig.—*v.t.* smear with lard; insert strips of bacon in (meat); garnish (with). **lardaceous,** *a.* like lard. **lardon, lardoon,** *n.* strip of bacon for larding. **lardy,** *a.* (L. *lardum*)

larder, *n.* store-room for meat. (*lard*)

lardy-dardy, *a.* (*sl.*) affected, languidly foppish. (imit.)

Lārēs and Penātēs, household gods, home. (L.)

large, *a.* big; wide in range; liberal, generous; (*Shake.*) free, licentious. **at l.,** at liberty; at full length; as a body; broadcast. **in l.,** on a large scale. **l.-hearted,** *a.* generous. **largen,** *v.i.* and *t.* (*poet.*). **largely,** *adv.* to a great extent. **largish,** *a.* fairly big. (L. *largus*)

largess, largesse, *n.* money, gifts, scattered on occasion of rejoicing; bounty. (*large*)

largo, *adv.* and *n.* (*mus.*) slow and dignified (movement). (It.)

lariat, *n.* picketing-rope; lasso. (Sp. *la,* the; *reata,* rope)

larithmics, *n.pl.* study of population

statistics. (Gk. *laos*, people; *arithmos*, number)

lark, laverock, *n.* small brown singing-bird, skylark. **rise with the l.,** rise early. **l.-heel,** *n.* nasturtium. **larkspur,** *n.* delphinium. (O.E. *láferce*)

lark, *n.* prank; amusing incident.—*v.i.* play tricks, frolic. **larky,** *a.*

larrikin, *n.* (*Austral.*) young rough, hooligan.

larrup, *v.t.* (*colloq.*) thrash, flog.

larum, rare form of **alarum.**

larva, *n.* (*pl.* **larvae**) insect in first stage after leaving egg; caterpillar, grub. **larval,** *a.* (L.=ghost)

larynx, *n.* upper part of windpipe, organ of voice. **laryngeal, laryngic,** *aa.* **laryngitis,** *n.* inflammation of larynx. **laryngology,** *n.* science of larynx. **laryngologist,** *n.* **laryngoscope,** *n.* mirror apparatus for examining larynx. **laryngotomy,** *n.* cutting into larynx. (Gk. *larungx*)

Lascar, *n.* native E. Indian seaman.

lascivious, *a.* lustful; inciting to lust. (L. *lascivius*, wanton)

lash, *n.* flexible part of whip, thong; stroke with whip; eyelash.—*v.t.* and *i.* swing (tail); strike out violently; pour, rush; flog with whip; beat upon; castigate in words; goad; tie tightly, bind. **l. out,** give sudden blow or kick. **lashing,** *n.* flogging; cord used for binding; (*pl.*, *Ir. sl.*) plenty (of).

lasher, *n.* weir, water rushing over it, pool below it. (*lash*)

lashkar, *n.* body of armed Indian tribesmen. (Hind.=army)

laspring, *n.* young salmon.

lasque, *n.* ill-formed or veiny diamond.

lass, *n.* girl; sweetheart; (*Scot.*) maid-servant. **l.-lorn,** *a.* (*Shake.*) forsaken by one's mistress. **lassie, lassock,** *nn.* (*Scot.*) young girl. (M.E. *lasce*)

lassitude, *n.* weariness, languor, faintness. (L *lassus*, tired)

lasso, *n.* (*pl.* **lassos**) rope with running noose for catching cattle etc.—*v.t.* catch with one. (L. *laqueus*, noose)

last, *a.* after all others, at the end; most recent; least likely; utmost.—*n.* most recent, last-mentioned, thing; end, death.—*adv.* in the last place; the time next before the present. **at l.,** in the end; after much delay. **first and l.,** altogether. **l. day,** Day of Judgment; (*Scot.*) yesterday. **lastly,** *adv.* finally. (=latest)

last, *v.i.* go on; hold out, remain unimpaired.—*n.* stamina. **l. out,** not come to an end before. **lasting,** *a.* permanent; durable.—*n.* kind of hard cloth. (O.E. *læstan*, fulfil)

last, *n.* wooden model of foot on which shoes are made. **stick to one's l.,** not meddle outside one's own province. (O.E. *last*, footprint)

last, *n.* load; large measure of quantity or weight, about 4,000 lb. but varying with goods. (O.E. *hlæst*)

Latakia, *n.* fine kind of Turkish tobacco. (place)

latch, *n.* door-fastening of bar falling into catch and raised by lever from outside; small spring-lock. — *v.t.* fasten with latch; (*Shake.*) catch. **on the l.,** latched but not locked. **l.-key,** *n.* key of latch or front door.

latchet, *n.* shoe-strap. (O.F. *lachet*)

late, *a.* behindhand, after the right time; far on in day etc.; that was recently but now is not; now dead; recent.—*adv.* after the right time; recently; at or till a late hour. **of l.,** recently. **lately,** *adv.* recently, in recent times. (O.E. *læt*)

lateen, *a.* **l. sail,** triangular sail on long sloping yard. (*Latin*)

latent, *a.* hidden, not visible; dormant, undeveloped. **latency,** *n.* (L. *latēre*, lie hid)

lateral, *a.* of, from, towards, the side; (of branch of family) sprung from brother or sister of person in direct line.—*n.* lateral branch. (L. *latus*, side)

latex, *n.* milky juice of plants; crude rubber. (L.=liquid)

lath, *n.* thin, narrow strip of wood. **l. and plaster,** material of ceiling etc. **lathing,** *n.* (O.E. *lætt*)

lathe, *n.* machine for turning or shaping wood, metal etc.; potter's wheel.

lathe, *n.* a division of the county of Kent. (O.E. *læth*, district)

lather, *n.* froth of soap and water; frothy sweat of horse.—*v.t.* and *i.* cover with lather; (of soap) form lather; (*sl.*) thrash. **lathering,** *n.* (*sl.*) thrashing. (O.E. *léathor*)

lathi, *n.* (*Anglo-Ind.*) long heavy stick of Indian native policeman. (Hind.)

lathy, *a.* like lath; tall and thin.

Latin, *n.* language of ancient Rome; inhabitant of ancient Latium.—*a.* of, in, Latin; of ancient Rome or Latium; speaking language based on Latin, Romance; Roman Catholic. **classical L.,** that used 75 B.C.–A.D. 175; **late L.,** 175–600; **medieval L.,** 600–1500; **modern L.,** after 1500; **low L.,** medieval or late and medieval. **dog L.,** barbarous Latin. **thieves' L.,** secret lingo. **L. America,** where Latin languages are spoken. **L. Church,** Western Church. **L. languages, peoples,** those of Italy, France, Spain, and Portugal. *Latinè*, *adv.* in Latin. **latinist,** *n.* Latin scholar. **latinity,** *n.* Latin style or idiom. **latinize,** *v.t.* and *i.* give Latin form to; adopt, cause to adopt, Latin ideas. **latinization, latinizer,** *nn.* (*Latium*)

latitude, *n.* scope, full extent; freedom from restriction; angular distance N. or S. of equator; (*astron.*) angular distance from ecliptic; (*pl.*) regions. **high ll.,** far N. or S. **low ll.,** near equator. **latitudinal,** *a.* **latitudinarian,** *a.* and *n.* (person) claiming

or showing freedom of thought, esp. **in** religion; liberal. latitudinarianism, *n.* (L. *latus*, broad)

latrine, *n.* privy, convenience, in camp, barracks etc. (L. *lavare*, wash)

latten, *n.* kind of brass or bronze; sheet tin.—*a.* of this. (O.E. *laton*)

latter, *a.* mentioned second of two; recent; (*Shake.*) last; (*arch.*) later. **l.-day,** *a.* modern. **L.-day Saints,** Mormons. **latterly,** *adv.* in later time, lately. (variant of *later*)

lattice, *n.* screen etc. of crossed laths or bars with spaces between; (also **l. window**) window with small diamond panes set in lead. **latticed,** *a.* **latticing, l.-work,** *nn.* (*lath*)

laud, *n.* praise; song of praise; (*pl.*) church office following matins.—*v.t.* praise, extol. **laudable,** *a.* commendable. (L. *laus*)

laudanum, *n.* tincture of opium.

laudation, *n.* praising, panegyric. **laudative, laudatory,** *aa.* (*laud*)

laudator temporis acti, one who prefers the good old days. (L.=praiser of time past)

laugh, *v.i.* and *t.* make sound expressing amusement etc.; utter with laugh; (of sea etc.) sparkle, look bright.—*n.* sound, act, of laughing. **have, get, the l. of,** turn the tables on. **l. in one's sleeve,** be secretly amused. **l. off,** treat as trivial. **l. to scorn,** deride. **laughable,** *a.* amusing. **laugher,** *n.* **laughing-gas,** *n.* nitrous oxide used as anaesthetic. **laughing hyena,** striped hyena. **laughing jackass,** great kingfisher of Australia. **laughing-stock,** *n.* object of general derision. **laughingly,** *adv.* **laughter,** *n.* laughing. (O.E. *hlehhan*)

launch, *v.t.* and *i.* hurl; send, go, forth; set (ship) afloat; (*Shake.*) lance.—*n.* launching of ship. **l. out,** burst (into), expatiate. (*lance*)

launch, *n.* warship's largest boat; small power-driven pleasure-vessel. (Sp. *lancha*, pinnace)

laund, *n.* (*Shake.*) glade. (*lande*)

launder, *v.t.* wash and iron (linen). **laundress,** *n.* woman who launders, washerwoman. **laundry,** *n.* place for laundering; (*colloq.*) articles to be laundered. (L. *lavare*, wash)

laureate, *a.* crowned with, worthy of, laurel-wreath.—*n.* poet laureate. **poet l.,** salaried poet of royal household. **laureateship,** *n.* (*laurel*)

laurel, *n.* an evergreen shrub, bay-tree; its leaves, used as emblem of victory or merit. **rest on one's ll.,** seek no further glory. **laurelled,** *a.* crowned with laurel. (L. *laurus*)

laurustinus, laurestinus, *n.* an evergreen flowering shrub. (L. *laurus*, laurel; *tinus*, laurustinus)

lauwine, *n.* avalanche. (G. *lawine*)

lava, *n.* molten rock discharged by volcano and solidifying as it cools. (L. *lavare*, wash)

lavabo, *n.* ritual washing of hands; wash-basin. (L.=I will wash)

lavation, *n.* washing. **lavatory,** *n.* room for washing hands and face; water-closet and urinal. (*lave*)

lave, *v.t.* wash, bathe. (L. *lavare*)

lave, *n.* (*Scot.*) the rest, the others. (O.E. *láf*)

laveer, *v.i.* (*naut.*) tack. (*luff*)

lavement, *n.* (*med.*) injection, enema.

lavender, *n.* shrub with sweet-scented flowers; pale lilac colour.—*v.t.* put lavender among. **lay up in l.,** lay by carefully. **l.-water,** *n.* perfume made with it. (L.L. *lavendula*)

laver, *n.* an edible seaweed. (L.)

laver, *n.* (*arch.*) large vessel for washing. (*lave*)

laverock, see **lark.**

lavish, *a.* giving without stint, profuse; very abundant, excessive.—*v.t.* spend, bestow, profusely. **lavishment,** *n.* (O.F. *lavache*, downpour)

lavolt, lavolta, *n.* (*Shake.*) twirling capering dance for couples. (It. *la*, the; *volta*, turn)

law, *n.* rule, body of rules, binding community; legal science or profession, litigation; rule of procedure, principle; start given in race, respite. **go to l.,** start lawsuit. **have the l. of,** sue. **lay down the l.,** dictate. **common l.,** unwritten law of England. **written l.,** statute law. **l. merchant,** laws regulating trade. **l. of nations,** international law. **l. of the Medes and Persians,** unalterable rule. (O.E. *lagu*)

law, laws, *int.* (*vulg.*) of surprise.

law-abiding, *a.* obedient to the law.

lawcourt, *n.* place where justice is administered.

lawful, *a.* permitted or recognized by law, legitimate. **l. day,** working day.

lawgiver, *n.* maker of code of laws.

lawing, *n.* litigation; (*Scot.*) tavern-bill, reckoning.

lawk, lawks, *int.* (*vulg.*) of surprise. **lawk-a-mussy,** *int.* Lord have mercy.

lawless, *a.* without laws; disobedient to law; uncontrolled.

law-lord, *n.* member of House of Lords qualified for its legal work.

lawn, *n.* piece of close-mown turf in garden etc.; (*arch.*) glade. **l.-mower,** *n.* machine for mowing lawn. **l. tennis,** game for two or four, orig. on grass court, with net, rackets, and ball. **lawny,** *a.* (*lande*)

lawn, *n.* kind of fine plain-woven linen or cotton fabric. **lawny,** *a.*

lawsuit, *n.* prosecution of claim in lawcourt.

lawyer, *n.* one who practises law, solicitor; expert in law. **Penang l.,** walking-stick of Penang palm. (*law*)

lax, *n.* Norwegian salmon. (Scand.)

lax, *a.* loose, slack; not strict; vague. **laxative,** *a.* and *n.* (drug) loosening bowels. **laxity,** *n.* (L. *laxus*)

lay, *v.t.* and *i.* (*past, p.p.* laid) cause to

lie, level; place, deposit, impose; set, prepare; produce (egg); stake, bet; (*vulg.*) lie.—*n.* lie (of country etc.); (*sl.*) line of business. **l. about one,** hit out on all sides. **l. aside or by,** put away, save; discard. **l. bare,** reveal. **l. down,** give up; formulate; start building (ship); store (wine). **l. hold of,** grasp. **l. in,** get supply of. **l. into,** (*sl.*) beat. **l. on,** impose; strike; supply (water etc.). **l. out,** extend; dress (corpse); expend; plan. **l. to,** (*naut.*) bring ship to stop. **l. up,** store up; disable; (*naut.*) place in dock. **l. waste,** ravage. **layout,** *n.* arrangement. (O.E. *lecgan*)

lay, *a.* of the people, not clerical or professional. **l. brother, sister,** member of religious order exempted from religious duties. **l. lord,** peer not a law-lord. **l. reader,** layman licensed to conduct services. (*laic*)

lay, *n.* minstrel's song, ballad; poem. (O.F. *lai*)

lay, see lie.

layer, *n.* one who lays; stratum, row, thickness; shoot fastened down to take root.—*v.t.* propagate by layers.

layette, *n.* outfit for new-born child. (F.)

lay figure, artist's adjustable model; nonentity. (Du. *led,* joint)

laylock, *dial.* for lilac.

layman, *n.* ordinary person, not cleric or expert.

laystall, *n.* refuse-heap. (*lay*; *stall*)

lazar, *n.* diseased beggar, esp. leper. **lazaretto, lazaret,** *n.* public hospital; place of quarantine; after part of ship's hold. (*Lazarus* in Bible)

lazy, *a.* averse to work, slothful; sluggish. **l.-bones,** *n.* sluggard. **l.-tongs,** *n.pl.* scissor-like arrangement of levers for gripping objects at distance. **laze,** *v.i.* and *t.* (*colloq.*) pass (time) lazily.

lazzarone, *n.* (*pl. lazzaroni*) homeless street-idler of Naples. (It.)

lea, *n.* (*poet.*) meadow; grass land. **l.-rig,** *n.* (*Scot.*) grass ridge or field. (O.E. *leah*)

lea, *n.* measure of yarn, varying from 300 to 80 yds.

lead, *n.* soft heavy grey metal; lump of this for sounding depth of water; graphite; (*pl.*) lead covering of roof; (*print.*) metal strip to widen space. —*v.t.* cover, weight, or space out with lead. **heave the l.,** take soundings. **swing the l.,** (*sl.*) malinger. **black l.,** graphite, plumbago. **red, white, l.,** compounds of lead used as pigments. **l. pencil,** one of graphite enclosed in wood. **leaden,** *a.* of, like, lead; heavy, slow. (O.E. *léad*)

lead, *v.t.* and *i.* (*past, p.p.* **led**) guide, conduct; direct, command; induce; go, play, first; precede; pass (life).—*n.* leading; example; front or chief place; leash; channel in ice-field; (*electr.*) wire supplying current to instrument. **l. off,** begin. **l. on,** entice. **l. up to,** approach by degrees. (O.E. *lǽdan*)

leader, *n.* one who leads, commander; leading article. **leaderette,** *n.* small leading article. **leadership,** *n.*

leading, *a.* chief, principal. — *n.* guidance. **l. article,** expressing editorial views. **l. case,** legal decision forming precedent. **l. man, lady,** taking chief part in play. **l. note,** seventh note of scale. **l. question,** designed to prompt reply desired. **l. strings,** with which children were formerly taught to walk.

leadsman, *n.* sailor who heaves lead.

leaf, *n.* (*pl.* **leaves**) green blade on stem of tree or plant; foliage; petal; single sheet of paper, thin sheet of metal; flap of table, shutter etc.—*v.i.* put forth leaves. **leafage,** *n.* foliage. **leaflet,** *n.* small leaf; handbill. **leafy,** *a.* of leaf; having, abounding in, leaves. (O.E. *léaf*)

leaf, *n.* (*sl.*) leave, furlough. (*leave*)

league, *n.* measure of distance, us. 3 miles. (L.L. *leuga*)

league, *n.* compact for mutual help; alliance, association.—*v.t.* and *i.* unite in league. **L. of Nations,** established in 1919 for prevention of war. **leaguer,** *n.* member of league. (L. *ligare,* bind)

leaguer, *n.* (*arch.*) camp; siege. (Du. *leger*)

leak, *n.* hole or other defect through which liquid may pass in or out.—*v.i.* pass, let liquid pass, through leak. **l. out,** be divulged. **spring a l.,** develop one. **leakage,** *n.* what passes through leak; divulging of secrets; unexplained shortage. **leaky,** *a.* (O.N. *leka,* drip)

leal, *a.* (*Scot.*) true, loyal. **land of the l.,** heaven. **lealty,** *n.* (*loyal*)

leam, *n.* and *v.i.* (*obs.*) gleam, glow. (O.E. *leóma*)

lean, *v.i.* and *t.* (*past, p.p.* **leaned** or **leant**) be, put, in sloping position; incline, tend; rely (on).—*n.* slope. **l.-to,** *n.* shed built against side of house, penthouse. **leaning,** *n.* inclination. (O.E. *hlinian*)

lean, *a.* thin; without fat; meagre.—*n.* meat without fat. (O.E. *hlǽne*)

leap, *v.i.* and *t.* (*past, p.p.* **leaped** or **leapt**) jump.—*n.* jump. **l.-day,** *n.* 29 February. **l.-frog,** *n.* game in which players vault over one another. **l.-year,** *n.* year with 29 February as extra day. **leaper,** *n.* **leaping-house,** *n.* (*Shake.*) brothel. **leaping-time,** *n.* (*Shake.*) youth. (O.E. *hleapan*)

learn, *v.t.* and *i.* (*past, p.p.* **learnt** or **learned**) gain knowledge (of) or skill (in); find out, hear; (*arch.* or *vulg.*) teach. **l. by heart,** commit to memory. **learned,** *a.* having, requiring, much knowledge; erudite; versed in law. **learning,** *n.* knowledge got by study, scholarship. **new learning,** renaissance. (O.E. *leornian*)

lease, *n.* contract by which tenant rents land or property from owner.—*v.t.* rent by lease, let. **leasehold,** *n.* tenure, property held, by lease. **leaseholder,** *n.* (L. *laxare,* loose)

lease, *n.* (*weaving*) crossing of warp-threads in loom.

leash, *n.* thong for holding animal; a brace and a half, three.—*v.t.* hold in leash, control. (O.F. *lesse*)

leasing, *n.* (*arch.*) falsehood, lies. (O.E. *léas,* false)

least, *a.* (*superl.* of **little**) smallest. —*n.* smallest amount.—*adv.* in the smallest degree. **at l.,** at all events. **leastways** (*vulg.*), **leastwise,** *advv.* or at least. (O.E. *lǽst*)

leat, *n.* trench for bringing water to mill-wheel. (O.E. *lǽtan,* let)

leather, *n.* prepared skin of animal; thong; (*sl.*) cricket-ball, football; (*pl.*) leather leggings or breeches.—*v.t.* cover with leather; flog. **l. and prunella,** a difference in clothes only. **nothing like l.,** one's own goods will serve all purposes. **l.-head,** *n.* blockhead. **l.-hunting,** *n.* (*cricket sl.*) fielding. **l.-jacket,** *n.* grub of daddy-long-legs; kinds of fish. **l.-neck,** *n.* (*naut. sl.*) soldier. **patent l.,** with black varnished surface. **leatherette, leatheroid,** *nn.* kinds of imitation leather. **leathern,** *a.* made of leather. **leathery,** *a.* like leather, tough. (O.E. *lether*)

leave, *n.* permission; permission to be absent from duty; formal parting. **take l. of,** bid farewell to. (O.E. *léaf*)

leave, *v.t.* and *i.* (*past, p.p.* **left**) allow to remain; bequeath; commit; deposit; depart (from); abandon; cease from, desist.—*n.* (*billiards*) position in which player leaves the balls. **l. alone,** not interfere with. **l. go** (*vulg.*) let go. **l. off,** stop; cease using. **l. out,** omit. (O.E. *lǽfan*)

leaved, *a.* having leaves.

leaven, *n.* ferment to make dough rise, yeast; transforming influence.—*v.t.* treat with leaven; modify, temper. (L. *levare,* raise)

leaves, see **leaf.**

leavings, *n.pl.* what someone has left as worthless, refuse.

leavy, *a.* (*Shake.*) leafy.

lebensraum, n. space for a country's expanding population. (G.=living space)

lecher, *n.* (*arch.*) fornicator. **lecherous,** *a.* lustful. **lechery,** *n.* (O.F. *lecher,* lick)

lectern, *n.* reading-desk in church. **lection,** *n.* reading, scripture lesson; variant in text. **lectionary,** *n.* book, list, of scripture lessons for particular days. **lector,** *n.* (*fem.* **lectress**) reader. (L. *legere,* read)

lecture, *n.* instructional discourse; formal reproof.—*v.i.* and *t.* give, instruct by, lecture; admonish. **lecturer, lectureship,** *nn.* (L. *legere,* read)

led, see **lead.**

leden, *n.* (*Spens.*) dialect, speech. (O.E. *lǽden,* Latin)

ledge, *n.* flat projection, narrow shelf, on wall or rock; reef; (*min.*) metal-bearing stratum. **ledgy,** *a.*

ledger, *n.* chief account-book of firm, in which items from others are entered in summary form; horizontal timber in scaffolding; flat gravestone; (*Shake.*) ambassador. **l.-line,** *n.* (*angling*) fixed line; (*mus.*) short line for notes above or below stave.

lee, *n.* shelter; side (of ship etc.) away from wind.—*a.* on the lee. **l. shore, tide,** shore situated, tide running, in direction towards which wind is blowing. (O.E. *hleo*)

leech, *n.* blood-sucking worm used in bleeding; (*arch.*) physician. **leechcraft,** *n.* (O.E. *lǽce*)

leech, *n.* edge of sail at sides.

leek, *n.* herb like onion, national emblem of Wales. **eat the l.,** swallow affront. (O.E. *léac*)

lee-lang, *a.* (*Scot.*) livelong.

leer, *v.i.* and *n.* glance with sly, immodest, or malign expression. **leery,** *a.* (*sl.*) knowing, sly.

leer, *n.* (*Shake.*) complexion, face. (O.E. *hléor*)

leer, *n.* annealing-furnace for glass.

lees, *n.pl.* sediment of liquor, dregs; basest part. (L.L. *lia*)

leesome, *a.* (*Scot.*) pleasant.

leet, *n.* (*Scot.*) selected list of candidates for office. **short l.,** small list for final choice. (*lot*)

leet, *n.* an ancient English court; its jurisdiction or district.

leeward, *a.* and *adv.* on, towards, the lee.—*n.* this direction. **leewardly,** *a.* (of ship) apt to fall to leeward.

leeway, *n.* drift of ship to leeward; arrears of work.

left, see **leave.**

left, *a.* opposite to right.—*n.* left side; (in politics) advanced or radical party.—*adv.* on, towards, left. **l.-handed,** *a.* using left hand in preference to right; adapted for, made with, left hand; clumsy; two-edged (compliment); morganatic (marriage); (*arch.*) ill-omened. **l.-hander,** *n.* left-handed person or blow. **leftward,** *a.* and *adv.* **leftwards,** *adv.* (O.E.)

leg, *n.* limb used for walking; support of chair, table etc.; (*cricket*) part of field behind batsman; (*naut.*) run made on one tack; (*arch.*) bow, scrape. **a l. up,** assistance. **have the ll. of,** be faster than. **l. it,** run hard. **on one's last ll.,** near end, worn out. **pull one's l.,** (*colloq.*) hoax, fool. **shake a l.,** dance. **show a l.,** get out of bed. **l.-bail,** *n.* decamping. **l.-before-wicket,** *a.* (*abbr.* **l.b.w.**) (of batsman) out for stopping with leg ball that would have hit wicket. **l.-bye,** *n.* run made when ball touches any part of batsman except hand. **l.-**

guard, **l.-iron**, *nn.* pad, fetter, for leg. **l.-pull**, *n.* hoax. (O.N. *leggr*, limb)

legacy, *n.* gift left by will; thing handed down by predecessor. (*legate*)

legal, *a.* of, according to, authorized or created by, law; lawful. **l. tender**, money that can be used in paying a debt. **legalism**, *n.* observance of letter rather than spirit of law, red tape; doctrine of justification by works. **legalist**, *n.* **legality**, *n.* lawfulness. **legalize**, *v.t.* make legal, sanction. **legalization**, *n.* (L. *lex*, law)

legate, *n.* papal ambassador; (*arch.*) envoy. **legateship**, *n.* (L. *legatus*)

legate, *v.t.* bequeath. **legatee**, *n.* one who receives a legacy. **residuary legatee**, who receives remainder of property after all claims are discharged. (L. *legare*)

legatine, *a.* of a legate.

legation, *n.* diplomatic minister and his suite; his residence. (*legate*)

legato, *adv.* (*mus.*) smoothly. (It.)

legend, *n.* traditional story, myth; life-story of saint; inscription, motto. **legendary**, *a.* fabulous, romantic. **legendary**, *n.* collection, compiler, of legends. (L. *legere*, read)

legerdemain, *n.* sleight of hand; jugglery; trickery. (F.=light of hand)

legerity, *n.* (*Shake.*) nimbleness. (L. *levis*, light)

leger-line, same as **ledger-line.**

legged, *a.* having legs. **legger**, *n.* man who pushes barge through canal tunnel by pressing with legs on walls.

leggings, *n.pl.* leather coverings for legs. **leggy**, *a.* lanky-legged.

leghorn, *n.* (hat of) fine plaited straw; breed of fowl. (town)

legible, *a.* easily read; decipherable. **legibility**, *n.* (L. *legere*, read)

legion, *n.* body of 3,000–6,000 Roman soldiers; vast host. **British L.**, association of ex-service men. **Foreign L.**, body of foreign volunteers in French colonial army. **L. of Honour**, a French decoration. **their name is l.**, they are countless. **legionary**, *a.* and *n.* (soldier) of legion. **legioned**, *a.* (*poet.*) in legions. (L. *legio*)

legislate, *v.i.* make laws. **legislation**, *n.* law-making; laws. **legislative**, *a.* **legislator**, *n.* (*fem.* **legislatress**) lawgiver; member of legislature. **legislature**, *n.* body that makes laws of a state, parliament. (L. *lex*, law; *ferre*, bring)

legist, *n.* one versed in law.

legitimate, *a.* lawful; born in wedlock; genuine; justifiable.—*v.t.* legitimize. **l. drama**, plays of accepted merit. **legitimacy**, *n.* **legitimatize**, **legitimize**, *vv.t.* make, prove, legitimate; justify. **legitimation**, **legitimization**, *nn.* **legitimist**, *n.* supporter of hereditary title to a monarchy. **legitimism**, *n.* (L. *lex*, law)

legume, **legumen**, *n.* pod (of pea etc.). **leguminous**, *a.* pod-bearing. (L.)

lehr, same as **leer.**

lei, *n.* Hawaiian garland of flowers. (Hawaiian)

lei, see **leu.**

leiotrichous, *a.* smooth-haired. (Gk. *leios*, smooth; *thrix*, hair)

leister, *n.* pronged salmon-spear.—*v.t.* spear with one. (O.N. *lióstr*)

leisure, *n.* freedom from employment or occupation; spare time. **at l.**, unoccupied; deliberately. **at one's l.**, when one has time. **leisured**, *a.* having plenty of leisure. **leisurely**, *a.* deliberate, unhurried.—*adv.* without haste. (L. *licēre*, be allowed)

leit-motif, *leit-motiv*, *n.* (*mus.*) theme associated throughout piece with some idea, person etc. (G.)

leman, *n.* (*arch.*) sweetheart; unlawful lover or mistress. (*lief*; *man*)

lemma, *n.* (*pl.* **lemmata** or **lemmas**) assumption or auxiliary proposition used in proof; theme, argument, annotation, used as heading. (Gk.)

lemming, *n.* small Arctic burrowing mouse-like animal. (Norwegian)

lemniscate, *n.* curve like figure 8. (Gk. *lēmniskos*, fillet)

lemon, *n.* pale-yellow acid fruit; its colour; tree bearing it; (*Amer. sl.*) unattractive girl. **l.-drop**, *n.* lemon-flavoured sweet. **l.-grass**, *n.* a fragrant Indian grass. **l. kali**, an effervescing drink. **l. squash**, lemon juice and soda-water. **lemonade**, *n.* drink made or flavoured with lemon. **lemony**, *a.* (Pers. *limun*)

lemon, *n.* (us. **l. sole**, **dab**) a kind of plaice. (F. *limande*)

lemur, *n.* nocturnal monkey-like animal of Madagascar. **lemurine**, **lemuroid**, *aa.* (L. *lemures*, spirits of the dead)

lend, *v.t.* and *i.* (*past*, *p.p.* **lent**) give temporary use of, give loan; let out at interest or for hire; give, bestow. **l. an ear**, listen. **l. a hand**, help. **l. itself to**, be adapted to. **lender**, *n.* (O.E. *lǣnan*)

length, *n.* measure from end to end, extent, duration; vowel quantity; long stretch; piece of standard extent. **at l.**, in detail; at last. **at full l.**, stretched out. **go to all ll.**, use utmost effort. **lengthen**, *v.t.* and *i.* make, become, longer; make (vowel) long. **lengthways**, *adv.*, **lengthwise**, *a.* and *adv.* in the direction of the length. **lengthy**, *a.* of unusual length; prolix. (*long*)

lenient, *a.* tolerant, mild, not severe; (*arch.*) emollient. **lenience**, **leniency**, *nn.* (L. *lenis*, gentle)

lenitive, *a.* softening, mitigating.—*n.* (*med.*) drug for easing pain; mild laxative. **lenity**, *n.* clemency, mercy. (L. *lenis*, gentle)

leno, *n.* kind of cotton gauze.

lenocinium, *n.* (*Scots law*) husband's connivance at wife's adultery. (L.)

lens, *n.* glass, combination of glasses

with curved surface, used in camera, spectacles, telescope etc.; magnifying-glass; (also **crystalline l.**) transparent focusing part of eye. **lensed,** *a.* (L.=lentil, from shape)

Lent, *n.* fast of 40 days from Ash Wednesday to Easter in commemoration of Christ's fast in the wilderness. **L. lily,** daffodil. (O.E. *lencten,* spring)

lent, see **lend.**

-lent, *adj.suf.* full of, as in **pestilent.**

lentamente, adv. (*mus.*) slowly. (It.)

lenten, *a.* of, suited to, Lent; spare, meagre; sombre. (*Lent*)

lenticular, lentiform, *aa.* lens-shaped, double-convex. (*lens*)

lentigo, *n.* a skin eruption; freckle. **lentiginous,** *a.* freckly. (L.)

lentil, *n.* a leguminous plant; its edible seed. (L. *lenticula*)

lentisk, *n.* mastic tree. (L. *lentiscus*)

lentitude, *n.* sluggishness. **lentous,** *a.* viscous, tenacious. *lento, adv.* (*mus.*) slowly. (L. *lentus,* slow)

lentoid, *a.* lens-shaped. (*lens*)

Leo, *n.* the Lion, 5th sign of zodiac, which the sun enters on 23 July. **Leonids,** *n.pl.* recurrent shower of meteors that seem to radiate from it.

leonine, *a.* of, like, a lion. (L.)

Leonine verse, Leonine, medieval Latin verse with internal rhyme, e.g. 'Qui bona vina bibit Paradiso fortius ibit.'

leopard, *n.* (*fem.* **leopardess**) large spotted animal of cat kind, panther; (*heraldry*) lion passant guardant, as in arms of England. **American l.,** jaguar. **hunting l.,** cheetah. **snow l.,** ounce. **can the l. change his spots?** character persists. (*lion*; *pard*)

leper, *n.* person afflicted with leprosy; outcast. (Gk. *lepros,* scaly)

lepid, *a.* pleasant, merry. (L. *lepidus*)

Lepidoptera, *n.pl.* order of insects having four wings covered with fine scales like powder, as butterflies and moths. **lepidopterous,** *a.* (Gk. *lepis,* scale; *pteron,* wing)

leporine, *a.* of, like, a hare. (L. *lepus,* hare)

leprechaun, *n.* (*Ir.*) sprite, brownie.

leprosy, *n.* loathsome disease forming silvery scales on skin and eating away parts affected; moral corruption. **leprous,** (*Shake.*) **leperous,** *aa.* (*leper*)

lepto-, from Gk. *leptos,* fine, used in **leptocephalic,** *a.* narrow-skulled; **leptodactylic,** *a.* having slender toes; **leptology,** *n.* minute discourse.

Lesbian, *a.* of Lesbos. **L. vice, Lesbianism,** *n.* Sapphism. (*Lesbos*)

lese-majesty, *lèse-majesté,* *n.* high treason. (F.)

lesion, *n.* injury; (*med.*) morbid change in organ or tissue. (L. *laedere,* hurt)

less, *a.* (*compar.* of **little**) smaller; inferior, minor; not so much, fewer. —*n.* smaller amount or number.—*adv.* to a smaller extent.—*prep.* minus, omitting. (O.E. *læs*)

-less, *adj.suf.* without, not having, as in **hopeless**; not subject to (action of verb) as in **tireless.**

lessee, *n.* one to whom a lease is granted. **lesseeship,** *n.* (*lease*)

lessen, *v.i.* and *t.* diminish, weaken.

lesser, *a.* smaller; inferior. (*less*)

lesson, *n.* portion of Scripture read in church; thing to be learnt; part of teaching course; warning experience; lecture.—*v.t.* admonish, discipline. (L. *legere,* read)

lessor, *n.* one who grants a lease.

lest, *conj.* in order that . . . not, for fear that; (of fears) that. (O.E. *thý læs the,* whereby less)

let, *v.t.* and *i.* allow, permit, cause; grant use of for rent or hire; (*arch.*) allow (blood etc.) to escape. **l. alone,** not meddle with; not to mention. **l. down,** lower; fail at need. **l. drive,** hit, shoot, at. **l. fly,** throw, shoot; use invective. **l. go,** loose hold (of). **l. in,** admit; (*sl.*) involve in loss. **l. into,** admit; insert. **l. loose,** release. **l. off,** discharge; pardon. **l. on,** (*sl.*) reveal (secret). **l. out,** let escape; make (dress) looser; hire out; hit out. **l. slip,** unleash; miss. **l. up** (on), forbear, diminish. (O.E. *lǽtan*)

let, *v.t.*(*arch.*; *past, p.p.* **letted** or **let**) hinder, prevent.—*n.* (*arch.*) hindrance; (*lawn tennis etc.*) obstruction causing point to be replayed. (O.E. *lettan*)

-let, *n.suf.* forming diminutive, as in **lakelet.**

lethal, *a.* death-dealing, deadly. **l. chamber,** for killing animals by poisonous gas. (L. *letum,* death)

lethargy, *n.* unnatural drowsiness; apathy, want of energy. **lethargic, lethargical,** *aa.* torpid, dull. **lethargize,** *v.t.* (Gk. *lēthē,* oblivion)

Léthē, *n.* (*myth.*) river of Hades giving forgetfulness to those who drank of it; oblivion. **Lethean,** *a.* **letheon,** *n.* sulphuric ether as anaesthetic. (Gk.)

letter, *n.* alphabetical symbol, character; printing type; written message, missive; (*pl.*) literature, authorship, learning.—*v.t.* stamp, mark, letters on. **the l.,** literal meaning, precise terms (opp. to spirit). **to the l.,** literally. **l. of attorney,** appointing another to act for one. **l. of credit,** authorizing sum to be paid to bearer. **ll. of administration,** authority to administer estate of intestate. **ll. of marque,** commission authorizing privateering. **ll. patent,** from sovereign conferring title or privilege. **l.-perfect,** *a.* knowing part in play perfectly. **l.-weight,** *n.* balance for weighing letters; weight to keep papers still. (L. *lītera*)

lettered, *a.* well-read. **lettering,** *n.* making letters, titling; letters. **letterless,** *a.* knowing no literature.

letterpress, *n.* printed matter of book, as distinct from illustrations.

lettre de cachet, royal warrant of imprisonment without trial. (F.)

lettuce, *n.* garden vegetable used in salads. (L. *lactuca*)
leu, *n.* (*pl.* lei) coin and monetary unit of Rumania. (Rumanian)
leuco-, from Gk. *leukos*, white, used in **leucocyte,** *n.* white corpuscle of blood or lymph; **leucoma,** *n.* opacity of the cornea; **leucopathy,** *n.* albinism; **leucorrhoea,** *n.* mucous discharge from vagina, the whites; **leucosis,** *n.* whiteness of skin, pallor.
lev, *n.* (*pl.* **leva**) coin and monetary unit of Bulgaria. (Bulgarian)
Levant, *n.* eastern coasts of Mediterranean. **levanter,** *n.* inhabitant, strong easterly wind, of Levant. **Levantine,** *a.* and *n.* (F.=sunrise)
levant, *v.i.* abscond, decamp, esp. to avoid paying bets. **levanter,** *n.*
levator, *n.* muscle that raises. (L.L.)
levee, *n.* sovereign's reception for men only; gathering of guests; (formerly) reception held by personage on rising from bed. (F. *lever*, rise)
levee, *n.* (*Amer.*) artificial bank against river floods; quay. (F.)
level, *n.* horizontal line or surface; instrument showing horizontal; plane, standard; flat country.—*a.* horizontal, flat; on equality (with); even, equable, well-balanced.—*v.t.* and *i.* make level; bring to a level (with); lay low, raze; aim (gun). **find one's l.,** take proper place among others. **one's l. best,** utmost effort. **on the l.,** straightforward; truly. **l. crossing,** of road and railway without bridge. **l.-headed,** *a.* not liable to be carried away. **leveller,** *n.* one who levels; advocate of social equality. **levelly,** *adv.* (L. *libra*, balance)
lever, *n.* bar forming with fulcrum a mechanical aid to raise weight; crowbar for prizing.—*v.i.* and *t.* use lever (on); prize up, move, with one. **leverage,** *n.* action, power, of lever; influence. (L. *levare*, raise)
lever de rideau, curtain-raiser. (F.)
leveret, *n.* young hare. (L. *lepus*, hare)
leviable, *a.* able to be levied.
leviathan, *n.* sea monster; anything huge or formidable. (Heb. *livyathan*)
levigate, *v.t.* smooth; grind to fine impalpable powder. **levigable,** *a.* **levigation,** *n.* (L. *lēvis*, smooth)
levin, *n.* (*poet.*) lightning. (M.E. *leven*)
levitate, *v.i.* (*spiritualism*) rise and float in the air.—*v.t.* cause to do this. **levitation,** *n.* (L. *levis*, light)
levity, *n.* frivolity, thoughtlessness; disposition to trifle, flightiness; lightness of weight. (L. *levis*, light)
levulose, same as **laevulose.**
levy, *n.* collecting of tax; enrolling of troops; amount, number, levied; (*pl.*) troops.—*v.t.* raise, impose, by compulsion. **capital l.,** a tax on capital instead of income. **l. war,** make war. (L. *levare*, raise)
lewd, *a.* indecent, lustful, unchaste; (*arch.*) vile, worthless. (O.E. *lǣwede*, ignorant, lay)
lewis, *n.* appliance for lifting heavy blocks of stone.
Lewis gun, kind of machine-gun. (*Lewis*, inventor)
lewisite, *n.* blistering liquid got from arsenic and acetylene, used in chemical warfare. (W. L. *Lewis*)
lewisite, *n.* mineral containing calcium, titanium, and antimony. (W. J. *Lewis*)
lexicon, *n.* dictionary; word-making game. **lexical,** *a.* of words; of a lexicon. **lexicographer,** *n.* compiler of lexicon. **lexicography,** *n.* **lexicographical,** *a.* (Gk. *lexis*, word)
lexigraphy, *n.* system of writing in which each character represents a word. (Gk. *lexis*, word; *graphein*, write)
lex talionis, law of retaliation, an eye for an eye. (L.)
Leyden jar, kind of electrical condenser. (*Leyden* in Holland)
li, *n.* Chinese mile (about 633 yds.); Chinese weight (about $\frac{4}{5}$ gr.). (Chin.)
liable, *a.* legally bound, responsible (for); subject (to); apt (to). **liability,** *n.* state of being liable, obligation; (*pl.*) debts opp. to assets).
liaison, *n.* illicit amour; (*gram.*) sounding of mute final consonant before following vowel; (*military*) connection, touch. **l. officer,** acting as go-between for troops under different commands. (L. *ligare*, bind)
liana, liane, *n.* climbing plant of tropical forests. (F.)
liar, *n.* one who lies. (*lie*)
liart, *a.* (*Scot.*) grey. (O.F. *liard*)
Lias, *n.* (*geol.*) a blue limestone, lowest strata of Jurassic series. **Liassic,** *a.* (O.F. *liois*)
libation, *n.* drink-offering; pouring of one to a god; (*joc.*) drinking. **libatory,** *a.* (L. *libatio*)
libbard, *n.* (*Spens.*) leopard.
libel, *n.* false defamatory statement or representation; (*law*) published statement damaging to person's reputation; (*civil law*) plaintiff's written declaration.—*v.t.* defame falsely, misrepresent; (*law*) publish libel against, bring suit against. **libeller, libellist,** *nn.* **libellous,** *a.* defamatory. (L. *libellus*, pamphlet)
liberal, *a.* generous; ample; open-minded, candid; (of education) fit for a gentleman, general; (of political party) favouring democratic reforms. —*n.* member of Liberal Party. **Liberalism,** *n.* Liberal political principles. **liberality,** *n.* generosity; breadth of mind. **liberalize,** *v.t.* free from narrowness. **liberalization,** *n.* (L. *līber*, free)
liberate, *v.t.* set free, release. **liberation, liberator,** *nn.* **liberationism,** *n.* policy of Church disestablishment. (L. *līber*, free)

libertarian, *a.* and *n.* (person) believing in free will. **libertarianism,** *n.*

liberticide, *n.* destroyer of liberty. (L. *caedere*, kill)

libertine, *n.* dissolute person; freethinker.—*a.* licentious; antinomian. **libertinage, libertinism,** *nn.* conduct, views, of libertine. (*liberty*)

liberty, *n.* freedom, being free; right or power to do as one pleases; piece of presumption; (*pl.*) privileges, immunities. **at l.,** free; disengaged. **take ll.,** be unduly familiar (with). **l. of conscience,** religious liberty. **l. hall,** house where guests do as they please. **l.-man,** *n.* sailor ashore on leave. (L. *līber*, free)

libido, *n.* (*psycho-anal.*) life-force, will to live; sexual urge. **libidinous,** *a.* lustful. (L.=lust)

Libra, *n.* the Scales, 7th sign of zodiac, which the sun enters on 23 Sept.; (*abbr.* **lb.**) pound weight; (*abbr.* **£**) pound sterling. (L.)

library, *n.* room, building, where books are kept; collection of books; publisher's uniform series of books. **librarian,** *n.* keeper of library. **librarianship,** *n.* (L. *līber*, book)

librate, *v.i.* and *t.* balance, poise; quiver. **libration,** *n.* (*libra*)

libretto, *n.* (*pl.* **libretti, librettos**) words of opera or musical play. **librettist,** *n.* writer of libretto. (It.)

lice, see **louse.**

licence, *n.* permission; document granting this, permit; excess, abuse, of freedom. **poetic l.,** poet's irregularities of grammar, metre etc. **special l.,** permitting marriage without banns. **license, licence,** *v.t.* grant permit to, authorize. **licensed victualler,** innkeeper licensed to sell alcohol. **licensee,** *n.* holder of licence. **licenser,** *n.* official granting licence. (L. *licēre*, be lawful)

licentiate, *n.* holder of certificate of competence in profession; degree between bachelor and doctor. (*licence*)

licentious, *a.* dissolute, immoral; using poetic licence. (*licence*)

lich, lych, *n.* (*obs.*) corpse. **l.-gate,** *n.* roofed churchyard gate, where coffin may be stood on **l.-stone,** *n.* **l.-house,** *n.* mortuary. **l.-owl,** *n.* screech-owl. (O.E. *līc*)

lichen, *n.* small fungoid plant forming crust on rocks, trees etc. **lichened,** *a.* **lichenology,** *n.* (Gk. *leichen*)

licit, *a.* lawful, permitted. (L. *licēre*, be lawful)

lick, *v.t.* and *i.* pass tongue over; take up by tongue; play lightly over; (*sl.*) beat.—*n.* act of licking; small quantity; sharp blow; salt-lick; (*sl.*) pace. **l. into shape,** mould, make efficient. **l. the dust,** be humbled or killed. (O.E. *liccian*)

lickerish, *a.* dainty about food; greedy; lustful. (form of *lecherous*)

lickety-split, *adv.* (*Amer.*) at full speed.

licking, *n.* (*sl.*) beating. **lickpenny,** *n.* (*Scot.*) miser. **lickspittle,** *n.* servile flatterer, toady. (*lick*)

licorice, same as **liquorice.**

lictor, *n.* officer attending Roman magistrate, bearing fasces. (L.)

lid, *n.* movable cover closing aperture; eyelid; operculum; (*sl.*) hat. **put the l. on,** (*sl.*) put finishing touch to. **lidded,** *a.* (O.E. *hlid*)

lido, *n.* bathing-beach. (place)

lie, *n.* falsehood, untruth; false belief; imposture.—*v.i.* (*pres.part.* **lying**) tell lie, speak falsely; (of things) deceive. **give the l. to,** accuse of lying; belie. **l. like a gas-meter,** lie freely. **white l.,** told for good purpose. (O.E. *lyge*)

lie, *v.i.* (*past* **lay**; *p.p.* **lain,** *arch.* **lien**; *pres.part.* **lying**) be horizontal, recline, rest; be situated, remain; lodge, be encamped; consist; (*law*, of action) be sustainable.—*n.* way thing lies, position. **l. by,** be unused. **l. in,** be in childbed. **l. in wait,** be in ambush. **l. low,** (*sl.*) keep out of the way. **l. over,** be deferred. **l. up,** take to one's bed; (of ship) go into dock. **l.-abed,** *n.* late riser. **lying-in hospital,** for women in childbed. **take it lying down,** submit tamely. (O.E. *licgan*)

lied, *n.* (*pl. lieder*) German song or ballad. (G.)

lief, *a.* (*arch.*) loved, dear.—*adv.* willingly. (O.E. *léof*)

liege, *n.* sovereign or subject by feudal tenure; faithful.—*n.* lord, superior; vassal, subject. **l. lord, liegeman,** *nn.* liege. (O.F. *lige*)

lien, *n.* right to hold another's property till debt on it is paid. (F.)

lien, see **lie.**

lierne, *n.* (*archit.*) cross-rib or branch-rib in vaulting. (F.)

lieu, *n.* **in l.,** instead, in place (of). (L. *locus*, place)

lieutenant, *n.* substitute or subordinate commander; rank below commander (navy), below captain (army). **l.-general,** *n.* rank below general. **lieutenancy,** *n.* (*lieu*; *tenant*)

life, *n.* (*pl.* **lives**) vital principle; animate existence; living beings; vigour, vivacity; individual's experiences, biography; way of living; human affairs. **bring, come, to l.,** recover from faint. **good, bad, l.,** person considered likely, unlikely, to live long. **high l.,** upper classes. **to the l.,** accurately. **l.-assurance, l.-insurance,** *nn.* insurance on person's life. **L. Guards,** regiment of household cavalry. **l.-guard,** *n.* bodyguard. **l. interest,** share for life (in). **l.-line,** *n.* line used in life-saving or to hold on by in rough weather; diver's signalling cord. **l.-preserver,** *n.* lifebelt; bludgeon. **l.-spring,** *n.* source of life. **l.-work,** *n.* task to which life is devoted. (O.E. *līf*)

lifebelt, *n.* cork or inflated belt for keeping person afloat.

lifeblood, *n.* blood necessary to life; what gives strength.
lifeboat, *n.* strong, buoyant boat for saving lives in cases of shipwreck.
lifebuoy, *n.* buoyant ring to support person who has fallen into water.
lifeless, *a.* dead; inert, spiritless.
lifelike, *a.* realistic, vivid.
lifelong, *a.* lasting through life.
lifer, *n.* (*sl.*) convict condemned to imprisonment for life.
lifetime, *n.* duration of a life.
lift, *v.t.* and *i.* raise, take up, elevate; steal, plagiarize; (of cloud) disperse; (*Amer.*) take up (mortgage).—*n.* lifting; lifting-machine, elevator. **give l. to,** convey in vehicle; help. **l. hand against,** strike; oppose. **l. up voice,** cry aloud. (O.N. *lypta*)
lift, *n.* (*Scot.*) sky, air. (O.E. *lyft*)
lig, ligge, *v.i.* (*Spens.*) lie. (*lie*)
ligament, *n.* (*arch.*) tie; (*anat.*) membrane connecting movable bones. **ligamental, ligamentary, ligamentous,** *aa.* (L. *ligare,* bind)
ligan, *n.* (*law*) goods sunk in the sea with a buoy attached. (*ligate*)
ligate, *v.t.* (*med.*) tie up. **ligation,** *n.*
ligature, *n.* bandage; (*med.*) cord used to tie up artery etc.; (*mus.*) line connecting notes, slur; (*print.*) two or more letters joined, as *æ, ffl.*—*v.t.* bind, connect, with ligature. (L. *ligare,* bind)
light, *n.* agent causing visibility; source of this, lamp, window, etc.; source of fire, match; vision, enlightenment; aspect; light part of picture; (in acrostic) clue.—*a.* bright; (of colour) pale, not dark.—*v.t.* and *i.* (*past, p.p.* **lighted** or **lit**) give light to, brighten; kindle, go on fire. **ancient ll.,** acquired right of windows being unobstructed. **bring, come, to l.,** reveal, be revealed. **l. of nature,** inborn intelligence. **l. of one's countenance,** favour. **l. of one's eyes,** adored one. **l. up,** light pipe or lamp. **lit up,** (*Amer. sl.*) drunk. **l. year,** (*astron.*) distance light travels in a year, about 6 million million miles. **northern ll.,** aurora borealis. **see the l.,** come into view, be born; be converted. (O.E. *léoht*)
light, *a.* of little weight, not heavy; of short weight; intended for small load; unladen; easy to perform, digest etc.; trifling; gentle; agile; gay, amusing; giddy; wanton; (of soil) loose.—*adv.* lightly, cheaply.—*v.i.* (*past, p.p.* **lit** or **lighted**) come by chance (upon); alight, settle. **make l. of,** treat as of little consequence. **l.-armed,** *a.* with light equipment. **l. engine,** with no train. **l.-fingered,** *a.* thievish. **l.-headed,** *a.* delirious, giddy. **l.-hearted,** *a.* untroubled, gay. **l. heavy,** (*boxing*) 11 st. 6 lb. to 12 st. 7 lb. **l. horse, l. infantry,** light-armed soldiers. **l.-minded,** *a.* flighty, irresponsible. **l.-o'-love,** *n.* wanton. **l. railway,** for light traffic. (O.E. *léoht*)
lighten, *v.t.* and *i.* shed light on, illuminate; make, become, bright; emit lightning; flash. (*light*)
lighten, *v.t.* and *i.* make, grow, lighter; relieve, mitigate. (*light*)
lighter, *n.* boat, barge, for shifting goods between ship and land.—*v.t.* remove in lighter. **lighterage,** *n.* unloading or price paid for it.
lighthouse, *n.* tower with beacon light for guiding ships or aircraft. **lightkeeper,** *n.* keeper of one.
lightly, *adv.* in a light manner; carelessly; (*Shake.*) commonly.—*v.t.* (*Scot.*) undervalue, slight.
lightning, *n.* flash, discharge, of electricity from cloud to cloud or earth. **forked l.,** in zigzag flashes. **sheet l.,** of diffused brightness. **summer l.,** without thunder. **like l.,** with great speed. **l.-conductor, l.-rod,** *nn.* rod fixed to building to give lightning harmless passage. **l. strike,** strike of workers without notice given. (=lightening)
lights, *n.pl.* lungs of animal as food. (from their lightness)
lightship, *n.* anchored ship with beacon light.
lightsome, *a.* light, gay, lively; graceful, nimble.
lightsome, *a.* luminous, bright.
lightweight, *n.* and *a.* (person) below average weight; (*boxing*) 9 st. to 9 st. 9 lb.
lign-aloes, *n.* aloes-wood; the drug aloes. (L.L. *lignum aloes*)
ligneous, *a.* of, like, wood; (of plant) having wood, woody. **ligniferous,** *a.* wood-producing. **ligniform,** *a.* like wood. **lignify,** *v.t.* and *i.* make, become, wood or woody. **lignification,** *n.* **lignite,** *n.* coal of woody texture, brown coal. **lignum vitae,** guaiacum, a tropical tree; its hard wood. (L. *lignum,* wood)
ligulate, *a.* (*bot.*) strap-shaped. (L. *ligula,* strap)
like, *a.* similar, resembling; characteristic of; in condition or mood for.—*adv.* in the same manner; probably; (*vulg.*) so to speak.—*prep.* in the same manner or degree as.—*n.* counterpart, equal; (*pl.*) preferences.—*v.t.* and *i.* find agreeable, enjoy; (*arch.*) be pleasing to; (*Shake.*) compare. **and the l.,** etcetera. **had l.** (*arch.*) was likely (to). **l. anything, blazes, fun, mad,** (*colloq.*) very vigorously. **l. a shot,** (*colloq.*) readily; at once. **such l.,** others of that kind. **l.-minded,** *a.* agreeing in opinions. **likable, likeable,** *a.* (O.E. *gelic*)
-like, *adj.suf.* like, as in **godlike.**
likely, *a.* probable, to be expected; liable; promising, apt-looking.—*adv.* probably. **likelihood,** *n.*
liken, *v.t.* compare; make like to.

likeness, *n.* resemblance; semblance; portrait.

likewise, *conj.* also, too.—*adv.* (*arch.*) similarly. (*in like wise*)

likin, *n.* provincial transit duty in China. (Chin.)

liking, *n.* taste, regard (for).

lil, *Amer. dial.* for little.

lilac, *n.* a garden shrub, its fragrant flowers or their pale pinkish-violet colour.—*a.* of this colour. (Pers. *nil*, blue)

liliaceous, *a.* of the lily kind.

lill, *v.i.* (*Spens.*) loll.

lilt, *v.t.* and *i.* sing in lively rhythm; move lightly.—*n.* marked rhythm, swing; song with this.

Lillibullero, Lilliburlero, *n.* a popular 17th-cent. song. (refrain)

Lilliputian, *a.* and *n.* midget, pygmy. (*Lilliput* in 'Gulliver's Travels')

lily, *n.* bulbous plant; its large fragrant flower; fleur-de-lis.—*a.* white, pallid; pure. **l. of the valley**, with small white bell-shaped flowers. **madonna l.**, common white kind. **l.-livered**, *a.* cowardly. **l.-white, lilied**, *aa.* (L. *lilium*)

limaceous, *a.* of the slug kind. **limaciform**, *a.* (L. *limax*, slug)

limation, *n.* filing, polishing. (L. *lima*, file)

limb, *n.* leg, arm, wing; projecting part, branch; mischievous child.—*v.t.* disable; dismember. **l. of Satan**, scamp. **l. of the law**, policeman, lawyer. (O.E. *lim*)

limb, *n.* (*astron.*) edge of sun or moon; edge of sextant etc. **limbate**, *a.* (*bot.*) bordered with different colour. (L. *limbus*, hem)

limbec, same as **alembic**.

limber, *n.* wheels and shaft forming detachable front of gun-carriage.—*v.t.* attach (gun) to limber.

limber, *a.* flexible; lithe, agile.

limber, *n.* drainage-hole in ship's flooring above keelson.

limbo, *n.* region on border of hell for those who had no opportunity to accept Christianity, such as good people who lived before Christ and unbaptized infants; prison; place of forgotten or unwanted things. (*limb*)

lime, *n.* white caustic earth got by burning limestone and used for mortar, quicklime; sticky substance, bird-lime.—*v.t.* smear, catch, with bird-lime; cement, manure, with lime. **slaked l.**, lime treated with water. **l.-twig**, *n.* one smeared with bird-lime. **limekiln**, *n.* furnace for making lime. **limelight**, *n.* intense white light got by heating lime; glare of publicity. **limestone**, *n.* kinds of rock. (O.E. *lim*)

lime, *n.* small acid fruit like lemon. **l.-juice**, *n.* used as antiscorbutic. **l.-juicer, limey**, *nn.* (*Amer. sl.*) British sailor. (Pers. *limun*)

lime, *n.* the linden, a tree. (O.E. *lind*).

limen, *n.* (*psychology*) point where effect of stimulus is just discernible. **liminal**, *a.* (L.=threshold)

limerick, *n.* nonsensical or witty five-lined stanza of this form:

There was an old man of the Cape,
Who made himself garments of crêpe.
When asked, 'Do they tear?'
He replied, 'Here and there,
But they're perfectly splendid for shape!'

lime-wort, *n.* brooklime, kind of speedwell. (O.E. *hleomoc*)

limey, see **lime**.

limy, *a.* of, like, lime; sticky.

limit, *n.* boundary; utmost extent; restriction.—*v.t.* set bounds to; restrain. **the l.**, the last straw. **l. man**, competitor with maximum handicap. **limitarian**, *n.* holder of doctrine that only part of mankind is to be saved. **limitary, limitative**, *aa.* restrictive. **limitation**, *n.* restriction; disability; (*law*) specified period beyond which action cannot be brought. **limited**, *a.* scanty, restricted. **limited, limited-liability, company**, in which shareholders' liability is limited in proportion to their holdings. **limited monarchy**, with constitutional restrictions. **limitless**, *a.* boundless, immense. (L. *limes*)

limitrope, *a.* bordering, on frontier. (L. *limes*, limit. Gk. *trephein*, feed)

limmer, *n.* (*Scot.*) mongrel; hussy; idler. (O.F. *liem*, leash)

limn, *v.t.* paint, draw; portray. **limner**, *n.* (L. *illuminare*, illuminate)

limnology, *n.* science of pond life. (Gk. *limnē*, lake; *legein*, speak)

limousine, *n.* a closed type of motor-car. (*Limoges* in France)

limp, *v.i.* walk lamely, halt.—*n.* lame gait. **limpingly**, *adv.*

limp, *a.* without stiffness, pliant, flaccid; lacking energy.

limpet, *n.* tent-shaped shell-fish that sticks tightly to rocks. (O.E. *lempedu*, lamprey)

limpid, *a.* clear, pellucid, transparent. **limpidity**, *n.* (L. *limpidus*)

limpkin, *n.* kinds of bird between cranes and rails. (*limp*)

limp-wort, same as **lime-wort**.

lin, *v.i.* and *t.* (*Spens.*) cease, desist. (O.E. *linnan*)

linage, *n.* number of lines in printed matter; payment by this. (*line*)

linament, *n.* tent for a wound; lint. (L. *linum*, flax)

linch, *n.* (*dial.*) ridge of land, ledge; cliff. **linchet**, *n.* terrace, ridge, on face of chalk down. (O.E. *hlinc*)

linchpin, *n.* pin through axle-end to keep wheel on. (O.E. *lynis*, axle)

Lincoln, *n.* **L. green**, bright green cloth made at Lincoln; its colour.

lincture, *n.* medicine to be sucked up. (L. *lingere*, lick)

linden, *n.* tree with heart-shaped leaves and fragrant yellow flowers, lime. (O.E. *lind*)

line, *n.* cord, wire; long narrow mark, wrinkle; outline, limit; row of soldiers or words, verse, short letter; series of ships, generations etc.; track, course; province, class; measure of $\frac{1}{12}$ in.; (*pl.*) marriage certificate; actor's part; imposition; row of field works or tents; (*Amer.*) reins. **the L.,** equator; regular numbered regiments.—*v.t.* and *i.* mark with lines; form line (along). **come into l.,** conform. **draw the l.,** set limit. **hard ll.,** undeserved bad luck. **l. of battle,** battle formation. **l.-of-battle ship,** (*arch.*) one of 74 guns or more. **l. of beauty,** like elongated S. **l. of fire,** path of shot. **l. in,** fill in details of (plan). **l. up,** form (into) a line. **on the l.,** (of picture) at eye-level. **l.-drawing,** *n.* drawing in ink or pencil. **l.-engraving,** *n.* with incised lines. (L. *linea*)

line, *n.* flax.—*v.t.* cover inside of; fill; (of dog) impregnate; (*Shake.*) reinforce. (O.E. *lin*)

lineage, *n.* lineal descent, ancestry.

lineal, *a.* in direct line of descent; linear.

lineament, *n.* (us. *pl.*) feature, characteristic, esp. of face. (*line*)

linear, *a.* of, in, lines; (*math.*) involving only one dimension.

lineate, *a.* marked with lines. **lineation,** *n.* drawing, arrangement, of lines. (L. *linea*, line)

linen, *n.* cloth made of flax; sheets, table-cloths etc.—*a.* of flax or linen. **wash dirty l. in public,** reveal domestic quarrels. **l.-draper,** *n.* dealer in linen. (O.E.)

linesman, *n.* soldier of line regiment; umpire's assistant watching line.

liner, *n.* large ship of passenger line; large passenger aeroplane; removable lining for gun etc.

ling, *n.* heather. (O.N. *lyng*)

ling, *n.* slender sea-fish like cod.

-ling, *n.suf.* little, as in **duckling;** petty, as in **princeling.**

lingam, linga, *n.* the phallus in Hindu mythology. (Sanskr.)

linger, *v.i.* and *t.* be slow to depart, delay, tarry; be protracted; (*Shake.*) prolong. **lingerer,** *n.* (*long*)

lingerie, *n.* linen goods, esp. women's underwear. (F.)

lingo, *n.* (*pl.* **lingoes**) (us. contemptuous) language, speech; jargon. **lingua franca,** mixed dialect used between Europeans and Arabs, Moors etc.; international dialect. (L. *lingua*, tongue).

lingual, *a.* of, formed by, the tongue. —*n.* lingual letter, e.g. *l.* **lingualize,** *v.t.* **linguiform,** *a.* tongue-shaped. (L. *lingua*, tongue)

linguist, *n.* person skilled in foreign languages. **linguistic,** *a.* of languages or their study.—*n.pl.* science of languages. (*lingual*)

linguodental, *a.* (of sounds) made with tongue and teeth.

lingy, *a.* heathery. (*ling*)

linhay, *n.* (*dial.*) farm-shed open in front.

liniment, *n.* liquid for rubbing into skin, embrocation. (L. *linire*, smear)

lining, *n.* inside covering.

link, *n.* single ring of chain, loop; thing that connects, member of series; $\frac{1}{100}$ part of surveying chain, 7·92 in.—*v.t.* and *i.* connect, join; intertwine. **missing l.,** between ape and man. **linkage,** *n.* (O.N.)

link, *n.* torch of tow and pitch. **l.-boy, l.-man,** *nn.* bearer of link.

link, *v.i.* (*Scot.*) go quickly.

links, *n.pl.* sandy stretch of ground near sea; golf-course. (O.E. *hlinc*)

linn, *n.* waterfall; pool below this; ravine. (Gael. *linne*)

linnet, *n.* small brown or grey songbird. (F. *lin*, flax, its food)

linney, linny, same as **linhay.**

linocut, *n.* design cut in relief on block of linoleum; print from this.

linoleum, *n.* floorcloth with surface of hardened linseed oil. so **lino,** *n.* **linoleumed,** *a.* (L. *linum*, flax; *oleum*, oil)

linotype, *n.* type-setting machine casting lines in one piece. (=line of type)

linsang, *n.* striped civet-cat of Borneo and Java. (Javanese)

linseed, *n.* seed of flax. **l.-cake,** *n.* cake made of this with l. oil pressed out. (O.E. *lin*, flax)

linsey-woolsey, *n.* fabric of wool woven with cotton; (*Shake.*) medley, gibberish. (*line*; *wool*)

linstock, *n.* staff holding match to fire old cannon. (Du. *lont*, match)

lint, *n.* linen with fluffy surface used for dressing wounds. (*line*)

lintel, *n.* horizontal timber or stone over door or window. **lintelled,** *a.* (O.F.=threshold)

lintie, lintwhite, same as **linnet.**

lion, *n.* (*fem.* **lioness**) large tawny animal of cat kind, noted for courage; celebrity; (*astron.*) Leo, 5th sign of zodiac; (*pl.*) sights. **British L.,** Britain personified. **l.'s mouth,** dangerous position. **l.'s share,** largest part. **l.-hearted,** *a.* very brave. **lionesque, lionlike,** *aa.* **lionet,** *n.* young lion. **lionize,** *v.t.* and *i.* treat as celebrity; see, show, sights (of). (Gk. *leōn*)

lip, *n.* fold of skin round mouth; edge, brim; pouring-channel; (*sl.*) insolence.—*v.t.* touch with lip; just touch; murmur. **hang on one's ll.,** listen admiringly to. **make a l.,** (*Shake.*) make a face. **l.-reading,** *n.* understanding speech from movements of lips (used by deaf). **l.-salve,** *n.* ointment for sore lips;

flattery. **l.-service,** *n.* insincere devotion. **lipped,** *a.* having lips. **lipstick,** *n.* cosmetic stick for reddening lips. (O.E. *lippa*)

lip(o)-, from Gk. *lipos,* fat, used in **lipaemia,** *n.* excessive fat in blood; **lipoma,** *n.* (*pl.* **lipomata**) tumour of fatty tissue; **lipomatosis,** *n.* excessive growth of fatty tissue.

lipogram, *n.* composition avoiding all words containing a given letter. **lipography,** *n.* haplography. (Gk. *leipein,* omit; *graphein,* write)

lippen, *v.i.* (*Scot.*) trust (to); rely (on).

lipper, *n.* (*naut.*) slight roughness of sea.

lippitude, *n.* soreness of eyes. (L. *lippus,* blear-eyed)

liquate, *v.t.* melt (metals) to separate or purify them. **liquation,** *n.* (L. *liquare*)

liquefy, *v.t.* amd *i.* make, become, liquid. **liquefacient, liquefactive,** *aa.* **liquefaction, liquefier,** *nn.* **liquescent,** *a.* becoming liquid.

liqueur, *n.* delicately flavoured alcoholic drink, cordial. **l.-glass,** *n.* very small glass for this. (F.)

liquid, *a.* fluid; watery, translucent, clear, unstable; (of sound) flowing, not grating; (of securities) easily convertible into cash.—*n.* fluid; letter *l, r, m,* or *n.* **liquidity,** *n.* **liquidize,** *v.t.* (*liquor*)

liquidate, *v.t.* settle (account); wind up (company); (*colloq.*) suppress, stamp out. **liquidation, liquidator,** *nn.* **go into liquidation,** become bankrupt. (*liquid*)

liquor, *n.* liquid; strong drink.—*v.t.* steep in water; rub with oil. **in l.,** partly drunk. **l. up,** have drink. **liquorish,** *a.* fond of liquor; lickerish. (L.)

liquorice, *n.* black substance used as sweetmeat or in medicine; plant whose root yields this. (Gk. *glukus,* sweet; *rhiza,* root)

lira, *n.* (*pl.* lire) a silver coin, monetary unit of Italy. (It.)

lirk, *n.* (*Scot.*) fold.—*v.i.* hang in creases.

lisp, *v.i.* and *t.* speak, say, giving *s* and *z* sound of *th*; (of child) speak imperfectly.—*n.* such utterance. (O.E. *wlisp,* stammering)

lissom, lissome, *a.* supple, lithe. (=lithesome)

lissotrichous, *a.* smooth-haired. (Gk. *lissos,* smooth; *thrix,* hair)

list, *n.* selvage, border or strip of cloth; catalogue, roll; (*pl.*) tilting ground; scene of contest.—*v.t.* and *i.* edge with strips of cloth; place on list; enlist. (O.E.)

list, *v.i.* (of ship) lean over to one side, heel.—*n.* such inclination.

list, *v.i.* (*past* **list** or **listed**) (*arch.*) desire, choose; be pleasing to. (O.E. *lystan*)

list, *v.i.* (*arch.*) listen. (O.E. *hlystan*)

listen, *v.i.* try to hear, hearken; attend (to advice etc.). **l. in,** tap telephone message; listen to wireless. **listener,** *n.* (*list*)

listerine, *n.* an antiseptic. **listerism,** *n.* antiseptic method introduced by Lord Lister. **listerize,** *v.t.* treat (wound) thus. (name)

listless, *a.* languid, indifferent, without energy. (*lust*)

lit, see **light.**

litany, *n.* series of short prayers, with responses from the congregation. (Gk. *litē,* prayer)

litchi, *n.* a Chinese tree; its fruit. (Chin, *li-chi*)

literacy, *n.* ability to read and write. (*literate*)

literae humaniores, Oxford course for honours degree in classics, 'Greats.' (L.=polite letters)

literal, *a.* of, expressed by, letters; (of meaning) giving words their exact sense, not figurative; (of translation) word for word; (of person) matter-of-fact.—*n.* misprint. **literalism,** *n.* adherence to the letter. **literalist, literality,** *nn.* **literalize,** *v.t.* take in literal sense. **literally,** *adv.* in exact sense of the word. (L. *lītera,* letter)

literary, *a.* of, concerned with, literature or writers; (of word) not colloquial. **literarily,** *adv.*

literate, *a.* and *n.* (person) able to read and write; one admitted to holy orders without university degree. (L. *līteratus,* learned)

literati, *n.pl.* men of letters. **literatim,** *adv.* letter for letter; with exact correspondence. **literator,** *n.* literary man. (L.)

literature, *n.* books, writings, collectively; artistic or imaginative writing; writing profession; (*arch.*) literary culture; (*colloq.*) printed matter. (L. *lītera,* letter)

lith, *n.* joint, segment. (O.E.)

litharge, *n.* protoxide of lead. (Gk. *lithos,* stone; *arguros,* silver)

lithe, *a.* supple, pliant. **lithesome,** *a.* lissom, lithe. (O.E.=soft)

lithe, *v.i.* (*arch.*) listen.

lither, *a.* (*Shake.*) yielding; (*obs.*) worthless. (O.E. *lýthre,* evil)

lithia, *n.* oxide of lithium.

lithic, *a.* (*chem.*) of lithium.

lithic, *a.* of the stone; of stone. (Gk. *lithos,* stone)

lithium, *n.* an element, lightest of the metals. (Gk. *lithos,* stone)

lith(o)-, from Gk. *lithos,* stone, used in **lithocarp,** *n.* fossil fruit; **lithodome,** *n.* shellfish that bores in rocks; **lithofracteur,** *n.* a blasting explosive; **lithogenous,** *a.* forming stone; **lithoglyph,** *n.* a carving on stone or gem; **lithography,** *n.* process of drawing on stone and printing impressions from it, hence **lithograph,** *n.* and *v.t.* print from stone, **lithographer,** *n.,* **lithographic,** *a.*; **lithoid,** *a.* stone-like; **litholatry,** *n.* worship of stones;

lithology, *n.* science of rocks and their structure, hence **lithological,** *a.*; **lithontriptic,** *a.* and *n.* (drug) that breaks up stone in bladder; **lithophyl,** *n.* fossil leaf; **lithophyte,** *n.* stony polyp, plant growing on rock; **lithosphere,** *n.* solid part of earth, opp. to atmosphere; **lithotomy,** *n.* operation of cutting for stone in bladder, hence **lithotomic, lithotomical,** *aa.*, **lithotomist,** *n.*, **lithotomize,** *v.t.*; **lithotrity,** *n.* operation of crushing stone in bladder, hence **lithotritist,** *n.*, **lithotritize,** *v.t.*; **lithotype,** *n.* a kind of stereotype plate or print from it.

litigate, *v.i.* and *t.* go to law; contest at law. **litigable,** *a.* **litigant,** *a.* and *n.* party to lawsuit. **litigation,** *n.* **litigious,** *a.* fond of going to law, contentious; disputable at law; of lawsuits. (L. *lis*, strife; *agere*, carry on)

litmus, *n.* blue dye got from lichens, turned red by acid and restored to blue by alkali. **l.-paper,** *n.* stained with litmus, used in chemical testing. (Du. *lak*, lac; *moes*, pulp)

litotēs, *n.* rhetorical understatement, meiosis, e.g. 'a citizen of no mean city.' (Gk. *litos*, plain)

litre, *n.* unit of capacity in metric system, =about 1¾ pints. (F.)

litter, *n.* untidy refuse, odds and ends; straw etc. as bedding; portable curtained couch; stretcher for wounded; young brought forth at a birth.—*v.t.* and *i.* make untidy; provide with litter; bring forth (young). **littery,** *a.* covered with litter, untidy. (L. *lectus*, bed)

litterae, same as *literae*.

littérateur, *n.* literary man. (F.)

little, *a.* (*compar.* **less,** *superl.* **least**) small; short; unimportant; paltry, mean. — *n.* small amount. — *adv.* slightly. **a l.,** somewhat. **in l.,** on a small scale. **L. Bear,** a group of stars. **l. by little,** gradually. **L.-Englander,** *n.* advocate of loose relations between Britain and her colonies. **l. Mary,** (*colloq.*) stomach. **l. people,** fairies. (O.E. *lýtel*)

littoral, *a.* of, on, the shore.—*n.* coastal region. (L. *litus*, shore)

liturgy, *n.* form of public worship, established ritual of church. **liturgical,** *a.* **liturgics,** *n.pl.* science of liturgies. **liturgist,** *n.* (Gk. *leōs*, people; *ergon*, work)

livable, *a.* fit to live in or with; worth living.

live, *v.i.* and *t.* have life; survive; pass (one's life), dwell; subsist.—*a.* living; actual; not obsolete; (of coal) glowing; (of wire) charged with electricity; (*Amer.*) energetic. **l. down,** live so that (scandal etc.) is forgotten. **l. well,** feed luxuriously. **l. wire,** forceful person. **l.-bait,** *n.* living fish or worm as bait. **l.-stock,** *n.* domestic animals. (O.E. *libban*)

livelihood, *n.* means of living; support. (O.E. *líf*, life; *lád*, course)

livelong, *a.* whole length of.

lively, *a.* full of life, active, vivid; lifelike, realistic; (of colour) gay; (*joc.*) exciting.

liven, *v.t.* and *i.* brighten up.

liver, *n.* one who lives in a certain way, as **good, evil, l.**

liver, *n.* large organ secreting bile and purifying blood; disordered state of this.—*a.* reddish-brown. **l. wing,** cooked fowl's right wing. **white-livered,** *a.* cowardly. **liverish, livery,** *aa.* with disordered liver; irritable. **liverwort,** *n.* a cryptogamous plant. (O.E. *lifer*)

Liverpudlian, *a.* and *n.* (citizen) of Liverpool.

livery, *n.* allowance of food for horses; distinctive dress of city company or person's servants; (*Amer.*) livery stables. **at l.,** (of horse) looked after for owner at fixed charge. **l. stable,** where horses are kept at livery or let out on hire. **liveryman,** *n.* member of livery company or keeper of livery stables. (L. *liberare*, free)

livid, *a.* of leaden colour; discoloured, as by bruise. **lividity,** *n.* (L. *lividus*)

livraison, *n.* an instalment of a book published in parts. (F.)

livre, *n.* old French coin, =about a franc. (L. *libra*)

lixiviate, *v.t.* separate soluble from insoluble by means of water or other solvents. **lixiviation,** *n.* (L. *lixivium*, lye)

lizard, *n.* kinds of four-footed scaly reptiles; fancy variety of canary. (L. *lacertus*)

llama, *n.* S. American camel-like animal without hump; its wool or material made from it. (Sp.)

llano, *n.* vast level S. American plain or steppe. **llanero,** *n.* inhabitant of this. (L. *planus*, plain)

Lloyd's, *n.* London corporation dealing with marine insurance etc. **L. register,** annual classified list of ships.

lo, *int.* (*arch.*) look! behold! (O.E. *lá* and M.E. *lo*)

loach, *n.* small river-fish. (F. *loche*)

load, *n.* burden, weight; freight; amount that cart etc. can carry; amount of electrical energy drawn from mains; (*pl.*, *colloq.*) plenty, lots. —*v.t.* and *i.* put load on or into; take load aboard; charge (gun); weight down, weight; overwhelm (with praise etc.); (*insurance*) add extra charge or loading to premium. **loaded dice,** weighted so as to fall with certain face up. **loadline,** *n.* ship's water-line when laden, Plimsoll mark. (O.E. *lád*, way)

loadstone, lodestone, *n.* magnetic oxide of iron; magnet. **loadstar,** see **lodestar.** (O.E. *lád*, way, hence the stone that leads)

loaf, *n.* (*pl.* **loaves**) shaped piece of bread; cone of sugar; lump; rounded head of cabbage etc.—*v.i.* (of cabbage) form loaf. **l. sugar,** cone of sugar; lump sugar. (O.E. *hláf*)

loaf, *v.i.* and *t.* spend (time) idly, loiter. **loafer,** *n.*

loam, *n.* fertile soil of sand, clay, and vegetable mould; clay paste for making bricks etc. **loamy,** *a.* (O.E. *lám*)

loan, *n.* (*Scot.*) lane; enclosure where cows are milked.

loan, *n.* thing lent, esp. money lent for interest; act of lending or being lent. —*v.t.* grant loan of. **on l.,** lent. **loanable,** *a.* **loanee, loaner,** *nn.* (O.E. *lán*)

loath, loth, *a.* reluctant, unwilling. **nothing l.,** readily. (O.E. *láth*)

loathe, *v.t.* feel disgust at, detest. **loathing,** *n.* extreme disgust. **loathly,** *a.* (*arch.*) loathsome. **loathsome,** *a.* exciting disgust or nausea, repulsive. (O.E. *láthian*)

loaves, see loaf.

lob, *n.* (*cricket*) ball bowled underhand; (*lawn tennis*) ball hit high in air; (*Shake.*) lout, bumpkin.—*v.i.* and *t.* deliver lob; move slowly or clumsily; (*Shake.*) droop.

lobar, *a.* of a lobe. **lobate,** *a.* having lobes. **lobation,** *n.* (*lobe*)

lobby, *n.* entrance-hall; corridor; anteroom of legislative chamber. **division l.,** into which members pass to vote. **lobbying,** *n.* frequenting lobby to obtain news or solicit votes. **lobbyist,** *n.* (L.L. *lobia,* portico)

lobe, *n.* lower hanging part of ear; (*anat.*) division of lung etc.; (*bot.*) division of leaf. **lobed,** *a.* **lobelet,** *n.* little lobe. (Gk. *lobos*)

lobelia, *n.* small bright-flowered border plant. (*Lobel,* botanist)

loblolly, *n.* (*obs.*) water-gruel. **l. boy,** attendant on ship's surgeon.

lobscouse, *n.* sailor's dish of meat, vegetables, and ship's biscuit.

lobster, *n.* edible blue-black shell-fish with long claws, red after boiling; (*sl.*) soldier, marine. **l.-pot,** *n.* wicker trap for lobsters. (L. *locusta*)

lobule, *n.* small lobe. **lobular,** *a.* lobe-shaped. (*lobe*)

lobworm, *n.* large worm used as bait, lugworm. (*lob*)

local, *a.* of place; belonging, confined, to a particular place; (*math.*) of a locus.—*n.* short-distance train; (*pl.*) local examinations. **l. colour,** details in story giving convincing background. **l. examination,** set by universities but held at local centres. **l. government,** by local authorities. **l. option, veto,** power of a district to prohibit local sale of intoxicants. **l. time,** as fixed by the sun. (*locus*)

locale, local, *n.* locality, scene, of event etc. (F.)

localism, *n.* local idiom or custom; great attachment to a place; resulting narrow outlook.

locality, *n.* position, site; district; faculty of finding one's way.

localize, *v.t.* restrict to, identify with, a particular place; decentralize. **localization,** *n.*

locate, *v.t.* and *i.* establish in a place; find, state, position of; (*Amer. colloq.*) settle. **location,** *n.* locating; situation; place marked off, native reserve etc.; (*cinema*) place outside studio where scene is shot. **locator,** *n.*

locative, *a.* and *n.* (grammatical case) indicating place where.

loch, *n.* Scottish lake or arm of the sea. **lochan,** *n.* little loch. (Gael.)

Lochaber-axe, *n.* highland battle-axe with hook. (place)

lock, *n.* device to fasten door etc.; check for wheel; wrestling hold; traffic jam; mechanism firing gun; enclosure in canal for moving boats from one level to another; angle to which fore-wheels of car can be turned; lock hospital.—*v.t.* and *i.* fasten with lock, shut (up); make, become, fixed; catch, entwine; convey, pass, through canal lock. **l. hospital,** for venereal disease. **l., stock, and barrel,** wholly, completely. **l.-keeper,** *n.* keeper of canal lock. **l.-stitch,** *n.* by which two threads are locked together. **l.-up,** *n.* time for locking up for night; place of detention. (O.E. *loc*)

lock, *n.* tuft of hair or wool, ringlet, tress. (O.E. *loc*)

lockage, *n.* system of canal locks; dues paid for using them; amount of rise or fall effected by them.

locker, *n.* small cupboard with lock. **shot in the l.,** last reserve.

locket, *n.* small hinged pendant case for portrait etc.; metal band on scabbard. (*lock*)

lockjaw, *n.* kind of tetanus in which jaws are rigidly closed.

lockman, *n.* (*Scot.*) hangman; (*Isle of Man*) under-sheriff.

lockout, *n.* exclusion of workers by employers as means of coercion.

lockram, *n.* a kind of coarse linen. (*Locrenan* in Brittany)

locksman, *n.* lock-keeper; turnkey.

locksmith, *n.* maker and mender of locks.

loco, *n.* American plant causing brain disease in cattle.—*a.* (also **locoed**) poisoned with this; crazy. **l.-disease,** *n.* (Sp.=insane)

loco, *n.* locomotive engine. (abbr.)

loco citato, (*abbr. loc. cit.* or *l.c.*) in the passage quoted. (L.)

locomotion, *n.* motion from place to place; power of this. **locomote,** *v.i.* move from place to place. **locomotive,** *a.* of, having, effecting, locomotion.—*n.* engine that travels under its own power, railway engine. **locomotor, locomotory,** *aa.* **locomotor ataxy** or **ataxia,** nervous disease causing disordered gait. (L. *locus,* place; *movēre,* move)

loculus ,*n.* (*pl.* **loculi**) small cavity or

cell. **locular, loculous,** *aa.* (dim. of *locus*)

locum tenens, (*colloq.*) **locum,** deputy for doctor or clergyman in his absence. **locum-tenency,** *n.* (L. *locus,* place; *tenēre,* hold)

locus, *n.* (*pl.* **loci**) place, locality; (*math.*) line traced by point, surface traced by line, moving according to defined conditions. ***l. classicus,*** most authoritative passage on subject. ***l. standi,*** recognized position; right to appear in court. (L.)

locust, *n.* destructive migratory winged insect like grasshopper; kinds of tree, esp. carob and false acacia. (L. *locusta*)

locution, *n.* style of expression; phrase. **locutory,** *n.* parlour, grille for interviews with visitors, in monastery. (L. *loqui,* speak)

lode, *n.* vein of metallic ore; watercourse. **lodestar, loadstar,** *n.* guiding star or principle, pole-star. **lodestone,** see **loadstone.** (=load)

lodge, *n.* gate-keeper's cottage or room; beaver's den; wigwam; branch of a society or its place of meeting; (*arch.*) small house.—*v.t.* and *i.* receive as inmate, accommodate; dwell for a time; deposit, place; fix in, settle. **grand l.,** governing body of freemasons. **lodger,** *n.* one who resides in lodgings. **lodging,** *n.* temporary habitation; (*pl.*) room or rooms hired in house of another. **lodging-house,** *n.* one where rooms are let. **lodgment, lodgement,** *n.* foothold; temporary work to hold captured position; deposit, material lodged in a place. (L.L. *lobia,* portico)

loess, *n.* deposit of fine loam in certain river-valleys. (G. *löss*)

loft, *n.* room directly under roof, attic; gallery in church or hall; pigeon-house; (*golf*) slope of club-face.—*v.t.* (*golf*) send (ball) high, clear (obstacle) thus. **lofty,** *a.* high, elevated; haughty, superior; stately, grandiose. (O.N.=sky)

log, *n.* unhewn piece of timber; float attached to line wound on reel for measuring ship's speed; log-book.—*v.t.* and *i.* enter in log-book; (*Amer.*) cut and transport (timber). **l.-book,** *n.* ship's journal, with record of voyage. **l. cabin, hut,** one built of logs. **l.-roll,** *v.i.* engage in mutual aid or advertisement. (M.E. *logge*)

log, *n.* logarithm. (abbr.)

logan, logan-stone, *nn.* poised boulder easily rocked. (dial. *log,* rock)

loganberry, *n.* cross between raspberry and blackberry. (Judge *Logan*)

logaoedic, *a.* and *n.* (verse) composed of dactyls and trochees. (Gk. *logos,* prose; *aoidē,* song)

logarithm, *n.* a number expressed as a power of another, us. 10; logarithm tables simplify reckoning by substituting addition for multiplication and subtraction for division. **logarithmic,** *a.* (Gk. *logos,* reckoning; *arithmos,* number)

loge, *n.* box, stall, in theatre. (F.)

loggats, loggets, *n.pl.* (*Shake.*) game like quoits.

loggerhead, *n.* (*arch.*) dolt. **be at ll.,** dispute (with). (dial. *logger,* block)

loggia, *n.* (*pl.* **loggias** or **loggie**) covered gallery or arcade with one side open. (It.)

logic, *n.* science of reasoning or thought; ability in argument. **logical,** *a.* of logic; according to reason, consistent; able to reason well. **logicality,** *n.* **logician,** *n.* one skilled in logic. (Gk. *logos,* reason)

logion, *n.* (*pl.* **logia**) saying of Jesus recorded not in Bible but elsewhere. (Gk.=oracle)

-logist, *n.suf.* one versed in, student of, as in astrologist. (*-logy*)

logistics, *n.pl.* science of moving and supplying armies. (*lodge*)

logo-, from Gk. *logos,* word, used in **logogram,** *n.* sign, letter, standing for word, as £; **logograph,** *n.* logogram, logotype; **logographer,** *n.* ancient Greek annalist or professional speech-writer; **logogriph,** *n.* word-puzzle based on anagram. **logomachy,** *n.* dispute about, battle of, words; **logotype,** *n.* (*print.*) type containing more letters than one.

Logos, *n.* the Word of God incarnate, Christ. (Gk.=word)

logwood, *n.* American tree yielding dye.

-logy, *n.suf.* science or study of, as in demonology, zoology. (Gk. *-logia*)

loimic, *a.* of the plague. **loimography, loimology,** *nn.* (Gk. *loimos,* plague)

loin, *n.* cut of meat from back; (*pl.*) back between ribs and hip. **gird up one's ll.,** prepare for energetic action. **l.-cloth,** *n.* cloth worn round middle. (L. *lumbus*)

loir, *n.* the fat dormouse. (L. *glis*)

loiter, *v.i.* and *t.* delay, linger, dawdle; idle away. **loiterer,** *n.* (Du. *leuteren*)

loll, *v.i.* and *t.* lean or rest lazily, lounge; (of tongue) hang out.

Lollard, *n.* follower of Wyclif, 14th-century church reformer. **Lollardism,** *n.* (M.Du. *lollen,* mumble)

lollipop, *n.* kind of sweet.

lollop, *v.i.* (*colloq.*) flop about, sprawl, move heavily. (*loll*)

Lombard Street, money market. **L. S. to a China orange,** practical certainty. (London banking centre)

loment, *n.* pod that breaks at maturity into one-seeded joints. **lomentaceous,** *a.* (L. *lomentum,* bean-meal)

London, *n.* **L. particular,** very thick fog. **L. pride,** kind of saxifrage. **Londoner, Londonism,** *nn.*

lone, *a.* (*poet.*) solitary, alone, unfrequented; (of woman) single or widowed. **lonely,** *a.* solitary, alone; isolated, unfrequented; sad because alone. **loneliness,** *n.* **lonesome,** *a.* solitary; feeling, making feel, lonely. (*alone*)

long, *a.* of great extent; of stated length; tedious, dilatory; distant, far-reaching; (of price) high; (of syllable) having greater of two durations, stressed. — *n.* long period, vowel, or vacation.—*adv.* for, by, a long time; throughout.—*v.i.* wish earnestly, yearn (for). **by a l. chalk,** by a long way. **in the l. run,** ultimately. **l. and short of it,** sum of the matter. **l. dozen,** 13. **l. face,** dismal look. **l. firm,** swindlers who obtain goods and do not pay. **l. hop,** (*cricket*) short-pitched ball. **l. hundred,** 120. **l. jump,** horizontal jump. **l. measure,** linear measure. **l. metre,** hymn stanza of four 8-syllable lines. **l. pig,** cannibal's name for human flesh. **l. primer,** 10-point printing type. **l. robe,** legal dress. **l. suit,** person's speciality. **l. vacation,** summer vacation. **l. wave,** (*wireless*) about 1,000 metres and over. (O.E. *lang*)

long, *v.i.* (*Shake.*) belong.

longaeval, same as **longeval.**

long-ago, *a.* and *n.* (in) the far past.

longanimity, *n.* long-suffering, forbearance. (L. *animus,* mind)

long-bill, *n.* snipe.

longboat, *n.* largest boat of sailing-ship.

long-bow, *n.* bow held vertically and drawn by hand. **draw the l.,** exaggerate.

longcloth, *n.* kinds of calico.

long-clothes, *n.pl.* baby's clothes, stretching beyond feet.

longe, same as **lunge.**

longeron, *n.* longitudinal spar of aeroplane's fuselage. (F.)

longeval, *a.* long-lived. **longevity,** *n.* long life. (L. *aevum,* age)

longhand, *n.* ordinary handwriting.

long-headed, *a.* shrewd, discerning.

longing, *n.* strong desire, yearning.

longi-, from L. *longus,* used in **longicaudate,** *a.* long-tailed; **longicorn,** *n.* kinds of beetle with long antennae; **longipennate,** *a.* long-winged; **longirostral,** *a.* long-beaked.

longitude, *n.* distance east or west of Greenwich or other standard meridian, measured in degrees; (*astron.*) angular distance on ecliptic eastward from vernal equinox. **longitudinal,** *a.* of length or longitude; lengthwise. (L. *longitudo,* length)

long-off, long-on, *nn.* (*cricket*) fielder at bowler's left, right, rear.

longshanks, *n.* kind of plover.

longshore, *a.* found, employed, on the shore. **longshoreman,** *n.* wharf-labourer, man employed about shore. (*along shore*)

long-sighted, *a.* able to see at a long distance; prudent.

long-standing, *a.* that has long existed.

longstop, *n.* (*cricket*) fielder behind wicket-keeper.

long-suffering, *a.* patient, forbearing.

longue haleine, long wind. **work of** *l. h.,* needing persistent effort. *longueur, n.* tedious passage in book or play. (F.)

longways, longwise, *advv.* in the direction of thing's length.

long-winded, *a.* long-breathed; verbose.

loo, *n.* round card-game.—*v.t.* subject to forfeit at loo. (F. *lanturelu*)

looby, *n.* clumsy stupid fellow.

loof, *n.* (*Scot.*) palm of the hand. (O.N. *lófi*)

loofah, *n.* fibrous skeleton of pod of an Egyptian plant, used as flesh-brush. (Arab. *lufah,* this plant)

look, *v.i.* and *t.* direct the eyes, gaze (at); direct attention to; make search; take care; show by look; seem; face.—*n.* glance; expression; aspect; appearance. **l. after,** attend to. **l. alive, sharp,** hurry. **l. down on,** despise. **l. for,** seek; expect. **l. into,** investigate. **l. on,** regard. **l. out,** watch; select. **l. to,** take care about; depend on; expect. **l. up,** improve; call on; search for in book. **l. up to,** respect. **l. upon,** regard. **good ll.,** beauty. **l.-in,** *n.* casual visit; chance (of winning etc.). **l.-out,** *n.* watch, watcher; observation-post; prospect; person's own concern. **l.-see,** *n.* survey, look round. (O.E. *lócian*)

looker, *n.* one who looks; (*Amer. sl.*) good - looking person. **l. - on,** *n.* spectator.

looking-glass, *n.* mirror.

lookit, *int.* (*Amer. sl.*) listen to me.

loom, *v.i.* appear faintly or at a distance; show larger than real size. —*n.* first hazy appearance of land at sea.

loom, *n.* frame or machine for weaving cloth; part of oar inside rowlock. (O.E. *gelóma,* tool)

loom, *n.* kinds of guillemot and diver. (O.N. *lómr*)

loon, *n.* rascal; boor; (*Scot.*) lad.

loon, *n.* kinds of diving-bird.

loony, *a.* and *n.* (*sl.*) lunatic, crazy. **l. bin,** (*sl.*) madhouse. (abbr.)

loop, *n.* folding or doubling of rope etc., noose; ornament, handle, so formed.—*v.t.* and *i.* make loop in; form, fasten with, loops. **l. the l.,** trace vertical loop with aeroplane, bicycle etc. so that it turns a somersault. **l.-line,** *n.* one that leaves and then rejoins main line. **looper,** *n.* caterpillar that crawls by arching itself into loops.

loophole, *n.* narrow vertical slit in wall for defence; means of evasion. —*v.t.* make loopholes in.

loopy, *a.* (*sl.*) slightly mad, cracked.

loord, *n.* (*Spens.*) lout. (F. *lourd,* heavy)

loose, *a.* released from bonds; slack, not fixed; not exact or literal; careless; licentious; (*chem.*) uncombined.

—*v.t.* and *i.* untie, free, detach; discharge (gun, arrow). **at a l. end,** without occupation. **break l.,** escape. **give a l. to,** give free vent to. **let l.,** set free. **l. ball, bowling,** (*cricket*) inaccurately pitched. **l. bowels,** inclined to diarrhoea. **l. stall,** in which horse is kept untied. **on the l.,** having a spree. (O.N. *lauss*)

loosen, *v.t.* and *i.* loose, relax; make, become, less tight or firm. **l. up,** (*Amer. sl.*) throw off restraint, show generosity.

loosestrife, *n.* kinds of plant with golden or purple flowers. (Gk. *Lusimachos*, a proper name, but taken in error as *luein*, loose; *machē*, battle)

loot, *n.* booty, spoil; sack (of city).—*v.t.* and *i.* plunder; carry off as plunder. (Hind. *lut*)

lop, *v.t.* cut branches off (tree), prune; cut off (top, limb etc.).—*n.* trimmings of tree.

lop, *v.i.* hang limply; slouch. **l.-ear,** *n.* drooping ear; rabbit with such ears. **l.-eared,** *a.* **lopsided,** *a.* heavier, lower, on one side.

lop, *v.i.* (of water) break in short waves.—*n.* this motion. (imit.)

lope, *v.i.* move easily with long bounding steps.—*n.* this gait. (O.N. *hloupa*)

lopho-, from Gk. *lophos*, crest, used in **lophobranchiate,** *a.* with gills arranged in tufts; **lophodont,** *a.* with transverse ridges on crowns of molar teeth.

loquacious, *a.* talkative; chattering. **loquacity,** *n.* (L. *loquax*)

loquat, *n.* an Asiatic tree; its edible fruit. (Chin. *luh kwat*, rush orange)

loquitur, *v.i.* (*abbr.* *loq.*) speaks (as stage direction). (L.)

lor, lor', *int.* (*vulg.*) Lord!

loranthaceous, *a.* of the mistletoe family. (L. *lorum*, strap. Gk. *anthos*, flower)

lorcha, *n.* vessel of European build, rigged like Chinese junk. (Port.)

lord, *n.* master, ruler; peer, nobleman; husband; God, Christ; personal style of marquis, viscount, earl, or baron; courtesy title of younger son of duke or marquis.—*v.i.* and *t.* domineer (over); ennoble. **drunk as a l.,** very drunk. **House of Ll.,** upper chamber of Parliament. **l. in waiting, of the bedchamber,** nobleman attending reigning queen, king. **L. Lieutenant,** head of magistracy in a county. **L. of Misrule,** medieval leader of Christmas revels. **L.'s day,** Sunday. **L.'s supper,** sacrament of communion. **L.'s table,** communion table. **ll. and ladies,** wild arum. **Ll. of Session,** judges of the Scottish Court of Session. **Ll. Spiritual, Temporal,** bishops, lay members, of House of Lords. **my l.,** respectful address for peer, bishop, or judge of supreme court. (O.E. *hláford*, lit. loaf-keeper)

lordling, *n.* young or petty lord.

lordly, *a.* of, fit for, a lord; haughty, imperious, grand.

lordolatry, *n.* worship of nobility.

lordosis, *n.* forward curvature of the spine. (Gk.)

Lord's, *n.* cricket-ground, headquarters of M.C.C. (T. *Lord*, maker)

lordship, *n.* dominion; domain. **his, your, l.,** deferential form for lord.

lore, *n.* body of traditions and facts on subject; (*arch.*) learning, doctrine. (O.E. *lár*)

lore, *n.* (*zool.*) space between eye and bill in birds; similar surface in reptiles. (L. *lorum*, strap)

lorette, *n.* prostitute. (F.)

lorgnette, *n.* eyeglasses with long handle; opera-glass. (F.)

loricate, *a.* (*zool.*) with protective armour of bone, plates, or scales. (L. *lorica*, cuirass)

lorikeet, *n.* small brightly coloured parrot. (dim. of *lory*)

lorimer, loriner, *n.* maker of bits and bridles, spurrier. (L. *lorum*, thong)

loriot, *n.* golden oriole. (F.)

loris, *n.* small tailless nocturnal climbing animal of Ceylon; kinds of slow-moving lemur. (F.)

lorn, *a.* (*poet.*) forlorn, wretched. (M.E. *lesen*, lose)

lorry, *n.* four-wheeled wagon without sides; truck.

lory, *n.* parrot-like bird with brilliant plumage. (Malay *luri*)

lose, *v.t.* and *i.* (*past, p.p.* **lost**) be deprived of, forfeit; fail to keep or get; be defeated in; waste; suffer loss. **l. ground,** recede, decline. **l. heart,** be discouraged. **l. one's heart (to),** fall in love (with). **l. oneself,** go astray; be absorbed (in). **l. one's temper,** grow angry. **lost,** *p.p.* astray; missing, vanished; destroyed, dead; damned. **lost to,** insensible to. **lost upon,** not appreciated by. (O.E. *losian*, perish)

losel, *n.* (*arch.*) ne'er-do-well, scamp, rake.

loser, *n.* one who loses, esp. in race etc.; (*billiards*) losing hazard.

losh, *int.* (*Scot.*) of surprise.

loss, *n.* deprivation, defeat; what is lost; detriment resulting from losing. **at a l.,** puzzled. (O.E. *los*)

lost, see **lose.**

lot, *n.* chance selection or object used in making it; destiny; share; collection; item at auction, plot of ground; (*colloq.*) large quantity.—*v.t.* divide into lots. **bad l.,** rascal. **cast, draw, ll.,** make chance selection. **the l.,** whole amount. (O.E. *hlot*)

lota, lotah, *n.* (*Anglo-Ind.*) brass or copper water-pot. (Hind.)

loth, see **loath.**

Lothario, *n.* libertine. (name in play)

lotion, *n.* liquid for washing wounds, bathing skin etc. (L. *lavare*, wash)

lottery, *n.* gamble in which prizes are distributed by chance. (*lot*)

lotto, *n.* game of chance, decided by drawing prize-numbers. (*lot*)
lotus, *n.* fabulous plant inducing indolence; Egyptian water-lily. **l.-eater, l.-land,** *nn.* person, place, given to slothful ease. (Gk. *lōtos*)
loud, *a.* full-sounding, noisy; ostentatious, showy.—*adv.* loudly. **loud-speaker,** *n.* instrument magnifying sound of wireless set etc. **louden,** *v.i.* grow loud. (O.E. *hlúd*)
lough, *n.* Irish lake or arm of sea.
louis, louis-d'or, *nn.* obsolete French gold coin, worth 20 francs. (king)
lounder, *v.t.* (*Scot.*) beat.—*n.* heavy blow.
lounge, *v.i.* loll, recline; saunter.—*n.* lounging; place for lounging, smoking-room; sofa. **l.-lizard,** *n.* (*Amer. sl.*) professional dance-partner, gigolo. **lounger,** *n.* loafer.
loup, *v.i.* and *n.* (*Scot.*) leap.
lour, lower, *v.i.* frown, scowl; (of sky) look gloomy and threatening.—*n.* scowl; gloominess. **louring, lowering,** *a.* sullen; overcast. **loury,** *a.* cloudy. (M.E. *louren*)
louse, *n.* (*pl.* **lice**) wingless parasitic insect. **lousy,** *a.* infested with lice; (*sl.*) bad, poor. (O.E. *lús*)
lout, *n.* hulking or awkward fellow, bumpkin. **loutish,** *a.*
lout, *v.i.* (*arch.*) bow. (O.E. *lutan*)
louver, louvre, *n.* ancient roof lantern or turret for ventilation or light; set of overlapping slats or panes admitting air but not rain. **louvered,** *a.* (L.L. *lodium*)
lovable, *a.* worthy of love, amiable.
lovage, *n.* kinds of herb. (L.L. *levisticum*)
love, *n.* strong affection, fondness; sexual passion; sweetheart, beloved; amour; god of love, Cupid; (*tennis etc.*) score of nothing.—*v.t.* and *i.* be in love (with); be fond of, delight in. **fall in l. with,** become enamoured of. **l. all,** no score. **l. game,** in which loser fails to score. **make l. to,** court, caress. **play for l.,** without money stakes. **l.-apple,** *n.* tomato. **l.-bird,** *n.* kind of small parrot. **l.-child,** *n.* bastard. **l.-feast,** *n.* religious feast like agape. **l.-in-a-mist,** *n.* garden plant with pale-blue or white flowers. **l.-in-idleness,** *n.* heartsease. **l.-knot,** *n.* kind of bow. **l.-lies-bleeding,** *n.* garden plant with red spike. **l.-match,** *n.* marriage for love. (O.E. *lufu*).
loveless, *a.* without love, unloving.
lovelock, *n.* curl worn on forehead.
lovelorn, *a.* forsaken by one's love; pining for love.
lovely, *a.* exquisitely beautiful; (*colloq.*) delightful. **loveliness,** *n.*
lover, *n.* sweetheart, suitor; admirer; paramour; (*pl.*) courting couple. **loverly,** *a.* like a lover.
lovesick, *a.* languishing with love.
lovesome, *a.* (*arch.*) lovely; loving.
loveworthy, *a.* deserving love.
loving, *a.* affectionate, showing love. **l.-cup,** *n.* large drinking-vessel passed round at banquet. **l.-kindness,** *n.* tender regard.
low, *a.* not high or tall or elevated; of humble position; not exalted, vulgar; not loud or shrill; dejected; (of dress) décolleté.—*adv.* in, to, a low position. **bring, lay, l.,** humble, overthrow. **lie l.,** be prostrate or dead; (*sl.*) keep quiet. **l. comedy,** tending to farce, hence **l. comedian. L. Countries,** Netherlands. **l. latitudes,** near equator. **l. mass,** without music. **l. relief,** bas-relief. **L. Sunday,** first after Easter. **l. water,** low tide. **l.-water-mark,** *n.* point then reached. (O.N. *lagr.*)
low, *v.i.* and *t.* bellow, moo.—*n.* cry of cow, bellow. (O.E. *hlówan*)
low, *n.* (*Scot.*) flame.—*v.i.* blaze.
low-born, *a.* of humble birth.
low-boy, *n.* (*Amer.*) low chest of drawers.
lowbrow, *a.* and *n.* (*Amer. sl.*) (person, book) of unintellectual type.
Low-Church, *a.* of the less sacerdotal and ritualistic party in the Church of England. **Low-Churchman,** *n.*
low-down, *a.* mean, underhand.—*n.* (*Amer. sl.*) true facts.
lower, *v.t.* and *i.* bring, let, down degrade; lessen, reduce; sink, fall.—*a.* (*compar.* of low). **l. case,** (*print.*) small letters. **l. deck,** petty officers and men. **L. Empire,** Byzantine Empire. **L. House,** House of Commons. **l. orders,** people of inferior social rank. **l. school,** junior forms. **lowermost,** *a.* very lowest.
lower, lowering, see lour.
lowland, *a.* of, in, low country.—*n.pl.* low country, esp. SE. Scotland. **lowlander,** *n.* inhabitant of lowlands.
lowly, *a.* humble, modest, unpretending. **lowly, lowlily,** *advv.* (*low*)
lown, *a.* (*Scot.*) sheltered, calm.
loxodromic, *a.* pertaining to oblique sailing by rhumb-lines.—*n.* rhumb-line; (*pl.*) art of oblique sailing. (Gk. *loxos,* oblique; *dromos,* course)
loyal, *a.* faithful; true to allegiance. **loyalty,** *n.* **loyalist,** *n.* adherent of legitimate sovereign. **loyalism,** *n.* (L. *legalis,* legal)
lozenge, *n.* diamond-shaped figure, rhombus; shield, pane, facet, of this shape; sweet, esp. for soothing throat; tablet of medicine or essence. (O.F. *losenge*)
lubber, *n.* clumsy fellow, lout; unskilled seaman. **l.'s hole,** hole in top giving access to masthead. **l.'s line,** vertical line inside compass-case showing direction of ship's head. **lubberly,** *a.* awkward.
lubra, *n.* aboriginal Australian woman.
lubricate, *v.t.* make slippery; oil, grease (machinery). **lubricant,** *n.* oil or other substance for reducing friction. **lubrication, lubricator,** *nn.* (L. *lubricus,* slippery)

lubricity, *n.* slipperiness; evasiveness; lewdness. **lubricious, lubricous,** *aa.* (*lubricate*)

lucarne, *n.* dormer-window, esp. in spire. (L. *lucerna,* lamp)

luce, *n.* pike, esp. when full-grown. (L.L. *lucius*)

lucent, *a.* bright, shining; clear. **lucency,** *n.* (L. *lux,* light)

lucerne, lucern, *n.* plant like clover used for fodder. (F. *luzerne*)

lucid, *a.* clear, easily understood, free from obscurity; bright, shining. **l. interval,** period of sanity between attacks of madness. **lucidity,** *n.* (L. *lux,* light)

Lucifer, *n.* Venus as morning star; Satan; (also **l. match**) friction match. (L. *lux,* light; *ferre,* bear)

lucifugous, *a.* shunning light. **lucigen,** *n.* powerful lamp burning oil-spray under pressure. **lucimeter,** *n.* photometer. (L. *lux,* light)

luck, *n.* fortune, chance; good fortune. **down on one's l.,** unhappy, unfortunate. **in l.,** fortunate. **out of l.,** unfortunate. **worse l.!** more 's the pity! **l.-penny,** *n.* trifle returned for luck from seller to buyer. **luckless,** *a.* unfortunate; ill-starred. **lucky,** *a.* fortunate; due to luck, fluky; well-omened. **lucky-bag, lucky-dip,** *nn.* bag of articles of which one makes blind choice. **luckily,** *adv.* fortunately. (L.G. *luk*)

lucky, *n.* (*sl.*) departure. **cut one's l.,** make off.

lucky, luckie, *n.* (*Scot.*) woman, esp. an elderly one.

lucre, *n.* gain in money, esp. as sordid motive. **lucrative,** *a.* profitable. (L. *lucrum,* gain)

luctation, *n.* struggle, contest. (L. *luctari,* struggle)

lucubrate, *v.i.* study by lamplight; write learnedly. **lucubration,** *n.* nocturnal study; dissertation, laboured or pedantic literary work. **lucubrator,** *n.* (L. *lucubrare*)

luculent, *a.* clear, transparent, lucid. (L. *lux,* light)

lucus a non lucendo, contradictory explanation. (L.=*lucus,* grove, is derived from *lucēre,* shine, because there is no shining in it)

ludicrous, *a.* absurd, laughable, ridiculous. (L. *ludicrus*)

ludo, *n.* game played with dice and counters. (L.=I play)

lues, *n.* plague, contagion. ***l. venerea,*** syphilis. **luetic,** *a.* (L.)

luff, *v.i.* and *t.* (*naut.*) turn (ship) nearer to the wind; (*yacht-racing*) get windward side of (opponent).

Luftwaffe, *n.* German Air Force. (G.)

lug, *v.t.* and *i.* drag with effort, tug; pull hard.—*n.* strong or rough pull. (cf. Swed. *lugga,* pull by hair)

lug, *n.* (*Scot.*) ear; projection, handle.

lug, for lugsail or lugworm.

luge, *n.* small raised toboggan.—*v.i.* toboggan in one. (F.)

luggage, *n.* traveller's trunks and other baggage. (*lug*)

lugger, *n.* small vessel with two or three masts and lugsails. **lugsail,** *n.* square sail bent on an unequally slung yard.

luggie, *n.* (*Scot.*) wooden dish with handle. (*lug*)

lugworm, *n.* large worm used as bait, lobworm.

lugubrious, *a.* mournful, doleful. (L. *lugēre,* mourn)

lukewarm, *a.* moderately warm, tepid; half-hearted. (M.E. *luke,* tepid)

lull, *v.t.* and *i.* soothe, sing to sleep; quiet, allay; subside.—*n.* brief cessation of storm. **lullaby,** *n.* song to lull to sleep, cradle-song.—*v.t.* sing to sleep. (imit.)

lum, *n.* (*Scot.*) chimney.

lumbago, *n.* rheumatism in the loins. **lumbaginous,** *a.* **lumbar,** *a.* of, in, the loins. (L. *lumbus,* loin)

lumber, *n.* anything useless or cumbersome; sawn timber.—*v.t.* and *i.* cumber, obstruct; heap together in disorder; cut and prepare timber. **l.-room,** *n.* for keeping disused articles. **lumberer, lumberjack, lumberman,** *nn.* one who cuts and dresses timber.

lumber, *v.i.* move heavily and clumsily; rumble. **lumbering, lumbersome,** *aa.* (M.E. *lomere*)

lumbrical, *a.* wormlike.—*n.* muscle of the fingers and toes. (L. *lumbricus,* earthworm)

lumen, *n.* unit of light-flux; amount of light emitted by a source of 1 candle-power through a square centimetre 1 centimetre distant. (L.=light)

luminary, *n.* body emitting light, esp. sun or moon; leader of thought. **luminiferous,** *a.* transmitting or producing light. **luminous,** *a.* emitting light, shining; perspicuous; enlightening. **luminous paint,** phosphorescent, visible in darkness. **luminosity,** *n.* (L. *lumen,* light)

lumme, *int.* (*vulg.*) of astonishment. (corrupt. of Lord *love me*)

lump, *v.t.* put up with though displeased (in **like it or l. it**).

lump, *n.* shapeless piece or mass; aggregate, large quantity; swelling; dull person.—*v.t.* and *i.* heap (together) in one mass, treat alike; form lumps; go, sit, heavily. **in the l.,** taken as a whole. **l. sugar,** in cubes. **l. sum,** covering several items or payments. **lumper,** *n.* docker; militiaman; small contractor. **lumpfish, lumpsucker,** *nn.* clumsy sea-fish clinging to objects by means of sucker. **lumping,** *a.* (*colloq.*) big, heavy. **lumpish,** *a.* heavy, gross, dull. **lumpy,** *a.* full of lumps.

lunacy, *n.* insanity, mental unsoundness; great folly. (*lunatic*)

lunar, *a.* of, depending on, caused by,

the moon. **l. caustic,** nitrate of silver fused. **l. month,** time of moon's revolution, 29½ days. **l. nodes,** at which moon's orbit cuts ecliptic. **lunarian,** *n.* student of, dweller in, the moon. **lunate,** *a.* crescent-shaped. **lunation,** *n.* moon's changes from one new moon to the next. (L. *luna,* moon)

lunatic, *a.* insane; crazy.—*n.* madman. **l. asylum,** institution for care of the insane. (*luna,* moon, once supposed to cause madness)

lunch, *n.* light meal taken at midday or between breakfast and midday dinner.—*v.i.* and *t.* have, provide with, lunch. **luncheon,** *n.* lunch; midday banquet.

lune, *n.* (*geom.*) figure formed on plane or sphere by two intersecting arcs of circles. **lunette,** *n.* arched opening in vaulted roof to admit light; crescent-shaped space in ceiling with painting etc.; hole for neck in guillotine; watch-glass flattened in centre. (L. *luna,* moon)

lung, *n.* breathing-organ; open space in city. **l.-fish,** *n.* with lungs as well as gills. **l.-power,** *n.* strength of voice. **lunger,** *n.* (*Amer. sl.*) consumptive. **lungwort,** *n.* plant with spotted leaves like diseased lung; a lichen. (O.E. *lungen*)

lunge, *n.* thrust with weapon, pass; sudden forward movement, plunge.—*v.i.* and *t.* make lunge; shoot out in lunge. (F. *allonger,* lengthen)

lunge, *n.* long halter; exercise-ground, for training horses.—*v.t.* train with lunge. (F. *longe,* halter)

lungi, *n.* (*Anglo-Ind.*) loin-cloth. (Urdu)

lunisolar, *a.* of sun and moon, caused by them in unison. **l. period,** of 532 years between agreement of solar and lunar cycles, bringing repetition of eclipses. (L. *luna,* moon; *sol,* sun)

lunkah, *n.* kind of Indian cheroot. (Hind. *lanka,* islands, source)

lunt, *n.* (*Scot.*) smoke; match.

luny, same as **loony.**

lupin, lupine, *n.* kinds of garden and fodder plant with flowers on long spikes. (L. *lupinus*)

lupine, *a.* of wolves, wolf-like. (L. *lupus,* wolf)

lupus, *n.* a tuberculous skin disease. **lupoid, lupous,** *aa.* (L.=wolf)

lurch, *n.* losing position in cribbage. **leave in the l.,** desert when in difficulties. (F. *lourche,* a game)

lurch, *n.* sudden roll to one side.—*v.i.* give lurch, stagger.

lurch, *v.i.* and *t.* (*Shake.*) lurk; rob, cheat. **lurcher,** *n.* spy; swindler; cross between collie and greyhound.

lurdan, lurdane, *a.* and *n.* (*arch.*) lazy, stupid (person). (F. *lourd,* heavy)

lure, *n.* bait, enticement; falconer's device for recalling hawk.—*v.t.* entice, allure; recall (hawk) with lure. (O.F. *leurre*)

lurid, *a.* wan, ghastly pale, gloomy; glaring or terrible in colour; sensational. (L. *luridus,* pale-yellow)

lurk, *v.i.* lie in wait; be concealed; exist unobserved. **on the l.,** spying.

luscious, *a.* richly sweet, delicious; cloying, over-rich.

lush, *a.* (of grass etc.) luxuriant, juicy, rank.

lush, *n.* (*sl.*) liquor.—*v.t.* and *i.* ply with liquor; drink. **lushy,** *a.* (*sl.*) drunk.

lust, *n.* carnal appetite, sexual desire; eagerness to possess or enjoy; (*Shake.*) pleasure.—*v.i.* have strong or inordinate desire. **lustful,** *a.* lascivious. **lustless,** *a.* (*Spens.*) listless. (O.E.)

lustral, *a.* of, used in, lustration. **lustrate,** *v.t.* purify by sacrifice or ceremonial washing. **lustration,** *n.* such cleansing. (*lustrum*)

lustre, *n.* sheen, gloss; brightness, splendour; renown; candlestick with pendants of cut glass; kinds of fabric with lustrous surface.—*v.t.* put lustre on. (L. *lustrare,* illuminate)

lustre, same as **lustrum.**

lustrine, *n.* glossy silk fabric.

lustrous, *a.* having sheen, shining; luminous. (*lustre*)

lustrum, *n.* (*pl.* **lustra, lustrums**) period of 5 years. (L., orig.=sacrifice at quinquennial census)

lusty, *a.* strong, healthy, vigorous. **lustihood,** *n.* (*lust*)

lusus naturae, freak of nature, sport. (L.)

lute, *n.* old round-backed stringed instrument played with the fingers. **lutanist, lutist,** *n.* lute-player. (*Arab. al,* the; *'ud,* wood)

lute, luting, *nn.* clay or cement used to make joints air-tight etc.—*v.t.* treat with lute. (L. *lutum,* mud)

luteous, *a.* deep orange-yellow. (L. *lutum,* weld)

lutestring, *n.* a lustrous silk.

Lutetian, *a.* Parisian. (L. *Lutetia,* ancient name of Paris)

lutrine, *a.* of, like, an otter. (L. *lutra,* otter)

luxate, *v.t.* put out of joint. **luxation,** *n.* dislocation. (L. *luxare*)

luxury, *n.* indulgence in choice and costly pleasures; comfortable surroundings; anything desirable but not necessary; sensuality. **luxuriant,** *a.* prolific; rank, abundant; (of style) florid. **luxuriance,** *n.* **luxuriate,** *v.i.* live luxuriously; grow exuberantly; delight, revel (in). **luxurious,** *a.* full of, given to, luxury; very comfortable; self-indulgent. (L. *luxus,* excess)

-ly, *adj.suf.* having the qualities of, as in **princely.** (O.E. *-lic*)

-ly, *suf.* forming adverbs from adjectives, as in **badly.** (O.E. *-lice*)

lycanthrope, *n.* sufferer from lycanthropy; werewolf. **lycanthropy,** *n.* form of insanity in which patient thinks himself some animal; supposed power of changing into a wolf. (Gk. *lukos*, wolf; *anthrōpos*, man)

lycée, *n.* state secondary school in France. (F.)

lyceum, *n.* lecture-hall. (Gk. *Lukeion*, grove where Aristotle taught)

lych, see **lich.**

lychnis, *n.* kinds of plant incl. campion and ragged robin. (Gk. *luchnis*)

lycopod, *n.* kind of moss. **lycopodium**, *n.* lycopod; inflammable powder in its spores, used in making stage lightning etc. (Gk. *lukos*, wolf; *pous*, foot)

lyddite, *n.* high-explosive made from picric acid. (*Lydd* in Kent)

lye, *n.* water made alkaline with wood ashes etc. for washing. (O.E. *léog*)

lye, *n.* railway siding. (*lie*)

lying, *a.* false, misleading.—*n.* untruthfulness. (*lie*)

lyke-wake, *n.* watch kept at night over corpse. (O.E. *lic*, corpse)

lymph, *n.* (*poet.*) pure water; (*anat.*) a colourless fluid in animal bodies; (*med.*) vaccine. **lymphoid, lymphous,** *aa.* **lymphatic**, *a.* (of glands) secreting or conveying lymph; (of persons) flabby, sluggish; pale-skinned.—*n.* duct conveying lymph. (L. *lympha*)

lyncean, *a.* lynx-eyed, sharp-sighted; of the lynx. (*lynx*)

lynch, *v.t.* execute or punish without trial. **Judge L.**, imaginary authority for this. **l. law**, mob law, summary justice without legal forms.

lynx, *n.* small fierce spotted animal of cat kind, noted for keen sight; its fur. **l.-eyed**, *a.* keen-sighted. (Gk. *lungx*)

lyre, *n.* stringed instrument like smal harp, used by ancients to accompany poetry. **l.-bird**, *n.* Australian bird with tail like lyre. **lyrate**, *a.* lyre-shaped. (Gk. *lura*)

lyric, *a.* of, for, the lyre; of the nature of song.—*n.* lyric poem. **l. poem**, expressing personal thought and emotion, usually short and written in stanzas. **l. poet**, writer of lyric poetry. **lyrical**, *a.* using language suited to lyric poetry, impassioned, high-flown; lyric. **lyricism**, *n.* lyrical quality or expression.

lyrist, *n.* lyric poet; lyre-player.

lysis, *n.* (*med.*) gradual abatement of acute disease, opp. to crisis. (Gk. *luein*, loose)

lysol, *n.* a disinfectant. (Gk. *luein*, loose)

lyssa, *n.* rabies. (Gk. *lussa*)

M

M, (*roman numerals*) 1,000; (*print.*) m or em, unit of measurement, $\frac{1}{6}$ in.

ma, *n.* (*vulg.*) mamma. (abbr.)

ma'am, same as madam.

macabre, *a.* gruesome, ghastly. (F.)

macaco, *n.* kind of monkey. (Port.)

macaco, *n.* kinds of lemur.

macadam, *n.* road surface of broken stone pressed down in layers. **macadamize**, *v.t.* cover (road) with this. **macadamization**, *n.* (J. L. *McAdam*)

macaroni, *n.* wheaten paste made into long thin tubes; 18th-century fop. **macaronic**, *a.* and *n.* (burlesque verse) of words from more than one language, or modern words with Latin endings, e.g. 'Trumpeter unus erat qui coatum scarlet habebat.' (It. *maccaroni*)

macaroon, *n.* small cake made of almonds, sugar etc. (*macaroni*)

macartney, *n.* kind of pheasant found in Far East. (Lord *Macartney*)

macassar oil, an oil for the hair. (*Macassar* in Celebes)

macaw, *n.* large handsome kind of parrot. (Port. *macao*)

macaw, *n.* kinds of palm.

maccaboy, maccabaw, *n.* kind of snuff, us. scented. (*Macouba* in Martinique)

mace, *n.* staff as emblem of authority; large billiard cue; (formerly) heavy spiked club. (O.F.)

mace, *n.* spice made from husk of nutmeg. (F. *macis*)

macédoine, *n.* dish of mixed fruits or vegetables, us. in jelly. (F.)

macerate, *v.t.* and *i.* make, become, soft by steeping; waste by fasting. **maceration**, *n.* (L. *macerare*)

machair, *n.* low-lying sandy beach affording some pasturage. (Gael.)

machairodus, *n.* sabre-toothed tiger, now extinct. (Gk. *machaira*, sword; *odous*, tooth)

machan, *n.* (*Anglo-Ind.*) shooting-platform in tree. (Hind.)

machete, *n.* broad-bladed knife of Spanish America. (Sp.)

Machiavellian, *a.* politically unprincipled, crafty, perfidious; deep-laid. (*Machiavelli*, statesman)

machicolation, *n.* (*archit.*) projecting parapet with openings for dropping stones etc. on assailants; such opening. **machicolated**, *a.* (L.L. *machicolare*)

machinate, *v.i.* plot. **machination**, *n.* (us. *pl.*) artful device. intrigue. **machinator**, *n.* (*machine*)

machine, *n.* mechanical apparatus,

engine; vehicle; methodical or unfeeling person; controlling organization.—*v.t.* sew, print, with machine. **m.-gun,** *n.* one that fires continuously and automatically. **machinery,** *n.* machines or their parts; framework of story or play. **machinist,** *n.* machine operator or maker. (Gk. *mēchanē*)

machtpolitik, n. doctrine that the State should use force if necessary to gain its ends. (G.)

mack, *n.* (*colloq.*) mackintosh. (abbr.)

mackerel, *n.* edible sea-fish barred with blue and silver. **m. sky,** one dappled with small fleecy clouds. (O.F. *makerel*)

mackinac, mackinaw, *n.* (*Amer.*) a heavy woollen cloth; blanket made of it.

mackintosh, *n.* waterproof overcoat or material. (C. *MacIntosh,* patentee)

mackle, *n.* and *v.t.* (*print.*) spot, blur with double impression. (*macula*)

macle, *n.* twin crystal; spot in mineral. **macled,** *a.* spotted. (*macula*)

maconochie, *n.* tinned stew as army ration. (maker's name)

macramé, *n.* fringe-work of knotted cord.

macr(o)-, from Gk. *makros,* long, used in **macrocephalic,** *a.* long-headed; **macrocosm,** *n.* the universe, great whole; **macrodactylic,** *a.* long-toed; **macrology,** *n.* redundancy; prolixity; **macrometer,** *n.* instrument for measuring distant objects; **macropod,** *n.* spider-crab; **macropterous,** *a.* long-winged; **macroscopic,** *a.* visible to the naked eye; **macrurous,** *a.* long-tailed.

macron, *n.* mark over vowel to show it is long, as ē. (Gk. *makros,* long)

macula, *n.* (*pl.* **maculae**) spot in sun, mineral, or skin. **macular,** *a.* **maculate,** *v.t.* spot, defile. **maculation,** *n.* (L.)

mad, *a.* (*compar.* **madder,** *superl.* **maddest**) disordered in mind, insane; rabid; wildly excited; very foolish; (*colloq.*) annoyed.—*v.t.* and *i.* make, be, mad. **like m.,** furiously. **madcap,** *n.* wild, irresponsible person. **madhouse,** *n.* lunatic asylum. **madman, madwoman,** *nn.* maniac. **madwort,** *n.* plant believed to cure hydrophobia. (O.E. *gemǣdan,* drive mad)

madam, *n.* polite form of address to a lady. *madame, n.* (*pl. mesdames*) French form for Mrs. or madam. (O.F. *ma dame,* my lady)

madar, same as **mudar.**

madarosis, *n.* falling of hair, esp. of eyelashes. (Gk. *madaros,* bald)

madden, *v.t.* and *i.* make, become, mad.

madder, *n.* yellow-flowered climbing-plant; red dye got from its root. (O.E. *mædere*)

made, see **make.**

Madeira, *n.* rich white wine. **M. cake,** kind of sponge-cake. (place)

mademoiselle, n. (*pl. mesdemoiselles*) French form of address to unmarried lady, miss. (F.)

madia, *n.* plant like sunflower, whose seeds yield oil. (Chilian *madi*)

Madonna, *n.* Virgin Mary; picture, statue, of her. **M. lily,** white lily. (It.=my lady)

madoqua, *n.* small Abyssinian antelope. (native)

Madras, *n.* coloured handkerchief worn as head-dress in W. Indies. (town)

madrepore, *n.* kind of coral; animal producing this. **madreporic, madreporiform,** *aa.* (It. *madre,* mother; *poro,* a coral-like substance)

madrigal, *n.* love song or poem; (*mus.*) part-song without accompaniment. **madrigalian,** *a.* (It. *madrigale*)

maduro, *a.* (of cigars) full-flavoured. (Sp.)

maelstrom, *n.* great whirlpool. (Du. *malen,* grind; *stroom,* stream)

maenad, *n.* Bacchante, female votary of Bacchus. (Gk. *mainesthai,* rave)

maestoso, adv. (*mus.*) majestically. (It.)

maestro, n. (*pl. maestri*) great musical composer or conductor. (It.)

Mae West, kind of lifebelt. (name of film actress)

mafficking *n.* riotous rejoicing. **maffick,** *v.i.* (relief of *Mafeking*)

mafia, *n.* lawless secret society in Sicily etc. (Sicilian)

mag, *v.t.* (*sl.*) steal.

mag, *n.* (*sl.*) halfpenny.

mag, *n.* (*sl.*) magneto. (abbr.)

magazine, *n.* store, esp. for arms or explosives; compartment in rifle feeding cartridges to breech; miscellaneous literary periodical.—**m. rifle,** one firing several shots without reloading. (Arab. *makhzan*)

Magdalen, Magdalene, *n.* reformed prostitute. (Mary *Magdalene*)

mage, *n.* (*arch.*) magician. (*magus*)

magenta, *n.* purple-red aniline dye.—*a.* of this colour. (battle)

maggot, *n.* larva of fly, grub; whim. **maggoty,** *a.*

magian, *n.* magician, wizard; magus. —*a.* of the Magi. (*magus*)

magic, *n.* witchcraft, sorcery; mysterious agency.—*a.* used in, done by, magic. **black, white, m.,** with, without, aid of devils. **m. lantern,** optical instrument throwing enlarged image of glass picture on darkened screen. **magical,** *a.* **magician,** *n.* one skilled in magic, wizard. (*magus*)

magilp, same as **megilp.**

magistrate, *n.* civil officer administering law; justice of the peace. **magisterial,** *a.* of a magistrate; dictatorial. **magistral,** *a.* of masters; (*med.*) specially prescribed. **magistracy,** *n.* office of magistrate; magistrates collectively. **magistrateship, magistrature,** *nn.* (L. *magister,* master)

magma, *n.* pasty mixture of mineral matter; molten stratum within earth's crust. (Gk. *massein,* knead)

magnalium, *n.* light tough alloy of *magn*esium and *al*uminium.
magnanimous, *a.* great-souled, above petty resentment. **magnanimity,** *n.* (L. *magnus,* great; *animus,* soul)
magnate, *n.* wealthy or eminent man. (L. *magnus,* great)
magnesia, *n.* oxide of magnesium; a carbonate of magnesium used as antacid and purgative. **magnesian,** *a.* **magnesium,** *n.* a metallic element, giving brilliant light when ignited. (place)
magnet, *n.* piece of iron having property of attracting iron and pointing north, loadstone; thing that attracts. **magnetic,** *a.* having, produced by, magnetism; exercising attraction; mesmeric.—*n.pl.* science of magnetism. **magnetic north,** as indicated by compass. **magnetism,** *n.* properties of a magnet; science of these; attraction, personal charm. **animal magnetism,** mesmerism. **magnetite,** *n.* magnetic iron oxide. **magnetize,** *v.t.* make magnetic; attract. **magnetization,** *n.* (Gk. *magnēs*)
magneto, *n.* igniting apparatus of petrol engine. **m.-electricity,** *n.* electric phenomena produced by magnetism. **magnetograph,** *n.* instrument recording movements of **magnetometer,** instrument measuring magnetic force, esp. of the earth. **magneton,** *n.* unit of magnetic moment. (*magnet*)
magnific, magnifical, *aa.* (*arch.*) splendid, magnificent.
Magnificat, *n.* hymn of Virgin Mary in Luke i. 46–55, used as canticle. (opening word in Vulgate)
magnificent, *a.* grand, splendid, imposing; (*colloq.*) excellent. **magnificence,** *n.* (*magnify*)
magnifico, *n.* Venetian nobleman; grandee.
magnify, *v.t.* cause to appear greater, as with lens; exaggerate; (*arch.*) exalt. **magnification, magnifier,** *nn.* (L. *magnus,* great; *facere,* make)
magniloquent, *a.* pompous in speech, bombastic. **magniloquence,** *n.* (L. *magnus,* great; *loqui,* speak)
magnitude, *n.* greatness, size; importance; (of star) order of brilliance. (L. *magnus,* great)
magnolia, *n.* a handsome flowering tree. (P. *Magnol,* botanist)
magnum, *n.* two-quart wine-bottle. **m. bonum,** kinds of plum and potato. *m. opus,* great or chief work. (L. *magnus,* great; *bonus,* good; *opus,* work)
magpie, *n.* chattering black and white bird like crow; chatterer; ring on target between outer and inner. (*mag,* abbr. of Margaret+*pie*)
magsman, *n.* street swindler. (*mag*)
magus, *n.* (*pl.* magi) priest of ancient Persia; sorcerer; (*pl.*) the three ' wise men from the East ' (Matt. ii. 1). (O. Pers.)
Magyar, *n.* and *a.* (member, tongue) of dominant race in Hungary. (native)
maharajah, maharaja, *n.* title of some Indian princes. **maharanee,** *n.* maharajah's wife. (Hind. *maha,* great)
mahatma, *n.* priest of inner cult of Buddhism; sage. (Sanskr. *maha,* great; *atman,* soul)
Mahdi, *n.* expected leader, saviour, of Mohammedans. **Mahdism, Mahdiism,** *n.* (Arab. *mahdiy,* the guided one)
mah-jongg, *n.* Chinese table game for four, with 144 pieces or ' tiles.'
mahlstick, same as **maulstick.**
mahogany, *n.* a tropical American tree; its reddish-brown wood; dinner-table.
Mahomedan, Mahometan, see **Mohammedan.**
Mahound, *n.* (*arch.*) Mohammed. (O.F. *Mahun*)
mahout, *n.* elephant-driver. (Hind. *mahaut*)
mahseer, *n.* large Indian freshwater fish. (Hind. *mahāsir*)
maid, *n.* girl; virgin, spinster; female servant. **m. of honour,** unmarried lady attending queen; kind of cake. **M. Marian,** May Queen; grotesque character in morris-dance. (*maiden*)
maidan, *n.* (*Anglo-Ind.*) parade-ground. (Pers.)
maiden, *n.* girl; spinster; old kind of guillotine.—*a.* unmarried; untried, with blank record. **m. name,** surname of woman before marriage. **m. over,** (*cricket*) in which no runs are scored. **m. speech,** person's first speech in assembly. **maidenhair,** *n.* a delicate fern. **maidenhead,** *n.* virginity; hymen. **maidenhood,** *n.* **maidenlike, maidenly,** *aa.* modest, becoming a maiden. (O.E. *mægden*)
maidservant, *n.* female servant.
maieutic, *a.* of Socratic method of teaching by means of questions; obstetric. Gk. *maia,* midwife)
maigre, *a.* without meat; of a fast-day. (F.=lean)
maik, same as **mag.**
mail, *n.* armour of rings or plates.—*v.t.* clothe in this. **mailed fist,** physical force. (L. *macula,* mesh)
mail, *n.* post-bag; the post; letters.—*v.t.* send by post. **m.-coach, m.-train,** *n.* those carrying mails. **m.-cart,** *n.* mail-coach; light perambulator. (O.F. *male,* bag)
maim, *v.t.* cripple; mutilate. (O.F. *mahaignier*)
main, *n.* hand at dice, number called by caster; match at cock-fighting.
main, *n.* strength; principal channel or part; (*poet.*) ocean.—*a.* chief, principal. **in the m.,** generally. **m. chance,** private advantage. **m. force,** physical strength. **Spanish M.,** north coast of S. America. **m.-brace,** *n.* rope working main yard. **splice the m.-brace,** have drink.

mainland, mainmast, mainsail, mainspring, *nn.* principal land etc. **mainly,** *adv.* chiefly. **mainstay,** *n.* stay from maintop to deck; chief support. **maintop,** *n.* platform on mainmast. (O.E. *mægen*)
mains, *n.* (*Scot.*) home farm.
maintain, *v.t.* keep going, support; keep up, sustain; keep in repair; affirm. **maintenance,** *n.* maintaining; means of support; (*law*) aiding party in lawsuit without lawful cause. (L. *manu tenēre,* hold in hand)
maiolica, same as **majolica.**
mair, *Scot.* form of **more.**
maisonette, maisonnette, *n.* small house; part of house let separately. (F.)
maist, *a.* (*Scot.*) most.—*adv.* almost.
maistry, *n.* (*Anglo-Ind.*) foreman; skilled workman; cook. (Port. *mestre,* master)
maître, *n.* master. *m. d'hôtel,* house-steward; hotel manager. (F.)
maize, *n.* Indian corn. **maizena,** *n.* maize starch as food. (Sp. *maiz*)
majesty, *n.* stateliness; sovereignty. **His, Her, Your, M.,** title of king, queen. **majestic,** *a.* stately, imposing. (L. *majestas*)
majolica, *n.* enamelled pottery of Italian origin. (It.)
major, *n.* person of full age; army officer above captain; (*logic*) major premiss; (*sl.*) sergeant-major.—*a.* greater of two; senior; (*mus.*) greater by a semitone. **m. in,** (*Amer.*) take as chief subject of studies. **m. key,** (*mus.*) in which semitones lie between 3rd and 4th, and 7th and 8th. **m. premiss,** (*logic*) principal statement in syllogism. **m. prophets,** Isaiah, Jeremiah, Ezekiel, Daniel. **m.-general,** *n.* rank below lieutenant-general.
majordomo, *n.* house-steward.
majority, *n.* greater number; more than half; excess of winning over losing vote; legal age (21); majorship. **join the majority,** die. **majorship,** *n.* rank of major. (L.=greater)
majuscule, *a.* and *n.* capital, uncial (letter). **majuscular,** *a.* (L. *majusculus,* somewhat larger)
make, *n.* (*obs.*) mate; match. **makeless,** *a.* matchless; (*Shake.*) husbandless. (O.E. *gemaca*)
make, *v.t.* and *i.* (*past, p.p.* made) create, cause; establish, construct; perform, effect; accomplish. reach; become, amount to; consider; earn; proceed, tend; eat (meal); shuffle (cards); (of tide) rise.—*n.* form, structure. **m. at,** attack. **m. away with,** destroy. **m. believe,** feign, **m. bold, free,** take liberty. **m. face,** grimace. **m. for,** move towards. **m. good,** fulfil; prove; compensate; (*colloq.*) succeed. **m. head,** advance. **m. much of,** pet. **m. out,** draw up; decipher; establish; (*Amer. sl.*) succeed. **m. over,** transfer. **m. sail,** set (more) sail. **m. up,** compose, compile; constitute; compensate; paint (face). **m. up to,** curry favour with. **on the m.,** intent on gain. **m.-believe,** *n.* pretence.—*a.* sham. **m.-up,** *n.* composition, style; cosmetics. **a made man,** one whose success is assured. (O.E. *macian*)
maker, *n.* creator; poet.
makeshift, *n.* temporary expedient.
makeweight, *n.* what is thrown into scale to make up weight; stop-gap.
making, *n.* creation; (*pl.*) earnings; needful qualities; (*Amer. sl.*) materials for rolling cigarette.
mako, *n.* large Australasian shark. (Maori)
mal-, *pref.* bad, badly, as in **maltreat.** (L. *male,* badly)
Malacca cane, brown walking-stick of Malacca palm.
malachite, *n.* carbonate of copper, a green mineral taking a high polish. (Gk. *malachē,* mallow)
malaco-, from Gk. *malakos,* soft, used in **malacoderm,** *n.* soft-skinned animal; **malacology,** *n.* science of molluscs; **malacopterygian,** *a.* soft-finned; **malacostracan,** *a.* soft-shelled, of a class of crustaceans.
maladdress, *n.* awkwardness.
maladjustment, *n.* faulty adjustment.
maladministration, *n.* bad management.
maladroit, *a.* clumsy, unskilful. (F.)
malady, *n.* illness, disease. (L. *male,* badly; *habēre,* have)
mala fidē, in bad faith. (L.)
Malaga, *n.* a white wine. (place)
Malagasy, *a.* and *n.* (language, inhabitant) of Madagascar.
malaise, *n.* vague feeling of bodily discomfort. (F.)
malamute, *n.* Eskimo dog. (tribe)
malanders, *n.* scabs behind horse's knee. (L. *malandria*)
malapert, *a.* (*arch.*) impudent. (O.F.)
malapropism, malaprop, *nn.* ludicrous misuse of word, e.g. 'comparisons are odorous.' **malapropian,** *a.* (Mrs *Malaprop* in play)
malapropos, *adv.* and *a.* out of place, ill-timed.—*n.* inopportune thing. (F. *mal à propos*)
malar, *a.* of cheek.—*n.* cheek-bone. (L. *mala,* jaw)
malaria, *n.* intermittent fever caused by mosquito bite; miasma. **malarial, malarious,** *aa.* (It. *mal' aria,* bad air)
Malay, Malayan, *a.* and *n.* (native) of Malay Peninsula. (native *malayu*)
Malayalam, *n.* language of Malabar. (native)
malcontent, *a.* and *n.* disaffected, discontented (person).
mal de mer, seasickness. (F.)
male, *a.* of the sex that begets young, masculine; (*bot.*) having stamens.—*n.* male person or animal. (L. *mas*)
malediction, *n.* curse, imprecation; slander. **maledictory,** *a.* (L. *male,* ill; *dicere,* speak)

malefactor, *n.* criminal, evil-doer. **malefaction,** *n.* **malefic,** *a.* (of magic) baleful. **maleficent,** *a.* harmful; criminal. **maleficence,** *n.* (L. *male,* ill; *facere,* do)
malemute, same as **malamute.**
malevolent, *a.* ill-disposed, spiteful. **malevolence,** *n.* (L. *male,* ill; *velle,* wish)
malfeasance, *n.* (*law*) illegal action, official misconduct. **malfeasant,** *a.* and *n.* (O.F. *malfaisance*)
malgré, prep. in spite of. *m. lui,* against one's desires. (F.)
mali, *n.* (*Anglo-Ind.*) native gardener. (Hind.)
malic, *a.* (of acid) got from fruit. (L. *malum,* apple)
malice, *n.* deliberate ill will, spite; (law) intention to injure. **malicious,** *a.* (L. *malus,* bad)
malign, *a.* hurtful; (of disease) malignant.—*v.t.* slander, misrepresent. **malignant,** *a.* feeling extreme ill will; (of disease) of virulent type. —*n.* supporter of Charles I against Parliament. **malignancy, malignity,** *nn.* (L. *malus,* bad; *genus,* sort)
malinger, *v.i.* feign illness to evade duty. **malingerer,** *n.* (F. *malingre,* sickly)
malism, *n.* doctrine that evil exceeds good in the world. (L. *malus,* bad)
malison, *n.* (*arch.*) curse, execration. (*malediction*)
malkin, *n.* (*Shake.*) slut. (dim. of *Matilda*)
mall, *n.* public shaded walk; (formerly) pall-mall; alley, mallet, for this; maul. (L. *malleus,* hammer)
mallard, *n.* wild drake or duck. (O.F. *malard*)
malleable, *a.* that can be shaped by hammering; pliable, adaptable. **malleability,** *n.* (L. *malleus,* hammer)
mallee, *n.* dwarf kind of eucalyptus. (native Australian)
mallee, same as **mali.**
mallemuck, *n.* fulmar petrel. (Du. *mal,* foolish; *mok,* gull)
mallenders, same as **malanders.**
mallet, *n.* wooden hammer; stick used in croquet or polo. (F. *maillet*)
mallow, *n.* kinds of plant incl. hairy-leaved weed with purple flowers. (L. *malva*)
malm, *n.* soft friable rock; loamy soil used for making bricks. (O.E. *mealm*)
malmaison, *n.* kind of carnation. (place)
malmsey, *n.* a strong sweet wine. (*Monembasia* in Greece)
malnutrition, *n.* underfeeding.
malodorous, *a.* ill-smelling.
malpractice, *n.* wrongdoing; abuse of position by doctor or trustee.
malt, *n.* barley etc. prepared for brewing.—*a.* made from malt.—*v.t.* and *i.* turn into malt. **m.-worm,** *n.* toper. (O.E. *mealt*)
Maltese, *a.* and *n.* (inhabitant) of Malta. **M. cat,** blue with short hairs. **M. cross,** with equal arms expanded at end and indented. **M. dog,** small silky-haired spaniel.
maltha, *n.* kinds of cement; mineral tar. (Gk.)
Malthusian, *a.* and *n.* (follower) of T. R. Malthus, who maintained that population tends to outgrow means of subsistence and should be checked. **Malthusianism,** *n.*
maltreat, *v.t.* ill-use, treat roughly. **maltreatment,** *n.*
maltster, *n.* maker of malt.
malvaceous, *a.* of mallows. (*mallow*)
malversation, *n.* corrupt handling of public or trust funds. (L. *male,* badly; *versari,* behave)
malvoisie, same as **malmsey.**
mama, same as **mamma.**
mamelon, *n.* rounded hill, mound. (F.=nipple)
Mameluke, *n.* member of former ruling class in Egypt; (in Mohammedan countries) slave. (Arab. *mamluk*)
mamilla, *n.* nipple; nipple-shaped thing. **mamillary,** *a.* of, like, nipple. **mamillate, mamillated,** *aa.* having nipples. (L.)
mamma, *n.* mother.
mamma, *n.* (*pl.* **mammae**) breast, milk gland. **mammary,** *a.* **mammal,** *n.* animal that suckles its young. **Mammalia,** *n.pl.* (*zool.*) class of mammals. **mammalian,** *a.* **mammaliferous,** *a.* (*geol.*) containing mammalian remains. **mammalology,** *n.* science of mammals **mammalologist,** *n.* (L.)
mammee, *n.* tropical American tree with edible fruit. (Sp. *mamey*)
mammer, *v.i.* (*Shake.*) stammer; waver.
mammet, *n.* (*Shake.*) doll, puppet.
mammifer, *n.* animal with breasts, mammal. **mammiferous,** *a.* (*mamma*)
mammock, *v.t.* (*Shake.*) break in pieces.
mammon, *n.* riches, wealth personified. **mammonism,** *n.* worldliness, worship of wealth. **mammonist, mammonite,** *nn.* **mammonish,** *a.* (Aram. *mamon*)
mammoth, *n.* huge extinct elephant. —*a.* gigantic. (Russ. *mammot*)
mammy, *n.* mamma; (*Amer.*) negro nurse.
man, *n pl.* **(men)** human being, person; adult male; husband; valet, workman, follower; mankind; (*chess* etc.) piece; (*pl.*) soldiers.—*v.t.* (*past, p.p.* **manned**) furnish with men; fortify. **best m.,** groomsman. **inner m.,** soul; (*joc.*) stomach. **m. about town,** society idler. **m. Friday,** servile attendant, factotum. **m. in the street,** ordinary person. **m. of business,** agent. **m. of letters,** scholar, writer. **m. of straw,** of no substance, imaginary. **m. of the world,** tolerant, experienced. **m. to m.,** openly. **m.-at-arms,** *n.* medieval soldier. **m.-eater,** *n.* cannibal; man-eating tiger;

biting horse. **manhandle,** *v.t.* manipulate; hustle. **m.-of-war,** *n.* warship. (O.E.)

manacle, *n.* (us. *pl.*) fetter, handcuff. —*v.t.* shackle. (L. *manus*, hand)

manage, *v.t.* and *i.* conduct, control, take charge of; cajole; wield; contrive (to), succeed.—*n.* (*arch.*) training of horse, manège. **manageable,** *a.* **management,** *n.* managing; trickery; governing body. **manager,** *n.* (*fem.* **manageress**). **managerial,** *a.* **managership,** *n.* **managing,** *a.* interfering, officious. (L. *manus*, hand)

manakin, same as **manikin.**

mañana, *adv.* and *n.* to-morrow, by and by; dilatoriness. (Sp.)

manatee, *n.* a large aquatic animal, sea-cow. (Carib. *manattoui*)

manavilins, manavlins, *n.pl.* (*naut. sl.*) odds and ends, scraps.

manche, *n.* (*heraldry*) sleeve. (F.)

Manchester, *n.* **M. school,** advocates of free trade and *laissez-faire.*

manchet, *n.* small loaf of fine bread.

manchineel, *n.* a poisonous tropical American tree. (L. name *Matia*)

manciple, *n.* catering official, steward. (L. *manus*, hand; *capere*, take)

Mancunian, *a.* and *n.* (citizen) of Manchester. (L. *Mancunium*, Manchester)

-mancy, *suf.* divination by, as in **oneiromancy.** (Gk. *manteia*)

mandamus, *n.* (*law.*) order by superior to inferior court. (L.=we bid)

mandarin, *n.* Chinese official or magistrate. **mandarinate,** *n.* body of these. (Sanskr. *mantra*, counsel)

mandarin, mandarine, *n.* a small sweet orange; its colour; a liqueur. (F.)

mandate, *n.* authoritative command; papal rescript; electorate's instructions as inferred from its votes; commission to act for another, esp. from League of Nations to govern a backward country.—*v.t.* entrust by mandate. **mandatary,** *n.* one to whom mandate is given. **mandatory,** *a.* of a command.—*n.* mandatary. (L. *manus*, hand; *dare*, give)

mandible, *n.* (*zool.*) jaw, esp. lower; either part of beak. **mandibular,** *a.* of, like, mandible. **mandibulate,** *a.* having mandibles. (L. *mandere*, chew)

mandora, mandola, *n.* small kind of lute. **mandoline, mandolin,** *n.* wire-stringed instrument of lute type played with plectrum. (It.)

mandragora, *n.* (*Shake.*) mandrake.

mandrake, *n.* a narcotic plant, fabled to shriek when uprooted. (Gk. *mandragoras*)

mandrel, mandril, *n.* spindle of lathe, to which work is fixed while turned; core round which metal is forged.

mandrill, *n.* blue-faced baboon.

manducate, *v.t.* chew, eat. **manducation,** *n.* **manducatory,** *a.* (L. *mandere*, chew)

mane, *n.* long hair on neck of horse, lion etc. (O.E. *manu*)

manège, manege, *n.* training of horse; horsemanship, riding-school. (F.)

mānēs, *n.pl.* ancestral spirits, shades; gods of lower world. (L.)

manful, *a.* courageous, resolute.

mangabey, *n.* a slender African monkey. (place)

manganese, *n.* a brittle reddish-grey metallic element; its black oxide, used in making glass. **manganesian, manganic,** *aa.* (*magnesia*)

mange, *n.* skin-disease of dogs etc. (O.F. *manjuer*, eat)

mangel-wurzel, mangel, *n.* large kind of beet. (G. *mangold*, beet; *wurzel*, root)

manger, *n.* eating-trough for horses or cattle. (L. *mandere*, chew)

mangle, *v.t.* hack, mutilate; spoil by blunders. (O.F. *mahaignier*, maim)

mangle, *n.* rolling-press for smoothing linen.—*v.t.* press in mangle. (Du. *mangel*)

mango, *n.* an E. Indian tree; its fleshy fruit. **m.-fish,** *n.* a gold-coloured fish. (Tamil *man*, mango; *kay*, fruit)

mangold, same as **mangel.**

mangonel, *n.* ancient engine for hurling stones. (Gk. *mangganon*)

mangosteen, *n.* an E. Indian tree; its red-brown juicy fruit. (Malay *mangustan*)

mangrove, *n.* tropical tree whose bark is used for tanning.

mangy, *a.* scabby; squalid, shabby. (*mange*)

manhattan, *n.* kind of cocktail. (place)

manhole, *n.* hole giving access to sewer, boiler etc.

manhood, *n.* state of being man; manliness. **m. suffrage,** enfranchisement of all adult males.

mania, *n.* acute or violent insanity; great enthusiasm. **maniac,** *a.* raving mad.—*n.* madman. **maniacal,** *a.* (Gk.)

Manichee, *n.* one of sect believing in two eternal equal principles of good and evil. **Manichaean, Manichean,** *aa.* **Manichaeism, Manicheism,** *nn.* (*Manichaios*, founder)

manicure, *n.* treatment of hands and nails; one who gives this.—*v.t.* give manicure to. **manicurist,** *n.* (L. *manus*, hand; *cura*, care)

manifest, *a.* clear, apparent, plain.—*v.t.* and *i.* show clearly, evince; record in manifest; (of ghost) appear. —*n.* invoice of cargo for customs. **manifestation,** *n.* disclosure. **manifestative,** *a.* **manifesto,** *n.* public declaration of political measures or intentions. (L. *manifestus*)

manifold, *a.* various in kind or quality; numerous.—*n.* (*mech.*) pipe with several outlets.—*v.t.* multiply copies of (letter etc.). **m. writer,** copying machine. (*many*; *fold*)

manikin, *n.* little man, dwarf; anatomical model of body; small tropical American bird. (Du. *manneken*)

manilla, manila, *n.* hemp for ropes; kind of cheroot. **m. paper,** kind of stout wrapping-paper. (place)
manilla, *n.* metal ring used as currency in W. Africa. (Sp.)
manille, *n.* highest card but one in quadrille or ombre. (F.)
manioc, *n.* cassava; meal made from it. (native)
maniple, *n.* company (60–120 men) of Roman legion; scarf worn on left arm by priest at mass. (L. *manus,* hand; *plēre,* fill)
manipulate, *v.t.* operate by hand; treat skilfully, manage. **manipulation, manipulator,** *nn.* **manipulative, manipulatory,** *aa.* (*maniple*)
manitou, manito, *n.* (*Amer. Ind.*) spirit of good or evil. (Algonquin)
mankind, *n.* human race, humanity.
manly, *a.* having qualities of a man, brave, firm. **manliness,** *n.*
manna, *n.* miraculous food of Israelites in wilderness; spiritual food; sweet juice of tree. (Heb. *man*)
mannequin, *n.* woman employed to show off costumes. (F.=lay figure)
manner, *n.* way a thing happens or is done; sort; style; (*pl.*) social behaviour; mode of life. **mannered,** *a.* affected, elaborate. **mannerism,** *n.* peculiarity, trick, of style, behaviour, or gesture. **mannerless,** *a.* rude. **mannerly,** *a.* polite, respectful.—*adv.* politely. (L. *manus,* hand)
mannish, *a.* masculine, aping men.
mannite, *n.* sugar got from manna. **mannitose,** *a.*
manœuvre, *n.* military or naval evolution; skilful plan, artifice.—*v.i.* and *t.* execute, put through, manœuvre; adroitly work into or out of a position. **manœuvrer,** *n.* (L. *manus,* hand; *opera,* work)
manometer, *n.* pressure-gauge showing density of gases. **manometric,** *a.* (Gk. *manos,* thin)
ma non troppo, (*mus.*) but not too much. (It.)
manor, *n.* feudal unit of land; holding of nobleman. **m.-house, m.-seat,** *nn.* house of manor. **manorial,** *a.* (L. *manēre,* remain)
manqué, *a.* spoiled, that might have been but is not. (F.)
mansard, *n.* (also **m. roof**) roof with break in its slope, lower part being steeper than upper. (inventor)
manse, *n.* (*Scot.*) minister's house. (L. *manēre,* remain)
mansion, *n.* large house; (*pl.*) block of flats. **m.-house,** *n.* manor-house; residence of Lord Mayor of London. (L. *mansio*)
manslaughter, *n.* (*law*) criminal homicide without malice.
mansuetude, *n.* gentleness, mildness. (L. *mansuetus,* tame)
mantel, *n.* structure round fireplace. **m.-board, m.-shelf,** *nn.* ornamental shelf at top of mantel. (=*mantle*)
mantelet, same as **mantlet.**
mantelpiece, *n.* mantel; mantel-shelf.
mantic, *a.* of divination. (Gk. *mantis,* prophet)
manticore, *n.* fabulous beast with human head, body of lion, and tail of scorpion. (Gk. *mantichoras*)
mantilla, *n.* kind of scarf worn as head-dress; light cape. (Sp.)
mantis, *n.* insect like locust. **praying m.,** kind that holds forelegs like folded hands when waiting for prey. (Gk. =prophet)
mantissa, *n.* decimal part of logarithm. (L.=addition)
mantle, *n.* loose sleeveless cloak; covering; incandescent hood for gas-jet.—*v.t.* and *i.* cover, envelop; conceal; (of blood) mount to cheeks; (of face) blush. **mantlet,** *n.* short cape; movable screen protecting besiegers or gunners. (L. *mantellum*)
mantology, *n.* divination. (*mantic*)
mantrap, *n.* trap to catch trespassers.
mantua, *n.* woman's loose gown of 18th century. **m.-maker,** *n.* dressmaker. (F. *manteau,* mantle)
manual, *a.* of, done with, hands.—*n.* handbook, textbook; R.C. service-book; organ keyboard. **m. alphabet,** finger-letters for deaf and dumb. **m. exercise,** drill in handling rifle. (L. *manus,* hand)
manufacture, *v.t.* make from raw materials, esp. in quantity; fabricate.—*n.* making, mechanical production or product. **manufacturer,** *n.* **manufactory,** *n.* factory, workshop. (L. *manus,* hand; *facere,* make)
manumit, *v.t.* release from slavery; free. **manumission,** *n.* (L. *manus,* hand; *mittere,* send)
manure, *n.* dung, compost, used to fertilize soil.—*v.t.* apply manure to. **manurial,** *a.* (*manœuvre*)
manuscript, *a.* hand-written.—*n.* (*abbr.* **MS.,** *pl.* **MSS.**) manuscript book or document; copy for printing. (L. *manus,* hand; *scribere,* write)
Manx, *a.* and *n.* (language, people) of Isle of Man. **M. cat,** tailless kind. **Manxman,** *n.*
many, *a.* (*compar.* **more,** *superl.* **most**) numerous.—*n.* great number, multitude. **one too m.,** not wanted; too clever. **the m.,** the populace. **m.-sided,** *a.* with many aspects; versatile. **manyplies,** *n.* ruminant's third stomach. (O.E. *manig*)
Manzanilla, *n.* a light dry sherry. (Sp.)
Maori, *n.* member, language, of New Zealand native race. (native)
map, *n.* flat representation of earth's surface, chart; (*sl.*) face.—*v.t.* represent on map. **m. out,** arrange in detail. **off the m.,** (*colloq.*) of no account. (L. *mappa,* napkin)
maple, *n.* kinds of tree. **m.-leaf,** *n.* emblem of Canada. (O.E. *mapeltréow*)
mappery, *n.* (*Shake.*) map-making.

mar, *v.t.* damage, disfigure; ruin. (O.E. *merran*)
marabou, *n.* large stork; adjutant; its down as trimming etc. (F.)
marabout, *n.* Mohammedan hermit or his shrine. (Arab. *murabit*)
maraschino, *n.* liqueur made from cherries. (L. *amarus*, bitter)
marasmus, *n.* emaciation, atrophy. **marasmic**, *a.* (Gk. *marainein*, wither)
marathon, *n.* long-distance race (us. about 25 miles). (place)
maraud, *v.i.* and *t.* make plundering raid; pillage. **marauder**, *n.* (F. *maraud*, rogue)
maravedi, *n.* Spanish coin, copper (⅙*d.*) or gold (14*s.*). (Arab. *Murabitin*, a Moorish dynasty)
marble, *n.* hard limestone capable of taking polish; small stone ball; (*pl.*) marble sculptures; boy's game with marbles.—*a.* of marble; hard, unfeeling.—*v.t.* colour like veined marble. **marbly**, *a.* (Gk. *marmaros*)
marc, *n.* refuse from pressed fruit. (F.)
marcando, *marcato*, *aa.* and *advv.* (*mus.*) with distinctness. (It.)
marcasite, *n.* white iron pyrites. (L.L. *marcasita*)
marcel wave, kind of artificial wave in hair. (inventor)
marcescent, *a.* (*bot.*) withering without falling off. **marcescence**, *n.* (L. *marcēre*, fade)
March, *n.* third month of year. (L. *Martius*, of Mars)
march, *n.* border, frontier; borderland.—*v.i.* have common boundary (with). (F. *marche*)
march, *v.i.* advance in military order or with regular paces; proceed steadily; progress.—*v.t.* cause to go. —*n.* marching, stately walk; progress; military step or music to accompany it. **marcher**, *n.* **marching orders**, directions to depart. (F. *marcher*)
marchioness, *n.* wife of marquis; lady of equal rank. (L.L. *marchionissa*)
marchpane, same as **marzipan**.
marconi, *v.t.* and *i.* and *n.* cable. **marconigram**, *n.* wireless message. (inventor)
mardi gras, Shrove Tuesday; last day of carnival. (F.=fat Tuesday)
mare, *n.* female horse. **grey m. is the better horse**, wife rules her husband. **m.'s-nest**, *n.* fancied discovery, hoax. **m.'s-tail**, *n.* cirrus cloud; an aquatic plant. **Shanks's m.**, one's own legs. (O.E. *mere*)
mārĕ, *n.* sea. *m. clausum*, under a country's jurisdiction. *m. liberum*, open to all. (L.)
maremma, *n.* unhealthy marshy coastal district. (It.)
mareschal, *arch.* for **marshal**.
margarine, *n.* imitation butter. (Gk. *margaron*, pearl)
margarite, *n.* pearl mica; (*arch.*) pearl. (Gk. *margaron*)
margay, *n.* S. American tiger-cat. (native *mbaracaia*)
marge, *poet.* for **margin**.
margin, *n.* border, strip near edge; blank space round printed page; amount allowed beyond what is necessary; sum deposited with stockbroker to cover risk of loss on speculation.—*v.t.* furnish with margins; deposit margin on. **marginal**, *a.* **marginalia**, *n.pl.* notes written on margin. **marginate, marginated**, *aa.* having margin. (L. *margo*)
margosa, *n.* Indian neem-tree. (native)
margrave, *n.* (*fem.* **margravine**) former German title of nobility. **margravate**, *n.* margrave's domain. (Du. *markgrave*, border count)
marguerite, *n.* kinds of large daisy. (Gk. *margaron*, pearl)
mariage de convenance, marriage for worldly motives, not love. (F.)
Marian, *a.* of Virgin Mary or Queen Mary.
maricolous, *a.* inhabiting the sea. (L. *mare*, sea; *colere*, inhabit)
marigold, *n.* yellow-flowered plant. (*Mary*; *gold*)
marimba, *n.* musical instrument of the xylophone type.
marinade, *n.* pickle of wine, vinegar, and spices; fish, meat, so pickled. (Sp. *marinar*, pickle in brine)
marine, *a.* of, found in, formed by, the sea; of shipping.—*n.* shipping, fleet; soldier serving on warship. **blue, red m.**, of artillery, of infantry. **m. stores**, old ships' materials, junk. **tell that to the mm.**, expression of disbelief.
mariner, *n.* sailor. (L. *mare*, sea)
Mariolatry, *n.* worship of Virgin Mary.
marionette, *n.* puppet worked by strings. (F. *marionnette*)
marish, *n.* (*poet.*) marsh.—*a.* marshy. (L.L. *mariscus*, marsh)
marital, *a.* of a husband; of marriage. (L. *marītus*, husband)
maritime, *a.* near, connected with, the sea; naval. (L. *mare*, sea)
marjoram, *n.* an aromatic plant. **pot, sweet, m.**, kinds used in cookery. (L.L. *marjorana*)
mark, *n.* target, objective; token, sign; line, dot, scar etc.; standard, unit of merit; (formerly) district; (*athletics*) starting-point; (*boxing*) pit of stomach; (*naut.*) point on lead-line marking 2, 3, 5, 7, 10, 15, 17, 20, or 25 fathoms; (*Rugby football*) heel-mark for fair catch.—*v.t.* and *i.* make mark on; indicate, be token of; watch, take notice; grade in merit. **beside the m.**, irrelevant. **easy m.**, (*sl.*) gullible person. **make one's m.**, attract notice. **m. down, up**, lower, raise (price). **m. off**, delimit. **m. out**, indicate. **m. time**, move feet without advancing; wait expectantly. **of m.**, noteworthy. **save the m.!** expression of scorn. **trade m.**, firm's sign. **up to the m.**, good enough; well. (O.E. *mearcian*)

mark, *n.* German coin (formerly about 1*s.*); obsolete English coin (13*s.* 4*d.*); (O.E. *marc*)

marked, *a.* noticeable. **markedly,** *adv.* unmistakably.

marker, *n.* scorer at billiards; man who marks game-birds; ribbon etc. to mark place in book.

market, *n.* place, gathering, for sale and purchase of commodities; centre of trade; demand, rate of sale.—*v.i.* and *t.* buy, sell, in market. **come into, be put on, the m.,** be offered, offer, for sale. **m.-day,** *n.* day of public market. **m. garden,** growing vegetables for sale. **m.-place, m. town,** *n.* where market is held. **m. price,** current price. **marketable,** *a.* in demand. (L. *mercari,* trade)

markhor, *n.* large wild goat of N. India. (Pushtu=snake-eater)

marking, *n.* mark; colouring. **m.-ink,** *n.* indelible ink.

marksman, *n.* crack shot. **marksmanship,** *n.* skill in shooting.

marl, *n.* rich limy clay.—*v.t.* manure with marl. (L. *marga*)

marline, *n.* (*naut.*) two-stranded cord. **m.-spike, marlinspike,** *n.* pointed tool for unravelling rope in splicing. (Du. *marren,* bind; *lijn,* line)

marlite, *n.* kind of marl resisting action of air. **marly,** *a.* like, full of, marl.

marmalade, *n.* jam made from oranges. **lemon, grape-fruit, m.** etc., made from these fruits. (Gk. *meli,* honey; *mēlon,* apple)

marmolite, *n.* pale-green laminated serpentine. (Gk. *marmairein,* shine)

marmoreal, marmorean, *aa.* of, like, marble. (L. *marmor,* marble)

marmoset, *n.* small American monkey. (O.F. *marmouset,* grotesque figure)

marmot, *n.* short-tailed rodent like squirrel; its fur; kind of bathing-cap. (F. *marmotte*)

marocain, *n.* dress material with grain surface. (F.=Moroccan)

maroon, *n.* marooned person; (orig.) fugitive slave.—*v.t.* abandon (person) on desolate island or coast. (F. *marron*)

maroon, *n.* and *a.* brownish crimson; signal-rocket with loud report. (F. *marron,* chestnut)

marplot, *n.* officious frustrator of plans. (*mar; plot*)

marque, *n.* **letters of m.,** privateer's licence to plunder enemy's merchant shipping. (F.)

marquee, *n.* large field-tent. (*marquise*)

marquess, same as **marquis.**

marquetry, marqueterie, *n.* inlaid work, wood mosaic. (F.)

marquis, *n.* noble ranking between duke and earl or count. **marquisate,** *n.* lordship of marquis. **marquise,** *n.* foreign marchioness; ring set with oval pointed group of gems; (*arch.*) tent. (O.F. *marchis*)

marquois, *n.* **m. scale,** device for drawing equidistant parallel lines.

marram, *n.* bent-grass. (O.N. *marr,* sea; *halmr,* haulm)

marriage, *n.* wedlock; wedding; union. **companionate m., trial marriage. m. licence,** authorizing marriage. **m. lines,** marriage certificate. **m. market,** supply of eligible partners. **m. settlement,** securing property to wife. **marriageable,** *a.* of an age to marry. (L. *marītus,* husband)

marron glacé, chestnut coated with sugar. (F.)

marrow, *n.* (*dial.*) mate, consort; match.

marrow, *n.* fatty substance inside bones; essence, inner meaning; marrowfat. **vegetable m.,** kind of gourd. **m.-bone,** *n.* bone containing marrow; (*pl.*) knees. **marrowfat,** *n.* kind of large pea. **marrowy,** *a.* (O.E. *mearg*)

marry, *v.t.* and *i.* (*past, p.p.* **married**) take, give, in marriage; wed; join as husband and wife; unite closely. (L. *marītus,* husband)

marry, *int.* (*arch.*) indeed, forsooth. **m. come up!** hoity-toity! (Virgin *Mary*)

Mars, *n.* Roman god of war; planet next beyond earth. (L.)

Marsala, *n.* light wine like sherry. (place)

Marseillaise, *n.* French national anthem. (*Marseilles*)

marsh, *n.* low-lying wet land, swamp. **m. gas,** firedamp. **m. mallow,** red-flowered shrubby herb; kind of sweet. **m. marigold,** yellow-flowered plant, kingcup. (O.E. *mersc*)

marshal, *n.* steward at assembly; herald; highest military rank, Field Marshal; (*Amer.*) civil officer of district.—*v.t.* arrange in due order; conduct ceremoniously. **marshaller, marshalship,** *nn.* **Marshalsea,** *n.* former Southwark prison. (O.H.G. *marahscalh,* horse servant)

marshy, *a.* swampy; produced in marshes.

marsupial, *a.* (*zool.*) of, like, pouch; having pouch for carrying young.—*n.* marsupial animal, e.g. kangaroo. (Gk. *marsupion,* pouch)

mart, *n.* place of trade, market. (L. *mercari,* trade)

Martello tower, small round fort for coast defence. (Cape *Mortella*)

marten, *n.* weasel-like animal; its fur. (O.F. *martrine,* of marten)

martial, *a.* of, suited to, war; military; brave. **m. law,** military government in place of ordinary law. **Martian,** *a.* and *n.* (inhabitant) of Mars. (*Mars*)

martin, *n.* (also **house-m.**) bird like swallow. (name)

martinet, *n.* strict disciplinarian. **martinettism,** *n.* **martinettish,** *a.* (French drill-master)

martingale, *n.* check-strap preventing horse from rearing or throwing up head; gambling system of doubling successive stakes; (*naut.*) short spar under bowsprit. (F.)

martini, *n.* cocktail of gin, vermouth, orange bitters etc.

martini, *n.* Martini-Henry rifle. (inventor)

Martinmas, *n.* St. Martin's Day, 11th November.

martlet, *n.* swift; (*heraldry*) bird without feet. (F. *martelet*)

martyr, *n.* one put to death for adherence to religion; sufferer for a cause; victim.—*v.t.* put to death for belief; make martyr of. **martyrdom,** *n.* martyr's death or sufferings; torment. **martyrize,** *v.t.* martyr. **martyrolatry,** *n.* worship of martyrs. **martyrology,** *n.* history, list, of martyrs. **martyrological,** *a.* **martyry,** *n.* shrine in honour of martyr. (Gk. *martus,* witness)

marvel, *n.* wonderful thing, wonder.—*v.i.* wonder, feel astonishment. **marvellous,** *a.* wonderful, amazing; improbable. (L. *mirari,* wonder at)

Marxian, *a.* and *n.* (adherent) of the socialist doctrines of Karl Marx. **Marxism,** *n.*

mary-bud, *n.* (*Shake.*) bud of marigold.

marzipan, *n.* paste, cake, of pounded almonds, sugar etc. (G.)

mascara, *n.* cosmetic for eyelashes etc.

mascot, *n.* person, thing, that brings luck; talisman. (F. *mascotte*)

masculine, *a.* male; manly, vigorous; mannish; (*gram.*) of male gender. **m. rhyme, m. ending,** of words ending in stressed syllable.—*n.* masculine gender or word. **masculinity,** *n.* (L. *mas,* male)

mash, *n.* soft pulpy mass; mess of bran, meal etc. and hot water; malt and hot water for brewing; (*sl.*) mashed potatoes.—*v.t.* beat into mash, bruise; mix with hot water. (O.E. *másc-*)

mash, *v.t.* (*sl.*) flirt with. **be mashed on,** be enamoured of. **masher,** *n.* lady-killer, dandy.

mashie, mashy, *n.* (*golf*) short lofted iron club.

mashlum, *n.* (*Scot.*) mixed grain.

masjid, *n.* mosque. (Arab.)

mask, *n.* covering to hide or protect face; false face; likeness moulded from face; disguise; fox's head; masque.—*v.t.* cover with mask; conceal, screen, disguise; hold in check; hamper by being in line of fire. **masker,** *n.* masked person; masquer. (L.L. *mascus*)

mask, *v.t.* and *i.* (*Scot.*) steep, infuse. (*mash*)

maskinonge, *n.* large N. American pike. (Amer. Indian)

masochism, *n.* sexual perversion in which pleasure is got from being dominated or tortured. **masochist,** *n.* **masochistic,** *a.* (von Sacher-*Masoch,* novelist)

mason, *n.* builder in stone; freemason.—*v.t.* strengthen with masonry. **masonic,** *a.* of freemasons. **masonry,** *n.* art of mason; stonework. (L.L. *machio*)

masque, *n.* kind of poetic drama with pageantry. **masquer,** *n.* one taking part in masque or masquerade. **masquerade,** *n.* masked or fancy-dress ball etc.; disguise, pretence.—*v.i.* appear in disguise. (*mask*)

mass, *n.* lump, body; dense collection of objects; large quantity, bulk; quantity of matter in a body.—*v.t.* and *i.* form into mass; (of troops) concentrate. **in the m.,** collectively. **m. meeting,** large public meeting. **m. production,** of standardized articles in bulk. **the mm.,** the lower classes. (L. *massa*)

mass, *n.* celebration of eucharist in R.C. Church; office, musical setting, for this. **high, low, m.,** with, without, music and incense. (L. *mittere,* send)

massa, *negro dial.* for master.

massacre, *n.* wholesale slaughter, esp. of unresisting people.—*v.t.* slaughter savagely, kill in large numbers. (O.F. *maçacre*)

massage, *n.* rubbing, kneading, of muscles as curative treatment.—*v.t.* give massage to. (F.)

massé, *n.* (*billiards*) stroke with cue upright. (F.)

masseur, *n.* (*fem.* **masseuse**) one who gives massage treatment. (F.)

massif, *n.* central mountain mass. (F.)

massive, *a.* large and heavy, weighty; substantial. **massy,** *a.* weighty, massive. (*mass*)

mast, *n.* pole supporting ship's sails; upright post for aerial etc. **before the m.,** as ordinary seaman. **masthead,** *n.* top of mast.—*v.t.* send to this. (O.E. *mæst*)

mast, *n.* fruit of beech, oak etc. esp. as pigs' food. (O.E. *mæst*)

mastaba, *n.* early Egyptian tomb with flat roof. (Arab. *maçtaba,* bench)

master, *n.* ruler, owner, employer; head of household or college; captain of ship; teacher; great artist, expert; young Mr.; (*Scot.*) eldest son of viscount or baron.—*a.* head, controlling.—*v.t.* overcome; acquire skill in. **be one's own m.,** be independent. **little mm.,** school of Dürer. **old m.,** painter, painting, of a century or more ago, esp. of Renaissance period. **M. of Arts,** (*abbr.* M.A.) holder of higher university degree. **m. of ceremonies,** (*abbr.* M.C.) person responsible for procedure on public occasion. **m. of foxhounds,** (*abbr.* M.F.H.) manager of hunt. **M. of the Horse,** official of royal household. **m.-at-arms,** *n.* warship's officer of police. **m.-builder,** *n.* chief builder. **m.-key,**

n. one serving different locks. (L. *magister*)
masterful, *a.* imperious, domineering.
masterless, *a.* without a master; unsubdued.
masterly, *a.* of consummate skill.
masterpiece, *n.* best or very fine work of artist.
mastership, *n.* office of master.
mastersinger, same as **meistersinger.**
masterstroke, *n.* brilliant stroke of policy.
mastery, *n.* dominion, the upper hand; great skill, full control.
mastic, *n.* a resin used for varnish, cement, and liquor; tree yielding it; pale yellow. (Gk. *mastichē*)
masticate, *v.t.* chew, grind with teeth. **mastication, masticator,** *nn.* **masticatory,** *a.* (L. *masticare*)
mastiff, *n.* large thick-set dog, used as watch-dog. (L. *mansuetus,* tame)
mastitis, *n.* inflammation of female breast. (Gk. *mastos,* breast)
mastodon, *n.* extinct animal like elephant. **mastodontic,** *a.* (Gk. *mastos,* breast; *odous,* tooth)
mastoid, *a.* (*anat.*) like female breast. **m. process,** of bone behind ear. (Gk. *mastos,* breast)
masturbate, *v.i.* stimulate genital organs artificially. **masturbation,** *n.* (L. *masturbari*)
mat, *n.* small rug; piece of material to protect floor, table etc.; tangled mass.—*v.t.* and *i.* cover with mats; tangle, be tangled. (L.L. *matta*)
mat, matt, *a.* dull, without lustre.—*n.* dull finish; roughened groundwork.—*v.t.* dull (metal); frost (glass). (Arab. =helpless)
matador, *n.* man who kills bull in bull-fight. (L. *mactare,* kill)
match, *n.* person, thing, corresponding or similar to another; equal; contest; marriage.—*v.t.* and *i.* set against, oppose; correspond (to), tally; join in marriage. **be m. for,** be able to cope with. **good m.,** well worth marrying. (O.E. *gemæca*)
match, *n.* small stick with head that ignites when rubbed; fuse. **m.-box,** *n.* **m.-lock,** *n.* ancient type of musket fired with fuse. (O.F. *mesche*)
matchboarding, *n.* thin planks tongued and grooved to fit together.
matchet, same as **machete.**
matchless, *a.* incomparable.
matchmaker, *n.* one who schemes to bring about marriages.
matchwood, *n.* small wood splinters.
mate, *n.* one of pair of birds etc.; marriage partner; fellow worker, equal; officer of merchant ship; assistant.—*v.t.* and *i.* pair, marry.
mate, *n.* and *v.t.* (*chess*) checkmate. **fool's m.,** at second move.
maté, *n.* an evergreen shrub; infusion of its leaves, Paraguay tea. (native *mati*)
matelot, *n.* (*sl.*) sailor. ***matelote,*** *n.* stew of fish with wine etc. (F.)
mater, *n.* (*sl.*) mother. **materfamilias,** *n.* mistress of house, matron. (L.)
material, *a.* of matter; corporeal, unspiritual; relevant, important.—*n.* substance of which thing is made; stuff, fabric. **materialism,** *n.* doctrine that matter is the only ultimate reality; absorption in material interests. **materialist,** *n.* and *a.* **materialistic,** *a.* **materialize,** *v.t.* and *i.* make material or materialistic; appear, cause to appear; become fact. **materially,** *adv.* essentially; considerably. ***materia medica,*** (science of) substances used in medicine. ***matériel,*** *n.* equipment, stores (opp. to personnel). (*matter*)
maternal, *a.* of mothers, motherly; on the mother's side. **maternity,** *n.* motherhood, childbirth. **maternity benefit,** payment to confined woman under Insurance Act. (*mater*)
matey, *a.* sociable, friendly. (*mate*)
mathematics, *n.* science of number and space. **mathematical,** *a.* of mathematics; very accurate. **mathematician,** *n.* one versed in mathematics. (Gk. *manthanein,* learn)
matico, *n.* Peruvian plant, used as styptic. (Sp.)
matin, *a.* of morning.—*n.pl.* (also **mattins**) morning prayers or service; (*poet.*) birds' morning song.
matinée, *n.* afternoon performance in theatre. (L. *matutinus*)
matlo, matlow, same as *matelot.*
matrass, *n.* round glass vessel with tapering neck. (F. *matras*)
matriarch, *n.* mother who is head and ruler of family. **matriarchal,** *a.* **matriarchy,** *n.* society with matriarchal government and descent reckoned in female line. (*mater*)
matricide, *n.* killing one's mother; person guilty of this. **matricidal,** *a.* (L. *mater,* mother; *caedere,* kill)
matriculate, *v.t.* and *i.* admit, be admitted, as student in university. **matriculation,** *n.* **matriculatory,** *a.* (L.L. *matricula,* register)
matrimony, *n.* marriage, wedlock; a card game. **matrimonial,** *a.* (*mater*)
matrix, *n.* (*pl.* **matrices, matrixes**) womb; medium in which thing develops; mould for casting type etc.; substance in which mineral is found; (*dyeing*) five simple colours, black, white, blue, red, yellow. (L.)
matron, *n.* married woman, us. elderly; manageress of hospital, woman superintendent. **matronage,** *n.* body of matrons; matronhood. **matronal,** *a.* **matronhood, matronship,** *nn.* **matronly,** *a.* matron-like, sedate. (L. *matrona*)
matronymic, *n.* name derived from mother or ancestress. (Gk. *mētēr,* mother; *onoma,* name)
matt, see **mat.**
mattamore, *n.* underground dwelling or storehouse. (Arab. *tamara,* store)

matter, *n.* physical substance; material; subject, occasion; affair, case, thing; importance; pus; (*print.*) set-up type, copy.—*v.i.* signify, be of importance; suppurate. **as a m. of fact,** in reality. **in the m. of,** as regards. **m. of course,** natural occurrence. **no m.,** it makes no difference. **what is the m.?** what is wrong? **m.-of-fact,** *a.* prosaic, practical, unimaginative. **mattery,** *a.* purulent, festering. (L. *materia*)

matting, *n.* fabric used for mats; mat-work.

mattins, see **matin.**

mattock, *n.* kind of pick with one head like axe, other like adze. (O.E. *mattuc*)

mattoid, *n.* person of abnormal mind, blend of genius and idiot. (It. *matto,* mad)

mattress, *n.* flat stuffed case on which bedclothes rest. **spring m.,** frame of stretched wires supporting this. (Arab. *matrah,* place where anything is thrown)

mature, *a.* ripe, full-grown; fully developed; (of bill) due.—*v.i.* and *t.* bring, come, to maturity, ripen; perfect; (of bill) fall due. **maturate,** *v.t.* and *i.* (*med.*) bring, come, to maturation. **maturation,** *n.* ripening of fruit or (*med.*) of morbific matter. **maturative,** *a.* and *n.* (application) promoting suppuration. **maturity,** *n.* matureness. (L. *maturus*)

matutinal, matutine, *aa.* morning, early. (L. *matutinus*)

maud, *n.* Scottish shepherd's woollen plaid; travelling-rug.

maudlin, *a.* sickly-sentimental; tearful, esp. from drink.—*n.* mawkish sentiment. (*Magdalen*)

maugre, *prep.* (*arch.*) in spite of. (L. *malus,* bad; *gratus,* pleasing)

maul, *n.* large wooden hammer.—*v.t.* bruise, mangle, handle roughly; (*Amer.*) split (rail) with wedge. (L. *malleus*)

mauley, *n.* (*sl.*) fist.

maulstick, *n.* stick held in painter's left hand as rest for right. (Du. *malen,* paint; *stok,* stick)

maun, *v.i.* (*Scot.*) must.

maund, *n.* (*Anglo-Ind.*) varying measure of weight, 25–82 lb. (Hind. *man*)

maunder, *v.i.* drivel, mutter; move listlessly.

maundy, *n.* religious ceremony of washing feet of poor. **m. money,** alms distributed by royal almoner on **M. Thursday,** day before Good Friday. (L. *mandare,* command)

Mauser, *n.* kind of magazine rifle or pistol. (inventor)

mausoleum, *n.* building erected as tomb and monument. (*Mausolus,* King of Caria)

mauvais, *a.* bad. *m. sujet,* worthless fellow. *m. quart d'heure,* short but trying experience (lit. bad quarter of an hour). *mauvaise honte,* bashfulness (lit. ill shame). (F.)

mauve, *n.* and *a.* pale purple. (L. *malva,* mallow)

maverick, *n.* unbranded calf; masterless person.—*v.i.* stray. (person)

mavis, *n.* song-thrush. (F. *mauvis*)

mavourneen, *n.* and *int.* (*Ir.*) my darling. (Ir. *mo mhuirnin*)

maw, *n.* stomach, crop. (O.E. *maga*)

mawkish, *a.* of sickly taste; feebly sentimental, maudlin. (O.N. *madkr,* maggot)

mawn, *n.* (*Scot.*) basket.

mawseed, *n.* poppy-seed. (G. *moh,* poppy; *samen,* seed)

mawworm, *n.* threadworm; hypocrite. (*maw*)

maxilla, *n.* (*pl.* **maxillae**) upper jawbone, jaw. **maxillary,** *a.* (L.)

maxim, *n.* general truth, proverb; principle. (L. *maximus,* greatest)

maxim, *n.* kind of machine-gun. (inventor)

maximum, *n.* (*pl.* **maxima**) greatest number or degree attainable.—*a.* greatest. **maximal,** *a.* **maximalist,** *n.* one who insists on maximum demands; Bolshevik. **maximize,** *v.t.* and *i.* magnify to utmost; interpret rigorously. **maximus,** *a.* eldest. (L. *maximus,* greatest)

maxixe, *n.* round dance like two-step in rhythm. (Port.)

maxwell, *n.* unit of magnetic flux. (person)

May, *n.* fifth month of year; hawthorn blossom; prime, bloom.—*v.i.* gather May flowers. **M. Day,** spring festival on 1 May. **M. Queen,** girl chosen as queen of May Day revels. (L. *Maius*)

may, *v.i.* (*past* **might**) be able; be allowed; be possible; be free to. **might-have-been,** *n.* failure. (O.E. *mæg*)

may, *n.* (*poet.*) maiden.

maya, *n.* (in Buddhist philosophy) illusion. (Sanskr.)

maybe, *adv.* perhaps.

Mayfair, *n.* fashionable part of London between Park Lane and Bond Street.

mayfly, *n.* an ephemeral insect.

mayhap, *adv.* (*arch.*) perhaps.

mayhem, *n.* (*law*) criminal maiming of person. (*maim*)

mayonnaise, *n.* (dish with) dressing of egg yolks beaten up with olive oil and seasoned. (F.)

mayor, *n.* head of town corporation. **mayoral,** *a.* **mayoralty,** *n.* office of mayor. **mayoress,** *n.* mayor's wife; female mayor. (*major*)

maypole, *n.* flower-decked pole for dancing round on May Day.

mazard, *n.* small black cherry; (*arch.*) head.

mazarine, *n.* and *a.* deep rich blue.

maze, *n.* labyrinth, network of windings.—*v.t.* bewilder.

mazer, *n.* a hard wood; drinking-cup of this.
mazuma, *n.* (*Amer. sl.*) money. (Yiddish)
mazurka, *a.* Polish dance like polka; music for it. (Pol.)
mazy, *a.* winding, intricate. (*maze*)
mazzard, same as **mazard.**
me, *n.* third note in sol-fa notation.
me, see **I.**
meacock, *a.* (*Shake.*) effeminate, cowardly.
mead, *n.* liquor of fermented honey and water. (O.E. *meodu*)
mead, *n.* (*poet.*) meadow. (O.E. *mǣd*)
meadow, *n.* field on which grass is grown for hay, grassland. **m.-lark,** *n.* American field-lark. **m.-sweet,** *n.* a fragrant white-flowered plant. **meadowy,** *a.* (*mead*)
meagre, *a.* thin, lean, scanty; jejune. (L. *macer*)
meal, *n.* grain or pulse ground to powder. (O.E. *melo*)
meal, *n.* food taken at one time, repast; occasion for this.—*v.i.* have meal. **square m.,** full meal. (O.E. *mǣl*, stated time)
mealie, *n.* (*S. Afr.*; us. *pl.*) maize. (Port. *milho*, millet)
mealy, *a.* of, like, meal; (of complexion) pale; (of potato) dry and powdery. **m.-bug,** *n.* red insect infesting vines. **m.-mouthed,** *a.* soft-spoken, euphemistic.
mean, *a.* middle, intermediate; average.—*n.* middle point, quantity, degree etc.; (*pl.*) that by which result is obtained; income, resources. **by all mm.,** certainly, of course. **by no mm.,** certainly not. (L. *medius*, middle)
mean, *v.t.* and *i.* (*past, p.p.* meant) intend, purpose; signify. (O.E. *mǣnan*)
mean, *a.* inferior, low; base, sordid; stingy; small-minded; (*Amer. colloq.*) ashamed, small. **m. white,** landless white man in U.S.A. (O.E. *gemǣne*, common)
mean, *v.i.* (*Shake.*) lament. (*moan*)
meander, *n.* winding course, circuitous path.—*v.i.* wind about, wander aimlessly. **meandrine,** *a.* (Gk. river *Maiandros*)
meaning, *n.* sense, significance.—*a.* significant, expressive. (*mean*)
meantime, meanwhile, *advv.* in the intervening time; at the same time.
measles, *n.pl.* infectious fever with red rash; a swine disease. **German m.,** disease like mild measles. **measly,** *a.* of, having, measles; (*sl.*) poor, worthless; stingy. (M.E. *maseles*)
measure, *n.* size, quantity, extent; unit, system, appliance, for measuring; limit, moderation; rhythm, musical time; parliamentary bill; (*math.*) number dividing another without remainder; (*arch.*) dance; (*pl.*) steps, means; strata.—*v.t.* ascertain size or quantity of; estimate, allot; amount to; test by competition. **greatest common m.,** (*abbr.* **G.C.M.**) highest factor common to two or more numbers. **beyond m.,** excessively. m. one's length, fall prostrate. **m. swords** try contest (with). **take one's m.,** gauge his character. **measurable,** *a.* that may be measured; moderate. **measured,** *a.* rhythmical; carefully weighed. **measureless,** *a.* infinite. **measurement,** *n.* measuring, size; (*pl.*) dimensions. (L. *metiri*, measure)
meat, *n.* animal flesh as food; any food. **m.-fly,** *n.* blow-fly. **m.-offering,** *n.* Jewish sacrifice of flour and oil. **m.-safe,** *n.* cupboard for storing meat. (O.E. *meta*)
mĕātus, *n.* (*pl.* **meatus, meatuses**) (*anat.*) passage in the body. (L.)
meaty, *a.* full of, like, meat; full of matter, pithy.
mecca, *n.* place of pilgrimage, goal of aspiration. (birthplace of Mohammed)
meccano, *n.* toy engineering materials. (trade name)
mechanic, *a.* mechanical.—*n.* skilled workman, esp. one using machinery; (pl.) science of matter and motion or of machinery. **mechanical,** *a.* of machines, mechanism, or mechanics; made by, like, a machine; automatic, done by habit. **mechanical drawing,** done by instruments. **mechanical philosophy,** explaining phenomena by mechanical principles. **mechanical powers,** lever, wheel and axle, pulley, inclined plane, wedge, screw. **mechanicalism,** *n.* mechanical philosophy. **mechanician,** *n.* maker of machinery. **mechanism,** *n.* structure of machine; piece of machinery; artistic technique. **mechanist,** *n.* expert in mechanics; advocate of mechanical philosophy. **mechanistic,** *a.* **mechanize,** *v.t.* make mechanical; (*army*) substitute tanks for cavalry etc. **mechanization,** *n.* (Gk. *mēchanē*, contrivance)
Mechlin, *n.* kind of lace. (place)
mecometer, *n.* length-measuring instrument. (Gk. *mēkos*, length; *metron*, measure)
meconium, *n.* juice of poppy, opium. **meconic acid,** acid got from opium. (Gk. *mēkōn*, poppy)
medal, *n.* metal disk with inscription to commemorate event or reward merit. **m. play,** (*golf*) stroke competition. **reverse of the m.,** other side of the picture. **medalled,** *a.* wearing medals. **medallic,** *a.* **medallion,** *n.* large medal; tablet with figures in relief etc. **medallist,** *n.* winner of prize medal; engraver of medals. (L. *metallum*, metal)
meddle, *v.i.* interfere, busy oneself unduly (with). **meddler,** *n.* **meddlesome,** *a.* (L. *miscēre*, mix)
mediaeval, mediaevalism etc., see **medieval.**
medial, *a.* of, in, middle; mean,

average. **median**, *a.* middle, medial. —*n.* (*anat.*) middle artery etc.; (*geom.*) line from angular point of triangle to middle of opposite side. **mediant**, *n.* (*mus.*) third of any scale. **mediastinum**, *n.* (*anat.*) membranous partition, esp. that between lungs. (L. *medius*, middle)

mediate, *a.* involving an intermediary, not direct or immediate.—*v.i.* intervene to reconcile; form connecting link or medium. **mediation**, *n.* **mediatize**, *v.t.* annex (state) while leaving its ruler his title. **mediatization**, *n.* **mediator**, *n.* (*fem.* **mediatrix**) intercessor. **mediatorial**, **mediatory**, *aa.* (L. *medius*, middle)

medic, **medick**, *n.* a leguminous clover-like plant. (Gk. *Mēdikos*, Median)

medical, *a.* of the healing art; of medicine as opp. to surgery. **m. jurisprudence**, medical science applied to questions of law. **medicable**, *a.* that may be cured. **medicament**, *n.* healing application, medicine. **medicaster**, *n.* quack doctor. **medicate**, *v.t.* impregnate with medicinal substance; treat with medicine. **medication**, *n.* **medicative**, *a.* (L. *medicus*, doctor)

medicine, *n.* art of healing, esp. by remedies and diet; substance used in this, drug; charm, fetish; purge; (*Shake.*) doctor; poison.—*v.t.* treat, cure, with medicine. **take one's m.**, accept disagreeable consequences. **m.-ball**, *n.* heavy ball thrown about for exercise. **m.-man**, *n.* witch-doctor. **medicinal**, *a.* of medicine, curative. **medico**, *n.* (*sl.*) doctor, medical student. **medico-botanical**, **medico-legal**, *aa.* of botany, law, relating to medicine. (L. *medicus*, doctor)

medieval, **mediaeval**, *a.* of the Middle Ages (roughly 1100–1500). **medievalism**, **mediaevalism**, *n.* medieval spirit, cult, or relic. **medievalist**, **mediaevalist**, *n.* student, admirer, of Middle Ages. **medievalize**, **mediaevalize**, *v.t.* and *i.* make medieval; favour medievalism. (L. *medius*, middle; *aevum*, age)

mediocre, *a.* middling, neither good nor bad. **mediocrity**, *n.* middle condition; mediocre person. (L. *medius*, middle)

meditate, *v.i.* and *t.* think deeply, ponder (upon); plan. **meditation**, *n.* reflection. **meditative**, *a.* **meditator**, *n.* (L. *meditari*)

mediterranean, *a.* landlocked; inland; of the Mediterranean Sea. (L. *medius*, middle; *terra*, land)

medium, *n.* (*pl.* **media**, **mediums**) mean, middle quality; intervening thing, vehicle; agency, means; person through whom communication is said to be held with spirit world.—*a.* intermediate, moderate. **m. of circulation**, currency. **m. wave**, (*wireless*) about 200–1,000 metres. **mediumistic**, *a.* of a spiritualistic medium. (L. *medius*, middle)

medlar, *n.* a small tree; its apple-like fruit, eaten when decayed. (Gk. *mespilon*)

medley, *n.* mixture, jumble; literary or musical miscellany.—*a.* mixed, motley.—*v.t.* intermix. (*meddle*)

Médoc, *n.* a French wine. (place)

medulla, *n.* marrow, pith, inner tissue. **m. oblongata**, posterior part of brain. **medullary**, *a.* (L.)

medusa, *n.* jelly-fish. **medusal**, **medusan**, **medusoid**, *aa.* (Gk. *Medousa*, one of the Gorgons)

meed, *n.* (*poet.*) recompense, reward; due amount (of). (O.E. *mēd*)

meek, *a.* submissive, mild; spiritless. (O.N. *miukr*, gentle)

meerkat, *n.* S. African mongoose. (Du.=monkey)

meerschaum, *n.* kind of creamy clay; tobacco-pipe with bowl of this. (G. *meer*, sea; *schaum*, foam)

meet, *a.* (*arch.*) fit, suitable. (M.E. *mēte*)

meet, *v.t.* and *i.* (*past*, *p.p.* met) come face to face (with); encounter, confront; assemble, join; satisfy (demand), pay (debt).—*n.* meeting for hunt. **m. half-way**, compromise with. **m. the case**, be adequate. **m. with**, come upon; experience. **meeting**, *n.* assembly; sporting event; duel. **meeting-house**, *n.* nonconformist chapel. (O.E. *mētan*)

mega-, **megalo-**, from Gk. *megas*, great, used in **megacephalic**, **megacephalous**, *aa.* large-headed; **megafarad**, *n.* a million farads; **megafog**, *n.* fog-signalling apparatus with megaphones; **megalith**, *n.* huge stone, esp. of prehistoric monument, hence **megalithic**, *a.*; **megalomania**, *n.* insane conceit, delusion of grandeur, hence **megalomaniac**, *n.*, **megalomaniacal**, *a.*; **megalosaurus**, *n.* gigantic extinct lizard; **megaphone**, *n.* long-distance speaking-trumpet.—*v.t.* announce with this; **megapode**, **megapod**, *n.* kind of mound-building bird; **megascope**, *n.* kind of magic lantern, enlarging camera; **megascopic**, *a.* visible to the naked eye.

megass, *n.* residue after extraction of sugar from cane.

megatherium, *n.* extinct animal like gigantic sloth. (Gk. *megas*, great; *thērion*, wild beast)

megavolt, *n.* a million volts. (*mega-*)

megerg, *n.* a million ergs. (*mega-*)

megger, *n.* apparatus for measuring electrical resistance. (trade name)

megilp, *n.* a vehicle for oil colours.

megohm, *n.* a million ohms. (*mega-*)

megrim, *n.* migraine, sick headache; whim; (*pl.*) low spirits, vapours; staggers in horses. (Gk. *hemi-*, half; *kranion*, skull)

megrim, *n.* kinds of flat-fish.

meiosis, *n.* rhetorical understatement,

litotes, e.g. 'a citizen of no mean city.' (Gk.)

meistersinger, *n.* one of the burgher poets and musicians of Germany in the 14th–16th centuries. (G.)

mekometer, *n.* range-finder for rifle fire. (Gk. *mēkos*, length; *metron*, measure)

melancholy, *n.* gloom, defection; pensiveness.—*a.* gloomy, sad; depressing. **melancholia,** *n.* form of insanity marked by depression. **melancholic,** *a.* subject to, caused by, melancholy. (Gk. *melas*, black; *cholē*, bile)

mélange, *n.* mixture, medley. (F.)

melanism, *n.* excess of dark colour in skin (opp. to albinism). **melanistic,** *a.* **melanóchrōī,** *n.pl.* type of men with dark smooth hair and pale complexion. **melanochroous,** *a.* **melanosis,** *n.* abnormal deposit of black pigment in tissue; black cancer. **melanotic,** *a.* (Gk. *melas*, black)

melder, *n.* (*Scot.*) quantity of oats ground at one time.

mêlée, *n.* confused fight or crowd, scuffle. (F.)

melic, *a.* (of poem) meant to be sung. (Gk. *melos*, song)

melichroous, *a.* honey-coloured. (Gk. *meli*, honey; *chroa*, colour)

melinite, *n.* French explosive like lyddite. (Gk. *mēlon*, apple)

meliorate, *v.t.* and *i.* improve. **melioration,** *n.* **meliorism,** *n.* doctrine that world may be improved by human effort. **meliorist,** *n.* (L. *melior*, better)

melittology, *n.* study of bees. (Gk. *melitta*, bee; *legein*, speak)

mell, *v.i.* (*Spens.*) meddle; (*Scot.*) be intimate.

mellay, *arch.* for *mêlée.*

melliferous, *a.* yielding honey. (L. *mel*, honey; *ferre*, bear)

mellifluent, mellifluous, *aa.* (of voice) sweetly flowing, smooth. (L. *mel*, honey; *fluere*, flow)

mellow, *a.* ripe; soft and rich in flavour, colour, or sound; softened by experience; genial, half-tipsy.—*v.t.* and *i.* make, become, mellow; ripen.

melodeon, melodion, melodium, *n.* kind of accordion; old type of American organ. (*melody*)

melodious, *a.* full of melody, sweet-sounding. **melodize,** *v.i.* and *t.* make melody; make melodious. **melodist,** *n.* singer, composer. (*melody*)

melodrama, *n.* sensational play with crude appeals to emotion, formerly intermixed with songs; theatrical behaviour. **melodramatic,** *a.* of melodrama; sensational, theatrical. **melodramatist,** *n.* **melodramatize,** *v.t.* (Gk. *melos*, song; *drama*, play)

melody, *n.* sweet sound; agreeable succession of single tones; air, tune, of musical piece. (Gk. *melos*, song; *aeidein*, sing)

melon, *n.* a large fleshy fruit. **cut up the m.,** share profits. (Gk. = apple)

Melpómenē, *n.* muse of tragedy. (Gk.)

melt, *v.i.* and *t.* (*p.p.* **melted, molten**) become, make, liquid by heat; soften, be softened; dwindle, vanish. —*n.* melted metal. **melting-point,** *n.* temperature at which solid becomes liquid. **melting-pot,** *n.* crucible. (O.E. *meltan*)

melton, *n.* kind of woollen cloth. (*Melton* Mowbray in England)

melvie, *v.t.* (*Scot.*) soil with meal.

member, *n.* limb, organ, of animal; distinct part of complex whole, branch; one of a society. **unruly m.,** tongue. **membership,** *n.* state of being a member; number of members. (L. *membrum*)

membrane, *n.* thin flexible layer of tissue in animal or plant. **mucous m.,** that lining channels of body. **membranaceous, membraneous, membranous,** *aa.* (L. *membrana*)

membrum virīlē, penis. (L.=male member)

memento, *n.* (*pl.* **mementoes, mementos**) object kept as reminder; souvenir, keepsake. *m. mori*, reminder of death. (L.=remember)

memoir, *n.* personal history, short biography; (*pl.*) reminiscences; record of researches; transactions of society. (L. *memor*, mindful)

memorabilia, *n.pl.* things worth remembering. (L.)

memorable, *a.* worthy of remembrance, remarkable.

memorandum, *n.* (*pl.* **memoranda, memorandums;** *abbr.* **memo., mem.**) note to help memory; summary, outline; informal letter. (L.=to be remembered)

memorial, *a.* of memory, commemorative.—*n.* commemorative monument, custom etc.; written representation made to authorities. **M. Day,** (*Amer.*) 30 May, commemorating those who fell in the Civil War. **memorialist,** *n.* signatory of memorial. **memorialize,** *v.t.* petition by memorial; commemorate. (*memory*)

memoria technica, system to aid memory (lit. artificial memory). *memoriter,* *adv.* from memory. (L.)

memory, *n.* faculty of remembering; recollection, remembrance; posthumous repute; limit to which personal experience goes back. **in m. of,** as record of. **memorize,** *v.t.* learn by heart; commemorate. (L. *memoria*)

memsahib, *n.* European married woman in India. (*ma'am*; *sahib*)

men, see **man.**

menace, *n.* threat; source of danger. —*v.t.* threaten. **menacingly,** *adv.* (L. *minari*, threaten)

ménage, *n.* household; housekeeping. (F.)

menagerie, menagery, *n.* collection, show, of wild animals. (*ménage*)
mend, *v.t.* and *i.* repair, patch; put right, reform; improve, regain health; quicken (pace).—*n.* mended place. **on the m.,** improving. (*amend*)
mendacious, *a.* lying, untruthful; false. **mendacity,** *n.* (L. *mendax*)
Mendelism, *n.* principle that inherited characteristics follow numerical law. **Mendelian,** *a.* (G. F. *Mendel*)
mendicant, *n.* beggar.—*a.* begging. **m. friar,** one who lives on alms. **mendicancy, mendicity,** *nn.* (L. *mendicus*)
menhaden, *n.* fish like herring. (Amer. Ind. *munnawhatteaug*)
menhir, *n.* tall upright monumental stone, monolith. (Breton *men,* stone; *hir,* high)
menial, *a.* fit only for a servant, servile; (of servant) domestic.—*n.* household servant; servile person. (O.F. *mesnie,* household)
meninx, *n.* (*pl.* **meninges**) membrane enclosing brain. **meningeal,** *a.* **meningitis,** *n.* inflammation of meninges. **cerebro-spinal meningitis,** spotted fever. **meningocele,** *n.* rupture of meninges. (Gk.)
meniscus, *n.* lens concave on one side, convex on other. (Gk. *mēnē,* moon)
menology, *n.* calendar of saints, esp. of Greek Church. (Gk. *mēn,* month; *logos,* account)
menopause, *n.* cessation of menses at climacteric. **menorrhagia,** *n.* excessive flow, **menorrhoea,** *n.* ordinary flow, of menses. (Gk. *mēn,* month)
mens, *n.* mind. *m. conscia recti,* a mind conscious of rectitude, a clear conscience. *m. sana in corpore sano,* a sound mind in a sound body. (L.)
mense, *n.* (*Scot.*) good manners; credit. —*v.t.* grace, set off. **menseful,** *a.* civil; respectable. **menseless,** *a.* uncivil; graceless.
menses, *n.pl.* monthly discharge from womb. (L. *mensis,* month)
Menshevik, *n.* Russian socialist of more moderate party. (Russ.=minority)
menstrual, *a.* of the menses; (*astron.*) monthly. **menstruate,** *v.i.* discharge menses. **menstruation,** *n.* (L. *menstruus,* monthly)
menstruum, *n.* (*pl.* **menstrua**) solvent. (L. *menstruus,* monthly)
mensurable, *a.* measurable; (*mus.*) having fixed rhythm. **mensural,** *a.* of measure. **mensuration,** *n.* science of measurement; measuring. (L. *mensura,* measure)
ment, *p.p.* (*Spens.*) mixed. (O.E. *mengan,* mix)
-ment, *n.suf.* indicating action, result, means, product, as in **concealment, astonishment, impediment, abridgment.** (L. *-mentum*)
mental, *a.* of the chin. (L. *mentum,* chin)
mental, *a.* of, done by, the mind; (*colloq.*) feeble-minded. **mentality,** *n.* intellectual power; disposition, character. **mentation,** *n.* working of the mind. (L. *mens,* mind)
menthol, *n.* camphor-like substance got from peppermint etc. (L. *mentha,* mint)
mention, *n.* brief notice, reference.—*v.t.* speak briefly of, notice casually, name. **honourable m.,** award of distinction to unsuccessful candidate. (L. *mentio*)
mentor, *n.* wise counsellor, adviser. (Homeric character)
menu, *n.* bill of fare; dishes served. (F.)
Mephistophelean, Mephistophelian, *a.* cynically wicked, fiendish. (*Mephistopheles,* devil in legend)
mephitis, *n.* noxious exhalation from ground; foul stench. **mephitic,** *a.* (L.)
mercantile, *a.* of merchants, commercial; mercenary. **m. marine,** ships and men engaged in commerce. **m. theory,** that money is the only wealth, so that it is best for exports to exceed imports. **mercantilism,** *n.* commercialism; mercantile theory. **mercantilist,** *n.* (L. *merx,* merchandise)
Mercator's projection, method of map-making with all parallels and meridians as straight lines. (inventor)
mercenary, *a.* serving merely for pay, hired; grasping; venal.—*n.* soldier hired into foreign service. (L. *merces,* reward)
mercer, *n.* dealer in textiles, esp. silk and velvet. **mercery,** *n.* trade, goods, of mercer. (L. *merx,* goods)
mercerized, *a.* (of cotton) treated so as to have silky lustre. (J. *Mercer*)
merchandise, *n.* goods for sale, wares. (*merchant*)
merchant, *n.* wholesale dealer; trader; (*Scot.* and *Amer.*) shopkeeper. **m. prince,** wealthy merchant. **m. ship,** merchantman. **m. tailor,** tailor who supplies his own materials. **merchantable,** *a.* marketable. **merchantman,** *n.* (*pl.* **merchantmen**) trading ship. (L. *merx,* merchandise)
merciful, *a.* compassionate, humane. **merciless,** *a.* cruel, pitiless. (*mercy*)
mercury, *n.* a white liquid metal, quicksilver; the innermost planet; Roman god of thieves, traders etc.; messenger. **mercurial,** *a.* of, containing, mercury; lively, sprightly; flighty.—*n.* drug containing mercury. **mercuric, mercurous,** *aa.* (*chem.*). (L. *Mercurius*)
mercy, *n.* forbearance from injuring or punishing; clemency, compassion; blessing. **at the m. of,** wholly in the power of. **Sister of M.,** woman of religious community. **m.-seat,** *n.* covering of Ark of Covenant; throne of God. (L. *merces,* reward)

merdivorous, *a.* feeding on dung. (L. *merda,* dung; *vorare,* devour)
mere, *n.* lake, pool. (O.E.)
mere, *a.* nothing other than; simple, unmixed. **merely,** *adv.* only, just. (L. *merus*)
meretricious, *a.* of, suited to, a harlot; showily attractive, tawdry. (L. *meretrix,* prostitute)
merganser, *n.* diving fish-eating duck. (L. *mergus,* diver; *anser,* goose)
merge, *v.t.* and *i.* absorb, be absorbed; lose, cause to lose, identity (in). **mergence,** *n.* **merger,** *n.* absorption; business combine. (L. *mergere,* dip)
meridian, *n.* highest altitude of sun or star; highest point, acme; line from N. to S. pole on which noon is simultaneous; great circle of earth or heavens passing through poles.—*a.* of, at, noon; of highest point, culminating. **meridional,** *a.* and *n.* (inhabitant) of the south; of a meridian. (L. *medius,* middle; *dies,* day)
meringue, *n.* light sweet or cake of sugar and white of eggs. (F.)
merino, *n.* breed of sheep; their fine wool; fabric of this; fine woollen yarn. (Sp.)
merit, *n.* commendable quality, worth, excellence; (*pl.*) rights and wrongs (of case).—*v.t.* deserve. **meritorious,** *a.* praiseworthy, well-deserving. (L. *merēri,* earn)
merk, *n.* old Scots silver coin, worth 13½*d.* (*mark*)
merle, *n.* (*arch.*) blackbird. (L. *merula*)
merlin, *n.* kind of small hawk. (O.F. *esmerillon*)
merlon, *n.* part of battlement between two embrasures. (It. *merlo,* battlement)
mermaid, *n.* (*masc.* **merman**) fabulous sea-woman with tail of fish. **mermaiden,** *n.* (*mere*)
mero-, from Gk. *meros,* part, used in **meroblast,** *n.* ovum only partly germinal; **merohedral,** *a.* (of crystal) with less than full number of facets.
merriment, *n.* gaiety with laughter and noise, mirth, fun. (*merry*)
merry, *n.* wild black cherry. (F. *merise*)
merry, *a.* gay, mirthful, jovial; festive. **make m.,** enjoy oneself; make fun. **m. dancers,** aurora borealis. **m. monarch,** Charles II. **m.-andrew,** *n.* buffoon, clown. **m.-go-round,** *n.* revolving ring of hobby-horses, roundabout. **merrymaking,** *n.* festivity. **merrythought,** *n.* wish-bone. (O.E. *myrge*)
mesa, *n.* (*Amer.*) rocky plateau with steep sides. (Sp.=table)
mésalliance, *n.* marriage with social inferior, misalliance. (F.)
mesdames, mesdemoiselles, see *madame, mademoiselle.*
meseems, *v.i.* (*arch.*) it seems to me.
mesembryanthemum, mesembrianthemum, *n.* kinds of flowering plant, incl. fig-marigold. (Gk. *mesēmbria,* noon; *anthemon,* flower)
mesentery, *n.* membrane attaching intestines to abdominal wall. **mesenteric,** *a.* (Gk. *mesos,* middle; *enteron,* intestine)
mesh, *n.* opening between cords of net; (*pl.*) network; snare. *v.t.* and *i.* catch in net; (of teeth of gear) interlock. (O.E. *max,* net)
mesial, *a.* in, towards, middle line of body. (Gk. *mesos,* middle)
mesmerism, *n.* system by which one person can impose his will on another, hypnotism. **mesmeric,** *a.* **mesmerist,** *n.* **mesmerize,** *v.t.* (A. *Mesmer*)
mesne, *a.* (*law*) intervening, intermediate. **m. lord,** one tenant to a superior. (F.=mean)
meso-, from Gk. *mesos,* middle, used in **mesoblast,** *n.* (*zool.*) middle germinal layer of embryo; **mesocarp,** *n.* middle layer of seed-vessel; **mesocephalic,** *a.* having skull of medium proportions; **mesoderm,** *n.* mesoblast; **mesogaster,** *n.* membrane attaching stomach to abdominal wall; **mesohippus,** *n.* extinct three-toed horse; **Mesolithic,** *a.* between Palaeolithic and Neolithic; **mesophyll,** *n.* inner tissue of leaf; **mesophyte,** *n.* plant requiring average water-supply; **mesoplast,** *n.* nucleus of a cell; **mesothorax,** *n.* middle ring of insect's thorax; **Mesozoic,** *a.* of second geological period.
Mespot, *sl. abbr.* of **Mesopotamia.**
mesprize, mesprise, (*Spens.*) same as **misprize.**
mesquite, mesquit, *n.* pod-bearing American tree. (Sp. *mezquite*)
mess, *n.* portion of food; group who eat together regularly, their meal or room; untidy or dirty state; muddle.—*v.t.* and *i.* make mess (of), bungle; eat in company; potter (about). (L. *mittere,* send)
message, *n.* communication sent; divinely inspired communication; errand.—*v.t.* transmit, send as message. **messenger,** *n.* bearer of message; forerunner; paper sent up kite-string. **king's messenger,** official who carries dispatches. (L. *mittere,* send)
Messiah, Messias, *n.* promised saviour of Jewish race; Jesus Christ. **Messianic,** *a.* (Heb. *mashah,* anoint)
messieurs, see *monsieur.*
messin, *n.* (*Scot.*) mongrel dog.
messmate, *n.* member of same mess.
Messrs., see **mister.**
messy, *a.* sloppy, dirty; untidy.
messuage, *n.* dwelling-house with outbuildings and land. (O.F.)
mestee, *n.* offspring of white person and quadroon.
mestizo, *n.* half-breed, esp. child of Spaniard and American Indian. (Sp.)

met, see **meet.**

meta-, met-, meth-, *pref.* after, with, or implying change. (Gk.)

metabolism, *n.* chemical change by which food is built up into living organism (constructive), or protoplasm broken down into simpler substances (destructive). **metabolic,** *a.* **metabolize,** *v.t.* alter by metabolism, assimilate. (Gk. *metabolē*, change)

metacarpus, *n.* hand between wrist and fingers. **metacarpal,** *a.* (Gk. *karpos*, wrist)

metacentre, *n.* point in floating body through which upward thrust of fluid always passes when body is slightly displaced from vertical. **metacentric,** *a.*

metage, *n.* official weighing or measuring; duty paid for this. (*mete*)

metagenesis, *n.* alternation of sexual and asexual generation. **metagenetic,** *a.* (*genesis*)

metagrobolize, metagrabolize, *v.t.* (*joc.*) puzzle; puzzle out. **metagrobolism,** *n.* mystification. (O.F. *metagraboulizer*)

metal, *n.* solid bright opaque substance such as gold, iron etc.; broken stone for road-making; molten glass; gun-power of warship; mettle; (*pl.*) rails of railway.—*v.t.* make, mend (road), fit, with metal. (Gk. *metallon*, mine)

metalepsis, *n.* uniting of two or more figures of speech in same word. (Gk.)

metallic, *a.* of, like, metal. **metalliferous,** *a.* yielding metal. **metalline,** *a.* metallic; impregnated with, yielding, metal. **metallize,** *v.t.* give metallic qualities to. **metallography,** *n.* science, description, of structure of metals. **metalloid,** *a.* like metal.—*n.* non-metallic element. **metallurgy,** *n.* art of working metals or of separating them from their ores. **metallurgic, metallurgical,** *aa.* **metallurgist,** *n.*

metamere, *n.* one of several similar segments of a body. **metameric,** *a.* of a metamere; (*chem.*) having same elements and molecular weight, but different properties. **metamerism,** *n.* (Gk. *meros*, part)

metamorphic, *a.* of, caused by, metamorphism or metamorphosis. **metamorphism,** *n.* change of rock's structure through heat, pressure etc. **metamorphose,** *v.t.* transform; transmute. **metamorphosis,** *n.* (*pl.* **metamorphoses**) change of form or character; magic transformation. (Gk. *morphē*, form)

metaphor, *n.* use of word or phrase for another of which it is an image, implied simile, e.g. ' a frowning sky,' ' blowing his own trumpet.' **mixed m.,** combination of inconsistent metaphors, e.g. ' I smell a rat, but I shall nip it in the bud.' **metaphorical,** *a.* figurative. (Gk. *metapherein*, transfer)

metaphrase, *n.* word-for-word translation (opp. to paraphrase).—*v.t.* alter in wording. **metaphrast,** *n.* literal translator. **metaphrastic,** *a.* (Gk. *metaphrazein*, translate)

metaphysics, *n.pl.* philosophy of being and thought, ontology; abstract speculation. **metaphysical,** *a.* of metaphysics; abstract, abstruse; supernatural; (of poet) fantastic, over-subtle in style. **metaphysician,** *n.* one versed in metaphysics. **metaphysicize,** *v.t.* (Gk. *meta phusika*, after physics—in Aristotle's works)

metaplasm, *n.* part of contents of cell consisting of lifeless matter, esp. formative material; (*gram.*) change in word by adding or dropping a letter. **metaplasmic,** *a.* (Gk. *plassein*, mould)

metapolitics, *n.pl.* abstract or impractical political theory. **metapolitical,** *a.* **metapolitician,** *n.*

metapsychics, *n.pl.* psychical research.

metastasis, *n.* change in the seat of a disease; metabolism; transformation. **metastatic,** *a.* (Gk.=change)

metatarsus, *n.* foot between tarsus and toes. **metatarsal,** *a.*

metathesis, *n.* transposition of letters or syllables of a word, as in ' bird ' from O.E. ' bridd.' (Gk. *metatithenai*, transpose)

metathorax, *n.* hindmost segment of insect's thorax.

métayer, *n.* farmer who pays rent in produce. ***métayage***, *n.* land tenure of this kind. (F.)

mete, *n.* boundary. (L. *meta*, goal)

mete, *v.t.* measure; allot. **m.-wand, m.-yard,** *nn.* measuring-rod. (O.E. *metan*)

metempiric, *a.* beyond, outside of, experience.—*n.* philosophy of such things. **metempirical,** *a.* **metempiricist,** *n.* (*empiric*)

metempsychosis, *n.* transmigration of soul after death to some other body. **metempsychosist,** *n.* believer in this. (Gk. *meta-*, indicating change; *en*, in; *psuchē*, soul)

meteor, *n.* meteoroid made incandescent by friction of earth's atmosphere, shooting star; atmospheric phenomenon. **meteoric,** *a.* of, like, a meteor; dazzling, transitory. **meteorite,** *n.* fallen meteor, meteoric stone. **meteorograph,** *n.* weather-recording instrument. **meteoroid,** *n.* small body moving through space. **meteorolite,** *n.* meteorite. **meteorology,** *n.* science of weather. **meteorologic, meteorological,** *aa.* **meteorologist,** *n.* (Gk. *meteōros*, up in the air)

meter, *n.* measuring instrument; device recording consumption of gas etc. (*mete*)

-meter, *n.suf.* measuring instrument, as in **thermometer.** (Gk. *metron*, measure)

methane, *n.* marsh gas. (G. *methan*)

metheglin, *n.* kind of spiced mead. (W. *meddyg*, healing; *llyn*, liquor)

methinks, *v.i.* (*arch.*; *past* **methought**) it seems to me. (O.E. *thyncan,* seem)
method, *n.* way, procedure; orderliness, system. **methodical,** *a.* systematic. **methodize,** *v.t.* systematize. **methodology,** *n.* science of method or classification. (Gk. *methodos*)
Methodist, *n.* member of any of the churches originated by Wesley and Whitefield. **Methodism,** *n.* doctrine of Methodists. **methodistic, methodistical,** *aa.* (*method*)
methought, see **methinks.**
Methuselah, *n.* very old person. (name in Bible)
methyl, *n.* base of wood spirit. **m. alcohol,** wood alcohol. **methylated spirit,** mixture of alcohol and wood spirit. (Gk. *methu,* wine; *hulē,* wood)
metic, *n.* immigrant, resident alien. (Gk. *meta-,* indicating change; *oikos,* house)
meticulous, *a.* finically accurate or proper, excessively careful of detail. (L. *metus,* fear)
métier, *n.* calling, trade; forte. (F.)
metif, *n.* offspring of white and quadroon. **metis,** *n.* offspring of white and Red Indian. (L. *miscēre,* mix)
metol, *n.* a photographic developer. (trade name)
metonymy, *n.* figure of speech in which a thing is replaced by its attribute, e.g. 'the pen is mightier than the sword.' **metonymical,** *a.* (Gk. *meta-,* indicating change; *onoma,* name)
metope, *n.* (*arch.*) space between triglyphs of Doric frieze. (Gk.)
metre, *n.* French unit of length, 39·37 in. **metric,** *a.* **metric system,** decimal system of weights and measures. (Gk. *metron,* measure)
metre, *n.* poetical measure, rhythm; verse. **metrical,** *a.* of, in, metre or measurement. **metrics,** *n.pl.* art of measurement; art of composing verse. **metrology,** *n.* science of weights and measures. **metronome,** *n.* musician's pendulum beating time at required pace. **metronomic,** *a.* (Gk. *metron,* measure)
metronymic, *a.* and *n.* (name) derived from mother or female ancestor. (Gk. *mētēr,* mother; *onoma,* name)
metropolis, *n.* capital, chief centre; chief ecclesiastical city. **metropolitan,** *a.* of metropolis.—*n.* bishop presiding over other bishops of province. **metropolitanate,** *n.* see of metropolitan. (Gk. *mētēr,* mother; *polis,* city)
-metry, *n.suf.* science of measurement of, as in **geometry.** (*metre*)
mettle, *n.* temperament; spirit, courage. **be on one's m.,** be roused to do one's utmost. **mettled, mettlesome,** *aa.* high-spirited, full of fire. (*metal*)
meum and tuum, mine and thine. (L.)
meuse, *n.* gap in hedge through which wild animal's track passes. (O.F. *muce*)
mew, *v.t.* and *i.* shed (feathers), moult; put in mew, confine.—*n.* cage for hawks; (*pl.*) stables for carriage horses. (L. *mutare,* change)
mew, *n.* cry of cat, gull etc.—*v.i.* utter this. (imit.)
mew, *n.* gull, sea-mew. (O.E. *mæw*)
mewl, *v.i.* cry feebly, whimper; mew. (imit.)
mezzanine, *n.* (also **m. floor**) low storey between two higher ones; floor under theatre stage. (*mezzo*)
mezzo, *a.* (*mus.*) half, middle. *m.-rilievo,* *n.* half-relief, figures projecting half from background. **m.-soprano,** *n.* singer, part, between soprano and contralto. **mezzotint,** *n.* mode of engraving in which lights are made by scraping a roughened surface; print so made. (It.)
mho, *n.* (*electr.*) unit of conductivity. (*ohm* reversed)
mi, (*mus.*) same as **me.**
mia-mia, *n.* (*Austral.*) native hut. (native)
miaow, *n.* and *v.i.* mew. (imit.)
miasma, *n.* (*pl.* **miasmata,** *miasmas*) harmful exhalation from marsh etc. **miasmal, miasmatic,** *aa.* (Gk.)
miaul, *v.i.* cry like cat. (imit.)
mica, *n.* a mineral divisible into thin transparent plates. **micaceous,** *a.* (L.=crumb)
Micawber, *n.* optimistic idler. (name in Dickens)
mice, see **mouse.**
mich, *v.i.* skulk, sneak; play truant. **micher,** *n.* (M.E. *muchen,* pilfer)
Michaelmas, *n.* St. Michael's day, 29 Sept. **M. daisy,** aster with light-purple flowers. (*mass*)
Mick, *n.* (*Amer.*) Irishman. (name)
mickey mouse (*R.A.F. sl.*) electrical distributor releasing bombs from aircraft. (figure in cartoon)
mickle, *a.* (*arch.*) great. (O.E. *micel*)
micr(o)-, from Gk. *mikros,* small, used in **micranthous,** *a.* small-flowered; **micro-organism,** *n.* minute plant or animal; **micro-ampere, micro-farad, micro-gramme, micro-litre, micrometre, micro-millimetre, micro-volt,** *nn.* millionth part of an ampere, farad etc.
microbe, *n.* minute organism; germ of disease. **microbial,** *a.* **microbicide,** *n.* agent for killing bacteria. **microbiology,** *n.* science of microbes. (Gk. *mikros,* small; *bios,* life)
microcephalic, microcephalous, *aa.* small-headed. (Gk. *kephalē,* head)
micrococcus, *n.* (*pl.* **micrococci**) kind of round microbe. (Gk. *kokkos,* grain)
microcosm, *n.* man as epitome of universe; miniature community; analogue on small scale. **microcosmic,** *a.* (Gk. *kosmos,* world)
microcyte, *n.* small kind of corpuscle. (Gk. *kutos,* vessel)
micrograph, *n.* pantograph for minute engraving; picture of object as seen

by microscope. **micrography,** *n.* (Gk. *graphein,* write)

microhm, *n.* millionth of an ohm.

microlithic, *a.* made of small stones; marked by monuments so made. (Gk. *lithos,* stone)

micrology, *n.* hair-splitting; micrography. (Gk. *legein,* speak)

micrometer, *n.* instrument for measuring minute distances or angles. **micrometry,** *n.* (Gk. *metron,* measure)

micron, *n.* millionth of a metre. (Gk. *mikros,* small)

microphone, *n.* instrument for intensifying faint sounds; mouthpiece for broadcasting. (Gk. *phōnē,* sound)

microphotograph, *n.* photograph taken through a microscope or of microscopic size. **microphotography,** *n.*

microphyllous, *a.* small-leaved. (Gk. *phullon,* leaf)

microphyte, *n.* microscopic plant, esp. parasite. (Gk. *phuton,* plant)

microscope, *n.* optical instrument for magnifying and making visible minute objects. **microscopic, microscopical,** *aa.* of, with, like, a microscope; visible only through a microscope, very small. **microscopist,** *n.* **microscopy,** *n.* use of microscope. (Gk. *mikros,* small; *skopein,* look at)

microseism, *n.* faint earthquake tremor. **microseismic,** *a.* **microseismograph,** *n.* instrument recording this. (Gk. *seismos,* earthquake)

microspore, *n.* small asexual spore.

microtome, *n.* instrument for cutting thin sections for microscopic examination. (Gk. *temnein,* cut)

microzyme, *n.* microbe causing fermentation. (Gk. *zumē,* leaven)

micturition, *n.* morbid desire to pass water; (*incorrectly*) urination. (L. *mingere,* make water)

mid, *a.* intermediate, the middle of.—*prep.* (*poet.*) amid. **m.-off, m.-on,** *nn.* (*cricket*) fieldsman level with bowler's wicket on off, on, side. **midday,** *n.* and *a.* noon. (O.E. *midd*)

midden, *n.* dunghill, refuse-heap.

middle, *a.* equidistant from extremes, medial; intermediate; (*gram.*) of middle voice.—*n.* middle point, term, article etc.; waist.—*v.t.* place in middle, centre. **in the m. of,** while, during. **m. age,** about 40–60. **M. Ages,** about 1100–1500. **m. article,** newspaper article on general topic. **m. class,** between nobility and working class, bourgeoisie. **m. distance,** between foreground and background. **M. English,** that used about 1150–1500. **M. Kingdom,** China. **m. term,** (*logic*) that common to both premisses. **m. voice,** (*gram.*) verbal form with reflexive meaning. **m. watch,** midnight to 4 a.m. **m.-weight,** *n.* (*boxing*) 10 st. 7 lb. to 11 st. 6 lb. (O.E. *middel*)

middleman, *n.* dealer between producer and consumer.

middlemost, *a.* nearest the middle.

middling, *a.* of medium quality, size etc.; second-rate; fairly well.—*n.pl.* the coarser part of flour.—*adv.* moderately.

middy, *n.* midshipman. (abbr.)

midge, *n.* small fly, gnat; small person. (O.E. *mycg*)

midget, *n.* very small person, dwarf; tiny photograph. (*midge*)

midinette, *n.* Parisian shop-girl. (F.)

midland, *n.* middle part of country; (*pl.*) central England.—*a.* of, in, midland; inland.

midmost, *a.* nearest the middle.

midnight, *n.* twelve o'clock at night. —*a.* at, dark as, midnight. **m. sun,** shining all night in Arctic summer.

midrash, *n.* (*pl.* **midrashim**) Hebrew commentary on part of Old Testament. (Heb.)

midrib, *n.* central rib of leaf.

midriff, *n.* membrane separating chest from stomach, diaphragm. (O.E. *hrif,* belly)

midship, *n.* middle part of ship. **midshipman,** *n.* naval officer below sub-lieutenant. **midshipmite,** *n.* (*colloq.*) midshipman. **midships,** *adv.* amidships.

midst, *n.* middle.—*prep.* amidst, among. (*mid*)

midsummer, *n.* the height of summer, about 21 June. **M. Day,** 24 June. **m. madness,** utter folly.

midway, *a.* and *adv.* about halfway.

midwife, *n.* (*pl.* **midwives**) woman who assists at childbirth, accoucheuse. **midwifery,** *n.* obstetrics.

mien, *n.* air, bearing, look.

miff, *n.* (*colloq.*) petty quarrel, tiff.—*v.i.* and *t.* take offence, offend. **miffy,** *a.* touchy, huffy.

might, see **may.**

might, *n.* great strength or force; power. **with m. and main,** with all one's power. **mighty,** *a.* powerful, strong; massive, huge; (*colloq.*) considerable.—*adv.* (*colloq.*) very. (O.E. *miht*)

mignon, *a.* (*fem.* ***mignonne***) daintily small, delicately pretty. (F.)

mignonette, *n.* sweet-scented plant; greyish-green colour. (*mignon*)

migraine, *n.* sick headache, megrim. (F.)

migrant, *a.* migratory.—*n.* colonist; migrating bird. (*migrate*)

migrate, *v.i.* remove for residence from one region to another. **migration, migrator,** *nn.* **migratory,** *a.* (L. *migrare*)

mikado, *n.* Emperor of Japan. (Jap. *mi,* august; *kado,* door)

mike, *v.i.* loaf, shirk work.—*n.* idling.

mike, *n.* (*sl.*) microphone. (abbr.)

mil, *n.* $\frac{1}{1000}$ in.; £$\frac{1}{1000}$. **per m.,** per thousand. (L. *mille,* thousand)

milady, *n.* French word for English lady. (*my*; *lady*)

milage, same as **mileage.**

milch, *a.* yielding milk. **m. cow,** ready source of gain. (M.E. *mielch*)
mild, *a.* gentle, placid; not severe or strong or sour; (of weather) calm and warm; (of steel) tough and malleable. **milden,** *v.t.* and *i.* (O.E. *milde*)
mildew, *n.* mould, fungoid growth on plant, leather etc. exposed to damp.—*v.t.* and *i.* taint, be tainted, with this. **mildewy,** *a.* (O.E. *meledéaw*)
mile, *n.* measure of length, 1,760 yd. **nautical m.,** one-sixtieth of a mean degree of longitude, 6,080 ft. **mileage,** *n.* distance in miles; cost, allowance, per mile; (*Amer.*) book of railroad tickets. (L. *mille* passuum, a thousand paces)
Milesian, *a.* and *n.* Irish, Irishman. (*Milesius,* fabled king)
milestone, *n.* stone marking distance in miles; stage in progress.
milfoil, *n.* yarrow. (L. *mille,* thousand; *folium,* leaf)
miliary, *a.* like millet-seed. **m. fever,** with eruption like this. (L. *milium,* millet)
milieu, *n.* environment, condition in life. (F.)
militant, *a.* fighting; combative. **militancy,** *n.* (*militate*)
military, *a.* of soldiers or war.—*n.* soldiery. **m. fever,** typhoid. **militarism,** *n.* military spirit, policy, or government. **militarist,** *n.* believer in militarism; student of military science; (*Shake.*) soldier. **militarize,** *v.t.* (L. *miles,* soldier)
militate, *v.i.* be argument or influence (against). (L. *miles,* soldier)
militia, *n.* British conscript army, founded 1939; (formerly) citizen army for home service. **militiaman,** *n.* (L. *miles,* soldier)
milk, *n.* white fluid with which animals feed young; milk-like juice or liquid.—*v.t.* draw milk from; exploit; (*sl.*) tap (telegraph wires). **m. pudding,** of rice, sago etc. baked with milk. **m. punch,** of spirits and milk. **m.-and-water,** *a.* insipid, feeble. **m.-float,** *n.* milkman's low flat cart. **m.-tooth,** *n.* one of set shed in childhood. **m.-walk,** *n.* milkman's round. **m.-white,** *a.* pure white. **milkmaid,** *n.* girl who milks cows; dairymaid. **milkman,** *n.* seller of milk. **milksop,** *n.* weak, unmanly fellow. **milkweed, milkwort,** *nn.* kinds of plant. **milky,** *a.* of, like, containing, milk; cloudy; effeminate. **Milky Way,** the galaxy. (O.E. *meolc*)
mill, *n.* building where corn is ground; grinding apparatus; kinds of manufacturing machine; factory; fight with fists.—*v.t.* and *i.* grind, press, stamp, in mill; put raised furrowed edge on (coin); full (cloth); beat, fight; (of cattle etc.) move in circle. **go through the m.,** undergo training or testing experience. **m.-hand,** *n.* factory worker. **m.-pond,** *n.* pond for water-mill. **m.-race,** *n.* current driving mill-wheel. (L. *mola*)
mill, *n.* (*Amer.*) one-thousandth of a dollar. (L. *mille,* thousand)
millboard, *n.* thick pasteboard. (*mill*)
millenary, *a.* consisting of a thousand (years).—*n.* thousandth anniversary; millenarian. **millenarian, millennarian,** *a.* of, expecting, the millennium.—*n.* believer in the millennium. **millenarianism,** *n.* (L. *mille,* thousand)
millennium, *n.* period of a thousand years; Christ's second coming; coming time of happiness. **millennial,** *a.* of millennium; every thousand years. (L. *mille,* thousand; *annus,* year)
millepede, *n.* worm-like animal with many legs; woodlouse. (L. *mille,* thousand; *pes,* foot)
miller, *n.* one who grinds corn. **m.'s thumb,** a small fish, bull-head.
millesimal, *a.* and *n.* thousandth; consisting of a thousand parts. (L. *mille,* thousand)
millet, *n.* kind of cereal; its minute seed. **m.-grass,** *n.* a tall grass. (L. *milium*)
milliard, *n.* a thousand millions. **milligram, milligramme,** *n.* thousandth of a gramme (·0154 grain). **millilitre,** *n.* thousandth of a litre (·061 cubic in.). **millimetre,** *n.* thousandth of a metre (·0393 in.). (L. *mille,* thousand)
milliner, *n.* one who makes or deals in women's hats, ribbons etc. **millinery,** *n.* his goods. (*Milan,* town)
million, *n.* a thousand thousand. **the m.,** ordinary people. **millionaire,** *n.* one who owns a million pounds, dollars etc.; very wealthy man. **millionary,** *a.* of, having, millions. **millionth,** *a.* (L. *mille,* thousand)
millipede, same as **millepede.**
Mills bomb, kind of hand grenade. (inventor)
millstone, *n.* flat stone used for grinding.
millwright, *n.* mechanic who builds and repairs mills.
milord, milor, *n.* French word for noble or rich Englishman. (*my; lord*)
milt, *n.* spleen; roe of male fish.—*v.t.* impregnate (spawn of female fish). **milter,** *n.* male fish in breeding season. (O.E. *milte*)
mim, *a.* (*prov.*) demure, precise.
mime, *n.* ancient comedy of ordinary life; actor, dialogue, in this; mimic, buffoon.—*v.i.* act with gestures. (Gk. *mimos*)
mimeograph, *n.* kind of stencil copying device. (Gk. *mimeisthai,* imitate; *graphein,* write)
mimesis, *n.* mimicry, resemblance of animal to its environment etc. **mimetic,** *a.* of, given to, imitation or mimicry. (Gk.)
mimic, *a.* feigned, sham; imitative

—*n.* one good at ludicrous imitation.—*v.t.* (*past, p.p.* **mimicked**) ridicule by imitating, burlesque; copy, resemble, closely. **mimicry,** *n.* mimicking; close external likeness, mimesis. (*mime*)
miminy-piminy, *a.* over-refined, finicking. (imit.)
mimosa, *n.* kinds of shrub, including sensitive plant. (*mime*)
mina, *n.* ancient Greek money or weight of 100 drachmae (about £4 or 1 lb.). (Gk. *mna*)
mina, *n.* Indian bird like starling. (Hind. *maina*)
minacious, *a.* threatening. **minacity,** *n.* (L. *minax*)
minar, *n.* lighthouse, tower. **minaret,** *n.* slender turret of mosque, from which muezzin calls to prayer. (Arab. *nar*, fire)
minatory, *a.* threatening. (L. *minari*, threaten)
mince, *v.t.* and *i.* cut small, chop fine; make little of, palliate; speak, walk, with affected elegance.—*n.* minced meat; **m.-pie,** *n.* pie containing mincemeat or mince; **mincemeat,** *n.* currants, spices, mixed with chopped peel etc. **make mincemeat of,** demolish. (O.F. *mincier*)
Mincing Lane, wholesale tea trade. (London centre)
mind, *n.* thinking faculty, intellect; memory; attention; intention; taste; opinion.—*v.t.* attend to, heed; take care (that); object (to); (*Shake.*) intend; (*Scot.*) remember. **in two mm.,** irresolute. **make up one's m.,** resolve. **m. one's p's and q's,** be careful how one behaves. **m.'s eye,** mental view. **m. your eye,** (*sl.*) look out! **never m.,** do not concern yourself. **out of one's m.,** insane. **minded,** *a.* disposed, inclined. **minder,** *n.* caretaker. **mindful,** *a.* not forgetful; heedful. **mindless,** *a.* unthinking, stupid. (M.E. *mynd*)
mine, see **I.**
mine, *n.* deep hole for digging out coal, metals etc.; rich source; explosive charge in sea or underground; excavation under enemy's position. —*v.t.* and *i.* make mine in or under; dig from, work in, mine. **magnetic m.,** detonated without contact by effect on magnet of ship's metal parts. **minefield,** *n.* area sown with explosive mines. **m.-layer, m.-sweeper,** *nn.* ship for placing, gathering up, mines. **m.-thrower,** *n.* trench mortar. **miner,** *n.* one who works in or lays mines. (F.)
minenwerfer, *n.* trench mortar. (G.)
mineral, *n.* inorganic substance; ore; (*pl.*) mineral waters.—*a.* of, like, impregnated with, minerals; inorganic, not animal or vegetable. **m. oil,** got from earth, petroleum etc. **m. water,** impregnated with minerals; effervescent drink, soda-water, ginger-beer etc. **mineralize,** *v.t.* impregnate with, change into, mineral. **mineralogy,** *n.* science of minerals. **mineralogical,** *a.* **mineralogist,** *n.* (L.L. *minera*, mine)
Minerva, *n.* Roman goddess of wisdom.
minever, *n.* white fur of judge's robe etc., ermine. (F. *menu*, small; *vair*, kind of fur)
mingle, *v.i.* and *t.* mix, blend, be united (with). (O.E. *mengan*)
mingy, *a.* (*colloq.*) mean, stingy.
miniate, *v.t.* colour with vermilion, illuminate. (*minium*)
miniature, *n.* very small painting; small-scale representation.—*a.* small-scale, minute. **miniaturist,** *n.* painter of miniatures. (*miniate*)
minibus, *n.* small four-wheeled carriage.
minify, *v.t.* represent as smaller than it is; lessen. (L. *minor*, less; *facere*, make)
minikin, *n.* tiny creature.—*a.* tiny; affected, mincing. (Du. *minne*, love)
minim, *n.* smallest liquid measure, drop, one-sixtieth of drachm; single downstroke in letter; (*mus.*) half a semibreve. (L. *minimus*, smallest)
minimum, *n.* (*pl.* **minima**) least amount possible or recorded. **minimal,** *a.* very minute; least possible. **minimalist,** *n.* one ready to accept minimum; moderate socialist. **minimize,** *v.t.* render as small as possible, belittle. **minimus,** *n.* small creature. —*a.* youngest. (L.)
minion, *n.* darling, favourite; servile dependant; (*Shake.*) hussy; (*print.*) 7-point type, between brevier and nonpareil. (F. *mignon*)
minish, *v.t.* and *i.* (*arch.*) diminish.
minister, *n.* servant, agent; head of state department; ambassador, state envoy; clergyman.—*v.i.* and *t.* render aid; serve, contribute; (*arch.*) supply. **prime m.,** chief minister of state. **ministerial,** *a.* of minister; of, on the side of, the government. **ministerialist,** *n.* government supporter. **ministrant,** *a.* ministering.—*n.* officiating clergyman. **ministration,** *n.* priestly service; rendering help, esp. to the sick. **ministrative,** *a.* **ministry,** *n.* clergy, clerical profession; body of ministers forming government; their term of office; state department. (L.)
minium, *n.* red oxide of lead, cinnabar, vermilion. (L.)
miniver, same as **minever.**
mink, *n.* small animal like weasel; its brown fur.
minnesinger, *n.* one of German court poets and musicians of 12th–13th centuries. (G.)
minnie, *n.* (*Scot.*) mother.
Minnie, *n.* (*army sl.*) trench mortar. (G. *minenwerfer*)
minnow, *n.* small freshwater fish, stickleback. (O.E. *myne*)
Minoan, *a.* of ancient Cretan civilization (3000–1400 B.C.). (King *Minos*)

minor, *a.* lesser; younger; unimportant; (*mus.*) less by a semitone.—*n.* person under 21; minor term. **m. canon,** cathedral clergyman not member of chapter. **m. key,** (*mus.*) in which scale has a minor third; plaintive or doleful tone. **m. premiss,** (*logic*) that containing minor term. **m. prophets,** twelve from Hosea to Malachi. **m. suit,** (*bridge*) diamonds or clubs. **m. term,** (*logic*) term of syllogism forming subject of conclusion. **Minorite,** *n.* Franciscan friar. **minority,** *n.* smaller number, less than half; state, period, of being a minor. (L.)

Minorca, *n.* (also **M. fowl**) black kind of Spanish fowl. (place)

Minotaur, *n.* fabled monster, half bull, half man. (Gk. *Minōtauros*)

minster, *n.* church of a monastery; large church, cathedral. (O.E. *mynster*)

minstrel, *n.* medieval singer or musician; poet. **nigger mm.,** entertainers with faces blacked. **minstrelsy,** *n.* art, body, of minstrels; collection of songs. (O.F. *menestral*)

mint, *n.* place where money is coined; source of supply.—*v.t.* coin, invent. **in m. condition,** new, unused. **mintage,** *n.* what is minted; duty paid for minting. (L. *moneta,* money)

mint, *n.* an aromatic plant. **m. julep,** spirits and sugar etc. flavoured with mint. (Gk. *minthē*)

mint, *v.i.* and *n.* (*Scot.*) try, aim; hint. (O.E. *myntan,* mean)

minuend, *n.* number from which another is to be subtracted. (L. *minuere,* lessen)

minuet, *n.* slow stately dance for two; music for this. (F. *menuet*)

minus, *n.* sign (−) of subtraction.—*prep.* less, deprived of.—*a.* negative. (*minor*)

minuscule, *a.* minute.—*n.* small letter; small cursive script of about years 600–900. (L. *minusculus*)

minute, *n.* one-sixtieth of hour or degree; short time, moment; draft, memorandum; (*pl.*) short summary of proceedings.—*v.t.* make note or record of. **m.-gun,** *n.* gun fired every minute. **m.-hand,** *n.* hand indicating minutes on dial. **m.-man,** *n.* American militiaman of revolutionary period. (L. *minuere,* lessen)

minute, *a.* very small; precise, detailed. (L. *minuere,* lessen)

minutely, *a.* and *adv.* (occurring) every minute.

minutely, *adv.* in a minute manner; precisely.

minutiae, *n.pl.* minor details. (L.)

minx, *n.* pert or sly girl; flirt.

Miocene, *a.* (*geol.*) of the middle division of Tertiary strata. (Gk. *meiōn,* less; *kainos,* new)

mir, *n.* Russian village community. (Russ.)

mirable, *a.* (*Shake.*) marvellous. (L. *mirari,* wonder at)

miracle, *n.* supernatural event or act; marvel, prodigy. **m. play,** medieval play on sacred subject. **miraculous,** *a.* supernatural; wonderful; able to work miracles. (L. *miraculum*)

mirador, *n.* watch-tower, gallery. (Sp.)

mirage, *n.* illusory image in atmosphere. (F.)

mire, *n.* swampy ground, bog; mud.—*v.t.* stick in, dirty with, mud. (O.N. *mýrr*)

mirific, mirifical, *aa.* wonder-working; marvellous. (L. *mirus,* wonderful; *facere,* make)

mirk, *Scot.* form of **murk.**

mirror, *n.* surface reflecting image, looking-glass; pattern.—*v.t.* reflect. **m. writing,** reversed, as seen in mirror. (L. *mirari,* wonder at)

mirth, *n.* merriment, noisy gaiety; gladness; laughter. **mirthful, mirthless,** *aa.* (O.E. *myrigth*)

miry, *a.* muddy; vile. (*mire*)

mirza, *n.* title of respect in Persia. (Pers.)

mis-, *pref.* amiss, wrongly, badly, as in **mis-cue,** *n.* and *v.i.* (make) false stroke or slip with billiard cue. (O.E. *mis-* and L. *minus,* less)

misadventure, *n.* unlucky accident, disaster; bad luck. **misadventured,** *a.* (*Shake.*) unfortunate.

misadvertence, *n.* want of proper care. (*advert*)

misalliance, *n.* bad alliance; unsuitable marriage.

misandry, *n.* hatred of men by women. (Gk. *misein,* hate; *anēr,* man)

misanthrope, misanthropist, *nn.* hater of mankind. **misanthropic, misanthropical,** *aa.* **misanthropy,** *n.* (Gk. *misein,* hate; *anthrōpos,* man)

misapply, *v.t.* use wrongly. **misapplication,** *n.*

misapprehend, *v.t.* misunderstand. **misapprehension,** *n.* **misapprehensive,** *a.*

misappropriate, *v.t.* use, appropriate, wrongly (esp. other's money). **misappropriation,** *n.*

misbecome, *v.t.* suit ill.

misbegotten, *a.* illegitimate.

misbehave, *v.i.* behave badly. **misbehaviour,** *n.*

misbelief, *n.* wrong religious belief, false opinion. **misbeliever,** *n.*

misbeseem, *v.i.* suit ill.

miscalculate, *v.t.* and *i.* calculate wrongly. **miscalculation,** *n.*

miscall, *v.t.* call by wrong name; abuse, revile.

miscarry, *v.i.* go wrong, fail; bring forth young prematurely; (of letter) fail to reach address; (*Shake.*) perish. **miscarriage,** *n.* miscarrying, failure; premature delivery, abortion.

miscast, *v.t.* and *i.* reckon wrongly; allot acting parts unsuitably.

miscegenation, *n.* interbreeding of races, esp. whites and negroes. (L. *miscēre,* mix; *genus,* race)
miscellaneous, *a.* made up of several kinds, mixed. **miscellanea,** *n.pl.* odds and ends. **miscellany,** *n.* mixed collection, medley, of writings etc. **miscellanist,** *n.* compiler of miscellany. (L. *miscēre,* mix)
mischance, *n.* unlucky event, bad luck. **mischancy,** *a.* (*Scot.*) unlucky.
mischief, *n.* evil consequence; harm, injury; annoying conduct, pranks; playful malice. **make m.,** stir up strife. **play the m. with,** trouble greatly. **mischievous,** *a.* hurtful; prone to mischief. (O.F. *mes-,* ill; *chief,* end)
misconceive, *v.t.* have wrong idea (of), mistake. **misconception,** *n.*
miscible, *a.* that may be mixed. (L. *miscēre,* mix)
misconduct, *n.* wrong conduct or management; adultery.—*v.t.* conduct ill.
misconstrue, *v.t.* put wrong construction on, interpret wrongly. **misconstruction,** *n.*
miscount, *n.* wrong counting, esp. of votes.—*v.t.* count wrongly.
miscreant, *n.* (*arch.*) vile wretch, villain; infidel.—*a.* depraved; heretical. **miscreance,** *n.* (*Spens.*) misbelief. (L. *credere,* believe)
miscreated, *a.* deformed. **miscreation,** *n.* **miscreate,** *a.* (*Shake.*) illegitimate.
misdeal, *n.* wrong deal at cards.—*v.t.* and *i.* deal, allot, wrongly.
misdeed, *n.* wrong action, crime.
misdeem, *v.t.* and *i.* think wrongly, misjudge; mistake (one for another).
misdemean, *v.t.* behave (oneself) ill. **misdemeanant,** *n.* one guilty of petty crime. **misdemeanour,** *n.* offence; (*law*) crime less than felony.
misdirect, *v.t.* direct wrongly. **misdirection,** *n.*
misdoing, *n.* misdeed.
misdoubt, *v.t.* (*arch.*) have doubts or misgivings (about); suspect.
mise, *n.* arbitral award. *m.-en-scène,* *n.* staging of play; surroundings of event. (L. *mittere,* send)
miser, *n.* hoarder of wealth, avaricious or grasping person. (L.=wretched)
miser, *n.* large tubular boring tool.
miserable, *a.* wretched, very unhappy; paltry, poor; pitiable. (*miser*)
Miserere, *n.* 51st Psalm; musical setting for it. (opening word)
misericord, misericorde, *n.* projection under hinged seat in choir stall to support person standing; small dagger for giving death-thrust. (L. *misereri,* pity; *cor,* heart)
miserly, *a.* like a miser, stingy.
misery, *n.* extreme pain, unhappiness, or poverty. (*miser*)
misfeasance, *n.* (*law*) transgression; doing of lawful act in wrongful manner. (L. *facere,* do)
misfire, *v.i.* (of gun, engine etc.) fail to go off or start.
misfit, *n.* garment, thing, that fits badly.—*v.t.* and *i.* fit badly.
misfortune, *n.* bad luck; calamity.
misgive, *v.t.* (*past* **misgave**) fill with doubt or apprehension. **misgiving,** *n.* foreboding, mistrust.
misgovern, *v.t.* govern badly. **misgovernment,** *n.*
misguide, *v.t.* mislead, lead astray.
mishandle, *v.t.* handle roughly, maltreat.
mishap, *n.* minor unlucky accident.
mishit, *v.t.* and *n.* (make) faulty stroke.
mishmash, *n.* hotch-potch, jumble. (*mash*)
mishna, mishnah, *n.* body of precepts forming basis of Talmud. **mishnic,** *a.* (Heb. *shanah,* repeat)
misimprove, *v.t.* misuse, abuse.
misinform, *v.t.* give untrue information to, mislead. **misinformation,** *n.*
misinterpret, *v.t.* explain wrongly, make wrong inference from. **misinterpretation,** *n.*
misjudge, *v.t.* form wrong opinion of.
misken, *v.t.* (*Scot.*) be, seem, ignorant of; take no notice of. (*ken*)
mislay, *v.t.* (*past, p.p.* **mislaid**) put in wrong place or one not remembered.
mislead, *v.t.* (*past, p.p.* **misled**) lead astray; deceive.
misleared, *a.* (*Scot.*) ill-bred; misinformed. (*lore*)
mislike, *v.t.* (*arch.*) dislike.
mislippen, *v.t.* (*Scot.*) disappoint; neglect to pay attention to.
mismanage, *v.t.* manage badly or wrongly. **mismanagement,** *n.*
mismated, *a.* ill-matched.
misname, *v.t.* call by wrong name.
misnomer, *n.* misnaming; wrong name or term. (L. *nomen,* name)
miso-, from Gk. *misos,* hatred, used in **misocapnic,** *a.* hating (tobacco) smoke; **misogamy,** *n.* hatred of marriage, hence **misogamist,** *n.*; **misogyny,** *n.* hatred of women, hence **misogynist,** *n.* woman-hater, **misogynic,** *a.*; **misology,** *n.* hatred of reason, hence **misologist,** *n.*; **misoneism,** *n.* hatred of novelty, hence **misoneist,** *n.*; **misopaedia,** *n.* hatred of children, hence **misopaedist,** *n.*; **misotheism,** *n.* hatred of God or of gods.
misplace, *v.t.* put in wrong place; set on improper or unworthy object; time badly. **misplacement,** *n.*
mispraise, *v.t.* praise falsely.
misprint, *n.* error in printing.—*v.t.* print wrongly.
misprision, *n.* (*law*) criminal neglect in respect of another's crime. **m. of treason,** concealment of treason without assenting to it. (O.F. *mesprison,* mistake)
misprision, *n.* (*arch.*) contempt; undervaluation. (*misprize*)
misprize, *v.t.* slight, undervalue.

mispronounce, *v.t.* pronounce wrongly. **mispronunciation,** *n.*
misquote, *v.t.* quote wrongly. **misquotation,** *n.*
misread, *v.t.* read, interpret, wrongly.
misrepresent, *v.t.* give false account of; falsify. **misrepresentation,** *n.*
misrule, *n.* bad government. **Abbot, Lord, of M.,** leader of old Christmas revels.
miss, *v.t.* and *i.* fail to hit, reach, find, catch, or notice; be too late for; omit, pass over; regret absence of; misfire.—*n.* failure to hit etc. **give a m. to,** leave out. **m. fire,** fail to explode. **m. stays,** (*naut.*) fail in going about from one tack to another. (O.E. *missan*)
miss, *n.* title of unmarried woman; girl. (abbr. of *mistress*)
missal, *n.* book containing service of the mass. (L.L. *missale*)
missay, *v.t.* and *i.* say or speak incorrectly; abuse.
missel, *n.* (also **m.-thrush**) largest British thrush. (O.E. *mistel,* mistletoe, on which it feeds)
misshapen, *a.* ill-shaped, deformed.
missile, *a.* for throwing.—*n.* weapon, thing, thrown to do damage. (L. *mittere,* send)
missing, *a.* absent, wanting, lost. **m. link,** intermediate form, esp. between man and ape.
mission, *n.* body, organization, post or field of work of missionaries; body of envoys, embassy; calling in life, vocation; errand, commission. **missionary,** *n.* one sent to preach religion, esp. abroad; person attached to police court to help offenders.—*a.* of religious mission. **missionary-box,** *n.* box to collect funds for missions. **missioner,** *n.* missionary; one in charge of parochial mission. (L. *mittere,* send)
missis, *n.* mistress; (*joc.*) wife.
missish, *a.* prim, schoolgirlish. (*miss*)
missive, *n.* letter; (*Shake.*) messenger.—*a.* meant to be sent. (L. *mittere,* send)
misspell, *v.t.* (*past, p.p.* **misspelt**) spell incorrectly.
misspend, *v.t.* (*past, p.p.* **misspent**) waste, squander.
misstate, *v.t.* state wrongly. **misstatement,** *n.*
missus, same as **missis.**
missy, *a.* namby-pamby.—*n.* miss.
mist, *n.* water vapour visible in air, haze; anything that obscures vision. —*v.t.* and *i.* cover, be covered, as with mist. **Scotch m.,** thick wetting mist, drizzle. (O.E.)
mistake, *v.t.* and *i.* (*past* **mistook,** *p.p.* **mistaken**) misunderstand, misapprehend; form wrong opinion (about); take (one for another).—*n.* misconception; error, blunder. **and no m.,** undoubtedly. **mistaken,** *a.* guilty of mistake; erroneous, ill-judged. **mistakenly,** *adv.*
mister, *n.* (*abbr.* **Mr.**) title of courtesy to man; sir.—*v.t.* address thus. (*master*)
mister, *n.* (*Spens.*) manner, kind; (*Scot.*) necessity.—*v.i.* (*Spens.*) need; be necessary. (*minister*)
mistigris, *n.* (*cards*) kind of poker. (F. *mistigri,* knave of spades)
mistime, *v.t.* do or say at wrong time; time wrongly. **mistimed,** *a.* ill-timed.
mistletoe, *n.* evergreen parasitic plant with sticky white berries. (O.E. *mistel,* mistletoe; *tán,* twig)
mistral, *n.* cold dry northerly wind of S. France. (F.)
mistranslate, *v.t.* translate incorrectly. **mistranslation,** *n.*
mistress, *n.* female head of household, school etc.; woman having authority or skill; female teacher; sweetheart; paramour; (*abbr.* **Mrs.**) title of married woman, madam; (*Shake.*) jack at bowls. **M. of the Robes,** lady in charge of Queen's wardrobe. **m.-ship,** *n.* (O.F. *maistresse*)
mistrial, *n.* (*law*) trial rendered invalid by error.
mistrust, *v.t.* regard with suspicion; doubt.—*n.* want of confidence or trust. **mistrustful,** *a.*
mistryst, *v.t.* (*Scot.*) fail to keep engagement with.
misty, *a.* full of mist; dim, obscure.
misunderstand, *v.t.* (*past, p.p.* **misunderstood**) take in wrong sense, mistake. **misunderstanding,** *n.*
misuse, *v.t.* use for wrong purpose or in wrong way; ill-treat.—*n.* improper use.
mite, *n.* very small child or person; small coin, half-farthing; bit, jot. (O.Du.)
mite, *n.* tiny animal of arachnid class breeding in cheese etc. (O.E.)
mithridatism, *n.* immunity from poison, got by taking gradually increasing doses of it. **mithridatic,** *a.* **mithridatize,** *v.t.* (King *Mithridates*)
mitigate, *v.t.* make less severe; alleviate; moderate. **mitigation,** *n.* **mitigatory,** *a.* (L. *mitis,* mild)
mitosis, *n.* (*pl.* **mitoses**) process by which plant or animal cells divide. **mitotic,** *a.* (Gk. *mitos,* thread)
mitrailleuse, *n.* machine-gun with several barrels. (F.)
mitre, *n.* bishop's head-dress; episcopal rank; joint of mouldings etc. at right angles, line of junction being at 45°.—*v.t.* put mitre on; join with, shape for, mitre-joint. **m.-box,** *n.* guide for saw in cutting mitre-joint. **mitral,** *a.* of, like, mitre. **mitral valve,** a valve of the heart. (Gk. *mitra,* headband)
mitt, *n.* glove covering wrist and palm but not fingers; mitten; (*sl.*) hand, fist. (abbr. of *mitten*)
mitten, *n.* glove with one compartment for four fingers; mitt; (*pl., sl.*)

boxing-gloves. **get the m.**, be dismissed. (F. *mitaine*)

mittimus, *n.* (*law*) warrant for commitment to prison; dismissal. (L.= we send)

mix, *v.t.* and *i.* unite in one mass, blend, mingle; make by mixing; associate (with). **m. up**, confuse; mistake (one for another). **m.-up**, *n.* medley; (*colloq.*) free fight. **mixed**, *a.* made up of different things; not select; of both sexes. **mixed doubles**, (*lawn tennis*), **mixed foursome**, (*golf*) with man and woman on each side. (L. *miscēre*)

mixen, *n.* dung-heap. (O.E. *meox*, dung)

mixer, *n.* person, thing, that mixes. **good, bad, m.**, (*Amer.*) person sociable, unsociable, with casual acquaintances. **mixture**, *n.* mixing; mixed mass, compound; medicine. **mixty-maxty**, *a.* (*Scot.*) jumbled together.

mizzen, mizen, *n.* lowest sail on mizzen-mast; spanker. **m.-mast**, *n.* aftermost mast when there are three. (F. *misaine*)

mizzle, *v.i.* and *n.* drizzle.

mizzle, *v.i.* (*sl.*) go, decamp.

mnemonic, *a.* of, aiding, memory.—*n. pl.* art, system, of developing memory. **mnemonist**, *n.* **Mnemosyne**, *n.* Greek goddess of memory. **mnemotechny**, *n.* mnemonics. **mnemotechnic**, *a.* (Gk. *mnēmōn*, mindful)

mo, *vulg. abbr.* for **moment.**

mo, same as **moe.**

moa, *n.* large extinct flightless New Zealand bird like ostrich. (native)

moan, *n.* low sound of pain or grief. —*v.i.* utter moan; lament (for). **make m.**, (*arch.*) complain. **moanful**, *a.* (M.E. *mone*)

moat, *n.* defensive ditch round castle or fort.—*v.t.* surround with moat. (O.F. *mote*, mound)

mob, *n.* populace; rabble, riotous crowd.—*v.t.* crowd about and hustle. **m. law**, lynch law. **swell m.**, mobsman class. (L. *mobile vulgus*, fickle crowd)

mob-cap, *n.* woman's indoor cap.

mobile, *a.* movable, not fixed; easily changing. **mobility**, *n.* **mobilize**, *v.t.* and *i.* call up (forces) for active service. **mobilization**, *n.* (L. *movēre*, move)

moble, *v.t.* (*Shake.*) muffle, cover head of.

mobocracy, *n.* rule by the mob. (Gk. *kratos*, power)

mobsman, *n.* well-dressed thief. (*mob*)

moccasin, *n.* soft deerskin shoe of American Indian; venomous American snake, copperhead. (native)

mocha, *n.* fine quality of coffee. (place)

mocha, *n.* kind of chalcedony.

mock, *v.t.* and *i.* ridicule, deride; scoff (at); mimic; impose upon.—*n.* ridicule, sneer; laughing-stock.—*a.* sham, imitation. **m. duck**, pork with duck stuffing. **m. sun, moon**, parhelion, paraselene. **m.-heroic**, *a.* parodying heroic style.—*n.* burlesque epic. **m.-turtle soup**, us. of calf's head. **mockery**, *n.* derision; laughing-stock; false show. **mocking-bird**, *n.* American bird that mimics others. (O.F. *mocquer*)

mod, *n.* annual festival for encouraging national poetry and art. (Gael.)

mode, *n.* way, method, form; prevailing fashion; (*mus.*) arrangement of intervals in the scale. **modal**, *a.* of mode or form, not substance; (*gram.*) of mood. **modal proposition**, (*logic*) in which assertion is made with a qualification. (L. *modus*)

model, *n.* miniature representation, copy; design, pattern; example for imitation; one who poses for painter; one who displays clothes for draper. —*a.* serving as a model.—*v.t.* mould, fashion; make to a model. **modeller, modelling**, *nn.*

modena, *n.* deep purple. (place)

moderate, *a.* not extreme or excessive; temperate, restrained; medium.—*n.* person of moderate views.—*v.t.* and *i.* make, become, less violent or vehement; lessen; act as moderator. **moderation**, *n.* moderateness, freedom from excess; (*pl.*, *abbr.* **mods**) first public examination for B.A. at Oxford. *moderato*, *adv.* (*mus.*) moderately. **moderator**, *n.* mediator; president of a Presbyterian council; lamp with device regulating flow of oil. **moderatism**, *n.* moderate opinion. (L. *modus*, measure)

modern, *a.* of present or recent times; new-fashioned; (*Shake.*) commonplace.—*n.* person of modern times. **m. side**, division of school specializing in modern languages and science (opp. to classical). **modernism**, *n.* modern views, methods, or usage; rationalistic theology. **modernist**, *n.* **modernity**, *n.* state of being modern. **modernize**, *v.t.* adapt to modern ways or views. **modernization**, *n.* (L. *modo*, just now)

modest, *a.* unassuming, not boastful or forward; pure-minded, decorous; moderate, unpretentious. **modesty**, *n.* (L. *modestus*)

modicum, *n.* small quantity. (L. *modus*, measure)

modify, *v.t.* change slightly; tone down, qualify. **modification**, *n.* **modifiable, modificatory**, *aa.* (L. *modus*, measure; *facere*, make)

modillion, *n.* (*archit.*) ornamental bracket under cornice in Corinthian order. (It. *modiglione*)

modish, *a.* fashionable. **modiste**, *n.* fashionable dressmaker. (*mode*)

mods, see **moderate.**

modulate, *v.t.* and *i.* regulate; vary intonation or pitch of, attune; (*mus.*) change key. **modulation, modulator**, *nn.* **module**, *n.* unit of measure;

(*archit.*) semi-diameter of shaft etc. as standard for regulating other proportions; (*Shake.*) image. **modulus,** *n.* (*pl.* **moduli**) quantity expressing measure of some function or property, e.g. elasticity. (L. *modus,* measure)

modus, *n.* way, mode; compensation in lieu of tithes. *m. operandi,* plan of working, way thing works. *m. vivendi,* working arrangement, compromise, between differing parties. (L.)

moe, *a.* (*Shake.*) more in number. (O.E. *mā*)

mofette, *n.* exhalation of mephitic gas; fissure from which it issues. (F.)

mofussil, *n.* (*Anglo-Ind.*) provincial districts, the country. (Arab. *faççala,* divide)

Mogul, *n.* and *a.* Mongol; great personage. **Great, Grand, M.,** ruler of former Mogul Empire at Delhi. (Pers. *mugul*)

mohair, *n.* fine silken hair of Angora goat; cloth of this. (Arab. *mukhayyar,* select)

Mohammedan, Mahometan, Mahomedan, *n.* and *a.* (follower) of Mohammed or the Moslem religion. **Mohammedanism,** *n.* Islam. **Mohammedanize,** *v.t.* convert to Islam.

Mohawk, Mohican, *nn.* names of two N. American Indian tribes. (native)

Mohock, *n.* London street ruffian of 18th century. (*Mohawk*)

mohr, *n.* small African gazelle.

mohur, *n.* (also **gold m.**) Indian gold coin worth 15 rupees. (Pers. *muhr*)

moider, *v.t.* and *i.* weary, bewilder; toil hard.

moidore, *n.* ancient Portuguese gold coin worth 27*s.* (Port. *moeda,* money; *ouro,* gold)

moiety, *n.* half; one of two parts, share. (L. *medius,* middle)

moil, *v.i.* and *t.* drudge; (*arch.*) daub, defile; soil oneself. (L. *mollis,* soft)

moire, *n.* (also **m. antique**) watered fabric, us. silk. **moiré,** *a.* watered; having clouded appearance. (F.)

moist, *a.* slightly wet, damp; rainy, humid. **moisten,** *v.t.* and *i.* make, become, damp. **moisture,** *n.* liquid in diffused or absorbed state. (O.F. *moiste*)

moke, *n.* (*sl.*) donkey.

moko, *n.* Maori method of tattooing. (Maori)

molar, *a.* for grinding.—*n.* molar tooth, back tooth. (L. *mola,* mill)

molar, *a.* of or in the whole mass (opp. to molecular). (L. *moles,* mass)

molasses, *n.* syrup drained from raw sugar; treacle. (L. *mel,* honey)

mole, *n.* massive work of masonry, breakwater, pier, causeway; harbour within this. (L. *moles,* mass)

mole, *n.* small dark-furred burrowing animal. (M.E. *molle*)

mole, *n.* small dark protuberant spot on skin. (O.E. *māl*)

molecule, *n.* smallest part of a substance that retains the distinctive properties of that substance; any minute particle. **molecular,** *a.* of, inherent in, molecules. **molecular weight,** weight of a molecule of any substance relative to one of hydrogen. (L. *moles,* mass)

molehill, *n.* mound thrown up by burrowing mole. **make mountain out of m.,** exaggerate difficulty.

moleskin, *n.* fur of mole; kind of fustian; (*pl.*) trousers of the fustian.

molest, *v.t.* interfere with so as to annoy or injure. **molestation,** *n.* (L. *molestus,* troublesome)

moll, *n.* (*sl.*) wench; mistress (of thief etc.). (dim. of *Mary*)

mollify, *v.t.* calm down, appease; soften. **mollification,** *n.* (L. *mollis,* soft; *facere,* make)

mollusc, *n.* soft-bodied and (us.) hard-shelled animal, e.g. snail, oyster etc. **molluscan, molluscoid, molluscous,** *aa.* (L. *mollis,* soft)

molly, *n.* milksop. **mollycoddle,** *n.* soft, effeminate, person.—*v.t.* and *i.* coddle (oneself). (dim. of *Mary*)

mollymawk, same as **mallemuck.**

Moloch, *n.* Semitic fire-god, to which children were sacrificed; kind of Australian lizard.

molossus, *n.* three-syllabled foot, long-long-long. (Gk. *molossos*)

Molotov breadbasket, case with large number of incendiary bombs which it empties out in mid-air. **Molotov cocktail,** makeshift bomb of bottle filled with inflammable mixture, used against tanks. (person)

molten, see **melt.**

molto, *adv.* very. (It.)

moly, *n.* fabulous herb warding off enchantment; wild garlic. (Gk. *mōlu*)

molybdenum, *n.* rare silvery-white metal. **molybdenous, molybdic,** *aa.* (Gk. *molubdos,* lead)

moment, *n.* point or short space of time, instant; importance; (*mech.*) measure of force's power to cause rotation. **at the m.,** just now. **man of the m.,** now in public eye. **momentary,** *a.* lasting only a moment, transitory. **momentarily,** *adv.* **momently,** *adv.* from moment to moment; every moment; for a moment. **momentous,** *a.* very important, weighty. **momentum,** *n.* (*pl.* **momenta**) impetus; (*mech.*) product of body's mass and velocity. (L. *movēre,* move)

Momus, *n.* Greek god of raillery; wag, fault-finder. (Gk. *Mōmos*)

monachal, monacal, *a.* of monks, monastic. **monachism,** *n.* monasticism. (L. *monachus,* monk)

monad, *n.* unit, number one; ultimate unit of being or evolution; (*chem.*) element, radical, with valency of one.

monadic, *a.* **monadism,** *n.* theory that universe is composed of monads. (Gk. *monos*, alone)
monadelphous, *a.* (*bot.*) having stamens in one bundle. (Gk. *monos*, alone; *adelphos*, brother)
monandrous, *a.* (*bot.*) having one stamen only. **monandry,** *n.* possession of only one husband at a time. (Gk. *monos*, alone; *anēr*, man)
monarch, *n.* supreme ruler, sovereign; large red and black butterfly. **monarchal,** *a.* of, befitting, a monarch. **monarchic, monarchical,** *aa.* of, favouring, monarchy. **monarchism,** *n.* principles of, devotion to, monarchy. **monarchist,** *n.* **monarchy,** *n.* monarchical system or state, kingdom. **absolute, limited, monarchy,** without, with, constitutional restrictions. (Gk. *monos*, alone; *archein*, rule)
monastery, *n.* house of religious retirement for monks. **monastic, monastical,** *aa.* of monks or monasteries; recluse; (of binding) finished by tooling without gold. **monasticism,** *n.* monastic life or system. (Gk. *monos*, alone)
mondaine, *n.* society or worldly woman. (F.)
Monday, *n.* second day of week. **mondayish,** *a.* (*colloq.*) feeling slack after week-end. (O.E. *mona*, moon)
monde, *n.* fashionable world. **mondial,** *a.* worldwide. (F.)
money, *n.* coin, currency; medium of exchange; wealth; (*pl.*, *arch.*) sums of money. **coin m.,** (*sl.*) make it quickly. **m. of account,** monetary unit not necessarily actual coin, e.g. guinea. **m.-box,** *n.* closed box with slit for savings. **m.-changer,** *n.* one who changes money into other coinage at fixed rate. **m.-grubber,** *n.* avaricious person. **m.-lender,** *n.* usurer. **m.-market,** *n.* operations of dealers in stocks and bills. **m. order,** Post Office cheque for remitting money. **m.-spinner,** *n.* kind of small spider. **monetary,** *a.* of coinage or money. **monetize,** *v.t.* make into, recognize as, money. **monetization,** *n.* **moneyed,** *a.* wealthy; consisting of money. (L. *moneta*, mint)
monger, *n.* dealer. (L. *mango*)
Mongol, *n.* and *a.* (inhabitant) of Mongolia. **Mongolian,** *a.* and *n.* Mongol; of yellow-skinned, straight-haired type of mankind.
mongoose, *n.* small Indian animal that preys on snakes, ichneumon; kind of lemur. (native *mangus*)
mongrel, *n.* dog, person, of mixed breed; hybrid.—*a.* of mixed breed or origin. **mongrelize,** *v.t.* **mongrelly,** *adv.*
monial, *n.* mullion. (O.F.)
moniker, *n.* (*Amer. sl.*) name; nickname.
moniliform, *a.* shaped like a necklace. (L. *monīle*, necklace)
monism, *n.* philosophical theory that there is only one kind of being and that matter and mind are ultimately identical. **monist,** *n.* believer in this. **monistic,** *a.* (Gk. *monos*, alone)
monition, *n.* admonition; formal notice from ecclesiastical court to offender; summons. **monitor,** *n.* (*fem.* **monitress, monitrix**) one who admonishes; senior schoolboy assisting master; turreted ironclad with low freeboard; kind of lizard. **monitorial,** *a.* **monitorship,** *n.* **monitory,** *a.* warning.—*n.* papal letter of admonition. (L. *monēre*, warn)
monk, *n.* one of religious community of men living apart under vows. **m.-fish,** *n.* angel-fish. **m.'s-hood,** *n.* a poisonous plant, aconite. **monkdom, monkhood,** *nn.* **monkery,** *n.* life, practices, of monks; monastery. (Gk. *monos*, alone)
monkey, *n.* manlike animal with prehensile feet; ape; mischievous child; striker of pile-driver; (*sl.*) £500.—*v.i.* and *t.* play tricks; ape, mock. **get one's m. up,** lose one's temper. **m.-bread,** *n.* fruit of baobab tree. **m.-cup,** *n.* pitcher-plant. **m.-jacket,** *n.* short close-fitting jacket. **m.-meat,** *n.* (*Amer. sl.*) tinned beef. **m.-nut,** *n.* peanut. **m.-puzzle,** *n.* Chile pine. **m.-shines,** *n.pl.* (*Amer.*) monkey-tricks. **m.-wrench,** *n.* spanner with movable jaw.
monkish, *a.* of, like, monks; monastic.
mono-, *pref.* alone, sole, single. (Gk. *monos*, alone)
monobasic, *a.* (*chem.*) having one base or atom of a base.
monocarp, *n.* annual. **monocarpic, monocarpous,** *aa.* bearing fruit only once. (Gk. *karpos*, fruit)
monocephalous, *a.* (*bot.*) single-headed. (Gk. *kephalē*, head)
monochord, *n.* one-stringed instrument; one-stringed appliance for determining musical intervals.
monochrome, *n.* painting in single colour. **monochromatic,** *a.* of one colour only. (Gk. *chrōma*, colour)
monocle, *n.* single eyeglass. (L. *oculus*, eye)
monoclinal, *a* (*geol.*) tilted one way only. (Gk. *klinein*, incline)
monocotyledon, *n.* plant with one seed-leaf. **monocotyledonous,** *a.*
monocrat, *n.* one who governs alone. **monocracy,** *n.* (Gk. *kratos*, power)
monocular, *a.* for one eye only.—*n.* single field-glass.
monocycle, *n.* one-wheeled velocipede.
monodactylous, *a.* having only one finger or toe. (Gk. *daktulon*, finger)
monodrama, *n.* piece for one actor.
monody, *n.* dirge, elegy; song for one voice. **monodic,** *a.* **monodist,** *n.* (Gk. *aeidein*, sing)
monoecious, *a.* having stamens and pistils on same plant, hermaphrodite. (Gk. *oikos*, house)

monogamy, *n.* possession of only one wife, husband, or mate at a time; marrying only once. **monogamist,** *n.* **monogamous,** *a.* (Gk. *gamos,* marriage)

monogenesis, *n.* derivation from single cell. **monogenetic,** *a.* **monogeny,** *n.* descent of mankind from one pair.

monoglot, *n.* and *a.* (one) who uses only one language. (Gk. *glōtta,* tongue)

monogony, *n.* asexual propagation by fission. (Gk. *gonos,* seed)

monogram, *n.* two or more letters, esp. initials, interwoven. **monogrammatic,** *a.* (Gk. *graphein,* write)

monograph, *n.* special treatise on single subject. **monographer, monographist,** *nn.* **monographic,** *a.* (Gk. *graphein,* write)

monolatry, *n.* worship of only one god, without necessarily disbelieving in others. (Gk. *latreia,* worship)

monolith, *n.* monument consisting of single stone. **monolithic,** *a.* (Gk. *lithos,* stone)

monologue, *n.* soliloquy; dramatic composition with only one speaker. **monological,** *a.* **monologist, monologuist,** *nn.* **monologize,** *v.i.* soliloquize. (Gk. *legein,* speak)

monomachy, *n.* single combat. (Gk. *machē,* fight)

monomania, *n.* madness on single subject. **monomaniac,** *n.* **monomaniacal,** *a.*

monometallism, *n.* use of single metal as standard of currency. **monometallic,** *a.* **monometallist,** *n.*

monomial, *n.* and *a.* (*math.*) (expression) consisting of one term. (*binomial*)

monomorphic, monomorphous, *aa.* of same type or structure; unchanging in shape. (Gk. *morphē,* form)

monopetalous, *a.* (*bot.*) having corolla in one piece. (*petal*)

monophobia, *n.* morbid fear of being alone. (Gk. *phobos,* fear)

monophthong, *n.* simple vowel-sound. **monophthongal,** *a.* (Gk. *phthonggos,* sound)

monophyllous, *a.* composed of single leaf. (Gk. *phullon,* leaf)

Monophysite, *n.* one who holds that Christ had only one nature, both human and divine. **Monophysitism,** *n.* (Gk. *phusis,* nature)

monoplane, *n.* aeroplane with one plane.

monopoly, *n.* sole right of dealing in a thing; sole possession or control; thing monopolized. **monopolist,** *n.* **monopolize,** *v.t.* possess, control, exclusively; engross the whole of. (Gk. *pōlein,* sell)

monopolylogue, *n.* entertainment in which there is only one performer who plays many parts. (Gk. *monos,* alone; *polus,* many; *legein,* speak)

monopsychism, *n.* theory that all souls are one. (Gk. *psuchē,* soul)

monopteral, *a.* one-winged; with one ring of supporting columns. **monopteron,** *n.* monopteral temple. (Gk. *pteron,* wing)

monorail, *n.* railway with single rail and balanced or hanging cars.

monorhyme, *n.* poem in which all lines have same rhyme.

monosepalous, *a.* (*bot.*) having calyx undivided. (*sepal*)

monospermous, *a.* one-seeded. (*sperm*)

monostich, *n.* poem in one line. **monostichous,** *a.* (*bot.*) consisting of one layer or row. (Gk. *stichos,* line)

monostrophic, *a.* with stanzas all of same metric form. (*strophe*)

monosyllable, *n.* word of one syllable. **monosyllabic,** *a.*

monotheism, *n.* doctrine that there is only one God. **monotheist,** *n.* **monotheistic,** *a.* (Gk. *theos,* god)

monotone, *n.* succession of sounds on same pitch; unvaried tone or style. —*v.t.* recite on single note. **monotonic,** *a.* (*mus.*). **monotonous,** *a.* unvarying in tone; with dull uniformity, wearisome. **monotony,** *n.* want of variety, irksome sameness.

monotreme, *n.* one of the lowest orders of mammals, with single vent for digestive, urinary, and genital organs. (Gk. *trēma,* hole)

monotype, *n.* type-setting machine casting each letter separately. **monotypic,** *a.* represented by only one type or species.

monovalent, *a.* (*chem.*) having valency of one. **monovalency, monovalence,** *nn.*

monoxide, *n.* oxide with one oxygen atom in each molecule.

Monroe doctrine, Monroeism, *n.* principle of non-intervention of Europe in affairs of American continents. (laid down by U.S. President *Monroe*)

monseigneur, *n.* (*pl. messeigneurs*) French title given to princes, prelates etc. *monsieur,* *n.* (*pl. messieurs*) French equivalent of Mr., sir. *monsignor,* *n.* Italian title of prelates etc.

monsoon, *n.* seasonal wind, esp. that from SW. in summer, NE. in winter, in Indian Ocean; rainy season. (Arab *mausim,* season)

monster, *n.* thing out of the course of nature, prodigy; misshapen, huge, animal or thing; very wicked person. —*a.* huge. (L. *monstrum*)

monstrance, *n.* vessel in which host is exposed for veneration. (L. *monstrare,* show)

monstrous, *a.* like a monster; huge; outrageous, atrocious.—*adv.* (*arch.*) extremely. **monstrosity,** *n.* unnatural being, abortion; monstrousness.

montage, *n.* cutting and assembling of shots taken in making film. (F.)

montane, *a.* of, inhabiting, mountains. (L. *mons*, mountain)
montbretia, *n.* orange-flowered plant. (de *Montbret*, botanist)
mont de piété, public pawnshop. (F.)
móntĕ, *n.* a gambling card-game. (Sp.)
Montessori system, of educating very young children, based on free discipline. (Dr. Maria *Montessori*)
month, *n.* any of year's twelve divisions (also **calendar m.**). **lunar m.**, period of moon's revolution, about 29½ days. **m. of Sundays**, very long period. **m.'s mind**, commemoration by requiem mass a month after death; fancy. **monthly**, *a.* and *adv.* (done etc.) once a month or in a month.—*n.* monthly magazine; (*pl.*) menses. **monthly nurse**, attending mothers for a month after confinement. **monthly rose**, China rose. (O.E. *mónadh*)
monticule, *n.* hillock; small excrescence. (L. *monticulus*)
monument, *n.* commemorative building, stone etc.; written record. **the M.**, in London, of the Great Fire. **monumental**, *a.* of monuments; colossal; lasting. **monumental mason**, tombstone maker. **monumentalize**, *v.t.* record, commemorate. (L. *monumentum*)
moo, *n.* cry of cow.—*v.i.* low. (imit.)
mooch, *v.i.* and *t.* (*sl.*) loaf, loiter, slouch; steal. **moocher**, *n.*
mood, *n.* (*gram.*) form of verb indicating mode of action; (*logic*) a subdivision of the figures; (*mus.*) arrangement of intervals in the scale, mode. (*mode*)
mood, *n.* state of mind or feelings, humour. **in the m.**, inclined. **moody**, *a.* changeable in mood; out of temper; pensive, gloomy. (O.E. *mód*)
mool, *n.* (*Scot.*) mould; (*pl.*) earth of grave.
moollah, same as **mullah**.
moolvie, *n.* Mohammedan doctor of law; learned man, teacher. (Arab. *maulawiyy*, judicial)
moon, *n.* satellite of earth or other planet; crescent-shaped thing; (*poet.*) month.—*v.i.* wander aimlessly, gaze vacantly. **full m.**, with whole disk illuminated. **new m.**, when first visible as crescent. **once in a blue m.**, very seldom. **shoot the m.**, decamp by night. **m.-flower**, *n.* ox-eye daisy. **m.-raker**, *n.* simpleton. (O.E. *móna*)
moonbeam, *n.* ray of moonlight.
mooncalf, *n.* monster; born fool.
moong, *n.* kind of Indian vetch; its fibre, used for mats.
moonglade, *n.* (*Amer.*) track of moonlight on water.
moonlight, *n.* light of moon. **m. flitting**, night removal to evade rent. **moonlighter**, *n.* Irish night-raider. **moonlit**, *a.* illuminated by the moon.
moonshee, *n.* Indian native secretary or interpreter. (Arab. *munshi*)
moonshine, *n.* visionary talk, empty show; smuggled spirits. **moonshiner**, *n.* spirit-smuggler; illicit distiller.
moonstone, *n.* translucent pearly kind of feldspar.
moonstruck, *a.* lunatic.
moonwort, *n.* crescent-shaped fern.
moony, *a.* crescent-shaped; round; listless, dreamy, tipsy.
moop, *v.i.* (*Scot.*) nibble.
Moor, *n.* native of Morocco; N. African Mohammedan. **Moorish**, *a.* (Gk. *Mauros*)
moor, *n.* large tract of waste land, heath. **moorcock, moorfowl**, *nn.* red grouse. **moorhen**, *n.* water-hen; hen grouse. **moorland**, *n.* heath-land. **moorstone**, *n.* kind of granite. (O.E. *mór*)
moor, *v.t.* and *i.* secure (ship) by cable to shore etc. **moorage**, *n.* place, charge, for mooring. **mooring**, *n.* (us. *pl.*) anchors, chains etc. for mooring ship to. **mooring-mast**, *n.* tower for mooring airship.
moose, *n.* N. American elk. (native *moos*)
moot, *n.* ancient assembly; students' practice debate.—*a.* debatable.—*v.t.* and *i.* propose for discussion; argue for practice. (O.E. *gemót*)
mop, *n.* bunch of yarn, rags etc. on stick; unruly mass (of hair); hiring-fair.—*v.t.* clean with mop, wipe. **m. up**, wipe up; (*sl.*) wipe out; (*sl.*) absorb, drink up. (L. *mappa*, napkin)
mop, *v.i.* and *n.* grimace.
mope, *v.i.* and *t.* be, make, dispirited or dull.—*n.* one who mopes; (*pl.*) dumps. **mopish**, *a.* spiritless.
mopoke, same as **morepork**.
moppet, *n.* rag doll; pet name for child. **moppy**, *a.* like a mop; tipsy. **mopsy**, *n.* untidy woman. (*mop*)
moquette, *n.* material for carpets, with short velvety pile. (F.)
mora, *n.* ancient guessing game played with fingers. (It.)
mora, *n.* a S. American tree. (It.)
mora, *n.* (*Scots law*) delay. (L.)
moraine, *n.* mass of earth, stones etc. deposited by glacier. (F.)
moral, *a.* of character or conduct; concerned with, understanding, right and wrong; good, virtuous.—*n.* moral lesson or maxim; morale; (*vulg.*) likeness; (*pl.*) moral habits, esp. in matters of sex. **m. certainty**, reasonable certainty. **m. courage**, to face ridicule etc. for one's principles. **m. law**, law of conscience. **m. philosophy**, ethics. **m. sense**, knowledge of right and wrong. **m. victory**, one that seems defeat. **morale**, *n.* spirit, discipline. **moralism**, *n.* moral system. **moralist**, *n.* teacher of morals; one for whom morality needs no religious sanction. **moralistic**, *a.* **morality**, *n.* moral conduct, quality, or science; virtue; kind of medieval allegorical play; (*pl.*) moral princi-

ples. **moralize,** *v.i.* and *t.* make moral reflections; interpret morally. **moralization,** *n.* **morally,** *adv.* in a moral manner, ethically; virtually. (L. *mos,* custom)
morass, *n.* swamp, marsh, slough. (L.L. *mariscus*)
morat, *n.* drink of honey and mulberry juice. (L. *morum,* mulberry)
moratorium, *n.* governmental permission to delay payment of debts. (*mora*)
morbid, *a.* unwholesome, sickly; (*med.*) of, indicating, disease. **morbidity,** *n.* morbidness; amount of disease (in district). **morbific,** *a.* causing disease (L. *morbus,* disease)
morbidezza, *n.* soft delicate flesh-tints in painting. (It.)
morceau, *n.* small piece, short composition. (F.)
mordacious, *a.* biting; sarcastic. **mordacity,** *n.* (L. *mordēre,* bite)
mordant, *a.* biting, corrosive; caustic, sarcastic, keen.—*n.* substance used to fix dyes or make gold-leaf adhere. **mordancy,** *n.* (L. *mordēre,* bite)
mordent, *n.* (*mus.*) kind of trill. (It. *mordente*)
more, *a.* and *pron.* greater, additional, quantity or number (of).—*adv.* to a greater extent; again. **be no m.,** be dead. **m. and m.,** continually increasing. **m. or less,** about. (O.E. *māra*)
mōrĕ, *prep.* in the manner of. (L.)
moreen, *n.* stout woollen stuff used for curtains.
morel, *n.* an edible mushroom. (F. *morille*)
morel, *n.* kinds of nightshade, esp. black. (O.F. *morele*)
morello, *n.* a dark-red cherry.
moreover, *adv.* further, besides.
morepork, *n.* (*New Zealand*) owl; (*Tasmania*) nightjar. (imit. of cry)
Moresque, *a.* Moorish in style or design.—*n.* arabesque. (F.)
morganatic, *a.* **m. marriage,** between royal person and one of inferior rank; the children are legitimate, but neither they nor the **m. wife** (or **m. husband**) share royal rank or property. **morganatically,** *adv.* (L.L. *morganatica,* morning gift)
morgue, *n.* public mortuary where unknown bodies are laid out for identification. (F.)
morgue, *n.* hauteur. *m. anglaise,* traditional English aloofness. (F.)
moribund, *a.* in a dying state, near death. (L. *mori,* die)
morion, *n.* hat-shaped helmet, without beaver or visor. (F.)
morisco, *a.* and *n.* Moorish, Moor; Moorish dance. (Sp.)
mormo, *n.* bugbear; kind of moth. (Gk.)
Mormon, *n.* member of religious sect in Utah, the Latter-day Saints; formerly practising polygamy. **Mormonism,** *n.*
morn, *n.* (*poet.*) morning. **the m.,** (*Scot.*) to-morrow. **the m.'s m.,** to-morrow morning. (O.E. *morgen*)
morning, *n.* early part of day, forenoon; dawn, time near daybreak.—*a.* of, in, the morning. **m. call,** (esp.) afternoon visit. **m. coat,** tailcoat with cutaway front. **m. dress,** ordinary (not evening) dress. **m. gift,** from husband to bride the morning after marriage. **m. glory,** kind of convolvulus. **m. performance,** matinée. **m. prayer,** matins. **m. star,** planet, esp. Venus, rising before sun. **m. watch,** (*naut.*) 4–8 a.m. (M.E. *morwening*)
morocco, *n.* fine kind of leather made from goatskin. (place)
moron, *n.* one with mental development of a child, feeble-minded person. (Gk. *mōros,* dull)
morose, *a.* sullen, sulky, unsociable; gloomy. (L. *morosus*)
Morpheus, *n.* god of dreams. **in the arms of M.,** asleep. (Gk.)
morphia, morphine, *nn.* narcotic part of opium, drug used to relieve pain. **morphinism,** *n.* state caused by excessive use of morphia. **morphinomaniac, morphiomaniac,** *nn.* morphia addict. (*Morpheus*)
morphology, *n.* science of form of living things or words. **morphological,** *a.* **morphologist,** *n.* (Gk. *morphē,* form; *legein,* speak)
morra, same as **mora.**
morris, *n.* (also **m.-dance**) grotesque dance in costumes representing Robin Hood legend etc. **m.-pike,** *n.* (*Shake.*) Moorish pike. (*Morisco*)
morris, *n.* **nine men's m.,** (*Shake.*) kind of open-air draughts; ground for playing this.
morris tube, small-bore tube by which rifle is adapted for miniature range. (inventor)
morrow, *n.* next day; time just after. (M.E. *morwen,* morn)
morse, *n.* jewelled clasp of cope. (L. *mordēre,* bite)
morse, *n.* walrus. (Lapp *morsa*)
Morse, *n.* (*colloq.*) Morse code.—*v.t.* signal by this. **M. alphabet, code, signals,** in which letters are represented by dots and dashes, used in telegraphy etc. (inventor)
morsel, *n.* bite, mouthful; small piece, bit. (L. *mordēre,* bite)
mort, *n.* note sounded on hunting-horn at a kill. (L. *mors,* death)
mort, *n.* salmon in third year.
mort, *n.* (*dial.*) great amount or number (of).
mortal, *a.* subject to death; causing death, fatal; implacable, deadly; (*sl.*) very great, tedious.—*n.* man, human being. **mortality,** *n.* mortal nature; human race; death-rate. **mortality tables,** giving expectation of life. (L. *mors,* death)
mortar, *n.* vessel in which substances

are pounded with pestle; short gun throwing shells at high angle; cement of lime, sand, and water.—*v.t.* plaster, join with mortar. **m.-board,** *n.* board for holding mortar; square college cap. (L. *mortarium*)

mortgage, *n.* assignment of property to creditor as security for payment of debt; deed effecting this.—*v.t.* make over as security, pledge. **mortgagee,** *n.* one to whom mortgage is given. **mortgager, mortgagor,** *nn.* one who grants mortgage. (O.F.= dead pledge)

mortician, *n.* (*Amer.*) undertaker. (L. *mors,* death)

mortify, *v.t.* subdue, chasten (flesh, appetites) by repression or penance; humiliate, chagrin.—*v.i.* (of flesh) be affected with gangrene. **mortification,** *n.* mortifying; (*Scots law*) charitable bequest. (L. *mors,* death; *facere,* make)

mortise, mortice, *n.* hole in piece of wood to receive projection (tenon) of other piece made to fit.—*v.t.* join by this. (F. *mortaise*)

mortmain, *n.* (*law*) tenure of land held by corporation, which cannot transfer ownership. (O.F.=dead hand)

mortuary, *a.* of death or burial.—*n.* building where corpses are kept pending burial. (L. *mortuus,* dead)

mosaic, *n.* pattern, picture, made with small bits of coloured stone or glass; diversified whole.—*a.* of, made of, mosaic.—*v.t.* (*past, p.p.* **mosaicked**) adorn with, make into, mosaic. (Gk. *mousa,* a muse)

Mosaic, *a.* of Moses.

mosasaurus, *n.* large extinct marine reptile. (L. *Mosa,* Meuse, where it was found. Gk. *sauros,* lizard)

moschatel, *n.* plant with pale-green flower and musky smell. (It. *moscato,* musk)

moselle, *n.* a light white wine. (river in France)

mosey, *v.i.* (*Amer. sl.*) go off, go.

Moslem, *a.* and *n.* Mohammedan. **Moslemism,** *n.* (Arab. *salama,* submit to God)

mosque, *n.* Mohammedan temple. (Arab. *masgid*)

mosquito, *n.* kinds of biting gnat, some carrying malaria. **m.-craft,** *n.* small light vessels, torpedo-boats etc. **m.-curtain, m.-net,** *nn.* netting to keep off mosquitoes. (L. *musca,* fly)

moss, *n.* small plant growing in masses on a surface; lichen; soft peaty ground, swamp.—*v.t.* cover with moss. **m.-back,** *n.* (*sl.*) out-of-date person. **m.-hag,** *n.* broken ground from which peat has been cut. **m.-rose,** *n.* kind with moss-like growth on calyx. **m.-trooper,** *n.* freebooter of Scottish borders. **mossy,** *a.* overgrown with, like, moss. (O.E. *mos*)

most, *a.* greatest in number or degree, the greater part of.—*pron.* greatest part, majority.—*adv.* to great or greatest degree or extent, very. **at m.,** at the utmost. **make the m. of,** use to best advantage. **mostly,** *adv.* for the most part, generally. (O.E. *mæst*)

-most, *adj.suf.* forming superlative, as in hindmost. (O.E. *-mest*)

mot, *n.* witty remark. ***m. juste,*** exactly right word. (F.)

mote, *n.* particle of dust, speck. (O.E. *mot*)

mote, *arch.* for might or must.

motet, *n.* (*mus.*) short sacred vocal composition. (F).

moth, *n.* nocturnal winged insect like butterfly; type of light aeroplane. **m.-ball,** *n.* ball of camphor etc. to keep moths from clothes. **m.-eaten,** *a.* eaten into holes by moth's larva; old, shabby; time-worn. (O.E. *moththe*)

mother, *n.* female parent; producer, source; mother superior; (*arch.*) hysteria.—*v.t.* give birth, act as mother, to. **M. Carey's chicken,** stormy petrel. **M. Church,** Church personified; one from which others have sprung. **M. Earth,** earth personified. **Mothers' Day,** (*Amer.*) for honouring mothers, 2 May. **m. ship,** in charge of smaller craft. **m. superior,** head of convent. **m. tongue,** native language. **m. wit,** innate common sense. **m.-in-law,** *n.* mother of one's wife or husband. **m.-of-millions,** *n.* ivy-leaved toadflax. **m.-of-pearl,** *n.* iridescent lining of pearl-shell.

mother, *n* (also **m. of vinegar**) thick slimy substance formed in vinegar during fermentation.

mothercraft, *n.* art of rearing children.

motherhood, *n.* state of being a mother.

mothering, *n.* custom of visiting parents on **M. Sunday,** in mid-Lent.

motherland, *n.* native land.

motherly, *a.* like a mother, homely, tender.

mothery, *a.* like mother; concreted.

motif, *n.* dominant idea or theme in artistic composition; ornament sewn on dress. (F.)

motile, *a.* able to move. **motility,** *n.* (L. *movēre,* move)

motion, *n.* moving, movement; gesture; proposal in meeting; applicaton to judge; evacuation of bowels.—*v.i.* and *t.* sign, direct by sign. **in m.,** moving, working. **m. picture,** cinema film. **motionless,** *a.* still. (L. *movēre,* move)

motive, *a.* causing motion or action. —*n.* what impels to action, inducement; motif.—*v.t.* motivate. **m. power,** steam, water, wind etc. used to drive machinery. **motivity,** *n.*

power of producing motion. **motivate,** *v.t.* supply motive to, instigate; be motif of. (L. *movēre,* move)
motley, *a.* chequered, particoloured; heterogeneous, of diverse parts.—*n.* jester's particoloured dress; mixture.
motmot, *n.* tropical American bird like jay. (imit. of note)
motor, *n.* what imparts movement; machine supplying motive power, esp. internal - combustion engine; motor-car.—*a.* (*anat.*) causing, transmitting, motion.—*v.i.* and *t.* go, convey, by motor-car. **m. bandit,** thief using motor-car for raids. **m.-bicycle, m.-boat, m.-bus, m.-car,** *nn.* bicycle etc. driven by motor. **m.-garage,** *n.* for housing motor-cars. **motordrome,** *n.* testing track for motor-vehicles. **motorial, motory,** *aa.* (*anat.*) motor. **motorist,** *n.* user of motor-car. **motorize,** *v.t.* provide (army unit) with motor transport. **motorman,** *n.* driver of tram etc. (L.)
mottle, *v.t.* mark with coloured blotches or spots, variegate.—*n.* such marking.
motto, *n.* (*pl.* **mottoes**) phrase, maxim, chosen as rule of conduct; slogan on heraldic crest; quotation prefixed to book etc.; verses etc. in Christmas cracker. (It.)
mouch, same as **mooch.**
mouchard, *n.* police spy. (F.)
mouchoir, *n.* handkerchief. (F.)
moue, *n.* pout, grimace. (F.)
moufflon, mouflon, *n.* wild mountain sheep of S. Europe. (L.L. *mufron*)
mouillé, *a.* softened in sound, palatalized, as *gl* in 'seraglio.' (F.)
moujik, *n.* Russian peasant. (Russ. *muzhiku*)
mould, *n.* pattern, templet, for shaping; matrix in which metal is cast; make, form, shape.—*v.t.* fashion, shape to pattern. (M.E. *molde*)
mould, *n.* loose earth; soil rich in decayed matter. **man of m.,** mere mortal. (O.E. *molde*)
mould, *n.* minute fungoid growth caused by dampness.
moulder, *n.* one who moulds or casts, esp. metal.
moulder, *v.i.* decay, rot, crumble to dust.
moulding, *n.* moulded object: decoration, ornamental edging.
mouldwarp, *n.* mole. (M.E. *werpen,* throw up)
mouldy, *a.* musty, stale; antiquated; (*sl.*) dull, boring. (*mould*)
mouldy, *n.* (*naut. sl.*) torpedo.
moulin, *n.* crevasse, shaft, in glacier through which water drains. (F.)
moult, *v.t.* and *i.* (of birds) cast, shed (feathers); change feathers.—*n.* moulting. (L. *mutare,* change)
moulvie, same as **moolvie.**
mound, *n.* heap of earth or stones; rampart; hillock, knoll; (*baseball*) pitcher's box.—*v.t.* fortify with mound. **m.-builders,** *n.pl.* prehistoric race in N. America.
mound, *n.* ball or globe surmounted by cross etc., heraldic symbol of empire. (L. *mundus,* world)
mount, *n.* mountain, hill: margin round picture, card on which it is mounted; riding-horse.—*v.i.* and *t.* go up, ascend; get on (horse); rise in amount, rank etc.; provide with horse; furnish with setting or support. **m. guard,** act as sentry. (L. *mons*)
mountain, *n.* high hill; large pile; (also **m. wine**) kind of Malaga. **m. ash,** rowan-tree. **m. dew,** Scotch whisky. **m. lion,** cougar. **m. railway,** light railway with centre rail cogged. **m. sickness,** caused by rarefied air. **the M.,** extremists in French Revolution. **mountaineer,** *n.* dweller on, climber of, mountains. **mountainous,** *a.* full of mountains; very high. (L. *mons,* mountain)
mountant, *n.* paste for mounting photographs.
mountebank, *n.* itinerant quack doctor; boastful pretender, charlatan. **mountebankery,** *n.* (It. *monta in banco,* mount on bench)
mourn, *v.i.* and *t.* grieve, feel sorrow (for), bewail; wear mourning. **mourner,** *n.* one who mourns or attends at funeral. **mournful,** *a.* doleful, sad. **mourning,** *n.* grieving; black dress of mourner. **mourning-paper,** *n.* note-paper with black edge. (O.E. *murnan*)
mouse, *n.* (*pl.* **mice**) small rodent infesting houses; sash-window counterweight; (*sl.*) black eye.—*v.i.* hunt, catch, mice; search about, prowl. **m.-colour,** *n.* dark grey with brownish tinge. **m.-ear,** *n.* kind of hawkweed etc. **mouser,** *n.* cat that catches mice. (O.E. *mús*)
mousmee, *n.* unmarried girl in Japan; waitress in tea-garden. (Jap.)
mousse, *n.* dish of flavoured cream whipped and frozen. (F.=froth)
mousseline, *n.* fine French muslin. *m.-de-laine,* *n.* material of wool and cotton. *m.-de-soie,* *n.* a thin silk fabric. (F.)
moustache, *n.* hair of upper lip. **m.-cup,** *n.* one with half-cover to protect moustache. (Gk. *mustax*)
mousy, *a.* like a mouse; quiet, timid; smelling of mice.
mouth, *n.* opening in head for eating etc.; opening, entrance; outfall of river; grimace; (*sl.*) impudence.—*v.t.* and *i.* take in mouth; utter pompously, declaim, rant. **down in the m.,** despondent. **laugh on wrong side of one's m.,** lament. **m.-honour,** *n.* (*Shake.*) insincere civility. **m.-organ,** *n.* harmonica, Jew's harp, or pan-pipes. **mouthful,** *n.* as much as mouth contains; small quantity; mouth-filling word; (*Amer. sl.*) important statement, **lot. mouthpiece,**

n. end of pipe, instrument etc. placed between lips; spokesman. **mouthy,** *a.* ranting, bombastic. (O.E. *múth*)

move, *v.t.* and *i.* change position (of); stir, rouse, affect with emotion; propose (resolution); take action.—*n.* moving, motion; step. **get a m. on,** hurry, get started. **m. in,** remove to new home. **on the m.,** moving about. **movable,** *a.* that may be moved.—*n.pl.* personal property. **movable feast,** one that varies its date. **movement,** *n.* moving; moving part of machine; policy and activities of group; division of musical work; tempo. **mover,** *n.* one who moves. **prime mover,** originator; driving force. **movies,** *n.pl.* (*sl.*) cinema films. **movietone,** *n.* a form of sound film. **moving,** *a.* affecting, pathetic. **moving staircase,** escalator. (L. *movēre*)

mow, *v.t.* and *i.* (*p.p.* **mown**) cut down (grass) with scythe or machine; cut down in great numbers. **mower,** *n.* man who mows; mowing-machine. (O.E. *máwan*)

mow, *n.* heap of corn, hay etc.; place in barn for this. (O.E. *múga*)

mow, *n.* wry face.—*v.i.* grimace. (*moue*)

moxa, *n.* down from plant used for cauterizing by burning on skin. (Jap. *moe kusa,* burning herb)

moya, *n.* volcanic mud.

Mpret, *n.* former title of Albanian ruler. (L. *imperator,* emperor)

mu, *n.* Greek letter M.

much, *a.* (*compar.* **more,** *superl.* **most**) a great amount of.—*n.* a great deal. —*adv.* to a great degree; by far; nearly. **m. of a muchness,** just about the same. **muchly,** *adv.* (*joc.*) much. (O.E. *micel*)

mucilage, *n.* adhesive, gum; sticky substance from plants or animals, mucus. **mucilaginous,** *a.* sticky; secreting mucilage. (L.L. *mucilago*)

muck, *n.* moist dung; dirt, filth; (*colloq.*) untidy state.—*v.t.* and *i.* manure; make dirty; (*sl.*) bungle; dawdle, loaf (about). **mucker,** *n.* heavy fall. (M.E. *muk*)

muckle, *a.* (*Scot.*) much; large.—*n.* a large amount. (O.E. *micel*)

muckna, *n.* (*Anglo-Ind.*) male elephant without tusks.

mucky, *a.* miry, filthy.

mucro, *n.* (*bot.*) sharp point. **mucronate,** *a.* narrowed to a point. (L.)

mucus, *n.* slimy substance from nose, viscous secretion of mucous membrane. **mucous,** *a.* slimy, sticky. **mucous membrane,** lining of channels of body. **mucosity,** *n.* mucousness. (L.)

mud, *n.* soft wet earth, mire.—*v.t.* muddy. **throw m. at,** vilify. (M.E. *mode*)

mudar, *n.* an E. Indian shrub whose root yields medicine. (Hind.)

muddle, *v.t.* and *i.* confuse, fuddle; mix up; bungle, mismanage.—*n.* confused state. **m. on,** proceed haphazard. **m. through,** succeed in spite of lack of system. **m.-headed,** *a.* stupid. (*mud*)

muddy, *a.* like, covered with, mud; (of colour) not clear or bright; (of voice) thick.—*v.t.* make muddy.

mudguard, *n.* screen on bicycle-wheel to catch mud-splashes.

mudir, *n.* Turkish local governor. (Turk.)

mudlark, *n.* one who works or dabbles in mud; street arab.

muezzin, *n.* Mohammedan crier who calls hours of prayer from minaret. (Arab. *adhana,* proclaim)

muff, *n.* warm soft cover for hands in winter. **muffettee,** *n.* small muff for wrist.

muff, *n.* duffer, milksop.—*v.t.* bungle, fail in, miss. **muffish,** *a.*

muffin, *n.* soft round spongy cake. **m.-bell,** *n.* one rung by **m.-man,** *n.* seller of muffins. **muffineer,** *n.* cruet for sprinkling salt or sugar on muffins.

muffle, *n.* bare end of nose of ruminant or rodent. (F. *mufle*)

muffle, *v.t.* wrap up warmly; deaden (sound) by wrapping up.—*n.* mitten; clay oven for baking pottery. **muffler,** *n.* scarf, thick neckerchief; boxing-glove; thing used to deaden sound. (L.L. *muffula,* mitten)

mufti, *n.* Mohammedan priest; civilian dress, plain clothes, of soldier etc. (Arab.)

mug, *n.* drinking-cup, us. without handle; its contents; (*sl.*) face.

mug, *n.* (*sl.*) simpleton, dupe.

mug, *v.i.* (*sl.*) study hard.—*n.* swot. **m. up,** get up (subject)

mugger, *n.* broad-snouted Indian crocodile. (Hind. *magar*)

muggins, *n.* simpleton; game at cards or dominoes.

muggy, *a.* warm, damp, and close; stuffy; mouldy.

mugwump, *n.* (*Amer.*) boss, bigwig; independent in politics. (Amer. Ind. *mugquomp,* great chief)

Muhammadan, same as **Mohammedan.**

mulatto, *n.* offspring of white and negro.—*a.* tawny. (Sp.)

mulberry, *n.* tree on whose leaves silkworms feed; its berry. (L. *morum,* mulberry)

mulch, *n.* half-rotten straw, litter, used to protect roots of plants.—*v.t.* treat with this.

mulct, *n.* fine, penalty.—*v.t.* fine (in), deprive (of). (L. *mulcta*)

mule, same as **mewl.**

mule, *n.* heelless slipper. (F.)

mule, *n.* offspring of ass and horse, esp. of he-ass and mare; hybrid; stubborn person; machine for cotton-spinning. **muleteer,** *n.* mule-driver. (O.E. *múl*)

muliebrity, *n.* womanhood; effeminacy. (L. *mulier,* woman)
mulish, *a.* like a mule; sullen, stubborn.
mull, *v.t.* warm, spice, and sweeten (wine, ale).
mull, *v.t.* bungle.—*n.* muddle.
mull, *n.* a thin muslin. (Hind. *malmal*)
mull, *n.* (*Scot.*) snuff-box. (=*mill*)
mull, *n.* (*Scot.*) promontory, headland. (Icelandic *múli*)
mull, *v.i.* and *t.* (*Amer. colloq.*) cogitate, turn (over) in mind.
mullah, *n.* Mohammedan theologian; fanatic. (Arab. *maula*)
mullein, *n.* plant with woolly leaves and yellow flowers.
muller, *n.* flat-bottomed pestle for grinding drugs etc. on slab.
mullet, *n.* kinds of sea-fish used as food. (L. *mullus*)
mulligatawny, *n.* (also **m. soup**) kind of Indian soup made with curry-powder. (Tamil *milagu-tannir,* pepper-water)
mulligrubs, *n.pl.* the dumps; colic.
mullion, *n.* upright division between lights of window. **mullioned,** *a.*
mullock, *n.* (*Austral.*) rock containing no gold or from which gold has been extracted; rubbish.
mult(i)-, from L. *multus,* many, used in **multangular,** *a.* many-angled; **multeity,** *n.* multiplicity; **multicolour, multicoloured,** *aa.* many-coloured; **multifarious,** *a.* of great variety, manifold; **multifid,** *a.* cleft into many parts; **multiflorous,** *a.* bearing more than three flowers; **multifoil,** *a.* and *n.* (*archit.*) (ornament) with over five leaf-like divisions; **multiform,** *a.* having many shapes, of many kinds, hence **multiformity,** *n.*; **multigraph,** *n.* combined type-setting and printing machine; **multilateral,** *a.* having many sides; **multilineal, multilinear,** *aa.* having many lines; **multimillionaire,** *n.* person with two or more millions of money; **multinomial,** *a.* and *n.* (*math.*) (expression) of more than two terms; **multiparous,** *a.* producing many at a birth; **multipartite,** *a.* divided into many parts. **multiplane,** *n.* aeroplane with three or more planes.
multiple, *a.* of many parts, manifold; repeated many times.—*n.* (*math.*) number exactly divisible by another. **least common m.,** (*abbr.* L.C.M.) smallest multiple of given numbers. **m. shop,** with branches in various places. **m.-poinding,** *n.* (*Scots law*) process to determine rights of property. (L. *multus,* many; *plicare,* fold)
multiply, *v.t.* and *i.* increase in number; breed, spread, produce; (*math.*) find product of two numbers. **multiplex,** *a.* manifold, multiple. **multipliable, multiplicable,** *aa.* able to be multiplied. **multiplicand,** *n.* (*math.*) number to be multiplied. **multiplication,** *n.* multiplying. **multiplicative,** *a.* **multiplicity,** *n.* state of being multiplied or various; great number. **multiplier,** *n.* (*math.*) number that is multiplied by; (*electr.*) instrument for multiplying intensity of current. (L. *multus,* many; *plicare,* fold)
multipotent, *a.* (*Shake.*) most mighty.
multipresent, *a.* present in several places at once. **multipresence,** *n.*
multitude, *n.* numerousness; great number, crowd; populace. **multitudinism,** *n.* principle of setting general before individual interest. **multitudinous,** *a.* of a multitude; very numerous. (L. *multus,* many)
multiversant, *a.* turning into many shapes. (L. *vertere,* turn)
multivocal, *a.* and *n.* ambiguous, equivocal (word).
multocular, *a.* having more than two eyes. **m. microscope,** allowing several persons to observe at once.
multum in parvo, much in small compass, compendious. (L.)
multungulate, *a.* and *n.* (animal) with hoof divided into more than two parts.
multure, *n.* toll paid in kind for grinding at mill. (L. *molere,* grind)
mum, *a.* silent.—*n.* and *int.* silence. —*v.i.* act in dumb-show. (imit.)
mum, *n.* kind of strong beer. (G. *mumme*)
mum, *n.* mamma. (abbr. of *mummy*)
mumble, *v.i.* and *t.* speak indistinctly, mutter; chew without using teeth.—*n.* indistinct talk. (*mum*)
Mumbo Jumbo, negro idol, bogy; object of foolish worship or fear.
mumchance, *a.* (*arch.*) silent; tongue-tied. (*mum*)
mummer, *n.* masker, buffoon; actor. **mummery,** *n.* buffoonery; ridiculous ceremonial, empty parade. (O.F. *momer,* mum)
mummy, *n.* corpse preserved by Egyptian art of embalming; rich brown colour. **beat to a m.,** beat into pulp. **mummify,** *v.t.* embalm; shrivel, desiccate. **mummification,** *n.* (Arab. *mum,* wax)
mummy, *n.* mother. (=mamma)
mump, *v.i.* beg, play the beggar; cheat.
mump, *v.i.* be silent, sulk; mumble. **mumping, mumpish,** *aa.* sullen. **mumps,** *n.* sulks; infectious disease with swelling of face and neck. (imit.)
mumpsimus, *n.* error in which one persists after correction. (ignorant priest's mistake for *sumpsimus*)
munch, *v.t.* and *i.* chew vigorously or noisily; crunch. (imit.)
Munchausen, *n.* lying braggart; tall story. (Baron *Munchausen* in book)
mundane, *a.* of the world, earthly; of the universe. (L. *mundus,* world)

mundungus, *n.* (*arch.*) bad-smelling tobacco. (Sp. *mondongo,* tripe)
munerary, *a.* of the nature of a gift. (L. *munus,* gift)
mung, same as **moong.**
mungo, *n.* cloth waste; cheap cloth like shoddy.
mungoose, same as **mongoose.**
municipal, *a.* of town or corporation. **m. law,** law of state, opp. to international law. **municipality,** *n.* town, district, having local self-government; its governing body. **municipalize,** *v.t.* bring under municipal control. **municipalization,** *n.* (L. *munia,* civic duties; *capere,* take)
munificent, *a.* magnificently generous, bountiful. **munificence,** *n.* (L. *munus,* gift; *facere,* make)
munifient, *n.* (*Spens.*) fortification. (L. *munire,* fortify)
muniment, *n.* defence; (*pl.*) deeds, charters, and papers for proving title. (L. *munire,* fortify)
munition, *v.t.* equip with arms.—*n.pl.* war stores, guns, shells etc. **m.-worker, munitioneer, munitioner,** *nn.* (*fem.* **munitionette**) one who makes munitions. (L. *munire,* fortify)
munnion, same as **mullion.**
munshi, same as **moonshee.**
muntjak, *n.* small Asiatic deer. (native *minchak*)
Muntz metal, a copper alloy. (inventor)
mural, *a.* of, like, on, a wall. **m. crown,** awarded to Roman soldier who was first up wall of besieged town. **murage,** *n.* tax for maintenance of town fortifications. (L. *murus,* wall)
murder, *n.* unlawful and deliberate killing of human being.—*v.t.* and *i.* commit murder (upon), kill; mangle, mar. **the m. is out,** the secret is revealed. **murderer,** *n.* (*fem.* **murderess**). **murderous,** *a.* capable of, bent on, murder; deadly. (O.E. *mordhor*)
mure, *v.t.* shut up, immure.—*n.* (*Shake.*) wall. (L. *murus,* wall)
murex, *n.* (*pl.* **murices, murexes**) shellfish yielding purple dye. (L.)
muriate, *n.* chloride. **muriatic,** *a.* got from brine. **muriatic acid,** hydrochloric acid. (L. *muria,* brine)
murk, *a.* dark.—*n.* gloom. **murky,** *a.* dark, gloomy, thick with darkness. (O.E. *mirce*)
murmur, *n.* low indistinct sound; low complaint, grumble; hushed speech. —*v.i.* and *t.* make, utter, murmur; speak softly. **murmurous,** *a.* (L.)
murphy, *n.* (*sl.*) potato. (Irish name)
murrain, *n.* infectious disease of cattle, foot-and-mouth disease. **a m!** (*arch.*) plague! (F. *morine*)
murrey, *a.* and *n.* (*arch.*) purple-red, mulberry-colour. (L. *morum,* mulberry)
murther, murtherer, same as **murder, murderer.**
muscadel, muscadine, same as **muscatel.**
muscae volitantes, specks that seem to float before eyes, due to small bodies in the vitreous humour. (L. = flitting flies)
muscardine, *n.* a disease of silkworms; fungus causing this. (F.)
muscatel, muscat, *nn.* a rich spicy wine; the musk-flavoured grape from which it is made. (L. *muscus,* musk)
muscle, *n.* fibrous band producing movement in body; muscular tissue or strength. **m. in,** (*Amer. sl.*) intrude by force. **m.-bound,** *a.* with inelastic muscles. (L. *musculus*)
muscoid, *a.* moss-like. **muscology,** *n.* science of mosses, bryology. **muscologist,** *n.* (L. *muscus,* moss)
muscovado, *n.* raw sugar. (Sp. *mascabado,* unrefined)
Muscovy, *n.* (*arch.*) Russia. **M. duck,** musk-duck. **M. glass,** mica. **Muscovite,** *a.* and *n.* Russian; mica. (Russ. *Moskova,* Moscow)
muscular, *a.* of muscles; strong, brawny. **muscularity,** *n.* **musculature,** *n.* muscular system. (*muscle*)
muse, *n.* poetry, poetic inspiration; one of the nine goddesses of art—Calliope (epic), Clio (history), Erato (love-poetry), Euterpe (lyric), Melpomene (tragedy), Polyhymnia (hymn), Terpsichore (dancing), Thalia (comedy), Urania (astronomy). (Gk. *Mousa*)
muse, *v.i.* ponder, reflect; be lost in thought.—*n.* fit of abstraction. (F. *muser*)
muset, (*obs.*) same as **meuse.**
musette, *n.* kind of bagpipe; soft pastoral melody; rustic dance. (F.)
museum, *n.* collection of natural, scientific, or artistic objects of interest. **m. piece,** antique, curio. (Gk. *mouseion,* temple of the muses)
mush, *n.* soft pulp; (*Amer.*) porridge of maize meal.
mush, *n.* (*sl.*) umbrella. (*mushroom*)
mush, *v.i.* and *n.* (*Amer.*) journey on snow by dog-sledge.
mushroom, *n.* edible kind of fungus; upstart.—*a.* of rapid growth, ephemeral.—*v.i.* gather mushrooms; take shape of mushroom. (F. *mousseron*)
mushy, *a.* soft, pulpy; (*sl.*) sentimental, soppy. (*mush*)
music, *n.* melody, harmony; laws of this; musical composition or score; pleasant sound. **face the m.,** face critics etc. **m. of the spheres,** supposed ethereal harmony caused by planetary motion. **set to m.,** compose music for. **m.-hall,** *n.* variety theatre. **m.-stool,** *n.* one with adjustable seat. **musical,** *a.* of music, melodious; skilled in, set to, music. **musical chairs,** a drawing-room game. **musical glasses,** set of glass bowls as

musical instrument. **musical-box,** *n.* box with mechanism that plays tunes. **musicale,** *n.* (*Amer.*) musical party. **musicality,** *n.* musicalness. **musician,** *n.* student, performer, of music. (Gk. *mousikē*, art of muses)

musk, *n.* scent obtained from gland of musk-deer; plants with similar scent. **m.-deer, m.-duck, m.-melon, m.-ox, m.-rose, m.-tree,** *nn.* named from their musky odour. **m.-rat,** *n.* large American water-rat, musquash. (Gk. *moschos*)

musket, *n.* infantryman's smooth-bore gun. **musketeer,** *n.* soldier armed with musket. **musketoon,** *n.* short musket. **musketry,** *n.* small-arm fire; practice in this. (It. *moschetto*, sparrow-hawk)

musky, *a.* like, smelling of, musk.

Muslim, same as **Moslem.**

muslin, *n.* fine cotton fabric. **m.-delaine,** *n.* material of wool and cotton. **muslined,** *a.* dressed in muslin. **muslinet,** *n.* coarse kind of muslin. (*Mussolo* in Mesopotamia)

musquash, *n.* fur of musk-rat; musk-rat. (Amer. Ind. *muskwessu*)

muss, *v.t.* (*Amer.*) disarrange, rumple. —*n.* state of disorder; scramble.

mussel, *n.* a bivalve shell-fish. (O.E. *muscle*)

mussuck, *n.* (*Anglo-Ind.*) skin water-bag. (Hind. *masak*)

Mussulman, *n.* (*pl.* **Mussulmans**) Mohammedan. (Pers. *musulmān*)

mussy, *a.* (*Amer.*) rumpled, tousled, untidy. (*muss*)

must, *n.* new wine; unfermented grape-juice. (L. *mustus*, new)

must, *n.* mustiness; mould.

must, *a.* (of male elephant) in state of dangerous frenzy.—*n.* this state. (Hind. *mast*, ruttish)

must, *v.i.* be obliged (to); be certain (to). (O.E. *móste*)

mustachio, *n.* (*arch.*) moustache. (Sp. *mostacho*)

mustang, *n.* half-wild horse of American prairies. (Sp. *mestengo*)

mustard, *n.* a plant; pungent seasoning made from its seeds; (*Amer. sl.*) zestful thing or person. **French m.,** mixed with vinegar, sugar etc. **m. gas,** an irritant poison gas. **m. plaster,** poultice made with mustard. (L. *mustum*, must)

mustee, same as **mestee.**

muster, *v.t.* and *i.* assemble for inspection, gather together; summon.—*n.* mustering, review; collection. **pass m.,** come up to standard. **m.-roll,** (*Shake.*) **m.-book,** *nn.* official list of men in regiment etc. (L. *monstrare*, show)

musty, *a.* mouldy, stale; antiquated.

mutable, *a.* changeable; fickle. **mutability,** *n.* **mutation,** *n.* alteration; sudden change in species; (*philol.*) umlaut. ***mutatis mutandis,*** with the necessary changes. (L. *mutare*, change)

mutch, *n.* (*Scot.*) woman's linen cap. (O. Du. *mutse*)

mutchkin, *n.* Scottish liquid measure of a pint. (*mutch*+dim.)

mute, *a.* silent, soundless; dumb.—*n.* dumb person; hired mourner; clip, pad, plug, for deadening sound of instrument; mute consonant.—*v.t.* deaden, muffle, sound of. **m. consonant,** one formed with stoppage of breath, esp. *t, p, k.* **m. letter,** written but not sounded, e.g. *k* in 'knit.' (L. *mutus*)

mute, *v.i.* and *t.* (of birds) void (dung). (O.F. *muetir*)

mutilate, *v.t.* injure, render imperfect, by removing part; maim, hack. **mutilation, mutilator,** *nn.* (L. *mutilus*, maimed)

mutiny, *n.* rebellion against authority, esp. of soldiers or sailors against officers; (*Shake.*) contention.—*v.i.* refuse to obey, revolt against, commander. **mutineer,** *n.* one who mutinies. **mutinous,** *a.* rebellious; seditious. (F. *mutin*, mutinous)

mutism, *n.* silence; dumbness. (*mute*)

muto-, from L. *mutare*, change, used in **mutograph,** *n.* primitive form of cine-camera; **mutoscope,** *n.* apparatus for showing pictures taken with this.

mutt, *n.* (*Amer. sl.*) fool.

mutter, *v.i.* and *t.* utter (words) in low tone or indistinctly; grumble.—*n.* muttering.

mutton, *n.* flesh of sheep; (*joc.*) sheep. **dead as m.,** quite dead. **laced m.,** (*Shake.*) strumpet. **return to one's mm.,** get back to subject. **m. chop,** rib of mutton chopped at small end. **m.-chop whiskers,** narrow at top, broad at bottom. **m.-head,** *n.* stupid person. **m.-headed,** *a.* (L.L. *multo*)

mutual, *a.* felt, done, by each to the other; reciprocal, interchanged; (*incorrectly*) common to two or more. **mutuality,** *n.* **mutualism,** *n.* doctrine that social interdependence is necessary to well-being. (L. *mutuus*)

mutule, *n.* (*archit.*) projecting block under corona of Doric cornice. (L. *mutulus*)

mux, *v.t.* spoil, botch.—*n.* mess.

muzhik, same as **moujik.**

muzz, *v.t.* (*sl.*) make muzzy.

muzzle, *n.* mouth and nose of animal, snout; open end of gun; cover for mouth to prevent biting.—*v.t.* secure mouth of with muzzle; gag, silence. **m.-loader,** *n.* gun loaded at muzzle. (L. *musus*)

muzzy, *a* dazed, fuddled, tipsy; dull.

my, see **I.**

myalgia, *n.* pain in the muscles. (Gk. *mus*, muscle; *algos*, pain)

myalism, *n.* sorcery of W. Indies.

myall, *n.* Australian acacia; black-fellow. (native *maial*)

myc(o)-, from Gk. *mukēs*, mushroom, used in **mycelium**, *n.* mushroom spawn; **mycetoma**, *n.* fungoid disease of feet; **mycology**, *n.* science of fungi, hence **mycologist**, *n.* **mycosis**, *n.* presence of, disease caused by, parasitic fungi.

mydriasis, *n.* excessive dilatation of eye-pupil. **mydriatic**, *a.* and *n.* (drug) causing this. (Gk. *mudriasis*)

myelitis, *n.* inflammation of spinal cord. (Gk. *muelos*, marrow)

mylodon, *n.* gigantic extinct sloth. (Gk. *mulē*, mill; *odous*, tooth)

mynheer, *n.* Dutchman. (Du. *mijnheer*, Mr., sir)

myo-, from Gk. *mus*, muscle, used in **myocardium**, *n.* muscular parts of heart; **myocarditis**, *n.* inflammation of these; **myodynamics**. *n.pl.* science of muscular force; **myography**, *n.* delineation of muscular system; **myology**, *n.* science of muscles.

myope, *n.* short-sighted person. **myopic**, *a.* **myopia**, **myopy**, *nn.* short sight. (Gk. *muein*, shut; *ōps*, eye)

myosis, *n.* abnormal contraction of eye-pupil. (Gk. *muein*, shut)

myositis, *n.* inflammation of a muscle. (Gk. *mus*, muscle)

myosote, *n.* forget-me-not. **myosotis**, *n.* kinds of small plant with blue, pink, or white flowers, incl. myosote. (Gk. *mus*, mouse; *ous*, ear)

myotic, *a.* and *n.* (drug) producing myosis.

myriad, *n.* ten thousand; vast number —*a.* countless. **myriagramme**, **myriagram**, **myrialitre**, **myriametre**, *nn.* ten thousand grammes, litres, metres. **myriapod**, *a.* and *n.* (animal) with many legs. (Gk. *murias*, ten thousand)

myrmeco-, from Gk. *murmex*, ant, used in **myrmecology**, *n.* science of ants; **myrmecophagous**, *a.* feeding on ants.

myrmidon, *n.* base or brutal follower. **mm. of the law**, police, bailiffs. (Gk. *Murmidones*, followers of Achilles)

myrobalan, *n.* dried astringent fruit like prune. (Gk. *muron*, unguent; *balanos*, acorn)

myrrh, *n.* an aromatic gum resin. **myrrhic**, **myrrhy**, *aa.* (Gk. *murra*)

myrrh, *n.* sweet cicely, an aromatic plant. (Gk. *murris*)

myrtle, *n.* evergreen shrub with fragrant white flowers; (*Amer.*) trailing periwinkle. **myrtaceous**, *a.* of the myrtle family. (Gk. *murtos*)

myself, *pron.* emphatic and refl. form of **I**, **me**; in my normal state.

mysophobia, *n.* mania for cleanness, (Gk. *musos*, uncleanness; *phobos*, fear)

mystagogue, *n.* one who initiates into or interprets religious mysteries. **mystagogic**, **mystagogical**, *aa.* (Gk. *mustēs*, initiate; *agein*, lead)

mystery, *n.* profound secret, inexplicable thing; secrecy, obscurity; religious truth beyond human understanding, sacrament; miracle play; (*pl.*) secret religious ceremonies of ancient Greeks. **m.-ship**, *n.* Q-boat. **mysterious**, *a.* obscure, incomprehensible; delighting in mystery. (Gk. *mustērion*)

mystery, *n.* (*arch.*) handicraft, trade. (L. *ministerium*, service)

mystic, *a.* of hidden (esp. religious) meaning; spiritually symbolic; occult; mysterious, awe-inspiring.—*n.* one who seeks direct knowledge of God or spiritual truths by self-surrender or contemplation. **mystical**, *a.* **mysticism**, *n.* doctrine of mystics; obscurity of doctrine. **mysticize**, *v.t.* interpret mystically. (*mystery*)

mystify, *v.t.* bewilder, puzzle. **mystification**, *n.* (*mystery*)

myth, *n.* legend expressing primitive beliefs, fable of supernatural; fiction, imaginary person. **mythic**, *a.* of, in, myths; mythical. **mythical**, *a.* imaginary, unreal; mythic. **mythicize**, *v.t.* treat as myth, interpret mythically. **mythographer**, *n.* writer of myths. **mythography**, *n.* representation of myths in plastic art. **mythology**, *n.* body, science, of myths. **mythologic**, **mythological**, *aa.* **mythologist**, *n.* student of myths. **mythopoet**, *n.* writer of myths. **mythopoeic**, **mythopoetic**, *aa.* making, productive of, myths. **mythus**, *n.* myth. (Gk. *muthos*)

myxoedema, *n.* physical and mental degeneration due to atrophy of thyroid gland. (Gk. *muxa*, mucus; *oidein*, swell)

N

N, (*math.*) an indefinite number; (*print.*) n or en, unit of measurement, size of average letter of type used.
na, *Scot.* form of **no.**
Naafi, *n.* organization providing canteens etc. for the services. (*N*avy, *A*rmy, and *A*ir *F*orce *I*nstitutes)
nab, *v.t.* (*sl.*) catch, arrest.
nabob, *n.* deputy ruler of the Mogul empire; wealthy man, esp. retired Anglo-Indian. (=*nawab*)
nacarat, *n.* bright orange-red colour or fabric. (F.)
nacelle, *n.* car of aircraft. (F.)
nacket, *n.* (*Scot.*) small cake, luncheon.
nacre, *n.* mother-of-pearl; shell-fish that yields it. (Sp. *nacar*)
nadir, *n.* point opposite zenith; lowest point. (Arab.=opposite)
naeve, naevus, *n.* birth-mark, mole. (L.)
nag, *n.* small riding-horse; (*colloq.*) horse.
nag, *v.t.* and *i.* find fault constantly, scold. (cf. Scand. *nagga,* gnaw)
nagana, *n.* (*S. Afr.*) disease caused by tsetse-fly. (Zulu *nakane*)
nagor, *n.* Senegal antelope.
naiad, *n.* water-nymph. (Gk. *naias*)
naïf, less usual form of **naïve.**
naik, *n.* Indian native corporal; lord or governor. (Urdu)
nail, *n.* horny plate at outer end of human finger or toe; animal's claw; metal spike for fastening or hanging; measure of length (2¼ in.).—*v.t.* fasten with nails; fix, secure. **hit n. on the head,** seize or speak to the point. **on the n.,** at once. (O.E. *nægel*)
nainsell, *n.* (*Scot.*) own self.
nainsook, *n.* kind of closely woven muslin, orig. Indian. (Hind.)
naïve, naive, *a.* unaffected; simple to excess. **naïveté, naïvety, naivety,** *n.* (F.)
naja, *n.* venomous Indian snake, cobra. (Hind. *nag,* snake)
naked, *a.* nude, uncovered; defenceless; without addition or ornament. (O.E. *nacod*)
naker, *n.* kettledrum. (Arab.)
namby-pamby, *a.* insipid, weakly sentimental.—also *n.* (*Ambrose Philips,* pastoral poet)
name, *n.* word by which a person or thing is called; family; reputation, fame.—*v.t.* call by name; designate. **nameless,** *a.* without a name; obscure; unspeakable. **namely,** *adv.* that is to say; (*Spens.*) especially. **namesake,** *n.* one with the same name as another. (O.E. *nama*)
nancy, *n.* effeminate youth. (name)
nancy pretty, *n.* kind of saxifrage, London pride. (corrupt. of *none-so-pretty*)
nandu, *n.* S. American ostrich.
nanism, *n.* dwarfishness. **nanoid,** *a.* (Gk. *nanos,* dwarf)
nankeen, *n.* buff-coloured cotton cloth; (*pl.*) trousers made of it. (*Nanking* in China)
nanny, *n.* she-goat; child's nurse. (name)
nap, *n.* short sleep, doze.—*v.i.* take nap. **catch napping,** take unawares, detect in error. (O.E. *knappian*)
nap, *n.* a card-game. **go n.,** undertake to win all tricks at nap; stake one's all (on). (*Napoleon*)
nap, *n.* woolly or downy surface o cloth or plants. (Du. *noppe*)
nape, *n.* back of the neck.
napery, *n.* household linen, esp. for table. (O.F. *naperie*)
naphtha, *n.* inflammable liquid distilled from coal, etc. **naphthaline,** *n.* disinfectant made from coal-tar. (Gk.)
napiform, *a.* turnip-shaped. (L. *napus,* turnip)
napkin, *n.* cloth for wiping fingers or lips or protecting clothes at table, serviette; sanitary towel. (F. *nappe* +dim.)
napoleon, *n.* French gold coin worth 20 francs; kind of top-boot. **Napoleonic,** *a.* of or like Emperor Napoleon. (*Napoleon I*)
napoo, *int.* and *a.* (*sl.*) finished, done. (F. *il n'y a plus,* there is no more)
nappy, *a.* (*Scot.*) heady, strong; drunk. —*n.* strong ale.
nappy, *a.* (*Scot.*) brittle.
napron, *n.* (*Spens.*) apron. (O.F. *naperon*)
narceine, *n.* sedative got from opium. (Gk. *narkē,* numbness)
narcissus, *n.* (*pl.* **narcissuses, narcissi**) kind of flowering plant, including daffodil. **narcissism,** *n.* (*psycho-anal.*) excessive love and admiration of oneself. **narcissist,** *n.* **narcissistic,** *a.* (Gk. *Narkissos,* youth who fell in love with his reflection).
narcotic, *a.* producing torpor, sleep, or insensibility.—*n.* narcotic drug. **narcosis,** *n.* narcotic effect, insensibility. **narcotize,** *v.t.* use narcotic upon. **narcotism,** *n.* morbid dependence on narcotics. (Gk. *narkē,* numbness)
nard, *n.* spikenard, an aromatic plant; ointment made from it. (Gk. *nardos*)
nardoo, *n.* Australian pillwort, the spore-case of which is eaten by the natives. (native)
narghile, *n.* Eastern tobacco-pipe in which the smoke is passed through water, hookah. (Pers.=coco-nut)
nark, *n.* (*sl.*) police spy or decoy. (Romany *nak,* nose)

narrate, *v.t.* tell as a story, give an account of. **narration, narrator**, *nn.* **narrative**, *a.* related to narration, story-telling.—*n.* continued account of occurrence, story. (L. *narrare*)
narre, *adv.* (*Spens.*) nearer.
narrow, *a.* of little breadth; of little extent, confined; with little margin; bigoted, illiberal; careful, exact.—*n.* (us. *pl.*) narrow part of pass, street, or channel.—*v.t.* and *i.* make or grow narrow, contract. **narrowly**, *adv.* closely, carefully. (O.E. *nearu*)
narthex, *n.* western portico in early Christian church. (Gk.=giant fennel)
narwhal, *n.* sea-unicorn, kind of dolphin with projecting tusk. (Da. *narhval*)
nary (*prov.*) for **ne'er a, never a.**
nas (*obs.*) for **ne has, ne was.**
nasal, *a.* of the nose; sounded through the nose.—*n.* nasal letter, such as *m* or *n.* (L. *nasus*)
nascent, *a.* beginning to exist or grow; springing up. (L. *nasci*, be born)
naseberry, *n.* sapodilla plum tree. (Sp. *néspera*, medlar)
nasturtium, *n.* kinds of plant incl. watercress; garden plant with bright flowers. (L. *nasus*, nose; *torquēre*, twist)
nasty, *a.* filthy, obscene; disagreeable, unpleasant; hard to deal with, ill-natured.
natal, *a.* of birth. **natality**, *n.* birth-rate. (L. *natalis*)
natation, *n.* swimming. **natant, natatorial, natatory**, *aa.* (L. *natare*, swim)
nātēs, *n.pl.* (*anat.*) buttocks. (L.)
natheless, nathless, *adv.* (*arch.*) nevertheless. (O.E.)
nathmore, *adv.* (*Spens.*) not or never the more. (O.E. *ná thy mara*)
nation, *n.* people of same descent, country, or government. (L. *natio*)
national, *a.* of a nation; common to whole nation, general.—*n.* member of nation, fellow countryman. **nationalism**, *n.* patriotic feeling; policy of national independence; policy of nationalizing industry. **nationalist**, *n.* supporter of nationalism. **nationality**, *n.* existence as nation; national quality; nation. **nationalize**, *v.t.* make national; naturalize; convert into national property.
native, *a.* by birth, inborn, inherent; simple, unadorned; of one's birth or country; born in a place, indigenous; (of metals, etc.) found in pure state.—*n.* one born in a place, original inhabitant, esp. black man or non-European; superior or British-reared oyster. **nativity**, *n.* birth; horoscope. **the Nativity**, birth of Christ, hence Christmas Day. (L. *nativus*)
natron, *n.* a native carbonate of soda. (Gk. *nitron*, nitre)
natter, *v.t.* and *i.* (*prov.*) find fault. **nattered, nattery**, *aa.* peevish.
natterjack, *n.* yellow-striped running toad.
natty, *a.* spruce, neat; deft.
natural, *a.* of, produced by, or according to, nature, normal; physically existing, not fictitious; unaffected, not artificial or acquired; lifelike; (*mus.*) not flat or sharp.—*n.* idiot; (*mus.*) natural note or sign indicating one. **n. child**, illegitimate. **n. history**, study of nature, esp. animal life. **n. law**, based on innate moral sense. **n. magic**, with no use of personal spirits. **n. order**, (*bot.*) classification by likeness. **n. philosophy**, physics. **n. religion**, without revelation. **n. science**, study of material things. **n. selection**, principle of the survival of the fittest. (L. *naturalis*)
naturalism, *n.* religion or philosophy based on nature alone, and excluding the spiritual; realism.
naturalist, *n.* student of natural history; taxidermist; believer in naturalism.
naturalize, *v.t.* confer (on alien) rights of a native subject; introduce foreign word, plant etc. rationalize.
naturally, *adv.* by nature, in a natural manner; of course.
nature, *n.* material world as a whole, or forces observable in it; essential qualities of thing, innate character of person; general characteristics of mankind; kind, class; vital force or functions. **debt of n.**, death. **state of n.**, rude or uncultivated condition; nakedness. (L. *natura*)
naught, (*arch.*) *n.* nothing, figure 0.—*a.* of no value, worthless. **set at n.**, despise. **naughty**, *a.* (used of or to children) bad, disobedient. (O.E. *náwiht*)
naumachy, *n.* sea-fight; show representing one. (Gk. *naus*, ship; *machē*, fight)
nausea, *n.* tendency to vomit; loathing. **nauseate**, *v.i.* feel nausea.—*v.t.* loathe; disgust. **nauseous**, *a.* causing nausea, disgusting. (Gk. *nausia*, sea-sickness)
nautch, *n.* performance by Indian dancers known as **n.-girls.** (Hind. *nach*)
nautical, *a.* of ships or sailors, marine. **n. mile**, one-sixtieth of a mean degree of longitude, 6,080 ft. (Gk. *nautikos*)
nautilus, *n.* (*pl.* **nautiluses, nautili**) shell-fish with webbed arms once supposed to sail upon the sea. (Gk. *nautilos*, sailor)
naval, *a.* of the navy; of ships, marine. (L. *navis*, ship)
navarch, *n.* admiral. **navarchy**, *n.* (Gk. *nauarchos*)
nave, *n.* main part of church, distinct from chancel and aisles. (L. *navis*, ship)
nave, *n.* central block of wheel, hub. (O.E. *nafu*)
navel, *n.* depression in middle of belly;

any central point. **n.-string,** *n.* umbilical cord. (O.E. *nafela*)

navicert, *n.* certificate given in neutral port by British consul to show that ship's cargo has been examined and contains no contraband. (*naviga*tion *cert*ificate)

navicular, *a.* boat-shaped. **n. bone,** a bone in the foot or hand. **n. disease,** disease of this bone. (L. *navicula,* little ship)

navigable, *a.* that may be sailed upon; (of ship) seaworthy; (of balloon) steerable.

navigate, *v.t.* steer, direct course of; sail upon or through.—*v.i.* sail, voyage. **navigator,** *n.* (L. *navis,* ship; *agere,* drive)

navigation, *n.* act, art, or science of navigating; method of calculating ship's position by nautical astronomy.

navvy, *n.* labourer on roads, railways, etc. **steam n.,** mechanical excavator. (short for *navigator,* because orig. worker on canals)

navy, *n.* sea defence force of a nation; (*poet.*) fleet. **n. blue,** dark blue. **n. cut,** cake tobacco finely sliced. (L. *navis,* ship)

nawab, *n.* Indian native governor, nabob. (Arab. *nā'ib,* deputy)

nay, *adv.* no (*arch.*); or rather, and even.—*n.* denial, refusal. (O.N. *ne,* not; *ei,* ever)

nayword, *n.* (*Shake.*) byword; watchword.

Nazarene, *n.* native of Nazareth; Christian (Jewish use); member of early Christian sect.

Nazarite, *n.* native of Nazareth.

Nazarite, *n.* Hebrew vowed to abstinence. (Heb. *nazar,* separate oneself)

naze, *n.* headland. (=*ness*)

Nazi, *n.* and *a.* (member) of German National Socialist party. **Nazism, Naziism,** *nn.* (G.)

ne, *adv.* (*arch.*) not; *conj.* (*arch.*) nor. (O.E.)

neaf, *n.* (*Shake.*) fist.

neal, *v.t.* temper by heat; anneal.

Neanderthal, *a.* **N. man,** people inhabiting Europe in the Stone Age. (name of valley near Düsseldorf where Neanderthal skull was found)

neap, *a.* and *n.* **n. (tide),** tide at beginning of moon's second or fourth quarter, when high water is at lowest. —*v.i.* (of tides) tend towards neap; (of tide) reach highest point of neap. **neaped,** *a.* (of ship) left aground by neap. (O.E. *nep*)

Neapolitan, *a.* of Naples. **N. ice,** ice with layers of different flavour and colour. (Gk. *Neapolis,* Naples)

near, *a.* close, not distant; closely related, intimate; (of road) direct; (of side of horse, etc.) left; stingy.—*adv.* at a little distance, almost.—*prep.* close to.—*v.t.* and *i.* draw near, approach. **n.-sighted,** *a.* short-sighted. (O.E. *néar,* nigher)

nearby, *a.* neighbouring.

nearly, *adv.* almost, closely.

neat, *n.* (*pl.* same) ox, cow; cattle. **n.-herd,** *n.* cowherd. (O.E. *néat*)

neat, *a.* tidy, trim, well made; undiluted, pure; deft, skilful. (L. *nitidus,* shining)

neath, *prep.* (*poet.*) beneath.

neb, *n.* (*Scot.*) beak, nose, point. (O.E. *nebb*)

nebris, *n.* fawn-skin worn by votaries of Bacchus. (Gk.)

nebula, *n.* (*pl.* **nebulae**) gaseous mass or star-cluster appearing as luminous patch in sky. **nebular,** *a.* **nebular theory,** theory that stars and planets were formed from nebulae. (L.= cloud)

nebulium, *n.* element known only as producing green line in spectrum of gaseous nebulae.

nebulous, *a.* of or like nebula; indistinct, vague.

necessary, *a.* unavoidable; indispensable.—*n.* (chiefly *pl.*) essential need. **necessarian,** *n.* determinist. (L. *necesse*)

necessity, *n.* indispensability; necessary thing; compulsion; need; poverty. **necessitarian,** *n.* necessarian. **necessitate,** *v.t.* make necessary, compel. **necessitous,** *a.* poor, destitute. **physical, moral,** etc. **n.,** constraint regarded as universal law.

neck, *n.* part of body connecting head and trunk; narrow part of land, bottle, etc.—*v.i.* (*Amer. sl.*) cuddle. **neckcloth, neckerchief,** *nn.* cloth worn round the neck. **necklace,** *n.* string of precious stones or beads worn on neck. **necklet,** *n.* neck ornament or fur. **necktie,** *n.* tie worn round neck. **n. and crop,** completely. **n. and n.,** side by side. **n. or nothing,** risking all. (O.E. *hnecca*)

necr(o)-, from Gk. *nekros,* corpse, used in **necrobiosis,** *n.* decay of living tissue; **necrology,** *n.* death-roll; **necromancy,** *n.* art of predicting by communicating with the dead, magic; **necromancer,** *n.* wizard; **necrophagous,** *a.* feeding on carrion; **necropolis,** *n.* cemetery; **necropsy, necroscopy,** *nn.* post-mortem; **necrosis,** *n.* mortification of bone, gangrene.

nectar, *n.* drink of the gods; delicious drink; sweet fluid secreted by plants. **nectarean, nectared, nectareous, nectarous,** *aa.* **nectarine,** *n.* smooth-skinned peach. **nectary,** *n.* plant's nectar-secreting organ. (Gk. *nektar*)

neddy, *n.* (*colloq.*) donkey. (name)

née, *a.* born (used to indicate married woman's maiden name, e.g. 'Mrs. Browning, *née* Barrett'). (F.)

need, *n.* want, necessity; state of want, destitution; thing wanted, requirement.—*v.t.* have a necessity for, require.—*v.i* be under necessity or obligation to (do etc.); (*arch.*) be necessary. **needful,** *a.* necessary, requisite. **the needful** (*sl.*), money required. **needless,** *a.* not needed, unnecessary. **needs,** *adv.* (in phr. **needs must** or **must needs**) of necessity. **needy,** *a.* in need, very poor. (O.E. *nied, néod*)

needle, *n.* small pointed tool, pierced with eye for thread, used in sewing; similar things, such as bar of compass, indicator on dial, etcher's tool; obelisk; pinnacle of rock; slender crystal; fir or pine leaf. **n.-bath,** *n.* shower-bath with fine spray. **n.-fish,** *n.* garfish. **needleful,** *n.* sewing-length of thread. **n.-gun,** *n.* gun with cartridge exploded by needle. **needlewoman,** *n.* user of needle, sempstress. **needlework,** *n.* sewing, embroidery. (O.E. *nǽdl*)

neem, *n.* margosa, an Indian tree.

neep, *n.* (*Scot.*) turnip. (O.E. *næp*)

ne'er, *adv.* (*poet.*) never. **n.-do-well,** *a.* and *n.* good-for-nothing. (contr.)

neeze, *v.i.* (*arch.*) sneeze.

nef, *n.* case for table requisites in form of a ship. (*nave*)

nefarious, *a.* wicked, abominable. (L. *nefas,* wrong)

negate, *v.t.* nullify, be negation of. (L. *negare,* deny)

negation, *n.* negative statement, denial; contradiction; negative or unreal thing. **negationist,** *n.* destructive critic.

negative, *a.* indicating denial or refusal, opposite to affirmative; lacking positive qualities, opposite to positive; (of electricity) of kind produced by friction on resin, as opposed to positive, produced on glass; (*algebra*) minus; (*phot.*) showing light for dark and vice versa.—*n.* negative statement or quality; (*algebra*) minus quantity; (*phot.*) plate etc. with negative image. **in the n.,** no.—*v.t.* disprove, contradict; veto. (*negate*)

neglect, *v.t.* leave uncared for; disregard, slight; leave undone.—*n.* careless treatment; slight; omission. **neglectful,** *a.* (L. *neg-,* not; *legere,* pick up)

négligé, *n.* free and easy attire. negligee, *n.* loose gown. (F.)

negligence, *n.* want of proper care; act of carelessness; disregard of precision. **negligent,** *a.* careless, heedless. **negligible,** *a.* that need not be regarded, very unimportant. (*neglect*)

negotiate, *v.i.* bargain, confer with view to mutual arrangement.—*v.t.* arrange, bring about by such conference; obtain or give money value for (bill); overcome (obstacle etc.). **negotiable,** *a.* **negotiation,** *n.* act of negotiating. **negotiant, negotiator, negotiatress, negotiatrix,** *nn.* one who negotiates. (L. *negotium,* business)

negrillo, *n.* dwarf negro found in Africa, pygmy. **negrito,** *n.* dwarf negro of Philippines and Polynesia. (Sp. dim. of *negro*)

negro, *n.* and *a.* (member) of black, woolly-haired, thick-lipped African race, (*fem.* **negress**). **negrohead,** *n.* plug tobacco that has been soaked in molasses. **negroid,** *a.* of partly negro type, like a negro. **negrophile,** *n.* supporter of the cause of negroes. **negrophobia,** *n.* fear of negroes. (L. *niger,* black)

Negus, *n.* ruler of Abyssinia. (native)

negus, *n.* hot sweetened wine and water. (Colonel *Negus,* who first made it)

neigh, *n.* cry of horse.—*v.i.* utter this cry. (O.E. *hnægan*)

neighbour, *n.* dweller next door or close by; person or thing near or next to another.—*v.t.* and *i.* be near, adjoin. **neighbourhood,** *n.* vicinity, people of district. **neighbourly,** *a.* becoming a neighbour, friendly. (O.E. *néahgebúr*)

neist, *dial.* form of **next.**

neither, *adv.* not on the one hand.—*conj.* nor, nor yet.—*a.* and *pron.* not one nor the other. (O.E. *nahwæther*)

neive, same as **nieve.**

nek, *n.* (*S. Afr.*) depression or pass in mountain range. (Du.=neck)

nekton, *n.* collective term for forms of organic life found at various depths in sea and lakes. (Gk. *nēchein,* swim)

nelly *n.,* largest kind of petrel.

nema-, nemato-, from Gk. *nēma,* thread, fibre, used in **nemalite,** *n.* fibrous hydrate of magnesia; **nematocerous,** *a.* having long thready antennae; **nematocyst,** *n.* cell of jellyfish with fibrous sting; **nematode, nematoid,** *a.* thread-like.—*n.* threadworm.

Nemesis, *n.* goddess of retribution; retributive justice. (Gk.)

nemine contradicente or *dissentiente* (*abbr. nem. con.* or *diss.*) unanimously. (L.=no one contradicting or dissenting)

nemoral, *a.* of a wood or grove. **nemorose,** *a.* growing in woodland. **nemorous,** *a.* woody. (L. *nemus,* grove)

nempt, *a.* (*Spens.*) named.

nenuphar, *n.* water-lily. (Sanskr. *nil,* blue; *utpala,* lotus)

neo-, from Gk *neos,* new, used in **neo-Catholic,** *a.* of Anglican party which imitates Roman Catholic doctrine and ritual; **neo-Hellenism,** *n.* revival of Greek ideals; **Neolithic,** *a.* of the later Stone Age; **neologism, neology,** *nn.* introduction of new words or new doctrines, new-coined word, hence **neologian, neologist,** *nn.,* **neologize,** *v.t.*; **neo-Malthusianism,** *n.* use of contraceptives; **neo-paganism,** *n.* revival of pagan ideas; **neophyte,** *n.* new convert, novice; **neo-Platonism,** *n.* mixture of Platonic teaching with oriental mysticism in third century; **neoteric,** *a.* newfangled, modern; **neotropical,** *a.* of tropical or South America.

neodymium, *n.* a metallic element. *neo-+didymium*)

neon, *n.* an atmospheric gas. (Gk. *neos*, new)

neophron, *n.* white Egyptian vulture. (man's name)

nepenthe, *n.* drug that brings forgetfulness of grief. **nepenthes,** *n.* nepenthe; pitcher-plant. (Gk. *nē-*, not; *penthos*, grief)

nephew, *n.* brother's or sister's son. (L. *nepos*)

nephology, *n.* study of the clouds. (Gk. *nephos*, cloud; *legein*, speak)

nephr(o)-, from Gk. *nephros*, kidney, used in **nephralgia,** *n.* pain or disease of kidneys; **nephritic,** *a.* of kidneys; of or for kidney disease; **nephritis,** *n.* inflammation of the kidneys; **nephroid,** *a.* kidney-shaped; **nephrology,** *n.* study of the kidneys; **nephropathy,** *n.* diseases of the kidneys; **nephroptosis,** *n.* floating kidney; **nephrotomy,** *n.* incision into the kidney.

ne plus ultra, farthest attainable point; acme. (L.=not more beyond)

nepotism, *n.* undue favour to relatives in bestowing offices. (L. *nepos*, nephew)

Neptune, *n.* god of the sea; outer planet. **Neptunian,** *a.* caused by water action. (L. *Neptunus*)

nereid, *n.* sea-nymph; (*zool.*) sea-worm. (Gk. *Nērēis*)

nero antico, *n.* deep-black marble found in Roman ruins. (It.)

neroli, *n.* essential oil of orange-flowers. (Princess *Neroli*)

Neronian, *a.* of or like the cruel and sensual Emperor Nero.

nerts, *int.* (*Amer.*) of contempt.

nerve, *n.* sinew; vigour, energy; courage, assurance; (*colloq.*) impudence; (*anat.*) one of the fibres conveying sensation from body to brain; (*bot.*) rib of leaf; (*pl.*) sensitiveness, irritability.—*v.t.* give strength or courage to. **nervate,** *a.* (*bot.*) ribbed. **nerveless,** *a.* wanting in vigour. **nervine,** *a.* acting on nerves.—*n.* medicine for nerves. (L. *nervus*)

nervous, *a.* sinewy, muscular; (of style) terse, vigorous; having delicate nerves, highly strung, excitable, timid. **n. system,** brain, spinal cord, and nerves.

nervure, *n.* vein of leaf; tube of insect's wing-frame.

nervy, *a.* fidgety, nervous; (*poet.*) sinewy; (*sl.*) impudent; trying to the nerves.

nescience, *n.* ignorance. **nescient,** *a.* ignorant, agnostic. (L. *ne-*, not; *scire*, know)

nesh, *a.* soft, tender. (O.E. *hnesce*)

nesiote, *a.* insular. (Gk. *nēsos*, island)

ness, *n.* headland, cape. (O.E. *næs*)

-ness, *n.suf.* state, quality, of being, as in oddness, half-wittedness.

nest, *n.* bird's home; breeding-place, lair; snug residence, haunt; swarm, brood; set of boxes or cases inserted each inside next larger.—*v.i.* make or have nest.—*v.t.* place in nest. **n.-egg,** *n.* real or sham egg left in nest to prevent the hen from forsaking it; sum laid by. (O.E.)

nestitherapy, *n.* medical treatment by fasting, hunger cure. (Gk. *nēstis*, fasting)

nestle, *v.i.* and *t.* lie snugly, half hidden, or embedded; settle comfortably. **nestling,** *n.* and *a.* (bird) too young to leave nest.

Nestor, *n.* wise old man. (Homeric hero)

net, *n.* instrument of twine, wire etc., knotted into meshes; snare.—*v.t.* and *i.* take or cover with net; make or make with netting. **netting,** *n.* fabric of net form. **network,** *n.* netting; complicated system. **netball,** *n.* girls' game in which a ball has to be thrown through an elevated horizontal ring. (O.E.)

net, nett, *a.* clear of deductions or charges.—*v.t.* gain, yield, as clear profit. (F. *net*, clear)

nether, *a.* lower. **nethermost,** *a.* lowest. (O.E. *neothera*)

netsuke, *n.* Japanese buttonlike ornament. (Jap.)

nettle, *n.* plant covered with stinging hairs.—*v.t.* irritate, provoke. **n.-rash,** *n.* skin eruption like nettle-stings. (O.E. *netele*)

neur(o)-, from Gk. *neuron*, nerve, used in **neural,** *a.* of the nerves; **neuralgia,** *n.* pain of the nerves; **neurasthenia,** *n.* weakness of the nerves; **neuration,** *n.* arrangement of the nervures of insect's wing; **neurectomy,** *n.* excision of nerve; **neurine,** *n.* nerve-tissue; **neuritis,** *n.* inflammation of nerves; **neurology,** *n.* science of the nerves; **neuroma,** *n.* tumour in nerve-tissue; **neurone, neuron,** *n.* nerve-cell; **neuropath,** *n.* person affected by nervous disease, hence **neuropathic,** *a.*, **neuropathology, neuropathy,** *nn.*; **neuropathist,** *n.* specialist in neuropathy; **neuropterous,** *a.* with four wings marked with a network of nerves.

neurosis, *n.* functional disease due to nervous disorder.

neurotic, *a.* suffering from nervous disorder; highly strung; of or acting upon the nerves.—*n.* neurotic person or drug.

neuter, *a.* neutral; (*gram.*) neither masculine nor feminine, (of verb) intransitive; (*bot.* and *zool.*) asexual. —*n.* neuter person, word, plant, or animal. (L.=neither)

neutral, *a.* taking neither side in war or dispute, impartial; indeterminate; (*chem.*) neither acid nor alkaline; (*bot.*) asexual.—*n.* neutral state or person. **neutrality,** *n.* **neutralize,** *v.t.* exclude (place) from hostilities; counterbalance, render ineffective. (L. *neutralis*)

neutrodyne, *n.* device for neutralizing

capacity between plate and grid in a valve of a radio set. (L. *neuter*, neither. Gk. *dunamis*, power)
neutron, *n.* electrically neutral particle. (*neuter*)
névé, *n.* the granular snow that feeds a glacier. (F.)
never, *adv.* at no time, not ever; not at all; (*colloq.*) surely not. **N. N. (Land),** north Queensland. **nevermore,** *adv.* never again. **nevertheless,** *adv.* all the same, notwithstanding. (O.E. *næfre*)
new, *a.* recently made or experienced; seen, known, or used for the first time, unfamiliar; fresh, additional; different, changed; modern; unaccustomed.—*adv.* newly (us. in compound, as **n.-laid,** *a.* newly laid, **n.-born,** *a.* born anew). **newcomer,** *n.* one who has recently arrived. **N. Deal,** economic and social measures introduced in U.S. by President Roosevelt in 1933 to combat great economic crisis which began in 1929. **N. England,** six NE. states of the U.S.A. **n. learning,** renaissance. **n. moon,** moon when first visible as crescent. **N. World,** America. **N. Year's Day,** first day of the new year. (O.E. *niwe*)
newel, *n.* central pillar of spiral staircase; end post of banisters. (L. *nux*, nut)
newel, *n.* (*Spens.*) new thing, novelty.
newfangled, *a.* newly devised, objectionably novel; fond of new things. (O.E. *fangen*, seize)
Newfoundland, *n.* large kind of water-spaniel. (place of origin)
Newgate, *n.* London prison. **N. Calendar,** list of Newgate prisoners and their crimes. **N. fringe** or **frill,** beard grown under chin and jaw, face remaining shaven.
Newmarket, *n.* close-fitting overcoat; card-game. (town)
news, *n.* fresh information of anything that has just happened, tidings. **newsy,** *a.* (*colloq.*) full of news. **newsagent,** *n.* newspaper dealer. **newsboy, newsman,** *nn.* one who sells newspapers in the street. **newsmonger,** *n.* gossip. **newspaper,** *n.* printed periodical containing news. **n.-room,** *n.* room for reading newspapers. **newsvendor,** *n.* seller of newspapers.
newt, *n.* water-lizard, eft. (O.E. *efeta*, with *n* transferred from indef. article)
next, *a., adv.,* and *prep.,* nearest, nearest to; immediately after or before. (superl. of *nigh*)
nexus, *n.* connecting principle or link. (L. *nectere*, bind)
nib, *n.* split pen-point; bird's bill; (*pl.*) crushed cocoa-beans.—*v.t.* cut, insert, pen-nib. (=*neb*)
nibble, *v.t.* and *i.* take small bites at, bite cautiously; dally with.—*n.* act of nibbling; small amount.
niblick, *n.* golf-club with heavy lofted head.
nibs, *n.* (*sl.*). **his n.,** burlesque title.
nice, *a.* particular, fastidious; delicately sensitive; requiring care or tact; subtle, exact; pleasing, agreeable, kind. **n. and,** satisfactorily. **n.-looking,** *a.* pretty, handsome. (L. *nescius*, ignorant)
nicety, *n.* delicacy, punctiliousness; precision; subtlety; unimportant detail. **to a n.,** exactly.
niche, *n.* shallow recess for statue, etc.; person's appropriate place.—*v.t.* place in niche. (It. *nicchia*)
nichevo, *int.* it does not matter. (Russ.)
nick, *n.* notch, score; opportune moment. *v.t.* make nick in, indent; hit upon; catch, nab. *v.i.* cut in (at race etc.); unite.
Nick, *n.* (esp. **Old N.**) the devil.
nickel, *n.* silvery-white metal much used in alloys and plating; (*Amer.*) five-cent piece of nickel.—*v.t.* coat with nickel. **n.-silver,** *n.* alloy like German silver. (abbr. of G. *kupfernickel*)
nicker, *n.* and *v.i.* neigh, snigger.
nick-nack, same as knick-knack.
nickname, *n.* name used familiarly in place of or in addition to regular name.—*v.t.* call by nickname. (*ekename*, with *n* transferred from indef. article)
nicotine, *n.* poisonous oily liquid extracted from tobacco. **nicotian,** *a.* of tobacco.—*n.* smoker. **nicotiana,** *n.pl.* literature of tobacco. (Jean *Nicot*, who introduced tobacco to France in 1560)
nictate, nictitate, *v.i.* wink. (L. *nictare, nictitare*)
niddering, *a.* and *n.* coward (misreading of obs. *nithing*, from O.N. *nith*, satire)
niddle-noddle, *a.* unsteady; vacillating. *v.t.* and *i.* keep nodding; totter. (*nod*)
nide, nid, *n.* brood of pheasants. (*nidus*)
nidge, *v.t.* dress stones with pointed hammer.
nidificate, nidify, *vv.i.* build nest. (L. *nidificare*)
nid-nod, *v.t.* and *i.* keep nodding.
nidor, *n.* odour of cooked food. **nidorous,** *a.* (L.)
nidus, *n.* (*pl.* **nidi, niduses**) developing-place of spores, seeds, germs, insects' eggs etc.; accumulation of eggs, tubercles etc. (L.=nest)
niece, *n.* daughter of brother or sister. (L. *neptis*)
niello, *n.* (*pl.* **nielli, niellos**) ornamental engraving in black on silver or gold; black alloy used in this. (It.)
niest, *a.* (*Scot.*) next.
nieve, *n.* (*Scot.*) fist. **nieve-fu',** *n.* handful. **nievie-nievie-nick-nack,** *n.* children's guessing game. (*neaf*)
niffer, *v.t.* (*Scot.*) barter.—*n.* an exchange.

Niflheim, *n.* (*Scand. myth.*) region of primeval cold and mist. (O.N.= cloud-home)
nifty, *a.* (*sl.*) neat, stylish.
nigella, *n.* kinds of plant incl. love-in-a-mist. (L. *niger*, black+dim.)
niggard, *n.* stingy person, miser.—also *a.* **niggardly,** *a.* sparing, giving grudgingly.—*adv.* sparingly.
nigger, *n.* (*colloq.*) negro, black man; black turnip caterpillar. **n. in the woodpile,** (*Amer. sl.*) something that spoils a good thing. (*negro*)
niggle, *v.i.* fiddle, waste time on petty details. **niggling,** *a.* finicking; (of writing) cramped.
nigh, *adv.* and *prep.* (*arch., poet.,* or *dial.*) near. (O.E. *néah*)
night, *n.* time from sunset to sunrise; darkness, the dark. **n.-bird,** *n.* owl etc.; prowler by night. **nightcap,** *n.* cap worn in bed; alcoholic drink taken last thing at night. **n.-club,** *n.* club open through the night. **night-dress, nightgown,** (*colloq.*) **nighty,** *nn.,* woman's night attire. **n.-flower,** *n.* one that opens at night. **n.-glass,** *n.* short telescope for night use. **n.-light,** *n.* short thick candle giving dim light through night. **n.-line,** *n.* baited line left to catch fish by night. **n.-long,** *a.* lasting through the night. **n.-piece,** *n.* painting of night scene. **nightshirt,** *n.* man's sleeping suit. **n.-stool,** *n.* commode for use at night. **n.-time,** *n.* period of night. **n.-watch,** *n.* watch by night or person keeping it; (*pl.*) night-time. (O.E. *niht*)
nightchurr, see **nightjar.**
nightfall, *n.* beginning of night.
nightingale, *n.* small brown bird that sings sweetly at night as well as by day. (O.E. *galan,* sing)
nightjar, nightchurr, *n.* goatsucker. (imit. of its cry)
nightly, *a.* happening or done by night or every night.—*adv.* every night.
nightmare, *n.* terrifying or oppressive dream, incubus. **nightmarish,** *a.* (*night*+O.E. *mara,* nightmare)
nightshade, *n.* plant. **black n.,** with white flowers and black poisonous berries. **woody n.,** with purple flowers and bright red berries. **deadly n.,** belladonna.
nigrescent, *a.* blackish, growing black. **nigritude,** *n.* blackness. (L. *niger,* black)
nihil ad rem, irrelevant. (L.)
nihilism, *n.* doctrine of Russian revolutionaries who rejected all constituted authority; (*philos.*) belief that nothing has real existence, scepticism. **nihilist,** *n.* **nihility,** *n.* non-existence; trifle. (L. *nihil,* nothing)
nil, *n.* nothing, no amount. *n. admirari,* nonchalance. (L.)
nilgai, nilgau, same as **nylghau.**
nill, *v.i.* and *t.* (*Spens.*) refuse, be unwilling. (O.E. *ne,* not; *willan,* will)
Nilometer, *n.* gauge showing height to which Nile rises; river-gauge. **Nilotic,** *a.* of the Nile.
nimble, *a.* quick, agile, dexterous. (O.E. *niman,* take)
nimbus, *n.* (*pl.* **nimbi**), bright cloud or halo, aureole; rain-cloud. (L.= cloud)
nimiety, *n.* excess. (L. *nimis,* too much)
niminy-piminy, *a.* mincing, prim. (imit.)
Nimrod, *n.* great hunter. (Biblical name)
nincompoop, *n.* simpleton, ninny.
nine, *a.* and *n.* one more than eight. **The N.,** the muses. **n. days' wonder,** novelty viewed with keen but brief interest. **up to the nn.,** elaborately. **ninefold,** *a.* nine times repeated. **ninepins,** *n.pl.* skittles. **ninth,** *a.* next after eighth.—*n.* one of nine equal parts. **ninthly,** *adv.* in the ninth place. (O.E. *nigon*)
nineteen, *a.* and *n.* nine and ten. **n. to the dozen,** volubly. **nineteenth,** *a.* and *n.* **nineteenth hole,** (*colloq.*) golf clubhouse bar.
ninety, *a.* and *n.* nine times ten. **ninetieth,** *a.* and *n.*
ninny, *n.* person of weak character or mind. so **ninny-hammer,** *n.*
ninon, *n.* light silk material.
Niobe, *n.* inconsolable bereaved woman. (Gk. legendary heroine who was turned to stone while weeping for her slain children)
niobium, *n.* rare steel-grey metallic element. (*Niobe*)
nip, *v.t.* pinch, pinch off; check growth of, destroy.—*v.i.* (*sl.*) move nimbly; take nip of spirits.—*n.* pinch, sharp squeeze; cold air, injury by frost; small quantity, sip. **nipper,** *n.* small boy; crab's claw; horse's incisor tooth; (*pl.*) small pincers; pince-nez. **nippy,** *a.* cold; (*sl.*) nimble. (cf. Du. *nijpen*)
nipa, *n.* E. Indian palm. (Malay *nipah*)
nipple, *n.* point of female breast, teat; projection resembling it, on mountain, lock of gun etc. **nipplewort,** *n.* yellow-flowered weed.
nipter, *n.* ecclesiastical ceremony of washing the feet. (Gk. *niptein,* wash)
nirles, nirls, *n.* (*Scot.*) kind of rash.
Nirvana, *n.* highest aspiration of the Buddhist faith, when the individual is merged in the supreme spirit. (Sanskr.=blown out)
nis, (*Spens.*) is not. (contr. of *ne is*)
nisi, *adv.* **decree (order, rule** etc.) **n.,** decree valid unless cause is shown to the contrary by a fixed date, at which it is 'made absolute.' **n. prius,** trial of civil causes by judges of assize. (L.=unless)
nit, *n.* egg of louse or other parasite; (*Amer.*) insignificant person. (O.E. *hnitu*)
nit, *adv.* (*Amer.*) not at all, no.

nitchevo, same as *nichevo*.
nitid, *a.* shining, gay. (L. *nitēre*, shine)
niton, *n.* gaseous radioactive element, radon. (L. *nitēre*, shine)
nitre, *n.* potassium nitrate, saltpetre. **nitrate,** *n.* a salt of nitric acid. **nitric, nitrous,** *aa.* **nitric acid,** corrosive, caustic liquid, aqua-fortis. **nitrous acid,** containing less oxygen than nitric. **nitrous oxide,** laughing gas. **nitrite,** *n.* a salt of nitrous acid. **nitrify,** *v.t.* and *i.* make or become nitrous. **nitro-,** made with nitric acid, e.g. **nitro-glycerine,** *n.* violent explosive made by adding glycerine to a mixture of nitric and sulphuric acids. (Gk. *nitron*)
nitrogen, *n.* gas forming nearly four-fifths of common air, so called from being an essential constituent of nitre.
nitter, *n.* bot-fly, horse-bot.
nitwit, *n.* (*Amer. sl.*) blockhead.
nival, niveous, *aa.* snowy. (L. *nix*, snow)
nix, *int.* (*sl.*) look out! cave!
nix, *n.* (*fem.* nixie), water-elf. (G.)
nix, *n.* (*sl.*) nothing. (G. *nichts*)
Nizam, *n.* ruler of Hyderabad; Turkish army, soldier. (Arab. *nidam*, order)
no, *adv.* word of refusal or denial; not at all; by no amount; not.—*a.* not any, none; by no means. —*n.* denial; negative vote or voter. **no man's land,** unclaimed waste region; debatable ground between hostile trenches. **no one,** nobody. **no-ball,** *n.* unfairly delivered ball at cricket. (O.E. *nā*)
Noachian, Noachic, *a.* of Noah or his time.
nob, *n.* (*sl.*) head; (at cribbage) knave of suit of turn-up card.
nob, *n.* (*sl.*) member of upper classes. **nobby,** *a.* smart, stylish.
nobble, *v.t.* (*sl.*) tamper successfully with (racehorse, etc.); secure dishonestly; catch (criminal).
nobiliary, *a.* of nobility.
nobility, *n.* noble rank, birth, character, or mind. **the n.,** the peerage.
noble, *a.* illustrious, exalted in rank or birth; of lofty character, magnanimous; magnificent, imposing; excellent.—*n.* man of high rank, peer; obsolete coin=6*s.* 8*d.* **nobleman,** *n.* peer. **noblesse,** *n.* (*Spens.*) nobility; class of nobles. **noblesse oblige,** rank has its obligations. (L. *noscere*, know)
nobody, *n.* no one; person of no importance.
nock, *n.* notch in bow or arrow for string; forward upper corner of some sails.—*v.t.* fit (arrow) to string.
noct(i)-, from L. *nox*, night, used in **noctambulant,** *a.* night-walking; **noctiflorous,** *a.* night-flowering; **noctiluca,** *n.* phosphorescent animalcule; **noctivagant, noctivagous,** *aa.* night-wandering; **noctograph,** *n.* writing-frame for the blind.
noctule, *n.* largest British kind of bat. (L. *nox*, night)
nocturnal, *a.* of night; active by night.
nocturne, *n.* dreamy musical piece, serenade; picture of night-scene.
nocuous, *a.* hurtful. (L. *nocēre*, hurt)
nod, *v.i.* incline head quickly; be drowsy, make sleepy mistake; incline; (of plumes) dance.—*v.t.* indicate by nod.—*n.* nodding of head; sign of assent or command.
noddle, *n.* back of head; head.—*v.t.* nod or wag (head).
noddy, *n.* simpleton, noodle; tropical sea-bird; four-wheeled carriage with door at back.
node, *n.* knob, knot, point of intersection; (*med.*) hard tumour, esp. on gouty or rheumatic joint; (*bot.*) joint of a stem; (*astron.*) two points at which the orbit of a planet intersects the ecliptic; (*math.*) point at which a curve crosses itself; point of rest in vibrating body. **nodal,** *a.* **nodical,** *a.* (*astron.*). **nodose,** *a.* knotty, knobbed. **nodule,** *n.* small lump or tumour. **nodus,** *n.* (*pl.* **nodi**) knotty point, complication in plot of story etc. (L. *nodus*, knot)
Noel, *n.* Christmas. (F.)
noetic, *a.* intellectual, abstract.—*n.* science of the intellect.—also **noemics,** *n.pl.* (Gk. *noein*, perceive)
nog, *n.* wooden peg or block; stump. *v.t.* secure with nogs. **nogging,** *n.* brickwork etc. in timber frame.
nog, *n.* East Anglian strong beer.
noggin, *n.* small mug; measure, us. quarter-pint.
nohow, *adv.* in no way, by no means; (*colloq.*) out of sorts.
noils, *n. pl.* short wool-combings.
noise, *n.* sound of any kind; outcry, din; frequent talk.—*v.t.* spread by rumour.—*v.i.* make noise. **big n.,** person of importance, local celebrity. **noiseless,** *a.* silent. **noisy,** *a.* making much noise; clamorous, turbulent. (F.)
noisette, *n.* rose, cross between China and musk. (grower's name)
noisette, *n.* piece of meat cooked with special sauce (F.)
noisome, *a.* harmful, noxious ill-smelling, offensive. (M.E. *noy*, annoy)
nolens volens, willing or unwilling, willy-nilly. (L.)
noli me tangere, *n.* warning not to meddle; erosive ulcer, lupus; wild cucumber; picture of Christ as He appeared to Mary Magdalen at sepulchre. (L.=do not touch me)
noll, *n.* head. (O.E. *hnoll*)
nolle prosequi, English legal term indicating plaintiff's abandonment of his suit. (L.=to refuse to pursue)
nolo episcopari, unwillingness to accept office. (L.=I am unwilling to be a bishop)

nomad, *n.* member of tribe roaming in search of pasture.—*a.* of nomads; leading a wandering life. **nomadic,** *a.* (Gk. *nemein,* pasture)

nomarch, *n.* governor of a **nome,** or administrative district in Greece. (Gk. *nomos,* district, *archē,* rule)

nom de guerre, pseudonym, assumed name. (F.=war-name)

nom de plume, writer's pseudonym, pen-name. (English use of F. words)

nomenclator, *n.* ancient Roman slave who named persons met; giver of names. **nomenclature,** *n.* system of names, terminology; catalogue. (L. *nomen,* name; *calare,* call)

nomic, *a.* customary. (Gk. *nomos,* custom)

nominal, *a.* of names; existing only in name, not real. **nominalism,** *n.* belief that abstract concepts are mere names (opp. to realism). (L. *nomen,* name)

nominate, *v.t.* name, appoint; propose as candidate. **nomination,** *n.* act or right of nominating; state of being nominated. **nominative,** *a.* (*gram.*) of the subject.—*n.* nominative case or word in it. **nominee,** *n.* one who is nominated. (L. *nominare*)

nom(o)-, from Gk. *nomos,* law, used in **nomocracy,** *n.* government according to a code of laws; **nomogeny,** *n.* origin of life according to natural law, not miracle; **nomography,** *n.* art of drawing up laws; **nomology,** *n.* science of the laws of the mind; **nomothetic,** *a.* legislative, founded on a system of laws.

non, adv. not. *n. compos* (*mentis*), mad, not responsible (lit. not in possession of his mind). *n. est inventus, n. est, n. inventus,* missing (lit. he has not been found). *n. liquet,* verdict deferring decision (lit. it is not clear). *n. nobis,* giving praise to God, not ourselves, song of rejoicing (lit. not to us, first words of Psalm cxv). *n. placet,* negative vote (lit. it does not please). *n. plus ultra,* same as *ne plus ultra.* *n. possumus,* statement of inability, refusal to act (lit. we cannot). *n. sequitur,* illogical inference (lit. it does not follow). (L.)

non-, *pref.* reversing the meaning of a word, as in **non-attendance.**

non-access, *n.* (*law*) absence of opportunity for marital commerce.

nonage, *n.* minority, legal infancy; early stage. (*non; age*)

nonagenarian, *n.* person ninety years old. (L. *nonagenarius*)

nonagon, *n.* (*math.*) plane figure of nine sides. (L. *novem,* nine. Gk. *gonia,* angle)

non avenu, (regarded as) not having happened. (F.)

nonce, *n.* for the n., for this time only. **n.-word,** *n.* word coined for one occasion. (M.E. *than anes,* the once, with *n* transferred)

nonchalant, *a.* unexcited, indifferent, cool. **nonchalance,** *n.* (L. *non,* not; *calēre,* be warm)

non-collegiate, *a.* (of student) not belonging to a college; (of university) not having colleges.

non-combatant, *n.* person in fighting service who does not fight, e.g. surgeon, chaplain; civilian.

non-commissioned, *a.* of grade below those with commissions.

non-committal, *a.* avoiding definite preference or pledge.

non-conductor, *n.* substance that will not conduct electricity or heat.

nonconformist, *n.* Protestant dissenter from Church of England. **nonconformity,** *n.* body or principles of nonconformists; want of conformity, irregularity.

non-content, *n.* negative vote or voter in the House of Lords.

non-co-operation, *n.* (Indian politics) refusal to co-operate with the British Government.

nondescript, *a.* hard to classify, indeterminate; odd.—*n.* nondescript person or thing. (L. *non; describere,* describe)

none, *a.* and *pron.* not one; not any; no amount.—*adv.* by no amount. **n.-so-pretty,** *n.* kind of saxifrage, London pride. **n. the less,** nevertheless. (O.E. *ne,* not; *an,* one)

non-effective, *n.* and *a.* (soldier, sailor) not qualified for active service.

nonentity, *n.* non-existence; non-existent thing; person of no account.

nones, *n.pl.* ninth day before ides in ancient Roman calendar, i.e. the 7th of March, May, July, October, and the 5th of the other months; three-o'clock (ninth-hour) church service. (L. *novem,* nine)

nonesuch, see **nonsuch.**

nonet, nonette, *n.* musical piece for nine players. (L. *nonus,* ninth)

non-feasance, *n.* (*law*) omission of obligatory act.

non-ferrous, *a.* containing no iron.

nonillion, *n.* ninth power of million (1 with 54 ciphers); (in U.S. and France) tenth power of thousand (1 with 30 ciphers).

non-intervention, *n.* keeping aloof from others' disputes, esp. in international affairs.

nonius, *n.* early kind of vernier (*Nuñez,* inventor)

nonjuror, *n.* one who would not swear allegiance to William and Mary at the revolution of 1689.

non-moral, *a.* unconcerned with morality, without moral standards.

nonny, *int.* a meaningless refrain, often **hey, nonny.**

nonpareil, *n.* and *a.* unrivalled matchless (person or thing); kinds of apple, bird, moth, wheat etc.; (*print.*) 6-point type. (L. *par,* equal)

non-party, *a.* free from party obligations.

nonplus, *n.* state of perplexity, standstill.—*v.t.* throw into complete perplexity. (L.=not more)

non-rigid, *a.* (of airships) having gasbag with no rigid framework or keel.

nonsense, *n.* absurd language or ideas; trifles; foolish conduct. **nonsensical,** *a.*

non-stop, *a.* not stopping at intermediate stations; made without a stop.—*adv.* without a stop.

nonsuch, nonesuch, *n.* unrivalled person or thing; kind of lucerne.

nonsuit, *n.* stoppage of suit by judge as unsustainable. —*v.t.* pronounce nonsuit against.

non-union, *a.* not belonging to a trade union.

noodle, *n.* simpleton. **noodledom,** *n.*

noodle, *n.* strip of dough made with eggs and served in soup.

nook, *n.* secluded corner, retreat. **n.-shotten,** *a.* full of nooks and corners. **nooky,** *a.*

noon, *n.* twelve o'clock in the day, midday.—also *a.* **noonday, noontide,** *nn.* midday.—also *aa.* (L. *nonus,* ninth; orig.=3 p.m.)

noose, *n.* loop with running knot; snare.—*v.t.* catch, enclose in noose. (L. *nodus,* knot

nopal, *n.* American cactus, the food of the cochineal insect. (Mex. *nopalli*)

nope, *adv.* (*Amer. sl.*) no.

nor, *adv.* and not, not either. (contr. of obs. *nother*=neither)

Nordenfelt, *n.* kind of machine-gun. (inventor)

Nordic, *a.* of the tall blond dolichocephalic race found in Scandinavia etc. (G. *nord,* north)

Norfolk, *n.* **N. capon,** red herring. **N. dumpling** or **turkey,** Norfolk person. **N. Howard** (*sl.*) bed-bug. **N. jacket,** man's loose jacket with belt.

noria, *n.* water-raising apparatus in Spain etc.; flush-wheel. (Sp.)

norm, *n.* standard, type. (L. *norma,* carpenter's square)

normal, *a.* conforming to type, regular, usual; perpendicular. *n.* usual state; perpendicular line. **normality,** *n.* **normalize,** *v.t.* **normalization,** *n.* **n.-school,** *n.* training college for teachers.

Norman, *n.* native of Normandy.—*a.* (also **Normanesque**) in the Norman style of architecture. (*Northman*)

Norn, *n.* one of the three fates in Scandinavian mythology—**Urd, Verdande,** and **Skuld.**

Norse, *n.* the Norwegian language.—*a.* Norwegian. **Norseland, Norseman,** *nn.*

north, *n.* point opposite the sun at noon; northern part of a country.—*a., ad.* towards or in the north. **n.-east,** *n.* point midway between north and east. **n.-easter,** *n.* northeast wind. **n.-easterly,** *a.* towards or coming from the north-east. **n.-eastern,** *a.* belonging to the northeast, or in that direction. **n.-eastward,** *adv.* towards the north-east. **n. star,** the polar star. **n.-west** etc., like **n.-east** etc. **norther,** *n.* wind or storm from the north. **northerly,** *a.* towards or coming from the north. **northern,** *a.* in or of the north. **northern lights,** aurora borealis. **northerner,** *n.* native of the north. **northward,** *a.* and *adv.* towards the north. **northwards,** *adv.*

nose, *n.* organ of smell; end of nozzle; projecting part, prow.—*v.t.* smell at, detect by smell; thrust nose into, pry. **n.-dive,** *n.* downward swoop of aeroplane.—*v.i.* and *t.* make, cause (aircraft) to make, this. **nosebag,** *n.* bag with fodder hung on horse's head. **nosegay,** *n.* bunch of flowers. **nosing,** *n.* rounded edge of step etc. or metal shield for it. (O.E. *nosu*)

nosism, *n.* egotism of a group of persons; use of 'we' in speaking about oneself. (L. *nos,* we)

noso-, from Gk. *nosos,* disease, as in **nosography,** *n.* systematic description of diseases; **nosology,** *n.* classification of diseases.

nostalgia, *n.* homesickness. (Gk. *nostos,* return; *algos,* pain)

nostology, *n.* study of senility or second childhood. (Gk. *nostos,* return; *legein,* speak)

Nostradamus, *n.* prediction-monger. (Dr. de *Nostredame,* 1555)

nostril, *n.* breathing-hole in nose. (O.E. *nosthyrl*)

nostrum, *n.* quack remedy, patent medicine. (L.=our)

nosy, nosey, *a.* long-nosed; inquisitive; ill-smelling.

not, *adv.* expressing denial, refusal, or negation.

nota bene (*abbr.* **N.B.**), note this. (L.=note well)

notable, *a.* worthy of note, remarkable, eminent.—*n.* eminent person. **notability,** *n.* worthiness of notice; notable person or thing.

notanda, *n.pl.* things to be specially noted. (L.)

notary, *n.* registered officer who certifies deeds, contracts etc. (L. *notarius,* secretary)

notation, *n.* use of symbols to represent quantities etc.; system of such symbols. (*note*)

notch, *n.* nick, indentation; run scored at cricket.—*v.t.* make notch in. **notchy,** *a.* (F. *hoche,* with *n* transferred from indef. article)

note, *n.* sign, characteristic; brief record (us. *pl.*); explanation, comment; short letter; diplomatic paper; (*mus.*) mark representing sound or the sound itself.—*v.t.* observe, notice; record in writing. **noted,** *p.p.* celebrated, well-known. **notebook,** *n.* memorandum-book. **notepaper,** *n.*

writing-paper. **noteworthy,** *a.* worthy of notice. **n. of hand,** written promise to pay sum by certain time. (L. *nota,* mark)
note, (*Spens.*) know not; could not. (contr. of *ne wot* or *ne mote*)
nothing, *n.* no thing; no amount; thing of no importance, trifle.—*adv.* in no way, not at all. **nothingness,** *n.* (*no; thing*)
notice, *n.* attention, observation; intimation, warning; remark, comment. —*v.t.* perceive, regard; mention, remark upon. **noticeable,** *a.* (L. *noscere,* know)
notify, *v.t.* inform; give notice of. **notifiable,** *a.* that must be notified. **notification,** *n.* act of notifying; notice or paper bearing it.
notion, *n.* idea, belief, view. **notional,** *a.* of notion, fanciful. (L. *notio*)
noto-, from Gk. *noton,* back, used in **notobranchiate,** *a.* having dorsal gills; **notochord,** *n.* band forming basis of spinal column; **notonectal,** *a.* swimming on the back (of certain insects etc.).
noto-, from Gk. *notos,* south, used in **notornis,** *n.* gigantic New Zealand wading-bird; **nototherium,** *n.* gigantic fossil kangaroo-like Australian animal.
notorious, *a.* publicly known; infamous. **notoriety,** *n.* publicity, public exposure.
not-pated, *a.* (*Shake.*) having the hair cropped close. (O.E. *hnot,* shorn)
notwithstanding, *prep.* in spite of.—*adv.* nevertheless.—*conj.* although.
nougat, *n.* confection of sugar and almonds. (L. *nux,* nut)
nought, *n.* nothing; figure 0.—*adv.* in no degree. (O.E. *nōwiht*)
noul, *n.* (*Spens.*) top of the head.
nould, (*Spens.*) would not. (contr. of *ne would*)
noumenon, *n.* object of purely intellectual intuition; the real under the phenomenal. (Gk.)
noun, *n.* (*gram.*) word used as name of person or thing, substantive. (L. *nomen,* name)
nourice, *n.* (*Spens.*) nurse.
nourish, *v.t.* feed, sustain with food; cherish, nurse. **nourishing,** *a.* containing nourishment. **nourishment,** *n.* food; act of nourishing. (L. *nutrire*)
nous, *n.* pure intellect; common sense. (Gk.)
nouveau riche (*pl. nouveaux riches*), new rich, parvenu.
nova, *n.* new star. (L *novus,* new)
novel, *a.* new, strange, hitherto unknown. *n.* fictitious tale. **novelette,** *n.* short novel. **novelist,** *n.* writer of novels. **novelize,** *v.t.* turn (play etc.) into novel. **novelty,** *n.* novel thing or occurrence; newness. (L. *novus,* new)
November *n.* eleventh month. (L. *novem,* nine, because ninth month of Roman year)
novena, *n.* prayer lasting nine days to obtain a request through intercession of the Virgin or saint. **novenary,** *a.* of the number nine. **novennial,** *a.* done every ninth year. (L. *novem,* nine)
novercal, *a.* stepmotherly. (L. *noverca,* stepmother)
novice, *n.* beginner, tiro; probationary member of religious order. **novitiate, noviciate,** *n.* probationary period or initiation; novice. (L. *novicius*)
novus homo, one risen from low position, upstart. (L.=new man)
now, *adv.* at the present time; in the immediate past; by that time.—*conj.* it being the case that.—*n.* the present time. **n. and then,** occasionally. **now . . ., now . . .,** at one time . . ., at another time . . . **nowaday,** *a.* **nowadays,** *adv.* in our time, at present.—*n.* these times. (O.E. *nu*)
Nowel, *n.* Christmas.—*int.* in Christmas carols. (L. *natalis*)
nowhere, *adv.* in, at, to, no place. **nowhither,** *adv.* to no place. **nowise,** *adv.* in no way or degree.
nowt, *n.* (*Scot.*) cattle. (*neat*)
noxious, *a.* harmful, unhealthy. (L. *noxa,* harm)
noyade, *n.* wholesale execution by drowning. (F.)
noyance, *n.* (*Shake.*) harm. (*annoyance*)
noyau, *n.* liqueur of brandy and kernels. (L. *nux,* nut)
noyous, noysome, *aa.* (*Spens.*) troublesome, hurtful. (*annoy*)
nozzle, *n.* mouthpiece, open end of hose etc.; snout. (*nose*)
nuance, *n.* delicate difference, shade. (F. *nuer,* shade)
nub, *n.* knob, lump; point, gist. **nubbly,** *a.* in small lumps. **nubby,** *a.* lumpy, dirty. (=knob)
nubbin, *n.* (*Amer.*) small imperfect ear of maize.
nubecula, *n.* cloudy appearance; light film on the eye. (L.=little cloud)
nubile, *a.* marriageable. (L. *nubere,* become wife)
nubilous, *a.* cloudy; obscure. (L. *nubes,* cloud)
nuci-, from L. *nux,* nut, used in **nuciform,** *a.* nut-shaped; **nucivorous,** *a.* nut-eating.
nucleus, *n.* central part; core round which other parts accumulate; (*astron.*) head of comet. (L. *nux,* nut)
nucule, *n.* little nut. (L. *nucula*)
nude, *a.* naked, unclothed.—*n.* picture or sculpture in the nude. **nudist,** *n.* one who believes in going naked. —also *a.* (L. *nudus,* naked)
nudge, *v.t.* touch gently with elbow. —*n.* light push.
nugae, *n.pl.* trifles. **nugatory,** *a.* trifling, worthless; inoperative, not valid. (L.)

nuggar, *n.* flat-bottomed barge on the Nile. (native)
nugget, *n.* lump of native gold.
nuisance, *n.* annoying or offensive thing, esp. one for which legal remedy may be had; anything disagreeable. (L. *nocēre,* hurt)
null, *a.* of no force, invalid; expressionless.—*n.* dummy letter in cipher. (L. *nullus,* none)
nullah, *n.* water-course, ravine. (Hind.)
nulla-nulla, *n.* hard wooden club of Australian natives. (native)
nullify, *v.t.* make null, cancel. **nullification,** *n.* **nullity,** *n.* invalidity (esp. of marriage); lack of force; nonentity.
nullipara, *n.* woman who has never given birth to a child, esp. if not a virgin. (L. *nullus,* none; *parere,* bring forth)
numb, *a.* deprived of sensation or motion; stupefied.—*v.t.* make numb, paralyse. (O.E. *niman,* take)
number, *n.* collection of things, company; symbol in counting; (*gram.*) class of word-form (singular, plural etc.); (*pl.*) groups of musical notes; metre, verse.—*v.t.* count; mark with a number; amount to. **numberless,** *a.* innumerable. (L. *numerus*)
numbles, *n.pl.* (*arch.*) entrails of a deer. (O.F. *nombles*)
numdah, numnah, *n.* kind of felt; saddle-cloth or pad made of this. (Pers. *namad,* carpet)
numerable, *a.* countable.
numeral, *a.* of number.—*n.* figure or group of figures denoting a number.
numerary, *a.* belonging to a certain number.
numerate, *v.t.* point off and read as figures. **numeration,** *n.* act or method of numbering; reading of numerals as words. **numerator,** *n.* one who counts; upper number of a vulgar fraction.
numerical, *a.* of, in, denoting, number.
numerous, *a.* of a great number; many; rhythmic, harmonious.
numismatic, *a.* of coins. **numismatics, numismatology,** *nn.* science of coins and medals. **numismatist,** *n.* student of coins. (Gk. *nomisma,* coin)
nummary, nummulary, *aa.* of, in, coin. **nummulite,** *n.* fossil shell resembling a coin. (L. *nummus,* coin)
nummet, *n.* (*dial.*) lunch. (=noon meat)
numnah, see **numdah.**
numskull, *n.* dolt, blockhead.
nun, *n.* woman who has taken religious vows and lives in a convent; breed of domestic pigeon; kinds of bird and moth. **n.'s cloth, thread, veiling,** fine kinds of each. **n.-buoy,** *n.* shuttle-shaped buoy. (L. *nonna*)
Nunc dimittis, a canticle. **sing N. d.,** be glad to depart or die. (L.=now lettest thou go)
nuncheon, *n.* midday or afternoon refreshment. (O.E. *nón,* noon; *scencan.* pour)
nuncio, *n.* pope's envoy at foreign court. **nunciature,** *n.* office of nuncio; tenure of it. (L. *nuncius,* messenger)
nuncle, (*Shake.*) contr. for **mine uncle.**
nuncupate, *v.t.* declare, make will, verbally, not in writing. **nuncupation, nuncupator,** *nn.* **nuncupative, nuncupatory,** *aa.* verbal, not written. (L. *nomen,* name; *capere,* take)
nundinal, *a.* of fair or market.—*n.* (also **n. letter**) one of the first eight letters, A–H. (L. *nundinae,* market-day held every eighth day)
nunnery, *n.* convent for nuns.
nuphar, *n.* yellow water-lily. (for *nenuphar*)
nuptial, *a.* of marriage; *n.pl.* wedding. (L. *nubere,* become wife)
nurl, same as **knurl.**
nurse, *n.* woman who suckles an infant; one who has care of infants or the sick; shrub or tree that protects a young plant.—*v.t.* suckle; tend, as an infant or sick person; foster; tend with an eye to the future. **nurseling, nursling,** *n.* infant; one who is nursed. **nursemaid,** *n.* girl in charge of children. **nursing home,** establishment for those taking medical treatment. **nursery,** *n.* children's quarters; plot where plants are reared; place where the growth of anything is promoted. (L. *nutrire,* nourish)
nurse, nurse-hound, *n.* small shark.
nurture, *n.* act of nursing or nourishing; nourishment; education, upbringing. —*v.t.* nourish, bring up, educate.
nut, *n.* fruit consisting of a kernel in a hard shell; small block of metal screwed on end of bolt to secure it; (*sl.*) head; (*sl.*) overdressed young man; (*Amer.*) blockhead, lunatic; (*pl.*) small lumps of coal.—*v.i.* gather nuts. **nutty,** *a.* **n.-brown,** *a.* coloured like ripe hazel-nut. **n.-cracker,** *n.* tool for cracking nuts (us. *pl.*); kind of bird. **nuthatch,** *n.* small climbing bird feeding on nuts. **nutshell,** *n.* hard covering on nut; tiny receptacle; compact way of expression. **nutting,** *n.* nut-gathering. **n. to crack,** hard problem to solve. **be nn. on,** (*sl.*) be fond of. (O.E. *hnutu*)
nutate, *v.i.* (*bot.*) nod, droop. **nutant,** *a.* **nutation,** *n.* nodding; periodic oscillation of earth's axis; (*bot.*) turning of flowers towards the sun. (L. *nutare,* nod)
nutmeg, *n.* aromatic kernel of an E. Indian tree, used as spice and in medicine. **n.-grater,** *n.* appliance for grating nutmeg. (L.L. *nux muscata,* musky nut)
nutria, *n.* fur of the coypu, a S. American beaver. (Sp.=otter)
nutrient, *a.* nourishing. **nutriment,** *n.*

nourishing food. **nutrition,** *n.* supplying or receiving of food; nourishment. **nutritious,** *a.* efficient as food. **nutritive,** *a.* serving as food. —*n.* article of food. (L. *nutrire,* nourish)
nux vomica *n.* seed yielding strychnine. (L.L. *nux,* nut; *vomere,* vomit)
nuzzer, *n.* present made to one of higher rank. (Hind. *nuzar*)
nuzzle, *v.i.* and *t.* burrow or sniff with nose; nestle, thrust head forward as a child at its mother's breast; root up with nose. (*nose*)
nyaff, *n.* (*Scot.*) insignificant or contemptible person.
nyctalopia. nyctalopy, *n.* night-blindness; inability to see clearly except at night. (Gk. *nux,* night; *alaos,* blind; *ops,* eye; incorrect second sense due to overlooking of *al*)
nyctitropism, *n.* so-called sleep of plants, turning in certain direction at night. **nyctitropic,** *a.* (Gk. *nux,* night; *tropos,* turn)
nye, *n.* flock of pheasants.
nylghau, *n.* short-horned Indian antelope. (Pers. *nil,* blue; *gaw,* ox)
nymph, *n.* (*myth.*) semi-divine maiden of sea, rivers, hills, woods, or trees; (*poet.*) maiden; chrysalis of insect (so also nympha). **nymphean,** *a.* **nympholepsy,** *n.* frenzy caused by desire of the unattainable. **nympholept,** *n.* one inspired by violent enthusiasm for an ideal. **nymphomania,** *n.* uncontrollable sexual desire in women. (Gk. *numphē,* bride)
nys, (*Spens.*) same as nis.
nystagmus, *n.* eye-disease common among miners, with spasmodic movement of the eyeballs. (Gk. *nustazein,* nod)

O

O, *int.* (oh before punctuation mark) of surprise, used with vocative etc.
o, *n.* (*pl.* **oes, o's**) cipher, nought; (*Shake.*) circle.
o', for of or on.
oaf, *n.* (*pl.* **oafs, oaves**) awkward fellow, lout; deformed child, changeling. **oafish,** *a.* (O.N. *álfr,* elf)
oak, *n.* kinds of tree; its wood.—*a.* of oak. **sport one's o.,** (*Oxford sl.*) close outer door to exclude visitors. **the Oo.,** horse-race at Epsom. **o.-apple, o.-gall,** *nn.* swellings produced on oak by gall-fly. **o.-apple day.** 29 May, anniversary of Restoration. **oaken,** *a.* (*arch.*). **oakling,** *n.* young oak. (O.E. *ác*)
oakum, *n.* loose fibre got by unpicking old rope and used for caulking. (O.E. *ácumba,* tow)
oar, *n.* flat-bladed pole for rowing; rower.—*v.t.* and *i.* row. **put one's o. in,** meddle. **rest on one's oo.,** suspend effort. **toss oo.,** raise them vertically in salute. **oarsman,** *n.* rower. **oarsmanship,** *n.* art of rowing. (O.E. *ár*)
oasis, *n.* (*pl.* **oases**) fertile place in desert. (Gk.)
oast, *n.* kiln for drying hops. **o.-house,** *n.* (O.E. *ást*)
oat, *n.* shepherd's pipe; pastoral song; (*pl.*) a cereal plant; its grain. **sow one's wild oo.,** have youthful dissipations. **oaten,** *a.* **oatcake,** *n.* thin broad cake of **oatmeal.** (O.E. *áte*)
oath, *n.* solemn affirmation or promise with appeal to God as witness; formula for this; curse, imprecation. (O.E. *óth*)
ob-, *pref.* denoting exposure, as in **obtrude**; meeting, as in **occur**; hostility, as in **oppose**; hindrance, as in **obtuse**; completeness, as in **obtain** inversion, as in **obconical.** (L.)
obbligato, *a.* and *n.* (accompaniment) forming integral part of musical composition. (It.)
obconical, *a.* like inverted cone.
obdormition, *n.* numbness, going to sleep, of limb. (L. *dormire,* sleep)
obdurate, *a.* hard-hearted, unyielding, stubborn. **obduracy,** *n.* (L. *durus,* hard)
obeah, *n.* negro witchcraft or fetish. (W. Afr.)
obedient, *a.* obeying, submissive to authority, dutiful. **obedience,** *n.* **obedientiary,** *n.* office-holder in monastery under superior. (*obey*)
obeisance, *n.* bow, curtsy, act of reverence; homage. (F. *obéissance*)
obelisk, *n.* four-sided tapering pillar, us. with pyramidal top; (also obelus) mark (—, ÷) to denote spurious passage; dagger (†) as mark of reference. **obelize,** *v.t.* mark with obelus. (Gk. *obelos,* spit)
obese, *a.* stout, corpulent. **obesity,** *n.* (L. *obesus*)
obey, *v.t.* and *i.* do commands, submit to authority (of). (L. *obedire*)
obfuscate, *v.t.* darken; confuse. **obfuscation,** *n.* (L. *fuscus,* dark)
obi, *n.* Japanese woman's sash. (Jap.)
obi, same as **obeah.**
obit, *n.* (*arch.*) memorial service, requiem. *obiit,* (*abbr.* *ob.*) died. (L. *obire,* die)
obiter, *adv.* in passing. *o. dictum,* (*pl.* *o. dicta*) casual remark, esp. judge's opinion expressed incidentally. (L. *ob iter.* by the way)
obituary, *a.* of death of person.—*n.* obituary notice with biography; death-roll. **obituarist,** *n.* (*obit*)

object, *n.* material thing; that to which feeling or action is directed; aim, purpose; oddity, deplorable sight; (*gram.*) noun governed by verb or preposition.—*v.t.* and *i.* feel, express, disapproval of; protest against; state as objection. **o. ball,** (*billiards*) that meant to be hit by cue ball. **o. glass,** lens of telescope nearest object. **o. lesson,** (with) practical and concrete illustration. (L. *jacere*, throw)

objectify, *v.t.* render objective; embody; materialize. **objectification,** *n.*

objection, *n.* objecting; ground, expression, of disapproval; (*Shake.*) accusation. **objectionable,** *a.* open to objection; disagreeable.

objective, *a.* of, concerned with, outward things, not thoughts or feelings; (*gram.*) of, appropriate to, object; (*philos.*) having an independent existence of its own, real.—*n.* thing or place aimed at; (*gram.*) objective case. **objectivism,** *n.* theory stressing the objective. **objectivist,** *n.* **objectivity,** *n.* objectiveness.

objector, *n.* one who objects.

objet d'art, thing of artistic value. (F.)

objurgate, *v.t.* reprove, scold. **objurgation,** *n.* **objurgatory,** *a.* (L. *jurgare*, quarrel)

oblate, *n.* one dedicated to monastic or religious life. **oblation,** *n.* offering to God, esp. of eucharist; pious gift. **oblational, oblatory,** *aa.* (L. *oblatus*, offered)

oblate, *a.* (of spheroid) flattened at poles. (opp. to *prolate*)

obligate, *v.t.* bind, put under obligation. **obligation,** *n.* duty or its binding power; favour, debt of gratitude; (*law*) written agreement. **obligatory,** *a.* binding, not optional. (*oblige*)

oblige, *v.t.* constrain, compel; do favour to, gratify. **obligee,** *n.* (*law*) person in whose favour a bond is made by **obligor. obligement,** *n.* favour. **obliging,** *a.* complaisant, civil. (L. *ligare*, bind)

oblique, *a.* slanting, diverging from straight; indirect, allusive.—*v.i.* advance obliquely. **o. cases,** (*gram.*) all but nominative and vocative. **o. narration,** giving substance, not actual words. **obliquity,** *n.* obliqueness; deviation from moral code. (L. *obliquus*)

obliterate, *v.t.* blot out, make illegible; efface. **obliteration, obliterator,** *nn.* (L. *litera*, letter)

oblivion, *n.* forgetting, being forgotten; amnesty. **oblivious,** *a.* forgetful, unheeding; (*poet.*) inducing oblivion. (L. *oblivisci*, forget)

oblong, *a.* longer than broad; (*geom.*) rectangular with unequal sides.—*n.* oblong figure. (*long*)

obloquy, *n.* reproach, detraction; disgrace. (L. *obloqui*, gainsay)

obmutescence, *n.* persistent silence. **obmutescent,** *a.* (*mute*)

obnoxious, *a.* offensive, objectionable; (*arch.*) liable (to). (L. *noxa*, harm)

oboe, *n.* a wood-wind instrument, hautboy. **oboist,** *n.* (F. *hautbois*)

obol, *n.* ancient Greek silver coin, worth about 1½*d.* (Gk. *obolos*)

obscene, *a.* indecent, lewd; (*arch.*) repulsive, filthy. **obscenity,** *n.* (L. *obscenus*)

obscurant, *a.* and *n.* (person) opposed to enlightenment, reactionary. **obscurantism, obscurantist,** *nn.*

obscuration, *n.* obscuring; occultation.

obscure, *a.* dim, indistinct, not bright; not clear, puzzling; unimportant, humble.—*n.* (*poet.*) darkness.—*v.t.* darken, conceal; make unintelligible. **obscurity,** *n.* (L. *obscurus*)

obsecrate, *v.t.* (*arch.*) implore. **obsecration,** *n.* supplication; litany petition beginning with 'by.' (L. *sacer*, sacred)

obsequies, *n.pl.* funeral rites, funeral. **obsequial,** *a.* (L.L. *obsequiae*)

obsequious, *a.* servile, cringing; (*arch.*) submissive. (L. *sequi*, follow)

observance, *n.* observing; ceremony, religious rite; (*arch.*) deference. **observant,** *a.* mindful, attentive; alert, vigilant.—*n.* member of stricter branch of Franciscans.

observation, *n.* act, faculty, of observing; surveillance; remark, comment. **o. car,** at end of train giving view of scenery. **o. post,** (*abbr.* **O pip**) advanced post for watching gunfire. **observational,** *a.* **observatory,** *n.* building for astronomical observation.

observe, *v.t.* and *i.* keep, follow, perform duly; watch, notice, be attentive (of); remark, say; (*Shake.*) pay court to. **observer,** *n.* one who observes; member of aircraft's crew employed in reconnaissance. **observed of all observers,** centre of attention. (L. *servare*, keep)

obsess, *v.t.* possess, haunt, mind of; preoccupy. **obsession,** *n.* fixed idea, monomania. (L. *sedēre*, sit)

obsidian, *n.* hard dark-coloured glassy lava. (*Obsius*, discoverer)

obsidional, *a.* of sieges. (L. *obsidio*, siege)

obsolete, *a.* disused, out of date; (*zool.*) indistinct, rudimentary. **obsolescent,** *a.* becoming obsolete. **obsolescence,** *n.* (L. *obsoletus*)

obstacle, *n.* hindrance, impediment. **o. race,** in which barriers have to be crossed. (L. *stare*, stand)

obstetrics, *n.pl.* science of midwifery. **obstetric, obstetrical,** *aa.* **obstetrician,** *n.* specialist in obstetrics. (L. *obstetrix*, midwife)

obstinate, *a.* stubborn, self-willed; intractable. **obstinacy,** *n.* (L. *stare*, stand)

obstreperous, *a.* unruly, turbulent; clamorous. (L. *strepere*, make noise)

obstruct, *v.t.* and *i.* block up, bar; prevent, hinder; retard progress (of). **obstruction,** *n.* obstructing; obstacle, hindrance. **obstructionism,** *n.* systematic hindering of political business etc. **obstructionist,** *n.* **obstructive,** *a.* **obstruent,** *a.* and *n.* (medicine) blocking up body passage. (L. *struere,* build)

obtain, *v.t.* and *i.* gain, acquire, have granted; be prevalent, hold good. **obtainable,** *a.* procurable. **obtainment,** *n.* (L. *tenēre,* hold)

obtected, *a.* (of pupa) protected by hard outer case. (L. *tegere,* cover)

obtest, *v.t.* and *i.* (*arch.*) supplicate, call to witness; protest. **obtestation,** *n.* (L. *testis,* witness)

obtrude, *v.t.* and *i.* thrust forward (opinion etc.) uninvited; intrude. (L. *trudere,* thrust)

obtruncate, *v.t.* lop top off, behead. (L. *truncus,* maimed)

obtrusion, *n.* obtruding. **obtrusive,** *a.* apt to obtrude, pushing.

obtund, *v.t.* (*med.*) blunt, deaden. (L. *tundere,* pound)

obturate, *v.t.* stop, seal up; close (gun-breech). **obturation, obturator,** *nn.* (L. *obturare*)

obtuse, *a.* blunt, not pointed; dull, stupid; (*geom.*) greater than right angle. (*obtund*)

obverse, *a.* facing observer; with top wider than base; answering to.—*n.* front or top side (opp. to reverse); (of coin) head; counterpart. (*obvert*)

obvert, *v.t.* (*logic*) infer by obversion. **obversion,** *n.* immediate inference by which we deny the opposite of anything affirmed. (L. *vertere,* turn)

obviate, *v.t.* prevent, clear away. (L. *via,* way)

obvious, *a.* easily seen or understood, evident, manifest; lacking subtlety. (L. *ob viam,* in the way)

oc-, form of ob- before *c.*

ocarina, *n.* egg-shaped instrument played like flute. (It.)

occasion, *n.* time when thing happens; favourable juncture, opportunity; special occurrence; ground, need; subsidiary cause; (*pl.*) affairs, business.—*v.t.* give rise to. **on o.,** now and then. **rise to the o.,** be equal to emergency. **occasional,** *a.* not continuous, infrequent; produced for some special event; (of cause) incidental. **occasionalism,** *n.* Cartesian doctrine that apparent action of mind on matter is due to intervention of God. **occasionalist,** *n.* **occasionality,** *n.* occasionalness. **occasionally,** *adv.* intermittently. (L. *occasio*)

occident, *n.* the west; Europe; western hemisphere. **occidental,** *a.* **occidentalism,** *n.* western as opp. to oriental culture. **occidentalist,** *n.* **occidentalize,** *v.t.* (L. *occidens,* setting)

occiput, *n.* back of head. **occipital,** *a.* (L.)

occlude, *v.t.* stop up, close; (*chem.*) absorb and retain (gas). **occlusion,** *n.* (L. *claudere,* shut)

occult, *a.* supernatural, magical; secret, esoteric.—*v.t.* and *i.* conceal, hide from sight. **occulting light,** flashing light. **occultation,** *n.* eclipse of star or planet by moon etc. **occultism,** *n.* mysticism, theosophy, spiritualism etc. **occultist,** *n.* (L. *occulere,* cover)

occupy, *v.t.* take, have, possession of; inhabit; fill, take up; employ, busy. **occupant,** *n.* one who occupies; resident. **occupancy,** *n.* having possession. **occupation,** *n.* occupying, tenure; employment, business, pursuit. **army of occupation,** left to hold captured territory. **occupational,** *a.* caused by occupation. **occupier,** *n.* person in possession; tenant. (L. *capere,* take)

occur, *v.i.* happen; be met with; come into the mind. **occurrence,** *n,* happening, incident, event. (L. *currere,* run)

ocean, *n.* the sea; large division of it; immense expanse. **o. greyhound,** swift liner. **Oceania,** *n.* Pacific Islands. **oceanic,** *a.* of, found in, ocean; of Oceania. **Oceanid,** *n.* sea-nymph. **oceanography,** *n.* science of ocean and its phenomena. **oceanographic, oceanographical,** *aa.* **oceanographer,** *n.* (Gk. *ōkeanos*)

ocellus, *n.* (*pl.* **ocelli**) facet of compound eye; eye-like spot on peacock's tail etc. **ocellate,** *a.* marked with ocelli. (L.=little eye)

ocelot, *n.* S. American animal like leopard, tiger-cat. (Mex. *tlalocelotl,* field jaguar)

och, *int.* (*Ir.*) oh.

ochl(o)-, from Gk. *ochlos,* mob, used in **ochlesis,** *n.* unhealthy condition due to overcrowding; **ochlocracy,** *n.* mob-rule, hence **ochlocratic,** *a.,* **ochlocrat,** *n.*; **ochlophobia,** *n.* fear of crowds.

ochone, *int.* (*Ir.*) of lamentation.

ochre, *n.* an earthy oxide of iron; yellow-brown pigment from this. **ochreous, ochrous, ochry,** *aa.* (Gk. *ōchros,* yellow)

o'clock, see **clock.**

octa-, from Gk. *oktō,* eight, used in **octachord,** *n.* eight-stringed instrument, series of eight notes, diatonic scale, hence **octachordal,** *a.*; **octad,** *n.* group of eight, number eight, (*chem.*) element or radical with valency of eight. **octagon,** *n.* eight-sided plane figure, hence **octagonal,** *a.*; **octahedron,** *n.* solid with eight plane faces, us. triangles, hence **octahedral,** *a.*; **octameter,** *n.* eight-foot verse; **octant,** *n.* eighth part of circle, instrument for measuring angles, (*astron.*) aspect of two planets etc.

when 45° apart; **octarchy,** *n.* aggregate of eight petty kingdoms; **octaroon,** *n.* octoroon; **octastyle,** *a.* and *n.* (building) with eight columns at end; **octateuch,** *n.* first eight books of Old Testament; **octavalent,** same as **octovalent.**

octave, *n.* day week of festival; the eight days from festival to this; eight-line stanza, octet; a fencing guard; (*mus.*) eighth tone above or below a note; interval, notes, between note and its octave. **o.-flute,** *n.* piccolo. (L. *octavus,* eighth)

octavo, *n.* (*abbr.* **8vo**) book of sheets folded into eight leaves; this size, average 9½ × 6 in. (*octave*)

octennial, *a.* lasting, happening every eight years. (L. *octo,* eight; *annus,* year)

octet, octette, *n.* composition for eight singers or players; group of eight lines, esp. first eight of sonnet. (L. *octo,* eight)

octillion, *n.* eighth power of million (1 with 48 ciphers); (in U.S. and France) ninth power of thousand (1 with 27 ciphers).

octingentenary, *n.* 800th anniversary. (L. *octingenti,* 800)

octo-, from L. *octo,* eight, used in **October,** *n.* tenth month of year (eighth in Roman calendar); **Octobrists,** *n. pl.* moderate reforming party in Czarist Russia; **octocentenary,** *n.* 800th anniversary, hence **octocentennial,** *a.*; **octodecimo,** *n.* (*abbr.* **18mo**) book of sheets folded into eighteen leaves, this size; **octogenarian,** *a.* and *n.* eighty-year-old (person); **octonal,** *a.* counted in eights; **octonarian,** *a.* and *n.* (verse) with eight feet; **octonary,** *a.* octonal.—*n.* eight-line stanza; **octopod,** *a.* and *n.* eight-armed (mollusc); **octopus,** *n.* (*pl.* **octopuses**) mollusc with eight arms furnished with suckers, cuttle-fish, wide-branching organization; **octoroon,** *n.* offspring of white and quadroon, person one-eighth negro; **octosyllable,** *n.* word, verse, of eight syllables, hence **octosyllabic,** *a.* and *n.*; **octovalent,** *a.* having valency of eight.

octroi, *n.* municipal customs duty; place, officials, for its collection. (F.)

octuple, *a.* eightfold.—*v.t.* multiply by eight. (L. *octo,* eight)

ocular, *a.* of, by, sight; visual.—*n.* eyepiece. **ocularist,** *n.* maker of artificial eyes. **oculate,** *a.* ocellate. **oculist,** *n.* eye specialist. **oculistic,** *a.* **oculo-motor,** *a.* (*anat.*) moving the eye. (L. *oculus,* eye)

od, *n.* hypothetical natural force once used to explain magnetism, mesmerism etc. (coined)

Od, (*Shake.*) minced form of **God. Od's-bodikins,** *int.* God's body.

odalisque, *n.* slave, concubine, in harem. (Turk. *odah,* chamber)

odd, *a.* not divisible by two, not even; surplus, extra; casual, occasional; peculiar, queer; eccentric; (after numeral) and a few more.—*n.pl.* inequality, difference; balance of advantage, handicap; excess of one number over another, esp. in betting. **at oo.,** at variance. **o. man out,** left when others pair off. **oo. and ends,** miscellaneous articles, scraps. **the o.,** (*golf*) one stroke more than opponent. **Oddfellows,** *n.pl.* a friendly society like freemasons. **oddity,** *n.* queerness; odd trait or person. **oddment,** *n.* remnant. (O.N. *oddi,* triangle)

ode, *n.* lyric poem of exalted style, often in form of address; (formerly) song. (Gk. *aeidein,* sing)

odeum, *n.* (*pl.* **odeums, odea**) hall for musical performances. (L.)

odium, *n.* general dislike; stigma. **odious,** *a.* hateful, repulsive. (L.)

odometer, same as **hodometer.**

odont(o)-, from Gk. *odous,* tooth, used in **odontalgia,** *n.* toothache; **odontiasis,** *n.* cutting of teeth; **odontic,** *a.* dental; **odontoglossum,** *n.* a tropical orchid; **odontoid,** *a.* tooth-shaped; **odontology,** *n.* dental science; **odontorhyncous,** *a.* with serrated bill.

odour, *n.* smell, perfume; trace; repute. **in good, bad, o.,** in, out of, favour. **o. of sanctity,** reputation for holiness. **odoriferous,** *a.* diffusing fragrance; (*joc.*) smelly. **odorous,** *a.* scented, fragrant. (L. *odor*)

odyl, *n.* od.

Odyssey, *n.* Homer's epic describing return of Odysseus from Troy; any long adventurous journey.

oe, *n.* (*Scot.*) grandchild.

oecist, *n.* founder of colony. (Gk. *oikos,* house)

oecology, same as **ecology.**

oecumenical, *a.* of the whole Christian world or church; universal, world-wide. **oecumenicity,** *n.* (Gk. *oikein,* inhabit)

oedema, *n.* dropsical swelling. **oedematous,** *a.* (Gk. *oidein,* swell)

Oedipus, *n.* solver of riddles. **O. complex** (*psycho-anal.*) arising from relations of son to parents. (name)

œillade, *n.* glance, ogle. *œil-de-bœuf,* *n.* small round window. (F.)

oen(o)-, from Gk. *oinos,* wine, used in **oenanthic,** *a.* having odour of wine; **oenology,** *n.* science of wines; **oenomania,** *n.* dipsomania; **oenometer,** *n.* instrument for measuring alcoholic strength of wines.

o'er, *contr.* of over.

oesophagus, *n.* (*pl.* **oesophagi, oesophaguses**) canal from mouth to stomach, gullet. **oesophageal,** *a.* (Gk. *oisophagos*)

oestrum, oestrus, *n.* violent desire, frenzy. (Gk. *oistros,* gadfly)

of, *prep.* belonging, relating, to; from; concerning; among; by; during. **of purpose,** intentionally. (O.E.)

of-, form of **ob-** before *f.*

off, *adv.* away, from; detached, gone; discontinued; out of condition; entirely.—*prep.* away from; not on.—*a.* farther; (of horse) right; (*cricket*) in front of batsman.—*n.* (*cricket*) off side. **o. and on,** intermittently. **o. chance,** remote possibility. **o. colour,** unfit. **o. day,** when disengaged or in poor form. **o. one's head,** crazy. **well, badly, o.,** well-to-do, poor. (orig. same word as *of*)

offal, *n.* entrails of animal, waste parts, husks; garbage. (*off*; *fall*)

offend, *v.i.* and *t.* do wrong, transgress; annoy, hurt feelings of, outrage; (*arch.*) lead astray; (*Shake.*) harm. **offender**, *n.* one who offends; delinquent. **offence**, *n.* transgression, crime; affront, insult; displeasure; attack. **offensive**, *a.* repulsive, disagreeable; insulting; aggressive.—*n.* attack. (L. *offendere*, dash against)

offer, *v.t.* and *i.* present for acceptance or refusal; tender in sacrifice; express willingness; attempt; bid (price); occur.—*n.* act of offering; proposal, esp. of marriage; bid. **offering**, *n.* sacrifice; present. **offertory**, *n.* church collection; part of service when it is taken. (L. *ferre*, bring)

offhand, *a.* without preparation; unceremonious; curt, brusque.—*adv.* extempore. **offhanded**, *a.*

office, *n.* task, function; service; position of trust or authority; state department; place of business, counting-house; religious service, rite; (*sl.*) tip, signal; (*pl.*) parts of house for domestic work etc. **Holy O.,** Inquisition. **last oo.,** funeral rites. **o.-bearer**, *n.* holder of office. **officer**, *n.* functionary, office-bearer; constable; holder of authority in army, navy, mercantile marine etc.; (*Shake.*) household servant. (L. *officium*)

official, *a.* of an office or its tenure; properly authorized; formal; (*chem.*) according to pharmacopoeia.—*n.* holder of public office. **o. principal,** presiding judge of archdeacon's court. **officialdom**, *n.* body of officials. **officialism**, *n.* official system, red tape. **officialize**, *v.t.*

officiate, *v.i.* discharge duty, act (as); perform divine service. **officiant**, *n.* officiating clergyman.

officinal, *a.* (of drug) stocked by apothecaries, official; used in medicine or the arts. (L. *officina*, workshop)

officious, *a.* interfering, meddlesome; (*arch.*) obliging. (*office*)

offing, *n.* position at distance from shore but above horizon. (*off*)

offish, *a.* (*colloq.*) distant, stiff.

off-licence, *n.* licence to sell alcohol for consumption off premises.

off-print, *n.* separately printed copy or part of publication.

offscourings, *n.pl.* refuse, dregs.

offset, *n.* side branch; compensation; (*archit.*) sloping ledge on face of wall; (*print.*) smudging of clean sheet from freshly printed surface.—*v.t.* compensate for. **o. printing,** in which impression is transferred from plate to rubber surface and then to paper.

offshoot, *n.* branch from main stem, family etc.; derivative.

offside, *a.* (*football*) illegally between ball and opponents' goal.

offspring, *n.* child, progeny; result.

often, *adv.* frequently.—*a.* (*arch.*) frequent. **oft, oftentimes,** *advv.* (*arch.*) often. (O.E.)

ogdoad, *n.* eight, set of eight. (Gk. *oktō*, eight)

ogee, *a.* and *n.* S-shaped (moulding, line). **ogee'd**, *a.*

ogham, ogam, *n.* ancient British alphabet of notches; character in it. **oghamic, ogamic**, *a.* (O.Ir.)

ogive, *n.* diagonal groin of vault; pointed arch. **ogival**, *a.* (F.)

ogle, *v.i.* and *t.* make eyes (at).—*n.* amorous glance. **ogler**, *n.*

Ogpu, *n.* secret police of Soviet Russia. (Russ.)

ogre, *n.* (*fem.* ogress) man-eating giant; hideous person. **ogreish, ogrish**, *aa.* (F.)

oh, see **O.**

ohm, *n.* unit of electrical resistance. **ohmmeter**, *n.* instrument for measuring resistance. (person)

oho, *int.* of surprise.

-oid, *adj.* and *n.suf.* (thing) like, as in **negroid.**

oil, *n.* light inflammable viscous liquid; (*pl.*) oil-colours.—*v.t.* smear with oil, lubricate. **o. one's tongue,** flatter. **o. palm of,** bribe. **strike o.,** find petroleum by sinking shaft; attain success. **o.-colour**, *n.* in which oil is used as vehicle for pigment. **o.-painting**, *n.* painting in oils. **oilcake**, *n.* cattle-food of linseed. **oilcloth**, *n.* canvas coated with oil, linoleum. **oiled**, *a.* (*sl.*) tipsy. **oiler**, *n.* oil-can; greaser. **oilman**, *n.* dealer in oils. **oilskin**, *n.* cloth made waterproof with oil; (*pl.*) coat of this. **oily**, *a.* like, covered with, oil; unctuous, fawning; evasive. (L. *oleum*)

ointment, *n.* oily substance used for healing skin or as cosmetic, unguent. (L. *unguere*, smear)

Oireachtas, *n.* legislature of Eire, consisting of the President, Dáil Eireann (Chamber of Deputies), and Seanad Eireann (Senate). (Ir.)

O.K., okay, *adv.* and *a.* (*Amer.*) all right.—*v.t.* pass as O.K. **oke, okey-doke**, *adv.* and *a.* (*Amer. sl.*) all right. (Orl K'rect)

okapi, *n.* African animal like short-necked giraffe. (native)

okra, *n.* W.Indian plant whose seed-pods are used for soup. (W.Afr.)

old, *a.* aged; elderly, not young; long used, not new; of the past, not modern; experienced; worn out; (*sl.*) familiar or intensive use, as in **o. chap, o. thing, friend, high o. time,** very good time. **of o.,** of old time; formerly. **o. age,** over 60. **o.-age pension,** state allowance to aged people. **O. Glory,** the Stars and Stripes. **O. Harry, Nick, Scratch,** the devil. **O. Lady of Threadneedle Street,** Bank of England. **o. maid,** confirmed spinster; a card game. **o. man,** (*sl.*) skipper, governor; husband, father. **o. master,** painter, painting, of a century or more ago, esp. of Renaissance period. **o. stuff,** stale news, hackneyed material. **O. Tom,** a kind of gin. **o. woman,** (*sl.*) one's wife; fussy man. **O. World,** Europe, Asia, and Africa. **o.-fashioned,** *a.* out of date. **o.-gold,** *a.* the colour of tarnished gold. **o.-man's-beard,** *n.* a moss; wild clematis. **o.-world,** *a.* antiquated. (O.E. *ald*)

olden, *a.* ancient, of past times.

oldster, *n.* (*colloq.*) old person.

oleaginous, *a.* oily, greasy; unctuous. (L. *oleum,* oil)

oleander, *n.* an evergreen poisonous shrub. (L.L. *lorandrum*)

oleaster, *n.* wild olive; yellow-flowered shrub like it. (L.)

oleo-, from L. *oleum,* oil, used in **oleograph,** *n.* lithograph in oil-colours; **oleo-margarine,** *n.* a butter-substitute of animal fats; **oleometer,** *n.* instrument for measuring density of oils.

olfaction, *n.* smelling. **olfactology,** *n.* science of smells. **olfactory,** *a.* of sense of smell. (L. *olēre,* smell; *facere,* make)

olibanum, *n.* gum resin used in incense. (Gk. *libanos,* frankincense)

olid, *a.* rank-smelling. (L. *olēre,* smell)

olig(o)-, from Gk. *oligos,* few, small, used in **oligarch,** *n.* member of **oligarchy,** *n.* government by the few, hence **oligarchic, oligarchical,** *aa.*; **Oligocene,** *a.* (*geol.*) between Eocene and Miocene.

olio, *n.* hotch-potch, stew; miscellany. (L. *olla,* pot)

olive, *n.* an evergreen tree; its oval hard-stoned fruit; its wood; (*pl.*) slices of meat rolled and stuffed.—*a.* brownish-green. **o.-branch,** *n.* offer of peace. **o.-drab,** *a.* (*Amer.*) colour of U.S. service uniform. **o. oil,** oil from olives. **olivaceous,** *a.* olive-green. **olivary,** *a.* olive-shaped, oval. (L. *oliva*)

oliver, *n.* small hammer worked by treadle.

olivine, *n.* chrysolite. (*olive*)

olla podrida, hash, medley, olio. (Sp.=rotten pot)

ology, *n.* (*joc.*) science. (*-logy*)

Olympian, *a.* of Olympus, home of the Greek gods; stately; condescending. —*n.* great person. **olympiad,** *n.* four-year period between Olympic Games. **Olympic,** *a.* of Olympia in Greece, scene of **Olympic Games,** ancient athletic festival revived in 1900 as international meeting.

om, *n.* Hindu symbol equivalent to amen.

omasum, *n.* third stomach of ruminant, manyplies. (L.=tripe)

ombre, *n.* old card game for three. (L. *homo,* man)

ombro-, from Gk. *ombros,* rain, used in **ombrology,** *n.* study of rain; **ombrograph, ombrometer,** *nn.* rain-gauge.

omega, *n.* last letter of Greek alphabet, long o; end. (Gk.)

omelet, omelette, *n.* eggs beaten up and fried with seasoning. (F.)

omen, *n.* sign of coming event, portent.—*v.t.* give warning of. (L.)

omentum, *n.* (*pl.* **omenta**) fold of peritoneum connecting viscera. **omental,** *a.* (L.)

ominous, *a.* of ill omen, foreboding evil; portentous. (*omen*)

omit, *v.t.* leave out; neglect, leave undone. **omission,** *n.* omitting, what is omitted; neglect. **omissive,** *a.* **omittance,** *n.* (*Shake.*). (L. *ob-*+*mittere,* send)

omnibus, *n.* large closed passenger vehicle, bus; volume containing several works, us. by one author.—*a.* embracing several cases or items, inclusive. **omnicompetent,** *a.* having jurisdiction in every matter. **omnifarious, omnigenous,** *aa.* of all kinds. **omnipotent,** *a.* all-powerful, almighty. **omnipotence,** *n.* **omnipresent,** *a.* present everywhere, ubiquitous. **omnipresence,** *n.* **omniscient,** *a.* all-knowing. **omniscience,** *n.* **omnium gatherum,** miscellaneous collection. **omnivorous,** *a.* devouring all things; not fastidious; (*zool.*) eating both animal and vegetable food. (L. *omnis,* all)

omophagous, *a.* eating raw flesh. **omophagia, omophagy,** *nn.* (Gk. *ōmos,* raw; *phagein,* eat)

omoplate, *n.* shoulder-blade. (Gk.)

omphalos, *n.* centre, hub; boss on ancient Greek shield. **omphalic,** *a.* of the navel. **omphalocele,** *n.* umbilical hernia. **omphalotomy,** *n.* dividing of umbilical cord. (Gk.= navel)

on, *prep.* upon; at, near, in direction of; during; concerning, about.—*adv.* forward; functioning; (*sl.*) willing.—*a.* (*cricket*) behind batsman; (*sl.*) tipsy.—*n.* (*cricket*) on side. **on and off,** intermittently. **on high,** in heaven. **on time,** punctually. **on to,** upon. (O.E.)

onager, *n.* wild ass. (Gk. *onos,* ass; *agrios,* wild)

onanism, *n.* masturbation. (*Onan,* person in Bible)

once, *adv.* on one occasion only; formerly; at some time.—*conj.* as soon

as.—*n.* one time. **at o.,** immediately; at the same time. **o. for all,** finally. **o. in a way,** on rare occasions. **o.-over,** *n.* (*Amer.*) preliminary survey. **oncer,** *n.* (*joc.*) person who does thing once. (*one*)
onco-, from Gk. *ongkos,* swelling, used in **oncology,** *n.* science of tumours; **oncotomy,** *n.* incision into tumour.
oncoming, *a.* and *n.* approaching.
oncost, *n.* upkeep and overhead charges of mine, opp. to wages. (*on; cost*)
on dit, piece of gossip. (F.=they say)
ondo-, from L. *unda,* wave, used in **ondograph,** *n.* instrument recording variations in waves of electric current; **ondogram,** *n.* record made by it; **ondometer,** *n.* wave-meter.
one, *a.* single; undivided; the same; a certain.—*n.* unity; single specimen.—*pron.* a person, someone. **all o.,** immaterial. **at o.,** agreed. **o. and all,** every one. **o. by o.,** singly. **o.-eyed,** *a.* (*sl.*) unfair. **o.-horse,** *a.* (*sl.*) paltry. **o.-sided,** *a.* lopsided; partial. **o.-step,** *n.* a ballroom dance. **o.-track,** *a.* with single line of rails; with room for only one idea at a time. **o.-way,** *a.* restricted to one direction. (O.E. *án*)
oneiro-, from Gk. *oneiros,* dream, used in **oneirocritic,** *n.* interpreter of dreams; **oneirology,** *n.* science of dreams; **oneiromancy,** *n.* divination by dreams.
oneness, *n.* unity, singleness, concord.
oner, *n.* remarkable person or thing; severe blow.
onerous, *a.* burdensome, oppressive; troublesome. (*onus*)
oneself, *pron.* refl. form of **one.**
onfall, *n.* attack, onset.
onflow, *n.* onward flow.
onion, *n.* edible bulb with strong flavour; (*sl.*) native of Bermuda. **off one's o.,** (*sl.*) crazy. **flaming o.,** anti-aircraft shell bursting in series of fire-balls designed to set aircraft on fire. **o.-eyed,** *a.* (*Shake.*) tearful. (L. *unio*)
onlooker, *n.* spectator.
only, *a.* single, sole.—*adv.* solely, merely.—*conj.* except that. **one and o.,** unique. (*one*)
onoma-, from Gk.=name, used in **onomancy,** *n.* divination by names; **onomastic,** *a.* of names; **onomasticon,** *n.* list of words, dictionary; **onomatology,** *n.* science of names; **onomatope, onomatop,** *nn.* onomatopoeic word; **onomatopoeia,** *n.* formation of word in imitation of sound, e.g. 'bang,' representation of sense by sound, e.g. 'the moan of doves in immemorial elms.' hence **onomatopoeic, onomatopoetic,** *aa.*
onset, *n.* attack, beginning. (*set*)
onslaught, *n.* onset, fierce attack.
onstead, *n.* (*Scot.*) farmstead. (O.E. *wunian,* dwell; *stede,* place)
onto, *prep.* on to, upon.
onto-, from Gk. *ōn,* being, used in **ontogenesis, ontogeny,** *nn.* life history of individual development, hence **ontogenetic,** *a.*; **ontology,** *n.* science of being or reality, hence **ontological,** *a.*, **ontologist,** *n.*
onus, *n.* burden, responsibility, *o. probandi,* burden of proof. (L.)
onward, *a.* advancing, forward.—*adv.* (also **onwards**) ahead, forward.
onychia, *n.* abscess round finger-nail, whitlow. **onychitis,** *n.* inflammation of nail. (Gk. *onux,* nail)
onym, *n.* scientific name. **onymal,** *a.* **onymous,** *a.* not anonymous. (Gk. *onoma,* name)
onyx, *n.* kind of quartz with layers of different colours. (Gk. *onux*)
oo-, from Gk. *ōon,* egg, used in **oogamous,** *a.* heterogamous; **oogenesis,** *n.* formation of ovum; **oolite,** *n.* granular limestone, (*geol.*) rocks between chalk and Lias, hence **oolitic,** *a.*; **oology,** *n.* study of birds' eggs.
oodles, *n.pl.* (*colloq.*) abundance.
oof, *n.* (*sl.*) money. **oofy,** *a.* rich. (G. *auf dem tische,* on the table)
oolong, *n.* kind of black tea. (Chin. *wu,* black; *lung,* dragon)
oom, *n.* (*S. Afr.*) uncle. (Du.)
oomiak, same as **umiak.**
oont, *n.* (*Anglo-Ind. sl.*) camel. (Hind.)
oorie, *a.* (*Scot.*) chilly, shivering.
ooss, *n.* (*Scot.*) fluff.
oosperm, *n.* fertilized ovum. (*oo-*)
oot, *Scot.* form of out.
ootocous, *a.* egg-laying, oviparous. (Gk. *ōon,* egg; *tokos,* bringing forth)
ooze, *n.* liquid mud, slime; exudation; liquor of tanning-vat.—*v.i.* and *t.* flow slowly out, exude (moisture); leak out or away. **oozy,** *a.* (O.E. *wáse,* mud and *wos,* juice)
op-, form of **ob-** before *p.*
opacity, *n.* opaqueness, obscurity.
opah, *n.* bright-coloured sea-fish like mackerel. (W. Afr.)
opal, *n.* white or bluish stone with changing colours; opaline. **opalescent,** *a.* like opal, iridescent. **opalescence,** *n.* **opaline,** *n.* semi-translucent white glass.—*a.* opalescent. **opalize,** *v.t.* make like opal. (Sanskr. *upala,* gem)
opaque, *a.* not allowing passage of light; obscure; stupid, obtuse. (L. *opacus,* shady)
ope, *v.t.* and *i.* (*poet.*) open.
open, *a.* not shut, unfastened; unfenced, uncovered, clear; spread out, unfolded; accessible, free to all; generous, unprejudiced; frank, not secret; not settled; (of consonant) pronounced without closure of air-passage, e.g. *s, v.*—*v.t.* and *i.* make, become, open; expand, unfold; begin, make start; have opening (into); (of dog) give tongue.—*n.* open space or air. **o. air,** outdoors. **o. book,** easily understood. **o. fire,**

begin shooting. **o. letter,** printed in newspaper but addressed to individual. **o. one's eyes,** surprise; undeceive. **o. out,** expand; speak freely; accelerate. **o. syllable,** ending in vowel. **o. up,** make accessible; reveal. **o. verdict,** without naming criminal. **with o. arms,** cordially. **o.-eyed,** *a.* vigilant. **o.-handed,** *a.* generous. **o.-hearted,** *a.* frank, generous. **o.-work,** *n.* pattern with interstices. (O.E.)

opening, *n.* gap, aperture; beginning; chance.—*a.* initial.

openly, *adv.* frankly; publicly.

opera, *n.* drama set to music. **grand o.,** wholly sung, us. with tragic theme. **comic o.,** light, with dialogue. **o. bouffe,** farcical opera. **o.-cloak,** *n.* lady's evening cloak. **o.-glass,** *n.* small binocular. **o.-house,** *n.* theatre for opera. (L.=work)

operate, *v.i.* and *t.* work, function; produce, effect; perform surgical operation; deal in stocks. **operating theatre,** room in hospital for operations. (L. *operari,* work)

operatic, *a.* of, like, opera.

operation, *n.* action, working; piece of surgery; business transaction; military movement. **operative,** *a.* in force, effective; of, by, surgery.—*n.* factory worker, artisan. **operator,** *n.* one who works machine or conducts operation. (*operate*)

operculum, *n.* gill-cover of fish; lid-like organ of mollusc etc. **opercular,** *a.* **operculate,** *a.* having operculum. (L.=cover)

operetta, *n.* short light opera. (It.)

operose, *a.* laborious; hard-working. (L. *opus,* work)

ophicleide, *n.* keyed brass wind-instrument consisting of tube bent double. (Gk. *ophis,* snake; *kleis,* key)

ophi(o)-, from Gk. *ophis,* snake, used in **ophidian,** *a.* and *n.* (reptile) of the order including snakes; **ophiolatry,** *n.* snake-worship; **ophite,** *n.* serpentine (marble).

ophthalmia, ophthalmitis, *nn.* inflammation of the eyes. **ophthalmic,** *a.* of the eyes; having opthalmia. **ophthalmology,** *n.* science of the eye. **ophthalmologist,** *n.* eye specialist. **ophthalmoscope,** *n.* instrument for examining retina. (Gk. *ophthalmos,* eye)

opiate, *a.* and *n.* (drug) containing opium, for relieving pain or inducing sleep; narcotic.—*v.t.* mix, treat, with opium. (*opium*)

opine, *v.t.* hold, express, opinion (that). **opinion,** *n.* what one thinks about something; belief, judgment; professional advice; (*Shake.*) reputation; self-confidence. **opinionated, opinionative,** *aa.* unduly confident in one's opinions, dogmatic. (L. *opinari*)

opisometer, *n.* instrument for measuring curved lines on map. (Gk. *opisō,* backwards)

opisthograph, *n.* slab, parchment, inscribed on both sides. (Gk. *opisthen,* behind; *graphein,* write)

opium, *n.* narcotic drug got from white poppy.—*v.t.* drug, treat, with it. **o. den,** haunt of opium-smokers. **o.-eater,** *n.* opium addict. **opiumism,** *n.* opium habit. (Gk. *opos,* sap)

opodeldoc, *n.* soap liniment.

opoponax, *n.* gum resin used in medicine and perfumery. (Gk. *opos,* sap; *pas,* all; *akos,* cure)

opossum, *n.* American nocturnal pouched animal; (*Austral.*) phalanger. **play possum,** sham dead. (Amer. Ind.)

oppidan, *n.* townsman; Eton schoolboy boarded in town. (L. *oppidum,* town)

oppilate, *v.t.* (*med.*) block up, obstruct. **oppilation,** *n.* (L. *pilare,* ram)

opponent, *n.* antagonist, adversary.—*a.* opposing. **opponency,** *n.* (*oppose*)

opportune, *a.* well-timed; convenient. **opportunism,** *n.* policy of adapting principles to circumstances. **opportunist,** *n.* time-server. **opportunity,** *n.* favourable chance; convenient time. (L. *opportunus*)

oppose, *v.t.* place in opposition, pit against, place front to front; contend against, resist. **opposable,** *a.* **opposability,** *n.* **opposeless,** *a.* (*poet.*) irresistible. (L. *pausare,* halt + confusion with *ponere,* place)

opposite, *a.* facing; diametrically different, contrary.—*n.* contrary.—*adv.* and *prep.* in opposite position (to). **o. prompter,** (*abbr.* **O.P.**) to actor's left. (L. *ponere,* place)

opposition, *n.* resistance; antithesis; hostility; party opposing government; (*astron.*) diametrically opposite position of two heavenly bodies. **oppositional,** *a.*

oppositive, *a.* adversative; fond of opposing.

oppress, *v.t.* treat unjustly, tyrannize over; weigh down; overwhelm. **oppression,** *n.* oppressing, being oppressed; lassitude. **oppressive,** *a.* tyrannical; burdensome; (of weather) sultry, close. **oppressor,** *n.* (L. *premere,* press)

opprobrium, *n.* reproach; disgrace. **opprobrious,** *a.* abusive; infamous. (L.)

oppugn, *v.t.* reason against, controvert; resist. **oppugnant,** *a.* and *n.* **oppugnancy, oppugnation,** *nn.* (L. *pugnare,* fight)

opsimath, *n.* one who learns late in life. **opsimathy,** *n.* (Gk. *opse,* late; *manthanein,* learn)

opso-, from Gk. *opson,* cooked meat, used in **opsomania,** *n.* morbid liking for some special food; **opsonin,** *n.* substance of blood serum making bacteria vulnerable to phagocytic action, hence **opsonic,** *a.*, **opsonology,** *n.*

opt, *v.i.* exercise option, make choice. **optative,** *a.* (*gram.*) expressing wish. —*n.* optative mood or form of verb. (L. *optare,* choose)

optic, *a.* (*anat.*) of eye or sight.—*n.* (*joc.*) eye; (*pl.*) science of vision and laws of light. **optical,** *a.* visual; aiding sight; of, according to, optics. **optician,** *n.* maker, seller, of optical instruments, esp. spectacles. (Gk. *optikos*)

optimism, *n.* disposition to look on bright side; (*philos.*) doctrine that this is the best possible world; belief that good must ultimately prevail over evil. **optimist,** *n.* hopeful person; adherent of optimism. **optimistic, optimistical,** *aa.* (L. *optimus,* best)

optimum, *n.* best, most favourable, condition. (L. *optimus,* best)

option, *n.* choice, right of choosing; purchased right of acquiring stock etc. at fixed price and within certain period. **local o.,** right of district to decide to what extent alcohol is to be sold in it. **optional,** *a.* not obligatory. (*opt*)

optometer, *n.* eye-testing instrument. **optophone,** *n.* instrument converting light into sound, and so enabling blind to read print by ear. (*optic*)

opulent, *a.* wealthy; luxuriant, copious. **opulence,** *n.* riches, abundance. (L. *ops.* plenty)

opus, *n.* (*abbr.* **op.**) musician's separate composition. *magnum o.,* writer's chief work. **opuscule,** *n.* minor work. (L.=work)

or, *n.* (*heraldry*) gold. (L. *aurum*)

or, *conj.* introducing alternative; (*Shake.*) either. (M.E. *other*)

or, *prep.* and *conj.* (*arch.*) ere, before. **or ever,** (*poet.*) before. (O.E. *ár*)

ora pro nobis, pray for us. (L.)

orach, *n.* mountain spinach. (Gk. *atraphaxus*)

oracle, *n.* place where ancient Greeks consulted a deity; response given (often ambiguous); priest giving it; holy of holies; divine revelation; guide supposed infallible; wise advice or adviser. **work the o.,** arrange things by wirepulling. **oracular,** *a.* prophetic; obscure, ambiguous; dogmatic, sententious. **oracularity,** *n.* (L. *oraculum*)

oral, *a.* spoken, verbal; (*anat.*) of mouth. (L. *os,* mouth)

orange, *n.* round juicy golden fruit; tree bearing it; its colour.—*a.* reddish-yellow. **mock o.,** syringa. **oo. and lemons,** a children's game. **o.-blossom,** *n.* worn by bride. **orangeade,** *n.* drink made with orange juice. **orangery,** *n.* hothouse for growing oranges; orange garden. (Arab. *naranj,* with *n* dropped)

Orangeman, *n.* member of Irish Protestant party, named after William of Orange. **Orange,** *a.* **orangism,** *n.*

orang-outang, orang-utan, *n.* large long-armed manlike E. Indian ape. (Malay=man of the woods)

oration, *n.* formal or public speech. **direct, indirect, o.,** (*gram.*) report in actual words used, in third person. **orate,** *v.i.* (*joc.*) hold forth. **orator,** *n.* eloquent, public, or official speaker. (L. *oratio*)

oratorian, *a.* and *n.* (member) of the Oratory.

oratorical, *a.* of oratory, rhetorical.

oratorio, *n.* sacred story set to music but without scenery, costumes, or acting. (It.)

oratory, *n.* art of public speaking; eloquence; small chapel for private prayer. **the O.,** a Roman Catholic religious society. (L. *orare,* pray)

oratress, *n.* female orator.

orb, *n.* sphere, globe; golden globe with cross forming part of regalia; (*poet.*) eyeball. **orbed,** *a.* rounded; bearing orb. **orbicular, orbiculate,** *aa.* ring-shaped; spherical. **orbit,** *n.* path of one celestial body round another; sphere of action; eye-socket. **orbital,** *a.* (L. *orbis,* circle)

orc, orca, *n.* grampus; killer-whale; sea-monster. (L. *orca*)

Orcadian, *a.* and *n.* (inhabitant) of Orkney. (L. *Orcades,* Orkneys)

orchard, *n.* garden of fruit-trees. **orchardman, orchardist,** *nn.* fruit-grower. (O.E. *ortgeard*)

orchestic, *a.* of dancing.—*n.pl.* art of dancing. (Gk. *orcheisthai,* dance)

orchestra, *n.* band of musicians; place for it in theatre; place in ancient Greek theatre where chorus danced and sang. **orchestral,** *a.* **orchestrate,** *v.t.* arrange (music) for performance by orchestra. **orchestration,** *n.* **orchestrina, orchestrion,** *nn.* large automatic barrel-organ. (Gk.)

orchid, *n.* kinds of exotic plant with showy flower. **orchidaceous,** *a.* **orchidist,** *n.* collector of orchids. **orchis,** *n.* wild English orchid. (Gk.)

orchil, *n.* red or violet dye from lichen. (O.F. *orchel*)

orchitis, *n.* inflammation of testicles. (Gk. *orchis,* testicle)

orcin, *n.* substance from lichens yielding dye. (*orchil*)

ordain, *v.t.* decree, enact; admit to holy orders, appoint as minister. **ordainment,** *n.* (L. *ordo,* order)

ordeal, *n.* ancient form of trial by fire, water, poison, combat etc., endurance being taken as proof of innocence; severe trial, searching experience. (O.E. *ordál*)

order, *n.* relative position, sequence; method, tidiness; rules of procedure; efficient state; class, group, sort; style of architecture; honour or decoration, possessors of this; friendly society; religious fraternity; grade of Christian ministry; form of divine service; request to supply goods; (*bot., zool.*) divisions between class and family or genus.—*v.t.* arrange, dispose; command, prescribe; send for (goods). **by o.,** by authoritative command. **holy oo.,** bishop, priest, or deacon; ministry. **in o.,** according to rule; relevant. **in oo.,** ordained. **keep o.,** prevent disturbance. **lower oo.,** working classes. **o. about,** dictate to. **o. arms,** hold rifle vertically with butt on ground. **O. in Council,** order by sovereign with Privy Council's advice. **oo. of the day,** day's programme. **postal o.,** kind of post-office cheque. **standing oo.,** rules of parliamentary procedure. **take o.,** (*Shake.*) take measures. **take oo.,** be ordained. (L. *ordo*)

orderly, *a.* methodical, tidy; not unruly.—*n.* soldier attending officer; hospital attendant. **o. room,** business room of barracks.

ordinal, *a.* showing position in series. —*n.* ordinal number, e.g. 'fifth'; ordination ceremony or service-book. (*order*)

ordinance, *n.* decree, enactment; religious rite. (*ordain*)

ordinary, *a.* normal, usual, average; commonplace, plain.—*n.* archbishop in province, bishop in diocese; prescribed form of service; meal at fixed price and time, inn providing this; (*heraldry*) one of the simple charges. **in o.,** by permanent appointment. **Lords O.,** (*Scot.*) judges of outer house of Court of Session. **o. seaman,** (*abbr.* **O.S.**) one not fully skilled. **out of the o.,** exceptional. (L. *ordo*, order)

ordinate, *n.* (*geom.*) one of the coordinates of a point. (L.=parallel)

ordination, *n.* classification; admission to ministry. **ordinee,** *n.* newly ordained deacon. (*ordain*)

ordnance, *n.* big guns, artillery; military stores. **o. survey,** official geographical survey of British Isles. (=*ordinance*)

Ordovician, *a.* (*geol.*) of period between Cambrian and Silurian. (L. *Ordovices*, a Welsh tribe)

ordure, *n.* dung; obscenity. (L. *horridus*, rough)

ore, *n.* native mineral yielding metal; (*poet.*) precious metal.

oread, *n.* mountain nymph. (Gk. *oros*, mountain)

orectic, *a.* appetitive. (Gk. *oregein*, stretch out)

oreide, same as **oroide.**

oreography, oreology, same as **orography, orology.**

orfe, *n.* kind of goldfish. (Gk. *orphos*, sea-perch)

orfray, same as **orphrey.**

organ, *n.* member of animal or plant performing vital function; medium of opinion, journal; keyboard wind-instrument with pipes and stops. **American o.,** harmonium. **o.-blower,** *n.* working organ bellows. **o.-grinder,** *n.* player of barrel-organ. **o.-loft,** *n.* gallery for organ. (Gk. *organon*, tool)

organdie, *n.* light transparent muslin. (F. *organdi*)

organic, *a.* structural; organized; having vital organs; (*chem.*) of, derived from, living organisms; (*med.*) of, affecting, organ of body. **organism,** *n.* organized body; animal, plant. **organist,** *n.* organ-player. **organize,** *v.t.* furnish with organs; make into living tissue; give definite structure to, systematize; get up, arrange. **organization,** *n.* organizing; organized body, association.

organon, organum, *n.* method of thought, logical system. (Gk.=tool)

organotherapy, *n.* treatment of disease with organic extracts. (Gk. *therapeia*, service)

organzine, *n.* strong silk thread with double twist. (It. *organzino*)

orgasm, *n.* emotional paroxysm, esp. in coition. **orgastic,** *a.* (Gk. *orgaein*, swell)

orgeat, *n.* barley-water flavoured with almonds. (L. *hordeum*, barley)

orgy, *n.* drunken carousal, debauch. **orgiastic,** *a.* (Gk. *orgia*, Bacchic rites)

oricalche, *n.* (*Spens.*) alloy like brass. (Gk. *oros*, mountain; *chalkos*, copper)

oriel, *n.* projecting angular recess with window; the window. (O.F. *oriol*)

orient, *n.* east; eastern lands, Asia; lustre of finest pearls.—*a.* rising, being born; lustrous, brilliant; (*poet.*) oriental.—*v.t.* lay out (church) with altar end eastwards; take bearings of. **o. oneself,** see how one stands. **oriental,** *a.* and *n.* (inhabitant) of the East. **orientalism,** *n.* eastern culture. **orientalist,** *n.* expert in eastern languages and history. **orientalize,** *v.t.* **orientate,** *v.t.* orient. **orientation,** *n.* (L. *oriri*, rise)

orifice, *n.* opening, mouth, of pipe etc. (L. *os*, mouth; *facere*, make)

oriflamme, *n.* ancient French standard, red with streamers; party symbol; blaze of colour. (L. *aurum*, gold; *flamma*, flame)

origan, origanum, *n.* wild marjoram. (Gk. *origanon*)

origin, *n.* starting-point, beginning; birth, parentage. **original,** *a.* earliest, primitive; first-hand, new; inventive, creative.—*n.* picture etc. from which copy, book from which translation, is made; eccentric person. **original sin,** innate sin inherited from Adam. **originality,** *n.* **originate,** *v.t.* and *i.* bring into being, initiate; take rise. **origination, originator,** *nn.* **originative,** *a.* (L. *origo*)

orinasal, *a.* and *n.* (vowel) sounded with both mouth and nose. (L. *os*, mouth; *nasus*, nose)

oriole, *n.* kinds of yellow black-winged bird. (L. *aureus*, golden)

orison, *n.* (*arch.*) prayer. (O.F.)

Orleans, *n.* a purple plum; fabric of worsted and cotton. (city)

orlop, *n.* lowest deck of ship with three or more decks. (Du. *overloop*, covering)

ormer, *n.* a mollusc, sea-ear. (F. *oreille-de-mer*, ear of sea)

ormolu, *n.* gilded bronze; alloy imitating gold; articles of these.—*a.* (*navy sl.*) gorgeous. (F. *or moulu*, ground gold)

ornament, *n.* decoration; decorative object, vase, jewel etc.; embellishment; (*pl.*) church accessories—*v.t.* adorn, beautify. **ornamental,** *a.* **ornamentalist,** *n.* decorator. **ornamentation,** *n.* (L. *ornare*, adorn)

ornate, *a.* richly adorned; (of style) highly elaborate. (L. *ornare*, adorn)

ornery, *a.* (*Amer. dial.*) of bad disposition, hard to manage. (*ordinary*)

ornitho-, from Gk. *ornis*, bird, used in **ornithoid,** *a.* birdlike ; **ornithology,** *n.* study of birds, hence **ornithological** *a.*, **ornithologist,** *n.*; **ornithomancy,** *n.* divination by birds; **ornithopter,** *n.* flying-machine with flapping wings; **ornithorhyncus,** *n.* duck-billed platypus. **ornithoscopy,** *n.* augury.

oro-, from Gk. *oros*, mountain, used in **orogeny,** *n.* formation of mountains; **orography,** *n.* geography of mountains, hence **orographic, orographical,** *aa.*; **orohippus,** *n.* fossil ancestor of horse; **orology,** *n.* study of mountains, hence **orological,** *a.*; **orometer,** *n.* barometer giving height above sea-level.

oroide, *n.* gold-coloured alloy. (L. *aurum*, gold. Gk. *eidos*, form)

orotund, *a.* (of voice) full, resonant; (of style) pompous, high-flown. (L. *ore rotundo*, with round mouth)

orphan, *n.* and *a.* (child) bereaved of one or both parents.—*v.t.* render orphan. **orphanage,** *n.* institution for orphans; orphanhood. (Gk. *orphanos*, bereaved)

Orphean, *a.* of Orpheus; like his music, melodious. **Orphic,** *a.* of Orpheus or his cult, mystical. **Orphism,** *n.*

orphrey, *n.* gold-embroidered band on cope etc. (L. *aurum*, gold; *Phrygius*, Phrygian)

orpiment, *n.* yellow compound of arsenic, used as pigment. (L. *aurum*, gold; *pigmentum*, pigment)

orpine, orpin, *n.* a purple-flowered plant. (F.)

Orpington, *n.* a breed of poultry. (village)

orra, *a.* (*Scot.*) odd, not matched. **o. man,** man of all work.

orrery, *n.* moving model of solar system. (Earl of *Orrery*)

orris, *n.* kind of iris. **o.-root,** *n.* used in perfumery and medicine.

orris, *n.* kinds of gold or silver lace.

ort, *n.* (us. *pl.*) leavings after meal, scraps.

orthocephalic, orthocephalous, *aa.* with skull of medium proportions, between brachycephalic and dolichocephalic. (Gk. *orthos*, right; *kephalē*, head)

orthochromatic, *a.* (*phot.*) giving correct relative tones to colours, isochromatic. (Gk. *orthos*, right; *chrōma*, colour)

orthoclase, *n.* potash feldspar. **orthoclastic,** *a.* having cleavage at right angles. (Gk. *orthos*, right; *klaein*, cleave)

orthodox, *a.* correct in opinion or doctrine; not heretical; generally accepted, conventional. **O. Church,** eastern branch of Catholic Church with centre at Constantinople. **orthodoxy,** *n.* orthodoxness. (Gk. *orthos*, right; *doxa*, opinion)

orthodromy, *n.* navigation by great circle. (Gk. *orthos*, straight; *dromos*, course)

orthoepy, *n.* science of correct pronunciation. **orthoepic,** *a.* **orthoepist,** *n.* (Gk. *orthos*, right; *epos*, word)

orthogenesis, *n.* evolution following a definite line, determinate variation. **orthogenetic,** *a.* (Gk. *orthos*, right; *genesis*, birth)

orthognathous, *a.* having upright jaw, neither receding nor protruding. (Gk. *orthos*, straight; *gnathos*, jaw)

orthogon, *n.* rectangular figure. **orthogonal,** *a.* rectangular. (Gk. *orthos*, right; *gōnia*, angle)

orthography, *n.* spelling, science of spelling; map projection with point of sight supposed infinitely distant. **orthographic, orthographical,** *aa.* **orthographer,** *n.* (Gk. *orthos*, right; *graphein*, write)

orthopaedy, orthopaedics, *nn.* curing of deformities, esp. in children. **orthopaedic,** *a.* **orthopaedist,** *n.* (Gk. *orthos*, right; *pais*, child)

orthophony, *n.* correct speaking; voice culture. (Gk. *orthos*, right; *phōnē*, voice)

orthopterous, *a.* with wings folded down the back, as in grasshoppers. (Gk. *orthos*, right; *pteron*, wing)

orthoptic, *a.* of correct seeing.—*n.* peep-sight of rifle. (Gk. *orthos*, right; *optikos*, of sight)

orthotropism, *n.* vertical growth in plants. **orthotropal, orthotropous,** *aa.* (Gk. *orthos*, straight; *trepein*, turn)

ortolan, *n.* garden bunting; (*Amer.*) bobolink. (L. *hortus*, garden)

ortyx, *n.* American partridge or quail. (Gk. *ortux*, quail)

oryx, *n.* straight-horned African antelope. (Gk. *orux*)

os, *n.* (*pl. ossa*) bone. (L.)

oscillate, *v.i.* swing to and fro; waver, vacillate; (*wireless*) set up disturbing wave-motion. **oscillation, oscillator,** *nn.* **oscillatory,** *a.* (L. *oscillare*, swing)

oscitation, *n.* yawning, dullness; negligence. (L. *oscitare*, gape)

osculate, *v.t.* and *i.* (of species) have features in common; (*geom.*) make contact (with); (*joc.*) kiss. **osculant,** *a.* osculating. **oscular,** *a.* (*joc.*) of, for, kissing. **osculation,** *n.* **osculatory,** *a.* (L. *osculum*, kiss)

-ose, *adj.suf.* full of, as in **jocose.** (L. *-osus*)

osier, *n.* willow used in basket-work; shoot of it.—*a.* of osier. (F.)

Osmanli, *a.* and *n.* Ottoman. (Turk.)

osmium, *n.* a greyish metal, the heaviest substance known. **osmic,** *a.* (Gk. *osmē*, smell)

osmo-, from Gk. *osmē*, smell, used in **osmology,** *n.* scientific study of smells; **osmometry,** *n.* measurement of smells.

osmosis, osmose, *n.* percolation and intermixture of fluids separated by porous membrane. **osmotic,** *a.* (Gk. *ōthein*, push)

osmund, *n.* the flowering fern.

osprey, *n.* large bird of prey, sea-eagle; egret's plume.

osseous, *a.* of bone, bony. **ossicle,** *n.* small bone, esp. of ear. **ossifrage,** *n.* lammergeyer. **ossify,** *v.t.* and *i.* form, change, into bone; harden, grow rigid or unprogressive. **ossification,** *n.* **ossuary,** *n.* charnel-house, bone-urn. (L. *os*, bone)

osteal, *a.* osseous. **osteitis,** *n.* inflammation of bone. (Gk. *osteon*, bone)

ostensible, *a.* pretended, professed, used as a blind. **ostensory,** *n.* receptacle for displaying the host, monstrance. **ostent,** *n.* (*Shake.*) display. **ostentation,** *n.* showing off; pretentious display, parade. **ostentatious,** *a.* (L. *ostendere*, show)

osteo-, from Gk. *osteon*, bone, used in **osteogenesis,** *n.* formation of bone; **osteography,** *n.* descriptive osteology; **osteoid,** *a.* bone-like; **osteology,** *n.* anatomy of bones; bony structure; **osteoma,** *n.* bone tumour; **osteomalacia,** *n.* softening of bones; **osteopath,** *n.* bone-setter; **osteopathy,** *n.* manipulative surgery; **osteophone,** *n.* instrument enabling deaf to hear through cranial bones.

ostiary, *n.* church door-keeper. (L. *ostium*, door)

ostler, *n.* stableman at inn. (*hostel*)

ostracize, *v.t.* banish from society, send to Coventry. **ostracism,** *n.* (Gk. *ostrakizein*, banish by popular vote)

ostreiculture, *n.* oyster-breeding. **ostreoid,** *a.* oyster-like. **ostreophagous,** *a.* eating oysters. (Gk. *ostreon*, oyster)

ostrich, *n.* large swift-running flightless African bird, prized for its feathers. **digestion like o.,** very strong. **o. policy,** self-delusive one. (Gk. *strouthos*)

otacoustic *a.* and *n.* (instrument) aiding hearing. **otalgia,** *n.* earache. (Gk. *ous*, ear; *akouein*, hear; *algos*, pain)

other, *a.* different; distinct in kind; alternative, additional.—*pron.* other person or thing.—*adv.* otherwise. **every o.,** each alternate. **the o. day,** quite recently. **the o. world,** future life. **o.-guess,** *a.* of another kind. **o.-worldly,** *a.* spiritual; unworldly. **otherness,** *n.* diversity. **otherwhere,** *adv.* elsewhere. **otherwhile,** *adv.* (*arch.*) at another time. **otherwise,** *adv.* in another manner; if not, else. (O.E.)

otic, *a.* of the ear. **otitis,** *n.* inflammation of ear. (Gk. *ous*, ear)

otiose, *a.* superfluous, serving no practical purpose; at leisure. *otium cum dignitate*, dignified leisure. (L. *otium*, leisure)

oto-, from Gk. *ous*, ear, used in **otolith,** *n.* chalky concretion in ear; **otology,** *n.* science of the ear; **otoscope,** *n.* instrument for examining inner ear.

ottava rima, stanza of eight five-foot lines rhyming abababcc, as in Byron's 'Don Juan.' (It.)

otter, *n.* fish-eating animal like weasel; its dark-brown fur; kind of fishing tackle. (O.E. *oter*)

otto, same as **attar.**

Ottoman, *a.* of dynasty or empire founded by Othman, Turkish.—*n.* Turk; backless cushioned settee.

oubit, same as **woobut.**

oubliette, *n.* dungeon with entrance in roof. (F. *oublier*, forget)

ouch, *n.* clasp, jewel; setting of gem. (O.H.G. *nuscha*, with loss of *n*, *a nouch* being taken as *an ouch*)

ouch, *int.* of pain or annoyance.

ought, *v.i.* be bound, be obliged (to). (O.E. *ahte*, owed)

ought, *n.* (*vulg.*) nought, cipher.

ought, same as **aught.**

ouija, *n* (also **o.-board**) board with letters and symbols used to obtain messages at seances. (F. *oui*, yes. G. *ja*, yes)

ounce, *n* (*abbr.* **oz.**) unit of weight, $\frac{1}{16}$ lb. avoirdupois, $\frac{1}{12}$ lb. troy; small amount. **fluid o.** $\frac{1}{20}$ pint. (L. *uncia*)

ounce, *n.* snow-leopard; (*poet.*) lynx or animal like it. (L. *lyncea*, O.F. *lonce* being misdivided as *l'once*)

our, *a.* belonging to us. **ours,** *pron.* and *a.* our (one). **ourselves,** *pron.* emphatic and refl. form of we (**ourself,** *sing.*, used in regal style). (O.E. *ūre*, of us)

ourie, same as **oorie.**

-ous, *adj.suf.* full of, as in **joyous;** (*chem.*) containing in lower proportion, as in **ferrous,** opp. to ferric. L. *-osus*)

ousel, same as **ouzel.**

oust, *v.t.* expel, esp. by underhand means; seize place of. **ouster,** *n.*

(*law*) dispossession. (O.F. *oster*, take away)
out, *adv.* not in; from within, away; in the open; at an end; in error; in revolt, on strike; (of girl) introduced to society; (*cricket*) no longer batting. —*prep.* out of; outside.—*n.* one out of office.—*v.t.* put, knock, out.—*int.* begone; (*arch.*) fie. **all o.,** striving hard. **down and o.,** ruined. **o. and away,** by far. **o. and o.,** thorough; completely. **o. for, to,** striving for, to. **o. of,** from within; outside; beyond; because of; by use of. **o. of hand,** at once; out of control. **o. of it,** neglected; mistaken. **o. of one's mind,** mad. **o. of sorts,** indisposed. **o. upon,** (*Shake.*) confound. **o. with it,** say it openly. (O.E. *út*)
out-, *pref.* out, outside, as in **outroot, outpost**; more, longer, as in **outnumber, outlive.**
out-at-elbows, *a.* threadbare; needy.
outback, *n.* (*Austral.*) more remote settlements, back-country.
outbalance, *v.t.* exceed in weight.
outbid, *v.t.* bid higher than.
outboard, *a.* outside of ship.
outbrave, *v.t.* excel in bravery; defy.
outbreak, *n.* breaking out; outburst.
outbuilding, *n.* detached subsidiary building.
outburst, *n.* bursting out; forcible expression of feeling.
outcast, *a.* and *n.* homeless and friendless (person); vagabond.
outcaste, *n.* one who has lost caste, pariah.—*v.t.* expel from caste.
outclass, *v.t.* surpass, excel, widely.
outcome, *n.* upshot, consequence.
outcrop, *n.* emergence of stratum; edge of it appearing at surface.
outcry, *n.* cry of distress or alarm, clamour; strong protest.
outdistance, *v.t.* get well ahead of.
outdo, *v.t.* surpass, do more than.
outdoor, *a.* open-air. **o. relief,** to people not resident in workhouse. **outdoors,** *adv.* in the open air.—*n.* outdoor world.
outer, *a.* further from centre or inside; external.—*n.* outer circle of target, hit on this. **o. man,** personal appearance. **o. world,** beyond one's own circle. **outermost,** *a.* farthest outward. (*out*)
outface, *v.t.* stare down or out of countenance; defy.
outfall, *n.* mouth of river or sewer.
outfield, *n.* outlying land; (*cricket*) ground, fielders, farthest from pitch.
out-fighting, *n.* boxing at arm's length.
outfit, *n.* equipment; (*Amer.*) gang of workmen, army company. **outfitter,** *n.* supplier of equipment; draper.
outflank, *v.t.* get round side of (enemy); circumvent.
outflow, *n.* what flows out.
outgeneral, *v.t.* outdo in strategy.
outgo, *v.t.* surpass.—*n.* expenditure. **outgoing,** *a.* departing.—*n.* outlay.
outgrow, *v.t.* become too big for; grow taller than; grow out of. **outgrowth,** *n.* offshoot.
outhouse, *n.* shed etc. adjoining main house.
outing, *n.* excursion, airing.
outjockey, *v.t.* overreach.
outlandish, *a.* foreign, strange; barbarous.
outlast, *v.t.* last longer than.
outlaw, *v.t.* deprive of protection of law.—*n.* outlawed person, bandit; social outcast. **outlawry,** *n.* being outlawed.
outlay, *n.* expenditure.
outlet, *n.* way out, vent.
outline, *n.* contour line, boundary; unshaded sketch; summary; (*pl.*) main features.—*v.t.* draw, describe, in outline.
outlive, *v.t.* live longer than, survive.
outlook, *n.* prospect, view; point of view.
outlying, *a.* detached; remote.
outmanœuvre, *v.t.* outdo in tactics.
outmarch, *v.t.* march faster or farther than.
outmatch, *v.t.* be more than match for.
outmost, *a.* outermost.
outness, *n.* (*philos.*) externality; objectivity.
outnumber, *v.t.* exceed in number.
out-of-the-way, *a.* uncommon; secluded.
outpace, *v.t.* be quicker than.
out-patient, *n.* one treated at, but not lodged in, hospital.
outpeer, *v.t.* (*Shake.*) surpass.
outpost, *n.* post, detachment, at distance from main body.
outpouring, *n.* effusion, emotional speech.
output, *n.* goods produced.
outrage, *n.* gross violation of right or decency; injurious violence; rape. —*v.t.* do violence to, injure, shock; ravish. **outrageous,** *a.* flagrant, monstrous, atrocious. (L. *ultra*, beyond)
outrange, *v.t.* have longer range than.
outré, *a.* outraging decorum, eccentric; extravagant. (F.)
out-relief, *n.* outdoor relief.
outride, *v.t.* ride faster or farther than; keep afloat through (storm). **outrider,** *n.* mounted servant attending carriage.
outrigger, *n.* projecting spar for sail etc.; projection with float to prevent canoe from capsizing; outboard support for rowlock, boat with this.
outright, *adv.* openly; at once; entirely.—*a.* downright, thorough.
outrival, *v.t.* surpass, excel.
outrun, *v.t.* run faster than; exceed, go beyond. **o. the constable,** let expenses exceed income.
outsail, *v.t.* sail faster than.
outset, *n.* start, beginning.
outshine, *v.t.* outdo in brilliance.
outside, *n.* external part, surface;

outward aspect.—*a.* external, outer; outdoor.—*adv.* on, to, the outside; not inside.—*prep.* on exterior, beyond limits, of; apart from. **at the o.,** at the utmost. **outsider,** *n.* non-member; horse not known to have chance in race; (*sl.*) bounder.

outskirts, *n.pl.* outer border, fringe.

outsmart, *v.t.* (*Amer.*) outwit.

outspan, *v.t.* and *i.* (*S.Afr.*) unharness (oxen); encamp.—*n.* halting-place.

outspoken, *a.* frank, blunt.

outstanding, *a.* prominent, conspicuous; still to be done; (of debt) unsettled.

outstay, *v.t.* stay longer than. **o. one's welcome,** stay too long.

outstrip, *v.t.* outrun, leave behind; surpass. (obs. *strip,* run)

out-talk, *v.t.* talk down.

outvie, *v.t.* surpass in competition.

outvote, *v.t.* defeat by number of votes. **out-voter,** *n.* non-resident voter.

outward, *a.* directed towards outside; external; bodily.—*adv.* towards outside.—*n.* outside. **o. bound,** sailing from port. **o. man,** body; (*joc.*) clothes. **outwardly,** *adv.* externally. **outwardness,** *n.* external existence; objectivity. **outwards,** *adv.* outward.

outwatch, *v.t.* keep awake longer than.

outwear, *v.t.* outlast; wear out.

outweigh, *v.t.* count for more than, exceed in value.

outwin, *v.t.* (*Spens.*) get out of.

outwit, *v.t.* get the better of by cunning, overreach.

outwith, *prep.* (*Scot.*) outside of.

outwork, *n.* outlying defensive work; work done outside factory.

outworn, *a.* worn out, hackneyed.

ouzel, *n.* kinds of small bird; blackbird. (O.E. *ósle*)

ova, see **ovum.**

oval, *a.* egg-shaped; elliptical.—*n.* oval curve. **the O.,** Surrey cricket ground in London. (*ovum*)

ovary, *n.* female reproductive organ, producing ova or eggs. **ovarian,** *a.* **ovariotomy,** *n.* removal of ovary or tumour in it. **ovaritis,** *n.* inflammation of ovary. (*ovum*)

ovate, *a.* (*bot.*) oval.

ovation, *n.* burst of applause; enthusiastic reception; minor Roman triumph. (L. *ovare,* exult)

oven, *n.* chamber in contact with fire for baking or heating. **o.-bird,** *n.* kind with dome-shaped nest. (O.E. *ofn*)

over, *prep.* higher than; on the (whole) surface of; across; concerning; more than.—*adv.* above; across; in every part; completed; in addition; too.—*n.* (*cricket*) number of balls (now eight) bowled before changing ends. **o. again,** once more. **o. against,** opposite to. **o. and above,** besides. **o. and o.** (again), repeatedly. **o. head and ears,** completely. **o. one's head,** without consulting him; beyond his comprehension. **o. the top,** emerging to attack. **o. the way,** across the street. (O.E. *ofer*)

over-, *pref.* in excess, too much, as in **overwork**; above, as in **overcoat.**

overact, *v.t.* and *i.* act in exaggerated manner, overdo part.

overall, *n.* loose working garment.—*adv.* (*Spens.*) over whole surface.

overarch, *v.t.* and *i.* form arch (over).

overarm, *a.* (*cricket*) with arm raised above shoulder.

overawe, *v.t.* restrain by awe, daunt.

overbalance, *v.i.* and *t.* fall over; upset; outweigh.—*n.* surplus.

overbear, *v.t.* dominate, repress, bear down. **overbearing,** *a.* domineering.

overboard, *adv.* over side of ship into water. **throw o.,** discard.

overbold, *a.* foolhardy, rash; insolent.

overbrim, *v.t.* and *i.* overflow; be too full.

overburden, *v.t.* load too heavily.

overcall, *v.t.* and *i.* (*bridge*) bid more on (hand) than it is worth; take bid away from (partner).

over-capitalize, *v.t.* float (company) with too great a capital.

overcast, *v.t.* cover with cloud; stitch over edge of.—*a.* cloudy.

overcharge, *v.t.* and *i.* overload, fill to excess; demand too high price (from).—*n.* excessive or exorbitant charge.

overcoat, *n.* outdoor coat worn over other.

overcolour, *v.t.* exaggerate details of.

overcome, *v.t.* and *i.* prevail over; master, surmount; be victorious.—*p.p.* exhausted, deprived of self-control.

over-compensation, *n.* (*psycho-anal.*) excess of compensation, often resulting in overbearing manner.

overcrop, *v.t.* exhaust (land) by excessive cultivation.

overdight, *v.t.* (*Spens.*) deck all over.

overdo, *v.t.* do to excess; overact; cook too much. **o. it,** overtax one's strength.

overdose, *n.* excessive dose.

overdraft, *n.* overdrawing, amount overdrawn, at bank.

overdraw, *v.t.* and *i.* draw cheque in excess of (credit balance); exaggerate in describing.

overdress, *v.t.* and *i.* dress too showily.

overdrive, *v.t.* drive too hard, overtax.

overdue, *a.* behind time; in arrears.

overeat, *v.i.* and *refl.* eat too much.

overestimate, *v.t.* put value or amount of too high.—*n.* excessive estimate.

overflow, *v.t.* and *i.* flow over, flood; exceed bounds (of); be filled abundantly (with).—*n.* overflowing; surplus, excess. **o. meeting,** for those excluded from main meeting.

overgo, *v.t.* exceed; overcome.

overgrow, *v.t.* and *i.* cover with growth; grow too big or fast (for);

outgrow. **overgrown,** *a.* rank; ungainly. **overgrowth,** *n.*
overhand, *a.* and *adv.* (struck, made) with hand above shoulder.
overhang, *v.t.* and *i.* jut, project (over). —*n.* projecting part.
overhaul, *v.t.* examine and set in order; overtake.—*n.* repair.
overhead, *adv.* above, aloft; on floor above.—*a.* placed overhead.—*n.* (also **o. charges**) general expenses that do not vary with output or profit.
overhear, *v.t.* hear accidentally or when not meant to.
overjoyed, *a.* highly delighted.
overladen, *a.* too heavily loaded.
overlaid, *p.p.* of **overlay.**
overland, *adv.* and *a.* by land, not sea.
overlap, *v.t.* and *i.* partly cover; extend over and beyond; partly coincide.
overlay, *v.t.* cover with coating, spread over; (incorrectly) overlie.—*n.* coating.
overleaf, *adv.* on the other side of leaf of book.
overleap, *v.t.* surmount; skip, omit.
overlie, *v.t.* lie on top of; stifle (baby) thus.
overload, *v.t.* overburden; (*electr.*) charge with too much current.
overlook, *v.t.* have view over; oversee; fail to notice; slight; excuse; cast spell upon.
overlord, *n.* supreme lord, suzerain.
overman, *n.* superman; foreman.
overmantel, *n.* mirror over mantelpiece, with shelves for ornaments.
overmaster, *v.t.* dominate wholly, overpower.
overmatch, *v.t.* be too strong for.—*n.* superior in strength or skill.
overmuch, *adv.* and *a.* too much.
over-nice, *a.* too particular.
overnight, *adv.* on, during, previous night; through the night.
overpass, *v.t.* pass beyond, overstep; surpass. **overpast,** *a.* gone by.
over-persuade, *v.t.* persuade (person) against his judgment.
overpitch, *v.t.* (*cricket*) bowl so that ball pitches too near wicket.
overplus, *n.* surplus, excess.
overpower, *v.t.* bear down by superior force, subdue; overwhelm.
overproduction, *n.* production in excess of demand.
over-proof, *a.* containing more alcohol than proof spirit contains.
overrate, *v.t.* estimate too highly.
overreach, *v.t.* and *i.* extend beyond; circumvent, outwit; (of horse) strike forefoot with hind hoof. **o. oneself,** fail through trying too much or being too subtle.
override, *v.t.* trample down; set aside; annul; ride too much; (of fractured bone) overlap.
overrule, *v.t.* set aside by superior authority; prevail over.
overrun, *v.t.* swarm over, infest; ravage; exceed (limit).
oversea, overseas, *adv.* and *a.* across or beyond sea.
oversee, *v.t.* superintend. **overseer,** *n.* supervisor.
overset, *v.t.* and *i.* upset; overthrow.
overshadow, *v.t.* throw shade over; outshine.
overshoe, *n.* galosh.
overshoot, *v.t.* send, go, beyond. **o. the mark, oneself,** go too far; exaggerate. **overshot wheel,** turned by water flowing on it from above.
overside, *adv.* and *a.* over the side of ship.
oversight, *n.* failing to notice; slip, inadvertence; supervision.
overslaugh, *n.* passing over ordinary military duty because of special one. (Du. *overslaan,* omit)
oversleep, *v.i.* and *refl.* sleep beyond intended time.
overspread, *v.t.* cover surface of.
overstate, *v.t.* state too strongly, exaggerate. **overstatement,** *n.*
overstep, *v.t.* exceed, transgress.
overstock, *v.t.* lay in too large a stock of or for, glut.
overstrung, *a.* too highly strung; (of piano) with strings in sets crossing each other diagonally.
oversubscribe, *v.t.* apply for more shares in than can be allotted.
overt, *a.* openly done, unconcealed. (L. *aperire,* open)
overtake, *v.t.* catch up with; come suddenly upon.
overtax, *v.t.* make too great demands on; tax too heavily.
overthrow, *v.t.* upset, overturn; vanquish; destroy.—*n.* defeat, ruin; (*cricket*) fielder's return missed at wicket and so allowing further runs.
overtime, *adv.* beyond regular working hours.—*n.* extra time worked.
overtone, *n.* harmonic.
overtop, *v.t.* be higher than, tower above.
overtrain, *v.t.* and *i.* train too hard.
overtrump, *v.t.* play higher trump than (card that has trumped another).
overture, *n.* opening of negotiations, formal offer; (*mus.*) orchestral introduction.
overturn, *v.t.* and *i.* and *n.* upset, overthrow.
overwatched, *a.* wearied by keeping awake.
overweening, *a.* arrogant, presumptuous. **overween,** *v.i.* (*Shake.*) think too much of oneself. (*ween*)
overweight, *n.* excess weight.—*a.* beyond proper weight. **overweighted,** *a.* overburdened.
overwhelm, *v.t.* submerge, engulf; crush, overpower; abash. **overwhelming,** *a.* irresistible.
overwork, *v.t.* and *i.* work too hard.—*n.* excessive work.
overwrought, *a.* over-excited; too elaborate.
ovi-, from L. *ovis,* sheep, used in

ovibovine, *a.* and *n.* (animal) between sheep and ox, musk-ox; **ovicide,** *n.* (*joc.*) sheep-killing; **oviform,** *a.* sheep-like; **ovine,** *a.* of, like, sheep.

ovi-, from L. *ovum*, egg, used in **oviduct,** *n.* passage for ova from ovary; **oviform,** *a.* egg-shaped; **oviparous,** *a.* laying eggs; **oviposit,** *v.t.* deposit eggs with **ovipositor,** *n.* insect's egg-laying organ.

ovum, *n.* (*pl.* **ova**) female germ-cell. **ovoid,** *a.* egg-shaped. **ovolo,** *n.* (*archit.*) convex moulding. **ovology,** *n.* science of animals' ova. **ovoviviparous,** *a.* hatching eggs within the body. **ovule,** *n.* seed before it is fertilized. (L.=egg)

owe, *v.t.* and *i.* (*past, p.p.* **owed,** *Shake.* **ought**) be bound to pay; be indebted or under obligation (for); (*Shake.*) own. **owing,** *a.* owed, due. **owing to,** because of. (O.E. *ágan*)

ower, *Scot.* form of **over. owercome,** *n.* refrain; hackneyed phrase.

own, *a.* possessed by, peculiar to, oneself.—*v.t.* and *i.* possess; acknowledge, admit. **get one's o. back,** get even with. **hold one's o.,** maintain position. **o. brother, sister,** with both parents same. **o. cousin,** first cousin. **o. up,** confess. **owner,** *n.* possessor; (*naut. sl.*) skipper. **ownership,** *n.* (*owe*)

owl, *n.* a night bird; solemn fool. **owlet,** *n.* young owl. **owlish,** *a.* (O.E. *úle*)

ox, *n.* (*pl.* **oxen**) male of cow, esp. when castrated; animal of this genus. **o.-bird,** *n.* dunlin. **o.-bow,** *n.* U-shaped collar of yoke; (*Amer.*) horse-shoe loop in stream. **o.-eye,** *n.* large eye; kinds of flower. (O.E. *oxa*)

oxalis, *n.* wood-sorrel. **oxalic acid,** poisonous acid got from it. (Gk.)

oxer, *n.* cattle-fence, us. of quickset hedge, single rail, and ditch.

Oxford, *n.* **O. bags,** very wide trousers. **O. blue,** dark blue with purple tinge. **O. frame,** picture-frame with cross at each corner. **O. Group,** Buchmanism, evangelical movement emanating from America. **O. mixture,** dark-grey cloth. **O. movement,** High Church movement begun at Oxford in 1833. **O. shoes,** low shoes laced over instep.

oxide, *n.* compound of oxygen with element or organic radical. **oxidize,** *v.t.* and *i.* combine with oxygen; cover with oxide, rust. **oxidization,** *n.* (*oxygen*)

oxlip, *n.* kind of primula; hybrid between primrose and cowslip.

Oxonian, *a.* of Oxford.—*n.* Oxford man.

oxter, *n.* (*Scot.*) arm-pit. (O.E. *óxta*)

oxy-, from Gk. *oxus*, sharp, used in **oxyacanthous,** *a.* with sharp thorns; **oxyblepsia, oxyopia,** *nn.* keen-sightedness.

oxygen, *n.* colourless scentless gas forming part of air, water etc. **oxygenate, oxygenize,** *vv.t.* combine, treat, with oxygen. **oxygenation,** *n.* **oxygenous,** *a.* **oxy-acetylene, oxy-hydrogen,** *nn.* mixture of oxygen with acetylene, hydrogen, used in blow-lamp etc. (Gk. *oxus*, sharp; *genesis*, origin)

oxymel, *n.* mixture of vinegar and honey. (Gk. *oxus*, sharp; *meli*, honey)

oxymoron, *n.* figure of speech combining contradictory words, e.g. 'faith unfaithful kept him falsely true.' (Gk. *oxus*, sharp; *mōros*, foolish)

oxytone, *a.* and *n.* (word) with acute accent on last syllable. (Gk. *oxus*, sharp)

oyer and terminer, (*law*) authority to hold courts. (L. *audire*, hear; *terminare*, determine)

oyez, oyes, *int.* of public crier demanding attention. (O.F.=hear)

oyster, *n.* bivalve shell-fish us. eaten alive. **o.-catcher,** *n.* a wading sea-bird. **o.-knife,** *n.* for opening oysters. (Gk. *ostreon*)

ozocerite, ozokerit, *n.* waxy fossil resin used for candles. (Gk. *ozein*, smell; *kēros*, wax)

ozone, *n.* bracing air of seaside etc.; (*chem.*) condensed form of oxygen. **ozonic,** *a.* **ozonize,** *v.t.* (Gk. *ozein*, smell)

P

P. mind one's p's and q's, be on one's best behaviour.

pa, *n.* (*colloq.*) father. (*papa*)

pa, same as **pah.**

pabulum, *n.* food. (L.)

paca, *n.* large spotted S. American rodent like guinea-pig. (native)

pace, *n.* step, stride; length of this, about 30 in.; gait; rate of speed; horse's gait in which legs on same side are lifted together, amble.—*v.i.* and *t.* walk (over) with measured tread; amble; measure by paces; set pace for. **go the p.,** live extravagantly. **keep p. with,** keep up with. **put one through his pp.,** test his abilities. **p.-maker,** *n.* one who sets the pace. (L. *passus*)

pācĕ, *prep.* by leave of, with all due deference to. *p. tua*, by your leave. (L.)

pacer, *n.* horse that paces; pace-maker.

pacha, same as **pasha.**

pachisi, *n.* Indian game like backgammon. (Hind. *pachis,* 25)

pachy-, from Gk. *pachus,* thick, used in **pachyderm,** *n.* thick-skinned animal, esp. elephant; **pachydermatous,** *a.* thick-skinned, stolid; **pachyglossal,** *a.* thick-tongued; **pachymeter,** *n.* instrument for measuring thickness.

pacify, *v.t.* appease, calm; establish peace in. **pacific,** *a.* promoting peace; mild, conciliatory. **Pacific (Ocean)** between Asia and America. **pacification,** *n.* pacifying. **pacificatory,** *a.* **pacifier,** *n.* peace-maker. **pacifist, pacificist,** *n.* one who advocates abolition of war, anti-militarist. **pacifism, pacificism,** *n.* (L. *pax,* peace; *facere,* make)

pack, *n.* bundle for carrying; bale; set of hounds or wolves; lot, gang; set of playing-cards; pack-ice; (*Rugby football*) forwards.—*v.t.* and *i.* put in, fill, box or bag for transport or storage; cram, crowd; depart in haste; (*med.*) wrap in wet sheets. **p. off,** send away hurriedly. **p.-animal, p.-horse, p.-saddle,** *nn.* for carrying goods. **p.-drill,** *n.* punishment drill in full marching order. **p.-ice,** *n.* mass of floating pieces of ice. (M.E. *packe*)

pack, *v.t.* and *i.* fill (jury etc.) with partisans; (*Shake.*) conspire; shuffle (cards) unfairly.

pack, *a.* (*Scot.*) confidential, intimate.

package, *n.* compact bundle, parcel.

packet, *n.* small package; (*sl.*) considerable sum; (also **p.-boat**) mail-boat.

packing, *n.* material to prevent shifting or jarring. **p.-case,** *n.* rough wooden case. **p.-needle,** *n.* large needle for sewing up packages.

packman, *n.* pedlar.

packthread, *n.* strong thread.

pact, *n.* agreement, compact. **paction,** *n.* bargain, pact. (L. *pactum*)

pad, *n.* (*sl.*) road; easy-paced horse.—*v.t.* and *i.* trudge, tramp (along). **p. the hoof,** (*sl.*) walk. (Du.)

pad, *n.* basket used as measure for fruit.

pad, *n.* anything stuffed with soft material; guard for leg; soft saddle; fleshy cushion on sole of dog's foot; paw of fox; floating leaf of water-lily; block of sheets of paper.—*v.t.* stuff; protect with pad. **padding,** *n.* stuffing; literary matter used merely to fill out space.

paddle, *v.i.* walk with bare feet in shallow water, dabble; toy, fidget; toddle.

paddle, *n.* short oar with broad blade at one or both ends; float of paddle-wheel; flipper.—*v.i.* and *t.* propel (boat) with paddle; row gently. **p.-box,** *n.* casing over **p.-wheel,** *n.* propelling ship by floats striking on water.

paddock, *n.* small field in which horses are exercised or assembled for race; (*Austral.*) fenced-in area.

paddock, *n.* (*arch.*) toad, frog. (O.E. *pade,* toad+dim.)

Paddy, *n.* nickname for Irishman. (*Patrick*)

paddy, *n.* rice growing or in the husk. **p.-bird,** *n.* (*Anglo-Ind.*) kind of white egret. (Malay *padi*)

paddy, paddywhack, *nn.* (*colloq.*) rage, fit of temper.

paddymelon, pademelon, *n.* (*Austral.*) small wallaby.

padishah, padshah, *n.* title (in Persia) of Shah, (in India) of British Emperor. (Pers.)

padlock, *n.* detachable lock with loop fastening through staple or ring.—*v.t.* fasten with this.

padouk, *n.* a Burmese tree; its wood. (native)

padre, *n.* (*sl.*) army or navy chaplain; parson. (Port.=father)

padrónĕ, *n.* (*pl.* **padroni**) Italian innkeeper, contractor, employer of street musicians etc. (It.)

paduasoy, *n.* kind of corded silk. (F. *pou-de-soie*)

paean, *n.* song of triumph or thanksgiving. (Gk. *paian*)

paed(o)-, from Gk. *pais,* boy, used in **paedarchy,** *n.* government by children; **paederasty,** *n.* sodomy; **paedeutics,** *n.pl.* science of education; **paediatrics,** *n.pl.* study of children's diseases; **paedobaptism,** *n.* baptism of infants; **paedology,** *n.* child study; **paedophilia,** *n.* love of children.

paeon, *n.* four-syllabled foot, three short and one long in any order. **paeonic,** *a.* (Gk. *paiōn*)

pagan, *n.* and *a.* heathen, non-Christian. **paganish,** *a.* **paganism,** *n.* heathen beliefs and practices. **paganize,** *v.t.* render pagan. (L. *pagus,* country district)

page, *n.* boy servant or attendant.—*v.t.* attend as, summon by, page. (O.F.)

page, *n.* one side of leaf of book.—*v.t.* number pages of; make up into pages. (L. *pagina*)

pageant, *n.* brilliant spectacle; representation in costume of historical events; empty show; (formerly) tableau on wheeled platform.—*v.t.* (*Shake.*) mimic. **pageantry,** *n.* what makes up a pageant; pomp.

paginal, *a.* of pages; page for page. **paginate,** *v.t.* number pages of. **pagination,** *n.* (*page*)

pagoda, *n.* Hindu or Chinese sacred tower, us. pyramidal in shape; obsolete Indian coin. (Port. *pagode*)

pagurian, *a.* and *n.* (of) the hermit-crab. (Gk. *pagouros,* kind of crab)

pah, *int.* of disgust.

pah, *n.* (*New Zealand*) native fort or fortified village. (Maori *pa*)

paid, see **pay.**

paideutics, same as **paedeutics.**
paik, *n.* (*Scot.*) beating.
pail, *n.* round open vessel for liquid, bucket. **pailful,** *n.*
paillasse, same as **palliasse.**
paillette, *n.* piece of metal foil, spangle. (F.)
pain, *n.* suffering, distress; ache, twinge; penalty; (*pl.*) trouble, exertion.—*v.t.* and *i.* cause pain to; ache. **on p. of,** subject to penalty of. **pained,** *a.* hurt, offended. **painful,** *a.* giving pain, distressing; (*arch.*) painstaking. **painstaking,** *a.* careful, laborious. (L. *poena,* penalty)
paint, *v.t.* and *i.* coat with pigment; portray, make pictures, in colours; depict (as); use cosmetics (on).—*n.* colouring matter, pigment; rouge. **p. out,** efface with paint. **p. the town red,** have riotous spree. **painted lady,** kind of butterfly. **painter,** *n.* one who paints pictures or houses. (L. *pingere*)
painter, *n.* rope used to fasten boat. **cut the p.,** sever connection.
painting, *n.* painted picture.
paintress, *n.* female artist.
pair, *n.* set of two; thing in two parts; married, engaged, or mated couple; flight (of stairs).—*v.t.* and *i.* form into pairs; mate; agree with M.P. of opposite party to abstain from voting. **one-p., two-p., front** or **back,** front or back room on first, second, floor. (L. *par,* equal)
pajamas, same as **pyjamas.**
pakeha, *n.* (*New Zealand*) white man, European. (Maori)
pal, *n.* (*sl.*) comrade, mate. **p. up,** make friends (with). (Gipsy)
palabra, *n.* word; palaver. (Sp.)
palace, *n.* residence of sovereign or bishop; splendid house or building. (L. *Palatium,* a hill in Rome)
paladin, *n.* knight-errant, chivalrous hero; medieval champion, esp. of Charlemagne's court. (F.)
palae(o)-, from Gk. *palaios,* old, used in **palaeoanthropic,** *a.* of earliest form of man; **palaeobiology,** *n.* study of fossil life; **palaeobotany,** *n.* study of fossil plants; **palaeocrystic,** *a.* frozen from remote ages; **palaeographer, palaeography,** *nn.* student, study, of ancient writing and inscriptions, hence **palaeographic, palaeographical,** *aa.*; **palaeolithic,** *a.* of the middle Stone Age; **palaeology,** *n.* archaeology; **palaeontologist, palaeontology,** *nn.* student, study, of past geological periods and fossils, hence **palaeontological,** *a.*; **palaeothere,** *n.* extinct animal like tapir; **palaeozoic,** *a.* of first geological period, containing earliest forms of life; **palaeozoology,** *n.* study of fossil animals.
palaestra, *n.* wrestling-school, gymnasium. (Gk. *palaiein,* wrestle)
palafitte, *n.* prehistoric Swiss lake dwelling. (It. *palo,* stake; *fitto,* fixed)
palanquin, palankeen, *n.* eastern box-like carriage on poles, covered litter. (Port.)
palate, *n.* roof of mouth; taste, liking. —*v.t.* (*Shake.*) savour, relish. **hard, soft, p.,** front, back, part of it. **palatable,** *a.* pleasant to taste. **palatal,** *a.* of palate; (of sound) made by placing tongue against palate.—*n.* palatal letter. (L. *palatum*)
palatial, *a.* of, like, a palace; magnificent, sumptuous. (*palace*)
palatine, *a.* with royal privileges and rights.—*n.* woman's fur tippet. **palatinate,** *n.* territory under count palatine. (*palace*)
palatine, *a.* of the palate.—*n.pl.* palatine bones.
palaver, *n.* conference, discussion; chatter; cajolery.—*v.i.* and *t.* talk idly; wheedle. (Port. *palavra,* word)
pale, *n.* narrow board for fence, stake; boundary; (*heraldry*) vertical stripe in middle of shield. **beyond the p.,** ruled out of polite society, impossible. (L. *palus*)
pale, *a.* whitish, wan; (of colour) faint; (of light) dim.—*v.i.* and *t.* grow, make, pale.—*n.* (*Shake.*) paleness. (L. *pallidus*)
paleaceous, *a.* chaff-like. (L. *palea,* chaff)
paled, *a.* having palings.
paleface, *n.* Red Indian name for white man.
paleoanthropic, paleography etc., same as **palaeoanthropic, palaeography** etc.
palestra, same as **palaestra.**
paletot, *n.* loose overcoat. (F.)
palette, *n.* artist's flat board for mixing colours on. **p.-knife,** *n.* thin knife for mixing colours. (F.)
palfrey, *n.* (*arch.*) saddle-horse, esp. for lady. (Gk. *para,* beside. L. *veredus,* post-horse)
palimpsest, *n.* manuscript which has been written upon twice, original writing being more or less visible in spite of erasure. (Gk. *palin,* again; *psaein,* rub)
palindrome, *n.* and *a.* (word, sentence) reading the same backwards as forwards, e.g. 'Able was I ere I saw Elba.' **palindromic,** *a.* (Gk. *palin,* again; *dromos,* run)
paling, *n.* fence; fencing. (*pale*)
palingenesis, *n.* regeneration, new birth; reincarnation, metempsychosis; exact reproduction of ancestral characteristics. **palingenetic,** *a.* (Gk. *palin,* again; *genesis,* birth)
palinode, *n.* poem retracting former one; recantation. (Gk. *palin,* again; *ōdē,* song)
palisade, *n* fence of stakes or railings; pointed stake.—*v.t.* protect with palisade. (L. *palus,* stake)
pall, *n.* heavy cloth spread over coffin; pallium; dark covering, mantle.

p.-bearer, *n.* one of those who attend coffin at funeral. (*pallium*)
pall, *v.i.* and *t.* become tiresome, cloy.
Palladian, *a.* (*archit.*) in the pseudo-classical style of Palladio.
palladium, *n.* (*pl.* **palladia**) object, principle, on which safety of something depends. (Gk. *palladion*, image of Pallas)
palladium, *n.* a hard white metal. (*Pallas*, one of the asteroids)
pallet, *n.* small mean bed; straw mattress. (L. *palea*, chaff)
pallet, *n.* potter's flat-bladed shaping-tool; regulating-valve of organ-pipe; palette. (*palette*)
palliament, *n.* (*Shake.*) robe of candidate for consulship. (*pallium*)
palliasse, *n.* hard under-mattress of straw etc. (*pallet*)
palliate, *v.t.* extenuate, excuse; alleviate without curing. **palliation, palliator,** *nn.* **palliative,** *a.* and *n.* (thing) that palliates. (L. *palliare*, cloak)
pallid, *a.* pale, wan. (L. *pallidus*)
pallium, *n.* (*pl.* **pallia**) white woollen scarf worn by archbishop; square mantle of ancient Greeks; mollusc's outer fold of skin. (L.=cloak)
pall-mall, *n.* game in which ball was driven through iron ring hung at end of alley; the alley. (It. *palla*, ball; *maglio*, hammer)
pallónē, *n.* Italian game like tennis with ball struck by arm-guard and three players a side. (It.)
pallor, *n.* paleness. (L.)
pally, *a.* (*sl.*) friendly, matey. (*pal*)
palm, *n.* tropical tree with branchless trunk and crown of leaves; leaf of this as symbol of victory; merit, success. **p. oil,** oil from palm; (*joc.*) bribe. **P. Sunday,** Sunday before Easter. (L. *palma*)
palm, *n.* inner part of hand.—*v.t.* conceal in, touch with, palm. **p. off,** impose by fraud, foist. (L. *palma*)
palmaceous, *a.* of the palm family.
Palma Christi, castor-oil plant. (L. =hand of Christ, from shape of leaf)
palmar, *a.* of, in, palm of hand.
palmary, *a.* deserving the palm, pre-eminent.
palmate, palmated, *aa.* like open hand; (of leaf) with lobes radiating from common point; (*zool.*) web-footed.
palmer, *n.* pilgrim returning from Holy Land, with palm leaf as token; itinerant monk under vow of poverty. **p.-worm,** *n.* kind of caterpillar.
palmetto, *n.* dwarf fan-palm.
palmiped, palmipede, *a.* and *n.* web-footed (bird). (L. *palma*, palm; *pes*, foot)
palmist, *n.* one who practises palmistry. **palmistry,** *n.* foretelling of future from lines of hand.
palmy, *a.* full of palm-trees; flourishing, successful.
palmyra, *n.* tall Indian palm, leaves of which are used for matting. (Port. *palmeira*)
palp, same as **palpus.**
palpable, *a.* that can be felt; obvious, manifest. **palpate,** *v.t.* examine by touch. **palpation,** *n.* (L. *palpare*, stroke)
palpal, *a.* of palpi.
palpebral, *a.* of the eyelids. (L. *palpebra*, eyelid)
palpitate, *v.i.* pulsate, throb; flutter. **palpitation,** *n.* throbbing; irregular quickened action of heart. (L. *palpitare*)
palpus, *n.* (*pl.* **palpi**) feeler attached to mouth-parts of insect. (L.)
palsgrave, *n.* (*fem.* **palsgravine**) count palatine. (Du. *paltsgrave*)
palstave, *n.* ancient weapon of bronze wedge in handle. (Icel. *pálstafr*)
palsy, *n.* paralysis; paralytic trembling.—*v.t.* paralyse; make helpless. (*paralysis*)
palter, *v.i.* trifle, shuffle; haggle.
paltry, *a.* petty, insignificant, contemptible.
paludal, *a.* of a marsh; malarial. (L. *palus*, marsh)
paly, *a.* (*poet.*) palish.
paly, *a.* (*heraldry*) divided by pales.
pam, *n.* knave of clubs at loo.
pampas, *n.pl.* treeless S. American plains. **p.-grass,** *n.* very tall grass with feathery spikes. (Sp.)
pamper, *v.t.* over-indulge, coddle.
pampero, *n.* cold west wind blowing from Andes across pampas. (Sp.)
pamphlet, *n.* small unbound book, us. on current topic. **pamphleteer,** *n.* writer of pamphlets.—*v.i.* write pamphlets.
pan, *n.* broad flat shallow vessel; tray; hollow; (*S. Afr.*) dried-up salt-marsh. **p. off,** wash (gold-bearing gravel) in pan. **p. out,** yield gold; turn out. (O.E. *panne*)
pan, *n.* betel leaf; mixture of this with lime etc. for chewing. (Hind.)
pan, *v.t.* (*Amer. sl.*) disparage, find fault with.
Pan, *n.* Greek god of woods; spirit of nature, paganism.
pan-, from Gk. *pas*, all, used in **pan-African, pan-American, pan-Anglican,** *aa.* of or for all Africans, Americans, branches of the English Church; **pan-Germanism, pan-Hellenism, pan-Slavism,** *nn.* movement for political union of all Germans, Greeks, Slavs; **pan-Islam,** *n.* union of Mohammedan world.
panacea, *n.* universal remedy, cure-all. (Gk. *pas*, all; *akos*, cure)
panache, *n.* plume; swaggering air. (F.)
panada, *n.* bread boiled to pulp and flavoured. (Sp.)
Panama, *n.* (also **P. hat**) hat of fine straw-like material. (place)
panatrope, *n.* electrical apparatus reproducing gramophone records through loud-speaker.

pancake, *n.* thin cake of eggs, flour, sugar, and milk fried in pan.—*v.i,* (of aeroplane) descend vertically in level position.
panchayat, *n.* Indian native village council. (Sanskr. *pañca,* five)
panchromatic, *a.* (*phot.*) sensitive to light of all colours. (Gk. *pas,* all; *chrōma,* colour)
pancosmism, *n.* doctrine that nothing exists beyond material universe. (Gk. *pas,* all; *kosmos,* universe)
pancratium, *n.* contest combining boxing and wrestling. **pancratiast, pancratist,** *nn.* competitor in this. **pancratic,** *a.* (Gk. *pas,* all; *kratos,* strength)
pancreas, *n.* digestive gland behind stomach. **pancreatic,** *a.* **pancreatin,** *n.* digestive principle of pancreatic juice. (Gk. *pas,* all; *kreas,* flesh)
panda, *n.* Indian animal like racoon, red bear-cat. **giant p.,** like black and white bear. (native)
pandal, *n.* (*Anglo-Ind.*) shed; arbour.
Pandean, Pandaean, *a.* of Pan.
pandect, *n.* (us. *pl.*) Justinian's digest of Roman civil law; any code of laws, (Gk. *pas,* all; *dechesthai,* receive)
pandemic, *a.* affecting a whole people; universal.—*n.* (also **pandemia**) pandemic disease. (Gk. *pas,* all; *dēmos,* people)
pandemonium, *n.* riotous uproar or place; abode, assembly, of evil spirits. (*pan-* +*demon*)
pander, *n.* go-between in illicit amours, procurer; tool in evil designs.—*v.i.* act as pander, minister basely. (*Pandarus,* name in story)
pandiculation, *n.* act of stretching oneself. (L. *pandere,* spread out)
pandit, same as **pundit.**
pandore, *n.* stringed instrument of cithern kind. (Gk. *pandoura*)
pandour, pandoor, *n.* brutal (orig. Croatian) soldier. (L.L. *banderius*)
pandy, *n.* (*Scot.*) stroke on hand with tawse. (L. *pandere,* hold out)
pane, *n.* single piece of glass in window; square in pattern. **paned,** *a.* made of strips of different materials. (L. *pannus,* piece of cloth)
panegyric, *n.* laudatory oration, eulogy.—*a.* (also **panegyrical**) laudatory. **panegyrize,** *v.t.* praise highly, extol. **panegyrist,** *n.* (Gk. *pas,* all; *agora,* assembly)
panel, *n.* compartment of surface, thin board let into door, vertical strip in dress; tall narrow picture; list of jurors, jury; list of Health Insurance doctors for district; (*Scots law*) prisoner at the bar.—*v.t.* fit, adorn, with panels. **panelling,** *n.* panelled work (*pane*)
pang, *n.* sudden sharp pain, twinge, throw.—*v.t.* (*Shake.*) torture.
pang, *v.t.* (*Scot.*) cram.
pangenesis, *n.* theory that reproductive cells contain particles from all parts of parents. **pangenetic,** *a.*
pangolin, *n.* scaly ant-eater. (Malay *peng-goling,* roller)
panhandle, *n.* narrow projecting tongue of land.
panic, *n.* kinds of grass incl. millet. (L. *panicum*)
panic, *n.* sudden overpowering fright. —*a.* (of fear) unreasoning, excessive. —*v.t.* and *i.* (*past, p.p.* **panicked**) affect, be affected, with panic. **p.-monger,** *n.* one who fosters panic. **panicky,** *a.* (*Pan*)
panicle, *n.* irregularly branched flower-cluster. **panicular, paniculate, paniculated,** *aa.* (L. *panicula*)
panification, *n.* bread-making. (L. *panis,* bread; *facere,* make)
panjandrum, *n.* burlesque potentate, pompous official. (coined word)
panlogism, *n.* doctrine that only the rational is real. **panlogistic,** *a.* (Gk. *pas,* all; *logos,* reason)
pannage, *n.* pigs' food in woods, acorns etc.; right of, fee for, pasturing pigs. (L. *pascere,* feed)
panne, *n.* soft fabric like velvet. (F.)
panner, *n.* (*Amer. sl.*) fault-finder.
pannier, *n.* basket carried (often in pairs) on back of pack-animal or person; part of skirt puffed out round hips, framework for this. (L. *panarium,* bread-basket)
pannier, *n.* (*colloq.*) robed waiter of Inner Temple.
pannikin, *n.* small metal drinking-cup. (*pan* +dim.)
panophobia, *n.* morbid fear of everything. (Gk. *pas,* all; *phobos,* fear)
panoply, *n.* full suit of armour. **panoplied,** *a.* (Gk. *pas,* all; *hopla,* arms)
panopticon, *n.* circular prison where all cells can be watched from central point; exhibition. (Gk. *pas,* all; *opsis,* sight)
panorama, *n.* continuous series of pictures unrolled before spectators; wide unbroken view. **panoramic,** *a.* **panoramically,** *adv.* (Gk. *pas,* all; *horaein,* see)
pan-pipe, *n.* wind-instrument of short hollow tubes, orig. made of reed, graduated in size. (*Pan*)
pansy, *n.* plant of violet family, heartsease; (*sl.*) effeminate man.—*a.* (*sl.*) womanish. (F. *pensée*)
pant, *v.i.* and *t.* breathe rapidly, gasp; yearn; throb.—*n.* short laboured breath.
pantagamy, *n.* communistic marriage; free love. (Gk. *pas* all; *gamos,* marriage)
pantagruelism, *n.* coarse satiric humour like that of Pantagruel in Rabelais. **pantagruelian,** *a.*
pantaloon, *n.* old dotard on whom clown plays tricks in harlequinade; breeches and stockings in one piece; (*pl.*) tight trousers. **pantaloonery,** *n.* buffoonery. **pantalettes, pantalets,** *n.pl.* women's long frilled drawers. (It. *pantalone,* buffoon)

pantechnicon, *n.* furniture van or depository. (Gk. *pas*, all; *technē*, art)

pantheism, *n.* doctrine that the whole universe is God; heathen worship of all gods. **pantheist,** *n.* **pantheistic, pantheistical,** *aa.* (Gk. *pas*, all; *theos*, god)

pantheon, *n.* temple of all gods; gods of a people collectively; building where nation's famous dead are buried or have memorials. (Gk. *pas*, all; *theos*, god)

panther, *n.* (*fem.* **pantheress**) leopard; (*Amer.*) cougar, puma. (Gk.)

pantile, *n.* roof-tile with S-shaped cross-section. (*pan*; *tile*)

pantisocracy, *n.* community in which all are equal and all rule. (Gk. *pas*, all; *isos*, equal; *kratos*, power)

pantler, *n.* (*Shake.*) servant in charge of pantry. (L. *panis*, bread)

pant(o)-, from Gk. *pas*, all, used in **pantochronometer,** *n.* combined compass and sun-dial, showing time in all parts of the world; **pantograph,** *n.* instrument for copying maps etc. on any scale, hence **pantographic,** *a.*; **pantology,** *n.* universal knowledge, hence **pantologic,** *a.*; **pantomorphic,** *a.* assuming all shapes; **pantopragmatic,** *a.* and *n.* (person) interfering with everything; **pantoscopic,** *a.* having wide range of vision, panoramic.

pantoffle, *n.* slipper. (F.)

pantomime, *n.* spectacular Christmas play for children, us. based on fairy tale; play in dumb show; ancient Roman mimic actor; language of gestures.—*v.i.* and *t.* use, express by, gestures. **pantomimic,** *a.* **pantomimist,** *n.* actor in pantomime. (Gk. *pas*, all; *mimos*, mimic)

pantoum, *n.* Malayan verse-form of four-lined rhyming stanzas. (Malay *pantun*)

pantry, *n.* room for storing food or keeping plate, table-linen etc. **pantryman,** *n.* butler or his assistant. (L. *panis*, bread)

pants, *n.pl.* men's drawers; (*Amer.*) trousers. (abbr. of *pantaloons*)

panurgic, *a.* adept at all kinds of work. (Gk. *pas*, all; *ergon*, work)

panzer, *a.* armoured. **p. division,** German self-contained mechanized division of all arms, incl. tanks and aeroplanes. (G.)

pap, *n.* nipple of breast, teat; round conical hill. (imit.)

pap, *n.* soft food for infants; mash, pulp. (imit.)

papa, *n.* father. (L.)

papacy, *n.* office and dignity of pope; papal system. **papal,** *a.* of the pope or papacy. **papalism, papalist,** *nn.* **papalize,** *v.t.* and *i.* convert, conform, to popery. **paparchy,** *n.* papal government. (L. *papa*, father)

papaveraceous, *a.* of the poppy family. **papaverous,** *a.* of, like, poppy. (L. *papaver*, poppy)

papaw, *n.* palm-like S American tree; its large orange-coloured fruit. (Sp. *papaya*)

paper, *n.* thin sheets made of pulp; document; essay, memorandum; newspaper; bank-notes, bills of exchange etc.; set of examination questions; (*sl.*) free passes to theatre; (*pl.*) documents establishing identity, credentials.—*a.* made of paper.—*v.t.* cover, decorate, with paper. **commit to p.,** write down. **on p.,** on form, judging by statistics. **p. money,** bank-notes. **send in one's pp.,** resign commission. **p.-hanger,** *n.* wall-paperer. **p.-knife,** *n.* blunt blade for cutting folded paper. **p.-weight,** *n.* heavy object to secure loose papers. **paperchase,** *n.* cross-country pursuit of runners who lay trail of pieces of paper. **papery,** *a.* like paper. (*papyrus*)

papier mâché, solid substance made of paper pulp. (F. =chewed paper)

papilionaceous, *a.* butterfly-shaped; having corolla like butterfly. (L. *papilio*, butterfly)

papilla, *n.* (*pl.* **papillae**) small nipple-like protuberance. **papillary,** *a.* of, like, papillae. **papillate, papillose,** *aa.* having papillae. (L. =nipple)

papist, *n.* supporter of papal supremacy; Roman Catholic (often used disparagingly). **papistic, papistical,** *aa.* **papistry,** *n.* (L. *papa*, father).

papoose, *n.* Red Indian baby. (native)

papoosh, papouche, same as **babouche.**

pappus, *n.* (*pl.* **pappi**) downy tuft on seed of dandelion etc.; down. **pappose,** *a.* (Gk. *pappos*)

pappy, *a.* semi-liquid, like pap.

paprika, *n.* Hungarian red pepper. (Hungarian)

papule, papula, *nn.* (*pl.* **papules, papulae**) pimple. **papular, papulose, papulous,** *aa.* (L.)

papyrus, *n.* marsh-plant like sedge; writing-material made from its stem; (with *pl.* **papyri**) manuscript written on this. **papyraceous,** *a.* like, thin as, papyrus. **papyrograph,** *n.* instrument for copying documents by means of paper stencil. **papyrologist, papyrology,** *nn.* student, study, of papyri. (Gk. *papuros*)

par, *n.* equality, equal footing; (of stocks or shares) face value; (*golf*) score of perfect player (less than 'bogey'). **above p.,** at a premium. **below p.,** at a discount; out of sorts. **p. of exchange,** normal relation between two currencies. (L. =equal)

par, *n.* (*colloq.*) paragraph. (abbr.)

par, same as **parr.**

para-, *pref.* beside, as in parallel, against, as in paradox. (Gk.)

parabasis, *n.* address of chorus to audience in old Greek comedy. (Gk).

parable, *n.* short story with moral lesson, allegory; (*arch.*) enigmatical saying; discourse. (Gk. *para*, beside; *ballein*, throw)

parablepsis, parablepsy, *nn.* false vision. **parableptic,** *a.* (Gk. *para,* beside; *bleptein,* see)
parabola, *n.* curve formed by cutting of cone by plane parallel to its side. (Gk. *para,* beside; *ballein,* throw)
parabolic, *a.* of, like, a parabola; parabolical. **parabolical,** *a.* of, expressed in, a parable; parabolic.
paraboloid, *n.* solid formed by revolution of parabola round its axis.
parachronism, *n.* error of chronology, esp. post-dating of event. (Gk. *para,* beside; *chronos,* time)
parachute, *n.* umbrella-like apparatus for descending safely from aircraft. **parachutist,** *n.* user of this. (F.)
paraclete, *n.* advocate (as title of the Holy Ghost). (Gk. *para,* beside; *kalein,* call)
parade, *n.* display, ostentation; muster of troops, review; ground for this; public walk, promenade.—*v.t.* and *i.* show off; assemble in military order; march (along) with display. (L. *parare,* prepare)
paradigm, *n.* example, model, esp. of grammatical inflexions. **paradigmatic,** *a.* (Gk. *para,* beside; *deiknunai,* show)
paradise, *n.* heaven; place of supreme beauty or happiness; garden of Eden; oriental park. **bird of p.,** bird of crow family with splendid plumage. **paradisaic, paradisaical, paradisean, paradisiac, paradisiacal, paradisial, paradisian, paradisic, paradisical,** *aa.* (Gk. *paradeisos*)
parados, *n.* rampart protecting rear of fortification, back wall of trench. (Gk. *para,* beside. L. *dorsum,* back)
paradox, *n.* statement apparently absurd but containing substratum of truth, e.g. 'The child is father of the man'; statement contrary to received opinion. **paradoxical,** *a.* **paradoxer, paradoxist, paradoxy,** *nn.* (Gk. *para,* against; *doxa,* opinion)
paradoxure, *n.* animal with long curving tail, palm-cat. (Gk. *paradoxos,* incredible; *oura,* tail)
paraesthesia, *n.* tingling sensation on skin. **paraesthetic,** *a.* (Gk. *para,* beside; *aisthanesthai,* perceive)
paraffin, *n.* white tasteless fatty substance got from shale, wood etc.; (also **p. oil**) oil of similar origin. (L. *parum,* little; *affinis,* related—because resistant to chemical union)
paragenesis, *n.* mutual effect of contact on development of minerals. **paragenetic,** *a.* (*para-* + *genesis*)
parageusia, *n.* perverted sense of taste. (Gk. *para,* beside; *geusis,* taste)
paragógē, *n.* addition of letter or syllable to word. **paragogic,** *a.* (Gk. *para,* beside; *agein,* lead)
paragon, *n.* model of perfection; supremely excellent person or thing; (*Spens.*) companion, equal; rivalry; (*print.*) 20-point type, twice size of long primer.—*v.t.* (*poet.*) compare; (*Shake.*) surpass. (It. *paragone*)
paragram, *n.* play upon words, pun. (Gk. *para,* beside; *graphein,* write)
paragraph, *n.* subdivision of writing or discourse; brief item in newspaper; reference mark (¶).—*v.t.* arrange in paragraphs. **paragraphic,** *a.* **paragrapher, paragraphist,** *nn.* writer of newspaper paragraphs. (Gk. *paragraphos,* stroke in margin)
paraguay, *n.* maté. (place)
paraheliotropism, *n.* plant's turning of its leaves parallel to sun's rays. **paraheliotropic,** *a.* (Gk. *para,* beside; *hēlios,* sun; *trepein,* turn)
parakeet, *n.* small kinds of parrot. (O.F. *paroquet*)
parakite, *n.* kite used as parachute; tailless kite used in meteorological observations. (*para-* + *kite*)
paraldehyde, *n.* a narcotic drug. (*para-* + *aldehyde*)
paraleipsis, paralipsis, *n.* figure in which emphasis is laid on something by professing to pass it over. (Gk. *para,* beside; *leipein,* leave)
parallax, *n.* apparent difference in object's position or direction as viewed from different points; angular amount of this. **parallactic,** *a.* (Gk. *para,* beside; *allassein,* change)
parallel, *a.* equidistant in all parts; side by side; similar, corresponding. —*n.* parallel thing, counterpart; comparison; imaginary line marking degree of latitude; (*print.*) reference-mark (‖).—*v.t.* find parallel, correspond, to; compare. **p. bars,** for gymnastic exercises. **parallelepiped,** *n.* regular solid contained by parallelograms. **parallelism,** *n.* being parallel; correspondence. **parallelogram,** *n.* four-sided plane figure whose opposite sides are parallel. (Gk. *para allēlous,* beside each other)
paralogism, *n.* illogical reasoning; fallacy. **paralogize,** *v.i.* (Gk. *para,* against; *logos,* reason)
paralyse, *v.t.* strike with paralysis; make helpless or ineffectual. **paralysation,** *n.* **paralysis,** *n.* loss of power to move or feel, palsy; utter helplessness. **paralytic,** *a.* and *n.* (person) affected with paralysis. (Gk. *para,* beside; *luein,* loose)
paramatta, *n.* light fabric of wool and cotton. (Australian town)
paramo, *n.* high bleak plateau in S. America. (Sp.)
paramount, *a.* highest in rank, chief; pre-eminent; superior. **paramountcy,** *n.* (O.F. *par,* by; *amont,* above)
paramour, *n.* illicit lover; mistress. (O.F. *par amour,* by love)
parang, *n.* heavy Malay sheath-knife. (Malay)
paranoia, paranoea, *n.* mental disease with delusions of grandeur and persecution. **paranoiac,** *a.* and *n.* (Gk. =madness)

parapet, *n.* low wall at edge of roof, bridge etc.; protective mound along front of trench. (L. *parare,* prepare; *pectus,* breast)

paraph, *n.* mark or flourish under signature. (*paragraph*)

paraphernalia, *n.pl.* trappings, accessories; personal belongings; (*law*) what wife possesses in her own right. (Gk. *para,* beside; *phernē,* dowry)

paraphrase, *n.* rendering of passage in other words; free translation; metrical version of scriptural passage.—*v.t.* express in other words. **paraphrastic,** *a.* **paraphrastically,** *adv.* (Gk. *para,* beside; *phrazein,* speak)

paraplegia, *n.* paralysis of lower half of body. **paraplegic, paraplectic,** *aa.* (Gk. *para,* beside; *plēssein,* strike)

parasang, *n.* ancient Persian measure of length, about 3½ miles. (Gk. *parasanggēs*)

paraselénē, *n.* bright spot on lunar halo; mock moon. (Gk. *para,* beside; *selēnē,* moon)

parasite, *n.* hanger-on, sponger; plant, animal, living in or on another. **parasitic, parasitical,** *aa.* **parasitism,** *n.* **parasiticide,** *n.* parasite-killer. **parasitize,** *v.t.* infest as parasite. **parasitology,** *n.* study of parasites. (Gk. *para,* beside; *sitos,* food)

parasol, *n.* sunshade. (It. *parare,* ward off; *sole,* sun)

parasynthesis, *n.* (*philol.*) derivation from a compound. **parasynthetic,** *a.* (*para-*+*synthesis*)

parataxis, *n.* (*gram.*) use of successive clauses without connecting words. **paratactic,** *a.* **paratactically,** *adv.* (Gk. *para,* beside; *tassein,* arrange)

parathyroid, *a.* and *n.* (gland) lying near thyroid gland. (*para-*)

paratroops, *n.pl.* invading troops landed by parachute.

paratyphoid, *a.* and *n.* (fever) closely resembling typhoid. (*para-*)

paravane, *n.* apparatus for cutting moorings of submerged mines. (*para-*+*vane*)

paravaunt, *adv.* (*Spens.*) beforehand, in front. (O.F. *par,* through; *avant,* before)

parboil, *v.t.* boil partially; scorch. (*per-,* wholly, confused with *part*)

parbuckle, *n.* rope sling for raising or lowering casks.—*v.t.* hoist or lower with this.

parcel, *n.* package of goods; (*arch.*) portion; (*Shake.*) item, particular.—*v.t.* wrap up; (*naut.*) wrap, cover, with canvas strips. **p. out,** distribute. **p.-gilt,** *a.* partly gilded. (L. *pars,* part)

parcener, *n.* coheir. **parcenary,** *n.* joint heirship. (L. *partitio,* division)

parch, *v.t.* and *i.* make, become, hot and dry; scorch, roast.

parchment, *n.* writing-material made from skin of sheep etc.; manuscript on this. (first used at *Pergamum*)

pard, *n.* (*arch.*) leopard. (Gk. *pardos*)

pard, *n.* (*Amer. sl.*) partner. (abbr.)

pardi, pardy, *adv.* (*arch.*) in truth, certainly. (F. *par Dieu,* by God)

pardon, *n.* forgiveness; papal indulgence; (*law*) official remission of penalty.—*v.t.* forgive, excuse. **pardonable,** *a.* excusable. **pardoner,** *n.* (formerly) one licensed to sell papal indulgences. (L. *per,* through; *donare,* give)

pare, *v.t.* remove skin from, peel; cut or trim edges of; whittle (down). (L. *parare,* prepare)

paregoric, *a.* and *n.* (drug) soothing pain, esp. tincture of opium. (Gk. *parēgorein,* console)

pareira, *n.* diuretic drug made from S. American shrub. (Port. *parreira,* vine)

parenchyma, *n.* fundamental cellular tissue of organ or plant. **parenchymal, parenchymatous,** *aa.* (Gk. *para,* beside; *en,* in; *chein,* pour)

parent, *n.* father or mother; forefather; organism producing another; origin. **parentage,** *n.* descent, extraction. **parental,** *a.* of a parent. (L. *parere,* bring forth)

parenthesis, *n.* (*pl.* **parentheses**) word, statement, inserted in sentence independently of grammatical sequence; round brackets marking this off. **parenthesize,** *v.t.* insert as parenthesis; enclose in brackets. **parenthetic, parenthetical,** *aa.* (Gk. *para,* beside; *en,* in; *tithenai,* put)

parergon, *n.* subsidiary work. (Gk. *para,* beside; *ergon,* work)

paresis, *n.* paralysis affecting movement but not feeling. **paretic,** *a.* (Gk. *parienai,* relax)

par excellence, pre-eminently, in the highest degree. (F.)

parget, *v.t.* and *n.* plaster, whitewash.

parhelion, *n.* brilliant spot on solar halo; mock sun. (Gk. *para,* beside; *hēlios,* sun)

pariah, *n.* member of lowest Hindu caste; social outcast. **p.-dog,** *n.* yellow ownerless dog in India. (Tamil *paraiyan,* drummer)

Parian, *a.* of the island of Paros.—*n.* a fine white porcelain.

parietal, *a.* of the wall of the body or its cavities. **p. bones,** forming top and sides of skull. (L. *paries,* wall)

pari mutuel, mechanical betting system by which losers' stakes (less a tax) are divided among winners. (F. =mutual stake)

paring, *n.* what is pared off, rind.

pari passu, with equal pace, together; in equal degree. (L.)

Paris, *n.* **P. doll,** dressmaker's lay figure. **P. green,** pigment and insecticide. **P. white,** fine whiting.

parish, *n.* subdivision of county with its own church and clergyman; (also **civil p.**) poor-law district. **go on the p.,** receive poor-relief. **p. council,** administering rural civil parish.

p. register, of births, marriages, and deaths. **parishioner,** *n.* inhabitant of parish. (Gk. *para*, beside; *oikos*, house)

Parisian, *a.* and *n.* (citizen) of Paris.

parity, *n.* equality; analogy; being at par. (*par*)

park, *n.* ornamental grounds for public recreation; large enclosed piece of ground attached to country house; collection of artillery, space occupied by it, in encampment; enclosure for motor-cars to wait in.—*v.t.* enclose as park; leave in place reserved for it; (*sl.*) deposit, plant. (O.F. *parc*)

parka, *n.* hooded skin jacket of Eskimos. (Eskimo)

parkin, *n.* biscuit of oatmeal, ginger, and treacle.

parky, *a.* chilly, nipping.

parlance, *n.* way of speaking, idiom.

parley, (*Shake.*) **parle,** *nn.* conference, discussion of terms with enemy.—*v.i.* and *t.* discuss (terms), treat; speak. **parleyvoo,** *n.* (*joc.*) Frenchman.—*v.i.* talk French. (F. *parler*, speak)

parliament, *n.* legislative assembly, composed of House of Lords and House of Commons; similar foreign legislature. **parliamentarian,** *n.* skilled parliamentary debater; supporter of Parliament against Charles I. **parliamentary,** *a.* of, used in, enacted by, parliament; (of language) decorous, civil; (of train) bound to carry passengers at rate of not above 1*d.* per mile. (F. *parler*, speak)

parlour, *n.* family sitting-room; private room in inn. **p.-car,** *n.* (*Amer.*) luxuriously fitted railway coach. **parlourmaid,** *n.* maid who waits at table. (F. *parler*, speak)

parlous, *a.* perilous; hard to deal with, trying; dangerously clever.—*adv.* extremely. (=*perilous*)

parmaceti, (*Shake.*) corrupt. of spermaceti.

Parmesan, *a.* and *n.* (cheese) of Parma.

Parnassus, *n.* realm of poetry; poetic fame. **Parnassian,** *a.* (mountain in Greece sacred to the muses)

parochial, *a.* of a parish; merely local; narrow, petty. **parochialism,** *n.* narrow-mindedness. (*parish*)

parody, *n.* burlesque imitation of an author's style; travesty.—*v.t.* ridicule by imitation. **parodist,** *n.* (Gk. *para*, beside; *ōdē*, song)

parole, *n.* word of honour, esp. prisoner of war's promise not to attempt escape or resume hostilities; password used by officers of guard.—*v.t.* put on parole. (F =word)

paronomasia, *n.* play on words, pun. **paronym,** *n.* paronymous word. **paronymous,** *a.* with same derivation; with same sound but different spelling and meaning, e.g. 'pail,' 'pale.' (Gk. *para*, beside; *onoma*, name)

paroquet, same as parakeet.

parotid, *a.* and *n.* (gland) beside the ear. **parotitis,** *n.* mumps. (Gk. *para*, beside; *ous*, ear)

paroxysm, *n.* fit, violent convulsion, of pain or emotion; periodic attack of disease. **paroxysmal,** *a.* (Gk. *para*, beyond; *oxus*, sharp)

paroxytone, *a.* and *n.* (word) with acute accent on last syllable but one. (*para-+oxytone*)

parpen, *n.* stone passing through wall, binding-stone. (O.F. *parpain*)

parquet, *n.* flooring of wooden blocks arranged in pattern.—*v.t.* floor thus. **parquetry,** *n.* (F.)

parr, *n.* young salmon.

parrot, *n.* kinds of bird with brilliant plumage and hooked beak, sometimes able to imitate speech; one who repeats another's words.—*v.t.* repeat mechanically. **parrotry,** *n.* unintelligent repetition.

parry, *v.t.* ward off, turn aside.—*n.* defensive movement in fencing etc. (L. *parare*, prepare)

parse, *v.t.* classify (word), analyse (sentence), in terms of grammar.

parsec, *n.* (*astron.*) unit of stellar distances, 3·26 light-years, about 19 billion miles. (*par*allax; *sec*ond)

Parsee, *n.* Indian adherent of Zoroastrianism. (Pers. *Pars*, Persia)

parsimony, *n.* extreme frugality; meanness, stinginess. **parsimonious,** *a.* sparing, niggardly. (L. *parcere*, spare)

parsley, *n.* herb with crinkly leaves used for seasoning. (Gk. *petra*, rock; *selinon*, parsley)

parsnip, *n.* plant with large yellow root cooked for food. (L. *pastinaca*)

parson, *n.* priest of parish, vicar; *colloq.*) any clergyman. **p.-bird,** *n.* a black New Zealand bird. **parsonic,** *a.* **parsonage,** *n.* incumbent's house. (L. *persona*, person)

part, *n.* portion, section; share; interest; duty, function; actor's role; side, party; organ, member; (*mus.*) one of the melodies of a harmony; (*Shake.*) act; (*pl.*) region; qualities, talent.—*adv.* partly.—*v.t.* and *i.* divide, sever; separate; (*arch.*) distribute; (*sl.*) pay money; (*Shake.*) depart (from). **for my p.,** as far as I am concerned. **for the most p.,** commonly. **in good, bad, p.,** amicably, resentfully. **p. and parcel,** an essential part. **p. of speech,** grammatical classification. **p. with,** give up. **p.-owner,** *n.* sharer of ownership. **p.-song,** *n.* with three or more vocal parts. (L. *pars*)

partake, *v.t.* and *i.* (*past* **partook,** *p.p.* **partaken**) take a share; eat or drink some (of); be suggestive, smack (of); (*Shake.*) impart. **partaker,** *n.* (*Shake.*) adherent. (*part*; *take*)

partan, *n.* (*Scot.*) crab. (Gael.)

parterre, *n.* ornamental arrangement of flower beds and paths; pit of theatre. (F.)

partheno-, from Gk. *parthenos,* virgin, used in **parthenocarpy,** *n* bearing of fruit without fertilization; **parthenogenesis,** *n.* reproduction without sexual union, virgin birth, hence **parthenogenetic,** *a.*

Parthian, *a.* of Parthia. **P. shot, shaft,** parting thrust, sally made at departure.

parti, *n.* person from match-making point of view. *p. pris,* preconceived view, bias. (F.)

partial, *a.* incomplete; prejudiced, unfair. **p. to,** fond of. **partiality,** *n.* biased judgment; liking. (*part*)

partible, *a.* that can be divided.

participate, *v.i.* and *t.* have share (in), partake. **participant, participator,** *nn.* sharer. **participation,** *n.* (L. *pars,* part; *capere,* take)

participle, *n.* adjectival part of verb. **participial,** *a.* (L. *participium*)

particle, *n.* minute portion of matter; very small part; (*gram.*) word that cannot be used alone, prefix, suffix. (L. *particula,* little part)

particoloured, *a.* differently coloured in different parts, variegated.

particular, *a.* relating to one, personal; individual, distinct; special, remarkable; minute, detailed; fastidious, hard to please.—*n.* detail, single item; (*Shake.*) personal concern; (*pl.*) detailed report. **in p.,** especially. **particularism,** *n.* exclusive devotion to party or sect; principle of political freedom for each state in a federation; doctrine that salvation is only for the elect. **particularist,** *n.* **particularity,** *n.* being particular. **particularize,** *v.t.* describe in detail, mention one by one. **particularly,** *adv.* very; especially; in detail. (*particle*)

parting, *n.* leave-taking; separation: dividing-line in combing hair. **p. of the ways,** cross-roads.

partisan, *n.* adherent, blind follower, of party or cause; guerrilla.—*a.* favouring one side. **partisanship,** *n.* (*part*)

partisan, *n.* long-handled pike, halberd. (It. *partesana*)

partition, *n.* division into parts; compartment, cell; interior wall.—*v.t.* divide into sections, cut up. **partite,** *a.* (*bot.*) divided almost to the base. **partitive,** *a.* and *n.* (word) denoting partition or part. (*part*)

partizan, same as **partisan.**

partner, *n.* associate, companion; one who shares the risks and profits of a business; one of a couple who dance or play together; husband, wife.—*v.t.* join as partners, be partner to. **partnership,** *n.*

partook, see **partake.**

partridge, *n.* a game-bird; (*Amer.*) ruffed grouse. (Gk. *perdix*)

parturient, *a.* about to give birth, in labour. **parturition,** *n.* childbirth. (L. *parere,* bring forth)

party, *n.* political group, faction; side in contest, lawsuit, or contract; small company, detachment; social gathering; person consenting, accessory; (*vulg.*) person. **p. wall,** common wall separating two houses. **p.-coloured,** *a.* particoloured. (*part*)

parvenu, *n.* vulgar newly rich person, upstart. (F.)

parvis, *n.* enclosed space in front of church. (O.F. *parevis*)

pas, *n.* step; precedence. *p. seul, de deux,* dance for one, two. (F.)

paschal, *a.* of the Passover; of Easter. (Heb. *pasakh,* pass over)

pash, *n.* (*sl.*) passion. (abbr.)

pash, *v.t.* (*Shake.*) smite; smash.

pash, *n.* (*Shake.*) head.

pasha, *n.* title of high Turkish or Egyptian official. **pashalic,** *n.* his province or jurisdiction. (Turk.)

pashm, *n.* under-fur of Cashmere goat, used for shawls. (Pers. =wool)

pasque-flower, *n.* kind of anemone. (F. *passefleur*)

pasquinade, *n.* lampoon, satire. (It. *Pasquino,* statue in Rome on which lampoons used to be posted)

pass, *v.i.* and *t.* proceed, go; elapse, happen; come to an end, die; change, be transferred; be accepted or known; go by, beyond, or through; be successful in (examination); outstrip, exceed; hand on, circulate; utter; void.—*n.* narrow passage, defile; free ticket; state of extremity; thrust, movement of hands; passing of examination; (*football*) passing of ball from one player to another. **bring, come, to p.,** cause to happen, happen. **p. away,** come to an end; die. **p. degree,** one without honours. **p. for,** be taken for. **p. off,** cease gradually; palm off. **p. out,** (*Amer. sl.*) lose consciousness. **p. over,** omit, disregard; die. **p. the time of day,** exchange greetings. **p. up,** (*Amer.*) let go by, renounce. (L. *passus,* pace)

passable, *a.* fairly good, tolerable; (of river) that can be crossed.

passado, *n.* (*Shake.*) forward thrust with sword.

passage, *n.* act or right of passing; transit, transition; crossing from port to port; channel; corridor; portion of book; (*pl.*) what passes between two persons.—*v.i.* and *t.* (of horse) go sideways, cause to do this. **bird of p.,** migratory bird; transient visitor. **north-east, north-west, p.,** ship-route round north of Asia, America. **p. of arms,** conflict.

passant, *a.* (*heraldry*) walking. (*pass*)

pass-book, *n.* book with depositor's copy of bank-account.

passé, *a.* (*fem.* *passée*) having lost youth's freshness; out of date. (F.)

passementerie, *n.* trimming of gold or silver lace, braid, beads etc. (F.)

passenger, *n.* traveller in public conveyance; wayfarer; man who does not pull his weight. (*passage*)

passe-partout, *n.* framing with picture, glass, and back held together by strips of paper or cloth; master-key. (F. =pass everywhere)

passerine, *a.* of the order of perching birds. (L. *passer*, sparrow)

passim, *adv.* here and there, throughout. (L.)

passimeter, *n.* automatic ticket-booking machine. (*pass*; *meter*)

passing, *a.* transient; casual.—*adv.* (*arch.*) very, exceedingly.—*n.* departure, death. **p.-bell,** *n.* bell tolled immediately after death.

passion, *n.* intense feeling; violent rage; sexual desire, ardour; the sufferings of Christ on the cross; (*Shake.*) grief.—*v.i.* (*poet.*) feel, express, passion. **P. Play,** mystery play of Christ's Passion. **P. Sunday,** 5th Sunday in Lent. **P. Week,** week before Easter. **p.-flower,** *n.* climbing plant with large flower resembling crown of thorns. **passional,** *a.* of passion.—*n.* book telling of sufferings of saints and martyrs. **passionate,** *a.* moved by, showing, passion; quick-tempered; ardent, fervid; (*Shake.*) sorrowful. **passionless,** *a.* cold, unemotional. (L. *pati*, suffer)

passive, *a.* acted upon, not acting; inert; unresisting; (*gram.*) expressing state of being acted upon.—*n.* passive form of verb. **passivity,** *n.* (L. *pati*, suffer)

pass-key, *n.* master-key; latch-key.

passman, *n.* one taking pass degree.

Passover, *n.* Jewish spring festival; sacrifice at it. (in memory of passing over of the Israelites when the Egyptians were smitten)

passport, *n.* official document showing one's identity and permitting travel abroad; thing that ensures admission. (*pass*; *port*)

password, *n.* word, phrase, to distinguish friend from enemy, countersign.

past, *a.* gone by, elapsed; just over; (*gram.*) expressing past action.—*n.* past time; past career, esp. discreditable one.—*prep.* beyond.—*adv.* by. **p. master,** former master; adept. (*pass*)

paste, *n.* soft plastic mixture; flour and water forming dough or adhesive; relish of pounded fish or meat; fine glass used for sham gems.—*v.t.* stick with paste; cover by pasting. **pasteboard,** *n.* thick stiff paper; (*sl.*) card. —*a.* flimsy. (O.F.)

pastel, *n.* dry pigment-paste, crayon of this; (art of) drawing with crayons; woad, dye from woad.—*a.* delicately coloured. **pastellist,** *n.* artist using pastels. (*paste*)

pastern, *n.* part of horse's foot between fetlock and hoof. (O.F. *pasturon*)

pasteurism, *n.* prevention or cure of hydrophobia etc. by successive inoculations. **pasteurize,** *v.t.* sterilize (milk) by heat. **pasteurization,** *n.* (L. *Pasteur*, scientist)

pastiche, pasticcio, *nn.* musical, literary, or artistic patchwork of borrowings; work in imitation of another's style. (F. and It.)

pastille, pastil, *n.* lozenge; aromatic cone burnt as fumigator. (L. *pastillus*, small roll)

pastime, *n.* recreation, diversion; game. (*pass*; *time*)

pastor, *n.* minister of congregation; spiritual adviser. **pastoral,** *a.* of shepherds or rural life; used for pasture; of spiritual pastors.—*n.* conventional poem of rural life; letter from bishop to clergy or minister to congregation. **pastoralism, pastorality,** *nn.* **pastorálě,** *n.* (*pl.* **pastorali**) musical composition with pastoral subject. **pastorate,** *n.* office of pastor; pastors collectively. **pastorium,** *n.* (*Amer.*) parsonage. (L. = shepherd)

pastry, *n.* baked flour-paste; cakes, tarts etc. **p.-cook,** *n.* baker of pastry.

pasture, *n.* grass for food of cattle; grazing land.—*v.i.* and *t.* feed (cattle) on grass, graze. **pasturage,** *n.* pasturing; pasture. (L. *pascere*, feed)

pasty, *n.* meat etc. enclosed in paste and baked without dish. (*paste*)

pasty, *a.* like paste; pale.

pat, *v.t.* and *i.* strike gently with palm of hand or flat object.—*n.* patting touch or sound; small moulded lump of butter. **p. on the back,** congratulation, approval. **p.-ball,** *n.* feeble lawn-tennis.

pat, *a.* apt, apposite.—*adv.* opportunely; fluently. **stand p.,** stick to decision; (*poker*) keep hand as first dealt.

Pat, *n.* nickname for Irishman. (*Patrick*)

patagium, *n.* (*pl.* **patagia**) wing-membrane of bat. (L. =gold edging)

patamar, same as **pattamar.**

patavinity, *n.* provincialism. (L. *Patavium*, Padua)

patch, *n.* piece of material used in mending; piece of plaster over wound; shield for injured eye; black spot of silk etc. worn on cheek to show off complexion; irregular spot on surface; plot of ground; shred, remnant; (*Shake.*) fool.—*v.t.* repair with patch; piece together. **not a p. on,** not comparable to. **p. up,** mend temporarily; smooth over (quarrel). **patchery,** *n.* patchwork; (*Shake.*) roguery. (M.E.)

patchouli, *n.* an Indian plant; perfume got from it. (native)

patchwork, *n.* work of variegated pieces sewn together; jumble.

patchy, *a.* not uniform, unequal.
pate, *n.* (*arch.*) head.
pâté, *n.* pie. *p. de foie gras,* rich paste of goose's liver. (F.)
patella, *n.* knee-cap. **patellar, patellate,** *aa.* (L. =small pan)
paten, *n.* plate for bread in the eucharist; (*Shake.*) thin plate. (L. *patina,* plate)
patent, *a.* plain, obvious; patented; (*colloq.*) ingenious.—*n.* exclusive right to make or sell something; invention, process, protected by this; letters patent.—*v.t.* secure by patent. **letters p.,** royal grant of title or special privilege. **p. leather,** with black varnished surface. **patentee,** *n.* holder of patent. (L. *patēre,* lie open)
pater, *n.* (*sl.*) father. **paterfamilias,** *n.* father of a family. **paternal,** *a.* of a father; fatherly; on the father's side. **paternalism,** *n.* system of fussy interference. **paternity,** *n.* fatherhood; paternal descent; authorship. **paternoster,** *n.* Lord's Prayer in Latin; every eleventh bead in rosary; fishing-line with hooks at intervals. (L.)
path, *n.* footway; track; line of movement, course. (O.E. *pæth*)
Pathan, *n.* Afghan tribesman of Indian frontier. (Hind.)
pathetic, *a.* causing pity or sorrow, touching; of the emotions. **p. fallacy,** artistic convention making nature share in human emotions. **pathetical,** *a.* (*Shake.*) affecting. (Gk. *paschein,* suffer)
pathic, *n.* catamite. (Gk. *pathikos,* passive)
patho-, from Gk. *pathos,* suffering, emotion, used in **pathogenesis, pathogeny,** *nn.* origin or development of disease; **pathogenetic, pathogenic,** *aa.* causing disease; **pathognomonic,** *a.* characteristic of particular disease; **pathognomy,** *n.* study of the expressions of emotions, hence **pathognomic,** *a.*; **pathology,** *n.* science of diseases; **pathological,** *a.* of pathology, of the nature of disease; **pathologist,** *n.* one versed in pathology.
pathos, *n.* quality that excites pity or sadness; expression of deep feeling. (Gk. =suffering)
patience, *n.* enduring or waiting with calmness; perseverance; a card-game for one; (*Shake.*) permission. **patient,** *a.* having or showing patience, not easily provoked.—*n.* person under medical treatment. (L. *pati,* suffer)
patin, patine, same as **paten.**
patina, *n.* green film on antique bronze. **patinated, patinous,** *aa.* (F. *patine*)
patio, *n.* open inner court in Spanish house. (Sp.)
pâtisserie, *n.* pastry-shop. (F.)
patois, *n.* dialect of lower classes. (F.)
patriarch, *n.* father and head of family or tribe; venerable old man; (in Roman Catholic and Greek Churches) bishop of highest rank. **patriarchal,** *a.* **patriarchate,** *n.* office or rank of patriarch. **patriarchy,** *n.* government by head of tribe; community under this. **patriarchism,** *n.* (Gk. *patēr,* father; *archē,* rule)
patrician, *n.* member of ancient Roman nobility; nobleman.—*a.* aristocratic. (L. *patricius*)
patricide, *n.* murder, murderer, of own father. **patricidal,** *a.* (L. *pater,* father; *caedere,* kill)
patrimony, *n.* property inherited from father or ancestors, heritage. (L. *patrimonium*)
patriot, *n.* one who loves and serves his native country. **patriotic,** *a.* **patriotism,** *n.* love for, loyalty to, one's country. (Gk. *patriōtēs,* fellow-countryman)
patristic, *a.* of the Fathers of the Church.—*n.pl.* study of their works. (L. *pater,* father)
patrol, *v.i.* and *t.* go the rounds (of) to keep watch and maintain order.—*n.* patrolling; man, detachment of troops or police, on patrol. **on p.,** patrolling. **patrolman,** *n.* (*Amer.*) policeman on beat. (F. *patrouiller,* go through puddles)
patron, *n.* (*fem.* **patroness**) one who gives moral or financial backing; regular customer; person having right of presentation to benefice. **p. saint,** tutelary saint. **patronage,** *n.* support given by patron; dispensing of appointments; patronizing manner.—*v.t.* (*Shake.*) uphold. **patronal,** *a.* of patron saint. **patronize,** *v.t.* support, encourage; frequent (shop); treat with condescension. **patronizing,** *a.* condescending. (L. *patronus*)
patronymic, *a.* and *n.* (name) derived from father or ancestor; surname. (Gk. *patēr,* father; *onoma,* name)
pattamar, *n.* Indian dispatch-boat; lateen-rigged Indian coaster.
patten, *n.* wooden sole for raising foot above wet; clog. (F. *patin*)
patter, *n.* quick tapping sound.—*v.i.* make, run with, patter. (*pat*)
patter, *v.t.* and *i.* utter rapidly and mechanically, mutter.—*n.* glib talk of cheap-jack, conjuror etc.; cant of class, jargon. (*paternoster*)
pattern, *n.* person or thing to be copied; model, example; sample of cloth; ornamental design; (*Shake.*) precedent.—*v.t.* model, design; decorate with pattern; (*Shake.*) be pattern for. (*patron*)
pattle, *n.* (*Scot.*) small long-handled spade.
patty, *n.* small pie. (*pâté*)
patulous, *a,* spreading, extended. (L. *patēre,* lie open)
paucity, *n.* fewness, smallness of amount. (L. *paucus,* few)

paughty *a.* (*Scot.*) haughty; insolent.
Pauline, *a.* of St. Paul.—*n.* boy, girl, of St. Paul's School.
paulo-post-future, *n.* (*gram.*) future perfect tense; (*joc.*) immediate future. (L. =future a little after)
paulownia, *n.* tree with showy purple flowers. (Princess Anna *Pavlovna*)
Paul Pry, inquisitive person. (name in play)
paunch, *n.* belly; first stomach of ruminant.—*v.t.* disembowel. **paunchy,** *a.* big-bellied. (L. *pantex*)
pauper, *n.* poor person; one who is supported by poor-rates. **pauperism,** *n.* destitution. **pauperize,** *v.t.* make pauper of, esp. through dole. **pauperization,** *n.* (L. =poor)
pause, *n.* temporary stop; break in speech or reading; (*mus.*) mark (⌒ or ◡) denoting prolongation of note.—*v.i.* cease temporarily, wait; hesitate; linger. (Gk. *pauein*, stop)
pavage, *n.* paving; tax for paving streets.
pavan, *n.* an old stately dance. (F. *pavane*)
pave, *v.t.* make hard level surface on, cover with pavement. **p. the way for,** lead up to. *pavé*, *n.* pavement; paved street; close setting for jewels. **pavement,** *n.* flat slabs, tiles etc. forming surface of road or floor; paved footway at side of street. (L. *pavire*, beat down)
pavid, *a.* timid. (L. *pavidus*)
pavilion, *n.* tent, esp. large one on posts; summer-house; club-house on playing-field; projecting subdivision of building.—*v.t.* enclose like, furnish with, pavilion. (L. *papilio*)
paviour, *n.* workman employed in paving.
pavonine, *a.* of, like, a peacock. *pavonazzo*, *a.* and *n.* peacock-coloured (marble). (L. *pavo*, peacock)
paw, *n.* animal's foot; (*sl.*) hand.—*v.t.* and *i.* feel with paw; scrape (ground) with hoof; handle clumsily or rudely. (O.F. *powe*)
pawky, *a.* (*Scot.*) sly, shrewd; (of humour) dry, ironical.
pawl, *n.* pivoted catch to prevent wheel, capstan, from running back.—*v.t.* secure with pawl.
pawn, *n.* piece of lowest value in chess; mere tool. (L. *pedo*, foot-soldier)
pawn, *v.t.* deposit as security for money received; offer (honour, word) as pledge.—*n.* thing pawned, pledge; state of being pledged. **p.-ticket,** *n.* receipt for pawned goods. **pawnbroker,** *n.* one who lends money on security of pawned goods. **pawnee,** *n.* one who accepts pledge as security. **pawnshop,** *n.* pawnbroker's shop. (O.F. *pan*, pledge)
pawpaw, same as **papaw.**
pax, *n.* tablet with crucifix, kissed at mass by priest and congregation.—*int.* (*school sl.*) asking for truce. **P. Romana, Britannica,** peace imposed by Roman, British, Empire. *p. vobiscum*, peace be with you. (L. = peace)
paxwax, *n.* strong tendon in neck of animals.
pay, *v.t.* and *i.* (*past, p.p.* **paid**) give as due; remunerate, requite; discharge (debt to); bear cost, suffer penalty; render, bestow; be profitable (to).—*n.* wages; hire. **p. off,** pay in full; discharge; (of ship) fall to leeward. **p. one's way,** have no debts. **p. out,** be revenged on: let out (rope). **p. round,** turn ship's head. **p. the piper,** bear cost. **p. through the nose,** pay dearly. **p.-dirt,** *n.* deposit containing enough gold to be worth working. **p.-roll, p.-sheet,** *nn.* list of employees and their wages. **paying guest,** lodger treated as one of household. (L. *pacare*, appease)
pay, *v.t.* (*naut.*) coat with pitch. (L. *pix*, pitch)
payable, *a.* that must be paid, due; profitable; (*rare*) that may be paid.
payee, *n.* one to whom money is paid.
paymaster, *n.* officer who pays troops.
payment, *n.* paying; amount paid; recompense.
paynim, *n.* (*arch.*) pagan; Mohammedan; heathendom. (L. *paganus*, pagan)
paysage, *n.* landscape; landscape-painting. **paysagist,** *n.* (F.)
pea, *n.* a climbing plant; its round fruit, contained in pods. **sweet p.,** with fragrant coloured flowers. **p.-shooter,** *n.* boy's blowpipe for peas. **p.-souper,** *n.* (*colloq.*) thick yellow fog. (false singular from *pease*)
peace, *n.* freedom from war; treaty securing this; law and order; calm, quiet, tranquillity. **hold one's p.,** keep silence. **keep the p.,** refrain from, prevent, strife. **make one' p. with,** become reconciled with **p.-offering,** *n.* propitiatory gift. **p.-pipe,** *n.* calumet. **peaceable,** *a.* disposed to peace; (*rare*) peaceful. **peaceful,** *a.* having peace, tranquil, quiet; (*rare*) peaceable. **peacemaker,** *n.* one who reconciles enemies. (L. *pax*)
peach, *n.* round stone-fruit with downy skin; tree bearing it; (*sl.*) pretty girl. **p.-colour,** *n.* soft pale red. (L. *Persicum* malum, Persian apple)
peach, *v.i.* and *t.* (*sl.*) tell tales, turn informer; (*Shake.*) denounce. (O.F. *empechier*, impeach)
peachick, *n.* young of peacock.
peacock, *n.* (*fem.* **peahen**) large bird with brilliant-coloured fanlike tail; vain person.—*v.i.* strut about. **p. blue,** a lustrous blue. **peacockery,** *n.* strutting vanity. **peacocky,** *a.* **peafowl,** *n.* peacock or peahen. (L. *pavo*, peacock+*cock*)
pea-jacket, *n.* seaman's short heavy

woollen jacket. (Du. *pij*, coat of coarse woollen stuff +*jacket*)
peak, *v.i.* waste away; look sickly. **peaked, peaky,** *aa.* drawn, emaciated.
peak, *n.* pointed top or end; mountain summit; maximum point in record; eyeshade of cap; (*naut.*) narrow part of hold at bow or stern; upper outer corner of sail extended by gaff.—*v.t.* and *i.* raise, rise, to perpendicular. **peaked, peaky,** *aa.* having, ending in, a peak. (=*pike*)
peal, *n.* loud continuous sound of bell, thunder etc.; set of bells, changes rung on them.—*v.i.* and *t.* resound, ring out.
peanut, *n.* plant with pod that ripens underground; its fruit, monkey-nut.
pear, *n.* juicy fruit of tapering oval shape; tree bearing it. (L. *pirum*)
pearl, *n.* one of a row of loops forming decorative edging of lace.
pearl, *n.* lustrous white gem found in oyster; mother-of-pearl; pearl-like or precious thing; (*print.*) 5-point type, between diamond and nonpareil.—*v.i.* and *t.* fish for pearls; form drops (on), bespangle. **p.-ash,** *n.* potassium carbonate. **p. barley, sago, tapioca,** ground down to small grains. **p. button,** made of mother-of-pearl. **p.-diver, p.-fisher,** *nn.* one who dives, fishes, for pearls. **p.-powder,** *n.* cosmetic for whitening skin. **pearly,** *a.* clear, lustrous, like pearl.—*n.pl.* costermonger's dress covered with pearl buttons. (L.L. *perla*)
pearmain, *n.* kind of apple. (O.F. *permain*)
peart, *a.* (*Amer. dial.*) lively, saucy, full of spirits. (=*pert*)
peasant, *n.* countryman, rustic; (*Shake.*) low fellow, rascal. **p. proprietor,** one who works his own farm. **peasantry,** *n.* peasants collectively. (L. *pagus*, district)
pease, *n.* (*arch.*) peas. **p.-pudding,** *n.* porridge of boiled pease. **peasecod, peascod,** *n.* (*arch.*) pea-pod. (Gk. *pison*, pea)
peat, *n.* (*Shake.*) pet, darling.
peat, *n.* decayed vegetable matter from bogs; turf of this as fuel. **p.-bog,** *n.* where peat is dug. **p.-reek,** *n.* smoke of peat; highland whisky.
pebble, *n.* small roundish stone; rock-crystal used for spectacles, lens of this; kinds of agate.
pébrine, *n.* epidemic disease of silk-worms. (F.)
peccable, *a.* liable to sin. **peccability,** *n.* **peccadillo,** *n.* trifling misdeed, indiscretion. **peccant,** *a.* sinful, wrong; forming source of trouble; (*med.*) morbid. (L. *peccare*, sin)
peccary, *n.* American wild animal allied to pig. (native *pakira*)
peccavi, *v.i.* I have sinned.—*n.* confession of guilt. (L.)
pech, *v.i.* (*Scot.*) pant, breathe hard. (imit.)
pechan, *n.* (*Scot.*) crop; stomach.
peck, *n.* measure of capacity, 2 gallons; large amount. (O.F. *pek*)
peck, *v.t.* and *i.* (*sl.*) shy (stones). (=*pitch*)
peck, *v.t.* and *i.* strike (at) with beak, dab; make, pick up, by pecking; (*colloq.*) nibble.—*n.* stroke with beak: (*joc.*) perfunctory kiss; (*sl.*) food. **pecker,** *n.* kind of hoe; (*sl.*) spirits. **peckish,** *a.* (*sl.*) hungry.
Pecksniff, *n.* unctuous hypocrite, humbug. (name in Dickens)
pecten, *n.* (*zool.*) comb-like organ. **pectinate, pectinated,** *aa.* **pectination,** *n.* (L.=comb)
pectin, *n.* substance in fruit causing jam to set. **pectic,** *a.* (Gk. *pēgnunai*, make solid)
pectoral, *a.* of, worn on, good for diseases of, the breast.—*n.* breast ornament, esp. that of Jewish high priest. (L. *pectus*, breast)
pectose, *n.* substance like cellulose, yielding pectin.
peculate, *v.t.* and *i.* pilfer money entrusted to one's care, embezzle. **peculation, peculator,** *nn.* (L. *peculium*, private property)
peculiar, *a.* belonging exclusively (to); individual; particular, special; odd, singular. **peculiarity,** *n.* distinctiveness; distinguishing feature; oddity. **peculiarly,** *adv.* (L. *peculium*, private property)
pecuniary, *a.* of, consisting of, money. (L. *pecunia*, money)
pedagogue, *n.* schoolmaster; pedant. **pedagogic, pedagogical,** *aa.* **pedagogism, pedagoguism,** *n.* occupation, manner, of a pedagogue. **pedagogy, pedagogics,** *nn.* science of teaching. (Gk. *pais*, boy; *agein*, lead)
pedal, *n.* treadle of bicycle, sewing-machine etc.; organ-key, lever varying tone of piano, worked by foot.—*a.* (*anat.*) of foot or feet.—*v.i.* and *t.* work, drive with, pedal. (L. *pes*, foot)
pedant, *n.* one who makes a vain display of learning; one who insists overmuch on adherence to formal rules, precisian; doctrinaire; (*Shake.*) schoolmaster. **pedantic,** *a.* **pedantry,** *n.* (It. *pedante*)
pedarchy, pederasty etc., same as **paedarchy, paederasty** etc.
pedate, *a.* (*zool.*) having feet; (*bot.*) divided like toes. (L. *pes*, foot)
peddle, *v.i.* and *t.* travel about selling small wares, hawk; potter, trifle. **peddling,** *a.* trumpery, petty.
pedestal, *n.* base of column; stand for statue etc.; foundation; movable cupboard for chamber-pot.—*v.t.* set on pedestal. (It. *piè*, foot; *di*, of; *stallo*, stall)
pedestrian, *a.* of walking; on foot; dull, commonplace.—*n.* walker. **pedestrianism,** *n.* (L. *pes*, foot)
pedicel, pedicle, *nn.* small or subor-

dinate stalk; stalk-like structure.
pedicellate, pediculate, *aa.* (L. *pes,* foot+dim.)
pedicular, pediculous, *aa.* of lice; lousy. **pediculosis,** *n.* infestation with lice. (L. *pediculus,* louse)
pedicure, *n.* treatment of corns etc. on feet; chiropodist. (L. *pes,* foot; *cura,* care)
pedigree, *n.* genealogical table; ancestry; ancient lineage; derivation.—*a.* having a known ancestry.
pediment, *n.* trangular part, often richly sculptured, crowning front of Greek temple etc. **pedimental,** *a.*
pedlar, *n.* travelling vendor of small wares. **pedlary,** *n.*
pedometer, *n.* instrument for measuring distance walked by recording number of steps. (L. *pes,* foot. Gk. *metron,* measure)
pedrail, *n.* fitment on wheel automatically accommodating itself to rough ground. (L. *pes,* foot+*rail*)
peduncle, *n.* flower-stalk, stem; stalk-like structure. **peduncular, pedunculate,** *aa.* (L. *pes,* foot+dim.)
peek, *v.i.* peer.—*n.* peep. **p.-a-boo,** *n.* bo-peep.
peel, *n.* small square defence tower on Scottish borders. (L. *palus,* stake)
peel, *n.* baker's long-handled shovel; fire-shovel. (L. *pala*)
peel, *v.t.* and *i.* strip skin or rind from; take, come, off in strips; (*sl.*) undress, —*n.* skin of fruit, rind. **peeled,** *a.* (*Shake.*) tonsured. **peeling,** *n.* piece peeled off. (L. *pilare,* deprive of hair)
peeler, *n.* (*sl.*) policeman. (Sir R. *Peel*)
peen, *n.* pointed or thin end of head of hammer.
peenge, *v.i.* (*Scot.*) whine, fret.
peep, *v.i.* and *n.* squeak, cheep, chirp. (=*pipe*)
peep, *v.i.* look hastily or slyly; peer through chink; begin to appear, emerge.—*n.* furtive or hurried glance, glimpse; first appearance (of day). **p.-hole,** *n.* small hole to spy through. **p.-show,** *n.* small show viewed through hole with lens. **p.-sight,** *n.* aperture sight on rifle. **peeper,** *n.* one who peeps; (*sl.*) eye.
peepul, *n.* sacred Indian fig-tree, bo-tree. (Hind. *pīpal*)
peer, *v.i.* look narrowly or intently; appear, peep.
peer, *n.* equal in rank or merit; member of House of Lords; nobleman.—*v.t.* and *i.* rank with, equal. **peerage,** *n.* rank of peer; peers collectively, book with list of them. **peeress,** *n.* wife of peer; female holder of peerage. (L. *par,* equal)
peerie, *n.* (*Scot.*) top. **p.-heided,** *a.* feather-brained.
peerless, *a.* unequalled, matchless.
peesweep, same as **pewit.**
peevish, *a.* querulous, irritable; (*Shake.*) silly; obstinate. **peeve,** *v.t.* (*Amer. sl.*) annoy. **peeved,** *a.* sulky, irritated.
peevers, *n.* (*Scot.*) hop-scotch.
peewit, see **pewit.**
peg, *n.* pin, bolt, us. of wood, for securing framework, hanging things on, adjusting violin-string, marking score etc.; theme, pretext for discourse; drink, brandy-and-soda.—*v.t.* and *i.* fasten with peg; keep (price of stock) steady by buying or selling; (*sl.*) throw, prod (at). **king's p.,** brandy and champagne. **p. away,** persevere. **p. down,** restrict. **p. out,** mark with pegs; (*croquet*) finish game by hitting peg; (*sl.*) die. **take down a p.,** humble. **p.-top,** *n.* top spun with string.
pegamoid, *n.* an artificial leather.
Pegasus, *n.* poetic inspiration. (Gk. myth)
peignoir, *n.* woman's dressing-gown or wrapper.
peinct, (*Spens.*) form of paint.
peise, peize, *v.t.* (*Shake.*) weigh (down); poise. (*poise*)
pejorate, *v.t.* worsen, depreciate. **pejorative,** *a.* and *n.* disparaging (word). (L. *pejor,* worse)
pekan, *n.* American kind of **marten** with dark brown fur. (native *pekane*)
peke, *n.* pekinese. (abbr.)
pekin, *n.* kind of silk; civilian. (Chinese town)
pekinese, pekingese, *n.* long-haired Chinese pug-dog. (*Pekin,* town)
pekoe, *n.* choice kind of black tea. (Chin. *pek,* white; *ho,* down)
pelage, *n.* animal's hair or wool. (F.)
Pelagian, *a.* and *n.* (follower) of Pelagius, who denied the doctrine of original sin. **Pelagianism,** *n.*
pelagian, *a.* and *n.* deep-sea (animal), **pelagic,** *a.* (Gk. *pelagos,* sea)
pelargonium, *n.* kinds of plant with brightly coloured flowers, commonly called geranium. (Gk. *pelargos,* stork)
pelerine, *n.* woman's cape with long ends in front. (F. *pèlerin,* pilgrim)
pelf, *n.* money, wealth. (O.F. *pelfre*)
pelican, *n.* large fish-eating water-bird. (Gk. *pelekan*)
pelisse, *n.* woman's long mantle; hussar's jacket; child's cloak. (F.)
pellagra, *n.* deficiency disease affecting skin and nervous system. **pellagrous,** *a.*
pellet, *n.* small ball, pill; small shot.—*v.t.* hit with, form into, pellets. (L. *pila,* ball)
pellicle, *n.* thin skin, film. **pellicular,** *a.* (L. *pellis,* skin+dim.)
pellitory, *n.* (also **p. of Spain**) plant with pungent root. (Gk. *purethron,* feverfew)
pellitory, *n.* (also **p. of the wall**) green-flowered wall-plant. (L. *paries,* wall)
pell-mell, *adv.* and *a.* in disorder; headlong.—*n.* confusion, mêlée. (F. *pêle-mêle*)
pellucid, *a.* clear, transparent; **lucid. pellucidity,** *n.* (*per-*+*lucid*)

pelma, *n.* sole of foot. **pelmatogram,** *n.* impression of this. (Gk.)

pelmet, *n.* canopy for window-frame, concealing curtain-rods; valance.

pelota, *n.* Basque game like tennis, played with ball and racket. (Sp.)

pelotherapy, *n.* (*med.*) treatment by mud baths. (Gk. *pēlos*, mud; *therapeuein*, heal)

pelt, *v.t.* and *i.* assail with missile; (of rain) beat violently; rush; (*Shake.*) storm.—*n.* pelting. **at full p.,** at full speed.

pelt, *n.* raw hide. (L. *pellis*, skin)

pelta, *n.* (*pl.* **peltae**) small shield. **peltast,** *n.* ancient Greek light-armed soldier. **peltate,** *a.* shield-shaped. (Gk. *peltē*)

pelting, *a.* (*Shake.*) mean, paltry.

peltry, *n.* furs and skins. (*pelt*)

pelvis, *n.* (*pl.* **pelves**) bony cavity forming lower part of abdomen. **pelvic,** *a.* (L. =basin)

pemmican, *n.* meat dried, pounded, and pressed into cakes; condensed literary matter. (Amer. Ind. *pimecan*)

pemphigus, *n.* skin-disease with watery vesicles. **pemphigoid, pemphigous,** *aa.* (Gk. *pemphix*, bubble)

pen, *n.* instrument for writing with ink. —*v.t.* write; compose. **p.-name,** *n.* literary pseudonym. (L. *penna*, feather)

pen, *n.* small enclosure for cattle, fowls etc.; (*W. Indies*) plantation.—*v.t.* enclose in pen, shut up. (O.E. *penn*)

pen, *n.* female swan.

pen, *n.* (*Amer. sl.*) prison. (*penitentiary*)

penal, *a.* of, involving (esp. legal) punishment; punitive. **p. servitude,** imprisonment for three years or more with hard labour. **penalize,** *v.t.* lay under penalty; put at a disadvantage. **penalty,** *n.* punishment attached to offence; forfeit; handicap; (*football etc.*) disadvantage imposed for breaking rule. (Gk. *poinē*, penalty)

penance, *n.* suffering submitted to as expression of penitence; Roman Catholic sacrament including contrition, confession, satisfaction, and absolution.—*v.t.* impose penance on. (L. *paenitēre*, regret)

Penates, *n.pl.* household gods. (L.)

pence, see **penny.**

penchant, *n.* inclination, liking. (F.)

pencil, *n.* writing-instrument of lead, slate etc.; fine paint-brush; artist's style; set of convergent rays or straight lines.—*v.t.* draw, write, with pencil; enter (horse's name) in betting-book. **penciller,** *n.* (*sl.*) bookmaker. (L. *penis*, tail+dim.)

pend, *n.* (*Scot.*) narrow close leading off street.

pendant, pendent, *n.* hanging ornament; earring, locket; chandelier; complement, match; pennant. **pendent, pendant,** *a.* hanging; projecting; undecided; (*gram.*) unattached. **pendency,** *n.* *pendente lite*, while suit is in progress. **pendentive,** *n.* (*archit.*) portion of dome supported by single pillar. **pending,** *a.* awaiting settlement; in process.—*prep.* during; until. (L. *pendēre*, hang)

pendragon, *n.* ancient British prince. (W. *pen*, head +*dragon* standard)

pendulum, *n.* suspended weight swinging to and fro to regulate clock etc. **compensation p.,** adjusting itself to changes of temperature. **pendulate,** *v.i.* swing like pendulum; waver. **penduline,** *a.* (of nest) hanging; (of bird) building such nest. **pendulous,** *a.* hanging loosely; swinging. (L. *pendēre*, hang)

peneplain, *n.* (*geol.*) tract that is almost a plain. (L. *paene*, almost)

penetrate, *v.t.* and *i.* go through, pierce; comprehend, fathom; saturate, imbue; make way (into). **penetrable,** *a.* **penetralia,** *n.* innermost shrine; secrets. **penetrating,** *a.* acute, discerning; (of voice) easily heard through other sounds. **penetration,** *n.* penetrating; insight. **penetrative,** *a.* **penetrator,** *n.* (L. *penetrare*)

penguin, *n.* large short-legged sea-bird using wings as paddles; (*sl.*) member of Women's Royal Air Force.

penial, *a.* of penis.

penicillate, *a.* having, forming, small tufts: streaked. (*pencil*)

penicillin, *n.* substance, got from mould, which inhibits growth of bacteria.

peninsula, *n.* piece of land almost surrounded by water. **the P.,** Spain and Portugal. **peninsular,** *a.* of, like, a peninsula. **peninsulate,** *v.t.* make into a peninsula. (L. *paene*, almost; *insula*, island)

penis, *n.* (*pl.* **penes**) male copulative organ. (L.)

penitent, *a.* repentant for sin, contrite. —*n.* repentant sinner; one who is doing penance. **penitence,** *n.* repentance. **penitential,** *a.* of penitence. **penitentiary,** *n.* papal court or official regulating penance, dispensations etc.; reformatory prison; institution for reclaimed prostitutes; (*Amer.*) prison.—*a.* of penance or reformatory treatment. (L. *paenitēre*, repent)

penknife, *n.* small pocket-knife.

penman, *n.* writer. **penmanship,** *n.* skill in, style of, handwriting; literary style.

pennant, *n.* long tapering flag flown at masthead of warship etc.; pennon. (mixture of *pendant* and *pennon*)

pennate, *a.* winged, feathered. **peniform,** *a.* like a feather. (L. *penna*, feather)

penniless, *a.* poor, destitute.

pennill, *n.* (*pl.* **pennillion**) improvised verse or stanza sung to harp at Welsh eisteddfod. (W.)

pennon, *n.* narrow pointed or swallow-tailed flag of lancer or medieval knight; flag. (O.F. *penon*)

penn'orth, *abbr.* of **pennyworth.**

penny, *n.* (*pl.* **pence** denoting sum, **pennies** separate coins) bronze coin worth $\frac{1}{12}$ shilling. **p. dreadful**, cheap shocker. **p. wedding**, at which guests contribute to expenses. **pretty p.**, considerable sum. **p.-a-liner**, *n.* hack journalist. (O.E. *pening*)
pennyroyal, *n.* kind of mint formerly used in medicine.
pennyweight, *n.* (*abbr.* **dwt.**) $\frac{1}{20}$ oz. troy.
pennywort, *n.* kinds of round-leaved plant growing on walls (**wall p.**) or in marshes (**water p.**).
pennyworth, *n.* a penny's worth; bargain; trifle.
penology, *n.* study of punishment and prevention of crime. **penological**, *a.* **penologist**, *n.* (Gk. *poinē*, punishment; *legein*, speak)
pensile, *a.* hanging; (of bird) building hanging nest. (L. *pendere*, hang)
pension, *n.* boarding-house. *en p.*, as boarder at inclusive charge. (F.)
pension, *n.* periodic payment in consideration of past services.—*v.t.* grant pension to. **old-age p.**, state allowance to aged people. **p. off**, dismiss with pension. **pensionable**, *a.* entitled, entitling, to pension. **pensionary**, *a.* by way of pension.—*n.* recipient of pension; hireling. **pensioner**, *n.* recipient of pension; dependant, retainer; ordinary undergraduate at Cambridge. (L. *pendere*, weigh)
pensive, *a.* thoughtful, musing; wistful, melancholy. (L. *pendere*, weigh)
penstock, *n.* sluice, floodgate. (*pen*; *stock*)
pent, *a.* shut in, cooped up. (*pen*)
penta-, from Gk. *pente*, five, used in **pentachord**, *n.* five-stringed instrument, scale of five tones; **pentacle**, **pentagram**, *nn.* five-pointed star used as magic symbol; **pentad**, *n.* number five, group of five; **pentadactyl**, *a.* and *n.* (animal) having five fingers or toes, hence **pentadactylic**, *a.*; **pentaglot**, *a.* and *n.* (work) in five languages; **pentagon**, *n.* five-sided plane figure, hence **pentagonal**, *a.*; **pentahedron**, *n.* solid with five faces, hence **pentahedral**, *a.*; **pentamerous**, *a.* (*bot.*, *zool.*) with five parts or five joints; **pentameter**, **pentapody**, *nn.* verse of five feet; **pentastich**, *n.* stanza of five lines; **pentasyllable**, *n.* word of five syllables, hence **pentasyllabic**, *a.*; **pentateuch**, *n.* first five books of the Old Testament; **pentathlon**, *n.* composite Olympic contest of 200-metre and 1,500-metre run, broad jump, and throwing javelin and discus; **pentatomic**, *a.* having five atoms to the molecule; **pentatonic**, *a.* of five notes; **pentavalent**, *a.* having valency of five.
Pentecost, *n.* Jewish harvest festival, fifty days after Passover; (*arch.*) Whit Sunday. **pentecostal**, *a.* (Gk. *pentēkonta*, fifty)
penthouse, (*arch.*) **pentice**, *n.* sloping roof, shed with this, projecting from main building; awning; (*Amer.*) small house on flat roof of another building. (L.L. *appendicium*, appendage)
pentstemon, *n.* bright-flowered garden plant. (Gk. *pente*, five; *stēmōn*, stamen)
penultimate, *a.* last but one.—*n.* (also **penult**) penultimate syllable. (L. *paene*, almost; *ultimus*, last)
penumbra, *n.* partly shaded region round total shadow, esp. in eclipse; lighter outer part of sun-spot. **penumbral**, *a.* (L. *paene*, almost; *umbra*, shadow)
penury, *n.* poverty; scarcity, want. **penurious**, *a.* grudging, stingy; scanty. (L. *penuria*)
peon, *n.* day-labourer; serf, enslaved debtor, in Mexico; native orderly or constable in India. **peonage**, *n.* (Sp.)
peony, *n.* plant with showy red, pink, or white flowers. (Gk. *paiōnia*)
people, *n.* (as *sing.*) race, nation, community; lower classes; (as *pl.*) inhabitants; subjects; relations; persons generally.—*v.t.* populate. **the good p.**, fairies. (L. *populus*)
pep, *n.* (*Amer. sl.*) energy, go. (*pepper*)
peperino, *n.* light porous volcanic rock. (It.)
pepper, *n.* hot pungent seasoning of powdered berry; plant bearing this; pungent thing.—*v.t.* sprinkle, flavour, with pepper; besprinkle; hit with small shot; pelt, beat; (*Shake.*) do for. **black, white, p.**, from unripe, ripe, berry. **p.-and-salt**, *a.* and *n.* (cloth) of dark and light threads interwoven. **p.-castor**, **p.-caster**, **p.-pot**, *nn.* box with perforated top for sprinkling pepper. **pepperbox**, *n.* pepper-castor; (*joc.*) small turret. **peppercorn**, *n.* dried pepper berry. **peppermint**, *n.* a kind of mint; oil from it; lozenge flavoured with this. **peppery**, *a.* of, like, full of, pepper; fiery; hot-tempered. (Gk. *peperi*)
pepsin, *n.* digestive ferment in gastric juice. **peptic**, *a.* of, promoting, digestion. **peptone**, *n.* substance formed from action of pepsin on proteids. **peptonize**, *v.t.* convert into peptone; pre-digest. (Gk. *pepsis*, digestion)
per, *prep.* by means of (**p. post**, **rail** etc.); for or in **each** (**p. man, dozen** etc.). **as p. usual**, (*joc.*) as usual. **p. annum**, *p. diem*, *mensem*, (of payment) each year, day, month. *p. caput*, *capita*, a head, each. **p. cent**, in every hundred. *p. contra*, on the other side of the account, as a set-off. *p. mille*, in every thousand. *p. procurationem*. (*abbr. per proc.*, *per pro.*, *p.p.*) by proxy (used when signing for someone else). *p. se*, by itself; by its very nature. (L.)
per-, *pref.* through, as in **perforate**; completely, as in **perturb**; to the bad,

as in **pervert**; (*chem.*) denoting maximum proportion of some element in compound, as in **peroxide.** (L.)

peradventure, *adv.* (*arch.*) perchance; by chance.—*n.* uncertainty. (O.F. *par aventure*)

perai, peraya, *n.* voracious S. American freshwater fish. (native)

perambulate, *v.t.* walk through, over, or round; traverse, survey (parish boundaries). **perambulation,** *n.* **perambulatory,** *a.* **perambulator,** *n.* one who perambulates; baby-carriage. (L. *per*, through; *ambulare*, walk)

percale, *n.* closely woven cambric. (F.)

perceive, *v.t.* apprehend through senses; discern, see; comprehend, grasp. **perceivable,** *a.* (L. *per-*, completely; *capere*, take)

percentage, *n.* rate per hundred; proportion. (*per cent*)

percept, *n.* (*philos.*) thing perceived. **perceptible,** *a.* perceivable. **perceptibility,** *n.* **perception,** *n.* act or faculty of perceiving; (*philos.*) referring of sensations to their external causes. **perceptional,** *a.* **perceptive,** *a.* having power of perceiving; of perception. **perceptivity,** *n.* (*perceive*)

perch, *n.* bird's resting-place, roost; high seat or position; measure of length, 5½ yds.—*v.i.* and *t.* alight, rest, on perch; balance (oneself) on; set in high position. (L. *pertica*, pole)

perch, *n.* spiny-finned freshwater fish. (Gk. *perkē*)

perchance, *adv.* (*arch.*) perhaps.

percheron, *n.* breed of strong swift draught horses. (F.)

percipient, *a.* perceiving; having perception.—*n.* one who perceives; (*telepathy*) one who receives communications otherwise than through the five senses. **percipience,** *n.* (*perceive*)

percolate, *v.i.* and *t.* pass through small openings or pores; ooze through, permeate; filter. **percolation,** *n.* **percolator,** *n.* coffee-pot with strainer; filtering-vessel. (L. *per*, through; *colare*, strain)

percuss, *v.t.* (*med.*) tap (body) gently to find condition of internal organ by sound. (L. *percutere*, strike)

percussion, *n.* impact, collision; shock, sound, caused by this; (*med.*) percussing. **p. cap,** small metal cap containing fulminating powder used to detonate charge of firearm. **p. instrument,** one played by striking, e.g. drum, cymbals. **percussive,** *a.*

percutaneous, *a.* done, acting, through the skin. (*per-*; *cutaneous*)

perdie, perdy, same as **pardie.**

perdition, *n.* utter destruction; damnation; hell. (L. *perdere*, destroy)

perdu, perdue, *a.* in ambush; out of sight, hidden.—*n.* (*Shake.*) man on a forlorn hope. (F.)

perdurable, *a.* very durable, lasting; eternal. **perdurability,** *n.* (*per-*)

père, *n.* father, senior. (F.)

peregall, *a.* and *n.* (*Spens.*) equal.

peregrinate, *v.i.* and *t.* travel, roam about.—*a.* (*Shake.*) exotic. **peregrination, peregrinator,** *nn.* (*peregrine*)

peregrine, *a.* (*arch.*) foreign, outlandish.—*n.* (also **p. falcon**) kind of falcon used in hawking. (L. *peregrinus*)

peremptory, *a.* imperious, dictatorial; not admitting discussion or refusal; final, decisive. (L. *perimere*, destroy)

perennial, *a.* perpetual, never-failing; (of plant) lasting several years.—*n.* perennial plant. **perenniality,** *n.* (L. *per*, through; *annus*, year)

perfect, *a.* faultless, supremely excellent; exact, without error; entire, not deficient; complete, utter; fully skilled; (*gram.*) expressing completed action; (*Shake.*) certain; satisfied.—*n.* perfect tense.—*v.t.* make perfect; complete; improve; (*Shake.*) instruct fully. **perfectible,** *a.* **perfectibility,** *n.* **perfection,** *n.* perfecting; being perfect; faultlessness, great excellence; highest manifestation; perfect person or thing; (*pl.*) accomplishments. **perfectionist,** *n.* one who holds that moral perfection may be attained in this world. **perfectionism,** *n.* **perfectly,** *adv.* thoroughly, quite; quite well; exactly. (L. *per-*, completely; *facere*, do)

perfecto, *n.* (*Amer.*) medium-sized cigar, tapered at both ends. (Sp.)

perfervid, *a.* very fervid, intense.

perfidy, *n.* breach of faith, treachery. **perfidious,** *a.* (L. *perfidia*)

perfoliate, *a.* (*bot.*) with stalk apparently passing through leaf. (L. *per*, through; *folium*, leaf)

perforate, *v.t.* and *i.* pierce, penetrate; make hole or row of holes in.—*a.* (of postage stamps) separated by perforation. **perforation,** *n.* perforating; hole; row of holes to facilitate tearing. **perforative,** *a.* **perforator,** *n.* (L. *per*, through; *forare*, bore)

perforce, *adv.* of necessity; (*Shake.*) by violence.—*n.* necessity. (*per*)

perform, *v.t.* and *i.* accomplish, carry out, do; go through, execute; act, give exhibition, do tricks. **performance,** *n.* execution, doing; achievement, feat; presentation of play or show. **performer,** *n.* executant; actor, artiste. **performing,** *a.* trained to do tricks. (O.F. *parformer*)

perfume, *n.* pleasant smell, fragrance; perfumed liquid, scent; any odour.—*v.t.* fill, saturate, with perfume. **perfumer,** *n.* seller of perfumes. **perfumery,** *n.* his shop, wares, or business. (L. *per-*, thoroughly; *fumare*, smoke)

perfunctory, *a.* done merely as matter of form, half-hearted; superficial, hasty. (L. *per-*, thoroughly; *fungi*, perform)

perfuse, *v.t.* sprinkle, pour over; shed over, suffuse. **perfusion,** *n.* **perfusive,** *a.* (L. *per-*, thoroughly; *fundere*, pour)

pergameneous, *a.* of, like, parchment. (*parchment*)

pergola, *n.* arbour or garden-walk arched over by climbing plants on trellis-work. (It.)

pergunnah, pergana, *n.* group of Indian villages forming territorial division. (Hind. *parganah*, district)

perhaps, *adv.* possibly, maybe. (*per*; *hap*)

peri, *n.* Persian fairy, descendant of fallen angels; beautiful being. (Pers.)

peri-, *pref.* round, about, as in **perimeter.** (Gk.)

periagua, same as **piragua.**

perianth, *n.* outer part of flower, calyx and corolla together. (Gk. *peri*, around; *anthos*, flower)

periapt, *n.* amulet. (Gk. *peri*, about; *haptein*, fasten)

pericardium, *n.* membrane enclosing heart. **pericardiac, pericardial,** *aa.* **pericarditis,** *n.* inflammation of pericardium. (Gk. *peri*, around; *kardia*, heart)

pericarp, *n.* seed-vessel of plant. **pericarpial,** *a.* (Gk. *peri*, around; *karpos*, fruit)

perichondrium, *n.* membrane covering cartilages. (Gk. *peri*, around; *chondros*, cartilage)

periclinal, *a.* (*geol.*) sloping on all sides from central point. (Gk. *peri*, around; *klinein*, slope)

pericopē, *n.* extract; portion of Scriptures read at public worship. (Gk. *peri*, around; *koptein*, cut)

pericranium, *n.* membrane surrounding skull; (*joc.*) skull. (*peri-*)

peridot, *n.* olivine, kind of chrysolite. (F.)

perigee, *n.* point of moon's or planet's orbit nearest earth. **perigean,** *a.* (Gk. *peri*, around; *gē*, earth)

perigynous, *a.* (with stamens) growing round pistil. (Gk. *peri*, around; *gunē*, female)

perihelion, *n.* point of planet's orbit nearest sun. (Gk. *peri*, around; *hēlios*, sun)

peril, *n.* danger; risk, hazard.—*v.t.* endanger. **perilous,** *a.* dangerous. (L. *periculum*)

perimeter, *n.* line bounding closed figure; length of this. (Gk. *peri*, around; *metron*, measure)

perineum, *n.* part between anus and genitals, fork. **perineal,** *a.* (L.L.)

period, *n.* portion of time; stage in history or life, epoch; circuit; full stop (.); complete sentence, us. with several clauses; (*astron.*) planet's time of revolution; (*med.*) time disease takes to run course; (*Shake.*) end, goal; (*pl.*) stately rhetoric; menses.—*v.t.* (*Shake.*) put an end to. **periodic,** *a.* relating to a period; recurring at regular intervals, cyclic; intermittent; (of style) with long close-knit complex sentences. **periodicity,** *n.* **periodical,** *a.* periodic. —*n.* magazine etc. issued at fixed times. (Gk. *peri*, around; *hodos*, way)

periosteum, *n.* membrane covering the bones. **periosteal,** *a.* **periostitis,** *n.* inflammation of periosteum. (Gk. *peri*, around; *osteon*, bone)

peripatetic, *a.* walking about, itinerant; of the school of Aristotle, who walked up and down as he taught.—*n.* follower of Aristotle; (*joc.*) walker. **peripateticism,** *n.* Aristotelian philosophy. (Gk. *peri*, about; *patein*, walk)

peripeteia, peripetia, *n.* sudden change of fortune, esp. in drama. (Gk.)

periphery, *n.* line forming boundary of round figure, circumference; surface, outside. **peripheral,** *a.* (Gk. *peri*, around; *pherein*, bear)

periphrasis, periphrase, *n.* (*pl.* **periphrases**) roundabout speech or phrase, circumlocution. **periphrastic,** *a.* **periphrastically,** *adv.* (Gk.)

periplus, *n.* circumnavigation. (Gk. *peri*, around; *plous*, voyage)

peripteral, *a.* (*archit.*) with row of columns on every side. (Gk. *peri*, around; *pteron*, row of columns)

perique, *n.* a strong Louisiana tobacco.

periscope, *n.* device of mirrors giving view over obstacle or (to observer in submarine) above water. **periscopic,** *a.* (Gk. *peri*, around; *skopein*, look)

perish, *v.i.* and *t.* pass away, die; be destroyed; decay; (of cold) distress, exhaust. **perishable,** *a.* liable to decay quickly.—*n.pl.* perishable foodstuffs. **perisher,** *n.* (*sl.*) blighter. **perishing,** *a.* (*sl.*) blinking. (L. *perire*)

perisperm, *n.* albumen round embryo-sac of seed. (Gk. *peri*, around; *sperma*, seed)

perispomenon, perispome, *a.* and *n.* (word) with circumflex accent on last syllable. (Gk. *perispaein*, mark with circumflex)

peristalith, *n.* prehistoric ring of standing stones. (Gk. *peri*, around; *histanai*, stand; *lithos*, stone)

peristalsis, *n.* rhythmic movement of intestines forcing contents onward. **peristaltic,** *a.* (Gk. *peri*, around; *stellein*, send)

peristeronic, *a.* of pigeons. (Gk. *peristera*, pigeon)

peristome, *n.* fringe round rim of capsule of moss; lip of spiral shell. (Gk. *peri*, around; *stoma*, mouth)

peristyle, *n.* surrounding range of pillars; court within this. (Gk. *peri*, around; *stulos*, pillar)

peritoneum, peritonaeum, *n.* membrane lining inside of abdomen. **peritoneal,** *a.* **peritonitis,** *n.* inflam-

mation of peritoneum. (Gk. *peritonaion*)
perityphlitis, *n.* inflammation of parts round caecum. (Gk. *peri,* around; *tuphlos,* blind)
periwig, *n.* wig. (*peruke*)
periwinkle, *n.* blue-flowered evergreen trailing shrub. (L. *pervinca*)
periwinkle, *n.* small edible shell-fish.
perjure, *v.refl.* swear falsely, commit perjury.—*n.* (*Shake.*) perjurer. **perjured,** *a.* guilty of perjury. **perjurer,** *n.* **perjury,** *n.* swearing to what is untrue, false statement by witness on oath. (L. *per-,* to the bad; *jurare,* swear)
perk, *n.* (*sl.*) perquisite. (abbr.)
perk, *v.i.* and *t.* (us. **p. up**) lift (head) jauntily; recover self-confidence or spirit; smarten, trim.—*a.* perky. **perky,** *a.* pert, cheeky; jaunty.
perlite, *n.* vitreous rock which looks as if made of pearly globules. (F.)
perm, *n.* (*colloq.*) permanent wave.
permanent, *a.* lasting, not subject to change (opp. to temporary). **p. wave,** artificial wave in hair lasting for months. **p. way,** bed of railway track. **permanence,** *n.* being permanent. **permanency,** *n.* permanent occupation; permanence. (L. *per,* through; *manēre,* remain)
permanganate, *n.* salt of an acid of manganese, esp. **p. of potash,** used as disinfectant. (*per-*)
permeate, *v.t.* and *i.* fill every part of, saturate; pervade, be diffused (through). **permeation,** *n.* **permeable,** *a.* admitting the passage of fluid. **permeability,** *n.* (L. *per,* through; *meare,* pass)
Permian, *a.* (*geol.*) of last Palaeozoic series, consisting of red sandstone and limestones. (*Perm* in Russia)
permit, *v.t.* and *i.* allow, give leave; make possible.—*n.* document giving official permission, warrant. **p. of,** admit of. **permissible,** *a.* allowable. **permission,** *n.* leave, sanction. **permissive,** *a.* allowing; licensing but not enjoining. (L. *per,* through; *mittere,* send)
permute, *v.t.* put in different order. **permutation,** *n.* change in order of a series; transformation. (L. *per-,* thoroughly; *mutare,* change)
pern, *n.* honey-buzzard. **pernine,** *a.* (Gk. *pternis,* kind of hawk)
pernicious, *a.* destructive, very harmful; (*Shake.*) villainous. (L. *per-,* thoroughly; *nex,* slaughter)
pernickety, *a.* (*colloq.*) fussy, fastidious; punctilious; ticklish.
pernoctation, *n.* passing the night; all-night vigil. (L. *per,* through; *nox,* night)
perorate, *v.i.* speak at length, harangue; make peroration. **peroration,** *n.* final part of speech, esp. if rhetorical. (L. *per,* through; *orare,* speak)
peroxide, *n.* an oxide containing maximum proportion of oxygen. **p.** (**of hydrogen**) colourless liquid used as antiseptic and to bleach hair. (*per-*)
perpend, *v.t.* and *i.* (*arch.*) ponder, reflect. (L. *per-,* thoroughly; *pendere,* weigh)
perpendicular, *a.* exactly upright, vertical; very steep; (*archit.*) late English Gothic; (*geom.*) at right angles (to).—*n.* perpendicular line, position, or style; plumb-line; (*sl.*) meal at which guests stand. **perpendicularity,** *n.* (L. *perpendiculum,* plumb-line)
perpetrate, *v.t.* commit, be guilty of. **perpetration, perpetrator,** *nn.* (L. *per-,* thoroughly; *patrare,* perform)
perpetual, *a.* lasting for ever, eternal; continuous, incessant; (*colloq.*) frequent. **perpetuate,** *v.t.* make perpetual; preserve from extinction or oblivion. **perpetuation, perpetuator,** *nn.* **perpetuity,** *n.* endless duration; perpetual continuance, possession, or annuity. **in perpetuity,** for ever. (L. *perpetuus*)
perplex, *v.t.* puzzle, bewilder; complicate, make intricate; entangle. **perplexity,** *n.* bewilderment, being at a loss; perplexing thing, dilemma. (L. *per-,* thoroughly; *plectere,* weave)
perquisite, *n.* casual profit in money or kind additional to regular payment; customary gratuity. (L. *per-,* thoroughly; *quaerere,* seek)
perron, *n.* flight of steps and platform before large entrance-door. (F.)
perruquier, *n.* wig-maker. (F.)
perry, *n.* cider-like drink made from pears. (L. *pirum,* pear)
perse, *a.* and *n.* (*arch.*) bluish grey. (L.L. *persus*)
persecute, *v.t.* ill-treat persistently; oppress for religious beliefs; worry, importune. **persecution, persecutor,** *nn.* (L. *per-,* thoroughly; *sequi,* follow)
persevere, *v.i.* persist, maintain effort; continue steadfastly. **perseverance,** *n.* (L. *perseverare*)
Persian, *a.* and *n.* (native, language) of Persia. **P.** (**cat**), kind with long silky hair.
persiennes, *n.pl.* outside window-shutters like Venetian blinds. (F.)
persiflage, *n.* frivolous talk, banter, chaff. (F.)
persimmon, *n.* an American tree; its hard wood; its fruit, date-plum. (Amer. Ind.)
persist, *v.i.* continue in spite of obstacles or opposition, persevere. **persistence, persistency,** *nn.* persisting; tenacity of purpose. **persistent,** *a.* persisting, pertinacious; (*bot.*) permanent (opp. to deciduous). (L. *per,* through; *sistere,* stand)
person, *n.* human being, individual; one of the three modes of being of the Godhead; human body, bodily

presence; character in play. **first, second, third, p.,** (*gram.*) denoting person speaking, spoken to, spoken of. **in p.,** oneself, not by deputy. (*persona*)

persona, n. (*pl. personae*) person. *p. grata, non grata,* welcome, unwelcome, person. *dramatis pp.,* characters of play. (L.)

personable, *a.* good-looking.

personage, *n.* person of rank or importance; character in play; person.

personal, *a.* individual, private; done in person; directed against an individual; (*gram.*) denoting person; (*Shake.*) physical. **p. estate, property,** (*law*) movables, not land. **personality,** *n.* personal identity; distinctive character; personage; (*pl.*) remarks aimed at individual. **multiple personality,** (*psycho-anal.*) existence of two or more distinct personalities in one individual. **personalize,** *v.t.* personify. **personalization,** *n.* **personally,** *adv.* in person; for one's own part. **personalty,** *n.* personal property.

personate, *v.t.* play part of; pretend to be.—*a.* (*bot.*) mask-like. **personation, personator,** *nn.*

personify, *v.t.* think of, represent, as person; typify, be example of. **personification,** *n.* personifying; embodiment, type.

personnel, *n.* collective body of men in a service, business etc. (F.)

perspective, *n.* art of drawing so as to give impression of relative distance; picture so drawn; relation, proportion, between parts of subject; vista, prospect; (*Shake.*) instrument, drawing, producing optical illusion.—*a.* of, in, perspective. **in p.,** according to its rules. (L. *per,* through; *specere,* look)

perspicacious, *a.* of clear understanding, shrewd, discerning. **perspicacity,** *n.* **perspicuous,** *a.* clearly expressed, lucid. **perspicuity,** *n.* (L. *per,* through; *specere,* look)

perspire, *v.i.* and *t.* excrete (moisture) through pores of skin, sweat. **perspiration,** *n.* sweating; sweat. **perspiratory,** *a.* (L. *per,* through; *spirare,* breathe)

persuade, *v.t.* induce, prevail upon; convince by argument; (*Shake.*) urge. **persuader,** *n.* **persuadable, persuasible,** *aa.* **persuasion,** *n.* persuading; conviction; religious belief or sect; (*joc.*) sort, class. **persuasive,** *a.* efficacious in persuading; winning.—*n.* inducement. (L. *per-,* thoroughly; *suadēre,* advise)

persue, *n.* (*Spens.*) track of blood left by wounded beast.

persulphate, *n.* sulphate containing maximum proportion of acid. (*per-*)

pert, *a.* impudent, cheeky; (*Shake.*) lively, brisk. (L. *apertus,* open)

pertain, *v.i.* belong; be appropriate; relate, have reference (to). (L. *per-,* thoroughly; *tenēre,* hold)

pertinacious, *a.* persistent, resolute, dogged. **pertinaciousness, pertinacity,** *nn.* (*per-*; *tenacious*)

pertinent, *a.* relevant, apposite; to the point.—*n.* (us. *pl.*) accessory. **pertinence, pertinency,** *nn.* (*pertain*)

perturb, *v.t.* trouble greatly, disquiet; throw into confusion. **perturbation,** *n.* mental agitation; (*astron.*) irregularity or deviation in planet's motion in its orbit. **perturbative,** *a.* (L. *per-,* thoroughly; *turbare,* disturb)

peruke, *n.* wig. (It. *perruca*)

peruse, *v.t.* read; examine scan. **perusal,** *n.* (*per-*; *use*)

Peruvian, *a.* of Peru. **P. bark,** of cinchona-tree.

pervade, *v.t.* pass into all parts of, spread through; be rife among. **pervasion,** *n.* **pervasive,** *a.* able or tending to pervade. (L. *per,* through; *vadere,* go)

perverse, *a.* persisting in error; wayward, contrary; wicked; vexatious. **perversity,** *n.* (*pervert*)

pervert, *v.t.* turn from proper use or meaning, misapply, misinterpret; turn from true belief, lead astray.—*n.* one who adopts another religion, apostate; abnormal person, degenerate. **perversion,** *n.* perverting; abnormality. **perversive,** *a.* (L. *per-,* to the bad; *vertere,* turn)

pervious, *a.* giving passage, penetrable; open (to ideas). (L. *per,* through; *via,* way)

peseta, *n.* Spanish silver coin worth about $9\frac{1}{2}$*d.* (Sp.)

pesky, *a.* (*Amer.*) troublesome, annoying.

peso, *n.* S. American silver coin formerly worth about 4*s.* (Sp.)

pessary, *n.* surgical appliance or suppository introduced into vagina. (Gk. *pessos,* oval stone)

pessimism, *n.* disposition to look on dark side; (*philos.*) doctrine that world is essentially bad, and that all things tend to evil. **pessimist,** *n.* one who tends to expect misfortune; adherent of pessimism. **pessimistic,** *a.* **pessimistically,** *adv.* (L. *pessimus,* worst)

pest, *n.* troublesome thing, nuisance; destructive insect or weed; (*arch.*) plague. **p.-house,** *n.* (formerly) fever hospital. (L. *pestis*)

pester, *v.t.* worry, harass, plague.

pestiferous, *a.* spreading infection, noxious; morally harmful, pernicious. (L. *pestis,* plague; *ferre,* carry)

pestilence, *n.* any fatal epidemic disease; bubonic plague. **pestilent,** *a.* destructive to life, deadly; harmful to morals, corrupt; (*colloq.*) vexatious, annoying. **pestilential,** *a.* of the nature of, conveying, pestilence; foul-smelling. (*pest*)

pestle, *n.* club-shaped tool for pounding substances in a mortar.—*v.t.* and *i.* pound with, use, pestle. (L. *pinsere*, pound)

pestology, *n.* study of insect pests.

pet, *n.* tame animal kept as companion; favourite, darling. — *v.t.* fondle, caress. **p. aversion,** thing specially disliked. **p. name,** one used in affection.

pet, *n.* fit of sulks or ill humour.

petal, *n.* coloured leaf of flower, single part of corolla. **petalled, petaled,** *a.* having petals. **petaline, petaloid,** *aa.* of, like, petals. (Gk. *petalon*, leaf)

petard, *n.* small bomb formerly used to blow in door; kind of fire-cracker. (L. *pedere*, break wind)

petasus, *n.* ancient Greek broad-brimmed hat; winged hat of Hermes. (Gk. *petasos*)

petaurist, *n.* kinds of flying marsupial. (Gk. *petauron*, spring-board)

peter, *v.i.* **p. out,** (of vein of ore etc.) be exhausted, come to an end.

Peter, *n.* **rob P. to pay Paul,** pay one debt by incurring another. **P.-penny, P.'s penny, P.'s pence,** voluntary contribution to papal treasury.

petersham, *n.* thick shaggy cloth; overcoat of this. (Lord *Petersham*)

petiole, *n.* leaf-stalk. **petiolar,** *a.* of, growing on, petiole. **petiolate,** *a.* having petiole. (L. *petiolus*, little foot)

petit, *a.* (*fem. petite*) small, dainty. *p. mal*, mild form of epilepsy. *p. point*, kind of open-work embroidery. *petits soins*, small attentions. *p. verre*, glass of liqueur. *p.-maître*, *n.* fop, dandy. *petits-chevaux*, *n.* kind of gambling game. (F.)

petition, *n.* entreaty, prayer; written supplication presented to sovereign etc.; formal application to lawcourt. —*v.t.* and *i.* address petition to; ask humbly. **petitionary,** *a.* **petitioner,** *n.* (L. *petere*, seek)

petitio principii, begging the question. (L.)

petrel, *n.* small black-and-grey sea-bird. **stormy p.,** one kind, smallest web-footed bird; harbinger of trouble.

petrify, *v.t.* and *i.* turn to stone; stupefy, stun; render callous. **petrifaction,** *n.* (L. *petra*, rock; *facere*, make)

petro-, from Gk. *petra*, rock, used in **petroglyph,** *n.* rock-carving; **petrograph,** *n.* rock-inscription; **petrography,** *n.* scientific description and classification of rocks, hence **petrographer,** *n.*, **petrographic, petrographical,** *aa.*; **petrolithic,** *a.* as hard as rock; **petrology,** *n.* science of rocks and their structure.

petroleum, *n.* a mineral oil. **petrol,** *n.* refined petroleum used in motor-cars etc. ***pétroleur,*** *n.* (*fem. pétroleuse*) incendiary who uses petroleum. **petrolic,** *a.* of petrol or petroleum. **petrolin,** *n.* oil got from petroleum. (L. *petra*, rock; *oleum*, oil)

petronel, *n.* large horse-pistol, small carbine. (L. *pectus*, breast)

petrous, *a.* of, like, rock. (Gk. *petra*, rock)

petticoat, *n.* underskirt; (*sl.*) woman. **p. government,** rule by women. (*petty*; *coat*)

pettifog, *v.i.* play the pettifogger. **pettifogger,** *n.* inferior or rascally lawyer; paltry or crooked dealer. **pettifogging,** *a.* quibbling; paltry, trumpery. (*petty*)

pettish, *a.* peevish, sulky. (*pet*)

pettitoes, *n.pl.* pig's feet as food, trotters.

pettle, *v.t.* (*Scot.*) indulge, pet.

petto, *n.* breast. *in p.*, in secret thoughts. (It.)

petty, *a.* unimportant, trifling; small-minded, ungenerous; inferior, minor. **p. cash,** small items of expenditure. **p. jury,** common jury. **p. larceny,** pilfering. **p. officer,** N.C.O. in Navy. **p. sessions,** court of justices of the peace trying minor offences without jury. (*petit*)

petulant, *a.* capriciously peevish, irritable. **petulance,** *n.* (L. *petere*, attack)

petunia, *n.* plant with funnel-shaped purple or white flowers; deep violet colour. (Brazilian *pety*, tobacco)

petúntsĕ, *n.* fine white clay used in making Chinese porcelain. (Chin. *pai*, white; *tun*, stone)

pew, *n.* long fixed bench in church, often enclosed; (*colloq.*) chair.—*v.t.* furnish with, enclose in, pews. **p.-rent, pewage,** *nn.* church seat-rent. (Gk. *podion*, pedestal)

pewit, peewit, *n.* lapwing. (imit. of cry)

pewter, *n.* alloy of tin and lead; tankard, vessels, of this; (*sl.*) prize-money. (O.F. *peutre*)

pfennig, pfenning, *n.* small German bronze coin, $\frac{1}{100}$ mark. (G.)

phacitis, *n.* inflammation of crystalline lens of eye. **phacoid,** *a.* lentil-shaped. (Gk. *phakos*, lentil)

phaeton, *n.* light open four-wheeled carriage. (*Phaëthon* in Gk. myth)

phagedaena, phagedena, *n.* spreading ulcer; gangrene. **phagedaenic, phagedenic,** *a.* (Gk. *phagein*, eat)

phagocyte, *n.* white corpuscle which devours harmful microbes, leucocyte. **phagocytosis,** *n.* this devouring process. (Gk. *phagein*, eat; *kutos*, cell)

-phagous, *adj.suf.* eating, as in **anthropophagous.** (Gk. *phagein*, eat)

phalange, *n.* single bone of finger or toe; bundle of stamens joined by filaments. **phalangeal,** *a.* (*phalanx*)

phalanger, *n.* kinds of tree marsupial, incl. flying squirrel. (*phalanx*)

phalanx, *n.* (*pl.* **phalanxes, phalanges**) closely ranked oblong infantry

formation; massed body, closely knit party; phalange. (Gk. *phalangx*)
phalarope, *n.* small wading bird like sandpiper, but with lobed feet. (Gk. *phalaris,* coot; *pous,* foot)
phallus, *n.* (*pl.* **phalli**) penis; symbol of it used in primitive rites. **phallic,** *a.* **phallicism, phallism,** *nn.* worship of generative power of nature symbolized by phallus. (L.)
phanerogam, *n.* plant with pistils and stamens, flowering plant. **phanerogamic, phanerogamous,** *aa.* (Gk. *phaneros,* visible; *gamos,* marriage)
phansigar, *n.* thug. (Hind.)
phantasm, *n.* illusion, phantom; vision of absent person. **phantasmal, phantasmic,** *aa.* **phantasmagoria,** *n.* series of shifting images, shadow-show. **phantasmagoric,** *a.* **phantasy,** same as **fantasy. phantasime,** *n.* (*Shake.*) fantastic being. **phantom,** *n.* spectre, ghost; vain show, illusion; vision.—*a.* illusive; spectral. (Gk. *phainein,* show)
Pharaoh, *n.* title of ancient Egyptian kings. (Egyptian *pr'o,* great house)
Pharisee, *n.* member of strict Jewish religious sect; formalist; self-righteous person, hypocrite. **pharisaic, pharisaical,** *aa.* **pharisaism,** *n.* (Heb. *parush,* separated)
pharmacy, *n.* preparation and dispensing of drugs; chemist's shop, dispensary. **pharmacist, pharmaceutist,** *nn.* apothecary. **pharmaceutical,** *a.* of, engaged in, pharmacy. **pharmaceutics,** *n.pl.* science of pharmacy. **pharmacology,** *n.* science of drugs and their properties. **pharmacologist,** *n.* **pharmacopoeia,** *n.* book with list of drugs and directions for their use; stock of drugs. **pharmacopoeial,** *a.* (Gk. *pharmakon,* drug)
pharos, *n.* lighthouse, beacon. (Gk.)
pharynx, *n.* part between mouth and gullet, throat. **pharyngal, pharyngeal,** *aa.* **pharyngitis,** *n.* inflammation of pharynx. **pharyngology,** *n.* study of throat. **pharyngoscope,** *n.* instrument for viewing throat. **pharyngotomy,** *n.* incision into pharynx. (Gk. *pharungx*)
phase, *n.* amount of moon's or planet's surface illuminated, aspect; stage in development or change. **phasic,** *a.* (Gk. *phasis,* appearance)
pheasant, *n.* game-bird with brilliant plumage. (river *Phasis*)
pheeze, *v.t.* (*Shake.*) do for, settle. (O.E. *fýsian,* chase)
phellem, *n.* cork. **phellogen,** *n.* cork-producing tissue. **phelloplastics,** *n.pl.* modelling in cork. (Gk. *phellos,* cork)
phenacetin, *n.* antipyretic drug used for headache etc. (Gk. *phainos,* shining. L. *acetum,* vinegar)
phenakistoscope, *n.* form of zoetrope. (Gk. *phenax,* cheat; *skopein,* look)
phenix, same as **phoenix.**
phenol, *n.* carbolic acid. (Gk. *phainos,* shining)
phenology, *n.* study of the influence of climate on animal and plant life. (*phenomenon*)
phenomenon, *n.* (*pl.* **phenomena**) observed object or event, esp. one of scientific interest; remarkable thing or person, wonder; (*philos.*) object of perception. **phenomenal,** *a.* of, concerned with, phenomena; perceptible by senses; remarkable, prodigious. **phenomenalism, phenomenism,** *nn.* doctrine that all knowledge is derived from sense impressions. **phenomenalist, phenomenist,** *nn.* **phenomenalistic, phenomenistic,** *aa.* (Gk. *phainein,* show)
phenyl, *n.* radical found in phenol, benzene etc.
phew, *int.* of disgust, relief etc.
phial, *n.* small bottle for drugs etc. (Gk. *phialē,* broad flat cup)
Phi Beta Kappa, oldest of American college fraternities. (initials of Gk. *philosophia biou kubernētēs,* philosophy is the guide of life)
-phil, -phile, *adj.* and *n.suf.* lover of, loving, as in **bibliophil, bibliophile.** (Gk. *philos,* loving)
philabeg, see **filibeg.**
philander, *v.i.* make love for amusement, flirt. **philanderer,** *n.* (Gk. *philos,* loving; *anēr,* man)
philanthropy, *n.* love of mankind; practical benevolence. **philanthropist, philanthrope,** *nn.* one who loves and tries to benefit his fellow men. **philanthropic,** *a.* **philanthropize,** *v.i.* and *t.* practise philanthropy (upon). Gk. *philos,* loving; *anthrōpos,* man)
philately, *n.* stamp-collecting. **philatelic,** *a.* **philatelist,** *n.* (Gk. *philos,* loving; *atelēs,* toll-free)
-phile, see **-phil.**
philharmonic, *a.* and *n.* (person) fond of music. (Gk. *philos,* loving)
philhellene, *n.* lover, supporter, of Greece. **philhellenic,** *a.* **philhellenism, philhellenist,** *nn.* (Gk. *philos,* loving; *Hellēn,* Greek)
philibeg, see **filibeg.**
philippic, *n.* diatribe, invective; (*pl.*) speeches of Demosthenes against Philip or of Cicero against Antony.
philippine, philippina, *n.* twin-kernelled nut; forfeit-game played with this, forfeit or player in it.
Philistine, *n.* member of warlike race hostile to Israel; person with no artistic feeling. — *a.* uncultured. **philistinism,** *n.*
phil(o)-, from Gk. *philos,* loving, used in **philobiblic,** *a.* fond of literature; **philogyny,** *n.* fondness for women, hence **philogynist,** *n.*; **philology,** *n.* science of language, (*arch.*) love of literature, hence **philological,** *a.*; **philologist, philologian,** *nn.* student of philology; **philologize,** *v.i.* study philology; **philomath,** *n.* lover of

learning, esp. mathematics, hence **philomathy**, *n.*, **philomathic**, *a.*; **philoprogenitive**, *a.* prolific, fond of one's children.

Philomel, Philomela, *n.* (*poet.*) nightingale. (name in myth)

philopoena, same as **philippine.**

philosophy, *n.* pursuit of wisdom; study of ultimate reality; body of laws and principles belonging to a branch of knowledge; system for conduct of life; mental balance, serenity. **moral p.**, ethics. **natural p.**, physics. **philosopher**, *n.* student of philosophy; one who acts calmly and rationally. **philosophers' stone**, fabled substance for turning base metals into gold. **philosophic, philosophical**, *aa.* of, devoted to, philosophy; serene, temperate, resigned. **philosophism**, *n.* sophism. **philosophist**, *n.* **philosophize**, *v.i.* reason like a philosopher; speculate, moralize. (Gk. *philos*, loving; *sophia*, wisdom)

philtre, philter, *n.* love-potion. (Gk. *philein*, love)

phiz, *n.* (*colloq.*) face, expression. (abbr. of *physiognomy*)

phlebitis, *n.* inflammation of a vein. **phlebitic**, *a.* **phlebolith**, *n.* concretion formed in a vein. **phlebology**, *n.* science of veins. **phlebotomy**, *n.* blood-letting. **phlebotomist**, *n.* **phlebotomize**, *v.i.* and *t.* practise phlebotomy; bleed. (Gk. *phleps*, vein)

phlegm, *n.* slimy matter coughed up, bronchial mucus; calmness, impassivity; apathy; (*arch.*) one of the four humours of the body. **phlegmatic**, *a.* unemotional, composed; sluggish. (Gk. *phlegein*, burn)

phlegmon, *n.* inflammatory tumour, boil. **phlegmonic, phlegmonous**, *aa.* (Gk. *phlegein*, burn)

phloem, *n.* soft inner tissue of bark, bast. (Gk. *phloos*, bark)

phlogiston, *n.* inflammatory element once supposed to exist in all combustible bodies. **phlogistic**, *a.* of phlogiston; (*med.*) inflammatory. (Gk. *phlox*, flame)

phlox, *n.* kinds of bright-coloured flowering plant. (Gk. =flame)

-phobe, *adj.* and *n.suf.* (person) afraid of, hostile to, as in **Gallophobe. -phobia**, *n.suf.* fear of, as in **agoraphobia.** (Gk. *phobos*, fear)

phocine, *a.* of the seal kind. (Gk. *phōkē*, seal)

Phoebus, *n.* (*poet.*) sun. (Gk. *Phoibos*, sun-god)

phoenix, *n.* fabulous Arabian bird that burned itself on a pyre every 500 years and rose renewed from the ashes; paragon. (Gk. *phoinix*)

phon, *n.* unit of loudness.

phone, *n.* single speech-sound, vowel or consonant. **phonate**, *v.i.* utter vocal sound. **phonation**, *n.* **phonatory**, *a.* **phonautograph**, *n.* apparatus recording vibrations of sound. **phonendoscope**, *n.* kind of stethoscope for making small sounds audible. (Gk. *phōnē*, sound)

phone, *colloq.* for **telephone.**

phonetic, *a.* of, in accordance with, vocal sounds. — *n.pl.* science of speech-sounds. **p. spelling**, simplified, following pronunciation. **phonetically**, *adv.* **phonetician**, *n.* student of phonetics. **phoneticize**, *v.t.* represent phonetically. **phoneticist, phonetist**, *nn.* phonetician; advocate of phonetic spelling. (*phone*)

phoney, *a.* (*Amer. sl.*) false, bogus.

phonic, *a.* of sound; phonetic.—*n.pl.* acoustics; phonetics. **phoniatrics**, *n.pl.* correction of speech defects.

phono-, from Gk. *phōnē*, sound, used in **phonofilm**, *n.* film for talking pictures; **phonogram**, *n.* phonograph record, sound-symbol in shorthand; **phonograph**, *n.* gramophone using cylinder instead of disk,—*v.t.* record by this, hence **phonographic**, *a.*; **phonographer, phonographist**, *nn.* shorthand-writer; **phonography**, *n.* recording by phonograph, kind of shorthand; **phonolite**, *n.* volcanic rock that rings when struck; **phonology**, *n.* study of speech-sounds and their development, system of sounds in a language, hence **phonologic, phonological**, *aa.*, **phonologist**, *n.*; **phonometer**, *n.* instrument measuring intensity of sounds; **phonopore, phonophore**, *n.* device for telephoning and telegraphing simultaneously along same wire; **phonoscope**, *n.* instrument representing sound-vibrations in visible form; **phonotype**, *n.* printing-type of phonetic alphabet, hence **phonotypic, phonotypical**, *aa.*, **phonotypist, phonotypy**, *nn.*

phony, same as **phoney.**

phooka, same as **pooka.**

phormium, *n.* New Zealand flax. (Gk. *phormos*, basket)

phosgene, *n.* irritant poison-gas with deadly delayed action. (Gk. *phōs*, light; *genesis*, origin)

phosphate, *n.* a salt of phosphoric acid; fertilizer containing this.

phosphene, *n.* luminous rings seen when closed eye is pressed. (Gk. *phōs*, light; *phainein*, show)

phosphide, *n.* compound of phosphorus and some other element.

phosphite, *n.* a salt of phosphorous acid.

phosphorus, *n.* non-metallic wax-like element, inflammable, poisonous, and luminous in the dark. **p. necrosis**, (*colloq.*) **phossy-jaw**, *n.* gangrene of jawbone due to phosphorus fumes. **phosphorate**, *v.t.* combine, impregnate, with phosphorus. **phosphor-bronze**, *n.* hard tough alloy of copper, tin, and phosphorus. **phosphoresce** *v.i.* glow in the dark; emit light without sensible heat. **phosphorescence**, *n.* phosphorescing; luminosity in darkness. **phosphorescent,** *a.* **phosphoric, phosphorous,** *aa.* containing phosphorus in lower, higher, proportion. **phosphorism,** *n.* chronic phosphorus poisoning. **phosphorite,** *n.* kind of phosphate of lime. **phosphorogenic,** *a.* causing phosphorescence. **phosphorograph,** *n.* evanescent picture on phosphorescent surface. **phosphoroscope,** *n.* instrument for measuring duration of phosphorescence. **phosphuretted, phosphureted,** *a.* combined with phosphorus.

photic, *a.* of, penetrated by, light. —*n.pl.* study of light. **photism,** *n.* illusory sensation of light. (Gk. *phōs,* light)

photo, *n.* and *v.t.* photograph. (abbr.)

photochromy, *n.* colour-photography. **photochromatic, photochromic,** *aa.*

photo-engraving, *n.* any process of making printing-blocks by photography.

photogen, *n.* light-producing organ; kind of paraffin. **photogenic,** *a.* generating light. (Gk. *phōs,* light; *genesis,* origin)

photoglyph, *n.* plate engraved by photography. **photoglyphy,** *n.* (Gk. *phōs,* light; *gluphein,* carve)

photograph, *n.* picture taken by photography.—*v.t.* take photograph of. **photographer,** *n.* **photographic,** *a.* of, by, photography; minutely accurate like a photograph. **photographically,** *adv.* **photography,** *n.* process, art, of taking pictures by chemical action of light on sensitive film. (Gk. *phōs,* light; *graphein,* write)

photogravure, *n.* process of printing from photograph etched on plate; print made by this. —*v.t.* reproduce by photogravure. (F. *gravure,* engraving)

photolithography, *n.* process of printing from photographs transferred to stone. **photolithograph,** *n.*

photology, *n.* science of light. (Gk. *phōs,* light; *legein,* speak)

photomechanical, *a.* producing pictures by mechanical printing from photographically prepared plate.

photometer, *n.* instrument for measuring intensity of light. **photometric,** *a.* **photometry,** *n.* (Gk. *phōs,* light; *metron,* measure)

photomicrograph, *n.* photograph taken through microscope. **photomicrography,** *n.*

photon, *n.* unit of light-intensity; light-quantum. (Gk. *phōs,* light)

photophobia, *n.* (*med.*) morbid dread of light. (Gk. *phōs,* light; *phobia,* fear)

photophone, *n.* instrument for transmitting sound by means of light. (Gk. *phōs,* light; *phōnē,* sound)

photo-play, *n.* (*Amer. colloq.*) cinema play.

photosphere, *n.* bright hot envelope of sun or star. (Gk. *phōs,* light)

photosynthesis, *n.* formation of carbohydrates by chlorophyll-containing cells of plant under influence of sunlight. (Gk. *phōs,* light)

phototelegraphy, *n.* telegraphic transmission of photographs and drawings.

phototherapy, *n.* medical treatment, esp. of skin disease, by action of light. (Gk. *phōs,* light; *therapeuein,* heal)

phototropism, *n.* movement directed by light; heliotropism. (Gk. *phōs,* light; *trepein,* turn)

phototype, *n.* process-block made by photographic process; picture from this. **phototypy,** *n.*

photozincography, *n.* process of printing from photograph etched on zinc.

phrase, *n.* small group of words; pointed saying; diction, phraseology; (*mus.*) short distinct passage.—*v.t.* express in words, put. **phraseogram,** *n.* shorthand symbol for phrase. **phraseology,** *n.* mode of expression, wording. **phraseological,** *a.* (Gk. *phrazein,* speak)

phratry, *n.* subdivision of tribe, clan. (Gk. *phratēr,* clansman)

phrĕătic, *a.* of wells or subterranean water. (Gk. *phrear,* well)

phrenetic, *a.* wild, frenzied, frantic.

phrenic, *a.* (*anat.*) of the diaphragm.

phrenitis, *n.* inflammation of the brain. (Gk. *phrēn,* midriff, mind)

phrenology, *n.* study of outline of skull giving supposed indication of character and mental abilities. **phrenological,** *a.* **phrenologist,** *n.* (Gk. *phrēn* mind; *legein,* speak)

phrontistery, *n.* (*joc.*) place for study, 'reflectory.' (Gk. *phrontistērion*)

phthisis, *n.* consumption, tuberculosis; wasting disease. **phthisical,** *a.* (Gk. =wasting)

phut, *n.* sound of bullet etc. **go p.,** collapse. (Hind. *phatna,* burst)

phycology, *n.* science of seaweeds. (Gk. *phukos,* seaweed; *legein,* speak)

phylactery, *n.* small case containing Hebrew texts, worn by pious Jews; amulet. (Gk. *phulassein,* guard)

phyletic, *a.* of phylum, racial.

phyllo-, from Gk. *phullon,* leaf, used in **phyllode,** *n.* petiole with functions of a leaf; **phylloid,** *a.* leaf-like; **phyllophagous,** *a.* leaf-eating; **phyllophorous,** *a.* leaf-bearing; **phyllopod,** *a.* and *n.* leaf-footed (crustacean); **phyllostome,** *n.* leaf-nosed bat; **phyllotaxis,** *n.* arrangement of leaves on stem; **phylloxera,** *n.* plant-louse injurious to vines.

phyl(o)-, from Gk. *phulon,* race, used in **phylogenesis, phylogeny,** *nn.* racial evolution of animal or plant type, hence **phylogenetic, phylogenic,** *aa.*; **phylum.** *n.* (*pl.* phyla) primary division of animal or vegetable kingdom.

physic, *n.* medicine; medical profession; (*pl.*) see **physics**.—*v.t.* (*past, p.p.* **physicked**, *pres. part.* **physicking**) dose, esp. with purgatives. **p. garden**, botanic garden. (Gk. *phusis*, nature)
physical, *a.* material, of the body; of, according to, nature; of physics; (*Shake.*) curative. **p. geography**, dealing with natural features. **p. jerks**, (*sl.*) gymnastics.
physician, *n.* medical doctor, esp. consultant; healer. (*physic*)
physicist, *n.* student of physics; believer in natural origin of life, without creator. **physicism**, *n.*
physicky, *a.* like physic.
physics, *n.* science of matter and energy, embracing mechanics, electricity, light, heat, and sound. (Gk. *phusis*, nature)
physio-, from Gk. *phusis*, nature, used in **physiocracy**, *n.* government according to supposed natural order, **physiocrat**, *n.* advocate of this, esp. in 18th-century France; **physiogeny**, *n.* development of vital activities; **physiolatry**, *n.* nature-worship.
physiognomy, *n.* art of judging character from features or form; facial expression, face; physical features of country. **physiognomic, physiognomical**, *aa.* **physiognomist**, *n.* expert at, believer in, physiognomy. (Gk. *phusis*, nature; *gnōmōn*, judge)
physiography, *n.* description of natural phenomena; physical geography. (Gk. *phusis*, nature; *graphein*, write)
physiology, *n.* science of vital processes of living organisms. **physiological**, *a.* **physiologist**, *n.* (Gk. *phusis*, nature; *legein*, speak)
physique, *n.* bodily structure and development. (F.)
phyto-, from Gk. *phuton*, plant, used in **phytogenesis, phytogeny**, *nn.* plant evolution; **phytography**, *n.* descriptive botany; **phytoid**, *a.* plant-like; **phytolithology**, *n.* science of fossil plants; **phytology**, *n.* botany; **phytomer, phyton**, *nn.* smallest unit of plant that can grow into new individual; **phytophagous**, *a.* feeding on plants; **phytotomy**, *n.* dissection of plants; **phytozoon**, *n.* (*pl.* **phytozoa**) plant-like animal, zoophyte.
pi, *n.* Greek letter (π) used as symbol of ratio of circumference to diameter of circle (about $3\frac{1}{7}$, better $\frac{355}{113}$ or 3·14159).
pi, *a.* (*school sl.*) pious, goody-goody. **pi-jaw**, *n.* moral lecture. (abbr.)
piacular, *a.* expiatory; sinful. (L. *piare*, appease)
piaffe, *v.i.* (of horse) move at **piaffer**, *n.* slow trot. (F.)
pia mater, inner membrane enclosing brain; (*Shake.*) brain. (L. =tender mother)
piano, *n.* (in full **pianoforte**) keyboard musical instrument with wires struck by hammers. **upright, grand, cottage, p.**, with vertical, horizontal, sloping wires. **p.-organ**, *n.* mechanical piano like barrel-organ. **p.-player**, *n.* pianola. **p.-stool**, *n.* adjustable stool for pianist. **pianette, pianino**, *nn.* small kinds of upright piano. **pianist**, *n.* player of piano. **pianola**, *n.* (*trade name*) mechanical device for playing piano. (It. *piano*, soft; *forte*, loud)
piano, *adv.* (*mus.*) softly. *pianissimo*, *adv.* (*mus.*) very softly. (It.)
piastre, piaster, *n.* small silver coin, $\frac{1}{100}$ Turkish or Egyptian pound; Spanish dollar. (F.)
piazza, *n.* public square in Italian town; (*Amer.*) veranda. (It.)
pibroch, *n.* kind of bagpipe music, us. warlike. (Gael. *piobaireachd*)
pica, *n.* (*med.*) craving for unnatural food. (L. =magpie)
pica, *n.* (*print.*) 12-point type; **small p.**, 11-point type (sizes between English and long primer).
picador, *n.* mounted bull-fighter with lance. (Sp.)
picamar, *n.* bitter oil got from wood-tar. (L. *pix*, pitch; *amarus*, bitter)
picaroon, *n.* rogue; pirate; pirate's ship.—*v.i.* live by one's wits or piracy. **picaresque**, *a.* (of novel) with rogue for hero. (Sp. *picaron*)
picayune, *n.* (*Amer.*) small coin, esp. Spanish half-real; trifle.—*a.* paltry, mean.
piccalilli, *n.* highly seasoned pickle of chopped vegetables.
piccaninny, *n.* negro child; baby.—*a.* tiny. (Sp. *pequeño*, small + dim.)
piccolo, *n.* small shrill flute. (It.)
pice, *n.* Indian coin, ¼ anna. (Hind. *paisa*)
piceous, *a.* of, like, pitch. (L. *pix*, pitch)
pichiciago, *n.* S. American burrowing animal like armadillo. (Sp. *pichiciego*)
pick, *v.t.* (*Shake.*) pitch.
pick, *v.t.* and *i.* break surface of, pierce, with pointed thing; probe, poke; open (lock) with wire etc.; strip (bone) of flesh; rifle (pocket) by stealth; gather, pluck; select; nibble (at); contrive (quarrel).—*n.* heavy tool with shaft and pointed crossbar for breaking up ground; choice; best (of). **p. holes in**, carp at. **p. oakum**, untwist old rope into fibre. **p. off**, shoot one by one. **p. on**, single out and pester. **p. out**, select, identify; relieve (with different colour). **p. to pieces**, criticize captiously. **p. up**, lift, acquire; call for; recover; (*colloq.*) make acquaintance of casually. **p.-a-back**, *adv.* on shoulders like pack. **p.-me-up**, *n.* stimulant, tonic. **p.-thank**, *n.* (*Shake.*) sycophant.
pickaninny, same as **piccaninny**

pickaxe, pickax, *n.* pick.—*v.t.* and *i.* break up with, use, pickaxe.
pickelhaube, *n.* spiked helmet. (G.)
pickerel, *n.* young pike. (*pike*)
picket, *n.* pointed stake, peg; outpost, patrol; man, men, posted by strikers to dissuade others from going to work.—*v.t.* and *i.* enclose with palisade; tether to post; station at intervals; beset with pickets. (F. *piquer*, prick)
pickings, *n.pl.* gleanings, perquisites.
pickle, *n.* brine, vinegar etc. for preserving; plight, mess; scapegrace; (us. *pl.*) vegetables in vinegar.—*v.t.* preserve in, treat with, vinegar. **rod in p.,** punishment in store.
pickle, *n.* (*Scot.*) small quantity.
picklock, *n.* lock-picker.
pickpocket, *n.* one who steals from pockets.
picksome, *a.* fastidious. (*pick*)
pickwick, *n.* kind of cigar. **in a Pickwickian sense,** not to be taken too literally. (name in Dickens)
picnic, *n.* excursion with meal out of doors.—*v.i.* have picnic. **picnicker,** *n.* (F. *piquenique*)
picot, *n.* small loop of thread as edging to lace. (F.)
picotee, *n.* kind of small carnation. (F. *picoté*)
picquet, same as **picket.**
picric, *a.* **p. acid,** used as dye-stuff and basis of high explosives. (Gk. *pikros*, bitter)
Pict, *n.* member of ancient race of N. Scotland. **Picts' houses,** rude earth-houses. **Pictish,** *a.*
pictograph, *n.* pictorial symbol; primitive writing in these. **pictographic,** *a.* **pictography,** *n.* (L. *pingere*, paint. Gk. *graphein*, write)
pictorial, *a.* of, expressed in, pictures; picturesque.—*n.* illustrated paper.
picture, *n.* drawing, painting; portrait; beautiful or striking thing; vivid description; type, embodiment; (*pl.*) cinema show.—*v.t.* portray, describe; visualize. **p. hat,** woman's large-brimmed hat. **p. house, palace, theatre,** cinema. **p.-card,** *n.* court card. **p.-gallery,** *n.* room, building, housing collection of pictures. **p.-writing,** *n.* pictographic script. **picturedrome,** *n.* cinema. **picturesque,** *a.* charmingly pretty, making an effective picture; (of language) graphic, forcible. (L. *pingere*, paint)
picul, *n.* a Chinese weight, 133⅓ lb. (Malay)
piddle, *v.i.* (*arch.*) trifle, potter; (*colloq.*) make water. **piddling,** *a.* insignificant.
piddock, *n.* bivalve boring shell-fish.
pidgin, *n.* (*colloq.*) business. **p. English,** Chinese broken English. (corrupt. of *business*)
pie, *n.* meat or fruit covered with paste and baked. **have a finger in the p.,** be concerned in the matter.
pie, *n.* magpie; kind of woodpecker. (L. *pica*)
pie, *n.* small Indian copper coin, $\frac{1}{12}$ anna. (Sanskr. *pad*, quarter)
pie, *n.* (*print.*) jumble of type.—*v.t.* mix, disarrange (type).
piebald, *a.* having patches of two different colours, esp. black and white. (*pie*, magpie; *bald*)
piece, *n.* part, bit; item; specimen; literary or musical composition, picture; fire-arm; man at chess, draughts etc.; (*sl.*) girl; (*Scot.*) slice of bread with butter, jam etc.—*v.t.* fit together, join; eke or make (out). **in pp.,** broken. **of a p.,** of same nature. **p. of eight,** Spanish dollar of eight reals. **p. together,** join together bit by bit. **p.-goods,** *n.pl.* textiles woven in standard lengths. (O.F. *pece*)
pièce de résistance, most important dish or item. (F.)
piecemeal, *adv.* and *a.* a bit at a time. into pieces. (*piece*; *meal*)
piecework, *n.* work paid by amount done, not time taken.
pied, *a.* of mixed colours, mottled. (*pie*, magpie)
pied-à-terre, *n.* temporary lodging, place to stay. (F.)
piedog, same as **pyedog.**
pier, *n.* structure projecting into sea as landing-stage, breakwater, or ornamental promenade; support for span of bridge; pillar; solid part of wall between windows. **p.-glass,** *n.* tall mirror. **pierage,** *n.* pier dues. (L.L. *pera*)
pierce, *v.t.* and *i.* pass through, perforate, penetrate; make hole through, bore. **piercing,** *a.* penetrating, keen. (O.F. *percer*)
Pierian, *a.* of the muses. (*Pieria*, their shrine in Thessaly)
pierrot, *n.* (*fem.* **pierrette**) member of seaside concert party, us. in loose white dress; traditional character of French pantomime. (F.)
pietà, *n.* picture, sculpture, of Virgin Mary mourning over dead Christ. (It.)
piety, *n.* piousness, devoutness; reverence for God or parents. **pietism,** *n.* exaggeration or affectation of piety. **pietistic, pietistical,** *aa.*
piezo-. from Gk. *piezein*, press, used in **piezochemistry,** *n.* study of chemical effects of pressure; **piezometer,** *n.* instrument for measuring compressibility of fluids.
piffle, *n.* (*sl.*) silly stuff, twaddle.—*v.i.* trifle. **piffling,** *a.* trivial.
pig, *n.* (*Scot.*) earthenware hot-water bottle.
pig, *n.* swine; its flesh; oblong mass of unforged metal; (*colloq.*) greedy, dirty, or disobliging person.—*v.i.* farrow; live in squalor. **p.-headed,** *a.* stupidly obstinate. **p.-iron,** *n.* iron in pigs or rough bars.

pigeon, same as **pidgin.**
pigeon, *n.* dove; dupe, gull.—*v.t.* cheat. **clay p.**, shooting-target of clay disk thrown into air from trap. **p.-breasted**, *a.* having constricted chest with prominent breast-bone. **p.-hole**, *n.* small compartment in desk.—*v.t.* file in this, classify; put aside for consideration, shelve. **p.-toed**, *a.* with toes turned in. **pigeonry**, *n.* dovecot. (L. *pipire*, chirp)
piggery, *n.* place for breeding pigs; pigsty.
piggish, *a.* greedy, dirty, selfish, like a pig.
pight, *obs. past* and *p.p.* of **pitch.**
piglet, pigling, *nn.* young pig.
pigment, *n.* colouring-matter, paint. **pigmental, pigmentary**, *aa.* **pigmentation**, *n.* coloration. (L. *pingere*, paint)
pigmy, see **pygmy.**
pignut, *n.* earthnut.
pigskin, *n.* leather from skin of pig; (*Amer. sl.*) football.
pigsticking, *n.* hunting of wild boar with spear, us. on horseback. **pigsticker**, *n.*
pigsty, *n.* sty for pig; dirty hovel.
pigtail, *n.* plait of hair hanging down back; roll of twisted tobacco.
pike, *n.* kind of spear now superseded by bayonet; mountain peak.—*v.t.* pierce, kill, with pike. (F. *pique*)
pike, *n.* large voracious freshwater fish.
pike, *n.* toll-gate; turnpike. (abbr.)
pikelet, *n.* small round tea-cake. (W. bara *pyglyd*, pitchy bread)
piker, *n.* (*Amer. colloq.*) timid gambler, poor sport; untrustworthy person.
pikestaff, *n.* shaft of pike. **plain as a p.**, easy to understand.
pikul, same as **picul.**
pilaster, *n.* rectangular pillar, us. set in wall. (L. *pila*, pillar)
pilau, pilaw, pilaff, *n.* boiled rice and meat with spices etc. (Pers.)
pilch, *n.* triangular flannel wrap for baby. (O.E. *pylece*)
pilchard, (*Shake.*) **pilcher**, *n.* small sea-fish like herring.
pilcher, *n.* (*Shake.*) scabbard.
pile, *n.* heap; lofty building; electric battery of superimposed metal plates; (*sl.*) fortune.—*v.t.* heap, stack; load. **funeral p.**, pyre. **p. arms**, stand rifles in pyramids of four. **p. it on**, exaggerate. (L. *pila*, pillar)
pile, *n.* vertical beam driven into river-bed etc. as foundation for building.—*v.t.* support with piles; drive piles into. **p.-driver**, *n.* machine for driving in piles. (L. *pilum*, javelin)
pile, *n.* soft surface of velvet, nap; soft hair, down. (L. *pilus*, hair)
pile, *n.* (*arch.*) reverse of coin, tails. (part of minting machine)
pile, *n.* (us. *pl.*) tumours of veins of rectum, haemorrhoids. **pilewort**, *n.* lesser celandine. (L. *pila*, ball)
pileate, *a.* having a cap, crested; cap-shaped. (L. *pileus*, cap)
pilfer, *v.t.* and *i.* steal in small quantities. **pilferage, pilferer**, *nn.* (O.F. *pelfrer*)
pilgrim, *n.* maker of pilgrimage; wayfarer. **P. Fathers**, first Puritan settlers in New England. **pilgrimage**, *n.* journey to sacred place as act of devotion; life's journey. (L. *peregrinus*, foreigner)
piliferous, *a.* hairy. **piliform**, *a.* like hair. (L. *pilus*, hair)
pill, *n.* small ball of medicine to be swallowed whole; (*pl.*, *sl.*) billiards. —*v.t.* (*sl.*) blackball. **p.-box**, *n.* small round box for pills; small concrete fort. (*pilule*)
pill, *v.t.* (*arch.*) plunder; (*dial.*) peel. **pillage**, *n.* plundering, plunder.—*v.t.* sack, despoil. (F. *piller*)
pillar, *n.* detached support, column; main supporter. **driven from p. to post**, from one resource to another. **p.-box**, *n.* hollow pillar with slit for posting letters in. (L. *pila*)
pillion, *n.* cushion behind saddle for second rider; luggage-bracket of motor-cycle. (L. *pellis*, skin)
pilliwinks, *n.* kind of thumbscrew.
pillory, *n.* framework enclosing neck and wrists in which offender was exposed to pelting and ridicule.—*v.t.* set in pillory; hold up to contempt. (O.F. *pellori*)
pillow, *n.* cushion to support head in bed.—*v.t.* and *i.* rest on, serve as, pillow. **p.-case, p.-slip**, *nn.* detachable cover for pillow. **pillowy**, *a.* (O.E. *pyle*)
pilose, pilous, *aa.* hairy. **pilosity**, *n.* (L. *pilus*, hair)
pilot, *n.* one who conducts ships in and out of harbour or where local knowledge is needed; person navigating aircraft; guide; (*arch.*) steersman.—*v.t.* direct course of; guide. **p.-cloth**, *n.* a thick blue cloth. **p.-engine**, *n.* one sent ahead of train to see that line is clear. **p.-fish**, *n.* small fish of mackerel family. **p.-jacket**, *n.* pea-jacket. **pilotage**, *n.* work, fee, of pilot. (It. *pilota*)
pilule, pillule, *n.* small pill; pill. **pilular, pilulous**, *aa.* (L. *pilula*, little ball)
pimelitis, *n.* inflammation of fatty tissue. **pimelode**, *n.* catfish. (Gk. *pimelē*, fat)
pimento, *n.* Jamaica pepper, allspice. (Sp. *pimienta*)
pimp, *n.* and *v.t.* pander.
pimpernel, *n.* plant with small scarlet, blue, or white flowers. (L.L. *pipinella*)
pimping, *a.* small, petty; puny.
pimple, *n.* small round swelling on skin. **pimpled, pimply**, *aa.*
pin, *n.* small piece of wire with point and head; peg, short bar; 4½-gallon cask; (*golf*) stick marking hole; (*pl.*, *sl.*) legs.—*v.t.* fasten with pin; hold,

fix; transfix. **p.** and **web,** (*Shake.*) an eye-disease. **p. one's faith to,** trust in. **pp. and needles,** tingling when feeling returns after numbness. **p.-fire** cartridge, exploded by means of pin. **p.-money,** *n.* dress allowance. **p.-prick,** *n.* trifling irritation. (O.E. *pinn*)

pinafore, *n.* child's apron or overall. (*pin*; *afore*)

pinaster, *n.* the cluster pine. (L.)

pince-nez, *n.* eyeglasses clipped to nose with spring. (F. =pinch-nose)

pincers, *n.pl.* gripping-tool with jaws working on pivot; (*zool.*) claw like this. (*pinch*)

pinch, *v.t.* and *i.* nip between finger and thumb, squeeze; afflict; make thin; stint; (*sl.*) steal; arrest.—*n.* nip, squeeze; very small quantity; stress, emergency. (F. *pincer*)

pinchbeck, *n.* copper and zinc alloy imitating gold; tawdry jewellery.—*a.* sham, flashy. (inventor's name)

pincushion, *n.* pad for holding pins.

Pindaric, *a.* of the Greek poet Pindar. —*n.* (also **P. ode**) irregular ode.

pine, *v.i.* and *t.* languish, waste away; be eager, yearn; (*Shake.*) starve. —*n.* (*Spens.*) suffering, distress. (L. *poena*, punishment)

pine, *n.* an evergreen coniferous tree; its wood. **p.-beauty,** *n.* moth infesting pines. **p.-cone,** *n.* fruit of pine. **p.-needle,** *n.* leaf of pine. (L. *pinus*)

pineal, *a.* (*anat.*) shaped like pine-cone. **p. gland,** eye-like gland in brain.

pineapple, *n.* yellow fruit shaped like pine-cone; tropical tree yielding it, ananas; (*sl.*) bomb. (shape)

pinery, *n.* plantation of pines; place for growing pineapples.

pinfold, *n.* pound for stray cattle.—*v.t.* shut in this. (*pound*; *fold*)

ping, *n.* sharp ringing sound.—*v.i.* emit ping. **p.-pong,** *n.* old name for table tennis. (imit.)

pinguid, *a.* fat, oily; rich. (L. *pinguis*, fat)

pinguin, *n.* W. Indian plant, fruit, of pineapple family.

pinion, *n.* outer joint of bird's wing; flight-feather; (*poet.*) wing.—*v.t.* cut off one pinion of; bind (arms) to sides, confine thus. (L. *penna*, feather)

pinion, *n.* small cog-wheel. (L. *pinna*, battlement)

pink, *n.* garden plant with clove-scented flowers; light red colour; huntsman's red coat; highest type, acme.—*a.* pink-coloured. **in the p.,** (*sl.*) very fit. **p.-eye,** *n.* kinds of ophthalmia and horse-fever.

pink, *v.t.* pierce, transfix; decorate with holes or scallops.

pink, *v.i.* (of petrol engine) make metallic noise like knocking. (imit.)

pink, *n.* sailing-vessel with pointed stern.

pink, *n.* young salmon; (*dial.*) minnow.

pink, *a.* (*Shake.*) half-shut (of eyes).

pinkie, *n.* (*Scot.*) the little finger.

pinkster, *n.* (*Amer.*) Whitsuntide. **p. flower,** pink azalea. (*Pentecost*)

pinnace, *n.* warship's eight-oared boat; (formerly) light sailing-vessel used as tender. (F. *pinasse*)

pinnacle, *n.* slender turret crowning roof etc.; slender peak; highest point, climax.—*v.t.* adorn with pinnacles; set on high. (L. *pinna*, battlement +dim.)

pinnate, pinnated, *aa.* feather-shaped; (*bot.*) with leaflets on either side of a stem. (L. *pinna*, feather)

pinner, *n.* head-dress, coif, with long side-flaps. (*pin*)

pinnet, *n.* pinnacle.

pinniped, *a.* with fin-like feet or flippers. (L. *pinna*, fin; *pes*, foot)

pinny, *n.* child's word for pinafore.

pinochle, pinocle, *n.* card-game like bezique.

pinole, *n.* parched maize, ground and sweetened. (Aztec *pinolli*)

pint, *n.* liquid measure, ⅛ gallon. (F. *pinte*)

pintado, *n.* (us. **p. bird**) kind of petrel; guinea-fowl. (Port. =painted)

pintail, *n.* kinds of duck and grouse.

pintle, *n.* pivot-pin, esp. of rudder. (O.E. *pintel*, penis)

pinto, *a.* and *n.* (*Amer.*) piebald (horse). (Sp.)

pinxit, *v.t.* (*abbr.* *pinx.*, *pnxt.*, *pxt.*) painted (used with artist's signature). (L.)

piolet, *n.* climber's ice-axe. (F.)

pioneer, *n.* man of corps that prepares roads, sinks mines etc.; explorer, early settler; beginner of enterprise. —*v.i.* and *t.* act as pioneer (to); open up (road) . (L. *pedo*, foot-soldier)

pioupiou, *n.* (*sl.*) French soldier. (F.)

pious, *a.* devout, religious; (*arch.*) dutiful. (L. *pius*)

pip, *n.* throat-disease of fowls; (*sl.*) fit of depression, hump.

pip, *n.* seed of apple, orange etc.

pip, *n.* spot on playing-card, dice etc.; star showing officer's rank.

pip, *v.t.* (*colloq.*) blackball; thwart, frustrate; hit with shot.

pip, *v.i.* chirp, peep.

pip, *n.* signallers' letter P. **p. emma,** (*sl.*) p.m., afternoon.

pipal, same as **peepul.**

pipe, *n.* hollow tube; wind instrument of tube with holes; boatswain's whistle; shrill sound, bird's note; tube with bowl for smoking tobacco; cask of wine, measure of 105 gallons; (*pl.*) bagpipes.—*v.i.* and *t.* play on pipe; whistle, chirp; lead, summon, with sound of pipe; convey through pipe; trim with piping; (*Amer. sl.*) watch, look at. **p. down,** dismiss; be less cocksure. **p. major,** N.C.O. commanding pipe band. **p. of peace,** calumet. **p. one's eye,** (*colloq.*) weep.

P. Roll, old annual record of Exchequer. **p. up**, begin to sing. **p.-fish**, *n.* long tube-like fish. **p.-rack**, *n.* rack for tobacco-pipes. (O.E. *pipe*)

pipeclay, *n.* clay used to make tobacco-pipes and for whitening leather etc.—*v.t.* whiten with this.

piper, *n.* player of pipe; bagpiper; gurnard; broken-winded horse. **pay the p.**, stand the expense.

piperaceous, *a.* of the pepper kind. (L. *piper*, pepper)

pipette, *n.* chemist's glass tube into which liquids are sucked for measurement etc. (F.)

piping, *n.* tube-like ornament along seam. **p. hot**, hissing hot. **p. times**, merry times. (*pipe*)

pipistrelle, pipistrel, *n.* small brown bat. (F.)

pipit, *n.* bird like lark.

pipkin, *n.* small earthenware pot.

pippin, *n.* kinds of apple. (O.F. *pepin*, seed)

pip-squeak, *n.* (*army sl.*) kind of shell; contemptible person.

piquant, *a.* racy, stimulating; pungent, sharp. **piquancy**, *n.* (*pique*)

pique, *v.t.* wound pride of, nettle; stimulate (curiosity); plume (oneself).—*n.* hurt resentment, pettishness; baffled curiosity. (F. *piquer*, prick)

pique, *n.* making of 30 points at piquet before opponent scores.—*v.t.* and *i.* score this (against). (F. *pic*)

piqué, *n.* a corded cotton fabric. (F.)

piquet, *n.* card-game for two using 32 cards. (F.)

piquet, same as **picket**.

piracy, *n.* armed robbery at sea; infringement of copyright. (*pirate*)

piragua, *n.* dug-out canoe; two-masted sailing vessel. (Sp.)

pirate, *n.* sea-robber, corsair; bus etc. outside of regular combine; one who pirates books.—*v.t.* and *i.* plunder; publish, reproduce, regardless of copyright. **piratic, piratical**, *aa.* (Gk. *peiraein*, attempt)

pirn, *n.* (*Scot.*) reel, bobbin.

pirogue, same as **piragua**.

pirouette, *v.i.* and *n.* spin round on single toe. (F.)

pis aller, makeshift. (F.)

Pisces, *n.pl.* the Fishes, 12th sign of zodiac, entered by sun about 20 Feb. **piscary**, *n.* fishing rights. **piscatology**, *n.* science of fishing. **piscatorial, piscatory**, *aa.* of fishing. **pisciculture**, *n.* fish-breeding. **piscicultural**, *a.* **pisciculturist**, *n.* **pisciform**, *a.* fish-shaped. **piscina**, *n.* (*pl.* **piscinas, piscinae**) fish-pond; ancient Roman bathing-pond; stone basin with drain in church wall, used for rinsing sacred vessels. **piscine**, *a.* of fish.—*n.* bathing-pond. **piscivorous**, *a.* fish-eating. (L. *piscis*, fish)

pisé, *n.* earth or clay rammed between boards to make floor etc. (F.)

pish, *int* of contempt.

pishogue, *n.* (*Ir.*) witchcraft; charm, spell. (Ir. *pisreog*)

pisiform, *a.* pea-shaped. (L. *pisum*, pea)

pismire, *n.* ant. (*piss*, from smell of ant-hill+M.E. *mire*, ant)

piss, *v.i.* and *t.* make water (on).—*n.* urine. **pissed**, *a.* (*sl.*) drunk. (O.F. *pissier*)

pistachio, *n.* an Asiatic tree; its almond-flavoured nut; green colour of this. (Gk. *pistakion*)

pistil, *n.* female organ of flower, containing seed. **pistillary, pistilline**, *aa.* **pistillate, pistilliferous**, *aa.* having a pistil; with pistil but no stamens. (L. *pistillum*, pestle)

pistol, *n.* small firearm for one hand.—*v.t.* shoot with one. (F. *pistole*)

pistole, *n.* Spanish coin worth about 18*s.* (F.)

piston, *n.* plug working up and down within cylinder by steam pressure etc.; (*mus.*) sliding valve in cornet. **p.-rod**, *n.* rod connecting piston with other machinery. (It. *pistone*)

pit, *n.* hole in ground; mine or its shaft; depression, hollow; pitfall; ground floor of theatre behind stalls; (*Amer.*) part of exchange used for special business.—*v.t.* store in pit; mark with small hollows, scar; match (against). **the p.**, hell. (L. *puteus*, well)

pit, *n.* (*Amer.*) fruit-stone.

pit-a-pat, *adv.* with quick light steps or beats, palpitatingly. (imit.)

pitch, *v.t.* and *i.* throw, hurl; set up, fix in position; set in key, express in style; fall heavily, plunge; encamp; (of ship) seesaw lengthwise.—*n.* pitching; height, intensity; musical tone; distance between threads (of screw); station of street-vendor; (*archit.*) amount of slope; (*cricket*) prepared ground between wickets. **p. and pay**, (*Shake.*) pay cash down. **p. into**, attack, scold; devour. **p. upon**, happen to select. **queer the p.**, spoil plans. **p.-and-toss**, *n.* game in which coins are pitched at mark. **p.-pipe**, *n.* small pipe giving pitch for singing. (M.E. *pichen*)

pitch, *n.* black sticky substance got from tar or turpentine.—*v.t.* coat, caulk, with pitch. **p.-dark**, *a.* completely dark. (L. *pix*)

pitchblende, *n.* mineral composed largely of uranium oxide, yielding radium. (*pitch*; *blende*)

pitched, *a.* (of battle) set, not casual.

pitcher, *n.* large jug, ewer. **p.-plant**, *n.* plant with pitcher-shaped leaves. (L.L. *picarium*, vessel)

pitcher, *n.* (*baseball*) player who delivers ball to batter.

pitchfork, *n.* long-handled fork for hay etc.—*v.t.* lift with this; thrust suddenly or willy-nilly (into)

pitchy, *a.* of, like, black as, pitch.

piteous, *a.* arousing pity, heart-rending; lamentable.

pitfall, *n.* concealed pit as trap; unexpected difficulty.
pith, *n.* soft inner tissue of stem; spinal cord; essence; force, vigour. —*v.t.* kill by piercing spinal cord. (O.E. *pitha*)
pithecanthrope, *n.* ape-man, 'missing link.' **pithecoid,** *a.* ape-like. (Gk. *pithēkos,* ape; *anthrōpos,* man)
pithless, *a.* spineless, flaccid.
pithy, *a.* like, full of, pith; forcible; concise, terse.
pitiable, *a.* deserving pity, lamentable, wretched.
pitiful, *a.* showing pity, compassionate; causing pity, touching; contemptible, paltry.
pitiless, *a.* without pity, ruthless.
pitman, *n.* miner; (*Amer.*) connecting-rod.
pitpan, *n.* Central American dug-out.
pittance, *n.* scanty wages or allowance. (O.F. *pitance*)
pittite, *n.* occupant of theatre pit.
pituitary, *a.* of, secreting, mucus. **p. gland, body,** ductless gland at base of brain affecting growth. **pituitrin,** *n.* hormone of this. **pituitous,** *a.* mucous. L. *pituita,* phlegm)
pity, *n.* sympathy with distress, compassion; regrettable fact.—*v.t.* feel pity for. (L. *pietas*)
pityriasis, *n.* a scaly skin-infection. (Gk. *pituron,* bran)
pivot, *n.* pin on which thing turns; soldier on whom company wheels; cardinal point or factor.—*v.i.* and *t.* turn, hinge (on); furnish with, attach by, pivot. **pivotal,** *a.* of pivot; of first importance. (F.)
pixy, pixie, *n.* small fairy, elf.
pizzicato, *a.* and *n.* (*mus.*) (note, passage) played by plucking string of violin or other bowed instrument with finger. (It.)
pizzle, *n.* penis of animal, esp. bull.
placable, *a.* easy to appease, forgiving. (*placate*)
placard, *n.* printed bill pasted up, poster.—*v.t.* post placard on; advertise by placards. (Du. *plakken,* glue)
placate, *v.t.* appease, pacify; conciliate. (L. *placare*)
place, *n.* locality, spot; town, village; building, residence; short street, square; position, space; rank, precedence; station in life; post, situation; office, duty; (*racing*) first, second, or third position at finish.—*v.t.* put, set; rank, arrange; invest, sell; size up, identify; kick (goal) with place-kick. **give p.,** make room, yield. **in, out of, p.,** in right, wrong, place. **in p. of,** instead of. **take p.,** happen. **p.-kick,** *n.* kicking of football placed by other player. (Gk. *plateia,* street)
place aux dames, (make) room for the ladies. (F.)
placēbo, *n.* first antiphon of Roman Catholic vespers for dead; (*med.*) medicine given to humour patient. (L. = I shall please)
placeman, *n.* holder of public office; jack-in-office.
placement, *n.* placing.
placenta, *n.* (*pl.* **placentae**) organ connecting foetus with womb, afterbirth; (*bot.*) part of carpel to which seeds are attached. **placental,** *a.* (L. = cake)
placer, *n.* deposit yielding gold etc. by washing. (Sp.)
placet, *n.* vote of assent. *non p.* vote against. (L. = it pleases)
placid, *a.* calm, unruffled, serene. **placidity,** *n.* (L. *placidus*)
plack, *n.* old Scottish copper coin worth ⅓*d.*
placket, *n.* slit or pocket in woman's skirt; (*Shake.*) petticoat.
placoid, *a.* plate-like; with plate-like scales. (Gk. *plax,* plate)
plafond, *n.* ceiling, esp. one of elaborate design. (F.)
plage, *n.* sea-beach, esp. at fashionable resort. (F.)
plagiarize, *v.t.* and *i.* copy (ideas, expressions) from another and pass them off as one's own. **plagiarism,** *n.* such literary theft. **plagiarist,** *n.* one who plagiarizes. **plagiary,** *n.* (*arch.*) plagiarism; plagiarist. (L. *plagiare,* kidnap)
plagio-, from Gk. *plagios,* oblique, used in **plagiocephalic,** *a.* having skull differently developed on either side; **plagioclastic,** *a.* (*min.*) having slanting cleavage; **plagiostome,** *n.* fish with mouth placed transversely beneath snout, e.g. shark, ray.
plague, *n.* pestilence; bubonic plague; affliction, nuisance.—*v.t.* afflict with plague; harass, pester. **bubonic p.,** a malignant infectious fever. **p.-spot,** *n.* centre of infection. **plaguy,** *a.* annoying, confounded.—*adv.* (*colloq.*) very, remarkably. (L. *plaga,* blow)
plaice, *n.* flat-fish like flounder. (L.L. *platessa*)
plaid, *n.* long wide piece of woollen cloth used as cloak by Scottish highlanders; cloth with tartan or chequered pattern. (Gael. *plaide*)
plain, *a.* clear, distinct; straightforward, blunt; simple, without ornament, not luxurious; homely, ugly.—*adv.* clearly, intelligibly.—*n.* large tract of level country. **p. clothes,** mufti. **p. dealing,** honesty. **p. sailing,** easy course of action. **p.-song,** *n.* unison singing resembling recitative, as in Gregorian chants. **p.-spoken,** *a.* frank, outspoken. (L. *planus*)
plain, *v.i.* (*arch.*) lament; complain. (L. *plangere,* beat breast)
plainsman, *n.* dweller in plain.
plainstanes, *n.pl.* (*Scot.*) flagstones, pavement.
plaint, *n.* (*poet.*) lamentation, sad

song; (*law*) formal statement of grievance, accusation. **plaintiff,** *n.* (*law*) person bringing action, prosecutor. **plaintive,** *a.* melancholy, mournful; mildly querulous. (*plain*)

plaister, *obs.* form of **plaster.**

plait, *n.* interlaced strands of hair, straw etc.; braid; flattened fold, pleat.—*v.t.* weave into plait; pleat. (L. *plicare*, fold)

plan, *n.* drawing of horizontal section of building etc.; diagram, map; scheme, design.—*v.t.* make plan of, design; arrange beforehand. (L. *planus*, flat)

planarian, *n.* kinds of flat worm. (L. *planarius*, flat)

planch, *v.t.* (*Shake.*) cover with planks. (F. *planche*, plank)

planchet, *n.* plain metal disk from which coin is made. (*planch*)

planchette, *n.* small board supported on pencil and wheels, supposed to write automatically when fingers are rested on it. (F.)

plane, *n.* a tree with broad leaves. (Gk. *platus*, broad)

plane, *n.* tool with blade projecting from flat bottom for smoothing surface.—*v.t.* smooth with plane. (L. *planus*, flat)

plane, *n.* flat surface; supporting surface of aeroplane; aeroplane; facet of crystal; level, pitch.—*a.* completely flat; lying in a plane. —*v.i.* glide in aeroplane. **p. geometry,** dealing with plane figures, not solids. **p. sailing,** navigating as if earth's surface were flat; plain sailing. (L. *planus*, flat)

planet, *n.* celestial body revolving round sun. **minor p.,** asteroid. **secondary p.,** moon, satellite. **p.-struck, p.-stricken,** *aa.* blasted; terrified. **planetarium,** *n.* model of solar system. **planetary,** *a.* of planets; mundane; wandering. **planetesimal,** *a.* and *n.* (one) of minute bodies in space, supposed by some to have joined to form planets. **planetoid,** *n.* asteroid. (Gk. *planētēs*, wanderer)

plangent, *a.* beating with noise, resounding. **plangency,** *n.* (L. *plangere*, beat breast)

plani-, from L. *planus*, level, used in **planimeter,** *n.* instrument for measuring area of irregular plane figure; **planimetry,** *n.* measurement of plane surfaces, hence **planimetric, planimetrical,** *aa.*; **planipennate,** *a.* with flat broad wings; **planisphere,** *n.* sphere projected on plane, map of heavens, hence **planispheric,** *a.*

planish, *v.t.* smooth, flatten, with hammer or between rollers. (*plane*)

plank, *n.* long flat piece of wood; item of political programme.—*v.t.* cover with planks. **p. down,** pay. **walk the p.,** be forced blindfold into sea along plank projecting from ship. **p.-bed,** *n.* of boards without mattress. **planking,** *n.* set of planks. (L.L. *planca*)

plankton, *n.* minute floating or swimming organisms found in ocean. **planktic,** *a.* (Gk. *planktos*, wandering)

plano-, from L. *planus*, level, used in **plano-concave, plano-convex,** *aa.* (of lens) with one side flat, the other concave, convex; **planography,** *n.* map-making; **planometer,** *n.* flat plate used as gauge for plane surfaces.

plant, *n.* vegetable organism, esp. one smaller than tree; cutting; growth; industrial machinery and equipment; (*sl.*) hoax, swindle.—*v.t.* set in ground to grow; furnish with plants; settle; fix firmly, establish; deliver (blow); (*sl.*) palm off, insert to mislead; bury. (L. *planta*)

plant, *n.* (*Shake.*) sole of foot. (L. *planta*)

plantain, *n.* low-growing weed with tough leaves. (L. *plantago*)

plantain, *n.* tropical tree and fruit like banana. (Sp. *plantano*)

plantar, *a.* (*anat.*) of sole. (*plant*)

plantation, *n.* group of planted trees; estate for cultivation of cotton etc.; (formerly) colonizing, colony.

planter, *n.* one who cultivates tea, cotton, or other tropical produce.

plantigrade, *a.* and *n.* (animal) walking on sole of foot. (L. *planta*, sole; *gradi*, walk)

plantocracy, *n.* dominant class of planters in W. Indies. (*-cracy*)

planxty, *n.* Irish dance tune on harp.

plaque, *n.* ornamental tablet or disk; (*med*). small patch. **plaquette,** *n.* small plaque. (F.)

plash, *v.t.* bend and intertwist (branches) to form hedge; make, repair (hedge), thus. (L. *plectere*, weave)

plash, *n.* marshy pool, puddle. **plashy,** *a.* (O.E. *plæsc*)

plash, *v.i.* and *n.* splash. **plashy,** *a.* (imit.)

plasma, plasm, *nn.* living matter of cell, protoplasm; colourless liquid part of blood, milk, or lymph; green kind of quartz. **plasmatic, plasmic,** *aa.* **plasmin,** *n.* protein got from blood plasma. **plasmocyte,** *n.* leucocyte. **plasmodium,** *n.* (*pl.* **plasmodia**) mass of protoplasm formed by union of single-cell organisms. **plasmogen,** *n.* true or formative protoplasm. **plasmogeny, plasmogony,** *nn.* origin of protoplasm from inorganic substances, spontaneous generation. **plasmology,** *n.* study of ultimate elements of living matter. **plasmolysis,** *n.* shrinking of protoplasm of plant cell under action of certain reagents. **plasmolyse,** *v.t.* subject to this. **plasmolytic,** *a.* **plasmosome,** *n.* true nucleus of cell. (Gk. *plassein*, mould)

plaster, *n.* mixture of lime, sand, and water for coating walls; plaster of Paris; curative or irritant substance spread on cloth and applied to body; adhesive fabric to protect cut, sticking-plaster.—*v.t.* coat with plaster; smear, bedaub; load to excess. **p. of Paris**, powdered gypsum used for moulds and as cement. (Gk. *emplastron*)

plastic, *a.* giving shape, formative; produced by moulding; able to be moulded; pliant, impressionable. **p. arts**, sculpture and pottery. **p. surgery**, restoration of lost or damaged parts by grafting. **plastically**, *adv.* **plasticity**, *n.* (Gk. *plassein*, mould)

plastron, *n.* chest-pad, breast-cloth, for protection or ornament; shirt-front. (F.)

plat, *n.* and *v.t.* braid. (=*plait*)

plat, *n.* patch of ground. (=*plot*)

plat, *n.* dish, item on menu. (F.)

platan, *n.* oriental plane-tree. (Gk. *platus*, broad)

plate, *n.* flat shallow dish; thin sheet of metal or glass; engraved metal sheet, illustration printed from it; full-page illustration separate from text; silver trophy as prize at race, the race; utensils of gold or silver; plated ware; plate-armour; set of false teeth; (*baseball*) home base, at which batter stands; (*phot.*) glass with sensitized film.—*v.t.* cover with metal plates; coat with deposit of gold, silver etc. **selling p.**, horse-race of which winner must be sold at fixed price. **p.-glass**, *n.* fine thick kind. **p.-powder**, *n.* for cleaning silver. **whole-p.**, **half-p.**, **quarter-p.**, photographic sizes, $8\frac{1}{2}\times6\frac{1}{2}$, $6\frac{1}{2}\times4\frac{3}{4}$, $4\frac{1}{4}\times3\frac{1}{4}$ in. (O.F. *plat*, flat)

plateau, *n.* (*pl.* **plateaus**, **plateaux**) elevated plain, tableland; large ornamental centre-dish. (F.)

platelayer, *n.* workman who lays and repairs railway track.

platen, *n.* roller of typewriter; (*print.*) plate that presses paper against type. (O.F. *platine*, flat piece)

plater, *n.* horse run in inferior races; workman who fits plates on ship.

platform, *n.* raised flooring, stage, for speaker, gun, passenger boarding train etc.; party programme; (*Shake.*) plan.—*v.t.* and *i.* place, speak, on platform. (F. *plateforme*, flat form)

platinum, *n.* heavy grey metallic element. **p. blonde**, girl with silvery-coloured hair. **platinic**, **platinous**, *aa.* **platinize**, *v.t.* coat with platinum. **platinoid**, *n.* metal found associated with platinum, e.g. iridium; alloy like platinum. **platinotype**, *n.* photographic print made with platinum; this process. (Sp. *plata*, silver)

platitude, *n.* trite remark, dull truism; commonplaceness. **platitudinize**, *v.i.* utter platitudes. **platitudinous**, *a.* **platitudinarian**, *n.* dealer in platitudes. (F.)

Platonic, *a.* of Plato or his philosophy; (of love) purely spiritual; theoretical, not put into practice.—*n.* Platonist. **Platonically**, *adv.* **Platonism**, *n.* Platonic doctrines. **Platonist**, *n.* follower of Plato.

platoon, *n.* subdivision of company under lieutenant; (formerly) squad firing simultaneously. (F. *peloton*)

platten, same as **platen**.

platter, *n.* (*arch.*) dish, plate. (O.F. *plater*)

platy-, from Gk. *platus*, broad, flat, used in **platycephalous**, *a.* with flat-crowned head; **platyhelminth**, *n.* flat worm; **platypus**, *n.* Australian egg-laying furred mammal with webbed feet and bill, ornithorhyncus; **platyrrhine**, **platyrhine**, *a.* (of monkeys) broad-nosed.

plaudit, *n.* (us. *pl.*) hand-clapping, applause; commendation. (L. *plaudere*, applaud)

plausible, *a.* having appearance of truth, specious; fair-spoken, inviting confidence; (*Shake.*) laudable. **plausibility**, *n.* **plausive**, *a.* applauding; (*Shake.*) plausible. (L. *plaudere*, applaud)

play, *v.i.* and *t.* amuse oneself, sport; engage in (game), compete with; gamble; move freely, flutter, flicker; perform (tune) on instrument; act part (of); strike (ball), put forward (card), move (piece); discharge, direct (hose); give line to (fish).—*n.* trifling, fun; recreation, diversion; gaming; light rapid movement, flicker; scope, freedom to move; dramatic piece. **hold in p.**, keep attention of. **p. at**, perform amateurishly or casually. **p. high**, gamble for big stakes. **p. into the hands of**, give away advantage to. **p. off**, decide by final contest after tie; oppose against each other to one's own advantage; (*Shake.*) toss off (liquor). **p. on words**, pun. **p. the game**, keep the rules. **p. the market**, (*Amer. colloq.*) speculate. **p. up**, exert oneself. **p. up to**, humour. **p. with**, treat casually. **played out**, exhausted; out of date. (O.E. *plegan*)

playable, *a.* able to be played or played on.

play-bill, *n.* theatre poster.

playboy, *n.* one who lives for pleasure.

player, *n.* one who plays; actor; musician; professional cricketer.

playfellow, *n.* companion in play.

playful, *a.* sportive; jocular.

playground, *n.* school recreation-ground.

playhouse, *n.* theatre.

playing-card, *n.* one of set of 52 cards used in games.

playlet, *n.* short dramatic piece.

playmate, *n.* companion in play.

plaything, *n.* toy.

playtime, *n.* time for recreation.

playwright, *n.* dramatist.
plaza, *n.* public square, market-place, in Spain. (Sp.)
plea, *n.* excuse, apology; entreaty; (*law*) defendant's answer to charge, defence. (L. *placēre*, please)
pleach, *v.t.* bend and interlace (branches), plash; (*poet.*) plait. (*plash*)
plead, *v.i.* and *t.* (*past, p.p.* **pleaded,** *colloq.* **pled**) beg, implore; offer as excuse; give as answer to charge; address court, argue at bar. **pleader,** *n.* advocate. **pleading,** *n.* formal statement of either side in lawsuit. **special pleading,** biased reasoning, unfair argument. (*plea*)
pleasance, *n.* (*arch.*) pleasure-ground, ornamental garden; enjoyment.
pleasant, *a.* agreeable, gratifying; affable; (*arch.*) jocular. **pleasantry,** *n.* jocularity; humour, joke.
please, *v.t.* and *i.* give pleasure (to), delight; satisfy; be willing, choose. **(if you) p.,** polite form of request. **(may it) p. you,** (*arch.*) formal address to superior. **p. God,** God willing. **p. yourself,** do as you like. **pleasing,** *a.* agreeable. (L. *placēre*)
pleasure, *n.* enjoyment, delight; satisfaction; will. choice.—*a.* for pleasure, not business.—*v.t.* and *i.* (*arch.*) give or take pleasure. **pleasurable,** *a.* (*please*)
pleat, *n.* flattened fold.—*v.t.* gather into pleats. (*plait*)
plebeian, *a.* of lower classes, low-born; base, vulgar.—*n.* commoner of ancient Rome; (also *sl.* **pleb**) member of lower orders, proletarian. **plebeianize,** *v.t.* make plebeian. **plebiscite,** *n.* direct vote of entire community on specified issue. (L. *plebs*, the common people)
plectrum, *n.* (*pl.* **plectra**) quill, small rod, for plucking strings of lyre etc. (L.)
pled, see **plead.**
pledge, *n.* thing given as security; thing pawned; token, earnest; promise; toast.—*v.t.* deposit as pledge; pawn; engage, plight; drink health of. **the p.,** undertaking to abstain from alcohol. **p. of love,** child. **pledgee,** *n.* person to whom pledge is given. (O.F. *plege*)
pledget, *n.* small pad of lint etc.
Pleiadēs, Pleiads, *n.pl.* a group of seven stars in Taurus. **Pleiad,** *n.* brilliant group, esp. of seven 16th-century French poets. (L.)
plein-air, *a.* open-air, outdoor. (F.)
Pleistocene, *a.* (*geol.*) early post-Tertiary.—*n.* glacial period or formation. (Gk. *pleistos*, most; *kainos*, new)
plenary, *a.* full, complete, absolute; (of meeting) fully attended. **p. indulgence,** entire remission of penance. (L. *plenus*, full)
plenipotentiary, *a.* possessing full powers.—*n.* envoy with authority to act at his own discretion. (L. *plenus*, full; *potens*, powerful)
plenish, *v.t.* (*arch.*) furnish. **plenishing,** *n.* (*Scot.*) furniture, stock. (L. *plenus*, full)
plenitude, *n.* fullness; abundance; entirety. (L. *plenus*, full)
plenty, *n.* abundance; more than enough.—*adv.* (*colloq.*) quite. **plentiful, plenteous,** *aa.* abundant, copious. (L. *plenus*, full)
plenum, *n.* space filled with matter; full assembly. (L. *plenus*, full)
pleonasm, *n.* use of unnecessary words, redundancy, e.g. 'he is blind and cannot see.' **pleonastic,** *a.* **pleonastically,** *adv.* (Gk. *pleon*, more)
plesiosaurus, *n.* large extinct long-necked swimming reptile. (Gk. *plēsios*, near; *sauros*, lizard)
plethora, *n.* over-abundance, glut; (*med.*) excess of red corpuscles in blood. **plethoric,** *a.* **plethorically,** *adv.* (Gk. *plēthein*, be full)
pleura, *n.* (*pl.* **pleurae**) membrane enclosing lung. **pleural,** *a.* **pleurisy,** *n.* inflammation of pleura. **pleuritic,** *a.* **pleurodynia,** *n.* neuralgia of chest muscles. **pleuro-pneumonia,** *n.* inflammation of both pleura and lung. (Gk.=rib)
plexal, *a.* of plexus.
plexor, *n.* (*med.*) small hammer used in percussion. **pleximeter,** *n.* small plate placed over part of body to be percussed. (Gk. *plēssein*, strike)
plexus, *n.* network, esp. of nerves or blood-vessels. **solar p.,** one at pit of stomach. (L. *plectere*, plait)
pliable, pliant, *aa.* easily bent or influenced, flexible, yielding; compliant. **pliability, pliancy,** *nn.* (L. *plicare*, fold)
plicate, plicated, *aa.* folded; pleated. **plication,** *n.* folding; fold. (L. *plicare*, fold)
pliers, *n.pl.* small pincers. (*ply*)
plight, *v.t.* pledge, vow solemnly; betroth.—*n.* engagement. (O.E. *pliht*, danger)
plight, *n.* state, condition; fix, predicament. (*plait*)
plight, *v.t.* (*Spens.*) weave, plait.—*n.* (*Spens.*) plait. (L. *plicare*)
plim, *v.i.* and *t.* (*dial.*) swell.
plimsoll, *n.* (*Austral.*) rubber-soled canvas shoe.
Plimsoll line, mark, statutory load-line on British ships. (person)
plinth, *n.* square slab at base of column or pedestal; projecting face at bottom of wall. **plinthite,** *n.* kind of brick-red clay. (Gk. *plinthos*, brick)
Pliocene, *a.* and *n.* (*geol.*) (of) latest division of Tertiary period. (Gk. *pleiōn*, more; *kainos*, new)
pliskie, *n.* (*Scot.*) mischievous trick; plight.
plod, *v.i.* and *t.* walk laboriously

trudge; work doggedly, drudge.—*n.* plodding. **plodder,** *n.*

plop, *v.i.* and *t.* fall into water without splash; plump.—*n.* sound of this.—*adv.* with a plop. (imit.)

plot, *n.* conspiracy, intrigue; scheme; plan, main story, of play or novel. —*v.i.* and *t.* contrive secretly, conspire. **plotter,** *n.*

plot, *n.* small piece of ground, patch. —*v.t.* mark out, chart.

plot, *v.t.* (*Scot.*) scald, steep in very hot water.

plough, plow, *n.* horse-drawn implement for turning up soil; ploughed land; the Great Bear.—*v.t.* and *i.* turn up with plough; make furrow (in), wrinkle; cleave (way); (*sl.*) reject in examination. **P. Monday,** first after Epiphany. **put one's hand to the p.,** start undertaking. **p.-tail,** *n.* handles for guiding plough. **ploughboy,** *n.* boy leading plough horses. **ploughman,** *n.* man guiding plough. **ploughshare,** *n.* blade of plough. (O.E. *plóh*)

plover, *n.* kinds of wading-bird; (also **green p.**) lapwing. (L. *pluvia,* rain)

plow, see **plough.**

ploy, *n.* (*Scot.*) adventure, escapade; occupation, job.

pluck, *v.t.* and *i.* strip of feathers; swindle, cheat; gather, pick (flowers); pull, snatch at, twitch; (*sl.*) reject in examination. — *n.* tug, twitch; heart, liver, and lungs of animal; courage, spirit. **p. up courage,** take heart. **plucky,** *a.* courageous, spirited. (O.E. *pluccian*)

plug, *n.* thing used to fill hole, bung, stopper; handle for flushing water-closet; fire-plug; compressed tobacco, cake of this; (*Amer. sl.*) worn-out horse.—*v.t.* and *i.* stop (up) with plug; (*colloq.*) shoot, punch; plod. **p.-ugly,** *n.* (*Amer. sl.*) street rowdy.

plum, *n.* a sweet stone-fruit; tree bearing it; dark purple colour; raisin, currant, in cake; choice thing, prize; (*sl.*) £100,000. **p. cake, duff, pudding,** cake, pudding, with raisins. **p.-pudding dog,** Dalmatian. (O.E. *plúme*)

plumage, *n.* bird's feathers collectively.

plumassier, *n.* dealer in ornamental feathers. (*plume*)

plumb, *n.* lump of lead, weight, for plumb-line; sounding-lead.—*a.* vertical; level, true; absolute, utter.—*adv.* vertically; exactly; (*Amer. sl.*) quite.—*v.t.* and *i.* make vertical; measure depth of, sound; get to bottom of, fathom; work as plumber. **out of p.,** not vertical. **p.-line,** *n.* weighted string for showing perpendicular; criterion. (L. *plumbum,* lead)

plumbago, *n.* graphite, black-lead; a blue-flowered plant, leadwort. **plumbaginous,** *a.* (L.)

plumbeous, *a.* of, like, lead; lead-glazed. (*plumb*)

plumber, *n.* man who fits and repairs pipes. **plumbing, plumbery,** *nn.* his work. (L. *plumbum,* lead)

plumbic, *a.* combined with, caused by, lead. **plumbism,** *n.* lead-poisoning.

plume, *n.* feather, esp. large one; feathery ornament.—*v.t.* trim, preen (feathers); furnish with plumes; pride (oneself). **plumelet,** *n.* small plume. (L. *pluma,* down)

plummet, *n.* sounding-lead; plumb-line or its weight; weight on fishing-line. (L. *plumbum,* lead + dim.)

plummy, *a.* like, full of, plums; (*colloq.*) rich, desirable.

plumose, *a.* feathered; feathery. (*plume*)

plump, *n.* (*arch.*) company, group.

plump, *a.* rounded, sleek, chubby.—*v.t.* and *i.* fatten, swell. **plumper,** *n.* disk carried in mouth to swell out cheeks.

plump, *v.i.* and *t.* drop, sit down, abruptly; cast exclusive vote, declare strong preference (for).—*n.* sudden drop or plunge; heavy shower.—*adv.* abruptly; bluntly.—*a.* downright. **plumper,** *n.* unsplit vote; downright lie.

plumule, *n.* down-feather; (*bot.*) rudimentary stem of embryo. **plumular, plumulaceous,** *aa.* (L. *plumula*)

plumy, *a.* feathery; plumed.

plunder, *v.t.* and *i.* seize by force, loot, despoil; steal, embezzle.—*n.* pillage; booty, spoils. **plunderage,** *n.* plundering; embezzlement of goods on board ship. (G. *plündern*)

plunge, *v.t.* and *i.* immerse, dive, suddenly; thrust, drive, forcibly; rush, hurl oneself; (of horse) start violently forward; (*sl.*) gamble recklessly.—*n.* plunging, dive. **take the p.,** take critical step. **plunger,** *n.* piston of pump; (*sl.*) rash gambler or speculator. (L. *plumbum,* lead)

plunk, *v.t.* and *i.* (*Amer.*) throw or fall heavily, plump.—*n.* dull hard blow; (*sl.*) dollar. (imit.)

pluperfect, *a.* and *n.* (tense) denoting action completed before a past point of time. (L. *plus quam perfectum,* more than perfect)

plural, *a.* consisting of, denoting, more than one.—*n.* (*gram.*) plural number or form. **p. vote, voter,** one person voting in more than one constituency. **pluralism,** *n.* simultaneous holding of more than one office or benefice; (*philos.*) belief that ultimate reality is of several kinds. **pluralist,** *n.* **pluralistic,** *a.* **plurality,** *n.* being plural; large number; majority; pluralism in office etc. **pluralize,** *v.t.* make plural. (L. *plus,* more)

plur(i)-, from L. *plus,* more, used in **plurilateral,** *a.* of more than two sides or parties; **pluriliteral,** *a.* of more than three letters; **pluriparous,** *a.* having several young at a birth; **plurisy,** *n.* (*Shake.*) superabundance.

plus, *n.* (*pl.* **plusses**) symbol of addition (+).—*a.* to be added; positive. —*prep.* with additfon of. **p. one, two,** etc. (*golf*) handicapped one, two, better than scratch. **p.-fours,** *n.pl.* long loose knickerbockers. (L. =more)

plush, *n.* cloth with long nap, long-piled velvet; (*pl.*) footman's breeches of this. (L. *pilus,* hair)

Pluto, *n.* Greek god of Hades; outermost planet, beyond Neptune. **Plutonic, Plutonian,** *aa.* of Pluto or Hades; (*geol.*) igneous, due to volcanic action. **Plutonic theory, Plutonism,** *n.* theory that geological changes are due to heat. (Gk. *Ploutōn*)

plut(o)-, from Gk. *ploutos,* wealth, used in **plutarchy, plutocracy,** *nn.* government by the rich, state with this, wealthy class; **plutocrat,** *n.* one who has power through wealth, rich man, hence **plutocratic,** *a.*; **plutolatry,** *n.* worship of wealth; **plutology,** *n.* science of wealth; **plutonomy,** *n.* economics, hence **plutonomic,** *a.,* **plutonomist,** *n.*

pluvial, *a.* (*geol.*) caused by action of rain; pluvious.—*n.* cope. **pluviometer,** *n.* rain-gauge. **pluvious,** *a.* of rain, rainy. (L. *pluvia,* rain)

ply, *v.t.* and *i.* wield, work with; work at; supply or assail persistently; go to and fro, run regularly. (*apply*)

ply, *n.* fold, thickness; strand; bias. (L. *plicare,* fold)

Plymouth, *n.* **P. Brethren,** a Calvinistic sect. **P. Rock,** breed of fowls.

pneumatic, *a.* of air or gases; inflated, worked, by compressed air; spiritual. —*n.* pneumatic tyre; (*pl.*) mechanics of gases. **pneumatically,** *adv.* **pneumaticity,** *n.* **pneumatocyst,** *n.* air-bladder of bird etc. **pneumatology,** *n.* doctrine of the Holy Spirit; science of spiritual essences; pneumatics. **pneumatometer,** *n.* instrument for measuring force of respiration. **pneumatophore,** *n.* marsh-plant's breathing-organ; air-bladder of marine animal. (Gk. *pneuma,* wind)

pneumonia, *n.* inflammation of lung. **pneumonic,** *a.* **pneumogastric,** *a.* of lungs and stomach. (Gk.)

Pnyx, *n.* ancient Athenian assembly's open-air meeting-place. (Gk. *Pnux*)

po, *n.* (*pl.* **pos**) chamber-pot. (F. *pot*)

poa, *n.* meadow-grass. **poaceous,** *a.* of the grass family. (Gk.)

poach, *v.t.* cook (egg) by breaking it into boiling water. (F. *poche,* pouch)

poach, *v.i.* and *t.* steal game or fish; trespass (on) for this purpose; encroach, be interloper; trample, cut up (turf). **poacher,** *n.*

pochard, *n.* kind of red-headed duck.

pock, *n.* eruptive spot in smallpox etc. (O.E. *poc*)

pocket, *n.* small pouch in clothing; cavity in earth or rock; air-pocket; billiard-table bag; measure of hops, $1\frac{1}{2}$ cwt.—*a.* small enough to put in pocket.—*v.t.* put in pocket; take, steal; put up with (insult); (*billiards*) drive (ball) into pocket. **in, out of, p.,** gainer, loser. **out-of-p. expenses,** actual outlay. **p. borough,** where election was controlled by single person. **p.-book,** *n.* note-book; case for letters or bank-notes. **p.-money,** *n.* money for occasional expenses; child's allowance. (F. *poche,* pouch +dim.)

pockmanty, *n.* (*Scot.*) portmanteau.

pocky, *a.* marked with pocks; affected with pox; vile, contemptible.

poco, adv. (*mus.*) a little, rather. (It.)

pococurante, *a.* and *n.* (person) caring little. **pococurantism, pococurante-ism,** *n.* apathy. (It.)

pod, *n.* seed-case of bean or pea; cocoon of silkworm.—*v.i.* and *t.* bear pods; shell (peas etc.).

pod, *n.* small herd of seals or whales.

pod, *n.* socket of brace and bit.

podagra, *n.* gout, esp. in feet. **podagral, podagric, podagrous,** *aa.* (Gk. *pous,* foot; *agra,* catching)

podded, *a* (*sl.*) well-off, snug. (*pod*)

podestà, *n.* mayor, magistrate, of Italian town. (It.)

podge, *n.* short fat person. **podgy,** *a.*

podium, *n.* (*pl.* **podia**) low wall round arena of amphitheatre; continuous base for two or more pillars. (L.)

podo-, from Gk. *pous,* foot, used in **podocarp,** *n.* fruit-stalk; **podophthalmate,** *a.* stalk-eyed; **podophyllin,** *n.* purgative resin got from wild mandrake.

póě, *n.* (also **p.-bird**) parson-bird. (Otaheitan = earring)

poem, *n.* a composition in verse, us. showing beauty of thought and language; prose piece with poetic tone; poetic thing. (Gk. *poiein,* make)

poesy, *n.* poetry; poems. (*poem*)

poet, *n.* (*fem.* **poetess**) writer of poems; person with great imaginative power and sense of beauty. **p. laureate,** official court poet. **poetaster,** *n.* petty versifier. (Gk. *poiein,* make)

poetic, *a.* of poets or poetry; imaginative, romantic, like poetry; poetical. —*n.pl.* theory of poetry; high-flown talk. **p. justice,** ideal justice found in fiction. **p. licence,** latitude allowed to poet in grammar, facts etc. **poetical,** *a.* written in verse; poetic. **poeticize,** *v.t.* make poetic. **poetize,** *v.i.* and *t.* write poetry (about); treat poetically.

poetry, *n.* expression of emotion in metre with appropriate diction;

verse of any kind: poetic quality or spirit.

pogo, *n.* (also **p.-stick**) toy consisting of stilt with spring.

pogrom, *n.* organized massacre and plunder, esp. of Jews in Russia. (Russ.)

poh, *int.* of contempt.

poi, *n.* paste made from taro root. (Hawaiian)

poignant, *a.* gripping, moving; pointed, biting; pungent. **poignancy,** *n.* (L. *pungere,* prick)

poilu, *n.* (*sl.*) French soldier. (F.)

poind, *v.t.* (*Scots law*) seize (debtor's goods) in satisfaction of debt, distrain. **poinding,** *n.* (*pound*)

poinsettia, *n.* S. American plant with gorgeous red bracts and small yellow flowers. (J. R. *Poinsett*)

point, *n.* sharp end, tip; pointed tool; promontory; dot, full stop; spot; exact place or time; crisis; chief feature, force; item, detail; unit; division of compass; physical characteristic; fine lace made with needle; tagged lace for fastening doublet and hose; (*boxing*) tip of jaw; (*cricket*) position, fielder, square with wicket on off side; (*print.*) unit of type size, $\frac{1}{72}$ in.; (*pl.*) railway switch.—*v.t.* and *i.* furnish with point, sharpen; punctuate; indicate; aim; (of dog) indicate game by looking at it; fill joints of (wall) with mortar. **at, on, the p. of,** on the verge of. **carry one's p.,** prevail in argument. **give pp. to,** be easily superior to. **make a p. of,** attach special importance to. **p. of order,** question of procedure. **to the p.,** apposite, relevant. (L. *pungere,* prick)

point-blank, *a.* aimed straight at mark; direct, blunt.—*adv.* with flat trajectory; flatly.

point-device, *a.* (*arch.*) scrupulously exact or neat. — *adv.* perfectly, exactly.

point-duty, *n.* post of stationary policeman controlling traffic.

pointed, *a.* sharp; aimed at someone; emphatic, incisive; (of style) epigrammatic; (*archit.*) using pointed arch, Gothic.

pointer, *n.* stick for pointing; index of dial; breed of dog trained to point at game.

pointillism, *n.* method of painting in dots of colour. **pointillist,** *n.* and *a.* (F. *pointillisme*)

pointless, *a.* without a point; irrelevant, unmeaning, aimless.

pointsman, *n.* man working railway switch.

point-to-point, *n.* race over course defined by landmarks, steeplechase.

poise, *v.t.* and *i.* balance, hold steady; hang suspended, hover; (*Shake.*) weigh.—*n.* balance; bearing, carriage; serenity, composure; (*Shake.*) weight. (L. *pendere,* weigh)

poison, *n.* substance destructive to life or health; baneful influence.—*v.t.* give poison to; kill by poison; infect, smear, with poison; pervert, spoil; fill (mind) with prejudice. **poisoner,** *n.* **poisonous,** *a.* (L. *potio,* draught)

poitrel, *n.* armour for breast of horse. (L. *pectus,* breast)

poke, *n.* bag, sack; (*Shake.*) pocket. **pig in a p.,** blind bargain. (M.E.)

poke, *v.t.* and *i.* prod, thrust (at); push forward.—*n.* prod, nudge; projecting brim of bonnet. **p. about,** pry; potter. **p. fun at,** ridicule, tease. **p.-bonnet,** *n.* large bonnet with projecting front.

poker, *n.* metal rod for poking fire. **red-hot p.,** plant with spikes of flame-coloured flowers. **p.-work,** *n.* design burned on white wood; art of this.

poker, *n.* card-game in which two or more players bet on value of hands. **p.-face,** *n.* expressionless face.

poky, *a.* small, cramped; petty, shabby.

polacca, polacre, *n.* three-masted Mediterranean merchantman. (It.)

Polack, *n.* (*Shake.*) Pole.—*a.* Polish.

polar, *a.* of, near, N. or S. Pole; of magnetic pole; magnetic; having positive and negative electricity; directly opposed.—*n.* (*geom.*) line joining points of contact of tangents to a curve from point called pole. **p. bear,** large white bear. **p. circle,** parallel of latitude 23° 28′ from N. or S. Pole. **polarimeter, polariscope,** *nn.* instruments for measuring, studying, the polarization of light. **Polaris,** *n.* pole-star. **polarity,** *n.* being polar; magnet's property of pointing to north. **polarize,** *v.t.* give polarity to; modify radiation of (light, heat) so that its vibrations take up a definite conformation; deposit (hydrogen etc.) on electrode, checking flow of current in cell; concentrate in one direction. **polarization,** *n.*

polatouche, *n.* small flying-squirrel. (Russ. *poletuchii,* flying)

polder, *n.* piece of land reclaimed from sea in Netherlands. (Du.)

Pole, *n.* native of Poland.

pole, *n.* long slender rounded piece of wood etc.; shaft of carriage; flagstaff; measure of length, 5½ yds., or area, 30¼ sq. yds.—*v.t.* propel, support, with pole. **under bare pp.,** with no sails set. **up the p.,** (*sl.*) crazy; in a fix. **p.-clipt,** *a.* (*Shake.*) hedged in with poles. **p.-jump,** *n.* and *v.i.* jump with aid of pole held in hands. (O.E. *pál*)

pole, *n.* either end of axis, esp. of earth or celestial sphere; area round this; terminal of electric battery or magnet; either of two opposed principles; (*arch.*) sky; (*geom.*) point of reference of polar. **magnetic pp.,**

where needle dips vertically. **pp. asunder,** in extreme opposition. **p.-star,** *n.* star marking approximate north; guide, lodestar. (Gk. *polos*, pivot)

pole-axe, pole-ax, *n.* long-handled battle-axe; halberd; butcher's slaughtering axe.—*v.t.* kill, strike, with this. (*poll*; *axe*)

polecat, *n.* small dark-brown evil-smelling animal of weasel kind; (*Amer.*) skunk.

pŏlĕmarch, *n.* ancient Greek magistrate or commander. (Gk. *polemarchos*)

polemic, *a.* disputatious, controversial.—*n.* war of words; controversialist; (*pl.*) art of controversy. **polemical,** *a.* **polemize,** *v.i.* (Gk. *polemos*, war)

polenta, *n.* Italian porridge of maize, barley, or chestnut meal. (It.)

police, *n.* body of men to preserve law and order; internal regulation of a state.—*v.t.* control with police, maintain order in; (*Amer. army*) clean up, put (camp) in order. **p.-constable, p.-officer, policeman,** *nn.* member of police force. **p.-court, p.-magistrate,** *nn.* dealing summarily with minor offences. **p.-station,** *n.* local headquarters of police. (Gk. *polis*, city)

policlinic, *n.* out-patient department of hospital. (Gk. *polis*, city+*clinic*)

policy, *n.* political wisdom, statecraft; scheme of government, political ideals; plan or course of action; worldly wisdom, prudence; (*Shake.*) stratagem; (*pl., Scot.*) grounds of country house. (Gk. *polis*, city)

policy, *n.* insurance contract. (Gk. *apodeixis*, proof)

poligar, *n.* village chieftain of S. India; one of his followers. (Tamil *palaiyam*, feudal estate)

poliomyelitis, *n.* inflammation of spinal cord, infantile paralysis. (Gk. *polios*, grey; *muelos*, marrow)

polish, *v.t.* and *i.* make, become, smooth and glossy by rubbing; smarten (up), perfect; give refinement or culture to.—*n.* smoothness, glossiness; refinement, elegance of manners; substance for polishing. **p. off,** finish off quickly; kill. (L. *polire*)

Polish, *a.* and *n.* (language) of Poles.

polite, *a.* well-bred, courteous; refined, cultured. (*polish*)

politic, *a.* prudent, judicious; crafty; (*arch.*) political.—*n.pl.* science and art of government; political affairs or opinions; party strife. **body p.,** state. (Gk. *polis*, city)

political, *a.* of politics or government; of the state or its affairs. **p. agent, resident,** government official advising native Indian ruler. **p. economy,** science of production and distribution of wealth. **p. geography,** dealing with frontiers etc. of states. **p. science,** science of government.

politician, *n.* one engaged in politics, statesman; one who makes a trade of politics. **politicaster,** *n.* petty politician. **politicize,** *v.i.* and *t.* talk, dabble in, politics; treat, discuss, politically.

politico - commercial, politico - economical, *aa.* of commerce, economics, in its political aspect. **politico-ethical, politico-religious,** *aa.* of politics as affected by or affecting morals, religion.

polity, *n.* form of government, constitution; organized state.

polka, *n.* lively round dance in 2-4 time; music for it. **polk,** *v.i.* (*colloq.*) dance polka. (Pol.)

poll, *n.* head; voting, place of voting, counting or number of votes, at election; poll-beast.—*v.t.* and *i.* cut top off (tree), pollard; clip horns of (cattle); crop hair of; count, receive, votes of; register (vote). **p.-beast,** *n.* hornless ox. **p.-tax,** *n.* tax levied on each person. **polling-booth,** *n.* voting-place at election. (M.E. *polle*)

poll, *n.* (*sl.*) passmen, ordinary degree, at Cambridge.

Poll, *n.* parrot. **p.-parrot,** *n.* parrot; chatterer. (*Polly*)

pollack, *n.* sea-fish allied to cod.

pollan, *n.* Irish freshwater fish.

pollard, *n.* tree with crown cut off so that a close thick head grows from top of trunk; hornless animal; fine bran, bran mixed with meal.—*v.t.* make pollard of (tree). (*poll*)

pollen, *n.* a yellowish dust, fertilizing element of plants.—*v.t.* cover with pollen. (L.=fine flour)

pollex, *n.* (*pl.* **pollices**) thumb. (L.)

pollicitation, *n.* (*civil law*) promise not yet formally accepted. (L. *pollicēri*, promise)

pollinate, *v.t.* fertilize with pollen. **pollination,** *n.* **pollinic,** *a.* of pollen. **polliniferous,** *a.* bearing pollen.

polliwog, *n.* tadpole. (M.E. *polwigle*)

pollock, same as **pollack.**

pollute, *v.t.* defile, make foul; desecrate, profane; corrupt. **pollution,** *n.* (L. *polluere*)

polo, *n.* game like hockey between teams of four players mounted on ponies. **p.-stick,** *n.* long-handled mallet for polo. **water p.,** played by swimmers with inflated ball, seven men a side. (native)

polonaise, *n.* slow stately dance in 3-4 time; music for it; one-piece bodice and skirt looped up at sides. (F.=Polish)

polonium, *n.* a radioactive element. (L.L. *Polonia*, Poland)

polony, *n.* kind of pork sausage.

poltergeist, *n.* noisy ghost that raps and moves furniture etc. about. (G.)

poltroon, *n.* coward, craven. **poltroonery,** *n.* (It. *poltro,* lazy)

poly-, from Gk. *polus,* many, as in polygamy.

polyadelphous, *a.* having stamens in three or more bundles. (Gk. *polus,* many; *adelphos,* brother)

polyandry, *n.* custom of women having more than one husband; (*bot.*) having 20 or more stamens. **polyandrous,** *a.* **polyandrist,** *n.* woman with several husbands. (Gk. *polus,* many; *anēr,* man)

polyanthus, *n.* kinds of primula. (Gk. *polus,* many; *anthos,* flower)

polyarchy, *n.* government by many. (Gk. *polus,* many; *archē,* rule)

polyatomic, *a.* with more than one atom in the molecule.

polybasic, *a.* (*chem.*) having more than two bases or atoms of a base.

polycarpellary, polycarpous, *aa.* having several carpels.

polychaete, *n.* kinds of marine worm. **polychaetan, polychaetous,** *aa.* (Gk. *polus,* many; *chaitē,* hair)

polychrome, *n.* work of art in several colours, coloured statue.—*a.* (also **polychromatic, polychromic, polychromous**) many-coloured. **polychromy,** *n.* art of decorating in many colours. (Gk. *polus,* many; *chrōma,* colour)

polyclinic, *n.* general hospital. (Gk. *polus,* many+*clinic*)

polydactyl, *a.* and *n.* (animal, person) with more than normal number of fingers or toes. (Gk. *polus,* many; *daktulos,* finger)

polydipsia, *n.* morbid thirst. (Gk. *polus,* much; *dipsa,* thirst)

polygamy, *n.* having more than one wife or (*rare*) husband at a time; (*bot.*) having staminate, pistillate, and hermaphrodite flowers on one plant. **polygamous polygamic,** *aa.* **polygamist,** *n.* one who practises or upholds polygamy. (Gk. *polus,* many; *gamos,* marriage)

polygastric, *a.* with many stomachs.

polygenesis, *n.* derivation from many origins. **polygenesic, polygenetic,** *aa.* **polygenic, polygenous,** *aa.* (*chem.*) forming more than one compound with hydrogen etc.; (*geol.*) composed of various kinds of rock. **polygeny,** *n.* descent of mankind from more than one pair of ancestors. **polygenism, polygenist,** *nn.* theory of, believer in, polygeny. (*poly-*; *genesis*)

polyglot, *a.* of, in, speaking, several languages.—*n.* book, esp. Bible, with versions of the text in several languages; one who speaks several languages. **polyglottal, polyglottic,** *aa.* (Gk. *polus,* many; *glōtta,* tongue)

polygon, *n.* many-sided plane figure. **polygonal,** *a.* (Gk. *polus,* many; *gōnia,* angle)

polygonum, *n.* kinds of plant incl. knotgrass. (Gk. *polus,* many; *gonu,* knee)

polygram, *n.* figure, design, with many lines. **polygraph,** *n.* kind of copying-machine. **polygraphy,** *n.* voluminous writing. **polygraphic,** *a.* (Gk. *polus,* many: *graphein,* write)

polygyny, *n.* custom of men having more than one wife; (*bot.*) having many pistils. **polygynous,** *a.* (Gk. *polus,* many; *gunē,* wife)

polyhedron, *n.* solid with many (us. more than six) plane faces. **polyhedral, polyhedric,** *aa.* (Gk. *polus,* many; *hedra,* base)

polyhistor, *n.* man of wide learning. (Gk. *polus,* much; *histōr,* knowing)

polymath, *n.* man versed in many arts and sciences. **polymathy,** *n.* (Gk. *polus,* many; *manthanein,* learn)

polymeric, *a.* (*chem.*) composed of same elements in same proportions, but of different molecular weights. **polymerous,** *a.* (*bot.*) having many parts. **polymerism,** *n.* **polymerize,** *v.t.* (Gk. *polus,* many; *meros,* part)

polymorphous, polymorphic, *aa.* having, assuming, many different forms. **polymorph,** *n.* polymorphous organism. (Gk. *polus,* many; *morphē,* form)

Polynesia, *n.* Pacific islands E. of Australia. **Polynesian,** *a.* and *n.* (Gk. *polus,* many; *nēsos,* island)

polynia, *n.* open water in ice-field. (Russ. *poluinya*)

polynomial, *a.* and *n.* (algebraic expression) of more than one term. (Gk. *polus,* many. L. *nomen,* name)

polyonymous, *a.* having several names. **polyonymy,** *n.* (Gk. *polus,* many; *onoma,* name)

polyopia, *n.* multiple vision. (Gk. *polus,* many; *ōps,* eye)

polyp, polype, *n.* tube-like tentacled marine invertebrate, e.g. sea-anemone; zooid; polypus. **polypary,** *n.* common structure of polyp colony. (*polypus*)

polyphagous, *a.* voracious; (*zool.*) feeding on various kinds of food. (Gk. *polus,* many; *phagein,* eat)

polyphonic, polyphonous, *aa.* many-voiced; (*philol.*) representing more than one sound; (*mus.*) contrapuntal. **polyphone,** *n.* polyphonic letter or symbol. **polyphony,** *n.* being polyphonic; counterpoint. (Gk. *polus,* many; *phōnē,* voice)

polyphyletic, *a.* having more than one original type, polygenetic. (Gk. *polus,* many; *phulē,* tribe)

polyphyllous, *a.* having many leaves. (Gk. *polus,* many; *phullon,* leaf)

polypite, *n.* individual polyp in coral.

polypod, *a.* and *n.* (animal) with many legs. (*polypus*)

polypody, *n.* kinds of fern. (*polypus*)

polypoid, polypous, *aa.* polyp-like.

polypus, *n.* (*pl.* **polypi, polypuses**) tumour with branching roots in nose

or womb. (Gk. *polus*, many; *pous*, foot)
polysepalous, *a.* with separate sepals.
polystome, *a.* and *n.* (animal) with many mouths. **polystomatous, polystomous,** *aa.* (Gk. *polus*, many; *stoma*, mouth)
polysyllable, *n.* word of many or of more than three syllables. **polysyllabic,** *a.* **polysyllabically,** *adv.*
polysyndeton, *n.* repetition of conjunction for emphasis. (Gk. *polus*, many; *sun*, with; *dein*, bind)
polysynthetic, *a.* (of language) combining several words into one. **polysynthetism,** *n.*
polytechnic, *a.* of many arts or sciences.—*n.* technical school; combined college and club. (Gk. *polus*, many; *technē*, art)
polytheism, *n.* belief in many gods or more than one god. **polytheist,** *n.* **polytheistic,** *a.* (Gk. *polus*, many; *theos*, god)
polyzoa, *n.pl.* class of minute animals forming crust on stones under water. **polyzoan,** *a.* (Gk. *polus*, many; *zōon*, animal)
pom, *n.* Pomeranian dog. (abbr.)
pomace, *n.* crushed apples for making cider; refuse pulp after oil is extracted from fish. (L. *pomum*, apple)
pomade, *n.* scented ointment for hair, hair-grease.—*v.t.* smear with this. (L. *pomum*, apple)
pomander, *n.* aromatic ball or powder formerly carried as protection against infection; box for this. (O.F. *pomme d'ambre*, apple of amber)
Pomard, same as **Pommard.**
pomatum, same as **pomade.**
pombe, *n.* native African beer. (native)
pome, *n.* any fruit of same structure as apple; (*poet.*) apple. (L. *pomum*)
pomegranate, *n.* fruit like orange, with thick rind; tree bearing it. (L. *pomum*, apple; *granatum*, seeded)
pomelo, *n.* grape-fruit; shaddock.
Pomeranian, *n.* breed of small dogs, spitz. (*Pomerania* in Prussia)
pomfret, *n.* large black edible sea-fish.
pomfret-cake, *n.* liquorice cake. (*Pontefract* in Yorkshire)
pomiculture, *n.* fruit-growing. **pomiferous,** *a.* pome-bearing. (*pome*)
Pommard, *n.* a red burgundy. (place)
pommel, *n.* knob of sword-hilt; raised front part of saddle.—*v.t.* pound repeatedly, beat with fists. (L. *pomum*, apple + dim.)
pomology, *n.* science of fruit-growing. **pomological,** *a.* **pomologist,** *n.* (L. *pomum*, fruit. Gk. *legein*, speak)
Pomona, *n.* goddess of fruits. (L.)
pomp, *n.* splendid display; splendour; pageant. (Gk. *pempein*, send)
pompadour, *n.* hair brushed straight up from forehead; low square-cut corsage. (Marquise de *Pompadour*)
pompano, *n.* an edible American sea-fish. (Sp. *pampano*)
pompelmoose, *n.* shaddock, esp. larger kind.
pom-pom, *n.* quick-firing gun with one-pound shells. (imit.)
pompon, *n.* ornamental tuft of feathers, ribbons etc. on cap or shoe. (F.)
pompous, *a.* stately, grand; self-important, high and mighty; (of language) stilted. **pomposity,** *n.*
ponceau, *n.* poppy-red. (F.)
poncho, *n.* cloak or cape like blanket with slit in middle for head. (Sp.)
pond, *n.* pool of standing water; small artificial lake.—*v.t.* and *i.* dam (up); form pool. **pondage,** *n.* capacity of pond.
ponder, *v.t.* and *i.* weigh in mind, think over; cogitate, muse. **ponderable,** *a.* having weight; tangible.—*n.* material thing. **ponderability,** *n.* **ponderation,** *n.* weighing. **ponderous,** *a.* heavy, massive; dull, boring. **ponderosity,** *n.* (L. *pondus*, weight)
pone, *n.* (*Amer.*) maize bread. (Amer. Ind.)
pongee, *n.* a soft unbleached Chinese silk.
pongo, *n.* large African anthropoid ape. (native)
poniard, *n.* dagger.—*v.t.* stab with one. (L. *pugnus*, fist)
pons asinorum, nickname of an early proposition of Euclid; any hard test for beginners. (L. =asses' bridge)
pontiff, *n.* pope; bishop; chief priest. **pontifical,** *a.* of pontiff; pompously dogmatic.—*n.* book of episcopal rites; (*pl.*) bishop's vestments. **pontificate,** *n.* office, term of office, of pontiff. **pontify,** *v.i.* play the pontiff; speak sententiously. (L. *pontifex*)
pont-levis, *n.* drawbridge. (F.)
pontoon, *n.* flat-bottomed boat; boat, cylinder, forming support of bridge; caisson.—*v.t.* cross by pontoons. **p.-bridge,** *n.* bridge of boats. **pontoneer,** *n.* engineer in charge of pontoons. (L. *pons*, bridge)
pontoon, *n.* gambling card-game, *vingt-et-un.*
ponty, same as **punty.**
pony, *n.* horse of small breed; (*sl.*) £25; (*Amer. sl.*) translation, crib.
pood, *n.* Russian measure of weight, 36 lb. (Russ. *pud*)
poodle, *n.* pet dog with long curling hair. **p.-faker,** *n.* young ladies' man. **p.-faking,** *n.* (G. *pudel*)
poogye, *n.* Indian nose-flute. (Hind.)
pooh, *int.* of contempt. **P.-Bah,** *n.* person who holds several offices at once. **p.-p.,** *v.t.* make light of.
pooja, *n.* Hindu religious rite or ritual. (*Sanskr. pūjā*)
pooka. *n.* Irish hobgoblin. (Ir. *púca*)
pookoo, *n.* red antelope of Central Africa. (Zulu *mpuku*)
pool, *n.* small body of still water; deep part of stream. (O.E. *pól*)
pool, *n.* collective stakes in certain

games; receptacle for these; common fund or store; commercial combine to cut out competition; kind of billiards.—*v.t.* contribute to common fund, share.

poon, *n.* an E. Indian tree whose seeds yield oil. (Cingalese *puna*)

poonah, *a.* (of painting) in style imitating oriental art. (Indian city)

poop, *n.* stern of ship; raised deck there.—*v.t.* (of wave) break heavily over stern of. (L. *puppis*)

poop, *n.* silly or inane person. (*nincompoop*)

poop, same as **pope.**

poor, *a.* having little money; deficient (in), feeble; of inferior quality, paltry; without fertility; scanty; unfortunate, deserving pity. **P. Clares,** female branch of Franciscans. **p.-box,** *n.* for offerings for the poor. **p.-john,** *n.* (*Shake.*) salted hake. **p.-law, p.-rate,** *nn.* for relief of paupers. **p.-spirited,** *a.* cowardly, base. **poorhouse,** *n.* workhouse. **poorly,** *adv.* insufficiently, badly; (*Shake.*) meanly.—*a.* out of sorts, unwell. (L. *pauper*)

poortith, *n.* (*Scot.*) poverty.

pop, *n.* short explosive sound; effervescing drink; (*colloq.*) shot.—*v.i.* and *t.* make, cause to make, sound of pop; go quickly, dart, thrust suddenly; (*sl.*) pawn; (*Amer.*) parch (maize) till it bursts open.—*adv.* with a pop; suddenly. **p. at,** shoot at. **p. off,** depart; die. **p. the question,** propose marriage. **p.-corn,** *n.* (*Amer.*) popped maize. **p.-eyed,** *a.* (*Amer. colloq.*) with bulging eyes. **popping crease,** (*cricket*) line marking batsman's ground. (imit.)

pop, *n.* (*sl.*) popular concert. (abbr.)

pop, *n.* (*Amer. colloq.*) father. (*papa*)

Pop, *n.* exclusive club at Eton. (L. *popina,* cook-shop, where it met)

pope, *n.* kind of perch.

pope, *n.* place on thigh where blow is disabling.—*v.t.* strike on pope.

pope, *n.* bishop of Rome, head of Roman Catholic Church; parish priest of Greek Church; person claiming infallibility. **P. Joan,** a card game. **p's eye,** fat in middle of leg of mutton. **popedom,** *n.* office of pope, papacy. **popery,** *n.* Roman Catholic doctrines (us. hostile). (L. *papa,* father)

popgun, *n.* toy firing pellets with pop.

popinjay, *n.* conceited person, fop; (formerly) shooting-mark in shape of bird; (*arch.*) parrot. (O.F. *papegai*)

popish, *a.* of popery, papistical.

poplar, *n.* a slender quick-growing tree. (L. *pōpulus*)

poplin, *n.* ribbed fabric with silk warp and worsted weft. (made at *papal* town of Avignon)

popliteal, *a.* of back of knee. (L. *poples,* ham)

poppa, *n.* (*Amer.*) papa.

poppet, *n.* darling; head of lathe. **p. valve,** valve opened by being lifted from its seat. (=*puppet*)

popple, *v.i.* (of water) tumble; ripple, bubble.—*n.* choppy motion; ripple.

poppy, *n.* kinds of showy-flowered plant one of which yields opium; vivid scarlet. **Flanders p.,** sacred to dead of Great War. (L. *papaver*)

poppycock, *n.* (*Amer. sl.*) nonsense.

populace, *n.* common people. (*popular*)

popular, *a.* of, by, for, the common people; easy to understand; generally admired or liked; (*Shake.*) vulgar. **popularity,** *n.* **popularize,** *v.t.* make popular; present in popular form. **popularization,** *n.* **populate,** *v.t.* inhabit; supply with inhabitants. **population,** *n.* populating; inhabitants collectively. **populist,** *n.* member of U.S. People's Party aiming at public control of railways etc. **populism,** *n.* **populistic,** *a.* **populous,** *a.* thickly inhabited; (*Shake.*) numerous. (L. *populus,* people)

porbeagle, *n.* mackerel-shark.

porcelain, *n.* fine white earthenware, china.—*a.* of this; fragile. **porcelainous, porcellaneous, porcellanic, porcellanous,** *aa.* (It. *porcellana,* kind of shell with polished surface)

porch, *n.* projecting covered entrance to building. **the P.,** Stoic school of philosophy. (L. *porticus*)

porcine, *a.* of, like, pigs. (L. *porcus,* pig)

porcupine, *n.* large rodent covered with long pointed quills. (L. *porcus,* pig; *spina,* thorn)

pore, *n.* minute opening, esp. in skin for passage of sweat. (Gk. *poros*)

pore, *v.i.* and *t.* look with steady attention; study closely. **p. over,** be absorbed in. (M.E. *puren*)

porge, *v.t.* (*Jewish*) make (slaughtered beast) ceremonially clean.

porgy, *n.* an edible sea-fish; sea-bream.

pork, *n.* pig's flesh as food. **porker,** *n.* fattened pig. **porky,** *a.* like pork; paunchy. (L. *porcus,* pig)

porno-, from Gk. *pornos,* harlot, used in **pornocracy,** *n.* government dominated by courtesans; **pornography,** *n.* indecent writing, obscenity, treatise on prostitutes, hence **pornographer,** *n.*, **pornographic,** *a.*

porous, *a.* having pores; permeable by liquids. **porosity,** *n.*

porpentine, *n.* (*Shake.*) porcupine.

porphyry, *n.* a hard reddish rock with embedded crystals; any rock of like composition. (Gk. *porphuros,* purple)

porpoise, *n.* sea-mammal like dolphin with blunt snout. (L. *porcus,* pig; *piscis,* fish)

porraceous, *a.* greenish like leek. (L. *porrum,* leek)

porrect, *a.* stretched out.—*v.t.* tender, hand. (L. *porrigere,* extend)

porridge, *n.* oatmeal etc. boiled in water or milk; (*Shake.*) soup. (=*pottage*)

porrigo, *n.* scaly eruption on scalp, scurf. **porriginous,** *a.* (L.)

porringer, *n.* small bowl for porridge, soup etc. (*porridge*)

port, *n.* harbour; town with harbour; refuge, haven. (L. *portus*)

port, *n.* gate, gateway; opening in ship's side for loading cargo; port-hole; (*mech.*) passage-way for steam etc. **porthole,** *n.* hole in ship's side for light and air. (L. *porta*)

port, *n.* bearing, mien; (*Shake.*) social station.—*v.t.* hold (rifle etc.) diagonally in front of body. (L. *portare,* carry)

port, *n.* and *a.* left of ship looking forward.—*v.t.* and *i.* turn (helm, ship) to port.

port, *n.* (also **p. wine**) a strong sweet red wine. (*Oporto* in Portugal)

portable, *a.* able to be carried by hand; movable. (L. *portare,* carry)

portage, *n.* transport of goods; price of this; carrying (of boat etc.) overland between rivers or past rapids; place for this.—*v.t.* convey over portage. (L. *portare,* carry)

portal, *n.* gate, doorway, esp. imposing one. **p. vein,** conveying blood to liver. (L. *porta,* gate)

portamento, *n.* (*mus.*) continuous glide from one note to another. (It.)

portance, *n.* (*Shake.*) behaviour. (*port*)

portative, *a.* serving to carry. (L. *portare,* carry)

portcrayon, *n.* crayon-holder. (F.)

portcullis, *n.* grating to defend castle gateway, raised and lowered in grooves. (O.F. *porte coleïce,* sliding door)

Porte, *n.* (also **Sublime P.**) old Turkish government at Constantinople. (F.)

porte-cochère, *n.* covered gateway for carriage through house into court-yard. (F.)

porte-monnaie, *n.* flat purse. (F.)

portend, *v.t.* foreshadow, presage, betoken; (*Shake.*) signify. **portent,** *n.* omen, warning; prodigy. **portentous,** *a.* ominous; imposing, prodigious; pompous. (L. *portendere*)

porter, *n.* door-keeper, gate-keeper; (*Amer.*) attendant in Pullman car. (L. *porta,* gate)

porter, *n.* railway servant handling luggage; man who carries burdens for hire; heavy dark-brown beer. **p.-house,** *n.* (*Amer.*) eating-house. **porterhouse steak,** choice cut of beef-steak next sirloin. **porterage,** *n.* hire of porter. (L. *portare,* carry)

portesse, *n.* (*Spens.*) portable breviary. (L. *portare,* carry; *foris,* out of doors)

portfire, *n.* device for igniting fire-works or rockets. (L. *portare,* carry)

portfolio, *n.* flat case for drawings, papers etc.; office of minister of state. **minister without p.** not in charge of a department. (L. *portare,* carry; *folium,* leaf)

portico, *n.* covered walk, entrance, enclosed by pillars. (L. *porticus*)

portière, *n.* heavy curtain over door or doorway. (F.)

portion, *n.* part; share, helping; dowry; destiny, lot.—*v.t.* divide (out); give share or dowry to. **portionless,** *a.* without dowry. (L. *portio*)

portly, *a.* corpulent, stout; of dignified mien. (*port*)

portmanteau, *n.* (*pl.* **portmanteaus, portmanteaux**) large oblong travelling-case with two compartments. **p. word,** combining sense and sound of two, e.g. 'brunch.' (F.)

portrait, *n.* likeness of person or face; vivid description; type. **portraitist,** *n.* portrait-painter. **portraiture,** *n.* portrait-painting; portrait; depicting (*portray*)

portray, *v.t.* paint, draw, likeness of; depict. **portrayal,** *n.* (L. *pro-,* forth; *trahere,* draw)

portreeve, *n.* (*obs.*) chief officer of a town. (*port*; *reeve*)

portress, *n.* female door-keeper.

Portuguese, *a.* and *n.* (native, language) of Portugal. **P. man-of-war,** kind of jelly-fish.

posada, *n.* inn. (Sp.)

pose, *v.t.* and *i.* propound, assert; place in, assume, an attitude for effect; exhibit oneself (as).—*n.* attitude; artificial posture. (L. *pausare,* halt+confusion with *ponere,* place)

pose, *v.t.* puzzle, cause to be at a loss. **poser,** *n.* puzzling question or problem. (short for *oppose*)

poseur, *n.* (*fem.* *poseuse*) one who poses, affected person. (F.)

posh, *a.* (*sl.*) smart, stylish.—*v.t.* trim (up), decorate.

poshteen, incorrect form of **posteen.**

posit, *v.t.* assume as fact, postulate; put in position. (L. *ponere,* place)

position, *n.* place, situation; attitude, posture; rank, place in society; office; strategic point; state of affairs; (*Shake.*) assertion.—*v.t.* place in position; locate. **in a p. to,** enabled by circumstances to. **in, out of, p.,** rightly, wrongly, placed. **positional,** *a.* (L. *ponere,* place)

positive, *a.* marked by presence, not absence, of qualities; practical, real; greater than zero, plus; definite, explicit; certain, confident; over-confident, cocksure; absolute, downright; (of electricity) of kind generated by friction on glass; (*gram.*) denoting simple form of adjective; (*phot.*) having light and shade as in original.—*n.* positive adjective, quantity, or photograph. **positively,** *adv.* in a positive way; decidedly. **positivism,** *n.* philosophy recognizing only matters of fact and experience. **positivist,** *n.* adherent of this. **positivity,** *n.* positiveness. (L. *ponere,* place)

positron, *n.* positive electron.
posology, *n.* science of medical doses. (Gk. *posos*, how much; *legein*, speak)
posse, *n.* force, company; (also *p. comitatus*) force of citizens called out by sheriff to aid in enforcing law. (L.=be able)
possess, *v.t.* own, have, keep; dominate, have mastery of; have sexual intercourse with; (*Shake.*) inform. **p. oneself of,** acquire. **possessed,** *a.* mad. **possessed of,** having. **possession,** *n.* possessing; ownership, occupancy; thing possessed; (*pl.*) property. **possessive,** *a.* of ownership; tending to possess; (*gram.*) denoting possession.—*n.* possessive case or pronoun. **possessor,** *n.* owner; proprietor. **possessory,** *a.* (L. *possidēre*)
posset, *n.* hot spiced drink of milk and ale or wine. (M.E. *poshote*)
possible, *a.* that may exist, happen, or be done; (*colloq.*) tolerable.—*n.* highest possible score. **possibilist,** *n.* member of political party which aims only at immediately practicable reforms. **possibility,** *n.* being possible; possible occurrence, contingency. **possibly,** *adv.* according to what is possible; perhaps. (L. *posse*, be able)
possum, *colloq.* for **opossum.**
post, *n.* fixed upright of wood or metal; starting, finishing, point in race; block of coal left as prop in mine.—*v.t.* stick (up), affix (notice); place in list, announce; placard. (L. *postis*)
post, *n.* place of duty; situation, job; outpost, fort; trading station.—*v.t.* station (sentry etc.). **last p.,** final bugle-call for retiring at night, also sounded at military funerals. **p. captain,** (*obs.*) full captain. (L. *ponere*, place)
post, *n.* official conveyance of letters and parcels, mail; postal collection or delivery; size of paper, 19½ × 15½ in.; (formerly) stage on road with relays of horses; courier; (*Shake.*) post-horse.—*v.t.* put (letter) in post; keep informed; (*book-keeping*) transfer (entry) from daybook to ledger. —*v.i.* go with speed, hurry; (formerly) travel with relays of horses.—*adv.* with post-horses, express. **p. office,** office for business connected with mails; the postal department. **p. up,** (*book-keeping*) bring entries in (ledger) up to date. (L. *ponere*, place)
post, *prep.* after. *p. hoc, ergo propter hoc*, after this, so owing to this; fallacy that event following another must be the result of it. *p. meridiem*, (*abbr.* **p.m.**) after noon. *p. mortem*, after death. (L.)
post-, *pref.* after, as in **postpone.**
postage, *n.* fee for conveyance by post. **p. stamp,** adhesive label prepaying this.
postal, *a.* of the post. **p. order,** kind of post-office cheque. **P. Union,** union of countries for regulating international postage.
post-boy, *n.* postilion.
postcard, *n.* card conveying message by post at cheaper rate than letter.
post-chaise, *n.* light closed carriage for travelling post.
post-classical, *a.* after the classical period.
post-communion, *n.* part of eucharistic service following communion.
post-date, *v.t.* date after the actual time; make (cheque) payable at date later than signature.
post-diluvian, post-diluvial, *aa.* after the Flood.
posteen, *n.* (*Anglo-Ind.*) Afghan leather jacket. (Pers. *postīn*)
poster, *n.* bill, placard; one who posts bills.
poster, *n.* (*Shake.*) swift traveller.
poste restante, department of post office holding letters till they are called for. (F.)
posterior, *a.* later in time or order; hinder.—*n.* backside. **posteriority,** *n.* **posterity,** *n.* later generations; descendants. (L.)
postern, *n.* back or side entrance; small private door. (L. *posterus*, behind + dim.)
post-exilian, post-exilic, *aa.* after the Babylonian captivity of the Jews.
postfix, *n.* suffix.—*v.t.* append as suffix.
post-free, *a.* without charge for postage.
post-glacial, *a.* after the glacial period.
post-graduate, *a.* (of study) carried on after taking of degree.
post-haste, *adv.* with utmost speed.—*n.* (*Shake.*) great haste.
post-horn, *n.* simple brass wind-instrument formerly used by guard of mail-coach.
post-horse, *n.* one of the relays kept at stage for those travelling post.
posthumous, *a.* born after father's death; published after author's death; occurring after death. (L. *postumus*, last + confusion with *humus*, ground)
postiche, *a.* artificial; superfluous.—*n.* ornament added, esp. inappropriately, to finished work; wig, false front. (F.)
posticous, *a* (*bot.*) hinder; turned away from axis. (L. *posticus*)
postil, *n.* (*arch.*) marginal note, esp. on text of Scripture. (L.L. *postilla*)
postilion, postillion, *n.* man riding on one of the horses of a carriage and guiding team. (It. *postiglione*)
post-impressionism, *n.* recent school of painting which seeks to express the artist's conception of things rather than their outward appearance; extreme subjectivity in art. **post-impressionist,** *n.* and *a.*
postliminy, *n.* right of prisoner of war or exile to resume privileges on return

to his own country. (L. *post*, after; *limen*, threshold)

postlude, *n.* (*mus.*) following movement (opp. to prelude). (L. *ludere*, play)

postman, *n.* official who collects and delivers letters.

postmark, *n.* official mark cancelling postage stamp.—*v.t.* mark with this.

postmaster, *n.* (*fem.* **postmistress**) official in charge of post office. **P.-General,** *n.* administrative head of postal service.

postmaster, *n.* scholar of Merton College, Oxford. **postmastership,** *n.*

post-mortem, *n.* medical examination of dead body. (L. = after death)

post-natal, *a*, after birth.

post-nuptial, *a.* after marriage.

post-obit, *a.* taking effect after death. *n.* bond in which borrower undertakes to repay loan on death of someone from whom he has expectations. (L. *post*, after; *obitus*, death)

postpone, *v.t.* put off, defer; subordinate. **postponement,** *n.* (L. *post*, after; *ponere*, place)

postposition, *n.* word or particle placed after another, e.g. '-wards.'

postprandial, *a.* after dinner.

postscript, *n.* (*abbr.* **P.S.**) addition made as afterthought at end of letter or book.

postulate, *v.t.* and *i.* assume, lay down as self-evident; demand, stipulate; nominate (to benefice) subject to superior sanction.—*n.* thing taken for granted, prerequisite; (*geom.*) construction the possibility of which is assumed. **postulation,** *n.* **postulant,** *n.* petitioner; candidate for admission to religious order. (L. *postulare*)

posture, *n.* position of body, attitude; condition (of affairs).—*v.i.* and *t.* take up posture for effect; pose. (L. *ponere*, place)

posy, *n.* motto, verse, inscribed inside ring etc.; bunch of flowers, nosegay. (=*poesy*)

pot, *n.* round vessel; cooking vessel; contents of pot; chamber-pot; flower-pot; trophy; pot shot; pott. —*v.t.* and *i.* preserve, plant, in pot; shoot (at): (*billiards*) pocket (ball) by hitting it with one's own. **big p.,** (*colloq.*) personage. **go to p.,** (*colloq.*) be ruined. **p. hat,** bowler. **p. luck,** whatever is to be had for meal. **p. of money,** (*sl.*) large sum. **p. shot,** easy or random shot. (O.E. *pott*)

potable, *a.* drinkable. (*potation*)

potamic, *a.* of rivers. **potamology,** *n.* science of rivers. (Gk. *potamos*, river)

potash, (*arch.*) **potass,** *n.* crude potassium carbonate, a powerful alkali; (also **p.-water**) an aerated water. **potassium,** *n.* a silvery-white metallic element. (=*pot ashes*)

potation, *n.* drinking; draught. **potatory,** *a.* (L. *potare*, drink)

potato, *n.* (*pl.* **potatoes**) tuber used for food; plant bearing it. **p. beetle,** Colorado beetle. **small pp.,** (*Amer. sl.*) petty, trifling. (Sp. *patata*)

pot-belly, *n.* (person with) protuberant belly. **pot-bellied,** *a.*

potboiler, *n.* literary or artistic work done simply to earn a living.

pot-boy, *n.* barman's assistant.

potch, *v.i.* (*Shake.*) thrust.

poteen, *n.* illicitly distilled Irish whisky. (Ir. *pota*, pot + dim.)

potent, *a.* powerful, mighty; forceful, cogent; intoxicating. **potency,** *n.* **potentate,** *n.* ruler, sovereign. **potential,** *a.* existing in possibility only, latent: powerful; (*gram.*) expressing possibility.—*n.* possibility; potential energy or mood; degree of electrification. **potential energy,** power of doing work which a body possesses in virtue of its position. **potentiality,** *n.* latent capacity; possibility. **potentialize,** *v.t.* make potential. **potentialization,** *n.* **potentiate,** *v.t.* make possible; give power to. (L. *posse*, be able)

potentilla, *n.* kinds of plant of rose family. (*potent*+dim.)

potentiometer, *n.* instrument for measuring electric potential.

potheen, same as **poteen.**

pother, *n.* bustle, turmoil; fuss.—*v.t.* and *i.* fluster; fuss.

pot-hole, *n.* hole worn in road by traffic; (*geol.*) deep hole in rock caused by water-action.

pot-hook, *n.* hook for hanging pots over fire; curved stroke used in teaching writing.

pot-house, *n.* low public-house.

pot-hunter, *n.* one who thinks more of prize or bag than of game or sport.

potichomania, *n.* imitation of porcelain by means of painted paper glued to inside of glassware. (F. *potiche*, porcelain vase; *manie*, madness)

potion, *n.* dose of medicine or poison. (L. *potare*, drink)

pot-metal, *n.* an alloy of lead and copper; a kind of stained glass.

pot-pourri, *n.* mixture of dried rose-leaves and spices kept in jar to scent room; musical or literary medley. (F.)

potsherd, *n.* piece of broken earthenware.

pot-still, *n.* still to which heat is applied directly.

pott, *n.* size of paper, $15 \times 12\frac{1}{2}$ in. (form of *pot*)

pottage, *n.* (*arch.*) broth, stew. (*pot*)

pottah, *n.* (*Anglo-Ind.*) lease.

potted, *a.* preserved; concentrated; abridged.

potter, *v.i.* and *t.* work in a feeble way, trifle; dawdle; fritter (away).

potter, *n.* maker of earthenware vessels. **pottery,** *n.* earthenware; potter's workshop. (*pot*)

pottle, *n.* old liquid measure, four pints; pot containing this; small fruit-basket. (*pot*)

potto, *n.* W. African lemur; kinkajou. (native)

potty, *a.* (*sl.*) trivial, petty; crazy, cracked.

pot-valiant, *a.* having the courage given by drink.

potwalloper, *n.* (*naut.*) cook's assistant; (also **potwaller**) holder of household franchise before Reform Act.

pouch, *n.* small bag; pocket, wallet; (*zool.*) sac for carrying young.—*v.t.* and *i.* put into pouch, pocket; hang, cause to hang, like pouch. **pouchy,** *a.* (F. *poche*)

poudrette, *n.* manure of dried excrement and charcoal. (F.)

pouffe, pouf, *n.* large solid cushion as seat, hassock; puffed way of dressing hair. (F.)

poulp, poulpe, *n.* octopus. (F.)

poult, *n.* young fowl, esp. turkey. (L. *pullus*, young of animal)

poult-de-soie, *n.* a fine corded silk. (F.)

poulterer, (*Shake.*) **poulter,** *n.* dealer in poultry.

poultice, *n.* moist, us. hot, mass of linseed etc. spread on cloth and applied to sore or inflamed part. —*v.t.* put poultice on. (L. *puls*, porridge)

poultry, *n.* domestic fowls. (*poult*)

pounce, *v.i.* and *t.* spring, dart, suddenly (upon); swoop (upon) and seize.—*n.* pouncing, swoop; talon of bird of prey.

pounce, *n.* fine powder used to prevent ink from spreading on unsized paper or in pattern-making.—*v.t.* prepare, dust, with pounce. **pouncet-box,** *n.* (*arch.*) small perforated box for perfumes. (F. *ponce*, pumice)

pound, *n.* (*abbr.* **lb.**) measure of weight (avoirdupois) 16 oz. or 7,000 grains, (troy) 12 oz. or 5,760 grains; (*abbr.* £ or *l.*) monetary unit, 20*s.* **p. Scots,** about 1*s.* 8*d.* **p. sterling,** £. **p.-cake,** *n.* rich fruit-cake containing 1 lb. of each chief ingredient. (L. *pondo*)

pound, *v.t.* and *i.* beat, thump; crush to pieces or powder; run, ride, heavily. (O.E. *púnian*)

pound, *n.* enclosure for cattle found straying.—*v.t.* shut in pound. (O.E. *pund*)

poundage, *n.* commission, rate, tax, per pound.

poundal, *n.* unit of force, giving to mass of 1 lb. an acceleration of 1 ft. per second per second.

pounder, *n.* fish, gun firing projectile, weighing 1 lb.

pour, *v.t.* and *i.* cause to flow, shower; give vent to, utter; flow, stream; rain heavily.—*n.* pouring, esp. of molten metal. (M.E. *pouren*)

pour, prep. for. *p. rire*, not serious. *pourboire, n.* tip. *pourparler, n.* (us. *pl.*) preliminary diplomatic talks. (F.)

pourpoint, *n.* 14th-century quilted doublet. (O.F.)

poussette, *v.i.* and *n.* swing round with hands joined, in country dance. (F.)

pou sto, standing-ground, base for operations. (Gk. = where I may stand)

pout, *n.* kinds of fish. (O.E. *púta*)

pout, *v.i.* and *t.* push out (lips), look sulky.—*n.* pouting; sullen fit. **pouter,** *n.* one who pouts; breed of pigeon with prominent crop.

poverty, *n.* being poor, indigence; deficiency, lack. **p.-stricken,** *a.* poor; shabby. (L. *pauper*, poor)

pow, *n.* (*Scot.*) head. (=*poll*)

powan, *n.* (*Scot.*) a fresh-water fish.

powder, *n.* small dry particles, dust; drug in this form; gunpowder; face-powder.—*v.t.* reduce to, sprinkle with, powder; salt. **p.-closet,** *n.* small room where hair was powdered. **p.-flask, p.-horn,** *nn.* for carrying gunpowder. **p.-magazine,** *n.* store for gunpowder. **p.-monkey,** *n.* boy carrying powder to gunners on old man-of-war. **p.-puff,** *n.* pad for applying face-powder. **powdery,** *a.* like, covered with, powder. (L. *pulvis*, dust)

power *n.* ability, faculty; strength, force; authority; ascendancy, influence; deity; state, nation; mechanical energy; magnifying capacity; (*colloq.*) large amount; (*math.*) result of continued multiplication of quantity by itself a specified number of times; (*Shake.*) fighting force; (*pl.*) sixth rank of angels. **p.-house, p.-station,** *nn.* where electrical power is generated. **powerful,** *a.* very strong. **powerless,** *a.* feeble; helpless. (L. *posse*, be able)

pow-wow, *n.* Red Indian conference; (*joc.*) discussion.—*v.i.* confer, chat. (*Amer. Ind.*)

pox, *n.* smallpox, chicken-pox; (*vulg.*) syphilis.—*int.* (*obs.*) plague!

pozzy, *n.* (*army sl.*) jam.

praam, same as **pram.**

practice, *n.* action, execution (opp. to theory); habit, custom, established procedure; systematic exercise, training; professional business of doctor or lawyer; (*arch.*) stratagem, plot; (*math.*) compendious method of multiplying expressions of several denominations. **sharp p.,** barely honest dealing. **practic,** *a.* (*Shake.*) practical; (*Spens.*) skilful; artful, crafty. **practicable,** *a.* possible, feasible. **practicability,** *n.* **practical,** *a.* of, concerned with, disposed to, action, not speculation; trained, got, by practice; workable, useful; virtual, in effect. **practicality,** *n.* **practically,** *adv.* in a practical manner; virtually. (Gk. *prassein*, do)

practise, *v.t.* and *i.* do habitually; perform; follow (profession); exercise oneself (in); (*Shake.*) plot. **p. upon,** impose upon. **practisant,** *n.*

(*Shake.*) conspirator. **practised,** *a.* expert. **practiser,** *n.* (*Shake.*) practitioner. (Gk. *prassein,* do)

practitioner, *n.* one who follows profession, esp. medicine or law. **general p.,** (*abbr.* **G.P.**) doctor with general practice. (*practice*)

praecocial, *a.* (of birds) whose young are able to look after themselves as soon as hatched. (*precocious*)

praemunirē, *n.* (*law*) offence of introducing papal authority into England; statute, writ, penalty, for this. (L. *praemonēre,* warn)

praenomen, *n.* first or personal name of a Roman. (L.)

praeposter, *n.* school prefect. (L. *prae,* before; *ponere,* place)

praetor, *n.* ancient Roman magistrate below consul. **praetorian,** *a.* and *n.* of praetor; (man) of **praetorian guard,** bodyguard of Roman emperor. (L.)

pragmatic, *a.* of, related to, pragmatism; practical, matter-of-fact; of state affairs; pragmatical. **pragmatical,** *a.* officious, meddlesome; dogmatic, dictatorial; pragmatic. **pragmatism,** *n.* judging a thing by its results; philosophy which judges the truth of a doctrine by the conduct resulting from belief in it; officiousness; pedantry. **pragmatist,** *n.* **pragmatistic,** *a.* **pragmatize,** *v.t.* represent as real. (Gk. *pragma,* deed)

prairie, *n.* wide level tract of treeless grass-land. **p. oyster,** pick-me-up of raw egg, Worcester sauce, pepper, and salt. **p.-chicken,** *n.* kind of grouse. **p.-dog,** *n.* burrowing rodent like squirrel. **p.-schooner,** *n.* emigrant wagon with canvas cover. (L. *pratum,* meadow)

praise, *v.t.* express approval of, commend; glorify, worship.—*n.* praising; commendation, eulogy. **praiseful,** *a.* **praiseworthy,** *a.* meritorious. (L. *pretium,* price)

praline, *n.* confection of nuts and sugar. (F.)

pram, *n.* flat-bottomed boat; Norwegian dinghy. (Du. *praam*)

pram, *n.* (*colloq.*) perambulator. (abbr.)

prance, *v.i.* (of horse) spring on hind legs, bound; (of person) walk, ride, in showy or warlike manner; swagger. —*n.* prancing; caper.

prandial, *a.* (*joc.*) of dinner. (L. *prandium,* lunch)

prang, *v.t.* (*R.A.F. sl.*) crash, damage, wreck.

prank, *v.t.* and *i.* adorn, deck; dress up showily.

prank, *n.* escapade, frolic; mischievous trick. **prankful, prankish,** *aa.*

prase, *n.* kind of leek-green transparent quartz. (Gk. *prason,* leek)

praseodymium, *n.* a metallic element. (Gk. *prason,* leek+*didymium*)

prate, *v.i.* and *t.* chatter, talk foolishly; blab.—*n.* idle talk. **prater,** *n.*

praties, *n.pl.* (*Ir. colloq.*) potatoes. (corrupt.)

pratincole, *n.* bird like swallow. (L. *pratum,* meadow; *incola,* inhabitant)

pratique, *n.* permission given to ship after satisfying health regulations to disembark passengers or goods. (F.)

prattle, *v.i.* talk like child; babble.—*n.* childish or artless talk. **prattler,** *n.* young child; babbler. (*prate*)

pravity, *n.* wickedness; badness (of food etc.). (L. *pravus,* crooked)

prawn, *n.* edible shell-fish like shrimp but larger.—*v.i.* fish for prawns. (M.E. *prane*)

praxis, *n.* practice; set of examples for exercise. (Gk.=doing)

pray, *v.t.* and *i.* offer prayer to God; ask earnestly, entreat. **prayer,** *n.* one who prays. (L. *prex,* prayer)

prayer, *n.* supplication to God, form of this; praying, entreaty; thing prayed for. **p. book,** manual of devotion, esp. liturgy of English Church. **p.-meeting,** *n.* religious meeting where several offer prayers. **p.-wheel,** *n.* revolving wheel inscribed with prayer, used in Tibet. **prayerful,** *a.* given to prayer; devout.

pre-, *pref.* before, beforehand, as in **predict, pre-war,** (attachable to any noun or verb). (L. *prae*)

preach, *v.i.* and *t.* deliver (sermon); give moral advice unasked; advocate, urge.—*n.* (*colloq.*) sermon. **preacher, preachment,** *nn.* **preachify,** *v.i.* hold forth tediously. **preachy,** *a.* (*colloq.*) fond of preaching. (L. *praedicare,* proclaim)

pre-Adamite, *a.* and *n.* (man) existing before Adam.

preamble, *n.* introductory part of document, speech, or story.—*v.i.* make preamble. (L. *ambulare,* walk)

pre-arrange, *v.t.* arrange beforehand.

pre-audience, *n.* (of lawyers) right of precedence at the bar.

prebend, *n.* stipend of canon or member of chapter. **prebendal,** *a.* **prebendary,** *n.* holder of prebend. (L. *praebēre,* afford)

precarious, *a.* held during the pleasure of another; dependent on chance; uncertain, insecure; based on uncertain premisses. (L. *prex,* prayer)

precatory, *a.* suppliant, expressing a wish. (L. *prex,* prayer)

precaution, *n.* preventive measure; careful foresight. **precautionary,** *a.*

precede, *v.t.* and *i.* be or go before in time, place, rank, or importance. **precedence, precedency,** *nn.* priority; superiority, higher place; right to this. **precedent,** *a.* preceding; previous.—*n.* previous and parallel case; (*law*) decision etc. serving as rule. (L. *cedere,* go)

precent, *v.i.* and *t.* lead choir or congregation in singing. **precentor,** *n.* (L. *canere,* sing)

precept, *n.* rule of conduct; exhortation, maxim; (*law*) kinds of writ or warrant. **preceptive,** *a.* of, using, precepts. **preceptor,** *n.* (*fem.* **preceptress**) instructor, teacher. **preceptorial,** *a.* (L. *praecipere,* direct)

precession, *n.* going forward. **p. of the equinoxes,** gradual westward shift of equinoctial points along ecliptic; resulting earlier occurrence of equinoxes each sidereal year. **precessional,** *a.* (*precede*)

precinct, *n.* space enclosed by walls of sacred or official building or place; (*Amer.*) electoral district; (*pl.*) environs. (L. *cingere,* gird)

precious, *a.* valuable; very dear; affectedly refined, mannered; (*colloq.*) out-and-out, fine.—*adv.* (*colloq.*) uncommonly. **p. metals,** gold, silver, platinum. **p. stone,** gem. **preciosity,** *n.* affected refinement, excessive elegance (in literary style or art). (L. *pretium,* price)

precipice, *n.* upright or overhanging face of rock, very steep cliff. (L. *praeceps,* headlong)

precipitate, *v.t.* throw headlong; hurl, fling; cause to happen suddenly or too soon; condense (vapour); (*chem.*) cause (substance in solution) to be deposited.—*a.* headlong; hasty, impetuous; done too soon.—*n.* substance precipitated. **precipitance, precipitancy,** *nn.* rash haste, headlong hurry. **precipitant,** *n.* (*chem.*) substance causing precipitation. **precipitation,** *n.* precipitating; rash haste; falling of rain, snow, dew etc.; depositing of solid matter from solution. (L. *praeceps,* headlong)

precipitous, *a.* of, like, a precipice; sheer, steep; (*rare*) precipitate.

précis, *n.* summary, abstract. (F.)

precise, *a.* exact, definite; punctilious, particular. **precisely,** *adv.* exactly; just so. **precisian,** *n.* one given to minute observance of rules, purist, pedant. **precisianism,** *n.* **precision,** *n.* accuracy. **arms of precision,** fitted with sights etc. (L. *praecīdere,* cut off)

preclude, *v.t.* make impossible; prevent, debar. **preclusion,** *n.* **preclusive,** *a.* (L. *claudere,* shut)

precocious, *a.* prematurely ripe or developed; showing precocity, too forward. **precocity,** *n.* (L. *praecox*)

precognition, *n.* previous knowledge; (*Scots law*) preliminary examination of witnesses to see if there is ground for trial.

preconceive, *v.t.* form idea or opinion of beforehand. **preconception,** *n.*

preconcert, *v.t.* agree upon beforehand.

preconize, *v.t.* proclaim, publish; extol; (of pope) publicly approve appointment of (bishop). **preconization,** *n.* (L. *praeco,* crier)

pre-Conquest, *a.* before the Norman Conquest.

precordial, *a.* in front of, about, the heart. (L. *cor,* heart)

precostal, *a.* in front of the ribs.

precursor, (*Shake.*) **precurrer,** *nn.* person, thing, indicating another's approach; forerunner. **precursive, precursory,** (*Shake.*) **precurse,** *aa.* heralding. (L. *currere,* run)

predacious, *a.* living on prey; of predacious animals. **predacity,** *n.* **predatory,** *a.* plundering, pillaging; living on prey. (L. *praeda,* booty)

predate, *v.t.* antedate.

predecease, *v.t.* die before.—*n.* prior death.

predecessor, *n.* former holder of office or position. (L. *decedere,* withdraw)

predella, *n.* platform for, shelf behind, altar; painting, sculpture, on this. (It.)

predestine, *v.t.* destine beforehand, foreordain. **predestinate,** *v.t.* predestine.—*a.* predestined. **predestination,** *n.* predestining; destiny; doctrine that God has from all eternity decreed the salvation or damnation of each soul. **predestinarian,** *a.* of predestination.—*n.* believer in it.

predetermine, *v.t.* decide beforehand; predestine. **predeterminate,** *a.* **predetermination,** *n.*

predial, *a.* of land or landed property; agrarian. (L. *praedium,* farm)

predicate, *v.t.* assert, state; connote. —*n.* (*gram., logic*) that which is stated about the subject. **predication,** *n.* **predicative,** *a.* **predicable,** *a.* able to be predicated.—*n.* predicable thing, attribute. **predicability,** *n.* **predicament,** *n.* trying position, awkward fix. **predicamental,** *a.* **predicant,** *a.* and *n.* preaching (friar). **predicatory,** *a.* of, given to, preaching. (L. *praedicare,* proclaim)

predict, *v.t.* and *i.* foretell, prophesy. **predictable, predictive,** *aa.* **prediction, predictor,** *nn.* (L. *dicere,* say)

predigest, *v.t.* digest (food) artificially before consumption.

predikant, *n.* Dutch or Boer Protestant minister. (Du.)

predilection, *n.* prepossession, partiality. (L. *diligere,* choose)

predispose, *v.t.* incline beforehand; make susceptible to (disease etc). **predisposition,** *n.*

predominate, *v.i.* be chief element or factor (in), preponderate; have control, prevail (over). **predominance,** *n.* preponderance; ascendancy. **predominant,** *a.*

predorsal, *a.* in front of the spine.

pree, *v.t.* (*Scot.*) prove, taste.

pre-eminent, *a.* surpassing all others, outstanding. **pre-eminence,** *n.*

pre-empt, *v.t.* acquire by pre-emption; appropriate beforehand. **pre-emption,** *n.* buying, right to buy, before opportunity **is** given to others. **pre-emptive,** *a.* **pre-emptive bid,** (*auction bridge*) high bid to exclude bids from opponents. (L. *emere*, buy)

preen, *v.t.* trim (feathers) with beak; trim, plume (oneself).

preen, *n.* (*Scot.*) pin.

pre-exilian, pre-exilic, *aa.* before the Babylonian captivity of the Jews.

pre-exist, *v.i.* exist beforehand. **pre-existence** *n.* prior existence, esp. of the soul before birth.

preface, *n.* introductory remarks prefixed to book, foreword; preamble.—*v.t.* furnish with preface; introduce. **prefatory,** *a.* of preface; introductory. (L. *fari*, speak)

prefect, *n.* governor of French department; senior schoolboy maintaining discipline; ancient Roman magistrate. **prefectoral, prefectorial,** *aa.* **prefecture,** *n.* prefect's office, district, residence, or tenure. (L. *praefectus*)

prefer, *v.t.* like better, choose rather; promote; submit (charge). **preferable,** *a.* deserving preference, superior. **preferably,** *adv.* for choice. **preference,** *n.* preferring; thing preferred, choice; prior right; concession to favoured country of lowered import duties. **preference, preferred, shares,** on which dividend is paid before ordinary shares. **preferential,** *a.* giving or receiving a preference. **preferment,** *n.* advancement, promotion. (L. *ferre*, bear)

prefigure, *v.t.* symbolize or typify in advance, foreshadow; imagine beforehand. **prefiguration, prefigurement,** *nn.* **prefigurative,** *a.*

prefix, *v.t.* put before or at beginning of; put as introduction.—*n.* syllable, particle, word, prefixed to another to affect its meaning, e.g. 'un-,' 'anti-,' 'Sir.' **prefixion, prefixture,** *nn.*

preform, *v.t.* shape beforehand. **preformation,** *n.* **theory of preformation,** old belief that all parts of complete organism exist in little in the germ cell. **preformative,** *a.* and *n.* (syllable, word) prefixed as formative element.

preglacial, *a.* before the glacial period.

pregnable, *a.* capable of being taken by assault. (L. *prehendere*, take)

pregnant, *a.* with child; fertile, inventive; full of importance or hidden meaning; (*Shake.*) receptive, inclined; clear, obvious. **pregnancy,** *n.* (L. *praegnans*)

prehensile, *a.* (*zool.*) capable of grasping. **prehensility,** *n.* **prehension,** *n.* power of grasping.

prehistoric, *a.* before written history begins; (*colloq.*) very old-fashioned. **prehistory,** *n.* prehistoric events or study.

pre-human, *a.* before the existence of man.

prejudge, *v.t.* pass judgment on before trial; form premature opinion on. **prejudgment, prejudgement,** *nn.*

prejudice, *n.* bias, partiality, preconceived opinion; (*law*) injury, disadvantage, due to another's action.—*v.t.* bias, prepossess; injure; impair validity of. **without p.,** (*law*) without impairing existing right or claim. **prejudicial,** *a.* detrimental, damaging. (L. *judex*, judge)

prelate, *n.* church dignitary, bishop; (formerly) abbot, prior. **prelatess,** *n.* abbess, prioress. **prelatic, prelatical,** *aa.* **prelacy,** *n.* office, rank, of prelate; prelates collectively; church government by prelates, episcopacy. **prelatize,** *v.t.* bring under rule of prelates. **prelature,** *n.* prelacy. (L. *latus*, borne)

prelect, *v.t.* discourse publicly, lecture at university. **prelection, prelector,** *nn.* (L. *legere*, read)

prelibation, *n.* foretaste.

preliminary, *a.* preceding and preparing for main business, introductory.—*n.* preliminary step or measure. **p. examination,** entrance examination. **prelim,** *n.* (*sl.*) preliminary examination; (*pl.*, *print.*) preliminary matter. (L. *limen*, threshold)

prelude, *n.* introductory act or event, preface; (*mus.*) introductory movement.—*v.t.* and *i.* serve as prelude to, usher in; play prelude. **prelusion,** *n.* **prelusive, prelusory,** *aa.* (L. *ludere*, play)

premature, *a.* done before the proper time, too early, hasty; (of report) unauthenticated. **prematurity,** *n.*

premeditate, *v.t.* plan beforehand. **premeditation,** *n.* set purpose.

premier, *a.* first, principal.—*n.* prime minister. **premiership,** *n.* (L. *primus*)

première, *n.* first night of play. *p. danseuse,* leading dancer. (F.)

premillennial, *a.* before the millennium. **premillennialism,** *n.* belief that Christ's second coming will precede the millennium. **premillenarian, premillennialist,** *nn.*

premise, *n.* (*logic*) proposition from which an inference is drawn; (*pl.*) a building and its grounds; (*Shake.*) conditions.—*v.t.* state beforehand; presuppose. **the pp.,** (*law*) the aforesaid (property). (L. *mittere*, send)

premiss, alternative form of **premise** (*logic*).

premium, *n.* reward; bounty, bonus; periodical payment for insurance; fee for apprenticeship. **at a p.,** above par or nominal value; in great demand. **put a p. on,** act as incentive to. (L. *praemium*)

premonition, *n.* presentiment, foreboding; previous warning. **premonitor,** *n.* **premonitory,** *a.*

premorse, *a.* (*bot.*) as if bitten off short. (L. *mordēre*, bite)

prenatal, *a.* previous to birth.
prenominate, *v.t.* (*Shake.*) name beforehand.
prentice, *arch.* **for apprentice. p. hand,** unskilled hand.
preoccupy, *v.t.* take possession of beforehand; engross, fill thoughts of. **preoccupied,** *a.* absent-minded, lost in thought. **preoccupation,** *n.* prior occupation; business that takes precedence; mental absorption; prejudice.
preocular, *a.* in front of the eye.
preordain, *v.t.* appoint beforehand, foreordain. **preordination,** *n.*
prep, *n.* (*school sl.*) preparation.
prepaid, see **prepay.**
prepare, *v.t.* and *i.* make or get ready; fit out, equip; cook, compound; instruct, learn. **preparation,** *n.* preparing; readiness; specially prepared food, medicine etc.; time for learning school lessons; (*mus.*) notes leading up to discord; (us. *pl.*) previous arrangements. **preparative,** *a.* preparatory.—*n.* thing that paves the way. **preparatory,** *a.* serving to prepare; introductory (to).—*adv.* by way of preliminary. **preparatory (school),** where pupils are prepared for advanced one. (L. *parare,* make ready)
prepay, *v.t.* (*past, p.p.* **prepaid**) pay in advance. **prepayment,** *n.*
prepense, *a.* deliberate (us. in phrase **malice p.**).—*v.t.* (*Spens.*) consider beforehand. (L. *pendere,* weigh)
preponderate, *v.i.* exceed in number, amount, influence etc.; predominate; be heavier. **preponderance,** *n.* **preponderant,** *a.* (L. *pondus,* weight)
preposition, *n.* word placed before noun or pronoun to express relations of time, place etc. **prepositional,** *a.* **prepositive,** *a.* and *n.* (particle, word) which can be prefixed to word.
prepossess, *v.t.* imbue, take possession of; impress favourably; prejudice. **prepossession,** *n.* preoccupation; inclination, prejudice.
preposterous, *a.* contrary to nature or reason; utterly absurd or foolish. (L. *prae,* before; *post,* after)
prepotent, *a.* very or more powerful; (of parent) having dominant hereditary influence. **prepotence, prepotency,** *nn.*
pre-preference, *a.* ranking before preference shares.
prepuce, *n.* loose skin ensheathing end of penis, foreskin. **preputial,** *a.* (L. *praeputium*)
Pre-Raphaelite, *a.* and *n.* (member) of school of artists imitating early Italian style before Raphael's time, using brilliant colour and minute detail. **Pre-Raphaelitism,** *n.*
prerequisite, *a.* needed beforehand.—*n.* necessary preliminary.
prerogative, *n.* right or power peculiar to person or office; (also **royal p.**) right of sovereign to act at his own discretion.—*a.* privileged, held by privilege. (L. *rogare,* ask)
presage, *n.* omen; foreboding.—*v.t.* portend, foretell; have presentiment of. (L. *sagire,* discern acutely)
presbyopia, *n.* indistinct vision of near objects in old age. (Gk. *presbus,* old man; *ōps,* eye)
presbyter, *n.* elder of Presbyterian or early Christian Church; priest of Episcopal Church; member of presbytery. **presbyteral, presbyterial,** *aa.* **presbyterate, presbytership,** *nn.* (Gk. *presbuteros,* elder)
Presbyterian, *a.* and *n.* (member) of Presbyterian church. **P. church,** one governed by elders, all of equal rank. **United P. Church,** formed in Scotland by union of Secession and Relief Churches in 1847, and merged with Free Church in 1900. **Presbyterianism,** *n.* **Presbyterianize,** *v.t.*
presbytery, *n.* Presbyterian church court composed of ministers and one elder from each church of district; eastern part of chancel; house of Roman Catholic priest.
prescient, *a.* knowing things beforehand. **prescience,** *n.* foreknowledge. (L. *scire,* know)
pre-scientific, *a.* before knowledge was systematized.
prescind, *v.t.* and *i.* cut off, abstract; withdraw attention (from). **prescission,** *n.* (L. *scindere,* cleave)
prescribe, *v.t.* and *i.* ordain, lay down (rules); suggest remedy (for); (*med.*) order, advise (medicine, treatment). **prescript,** *n.* ordinance, decree. **prescription,** *n.* prescribing; thing prescribed; recipe for medicine; (*law*) establishment of right or title through long use of it. **prescriptive,** *a.* prescribing; based on long use, traditional. (L. *scribere,* write)
presence, *n.* being present; place where person is; nearness; bearing, stately mien; ghostly influence; (*Shake.*) assembly; presence-chamber. **p. of mind,** readiness of resource. **p.-chamber,** *n.* ruler's audience-room.
present, *a.* at hand, here; existing or happening now; (*arch.*) ready, unfailing; (*gram.*) denoting present action.—*n.* present time or tense. **at p.,** now. **by these pp.,** (*law*) by this document. (L. *praesens*)
present, *v.t.* and *i.* introduce formally, esp. at court; nominate for appointment to benefice; submit, set forth; exhibit, display; offer, give; point (weapon).—*n.* gift. **p. arms,** hold rifle upright as salute. **p. oneself,** come forward, appear. **p. one with,** give one. **presentable,** *a.* fit to go into company; of decent appearance. **presentation,** *n.* presenting; formal introduction or bestowal; right, act, of presenting to benefice; (*med.*) position of child at parturition.

presentation copy (of book), free copy. **presentative,** *a.* (of benefice) admitting presentation by patron. **presentee,** *n.* person presented to benefice etc.; recipient of present. (L. *praesentare*)

presentient, *a.* having a presentiment. **presentiment,** *n.* foreboding, apprehension (esp. of evil).

presentive, *a.* bringing an idea directly to the mind (opp. to symbolic).

presently, *adv.* soon, shortly; (*arch.*) at once.

presentment, *n.* presentation; portrait, delineation; laying of formal statement before court or authority.

preserve, *v.t.* keep safe, protect; maintain, retain; save up; keep from decay, pickle; keep (game) for private use.—*n.* bottled fruit; jam; place where game is preserved; (*pl.*) goggles to protect from dust etc. **preservation,** *n.* preserving; state of repair. **preservative,** *a.* and *n.* (substance) preserving from decay. **preservatize,** *v.t.* treat with this. **preserver,** *n.* rescuer. (L. *servare*, keep)

preses, *n.* (*Scot.*) chairman.

preside, *v.i.* take the chair, be president; take control, be supreme. **president,** *n.* (*fem.* **presidentess**) head of assembly, corporation, college etc.; chairman; elective head of republic. **presidential,** *a.* **presidency,** *n.* office, term, of president; one of the three greater divisions of India (Bengal, Bombay, Madras). (L. *sedēre*, sit)

presidial, *a.* of guard or garrison. **presidium,** *n.* presiding body in various communist organizations. *presidio*, *n.* Spanish fort or military station. (L. *praesidium*, garrison)

press, *v.t.* carry off forcibly to serve in navy or army; requisition.—*n.* compulsory enlistment. **p.-gang,** *n.* detachment for pressing men. (L. *praestare*, furnish)

press, *v.t.* and *i.* push, bear upon; squeeze (out), flatten; hug; crowd, throng; oppress; urge, entreat; hasten; (*golf*) overswing.—*n.* pressing-machine; crowd, crush; stress; cupboard; printing, machine or establishment for this; newspapers collectively. **go to p.,** start printing (newspaper). **have good, bad, p.,** get favourable, unfavourable, comment in newspapers. **in the p.,** being printed. **p. of sail** as much as can be carried. **p.-agent,** *n.* publicity manager. **p.-box,** *n.* reporters' stand. **p.-cutting,** *n.* clipping from newspaper. **p.-mark,** *n.* number showing book's place in library. **be pressed for,** have barely enough. (L. *premere*)

pressing, *a.* urgent; importunate.

pressman, *n.* journalist; operator of printing-press.

pressure, *n.* pressing, thrust; urgency; constraint; (*mech.*) force per unit area.

prest, *a.* (*Shake.*) ready. (L. *praesto*)

prestidigitation, *n.* sleight of hand. **prestidigitator,** *n.* conjurer; juggler. (L. *praesto*, ready; *digitus*, finger)

prestige, *n.* reputation, influence, due to past achievements. (F.)

presto, *a.*, *adv.*, and *n.* (*mus.*) quick (passage). **hey p.!** conjurer's formula. *prestissimo*, *a.*, *adv.*, and *n.* (*mus.*) very quick (passage). (It.)

presume, *v.t.* and *i.* take for granted, suppose, infer; venture without leave; take liberties. **p. upon,** take advantage of. **presumable,** *a.* **presumably,** *adv.* as may be presumed. **presumption,** *n.* presuming; thing presumed; strong probability; effrontery, assurance. **presumptive,** *a.* assumed in absence of contrary evidence; probable. **presumptuous,** *a.* impudent, presuming; over-confident. (L. *sumere*, take)

presuppose, *v.t.* assume beforehand. **presupposition,** *n.*

pretend, *v.t.* and *i.* profess falsely; simulate, feign, make believe; lay claim (to); (*Spens.*) attempt; stretch out; offer. **pretence,** *n.* pretending; hypocritical show; fraud, sham; claim. **pretender,** *n.* claimant to title. **Old, Young, Pretender,** son, grandson, of James II. **pretension,** *n.* claim; justification for claim; assumption of superiority. **pretentious,** *a.* claiming great importance, ostentatious. (L. *praetendere*)

preter-, *pref.* beyond, more than, as in **preternatural.** (L. *praeter*)

preterhuman, *a.* more than human.

preterite, preterit, *a.* (*gram.*) denoting past action; (*joc.*) bygone.—*n.* past tense. **preterition,** *n.* omission; doctrine of passing over of non-elect by God. (L. *praeter*, past; *ire*, go)

pretermit, *v.t.* leave out; neglect; leave off for a time, interrupt. **pretermission,** *n.* (L. *praeter*, past; *mittere*, send)

preternatural, *a.* out of the regular course of things, abnormal.

pretersensual, *a.* not apprehensible by the senses.

pretext, *n.* excuse, pretended motive. —*v.t.* allege as pretext. (L. *texere*, weave)

pretone, *n.* syllable, vowel, before stressed syllable. **pretonic,** *a.* (*pre-*; *tone*)

pretor, same as **praetor.**

pretty, *a.* having beauty that is attractive rather than imposing; fine, good, stylish; considerable; (*arch.*) stout, brave.—*adv.* (*colloq.*) somewhat, fairly; rather.—*n.* fluted part of tumbler; (*golf*) fairway. **p. much,** nearly. **p.-p.,** *a.* insipidly attractive, namby-pamby.—*n.* knick-knack. **prettify,** *v.t.* (O.E. *prættig*, tricky)

pretzel, *n.* crisp biscuit, cracknel. (G.)

preux chevalier, gallant knight. (F.)

prevail, *v.i.* gain mastery, triumph; be general, predominate; be current, exist. **p. upon,** persuade, induce. **prevalent,** *a.* widely practised or experienced, in vogue, rife. **prevalence,** *n.* (L. *valēre,* have power)

prevaricate, *v.i.* make evasive or misleading statement, quibble. **prevarication, prevaricator,** *nn.* (L. *varus,* crooked)

prevenient, *a.* preceding, anticipatory; aiming at prevention. (*prevent*)

prevent, *v.t.* stop, hinder, make impossible; (*arch.*) go before, guide (*Shake.*) forestall, anticipate. **preventable, preventible,** *a.* **prevention,** *n.* **preventive, preventative,** *aa.* serving to prevent, precautionary. —*nn.* precaution; preventive drug, prophylactic. **preventive service,** coastguards. (L. *venire,* come)

previous, *a.* coming before in time or order, prior; (*colloq.*) too hasty, precipitate. **move the p. question,** move that the question be not now put (formula for shelving debate). (L. *via,* way)

previse, *v.t.* foresee, forecast; warn. **prevision,** *n.* **previsional,** *a.* (L. *vidēre,* see)

pre-war, *a.* before the Great War of 1914–18, or that of 1939–45

prex, prexy, *nn.* (*Amer. sl.*) president of college. (corrupt.)

prey, *n.* animal hunted for food by another; victim; (*arch.*) booty.—*v.i.* (**p. on, upon**) seize habitually for food; plunder; afflict, wear out. (L. *praeda*)

priapism, *n.* lustfulness. (Gk. *Priapos,* god of procreation)

price, *n.* amount paid for anything, cost; betting odds; (*arch.*) value, worth. — *v.t.* set price on, value. **beyond, without, p.,** invaluable. **what p.?** (*sl.*) what chance of? **priceless,** *a.* invaluable; (*sl.*) exquisitely funny or delightful. (L. *pretium*)

prick, *n.* sharp-pointed object, goad; pricking, puncture; dot, tick; qualm (of conscience); (*vulg.*) penis.—*v.t.* and *i.* make small hole in, pierce slightly; cause sharp pain to; spur, goad; tick (off) in list, mark (out); rise (up) in point; (*arch.*) ride fast; (*Shake.*) dress up. **p. off, out,** plant (seedlings). **p. up the ears,** listen intently. **p.-eared,** *a.* with ears sticking up (esp. of close-cropped Roundheads). **p.-song,** *n.* (*Shake.*) written music. (O.E. *prica*)

pricker, *n.* bradawl. **yeomen pp.,** huntsmen of royal hunt.

pricket, *n.* buck in its second year.

prickle, *n.* thorn, spine, bristle.—*v.i.* and *t.* feel, cause to feel, prickly. (O.E. *pricel*)

prickle, *n.* kinds of wicker basket.

prickly, *a.* full of prickles; tingling as if pricked. **p. heat,** skin disease of tropics, with great itching and prickling. **p. pear,** kind of cactus; its fruit.

pride, *n.* too high an opinion of oneself; arrogance, disdain; lofty self-respect; elation due to success, source of this; highest pitch, prime; herd (of lions); (*Shake.*) pomp, show; mettle; sexual desire.—*v.refl.* (**p. oneself on, upon**) be proud of; take credit for. **prideful,** *a.* (O.E. *prút,* proud)

prie-dieu, *n.* kneeling-desk. (F., lit. pray God)

prief, (*Spens.*) form of **proof.**

priest, *n.* clergyman, esp. second order in English or Roman Catholic Church, between deacon and bishop; (*fem.* **priestess**) one who performs sacred rites of heathen; mallet for killing fish.—*v.t.* ordain as priest. **p.-ridden,** *a.* dominated by priests. **priestcraft,** *n.* priestly policy; schemes of priesthood to get power. **priesthood,** *n.* rank of priest; priests collectively. **priestlike,** *a.* **priestly,** *a.* of, befitting, a priest. (L. *presbyter,* elder)

prig, *n.* (*sl.*) thief.—*v.t.* steal, pinch; (*Scot.*) plead; haggle.

prig, *n.* one who ostentatiously cultivates virtue or propriety; conceited precisian. **priggery, priggism,** *nn.* **priggish,** *a.* tiresomely precise; strait-laced, goody-goody.

prill, *n.* better part of ore.

prim, *a.* formally neat, stiffly decorous; prudish.—*v.t.* make prim.

primacy, *n.* office of primate; state of being first, pre-eminence.

prima donna, (*pl.* **prima donnas,** *primē dónnē*) chief woman singer in opera. (It.)

primaeval, see **primeval.**

prima facie, on the face of it; seeming true at first sight. (L.)

primage, *n.* charge in addition to freight for loading and unloading. (L.L. *primagium*)

primage, *n.* amount of water carried off from boiler in steam. (*prime*)

primal, *a.* of the earliest age, primitive; chief, fundamental. (*prime*)

primary, *a.* chief, principal; first in order of time; not derived, original. — *n.* primary colour or planet. (*Amer.*) party meeting to choose candidates for election, delegates to convention etc. **p. battery,** in which current is produced. **p. colours,** red, yellow, blue, or red, green, violet. **p. planets,** those revolving round sun as opp. to satellites. **p. school,** one teaching rudiments. **p. tenses,** present, future, and perfect. **primarily,** *adv.* in the first place; originally. (*prime*)

primate, *n.* archbishop. **primatial,** *a.* (*prime*)

primātēs, *n.pl.* highest order of mammals, incl. man and monkey. (*prime*)

prime, *a.* first in time, rank, or quality; (of number) divisible only by itself and 1, e.g. 7, 13.—*n.* first or best part of thing; state of highest perfection, full maturity; religious service at sunrise; first guard in fencing; (*arch.*) dawn; (*Shake.*) spring. **p. cost,** initial cost apart from overhead charges or profit. **P. Minister,** head of British government. **p. mover,** first promoter; (*mech.*) primary source of power, e.g. water. (L. *primus*, first)

prime, *v.t.* and *i.* fill up (with information or liquor); wet (pump) to start it working; coat (wood) with size before painting; (of engine) carry water into cylinder with the steam; (formerly) put powder in touch-hole of (gun).

primer, *n.* elementary school-book; introductory text-book, manual. **great p.,** 18-point type, between double pica and English. **long p.,** 10-point type, between small pica and bourgeois.

primero, *n.* old gambling card-game. (Sp. *primera*)

primeur, *n.* early vegetables, fruit etc.; advance news. (F.)

primeval, primaeval, *aa.* of the earliest age of the world; primitive. (L. *primus*, first; *aevum*, age)

priming, *n.* powder exploding charge; preliminary coating. (*prime*)

priming, *n.* acceleration of time of high water between neap and spring tides. (L. *primus*, first)

primipara, *n.* woman bearing or having borne first child. **primiparous,** *a.* (L. *primus*, first; *parere*, bear)

primitive, *a.* of early times, ancient; old-fashioned, simple, rude; radical, not derived or compounded. — *n.* painter, picture, of period before Renaissance; word, colour, not derived. **P. Methodists,** Wesleyan sect united with Methodists in 1932. (*prime*)

primo, *n.* (*mus.*) first or principal part. (It.)

primo, *adv.* (*abbr.* 1°) in the first place. (L.)

primogeniture, *n.* fact of being first-born; (also **right of p.**) principle of inheritance by eldest child. **primogenital, primogenitary,** *aa.* **primogenitor,** *n.* earliest ancestor; forefather (L. *primus*, first; *gignere*, beget)

primordial, *a.* existing from beginning, original, primary; (*bot.*) first formed. **primordiality,** *n.* (L. *primus*, first; *ordiri*, begin)

primp, *v.t.* and *i.* (*Scot.*) prink.

primrose, *n.* pale-yellow spring flower. —*a.* pale-yellow; flowery, gay. **P. Day,** 19 April, anniversary of Lord Beaconsfield's death. **P. League,** a Conservative association. (*prime*)

primsie, *a.* (*Scot.*) prim, demure.

primula, *n.* kinds of plant incl. primrose, cowslip etc. **primulaceous,** *a.* of this family. (L.L.=primrose)

primum móbilè, outermost sphere of Ptolemaic astronomy, carrying others with it. (L.=first movable thing)

primus, *a.* first; eldest.—*n.* presiding bishop of Scottish Episcopal Church. *p. inter pares,* first among equals. (L.)

primus, *n.* kind of stove burning vaporized oil. (trade name)

primy, *a.* (*Shake.*) blooming. (*prime*)

prince, *n.* son of king or emperor; ruler, sovereign; great foreign noble; chief, greatest (of). **p. consort,** husband of reigning queen. **p. of darkness,** Satan. **P. of Peace,** Christ. **P. of Wales,** heir apparent to British throne. **P. of Wales's feathers,** triple ostrich plumes. **p.'s feather,** plant with tall red spikes. **princedom,** *n.* **princelet, princeling,** *nn.* young prince; petty ruler. **princely,** *a.* of, like, a prince; august; magnificent, lavish. (L. *princeps*)

princeps, *a.* first, principal. *editio p.,* first edition. *fácilè p.,* easily first. (L.)

princess, *n.* female prince, woman ruler; wife of prince. **p. royal,** sovereign's eldest daughter. **p. dress,** with bodice and skirt in one piece.

principal, *a.* chief, leading, main.—*n.* head of college, school, business etc.; person for whom another acts as agent or surety; chief actor; capital sum lent or invested; main beam or rafter; an organ-stop. (L. *princeps*, prince)

principality, *n.* rank, territory, of prince; (*pl.*) fifth rank of angels.

principate, *n.* rule of early Roman emperors retaining republican forms.

principia, *n.pl.* first principles. (L. =beginnings)

principle, *n.* general truth or law; rule of action or conduct, tenet; ultimate source, primary element; chemical constituent. **on p.,** from settled conviction. (L. *principium*, beginning)

princox, *n.* (*Shake.*) pert saucy boy.

prink, *v.t.* and *i.* smarten, dress showily; preen. (*prank*)

print, *n.* impression, stamp; printed reading-matter or letters; reproduction, engraving, photograph; cotton fabric stamped in colours.—*v.t.* impress, mark, stamp; produce by means of inked types; publish; write like print; (*phot.*) make print from (negative). **in p.,** in printed form; stated in book; still on sale by publisher; (*Shake.*) with exactness. **out of p.,** no longer on sale by publisher. **p.-seller,** *n.* dealer in engravings. **p.-works,** *n.pl.* cloth-printing factory. **printable,** *a.* able or fit to be printed. (L. *premere*, press)

printer, *n.* one engaged in printing. **p.'s devil,** compositors' errand-boy. **p.'s pie,** jumbled type.
printery, *n.* cloth-printing works.
prior, *a.* earlier, previous; more important.—*n.* (fem. **prioress**) superior of priory; officer next below abbot. **p. to,** before. **priorate, priorship,** *nn.* office of prior. **priority,** *n.* being earlier; precedence. **priory,** *n.* monastery under prior; nunnery under prioress. (L.)
prise, see **prize.**
prism, *n.* (*geom.*) solid whose ends are similar, equal, and parallel plane figures, and whose sides are parallelograms; (*optics*) transparent body of this form, us. with triangular ends; spectrum produced by this. **prismatic,** *a.* of, like, a prism; (of colours) formed by prism, brilliant, rainbow-like. **prismatically,** *adv.* **prismoid,** *n.* prism-like body with unequal ends. **prismoidal,** *a.* (Gk. *prisma*)
prison, *n.* building for confinement of criminals, jail; place of captivity; custody.—*v.t.* imprison. **prisoner,** *n.* person in prison or under arrest; captive. **prisoner at the bar,** person under trial. **prisoners' base,** boys' chasing game. (L. *prehendere,* seize)
pristine, *a.* primitive, ancient, good old. (L. *pristinus*)
prithee, *int.* (*arch.*) pray, please. (=I pray thee)
privacy, *n.* being private; seclusion. secrecy.
private, *a.* of an individual, personal, not public; secluded, retired; secret, confidential; not holding public office.—*n.* common soldier; (*Shake.*) private message, privacy; (*pl.*) genitals. **in p.,** confidentially; alone; in private life. **p. bill,** affecting only individual or corporation. **p. house,** dwelling-house. **p. parts,** genitals. **p. school,** owned and managed by individual. **p. view,** to which only those invited are admitted. (L. *privatus*)
privateer, *n.* privately owned ship commissioned by government to seize and plunder enemy vessels; captain of this. **privateering,** *a.* and *n.*
privation, *n.* being deprived; want of comforts or necessaries; hardship. **privative,** *a.* depriving; consisting in, denoting, the absence of something; negative.—*n.* privative affix. (L. *privare,* deprive)
privet, *n.* white-flowered evergreen shrub used for hedges.
privilege, *n.* right, immunity, confined to person or class; advantage, favour, enjoyed by few.—*v.t.* invest with privilege; exempt. **breach of p.,** infringement of rights of parliament. **privileged communication,** (*law*) disclosure of which cannot be compelled in evidence. (L. *privus,* single; *lex,* law)
privy, *a.* (*arch.*) private, confidential; hidden, secret.—*n.* (*arch.*) latrine, water-closet; (*law*) person having interest in an action. **p. to,** having private knowledge of. **P. Council,** body appointed by Crown, advising on occasions of state emergency. **p. councillor,** (*abbr.* **P.C.**) member of this. **p. purse,** allowance from revenue for sovereign's personal expenses. **p. seal,** state seal affixed to documents of minor importance etc. **privity,** *n.* private knowledge; connivance. (F. *privé,* private)
prize, *n.* reward given for merit; award in competition or lottery; thing worth striving for; (*Shake.*) contest.—*a.* given as, rewarded by, prize; (*colloq.*) champion.—*v.t.* value highly. **p.-fight,** *n.* professional boxing match. **p.-fighter,** *n.* **p.-ring,** *n.* enclosure for, practice of, prize-fighting. (L. *pretium,* price)
prize, *n.* ship captured in war; windfall. **make p. of,** capture as prize. **p.-court,** *n.* admiralty court dealing with prizes. **p.-money,** *n.* money awarded for capture or destruction of an enemy vessel. (L. *prehendere,* seize)
prize, *v.t.* force (open, up) with lever.—*n.* leverage, purchase. (L. *prehendere,* seize)
prizeman, *n.* winner of prize.
prizer, *n.* (*Shake.*) one who fights in a match.
pro, *n.* (*sl.,* *pl.* **pros**) professional.
pro, *prep.* for. **p. and con,** (argument) for and against. *p. bono publico,* for the public good. *p. forma,* for form's sake. *p. patria,* for one's country. *p. rata,* in proportion. *p. re nata,* as occasion may arise. *p. tanto,* to that extent. *p. tempore,* (*abbr.* **pro tem.**) for the time being. (L.)
pro-, *pref.* for, acting-, vice-, as in **pronoun, pro-proctor**; favouring (opp. to anti-) as in **pro-Boer** (in both these senses used freely with many nouns); before, as in **propose**; forth, as in **proceed**; according to, as in **proportion.** (L. or Gk.)
proa, *n.* Malay sailing canoe with outrigger. (Malay *prau*)
probable, *a.* likely, to be expected. **probability,** *n.* likelihood; (*math.*) ratio of chances in favour of event to total number. **probabilism,** *n.* (*philos.*) theory recognizing no certain knowledge but only probability. **probabilist,** *n.* (L. *probare,* prove)
probang, *n.* flexible rod with sponge for clearing obstructions from gullet.
probate, *n.* official admission of will's validity; certified copy of will.—*v.t.* (*Amer.*) prove (will). (L. *probare,* prove)
probation, *n.* trial, test, of character or skill; period of this, novitiate; (*Shake.*) proof. **p. officer,** supervising first offenders etc. released on sus-

pended sentence under **p. system. probational, probationary,** *aa.* **probationer,** *n.* one undergoing probation; junior hospital nurse; (*Scot.*) one licensed to preach but not ordained. **probative,** *a.* serving as proof. (L. *probare*, prove)

probe, *n.* blunt-ended surgical instrument for exploring wound.—*v.t.* explore with probe; examine closely, search. (L. *probare*, prove)

probity, *n.* honesty, integrity, uprightness. (L. *probus*, good)

problem, *n.* question for solution; difficult matter, puzzle; (*math.*) proposition requiring something to be done. **p. play,** treating of social problem. **problematic, problematical,** *aa.* presenting a problem; questionable; uncertain. **problematist, problemist,** *nn.* student or composer of problems. (Gk. *problēma*)

pro-Boer, pro-Bolshevik, *nn.* one on the side of the Boers, Bolsheviks.

proboscis, *n.* elephant's trunk; long snout; insect's sucking-organ; (*joc.*) nose. **proboscidean, proboscidian,** *aa.* and *nn.* (animal) with proboscis, elephant. (Gk. *pro*, before; *boskein*, feed)

procacious, *a.* petulant, insolent. **procacity,** *n.* (L. *procax*)

proceed, *v.i.* pass, progress; go on, continue; be carried on; issue; take action; go to law.—*n.pl.* amount realized by sale etc. **proceeding,** *n.* piece of conduct; (*pl.*) action, steps, in lawsuit; published records of society etc. **procedure,** *n.* proceeding; mode of conducting business, practice. (L. *cedere*, go)

proceleusmatic, *a.* animating.—*n.* foot with four short syllables. (Gk. *pro*, before; *keleuein*, order)

procellarian, *a.* and *n.* (bird) of stormy petrel family. (L. *procella*, storm)

procerity, *n.* tallness. (L. *procērus*, tall)

process, *n.* course, state of going on; series of operations; mode of manufacture; making of printing-blocks by photography; (*law*) proceedings in action; summons, writ; (*bot., zool.*) projecting part, outgrowth; (*Shake.*) narrative; formal command. *v.t.* subject to, reproduce by, process. **p.-block,** *n.* printing-block made by photo-mechanical process. **p.-server,** *n.* sheriff's officer. (*proceed*)

process, *v.i.* (*colloq.*) walk in procession.

procession, *n.* train of persons etc. in formal march; ceremonious progress; one-sided race; emanation of the Holy Ghost.—*v.i.* and *t.* go along in procession. **processional,** *a.* of, used, sung, in processions.—*n.* processional hymn or hymn-book. **processionary,** *a.* **processionist,** *n.* one who goes in procession. (*proceed*)

procès-verbal, *n.* (*pl.* *procès-verbaux*) official report, minutes; summary of charges and evidence. (F.)

prochronism, *n.* assigning of event to date before real one. (Gk. *pro*, before; *chronos*, time)

proclaim, *v.t.* announce publicly and officially; tell openly; declare, show (to be); place under ban, prohibit. **proclamation,** *n.* proclaiming; official notice to public. **proclamatory,** *a.* (L. *clamare*, cry out)

proclitic, *a.* and *n.* (word) so closely connected with following word as to lose its accent. (Gk. *proklinein*, lean forward)

proclivity, *n.* tendency, inclination, esp. bad one. (L. *clivus*, slope)

proconsul, *n.* governor of colony or province. **proconsular,** *a.* **proconsulate, proconsulship,** *nn.* (L.)

procrastinate, *v.i.* and *t.* defer action, be dilatory; put off. **procrastination, procrastinator,** *nn.* **procrastinative, procrastinatory,** *aa.* (L. *cras*, tomorrow)

procreate, *v.t.* beget, generate. **procreant, procreative,** *aa.* **procreation,** *n.*

Procrustean, *a.* compelling uniformity by violent means. (*Prokroustēs* in Gk. legend)

proctor, *n.* university officer in charge of discipline; attorney in ecclesiastical courts. **King's P.,** Crown's representative in divorce suits, who intervenes in cases of collusion. **proctorial,** *a.* **proctorize,** *v.t.* (of proctor) arrest, summon (undergraduate). **proctorship,** *n.* (*procurator*)

procumbent, *a.* lying face down, prone; (*bot.*) trailing. (L. *procumbere*, fall forward)

procurable, *a.* obtainable.

procuration, *n.* procurement; acting for another, authorization to do this. **procurator,** *n.* agent, proxy; ancient Roman provincial treasurer. **procurator-fiscal,** *n.* (*Scot.*) public prosecutor. **procuratorial,** *a.* **procuratorship,** *n.* **procuratory,** *n.* authorization to act for another. **procuratrix,** *n.* business manageress of nunnery.

procure, *v.t.* acquire, obtain; act as procurer; (*arch.*) effect, contrive. **procurement,** *n.* **procurer,** *n.* (*fem.* **procuress**) person who supplies prostitutes, pander. (L. *curare*, see to)

prod, *v.t.* and *n.* thrust with pointed instrument, poke, jog; goad.

prodelision, *n.* elision of initial vowel, as in 'I 'm.' (*pro-*)

prodigal, *a.* extravagant, improvident; lavish, open-handed.—*n.* spendthrift, wastrel. **prodigality,** *n.* **prodigalize,** *v.t.* spend lavishly. (L. *pro-*, forth; *agere*, drive)

prodigy, *n.* marvellous thing or event; wonderful person, precocious child. **prodigious,** *a.* immense, vast; marvellous. (L. *prodigium*, portent)

prodrome, *n.* preliminary treatise; (*med.*) warning symptom. **prodromal, prodromic,** *aa.* (Gk. *dromos,* run)

produce, *v.t.* bring forward, show; bring forth, yield; bring about, cause; manufacture, make; extend in length; put (play) before public.—*n.* yield; natural products. **producer,** *n.* one who produces, esp. articles of consumption (opp. to consumer); one who stages a play. **producible,** *a.* (L. *ducere,* lead)

product, *n.* thing produced by growth or manufacture; outcome; (*chem.*) substance produced by chemical change; (*math.*) result of multiplying quantities together. **production,** *n.* producing; products; literary or artistic work. **productive,** *a.* producing, tending to produce; fertile. **productivity,** *n.* (*produce*)

proem, *n.* prelude; preface. **proemial,** *a.* (Gk. *prooimion*)

profane, *a.* secular, not sacred; heathen, unhallowed; blasphemous, irreverent; uninitiated.—*v.t.* desecrate, pollute; violate. **profanity,** *n.* profane act; blasphemy, swearing. (L. *pro,* in front of; *fanum,* temple)

profess, *v.t.* and *i.* declare, avow; affirm belief in; lay claim to, pretend; practise as trade or profession; be professor of. **professed,** *a.* self-acknowledged, ostensible. (L. *fatēri,* admit)

profession, *n.* affirmation; avowal of faith, entry into religious order; vocation, learned or artistic occupation; followers of this. **the p.,** theatrical profession. **professional,** *a.* of, following, a profession; practising, playing, played, for money.—*n.* one who makes his living by what to others is a pastime. **professionalism,** *n.* methods of professionals; use of professionals in games. **professionalize,** *v.t.*

professor, *n.* one who professes; teacher of highest rank, holder of university chair. **professorate,** *n.* professorship; professoriate. **professorial,** *a.* **professoriate,** *n.* body of professors. **professorship,** *n.* office of professor.

proffer, *v.t.* and *n.* offer. (*pro-*)

proficient, *a.* thoroughly qualified or skilled.—*n.* expert. **proficiency,** *n.* (L. *proficere,* progress)

profile, *n.* outline, esp. of face, as seen from side; drawing of this, silhouette.—*v.t.* draw in profile. **profilist,** *n.* (L. *filum,* thread)

profit, *n.* benefit, advantage; gain in money, excess of returns over outlay.—*v.t.* and *i.* be of advantage (to), benefit; gain. **p.-sharing,** *n.* system by which employees share in profits. **profitable,** *a.* yielding profit, lucrative; useful. **profiteer,** *v.i.* make exorbitant profits, esp. in war-time.—*n.* one who profiteers. **profitless,** *a.* useless. (L. *proficere,* progress)

profligate, *a.* dissolute, vicious; recklessly extravagant.—*n.* profligate person, libertine. **profligacy,** *n.* (L. *profligare,* dash down)

profound, *a.* very deep; heartfelt, intense; abstruse, mysterious; very learned.—*n.* deep sea; abyss. **profundity,** *n.* profoundness; great depth. (L. *fundus,* bottom)

profuse, *a.* abundant, plentiful; liberal, lavish; extravagant, excessive. **profusion,** *n.* (L. *fundere,* pour)

prog, *n.* (*sl.*) food, grub.

prog, *n.* (*sl.*) university proctor.—*v.t.* proctorize. (abbr.)

progenitor, *n.* (*fem.* **progenitress, progenitrix**) forefather, ancestor; predecessor, original. **progenitorial,** *a.* **progenitive,** *a.* reproductive. **progeniture,** *n.* begetting; offspring. **progeny,** *n.* offspring; descendants; outcome. (L. *gignere,* beget)

proggins, *n.* (*sl.*) university proctor.

proglottis, *n.* (*pl.* **proglóttidēs**) section of tapeworm capable of breeding. (Gk. *pro,* before; *glōtta,* tongue)

prognathous, prognathic, *aa.* having projecting jaws; (of jaw) projecting. **prognathism,** *n.* (Gk. *gnathos,* jaw)

prognosis, *n.* (*pl.* **prognoses**) foretelling; (*med.*) forecast of course of disease. **prognostic,** *a.* predictive of).—*n.* prediction; omen; forewarning symptom. **prognosticate,** *v.t.* predict; presage. **prognostication, prognosticator,** *nn.* **prognosticative, prognosticatory,** *aa.* (Gk. *gignōskein,* learn)

programme, program, *n.* list of items in performance; plan of intended proceedings, schedule; electoral policy.—*v.t.* make definite plan of. **p. music,** music suggesting objects or events without words. (Gk. *graphein,* write)

progress, *n.* forward motion, advance; improvement, development; ceremonial tour.—*v.i.* move forward, advance; improve. (L. *gradi,* walk)

progression, *n.* progressing; locomotion. **arithmetical p.,** series of numbers increasing or decreasing by fixed quantity, e.g. 3, 6, 9, 12. **geometrical p.,** where the increase is by common ratio, e.g. 3, 6, 12, 24. **harmonic p.,** series of numbers whose reciprocals are in arithmetical progression, e.g. $\frac{1}{2}, \frac{1}{4}, \frac{1}{6}, \frac{1}{8}$. **progressional,** *a.* **progressionist,** *n.* believer in progress of mankind; (also **progressist**) progressive.

progressive, *a.* advancing, improving; proceeding by degrees; continuously increasing; aiming at reforms.—*n.* member of progressive party. **p. bridge, whist,** in which partners are changed after each game. **progressivism,** *n.*

prohibit, *v.t.* forbid; prevent, debar.

prohibiter, prohibitor, *nn.* **prohibition,** *n.* forbidding; order that forbids; veto on sale of intoxicants. **prohibitionary,** *a.* **prohibitionist,** *n.* supporter of alcoholic prohibition. **prohibitive,** *a.* forbidding; (of price) so high as to prevent purchase. **prohibitory,** *a.* (L. *habēre,* hold)

project, *v.t.* and *i.* throw forward; propel, hurl, cast; make plans for, contrive; produce outline of on distant surface, make projection of; stick out, protrude.—*n.* plan, scheme. **projectile,** *a.* impelling; for throwing. —*n.* missile; shell, ball. **projection,** *n.* projecting, casting; part jutting out; representation on plane surface of part of earth's surface; mental image externalized; (*psycho-anal.*) unconscious attribution to another of our own feelings and motives. **projective,** *a.* **projector,** *n.* framer of schemes; instrument for projecting rays of light. (L. *jacere,* throw)

prolapse, *n.* (*med.*) slipping down, displacement, of internal part.—*v.i.* have prolapse. (L. *prolapsus*)

prolate, *a.* extended; (of spheroid) elongated in direction of polar diameter (opp. to oblate); prolative. **prolative,** *a.* (*gram.*) completing a predicate. (L. *latus,* brought)

prolegomenon, *n.* (*pl.* **prolegomena**) introductory treatise, preface. **prolegomenary, prolegomenous,** *aa.* (Gk.)

prolepsis, *n.* anticipation; figure in which word is used before its sense is due, e.g. 'the fairest of her daughters, Eve.' **proleptic,** *a.* **proleptically,** *adv.* (Gk.)

proletarian, *a.* and *n.* (member) of the proletariat. **proletarianism, proletairism,** *nn.* condition of, government by, the proletariat. **proletariat, proletariate,** *n.* common people, working class. **proletary,** *a.* (L. *proles,* offspring, his only wealth)

prolicide, *n.* killing, killer, of own offspring. **prolicidal,** *a.* (L. *proles,* offspring; *caedere,* kill)

proliferate, *v.i.* and *t.* reproduce by process of budding or cell division. **proliferation,** *n.* **proliferative, proliferous,** *aa.* (L. *proles,* offspring; *ferre,* bear)

prolific, *a.* producing offspring; fertile, fruitful; abounding (in). **prolificacy, prolificity,** *nn.* (L. *proles,* offspring; *facere,* make)

proligerous, *a.* bearing offspring. (L. *proles,* offspring; *gerere,* bear)

prolix, *a.* verbose, long-winded, tedious. **prolixity,** *n.* **prolixious,** *a.* (*Shake.*) tedious. (L. *prolixus*)

prolocutor, *n.* chairman of lower house of convocation; spokesman. (L. *loqui,* speak)

prologue, *n.* poem recited as introduction to play; reciter of it; preface —*v.t.* provide with prologue; usher in. **prologize, prologuize,** *v.i.* and *t.* speak, write. prologue (to). (Gk. *logos,* speech)

prolong, *v.t.* extend, lengthen; spin out. **prolongation,** *n.*

prolusion, *n.* preliminary essay or article; trial performance. **prolusory,** *a.* (L. *ludere,* play)

prom, *n.* (*colloq.*) promenade concert.

promenade, *n.* walk for exercise, pleasure, or parade; place for this, esplanade; foyer.—*v.i.* and *t.* take promenade (along); lead about. **p. concert,** at which audience may walk about. (F.)

prominent, *a.* jutting, projecting; standing out, conspicuous; distinguished. **prominence,** *n.* being prominent; projection. (L. *prominēre,* jut out)

promiscuous, *a.* mixed without order, indiscriminate; haphazard, casual; not restricted to one. **promiscuity,** *n.* (L. *miscēre,* mix)

promise, *n.* undertaking to do or not do something; likelihood of success, good hopes.—*v.t.* and *i.* make promise (to); undertake to give; excite hope (of), point to. **promised land,** Canaan; better world, heaven. **promisee, promisor,** *nn.* (*law*) person to, by, whom promise is made. **promising,** *a.* likely to turn out well, hopeful. **promissory,** *a.* of the nature of, containing, a promise. **promissory note,** signed promise to pay, I O U. (L. *mittere,* send)

promontory, *n.* headland, high cape; (*anat.*) protuberance. (L. *promunturium*)

promote, *v.t.* help forward, further, encourage; give higher rank to, prefer; initiate making of. **promoter,** *n.* supporter, patron; inciter; organizer of business. **promotion,** *n.* promoting; preferment. **promotive,** *a.* (L. *movēre,* move)

prompt, *a.* ready and quick to act; done at once, immediate; (*Shake.*) inclined.—*v.t.* instigate, inspire; suggest, dictate; remind (actor) of forgotten words. **p. side,** (*abbr.* **P.S.**) right of stage as seen by audience. **p.-box,** *n.* where stage prompter sits. **prompter,** *n.* **promptitude,** *n.* promptness, alacrity. **prompture,** *n.* (*Shake.*) prompting. (L. *promptus*)

promulgate, (*arch.*) **promulge,** *vv.t.* publish, spread abroad; proclaim as coming into force. **promulgation, promulgator,** *nn.* (L. *promulgare*)

pronaos, *n.* porch, vestibule, of Greek temple. (Gk.)

pronate, *v.t.* turn (hand, arm) so that palm is downward. **pronation,** *n.* **pronator,** *n.* pronating muscle. (*prone*)

prone, *a.* face downwards; prostrate; sloping downwards, steep; inclined, disposed. (L. *pronus*)

prôneur, **n.** (*fem. prôneuse*) eulogist. (F.)
prong, *n.* spike of fork, trident, antler etc.; fork.—*v.t.* pierce with prong.
pronominal, *a.* of, of the nature of, a pronoun. (L. *nomen*, noun)
pronoun, *n.* word used to represent a noun.
pronounce, *v.t.* and *i.* utter, articulate; speak officially, pass (judgment); declare or affirm formally. **pronounceable**, *a.* **pronounced**, *a.* strongly marked, decided. **pronouncement**, *n.* pronouncing; declaration, formal announcement. (L. *nuntius*, messenger)
pronto, *adv.* (*Amer. sl.*) quickly. (Sp.)
pronunciamento, *n.* proclamation; manifesto of insurrectionists; rising. (Sp. *pronunciamiento*)
pronunciation, *n.* articulation; way word is pronounced.
proof, *n.* demonstration; convincing evidence, thing that proves; test, trial; sample from type for correction; trial impression from engraved plate; standard strength of alcoholic spirit; (*law*) copy of testimony; (*Scots law*) trial by judge alone; (*arch.*) resisting power.—*a.* resistant, impenetrable. — *v.t.* make proof against (water). **p.-reader**, *n.* man who corrects printer's proofs. (L. *probare*, prove)
prop, *n.* support, stay; upholder.—*v.t.* and *i.* furnish with, act as, prop; sustain.
propaedeutic, *a.* and *n.* preliminary (course of study). **propaedeutical**, *a.* (Gk. *paideuein*, teach)
propaganda, *n.* organized spreading of doctrine or opinions; means used for this; committee of cardinals in charge of foreign missions. **propagandist**, *n.* agent of propaganda. **propagandism**, *n.* **propagandize**, *v.i.* and *t.* employ propaganda (among); proselytize. (L. *propagandus*, to be propagated)
propagate, *v.t.* and *i.* multiply by reproduction, breed; spread abroad, disseminate; transmit. **propagation**, **propagator**, *nn.* **propagative**, *a.* (L. *propagare*)
proparoxytone, *a.* and *n.* (word) with acute accent on last syllable but two. (*pro-*)
propel, *v.t.* drive, press, forward; give motion to. **propellent**, *a.* and *n.* propelling (agent). **propeller**, *n.* that which propels; screw propelling ship or aircraft. (L. *pellere*, drive)
propensity, (*Shake.*) **propension**, *nn.* inclination, tendency. **propend**, *v.i.* (*Shake.*) incline. (L. *pendere*, hang)
proper, *a.* own, individual, peculiar; appropriate, fit; correct, conventional; decent, respectable; real, strictly so called (us. after noun); (*colloq.*) thorough; (*heraldry*) in its natural colours; (*arch.*) handsome, fine. **p. fraction**, less than 1. **p. name**, **noun**, name of person, place etc. (L. *propius*)
properispomenon, *a.* and *n.* (word) with circumflex on last syllable but one. (*pro-*)
properly, *adv.* in the right way; justifiably; (*colloq.*) thoroughly.
property, *n.* thing owned, possessions; estate; quality, attribute; (*pl.*) articles, dresses, used on stage.—*v.t.* (*Shake.*) make tool of; appropriate. (*proper*)
prophet, *n.* (*fem.* **prophetess**) one who foretells the future, seer; interpreter of God's will, great religious teacher. **prophecy**, *n.* power of prophesying; prediction. **prophesy**, *v.i.* and *t.* foretell future, predict; speak, teach, as prophet. **prophetic**, **prophetical**, *aa.* of prophet or prophecy; predictive. (Gk. *phanai*, speak)
prophylactic, *a.* and *n.* (medicine) tending to prevent disease. **prophylaxis**, *n.* preventive treatment. (Gk. *phulassein*, guard)
propinquity, *n.* nearness, proximity; close kinship. (L. *prope*, near)
propitiate, *v.t.* appease, conciliate; render favourable. **propitiation**, **propitiator**, *nn.* **propitiatory**, *a.* **propitious**, *a.* favourable, kind; auspicious. (L. *propitius*, propitious)
propolis, *n.* resin of tree-buds collected by bees, bee-glue. (Gk.)
proponent, *n.* one who makes proposal or proposition. (*propound*)
proportion, *n.* relation in size, quantity, or degree; ratio; symmetry, balance; comparative part, share; (*math.*) equality of ratios; (*Shake.*) form, shape; rhythm; (*pl.*) dimensions; (*Shake.*) forces for war.—*v.t.* make proportionate (to). **proportionable**, *a.* proportionate. **proportional**, *a.* of proportion; aiming at due proportion; proportionate. — *n.* (*math.*) any term of a proportion. **proportional representation**, (*abbr.* P.R.) electoral system arranged so that minorities are represented in proportion to their strength. **proportionality**, *n.* **proportionate**, *a.* in due proportion, corresponding in amount. **proportionment**, *n.* (*pro-*)
propose, *v.t.* and *i.* submit, offer, suggest; move as resolution; form plans, intend; make offer of (marriage); (*Shake.*) confront; discourse. —*n.* (*Shake.*) intention. **proposal**, *n.* proposing; scheme, plan, suggestion; marriage offer. (*pose*)
proposition, *n.* statement, assertion; offer of terms; (*colloq.*) affair, job, prospect; (*math.*) theorem, problem. **propositional**, *a.*
propound, *v.t.* put (question), submit (problem); (*law*) produce (will) for probate. (L. *ponere*, place)
propraetor, *n.* governor of ancient Roman non-military province. (L.)
proprietor, *n.* (*fem.* **proprietress**,

proprietrix) owner. **proprietorial,** *a.* **proprietorship,** *n.* **proprietary,** *a.* of owner; held in private ownership. —*n.* proprietorship; body of proprietors. (L. *proprius,* one's own)
propriety, *n.* fitness, suitability; correctness of conduct or taste; (*Shake.*) individuality. **the pp.,** social conventions. (*proper*)
pro-proctor, *n.* deputy university proctor.
props, *n.pl.* (*sl.*) stage properties.
proptosis, *n.* prolapse, esp. of eyeball. **proptosed,** *a.* (Gk.)
propugnation, *n.* (*Shake.*) defence. (L. *pugnare,* fight)
propulsion, *n.* propelling. **propulsive,** *a.* having power to propel. (*propel*)
propylaeum, *n.* (*pl.* **propylaea**) porch, gateway, of temple etc. **propylite,** *n.* kind of volcanic rock. **propylon,** *n.* (*pl.* **propylons, propyla**) propylaeum. (Gk. *pulē,* gate)
prorogue, *v.t.* and *i.* terminate session of (parliament) without dissolution; be prorogued; (*Shake.*) prolong, defer. **prorogation,** *n.* (L. *prorogare*)
prosaic, *a.* commonplace, matter-of-fact, unromantic. **prosaically,** *adv.* **prosaist,** *n.* prosaic writer; writer of prose. **prosaism,** *n.*
proscenium, *n.* (*pl.* **proscenia**) part of stage in front of curtain; ancient Greek or Roman stage. (L.)
proscribe, *v.t.* publish name of as outlawed or condemned; banish; ostracize; denounce (practice). **proscription,** *n.* **proscriptive,** *a.* (L. *scribere,* write)
prose, *n.* ordinary language without metre; humdrum experiences.—*a.* in prose.—*v.i.* and *t.* talk tediously; turn into prose. **p. poem,** prose work of poetic style. (L. *prosa* oratio, straightforward speech)
prosector, *n.* one who makes preliminary dissections for anatomical lectures. (L. *secare,* cut)
prosecute, *v.t.* and *i.* follow, carry on; take legal proceedings (against). **prosecution,** *n.* prosecuting; prosecuting party. **prosecutor,** *n.* (*fem.* **prosecutrix,** *pl.* **prosecutrices**) one who prosecutes, esp. in criminal court. **public prosecutor,** official taking criminal proceedings in public interest. (L. *sequi,* follow)
proselyte, *n.* and *v.t.* convert, esp. to Jewish faith. **proselytism,** *n.* **proselytize,** *v.t.* and *i.* convert, seek proselytes. (Gk. *pros,* to; *eltheïn,* come)
prosenchyma, *n.* (*bot.*) tissue of elongated cells with little protoplasm. **prosenchymatous,** *a.* (Gk. *pros,* to; *en,* in; *chein,* pour)
prosify, *v.t.* and *i.* turn into, write, prose. (L. *facere,* make)
prosit, int. good health! (L.=may it benefit you)
prosody, *n.* science of versification, principles of metre. **prosodiacal, prosodial, prosodic,** *aa.* **prosodist,** *n.* (Gk. *prosōidia*)
prosopopoeia, *n.* figure in which the absent, dead, or inanimate is represented as present and speaking; personification. (Gk. *prosōpon,* person; *poiein,* make)
prospect, *n.* wide outlook, vista; expectation, probable fate or fortune. —*v.i.* and *t.* look round, make search; go on exploring expedition, esp. for minerals; (of mine) promise. **prospective,** *a.* anticipated; applying to the future. **prospector,** *n.* one who prospects for gold etc. **prospectus,** *n.* circular describing joint-stock company, literary work, school etc. (L. *specere,* look)
prosper, *v.i.* and *t.* flourish, succeed; be favourable to. **prosperity,** *n.* success, welfare. **prosperous,** *a.* successful, fortunate; favourable. (L. *prosperus,* prosperous)
prostate, *n.* (also **p. gland**) gland accessory to male generative organs. **prostatic,** *a.* **prostatitis,** *n.* inflammation of prostate. (Gk. *histanai,* set)
prosthesis, *n.* (*gram.*) addition of letter or syllable at beginning of word; (*med.*) replacement of lost limb, tooth etc., with artificial one. **prosthetic,** *a.* (Gk.=addition)
prostitute, *n.* woman who hires herself for sexual purposes, harlot.—*v.t.* make prostitute of; put to base use. **prostitution, prostitutor,** *nn.* (L. *prostituere,* expose for sale)
prostrate, *a.* lying flat; completely crushed, submissive; overcome, spent.—*v.t.* cast down, lay flat; exhaust. **p. oneself,** bow to the ground; show servility. **prostration,** *n.* (L. *sternere,* strew)
prostyle, *n.* and *a.* (temple) with pillared portico. (Gk. *stulos,* pillar)
prosy, *a.* dull, dry, tedious. (*prose*)
protagonist, *n.* principal actor in play; leading character. (Gk. *prōtos,* first; *agōnistēs,* actor)
protasis, *n.* (*pl.* **protases**) introductory clause of conditional sentence; introductory part of drama. **protatic,** *a.* (Gk.=premiss)
protean, *a.* able to assume many shapes, variable; versatile. (*Proteus*)
protect, *v.t.* guard from injury, defend; put protective tariff on. **protection,** *n.* protecting; shelter, defence; patronage; safe-conduct; system of fostering home industries by taxing competing imports. **protectionism, protectionist,** *nn.* doctrine, advocate, of economic protection. **protective,** *a.* serving to protect. **protector,** *n.* (*fem.* **protectress**) person, thing, that protects; regent. **protectorial,** *a.* **protectorate,** *n.* regency; administration of weaker state by powerful one; state so controlled. **protectory,**

n. Roman Catholic institution for destitute children. (L. *tegere*, cover)
protégé, *n.* (*fem.* **protégée**) one under care and protection of another. (F.)
protein, proteid, *n.* one of complex organic compounds forming essential constituent of food. **proteinic, proteinous**, *aa.* **proteolysis**, *n.* disintegration of protein, esp. in digestion. **proteolytic**, *a.* **proteose**, *n.* substance formed by proteolysis. (Gk. *prōtos*, first)
proter(o)-, from Gk. *proteros*, former, used in **proterandrous**, *a.* having stamens mature before pistil; **proteranthous**, *a.* with flowers appearing before leaves; **proterogynous**, *a.* having pistil mature before stamens.
protervity, *n.* peevishness; waywardness. (L. *protervus*, pert)
protest, *v.t.* and *i.* affirm solemnly, declare; raise objection, remonstrate; formally declare (bill of exchange) unaccepted or unpaid.—*n.* expression of dissent, remonstrance; formal petition (against); protesting of bill. **protestant**, *a.* and *n.* (person) making protest; (member) of one of the Churches founded at the Reformation, Christian who is not a Roman Catholic. **Protestantism**, *n.* Protestant doctrine and principles. **Protestantize**, *v.t.* convert to Protestantism. **protestation**, *n.* solemn declaration; protest. (L. *testis*, witness)
Proteus, *n.* person or thing that takes many shapes; kinds of bacillus and amphibian. (Gk. sea-god)
prothalamium, prothalamion, *n.* (*pl.* **prothalamia**) marriage song. (Gk. *thalamos*, bridal chamber)
prothesis, *n.* setting out of eucharistic elements before consecration; place for this, credence-table; (*gram.*) prosthesis. (Gk.=placing before)
prothonotary, same as **protonotary**.
protist, *n.* single-celled organism, neither animal nor plant. **protistan**, *a.* (Gk. *prōtistos*, very first)
proto-, *pref.* first, original, primitive, as in **proto-Celtic, protomartyr**; (*chem.*) denoting minimum proportion of an element in compound, as in **protoxide**. (Gk. *prōtos*, first)
proto-Celtic, *a.* of the original Celts.
protocol, *n.* preliminary draft of treaty, us. signed by negotiators; formulas at beginning and end of charter etc. —*v.i.* and *t.* draw up, record in, protocol. **the P.**, etiquette department of French Foreign Office. (Late Gk. *prōtokollon*, fly-leaf glued on)
protogenic, protogenetic, *aa.* of earliest period of formation. **protogine**, *n.* kind of granite found in Alps. (Gk. *prōtos*, first; *genesis*, origin)
protohippus, *n.* extinct ancestor of horse. (Gk. *prōtos*, first; *hippos*, horse)
protomartyr, *n.* first martyr. (*proto-*)
proton, *n.* particle forming constituent of nucleus of atom, and identified with unit charge of positive electricity. (Gk. *prōtos*, first)
protonotary, *n.* chief clerk of some law courts. **pp. apostolic**, Roman Catholic officials who keep records of canonization etc. (*proto-*)
protophyte, *n.* microscopic unicellular plant. **protophytic**, *a.* (Gk. *prōtos*, first; *phuton*, plant)
protoplasm, *n.* a semifluid colourless jelly, the physical basis of living matter. **protoplasmatic, protoplasmic**, *aa.* **protoplast**, *n.* original model or ancestor; all protoplasm of a cell regarded as a unit. (Gk. *prōtos*, first; *plasma*, form)
Prototheria, *n.pl.* most primitive division of mammals. (Gk. *prōtos*, first; *thēr*, wild beast)
prototype, *n.* original model or type. **prototypal, prototypic, prototypical**, *aa.* (*proto-*)
protoxide, *n.* oxide containing minimum of oxygen. (*proto-*)
protozoon, *n.* (*pl.* **protozoa**) microscopic unicellular animal. **protozoal, protozoan**, *aa.* **protozoic**, *a.* protozoal; (of strata) containing remains of earliest forms of life. **protozoology**, *n.* science of protozoa. (Gk. *prōtos*, first; *zōon*, animal)
protract, *v.t.* draw out, prolong; put off, delay; draw to scale; (*zool.*) extend. **protraction**, *n.* **protractile**, *a.* (*zool.*) able to be extended. **protractive**, *a.* (*Shake.*) long-drawn-out. **protractor**, *n.* instrument for measuring angles; muscle that extends limb. (L. *trahere*, draw)
protrude, *v.t.* and *i.* thrust forth; stick out, project; obtrude. **protrudent, protrusive**, *aa.* **protrusion**, *n.* **protrusible, protrusile**, *aa.* able to be thrust forth. (L. *trudere*, thrust)
protuberant, *a.* bulging out, prominent. **protuberance**, *n.* swelling, prominence. (L. *tuber*, hump)
protyle, *n.* hypothetical primitive substance from which chemical elements may have been derived. (Gk. *prōtos*, first; *hulē*, substance)
proud, *a.* having too high an opinion of oneself; arrogant, haughty; having proper self-respect; elated, honoured; splendid, magnificent; (of stream) swollen; (*Shake.*) mettlesome; lustful. **do one p.**, (*sl.*) do him great honour. **p. flesh**, granulated growth of flesh round healing wound. (O.E. *prūt*)
provable, *a.* able to be proved.
provand, *n.* (*Shake.*) provender.
prove, *v.t.* and *i.* (*p.p.* **proved, proven**) try out, test by experiment; suffer, experience; demonstrate, show; verify (calculation); establish validity of (will); turn out (to be). **not proven**, (*Scots law*) verdict implying guilt but not enough evidence to prove it. (L. *probare*)

proveditor, provedore, *nn.* steward, purveyor. (It. *proveditore*)
provenance, *n.* place of origin, source. (L. *venire,* come)
provender, *n.* fodder for cattle; (*joc.*) provisions. (L. *praebēre,* afford)
provenience, *n.* provenance.
proverb, *n.* short traditional saying, adage; notorious thing, byword. **proverbial,** *a.* of proverb; generally admitted, notorious. **proverbiality,** *n.* (L. *verbum,* word)
proviant, *n.* food supply, commissariat. (G.)
provide, *v.t.* and *i.* furnish, supply; prepare. take measures; stipulate. **provided, providing,** *conjj.* on condition (that). **providence,** *n.* foresight, prudence; the provisions of nature, God's care; the power that controls the world. **provident,** *a.* far-seeing, thrifty. **providential,** *a.* arranged by providence; very opportune or lucky. (L. *vidēre,* see)
province, *n.* region, district; department, sphere; (*pl.*) parts of a country outside its capital. **provincial,** *a.* of province or provinces; countrified, local.—*n.* inhabitant of the provinces; chief of heads of religious houses in province; metropolitan. **provinciality,** *n.* **provincialism,** *n.* provincial speech, phrase, or point of view; narrowness. **provincialize,** *v.t.* (L. *provincia*)
provision, *n.* providing; amount provided; stipulation, condition; (formerly) appointment to benefice not yet vacant; (*pl.*) supplies of food, stores.—*v.t.* supply with stores. **provisional,** *a.* temporary, makeshift. **provisionality,** *n.* **provisionment,** *n.* provisioning. **proviso,** *n.* (*pl.* **provisoes**) condition, stipulation; limiting clause in document. **provisor,** *n.* vicar general; holder of ecclesiastical provision. **provisory,** *a.* conditional; making provision; temporary. (*provide*)
provoke, *v.t.* give rise to, cause; stir up, excite, urge; irritate, annoy. **provoking,** *a.* exasperating. **provocation,** *n.* provoking, being provoked; resentment or ground for it. **provocative,** *a.* provoking; intentionally irritating. (L. *vocare,* call)
provost, *n.* head of various colleges and religious communities; chief magistrate of burgh, Scottish mayor; (*Shake.*) keeper of prison. **p. marshal,** chief of military police. **provostship,** *n.* (L. *prae,* before; *ponere,* place)
prow, *n.* forepart of ship, bow; prow-like projection; (*poet.*) ship. (Gk. *prōira*)
prowess, *n.* bravery, gallantry; skill, success. **prow,** *a.* (*arch.*) brave, valiant. (O.F. *prou,* valiant)
prowl, *v.i.* and *t.* go furtively, roam stealthily, esp. in search of prey or booty.—*n.* prowling. **prowler,** *n.* (M.E. *prollen*)
proximate, *a.* nearest, next; approximate; (of cause) direct, immediate. **proximal,** *a.* (*anat.*) at the inner end, towards centre of body. *proxime accessit,* (*pl. proxime accesserunt*) (competitor who) came very near winner. **proximity,** *n.* nearness. **proximo,** *adv.* (*abbr.* **prox.**) of next month. (L. *proximus*)
proxy, *n.* authority to act for another; authorized deputy; agency, vote, of such.—*a.* done by proxy. (L. *procuratio,* management)
prude, *n.* woman who affects excessive modesty; easily shocked person. (F.)
prudent, *a.* careful, cautious; discreet, sensible. **prudential,** *a.* marked by, arising from prudence.—*n.pl.* prudential matters. (*provident*)
prudery, *n.* affected modesty, prudishness.
prud'homme, *n.* member of French local board of labour arbitrators. (F.)
prudish, *a.* like a prude, morbidly proper.
pruinose, *a.* covered with whitish dust or bloom, frosted. (L. *pruina,* rime)
prune, *n.* dried plum; deep purple; (*Amer. sl.*) spiritless person, simpleton. (Gk. *prounon,* plum)
prune, *v.t.* cut off (superfluous branches); trim (tree) thus; rid of needless parts. (O.F. *prooingier*)
prune, *v.t.* preen.
prunella, *n.* fever of throat, quinsy; kinds of plant incl. self-heal. (L.L. *brunus,* brown+dim.)
prunella, *n.* strong silk or worsted fabric.
prunello, *n.* kind of prune. (dim.)
prurient, *a.* itching with lewd desire; given to, springing from, unclean thoughts. **prurience, pruriency,** *nn.* (L. *prurire,* itch)
prurigo, *n.* skin disease with violent itching. **pruriginous,** *a.* **pruritus,** *n.* itching. (L. =itching)
Prussian, *a.* and *n.* (native) of Prussia. **P. blue,** a deep blue. **prussianize,** *v.t.* render Prussian; militarize. **prussiate,** *n.* a salt of prussic acid. **prussic acid,** hydrocyanic acid, a deadly poison.
pry, *v.i.* look with curiosity, peer; inquire impertinently. **prying,** *a.* inquisitive. (M.E. *prien*)
pry, *v.t.* raise with lever, prize.
prytaneum, *n.* ancient Greek town hall. (Gk. *prutaneion*)
psalm, *n.* sacred song, esp. one from Book of Psalms in Bible. **psalmist,** *n.* writer of psalms. **psalmody,** *n.* act or art of singing psalms; collection of psalms. **psalmodic,** *a.* **psalmodist,** *n.* singer of psalms. **psalter,** *n.* the Book of Psalms; version of this with tunes. **psaltery,** *n.* ancient instrument like zither. (Gk. *psallein,* play on harp)

psammite, *n.* sandstone. (Gk. *psammos*, sand)

psephite, *n.* conglomerate. (Gk. *psēphos*, pebble)

pseud(o)-, from Gk. *pseudēs*, false, used in **pseudo-archaic, pseudo-Christian, pseudo-classical** etc., *aa.* sham, pretending or wrongly held to be, archaic, Christian, classical etc.; **pseudaesthesia,** *n.* imaginary feeling; **pseudechis,** *n.* kinds of venomous snake; **pseudepigrapha,** *n.pl.* spurious Biblical writings not in Apocrypha; **pseudepigraphy,** *n.* false attribution of authorship; **pseudocarp,** *n.* fruit formed from parts other than ovary, hence **pseudocarpous,** *a.*; **pseudograph,** *n.* literary forgery; **pseudologer,** *n.* (*joc.*) systematic liar, hence **pseudological,** *a.* wildly untrue; **pseudomorph,** *n.* false shape, mineral with crystalline form of another mineral, hence **pseudomorphic, pseudomorphous,** *aa.*, **pseudomorphism, pseudomorphosis,** *nn.*; **pseudonym,** *n.* fictitious name. nom de plume; **pseudonymous,** *a.* written, writing, under an assumed name, hence **pseudonymity,** *n.*; **pseudoscope,** *n.* optical intrument making convex seem concave and vice versa.

pshaw, *int*, of contempt.

psilanthropism, psilanthropy, *nn.* doctrine that Christ was a mere man. **psilanthropic,** *a.* **psilanthropist,** *n.* (Gk. *psilos*, bare; *anthrōpos*, man)

psilosis, *n.* falling of hair; sprue. (Gk. *psilos*, bare)

psittacine, *a.* of, like, parrots. **psittacosis,** *n.* contagious parrot disease causing kind of influenza in man. (L. *psittacus*, parrot)

psoas, *n.* a loin muscle. (Gk. *psoa*)

psora, *n.* a contagious skin disease, itch. **psoriasis,** *n.* chronic skin disease with red scaly patches. (Gk.)

psȳchē, *n.* soul, spirit; mind; kinds of moth. (Gk. *psuchē*)

psychiatry, *n.* study and treatment of mental disorders. **psychiatrist, psychiater,** *nn.* specialist in this. **psychiatric, psychiatrical,** *aa.* (Gk. *psuchē*, mind; *iatros*, doctor)

psychic, psychical, *aa.* of the soul or spirit; of the mind; of, having, extra-physical powers such as clairvoyance; spiritualistic. **psychic,** *n.* person with psychic powers, medium; (*pl.*) psychology. **psychical research, psychicism,** *n.* study of psychic phenomena. **psychicist,** *n.*

psycho-analysis, *n.* Freud's system of psychiatry, tracing neuroses, obsessions etc. to desires consciously rejected but unconsciously persistent. **psycho-analyse,** *v.t.* treat by this. **psycho-analyst,** *n.* **psychoanalytic, psycho-analytical,** *aa.*

psychodynamic, *a.* of mental action. —*n.pl.* science of this.

psychogenesis, psychogony, *nn.* evolution of soul or mind. **psychogenetic, psychogenetical, psychogonical,** *aa.*

psychogram, *n.* spirit-message. **psychograph,** *n.* instrument for recording spirit-message; spirit-photograph. **psychography,** *n.* spirit-writing; descriptive psychology. (Gk. *psuchē*, spirit; *graphein*, write)

psychology, *n.* science of the mind; treatise on this; mental equipment or state. **psychological,** *a.* of psychology or mind. **psychological moment,** (*joc.*) nick of time. **psychologist,** *n.* **psychologize,** *v.t.* and *i.* (Gk. *psuchē*, mind; *legein*, speak)

psychomachy, *n.* conflict between soul and body. (Gk. *psuchē*, soul; *machē*, battle)

psychomancy, *n.* occult communication with spirits, necromancy. (Gk. *psuchē*, spirit; *manteia*, divination)

psychometry, *n.* scientific measurement of mental powers; supposed faculty of divining unknown person's qualities by handling some object belonging to him. **psychometric, psychometrical,** *a.* **psychometrist,** *n.* (Gk. *psuchē*, mind; *metron*, measure)

psychomotor, *a.* of physical action induced by mental condition.

psychoneurosis, *n.* mental disease showing loss of balance between instincts and controlling power.

psychopathy, *n.* minor mental disorder. **psychopath,** *n.* victim of this. **psychopathic,** *a.* of psychopathy; morbidly emotional. **psychopathist, psychopathology,** *nn.* (Gk. *psuchē*, mind; *pathein*, suffer)

psychophysics, *n.pl.* science of general relations between mind and body. **psychophysical,** *a.* **psychophysicist,** *n.*

psychophysiology, *n.* branch of physiology dealing with mental phenomena. **psychophysiological,** *a.* **psychophysiologist,** *n.*

psychosis, *n.* (*pl.* **psychoses**) mental derangement not due to brain injury or disease. (Gk. *psuchē*, mind)

psychotherapy, psychotherapeutics, *nn.* treatment of disease by mental influence. **psychotherapeutic, psychotherapeutical,** *aa.* (Gk. *psuchē*, mind; *therapeuein*, heal)

psychro-, from Gk. *psuchros*, cold, used in **psychrometer,** *n.* wet-and-dry-bulb hygrometer; **psychrophilic,** *a.* thriving in cold; **psychrophobia,** *n.* morbid impressibility to cold.

ptarmigan, *n.* kind of grouse. (Gael. *tarmachan*+*p* from analogy with Gk.)

pteridology, *n.* study of ferns. **pteridological,** *a.* **pteridologist,** *n.* (Gk. *pteris*, fern; *legein*, speak)

pter(o)-, from Gk. *pteron*, wing, used in **pterocarpous,** *a.* having winged seeds; **pterodactyl,** *n.* extinct flying reptile with wings like bat; **pterography**, *n.* description of feathers, hence **pterographic**, **pterographical**, *aa.*: **pteropod**, *n.* small swimming mollusc with wing-like lobes on foot; **pteropus**, *n.* (*pl.* **pteropi**) flying fox; **pterosaur**, *n.* extinct flying reptile; **pterylosis**, *n.* arrangement of birds' feathers; **pterylology**, *n.* science of this.

pterygium, *n.* generalized limb (arm, leg, fin, wing). **pterygoid**, *a.* wing-like. (Gk. *pterux*, wing)

ptilosis, *n.* plumage; pterylosis. (Gk. *ptilon*, feather)

ptisan, *n.* decoction of herbs; barley-water. (Gk. *ptisanē*, peeled barley)

ptochocracy, *n.* government by paupers. (Gk. *ptōchos*, beggar; *kratos*, power)

Ptolemaic, *a.* of the Ptolemies, ancient rulers of Egypt. **P. system**, astronomy taking earth as centre of universe.

ptomaine, *n.* kinds of alkaloid, often poisonous, found in decaying matter. (Gk. *ptōma*, corpse)

ptosis, *n.* drooping of eyelid due to paralysis. (Gk.=falling)

ptyalin, *n.* digestive ferment in saliva. **ptyalism**, *n.* excessive flow of saliva. (Gk. *ptualon*, spittle)

pub, *n.* public-house; (*sl.*) hotel.

puberty, *n.* age at which generative powers begin, us. taken as 14 in boys, 12 in girls. **puberal**, *a.* **pubescent**, *a.* arriving, having arrived, at puberty; (*bot.*) downy. **pubescence**, *n.* (L. *pubes*, genitals, hair growing on them)

public, *a.* of, for, by, the people generally; open or known to all.—*n.* community at large; audience, body of readers etc.; public-house. **in p.**, openly, under general observation. **p. orator**, official speaker of university. **p. school**, large boarding-school for giving liberal education; free school maintained by local authorities. **p. spirit**, wish to promote common welfare. **p.-house**, *n.* place selling alcoholic liquor. **publican**, *n.* keeper of public-house; ancient Roman tax-gatherer. **publication**, *n.* publishing; thing published, book, periodical. **publicist**, *n.* writer on public affairs; political journalist. **publicity**, *n.* notoriety; advertisement. (L. *publicus*)

publish, *v.t.* make generally known; proclaim, announce formally; issue (book) for sale to public; (*law*) put (slander) into circulation. **publisher**, *n.* one who publishes; one who prints and issues books. (*public*)

puccoon, *n.* N. American plant yielding red or yellow dye. (native)

puce, *a.* purple-brown. (L. *pulex*, flea)

puck, *n.* mischievous goblin or child; Robin Goodfellow. (O.E. *púca*)

puck, *n.* flat rubber disk used instead of ball in ice-hockey.

puck, *n.* nightjar; cattle disease said to be caused by it.

pucka, same as **pukka**.

pucker, *v.i.* and *t.* draw together in creases, wrinkle.—*n.* wrinkle, fold.

puckish, *a.* impish, irresponsible.

pud, *n.* (*colloq.*) paw, hand.

puddening, same as **pudding** (*naut.*).

pudder, *n.* pother, bustle.—*v.i.* and *t.* make pudder; perplex. (*pother*)

pudding, *n.* kinds of dish served in soft mass, often as dessert; meat or fruit cooked in covering of flour; skin stuffed with seasoned chopped meat; (*naut.*) pad, tow binding, used as fender. **p.-face**, *n.* large flat expressionless face. **p.-head**, *n.* blockhead. **p.-stone**, *n.* conglomerate made of rounded pebbles.

puddle, *n.* small dirty pool; rough cement of kneaded clay; (*colloq.*) mess.—*v.i.* and *t.* dabble in mud, make muddy; make, line with, puddle; stir (molten iron) to free it from carbon. **puddler**, *n.* (M.E. *podel*)

puddock, same as **paddock**.

pudency, *n.* modesty, sense of shame. **pudenda**, *n.pl.* private parts, esp. of woman. **pudendal**, *a.* (L. *pudēre*, be ashamed)

pudge, *n.* (*colloq.*) short thick person or thing. **pudgy**, *a.*

pudic, *a.* of the pudenda. **pudicity**, *n.* modesty; chastity.

pudsy, *a.* plump, pudgy.

pueblo, *n.* Indian settlement in Mexico etc.; inhabitant of this. (Sp.)

puerile, *a.* boyish, childish; foolish, trivial. **puerility**, *n.* (L. *puer*, boy)

puerperal, *a.* of, caused by, child-birth. (L. *puer*, boy; *parere*, bear)

puff, *n.* sudden short blast of breath or wind; whiff; small pad for applying face-powder; loose roll of hair or of cloth in dress; light pastry; flattering notice or advertisement. —*v.i.* and *t.* emit puff; go, drive, inflate, utter, with puff; breathe hard, pant; put out of breath; praise with exaggeration. **p. up**, elate, swell. **p.-adder**, *n.* venomous African viper. **p.-ball**, *n.* round fungus emitting powder when broken. **p.-box**, *n.* for face-powder and puff. **p.-p.**, *n.* child's word for train. **puffer**, *n.* one who puffs; globe-fish. **puffery**, *n.* advertisement, puffing. (imit.)

puffin, *n.* sea-bird of auk family with short thick beak.

puffy, *a.* inflated, swollen; panting; gusty; bombastic.

pug, *n.* (also **p.-dog**) breed of dog like small bull-dog; (also **p.-nose**) snub nose.

pug, *v.t.* mix (clay for brickmaking); fill in (space) with mortar to deaden sound.—*n.* pugged clay.

pug, *n.* (*Anglo-Ind.*) footprint of beast. —*v.t.* track by pugs. (Hind. *pag*)

pug, *n.* (*sl.*) prize-fighter. (*pugilist*)
puggaree, puggree, *n.* Indian's light turban; scarf worn round hat as protection from sun. (Hind. *pagri*)
pugging, *a.* (*Shake.*) thieving.
pugh, *int.* of contempt.
pugilist, *n.* boxer; prize-fighter. **pugilism,** *n.* boxing. **pugilistic,** *a.* **pugilistically,** *adv.* (L. *pugil*)
pugnacious, *a.* fond of fighting, combative. **pugnacity,** *n.* (L. *pugnare,* fight)
puisne, *a.* (*law*) junior; later; (*Shake.*) petty.—*n.* junior judge. (O.F.)
puissant, *a.* (*arch.*) powerful, mighty. **puissance,** *n.* power; (*Shake.*) armed force. (L. *posse,* be able)
puja, same as **pooja.**
pukaki, same as **pukeko.**
puke, *v.i.* and *t.* and *n.* vomit.
puke, *n.* (*Shake.*) kind of woollen cloth.
pukeko, *n.* (*New Zealand*) swamp-hen.
pukka, *a.* (*Anglo-Ind.*) genuine, real; reliable, sound. (Hind. *pakka,* ripe)
puku, same as **pookoo.**
pulchritude, *n.* beauty. (L. *pulcher,* beautiful)
pule, *v.i.* whine, whimper. (imit.)
pulicine, *a.* of fleas. **pulicide,** *n.* flea-killer. **pulicose, pulicous,** *aa.* infested with fleas. (L. *pulex,* flea)
pull, *v.t.* and *i.* draw, tug; remove by pulling; pluck, gather; twitch; row; check (horse) with rein; (*cricket*) hit (ball) from off to on side of wicket; (*golf*) hit (ball) so that it curls to left; (*print.*) take (proof).—*n.* pulling, tug; draught; advantage, influence; handle, lever, for pulling; (*print.*) proof. **p. at,** suck at; drink deep of. **p. down,** demolish; weaken. **p. faces,** grimace. **p. off,** effect, be successful in. **p. one's leg,** tease, hoax. **p. one's weight,** do full share of work. **p. through,** get safely through (illness etc.). **p. together,** recover (oneself); co-operate. **p. to pieces,** criticize destructively. **p. up,** check, stop; gain ground; uproot. **p. up one's socks,** (*sl.*) prepare for effort. **p.-through,** *n.* cord with rag for cleaning rifle-barrel. (O.E. *pullian*)
pullet, *n.* young hen before first moult. (L. *pullus,* young animal)
pulley, *n.* wheel with groove in rim for cord, used to raise weights by downward pull; group of these used to increase applied force; wheel driven by belt.—*v.t.* hoist, work, by pulley. (O.F. *polie*)
Pullman, *n.* (also **P. car**) railway saloon carriage, often with sleeping accommodation. (designer)
pullover, *n.* buttonless jersey pulled over head.
pullulate, *v.i.* sprout, grow; spread abroad, spring up; multiply quickly, teem. **pullulant,** *a.* **pullulation,** *n.* (L. *pullus,* sprout+dim).
pulmonary, *a.* of, affecting, the lungs; having lungs; affected with lung disease. **pulmo-branchiate,** *a.* with gills modified for air-breathing. **pulmo-gastric,** *a.* of lungs and stomach. **pulmometer,** *n.* instrument measuring capacity of lungs. **pulmonate,** *a.* having lungs. **pulmonic,** *a.* consumptive; pulmonary.—*n.* medicine for, person with, lung disease. (L. *pulmo,* lung)
pulp, *n.* fleshy part of fruits; any soft coherent mass; crushed vegetable tissue for paper-making.—*v.t.* and *i.* reduce to, become, pulp; rid of pulp. (L. *pulpa*)
pulpit, *n.* raised enclosed platform for preacher in church; preachers as a class. **pulpiteer,** *n.* professional preacher.—*v.i.* hold forth. **pulpitarian,** *a.* (L. *pulpitum,* stage)
pulpy, *a.* of, like, pulp.
pulque, *n.* Mexican drink of fermented juice of agave. (Sp.)
pulse, *n.* beating of heart; place where this is felt, esp. in wrist; regular beat, vibration; trend of feeling—*v.i.* throb, pulsate. **pulsate,** *v.i.* and *t.* expand and contract rhythmically; vibrate, quiver; thrill. **pulsatile,** *a.* capable of pulsation; (*mus.*) played by percussion. **pulsatilla,** *n.* pasque-flower. **pulsation,** *n.* pulsating; single beat or throb. **pulsatory,** *a.* (L. *pellere,* drive)
pulse, *n.* seeds of pod-bearing plant, beans, peas etc. (L. *puls,* porridge)
pulsimeter, *n.* instrument for measuring pulse-beat, sphygmograph.
pulsometer, *n.* vacuum pump for raising water by steam.
pultaceous, *a.* pulpy; like porridge. (L. *puls,* porridge)
pultun, pultan, pultoon, *n.* Indian native infantry regiment.
pulverize, *v.t.* and *i.* reduce to fine powder, dust, or spray; demolish, smash; crumble. **pulverization,** *n.* **pulverulent,** *a.* of, covered with, dust; powdery; crumbling. (L. *pulvis,* dust)
pulvinate, pulvinated, *aa.* (*archit.*) curved convexly; (*bot.*) having cushion-like pad or swelling. (L. *pulvinus,* cushion)
pulwar, *n.* light keelless Bengal river-boat. (Hind. *palwar*)
puma, *n.* large tawny S. American animal of cat kind, cougar. (Peruvian)
pumice, *n.* (also **p.-stone**) light porous grey lava used for rubbing off stains, polishing etc.—*v.t.* clean with this. **pumiceous,** *a.* (L. *pumex*)
pummel, *v.t.* strike repeatedly with fists, thump. (*pommel*)
pump, *n.* light low shoe or slipper, us. of patent leather.
pump, *n.* appliance for raising water, putting in or taking out air etc. by suction or compression.—*v.t.* and *i.* raise, drive, make (full, empty) by pump; work pump; instil with

effort; (*colloq.*) **ply with questions,** extract information from; exhaust, puff. **p. up,** raise by pumping; inflate. **p.-handle,** *n.* for working pump.—*v.t.* (*colloq.*) shake hands effusively with. **p.-room,** *n.* room in spa where waters are drunk. (M.E. *pumpe*)

pumpernickel, *n.* kind of rye bread. (G.)

pumpkin, (*Shake.*) **pumpion,** *nn.* plant, fruit, of gourd kind; squash. (Gk. *pepōn,* kind of melon+dim.)

pumpship, *v.i.* (*colloq.*) make water.

pun, *n.* play on words of same sound but different meanings, or on different applications of a word, e.g. 'A brown man oft deep read we see, a black a wicked wight.'—*v.i.* make pun.

pun, *v.t.* make solid by ramming; (*Shake.*) pound. (*pound*)

puna, *n.* dry cold table-land in Andes; difficulty in breathing at high altitudes, mountain sickness. (Peruvian)

punch, *n.* tool, machine, for stamping holes, impressing design etc.—*v.t.* perforate, stamp, with punch; drive (nail) in or out with punch.

punch, *v.t.* strike with fist.—*n.* blow with fist; (*sl.*) vigour, pungency.

punch, *n.* drink of spirits or wine mixed with hot water, sugar, lemon, spices etc. **p.-bowl,** *n.* bowl for mixing this; bowl-shaped hollow.

punch, *n.* thickset breed of draught horse; short stout man.

punch, *n.* Indian native council of five persons. (*panchayat*)

Punch, *n.* grotesque hero of puppet-play **P. and Judy.** (*Punchinello*)

puncheon, *n.* large cask holding 72–120 gallons.

puncheon, *n.* short upright in mine etc.; punch. (L. *pungere,* prick)

Punchinello, *n.* clown of Italian puppet-show; grotesque figure, buffoon. (It. *Polichinello*)

punctate, punctated, *aa.* (*bot.*) marked with dots or points. **punctation,** *n.* (L. *punctum,* point)

punctilio, *n.* nice point of etiquette; petty formality. **punctilious,** *a.* precise in conduct; scrupulously exact. (It. *puncto,* point+dim.)

punctual, *a.* adhering to appointed time, not late; (*arch.*) punctilious; (*geom.*) of a point. **punctuality,** *n.* (L. *punctum,* point)

punctuate, *v.t.* divide up with stops, commas etc.; mark, interrupt, recurrently. **punctuation,** *n.* punctuating; system of stops. **punctuative,** *a.* **punctuator,** *n.* (L. *punctum,* point)

punctum, *n.* (*pl.* **puncta**) speck, dot. **punctule,** *n.* minute spot. **punctulate,** *a.* bearing small spots. (L.)

puncture, *n.* small hole, prick, esp. in pneumatic tyre; perforation.—*v.t.* make puncture in, perforate; have puncture. (L. *pungere,* prick)

pundit, *n.* one versed in Hindu learning and religion; (*joc.*) very learned man, authority. (Hind. *pandit*)

pung, *n.* (*Amer.*) kind of box-sleigh.

pungent, *a.* stinging, acrid; sharp, full-flavoured; (of wit) biting, caustic. **pungency,** *n.* (L. *pungere,* prick)

Punic, *a.* Carthaginian. **P. apple,** pomegranate. **P. faith,** treachery. (L. *Punicus*)

punish, *v.t.* inflict penalty on or for, chastise; handle roughly, maul. **punishable,** *a.* liable to legal punishment. **punishment,** *n.* punishing; penalty. **punitive, punitory,** *aa.* of, inflicting, punishment. (L. *punire*)

punk, *n.* (*Amer.*) rotten wood; worthless stuff.—*a.* (*Amer. sl.*) poor, useless; seedy.

punk, *n.* (*Shake.*) harlot.

punkah, punka, *n.* large swinging fan, us. worked by rope. (Hind. *pankha*)

punkie, *n.* (*Amer.*) a small biting fly.

punner, *n.* rammer. (*pun*)

punnet, *n.* small shallow wooden basket for fruit.

punster, *n.* one who makes puns.

punt, *n.* long flat-bottomed square-ended river boat propelled by pole. —*v.i.* and *t.* propel, convey in, punt. **punter, puntist,** *nn.* (L. *ponto*)

punt, *v.t.* kick (football) after dropping it from hands, before it reaches ground.—*n.* such kick. **p.-about,** *n.* practice kicking.

punt, *v.i.* (*cards*) lay stake against bank; (*colloq.*) bet on horse.—*n.* punter. (F. *ponter*)

punto, *n.* (*Shake.*) thrust. (It.)

punty, *n.* iron rod used in glass-blowing.

puny, *a.* inferior in strength or size, feeble; petty. (=*puisne*)

pup, *n.* puppy.—*v.i.* bring forth whelps. **sell one a p.,** swindle him.

pupa, *n.* (*pl.* **pupae**) chrysalis. **pupal,** *a.* **pupate,** *v.i.* become pupa. **pupation,** *n.* (L.=girl, doll)

pupil, *n.* person being taught; opening in iris of eye through which light passes; (*law*) child under guardianship. **p.-teacher,** *n.* young person teaching in elementary school while still under instruction himself. **pupillage, pupilage,** *n.* nonage, minority; being a pupil. **pupillar, pupilar, pupillary, pupilary,** *aa.* **pupillarity, pupilarity,** *nn.* **pupillize, pupilize,** *v.i.* and *t.* take pupils, coach. (L. *pupillus*)

pupiparous, *a.* (of fly) producing young in pupal state. (L. *parere,* bear)

puppet, *n.* small figure or doll moved by wires, marionette; one who acts just as another tells him. **p.-play, p.-show,** *nn.* **puppetry,** *n.* mummery. affectation. (L. *pupa,* doll+dim.)

puppy, *n.* young dog, whelp; conceited young man. **puppydom, puppyhood,** *nn.*

purana, *n.* book of Hindu scriptures. (Sanskr. *pura,* formerly)

purblind, *a.* half-blind, dim-sighted; obtuse, dull; (*Shake.*) wholly blind.

purchase, *v.t.* buy; obtain by effort or suffering. — *n.* buying; thing bought; value, esp. reckoned in annual yield; leverage, grip; (*Shake.*) obtaining; booty. (O.F. *pur*, for; *chacier*, chase)

purdah, *n.* curtain screening Indian women of rank from strangers; this system of seclusion; striped Indian cloth for curtains. (Hind. *pardah*)

pure, *a.* clean, uncontaminated; chaste, innocent; unmixed, unalloyed; mere, sheer; abstract, theoretical (opp. to applied); (of sound) not discordant, perfectly in tune; (of taste) rejecting the gaudy or conventional. **purely,** *adv.* solely, entirely. (L. *purus*)

purée, *n.* vegetables etc. boiled to pulp and sieved; thick soup. (F.)

purfle, *n.* embroidered edge of garment; (*archit.*) crocketed parapet.—*v.t.* finish with purfle, edge; beautify. (L. *pro*, before; *filum*, thread)

purge, *v.t.* cleanse, purify; clear away; clear (oneself) of charge; clear out bowels of; (*law*) expiate (offence) by suffering punishment.—*n.* purging; purgative. **purgation,** *n.* purging. **purgative,** *a.* and *n.* purging (medicine). **purgatory,** *n.* place of suffering or purification; (*Roman Catholic*) place intermediate between death and heaven where venial sins are purged.—*a.* purifying. (L. *purgare*)

puriform, *a.* like pus. (*pus*)

purify, *v.t.* make pure, cleanse; make ceremonially clean; free (language) from barbarisms. **purification, purificator,** *nn.* **purificatory,** *a.* (L. *purus*, pure; *facere*, make)

purine, purin, *n.* white crystalline compound from which uric acid etc. is derived. (*pure*; *uric*)

purist, *n.* stickler for correctness in language, style etc. **purism,** *n.* **puristic, puristical,** *aa.*

puritan, *n.* one who professes extreme strictness in religion or morals; extreme Protestant of Elizabethan or Stuart times.—*a.* of, like, a puritan; of the Puritans. **puritanical, puritanic,** *aa.* **puritanism,** *n.* **puritanize,** *v.i.* and *t.*

purity, *n.* pureness.

purl, *n.* edging of gold or silver wire or small loops; (*knitting*) inversion of stitches, producing ribbed appearance.—*v.t.* and *i.* attach purl to; invert (stitches).

purl, *v.i.* flow with whirling motion, swirl.—*n.* purling; babble.

purl, *n.* old drink of hot ale flavoured with wormwood.

purl, *v.t.* and *n.* (*colloq.*) spill, upset. **purler,** *n.* (*colloq.*) heavy fall head foremost, cropper.

purlicue *n.* (*Scot.*) curl or flourish in writing.

purlieu, *n.* (formerly) disafforested tract on fringe of forest; (*pl.*) outlying parts, outskirts; slums.

purlin, *n.* (*archit.*) main horizontal beam supporting rafters.

purloin, *v.t.* steal, filch. (L. *prolongare*, prolong, keep back)

purple, *n.* colour of mixed blue and red; imperial or royal rank: cardinalate; (*pl.*) swine fever; a disease of wheat.—*a.* purple-coloured; (*poet.*) deep red.—*v.t.* and *i.* make, become, purple. **p. emperor,** large kind of butterfly. **Tyrian p.,** crimson. (Gk. *porphura*)

purpoint, same as **pourpoint.**

purport, *v.t.* signify, convey; profess, be intended to seem.—*n.* significance, substance; apparent meaning. (L. *pro*, before; *portare*, carry)

purpose, *n.* intention, object; resolution, determination; effect; (*Shake.*) proposal; (*Spens.*) conversation, discourse.—*v.t.* and *i.* intend, design. **on p.,** deliberately. **to no p.,** in vain. **to the p.,** relevant. **purposeful,** *a.* determined, resolute; intentional. **purposeless,** *a.* aimless. **purposely,** *adv.* on purpose. **purposive,** *a.* done with, indicating, purpose; purposeful. (O.F. *purposer*, propose)

purpura, *n.* disease marked by livid spots; kinds of shell-fish incl. murex. **purpuric,** *a.* **purpurin,** *n.* red dyestuff got from madder. (L.)

purr, *n.* low murmuring sound of cat when pleased.—*v.i.* and *t.* utter this; say in tone like purr. (imit.)

purree, *n.* yellow Chinese pigment. **purreic,** *a.* (Hind. *peori*)

pur sang, pure-blooded, genuine. (F.)

purse, *n.* small pouch or case for money; sum given as prize etc.; funds, treasury.—*v.t.* and *i.* pucker, wrinkle up; (*arch.*) pocket. **p.-proud,** *a.* arrogant because of wealth. **p.-strings,** *n.pl.* for closing mouth of purse. **purser,** *n.* ship's officer who has charge of accounts. (Gk. *bursa*, hide)

purslane, *n.* succulent herb used in salads. (L. *portulaca*)

pursue, *v.t.* and *i.* chase, follow after; attend closely, dog; prosecute, engage in; conduct. **pursuance,** *n.* pursuing, performance. **pursuant,** *a.* following; according.—*adv.* conformably. **pursuer,** *n.* one who pursues; (*Scots law*) plaintiff. **pursuit,** *n.* pursuing, chase; quest; employment, occupation. (L. *pro-*, forth; *sequi*, follow)

pursuivant, *n.* inferior officer of College of Heralds; (*poet.*) follower. (*pursue*)

pursy, *a.* short-winded; stout. (L. *pulsare*, beat)

pursy, *a.* puckered. (*purse*)

purtenance, *n.* (*arch.*) heart, liver, and lungs of slaughtered animal; belongings. (=*pertinence*)

purulent, *a.* discharging pus, septic. **purulence, purulency,** *nn.* (*pus*)

purvey, *v.t.* and *i.* procure and supply (provisions). **purveyance,** *n.* purveying; supplies; former royal right of pre-empting necessaries. **purveyor,** *n.* (L. *providēre*, provide)

purview, *n.* enacting clauses, provisions, of statute; scope, range, limit. (*purvey*)

pus, *n.* yellowish matter produced by suppuration. (L.)

Puseyism, *n.* Tractarianism. **Puseyite,** *n.* (Dr. E. B. *Pusey*)

push, *v.t.* and *i.* impel forward, shove; thrust; press (against); urge claims of.—*n.* thrust, shove; attack; emergency; (*colloq.*) energy, enterprise; (*sl.*) set, crowd. **p. off,** leave, cause to leave, shore; go away. **p. on,** hurry on. **the p.,** (*sl.*) the sack. **p.-ball,** *n.* game with ball like enormous football, pushed by 11 players a side. **p.-bike,** *n.* (*sl.*) pedal cycle. **p.-cart,** *n.* hand-cart. **pusher,** *n.* aeroplane with propeller behind. **pushing, pushful,** *aa.* go-ahead, energetic; assertive. (L. *pellere*, drive)

Pushtu, Pushtoo, *n.* Afghan language. (Pers. *Pashto*)

pusillanimous, *a.* faint-hearted, cowardly; mean-spirited. **pusillanimity,** *n.* (L. *pusillus*, very small; *animus*, spirit)

puss, *n.* cat; hare; (*colloq.*) mischievous young girl. **p.-in-the-corner,** *n.* a children's game. **p.-moth,** *n.* large light-coloured moth. **pussy,** *n.* cat; willow or hazel catkin; soft furry thing. **pussyfoot,** *n.* (*sl.*) supporter of liquor-prohibition.

pustule, *n.* pimple containing pus; wart-like excrescence. **pustular, pustulous,** *aa.* **pustulate,** *v.i.* and *t.* form into pustules.—*a.* covered with pustules. **pustulation,** *n.* (L. *pustula*)

put, *v.t.* and *i.* (*past* **put**; *p.p.* **put,** *arch.* **putten**) place, set; apply; direct; bring into specified state; express; submit; estimate, rate; stake; hurl (weight); putt; (*naut.*) take course.—*n.* throw (of weight). **p. about,** change course of (ship); worry. **p. across,** effect successfully. **p. and take,** a gambling game. **p. away,** remove; lay by; (*sl.*) consume; (*arch.*) divorce. **p. back,** replace; return to land. **p. by,** thrust aside; store up. **p. down,** suppress; silence; write, enter; reckon; assign. **p. forth,** exert; bud, shoot; set out. **p. in,** interpose; spend (time); apply (for); call (at). **p. it past one,** (*Amer. colloq.*) consider him incapable of it. **p. off,** doff, discard; postpone; evade, get rid of; discourage, repel; foist (upon); leave shore. **p. on,** don; assume, pretend; increase; add; advance. **p. out,** eject; extend; exert; dislocate; quench; place at interest; disconcert, anger; leave shore. **p. over,** (*Amer.*) succeed in, carry through. **p. to it,** in difficulties, pressed. **p. up,** rouse; offer (prayer); propose as candidate; pack; sheathe; lodge; (*sl.*) concoct; (*Shake.*) pocket. **p. one up to,** reveal; instigate. **p. up with,** endure, tolerate. **p. upon,** impose upon. **p. wise,** (*Amer. sl.*) disabuse, enlighten. **stay p.,** (*colloq.*) stay as it is. (M.E. *putten*)

put, *n.* (*arch. sl.*) clown, rustic, queer person.

putamen, *n.* stone of fruit; membrane lining egg-shell. (L.)

putative, *a.* supposed, reputed. (L. *putare*, think)

pute, *a.* (*arch.*) mere. (L. *putus*)

puteal, *n.* stone kerb round mouth of well. (L.)

putid, *a.* rotten, stinking; worthless. (L. *putidus*)

putlog, putlock, *n.* cross-piece in scaffolding.

putrefy, *v.i.* and *t.* become or make rotten, decompose; suppurate. **putrefacient, putrefactive,** *aa.* and *nn.* (substance) causing putrefaction. **putrefaction,** *n.* putrefying, decomposition. **putrescent,** *a.* decaying, tending to decay. **putrescence,** *n.* **putrid,** *a.* rotten, decayed; foul; (*sl.*) bad, poor. **putrid fever,** typhus. **putridity,** *n.* (L. *puter*, rotten; *facere*, make)

putsch, *n.* rising, revolt. (G.)

putt, *v.i.* and *t.* (*golf*) play (ball) on putting-green; (*Scot.*) throw.—*n.* putting stroke. **putting-green,** *n.* smooth area of turf round hole. (*put*)

puttee, puttie, *n.* legging of strip of cloth wound spirally from ankle to knee. (Hind. *patti*, bandage)

putter, *n.* (*golf*) short stiff-shafted club for putting; one who putts.

putter, *n.* one who puts. **p.-on,** *n.* (*Shake.*) instigator.

puttock, *n.* (*Shake.*) kite, buzzard.

puttoo, *n.* fabric made from coarse hair of Cashmere goat. (native)

putty, *n,* cement of whiting and linseed oil, used in glazing windows; (also **plasterers' p.**) cement of lime and water; (also **jewellers' p.**) polishing powder of tin and lead.—*v.t.* fix, fill, with putty. (F. *potée*)

puzzel, *n.* (*Shake.*) slut. (F. *pucelle*, maid)

puzzle, *v.t.* and *i.* perplex, bewilder; think hard (over).—*n.* bewilderment; perplexing question; verbal or mechanical problem, conundrum. **p. out,** solve by hard thought. **puzzledom, puzzlement,** *nn.* **puzzler,** *n.*

pyaemia, *n.* blood-poisoning with widespread abscesses. **pyaemic,** *a.* (Gk. *puon*, pus; *haima*, blood)

pycno-, from Gk. *puknos*, dense, used in **pycnometer,** *n.* instrument for measuring densities or specific gravities; **pycnostyle,** *a.* and *n.* (building) with columns closely arranged, us. at intervals of $1\frac{1}{2}$ diameters.

pyedog, *n.* (*Anglo-Ind.*) pariah dog. (Hind. *pahi*, outsider+*dog*)

pygal, *a.* of the rump. (Gk. *pugē*, rump)

pygmy, pigmy, *n.* member of dwarf race; small person or thing; elf.—*a.* of the pygmies; dwarfish, insignificant. **pygmean,** *a.* (Gk. *pugmē*, cubit)

pyjamas, *n.pl.* sleeping-suit of jacket and trousers; loose silk drawers worn by Mohammedans. (Pers. *pae*, leg; *jamah*, clothing)

pyle, *n.* (*Scot.*) single grain of corn.

pylon, *n.* gateway of Egyptian temple; tower-like erection to mark out aerodrome, carry electric cables etc. (Gk. *pulōn*, gateway)

pylorus, *n.* opening from stomach into intestine. **pyloric,** *a.* (Gk. *pulōros*, gate-keeper)

pyo-, from Gk. *puon*, pus, used in **pyogenic,** *a.* forming pus; **pyoid,** *a.* like pus; **pyorrhoea,** *n.* discharge of pus, esp. in inflammation of tooth-sockets.

pyracanth, *n.* small white-flowered red-berried evergreen shrub. (Gk. *purakantha*)

pyramid, *n.* solid figure with square, triangular, or polygonal base and sloping sides meeting at apex; Egyptian stone tomb of this shape; tapering pile; (*pl.*) a billiard-table game. **pyramidal,** *a.* **pyramidist,** *n.* student of Egyptian pyramids. (Gk. *puramis*)

pyre, *n.* pile of wood for burning corpse ceremonially. (Gk. *pur.* fire)

pyrene, *n.* a hydrocarbon got from coal-tar. (Gk. *pur*, fire)

pyrene, *n.* stone, putamen. **pyrenocarp,** *n.* drupe. (Gk. *purēn*)

pyrethrum, *n.* kinds of composite plant, feverfew. (Gk. *purethron*)

pyretic, *a.* of, causing, good for, fever. **pyretology,** *n.* science of fevers. **pyrexia,** *n.* fever. **pyrexial, pyrexic, pyrexical,** *aa.* (Gk. *puretos*, fever)

pyrheliometer, *n.* instrument for measuring sun's heat. (Gk. *pur*, fire; *hēlios*, sun; *metron*, measure)

pyridine, *n.* liquid alkaloid used as antiseptic. (Gk *pur*, fire)

pyriform, *a.* pear-shaped. (L. *pirum*, pear)

pyrītēs, *n.* sulphide of a metal, esp. **iron p.,** which resembles gold. **pyritic, pyritous,** *aa.* **pyritiferous,** *a.* yielding pyrites. (Gk. *pur*, fire)

pyro, *n.* pyrogallic acid. (abbr.)

pyro-, from Gk. *pur*, fire, used in **pyrogallic acid,** got from gallic acid by heat and used as photographic developer; **pyrogenetic,** *a.* productive of heat or fever; **pyrogenic,** *a.* productive of fever; **pyrogenous,** *a.* produced by combustion, (*geol.*) igneous; **pyrography,** *n.* poker-work, hence **pyrographer, pyrographist,** *nn.*, **pyrographic,** *a.*; **pyrogravure,** *n.* piece of poker-work; **pyrolatry,** *n.* fire-worship; **pyroligneous,** *a.* got by action of heat on wood; **pyrology,** *n.* science of heat, blowpipe analysis; **pyrolysis,** *n.* decomposition by heat; **pyromancy,** *n.* divination by fire; **pyromania,** *n.* incendiary mania; **pyrometer,** *n.* instrument for measuring very high temperatures. **pyrope,** *n.* deep-red garnet; **pyrophobia,** *n.* morbid fear of fire; **pyrophorus,** *n.* substance igniting when exposed to air, hence **pyrophoric, pyrophorous,** *aa.*; **pyrosis,** *n.* heartburn; **pyrotechnics, pyrotechny,** *nn.* manufacture, display, of fireworks, hence **pyrotechnic, pyrotechnical,** *aa.*, **pyrotechnist,** *n.*; **pyrotoxin,** *n.* toxin causing fever; **pyroxylin,** *n.* kinds of explosive, incl. gun-cotton.

pyrrhic, *n.* two-syllabled foot, short-short; (also **p. dance**) ancient Greek military dance. (Gk. *Purrhichos*, inventor of them)

Pyrrhic, *a.* of Pyrrhus. **P. victory,** so costly as to be equal to defeat.

Pyrrhonism, *n.* sceptic philosophy of Pyrrho of Elis; scepticism. **Pyrrhonian, Pyrrhonic,** *aa.* **Pyrrhonist,** *n.*

pyrus, *n.* kinds of tree incl. pear. (L. *pirus*, pear-tree)

Pythagorean, *a.* and *n.* (adherent) of the philosopher Pythagoras and his doctrine of the transmigration of souls. **Pythagoreanism,** *n.*

Pythian, *a.* of Delphi or its oracle. **the P.,** Apollo or his priestess. (Gk. *Putho*, old name of Delphi)

pythogenic, *a.* due to, causing, filth or decay. **pythogenesis,** *n.* (Gk. *puthein*, rot; *genesis*, origin)

python, *n.* large non-poisonous snake that crushes its prey. **pythonic,** *a.* (Gk. *Puthōn*, serpent slain by Apollo)

python, *n.* familiar spirit; soothsayer, sorcerer. **pythoness,** *n.* priestess of Apollo at Delphi; sorceress, witch. **pythonic,** *a.* (Gk. *puthōn*)

pyuria, *n.* discharge of pus into urine. (Gk. *puon*, pus; *ouron*, urine)

pyx, *n.* vessel in which consecrated bread is kept; box in mint holding coins kept for trial.—*v.t.* test weight and fineness of (coin). **pyxidium,** *n.* (*pl.* **pyxidia**) seed-capsule of which top comes off like lid. **pyxis,** *n.* casket; pyxidium; vase with cover. (Gk. *puxos*, box-tree)

Q

Q-boat, ***n.*** warship disguised as merchantman, mystery ship.

qua, conj. as, in the capacity of. (L.)

quack, ***n.*** cry of duck.—*v.i.* utter this; gabble, chatter. (imit.)

quack, ***n.*** unqualified pretender to medical or other skill, charlatan.—*a.* of, used by, quack.—*v.i.* and *t.* practise as quack; puff, advertise. **quackery,** ***n.*** (*quacksalver*)

quacksalver, ***n.*** itinerant vendor of drugs, quack. (*quack*, cry; *salve*)

quad, *abbr.* of **quadrangle, quadrat,** or **quadruplet.**

quadra, *n.* square frame, esp. enclosing bas-relief. (L. *quadras*, square)

quadrable, *a.* (*math.*) able to be squared or to be represented by an equivalent square. (*quadrate*)

quadragenarian, *a.* and *n.* (person) forty years old. **quadragene,** *n.* papal indulgence of forty days. (L. *quadraginta*, forty)

Quadragesima, *n.* (also **Q. Sunday**) first Sunday in Lent. **quadragesimal,** *a.* lasting forty days; of Lent. (L. *quadraginta*, forty)

quadrangle, *n.* court enclosed by buildings; (*geom.*) four-sided figure; square, rectangle. **quadrangular,** *a.* (L. *quattuor*, four)

quadrant, *n.* quarter of circle or sphere; arc of 90°; instrument for measuring altitudes or elevations; curved street. **quadrantal,** *a.* (L. *quadrans*, quarter)

quadrat, *n.* (*print.*) block of type-metal used in spacing. (*quadrate*)

quadrate, *v.t.* and *i.* square; cause to conform; correspond.—*a.* square, rectangular.—*n.* quadrate bone or muscle. **quadratic,** *a.* square; (*math.*) containing square but not higher power.—*n.* quadratic equation; (*pl.*) branch of algebra dealing with them. **quadrature,** *n.* (*astron.*) relation of two heavenly bodies when distant 90° from each other; (*math.*) finding of square with area exactly equal to circle etc. (L. *quadrare*)

quadrennial, *a.* lasting, occurring every, four years. (L. *quattuor*, four; *annus*, year)

quadri-, from L. *quattuor*, four, used in **quadricentennial,** *n.* and *a.* (of) four hundredth anniversary; **quadrified,** *a.* cleft in four; **quadriga,** *n.* (*pl.* **quadrigae**) four-horse chariot; **quadrilateral,** *a.* and *n.* four-sided (figure); **quadrilingual,** *a.* in, using, four languages; **quadriliteral,** *a.* of four letters; **quadrillion,** *n.* fourth power of million (1 with 24 ciphers), (U.S. and France) fifth power of thousand (1 with 15 ciphers); **quadrinomial,** *a.* and *n.* (algebraic expression) consisting of four terms; **quadripartite,** *a.* of four parts, shared by four; **quadrireme,** *n.* galley with four banks of oars; **quadrisyllable,** *n.* word of four syllables, hence **quadrisyllabic,** *a.*; **quadrivalent,** *a.* (*chem.*) with valency of four; **quadrivial,** *a.* leading in four ways; **quadrivium,** *n.* medieval course of study comprising arithmetic, geometry, astronomy, and music.

quadrille, *n.* square dance with five figures, us. for four couples; music for this. (F.)

quadrille, *n.* old card game for four, using pack of forty cards. (F.)

quadroon, *n.* offspring of white and mulatto, person one-fourth negro. (Sp. *cuarto*, fourth)

quadru-, from L. *quattuor*, four, used in **quadrumanous,** *a.* four-handed, of the monkey kind; **quadruped,** *n.* four-footed animal.—*a.* (also **quadrupedal**) four-footed.

quadruple, *a.* fourfold; of four parts or parties; four times greater than.—*n.* quadruple amount or number.—*v.t.* and *i.* multiply by four. **quadruplet,** *n.* one of four children born at a birth; bicycle for four. **quadruplicate,** *v.t.* multiply by four; make four copies of.—*a.* fourfold.—*n.pl.* four similar examples. **quadruplication,** *n.* **quadruplicity,** *n.* fourfold nature. (L. *quadruplus*)

quaere, v.t. imperative and *n.* (*abbr.* **qu., qy**) question, query. (L.=inquire)

quaestor, *n.* ancient Roman magistrate in charge of public funds etc. **quaestorial,** *a.* **quaestorship** *n.* (L.)

quaff, *v.t.* and *i.* take large draughts (of), drain.

quag, *n.* bog, quagmire. (imit.)

quagga, *n.* extinct striped S. African animal like zebra. (S. Afr.)

quaggy, *a.* boggy, marshy.

quagmire, *n.* bog, swamp, marshy ground. (*quag*; *mire*)

quahog, quahaug, *n.* edible N. American clam. (Amer. Ind. *poquauhock*)

quaich, quaigh, *n.* (*Scot.*) kind of drinking-cup, us. of wood. (Gael. *cuach*, cup)

Quai d'Orsay, French Foreign Office. (place)

quail, *v.i.* and *t.* flinch, cower, give way; daunt; (*Shake.*) fail; overpower; (*Spens.*) wither.

quail, *n.* bird like partridge; (*Shake.*) whore. (O.F. *quaille*)

quaint, *a.* odd, whimsical; pleasing through strangeness; (*Shake.*) fine, elegant; clever. (L. *cognoscere*, learn)

quair, *obs.* form of **quire.**

quake, *v.i.* shake, tremble, shiver.—*n.*

tremor. **q.-grass, quaking-grass,** *nn.* a kind that trembles in wind. (O.E. *cwacian*)

Quaker, *n.* (*fem.* **Quakeress**) member of Society of Friends, religious sect cultivating peace and simplicity; (*Amer.*) dummy gun. **quakerish,** *a.* sober, strait-laced, like a Quaker. **quakerism,** *n.* (nickname from phrase 'quake at the word of the Lord')

qualify, *v.t.* and *i.* modify, limit; moderate, temper; describe (as); make, become, fit (for); fulfil conditions. **qualification,** *n.* qualifying; thing that qualifies; acquirement fitting one for post etc.; modification. **qualificatory,** *a.* (L. *qualis*, of what sort; *facere*, make)

quality, *n.* attribute, characteristic, property; kind, grade; timbre; excellence, high rank; (*Shake.*) profession; cause. **the q.,** the upper classes. **qualitative,** *a.* of, depending on, quality; (*chem.*) determining the nature of components (opp. to quantitative). (L. *qualis*, of what sort)

qualm, *n.* feeling of faintness, nausea; misgiving, scruple. **qualmish,** *a.* squeamish.

quandary, *n.* state of perplexity, dilemma.

quand même, all the same, whatever may happen. (F.)

quant, *n.* punting-pole with disk on end to prevent it from sinking in mud.—*v.t.* and *i.* punt with quant.

quantify, *v.t.* express as quantity; determine amount of; (*logic*) define application of. **quantification,** *n.*

quantity, *n.* amount, number, bulk; length of vowel sound, duration of tone; (*Shake.*) fragment; proportion; (*pl.*) profusion. **quantitative,** *a.* of, measured by, quantity; (*chem.*) determining relative proportions of components (opp. to qualitative). (L. *quantus*, how much)

quantivalency, quantivalence, *n.* (*chem.*) old term for valency. (L. *quantus*, how much; *valēre*, be worth)

quantum, *n.* (*pl.* **quanta**) share, portion; fundamental unit of radiation. *q. libet*, (*abbr. quant. lib.* or *q.l.*) as much as you please. *q. sufficit*, (*abbr. quant. suff.* or *q.s.*) a sufficient quantity. **q. theory,** theory that in radiation the energy of electrons is discharged not continuously but in discrete units or quanta. (L. *quantus*, how much)

quaquaversal, *a.* (*geol.*) pointing in every direction. (L. *quaqua*, wheresoever; *versus*, towards)

quarantine, *n.* isolation imposed on ship, traveller etc., suspected of infection; time of this (formerly forty days).—*v.t.* put, keep, in quarantine. (L. *quadraginta*, forty)

quare impedit, writ in action over disputed presentation to benefice. (L.=why does he hinder?)

quarenden, quarender, *n.* kind of dark-red apple.

quarrel, *n.* short heavy arrow for crossbow; diamond-shaped pane of glass. (L. *quadrus*, square)

quarrel, *n.* angry dispute, altercation; breach of friendship; ground of complaint.—*v.i.* fall out (with); become estranged; find fault (with). **pick a q.,** seek occasion for hostilities. **quarrelsome,** (*Shake.*) **quarrelous,** *aa.* contentious. (L. *queri*, complain)

quarry, *n.* hunted animal; object of pursuit, prey; (orig.) deer's entrails given to hounds after chase; (*Shake.*) heap of dead. (L. *corium*, hide)

quarry, *n.* place from which stone is excavated; source of information etc.—*v.t.* and *i.* dig (stone) from quarry; make research. **quarryman,** *n.* worker in quarry. (L. *quadrare*, square)

quart, *n.* liquid measure, ¼ gallon; pot or bottle holding this. (L. *quartus*, fourth)

quart, *n.* position in fencing, carte; sequence of four cards of a suit. (F. *quarte*)

quartan, *a.* and *n.* (fever, ague) recurring every third day. (L. *quartus*, fourth, counting inclusively)

quarter, *n.* fourth part, fourth (of); fourth of hundredweight, 28 lb., (*Amer.*) 25 lb.; fourth of year, between quarter-days; fourth of moon's period, hour, carcass etc.; dry measure of 8 bushels; side of ship between mainmast and stern; point of compass, direction; district, area; life granted to enemy, mercy; (*Amer.*) fourth of dollar, 25-cent piece; (*pl.*) lodgings, esp. for troops; action stations; haunches.—*v.t.* and *i.* divide into quarters; lodge, billet; range over (ground) in search; (*heraldry*) bear quarterly or among quarterings. **at close qq.,** close together. **bad q. of an hour,** short unpleasant ordeal. **q. sessions,** court held quarterly in county or borough with limited jurisdiction. (L. *quartus*, fourth)

quarterage, *n.* quarterly payment.

quarter-back *n.* (*Amer. football*) player directly behind forwards.

quarter-binding, *n.* binding of leather etc. on back only. **quarter-bound,** *a.*

quarter-day, *n.* day marking quarter of legal year, in England 25 March, 24 June, 29 Sept., 25 Dec.; in Scotland 2 Feb., 15 May, 1 Aug., 11 Nov.

quarter-deck, *n.* after part of upper deck reserved for ship's officers.

quarter-evil, quarter-ill, *nn.* an infectious disease of cattle.

quartering, *n.* (*heraldry*) division of shield that contains several coats, denoting family's alliances

quarterly, *a.* and *adv.* (occurring) every quarter of a year; (*heraldry*) in four, or two diagonally opposite, quarters of shield.—*n.* quarterly periodical.

quartermaster, *n.* (*abbr.* **Q.M.**) army officer in charge of stores; (*naut.*) petty officer in charge of steering etc. **q.-general,** *n.* (*abbr.* **Q.M.G.**) War Office official in charge of army supplies. **q.-sergeant,** *n.* N.C.O. assisting quartermaster.

quartern, *n.* fourth part of pint or peck; (also **q.-loaf**) four-pound loaf.

quarter-plate, *n.* plate, photograph, size $4\frac{1}{4} \times 3\frac{1}{4}$ in.

quarterstaff, *n.* staff 6 to 8 ft. long, used as two-handed weapon.

quartet, quartette, *n.* group of four; set of four singers or players; composition for four voices or instruments. (L. *quartus*, fourth)

quartile, *n.* (*astrol.*) aspect of planets separated by 90° longitude. (L. *quartus*, fourth)

quarto, *n.* (*abbr.* **4to**) book of sheets folded into four leaves; this size, commonly about 12 × 9 in. (L. *quartus*, fourth)

quartz, *n.* a mineral composed of pure crystalline silica. **quartzite,** *n.* quartz rock. (G. *quarz*)

quash, *v.t.* annul, make void; quell, suppress. (L. *quatere*, shake)

Quashee, *n.* nickname for negro. (common Ashantee name *Kwasi*)

quasi, *conj.* as it were.—*pref.* almost, apparently. (L.=as if)

quassia, *n.* a bitter tonic drug; S. American tree yielding it. (G. *Quassi*, who discovered its virtues)

quat, *n.* (*Shake.*) pimple.

quater-, *pref.* four times, used in **quatercentenary,** *n.* 400th anniversary; **quaternary,** *a.* of the number four, having four parts, (*geol.*) of most recent period, after Tertiary.—*n.* set of four things, the number four; **quaternion,** *n.* set of four; **quaternity,** *n.* four persons regarded as one. (L.)

quatorzain, *n.* fourteen-line poem, Shakespearian form of sonnet. (L. *quattuordecim*, fourteen)

quatrain, *n.* four-line stanza, rhymed alternately. (L. *quatuor*, four)

quatrefoil, *n.* (*archit.*) ornament like flower with four petals. (L. *quattuor*, four; *folium*, leaf)

quattrocento, *n.* fifteenth century in Italian art. **quattrocentist,** *n.* artist of this period. (It.=four hundred, used for 1400)

quaver, *v.i.* and *t.* tremble, vibrate; trill; say in tremulous tones.—*n.* quavering, trill; (*mus.*) note equal to half a crotchet. **quavery,** *a.*

quay, *n.* wharf, landing-place. **quayage,** *n.* quay dues or accommodation. (O.F. *kay*)

queachy, *a.* shaky, yielding under feet like bog. (O.E. *cweccan*, shake)

quean, *n.* brazen woman, hussy; (*Scot.*) girl. (O.E. *cwene*, woman)

queasy, *a.* inclined to, producing, nausea; easily upset; over-scrupulous.

quebracho, *n.* S. American tree with hard timber; its medicinal bark. (Sp. *quebrar*, break; *hacha*, axe)

quebrada, *n.* ravine. (Sp.)

queen, *n.* female sovereign; king's wife; best of her kind, belle; perfect female of bee, wasp etc.; a court-card; a piece at chess; (*Amer. sl.*) lady.—*v.t.* and *i.* make queen; (*chess*) become queen. **Q. Anne is dead,** stale news. **Q. Anne's Bounty,** fund for augmenting incomes of poor English clergy. **q. consort,** king's wife, **q. dowager,** king's widow. **q. it,** play the queen. **q. mother,** queen dowager who is mother of king or queen. **q. of the meadows,** meadow-sweet. **Q.'s Bench, Counsel** etc., corresponding to King's when queen is reigning. **q.'s metal,** alloy of tin etc. like pewter. **q.-cake,** *n.* small currant cake. **q.-post,** *n.* upright from tie-beam to rafters. **queendom, queenhood, queenship** *nn.* **queening,** *n.* kind of apple. **queenly,** *a.* like a queen, regal. (O.E. *cwén*)

queer, *a.* odd, strange, curious; suspicious, shady; out of sorts, giddy; (*sl.*) drunk.—*v.t.* put out of order. **in Q. Street,** (*sl.*) in trouble. **q. the pitch,** spoil chance of success.

queet, *n.* (*Scot.*) ankle. (*coot*)

quell, *v.t.* and *i.* put down, suppress, crush; restrain; (*Spens.*) kill; perish. —*n.* (*Shake.*) slaying. (O.E. *cwellan*)

quench, *v.t.* put out, extinguish; cool; suppress; slake (thirst). **quencher,** *n.* (*sl.*) drink. **quenchless,** *a.* (*poet.*) unquenchable.

quenelle, *n.* ball of savoury meat or fish paste. (F.)

quercetum, *n.* oak plantation. **quercine,** *a.* of the oak. **quercite,** *n.* sweet crystalline compound got from acorns. (L. *quercus*, oak)

querimonious, *a.* querulous, complaining. (L. *queri*, complain)

querist, *n.* one who asks questions. (*query*)

quern, *n.* hand-mill for grinding corn etc. (O.E. *cweorn*)

querulous, *a.* complaining, fretful, peevish. (L. *queri*, complain)

query, *n.* question; interrogation-mark.—*v.t.* and *i.* inquire, ask; call in question, dispute accuracy of. (L. *quaerere*, inquire)

quesal, same as **quetzal.**

quest, *n.* search, pursuit; (*arch.*) inquest.—*v.i.* and *t.* search (about) for, seek. (L. *quaerere*, seek)

question, *n.* inquiry; interrogative sentence; subject of discussion; problem, concern, affair; (*Shake.*) conversation. — *v.t.* and *i.* ask questions (of); call in question. **be a q. of,** be dependent on. **call in q.,** challenge truth of. **in q.,** under discussion. **open q.,** still unsettled. **out of the q.,** that cannot be considered. **pop the q.,** (*sl.*) propose marriage. **put the q.,** take vote. **put to the q.,** (*arch.*) torture to extort confession. **q.-mark,** *n.* mark of interrogation (?). **questionable,** *a.* disputed, doubtful; not clearly true or honest. **questioner,** *n.* **questionless,** *a.* undoubted.—*adv.* indubitably. **questionnaire, questionary,** *nn.* series of formal questions, interrogatory. (L. *quaerere*, seek)

quetzal, *n.* large brilliantly coloured Central American bird, national emblem of Guatemala. (Aztec *quetzalli*, its green tail-feather)

queue, *n.* hanging plait of hair, pigtail; line of people, vehicles etc. awaiting turn.—*v.i.* form, wait in, queue. (L. *cauda*, tail)

quey, *n.* (*Scot.*) young cow, heifer.

quhat, quhilk, *Old Scots* spelling of **what, whilk.**

quibble, *n.* petty evasion; merely verbal point; play on words.—*v.i.* use quibbles; trifle in argument, shuffle.

quich, *v.i.* (*Spens.*) stir, move. (O.E. *cweccan*, cause to quake)

quick, *a.* rapid, speedy; hasty; lively, alert, sensitive; (*arch.*) living.—*adv.* quickly.—*n.* sensitive flesh below nails or sore; seat of feeling. **q. march, time,** ordinary military marching step, about 3½ miles an hour. **q.-change,** *a.* changing costume quickly. **q.-firing,** *a.* shooting in rapid succession. **q.-firer,** *n.* machine-gun. **q.-tempered,** *a.* irascible. (O.E. *cwicu*)

quickbeam, *n.* rowan-tree.

quicken, *v.t.* and *i.* make alive, come to life; stir, stimulate; hasten, accelerate.

quicklime, *n.* unslaked lime.

quickly, *adv.* speedily; without delay.

quicksand, *n.* loose sand mixed with water, in which man, animal, ship etc. may be swallowed up.

quickset, *a.* (of hedge) made of living plants, esp. hawthorn.—*n.* live slip set in ground, hedge of these.

quicksilver, *n.* mercury; mercurial temperament.—*v.t.* coat with mixture of mercury and tin.

quickstep, *n.* fast foxtrot.

Quicunque vult, Athanasian creed. (L. =whoever will, opening words)

quid, *n.* lump of tobacco for chewing. (*cud*)

quid, *n.* (*sl., pl.* same) pound, £1.

quiddity, *n.* essence of a thing; captious subtlety, quibble. **quiddle,** *v.i.* waste time in trifling. (L. *quid*, what)

quidnunc, *n.* gossip, busybody, newsmonger. (L.=what now)

quid pro quo, thing given as compensation. (L.=something for something)

quien sabe? who knows? (Sp.)

quiesce, *v.i.* become quiet or still. **quiescent,** *a.* dormant, inactive, inert; silent. **quiescence, quiescency,** *nn.* (*quiet*)

quiet, *a.* silent, not noisy; still, not moving; gentle, not boisterous; unobtrusive, not showy; placid, calm; monotonous, uneventful.—*n.* stillness, peace; undisturbed state.—*v.t.* and *i.* make, become, quiet; calm, soothe. **quieten,** *v.t.* and *i.* quiet. **quietism,** *n.* passive attitude towards life, esp. as form of religious mysticism. **quietist,** *n.* adherent of this. **quietistic,** *a.* **quietude,** *n.* quietness, repose. **quietus,** *n.* final riddance; (*arch.*) quittance, receipt; (*sl.*) death-blow. (L. *quies*)

quiff, *n.* curl plastered down on forehead.

Qui hi, nickname for Anglo-Indian, esp. in Bengal. (Urdu *koi hai?* is any one there?)

quill, *n.* large feather; hollow stem of this; pen made of it; plectrum; musical pipe of reed; weaver's spindle; spine of porcupine.—*v.t.* wind on spindle; crimp. **q.-driver,** *n.* writer.

quillet, *n.* verbal subtlety, quibble.

quilt, *n.* coverlet of two cloths sewn together with padding between; counterpane.—*v.t.* stitch together like quilt; pad; (*sl.*) thrash. (L. *culcita*, cushion)

quin, *abbr.* of **quintuplet.**

quinary, *a.* of the number five; having five parts. **quinate,** *a.* (of leaf) having five leaflets. (L. *quinque*, five)

quince, *n.* yellowish pear-shaped fruit with acid taste; tree bearing it. (*Cydonia* in Crete)

quincentenary, *n.* 500th anniversary. (irregular for *quingentenary*)

quinch, *v.i.* (*Spens.*) stir.

quincunx, *n.* arrangement of five things in form of four corners and centre of square. **quincuncial,** *a.* (L.)

quingentenary, *a.* of, in, 500th year. —*n.* 500th anniversary. (L. *quingenti*, 500)

quinine, (*med.*) **quinia,** *n.* bitter alkaloid found in bark of cinchona; its sulphate, used as febrifuge and tonic. **quinize,** *v.t.* saturate, overdose, with quinine. **quinism,** *n.* (Peruvian *kina*, bark)

quinquagenarian, *a.* and *n.* (person) fifty years old. **quinquagenary,** *n.* fiftieth anniversary. (L. *quinquaginta*, fifty)

Quinquagesima, *n.* (also **Q. Sunday**) Sunday before Lent. (L. *quinquaginta*, fifty)

quinqu(e)-, L.=five, used in **quinquangular** *a.* five-angled; **quinque-**

costate, *a.* five-ribbed; **quinquennial,** *a.* lasting, occurring every, five years; **quinquenniad, quinquennium,** *nn.* period of five years; **quinquelateral,** *a.* and *n.* five-sided (figure); **quinquepartite,** *a.* of five parts, shared by five; **quinquereme,** *n.* galley with five banks of oars; **quinquifid,** *a.* cleft in five; **quinquivalent,** *a.* (*chem.*) having a valency of five.

quinquina, *n.* cinchona bark; tree producing it. (Peruvian *kinkina*)

quinsy, *n.* inflammation of throat, suppurative tonsillitis. (Gk. *kuōn*, dog; *angchein*, throttle)

quint, *n.* sequence of five cards of same suit in piquet; (*mus.*) interval of fifth. (L. *quintus*, fifth)

quintain, *n.* post with sandbag on pivot, used for practising tilting; tilting at this. (O.F. *quintaine*)

quintal, *n.* measure of weight, 112 or 100 lb. (Arab. *qintār*)

quintan, *a.* and *n.* (fever, ague) recurring every fourth day. (L. *quintus*, fifth, counting inclusively)

quinte, *n.* fifth fencing thrust or parry. (F.)

quintessence, *n.* concentrated extract; purest form, embodiment. **quintessential,** *a.* most typical. (L.L. *quinta essentia*, fifth essence)

quintet, quintette, *n.* group of five; set of five singers or players; composition for five voices or instruments. (L. *quintus*, fifth)

quintillion, *n.* fifth power of million (1 with 30 ciphers); (U.S. and France) sixth power of thousand (1 with 18 ciphers)

quintroon, *n.* offspring of white and octoroon, person one-sixteenth negro. (Sp. *quinterón*)

quintuple, *a.* fivefold; of five parts or parties; five times greater than.—*v.t.* and *i.* multiply by five. **quintuplet,** *n.* one of five children born at a birth. **quintuplicate,** *v.t.* multiply by five; make five copies of.—*a.* fivefold.—*n.pl.* five similar examples. **quintuplication,** *n.* (L. *quintus*, fifth)

quip, *n.* witty saying, epigram; clever hit, repartee; quibble.

quipu, *n.* knotted cord of various colours used by ancient Peruvians in place of writings. (Peruvian=knot)

quire, *n.* 24 sheets of writing-paper, $\frac{1}{20}$ ream; one of the folded sheets sewn together in bookbinding; (*obs.*) small book. (L. *quattuor*, four)

quire, *arch.* for choir.

Quirinal, *n.* Italian Court or Government. (name of palace)

quirk, *n.* quip, quibble; trick of gesture, flourish in writing; (*archit.*) groove in moulding.

quirt, *n.* (*Amer.*) riding-whip of plaited leather.—*v.t.* lash with this.

quisling, *n.* traitor who aids invading enemy, esp. by forming puppet government to regularize their conquest of his country. (person)

quit, *v.t.* and *i.* (*past, p.p.* **quitted** or **quit**) leave, go away from; give up, abandon; behave (oneself); (*poet.*) requite; (*Shake.*) absolve, acquit.—*a.* rid (of); discharged. **q.-rent,** *n.* payment by landholder in place of service. **quits,** *a.* on equal terms by payment or revenge. **cry quits,** abandon quarrel etc. (L. *quies*, quiet)

quitch, *n.* couch-grass. (O.E. *cwice*)

quite, *adv.* entirely, completely. **q. so,** I entirely agree. **q. the thing,** fashionable. (*quit*)

quits, see **quit.**

quittance, *n.* release from obligation; receipt; requital. **quitter,** *n.* one who deserts post, shirker. (*quit*)

quiver, *v.i.* and *t.* tremble, shake, shiver.—*n.* vibration.

quiver, *n.* case for holding arrows. (O.F. *cuivre*)

qui vive? who goes there? **on the** *q. v.*, on the alert. (F.=long live who? i.e. on which side are you?)

quixotic, *a.* extravagantly generous and chivalrous like Don Quixote. **quixotism, quixotry,** *nn.* quixotic conduct or ideals.

quiz, *v.t.* and *i.* make fun of, banter; puzzle; stare impudently (at); (*Amer.*) examine, coach.—*n.* practical joke or joker; riddle, puzzle; odd person, queer fish. **quizzing-glass,** *n.* single eyeglass, often with handle. **quizzical,** *a.* bantering, chaffing; comical, eccentric.

quoad, adv. as regards. *q. hoc*, in this respect. (L.)

quod, *n.* (*sl.*) prison.—*v.t.* imprison.

quod, pron. which. *q. erat demonstrandum*, (*abbr.* **Q.E.D.**) which was to be proved. *q. erat faciendum*, (*abbr.* **Q.E.F.**) which was to be made. *q. vide*, (*abbr. q.v.*) which see (in cross-references etc.). **quodlibet,** *n.* subtle or moot point; pedantic argument; (*mus.*) medley. (L.)

quoif, same as **coif.**

quoin, *n.* external angle of building; corner-stone; wedge.—*v.t.* fix, wedge, with quoin. (*coin*)

quoit, *n.* ring or disk of iron, rope etc.; (*pl.*) game of throwing these near or on to peg.

quondam, *a.* that was, former. (L.= formerly)

quorum, *n.* number that must be present at a meeting to make its proceedings valid. (L.=of whom)

quota, *n.* part, share, to be contributed or received. (L. *quotus*, how many)

quote, *v.t.* and *i.* repeat, copy (passage from); adduce by way of authority, cite; name current price, make estimate; (*print.*) enclose within quotation-marks; (*Shake.*) mark, set down. —*n.* (*colloq.*) passage quoted; (*pl.*) quotation-marks. **quotable,** *a.* worthy, fit, to be quoted. **quotation,**

n. quoting: passage or price quoted. **quotation-marks,** *n.pl.* punctuation-marks (' ' or " ") marking off quotation. **quotative,** *a.* of quotation. (L. *quotus,* how many)
quoth, *v.t.* said. **quotha,** *int.* (*arch.*) forsooth. (O.E. *cwethan,* say)
quotidian, *a.* daily; recurring every day; commonplace, trivial.—*n.* quotidian fever or ague. (L. *quotidie,* daily)
quotient, *n.* result got when one number is divided by another. **quotiety,** *n.* number as a category; numerical relationship. (L. *quot,* how many)
quo vadis? whither goest thou? (L.)
quo warranto, writ requiring person to show by what right he holds office etc. (L.L.=by what warrant)
Quran, same as **Koran.**

R

R. the three **R's,** reading, writing, and arithmetic.
Ra, *n.* Egyptian sun-god.
rabat, rabato, *n.* kind of ruff or neckband. (F.)
rabbet, *n.* groove cut lengthways on edge of board to receive projection of another.—*v.t.* cut rabbet in. (O.F. *rabat,* abatement)
rabbi, rabbin, *nn.* Jewish doctor of laws. **rabbinate,** *n.* status of rabbi; rabbis collectively. **rabbinic, rabbinical,** *aa.* **rabbinism,** *n.* teaching of rabbis and Talmud; rabbinic idiom. **rabbinist,** *n.* (Heb.=my master)
rabbit, *n.* burrowing animal of hare family; (*sl.*) duffer.—*v.i.* hunt rabbits. **Welsh r.,** toasted cheese.
rabbit, *v.t.* (*vulg.*) confound, drat.
rabble, *n.* iron bar for puddling. (L. *rutabulum,* fire-shovel)
rabble, *n.* disorderly crowd, mob; common herd. **rabblement,** *n.* tumult.
Rabelaisian, Rabelaesian, *a.* of Rabelais; coarsely and exuberantly humorous.—*n.* student of Rabelais.
rabid, *a.* furious, raging; fanatical; having rabies, mad. **rabidity,** *n.*
rabies, *n.* canine madness, hydrophobia. (L. *rabere,* rave)
raca, *a.* worthless, a Jewish term of reproach. (Chaldee *rēkā*)
raccoon, same as **racoon.**
race, *n.* root, esp. of ginger. (L. *radix*)
race, *n.* descendants of common ancestor; distinct variety, breed; noble birth; peculiar flavour; (*Shake.*) natural disposition. **r. suicide,** diminution of population by restriction of birth-rate. (It. *razza*)
race, *n.* contest of speed; swift current of water; current driving mill-wheel; course (of life).—*v.i.* and *t.* compete (with), enter, in race; go at full speed or too fast. **r.-card,** *n.* programme of races. **r.-meeting,** *n.* horse-racing fixture. **racecourse,** *n.* ground for horse races. **racehorse,** *n.* one bred for racing. (O.N. *rás*)
raceme, *n.* cluster of small separate flowers growing on stalks along central stem. **racemose,** *a.* (L. *racemus,* bunch of grapes)
rachis, *n.* (*pl.* **rachides**) spine; central axis of leaf etc. **rachitic,** *a.* **rachitis,** *n.* inflammation of spine, rickets. (Gk. *rhachis*)
racial, *a.* of race.
rack, *n.* stand or holder for hats, plates, fodder etc.; shelf in railway carriage; instrument for torture by stretching; bar with teeth fitting to cog-wheel.—*v.t.* and *i.* torture on rack; torment, strain; oppress. **r. one's brains,** think hard. **r.-railway,** *n.* one with cogged central rail. **r.-rent,** *n.* utmost or extortionate rent.—*v.t.* impose this on. **r.-renter,** *n.*
rack, *n.* driving clouds; destruction.
rack, *n.* horse's gait in which two feet on each side are lifted at same time. —*v.i.* go thus.
rack, *v.t.* pour off (wine) from lees. (Provençal *arracar*)
rack, *n.* arrack. (abbr.)
racket, racquet, *n.* bat with network of gut used in tennis; snow-shoe; (*pl.*) game like tennis played in four-walled court. (F. *raquette*)
racket, *n.* noise, din; bustle; (*sl.*) scheme, esp. for getting money illegally.—*v.i.* lead gay life; frolic. **stand the r.,** be answerable, pay. **racketeering,** *n.* (*Amer. sl.*) organized blackmail of traders by threats of violence. **racketeer,** *n.* **rackety,** *a.* rowdy; dissipated.
raconteur, *n.* (*fem. raconteuse*) teller of anecdotes. (F.)
racoon, *n.* furred climbing American animal allied to bear. (Algonquin)
racquet, see **racket.**
racy, *a.* strongly flavoured; piquant, spicy; spirited. (*race*)
rad, *n.* (*sl.*) radical. (abbr.)
raddle, *n.* red ochre.—*v.t.* plaster with rouge. (*ruddle*)
radial, *a.* of ray, radius, or radium; branching from centre like spokes of wheel. **radialize,** *v.t.* arrange radially. **radialization,** *n.*
radian, *n.* angle subtended at centre of circle by arc equal to radius, 57·2958°.
radiant, *a.* shining, brilliant; gay, beaming; emitting rays; transmitted by radiation.—*n.* point from which heat or light radiates. **radiance, radiancy,** *nn.* radiantness; brilliant light; dazzling beauty. (*radius*)

radiate, *v.t.* and *i.* emit (light, heat etc.) in rays; issue, spread abroad; branch out like spokes.—*a.* arranged radially. **radiation,** *n.* **radiative,** *a.* **radiator,** *n.* apparatus of hot pipes etc. for heating room; cooling device for motor-car engine. (*radius*)

radical, *a.* of, going to, root; basic, fundamental; inherent; thorough; of advanced liberal views.—*n.* radical politician; simple underived word; (*chem.*) base of a compound; (*math.*) root or root sign. **radicalism,** *n.* radical political doctrine. **radicle,** *n.* part of seed that develops into root; root-like subdivision of nerve or vein. (L. *radix,* root)

radio, *n.* wireless telegraphy, telephony, message, or receiving-set; X-rays.—*v.t.* telegraph by wireless, broadcast; photograph by X-rays; treat with radium. (L. *radius,* ray)

radioactive, *a.* emitting invisible rays that penetrate matter. **radioactivity,** *n.* (L. *radius,* ray)

radiocarpal, *a.* (*anat.*) of radius and wrist. (L. *carpus,* wrist)

radiochemistry, *n.* chemistry of the radioactive elements.

radiogoniometer, *n.* wireless direction-finding apparatus.

radiogram, *n.* wireless telegram. **radiograph,** *n.* X-ray photograph; sunshine-recording instrument.—*v.t.* photograph by X-rays. **radiographer, radiography,** *nn.* **radiographic, radiographical,** *aa.* (Gk. *graphein,* write)

radiolocation, *n.* system of detecting approach of aircraft by means of wireless. **radiolocator,** *n.*

radiology, *n.* science of X-rays and their medical application. **radiologist,** *n.* (Gk. *legein,* speak)

radiometer, *n.* instrument showing motion caused by action of light or measuring radiant energy.

radiophone, *n.* wireless telephone; instrument for producing sound by radiant energy. **radiophony,** *n.*

radioscopy, *n.* examination by X-rays. (Gk. *skopein,* view)

radiotelegram, *n.* wireless telegram. **radiotelegraphy,** *n.*

radiotelephone, *n.* wireless telephone. **radiotelephony,** *n.*

radiotherapeutics, radiotherapy, *nn.* medical treatment by X-rays.

radish, *n.* plant with fleshy root of pungent flavour. (L. *radix,* root)

radium, *n.* rare radioactive metallic element. (L. *radius,* ray)

radius, *n.* (*pl.* radii) straight line from centre of circle to circumference; thing like this, spoke; distance from given centre; sphere of activity; (*anat.*) thicker of the two forearm bones; (*bot.*) ray of flower. (L.=ray)

radix, *n.* (*pl.* **radices**) source, origin; (*math.*) basic number of numerical system. (L.=root)

radon, *n.* gaseous emanation of radium.

radula, *n.* rasp-like band forming tongue of mollusc. **radular,** *a.* (L. *radere,* scrape)

raffia, *n.* kind of palm; fibre from its leaves, used in basket-making etc. (Malagasy)

raffish, *a.* disreputable, fast-looking. (riff-*raff*)

raffle, *n.* kind of lottery in which those who have subscribed together for something decide by lot who is to have it.—*v.t.* and *i.* sell by, enter for, raffle. (O.F. *rafle,* a dice-game)

raffle, *n.* rubbish, lumber.

raft, *n.* (*Amer. colloq.*) large collection, crowd.

raft, *n.* flat floating structure of planks, logs etc.—*v.t.* and *i.* form into, convey on, work, raft. **rafter, raftsman,** *nn.* lumberman. (O.N. *raptr,* rafter)

rafter, *n.* one of the inclined beams supporting a roof.—*v.t.* furnish with these. (O.E. *ræfter*)

rag, *n.* shred of cloth; remnant, wisp; worthless newspaper: (*pl.*) tattered or shabby clothes. **r.-and-bone man,** dealer in household refuse. **r.-bag,** *n.* bag for odd scraps. **r.-bolt,** *n.* one with barbs to keep it tight. **r.-fair,** *n.* old-clothes sale. **r.-tag and bobtail,** riff-raff. (O.N. *rogg,* tuft of fur)

rag, *n.* a hard limestone; rough kind of slate.

rag, *v.t.* and *i.* (*colloq.*) play practical joke (on), be riotous; chaff, tease; scold.—*n.* rowdy scrimmage; joke, lark.

ragamuffin, *n.* ragged dirty person, gutter-snipe. **ragamuffinly,** *a.*

rage, *n.* violent anger, fury; frenzy, ardour; craze, fashion.—*v.i.* exhibit rage; rave, storm; be very prevalent or violent. **all the r.,** very popular. (L. *rabere,* rave)

ragged, *a.* jagged, frayed; rough, shaggy; torn, tattered; wearing rags; slipshod, lacking finish. **r. robin,** a pink-flowered wild plant. **r. school,** (*obs.*) free school for poor.

raggee, ragee, *n.* Indian millet. (Hind. *rāgī*)

Raglan, *n.* kind of loose overcoat. (Lord *Raglan*)

ragout, *n.* highly seasoned stew of meat and vegetables. (F. *ragoût*)

ragtime, *n.* strongly syncopated music, jazz.—*a.* farcical.

ragweed, ragwort, *nn.* a yellow-flowered wild plant.

rahat lakoum, Turkish delight. (Turk.)

raid, *n.* sudden incursion, foray; surprise visit by police.—*v.t.* and *i.* make raid (upon), plunder. **raider,** *n.* (O.E. *rād,* road)

rail, *n.* bar of fence etc.; one of lines forming track; (*pl.*) fence; railway shares.—*v.t.* furnish with rail, fence; send by rail. **by r.,** by railway. **off the rr.,** out of order. **r.-car,** *n.*

railway motor-car. **r.-chair,** *n.* metal clamp fixing rail to sleeper. (L. *regula,* rule)
rail, *v.i.* utter abuse, scoff. (F. *railler*)
rail, *n.* kinds of bird. **land-r.,** *n.* corncrake. **water-r.,** *n.* a wading-bird. (F. *râle*)
rail, *v.i.* (*Spens.*) flow, pour down.
railhead, *n.* terminus of railway, esp. one under construction.
railing, *n.* fence of rails and posts.
raillery, *n.* banter, chaff; good-humoured ridicule. (*rail*)
railroad, *n.* (*Amer.*) railway.—*v.t.* and *i.* send, go, by rail; (*colloq.*) push forward fast.
railway, *n.* track for trains; system of these, with rolling-stock, buildings etc.—*a.* of, used on, railway.
raiment, *n.* clothing, dress. (*array*)
rain, *n.* water falling from clouds in drops; shower, stream; (*pl.*) rainy season in tropics.—*v.i.* and *t.* fall in drops; pour down, shower upon. **r. cats and dogs,** rain violently. **r.-gauge,** *n.* instrument measuring rainfall. **rainbow,** *n.* arch of prismatic colours formed by sun's rays in rain, spray etc.—*a.* many-coloured. **rainbow trout,** Canadian kind. **raincoat,** *n.* rainproof. **rainfall,** *n.* amount of rain in given area. **rainproof,** *a.* and *n.* rain-resisting (overcoat). **rainy,** *a.* full of rain, wet. **rainy day,** time of need. (O.E. *regn*)
raise, *v.t.* cause to rise, elevate; lift, hold up; set upright; stir up, rouse; heighten, increase; originate, produce; evoke, conjure; breed, bring up; levy, collect; utter loudly; abandon (siege); (*naut.*) come within sight of.—*n.* (*Amer.*) rise in wages. **r. a dust,** (*colloq.*) make a row. **r. Cain, the devil, hell,** make a scene. **r. the wind,** (*sl.*) obtain money. (O.N. *reisa*)
raisin, *n.* dried grape. (L. *racemus,* bunch of grapes)
raison d'être, reason for existence, justification. *raisonné,* *a.* arranged systematically. (F.)
rait, same as **ret.**
raj, *n.* (*Anglo-Ind.*) rule, sway. **rajah,** *n.* Indian prince or ruler. **Rajput, Rajpoot,** *n.* member of Hindu warrior caste. (Hind.)
rake, *n.* long-handled pronged tool for gathering hay etc.; croupier's money-raking tool.—*v.t.* and *i.* use rake (on); scrape (together); ransack; sweep with gaze or shot, enfilade. **r. up,** stir up, revive (scandal etc.); (*Shake.*) cover up. **r.-off,** *n.* commission, esp. if illegal. (O.E. *raca*)
rake, *v.i.* and *t.* (of ship) project at upper part of bow or stern; (of mast etc.) incline, slope.—*n.* raking.
rake, *n.* dissolute or dissipated man, libertine. (*rakehell*)
rakehell, *n.* (*arch.*) rake, debauchee. **rakehelly,** *a.* (*rake; hell*)
rakish, *a.* dissolute, raffish; (of ship) smart, speedy-looking.
râle, *n.* rattling sound in lungs. (F).
rallentando, *a.* and *n.* (*mus.*) (passage played) gradually slower. (It.)
ralli car, ralli cart, light two-wheeled trap. (*Ralli,* first user)
ralline, *a.* of rail family of birds. (Mod. L. *rallus,* rail)
rally, *v.t.* and *i.* gather together; reassemble (scattered troops etc.); recover (strength), revive.—*n.* rallying, recovery; assembly, gathering; horseplay in pantomime; (*lawn tennis*) exchange of strokes. (F. *rallier*)
rally, *v.t.* chaff, tease. (*rail*)
ram, *n.* male sheep; battering engine; underwater beak on bow, warship with this; first sign of zodiac, which sun enters 21 March.—*v.t.* assail, pierce, with ram; press down, pack hard; crush, cram; butt. (O.E.)
Ramadan, *n.* ninth month of Mohammedan year; great fast in it. (Arab.)
ramal, *a.* of a branch. (L. *ramus,* branch)
ramble, *v.i.* walk without definite route, stroll about; talk, write, in desultory way; be delirious.—*n.* casual walk; discursive study. **rambler,** *n.* one who rambles; kinds of climbing rose. **rambling,** *a.* spread out, straggling; disconnected.
rambunctious, *a.* (*Amer.*) cantankerous, unruly.
rambutan, *n.* red fruit of an Indian tree. (Malay)
rameal, rameous, same as **ramal.**
ramekin, ramequin, *n.* dish of cheese, bread-crumbs etc., baked in small mould. (F.)
ramfeezle, *v.t.* (*Scot.*) weary out.
ramgunshock, *a.* (*Scot.*) rough.
ramie, *n.* Chinese stingless nettle; fibre from it. (Malay *rāmī*)
ramify, *v.i.* and *t.* spread in branches, subdivide. **ramification,** *n.* ramifying; system of branches. (L. *ramus,* branch; *facere,* make)
rammer, *n.* ramming-instrument, esp. paviour's.
rammish, *a.* rank-smelling. (*ram*)
ramose, *a.* (*bot.*) branching. (L. *ramus,* branch)
ramp, *v.i.* and *t.* rage, rampage; (of lion) stand on hind legs with fore-paws in air; (*archit.*) ascend to different level, furnish with ramp.—*n.* inclined plane, slope. (O.F. *ramper*)
ramp, *n.* and *v.i.* (*sl.*) attempt to get money under false pretences, swindle.
ramp, *n.* (*Shake.*) drab.
rampage, *v.i.* rage, rush about.—*n.* violent behaviour. **rampageous,** *a.*
rampallian, *n.* (*Shake.*) ruffian.
rampant, *a.* violent, dominant, rife; luxuriant; (*archit.*) with one abutment higher than other; (*heraldry*) reared up on hind legs, ramping. **rampancy,** *n.* (*ramp*)
rampart, *n.* defensive mound or wall;

protection.—*v.t.* defend with rampart. (L. *re-*, again; *ante*, before; *parare*, prepare)
rampion, *n.* campanula with edible root.
rampire, *arch.* form of **rampart.**
ramrod, *n.* rod for ramming home charge in muzzle-loading gun.
ramshackle, *a.* rickety, tumbledown.
ramson, *n.* (us. *pl.*) broad-leaved garlic; its root. (O.E. *hramsa*)
ramstam, *a.* (*Scot.*) reckless, headstrong.—*adv.* headlong.
ramulose, *a.* having many small branches. (L. *ramulus*, small branch)
ran, *n.* hank of twine 20 yds. long.
ran, see **run.**
rance, *n.* dark-red marble with blue and white veins.
ranch, *n.* American cattle farm; (*Amer. colloq.*) any farm.—*v.i.* manage ranch. **rancher, ranchman,** *nn.* one who runs or works on ranch. (Sp. *rancho*, mess)
rancid, *a.* (of fat etc.) having offensive taste, stale. **rancidity,** *n.* (L. *rancere*, be putrid)
rancour, *n.* inveterate hate, bitter spite. **rancorous,** *a.* malicious, malignant. (*rancid*)
rand, *n.* thin inner sole; (*S. Afr.*) ridge bordering valley of river. (O.E.=bank)
randan, *n.* boat for one sculler and two oarsmen.
randan, *n.* (*sl.*) spree.
randem, *adv.* and *n.* (carriage, team) with three horses in single file.
random, *a.* done haphazard, left to chance. **at r.,** haphazard, without aim. (O.F. *randon*, haste)
randy, *a.* boisterous, rowdy; lustful.—*n.* coarse-mannered woman, scold.
ranee, *n.* Indian princess, wife of rajah. (Hind. *rani*)
rang, see **ring.**
range, *v.t.* and *i.* set, arrange, in row; place in proper order; rove over, roam; reach, extend, run; vary between limits.—*n.* row, series, of mountains etc.; scope, compass; intellectual grasp; distance gun can fire, or from gun to target; practice-ground for shooting; kitchen stove. **r.-finder,** *n.* instrument for finding distance of target. **ranger,** *n.* rover; keeper of forest or park; senior Girl Guide; (*pl.*) mounted force. **rangy,** *a.* (*Amer.*) long and slender. (O.F. *rang*, rank)
rani, same as **ranee.**
ranine, *a.* of, like, frogs. (L. *rana*, frog)
rank, *n.* line of soldiers side by side; row of cabs; social class, grade, station.—*v.t.* and *i.* arrange in line; assign rank to, classify; hold position. **r. and fashion,** high society. **r. and file, the rr.,** common soldiers, ordinary people. **r. with,** be counted among. (O.F. *ranc*)
rank, *a.* over-luxuriant, coarse; flagrant, gross; foul-smelling, rancid; (*Shake.*) lustful. (O.E. *ranc*)
ranker, *n.* commissioned officer who has been promoted from the ranks.
rankle, *v.i.* fester; keep causing bitterness or resentment. (L. *draco*, serpent)
ransack, *v.t.* search thoroughly; plunder. (O.N. *rann*, house; *sækja*, seek)
ransom, *n.* release from captivity by payment; the price paid; compensation for immunity, blackmail.—*v.t.* secure release of by payment, redeem; expiate. **ransomer,** *n.* (L. *redemptio*)
rant, *v.i.* and *t.* use extravagant language, declaim theatrically; preach noisily.—*n.* bombast; (*Scot.*) rowdy frolic. **ranter,** *n.* noisy preacher; nickname for Primitive Methodist. (O.Du. *randten*, rave)
ranunculus, *n.* kinds of plant incl. buttercup. **ranunculaceous,** *a.* (L.)
ranz-des-vaches, *n.* Swiss herdsman's melody on Alpine horn. (Swiss F.)
rap, *n.* light blow, tap.—*v.t.* and *i.* strike lightly. **r. on the knuckles,** reproof. **r. out,** utter sharply. **take the r.,** (*Amer. sl.*) receive punishment.
rap, *n.* skein of yarn, about 120 yds.
rap, *n.* worthless thing, least bit.
rap, *v.t.* (*Shake.*) affect with rapture; seize.
rapacious, *a.* grasping, extortionate; greedy. **rapacity,** *n.* (L. *rapax*)
rape, *v.t.* seize and carry off by force; assault sexually, ravish.—*n.* raping.
rape, *n.* cabbage-like forage plant with oil-producing seeds. (L. *rapum*, turnip)
rape, *n.* grape-refuse, used in making vinegar. (F. *râpe*)
rape, *n.* division of Sussex.
rāphē, *n.* (*anat.*) seam-like junction. (Gk. *rhaphē*, seam)
raphia, same as **raffia.**
rapid, *a.* swift, quick; sudden, steep.—*n.* (us. *pl.*) part of river where current flows swiftly. **rapidity,** *n.* speed. (L. *rapidus*)
rapier, *n.* slender pointed sword for thrusting only. (F. *rapière*)
rapine, *n.* plundering, pillage. (L. *rapere*, seize)
raploch, *a.* and *n.* (*Scot.*) homespun.
rapparee, *n.* Irish irregular soldier or freebooter. (Ir. *rapaire*, pike)
rappee, *n.* coarse kind of snuff. (F. *râpé*, grated)
rapport, *n.* intimate relation, accord. *en r.*, in harmony. (F.)
rapprochement, *n.* re-establishment of cordial relations between states. (F.)
rapscallion, *n.* rascal, scamp.
rapt, *a.* carried away, enraptured; absorbed, intent. **raptorial,** *a.* predatory; (*zool.*) of the order of birds of prey. **rapture,** *n.* intense delight, ecstasy; (*Shake.*) plundering; fit. **raptured,** *a.* enraptured. **rapturous,** *a.* ecstatic. (L. *rapere*, seize)
rara avis, person, thing, of type seldom met with. (L.=rare bird)

rare, *a.* thin, not dense; scattered, infrequent; scarce, uncommon; exceptionally good. **r. earths**, oxides of certain metals. (L. *rarus*)
rare, *a.* (*Amer.*) underdone. (O.E. *hrér*, half-cooked)
rarebit, incorrect form of Welsh **rabbit.**
raree-show, *n.* portable peep-show.
rarefy, *v.t.* and *i.* make, become, less dense; refine, spiritualize. **rarefaction**, *n.* **rarefactive**, *a.* (L. *rarus*, rare; *facere*, make)
rarely, *adv.* seldom; uncommonly.
rarity, *n.* rareness; rare object.
rascal, *n.* rogue, knave; (*Shake.*) young or inferior deer.—*a.* (*arch.*) of the mob. **rascaldom**, *n.* rascals collectively. **rascalism, rascality**, *nn.* knavery. **rascally**, *a.* dishonest, base. (O.F. *rascaille*, rabble)
rase, see **raze.**
rash, *a.* reckless, incautious, hasty; precipitate; (*Shake.*) pressing; quick-acting.
rash, *n.* eruption on skin.
rash, *v.t.* (*Shake.*) stick, dash.
rasher, *n.* thin slice of bacon or ham.
rasorial, *a.* of the order of birds that scratch for food, gallinaceous. (L. *radere*, scrape)
rasp, *colloq.* for **raspberry.**
rasp, *n.* coarse file.—*v.t.* and *i.* rub with rasp; scrape roughly; sound harshly; grate (on), irritate. **raspatory**, *n.* surgical rasp. (O.F. *raspe*)
raspberry, *n.* red or yellow fruit; shrub yielding it; (*sl.*) gesture, sound, of dislike or derision. **r. cane**, raspberry plant.
rasse, *n.* kind of civet-cat. (Javanese *rase*)
rat, *n.* long-tailed rodent like large mouse; cowardly person; turncoat; (*Amer. sl.*) blackleg.—*v.i.* hunt rats; desert cause or political party. **ratter**, *n.* (O.E. *ræt*)
rat, same as **drat.**
rata, *n.* New Zealand tree with hard red wood. (Maori)
ratable, *a.* liable to payment of rates; (*arch.*) proportional.
ratafia, ratafee, *n.* liqueur, biscuit, flavoured with fruit-kernels. (F.)
ratal, *n.* amount on which rates are assessed.
ratan, see **rattan.**
rataplan, *n.* sound of drum.—*v.i.* and *t.* beat, play on, drum. (F.)
rat-a-tat, same as **rat-tat.**
ratchet, ratch, *nn.* set of teeth in bar or wheel with catch allowing motion in one direction only.—*v.t.* fit with ratchet. **r.-wheel**, *n.* wheel with ratchet. (F. *rochet*, bobbin)
rate, *n.* amount of one thing measured per unit of something else; standard of reckoning; tariff, charge; degree, quality; speed; (*pl.*) municipal taxes.—*v.t.* and *i.* estimate value of; assess, rank; consider, regard as. **at any r.**, in any case. **at that r.**, if that is so. (L. *reri*, reckon)
rate, *v.t.* scold, chide.
rate, same as **ret.**
ratel, *n.* S. African carnivorous animal, honey-badger. (S. Afr. Du.)
ratepayer, *n.* one who pays rates, householder.
rath, *n.* Celtic hill-fort. (Ir.)
rathaus, *n.* town hall. (G.)
rathe, *a.* (*arch.*) early-blooming, early. (O.E. *hrathe*, quickly)
rather, *adv.* more truly, to a greater extent; preferably, more readily; somewhat, slightly; (*colloq.*) yes, certainly. (O.E. *hrathe*, quickly)
rathskeller, *n.* (*Amer.*) beer-saloon or restaurant in basement. (G.=town hall cellar)
ratify, *v.t.* confirm formally, make valid by signature. **ratification**, *n.* (L. *reri*, reckon; *facere*, make)
ratine, *n.* fabric like sponge-cloth. (F.)
rating, *n.* assessment; (*naut.*) man's grading on ship's books; tonnage-class of racing yacht; (*pl.*) ship's crew.
rating, *n.* reprimand, scolding.
ratio, *n.* number of times one thing contains another, quantitative relation. (L.=reckoning, reason)
ratiocinate, *v.i.* reason, deduce conclusions. **ratiocination**, *n.* **ratiocinative**, *a.* (*ratio*)
ration, *n.* fixed daily allowance of food; (*pl.*) provisions.—*v.t.* limit to fixed quantity. (*ratio*)
rational, *a.* able to reason; sane, sensible, reasonable; of, based on, reasoning; (*math.*) expressible without radical sign, opp. to surd.—*n.pl.* women's knickerbockers. (*ratio*)
rationale, *n.* logical basis; reasoned theory.
rationalism, *n.* religion based on reason and rejecting revelation; doctrine that reason is only source of certain knowledge. **rationalist**, *a.* and *n.* (adherent) of rationalism. **rationalistic**, *a.* **rationality**, *n.* rationalness.
rationalize, *v.t.* and *i.* bring into conformity with reason; explain (away) by rationalism; rely solely or unduly on reason; reorganize (industry) scientifically so as to avoid waste; (*math.*) clear of surds; (*psycho-anal.*) supply reasonable cause for (apparently unreasonable emotion). **rationalization**, *n.*
ratite, *a.* (*zool.*) of ostrich kind, with keelless breast-bone. (L. *ratis*, raft)
ratline, ratlin, ratling, *n.* (us. *pl.*) one of pieces of rope fastened across shrouds forming steps of rigging.
ratoon, *n.* shoot from root-stock of sugarcane which has been cut. (Sp. *retoño*, sprout)
ratsbane, *n.* rat-poison, esp. white arsenic.
rattan, ratan, *n.* climbing palm with jointed stem; cane made of this. (Malay *rotan*)

rat-tat, *n.* rapping sound. (*imit.*)

ratten, *v.t.* molest (non-union worker etc.) by taking away or damaging his tools.

rattle, *v.i.* and *t.* make, cause to make, series of sharp noises, clatter; recite rapidly, chatter; move, ride, briskly; (*sl.*) disconcert, fluster.—*n.* rattling sound; instrument making it; voluble talk or talker. **r.-brain, r.-pate,** *nn.* empty-headed person. **rattler,** *n.* (*sl.*) first-rate specimen; (*Amer. sl.*) rattlesnake. **rattlesnake,** *n.* venomous snake with rattle in tail. **rattletrap,** *n.* rickety vehicle; knick-knack. **rattling,** *a.* (*sl.*) brisk, spanking; first-rate.—*adv.* extremely.

ratty, *a.* full of, like, rats; (*sl.*) angry, irritable, snappish.

raucle, *a.* (*Scot.*) rough; fearless.

raucous, *a.* hoarse, harsh-sounding. (L. *raucus*)

raught, (*Spens.*) *past* of **reach.**

raughty, *a.* (*sl.*) jolly, first-class.

raupo, *n.* New Zealand bulrush used for thatching roofs.

rauque, *a.* raucous. (F.)

ravage, *v.t.* and *i.* plunder, lay waste; ruin, make havoc.—*n.* devastation; (*pl.*) effects of this. **ravager,** *n.* (L. *rapere*, seize)

rave, *v.i.* speak wildly, incoherently, or rapturously; (of storm) roar, rage.

rave, *n.* rail of cart; (*pl.*) side-pieces to increase cart's capacity.

ravel, *v.t.* and *i.* entangle or disentangle; fray out; make, become, complicated. — *n.* entanglement, knot; frayed end; complication.

ravelin, *n.* outwork with two faces forming salient angle. (F.)

raven, *n.* large bird like crow with glossy black feathers.—*a.* jet-black. (O.E. *hræfn*)

raven, *v.i.* and *t.* prowl for prey; seek plunder; be ravenous, eat voraciously. **ravenous,** *a.* voracious; famished. **ravin,** *n.* (*arch.*) plunder, rapine; spoil. (L. *rapina*, rapine)

ravine, *n.* deep narrow gorge, large gully. (F.)

ravish, *v.t.* transport with delight, enrapture; seize and carry off; commit rape upon; (*Shake.*) pollute. **ravishing,** *a.* entrancing, captivating. **ravishment,** *n.* (L. *rapere*)

raw, *a.* uncooked; in natural state, crude; untrained, inexperienced; sore, skinned; damp, chilly; (*Amer. colloq.*) angry.—*n.* galled place, sore.—*v.t.* rub into rawness. **r. deal,** (*Amer.*) unfair treatment. **r. material,** out of which finished article is made. **r.-bones,** *a.* gaunt. **rawhide,** *a.* of untanned hide.—*n.* rawhide whip. (O.E. *hréaw*)

rax, *v.t.* (*Scot.*) reach out, hand.

ray, *n.* single line, narrow beam, of light or heat; line of radiation; glimmering, remnant (of hope etc.); outer part of composite flower.—*v.i.* and *t.* issue in rays, radiate. **Röntgen rr., X-rr.,** *n.* kind emitted by radioactive substances and able to penetrate opaque matter. (L. *radius*)

ray, *n.* large sea-fish with broad flat body. (L. *raia*)

ray, *n.* second note in sol-fa notation.

ray, *v.t.* (*Shake.*) befoul. (*array*)

rayah, *n.* non-Moslem Turkish subject. (Arab. *ra'iyah*, flock)

rayon, *n.* artificial silk. (F.)

raze, rase, *v.t.* level to the ground, destroy; wipe out, erase; graze. (L. *radere*, scrape)

razee, *n.* ship with upper deck cut away. (*raze*)

razor, *n.* instrument for shaving.—*v.t.* shave, cut, close. **r.-back,** *n.* sharp ridge: rorqual; (*Amer.*) kind of hog. **razorbill,** *n.* a sea-bird. **r.-fish, r.-shell,** *nn.* shell-fish resembling handle of razor. (*raze*)

razure, *n.* (*Shake.*) effacement. (*raze*)

razzia, *n.* raid, slave-collecting expedition. (Arab. *ghasw*, make war)

razzle-dazzle, razzle, *n.* (*sl.*) spree; excitement; kind of merry-go-round.

re, (*mus.*) same as **ray.**

re, prep. in the matter of, concerning. *re infecta*, with one's object unaccomplished. (L. *res*, thing)

re-, *pref.* again, afresh, as in **rejoin, re-reckon** (in this sense attachable to any verb); in return, as in **recompense**; against, as in **resist**; behind, as in **remain**; secretly, as in **recluse**; off, away, as in **relax**; intensive, as in **redolent**; un-, as in **reprobate.**

reach, *v.t.* and *i.* stretch out, extend; pass, hand over; arrive at, get as far as; attain, realize.—*n.* act, power, of reaching; grasp, mental range; compass, scope; straight stretch of river. **r.-me-down,** *a.* and *n.* (*sl.*) ready-made (suit). (O.E. *rǽcan*)

re-act, *v.t.* perform a second time.

react, *v.i.* respond to stimulus; have mutual or reverse effect; revolt; (*chem.*) cause, undergo, change. **reactance,** *n.* (*electr.*) inductive resistance. **reaction,** *n.* reacting; revulsion of feeling; exhaustion after excitement etc.; opposition to new ideas; (*chem.*) action set up by one substance in another. **reactionary,** *a.* and *n.* (person) opposed to progress. **reactionist,** *n.* **reactive,** *a.* **reactivity,** *n.*

read, same as **rede.**

read, *v.t.* and *i.* (*past, p.p.* **read**) comprehend, utter (written or printed matter); find in print; study by reading; interpret, divine; register; (*Spens.*) guess; discern; take (for). —*n.* spell of reading.—*a.* versed, instructed. **r. into,** take to be implicit in. **r. lesson to,** admonish. **r. oneself in,** hold first service in parish. **r. up,** study carefully. **readable,** *a.* legible; interesting. **readability,** *n.* (O.E. *rǽdan*)

readdress, *v.t.* change address on (letter) when forwarding it.

reader, *n.* one who reads; publisher's private critic; printer's proof-corrector; university lecturer; reading-book. **readership,** *n.* lectureship.

readily, *adv.* in a ready manner; willingly, easily. **readiness,** *n.* prepared state; quickness; prompt compliance.

reading, *n.* perusal; matter to be read; book-knowledge; public recital; text of passage; interpretation, view; presentation of bill in parliament. **r.-book,** *n.* one for teaching reading. **r.-glass,** *n.* magnifying-glass for hand.

readjourn, *v.t.* adjourn again.

readjust, *v.t.* make fresh adjustment in. **readjustment,** *n.*

readmit, *v.t.* admit again. **readmission, readmittance,** *nn.*

ready, *a.* prepared, fit for use; willing; inclined, apt; prompt, quick; handy. *adv.* beforehand; quickly.—*n.* (*sl.*) ready money.—*v.t.* get ready. **r. money,** cash. **r. reckoner,** book of tables for use in commerce etc. **r.-made,** *a.* made in standard sizes, not to measure.

reaffirm, *v.t.* affirm over again.

reagent, *n.* (*chem.*) substance used to detect presence of another by reaction. **reagency,** *n.* reacting.

real, *n.* Spanish monetary unit, about 2½*d.*; old Spanish silver coin, worth about 6*d.* (Sp.)

real, *a.* actual, existing, not imaginary; genuine, natural, not artificial; (*law*) immovable, consisting of land or houses.—*adv.* (*Amer. colloq.*) really. **R. Presence,** actual presence of the body and blood of Christ in the eucharist. **the r. thing,** not a makeshift. (L. *res*, thing)

realgar, *n.* red arsenic, used as pigment and in fireworks. (Arab. *rahj al-ghār*, powder of the mine)

realism, *n.* practical outlook, freedom from prejudice; (*art, fiction*) representation of things, often in minute detail, as they really are, without concealing what is ugly or sordid; (*philos.*) doctrine that physical world has objective existence (opp. to idealism); (*scholasticism*) doctrine that general ideas have objective existence (opp. to nominalism). **realist,** *a.* and *n.* (adherent) of realism; practical (person). **realistic,** *a.* matter-of-fact, not visionary; lifelike; of realism.

reality, *n.* being real; actual fact or thing; likeness to original; real nature. **in r.,** in fact.

realize, *v.t.* be fully conscious of, apprehend; make (hope etc.) accomplished fact; cause to appear real; convert into money, be sold for. **realization,** *n.*

really, *adv.* in fact, actually; positively. **r.?** is that so?

realm, *n.* kingdom, country; domain, region. (L. *regalis*, royal)

realpolitik, *n.* doctrine that state's policy should be determined entirely by its material interests. (G.)

realtor, *n.* (*Amer.*) real-estate agent, dealer in land for development. **realty,** *n.* real estate (opp. to personalty).

ream, *n.* 20 quires, 480 sheets, of paper; (*pl.*) vast quantity. **long, printer's, r.,** 516 sheets. (Arab. *rizmah*, bundle)

ream, *v.t.* bore out (hole in metal) to wider diameter; (*naut.*) open (seam) for caulking. **reamer,** *n.* tool for reaming. (O.E. *rýman*)

ream, *n.* and *v.t.* and *i.* (*Scot.*) cream; froth.

reanimate, *v.t.* revive; infuse new spirit into. **reanimation,** *n.*

reap, *v.t.* cut (grain), gather (harvest); obtain as fruit of labour. **reaping-hook,** *n.* sickle. **reaper,** *n.* harvester, reaping-machine. (O.E. *rípan*)

reappear, *v.i.* appear again. **reappearance,** *n.*

reappoint, *v.t.* appoint again. **reappointment,** *n.*

rear, *v.t.* and *i.* raise aloft; erect, build; breed, grow, bring up; (of horse) stand up on hind legs. (O.E. *ræran*)

rear, *n.* back part or position, esp. of army; (*colloq.*) rump; water-closet.—*a.* hinder. **r.-admiral,** *n.* rank below vice-admiral. **r.-arch,** *n.* inner arch of doorway when differing from outer. **rearguard,** *n.* troops protecting rear. (*arrear*)

rearm, *v.t.* and *i.* equip (oneself) with weapon of new pattern; take up arms afresh. **rearmament,** *n.*

rearmost, *a.* farthest back.

rearmouse, same as **reremouse.**

rearrange, *v.t.* arrange anew. **rearrangement,** *n.*

rearward, *a.* and *n.* (position) in the rear.—*adv.* (also **rearwards**) towards the rear.

reason, *n.* thinking faculty; sanity, common sense; motive, cause; (*Shake.*) account, talk.—*v.i.* and *t.* think, express, logically; draw conclusions, conclude; use argument (with), persuade by argument. **by r. of,** because of. **in r.,** within moderation. **listen to r.,** let oneself be persuaded. **stand to r.,** follow logically. **reasonable,** *a.* able to reason; sensible; not exorbitant, moderate, fair. (L. *ratio*)

reassemble, *v.i.* and *t.* come, bring, together again.

reassert, *v.t.* assert again. **reassertion,** *n.*

reassure, *v.t.* restore to confidence, free from anxiety; (us. **re-assure**) reinsure. **reassurance,** *n.*

Réaumur, *a.* (*abbr.* **R.**) using thermometer-scale with freezing-point 0°, boiling-point 80°. (inventor)

reave, *v.t.* and *i.* (*past, p.p.* **reft**) deprive, take by violence; plunder, reive. (O.E. *réafian*)

rebaptize, *v.t.* baptize anew.
rebate, *n.* deduction from sum to be paid, discount.—*v.t.* diminish, deduct from; blunt, dull. (L. *battuere*, beat)
rebate, same as **rabbet.**
rebato, same as **rabato.**
rebec, rebeck, *n.* ancient three-stringed fiddle. (Arab. *rebab*)
rebel, *v.i.* take arms against ruling power, revolt; resist control or authority.—*n.* one who rebels, insurgent.—*a.* rebellious. **rebellion,** *n.* armed resistance to established government, insurrection; defiance of authority. **rebellious,** *a.* of, engaged in, rebellion; (*med.*) difficult to treat, refractory. (L. *bellum*, war)
rebellow, *v.i.* and *t.* re-echo loudly.
rebind, *v.t.* put new binding on.
rebirth, *n.* being born again spiritually; reincarnation.
rebite, *v.t.* apply acid to etched plate to remedy defects.
reboant, *a.* resounding, reverberating. (L. *boare*, cry aloud)
rebound, *v.i.* spring back after impact.—*n.* recoil; emotional reaction.
rebuff, *n.* check to one who makes advances, repulse, snub.—*v.t.* give rebuff to. (It. *buffo*, puff)
rebuild, *v.t.* build again, reconstruct.
rebuke, *v.t.* reprimand, chide; (*Shake.*) check.—*n.* reproof. (O.F. *bucher*, beat)
rebus, *n.* puzzle with words represented by pictures; (*heraldry*) design with allusion to person's name.
rebut, *v.t.* refute, disprove; force back; (*law*) oppose by argument or proof. **rebutment, rebuttal,** *nn.* **rebutter,** *n.* that which rebuts; defendant's answer to plaintiff's surrejoinder. (O.F. *buter*, thrust)
recalcitrate, *v.i.* kick (at), refuse compliance. **recalcitrant,** *a.* actively disobedient, refractory. **recalcitrance,** *n.* (L. *calx*, heel)
recalescence, *n.* sudden renewal in glow as metal cools from white heat. **recalesce,** *v.i.* show this. (L. *calescere*, grow hot)
recall, *v.t.* call, summon, back; restore, revive; bring back to mind, recollect; cancel appointment of; annul, withdraw.—*n.* summons to return; (*Amer.*) removal from office by popular vote.
recant, *v.t.* and *i.* repudiate, retract (opinion, doctrine); renounce as heretical. **recantation,** *n.* (L. *cantare*, sing)
recapitulate, *v.t.* relate again briefly; summarize, give epitome **recapitulation, recapitulator,** *nn.* **recapitulative, recapitulatory,** *aa.* (L. *caput*, head)
recaption, *n.* (*law*) peaceable retaking of property wrongfully seized.
recapture, *v.t.* capture again.—*n.* recapturing, thing recaptured.
recast, *v.t.* mould, cast, again; put into new shape, reconstruct.
recede, *v.i.* move back; withdraw, retreat; slope backwards; decline in value. (L. *cedere*, go)
re-cede, *v.t.* cede back, restore, to former owner.
receipt, *n.* act of receiving; writing acknowledging this; recipe; place of receiving; (us. *pl.*) amount received.—*v.t.* mark (account) as paid. (*receive*)
receive, *v.t.* and *i.* accept, be given; experience, be subjected to; admit, allow; greet, give reception to; accept as true; take in (stolen goods). **received,** *a.* accepted, recognized. **receiver,** *n.* one who receives; receptacle; earpiece of telephone; wireless receiving-set; (*law*) one appointed to administer debtor's or disputed property. (L. *capere*, take)
recency, *n.* recentness.
recension, *n.* revision of, revised, text. (L. *censēre*, review)
recent, *a.* that has lately happened, fresh; not long established, modern. (L. *recens*)
recept, *n.* mental image formed by succession of sensuous impressions.
receptacle, *n.* vessel space, for containing things; (*bot.*) basis of flower. **receptacular,** *a.* (*bot.*). (*receive*)
reception, *n.* receiving; welcome; assembly for receiving guests. **r. clerk,** (*Amer.*) hotel booking-clerk. **r. order,** official order for detention in lunatic asylum. **r.-room,** *n.* living-room. **receptionist,** *n.* one who receives clients. (*receive*)
receptive, *a.* able or quick to take in ideas or impressions. **receptivity,** *n.*
recess, *n.* niche, alcove, hollow; withdrawn place; suspension of business, vacation; receding; (*anat.*) fold in organ.—*v.t.* set back from line. **recession,** *n.* withdrawal. **recessional,** *a.* of parliamentary recess; (of hymn) sung while clergy withdraw after service.—*n.* such hymn. **recessive,** *a.* tending to recede. (*recede*)
réchauffé, *n.* warmed-up dish, rehash. (F.)
recheat, *n.* (*Shake.*) signal on horn to recall hounds. (O.F. *recet*, retreat)
recherché, *a.* choice, of rare quality; far-fetched. (F.)
rechristen, *v.t.* christen afresh.
recidivism, *n.* habitual relapse into crime. **recidivist,** *n.* incorrigible criminal. (L. *cadere*, fall)
recipe, *n.* formula for dish or drink; prescription; expedient. (L.=take)
recipient, *a.* receptive.—*n.* one who receives. **recipiency,** *n.* (*receive*)
reciprocal, *a.* done by each to the other, mutual; complementary; interchangeable; (*gram.*) expressing mutual relation.—*n.* (*math.*) expression so related to another that their product is 1. **reciprocate,** *v.t.* and *i.* requite in kind, return; interchange;

move alternately backwards and forwards. **reciprocation,** *n.* **reciprocity,** *n.* being reciprocal; give-and-take. (L. *reciprocus*)

recite, *v.t.* and *i.* repeat aloud from memory, declaim; recount, enumerate; (*Amer.*) repeat (lesson). **recital,** *n.* reciting; detailed account, narrative; (*law*) statement of facts; (*mus.*) performance by one person or of one person's works (opp. to concert). **recitation,** *n.* reciting; piece recited. **recitative,** *n.* musical declamation in opera etc. **reciter,** *n.* one who recites; book of pieces for recitation. (L. *citare,* call)

reck, *v.i.* and *t.* heed, take account (of); concern (oneself). **reckless,** *a.* rash, incautious; heedless. (O.E. *reccan*)

reckon, *v.t.* and *i.* count, calculate; regard as; rely (on); (chiefly *Amer.*) suppose, think. **r. with,** settle accounts with; take into consideration. **r. without one's host,** underestimate difficulties. **reckoner,** *n.* one who reckons; book of arithmetical tables. **reckoning,** *n.* calculation, esp. of ship's position; retribution; (*arch.*) tavern bill. (O.E. *gerecenian,* explain)

reclaim, *v.t.* and *i.* recover (land) from wild state or sea; win back from vice, reform; tame, civilize; make protest.—*n.* reclamation. **reclamation,** *n.* reclaiming; reformation.

réclame, *n.* notoriety, self-advertisement. (F.)

recline, *v.i.* and *t.* sit or lie with back supported on slope; rest, repose; rely, depend. **reclinate,** *a.* (*bot.*) curving downwards. (L. *clinare,* bend)

recluse, *n.* solitary person, hermit.—*a.* living in retirement. **reclusive,** *a.* (*Shake.*) retired. (L. *claudere,* shut)

recoal, *v.i.* and *t.* take or put in fresh supply of coal.

recognition, *n.* recognizing, identification; acknowledgment, admission. **recognitory,** *a.* (*recognize*)

recognize, *v.t.* know again, identify; acknowledge formally; accept, admit. **recognizable,** *a.* **recognizance,** *n.* (*law*) bond by which person undertakes before court or magistrate to observe some condition; sum pledged as surety for this. **recognizant,** *a.* showing recognition, conscious (of). (L. *cognoscere,* know)

recoil, *v.i.* start back, shrink; retreat; (of gun) spring back, kick.—*n.* recoiling. (L. *culus,* hinder part)

re-collect, *v.t.* gather together again, rally; compose (oneself).

recollect, *v.t.* recall to mind, remember. **recollection,** *n.* remembrance; reminiscence. **recollective,** *a.*

recomfort, *v.t.* hearten; console. **recomforture,** *n.* (*Shake.*).

recommence, *v.t.* and *i.* start afresh. **recommencement,** *n.*

recommend, *v.t.* introduce favourably, make acceptable; commit, entrust; advise. **recommendation,** *n.* recommending; statement, quality, that recommends. **recommendatory,** *a.*

recommit, *v.t.* send back to custody; refer back to parliamentary committee. **recommitment, recommittal,** *nn.*

recompense, *v.t.* requite, reward; compensate, make amends to.—*n.* requital; compensation. (L. *compensare,* compensate)

recompose, *v.t.* compose anew; rearrange. **recomposition,** *n.*

reconcile, *v.t.* restore to friendship; bring to agreement, make compatible; make resigned (to); adjust, compose (quarrel); purify by special service after desecration. **reconcilement, reconciliation,** *nn.* **reconciliatory,** *a.* (L. *conciliare,* conciliate)

recondite, *a.* little known; abstruse, obscure. (L. *condere,* hide)

recondition, *v.t.* repair, refit.

reconduct, *v.t.* conduct back or anew.

reconnaissance, *n.* reconnoitring survey or party; spying out the land.

reconnoitre, *v.t.* and *i.* survey (enemy's position, district) with view to military operations. (F.)

reconquer, *v.t.* win back.

reconsecrate, *v.t.* consecrate second time, after profanation etc.

reconsider, *v.t.* consider afresh, review; modify **reconsideration,** *n.*

reconstitute, *v.t.* piece together to form whole; reconstruct (crime). **reconstituent,** *a.* and *n.* rebuilding (medicine).

reconstruct, *v.t.* rebuild; build up, supply missing parts by conjecture. **reconstruction,** *n.* **reconstructive,** *a.*

record, *v.t.* and *i.* preserve evidence of, put in writing; register, enroll; celebrate; warble in undertone.—*n.* recording; register; report of proceedings, account of events; known facts of man's career; disk with indentations which gramophone transforms into sound; best performance in particular sport etc., limit so far attained. **beat r.,** surpass this. **off the r.,** (*colloq.*) not for publication. **R. Office,** in which state papers are stored. **recordation,** *n.* (*Shake.*) recollection. **recorder,** *n.* magistrate presiding over court of quarter sessions of borough; old instrument like flute. (L. *cor,* heart)

re-count, *v.t.* count again.—*n.* second counting of votes at election.

recount, *v.t.* narrate, tell in detail. **recountal,** *n.*

recoup, *v.t.* and *i.* compensate, indemnify; (*law*) deduct (part of sum due). **recoupment,** *n.* (*coup*)

recourse, *n.* resort, going to for aid; (*Shake.*) access; flowing.—*v.i.* (*Spens.*) recur, return.

re-cover, *v.t.* put new cover on.

recover, *v.t.* and *i.* get back, regain;

retrieve, make up for; get well again, revive; (*fencing*) withdraw (sword) after thrust; (*law*) obtain (damages, restitution); (*Shake.*) reconcile.—*n.* position to which sword is brought back in fencing. **recoverable,** *a.* **recovery,** *n.* recovering; restoration to health. (L. *recuperare*)

recreant, *a.* cowardly, craven; false, traitorous, apostate. — *n.* mean-spirited wretch; renegade. **recreancy,** *n.* (L.L. *recredere,* recant)

re-create, *v.t.* create over again.

recreate, *v.t.* and *i.* refresh, entertain; take recreation. **recreation,** *n.* relaxation, amusement; sport, pastime. **recreative,** *a.*

recrement, *n.* waste product, dross; secretion of body reabsorbed by it, e.g. saliva. **recrementitious,** *a.* (L. *cernere,* sift)

recriminate, *v.i.* and *t.* make counter-charge, accuse in return. **recrimination,** *n.* mutual accusation or abuse. **recriminative, recriminatory,** *aa.*

recrudesce, *v.i.* break out again, be renewed. **recrudescent,** *a.* **recrudescence,** *n.* (L. *crudus,* raw)

recruit, *n.* newly enlisted soldier; new member, tyro.—*v.t.* and *i.* enlist (recruits); supply with recruits; restore, reinvigorate; recover health. **recruital, recruitment,** *nn.* (L. *crescere,* grow)

rectal, *a.* of, by, rectum.

rectangle, *n.* four-sided plane figure with four right angles. **rectangular,** *a.* shaped like rectangle; right-angled. **rectangularity,** *n.* (L. *rectus,* straight)

rectify, *v.t.* put right, correct; remedy, amend; (*chem.*) refine by repeated distillation; (*geom.*) find straight line equal to (curve). **rectifiable,** *a.* **rectification,** *n.* **rectifier,** *n.* thing that rectifies; (*wireless*) valve transforming alternating into direct current. (L. *rectus,* right, straight; *facere,* make)

rectilinear, rectilineal, *aa.* of, bounded by, straight lines; straight. **rectilinearity,** *n.* (L. *rectus,* straight; *linea,* line)

rectitude, *n.* moral uprightness, probity. (L. *rectus,* right)

recto, *n.* right-hand page of open book, front of leaf (opp. to verso). (L. *rectus,* right)

rector, *n.* clergyman of parish retaining tithes; title of some college or school heads; (*Scot., Amer.*) Episcopal clergyman of parish. **Lord R.,** elective president of Scottish university. **R. Magnificus,** head of German university. **rectorate, rectorship,** *nn.* **rectoress, rectress,** *n.* headmistress. **rectorial,** *a.* of rector. **rectory,** *n.* parish rector's benefice or house. (L.=ruler)

rectrix, *n.* (*pl.* **rectrices**) quill-feather of bird's tail. (L.)

rectum, *n.* last part of large intestine, leading to anus. (L. *rectus,* straight)

recumbent, *a.* reclining, lying back or down. **recumbency,** *n.* (L. *recumbere*)

recuperate, *v.t.* and *i.* restore, be restored, to health; recover, convalesce. **recuperation,** *n.* **recuperative,** *a.* (L. *recuperare*)

recur, *v.i.* occur again, be repeated; return to mind; go back in thought or speech. **recurring decimal,** in which same figures recur unendingly. (L. *currere,* run)

recure, *v.t.* (*Shake.*) cure, make whole.

recurrence, *n.* repetition, return; recourse. **recurrent,** *a.* returning periodically; (*anat.*) turning back in direction. (*recur*)

recurve, *v.t.* and *i.* bend backwards. **recurvate,** *a.* **recurvature,** *n.*

recuse, *v.t.* refuse to acknowledge authority of (judge etc.). **recusant,** *a.* recusing; refusing to conform to English Church ritual.—*n.* dissenter. **recusance, recusancy,** *nn.* (L. *recusare,* refuse)

red, *a.* of colour like blood; of, connected with, bloodshed or revolution.—*n.* red colour; revolutionary, communist; (*billiards*) red ball. **paint the town r.,** have riotous spree. **r. admiral,** a bright-coloured butterfly. **r. bark,** cinchona. **r. cent,** (*Amer.*) copper cent; trifle. **r. cross,** symbol of crusaders or ambulance. **r. currant,** a red clustered fruit. **r. deer,** largest British deer, stag. **r. ensign,** flag of merchant service. **r. flag,** symbol of revolution; danger-signal; a revolutionary song. **r. gum,** teething-rash; kind of eucalyptus or its resin. **r. hat,** cardinal's hat; staff officer. **r. herring,** smoked herring; topic to divert attention from main issue. **R. Indian,** N. American aboriginal. **r. lattice,** (*Shake.*) sign of alehouse. **r. lead,** red oxide of lead used in pigments. **r. man,** Red Indian. **r. meat,** beef, mutton. **R. Ribbon,** Order of the Bath. **r. tape,** excessive adherence to official rules. **r. triangle,** emblem of Y.M.C.A. **see r.,** be blinded with rage. (O.E. *réad*)

red-, same as **re-.**

redact, *v.t.* put into literary form, edit. **redaction,** *n.* redacting; new edition. (L. *agere,* drive)

redan, *n.* fieldwork with two faces forming salient angle. (F.)

redargue, *v.t.* (*scot.*) disprove.

redbreast, *n.* robin.

redcap, *n.* goldfinch.

redcoat, *n.* English soldier.

redd, *v.t.* (*Scot.*) put in order, make tidy; compose (dispute).

redden, *v.t.* and *i.* make, become, red; blush.

reddition, *n.* rendering; surrender. (L. *reddere,* render)

reddle, same as **ruddle.**

rede, *n.* (*arch.*) counsel, advice; tale, story; proverb.—*v.t.* advise; explain (riddle). (O.E. *rǣd*)
redecorate, *v.t.* decorate again.
redeem, *v.t.* regain by payment or effort; compound for; atone, make up, for; ransom, reclaim; save from damnation; take out of pawn; fulfil (promise). **redeemer**, *n.* one who redeems. **the Redeemer**, Jesus Christ. (L. *emere*, buy)
redeless, *a.* without counsel, witless.
redeliver, *v.t.* deliver again.
redemption, *n.* redeeming, being redeemed. **redemptive**, *a.* (*redeem*)
red-eyed, *a.* with bloodshot or red-rimmed eyes.
red-handed, *a.* in the act of crime.
red-hot, *a.* heated to redness; excited, furious. **r. poker**, plant with spikes of flame-coloured flowers.
redif, *n.* reserve, reservist, of Turkish army. (Turk.)
redingote, *n.* woman's long double-breasted skirted overcoat. (F. corrupt. of *riding-coat*)
redintegrate, *v.t.* make whole or united again; re-establish, renovate. **redintegration**, **redintegrator**, *nn.*
redirect, *v.t.* direct again, readdress. **redirection**, *n.*
rediscover, *v.t.* discover anew.
redistribute, *v.t.* distribute afresh, apportion differently. **redistribution**, *n.* redistributing; rearrangement of political constituencies.
redivide, *v.t.* and *i.* divide again.
redivivus, *a.* come to life again. (L.)
red-letter, *a.* (of day) marked in calendar with red; memorable.
redo, *v.t.* do over again.
redolent, *a.* having a strong scent, fragrant; reminiscent (of). **redolence**, *n.* (L. *olēre*, smell)
redouble, *v.t.* and *i.* double a second time; increase, intensify, multiply.
redoubt, *n.* detached outwork of fortification. (L. *reducere*, bring back)
redoubtable, *a.* formidable, dreaded. **redoubted**, *a.* (*arch.*). (*doubt*)
redound, *v.i.* contribute, conduce (to); recoil, react (upon). (L. *unda*, wave)
redpoll, *n.* song-bird like linnet.
redraft, *n.* second draft or copy.—*v.t.* draw or draft anew.
redress, *v.t.* remedy, make up for; adjust, set right.—*n.* reparation, amends.
redshank, *n.* kind of sandpiper.
redskin, *n.* Red Indian.
redstart, *n.* a migratory song-bird.
reduce, *v.t.* diminish, lessen; bring down, lower; weaken, make thin; subdue, capture; bring, convert (to other state or form); (*chem.*) deoxidize; (*med.*) adjust (dislocation) by replacing bone; (*phot.*) lessen density of; (*Scots law*) annul. **reducer**, **reduction**, *nn.* **reducible**, *a.* (L. *ducere*, bring)
reductio ad absurdum, proof of proposition by assuming its opposite and showing that the consequences are absurd. (L.)
reduit, *n.* small inner work for resistance when outer fortifications are carried. (F. *réduit*, redoubt)
redundant, *a.* superfluous, pleonastic; copious, luxuriant. **redundance**, **redundancy**, *nn.* (L. *unda*, wave)
reduplicate, *v.t.* make double, repeat; (*gram.*) repeat (syllable or letter), form (word) thus. **reduplication**, *n.* **reduplicative**, *a.*
redwing, *n.* kind of thrush.
redye, *v.t.* dye a second time.
ree, *n.* (*Scot.*) enclosure.
ree, see **reeve**.
reebok, *n.* small S. African antelope. (Du.=roebuck)
re-echo, *v.i.* and *t.* echo, go on echoing, reverberate.
reechy, *a.* (*Shake.*) dirty, filthy.
reed, *n.* tall jointed marsh-grass; its hollow stem; shepherd's pipe; sounding part of clarinet, oboe, bagpipe etc.; weaver's instrument for beating up weft; (*archit.*, us. *pl.*) convex moulding like reeds.—*v.t.* thatch, fit, ornament, with reeds. **broken r.**, unreliable person or thing. **r.-bird**, *n.* bobolink. **r.-bunting**, **r.-sparrow**, *nn.* small marsh-bird with black head and white neck. **r.-mace**, *n.* bulrush. **r.-pheasant**, *n.* reedling. **r.-pipe**, *n.* shepherd's pipe; organ pipe fitted with reed. **r.-stop**, *n.* set of reed-pipes worked by single stop. **r.-warbler**, **r.-babbler**, *nn.* small brown marsh-bird. (O.E. *hréod*)
re-edify, *v.t.* build up again.
re-edit, *v.t.* edit afresh.
reedling, *n.* bearded titmouse.
reedy, *a.* full, made, of reeds; long and thin; shrill, piping.
reef, *n.* ridge of rock at or just below surface of water; (*min.*) lode of gold-bearing quartz. (Du. *rif*)
reef, *n.* part of sail that can be rolled up to reduce area.—*v.t.* take in reefs of (sail). **r.-knot**, *n.* a symmetrical double knot. **reefer**, *n.* thick double-breasted jacket; reef-knot; (*sl.*) midshipman. (O.N. *rif*)
reek, *n.* foul smell, fumes; (*Scot.*) smoke.—*v.i.* emit fumes, steam, or smoke; stink; savour unpleasantly. **reeky**, *a.* smoky. **Auld Reekie**, Edinburgh. (O.E. *réc*)
reel, *n.* winding device; bobbin; thread wound on this; length of cinema film, about 1,000 ft.—*v.t.* wind on reel; draw (in) by means of reel. **off the r.**, straight off, without hitch. **r. off**, recite rapidly. (O.E. *hréol*)
reel, *v.i.* stagger, sway, rock; be dizzy or in a whirl.—*n.* reeling. **r.-rall**, *a.* (*Scot.*) topsy-turvy.
reel, *n.* lively Scottish dance; music for it.—*v.i.* dance reel. **foursome**, **eightsome**, **r.**, for two, four, couples.
re-elect, *v.t.* elect again. **re-election**, *n.*

re-embark, *v.i.* and *t.* embark again.
re-enact, *v.t.* enact over again. **re-enactment,** *n.*
re-enter, *v.i.* and *t.* enter again.
re-entrant, *a.* and *n.* (angle) directed inwards (opp. to salient).
reest, *v.i.* (*Scot.*) refuse to move, balk.
re-establish, *v.t.* establish afresh.
reeve, *n.* ancient chief magistrate of town or district; (*Canada*) president of village or town council. (O.E. *geréfa*)
reeve, *v.t.* (*past, p.p.* **rove, reeved**) pass (rope through ring etc.); fasten thus; (of ship) thread (shoals).
reeve, ree, *n.* female ruff.
re-export, *v.t.* export after importing. —*n.* re-exporting; imported goods exported.
refection, *n.* refreshment; light meal. **refectory,** *n.* dining-hall of monastery. (L. *facere,* make)
refel, *v.t.* (*Shake.*) refute. (L. *fallere,* deceive)
refer, *v.t.* and *i.* attribute, assign (to); submit; direct, have recourse (to authority); allude, relate. **r. to drawer,** (*abbr.* **R.D.**) banker's note suspending payment of cheque. **referable,** *a.* (L. *ferre,* carry)
referee, *n.* adjudicator, arbitrator; (in games) umpire, judge. (*refer*)
reference, *n.* referring, looking up; direction to passage in book; respect, relation; allusion; testimonial, person giving it. **cross-r.,** *n.* to another passage in same book. **r. bible,** indicating parallel passages. **r. library,** for consultation, not borrowing. **with r. to,** regarding. **without r. to,** irrespective of.
referendary, *n.* referee, adviser; medieval court official receiving petitions. (*refer*)
referendum, *n.* reference of political measure to vote of whole electorate, plebiscite. (*refer*)
referential, *a.* of reference.
refill, *v.t.* fill again.
refine, *v.t.* and *i.* free from impurities or dross; free from coarseness, make or become cultured; affect subtlety of thought or language. **r. on,** improve on. **refined,** *a.* polished, cultured; affected. **refinement,** *n.* fineness of manners or taste; nicety, elaboration; fine distinction, hair-splitting. **refiner,** *n.* one who refines (sugar etc.). **refinery,** *n.* refining plant.
refit, *v.t.* and *i.* restore by, undergo, renewal and repairs.—*n.* refitting. **refitment,** *n.*
reflation, *n.* inflation of currency after deflation.
reflect, *v.t.* and *i.* throw back (light, sound, heat); (of mirror) show image of; reproduce to eye or mind; redound with (credit etc.); consider, ponder. **r. on,** discredit, disparage. **reflecting telescope,** with mirror for object-glass. **reflection,** *n.* reflecting; reflected image; meditation, thought; reconsideration; aspersion, reproach. **reflectional,** *a.* **reflective,** *a.* meditative; concerned with ideas; (*gram.*) reflexive. **reflector,** *n.* mirror; reflecting telescope. (L. *flectere,* bend)
reflet, *n.* brilliance of surface, lustre. (F.)
reflex, *n.* reflected light or image; outward manifestation, reproduction; reflex action, reaction; (*art*) part of picture represented as illuminated by light from another part.—*a.* bent back; reactive, introspective; (*anat.*) involuntary; (*gram.*) reflexive. **conditioned r.,** (*psycho-anal.*) reaction due to some association, e.g. horror of thing that caused previous shock. **r. action,** involuntary muscular response to outside stimulus. **r. camera,** with full-size view-finder using main lens. **reflexed,** *a.* (*bot.*) recurved. **reflexible,** *a.* able to be reflected. **reflexibility,** *n.* **reflexion,** same as **reflection. reflexive,** *a.* and *n.* (verb) denoting action that comes back on doer; (pronoun) referring back to subject. (*reflect*)
refluent, *a.* flowing back, ebbing. **refluence, reflux,** *nn.*
refoot, *v.t.* put new foot on (stocking).
re-form, *v.t.* and *i.* form anew.
reform, *v.t.* and *i.* make, become, better by removal of faults; amend, abolish (abuse).—*n.* amendment, improvement. **R. Bill, Act,** amending electoral system in 1831–2. **Reformed Churches,** Protestant Churches, esp. Calvinistic Churches of Continent. **reformation,** *n.* reforming; change for the better; sixteenth-century religious revolt resulting in formation of Protestant Churches. **reformational,** *a.* of the Reformation. **reformative,** *a.* tending to reform. **reformatory,** *a.* reformative.—*n.* institution for reforming young criminals. **reformer, reformist,** *nn.*
refract, *v.t.* deflect (light) from straight path. **refracting telescope,** with lens for object-glass. **refraction,** *n.* **refractable, refractional, refractive,** *aa.* **refractor,** *n.* refracting medium or telescope. (L. *frangere,* break)
refractory, *a.* stubborn, unmanageable; difficult to treat or work. (L. *frangere,* break)
refrain, *v.i.* and *t.* abstain, forbear; hold aloof; (*arch.*) restrain, check. (L. *frenum,* bridle)
refrain, *n.* recurring words in song or poem, esp. at end of stanza; chorus. (L. *frangere,* break)
refrangible, *a.* able to be refracted. **refrangibility,** *n.* (*refract*)
refresh, *v.t.* and *i.* revive, reinvigorate; make cool; freshen up (memory);

(*sl.*) have drink. **refresher,** *n.* (*sl.*) cooling drink; (*law*) additional fee paid to counsel in prolonged cases. **refreshing,** *a.* pleasing through rarity, engaging. **refreshment,** *n.* refreshing; restorative; (*pl.*) light meal.

refrigerate, *v.t.* and *i.* make, become, cold or frozen; preserve by freezing. **refrigeration,** *n.* **refrigerant, refrigerative,** *aa.* and *nn.* cooling (medicine, preparation). **refrigerator,** *n.* chamber for cold storage, ice-box. **refrigeratory,** *a.* refrigerant.—*n.* cold-water vessel attached to still for condensing vapour; refrigerator. (L. *frigus,* cold)

reft, see **reave.**

refuge, *n.* shelter, protection; retreat, sanctuary; street-island; expedient. **refugee,** *n.* one who goes abroad to escape religious or political persecution. (L. *fugere,* flee)

refulgent, *a.* shining, radiant. **refulgence,** *n.* splendour, brightness. (L. *fulgēre,* shine)

refund, *v.t.* and *i.* pay back, make repayment; reimburse.—*n.* repayment. **refundment,** *n.*

refurbish, *v.t.* renovate.

re-fuse, *v.t.* fuse over again.

refuse, *a.* discarded, waste.—*n.* rubbish, garbage.

refuse, *v.t.* and *i.* decline, reject; withhold, deny; (of horse) decline to jump. **refusal,** *n.* refusing; chance of taking a thing before it is offered to others, option. (L. *fundere,* pour)

refute, *v.t.* prove falsity or error of, rebut. **refutable,** *a.* **refutation,** *n.* (L. *refutare*)

regain, *v.t.* get back, recover; reach again.

regal, *a.* of a king, royal; kingly, magnificent. (L. *rex,* king)

regal, *n.* old kind of portable organ. (F.)

regale, *v.t.* and *i.* entertain, feast, choicely; gratify, delight.—*n.* choice repast, dish, or flavour. **regalement,** *n.* (F. *régaler*)

regalia, *n.pl.* royal insignia (crown, sceptre, orb etc.); insignia of an order; royal prerogatives. (L.)

regalia, *n.* superior kind of cigar. (Sp.=royal privilege)

regalism, *n.* doctrine of royal supremacy in church matters. **regalist,** *n.* (*regal*)

regality, *n.* kingship; royal privilege; sovereign right. (*regal*)

regard, *v.t.* and *i.* gaze at, observe; contemplate, consider; heed, take into account; have respect for; concern.—*n.* gaze; heed, concern; esteem; reference; (*pl.*) good wishes. **in, with, r. to, as regards, regarding,** with respect to, about. **r.-ring,** *n.* set with ruby, emerald, garnet, amethyst, ruby, diamond, or other stones whose initials form 'regard.' **regardant,** *a.* (*heraldry*) looking backwards. **regardful,** *a.* heedful. **regardless,** *a.* heedless (of); (*sl.*) recklessly lavish.—*adv.* (*sl.*) without heeding cost, consequences etc. (F. *garder,* guard)

regatta, *n.* meeting for yacht or boat races. (It.)

regelate, *v.i.* freeze together again. **regelation,** *n.* (L. *gelare,* freeze)

regency, *n.* status, authority, of regent; regent's period of office; body entrusted with duties of regent; rule.

regenerate, *v.t.* and *i.* cause to be spiritually reborn, reform morally; give new life to; reorganize; produce anew.—*a.* regenerated. **regeneration,** *n.* **regenerative,** *a.* **regenerator,** *n.* device conserving fuel in furnace by heating incoming air.

regenesis, *n.* rebirth, renewal.

regent, *n.* one who governs during minority, absence, or incapacity of sovereign; (*Amer.*) member of governing board of some universities; (*Shake.*) ruler.—*a.* exercising vicarious authority. (L. *regere,* rule)

regicide, *n.* killer, killing, of king. **regicidal,** *a.* (L. *rex,* king; *caedere,* kill)

régie, *n.* state monopoly or control of tobacco, salt etc. (F.)

regime, régime, *n.* method of government; prevailing system; regimen. *ancien régime,* old order, esp. pre-revolutionary French system. (F.)

regimen, *n.* prescribed diet, health system; rule; (*gram.*) government of cases etc. (L.)

regiment, *n.* military unit, us. of several battalions, troops, or batteries, commanded by a colonel; legion, swarm; (*arch.*) rule, government.—*v.t.* form into regiments; organize in groups, systematize. **regimentation,** *n.* **regimental,** *a.* of regiment.—*n.pl.* uniform. (L. *regere,* rule)

Regina, *n.* (*abbr.* **R.**) title of reigning queen. **reginal,** *a.* queenly. (L.)

region, *n.* tract of country; district, area; part of body; (*Shake.*) air, heaven; rank. **regional,** *a.* local. (L. *regio*)

register, *n.* official list or record; compass of voice or instrument; exact adjustment, alignment; speed-indicator; plate regulating draught.—*v.t.* and *i.* enter in, sign, register; record; correspond exactly; entrust (letter) to post office with special precautions for safety; (*Amer.*) express (emotion) facially. **Lloyd's R.,** shipping list. **parish r.,** of births, marriages, and deaths. **registrar,** *n.* keeper of register, esp. official who performs civil marriages. **registrary,** *n.* registrar of Cambridge University. **registration,** *n.* registering. **registry,** *n.* registration; office where registers are kept, esp. of births, marriages, and deaths; domestic service agency. (L. *gerere,* carry)

Regius, *a.* (of professor) holding chair

founded by Crown, esp. those instituted by Henry VIII. (L.=royal)

reglet, *n.* (*archit.*) flat narrow moulding; (*print.*) kind of thick lead. (F.)

regnal, *a.* of a reign. **r. year,** beginning with sovereign's accession or its anniversary. (*reign*)

regnant, *a.* reigning; predominant, prevalent. **queen r.,** in own right (opp. to queen consort). (*reign*)

regorge, *v.t.* and *i.* vomit, disgorge; swallow again; flow back from hole.

regrate, *v.t.* buy and sell again in same market, thus raising price (formerly a criminal offence). **regrater, regrator,** *nn.* (O.F. *regrater*)

regreet, *v.t.* (*Shake.*) salute.—*n.* greeting.

regress, *n.* going back, falling-off (opp. to progress).—*v.i.* move backwards. **regression,** *n.* regressing; relapse, reversion; (*psycho-anal.*) retreat of personality when person is unable to face a situation. **regressive,** *a.* (L. *gradi,* step)

regret, *v.t.* be sorry for, deplore; remember with longing, miss; repent of, grieve at.—*n.* sorrow, concern; remorse. **regretful,** *a.* **regrettable,** *a.* to be regretted; deserving reproof). (F. *regretter*)

reguerdon, *v.t.* and *n.* (*Shake.*) reward.

regular, *a.* orderly, systematic; uniform, consistent; habitual, not casual; correct, normal; symmetrical; fully qualified: of standing army; of religious order (opp. to secular); (*colloq.*) downright, out-and-out.—*n.* professional soldier; one of regular clergy. **r. fellow, guy,** (*Amer. sl.*) all-round good fellow. **regularity,** *n.* **regularize,** *v.t.* make regular. **regularization,** *n.* (L. *regula,* rule)

regulate, *v.t.* control by rule; cause to conform to standard or needs; put in good order, adjust. **regulation,** *n.* regulating; rule, ordinance.—*a.* normal, standard. **regulative,** *a.* **regulator,** *n.* regulating device; lever of watch. (L. *regula,* rule)

regulus, *n.* partially purified metal sinking to bottom when ore is smelted; antimony; golden-crested wren; brightest star in Leo. **reguline,** *a.* (L.=little king)

regurgitate, *v.i.* and *t.* pour back, cast up again, esp. from stomach to mouth. **regurgitation,** *n.* (L. *gurges,* whirlpool)

rehabilitate, *v.t.* restore to rights or privileges, reinstate. **rehabilitation, rehabilitator,** *nn.*

rehash, *v.t.* dish up again.—*n.* old materials put in new form.

rehear, *v.t.* hear (lawsuit) over again.

rehearse, *v.t.* and *i.* recount, narrate in detail; enumerate; try over, practise (play etc.). **rehearsal,** *n.* trial performance. (O.F. *rehercer*)

rehouse, *v.t.* provide with new houses.

Reich, *n.* German Republic. **Reichstag,** *n.* German Parliament. **Reichswehr,** *n.* German standing army. (G.)

reify, *v.t.* make concrete or real. **reification,** *n.* materialization. (L. *res,* thing; *facere,* make)

reign, *n.* rule, sway, of sovereign; period of this; sphere.—*v.i.* be sovereign, rule; be supreme; prevail. (L. *regere,* rule)

reimburse, *v.t.* pay back, refund. **reimbursement,** *n.* (L.L. *bursa,* purse)

reimport, *v.t.* import after exporting.—*n.* reimporting; exported goods imported.

reimpose, *v.t.* impose (tax) again.

rein, *n.* strap fastened to bit for guiding horse; means of control.—*v.t.* manage, hold in, with rein; govern. **draw r.,** pull up. **give r. to,** allow free scope to. (O.F. *resne*)

reincarnate, *v.t.* embody again in flesh. **reincarnation,** *n.* re-embodiment; passage of soul after death into another body, metempsychosis. **reincarnationist,** *n.*

reindeer, *n.* a deer of cold climates. (O.N. *hreinn,* reindeer+*deer*)

reinforce, *v.t.* strengthen (force) with fresh troops; add to strength of (material).—*n.* thicker part of gun near breech. **reinforced concrete,** with metal bars, wire etc. inserted in it. **reinforcement,** *n.* reinforcing; additional troops or support.

reins, *n.pl.* (*arch.*) kidneys; loins. (L. *ren*)

reinstate, *v.t.* restore to former state, re-establish. **reinstatement,** *n.*

reinsure, *v.t.* and *i.* insure against insurance risk. **reinsurance,** *n.*

reinter, *v.t.* bury again.

reinvest, *v.t.* place in fresh investment; re-endow. **reinvestment,** *n.*

reis, *n.* Portuguese money of account, about $\frac{1}{20}$*d.* (Port.)

reissue, *v.t.* issue again; republish.—*n.* new issue; reprint.

reiterate, *v.t.* say, do, again or many times; repeat again and again. **reiteration, reiterator,** *nn.* **reiterative,** *a.*

reive, *v.i.* and *t.* commit ravages; reave. **reiver,** *n.* freebooter. (form of *reave*)

reject, *v.t.* throw away, discard; refuse to accept, decline. **rejection, rejector,** *nn.* *rejectamenta, n.pl.* refuse, waste matter; flotsam and jetsam. (L. *jacere,* throw)

rejoice, *v.t.* and *i.* make, be, glad; make merry. **r. in,** (*joc.*) have. **rejoicings,** *n.pl.* festivities. (*joy*)

rejoin, *v.t.* and *i.* join again, return to; say in answer, reply. **rejoinder,** *n.* retort, reply; (*law*) reply to replication. **rejoindure,** *n.* (*Shake.*) reunion.

rejuvenate, *v.t.* and *i.* make, become, young again. **rejuvenation, rejuvenator,** *nn.* **rejuvenesce,** *v.i.* and *t.* grow young again; renew vitality (of). **rejuvenescent,** *a.* **rejuven-**

escence, *n.* renewal of youth; formation of new cells from protoplasm of old. **rejuvenize,** *v.t.* and *i.* rejuvenate. (L. *juvenis,* young)
rekindle, *v.t.* and *i.* kindle again.
relapse, *v.i.* fall back into worse state after improvement; return to former vice, backslide.—*n.* relapsing.
relate, *v.t.* and *i.* narrate, recount; bring into relation, establish relation between; refer. **related,** *a.* connected, allied; akin. **relation,** *n.* narration, narrative; how one stands to another, footing; feeling between persons or countries; correspondence, connection; reference; kinsman, kinswoman; kinship; (*law*) information laid before Attorney-General. **relational,** *a.* **relationship,** *n.* tie, degree, of kindred; affinity. (L. *ferre,* carry)
relative, *a.* having, expressing relation; relevant, pertinent; comparative, conditional; (*gram.*) referring to antecedent.—*n.* kinsman, relation; (*gram.*) relative word. **relatival,** *a.* (*gram.*) **relativism,** *n.* theory that all knowledge is relative, not absolute. **relativity,** *n.* Einstein's theory, based on the principle that all motion is relative, that space and time are mutually inseparable.
relator, *n.* (*law*) one who lays information. (L.)
relax, *v.t.* and *i.* loosen, slacken; make, become, less severe or strict. **relaxing,** *a.* enervating (opp. to bracing). **relaxation,** *n.* relaxing; recreation. (L. *laxus,* loose)
re-lay, *v.t.* lay again.
relay, *n.* set of fresh horses, men etc. to relieve tired ones; (*telegraphy*) device reinforcing long-distance current so that it can work instruments; (*wireless*) broadcasting another station.—*v.t.* replace by, provide with, substitutes; pass on, re-broadcast. **r. race,** race between teams in which each runner does part of distance. (O.F. *relais*)
re-lease, *v.t.* grant new lease of.
release, *v.t.* let go, discharge, unfasten; set free, relieve; permit public exhibition of (cinema film); (*law*) remit, make over to another (debt, property).—*n.* releasing, liberation; catch to hold or release mechanism; (*law*) discharge, receipt, conveyance. **releasee, releasor,** *nn.* (*law*) person to, by, whom release is made. (L. *laxare,* relax)
relegate, *v.t.* banish; consign (to inferior position); assign, refer; transfer (team) to lower section of league. **relegation, relegator,** *nn.* (L. *legare,* send)
relent, *v.i.* become less severe or harsh; yield to pity or entreaty; (*Shake.*) dissolve. **relentless,** *a.* pitiless; unremitting. (L. *lentus,* soft)
re-let, *v.t.* let again, sublet.
relevant, *a.* bearing upon the matter in hand, pertinent, to the point. **relevance, relevancy,** *nn.* (L. *relevare,* relieve)
reliable, *a.* dependable, trustworthy. **reliability,** *n.* **reliance,** *n.* confidence, trust; thing depended on. **reliant,** *a.* confident. (*rely*)
relic, *n.* object, custom, surviving from past; trace, remnant; memorial, memento; part of saint's body or belongings; (*pl.*) remains of dead. (L. *linquere,* leave)
relict, *n.* widow. (*relic*)
relief, *n.* alleviation of pain or distress; redress of grievance; break in monotony; assistance given to poor or victims of disaster; raising of siege; (persons) taking place of those on duty; projection of carved design from its ground, such design; distinctness, vividness. **high, low, r.,** projection of design by more, less, than half true depth. **indoor, outdoor, r.,** given in workhouse, at home. **r. map,** showing mountains by raised surface. (*relieve*)
relieve, *v.t.* lighten, assuage; free from pain or anxiety, ease; break monotony of; bring assistance to; release from post or duty; raise siege of; deprive (of); bring into relief, show up. **r. nature,** empty bladder or bowels. **relieving officer,** poor-law official. (L. *levis,* light)
relievo, *n.* (*art*) relief. (It.)
religieuse, *n.* nun. *religieux,* *n.* monk. (F.)
religion, *n.* belief in God; system of faith and worship; monastic state; object of devotion; (*Shake.*) conscientiousness. **get r.,** (*vulg.*) be converted. **religioner,** *n.* religious; religionist. **religionism,** *n.* excessive religious zeal; affectation of religion. **religionist,** *n.* **religionize,** *v.t.* and *i.* imbue with, make profession of, religion. **religiose,** *a.* morbidly religious. **religiosity,** *n.* being religious or religiose. **religious,** *a.* of, conforming to, religion; devout, pious; of a monastic order; scrupulous, conscientious.—*n.* member of religious order. **religiously,** *adv.* piously; scrupulously, exactly. (L. *religio*)
reline, *v.t.* put new lining in.
relinquish, *v.t.* give up, abandon, surrender; let go. **relinquishment,** *n.* (L. *linquere,* leave)
reliquary, *n.* casket, shrine, for holy relics. (*relic*)
reliquiae, *n.pl.* fossil or literary remains; (*bot.*) withered leaves decaying on stem. (L.=remains)
relish, *n.* flavour, distinctive taste; spice, tinge; sauce, condiment; keen appetite, gusto, zest.—*v.t.* and *i.* enjoy, like; smack (of); give relish to. (O.F. *reles,* aftertaste)
relive, *v.i.* and *t.* live again.
reload, *v.t.* and *i.* load again.

relucent, *a.* shining, bright.
reluct, reluctate, *v.i.* make resistance. **reluctation,** *n.* **reluctant,** *a.* unwilling, loath; offering resistance. **reluctance,** *n.* (L. *luctari,* struggle)
relume, *v.t.* rekindle; make bright again. (L. *lumen,* light)
rely, *v.i.* trust, depend with confidence (on). (L. *ligare,* bind)
remain, *v.i.* stay, continue; survive, last; be left over or behind.—*n.pl.* surviving parts, relics; dead body; writings left unpublished at death. **remainder,** *n.* what is left, rest; unsold stock, esp. of books; (*law*) residual interest in estate; right of succession to title on holder's decease; (*math.*) result of subtraction; quantity left over after division.—*v.t.* treat as remainder, sell off at low price. (L. *manēre,* stay)
remake, *v.t.* make again.
reman, *v.t.* furnish with fresh men; restore to courage.
remand, *v.t.* reconsign; (*law*) send back into custody for further evidence.—*n.* such recommittal. (L. *mandare,* order)
remanent, *a.* remaining, surviving. **remanet,** *n.* residue; lawsuit, parliamentary bill, carried over to another session. (*remain*)
remark, *v.t.* and *i.* notice, perceive; say, observe; make comment.—*n.* observation; comment. **remarkable,** *a.* striking, unusual, noteworthy.
remarque, *n.* marginal design etc. indicating stage of engraved plate. (F.)
remarry, *v.t.* and *i.* marry again. **remarriage,** *n.*
remblai, *n.* materials of rampart or embankment. (F.)
remedy, *n.* cure for disease or evil; healing treatment or medicine; redress, reparation.—*v.t.* set right, mend; redress. **remediable,** *a.* curable. **remedial,** (*Shake.*) **remediate,** *aa.* affording remedy. (L. *medēri,* heal)
remember, *v.t.* and *i.* recall to mind, recollect; retain in mind, not forget; make present to; (*Shake.*) remind. **remembrance,** *n.* remembering; keepsake, memorial; message of goodwill. **remembrancer,** *n.* person, thing, that reminds. **King's Remembrancer,** officer of the Supreme Court who collects debts due to Crown. (L. *memor,* mindful)
remiform, *a.* oar-shaped. **remex,** *n.* (*pl.* **remiges**) quill-feather of bird's wing. (L. *remus,* oar)
remind, *v.t.* recall to memory; put in mind (of). **reminder,** *n.* thing that reminds.
reminiscence, *n.* recollection; remembered incident, memory; (*pl.*) memoirs. **reminiscent,** *a.* reminding, suggestive (of); recalling the past. (L. *reminisci,* recollect)
remise, *n.* (*fencing*) second thrust in same lunge, without recovery; (*arch.*) coach-house; carriage for livery stable. (F.)
remise, *n.* (*law*) surrender, quittance. —*v.t.* make over (property). (*remit*)
remiss, *a.* negligent, slack; not energetic. (L. *remissus*)
remission, *n.* remitting; pardon, forgiveness; abatement, diminution. **remissible,** *a.* capable of being remitted or forgiven. **remissive,** *a.* remitting, abating; forgiving.
remit, *v.t.* and *i.* forgive; refrain from exacting (debt) or inflicting (punishment); abate, moderate; send, transmit; refer; adjourn; (*law*) send (case) to inferior court. **remittal,** *n.* **remittance,** *n.* forwarding of money; sum forwarded. **remittance man,** living in colonies on allowance from home. **remittee, remitter,** *nn.* receiver, sender, of remittance. **remittent,** *a.* and *n.* (fever) abating at intervals. (L. *mittere,* send)
remnant, *n.* small remaining fragment or number; oddment, scrap; relic, trace. (*remain*)
remodel, *v.t.* fashion afresh, recast.
remonetize, *v.t.* restore (metal, currency) to use as legal tender. **remonetization,** *n.*
remonstrate, *v.i.* and *t.* expostulate (with); protest, make complaint (against). **remonstrant,** *a.* and *n.* (person) who remonstrates. **remonstrance,** *n.* remonstrating; formal protest. **remonstrative,** *a.* **remonstrator,** *n.* (L. *monstrare,* show)
remontant, *a.* and *n.* (rose) flowering more than once in a season. (F.)
remora, *n.* sucking-fish (once supposed to have power of stopping ships); hindrance. (L. *mora,* delay)
remorse, *n.* pain caused by sense of guilt; compunction; (*Shake.*) pity. **remorseful,** *a.* repentant. **remorseless,** *a.* ruthless, cruel; relentless. (L. *mordēre,* bite)
remote, *a.* far apart or distant; not closely related; secluded, aloof; vague, faint. **remotion,** *n.* (*Shake.*) keeping aloof. (L. *movēre,* move)
remount, *v.t.* and *i.* mount (horse), ascend (hill), again; provide with fresh horse.—*n.* reserve horse.
remove, *v.t.* and *i.* take away, shift elsewhere; take off, withdraw; dismiss, get rid of; go away, move house.—*n.* stage in gradation; degree in relationship; promotion to higher class at school; course, principal dish; (*Shake.*) removal. **cousin once removed,** cousin's child or parent's cousin; **cousin twice removed,** cousin's grandchild or grandparent's cousin. **removable,** *a.* **removal,** *n.* removing, abolition; shifting to new house.
remunerate, *v.t.* pay for service, reward. **remuneration,** *n.* remunerating; pay, salary. **remunerative,** *a.* paying, profitable. **remunerator,** *n.* (L. *munus,* reward)

renaissance, *n.* artistic or spiritual revival. **the R.,** revival of art and literature under influence of classical study in fourteenth–sixteenth centuries. (F.)

renal, *a.* of the kidneys. (*reins*)

rename, *v.t.* give new name to.

renascence, *n.* rebirth; renaissance. **renascent,** *a.* springing again into being or vigour.

Renard, same as **Reynard.**

rencounter, rencontre, *n.* encounter, skirmish, duel; casual meeting. (F.)

rend, *v.t.* and *i.* (*past, p.p.* **rent**) tear, wrench (apart); shiver, divide. (O.E. *rendan*)

render, *v.t.* and *i.* give in return; deliver, furnish, present; cause to become, make; express, depict; translate, interpret; melt down (fat); cover (wall) with first coat of plaster. —*n.* (*Shake.*) account. **rendering,** *n.* interpretation, translation. (L. *reddere*)

rendezvous, *n.* (*pl.* same) meeting-place; place of assembly for troops; assignation.—*v.i.* meet by appointment. (F.=betake yourselves)

rendition, *n.* rendering; handing over. (*render*)

renege, renegue, *v.i.* and *t.* revoke at cards; (*arch.*) deny, break promise. **renegade,** *n.* apostate, esp. from Christianity to Islam; deserter, turncoat.—*v.i.* turn renegade. **renegation,** *n.* **renegado,** *n.* (*Shake.*) renegade. (L. *negare,* deny)

renew, *v.t.* and *i.* renovate; restore to freshness or vigour; cause spiritual rebirth of; begin again, make or get anew; patch, replace; grant, obtain, extension of. **renewal,** *n.*

reniform, *a.* kidney-shaped. (*reins*)

renig, *Amer. colloq.* form of **renege.**

rennet, *n.* kind of eating apple. (F. *reinette*)

rennet, *n.* membrane of calf's stomach or artificial preparation used for curdling milk. **rennin,** *n.* enzyme forming active principle of rennet. (M.E. *rennen,* run)

renounce, *v.t.* and *i.* abandon formally, give up; cast off; disown; (*cards*) fail to follow suit, (*law*) decline to act as executor or trustee.—*n.* (*cards*) renouncing. **renouncement,** *n.* (L. *nuntius,* messenger)

renovate, *v.t.* restore to good condition, do up, repair. **renovation, renovator,** *nn.* (L. *novus,* new)

renown, *n.* fame, celebrity; (*Shake.*) reputation. **renowned,** *a.* famous, illustrious. (L. *nomen,* name)

rent, see **rend.**

rent, *n.* tear in cloth etc.; cleft, fissure; schism. (*rend*)

rent, *n.* periodical payment by tenant to owner or landlord for use of house, room, or land; hire for machinery etc.—*v.t.* and *i.* occupy as tenant, lease; hire, let, for rent. **r.-charge,** *n.* periodical charge on land paid to one not its owner. **r.-free,** *a.* and *adv.* without paying rent. **r.-roll,** *n.* register of estate and its rents. **rental,** *n.* amount of rent. **renter,** *n.* wholesaler in film trade. (L. *reddere,* render)

rente, *n.* French Government stock; income from investments or annuity. *rentier,* *n.* person living on this, who does not need to work. (F.)

renumber, *v.t.* number over again.

renunciation, *n.* formal abandonment, giving up; disavowal, repudiation. **renunciative, renunciatory,** *aa.* (*renounce*)

reoccupy, *v.t.* occupy again. **reoccupation,** *n.*

rep, repp, reps, *n.* thick corded material used for upholstery. (F.)

rep, *n.* (*sl.*) dissolute person.

rep, *n.* (*school sl.*) repetition. (abbr.)

repaid, see **repay.**

repair, *v.t.* restore to good condition, mend; remedy, make good.—*n.* repairing; condition as to soundness. **repairable,** *a.* (L. *parare,* prepare)

repair, *v.i.* resort, go; have recourse.—*n.* haunt, resort. (L. *patria,* native land)

repand, *a.* (*bot.*) with wavy margin. (L. *pandus,* bent)

repaper, *v.t.* put fresh paper on (wall).

reparable, *a.* that can be made good. **reparation,** *n.* compensation, amends. (*repair*)

repartee, *n.* witty retort; skill in making such. (F. *repartir,* reply)

repast, *n.* meal.—*v.t.* (*Shake.*) feed. **repasture,** *n.* (*Shake.*) food. (L. *pascere,* feed)

repatriate, *v.t.* restore to native country. **repatriation,** *n.* (L. *patria,* native land)

repay, *v.t.* and *i.* (*past, p.p.* **repaid**) pay back, refund; make return (for), requite. **repayment,** *n.*

repeal, *v.t.* annul, revoke (law); (*Shake.*) recall from exile.—*n.* repealing. (L. *appellare,* call)

repeat, *v.t.* and *i.* say again, reiterate; say piece learnt by heart, recite; do over again, reproduce; recur.—*n.* repetition, encore; (*mus.*) passage to be repeated, sign for this. **r. oneself,** say or do same thing over again. **repeating decimal,** in which same figures recur unendingly. **repeating rifle,** firing several times without reloading. **repeating watch,** striking hour when spring is pressed. **repeater,** *n.* repeating decimal, rifle, or watch; (*Amer. sl.*) fraudulent voter. (L. *petere,* seek)

repel, *v.t.* drive back, beat off; reject, spurn; excite aversion in. **repellent,** *a.* distasteful, unattractive; unsociable, forbidding. (L. *pellere,* drive)

repent, *a.* (*bot.*) creeping, trailing. (L. *repere,* creep)

repent, *v.t.* and *i.* wish one had not done something; feel penitence (for); regret and change from evil ways. **repentance,** *n.* penitence, contrition. **repentant,** *a.* repenting; sorry for sin. (L. *paenitēre,* make sorry)

repeople, *v.t.* people anew.

repercussion, *n.* rebound, recoil; reverberation; indirect effect, reaction. **repercussive,** *a.*

repertoire, *n.* stock of plays, songs etc. that actor or company can perform. **repertory,** *n.* storehouse, collection; repertoire. **repertory theatre,** with permanent company and constant change of plays. (F.)

repetend, *n.* recurring figures of repeating decimal; refrain. (*repeat*)

repetition, *n.* repeating; thing repeated, copy; piece spoken from memory, recitation. **repetitional, repetitionary, repetitious, repetitive,** *aa.* (*repeat*)

repine, *v.i.* fret, complain; be discontented.—*n.* (*Shake.*) dissatisfaction.

repique, *n.* (*piquet*) scoring 30 points from hand alone before beginning play.—*v.t.* and *i.* score repique (against).

replace, *v.t.* and *i.* put back, restore; take place of, substitute for, supersede. **replaceable,** *a.* **replacement,** *n.*

replant, *v.t.* plant again.

replenish, *v.t.* fill up again, restock; stock abundantly. **replenishment,** *n.* (L. *plenus,* full)

replete, *a.* filled, well provided; stuffed, gorged. **repletion,** *n.* complete or undue fullness. (L. *plēre,* fill)

replevy, *v.t.* (*law*) recover by replevin. **replevin,** *n.* recovery of goods wrongfully taken, with pledge to return them if defeated in lawsuit on the matter; writ for this. (O.F. *replevir*)

replica, *n.* duplicate of work made by original artist; exact copy, facsimile. **replicate,** *v.t.* make replica of; fold back.—*a.* (*bot.*) folded back on itself. —*n.* (*mus.*) tone one or more octaves from given tone. **replication,** *n.* making of copies; copy; echo; folding back; (*law*) plaintiff's reply to defendant's plea. **replicative,** *a.* (L. *plicare,* fold)

reply, *v.t.* and *i.* answer, respond.—*n.* answer. (L. *plicare,* fold)

répondez s'il vous plaît, (*abbr.* **R.S.V.P.**) please reply (appended to invitations). (F.)

repopulate, *v.t.* repeople.

report, *v.t.* and *i.* give account (of), tell as news; take down, describe, for publication; make official statement (on); inform against.—*n.* hearsay, rumour; account, description; formal statement or opinion after investigation; noise of explosion, bang. **r. (oneself),** announce one's arrival. **reported speech,** using third person, not actual words. **reporter,** *n.* one who reports for newspaper. (L. *portare,* carry)

repose, *v.t.* put, set (trust etc. in). **reposal,** *n.* (L. *ponere,* place)

repose, *v.t.* and *i.* rest; incline, lie; rely, be based (on).—*n.* rest, sleep; stillness, peace; composure, serenity. **reposeful,** *a.* restful. (L. *pausare,* pause)

repository, *n.* storehouse, warehouse, shop; receptacle. (*repose*)

repossess, *v.t.* possess again.

repoussé, *a.* hammered into relief from reverse side.—*n.* metal work so produced. **repoussage,** *n.* art of this. (F.)

repp, see **rep. repped,** *a.* ribbed like rep.

reprehend, *v.t.* rebuke, find fault with. **reprehensible,** *a.* blameworthy, culpable. **reprehension,** *n.* reproof, censure. (L. *prehendere,* seize)

represent, *v.t.* bring before mind; portray, describe (as); allege; stand for, symbolize; personate (character); act, deputize (for).

representation, *n.* representing; portrait, reproduction. **make rr.,** urge that something should be done. **proportional r.,** (*abbr.* **P.R.**) electoral system arranged so that minorities are represented in proportion to their strength. **representational,** *a.*

representative, *a.* portraying, typical. —*n.* agent, delegate; parliamentary deputy. **House of Rr.,** Lower House of U.S. Congress etc. **r. government,** in which people are represented by elected deputies.

repress, *v.t.* restrain, curb; quell, put down. **repressible, repressive,** *aa.* **repression,** *n.* restraint; (*psychoanal.*) involuntary exclusion from the conscious mind of processes painful to it. **repressor,** *n.*

reprieve, *v.t.* postpone execution of; give respite to.—*n.* cancelling of death sentence; respite.

reprimand, *n.* official reproof.—*v.t.* rebuke officially. (L. *premere,* press)

reprint, *v.t.* print again.—*n.* book, article, reprinted.

reprisal, *n.* act of retaliation for injury done, esp. internationally. **letters of r.,** official licence for this. **reprise,** *n.* resumption; (*fencing*) renewal of attack; (*law*) yearly deduction, rent-charge. (L. *prehendere,* seize)

reproach, *v.t.* upbraid, reprove; charge (with).—*n.* censure, blame; cause of discredit; disgrace, shame. **reproachful,** *a.* conveying reproach; shameful. (F. *reprocher*)

reprobance, *n.* (*Shake.*) reprobation.

reprobate, *v.t.* disapprove of, censure; exclude from salvation.—*a.* damned; abandoned, depraved.—*n.* hardened sinner, scoundrel. **reprobation,** *n.* (L. *reprobare,* reprove)

reproduce, *v.t.* and *i.* form anew; make

likeness or copy of, represent; propagate (one's kind). **reproducible,** *a.* **reproduction,** *n.* reproducing; breeding; copy, likeness. **reproductive,** *a.* used in reproduction; fertile; yielding profits.

reproof, *n.* blame; rebuke. **reprove,** *v.t.* rebuke, censure.

reps, see **rep.**

reptant, *a.* (*zool.*) creeping. (L. *repere,* crawl)

reptile, *n.* crawling animal, e.g. snake, lizard etc.; grovelling person.—*a.* crawling, moving on belly; grovelling, low. **reptilian,** *a.* of reptile class. **reptiliferous, reptiliform,** *aa.* (L. *repere,* crawl)

republic, *n.* government in which citizens elect head of state, usually called president; country with this; society in which all are equal. **republican,** *a.* of, characteristic of, supporting, republic; of U.S. Republican Party.—*n.* advocate of republican government; member of U.S. party favouring extension of federal power (opp. to Democrat). **republicanism,** *n.* republican principles. **republicanize,** *v.t.* (L. *respublica,* commonwealth)

republish, *v.t.* publish again; issue new edition of. **republication,** *n.*

repudiate, *v.t.* and *i.* disown, cast off, reject; refuse to acknowledge or pay (public debt); divorce. **repudiation, repudiator,** *nn.* (L. *repudium,* divorce)

repugn, *v.i.* and *t.* strive (against), oppose. **repugnant,** *a.* distasteful, offensive; inconsistent, contradictory; refractory. **repugnance,** *n.* aversion, disgust; inconsistency, incompatibility. (L. *pugnare,* fight)

repulse, *v.t.* repel, drive off; rebut; rebuff, reject.—*n.* defeat, check; rebuff, rejection. **repulsion,** *n.* aversion, disgust; repulsing; tendency of bodies to repel each other (opp. to attraction). **repulsive,** *a.* loathsome, disgusting; exercising repulsion; (*arch.*) repellent, cold. (L. *pellere,* drive)

repurchase, *v.t.* buy back.—*n.* buying back.

reputable, *a.* of good repute, respectable.

reputation, *n.* estimation in which one is held; good name, honour. **repute,** *n.* reputation. general belief.—*v.t.* deem, consider. **reputed,** *a.* generally reported; supposed, putative. **reputedly,** *adv.* in common estimation. (L. *putare,* think)

request, *v.t.* ask for earnestly; desire. —*n.* requesting, entreaty; demand; thing asked for, want. **in r.,** sought after.

requicken, *v.t.* reanimate.

requiem, *n.* dirge; mass for dead, music for this. (L.=rest, opening word of mass)

requiescat, *n.* wish for repose of dead. (L.)

require, *v.t.* and *i.* need, call for; claim as right, demand authoritatively; order, command. **requirement,** *n.* need, want; essential condition. (L. *quaerere,* seek)

requisite, *a.* needed, necessary.—*n.* thing required. **requisition,** *n.* formal demand; exaction of supplies for military purposes. —*v.t.* demand supply of or from; press into service. (*require*)

requite, *v.t.* repay, make return for; reward, recompense; avenge, punish. **requital,** *n.* (*quit*)

re-read, *v.t.* read over again.

rere-arch, same as **rear-arch.**

rerebrace, *n.* plate-armour for upper part of arm. (*rear*; *brace*)

reredos, *n.* ornamental screen behind altar. (*rear*+L. *dorsum,* back)

reremouse, *n.* bat. (O.E. *hréran,* move; *mús,* mouse)

res, *n.* thing. *r. angusta domi,* straitened circumstances. *r. judicata,* thing already settled. (L.)

rescind, *v.t.* repeal, annul. **rescission,** *n.* (L. *scindere,* cleave)

rescript, *n.* official ruling of pope or Roman emperor on legal point submitted; edict, decree; rewriting, thing rewritten.

rescue, *v.t.* deliver from captivity, violence, or danger; (*law*) unlawfully liberate; recover (property) by force.—*n.* rescuing; deliverance, succour. (L. *re-,* back; *ex,* out; *quatere,* shake)

research, *n.* diligent search; systematic investigation, scientific study.—*v.i.* make research. **researcher,** *n.*

reseat, *v.t.* seat again; put new seats in.

réseau, *n.* network; (*astron.*) squared lines on star photograph to facilitate measurement. (F.)

resect, *v.t.* pare down (bone etc.). **resection,** *n.* (L. *secare,* cut)

reseda, *n.* kinds of plant incl. mignonette; its pale-green colour. (L.)

resell, *v.t.* sell soon after buying.

resemble, *v.t.* be like, have similarity to; (*arch.*) liken. **resemblance,** *n.* **resemblant,** *a.* (L. *similis,* like)

resent, *v.t.* feel, show, indignation at; view as affront, take ill. **resentful,** *a.* **resentment,** *n.* indignant displeasure, sense of injury. (L. *sentire,* feel)

reserve, *v.t.* keep for future use, hold over; retain, set apart (for).—*n.* extra supply or stock; forces supplementary to standing army, member of these; spare man; tract reserved for natives or wild animals; restriction, qualification; caution, reticence; self-restraint in art; (us. *pl.*) troops in support. **in r.,** for use in emergency. **r. price,** least that will be accepted. **without r.,** fully; not subject to reserve price. **reserved,** *a.* set apart, booked; uncommunicative, lacking cordiality. **reservist,** *n.* man serving in reserve. (L. *servare,* keep)

reservation, *n.* reserving; thing reserved; limitation, proviso; tract reserved for American Indians; retention after eucharist of part of consecrated elements for adoration. **mental r.,** silent qualification of words of oath or statement.

reservoir, *n.* artificial lake for storing water; holder for fluid; store.—*v.t.* store in reservoir. (F.)

reset, *v.t.* set (bone, gem, type) over again; place in new setting.

reset, *v.t.* and *i.* (*Scots law*) receive (stolen goods). **resetter,** *n.* (L. *recipere,* receive)

resettle, *v.t.* settle again.

reshape, *v.t.* and *i.* shape anew.

reship, *v.t.* put on board again; transfer to other ship. **reshipment,** *n.*

reshuffle, *v.t.* shuffle afresh; redistribute.—*n.* rearrangement.

reside, *v.i.* live permanently, have home (in); be vested or present (in). **residence,** *n.* residing; dwelling, house. **in residence,** at official abode. **residency,** *n.* house of political resident. **resident,** *a.* residing, domiciled; living on the spot.—*n.* permanent inhabitant; British government agent at court of native ruler. **residenter,** *n.* (*Scot.*) inhabitant. **residential,** *a.* based on residence; used for private dwellings. **residentiary,** *a.* and *n.* (canon etc.) bound to occupy official residence. (L. *sedēre,* sit)

residue, *n.* remainder, part left over; what is left of estate after payment of debts and legacies; residuum. **residual,** *a.* and *n.* (substance) left as residuum; (quantity) resulting from subtraction. **residuary,** *a.* of the residue of an estate; residual. **residuent,** *n.* by-product. **residuum,** *n.*(*pl.* **residua**) amount not accounted for in calculations; substance left after combustion or evaporation; dregs of population. (L. *residuus,* remaining)

re-sign, *v.t.* sign again.

resign, *v.t.* and *i.* give up (office), retire; hand over, submit; reconcile (oneself). **resignation,** *n.* resigning of office; patient endurance. **resigned,** *a.* submissive, acquiescent; accepting the inevitable. (L. *re-,* un-; *signare,* seal)

resile, *v.i.* recoil, rebound. **resilient,** *a.* elastic, springing back; buoyant, with recuperative power. **resilience, resiliency,** *nn.* (L. *salire,* leap)

resin, *n.* sticky substance, insoluble in water, exuded by trees as liquid. —*v.t.* rub, treat, with resin. **resinaceous, resinous,** *aa.* **resinify,** *v.t.* and *i.* form into resin; become resinous. **resinoid,** *a.* and *n.* (substance) like resin. (L. *resina*)

resipiscence, *n.* return to wisdom; recognition of error. **resipiscent,** *a.* (L. *sapere,* be wise)

resist, *v.t.* and *i.* withstand, oppose; obstruct, bar; drive back, repel; offer opposition; be proof against; abstain from. **resistance,** *n.* resisting; opposition, hindrance; (*electr.*) non-conductivity, part of apparatus offering opposition to current; (*psycho-anal.*) opposition to making unpleasant complexes conscious. **passive resistance,** refusal to comply. **resistant, resistent, resistive,** *aa.* **resistible,** *a.* able to be resisted. **resistivity,** *n.* (*electr.*) capacity for for resistance (opp. to conductivity). **resistless,** *a.* irresistible; (*rare*) unresisting. (L. *sistere,* cause to stand)

resole, *v.t.* put new sole on (shoe).

resoluble, *a.* capable of being resolved or analysed.

resolute, *a.* determined; firm of purpose, steadfast. **resolution,** *n.* resolving; firmness of purpose; fixed intention, resolve; proposal, statement of opinion, at public meeting; analysis, disintegration; substitution of two short syllables for one long one; (*med.*) dispersion of tumour etc.; (*mus.*) relieving of discord by following concord. (*resolve*)

resolve, *v.t.* and *i.* break into component parts, dissolve; convert, be converted (into); determine, make up one's mind; solve, settle; vote by resolution; (*med.*) disperse (tumour); (*mus.*) convert (discord) into concord.—*n.* fixed intention; resolution, courage. **resolved,** *a.* resolute. **resolvent,** *a.* and *n.* (drug) having power to dissolve or disperse.

resonant, *a.* sonorous, ringing; resounding, echoing. **resonance,** *n.* **resonate,** *v.i.* resound. **resonator,** *n.* device for analysing sound; sounding-box. (L. *sonare,* sound)

resorb, *v.t.* absorb again. **resorbence,** *n.* **resorbent,** *a.* (L. *sorbēre,* swallow)

resorcin, *n.* crystalline compound got from resin and used in dyeing. (*resin*; *orcin*)

resorption, *n.* resorbing, resorbence.

resort, *v.i.* go, betake oneself; have recourse, apply (to).—*n.* recourse; expedient; frequenting, place frequented. **in the last r.,** if all else fails. (F. *sortir,* go out)

re-sort, *v.t.* sort over again.

resound, *v.i.* and *t.* ring, echo, reverberate; go on sounding; be much talked of; spread (fame).

resource, *n.* shift, expedient; ability to cope with a situation; means of diversion; (*pl.*) source of help or supply; funds, means. **resourceful,** *a.* fertile in expedients, ingenious. (L. *surgere,* rise)

respect, *n.* deferential regard, esteem; consideration, heed; reference, aspect; (*pl.*) good wishes.—*v.t.* regard with deference; pay heed to, obey; avoid injuring, spare. **have r. to,** be concerned with. **r. of persons,** favour shown to great etc. **respectable,** *a.* decent, well-conducted; of fair social standing; moderate, of some size; pretty good. **respectability,** *n.* **respectful,** *a.* deferential. **respective,** *a.* proper to each, several; (*Shake.*) considerate. **respectively,** *adv.* severally. (L. *specere*, look)

respire, *v.i.* and *t.* breathe; inhale and exhale (air); have respite, recover hope. **respiration,** *n.* breathing; single breath. **respirator,** *n.* appliance worn over mouth to filter air; gas-mask. **respiratory,** *a.* of respiration. (L. *spirare*, breathe)

respite, *n.* period of rest or relief; postponement of penalty.—*v.t.* grant respite to, relieve temporarily; postpone execution of; withhold (pay from). (L. *respectus*, respect)

resplendent, *a.* very bright, dazzling; magnificent. **resplendence, resplendency,** *nn.* (L. *splendēre*, shine)

respond, *v.i.* speak in return, reply; act in answer, react, retaliate; (*Amer.*) be liable for payment.—*n.* responsory; (*archit.*) half-column attached to wall to support arch. **respondent,** *a.* and *n.* defendant, esp. in divorce suit. **respondentia,** *n.* loan on security of ship's cargo. (L. *spondēre*, promise)

response, *n.* responding, answer; responsive act or feeling; answer made by congregation to priest during service. **responsible,** *a.* liable to be called to account, answerable; capable of rational conduct; trustworthy; involving responsibility. **responsibility,** *n.* being responsible; moral obligation, duty; charge, trust. **responsions,** *n.pl.* first examination for Oxford B.A., smalls. **responsive,** *a.* responding; sensitive to influence or stimulus. **responsory,** *n.* anthem sung by choir after lesson. (*respond*)

ressalah, *n.* squadron of Indian native cavalry. **ressaldar,** *n.* native captain of this. (Hind. *risalah*)

rest, *n.* cessation from motion; repose, sleep; support, prop; pause in music, metre etc.; place of quiet, shelter; (*Shake.*) restored vigour.—*v.i.* and *t.* take rest, give rest to; be still; lie, be fixed (on); lean, support, rely. **at r.,** still, tranquil; dead. **day of r.,** Sunday. **lay to r.,** bury. **set at r.,** settle; relieve. **r.-balk,** *n.* ridge left unploughed between furrows. **r.-cure,** *n.* in bed, avoiding all exertion. **r.-house,** *n.* shelter for travellers. (O.E. *ræst*)

rest, *v.i.* remain. — *n.* remainder, others; reserve fund of bank; (*tennis*) rally. **r. with,** be in the hands of. (L. *re-*, behind; *stare*, stand)

rest, *n.* projection on armour to hold butt of lance when jousting. (*arrest*)

restart, *v.i.* and *t.* start again.

restate, *v.t.* state over again; put differently. **restatement,** *n.*

restaurant, *n.* public eating-house. *restaurateur*, *n.* keeper of one. (F.)

restful, *a.* quiet, peaceful, soothing.

rest-harrow, *n.* plant with tough roots, cammock. (*arrest*)

restiff, *arch.* for **restive.**

restitute, *v.t.* and *i.* make restitution (of). **restitution,** *n.* restoring of property to owner; reparation, compensation. (L. *statuere*, set up)

restive, *a.* impatient of control; fidgety; (of horse) inclined to jib, refractory. (L. *restare*, remain)

restless, *a.* continually moving; uneasy, unsettled.

restore, *v.t.* give back, return; replace, reinstate; re-establish; renovate; heal; bring back (ruined building etc.) to original form, reconstruct. **restoration,** *n.* restoring, recovery. **the Restoration,** re-establishment of British monarchy under Charles II. **restorative,** *a.* tending to restore health or strength.—*n.* reinvigorating medicine or food. (L. *restaurare*)

restrain, *v.t.* hold back; control, repress, check; confine, imprison. **restrained,** *a.* moderate, without exuberance. **restraint,** *n.* control, restriction, curb; avoidance of excess, austerity; confinement in asylum. (L. *stringere*, bind)

restrict, *v.t.* impose limits on, confine. **restricted,** *a.* circumscribed. **restriction,** *n.* restricting; limitation. **restrictive,** *a.* (*restrain*)

resty, *a.* (*Shake.*) inactive, sluggish.

result, *v.i.* happen, follow, as consequence; end (in); (*arch.*) spring up. —*n.* consequence, outcome; answer to calculation. **resultant,** *a.* arising as result.—*n.* combined effect of two or more forces. (L. *salire*, leap)

resume, *v.t.* and *i.* take again, reoccupy; begin again, continue after interruption; summarize. *résumé*, *n.* summary, abstract. **resumption,** *n.* resuming. **resumptive,** *a.* (L. *sumere*, take)

resupinate, *a.* (*bot.*) upside-down. **resupination,** *n.* inverted position. (*supine*)

resurge, *v.i.* rise again. **resurgence,** *n.* revival, renewal. **resurgent,** *a.* rising again or from dead. (*surge*)

resurrect, *v.t.* bring back into use, revive (custom); (*sl.*) exhume. **resurrection,** *n.* rising from the dead, esp. that of Christ; revival; (*sl.*) exhumation. **resurrection-man, resurrectionist,** *nn.* one who disinterred bodies for sale to anatomists, body-snatcher. (L. *surgere*, rise)

resuscitate, *v.t.* and *i.* restore to life or consciousness; revive, be reanimated. **resuscitation, resuscitator,** *nn.* **resuscitative,** *a.* (L. *re-*, back; *sub*, under; *citare*, rouse)

ret, *v.t.* and *i.* soften (flax) by steeping; (of hay) be spoilt by wet, rot.

retable, *n.* shelf, ledge, above back of altar. (F.)

retail, *n.* sale in small quantities.—*adv.* by retail.—*v.t.* and *i.* sell, be sold, retail; tell to many, recount. **retailer,** *n.* (O.F. *tailler,* cut)

retain, *v.t.* keep possession of, hold; keep in mind or use; keep in place, support; engage services of (barrister). **retainer,** *n.* dependant, follower; fee to retain barrister; (*law*) formal retention. (L. *tenēre,* hold)

retake, *v.t.* take again, recapture.

retaliate, *v.t.* and *i.* repay (injury) in kind, return like for like; cast back (accusation); tax imports by way of reprisal. **retaliation,** *n.* **retaliative, retaliatory,** *aa.* (L. *talis,* such)

retard, *v.t.* and *i.* make slow or late; keep back; happen after normal time. **retardation, retardment,** *nn.* **retardative, retardatory,** *aa.* (L. *tardus,* slow)

retch, *v.i.* make effort to vomit.—*n.* retching. (O.E. *hrǣcan,* spit)

retention, *n.* retaining. **retentive,** *a.* having power of retaining; tenacious, not forgetful. (*retain*)

retenue, *n.* reserve, self-control. (F.)

retiarius, *n.* Roman gladiator armed with net and trident. **retiary,** *a.* and *n.* net-making (spider). (L.)

reticent, *a.* reserved in speech, uncommunicative. **reticence,** *n.* (L. *tacēre,* be silent)

reticle, *n.* network of fine lines on object-glass of telescope to help accurate observation. **reticulate,** *v.t.* and *i.* divide, mark, like network.—*a.* reticulated. **reticulation,** *n.* **reticule,** *n.* lady's hand-bag, esp. of net; reticle. **reticulum,** *n.* second stomach of ruminant. **retiform,** *a.* net-shaped. (L. *rete,* net)

retina, *n.* (*pl.* **retinas, retinae**) membrane at back of eye receiving image. **retinal,** *a.* **retinitis,** *n.* inflammation of retina. (L.L.)

retinue, *n.* train of attendants, suite. (*retain*)

retire, *v.i.* withdraw, retreat; give up office or work; go to bed; (*Shake.*) return.—*v.t.* order, compel, to retire. —*n.* signal to retire. **r. into oneself,** become reserved. **retired,** *a.* secluded; withdrawn from active duty. **retirement,** *n.* being retired; privacy, seclusion. **retiring,** *a.* unobtrusive, shy. (F. *tirer,* draw)

retort, *v.t.* and *i.* reply sharply; cast back (accusation etc.); requite in kind.—*n.* sharp or witty reply; vessel with funnel bent downwards used in distilling; kinds of receptacle used in making gas and steel. **retorted,** *a.* recurved, bent back. **retortion,** *n.* bending back; retaliation by state on subjects of another. (L. *torquēre,* twist)

retouch, *v.t.* touch up, improve with new touches.

retrace, *v.t.* go back over; trace back to source.

retract, *v.t.* and *i.* draw back or in; withdraw, disavow, unsay; recant. **retractable, retractile,** *aa.* able to be drawn back. **retractility,** *n.* **retractation,** *n.* disavowal, revoking. **retraction,** *n.* drawing back; withdrawing (of charge etc.). **retractive,** *a.* **retractor,** *n.* muscle that retracts limb. (L. *trahere,* draw)

retrad, *adv.* backwards. **retral,** *a.* back, posterior. (L. *retro*)

retranslate, *v.t.* translate again or back into original language. **retranslation,** *n.*

retread, *v.t.* walk over again.

re-tread, *v.t.* put new tread on (tyre).

retreat, *v.i.* and *t.* go back, withdraw, retire; recede.—*n.* withdrawal, esp. of troops; quiet or secluded place, refuge; seclusion for religious devotion; signal for retiring, sunset call on bugle. **beat a r.,** give signal for retiring; abandon undertaking. (L. *trahere,* draw)

retree, *n.* paper damaged or left imperfect in course of manufacture.

retrench, *v.t.* and *i.* cut down, shorten; reduce expenditure, economize. **retrenchment,** *n.* retrenching; inner trench to prolong defence.

retrial, *n.* fresh or second trial.

retribution, *n.* punishment for wickedness; vengeance, requital. **retributive,** *a.* (L. *tribuere,* assign)

retrieve, *v.t.* and *i.* recover, get back; restore (fortunes); re-establish (character); atone for (misdeed); rescue (from ruin); (of dog) find and bring in (shot game). **past r.,** irretrievably. **retrieval,** *n.* **retriever,** *n.* breed of dog trained for retrieving. (F. *trouver,* find)

retro-, *pref.* backwards, as in **retrograde**; behind, as in **retrochoir.**

retroact, *v.i.* react; act in opposite direction; apply to past. **retroaction,** *n.* **retroactive,** *a.* operating backwards; retrospective.

retrocede, *v.i.* move back, recede; (*med.*) strike inwards. **retrocedence, retrocession,** *nn.* **retrocedent, retrocessive,** *aa.* (L. *cedere,* go)

retrocede, *v.t.* cede back again. **retrocession,** *n.* **retrocessive,** *a.*

retrochoir, *n.* space in church behind high altar. (*retro-*; *choir*)

retroflected, retroflex, retroflexed, *aa.* (*anat.*) turned backwards. **retroflexion,** *n.* (L. *flectere,* bend)

retrograde, *a.* backward, reversed; passing from better to worse; reactionary; (*astron.*) of, showing, retrogradation.—*n.* degenerate; backward tendency.—*v.i.* move backwards, recede; decline, revert; (*astron.*) show retrogradation. **retrogradation,** *n.* retrogression; (*astron.*) apparent backward movement of planet in zodiac. (L. *gradi,* walk)

retrogress, *v.i.* move backwards; deteriorate. **retrogression,** *n.* **retro-**

gressing; reversal of development; deterioration; retrogradation. **retrogressive,** *a.* (L. *gradi,* walk)

retroject, *v.t.* cast back (opp. to project). (L. *jacere,* throw)

retropulsion, *n.* (*med.*) transfer of disease from external to internal part. (L. *pellere,* drive)

retrorse, *a.* (*bot.*) turned back or downward. (L. *retro,* backwards; *vertere,* turn)

retrospect, *n.* mental review of past. **retrospection,** *n.* meditation on past. **retrospective,** *a.* of, in, retrospection: lying behind one; applicable to what has already happened, licensing or punishing past action. (L. *specere,* look)

retroussé, *a.* turned upwards. (F.)

retrovert, *v.t.* turn backwards. **retroversion,** *n.* (L. *vertere,* turn)

retry, *v.t.* try a second time.

rettery, *n.* place for retting flax.

return, *v.i.* and *t.* come, go, back; revert, recur; give back, restore; repay, reciprocate; say in reply; yield as profit; elect as M.P.—*n.* returning; what is returned; requital, repayment; profit, increase; formal report. **many happy rr.** (**of the day**), birthday greeting. **r. match,** second match between same opponents. **r. one's lead,** lead from same suit as one; back one up. **r. thanks,** say grace; respond to toast. **r. ticket,** for there-and-back journey. **returning officer,** officer conducting election.

retuse, *a.* (*bot.*) having round end with notch in centre. (L. *tundere,* pound)

reunion, *n.* reuniting; social gathering. **reunite,** *v.i.* and *t.* join again.

rev, *n.* (*colloq.*) revolution.—*v.t.* and *i.* (*past, p.p.* **revved**) run (engine) quickly. (abbr.)

revalenta, *n.* preparation of lentil-meal. (L. *ervum,* vetch; *lens,* lentil)

revalorize, *v.t.* restore (currency) to its original value. **revalorization,** *n.*

revamp, *v.t.* patch up again.

revanche, *n.* return match, revenge. (F.)

reveal, *v.t.* disclose, make known; divulge, betray; manifest by supernatural agency. (L. *velum,* veil)

reveal, *n.* (*archit.*) vertical side of doorway or recess. (O.F. *valer,* lower)

reveillé, *n.* morning bugle-call to awaken soldiers. (F. *réveillez,* wake ye)

revel, *v.i.* make merry, carouse; take delight (in).—*n.* festivity; (*pl.*) entertainment. (L. *rebellare,* rebel)

revelation, *n.* revealing; communication by God to man, divine truth; striking or sensational disclosure; (also *pl.*) last book of New Testament, Apocalypse. **revelational,** *a.* **revelationist,** *n.* author of the Revelation; believer in divine revelation. (*reveal*)

reveller, *n.* one who revels. **revelry,** *n.* revelling, noisy festivity.

revenant, *n.* one returned from death or exile; spectre. (F.)

revendication, *n.* formal claiming, recovery, of lost territory etc. (F.)

revenge, *v.t.* and *i.* inflict injury in return for (wrong); satisfy (oneself) by retaliation; avenge (person).—*n.* revenging, retaliation; vindictive feeling; return match. **revengeful,** *a.* vindictive. **revengement,** *n.* (*Shake.*) retribution. (L. *vindicare,* lay claim to)

revenons à nos moutons, let us get back to the subject in hand (lit. let us return to our sheep). (F.)

revenue, *n.* annual income, esp. of state; government department collecting this. **r. cutter, officer,** employed by customs to prevent smuggling. (L. *venire,* come)

reverberate, *v.t.* and *i.* throw back, echo, reflect; resound, cause to resound. **reverberant, reverberative,** *aa.* **reverberation,** *n.* echo, rolling sound. **reverberator,** *n.* reflector, reflecting lamp. **reverberatory,** *a.* of, acting by, reverberation. **reverberatory furnace,** kiln in which flame is reflected from roof. (L. *verberare,* beat)

revere, *v.t.* venerate, regard with awe. **reverence,** *n.* revering; deep respect, veneration; (*arch.*) obeisance, bow.—*v.t.* revere, venerate. **his, your, reverence,** (*arch.*) title of clergyman. **saving your reverence,** (*arch.*) apology for using coarse term. **reverend,** *a.* venerable; deserving reverence; (*abbr.* **Rev.**) title of clergyman. **Very, Right, Most, Reverend,** used of dean, bishop, archbishop. **reverent,** *a.* feeling, showing, reverence. **reverential,** *a.* marked by, due to, reverence. (L. *verēri,* fear)

reverie, *n.* day-dream, brown study; (*mus.*) dreamy piece; (*arch.*) extravagant fancy, delusion. (O.F. *resver,* dream)

revers, *n.* (*pl.* same) part of coat or dress turned back, lapel. (F.)

reverse, *a.* turned round, upside-down; opposite, contrary.—*n.* opposite; check, set-back, defeat; back of coin (opp. to obverse).—*v.t.* and *i.* turn other way round or backwards or inside out; invert, transpose; revoke, recall; work backwards. **r. arms,** hold rifles butt upwards. **reversal,** *n.* (L. *vertere,* turn)

reversi, *n.* game with 64 counters on draught-board. (F.)

reversible, *a.* with both sides usable. **reversibility,** *n.*

reversion, *n.* reverting; return to former condition or type; right to future possession; return of estate to grantor or his heirs, us. on death of original grantee. **reversional, reversionary,** *aa.* **reversioner,** *n.* holder of reversionary right.

revert, *v.i.* and *t.* direct attention to, refer to, again; return to former or wild state; turn backwards; (*law*) fall in by reversion.—*n.* one who readopts his original faith. **revertible,** *a.* (L. *vertere,* turn)

revet, *v.t.* face (slope) with stone, sandbags etc. **revetment,** *n.* retaining-wall. (L. *vestire,* clothe)

review, *v.t.* and *i.* look back on; examine critically; inspect (troops); write review of (book).—*n.* reflective survey; reconsideration; military inspection; critical notice of book; periodical containing critical essays. **pass in r.,** inspect. **r. order,** ceremonial uniform. **reviewal,** *n.* reviewing. **reviewer,** *n.* writer of reviews.

revile, *v.t.* and *i.* call by ill names, speak abusively (of). **reviler, reviling,** *nn.* (*vile*)

revise, *v.t.* look over and correct; change after consideration.—*n.* revision; (*print.*) proof embodying corrections. **Revised Version,** translation of Bible made in 1870–84. **revisal, revision,** *nn.* **revisional, revisionary, revisory,** *aa.* (L. *vidēre,* see)

revisit, *v.t.* return to after absence.

revitalize, *v.t.* give fresh life to, reanimate.

revival, *n.* reviving; restoration to vigour or consciousness; coming back into vogue; religious awakening. **R. of Learning,** Renaissance. **revivalism,** *n.* spirit of religious revivals. **revivalist,** *n.* preacher at revivals.

revive, *v.i.* and *t.* return, restore, to life, consciousness, or vigour; recover from neglect or disuse. **reviver,** *n.* preparation for restoring colour; (*sl.*) stimulant. **revivify,** *v.t.* reanimate, quicken. **revivification,** *n.* **reviviscence,** *n.* returning to life or vigour. **reviviscent,** *a.* (L. *vivere,* live)

revoke, *v.t.* and *i.* repeal, reverse (decree); (*cards*) fail to follow suit when one could.—*n.* revoking. **revocation,** *n.* revoking, repeal. **revocatory,** *a.* (L. *vocare,* call)

revolt, *v.i.* and *t.* rebel (against); desert (from); feel disgust or revulsion; nauseate.—*n.* rebellion, insurrection; loathing. **revolting,** *a.* loathsome, disgusting. (L. *volvere,* roll)

revolute, *a.* (*bot.*) with margin rolled backwards. (*revolve*)

revolute, *v.i.* (*sl.*) take part in political revolution. (*revolution*)

revolution, *n.* revolving; movement round centre or axis; single completion of orbit or rotation, turn; regular recurrence; great change; forcible overthrow of system of government by subjects. **revolutionary,** *a.* of revolution; involving great changes.—*n.* revolutionist. **revolutionism,** *n.* advocacy of revolution. **revolutionist,** *n.* one who organizes or takes part in a revolution. **revolutionize,** *v.t.* change fundamentally. (*revolve*)

revolve, *v.i.* and *t.* turn round, roll on; move in orbit; rotate; turn over in mind, ponder. **revolver,** *n.* pistol firing several shots without reloading. (L. *volvere,* roll)

revue, *n.* spectacular loosely connected variety entertainment; satirical burlesque. (F.)

revulsion, *n.* sudden violent change, reversal (of feeling); (*med.*) diversion of pain from one part to another. **revulsive,** *a.* and *n.* (*med.*) counter-irritant. (L. *vellere,* pull)

reward, *n.* return given for service or merit, recompense; retribution; sum offered for return of lost property etc.—*v.t.* give in return for; recompense, requite. (O.F. *regarder,* regard)

reword, *v.t.* word differently, redraft.

rewrite, *v.t.* write afresh, revise.

Rex, *n.* (*abbr.* **R.**) reigning king. (L.)

rexine, *n.* kind of imitation leather used for bookbinding and other purposes. (Trade mark of Imperial Chemical Industries Ltd.)

Reynard, *n.* proper name for fox; fox. (name in medieval epic)

rhabdomancy, *n.* divination by means of rod, dowsing. (Gk. *rhabdos,* rod; *manteia,* divination)

Rhadamanthus, *n.* stern judge. **Rhadamanthine,** *a.* sternly just and inflexible. (name in Greek myth)

rhamphoid, *a.* beak-shaped. (Gk. *rhamphos,* beak)

rhapsode, *n.* ancient Greek professional reciter of epic. **rhapsodic, rhapsodical,** *aa.* of rhapsody; ecstatic, gushing. **rhapsodist,** *n.* one who rhapsodizes; rhapsode. **rhapsodize,** *v.i.* and *t.* utter or write rhapsody; recite (epic). **rhapsody,** *n.* enthusiastic high-flown utterance; emotional irregular piece of music; section of epic recited by rhapsode. (Gk. *rhaptein,* stitch; *ōdē,* song)

rhatany, *n.* a S. American shrub; its astringent juice, used to colour port wine. (native *rataña*)

rhea, *n.* S. American three-toed ostrich. (name of Greek goddess)

rhea, *n.* ramie. (Assamese)

Rhenish, *a.* and *n.* (*arch.*) Rhine (wine). (L. *Rhenus,* Rhine)

rhenium, *n.* rare metallic element.

rheo-, from Gk. *rheos,* stream, used in **rheology,** *n.* study of the flow of matter; **rheometer,** *n.* instrument measuring currents, galvanometer; **rheoscope,** *n.* instrument for detecting electric current; **rheostat,** *n.* instrument for regulating electric current; **rheotome,** *n.* device for interrupting electric current; **rheotrope,** *n.* commutator reversing electric current.

rhesus, *n.* small long-tailed Indian monkey. (king in Greek myth)

rhetor, *n.* ancient Greek teacher of

rhetoric; professional orator. **rhetoric,** *n.* art of elegant and persuasive speaking, oratory; flowery or artificial speech, showy declamation. **rhetorical,** *a.* of oratory; high-flown, bombastic; (of question) asked for effect only. **rhetorician,** *n.* rhetorical speaker; rhetor. (Gk.)

rheum, *n.* (*arch.*) watery discharge from throat or nose, mucus; catarrh. (Gk. *rhein,* flow)

rheumatism, *n.* disease causing pain in muscles and joints. **rheumatic,** *a.* of, caused by, affected with, rheumatism.—*n.* rheumatic patient; (*pl.*) rheumatism. **rheumaticky,** *a.* (*colloq.*) like, having, rheumatism. **rheumatiz,** *n.* (*vulg.*) rheumatism. **rheumatoid,** *a.* of, like, rheumatism. (*rheum*)

rheumy, *a.* affected with rheum; (of air) damp, raw.

rhinal, *a.* of the nose. (Gk. *rhis,* nose)

rhine, *n.* large open ditch.

rhinestone, *n.* kind of rock-crystal; paste imitation of diamond. (*Rhine*)

rhino, *n.* (*sl.*) rhinoceros. (abbr.)

rhino, *n.* (*sl.*) money.

rhino-, from Gk. *rhis,* nose, used in **rhinoceros,** *n.* large thick-skinned animal with horn on nose, hence **rhinocerotic,** *a.*; **rhinology,** *n.* study of the nose; **rhinoplasty,** *n.* plastic surgery of the nose; **rhinoscope,** *n.* instrument for examining nose.

rhizo-, from Gk. *rhiza,* root, used in **rhizocarp,** *n.* plant with perennial root but annual stem, hence **rhizocarpous,** *a.*; **rhizogenic,** *a.* root-producing; **rhizoid,** *a.* and *n.* rootlike (filament); **rhizome,** *n.* stem on or below ground producing roots below and shoots above, rootstock.

Rhodes scholar, holder of one of the scholarships founded by Cecil Rhodes and tenable at Oxford by students from British Dominions and U.S.A.

rhodium, *n.* hard metal like platinum. **rhodic, rhodous,** *aa.* (Gk. *rhodon,* rose, from colour of its salts)

rhodium, *n.* scented wood of Canary convolvulus, rosewood. (Gk. *rhodon,* rose)

rhododendron, *n.* evergreen shrub with large handsome flowers. (Gk. *rhodon,* rose; *dendron,* tree)

rhodomontade, same as **rodomontade.**

rhomb, *n.* rhombus, diamond-shaped figure. **rhombohedron,** *n.* solid bounded by six rhombic planes. **rhombohedral,** *a.* **rhombic,** *a.* of, like, a rhombus; diamond-shaped. **rhomboid,** *a.* nearly resembling a rhombus.—*n.* figure like rhombus but with only opposite sides equal. **rhomboidal,** *a.* **rhombus,** *n.* (*pl.* **rhombi, rhombuses**) oblique-angled parallelogram with all sides equal; kinds of flat-fish. (Gk. *rhombos*)

rhotacism, *n.* excessive pronunciation of *r,* burring; conversion of *s* etc. into *r.* **rhotacize,** *v.t.* (Gk. *rho,* r)

rhubarb, *n.* a garden herb; its leaf-stocks, used in cooking; purgative made from root of an allied oriental plant. (Gk. *rha,* rhubarb; *barbaros,* foreign)

rhumb, *n.* any of the 32 points of the compass; angle separating them, 11° 15′; (also **r.-line**) line cutting all meridians at same angle. (*rhombus*)

rhyme, rime, *n.* correspondence in sound between final syllables of words or verses; rhymed verse, poem.—*v.i.* and *t.* make rhyme (with); versify, put into rhyme. **single, male, masculine, r.,** e.g. 'moon' and 'spoon.' **double, female, feminine, r.,** e.g. 'cricket' and 'wicket.' **treble, triple, r.,** e.g. 'national' and 'rational.' **r. royal,** stanza of seven ten-syllabled lines rhyming ababbcc. **riding r.,** old name for heroic couplet. **without r. or reason,** unaccountable; thoughtlessly. **rhymer, rhymester,** *nn.* writer of rhymes; poetaster. (Gk. *rhuthmos,* rhythm)

rhyparography, *n.* *genre* or still-life pictures, esp. of low subjects. (Gk. *rhuparos,* dirty; *graphein,* write)

rhysimeter, *n.* instrument for measuring speed of current or ship. (Gk. *rhusis,* flowing; *metron,* measure)

rhythm, *n.* measured flow, timed movements, esp. of words or music; cadence; regular recurrence; symmetry. **rhythmic, rhythmical,** *aa.* **rhythmist,** *n.* adept in rhythm. (Gk. *rhuthmos*)

riant, *a.* gay, smiling. (F.)

rib, *n.* one of the bones extending from spine round chest; ridge, raised strip; curved timber of ship's frame-work; rod of umbrella-frame; vein of leaf or ore; (*archit.*) raised moulding across ceiling.—*v.t.* furnish with ribs; (*Shake.*) enclose. **false, floating, short, rr.,** those not attached to breast-bone. **r.-grass,** *n.* narrow-leaved plantain. (O.E.)

ribald, *a.* irreverent, scurrilous, foul-mouthed.—*n.* ribald person. **ribaldry,** *n.* ribald talk, obscenity. (O.F. *ribaut*)

riband, see **ribbon.**

ribband, *n.* narrow strip, scantling, to hold ship's ribs in position during construction; riband.

ribbon, riband, *n.* silk, satin, or velvet woven into narrow band; piece of this; narrow strip; (*pl., sl.*) reins. **Blue R.,** Order of the Garter; badge of teetotalism; highest distinction, e.g. for record Atlantic crossing. **Red R.,** Order of the Bath. **r. building,** along main roads leading out of towns. **r.-fish, r.-grass,** *nn.* long slender kinds. (O.E. *riban*)

ribēs, *n.* (*bot.*) currant or gooseberry plant. (Arab. *ribas,* sorrel)

Ribston pippin, kind of apple. (place)

ribwort, *n.* rib-grass.

rice, *n.* an Eastern cereal plant; its

white seeds. **r.-bird,** *n.* bobolink; Java sparrow. **r.-milk,** *n.* milk thickened with rice. **r.-paper,** *n.* delicate fabric of pith used by Chinese for painting on. **r. pudding,** milk pudding made with rice. (Gk. *oruza*)

rich, *a.* having much money, wealthy; abounding (in), fertile; copious; fine, costly; mellow; (of food) full of fat, highly flavoured; (*colloq.*) full of humour. **riches,** *n.* wealth; abundance. richly, *adv.* in a rich manner; thoroughly. (O.E. *rice*)

rick, *n.* stack, large pile, of hay etc. (O.E. *hréac*)

rick, see **wrick.**

rickets, *n.* children's disease marked by softening of bones, bandy legs etc.; rachitis. **rickety,** *a.* like, having, rickets; shaky, insecure.

rickle, *n.* (*Scot.*) loose heap.

rickshaw, ricksha, *abbr.* **of jinricksha.**

ricochet, *n.* glancing rebound of bullet etc. along ground or water; hit made after this.—*v.i.* and *t.* (*past, p.p.* **ricocheted** or **ricochetted**) skip, hit, with ricochet. (F.)

rictus, *n.* vertical width of open mouth or beak, gape. (L.)

rid, *v.t.* (*past* **ridded** or **rid,** *p.p.* **rid**) free, clear, relieve (of); (*Shake.*) kill. **get r. of,** be freed from; dismiss. **riddance,** *n.* (O.N. *rydhja*)

riddel, same as **ridel.**

ridden, see **ride.**

riddle, *n.* coarse sieve.—*v.t.* screen with riddle; make many holes in; demolish (theory). (O.E. *hridder*)

riddle, *n.* puzzling question, obscure description, enigma; mysterious thing or person.—*v.i.* and *t.* speak in, put, riddles; guess. **riddlemeree,** *n.* rigmarole. (O.E. *rǣdels*)

ride, *v.i.* and *t.* (*past* **rode,** *p.p.* **ridden**) go on horseback or in vehicle; manage horse; be borne along, float (on); lie (at anchor); overlap; oppress, dominate; give ride to.—*n.* journey on horseback, in vehicle etc.; riding-track. **r. and tie,** when two travel with one horse, each riding alternately and leaving horse tethered for the other. **r. down,** overtake by riding; make horse trample on. **r. for a fall,** ride or act recklessly. **r. out,** keep afloat through (storm). **r. to death,** overdo. **r. to hounds,** hunt fox. **take for a r.,** (*Amer. sl.*) kidnap and murder in car. (O.E. *rīdan*)

rideau, *n.* mound of earth, esp. as protection. (F.)

ridel, *n.* altar-curtain. (O.F.)

rident, *a.* laughing. (L. *rīdēre,* laugh)

rider, *n.* one who rides; addition to document, amending clause; (*geom.*) subsidiary problem.

ridge, *n.* line where two slopes meet, crest; raised strip; long narrow hilltop; earth between furrows.—*v.t.* and *i.* form into ridges, wrinkle. **r.-piece, r.-pole,** *nn.* beam along crest of roof. **ridgeway,** *n.* road along crest of hill. (O.E. *hrycg*)

ridicule, *n.* mockery, derision; (*arch.*) butt.—*v.t.* make fun of, deride. **ridiculous,** *a.* absurd, grotesque; preposterous. (L. *rīdēre,* laugh)

riding, *n.* one of the three divisions of Yorkshire. (for *thriding,* third part, *th* being dropped owing to preceding *t* of East etc.)

riding, *n.* track for riders. **r.-habit,** *n.* lady's riding-dress. **r.-light,** *n.* one shown by ship at anchor. **r.-master,** *n.* teacher of riding.

ridotto, *n.* gaming-house; public entertainment or dance. (It.)

rifacimento, *n.* recasting of literary work. (It.)

rife, *a.* prevalent, common, numerous; well provided (with). (O.E. *rýfe*)

riffle, *n.* (*min.*) groove in sluice to catch free particles of gold. (*rifle*)

riffle, *v.t.* (*Amer.*) ruffle slightly; turn over (pages).

riff-raff, *n.* rabble, lowest part of community. (F. *rif et raf*)

rifle, *v.t.* and *i.* search and rob, plunder; make spiral grooves in.—*n.* gun with rifled barrel; (*pl.*) troops armed with rifles. **R. Brigade,** certain British regiments. **R. Corps,** old corps of volunteers. **r.-green,** *a.* dark green. **rifleman,** *n.* man armed with rifle; member of Rifle Brigade or Rifle Corps. **rifling,** *n.* arrangement of grooves in gun-barrel. (O.F. *rifler,* graze)

rift, *n.* cleft, crack; opening (in clouds). —*v.t.* cleave. **r. in the lute,** first sign of coming discord.

rig, *v.t.* equip (ship) with sails and tackling.—*n.* arrangement of ship's masts and sails; dress, style; (*Amer.*) equipage, turn-out. **r. out,** fit out. **r. up,** contrive as makeshift.

rig, *n.* trick, dodge; corner in goods.—*v.t.* manipulate dishonestly. **run a r.,** (*arch.*) play prank. **r. the market,** raise or lower prices artificially.

rig, *n.* (*Scot.*) ridge; path.

Riga balsam, medicinal oil got from pine. (town)

rigadoon, *n.* a lively dance for two; music for it. (F. *rigaudon*)

rigescent, *a.* becoming rigid; rather stiff. **rigescence,** *n.* (L. *rigēre,* be stiff)

rigging, *n.* ropes for supporting masts and working sails. (*rig*)

riggish, *a.* (*Shake.*) wanton.

right, *a.* just, virtuous; correct, true; normal; fit, recovered; right-hand; straight; (*arch.*) genuine. — *adv.* directly; completely, exactly; correctly, properly; to right hand.—*n.* rectitude, virtue; what is just, fairness; privilege; justification, claim; right-hand side; conservative party; (*pl.*) right condition.—*v.t.* and *i.* set, become, upright; make reparation to or for; correct. **all r.**, satisfactory; very well. **in her own r.**, not by marriage. **in the r.**, not mistaken or unjust. **put, set, to rr.**, set in order. **r. angle**, one of 90°. **r. away, off**, at once. **r. bank**, on right of person facing down stream. **r. hand**, that opposite heart. **r. of way**, public path over private ground. **serve one r.**, be well deserved. (O.E. *riht*)

right-about, *a.* to opposite direction. **send to the r.**, dismiss abruptly.

right-down, *a.* thorough.

righten, *v.t.* set right, amend.

righteous, *a.* virtuous, good, just.

rightful, *a.* legitimate; having just claim.

right-hand, *a.* on, to, right hand. **r. man**, chief assistant. **right-handed**, *a.* fitted for, using, right hand.

rigid, *a.* stiff, not flexible; stern, severe; unadaptable. **rigidity**, *n.* (L. *rigidus*)

rigmarole, *n.* long rambling statement; meaningless string of words.

rigol, *n.* (*Shake.*) ring, circle. (It. *rigolo*)

rigor, *n.* (*med.*) fit of shivering. *r. mortis*, stiffening of body after death. **rigorism**, *n.* rigidity of principle. austerity. **rigorous**, *a.* stern, severe, strict. **rigour**, *n.* severity, strictness; harshness. (L.)

Rigsdag, *n.* Danish Parliament. (Da.)

Riksdag, *n.* Swedish Parliament. (Swed.)

rile, *v.t.* (*sl.*) anger, irritate. (*roil*)

rilievo, *n.* (*art*) relief. (It.)

rill, *n.* small brook, streamlet. **rille**, *n.* (*astron.*) furrow on moon's surface. **rillet**, *n.* small rill.

rim, *n.* raised edge; border, margin; outer circle of wheel.—*v.t.* supply, surround, with rim. (O.E. *rima*)

rim, *n.* (*arch.*) midriff. (O.E. *réoma*)

rime, *n.* hoar-frost.—*v.t.* cover with rime. (O.E. *hrim*)

rime, see **rhyme.**

rimer, same as **reamer.**

rimose, rimous, *aa.* full of chinks or fissures. (L. *rima*, chink)

rimy, *a.* covered with hoar-frost.

rind, *n.* hard outer coating of fruit, cheese, bacon etc.; bark, peel. (O.E.)

rinderpest, *n.* cattle-plague. (G.)

ring, *n.* metal hoop for finger; circular thing, band; round enclosure, arena; clique to control market etc.—*v.t.* and *i.* encircle, surround; put ring through nose of (bull); cut circular groove in bark of (tree); (of hawk) rise in spirals. **make rr. round**, excel, outstrip, very easily. **the r.**, pugilism; bookmakers collectively. **r.-bark**, *v.t.* ring (tree). **r.-bolt**, *n.* bolt with ring attached. **r.-bone**, *n.* bony growth on horse's pastern-bone. **r.-dove**, *n.* wood-pigeon. **r.-fence**, *n.* fence completely enclosing estate, **r.-finger**, *n.* third, esp. of left hand. **ringmaster**, *n.* manager of circus performance. **r.-ouzel**, *n.* kind of thrush. **r.-velvet**, *n.* fine supple velvet. (O.E. *hring*)

ring, *v.i.* and *t.* (*past* **rang or rung**, *p.p.* **rung**) sound resonantly, peal; resound, re-echo; cause (bell) to sound; announce, summon, by bell. —*n.* ringing; resonant note; set (of church bells). **r. down**, lower (curtain). **r. false, true**, sound or seem counterfeit, genuine. **r. off**, end telephone call. **r. the changes on**, repeat with variations. **r. knell of**, indicate death or end of. **r. up**, raise (curtain); call on telephone. (O.E. *hringan*)

ringent, *a.* (*bot.*) gaping, opened wide. (L. *ringi*, gape)

ringer, *n.* quoit that falls round pin; fox taking circular course; (*Austral.*) man who shears most sheep in a day.

ringleader, *n.* organizer of riot, mutiny etc.

ringlet, *n.* curl of hair; small ring.

ringtail, *n.* kinds of hawk, eagle, and opossum.

ringworm, *n.* skin-disease appearing in circular patches, us. on scalp.

rink, *n.* sheet of ice for skating, curling etc.; floor for roller-skating.—*v.i.* roller-skate.

rinse, *v.t.* cleanse with water by dipping or swilling; wash lightly.—*n.* rinsing. (O.F. *raincer*)

riot, *n.* disturbance of public peace by crowd; tumult, disorder; loose living; unrestrained profusion.—*v.i.* raise uproar, brawl; indulge in dissipation; revel. **R. Act**, on reading of which crowd must disperse or be guilty of felony. **riotous**, *a.* tumultuous, seditious; luxurious, wanton. (O.F. *riote*)

rip, *v.t.* and *i.* tear, slash; strip (off), open (up), by tearing; rush along.—*n.* ripping; tear, rent. **let her r.**, do not check speed.

rip, *n.* worn-out horse, screw; dissolute person, reprobate.

rip, *n.* stretch of broken water.

riparian, *a.* and *n.* (proprietor) of bank of river. (L. *ripa*, bank)

ripe, *v.t.* (*Scot.*) rummage, search.

ripe, *a.* ready for harvest; mature, fully developed; fit for use, ready.—*v.t.* and *i.* ripen. **ripen**, *v.t.* and *i.* make, become, ripe. (O.E. *ripe*)

riposte, *n.* quick lunge after parry; counterstroke, retort.—*v.i.* make riposte. (F.)

ripper, *n.* tool for ripping; (*sl.*) first-rate person. **ripping**, *a.* (*sl.*) splendid, capital.

ripple, *n.* comb for stripping seeds from flax.—*v.t.* cleanse (flax) thus.

ripple, *n.* small wave or undulation; sound of this, babble.—*v.i.* and *t.* form ripples (in). **r.-cloth**, *n.* woollen fabric with crinkled surface. **r.-mark**, *n.* ridge left on sand etc. by water or wind. **ripplet,** *n.* small ripple. **ripply,** *a.*

riprap, *n.* loose foundation of broken stones.

Rip van Winkle, person much behind the times. (name in story)

rise, *v.i.* and *t.* (*past* **rose,** *p.p.* **risen**) get up, become erect; go up, mount; become higher; swell, increase; have origin; revolt, be stirred; close session; ascend from grave; (of fish) come, lure, to surface.—*n.* rising; degree of elevation; upward slope; increase in price, salary, rank etc.; riser of stair. **give r. to,** cause. **on the r.,** increasing. **r. to the occasion,** be equal to emergency. **take a r. out of,** fool; anger deliberately. (O.E. *risan*)

riser, *n.* one who rises; upright face of step, between treads.

risible, *a.* of laughter; inclined to laugh; (*rare*) laughable. **risibility,** *n.* (L. *ridēre,* laugh)

rising, *a.* mounting; increasing.—*n.* insurrection; boil, tumour. **r. generation,** those now growing up. **r. ten, twelve** etc., nearing that age.

risk, *n.* chance of loss; hazard, danger; amount covered by insurance, person insured.—*v.t.* expose to danger; take chance of; venture on. **risky,** *a.* dangerous; *risqué.* (It. *risco*)

risorgimento, *n.* Italian Renaissance; Italian nineteenth-century national movement. (It.)

risorial, *a.* of, exciting, laughter. (L. *ridēre,* laugh)

risotto, *n.* stew of onions, rice, and butter. (It.)

risp, *v.t.* and *n.* (*Scot.*) rasp.

risqué, *a.* verging on indecency. (F.)

rissole, *n.* ball of minced meat etc. rolled in bread-crumbs and fried. (F.)

ritardando, *a.* and *n.* (*mus.*) (passage played) gradually slower. (It.)

rite, *n.* formal usage; religious ceremony. **ritual,** *a.* of, with, rites.—*n.* body of rites; prescribed order of divine service, book giving this. **ritualism,** *n.* elaborate use of ceremonial and symbolism in religion. **ritualist,** *n.* advocate of ritualism. **ritualistic,** *a.* **ritualize,** *v.t.* and *i.* make, become, ritualistic. (L. *ritus*)

rivage, *n.* (*poet.*) shore, bank. (F.)

rival, *n.* one who strives to equal or excel another, competitor; (*Shake.*) partner.—*v.t.* and *i.* vie with, emulate; be comparable to; compete. **without a r.,** unequalled. **rivality,** *n.* (*Shake.*) partnership. **rivalry,** *n.* emulation; competition. (L. *rivalis,* lit. on same stream)

rive, *v.t.* and *i.* (*past* rived, *p.p.* riven or rived) split, cleave; rend asunder, wrench. (O.N. *rifa*)

rivel, *v.i.* and *t.* (*arch.*) wrinkle, shrivel.

river, *n.* large natural stream of water; copious flow. **r.-basin,** *n.* land drained by river. **r.-horse,** *n.* hippopotamus. **riverain, riverine,** *aa.* of, near, river, riparian. **riverside,** *a.* and *n.* (on) bank of river. (L. *ripa,* bank)

rivet, *n.* short bolt for holding metal plates together, the headless end being hammered flat.—*v.t.* fasten with rivets; fix (eyes upon); engross (attention). **riveter,** *n.* (O.F. *river,* clinch)

rivière, *n.* necklace of gems, esp. one of several strings. (F.)

rivulet, *n.* small stream, brook; kinds of moth. (L. *rivus,* stream)

rix-dollar, *n.* old silver coin of Germany, Holland etc. (G. *reichstaler*)

rizzer, *v.t.* (*Scot.*) dry in sun.

roach, *n.* small freshwater fish like carp. (O.F. *roche*)

roach, *n.* (*naut.*) upward curve in foot of square sail.

roach, *n.* cockroach. (abbr.)

road, *n.* prepared track; way, route; (*Shake.*) raid; (*pl.*) roadstead. **on the r.,** travelling. **r.-book,** *n.* guide-book. **r.-hog,** *n.* reckless or inconsiderate motorist. **r.-metal,** *n.* broken stones for making road. **r.-sense,** *n.* ability to drive safely. **roadhouse,** *n.* country restaurant. **roadman,** *n.* man employed in repair of roads. **roadstead,** *n.* anchorage less enclosed than harbour. **roadster,** *n.* horse, bicycle, for road journeys; touring motor-car. **roadway,** *n.* main part of road. **roadworthy,** *a.* fit to be used on road. (O.E. *ridan,* ride)

roam, *v.i.* and *t.* wander about, rove. —*n.* ramble. **roamer,** *n.*

roan, *a.* with coat of mixed colour, bay or chestnut mixed with white or grey.—*n.* roan horse. (O.F.)

roan, *n.* grained sheepskin leather.

roar, *n.* loud deep hoarse sound.—*v.i.* and *t.* utter roar, bellow; guffaw. **roarer,** *n.* horse with roaring. **roaring,** *a.* boisterous, rough; brisk.—*n.* respiratory disease of horses. **roaring game,** curling. (O.E. *rárian,* bellow)

roast, *v.t.* and *i.* cook before open fire; cook in oven, bake; expose to extreme heat; (*arch. sl.*) chaff, ridicule.—*a.* roasted.—*n.* joint of roast meat. **rule the r.,** be master. **roasting-jack,** *n.* device for turning roasting meat. (O.F. *rostir*)

rob, *v.t.* deprive (of) by force or threats; steal, plunder; dispossess (of). **robber, robbery,** *nn.* (O.F. *rober*)

robe, *n.* loose outer garment, gown; (*Amer.*) wrap of dressed skin; (*pl.*) ceremonial vestments.—*v.t.* and *i.* dress, array; put on robes. **gentlemen of the r.,** lawyers. *r.-de-chambre,* *n.* dressing-gown. (F.)

robin, *n.* small brown bird with red breast; (*Amer.*) kind of thrush. **R. Goodfellow,** a mischievous elf. **R. Hood,** ancient forest outlaw.

r.-redbreast, *n.* robin. **r.-run-the-hedge,** *n.* ground-ivy. (*Robert*)
robinia, *n.* false acacia. (J. *Robin*)
róblē, *n.* American white oak. (Sp.)
roborant, *a.* and *n.* (*med.*) restorative, tonic. (L. *robur*, strength)
robot, *n.* mechanical man, automaton; machine-like person. (term in play)
Rob Roy, canoe with double-bladed paddle. (inventor's pen-name)
roburite, *n.* a flameless explosive. (L. *robur*, strength)
robust, *a.* strong, sturdy; vigorous. **robustious,** *a.* boisterous, hearty. (L. *robur*, strength)
roc, *n.* fabulous gigantic bird. (Arab. *rokh*)
rocambole, *n.* kind of leek, Spanish garlic. (F.)
rochet, *n.* bishop's linen vestment like surplice. (O.F.)
rock, *n.* stone; crag, boulder; a hard sweet; (*geol.*) natural mineral deposit, incl. sand, clay etc. **on the rr.,** (*sl.*) hard up. **R. scorpion,** native of the R., Gibraltar. **r.-bottom,** *a.* very lowest. **r.-bound,** *a.* hemmed in by rocks. **r.-cake,** *n.* a hard rough cake. **r.-cork, r.-paper, r.-wood,** *nn.* kind of asbestos. **r.-crystal,** *n.* transparent quartz. **r.-dove, r.-pigeon,** *nn.* kinds haunting rocks. **r.-goat,** *n.* ibex. **r.-hewn,** *a.* cut out of solid rock. **r.-rabbit,** *n.* hyrax. **r.-rose,** *n.* kind of cistus. **r.-salt,** *n.* kind found stratified in free state. **r.-tar,** *n.* petroleum. **r.-work,** *n.* rockery. (O.F. *roke*)
rock, *v.t.* and *i.* move, sway, to and fro; totter, oscillate; lull by swaying. —*n.* rocking. **rocking-chair, rocking-horse,** *nn.* chair, toy horse, fixed on rockers. **rocking-stone,** *n.* poised boulder easily rocked. (O.E. *roccian*)
rock, *n.* distaff.
rocker, *n.* curved support on which cradle etc. rocks; (*Amer.*) rocking-chair. **off his r.,** (*sl.*) mad.
rockery, *n.* pile of stones with pockets of earth for growing plants in.
rocket, *n.* kinds of flowering plant. (F. *roquette*)
rocket, *n.* firework on stick projected through air for display, signalling, or conveying line to wrecked ship. —*v.t.* and *i.* bombard with rockets; (of bird) fly straight upwards; (of horse) dart swiftly forward. **rocketer,** *n.* rocketing bird. (F. *roquet*)
rocky, *a.* full of rocks; rugged, hard, like rock.
rocky, *a.* unsteady, shaky.
rococo, *a.* with elaborate ornamentation, tastelessly florid; out of date. —*n.* rococo style. (F.)
rod, *n.* slender stick or bar; wand, switch; cane for flogging; fishing-rod, angler; measure of length, $5\frac{1}{2}$ yds.; (*Amer. sl.*) revolver. **kiss the r.,** take punishment meekly. (O.E. *rodd*)
rode, *n.* (*Spens.*) raid. (*road*)
rode, see **ride.**
rodent, *a.* gnawing.—*n.* gnawing animal, incl. rat, mouse, squirrel etc. (L. *rodere*, gnaw)
rodeo, *n.* rounding-up of cattle for branding; exhibition of cowboys' skill. (Sp.)
rodomontade, *n.* boastful talk, brag. —*v.i.* boast, bluster. (*Rodomonte* in Ariosto)
roe, *n.* (also **hard r.**) eggs or spawn of fish. **soft r.,** milt of male fish. **r.-stone,** *n.* oolite.
roe, *n.* (also **r.-deer**) small reddish-brown deer. **roebuck,** *n.* male roe. (O.E. *ráha*)
roer, *n.* (*S. Afr.*) long-barrelled gun for elephant-hunting.
rogation, *n.* (us. *pl.*) form of litany, supplication. **R. Days,** three days preceding Ascension Day. **r. flower,** milkwort. **R. Sunday,** begins **R. Week,** in which Rogation Days fall. (L. *rogare*, ask)
Roger, *n.* a name. **jolly R.,** black flag of pirate. **(Sir) R. de Coverley,** a country dance.
rogue, *n.* scoundrel, rascal; vagrant; mischievous or sly person; shirking racehorse; (also **r. elephant**) elephant living apart from herd and of savage temper. **rogues' gallery,** photographs of criminals at police headquarters. **roguery,** *n.* dishonesty, cheating; mischief. **roguish,** *a.* playfully mischievous; knavish.
roi, *n.* king. *r. fainéant,* ruler who is mere figurehead (lit. King Do-nothing). *le r. le veult, le r. s'avisera,* forms of giving, refusing, royal assent to parliamentary measure (lit. the king wills it, the king will consider). (F.)
roil, *v.t.* (*Amer.*) make (water) turbid; exasperate, annoy. **roily,** *a.* turbid.
roinek, same as *rooinek.*
roister, *v.i.* be jovially convivial, swagger. **roisterer,** *n.* noisy reveller. (L. *rusticus*, rustic)
Roland, *n.* a medieval hero. **a R. for an Oliver,** tit for tat.
role, rôle, *n.* dramatic part; function, task. (F.)
roll, *v.i.* and *t.* move by turning over and over; revolve; move smoothly or on wheels; sway, reel, wallow; undulate; wind round, make by winding; flatten with roller; sound with trill.—*n.* rolling motion; deep continuous sound of drum, thunder etc. **r. in,** come in quantities. **r. out,** flatten with roller; utter impressively. **r. up,** wind into cylinder; enwrap; (*sl.*) assemble. **r.-top desk,** with flexible sliding cover. **rolled gold,** thin coating of gold. **rolled into one,** made into single thing. (L. *rota*, wheel)
roll, *n.* piece of paper etc. rolled up; document in this form; register, list;

cylinder; turned-over edge; small loaf; (*Amer.*) bundle of paper money. **Master of the Rr.**, judge in charge of certain public records. **r. of honour**, list of those who have died for their country. **strike off the rr.**, remove from official list of solicitors. **r.-call**, *n.* calling over of list to see who is absent. (L. *rota*, wheel)

roller, *n.* thing that rolls; cylinder for smoothing or pressing, shifting heavy objects etc.; long heavy wave; (also **r.-bandage**) long narrow bandage. **r.-skate**, *n.* skate with wheels instead of runner.—*v.i.* go on these. **r.-towel**, *n.* endless towel on roller.

rolley, same as **rulley.**

rollick, *v.i.* be jovially boisterous.—*n.* boisterous gaiety; frolic.

rolling, *a.* undulating; swaying. **r. in**, having plenty of. **r. stone**, person constantly on move. **r.-mill**, *n.* for rolling metal into sheets. **r.-pin**, *n.* wooden roller for making pastry. **r.-stock**, *n.* railway carriages, engines etc.

roly-poly, *a.* round and plump.—*n.* (also **r. pudding**) pudding of paste covered with jam and rolled up.

Rom, *n.* (*pl.* **Roma**) male gipsy. (Romany)

Romaic, *a.* and *n.* (of) modern Greek language. **romaika**, *n.* Greek national dance. (Gk. *Romaikos*)

romage, *n.* (*Shake.*) bustle. (*rummage*)

romal, *n.* Indian silk or cotton fabric; handkerchief of this.

Roman, *a.* and *n.* (inhabitant) of Rome or its ancient empire; Roman Catholic; (*print.*) ordinary type, not italic. **R. candle**, firework discharging coloured balls. **R. Catholic**, (member) of Christian Church governed by pope. **R. Catholicism**, its doctrine. **R. fever**, kind of malaria. **R. nose**, with high arched bridge. **r. numerals**, letters for figures, III=3, XV=15 etc. **R. school**, painting school of Raphael.

roman, *n.* romance, novel; romaunt. *r. policier*, detective story. (F.)

Romance, *a.* and *n.* (language) developed from Latin, e.g. Old French, Old Spanish etc. (*Roman*)

romance, *n.* medieval tale of chivalry; series of unusual adventures; novel, literature, dealing with this; atmosphere of awe or wonder; idealized love, love-affair; picturesque falsehood.—*v.i.* exaggerate, embroider. **romancer**, *n.* (*Romance*)

Rómanĕs, *n.* gipsy language. (Romany)

Romanesque, *a.* and *n.* (in) style of round-arched and vaulted architecture prevalent between classical and Gothic periods; Romance.

romanic, *a.* Romance; inheriting Roman civilization, Romance-speaking.—*n.* Romance languages.

Romanism, *n.* Roman Catholicism. **Romanist**, *n.* Roman Catholic.

Romanity, *n.* civilization and influence of the Roman Empire.

Romanize, *v.t.* and *i.* bring, come, under ancient Rome's civilizing influence; convert, conform, to Roman Catholic religion. **Romanization**, *n.*

Romansh, Romansch, *n.* a Romance dialect of Switzerland, Rhaeto-Romanic.

romantic, *a.* of, given to, romance; strange and picturesque; imaginative, sentimental; (*art, literature*) preferring passion and imagination to proportion and finish, subordinating form to content (opp. to classical). **R. Revival**, nineteenth-century revolt against eighteenth-century classicism. **romanticism**, *n.* romantic character or style. **romanticist**, *n.* writer of romantic school.

Romany, *n.* gipsy; gipsy language or race.—*a.* gipsy. (*Rom*)

romaunt, *n.* (*arch.*) ancient romance in verse. (O.F. *romant*)

Rome, *n.* the city or its empire. **Church of R.**, Roman Catholic Church. **Romish**, *a.* papist. **Romeward, Romewards**, *advv.* towards Roman Catholicism.

romp, *v.i.* play boisterously.—*n.* romping; boisterous girl, tomboy. **r. home**, win easily. **romper**, *n.* child's overall.

rondeau, rondel, *nn.* forms of lyric with 10, 13, or 15 lines, only two rhymes throughout, and divided into three parts, the opening words being repeated in middle and at end. (F.)

rondo, *n.* piece of music with leading theme to which return is made. (It.)

rondure, *n.* (*poet.*) roundness, round object. (*round*)

rone, *n.* (*Scot.*) gutter of roof.

rone, *n.* (*Scot.*) shrub; thicket.

Röntgen rays, X-rays. **röntgenogram**, *n.* X-ray photograph. (discoverer)

ronyon, *n.* (*Shake.*) scurvy wretch.

rood, *n.* cross of Christ, crucifix; quarter of an acre. **r.-arch, r.-screen**, *nn.* those separating nave from choir. **r.-loft**, *n.* gallery on rood-screen. (O.E. *ród*, cross)

roof, *n.* covering of building; top of vehicle. —*v.t.* provide with roof, cover. **r.-tree**, *n.* main beam of roof, ridge-pole. **roofer**, *n.* (*colloq.*) letter of thanks sent after visit. **roofing**, *n.* materials for roof. (O.E. *hróf*)

rooinek, *n.* (*S. Afr.*) European immigrant, greenhorn; Boer nickname for British soldier. (S. Afr. Du.=redneck)

rook, *n.* (*chess*) castle. (Pers. *rukh*)

rook, *n.* black bird like crow; cardsharper.—*v.t.* swindle, esp. at cards; overcharge. **r.-rifle**, *n.* small-bore rifle. **rookery**, *n.* colony of rooks; crowded tenement. (O.E. *hróc*)

rookie, *n.* (*army sl.*) recruit. (corrupt.)

rooky, *a.* full of rooks.

room, *n.* division of house, chamber; unoccupied or adequate space; place (of another); scope, opportunity; (*pl.*) lodgings.—*v.i.* (*Amer.*) lodge. **make r.,** withdraw; remove obstructions. **roomful,** *n.* **roomy,** *a.* spacious. (O.E. *rúm*)

roomaul, same as **romal.**

roop, *n.* hoarseness. **roopy,** *a.* hoarse. (O.E. *hrópan*, roar)

roose, *v.t.* (*Scot.*) praise highly. (O.N. *hrósa*, praise)

roose, see **rouse.**

roost, *n.* tidal race off Orkneys and Shetlands. (O.N. *rost*)

roost, *n.* bird's perch or sleeping-place. —*v.i.* settle for sleep. **go to r.,** retire for night. **rooster,** *n.* domestic cock. (O.E. *hróst*)

root, *n.* part of plant that grows down into ground; root-like part of organ etc.; scion; source, origin; basis, bottom; word-form from which words are made, base; (*math.*) factor of a quantity which multiplied by itself gives the quantity; (*mus.*) fundamental note of chord; (*pl.*) plants with edible root.—*v.t.* and *i.* plant, establish, be established; tear (up), eradicate. **r. and branch,** completely, radically. **take r.,** be established. (O.N. *rót*)

root, rout, *v.i.* and *t.* (of pig etc.) dig, turn up, with snout; search, rummage. (O.E. *wrótan*)

root, *v.i.* (*Amer. sl.*) shout encouragement (for), cheer.

rooted, *a.* firmly fixed.

rootery, *n.* pile of roots for growing ferns etc. in.

rootle, *v.i.* root, burrow.

rootlet, *n.* small root.

rootstock, *n.* underground stem, rhizome.

rooty, *n.* (*army sl.*) bread. (Hind. *rōṭī*)

rope, *n.* thick cord, small cable; halter; viscous thickening in liquid. —*v.t.* and *i.* tie, fasten, mark off, with ropes; lasso; become ropy. **give one r.,** allow him latitude. **know the rr.,** understand ways of place. **r. in,** secure as supporter. **the r.,** hanging. **the rr.,** round boxing-ring. **r.-dancer, r.-walker,** *nn.* performer on tight-rope. **r.-ladder,** *n.* one made of ropes. **r's.-end,** *n.* short piece of rope for flogging. **r.-walk,** *n.* long shed in which rope is twisted. **ropy,** *a.* (of liquid) stringy, glutinous. (O.E. *ráp*)

Roquefort, *n.* French cheese made from ewes' and goats' milk. (*place*)

roquelaure, *n.* cloak reaching to knees, worn in 18th century. (F.)

roquet, *v.t.* and *i.* (*croquet*) hit (another ball) with one's own.—*n.* roqueting. (*croquet*)

roric, *a.* of dew. (L. *ros*, dew)

rorqual, *n.* large kind of whale, finback. (Norwegian *raud*, red; *kval*, whale)

rorty, same as **raughty.**

rosace, *n.* rose window; rose-shaped design. **rosaceous,** *a.* of the rose family. **rosaniline,** *n.* a red aniline dye-stuff. **rosarian,** *n.* rose-grower. *rosarium*, *n.* rose-garden.

rosary, *n.* string of beads for keeping count of prayers; series of Aves, Paternosters, and Glorias; rose garden, bed, or arbour. (*rose*)

rose, see **rise.**

rose, *n.* a beautiful red, pink, white, or yellow flower; shrub bearing it; pink colour; rosette; perforated nozzle for watering-can.—*a.* warm pink. **r. diamond,** with flat back and curved face cut into triangular facets. **r. noble,** old English coin worth 6*s.* 8*d.* **r. window,** circular with branching compartments. **the r.,** erysipelas. **under the r.,** secretly, in confidence. **Wars of the Rr.,** in 15th century between Yorkists and Lancastrians. **rosebud,** *n.* bud of rose; (*Amer.*) débutante. **r.-coloured,** *a.* rosy; optimistic. **r.-leaf,** *n.* petal of rose. **r.-water,** *n.* scent made from roses; gentle handling. (L. *rosa*)

roseate, *a.* rose-coloured.

rosemary, *n.* sweet-scented blue-flowered evergreen shrub. (L. *ros*, dew; *mare*, sea)

roseola, *n.* German measles; red rash. **roseolar, roseolous,** *aa.* (*rose*)

rosette, *n.* rose-shaped bunch of ribbon, carving etc.

rosewood, *n.* kinds of cabinet wood.

Rosicrucian, *a.* and *n.* (member) of a secret society for studying occult. **Rosicrucianism,** *n.* (*Rosenkreuz*, reputed founder)

rosin, *n.* resin, esp. in solid form.—*v.t.* rub, smear, with it. (*resin*)

Rosinante, *n.* worn-out horse, jade. (Don Quixote's horse)

rosland, *n.* (*prov.*) heathy or moorish land. (W. *rhos*, moor)

rosolio, *n.* sweet cordial made from raisins. (L. *ros solis*, sundew)

roster, *n.* list showing turns of duty, roll. (Du. *rooster*, list)

rostrum, *n.* (*pl.* **rostra, rostrums**) platform, pulpit; prow of war-galley; (*zool.*) beak, beak-like part. **rostral,** *a.* of, like, beak; adorned with beaks of captured ships. **rostrate, rostrated,** *aa.* beaked. **rostriform,** *a.* beak-shaped. (L.)

rosulate, *a.* (*bot.*) with leaves arranged in clusters like rose-petals.

rosy, *a.* warm pink; rose-strewn; (of prospects) favourable.

rot, *v.i.* and *t.* decay, decompose, putrefy; (*sl.*) talk ironically, chaff. —*n.* decay, putrefaction; sudden collapse; liver-disease in sheep; (*sl.*) rubbish, nonsense. **r.-gut,** *n.* bad liquor. (O.E. *rotian*)

rota, *n.* turn in succession; roster. (L.=wheel)

rotary, *a.* (of engine) turning like

wheel (opp. to reciprocating). (**R.**) **Clubs**, local business clubs for mutual service. **Rotarian**, *n.* member of Rotary Club. (*rota*)
rotate, *v.i.* and *t.* turn round centre like wheel, spin.—*a.* (*bot.*) wheel-shaped. **rotation**, *n.* rotating; regular succession. **rotation of crops**, growing them in scientific order to avoid exhausting soil. **rotational**, *a.* **rotator**, *n.* revolving part. **rotative**, **rotatory**, *aa.* (*rota*)
rotche, rotch, *n.* little auk.
rote, *n.* mechanical repetition. **by r.**, by heart.
rote, *n.* (*Spens.*) stringed instrument of lyre type. (O.F.)
rother, *n.* (*Shake.*) ox. (O.E. *hrýther*)
rôti, *n.* roast. ***rôtisserie***, *n.* shop where meat is roasted in view of diners. (F.)
rotifer, *n.* minute water-animal with rotating swimming-organs, wheel-animalcule. (L. *rota*, wheel; *ferre*, bear)
rotl, *n.* Arabian pound of 12 ounces. (Arab. *ratl*)
rotograph, *n.* photograph of MS. etc. made direct without negative. (L. *rota*, wheel. Gk. *graphein*, write)
rotor, *n.* rotary part of dynamo; upright revolving cylinder used instead of sails for driving ship. (*rota*)
rotten, *a.* putrid, decaying; perished, unsound; corrupt, unprincipled; inefficient; (*sl.*) bad, beastly. **rotter**, *n.* (*sl.*) useless person, good-for-nothing. (*rot*)
rotund, *a.* rounded, plump; sonorous, grandiloquent; round. **rotunda**, *n.* circular domed building or chamber. **rotundity**, *n.* (L. *rotundus*)
roturier, *n.* commoner, plebeian. (F.)
rouble, *n.* Russian coin and monetary unit. (Russ. *ruble*)
roucou, *n.* orange dye; W. Indian tree yielding it. (Brazilian *urucú*)
roué, *n.* fashionable profligate, rake. (F.)
rouge, *n.* red cosmetic; polishing powder.—*v.i.* and *t.* colour (face) with rouge. *r.-et-noir*, *n.* gambling game with cards, *trente-et-quarante*. (F.=red)
rouge, *n.* scrummage or touch-down in Eton football.
rough, *a.* uneven, coarse in texture, not smooth; shaggy; violent, boisterous, stormy; harsh, discordant; rude, unpolished; crude, unfinished; approximate.—*adv.* in rough manner. —*n.* rough thing; rowdy, hooligan; (*golf*) uncut ground beside fairway. —*v.t.* make rough; insert spikes in (shoe of horse). **cut up r.**, become quarrelsome. **in the r.**, in unfinished state. **r. and ready**, hastily made; roughly efficient. **r. in, out**, design roughly, outline. **r. it**, submit to hardships. **r. luck**, (*sl.*) undeserved ill-luck. **r. on**, unlucky for; harsh to. (O.E. *rúh*)
roughage, *n.* coarse fibrous part of food promoting intestinal action.
rough-and-tumble, *a.* scrambling and confused.—*n.* scuffle.
roughcast, *n.* mixture of lime and gravel.—*v.t.* coat with this; rough out.
rough-dry, *v.t.* dry (linen) without ironing.
roughen, *v.t.* and *i.* make, become, rough.
rough-hew, *v.t.* shape roughly.
rough-house, *n.* (*sl.*) horse-play.
roughneck, *n.* (*Amer. sl.*) coarse vulgar person.
rough-rider, *n.* horsebreaker; irregular mounted soldier.
roughshod, *a.* with shoes roughed to prevent slipping. **ride r. over**, treat in overbearing manner.
roulade, *n.* quick succession of notes, run. **rouleau**, *n.* (*pl.* **rouleaus, rouleaux**) little roll, esp. of coins wrapped in paper. **roulette**, *n.* gambling game played with revolving wheel and ball; toothed wheel for making dots or perforations. (F.)
Roumansh, same as **Romansh.**
round, *v.i.* and *t.* (*arch.*) whisper. (O.E. *rúnian*)
round, *a.* circular, spherical; curved, plump; full, not fractional; considerable; candid; (of style) flowing, balanced; (of vowel) pronounced with rounded lips.—*n.* round object; circuit, beat; cycle, series; bout, turn; single shot, ammunition for it; rung; (*golf*) circuit of course; (*mus.*) kind of canon.—*v.t.* and *i.* make, become, round; go round, turn; finish.—*adv.* circularly; on all sides; from one side to another; by indirect way. — *prep.* encircling, about. **ask r.**, invite to house. **get r.**, cajole. **r. about**, on all sides; in vicinity. **r. and r.**, several times round. **r. dance**, in which couples move round room. **r. game**, without sides or partners. **r. numbers**, roughly correct. **r. off**, make symmetrical; smooth away. **r. out**, fill out. **r. robin**, petition with signatures in circle to conceal order. **R. Table**, of King Arthur and his knights, none having precedence. **r.-table conference**, with all parties on equal footing. **r. up**, drive (cattle) together; collect and arrest. **r. upon**, turn unexpectedly upon; inform against. (L. *rotundus*)
roundabout, *a.* indirect, circuitous; gyratory.—*n.* indirect way; circumlocution; cross-roads where traffic circulates in one direction only; merry-go-round.
round-arm, *a.* (of bowling) with arm swung horizontally.
roundel, *n.* small disk; rondeau, rondel. **roundelay**, *n.* simple song with refrain. (*round*)
rounder, *n.* complete run round bases in rounders; (*Amer. sl.*) habitual

loafer; (*pl.*) game between two sides, with bat and soft ball.

Roundhead, *n.* supporter of Parliament against Charles I. (cropped hair)

round-house, *n.* cabin in after-part of ship's deck; (formerly) lock-up.

roundly, *adv.* bluntly, plainly; vigorously.

round-shot, *n.* cannon-ball.

round-shouldered, *a.* with bent shoulders, stooping.

roundsman, *n.* tradesman's messenger; (*Amer.*) policeman below sergeant, who makes rounds of inspection.

roup, *n.* and *v.t.* (*Scot.*) auction.

roup, *n.* an infectious disease of poultry. **roupy,** *a.*

rouse, *v.t.* and *i.* awake; stir up, provoke; become active; start (game); stir (liquid).—*n.* reveille.

rouse, *n.* (*arch.*) draught; toast; carouse.

rouse, roose, *v.t.* pickle in salt. (L. *adrorare,* bedew)

rouseabout, same as **roustabout.**

Roussillon, *n.* a red wine. (place)

roustabout, *n.* (*Amer.*) idler, loafer; deck-hand; (*Austral.*) odd-job man.

rout, *n.* disorderly retreat; tumultuous crowd, troop; (*arch.*) large evening party; (*law*) three or more persons engaged in unlawful act.—*v.t.* defeat and put to flight. (L. *rumpere,* break)

rout, *v.i.* and *n.* (*Scot.*) bellow; snore. (O.E. *hrútan,* roar)

rout, see **root.**

route, *n.* way or road travelled; marching orders. **column of r.,** marching formation. *en r.,* on the way. **r.-march,** *n.* practice march. (F.)

routh, *n.* (*Scot.*) plenty.—*a.* abundant. **routhie,** *a.*

routine, *n.* regular course of procedure; unvarying round.—*a.* done by rule. **routinism,** *n.* blind adherence to routine. **routinist,** *n.* (*route*)

rove, see **reeve.**

rove, *n.* slightly twisted strand of cotton etc.—*v.t.* form into roves.

rove, *n.* small metal plate or ring for rivet to pass through. (O.N. *ró*)

rove, *v.i.* and *t.* wander, roam (over); troll with live bait; (*archery*) aim at casual mark. **rover,** *n.* wanderer; fickle person; sea robber, pirate; senior boy-scout; (*archery*) casual mark; (*croquet*) ball, player, that has passed all hoops.

row, *v.i.* and *t.* propel (boat) by oars; transport by rowing.—*n.* trip in rowing-boat. **r.-boat, rowing-boat,** *nn.* (O.E. *rówan*)

row, *n.* line, rank; line of houses, plants etc. **hard r. to hoe,** difficult task. **the R.,** riding-track in Hyde Park. (O.E. *ráw*)

row, *n.* (*colloq.*) noise, disturbance; noisy quarrel, shindy; scolding.—*v.i.* and *t.* brawl; scold, rate. **get into a r.,** incur blame. **make a r.,** raise noise; protest strongly.

row, *v.t.* and *n.* (*Scot.*) roll.

rowan, *n.* a native tree, mountain-ash; its red berry. (cf. Swed. *rön*)

rower, *n.* one who rows, oarsman.

row-de-dow, *n.* hubbub, din. (imit.)

rowdy, *a.* rough and noisy.—*n.* hooligan. **rowdyism,** *n.*

rowel, *n.* spiked revolving wheel at end of spur.—*v.t.* urge with this. (L. *rota,* wheel)

rowlock, *n.* pair of pegs on gunwale against which oar works.

royal, *a.* of king or queen; kingly; patronized, founded, by sovereign; first-rate.—*n.* sail above topgallant sail; stag with head of twelve points or more; size of paper, 25 × 20 in. **r. blue,** deep rich blue. **r. road,** easy effortless way. **r. standard,** king's flag with royal arms. **royalist,** *n.* adherent of king or monarchy. **royalism,** *n.* **royalty,** *n.* royal rank or power; royal person; payment to landowner for right to work mine or to patentee for use of patent; percentage on sales of book, paid to author. (L. *rex,* king)

royne, *v.i.* (*Spens.*) growl.

roynish, *a.* (*Shake.*) scurvy, coarse.

Rozinante, same as **Rosinante.**

rub, *v.t.* and *i.* move (hand, cloth etc.) over surface with pressure; wipe, scour; smear; chafe, fret; take rubbing of; (*Shake.*) meet obstacle.—*n.* rubbing; pinch, drawback; (*bowls*) irregularity in green. **r. along,** manage somehow. **r. down,** rub vigorously with towel; curry (horse); smooth down. **r. in,** emphasize, keep harping on. **r. of the green,** (*golf*) chance deflection of moving ball. **r. out,** erase. **r. shoulders,** meet. **r. the wrong way,** irritate. **r. up,** polish; freshen, renew.

rub-a-dub, *n.* sound of drum.

rubato, *a.* and *n.* (*mus.*) (time) modified for expression. (It.)

rubber, *n.* group of three games at whist etc.; the deciding game.

rubber, *n.* tough elastic substance, the coagulated juice of certain plants, indiarubber; eraser made of this; thing for rubbing; masseur; (*pl.*) galoshes.—*v.t.* coat with rubber. —*v.i.* (*Amer.*) stare (at). **rubberneck,** *n.* (*Amer. sl.*) inquisitive person, sightseer; trippers' motor-coach.—*v.i.* stare curiously. (*rub*)

rubbing, *n.* copy of inscribed stone got by rubbing heelball etc. on paper laid over it.

rubbish, *n.* waste matter, refuse; trash; nonsense. **rubbishy,** *a.* worthless. (M.E. *robows*)

rubble, *n.* rough broken stone, brick etc.; builders' rubbish.

rube, *n.* (*Amer.*) bumpkin.

rubefy, rubify, *v.t.* redden. **rubefaction,** *n.* **rubefacient,** *a.* and *n.*

(application) causing redness of skin. (L. *rubēre*, be red; *facere*, make)
rubella, rubeola, *nn.* German measles. (L. *rubellus*, reddish)
rubescent, *a.* reddening, flushing. **rubescence,** *n.* (L. *rubēre*, be red)
rubiaceous, *a.* of the madder family. (L. *rubia*, madder)
rubicelle, *n.* orange-red gem, kind of spinel ruby. (F.)
rubicon, *v.t.* and *n.* (*piquet*) defeat, winning, before opponent has scored 100. **cross the R.,** take irrevocable step. (stream bounding ancient Italy)
rubicund, *a.* ruddy, red-faced. **rubicundity,** *n.* (L. *rubēre*, be red)
rubidium, *n.* soft silvery metallic element. (L. *rubidus*, red)
rubify, see **rubefy.**
rubiginous, *a.* brownish-red, rust-coloured. (L. *rubigo*, rust)
rubious, *a.* ruby-coloured.
rubric, *n.* chapter-heading, line, marked out in red; directions in prayer book for conduct of divine service; form settled by authority. **rubrical,** *a.* **rubricate,** *v.t.* mark in red; fix like ritual. **rubrication, rubricator,** *nn.* **rubricism,** *n.* strict adherence to rubrics, formalism. **rubricist,** *n.* (L. *ruber*, red)
ruby, *n.* dark-red precious stone; its colour; 5½-point type, between pearl and nonpareil; (*boxing sl.*) blood.—*a.* dark-red.—*v.t.* dye ruby. (O.F. *rubi*)
ruche, *n.* plaited frilling. (F.)
ruck, *n.* common run, undistinguished crowd; bunch of losers in race.
ruck, ruckle, *vv.i.* and *t.* and *nn.* crease, wrinkle. (O.N. *hrukka*)
ruckle, *n.* gurgling sound, death-rattle.—*v.i.* utter this.
rucksack, *n.* pack carried on back, knapsack. (G.)
ruction, *n.* (*sl.*) disturbance, row.
rudbeckia, *n.* composite plant like aster. (O. *Rudbeck*)
rudd, *n.* freshwater fish like carp.
rudder, *n.* flat piece hinged to stern of boat or rear of aeroplane to steer by; guiding principle. **r.-fish,** *n.* kind that follows ships. (O.E. *róther*)
ruddle, *n.* red ochre.—*v.t.* mark with this.
ruddock, *n.* robin. (O.E. *rudduc*)
ruddy, *a.* red, rosy; florid; (*vulg. sl.*) bloody, confounded.—*v.t.* and *i.* make, grow, ruddy. (O.E. *rudig*)
rude, *a.* uncivil, ill-mannered; uncultured, barbarous; coarse, brutal; roughly made; in natural state, primitive; vigorous, hearty. **rudesby,** *n.* (*Shake.*) uncivil fellow. (L. *rudis*)
Rudesheimer, *n.* a white Rhine wine. (G.)
rudiment, *n.* imperfectly developed organ; (*pl.*) elements, first principles. **rudimentary,** *a.* elementary; undeveloped, vestigial. (*rude*)
rue, *n.* evergreen shrub with strong-smelling bitter leaves. (Gk. *rhutē*)
rue, *v.t.* and *i.* regret, wish undone; (*arch.*) grieve for, pity.—*n.* (*arch.*) pity, ruth; repentance. **rueful,** *a.* dejected; showing quizzical self-pity. (O.E. *hréowan*)
rue-raddy, *n.* rope slung over shoulders to drag something with.
ruff, *n.* large stiff projecting frill worn round neck in Elizabethan times; (*zool.*) fringe of hair or feathers like this; kind of pigeon.
ruff, *n.* small freshwater fish like perch.
ruff, *n.* bird like sandpiper.
ruff, *n.* trumping at whist or bridge. —*v.t.* and *i.* trump.
ruffian, *n.* brutal lawless person, blackguard. **ruffianism,** *n.* **ruffianly,** *a.* (O.F.)
ruffle, *v.t.* and *i.* disturb smoothness of, disarrange, flutter; upset temper of; swagger about, be quarrelsome. —*n.* pleated frill at neck or wrist; bird's ruff; ripple; dispute, bustle; low roll of drum. **r. it,** cut a dash. **ruffler,** *n.* swaggerer.
rufous, *a.* brownish-red. (L. *rufus*)
rug, *n.* floor-mat with deep pile; thick woollen wrap or coverlet.
Rugby, *n.* (also **R. football**) football played with elliptical ball which may be carried. (school)
rugged, *a.* rough, uneven; unpolished; harsh, austere; (*Amer. colloq.*) vigorous, robust.
rugger, *n.* (*sl.*) Rugby.
rugose, rugous, *aa.* wrinkled, corrugated. **rugosity,** *n.* (L. *ruga*, wrinkle)
ruin, *n.* destruction, downfall, wrecked state; cause of this; loss of fortune; dilapidated building.—*v.t.* and *i.* destroy, wreck; impoverish; seduce (woman); (*arch.*) fall headlong. **ruination,** *n.* perdition. **ruinous,** *a.* tumbledown; disastrous. (L. *ruere*, fall)
rule, *n.* regulation, precept; principle, standard; habitual practice; government, sway; code of religious order; measuring-stick; (*print.*) thin metal strip separating columns; dash in punctuation.—*v.t.* and *i.* govern, control; guide, dominate; decide authoritatively; draw (lines) with ruler; (of prices) range. **as a r.,** usually. **r. of three,** arithmetical proportion. **r. of thumb,** method based on experience. **r. out,** exclude. **ruler,** *n.* sovereign, governor; stick for ruling lines. **ruling,** *n.* authoritative pronouncement.—*a.* dominant. (L. *regula*)
rulley, *n.* flat dray, lorry.
rum, *n.* spirit distilled from sugar-cane; (*Amer. colloq.*) any intoxicating liquor. **r.-runner,** *n.* (*Amer. sl.*) smuggler of intoxicants.
rum, *a.* (*sl.*) odd, queer.
Rumansh, same as **Romansh.**
rumba, *n.* Cuban dance with complex rhythm. (Sp.)
rumble, *n.* dull deep vibrant noise of thunder, heavy cart etc.; hind part

of carriage as extra seat or receptacle for luggage.—*v.i.* and *t.* make: move with sound of rumble; (*colloq.*) see through, find out. **r.-tumble,** *a.* and *n.* jolting (motion or vehicle).

rumbustious, *a.* boisterous, turbulent.

rumen, *n.* first stomach of ruminant. (L.=throat)

rumgumption, *n.* (*Scot.*) homely common sense, shrewdness.

ruminant, *a.* chewing the cud; thoughtful.—*n.* ruminant animal. **ruminate,** *v.i.* and *t.* regurgitate food after it has been swallowed, chew cud; ponder deeply, muse (over). **rumination, ruminator,** *nn.* **ruminative,** *a.* (*rumen*)

rummage, *v.i.* and *t.* make search (in), ransack; fish (out).—*n.* careful search; lumber. **r.-sale,** *n.* bazaar of discarded odds and ends; sale of unclaimed goods at docks. (O.F. *arrumage,* stowage)

rummer, *n.* large drinking-glass. (Du. *romer*)

rummy, *a.* (*sl.*) rum, queer.

rummy, *n.* simple card game for 4–6 players played with two packs.

rumour, *n.* common talk, hearsay; unverified report.—*v.t.* report by way of rumour. (L. *rumor*)

rump, *n.* hind quarters, backside; fag-end.

rumple, *v.t.* crease, wrinkle; disarrange, tousle.

rumpus, *n.* (*sl.*) disturbance, row.

rumpy, *n.* Manx tailless cat. (*rump*)

rum-tum, *n.* light sculling-boat.

run, *v.i.* and *t.* (*past* **ran,** *p.p.* **run**) move rapidly on legs; flee; go quickly or smoothly; race, enter for race; work, ply; flow, melt; extend, lie; pass, be current; be worded; drive, thrust; manage, direct; smuggle; hunt (fox).—*n.* running; trip; single score at cricket; sequence, course; rhythm, trend; type, kind; strong demand; enclosure for fowls, range of pasture; freedom (of); (*mus.*) roulade; (*Amer.*) watercourse. **in the long r.,** on the whole. **on the r.,** in flight. **r. away with,** elope with; accept (idea) hastily; (of emotion) overpower. **r. down,** overtake; drive over; disparage; (of clock) become unwound; in poor health. **r. for it,** (*colloq.*) flee for safety. **r. in,** (*colloq.*) arrest. **r. on,** ramble on; dwell on; (*print.*) continue in same line. **r. out of,** exhaust one's stock of. **r. over,** recapitulate; drive over. **r. through,** transfix; examine cursorily; spend rapidly. **r. to,** amount to; be enough for. **r. to extremes,** lack moderation. **r. up,** accumulate (debt); erect (building). (O.E. *rinnan*)

runabout, *a.* roving.—*n.* light motor-car.

runagate, *n.* vagabond, fugitive. (*renegade*+confusion with *run*)

runaway, *n.* fugitive; bolting horse.

runch, *v.t.* (*Scot.*) grind.

runcinate, *a.* (*bot.*) saw-toothed, with teeth pointing backwards. (L. *runcina,* plane)

rundale, *n.* land-tenure in which each holder has several detached strips. (*run*; *dole*)

rune, *n.* letter of primitive Teutonic alphabet; magic mark or sign. (O.N. *rún*)

rung, *n.* cross-bar of ladder or chair. (O.E. *hrung*)

rung, see **ring.**

runic, *a.* of, written in, inscribed with, runes.—*n.* kind of ornamental thick type.

runlet, *n.* small stream, rill. (*run*)

runlet, *n.* small wine-cask. (O.F. *rondelet*)

runnel, *n.* rill; small channel, gutter. (*run*)

runner, *n.* racer; messenger; blade of sledge or skate; moving stone of mill; rooting stem that runs along ground; kinds of twining plant; (*arch.*) constable. **r.-up,** *n.* competitor beaten in final.

running, *a.* successive; flowing, cursive; discharging pus. **in, out, of the r.,** having chance, no chance, of success. **make the r.,** set the pace. **r. powers,** right granted by one railway to another to run trains over its line. **r.-board,** *n.* footboard of car.

runrig, *n.* (*Scot.*) rundale. (*run*; *rig*)

runt, *n.* ox, cow, of small breed; dwarf; kind of pigeon; stump; stem of cabbage.

runway, *n.* beaten track of animal; incline for sliding logs etc.

rupee, *n.* Indian silver coin worth about 1*s.* 6*d.* (Sanskr. *rupya,* wrought silver)

rupture, *n.* breaking, breach; severance, quarrel; protrusion of bowel through containing membrane, hernia.—*v.t.* and *i.* burst; sever; cause hernia in. (L. *rumpere,* break)

rural, *a.* of country or agriculture, rustic. **r. dean,** head of clergy in group of parishes. **rurality,** *n.* **ruralize,** *v.t.* and *i.* make, become, rural. **ruralization,** *n.* **ruridecanal,** *a.* of rural dean or deanery. (L. *rus,* country)

rusa, *n.* large E. Indian deer. (Malay)

ruse, *n.* trick, stratagem. *rusé, a.* (*fem.* **rusée**) wily, cunning. (F.)

rush, *v.i.* and *t.* move, flow, run, impel, fast or violently; act, cause to act, with undue haste; take by sudden onset; (*sl.*) charge (customer); (*Amer. sl.*) entertain (candidate for election to college fraternity).—*n.* rushing, run; violent flow, spurt; charge, stampede. (O.F. *rehusser*)

rush, *n.* a marsh-plant; its slender pithy stem; worthless thing. **r.**

candle, **rushlight,** *n.* candle with pith of rush as wick; feeble light. **rushy,** *a.* full of rushes. (O.E. *risc*)
rusk, *n.* piece of bread rebaked and sweetened. (Sp. *rosca,* roll)
Russ, *n.* and *a.* (*arch.*) Russian.
russet, *a.* reddish-brown.—*n.* russet colour; homespun russet cloth; kind of apple. **r.-pated,** *a.* (*Shake.*) grey-headed. (L. *russus,* red)
Russia, *n.* **R. leather,** fine leather scented with birch-bark. **Russian,** *a.* and *n.* (native, language) of Russia. **russianize, russify,** *vv.t.* give Russian character to. **Russophil, Russophobe,** *nn.* one who loves, fears, Russia. **Russophilism, Russophobia,** *nn.*
rust, *n.* reddish coating formed on iron exposed to moisture; any metallic oxide so formed; red mould on plants, fungus causing this.—*v.i.* and *t.* become, make, rusty; lose efficiency through disuse or inactivity. (O.E.)
rustic, *a.* of the country or country people, rural; unsophisticated, uncouth; made of untrimmed branches. —*n.* peasant. **rusticity,** *n.* **rusticate,** *v.i.* and *t.* live country life; expel temporarily from university. **rustication,** *n.* (L. *rus,* country)
rustle, *n.* soft whispering sound of leaves, rain etc.—*v.i.* and *t.* make, move with, rustle; (*Amer. colloq.*) steal (cattle); hustle. (imit.)
rusty, *a.* coated with rust; rust-coloured, faded; out of practice; antiquated; (of voice) croaking. **turn r.,** take offence.
rusty, *a.* rancid. (O.F. *resté,* stale)
rut, *n.* wheel-track; mechanical routine, groove.—*v.t.* mark with ruts.
rut, *n.* seasonal sexual excitement of male animal.—*v.i.* be in heat. (L. *rugire,* roar)
rut, ruth, *n.* (*Anglo-Ind.*) native vehicle or carriage.
ruth, *n.* (*arch.*) pity, compassion; tenderness. (*rue*)
ruthenium, *n.* rare metallic element found in platinum ores. (L.L. *Ruthenia,* Russia)
ruthful, *a.* merciful; piteous. **ruthless,** *a.* pitiless, cruel. (*ruth*)
ruttish, *a.* lustful, lewd. (*rut*)
rutty, *a.* full of ruts.
rux, *n.* (*school sl.*) temper.
rye, *n.* a cereal plant; its grain; (*Amer. colloq.*) whisky made from it. **r.-grass,** *n.* kinds of fodder grass. (O.E. *ryge*)
rye, *n.* young man. (Romany)
ryke, *v.t.* (*Scot.*) reach.
ryot, *n.* Indian peasant. **ryotwary,** *n.* land-tenure arranged directly between government and cultivators. (Hind. *raiyat*)

S

sab, *Scot.* form of **sob.**
Sabaoth, *n.pl.* armies. (Heb. *çaba,* host)
sabbath, *n.* seventh day of Jewish week, set apart for rest from work; Christian Sunday. **break the s.,** work or play on it. **witches' s.,** witches' midnight orgy. **sabbatarian,** *a.* of the sabbath or its observance. —*n.* strict observer of sabbath. **sabbatarianism,** *n.* **sabbatic, sabbatical,** *aa.* of, like, sabbath; bringing rest. **sabbatize,** *v.i.* and *t.* keep (as) sabbath. (Heb. *shabāth,* rest)
sabicu, *n.* a Cuban tree; its hard wood. (Sp.)
sable, *n.* small animal like marten; its dark-brown fur. (O.F.)
sable, *a.* black, dusky.—*n.* black; (*pl.*) mourning garments. **s. antelope,** large black African antelope. (F.)
sabot, *n.* shoe made from single piece of wood; wooden-soled shoe, clog. **sabotage,** *n.* deliberate damage done to machinery etc. by workmen or spies.—*v.t.* damage thus. (F.)
sabre, *n.* heavy curved cavalry sword. *v.t.* cut down, wound, with sabre. **s.-bill, s.-wing,** *nn.* kinds of bird. **s.-toothed tiger,** extinct kind with very long canine teeth. **sabretache,** *n.* leather satchel hung from cavalry officer's sword-belt. *sabreur, n.* cavalryman with sabre. (G. *sabel*)
sabulous, *a.* sandy; gritty. (L. *sabulum,* sand)
saburra, *n.* foul granular deposit in stomach. (L.=sand)
sac, *n.* bag-like part, cavity, in animal or plant. **saccate,** *a.* pouched, bag-like. (L. *saccus,* sack)
saccharin, *n.* intensely sweet substance got from coal-tar. **saccharine,** *a.* of sugar; very sweet, cloying.—*n.* saccharin. **sacchariferous,** *a.* sugar-producing. **saccharify,** *v.t.* convert (starch) into sugar. **saccharimeter, saccharometer,** *nn.* instruments for measuring amount of sugar in a solution. **saccharoid,** *a.* (*geol.*) granular like sugar.—*n.* sugar-like substance. **saccharose,** *n.* cane or beet sugar, not glucose. (Gk. *sakcharon,* sugar)
sacciform, *a.* sac-shaped.
saccule, *n.* small sac. **saccular, sacculate,** *aa.* **sacculation,** *n.* division into saccules. (*sac*+dim.)
sacerdotal, *a.* of priests or priesthood. **sacerdotalism,** *n.* priestly system, priestcraft; undue influence of,

superstitious reverence for, priests. **sacerdotalist,** *n.* **sacerdocy,** (*joc.*) **sacerdotage,** *nn.* sacerdotalism. (L. *sacerdos*, priest)

sachem, *n.* Red Indian chief; bigwig, boss. (Amer. Ind.)

sachet, *n.* small perfumed bag or pad. (F.)

sack, *n.* large bag of coarse cloth; contents of this; kinds of loose gown or coat; (*baseball*) bag serving as base; (*colloq.*) dismissal.—*v.t.* put into sacks; (*colloq.*) dismiss. (Heb. *saq*)

sack, *v.t.* plunder, pillage, loot (town). —*n.* act of sacking. (F. *sac*, spoil)

sack, *n.* a white Spanish wine. (L. *siccus*, dry)

sackbut, *n.* old name for trombone; (in Bible) kind of stringed instrument. (F. *saquebute*)

sackcloth, *n.* coarse fabric of jute etc.; penitential garb.

sacking, *n.* material for sacks.

sackless, *a.* (*arch.*, *Scot.*) guiltless; harmless, guileless. (O.E. *sacu*, strife)

sacque, *n.* sack dress or coat.

sacral, *a.* of religious rites; (*anat.*) of the sacrum.

sacrament, *n.* religious ceremony forming outward and visible sign of inward and spiritual grace, esp. baptism and the eucharist; sacred symbol or pledge. **sacramental,** *a.* of sacraments. — *n.* rite similar to sacrament, e.g. use of holy water. **sacramentalism,** *n.* ascription of great importance to sacraments. **sacramentalist,** *n.* **sacramentarian,** *n.* sacramentalist; (*obs.*) one who holds the sacraments to be simply symbols. (L. *sacer*, sacred)

sacrarium, *n.* (*pl.* **sacraria**) part of church within altar-rails, sanctuary. (L.=shrine)

sacred, *a.* consecrated, dedicated (to); regarded as holy; religious; inviolable. (L. *sacer*)

sacrifice, *v.t.* and *i.* slaughter ceremonially as offering to deity; give up, allow to be destroyed, for the sake of something else; sell at a loss. —*n.* act of sacrificing; thing sacrificed, offering. **sacrificial,** *a.* (L. *sacer*, sacred; *facere*, make)

sacrilege, *n.* profanation of sacred place or thing; (*law*) breaking into, stealing from, a consecrated building. **sacrilegious,** *a.* guilty of sacrilege; irreverent, impious. (L. *sacer*, sacred; *legere*, gather)

sacring, *n.* consecration, esp. of sacramental elements. **s.-bell,** *n.* rung at elevation of the host. **sacrist,** *n.* official in charge of sacred vessels and vestments of a church. **sacristan,** *n.* sacrist; (*arch.*) sexton. **sacristy,** *n.* room for church vessels etc.; vestry. (L. *sacer*, sacred)

sacrosanct, *a.* secured by religious sanction against violation, very sacred. **sacrosanctity,** *n.* (L. *sacer*, sacred; *sancire*, consecrate)

sacrum, *n.* (*pl.* **sacra**) compound bone at base of spine forming back of pelvis. (L. os *sacrum*, sacred bone)

sad, *a.* feeling or causing sorrow, sorrowful; (of colour) dark; (of bread) heavy; (*colloq.*) bad, incorrigible; (*arch.*) serious, sober. **sadden,** *v.t.* and *i.* make, become, sad. (O.E. *sæd*)

saddle, *n.* seat, us. of leather, for rider on horse or bicycle; part of draught horse's harness fitting on back; joint of mutton or venison consisting of two loins; ridge between mountain-peaks, col.—*v.t.* put saddle on; burden, encumber. **in the s.,** mounted; in office. **s.-bag,** *n.* bag hung across behind saddle on either side; carpet-like cloth used in upholstery. **s.-bow,** *n.* arched front of saddle. **s.-cloth,** *n.* cloth placed under saddle. **s.-pillar,** *n.* support of bicycle saddle. **s.-tree,** *n.* frame of saddle. **saddleback,** *n.* sloping roof between two gables; kinds of bird and seal. **saddler,** *n.* maker of saddles and harness. **saddlery,** *n.* his trade or wares. (O.E. *sadol*)

Sadducee, *n.* member of ancient Jewish sect which denied resurrection.

sadhu, *n.* Hindu holy man. (Sanskr.)

sadism, *n.* sexual perversion in which pleasure is got from infliction of pain on another; inhuman cruelty. **sadist,** *n.* **sadistic,** *a.* (Marquis de *Sade*)

sae, *Scot.* form of so.

safari, *n.* hunting expedition; its carriers. (Arab. *safar*, journey)

safe, *a.* out of danger, secure; unhurt; conferring safety, reliable; prudent; sure; incapable of doing harm.—*v.t.* (*Shake.*) make safe.—*n.* steel box for valuables; ventilated cupboard for meat. **s.-conduct,** *n.* permit enabling holder to travel safely, esp. through enemy's country; convoy. **s.-deposit,** *n.* building with safes for renting. (L. *salvus*)

safeguard, *n.* protection, proviso, against foreseen risks.—*v.t.* secure by safeguard. (*safe*; *guard*)

safety, *n.* safeness, freedom from danger. **s.-bicycle,** *n.* modern bicycle, not old high type. **s.-bolt, s.-catch,** *nn.* catch preventing discharge of gun. **s.-lamp,** *n.* miner's lamp with gauze cover to prevent flame exploding gas. **s.-match,** *n.* kind striking only on box. **s.-pin, s.-razor,** *nn.* kinds with guard. **s.-valve,** *n.* automatic valve relieving excess pressure of steam etc.; harmless outlet for emotion.

saffian, *n.* brightly dyed goatskin or sheepskin leather. (Russ. *safiyanu*)

safflower, *n.* herb like thistle; red dye made from it. (O.F. *saffleur*)

saffron, *n.* plant of crocus kind, orange-red colouring-matter got from its flowers. — *a.* saffron - coloured.

safranin, safranine, *n.* synthetic saffron made from coal-tar. (Arab. *za'faran*)

sag, *v.i.* and *t.* bend downwards in middle, sink unevenly, under pressure; (of prices) decline; (of ship) drift from course.—*n.* sagging, droop.

saga, *n.* ancient Norse prose epic; tale of heroism. (O.N.=tale)

sagacious, *a.* mentally acute, shrewd, wise; (of animal) intelligent. **sagacity,** *n.* (L. *sagax*)

sagamore, *n.* Red Indian chief, sachem. (Amer. Ind. *sagamo*)

sage, *a.* wise, judicious, shrewd; wise-looking, solemn.—*n.* very wise man. (L. *sapere*, be wise)

sage, *n.* shrubby aromatic herb used for stuffing. **s.-brush,** *n.* low shrub of N. American alkali plains. **s.-green,** *a.* greyish-green. (L. *salvia*)

saggar, sagger, *n.* case of fireproof clay in which porcelain is enclosed for baking.

sagittal, *a.* of, like, an arrow. **Sagittarius,** *n.* the Archer, ninth sign of zodiac, which sun enters about 23 Nov. **sagittate, sagittated,** *aa.* shaped like arrow-head. (L. *sagitta*, arrow)

sago, *n.* (*pl.* **sagos**) kinds of E. Indian palm; their starchy pith, used for milk puddings. (Malay *sagu*)

sahib, *n.* title of respect used to Europeans by Indian natives; gentleman. (Arab. *çahib*, friend)

said, see **say** or **sayyid.**

saiga, *n.* antelope of steppes. (Russ.)

sail, *n.* piece of canvas spread to catch wind and propel vessel; ship, ships; cruise; arm of windmill.—*v.i.* and *t.* be moved by sails; travel by water; begin voyage; navigate (ship); glide, fly, pass smoothly; walk in stately manner. **full s.,** with all sails set. **make s.,** set more sails. **s. into** (*colloq.*) attack. **set s.,** spread sails; begin voyage. **under s.,** with sails set. **sailcloth,** *n.* canvas used for sails. **sailer,** *n.* sailing vessel. (O.E. *segel*)

sailor, *n.* seaman. **good, bad, s.,** one who is not, is, liable to sea-sickness. **s. hat,** child's straw hat. **s.'s knot,** slip-knot used for tying necktie. **sailoring,** *n.* sailor's life. **sailorly,** *a.* like a sailor. **sailorman,** *n.* sailor.

sailplane, *n.* glider.

sain, *v.t.* (*arch.*) make sign of cross on; bless to protect from evil. (L. *signum*, sign)

sain, *p.p.* (*Shake.*) said.

sainfoin, *n.* pink-flowered forage plant. (L. *sanus*, sound; *faenum*, hay)

saint, *n.* (*abbr.* **St.** or **S.**) person canonized by the Church; one of the company of heaven; very virtuous person. **s.'s day,** festival in memory of saint. **St. Andrew, David, George, Patrick,** patron saints of Scotland, Wales, England, Ireland. **St. Bernard (dog),** breed of large dog. **St. John's wort,** a yellow-flowered plant. **St. Stephen's,** Parliament. **sainted,** *a.* canonized; holy, hallowed; dead. **sainthood, saintship,** *nn.* **saintlike, saintly,** *aa.* (L. *sanctus*, holy)

sair, *Scot.* form of **sore.**

saith, see **say.**

sake, *n.* behalf. **for the s. of,** out of consideration for, on account of; in order to get. (O.E. *sacu*, strife)

sákē, *n.* Japanese rice beer. (Jap.)

saker, *n.* large falcon; ancient kind of cannon. (F. *sacre*)

saki, *n.* S. American monkey with white ruff and long tail. (native)

sakia, *n.* oriental wheel with buckets for raising water. (Arab. *sāqiya*)

sal, *n.* an Indian timber tree. (Hind.)

sal, *n.* salt. **s. volátilĕ,** ammonium carbonate; aromatic solution of this as restorative for faintness. **s.-ammoniac,** *n.* ammonium chloride. (L.)

salaam, *n.* oriental word of greeting or low bow with palm to forehead.—*v.i.* and *t.* make salaam (to). (Arab. *salam*)

salable, *a.* marketable; in good demand.

salacious, *a.* lustful, lewd. **salacity,** *n.* (L. *salire*, leap)

salad, *n.* dish of uncooked vegetables, variously prepared; lettuce etc. used for this. **s. days,** inexperienced youth. **s.-dressing, s.-oil,** *nn.* sauce, olive oil, for salads. (*sal*)

salamander, *n.* lizard-like amphibian once fabled to live in fire; fire-spirit; person who loves fire; plate for browning meat. **salamandrian, salamandrine,** *aa.* (Gk. *salamandra*)

salámĕ, *n.* Italian salted sausage. (It.)

salangane, *n.* Chinese swallow building edible nest. (F.)

salary, *n.* fixed periodical payment for non-manual work, commonly made monthly. **salaried,** *a.* (L. *salarium*, salt-money)

sale, *n.* exchange of anything for money; act of selling; auction; disposal of goods at reduced prices. **saleable,** same as **salable.** (O.E. *sala*)

salep, *n.* dried tubers of kinds of orchis, used as food. (Arab. *tha'leb*)

saleratus, *n.* (*Amer.*) baking soda. (Mod. L. *sal aeratus*, aerated salt)

salesman, *n.* (*fem.* **saleswoman**) shop assistant. **salesmanship,** *n.* art of selling.

salewe, (*Spens.*) form of **salute.**

Salic, *a.* Frankish. **S. law,** excluding women from succession to throne.

salicaceous, *a.* of the willow family. **salicin,** *n.* bitter white crystalline substance got from willow bark. **salicyl,** *n.* radical of **salicylic acid,**

antiseptic acid got from salicin or phenol. (L. *salix*, willow)

salient, *a.* projecting outwards; conspicuous, noteworthy; leaping, gushing.—*n.* projection, esp. in line of trenches. **salience, saliency,** *nn.* (L. *salire*, leap)

saline, *a.* of, impregnated with, salt or salts; salty.—*n.* salt spring; solution of salt and water; saline aperient. **salinity,** *n.* **salinometer,** *n.* device measuring amount of salt in a solution. **saliferous,** *a.* salt-producing. **salify,** *v.t.* make salty; (*chem.*) convert into a salt. **salification,** *n.* (*sal*)

Salique, same as **Salic.**

saliva, *n.* liquid secreted in mouth, spittle. **salivary,** *a.* **salivate,** *v.t.* and *i.* produce abnormal flow of saliva (in). **salivation,** *n.* (L.)

salle, n. large room. *s.-à-manger, n.* dining-room. *s. d'attente,* waiting-room. (F.)

sallenders, *n.pl.* dry eruption on horse's hock.

sallet, *n.* medieval light helmet. (L. *caelata* cassis, ornamented helmet)

sallet, (*Shake.*) form of salad.

sallow, *a.* and *n.* (of) sickly-yellow or pale-brown colour.—*v.t.* and *i.* turn sallow. (O.E. *salo*)

sallow, *n.* low shrubby kind of willow; shoot, wood, of this. (O.E. *sealh*)

sally, *n.* sudden attack made by besieged on besiegers, sortie; outburst; lively remark, quip.—*v.i.* make sally; go (forth). **s.-port,** *n.* postern gate for making sallies from. (L. *salire*, leap)

Sally Lunn, a sweet tea-cake.

salmagundi, *n.* highly seasoned dish of chopped meat, eggs etc.; medley. (F. *salmigondis*)

salmi, *n.* ragout, esp. of game. (F.)

salmon, *n.* (*pl.* same) large silvery fish that ascends rivers to spawn; colour of its flesh, orange-pink.—*a.* orange-pink. **s. trout,** fish like small salmon. (L. *salmo*)

salon, n. drawing-room; reception at which celebrities are present; annual exhibition of pictures in Paris. (F.)

saloon, *n.* large reception-room; main or first-class cabin on passenger ship; railway carriage, closed motor-car, with no internal partitions; (*Amer.*) public-house. **s. bar,** first-class bar. **s. pistol, rifle,** adapted for short-range practice. (*salon*)

saloop, *n.* hot drink of salep or sassafras tea. (=*salep*)

Salopian, *a.* and *n.* (native) of Shropshire; (member) of Shrewsbury School. (O.E. *Scrobbesbyrig*, Shrewsbury)

salpiglossis, *n.* plant like petunia. (Gk. *salpingx*, trumpet; *glōssa*, tongue)

salsify, salsafy, *n.* purple-flowered plant with edible root, oyster-plant. (It. *sassefrica*)

salt, *a.* (*Shake.*) lecherous.

salt, *n.* sodium chloride, used as seasoning and preservative; piquancy; wit; (*chem.*) compound of acid and base; (*pl.*) mineral salt as aperient.—*a.* containing, tasting of, preserved in, salt; pungent.—*v.t.* flavour, pickle, sprinkle, with salt; fake (mine) by inserting ore in it. **above, below, the s.,** at upper, lower, end of table. **eat one's s.,** be his guest. **not worth his s.,** not worth his keep. **old s.,** old sailor. **s., ss., of lemon,** citric acid. **s. of the earth,** person of highest worth. **take with a grain of s.,** believe only part of. **s.-bush,** *n.* an Australian forage plant. **s.-cellar,** *n.* vessel for salt at table. **s.-lick,** *n.* outcrop of salt licked by animals. **s.-pan,** *n.* vessel, hollow, where salt is made by evaporation. **s.-water,** *a.* of sea. (O.E. *sealt*)

saltant, *a.* leaping. *saltarello, n.* Italian skipping dance. **saltation,** *n.* leaping, dancing; abrupt variation. **saltatory, saltatorial,** *aa.* (L. *salire*, leap)

salter, *n.* dealer in, maker of, salt; drysalter. **saltern,** *n.* salt works. **salting,** *n.* salt marsh.

saltire, *n.* (*heraldry*) X-shaped cross dividing shield etc. into four compartments. (O.F. *sautoir*, stile)

saltpetre, *n.* potassium nitrate, used in making gunpowder etc. (L. *sal*, salt. Gk. *petra*, rock)

salubrious, *a.* favourable to health, health-giving. **salubrity,** *n.* (L. *salus*, health)

Saluki, *n.* Arabian gazelle-hound.

salutary, *a.* beneficial, wholesome. (L. *salus*, health)

salute, *n.* gesture of respect, greeting; motion of hand or rifle, discharge of guns etc., as military mark of honour; (*arch.*) kiss.—*v.t.* and *i.* make salute (to); greet; kiss. **salutation,** *n.* greeting, words used in it. **salutational, salutatory,** *aa.* (L. *salus*, health)

salvage, *n.* saving of ship or property from peril of sea, fire etc.; reward paid for this; thing salvaged.—*v.t.* save from wreck, fire etc. (L. *salvare*, save)

salvarsan, *n.* drug used for syphilis. (proprietary name)

salvation, *n.* saving, being saved; redemption from sin and its consequences; means of preservation. **find s.,** be converted. **S. Army,** organization for spread of religion among the masses. **salvationist,** *n.* member of Salvation Army; revivalist. **salvationism,** *n.* (L. *salvare*, save)

salve, *n.* healing ointment; soothing influence.—*v.t.* apply salve to, soothe; smooth over. (O.E. *sealf*)

salve, *v.t.* salvage. (*salvage*)

sálvē, *int.* hail.—*n.* (also *S. Regina*) a Roman Catholic hymn. (L.)
salver, *n.* small tray. (Sp. *salva*, tasting of food as precaution)
salvia, *n.* kinds of plant incl. sage. (L.)
salvo, *n.* (*pl.* salvos) exception, reservation. (L. *salvo* jure, the right being reserved)
salvo, *n.* (*pl.* salvoes) simultaneous discharge of guns; combined shout. (It. *salva*, salutation)
salvor, *n.* person effecting salvage.
sam, *adv.* (*Spens.*) together. (*same*)
Sam, *n.* **S. Browne**, army officer's belt and straps. **stand S.**, (*sl.*) bear expense. **Uncle S.**, typical U.S. citizen. **upon my S.**, upon my word.
samara, *n.* winged fruit, as of ash. (L.=elm seed)
Samaritan, *a.* and *n.* (inhabitant) of Samaria. **good S.**, one who helps those in need, hence **Samaritanism**, *n.*
sambo, *n.* offspring of negro and mulatto. (Sp. *zambo*)
Sambo, *n.* nickname for negro.
sambur, *n.* Indian elk. (Hind. *sambar*)
same, *a.* identical; exactly similar; unchanged; uniform, monotonous; previously mentioned. **all the s.**, **at the s. time**, nevertheless. (O.N. *samr*)
Samian, *a.* of Samos. **S. ware**, fine glazed Roman pottery.
samisen, *n.* kind of Japanese guitar. (Chin. *san*, three; *hsien*, string)
samite, *n.* rich medieval silk fabric. (Gk. *hex*, six; *mitos*, thread)
samlet, *n.* young salmon, parr. (dim.)
samovar, *n.* Russian tea-urn. (Russ. *samovaru*, lit. self-boiler)
Samoyed, *n.* member of Siberian Mongol race; white sledge-dog. **Samoyedic**, *a.*
samp, *n.* (*Amer.*) coarsely ground Indian meal; porridge of this.
sampan, *n.* small Chinese river-boat. (Chin. *san*, three; *pan*, board)
samphire, *n.* fleshy cliff plant used in pickles. (F. *saint Pierre*, St. Peter)
sample, *n.* part to show quality of the whole, specimen.—*v.t.* and *i.* take samples of; test quality of, taste. (L. *exemplum*)
sampler, *n.* piece of ornamental embroidery containing figures, texts etc.
Samson, *n.* very strong man. **samsonite**, *n.* an explosive. (name in Bible)
samurai, *n.* (*pl.* same) member of ancient Japanese warrior caste. (Jap.)
sanable, *a.* curable. **sanative**, **sanatory**, *aa.* curative. sanatorium, *n.* (*pl.* **sanatoria**) hospital, esp. for consumptives or convalescents; health resort. (L. *sanare*, cure)
sanbenito, *n.* penitential robe put on heretic in Spanish Inquisition. (Sp.)
sanctify, *v.t.* consecrate, make holy; purify from sin; give sanction to. **sanctification**, *n.* **sanctified**, *a.* hallowed; sanctimonious. **sanctimonious** *a.* hypocritically pious; (*Shake.*) sacred. **sanctimony**, *n.* **sanction**, *n.* authorization, express permission; binding influence; penalty by which law is enforced.—*v.t.* give sanction to. **sanctitude**, *n.* saintliness. **sanctity**, *n.* holiness, saintliness; inviolability. **sanctuary**, *n.* sacred place, shrine; part of church round altar; place where fugitive was safe from arrest or violence, asylum; refuge. **sanctuarize**, *v.t.* (*Shake.*) afford sanctuary to. **sanctum**, *n.* holy place; private room, study. **sanctum sanctorum**, holy of holies; most private place. *Sanctus*, *n.* hymn 'Holy, holy, holy' in the communion. (L. *sanctus*, holy; *facere*, make)
sand, *n.* powder of fine particles of rock; (*Amer. colloq.*) pluck; (*pl.*) stretch of sand.—*v.t.* sprinkle, overlay, adulterate, with sand. **the ss. are running out**, time is nearly up. **sandbank**, *n.* shoal of sand. **s. blast**, *n.* jet of sand for roughening glass etc. **s. glass**, *n.* instrument measuring time by running of sand. **sandhill**, *n.* dune. **s.-hopper**, *n.* small marine crustacean. **s.-shoe**, *n.* canvas shoe for beach wear. (O.E.)
sandal, *n.* sole without upper, attached to foot by straps. (Gk. *sandalion*)
sandalwood, **sandal**, *nn.* a yellow scented wood. (L.L. *sandalum*)
sandarac, *n.* a resin used in making varnish; realgar. (Gk. *sandarakē*)
sandbag, *n.* bag filled with sand.—*v.t.* fortify, surround, with sandbags; stun with sandbag.
sand-blind, *a.* (*arch.*) dim-sighted.
sanderling, *n.* a small wading-bird.
Sandhurst, *n.* the Royal Military College for army cadets. (place)
sandiver, *n.* salty scum formed in glass-making.
sandman, *n.* mythical man who makes children's eyes smart towards bedtime.
sandpaper, *n.* paper covered with sand.—*v.t.* polish, smooth, with this.
sandpiper, *n.* shore bird like plover.
sandstone, *n.* rock of compacted sand. **old red s.**, (*geol.*) strata below carboniferous.
sandstorm, *n.* storm of wind on desert carrying clouds of sand.
sandwich, *n.* two slices of bread with meat, egg etc., between.—*v.t.* insert, squeeze in. **sandwichman**, *n.* man who parades street with placards hung before and behind him.
sandy, *a.* like, covered with, sand; yellowish-brown.
Sandy, *n.* nickname for Scotsman. (*Alexander*)
sane, *a.* mentally normal, not mad; reasonable, sensible. (L. *sanus*, healthy)
san fairy ann, (*army sl.*) that does not matter, never mind. (F. *ce ne fait rien*)
sang, see sing.

sangar, sanga, *n.* breastwork of loose stones. (Hind. *sunga*)
sangaree, *n.* drink of spiced wine and water. (Sp. *sangria*, lit. bleeding)
sang-froid, *n.* coolness in danger, imperturbability. (F.=cold blood)
sangrail, sangreal, *n.* the holy grail. (*saint*; *grail*)
sanguine, *a.* blood-red; ruddy; confident, hopeful. **sanguification,** *n.* conversion of food into blood. **sanguinary,** *a.* bloody; blood-stained; bloodthirsty. **sanguineous,** *a.* of blood; full-blooded; blood-red. (L. *sanguis*, blood)
sanhedrim, sanhedrin, *n.* supreme council and court of justice in ancient Jerusalem. (Gk. *sun*, together; *hedra*, seat)
sanicle, *n.* herb once supposed to have healing powers. (L. *sanare*, heal)
sanies, *n.* (*med.*) thin discharge from ulcer etc. (L.)
sanify, *v.t.* make healthy. (L. *sanus*, healthy; *facere*, make)
sanitary, *a.* of, promoting, health; of drains. **sanitarian,** *n.* and *a.* (promoter) of public health and hygiene. **sanitarium,** same as **sanatorium. sanitate,** *v.t.* provide with drainage. **sanitation,** *n.* sanitary measures or appliances; drainage. (L. *sanus*, healthy)
sanity, *n.* saneness.
sanjak, *n.* subdivision of Turkish vilayet or province. (Turk.)
sank, see **sink.**
sannup, *n.* Red Indian warrior, brave. (Amer. Ind.)
sans, *prep.* (*arch.*) without. *s. cérémonie*, without formality. *s. doute*, doubtless. *s. façon*, bluntly. *s. gêne*, without constraint. *s. peur et s. reproche*, without fear and without reproach. *s. phrase*, without qualification. *s. souci*, free from care. (F.)
Sanscrit, same as **Sanskrit.**
sansculotte, *n.* violent or low-class French revolutionary. **sansculotterie, sansculottism,** *nn.* **sansculottic,** *a.* (F.=without breeches)
sanserif, *a.* and *n.* (type) without serifs.
Sanskrit, *n.* and *a.* (of, in) ancient language of India. **Sanskritic,** *a.* (Sanskr. *sam*, together; *kṛ*, make)
Santa Claus, nursery hero who brings children presents on Christmas Eve. (Du. *Sint Klaas*, St. Nicholas)
santon, *n.* Mohammedan monk or dervish. (L. *sanctus*, holy)
santonica, *n.* kind of wormwood. **santonin,** *n.* extract of this. (L.)
Saorstat Eireann, the Irish Free State. (Ir.)
sap, *n.* vital juice of plants; vitality; sap-wood.—*v.t.* drain of sap; exhaust vigour of. **s.-wood,** *n.* part of wood next bark. (O.E. *sæp*)
sap, *n.* narrow or covered siege-trench; digging of this, undermining.—*v.t.* and *i.* attack by, dig, sap; undermine insidiously. (F. *sappe*, spade)
sap, *v.i.* (*school sl.*) study hard.—*n.* hard task; plodding student, swot.
sapajou, *n.* capuchin monkey. (F.)
sapan-wood, *n.* Asiatic wood yielding a red dye. (Malay *sapan*)
saphead, *n.* (*Amer. sl.*) stupid person.
sapid, *a.* pleasantly flavoured; not tasteless; interesting, not insipid. **sapidity,** *n.* (L. *sapere*, taste)
sapient, *a.* wise, sagacious (often used ironically). **sapience,** *n.* **sapiential,** *a.* of wisdom. (L. *sapere*, be wise)
sapless, *a.* without sap; effete.
sapling, *n.* young tree; youth; greyhound in its first year. (*sap*+dim.)
sapodilla, *n.* large tropical evergreen tree yielding chicle. (Mex. *zapotl*)
saponaceous, *a.* of or containing soap, soapy; unctuous. **saponify,** *v.t.* and *i.* turn into soap. **saponification,** *n.* (L. *sapo*, soap)
sapor, *n.* taste, flavour. (L.)
sappan-wood, same as **sapan-wood.**
sapper, *n.* one who saps; private of the Royal Engineers.
Sapphic, *a.* of the Greek poetess Sappho.—*n.* stanza form used by her. **Sapphism,** *n.* homosexuality in women.
sapphire, *n.* a transparent blue precious stone; deep pure blue.—*a.* of this colour. **sapphirine,** *a.* (Gk. *sappheiros*, lapis lazuli)
sapples, *n.pl.* (*Scot.*) soapsuds.
sappy, *a.* full of sap, juicy; (*sl.*) soft, silly.
sapr(o)-, from Gk. *sapros*, rotten, used in **sapraemia,** *n.* septic poisoning; **saprodontia,** *n.* decay of teeth; **saprogenic,** *a.* causing, caused by, putrefaction; **saprophagous, saprophilous,** *aa.* feeding on, flourishing in, decaying matter; **saprophyte,** *n.* saprophagous plant.
sar, *n.* a fish, sea-bream. (L. *sargus*)
saraband, sarabande, *n.* a slow Spanish dance. (Sp. *zarabanda*)
Saracen, *n.* and *a.* medieval name for Arab or Moslem. **Saracenic,** *a.* (L.L. *Saracenus*)
Saratoga trunk, large travelling trunk. (*Saratoga* Springs in U.S.)
sarcasm, *n.* wounding or satirical remark, veiled sneer; use of this. **sarcastic,** *a.* **sarcastically,** *adv.* **sarcast,** *n.* sarcastic person. (Gk. *sarkazein*, tear flesh)
sarcelle, *n.* kinds of small duck. (L. *querquedula*)
sarcenet, same as **sarsenet.**
sarco-, from Gk. *sarx*, flesh, used in **sarcocarp,** *n.* pulpy part of fruit; **sarcode,** *n.* animal protoplasm; **sarcology,** *n.* anatomy of flesh; **sarcoma,** *n.* (*pl.* **sarcomata**) malignant tumour in connective tissue, cancer; **sarcous,** *a.* of flesh or muscle.
sarcophagus, *n.* (*pl.* **sarcophagi**) stone coffin. (Gk. *sarx*, flesh; *phagein*, eat)
sard, *n.* yellow or orange cornelian. (*Sardis* in Lydia)

sardine, *n.* kind of pilchard preserved in oil. **sardelle,** *n.* fish like sardine. (Gk. *sardē*)

sardonic, *a.* (of smile etc.) derisive, grimly mocking, maliciously jocular. **sardonically,** *adv.* (Gk. *sardanios*)

sardonyx, *n.* onyx with layers of sard.

saree, sari, *n.* Hindu woman's robe. (Hind.)

sargasso, *n.* kinds of floating seaweed. (Port. *sargaço*)

sarissa, *n.* (*pl.* sarissae) ancient Macedonian lance. (Gk.)

sark, *n.* (*Scot.*) shirt. (O.N. *serkr*)

sarmentose, sarmentous, *aa.* (*bot.*) with trailing shoots or runners. (L. *sarmentum*, twig)

sarong, *n.* skirt worn by Malays. (Malay *sārung*)

sarrusophone, *n.* brass instrument of oboe family. (*Sarrus*, inventor)

sarsaparilla, *n.* kinds of smilax; medicinal preparation, drink, made from their roots. (Sp. *zarzaparrilla*)

sarsenet, *n.* thin tissue of fine silk. (made by *Saracens*)

sartorial, *a.* of tailor or men's clothes. (L. *sartor*, tailor)

sash, *n.* ornamental scarf or band worn round waist or over shoulder. (Arab. *shash*, muslin)

sash, *n.* frame holding glass of window, sliding vertically. **s.-cord,** *n.* attaching this to **s.-weight,** *n.* which balances sash. (corrupt. of *chassis*)

sashay, *v.i.* (*Amer., vulg.*) move back and forward, dance about. (corrupt. of *chassé*)

sasin, *n.* Indian antelope. (*Nepalese*)

sassafras, *n.* kind of laurel; its root-bark, used medicinally. (Sp. *sasafras*)

Sassenach, *n.* (*Scot., Ir.*) Englishman. (*Saxon*)

sassy, *Amer. colloq.* for **saucy.**

sat, see **sit.**

Satan, (*arch.*) **Satanas,** *n.* the devil. **satanic, satanical,** *aa.* fiendish, diabolical; of Satan. **satanic school,** Byron and his followers. **satanism,** *n.* devil worship; deliberate wickedness. (Heb.=adversary)

satchel, *n.* small bag for papers etc.; school-bag. (L. *saccellus*)

sate, *v.t.* satisfy to repletion, glut. (O.E. *sadian*)

sate, see **sit.**

sateen, *n.* cotton or woollen fabric with glossy surface. (*satin*)

satellite, *n.* attendant, hanger-on; planet revolving round another, moon. **satellitic,** *a.* (L. *satelles*)

satiate, *v.t.* sate, surfeit.—*a.* (*poet.*) sated. **satiation,** *n.* **satiable,** *a.* **satiety,** *n.* state of being sated; feeling of having had too much. (L. *satis*, enough)

satin, *n.* silk fabric with glossy surface on one side; (*sl.*) gin.—*a.* of, like, satin.—*v.t.* give glossy surface to. **white s.,** the plant honesty. **satinet, satinette,** *n.* imitation satin of cotton and wool. **satinwood,** *n.* a fine hard tropical wood or tree. **satiny,** *a.* (F.)

satire, *n.* literary composition holding up vice or folly to ridicule, invective poem; trenchant wit, sarcasm. **satiric, satirical,** *aa.* **satirist,** *n.* writer of satires. **satirize,** *v.t.* attack with satire. (L. *satira*, medley)

satis, adv. enough. (L.)

satisfy, *v.t.* be enough for, render content; make reparation to; fulfil, discharge, pay; convince. **satisfaction,** *n.* act of satisfying; that which satisfies; atonement, reparation. **satisfactory,** *a.* giving satisfaction; good enough, adequate. (L. *satis*, enough; *facere*, make)

satrap, *n.* provincial governor of ancient Persia; petty despot. **satrapy,** *n.* district, office, of satrap. (Old Pers. *khsatra*, province; *pā*, protect)

Satsuma, *n.* (also **S. ware**) glazed yellow Japanese pottery. (province)

saturate, *v.t.* soak thoroughly, steep; (*chem.*) cause to absorb or dissolve the greatest amount possible of another substance.—*a.* (*poet.*) saturated. **saturation,** *n.* **saturable,** *a.* (L. *satur*, full)

Saturday, *n.* seventh day of week. (*Saturn's day*)

Saturn, *n.* ancient Roman god of agriculture, who reigned in the golden age; second largest planet. **saturnalia,** *n.* ancient festival of Saturn; noisy revelry, orgy. **saturnalian,** *a.* **Saturnian,** *a.* of Saturn. **Saturnian verse,** old native Roman metre, scanned like 'The queen was in the parlour, eating bread and honey.' **saturnine,** *a.* gloomy, morose; of lead or lead poisoning. (L. *Saturnus*)

satyr, *n.* woodland deity, half man, half goat; lustful man. **satyric,** *a.* **satyriasis,** *n.* sexual mania in male. (Gk. *saturos*)

sauce, *n.* liquid seasoning for food; (*colloq.*) impudence; (*Amer.*) compote of fruit.—*v.t.* season with sauce; make piquant; (*colloq.*) cheek; (*Shake.*) make suffer. **s.-alone,** *n.* weed used for flavouring. **s.-boat,** *n.* vessel for serving sauce. **s.-box,** *n.* impudent person. **saucepan,** *n.* cooking-pan with lid. (L. *salsus*, salted)

saucer, *n.* small flat dish placed under cup; shallow depression. **s.-eyed,** *a.* with large round eyes. (*sauce*)

saucy, *a.* pert, cheeky; (*sl.*) smart, stylish; (*Shake.*) lascivious.

sauerkraut, n. German dish of pickled cabbage. (G.)

saul, same as **sal.**

saunter, *v.i.* walk in leisurely way.—*n.* stroll. **saunterer,** *n.*

saurian, *a.* and *n.* (animal) of lizard order. (Gk. *sauros*, lizard)

saury, *n.* kinds of fish with long beak.

sausage, *n.* minced meat in tubular bag of gut; (*army sl.*) kite-balloon. **s.-meat,** *n.* minced and seasoned meat. **s.-roll,** *n.* sausage-meat cooked in roll of pastry. (L. *salsus*, salted)

sauté, *a.* fried lightly and quickly. (F.)

Sauterne, *n.* a light sweet white wine. (place in France)

sauve-qui-peut, *n.* precipitate flight, general stampede. (F.=save himself who can)

savage, *a.* uncivilized, primitive, wild; fierce, ferocious, brutal; (*colloq.*) furious.—*n.* primitive man; brutal or barbarous person.—*v.t.* bite and worry. **savagery,** *n.* savageness; (*Shake.*) wild vegetation. (L. *silva*, wood)

savannah, savanna, *n.* open grassy plain, prairie, of tropical America. (Sp. *zavana*)

savant, *n.* man of learning. (F. *savoir*, know)

save, *v.t.* and *i.* rescue from danger, preserve from harm; effect spiritual salvation of; keep unused, hoard, put by; avoid loss of, prevent waste (of).—*n.* (*football etc.*) preventing opponents from scoring.—*prep.* except.—*conj.* but. **s. appearances,** avoid public exposure. (L. *salvus*, safe)

saveloy, *n.* highly seasoned dried sausage. (L. *cerebrum*, brain)

savin, *n.* kind of juniper yielding medicinal oil. (L. *sabina*)

saving, *a.* thrifty, economical; (of clause) containing reservation. *n. pl.* money saved.—*prep.* (*arch.*) except; with apology to. **savings-bank,** *n.* bank receiving small deposits at interest.

saviour, *n.* one who saves; the Redeemer, Christ.

savoir faire, knowing the right thing to do, tact. *savoir vivre*, social knowledge, good breeding. (F.)

savory, *n.* aromatic herb used in cooking. (L. *satureia*)

savour, *n.* taste, flavour; odour, fragrance; smack, spice.—*v.t.* and *i.* season; taste, smack (of); relish, appreciate critically. **savourless,** *a.* insipid. **savoury,** *a.* tasty, appetizing; fragrant; reputable; of salt, not sweet, flavour.—*n.* savoury dish at beginning or end of dinner. (L. *sapere*, taste)

savoy, *n.* kind of cabbage with curled leaves. (province of France)

savvy, *v.t.* (*sl.*) understand.—*n.* wits. (Sp. *saber*, know)

saw, see see.

saw, *n.* traditional saying, proverb. (O.E. *sagu*)

saw, *n.* tool with toothed edge for cutting wood etc.—*v.t.* and *i.* (*p.p.* **sawn, sawed**) cut, shape, with saw; use saw; make to-and-fro motion. **s.-horse,** (*Amer.*) **s.-buck,** *nn.* rack for holding logs being sawn. **s.-mill,** *n.* for mechanical sawing. **s.-pit,** *n.* in which lower of two men working two-handed saw stands. (O.E. *saga*)

sawbones, *n.* (*joc.*) surgeon.

sawder, *n.* **soft s.,** flattery, blarney. (=*solder*)

sawdust, *n.* small particles of wood.

sawfish, *n.* fish with toothed snout.

Sawney, *n.* nickname for Scotsman; softy. (*Sandy*)

sawyer, *n.* one who saws; kind of beetle; (*Amer.*) uprooted tree floating in river.

sax, *n.* slate-cutter's hammer; dagger. (O.E. *seax*, knife)

saxatile, *a.* rock-inhabiting. (L. *saxum*, rock)

saxe, *n.* a bright blue. (*Saxony*)

saxhorn, *n.* instrument of trumpet kind. (A. *Sax*, inventor)

saxicoline, saxicolous, *aa.* rock-inhabiting. (L. *saxum*, rock; *colere*, inhabit)

saxifrage, *n.* kinds of rock plant. (L. *saxum*, rock; *frangere*, break)

Saxon, *n.* and *a.* (member, language) of a Teutonic people who occupied parts of England in 5th century (native) of Saxony. **saxony,** *n.* kind of wool; cloth made from it. (L. *Saxo*)

saxophone, *n.* brass reed instrument with about 20 finger-keys. **saxtuba,** *n.* bass saxhorn. (A. *Sax*, inventor)

say, *v.t.* and *n.* (*Shake.*) assay.

say, *n.* fine cloth like serge. (L. *sagum*, military cloak)

say, *v.t.* and *i.* (*past*, *p.p.* **said**; *2nd sing. pres.* **sayst** or **sayest**; *arch. 3rd sing.* **saith**; *2nd sing. past* **saidst** or **saidest**) utter, express in words; allege, report; repeat, recite; speak. —*n.* what one has to say; share in decision. **hear s.,** hear it reported. **that is to s.,** in other words. **they s.,** it is commonly reported. **s.-so,** *n.* (*Amer. colloq.*) assertion; dictum. **says you,** (*Amer. sl.*) expression of incredulity. **go without saying,** be self-evident. **saying,** *n.* common remark, proverb. (O.E. *secgan*)

sayyid, sayid, said, seid, *n.* Moslem title of honour applied to supposed descendants of Mohammed's daughter Fatima; chief, lord. (Arab.)

'sblood, *int.* (*obs.*) God's blood.

scab, *n.* dry crust formed on healing wound; skin disease, itch; workman who refuses to join strike, blackleg. —*v.i.* form scab. **scabbed, scabby,** *aa.* (Da. *skab*)

scabbard, *n.* sheath of sword or dagger.

scabies, *n.* the itch. **scabious,** *a.* having itch; scabby.—*n.* plant with pink, red, or blue flowers. **scabrous,** *a.* rough-surfaced; scurfy; indelicate, ticklish. (L.)

scad, *n.* horse-mackerel.

scaffolage, *n.* (*Shake.*) stage.

scaffold, *n.* raised platform for use of workmen erecting building etc., or for execution of criminal; capital punishment; (*Shake.*) stage.—*v.t.*

furnish with scaffold. **scaffolding,** *n.* structure of, materials for, scaffold. (O.F. *escadafault*)

scagliola, *n.* Italian plaster-work imitating stone. (It. *scagliuola*)

scalariform, *a.* ladder-shaped. (L. *scala,* ladder)

scalawag, same as **scallywag.**

scald, *v.t.* burn with hot liquid or steam; rinse with boiling water; bring (milk) to just below boiling-point.—*n.* injury from scalding. (L. *ex-,* entirely; *calidus,* hot)

scald, *n.* ancient Scandinavian bard. **scaldic,** *a.* (O.N. *skáld*)

scald, *a.* (*Shake.*) scurvy. **s.-head,** *n.* disease of scalp. (*scall*)

scale, *n.* pan of balance; (*pl.*) balance; Libra, seventh sign of zodiac.—*v.t.* and *i.* weigh in scales. **turn the s.,** be decisive. (O.N. *skál,* bowl)

scale, *n.* one of the plates covering fish or reptile; flake, film; scab; incrustation on teeth etc.—*v.t.* and *i.* scrape scales from; peel (off) in scales. (O.F. *escale*)

scale, *n.* a graduated measure; system of grading, series of degrees; proportion, relative dimensions; (*math.*) basis for a numerical system, 10 being that in general use; (*mus.*) series of tones from keynote to its octave, in order of pitch; (*arch.*) flight of steps.—*v.t.* climb by ladders; mount; reproduce to scale. **to s.,** with uniform reduction or enlargement. **scaling-ladder,** *n.* one used in escalade. (L. *scala,* ladder)

scalene, *a.* with unequal sides. (Gk. *skalēnos*)

scall, *n.* (*arch.*) scaly disease of skin. (O.N. *skalle,* bare head)

scallawag, same as **scallywag.**

scallion, *n.* Welsh onion. (*shallot*)

scallop, *n.* an edible shell-fish; one of a series of curves in edging; shallow baking-pan.—*v.t.* cut into scallops; cook in scallop. (O.F. *escalope*)

scallywag, *n.* scamp, scapegrace; undersized animal.

scalp, *n.* skin and hair of top of head; this torn off as trophy by Red Indians.—*v.t.* and *i.* tear scalp from; criticize savagely; (*Amer. sl.*) make small quick profit by speculation.

scalpel, *n.* small surgical knife. **scalper,** *n.* engraver's gouge. **scalpriform,** *a.* chisel-shaped. (L. *scalprum,* chisel+dim.)

scaly, *a.* like, covered with, scales; (*sl.*) mean, shabby.

scamble, *v.i.* (*Shake.*) scramble.

scammony, *n.* kind of Asiatic convolvulus; purgative gum-resin got from it. (Gk. *skammōnia*)

scamp, *n.* worthless fellow, rogue.

scamp, *v.t.* perform carelessly or imperfectly.

scamper, *v.i.* run quickly or friskily; hasten away.—*n.* brisk run. (L. *ex,* out of; *campus,* field)

scan, *v.t.* and *i.* look at closely, scrutinize; count feet in (verse); (of verse) be metrically correct. (L. *scandere,* climb)

scandal, *n.* offence to sense of decency; thing or person causing this; injury to reputation; malicious gossip. **scandalize,** *v.t.* shock moral feelings of; defame. **scandalmonger,** *n.* spreader of malicious gossip. **scandalous,** *a.* outrageous, disgraceful; defamatory; fond of scandal. *scandalum magnatum,* defamation of high personages. (Gk. *skandalon,* stumbling-block)

scandalize, *v.t.* (*naut.*) reduce area of (sail). (*scant*)

Scandinavian, *a.* and *n.* (native, language) of region including Denmark, Norway, Sweden, and Iceland.

scandium, *n.* a metallic element. (*Scandinavia*)

scansion, *n.* act or mode of metrical scanning.

scansorial, *a.* climbing; used for climbing. (L. *scandere,* climb)

scant, *a.* barely sufficient, inadequate; grudging.—*v.t.* stint, provide grudgingly. (O.N. *skamt,* short)

scantling, *n.* small beam, esp. one under 5 in. square; small quantity, modicum; size to which stone or wood is to be cut. (O.F. *escantillon*)

scanty, *a.* barely sufficient, meagre, small. (*scant*)

scape, *n.* long leafless flower-stalk springing from root; shaft of column where it leaves base. (Gk. *skapos*)

scape, *arch.* for **escape. scapegoat,** *n.* one who bears blame due to another. **scapegrace,** *n.* graceless hare-brained person, scamp.

scaphoid, *a.* boat-shaped. (Gk. *skaphē,* boat; *eidos,* form)

scapula, *n.* (*pl.* **scapulae**) shoulder-blade. **scapular,** *a.* of scapula.—*n.* (also **scapulary**) two squares of cloth worn on shoulders under ordinary clothes as badge of religious order; short sleeveless vestment. (L.)

scar, *n.* mark left after healing of wound.—*v.t.* and *i.* (*past, p.p.* **scarred**) mark with, form, scar. (Gk. *eschara,* hearth, burn)

scar, see **scaur.**

scarab, *n.* dung-beetle held sacred in ancient Egypt; gem or seal in shape of this. (L. *scarabaeus*)

scaramouch, *n.* idler, ne'er-do-well; (*arch.*) boastful poltroon. (*Scaramuccia,* character in Italian farce)

scarce, *a.* not plentiful, scanty; rare, hard to find.—*adv.* (*arch.*) scarcely. **make oneself s.,** decamp. **scarcely,** *adv.* hardly, barely. **scarcity,** *n.* dearth. (O.F. *escars*)

scare, *v.t.* strike with sudden terror, affright; drive away by frightening. —*n.* sudden panic; false alarm. **scarecrow,** *n.* dummy for scaring birds from crops; tattered or miserable-looking person, guy. **scaremonger,** *n.* alarmist. (O.N. *skirra*)

scarf, *v.t.* join endwise by bevelling or notching.—*n.* joint so made.

scarf, *n.* (*pl.* **scarves, scarfs**) long narrow strip of material worn round neck etc.; necktie.—*v.t.* cover as with scarf. **s.-pin, s.-ring,** *nn.* worn as ornaments with necktie. **s.-skin,** *n.* outer skin, epidermis.

scarify, *v.t.* scratch, lacerate; loosen surface of (soil); harrow feelings of, criticize savagely. **scarification,** *n.* (Gk. *skariphos*, style)

scarious, *a.* (*bot.*) dry, shrivelled; membranous. (Mod. L. *scariosus*)

scarlatina, *n.* scarlet fever. (It. *scarlattina*)

scarlet, *n.* bright red with tinge of orange; scarlet cloth or clothes.—*a.* of this colour. **s. fever,** highly infectious fever with scarlet rash. **s. hat,** cardinal's hat. **s. runner,** climbing bean with scarlet flowers. **s. woman,** Protestant name for Church of Rome. (Pers. *saqalat*)

scarp, *n.* inner face of ditch in fortification; steep slope.—*v.t.* make steep or perpendicular; provide with scarp. (It. *scarpa*)

scart, *v.t.* and *i.* (*Scot.*) scratch; scrape. —*n.* scratch; niggard.

scarus, *n.* bright-coloured fish with beak, parrot-fish. (Gk. *skaros*)

scary, *a.* (*colloq.*) timid; alarming.

scat, *int.* be off.—*v.t.* scare away.

scathe, *n.* harm, injury.—*v.t.* injure; sear, blast. **scatheless,** *a.* unharmed. **scathing,** *a.* cutting, withering. (O.N. *skathe*)

scatology, *n.* science of fossil dung; obscene literature. **scatological,** *a.* **scatophagous,** *a.* dung-eating. (Gk. *skatos*, dung; *legein*, speak)

scatter, *v.t.* and *i.* cast here and there, strew, sprinkle; dissipate; put or take to flight, disperse. **s.-brain,** *n.* flighty heedless person. **s.-brained,** *a.* **scattered,** *a.* spaced out, straggling. (M.E. *scateren*)

scaud, *v.t.* (*Scot.*) scald; scold.

scauper, same as **scalper.**

scaur, scar, *n.* rocky part of hillside, precipitous crag. (O.N. *sker*)

scavenger, *n.* one employed to clean streets, remove refuse etc.; animal that feeds on carrion.—*v.i.* (also **scavenge**) act as scavenger. (O.F. *scavage*, inspection)

scazon, *n.* iambic line of which last foot is trochee or spondee. (Gk. *skazein*, limp)

scend, *v.i.* and *n.* (of ship) heave upward on wave, plunge.

scene, *n.* stage of theatre; painted screen etc. used on this; section of play, division of act; place in which anything occurs; view, spectacle; incident, episode; unseemly display of strong feeling. **behind the ss.,** out of sight of audience; wielding influence secretly. **s.-painter, s.-shifter,** *nn.* one who paints, shifts, stage scenery. **scenario,** *n.* written version of cinema play; libretto. **scenery,** *n.* stage setting of play, scenes; aspect of landscape. **scenic,** *a.* of, used on, the stage; picturesque. **scenically,** *adv.* **scenography,** *n.* art of drawing in perspective. **scenograph, scenographer,** *nn.* **scenographic,** *a.* (Gk. *skēnē*)

scent, *v.t.* perceive, track, by smell; impart odour to, perfume; get wind of, detect.—*n.* odour, smell; artificial perfume; smell left by animal in passing; paper trail in paperchase; line of pursuit; sense of smell; instinct for detecting, flair. **put off the s.,** mislead. **s.-bottle,** *n.* for holding perfume. **scentless,** *a.* (L. *sentire*, perceive)

sceptre, *n.* rod forming symbol of sovereignty. (Gk. *skēptron*)

sceptic, *n.* one who questions received opinions, doubter; one who doubts the truth of religion, agnostic, unbeliever; (*philos.*) adherent of scepticism.—*a.* sceptical. **sceptical,** *a.* doubtful, incredulous; of the Sceptics. **scepticism,** *n.* attitude of questioning criticism, doubt; (*philos.*) doctrine that absolute knowledge is unattainable. (Gk. *skeptesthai*, consider)

schadenfreude, *n.* malicious pleasure got from others' misfortunes. (G.)

schedule, *n.* tabulated statement, list, time-table; (*Shake.*) document.—*v.t.* put in schedule. (L. **sceda,** strip of papyrus+dim.)

schema, *n.* (*pl.* **schemata**) synopsis; figure of speech; (*logic*) syllogistic figure; (*philos.*) image giving form or generality to sense-perception. **schematic,** *a.* **schematically,** *adv.* (Gk.=shape)

scheme, *n.* plan, project; underhand design, plot; systematic arrangement, tabulated statement.—*v.i.* and *t.* make plans, design; plot, intrigue. **schemer,** *n.* plotter. (*schema*)

scherzo, *n.* (*pl.* **scherzos**) light playful movement in sonata etc. *scherzando*, *adv.* (*mus.*) playfully. (It.)

Schiedam, *n.* Hollands gin. (place)

schipperke, *n.* small black short-haired tailless dog. (Du.)

schism, *n.* division, esp. of Church, into two parties; sin of causing this. **schismatic,** *a.* of, causing, guilty of, schism.—*n.* schismatic person, member of seceded Church. **schismatical,** *a.* (Gk. *schizein*, split)

schist, *n.* crystalline rock which splits into layers. **schistose,** *a.* (Gk. *schizein*, split)

schiz(o)-, from Gk. *schizein*, split, used in **schizanthus,** *n.* flowering plant with much-divided leaves; **schizocarp,** *n.* compound fruit splitting into several one-seeded ones; **schizogenesis,** *n.* reproduction by fission;

schizoid, *a.* mildly schizophrenic; **schizomycete,** *n.* unicellular organism reproducing by fission, e.g. microbe; **schizophrenia,** *n.* mental disorder with split personality, dementia praecox, hence **schizophrenic,** *a.*

schnapps, schnaps, *n.* kind of Hollands gin. (G.)

schloss, *n.* castle. (G.)

scholar, *n.* schoolboy, schoolgirl; pupil, learner; man of learning; holder of scholarship; (*vulg.*) one able to read and write. **scholarly,** *a.* learned, erudite. **scholarship,** *n.* learning, esp. in the classics; annual grant for scholar or student, us. won by competitive examination. **scholastic,** *a.* of schools or education; academic, donnish; of the schoolmen, dealing in logical subtleties.—*n.* schoolman. **scholasticism,** *n.* scholastic philosophy of Middle Ages. (*school*)

scholium, *n.* (*pl.* **scholia**) marginal note of scholiast. **scholiast,** *n.* ancient grammarian who annotated classical texts; commentator. (Gk. *scholē,* school)

school, *n.* shoal of fish.—*v.i.* form school. (Du.)

school, *n.* educational establishment; its pupils; place or means of discipline; group of thinkers, artists, writers, holding similar principles; (*Oxford*) branch of study, lecture hall, (*pl.*) degree examination.—*v.t.* train, discipline; (*arch.*) send to school. **s.-board,** *n.* local authority in charge of board-schools. **s.-house,** *n.* school building. **s.-ma'am, s.-marm,** *n.* (*Amer. colloq.*) schoolmistress. **schoolboy, schoolgirl,** *nn.* one attending school. **schoolfellow,** *n.* member of same school. **schoolman,** *n.* philosopher or divine of the Middle Ages. **schoolmaster,** *n.* (*fem.* **schoolmistress**) school-teacher. **schoolmate,** *n.* contemporary at school. **schoolroom,** *n.* lesson room. (Gk. *scholē,* leisure, school)

schooner, *n.* fore-and-aft rigged vessel with two or more masts; large drinking-glass.

schorl, *n.* black tourmaline. (G. *schörl*)

schottische, *n.* lively round dance like polka; music for it. (G. *Schottisch,* Scottish)

scia-, from Gk. *skia,* shadow, used in **sciagraph,** *n.* vertical section of building showing interior, skiagraph, hence **sciagrapher,** *n.,* **sciagraphic,** *a.*; **sciagraphy,** *n.* delineation of shadows, finding of time by shadows, sciagraph, skiagraphy; **sciamachy,** *n.* fighting with shadows, sham fight.

sciatic, *a.* of the hip; of, having, sciatica. **sciatica,** *n.* neuralgia of sciatic nerve. (Gk. *ischion,* hip-joint)

science, *n.* knowledge systematically arranged; any branch of this; natural science; expert skill; (*arch.*) knowledge. **applied s.,** science exemplified in concrete phenomena. **exact s.,** one admitting of quantitative treatment. **natural, physical, s.,** that dealing with the physical world. **pure s.,** one depending on deductions from self-evident truths, e.g. logic. **the dismal s.,** political economy. **scienter,** *adv.* (*law*) wittingly. **sciential,** *a.* of, by, knowledge. **scientific,** *a.* of, concerned with, science; systematic, exact; having or showing expert skill. **scientifically,** *adv.* **scientism,** *n.* methods, outlook, of scientists. **scientist,** *n.* one learned in a natural science. (L. *scire,* know)

scilicet, *adv.* (*abbr. sc., scil.*) that is to say. (L.)

scimitar, scimetar, *n.* oriental curved sword broadest at point. (It. *scimitarra*)

scintilla, *n.* spark; particle, atom. **scintillant,** *a.* sparkling. **scintillate,** *v.i.* sparkle. **scintillation,** *n.* (L.)

sciolism, *n.* superficial knowledge; conceit due to this. **sciolist,** *n.* pretender to knowledge, smatterer. **sciolistic,** *a.* (L. *scius,* knowing + dim.)

sciolto, *a.* (*mus.*) free, unrestrained. (It.)

sciomachy, same as **sciamachy.**

scion, *n.* shoot; slip for grafting; young member of family, descendant. (F.)

scire facias, writ to enforce or annul judgment etc. (L. = cause to know)

scirocco, same as **sirocco.**

scirrhus, *n.* (*pl.* **scirrhi**) hard cancerous tumour. **scirrhous,** *a.* **scirrhosity,** *n.* (Gk. *skiros,* hard)

scissel, *n.* waste clippings of metal. (L. *caedere,* cut)

scissile, *a.* able to be cut. **scission,** *n.* cutting, cleavage. (L. *scindere,* cleave)

scissor, *v.t.* cut with scissors, clip.—*n.pl.* cutting instrument of two blades fastened in middle. **s.-bill,** *n.* skimmer. **s.-bird, s.-tail,** *nn.* fork-tailed flycatcher. (L. *caedere,* cut)

sciurine, *a.* of the squirrel kind. (Gk. *skiouros,* squirrel)

sclaff, *v.t.* (*golf*) mishit by scraping ground before hitting ball. (imit.)

sclera, *n.* white coating of eyeball. **sclerenchyma,** *n.* hard woody tissue of plants. **sclerodermatous, sclerodermous,** *aa.* (*zool.*) with hard outer skin. **sclerogen,** *n.* hard matter deposited on inner surface of plant-cell. **scleroid,** *a.* of hard texture. **scleroma,** *n.* (*pl.* **scleromata**) sclerosis. **scleromeninx,** *n.* dura mater. **sclerosis,** *n.* (*pl.* **scleroses**) morbid hardening of tissue. **sclerosed,** *a.* **sclerotic,** *a.* hard, indurated; of sclera.—*n.* sclera. **sclerous,** *a.* indurated, bony. (Gk. *sklēros,* hard)

scobs, *n.* sawdust, filings. (L.)

scoff, *n.* mocking words, taunt. *v.i.* jeer, mock. (M.E. *scof*)

scoff, *n.* (*sl.*) food, grub.—*v.t.* devour. (Du. *schoft,* meal)

scogie, *n.* (*Scot.*) kitchen drudge.

scold, *v.t.* and *i.* reprove angrily, find fault noisily, rate.—*n.* nagging woman. (*skald*)

scolex, *n.* (*pl.* **scoleces**) embryo stage of tapeworm. (Gk. *skōlēx,* worm)

scoliosis, *n.* lateral curvature of spine. **scoliotic,** *a.* (Gk. *skolios,* crooked)

scollop, same as **scallop.**

scolopaceous, scolopacine, scolopacoid, *aa.* of the snipe kind. (Gk. *skolopax,* woodcock)

scolopendrine, *a.* of the centipede family. **scolopendrium,** *n.* kinds of fern incl. hart's-tongue. (Gk. *skolopendra,* millepede)

scomber, *n.* kinds of fish incl. mackerel. **scombroid,** *a.* (Gk. *skombros*)

scomfish, *v.t.* and *i.* (*Scot.*) suffocate with bad air.

scon, same as **scone.**

sconce, *n.* wall-bracket for candles or lamp; socket of candlestick. (L. *abscondere,* conceal)

sconce, *n.* small fort or earthwork. (Du. *schans*)

sconce, *n.* forfeit for breach of table etiquette.—*v.t.* fine thus.

sconce, *n.* (*sl.*) crown of head.

scone, *n.* (*Scot.*) small flat cake baked on griddle.

scoop, *n.* kind of shovel or ladle; small gouge; act of scooping; (*sl.*) large profit made quickly; piece of exclusive news.—*v.t.* shovel, lift, hollow out, with scoop; (*sl.*) obtain as scoop; forestall (rival paper) with news item.

scoot, *v.i.* and *t.* run quickly; make off; (*Scot.*) squirt. **scooter,** *n.* two-wheeled board on which child stands with one foot while propelling it with the other.

scopa, scopula, *nn.* (*pl.* **scopae, scopulae**) small tuft of hairs on bee's leg etc. **scopate, scopulate,** *aa.* brush-like. (L. *scopae,* broom)

scope, *n.* range of activity or application; outlet, opportunity; (*rare*) aim, purpose. (Gk. *skopein,* view)

-scope, *n.suf.* instrument for observing, as in **telescope.** (*scope*)

scorbutic, *a.* of, like, affected with, scurvy. (F. *scorbut,* scurvy)

scorch, *v.t.* and *i.* burn, be burnt, on surface; wither, blast; (*sl.*) cycle, drive, furiously. **scorcher,** *n.* (*sl.*) very hot day; striking thing.

score, *n.* notch, scratch; line; bill, reckoning; points made in game; account, reason; set of twenty; copy of musical work showing different parts; (*sl.*) piece of luck; telling retort.—*v.t.* and *i.* mark with scores, furrow; enter, record; make (points in game); gain advantage; write out in score, orchestrate. **pay off old ss.,** take revenge. **s. off,** (*sl.*) gain advantage over. **s.-book, s.-card, s.-sheet,** *nn.* for recording score. (O.N. *skor*)

scoria, *n.* (*pl.* scoriae) slag; (us. *pl.*) slag-like lava. **scoriaceous,** *a.* **scorify,** *v.t.* reduce to dross. **scorification,** *n.* (Gk. *skōr,* dung)

scorn, *n.* extreme contempt, disdain; object of this.—*v.t.* treat with scorn, despise; reject, refuse, as unworthy. **scornful,** *a.* contemptuous. (O.F. *escarn*)

scorpion, *n.* small lobster-like animal with sting at end of jointed tail; Scorpio. **rock s.,** (*army sl.*) native of Gibraltar. **scorpioid,** *a.* **Scorpio,** *n.* 8th sign of zodiac, entered by sun about 22 Oct. (Gk. *skorpios*)

scorse, *v.t.* (*Spens.*) exchange.

scorse, *v.t.* (*Spens.*) chase. (L. *excurrere,* run out)

scorzonera, *n.* narrow-leaved plant with edible root, black salsify. (It.)

scot, *n.* tax, rate. **s. and lot,** share of parish payments. **s.-free,** *a.* unharmed; exempt from payment. (O.N. *skot,* payment)

Scot, *n.* native of Scotland. (L.L. *Scottus*)

scotch, *v.t.* (*arch.*) wound, maim.—*n.* score, mark.

scotch, *n.* wedge, chock, to prevent wheel rolling.—*v.t.* check with this.

Scotch, *a.* and *n.* (people, language) of Scotland, Scots; Scotch whisky. **S. broth,** broth with barley and various vegetables. **S. collops,** minced beef stewed with onions. **S. mist,** fine rain, drizzle. **S. pebble,** kind of agate, cairngorm etc. **S. terrier,** short-legged rough-coated breed of dog. **Scotchman, Scotchwoman,** *nn.*

scoter, *n.* large sea-duck.

scotia, *n.* hollow moulding in base of column. (Gk.=darkness)

scoticè, **scoticism, scoticize,** same as *scotticè* etc.

Scotism, *n.* scholastic philosophy of Duns Scotus.

scoto-, from Gk. *skotos,* darkness, used in **scotodinia,** *n.* giddiness; **scotograph,** *n.* instrument enabling blind to write; **scotoma,** *n.* (*pl.* **scotomata**) blind spot; **scotophobia,** *n.* fear of darkness.

Scots, *a.* and *n.* Scottish (language). **Scotsman, Scotswoman,** *nn.* *scotticè,* *adv.* in Scots. **scotticism,** *n.* Scottish phrase. **scotticize,** *v.i.* and *t.* imitate, render like, the Scots. **Scottish,** *a.* of Scotland.

scoundrel, *n.* dishonourable person, blackguard. **scoundrelism,** *n.* **scoundrelly,** *a.*

scour, *v.t.* clean, polish, by hard rubbing; flush out; purge.—*n.* act, process, of scouring.

scour, *v.t.* and *i.* hasten over or along, range, esp. in search or pursuit.

scourge, *v.t.* flog, whip; afflict greatly.

—**n.** whip of leather thongs; instrument of punishment; pest. (L. *excoriare,* excoriate)
scout, *v.t.* reject with scorn, flout.
scout, *n.* man sent out to observe the enemy; Boy Scout; (*Oxford*) college servant.—*v.i.* act as scout, reconnoitre. **Boy Ss.,** organization for training boys in self-reliance etc. **scoutmaster,** *n.* leader of group of Boy Scouts. (L. *auscultare,* listen to)
scouth, *n.* (*Scot.*) room; scope.
scouther, *v.t.* (*Scot.*) scorch.
scouther, *n.* (*Scot.*) flying shower.
scow, *n.* kind of flat-bottomed boat. (Du. *schouw,* ferry-boat)
scowl, *n.* angry frown, sullen expression. — *v.i.* wear scowl, look sullen.
scrabble, *v.i.* scratch or grope about; (*arch.*) scrawl. (Du. *schrabben,* scrape+dim.)
scrag, *n.* skinny creature; inferior end of neck of mutton; (*sl.*) neck.—*v.t.* wring neck of, throttle; hang. **scraggy,** *a.* thin and bony.
scraich, scraigh, *v.i.* and *n.* (*Scot.*) screech.
scram, *v.i.* (*Amer. sl.*) clear out, make off.
scramble, *v.i.* and *t.* make way with difficulty, clamber, crawl; scuffle with others (for); throw (coin) to be scrambled for; cook (eggs) beaten up with butter.—*n.* act of scrambling; rough climb or walk.
scran, *n.* (*sl.*) scraps. **bad s. to you!** (*Ir.*) bad luck to you!
scrannel, *a.* (*arch.*) grating, squeaky.
scranny, same as **scrawny.**
scrap, *n.* (*sl.*) informal fight, rough-and-tumble.—*v.i.* have scrap.
scrap, *n.* small piece; waste material, refuse; (*pl.*) odds and ends of food; newspaper cuttings etc.—*v.t.* throw out, discard. **s.-book,** *n.* for pasting scraps in. **s.-heap,** *n.* pile of scrap. (O.N. *skrap,* scrapings)
scrape, *v.t.* and *i.* rub with something sharp; clean or smooth thus; draw along with grating or vibration; get narrowly past, graze; draw back foot in making bow; amass in small portions, be miserly.—*n.* act of scraping; grating sound; abrasion, scratch; awkward predicament. **s. acquaintance with,** thrust one's acquaintance on. **scraper,** *n.* grating, edge, for scraping mud from boots. (O.N. *skrapa*)
scrappy, *a.* fragmentary; full of gaps.
Scratch, *n.* **Old S.,** the devil. (O.N. *skratta,* goblin)
scratch, *v.t.* and *i.* score, tear, with nails or something pointed; hollow (out) thus, scrape; rub to relieve itching; scrawl; withdraw from race. —*n.* act of scratching; mark, sound, made by this; slight wound; starting-line for race; scribble; scratch-wig; (*pl.*) a disease of horses' heels.—*a.* taken at random, haphazard, impromptu; without handicap. **come up to the s.,** not back out. **s. out,** erase. **s.-wig,** *n.* small short wig. **scratchy,** *a.* making scratching noise; uneven, ragged; (of drawing) unskilful.
scrawl, *v.i.* and *t.* write hastily or illegibly. — *n.* scrawled writing, scribble.
scrawny, *a.* scraggy, raw-boned. (*scran*)
scray, *n.* sea-swallow, tern.
screak, *v.t.* and *n.* screech; creak.
scream, *v.i.* and *t.* utter shrill cry, shriek.—*n.* screaming cry; burst of laughter; (*sl.*) ludicrous affair or person. **screamer,** *n.* kinds of bird; ludicrous joke; (*golf*) very long hit. (M.E. *scremen*)
scree, *n.* loose shifting stones; slope covered with these. (O.N. *skritha,* glide)
screech, *n.* harsh shrill cry.—*v.i.* and *t.* utter this, shriek. **s.-owl,** *n.* barn-owl. (imit.)
screed, *n.* long tedious letter or speech; (*Scot.*) strip; tear. (O.E. *scréade,* shred)
screen, *n.* partition, framework, to protect or conceal; shelter, shield; board to display cinema pictures, notices, etc.; structure separating nave of church from choir; coarse riddle for sorting coal into sizes.—*v.t.* shelter, conceal; protect from censure; put on screen; make film of; grade by passing through screen.
screeve, *v.i.* write begging letters; be pavement artist. **screever,** *n.* (L. *scribere,* write)
screw, *n.* worthless or broken-down horse.
screw, *n.* cylinder with spiral groove running round it; male screw with slotted head; twist, turn; pressure; screw propeller; twisted-up piece of paper; skinflint; (*sl.*) salary.—*v.t.* and *i.* turn or twist round; swerve; fasten, press, with screw; make tense; oppress, extort; be miserly. **have a s. loose,** be slightly crazy. **interrupted s.,** with parts of thread cut away. **male, female, s.,** with thread outside, inside. **s. propeller,** revolving blades on shaft driving **s. steamer. s.-eye,** *n.* screw with loop instead of head. **screwdriver,** *n.* tool like blunt chisel for turning screws. **screwed,** *a.* (*sl.*) drunk. **screwjack,** *n.* weight-lifting device acting by screw. **screwy,** *a.* (*Amer. sl.*) slightly mad. (O.F. *escroue*)
scribacious, *a.* given to writing. (L. *scribere,* write)
scribble, *v.t.* and *i.* write hastily or carelessly; be writer.—*n.* hasty writing, scrawl. **scribblement,** *n.* (L. *scribere,* write+dim.)
scribble, *v.t.* card (wool) roughly.
scribe, *n.* writer; amanuensis, copyist;

Jewish expounder of law in time of Christ. (L. *scribere*, write)
scrieve, *v.i.* (*Scot.*) glide swiftly.
scrike, *v.i.* (*Spens.*) shriek.
scrim, *n.* cloth for linings etc.
scrimer, *n.* (*Shake.*) fencer. (F. *escrimer*, fence)
scrimmage, *n.* confused struggle, rough-and-tumble; scrummage.—*v.i.* have scrimmage, brawl. (*skirmish*)
scrimp, *v.t.* and *i.* make too small, skimp. **scrimpy,** *a.*
scrimshank, *v.i.* (*army sl.*) shirk duty. **scrimshanker,** *n.*
scrimshaw, *v.t.* and *i.* (*naut.*) decorate (shells, bone etc.) with design.—*n.* such work.
scrine, *n.* (*Spens.*) chest for safe-keeping of books. (*scrinium*)
scrinium, *n.* (*pl.* **scrinia**) medieval box for rolled manuscript. (L.)
scrip, *n.* temporary certificate of stock or shares held. (*subscription*)
scrip, *n.* (*Shake.*) piece of paper with writing on it. (*script*)
scrip, *n.* (*arch.*) wallet. **scrippage,** *n.* (*Shake.*) contents of scrip.
script, *n.* handwriting; style of writing; (*print.*) type like handwriting.
scriptorium, *n.* (*pl.* **scriptoriums, scriptoria**) writing-room, esp. of monastery. (L. *scribere*, write)
scripture, *n.* the Bible; sacred writings; (*arch.*) inscription.—*a.* contained in, quoted from, the Bible. **the Ss.,** the Bible. **scriptural,** *a.* of, based on, the Bible. **scripturalism,** *n.* adherence to letter of the Scriptures. **scripturalist,** *n.* (*script*)
scritch, (*Shake,*) form of **screech.**
scrivello, *n.* elephant's tusk, esp. one of less than 20 lb. weight.
scrivener, *n.* professional writer, notary. **s.'s palsy,** writer's cramp. (L. *scribere*, write)
scrobiculate, scrobiculated, *aa.* pitted. (L. *scrobis*, ditch+dim.)
scrofula, *n.* constitutional disease marked by swelling of glands of neck. **scrofulous,** *a.* (L. *scrofulae*)
scroggie, *a.* (*Scot.*) covered with underwood.
scroll, *n.* roll of parchment or paper; ornament like this, spiral design, volute; (*heraldry*) ribbon with motto; (*arch.*) list.—*v.t.* adorn with scrolls. (O.F. *escroue*+dim.)
scroop, *n.* grating noise.—*v.i.* make this. (imit.)
scrotum, *n.* (*pl.* **scrota**) pouch containing testicles. **scrotal,** *a.* (L.)
scrounge, *v.t.* and *i.* (*sl.*) cadge, pilfer. **scrounger,** *n.*
scroyle, *n.* (*Shake.*) scoundrel.
scrub, *v.t.* and *i.* wash vigorously, scour; rub hard.—*n.* scrubbing.
scrub, *n.* stunted trees, brushwood; anything small or mean. **scrubby,** *a.* stunted; paltry; unkempt. (*shrub*)
scruff, *n.* back of neck, nape.
scruffy, same as **scurfy.**
scrummage, *n.* scrimmage; (*Rugby football, abbr.* **scrum**) tussle between rival forwards in compact mass.
scrumptious, *a.* (*sl.*) delightful, delicious.
scrunch, *v.t.* crush, crunch.—*n.* act, sound, of scrunching. (*crunch*)
scrunt, *n.* (*Scot.*) niggardly person.
scruple, *n.* measure of weight, 20 grains; conscientious objection, qualm; (*arch.*) very small amount.—*v.i.* hesitate owing to scruples, feel compunction. **scrupulous,** *a.* extremely conscientious, strictly upright; attentive to details, thorough; (*Shake.*) cautious. (L. *scrupulus*)
scrutiny, *n.* careful examination, critical gaze; official inspection of votes cast in election. **scrutator,** *n.* careful investigator. *scrutin d'arrondissement, de liste,* polling in France by single, multiple, constituencies. **scrutineer,** *n.* inspector of ballot papers. **scrutinize,** *v.t.* look closely at, examine narrowly. (L. *scrutari*, examine)
scruze, *v.t.* (*Spens.*) squeeze, crush.
scry, *v.i.* practise crystal-gazing; (*Spens.*) descry. (*descry*)
scry, *v.t.* (*Scot.*) proclaim.—*n.* clamour; proclamation.
scud, *v.i.* and *t.* run fast; (*naut.*) run before the wind; (*Scot.*) slap.—*n.* scudding; light clouds driven by wind; (*Scot.*) slap.
scudo, *n.* (*pl.* **scudi**) old Italian coin worth about 4*s.* (It.)
scuff, *v.i.* and *t.* walk with scraping movement, shuffle; (*Scot.*) graze slightly.
scuff, same as **scruff.**
scuffle, *v.i.* struggle closely, fight confusedly.—*n.* rough-and-tumble.
scug, *n.* (*school sl.*) unsporting, unsociable, or spiritless person.
sculduddery, *n.* (*Scot.*) obscenity; fornication.—*a.* bawdy.
scull, *n.* light oar pulled with one hand; oar used in stern like propeller. —*v.t.* and *i.* propel (boat) with sculls or scull. **sculler,** *n.* person, boat, using sculls.
scullery, *n.* room off kitchen for washing dishes etc. **s.-maid,** *n.* (L. *scutra*, tray+dim.)
sculp, *v.t.* (*colloq.*) carve. *sculpsit, v.t.* (*abbr. sculps., sc.*) carved (used with sculptor's signature).
sculpin, *n.* small American sea-fish with large spiny head.
sculptor, *n.* (*fem.* **sculptress**) one who carves sculptures. **sculpture,** *n.* art of carving figures or designs in stone, wood etc.; work so carved.—*v.t.* and *i.* carve, adorn or portray with, sculptures. **sculptural, sculpturesque,** *aa.* (L. *sculpere*, carve)
scum, *n.* impurities that rise to surface of liquid; refuse, riff-raff.—*v.t.* and *i.* remove scum from; form scum. **scummy,** *a.* (Da. *skum*, froth)

scumble, *v.t.* cover (painting) with thin wash of opaque colour to soften effect.—*n.* the wash or effect. (*scum*)
scun, *v.t.* (*Scot.*) skip (stone).
scuncheon, *n.* stones across angles of square tower supporting octagonal spire. (O.F. *escoinson*)
scunner, *n.* (*Scot.*) loathing; object of disgust.—*v.i.* be nauseated.
scupper, *n.* hole in ship's side letting water run from deck into sea.—*v.t.* (*sl.*) sink; do for.
scurf, *n.* white scales on skin, dandruff; scaly incrustation on metal etc. **scurfy,** *a.* (O.E.)
scurrilous, (*arch.*) **scurrile, scurril,** *aa.* coarsely abusive, befitting a vulgar buffoon. **scurrility,** *n.* (L. *scurra,* buffoon)
scurry, *v.i.* hurry with quick short steps, scuttle.—*n.* scurrying, flurry.
scurvy, *a.* base, contemptible.—*n.* deficiency disease due to lack of fresh vegetable food. **s.-grass,** *n.* plant of mustard family. (*scurf*)
scuse, (*Shake.*) form of **excuse.**
scut, *n.* short tail of rabbit etc.
scutage, *n.* money paid by feudal landowner in place of military service. (L. *scutum,* shield)
scutal, *a.* of a scutum. **scutate,** *a.* shield shaped.
scutch, *v.t.* separate coarse tow from (flax) by beating.—*n.* instrument for this, swingle; tow separated.
scutcheon, *n.* escutcheon; name-plate; pivoted keyhole-cover. (*escutcheon*)
scute, same as **scutum.**
scutellum, *n.* (*pl.* **scutella**) small scale or plate. **scutellar, scutellate,** *aa.* (dim. of *scutum*)
scutter, *v.i.* run hastily or in startled way, scurry. (*scuttle*)
scuttle, *v.i.* run quickly, hurry away.—*n.* scuttling, hasty flight. (*scud*)
scuttle, *n.* vessel for small supply of coals. (L. *scutra*+dim.)
scuttle, *n.* hole with cover in ship's deck, side, or hatchway.—*v.t.* make holes in, sink (ship). **s.-butt,** *n.* ship's water-cask with hole for dipper.
scutum, *n.* (*pl.* **scuta**) knee-cap; (*zool.*) horny plate or scale. (L.= shield)
Scylla, *n.* a fabled monster; Scylla and the whirlpool Charybdis threatened a narrow sea-passage from either side, hence **between S. and Charybdis,** between two dangers.
scyphus, *n.* (*pl.* **scyphi**) (*bot.*) cup-shaped part. **scyphose,** *a.* (L.=cup)
scythe, *n.* two-handed mowing-tool with large curved blade.—*v.t.* mow down. (O.E. *sithe*)
'sdeath, *int.* (*arch.*) God's death.
se-, *pref.* apart, without, as in **segregate, secure.** (L.)
sea, *n.* the ocean; a section of this; ocean swell, great wave; vast expanse.—*a.* marine. **at s.,** away from land; perplexed. **go to s.,** become sailor. **put to s.,** start voyage. **s. front,** part of town facing sea. **s. lawyer,** (*naut.*) argumentative person. **s. legs,** ability to walk on heaving deck. **S. Lord,** naval member of Board of Admiralty. **s. mile,** nautical mile. **s. pie,** made with salt meat. **S. Scouts,** maritime branch of Boy Scouts. **s. wall,** to check encroachment of sea. **Seven Ss.,** Arctic, Antarctic, N. and S. Atlantic, N. and S. Pacific, and Indian Oceans. (O.E. *sǽ*)
sea-anchor, *n.* floating anchor to keep ship's head to wind.
sea-bells, *n.* kind of bindweed.
seaboard, *n.* coast line, seashore.
sea-calf, *n.* common seal.
sea-coal, *n.* coal as opp. to charcoal.
sea-coast, *n.* land adjacent to sea.
sea-cock, *n.* valve communicating with sea through ship's hull.
sea-cow, *n.* dugong; walrus.
sea-cucumber, *n.* trepang.
sea-dog, *n.* dogfish; kinds of seal; experienced sailor.
sea-ear, *n.* ormer, abalone.
sea-elephant, *n.* largest of the seals.
sea-fan, *n.* kind of coral.
seafarer, *n.* (*poet.*) traveller by sea, sailor. **seafaring,** *a.* and *n.*
sea-fennel, *n.* samphire.
sea-fox, *n.* thrasher shark.
sea-gauge, *n.* ship's draught.
sea-girt, *a.* surrounded by sea.
sea-green, *a.* and *n.* pale bluish-green.
seagull, *n.* gull.
sea-horse, *n.* walrus; hippocampus; fabled monster, horse with tail of fish.
sea-kale, *n.* a table vegetable.
sea-king, *n.* old Norse pirate chief.
seal, *n.* engraved stamp for impressing wax; wax so impressed; that which closes or secures; that which authenticates, token.—*v.t.* fix seal to; close, secure, by seal; shut up; mark as settled, confirm. **Great S.,** state seal of Great Britain. **sealed orders,** to be opened at stated time or place. **sealing-wax,** *n.* mixture of shellac and resin used for seals. (L. *sigillum*)
seal, *n.* amphibious marine animal with flippers for limbs; sealskin.—*v.i.* hunt seal. **sealer,** *n.* man, ship, engaged in sealing. **sealery,** *n.* seal-fishery. (O.E. *seolh*)
sea-lion, *n.* kinds of large seal.
sealskin, *n.* fur of seal; coat of this.
Sealyham, *n.* short-legged wire-haired terrier with long body. (place)
seam, *n.* line where two pieces of cloth are sewn together; junction of ship's boards; line, wrinkle; vein; piece of needlework; (*geol.*) thin stratum between thicker ones.—*v.t.* furrow, scar; unite by seam. (O.E. *séam*)
seam, *n.* (*Shake.*) grease. (L. *sagina*)
seaman, *n.* sailor. **seamanlike, seamanly,** *aa.* like a good sailor. **seamanship,** *n.*
sea-mark, *n.* guide for ships, beacon.

seamew, *n.* gull.
sea-mouse, *n.* kind of marine worm.
seamstress, sempstress, *n.* sewing-woman (*seam*)
seamy, *a.* showing seams. **s. side,** less pleasant aspect.
Seanad Eireann, Irish Senate or Upper House. (Ir.)
séance, *n.* sitting of public body; meeting of spiritualists for evoking manifestations. (F.)
seannachie, *n.* Scottish highland bard. (Gael. *seanachaidh*)
sea-pen, *n.* feather-shaped polyp.
sea-piece, *n.* seascape.
sea-pink, *n.* thrift, a plant.
seaplane, *n.* aeroplane with floats for alighting on sea. **s.-carrier,** *n.* warship that carries seaplanes.
seaport, *n.* town with harbour.
sea-purse, *n.* egg-case of skate.
seaquake, *n.* seismic disturbance of bed of sea.
sear, *v.t.* wither; scorch, brand; make (feelings) callous.—*a.* sere. (*sere*)
sear, *n.* catch in gun-lock by which it is held at full or half cock. (L. *sera,* bar)
searce, *v.t.* (*Scot.*) sift.—*n.* sieve.
search, *v.t.* and *i.* look round to find something, explore, examine; probe into; (*arch.*) test.—*n.* act of searching, quest. **right of s.,** right of belligerent to stop neutral ships and search them for contraband. **s. me!** (*Amer. sl.*) I don't know. **s.-warrant,** *n.* entitling police to search house. **searching,** *a.* keen, piercing. **searchlight,** *n.* powerful ray used to discover hostile aircraft etc. (L. *circus,* circle)
sea-room, *n.* free space for ship to navigate.
sea-rover, *n.* pirate.
seascape, *n.* picture of scene at sea.
sea-serpent, *n.* supposed huge sea-monster of snake-like form.
seashore, *n.* beach; sea-coast; (*law*) land between high and low water marks.
seasick, *a.* suffering from nausea brought on by ship's motion.
seaside, *n.* land beside the sea.
sea-slug, *n.* trepang.
season, *n.* one of four divisions of the year; time when something is plentiful or in use; suitable time; period; (*colloq.*) season-ticket.—*v.t.* and *i.* make, become, mature or fit for use; give relish to, flavour; qualify, temper. **s.-ticket,** *n.* ticket valid for a period. **seasonable,** *a.* suited to the season; opportune. **seasonal,** *a.* of, occurring at, season. **seasoning,** *n.* flavouring, spice. (L. *satio,* sowing)
sea-squirt, *n.* ascidian.
sea-swallow, *n.* tern; stormy petrel.
seat, *n.* thing for sitting on, chair; way of sitting; right to sit, membership; buttocks, part of trousers covering them; site, location; large country house.—*v.t.* place in, furnish with, seat; settle, fix. (O.N. *sæti*)
sea-urchin, *n.* echinus.
seaward, *a.* and *adv.* toward the sea. **seawards,** *adv.*
seaway, *n.* rough sea; ocean traffic lane.
seaweed, *n.* plant growing in sea.
seaworthy, *a.* fit to go to sea.
sebaceous, *a.* secreting oily matter; fatty. (L. *sebum,* tallow)
sebundy, *n.* class of irregular soldiers in Indian army; one of this class. (Hind. *sebandi*)
sec, *a.* (of wine) dry, unsweetened. (F.)
secant, *n.* (*trigonometry, abbr.* **sec**). **s. of an angle,** reciprocal of its cosine.
sécateur, sécateurs, *n.* pair of pruning shears. (F.)
secede, *v.i.* withdraw formally from federation, Church, etc. (L. *se-,* apart; *cedere,* go)
secernent, *a.* and *n.* secreting (organ); drug promoting secretion. (*secrete*)
secession, *n.* seceding. **secessionism, secessionist,** *nn.*
seckel, *n.* (*Amer.*) kind of small juicy pear. (person)
seclude, *v.t.* shut up apart, keep apart. **secluded,** *a.* retired, remote. **seclusion,** *n.* secluding; retirement. (L. *se-,* apart; *claudere,* shut)
second, *a.* next after first; inferior, subordinate; other, of the same kind. —*n.* person or thing coming second; another; one who attends principal in duel or prize-fight; sixtieth part of minute or angular degree; (*colloq.*) moment; (*pl.*) goods of second quality; coarse flour.—*v.t.* back up, further; support (motion) by adding one's voice to that of proposer; place (officer) on temporary service. **S. Advent,** second coming of Christ. **s. chamber,** upper house of legislature. **s. childhood,** dotage, senility. **s. nature,** long-established habit. **s. sight,** supposed faculty of seeing events before they occur. **s.-best,** *a.* best after first. **s.-class,** *a.* of second quality; mediocre. **s.-hand,** *a.* bought after use by another; derived, not original. **s.-rate,** *a.* of inferior quality. (L. *secundus*)
secondary, *a.* second in rank or importance; in the second stage; (of education) between elementary school and university; (*geol.*) Mesozoic. — *n.* delegate, deputy. **s. (planet),** planet's satellite.
seconde, *n.* a guard in fencing. (F.)
secondly, *adv.* in the second place.
secret, *a.* kept from general knowledge; hidden, concealed; private; secluded; reticent. — *n.* thing kept secret; hidden cause, mystery. **in s.,** secretly. **open s.,** nominal secret, known to all. **s. service,** intelligence department or its work, espionage. **secrecy,** *n.* secretness; ability to keep secret. (L. *se-,* apart; *cernere,* separate)

secretaire, *n.* escritoire. (F. *secrétaire*)
secretary, *n.* person employed to deal with letters and papers of person or association; head of a state department; escritoire. **s.-bird,** *n.* large long-legged African bird. **secretarial,** *a.* **secretariat,** *n.* administrative office or officials. **secretariate,** *n.* secretaryship; body of secretaries. (*secret*)
secrete, *v.t.* hide, conceal; (of gland etc.) produce (substance) by elaboration out of blood or sap. **secretion,** *n.* secreting; substance secreted. **secretive,** *a.* uncommunicative, reticent; promoting secretion. **secretory,** *a.* of glandular secretion.
sect, *n.* party within a Church; any religious denomination; philosophical school; party, faction; (*Shake.*) class. **sectarian,** *a.* of, confined to, a religious sect; bigoted.—*n.* adherent of sect. **sectarianism,** *n.* devotion to a sect; religious narrowness. **sectary,** *n.* (*arch.*) sectarian. (L. *sequi*, follow)
section, *n.* act of cutting; severed or separable part; distinct portion, division; subdivision of platoon; representation of anything cut through to show its interior; (*geom.*) cutting of solid by plane, plane figure formed by this; (*zool.*) group, subgenus. **s. mark,** symbol (§) marking subdivision of book. **sectional,** *a.* **sectionalism,** *n.* spirit of a class. **sectile,** *a.* capable of being cut. **sector,** *n.* section of battle front; (*geom.*) space enclosed by two radii of circle and the arc they cut off. **sectorial,** *a.* and *n.* (tooth) adapted for cutting. (L. *secare*, cut)
secular, *a.* worldly, temporal; lay, not monastic; lasting for ages; occurring once in an age or century.—*n.* member of secular clergy, parish priest; layman. **s. clergy,** clergy not bound by monastic vows. **secularity,** *n.* **secularist,** *n.* one who opposes teaching of religion in state schools; one who maintains that the basis of morality should be non-religious. **secularism,** *n.* **secularize,** *v.t.* make secular; transfer from ecclesiastical to civil possession or use. **secularization,** *n.* (L. *saeculum*, age)
secund, *a.* (*bot.*) arranged on one side only. (L. *secundus*, following)
secundum, *prep*, according to. *s. artem*, according to art. *s. legem*, legally. *s. naturam*, according to nature. (L.)
secundus, *a.* second of the name. (L.)
secure, *a.* safe; firm, stable; free from care; confident, assured (of).—*v.t.* make safe; fasten firmly; confine; fortify; gain possession of; (*Shake.*) give confidence to. (L. *se-*, without; *cura*, care)
securiform, *a.* axe-shaped. (L. *securis*, axe)
security, *n.* secureness, safety; protection, safeguard; confidence, want of caution; financial guarantee, surety; any form of bond, stock, or share.
sedan, *n.* closed-in motor-car with no division between driver and passengers; (also **s. chair**) covered chair with poles carried by two bearers.
sedate, *a.* composed, staid, serious. **sedative,** *a.* and *n.* calming, soothing (drug). (L. *sedare*, settle)
se defendendo, plea of self-defence in case of homicide. (L.)
sedentary, *a.* sitting; accustomed to, involving, much sitting; not migratory. **sederunt,** *n.* sitting of court or of company in conversation. (L. *sedēre*, sit)
sedge, *n.* plant like coarse grass growing in marshy places. **s.-warbler,** *n.* small brown and white bird. (O.E. *secg*)
sedilia, *n.pl.* clergy's stone seats in chancel wall. (L. *sedile*, seat)
sediment, *n.* matter that settles to bottom of liquid, dregs. **sedimentary,** *a.* **sedimentation,** *n.* depositing of sediment. (L. *sedimentum*)
sedition, *n.* conduct or speech inciting to rebellion. **seditious,** *a.* (L. *se-*, apart; *ire*, go)
seduce, *v.t.* lead astray, corrupt; entice; induce to surrender chastity. **seduction,** *n.* seducing; temptations, blandishments; attraction. **seductive,** *a.* enticing, alluring. (L. *se-*, apart; *ducere*, lead)
sedulous, *a.* persistent, assiduous. **sedulity,** *n.* (L. *sedulus*)
see, *n.* seat or jurisdiction of bishop, diocese. **Holy S.,** papacy. (L. *sedēre*, sit)
see, *v.t.* and *i.* (*past* **saw,** *p.p.* **seen**) perceive with eyes, have sight; grasp with intelligence, understand; experience; have interview with; accompany; take care (that); consider, reflect; make inquiry; (*Shake.*) meet. **s. about,** attend to. **s. after,** take care of. **s. good,** think fit. **s. into,** investigate. **s. off,** accompany on departure. **s. out,** wait till end of. **s. over,** inspect. **s. through,** detect falsity of; finish (undertaking). **s. to,** attend to. **seeing that,** inasmuch as, since. **well seen,** (*Shake.*) versed (in). (O.E. *séon*)
seecatch, seecatchie, *n.* (*Amer.*) male fur seal. (Russ. *syekach*)
seed, *n.* reproductive germ of flowering plant; quantity of these; male fertilizing fluid, semen; descendants; race; source, origin.—*v.i.* and *t.* produce or shed seed; sprinkle with seed; remove seeds from; (*lawn tennis*) arrange (draw) so that best players cannot meet till late rounds. **run to s.,** develop seed at expense of leaves; waste talents; become shabby. **s.-bed, s.-plot,** *nn.* nursery bed for plant. **s.-cake,** *n.* containing caraway seeds. **s.-corn,** *n.* corn kept for

sowing. **s.-pearl,** *n.* very small pearl. **s.-time,** *n.* time for sowing. **s.-vessel,** *n.* pod, case, holding seeds. **seedling,** *n.* young plant raised from seed and not from cutting. **seedsman,** *n.* dealer in seeds. **seedy,** *a.* full of seeds; out of sorts, indisposed; shabby. (O.E. *sǽd*)

seek, *v.t.* and *i.* (*past, p.p.* **sought**) look for, try to obtain; search; endeavour; resort (to). **s. out,** try to secure society of. **to s.,** (*arch.*) lacking, not yet found. **sought-after,** *a.* in demand, popular. (O.E. *sécan*)

seel, *v.t.* (*arch.*) sew up eyes of (hawk); blindfold. (L. *cilium,* eyelash)

seem, *v.i.* appear (to be); appear to oneself. **seeming,** *a.* ostensible, apparent. — *n.* appearance; false show. **seemingly,** *adv.* apparently. **seemly,** *a.* decent, becoming. (M.E. *seme*)

seen, see **see.**

seep, *v.i.* ooze, leak. **seepage,** *n.* (O.E. *sipian,* soak)

seer, *n.* one who sees visions, prophet. (*see*)

seer, *n.* Indian measure of weight, us. about 2 lb. (Hind. *ser*)

seerfish, *n.* Indian fish of mackerel kind. (Port. *serra,* saw)

seersucker, *n.* blue-and-white striped linen, orig. from India. (Pers. *shīr o shakkar,* milk and sugar)

seesaw, *n.* plank balanced across central support; up-and-down motion like that of ends of this; vacillation. —*v.i.* move up and down; fluctuate. —*a.* and *adv.* alternately rising and falling. (motion of *saw*)

seethe, *v.i.* and *t.* (*past* **seethed,** *arch.* **sod;** *p.p.* **seethed,** *arch.* **sodden**) boil, cook by boiling; bubble up; be violently agitated. (O.E. *séothan*)

segar, *obs.* form of **cigar.**

segment, *n.* part cut off, section; (*geom.*) part cut off from figure by line or plane, esp. part enclosed between arc and chord of circle.—*v.t.* and *i.* separate into segments. **segmental, segmentary,** *aa.* **segmentation,** *n.* (L. *secare,* cut)

segnitude, *n.* sluggishness. (L. *segnis,* slow)

segregate, *v.t.* and *i.* separate from others, isolate.—*a.* set apart; solitary. **segregation,** *n.* **segregative,** *a.* (L. *se-,* apart; *grex,* flock)

seguidilla, *n.* old Spanish dance in triple time. (Sp.)

Seidlitz powder, saline aperient of two powders dissolved separately and drunk as they mix and effervesce. (village in Bohemia)

seigneur, seignior, *n.* feudal lord, lord of manor. **grand seigneur,** great nobleman; distinguished person. **seigniorial, seignorial,** *a.* **seigniorage, seignorage,** *n.* Crown's right to percentage on minted bullion; mining royalty. **seigniory, seignory,** *n.* feudal lordship or domain; manorial rights. (F.)

seine, *n.* large vertical fishing-net.—*v.t.* and *i.* catch (fish) with seine. (Gk. *sagēnē,* fishing-net)

seise, *v.t.* (*law*) put in possession of, confiscate by warrant. **seisin,** *n.* freehold possession of land. (*seize*)

seismic, *a.* of earthquake. **seismogram,** *n.* record made by **seismograph,** *n.* instrument recording earthquake shock. **seismographer, seismography,** *nn.* **seismographic, seismographical,** *aa.* **seismology,** *n.* science of earthquakes. **seismological,** *a.* **seismologist,** *n.* **seismometer, seismoscope,** *nn.* kinds of seismograph. (Gk. *seismos,* earthquake)

seity, *n.* selfhood. (L. *se,* oneself)

seize, *v.t.* and *i.* lay hold of suddenly and forcibly, grasp, clutch; comprehend fully; seise; (of machinery) jam from excessive heat etc.; (*naut.*) lash with several turns of small cord. **seizin,** same as **seisin. seizor,** *n.* one who seises. **seizure,** *n.* seizing; sudden attack of illness, apoplectic stroke. (L.L. *sacire*)

sejant, *a.* (*heraldry*) sitting. (L. *sedēre,* sit)

sekos, *n.* sacred enclosure of Greek temple. (Gk.)

selachian, *a.* and *n.* (fish) of shark family. (Gk. *selachos,* shark)

seladang, *n.* Malayan wild ox or tapir. (native)

selah, *n.* unknown word us. taken as musical sign for pause. (Heb.)

seldom, (*Shake.*) **seld,** *adv.* rarely, not often. (O.E. *seldan*)

select, *v.t.* pick out by preference, choose.—*a.* choice, of special excellence; fastidious, exclusive. **selection,** *n.* selecting; what is selected; process by which certain types of animal or plant survive while others are eliminated. **selective,** *a.* having power of selection. **selectivity,** *n.* (*wireless*) degree to which set can receive one wave-length while excluding others. (L. *se-,* apart; *legere,* pick)

selenium, *n.* non-metallic element allied to sulphur. **s. cell,** whose electrical resistance varies according to amount of light falling on it. **selenic, selenous,** *aa.* (Gk. *selēnē,* moon)

seleno-, from Gk. *selēnē,* moon, used in **selenocentric,** *a.* as seen from centre of moon; **selenodont,** *a.* and *n.* (mammal) with crescent-shaped ridges on its molars; **selenograph,** *n.* chart of moon's surface, hence **selenography,** *n.,* **selenographic,** *a.*; **selenology,** *n.* study of the moon; **selenomancy,** *n.* divination by the moon; **selenotropism,** *n.* (*bot.*) tendency to curve upwards under moonlight.

self, *n.* (*pl.* **selves**) one's own personality, ego; one's own interests, advantage; myself, yourself, himself.—*a.*

(of colour) uniform; (*Shake.*) one's own; selfsame. (O.E.)
self-absorbed, *a.* absorbed in one's own affairs.
self-abuse, *n.* abuse of oneself; masturbation; (*Shake.*) self-deception.
self-acting, *a.* automatic.
self-admission, *n.* (*Shake.*) self-approbation.
self-assertive, *a.* pushing, bumptious. **self-assertion,** *n.*
self-binder, *n.* reaping-machine that binds automatically; portfolio for holding together loose sheets.
self-centred, *a.* preoccupied with one's own affairs.
self-coloured, *a.* of the same colour all over.
self-command, *n.* power of controlling one's feelings, self-control.
self-complacent, *a.* self-satisfied. **self-complacency,** *n.*
self-conceit, *n.* over-high opinion of oneself.
self-confident, *a.* sure of one's own powers. **self-confidence,** *n.*
self-conscious, *a.* embarrassed or awkward in the presence of others; (*philos.*) conscious of the ego as both subject and object of experience.
self-contained, *a.* complete in itself; uncommunicative.
self-contradictory, *a.* inconsistent.
self-control, *n.* control of one's emotions or temper by the will.
self-deceit, self-deception, *nn.* state, act, of deceiving oneself.
self-defence, *n.* defence of oneself. **in s.,** not as an aggressive action.
self-denial, *n.* abstention from pleasure; unselfishness. **self-denying,** *a.*
self-destruction, *n.* suicide.
self-determination, *n.* free will; right of a nation to choose its own government.
self-devotion, *n.* giving up of oneself to a cause.
self-esteem, *n.* good opinion of oneself.
self-evident, *a.* evident without proof.
self-examination, *n.* introspection.
self-existent, *a.* not derived from anything else.
self-fertilizing, *a.* fertilized by action of its own pollen.
self-forgetful, *a.* unselfish.
self-glorious, *a.* (*Shake.*) boastful.
self-governing, *a.* autonomous; (of colony) having an elective legislature. **self-government,** *n.*
self-heal, *n.* a blue-flowered plant.
self-help, *n.* fending for oneself.
selfhood, *n.* existence as a separate self; conscious personality.
self-importance, *n.* exaggerated estimate of one's own worth; pompousness. **self-important,** *a.*
self-indulgence, *n.* undue gratification of one's appetites or desires. **self-indulgent,** *a.*
self-inflicted, *a.* caused to a person by himself.
self-interest, *n.* regard to one's own advantage. **self-interested,** *a.*
selfish, *a.* regardful of one's own interests solely or chiefly, lacking in consideration for others.
self-knowledge, *n.* knowledge of one's own character.
selfless, *a.* with no thought of self, unselfish.
self-love, *n.* desire for one's own happiness.
self-made, *a.* having risen in wealth or position by one's own efforts.
self-mastery, *n.* self-command.
self-neglect, *n.* neglect of one's person, uncleanliness.
self-opinionated, self-opinioned, *aa.* sticking obstinately to one's own opinions.
self-pity, *n.* pity for oneself.
self-possessed, *a.* cool, collected. **self-possession,** *n.* composure.
self-preservation, *n.* saving of oneself from death or injury.
self-raising, *a.* (of flour) containing a proportion of baking-powder.
self-realization, *n.* development of one's own powers to their full extent.
self-registering, *a.* recording automatically.
self-reliant, *a.* relying on one's own powers. **self-reliance,** *n.*
self-respect, *n.* due regard for one's own dignity and worth. **self-respecting, self-respectful,** *aa.*
self-restraint, *n.* restraint over one's own desires.
self-righteous, *a.* thinking oneself better than others, priggish.
self-sacrifice, *n.* forgoing advantage for the sake of others.
selfsame, *a.* identical.
self-satisfied, *a.* smugly conceited.
self-seeking, *a.* seeking one's own advantage only. **self-seeker,** *n.*
self-sown, *a.* sprung from seed sown naturally, not by human agency.
self-starter, *n.* electric device for starting motor-car.
self-styled, *a.* called by oneself, pretended.
self-sufficient, *a.* bumptious, presumptuous. **self-sufficing,** *a.* independent.
self-will, *n.* wilfulness, obstinacy. **self-willed,** *a.*
sell, *v.t.* and *i.* (*past, p.p.* **sold**) dispose of in exchange for money or other equivalent; deal in; betray for money or reward; (*sl.,* us. *pass.*) disappoint, hoax.—*n.* (*sl.*) disappointment, hoax. **s. off,** clear out (stock) at bargain prices. **s. one a pup.** (*sl.*) swindle him. **s. one's life dearly,** kill many before one is killed. **s. out,** sell completely. **s. the pass,** be unfaithful to one's trust. **s. up,** sell goods of (debtor). **selling race,** horse-race in which winner must be auctioned. (O.E. *sellan*)
sell, *n.* (*Spens.*) seat; saddle. (L. *sella*)

sellanders, same as **sallenders.**
selliform, *a.* saddle-shaped. (*sell*)
seltzer, *n.* (also **s.-water**) a mineral water. **seltzogene,** *n.* gazogene. (*Selters* in Germany)
selvage, selvedge, *n.* edge of cloth so finished as to prevent unravelling. (*self*; *edge*)
selves, see **self.**
semantics, *n.pl.* semasiology. (Gk. *sēmainein*, mean)
semaphore, *n.* signalling device of post with movable arms; system of signalling with operator's arms, flags etc.—*v.t.* and *i.* signal by semaphore. **semaphoric,** *a.* **semaphorically,** *adv.* (Gk. *sēma*, sign; *pherein*, bear)
semasiology, *n.* science of meanings of words. **semasiological,** *a.* (Gk. *sēmainein*, mean; *legein*, speak)
sematic, *a.* serving as a sign of warning. (Gk. *sēma*, sign)
semblance, *n.* outward aspect; likeness, similitude. **semblable,** *a.* (*arch.*) seeming; (*Shake.*) similar.—*n.* (*Shake.*) (one's) like. **semblative,** *a.* (*Shake.*). (L. *similis*, like)
semeiology, semeiotics, *nn.* art of using symbols; (*med.*) study of symptoms. **semeiological,** *a.* **semeiologist,** *n.* (Gk. *sēmeion*, mark; *legein*, speak)
semen, *n.* generative fluid of males. (L.=seed)
semester, *n.* college half-year in U.S. (L. *sex*, six; *mensis*, month)
semi-, *pref.* half, as in **semicircle;** partly, as in **semi-official.** (L.)
semi-annual, *a.* half-yearly.
semi-barbarian, *a.* half-civilized.
semibreve, *n.* (*mus.*) note equal to two minims, whole note.
semichorus, *n.* part of choir or chorus, passage to be sung by it.
semicircle, *n.* half-circle. **semicircular,** *a.*
semicolon, *n.* punctuation-mark (;) of intermediate value between comma and full stop.
semidemisemiquaver, *n.* (*mus.*) half a demisemiquaver.
semi-detached, *a.* (of house) with another joined to it on one side.
semifinal, *a.* and *n.* (match, round) before the final. **semifinalist,** *n.*
semi-fluid, *a.* and *n.* viscous (fluid).
semilunar, *a.* shaped like half-moon.
seminal, *a.* of seed or semen; germinal, reproductive. (*semen*)
seminar, *n.* group of students engaged in research under supervision. (G.)
seminary, *n.* academy; training-college for Roman Catholic priests; breeding-ground, nursery. (*semen*)
semination, *n.* (*bot.*) process, plant's method, of seeding. (*semen*)
semi-official, *a.* coming from official source but not fully authorized.
semiquaver, *n.* (*mus.*) half a quaver.
Semite, *n.* member of race incl. Jews and Arabs. **Semitic,** *a.* and *n.* (language) of Semites. (Gk. *Sem*, Shem)
semitone, *n.* (*mus.*) interval equal to half a tone.
semitropical, *a.* between tropical and temperate.
semivocal, *a.* of semivowel.
semivowel, *n.* sound, letter, partly vowel and partly consonant, e.g. *y*.
semmit, *n.* (*Scot.*) undervest.
semolina, semola, *n.* coarse particles of grain left after sifting of wheat. (L. *simila*, fine flour)
semper fidelis, always faithful. *semper idem*, always the same. (L.)
sempiternal, *a.* eternal, everlasting. (L. *semper*, always; *aeternus*, eternal)
semplice, *a.* (*mus.*) simple, without embellishments. (It.)
sempre, *adv.* (*mus.*) throughout. (It.)
sempstress, see **seamstress.**
sen, *n.* Japanese copper coin, $\frac{1}{100}$ of yen. (Jap.)
senarius, *n.* (*pl.* **senarii**) Latin verse of six, us. iambic, feet. (L.)
senary, *a.* of the number six; having six parts. (L. *sex*, six)
senate, *n.* state council of ancient Rome; Upper House of U.S. and French legislatures; any legislature; governing body of some universities. **senator,** *n.* member of senate. **senatorial,** *a.* (L. *senatus*)
send, same as **scend.**
send, *v.t.* and *i.* (*past*, *p.p.* **sent**) cause to go; have conveyed; dispatch message or messenger; cause to move, propel; grant; cause to be. **s. down,** expel from university. **s. for,** order to be brought, summon. **s. forth,** send out; emit. **s.-off,** *n.* friendly demonstration at departure. (O.E. *sendan*)
sendal, *n.* fine medieval silk stuff. (L.L. *cendalum*)
senega, seneka, *n.* American plant, drug made from its root. (*Seneca* Indians)
senescent, *a.* growing old. **senescence,** *n.* (L. *senex*, old)
seneschal, *n.* steward, majordomo, of medieval palace or castle. (O.F.)
sengreen, *n.* (*arch.*) house-leek. (O.E. *singréne*, evergreen)
senhor, *senhora*, *senhorita*, *nn.* Portuguese equivalents of Mr., Mrs., Miss.
senile, *a.* of, attendant on, old age; aged; feeble from age, doting. **senility,** *n.* (L. *senex*, old)
senior, *a.* older in years or standing; of higher rank.—*n.* one's elder or superior in standing; person of advanced age. **s. partner,** head of firm. **s. service,** Navy. **seniority,** (*Shake.*) **seniory,** *nn.* (L.)
senna, *n.* aperient made from cassia. (Arab. *sanā*)
sennet, *n.* (*Shake.*) trumpet-call. (*signet*)
sennight, se'nnight, *n.* week. (*seven night*)

sennit, *n.* kind of braided cordage.

señor, señora, señorita, nn. Spanish equivalents of Mr., Mrs., Miss.

sensation, *n.* operation of a sense, feeling; state of excited interest or feeling, cause of this. **sensational,** *a.* of sensation; exciting; melodramatic. **sensationalism,** *n.* use of sensational writing or language; doctrine that all knowledge is got from sense-impressions.

sense, *n.* any of the bodily faculties by which we perceive or feel; perception, feeling, consciousness; sound appreciation; good judgment, wisdom; meaning, intelligibility; (*Shake.*) sensual nature; (*pl.*) wits. —*v.t.* perceive by sense; (*Amer. colloq.*) understand. **five ss.,** sight, hearing, smell, taste, and touch. **in a s.,** considered in a certain way. **in, out of, one's ss.,** sane, mad. **make s.,** be intelligible. **sixth s.,** special insight or intuition. (L. *sentire,* feel)

senseless, *a.* unconscious; stupid, foolish.

sensible, *a.* wise, judicious, reasonable; perceptible by the senses, appreciable; conscious (of); sensitive. **sensibility,** *n.* capacity to feel; over-sensitiveness; susceptibility.

sensitive, *a.* feeling readily and acutely, keenly perceptive; easily hurt or shocked, tender, touchy; responsive to slight changes; sensory; (*phot.*) reacting to light rays. **s. plant,** whose leaves curl up when touched. **sensitivity,** *n.* **sensitize,** *v.t.* render sensitive. **sensitization,** *n.*

sensory, sensorial, *aa.* of senses, sensation, or sensorium. **sensorium,** *n.* (*pl.* **sensoria, sensoriums**) seat of sensation in brain.

sensual, *a.* of the body, carnal; given to gratifying the appetites, self-indulgent; licentious; (*rare*) sensory. **sensualism,** *n.* sensuality; (*philos.*) sensationalism. **sensualist,** *n.* voluptuary; debauchee; adherent of sensualism. **sensuality,** *n.* pursuit of fleshly gratification. **sensualize,** *v.t.* make sensual.

sensuous, *a.* of, acting on, the senses; aesthetic.

sent, see **send.**

sentence, *n.* word, series of words, conveying complete thought; (*law*) judgment declaring punishment to be inflicted, punishment so declared; (*arch.*) opinion; pithy saying.—*v.t.* pass sentence upon; condemn (to). **pass s.,** declare decision of court; express opinion. **sentential,** *a.* of sentence. **sententious,** *a.* full of aphorisms; pithy; pompously moralizing. (L. *sentire,* feel)

sentient, *a.* feeling or capable of feeling. **sentience,** *n.* (L. *sentire,* feel)

sentiment, *n.* feeling, sum of feelings, attitude of mind; tendency to be swayed by feeling rather than reason; maudlin emotion, sentimentality; thought expressed in words, motto. **sentimental,** *a.* of, arising from, feelings; foolishly emotional. **sentimentalism, sentimentality,** *nn.* being sentimental; affected or morbid tenderness. **sentimentalist,** *n.* **sentimentalize,** *v.i.* and *t.* think or talk sentimentally; render sentimental. (L. *sentire,* feel)

sentinel, *n.* guard, sentry.—*v.t.* keep guard over. (It. *sentinella*)

sentry, *n.* soldier on watch; guard. **s.-box,** *n.* small shelter for sentry. **s.-go,** *n.* sentry duty.

sepal, *n.* leaf of flower's calyx. (L. *separ,* separate)

separable, *a.* able to be separated; (*Shake.*) causing separation. **separability,** *n.*

separate, *v.t.* and *i.* divide, part; put apart, sever; occupy place between; come asunder, part company.—*a.* disconnected; distinct, individual. **separation,** *n.* separating; formal arrangement of husband and wife to live apart. **separatist,** *n.* one who advocates withdrawal from Church or political union; home-ruler. **separatism,** *n.* **separative, separatory,** *aa.* **separator,** *n.* one who separates; machine for separating cream from milk. (L. **se-,** apart; *parare,* put)

sepia, *n.* inky fluid secreted by cuttle-fish; dark-brown pigment made from this. (Gk.=cuttle-fish)

sepoy, *n.* native soldier in Indian army. (Pers. *sipah,* army)

seps, *n.* a snake-like lizard. (Gk.)

sepsis, *n.* septic state or agency, blood-poisoning. (Gk.=putrefaction)

sept, *n.* clan, tribe, esp. in Ireland. **septal,** *a.* (*sect*)

sept-, from L. *septem,* seven, used in **septan,** *a.* (of fever) recurring every sixth day (seventh by inclusive reckoning); **septangle,** *n.* heptagon; **septavalent, septivalent,** *a.* having a valency of seven; **September,** *n.* ninth month of year (seventh in Roman calendar); **septempartite,** *a.* divided into seven parts; **septenarius,** *n.* verse of seven feet; **septenary,** *a.* of the number seven, having seven parts; **septennium, septennate,** *nn.* period of seven years; **septennial,** *a.* lasting, occurring every, seven years; **septet, septette,** *n.* set of seven singers or players, composition for seven voices or instruments, group of seven, **septilateral,** *a.* seven-sided; **septillion,** *n.* seventh power of million (1 with 42 ciphers), (in U.S. and France) eighth power of thousand (1 with 24 ciphers).

septa, see **septum. septal,** *a.* of septum. **septate,** *a.* having septum, partitioned. **septation,** *n.*

septic, *a.* causing, caused by, putre-

faction; involving sepsis. **septicity,** *n.* **septicaemia,** *n.* blood-poisoning.
septime, *n.* a guard in fencing. (F.)
septimus, *a.* seventh of the name. (L.)
septisyllable, *n.* word of seven syllables. (L. *septem,* seven)
septuagenarian, *a.* and *n.* (person) in his seventies. **septuagenary,** *a.* of seventy. **Septuagesima (Sunday),** Sunday before Sexagesima. **Septuagint,** *n.* Greek version of Old Testament (traditionally by seventy translators). (L. *septuaginta,* seventy)
septum, *n.* (*pl.* **septa**) dividing membrane, partition. (L.=fence)
septuple, *a.* sevenfold.—*v.t.* multiply by seven. (L. *septem,* seven)
sepulchre, *n.* tomb, burial vault.—*v.t.* inter. **Holy S.,** in which Christ was laid. **whited s.,** hypocrite. **sepulchral,** *a.* of tomb; dismal, funereal. **sepulture,** *n.* burial. (L. *sepelire,* bury)
sequacious, *a.* easily led or moulded; logical. **sequacity,** *n.* (L. *sequi,* follow)
sequel, *n.* what comes after; continuation of story; consequence, upshot. **sequela,** *n.* (*pl.* **sequelae**) disease etc. consequent on another disease. (L. *sequi,* follow)
sequence, *n.* succession; series of succeeding things; three or more cards of same suit in order of value; scene in cinema play. **s. of tenses,** regulation of tenses in subordinate clause by those in principal clause. **sequent,** *a.* following in sequence or as consequence. — *n.* (*Shake.*) follower. *sequentes, sequentia, nn.pl.* (*abbr. seq.* or *seqq.*) what follows. **sequential,** *a.* forming sequel (to); in succession, continuous. (L. *sequi,* follow)
sequester, *v.t.* seclude, set apart; (*law*) sequestrate.—*n.* (*Shake.*) separation. **sequestrable,** *a.* liable to sequestration. **sequestrate,** *v.t.* confiscate; (*law*) set apart income of (estate) to meet claims against its owner. **sequestration,** *n.* **sequestrator,** *n.* person administering sequestrated estate. (L.=trustee)
sequin, *n.* small bright metal disk, spangle, sewn on dress; old Venetian coin worth about 9*s.* (Arab. *sikka,* die for coins)
sequoia, *n.* lofty coniferous Californian tree. (Indian chief *Sequoiah*)
sérac, *n.* ice pinnacle among glacier crevasses. (F.)
seraglio, *n.* harem; palace of sultan. (L. *sera,* bolt)
serai, *n.* oriental inn, caravanserai. (Pers.=palace)
serang, *n.* boatswain of lascar crew. (Pers. *sarhang,* commander)
seraph, *n.* (*pl.* **seraphim, seraphs**) angel of highest order. **seraphic,** *a.* of seraphs; angelic; sublime. **seraphically,** *adv.* **seraphine, seraphina,** *n.* old kind of harmonium. (Heb.)
sere, *a.* shrivelled, withered. (O.E. *séar*)
sere, same as **sear.**
serenade, *n.* music sung or played at night under person's window, esp. by lover.—*v.t.* entertain with serenade. (It. *serenata*)
serendipity, *n.* faculty of making happy chance finds. (*Serendip,* place in fairy-tale)
serene, *a.* calm, placid, tranquil; clear, unclouded,—*n.* serene expanse. **His S. Highness,** title of certain princes. **serenity,** *n.* (L. *serenus*)
serf, *n.* labourer who was bound to, and could be sold with, the land he tilled; drudge. **serfage, serfdom, serfhood,** *nn.* (L. *servus,* slave)
serge, *n.* hard-wearing twilled woollen fabric. (L. *sericus,* silken)
sergeant, *n.* non-commissioned officer ranking above corporal; police-officer ranking between inspector and constable; (*Shake.*) bailiff. **s.-at-arms,** same as **serjeant-at-arms. s.-fish,** *n.* sea-fish like mackerel. **s.-major,** *n.* warrant officer ranking above sergeant. (L. *servire,* serve)
sergette, *n.* thin serge. (F.)
serial, *a.* of, forming, a series; published by instalments.—*n.* serial story. **seriality,** *n.* **seriate,** *v.t.* arrange in series.—*a.* seriated. **seriation,** *n.* **seriatim,** *adv.* point by point, in order.
Seric, *a.* Chinese. **sericeous,** *a.* (*bot., zool.*) silky; bearing silky hairs. **sericulture, sericiculture,** *n.* breeding of silkworms for silk production. (Gk. *Sēr,* Chinese)
seriema, *n.* long-legged crested Brazilian bird. (native)
series, *n.* (*pl.* same) succession of things connected by some likeness, sequence, set; (*math.*) progression of numbers or quantities according to a certain law. (L.)
serif, *n.* minute cross-line finishing off stroke of letter.
serin, *n.* kind of small finch. (F.)
seringa, *n.* Brazilian rubber-tree. (Port.)
serious, *a.* grave, solemn, not frivolous; meaning what one says, sincere; important, critical; demanding thought. **serio-comic,** *a.* half serious, half comic. (L. *serius*)
serjeant, *n.* (formerly) lawyer of high rank. **common s.,** a judicial officer of the City of London. **s.-at-arms,** *n.* ceremonial official responsible for discipline in Houses of Parliament. (*sergeant*)
sermon, *n.* religious discourse delivered from pulpit; moral lecture; tedious harangue. **sermonette, sermonet,** *nn.* short sermon. **sermonize,** *v.t.* and *i.* preach (at). (L. *sermo,* discourse)
serosity, *n.* serousness.
serotine, *n.* small brown bat. **sero-**

tinous, *a.* flowering late. (L. *serus,* late)

serous, *a.* of the nature of, secreting, serum; thin and watery.

serpent, *n.* snake; venomous or treacherous person; obsolete wind-instrument; kind of firework. **s.-eater,** *n.* secretary-bird. **serpentine,** *a.* like a serpent; twisting, tortuous; crooked, treacherous.—*n.* kinds of rock with mottled appearance.—*v.i.* meander. (L. *serpere,* creep)

serpigo, *n.* ringworm; shingles. **serpiginous,** *a.* having shingles; (of disease) spreading from one part to another. (L. *serpere,* creep)

serpolet, *n.* wild thyme. (F.)

serra, *n.* (*pl.* **serrae**) saw-like organ. **serradilla,** *n.* kind of clover. **serrate, serrated,** *aa.* (of leaf) having edge notched like teeth of saw. **serration,** *n.* **serricorn,** *n.* kind of beetle. **serriferous,** *a.* having a saw-like organ. **serriform,** *a.* saw-shaped. **serrulate,** *a.* finely serrated. **serrulation,** *n.* (L.=saw)

serried, *a.* packed closely, in compact order. (L. *sera,* bolt)

serum, *n.* (*pl.* **serums, sera**) watery part of bodily fluid, esp. liquid that separates out from blood when it coagulates; such fluid containing anti-toxin and used for inoculation; whey. (L.)

serval, *n.* African wild cat; its tawny black-spotted fur. (F.)

servant, *n.* personal or domestic attendant; one in the service of another. **civil s.,** member of civil service. **public s.,** state official. **your obedient s.,** form of signature in official letters. **s.-girl, s.-maid,** *nn.* maidservant. (*serve*)

serve, *v.t.* and *i.* work under (another); do service (for), be useful to; meet needs (of), suffice, suit; wait upon, hand round; treat; undergo (sentence); be soldier or sailor; (*law*) deliver (summons etc.); (*naut.*) bind (rope) with small cord to prevent fraying; (*tennis*) put (ball) in play.—*n.* tennis service. **s. one right,** be only what one deserves. **s. one's time,** go through apprenticeship. **s. out,** distribute; retaliate upon. **s. the turn,** suffice for the purpose. **s. time,** undergo imprisonment. (L. *servire*)

service, *n.* (us. **s.-tree**) tree like rowan. (L. *sorbus*)

service, *n.* act of serving; state of being servant; domestic employment; department of royal or state employ, persons engaged in it; military duty; work done for another; use, assistance; attendance in hotel; regular supply of trains etc.; set of dishes; liturgical form or office; meeting for religious worship. **at your s.,** ready to do as you wish. **see s.,** take part in warfare; have experience. **s. dress,** ordinary uniform. **s. flat,** where meals and attendance are provided. **take s. with,** become servant to. **serviceable,** *a.* useful; durable; (*Shake.*) diligent in service.

serviette, *n.* table-napkin. (F.)

servile, *a.* of, like, a slave; abjectly submissive, cringing; menial. **servility,** *n.* slavery; obsequiousness. (L. *servus,* slave)

servitor, *n.* male servant, henchman; (formerly) Oxford undergraduate assisted from college funds and doing menial services in return. (*serve*)

servitude, *n.* slavery, bondage. (L. *servus,* slave)

sesame, *n.* an E. Indian plant; its oil-yielding seeds. **open s.,** magic formula opening door. (Gk.)

sesqui-, *pref.* one and a half, used in **sesquialteral,** *a.* half as big again; **sesquicentennial,** *a.* of a century and a half.—*n.* 150th anniversary; **sesquipedalian,** *a.* a foot and a half long, (of word) cumbrous, pedantic; **sesquiplicate,** *a.* in ratio of cube to square. (L.)

sess, same as **cess.**

sessile, *a.* (*bot.*) attached directly without stalk. (L. *sedēre,* sit)

session, *n.* sitting; meeting, assembly; continuous series of these; period between meeting and prorogation of Parliament; university year; (*Scot.*) minister and elders, deciding church business; (*pl.*) meetings of courts of justice. **Court of S.,** supreme civil court of justice in Scotland. **in s.,** sitting. **sessional,** *a.* (L. *sedēre,* sit)

sesterce, *n.* ancient Roman coin worth about 2*d.* (L. *sestertius*)

sestet, *n.* last six lines of sonnet; sextet. (L. *sextus,* sixth)

sestina, *n.* poem of six six-line stanzas and envoy, each stanza having the same words ending its lines, but in a different order. (It.)

set, *v.t.* and *i.* (*past, p.p.* same) put, place; fix, affix; cause to stand, station; sow, plant; fix in framework, mount; adorn, variegate; prepare for use, adjust; make or become stiff, congeal; appoint; cause to be; stake; clench (teeth); spread (sail); compose (type); give edge to (razor); restore (broken bone) to position; provide (words) with music; tend; start; (of sun) go down; (of dog) indicate game by crouching. **s. about,** begin. **s. aside,** reserve; disregard. **s. at naught,** treat as of no account. **s. back,** impede; (*Amer. sl.*) cost. **s. down,** put in writing; attribute (to). **s. in,** begin. **s. little, much, by,** esteem little, much. **s. off,** discharge; enhance; weigh against; start. **s. on,** attack, make (dog) attack. **s. out,** state; start journey. **s. to,** apply oneself vigorously. **s. up,** erect; establish; begin uttering; develop; start in business; put in type; pretend (to be). (O.E. *settan*)

set, *n.* number of similar things used or classed together; group, clique; clutch of eggs; arrangement of stage scenery; setting of sun; tendency, drift; fit, hang; slip for planting; sett; (*lawn tennis*) series of games forming unit of match.—*a.* fixed, immovable; obstinate, determined; prescribed, established; (*sl.*) ready. **make dead s. at,** combine to attack. **s. fair,** (of weather) fine and settled. **setback,** *n.* check. **s.-down,** *n.* rebuff. **s.-off,** *n.* counterpoise. **s.-square,** *n.* flat triangular piece of wood for drawing angles. **s.-to,** *n.* fight, dispute.

seta, *n.* (*pl.* **setae**) bristle. **setaceous, setose, setous,** *aa.* bristly. **setiferous,** *a.* bearing bristles. **seton,** *n.* thread drawn through skin and left to draw off discharge. (L.)

sett, *n.* stone block for paving; tennis set. (*set*)

settee, *n.* seat for two or more.

settee, *n.* lateen-sailed Mediterranean vessel. (L. *sagitta,* arrow)

setter, *n.* breeds of long-haired dog trained to set or point.

setting, *n.* music of song; mounting, framework; environment.

settle, *n.* bench with back and arms. (O.E. *setl*)

settle, *v.t.* and *i.* establish, become established, in place, business, home etc.; colonize (country); make, become, firm; calm, become calm; deal with, dispose of; decide, come to agreement; balance, pay (account); bestow legally for life; sink gradually; (of dregs) fall to bottom; (of bird) alight. **s. down,** become established (in); adopt regular mode of life. **s. up,** pay (what is owing). **s. upon,** decide upon. **settlement,** *n.* act of settling; sum settled, esp. on woman at her marriage; colony; mission centre in poor district; (*Amer.*) small village. **settler,** *n.* early colonist. (O.E. *setlan*)

setwall, *n.* valerian. (Arab. *zedwār*)

seven, *a.* and *n.* one more than six. **sevenfold,** *a.* and *adv.* seven times repeated. **seventh,** *a.* next after sixth.—*n.* one of seven equal parts. **seventh heaven,** state of extreme happiness. **seventhly,** *adv.* in the seventh place. **seventeen,** *a.* and *n.* seven and ten. **seventeenth,** *a.* and *n.* **seventy,** *a.* and *n.* seven times ten. **seventy-four,** *n.* old line-of-battle ship with 74 guns. **seventy-five,** *n.* French 75 mm. field-gun. **seventieth,** *a.* and *n.* (O.E. *seofon*)

sever, *v.t.* and *i.* separate, disjoin; cut or break off. (*separate*)

several, *a.* more than two but not very many; separate, distinct; respective; (*Shake.*) private.—*pron.* several persons or things. **severally,** *adv.* separately; respectively. **severals,** *n.pl.* (*Shake.*) individuals; particulars.

severalty, *n.* sole tenancy of property. (L. *separ,* separate)

severance, *n.* act of severing.

severe, *a.* stern, strict; harsh, not lenient; censorious; exacting, trying; violent, not slight; (*art*) plain, not florid. **severity,** *n.* (L. *severus*)

severy, *n.* compartment of vaulted ceiling. (*ciborium*)

Sèvres, *n.* kind of porcelain. (place)

sew, *v.t.* and *i.* (*p.p.* **sewn, sewed**) fasten by stitches, work with needle and thread. **sewing-machine,** *n.* (O.E. *siwian*)

sewage, *n.* waste matter, excrement, conveyed in sewer.

sewellel, *n.* small American burrowing rodent. (Amer. Ind.)

sewer, *n.* seamstress.

sewer, *n.* medieval servant who set out table, carried dishes etc. (L. *ad,* to; *sedēre,* sit)

sewer, *n.* main drain.—*v.t.* furnish with drains. **sewerage,** *n.* system of, drainage by, sewers. (L. *ex,* out; *aqua,* water)

sewin, sewen, *n.* kind of sea trout.

sewn, see **sew.**

sex, *n.* state of being male or female; males or females collectively. **the (fair, weaker) s.,** women. **the sterner s.,** men. **s.-appeal,** *n.* what makes a person sexually desirable. (L. *sexus*)

sex(i)-, from L. *sex,* six, used in **sexagenarian,** *a.* and *n.* (person) in his sixties; **sexagenary,** *a.* of sixty, by sixties; **Sexagesima (Sunday),** second Sunday before Lent; **sexagesimal,** *a.* of, based on, the number sixty; **sexangle,** *n.* hexagon; **sexcentenary,** *n.* and *a.* (of) the 600th anniversary; **sexdigitate,** *a.* six-toed; **sexennial,** *a.* lasting, occurring every, six years; **sexisyllable,** *n.* word of six syllables, hence **sexisyllabic,** *a.*; **sexivalent, sexavalent,** *a.* (*chem.*) having a valency of six. **sexpartite,** *a.* divided into six parts; **sext, sexte,** *n.* canonical office of sixth hour or noon; **sextain,** *n.* six-line stanza; **sextan,** *a.* (of fever) recurring every fifth day (sixth by inclusive reckoning); **sextant,** *n.* navigator's instrument for measuring altitudes; **sextet, sextette,** *n.* set of six, (composition for) six singers or players; **sextillion, sexillion,** *n.* sixth power of million (1 with 36 ciphers), (in U.S. and France) seventh power of thousand (1 with 21 ciphers); **sexto,** *n.* book of sheets folded in six; **sextodecimo,** *n.* (*abbr.* **16mo**) book of sheets folded into sixteen leaves, this size, average 6 × 4¾ in.

sexton, *n.* officer in charge of church, who rings bell, digs graves etc. (corrupt. of *sacristan*)

sextuple, *a.* sixfold.—*v.t.* multiply by six. (L. *sex,* six)

sextus, *a.* sixth of the name. (L.)

sexual, *a.* of sex or sexes; having sex.

s. classification, (*bot.*) by number of stamens. **sexuality,** *n.*
sexvalent, same as **sexivalent.**
sez you, same as **says you.**
'sfoot, *int.* (*Shake.*) God's foot.
sforzando, adv. (*mus.*) with sudden emphasis. (It.)
sgraffito, same as *graffito.*
shabash, *int.* bravo. (Pers.)
shabby, *a.* wearing old or worn-out clothes; worn, ragged; mean, stingy; scurvy, despicable. (*scabby*)
shabrack, *n.* cavalry saddle-cloth. (G. *schabracke*)
shack, *n.* (*Amer.*) hut, shanty.
shack, *v.t.* (*Amer.*) chase after, retrieve (ball).
shackle, *n.* link joining rings on wrists or ankles so as to allow some movement; staple; (*pl.*) fetters; anything that confines. — *v.t.* fasten with shackles; hamper. (O.E. *sceacul,* loose bond)
shad, *n.* sea-fish of herring family. (O.E. *sceadd*)
shaddock, *n.* kinds of tropical fruit incl. grape-fruit. (person)
shade, *n.* partial darkness; darker parts of anything; shadow; ghost, spirit; screen, shelter; variety of colour, esp. one made by admixture of black; minute difference.—*v.t.* and *i.* screen from light; make dark; pass by degrees into another colour. (O.E. *sceadu*)
shadoof, *n.* pole with bucket and counterpoise used for raising water in the East. (Arab. *shādūf*)
shadow, *n.* patch of shade; darkness, obscurity; darker parts of picture; shelter, protection; inseparable companion; unsubstantial thing, phantom; mere remnant, slight trace; (*Shake.*) reflection, likeness.—*v.t.* cast shadow over; set (forth) vaguely; follow and watch, dog; (*Shake.*) conceal, shelter. **shadowy,** *a.* full of shadows; dim, indistinct; unreal. (*shade*)
shady, *a.* giving, standing in, shade; of doubtful honesty, disreputable.
shaft, *n.* straight rod, pole; stem, shank; main part of column; arrow; ray of light, stroke of lightning; one of the poles between which horse is harnessed; revolving rod for transmitting power; hole giving access to mine. **s.-horse,** *n.* one between shafts. (O.E. *sceaft*)
shag, *n.* crested cormorant.
shag, *n.* kind of coarse fine-cut tobacco; rough mop of hair; (*arch.*) coarse long-napped cloth. — *a.* (*Shake.*) shaggy. **shagbark,** *n.* (*Amer.*) white hickory. **shaggy,** *a.* covered with rough hair, unkempt; overgrown with brushwood; villous.
shagreen, *n.* kinds of untanned leather with roughened surface; shark-skin. (Turk. *saghri*)
shah, *n.* ruler of Persia. (Pers.)
shaitan, *n.* evil spirit, devil. (Arab.)
shakable, *a.* able to be shaken.
shake, *v.t.* and *i.* (*past* **shook,** *Shake.* **shaked**; *p.p.* **shaken,** *Shake.* **shook, shaked**) move to and fro with quick short motions, agitate; tremble, vibrate, rock; jar, jolt; brandish; weaken, unsettle.—*n.* act of shaking, jolt; (*mus.*) rapid alternation of two notes, trill; (*colloq.*) moment. **no great ss.,** (*sl.*) not much good. **s. down,** cause to subside by shaking; get makeshift accommodation. **s. hands,** clasp hands (with). **s. off,** get rid of. **s. out,** empty by shaking; spread (sail). **s. up,** shake together, mix; upset. **shakedown,** *n.* makeshift bed. **shaker,** *n.* one who shakes; (*fem.* **Shakeress**) member of religious sect with dancing as part of ritual. **Shakerism,** *n.* (O.E. *scacan*)
Shakespearian, Shaksperian, *a.* of, in the style of, Shakespeare.
shako, *n.* tall flat-topped military cap with plume. (Hungarian *csákó*)
shaky, *a.* unsteady; infirm; unreliable.
shale, *n.* kinds of clay rock like slate but softer.
shale, *n.* (*Shake.*) shell. (O.E. *sceale*)
shall, *v.aux.* (*2nd sing. pres.* **shalt**; *past,* **should,** *2nd sing.* **shouldest** or **shouldst**) expressing intention, compulsion, or promise; (in 1st pers. only) forming future tense. (O.E. *sceal*)
shalloon, *n.* light kind of woollen stuff. (*Chalons* in France)
shallop, *n.* (*poet.*) light open boat. (F. *chaloupe*)
shallot, shalot, *n.* plant of onion family. (*Ascalon* in Palestine)
shallow, *a.* having little depth; superficial, trivial.—*n.* shallow place, shoal.—*v.t.* and *i.* make, become, shallow. (M.E. *schalowe*)
shalt, see **shall.**
sham, *v.t.* and *i.* feign, pretend (to be). —*n.* counterfeit, fake; imposture, impostor.—*a.* bogus, feigned.
shama, *n.* Indian cereal like millet. (Hind. *çāmā*)
shama, *n.* Indian song-bird. (Hind. *çāmā*)
shaman, *n.* Siberian wizard; medicine-man.
shamble, *n.* ungainly stumbling gait. —*v.i.* go with shamble, shuffle.
shambles, *n.pl.* butcher's slaughter-house; place of bloodshed. (L. *scamnum,* bench+dim.)
shame, *n.* painful emotion due to sense of guilt or impropriety; disgrace, dishonour; cause of this; (*colloq.*) piece of unfairness; (*Shake.*) modesty. —*v.t.* and *i.* make ashamed; bring disgrace on; force by shame (into); (*arch.*) be ashamed (to). **put to s.,** humiliate by showing superior qualities. (O.E. *scamu*)
shamefaced, *a.* bashful; sheepish; (*poet.*) modest. (O.E. *scam,* shame; *fæst,* fixed+confusion with *face*)

shameful, *a.* disgraceful; outrageous.
shameless, *a.* immodest; impudent, brazen.
shammy, shamoy, same as **chamois.**
shampoo, *v.t.* wash (scalp) with soapy fluid; massage (limbs) in hot bath.—*n.* shampooing; powder etc. for this. (Hind. *chāmpnā*)
shamrock, *n.* kinds of trefoil or clover, the national emblem of Ireland. (Ir. *seamrog*)
shandrydan, *n.* light two-wheeled cart; shabby old-fashioned vehicle.
shandygaff, *n.* mixture of ginger-beer and beer.
shangan, *n.* (*Scot.*) cleft stick.
shanghai, *v.t.* (*naut. sl.*) drug, put on board ship, and compel to serve as sailor.—*n.* (*Austral.*) catapult. (place)
shangie, *n.* (*Scot.*) shackle.
shank, *n.* leg from knee to ankle, shin; leg; shaft, stem, handle. **Shanks's mare,** one's own legs. (O.E. *scanca*)
shanny, *n.* small green sea-fish, smooth blenny.
shan't, *contr.* of **shall not.**
shantung, *n.* coarse kind of silk. (Chinese province)
shanty, *n.* small hut or shed. (F. *chantier,* workshop)
shanty, see **chanty.**
shape, *v.t.* and *i.* form, fashion; devise; assume form; (*Shake.*) adjust.—*n.* form; outward appearance, guise; orderly arrangement, proper condition; mould, pattern; blancmange. **shapeless,** *a.* lacking definite form; (*Shake.*) ugly. **shapely,** *a.* well proportioned. (O.E. *scieppan*)
shard, sherd, *n.* wing-case of beetle; fragment of broken pottery; (*Shake.*) patch of cow-dung. (O.E. *sceard*)
share, *n.* blade of plough. (O.E. *sceran,* shear)
share, *n.* allotted portion, part; one of the parts into which company's capital is divided, entitling holder to share of profits.—*v.t.* and *i.* distribute, apportion (out); have, experience, in common with others. **go ss.,** divide equally. **s. and s. alike,** take, taking, equal shares. **shareholder,** *n.* holder of shares in a company. (O.E. *sceran,* shear)
shark, *n.* large voracious sea-fish; swindling rogue, extortioner; (*Amer. sl.*) brilliant student.—*v.i.* and *t.* be swindler; gather (up) by dishonest means; swallow greedily.
sharp, *a.* having keen edge or fine point; pointed, not rounded; clear-cut; intense, piercing; shrill; keen, pungent; alert, quick; clever, artful; cutting, severe; (*mus.*) raised a semitone in pitch; out of tune by being too high; (*Shake.*) hungry.—*adv.* punctually; quickly. — *n.* (*colloq.*) swindler; (*mus.*) sharp note, symbol (♯) for this.—*v.t.* and *i.* sharpen; swindle. **s.-set,** *a.* hungry. **s.-sighted, s.-witted,** *aa.* **sharpen,** *v.t.* and *i.* make or become sharp, whet. **sharper,** *n.* swindler, cheat. **sharpshooter,** *n.* marksman. (O.E. *scearp*)
shatter, *v.t.* and *i.* break into fragments, smash; destroy utterly.
shauchle, *v.i.* (*Scot.*) shuffle.
shave, *v.t.* and *i.* (*p.p.* **shaved, shaven**) remove hair from (face) with razor; pare, whittle; miss narrowly, graze. —*n.* being shaved; shaving; narrow escape or miss. **shaveling,** *n.* (*arch.*) shaven person, monk. **shaver,** *n.* one who shaves; (*sl.*) youngster. **shavetail,** *n.* (*Amer. army sl.*) second lieutenant. **shaving,** *n.* thin slice, paring. (O.E. *scafan*)
Shavian, *a.* of, in the style of, G. B. Shaw, the playwright.
shavie, *n.* (*Scot.*) trick, prank.
shaw, *n.* (*poet.*) small wood, thicket; (*pl., Scot.*) leaves and stalks of potatoes, turnips etc. (O.E. *scaga*)
shawl, *n.* wrap of cloth or netted fabric worn over shoulders by women. —*v.t.* put shawl on. (Pers. *shāl*)
shawm, *n.* obsolete musical instrument like oboe. (Gk. *kalamos,* reed)
shay, *arch.* or *vulg.* for **chaise.**
she, *pron.* (*objective* **her,** *possessive* **her, hers**) the female person named before.—*n.* and *a.* female; (*Shake.*) mistress. (O.E. *séo*)
shea, *n.* W. African tree yielding **s.-butter,** *n.* an edible fat. (native)
sheaf, *n.* (*pl.* **sheaves**) bundle of stalks of grain bound together; any similar bundle.—*v.t.* put (corn) into sheaves. (O.E. *scéaf*)
sheal, *v.t.* (*Shake.*) shell. (shell)
shealing, same as **shieling.**
shear, *v.t.* and *i.* (*past* **sheared,** *arch.* **shore;** *p.p.* **shorn,** *rare* **sheared**) clip, cut (through); clip wool from (sheep), fleece; (*mech.*) distort, rupture, through shear; (*Scot.*) reap with sickle.—*n.* (*mech.*) stress acting sideways on rivet etc.; (*pl.*) large pair of scissors; (also **s.-legs**) sheers. **s.-hog, shearling,** *nn.* sheep after its first shearing. **shearman,** *n.* (*Shake.*) one who shears woollen cloth. **shearwater,** *n.* a sea-bird. (O.E. *sceran*)
sheat-fish, *n.* great catfish. (G. *scheidfisch*)
sheath, *n.* close-fitting cover, esp. for blade, scabbard; enveloping membrane. **s.-knife,** *n.* with fixed blade fitting into sheath. **sheathe,** *v.t.* put in sheath; encase, protect with casing. (O.E. *scǣth*)
sheave, *n.* grooved wheel of pulley.
sheave, *v.t.* sheaf. **sheaved,** *a.* (*Shake.*) made of straw.
shebang, *n.* (*Amer. sl.*) dwelling, shop; contrivance; concern.
shebeen, *n.* (*Ir.*) unlicensed liquor-shop. (Ir.)
Shechinah, same as **Shekinah.**
shed, *n.* roofed shelter, us. with one or more sides open. (*shade*)

shed, *v.t.* (*past, p.p.* same) let fall; slough off; allow, cause, to flow; diffuse, radiate.—*n.* parting in hair etc. (O.E. *scádan*)

sheeling, same as **shieling.**

sheen, *n.* gloss, lustre; brightness.—*a.* (*obs.*) bright, gleaming. **sheeny,** *a.* (O.E. *scéne,* beautiful+confusion with *shine*)

sheeny, *n.* (*colloq.*) Jew.

sheep, *n.* (*pl.* same) four-footed animal with woollen fleece; feeble bashful person; (*pl.*) pastor's flock. **black s.,** disreputable member of family. **s.'s eyes,** languishing glances. **s.-biter,** *n.* (*Shake.*) poor sneaking fellow. **s.-cote,** *n.* shelter for sheep. **s.-dip, s.-wash,** *nn.* preparation for cleansing sheep of vermin. **s.-dog,** *n.* kind used for herding sheep, esp. collie. **s.-hook,** *n.* shepherd's crook. **s.-run, s.-walk,** *nn.* tract of land on which sheep are pastured. **sheepfold,** *n.* enclosure for penning sheep in. **sheepish,** *a.* bashful, embarrassed. **sheepshank,** *n.* knot in rope to shorten it temporarily. **sheepskin,** *n.* rug, leather, parchment, made from skin of sheep. (O.E. *scéap*)

sheer, *a.* pure, unmixed; downright; perpendicular; (of fabrics) delicately fine, transparent.—*adv.* outright; perpendicularly. (M.E. *schere*)

sheer, *v.i.* (of ship) deviate from course; swerve.—*n.* act of sheering; upward curve of deck towards bow or stern. **s. off,** go away.

sheers, sheer-legs, *n.pl.* hoisting-apparatus of two poles joined together at top and fitted with tackle. **sheer-hulk,** *n.* dismantled ship fitted with sheers for harbour use.

sheet, *n.* rope at lower corner of sail for working it; (*pl.*) open space at bow or stern of open boat. **s. home,** extend (square sail) by sheets till it is as flat as possible. **three ss. in the wind,** (*sl.*) tipsy. (O.E. *scéat,* corner)

sheet, *n.* one of two broad pieces of linen etc. used as inner bed-clothes; piece (of paper); thin plate; broad flat expanse; newspaper.—*v.t.* furnish, cover, with sheets. O.E. *scéte*)

sheet-anchor, *n.* large anchor used only in emergencies; support in extremity. (*shoot*)

sheik, sheikh, *n.* Arab chief. (Arab. *shaikh*)

sheiling, same as **shieling.**

shekarry, same as **shikari.**

shekel, *n.* old Jewish weight or silver coin; (*pl., colloq.*) cash. (Heb. *shāqal,* weigh)

Shekinah, *n.* visible presence and glory of Jehovah. (Heb.)

sheldrake, *n.* (*fem.* **shelduck**) bright-plumaged wild duck; (*Amer.*) merganser.

shelf, *n.* (*pl.* **shelves**) board fixed on wall or in cupboard for holding articles; ledge on cliff-face; reef, shoal.

shell, *n.* hard outside covering of nut, egg, shell-fish etc.; framework; light inner coffin; kind of light racing boat; explosive projectile; intermediate form at school; outward show; (*poet.*) lyre; (*Amer.*) cartridge. —*v.t.* and *i.* take out of shell; remove pod from; cover with shells; bombard. **come out of one's s.,** throw off reserve. **s. out,** (*sl.*) pay up. **shell-fish,** *n.* aquatic animal with shell, e.g. oyster, crab. **s.-jacket,** *n.* kind of military undress jacket. **s.-lac,** *n.* shellac. **s.-shock,** *n.* nervous disorder caused by shock of bombardment. **shellback,** *n.* (*sl.*) old sailor. (O.E. *scell*)

shellac, *n.* lac prepared in thin plates for varnishing.—*v.t.* (*past, p.p.* **shellacked**) coat with this. (*shell; lac*)

Shelta, *n.* kind of secret back-slang used by Irish gipsies and tinkers.

shelter, *n.* protection, cover; place giving protection, refuge; shed, cabin.—*v.t.* and *i.* give shelter to, shield, cover; take shelter.

shelty, sheltie, *n.* Shetland pony.

shelve, *v.t.* place on shelf; put aside, defer consideration of.

shelve, *v.i.* slope gently, incline.

shelves, see **shelf.**

shemozzle, *n.* (*sl.*) rough-and-tumble, uproar.

shend, *v.t.* (*past, p.p.* **shent**) (*Spens.*) blame, reproach; disgrace; ruin. (O.E. *scendan*)

Sheol, *n.* the Hebrew Hades. (Heb.)

shepherd, *n.* (*fem.* **shepherdess**) one who tends sheep; pastor.—*v.t.* tend as shepherd; manœuvre, marshal, in particular direction. **the good S.,** Christ. **s.'s crook,** hooked staff. **s.'s pie,** of mince covered with mashed potatoes. **s.'s plaid,** cloth with black and white check. **s.'s-club, s.'s-knot, s.'s-purse,** *nn.* kinds of plant. (*sheep; herd*)

sheppy, *n.* sheep-cote. (*sheep*)

Sheraton, *n.* a severe 18th-century style of furniture. (designer)

sherbet, *n.* oriental drink of diluted fruit juice; effervescent drink made by mixing chemical powder with water. (Arab. *shariba,* drink)

sherd, see **shard.**

shereef, sherif, *n.* descendant of Mohammed through Fatima; title of certain Arab princes. **shereefian, sherifian,** *a.* (Arab. *sharīf,* lofty)

sheriff, *n.* chief administrative official of county; (*Scot.*) chief magistrate of county. **sheriffalty, sheriffdom, sheriffhood, sheriffship,** *nn.* (*shire; reeve*)

sherry, (*arch.*) **sherris,** *n.* a white Spanish wine. **s.-glass,** *n.* holding about four table-spoonfuls. (*Xeres* in Spain)

sheuch, *n.* (*Scot.*) ditch.—*v.t.* dig; plant temporarily.

shew, shewn, see **show.**

shewbread, *n.* unleavened bread used in ancient Jewish ritual. (*shew*)

shibboleth, *n.* word, custom, used to test a person's nationality, class, party etc.; party catchword. (Heb.)

shield, *n.* broad plate carried for defence, us. on left arm; protective covering, guard.—*v.t.* protect, defend, screen; (*Shake.*) forfend. (O.E. *sceld*)

shieling, *n.* (*Scot.*) highland shepherd's hut or shelter.

shier, shiest, same as **shyer, shyest.**

shift, *v.t.* and *i.* change position (of); remove, transfer; change form or character; contrive, manage; (*arch.*) change (clothing).—*n.* change in position; expedient, resource; trick, dodge; relay of workmen, time worked by them; (*arch.*) chemise. **make s.,** manage somehow, get along. **s. for oneself,** manage without help. **s. one's ground,** change position in argument. **shiftless,** *a.* incapable, feckless. **shifty,** *a.* tricky, evasive; (of wind) unreliable; (*rare*) resourceful. (O.E. *sciftan*, divide)

shikar, *n.* (*Anglo-Ind.*) hunting, sport; game.—*v.i.* and *t.* hunt. **shikari, shikaree,** *n.* hunter; sportsman's native attendant. (Hind.)

shillelagh, shillelah, *n.* (*Ir.*) stout cudgel, esp. of blackthorn. (place)

shilling, *n.* silver coin worth 12*d.* **cut off with a s.,** deprive of expected legacy. **take King's, Queen's, s.,** enlist. (O.E. *scilling*)

shilly-shally, *v.i.* vacillate, hesitate.—*n.* inability to make up one's mind. (*shall I?*)

shilpit, *a.* (*Scot.*) weak, puny; pale, sickly; insipid.

shily, same as **shyly.**

shim, *n.* thin slip used in machinery to make parts fit.—*v.t.* fit thus.

shimmer, *n.* fitful or faint light.—*v.i.* shine with this, glimmer. (O.E. *sciman*, shine)

shimmy, *n.* (*colloq.*) chemise. (corrupt.)

shimmy, *n.* and *v.i.* (*Amer.*) dance with wriggling movements.

shimosē, *n.* Japanese explosive made from picric acid. (inventor)

shin, *n.* front of leg below knee; shank.—*v.t.* and *i.* kick shins of, hack; climb or swarm (up). **s.-bone,** *n.* tibia. **s.-guard, s.-pad,** *nn.* to protect shin. (O.E. *scinu*)

shindig, *n.* (*Amer. sl.*) social function.

shindy, *n.* (*colloq.*) row, disturbance.

shine, *v.i.* (*past. p.p.* **shone**) emit light; be bright, glow; be brilliant or conspicuous.—*v.t.* (*past, p.p.* **shined**) polish (boots).—*n.* lustre, gloss; bright weather; (*sl.*) fuss, row; (*pl., Amer. sl.*) capers, tricks. **take a s. to,** (*Amer. sl.*) take a fancy for. **shiner,** *n.* (*sl.*) sovereign; (*Amer.*) freshwater fish like carp; (*pl.*) money. (O.E. *scinan*)

shingle, *n.* wooden roof-tile; style of cutting women's hair close at nape of neck; (*Amer.*) small signboard.—*v.t.* cover (roof) with shingles; cut (hair) in shingle. (L. *scandula*)

shingle, *n.* mass of pebbles on seashore.

shingles, *n.pl.* disease with eruptions often forming band round part of waist. (L. *cingere*, gird)

shinny, same as **shinty.**

Shinto, *n.* native Japanese religion, mainly ancestor-worship. **Shintoism,** *n.* its principles. **Shintoist,** *n.* (Chin. *shin tao*, way of the gods)

shinty, *n.* rough form of hockey; stick used in it.

shiny, *a.* glossy, polished; worn smooth.

-ship, *n.suf.* status of, as in **kingship**; skill of, as in **scholarship.**

ship, *n.* large sea-going vessel; (*naut.*) sailing-vessel with three or more square-rigged masts.—*v.t.* and *i.* send by ship; take, go, on board; engage for service on ship; fix (mast) in place for use; lay (oars) inside boat. **s. a sea,** have wave break over gunwale. **s. biscuit,** hard coarse kind. **s.'s husband,** (*naut.*) owner's agent in management of ship. **take s.,** embark. **s.-breaker,** *n.* one who buys old ships to dispose of the parts. **s.-broker,** *n.* agent for sale or insurance of ships. **s.-canal,** *n.* one large enough for sea-going vessels. **s.-chandler,** *n.* dealer in ship's requisites. **s.-money,** *n.* old tax for providing navy. **s.-tire,** *n.* (*Shake.*) kind of head-dress. (O.E. *scip*)

shipboard, *n.* **on s.,** on board ship.

shipbuilder, *n.* one who constructs ships.

shipload, *n.* full cargo of ship.

shipmaster, *n.* captain of merchant vessel.

shipmate, *n.* fellow sailor.

shipment, *n.* putting of goods on board; goods shipped.

shippen, *n.* (*prov.*) cowhouse. (O.E. *scypen*)

shipper, *n.* importer or exporter.

shipping, *n.* ships collectively. **s.-articles,** *n.pl.* articles of agreement between captain and crew.

shippon, same as **shippen.**

shipshape, *a.* in good order, tidy.

shipway, *n.* inclined way for building and launching of vessels.

shipwreck, *n.* loss of vessel at sea; vessel so lost; ruin, destruction.—*v.t.* and *i.* destroy by, suffer, shipwreck; cast ashore; ruin.

shipwright, *n.* shipbuilder's workman.

shipyard, *n.* place where ships are built.

shir, same as **shirr.**

shire, *n.* county. **s. horse,** large breed of draught horse. **the ss.,** midland counties; hunting district incl. Leicestershire, Rutland, and Northamptonshire. (O.E. *scir*)

shirk, *v.t.* and *i.* try to get out of, refuse to face (duty, danger etc.).—*n.* shirker.

shirr, *v.t.* (*Amer.*) gather (material) with parallel threads run through.—*n.* puckering made by shirring.

shirt, *n.* man's sleeved undergarment for upper part of body; woman's blouse with collar and cuffs. **boiled s.**, one with starched front. **keep one's s. on**, (*sl.*) keep one's temper. **put one's s. on**, bet all one can on. **s.-front**, *n.* starched front of shirt; dicky. **in one's s.-sleeves**, with jacket off. **s.-waist**, *n.* (*Amer.*) woman's blouse. **shirting**, *n.* material for shirts. **shirty**, *a.* (*sl.*) in a bad temper, angry. (O.E. *scyrte*)

shit, shite, *n.* (*vulg.*) excrement.—*v.i.* and *t.* evacuate bowels (on).

shive, *n.* (*Shake.*) slice.

shiver, *n.* small fragment, splinter.—*v.t.* break to shivers. **s. my timbers!** old nautical exclamation. (*shive*)

shiver, *v.i.* tremble with cold or fear, shudder.—*n.* act of shivering. (M.E. *chiveren*)

shoal, *n.* submerged sand-bank, esp. one that shows at low tide; shallow place; hidden danger.—*a.* shallow.—*v.i.* get shallower. (O.E. *sceald*)

shoal, *n.* large number of fish swimming together; crowd.—*v.i.* form shoals.

shock, *n.* group of sheaves set upright in field.—*v.t.* arrange in shocks.

shock, *n.* shaggy mass of hair. **s.-headed**, *a.*

shock, *n.* violent jolt or impact, abrupt forcible onset; agitation, surprise, offence, suddenly caused; event or experience causing this; physical prostration caused by injury; sensation caused by passage of electricity through body; (*colloq.*) paralytic stroke.—*v.t.* affect with horror or disgust, scandalize; (*Shake.*) meet in conflict. **s. tactics**, relying on weight and impact. **s. troops**, picked troops for attacking. **shocker**, *n.* (*sl.*) very bad specimen; sensational novel. **shocking**, *a.* revolting; scandalous, improper; very bad. (F. *choquer*, clash)

shod, see **shoe**.

shoddy, *n.* fibre got by shredding old cloth; cloth made partly of this.—*a.* made of shoddy; cheap and nasty, trashy.

shoe, *n.* (*pl.* **shoes**, *arch.* **shoon**) outer covering for foot not enclosing ankle; thing like shoe, drag for wheel, mast-socket, ferrule.—*v.t.* (*past, p.p.* **shod**) fit with shoes or shoe. **dead man's ss.**, expectation of inheritance. **in one's ss.**, in his position. **s.-buckle**, *n.* ornamental buckle on instep of shoe. **shoelace**, (*arch.*) **shoestring**, *nn.* lace for fastening shoe. **shoeblack**, *n.* one who polishes boots and shoes of passers-by. **shoehorn**, *n.* implement for easing heel into back of shoe. **shoemaker**, *n.* maker of boots and shoes. (O.E. *scóh*)

shog, *v.i.* and *t.* (*Shake.*) go away; (*Scot.*) shake, jog.

shogun, *n.* military governor of Japan in feudal times before 1868. **shogunate**, *n.* (Jap.=generalissimo)

shola, *n.* thicket or jungle in S. India. (Tamil)

shone, see **shine**.

shoo, *int.* for driving off birds.—*v.t.* scare away with this. (imit.)

shoogle, *v.t.* and *i.* (*Scot.*) shake, wobble. **shoogly**, *a.*

shook, *n.* set of staves and headings for cask.

shook, see **shake**.

shooldarry, *n.* (*Anglo-Ind.*) small tent with steep sloping roof. (Hind.)

shoon, see **shoe**.

shoot, *v.i.* and *t.* (*past, p.p.* **shot**) move swiftly, flash, dart; issue; put forth buds, sprout; jut (out); be carried swiftly over (rapids) or through (bridge); propel quickly; emit, thrust out; discharge (gun); hit, kill, with bullet etc.; shoot game in; slide (bolt) home; photograph (cinema scene); (*football*) kick at goal.—*n.* young branch; sloping trough for discharging goods from height, chute; shooting-party; (*Shake.*) shot.—*int.* (*Amer.*) say what is in your mind. **s. a line**, (*R.A.F. sl.*) brag, exaggerate. **s. cuffs**, shake them into view. **s. rubbish**, tilt it out of cart. **s. the moon**, (*sl.*) decamp by night. **s. the sun**, take its altitude at noon with sextant. **s. up**, grow rapidly; rise abruptly; (*Amer. sl.*) terrorize with firing. (O.E. *scéotan*)

shooting, *n.* tract of land where game is preserved, right of shooting over this. **s. star**, meteor. **s.-box**, *n.* small house for use in shooting season. **s.-gallery**, *n.* place for shooting at targets with miniature rifles. **s.-iron**, *n.* (*sl.*) revolver.

shop, *n.* room, building, for retail sale of goods; workshop, works building; talk about one's own work, technicalities.—*v.i.* and *t.* make purchases at shops; (*sl.*) get (person) arrested. **the S.**, (*sl.*) Woolwich Academy. **all over the s.**, (*sl.*) in disorder. **shut up s.**, abandon enterprise. **s. assistant, s.-girl**, *n.* employee in retail shop. **s.-soiled, s.-worn**, *aa.* tarnished from being exposed for sale. **s.-steward**, *n.* trade union official elected as spokesman by fellow workers. **shopkeeper**, *n.* one who keeps retail shop. **shoplifter**, *n.* one who steals from shop in guise of customer. **shoplifting**, *n.* **shopman**, *n.* shopkeeper; salesman. **shopper**, *n.* one who shops. **shoppy**, *a.* technical. **shopwalker**, *n.* overseer directing customers in large shop. (O.E. *sceoppa*, booth)

shore, *n.* land beside sea or large body of water.—*v.t.* (*Shake.*) put ashore. **in s.**, on water close to shore. **on s.**, on land. (M.E. *schore*)

shore, *n.* beam set obliquely as support. prop.—*v.t.* hold (up), support, with shore. (M.E. *schore*)

shore, *v.i.* (*Scot.*) threaten; offer.

shore, (*Shake.*) form of sewer.

shore, shorn, see **shear.**

short, *a.* not long or tall; brief; curt, abrupt; below standard; deficient, lacking; brittle, crumbling; (of vowel) not prolonged, unstressed; (*colloq.*) undiluted, neat.—*n.pl.* loose trousers cut above knee. — *adv.* abruptly; without reaching the end. —*v.i.* and *t.* (*electr.*) short-circuit; (*Shake.*) shorten. **be taken s.,** (*colloq.*) have sudden need to evacuate bowels. **bring up s.,** check abruptly. **come s. of,** fail to reach. **for s.,** as abbreviation. **in s.,** to sum up. **make s. work of,** dispose of, destroy, quickly. **run s.,** have or be too little. **sell s.,** sell securities which seller does not possess, but hopes to acquire at lower price before delivery is due. **s. of,** without going the length of. **s. time,** less than usual hours of work. **s. wave,** (*wireless*) from about 10 to 60 metres. **take up s.,** interrupt and contradict. (O.E. *sceort*)

shortage, *n.* deficiency.

shortbread, shortcake, *nn.* kind of rich short tea-cake.

short-circuit, *n.* deviation of electric current by a path of small resistance. —*v.t.* establish short-circuit in; cut off current from this; provide with short cut.

shortcoming, *n.* defect, inadequacy.

shorten, *v.t.* and *i.* make, become, short or shorter; reduce amount of (sail) spread.

shorthand, *n.* method of rapid writing by signs or contractions.

short-handed, *a.* not having the usual number of assistants.

shorthorn, *n.* one of breed of large heavy cattle.

short-lived, *a.* not living or lasting long.

shortly, *adv.* soon; briefly; curtly.

short-sighted, *a.* not able to see well at a distance; lacking foresight.

short-spoken, *a.* laconic.

short-tempered, *a.* easily angered.

short-waisted, *a.* with waist high up.

short-winded, *a.* easily made out of breath.

shot, *a.* woven with warp and woof of different colours so that colour changes with angle of view; variegated. (*shoot*)

shot, *n.* reckoning. **s.-free,** *a.* (*Shake.*) without having to pay. (*scot*)

shot, *n.* act of shooting; one who shoots, marksman; range of missile; attempt to hit; stroke; injection; part of cinema film taken at one time; (*colloq.*) attempt, guess; (*pl.* us. **shot**) solid projectile; one of small lead pellets in cartridge.—*v.t.* load, weight, with shot. **big s.,** (*Amer. colloq.*) important person. **s.-gun.** *n.* smooth-bore gun firing shot. **s.-tower,** *n.* for making shot by dropping molten lead through sieve.

shote, *n.* (*Amer.*) young hog.

shotten, *a.* (of herring) that has shed its roe.

shough, *n.* (*Shake.*) shaggy kind of dog.

should, see **shall.**

shoulder, *n.* part of body to which arm or foreleg is attached; part like shoulder, prominence; foreleg of animal as butcher's joint; (*pl.*) upper part of back.—*v.t.* push with shoulder, jostle; place on shoulder to carry; assume (responsibility). **rub ss. with,** meet. **set s. to the wheel,** make effort. **s. arms,** hold rifle upright at side. **s. to s.,** in close order; inseparably united. **s.-belt,** *n.* belt passing over shoulder and under other arm. **s.-blade,** *n.* broad flat bone of shoulder. **s.-shotten,** *a.* (*Shake.*) foundered in the shoulder. **s.-strap,** *n.* short strap on tip of shoulder. (O.E. *sculder*)

shout, *n.* loud cry.—*v.i.* and *t.* utter this, call out. **my s.,** (*sl.*) my turn to stand treat.

shove, *v.t.* and *i.* push; (*colloq.*) put. —*n.* push. **s.-halfpenny,** *n.* game in which coin is slid over marked board. (O.E. *scúfan*)

shovel, *n.* implement like large spade for lifting earth etc.; scoop.—*v.t.* and *i.* lift, move, with shovel. **s. hat,** broad-brimmed clerical hat. (*shove*)

shovelboard, *n.* shove-halfpenny; similar game played with large disks on ship's deck. (*shove*)

shoveller, *n.* spoonbill duck.

show, (*arch.*) **shew,** *v.t.* and *i.* (*p.p.* **shown,** *rare* **showed,** *arch.* **shewn, shewed**) present to view, exhibit; manifest, disclose; direct, guide, conduct; make clear, demonstrate; appear, be visible.—*n.* display, exhibition; parade, pomp; semblance, pretence; (*sl.*) concern, undertaking. **s. forth,** (*arch.*) display; expound. **s. off,** display to advantage; try to attract admiration. **s. up,** unmask; stand out; (*colloq.*) put in an appearance. (O.E. *scéawian,* see)

show-boat, *n.* river steamboat in which theatrical performances are held.

showbread, same as **shewbread.**

show-case, *n.* glass-topped case for displaying exhibits or goods.

show-down, *n.* revelation of truth.

shower, *n.* brief fall of rain; anything coming down like rain; great number. —*v.t.* and *i.* pour in copious flood; bestow liberally. **s.-bath,** *n.* in which water is showered from above. **showery,** *a.* rainy. (O.E. *scúr*)

show-girl, *n.* actress chosen for looks only.

showman, *n.* owner, manager, of travelling show, circus etc. **showmanship,** *n.* art of publicity.
shown, see **show.**
show-place, *n.* place that tourists go to see.
showroom, *n.* room for display of goods.
showy, *a.* gay, bright; ostentatious.
shram, *v.t.* (*dial.*) benumb with cold.
shrank, see **shrink.**
shrapnel, *n.* shell filled with bullets which it scatters on bursting; (incorrectly) shell-splinters. (inventor)
shred, *n.* small piece torn off, scrap; particle.—*v.t.* and *i.* (*past, p.p.* **shredded,** *arch.* **shred**) cut or tear to shreds. (O.E. *scréade*)
shrew, *n.* nagging woman; (also **s.-mouse**) mouse-like animal feeding on insects.—*v.t.* (*Shake.*) beshrew. (O.E. *scréawa*, shrew-mouse)
shrewd, *a.* astute, having common sense; keen, penetrating; (*arch.*) malicious, mischievous, grievous; (*Shake.*) shrewish. (*shrew*)
shrewish, *a.* sharp-tongued, nagging.
shriek, *n.* loud shrill cry, scream.—*v.i.* and *t.* scream, screech. (*screech*)
shrievalty, *n.* office, rank, of sheriff.
shrieve, *n.* (*Shake.*) sheriff. (*sheriff*)
shrift, *n.* (*arch.*) confession made to priest; shriving, absolution. **get short s.,** be treated summarily.
shright, *v.i.* and *n.* (*Spens.*) shriek.
shrike, *n.* butcher-bird.
shrill, *a.* high-pitched and piercing in sound; importunate.—*v.i.* and *t.* make shrill noise; utter shrilly. **s.-gorged,** *a.* (*Shake.*) high-voiced.
shrimp, *n.* small edible crustacean allied to lobster; small or puny person.—*v.i.* go catching shrimps.
shrine, *n.* casket holding sacred relics; tomb of saint, chapel for this; temple; place hallowed by associations.—*v.t.* enshrine. (L. *scrinium*, case for books)
shrink, *v.i.* and *t.* (*past* **shrank,** *p.p.* **shrunk, shrunken**) become smaller, contract; recoil (from), flinch; cause (flannel etc.) to contract by soaking. **shrinkage,** *n.* contraction, diminution. (O.E. *scrincan*)
shrive, *v.t.* (*arch.*; *past* **shrived** or **shrove,** *p.p.* **shriven**) hear confession of and absolve; confess (oneself). (O.E. *scrífan*)
shrivel, *v.i.* and *t.* contract into wrinkles, curl up with heat etc.
shroff, *n.* oriental money-changer or expert in detecting bad coins.—*v.t.* test (coin). (Arab. *çarrāf*)
shroud, *n.* sheet in which corpse is wrapped, winding-sheet; thing that conceals; (*Shake.*) shelter; (*pl., naut.*) supporting ropes from masthead to sides of ship.—*v.t.* and *i.* dress for burial; conceal, veil; (*arch.*) shelter. (O.E. *scrúd*, garment)
Shrovetide, *n.* confession and carnival time, three days preceding Lent. **Shrove Tuesday,** day before Ash Wednesday. (*shrive*)
shrow, (*Shake.*) form of **shrew.**
shrub, *n.* drink of rum etc. mixed with lemon and sugar. (Arab. *sharāb*)
shrub, *n.* woody plant smaller than tree with several stems rising from same root, bush. **shrubbery,** *n.* plantation of shrubs. (O.E. *scrybb*)
shrug, *v.t.* and *i.* (*past, p.p.* **shrugged**) draw up and contract (shoulders) as sign of doubt, indifference etc.—*n.* this movement.
shrunken, *a.* shrivelled, pinched. (*shrink*)
shuck, *n.* shell, husk, pod.—*v.t.* remove shucks from. **ss.,** *int.* (*Amer.*) of contempt.
shudder, *v.i.* tremble violently, shiver; feel strong repugnance.—*n.* violent tremor. (M.E. *schoderen*)
shuffle, *v.t.* and *i.* scrape (feet) along ground; walk with dragging steps; change order of, mix (cards in pack); intermingle, mix up; act or speak evasively.—*n.* act of shuffling; piece of equivocation or evasion. **s. off,** get rid of.
shuffleboard, same as **shovelboard.**
'shun, *abbr.* of **attention** as word of command.
shun, *v.t.* avoid, eschew. **shunless,** *a.* (*poet.*) inevitable. (O.E. *scunian*)
shunt, *v.t.* and *i.* move (train) from one line to another; put aside, shelve; (*electr.*) divert (current).—*n.* act of shunting; (*electr.*) conductor through which part of current can be diverted.
shut, *v.t.* and *i.* (*past, p.p.* same) close; close door or lid of; close up parts of, fold together; bar. **s. down,** stop working. **s. in,** enclose; block view from. **s. of,** (*sl.*) quit of. **s. off,** check flow of; debar. **s. out,** exclude. **s. up,** close securely; imprison; (*colloq.*) stop talking. **shutter,** *n.* screen for blocking window; (*phot.*) flap for regulating exposure of plate. (O.E. *scyttan*)
shuttle, *n.* cigar-shaped instrument holding weft-thread and carrying it between warp in loom. **shuttlecock,** *n.* cork stuck with feathers, hit with racket in badminton. (O.E. *scytel*, bolt)
shy, *a.* very self-conscious, bashful; chary (of); (of animals) timid; (*Amer. sl.*) short (of).—*v.i.* (of horse) start and swerve nervously.—*n.* act of shying. (O.E. *scéoh*)
shy, *v.t.* and *i.* and *n.* (*colloq.*) throw.
Shylock, *n.* merciless moneylender, grasping person. (name in play)
shyster, *n.* (*Amer. sl.*) twister; unprincipled lawyer.
si, same as **te.**
siamang, *n.* large black ape of Malaya. (Malay)

Siamese, *a.* and *n.* (native, language) of Siam. **S. cat,** cream-coloured kind with brown head and feet. **S. twins,** human twins joined together from birth; inseparables.

sib, *a.* related, kin. (O.E. *sibb*)

sibilant, *a.* hissing.—*n.* sibilant letter, e.g. *s, z.* **sibilance,** *n.* **sibilate,** *v.t.* and *i.* utter with hissing sound, hiss. **sibilation,** *n.* (L. *sibilare*, hiss)

sibyl, *n.* pagan prophetess; fortune-teller; old hag. **sibylline,** *a.* prophetic, occult. (Gk. *sibulla*)

sic, *adv.* so (used in brackets after erroneous or unusual expression in quotation to show that it is not writer's or printer's error). *s. vos non vobis,* thus you (toil) not for yourselves. (L.)

sic, siccan, *aa.* (*Scot.*) such.

siccar, same as **sicker.**

siccative, *a.* and *n.* (substance) that promotes drying. (L. *siccus*, dry)

sice, *n.* six at dice. (O.F. *sis*, six)

sice, same as **syce.**

sick, *v.t.* set upon; incite to attack. (*seek*)

sick, *a.* vomiting, suffering from nausea; ill; longing (for); utterly tired (of); (*sl.*) mortified; (*Shake.*) envious.—*v.i.* (*Shake.*) sicken. **s.-bed, s.-room,** *nn.* in which invalid lies. **s.-benefit,** *n.* allowance made to worker during illness. **s.-leave,** *n.* leave given because of illness. **sicken,** *v.i.* and *t.* become sick or nauseated; show signs of illness; nauseate. **sickening,** *a.* disgusting; (*colloq.*) very annoying. (O.E. *séoc*)

sicker, *a.* (*Scot.*) sure, certain; firm.—*v.t.* make sure.

sickle, *n.* reaping-hook with semicircular blade. (O.E. *sicol*)

sickly, *a.* inclined to be ill; unhealthy; causing nausea, mawkish; pale, feeble; (*Shake.*) of sickness.—*v.t.* (*Shake.*) make sickly.

sickness, *n.* being sick; disease.

side, *a.* (*Shake., Scot.*) wide, long.

side, *n.* surface, outer or inner face; border, edge; right or left portion of body; slope of hill; aspect; direction; party, faction, cause; team; line of descent; (*billiards*) side-spin, bias; (*colloq.*) swagger, conceit.—*a.* of or on side, lateral; incidental.—*v.i.* make common cause (with). **no s.,** (*Rugby football*) call of time. **off s.,** (*football*) between ball and opponent's goal. **on the s.,** in addition to one's regular work. **shake one's ss.,** laugh heartily. **s. by s.,** close together. **take s. of,** support; join party of. (O.E.)

side-arms, *n.pl.* swords or bayonets.

sideboard, *n.* long table or cabinet against dining-room wall; (*pl., sl.*) side-whiskers.

sideburns, *n.pl.* (*Amer.*) short side-whiskers.

sidecar, *n.* small car attached to side of motor-cycle; jaunting-car; kind of cocktail.

side-dish, *n.* extra dish at dinner.

side-glance, *n.* look directed to one side; slight reference.

side-issue, *n.* subsidiary matter.

sidelight, *n.* light coming from side; incidental information.

sideline, *n.* minor branch of business.

sidelong, *a.* oblique, not direct.—*adv.* obliquely.

side-piercing, *a.* (*Shake.*) heartrending.

sidereal, *a.* of, measured by, the fixed stars. (L. *sidus*, star)

sidero-, from Gk. *sidēros*, iron, used in **siderography,** *n.* steel engraving; **siderolite,** *n.* kind of meteorite.

side-saddle, *n.* woman's saddle on which rider sits with both feet on same side of horse.

sideshow, *n.* minor attraction at fair; subsidiary event.

side-slip, *v.i.* and *n.* slip to one side, skid (of car or aeroplane).

sidesman, *n.* churchwarden's assistant; usher in church.

side-splitting, *a.* uproariously funny.

side-step, *n.* and *v.i.* and *t.* step to one side; avoid (blow) thus.

side-track, *n.* railway siding.—*v.t.* shunt aside; shelve.

sidewalk, *n.* street pavement.

sideward, sidewards, *adv.* sideways.

sideways, *adv.* and *a.* towards, from, the side; edgewise.

sidewise, *adv.* sideways.

sidi, *n.* African negro; title given in India to African Moslems. (Urdu)

siding, *n.* short line beside main railway track for use in shunting.

sidle, *v.i.* move sideways, edge along.

sidy, *a.* (*colloq.*) swaggering.

siècle, *n.* century, age. *grand s.,* great age, esp. 17th century in France. (F.)

siege, *n.* surrounding of a place to compel its surrender, act of besieging; continued endeavour to gain possession; (*Shake.*) seat; rank; excrement.—*v.t.* (*arch.*) besiege. **lay s. to,** begin besieging. **raise s.,** abandon it. **s.-artillery, s.-gun,** *nn.* heavy kinds used in siege. **s.-train,** *n.* artillery and other siege appliances. (L. *sedēre*, sit)

sienna, *n.* an earthy pigment, either reddish-brown (**raw s.**) or yellowish-brown (**burnt s.**). (Italian town)

sierra, *n.* mountain-range with saw-like ridge. (Sp.)

siesta, *n.* midday nap taken in hot countries. (L. *sexta* hora, sixth hour)

sieve, *n.* utensil with network or perforated bottom for sifting; one who cannot keep secrets.—*v.t.* put through sieve, sift. (O.E. *sife*)

siffleur, *n.* (*fem. siffleuse*) whistling artiste. (F.)

sift, *v.t.* and *i.* separate coarser parts from finer with sieve; sort out;

examine critically; sprinkle (sugar etc.) from perforated spoon. (*sieve*)

sigh, *v.i.* and *t.* draw deep audible breath; make sound like this; pine, lament (for); utter with sigh.—*n.* act, sound, of sighing. (M.E. *sihen*)

sight, *n.* act or faculty of seeing; what is seen or worth seeing, spectacle; range of vision; pin etc. to guide eye in aiming fire-arm, aim taken with this; mental view, judgment; (*colloq.*) great quantity; (*Shake.*) pupil of eye; visor.—*v.t.* and *i.* catch sight of; aim, furnish, with sights. **at s.,** as soon as seen; on presentation for payment. **long, short, s.,** ability to see well only at long, short, distance. **lose s. of,** cease to see; fail to keep in mind. **s.-hole,** *n.* peep-hole. **sightless,** *a.* blind; invisible; (*Shake.*) ugly. **sightly,** *a.* comely. **sightseeing,** *n.* viewing objects of interest. **sightseer,** *n.* (O.E. *gesihth*)

sigillate, *a.* with impressed patterns; (*bot.*) bearing seal-like marks. (L. *sigillum*, seal)

sigma, *n.* Greek S. **sigmate, sigmoid,** *aa.* shaped like S or C. (Gk.)

sign, *n.* mark, symbol; gesture; indication, token, symptom (of); password; constellation; omen, miracle; signboard; (*Amer.*) spoor; (*Shake.*) standard.—*v.t.* and *i.* mark with sign; append signature to, ratify thus; make, indicate by, sign. **s. away,** relinquish by signing deed etc. **s. manual,** autograph signature, esp. of sovereign. **s. on,** formally accept employment. (L. *signum*)

signal, *n.* sign to convey message or order, esp. at a distance; message so conveyed; railway semaphore.—*a.* striking, notable.—*v.i.* and *t.* make signal; indicate, notify, by signal. **s.-book,** *n.* containing code of signals. **s.-box,** *n.* signalman's cabin. **signalize,** *v.t.* make notable, lend lustre to. **signaller,** *n.* soldier trained in signalling. **signalman,** *n.* man who works railway signals. (L. *signum*, sign)

signatory, *a.* and *n.* (party, state) that has signed an agreement or treaty.

signature, *n.* person's name written by himself; (*arch.*) characteristic mark; (*mus.*) flats and sharps after clef showing key; (*print.*) letter, figure, on first page of each sheet of book as guide to binder; such sheet after folding. **s. tune,** (*wireless*) tune used to announce particular band.

signboard, *n.* board with sign or inscription in front of shop or inn.

signet, *n.* private seal. **s.-ring,** *n.* ring with seal set in it. (O.F.)

signify, *v.t.* and *i.* mean; be sign of, portend; indicate, announce; matter. **significant,** *a.* full of meaning, highly expressive; momentous, important. —*n.* (*Shake.*) sign. **significance,** *n.* import; expressiveness; importance. **signification,** *n.* signifying; meaning, sense. **significative,** *a,* offering indications (of).

signor, signora, signorina, nn. Italian equivalents of Mr., Mrs., Miss.

signory, same as **seigniory.**

signpost, *n.* direction-post.

Sikh, *n.* member of military sect in Punjab. (Hind. = disciple)

silage, *n.* green fodder preserved for winter in silo, ensilage.—*v.t.* pack in silo.

silence, *n.* absence of sound, quiet; refraining from speech; secrecy, oblivion.—*v.t.* cause to be silent. **put to s.,** confute. **silencer,** *n.* device for deadening noise of fire-arm, motor-car exhaust etc. **silent,** *a.* not speaking; taciturn; noiseless, still. —*n.* (*Shake.*) stillness. (L. *silēre*, be silent)

silesia, *n.* kinds of thin linen or cotton cloth. (place)

silhouette, *n.* outline of object seen against light; portrait, picture, of this style, us. in solid black on white. —*v.t.* show up in outline; depict in silhouette. (person)

silica, *n.* hard mineral found in quartz and flint. **silicate,** *n.* salt of silicic acid. **siliceous, silicic,** *aa.* of, containing, silica. **silicify,** *v.t.* and *i.* turn into, impregnate with, silica; petrify. **silicification,** *n.* **silicon, silicium,** *nn.* non-metallic element found in silica. (L. *silex*, flint)

siliqua, silique, *n.* long narrow seed-pod. **siliquose, siliquous,** *aa.* (L.)

silk, *n.* fibre of silkworm's cocoon; thread, fabric, made from this; (*colloq.*) King's Counsel; (*pl.*) silk garments.—*a.* made of silk. **s. hat,** cylindrical hat covered with silk plush, top hat. **take s.,** become King's Counsel. **silken,** *a,* made of, like, silk; silky. **silkworm,** *n.* caterpillar that feeds on mulberry leaves. **silky,** *a.* soft and smooth like silk; suave. (O.E. *seolc*)

sill, *n.* slab of stone or wood at bottom of window or doorway. (O.E. *syll*)

sillabub, *n.* cream curdled with wine.

siller, *n.* (*Scot.*) money; silver.

Sillery, *n.* brand of champagne. (place)

silly, *a.* foolish, stupid, senseless; weak - minded; (*arch.*) innocent; simple; helpless; (*Shake.*) poor, hapless.—*n.* (*colloq.*) silly person. **s. point,** placed close to batsman. **s. season,** holiday period when there is dearth of serious news. (O.E. *sǣlig*, happy)

silo, *n.* pit for storing fodder in green compressed state. (Gk. *siros*, pit)

silt, *n.* mud or sand deposited by water. —*v.t.* and *i.* choke, be choked (up) with silt.

Silurian, *a.* and *n.* (of) division of Palaeozoic rocks between Ordovician and Devonian. **the Silurist,** the poet Henry Vaughan. (L. *Silures*, ancient tribe of Wales)

silvan, sylvan, *a.* of woods; wooded; rural. (L. *silva*, wood)

silver, *n.* a white metallic element; dishes, coins, made of this.—*a.* made of silver; silvery; (of hair) grey.—*v.t.* and *i.* plate with silver; make, become, silvery or grey; back (mirror-glass) with mercury. **s. age,** fabled age, literary period, showing slight decline from golden age. **s. fox,** kind with silver-tipped black fur. **s. Latin,** of silver age, about A.D. 14–180. **s. lining,** bright side of cloud or misfortune. **s. paper,** fine white tissue-paper; tinfoil. **s. point,** drawing with silver pencil on special paper. **s. sand,** fine white kind. **s. screen,** the cinema. **s. thaw,** slippery surface caused by sudden frost after thaw or rain. **s.-tongued,** *a.* plausible, eloquent. **silvern,** *a.* (*arch.*) silver. **silverside,** *n.* best side of round of beef. **silversmith,** *n.* worker in silver. **silverweed,** *n.* wayside plant with silvery leaves. **silvery,** *a.* white and lustrous like silver; (of sound) soft and clear. (O.E. *seolfor*)

silviculture, *n.* forestry. (*silvan*)

simian, *a.* and *n.* (of, like) ape or monkey; (*zool.*) (of) anthropoid ape. (L. *simia*, ape)

similar, *a.* having resemblance to, like; nearly corresponding. **similarity,** *n.* **simĭlĕ,** *n.* poetical comparison of two things, e.g. ' Errors, like straws, upon the surface flow.' **similitude,** *n.* guise, likeness; simile; counterpart. **similize,** *v.i.* and *t.* use, illustrate by, similes. (L. *similis*)

simkin, *n.* (*Anglo-Ind.*) champagne. (Urdu corrupt. of *champagne*)

simmer, *v.i.* and *t.* boil gently; be, keep, on point of boiling; be in state of suppressed rage or laughter.—*n.* simmering state. **s. down,** abate.

simnel-cake, *n.* rich spiced cake made at Christmas, Easter, or Mid-Lent. (L. *simila*, fine flour)

simoniac, *n.* person guilty of simony. **simoniacal,** *a.*

Simon Pure, genuine article or person. (name in play)

simony, *n.* crime of buying or selling church preferment. (*Simon* Magus in Bible)

simoom, *n.* dry hot dusty wind of deserts. (Arab. *samm*, poison)

simp, *n.* (*Amer. sl.*) fool. (*simpleton*)

simper, *v.i.* smile in silly way, smirk. —*n.* this expression.

simpkin, same as **simkin.**

simple, *a.* single, uncompounded; plain, not elaborate; clear, not intricate; easy to understand or solve; artless, not sophisticated; guileless, unsuspecting, credulous; of humble birth; sheer, mere.—*n.* medicinal herb, medicine made from it; ingredient in compound. **s. life,** without servants or luxuries. **s. interest,** charged on principal only. **simpleton,** *n.* foolish weak-minded person. *simpliciter*, *adv.* absolutely, not relatively. **simplicity,** *n.* simpleness. **simplify,** *v.t.* make simple or easy to understand. **simplification,** *n.* **simplism,** *n.* affected simplicity. **simply,** *adv.* in a simple manner; plainly; merely; utterly. (L. *simplex*)

simulacrum, *n.* (*pl.* **simulacra**) image, semblance; shadowy likeness, mere pretence, sham. (L.)

simulate, *v.t.* pretend to have or feel, feign; assume likeness of, mimic. **simulation,** *n.* **simulant,** *a.* **simular,** *a.* pretended, counterfeit.—*n.* pretender. (L. *similis*, like)

simultaneous, *a.* occurring at the same time. **simultaneity,** *n.* (L. *simul*, at the same time)

sin, *n.* wilful transgression of divine law, wicked act, offence; sinfulness. —*v.i.* commit sin; offend (against). **like s.,** (*sl.*) vigorously. **seven deadly ss.,** pride, covetousness, lust, gluttony, anger, envy, sloth. (O.E. *synn*)

sinapism, *n.* mustard plaster. (Gk. *sinapi*, mustard)

since, *adv.* from then till now; subsequently; ago.—*prep.* from the time of, after.—*conj.* from the time that; seeing that, because; (*Shake.*) when. (O.E. *siththan*, after that)

sincere, *a.* genuine, real, not pretended; honest, straightforward. **sincerity,** *n.* (L. *sincerus*)

sinciput, *n.* part of head from crown to forehead. (L. *semi*, half; *caput*, head)

sine, *n.* (*trigonometry*, *abbr.* **sin**). **s. of an angle,** ratio of the perpendicular subtending it in any right-angled triangle to the hypotenuse. (L. *sinus*, curve)

sīnĕ, *prep.* without. *s. dīĕ*, without date, indefinitely. *s. prōlĕ*, without issue. *s. qua non*, indispensable condition (lit. without which not). (L.)

sinecure, *n.* position, office, with salary but no duties. **sinecurist,** *n.* holder of sinecure. (L. *sine*, without; *cura*, care)

sinew, *n.* cord of fibrous tissue, tendon; (us. *pl.*) what gives power, mainstay; (*pl.*) muscles, brawn.—*v.t.* (*poet.*) join fast, sustain. **sinewy,** *a.* containing sinews; strong, vigorous. (O.E. *sinu*)

sinful, *a.* guilty of sin, wicked.

sing, *v.i.* and *t.* (*past* **sang,** *arch.* **sung;** *p.p.* **sung**) utter (words) with musical modulations; hum, ring; (of bird) pipe, twitter; (*poet.*) write poetry (about). **s. out,** (*sl.*) shout, bawl. **s. small,** behave humbly. (O.E. *singan*)

singe, *v.t.* and *i.* burn surface of, scorch; be so burned; remove hair or feathers from by burning.—*n.* singeing. (O.E. *sengan*)

Singh, *n.* great warrior (name used by all Sikhs). (Hind.)

singhara, *n.* water-chestnut of India.

single, *a.* one only, not double; alone, sole; separate; unmarried; for one; with one contestant on each side; simple, sincere; (of flower) with only one whorl of petals; (of ticket) for outward journey only; (*Shake.*) poor, weak.—*n.* single ticket; game between two players; hit scoring one.—*v.t.* choose (out). **s. blessedness,** (*joc.*) celibacy. **s.-breasted,** *a.* buttoning on one side only. **s.-foot,** *n.* (*Amer.*) horse's racking gait. **s.-handed,** *a.* and *adv.* without assistance. **s.-hearted,** *a.* free from duplicity or mixed motives. **s.-minded,** *a.* wholly devoted to one aim. **s.-soled,** *a.* (*Shake.*) mean, shabby. (L. *singuli,* individual)

singlestick, *n.* basket-hilted stick; fencing with this.

singlet, *n.* undervest. (*single*)

singleton, *n.* card which is the only one of its suit in a hand.

singly, *adv.* one by one; alone; (*Shake.*) uniquely.

sing-song, *n.* droning monotonous utterance; (*colloq.*) party where every one sings.—*a.* having monotonous rhythm.

singular, *a.* of, relating to, single person or thing; unusual, extraordinary; eccentric, odd; (*rare*) unique.—*n.* (*gram.*) singular number. **singularity,** *n.* being singular; peculiarity, odd trait. **singularize,** *v.t.* make singular; turn (word) into supposed singular form, e.g. 'Chinese' into 'Chinee.' (L. *singuli,* individual)

singule, *v.t.* (*Shake.*) single out.

Sinhalese, same as **Cingalese.**

sinister, *a.* inauspicious, ill-omened; evil-looking, malignant; wicked; left; (*heraldry*) on left side of shield, i.e. on right of observer facing it. **sinistral,** *a.* (of shell) with whorls going to left. **sinistrorse,** *a.* (*bot.*) twining spirally from right to left. (L.)

sink, *v.i.* and *t.* (*past* **sank,** *arch.* **sunk;** *p.p.* **sunk, sunken**) descend gradually; subside; be submerged, submerge, in water; droop, decline; grow weaker; become hollow; lower, degrade; send (ship) to bottom; make by digging out; engrave; invest; conceal, ignore; (*Shake.*) perish; ruin.—*n.* basin with outflow pipe in scullery etc.; cesspool. **s. in, into,** penetrate; thrust into. **s. of iniquity,** resort of scoundrels. **sinker,** *n.* weight used to sink line. **sinking** *n.* feeling of collapse. **sinking-fund,** *n.* money put aside for gradual payment of debt. (O.E. *sincan*)

sinke-a-pace, (*Shake.*) same as **cinque-pace.**

sinner, *n.* one who sins.

sinnet, same as **sennit.**

Sinn Fein, Irish political movement aiming at complete independence. (Ir.=we ourselves)

Sino-Japanese, *a.* of China and Japan.

sinology, *n.* study of Chinese history, literature etc. **sinologue, sinologist,** *nn.* one versed in sinology. **Sinophil, Sinophobe,** *nn.* and *aa.* (person) who admires, fears, China. (Gk. *Sinai,* Chinese)

sinter, *n.* siliceous deposit of mineral springs. (G.)

sinuate, *a.* wavy; (*bot.*) with wavy edge. **sinuation,** *n.* **sinuous,** *a.* winding, tortuous. **sinuosity,** *n.* sinuousness; bend. (*sinus*)

sinus, *n.* (*pl.* **sinuses, sinus**) cavity, esp. in bones of skull; fistula; (*bot.*) curve between lobes of leaf. **sinusitis,** *n.* inflammation of sinus. (L.=curve)

sip, *v.t.* and *i.* drink in small quantities. —*n.* small mouthful.

siphon, *n.* bent tube for drawing off liquids from higher to lower level by atmospheric pressure; bottle with internal tube and tap at top, for aerated water; (*zool.*) tubular organ for drawing in or ejecting fluid.—*v.t.* and *i.* draw off, be drawn off, with siphon. **siphonage,** *n.* action of siphon. **siphonal, siphonic,** *aa.* **siphonet, siphuncle,** *nn.* (*zool.*) kinds of siphon. (Gk.=tube)

sippet, *n.* one of the small pieces of toast served with mince etc.; sop.

sir, *n.* title of respect given to superiors or seniors; title preceding Christian name of knight or baronet; (*Shake.*) lord, gentleman.—*v.t.* address as sir. (*sire*)

sircar, *n.* (*Anglo-Ind.*) government or head of it; house-steward; native clerk. (Pers. *sar,* head; *kār,* work)

sirdar, *n.* chief, leader; British commander-in-chief of Egyptian army. (Pers. *sar,* head; *dār,* holding)

sire, *n.* father, male ancestor; male parent of animal; (*arch.*) Your Majesty.—*v.t.* (of animal) beget. (O.F.)

siren, *n.* fabled sea-nymph who lured sailors to destruction with sweet song; sweet singer; seductive or alluring woman; instrument producing sound by series of puffs of air or steam, hooter. (Gk. *seirēn*)

sirenian, *a.* and *n.* (member) of order of marine mammals incl. sea-cow. (*siren*)

sirgang, *n.* bright-green Asiatic bird allied to jackdaw. (native)

siriasis, *n.* sunstroke; sun-bath. (Gk. *seirios,* scorching)

sirkar, same as **sircar.**

sirloin, *n.* upper part of loin of beef. (F. *sur,* over; *longe,* loin)

sirocco, *n.* hot wind blowing across Italy from N. Africa. (Arab. *sharq,* East)

sirrah, *n.* (*arch.*) sir, fellow (used to inferior etc.). (*sir*)
sirree, *n.* (*Amer. colloq.*) sir.
sir-reverence, (*Shake.*) corrupt. of **save** (your) **reverence,** apology for unseemly expression.
sirup, see **syrup.**
sirvente, *n.* medieval form of lay, us. satirical. (F.)
sisal-grass, sisal-hemp, *nn.* fibre of American aloe. (*Sisal* in Yucatan)
siskin, *n.* small olive-green finch. (Pol. *czyż*+dim.)
sissoo, *n.* an Indian tree; its wood. (Hind. *sisū*)
sissy, *n.* (*Amer.*) sister, girl; effeminate boy or man. (*sister*)
sist, *v.t.* (*Scots law*) stay; summon.—*n.* act of staying execution on decrees for civil debts. (L. *sistere,* make to stand)
sister, *n.* daughter of same parents; female fellow-member or associate; member of sisterhood, nun; head nurse in hospital.—*a.* closely related, exactly similar.—*v.t.* (*Shake.*) resemble closely. **the three Ss.,** the Fates. **half-s.,** *n.* having one parent only in common. **s.-german,** *n.* full sister. **s.-in-law,** *n.* sister of husband or wife; wife of brother. **sisterhood,** *n.* female religious or charitable order; state of being sister. **sisterly,** *a.* like, befitting, affectionate as, a sister. (O.E. *swuster*)
sistrum, *n.* (*pl.* **sistra**) rattle used in ancient Egyptian rites. (Gk. *seiein,* shake)
Sisyphean, *a.* (of task) laborious and fruitless. (*Sisyphus,* who was condemned in Hades to push uphill a stone that always rolled down again)
sit, *v.i.* and *t.* (*past* **sat,** *arch.* **sate;** *p.p.* **sat**) rest on haunches; be in session; pose (for portrait); ride (horse); press, weigh (upon); fit, hang; rest, be situated; (of bird) remain covering eggs; perch. **s. down,** take seat. **s. down before,** begin siege of. **s. for,** represent in parliament; undergo examination for. **s. on,** hold meeting to discuss; (*sl.*) suppress, rebuke. **s. out,** sit through whole of; abstain from dancing. **s. pretty,** (*Amer. sl.*) be in favourable position. **s. tight,** (*sl.*) take no action. **s. under,** attend preaching of. **s. up,** straighten back while sitting; not go to bed; (*colloq.*) be astonished. (O.E. *sittan*)
sitar, *n.* kind of Indian guitar.
site, *n.* space occupied or to be occupied by building; situation. (L. *situs*)
sith, *n.* (*Spens.*) time. (O.E. *sith*)
sith, sithens, old forms of **since.**
sito-, sitio-, from Gk. *sitos,* food, used in **sitology, sitiology,** *n.* science of diet; **sitophobia, sitiophobia,** *n.* morbid aversion to food.
sitringee, *n.* (*Anglo-Ind.*) striped cotton carpet. (Bengali *satrangi*)
sitter, *n.* one who sits; (*colloq.*) easy shot or catch.
sitting, *n.* session; spell of work; seat rented in church; clutch (of eggs). **s.-room,** *n.* room other than bedrooms and kitchen; parlour.
situated, (*arch.*) **situate,** *aa.* placed. **situation,** *n.* place, position; state of affairs, circumstances; job, post. (*site*)
sitz-bath, *n.* hip-bath. (G. *sitzbad*)
six, *a.* and *n.* one more than five. **at ss. and sevens,** in confusion. **s.-shooter,** *n.* six-chambered revolver. **sixain,** *n.* six-line stanza. **sixer,** *n.* hit for six at cricket. **sixfold,** *a.* and *adv.* six times as much. **sixpence, sixpenny-bit,** *nn.* silver coin worth 6*d.* **sixte,** *n.* a guard in fencing. **sixteen,** *a.* and *n.* one more than fifteen. **sixteenth,** *a.* and *n.* **sixteenmo,** same as **sextodecimo. sixth,** *a.* next after fifth.—*n.* one of six equal parts. **sixthly,** *adv.* in the sixth place. **sixty,** *a.* and *n.* six times ten. **sixtieth,** *a.* and *n.* **sixty-four-mo,** (*abbr.* **64mo**) book of sheets folded into 64 leaves. (O.E.)
sizable, *a.* biggish.
sizar, *n.* undergraduate at Cambridge paying reduced fees. (*size*)
size, *n.* magnitude, dimensions; (formerly) standard of weight or measure; (*pl., Shake.*) allowances.—*v.t.* arrange according to size. **of a s.,** equal in size. **s. up,** take measure, form estimate, of. (*assize*)
size, *n.* thin kind of glue used to glaze paper, stiffen cloth etc.—*v.t.* treat with size. **sizy,** *a.* gluey.
sizzle, *n.* hissing spluttering noise.—*v.i.* make this. (imit.)
sjambok, *n.* heavy hide whip used in S. Africa.—*v.t.* flog with this. (Pers. *chābuk,* whip)
skail, *v.t.* and *i.* (*Scot.*) disperse, break up; empty; upset, spill.
skain, same as **skean.**
skald, same as **scald.**
skat, *n.* three-handed card game played with pack of 32. (G.)
skate, *n.* steel blade attached to boot for gliding over ice; roller-skate.—*v.i.* move on skates. (O.F. *eschace,* stilt)
skate, *n.* edible flat-fish of ray family. (O.N. *skata*)
skean, *n.* dirk. **s.-dhu,** *n.* dagger worn in stocking of highland dress. (Gael. *sgian,* knife; *dubh,* black)
skedaddle, *v.i.* (*sl.*) run away, make off.—*n.* hurried flight.
skee, same as **ski.**
skeely, *a.* (*Scot.*) skilful.
skeen, *n.* Himalayan ibex. (Tibetan *skyin*)
skeer, *Amer. sl.* form of **scare.**
skeeter, *n.* (*sl.*) mosquito.
skeigh, *a.* (*Scot.*) high-mettled, disdainful; skittish.
skein, *n.* folded coil of yarn, thread

etc.; tangle; flight of wildfowl. (O.F. *escaigne*)

skeleton, *n.* hard framework of animal or plant; bones separated from flesh and preserved in their natural position; framework; outline, abstract; very thin person. **s. at the feast,** thing that spoils pleasure. **s. in the cupboard,** disgrace kept secret from strangers. **s. key,** key with centre filed away, used for picking locks. **skeletal,** *a.* **skeletology,** *n.* scientific study of skeleton. **skeletonize,** *v.t.* reduce to skeleton or outline. (Gk. *skellein*, dry)

skelf, *n.* (*Scot.*) small splinter.

skelloch, *v.i.* and *n.* (*Scot.*) scream.

skellum, *n.* (*Scot.*) ne'er-do-well; scamp.

skelly, *v.i.* and *n.* (*Scot.*) squint.

skelp, *v.t.* and *i.* (*Scot.*) slap; spank; move quickly along.—*n.* slap.

skene, same as **skean.**

skep, *n.* straw beehive; wicker basket. (O.N. *skeppa*)

skepsis, skeptic, same as **scepsis, sceptic.**

skerry, *n.* rocky isle or reef. (O.N. *sker*)

sketch, *n.* rough drawing; preliminary draft; short play or essay.—*v.t.* and *i.* make sketch (of); plan roughly. **s.-map,** *n.* rough map. **sketchy,** *a.* vague; unfinished. (It. *schizzo*)

skew, *a.* slanting, oblique, set at an angle.—*adv.* aslant.—*n.* sloping top of buttress. **s.-eyed,** *a.* squinting. **s.-whiff,** *a.* (*colloq.*) askew. **skewback,** *n.* abutment which slopes to receive end of arch. **skewbald,** *a.* with patches of white and some colour other than black. (O.F. *eschever*, eschew)

skewer, *n.* wooden or metal pin for holding meat together; (*joc.*) sword. —*v.t.* fasten, transfix, with skewer.

ski, *n.* (*pl.* **ski, skis**) long wooden runner strapped to foot for moving over snow.—*v.i.* (*past, p.p.* **ski'd**) go on ski. **s.-joring,** *n.* sport in which skier is towed by horse. (Da.)

skiagraphy, *n.* X-ray photography. **skiagraph, skiagram,** *nn.* X-ray photograph. **skiagrapher,** *n.* **skiagraphic,** *a.* (Gk. *skia*, shadow; *graphein*, write)

skid, *n.* wooden support or fender; drag placed under wheel to reduce speed downhill; act of skidding, side-slip.—*v.t.* and *i.* support, protect, check, with skid; slide without rotating, slip sideways.

skier, *n.* one who skis.

skiff, *n.* small light row-boat. (F. *esquif*)

skiff, *v.i.* and *t.* (*Scot.*) glide, skim; graze.—*n.* act of skiffing.

skill, *n.* proficiency, expertness, dexterity.—*v.i.* (*arch.*) matter. **skilful,** *a.* proficient, adroit. **skilled,** *a.* having skill; trained, expert. (O.N. *skil*, distinction)

skillet, *n.* small metal cooking-pot with long handle and us. legs.

skill-less, *a.* (*rare*) without skill; knowing nothing (of).

skilly, *n.* thin gruel or soup served in prisons.

skim, *v.t.* and *i.* remove (cream, scum) from surface (of); glide lightly over, brush surface of; read superficially. **s.-milk,** *n.* milk from which cream has been skimmed.

skimble-skamble, *a.* rambling, incoherent.

skimmer, *n.* utensil for skimming milk; a long-winged sea-bird.

skimp, *v.t.* and *i.* give scanty measure (of), stint; be parsimonious. **skimpy,** *a.* scant, meagre.

skin, *n.* outer covering of animal body; hide; rind of fruit; outer layer; vessel for water etc. made of hide. —*v.t.* and *i.* remove skin from; abrade; peel; cover, become covered, with skin. **by the s. of one's teeth,** very narrowly. **save one's s.,** escape without injury. **s.-deep,** *a.* superficial. **s.-game,** *n.* (*Amer. sl.*) ruthless swindle. **skinflint,** *n.* stingy person, niggard. **skinful,** *n.* as much as one can drink or eat. (O.N. *skinn*)

skink, *n.* kind of lizard. (Gk. *skingkos*)

skink, *v.i.* and *t.* serve (liquor).—*n.* drink. **skinker,** *n.* tapster. (O.E. *scincan*, pour out)

skink, *n.* (*Scot.*) shin of beef.

skip, *v.i.* and *t.* leap lightly about, frisk; keep jumping rope as it is swung under one; make omissions, pass over, esp. in reading; (*sl.*) make off, bolt.—*n.* light jump, caper. **skipping,** *a.* flighty. **skipping-rope,** *n.* rope for skipping.

skip, *n.* cage, bucket, for hoisting men or materials in mine. (*skep*)

skip, *n.* captain of team at bowls or curling.

skip, *n.* servant at Trinity College, Dublin.

skipjack, *n.* jumping toy made from bird's wish-bone; kinds of jumping fish; impudent fellow, upstart.

skipper, *n.* captain of ship or team.—*v.t.* captain. (Du. *schip*, ship)

skipper, *n.* kinds of butterfly; (*Shake.*) flighty youngster.

skippet, *n.* round flat box for holding seal attached to parchment.

skippet, *n.* (*Spens.*) small boat. (O.E. *scip*, ship+dim.)

skirl, *n.* (*Scot.*) shrill sound, scream.—*v.i.* emit, utter, skirl.

skirmish, *n.* irregular fight between two small parties.—*v.i.* engage in desultory fighting. **skirmisher,** *n.* (O.H.G. *scirman*, fight)

skirr, *v.i.* and *t.* (*Shake.*) move rapidly, scour.

skirret, *n.* water-parsnip.

skirt, *n.* lower part of woman's dress or of long coat; outer edge, border; midriff of beef; (*sl.*) woman.—*v.t.*

and *i.* move, be, along edge (of). **skirting-board,** *n.* board running along bottom of room wall. (O.N. *skyrta,* shirt)

skit, *n.* light satirical literary work, burlesque, parody.

skit, *n.* (*colloq.*) crowd; (*pl.*) lots.

skite, *v.i.* (*Scot.*) glide, slip.

skitter, *v.i.* skim over water with splashes at intervals; fish by drawing bait along surface.

skittish, *a.* (of animal) frisky, frolicsome, easily frightened, fidgety; (of woman) given to flirting or gadding about.

skittles, *n.pl.* game like ninepins.—*int.* (*sl.*) of contempt. **skittle-alley,** *n.* for playing skittles in.

skiv, *n.* (*sl.*) sovereign.

skive, *v.t.* cut (leather) into slices; grind on skive.—*n.* wheel for polishing diamonds. (O.N. *skífa,* slice)

skivvy, *n.* (*colloq.*) maidservant.

sklent, *Scot.* form of **slant.**

skoal, *int.* good health! (O.N. *skál*)

skua, *n.* kinds of dark-brown gull. (O.N. *skúfr*)

skulk, *v.i.* sneak out of the way, lurk; shirk danger or duty.—*n.* skulker.

skull, *n.* bony case enclosing brain; bones of head. **s. and crossbones,** skull and thigh-bones as emblem of death. **s.-cap,** *n.* close-fitting brimless cap.

skunk, *n.* black-and-white striped American animal with offensive smell; its fur; (*sl.*) mean rascal.—*v.t.* (*Amer. sl.*) defeat (opponent) without his scoring. (Amer. Ind. *segongw*)

Skupshtina, *n.* parliament of Yugoslavia. (Serbian)

sky, *n.* (*pl.* **skies**) vault of heaven; upper atmosphere; weather, climate.—*v.t.* hit (ball) high in air; hang (picture) high on wall. **s.-blue,** *a.* and *n.* azure. **s.-high,** *a.* and *adv.* very high. **skyline,** *n.* outline of hill against sky. **s.-pilot,** *n.* (*sl.*) clergyman. **s.-writing,** *n.* writing in sky with aeroplane's smoke-trail. **skyer,** *n.* high hit at cricket. **skyey,** *a.* of, in, the sky; sky-blue. **skylark,** *n.* common lark.—*v.i.* caper about; play tricks. **skylight,** *n.* window in roof. **skysail,** *n.* sail above royals. **skyscape,** *n.* picture of sky and clouds. **skyscraper,** *n.* very tall building. **skyward,** *a.* and *adv.*, **skywards,** *adv.* toward the sky. (O.N. *ský,* cloud)

Skye, *n.* (also **S. terrier**) long-haired kind of Scotch terrier. (island)

slab, *n.* flat thick piece; outside piece sawn from log.—*v.t.* cut slabs from (log).

slab, *a.* (*arch.*) thick and sticky.—*n.* (*prov.*) slime.

slabber, same as **slobber.**

slack, *n.* small coal, coal-dust.

slack, *a.* loose, relaxed, not tight; slow, sluggish; inattentive, not keen; (of business) not brisk.—*n.* slack part of rope; (*colloq.*) spell of lazing; (*pl.*) trousers.—*v.t.* and *i.* slacken, loosen; slake (lime); (*colloq.*) work slowly, be lazy; (*Shake.*) neglect. **s. water,** at turn of tide. **slacken,** *v.t.* and *i.* make, become, slack or loose; diminish, abate. **slacker,** *n.* lazy person who scamps work, shirker. (O.E. *sleac*)

slag, *n.* dross or refuse left after smelting, clinkers; volcanic scoria.—*v.i.* form slag. (Swed. *slagg*)

slain, see **slay.**

slaister, *n.* (*Scot.*) dirty mess.—*v.i.* and *t.* make mess (of); bedaub.

slake, *v.t.* quench, satisfy (thirst etc.); mix (lime) with water. (*slack*)

slam, *v.t.* and *i.* shut, throw (down), violently; bang; (*sl.*) hit, beat; (*Amer. sl.*) criticize, censure.—*n.* sound of slamming, bang. **grand, little, s.,** (*cards*) winning of all, of all but one, tricks.

slander, *n.* false and malicious statement about a person; uttering of this, calumny; (*Shake.*) reproach, disgrace.—*v.t.* utter slander about, defame; (*Shake.*) reproach. **slanderous,** *a.* (*scandal*).

slang, *n.* word, expression, used in familiar speech but not regarded as standard English; jargon of a particular class etc.—*v.t.* (*sl.*) abuse with vulgar language. **slangy,** *a.* of, given to using, slang; (of dress) loud and flashy.

slank, see **slink.**

slant, *v.i.* and *t.* slope, incline.—*n.* oblique position; (*sl.*) view, line.—*a.* sloping. **slantindicular, slantendicular,** *a.* (*sl.*) slant. **slantwise,** *adv.* aslant. (Swed. *slinta,* slide)

slap, *n.* (*Scot.*) cleft between hills; gap in fence.

slap, *v.t.* strike with open hand.—*n.* such blow.—*adv.* directly, full. **s. in the face, rebuff. s.-bang,** *adv.* violently, headlong. **s.-up,** *a.* (*sl.*) smart, up-to-date. **slapdash,** *a.* impetuous; happy-go-lucky. **slapjack,** *n.* (*Amer.*) flapjack. **slapping,** *a.* (*sl.*) very large. **slapstick,** *n.* harlequin's wand; boisterous humour of knockabout kind. (imit.)

slash, *v.t.* and *i.* cut gashes in, slit; strike fiercely (at) with sword etc.—*n.* cutting blow; slit, gash. **slashing,** *a.* severe, destructive.

slat, *n.* thin flat narrow board, lath; (*pl., sl.*) ribs. (*slate*)

slat, *v.i.* and *t.* (of sail) flap, strike, noisily.

slate, *v.t.* (*colloq.*) criticize severely, rate.

slate, *n.* kinds of rock easily split into thin layers; flat plate of this for roofing, sheet of it in frame for writing on; its colour, bluish-grey.—*a.* made of slate.—*v.t.* cover with slates; (*Amer.*) suggest as political candidate. **clean s.**, unblemished record. **s.-club**, *n.* club providing Christmas dinners etc. from small weekly payments by members. **s.-pencil**, *n.* pencil of slate for writing on slate. **slater**, *n.* one who fixes slates; wood-louse. (O.F. *esclat*, splinter)

slattern, *n.* untidy slovenly woman, slut. **slatternly**, *a.*

slaughter, *n.* killing of animals for food; wholesale slaying. —*v.t.* butcher; massacre. **s.-house**, *n.* place where cattle are slaughtered, shambles. **slaughterous**, *a.* murderous. (O.N. *slátr*, meat)

Slav, *a.* and *n.* (member) of race incl. Russians, Poles, Bulgarians etc.

slave, *n.* person without freedom or personal rights, who is the legal property of another; drudge; victim of habit or vice.—*v.i.* and *t.* toil hard; (*Shake.*) make slave of. **s.-driver**, *n.* overseer of slaves at work; hard taskmaster. **s.-trade**, *n.* traffic in slaves. **slaver**, *n.* person, ship, engaged in slave-trade. (*Slav*)

slaver, *v.i.* and *t.* dribble, cover, with saliva; fawn upon, flatter.—*n.* saliva running from mouth; gross flattery. **slavery**, *a.* (Icel. *slafra*)

slavery, *n.* condition of slave, bondage; slave-owning as an institution; drudgery.

slavey, *n.* (*sl.*) maidservant. (*slave*)

Slavic, *a.* and *n.* (language) of Slavs.

slavish, *a.* servile, abject.

Slavism, *n.* common interests of Slav peoples; Slavic idiom. **Slavonian**, **Slavonic**, *aa.* Slavic. **Slavophil**, **Slavophobe**, *nn.* and *aa.* (person) who admires, fears, the Slavs.

slaw, *n.* (*Amer.*) salad of sliced cabbage. (*salad*)

slay, *v.t.* (*past* **slew**, *p.p.* **slain**) kill. (O.E. *sléan*)

sleave, *n.* (*Shake.*) floss-silk.

sleazy, *a.* thin and flimsy.

sledge, **sled**, *nn.* framework on runners for travelling over snow or ice, toboggan.—*v.i.* and *t.* go, convey, by sledge. (Du. *slede*)

sledge, *n.* (also **s.-hammer**) large heavy hammer for two hands. (O.E. *sléan*, smite)

slee, *a.* (*Scot.*) sly; skilful.

sleek, *a.* smooth, glossy; healthily plump; plausible.—*v.t.* make sleek by stroking. (O.N. *slikr*)

sleep, *n.* natural suspension of consciousness at night; spell of this.—*v.i.* and *t.* (*past*, *p.p.* **slept**) be or fall asleep; pass night, lodge; be inactive; be dead; have beds for; (of top) spin so rapidly as to seem motionless. **go to s.**, fall asleep. **s. in**, sleep on the premises; (*Scot.*) oversleep. **s. off**, get rid of by sleeping. **s. on**, have night's interval before deciding about. **s.-walker**, *n.* somnambulist. **let sleeping dogs lie**, do not make needless trouble. **sleeping partner**, who takes no part in management of business. **sleeping-bag**, *n.* for sleeping in the open. **sleeping-car**, *n.* railway carriage with sleeping berths. **sleeping-draught**, *n.* opiate. **sleeping-sickness**, *n.* tropical African disease spread by tsetse fly. **sleeper**, *n.* one who sleeps; timber supporting rails of railway-line; sleeping-car. **sleepless**, *a.* wakeful; vigilant; unremitting. **sleepy**, *a.* drowsy; lazy, not alert; (of pears) soft yet juiceless. **sleepy sickness**, inflammation of the brain, encephalitis lethargica. **sleepyhead**, *n.* sleepy person. (O.E. *slǽp*)

sleet, *n.* snow or hail mixed with rain. —*v.i.* rain sleet. **sleety**, *a.*

sleeve, *n.* part of garment enclosing arm; (*mech.*) tube fitting over part. **have up one's s.**, have unseen but ready to produce. **laugh in one's s.**, laugh secretly. **s.-hand**, *n.* (*Shake.*) cuff. **s.-link**, *n.* linked buttons for fastening cuff. **sleeveless**, *a.* (*Shake.*) futile. (O.E. *slýf*)

sleided, *a.* (*Shake.*) unwoven. (*sley*)

sleigh, *n.* sledge, esp. one drawn by horses or reindeer.—*v.i.* and *t.* drive in sleigh. (*sled*)

sleight, *n.* (*arch.*) dexterity, cunning. **s.-of-hand**, *n.* juggling, legerdemain. (O.N. *slægr*, sly)

slender, *a.* thin, slim; slight, scanty.

slept, see **sleep**.

sleuth, *n.* (also **s.-hound**) bloodhound; detective. (*slot*)

slew, **slue**, *v.t.* and *i.* and *n.* swing round, turn on pivot.

slew, see **slay**.

sley, *n.* weaver's reed. (O.E. *slǽ*)

slice, *n.* thin flat piece; part, share; broad knife for serving fish; fire-shovel; (*golf*) stroke making ball curl to right.—*v.t.* and *i.* cut into slices; strike (ball) with drawing motion, cut. (O.F. *esclice*, splinter)

slick, *a.* (*colloq.*) smooth-running; clever, deft; smart but unsound.—*adv.* full, clean. **slicker**, *n.* (*Amer.*) waterproof coat. (*sleek*)

'slid, *int.* (*Shake.*) by God's lid.

slid, see **slide**.

slidder, *v.i.* slip, slide. **sliddery**, *a.* slippery.

slide, *v.i.* and *t.* (*past*, *p.p.* **slid**) move smoothly over, slip, glide; pass gradually (into).—*n.* act of sliding; strip of smooth ice for sliding on; chute; buckle without tongue; picture on glass for magic-lantern, glass slip holding object for microscopic examination. **s.-rule**, **sliding rule**, *n.* ruler with graduated sliding part for making calculations. **sliding scale**, schedule for automatically varying one thing (e.g. wages) according to the fluctuations of another thing (e.g. cost of living). **slider**, *n.* one who slides; (*sl.*)

ice-cream between wafer biscuits. (O.E. *slidan*)

slight, *a.* small, inconsiderable; trivial; slim, fragile; (*Shake.*) careless.—*v.t.* disregard as insignificant; treat with disrespect.—*n.* intentional neglect, discourtesy. **slighting,** *a.* disparaging.

'slight, *int.* (*Shake.*) by God's light.

slily, same as slyly.

slim, *a.* slender, not stout; slight; (*sl.*) wily, cunning.—*v.i.* reduce one's weight by diet etc. (Du.=sly)

slime, *n.* sticky slippery half-liquid substance, glutinous mud, mucus.—*v.t.* smear with slime. **slimy,** *a.* like, covered with, slime; repulsive; fawning. (O.E. *slim*)

sling, *n.* (*Amer.*) drink of sweetened gin and water.

sling, *n.* pocket with string attached for hurling stone; hanging bandage for wounded arm; rope for hoisting weights.—*v.t.* (*past.* **slung,** *arch.* **slang;** *p.p.* **slung**) throw, lift, with sling; hurl; hang so as to swing, suspend. **s. ink,** (*sl.*) write. (O.N. *slyngva*, throw)

slink, *v.i.* (*past* slunk, *rare* **slank;** *p.p.* **slunk**) move stealthily or furtively, sneak. (O.E. *slincan*, creep)

slink, *v.t.* and *i.* (*past, p.p.* **slinked**) (of animal) give birth to prematurely, miscarry.—*n.* prematurely born calf etc. **slinky,** *a.* thin, lean.

slip, *v.i.* and *t.* slide, glide; lose one's foothold; go, put, quietly or quickly; let go, release; escape from; make mistake; (of animal) give birth (to) prematurely.—*n.* act of slipping; error, lapse; loose garment or cover; under-bodice; shoot for grafting, cutting; narrow strip; leash for dog; slipway; small sole; (*cricket*) position, fielder, behind wicket on off side; (*Shake.*) counterfeit coin. **give one the s.,** escape from him. **s.-carriage,** *n.* one which is uncoupled while the train is running. **s.-knot,** *n.* knot that slips along the rope round which it is made; knot that can be undone at a pull. (M.E. *slippen*)

slipper, *n.* loose indoor shoe; drag for wagon wheel.—*v.t.* spank with slipper. **s.-bath,** *n.* kind with cover over legs. **slippered,** *a.* wearing slippers. **slipperwort,** *n.* calceolaria. (*slip*)

slippery, *a.* so smooth as to cause slipping; difficult to hold or catch; evasive, unreliable, shifty. **slipper,** *a.* (*Shake.*) slippery. (O.E. *slipor*)

slippy, *a.* slippery. **look s.,** (*sl.*) make haste.

slipshod, *a.* having shoes down at heel; slovenly, careless.

slipslop, *n.* sloppy food; sentimental trashy work or talk. (*slop*)

slipstream, *n.* (*aviation*) stream of air driven astern by propeller.

slipway, *n.* inclined plane for launching ships; sloped landing-stage.

slit, *v.t.* and *i.* cut, tear, lengthwise or into strips; make slit in.—*n.* long cut; narrow opening. (O.E. *slitan*, tear)

slither, *v.i.* (*colloq.*) slide and bump. **slithery,** *a.* slippery. (*slidder*)

sliver, *n.* small narrow piece torn off, splinter.—*v.t.* and *i.* tear off as sliver; break into shivers. (O.E. *slifan*, split)

slob, *n.* mud, ooze; shiftless person.

slobber, *v.i.* and *t.* run at mouth, dribble; wet with saliva; bungle.—*n.* dribbling saliva: maudlin talk.

slocken, *v.t.* (*Scot.*) quench.

sloe, *n.* blackthorn; its bluish-black fruit. (O.E. *slá*)

slog, *v.i.* and *t.* hit hard and wildly; trudge doggedly.—*n.* hard random hit.

slogan, *n.* war-cry of highland clan; political watchword; catchy phrase used in advertising. (Gael. *sluagh*, army; *gairm*, cry)

sloid, *n.* system of manual training by wood-carving. (Swed. *slöjd*, skill)

sloop, *n.* one-masted fore-and-aft-rigged vessel like cutter. (Du. *sloep*)

slop, *n.* (*sl.*) policeman. (back-slang)

slop, *n.* spilt liquid; (*pl.*) dirty water; semi-liquid food for invalids etc.—*v.i.* and *t.* be spilt, spill. **s. over,** be maudlin. **s.-basin,** *n.* for dregs from tea-cups. **s.-pail,** *n.* for slops from bedroom. (M.E. *sloppe*, puddle)

slop-chest, slop-room, *nn.* chest, room, from which clothes are issued on ship. **slop-shop,** *n.* shop selling cheap clothes. (*slops*)

slope, *n.* inclined position, slant; sloping ground, declivity.—*v.i.* and *t.* incline, slant; (*sl.*) make off; saunter. **s. arms,** place rifle in sloping position on shoulder.

sloppy, *a.* semi-liquid, watery; slovenly, slipshod; maudlin.

slops, *n.pl.* cheap ready-made clothing; (*arch.*) wide trousers. (O.N. *sloppr*, gown)

slosh, *n.* slush; (*sl.*) heavy blow.—*v.t.* (*sl.*) hit hard, beat; spread (paint) thickly. (*slush*)

slot, *n.* track of animal, esp. deer. (O.F. *esclot*, hoof-print)

slot, *n.* slit, groove, for part of mechanism.—*v.t.* provide with slot. **s.-machine,** *n.* from which chocolate etc. can be got by insertion of coin. (O.F. *esclot*, hollow of breast)

sloth, *n.* laziness, indolence; slow-moving S. American animal living in trees. **s.-bear,** *n.* a black Indian bear. **s.-monkey,** *n.* kind of loris. **slothful,** *a.* (*slow*)

slouch, *n.* stooping slovenly posture or gait; downward droop of hat-brim; (*sl.*) poor performer or performance.—*v.i.* sit, walk, with slouch; droop. **s. hat,** soft hat with slouch.

slough, *n.* skin shed by snake; dead tissue separating from healing wound. —*v.t.* and *i.* shed (slough); drop off.

slough, *n.* swamp, bog. (O.E. *slóh*)

sloven, *n.* untidy dirty person. **slovenly,** *a.* negligent of neatness or cleanliness; slipshod. **slovenry,** *n.*

slow, *a.* moving at low speed, not quick; gradual; reluctant, backward; dull, sluggish; behind time; tedious, boring; (of surface) causing slowness. —*adv.* slowly.—*v.i.* and *t.* reduce speed (of). **s.-match,** *n.* slow-burning fuse for firing charge. **s.-motion,** *a.* (of film) showing movement greatly slowed down. **slow-coach,** *n.* laggard; dull person. (O.E. *sláw*)

slow-worm, *n.* small reptile between snake and lizard. (O.E. *slá-wyrm*)

sloyd, same as **sloid.**

slub, *n.* wool slightly twisted before spinning.—*v.t.* twist into slub.

slubber, *v.t.* and *i.* do in slovenly manner; slobber.

sludge, *n.* slush, ooze; sewage. (*slush*)

slue, see **slew.**

slug, *v.i.* and *t.* (*Amer.*) hit hard, slog.

slug, *n.* small roughly shaped bullet; line of type set by linotype.

slug, *n.* kinds of shell-less snail. **s.-abed,** *n.* (*arch.*) sluggard. **sluggard,** *n.* lazy person, habitual idler. **sluggish,** *a.* slow, inert; indolent.

slug-horn, *n.* trumpet. (corrupt. of *slogan,* mistakenly used)

sluice, *n.* gate regulating flow of water; water passing through this; artificial water-channel; sluicing.—*v.t.* and *i.* draw off with sluice; provide with sluice-gates; flush, wash out; stream out. **s.-gate,** *n.* (L. *excludere,* shut out)

sluit, *n.* (*S. Afr.*) narrow water-channel. (Du. *sloot,* ditch)

slum, *n.* low squalid street or district. —*v.i.* visit slum, esp. for charitable purpose.

slumber, *v.i.* and *t.* and *n.* sleep. **s.-suit,** *n.* pyjamas. **slumberer,** *n.* **slumberous, slumbrous,** *a.* drowsy; inducing sleep. (O.E. *slúma*)

slummock, *v.t.* and *i.* (*colloq.*) swallow greedily; move or speak awkwardly.

slump, *n.* sudden fall in value or slackening in demand.—*v.i.* undergo slump; sink down heavily.

slump, *v.t.* lump (together).—*n.* gross amount.

slung, see **sling.**

slunk, see **slink.**

slur, *v.t.* and *i.* pronounce, speak, indistinctly; run (letters, words) together; pass lightly (over), minimize; (*arch.*) disparage; (*mus.*) sing or play in gliding manner; mark with slur.—*n.* act of slurring; stigma, imputation of disgrace; (*mus.*) curved line over notes to be slurred. (obs. =thin mud)

slurry, *n.* liquid mixture for making Portland cement. (*slur*)

slush, *n.* liquid mud; melting snow; grease for lubricating; (*colloq.*) sentimental trash, twaddle.

slut, *n.* slovenly woman, slattern; (*joc.*) girl. **sluttish,** *a.* **sluttery,** *n.*

sly, *a.* secretively cunning, wily; arch, knowing. **on the s.,** surreptitiously. **slyboots,** *n.* sly or roguish person. **slyly,** *adv.* (O.N. *slægr*)

slype, *n.* covered passage from cathedral transept to chapter-house. (*slip*)

smack, *v.t.* and *i.* strike smartly, slap; part (lips) with noise; crack (whip). —*n.* hard blow; sharp report, crack; loud kiss.—*adv.* (*colloq.*) full. **have a s. at,** (*colloq.*) have a go at. **s. lips over,** gloat over.

smack, *n.* taste, flavour; tinge, dash (of).—*v.i.* taste, be suggestive, have a tinge (of). (O.E. *smæc*)

smack, *n.* small fishing-boat, sloop. (Du. *smak*)

small, *a.* little, not large; undersized; young; trivial, unimportant; ungenerous, petty; (*Shake.*) slender, fine; shrill.—*n.* slender part, esp. of back; (*pl.*) responsions. **feel s.,** be humiliated. **s. beer,** thin weak beer; unimportant person. **s. debt,** one recoverable in county court. **s. fry,** immature fish; young persons. **s. gross,** ten dozen. **s. holding,** small plot let by county council on special terms for cultivation by **s. holder. s. hours,** those immediately after midnight. **s. letter,** not capital. **s. talk,** light conversation. **s.-arms,** *n.pl.* hand fire-arms. **s.-clothes,** *n.pl.* (*arch.*) knee-breeches. **s.-minded,** *a.* petty. **s.-sword,** *n.* rapier. (O.E. *smæl*)

smallage, *n.* wild celery. (*small*+ L. *apium,* parsley)

smallpox, *n.* contagious disease with fever and eruptions on skin.

smalt, *n.* glass coloured blue with cobalt; pigment made by pulverizing this. (It. *smalto*)

smaragdine, *a.* emerald-green. (Gk. *smaragdos,* emerald)

smarm, *v.t.* smooth down (hair). **smarmy,** *a.* (*colloq.*) unctuous, fawning.

smart, *v.i.* feel tingling pain; be felt as painful, rankle; feel hurt or resentful.—*n.* tingling pain; wounded feeling.—*a.* sharp, severe; brisk, vigorous; alert, quick; superficially clever, witty; well-dressed; in the latest style, good form. **s. Aleck,** (*Amer.*) know-all. **s. for,** be punished for. **smarten,** *v.t.* and *i.* make, become, smart. (O.E. *smeortan*)

smash, *v.t.* and *i.* break in pieces, shatter; hit hard; destroy, crush; ruin, be ruined; crash (into); (*lawn tennis*) hit (ball) violently downwards; (*sl.*) pass counterfeit coin.— *n.* smashing; violent collision or fall; ruin; drink of spirits and water iced and **flavoured.**—*adv.* with a smash. **s.-up,** *n.* complete smash. **smasher,** *n.* smashing blow; clinching argument. **smashing,** *a.* crushing; dashing; (*sl.*) first-rate.

smatch, *n.* taste, smack. (*smack*)

smattering, *n.* slight superficial knowledge. **smatterer,** *n.* dabbler. **smatter,** *v.i.* (*Shake.*) chatter.

smear, *v.t.* and *i.* spread, rub, with grease; daub; make smear, be blurred.—*n.* greasy blotch. **smeary,** *a.* (O.E. *smeru,* fat)

smeddum, *n.* (*Scot.*) fine powder; spirit, mettle.

smeech, *n.* (*dial.*) smell of burning. (O.E. *sméc*)

smegma, *n.* soapy secretion of sebaceous gland. **smegmatic,** *a.* (Gk. =soap)

smell, *n.* odour; sense by which this is perceived through nose; act of smelling, sniff.—*v.t.* and *i.* (*past, p.p.* **smelt, smelled**) perceive by smell; sniff (at); emit odour; smack (of). **s. out,** hunt by scent; find out by prying. **s.-less,** *a.* lacking sense of smell; odourless. **smelling-bottle,** *n.* bottle filled with **smelling-salts,** *n.pl.* preparation of ammonium carbonate sniffed as restorative. **smeller,** *n.* (*sl.*) nose; severe blow or fall. **smelly,** *a.* having unpleasant smell. (M.E. *smel*)

smelt, *v.t.* melt (ore) to separate metal from it; extract (metal) thus.

smelt, *n.* small fish of salmon family. (O.E.)

smew, *n.* a diving-bird.

smilax, *n.* a climbing plant, greenbrier. (Gk.=bindweed)

smile, *v.i.* and *t.* curve or part lips in pleased or amused expression; look gay or happy; be favourable; express by smile; (*Shake.*) smile at.—*n.* act of smiling; bright aspect. **s. on,** be propitious to. **smilet,** *n.* (*Shake.*) little smile.

smirch, *v.t.* soil, sully.—*n.* stain.

smirk, *v.i.* smile fatuously, simper.—*n.* act of smirking.—*a.* neat, trim. (O.E. *smercian,* smile)

smirr, *n.* and *v.i.* (*Scot.*) drizzle.

smitch, same as **smeech.**

smite, *v.t.* and *i.* (*past* **smote,** *arch.* smit; *p.p.* smitten, *arch.* smit) strike (heavy blow); chastise, afflict; defeat; slay.—*n.* (*sl.*) hard hit. **smitten by,** infected, captivated, by. (O.E. *smitan*)

smith, *n.* worker in metal; one who forges iron, blacksmith. (O.E.)

smithereens, smithers, *nn.pl.* small fragments.

smithery, *n.* smith's work.

smithy, *n.* blacksmith's workshop.

smitten, see **smite.**

smock, *n.* loose outer garment like shirt with upper part smocked; (*arch.*) chemise.—*v.t.* stitch with small pleats forming honeycomb ornamentation. **s.-frock,** *n.* farm-labourer's smock. (O.E. *smoc*)

smoke, *n.* vapour from burning body; spell of tobacco-smoking; (*colloq.*) cigar.—*v.i.* and *t.* emit smoke; reek, steam; darken, fumigate, preserve, drive (out), with smoke; draw in and puff out smoke of (tobacco, pipe etc.); (of chimney) send smoke into room; (*school sl.*) blush; (*arch.*) have inkling of, detect; quiz, chaff. **Cape s.,** cheap kind of S. African brandy. **end in s.,** come to nothing. **s.-ball, s.-bomb,** *nn.* bomb emitting smoke to provide **s.-screen,** *n.* for concealing operations from enemy. **s.-box,** *n.* chamber between boiler and **s.-stack,** *n.* funnel. **smoking-carriage, smoking-concert, smoking-room,** *nn.* where smoking is allowed. **smoking-cap, smoking-jacket,** *nn.* light ornamental kinds. **smoker,** *n.* one who smokes tobacco; (*colloq.*) smoking-carriage, smoking-concert. **smoky,** *a.* emitting, filled with, coloured like, smoke. (O.E. *smoca*)

smolt, *n.* salmon older than parr and younger than grilse. (O.E.=serene)

smooth, *a.* with even surface, not rough; (of water) calm, unruffled; (of skin) not hairy; (of wine) not harsh or acrid; (of verse) flowing, rhythmical; (of manner) suave, plausible.—*n.* smooth or pleasant part.—*v.t.* and *i.* make smooth; calm (down); clear (away); (*Shake.*) flatter, gloss over. **s.-bore,** *n.* gun whose barrel is not rifled. **s.-faced,** *a.* clean-shaven; hypocritical. (O.E. *smóth*)

smote, see **smite.**

smother, *v.t.* and *i.* kill by stopping breath or excluding air, suffocate, stifle; suppress, conceal; enwrap wholly, overwhelm.—*n.* dense smoke, thick dust; obscurity caused by this. **smothery,** *a.* stifling. (O.E. *smorian*)

smoulder, *v.i.* burn slowly without flame; (of emotion) exist in stifled condition.—*n.* smouldering combustion. (M.E. *smolderen*)

smout, smowt, *n.* (*Scot.*) smolt; tiny object or person. (*smolt*)

smudge, *n.* blurred dirty mark, blot, smear.—*v.i.* and *t.* make smudge (on); blur, become blurred.

smudge, *n.* (*Amer.*) smoky fire to drive off mosquitoes.

smug, *a.* self-satisfied, complacent; affectedly or primly proper; (*arch.*) neat, trim.—*n.* (*school sl.*) unsociable over-studious person.

smuggle, *v.t.* and *i.* import or export (goods) secretly to avoid customs duties; convey by stealth. (L.G. *smuggeln*)

smut, *n.* flake of soot; spot, smudge, made by it; fungoid disease of wheat; obscene talk or writing.—*v.t.* and *i.* mark with smuts; infect with smut.

smutch, *v.t.* and *i.* blacken as with soot; smirch, sully; smudge.—*n.* dirty mark, stain; smudge.

smutty, *a.* soiled with smuts; obscene, filthy.

smytrie, *n.* (*Scot.*) number huddled together.

snack, *n.* slight hasty meal; share.

snaffle, *n.* light bridle-bit without curb.

snaffle, *v.t.* (*sl.*) steal, pinch.

snag, *n.* rough jagged projection, stump; tree or rock in river-bed impeding navigation; obstacle, drawback.—*v.t.* run (ship) on snag; clear of snags.

snail, *n.* slow-moving mollusc, us. with spiral shell; slow sluggish person. **snailery,** *n.* place for breeding edible snails. (O.E. *snægl*)

snake, *n.* scaly limbless reptile, serpent; treacherous person.—*v.t.* (*Amer.*) draw (log) along, out, or up. **s. in the grass,** lurking enemy. **s.-charmer,** *n.* one who charms snakes, esp. with music. **s.-fence,** *n.* of horizontal trunks laid zigzag. **s.-stone,** *n.* ammonite. **s.-weed,** *n.* bistort. **snaky,** *a.* like, full of, snakes; treacherous-looking. (O.E. *snaca*)

snap, *v.t.* and *i.* bite or snatch (at) suddenly; break sharply; make sharp sound, crack; shut with click; take snapshot of; speak crossly; (*cricket*) catch smartly at wicket.—*n.* act or sound of snapping; spring catch; energy, dash; snapshot; a simple card game; (*Amer. sl.*) easy task.—*adv.* with a snap. **cold s.,** short spell of cold weather. **s. division,** (in Parliament) one sprung on opponents by surprise. **s. fingers at,** make light of. **s. into it,** (*sl.*) make vigorous start. **s. up,** seize hastily or eagerly; interrupt rudely. (L.G. *snappen*)

snapdragon, *n.* a bright-flowered plant. antirrhinum; old Christmas game of picking raisins from dish of burning brandy.

snaphance, *n.* old form of flintlock gun. (Du. *snappen,* snap; *haan,* cock)

snappish, *a.* inclined to snap; irritable.

snappy, *a.* snappish; brisk, lively.

snapshot, *n.* shot fired without taking deliberate aim; instantaneous photograph.—*v.t.* take snapshot of.

snare, *n.* wire noose, trap, for catching animals; thing that tempts or deceives.—*v.t.* catch in snare; entangle, entrap. (O.N. *snara*)

snark, *n.* vague fabulous nonsensical creature. (coined by 'Lewis Carroll')

snarl, *v.i.* and *t.* growl showing teeth; speak, say, in harsh savage tone.—*n.* act, sound, of snarling.

snarl, *n.* (*arch.*) tangle.—*v.t.* and *i.* entangle, become entangled; produce raised pattern on (vase) by hammering inside with **snarling-iron,** *n.* (*snare*)

snash, *n.* (*Scot.*) insolence, impudent talk.—*v.i.* sneer, gibe.

snatch, *v.t.* and *i.* seize, take, suddenly or eagerly; make quick grab (at).—*n.* act of snatching, grab; short spell; disconnected fragment, scrap (of song etc.). **snatchy,** *a.* done in snatches. (M.E. *snacchen*)

snath, snathe, snead, *nn.* curved shaft of scythe. (O.E. *snǣd,* slice)

sneak, *v.i.* and *t.* go furtively, slink; (*sl.*) steal; (*school sl.*) inform against another.—*n.* underhand person; talebearer; (*cricket*) ball bowled to run along ground. **s.-thief,** *n.* one who steals from open doors or windows without breaking in. **sneakers,** *n.pl.* (*Amer.*) soft-soled shoes. **sneaking,** *a.* furtive, unavowed.

sneap, *n.* (*Shake.*) rebuke, rebuff.—*v.t.* pinch with cold.

sneb, same as **snib.**

sneck, *n.* and *v.t.* (*Scot.*) latch. **s. up,** (*Shake.*) go hang! (M.E.)

sned, *v.t.* (*Scot.*) lop off, prune.

snee, *n.* large knife.

sneer, *v.i.* show contempt by expression of face; utter derisive words, gibe; express by sneer.—*n.* derisive look or remark.

sneeshing, *n.* (*Scot.*) snuff.

sneeze, *v.i.* emit breath with sudden involuntary spasm and noise.—*n.* act of sneezing. **not to be sneezed at,** worth consideration. (O.E. *fnéosan, f* being mistaken for long *s* in M.E.)

snell, *n.* short piece of gut attaching hook to fishing-line.

snell, *a.* (*Scot.*) keen, sharp; cold. (O.E.=active)

snib, *v.t.* (*Spens.*) reprove. (*snub*)

snib, *n.* and *v.t.* (*Scot.*) bolt.

snick, *n.* small notch or cut; (*cricket*) stroke off edge of bat.—*v.t.* cut snick in; hit (ball) with snick.

snicker, *v.i.* and *n.* whinny, neigh; snigger. (imit.)

snickersnee, *n.* (*joc.*) long knife.

snide, *a.* (*sl.*) counterfeit; dishonest.—*n.* counterfeit coin or jewellery.

Snider, *n.* obsolete type of rifle. (inventor)

sniff, *v.i.* and *t.* inhale audibly through nose; express contempt thus; draw (up) into nose.—*n.* act or sound of sniffing. **s. at,** try smell of; sneer at. **sniffle,** *v.i.* snuffle. **sniffy,** *a.* (*colloq.*) smelly; disdainfully superior. **snifter,** *v.i.* (*Scot.*) sniff.—*n.* snuff; (*sl.*) heavy storm; drink; (*pl.*) nasal catarrh. (imit.)

snigger, *n.* half-suppressed laugh, giggle.—*v.i.* laugh furtively and slyly. (imit.)

sniggle, *v.i.* fish (for eels) by pushing baited hook into their holes. (dial. *snig,* eel)

snip, *v.t.* and *i.* cut with scissors, clip. —*n.* act of snipping; piece snipped off; (*colloq.*) tailor; (*racing sl.*) certainty.

snipe, *n.* (*pl.* same) bird with long bill and zigzag flight; simpleton.—*v.i.* and *t.* shoot snipe; shoot, pick off, with rifle from concealed position. **sniper,** *n.*

snippet, *n.* small piece snipped off, clipping; scrap. **snippety,** *a.* made of odds and ends. (*snip*+dim.)

snirtle, *v.i.* (*Scot.*) laugh slyly.

snitcher, *n.* (*sl.*) informer; sneak-thief; handcuff.

snivel, *v.i.* run at nose; whine, whimper.—*n.* running mucus; whining; canting talk. (O.E. *snofl*, mucus)

snob, *n.* one who puts exaggerated value on social position, wealth, or success; (*obs. sl.*) townsman of university town. **snobbery,** *n.* snobbishness. **snobbish,** *a.* **snobocracy,** *n.* government by snobs.

snod, *a.* (*Scot.*) neat, trim; snug.

snood, *n.* any of short lines attaching hooks to main line in sea-fishing; (*Scot.*) hair-ribbon formerly worn only by unmarried girls. (O.E. *snód*)

snook, *n.* kinds of fish, esp. sea-pike. (Du. *snoek*)

snook, *n.* (*sl.*) derisive gesture with thumb to nose and fingers spread out. **cock a s.,** make this.

snooker, *n.* game on billiard-table combining pool and pyramids.

snool, *v.i.* (*Scot.*) submit tamely to wrong; cringe. (*snivel*)

snoop, *v.i.* (*Amer. colloq.*) pry, meddle; sneak about.

snooze, *n.* short sleep, nap.—*v.i.* take snooze.

snore, *v.i.* breathe heavily with snorting noise during sleep.—*n.* act or sound of snoring.

snort, *v.i.* and *t.* make harsh sudden noise by drawing breath through nostrils; express anger, derision etc., by snort; say with snort.—*n.* act or sound of snorting. **snorter,** *n.* (*sl.*) something big or noisy; violent gale.

snot, *n.* (*vulg.*) mucus from nose. **snotter,** *n.* (*Scot.*) snot.—*v.i.* (*Scot.*) breathe with obstructed nose; snivel. **snotty,** *a.* (*vulg.*) foul with snot; (*colloq.*) annoyed, huffy.—*n.* (*naval sl.*) midshipman. (O.E. *gesnot*)

snout, *n.* projecting nose of animal, esp. pig; pointed front, nozzle.

snow, *n.* sailing-vessel like brig with supplementary mast. (Du. *snauw*)

snow, *n.* frozen vapour that falls in flakes; fall, layer, of this; white colour; (*sl.*) cocaine.—*v.i.* and *t.* rain snow; fall, shower, thickly. **s. under,** overwhelm with numbers. **s.-bird, s.-bunting,** *nn.* an Arctic finch. **s.-blind,** *a.* temporarily blind from glare of snow. **s.-blink,** *n.* reflection in sky from snow-field. **s.-boot,** *n.* over-boot for walking in snow. **s.-bound,** *a.* kept from travelling by snow. **s.-capped,** *a.* with snow on summit. **s.-field,** *n.* expanse of permanent snow. **s.-leopard,** *n.* ounce. **s.-line,** *n.* above which snow never melts. **s.-on-the-mountain,** *n.* plant with closely set white flowers. **s.-plough,** *n.* machine for clearing road of snow. **s.-shoe,** *n.* racket-shaped framework for going on surface of snow. **snowed in, up,** imprisoned, blocked, by snow. (O.E. *snáw*)

snowball, *n.* ball of snow as missile; guelder rose.—*v.t.* and *i.* pelt with, throw, snowballs.

snowdrift, *n.* bank of snow heaped up by wind.

snowdrop, *n.* white-flowered plant appearing in early spring.

snowfall, *n.* fall of snow; amount of this.

snowflake, *n.* flake of snow; plant resembling snowdrop.

snowk, *v.i.* (*Scot.*) sniff (of dog).

snowstorm, *n.* heavy fall of snow.

snowy, *a.* white as, covered with, snow; tending to snow. **s. owl,** the great white owl.

snub, *v.t.* check, rebuff, with rude remark or show of indifference; (*naut.*) check (cable) from running out, check (ship) with tautened rope. —*n.* snubbing, intentional slight.—*a.* (of nose) short and blunt and turned up. **s.-nosed,** *a.* (O.N. *snubba*, chide)

snuff, *v.t.* and *i.* sniff (up); take snuff. —*n.* sniff; grated tobacco for sniffing up nose; (*Shake.*) huff. **give person s.,** deal sharply with him. **take in s.,** (*Shake.*) take offence at. **up to s.,** (*sl.*) knowing, sharp. **s.-box, s.-mull,** *nn.* small box for carrying snuff. **s.-coloured,** *a.* dark yellowish-brown. **s.-mill,** *n.* machine for grinding tobacco into snuff. (M.Du. *snuffen*, clear nose)

snuff, *n.* charred part of candle's wick.—*v.t.* and *i.* trim snuff from (candle). **s. out,** extinguish (candle); suppress; (*sl.*) die. **snuffers,** *n.pl.* wick-trimming scissors.

snuffle, *v.i.* and *t.* sniff continually; speak, utter, with nasal whine.—*n.* act of snuffling; (*pl.*) kind of catarrh. (*snuff*)

snuffy, *a.* soiled with snuff; (*colloq.*) offended, cross.

snug, *a.* cosy, sheltered, comfortable; compact, trim. **snuggery,** *n.* snug retreat; bar-parlour. **snuggle,** *v.i.* and *t.* nestle, lie close; cuddle.

so, *adv.* in that or the same manner or degree; very; accordingly; as it seems; also.—*conj.* (*arch.*) provided that.—*int.* indeed; (*Shake.*) very well. **and so on,** etcetera. **just, quite, so,** exactly. **or so,** or thereabouts. **so long,** (*colloq.*) good-bye. **so long as,** provided that. **so please you,** (*arch.*) by your favour. **so what?** (*Amer.*) what about it? **so-and-so,** *n.* substitute for name of person. **so-called,** *a.* purporting to be. **so-so,** *a.* not very good, fair.—*adv.* tolerably. (O.E. *swá*)

soak, *v.t.* and *i.* draw, be drawn (up, in) by absorption; steep, be steeped; drench; drink to excess.—*n.* soaking; drenching rain; drinking-bout, hard drinker; (*Austral.*) depression where water can be found. **soakage,** *n.* process of soaking. (O.E. *socian*)

soap, *n.* cleansing agent made of alkali and oils or fats.—*v.t.* and *i.* apply soap (to). **soft s.,** semi-liquid kind made with potash; flattery. **s.-boiler,** *n.* maker of soap. **s.-bubble,** *n.* iridescent bubble made from soapsuds. **soapstone,** *n.* steatite. **soapsuds,** *n.pl.* froth of soapy water. **soapy,** *a.* like, full of, soap; flattering, unctuous. (O.E. *sápe*)

soar, *v.i.* fly high; hover; rise to, be at, great height. (L. *ex,* out; *aura,* air)

soave, soavemente, *advv.* (*mus.*) sweetly, softly. (It.)

sob, *v.i.* and *t.* catch breath convulsively, esp. in weeping; utter with sob.—*n.* short convulsive sigh. **s.-stuff,** *n.* (*sl.*) cheap pathos.

sober, *a.* not drunk; not given to drink, abstemious; moderate, sane; grave, calm; (of colour) subdued, quiet; (*Scot.*) weak, feeble.—*v.t.* and *i.* make, become, sober. **sobersides,** *n.* solemn serious person. (L. *sobrius*)

Sobranje, *n.* parliament of Bulgaria. (Bulgarian)

sobriety, *n.* soberness.

sobriquet, *n.* nickname. (F.)

soc, *n.* (*law*) right of holding a local court. **socage, soccage,** *n.* feudal tenure by money rent, not military service. (O.E.)

soccer, *n.* (*sl.*) association football. (abbr. of *association*)

sociable, *a.* fond of company, affable; giving opportunities for intercourse. —*n.* open carriage with facing side seats; tricycle for two side by side; S-shaped couch; (*Amer.*) informal reception, social. **sociability,** *n.*

social, *a.* of human intercourse, concerned with the mutual relations of men or classes; living in communities, gregarious; of, in, society; sociable, convivial.—*n.* (*colloq.*) social gathering. **s. contract,** agreement expressed or implied between governors and governed. **s. evil,** prostitution. **s. science,** science of man as member of community, sociology. (L. *socius,* companion)

socialism, *n.* political system aiming at a more equal distribution of property and the substition of co-operation for competition through state ownership of land, capital etc.; social equality. **socialist,** *a.* and *n.* (adherent) of socialism. **socialistic,** *a.* **socialistically,** *adv.*

sociality, *n.* state of being social.

socialize, *v.t.* make social; incorporate in a society; make socialistic, change from private to state ownership. **socialization,** *n.*

society, *n.* living in association with others; organized human community; civilized people collectively; upper classes, people of fashion; companionship, company; association, club. **S. of Friends,** Quakers. **S. of Jesus,** Jesuits. **s. verse,** of light topical witty kind. (*social*)

sociology, *n.* science of the nature and development of social institutions. **sociological,** *a.* **sociologist,** *n.* (L. *socius,* companion. Gk. *legein,* speak)

sock, *n.* short stocking; inner sole for shoe; (*arch.*) low-heeled shoe worn by comic actor. **pull up your ss.,** (*sl.*) make vigorous effort. (L. *soccus*)

sock, *v.t.* (*sl.*) fling; hit.—*n.* blow. **give one ss.,** thrash him soundly.

sock, *n.* (*school sl.*) eatables, tuck.

sockdologer, *n.* (*Amer. sl.*) knock-down blow; conclusive argument.

socker, same as **soccer.**

socket, *n.* hollow, recess, into which thing fits.—*v.t.* provide with, fix in, socket; (*golf*) hit with shank of club. (O.F. *soc,* ploughshare+dim.)

sockeye, *n.* the blue-back salmon. (Amer. Ind. *sukai*)

socle, *n.* (*archit.*) plain rectangular pedestal of statue or column. (F.)

socman, *n.* one who holds land by socage.

Socratic, *a.* of, like, the Greek philosopher Socrates. **S. irony,** feigned ignorance used to entrap opponent in argument. **S. method,** procedure by question and answer.

sod, *n.* flat square of earth with grass on it, turf; (*poet.*) surface of the earth.—*v.t.* cover with sods. **under the s.,** in the grave.

sod, *n.* (*vulg.*) sodomite. (abbr.)

sod, see **seethe.**

soda, *n.* (also **washing s.**) sodium carbonate; (also **baking s.**) sodium bicarbonate; (also **caustic s.**) sodium hydroxide; (also **s.-water**) water made effervescent with carbonic acid gas. **s.-fountain,** *n.* container for, (*Amer.*) store selling, soda-water. **sodalite,** *n.* rock-forming mineral containing soda.

sodality, *n.* fraternity, religious fellowship. (L. *sodalis,* comrade)

sodden, *a.* soaked, saturated; stupid with drink; (of bread) damp and soft.—*v.t.* and *i.* make, become, sodden. (*seethe*)

sodium, *n.* silver-white metallic alkaline element. **s. bicarbonate,** baking soda. **s. carbonate,** washing soda. **s. chloride,** common salt. **s. hydroxide,** caustic soda. **sodic,** *a.* (*soda*)

sodomy, *n.* unnatural sexual intercourse, esp. between males. **sodomite,** *n.* (city of *Sodom*)

-soever, *suf.* giving more general or indefinite sense, as in whosoever.

sofa, *n.* long padded seat or couch with back and raised end or ends. (Arab. *suffah*, bench)
soffit, *n.* (*archit.*) under side of arch, staircase etc. (L. *sub*, under; *figere*, fix)
sofi, same as **sufi.**
soft, *a.* yielding to pressure, not hard; easily cut or moulded; smooth, delicate; mild, balmy; gentle; tender, compassionate; flabby, weak; effeminate; half-witted; (of sound) low, not harsh; (of colour) subdued, not glaring; (of outline) not sharp; (of weather) rainy, moist; (*phonetics*) sibilant or voiced.—*n.* softy.—*adv.* softly.—*int.* (*arch.*) be quiet; stay, stop. **s. drink,** (*sl.*) non-alcoholic drink. **s. goods,** textiles. **s. job, thing,** (*sl.*) easy task. **s. water,** free from mineral salts and so forming lather easily. **s.-headed,** *a.* half idiotic. **s.-hearted,** *a.* merciful. **s.-spoken,** *a.* quiet-voiced; affable. (O.E. *sófte*)
softa, *n.* Moslem theological student. (Turk.)
soften, *v.t.* and *i.* make, become, soft or softer. **softening of the brain,** disease impairing mental faculties.
softy, *n.* weak silly person.
soggy, *a.* soaked with water, sodden.
soh, *n.* fifth note in sol-fa notation.
soho, *int.* sportsman's halloo.
soi-disant, *a.* self-styled. (F.)
soigné, *a.* (*fem.* *soignée*) well-groomed. (F.)
soil, *v.t.* fatten (cattle) with cut grass.
soil, *n.* ground, earth, mould. **native s.,** native land. (L. *solium*, seat, confused with *solum*, ground)
soil, *v.t.* and *i.* make dirty; tarnish, defile; show stains.—*n.* dirty mark, stain. **s.-pipe,** *n.* waste-pipe of water-closet. **soilure,** *n.* (*arch.*) defilement. (O.F. *soillier*)
soirée, *n.* evening party or social meeting with tea etc. (F.=evening)
soixante-quinze, *n.* French field-gun, seventy-five. (F.)
sojourn, *v.i.* stay for a time—*n.* temporary residence or stay. (L. *sub*, under; *dies*, day)
soke, same as **soc.**
sol, same as **soh.**
Sol, *n.* the sun. (L.)
sola, *n.* an Indian swamp-plant; pith of its stem. **s. topi,** sun-helmet made of sola pith. (Hind. *sholā*)
solace, *n.* comfort in distress, consolation; (*obs.*) amusement.—*v.t.* and *i.* bring solace to; (*Shake.*) be happy (in). (L. *solari*, console)
solan, *n.* (also **s. goose**) gannet. (O.N. *súla*)
solanum, *n.* genus of plants incl. potato and nightshade. (L.=nightshade)
solar, *a.* of, caused by, reckoned by, the sun. **s. myth,** symbolizing sun and its movements. **s. plexus,** network of nerves at pit of stomach. **s. system,** sun and planets. **solarism,** *n.* excessive use of solar myths in explaining mythology. **solarist,** *n.* **solarium,** *n.* (*pl.* **solaria**) room for treatment of patients by exposure to sun. **solarize,** *v.t.* and *i.* (*phot.*) spoil through over-exposure causing reversed image. **solarization,** *n.* (L. *sol*, sun)
solatium, *n.* (*pl.* **solatia**) sum given as compensation, esp. for injured feelings. (L.=solace)
sold, see **sell.**
soldan, same as **sultan.**
solder, *n.* easily melted alloy used for joining metals.—*v.t.* join with solder. (L. *solidus*, solid)
soldier, *n.* man serving in army, esp. private or non-commissioned officer; man of military skill; (*sl.*) red herring.—*v.i.* serve as soldier; (*naut. sl.*) shirk work. **s. ant,** one of fighting section of ant colony. **s. crab,** hermit crab. **s. of fortune,** military adventurer. **soldierlike, soldierly,** *aa.* **soldiership,** *n.* military ability. **soldiery,** *n.* soldiers collectively. (L. *solidus*, a coin, pay)
soldo, *n.* (*pl.* **soldi**) Italian coin=5 centesimi, worth about ½*d.* (It.)
sole, *n.* under surface of foot; under part of boot or shoe; bottom of plough, golf-club etc.—*v.t.* fit (boot) with sole. (L. *solea*)
sole, *n.* small flat-fish. (L. *solea*)
sole, *a.* one and only, single; (*arch.*) alone, solitary. (L. *solus*)
solecism, *n.* grammatical blunder, use of vulgar expression; breach of etiquette, impropriety. **solecist,** *n.* one guilty of solecism. **solecistic,** *a.* **solecistically,** *adv.* (Gk. *soloikos*, speaking incorrectly)
solemn, *a.* kept, performed, with ceremony; awe-inspiring; serious, grave; pompous. **solemnity,** *n.* solemness; formal rite. **solemnize,** *v.t.* keep (festival); perform (ceremony) with due rites; make solemn. **solemnization,** *n.* (L. *sollemnis*)
solen, *n.* a bivalve, razor-shell. (Gk. *sōlēn*, pipe)
solenoid, *n.* cylindrical coil of wire which acts as magnet when carrying a current. (Gk. *sōlēn*, pipe; *eidos*, form)
sol-fa, *n.* use of names (sol, fa etc.) for notes in singing.—*v.i.* and *t.* sing thus and not with words.
solfeggio, *n.* (*pl.* **solfeggi**) sol-fa, solmization. (It.)
solicit, *v.t.* and *i.* ask earnestly (for), beg; importune; request, invite; (of prostitute) accost.—*n.* (*Shake.*) solicitation. **solicitation,** *n.* **solicitor,** *n.* one who solicits; lawyer who advises clients and prepares their cases. **Solicitor-General,** *n.* law officer of Crown below Attorney-General. **solicitous,** *a.* eager, desirous; anxious. **solicitude,** *n.* (L. *sollicitus*, anxious)

solid, *a.* rigid, not fluid or gaseous; hard, compact; massive, substantial; of one material or shade throughout; not hollow; sound, trustworthy; unanimous; (*math.*) of three dimensions.—*n.* solid body or figure. **solidare,** *n.* (*Shake.*) a small coin. **solidarity,** *n.* united state; agreement in opinions or policy. **solidify,** *v.t.* and *i.* make, become, solid. **solidification,** *n.* **solidity,** *n.* solidness. **solidungular, solidungulate,** *aa.* solid-hoofed. **solidus,** *n.* (*pl.* **solidi**) stroke (/) standing for shilling as in 6/8; an ancient Roman gold coin. (L. *solidus*)

solifidian, *n.* one who believes in salvation by faith alone without works. **solifidianism,** *n.* (L. *solus,* alone; *fides,* faith)

soliloquy, *n.* talking to oneself; speech made by actor when alone on stage. **soliloquize,** *v.i.* utter soliloquy. (L. *solus,* alone; *loqui,* speak)

solipsism, *n.* (*philos.*) theory that the self can know nothing outside of its own states. **solipsist,** *n.* (L. *solus,* alone; *ipse,* self)

solitaire, *n.* single gem set by itself; earring etc. adorned with this; game played on board with marbles; card-game for one, patience; kinds of American thrush; (*rare*) recluse. (F.)

solitary, *a.* living or performed alone; unfrequented, lonely; single, sole.—*n.* recluse. **solitude,** *n.* loneliness; lonely place. (*solus*)

solleret, *n.* steel shoe worn in medieval armour. (O.F. *soler,* shoe+dim.)

solmizate, *v.i.* use names (sol, mi etc.) for musical notes, sol-fa. **solmization,** *n.*

solo, *a.* and *n.* (song, piece) sung or played by single performer, with or without subordinate accompaniment; (motor-cycle) without side-car; (aeroplane flight) by single person; (also **s. whist**) card game like whist. **soloist,** *n.* performer of solo. (It.)

Solomon, *n.* wise man. **S.'s seal,** six-pointed figure formed by two interlaced triangles; plant like lily of the valley. (name in Bible)

Solon, *n.* wise lawgiver. (person)

solstice, *n.* time at which sun attains greatest distance north or south of equator. **summer, winter, s.,** about 21 June, 22 Dec. **solstitial,** *a.* (L. *sol,* sun; *sistere,* make to stand)

soluble, *a.* dissolvable in fluid; solvable. **solubility,** *n.* (*solve*)

solus, *a.* (*fem.* sola) alone. (L.)

solution, *n.* act of dissolving or being dissolved; liquid with something dissolved in it; solving of, answer to, a problem; separation, disruption. **solutionist,** *n.* professional solver of newspaper puzzles. (*solve*)

solve, *v.t.* find answer to (problem); find way out of (difficulty); (*arch.*) loosen, untie. **solvable,** *a.* **solvent,** *a.* able to dissolve another substance; able to pay one's debts, having more assets than liabilities.—*n.* substance that dissolves another. **solvency,** *n.* being financially solvent. (L. *solvere*)

soma, *n.* ancient Indian intoxicating drink made from juice of **s. plant.** (Sanskr.)

somatic, *a.* of the body, corporeal. **somatism,** *n.* materialism. **somatology,** *n.* study of properties of substances, physics; study of human body, physiology. (Gk. *sōma,* body)

sombre, *a.* dark, dismal; gloomy. **sombrous,** *a.* (*poet.*) (F.)

sombrero, *n.* wide-brimmed felt hat (Sp.)

-some, *adj.suf.* apt to, as in **tiresome.**

some, *a.* one, a certain; a certain amount or number of; more or less, about; (*sl.*) an outstanding or surpassing.—*pron.* some people; a part or quantity.—*adv.* (*sl.*) rather; a good deal. **s. deal,** (*Shake.*) somewhat. **somebody, someone,** *nn.* some person; an important person. **somehow,** *adv.* in some way; by some means. **something,** *n.* some thing; a portion.—*adv.* somewhat. **sometime,** *adv.* formerly; at some time. **sometimes,** *adv.* occasionally; now and then. **somewhat,** *adv.* to some extent; rather.—*n.* (*arch.*) something. **somewhen,** *adv.* (*rare*) at some time. **somewhere,** *adv.* in or to some place. **somewhither,** *adv.* (*arch.*) to some place. (O.E. *sum*)

somersault, somerset, *n.* leap in which one turns head over heels.—*v.i.* perform this. (L. *supra,* above; *salire,* leap)

somite, *n.* segment of body of articulate or vertebrate animal. **somitic,** *a.* (Gk. *sōma,* body)

somnambulate, *v.i.* walk in one's sleep. **somnambulant,** *a.* **somnambulism,** *n.* sleep-walking. **somnambulist,** *n.* sleep-walker. **somnambulistic,** *a.* (L. *somnus,* sleep; *ambulare,* walk)

somniferous, *a.* inducing sleep. (L. *somnus,* sleep; *ferre,* bear)

somniloquence, somniloquy, *nn.* talking in one's sleep. **somniloquist,** *n.* one who talks in his sleep. **somniloquous,** *a.* (L. *somnus,* sleep; *loqui,* talk)

somnolent, *a.* half asleep, drowsy; inducing sleep. **somnolism,** *n.* hypnotic sleep. (L. *somnus,* sleep)

son, *n.* male child or descendant; native (of); disciple, devotee. **S. (of God),** Second Person of the Trinity, Christ. **s.-in-law,** *n.* daughter's husband. (O.E. *sunu*)

sonant, *a.* sounding; (*phonetics*) voiced.—*n.* voiced letter. **sonance, sonancy,** *nn.* (L. *sonare,* sound)

sonata, *n.* instrumental composition of three or more movements in contrasted rhythms but related keys. **sonatina,** *n.* short sonata. (It.)

song, *n.* singing; words set to music; poetry, poem; notes of birds. **for a s.,** for a trifle. **nothing to make a s. about,** of little importance. **s.-bird,** *n.* bird that sings. **songster,** *n.* (*fem.* **songstress**) singer; song-bird; poet. (*sing*)

sonnet, *n.* poem with 14 lines of ten syllables; (*rare*) any short poem.—*v.i.* and *t.* write sonnets (to). **regular, Petrarchan, s.,** with first eight lines rhymed abbaabba, last six variously. **Shakespearian s.,** rhymed ababcdcdefefgg. **sonneteer,** *n.* writer of sonnets; poetaster. (L. *sonus,* sound+dim.)

sonny, *n.* (*colloq.*) small boy. (*son*)

sonometer, *n.* instrument for measuring sounds or testing powers of hearing. (L. *sonus,* sound. Gk. *metron,* measure)

sonorous, *a.* loud-sounding, resonant; high-sounding, rhetorical. **sonority,** *n.* **sonorescent,** *a.* emitting sound under the influence of some radiation. **sonorescence,** *n.* **sonorific,** *a.* producing sound. (L. *sonare,* sound)

sonsy, sonsie, *a.* (*Scot.*) plump, buxom; good-natured.

sonty, *n.* (*Shake.*) sanctity. (*saint*)

soojee, *n.* flour from Indian wheat; food made from this. (Hind. *sūjī*)

soom, *Scot.* form of **swim.**

soon, *adv.* in a short time; readily, quickly; willingly. **s. at,** (*Shake.*) about. (O.E. *sóna*)

soop, *v.t.* (*Scot.*) sweep.

soorkee, *n.* (*Anglo-Ind.*) powdered brick. (Pers. *surkhī*)

soot, *n.* black powder deposited by smoke.—*v.t.* cover with soot. (O.E. *sót*)

sooth, *n.* (*arch.*) truth. (O.E. *sóth*)

soothe, *v.t.* calm down, quiet; alleviate; flatter, humour. **soother,** *n.* one who soothes; baby's rubber teat. (O.E. *gesóthian,* prove truth of)

soothfast, *a.* (*arch.*) truthful; honest; faithful. (O.E. *sóthfæst*)

soothsayer, *n.* prophet, diviner. **soothsay,** *v.i.* foretell future.

sooty, *a.* of, covered with, black like, soot.

sop, *n.* piece of bread dipped in milk, gravy etc.; thing given to pacify, bribe.—*v.t.* and *i.* soak (up); drench; be wet through. (O.E. *sopp*)

soph, *abbr.* of **sophister** or **sophomore.**

sophism, *n.* false argument meant to deceive, specious fallacy. **sophist,** *n.* ancient Greek teacher of philosophy; one who uses plausible but unsound arguments. **sophister,** *n.* (*obs.*) university student in second or third year; (*Shake.*) sophist. **sophistic,** *a.* of sophists; sophistical. **sophistical,** *a.* subtly deceptive, quibbling; sophistic. **sophisticate,** *v.t.* and *i.* use sophisms (about); spoil simplicity or naturalness of; corrupt, adulterate. **sophisticated,** *a.* (of persons) artificial, worldly-wise. **sophistication,** *n.* **sophistry,** *n.* use of sophisms; sophism. (Gk. *sophos,* wise)

sophomore, *n.* second-year man at American university. **sophomoric,** *a.* adolescent, immature.

Sophy, *n.* old name for Shah of Persia. (Pers. *Çafī,* name of dynasty)

soporific, *a.* and *n.* (drug) causing sleep. **soporiferous, soporose, soporous,** *aa.* soporific. (L. *sopor,* sleep; *facere,* make)

soppy, *a.* soaked; weakly sentimental, sloppy.

soprano, *n.* (*pl.* **sopranos, soprani**) highest female or boy's voice; part for, singer with, this. **sopranist,** *n.* soprano singer. (It.)

sora, *n.* a small American rail. (native)

sorb, *n.* service-tree; (also **s.-apple**) its fruit. (L. *sorbus*)

sorbefacient, *a.* and *n.* (drug) promoting absorption. (L. *sorbēre,* suck in; *facere,* make)

sorbet, *n.* water-ice. (F.)

sorcerer, *n.* (*fem.* **sorceress**) one who uses spells, magician. **sorcery,** *n.* witchcraft, magic. (L. *sors,* lot)

sordamente, adv. (*mus.*) in a muffled manner. (It.)

sordid, *a.* squalid, mean; ignoble, base; meanly avaricious, mercenary; (of colours) muddy. (L. *sordēre,* be dirty)

sordine, *n.* mute, damper, for stringed instrument. (L. *surdus,* deaf)

sore, *a.* painful to touch, tender; grieved, sad; wounded in feelings, aggrieved; severe, grievous.—*adv.* grievously.—*n.* sore place, ulcer; painful memory. **sorely,** *adv.* grievously; very much. (O.E. *sár*)

sorel, *n.* buck of third year. **sore,** *n.* (*Shake.*) buck of fourth year. (*sorrel*)

sorghum, *n.* kinds of grass incl. millet. (It. *sorgo*)

soricine, *a.* of, like, shrew-mouse. (L. *sorex,* shrew-mouse)

sorites, *n.* (*logic*) series of linked syllogisms, the predicate of each forming subject of the next. (Gk. *sōros,* heap)

sorn, *v.i.* (*Scot.*) obtrude oneself as uninvited guest; sponge. (Ir. *sorthan,* free quarters)

soroptimist, *n.* member of women's rotary club. (L. *soror,* sister+*optimist*)

sororal, *a.* of sisters. **sororicide,** *n.* killing, killer, of a sister. **sorority,** *n.* sisterhood; (*Amer.*) women's college society. (L. *soror,* sister)

sorosis, *n.* compound pulpy fruit, e.g. pineapple. (Gk. *sōros,* heap)

sorra, *n.* (*Ir.*) sorrow. **s. a bit,** (*sl.*) never a bit.

sorrel, *n.* sour-leaved plant allied to dock. (O.F. *sorele*)

sorrel, *a.* and *n.* reddish-brown (horse); sorel. (O.F. *sor,* sorel+dim.)

sorrow, *n.* grief, sadness; regret,

penitence; misfortune, affliction.—*v.i.* feel sorrow, mourn. **sorrowful,** *a.* feeling or causing sorrow. (O.E. *sorg*)
sorry, *a.* regretful, vexed; feeling pity (for); ridiculously bad, wretched; (*Shake.*) sorrowful. **sorrily,** *adv.* **sorriness,** *n.* (O.E. *sár*, sore; not connected with *sorrow*)
sort, *n.* kind, species; (*arch.*) manner, way; (*Shake.*) class, rank.—*v.t.* and *i.* arrange in sorts, classify; (*arch.*) consort, agree; (*Shake.*) choose; happen; (*Scot.*) adjust, put right; punish. **a good s.,** (*colloq.*) a pleasant fellow. **out of ss.,** in poor health. **s. of,** rather; as it were. **sortance,** *n.* (*Shake.*) agreement. **sorter,** *n.* one who sorts, esp. letters at post office for distribution. (L. *sors*, lot)
sort, *n.* (*Shake.*) lot. *sortes Virgilianae, Biblicae,* divination by random opening of Virgil, the Bible. (L. *sors*)
sortie, *n.* sally made by besieged troops. (F.)
sortilege, *n.* divination by drawing lots. **sortition,** *n.* casting of lots. (L. *sors*, lot; *legere*, choose)
sorus, *n.* (*pl.* sori) cluster of spore-cases on back of fern-frond. (Gk. *sōros*, heap)
sostenuto, *a.* (*mus.*) prolonged. (It.)
S O S, appeal for help, esp. by wireless.
sot, *n.* habitual drunkard; (*Shake.*) fool.—*v.i.* tipple. **sottish,** *a.* (O.F.)
sotto voce, in an undertone. (It.)
sou, *n.* five-centime piece, French halfpenny. (F.)
soubrette, *n.* pert maidservant, coquettish girl, in comedy. (F.)
soubriquet, same as **sobriquet.**
soucar, *n.* Hindu banker. (Hind. *sāhūkār*, great merchant)
souchong, *n.* fine quality of black Chinese tea. (Chin, *siao*, small; *chung*, sort)
souffle, *n.* (*med.*) low murmur. (F.)
soufflé, *n.* dish made with white of egg beaten to froth and baked. (F.)
sough, *n.* low murmuring or sighing sound: moaning of wind.—*v.i.* make this. (O.E. *swógan*, resound)
sought, see **seek.**
soukar, same as **soucar.**
soul, *n.* spiritual and immortal part of human being; seat of emotion and intellect; essence of a thing, moving spirit; person. **s. of honour,** honour personified. **soulful,** *a.* full of deep feeling or sentiment. **soulless,** *a.* without nobleness of mind; dull, prosaic. (O.E. *sáwl*)
sound, *a.* healthy, not diseased; not decayed or defective; wise, judicious; right, orthodox; valid; reliable, efficient; thorough; (of sleep) unbroken.—*adv.* soundly. (O.E. *sund*)
sound, *n.* narrow channel, strait; air-bladder of fish. (O.E. *sund*)
sound, *v.t.* and *i.* find depth of (water) by means of lead etc.; try to elicit views of; (of whale) dive down suddenly; (*med.*) examine with probe. —*n.* surgeon's probe. (F. *sonder*)
sound, *n.* what is heard; meaningless noise; earshot.—*v.i.* and *t.* emit, cause to emit, sound; appear on narration, seem; be spread abroad, publish: give signal for; pronounce; listen to (heart etc.) with stethoscope. **s.-box,** *n.* part of gramophone containing diaphragm. **s.-film,** *n.* cinema film with mechanically produced dialogue recorded on **s.-track,** *n.* **s.-wave,** *n.* air-vibration causing sound. (L. *sonus*)
sound, (*Spens.*) form of **swoon.**
sounder, *n.* (*arch.*) herd of wild swine; young boar. (O.F. *sundre*)
sounding, *a.* resonant. **s.-board,** *n.* horizontal board over pulpit etc. carrying speaker's voice towards audience; thin plate increasing resonance of musical instrument.
soundings, *n.pl.* parts shallow enough to admit of lead finding bottom.
soup, *n.* liquid food made by boiling meat, vegetables etc., in water. **in the s.,** (*sl.*) in trouble. **s.-and-fish,** *n.* (*Amer. sl.*) full evening dress. **s.-kitchen, s.-ticket,** *nn.* for supplying free soup to poor. (F. *souper*, sup)
soupçon, *n.* flavour, trace. (F.)
sour, *a.* acid: rancid, musty; crabbed, morose; (of soil) cold and wet.—*v.t.* and *i.* turn sour. (O.E. *súr*)
source, *n.* fount, spring; starting-point, origin. (L. *surgere*, rise)
sourdine, *n.* harmonium stop with soft effect; sordine. (L. *surdus*, deaf)
sourdough, *n.* (*dial.*) leaven; (*Canada*) old-timer. (*sour*; *dough*)
souse, *n.* salt pickle; thing steeped in this; drenching, ducking.—*v.t.* and *i.* steep in souse; drench; plunge in water, duck.—*adv.* with a splash. **soused,** *a.* (*sl.*) drunk. (O.H.G. *salzan*, salt)
souse, *v.i.* and *t.* (*Shake.*) swoop down (upon). (O.F. *sorse*, source)
soutane, *n.* Roman Catholic priest's cassock. (F.)
souteneur, *n.* man living with prostitute and on her earnings. (F.)
souter, soutar, *n.* (*Scot.*) cobbler. (L. *sutor*)
south, *n.* point directly opposite north; southern lands; southern states of U.S.—*a.* and *adv.* towards or in the south; (of wind) from the south.—*v.i.* move southward; (of moon) cross meridian. **s.-east,** *n.* point midway between south and east. **s.-easter,** *n.* south-east wind. **s.-easterly,** *a.* towards or coming from the south-east. **s.-eastern,** *a.* belonging to the south-east, or in that direction. **s.-eastward,** *a.* and *adv.* towards the south-east. **s.-eastwards,** *adv.* **s.-west** etc., like **s.-east** etc. **southdown,** *n.* breed of sheep from South Downs. **souther,** *n.*

wind or storm from the south. **southerly**, *a.* towards or coming from the south. **southern**, *a.* in or of the south. **Southern Cross**, a constellation. **southerner**, *n.* native of the south. **southernwood**, *n.* kind of wormwood with scented leaves. **southing**, *n.* southward progress. **southpaw**, *a.* and *n.* (*Amer. sl.*) left-handed (player). **southron**, *n.* (*Scot.*, *arch.*) Englishman. **southward**, *a.* and *adv.* toward the south. **southwards**, *adv.* (O.E. *suth*)

souvenir, *n.* memento, keepsake. (F.)

sou'wester, *n.* waterproof hat with flap behind to protect neck.

sovereign, *a.* supreme; having supreme power; efficacious.—*n.* sovereign ruler, king, obsolete gold coin for £1. **sovereignty**, *n.* state of being sovereign. (L. *supra*, above)

soviet, *n.* workers' council in Russia. **sovietism**, *n.* political system of which soviet is unit. **sovietist**, *n.* supporter of sovietism. **sovkhos**, *n.* Russian co-operative farm. **sovnarkom**, *n.* council of people's commissars. (Russ.)

sovran, *arch.* form of **sovereign.**

sow, *v.t.* and *i.* (*p.p.* **sown** or **sowed**) scatter (seed) on ground; plant (ground) with seed; disseminate; cover thickly. (O.E. *sáwan*)

sow, *n.* female pig; bar of cast iron from which pigs branch. **s.-bug**, *n.* wood-louse. **s.-thistle**, *n.* kinds of yellow-flowered plant. (O.E. *sugu*)

sowar, *n.* (*Anglo-Ind.*) trooper of Indian cavalry; mounted orderly. **sowarry**, *n.* high official's mounted attendant or retinue. (Pers. *sawār*, horseman)

sowbread, *n.* wild cyclamen.

sowens, *n.pl.* (*Scot.*) oat husks steeped in water and boiled.

sowl, *v.t.* (*Shake.*) drag by the ears.

sown, see **sow.**

sowne, (*Spens.*) form of **sound.**

sox, trade spelling of **socks.**

soy, *n.* sauce made from fermented soya-bean. **soya-bean**, **s.-bean**, *n.* an Asiatic bean. (Jap. *shoyu*)

sozzled, *a.* (*sl.*) very drunk.

spa, *n.* medicinal spring; health resort with one. (place in Belgium)

space, *n.* interval between things; all such intervals collectively; the expanse of the universe; empty place, room; period of time; (*print.*) interval between lines or words.—*v.t.* arrange with spaces between. **s. out**, set at wider intervals. **s.-bar**, *n.* bar in typewriter for making spaces between words. **s.-time**, *n.* four-dimensional system embracing both space and time. **spacious**, *a.* extensive, roomy; offering great opportunities; large, not petty. (L. *spatium*)

spade, *n.* digging-tool with broad blade attached to long shaft.—*v.t.* dig with spade. **call a s. a s.**, speak plainly. **s.-work**, *n.* preliminary drudgery. (O.E. *spadu*)

spade, *n.* card with leaf-like markings; (*pl.*) suit of these. **s. guinea**, guinea of George III, marked with shield. (Sp. *espada*, sword)

spadger, *n.* (*sl.*) sparrow. (corrupt.)

spadiceous, **spadicose**, *aa.* of, having, a spadix.

spadille, *n.* ace of spades in ombre or quadrille. (F.)

spadix, *n.* (*pl.* **spadices**) flower-spike with fleshy axis, us. covered with large leaf. (Gk.=palm-branch)

spado, *n.* (*law*) person incapable of procreation. (Gk. *spadōn*, eunuch)

spae, *v.t.* and *i.* (*Scot.*) foretell. **spaewife**, *n.* fortune-teller.

spaghetti, *n.* kind of thin macaroni. (It.)

spahi, *n.* Algerian cavalryman in French army. (Hind. *sipahi*, sepoy)

spake, see **speak.**

spall, *n.* (*Spens.*) shoulder. (It. *spalla*)

spall, *v.t.* and *i.* and *n.* splinter, chip. **spalder**, *n.* one who spalls.

spalpeen, *n.* (*Ir.*) rascal, scamp.

span, *n.* (*Amer.*) pair, team, of horses etc. (Du.)

span, *n.* distance between tips of thumb and little finger at utmost stretch; this as measure, 9 in.; short distance; extent from end to end; unsupported stretch of arch or roof.—*v.t.* and *i.* encircle with thumb and finger; measure by spans; stretch across, extend over; bridge. **s.-roof**, *n.* with two sloping sides. (O.E.)

spandrel, *n.* triangular space between curve of arch and right angle enclosing it; design in corner of stamp.

spang, *v.i.* and *n.* (*Scot.*) leap.

spangle, *n.* small piece of glittering metal used to ornament dress; small glittering object.—*v.t.* adorn, cover, with spangles. (O.E. *spange*, buckle)

Spaniard, *n.* native of Spain.

spaniel, *n.* breed of dogs with drooping ears; fawning person. (*Spain*)

Spanish, *a.* and *n.* (language) of Spain. **S. fly**, insect from which cantharides is made. **S. grass**, esparto grass. **S. Main**, north coast of S. America; (incorrectly) Caribbean Sea.

spank, *v.t.* and *i.* strike on buttocks with open hand; slap; go quickly or dashingly.—*n.* spanking, slap. **spanker**, *n.* fore-and-aft sail on mizzen-mast; horse with fast spirited action; (*sl.*) striking person or thing. **spanking**, *a.* (*sl.*) brisk; fine, big. (imit.)

spanless, *a.* (*poet.*) beyond measure.

spanner, *n.* tool for tightening nuts, wrench. (G.)

spar, *v.i.* make fighting motions with fists, box; engage in repartee or banter; (of cocks) fight with spurs.—*n.* act of sparring; boxing-match; cock-fight. **sparring-partner**, *n.* boxer with whom another practises.

spar, *n.* pole or beam forming mast,

yard etc.—*v.t.* furnish with spar. **s.-deck,** *n.* light upper deck extending from bow to stern. (M.E. *sparre*)

spar, *n.* kinds of crystalline mineral. (O.E. *spæren*, gypsum)

sparable, *n.* headless nail used in shoemaking. (*sparrow-bill*)

spare, *a.* scanty, meagre; lean, thin; additional, in reserve; not in use.—*n.* spare part for substitution in machine.—*v.t.* and *i.* refrain from using, grudge; do without, give away without inconvenience; show mercy to, refrain from killing or destroying; let off; (*arch.*) forbear. **s. rib,** ribs of pork with small amount of flesh. **s. room,** room kept for guests. **sparing,** *a.* frugal, saving. (O.E. *spær*)

sparge, *v.t.* sprinkle. **sparger,** *n.* sprinkling-apparatus used in brewing. (L. *spargere*)

spar-hawk, same as **sparrow-hawk.**

spark, *n.* small glowing or burning particle; animating principle; trace; (*motoring*) electric spark which ignites explosive mixture in cylinder; (*pl., naut. sl.*) wireless operator.—*v.i.* and *t.* emit sparks; apply electric spark to. (O.E. *spearca*)

spark, *n.* gay fellow, gallant.—*v.i.* and *t.* play the gallant, court.

sparkle, *v.i.* seem to emit sparks, flash, glitter.—*n.* sparkling, glitter. **sparkling wines,** effervescent kinds. **sparkler,** *n.* (*sl.*) diamond.

sparklet, *n.* small spark; minute trace.

sparling, *n.* smelt.

sparrow, *n.* small brown bird. **s.-bill,** *n.* sparable. **s.-grass,** *n.* (*vulg.*) asparagus. **s.-hawk,** *n.* small hawk that hunts sparrows. (O.E. *spearwa*)

sparry, *a.* of, like, rich in, spar.

sparse, *a.* thinly scattered. (*sparge*)

Spartan, *a.* and *n.* (native) of Sparta; hardy, frugal (person).

spasm, *n.* sudden violent involuntary contraction of muscles; violent access, fit, of emotion etc. **spasmodic,** *a.* of, subject to, spasms; occurring by fits and starts. **Spasmodic School,** group of poets incl. Bailey, Dobell, and Alexander Smith, whose work was often strained and unnatural. **spasmology,** *n.* study of spasms. **spastic,** *a.* (*med.*) spasmodic. **spasticity,** *n.* (Gk. *spaein*, draw)

spat, *n.* spawn of shell-fish, esp. oyster.—*v.i.* shed spat.

spat, *n.* short gaiter buttoning under boot. (*spatterdash*)

spat, *n.* (*Scot.*) petty quarrel; large drop (of rain).

spat, see spit.

spatchcock, *n.* fowl killed and cooked in a hurry.—*v.t.* cook thus; interpolate as afterthought, sandwich in.

spate, *n.* sudden flood, as in river after rain.

spathe, *n.* large sheathlike leaf enclosing flower-cluster. **spathose, spathous,** *aa.* (Gk. *spathē*, broad blade)

spathic, spathose, *aa.* of, like, spar. (G. *spath*, spar)

spatial, *a.* of, in, space. **spatiality,** *n.* (L. *spatium*, space)

spattee, *n.* woman's woollen legging worn over stockings. (*spat*)

spatter, *v.t.* and *i.* splash, cast drops over; fall in scattered drops.—*n.* slight splash, sprinkling. **spatterdashes,** *n.pl.* leggings, gaiters.

spatula, *n.* broad thin flexible edgeless blade for spreading ointment etc. **spatule,** *n.* (*zool.*) racket-shaped formation. **spatular, spatulate,** *aa.* (Gk. *spathē*, broad blade+dim.)

spaul, *n.* (*Scot.*) limb.

spavin, *n.* kind of tumour on horse's leg. **spavined,** *a.* (O.F. *esparvain*)

spawn, *n.* eggs of fish, frogs, molluscs etc.; (in contempt) progeny.—*v.i.* and *t.* produce, deposit (spawn); (of spawn) be produced; (in contempt) generate. (L. *expandere*, spread out)

spay, *v.t.* render (female animal) sterile. (O.F. *espee*, sword)

speak, *v.i.* and *t.* (*past* **spoke,** *arch.* **spake;** *p.p.* **spoken**) utter (words), pronounce; talk, converse; make speech; use (specified language) in talking; sound; (*naut.*) hail and communicate with in passing. **so to s.,** as it were. **s. fair,** be polite to. **s. for,** speak on behalf of. **s. of,** talk about. **s. out, up,** speak frankly, loud or louder. **s. to,** address; speak in confirmation of. **s. well for,** witness favourably to. **s. with,** (*arch.*) talk to. (O.E. *specan*)

speakeasy, *n.* (*Amer.*) illicit drinking-saloon.

speaker, *n.* one who speaks; orator; chairman of House of Commons.

speaking, *a.* used in speech. **not on s. terms,** estranged. **s. likeness,** lifelike portrait. **s.-trumpet,** *n.* instrument for conveying voice to a distance. **s.-tube,** *n.* for conveying voice from one room to another.

spear, *n.* weapon with shaft and sharp point for throwing or stabbing; (*poet.*) spearman.—*v.t.* pierce, wound, with spear. **s. side,** male line. **spearhead,** *n.* leader of movement. **spearman,** *n.* soldier armed with spear. **spearmint,** *n.* common mint. (O.E. *spere*)

spec, *sl. abbr.* for **speculation.**

special, *a.* particular, peculiar; designed for a particular purpose; exceptional, uncommon.—*n.* special constable; extra train or newspaper edition. **specialist,** *n.* one who devotes himself to a single subject or branch of a subject. **specialistic,** *a.* **specialism,** *n.* **speciality,** *n.* specialness; distinctive feature; thing in which one specializes. **specialize,** *v.t.* and *i.* make special, limit; develop in particular direction; be, become, specialist (in). **specialization,**

n. **specialty,** *n.* speciality; (*law*) sealed contract. (*species*)
specie, *n.* coin as opp. to paper money. (*species*)
species, *n.* (*pl.* same) class of things with common characteristics; subdivision of genus; sort, kind. (L.)
specific, *a.* characteristic of a species or class; clearly defined, precise, explicit; (of drugs) for some particular disease or organ.—*n.* specific drug. **specification,** *n.* act of specifying; detailed descriptive statement of contract or patent. **specify,** *v.t.* make particular mention of; include in specification.
specimen, *n.* individual example; part used to typify whole; (*colloq.*) eccentric person. (L.)
speciology, *n.* science of origin and development of species.
specious, *a.* having a fair appearance; plausible. **speciosity,** *n.* (L. *species*, appearance, kind)
speck, *n.* (*Amer.*) blubber. **specksioneer,** *n.* chief harpooner. (Du. *spek*, fat)
speck, *n.* small spot or mark, dot; particle.—*v.t.* mark with specks. **speckle,** *n.* small spot or mark distinct in colour from surrounding surface.—*v.t.* variegate with speckles, spot. **speckless,** *a.* spotless. (O.E. *specca*)
specs, *colloq. abbr.* of **spectacles.**
spectacle, *n.* sight; public show, noteworthy scene; (*pl.*) pair of lenses in frame to assist defective eyesight. **pair of ss.,** (*cricket sl.*) two ducks. **spectacled,** *a.* wearing spectacles. **spectacular,** *a.* of the nature of a show. **spectator,** *n.* (*fem.* **spectatress**) onlooker. **spectatorial,** *a.* (L. *spectare*, look at)
spectral, *a.* of or like a spectre, ghostly; of the spectrum.
spectre, *n.* ghost, apparition. **s. of the Brocken,** huge shadow of observer projected on mountain mists. (L. *spectrum*, image)
spectrum, *n.* (*pl.* **spectra**) band of colours into which beam of light is split up by passing through prism; after-image. **s. analysis,** chemical analysis by means of spectrum. **spectrogram,** *n.* reproduction of spectrum. **spectrograph,** *n.* instrument for making spectrograms. **spectrography,** *n.* **spectrology,** *n.* science of spectrum analysis. **spectrophone,** *n.* adaptation of spectroscope in which succession of sounds takes the place of observation by eye. **spectroscope,** *n.* instrument for forming and examining spectra. **spectroscopic, spectroscopical,** *aa.* **spectroscopy,** *n.* (L.=image)
specular, *a.* of a speculum; reflecting.
speculate, *v.i.* make theories or guesses; buy or sell stocks with a view to profiting by change of price, not as permanent investment; engage in risky business transactions. **speculation,** *n.* speculating; conjecture; (*Shake.*) power of seeing; scout. **speculative,** *a.* given to speculation; theoretical; risky; (*Shake.*) seeing. **speculator,** *n.* (L. *speculari*, spy out)
speculum, *n.* (*pl.* **specula**) mirror, esp. metal one in reflecting telescope; instrument for dilating cavities of the body for examination; coloured patch on bird's wing. (L.)
sped, see **speed.**
speech, *n.* act, faculty, of speaking; enunciation; remark; address, oration; language. **s.-day,** *n.* school prize-giving day. **speechify,** *v.i.* make speeches; hold forth tediously. **speechification,** *n.* **speechless,** *a.* dumb; unable to speak for emotion; (*sl.*) dead drunk. (*speak*)
speed, *n.* swiftness; rate of motion, velocity; (*arch.*) success.—*v.i.* and *t.* (*past, p.p.* **sped**) go fast, hasten; fare, prosper; wish or grant success to; (of motorist) exceed speed limit; (*arch.*) send off, kill. **s. up,** cause to work faster. **s.-boat,** *n.* fast motorboat. **s.-limit,** *n.* legal limit of vehicle's speed. **speedily,** *adv.* rapidly; promptly. **speedometer,** *n.* instrument indicating vehicle's speed. **speedway,** *n.* public track for motorcycle racing. **speedwell,** *n.* small blue-flowered plant. **speedy,** *a.* rapid; prompt. (O.E. *spēd*)
speel, *v.i.* and *n.* (*Scot.*) climb.
speer, *v.t.* and *i.* (*Scot.*) ask.
speiss, *n.* arsenical compound found in smelting certain ores. (G. *speise*, amalgam)
spelaean, *a.* of, inhabiting, a cave. **spelaeology,** *n.* scientific study of caves. (Gk. *speos*, cave)
spelican, spellican, same as **spillikin.**
spell, *v.t.* take turns with in working. —*n.* turn of activity; short period, interval. (O.E. *spelian*)
spell, *n.* magic formula, charm; strong fascination or attraction.—*v.t.* and *i.* (*past, p.p.* **spelt** or **spelled**) name, write, letters of (word); (of letters) form (word); involve, signify. **spelling-bee,** *n.* spelling competition. **spelling-book,** *n.* for teaching spelling. **spellbinder,** *n.* speaker who can hold audience spellbound. **spellbound,** *a.* fascinated, entranced. (O.E.=saying)
spelt, *n.* kind of wheat. (L.L. *spelta*)
spelter, *n.* zinc.
spence, *n.* (*arch.*) larder, pantry; (*Scot.*) spare room, parlour. (O.F.)
spencer, *n.* kind of short jacket or overcoat. (Earl *Spencer*)
spencer, *n.* (*naut.*) trysail.
Spencerian, *a.* and *n.* (follower) of Herbert Spencer and his synthetic philosophy. **Spencerism, Spencerianism,** *nn.*
spend, *v.t.* and *i.* (*past, p.p.* **spent**) give in payment; use up, consume; wear out, exhaust; pass (time); (*Shake.*)

utter. **spendthrift,** *n.* squanderer, prodigal.—*a.* extravagant, thriftless. (O.E. *spendan*)

spense, same as **spence.**

Spenserian, *a.* of the poet Edmund Spenser. **S. stanza,** eight ten-syllabled lines followed by alexandrine, rhymed ababbcbcc.

spent, *a.* exhausted; (of bullet) having lost speed; (of fish) having spawned.

sperm, *n.* (also **s.-whale**) cachalot. (*spermaceti*)

sperm, *n.* male generative fluid, semen. **spermary,** *n.* male germ-gland, testicle. **spermatic,** *a.* of sperm or spermary. **spermatize,** *v.i.* emit sperm. **spermatoblast, spermoblast,** *nn.* germ of spermatozoon. **spermatogenesis, spermatogeny,** *nn.* development of spermatozoa. **spermatogenous,** *a.* **spermatology,** *n.* scientific study of sperm. **spermatological,** *a.* **spermatologist,** *n.* **spermatorrhoea,** *n.* involuntary emission of semen. **spermatozoon,** *n.* (*pl.* **spermatozoa**) male sexual cell, fertilizing egg. **spermatozoal, spermatozoan,** *aa.* **spermology,** *n.* branch of botany dealing with seeds; spermatology. **spermological,** *a.* **spermologist,** *n.* (Gk. *sperma,* seed)

spermaceti, *n.* white waxy substance made from oil of sperm-whale. (Gk. *sperma,* seed. L. *cetus,* whale)

spew, spue, *v.t.* and *i.* vomit. (O.E. *spiwan*)

sphacelate, *v.t.* and *i.* affect with gangrene, mortify.—*a.* gangrenous. **sphacelation,** *n.* (Gk. *sphakelos,* gangrene)

sphagnum, *n.* (*pl.* **sphagna**) peat or bog moss. (Gk. *sphagnos,* moss)

sphenic, *a.* wedge-shaped. **sphenogram,** *n.* cuneiform character. **sphenography,** *n.* cuneiform writing. **sphenographic,** *a.* **sphenoid,** *a.* wedge-like.—*n.* (also **sphenoid bone**) large bone at base of skull. **sphenoidal,** *a.* (Gk. *sphēn,* wedge)

sphere, *n.* ball, globe; field of action, range; social circle; (*Ptolemaic astron.*) any of revolving transparent shells in which heavenly bodies were supposed to be set; (*Shake.*) eye-socket.—*v.t.* place in, form into, a sphere. **spheric,** *a.* (*poet.*) of the heavens, celestial; spherical.—*n.pl.* spherical geometry. **spherical,** *a.* of spheres; sphere-shaped. **sphericity,** *n.* **spheroid,** *n.* body which is nearly but not quite spherical. **spheroidal, spheroidic, spheroidical,** *aa.* **spheroidicity,** *n.* **spherometer,** *n.* instrument for measuring curvature of round surfaces and thickness of small bodies. **spherule,** *n.* small sphere. **spherular, spherulate,** *aa.* **spherulite,** *n.* vitreous globule found in certain rocks. **spherulitic,** *a.* **sphery,** *a.* of the celestial spheres, heavenly. (Gk. *sphaira*)

sphincter, *n.* ring-like muscle closing orifice of body. **sphincteral, sphincterial, sphincteric,** *aa.* (Gk. *sphinggein,* bind tight)

sphinx, *n.* fabulous monster, lion with woman's head, which slew all who could not solve a riddle put by it; enigmatic or inscrutable person; hawk-moth; kind of baboon. (Gk. *sphingx*)

sphragistics, *n.pl.* study of engraved seals. (Gk. *sphragis,* seal)

sphygmus, *n.* pulse. **sphygmic,** *a.* **sphygmogram,** *n.* record of pulse-beats made by **sphygmograph,** *n.* pulse-recording instrument. **sphygmographic,** *a.* **sphygmography,** *n.* **sphygmology,** *n.* study of the pulse. **sphygmometer, sphygmomanometer,** *nn.* instrument for measuring blood-pressure. **sphygmophone, sphygmoscope** *nn.* instruments for making pulse-beat audible, visible. (Gk. *sphugmos*)

spica, *n.* (*bot.*) spike; (*med.*) spiral bandage. **spicate, spicated,** *aa.* (*bot.*) having a spike. (L.=ear of corn)

spice, *n.* aromatic vegetable substance used for seasoning; spicery; trace, smack.—*v.t.* season with spices; flavour. **spicebush,** *n.* aromatic American shrub. **spicery,** *n.* spices collectively. **spicily,** *adv.* in a spicy manner. **spiciness,** *n.* (*species*)

spick and span, bright and clean, smart and fresh. (obs. *span new,* from O.N. *spán-nýr,* new as a chip)

spicule, *n.* small spike; small hard body found in sponges. **spicular, spiculate,** *aa.* (*spica*+dim.)

spicy, *a.* flavoured with spice; piquant, racy, improper.

spider, *n.* eight-legged animal that spins web to catch its prey; light dog-cart; trivet. **s.-crab, s.-monkey,** *nn.* kinds with long thin legs. **s.-line,** *n.* thread of spider's web. **s.-web,** *n.* spider's web. **spiderlike,** *a.* **spidery,** *a.* like, full of, spiders; very thin. (O.E. *spinnan,* spin)

spied, see **spy.**

spiegeleisen, *n.* kind of cast iron containing manganese. (G.)

spiel, *n.* (*Amer.*) speech; patter, yarn.—*v.i.* reel off spiel. (G.=game)

spiff, *a.* (*dial.*) smart, spruce. **spiffing,** *a.* (*sl.*) excellent.

spiflicate, spifflicate, *v.t.* (*sl.*) beat; disconcert; suffocate, kill. **spiflication, spifflication,** *n.*

spigot, *n.* plug for stopping air-hole in cask, vent-peg; part of tap by which flow is controlled. (*spica*)

spike, *n.* pointed projection; pointed piece of metal, large nail; ear of corn; (*bot.*) flower-cluster of many stalkless or short-stalked flowers arranged round a central column; (*sl.*) very High Church clergyman.—*v.t.* furnish, set, fasten, with spikes; pierce with spike, impale; make (cannon) useless by plugging touch-hole. **s. person's guns,** upset his schemes. **spikelet,** *n.* small or secondary spike. (O.N. *spik,* nail and L. *spica,* ear of corn)

spikenard, *n.* herb like valerian; aromatic substance got from it. (L. *spica nardi,* spike of nard)

spiky, *a.* set with spikes, bristling; (*sl.*) very High-Church.

spile, *n.* plug to stop vent, spigot; stake driven into ground as foundation, pile.—*v.t.* make vent-hole in (cask).

spill, *v.t.* and *i.* (*past, p.p.* **spilt** or **spilled**) allow to run out, esp. unintentionally; flow out; shed (blood); (*colloq.*) throw off, upset, be upset. (*naut.*) empty (sail) of wind; (*Shake.*) destroy.—*n.* (*colloq.*) upset, tumble. **s. the beans,** (*Amer. sl.*) divulge the matter. (O.E. *spillan*)

spill, *n.* thin strip of wood or paper for lighting pipes etc. (M.E.)

spiller, *n.* seine let down into larger one to take out fish.

spillikin, *n.* one of a set of small rods or pegs; (*pl.*) game played with these. (*spill*+dim.)

spillway, *n.* passage to carry off overflow of water from dam.

spilth, *n.* (*arch.*) overflow.

spin, *v.t.* and *i.* (*past* **span** or **spun,** *p.p.* **spun**) draw out and twist (wool, fibre) into threads; make (thread) thus; compose (story); revolve, whirl; go on wheels; (*mech.*) bend (sheet metal) into shape on lathe; (*sl.*) reject in examination.—*n.* rapid rotation, whirl; brisk run or ride. **s. a yarn,** tell a story. **s. out,** protract unduly. **spinning-jenny,** *n.* machine for spinning several threads at same time. **spinning-wheel,** *n.* machine for household spinning, us. driven by treadle. **spun glass,** stretched into threads while hot. **spun gold, silver,** gold, silver, thread. **spun silk,** cheap material made from short-fibred silk. **spun yarn,** rope of loosely twisted strands. (O.E. *spinnan*)

spinach, spinage, *n.* thick-leaved garden vegetable. **spinaceous,** *a.* (O.F. *espinache*)

spinal, *a.* of the spine. **s. column,** backbone. **s. cord,** cord of nerve matter filling cavity of spine.

spindle, *n.* rod on which thread from distaff is wound; pin, axis, on which anything revolves. **live, dead, s.,** revolving, non-revolving, spindle. **s.-shanks,** *n.* person with long thin legs. **s.-shanked,** *a.* **s.-shaped,** *a.* thick in middle and tapering at ends. **s.-tree,** *n.* shrub with hard wood. **spindly,** *a.* long and thin. (*spin*)

spindrift, *n.* spray blown along surface of sea.

spine, *n.* backbone; central ridge; back of book; thorn, prickle. (L. *spina*)

spinel, *n.* a crystalline mineral. (O.F. *espinelle*)

spineless, *a.* invertebrate; lacking strength of character.

spinet, *n.* small keyboard instrument, ancestor of harpsichord and piano.

spini-, from L. *spina,* thorn, backbone, used in **spinicerebrate,** *a.* having brain and spinal cord; **spiniferous,** *a.* producing spines; **spinifex,** *n.* kinds of pointed Australian grass; **spiniform,** *a.* thorn-shaped.

spinnaker, *n.* large extra sail used by racing yacht before wind. (*Sphinx,* yacht using it)

spinneret, *n.* thread-spinning organ of spider.

spinney, *n.* copse, thicket. (L. *spinetum,* thicket of thorns)

spinose, *a.* full of spines, prickly. **spinosity,** *n.* **spinous,** *a.* thorn-shaped; spinose.

spinster, *n.* unmarried woman; old maid. **spinsterhood,** *n.* (=one who spins)

spinthariscope, *n.* instrument showing by sparks the emission of rays from radium. (Gk. *spintharis,* spark; *skopein,* view)

spinule, *n.* small spine, prickle. **spinulose, spinulous,** *aa.*

spiny, *a.* prickly; perplexing, thorny.

spiracle, *n.* breathing-hole; blowhole of whale. **spiracular,** *a.* (L. *spirare,* breathe)

spiraea, *n.* garden plant allied to meadow-sweet. (Gk. *speira,* coil)

spiral, *a.* winding round a centre, like thread of screw; coiled.—*n.* spiral curve.—*v.t.* and *i.* make spiral; move in spiral. **spirality,** *n.* (Gk. *speira,* coil)

spirant, *a.* and *n.* (consonant) pronounced with friction of breath against part of mouth, e.g. *f, v.* (L. *spirare,* breathe)

spire, *n.* pointed part of steeple; peak, plant etc., of similar tapering form. —*v.i.* and *t.* shoot up like, furnish with, spire. (O.E. *spir*)

spire, *n.* spiral, coil; single twist of this. (Gk. *speira*)

spirillum, *n.* (*pl.* **spirilla**) bacterium of spiral structure. (*spire*)

spirit, *n.* life-principle animating body; soul; disembodied person, ghost; frame of mind, disposition; courage, liveliness; essential meaning (opp. to letter); liquid got by distillation; alcohol; (*pl.*) mood; exaltation; spirituous liquors.—*v.t.* carry (away) secretly; cheer. **the (Holy) S.,** the Holy Ghost. **in the s.,** in imagination. **s., ss., of wine,** pure alcohol. **s.-lamp,** *n.* one burning methylated spirit. **s.-level,** *n.* instrument showing deviation from level by movement of bubble in spirit. **s.-rapping,** *n.* supposed communication with spirits by rapping on a table at seances. **s.-room,** *n.* (*naut.*) paymaster's store-room. (L. *spirare,* breathe)

spirited, *a.* animated, lively; courageous.
spiritism, *n.* spiritualism. **spiritist,** *n.*
spiritless, *a.* lacking spirit; apathetic, abject.
spiritoso, *adv.* (*mus.*) with animation.
spiritual, *a.* concerned with the soul or religion; ecclesiastical; unworldly. —*n.* negro sacred song or hymn. **spiritualism,** *n.* belief that spirits of the dead communicate with the living; (*philos.*) doctrine that spirit is the only reality. **spiritualist,** *n.* and *a.* **spiritualistic,** *a.* **spirituality,** *n.* spiritual quality; that which belongs to the Church. **spiritualize,** *v.t.* make spiritual, elevate; animate. **spiritualization,** *n.*
spirituelle, *a. fem.* (*masc. spirituel*) refined, ethereal; sprightly. (F.)
spirituous, *a.* containing a large percentage of alcohol, distilled.
spirivalve, *a.* having spiral shell.
spirket, *n.* space between floor-timbers of ship.
spiro-, from Gk. *speira,* coil, used in **spirochaete,** *n.* spiral-shaped microorganism.
spiro-, from L. *spirare,* breathe, used in **spirograph,** *n.* instrument recording movements in breathing; **spirometer,** *n.* instrument recording volume of air taken in by lungs; **spirophone,** *n.* instrument for inducing artificial respiration.
spirt, see **spurt.**
spit, *v.i.* and *t.* (*past, p.p.* **spat,** *arch.* **spit**) eject (saliva) from mouth; eject, utter, violently; make spitting noise, sputter; rain in scattered drops.—*n.* spittle; spitting; frothy secretion of certain insects; counterpart, likeness. **s. it out,** (*sl.*) speak up. **s. upon,** show contempt for. (O.E. *spittan*)
spit, *n.* pointed rod on which meat is stuck for roasting; long narrow point of land running out into water.—*v.t.* pierce with spit; transfix. (O.E. *spitu*)
spit, *n.* depth of earth equal to blade of spade. (Du.)
spital, spital-house, *nn.* (*Shake.*) hospital. (*hospital*)
spitchcock, *v.t.* split and broil.—*n.* spitchcocked eel.
spitcher, *v.t.* (*naval sl.*) sink (submarine)
spite, *n.* petty hatred, malice; grudge; (*Shake.*) injury; vexation.—*v.t.* mortify intentionally. **in s. of,** notwithstanding. **spiteful,** *a.* meanly hostile, malicious. (*despite*)
spitfire, *n.* hot-tempered person.
spit-lock, *v.t.* mark out (lines of trench) with point of pick.
spittle, *n.* saliva.
spittoon, *n.* pan to spit into.
spitz, *n.* (also **s.-dog**) Pomeranian. (G.)
splanchnic, *a.* of the intestines, visceral. **splanchnology,** *n.* science of viscera. **splanchnotomy,** *n.* anatomy of viscera. (Gk. *splangchna,* entrails)
splash, *v.t.* and *i.* dash (liquid) about; spatter with water or mud; (of liquid) be flung about; go with splash (into).—*n.* act or sound of splashing; patch of colour; small amount of soda-water. **s.-board,** *n.* mudguard in front of driver in vehicle. (*plash*)
splatter, *v.i.* and *t.* make continuous splashing sound; spatter; jabber.
splay, *v.t.* and *i.* form with diverging sides, spread outwards; dislocate (horse's shoulder).—*a.* splayed.—*n.* splayed side of loophole etc. **s.-foot,** *n.* flat foot turned outwards. **s.-mouth,** *n.* wide mouth. (*display*)
spleen, *n.* organ near stomach which acts on blood; ill humour; melancholy; (*Shake.*) fit, mood. **spleenful, spleenish,** *aa.* peevish, fretful. **spleenwort,** *n.* kinds of fern. (Gk. *splēn*)
splendid, *a.* magnificent, sumptuous; glorious, grand; shining, brilliant; (*colloq.*) very satisfactory. **splendent,** *a.* lustrous, gleaming; illustrious. **splendiferous,** *a.* (*sl.*) magnificent; extremely good. **splendour,** *n.* great brightness, brilliance; magnificence, grandeur. (L. *splendēre,* shine)
splenetic, *a.* of the spleen; peevish.—*n.* medicine for, sufferer from, disease of the spleen. **splenetically,** *adv.* **splentic,** *a.* of, in, the spleen. **splenitis,** *n.* inflammation of the spleen. **splenitive,** *a.* fiery, passionate. **splenization,** *n.* conversion of lung into tissue like that of the spleen. **splenoid,** *a.* spleenlike. **splenology,** *n.* study of the spleen. **splenological,** *a.* **splenotomy,** *n.* incision into, dissection of, the spleen.
splenius, *n.* (*pl.* **splenii**) flat muscle on either side of back of neck. **splenial,** *a.* (Gk. *splēnion,* bandage)
spleuchan, *n.* (*Scot.*) pouch.
splice, *v.t.* join (ropes) by interweaving strands; join (pieces of wood) by overlapping; (*sl.*) join in marriage.—*n.* join made by splicing; part of handle of cricket-bat which fits into blade. **sit on the s.,** (*cricket sl.*) play cautious defensive game. (M.Du. *splissen*)
spline, *n.* flexible ruler used in drawing curves; square key fitting into shaft and hub to ensure that they revolve together.
splint, *n.* thin piece of wood for keeping broken bone in position; hard tumour on horse's leg; splint-bone. —*v.t.* hold in place with splints. **s.-bone,** *n.* minor bone of horse's leg; fibula. (L.G. *splinte,* iron pin)
splinter, *n.* thin sharp irregular fragment.—*v.t.* and *i.* break into splinters, shiver. **s.-bar,** *n.* crossbar supporting springs of vehicle; swingletree. **s.-bone,** *n.* fibula. **s.-proof,** *a.* giving projection from shell splinters. **splintery,** *a.* of, like, splinters; apt to splinter. (*splint*)
split, *v.i.* and *t.* (*past, p.p.* **split,** *rare* **splitted**) divide lengthwise; burst,

rend, be rent; suffer disunion, disunite; share; (*sl.*) betray secret.—*n.* splitting; fissure, rent; disunion, schism; (*sl.*) small bottle of soda-water; (*pl.*) **feat** of sitting on floor with legs spread flat sideways. **s. hairs,** make subtle distinctions. **s. infinitive,** with word separating 'to' from verb, e.g. 'try to always remember.' **s. on,** (*sl.*) betray. **s. one's sides,** laugh uproariously. **s. peas,** dried and split for cooking. **s. pin,** with divided end which springs apart to keep it in place. **s. ring,** kind on which keys are held. **s. shot, stroke,** (*croquet*) by which touching balls are driven in different directions. **s. the difference,** take mean between suggested amounts. (M.Du. *splitten*)

splodge, same as **splotch.**

splore, *n.* (*Scot.*) frolic, spree.

splosh, *n.* (*colloq.*) quantity of water thrown down; (*sl.*) money.

splotch, *n.* smear, blotch.

splurge, *n.* (*Amer.*) obtrusive display, ostentation.—*v.i.* make splurge.

splutter, *n.* sound, action, of repeated spitting.—*v.i.* and *t.* speak incoherently with splutter; emit splutter. (imit.)

Spode, *n.* a fine pottery. (maker)

spodomancy, *n.* divination by ashes. (Gk. *spodos,* ashes; *mantis,* seer)

spoffish, *a.* (*sl.*) officious, fussy.

spoil, *n.* goods taken by violence, plunder; emoluments of office; what is gained by effort; (*Shake.*) spoliation, ruin.—*v.t.* and *i.* (*past, p.p.* **spoilt or spoiled**) plunder, rob; injure, impair; treat with excessive indulgence, damage character or manners of thus; deteriorate, go bad; (*sl.*) maim, kill. **s.-sport,** *n.* one who interferes with others' enjoyment. **s.-five,** *n.* a card game. **spoiling for a fight,** eager for one. (L. *spolium*)

spoke, *n.* any of the bars joining hub of wheel to rim; rung of ladder; bar to prevent wheel from turning.—*v.t.* fit with spokes; check with spoke. **put s. in one's wheel,** thwart him. (O.E. *spáca*)

spoke, spoken, see **speak.**

spokeshave, *n.* blade with handle at each end for planing spokes.

spokesman, *n.* one who speaks as representative of others.

spolia opima, arms of hostile leader killed by Roman general in single combat; supreme achievement. (L.)

spoliation, *n.* act of spoiling, pillage; (*law*) destruction of document to prevent its use in evidence. **spoliator,** *n.* **spoliatory,** *a.*

spondee, *n.* two-syllabled foot, long-long. **spondaic,** *a.* (Gk. *spondeios*)

spondulicks, *n.pl.* (*Amer. sl.*) money.

spondyl, spondyle, *n.* joint of backbone. (Gk. *spondulos*)

sponge, *n.* kinds of marine animal; skeleton of this, used to absorb water; mop for cleaning bore of cannon; sponge cake; sponger; sot.—*v.t.* and *i.* wipe, wet, with sponge; be meanly dependent (on), cadge. **throw up the s.,** admit defeat. **s.-bag,** *n.* for holding sponge. **s.-bag trousers,** with black and white check. **s.-bath,** *n.* saucer-shaped bath. **s. cake,** soft light sweet cake. **s.-down,** *n.* sponging of the body. **sponging-house,** *n.* (formerly) house where debtors were kept before being imprisoned. **sponger,** *n.* one who sponges on others. **spongoid,** *a.* spongelike. **spongology,** *n.* science of sponges. **spongy,** *a.* like a sponge; of open texture, porous; moist and soft; marshy. (Gk. *sponggia*)

sponsal, *a.* of betrothal or marriage. **sponsion,** *n.* being surety for another. (L. *spondēre,* promise)

sponsible, *a.* (*Scot.*) reliable; respectable.

sponson, *n.* platform projecting from ship's side.

sponsor, *n.* one who makes himself responsible for another; introducer of person or thing; godparent. **sponsorial,** *a.* **sponsorship,** *n.* (L.)

spontaneous, *a.* voluntary, of one's own free will; self-produced, without external cause; not laboured. **s. generation,** production of living from non-living matter. **spontaneity,** *n.* (L. *sponte,* of one's own accord)

spontoon, *n.* ancient kind of halberd. (L. *pungere,* prick)

spoof, *v.t.* and *n.* (*sl.*) hoax, swindle.

spook, *n.* ghost. **spookish, spooky,** *aa.* (Du.)

spool, *n.* reel, bobbin.—*v.t.* wind on spool. (M.Du. *spoele*)

spoon, *n.* implement with shallow bowl at end of handle; spoon-shaped thing; (*golf*) club like brassy but with more loft, (formerly) wooden club with hollowed face.—*v.t.* and *i.* lift with spoon, scoop; (*cricket*) hit feebly upwards. **s.-bait,** *n.* bright spoon-shaped revolving piece of metal. **s.-bill,** *n.* kinds of wading bird. **s.-drift,** same as **spindrift. s.-fed,** *a.* artificially fed or fostered. **s.-meat,** *n.* infants' food, slops. (O.E. *spón*)

spoon, *n.* (*sl.*) person in love; silly person; love-making.—*v.i.* (*sl.*) make love (to). **be ss. on,** (*sl.*) be in love with.

spoonerism, *n.* involuntary transposition of sounds in successive words, e.g. 'I have in my breast a half-warmed fish.' (Dr. W. A. *Spooner*)

spoonful, *n.* amount a spoon holds.

spoony, spooney, *a.* amorous, sentimental.—*n.* weak-minded person.

spoor, *n.* track, trail, of wild animal. —*v.t.* and *i.* follow spoor (of). (Du.)

sporadic, sporadical, *aa.* occurring singly or in scattered instances. (Gk. *speirein,* sow)

spore, *n.* minute reproductive organism of flowerless plant or protozoan. **sporangium, sporange,** *nn.* spore-case of fern etc. **sporogenesis,** *n.* formation of, reproduction by, spores. **sporogenous,** *a.* (Gk. *speirein,* sow)

sporran, *n.* pouch worn in front of kilt. (Gael. *sporan*)

sport, *n.* pastime, outdoor recreation; fun, diversion; plant or animal varying from normal type, freak; (*sl.*) sporting person; (*pl.*) athletic meeting.—*v.i.* and *t.* frolic, dally; wear, display; (*bot., zool.*) become, produce, sport. **make s. of,** ridicule. **sporting,** *a.* of sport or sportsmen; ready to take risks. **sportive,** *a.* playful, frolicsome. **sportsman,** *n.* (*fem.* **sportswoman**) one engaged in sport; fair-minded person, good loser. **sportsmanlike,** *a.* **sportsmanship,** *n.* (*disport*)

sporule, *n.* small spore. **sporular,** *a.*

spot, *n.* small mark, speck; stain, blemish; pimple; locality, place; marked point on billiard-table, spot-ball; (*colloq.*) small quantity.—*v.t.* and *i.* mark, become marked, with spots; (*colloq.*) detect, identify.—*a.* for immediate delivery or payment. **on the s.,** at once; present; in good form. **put on the s.,** (*Amer. sl.*) arrange murder of. **s. cash,** money down. **s.-ball,** *n.* (*billiards*) white ball with spot on it. **s.-barred,** *a.* (*billiards*) limiting use of **s.-stroke,** *n.* in which red ball is pocketed from spot. **spotted dog,** (*sl.*) plum-duff. **spotted fever,** cerebro-spinal meningitis. **spotless,** *a.* scrupulously clean; pure, immaculate. **spotlight,** *n.* concentrated beam thrown on part of stage. **spotter,** *n.* person trained to watch for raiding aeroplanes. **spotty,** *a.* marked with spots; patchy. (M.E.)

spouse, *n.* husband or wife. **spousal,** *a.* nuptial.—*n.* (us. *pl.*) marriage. (L. *spondēre,* promise)

spout, *v.t.* and *i.* pour forth (liquid), gush; recite, declaim; (*sl.*) pawn.—*n.* projecting tube or lip for discharging liquid; jet. **up the s.,** (*sl.*) in pawn. (M.E. *spouten*)

sprachle, same as **sprauchle.**

sprack, *a.* vigorous, sprightly.

sprag, *n.* piece of wood to lock a wheel. —*v.t.* lock with this.

sprain, *v.t.* wrench, strain (ankle etc.). —*n.* such injury.

spraints, *n.pl.* otter's dung. (L. *exprimere,* press out)

sprang, see **spring.**

sprat, *n.* small fish of herring family. —*v.i.* fish for sprats. (O.E. *sprott*)

sprattle, *v.i.* and *n.* (*Scot.*) scramble.

sprauchle, *v.i.* (*Scot.*) clamber with difficulty.

sprawl, *v.i.* and *t.* lie, sit, in ungainly manner; spread out irregularly, straggle. — *n.* sprawling position. (O.E. *spreawlian*)

spray, *n.* small branch with leaves and flowers, sprig; ornament of this form. **sprayey,** *a.* (M.E.)

spray, *n.* liquid flying in fine drops; device for producing this.—*v.t.* scatter in, sprinkle with, spray. **sprayer,** *n.* spraying - apparatus. **sprayey,** *a.*

spread, *v.t.* and *i.* (*past, p.p.* same) stretch out, extend; unroll, unfurl; scatter abroad, overlay; diffuse, hand on; force apart.—*n.* extension, increase; amount of expansion; (*sl.*) feast. **s. eagle,** (*heraldry*) with wings and legs spread. **s. oneself,** (*sl.*) talk ostentatiously. **s.-eagle,** *v.t.* tie up with arms and legs spread out. —*a.* noisily patriotic. **s.-eagleism,** *n.* **s.-over,** *n.* system by which maximum legal hours of work are averaged over a period. **spreader,** *n.* bar for stretching. (O.E. *sprǣdan*)

spree, *n.* lively frolic; drinking-bout. —*v.i.* have spree.

sprent, *a.* (*arch.*) sprinkled. (O.E. *sprengan,* cause to spring)

sprig, *n.* small shoot, spray; spray-like ornament; scion; headless nail, brad. **sprigged, spriggy,** *aa.*

sprightly, *a.* gay, vivacious, lively.

spright, *arch.* form of **sprite. sprighted,** *a.* (*Shake.*) haunted. **sprightful,** *a.* (*Shake.*) high-spirited.

spring, *v.i.* and *t.* (*past* **sprang,** *p.p.* **sprung**) jump, leap; move suddenly; well up from source, rise; sprout up, grow; be descended (of); arise (from); set off or reveal suddenly; rouse (game); strain at joints, warp; develop (leak); provide with springs. —*n.* leap; metal spiral, elastic device; resilience; source, fount; small stream; motive, origin; strain, crack; season from March to May, (*astron.*) 21 March to 22 June; (*Shake.*) young shoot. **s. tide,** high tide occurring after new and full moon. **s. upon,** attack violently. **s. water,** water from spring. (O.E. *springan*)

springal, springald, *n.* (*arch.*) youth.

springal, springald, *n.* medieval engine for hurling stones. (O.F. *espringale*)

spring-balance, *n.* instrument measuring weight by action on a spring.

spring-board, *n.* resilient board for jumping or diving from.

springbok, *n.* small S. African gazelle. (S. Afr. Du.)

spring-cart, *n.* cart mounted on springs.

springe, *n.* snare with spring-noose, gin. (*spring*)

springer, *n.* breed of spaniel; (*archit.*) lowest part of curve of arch, rib of vaulted roof. (*spring*)

spring-gun, *n.* gun set to go off when trespasser etc. comes against wire.

spring-halt, *n.* disease of horse's leg, causing violent twitching.

spring-mattress, *n.* mattress made resilient with spiral springs.

springtime, (*poet.*) **springtide,** *nn.* season of spring.

springy, *a.* elastic, resilient.
sprinkle, *v.t.* and *i.* scatter, fall, in drops or particles; strew.—*n.* light shower. **sprinkling,** *n.* small quantity, a few here and there.
sprint, *v.i.* and *t.* run (short distance) at full speed.—*n.* such run.
sprit, *n.* (*Scot.*) joint-leaved rush.
sprit, *n.* small spar reaching diagonally to upper outer corner of fore-and-aft sail. **spritsail,** *n.* sail extended by sprit. (O.E. *spréot,* pole)
sprite, *n.* elf, fairy. (*spirit*)
sprocket, *n.* one of the projections on wheel engaging with links of chain.
sprog, *n.* (*army sl.*) recruit.
sprout, *v.i.* and *t.* put forth (shoot), begin to grow.—*n.* young shoot; (*pl.*) Brussels sprouts. (O.E. *sprútan*)
spruce, *a.* trim, smart, dapper.—*v.t.* smarten (up).
spruce, *n.* (also **s.-fir**) tree of pine family; its timber. **s.-beer,** *n.* beer made from its leaves. (*Prussia*)
sprue, *n.* tropical disease with ulcerated mouth and enteritis. (Du. *spruw,* thrush)
sprue, *n.* channel through which metal is poured into mould.
spruit, *n.* (*S. Afr.*) small stream flowing only in wet season. (Du.=sprout)
sprung, *a.* (*colloq.*) tipsy. **s. rhythm,** rhythm depending on number of stresses rather than number of syllables. (*spring*)
spry, *a.* active, agile; alert.
spud, *n.* small spade for digging up weeds; (*colloq.*) potato.—*v.t.* dip up with spud. **spuddy,** *a.* short and fat.
spue, see **spew.**
spulzie, *v.t.* and *n.* (*Scot.*) spoil.
spume, *n.* foam, froth. **spumescent, spumous, spumy,** *aa.* **spumescence,** *n.* (L. *spuma*)
spun, see **spin.**
spunge, *arch.* form of **sponge.**
spunk, *n.* (*Scot.*) spark; lucifer match; courage, spirit. **spunky,** *a.* spirited.
spur, *n.* pricking instrument worn on horseman's heel; spine on leg of cock; hollow spur-like part of flower; lateral mountain-range or root; stimulus, incitement.—*v.t.* and *i.* prick with spur, urge on; equip with spurs; ride fast. **on the s. of the moment,** without previous preparation. **win one's ss.,** attain rank of knight; make a name, gain distinction. **s.-wheel,** *n.* wheel with toothed rim. (O.E. *spura*)
spurge, *n.* kinds of plant with acrid milky juice. (L. *expurgare,* purge)
spurious, *a.* false, sham, not genuine; (*zool.*) like an organ but not having its functions. (L. *spurius*)
spurn, *v.t.* and *i.* thrust at with foot, kick; repel roughly; reject with scorn.—*n.* spurning. (O.E. *spurnan*)
spurrier, *n.* spur-maker.
spurry, spurrey, *n.* kinds of herb of pink family. (Du. *spurrie*)
spurt, spirt, *n.* short sudden effort or quickening of pace; violent gush, jet.—*v.i.* and *t.* make spurt, increase pace; gush or squirt out in jet.
spurtle, *n.* (*Scot.*) short stick for stirring porridge etc.
sputter, same as **splutter.**
sputum, *n.* (*pl.* **sputa**) saliva; expectorated matter. (L.)
spy, *v.t.* and *i.* discern, make out; act as spy.—*n.* (*pl.* **spies**) one who watches another secretly; one who enters hostile country in disguise to observe and report. **s. out,** explore secretly. **s.-glass,** *n.* small telescope. **s.-hole,** *n.* through which one can see without being seen. (O.F. *espier,* espy)
squab, *a.* short and plump, stumpy.—*n.* squab person; unfledged pigeon; thickly stuffed cushion, ottoman.
squabble, *n.* noisy or petty quarrel.—*v.i.* and *t.* have squabble, bicker; (*print.*) disarrange (type set).
squacco, *n.* small crested heron. (It. *sguacco*)
squad, *n.* small detachment of troops for drill; party employed together, gang. **awkward s.,** of raw recruits or learners. **squadron,** *n.* division of cavalry regiment consisting of two troops or 120–200 men; group of warships or aeroplanes forming unit. **squadron-leader,** *n.* R.A.F. rank corresponding to major in Army. (It. *squadra,* square)
squailer, *n.* weighted throwing-stick.
squalid, *a.* mean and dirty, filthy with neglect. **squalidity,** *n.* (L. *squalēre,* be stiff with dirt)
squall, *v.i.* and *t.* cry out violently, scream.—*n.* harsh piercing cry; sudden violent gust of wind. **look out for ss.,** beware of trouble. (imit.)
squaloid, *a.* of, like, a shark. (L. *squalus,* a sea-fish)
squalor, *n.* squalidity, filth.
squama, *n.* (*pl.* **squamae**) scale; scale-like feather etc. **squamiferous,** *a.* scale-bearing. **squamiform, squamoid,** *aa.* scale-like. **squamous, squamose,** *aa.* covered with scales, scaly. **squamule,** *n.* small scale. (L.)
squander, *v.t.* spend wastefully, dissipate. **squandering,** *a.* (*Shake.*) roving. **squandermania,** *n.* mania for spending.
square, *n.* rectangular figure with four equal sides; square thing; open space surrounded by buildings; gauge of L or T shape for testing right angles; (*math.*) number multiplied by itself. —*a.* square-shaped, forming a square; forming right angle (with); tallying, even (with); (*colloq.*) fair, honest; straightforward; (*naut.*) at right angles with mast and keel.—*adv.* squarely.—*v.t.* and *i.* make square; balance (accounts); bring into line, tally (with); (*sl.*) bribe into agreement or silence; (*math.*) multiply (quantity) by itself; (*Shake.*) quarrel.

all s., (*golf*) level in number of holes won. **on the s.,** honest. **s. dance,** with set figures for four couples. **s. inch, foot, yard,** area equal to that of square whose side is inch etc. **s. leg,** fielder level with batsman on leg side. **s. meal,** substantial meal. **s. measure,** measure of area. **s. root,** factor which makes given number when multiplied by itself. **s. sail,** rectangular sail extended on yard suspended at middle from mast. **s. the circle,** find exact area of circle in square measure; perform impossibility. **s. up,** put straight; assume boxing attitude. (L. *ex-*, entirely; *quadrare*, square)

square-face, *n.* (*S. Afr.*) gin.

squarehead, *n.* (*Amer.*) Scandinavian.

squarer, *n.* (*Shake.*) quarreller.

square-rigged, *a.* having chiefly square sails.

square-toes, *n.* prim conventional puritanical person.

squarrose, squarrous, *aa.* (*bot., zool.*) rough with projecting scales.

squarson, *n.* (*joc.*) squire and parson in one. (*squ*ire; p*arson*)

squash, *n.* kinds of gourd. (Amer. Ind. *askutasquash*)

squash, *v.t.* and *i.* squeeze, jam; crush to pulp, flatten; silence with retort, suppress; force one's way, crowd.—*n.* squashing, jam; packed crowd; juice of crushed fruit; squash rackets; (*Shake.*) unripe pea-pod. **s. hat,** soft felt hat. **s. rackets,** game played in walled court with soft ball and rackets. **squashy,** *a.* pulpy, soft. (*ex-*+*quash*)

squat, *v.i.* sit on ground with heels drawn up, or in crouching posture; settle on land without authorization; (*colloq.*) sit.—*a.* short and thick, stumpy. **squatter,** *n.* one who squats; (*Austral.*) sheep-farmer. (L. *ex-*, entirely; *cogere*, drive together)

squaw, *n.* Red Indian woman. **s.-man,** *n.* white married to squaw. (Amer. Ind. *squa*)

squawk, *n.* shrill harsh **cry.**—*v.i.* utter this. (imit.)

squdgy, *a.* soft and wet.

squeak, *n.* weak high-pitched cry; piercing grating sound.—*v.i.* and *t.* emit squeak; utter in squeak; (*sl.*) betray secrets, peach. **narrow s.,** narrow escape. (imit.)

squeal, *n.* shrill prolonged cry.—*v.i.* and *t.* emit, utter in, squeal; (*sl.*) protest excitedly; confess, betray by confession. (imit.)

squeamish, *a.* easily made sick; fastidious; over-scrupulous. (M.E. *squaimous*)

squeegee, *n.* kind of rubber broom for clearing water from deck, floor etc.; small rubber roller.—*v.t.* dry, smooth, with squeegee.

squeeze, *v.t.* and *i.* compress, press; hug; force, crush (into or through); extract by pressure, wring; subject to extortion; take squeeze of.—*n.* squeezing, compression; crush; impression of inscription taken by pressure on soft surface; forced exaction, illicit commission, of Asiatic official or servant.

squelch, *n.* (*colloq.*) splashing sucking sound made in walking through mud. —*v.i.* and *t.* make, walk with, squelch; suppress, squash. (imit.)

squib, *n.* small firework; short satire, lampoon.—*v.t.* and *i.* lampoon.

squid, *n.* kind of cuttle-fish; kind of artificial bait.—*v.i.* fish with squid.

squier, (*Shake.*) form of **square.**

squiffer, *n.* (*sl.*) concertina.

squiffy, *a.* (*sl.*) tipsy.

squiggle, *v.i.* (*Amer.*) squirm, wriggle.

squilgee, same as **squeegee.**

squill, *n.* plant of lily family; its bulb, used as purgative. (Gk. *skilla*)

squinch, *n.* arch across interior corner of tower. (*scuncheon*)

squint, *v.i.* and *t.* have eyes turned in different directions; look sideways or hastily (at); half-shut (eyes); give squint to.—*n.* act or condition of squinting; (*colloq.*) glance, peep; (*archit.*) hole in church wall giving view of altar from transept, hagioscope.—*a.* squinting. **s.-eyed,** *a.* malignant. (*asquint*)

squiny, *v.i.* (*Shake.*) look asquint.

squire, *n.* owner of country estate; chief landowner of village; man escorting woman; (formerly) knight's attendant. — *v.t.* escort (woman). **squirearchy,** *n.* country gentry; government by landed class. **squirearchal, squirearchical,** *aa.* **squireen,** *n.* small landowner, esp. in Ireland. **squirehood, squireship,** *nn.* **squirelet, squireling,** *nn.* petty squire. (*esquire*)

squirm, *v.i.* twist about, writhe; show or feel embarrassment.—*n.* wriggle; (*naut.*) kink in rope. (imit.)

squirrel, *n.* small bushy-tailed animal living in trees. **s.-monkey,** *n.* marmoset. **s.-tail,** *n.* kinds of grass like barley. (Gk. *skiouros*)

squirt, *v.t.* and *i.* eject (liquid), be ejected, in thin stream.—*n.* syringe; jet; (*colloq.*) bumptious upstart.

squish, *n.* (*sl.*) marmalade.

squit, *n.* (*sl.*) small insignificant person.

stab, *v.t.* and *i.* wound, pierce, thrust, with pointed weapon; stick, jab (into); inflict sharp pain on; roughen surface of (wall) before plastering.—*n.* blow, wound, with pointed weapon; throb of pain. **have a s. at,** (*sl.*) make attempt at. **s. in the back,** treacherous attack. **stabber,** *n.*

Stabat Mater, hymn describing Virgin Mary at the Cross. (L.=the mother was standing—first words of hymn)

stable, *a.* firmly established, steady; resolute, steadfast. **s. equilibrium,** (*mech.*) tendency of body to return to position of rest when moved.

stability, *n.* **stabilize,** *v.t.* make stable; fix value of (currency) in terms of gold. **stabilization,** *n.* **stabilizer,** *n.* thing that stabilizes; fixed horizontal tail-plane of aircraft. (L. *stare,* stand)

stable, *n.* building in which horses or cattle are kept; race-horses of particular stable.—*v.t.* and *i.* keep, be kept, in stable. **s.-companion,** *n.* horse of same stable; member of same school etc. **stabling,** *n.* stable accommodation. (L. *stare,* stand)

stablish, *arch.* form of **establish.**

staccato, a. and *adv.* (*mus.*) with notes sharply separated. (It.)

stack, *n.* large pile of hay or corn, rick; orderly heap; pyramidal pile of rifles; cluster of chimneys; tall chimney, detached shaft of rock; (*colloq.*) large quantity.—*v.t.* pile in stacks; arrange (cards) for cheating. (O.N. *stakkr*)

stáctē, *n.* spice used in ancient Jewish incense. (Gk. *stazein,* drip)

stactometer, *n.* tube for measuring liquid in drops. (Gk. *stazein,* drip; *metron,* measure)

stadium, *n.* (*pl.* **stadia**) athletic ground; (in ancient Greece) arena for foot-racing, measure of about 202 yds.; (*med.*) phase of disease. (Gk. *stadion*)

stadle, *n.* (*Spens.*) staff, prop. (O.E. *stathol*)

stadtholder, stadholder, *n.* (formerly) chief magistrate of United Provinces of Holland. (Du. *stadhouder,* deputy)

staff, *n.* (*pl.* **staffs,** *arch.* and *mus.* **staves**) strong stick, pole; wand of office; support, prop; body of officers attached to commander; personnel of a business; (*mus.*) the five lines on which notes are written; (*Shake.*) stanza.—*v.t.* provide with staff. **s. notation,** music using staff as opp. to sol-fa. **s. work,** organization and management. (O.E. *stæf*)

staff, *n.* kind of plaster composition used as building material.

stag, *n.* male of red deer or other large deer; castrated bull; (*stock exchange*) one who applies for allotment of shares in new company in order to sell at once at profit; (*Amer.*) man without woman partner at party.—*v.i.* (*stock exchange*) deal as stag. **s.-beetle,** *n.* kind with mandibles like antlers. **s.-evil,** *n.* lockjaw in horses. **s.-horn,** *n.* kinds of moss and coral. **s.-party,** *n.* for men only.

stage, *n.* raised platform, scaffold; platform of theatre; theatrical profession, dramatic literature; scene of action; period of development; stopping-place of bus, interval between stopping-places; (*Amer.*) stage-coach.—*v.t.* put (play) on stage; arrange with view to effect. **go on the s.,** become actor or actress. **s. direction,** instruction provided in play for its production and acting. **s. door,** actors' entrance to theatre. **s. fever,** passion to go on stage. **s. fright,** nervousness felt on facing an audience. **s. whisper,** loud whisper intended for audience to hear. **s.-manager,** *n.* person superintending production of play. **s.-struck,** *a.* smitten with stage fever. **stagecoach,** *n.* large public vehicle plying between places. **stagecraft,** *n.* practical knowledge of dramatic effects. **old stager,** person of experience. (L. *stare,* stand)

staggard, *n.* stag of fourth year.

stagger, *v.i.* and *t.* walk unsteadily, reel; waver, hesitate; disconcert, shock; place in zigzag order; arrange (holidays etc.) so that they come at different times.—*n.* staggering; zigzag arrangement; (*pl.*) giddiness; a disease of horses and cattle. **staggering,** *a.* overwhelming, astounding. (O.N. *staka,* push)

staghound, *n.* large swift breed of hound.

staging, *n.* temporary platform or scaffolding.

Stagirite, *n.* **the S.,** Aristotle. (native of *Stageira*)

stagnant, *a.* without current, standing; foul from being motionless; inactive, sluggish. **stagnate,** *v.i.* be stagnant. **stagnation,** *n.* **stagnicolous,** *a.* living in or near stagnant water. (L. *stagnum,* pool)

stagy, *a.* theatrical, melodramatic.

staid, *a.* steady, sober, sedate. (=*stayed*)

staig, *n.* (*Scot.*) young horse, stallion.

stain, *v.t.* and *i.* discolour, make foul, sully; tinge (substance) with colour penetrating it, dye; mar with guilt or infamy; be stainable; (*Shake.*) make dim, eclipse.—*n.* discoloration, dirty mark; liquid for staining, dye; moral blemish. **stainless,** *a.* spotless, immaculate; not liable to become stained. (L. *dis-,* away; *tingere,* dye)

stair, *n.* flight of steps connecting floors; single step of this. **below ss.,** in servants' quarters. **s.-rod,** *n.* for holding **s.-carpet,** *n.* in position. **staircase, stairway,** *nn.* series of stairs. (O.E. *stǣger*)

staith, staithe, *n.* waterside coal depot with wharf. (O.E. *stæth,* bank)

stake, *n.* post pointed at end for fixing in ground; post to which person is bound for burning; death by burning; money risked in wager; (*pl.*) prize in contest; horse-race for stakes.—*v.t.* secure, mark (out), with stakes; wager, hazard. **at s.,** involved, in jeopardy. **s. in the country,** material interest in its welfare. **s.-boat,** *n.* boat moored to mark course of race. **stakeholder,** *n.* person with whom stakes in wager are deposited. (O.E. *staca*)

stalactite, *n.* lime deposit hanging like icicle from roof of cave. **stalactic, stalactiform, stalactitic,** *aa.* **stalag-**

mite, *n.* lime deposit rising like inverted stalactite from floor of cave. **stalagmitic, stalagmitical,** *aa.* (Gk. *stalassein,* drip)

stale, *a.* musty, not fresh; hackneyed, trite; (of athlete) overtrained.—*v.t.* make stale.

stale, *n.* urine of horses or cattle.—*v.i.* (of horse etc.) urinate.

stale, *n.* (*arch.*) decoy; dupe, laughing-stock.

stale, *n.* (*Shake.*) harlot.

stalemate, *n.* deadlock, impasse; (*chess*) position in which one player cannot move without bringing his king into check.—*v.t.* subject to stalemate; bring to standstill.

stalk, *n.* stem of plant or flower or leaf: slender supporting shaft; tall slender chimney. **s.-eyed,** *a.* having eyes on stalks. (M.E. *stalke*)

stalk, *v.i.* and *t.* walk in stiff and stately manner; approach (game) stealthily or under cover. **stalking-horse,** *n.* horse used as cover in stalking; pretext. (O.E. *stealcian,* walk warily)

stall, *n.* pickpocket's accomplice who diverts victim's attention. —*v.i.* (*Amer.*) fence conversationally. (*stale*)

stall, *n.* compartment for one animal in stable etc.; erection for display and sale of goods, booth; seat in choir of church for officiating clergy; seat in front part of floor of theatre; sheath for finger.—*v.t.* and *i.* place in, furnish with, stalls; unintentionally stop (motor engine); (of aircraft) become unstable by loss of speed; (*Shake.*) keep close; install; dwell. **orchestra, pit, ss.,** front, back, rows of theatre stalls. **s.-feed,** *v.t.* fatten under shelter. **stallage,** *n.* space, rent, for stall in market. (O.E. *steall*)

stallion, *n.* uncastrated male horse. (*stall*)

stalwart, *a.* robust, strong; staunch, unflinching. (O.E. *stǣlwyrthe*)

stamen, *n.* male organ of flower, containing pollen. **stamina,** *n.* vitality, staying - power. **staminal,** *a.* of stamina or stamens. **stamineal, stamineous,** *aa.* of stamens. **staminate,** *a.* having stamens. (L.=thread)

stammer, *v.i.* and *t.* speak with repetition of syllables, stutter; utter with hesitation.—*n.* stammering utterance. (O.E. *stamerian*)

stamp, *v.t.* and *i.* put down (foot) with force, strike thus; crush with downward blows; impress (mark) on; distinguish (as); affix postage stamp to; cut (out) with die; (*Shake.*) give currency to.—*n.* act of stamping; design imprinted; official mark or label affixed to show that tax etc. has been paid, postage stamp; crushing-machine; kind, class, character. **s. out,** extirpate. **s.-album,** *n.* book in which **s.-collector,** *n.* keeps his postage stamps. **s.-duty,** *n.* tax levied on certain legal instruments. (M.E. *stampen*)

stampede, *n.* sudden panic-stricken rush.—*v.i.* and *t.* make, cause to make, stampede. (Sp. *estampida,* crash)

stance, *n.* (*golf, cricket*) position taken for stroke; (*Scot.*) site.

stanch, *v.t.* check flow of (blood, wound); (*Shake.*) quench (thirst).—*a.* staunch. (O.F. *estanchier*)

stanchion, *n.* upright bar, prop.—*v.t.* furnish, secure, with stanchions. (O.F. *estance,* prop+dim.)

stanck, *a.* (*Spens.*) weary. (It. *stanco*)

stand, *v.i.* and *t.* (*past, p.p.* stood) be, put, in upright position; rise up; become, remain, firm or stationary; be in specified state; remain valid, hold good; offer oneself as candidate (for); set up; endure, put up with; withstand; (*naut.*) sail in specified direction; (*colloq.*) treat to; (*arch.*) halt, stop.—*n.* halt, stoppage; parking-place; erection for spectators; stall for goods; pedestal, rack etc., for putting things on. **s. at ease, easy,** orders for semi-relaxed, relaxed, position in army drill. **s. by,** support; adhere to; (*naut.*) get ready. **s. down,** withdraw. **s. fast,** remain firm. **s. for,** be symbol of; acquiesce in. **s. good,** remain valid. **s. of arms,** set for one man. **s. off,** hold aloof; suspend (employee). **s. one in,** cost him. **s. out,** be prominent; refuse to yield. **s. over,** be left for later consideration. **s. to,** abide by; take up position for attack. **s. to win, lose,** be likely to win, lose. **s. up for,** champion. **s. up to,** confront boldly. **s. upon,** insist upon; (*Shake.*) be incumbent on; concern. **s.-by,** *n.* resource. **s.-in,** *n.* one who takes film actor's place till cameras are ready. **s.-offish,** *a.* aloof. (O.E. *standan*)

standard, *n.* distinctive flag, banner; flag of cavalry regiment; weight or measure to which others must conform; gauge, criterion; approved model; class in elementary school; upright post; tree or shrub not supported by wall.—*a.* in accordance with, serving as, standard. **s. lamp,** lamp on tall support. **s.-bearer,** *n.* one who carries standard; leader of party. **standardize,** *v.t.* reduce to standard. **standardization,** *n.* (O.F. *estandard*)

standing, *a.* permanent; stagnant; (*print.*) remaining set up.—*n.* position, reputation; duration. **s. army,** force maintained in peace time. **s. jump,** done without run. **s. orders,** fixed procedure. **s. part,** fixed end (of rope). **s. rigging,** fixed stays.

standish, *n.* (*arch.*) inkstand. (*stand; dish*)

standpoint, *n.* point of view.

standstill, *n.* halt.

stang, *n.* (*Scot.*) pole, post.

stanhope, *n.* kind of light open carriage. (inventor)

staniel, *n.* kestrel. (O.E. *stán*, stone; *gellan*, yell)

stank, *n.* (*Scot.*) ditch, drain.

stank, see **stink.**

stannary, *n.* tin-mine; tin-mining district. **stannic, stannous**, *aa.* (*chem.*) of tin in its higher, lower, valency. (L. *stannum*, tin)

stanza, *n.* group of four or more lines of verse. **stanzaic**, *a.* **stanze, stanzo**, *n.* (*Shake.*) stanza. (It.)

staple, *n.* iron loop for holding bolt, recess into which lock shoots; bent wire used in wire-stitching.—*v.t.* secure by staple. (O.E. *stapul*)

staple, *n.* chief product of district; leading factor, main element; raw material; fibre of wool or cotton; (formerly) settled market.—*a.* forming staple, principal.—*v.t.* grade according to fibre. (O.F. *estaple*)

star, *n.* heavenly body seen as point of light, esp. one that is self-luminous; planet as astrological influence, destiny; figure, badge, with five or more points; brilliant or attractive person; leading actor or actress in play; (*print.*) asterisk (*).—*v.t.* and *i.* mark, adorn, with stars; mark with asterisk; present, appear, as theatrical star. **S. Chamber**, ancient high court notorious for arbitrary methods. **s. of Bethlehem**, plant of lily family. **S. of India**, an order of knighthood. **Ss. and Stripes**, U.S. national flag. **s.-drift**, *n.* proper motion common to group of stars. **s.-finch**, *n.* redstart. **s.-gazer**, *n.* (*joc.*) astronomer. **s.-shell**, *n.* light shot into air to show enemy's night movements. **s.-spangled**, *a.* spangled with stars (esp. of U.S. flag). (O.E. *steorra*)

starboard, *a.* and *n.* (on) right-hand side of ship to one looking towards bow.—*v.t.* turn to starboard. (O.E. *stéor*, rudder; *bord*, board)

starch, *n.* substance forming main food element in bread, potatoes etc.; preparation of this in water for stiffening linen; stiffness of manner. —*a.* prim, starchy.—*v.t.* stiffen with starch. **starchy**, *a.* containing starch; formal, prim. (*stark*)

stare, *v.i.* and *t.* look with fixed gaze; (of eyes) be wide open; (*Shake.*, of hair) stand on end.—*n.* fixed gaze. **s. one in the face**, be very obvious. **s. out of countenance**, confuse by staring. **staring**, *a.* (of colour) conspicuous. (O.E. *starian*)

starfish, *n.* star-shaped marine animal allied to sea-urchin.

stark, *a.* stiff, rigid, esp. in death; utter, downright; (*poet.*) strong, firm, resolute. — *adv.* completely, thoroughly. (O.E. *stearc*)

stark naked, completely naked. (O.E. *steort*, tail)

starless, *a.* without stars.

starlet, *n.* small star.

starlight, *n.* light of stars.—*a.* starlit.

starling, *n.* kinds of speckled song-bird. (O.E. *stær*, starling+dim.)

starling, *n.* ring of piles supporting pier of bridge.

starlit, *a.* lighted by the stars.

starry, *a.* of, like, covered with, stars.

start, *v.i.* and *t.* make sudden involuntary movement, wince; dart, spring; begin, put in motion; set out; send off; rouse (game); displace, be displaced, warp; (*Shake.*) startle. —*n.* act of starting; starting-point; commencement, outset; sudden involuntary movement; handicap conceded in race, initial lead. **s. in**, (*colloq.*) set to work. **s. up**, rise suddenly. **starting-gate**, *n.* movable barrier to ensure fair start in horse-race. **starting-point**, *n.* **starter**, *n.* one who starts; person giving signal for start in race. (M.E. *sterte*)

startle, *v.t.* and *i.* alarm suddenly, scare; give shock of surprise to; start with fright. (*start*)

starve, *v.i.* and *t.* die, suffer greatly, from hunger; keep without or short of food, kill thus; cause to become atrophied; (*arch.*) suffer greatly from cold, freeze. **starving**, *a.* (*colloq.*) very hungry. **starvation**, *n.* **starveling**, *n.* underfed person or animal. —*a.* hungry, emaciated. (O.E. *steorfan*, die)

stasis, *n.* (*med.*) stoppage in circulation. (Gk.=standing)

state, *n.* condition; rank, status; ceremonial pomp; politically organized community; division of federal republic; civil government; (*Shake.*) estate, fortune; chair of state.—*a.* of the State; used on ceremonial occasions.—*v.t.* express in words, affirm; specify. **chair of s.**, (*Shake.*) canopied chair. **in a s.**, (*colloq.*) upset, excited. **lie in s.**, (of corpse) be laid out publicly. **Ss. General**, legislature of France before the Revolution. **s.-house**, *n.* (*Amer.*) capitol; meeting-place of state legislature. (*status*)

statecraft, *n.* art of government.

stately, *a.* dignified, imposing.

statement, *n.* expression in words; thing said; formal account.

stater, *n.* ancient Greek gold coin. (Gk.)

stateroom, *n.* private cabin on ship.

statesman, *n.* one who is skilled in public affairs, sagacious politician; (in northern England) small landowner. **statesmanlike, statesmanly**, *aa.* **statesmanship**, *n.*

static, *a.* motionless, at rest; of bodies at rest.—*n.* (*wireless*) atmospherics; (*pl.*) science of bodies at rest and forces in equilibrium. **statical**, *a.* static. (Gk. *histanai*, stand)

station, *n.* appointed place of thing or

person; place forming headquarters; stopping-place of railway trains, buildings attached to it; rank, status, walk in life; state of stillness; (*Austral.*) sheep or cattle farm; (*India*) military post or its residents; (*Shake.*) manner of standing.—*v.t.* assign station to. **Ss. of the Cross,** series of pictures depicting stages of Christ's passion. **s.-master,** *n.* official in charge of railway station. **stationary,** *a.* not in motion, fixed; not changing or progressive. (L. *stare*, stand)

stationer, *n.* dealer in stationery. **Stationers' Hall,** at which book is registered for copyright. **stationery,** *n.* writing materials. (L.L. *stationarius*, shopkeeper)

statist, *n.* statistician; statesman.

statistics, *n.pl.* numerical facts systematically collected and set out; science of compiling these. **statistic, statistical,** *aa.* **statistician,** *n.* one skilled in statistics. **statistology,** *n.* (*state*)

stator, *n.* (*electr.*) stationary part of generator. (L. *stare*, stand)

statoscope, *n.* instrument showing minute changes in atmospheric pressure. (Gk. *statos*, fixed; *skopein*, view)

statue, *n.* human or animal figure carved or modelled in the round, image. **statua,** *n.* (*Shake.*) statue. **statuary,** *a.* of statues.—*n.* sculpture; sculptor. **statuesque,** *a.* like a statue, immobile; having dignified serenity. **statuette,** *n.* small statue. (L. *statua*)

stature, *n.* bodily height. (L. *stare*, stand)

status, *n.* standing, rank; relation to others. *s. quo* (*ante*), previous position, unaltered condition. (L.)

statute, *n.* law enacted by legislature; ordinance of corporation or institution; (*Shake.*) bond. **s. law,** statutes as opp. to common law. **s.-book,** *n.* register of statutes. **s.-cap,** *n.* (*Shake.*) woollen cap ordered by act of parliament to be worn. **statutable, statutory,** *aa.* in accordance with statutes. (L. *statuere*, establish)

staumrel, *n.* (*Scot.*) blockhead.

staunch, *a.* trustworthy, loyal; water-tight.—*v.t.* stanch. (*stanch*)

stauroscope, *n.* instrument for examining effect of polarized light on crystals. (Gk. *stauros*, cross; *skopein*, view)

stave, *n.* one of the pieces forming side of cask; rung of ladder; fragment of song, stanza; (*mus.*) staff.—*v.t.* (*past, p.p.* **stove** or **staved**) furnish with staves. **s. in,** make dent, break hole, in. **s. off,** defer with effort. **s.-rhyme,** *n.* alliteration. (*staff*)

staves, see **staff.**

stavesacre, *n.* kind of larkspur. (Gk. *staphis*, dried grapes; *agrios*, wild)

staw, *Scot.* form of **stole.**

stay, *v.t.* and *i.* check, hold back; prop, support, sustain; last out, endure (through); remain, stop; reside for a time, lodge; (*law*) delay, defer; (*arch.*) await.—*n.* act of staying, halt, check; prop, support; (*pl.*) laced corset. **has come to s.,** (*colloq.*) must be regarded as permanent. **s. on,** prolong stay. **s. put,** (*colloq.*) stay in place. **s.-at-home,** *a.* and *n.* home-keeping (person). **s.-maker,** *n.* corset-maker.

stay, *n.* (*naut.*) rope supporting mast or spar. **in ss.,** going about. **miss ss.,** fail in trying to tack. (O.E. *stæg*)

stayer, *n.* person, animal, with great powers of endurance.

staysail, *n.* sail extended on stay.

stead, *n.* place.—*v.t.* (*Shake.*) help. **in his s.,** in place of him. **stand in good s.,** be of great service to. **s. up,** (*Shake.*) take place of. (O.E. *stede*)

steadfast, *a.* constant, unwavering. (*Spens.*) firmly fixed. (*stead; fast*)

steading, *n.* farmstead. (*stead*)

steady, *a.* firm, not shaky; constant, not wavering; regular, uniform; sober, temperate.—*v.t.* and *i.* make, become, steady.—*n.* rest, support, on machine; (*Amer. colloq.*) regular sweetheart. (*stead*)

steak, *n.* large thick slice of meat or fish for grilling, frying etc. (O.N. *steik*)

steal, *v.t.* and *i.* (*past* **stole,** *p.p.* **stolen**) take (another's property) without leave, thieve; gain by stealth, win subtly; go furtively or silently. **stealth,** *n.* secret or underhand procedure; (*Shake.*) theft. **stealthy,** *a.* done by stealth, furtive. (O.E. *stelan*)

steam, *n.* vapour of boiling water; exhalation.—*a.* worked by steam.—*v.i.* and *t.* give out steam; move, cook, by steam. **get up s.,** heat boilers for working engine; gather energy. **let off s.,** release steam not required; relieve one's feelings. **s.-box, s.-chest,** *nn.* chamber through which steam passes from boiler to cylinder. **s.-engine, s.-hammer, s.-launch, s.-whistle,** *nn.* driven or worked by steam. **s.-gauge,** *n.* gauge showing steam pressure. **s.-navvy,** *n.* excavating machine worked by steam. **s.-roller,** *n.* heavy steam-propelled roller for levelling roads; force for crushing opposition. **steamboat, steamship,** *nn.* vessel propelled by steam. **steamer,** *n.* steamship; utensil for cooking by steam. **steamy,** *a.* of, like, covered with, steam; misty, hazy. (O.E. *stéam*)

stearin, *n.* solid part of any fat; stearic acid, used in making candles. **stearic,** *a.* **steatite,** *n.* kind of talc, soapstone. **steatitic,** *a.* (Gk. *stear*, fat)

stech, *v.t.* (*Scot.*) cram.

steed, *n.* (*poet.*) horse. (O.E. *stéda*)

steek, *n.* (*Scot.*) stitch.—*v.t.* stitch; close (gate).

steel, *n.* hard metal made by mixing carbon in iron; weapon of this; steel rod for sharpening knives.—*a.* made of, like, steel.—*v.t.* overlay, tip, with steel; make hard or invulnerable. **cold s.,** sword or bayonet. **s.-clad,** *a.* clad in armour. **s. engraving,** engraving on steel plate, print made from this. **steely,** *a.* of, like, steel; hard, relentless. (O.E. *stýle*)

steelyard, *n.* kind of balance with single weight moving along graduated beam.

steenbok, *n.* small S. African antelope. (Du.)

steening, same as **steining.**

steep, *v.t.* wet thoroughly, soak in liquid; saturate, impregnate.—*n.* steeping. (M.E. *stepen*)

steep, *a.* having abrupt or decided slope, hard to climb; difficult; (*colloq.*) hard to believe; exorbitant. —*n.* steep slope. **steepen,** *v.t.* and *i.* make, become, steep or steeper. (O.E. *stéap*)

steeple, *n.* tower tapering to point, church tower with spire. **steeplechase,** *n.* cross-country horse-race over obstacles; similar race on foot. **steeplechaser,** *n.* horse, man, taking part in this. **steeplechasing,** *n.* **steeplejack,** *n.* man employed to climb steeples, tall chimneys etc. (O.E. *stépel*)

steepy, *a.* (*poet.*) steep, sheer.

steer, *Scot.* form of stir.

steer, *n.* young male ox, bullock. (O.E. *stéor*)

steer, *v.t.* and *i.* direct course of (vessel, motor-car) with rudder or steering-wheel; keep on definite course; guide, direct; answer helm. **s. clear of,** avoid. **steering-gear, steering-wheel,** *nn.* mechanism for steering. **steerable,** *a.* **steerage,** *n.* steering; way a vessel steers; accommodation for passengers paying cheapest fare. **steerage-way,** *n.* movement sufficient to let vessel answer helm. **steersman,** *n.* man steering vessel. **steersmanship,** *n.* skill in steering. (O.E. *stieran*)

steeve, *n.* (*naut.*) spar used in stowing cargo.—*v.t.* stow with this. (L. *stipare,* cram)

steeve, *n.* angle of elevation of bowsprit.—*v.i.* and *t.* slope (bowsprit).

steeve, *a.* (*Scot.*) firm, strong; stiff.

steganography, *n.* art of writing in cipher. (Gk. *stegein,* cover; *graphein,* write)

steinbock, *n.* Alpine ibex. (G.)

steining, *n.* lining of well. (*stone*)

stélē, *n.* (*pl.* stelae) ancient Greek carved stone pillar or slab. (Gk.)

stellar, *a.* of stars. **stellate, stellated,** *aa.* star-shaped, radiating. **stellular, stellulate,** *aa.* shaped like, set with, small stars. (L. *stella,* star)

stem, *v.t.* check, dam up; make headway against. (O.N. *stemma*)

stem, *n.* main body of tree or plant, trunk, stalk; branch of family; slender shaft; upright to which vessel's sides converge at bow; part of word to which inflexions are added. —*v.t.* remove stem of. **from s. to stern,** throughout. **stemlet,** *n.* small stem. (O.E. *stefn*)

stemma, *n.* (*pl.* **stemmata**) pedigree, genealogical tree; (*zool.*) simple eye, facet of compound eye. (Gk.= wreath)

stemple, *n.* crossbar in mine-shaft for ascending or descending.

stench, *n.* offensive smell. (O.E. *stenc,* smell)

stencil, *v.t.* mark with letters or pattern by passing brush over plate in which they are punched.—*n.* the letters or pattern; (also **s.-plate**) the plate. **stenciller,** *n.*

stend, stenn, *v.i.* (*Scot.*) rear.

stengah, *n.* small whisky and soda. (Malay=half)

steno-, from Gk. *stenos,* narrow, used in **stenochromy,** *n.* process of printing in several colours at one impression; **stenograph,** *n.* shorthand character or script; **stenography,** *n.* shorthand, hence **stenographic, stenographical,** *aa.*; **stenographer, stenographist,** *nn.* shorthand-writer.

stent, *Scot.* form of **stint.**

Stentor, *n.* loud-voiced person. **stentorian,** *a.* very loud. **stentorphone,** *n.* powerful loud-speaker. (name in Homer)

step, *v.t.* and *i.* move and set down foot; go, walk; measure in steps; insert (mast) in socket.—*n.* pace; footprint; tread; degree in scale, grade in rank; stair, rung; socket for mast; (*pl.,* also **pair of ss.**) stepladder with supporting prop. **in, out of, s.,** keeping, not keeping, step. **keep s. (with),** move corresponding foot at same time (as). **s. by s.,** gradually. **s. in,** visit casually; intervene. **s. on it,** (*Amer. sl.*) drive fast; hurry. **s. out,** lengthen stride. **s.-ladder,** *n.* with steps instead of rungs. **stepped,** *a.* having, forming, a series of steps. **stepping-stone,** *n.* one of row of stones for crossing stream; means of advancement. (O.E. *steppan*)

step-, *pref.* denoting nominal relation through remarriage of parent. **stepbrother, stepsister,** *nn.* son, daughter, of one's step-parent by former marriage. **stepdame,** *n.* (*arch.*) stepmother. **stepdaughter, stepson, stepchild,** *nn.* daughter, son, of one's wife or husband by a previous marriage. **stepfather,** *n.* one's mother's second or subsequent husband. **stepmother,** *n.* one's father's second or subsequent wife. **stepmotherly,** *a.* like a stepmother; unfeeling, neglectful. **step-parent,** *n.* (O.E. *stéop,* orphaned)

stephanotis, *n.* a fragrant hothouse flower. (Gk. *stephanos*, wreath)
stepney, *n.* extra rim and tyre for attaching to motor-car wheel whose tyre has collapsed. (place)
steppe, *n.* level treeless plain. (Russ. *stepi*)
stercoraceous, stercoral, *aa.* of, containing, dung. (L. *stercus*, dung)
stere, *n.* cubic metre (about 35·3 cubic ft.). (Gk. *stereos*, solid)
stereo, *abbr.* of **stereotype.**
stereo-, from Gk. *stereos*, solid, used in **stereobate,** *n.* solid platform on which building is erected; **stereochemistry,** *n.* chemical study of arrangement of atoms and molecules; **stereochromy,** *n.* wall-painting in colours fixed with water-glass; **stereography,** *n.* art of representing solids on plane surface, hence **stereographic, stereographical,** *aa.*, **stereogram,** *n.* stereographic drawing; **stereometer,** *n.* instrument for measuring solid bodies, hence **stereometric, stereometrical,** *aa.*, **stereometry,** *n.*; **stereoscope,** *n.* instrument with two lenses combining two photographs taken at slightly different angles to give effect of solidity, hence **stereoscopic,** *a.*, **stereoscopically,** *adv.*, **stereoscopy,** *n.*
stereotype, *n.* metal plate cast in mould taken from page of ordinary type.—*v.t.* make stereotype of; print from stereotypes; fix permanently, reduce to formula. **stereotyper, stereotypist, stereotypography, stereotypy,** *nn.* (Gk. *stereos*, solid)
sterile, *a.* not bearing seed or offspring; barren, unproductive; free from germs, sterilized; destitute of ideas. **sterility,** *n.* **sterilize,** *v.t.* deprive of reproductive power; rid of microbes. **sterilization,** *n.* (L. *sterilis*)
sterlet, *n.* kind of small sturgeon.
sterling, *a.* genuine, true; of solid worth; (of money) of standard British value.
stern, *a.* severe, strict; firm, steadfast. (O.E. *styrne*)
stern, *n.* back part of ship; rump; tail, esp. of foxhound. **s. chase,** in which pursuing vessel follows in wake of pursued. **s.-chaser,** *n.* gun mounted in stern. **s.-post,** *n.* upright supporting rudder. **s.-sheets,** *n.* space in boat between stern and rowers. **s.-wheeler,** *n.* steamboat with single paddle-wheel at stern. **to sternage of,** (*Shake.*) astern of. (O.N. *stjórn*, steering)
sternum, *n.* (*pl.* **sterna**) breast-bone. **sternal,** *a.* **sternalgia,** *n.* pain in chest. **sternocostal,** *a.* of sternum and ribs. (Gk. *sternon*, chest)
sternutation, *n.* sneezing, sneeze. **sternutatory,** *a.* and *n.* (substance) causing sneezing. **sternutative,** *a.* (L. *sternuere*, sneeze)
stertorous, *a.* making snore-like sounds. (L. *stertere*, snore)
stet, v.i. (*print.*) used to cancel correction in proof. (L.=let it stand)
stethoscope, *n.* instrument for listening to action of heart or lungs.—*v.t.* examine with it. **stethoscopic,** *a.* **stethoscopically,** *adv.* **stethoscopist, stethoscopy,** *nn.* (Gk. *stēthos*, breast; *skopein*, view)
stetson, *n.* slouch hat. (maker)
stevedore, *n.* dock labourer loading or unloading ship. (L. *stipare*, cram)
steven, *n.* (*Spens.*) voice, cry. (O.E. *stefn*)
stew, *n.* tank for keeping fish alive in, fishpond. (O.F. *estuier*, shut up)
stew, *v.t.* and *i.* cook by simmering in closed vessel with little liquid; swelter in hot atmosphere; (*sl.*) work for examination, swot.—*n.* stewed dish; (*sl.*) state of worry or agitation; (*arch.*) brothel. **s.-pan, s.-pot,** *nn.* for stewing. **stewed,** *a.* (*sl.*) drunk. (O.F. *estuve*, hot bath)
steward, *n.* one who manages another's estate; official in charge of meeting or show; (*fem.* **stewardess**) man in charge of catering in club or ship; attendant on ship's passengers. **stewardship,** *n.* charge committed to steward. (O.E. *stig*, house; *weard*, ward)
stey, *a.* (*Scot.*) steep.
sthenic, *a.* (*med.*) abnormally active. (Gk. *sthenos*, strength)
stich, *n.* line of verse. **stichic,** *a.* **stichomyth, stichomythia,** *nn.* question and answer in alternate lines, verse dialogue. (Gk. *stichos*)
stick, *n.* twig, rod; rod-shaped piece of chocolate etc.; set of bombs dropped in succession; (*colloq.*) stiff or dull person; (*print.*) composing-stick; (*pl., cricket*) wicket. **s.-insect.** *n.* kinds resembling twig. (O.E, *sticca*)
stick, *v.t.* and *i.* (*past, p.p.* **stuck**) thrust, jab; transfix, pierce; set, place; cause to adhere, attach, fasten; remain fixed, be held fast; adhere; cling closely, cleave; (*sl.*) tolerate; (*Amer.*) cheat. **s. at,** persist in; draw the line at. **s. out,** protrude; continue to resist. **s. out for,** persist in claiming. **s. to,** (*colloq.*) keep; persevere in. **s. up,** (*sl.*) stop for purpose of robbing. **s. up for,** (*colloq.*) defend, uphold. **s.-in-the mud,** *a.* and *n.* unprogressive, dull (person). **sticking-place,** *n.* highest pitch. **sticking-plaster,** *n.* plaster for small cuts. **stickit minister,** (*Scot.*) licentiate who never gets pastoral charge. (M.E. *steken*, pierce and O.E. *stician*, adhere)
sticker, *n.* one who sticks; persevering person; (*cricket*) stone-waller.
stickjaw, *n.* kind of sticky toffee.
stickleback, *n.* small fish with sharp spines on back.

stickler, *n.* **s. for,** person who insists on. **s.-like,** *a.* (*Shake.*) like an umpire.
sticky, *a.* tending to stick, adhesive; (*sl.*) painful.
stie, same as sty.
stiff, *a.* rigid, not flexible; hard to mould; not moving freely, painful when moved; lacking ease or grace; formal, distant; strong, severe; exorbitant; difficult; hard to bear; (*naut.*) not heeling over easily.—*n.* (*sl.*) negotiable paper; corpse; (*Amer.*) fool, bungler. **bore, scare, s.,** bore, scare, to death. **s.-necked,** *a.* stubborn, obstinate. **stiffen,** *v.t.* and *i.* make, become, stiff or stiffer; increase in force. (O.E. *stif*)
stifle, *v.t.* and *i.* smother, suffocate; extinguish; repress. **stifling,** *a.* stuffy, airless.
stifle, *n.* joint next above hock in horse's hind leg; disease of this. **s.-bone,** *n.* horse's knee-cap.
stigma, *n.* (*pl.* **stigmas**) moral reproach, mark of disgrace; (*arch.*) brand; (*pl.* **stigmas, stigmata**) visible sign of latent disease; small spot that bleeds periodically; (*bot.*) part of pistil that receives pollen. **stigmata,** *n.pl.* marks corresponding to Christ's five wounds. **stigmatic,** *a.* of, marked with, stigma; anastigmatic. **stigmatism,** *n.* condition of bearing the stigmata; (*optics*) correct focusing power of lens. **stigmatist,** *n.* one who bears the stigmata. **stigmatize,** *v.t.* hold up to disgrace, brand (as); mark with stigma or stigmata. **stigmatization,** *n.* **stigmatose,** *a.* having stigma. (Gk.)
stile, *n.* set of steps for climbing fence or wall. (O.E. *stigel*)
stile, *n.* upright piece in framing or panelling.
stiletto, *n.* small dagger; small boring tool. (It.)
still, *n.* apparatus for distilling esp. spirits.—*v.t.* and *i.* distil; (*poet.*) fall drop by drop. **s.-room,** *n.* housekeeper's store-room for home-made preserves. (L. *stillare*, drip)
still, *a.* motionless, at rest; silent, quiet; (of wine) not effervescent; (*Shake.*) constant. — *n.* stillness; ordinary photograph as opp. to motion picture.—*v.t.* and *i.* make, become, still; calm, hush.—*adv.* to this time, even now; even, yet; (*arch.*) constantly, always. **s. life,** inanimate objects as subject of picture. **s.-born,** *a.* dead when born. **s.-birth,** *n.* (O.E. *stille*)
stillage, *n.* frame on which things are laid.
stillitory, *n.* (*Shake.*) alembic, still.
stilly, *adv.* in a still manner.—*a.* (*poet.*) quiet.
stilp, *v.i.* (*Scot.*) go on crutches.
stilt, *n.* pole with foot-rest for walking raised from ground; kinds of long-legged wading-bird. **stilted,** *a.* (of style) stiff, pompous; (of arch) separated from impost by vertical members.
Stilton, *n.* kind of cheese. (place)
stime, *n.* (*Scot.*) ray of light, glimmer; faintest form of any object.
stimpart, *n.* (*Scot.*) quarter of a peck.
stimulus, *n.* (*pl.* **stimuli**) rousing influence, incentive; thing that evokes activity in tissues; (*bot.*) sting. **stimulate,** *v.t.* apply stimulus to; rouse to action, incite. **stimulation, stimulator,** *nn.* **stimulative,** *a.* **stimulant,** *a.* stimulating; (*med.*) producing temporary increase of vital energy.—*n.* stimulant agent or drug, esp. alcohol. (L.=goad)
stimy, same as **stymie.**
sting, *v.t.* and *i.* (*past, p.p.* **stung**) wound with sting; affect with, feel, sharp quick pain; wound feelings of; provoke, stimulate; be pungent; (*sl.*) cheat.—*n.* pointed organ, us. poisonous, of insect or plant; wound, pain, produced by it; any acute pain; bite, tang; (*Shake.*) carnal impulse. **s.-bull, s.-fish,** *nn.* weever. **stinging-nettle, s.-nettle,** *nn.* with stinging leaf. **s.-ray, stingaree,** *nn.* fish with sharp spines on whip-like tail. **stinger,** *n.* (*colloq.*) stinging blow. **stingo,** *n.* (*arch.*) strong beer. (O.E. *stingan*)
stingy, *a.* meanly avaricious, niggardly. (*sting*)
stink, *v.i.* and *t.* (*past,* **stank** or **stunk,** *p.p.* **stunk**) emit strong offensive smell.—*n.* stench; (*pl., sl.*) chemistry. **s. in the nostrils of,** be highly offensive to. **s. out,** drive out by stinking. **s.-ball, s.-pot,** *nn.* old kind of grenade emitting choking fumes. **s.-bomb,** *n.* bomb emitting nauseating smell. **s.-horn,** *n.* an evil-smelling fungus. **stinking,** *a.* (*sl.*) hateful. **stinkard,** *n.* stinking person; teledu. (O.E. *stincan*)
stint, *v.t.* and *i.* be chary of giving, supply on niggardly scale; (*arch.*) cease.—*n.* restriction, limitation; allotted amount of work. (O.E. *styntan*)
stint, *n.* small sandpiper.
stipate, *a.* (*bot.*) compressed, close-set. (L. *stipare*, cram)
stipe, *n.* stalk, stem. **stipel,** *n.* secondary stipule at base of leaflet in compound leaf. (L. *stipes*)
stipend, *n.* salary, esp. of clergyman. **stipendiary,** *a.* receiving pay.—*n.* paid magistrate in service of Crown. (L. *stipendium*)
stipes, *n.* stipe. **stipiform, stipitiform,** *aa.* stipe-shaped. **stipitate,** *a.* having a stipe. (L.)
stipple, *v.t.* and *i.* use dots instead of lines in painting or drawing.—*n.* stippled work. (Du. *stip*, point)
stipular, stipulary, *aa.* of stipule.
stipulate, *v.i.* and *t.* demand as part of one's terms. **s. for,** insist on as essential. **stipulation,** *n.* stipulating;

special condition. **stipulator,** *n.* (L. *stipulari*)

stipule, *n.* leaf-like appendage at base of leaf-stalk. **stipulate,** *a.* having stipule. **stipulation,** *n.* formation of stipules. (*stipe*)

stir, *n.* (*sl.*) prison.

stir, *v.t.* and *i.* move; give circular motion to with spoon etc.; rouse, excite.—*n.* stirring movement; disturbance, commotion. **s. up,** stir thoroughly, mix; instigate. **stirabout,** *n.* oatmeal porridge.—*a.* active, bustling. (O.E. *styrian*)

stirk, *n.* (*Scot.*) yearling ox or cow.

stirps, *n.* (*law*) person from whom family is descended; (*zool.*) classificatory group. **stirpiculture,** *n.* breeding of special stocks. (L.=stock)

stirrup, *n.* (also **s.-iron**) metal loop in which rider places foot; (also **s.-leather**) strap this hangs from. **s.-cup,** *n.* drink given to rider mounted for departure. **s.-pump,** *n.* kind of hand-pump. (O.E. *stirāp*)

stitch, *n.* single pass of needle; turn or loop of thread it leaves in fabric; style of sewing; sudden stabbing pain in side.—*v.t.* and *i.* fasten or ornament with stitches, sew. **drop a s.,** let loop fall off knitting-needle. **stitchwort,** *n.* kinds of plant incl. chickweed. (O.E. *stician,* pierce)

stithy, *n.* (*arch.*) anvil; forge, smithy. (O.E. *stethi*)

stiver, *n.* old Dutch coin of small value; trifle. (Du. *stuiver*)

stŏă, *n.* ancient Greek portico or covered colonnade. (Gk.)

stoat, *n.* small animal of weasel kind.

stoccado, stoccata, *nn.* (*Shake.*) thrust in fencing. (It.)

stock, *n.* stump, post; trunk; stem into which graft is inserted; main supporting or holding part; crossbar of anchor; family, breed; animals of farm; materials of business; supply, fund; liquid made by boiling bones etc. as foundation for soup; close-fitting neck-band; kinds of fragrant garden plant; money contributed as loan to form state fund or capital of company; (*Shake.*) stocking; (*pl.*) framework supporting ship while it is built; wooden frame in which legs of malefactors used to be confined. —*v.t.* provide with stock; keep regularly for sale; put in the stocks.—*a.* kept in stock; commonplace, hackneyed. **fat s.,** animals fit for slaughter as food. **have in s.,** have already in one's shop. **live s.,** domestic animals. **s. exchange,** place where stocks and shares are bought and sold; association of stockbrokers. **take s.,** make inventory of stock; form estimate (of); concern oneself (in). (O.E. *stocc*)

stockade, *n.* barrier, enclosure, of stakes.—*v.t.* surround, protect, with stockade. (Sp. *estaca,* stake)

stock-breeder, *n.* one who raises livestock.

stockbroker, *n.* agent for buying and selling stocks and shares. **stockbroking,** *n.*

stockdove, *n.* small wild pigeon.

stockfish, *n.* dried codfish.

stock-holder, *n.* owner of stock.

stocking, *n.* close-fitting covering for foot and lower leg; wind-indicator at aerodrome. **stockinged,** *a.* **stockinet,** *n.* elastic knitted fabric for undergarments. (*stock*)

stock-in-trade, *n.* goods, tools etc., needed for business or trade.

stockish, *a.* stupid.

stockjobber, *n.* one who speculates in stocks and shares. **stockjobbing,** *n.*

stockman, *n.* man in charge of cattle on farm.

stock-rider, *n.* (*Austral.*) mounted herdsman.

stock-still, *a.* absolutely motionless

stock-whip, *n.* whip with short handle and long lash.

stocky, *a.* short and thickset.

stodge, *n.* (*sl.*) heavy solid food.—*v.i.* (*sl.*) eat greedily, stuff. **stodgy,** *a.* heavy, indigestible; dull, uninteresting.

stoep, *n.* (*S. Afr.*) terraced veranda in front of house. (Du.)

stogie, stogy, *n.* (*Amer.*) kind of cheap cigar; heavy shoe. (*Conestoga* in U.S.)

stoic, *n.* person of great fortitude or impassivity; follower of Greek philosopher Zeno and his doctrine of indifference to pleasure and pain.—*a.* of, like, a Stoic. **stoical,** *a.* showing indifference to pain. **stoicism,** *n.* being stoical; Stoic doctrine. (*stoa* where Zeno taught)

stoit, *v.i.* (*Scot.*) stumble.

stoke, *v.t.* and *i.* feed (furnace) with fuel. **s. up,** (*sl.*) have meal. **s.-hole, stokehold,** *nn.* compartment from which steamer's fires are fed. **stoker,** *n.* (Du. *stoken*)

stole, *n.* long robe reaching to feet; long scarf with fringed ends worn by priest; woman's fur wrap for neck and shoulders. (Gk. *stolē*)

stole, same as **stolon.**

stole, stolen, see **steal.**

stolid, *a.* not easily excited, phlegmatic; dull and stupid; stubborn. **stolidity,** *n.* (L. *stolidus*)

stolon, *n.* runner of plant, sucker. **stolonate,** *a.* (L. *stolo*)

stoma, *n.* (*pl.* **stomata**) small mouth-like opening. (Gk.=mouth)

stomach, *n.* bag forming chief digestive organ; belly, abdomen; appetite; desire, inclination; (*arch.*) disposition, bearing; (*Shake.*) courage, pride, anger.—*v.t.* relish, manage to eat; put up with (insult); (*Shake.*) resent. **s.-ache,** *n.* abdominal pain. **s.-pump,** *n.* apparatus for washing out stomach. **stomachal,** *a.* **stomacher,** *n.* woman's ornamental breast-covering of 15th–17th centuries. **stomachic,** *a.* of stomach, digestive.—*n.* drug promoting digestion. (*stoma*+dim.)

stomatitis, *n.* inflammation of mouth.

stomatology, *n.* science of the mouth and its diseases. (*stoma*)

stone, *n.* rock; piece of rock; gem; hard seed of fruit; calculus; testicle; (*pl.* same) measure of weight, 14 lb. —*v.t.* pelt with stones; remove stones from (fruit). **leave no s. unturned,** use every resource. **S. Age,** prehistoric period in which tools were made of stone. **s.-blind, s.-cold, s.-dead, s.-deaf,** *aa.* quite blind, cold etc. **s.-boat,** *n.* (*Amer.*) runnerless sled for carrying stones. **s.-bow,** *n.* crossbow for shooting stones. **s.-break,** *n.* saxifrage. **s.-cast, s.'s-cast,** *nn.* as far as one can fling a stone. **s.-coal,** *n.* anthracite. **s.-fruit,** *n.* with seed in hard shell surrounded by pulp. **s.-pine,** *n.* umbrella-shaped Mediterranean pine. **s.-walling,** *n.* parliamentary obstruction; (*cricket*) purely defensive batting. **s.-waller,** *n.* **stonework,** *n.* masonry. (O.E. *stán*)

stonechat, *n.* kinds of small bird.

stonecrop, *n.* small creeping plant.

stoneware, *n.* heavy common pottery.

stonish, *v.t.* (*Shake.*) dismay, astonish.

stony, *a.* full of stones; like stone; hard, unfeeling. **s. broke,** (*sl.*) with no money left. **s.-hearted,** *a.* cruel.

stood, see **stand.**

stooge, *n.* (*Amer.*) butt, scapegoat.

stook, *n.* group of sheaves of corn, shock.—*v.t.* set up in stooks. (M.E. *stouk*)

stool, *n.* low backless seat for one; footstool, hassock; seat for evacuating bowels, solid matter evacuated; part of plant that remains alive but dormant between seasons. — *v.i.* throw up shoots from root; evacuate bowels. **fall between two ss.,** fail from hesitating between two choices. **s.-pigeon,** *n.* pigeon, person, acting as decoy. **stoolball,** *n.* primitive kind of cricket. (O.E. *stól*)

stoop, *v.i.* and *t.* lean, bend, forward and down; be round-shouldered; abase oneself, condescend; swoop, pounce.—*n.* act, position, of stooping. (O.E. *stúpian*)

stoop, same as **stoup.**

stoop, (*Amer.*) same as **stoep.**

stoor, *a.* (*Scot.*) stiff; harsh, hoarse.

stoor, same as **stour.**

stop, *v.t.* and *i.* stuff (up), obstruct; fill cavity of (tooth); stanch (wound); check, bring to halt; cease; withhold part of (wages etc.); punctuate; (*mus.*) change pitch of; (*colloq.*) stay.—*n.* act of stopping, halt; checking-device; punctuation-mark; (*mus.*) device in instrument to regulate pitch; set of organ pipes, key controlling it; (*phonetics*) consonant made by closure of organs concerned, e.g. *k, p, t*; (*phot.*) device reducing aperture of lens. **full s.,** period. **s.-press,** *n.* late news inserted in newspaper after printing has begun. **s.-volley,** *n.* (*lawn tennis*) volley that checks ball and drops it close to racket. **s.-watch,** *n.* watch with hands that can be stopped for exact timing of race. (O.E. *forstoppian*)

stopcock, *n.* tap.

stopgap, *n.* temporary substitute.

stoppage, *n.* blocked state; cessation.

stopper, *n.* plug for mouth of bottle. —*v.t.* close with stopper.

stopping, *n.* material to stop tooth.

stopple, *n.* and *v.t.* (*rare*) stopper.

storage, *n.* act of, place or charge for, storing.

storax, *n.* a vanilla-scented resin; tree yielding it. (Gk. *sturax*)

store, *n.* abundance; reserve supply, stock; place for keeping goods; (*Amer.*) shop; (*pl.*) large general shop.—*a.* (*Amer.*) bought, not home-made.—*v.t.* fill with supplies, stock; put away, reserve; deposit (furniture) in warehouse. **in s.,** about to come. **set s. by,** value greatly. **s. cattle,** cattle for fattening. **storekeeper,** *n.* man in charge of store; (*Amer.*) shopkeeper. **storehouse,** *n.* place where goods are stored, repository. (L. *instaurare*, renew)

storey, story, *n.* set of rooms on one level, floor. **upper s.,** (*joc.*) brain. **s.-post,** *n.* upright post supporting floor-beam.

stórgē, *n.* natural affection. (Gk.)

storied, *a.* celebrated in story; adorned with scenes from history. **storiette,** *n.* very short story. **storiology,** *n.* study of folklore.

stork, *n.* large wading-bird with long legs and neck. **s.'s-bill,** *n.* kind of geranium. (O.E. *storc*)

storm, *n.* violent wind or disturbance of atmosphere, tempest; violent agitation or upheaval; dense shower (of missiles etc.); military assault on fortified place.—*v.t.* and *i.* take by storm; talk violently, scold; rage. **s. in a tea-cup,** fuss about trifles. **s.-beaten, s.-tossed,** *aa.* **s.-bound,** *a.* delayed by storm. **s.-centre,** *n.* point of lowest pressure in cyclonic storm. **s.-cock,** *n.* fieldfare or missel-thrush. **s.-cone,** *n.* large canvas cone hoisted as storm-signal. **s.-sail,** *n.* heavy sail for rough weather. **s.-trooper,** *n.* member of semi-military nucleus of Nazi party. **stormy,** *a.* subject to storms; boisterous; violent, passionate. **stormily,** *adv.* **storminess,** *n.* (O.E.)

Storthing, Storting, *n.* Norwegian parliament. (Norwegian)

story, see **storey.**

story, *n.* (*pl.* **stories**) history, legends; narrative of fact or fiction, tale, anecdote; account of incident, report;

plot of novel or play; (*colloq.*) lie, fib. **s.-book,** *n.* **s.-teller,** *n.* reciter or writer of stories; (*colloq.*) liar. (*history*)

stot, *n.* (*dial.*) young ox, steer. (O.E.)

stot, *v.i.* and *n.* (*Scot.*) rebound, bounce.

stound, *n.* (*Spens.*) moment; time of trial; pang, shock. (O.E. *stund*)

stound, *v.t.* (*Spens.*) stupefy.—*n.* amazement. (*astound*)

stoup, *n.* (*arch.*) drinking-vessel, flagon; holy-water basin. (O.N. *staup*)

stour, *n.* (*Spens.*) tumult, disturbance; paroxysm; (*Scot.*) flying dust.

stout, *a.* fat, corpulent; strong, durable; brave, resolute; (*Shake.*) proud.—*n.* strong kind of porter. **s.-hearted,** *a.* courageous. (O.F. *estout*)

stovaine, *n.* a local anaesthetic. (F.)

stove, see **stave.**

stove, *n.* closed-in apparatus for heating or cooking. **s.-pipe,** *n.* chimney of stove. **s.-pipe hat,** (*Amer.*) tall silk hat.

stover, *n.* (*Shake.*) fodder for cattle. (O.F. *estover*, necessaries)

stow, *v.t.* pack closely or compactly; (*sl.*) be silent about. **stowage,** *n.* stowing; space or charge for this. **stowaway,** *n.* one who hides in vessel to obtain free passage. (O.E.=place)

strabismus, *n.* squint. **strabismal, strabismic,** *aa.* **strabotomy,** *n.* cutting operation to cure squint. (Gk. *strabos*, squinting)

Strad, *abbr.* for **Stradivarius.**

straddle, *v.i.* and *t.* stretch legs out widely; bestride thus; sit on fence, vacillate; drop shells over and short of.—*n.* straddling; (*stock exchange*) contract giving right of either calling for or delivering stock at fixed price. (*stride*)

Stradivarius, *n.* violin made by Antonio Stradivari of Cremona.

strae, *Scot.* form of **straw.**

strafe, *v.t.* (*sl.*) bombard heavily; damage, punish; scold severely.—*n.* act of strafing. (G.=punish)

straggle, *v.i.* wander from direct course, stray; lag behind; be dispersed, lack compactness. **straggly,** *a.*

straight, *a.* without bend or angle; correctly placed, in proper order; direct; frank; honest, sincere; (*cards*) forming regular sequence; (*Amer.*) undiluted, neat.—*n.* straightness; straight stretch; (*cards*) sequence.—*adv.* in a straight line, directly; without ambiguity; (*arch.*) immediately. **keep a s. face,** avoid smiling. **put things s.,** tidy up. **s. away,** (*colloq.*) at once. **s. off,** without hesitation. **s. ticket,** (*Amer.*) party programme without modification. **s. tip,** (*sl.*) reliable forecast. **s.-cut,** *a.* (of tobacco) of leaf cut lengthwise. **s.-edge,** *n.* ruler. **straighten,** *v.t.* and *i.* make, become, straight. **straightforward,** *a.* frank, candid; simple, not complicated. **straightway,** *adv.* (*arch.*) at once. (O.E. *streccan*, stretch)

strain, *n.* breed, stock. (O.E. *stréon*)

strain, *v.t.* and *i.* stretch tightly; exert (oneself) to utmost; injure by over-exertion, try too far; wrench, distort; tug (at); press closely, hug; filter, percolate; (*Shake.*) urge, constrain.—*n.* tension, tightness; severe effort; injury from over-exertion; cast of mind, disposition; tinge, streak; style, tone; song, tune; (*Shake.*) impulse, emotion. **s. a point,** go further than can be expected. **s. at,** be over-scrupulous about. **strained,** *a.* awkward, constrained; forced, unnatural. **strainer,** *n.* sieve, filter. (L. *stringere*)

strait, *n.* narrow channel connecting two large bodies of water; (us. *pl.*) awkward fix, perplexity.—*a.* (*arch.*) narrow, restricted; strict, scrupulous. **s. jacket, waistcoat,** coat confining arms of lunatic. **s.-laced,** *a.* strict, austere. **straiten,** *v.t.* put in difficulties, embarrass; (*arch.*) make narrow, confine. (L. *stringere*, draw tight)

strake, *n.* single breadth of planks or plates forming continuous strip through length of ship. (*streak*)

stramash, *n.* (*Scot.*) tumult, uproar.—*v.t.* wreck, destroy.

stramineous, *a.* (*arch.*) of, like, straw; valueless. (L. *stramen*, straw)

stramonium, *n.* narcotic drug used for asthma; kind of datura yielding it.

strand, *n.* shore, beach.—*v.t.* and *i.* run aground. **stranded,** *p.p.* left behind; in difficulties. (O.E.)

strand, *n.* single thread or fibre of rope etc.—*v.t.* break strand in.

strange, *a.* not known, unfamiliar; foreign, alien; unusual, singular, queer; inexperienced, raw; distant, reserved. **stranger,** *n.* person unknown to one; foreigner; person unaccustomed (to).—*a.* (*Shake.*) strange. (L. *extra*, outside)

strangle, *v.t.* kill by squeezing windpipe, choke; suppress, keep back. **s.-hold,** *n.* deadly grip. **strangulate,** *v.t.* compress, constrict (vein, intestine) so as to prevent circulation. **strangulation,** *n.* strangling; strangulating. (Gk. *stranggos*, twisted)

strangury, *n.* difficult and painful urination. **strangurious,** *a.* (Gk. *strangx*, drop; *ouron*, urine)

strap, *n.* leather strip for fastening or punishing; binding-strip of metal.—*v.t.* fasten, bind, punish, with strap; apply strapping to; strop. **s.-hanger,** *n.* person in tram etc. who cannot find seat and has to hold on to strap. **s.-work,** *n.* ornamentation of interlaced bands. **strapping,** *a.* tall and lusty, stalwart.—*n.* strips of adhesive plaster for surgical use; flogging. (O.E. *strop*)

strappado, *n.* torture in which victim was let fall the length of a rope tied to his wrists.—*v.t.* torture thus. (It. *strappare*, pull)

strass, *n.* paste for making sham gems. (J. *Strasser*, inventor)

strata, see **stratum.**

stratagem, *n.* ruse, clever trick; military artifice; (*Shake.*) deed of great violence. (*strategy*)

stratal, *a.* of strata.

strategy, *n.* art of conducting a military campaign (opp. to tactics). **strategic,** *a.* of, showing, dictated by, strategy. —*n.pl.* strategy. **strategical,** *a.* **strategist,** *n.* expert in strategy. (Gk. *stratos*, army; *agein*, lead)

strath, *n.* (*Scot.*) broad river-valley. (Gael. *srath*)

strathspey, *n.* Scottish dance like reel but slower. (place)

stratocracy, *n.* military government. (Gk. *stratos*, army; *kratos*, power)

stratosphere, *n.* upper layer of atmosphere beginning about seven miles above the earth, in which temperature remains constant. (*stratum*)

stratum, *n.* (*pl.* **strata**) layer, horizontal division; (*geol.*) layer of deposited rock. **straticulate,** *a.* arranged in thin layers. **stratiform,** *a.* having character of, forming, stratum. **stratify,** *v.t.* arrange, deposit, in strata. **stratification,** *n.* **stratigraphy,** *n.* study of geological strata. **stratigraphic,** *a.* **stratigraphically,** *adv.* (L. *sternere*, strew)

stratus, *n.* (*pl.* **strati**) low horizontal sheet of cloud. (*stratum*)

stravaig, *v.i.* (*Scot.*) go about aimlessly, wander.—*n.* ramble.

straw, *arch.* for **strew.**

straw, *n.* stalk of grain; dried mass of such stalks; straw hat.—*a.* made of straw. **man of s.,** imaginary person; unreliable or impecunious person. **not care a s.,** be indifferent. **s. vote,** (*Amer.*) unofficial ballot taken as test. **s.-boss,** *n.* (*Amer.*) assistant foreman. **s.-colour,** *n.* pale yellow. (O.E. *stréaw*)

strawberry, *n.* a red juicy fruit; plant bearing it. **crushed s.,** dull crimson. **s. leaves,** symbol of ducal rank. **s.-mark,** *n.* dull reddish birthmark. **s.-tree,** *n.* kind of arbutus. (*straw*)

strawboard, *n.* coarse cardboard.

strawy, *a.* of, like, straw.

stray, *v.i.* and *t.* wander from path, lose one's way; rove, roam; err, sin; (*Shake.*) lead astray.—*n.* strayed animal, lost child; (*pl.*, *wireless*) atmospherics.—*a.* wandering, lost; occurring here and there, scattered. **strayed,** *a.* having strayed. (O.F. *estraier*)

streak, *n.* long narrow mark or band, stripe; vein of character, strain.—*v.t.* and *i.* mark with streaks; move rapidly, flash. **yellow s.,** liability to panic. (O.E. *strica*, stroke)

stream, *n.* river, brook; steady flow, jet; current, trend; moving mass or crowd.—*v.i.* and *t.* flow freely, run (with); pour forth; trail. **streamer,** *n.* flag, ribbon, to stream in wind; ray shooting up in aurora. **streamlet,** *n.* small stream. **streamline,** *n.* shape that offers least possible resistance to air or water when passing through it.—*v.t.* design, make, with streamline. (O.E. *stréam*)

street, *n.* town or village road lined with houses. **not in the same s. with,** far inferior to. **on the ss.,** homeless; practising prostitution. **streetwalker,** *n.* prostitute. (L. *strata* via, paved way)

strength, *n.* quality of being strong, power; intensity, potency; amount of forces. **up to s.,** having full complement. **on the s. of,** on muster-roll of; relying on. **strengthen,** *v.t.* and *i.* make, become, strong or stronger; reinforce. (*strong*)

strenuous, *a.* energetic, vigorous; making or requiring great efforts. (L. *strenuus*)

strepitoso, *adv.* (*mus.*) boisterously, with impetuosity. (It.)

streptococcus, *n.* (*pl.* **streptococci**) bacterium of chain formation, as in pneumonia. (Gk. *strephein*, turn; *kokkos*, grain)

stress, *n.* impelling force; strain; emphasis; accent; (*mech.*) force exerted between contiguous bodies or parts of a body.—*v.t.* lay stress on, emphasize; accent. (L. *stringere*, draw tight)

stretch, *v.t.* and *i.* pull tight, strain; make, become, longer or larger by pulling; extend, reach; extend oneself or one's limbs; exaggerate; have elasticity.—*n.* act of stretching, strain; extent, expanse; unbroken period; (*sl.*) term of imprisonment. **at a s.,** continuously. **stretcher,** *n.* one who, that which, stretches; crosspiece against which rower braces feet; frame of two poles and canvas for carrying sick or wounded; brick laid lengthwise along line of wall. **stretcher-bearer,** *n.* (O.E. *streccan*)

strew, *v.t.* (*p.p.* **strewn** or **strewed**) scatter, spread. **strewment,** *n.* (*Shake.*). (O.E. *streawian*)

stria, *n.* (*pl.* **striae**) line, small groove, strip. **striate, striated,** *aa.* marked with striae. **striation, striature,** *nn.* (L.)

strich, *n.* (*Spens.*) screech-owl. (L. *strix*)

stricken, *a.* smitten; (*arch.*) wounded. **s. field,** pitched battle. **s. in years,** elderly. (*strike*)

strickle, *n.* rod for levelling grain in measure; templet. (*strike*)

strict, *a.* stern, severe; requiring implicit obedience; without exception, rigorously exact; tight. **stricture,** *n.* severe criticism, censure; (*med.*) constriction of urethra or other duct; (*Shake.*) strictness. (L. *stringere,* draw tight)

stride, *v.i.* and *t.* (*past* **strode,** *p.p. rare* **stridden, strid**) walk with long steps; pass (over) with one step; stand astride of.—*n.* single step; length of this. **get into one's s.,** settle steadily to work. (O.E. *stridan*)

strident, *a.* loud and harsh, jarring. **stridor,** *n.* harsh noise; whistling sound in breathing. **stridulate,** *v.i.* make shrill chirping or creaking noise. **stridulation, stridulator,** *nn.* **stridulant,** *a.* (L. *stridere,* creak)

strife, *n.* conflict, hostilities; quarrelling; (*Shake.*) endeavour. (O.F. *estrif*)

striga, *n.* (*pl.* **strigae**) plant's stiff bristle; stria. **strigose, strigous,** *aa.* having strigae. (L.=swath)

strigil, *n.* skin-scraper used by Romans after bath. (L. *strigilis*)

strike, *v.t.* and *i.* (*past* **struck;** *p.p.* **struck,** *arch.* **stricken**) hit, deal (blow); collide (with); impel with blow, dash; cause, produce, by stroke; make by stamping, mint; thrust (roots) in; light suddenly upon; come to (bargain); lower (flag), surrender thus; take down (tent); hook (fish); level (measure of grain) by smoothing top with rod; assume (attitude); impress mind of; take course, turn; (of clock) sound; (of ship) run aground; (of workman) go on strike; (*Shake.*) blast.—*n.* general stoppage of work to enforce workmen's demands; sudden successful find (of oil etc.); (*baseball*) act of striking at pitched ball. **s. down,** fell, prostrate. **s. in,** interpose; (of disease) affect internal parts. **s. off,** cut off, cancel; print. **s. out,** erase; devise (plan); start swimming; (*baseball*) be put out for not hitting ball fairly. **s. up,** begin to play or sing. (O.E. *strican,* go)

strike-breaker, *n.* worker brought in from outside to replace striker.

strike-measure, *n.* measure of grain with surface levelled off by rod.

strike-pay, *n.* allowance paid to strikers by trade-union.

striking, *a.* arresting, noteworthy.

string, *n.* fine cord, twine; piece of this, tape etc., for tying; stretched gut or wire for violin, piano etc.; chain; long succession; (*pl.*) stringed instruments.—*v.t.* and *i.* (*past, p.p.* **strung**) furnish with string or strings; link by string; put (facts) together; (*Amer. colloq.*) hoax. **first, second, s.,** athlete chosen to compete first, second, in team. **have one on a s.,** (*sl.*) have complete control over him. **pull ss.,** exert influence behind scenes. **s. band,** of stringed instruments. **s. out,** extend in long line. **s. quartet,** us. two violins, viola, and violoncello. **s. up,** bring to state of tension; (*sl.*) hang. **two ss. to one's bow,** choice of sweethearts or plans. **s.-board,** *n.* support for ends of steps in staircase. **s.-course,** *n.* projecting moulding running along wall. **s.-halt,** *n.* spring-halt. **stringed,** *a.* having strings. (O.E. *streng*)

stringendo, adv. (*mus.*) with increasing pace. (It.)

stringent, *a.* rigid, binding; leaving no discretion; (of money market) tight. **stringency,** *n.* (L. *stringere,* draw tight)

stringer, *n.* string-board.

stringy, *a.* fibrous, like strings; viscous, ropy.

strip, *v.t.* and *i.* tear off (outer covering), lay bare; deprive, divest; undress; dismantle; tear thread from (screw).—*n.* long narrow piece. **comic s.,** row of consecutive drawings in newspaper etc., presenting comic incident. **s.-tease,** *n.* turn in which actress divests herself of successive articles of dress. (O.E. *strýpan*)

stripe, *n.* long narrow band of different colour from background; chevron as symbol of military rank; stroke of rod or lash.—*v.t.* mark with stripe.

stripling, *n.* young man, youth. (dim. of *strip*)

strive, *v.i.* (*past* **strove,** *p.p.* **striven**) try hard, struggle; contend. (O.F. *estriver*)

stroan, *v.i.* (*Scot.*) urinate.

strob, *n.* angular velocity of one radian per second. **stroboscope,** *n.* apparatus for studying rapidly rotating objects by intermittent glimpses. (Gk. *strephein,* twist)

strobile, *n.* fir-cone. (Gk. *strobilos*)

strode, see **stride.**

stroke, *n.* act of striking, blow; sudden action; injury, affliction; attack of paralysis; mark of pen or pencil, dash; sweep of oar or wing, movement of piston; rower nearest stern, setting time for others.—*v.t.* row stroke in (boat). (*strike*)

stroke, *v.t.* pass hand lightly over, caress.—*n.* act of stroking. **s. the wrong way,** irritate. (O.E. *strácian*)

stroll, *n.* short leisurely walk.—*v.i.* saunter. **stroller,** *n.* one who strolls; strolling player. **strolling,** *a.* itinerant.

stroma, *n.* (*pl.* **stromata**) network of connective tissue forming framework of organ. **stromatic,** *a.* (Gk.= coverlet)

strond, (*Shake.*) form of **strand.**

strong, *a.* powerful, muscular; robust, healthy; having great force of character, masterful; not easily broken, durable; well fortified; drastic; intense, decided; potent, concentrated; having specified numbers; (*Shake.*) resolute.—*adv.* (*sl.*) strongly, vigorously. **going s.,** (*sl.*) in full vigour. **s. drink, waters,** alcoholic drink, spirits. **s. meat,** doctrine suited only to vigorous or instructed minds. **s. verb,** one that forms past by varying root vowel. **s.-box, s.-room,** *nn.* made secure for storing valuables. **s.-minded,** *a.* of determined or independent character. **stronghold,** *n.* fortified place, citadel. (O.E. *strang*)

strontium, *n.* yellowish metallic element. **strontian,** *a.* (*Strontian* in Argyllshire)

strop, *n.* leather strap for sharpening razor.—*v.t.* sharpen on strop. (*strap*)

strophanthus, *n.* kinds of tropical plant. **strophanthin,** *n.* poisonous drug made from its seeds. (Gk. *strephein,* twist; *anthos,* flower)

strŏphē, *n.* stanza or movement of Greek chorus with which antistrophe alternates. **strophic,** *a.* (Gk.)

stroup, *n.* (*Scot.*) spout, nozzle.

strove, see **strive.**

strow, *v.t.* (*p.p.* **strown or strowed;** *arch.*) strew.

stroy, *v.t.* (*Shake.*) destroy.

struck, see **strike.**

structure, *n.* formation, make; thing built, building; complex whole. **structural,** *a.* (L. *struere,* build)

struggle, *v.i.* move limbs violently in effort; offer resistance, fight; put forth great efforts, strive; make way with difficulty.—*n.* act of struggling, scuffle; strenuous effort, hard contest. (M.E. *strogelen*)

strum, *v.i.* and *t.* play on stringed instrument badly or carelessly.—*n.* spell of strumming. (imit.)

struma, *n.* (*pl.* **strumae**) goitre; scrofula. **strumose, strumous,** *aa.* (L.)

strumpet, *n.* prostitute.

strung, see **string.**

strunt, *n.* (*Scot.*) sulky fit.

strunt, *n.* (*Scot.*) spirits; dram.

strunt, *v.i.* (*Scot.*) strut.

strut, *v.i.* walk in stiff, pompous, or affected manner.—*n.* strutting gait. (O.E. *strútian,* project)

strut, *n.* rigid support, us. set obliquely; stay.—*v.t.* support with strut, brace.

struthious, *a.* of the ostrich family. (Gk. *struthion,* ostrich)

strychnine, strychnin, (*chem.*) **strychnia,** *nn.* highly poisonous alkaloid used as stimulant. **strychnic,** *a.* **strychninism, strychnism,** *nn.* strychnine poisoning. (Gk. *struchnos,* kind of nightshade)

stub, *n.* stump of tree; short remnant of pencil, cigar etc.; counterfoil of cheque.—*v.t.* clear of stumps; dig up (root); strike (toe) accidentally against something. (O.E. *stybb*)

stubble, *n.* short stiff stalks of grain left in ground after reaping; hairs of bristly beard. (L. *stipes,* stalk + dim.)

stubborn, *a.* unyielding, obstinate; not easily worked, refractory; (*Shake.*) rough. (M.E. *stoburn*)

stubby, *a.* squat, stumpy. (*stub*)

stucco, *n.* fine white plaster used as external coating for walls, for making architectural decorations etc.—*v.t.* coat with stucco. (It.)

stuck, *n.* (*Shake.*) thrust. (*stoccado*)

stuck, see **stick.**

stuck-up, *a.* (*colloq.*) conceited.

stud, *n.* movable double-headed button for two button-holes; large-headed projecting nail; ornamental knob, boss; upright to which laths are nailed.—*v.t.* cover with studs; encrust, bespangle. (O.E. *studu,* post)

stud, *n.* number of horses kept for breeding or racing. **at s.,** in use for breeding. **s.-book,** *n.* record of pedigrees of famous animals. **s.-farm,** *n.* where horses are bred. **s.-horse,** *n.* stallion. (O.E. *stód*)

studdie, *n.* (*Scot.*) anvil.

studding-sail, *n.* extra sail set out beyond square sail in light winds.

student, *n.* one who studies; person undergoing instruction at college or university; one devoted to learning; bookish person. **studentry,** *n.* students generally. **studentship,** *n.* kind of scholarship.

studio, *n.* workshop of artist or photographer; transmitting-room in broadcasting station. (It.)

study, *n.* process of acquiring knowledge; thoughtful attention or scrutiny; meditation; earnest endeavour; subject studied, branch of learning; excursus, essay; sketch; piece of artistic work done as exercise in technique; room to study in. —*v.t.* and *i.* apply mind to, read books with a view to learning; con over; scrutinize; have regard for, try earnestly (to). **s. for, be in course** of training for. **studied,** *a.* deliberate, premeditated; mannered, lacking spontaneity; (*Shake.*) practised. **studious,** *a.* given to study; careful (of); (of care etc.) painstaking. (L. *studium,* zeal)

stuff, *n.* material, substance; essential quality; woollen fabric, textiles; goods, furniture; nonsense, trash; (*sl.*) money.—*a.* of woollen cloth.—*v.t.* and *i.* fill tightly, cram (in); block up; pad out; fill with seasoning; fill skin of (dead animal) for preservation in natural form; overeat, guzzle; (*colloq.*) hoax. **do your s.,** (*sl.*) go through prearranged performance. **that 's the s.!** (*sl.*) excellent! **stuffing,** *n.* padding; minced seasoning. **knock the stuffing out of,** disconcert; unman; demolish. **stuffy,** *a.* ill-ventilated, close; (of person) dull, stodgy; (*sl.*) sulky. (O.F. *estoffe*)

stuggy, *a.* stocky.

stultify, *v.t.* cause to look foolish; undo the effect of. **stultification,** *n.* (L. *stultus,* foolish; *facere,* make)

stum, *n.* unfermented or partly fermented grape-juice.—*v.t.* prevent fermentation of. (Du. *stom*)

stumble, *v.i.* and *t.* trip and nearly

fall, miss footing; be guilty of moral lapse, err; speak haltingly, falter; (*arch.*) give pause to, perplex.—*n.* act of stumbling. **s. at,** feel scruples about. **s. on,** come upon by chance. **stumbling-block,** *n.* cause of error or hesitation, obstacle.

stumer, *n.* (*sl.*) worthless cheque; counterfeit note or coin.

stump, *n.* part of tree, limb etc., when main part has been cut away; remnant, stub; (*cricket*) any of the three uprights forming wicket; (*pl., sl.*) legs.—*v.i.* and *t.* walk with stiff heavy steps; puzzle, nonplus; (*cricket*) break wicket of (batsman out of his ground). **stir one's ss.,** (*sl.*) walk, hurry. **s. orator,** political agitator. **s. up,** (*sl.*) pay up. **stumper,** *n.* poser; (*sl.*) wicket-keeper. **stumpy,** *a.* short and thickset.

stun, *v.t.* knock senseless; stupefy by shock. **stunning,** *a.* (*sl.*) first-rate. **stunner,** *n.* (*sl.*) stunning specimen.

stung, see **sting.**

stunk, see **stink.**

stunkard, *a.* (*Scot.*) sullen; obstinate.

stunsail, *contr.* for **studding-sail.**

stunt, *v.t.* check growth of, dwarf. (O.E.=foolish)

stunt, *n.* showy feat of dexterity or daring; spectacular display; aerobatics.—*v.i.* perform stunt.

stupe, *n.* dressing of cloth wrung out of hot water; pledget.—*v.t.* foment. (L. *stupa,* tow)

stupe, *n.* (*sl.*) fool. (*stupid*)

stupefy, *v.t.* deprive of full sensibility; make stupid or torpid. **stupefaction,** *n.* **stupefacient,** *a.* and *n.* stupefying (substance), narcotic. (L. *stupēre,* be torpid; *facere,* make)

stupendous, *a.* prodigious, amazing; of vast size. (L. *stupendus*)

stupeous, *a.* with long loose scales. (L. *stupa,* tow)

stupid, *a.* slow-witted, foolish; uninteresting; with senses dulled, stupefied.—*n.* (*colloq.*) stupid person. **stupidity,** *n.* (L. *stupidus*)

stupor, *n.* partial insensibility; state of coma; helpless astonishment. **stuporous,** *a.* (L.)

stupose, *a.* with tufts of long hair. (L. *stupa,* tow)

stupration, *n.* rape. (L. *stuprare,* debauch)

sturdy, *a.* strongly built, robust, vigorous. (O.F. *estourdi,* amazed)

sturdy, *n.* disease causing vertigo in sheep. (O.F. *estourdi,* amazed)

sturgeon, *n.* large fish yielding caviare. (O.H.G. *sturjo*)

sturm und drang, storm and stress. (G.)

sturt, *n.* (*Scot.*) trouble, strife.

stutter, *v.i.* and *t.* speak with involuntary checks and repetitions, stammer. —*n.* stuttering utterance.

sty, *n.* enclosure for pig; filthy place, hovel.—*v.i.* keep in sty, coop up. (O.E. *sti*)

sty, *v.i.* (*Spens.*) ascend. (O.E. *stigan*)

sty, stye, *n.* small inflamed swelling on edge of eyelid.

Stygian, *a.* of the Styx or Hades; murky, gloomy.

style, *n.* pointed instrument for writing on waxed tablets; engraving-tool, etching-needle; manner of writing, of artistic expression, of playing game, of general behaviour; distinction, grace, shown in this; mode of dress, fashion; fashionable elegance; shape, make; sort, kind; mode of address, designation.—*v.t.* call, name. **old s.,** (*abbr.* **O.S.**) Julian calendar, superseded in 1752 by **new s.,** (*abbr.* **N.S.**) Gregorian calendar, which differed from it by a number of days. (L. *stilus*)

style, *n.* pointer of sun-dial, gnomon; (*bot.*) narrowed extension of ovary bearing stigma. (Gk. *stulos,* pillar)

stylet, *n.* slender probe; stiletto. (*stiletto*)

stylish, *a.* having good style, fashionable, smart.

stylist, *n.* master of style; one who pays more attention to style than to matter. **stylistic,** *a.* of literary style. **stylistically,** *adv.*

stylite, *n.* medieval hermit who lived on top of lofty pillar. (Gk. *stulos,* pillar)

stylize, *v.t.* (*art*) conform to rules of conventional style.

stylo, *n.* (*colloq.*) stylograph.

stylobate, *n.* continuous base below row of pillars. (Gk. *stulos,* pillar; *bainein,* go)

stylograph, *n.* fountain-pen with needle-like point. **stylography,** *n.* writing with a pointed instrument. **stylographic,** *a.* (L. *stilus,* style. Gk. *graphein,* write)

stymie, *n.* (*golf*) position on putting-green when one ball lies between the other and the hole.—*v.t.* impede by stymie; (*joc.*) get in way of.

styptic, *a.* and *n.* (substance) checking bleeding. (Gk. *stuphein,* contract)

styrax, *n.* kinds of tree yielding gums and resins. (Gk. *sturax*)

Styx, *n.* river bounding Hades. **cross the S.,** die. (Gk. *Stux*)

suable, *a.* capable of being sued.

suasion, *n.* persuasion. **suasive,** *a.* (L. *suadēre,* advise)

suave, *a.* smoothly courteous, bland. urbane. **suavity,** *n.* *suaviter in re, fortiter in modo,* gently but firmly, with iron hand in velvet glove. (L. *suavis,* sweet)

sub, *colloq.* for **subaltern, subscription, subsistence money, substitute.**

sub, prep. below. *s. finem* (*abbr. s.f.*) towards the end. *s. judice,* under consideration, awaiting decision. *s. rosa,* in confidence (lit. under the rose). *s. silentio,* tacitly. *s. specie,* under appearance (of). *s. voce* (*abbr. s.v.*) under the word (in references to dictionaries etc.).

sub-, *pref.* under, as in **subway**; inferior, lower, as in **subdivision, sublibrarian**; nearly, slightly, as in **subtropical.**

subacid, *a.* slightly acid.

subacute, *a.* (of disease) moderately acute.

subagent, *n.* agent's representative.

subahdar, *n.* (*Anglo-Ind.*) chief native officer of company of sepoys. (Hind. *subah*, province; *dār*, master)

subalpine, *a.* of zone next below timber-line.

subaltern, *n.* commissioned officer of lower rank than captain.—*a.* subordinate; (*logic*) particular, not universal. (L. *sub*, under; *alter*, other)

subaqueous, *a.* under-water.

subarctic, *a.* of region or climate bordering on the arctic.

subaudition, *n.* mental supplying of something implied though not expressed, reading between lines. *subaudi, v.t. imper.* supply thus.

subaxillary, *a.* below the armpit; (*bot.*) under the angle formed by branch or leaf.

subcaudal, *a.* beneath the tail.

subcentral, *a.* nearly central; beneath the centre.

subclass, *n.* subdivision of class.

subclavian, *a.* under the clavicle.

subcommittee, *n.* committee of a committee.

subconscious, *a.* partially conscious; unconsciously perceptive.

subcontinent, *n.* region large and important enough to be styled a continent if it were not part of one.

subcontract, *n.* arrangement by which one who has contracted to do work gets it done for him by others under contract.—*v.i.* and *t.* make subcontract (for); (*Shake.*) betroth for second time. **subcontractor,** *n.*

subcontrary, *a.* contrary in some respects only.

subcostal, *a.* under the ribs.

subcutaneous, *a.* under the skin.

subdeacon, *n.* member of order of ministry below deacon. **subdiaconate,** *n.* his office.

subdivide, *v.t.* and *i.* divide what has already been divided, divide further. **subdivision,** *n.*

subdominant, *n.* (*mus.*) fourth note of scale.

subdorsal, *a.* near the back.

subduce, subduct, *vv.t.* take away, withdraw. (L. *ducere*, lead)

subdue, *v.t.* overcome, conquer; bring into subjection, tame; tone down, soften. **subdual,** (*Shake.*) **subduement,** *nn.* **subduable,** *a.* (L. *subducere*, withdraw + confusion with *subdere*, put under)

subduplicate, *a.* expressed by the square root.

subedit, *v.t.* prepare (copy) for press by inserting headings etc. **subeditor,** *n.* journalist who subedits; assistant editor. **subeditorial,** *a.*

subequal, *a.* approximately equal.

subereous, suberic, suberose, *aa.* of, like, cork. (L. *suber*, cork-tree)

subfamily, *n.* (*zool.*) division of family.

subflavour, *n.* secondary flavour.

subfusc, subfuscous, *aa.* sober-hued, dark.

subgenus, *n.* division of genus.

subglacial, *a.* beneath a glacier; partially glacial.

subheading, *n.* heading below main heading.

subhuman, *a.* less than human.

subinfeudate, *v.t.* grant to another land held from superior. **subinfeudation, subinfeudatory,** *nn.*

subito, adv. (*mus.*) suddenly. (It.)

subjacent, *a.* situated below. (L. *jacēre*, lie)

subject, *a.* under power of another; owing allegiance, politically dependent; exposed, liable (to).—*n.* one owing allegiance or under authority; thing spoken or treated of, topic, theme; person of specified tendencies; body for dissection; (*gram., logic*) that of which anything is affirmed; (*philos.*) conscious self, ego; substance, substratum, as opp. to attributes; (*Shake.*) people of a state.—*v.t.* bring under authority; cause to undergo, submit. **s. to,** conditional upon. **s.-matter,** *n.* what is discussed. **subjection,** *n.* subjecting; dependence. (L. *jacere*, throw)

subjective, *a.* of, derived from, the mind or inner consciousness, not from external things; existing only in thought, imaginary; (*art*) expressing artist's own individuality; (*gram.*) of, appropriate to, subject. **subjectivism,** *n.* doctrine that all knowledge is subjective only. **subjectivist,** *n.* **subjectivity,** *n.* subjectiveness.

subjoin, *v.t.* add at the end, append.

subjugate, *v.t.* bring into subjection, conquer. **subjugation, subjugator,** *nn.* (L. *jugum*, yoke)

subjunctive, *a.* and *n.* (mood of verb) expressing wish or possibility, not fact. (L. *jungere*, join)

subkingdom, *n.* division of kingdom.

sublapsarian, *n.* Calvinist who held that the fall of man was permitted but not preordained by God. **sublapsarianism,** *n.* (L. *lapsus*, fall)

sublease, *n.* lease granted by tenant to another.—*v.t.* grant or take sublease of. **sublessee, sublessor,** *nn.*

sublet, *v.t.* let property held on lease or rented.

sublibrarian, *n.* assistant librarian.

sublieutenant, *n.* naval rank below lieutenant.

sublime, *a.* exalted, lofty; awe-inspiring.—*v.t.* and *i.* make sublime; sublimate, be sublimated; extract, transmute, purify, by sublimation.

sublimity, *n.* **sublimate,** *v.t.* vaporize (substance) and allow it to solidify; (*psycho-anal.*) direct (instinctive energy) to higher plane.—*a.* and *n.* (substance) refined by sublimation. **sublimation,** *n.* (L. *sublimis*)

subliminal, *a.* (*psychology*) beneath the level of consciousness, latent.

sublunary, sublunar, *aa.* of the world, terrestrial.

subluxation, *n.* partial dislocation.

sub-man, *n.* man of type beneath that of ordinary humanity.

submarine, *a.* below the sea.—*n.* submarine torpedo-boat.

submaxillary, *a.* under the lower jaw.

submediant, *n.* (*mus.*) sixth note of scale.

submental, *a.* under the chin.

submerge, *v.t.* and *i.* cause to plunge under water, sink; go under water, dive; cover with water. **submerged tenth,** completely destitute class. **submergence, submersion,** *nn.* **submerse,** *v.t.* (*rare*) submerge. **submersible,** (*rare*) **submergible,** *aa.*

submit, *v.t.* and *i.* put forward for consideration, suggest; yield, resign (oneself). **submission,** *n.* act of submitting; submissiveness; (*Shake.*) admission of fault. **submissive,** *a.* yielding, compliant, meek. (L. *mittere,* send)

submultiple, *n.* quantity dividing into another exactly.

subnormal, *a.* below normal.

suborder, *n.* division of an order.

subordinate, *a.* of lower rank or less importance.—*n.* one under the orders of another.—*v.t.* make, treat as, subordinate. **subordination,** *n.* **subordinative,** *a.* (L. *ordo,* order)

suborn, *v.t.* induce, bribe, to commit perjury or other crime. **subornation,** *n.* (L. *ornare,* equip)

suboval, subovate, *aa.* somewhat egg-shaped.

subpoena, *n.* writ summoning person to attend at court of law.—*v.t.* (*past, p.p.* **subpoenaed**) summon by subpoena. (L.=under penalty)

subpolar, *a.* just outside the polar regions; (*astron.*) directly below the celestial pole.

subprior, *n.* prior's assistant.

subreption, *n.* obtaining of advantage by fraudulent concealment; misrepresentation of fact. (L. *rapere,* seize)

subrogation, *n.* (*law*) substitution of one person for another.

subscribe, *v.t.* and *i.* write (one's name), sign (document), at foot; pay, promise to pay, contribute (to); assent, agree (to); (*Shake.*) admit, acknowledge. **subscriber,** *n.* contributor to fund; one who takes in periodical. **subscript,** *a.* written below. **subscription,** *n.* subscribing; sum subscribed; (*Shake.*) submission. (L. *scribere,* write)

subsection, *n.* division of section.

subsequent, *a.* posterior (to), later, coming after. **subsequence,** *n.*

subserve, *v.t.* serve as means towards, promote. **subservient,** *a.* subserving, ancillary; obsequious, servile. **subservience, subserviency,** *nn.*

subside, *v.i.* sink to lower level, settle; collapse, cave in; flop down; abate, die away; (*colloq.*) fall silent. **subsidence,** *n.* (L. *sīdere,* settle)

subsidy, *n.* government grant to assist commercial undertaking, subvention; grant from one state to another in return for support. **subsidiary,** *a.* supplementary, secondary.—*n.* accessory. **subsidize,** *v.t.* aid, support, by subsidy. (L. *subsidium,* reserve troops)

subsist, *v.i.* and *t.* remain in being, sustain life; provide food for. **subsistence,** *n.* subsisting; what one lives on or by. **subsistence money,** (*colloq.*) **sub,** *n.* advance of wages for immediate needs. (L. *sistere,* stand)

subspecies, *n.* division of a species.

substance, *n.* matter; reality, solidity; chief part, essence; gist, purport; wealth, property. **substantial,** *a.* material; real, not illusory; solid, firm; considerable, important; well-to-do; virtual. **substantiality,** *n.* **substantialism,** *n.* (*philos.*) doctrine that constant realities underlie phenomena. **substantialist,** *n.* **substantialize,** *v.t.* and *i.* endow with, acquire, reality. **substantiate,** *v.t.* give grounds for, make good, prove. **substantiation,** *n.* **substantive,** *a.* having independent existence; expressing existence.—*n.* noun. **substantival,** *a.* (L. *stare,* stand)

substitute, *n.* thing, person, put in place of another.—*v.t.* put, use, in place of another. **substitution, substitutor,** *nn.* **substitutional, substitutionary, substitutive,** *aa.* (L. *statuere,* place)

substractor, *n.* (*Shake.*) detractor.

substratum, *n.* (*pl.* **substrata**) lower stratum, underlying layer; basis.

substructure, *n.* lower part of structure; foundation, basement. **substructural,** *a.*

subsume, *v.t.* include (instance) under rule or class. **subsumption,** *n.* (L. *sumere,* take)

subtenant, *n.* tenant who rents from a tenant, sublessee. **subtenancy,** *n.*

subtend, *v.t.* (*geom.,* of line) be opposite to (angle, arc). **subtense,** *n.* subtending line. (L. *tendere,* stretch)

subter-, *pref.* under, less than (opp. to super-). (L.)

subterfuge, *n.* evasion, lying excuse, trick to escape censure. (L. *fugere,* flee)

subterminal, *a.* nearly at the end.

subterposition, *n.* state of being below. (*subter-*)

subterranean, subterraneous, *aa.* underground. (L. *terra,* earth)

subtil, subtile, *arch.* for subtle.

subtilize, *v.t.* and *i.* make subtle; make

subtle distinctions (in). **subtilization,** *n.*
subtitle, *n.* secondary title of book; film caption.
subtle, *a.* evasive, hard to grasp; delicate, nice; deft, ingenious; crafty, cunning; acute, discriminating; (*arch.*) tenuous, rarefied. **subtlety,** *n.* subtleness; fine distinction; (*Shake.*) illusion. **subtly,** *adv.* (L. *subtilis*)
subtract, *v.t.* take away, deduct. **subtraction,** *n.* **subtractive,** *a.* **subtrahend,** *n.* amount to be subtracted. (L. *trahere*, draw)
subtropical, *a.* just outside tropics.
subulate, *a.* awl-shaped, long and tapering. (L. *subula*, awl)
suburb, *n.* outlying district of town. **suburban,** *a.* (L. *urbs*, city)
subvention, *n.* grant of money in aid of institution etc., subsidy. (L. *venire*, come)
subvert, *v.t.* destroy, overthrow; corrupt. **subversion,** *n.* **subversive,** *a.* (L. *vertere*, turn)
subway, *n.* underground passage or railway.
suc-, form of **sub-** before *c.*
succedaneum, *n.* (*pl.* **succedanea**) substitute. **succedaneous,** *a.* (L. *succedaneus*, substituted)
succeed, *v.t.* and *i.* follow, come after; take the place of, be successor to; be heir (to); attain one's purpose, prosper; go well. (L. *cedere*, go)
succentor, *n.* precentor's deputy; leading bass in choir. (L. *canere*, sing)
succès, *n.* success. *s. d'estime*, applause accorded from respect rather than appreciation. *s. fou*, success marked by wild enthusiasm. *s. de scandale*, success (of book etc). due to its scandalous character. (F.)
success, *n.* attainment of one's aim; good fortune, favourable issue; person, thing, that turns out well; (*Shake.*) succession; issue, event. **successful,** *a.* attaining, producing, the desired effect; prosperous. (*succeed*)
successantly, *adv.* (*Shake.*) one after another.
succession, *n.* act of following in order; right of succeeding as heir or to throne; descendants, heirs; series, sequence. **successional,** *a.* of succession. **successive,** *a.* following in succession; consecutive. **successively,** *adv.* one after another; (*Shake.*) by right of succession. **successor,** *n.* person, thing, that succeeds another. (*succeed*)
succinct, *a.* concise, terse; (*arch.*) girded up. (L. *cingere*, gird)
succory, form of **chicory.**
succotash, *n.* (*Amer.*) beans and Indian corn boiled together. (Amer. Ind. *msiquatash*)
succour, *v.t.* help in difficulty or distress.—*n.* aid in time of need; (*pl.*, *arch.*) reinforcements. (L. *currere*, run)
succubus, succuba, *n.* (*pl.* **succubi, succubae**) female demon supposed to have sexual intercourse with sleeping men. (L. *cumbere*, lie)
succulent, *a.* juicy; (of plant) thick and fleshy. **succulence,** *n.* (L. *succus*, juice)
succumb, *v.i.* yield, give way (to); die. (L. *cumbere*, lie)
such, *a.* of that or similar kind.—*pron.* such person or thing. **s. as,** all who. **s.-and-s.,** *a.* certain unspecified. **suchlike,** *a.* and *pron.* (*vulg.*) similar (things). (O.E. *swylc*)
suck, *v.t.* and *i.* draw in, draw liquid from, by mouth; draw milk from breast; roll tongue round (sweet); absorb, imbibe; (of pump) draw air instead of water.—*n.* act of sucking; (*sl.*) mouthful, sip; hoax, sell. **give s.,** suckle. **s. in,** absorb; engulf. **s. up,** (*school sl.*) toady (to). **sucking,** *a.* not yet weaned; very young and inexperienced. **sucking-fish,** *n.* fish with adhesive organ. **sucking-pig,** *n.* **sucker,** *n.* organ, concave disk, that adheres by suction; piston of pump; shoot springing from plant's root beside stem; (*Amer. sl.*) greenhorn, mug. **suckle,** *v.t.* feed with milk from breast or udder. **suckling,** *n.* unweaned child or animal. (O.E. *súcan*)
sucrose, *n.* cane-sugar. (F. *sucre*, sugar)
suction, *n.* act of sucking; process of drawing fluid, causing adhesion, by exhausting air. **s.-pump,** *n.* **suctorial,** *a.* of, adapted for, sucking; (*zool.*) having a sucker.
sudation, *n.* sweating; sweat. **sudarium,** *n.* St. Veronica's handkerchief, said to bear image of Christ after she wiped His face with it. **sudatorium,** *n.* (*pl.* **sudatoria**) hot-air bath. **sudatory,** *a.* sweating; promoting perspiration.—*n.* sudatory substance; sudatorium. (L. *sudare*, sweat)
sudd, *n.* mass of weeds and trees forming floating island in Nile. (Arab. = barrier)
sudden, *a.* done or occurring unexpectedly; abrupt; hurried; (*Shake.*) immediate; rash. **all of a s.,** suddenly. (L. *subitus*)
sudoriferous, *a.* sweat-producing. **sudorific,** *a.* and *n.* (drug) promoting perspiration. (L. *sudor*, sweat; *ferre*, bear; *facere*, make)
suds, *n.pl.* soapy water, esp. when frothy.
sue, *v.t.* and *i.* take legal proceedings (against), prosecute; beseech, make petition. (L. *sequi*, follow)
suède, *n.* soft undressed leather of kid-skin. (F. = Sweden)
suet, *n.* hard fat surrounding kidneys of sheep, ox etc. (L. *sebum*, tallow)
suf-, form of **sub-** before *f.*
suffer, *v.t.* and *i.* undergo, be subjected to; feel pain; be injured; allow, per-

mit, tolerate; (*Shake.*) allow to continue; perish. **sufferance,** *n.* tacit consent; passive resignation, patient endurance; (*Shake.*) pain, distress; execution. **on sufferance,** merely tolerated. **sufferer,** *n.* one who suffers; sick person. **suffering,** *n.* pain; enduring of pain. (L. *ferre*, bear)

suffice, *v.i.* and *t.* be enough (for), meet needs of. **sufficient,** *a.* enough; (*arch.*) well qualified.—*n.* (*colloq.*) sufficient quantity. **sufficiency,** *n.* adequate amount; competence; (*arch.*) efficiency. (L. *facere*, make)

suffix, *n.* letter, syllable, added to end of word.—*v.t.* append thus.

suffocate, *v.t.* and *i.* kill or die by stoppage of breathing, stifle; impede breathing of, gasp for breath. **suffocation,** *n.* (L. *fauces*, throat)

suffrage, *n.* vote; right of voting at political elections; approval; intercessory prayer. **suffragan,** *a.* (of bishop) subordinate.—*n.* assistant bishop in charge of part of diocese. **suffragette,** *n.* woman who agitated for women's rights to parliamentary vote. **suffragist,** *n.* advocate of extending suffrage, esp. to women. (L. *suffragium*)

suffuse, *v.t.* well up and spread over, flood. **suffusion,** *n.* (L. *fundere*, pour)

sufi, *n.* Mohammedan pantheist. **sufic,** *a.* (Arab. *çūfī*, man of wool)

sugar, *n.* sweet crystalline substance got from sugarcane, beet etc.; sweet words, flattery; (*chem.*) kinds of soluble sweet fermentable carbohydrate.—*v.t.* and *i.* sprinkle, coat, with sugar; sweeten; flatter; (*sl.*) do less than one's share of work; (*Amer.*) make maple-sugar. **s. daddy,** (*Amer. sl.*) gold-digging girl's elderly admirer. **s.-basin,** *n.* for holding sugar at table. **s.-bush,** *n.* (*Amer.*) grove of sugar-maples. **s.-candy,** *n.* sugar crystallized in large lumps. **s.-maple,** *n.* maple whose sap yields sugar. **s.-tongs,** *n.pl.* for handling lump sugar. **sugarcane,** *n.* tall grass yielding sugar. **sugarloaf,** *n.* hard conical mass of sugar. **sugarplum,** *n.* kind of sweet. **sugary,** *a.* like, tasting of, sugar; honeyed, flattering. (Arab. *sukkar*)

suggest, *v t.* call up idea of; put forward, propose; insinuate, hint; (*Shake.*) tempt, prompt. **suggestible,** *a.* capable of being suggested; open to psychological suggestion. *suggestio falsi*, statement giving false impression. **suggestion,** *n.* act of suggesting; thing suggested, proposal, insinuation; (*psycho-anal.*) impressing of thing on subconscious, impression so made. **suggestionize,** *v.t.* influence by psychological suggestion. **suggestive,** *a.* calling up idea (of); stimulating, thought-provoking; smacking of indecency. (L. *sub*, under; *gerere*, carry)

suicide, *n.* one who kills himself, felo-de-se; killing of oneself; ruin of one's own interests. **suicidal,** *a.* of suicide; ruinous. (L. *se*, self; *caedere*, kill)

sui generis, unique. *sui juris*, of age to act for oneself. (L.)

suilline, *a.* of the pig family; piglike. (L. *sus*, pig)

suit, *n.* act of suing, request; courtship; action at law; set of clothes; set of armour or sails; one of the four sets in a pack of cards; (*Shake.*) service to feudal superior.—*v.t.* and *i.* be convenient or satisfactory (to); be appropriate or becoming to, befit; cause to conform, adapt; (*Shake.*) clothe, dress. **follow s.,** play card of suit led; follow another's example. **make s.,** (*arch.*) urge humble request. **suitcase,** *n.* flat oblong travelling-case. **suitable,** *a.* suited (to), fitted for the purpose. **suitability,** *n.* (*sue*)

suite, *n.* train, retinue; matched set, esp. of furniture; set of rooms; (*mus.*) series of dances. (F.)

suitor, *n.* wooer; petitioner; party in lawsuit. (*suit*)

sulcate, *a.* having grooves, furrowed. (L. *sulcus*, furrow)

sulk, *v.i.* be sulky.—*n.pl.* sulky mood. **sulky,** *a.* silent or unsociable from resentment, sullen.—*n.* light two-wheeled vehicle for one.

sullage, *n.* filth, refuse, sewage.

sullen, *a.* silent and ill-humoured, morose; passively resentful; dismal, dull; (*Shake.*) mournful.—*n.pl.* sulks; dumps. (L. *solus*, alone)

sully, *v.t.* and *i.* soil, tarnish; be a stain on, disgrace.

sulphanilamide, *n.* drug used in combating diseases caused by bacteria, esp. streptococcic infections. **sulphapyridine,** *n.* drug related to sulphanilamide, used esp. in cases of pneumonia.

sulphate, *n.* salt of sulphuric acid. **s. of copper,** blue vitriol. **s. of iron,** green vitriol. **s. of magnesium,** Epsom salts. **s. of sodium,** Glauber salts. **s. of zinc,** white vitriol.

sulphide, *n.* compound of sulphur with element or radical.

sulphite, *n.* salt of sulphurous acid.

sulphonal, *n.* an anaesthetic and hypnotic.

sulphur, *n.* yellow non-metallic inflammable element; kinds of yellow butterfly.—*a.* pale lemon-yellow.—*v.t.* treat, fumigate, with sulphur. **s.-spring,** *n.* spring impregnated with sulphur. **sulphurate,** *v.t.* impregnate, fumigate, with sulphur. **sulphuration, sulphurator,** *nn.* **sulphureous,** *a.* of, like, sulphur; infernal; profane; (*bot.*) sulphur-coloured. **sulphuretted,** *a.* combined with sulphur. **sulphuretted hydrogen,** an evil-smelling colourless gas. **sulphuric,** *a.* containing sulphur in its higher combining proportion. **sulphuric acid,** oil of vitriol. **sulphurize,** *v.t.* sulphurate.

sulphurization, *n.* **sulphurous,** *a.* containing sulphur in its lower combining proportion; sulphureous. **sulphury,** *a.* like sulphur. (L.)

sultan, *n.* Mohammedan sovereign; breed of small hen. **sweet, yellow, s.,** garden plant with purple, yellow, flowers. **sultana,** *n.* wife, daughter, sister, concubine, of sultan; kind of small raisin. **sultanate,** *n.* rank, domain, of sultan. **sultaness,** *n.* sultana (person). (Arab.)

sultry, *a.* hot and close, sweltering.

sum, *n.* total resulting from addition, aggregate; amount; arithmetical problem; summary.—*v.t.* and *i.* reckon. **s. up,** give total of; set out (facts) in brief review, recapitulate. (L. *summa*)

sumac, sumach, *n.* kinds of shrub; its dried leaves, used for tanning. (Arab. *summāq*)

sumless, *a.* (*Shake.*) incalculable.

summary, *a.* condensed; done without delay or formality.—*n.* brief account, abstract, *résumé*. **summarily,** *adv.* **summarist,** *n.* one who prepares summary. **summarize,** *v.t.* make summary of, epitomize. (*sum*)

summation, *n.* addition, computation.

summer, *n.* (also **s.-tree**) large supporting beam or stone. (*sumpter*)

summer, *n.* warm season from June to August, (*astron.*) 21 June to 21 Sept.; most flourishing period; (*pl.*) years of age.—*v.i.* spend summer. **Indian s.,** short spell of warm weather in autumn. **St. Luke's, St. Martin's, s.,** warm dry period about 18 Oct. (St. Luke's Day), 11 Nov. (St. Martin's Day). **s. lightning,** without thunder. **s. time,** time indicated by clocks advanced one hour in summer, noon being taken as one o'clock. **s.-house,** *n.* small outhouse for sitting in. **summertime,** *n.* season of summer. (O.E. *sumor*)

summersault, same as **somersault.**

summit, *n.* top of hill, peak; highest point, maximum. (L. *summus*, highest)

summon, *v.t.* send for; demand attendance of, bid (witness etc.) appear; call upon to surrender; muster up (courage etc.). **summons,** *n.* authoritative call; order to appear in court. —*v.t.* serve with summons. (L. *sub-*, secretly; *monēre*, warn)

summum bonum, supreme good. (L.)

sump, *n.* lowest part of mine etc., in which water collects; well in crankcase of motor-car for lubricating oil; cesspool. (L.G.=marsh)

sumph, *n.* (*Scot.*) soft sheepish fellow, blockhead.

sumpitan, *n.* blow-pipe for poisoned darts.

sumpter, *n.* (*arch.*, also **s.-horse, s.-mule**) beast of burden, pack-animal. (Gk. *sagma*, pack-saddle)

sumption, *n.* (*logic*) major premiss. (L. *sumere*, take)

sumptuary, *a.* of, regulating, expenditure. **sumptuous,** *a.* costly, lavish. (L. *sumptus*, cost)

sun, *n.* luminous body round which earth revolves; sunlight; star; (*poet.*) day or year.—*v.t.* and *i.* expose to, bask in, sun. **place in the s.,** favourable situation. **S. of Righteousness,** Christ. **touch of the s.,** slight sunstroke. **under the s.,** in the world. **with, against, the s.,** clockwise, counter-clockwise. (O.E. *sunne*)

sun-bath, *n.* exposure of body to sun.

sunbeam, *n.* shaft of sunlight.

sun-bird, *n.* kinds of brightly coloured song-bird.

sun-blind, *n.* movable shade outside window.

sunbonnet, *n.* bonnet with projecting brim to shade face.

sunburn, *n.* darkening of skin through exposure to sun. **sunburned, sunburnt,** *aa.*

sunburst, *n.* sudden flood of sunshine; piece of jewellery imitating sun and its rays.

sundae, *n.* ice-cream with crushed fruit, syrup, nuts etc.

Sunday, *n.* first day of week, kept as day of rest. **month of Ss.,** very long time. **S. best,** (*colloq*) clothes worn on Sunday. **S.-school,** *n.* children's classes for religious instruction held on Sunday. (*sun*; *day*)

sunder, *v.t.* and *i.* put or keep apart, sever. **sunderance,** *n.* (O.E. *sundrian*)

sundew, *n.* small bog-plant with sticky leaves by which it captures insects.

sundial, *n.* graduated plate showing hour by position of sun's shadow.

sun-dog, *n.* parhelion.

sundown, *n.* sunset. **sundowner,** *n.* (*Austral.*) tramp who times arrival for evening so as to get lodging for night; (*S. Afr.*) drink at sunset.

sundry, *a.* several, divers.—*n.pl.* odd items, odds and ends. **all and s.,** every one. (O.E. *syndrig*)

sun-fish, *n.* fish with nearly spherical body.

sunflower, *n.* plant with large yellow-rayed flowers.

sung, see **sing.**

sun-god, *n.* personification of sun worshipped as god.

sun-hat, *n.* large broad-brimmed hat.

sun-helmet, *n.* pith helmet with brim shading head and neck.

sunk, *a.* (*sl.*) in a hopeless fix. **s. fence,** one along bottom of ditch. **sunken,** *a.* hollow.

sunless, *a.* getting little or no sun.

sunlight, *n.* light of sun.

sunlit, *a.* illuminated by the sun.

sunn, *n.* (also **s.-hemp**) Indian hemp-like fibre. (Sanskr. *sana*)

sunnud, *n.* (*Anglo-Ind.*) grant, charter. (Hind. *sanad*, deed)

sunnyasee, sunnyasi, *n.* Brahmin in fourth stage of life; religious mendicant. (Hind. *sannyasi*)

sunrise, *n.* rising of sun; time of this; sky effects accompanying it.
sunset, *n.* setting of sun; time of this; sky effects accompanying it.
sunshade, *n.* light umbrella, parasol.
sunshine, *n.* light of sun; sunny weather; cheerfulness, bright influence. **s. roof,** sliding roof of saloon car.
sun-spot, *n.* dark spot appearing periodically on sun's surface; freckle.
sunstroke, *n.* acute prostration caused by excessive exposure to sun.
sun-up, *n.* (*Amer.*) sunrise.
sunward, *adv.* and *a.* towards the sun. **sunwards,** *adv.*
sunwise, *adv.* in the direction of the sun's course, clockwise.
sup, *v.t.* and *i.* take (liquid) in small mouthfuls; (*Scot.*) take with spoon. —*n.* small amount, mouthful, of liquid. (O.E. *súpan*)
sup, *v.i.* and *t.* have supper, make supper (off); (*Shake.*) feed. (*supper*)
sup-, form of **sub-** before *p*.
super, *n.* (*sl.*) supernumerary actor.—*a.* (of feet etc.) in square measure; (*sl.*) superfine, very good.
super-, *pref.* above, on top, as in **superimpose, superstructure**; more than, as in **superhuman**; exceedingly, as in **superfine.** (L.)
superable, *a.* capable of being overcome. (L. *superare*, overcome)
superabound, *v.i.* abound greatly; be more than enough. **superabundant,** *a.* **superabundance,** *n.*
superadd, *v.t.* add over and above.
superaltar, *n.* small consecrated slab for use on unconsecrated altar.
superannuate, *v.t.* dismiss, discard, as too old; pension off. **superannuation,** *n.* superannuating; pension given on retirement. (L. *annus*, year)
superb, *a.* magnificent, grand, stately; excellent. (L. *superbus*, proud)
supercalendered, *a.* (of paper) finished off with a high polish.
supercargo, *n.* ship's official superintending cargo and business affairs.
supercharger, *n.* apparatus for forcing extra amount of petrol vapour into cylinders of motor-car.
superciliary, *a.* of brows, over the eyes. **supercilious,** *a.* loftily superior, showing contemptuous indifference. (L. *cilium*, eyelid)
superclass, *n.* group containing more than one class.
supercolumniation, *n.* arrangement of one architectural order above another. **supercolumnar,** *a.*
supercool, *v.t.* (*chem.*) cool below freezing-point without solidifying.
superdreadnought, *n.* warship of dreadnought type with increased power.
super-ego, *n.* (*psycho-anal.*) that unconscious morality within the mind which directs action of the censor.
supereminent, *a.* supremely eminent. **supereminence,** *n.*
supererogation, *n.* doing more than duty requires or than is necessary for salvation. **supererogatory,** *a.* (L. *erogare*, expend)
superexcellent, *a.* supremely excellent. **superexcellence,** *n.*
superfamily, *n.* group containing more than one family.
superfatted, *a.* containing a large proportion of fat.
superfecundation, *n.* superfetation.
superfetate, *v.i.* conceive during pregnancy. **superfetation,** *n.* (L. *fetus*, offspring)
superficies, *n.* (*pl.* same) surface; surface area. **superficial,** *a.* of, on, surface; with no reserve of feeling, shallow; comprehending only the obvious. **superficiality,** *n.* (L.)
superfine, *a.* of extra quality; affecting great refinement.
superfluous, *a.* more than is wanted; unnecessary, useless; (*Shake.*) having more than enough. **superfluity,** *n.* superfluousness; surplus. **superflux,** *n.* (*Shake.*). (L. *fluere*, flow)
superheat, *v.t.* raise (steam) to temperature higher than that of boiling water.
superheterodyne, *n.* (*abbr.* superhet) powerful and highly selective wireless receiving-set.
superhuman, *a.* more than human.
superimpose, *v.t.* place on top, lay above.
superincumbent, *a.* lying on top.
superinduce, *v.t.* develop as addition, superadd; bring on (sleep) by external influence. **superinduction,** *n.*
superintend, *v.t.* have charge or management of, supervise. **superintendence,** *n.* **superintendent,** *n.* official manager; police officer above inspector. (*intend*)
superior, *a.* upper, higher; of higher rank; better in some respect; better than the average; affecting superiority, supercilious; (*print.*) set above the line.—*n.* person superior in rank or quality, better; head of religious house. **s. person,** snob, prig. **s. to,** unaffected by. **superiority,** *n.* **superiorly,** *adv.* in upper position. (L.)
superjacent, *a.* lying above. (L. *jacēre*, lie)
superlative, *a.* surpassing; (*gram.*) expressing highest or very high degree of a quality.—*n.* superlative degree or word. (L. *ferre*, bear)
superlunary, superlunar, *aa.* beyond the moon, not of this world.
superman, *n.* man of type above that of ordinary humanity; ideal man of Nietzsche's philosophy, superior to moral restrictions.
supermedial, *a.* above the middle.
supermundane, *a.* above the world; superior to earthly things.
supernaculum, *adv.* to the last drop.—*n.* very choice wine. **supernacular,** *a.* (G. *nagel*, nail)

supernal, *a.* (*poet.*) heavenly.
supernatant. *a.* floating on surface.
supernatural, *a.* beyond the powers or laws of nature, miraculous. **supernaturalism,** *n.* belief in existence of supernatural. **supernaturalist,** *n.* **supernaturalistic,** *a.*
supernumerary, *a.* beyond the usual or necessary number, extra.—*n.* extra person.
superorder, *n.* group containing more than one order.
superordinary, *a.* above the ordinary.
superorganic, *a.* beyond the organic, psychical; social.
superparasite, *n.* parasite of a parasite. **superparasitic,** *a.*
superpose, *v.t.* lay upon or above. **superposition,** *n.*
superscribe, *v.t.* write at top or outside of. **superscript,** *a.* written above line. — *n.* (*Shake.*) superscription. **superscription,** *n.* superscribed words; (*Shake.*) address. (L. *scribere,* write)
supersede, *v.t.* replace by another person or thing; set aside, supplant. **supersession,** *n.* (L. *sedēre,* sit)
supersensible, supersensual, supersensuous, *aa.* beyond the range of the senses. **supersensitive,** *a.* abnormally sensitive.
supersolid, *n.* solid of more than three dimensions.
supersonic, *a.* beyond the audible limit of vibrations. **supersonant,** *n.* supersonic vibration.
superstition, *n.* belief in magic or luck; opinion, act, practice, based on this; false religion. **superstitious,** *a.* (L. *sistere,* stand)
superstratum, *n.* overlying stratum.
superstructure, *n.* structure built on another. **superstructural,** *a.*
supersubtle, *a.* too subtle.
supertax, *n.* tax on large incomes in addition to ordinary income-tax.
supertemporal, *a.* beyond the limits of time; above temples of the head.
superterrestrial, superterranean, *aa.* above or on surface of the earth.
supertonic, *n.* (*mus.*) second note of scale.
supervene, *v.i.* occur in addition or unexpectedly; follow close upon. **supervention,** *n.* (L. *venire,* come)
supervise, *v.t.* watch or direct the work of, superintend; (*Shake.*) peruse.—*n.* (*Shake.*) inspection. **supervisor,** *n.* overseer, inspector. **supervisory,** *a.* (L. *vidēre,* see)
supine, *a.* lying on back, face upwards; indolent, inactive.—*n.* Latin verbal noun used in special construction. **supinate,** *v.t.* turn (hand) palm upward. **supination,** *n.* (L. *supinus*)
supper, *n.* meal taken at close of day. **Last S.,** Christ's meal with His disciples before the Crucifixion. **Lord's S.,** communion. (O.F. *soper*)
supplant, *v.t.* take the place of, oust, esp. by fraud. (L. *supplantare,* trip up)
supple, *a.* easily bent, pliant, lithe; compliant; obsequious.—*v.t.* and *i.* make, become, supple. **s.-jack,** *n.* kinds of climbing shrub; pliant cane. (L. *plicare,* fold)
supplement, *n.* something added to supply a deficiency; appendix of book, special number of periodical; (*math.*) quantity by which angle falls short of two right angles.—*v.t.* make addition to. **supplemental, supplementary,** *aa.* **supplementation,** *n.* (L. *plēre,* fill)
suppliant, *a.* (*Shake.*) auxiliary. **suppliance,** *n.* (*Shake.*) diversion. (*supply*)
suppliant, supplicant, *aa.* entreating, beseeching.—*n.* one who makes entreaty, petitioner. **suppliance,** *n.* **supplicate,** *v.t.* and *i.* ask humbly and earnestly (for), pray, petition. **supplication,** *n.* **supplicatory,** *a.* (L. *plicare,* fold)
supply, *adv.* in a supple manner.
supply, *v.t.* provide, furnish; produce, yield; make up for; fill (place) as substitute; (*Shake.*) reinforce; gratify. —*n.* act of supplying; store, stock; (*Shake.*) aid, relief; (*pl.*) necessaries; grant of money by parliament for cost of government. **supplyment,** *n.* (*Shake.*) supply. (L. *plēre,* fill)
support, *v.t.* hold up from below, prop up; endure, tolerate; sustain, maintain; supply with means of living; give aid to, back up; bear out, substantiate; keep up (part, character). —*n.* act of supporting; person or thing that supports. **supportable,** *a.* endurable. **supportance,** *n.* (*Shake.*) support. **supporter,** *n.* adherent, partisan; (*heraldry*) one of two figures placed on either side of escutcheon. (L. *portare,* carry)
suppose, *v.t.* assume as theory; imagine, think likely; require as condition, presuppose. — *n.* (*Shake.*) conjecture. **supposal,** *n.* (*Shake.*) opinion. **supposed,** *a.* reputed. **supposedly,** *adv.* (*pose*)
supposition, *n.* act of supposing; conjecture, assumption. **suppositional,** *a.* **suppositious,** *a.* hypothetical.
supposititious, *a.* put by trick in place of another; spurious, sham. (L. *ponere,* place)
suppository, *n.* medicinal cone or cylinder for introduction into rectum or other canal. (L. *ponere,* place)
suppress, *v.t.* restrain, keep back, stifle; put down by force, crush; forbid publication of, keep secret. **suppressible, suppressive,** *aa.* **suppression, suppressor,** *nn.* *suppressio veri,* concealment of truth.
suppurate, *v.i.* form pus, fester. **suppuration,** *n.* **suppurative,** *a.* (*pus*)
supra, *adv.* (*abbr. sup.*) above, previously (in book etc.). (L.)
supra-, from L.=above, used in **supraclavicular,** *a.* above collar-bone; **supralapsarian,** *n.* Calvinist who held

that the fall of man was preordained by God, hence **supralapsarianism,** *n.*; **supraliminal,** *a.* belonging to the conscious faculties; **supramaxillary,** *a.* and *n.* (bone) of upper jaw; **supramundane,** *a.* above the world or worldly things; **supraorbital,** *a.* above the eye-socket; **suprarenal,** *a.* above the kidneys.

supreme, *a.* highest in authority or rank; superior to all others; utmost. —*n.* (*Shake.*) chief. **S. Being,** God. **supremacy,** *n.* supremeness; supreme power, domination. (L. *supremus*)

sur-, *pref.* above, over. (*super*)

sura, *n.* fermented sap of kinds of palm. (Hind.)

sura, surah, *n.* chapter of Koran. (Arab.)

surah, *n.* kind of soft twilled silk.

sural, *a.* of calf of leg. (L. *sura,* calf)

surance, *n.* (*Shake.*) assurance.

surat, *n.* kind of coarse uncoloured cotton or cotton goods. (place)

surbase, *n.* (*archit.*) moulding above base of pedestal.

surbate, *v.t.* (*Spens.*) make footsore. (L. *battuere,* beat)

surcease, *n.* (*arch.*) cessation.—*v.i.* cease. (L. *supersedēre,* desist from)

surcharge, *n.* extra charge; additional charge on letter for understamping; overprinting on postage-stamp; excessive load.—*v.t.* exact surcharge from; overprint with surcharge; overload.

surcingle, *n.* band fastening anything on horse's back; girdle of cassock.—*v.t.* gird, fasten, with surcingle. (L. *cingere,* gird)

surcoat, *n.* loose coat worn over medieval armour.

surculose, surculous, *aa.* (*bot.*) producing suckers. (L. *surculus,* sucker)

surd, *a.* and *n.* (quantity) that cannot be exactly expressed as whole number or fraction, e.g. $\sqrt{2}$; (consonant, sound) uttered without vibration of vocal cords, e.g. *f, s.* (L. *surdus,* deaf; math. sense due to mistranslation of Gk. *alogos,* irrational)

sure, *a.* certain, convinced (of); reliable, unfailing; undoubtedly true; (*Shake.*) safe, harmless; firmly united.—*adv.* certainly; (*Amer.*) yes. **s. thing,** (*Amer.*) certainly, yes. **to be s.,** without doubt. **s.-footed,** *a.* not liable to slip. **surely,** *adv.* with certainty. **surety,** *n.* one who guarantees another's appearance in court or payment of sum; security against loss, pledge; (*arch.*) certainty.—*v.t.* (*Shake.*) be bail for. **suretyship,** *n.* (L. *securus,* secure)

surf, *n.* foam of breaking waves. **s.-board,** *n.* board on which one balances to be swept along by surf in **s.-riding,** *n.*

surface, *n.* outside, exterior; upper face; any of the faces of a solid; outward appearance; (*geom.*) that which has length and breadth but no thickness.—*v.t.* put special surface on. **s.-car,** *n.* (*Amer.*) tram-car. **s.-printing,** *n.* printing from plate with design in relief. **s.-tension,** *n.* property by which liquid surface behaves like elastic membrane, e.g. in bubble. **surfaceman,** *n.* workman keeping permanent way of railway in repair.

surfeit, *n.* excess, esp. in eating or drinking; satiety, repletion.—*v.t.* and *i.* indulge (oneself) to excess, overfeed; satiate, cloy. (L. *facere,* do)

surge, *v.i.* move in large waves, billow; swell, rise, tumultuously.—*n.* act of surging; mass of heaving water; (*poet.*) sea. (L. *surgere,* rise)

surgeon, *n.* medical man who performs or is qualified to perform operations; doctor in army or navy. **surgery,** *n.* treatment of diseases and injuries by manual operation; doctor's consulting-room and dispensary. **surgical,** *a.* of surgeons or their art. (Gk. *cheir,* hand; *ergon,* work)

suricate, *n.* S. African animal like mongoose. (native)

surly, *a.* sullen and gruff; churlishly morose. (*sir*; orig. sense masterful)

surmaster, *n.* second master in school.

surmise, *n.* conjecture, guess; suspicion.—*v.i.* and *t.* form surmise; suspect existence of. (L. *mittere,* send)

surmount, *v.t.* get over, overcome; be above, cap. **surmountable,** *a.*

surmullet, *n.* red mullet. (O.F. *surmulet*)

surname, *n.* family name.—*v.t.* give surname to.

surpass, *v.t.* outdo, excel. **surpassing,** *a.* pre-eminent, matchless.

surplice, *n.* long white loose-sleeved garment worn by officiating clergy and choristers. **s.-fee,** *n.* clergyman's fee for marriage, burial etc. (L.L. *superpellicium,* over-garment)

surplus, *n.* amount over and above what is required; excess of income over expenditure.—*a.* remaining as surplus. **surplusage,** *n.* excess.

surprise, *n.* act of taking unawares; feeling caused by the unexpected, astonishment; unexpected event.—*v.t.* affect with surprise, astonish; shock; take unawares, make unexpected attack on.—*a.* unexpected. **surprisal,** *n.* (L. *prehendere,* take)

surquedry, *n.* (*Spens.*) pride, arrogance.

surra, *n.* tropical disease of horses. (Marathi *sūra*)

surrealism, *n.* twentieth-century artistic and literary movement drawing inspiration from the unconscious and from dreams. **surrealist,** *n.* and *a.* **surrealistic,** *a.*

surrebutter, *n.* plaintiff's reply to defendant's rebutter. **surrebut,** *v.i.* make this.

surreined, *a.* (*Shake.*) overridden.
surrejoinder, *n.* plaintiff's reply to defendant's rejoinder. **surrejoin,** *v.i.* make this.
surrender, *v.t.* and *i.* hand over, give up; yield (oneself), cease to resist.—*n.* act of surrendering.
surreptitious, *a.* done secretly or stealthily, underhand, furtive. (L. *sub*, under; *rapere*, seize)
surrey, *n.* (*Amer.*) kind of four-wheeled two-seated carriage. (county)
surrogate, *n.* deputy, esp. of bishop or of his chancellor. (L. *rogare*, ask)
surround, *v.t.* be or come all round; encircle; hem in.—*n.* floor-covering between carpet and walls. **surroundings,** *n.pl.* environment. (L. *superundare*, overflow+confusion with *round*)
surtax, *n.* additional tax.—*v.t.* impose surtax on.
surtout, *n.* (*arch.*) kind of overcoat. (F.=over all)
surveillance, *n.* close observation, supervision, esp. of suspected person. (L. *vigilare*, watch)
survey, *v.t.* look over, view; scrutinize; inspect, examine condition of (building); measure, map (land); (*Shake.*) see.—*n.* general view or review; act of surveying (building, land), record then made. **surveyor,** *n.* official inspector (of); person employed in land-surveying. (L. *vidēre*, see)
survive, *v.t.* and *i.* live or exist longer than, outlive; come alive through; be still in existence or operation. **survival,** *n.* surviving; relic of the past. **survivor,** *n.* one who survives. (L. *vivere*, live)
surwan, *n.* (*Anglo-Ind.*) camel-driver.
sus-, form of **sub-** before *c* and *p*.
susceptible, *a.* sensitive, impressionable; touchy; easily made amorous; admitting (of). **s. to,** readily influenced by. **susceptibility,** *n.* **susceptive,** *a.* concerned with the receiving of emotional impressions. (L. *capere*, take)
susi, *n.* E. Indian cotton fabric with stripes of different-coloured silk. (Hind.)
suslik, *n.* kind of ground-squirrel. (Russ.)
suspect, *v.t.* have impression of the existence of, surmise; be inclined to think; mistrust, doubt; believe (person) guilty.—*a.* open to suspicion.—*n.* suspected person; (*Shake.*) suspicion. (L. *specere*, look)
suspend, *v.t.* hang up; hold floating in liquid; defer; stop temporarily; debar from duty for a time. **suspended animation,** temporary cessation of the outward signs and some of the functions of life. **suspender,** *n.* strap for supporting sock; (*pl.*, *Amer.*) braces. **suspense,** *n.* state of anxious uncertainty; undetermined state; (*law.*) temporary cessation of right etc. **suspensible,** *a.* **suspension,** *n.* suspending, being suspended. **suspension-bridge,** *n.* bridge with roadway hung from cables supported by towers. *suspensio per collum*, (*abbr. sus. per coll.*) execution by hanging. **suspensive, suspensory,** *aa.* (L. *pendere*, hang)
suspicion, *n.* act of suspecting; unconfirmed belief, impression, esp. that something is wrong; slight trace, hint.—*v.t.* (*Amer. sl.*) have suspicion that. **suspicious,** *a.* feeling suspicion, mistrustful; arousing or justifying suspicion.
suspire, *v.i.* (*poet.*) draw breath, sigh. **suspiration,** *n.* (L. *spirare*, breathe)
sustain, *v.t.* support, hold up; enable to last out; endure without giving way, stand; undergo, suffer; uphold, approve; substantiate; keep up, maintain; keep going continuously. **sustainment,** *n.* **sustenance,** *n.* nourishment, food; nourishing. **sustentation,** *n.* supporting of life, maintenance. (L. *tenēre*, hold)
susurration, *n.* soft whisper or rustle. **susurrant, susurrous,** *aa.* (L. *susurrus*, whisper)
sutler, *n.* camp-follower selling provisions. (Du. *zoetelaar*)
sutorial, *a.* of a cobbler. (L. *sutor*, cobbler)
suttee, *n.* Hindu widow who immolates herself on husband's funeral pyre; this custom. **sutteeism,** *n.* (Sanskr. *sati*, virtuous wife)
suture, *n.* stitching up of wound, thread or wire used for this; (*anat.*) seam-like joint of bones along their edges. **sutural,** *a.* **suturation,** *n.* (L. *suere*, sew)
suzerain, *n.* feudal lord; sovereign, state, exercising political control over semi-independent state. **suzerainty,** *n.* rights of suzerain, paramount authority. (L. *sursum*, upward)
svelte, *a.* slender and graceful, lissom. (F.)
swab, *n.* mop; absorbent pad for surgical work; (*naut. sl.*) clumsy fellow, lubber; epaulet.—*v.t.* clean, wash out, mop (up), with swab. **swabber,** *n.* one who uses swab. (Du. *zwabber*, ship-drudge)
swaddle, *v.t.* wrap (baby) tightly in clothes, swathe. **swaddling-band, swaddling-cloth,** *nn.* long strip of material formerly used for wrapping babies; (*pl.*) hindering influences. (*swathe*)
swadeshi, *n.* movement in India for boycotting British goods. (Bengali =own country)
swag, *n.* (*sl.*) burglar's booty; gains made by jobbery; (*Austral.*) tramp's bundle. **s.-bellied,** *a.* (*Shake.*) with pendulous paunch. (obs.=sway)
swage, *n.* metal-worker's grooved shaping-tool.—*v.t.* shape with swage. (O.F. *souage*)
swagger, *v.i.* walk or behave arro-

gantly, strut; talk boastfully, put on airs.—*n.* swaggering gait or talk.—*a.* fine, smart. **s.-cane,** *n.* small cane carried by soldiers when walking out. (*swag*)

swagger, swagman, *nn.* (*Austral. sl.*) tramp, bush-traveller. (*swag*)

swain, *n.* peasant, yokel; lover, admirer. (O.N. *sveinn*, lad)

swale, *v.t.* and *i.* (*dial.*) burn; be scorched; melt away. (O.E. *swǽlan*)

swale, *n.* hollow, small valley; marshy depression.

swallet, *n.* (*dial.*) underground stream; rock-fissure through which it flows.

swallow, *v.t.* and *i.* cause or allow to pass down one's throat; gulp; absorb, engulf; accept credulously; tolerate (insult); take back (one's words).—*n.* act of swallowing; amount swallowed at once; gullet. (O.E. *swelgan*)

swallow, *n.* migratory bird with forked tail and swift flight. **s.-dive,** *n.* with arms outstretched till near water. **swallowtail,** *n.* forked tail; kinds of humming-bird and butterfly; (also **s.-tailed coat**) man's evening dress coat. (O.E. *swalewe*)

swam, see **swim.**

swami, *n.* Hindu idol; title for Hindu religious teacher. (Sanskr. *svāmin*, master)

swamp, *n.* wet spongy land, marsh.—*v.t.* and *i.* entangle in swamp; sink by filling with water, founder; flood, soak; overwhelm.

swan, *n.* large graceful web-footed water-bird. **S. of Avon,** Shakespeare. **s.-shot,** *n.* large size of shot. **s.-song,** *n.* fabled song of swan before death; last work of poet or artist. **s.'s-down,** *n.* down of swan; cotton cloth with soft nap. **s.-upping,** *n.* annual taking up and marking of royal swans on Thames. **swannery,** *n.* place where swans are bred. (O.E.)

swank, *n.* (*sl.*) swagger, bounce.—*v.i.* show off.

swank, *s.* (*Scot.*) slender; agile. **swanky,** *n.* active youth.

swap, see **swop.**

swaraj, *n.* home-rule for India. **swarajist,** *n.* and *a.* (Sanskr. *svaraj*, self-ruling)

sward, *n.* grassy surface of land, turf. **swarded,** *a.* (O.E. *sweard*, rind)

sware, see **swear.**

swarf, *v.i.* and *n.* (*Scot.*) swoon.

swarm, *n.* large number of insects or birds; cluster of bees leaving hive with queen; large group, throng.—*v.i.* congregate, exist, in large numbers; be infested or crowded (with); (of bees) leave hive to form new colony. (O.E. *swearm*)

swarm, *v.t.* and *i.* climb (rope, pole) by clasping with hands and legs.

swarth, (*Shake.*) same as **swath.**

swarthy, (*arch.*) **swart,** (*Shake.*) **swarth,** dark-hued; sunburnt. (O.E. *sweart*)

swash, *n.* noise of splashing water.—*v.i.* and *t.* make swash, splash; (*arch.*) strike violently. **swashbuckler,** *n.* swaggering bully, braggart. **swasher,** *n.* (*Shake.*) bully. **swashing,** *a.* (*Shake.*) blustering. (imit.)

swastika, *n.* cross with equal arms, each of which is continued at right angles (卐); this as badge of Nazis. (Sanskr.=fortunate)

swat, *v.t.* (*colloq.*) hit smartly.

swatch, *n.* (*Scot.*) sample.

swath, *n.* grass cut, ground cleared, by single stroke of scythe or passage of mower. (O.E. *swalhu*, track)

swathe, *v.t.* cover with wraps or bandages.—*n.* bandage. (O.E. *swathian*)

sway, *v.i.* and *t.* swing unsteadily; rock, totter; influence; rule, govern.—*n.* swaying movement; influence; rule, dominion. (L.G. *swâjen*, be blown to and fro)

sweal, same as **swale.**

swear, *v.t.* and *i.* (*past* **swore,** *arch.* **sware;** *p.p.* **sworn**) take, cause to take, an oath; promise on oath, vow; assert emphatically; use profane language, curse; (*Shake.*) swear by.—*n.* profane oath. **s. by,** invoke as witness of oath; (*colloq.*) think very highly of. **s. in,** administer oath of office to. **s. off,** promise to abandon. **s. out,** (*Shake.*) forswear. **s. to,** affirm on oath. **s.-word,** *n.* (*colloq.*) profane oath. (O.E. *swerian*)

sweat, *n.* moisture from skin, perspiration; sweat-like exudation; process or state of sweating; (*colloq.*) toil, drudgery; (*Shake.*) sweating-sickness.—*v.i.* and *t.* exude sweat, perspire; emit like sweat; work hard, toil; cause to perspire freely; employ for unduly low wages. **s.-band,** *n.* strip of leather lining hat. **s.-cloth,** *n.* cloth under horse's saddle. **s.-duct, s.-gland,** *nn.* **sweating-sickness,** *n.* kind of fever epidemic in 15th and 16th centuries. **sweater,** *n.* athlete's woollen jersey; employer who sweats workers. **sweaty,** *a.* wet with sweat; laborious. (O.E. *swát*)

Swede, *n.* native of Sweden; Swedish turnip. **Swedish,** *a.* and *n.* (language) of Sweden.

sweeny, *n.* (*Amer.*) atrophy of muscle of horse.

sweep, *v.t.* and *i.* (*past, p.p.* **swept**) clear, clean, with broom; draw or pass rapidly over, brush; rake, scan; carry away or along violently; clear everything from; move with swiftness or force; go majestically; extend in wide curve; propel with sweeps.—*n.* sweeping with broom; sweeping movement or curve; range, reach; long heavy oar worked by standing rowers; chimney-sweep; (*colloq.*) sweepstake; (*sl.*) mean rascal, blackguard. **make a clean s. of,** abolish wholly. **s. the board,** win all stakes or rewards. **sweeping,** *a.*

comprehensive, thorough; wholesale, indiscriminate.—*n.pl.* refuse. (O.E. *swapan*, swoop)

sweepstake, sweepstakes, *n.* gamble on horse-race etc. in which winner takes stakes contributed by all.

sweir, sweer, *a.* (*Scot.*) unwilling; lazy.

sweet, *a.* having taste of sugar; fragrant; melodious; fresh; not sour or bitter; agreeable, pleasant; kind, gentle; beloved, dear; (*colloq.*) pretty, charming.—*n.* sweetmeat; sweet dish, pudding, tart etc.; darling; (*pl.*) delights. **be s. on,** (*sl.*) be in love with. **have a s. tooth,** be fond of sweets. **s. oil,** olive oil. **s. pea,** garden plant with fragrant coloured flowers. **s. potato,** tropical plant with edible tuberous root. **s.-sop,** *n.* tropical American plant; its sweet pulpy fruit. **s.-tempered,** *a.* good-natured. **s.-william,** *n.* garden flower of various colours. **sweetbread,** *n.* pancreas or thymus of animal as food. **sweetbrier,** *n.* wild rose-tree. **sweeten,** *v.t.* and *i.* make, become, sweet; render pleasant. **sweetheart,** *n.* lover.—*v.i.* court. **sweeting,** *n.* kind of apple; (*arch.*) darling. **sweetly,** *adv.* in a sweet manner; smoothly. **sweetmeat,** *n.* piece of confectionery. **sweetstuff,** *n.* sweetmeats. **sweety, sweetie,** *n.* sweetmeat; (*Amer. sl.*) sweetheart. (O.E. *swéte*)

swell, *v.i.* and *t.* (*past* **swelled**; *p.p.* **swollen,** *arch.* **swoln,** *rare* **swelled**) expand, dilate; increase in bulk, enlarge; grow or make louder; billow, bulge out; feel elation, puff up.—*n.* act or state of swelling; heaving of sea after storm; mechanism in organ to vary volume of sound; (*mus.*) *crescendo* followed by *diminuendo*; (*colloq.*) person of eminence, good social position, or fashionable appearance; expert (at).—*a.* (*colloq.*) finely dressed, smart; first-rate, excellent. **s. mob,** class of well-dressed thieves. **s.-mobsman,** *n.* **s.-fish,** *n.* kind that inflates itself. **swelled head,** (*sl.*) conceit. **swelldom,** *n.* (*sl.*) fashionable world. **swelling,** *n.* temporary protuberance due to injury; tumour. (O.E. *swellan*)

swelt, *v.i.* (*Spens.*) faint. (O.E. *sweltan*)

swelter, *v.i.* feel very hot; (of atmosphere) be oppressive with heat.—*n.* sweltering atmosphere. (O.E. *sweltan*, die)

swept, see **sweep.**

swerve, *v.i.* and *t.* change direction (of) during motion, deviate from straight; turn aside (from duty etc.).—*n.* act of swerving; twist of ball in air. (O.E. *sweorfan*, file)

swift, *a.* speedy, quick; prompt.—*adv.* (*poet.*) swiftly.—*n.* long-winged swift-flying bird like swallow; common newt; kinds of lizard, pigeon, and moth. (O.E.)

swig, *n.* (*sl.*) long draught of liquor, pull.—*v.t.* and *i.* (*sl.*) take swig (of).

swill, *v.t.* and *i.* wash (out) with water, flush; drink greedily.—*n.* act of swilling; inferior liquor; hogwash, slops. (O.E. *swilian*, wash)

swim, *v.i.* (*past* **swam** or **swum,** *p.p.* **swum**) support and move oneself in water; float; go with gliding motion; be flooded or drenched; feel giddy; appear to reel or whirl.—*v.t.* compel to swim; traverse by swimming.—*n.* act, spell, of swimming. **in the s.,** in the main current of affairs. **s.-suit,** *n.* bathing costume. **swimming-bath,** *n.* pond for swimming in. **swimming-bladder,** *n.* fish's air-bladder. **swimmingly,** *adv.* without hindrance, very successfully. **swimmer,** *n.* (O.E. *swimman*)

swindle, *v.t.* and *i.* cheat, defraud; obtain by fraud.—*n.* fraudulent scheme, imposition. **swindler,** *n.* (G. *schwindler*, swindler)

swine, *n.* (*pl.* same) pig; pigs collectively; dirty or degraded person. **s.-bread,** *n.* truffle. **s.-fever, s.-plague,** *nn.* infectious disease of swine. **s.-pox,** *n.* form of chicken-pox. **s.'s-snout,** *n.* dandelion. **swineherd,** *n.* man in charge of pigs. **swinery,** *n.* place where pigs are kept. (O.E. *swin*)

swing, *v.i.* and *t.* (*past* swung, *rare* **swang;** *p.p.* **swung**) wave to and fro, sway like pendulum, oscillate; turn on hinge, pivot, revolve; go with swinging gait; suspend; (*sl.*) be hanged.—*n.* act of swinging, oscillation; rhythmic movement or gait; seat slung by ropes for swinging on. **s. the lead,** (*sl.*) malinger. **s.-boat,** *n.* boat-shaped swing with seats. **s.-bridge,** *n.* bridge pivoting to let ships pass. **swinging,** *a.* vigorously rhythmical. (O.E. *swingan*)

swinge, *v.t.* (*arch.*) belabour. **s.-buckler,** *n.* (*Shake.*) roisterer. **swingeing,** *a.* (of damages etc.) very heavy, thumping. (O.E. *swengan*, shake)

swingle, *n.* swinging bar of flail; instrument for beating flax to separate wood from fibre.—*v.t.* beat with swingle. **swingletree,** *n.* pivoted crossbar to which traces of harnessed horse are attached. (*swing*)

swinish, *a.* of, like, befitting, swine; bestial, gross.

swink, *v.i.* and *n.* (*arch.*) toil. (O.E. *swinc*)

swipe, *v.i.* and *t.* hit hard and wildly (at); (*sl.*) steal by snatching.—*n.* reckless hit, slog; (*pl.*) washy or inferior beer. (*sweep*)

swirl, *n.* whirling motion, eddy; curl, twist.—*v.i.* and *t.* flow, carry, with swirl.

swish, *n.* hissing sound of flying missile, pelting rain etc.; movement causing this; stroke of cane etc.—*v.t.* and *i.* move, swing, with swish; flog, thrash. (imit.)

swish, *a.* (*colloq.*) smart, posh.

Swiss, *a.* and *n.* (native, language) of Switzerland. **S. roll,** layer of sponge cake rolled up with jam in it.

switch, *n.* flexible shoot cut from tree; tress of dead or false hair used in hairdressing; movable rail enabling train to pass from one line to another; (*electr.*) mechanism to make or break circuit.—*v.t.* and *i.* strike, whip, with switch; flick, whisk; shift (train) to other track; turn (thoughts) to other subject; (*electr.*) turn (off, on) with switch. **switchback,** *n.* zigzag railway for steep slopes; miniature railway with steep rises and descents. **switchboard,** *n.* set of switches at telephone exchange etc.

swith, *adv.* (*Scot.*) suddenly.

swither, *v.i.* (*Scot.*) hesitate.

swivel, *n.* ring and pivot connecting two parts so that one can revolve without the other.—*v.i.* and *t.* turn on or as on swivel. **s.-eye,** *n.* (*colloq.*) squinting eye. (O.E. *swifan*, move quickly)

swizzle, *n.* compounded drink. **s.-stick,** *n.* stick for frothing drinks.

swob, same as **swab.**

swollen, swoln, see **swell.**

swoon, *v.i.* faint.—*n.* fainting-fit. (M.E. *swounen*)

swoop, *v.i.* and *t.* come down with rush, pounce; make sudden attack (on).—*n.* swooping, pounce; snatching action carrying off several things at once. **swoopstake,** *adv.* (*Shake.*) indiscriminately. (O.E. *swápan*, rush)

swop, swap, *v.t.* and *i.* and *n.* (*sl.*) exchange.

sword, *n.* weapon with long blade for cutting or thrusting. **cavalry s.,** sabre. **cross, measure, ss. with,** oppose. **draw, sheathe, the s.,** begin, cease from, war. **put to the s.,** slaughter. **s. of state,** carried before sovereign on state occasions. **the s.,** military power; warfare. **s.-and-buckler,** *a.* (*Shake.*) ruffianly. **s.-arm, s.-hand,** *nn.* right arm, hand. **s.-bayonet,** *n.* of dagger shape, not conical. **s.-cane, s.-stick,** *nn.* hollow cane enclosing sword-blade. **s.-cut,** *n.* wound from sword; scar of this. **s.-dance,** *n.* dance with steps performed in and out of crossed swords laid on ground. **s.-flag,** *n.* iris. **s.-grass,** *n.* kinds of sedge. **s.-guard,** *n.* part of hilt protecting hand. **s.-knot,** *n.* ribbon or tassel attached to hilt. **s.-lily,** *n.* gladiolus. **s.-play,** *n.* fencing. (O.E. *sweord*)

swordbill, *n.* long-billed humming-bird.

sworder, *n.* (*Shake.*) gladiator.

swordfish, *n.* sea-fish with upper jaw prolonged into sword-like weapon.

swordsman, (*Shake.*) **swordman,** *n.* fencer. **swordsmanship,** *n.*

swore, see **swear.**

sworn, *a.* pledged; (*Shake.*) intimate.

swot, *v.i.* and *t.* (*school sl.*) study hard.—*n.* hard study, task requiring it; one who swots. (*sweat*)

swound, *arch.* form of **swoon.**

swounds, (*Shake.*) form of **zounds.**

swum, see **swim.**

swung, see **swing.**

sybarite, *n.* and *a.* luxurious and effeminate (person). **sybaritic,** *a.* **sybaritically,** *adv.* **sybaritism,** *n.* (*Sybaris* in ancient Italy)

sybo, *n.* (*Scot.*, *pl.* **syboes**) young onion, shallot.

sycamine, *n.* black mulberry-tree. (Gk. *sukaminos*)

sycamore, *n.* large tree of maple family; (also **s.-fig**) kind of fig-tree. (Gk. *sukon*, fig; *mōron*, mulberry)

syce, *n.* (*Anglo-Ind.*) groom. (Arab. *sā'is*)

sychnocarpous, *a.* (*bot.*) perennial. (Gk. *suchnos*, many; *karpos*, fruit)

syconium, *n.* (*pl.* **syconia**) fleshy fruit with seeds in hollow receptacle, e.g. fig. (Gk. *sukon*, fig)

sycophant, *n.* servile flatterer, toady. **sycophantic,** *a.* **sycophancy,** *n.* (Gk. *sukophantēs*, informer)

sycosis, *n.* barber's itch. (Gk. *sukōsis*, figlike ulcer)

syenite, *n.* kind of grey crystalline rock. (*Syene* in Egypt)

syllable, *n.* word or part of word forming one sound, unit of pronunciation.—*v.t.* pronounce syllable by syllable; (*poet.*) utter. **syllabary,** *n.* set of characters representing syllables. **syllabic,** *a.* of, in, syllables; representing a syllable. **syllabicate, syllabify, syllabize,** *vv.t.* divide into, utter by, syllables. **syllabication, syllabification,** *nn.* (Gk. *sun*, with; *lambanein*, take)

syllabub, same as **sillabub.**

syllabus, *n.* (*pl.* **syllabuses, syllabi**) list of subjects of lecture or course; programme of hours. (Gk. *sun*, with; *lambanein*, take)

syllepsis, *n.* (*pl.* **syllepses**) figure of speech in which the same word is used in two different senses at same time, e.g. 'a great taker of snuff as well as of towns.' **sylleptic,** *a.* **sylleptically,** *adv.* (Gk. *sun*, together; *lambanein*, take)

syllogism, *n.* (*logic*) formal statement of argument, consisting of major and minor premisses and conclusion. **syllogistic,** *a.* **syllogistically,** *adv.* **syllogize,** *v.i.* and *t.* reason by syllogisms; put into syllogistic form. (Gk. *sun*, together; *logos*, reason)

sylph, *n.* spirit of air; slim girl. **sylphlike,** *a.* slender and graceful.

sylvan, sylviculture, same as **silvan, silviculture.**

symbiosis, *n.* living together of two organisms of different kinds, esp. to their mutual benefit. **symbiotic,** *a.* **symbiotically,** *adv.* **symbion, symbiont,** *nn.* organism living in symbiosis. (Gk. *sun*, with; *bios*, life)

symbol, *n.* thing representing or typifying something else, emblem; written character, letter, figure. **symbolic, symbolical,** *aa.* **symbolism,** *n.* use of, representation by, symbols; literary and artistic movement of late nineteenth century forming revolt from realism and exalting the metaphysical and mysterious. **symbolist,** *n.* **symbolize,** *v.t.* be symbol of, typify; represent by symbol; treat as symbolic and not literal. **symbolization,** *n.* **symbology, symbolology,** *nn.* study of symbols. (Gk. *sun,* together; *ballein,* throw)

symmetry, *n.* balance, correspondence, between opposite sides of thing; due proportion between parts. **symmetrical,** (*rare*) **symmetric,** *aa.* **symmetrize,** *v.t.* make symmetrical. **symmetrization,** *n.* **symmetrian, symmetrist,** *nn.* one who insists on symmetry. **symmetrophobia,** *n.* dread of symmetry; avoidance of mechanical correspondence. (Gk. *sun,* together; *metron,* measure)

sympathy, *n.* feeling for another in pain, compassion; sharing of emotion or interest or sensation. **sympathetic,** *a.* feeling, expressing, sympathy; harmonious, congenial; able to sympathize or evoke sympathy; (of pain) caused by pain in some other part; (of sound) due to vibration of one object set up by that of another. **sympathetic ink,** kind that is invisible till exposed to heat or treated chemically. **sympathize,** *v.i.* and *t.* feel, express, sympathy; accord; (*Shake.*) feel sympathy for. **sympathized,** *a.* (*Shake.*) shared. (Gk. *sun,* with; *pathos,* suffering)

sympetalous, *a.* with petals united. (Gk. *sun,* together)

symphony, *n.* elaborate orchestral composition of several contrasted but related movements; instrumental introduction or ending to accompaniment of song; (*poet.*) harmony of sounds. **symphonic,** *a.* of, like, a symphony. **symphonious,** *a.* harmonious. (Gk. *sun,* together; *phōnē,* sound)

symphyllous, *a.* having leaves united. (Gk. *sun,* together; *phullon,* leaf)

symphysis, *n.* growing together, coalescence; junction between two bones, directly or by cartilage. **symphyseal, symphysial,** *a.* (Gk. *sun,* together; *phuein,* grow)

sympodium, *n.* apparent main stem consisting of a succession of branches, as in vine. **sympodial,** *a.* (Gk. *sun,* together; *pous,* foot)

symposium, *n.* (*pl.* **symposia**) drinking-party; meeting for philosophical discussion; collection of articles by different writers on one subject. **symposiac, symposial,** *aa.* (Gk. *sun,* together; *pinein,* drink)

symptom, *n.* change in body indicating disease; sign showing existence of something. **symptomatic,** *a.* of, like, a symptom; indicative (of). **symptomatically,** *adv.* **symptomatology,** *n.* science of symptoms. (Gk. *sumptōma*)

syn-, *pref.* with, together, alike, as in synthesis, synonym. (Gk. *sun*)

synaeresis, *n.* contraction of two vowels or syllables into one. (Gk. *hairein,* take)

synagogue, *n.* Jewish congregation or place of worship. **synagogical,** *a.* (Gk. *agein,* lead)

synallagmatic, *a.* bilateral, reciprocal. (Gk. *allassein,* change)

synaloepha, synalepha, *n.* elision of final vowel before following initial vowel, as in 'that th' opposed may beware of thee.' (Gk. *aleiphein,* smear)

synantherous, *a.* having anthers united.

synanthous, *a.* producing flowers and leaves at same time. (Gk. *anthos,* flower)

synaphea, synapheia, *n.* metrical continuity between lines of verse so that they are scanned together. (Gk. *haptein,* join)

synarthrosis, *n.* (*pl.* **synarthroses**) joint permitting no movement between its parts. (Gk. *arthron,* joint)

syncarp, *n.* multiple fruit, e.g. blackberry. **syncarpous,** *a.* (Gk. *karpos,* fruit)

synchondrosis, *n.* union of bones by layer of cartilage, forming nearly immovable joint. (Gk. *chondros,* cartilage)

synchro-mesh, *a.* with automatic gear-changing. (*synchronized mesh*)

synchronous, *a.* occurring at same moment, simultaneous; occurring at same date, contemporary. **synchronism, synchrony,** *nn.* **synchronize,** *v.i.* and *t.* be or make synchronous; set (clocks) to same time; show (events) to coincide in date. **synchronization,** *n.* (Gk. *chronos,* time)

synclastic, *a.* concave, convex, all over. (Gk. *klaein,* break)

synclinal, *a.* (*geol.*) dipping towards common line or point. (Gk. *klinein,* slope)

syncopate, *v.t.* shorten (word) by omission of letter or letters from middle, as in 'Gloster' for 'Gloucester'; (*mus.*) change rhythm of by displacement of beat or of normal accent. **syncopation,** *n.* **sy̌ncopě,** *n.* (*gram.*) syncopation; (*med.*) fainting. **syncopic, syncoptic,** *aa.* (Gk. *koptein,* cut off)

syncotyledonous, *a.* having cotyledons united.

syncretism, *n.* attempted reconciliation of opposing philosophical schools or sects; theological compromise. **syncretic, syncretistic,** *aa.* **syncretize,** *v.t.* and *i.* (Gk. *sungkrētizein,* unite against)

synd, *v.t.* (*Scot.*) rinse.

syndactyl, *n.* and *a.* (animal) with two or more digits joined together. **syndactylous,** *a.* (Gk. *daktulos,* digit)
syndesmosis, *n.* union of bones by ligaments. (Gk. *dein,* bind)
syndetic, *a.* of, using, conjunctions. (Gk. *dein,* bind)
syndic, *n.* business agent of corporation etc.; delegate; kinds of foreign magistrate. **syndicalism,** *n.* movement aiming at control of all industries by delegates of the workers. **syndicalist,** *n.* advocate of syndicalism. **syndicalistic,** *a.* **syndicate,** *n.* group of financiers or firms combining to carry out commercial enterprise; committee of delegates or syndics.—*v.t.* combine into syndicate; arrange to publish (news etc.) in several papers at same time. **syndication,** *n.* (Gk. *sundikos,* advocate)
syne, *adv.* (*Scot.*) since; long ago; then, afterwards.
synécdochě, *n.* figure of speech in which part is put for whole or whole for part, e.g. 'sail' for 'ship.' (Gk. *ek,* out; *dechesthai,* accept)
syneresis, same as **synaeresis.**
synesis, *n.* (*gram.*) construction in harmony with sense rather than with strict syntax, e.g. 'a large number were present.' (Gk. *sunesis,* understanding)
syngenesis, *n.* sexual reproduction.
syngnathous, *a.* (of fish) with jaws united into tubular snout. (Gk. *gnathos,* jaw)
synizesis, *n.* (*pl.* **synizeses**) union into one syllable of two vowels not forming a diphthong. (Gk. *hizein,* place)
synod, *n.* ecclesiastical assembly; Presbyterian church court intermediate between General Assembly and presbyteries; council, convention. **synodal, synodic, synodical,** *aa.* (Gk. *hodos,* way)
synoecious, synoicous, *aa.* having male and female flowers in same inflorescence. (Gk. *oikos,* house)
synonym, *n.* word identical or nearly identical in meaning with another, e.g. 'jest,' 'joke.' **synonymic,** *a.* of, using, synonyms. **synonymous,** *a.* having the same or almost the same meaning. **synonymity,** *n.* **synonymy,** *n.* synonymity; system, collection, of synonyms; use of synonyms for emphasis, e.g. 'in any shape or form.' (Gk. *onoma,* name)
synopsis, *n.* (*pl.* **synopses**) summary, outline. **synoptic, synoptical,** *aa.* giving a synopsis; taking the same view. **synoptic gospels,** those of Matthew, Mark, and Luke. **synoptist,** *n.* writer of one of these. (Gk. *opsis,* sight)
synosteology, *n.* science of joints. **synosteosis, synostosis,** *nn.* anchylosis. **synostotic,** *a.* (Gk. *osteon,* bone; *legein,* speak)
synovia, *n.* lubricating fluid secreted by certain membranes. **synovial,** *a.* **synovitis,** *n.* inflammation of synovial membrane.
syntax, *n.* part of grammar dealing with arrangement of words in sentence. **syntactic,** *a.* of, according to, syntax.—*n.pl.* mathematics of permutations and combinations. **syntactically,** *adv.* (Gk. *tassein,* arrange)
synthesis, *n.* (*pl.* **syntheses**) putting together, combination; combining of separate elements of thought to form whole, deducing of complex ideas from simple ones; system, theory, so formed; (*chem.*) uniting of elements to form compound (opp. to analysis); (*gram.*) making of compound and derivative words, preference of composition and inflexion to use of prepositions; (*med.*) joining of divided parts. **synthetic, synthetical,** *aa.* of, resulting from, synthesis; (of substance) artificial; (of language) inflexional. **synthesize, synthetize,** *vv.t.* and *i.* combine by, form, synthesis. **synthetist, synthesist,** *nn.* (Gk. *tithenai,* place)
syntonic, *a.* (*wireless*) tuned to same wave-length. **syntony,** *n.* **syntonize,** *v.t.* adjust to same wave-length. **syntonization,** *n.* (*tone*)
sypher, *v.t.* join (planks) with overlapping edges forming flush surface. **s.-joint,** *n.* (*cipher*)
syphilis, *n.* contagious venereal disease, pox. **syphilitic, syphilous,** *aa.* of, affected with, due to, syphilis. **syphiloid,** *a.* like syphilis. **syphilology,** *n.* study of syphilis. (*Syphilus,* name in poem)
syphon, syren, same as **siphon, siren.**
syrinx, *n.* (*pl.* **syrinxes, syringes**) panpipe; bird's song-organ; Eustachian tube; fistula; narrow rock-gallery in ancient Egyptian tomb. **syringa,** *n.* shrub with white scented flowers, mock orange. **syringe,** *n.* kind of small hand-pump or squirt.—*v.t.* spray, cleanse, with syringe. **syringeal,** *a.* of bird's song-organ. **syringitis,** *n.* inflammation of Eustachian tube. **syringotomy,** *n.* operation on fistula. (Gk. *suringx,* reed)
syrtis, *n.* (*pl.* **syrtes**) quicksand. (L.)
syrup, *n.* solution of sugar in water, simple, flavoured, or medicated; condensed sugarcane juice; treacle. **syrupy,** *a.* (Arab. *sharāb,* beverage)
syssarcosis, *n.* connection between bones by intervening muscle. (Gk. *sun,* together; *sarx,* flesh)
systaltic, *a.* alternately contracting and dilating, pulsatory. (Gk. *sun,* together; *stellein,* place)
system, *n.* assemblage of things or parts as connected whole; collection of related facts or principles; scheme of classification; orderly arrangement, regular method; the body considered as functional unit.

systematic, *a.* methodical, according to system. **systematically,** *adv.* **systematism,** *n.* use of, devotion to, system. **systematist,** *n.* **systematize,** *v.t.* reduce to system. **systematization,** *n.* **systemic,** *a.* of bodily system as a whole. **systemically,** *adv.* (Gk. *histanai*, place)

sȳstolĕ, *n.* contracting of heart in each beat, alternating with diastole.

systolic, *a.* (Gk. *sun*, together; *stellein*, place)

systyle, *a.* (*archit.*) having pillars two diameters apart. **systylous,** *a.* (*bot.*) having styles united. (Gk. *sun*, together; *stulos*, pillar)

syver, *n.* (*Scot.*) sewer, gutter.

syzygy, *n.* (*astron.*) point at which planet is in conjunction or opposition. (Gk. *sun*, together; *zugon*, yoke)

T

T. to a **T,** precisely, to a nicety. **T-square,** *n.* ruler with cross-piece for drawing parallel lines.

ta, *colloq.* for thanks.

Taal, *n.* Cape Dutch. (Du.=language)

tab, *n.* small flap, tag; (*colloq.*) tally, check.

tabard, *n.* herald's official dress; (formerly) garment worn over armour by knight, coarse cloak. (O.F.)

tabaret, *n.* fabric of satin and watered silk in alternate stripes.

tabasco, *n.* kind of pepper sauce. (trade-mark)

tabasheer, tabashir, *n.* siliceous substance from joints of bamboo, used by Hindus as tonic. (Hind.)

tabby, *n.* female cat; tabby-cat; spiteful old woman; coarse watered silk; kind of concrete.—*v.t.* water (silk). **t.-cat,** *n.* cat with dark stripes on brown or grey. **t.-moth,** *n.* kind with mottled wings. (Arab. *'attābiy*, a quarter in Bagdad)

tabefaction, *n.* emaciation due to disease. (L. *tabēre*, waste away; *facere*, make)

taberdar, *n.* scholar of Queen's College, Oxford. (*tabard*)

tabernacle, *n.* temporary habitation, tent; light portable temple of Israelites; nonconformist meeting-house; receptacle for pyx; soul's habitation, body; (*archit.*) niche with canopy; (*naut.*) socket of hinged mast; (*Amer.*) large church.—*v.t.* and *i.* provide with shelter; dwell temporarily. **tabernacular,** *a.* (L. *taberna*, hut+dim.)

tabes, *n.* (*med.*) emaciation. **dorsal t.,** locomotor ataxia. **tabescent,** *a.* wasting away. **tabescence,** *n.* **tabetic, tabic, tabid,** *aa.* of, affected with, tabes. **tabitude,** *n.* (L.)

tabinet, *n.* watered fabric of silk and wool.

tablature, *n.* (*arch.*) mental image, description, picture. (*table*)

table, *n.* article of furniture consisting of flat board on legs; people seated round this; food, fare; flat surface, level area; slab, tablet; inscription on this; set of facts or figures arranged systematically in columns; (*pl., arch.*) backgammon.—*v.t.* lay on table. **at t.,** while taking meal. **fence the tt.,** (*Scot.*) exhort against unworthy reception of communion. **good, liberal, t.,** generous meals. **lay, lie, on the t.,** postpone (parliamentary measure), be postponed, indefinitely. **the tt. of the law,** the ten commandments. **the twelve tt.,** early Roman law. **turn the tt. on,** put (opponent) in position of disadvantage lately held by oneself. (L. *tabula*, board)

tableau, *n.* (*pl.* **tableaux**) dramatic situation suddenly brought about; (also **t. vivant**) representation of historic scene etc. by posed group. (F.=picture)

table-book, *n.* note-book; ready-reckoner; ornamental book kept on table.

tablecloth, *n.* cloth for table.

table-d'hôte, *n.* meal at fixed price with limited choice of dishes. (F. =table of the host)

tableland, *n.* flat elevated area, plateau.

table-linen, *n.* tablecloths and napkins.

table-rapping, *n.* raps on table supposed to be signals of spirits.

tablespoon, *n.* large spoon for soup, four times size of teaspoon.

tablet, *n.* small flat slab for inscription etc.; small compressed cake of drug; lozenge; (often *pl.*) thin sheet of ivory etc. for writing notes on. (dim. of *table*)

table-talk, *n.* miscellaneous talk like that at meals.

table-turning, *n.* movement of table supposed to be caused by spirits.

tabloid, *n.* small compressed cake of drug or chemical (*trade-mark*); (*Amer.*) illustrated paper with compressed news. **in t. form,** compressed.

taboo, tabu, *n.* setting apart of thing or person as sacred or accursed and not to be touched, spoken of etc.; prohibition, ban.—*a.* subject to taboo; ruled out by convention.—*v.t.* put under taboo; prohibit. (Polynesian *tapu*)

tabor, tabour, *n.* (*arch.*) small drum. **taborer,** *n.* (*Shake.*) drummer. **tabor-**

in, tabourine, *n.* (*Shake.*) military drum. **tabouret,** *n.* low stool; embroidery-frame. **tabret,** *n.* small tabor. (O.F.)

tabula, *n.* (*anat.*; *pl.* **tabulae**) flat plate of bone. *t. rasa*, condition of mind free from impressions, complete blank. (L.=board)

tabular, *a.* like a table, flat; formed in thin plates; displayed systematically in columns. **tabulate,** *v.t.* make tabular; arrange (figures etc.) in tables. **tabulation,** *n.* **tabulator,** *n.* typewriter attachment for tabulating. (*table*)

tacamahac, *n.* an aromatic gum-resin; balsam poplar. (Aztec *tecomahiyac*)

tac-au-tac, *n.* (*fencing*) parry combined with riposte; rapid succession of attacks and parries. (F.)

tácē, *v.i.* (*imperative*) be silent. *tacet*, *v.i.* (*mus.*) direction for instrument to remain silent. (L.)

tach, tache, *n.* (*arch.*) clasp, link. (O.F.)

tacho-, tachy-, from Gk. *tachos*, speed, and *tachus*, swift, used in **tachometer,** *n.* velocity-measuring instrument, hence **tachometry,** *n.*; **tachycardia,** *n.* abnormally rapid action of heart; **tachygraphy,** *n.* shorthand writing, Greek or Roman stenography, hence **tachygraphic, tachygraphical,** *aa.*; **tachylyte,** *n.* a vitreous form of basalt, hence **tachylytic,** *a.*; **tachymeter,** *n.* surveyor's instrument for rapid location of points, tachometer, hence **tachymetry,** *n.*

tacit, *a.* unspoken, understood without being said, implicit. **taciturn,** *a.* habitually silent, of few words. **taciturnity,** *n.* (L. *tacēre*, be silent)

tack, *n.* short flat-headed nail; long stitches forming temporary fastening; lower forward corner of sail, rope attached to this; course of ship sailing obliquely to windward, change of this; course of action, policy; (*naut.*) food.—*v.t.* and *i.* fasten with tacks; stitch lightly; attach, link on; sail against wind in zigzag course; change from one tack to the other; change policy. **come down to brass tt.,** (*colloq.*) state facts. **hard t.,** ship's biscuit. **on port, starboard, t.,** with wind on port, starboard. **soft t.,** bread. **tacket,** *n.* hobnail. (O.F. *tache*, clasp)

tackle, *n.* ropes and pulleys for working sails, lifting weights etc.; gear, equipment; (*football*) act of tackling. —*v.t.* grapple with; deal with, undertake; (*football*) stop, seize (player with ball). (M.E. *takel*)

tacky, *a.* (of varnish etc.) nearly dry, but sticky. (*tack*)

tact, *n.* quick apprehension of the right thing to say or do, skill in avoiding offence; (*mus.*) stroke in beating time. **tactful,** *a.* (L. *tangere*, touch)

tactics, *n.pl.* (often as *sing.*) art of handling troops in battle or in presence of enemy; method of dealing with situation. **tactical,** *a.* **tactician,** *n.* one skilled in tactics. (Gk. *tassein*, arrange)

tactile, *a.* of, perceived by, connected with, the sense of touch; (*art*) producing effect of solidity. **tactility,** *n.* **tactual,** *a.* of touch. (L. *tangere*, touch)

tadpole, *n.* larva of frog or toad, esp. while it presents only round head and tail. (*toad*; *poll*)

taedium vitae, (*med.*) weariness of life with suicidal tendency. (L.)

tael, *n.* Chinese measure of weight, 1⅓ oz.; Chinese money of account, about 3*s.* (Malay *tahil*, weight)

ta'en, *poet. contr.* of **taken.**

taenia, *n.* (*pl.* **taeniae**) (*anat.*) ribbon-like part; tapeworm; (*archit.*) band above architrave in Doric column. **taenioid,** *a.* (L.=head-band)

tafferel, *n.* upper part of stern; taffrail. (Du. *tafereel*, panel)

taffeta, *n.* a fine smooth glossy fabric, us. of silk. (Pers. *taftan*, twist)

taffrail, *n.* rail round ship's stern. (*tafferel*+confusion with *rail*)

Taffy, *n.* nickname for Welshman. (*David*)

taffy, *Amer.* form of **toffee.**

tafia, *n.* W. Indian rum made from molasses. (native)

tag, *n.* appendage, flap; metal point at end of lace; loop for pulling on boot; tie-on label; loose or ragged end; refrain; epilogue; stock phrase.—*v.t.* and *i.* furnish with tag; add, tack (on); (*colloq.*) follow closely. **t.-rag,** same as **rag-tag.**

tag, *n.* children's chasing game, touch-last.—*v.t.* touch in this.

taiga, *n.* Siberian pine-forest. (Russ.)

taigle, *v.t.* and *i.* (*Scot.*) entangle, hinder; delay, loiter.

tail, *n.* (*law*) limitation of inheritance of estate to particular person or line. —*a.* limited by tail. (O.F. *taillier*, cut)

tail, *n.* loose projection of animal's spine; thing like this, plait, appendage; hindmost or lowest part; reverse side of coin; (*pl.*) tailcoat.—*v.t.* and *i.* provide with tail; remove stalk from; follow closely. **t. away, off,** diminish gradually, dwindle. **t. margin,** at foot of page. **t. of letter,** part below line. **t. of the eye,** outer end. **tt. up,** in good spirits. **turn t.,** run away. **with t. between legs,** cowed. **t.-board,** *n.* movable back of cart. **t.-end,** *n.* last part. **t.-light,** *n.* rear light of vehicle. **t.-piece,** *n.* ornamental design at end of chapter or book. **t.-skid,** *n.* runner beneath tail of aeroplane to take shock of landing. **t.-spin,** *n.* spinning dive of aeroplane. **tailcoat,** *n.* man's coat with skirt cut away in front and divided at back. (O.E. *tægel*)

tailor, *n.* (*fem.* **tailoress**) one who cuts out and makes men's clothes and ladies' costumes.—*v.t.* and *i.* make, furnish with, clothes. **t.-bird,** *n.* kind that stitches leaves to build nest. **t.-made,** *a.* (of woman's dress) made by tailor, close-fitting, plain. (O.F. *taillier*, cut)

tain, *n.* thin tinplate; tinfoil for backing mirrors. (F.)

taint, *n.* trace of decay or disease; blemish; corruption, infection.—*v.t.* and *i.* infect, be infected; contaminate, corrupt. **tainture,** *n.* (*Shake.*) defilement. (L. *tingere*, dye)

tait, *n.* (*Scot.*) small quantity.

taj, *n.* tall conical cap of Mohammedan dervish. (Pers.)

take, *v.t.* and *i.* (*past* **took,** *p.p.* **taken**) seize, capture; remove, steal; catch, come upon; gain, win; captivate, please; accept, obtain; select; use, consume; have recourse (to); require, demand; assume, adopt; regard, consider; ascertain, understand; infer; experience, feel; be infected with; tolerate; conduct, transport; photograph; (of vaccination) operate; (*Shake.*) strike; infect, bewitch; pretend; betake oneself to.—*n.* amount taken, catch. **t. after,** inherit likeness from. **t. down,** write down; humble. **t. for,** mistake for. **t. from,** detract, diminish. **t. in,** receive; entertain; shorten, furl; include; cheat; (*Shake.*) conquer, subdue. **t. it easy,** not exert oneself. **t. it out of,** exhaust; get even with. **t. off,** remove; mimic; start leap or aeroplane flight; (*Shake.*) destroy. **t. on,** undertake; engage; (*colloq.*) grieve. **t. out,** remove; have issued to one. **t. over,** succeed to charge of. **t. to,** take liking to; form habit of. **t. up,** lift; arrest; interrupt, correct; become friendly with; enter upon (study); (*Shake.*) levy; make up (dispute). **t. upon one,** assume; presume. (O.N. *taka*)

takin, *n.* heavy Asiatic animal between goat and antelope. (native)

taking, *a.* attractive, pleasing; (*Shake*). pernicious.—*n.* (*arch.*) state of agitation; (*Shake.*) malignant influence.

talapoin, *n.* Buddhist monk; small W. African monkey. (Port. *talapão*)

talaria, *n.pl.* winged sandals of Mercury. **talaric,** *a.* of the ankles. (L.)

talbot, *n.* extinct breed of hound like bloodhound.

Talbot House, (*abbr.* Toc H) society carrying on comradeship of the Great War. (Gilbert *Talbot*, killed 1915)

talc, *n.* magnesium silicate, a soft mineral with soapy feel; (*colloq.*) mica. **talcky, talcose, talcous,** *aa.* (Arab. *talq*)

tale, *n.* narrative, story; malicious report; (*arch.*) number, total. **tells its own t.,** is self-explanatory. **tell tt. (out of school),** betray confidences; act as informer. **talebearer,** *n.* informer. **talebearing,** *a.* (O.E. *talu*)

talegalla, *n.* (*Austral.*) brush turkey.

talent, *n.* ancient weight or sum of money varying in different countries, in Greece upwards of 56 lb. and £200; natural ability or power, persons having this. **talented,** *a.* gifted. (Gk. *talanton*)

talion, *n.* (also *lex talionis*) punishment in kind, an eye for an eye. **talionic,** *a.* (L. *talis*, such)

tálipēs, *n.* club-foot; distortion of feet. **taliped,** *a.* and *n.* club-footed (person); (animal) walking with feet twisted. (L. *talus*, ankle; *pes*, foot)

talipot, taliput, *n.* a fan-leaved palm. (Sanskr. *tala*, palm; *patra*, leaf)

talisman, *n.* thing believed to have magical power of protecting wearer, charm, amulet. **talismanic,** *a.* (Gk. *telein*, consecrate)

talk, *v.i.* and *t.* speak, converse; gossip; discuss; utter; make, persuade, by talking.—*n.* conversation; short lecture; rumour; mere words. **t. at,** aim remarks at one person while addressing another. **t. back,** answer defiantly. **t. big,** boast. **t. down,** silence by louder or more persistent talk. **t. out,** get rid of (parliamentary motion) by prolonging discussion till time of adjournment. **t. over,** discuss; persuade. **t. tall,** use bluff or exaggeration. **talking of,** with regard to. **talking-to,** *n.* scolding. **talkative,** *a.* fond of talking. **talkee-talkee,** *n.* broken English, lingo; chatter. **talkie,** *n.* (*sl.*) cinematograph picture with mechanical speech accompaniment, sound-film. (M.E. *talken*)

tall, *a.* high in stature; lofty; of specified height; (*sl.*) extravagant, boastful, hard to believe; (*Shake.*) goodly, fine, valiant. **t. order,** unreasonable demand.

tallage, talliage, *n.* a feudal tax. (O.F. *taillier*, cut)

tallboy, *n.* chest of drawers high in itself or raised on legs. (*tall; boy*)

tallith, *n.* scarf worn by Jews at prayer. (Heb.)

tallow, *n.* animal fat melted down.—*v.t.* grease with tallow. **t.-catch,** *n.* (*Shake.*) lump of tallow. **t.-chandler,** *n.* dealer in tallow candles. **t.-faced,** *a.* pasty-faced. (M.E. *talgh*)

tally, *n.* piece of wood notched to indicate items in account and afterwards split into halves of which each party kept one; either of the halves; account, score; counterpart, duplicate; ticket, label.—*v.i.* and *t.* correspond, conform exactly; reckon by tally. **tallier,** *n.* (L. *talea*, slip of wood)

tally-ho, *int.* and *n.* huntsman's view-halloo; (*Amer.*) large four-in-hand coach.—*v.i.* and *t.* utter, urge on with, tally-ho. (F. *taïaut*)

talma, *n.* kind of long cloak. (name of actor)

Talmud, *n.* body of Jewish law. **Talmudic, Talmudical,** *aa.* **Talmudist,** *n.* compiler, adherent, student, of the Talmud. (Heb.=instruction)

talon, *n.* claw of bird of prey; heel of sword-blade; cards left after deal; ogee moulding. (*talus*)

taluk, talook, *n.* revenue district, estate, in India. **talukdar,** *n.* native tax-collector, proprietor, of this. (Hind.)

talus, *n.* (*pl.* tali) ankle-bone; slope of face of earthwork; (*geol.*) rock debris at base of cliff. (L.)

tamable, *a.* capable of being tamed.

tamâlĕ, *n.* Mexican dish of crushed maize and meat, seasoned with pepper. (Sp. *tamal*)

tamandua, tamanoir, *nn.* kinds of American ant-eater. (Brazilian)

tamarack, *n.* American larch. (Amer. Ind.)

tamarin, *n.* S. American marmoset. (native)

tamarind, *n.* a tropical tree; its pods, containing sweet brownish pulp. (Arab. *tamr*, date; *Hind*, India)

tamarisk, *n.* evergreen shrub with feathery branches and minute leaves. (L.L. *tamariscus*)

tamasha, *n.* (*Anglo-Ind.*) show, entertainment, public function. (Arab.)

tambour, *n.* drum, esp. bass drum; circular frame for stretching embroidery work on, stuff so embroidered; cylindrical stone in column; vestibule to break draught in church porch; stockade protecting gateway; kinds of fish.—*v.t.* embroider on tambour. **tambourin,** *n.* old Provençal dance; music for it. **tambourine,** *n.* small shallow open hand-drum with jingling disks of metal in the hoop; kind of African pigeon. (F.)

tambreet, *n.* (*Austral.*) duck-billed platypus. (native)

tame, *a.* domesticated, made friendly or tractable; subdued, spiritless; dull, insipid.—*v.t.* make tame, domesticate; break in, subdue, curb. **tameless,** *a.* untamable. (O.E. *tam*)

Tamil, *a.* and *n.* (member, language) of a non-Aryan race of SE. India.

tamis, *n.* cloth for straining liquids. (F.=sieve)

Tammany, *n.* organization of Democratic Party in New York. **Tammanyism,** *n.* its principles; political and municipal corruption. (name of a Red Indian chief)

tam-o'-shanter, tammy, *nn.* round woollen cap with flat baggy top. (hero of Burns's poem)

tamp, *v.t.* plug (blasting-hole) with clay etc. to intensify force of explosion; ram down.

tampan, *n.* poisonous S. African tick. (native)

tamper, *v.i.* **t. with,** interfere, meddle with; make unauthorized changes in; corrupt, bribe. **tamperer,** *n.* (= *temper*)

tampion, *n.* plug for muzzle of gun.

tampon, *n.* and *v.t.* plug to stop haemorrhage. **tamponade, tamponage, tamponment,** *nn.* use of tampon on wounds. (O.F. *tape*, bung)

tamtam, same as **tomtom.**

tan, *n.* bark of oak crushed to extract tannic acid; refuse of this used as soft surface for riding-school etc.; yellowish brown; sunburn.—*a.* yellowish-brown.—*v.t.* and *i.* (*past, p.p.* **tanned**) make (hides) into leather by steeping in solution of tannic acid; make or become sunburnt; (*sl.*) thrash. **spent t.,** tan refuse. **the t.,** (*sl.*) the circus. **t.-liquor, t.-ooze, t.-pickle,** *nn.* liquid used in tanning. **t.-yard,** *n.* tannery. (F.)

tan, *abbr.* of **tangent.**

tana, *n.* police station, military post. in India. **tanadar,** *n.* chief officer of this. (Hind. *thāna*)

tanager, *n.* any of a family of American birds, us. brilliantly coloured, allied to finches. **tanagrine,** *a.* (Brazilian *tangara*)

tanagra, *n.* terra-cotta statuette of type found at Tanagra in Greece.

tandem, *adv.* (with horses) harnessed one behind another.—*n.* horses so harnessed, vehicle drawn by them; bicycle for two or more seated one behind another. (L.=**at** length)

tang, *n.* tapering part of knife or tool that fits into handle; strong pungent taste or smell; smack.—*v.t.* furnish (tool) with tang. (O.N. *tange*, point)

tang, *n.* and *v.i.* and *t.* twang, ring. (imit.)

tang, *n.* kind of seaweed.

tangent, *n.* (*geom.*) straight line touching curve at one point only.—*a.* meeting but not intersecting. **t. of an angle,** (*trigonometry*) ratio of the perpendicular subtending it in any right-angled triangle to the base. **go off at a t.,** change suddenly to different line of thought. **tangency,** *n.* **tangential,** *a.* (L. *tangere*, touch)

Tangerine, *a.* and *n.* (native) of Tangiers; kind of small orange.

tanghin, *n.* Madagascar tree with poisonous seed. (native *tangena*)

tangible, *a.* perceptible by touch; definite, real, concrete. **tangibility,** *n.* (L. *tangere*, touch)

tangle, *n.* kind of seaweed, tang.

tangle, *v.t.* and *i.* interweave, be involved, in confused mass; entangle. —*n.* tangled string, snarl; muddle. **tanglefoot,** *n.* (*Amer. sl.*) whisky. **tanglesome, tangly,** *aa.*

tango, *n.* (*pl.* tangos) a dance of S. American origin.

tangram, *n.* toy made by cutting

square into seven pieces which are fitted together to form other shapes.

tanistry, *n.* ancient Irish system by which chief's successor was chosen from his family by election. **tanist,** *n.* such successor. (Ir. *tanaiste,* heir)

tank, *n.* large receptacle for liquid or gas, cistern; reservoir; armoured motor-vehicle with endless bands over wheels enabling it to move over rough ground; (*Amer.*) small lake, pool. **t. engine,** railway engine carrying its own water and coal, without tender. **tankage,** *n.* storage in tanks; charge for this; capacity of tank; fertilizer got from refuse fats. (Port. *tanque*)

tankard, *n.* large drinking-vessel of metal or wood; contents of this.

tanker, *n.* cargo steamer for carrying oil in bulk.

tanling, *n.* (*Shake.*) one tanned by sun.

tanna, tannadar, same as **tana, tanadar.**

tanner, *n.* (*sl.*) sixpence.

tanner, *n.* one who tans. **tannery,** *n.* place where tanning is done. **tannic,** *a.* of, got from, bark. **tannin,** *n.* tannic acid, astringent substance used in tanning.

tanrec, same as **tenrec.**

tansy, *n.* yellow-flowered aromatic herb. (Gk. *athanasia,* immortality)

tantalize, *v.t.* torment by keeping something desired in view but just out of reach; raise and then dash hopes of. **tantalization,** *n.* **tantalum,** *n.* a metal used for electric-lamp filaments. **tantalus,** *n.* stand in which decanters are locked up but visible; wood-ibis. (*Tantalos* in Gk. myth)

tantamount, *a.* equivalent, amounting (to). (L. *tantus,* so great+*amount*)

tantara, *n.* series of notes on trumpet or horn. (imit.)

tantivy, *n.* (*arch.*) hunting cry; swift gallop; rush.—*a.* swift.—*adv.* swiftly. —*v.i.* gallop fast; hurry.

tantrum, *n.* fit of violent temper.

Taoism, *n.* religious doctrine of Lao-tsze, Chinese philosopher. (Chin. *tao,* way)

tap, *n.* short pipe for drawing off liquid; valve with handle to regulate flow in pipe, cock; brand of liquor; tap-room; tool for cutting internal screw-threads.—*v.t.* (*past, p.p.* **tapped**) fit tap into (cask) and draw liquor; draw off fluid by incision; obtain access to, make available; secretly take message from (telegraph or telephone wire); (*sl.*) borrow from. **on t.,** ready to be drawn; always available. **t.-room,** *n.* room in which liquor is drawn and served. **t.-root,** *n.* long tapering root growing directly downwards. (O.E. *tæppa*)

tap, *v.t.* and *i.* (*past, p.p.* **tapped**) strike lightly, rap; fix piece of leather on (heel of shoe).—*n.* light blow or sound; (*pl., Amer.*) military signal for putting lights out and going to bed. **t.-dancing,** *n.* solo dancing with rhythmical tapping of feet. (imit.)

tap, *Scot.* form of **top.**

tapa, *n.* bark of a Polynesian tree; fabric made from it. (native)

tape, *n.* narrow strip of woven material; length of this between winning-posts; strip of paper in tape-machine; tape-measure; (*sl.*) liquor. —*v.t.* join, fasten, with tape; (*sl.*) size up. **red t.,** excessive adherence to official rules. **t.-machine,** *n.* (*colloq.*) self-recording telegraph instrument. **t.-measure, t.-line,** *nn.* length of tape marked off in inches etc. (O.E. *tæppe*)

taper, *n.* wick thinly coated with wax, for lighting lamps; slender candle. —*a.* tapering.—*v.i.* and *t.* become, make, gradually thinner towards one end; fine (off). (O.E.)

tapestry, *n.* textile fabric with designs worked by hand, used for covering walls etc. **tapestried,** *a.* hung with tapestry. (Gk. *tapēs,* carpet)

tapeworm, *n.* long flat worm parasitic in animal or human intestine.

tapioca, *n.* granular food made from cassava-root. (Brazilian *tipi,* residue; *ok,* press out)

tapir, *n.* S. American pig-like animal with short flexible proboscis. **tapiroid,** *a.* (Brazilian *tapira*)

tapis, *n.* carpet. **on the** *t.,* under discussion. (F.)

tapotement, *n.* (*med.*) beating or tapping used in massage. (F.)

tappal, *n.* (*Anglo-Ind.*) mail, post.

tappet, *n.* small lever, rod, transmitting intermittent motion from one part of machine to another.

tappit, *a.* (*Scot.*) topped, crested. **t.-hen,** *n.* crested hen; vessel for liquor holding about three quarts.

tap rate, current price of Treasury additional paper. (initials)

tapsalteerie, *a.* (*Scot.*) topsyturvy.

tapster, *n.* person who draws and serves liquor.

tapu, same as **taboo.**

tar, *n.* (*colloq.*) sailor. (abbr. of *tarpaulin*)

tar, *n.* thick black viscous liquid distilled from wood or coal.—*v.t.* coat, treat, with tar. **t. and feather,** smear with tar and roll in feathers as punishment. **tarred with the same brush,** having same faults. **touch of the t.-brush,** slight admixture of negro blood. **t.-macadam,** *n.* mixture of tar and road metal giving smooth road surface. **t.-water,** *n.* cold infusion of tar, used as medicine. (O.E. *teoru*)

tara, *n.* (also **t.-fern**) edible fern of New Zealand. (native)

taradiddle, *n.* (*colloq.*) lie, fib.

tarantass, *n.* four-wheeled springless Russian carriage. (Russ. *tarantasu*)

tarantella, tarantelle, *n.* rapid whirling Italian dance for two; music for it. **tarantism,** *n.* dancing mania. (*Taranto* in Italy)

tarantula, *n.* large poisonous S. European spider. **tarantular,** *a.* (*Taranto* in Italy)

taratantara, *n.* trumpet or bugle call. (imit.)

taraxacum, *n.* kinds of plant incl. dandelion; laxative drug made from root of dandelion.

tarboosh, *n.* brimless tasselled felt cap worn by Turks. (Arab. *tarbūsh*)

tardamente, tardo, advv. (*mus.*) slowly. (It.)

tardy, *a.* slow, sluggish; dilatory; late, behind time.—*v.t.* (*Shake.*) delay. **tardily,** *adv.* **tardigrade,** *a.* and *n.* slow-moving (animal), e.g. sloth. (L. *tardus*)

tare, *n.* allowance made for weight of box, wrapping, cart, truck etc., when goods are weighed in it.—*v.t.* ascertain weight of (container). (Arab. *tarhah*, what is rejected)

tare, *n.* vetch; (*pl.*) noxious weeds among corn. (M.E.)

targe, *n.* (*arch.*) small round shield or buckler. (O.N. *targa*)

target, *n.* mark for shooting-practice; thing aimed at; object of criticism, butt; small circular railway signal at switch; targe. **targeteer,** *n.* soldier armed with targe. (*targe*)

tariff, *n.* duty imposed on imports or exports; schedule of these; list of charges at hotel etc.—*v.t.* make list of duties on; price. **t. reform,** protectionist policy. (Arab. *ta'rīf*, notification)

tarlatan, *n.* kind of thin muslin. (F. *tarlatane*)

tarmac, *n.* trade-mark name for tarmacadam.

tarn, *n.* small mountain lake. (O.N. *tjörn*)

tarn, same as **tern.**

tarnal, tarnation, (*Amer.*) mild forms of **eternal, damnation.**

tarnish, *v.t.* and *i.* diminish lustre of, lose lustre; discolour by oxidization; sully (reputation).—*n.* loss of brightness; discoloration on metal; blemish. (F. *terne*, dull)

taro, *n.* plant grown in Pacific islands; its edible root. (native)

taroc, tarot, *n.* early kind of playing-card, 78 to the pack; game played with these. (It. *tarocchi*)

tarpan, *n.* wild horse of Russian steppes. (Tartar)

tarpaulin, *n.* canvas treated with tar or oil; sheet of this; sailor's tarred hat. (*tar*; *pall*)

tarpon, *n.* large sea-fish of Florida coast.

tarradiddle, same as **taradiddle.**

tarragon, *n.* herb like wormwood, used for flavouring. (Arab. *tarkhūn*)

tarras, same as **trass.**

tarre, *v.t.* (*Shake.*) set on, incite (hound).

tarriance, *n.* (*arch.*) delay. (*tarry*)

tarrock, *n.* young kittiwake; tern; guillemot.

tarrow, *v.i.* (*Scot.*) complain.

tarry, *a.* smeared with tar.

tarry, *v.i.* and *t.* linger, delay; stop, stay; wait (for).

tarsal, *a.* of the tarsus.

tarsia, *n.* wood mosaic. (It.)

tarsier, *n.* large-eyed nocturnal E. Indian lemur. (F.)

tarsus, *n.* (*pl.* **tarsi**) ankle; bird's shank; insect's foot; gristly plate of eyelid. (Gk. *tarsos*, flat of foot)

tart, *a.* acid, sour; crabbed, snappish. (O.E. *teart*)

tart, *n.* fruit pie; pastry with jam or fruit in or on it; (*sl.*) prostitute; girl. (O.F. *tarte*)

tartan, *n.* woollen stuff with various coloured checks, each Scottish clan having its own distinctive pattern. —*a.* made of, like, tartan.

tartan, *n.* small Mediterranean coaster with lateen sail. (It. *tartana*)

Tartar, *n.* native of Tartary; Tatar; bad-tempered person. **catch a T.,** find intended victim too strong for one. **Tartarian,** *a.* (*Tatar*)

tartar, *n.* crust deposited in cask by wine; incrustation on teeth. **t. emetic,** a compound of potassium and antimony. **tartaric, tartarous,** *aa.* **tartarize,** *v.t.* treat with tartar. **tartarization,** *n.* (F. *tartre*)

Tartarus, *n.* lowest part of Hades; hell. **Tartarean,** *a.* (L).

tartlet, *n.* small open tart. (dim.)

tartrate, *n.* salt of tartaric acid.

Tartuffe, Tartufe, *n.* sanctimonious hypocrite. (name in Molière)

task, *n.* piece of work to be done.—*v.t.* assign task to; put strain on, tax; (*Shake.*) reproach. **take to t.,** find fault with. **taskmaster,** *n.* (*fem.* **taskmistress**) imposer of task, overseer. (L. *taxare*, rate)

taslet, *n.* piece of armour for thigh.

Tasmanian, *a.* of Tasmania. **T. devil,** savage cat-like marsupial, dasyure. **T. wolf,** wolf-like marsupial.

tass, *n.* (*Scot.*) drinking-cup; small draught. (O.F. *tasse*, cup)

tassel, *n.* ornament of hanging tuft of threads; flower or catkin like this; ribbon book-mark.—*v.t.* furnish with tassel. (O.F.)

tassel-gentle, *n.* (*Shake.*) tercel.

tasset, *n.* plate hanging from cuirass to protect thigh. (O.F. *tassette*)

tassie, *n.* (*Scot.*) drinking-cup. (*tass*)

taste, *v.t.* and *i.* detect or try flavour of; eat or drink small quantity of; experience, feel; have specified flavour; (*Shake.*) put to proof, test.—*n.* sense peculiar to tongue and mouth; act of tasting; savour, flavour; small portion, sample; preference, liking; artistic discernment or style; (*Shake.*)

trial. **in good, bad, t.,** pleasing, offensive, to aesthetic faculty. **tastable,** *a.* **tasteless,** *a.* insipid, flat; having, done in, bad taste. **taster,** *n.* one who tests quality of teas or wines by tasting; court official who tasted food to detect poison; (*colloq.*) publisher's reader. **tasty,** *a.* savoury, not insipid; (*vulg.*) stylish, smart. (L. *taxare*, rate)

tat, *v.i.* and *t.* do, make by, tatting.

tat, tatt, *abbr.* of **tattoo** or **tatty.**

ta-ta, *int.* (*colloq.*) good-bye.

Tatar, *a.* and *n.* (member) of race incl. Turks and Cossacks. (Pers.)

tatou, tatouay, *nn.* kinds of armadillo. (native)

tatter, *n.* torn fragment, shred; (*pl.*) torn state. **tattered,** *a.* ragged. **tatterdemalion,** *n.* ragged fellow.

Tattersall's, *n.* horse-dealing and betting rendezvous in London.

tatting, *n.* lace-like trimming of knotted and looped threads.

tattle, *v.i.* and *t.* gossip indiscreetly, talk scandal, chatter.—*n.* idle talk, gossip. **tattler,** *n.* one who tattles; sandpiper.

tattoo, *n.* drum-beat or bugle-call summoning soldiers to quarters at night; loud knocking; military pageant by night. **devil's t.,** drumming with fingers. (Du. *taptoe*, tap to or shut, orig. used of public-house)

tattoo, *v.t.* mark (skin) indelibly by pricking in colouring matter.—*n.* tattooing; tattooed pattern. (Tahitian *tatau*)

tattoo, *n.* native-bred Indian pony. (Hind. *tattū*)

tatty, *n.* (*Anglo-Ind.*) matting of woven grass hung in doorway or window and kept wet to cool the air. (Hind. *tatti*, wicker frame)

tau, *n.* Greek T; toad-fish. (Gk.)

taught, see **teach.**

taunt, *v.t.* reproach contemptuously, jeer at.—*n.* sneering remark, gibe. (F. *tant pour tant*, tit for tat)

taunt, *a.* (*naut.*, of mast) tall. (F. *autant*, as much)

taupie, same as **tawpie.**

Taurus, *n.* the Bull, second sign of zodiac, which sun enters on 21st April. **taurine,** *a.* of, like, a bull; of Taurus. **tauromachy,** *n.* bullfighting; bull-fight. (L.)

taut, *a.* (*naut.*) drawn tight; in good condition. **tauten,** *v.t.* and *i.* make, become, taut. (M.E. *togt*)

tautog, *n.* edible N. American sea-fish. (Amer. Ind.)

tautology, *n.* needless repetition of same thing in other words, e.g. 'free, gratis, and for nothing.' **tautologic, tautological,** *aa.* **tautologist,** *n.* **tautologize,** *v.i.* (Gk. *tauto*, the same; *legein*, speak)

tautophony, *n.* repetition of the same sound. (Gk. *tauto*, same; *phōnē*, sound)

tavern, *n.* (*arch.*) inn, public-house. (L. *taberna*)

taw, *v.t.* make (hides) into leather by steeping in solution of alum and salt. (O.E. *tawian*, prepare)

taw, *n.* large marble; game of marbles; line at which player stands in this.

tawdry, *a.* tastelessly showy, flashy.—*n.* cheap finery. (fair of *Saint Audry*)

tawie, *a.* (*Scot.*) tame.

tawny, *a.* light brownish-yellow, sand-coloured. (O.F. *tané*, tanned)

tawpie, *n.* (*Scot.*) foolish girl.

tawse, taws, *n.* (*Scot.*) teacher's strap for punishing.

tax, *n.* legally levied contribution to state revenue; strain, heavy burden; (*Shake.*) accusation.—*v.t.* impose tax on; make heavy demands on; charge (with), accuse; (*law*) examine and revise (bill of costs); (*arch.*) register for fiscal purposes. **direct t.,** imposed on persons or property. **indirect t.,** imposed on commodities and paid in form of higher prices. **t.-cart, taxed-cart,** *n.* light two-wheeled cart. **t.-collector,** (*arch.*) **t.-gatherer,** *nn.* official who receives taxes. **t.-free,** *a.* exempt from taxes. **t.-farmer,** *n.* one who buys from state the right to levy tax. **taxing-master,** *n.* law-court official who taxes costs. **taxable,** *a.* **taxability,** *n.* **taxation,** *n.* taxes or their imposition; (*Shake.*) demand; censure. (L. *taxare*, rate)

taxi, *n.* (also **t.-cab**) motor-cab for public hire.—*v.i.* and *t.* (*pres. part.* **taxying, taxi-ing**) go, convey, in taxi; (of aircraft) go along ground or water under its own power. (*taximeter*)

taxidermy, *n.* art of stuffing skins of animals in lifelike form. **taxidermal, taxidermic,** *aa.* **taxidermist,** *n.* (Gk. *taxis*, arrangement; *derma*, skin)

taximeter, *n.* automatic fare-indicator for cab. (F. *taxe*, tariff. Gk. *metron*, measure)

taxin, *n.* resinous substance got from leaves of yew. (L. *taxus*, yew)

taxiplane, *n.* light aeroplane for public hire. (*taxi*; *plane*)

taxis, *n.* arrangement, classification; (*med.*) replacement of displaced part by hand. **taxology,** *n.* science of classification. **taxonomy,** *n.* classification of animals and plants; principles of this. **taxonomic, taxonomical,** *a.* **taxonomist,** *n.* (Gk.)

taxpayer, *n.* one who pays taxes.

tazza, *n.* saucer-shaped cup or vase, esp. one mounted on foot. (It.)

tch, tcha, *intt.* of impatience.

tchick, *n.* sound made with tongue against roof of mouth to urge on horse.—*v.i.* make this. (imit.)

te, *n.* seventh note in sol-fa notation.

tea, *n.* dried leaves of tea-plant; drink made by soaking these in boiling water; meal at which tea is drunk. —*v.i.* take tea. **black t.,** roasted after fermentation. **green t.**, roasted while fresh. **high, meat, t.**, evening meal after midday dinner. **Russian t.**, with lemon instead of milk. **t.-caddy**, *n.* small box or tin for tea. **tea-cake**, *n.* a flat cake eaten hot with butter. **t.-chest**, *n.* lead-lined wooden chest in which tea is imported. **t.-cloth**, *n.* small tablecloth; dish-towel. **teacup**, *n.* small cup holding about ½ pint. **t.-fight**, *n.* (*sl.*) tea-party. **t.-garden, tearoom**, *nn.* where teas are purveyed. **t.-gown**, *n.* woman's loose afternoon gown. **t.-plant**, *n.* oriental shrub yielding tea. **t.-rose**, *n.* yellow tea-scented rose. **t.-service, t.-set, t.-things**, *nn.* set of cups, plates etc. for tea. **tea-spoon**, *n.* small spoon for use with teacup. (Chin. dial. *t'e*)

teach, *v.t.* and *i.* (*past, p.p.* **taught**) impart knowledge to, educate; train; give lessons (in); show; instil. **teach-able**, *a.* **teachability**, *n.* **teacher**, *n.* (O.E. *tǣcan*)

tead, *n.* (*Spens.*) torch. (L. *taeda*)

teak, *n.* an E. Indian tree; its hard durable yellowish-brown wood. (Malayalam *tēkka*)

teal, *n.* (*pl.* same) small freshwater duck. (M.E. *tele*)

team, *n.* two or more animals harnessed together; side at football etc.; group working together.—*v.t.* harness in team; give out (work) to gang under sub-contractor. **t.-work**, *n.* co-operation. **teamster**, *n.* driver of team. (O.E. *téam*, family)

teapot, *n.* vessel in which tea is made.

teapoy, *n.* three-legged stand; small tea-table. (Hind. *tīn*, three; Pers. *pae*, foot; +confusion with *tea*)

tear, *v.t.* and *i.* (*past* **tore**, *p.p.* **torn**) pull forcibly apart, rend, lacerate; drag (up, out); disunite; agitate; rush; suffer tearing.—*n.* rent. **t. him off a strip**, (*R.A.F. sl.*) reprimand him. **t. one's hair**, pull it out in grief etc. **t. up**, tear in pieces; regard as cancelled. **that 's torn it**, (*sl.*) that spoils things completely. **tearaway**, *a.* impetuous. **tearing**, *a.* violent, furious. (O.E. *teran*)

tear, *n.* drop of fluid from the eye; tear-like thing. **in tt.**, weeping. **t.-drop**, *n.* tear. **t.-gas**, *n.* poison gas causing violent watering of the eyes. **t.-shell**, *n.* shell containing this. **tearful**, *a.* weeping; given to tears. **tearless**, *a.* without tears; not weeping. (O.E. *téar*)

tease, *v.t.* mock at maliciously, bait; banter playfully; pester, importune; tear apart fibres of, card (wool etc.); teasel.—*n.* one who teases. (O.E. *tǣsan*, pluck)

teasel, *n.* a plant; its prickly head, used for teaseling; machine for this. —*v.t.* raise nap on (cloth) with teasel. **teaseler**, *n.* (*tease*)

teaser, *n.* one who teases; (*colloq.*) awkward problem or task.

teat, *n.* nipple through which milk passes; pap, dug. (O.F. *tete*)

teazel, teazle, same as **teasel.**

tec, *n.* (*sl.*) detective. (abbr.)

technic, *a.* technical.—*n.* technique; (*pl.*) branches of learning relating to the arts. **technical**, *a.* of, in, peculiar to, a particular art or craft; needing expert knowledge; of the mechanical arts; (of offence) legally such. **technicality**, *n.* being technical; technical term. **technician, technicist**, *nn.* one skilled in the technique of an art. **technique**, *n.* mechanical side of an art; style of execution. **technocracy**, *n.* system under which a country's resources and production would be managed by technical experts for the benefit of all. **technocrat**, *n.* advocate of, expert under, technocracy. **technocratic**, *a.* **technology**, *n.* science and history of the mechanical arts; scientific nomenclature. **technological**, *a.* **technologist**, *n.* (Gk. *technē*, art)

techy, same as **tetchy.**

tecnology, *n.* study of children. (Gk. *teknon*, child; *legein*, speak)

tectology, *n.* study of organisms as groups of structural units. **tectological**, *a.* **tectonic**, *a.* structural.—*n. pl.* science of design and structure. (Gk. *tektōn*, carpenter; *legein*, speak)

tectorial, *a.* covering. **tectrices**, *n.pl.* covering feathers of bird's wing or tail. (L. *tegere*, cover)

ted, *v.t.* (*past, p.p.* **tedded**) spread and turn (hay) to dry it. (Icel. *tedhja*, spread manure)

teddy bear, furry toy bear. (*Theodore* Roosevelt)

Te Deum, a thanksgiving hymn. (L. = thee, God—opening words)

tedious, *a.* tiresome, boring. **tedium**, *n.* tediousness, monotony. (L. *taedet*, it wearies)

tee, *n.* letter T; T-shaped thing.

tee, *n.* umbrella-shaped ornament on top of pagoda. (Burmese *h'ti*, umbrella)

tee, *n.* mark aimed at in quoits, bowls, and curling; (*golf*) mound of sand, peg, on which ball is placed for first stroke; teeing-ground.—*v.t.* place (ball) on tee. **teeing-ground**, *n.* (*golf*) space from which first stroke is played.

teem, *v.i.* and *t.* swarm (with), be prolific; abound; (*arch.*) bear (offspring). (O.E. *téam*, family)

teem, *v.t.* empty, pour out. (O.N. *tómr*, empty)

teen, *n.* (*arch.*) grief, woe; harm. (O.E. *téona*, injury)

-teen, *suf.* and ten, as in **sixteen.**

teens, *n.pl.* years of life from 13 to 19. (O.E. *téne*, tens)

teeny, *a.* (*sl.*) tiny. **t.-weeny**, *a.* (*sl.*) very tiny. (*tiny*)

teepee, same as **tepee.**

teeter, *v.i.* (*Amer.*) seesaw; vacillate.
teeth, see **tooth.**
teethe, *v.i.* grow one's teeth, esp. milk-teeth.
teetotal, *a.* abstaining entirely from intoxicants; temperance; (*colloq.*) complete. **teetotalism, teetotaller, teetotaler.** *nn.* (*total*)
teetotum, *n.* toy top twirled by fingers; kind with numbered or lettered sides, used in gaming. (*T*+L. *totus*, whole, from method of staking)
teg, *n.* sheep in its second year.
tegular, *a.* of, like, tiles. **tegulated,** *a.* having overlapping plates or scales. (L. *tegula*, tile)
tegument, *n.* natural covering of animal body or organ, skin. **tegumental, tegumentary,** *aa.* (L. *tegere*, cover)
tehee, *n.* and *v.i.* titter. (imit.)
teil, *n.* lime-tree. (L. *tilia*)
teind, *n.* (*Scot.*) tithe. (M.E. *tende*, tenth)
teinoscope, *n.* prism telescope. (Gk. *teinein*, stretch; *skopein*, view)
teknonymy, *n.* practice of naming parent from child. **teknonymous,** *a.* (Gk. *teknon*, child; *onoma*, name)
telaesthesia, *n.* direct perception of distant object or event by means other than the five senses. **telaesthetic,** *a.* (Gk. *tēle*, far; *aisthanesthai*, perceive)
telamon, *n.* (*archit.*) male figure supporting pillar. (name in Gk. myth)
telary, *a.* of webs; web-spinning. (L. *tela*, web)
telautograph, *n.* telegraph that reproduces writing. **telautography,** *n.* **telautogram,** *n.* message transmitted by this. (Gk. *tēle*, far; *autos*, self; *graphein*, write)
tele-, *pref.* at a distance, from far off, as in **telephone.** (Gk.)
tele-archics, *n.pl.* art of wireless control of aircraft from a distance. (Gk. *tēle*, far; *archē*, command)
telebarometer, *n.* barometer transmitting its readings to a distance.
teledu, *n.* stinking badger of Java. (native)
telegony, *n.* supposed influence of female's first mate on her offspring by other mates. **telegonic,** *a.* (Gk. *tēle*, far; *gonos*, offspring)
telegraph, *n.* electric apparatus for sending messages to distance by signals; semaphore, signalling by it; telegraph-board.—*v.i.* and *t.* send (message) by telegraph; make, convey by, signals. **t.-board,** *n.* scoreboard with large figures visible across ground. **t.-line, t.-pole, t.-post, t.-wire,** *nn.* forming telegraphic connection. **t.-plant,** *n.* Indian plant whose leaves jerk like semaphore. **telegram,** *n.* message sent by telegraph. **telegraphic,** *a.* of, sent by, telegraph; (of style) compressed by omission of words. **telegraphically,** *adv.* **telegraphese,** *n.* telegraphic style. **telegraphist,** *n.* telegraph operator. **telegraphy,** *n.* use or making of telegraph. (Gk. *tēle*, far; *graphein*, write)
telekinesis, *n.* causing objects to move by non-material means, esp. as spiritualistic phenomenon. **telekinetic,** *a.* (Gk. *tēle*, far; *kinēsis*, movement)
telemark, *n.* swinging turn in skiing. (district in Norway)
telemechanics, *n.pl.* mechanical control from distance by wireless.
telemeter, *n.* instrument for determining distances, range-finder. (Gk. *tēle*, far; *metron*, measure)
teleology, *n.* doctrine of final causes, belief that things happen because of the purpose or design that will be fulfilled by them. **teleologic, teleological,** *aa.* **teleologist,** *n.* (Gk. *telos*, end; *legein*, speak)
teleosaurus, *n.* genus of fossil crocodiles. (Gk. *teleos*, complete; *sauros*, lizard)
teleostean, *a.* of the order of bony fishes. (Gk. *teleos*, complete; *osteon*, bone)
telepathy, *n.* communication between mind and mind otherwise than by the senses, thought-transference. **telepathic,** *a.* **telepathically,** *adv.* **telepathist,** *n.* one who believes in or practises telepathy. **telepathize,** *v.t.* and *i.* influence, communicate, by telepathy. (Gk. *tēle*, far; *pathos*, feeling)
telephone, *n.* apparatus for transmitting speech or sounds to distant hearer, esp. by electricity.—*v.i.* and *t.* speak (to), convey (message), by telephone. **telephonic,** *a.* **telephonically,** *adv.* **telephonist,** *n.* telephone operator. **telephonograph,** *n.* instrument which records telephone messages for later reproduction. **telephony,** *n.* use or making of telephones. (Gk. *tēle*, far; *phōnē*, sound)
telephotography, *n.* photography with telescopic lens; phototelegraphy. **telephotograph,** *n.* **telephotographic, telephoto,** *aa.* (Gk. *tēle*, far)
teleprinter, *n.* apparatus by which typed messages can be transmitted over wire. (Gk. *tēle*, far)
telergy, *n.* supposed force effecting telepathy. (Gk. *tēle*, far+*energy*)
telescope, *n.* optical instrument of tube with lenses making distant objects appear larger.—*v.t.* and *i.* close up, open out, like sections of portable telescope; force, be forced, into one another. **telescopic,** *a.* of, made with, visible only through, telescope; with sections sliding inside one another. **telescopically,** *adv.* **telescopist,** *n.* user of telescope. **telescopy,** *n.* use or making of telescopes. (Gk. *tēle*, far; *skopein*, view)

teleseme, *n.* system of electric signalling with annunciator. (Gk. *tēle*, far; *sēma*, sign)

telestich, *n.* poem in which final letters of lines spell a name. (Gk. *telos*, end; *stichos*, line)

telethermometer, *n.* thermometer transmitting its readings to a distance.

television, *n.* seeing at a distance by wireless. **televise**, *v.t.* transmit by television. **televisor**, *n.* television apparatus. (Gk. *tēle* far. L. *vidēre*, see)

tell, *v.t.* and *i.* (*past, p.p.* **told**) narrate, utter; give account (of); make known, betray secret; make out, distinguish; order; have striking effect; (*arch.*) count. **t. off**, detach for special duty; (*sl.*) reprimand. **t. the tale**, (*sl.*) pitch hard-luck yarn. **t. the world**, (*Amer.*) assert emphatically. **all told**, including all. **teller**, *n.* bank official who pays out money; M.P. who counts votes in House of Commons. **telling**, *a.* having great effect. **telltale**, *n.* sneak, informer; automatic indicator.—*a.* revealing. (O.E. *tellan*)

tellurian, *a.* and *n.* (inhabitant) of the earth. **tellural**, *a.* **tellurion**, *n.* apparatus illustrating earth's motions. (L. *tellus*, earth)

tellurium, *n.* rare brittle lustrous element like sulphur. **telluric, tellurous**, *aa.* (L. *tellus*, earth)

telotype, *n.* telegraph instrument which prints automatically; message printed by it. (Gk. *tēle*, far)

telpher, *n.* electrically propelled light car on overhead cable. **telepherage**, *n.* this system of transport. (Gk. *tēle*, far; *pherein*, carry)

telson, *n.* last joint in abdomen of crustacean. (Gk.=limit)

temenos, *n.* (*pl.* **témenē**) precinct of Greek temple. (Gk.)

temerarious, *a.* reckless, rash. **temerity**, *n.* rashness; audacity. (L. *temere*, rashly)

temp., *prep.* in the time of. (abbr. of L. *tempore*, in the time)

temper, *v.t.* and *i.* mitigate severity of, qualify; moisten and knead (clay); toughen and harden (metal); (*arch.*) blend, compound.—*n.* disposition of mind, mood; anger; composure under provocation; consistency, toughness, got by tempering. **lose, keep, one's t.**, become, not become, angry. **out of t.**, irritable. (L. *temperare*)

tempera, *n.* distemper used in fresco painting. (It.)

temperament, *n.* mental and emotional constitution, disposition; passionate nature; (*mus.*) system of tuning piano etc. so that it can be used in all keys. **temperamental**, *a.* of temperament; moody. (*temper*)

temperance, *n.* avoidance of excess; moderation in use of intoxicants; total abstinence from intoxicants, teetotalism; (*Shake.*) temperature. —*a.* non-alcoholic; aiming at teetotalism. (*temper*)

temperate, *a.* moderate, not extreme; exercising self-restraint, abstemious; of mild temperature; (*Shake.*) chaste. **north, south, t. zone**, between tropic of Cancer and Arctic circle, tropic of Capricorn and Antarctic. (*temper*)

temperature, *n.* degree of heat or cold; (*med.*) internal heat of body, normally 98·4°. **have a t.**, (*colloq.*) be feverish. (*temper*)

tempest, *n.* violent storm; tumult. **tempestuous**, *a.* stormy; turbulent. (L. *tempestas*)

Templar, *n.* member of medieval military religious order of Knights Templars; member of the temperance society of Good Templars; one who has chambers in the Temple in London.

template, same as **templet**.

temple, *n.* place of worship; place regarded as abode of divinity; Christian church. **the T.**, temple of Jehovah at Jerusalem; two Inns of Court in London. (L. *templum*)

temple, *n.* flat part on either side of forehead. (L. *tempora*, temples)

temple, *n.* device for keeping cloth tight on loom. (F.)

templet, *n.* pattern, gauge, mould, used as guide in cutting metal, stone etc.; timber to distribute weight under beam or girder.

tempo, *n.* (*mus.*) rapidity of movement, time. (It.)

temporal, *a.* (*anat.*) of the temple.

temporal, *a.* of, limited by, time; of this life, earthly; secular, lay. **temporality**, *n.* secular possessions, esp. of the Church, (*law*) temporariness. **temporalty**, *n.* laity; temporality. **temporary**, *a.* lasting only for a time, not permanent. **temporize**, *v.i.* act so as to gain time, avoid committing oneself; yield to circumstances, trim. **temporization**, *n.* (L. **tempus**, time)

tempt, *v.t.* try to persuade, esp. to evil; entice, induce; attract, provoke; risk angering; (*arch.*) test, try. **temptation**, *n.* tempting; thing that tempts; attraction, inducement. **tempter**, *n.* (*fem.* **temptress**) one who tempts. **the tempter**, Satan. **tempting**, *a.* attractive. (L. *temptare*)

tempus fugit, time flies. (L.)

ten, *a.* and *n.* one more than nine. (O.E. *tien*)

tenable, *a.* capable of being held, maintained, or defended. **tenability**, *n.* (L. *tenēre*, hold)

tenace, *n.* (*bridge*, *whist*) best and third best (**major t.**) or second and fourth best (**minor t.**) cards of a suit; holding of these. (Sp. *tenaza*, pincers)

tenacious, *a.* grasping firmly; cohesive, adhesive; stubborn, unyielding; (of memory) retentive. **tenacity**, *n.* (L. *tenēre*, hold)

tenaculum, *n.* (*pl.* **tenacula**) surgeon's sharp hook for picking up arteries etc. (L.=holding instrument)

tenaille, tenail, *n.* outwork of fortification in main ditch between two bastions. (F.)

tenant, *n.* person who rents land or house from a landlord; occupant; (*law*) one who possesses real estate. —*v.t.* hold, occupy, as tenant. **tenantable,** *a.* fit to be occupied by a tenant. **tenancy,** *n.* act, period, of holding property as tenant. **tenantry,** *n.* body of tenants. (L. *tenēre,* hold)

tench, *n.* freshwater fish of carp family. (L.L. *tinca*)

tend, *v.t.* and *i.* look after, take care of; attend; (*naut.*) stand by. **tendance,** *n.* (*arch.*) tending, care. (contr. of *attend*)

tend, *v.i.* incline, have tendency; conduce, serve; move, be directed. **tendency,** *n.* inclination, proclivity; aptness to move or act in particular way. **tendentious,** *a.* (of writing etc.) having an underlying purpose, not impartial. (L. *tendere,* stretch)

tender, *n.* one who tends; small ship in attendance on larger one for landing passengers etc.; truck with coal and water attached to railway engine.

tender, *n.* offer; statement of sum for which one will contract to do work or supply goods.—*v.t.* make offer of, present; send in tender (for). **legal t.,** currency that cannot be refused in payment of debt. (L. *tendere,* stretch)

tender, *a.* easily chewed, not tough; easily hurt; soft, delicate; sensitive, susceptible; immature, young, weak; loving, compassionate, considerate; (*naut.*) somewhat crank; (*Shake.*) dear.—*n.* (*Shake.*) regard, care.—*v.t.* (*Shake.*) regard, care for. **t.-hearted,** *a.* easily touched. **tenderfoot,** *n.* newcomer in colonies, greenhorn. **tenderloin,** *n.* (*Amer.*) undercut of sirloin; (*sl.*) amusement district of New York etc. (L. *tener*)

tendon, *n.* cord of fibrous tissue joining muscle to bone etc., sinew. **tendinoús,** *a.* (Gk. *tenōn*)

tendresse, *n.* tender feeling, delicacy. (F.)

tendril, *n.* one of the slender curling shoots by which some climbing plants cling. **tendrillar,** *a.* (L. *tener,* tender)

tenebrae, *n.pl.* (in Roman Catholic Church) matins and lauds for last three days of Holy Week. **tenebrific,** *a.* making darkness. **tenebrous,** *a.* dark, gloomy. **tenebrosity,** *n.* (L.= darkness)

tenement, *n.* part of house or building forming separate dwelling, flat; dwelling-place, abode; tenement-house; (*law*) any kind of permanent property held of another. **t.-house,** *n.* house divided into tenements. **tenemental,** *a.* **tenementary,** *a.* (*law*). (L. *tenēre,* hold)

tenesmus, *n.* straining to void bowels or bladder without effect. (Gk. *teinein,* stretch)

tenet, *n.* principle, belief, dogma. (L.=he holds)

tenfold, *a.* and *adv.* ten times repeated.

tenner, *n.* (*colloq.*) ten-pound note.

tennis, *n.* ancient game for two or four played in walled court by striking ball over net with racket; (also **lawn t.**) game like this played in open. **table t.,** similar game played indoors on table. **t. elbow,** painful affection of arm caused by tennis.

tenon, *n.* projection of piece of wood made to fit into hole (mortise) in other piece.—*v.t.* fit, join, with tenons. **t.-saw,** *n.* small saw for fine work. (L. *tenēre,* hold)

tenor, *n.* settled course; general purport, drift; (*mus.*) highest adult male voice, between bass and alto; singer with, music for, this. (L.)

tenotomy, *n.* operation of cutting tendon. (Gk. *tenōn,* tendon; *temnein,* cut)

tenrec, *n.* insect-eating animal like hedgehog, found in Madagascar. (Malagasy *tràndraka*)

tense, *n.* (*gram.*) form taken by verb to indicate time of action. (L. *tempus,* time)

tense, *a.* tightly stretched; strained, keyed up.—*v.t.* make tense, brace. **tensible,** *a.* capable of being stretched. **tensibility,** *n.* **tensile,** *a.* of tension; tensible. **tensility,** *n.* **tension,** *n.* stretching; tenseness, strain; suppressed excitement; (*mech.*) stress produced by forces pulling against each other (opp. to compression). **tensional,** *a.* **tensity,** *n.* tenseness. (L. *tendere,* stretch)

tenson, *n.* contest in verse between troubadours; subdivision of poem composed for this. (F.)

tensor, *n.* muscle that tightens a part. (L. *tendere,* stretch)

tent, *n,* portable shelter of canvas.—*v.t.* and *i.* cover with, lodge in, tent. **bell t.,** circular kind with pole in middle. **t.-bed,** *n.* bed with arched canopy. **t.-peg,** *n.* one of the pegs fastening down ropes of tent. **t.-pegging,** *n.* cavalry exercise of riding at tent-peg and carrying it off on lance-point. **t.-pole,** *n.* pole supporting tent. **t.-stitch,** *n.* series of parallel diagonal stitches. (L. *tendere,* stretch)

tent, *n.* plug of lint or linen to keep wound etc. open.—*v.t.* dilate with tent. (L. *temptare,* probe)

tent, *n.* a sweet red Spanish wine. (L. *tingere,* dye)

tent, *n.* (*Scot.*) heed, attention.—*v.t.* and *i.* be careful (of). (*intent*)

tente d'abri, light shelter-tent. (F.)

tentacle, *n.* long slender flexible organ

for feeling, holding, or locomotion; feeler. **tentacled, tentaculate, tentaculated,** *aa.* furnished with tentacles. **tentacular,** *a.* of, like, tentacles. (L. *temptare,* feel)

tentative, *a.* experimental, done to feel the way.—*n.* tentative proposal or step. (L. *temptare,* try)

tenter, *n.* frame for stretching cloth to set or dry. **tenterhook,** *n.* hook in this to which cloth is fastened. **on tenterhooks,** in state of suspense. (L. *tendere,* stretch)

tenter, *n.* person in charge of machinery etc. (Scot. *tent*)

tenth, *a.* next after ninth.—*n.* one of ten equal parts. **tenthly,** *adv.* in the tenth place.

tenuous, *a.* fine, slender; thin, rarefied; subtle, over-refined. **tenuity,** *n.* (L. *tenuis*)

tenure, *n.* act of holding property or office; conditions, period, of such holding. **tenurial,** *a.* (L. *tenēre,* hold)

tenuto, a. (*mus.*) sustained. (It.)

tenzon, same as **tenson.**

teocalli, *n.* ancient Mexican temple, us. built on truncated pyramid. (Mex. *teotl,* god; *calli,* house)

tepee, *n.* Red Indian tent, wigwam. (Amer. Ind. *tipi*)

tepefy, *v.t.* and *i.* make, become, tepid. **tepefaction,** *n.* (L. *tepēre,* be lukewarm; *facere,* make)

tephrite, *n.* ash-coloured volcanic rock. (Gk. *tephra,* ashes)

tepid, *a.* slightly warm, lukewarm. **tepidity,** *n.* **tepidarium,** *n.* room of intermediate temperature in Roman baths. (L. *tepēre,* be lukewarm)

ter, adv. three times. (L.)

terai, *n.* wide-brimmed felt hat worn in hot climates. (region of India)

teraph, teraphim, *n.* (*pl.* **teraphim, teraphims, teraphs**) small image used as household oracle by ancient Jews. (Heb.)

terato-, from Gk. *teras,* monster, used in **teratogeny,** *n.* production of monsters, hence **teratogenic,** *a.*; **teratolite,** *n.* kind of clay once supposed to have medicinal properties; **teratology,** *n.* study of animal or plant monstrosities or abnormalities, hence **teratological,** *a.*, **teratologist,** *n.*

terbium, *n.* a rare metallic element. (*Ytterby* in Sweden)

terce, same as **tierce.**

tercel, *n.* male falcon. (L. *tertius,* third, from belief that every third egg produced a male)

tercentenary, *n.* and *a.* (of) the three hundredth anniversary. **tercentennial,** *a.* lasting, occurring every, three hundred years.—*n.* tercentenary. (*ter*; *centenary*)

tercet, *n.* triplet. (L. *tertius,* third)

terebinth, *n.* tree yielding turpentine. **terebinthine,** *a.* of terebinth; (also **terebic**) of turpentine. **terebene,** *n.* disinfectant made from turpentine. (Gk. *terebinthos*)

terebra, *n.* (*pl.* **terebrae**) boring egg-depositing organ of some insects. **terebrate,** *a.* having a terebra. (L. =borer.)

teredo, *n.* ship-worm, mollusc that attacks submerged timber. (Gk. *terēdōn*)

tergal, *a.* of the back. (L. *tergum,* back)

tergeminate, *a.* (of leaf) having a pair of leaflets at base and on each of two secondary leaf-stalks. (L. *ter,* thrice; *geminus,* double)

tergiversate, *v.i.* shuffle, be evasive; change sides, apostatize. **tergiversation, tergiversator,** *nn.* (L. *tergum,* back; *vertere,* turn)

term, *n.* limit; limited period; period during which lawcourts sit, school is open etc.; fixed day for payment of rent, quarter-day; word, expression, used in definite sense; (*algebra*) item of a compound quantity; (*logic*) any of the subjects or predicates in a syllogism; (*pl.*) conditions, stipulations; personal relations, footing; mode of expression, phraseology; charge, fee.—*v.t.* designate, call. **bring to tt.,** compel to accept conditions. **come to tt.,** conclude agreement; submit. **in tt. of,** in the language peculiar to. **tt. of reference,** points referred for decision, scope of inquiry. (*terminus*)

termagant, *n.* quarrelsome woman, scold.—*a.* turbulent, shrewish. **termagancy,** *n.* (It. *trivigante*)

terminable, *a.* able, liable, to be terminated. **terminability,** *n.*

terminal, *a.* at or forming an end; of, done, each term.—*n.* terminal part, extremity; (*electr.*) either end of conducting circuit of dynamo etc.; (*Amer.*) railway terminus. **terminally,** *adv.* at the end; finally; every term. (*terminus*)

terminate, *v.t.* and *i.* bring, come, to an end; bound; end (in).—*a.* coming to an end. **termination,** *n.* ending; last syllable of word; (*Shake.*) expression. **terminational, terminative, terminatory,** *aa.* **terminator,** *n.* one who terminates; (*astron.*) dividing line between light and dark part of moon etc. (*terminus*)

terminer, see **oyer.**

terminism, *n.* doctrine that each man has only a limited time to obtain divine grace; nominalism. **terminist,** *n.* (*terminus*)

terminology, *n.* set of words peculiar to a science or art, system of technical terms; nomenclature. **terminological,** *a.* **terminological inexactitude,** (*joc.*) lie. (L. *terminus,* limit. Gk. *legein,* speak)

terminus, *n.* (*pl.* **termini, terminuses**) station at end of railway line; farthest point to which thing extends; bust ending in square pillar. *t. ad quem, a quo,* goal, starting-point, of argument or policy. (L.=limit)

termite, *n.* ant-like insect, white ant. **termitary, termitarium,** *nn.* termites' nest. (L. *termes*)

termly, *a.* and *adv.* (occurring, done) every term.

termor, *n.* (*law*) one who holds estate for a term of years.

tern, *n.* set of three.—*a.* ternate. **ternary, ternal,** *aa.* consisting of three; proceeding in threes. **ternate,** *a.* arranged in threes; (*bot.*) having three leaflets. (L. *terni*, three each)

tern, *n.* sea-bird like gull.

terne, *n.* (us. **t.-plate**) an inferior tinplate alloyed with lead.

ternery, *n.* breeding-place of terns.

Terpsichorē, *n.* muse of dancing. **Terpsichorean,** *a.* (Gk.)

terra, *n.* earth. **t. firma,** dry land. *t. incognita,* unknown region. (L.)

terrace, *n.* raised flat space, shelf in hillside; row of houses; (*geol.*) raised beach.—*v.t.* form into, furnish with, terrace. (*terra*)

terra-cotta, *n.* a hard unglazed pottery; work of art in this; its brownish-red colour. (It.=baked earth)

terrain, *n.* tract of land, esp. as scene of event or operations. (F.)

terramara, *n.* earthy deposit containing bones etc., useful as fertilizer; deposit of prehistoric remains. (It.)

terraneous, *a.* growing on land. (*terra*)

terrapin, *n.* kinds of freshwater tortoise.

terraqueous, *a.* consisting of land and water. (L. *terra*, land; *aqua*, water)

terrene, *a.* consisting of earth; terrestrial. (*terra*)

terrestrial, *a.* of the earth (opp. to celestial); of this world; living on land. (*terra*)

terret, *n.* one of the rings or loops on harness-pad through which driving-reins pass. (O.F. *toret*)

terrible, *a.* causing, fitted to cause, terror; awful, frightful; (*colloq.*) very great. **terribly,** *adv.*

terricolous, *a.* living on or in the earth. (L. *terra*, earth; *colere*, inhabit)

terrier, *n.* kinds of active and hardy small dog. (L. *terra*, earth, because orig. used for burrowing)

terrier, *n.* book setting forth extent and boundaries of landed estate. (L. *terrarius* liber, book of lands)

Terrier, *n.* (*sl.*) man of Territorial Force. (abbr.)

terrific, *a.* striking terror, appalling; of tremendous intensity. **terrifically,** *adv.* to a terrific extent. **terrify,** *v.t.* frighten greatly. (L. *terrēre*, terrify; *facere*, make)

terrigenous, *a.* produced by the earth. (L. *terra*, earth; *gignere*, beget)

terrine, *n.* earthenware jar containing table delicacy and sold with it. (F.)

territ, same as **terret.**

territory, *n.* large tract of land; region under jurisdiction of ruler or state: part of a country separately organized but not admitted to full state rights; sphere. **territorial,** *a.* of territory; limited to a district.—*n.* man of **Territorial Army** or **Force,** British home defence force raised on local basis. **territorialism,** *n.* system of church polity which gives the ruler of a country control of its ecclesiastical affairs. **territorialize,** *v.t.* enlarge by addition of territory; reduce to status of territory. (L. *territorium*)

terror, *n.* extreme fear; person or thing inspiring this; (*colloq.*) pest, nuisance. **king of tt.,** death. **reign of t.,** period of ruthless oppression, esp. that of 1793–4 in French Revolution. **t.-stricken,** *a.* **terrorism,** *n.* systematic intimidation. **terrorist,** *n.* **terroristic,** *a.* **terrorize,** *v.t.* coerce by terror, intimidate. **terrorization,** *n.* (L.)

terry, *n.* pile fabric with uncut loops.

terse, *a.* brief and forcible, neatly concise, pithy. (L. *tergere*, wipe)

tertius, *a.* third of the name. *tertium quid,* third something, compromise, hybrid. **tertial,** *n.* flight-feather of third row on wing. **tertian,** *a.* and *n.* (fever, disease) with paroxysms every alternate day. **tertiary,** *a.* of the third degree, order, or rank; (*geol.*) of the era following the Mesozoic, Cainozoic.—*n.* Tertiary era; member of third order in monastic system; tertial. (L.=third)

tervalent, *a.* having a valency of three.

terza rima, triplets of ten or eleven syllables rhymed aba bcb cdc etc., the metre of Dante's 'Divina Commedia.' *terzetto,* *n.* composition for three voices. (It.)

tessellate, *v.t.* form of, pave with, tesserae; chequer. **tessellation,** *n.* mosaic work. **tessellar,** *a.* tessellated. **tessera,** *n.* (*pl.* **tesserae**) small square block used in mosaic. **tesseral,** *a.* (Gk. *tessares*, four)

tessitura, *n.* range, compass, of voice-part. (It.)

test, *n.* trial to ascertain quality, critical examination; means of trial, ordeal; standard, touchstone; (*chem.*) reagent, use of this to detect constituent of compound; (*colloq.*) test match.—*v.t.* make trial of; try severely, tax; refine (metal); (*chem.*) examine by use of reagents. **T. Act,** limited public office to members of Church of England. **t. case,** case chosen for trial in order to decide question affecting many others. **t. match,** cricket match of international series. **t.-tube,** *n.* small glass tube used by chemist. (L. *testum*, earthen pot)

test, *n.* shell, hard covering, of shellfish etc. **testaceous,** *a.* having test;

of shells or shell-fish; (*bot.*, *zool.*) brick-red. **testacean**, *a.* and *n.* testaceous (mollusc), shell-fish. **testaceology**, *n.* zoology of testaceans. (L. *testa*, potsherd)

testable, *a.* capable of witnessing; devisable by will. (*testate*)

testacy, *n.* being testate.

testament, *n.* will; (*colloq.*) copy of New Testament. **Old, New, T.,** divisions of the Bible. **testamentary**, *a.* of, by, in, a will. **testate**, *a.* leaving a will.—*n.* person who dies testate. **testator**, *n.* (*fem.* **testatrix**) maker of will. (L. *testis*, witness)

testamur, *n.* certificate that one has passed university examination. (L. =we testify)

tester, *n.* one who tests.

tester, *n.* canopy over a bed. (O.F. *teste*, head)

tester, *n.* (*arch.*) sixpence. **testern**, *v.t.* (*Shake.*) tip. (O.F. *teste*, head)

testicle, *n.* either of two male reproductive glands. **testicular**, *a.* **testiculate**, *a.* having, shaped like, testicles. (L. *testis*, testicle+dim.)

testify, *v.i.* and *t.* bear witness (to), give evidence (of); declare, affirm. (L. *testis*, witness; *facere*, make)

testimonial, *n.* certificate of character or qualifications; gift forming token of respect or gratitude for services. **testimonialize**, *v.t.* present with testimonial. (*testimony*)

testimony, *n.* evidence; statement under oath; solemn declaration or protest; the tables of the Mosaic law; (*pl.*) divine revelation, the Scriptures.—*v.t.* (*Shake.*) attest, prove. (L. *testis*, witness)

testril, (*Shake.*) same as **tester**.

testudo, *n.* screen of overlapping shields used by ancient Roman besieging troops. **testudinal**, *a.* of tortoise. **testudinarious**, *a.* like tortoise-shell, mottled. **testudinate**, *a.* arched like shell of tortoise. (L.=tortoise)

testy, *a.* irritable, short-tempered. (O.F. *teste*, head)

tetanus, *n.* disease marked by muscular spasms, lockjaw. **tetanic**, *a.* of, like, tetanus.—*n.* medicine acting on muscles through nerves, e.g. strychnine. **tetanize**, *v.t.* cause tetanus or tetanic contractions in. **tetanization**, *n.* (Gk. *teinein*, stretch)

tetchy, *a.* easily put out, peevish.

tête-à-tête, *adv.* and *a.* (of two people) together in private, confidential.—*n.* confidential talk, private meeting. (F.=head to head)

tether, *n.* rope by which grazing animal is kept from straying; extent of endurance or resources.—*v.t.* confine by tether.

tetra-, from Gk. *tessares*, four, used in **tetrachord**, *n.* scale of four notes: **tetrad**, *n.* number four, group of four; **tetradactyl**, *a.* and *n.* four-toed (animal); **tetragon**, *n.* four-sided plane figure, hence **tetragonal**, *a.*; **tetragram**, *n.* word of four letters, quadrilateral. **tetragrammaton**, *n.* four letters (JHWH) forming Hebrew name for God us. written Jehovah; **tetrahedron**, *n.* solid with four faces, triangular pyramid, hence **tetrahedral**, *a.*; **tetralogy**, *n.* series of four connected dramas; **tetramerous**, *a.* (*bot.*, *zool.*) with four parts or four joints; **tetrameter**, *n.* verse of four measures, each containing one or two feet according to the metre; **tetrapod**, *a.* and *n.* four-footed (insect); **tetrapody**, *n.* verse of four feet; **tetrarch**, *n.* Roman governor of fourth part of province, subordinate ruler, **tetrarchate, tetrarchy**, *nn.* his office or jurisdiction; **tetrastich**, *n.* stanza of four lines; **tetrastyle**, *a.* and *n.* four-pillared (building); **tetrasyllable**, *n.* word of four syllables, hence **tetrasyllabic**, *a.*; **tetravalent**, *a.* having valency of four.

tetter, *n.* skin disease, ringworm, eczema etc.—*v.t.* (*Shake.*) affect with this. (O.E. *teter*)

teuch, teugh, *Scot.* form of **tough.**

teuchat, teuchit, *n.* (*Scot.*) pewit.

Teuton, *n.* member of Germanic race; German. **Teutonic**, *a.* of the Germanic race, incl. Germans, Scandinavians, English, etc.; of the Germans.—*n.* primitive Germanic language. **teutonism, teutonicism**, *nn.* Teutonic idiom or custom; germanism. **teutonize**, *v.t.* render Teutonic; germanize. **teutonization**, *n.* **Teutophil, Teutophobe**, *nn.* one who admires, fears, the Teutons or Germans. (L. *Teutones*, Teutons)

tew, same as **taw.**

text, *n.* actual words of book, document, or passage, apart from notes or illustrations; verse or short passage of Scripture, esp. as subject of sermon; theme of discussion; (also **t. hand**) large style of handwriting. **textbook**, *n.* manual of instruction; book set for study. (L. *texere*, weave)

textile, *a.* woven; of weaving.—*n.* woven fabric. (L. *texere*, weave)

textual, *a.* of, in, based on, the text of an author; word for word. **textualist**, *n.* one who adheres rigidly to the letter of a text; ready quoter of scriptural texts. **textualism**, *n.* literalism.

texture, *n.* way in which threads of a fabric are arranged; arrangement of parts, structure. **textural**, *a.* (L. *texere*, weave)

-th, *n.suf.* expressing state or condition, as in **truth, youth.** (O.E.)

-th, *suf.* forming ordinal number from cardinal, as in **tenth.** (O.E. *-tha*)

thairm, *n.* (*Scot.*) intestine, fiddle-string.

thakur, thakoor, *n.* Indian title of respect, master. (Hind. *ṭhākur*)

thalamite, *n.* oarsman of lowest bank in trireme. (Gk. *thalamos*, hold)

thalamus, *n.* (*pl.* **thalami**) part of brain from which optic nerve springs; (*bot.*) receptacle of flower. (Gk. *thalamos*, chamber)

thalassic, *a.* of the sea. **thalassocracy,** *n.* sovereignty of the seas. **thalassocrat,** *n.* **thalassography,** *n.* study of the seas, oceanography. **thalassographer,** *n.* **thalassometer,** *n.* tide-gauge. **thalassotherapy,** *n.* medical treatment by sea-baths. (Gk. *thalassa*, sea)

thaler, *n.* old silver coin of Germany, worth about 3*s*. (G.)

Thalia, *n.* muse of comedy and pastoral poetry. **Thalian,** *a.* (Gk. *Thaleia*)

thallium, *n.* rare white metallic element. **thallic, thallous,** *aa.* (*thallus*, from green line in its spectrum)

thallus, *n.* (*pl.* **thalli**) stemless rootless body of **thallophyte,** *n.* kinds of lower plants incl. fungi and lichens. (Gk. *thallos*, young shoot)

than, *adv.* and *prep.* introducing second part of comparison. (orig. = *then*)

thanat(o)-, from Gk. *thanatos*, death, used in **thanatoid,** *a.* death-like, deadly; **thanatology,** *n.* scientific study of death; **thanatophobia,** *n.* morbid fear of death; **thanatopsis,** *n* view of, meditation on, death; **thanatosis,** *n.* necrosis; mimicry of death for protective purposes.

thane, *n.* holder of lands by military service in Anglo-Saxon times, ranking between nobility and freeman. **thanedom, thanehood, thaneship,** *nn.* (O.E. *thegn*)

thank, *v.t.* express gratitude to.—*n.pl.* expression of gratitude, grateful acknowledgment. **tt. to,** owing to. **no, t. you,** polite form of refusal. **t.-offering,** *n.* gift made in gratitude. **thankful,** *a.* grateful; (*Shake.*) worthy of thanks. **thankless,** *a.* not feeling or arousing gratitude; unprofitable. **thanksgiving,** *n.* act of rendering thanks, esp. for divine goodness. **Thanksgiving Day,** (*Amer.*) day set apart for this each year. **thankworthy,** *a.* deserving thanks. (O.E. *thanc*, thanks)

thar, *n.* goat-antelope of Nepal. (native)

that, *pron.* and *a.* (*demonstrative, pl.* **those**) the (one) there or then.—*pron.* (*relative*) who or which.—*conj.* introducing noun clause or adverbial clause of purpose or consequence. **t. far, t. much,** as far, much, as that. (O.E. *thæt*)

thatch, *n.* roofing of straw or rushes; (*colloq.*) hair of head.—*v.t.* cover with thatch. (O.E. *thæc*)

thaumat(o)-, from Gk. *thauma*, wonder, used in **thaumatology,** *n.* science of wonder-working; **thaumatrope,** *n.* kind of zoetrope; **thaumaturge, thaumaturgist,** *nn.* wonder-worker, magician, hence **thaumaturgic, thaumaturgical,** *aa.*, **thaumaturgy,** *n.*

thaw, *v.i.* and *t.* (of ice or snow) melt; (of weather) stop freezing; (of person) throw off reserve, become genial. —*n.* process of thawing. (O.E. *thawian*)

the, *a.* (termed the definite article) denoting a particular person or thing. —*adv.* by how much, by so much. (O.E.)

theandric, *a.* of, based on, the union of divine and human nature in Christ. (Gk. *theos*, god; *anēr*, man)

theanthropic, theanthropical, *aa.* both divine and human. **theanthropism,** *n.* belief in the embodiment of God in human form. **theanthropist,** *n.* (Gk. *theos*, god; *anthrōpos*, man)

thearchy, *n.* theocracy; government by, system of, gods. (Gk. *theos*, god; *archē*, rule)

theatre, *n.* place where plays are performed; room for lectures or surgical demonstrations; scene of action; dramatic literature. **t.-goer,** *n.* frequenter of plays. **theatrical,** *a.* of, suited to, the theatre; designed for effect, showy, affected.—*n.pl.* dramatic performance. **theatricality,** *n.* **theatricalize,** *v.t.* (Gk. *thea*, spectacle)

theca, *n.* (*pl.* **thecae**) spore-case, capsule; sheath. (Gk. *thēkē*)

thee, *v.i.* (*Spens.*) prosper, thrive. (O.E. *théon*)

thee, see **thou.**

theft, *n.* act of stealing; thing stolen. (*thief*)

thegn, same as **thane.**

theic, *n.* tea-drunkard. **theine,** *n.* caffeine. **theism,** *n.* morbid condition from excessive tea-drinking. (Mod. L. *thea*, tea)

their, theirs, see **they.**

theism, *n.* belief in the existence of God, without the denial of revelation characteristic of deism. **theist,** *n.* adherent of theism. **theistic, theistical,** *aa.* (Gk. *theos*, god)

them, see **they.**

theme, *n.* subject of discourse, topic; school essay; (*gram.*) stem of verb or noun; (*mus.*) leading melody in piece. **t. song,** recurring melody identified with one of the characters in musical play. **thematic,** *a.* **thematically,** *adv.* (Gk. *tithenai*, set)

Themis, *n.* Greek goddess of law. (Gk.)

themselves, *pron.* emphatic and refl. form of **they.**

then, *adv.* at that time; after that, next; in that case, therefore.—*a.* then-existing.—*n.* that time. (O.E. *thonne*)

then, (*Shake.*) form of **than.**

thenar, *n.* palm of hand, sole of foot. (Gk.)

thence, *adv.* from that place or time; for that reason; elsewhere. **thenceforth, thenceforward,** *advv.* from that time on. (O.E. *thanon*)

theobroma, *n.* kinds of tropical tree

incl. cacao. (Gk. *theos*, god; *brōma*, food)

theocentric, *a.* considering God as centre of the universe.

theocracy, *n.* government, state, in which God is the sovereign and religion the law. **theocrat,** *n.* ruler, subject, under theocracy. **theocratic, theocratical,** *aa.* (Gk. *theos*, god; *kratos*, power)

theocrasy, *n.* union of soul with God through contemplation; worship of a mixture of gods. (Gk. *theos*, god; *krasis*, mixture)

theodicy, *n.* vindication of divine justice in permitting existence of evil. (Gk. *theos*, god; *dikē*, right)

theodolite, *n.* surveyor's instrument for measuring angles.

theogony, *n.* genealogy of the gods; poem on this. **theogonic,** *a.* **theogonist,** *n.* (Gk. *theos*, god; *gonos*, offspring)

theology, *n.* science treating of God and His relation to man; science or system of religion. **theologian,** *n.* person learned in theology. **theological,** *a.* of, in, for, the study of theology. **theologize,** *v.t.* and *i.* treat theologically; indulge in theological speculations. **theologue,** *n.* (*arch.*) theologian. (Gk. *theos*, god; *legein*, speak)

theomachy, *n.* battle with or among the gods. (Gk. *theos*, god; *machē*, battle)

theomania, *n.* delusion that one is God; religious insanity. **theomaniac,** *n.* (Gk. *theos*, god+*mania*)

theomorphic, *a.* in the form of a god, godlike. (Gk. *theos*, god; *morphē*, form)

theopathy, *n.* mystical religious experience. (Gk. *theos*, god; *pathos*, suffering)

theophany, *n.* appearance, manifestation, of God to man. **theophanic,** *a.* (Gk. *theos*, god; *phainesthai*, appear)

theopneusty, *n.* divine inspiration. **theopneustic,** *a.* (Gk. *theos*, god; *pnein*, breathe)

theorbo, *n.* (*pl.* **theorbos**) large double-necked lute. (It. *tiorba*)

theorem, *n.* principle established by reasoning; (*math.*) proposition to be proved; algebraical rule. **theorematic, theorematical,** *aa.* **theorematist,** *n.* (*theory*)

theoric, *a.* of, for, public spectacles in ancient Greece. (Gk. *thea*, spectacle)

theory, *n.* supposition to account for something; view held; system of abstract principles of a science or art; speculation as opposed to practice. **theoretic, theoretical,** *aa.* of or based on theory, not facts; concerned with knowledge but not with its application. **theoretics,** *n.pl.* speculative parts of a science. **theoretician,** *n.* **theoric,** *n.* (*Shake.*) theory. **theorize,** *v.i.* form, propound, a theory. **theorization, theorist,** *nn.* (Gk. *theōrein*, contemplate)

theosophy, *n.* any mystical philosophy professing to attain knowledge of God by spiritual ecstasy or deductive speculation, esp. that of modern school following Buddhist theories and claiming to teach the essential truth of which all religions are expressions. **theosophic, theosophical, theosophistical,** *aa.* **theosophist, theosopher,** *nn.* adherent of theosophy. **theosophize,** *v.i.* (Gk. *theos*, god; *sophia*, wisdom)

therapeutic, *a.* of the art of healing, curative.—*n.pl.* curative branch of medicine. **therapeutist,** *n.* **therapy,** *n.* curative treatment. (Gk. *therapeuein*, attend)

there, *adv.* in or to that place or point. —*n.* that place. **get t.,** (*sl.*) succeed. **thereabout, thereabouts,** *adv.* near that place, time, or amount. **thereafter,** *adv.* after that; according to that. **thereanent,** *adv.* (*Scot.*) concerning that. **thereat,** *adv.* at that; at that place; on account of that. **thereaway,** *adv.* (*Scot.*) thence; in those parts. **thereby,** *adv.* by that means. **therefor,** *adv.* (*arch.*) for that. **therefore,** *adv.* for that reason, accordingly, consequently. **therefrom,** *adv.* (*arch.*) from that or it. **therein,** *adv.* (*arch.*) in that place; in that particular. **thereinafter,** *adv.* later in the same document. **thereof,** *adv.* (*arch.*) of that or it. **thereon,** *adv.* (*arch.*) on that or it. **thereout,** *adv.* (*arch.*) out from that or it. **thereto,** *adv.* (*arch.*) to that place; moreover. **thereunto,** *adv.* (*arch.*) to that or it. **thereupon,** *adv.* upon that; in consequence of, immediately after, that. **therewith,** *adv.* (*arch.*) with that; thereupon. **therewithal,** *adv.* (*arch.*) besides; therewith. (O.E. *thǣr*)

theriac, *n.* antidote to poisonous bites. (Gk. *thērion*, wild beast)

theri(o)-, from Gk. *thērion*, wild beast, used in **therianthropic,** *a.* of, worshipping, beings represented in combined human and animal form, hence **therianthropism,** *n.*; **theriatrics,** *n.pl.* veterinary medicine; **theriomorphic, theriomorphous,** *aa.* having animal form; **theriotomy,** *n.* anatomy of animals.

therm, *n.* British thermal unit (*abbr.* **B.Th.U.**) amount of heat required to raise 1 lb. of water at maximum density through 1° Fahr.; (as measure of gas-supply) 100,000 British thermal units. **thermae,** *n.pl.* ancient Roman baths. **thermal, thermic,** *aa.* of, due to, heat. **thermantidote,** *n.* apparatus for cooling the air. **thermion,** *n.* ion emitted by incandescent substance. **thermionic,** *a.* **thermionic valve,** appliance converting wireless waves into vibrations audible in wireless set. **thermite, thermit,** *n.* aluminium powder mixed with a metal oxide, giving out tremendous heat when ignited. (Gk. *thermos*, hot)

thermo-, from Gk. *thermos*, hot, used in **thermobarometer,** *n.* apparatus for measuring atmospheric pressure by the boiling-point of water; **thermodynamics,** *n.pl.* science of relationship between heat and mechanical energy; **thermoelectricity,** *n.* electricity produced by difference of temperature; **thermoelectrometer,** *n.* instrument for determining heating-power of electric current; **thermogenesis,** *n.* production of heat, esp. in human body; **thermogram,** *n.* record made by **thermograph,** *n.* self-registering thermometer; **thermology,** *n.* science of heat; **thermolysis,** *n.* disintegration by heat, loss of body heat; **thermometer,** *n.* instrument for measuring temperature, hence **thermometric, thermometrical,** *aa.*, **thermometry,** *n.*; **thermomotive,** *a.* of motion produced by heat; **thermos (flask),** proprietary name for vacuum flask; **thermostat,** *n.* apparatus for automatically regulating temperature, hence **thermostatic,** *a.*; **thermostatics,** *n.pl.* theory of the equilibrium of heat; **thermotherapy,** *n.* medical treatment by heat.

theroid, *a.* like a wild animal. **therology,** *n.* science of mammals. (Gk. *thēr*, wild beast)

thesaurus, *n.* (*pl.* **thesauri**) treasury (of knowledge etc.); lexicon, cyclopaedia. (Gk. *thēsauros*, treasure)

these, see **this.**

thesis, *n.* (*pl.* **theses**) proposition that one offers to prove; dissertation, esp. one presented for degree; unaccented syllable in foot. (Gk. *tithenai*, place)

Thespian, *a.* of drama or acting. —*n.* actor. (*Thespis*, founder of Greek drama)

theurgy, *n.* supernatural intervention in human affairs; art of securing this, magic worked by means of it. **theurgic, theurgical,** *aa.* **theurgist,** *n.* magician. (Gk. *theos*, god; *ergon*, work)

thews, *n.pl.* sinews, muscles; robustness, vigour; (*Spens.*) qualities, characteristics. **thewed, thewless, thewy,** *aa.* (O.E. *théaw*, habit)

they, *pron.* (*objective* **them,** *possessive* **their, theirs**) plural of **he, she,** or **it.** (O.N. *their*)

thick, *a.* having considerable thickness, not thin; of specified thickness; set closely, packed (with); dense, of stiff consistency; dull, stupid; (of voice) indistinct; (*sl.*) intimate.—*n.* thick or crowded part.—*adv.* thickly. **a bit t.,** (*sl.*) more than can be put up with. **lay it on t.,** flatter extravagantly. **t. ear,** (*sl.*) one swollen by blow. **t. 'un,** (*sl.*) sovereign. **through t. and thin,** in all circumstances. **t.-eyed, t.-sighted,** *aa.* (*Shake.*) dim-sighted. **t.-skinned,** *a.* insensitive. **t.-skulled, t.-witted,** *aa.* stupid. **thicken,** *v.t.* and *i.* make, become, thick or thicker. **thicket,** *n.* thick growth of shrubs and trees. **thickhead,** *n.* blockhead. **thickly,** *adv.* densely; indistinctly; in rapid succession. **thickness,** *n.* dimension through a thing at right angles to length and breadth; state of being thick; layer of material. **thickset,** *a.* heavy and sturdy, stocky; close-grown.—*n.* thickset hedge. (O.E. *thicce*)

thief, *n.* (*pl.* **thieves**) one who steals. **thieve,** *v.i.* and *t.* be a thief; steal. **thievery,** *n.* theft. **thievish,** *a.* given to stealing. (O.E. *théof*)

thieveless, *a.* (*Scot.*) spiritless; cold; shy.

thigh, *n.* thick part of leg above knee. (O.E. *théoh*)

thill, *n.* shaft of cart. **t.-horse, thiller,** *nn.* shaft-horse.

thimble, *n.* small cap to protect tip of finger when sewing. **thimbleful,** *n.* very small quantity. **thimblerig,** *n.* sharper's sleight-of-hand trick in which onlookers are invited to bet which of three thimbles covers pea. —*v.i.* play this. **thimblerigger,** *n.* (O.E. *thúma*, thumb)

thin, *a.* of little thickness; slender, lean; sparse, scattered; weak, lacking body; rarefied; (of voice) shrill; (of excuse) flimsy.—*v.t.* and *i.* make, become, thin or thinner. **t. out,** remove some to give the rest room. **t.-skinned,** *a.* sensitive, touchy. (O.E. *thynne*)

thine, see **thou.**

Thing, *n.* Icelandic parliament. (O.N.)

thing, *n.* any object of thought; material object; object of pity or contempt; (*pl.*) belongings, clothes. **the t.,** what is right or conventional. **know a t. or two,** be shrewd. **make a good t. of,** extract profit from. **thingummy, thingamy, thingumajig, thingumbob,** *nn.* thing or person whose name one forgets. (O.E.)

think, *v.i.* and *t.* (*past, p.p.* **thought**) exercise mind; reflect, consider; hold the opinion, judge; conceive, imagine; intend; (*Shake.*) have despondent thoughts. **t. better of,** reconsider. **t. badly, little, of,** have low opinion of. **t. much, well, of,** have high opinion of. **t. nothing of,** make light of. **t. of,** (*arch.*) **on,** consider, contemplate; hit upon. **t. out,** devise; solve. **t. over,** reflect on. **thinker,** *n.* philosopher. **thinking,** *a.* reasonable; reflective. (O.E. *thencan*)

third, *a.* next after second.—*n.* one of three equal parts. **t. degree,** (*Amer.*) severe cross-examination or treatment used to extort confession from prisoner. **t. man,** (*cricket*) fielder between point and short slip.

t.-rate, *a.* third in order of merit; inferior. **thirdly,** *adv.* in the third place. (*three*)

thirdborough, *n.* (*Shake.*) constable.

thirl, *v.t.* (*Scot.*) bind, subject. (*thrall*)

thirst, *n.* sensation caused by want of drink; desire for drink; drought; craving.—*v.i.* crave (for); (*arch.*) be thirsty. **thirsty,** *a.* feeling or causing thirst; parched; eager (for). (O.E. *thurst*)

thirteen, *a.* and *n.* three and ten. **thirteenth,** *a.* and *n.* **thirty,** *a.* and *n.* three times ten. **thirtieth,** *a.* and *n.* (*three*)

this, *a.* and *pron.* (*pl.* **these**) the (one) here or now. **thisness,** *n.* quality of being this. (O.E.)

thistle, *n.* purple-flowered prickly-leaved plant, the national emblem of Scotland. **Order of the T.,** a Scottish order of knighthood. **thistledown,** *n.* down on seeds of thistle. **thistly,** *a.* (O.E. *thistel*)

thither, *adv.* (*arch.*) to that place. **thitherward, thitherwards,** *adv.* (O.E. *thider*)

thlipsis, *n.* (*med.*) constriction of blood-vessel, esp. by external compression. (Gk. *thlibein*, press)

tho, *adv.* (*Spens.*) then. (O.E. *thá*)

tho', same as **though.**

thole, *n.* (us. **t.-pin**) one of two pegs between which oar works, pin of rowlock. (O.E. *thol*)

thole, *v.t.* (*arch.*) endure, undergo; tolerate, permit. (O.E. *tholian*)

thong, *n.* strip of leather, strap.—*v.t.* provide, strike, with thong. (O.E. *thwang*)

thorax, *n.* (*pl.* **thoraces**) part of body between neck and abdomen, chest. **thoracic,** *a.* (Gk.)

thorite, *n.* a black mineral. **thorium,** *n.* a radioactive metallic element. (*Thor*, Norse god)

thorn, *n.* prickle on plant, spine; kinds of prickly plant; Old English letter þ=th. **on tt.,** very uneasy. **t. in one's side,** constant source of annoyance. **thornbill, thorntail,** *nn.* kinds of humming-bird. **thorny,** *a.* full of thorns; difficult, painful; ticklish. (O.E.)

thorough, *a.* complete; unqualified.—*adv.* and *prep.* (*arch.*) through. **t.-bass,** *n.* bass part with figures over notes to indicate the harmony to be played to each; science of harmony. **t.-going,** *a.* uncompromising, out-and-out. **t.-paced,** *a.* practised, complete. **thoroughbred,** *a.* pure-bred; high-spirited, graceful; (of horse) of pedigree recorded for some generations in the stud-book.—*n.* thoroughbred animal or person. **thoroughfare,** *n.* road, passage, open at both ends. (=*through*)

thorp, thorpe, *n.* village, hamlet. (O.E.)

those, see **that.**

thou, *pron.* (*arch.*; *objective* **thee,** *possessive* **thy, thine**; *pl.* **ye,** *objective* **you**) 2nd personal pronoun, the person addressed. (O.E. *thú*)

though, *conj.* in spite of the fact that; even if.—*adv.* (*colloq.*) all the same, nevertheless. **as t., as if.** (M.E. *thogh*)

thought, see **think.**

thought, *n.* act, product, of thinking; reflection; faculty of reason; idea, conception; consideration, care; (*Shake.*) sorrow, melancholy. **on second tt.,** after thinking it over. **with a t.,** (*Shake.*) in an instant. **t.-executing,** *a.* (*Shake.*) swift as thought in operation. **t.-reading,** *n.* divining another's thought. **t.-reader,** *n.* **t.-transference,** *n.* telepathy. **thoughtful,** *a.* given to thought, pensive; showing original thought; mindful of others, considerate. **thoughtless,** *a.* heedless, careless; inconsiderate, unfeeling. (*think*)

thousand, *a.* and *n.* ten hundred; very large number. **one in a t.,** very exceptional. **thousandfold,** *a.* and *adv.* **thousandth,** *a.* last of a thousand.—*n.* one of a thousand equal parts. (O.E. *thúsend*)

thowless, *a.* (*Scot.*) pithless; lazy. (*thew*)

thrall, *n.* slave, bondman; bondage.—*v.t.* enslave.—*a.* (*arch.*) enslaved. **thraldom, thralldom,** *n.* bondage. (O.N. *thræll*)

thrang, *a.* (*Scot.*) thronged; **busy;** intimate. (*throng*)

thranite, *n.* oarsman of uppermost bank in trireme. (Gk. *thranos*, bench)

thrapple, *n.* (*Scot.*) windpipe.

thrash, *v.t.* beat, flog; plunge, toss; thresh; (*colloq.*) defeat. **t. out,** discuss thoroughly. **thrasher,** *n.* kind of shark; American thrush. (O.E. *therscan*)

thrasonical, *a.* boastful. (*Thraso*, name in play by Terence)

thrave, *n.* (*Scot.*) bundle; twenty-four sheaves of grain, making two stooks.

thraw, *v.t.* and *i.* (*Scot.*) twist, wrench; writhe; contradict. **heads and tt.,** side by side with head of one by feet of the other. **thrawn,** *a.* twisted; perverse, contrary.

thread, *n.* fine cord used for sewing; filament; spiral part of screw; train of thought.—*v.t.* pass thread through eye of (needle); string (beads); pick (one's way), go cautiously along. **t. and thrum,** all alike, good and bad. **threadbare,** *a.* with nap worn off, shabby; trite, hackneyed. **threaden,** *a.* (*Shake.*) made of thread. **threadworm,** *n.* thread-like worm, esp. parasitic kind. **thready,** *a.* made of, like, thread; thin, reedy; ropy. (O.E. *thrǽd*)

threap, same as **threep.**

threat, *n.* statement of intention to injure or punish, menace; indication of coming evil. **threaten,** *v.t.* and *i.* utter threats (against); intimidate (with); portend, seem to impend. (O.E. *thrēat*)

three, *a.* and *n.* one more than two. **t. times t.,** three cheers thrice repeated. **t.-bottle man,** hard drinker. **t.-colour process,** photo-mechanical process using yellow, red, and blue blocks. **t.-cornered,** *a.* triangular; with three contestants. **t.-decker, t.-master,** *nn.* ship with three decks, masts. **t.-ha'pence,** *n.* 1½*d.* **t.-pair,** *a.* of third floor. **t.-pile,** *n.* (*Shake.*) richest kind of velvet. **t.-ply,** *a.* of three strands.—*n.* boarding of three layers glued together with grain running in different directions. **t.-quarter,** *a.* (of portrait) going down to hips; between full-face and profile.—*n.* (*Rugby football*) man between full-back and half-backs. **threefold,** *a.* and *adv.* three times repeated. (O.E. *thrēo*)

threep, *v.t.* (*Scot.*) maintain persistently, urge.—*n.* obstinate assertion.

threepence, *n.* 3*d.* **threepenny-bit,** *n.* coin worth 3*d.*

threesome, *n* (*golf*) game played by one player against two who strike alternately.

thremmatology, *n.* science of breeding animals and plants. (Gk. *thremma,* nursling; *legein,* speak)

threnody, threnode, *nn.* song of lamentation, dirge. **threne,** *n.* (*Shake.*) dirge. **threnetic, threnetical, threnodial, threnodic,** *aa.* **threnodist,** *n.* composer of threnody. (Gk. *thrēnos,* lament; *ōidē,* song)

threpsology, *n.* science of, treatise on, diet. (Gk. *trephein,* nourish; *legein,* speak)

thresh, *v.t.* and *i.* beat grain out of (wheat); thrash. (=*thrash*)

threshold, *n.* stone or plank forming bottom of doorway; entrance. (O.E. *therscold*)

threw, see **throw.**

thrice, *adv.* three times; greatly.

thrid, *v.t.* (*arch.*) thread. (*thread*)

thridace, *n.* inspissated juice of lettuce. (Gk. *thridax,* lettuce)

thrift, *n.* saving methods, economy of expenditure; a plant, sea-pink; (*Shake.*) profit. **thriftless,** *a.* improvident; (*Shake.*) profitless. **thrifty,** *a.* frugal, saving; (*Shake.*) won by thrift. (*thrive*)

thrill, *n.* tremor, tingling, due to emotion; wave of sensation; throb, glow.—*v.t.* and *i.* stir thrills in, feel thrills; vibrate, throb; (*Spens.*) pierce. **thriller,** *n.* sensational novel or play. (O.E. *thyrlian,* pierce)

thrips, *n.sing.* genus of insects destructive to plants. (Gk.=woodworm)

thrive, *v.i.* (*past* **throve, thrived,** *p.p.* **thriven, thrived**) prosper, be successful; grow vigorously, flourish. (O.N. *thrifa,* grasp)

thro', thro, same as **through.**

throat, *n.* front of neck; gullet, windpipe; narrow passage or entrance. **cut one another's tt.,** engage in ruinous competition. **lie in the t.,** gross lie. **ram down one's t.,** force on his attention. **throaty,** *a.* guttural; having a prominent throat. (O.E. *throte*)

throb, *v.i.* pulsate; beat strongly, palpitate; quiver.—*n.* beat; strong pulsation. (M.E. *throbben*)

throe, *n.* spasm, pang; (*pl.*) pains of childbirth.—*v.i.* and *t.* be, put, in agony. **in the tt. of,** struggling with. (M.E. *throwe*)

thrombosis, *n.* formation of blood-clot. **thrombin,** *n.* substance in blood causing clotting. **thrombus,** *n.* (*pl.* **thrombi**) blood-clot. (Gk. *thrombos,* lump)

throne, *n.* chair of state for king etc.; sovereign power; (*pl.*) third order of angels.—*v.t.* and *i.* place on, occupy, throne. (Gk. *thronos,* chair)

throng, *n.* press of people, crowd.—*v.i.* and *t.* come in great numbers; flock into, crowd. (O.E. *thringan,* crowd)

throstle, *n.* song-thrush, mavis; kind of spinning-machine. (O.E.)

throttle, *v.t.* choke, strangle; check with throttle.—*n.* throat, windpipe; (also **t.-valve**) valve regulating supply of steam etc. in engine.

through, *prep.* from end to end or side to side of; between the sides of; over the whole extent of; by means or reason of.—*adv.* from one end or side to the other; from beginning to end; to the end; (*Amer. sl.*) finished; (*Shake.*) thoroughly.—*a.* clear, unobstructed; (of railway travel) going all the way without change. **carry t.,** accomplish. **t. and t.,** thoroughly. **t.-gang,** *n.* (*Scot.*) thoroughfare. **t.-ither,** *adv.* (*Scot.*) confusedly. **throughly,** *adv.* (*arch.*) thoroughly. **throughout,** *adv.* and *prep.* in every part (of). (O.E. *thurh*)

throve, see **thrive.**

throw, *v.t.* and *i.* (*past* **threw,** *p.p.* **thrown**) hurl, cast, fling; upset in wrestling; (of horse) dislodge (rider); (of snake) slough (skin); twist (silk) into thread; put, bring (into confusion etc.); (*Amer.*) intentionally lose (contest, point).—*n.* act of throwing, cast; wrestling-bout. **t. a fit,** have a fit. **t. a party** (*sl.*) give a party. **t. away,** waste; discard. **t. back,** revert to ancestral type. **t.-back,** *n.* **t. down,** overthrow. **t. in,** add as an extra. **t. off,** remove hastily; get rid of; improvise; make start at hunt. **t. oneself on,** commit one's fate to. **t. open,** make accessible. **t. out,** eject; discard; reject (bill); confuse (speaker). **t. over,** desert; jilt. **t. up,** abandon, resign; vomit. **throwster,** *n.* one who throws silk. (O.E. *thráwan*)

thrum, *v.i.* and *t.* play idly or carelessly on (instrument); pluck at (strings); drum with fingers.—*n.* thrumming sound. (imit.)

thrum, *n.* fringe of threads remaining attached to loom when web is cut off; loose thread, tuft.—*v.t.* make of thrums, fringe. **thrummy,** *a.* (M.E.)

thrush, *n.* kinds of song-bird. (O.E. *thrysce*)

thrush, *n.* ulcerous disease of mouth in children; foot-disease in horses.

thrust, *v.t.* and *i.* (*past, p.p.* same) push, shove; make lunge, stab; obtrude (oneself); force (one's way).—*n.* push, drive; stab; shaft of satire; (*mech.*) pressure of one thing against another. **t.-block,** *n.* block that receives thrust of ship's propeller. **thruster,** *n.* one who pushes forward regardless of others. (O.N. *thrýsta*)

thud, *n.* dull sound of heavy blow or fall.—*v.i.* make, fall with, thud.

thug, *n.* member of extinct Indian fraternity of assassins and robbers; cut-throat. **thuggee,** *n.* thugs' method of murder by strangling. **thuggery, thuggism,** *nn.* thuggee; ruffianism. (Hind.)

thumb, *n.* the short thick finger, which can be opposed to the others.—*v.t.* wear, dirty (book). **rule of t.,** rough and ready method. **tt. up!** (*sl.*) expression of success. **under one's t.,** dominated by him. **t.-nail sketch,** very brief description. **thumbscrew,** *n.* instrument of torture squeezing thumb. (O.E. *thúma*)

thummim, see **urim.**

thump, *n.* heavy blow; sound of this.—*v.t.* strike with thump; beat, pummel. **thumper,** *n.* big specimen; big lie. **thumping,** *a.* (*sl.*) big. (imit.)

thunder, *n.* loud noise accompanying lightning; sound like this, deep rumble; strong denunciation.—*v.i.* and *t.* emit thunder; utter loudly, roar. **t. against,** denounce vehemently. **t.-stone,** *n.* (*Shake.*) thunderbolt. **t.-struck,** *a.* astounded. **thunderbolt,** *n.* lightning flash; overwhelming surprise. **thunderclap,** *n.* peal of thunder. **the Thunderer,** Jove; 'The Times.' **thundering,** *a.* (*sl.*) very big.—*adv.* (*sl.*) very. **thunderous,** *a.* as loud as thunder. **thundery,** *a.* close, sultry. (O.E. *thunor*)

thurible, *n.* censer. **thurifer,** *n.* acolyte who carries censer. **thuriferous,** *a.* producing frankincense. **thurification,** *n.* burning of incense. (L. *thus,* frankincense)

Thursday, *n.* fifth day of week. (*Thor,* Norse god)

thus, *adv.* in this way; to this extent; consequently. **thusness,** *n.* (*joc.*) state of being thus. (O.E.)

thwack, *v.t.* beat, thrash.—*n.* blow, thump. (imit.)

thwaite, *n.* piece of wild land reclaimed and cultivated, clearing. (O.N. *thveit,* paddock)

thwart, *v.t.* frustrate, baffle; (*Shake.*) cross.—*n.* seat across boat for rower.—*a.* (*arch.*) transverse; (*Shake.*) perverse.—*adv.* and *prep.* (*arch.*) across. **thwartships,** *adv.* across ship's length. (O.N. *thvert,* across)

thy, see **thou.**

thylacine, *n.* Tasmanian wolf, a carnivorous marsupial. (Gk. *thulakos,* pouch)

thyme, *n.* kinds of herb with sweet-smelling leaves. **thymol,** *n.* oil from this used as antiseptic. (Gk. *thumos*)

thymus, *n.* (*pl.* **thymi**) ductless gland near base of neck. (Gk. *thumos,* thyme, from its shape)

thyroid, *a.* and *n.* **t.** (**cartilage**), chief cartilage of larynx, Adam's apple. **t.** (**gland**), ductless gland of neck which affects growth. (Gk. *thureos,* shield; *eidos,* form)

thyrsus, *n.* (*pl.* **thyrsi**) ivy-wreathed staff of Bacchus. (Gk. *thursos*)

thyself, *pron.* emphatic and refl. form of **thou.**

ti, *n.* kinds of Polynesian tree with edible roots. (native)

ti, *n.* (*Amer.*) te.

tiara, *n.* jewelled head-ornament, coronet; pope's triple crown; ancient Persian head-dress. (Gk.)

Tib, *n.* (*Shake.*) name for common woman.

tibia, *n.* (*pl.* **tibiae**) shin-bone. **tibial,** *a.* (L.)

tic, *n.* involuntary twitching. **t. douloureux,** neuralgia with twitching of facial muscles. (F.)

tical, *n.* Siamese silver coin worth about 1*s.* 8*d.* (Port.)

ticca, *a.* (*Anglo-Ind.*) hired. **t. gharry,** gharri, hired carriage. (Hind. *thīkā,* fare)

tice, *n.* (*cricket, arch.*) yorker. (*entice*)

tick, *n.* sound of clock or watch, recurrent tap; small mark; moment.—*v.i.* and *t.* make, mark with, tick. **t. off,** mark off; reprimand. **t. over,** (of motor-car engine) run very slowly with gear disconnected. **t.-tack,** *n.* hand-signals of bookmaker's assistant. **t.-t.,** *n.* (*sl.*) watch, clock, (M.E. *tek,* light touch)

tick, *n.* case, cover, of mattress; ticking. (Gk. *tithenai,* place)

tick, *n.* parasitic insect infesting dogs, sheep etc. (M.E. *teke*)

tick, *n.* (*colloq.*) credit.—*v.i.* give credit. (abbr. of *ticket*)

ticker, *n.* (*sl.*) tape-machine; watch; (*joc.*) heart.

ticket, *n.* marked card giving right of admission, of conveyance by train etc.; price-label; notice; list of party candidates; (*army sl.*) discharge.—*v.t.* attach label to. **the t.,** (*colloq.*) the correct thing. **t.-of-leave,** *n.* permit setting convict free under certain restrictions, before expiry of his sentence. (O.F. *etiquet*)

tickey, ticky, *n.* (*S. Afr. colloq.*) three-penny-bit.

tickle, *v.t.* and *i.* cause to itch by light touches, itch; poke in ribs etc. and cause laughter; rovoke sense of humour in ; please, gratify.—*n.* itching sensation.—*a.* (*Shake.*) unstable, insecure. **t.-brain,** *n.* (*Shake.*) strong liquor. **ticklish,** *a.* easily tickled; awkward to handle, needing tact; (*Shake.*) wanton. (M.E. *tikelle*)

tick-tack, same as **trick-track.**

ticpolonga, *n.* venomous Indian snake. (Cingalese *titpolongā*, spot-viper)

tidal, *a.* of, caused by, tide. **t. river,** up which tide runs. **t. wave,** great wave caused by tide, earthquake etc.; everwhelming burst of feeling.

tidbit, same as **titbit.**

tiddler, *n.* (*colloq.*) stickleback.

tiddley, tiddly, *a.* (*naval sl.*) smart.

tiddley, tiddly, *a.* (*sl.*) drunk.—*n.* any alcoholic drink.

tiddly-winks, tiddledy-winks, *nn.* parlour game in which disks are flipped from table into cup.

tiddy, *a.* (*dial.*) very small, tiny.

tide, *n*, alternate rise and fall of sea due to moon's attraction; trend, tendency; (*arch.*) period, season.—*v.i.* be carried by tide; (*arch.*) happen. **flood, high, t.,** rise of sea. **ebb, low, t.,** fall of sea. **spring, neap, t.,** maximum, minimum, tide due to sun's attraction working with, against, moon's. **t. over,** surmount, help over, for time being. **t.-rip,** *n.* rough water caused by opposing tides. **t.-waiter,** *n.* customs officer who boards incoming vessels to enforce regulations. **tidewater,** *n.* water affected by tide; seaboard. **tideway,** *n.* channel where tide runs. **tidology,** *n.* science of tides. (O.E. *tīd*, time)

tidings, *n.pl.* news. (*tide*)

tidy, *a.* orderly, neat; (*colloq.*) considerable.—*n.* antimacassar; receptacle for odds and ends.—*v.t.* make tidy, put in order. (M.E. =seasonable, from *tide*)

tie, *v.t.* and *i.* (*pres. part.* **tying**) fasten, bind; form (into) knot; restrict, hamper; make equal score, draw.—*n.* bond, link; connecting-piece; necktie, fur necklet; draw, dead heat; match; (*mus.*) curve over notes that represent one sound sustained; (*Amer.*) railway sleeper. **t. up,** fasten securely; annex conditions to (bequest etc.). **t.-up,** *n.* (*Amer.*) strike or lock-out. **t.-beam,** *n.* beam connecting rafters. **t.-wig,** *n.* wig tied behind with ribbon. **tied house,** public-house bound to deal with one brewer only. (O.E. *tīgan*)

tier, *n.* one of series of rows rising one behind another; (*New Zealand*) mountain range.—*v.t.* pile in tiers. (F. *tirer*, draw)

tierce, *n.* medium-size cask, ⅓ of a pipe; a position in fencing; third canonical hour, service at 9 a.m. (*tertius*)

tiercel, tiercet, same as **tercel, tercet.**

tiers état, third estate. (F.)

tiff, *n.* slight quarrel; huff.—*v.i.* be in a pet.

tiff, *n.* draught of liquor.—*v.t.* and *i.* sip, drink; (*Anglo-Ind.*) tiffin.

tiffany, *n.* light gauzy muslin. (L.L. *theophania*, manifestation of God, because orig. dress for Twelfth Night)

tiffin, *n.* (*Anglo-Ind.*) light meal, esp. of curried dishes and fruit; lunch.—*v.i.* and *t.* have tiffin. (*tiff*)

tig, same as **tag.**

tige, *n.* (*archit.*) shaft of pillar; (*bot.*) stalk, stem. (F.)

tiger, *n.* (*fem.* **tigress**) large striped beast of prey of cat tribe; cruel ruthless person; small groom in livery; (*colloq.*) first-class player; (*Amer. sl.*) supplementary cheer, final yell. **American t.,** jaguar, **red t.,** cougar. **t.-beetle, t.-moth,** *nn.* kinds with tiger-like markings. **t.-cat,** *n.* kinds of wild cat. **t.-lily,** *n.* with black-spotted orange flowers. **t.'s-eye,** *n.* a yellowish-brown gem. **tigerish, tigrish,** *aa.* like a tiger. (Gk. *tigris*)

tight, *a.* fully stretched, taut; gripping or fitting close; water-tight; compact, trim; too small, cramped; (of money) scarce; (*colloq.*) drunk; (*Shake.*) deft, smart.—*adv.* tightly. —*n.pl.* tight-fitting costume of dancer etc. **t. corner,** dangerous situation. **t.fisted,** *a.* mean. **tighten,** *v.t.* and *i.* make, become, tight or tighter. **tightrope,** *n.* stretched rope on which acrobat performs. **tightwad,** *n.* (*Amer.*) stingy person. (O.N. *théttr*)

tike, see **tyke.**

tikkie, same as **tickey.**

til, *n.* sesame. (Hind.)

tilbury, *n.* light two-wheeled carriage. (maker)

tildě, *n.* mark (˜) placed over *n* in Spanish to indicate a following *y* sound. (Sp.)

tile, *n.* flat slab of baked clay for roofing etc.; (*colloq.*) silk hat.—*v.t.* cover, face, with tiles; guard (masonic meeting) from intrusion; bind to secrecy. **have a t. loose,** (*colloq.*) be rather mad. **tiler,** *n.* one who lays tiles; (also *arch.* **tyler**) door-keeper of masonic lodge. (L. *tegula*)

tiliaceous, *a.* of the linden family of trees. (L. *tilia*, linden)

tilka, *n.* Hindu caste-mark on forehead. (Sanskr.)

till, *prep.* up to, as late as.—*conj.* up to the time when. (O.N. *til*)

till, *n.* glacial deposit of clay, gravel etc.; boulder-clay.
till, *n.* money-drawer in shop counter.
till, *v.t.* and *i.* cultivate (land). **tillage**, *n.* tilling; tilled land. **tiller**, *n.* (O.E. *tilian*)
tiller, *n.* lever or handle for turning rudder. (L. *tela*, web, through sense weaver's beam)
tiller, *n.* shoot, sucker, springing from bottom of original stalk.—*v.i.* put forth tillers. (O.E. *telgor*)
tilly-vally, *int.* (*Shake.*) nonsense!
tilt, *v.i.* and *t.* slope, cause to slope; heel over, tip; charge on horseback, thrust, with lance.—*n.* sloping position, cant; tilting, joust. **full t.**, at full speed. **t. at**, inveigh against, attack. **t.-hammer**, *n.* pivoted hammer used in forging. (O.E. *tealt*, unsteady)
tilt, *n.* canvas covering of wagon, hood; awning. (O.E. *teld*)
tilth, *n.* cultivation; tilled land.
timbal, timbul, *n.* kettledrum. (Arab. *al tabl*, the drum)
timber, *n.* wood, trees, regarded as building material; single piece of wooden framework, beam; rib of ship. **t.-toes**, *n.* wooden-legged or heavy-footed person. **t.-wolf**, *n.* large American grey wolf. **t.-yard**, *n.* (*cricket, sl.*) wicket. **timbered**, *a.* made with timber; wooded. (O.E.)
timbre, *n.* distinctive quality of a sound apart from its pitch and intensity. (F.)
timbrel, *n.* kind of hand-drum or tambourine. (L. *tympanum*, drum)
timbrology, *n.* study of postage stamps, philately. (F. *timbre*, postage stamp. Gk. *legein*, speak)
time, *n.* measure of duration, mode of reckoning this; period; age, epoch; lifetime; hour, season; appointed hour or interval; occasion; leisure; breathing-space; repetition; rhythm; tempo; hour of travail or death; (*pl.*) state of things at any period. —*v.t.* choose or appoint time for; do at proper moment; note time taken by. **at tt., from t. to t.**, now and then. **beat t.**, mark musical rhythm with hand etc. **do t.**, serve sentence. **Greenwich t.**, British standard time. **have t. of one's life**, (*sl.*) enjoy oneself greatly. **in t.**, eventually; soon enough. **pass the t. of day**, greet. **tell the t.**, read clock. **serve one's t.**, go through apprenticeship. **summer t.**, with clocks advanced so that day starts earlier in summer, 11 a.m. being reckoned as noon. **t. being**, present time. **t. enough**, sufficiently early. **what t.**, (*poet.*) while. (O.E. *tima*)
time-fuse, *n.* fuse calculated to burn for a given time.
time-honoured, *a.* venerable because of age.
timekeeper, *n.* one who keeps record of hours worked by men in factory.
time-lag, *n.* pause between a cause and its effect.
timeless, *a.* unending; untimely.
timely, *a.* opportune, well-timed.—*adv.* opportunely; (*Shake.*) early.
timeo Danaos et dona ferentes, distrust a conciliatory enemy. (L.= I fear the Greeks even bearing gifts)
timeous, timous, *a.* (*Scot.*) timely.
timepiece, *n.* clock.
time-server, *n.* selfish opportunist.
time-table, *n.* table of hours of work or times of trains etc.
time-work, *n.* work paid for by time.
timid, *a.* easily frightened; diffident, shy. **timidity**, *n.* (L. *timēre*, fear)
timocracy, *n.* form of government in which office is held by property qualification. (Gk. *timē*, honour; *kratos*, power)
timorous, *a.* faint-hearted, timid. (L. *timēre*, fear)
timothy, *n.* (also **t.-grass**) a grass grown for hay. (*Timothy* Hanson, who introduced it to America)
timous, see **timeous.**
tin, *n.* a white malleable metal; thin iron coated with it, tinplate; receptacle made of this, can; (*sl.*) money.—*a.* made of tin.—*v.t.* coat with tin; pack, preserve, in tin. **little t. god**, undeservedly idolized person. **t. fish**, (*sl.*) torpedo. **t. hat**, (*sl.*) steel helmet. **t. Lizzie**, nickname for Ford motor-car. **t. whistle**, penny whistle. (O.E.)
tinamou, *n.* S. American bird like quail. (F.)
tincal, *n.* crude borax. (Sanskr. *ṭankaṇa*)
tinct, *a.* (*arch.*) tinged.—*n.* (*arch.*) tint; (*Shake.*) elixir. **tinction**, *n.* process of dyeing. **tinctorial**, *a.* of dyeing; colouring. **tincture**, *n.* tinge, tint; trace, spice; veneer; (*med.*) solution of substance in alcohol.—*v.t.* tinge, flavour; affect slightly (with). (*tinge*)
tindal, *n.* Lascar petty officer. (Malayalam *taṇḍal*)
tinder, *n.* dry easily burning material, esp. for kindling fire from spark. **t.-box**, *n.* containing tinder, flint, and steel. (O.E. *tyndre*)
tine, *n.* prong of fork, spike of harrow, point of antler. (O.E. *tind*)
tine, *v.t.* (*Spens.*) kindle. (O.E. *tendan*)
tine, *v.t.* and *i.* (*Scot.*) lose; be lost, perish. (O.N. *týna*)
tine, same as **teen.**
tinea, *n.* kinds of skin disease, esp. ringworm. (L.=worm)
tinfoil, *n.* tin in thin leaves for wrapping.—*v.t.* cover with this.
ting, *n.* (*colloq.*) sound of bell, tinkle. —*v.i.* and *t.* tinkle. (imit.)
tinge, *v.t.* colour slightly; affect faintly. —*n.* trace of colour; flavour; slight admixture. (L. *tingere*, dye)
tingle, *v.i.* feel prickling or stinging sensation, thrill. (=*tinkle*)

tinkal, same as **tincal.**
tinker, *n.* one who mends pots and pans; rough and ready worker; act of tinkering.—*v.t.* and *i.* mend (pots etc.); mend roughly; work clumsily, fiddle (at). **tinkerly**, *a.*
tinkle, *n.* sound of small bell; jingle. —*v.i.* and *t.* make, cause (bell) to make, tinkle. **tinkler**, *n.* (*sl.*) small bell. (imit.)
tinkler, *Scot.* form of **tinker.**
tinnitus, *n.* (*med.*) ringing in the ears. (L.)
tinny, *a.* sounding like tin when struck.
tinplate, *n.* sheet iron coated with tin.
tinsel, *n.* glittering trimming of metal foil or threads; tawdry brilliance, sham splendour.—*a.* cheaply showy, flashy.—*v.t.* adorn with tinsel. (L. *scintilla*, spark)
tinsmith, *n.* worker in tin or tinplate.
tint, *n.* variety of colour, esp. one made by admixture of white; hue.—*v.t.* give (esp. slight) colour to, tinge. **tinter**, *n.* (L. *tingere*, dye)
tintack, *n.* tin-coated tack.
tintinnabulation, *n.* ringing of bells. **tintinnabular, tintinnabulary, tintinnabulous**, *aa.* of bells. (L. *tintinnabulum*, bell)
tintometer, *n.* instrument for determining tints.
tintype, *n.* positive photograph taken on tin plate, ferrotype.
tinware, *n.* vessels of tin.
tiny, *a.* very small.
tip, *n.* point, top, end; cap for this, ferrule.—*v.t.* cover tip of. **on the t. of one's tongue,** just about to be said. (M.E.)
tip, *v.t.* and *i.* strike lightly, tap; incline, tilt; empty (out) by tilting; give (gratuity) to.—*n.* light touch; gratuity; private information; useful hint or dodge; rubbish-dump. **t. off**, (*sl.*) give warning to. **t. over,** overturn. **t. the wink,** give secret signal. **t.-and-run**, *n.* cricket in which batsman must run if bat touches ball. **t.-cart**, *n.* one that tilts backwards to empty. **t.-cat**, *n.* game in which cigar-shaped piece of wood is flipped into the air by hitting one of the ends with a stick, and is then hit as far as possible. **t.-tilted**, *a.* (of nose) turned up at end.
tippet, *n.* short cape or scarf covering neck and shoulders.
tipple, *v.i.* and *t.* drink in small quantities; drink (intoxicants) habitually.—*n.* strong drink.
tipstaff, *n.* (*pl.* **tipstaves**) sheriff's officer; his metal-shod staff.
tipster, *n.* one who gives or sells racing tips.
tipsy, *a.* fuddled with drink, partly drunk. **t.-cake**, *n.* sponge cake soaked in wine and covered with custard. **tipsify**, *v.t.* fuddle.
tiptoe, *n.* point of toe.—*v.i.* walk on toes. **on t.,** with strained attention.
tiptop, *n.* highest point; height of excellence.—*a.* (*colloq.*) first-rate.
tirade, *n.* long violent speech or denunciation, rant. (It. *tirare*, draw)
tirailleur, *n.* sharpshooter, skirmisher. (F.)
tire, see **tyre.**
tire, *v.t.* (*Shake.*) tear as prey, feed ravenously on. (F. *tirer*, draw)
tire, *n.* (*Spens.*) rank; train. (*tier*)
tire, *n.* (*arch.*) dress; head-dress.—*v.t.* (*arch.*) attire, deck. **tiring-room**, *n.* (*arch.*) dressing-room in theatre. (*attire*)
tire, *v.t.* and *i.* make or become weary, exhaust, fatigue. **tired**, *a.* weary; exhausted; sick (of). **tireless**, *a.* unwearying, indefatigable. **tiresome**, *a.* annoying, worrying; tedious, dull. (O.E. *teorian*)
tirewoman, *n.* (*arch.*) lady's-maid.
tirl, *v.i.* and *t.* (*Scot.*) twirl; quiver; strip; strike ring on pin of old-fashioned knocker.—*n.* twirl; vibration. **tirlie-whirlie**, *n.* whirligig; involved ornamentation. (*twirl*)
tiro, same as **tyro.**
tirocinium, *n.* apprenticeship. (L. *tiro*, recruit)
tirr, *v.t.* (*Scot.*) tear off.
tirrivee, *n.* (*Scot.*) tantrum, pet.
'tis, *contr.* of **it is.**
tisane, *n.* decoction, ptisan. (F.)
tisick, *n.* (*Shake.*) consumptive cough. (*phthisis*)
tissue, *n.* woven fabric, esp. thin gauzy stuff; substance of animal body or plant; network (of lies etc.); (also **t.-paper**) thin soft semi-transparent paper. (L. *texere*, weave)
tit, *n.* kinds of small bird, incl. titmouse; (*arch.*) small child, chit; small or poor horse.
tit, *n.* **t. for tat,** blow for blow, retaliation.
tit, same as **teat.**
Titan, *n.* (*fem.* **Titaness**) giant; person of commanding genius; largest of Saturn's satellites; (*poet.*) the sun. **titanic**, *a.* enormous. **titanium**, *n.* a grey metallic element. (primeval earth-born Greek god)
titbit, *n.* choice morsel or item.
tithe, *n.* tenth part, esp. of agricultural produce allotted (now in form of tax) to the Church; small part.—*v.t.* tax to amount of a tenth. **tithable**, *a.* **tithing**, *n.* small administrative division in Saxon times. (O.E. *téotha*)
Titian, *a.* reddish-brown. (painter)
titillate, *v.t.* tickle; stimulate pleasurably. **titillation, titillator**, *nn.* (L. *titillare*)
titivate, *v.t.* and *i.* (*colloq.*) smarten (oneself) up. **titivation**, *n.*
titlark, *n.* meadow pipit. (*tit*)
title, *n.* name of book, picture etc.; heading; appellation indicating status; peerage; recognized claim or right; (*law*) right, proof, of owner-

ship. **t.-deed,** *n.* document proving ownership or title. **t.-page,** *n.* page at beginning of book with title and author's name. **t.-role,** *n.* part from which play is named, e.g. Hamlet. **titled,** *a.* having title. (L. *titulus*)

titmouse, *n.* (*pl.* **titmice**) a small active bird, tit. (*tit*+O.E. *máse*, kind of small bird)

titrate, *v.t.* determine strength of, analyse, by adding standard solutions until a certain definite effect is observed. **titration,** *n.* (F. *titre*, title)

titter, *n.* shrill partly-smothered laugh. *v.i.* emit this. (imit.)

tittivate, same as **titivate.**

tittle, *n.* small amount, particle; small mark over letter to indicate contraction etc. (*title*)

tittlebat, *n.* stickleback. (corrupt.)

tittle-tattle, *n.* and *v.i.* gossip. (*tattle*)

tittup, *v.i.* skip about, curvet; bob up and down; canter; (*naut. sl.*) toss for drinks.—*n.* tittuping movement, prance; canter.

titty, *n.* teat. (*tit*)

titty, *n.* (*Scot.*) sister.

titubate, *v.i.* reel, totter; stammer. **titubation,** *n.* titubating; fidgetiness. (L. *titubare*)

titular, *a.* of, having, giving, title; nominal, in name only.—*n.* nominal holder of office. (*title*)

tityrĕ-tu, *n.* one of the roughs infesting London streets in Charles II's time. (opening words of Virgil's first eclogue)

tizzy, *n.* (*sl.*) sixpence.

tmesis, *n.* separation of parts of a compound word by insertion of one or more words, e.g. 'brim in a flash full.' (Gk.=cutting)

to, *prep.* in the direction of; as far as; until; also used to introduce infinitive mood, indirect object etc.—*adv.* to normal or required position; closed. **to and fro,** backwards and forwards. (O.E. *tó*)

toad, *n.* amphibian like frog with warty skin; repulsive person. **t.-eater,** *n.* (*arch.*) toady. **t.-flax,** *n.* kinds of small plant allied to snapdragon. **t.-in-the-hole,** *n.* meat baked in batter. **toadstool,** *n.* fungus like mushroom but poisonous or inedible. **toady,** *n.* servile flatterer, fawning sycophant.—*v.i.* truckle (to), curry favour. **toadyism,** *n.* (O.E. *tádige*)

toast, *v.t.* dry and brown before fire; warm thus; drink health of.—*n.* toasted bread; drinking of health, person thus honoured. **on t.,** at one's mercy. **t.-master,** *n.* professional announcer of toasts. **t.-rack,** *n.* for holding slices of toast. **toasting-fork,** *n.* for toasting bread. (L. *torrēre*, parch)

toaze, *v.t.* (*Shake.*) tear, elicit.

tobacco, *n.* (*pl.* **tobaccos**) dried narcotic leaves used for smoking; plant yielding them. **t.-pipe,** *n.* for smoking tobacco. **tobacconist,** *n.* seller of tobacco. (Carib)

toboggan, *n.* sledge for sliding down snow-clad slope.—*v.i.* slide on toboggan; coast. (Amer. Ind.)

toby, *n.* beer-mug in shape of man with three-cornered hat. (name)

toccata, *n.* composition for piano or organ designed to practise or exhibit touch. **toccatella, toccatina,** *nn.* short or simple toccata. (It.)

tocher, *n.* and *v.t.* (*Scot.*) dowry. (Gael. *tochar*)

toco, same as **toko.**

tocology, *n.* obstetrics. (Gk. *tokos*, birth; *legein*, speak)

tocsin, *n.* alarm-bell, alarm-signal. (*touch*; *sign*)

tod, *n.* (*arch.*) bush; thick foliage; weight of wool, us. 28 lb.

tod, *n.* (*Scot.*) fox.

today, to-day, *adv.* on this day; nowadays.—*n.* present day or period.

toddle, *v.i.* walk with short uncertain steps like a child; (*joc.*) stroll.—*n.* toddling walk. **toddler,** *n.* child just beginning to walk.

toddy, *n.* mixture of whisky, sugar, and hot water; fermented juice of certain palms. (Hind. *tār*, palm)

to-do, *n.* fuss, ado.

tody, *n.* bright-coloured W. Indian bird allied to kingfisher. (L. *todus*, kind of small bird)

toe, *n.* digit of foot; fore part of foot or hoof; corresponding part of stocking or shoe; lower end, tip.—*v.t.* put toe on; (*sl.*) kick. **t. the line,** conform to discipline. **tread on one's tt.,** offend his feelings. **turn up one's tt.,** (*sl.*) die. **t.-nail,** *n.* **toed,** *a.* having toes. (O.E. *tá*)

to-fall, *n.* (*poet.*) close, decline.

toff, *n.* (*sl.*) well-dressed man, swell; gentleman.

toffee, toffy, *n.* sweetstuff of boiled sugar and butter.

tofore, *adv.* (*Shake.*) formerly, before.

toft, *n.* knoll, hillock; homestead. (O.N. *topt*)

tog, *v.t.* (*sl.*) dress (out).—*n.pl.* (*sl.*) clothes.

toga, *n.* loose flowing garment of ancient Roman citizen. **tog'd, togaed,** (*Shake.*) **toged,** *aa.* dressed in toga. (L.)

together, *adv.* in company; towards or with each other; simultaneously. (O.E. *tó*, to; *geador*, together)

togger, *n.* (*Oxford sl.*) torpid.

toggery, *n.* (*sl.*) clothes collectively.

toggle, *n.* (*naut.*) pin put through rope to prevent it from passing through loop or knot.—*v.t.* fasten by toggle.

tohu-bohu, chaos. (Heb.)

toil, *v.i.* and *t.* work hard, labour (at); go with effort; (*Shake.*) put to exertion.—*n.* labour, drudgery.

toil, *n.* net, snare. (L. *tela*, web)

toilet, toilette, *n.* process of dressing; dress and appearance; lavatory, water-closet.—*a.* used in toilet. **t. vinegar,** scented kind. **t.-cover,** *n.*

for t.-table, *n.* dressing-table. **t.-paper,** *n.* for water-closet. (F.)
toilful, toilsome, *aa.* involving toil, laborious. **toilless,** *a.* without labour. **toilworn,** *a.* worn by toil.
Tokay, *n.* a rich Hungarian wine; kind of grape. (place)
toke, *n.* (*vulg. colloq.*) food.
token, *n.* object serving as memorial or guarantee; symbol, sign; (*Shake.*) plague-spot. **by the same t.,** further in corroboration. **t. money,** whose face value exceeds its real value. (O.E. *tácen*)
toko, *n.* (*sl.*) beating, punishment.
tokology, same as **tocology.**
tola, *n.* Indian unit of weight, 180 grains troy. (Hind.)
tolbooth, same as **tollbooth.**
told, see **tell.**
tolerate, *v.t.* endure, put up with; permit, suffer. **toleration,** *n.* tolerating; allowing of freedom of opinion, esp. in religious matters. **tolerationist,** *n.* advocate of toleration. **tolerable,** *a.* endurable; fairly good. **tolerably,** *adv.* fairly. **tolerant,** *a.* forbearing, indulgent; broad-minded. **tolerance,** *n.* (L. *tolerare*)
toll, *v.t.* and *i.* sound (bell) with slow succession of strokes; strike (hour), mark (death) thus.—*n.* tolling sound. (M.E. *tollen*, draw)
toll, *n.* charge, tax, for using road or bridge; right to exact this; part of corn formerly kept by miller as payment for grinding.—*v.t.* and *i.* (*Shake.*) take (tribute). **take t. of,** abstract part of. **t.-bar, t.-gate,** *nn.* barrier where toll is exacted. **t.-house,** *n.* for keeper of toll-gate. **tollable,** *a.* subject to toll. **tollage,** *n.* payment of toll. **tollbooth,** *n.* (*Scot.*) town jail. (O.E.)
tol-lol, tol-lollish, *aa.* (*sl.*) fairly well, so-so. (*tolerable*)
tolly, *n.* (*school sl.*) candle.
Toltec, *n.* member of race preceding Aztecs in Mexico. **Toltecan,** *a.*
tolu, *n.* aromatic balsam got from a S. American tree. **toluene, toluol,** *nn.* a hydrocarbon got from coal-tar and used in explosives. (place)
tom, *n.* (also **t. cat**) male cat. **long t.,** long naval gun. **Old T.,** kind of gin. **T., Dick, and Harry,** persons taken at random. **T. Tiddler's ground,** a children's game; place where money can be had for picking up. **T. Thumb,** midget. (*Thomas*)
tomahawk, *n.* Red Indian war-axe.—*v.t.* kill or wound with this; criticize (book) savagely. (Amer. Ind.)
tomalley, tomally, *n.* part of lobster's flesh that turns green when boiled. (Carib)
toman, *n.* Persian gold coin worth about 7*s.* 2*d.* (Pers.)
tomato, *n.* (*pl.* **tomatoes**) juicy acid red or yellow fruit; trailing plant yielding it. (Mex. *tomatl*)
tomb, *n.* grave; burial vault; sepulchral monument.—*v.t.* entomb. (Gk. *tumbos*)
tombac, tombak, *n.* an alloy of copper and zinc. (Malay *tambāga*, copper)
tombola, *n.* kind of lottery. (It.)
tomboy, *n.* romping girl, hoyden; (*Shake.*) wanton. (*Tom*; *boy*)
tombstone, *n.* stone over grave.
tome, *n.* volume, esp. large heavy one. (Gk. *temnein*, cut)
tomentum, *n.* (*bot.*) covering of matted woolly hairs. **tomentose, tomentous,** *aa.* (L.=stuffing)
tomfool, *n.* complete fool; trifler. **tomfoolery,** *n.* buffoonery; nonsense.
tommy, *n.* kind of wrench or lever; (*sl.*) private soldier; food. **soft t.,** (*naut.*) fresh bread. **T. Atkins,** British soldier. **t. rot,** absurd nonsense. (*Thomas*)
tommy-gun, *n.* short-barrelled submachine-gun. (J. T. *Thompson*)
tomnoddy, *n.* puffin; blockhead.
tomorrow, to-morrow, *adv.* and *n.* (on) the day following today.
tompion, same as **tampion.**
tomtit, *n.* titmouse. (*Tom*; *tit*)
tomtom, *n.* native Indian drum; gong. —*v.i.* beat tomtom. (Hind. *tamtam*)
ton, *n.* measure of weight, 20 cwt.; unit of ship's cubic capacity, 100 cubic ft. (**register t.**), or of its carrying capacity, 40 cubic ft. (**freight t.**); (*pl., colloq.*) large amount. **metric t.,** 1,000 kilogrammes or 2,204·6 lb. (=*tun*)
ton, *n.* prevailing mode, fashion. (F.)
tonal, *a.* of tone or tonality. **tonality,** *n.* system of tones; correctness of pitch; colour-scheme.
to-name, *n.* (*Scot.*) nickname.
tone, *n.* musical sound; quality of this; inflexion of voice; shade, hue, colour-effect; atmosphere, spirit, style; healthy condition; (*mus.*) the larger interval between successive notes in scale.—*v.t.* and *i.* give tone to; modify tone of; tune; be in harmony (with). **t. down,** lessen vigour of, soften. **t.-arm,** *n.* arm connecting sound-box to horn of gramophone. **t.-poem,** *n.* piece of programme music conveying poetic idea. **toneless,** *a.* unmusical; expressionless, flat. (Gk. *tonos*, pitch)
tong, *n.* Chinese secret society. (Chin. *t'ang*, meeting-place)
tonga, *n.* light two-wheeled Indian carriage. (Hind. *tāngā*)
tongs, *n.pl.* gripping-tool of two connected bars for lifting coal, sugar etc. (O.E. *tange*)
tongue, *n.* organ in mouth used for tasting, speaking etc.; power, manner, of speaking; language; tongue-like projection, pointer of balance, spit of land, jet of flame, pin of buckle, flap inside shoe, clapper of bell.—*v.t.* and *i.* use tongue to check wind stream in playing wind-instru-

ment. (*Shake.*) utter; scold. **give t.**, bay. **hold one's t.**, be silent. **with one's t. in one's cheek**, insincerely, ironically. **t.-tied**, *a.* unable to speak because of malformed tongue or shyness. (O.E. *tunge*)

tonic, *a.* stimulating, bracing; of tones; (of accent) depending on pitch, not stress.—*n.* tonic medicine or agency; (*mus.*) key-note. **t. sol-fa**, musical notation using doh, ray, me etc. **tonically**, *adv.* **tonicity**, *n.*

tonight, to-night, *adv.* and *n.* (on) the night after this day, this night; (*Shake.*) last night.

tonish, *a.* modish, stylish. (*ton*)

tonite, *n.* a gun-cotton explosive. (L. *tonare*, thunder)

tonk, *v.t.* (*sl.*) hit hard; defeat easily.

tonka bean, a fragrant seed used in perfumes; plant yielding it. (native)

tonnage, *n.* ship's carrying capacity; ships collectively; charge per ton.

tonneau, *n.* part of motor-car containing back seat. (F.)

tonometer, *n.* instrument measuring pitch of tone.

tonsil, *n.* gland at either side of back of mouth. **tonsillar, tonsilar**, *a.* **tonsillitis, tonsilitis**, *n.* inflammation of tonsils. (L. *tonsillae*, tonsils)

tonsorial, *a.* of a barber or his work. (L. *tondēre*, clip)

tonsure, *n.* shaving of part of head as symbol of monkhood or priesthood; bare patch so made.—*v.t.* shave thus. (L. *tondēre*, clip)

tontine, *n.* annuity shared among a group of persons so that as each one dies his portion is divided among the remainder; this system. (Lorenzo *Tonti*, originator)

tony, *a.* (*sl.*) genteel, high-class. (*tone*)

tony, *n.* simpleton. (name)

too, *adv.* excessively, overmuch; as well, moreover. **t.-t.**, *a.* gushing. (=*to*)

took, see **take**.

tool, *n.* implement, utensil; cutting part of machine; person used as instrument by another.—*v.t.* and *i.* dress (stone) with chisel; impress design on (book-cover); (*sl.*) drive in carriage, bowl (along). (O.E. *tól*)

toom, *a.* (*Scot.*) empty. (O.N. *tómr*)

toon, *n.* Indian tree with red wood used for furniture. (Hind. *tun*)

toon, *Scot.* form of **town**.

toot, *n.* sound of horn or trumpet.—*v.i.* and *t.* sound (horn), hoot. (imit.)

toot, *v.i.* (*Spens.*) peer about. (O.E. *tótian*)

tooth, *n.* (*pl.* **teeth**) bone-like chewing-organ rooted in jaw; tooth-like projection, prong, cog. **cast in one's tt.**, reproach vehemently with. **have a sweet t.**, enjoy sweet things. **in the tt. of**, in defiance of. **long in the t.**, old. **set one's tt.**, be grimly determined. **show one's tt.**, threaten. **t. and nail**, with utmost effort. **t.-comb**, *n.* comb with fine close-set teeth. **toothpaste, t.-powder**, *nn.* for use with **toothbrush**, *n.* for cleaning teeth. **toothache**, *n.* pain in teeth. **toothful**, *n.* small drink. **toothpick**, *n.* quill etc. for picking fragments of food from teeth. **toothsome**, *a.* pleasing to taste. **toothy**, *a.* with many or prominent teeth. (O.E. *tóth*)

tootle, *v.i.* and *t.* toot, hoot, repeatedly. —*n.* sound of this. (*toot*)

tootsy, *n.* (*sl.*) foot.

top, *n.* toy spinning on tapering point. **t.-shaped**, *a.* pear-shaped.

top, *n.* highest part, summit, head; upper surface; highest rank or degree; cover, lid; platform on ship's mast.—*a.* highest; chief.—*v.t.* (*past*, *p.p.* **topped**) cover top of, crown; cut off top of (tree); surpass in height, excel; (*golf*) hit (ball) on top. **big t.**, main tent of circus. **old t.**, (*sl.*) old chap. **t. dog**, winning party. **t. off, up**, put finishing touch (to). **t.-boot**, *n.* long riding-boot with light-coloured band round top. **t.-coat**, *n.* overcoat. **t.-dress**, *v.t.* apply manure to surface of. **t.-hamper**, *n.* upper rigging of ship. **t.-hat**, *n.* tall silk hat. **t.-heavy**, *a.* with upper part too heavy for base. **t.-hole**, *a.* (*sl.*) first-rate. **t.-sawyer**, *n.* upper man of two working saw in pit; person of distinction. (O.E.)

topaz, *n.* precious stone of various colours, esp. yellow. (Gk. *topazos*)

tope, *n.* Buddhist monument containing relics. (Sanskr. *stūpa*, mound)

tope, *n.* (*Anglo-Ind.*) grove of trees, orchard. (Tamil *tōppu*)

tope, *n.* small shark, dogfish.

tope, *v.i.* and *t.* drink (intoxicants) to excess, tipple. **toper**, *n.*

topee, same as **topi**.

topgallant, *a.* and *n.* (mast, sail) above topmast and topsail.

Tophet, *n.* hell. (Heb. *topheth*)

tophus, toph, *n.* (*pl.* **tophi, tophs**) gouty concretion in joints etc. **tophaceous**, *a.* (L.=sandstone)

topi, *n.* pith helmet. **t. wallah**, European in Indian. (Hind.=hat)

topiary, *a.* of, made by, clipping live shrubs into ornamental shapes. **topiarist**, *n.* (L. *topiarius*, of ornamental gardening)

topic, *n.* theme, subject of talk. **topical**, *a.* of topic; of current or local interest. (Gk. *topos*, place)

topknot, *n.* tuft of hair, bow of ribbon, on top of head; crest.

topless, *a.* very lofty.

topmast, *n.* second mast from deck.

topmost, *a.* highest, chief.

topo-, from Gk. *topos*, place, used in **topography**, *n.* physical features of a district, local geography, hence **topographic, topographical**, *aa.*, **topographer, topographist**, *nn.*; **toponymy**, *n.* study of place-names of a region.

topper, *n.* (*colloq.*) good fellow; top-hat. **topping**, *a.* (*sl.*) excellent.

topping-lift, *n.* rope from masthead to end of boom.
topple, *v.i.* and *t.* fall or push (over, down); be on point of falling; overhang. (*top*)
topsail, *n.* sail on topmast.
topside, *n.* (*naut.*) upper side.—*adv.* on top.
topsyturvy, *adv.* and *a.* upside-down, in utter confusion.—*n.* confusion, muddle.—*v.t.* turn topsyturvy. **topsyturvify,** *v.t.* **topsyturvification, topsyturvydom,** *nn.*
toque, *n.* woman's small close-fitting brimless hat; kinds of monkey. (F.)
tor, *n.* high rocky hill, esp. on Dartmoor. (O.E.)
torah, *n.* Mosaic law; Pentateuch. (Heb.)
torc, see **torque.**
torch, *n.* burning stick or piece of rope as portable light; light of knowledge. **electric t.,** electric hand-lamp. **torcher,** *n.* (*Shake.*) torch-bearer. (F. *torche*)
torchon, *n.* (*also* **t. lace**) coarse loose kind of lace. (F.=dishcloth)
torcular, *n.* tourniquet. (L. *torquēre*, twist)
tore, see **tear.**
toreador, *n.* bullfighter, us. mounted. **torero,** *n.* bullfighter on foot. (Sp.)
toreutics, *n.pl.* carved or embossed work, esp. in metal. **toreutic,** *a.* (Gk. *toreuein*, bore)
torgoch, *n.* red-bellied char. (W.)
torii, *n.* Shinto temple gateway of posts and lintel only. (Jap.)
torment, *n.* extreme pain, anguish; source of worry.—*v.t.* cause torment to, torture; tease. **tormentor,** *n.* (*fem.* **tormentress**) one who torments. (L. *torquēre*, twist)
tormentil, *n.* yellow-flowered plant. (*torment*)
tormina, *n.pl.* (*med.*) colic. **(L.)**
torn, see **tear.**
tornado, *n.* (*pl.* **tornadoes**) violent whirlwind, cyclone; outburst. **tornadic,** *a.* (Sp. *tronar*, thunder)
torous, torose, *aa.* (*bot.*) cylindrical with bulges at intervals; (*zool.*) knobby. **torosity,** *n.* (*torus*)
torpedo, *n.* (*pl.* **torpedoes**) cigar-shaped self-propelling explosive under-water missile; kinds of explosive mine; fish that gives electric shocks, electric ray.—*v.t.* hit, sink, with torpedo; make ineffective. **aerial t.,** kind discharged from aircraft. **t.-boat,** *n.* small fast warship armed with torpedoes. **t.-boat destroyer,** large type of torpedo-boat. **t.-net,** *n.* steel net hung round ship as protection against torpedoes. **t.-tube,** *n.* from which torpedo is discharged. (L.)
torpid, *a.* numb, in a state of torpor; sluggish, dull.—*n.* eight-oared boat for Oxford college races in spring; (*pl.*) the races. **torpidity,** *n.* **torpify,** *v.t.* make torpid. **torpor,** *n.* suspended animation; apathy. **torporific,** *a.* numbing. (L. *torpēre*, be numb)
torque, *n.* twisting force; (also **torc**) twisted metal necklet of ancient Britons etc. **torquate, torquated,** *aa.* (*zool.*) having a collar. (L. *torquēre*, twist)
torrefy, *v.t.* parch with heat, scorch, roast. **torrefaction,** *n.* (L. *torrēre*, parch; *facere*, make)
torrent, *n.* rapid stream, violent rush; violent outburst. **torrential,** *a.* (L. *torrens*)
torrid, *a.* parched, intensely hot. **t. zone,** part of earth between tropics. (L. *torrēre*, parch)
torsel, *n.* twisted scroll.
torsion, *n.* twisting; state of being twisted. **t.-balance,** *n.* for measuring minute forces by torsion of a fine wire. **torsional, torsive,** *aa.* (L. *torquēre*, twist)
torsk, *n.* sea-fish of cod family. (Da.)
torso, *n.* (*pl.* **torsos**) human trunk; statue mutilated of head and limbs; unfinished piece of work. (It.)
tort, *n.* (*law*) private or civil wrong. (L. *torquēre*, twist)
torticollis, *n.* (*med.*) stiff neck. (L. *torquēre*, twist; *collum*, neck)
tortile, *a.* twisted, wreathed. **tortility,** *n.* (L. *torquēre*, twist)
tortilla, *n.* flat maize cake used by Mexicans for bread. (Sp.)
tortious, *a.* of tort, wrongful.
tortive, *a.* (*Shake.*) distorted.
tortoise, *n.* four-footed reptile encased in horny shell, land turtle. **t.-shell,** *n.* substance of the shell.—*a.* of its colour, mottled brown and yellow. (L.L. *tortuca*)
tortuous, *a.* full of twists, involved; crooked, not straightforward. **tortuosity,** *n.* (L. *torquēre*, twist)
torture, *n.* pain deliberately inflicted, esp. to extort something; anguish. —*v.t.* inflict torture on; distort. **torturous,** *a.* (L. *torquēre*, twist)
torula, *n.* (*pl.* **torulae**) kind of fungus; chain of bacteria; (*bot.*) small torus. (dim. of *torus*)
torus, *n.* (*pl.* **tori**) rounded moulding at base of pillar; (*anat.*) rounded ridge; (*bot.*) basis of flower. (L.= rounded swelling)
Tory, *a.* and *n.* (member) of political party opposed to change, Conservative. **Toryism,** *n.* (Ir. *toiridhe*, pursuer, used of royalist outlaws)
tosh, *n.* (*sl.*) rubbish, rot.
tosh, *a.* (*Scot.*) neat, trim.
tosher, *n.* (*sl.*) non-collegiate student. (corrupt. of *unattached*)
toss, *v.t.* and *i.* fling, throw in air; heave up and down, tumble about; jerk (head); spin (coin).—*n.* tossing, pitch. **take a t.,** be thrown from horse. **t. oars,** bring oars to upright position as salute. **t. off,** drain at gulp. **t. up,** spin coin to decide question by the side that falls

uppermost. **t.-up,** *n.* even chance.
tosspot, *n.* (*arch.*) toper.
tost, *poet.* form of **tossed.**
tot, *n.* small child; small portion of drink, dram; small mug.
tot, *v.t.* and *i.* (*colloq.*) add (up).—*n.* column of addition. (*total*)
total, *a.* entire; complete, utter.—*n.* whole amount.—*v.t.* and *i.* reckon total of; amount to as whole. **totalitarian,** *a.* controlling, involving, the entire resources of a country. **totality,** *n.* being total; (*astron.*) time when eclipse is total. **totalize,** *v.t.* combine into total; find total of. **totalization,** *n.* **totalizator, totalizer,** *nn.* machine for making bets, the total stakes (less a percentage) being divided among backers of the winner. (L. *totus,* whole)
tote, *n.* (*sl.*) totalizator. (abbr.)
tote, *v.t.* (*Amer.*) carry, lift.
totem, *n.* animal or plant, symbol of this, adopted as tribal badge or emblem. **totemic,** *a.* **totemism,** *n.* social system using totems. **totemist,** *n.* member of clan having totem. **totemistic,** *a.* (Amer. Ind.)
tother, t'other, forms of **the other. tell t. from which,** (*joc.*) tell one from the other.
totidem verbis, in these very words. *toties quoties,* as often as occasion arises. *toto caelo,* diametrically (lit. by the whole sky). (L.)
totter, *v.i.* walk with shaky or faltering steps; be on the point of falling, be shaky. **t.-grass,** *n.* quake-grass. **tottery,** *a.*
toucan, *n.* bright-coloured S. American bird with huge beak. (Brazilian *tucana*)
touch, *v.t.* and *i.* be in contact (with); put hand on, strike gently; reach (to); equal in merit; concern; stir pity in, soften; (*sl.*) borrow from; (*Shake.*) test.—*n.* act of touching; sense of feeling; stroke with brush or pen; trace, tinge; style of execution; responsiveness of instrument; (*football*) side of field outside touchlines; (*arch.*) test. **t. at,** (of ship) call at. **t. down,** (*Rugby football*) touch ball on ground behind goal-line. **t. on,** refer briefly to. **t. to the quick,** deeply wound feelings of. **t. up,** repair, amend; flick. **t.-and-go,** *a.* and *n.* precarious (situation). **t.-hole,** *n.* hole through which fire was communicated to powder in ancient guns. **t.-judge,** *n.* (*Rugby football*) linesman. **t.-last,** *n.* children's chasing game, tag. **t.-line,** *n.* (*football*) side boundary of ground. **t.-me-not,** *n.* garden balsam. **t.-paper,** *n.* paper steeped in nitre so as to burn slowly. (O.F. *tochier*)
touched, *a.* slightly mad.
toucher, *n.* (*sl.*) close shave; (*bowls*) bowl that touches jack.
touching, *a.* pathetic, moving.
touchstone, *n.* black jasper etc. used to test purity of gold or silver by streak they leave on it; test, criterion.
touchwood, *n.* dry rotten wood used as tinder.
touchy, *a.* morbidly sensitive, irritable.
tough, *a.* hard to chew or tackle or endure; not easily broken or torn; able to stand strain or hardship; tenacious, stubborn; (*Amer. sl.*) depraved, criminal, vicious.—*n.* street ruffian. **toughen,** *v.t.* and *i.* make tough. (O.E. *tóh*)
toupee, *n.* small patch, front, of false hair. (F. *toupet*)
tour, *n.* extensive journey, round of visits.—*v.i.* and *t.* make tour, travel (through). **the grand t.,** European travel to finish education. *t. de force,* feat of strength or skill. (F.)
touraco, *n.* crested African bird allied to cuckoo. (F.)
tourbillion, *n.* ornamental revolving firework. (F. *tourbillon,* whirlwind)
tourist, *n.* one who travels for pleasure.
tourmaline, tourmalin, *n.* mineral of various colours, used as gem. (G.)
tournament, *n.* contest between a number of competitors, sports meeting; series of tilting matches, medieval jousts. **tourney,** *n.* tournament. —*v.i.* take part in tournament. (L. *tornare,* turn)
tourniquet, *n.* device to stop bleeding, bandage twisted tight by stick etc. (F.)
tournure, *n.* grace, poise; contour; drapery at back of gown. (F.)
tousle, *v.t.* make untidy, rumple, ruffle. **touse,** *v.t.* (*Shake.*) tear. **tousy,** *a.* dishevelled, unkempt.
tout, *v.i.* solicit custom, cadge; spy on race-horses in training.—*n.* one who touts. (O.E. *tótian,* peep out)
tout, *v.i.* (*Scot.*) pout.—*n.* fit of sulks; sudden illness. **toutie,** *a.*
tout, *a.* all. *t. à fait,* entirely. *t. à l'heure,* in a moment. *t. court,* simply, without addition. *t. de suite,* immediately. *t. ensemble,* general effect. (F.)
tovarish, tovarisch, *n.* comrade. (Russ.)
tow, *n.* coarse fibre of hemp.
tow, *v.t.* draw (vessel) through water by rope; pull along behind one. *n.* act of towing. **take in t.,** begin towing; take charge of. **towing-line, towing-rope,** *nn.* for towing with. **towing-path,** *n.* towpath. **towage,** *n.* act of, fee for, towing. (O.E. *togian*)
toward, *a.* (*arch.*) about to happen, in train; compliant, docile.—*prep.* (also **towards**) in direction of; (of time) near. **towardly,** *a.* (*arch.*) propitious, promising. (*to*; *-ward*)
towel, *n.* cloth for drying after washing.—*v.t.* and *i.* rub (oneself) with towel; (*sl.*) thrash. **throw in the t.,** admit defeat. **t.-horse,** *n.* wooden frame for hanging towels on. **towelling,** *n.* material for making towels. (O.H.G. *twahan,* wash)

tower, *n.* tall strong structure standing alone or forming part of building; fortress.—*v.i.* rise aloft; stand very high. **t. above,** overtop; excel. **t. of strength,** person who can be relied on. **towering,** *a.* lofty; (of rage) violent. **towered,** *a.* having towers. (L. *turris*)

towline, *n.* rope for towing.

towmond, *n.* (*Scot.*) twelvemonth.

town, *n.* collection of houses larger than village; its people; nearest main centre, esp. London. **man about t.,** fashionable idler. **t. clerk,** secretary to corporation of town. **t. council,** elective body administering town. **t.-councillor,** *n.* member of this. **t. crier,** officer who makes public proclamations. **t. hall,** public hall for official business of town. **townee,** *n.* (*university sl.*) inhabitant of university town. **townlet,** *n.* little town. **townsfolk,** *n.* townspeople. **township,** *n.* territory of a town; parish; (*Amer.*) subdivision of county; (*Austral.*) site laid out for town. **townsman, townspeople,** *nn.* inhabitant, people, of town. (O.E. *tún*)

towpath, *n.* path for horse towing barge on canal.

towrope, *n.* rope for towing.

toxic, *a.* poisonous; due to poison. **toxicant,** *a.* and *n.* poisonous (agent). **toxaemia,** *n.* blood-poisoning. **toxicology,** *n.* study of poisons. **toxicological,** *a.* **toxicologist,** *n.* **toxicosis,** *n.* condition due to poisoning. **toxin,** *n.* poison of bacterial origin. **toxiphobia,** *n.* morbid fear of poisons. (Gk. *toxikon,* poison)

toxophilite, *n.* and *a.* (student) of archery. **toxophilitic,** *a.* (Gk. *toxon,* bow; *philein,* love)

toy, *n.* child's plaything; trinket, curiosity; thing of no importance, trifle; (*Shake.*) whim.—*a.* mimic, not for real use.—*v.i.* trifle, fiddle (with); dally amorously. **t. dog,** very small pet dog.

trabeated, *a.* constructed of horizontal beams, not arched. **trabeation,** *n.*

trabecula, *n.* (*pl.* **trabeculae**) (*anat.*) small rod, bundle of fibres; (*bot.*) beam-like projection. **trabecular, trabeculate,** *aa.* (L. *trabs,* beam)

tracasseries, *n.pl.* small vexations. (F.)

trace, *n.* either of the side straps or chains by which horse draws vehicle. **kick over the tt.,** break loose from discipline. **t.-horse,** *n.* one hitched on to help up hill etc. (L. *trahere,* draw)

trace, *v.t.* follow course or track of; traverse; detect by scrutiny, discern; mark out, delineate; form (letters); copy (drawing etc.) by marking lines on transparent sheet superimposed.—*n.* marks left by something; footprint; vestige; minute amount, tinge. **traceable,** *a.* **traceability,** *n.* **tracer bullet,** one that leaves visible trail so that aim can be checked. **tracery,** *n.* interlaced pattern; (*archit.*) stone openwork. (L. *trahere,* draw)

trachea, *n.* (*pl.* **tracheae**) windpipe; (*bot.*) duct; (*zool.*) insect's breathing-tube. **tracheal, trachean,** *aa.* **tracheate,** *a.* having trachea. **tracheitis,** *n.* inflammation of trachea. **tracheocele,** *n.* goitre. **tracheotomy,** *n.* making of incision into windpipe. (Gk. *trachus,* rough)

trachle, *v.t.* and *i.* (*Scot.*) draggle; tire; drudge.—*n.* tiring effort.

trachoma, *n.* disease causing roughness of inner surface of eyelid. **trachomatous,** *a.* (Gk.=roughness)

trachyte, *n.* light-coloured volcanic rock. (Gk. *trachus,* rough)

tracing, *n.* reproduction of drawing traced on **t.-paper,** *n.* thin transparent paper.

track, *n.* marks left by passage of something; rough road, path; prepared racing-path; line of railway; band on which military tank runs; transverse distance between vehicle's wheels; (*pl.*) footprints.—*v.t.* and *i.* follow track of, trail; trace by vestiges; tow by rope from bank; (of wheels) so run that hinder is exactly in track of fore. **in one's tt.,** just where one stands. **make tt.,** depart, go hurriedly. **off the t.,** on the wrong path. **the beaten t.,** usual route, ordinary methods. **trackage,** *n.* railway tracks collectively; towage. **trackless,** *a.* untrodden; not using rails. (O.F. *trac*)

tract, *n.* stretch of country, region; expanse; (*anat.*) area of organ or system; (*Shake.*) track, course. (L. *trahere,* draw)

tract, *n.* religious pamphlet; short treatise. (abbr. of *tractate*)

tractable, *a.* easily managed, docile; easily wrought, malleable. **tractability,** *n.* (L. *tractare,* handle)

Tractarian, *a.* and *n.* (adherent) of High Church movement begun at Oxford in 1833 by Newman and others. **Tractarianism,** *n.* (*tract*)

tractate, *n.* (*arch.*) treatise. (L. *tractare,* handle)

tractile, *a.* ductile. **tractility,** *n.* (L. *trahere,* draw)

traction, *n.* action of hauling, pull; transport. **t.-engine,** *n.* steam-engine for drawing heavy loads on road. **tractional, tractive,** *aa.* **tractor,** *n.* motor-vehicle for hauling, caterpillar; traction-engine; aeroplane with engine in front (opp. to pusher). (L. *trahere,* draw)

trade, *n.* business of buying and selling, commerce; shopkeeping; calling; handicraft; (*Shake.*) resort, traffic; (*pl.*) trade-winds.—*v.i.* and *t.* carry on trade; exchange. **Board of T.,** committee of Privy Council supervising commerce and industry. **the t.,** brewers; (*navy sl.*) submarine service. **t. show,** private advance show of film. **t. upon,** exploit, take advantage of. **t.-board,** *n.* statutory body representing employers and employees in a trade. **t. mark,** registered word or symbol used by manufacturer to distinguish his goods. **t. union, trades union,** organized association of workmen of a trade or industry for protection of their interests. **t.-unionism, t.-unionist,** *nn.* **t. wind,** wind blowing continuously from NE. on north side of equator or from SE. on south side. **traded,** *a.* (*Shake.*) experienced. (M.E.=path)

trader, *n.* merchant; trading vessel.

tradesman, *n.* shopkeeper; skilled workman.

tradespeople, *n.* tradesmen and their families.

tradition, *n.* belief, custom, story, handed down by word of mouth from generation to generation; this process of transmission; (*law*) formal delivery. **traditional, traditionary,** *aa.* consisting of, derived from, tradition. **traditionalism,** *n.* adherence to tradition. **traditionalist, traditionist,** *nn.* **traditionalistic,** *a.* (L. *tradere*, hand over)

traduce, *v.t.* slander, defame; misrepresent. **traducer, traducement,** *nn.* **traducible,** *a.* (L. *trans*, across; *ducere*, lead)

traducianism, *n.* doctrine that soul is procreated along with body. **traducian, traducianist,** *nn.* (*traduce*)

traffic, *v.i.* and *t.* (*past, p.p.* **trafficked**) trade, do business; barter.—*n.* trade; passage to and fro of people, vehicles, ships, etc.; intercourse. **trafficker,** *n.* **trafficator,** *n.* movable pointer by which driver of motor-car can signal when turning. (It. *trafficare*)

tragacanth, *n.* gum used in pharmacy; shrub yielding it. (Gk. *tragos*, goat; *akantha*, thorn)

tragedy, *n.* serious play with unhappy ending; this type of drama; sad or dreadful event. **tragic,** *a.* of tragedy; (also **tragical**) sad, distressing; calamitous. **tragedian,** *n.* writer of, actor in, tragedy. **tragedienne,** *n.* tragic actress. **tragi-comedy,** *n.* play, events, with both tragic and comic elements. **tragi-comic,** *a.* (Gk. *tragos*, goat; *aeidein*, sing)

tragopan, *n.* kinds of bright-coloured Asiatic pheasant. (Gk.=goat-Pan)

traik, *v.i.* (*Scot.*) wander about; get lost.—*n.* misfortune.

trail, *v.t.* and *i.* drag, be dragged, along behind; hang loosely, stream out; follow track of; walk wearily. —*n.* sign of passage, track, spoor; path through wild region; appendage; extended part of gun-carriage which rests on ground; trailing position of rifle. **t. arms,** carry rifle horizontally at arm's length. **t. one's coat,** give deliberate provocation. **trailer,** *n.* one who trails; trailing plant, creeper; vehicle drawn by another; extracts from cinema film shown in advance as advertisement. (L. *trahere*, draw)

train, *v.t.* and *i.* educate; discipline; instruct by exercise; make (oneself) physically fit; direct growth of (plant); aim (gun); (*rare*) draw along; (*colloq.*) travel by train; (*arch.*) entice.—*n.* retinue; procession, line; series; sequences of events; string of railway coaches or trucks; trailing prolongation of skirt; line of gunpowder for firing charge; (*Shake.*) tail; lure. **in t.,** in preparation. **t.-band,** *n.* company of citizen-soldiers of 16th–18th centuries. **t.-bearer,** *n.* one holding up train of another's dress. **t.-ferry,** *n.* vessel carrying railway train across water. **training-college,** *n.* for training teachers. **training-ship,** *n.* moored vessel on which boys are taught seamanship. (L. *trahere*, draw)

trainee, *n.* person being trained.

trainer, *n.* one who trains athletes or race-horses.

trainman, *n.* (*Amer.*) brakeman or porter on railway train.

train-oil, *n.* thick oil made from whale's blubber. (O. Du. *traen*, tear)

traipse, same as **trapes.**

trait, *n.* characteristic, feature; (*arch.*) stroke, touch. (F.)

traitor, *n.* (*fem.* **traitress**) one who betrays a person or cause; one who helps his country's enemies. **traitorous,** *a.* guilty of treachery, disloyal. (L. *tradere*, hand over)

trajectory, *n.* path of projectile. (L. *trans*, across; *jacere*, throw)

tram, *n.* double twisted thread used in some silks. (L. *trama*, weft)

tram, *n.* tram-car; tramway; four-wheeled wagon in coal-mine.—*v.t.* and *i.* convey, go, in tram-car. **t.-car,** *n.* large public vehicle running on rails. **t.-line,** *n.* tramway rail or route. (L.G. *traam*, beam)

trammel, *n.* anything that checks or restrains; fishing-net; shackle for teaching horse to amble; pot-hook; beam-compass. — *v.t.* hamper, restrain. (L.L. *tramacula*)

tramontane, *a.* (from) across the mountains, transalpine; foreign, barbarous.—*n.* tramontane person. *tramontana*, *n.* dry cold wind of Adriatic. (L. *trans*, beyond; *mons*, mountain)

tramp, *v.i.* and *t.* tread heavily; go on foot, walk (over); wander as vagrant; (*Scot.*) tread (clothes) in wash-tub.—*n.* homeless vagrant; sound of tramping; ramble; cargo steamer with no fixed trade route. (M.E. *trampen*)

trample, *v.t.* and *i.* tread under foot;

tread heavily. **t. on,** treat with contempt; domineer over. (*tramp*)

tramway, *n.* line of rails laid in road for tram-cars.

trance, *n.* abnormal state of suspended consciousness; profound abstraction, ecstasy; catalepsy. (L. *trans,* across; *ire,* go)

tranquil, *a.* calm, undisturbed; composed, unruffled. **tranquillity,** *n.* **tranquillize,** *v.t.* and *i.* make or become tranquil, calm down. **tranquillization,** *n.* (L. *tranquillus*)

trans-, *pref.* across, through, beyond, as in **transit, transfix, transatlantic;** into a different state or place, as in **transform, transpose.** (L.)

transact, *v.t.* and *i.* carry through, conduct, do (business). **transaction,** *n.* transacting; piece of business done; (*pl.*) proceedings; papers read before learned society. **transactor,** *n.* (*act*)

transalpine, *a.* beyond the Alps in regard to Rome, i.e. north of them (opp. to cisalpine).

transatlantic, *a.* across or beyond the Atlantic, American.

transcend, *v.t.* and *i.* go beyond, overstep; be too high for; surpass, excel. **transcendent,** *a.* surpassing, supreme; beyond the range of human knowledge; above human limitations. **transcendence, transcendency,** *nn.* **transcendental,** *a.* abstruse, visionary; not based on experience but concerned with its presuppositions, intuitive. — *n.* transcendentalist. **transcendentalism,** *n.* philosophy that emphasizes the limitations of the senses and holds true knowledge to be intuitive. **transcendentalist,** *n.* adherent of this. **transcendentalize,** *v.t.* (L. *scandere,* climb)

transcontinental, *a.* passing across a continent.

transcribe, *v.t.* copy out in writing. **transcript,** *n.* written copy. **transcription,** *n.* transcribing; transcript. **transcriptional, transcriptive,** *aa.* (L. *scribere,* write)

transcurrent, *a.* extending across. (L. *currere,* run)

transect, *v.t.* cut across. **transection,** *n.* cross-section. (L. *secare,* cut)

transept, *n.* part of cruciform church at right angles to and between nave and choir. (L. *septum,* enclosure)

transfer, *v.t.* and *i.* move from one place to another; convey from one surface to another; make over the possession of (to); change from one conveyance, regiment etc., to another.—*n.* transference; conveyance of property; coloured picture or design that can be transferred from paper on which it is sold to another surface. **transferable,** *a.* able to be transferred; negotiable. **transferable vote,** method of election in which voter indicates to which candidate his vote is to be transferred if his first choice has a surplus or is out of the running. **transferor, transferee,** *nn.* person by, to, whom stocks etc. are transferred. **transference,** *n.* transferring; (*psycho-anal.*) redirection of emotion under analysis, usually towards analyst. (L. *ferre,* bear)

transfigure, *v.t.* alter appearance of, transform; make beautiful or glorious. **transfiguration,** *n.* transfiguring; miraculous glorification of Christ's appearance when on the mount with Peter, James, and John; festival commemorating this on 6 Aug.

transfix, *v.t.* pierce through, impale; root (person) to spot; (*Shake.*) remove. **transfixion,** *n.*

transform, *v.t.* change appearance or character of, alter out of recognition; change into something else, transmute. **transformation,** *n.* transforming; woman's wig. **transformation-scene,** *n.* theatrical scene which changes before eyes of audience. **transformer,** *n.* one who transforms; (*electr.*) apparatus for changing voltage of alternating current supply. **transformism,** *n.* development of one species from another; theory of development of complex animals from free organisms united into colony and changed into organs of complex whole. **transformist,** *n.* **transformistic,** *a.*

transfuse, *v.t.* pour from one vessel into another; transfer (blood) from healthy person to ill one; penetrate deeply, imbue (with). **transfusion,** *n.* **transfusive,** *a.* (L. *fundere,* pour)

transgress, *v.t.* and *i.* go beyond, overstep; break (law); sin. **transgression,** *n.* transgressing; misdeed. **transgressional, transgressive,** *aa.* **transgressor,** *n.* sinner. (L. *gradi,* step)

tranship, *v.t.* and *i.* move from one ship to another. **transhipment,** *n.*

transient, *a.* passing, not permanent; fleeting, momentary. **transience, transiency,** *nn.* (L. *ire,* go)

transilient, *a.* leaping across; abruptly discontinuous. (L. *salire,* leap)

transilluminate, *v.t.* (*med.*) pass light through (body). **transillumination,** *n.*

transirė, *n.* custom-house warrant for passage of goods. (L.=go across)

trans-isthmian, *a.* across an isthmus.

transit, *n.* passing over, crossing; conveyance; (*astron.*) passage of planet across sun's disk, or of star across meridian. **transition,** *n.* passage from one place, condition, or style to another; change. **transitional, transitionary,** *aa.* **transitive,** *a.* (of verb) governing a direct object. **transitivity,** *n.* **transitory,** *a.* fleeting, transient. (L. *ire,* go)

translate, *v.t.* and *i.* turn from one

language into another; interpret, explain; move (bishop) from one see to another; convey direct to heaven without death; (*mech.*) impart motion without rotation to; (*arch.*) transform. **translation,** *n.* translating; thing translated; version. **translational, translative,** *aa.* **translator,** *n.* (*transfer*)

transliterate, *v.t.* write in letters of another alphabet. **transliteration, transliterator,** *nn.* (L. *litera,* letter)

translucent, *a.* allowing light to pass but not transparent. **translucence, translucency,** *nn.* (L. *lux,* light)

transmarine, *a.* beyond the sea.

transmigrate *v.i.* migrate; (of soul) pass at death into another body. **transmigration,** *n.* transmigrating; metempsychosis. **transmigrator,** *n.* **transmigratory,** *a.* **transmigrant,** *n.* alien passing through one country on way to another.

transmit, *v.t.* hand over, pass on; communicate; hand down to descendants; allow to pass, be medium for. **transmitter,** *n.* one who transmits; appliance for transmitting telegraphic or wireless messages. **transmissible,** *a.* **transmissibility,** *n.* **transmission,** *n.* transmitting. (L. *mittere,* send)

transmogrify, *v.t.* (*colloq.*) change completely, transform. **transmogrification,** *n.*

transmute, *v.t.* change into another substance or species; change nature of. **transmutation,** *n.* transmuting. **transmutation of metals,** conversion of metals into gold. **transmutative,** *a.* (L. *mutare,* change)

transoceanic, *a.* across or beyond an ocean.

transom, *n.* transverse beam or bar; lintel. (L. *transtrum*)

transpadane, *a.* north of the Po. (L. *Padus,* Po)

transparent, *a.* able to be seen through distinctly, letting light pass without distortion; candid, open; obvious; (of style) clear, lucid; (of excuse) flimsy. **transparence,** *n.* **transparency,** *n.* being transparent; picture made visible by light behind it. (L. *parēre,* appear)

transpierce, *v.t.* pierce through.

transpire, *v.t.* and *i.* emit, pass off, through pores of skin; exhale (moisture); (of news) become known, leak out; (*vulg.*) happen. **transpiration,** *n.* **transpiratory,** *a.* (L. *spirare,* breathe)

transplant, *v.t.* dig up and plant in another place; remove and settle elsewhere; (*med.*) transfer (living tissue) to another part or body. **transplantation, transplanter,** *nn.*

transpontine, *a.* of the part of London south of the Thames. **t. drama,** lurid melodramatic kind once popular there. (L. *pons,* bridge)

transport, *v.t.* carry, convey; deport (criminal) beyond sea; carry away by violent emotion, ravish; (*Shake.*) remove from the world.—*n.* conveyance, carrying; ship conveying troops or military stores; violent emotion, ecstasy. **transportable,** *a.* **transportation,** (*Shake.*) **transportance,** *nn.* (L. *portare,* carry)

transpose, *v.t.* put each in place of the other, interchange; alter order of; (*mus.*) put into different key. **transposal, transposition,** *nn.* **transpositional, transpositive,** *aa.* (L. *pausare,* halt and *ponere,* place)

trans-ship, same as **tranship.**

transubstantiate, *v.t.* change into another substance. **transubstantiation,** *n.* transubstantiating; conversion of eucharistic elements into the body and blood of Christ.

transude, *v.i.* pass through pores, be exuded. **transudation,** *n.* **transudatory,** *a.* (L. *sudare,* sweat)

transverse, *a.* set or acting across.—*n.* transverse muscle. **transversal,** *n.* line cutting a system of lines. **transversely,** *adv.* crosswise. (L. *vertere,* turn)

tranter, *n.* (*dial.*) carter, carrier, hawker. (L.L. *travetarius*)

trap, *v.t.* furnish with trappings.—*n.pl.* personal possessions; luggage. (F. *draper,* clothe)

trap, *n.* (also **t.-rock**) kinds of dark-coloured igneous rock. (Swed. *trapp*)

trap, *n.* device for catching animals, snare; scheme to entice or detect, stratagem; bend in drain-pipe retaining water and preventing gas from escaping; contrivance for throwing up ball etc. to be shot or struck at; two-wheeled horse-carriage; trap-door; (*sl.*) policeman.—*v.t.* and *i.* catch in trap, snare; beguile; supply (drain) with trap; work as trapper. **t.-ball,** *n.* old game played with trap and ball. **t.-door,** *n.* horizontal door in floor or roof. (O.E. *treppe*)

trapan, same as **trepan.**

trapes, *v.i.* tramp or trudge wearily; go about on errands.—*n.* slattern.

trapeze, *n.* short swinging cross-bar suspended by ropes; trapezium.

trapezium, *n.* quadrilateral with only two sides parallel; (*Amer.*) trapezoid. **trapeziform,** *a.* **trapezoid,** *n.* quadrilateral with no sides parallel; (*Amer.*) trapezium. **trapezoidal,** *a.* (Gk. *trapeza,* table)

trappean, *a.* of trap-rock.

trapper, *n.* one who traps animals for their skins.

trappings, *n.pl.* ornamental housings for horse; ceremonial dress; embellishments. (*trap*)

Trappist, *n.* member of Cistercian order of monks who observe strict silence. (La *Trappe* in France)

trappoid, trappose, *aa.* trappean.

trappy, *a.* (*colloq.*) full of snares.
trash, *n.* rubbish, refuse; riff-raff; loppings of trees; sugarcane waste. —*v.t.* strip of leaves; lop. **t.-ice,** *n.* broken ice mixed with water.
trash, *v.t.* (*Shake.*) slow down (hound) with weight attached to collar.
trass, *n.* a volcanic earth formerly used for cement. (Du. *tras*)
trattoria, *n.* Italian eating-house. (It.)
trauchle, same as **trachle.**
trauma, *n.* (*med.*, *pl.* **traumata**) injury; shock. **traumatic,** *a.* of, for, caused by, trauma. (Gk.=wound)
travail, *n.* (*arch.*) pains of childbirth; laborious effort.—*v.i.* (*arch.*) be in labour; toil. (L.L. *trepalium,* instrument of torture)
trave, *n.* frame to confine horse while being shod. (L. *trabs,* beam)
travel, *v.i.* and *t.* make journey (through); pass, proceed; be commercial traveller; (*colloq.*) get up great pace.—*n.* travelling, esp. abroad. (=*travail*)
traveller, *n.* one who travels; (*also* **commercial t.**) one who goes about to obtain orders for firm. **t.'s tale,** highly coloured story. **t.'s-joy,** *n.* wild clematis.
travelogue, *n.* lecture-narrative of travels; geographical film. (*travel*+Gk. *legein,* speak)
traverse, *v.t.* and *i.* go through or over, cross; take exception to, deny; move or turn laterally, swivel; make traverse of (cliff).—*n.* thing laid or built across; lateral movement; sideways crossing of cliff-face; zigzag turn in trench to prevent enfilading, earthwork screening approach; (*law*) formal denial of opponent's allegation.—*a.* and *adv.* (set) across. **t.-table, traverser,** *nn.* platform for shifting railway carriages from one line to another. (*transverse*)
travertine, travertin, *n.* limestone formed by deposit of springs. (L. *Tiburtinus,* of Tivoli)
travesty, *n.* comic imitation, burlesque; misrepresentation.—*v.t.* make or be travesty of, caricature. (L. *trans,* across; *vestire,* clothe)
trawl, *n.* (also **t.-net**) wide-mouthed net for dragging along sea-bottom after boat; (also **t.-line**) long line buoyed at ends and supporting short lines with hooks.—*v.i.* and *t.* fish, catch, with trawl-net. **trawler,** *n.* person, vessel, employed in trawling.
tray, *n.* flat board or metal plate with low rim. (O.E. *trig*)
tray-trip, *n.* (*Shake.*) a game at dice. (*trey*)
treacherous, *a.* disloyal, faithless; unreliable, deceptive. **treacher,** *n.* (*Shake.*) traitor. **treachery,** *n.* violation of faith, perfidy. (O.F. *trechier,* deceive)
treacle, *n.* thick syrupy substance got in refining sugar, molasses. **treacly,** *a.* thick and sticky; unctuous. (Gk. *thēriakē,* antidote)
tread, *v.i.* and *t.* (*past* **trod,** *p.p.* **trodden, trod**) walk, step (on); traverse; press by treading, trample; (of male bird) copulate with.—*n.* manner or sound of walking; upper surface of step; part of shoe or tyre which presses on ground; germ of chick, showing as white spot on yolk. **t. a measure,** (*arch.*) dance. **t. in one's footsteps,** follow his example. **t. on one's toes,** offend his prejudices. **t. on the heels of,** follow close after. **t. the boards,** be an actor. **t. water,** support oneself upright in water by trampling. **treadle,** *n.* lever worked by foot to turn wheel. **treadmill,** *n.* mill worked by walking on steps of wheel, formerly used as punishment in prisons; wearisome grind. O.E. *tredan*)
treason, *n.* treachery, disloyalty; (also **high t.**) violation of allegiance to sovereign or state by rebellion, aiding enemy, etc. **treasonous,** *a.* **treasonable,** *a.* involving, guilty of, treason. (L. *tradere,* hand over)
treasure, *n.* stored wealth or valuables; thing of great value; loved or useful person.—*v.t.* store, keep, as valuable; value highly, cherish fondly; (*Shake.*) enrich. **t. trove,** gold or silver found hidden, the owner being unknown. **treasurer,** *n.* officer in charge of funds of society etc. (Gk. *thēsauros*)
treasury, *n.* place where treasure is stored; funds of state or institution; state department of finance; literary collection, anthology; (*Shake.*) treasure. **T. bench,** front bench on Speaker's right in House of Commons, occupied by members of ministry. **t. note,** £1 or 10*s.* note issued by Treasury.
treat, *v.t.* and *i.* act or behave towards, use; deal with, subject to process; pay expenses of, regale; negotiate (with).—*n.* great pleasure or thing that gives it; entertainment, picnic. **stand t.,** bear expenses. **t. of,** discourse on. **treatise,** *n.* systematic written account, formal essay; (*Shake.*) discourse. **treatment,** *n.* way of treating, usage; mode of dealing with disease. **treaty,** *n.* formal agreement between states; negotiation. **treaty port,** one opened under treaty to foreign commerce. (L. *tractare,* handle)
treble, *a.* threefold, three times.—*n.* highest voice, soprano; singer with, music for, this.—*v.t.* and *i.* make, become, three times as much. **t.-dated,** *a.* (*Shake.*) living for three generations. (L. *triplus*)
trebuchet, trebucket, *n.* ancient military engine for hurling stones. (O.F.)
trecento, *n.* fourteenth century in Italian art. **trecentist,** *n.* painter,

writer, of this time. (It.=three hundred, used for 1300)

trechometer, *n.* instrument for registering distance run by vehicle. (Gk. *trechein,* run; *metron,* measure)

tree, *n.* large perennial plant with woody trunk; beam; family tree; (*arch.*) the cross of Christ.—*v.t.* chase up tree; place in dilemma; stretch (boot) on boot-tree. **family t.,** genealogical chart. **t. calf,** calf binding stained with tree-like markings. **up a t., in a fix. t.-creeper,** *n.* a small bird. **t.-fern,** *n.* large kinds with woody stem. **t.-frog,** *n.* kind that climbs trees. **t.-nail,** *n.* pin of hard wood used for securing planks.

treen, *a.* wooden. (O.E. *tréo*)

trefoil, *n.* plant with three-lobed leaf, esp. clover; (*archit.*) three-cusped ornament like this. (L. *tres,* three; *folium,* leaf)

trek, *v.i.* and *t.* travel by ox-wagon, migrate; (of ox) pull (load); (*sl.*) clear out.—*n.* trekking; organized migration. **trekker,** *n.* (Du.)

trellis, *n.* lattice or grating of light bars fixed crosswise.—*v.t.* furnish, support, with trellis. **t.-work,** *n.* (L. *trilix,* three-ply)

tremble, *v.i.* quiver, shake; be terrified, quail.—*n.* tremor, quiver. **all of a t.,** (*colloq.*) greatly agitated. **trembler,** *n.* automatic vibrator for making and breaking electric circuit. (L. *tremere*)

tremelloid, tremellose, *aa.* (*bot.*) jelly-like, shaking like jelly. (*tremble*)

tremendous, *a.* awful, terrific; (*colloq.*) great. (L. *tremere,* tremble)

tremolando, adv. (*mus.*) tremulously. *tremolo, n.* intentionally quavering effect in singing or playing. (It.)

tremor, *n.* shaking, quivering; thrill of fear, qualm. **tremulous,** *a.* shaky, trembling; timid, agitated. (L.)

trenail, same as **tree-nail.**

trench, *v.t.* and *i.* cut ditches in; dig deeply; furrow; encroach or verge (on).—*n.* deep ditch; excavation with parapet as shelter from enemy's fire; groove. **t. coat,** soldier's short waterproof coat. **t. feet,** disease of feet with sloughing, caused by continual standing in water. **t. fever,** an infectious fever propagated by lice. **t. mortar,** small smooth-bore gun throwing large shell short distance. (O.F. *trenchier,* cut)

trenchant, *a.* sharp, cutting; incisive, biting, severe. **trenchancy,** *n.* (*trench*)

trencher, *n.* wooden board for cutting bread on; (*Shake.*) plate. **t.-friend,** *n.* (*Shake.*) parasite. **t.-knight,** *n.* (*Shake.*) serving-man at table. **trencherman,** *n.* eater. (*trench*)

trend, *v.i.* take specified direction; tend.—*n.* inclination, course; tendency, drift. (O.E. *trendan*)

trental, *n.* series of thirty masses for dead. (L. *triginta,* thirty)

trente-et-quarante, n. a gambling card-game, *rouge-et-noir.* (F.)

trepan, *v.t.* cut out part of bone from (skull) to relieve pressure on brain.—*n.* surgeon's cylindrical saw for this. **trepanation,** *n.* (Gk. *trupa,* hole)

trepan, *v.t.* ensnare, beguile.

trepang, *n.* edible sea-slug, *bêche-de-mer.* (Malay *trīpang*)

trephine, *n.* improved kind of trepan. —*v.t.* operate upon with this. (L. *tres fines,* three ends)

trepidation, *n.* alarm, fluster, apprehension; involuntary twitching of limbs. (L. *trepidus,* agitated)

trespass, *v.i.* go unlawfully upon another's land; encroach, make unwarrantable demands (on); (*arch.*) transgress, sin.—*n.* act of trespassing; (*arch.*) sin, offence. **trespasser,** *n.* (L. *trans,* across; *passus,* step)

tress, *n.* lock or braid of hair.—*v.t.* arrange in tresses. (L.L. *tricia*)

tressure, *n.* (*heraldry*) double border round escutcheon, ornamented with fleurs-de-lis. (*tress*)

trestle, *n.* bar fixed on pairs of spreading legs and used as support; similar framework supporting **t.-bridge,** *n.* (L. *transtrum,* transom+dim.)

tret, *n.* extra allowance of 4 lb. on 100 lb. formerly made to buyers of certain goods for wastage in transit.

trews, *n.pl.* trousers, esp. of tartan cloth. (Gael. *triubhas,* trousers)

trey, *n.* three at dice or cards. (L. *tres,* three)

tri-, *pref.* thrice, threefold. (L. and Gk.)

triad, *n.* number three; group of three; element or radical with valency of three. (Gk. *treis,* three)

triadelphous, *a.* having stamens united in three bundles. (Gk. *treis,* three; *adelphos,* brother)

trial, *n.* test; probation; attempt; misfortune, affliction; judicial inquiry in court of law. **bring to t.,** prosecute. **t. trip,** short voyage to test ship. (*try*)

triandrous, *a.* with three stamens. (Gk. *treis,* three; *anēr,* man)

triangle, *n.* three-sided plane figure; percussion-instrument of steel rod bent into triangle and struck with another rod; set-square; tripod for hoisting etc. **the eternal t.,** married pair and lover of one of them. **triangular** *a.* triangle-shaped, three-cornered, involving three parties. **triangularity,** *n.* **triangulate,** *v.t.* divide (area) into triangles for surveying purposes. **triangulation,** *n.* (L. *tres,* three; *angulus,* angle)

triapsal, triapsidal, *aa.* with three apses. (*tri-*)

triarchy, *n.* government by three persons. (Gk. *treis,* three; *archē,* rule)

Trias, *n.* (*geol.*) earliest of Mesozoic periods, new red sandstone formation. **Triassic,** *a.* (*triad*)

tribadism, *n.* homosexuality in women. (Gk. *tribas,* lewd woman)
tribasic, *a.* with three replaceable univalent atoms in the molecule.
tribe, *n.* aggregate of families forming primitive community us. under a chief; class, group; (*zool.*) subdivision of order or family. **tribal,** *a.* of tribe. **tribalism,** *n.* tribal organization. **tribesman,** *n.* member of tribe. (L. *tribus*)
triblet, tribolet, *n.* mandrel for forging rings etc. (F. *triboulet*)
tribometer, *n.* apparatus for measuring sliding friction. (Gk. *tribein,* rub; *metron,* measure)
tribrach, *n.* foot of three short syllables. **tribrachic,** *a.* (Gk. *treis,* three; *brachus,* short)
tribrach, *n.* three-armed object or implement. **tribrachial,** *a.* (Gk. *treis,* three; *brachion,* arm)
tribulation, *n.* severe affliction; distress. (L. *tribulum,* threshing-sledge)
tribunal, *n.* seat of judge; court of justice; board hearing claims for exemption from military service. (L.)
tribune, *n.* plebeian magistrate of ancient Rome; champion of people's rights. **tribunate,** *n.* office of tribune. **tribunary, tribunicial, tribunitial, tribunician,** *aa.* (L. *tribunus*)
tribune, *n.* raised stand, platform, from which assembly is addressed; bishop's throne; apse of basilica. (L.L. *tribuna*)
tribute, *n.* payment made by one state or ruler to another in sign of dependence; personal contribution, thing done as mark of respect. **tributary,** *a.* paying tribute; auxiliary.—*n.* stream flowing into another; tributary state. (L. *tribuere,* assign)
tricapsular, *a.* with three capsules.
tricar, *n.* three-wheeled motor-car with single driving-wheel behind.
tricarpous, *a.* bearing three fruits or carpels. (Gk. *treis,* three; *karpos,* fruit)
trice, *v.t.* (*naut.*) haul (up) and make fast.—*n.* moment. **in a t.,** in an instant. (O. Du. *trisen,* hoist)
tricennial, *a.* lasting, occurring every, thirty years. (L. *tricennium,* thirty years)
tricentenary, same as **tercentenary.**
tricephalous, *a.* three-headed. (Gk. *treis,* three; *kephalē,* head)
triceps, *a.* three-headed.—*n.* extensor muscle at back of arm. (L. *tres,* three; *caput,* head)
trichinopoli, trichi, *n.* kind of Indian cheroot. (place)
trich(o)-, from Gk. *thrix,* hair, used in **trichiasis,** *n.* disease marked by hair-like filaments in urine, inward turning of eyelashes; **trichina,** *n.* (*pl.* **trichinae**) a minute parasitic worm, hence **trichinotic, trichinosed, trichinous,** *aa.*, **trichinize,** *v.t.* infect with trichinae, **trichinosis,** *n.* disease caused by trichinae; **trichocarpous,** *a.* hairy-fruited; **trichoclasis,** *n.* brittleness of hair; **trichogenous,** *a.* producing hair; **trichology,** *n.* scientific study of hair; **trichome,** *n.* hair or other outgrowth from epidermis of plant; **trichopathy,** *n.* treatment of hair-disease, hence **trichopathic,** *a.*; **trichophytosis,** *n.* ringworm; **trichosis,** *n.* any disease of hair.
trichord, *a.* three-stringed; having three strings to each note.—*n.* three-stringed instrument. (*tri-*)
trichotomy, *n.* threefold division, esp. of human nature into body, soul, and spirit. **trichotomous,** *a.* (Gk. *treis,* three; *temnein,* cut)
trichromatic, *a.* three-coloured.
trick, *n.* stratagem, artifice, deception; practical joke, prank; contrivance to puzzle, amuse, or annoy; feat of skill, knack; habit, mannerism; turn, spell; the cards played in one round.—*v.t.* impose on, cheat; deck. **do the t.,** (*sl.*) succeed, suffice. **t. out,** decorate, set off. **trickery,** *n.* fraud, knavery. (O.F. *trique*)
trickle, *v.i.* and *t.* flow, cause to flow, slowly or in thin stream.—*n.* thin flow. (M.E. *triklen*)
trickster, *n.* cheat, swindler.
tricksy, *a.* capricious, mischievous.
trick-track, *n.* complicated form of backgammon. (F. *trictrac*)
tricky, *a.* unreliable, shifty; ingenious; full of pitfalls, involved.
triclinic, *a.* (of crystal) having three unequal axes meeting at oblique angles. (Gk. *treis,* three; *klinein,* bend)
triclinium, *n.* (*pl. triclinia*) ancient Roman dining-room; horse-shoe of three couches round table in it. (L.)
tricolour, tricolor, *n.* French national flag of three vertical stripes, red, white, and blue.—*a.* (also **tricoloured**) three-coloured. (*tri-*)
tricorn, *a.* three-horned.—*n.* three-cornered hat. (L. *tres,* three; *cornu,* horn)
tricorporal, tricorporate, *aa.* having three bodies and one head. (L. *tres,* three; *corpus,* body)
tricot, *n.* knitted fabric. (F.)
tricrotic, *a.* (of pulse) with three beats. **tricrotism,** *n.* (Gk. *treis,* three; *krotos,* beat)
trictrac, same as **trick-track.**
tricuspid, *a.* with three cusps or points. (*tri-*)
tricycle, *n.* three-wheeled cycle.—*v.i.* ride on this. **tricyclist,** *n.*
tridactyl, tridactylous, *aa.* with three fingers or toes. (Gk. *treis,* three; *daktulos,* finger)
trident, *n.* three-pronged fish-spear borne as sceptre by Neptune and Britannia. **tridentate,** *a.* having three

teeth or prongs. (L. *tres*, three; *dens*, tooth)

tridigitate, *a.* tridactyl. (L. *tres*, three; *digitus*, finger)

tridimensional, *a.* of three dimensions.

triduum, *n.* three days' space or service of prayer. **triduan,** *a.* (L.)

tried, *a.* tested; trustworthy.

triennial, *a.* lasting three years; happening every third year.—*n.* third anniversary. (L. *tres*, three; *annus*, year)

trier, *n.* one who tries; judge; trior.

trifid, *a.* divided into three parts. (L. *tres*, three; *findere*, split)

trifle, *n.* thing of no value, paltry matter; small amount; cold sweet of sponge cake soaked in sherry and covered with whipped cream.—*v.i.* and *t.* act or talk with levity; amuse oneself, toy (with); fool (away); (*Shake.*) make insignificant. **a t.,** slightly. **trifling,** *a.* unimportant. (O.F. *trufle*, mockery)

trifloral, triflorous, *aa.* bearing three flowers. (L. *tres*, three; *flos*, flower)

trifoliate, *a.* having three leaves or leaflets; (*archit.*) trefoiled. (L. *tres*, three; *folium*, leaf)

triforium, *n.* (*pl.* **triforia**) gallery, arcade, above nave and choir. (L.L.)

triform, triformed, *aa.* having three forms or parts, triple. (*tri-*)

trifurcate, *a.* having three branches or forks.—*v.t.* and *i.* divide thus. (L. *tres*, three; *furca*, fork)

trig, *a.* smart, trim.—*v.t.* smarten.

trig, *n.* skid for wheel; mark for playing from at skittles etc.—*v.t.* wedge with trig.

trig, *n.* (*school sl.*) trigonometry.

trigamy, *n.* having three wives or husbands at a time. **trigamist,** *n.* **trigamous,** *a.* guilty of trigamy; (*bot.*) having male, female, and hermaphrodite flowers in same head. (Gk. *treis*, three; *gamos*, marriage)

trigeminal, *a.* triple. **trigeminous,** *a.* born three at a birth. (L. *tres*, three; *geminus*, twin)

trigger, *n.* lever releasing spring, esp. that which fires gun. (Du. *trekken*, pull)

triglot, *a.* written in, speaking, three languages. (Gk. *treis*, three; *glōtta*, tongue)

triglyph, *n.* grooved tablet alternating with metope in Doric frieze. **triglyphal, triglyphic, triglyphical,** *aa.* (Gk. *trigluphos*)

trigon, *n.* triangle; an ancient Greek ball-game; trine; (*astrol.*) group of three zodiacal signs. **trigonal, trigonic, trigonous,** *aa.* triangular. (Gk. *treis*, three; *gōnia*, angle)

trigoneutic, *a.* having three broods in a year. (Gk. *treis*, three; *goneuein*, beget)

trigonometry, *n.* branch of mathematics dealing with relations between sides and angles of triangles. **trigonometric, trigonometrical,** *aa.* (Gk. *trigōnon*, triangle; *metron*, measure)

trigraph, trigram, *nn.* group of three letters sounded as one, as in b*eau*, s*ch*ism. **trigrammatic,** *a.* (Gk. *treis*, three; *graphein*, write)

trigynous, *a.* having three pistils. (Gk. *treis*, three; *gunē*, woman)

trihedral, *a.* with three surfaces. (Gk. *treis*, three; *hedra*, seat)

trijugate, trijugous, *aa.* having three pairs of leaflets. (L. *tres*, three; *jugum*, yoke)

trike, *n.* (*colloq.*) tricycle. (abbr.)

trilabiate, *a.* three-lipped. (L. *tres*, three; *labium*, lip)

trilaminar, *a.* with three layers. (L. *tres*, three; *lamina*, plate)

trilateral, *a.* three-sided.—*n.* triangle. (L. *tres*, three; *latus*, side)

trilby, *n.* soft felt hat; (*pl.*, *sl.*) feet. (name in novel)

trilemma, *n.* dilemma-like position with three choices. (Gk. *treis*, three; *lēmma*, assumption)

trilinear, *a.* of, enclosed by, three lines. (*tri-*)

trilingual, *a.* of, in, speaking, three languages. (L. *tres*, three; *lingua*, tongue)

triliteral, *a.* and *n.* (word) of three letters. (L. *tres*, three; *litera*, letter)

trilith, *n.* monument of two upright stones with one across top. **trilithic,** *a.* (Gk. *treis*, three; *lithos*, stone)

trill, *n.* quavering or vibrating sound; (*mus.*) shake.—*v.i.* and *t.* utter, pronounce with, trill; warble. (It. *trillare*)

trill, *v.i.* (*Shake.*) trickle. (M.E. *trillen*, roll)

trilling, *n.* compound threefold crystal; triplet (child). (*tri-+-ling*)

trillion, *n.* a million million million (1 with 18 ciphers); (in U.S. and France) a million million (1 with 12 ciphers). (*tri-+million*)

trilobate, *a.* three-lobed. **trilobite,** *n.* fossil crustacean of the Palaeozoic age. **trilobitic,** *a.* (*tri-*)

trilocular, *a.* with three cells or cavities. (L. *tres*, three; *loculus*, little place)

trilogy, *n.* series of three plays, novels etc., with common theme. (Gk. *treis*, three; *logos*, discourse)

trim, *v.t.* and *i.* (*past*, *p.p.* **trimmed**) make neat, adjust; clip edges of, clip off, lop; decorate, adorn; arrange (sails) to suit wind; adjust balance of (ship, aircraft); fluctuate between parties, be time-server; (*colloq.*) reprove, thrash, worst; fleece.—*n.* order, adjustment; state of fitness or readiness; set of ship on water; (*Shake.*) trappings.—*a.* neat, compact; in good order. (O.E. *trymian*)

trimensual, *a.* happening every three months, quarterly. (L. *tres*, three; *mensis*, month)

trimerous, *a.* (*bot.*) having its parts in threes; (*zool.*) three-jointed. (Gk. *treis*, three; *meros*, part)
trimester, *n.* three-month period. **trimestrial,** *a.* (*trimensual*)
trimeter, *n.* verse of three measures each containing one or two feet according to the metre. **trimetric, trimetrical,** *aa.* (Gk. *treis*, three; *metron*, measure)
trimmer, *n.* one who trims; timeserver. **trimming,** *n.* border, frill; (*pl.*) accessories.
trimorphous, trimorphic, *aa.* existing, crystallizing, in three distinct forms. **trimorphism,** *n.* (Gk. *treis*, three; *morphē*, form)
trine, *a.* threefold, triple; in trine.—*n.* (*astrol.*) aspect of planets 120° apart. **trinal,** *a.* threefold. **trinary,** *a.* ternary. (L. *tres*, three)
trinervate, *a.* three-nerved. (*tri-*)
tringle, *n.* curtain-rod; bar on gun-platform to check recoil; (*archit.*) small square moulding. (F.)
trinitrotoluene, trinitrotoluol, *nn.* (*abbr.* **T.N.T.**) a high-explosive. (*tri-*+*nitre*+*toluene*)
trinity, *n.* whole consisting of three parts. **the T.,** the three Persons of the Godhead. **T. Brethren,** members of **T. House,** a corporation which has charge of lighthouses, pilots etc. **T. Sunday,** that after Whit Sunday. **Trinitarian,** *n.* believer in doctrine of the Trinity. **Trinitarianism,** *n.* (L. *tres*, three)
trinket, *n.* small ornament worn on the person; trifle. **trinketry,** *n.*
trinkgeld, *n.* tip, gratuity. (G.)
trinodal, *a.* having three joints. (L. *tres*, three; *nodus*, knot)
trinomial, *a.* composed of three terms. —*n.* (*math.*) trinomial expression. **trinomialism,** *n.* scientific system of naming by genus, species, and variety. (L. *tres*, three; *nomen*, name)
trio, *n.* set of three persons or performers; (*mus.*) composition for three parts; middle section of minuet or march. (It.)
trioecious, *a.* having male, female, and hermaphrodite flowers each on different plants. (Gk. *treis*, three; *oikos*, house)
triolet, *n.* poem of eight lines rhymed abaaabab, 4th and 7th lines being same as 1st, and 8th as 2nd. (F.)
trional, *n.* a hypnotic drug. (*tri-*+*sulphonal*)
trior, *n.* (*law*) person appointed to decide whether challenge to juror is valid. (*try*)
trioxide, *n.* oxide with three oxygen atoms to the molecule. (*tri-*)
trip, *v.i.* and *t.* (*past, p.p.* **tripped**) move with light quick steps; catch foot in obstacle; stumble, cause to stumble, thus; make, detect in, error; be guilty of moral lapse; loose (anchor) from bottom.—*n.* excursion, outing; slip, *faux pas*; act of tripping, stumble. **t.-hammer,** *n.* large tilt-hammer. (O.F. *triper*)
tripartite, *a.* divided into three parts; made between three parties. **tripartition,** *n.* (*tri-*)
tripe, *n.* part of stomach of ox etc. as food; (*sl.*) poor stuff, tosh; (*pl.*, *vulg.*) entrails. (O.F.)
tripedal, *a.* having three feet. (L. *tres*, three; *pes*, foot)
tripennate, same as **tripinnate.**
tripery, *n.* place where tripe is prepared and sold.
tripetalous, *a.* having three petals.
triphthong, *n.* three vowels forming compound sound, as in b*eau*ty; trigraph. **triphthongal,** *a.* (Gk. *treis*, three; *phthonggos*, sound)
triphyllous, *a.* (*bot.*) three-leaved. (Gk. *treis*, three; *phullon*, leaf)
tripinnate, *a.* with bipinnate leaves ranged on each side of a stem. (*tri-*)
triplane, *n.* aeroplane with three planes. (*tri-*)
triple, *a.* threefold; consisting of three parts; (*Shake.*) third.—*v.t.* and *i.* treble. **t. crown,** papal tiara. **t. expansion,** method of using steam in three cylinders of engine in succession. **t. time,** (*mus.*) of three or nine beats in a bar. **t.-turned,** *a.* (*Shake.*) thrice false. **triplet,** *n.* set of three; three lines rhyming together; one of three children born at a birth; (*mus.*) three notes played in time of two. (Gk. *triplous*)
triplex, *a.* threefold.—*n.* (*mus.*) triple time. **t. glass,** kind of unsplinterable glass (*proprietary term*). **triplicate,** *a.* threefold.—*v.t.* multiply by three; make three copies of.—*n.* each of a set of three copies. **triplication, triplicature,** *nn.* **triplicity,** *n.* state of being triple. (L.)
tripod, *n.* three-legged stand, table, or stool. **tripodal,** *a.* three-footed. (Gk. *treis*, three; *pous*, foot)
tripos, *n.* (*pl.* **triposes**) honours examination at Cambridge. (*tripod*)
tripper, *n.* excursionist. (*trip*)
triptych, *n.* picture, set of pictures on three panels hinged side by side, esp. as altar-piece; writing-tablet in three parts. (Gk. *treis*, three; *ptussein*, fold)
triptyque, *n.* customs pass for importing motor-car. (F.)
tripudiate, *v.i.* dance in triumph, exult. (L. *tripudium*, dance)
triquetrous, *a.* three-cornered; (*bot.*) having three acute angles. **triquetra,** *n.* (*pl.* **triquetrae**) ornament of three interlaced arcs. (L. *triquetrus*)
trireme, *n.* ancient galley with three banks of oars. (L. *tres*, three; *remus*, oar)
trisect, *v.t.* divide into three (esp. equal) parts. **trisection,** *n.* (L. *tres*, three; *secare*, cut)
triserial, triseriate, *aa.* arranged in three rows. (*tri-*)

triskelion, triskele, *nn.* device of three branches or legs radiating from centre, as in arms of Isle of Man. (Gk. *treis*, three; *skelos*, leg)

trismus, *n.* (*med.*) lockjaw. (Gk. *trizein*, gnash)

trisoctahedron, *n.* solid with 24 faces, every three corresponding to one face of an octahedron. (*tri-*)

triste, *a.* sad. *tristesse*, *n.* (F.)

tristful, *a.* (*arch.*) sad. (L. *tristis*)

tristich, *n.* group of three lines, triplet. **tristichous,** *a.* arranged in three rows. (Gk. *treis*, three; *stichos*, row)

tristigmatic, *a.* with three stigmas.

tristylous, *a.* (*bot.*) with three styles.

trisulcate, *a.* (*bot.*) three-grooved; (*zool.*) cleft into three divisions. (L. *tres*, three; *sulcus*, furrow)

trisyllable, *n.* word of three syllables. **trisyllabic,** *a.* **trisyllabically,** *adv.* (*tri-*)

tritagonist, *n.* third actor in Greek play. (Gk. *tritos*, third; *agōnistēs*, actor)

trite, *a.* used till it has lost interest, hackneyed. (L. *terere*, rub)

triternate, *a.* thrice ternate, having 27 leaflets. (*tri-*)

tritheism, *n.* heresy that the Persons of the Trinity are three distinct Gods. **tritheist,** *n.* **tritheistic, tritheistical,** *aa.* (Gk. *treis*, three; *theos*, god)

Triton, *n.* a minor sea-god; (*zool.*) kind of mollusc with spiral shell. **T. among the minnows,** person looking important among nonentities. (Gk.)

tritone, *n.* (*mus.*) interval of three whole tones. (*tri-*)

triturate, *v.t.* grind to powder, pulverize. **trituration, triturator,** *nn.* (L. *terere*, rub)

triumph, *n.* victory, great success; joy at success, exultation; ancient Roman procession in honour of victorious general; (*Shake.*) trump card.—*v.i.* win victory, prevail (over); exult; ride in triumph. **triumphal,** *a.* of the nature of a Roman triumph, celebrating victory. **triumphant,** *a.* victorious, successful; exultant. (L. *triumphus*)

triumvirate, *n.* board of three; coalition of three persons in office. **first t.,** Caesar, Pompey, Crassus. **second t.,** Octavian, Antony, Lepidus. **triumvir,** *n.* (*pl.* **triumvirs, triumviri**) member of triumvirate. **triumviral,** *a.* (L. *tres*, three; *vir*, man)

triune, *a.* three in one. **triunity,** *n.* (L. *tres*, three; *unus*, one)

trivalent, *a.* having a valency of three. (*tri-*)

trivet, *n.* three-legged iron stand, bracket hooking on to bars of grate, for kettle etc. **right as a t.,** all right. (L. *tres*, three; *pes*, foot)

trivial, *a.* unimportant, trifling; ordinary, everyday. **triviality,** *n.* being trivial; trifle; commonplace remark. **trivialize,** *v.t.* render trivial. (L. *trivium*, cross-roads)

trivium, *n.* initial course of study in medieval university, comprising grammar, rhetoric, and logic. (L. *tres*, three; *via*, road)

trocar, *n.* surgical instrument for withdrawing fluid from body. (F.)

trochee, *n.* two-syllabled foot, long-short. **trochaic,** *a.* of, composed in, trochees.—*n.pl.* trochaic verse. (Gk. *trechein*, run)

troch(o)-, from Gk. *trechein*, run, used in **trochal,** *a.* (*zool.*) wheel-shaped; **trochanter,** *n.* prominence at upper end of thigh-bone, second joint of insect's leg; **troche,** *n.* medicinal lozenge; **trochilus, trochil,** *nn.* humming-bird, crocodile bird; **trochlea,** *n.* (*anat.*, *pl.* **trochleae**) pulley-like structure or cartilage, hence **trochlear,** *a.*; **trochoid,** *a.* rotating on its own axis, top-shaped.—*n.* path traced by point in one curve that rolls on another; **trochometer,** *n.* trechometer.

trod, *n.* (*Spens.*) path. (*tread*)

trod, trodden, see **tread.**

troggs, *n.pl.* (*Scot.*) clothes. **troggin,** *n.* pedlar's wares.

troglodyte, *n.* cave-dweller; recluse; kinds of ape. **troglodytic, troglodytical,** *aa.* (Gk. *trōglē*, cave; *duein*, enter)

trogon, *n.* kinds of brilliantly coloured S. American bird incl. quetzal. (Gk. *trōgein*, gnaw)

troika, *n.* Russian carriage drawn by three horses abreast. (Russ.)

trois-temps, *a.* in triple time.—*n.* waltz. (F.)

Trojan, *a.* and *n.* (inhabitant) of Troy; steadfast or persevering person; (*Shake.*) boon companion.

troke, *n.* (*Scot.*) exchange; small wares. —*v.i.* barter, deal. (*truck*)

troll, *v.t.* and *i.* sing parts of (song) in succession; sing in casual manner; fish by dragging bait through water; (*arch.*) pass (bottle) round.—*n.* song trolled, catch. (O.F. *troller*, roll)

troll, *n.* giant or mischievous dwarf of Scandinavian folklore. (O.N.)

trolley, trolly, *n.* kinds of low truck; wheel on pole by which electric tram-car draws power from wire; (*Amer.*) electric tram-car.

troll-my-dames, *n.* (*Shake.*) kind of bagatelle. (F. *trou-madame*)

trollop, *n.* disreputable woman, slut; prostitute.—*v.i.* draggle.

trombone, *n.* deep-toned brass wind-instrument with sliding tube. **trombonist,** *n.* (It.)

trommel, *n.* revolving sieve used in cleansing ores. (G.=drum)

tromometer, *n.* instrument for measuring slight earth tremors. (Gk. *tromos*, trembling; *metron*, measure)

trompe, *n.* apparatus for making blast in furnace. (F.=trump)

tronc, *n.* system of pooling tips among waiters. (F.)

troop, *n.* number of people, assemblage; company of cavalry, us. about 60; (*pl.*) soldiers.—*v.i.* and *t.* move in large numbers, flock; form into troops. **t.-horse,** *n.* cavalry horse. **t.-ship,** *n.* transport. **trooping the colour,** elaborate military ceremony at public mounting of guards etc. **trooper,** *n.* cavalry private; troop-horse; troop-ship; (*Amer.*) member of state police-force. (L.L. *troppus*)

tropaeolum, *n.* kinds of S. American trailing plant incl. nasturtium. (Gk. *tropaion*, trophy)

trope, *n.* figure of speech, figurative use of word. (Gk. *trepein*, turn)

troph(o)-, from Gk. *trophē*, food, used in **trophesy,** *n.* disease due to disorder of trophic nerves; **trophic,** *a.* of, concerned with, nutrition; **trophology,** *n.* science of nutrition; **trophotropism,** *n.* movement of organs of plant towards nutrient substances.

trophy, *n.* memorial of victory; captured spoils of enemy; prize; memento. **trophied,** *a.* (Gk. *tropaion*)

tropic, *n.* parallel of latitude 23° 27′ north (**t. of Cancer**) or south (**t. of Capricorn**) of equator; (*astron.*) corresponding circles of celestial sphere; (*pl.*) region between tropics, torrid zone.—*a.* tropical. **t.-bird,** *n.* seabird with long tail-feathers. **tropical,** *a.* of, peculiar to, the tropics; very hot, sultry; fervid. (Gk. *trepein*, turn)

tropical, *a.* figurative. (*trope*)

tropism, *n.* direction of growth of plant etc. due to a stimulus. (Gk. *trepein*, turn)

tropist, *n.* one who uses figures of speech. **tropology,** *n.* figurative style of writing; figurative method of interpreting Scriptures. **tropological,** *a.* (*trope*)

troposphere, *n.* part of atmosphere, extending in temperate regions about seven miles up from earth's surface, in which temperature falls with height. **tropopause,** *n.* imaginary boundary between troposphere and stratosphere. (Gk. *tropos*, turn+*sphere*)

troppo, *adv.* (*mus.*) too much. (It.)

trot, *n.* horse's medium pace with feet lifted in diagonal pairs; man's gentle run, jog; spell of trotting; toddling child; (*Shake.*) old woman.—*v.i.* and *t.* (*past, p.p.* **trotted**) go, ride, cause to go, at trot; go fussily (about); (*joc.*) go on foot. **t. out,** show off, submit. **t. round,** (*colloq.*) conduct quickly round. (O.F.)

troth, *n.* (*arch.*) truth, faith. **plight one's t.,** pledge oneself, become engaged. (*true*)

trotter, *n.* trotting horse; (*joc.*) human foot; (*pl.*) feet of sheep or pig as food.

trottoir, *n.* pavement, side-walk. (F.)

trotyl, *n.* trinitrotoluol. (abbr.)

troubadour, *n.* medieval romantic poet of S. France; wandering minstrel. (F.)

trouble, *n.* agitation, distress; source of this, affliction; unrest; difficulty, inconvenience; pains taken; ailment.—*v.t.* and *i.* make or be anxious, worry; put, be put, to inconvenience; take pains; ruffle (water etc.). **ask for t.,** (*sl.*) show lack of caution. **get into t.,** incur blame; seduce. **troublesome,** *a.* giving trouble, difficult, harassing; unruly. **troublous,** *a.* (*arch.*) disturbed, unsettled. (L. *turba*, crowd)

trough, *n.* long narrow open vessel for water or fodder; hollow; depression between two waves. (O.E. *trog*)

trounce, *v.t.* beat soundly, thrash; criticize severely.

troupe, *n.* company of performers. **trouper,** *n.* member of this. (F.)

trousers, *n.pl.* loose two-legged outer garment reaching from waist to ankles; woman's long frilled drawers. **trouser-press, trouser-stretcher,** *nn.* for pressing trousers to preserve shape. **trousered,** *a.* wearing trousers. **trousering,** *n.* material for trousers. (Gael. *triubhas*)

trousseau, *n.* (*pl.* **trousseaus, trousseaux**) bride's outfit of clothing. (F.)

trout, *n.* freshwater fish allied to salmon but smaller. **troutlet, troutling,** *nn.* small trout. (Gk. *trōktēs*, a sea-fish)

trouvaille, *n.* lucky find. (F.)

trouvère, *n.* medieval epic poet of N. France. (F.)

trove, see **treasure.**

trover, *n.* (*law*) action to recover value of goods wrongfully taken or detained. (O.F.=find)

trow, *v.t.* (*arch.*) suppose, believe. (O.E. *trēowian*, trust)

trowel, *n.* small flat-bladed tool for spreading mortar; gardener's small rounded shovel.—*v.t.* apply with trowel. **lay it on with a t.,** flatter grossly. (L. *trua*, ladle+dim.)

troy, *n.* (also **t. weight**) system of weight used for gold, silver, and gems, in which 24 grains=1 pennyweight, 20 pennyweights=1 ounce, and 12 ounces=1 pound, $=\frac{144}{175}$ pound avoirdupois. (*Troyes* in France)

truant, *n.* one who absents himself from school or duty without leave.—*a.* shirking duty; wandering.—*v.i.* play truant. **truancy,** *n.* (O.F.=vagrant)

truce, *n.* suspension of hostilities by agreement, armistice; respite. (O.E. *trēow*, faith)

truck, *n.* railway wagon for goods or cattle; heavy lorry; porter's barrow; wheeled framework of railway coach; (*naut.*) wooden cap on top of mast.—

v.t. transport in trucks. (Gk. *trechein*, run)

truck, *v.i.* and *t.* exchange, trade.—*n.* barter, exchange; dealings; small wares; rubbish, nonsense; (*Amer.*) garden produce. **T. Acts,** suppressing **t. system,** of paying workmen in goods instead of money. (F. *troquer*)

truckle, *v.i.* yield obsequiously, cringe (to).—*n.* (us. **t.-bed**) low bed made to wheel under larger one. (L. *trochlea*, pulley)

truculent, *a.* ferociously aggressive or defiant, fierce. **truculence,** *n.* (L. *trux*)

trudge, *v.i.* and *t.* go on foot, toil along. —*n.* wearisome tramp.

trudgen, *n.* (also **t. stroke**) swimming stroke with arms brought over head alternately. (J. *Trudgen*)

true, *a.* in accordance with fact; genuine, authentic; exact, correct; faithful, loyal; (*arch.*) truthful; honest.—*adv.* truly.—*v.t.* adjust accurately, make straight. **come t.** happen as foretold. **t. bill,** grand jury's finding that there is a case for trial. **t. to type,** normal. **t.-blue,** *a.* thoroughgoing, loyal. **t.-born, t.-bred,** *aa.* native, genuine. **t.-hearted,** *a.* sincere. **t.-love,** *n.* sweetheart. **t.-love, t.-lover's, knot,** double knot of interlaced bows. **truepenny,** *n.* (*Shake.*) honest fellow. (O.E. *tréowe*)

truffle, *n.* round edible fungus growing below ground. (O.F. *trufle*)

trug, *n.* gardener's shallow wooden basket.

truism, *n.* self-evident truth, platitude.

trull, *n.* (*arch.*) harlot, trollop.

truly, *adv.* with truth, really; genuinely; sincerely, loyally.

trumeau, n. (*pl. trumeaux*) piece of wall between two openings. (F.)

trump, *n.* card of suit temporarily ranking above others; (*colloq.*) good fellow.—*v.t.* take with trump card. **t. card,** trump; valuable resource. **t. up,** fabricate, concoct. **turn up tt.,** (*colloq.*) turn out fortunately. (*triumph*)

trump, *n.* (*arch.*) trumpet; blast of this. **last t.,** that on Judgment Day. (F. *trompe*)

trumpery, *a.* showy but worthless; fallacious, feeble. — *n.* worthless finery; trash; nonsense. (F. *tromper*, deceive)

trumpet, *n.* wind-instrument of long straight or coiled tube with bell-shaped mouth; blast on this; trumpet-toned organ-stop; horn of gramophone; ear-trumpet; (*arch.*) herald with trumpet.—*v.i.* and *t.* blow trumpet; (of elephant) emit cry like trumpet; proclaim, noise abroad. **blow one's own t.,** praise oneself. **t. major,** head trumpeter of cavalry regiment. **t.-call,** *n.* signal with trumpet; call to action. **t.-flower, t.-leaf,** *nn.* trumpet-shaped kinds. **t.-tongued,** *a.* **trumpeter,** *n.* one who sounds trumpet; kinds of swan and pigeon. (*trump*+dim.)

truncal, *a.* of the trunk.

truncate, *v.t.* cut off the tip of, lop; maim.—*a.* truncated, ending abruptly. **truncation, truncature,** *nn.* (L. *truncus*, maimed)

truncheon, *n.* staff of authority; short club, baton.—*v.t.* cudgel. (O.F. *tronchon*)

trundle, *v.t.* and *i.* roll (hoop, truck etc.); (*cricket, colloq.*) bowl.—*n.* small broad wheel, castor; low truck. **t.-bed,** *n.* truckle-bed. **t.-tail,** *n.* (*Shake.*) curly-tailed dog. (O.E. *trendel*, circle)

trunk, *n.* main stem of tree; body excluding head and limbs; main part of structure; elephant's proboscis; large travelling box; (*pl.*) tight-fitting drawers for swimming etc. **t. call,** long-distance telephone call. **t.-hose,** *n.* old style of breeches reaching to middle of thigh. **t.-line,** *n.* main line of railway; telephone or telegraph line from town to town. **t.-road,** *n.* main road. (L. *truncus*, maimed)

trunnion, *n.* projection on either side of cannon by which it rests and pivots in carriage. (F. *trognon*, stump)

truss, *n.* bundle, package; compact cluster of flowers; supporting framework of timbers or girders; bandage used in cases of rupture; measure =56 lb. (old hay), 60 lb. (new hay), 36 lb. (straw).—*v.t.* make into trusses; support with truss; tie up (fowl) compactly for cooking; bind (person) similarly. (F. *trousse*)

trust, *n.* reliance, confidence, faith; credit; state of being relied on, responsibility; custody, charge; property held or administered for another; board of trustees; trusteeship; combination of producers to do away with competition.—*v.t.* and *i.* rely on, believe in; give credit to; commit, entrust; hope earnestly. **take on t.,** believe without testing. **t. deed,** document creating legal trust. **trustee,** *n.* person entrusted with administration of property for another's benefit. **trusteeship,** *n.* **trustful, trusting,** *aa.* disposed to trust, confiding. **trustless,** *a.* (*Shake.*) faithless. **trustworthy,** *a.* reliable, dependable. **trusty,** *a* faithful, staunch; (*arch.*) reliable. (O.N *traust*)

truth, *n.* trueness, veracity; truthfulness; accuracy; loyalty; what is true; true statement; established fact or principle. **in t.,** (*arch.*) **of a t.,** truly. **truthful,** *a.* habitually speaking the truth; true. **truthless,** *a.* false; faithless.

try, *v.t.* and *i.* (*past, p.p.* tried) attempt, endeavour; test, put to proof; put strain upon; conduct judicial inquiry into; (*Shake.*, of ship) lie to.—*n.* (*colloq.*) attempt; (*Rugby football*) touching-down of ball behind opponents' goal-line. **t. and,** (*colloq.*) endeavour to. **t. back,** hark back. **t. for,** aim at. **t. it on,** (*sl.*) see how much will be put up with. **t. on,** put on (garment) to test fit. **t. out,** put to test. **trying,** *a.* exhausting, hard to bear; provoking. (O.F. *trier*, pick out)

trypanosome, *n.* minute parasite transmitted by bite of tsetse-fly and causing sleeping-sickness. (Gk. *trupanon*, auger; *sōma*, body)

trypsin, *n.* pancreatic enzyme digesting protein. (Gk. *tripsis*, friction)

trysail, *n.* small fore-and-aft sail set with gaff, storm-sail. (*try*)

tryst, *n.* engagement to meet; appointed meeting-place.—*v.t.* and *i.* make tryst (with). (O.F. *triste*, watching-place)

tsar, see **czar.**

tsetse, *n.* (also **t.-fly**) S. African fly infecting men with sleeping-sickness and cattle with nagana. (S. Afr. Du.)

tuan, *n.* Malay title of respect, master. (Malay)

tub, *n.* open wooden vessel for washing etc.; box for conveying coal in mines; slow clumsy ship; boat used for practice rowing; (*colloq.*) bath.—*v.t.* and *i.* bathe in tub; plant or pack in tub; take (crew) in tub for practice. **t.-thumper,** *n.* ranting politician.

tuba, *n.* large low-pitched brass instrument; an organ reed-stop. (L. = trumpet)

tubal, tubar, *aa.* of a tube.

tubby, *a.* tub-shaped, fat and round.

tube, *n.* long hollow cylinder, pipe; underground railway; (*anat.*) pipe-shaped organ.—*v.t.* furnish with, enclose in, tube. (L. *tubus*)

tuber, *n.* swelling on underground stem containing buds for new plant; (*anat.*) swelling part. (L. = bump)

tubercle, *n.* small tumour formed in lungs etc. in consumption; small knob or outgrowth; small tuber. **tubercled,** *a.* **tubercular,** *a.* of, having, tubercles or tuberculosis. **tuberculin,** *n.* culture of tubercular bacillus used as test for tuberculosis. **tuberculize, tubercularize,** *vv.t.* infect with tuberculosis. **tuberculization,** *n.* **tuberculosis.** *n.* (*colloq. abbr.* **T.B.**) disease marked by tubercles and characteristic bacillus consumption. **tuberculous,** *a.* affected by tuberculosis, consumptive. (*tuber* + dim.)

tuberose, *a.* tuberous.—*n.* bulbous plant with creamy-white fragrant flowers. **tuberous,** *a.* of, like, having, tubers; knobby. **tuberosity,** *n.*

tubing, *n.* length, system, of tubes.

tubular, tubulous, *aa.* tube-shaped; having, consisting of, a tube or tubes.

tubule, *n.* small tube.

tuck, *n.* (*arch.*) blast of trumpet; (*Scot.*) beat of drum. (*touch*)

tuck, *n.* (*Shake.*) rapier. (It. *stocco*)

tuck, *v.t.* and *i.* gather or stitch in folds; draw, press, in or together; fold under; cover snugly, stow compactly.—*n.* horizontal fold sewn in garment; (*school sl.*) food, esp. pastry and sweets. **t. in,** (*sl.*) eat heartily. **t.-in, t-out,** *nn.* (*sl.*) feast. **t.-shop,** *n.* shop selling tuck. **tucker,** *n.* strip of linen or lace worn across bosom by women; (*sl.*) food. (M.E. *tukken*)

tucker, *v.t.* (*Amer. colloq.*) tire, weary.

tucket, *n.* (*arch.*) flourish on trumpet.

tucum, *n.* S. American palm yielding valuable fibre. (Brazilian)

Tudor, *a.* and *n.* (one) of the English sovereigns from Henry VIII to Elizabeth; (*archit.*) late Perpendicular.

Tuesday, *n.* third day of week. (O.E. *Tíw*, god of war)

tufa, *n.* porous rock formed as deposit from springs etc.; tuff. **tufaceous,** *a.*

tuff, *n.* friable volcanic rock. (L. *tofus*)

tuft, tuffet, *nn.* green knoll. (*toft*)

tuft, *n.* knot or cluster of threads, hairs etc.; imperial; ornamental tassel formerly worn by titled undergraduates; (*obs. sl.*) swell.—*v.t.* and *i.* furnish with, form, tufts. **t.-hunter,** *n.* hanger-on of persons of rank. **tufty,** *a.* (F. *touffe*)

tug, *v.t.* and *i.* pull strongly or jerkily, haul; tow.—*n.* strong pull or jerk; (also **tugboat**) small powerful steamboat for towing ships. **t.-of-war,** *n.* contest between teams pulling at opposite ends of rope; laborious contest. (M.E. *toggen*)

tui, *n.* parson-bird of New Zealand. (Maori)

tuilyie, tuilzie, same as **tulzie.**

tuism, *n.* (*philos.*) doctrine that all thought is addressed to a second person or to one's future self as this. (L. *tu*, thou)

tuition, *n.* teaching, instruction; (*Shake.*) protection. **tuitional, tuitionary,** *aa.* (L. *tuēri*, watch)

tula-work, *n.* kind of decoration in silver, niello. (*Tula* in Russia)

tulchan, tulchin, *n.* (*Scot.*) stuffed calf-skin set beside cow to make it give milk. **t. bishops,** in whose names revenues of Scottish sees were drawn by nobles after Reformation. (Gael.)

túlē, *n.* large American rush. (Mex.)

tulip, *n.* bulbous plant with brilliant bell-shaped flowers. **t.-root,** *n.* a disease of oats. **t.-tree,** *n.* tree with tulip-like flowers. (Pers. *dulband*, turban)

tulle, *n.* soft fine material for veils and dresses. (French town)

tulwar, *n.* Indian sabre. (Hind. *talwār*)

tulzie, *n.* and *v.i.* (*Scot.*) quarrel.
tumasha, same as **tamasha**.
tumble, *v.i.* and *t.* fall, go sprawling; turn somersaults; rush helter-skelter, toss to and fro; overturn, upset; disarrange, rumple.—*n.* act of tumbling, fall. **t. in**, (*sl.*) go to bed. **t. to**, (*sl.*) understand, twig. **t.-bug**, *n.* (*Amer.*) kinds of dung-beetle.
tumbledown, *a.* ruinous, ramshackle.
tumbler, *n.* acrobat; kind of pigeon; catch in lock lifted by key; drinking-glass without stem. (O.E. *tumbian*)
tumbrel, tumbril, *n.* tip-cart for rubbish; ammunition-cart; open cart for taking victims of French Revolution to guillotine. (O.F. *tomber*, fall)
tumefy, *v.t.* and *i.* cause to swell; swell up. **tumefaction**, *n.* **tumefacient**, *a.* **tumescent**, *a.* somewhat swollen. **tumescence**, *n.* (L. *tumēre*, swell; *facere*, make)
tumfie, *n.* (*Scot.*) stupid or awkward person.
tumid, *a.* swollen, inflated; pompous. **tumidity**, *n.* (L. *tumēre*, swell)
tummy, *n.* (*sl.*) stomach. (abbr.)
tumour, *n.* diseased swelling in any part of body. (L. *tumēre*, swell)
tum-tum, *n.* W. Indian dish of boiled plantains.
tum-tum, *n.* (*Anglo-Ind.*) dog-cart.
tumult, *n.* noisy commotion of crowd, riot; uproar; violent disturbance or agitation. **tumultuary**, *a.* disorderly, riotous. **tumultuous**, *a.* uproarious; vehement. (L. *tumultus*)
tumulus, *n.* (*pl.* **tumuli**) ancient burial mound, barrow. **tumular, tumulary**, *aa.* (L.)
tun, *n.* large cask; old measure, 252 gallons.—*v.t.* store in tun. **t.-dish**, *n.* (*Shake.*) funnel. (O.E. *tunne*)
tuna, *n.* the great tunny. (Sp.)
tuna, *n.* prickly pear. (Carib)
tundra, *n.* mossy treeless Arctic plain of N. Russia. (Lappish)
tune, *n.* air, melody; correct intonation in singing or playing; concord; (*Shake.*) tone, humour.—*v.t.* and *i.* bring into tune, adjust pitch of. **change one's t.**, alter one's attitude. **in, out of, t.**, harmonious, discordant. **to the t. of**, to the amount of. **t. in**, (*wireless*) adjust receiving-set to wave-length. **t. up**, begin to play. **tuning-fork**, *n.* two-pronged implement giving particular note when struck. **tuneful**, *a.* melodious, harmonious. **tuneless**, *a.* unmusical, harsh. **tuner**, *n.* one who tunes piano etc. (=*tone*)
tungsten, *n.* grey metallic element with very high melting-point. **tungstic, tungstous**, *aa.* (Swed. *tung*, heavy; *sten*, stone)
tunic, *n.* loose belted garment reaching to knees; soldier's close-fitting coat; tunicle; (*anat.*) membrane enclosing organ; (*bot.*, *zool.*) covering, husk. **tunicate**, *a.* covered with tunic or layers.—*n.* one of class of marine animals incl. ascidians. **tunicle**, *n.* close-fitting vestment like small dalmatic; (*bot.*, *zool.*) fine or delicate tunic. (L. *tunica*)
tunnel, *n.* underground passage, esp. for railway through hill; burrow of mole; main flue of chimney.—*v.i.* and *t.* make tunnel (through), make (one's way) thus. (O.F. *tonne*, tun +dim.)
tunny, *n.* large edible sea-fish of mackerel family. (Gk. *thunnos*)
tuny, *a.* having catchy tunes.
tup, *n.* male sheep, ram; striking-face of steam hammer.—*v.t.* (of ram) copulate with. (M.E. *tupe*)
tupelo, *n.* (*pl.* **tupelos**) N. American tree with red berries.
tuque, *n.* Canadian knitted cap for winter wear. (*toque*)
tu quoque, retort of ' you 're another.' (L.)
turacou, turako, same as **touraco**.
Turanian, *a.* Asiatic but neither Aryan nor Semitic; Ural-Altaic.
turban, *n.* head-dress of long strip of cloth wound round head or cap, worn by men in the East; kinds of woman's brimless hat; whole whorls of a shell. **turbaned**, *a.* wearing a turban. (Pers. *dulband*)
turbary, *n.* right to dig turf in another's ground; place where peat is dug. (L.L. *turba*, turf)
turbid, *a.* thick, muddy; not clear or limpid. **turbidity**, *n.* (L. *turba*, crowd)
turbine, *n.* wheel, rotary engine, driven by steam, water, or air playing on blades. **turbinate, turbinal**, *aa.* shaped, whirling, like a top; spirally rolled. **turbination**, *n.* (L. *turbo*, whirl)
turbit, *n.* domestic pigeon with short beak.
turbot, *n.* large flat sea-fish much prized for food. (O.F. *tourbout*)
turbulent, *a.* disturbed, in violent commotion; unruly, ill-controlled; insubordinate, riotous. **turbulence**, *n.* (L. *turba*, crowd)
Turco, *n.* French Algerian soldier. (F.)
Turcoman, same as **Turkoman**.
Turcophil, *n.* one who favours the Turks. **Turcophobe**, *n.* one who fears the Turks. (Gk. *philos*, loving; *phobos*, fear)
turd, *n.* ball of dung. (O.E. *tord*)
turdine, *a.* like a thrush. (L. *turdus*, thrush)
tureen, *n.* large deep dish for soup. (L. *terra*, earth)
turf, *n.* (*pl.* **turfs**, *obs.* **turves**) short grass with the earth matted together by its roots, sward; slab of this, sod; peat; racecourse, horse-racing.—*v.t.* cover with turf; (*sl.*) throw (out). **turfite, turfman**, *nn.* one devoted to horse-racing. (O.E.)

turgid, *a.* pompous, bombastic; morbidly swollen or enlarged. **turgidity,** *n.* **turgescent,** *a.* swelling; growing big. **turgescence,** *n.* (L. *turgēre,* swell)

turion, *n.* scaly shoot budded off underground stem. (L. *turio,* shoot)

Turk, *n.* inhabitant of Turkey, Ottoman; (*joc.*) unruly child. **T.'s-head,** *n.* kinds of knot, broom, and cooking-pan.

turkey, *n.* large bird bred for food. **talk t.,** (*Amer.*) tell plain truth. **T. carpet,** woollen kind with thick pile. **T. red,** a scarlet dye, cotton dyed with it. **t. trot,** a ragtime dance. **t.-buzzard,** *n.* kind of American vulture. **t.-cock,** *n.* male turkey; pompous person. **t.-poult,** *n.* young of turkey. (bird once supposed to come from *Turkey*)

Turkish, *a.* and *n.* (language) of Turks. **T. bath,** hot-air bath. **T. delight,** gelatine flavoured and coated with powdered sugar. **T. towel,** rough kind of bath towel.

Turkoman, *n.* (*pl.* **Turkomans**) member of certain Tartar tribes of Central Asia.

turmalin, turmaline, same as **tourmaline.**

turmeric, *n.* an Indian plant; powdered root of this used as dye and condiment. (F. *terre-mérite*)

turmoil, *n.* confusion and bustle; agitation, commotion.—*v.t.* (*arch.*) agitate, harass.

turn, *v.t.* and *i.* move round; revolve, rotate; reverse position, change direction (of); bend; deflect, direct; transform, change; translate; make, become; hinge, depend; have recourse (to); phrase (compliment); derange (brain); sicken (stomach); curdle (milk); shape in lathe; (*Shake.*) return; be fickle.—*n.* act of turning; bend, twist; marked change; stroll; spell, bout; single performance; opportunity; aptitude; (*mus.*) embellishment of note consisting of note above, note itself, note below, note itself; (*colloq.*) shock. **by tt.,** alternately. **do good, bad, t. to,** do service, disservice. **in t.,** in due order. **to a t.,** exactly, perfectly. **t. against,** make, become, hostile to. **t. away,** dismiss; avert one's face. **t. back,** return, cause to return. **t. down,** lower (light); (*colloq.*) reject. **t. in,** (*colloq.*) go to bed. **t. off,** shut off by tap; (*sl.*) hang; solemnize marriage of. **t. on,** set running; turn upon. **t. out,** expel; empty; produce; dress; extinguish; come forth; prove, be shown. **t. over,** transfer; consider. **t. to,** set to. **t. up,** bring to surface; refer to; arrive, happen; (*sl.*) nauseate. **t. upon,** suddenly attack. (L. *tornare,* turn in lathe)

turnbuckle, *n.* coupling with screw for regulating tension of the rod or wire whose two parts it links.

turncoat, *n.* person who changes sides, esp. from interested motives.

turncock, *n.* person in charge of public taps.

turner, *n.* one who works a lathe. **turnery,** *n.* his craft; turned articles.

turning, *n.* bend, deviation; corner, side road. **t.-point,** *n.* crisis.

turnip, *n.* plant of mustard family; its round fleshy root, used as food; (*sl.*) large clumsy silver watch. **t.-top,** *n.* leaves and stem of turnip. (L. *napus*)

turnkey, *n.* prison warder.

turn-out, *n.* gathering, assembly; equipage.

turnover, *n.* tart made by doubling piece of dough; amount of money passing through business.

turnpike, *n.* bar or gate across road for toll-collecting; road with this.

turnscrew, *n.* screwdriver.

turnsole, *n.* plant that turns with the sun, sunflower. (L. *sol,* sun)

turnspit, *n.* one who turns a spit, kitchen-boy; breed of dog with short legs and long body.

turnstile, *n.* revolving gate allowing only one person to pass at a time.

turn-table, *n.* revolving platform for turning locomotives round.

turn-up, *n.* (*colloq.*) row, fight.

turpentine, *n.* resin got from pine-tree etc.; oil or spirit made from this. **t.-tree,** *n.* terebinth. (Gk. *terebinthos,* terebinth)

turpeth, *n.* root of an Asiatic plant, used as purgative. (Pers. *turbid*)

turpitude, *n.* baseness; depravity, wickedness. (L. *turpis,* base)

turps, *n.* (*sl.*) turpentine spirit.

turquoise, *n.* opaque azure precious stone. **t. green,** colour between blue and green. (F. *turquois,* Turkish)

turret, *n.* small tower forming part of building; revolving armoured tower for guns on warship or fort. **turreted,** *a.* **turriculate, turriculated,** *aa.* (of shell) with long spiral. (L. *turris,* tower+dim.)

turtle, *n.* marine reptile with hard bony shell and flippers, sea-tortoise. **turn t.,** capsize, overturn. (L.L. *tortuca,* tortoise)

turtle, *n.* (us. **t.-dove,**) kind of wild dove with cooing note and great affection for mate. (L. *turtur*)

tush, *n.* horse's canine tooth; tusk. (=*tusk*)

tush, *int.* (*arch.*) of contempt or impatience.—*v.i.* utter this. **tushery,** *n.* use of literary archaisms.

tusk, *n.* long pointed tooth projecting from mouth as in elephant and walrus.—*v.t.* gore, tear up, with tusks. **tusker,** *n.* elephant whose tusks are grown. (O.E. *tusc*)

tusser, same as **tussore.**

tussive, *a.* (*med.*) of, caused by, a cough. (L. *tussis,* cough)

tussle, *n.* and *v.i.* struggle, wrestle. (*tousle*)

tussock, *n.* clump of grass; tuft.

t.-grass, *n.* tall tufted grass of Falkland Islands. **tussocky,** *a.*
tussore, *n.* kinds of Indian silkworm; their strong coarse silk; fabric made from it. (Sanskr. *tasara*, shuttle)
tut, *int.* of impatience.—*v.i.* utter this.
tut, *n.* (*mining*) piece of work.—*v.i.* work by the piece. **t.-work,** *n.*
tutania, *n.* kind of Britannia metal. (W. *Tutin*, inventor)
tutelage, *n.* guardianship; state of being under guardian. **tutelary, tutelar,** *aa.* of, acting as, guardian; protective. (L. *tuēri*, watch)
tutenag, *n.* alloy of copper, zinc, and nickel; zinc from China. (Marathi *tuttināg*)
tutor, *n.* (*fem.* **tutoress**) private teacher; college official directing studies of undergraduates; (*law*) guardian of a minor.—*v.t.* and *i.* act as tutor (to); discipline, school. **tutorial,** *a.* of tutor.—*n.* (*sl.*) hour of instruction by college tutor. **tutorship,** *n.* (L.)
tutsan, *n.* variety of St. John's wort. (L. *totus*, whole; *sanus*, sound)
tutti, *a.* and *n.* (*mus.*) (passage) for all voices or instruments together. (It.)
tutti-frutti, *n.* mixture of preserved fruits of many kinds. (It.)
tutty, *n.* crude zinc oxide used as polishing-powder. (Arab. *tūtiyā*)
tuum, *see* **meum.**
tu-whit tu-whoo, cry of owl. (imit.)
tuxedo, *n.* (*Amer.*) dinner-jacket. (place)
tuyère, *n.* blast-pipe in furnace. (F.)
twa, *Scot.* form of **two.**
twaddell, *n.* kind of hydrometer. (inventor)
twaddle, *n.* silly talk, piffle.—*v.i.* talk twaddle.
twain, *a.* and *n.* two. **in t.,** asunder. (O.E. *twégen*)
twal, *Scot.* form of **twelve.**
twang, *n.* ringing sound made by tense string when plucked; nasal utterance.—*v.i.* and *t.* emit, cause to emit. twang; speak with twang. **twangle,** *v.i.* and *t.* keep on twanging. (imit.)
twankay, *n.* kind of green tea. (*Tun-ki*, river in China)
'twas, *contr.* of **it was.**
tway, *a.* and *n.* (*Spens.*, *Scot.*) two. **twayblade,** *n.* kinds of orchid with single pair of leaves. (*twain*)
tweak, *v.t.* pinch, pull, twist, with sudden jerk; twitch.—*n.* sharp pinch, twitch; (*sl.*) dodge, device. **tweaker,** *n.* (*sl.*) boy's catapult. (=*twitch*)
tweed, *n.* a rough-surfaced cloth used for men's clothes. (misreading of *tweel*)
tweedle, *n.* sound of fiddle. **tweedledum and tweedledee,** things differing only or chiefly in name.
tweel, *Scot.* form of **twill.**
'tween, *contr.* of **between. 't.-decks,** *n.* space between decks. **tweeny,** *n.* (*colloq.*) between-maid, assisting both cook and housemaid.

tweet, *n.* and *v.i.* chirp. (imit.)
tweezers, *n.pl.* small tongs or pincers. (F. *étui*, small case)
twelfth, *a.* next after eleventh.—*n.* one of twelve equal parts. **the t.,** 12 Aug., when grouse-shooting starts. **T. Day,** Epiphany, 6 Jan. (twelve days after Christmas). **T. Night,** eve of this, 5 Jan.
twelve, *a.* and *n.* one more than eleven, a dozen. **the T.,** the Apostles. **twelvemo, 12mo,** *n.* duodecimo. **twelvemonth,** *n.* year. (O.E. *twelf*)
twenty, *a.* and *n.* twice ten, a score. **t.-five,** *n.* (*Rugby football*) cross-line 25 yards from goal, space within this. **twentieth,** *a.* and *n.* **twentymo, twentyfourmo,** *nn.* (*abbr.* **20mo, 24mo**) book of sheets folded into 20, 24, leaves. (O.E. *twentig*)
'twere, *contr.* of **it were.**
twerp, *n.* (*sl.*) contemptible person.
twibill, *n.* kind of mattock; (*arch.*) double-bladed battle-axe. (*two*)
twice, *adv.* two times, on two occasions; doubly. **twicer,** *n.* compositor who is also pressman; (*sl.*) one who goes to church twice on Sunday. (*two*)
twiddle, *v.t.* and *i.* twirl, twist.—*n.* twirl; flourish. **t. one's thumbs,** be idle.
twig, *v.t.* and *i.* (*colloq.*) understand, follow; observe.
twig, *n.* small branch, minor shoot; divining-rod. **hop the t.,** (*sl.*) die. **twiggen,** *a.* (*Shake.*) cased in wicker. (O.E.)
twilight, *n.* half light after sunset or before dawn, dusk; faint light; state of imperfect knowledge. **t. sleep,** partial insensibility induced to lessen pains of childbirth. (*two*)
twill, *n.* fabric in which warp is raised one thread and depressed two or more for passage of weft, thus giving ribbed appearance.—*v.t.* weave thus. (O.E. *twili*, two-threaded)
'twill, *contr.* of **it will.**
twin, *n.* one of two born at a birth; one of a pair, counterpart; (*pl.*) Gemini, third sign of zodiac.—*a.* born as twin; double, twofold; closely related or alike.—*v.t.* and *i.* join intimately together, pair. **t. steamer,** with two hulls and paddle-wheel between. **t.-screw,** *a.* with two propellers on separate shafts. **twinflower,** *n.* a slender creeping evergreen. (O.E. *twinn*, double)
twin, *v.i.* (*Scot.*) separate. (*two*)
twine, *n.* string; twist, coil; tangle.—*v.i.* and *t.* twist or wind (about), wreathe; form of twisted strands, weave. (O.E. *twin*, double thread)
twine, same as **twin.**
twinge, *n.* shooting pain, pang; qualm.—*v.t.* and *i.* affect with, feel, twinge. (O.E. *twengan*, pinch)
twink, *n.* (*Shake.*) twinkling.
twinkle, *v.i.* shine with quivering

light, sparkle; blink; appear intermittently, flicker.—*n.* act of twinkling; slight flash; gleam of amusement in eyes. **in a twinkling,** in an instant. (O.E. *twinclian*)

twire, *v.i.* (*Shake.*) twinkle.

twirl, *v.t.* and *i.* turn round lightly and rapidly, whirl; twiddle.—*n.* act of twirling; flourish.

twist, *v.t.* and *i.* wind or move spirally; unite, make, by winding together; wrench, distort; take curved course; shuffle, cheat.—*n.* twisted motion or state; act of twisting; bend, turn; moral obliquity, kink; kind of strong thread; rope-like tobacco; roll of bread; screw of paper; kinds of mixed drink; (*sl.*) keen hunger. **twister,** *n.* person, thing, that twists; difficult problem; dodger, crook. (O.E. = rope)

twit, *v.t.* taunt, reproach. (O.E. *æt*, at; *witan*, blame)

twitch, *v.t.* and *i.* pluck, pull, move, with sudden jerk; quiver or jerk involuntarily.—*n.* sharp light pull; slight muscular spasm; device for holding refractory horse during shoeing etc. (O.E. *twiccian*)

twitch, same as **quitch.**

twite, *n.* kind of linnet.

twitter, *n.* light broken sound, chirping of bird; nervous condition, flutter.—*v.i.* utter twitter; dither. **twitteration,** *n.* nervous twitter. (M.E. *twiteren*)

'twixt, *contr.* of **betwixt.**

two, *a.* and *n.* one more than one, a pair. **in t.,** asunder. **put t. and t. together,** draw obvious conclusion. **t.-edged,** *a.* double-edged; ambiguous. **t-faced,** *a.* with two faces; double-dealing. **t.-handed,** *a.* used with both hands; ambidextrous; (of game) for two players. **t.-pair,** *a.* of second floor. **t.-ply,** *a*, of two strands or layers. **t.-seater,** *n.* motor-car for two. **t.-step,** *n.* round dance in march or polka time; music for this. **twopence,** *n.* 2*d.* **twopenny,** *a.* costing twopence.—*n.* kind of beer; (*sl.*) one's head. **twopenny-halfpenny,** *a.* insignificant, trumpery. **twosome,** *n.* (*Scot.*) game, dance, for two. (O.E. *twégen*)

'twould, *contr.* of **it would.**

twyer, same as **tuyère.**

-ty, *n.suf.* state of being, as in **ability, piety.** (L. *-tas*)

-ty, *suf.* ten times, as in sixty. (O.E. *-tig*)

Tyburn, *n.* former place of execution in London. **T. tree,** gallows.

tycoon, *n.* a title of the shogun. (Jap. *taikun*, great prince)

tying, see **tie.**

tyke, tike, *n.* (*colloq.*) cur. **Yorkshire t.,** Yorkshireman. (O.N. *tik*, bitch)

tyler, see **tiler.**

tylopod, *a.* and *n.* (animal) with padded digits, e.g. camel. **tylopodous,** *a.* (Gk. *tulos*, knob; *pous*, foot)

tylosis, *n.* callosity; an inflammation of the eyelids; (*bot.*) kind of growth formed in cavity of a duct. **tylotic,** *a.* (Gk. *tulos*, knob)

tymbal, same as **timbal.**

tymp, *n.* crown of opening in front of blast-furnace hearth. (*tympanum*)

tympan, *n.* frame for equalizing pressure in printing-press. (*tympanum*)

tympanum, *n.* (*pl.* **tympana**) (*anat.*) ear-drum; middle ear; (*archit.*) face of pediment; space between arch and top of door. **tympanic,** *a.* of tympanum; of, like, a drum. **tympanitēs,** *n.* distension of abdomen by flatulence. **tympanitis,** *n.* inflammation of membrane of middle ear. (L. = drum)

type, *n.* class, group; features distinguishing this; characteristic example, specimen, symbol; block bearing letter used for printing; set, fount, of these; (*Shake.*) badge.—*v.t.* and *i.* typewrite; typify. **in t.,** set up for printing. **t.-founder,** *n.* one who casts printing-type. **t.-metal,** *n.* alloy of lead, antimony, and tin, used for making type. **t.-setter,** *n.* compositor. **typescript,** *n.* typewritten matter. **typewrite,** *v.t.* and *i.* write with typewriter. **typewriter,** *n.* writing-machine worked by fingers on keyboard; typist. (Gk. *tupos*)

typhlitis, *n.* inflammation of caecum. **typhlitic,** *a.* *k*Gk. *tuphlos*, blind)

typhoid, *a.* like typhus.—*n.* (also **t. fever**) infectious fever attacking intestines, enteric. **t. bacillus,** germ causing typhoid. **typhoidal,** *a.* (*typhus* + Gk. *eidos*, form)

typhomania, *n.* delirium characteristic of typhus.

typhoon, *n.* hurricane of China seas. **typhonic,** *a.* (Arab. *tūfān*, hurricane, and Chin. *tai fung*, big wind)

typhus, *n.* severe contagious fever carried by lice, jail fever. **typhous,** *a.* (Gk. *tuphos*, stupor)

typical, *a.* fit to serve as specimen; characteristic.

typify, *v.t.* be type of; represent by a type, prefigure. **typification,** *n.*

typist, *n.* user of typewriter.

typo, *n.* (*colloq.*) typographer. (abbr.)

typo-, from Gk. *tupos*, type, used in **typograph,** *n.* machine for making and setting type; **typographer,** *n.* printer; **typography,** *n.* art of printing, style and lay-out of printed matter, hence **typographic, typographical,** *aa.*; **typolite,** *n.* stone impressed with figure of plant or animal, fossil; **typology,** *n.* doctrine, interpretation, of scriptural types; **typonym,** *n.* name based on type as specimen of species, hence **typonymal, typonymic,** *aa.*

typtology, *n.* science of spirit-rapping. **typtological,** *a.* **typtologist,** *n.* (Gk. *tuptein*, strike; *legein*, speak)

tyrannosaurus, *n.* extinct carnivorous reptile about 47 ft. long. (Gk. *turannos,* tyrant; *sauros,* lizard)
tyrant, *n.* oppressive or cruel ruler or master; (in ancient Greece) usurping despot. **tyrannical, tyrannous,** *aa.* of or like a tyrant, unjustly severe; despotic. **tyrannicide,** *n.* killing, killer, of tyrant. **tyrannize,** *v.i.* and *t.* exercise tyranny (over). **tyranny,** *n.* cruel and arbitrary use of authority; oppressive rule; tyrannical act; office of Greek tyrant, despotism. (Gk. *turannos*)
tyre, tire, *n.* rim of wheel; rubber cushion or tubing surrounding this.
tyre, *n.* (*Anglo-Ind.*) curdled milk and cream. (Tamil *tayir*)
tyro, *n.* (*pl.* **tyros**) one learning an art, novice. (L. *tiro,* recruit)
tyr(o)-, from Gk. *turos,* cheese, used in **tyriasis,** *n.* elephantiasis, alopecia; **tyrotoxicon,** *n.* a ptomaine produced in milk or cheese.
tzar, see **czar.**
tzetze, same as **tsetse.**
tzigane, *a.* and *n.* Hungarian gipsy. (Magyar *czigány*)

U

U. **U-boat,** *n.* German submarine. **U-bolt,** *n.* one shaped like U.
uberous, *a.* copious; fertile. **uberty,** *n.* *uberrima fides* (*law*) complete good faith. (L. *uber*)
ubiety, *n.* local relation, whereness. (L. *ubi,* where)
ubiquity, *n.* omnipresence, ubiquitousness. **ubiquitarian,** *a.* and *n.* of, believer in, the omnipresence of Christ's body. **ubiquitarianism,** *n.* **ubiquitous,** *a.* being everywhere at once. (L. *ubique,* everywhere)
ubi supra, in the place above mentioned. (L.=where above)
udal, *n.* pre-feudal form of freehold tenure still existing in Orkney and Shetland. **udaller, udalman,** *nn.* holder of property by udal. (O.N. *óthal*)
udder, *n.* large milk-gland of cow etc. (O.E. *úder*)
udometer, *n.* rain-gauge. **udometric,** *a.* (L. *udus,* wet)
ugh, *int.* of disgust or horror.
ugly, *a.* hideous, offensive to the eye; repulsive, vile; menacing; ill-natured. **uglify,** *v.t.* make ugly. **ugsome,** *a.* (*Scot.*) disgusting. (O.N. *uggr,* fear)
uhlan, *n.* German lancer. (G.)
Uitlander, *n.* settler, incomer, in Transvaal. (Du.=outlander)
ukase, *n.* Russian imperial edict; official decree. (Russ. *ukaz*)
ukelélě, ukulélě, ukalélě, *n.* four-stringed Hawaiian instrument like guitar. (native)
ulcer, *n.* open sore discharging pus; corrupting influence. **ulcered, ulcerous,** *aa.* **ulcerate,** *v.i.* and *t.* become, make, ulcerous. **ulceration,** *n.* **ulcerative,** *a.* (L. *ulcus*)
-ule, *suf.* of diminutives, as in **granule.** (L. *-ulus*)
ulema, *n.* college of Moslem doctors of sacred law, esp. in Turkey. (Arab. *'alama,* know)
uliginose, uliginous, *aa.* oozy, slimy; growing in swamps. (L. *uligo,* moisture)
ulitis, *n.* inflammation of gums. (Gk. *oula,* gums)
ullage, *n.* quantity a cask lacks of being full; (*sl.*) lees, dregs. (O.F. *ouiller,* fill up)
ulmaceous, *a.* of the elm family. **ulmin,** *n.* brown gummy substance found in elm-bark and humus. **ulmic, ulmous,** *aa.* of ulmin. (L. *ulmus,* elm)
ulna, *n.* (*pl.* **ulnae**) larger of two bones of forearm. **ulnar,** *a.* (L.= elbow)
ulotrichous, *a.* woolly-haired. **ulotrichan,** *a.* and *n.* (Gk. *oulos,* woolly; *thrix,* hair)
ulster, *n.* long loose overcoat. (*place*)
ulterior, *a.* further; later in time; beyond what appears. (L.)
ultimate, *a.* furthest; last, final; fundamental, primary. *ultimā ratio,* final argument, force. *ultima Thūlē,* very remote place. **ultimatum,** *n.* (*pl.* **ultimatums, ultimata**) final proposals; terms whose rejection means war. **ultimo,** *adv.* (*abbr.* **ult.**) of last month. **ultimogeniture,** *n.* system by which youngest son inherits (opp. to primogeniture). (L. *ultimus,* last)
ultra, *n.* extremist. *u. vīrēs,* beyond one's power or authority. **u.-conservative, u.-fashionable, u.-modern** etc., *aa.* extremely or excessively conservative etc. **u.-microscope,** *n.* instrument for viewing particles that are **u.-microscopic** or too small to be visible under microscope. **u.-red,** *a.* infra-red. **u.-violet,** *a.* beyond violet in the spectrum. **ultraism,** *n.* extremism. **ultraist,** *n.* (L.=beyond)
ultramarine, *a.* beyond the sea.—*n.* blue pigment got from lapis lazuli. (L. *ultra,* beyond; *mare,* sea)
ultramontane, *a.* beyond, south of, the Alps; favourable to the absolute authority of the pope. **ultramontanism, ultramontanist,** *nn.* (L. *ultra,* beyond; *mons,* mountain)
ultramundane, *a.* beyond the world or the solar system. (L. *ultra,* beyond; *mundus,* world)

ultromotivity, *n.* power of spontaneous movement. (L. *ultro*, of one's own accord)

ulu, *n.* Eskimo domestic knife for general purposes. (Eskimo)

ululate, *v.i.* howl; hoot. **ululant,** *a.* **ululation,** *n.* (L. *ululare*)

umbel, *n.* umbrella-like flower-cluster with stalks springing from central point. **umbellal, umbellar, umbellate,** *aa.* **umbellet, umbellule,** *nn.* secondary umbel in compound umbel. **umbellifer,** *n.* plant of carrot family. **umbelliferous,** *a.* having umbels; of umbellifers. (L. *umbella*, sunshade)

umber, *n.* brownish mineral pigment; grayling; umbrette.—*a.* olive-brown.—*v.t.* colour with umber. **raw u.,** in its natural state. **burnt u.,** calcined and reddish. (F. *ombre*)

umbilicus, *n.* (*pl.* **umbilici**) navel; navel-like formation. **umbilical,** *a.* of, like, umbilicus; central; connected through female line. **umbilicate,** *a.* navel-shaped. **umbilicular,** *a.* of navel. (L.)

umbles, *obs.* form of **numbles.**

umbo, *n.* (*pl.* **umbos, umbōnēs**) boss of shield; (*bot., zool.*) knob, protuberance. **umbonal, umbonate, umbonic,** *aa.* (L.)

umbra, *n.* (*pl.* **umbrae**) part of shadow within which sun is entirely hidden during eclipse; central part of sun-spot. (L=shade)

umbraculum, *n.* (*bot.*) umbrella-shaped appendage. (L.=umbrella)

umbrage, *n.* sense of injury, offence; (*poet.*) shade, foliage. **umbrageous,** *a.* shady, giving shade. (*umbra*)

umbrella, *n.* screen folding on central stick, carried as shelter from rain; similar device as symbol of dignity; (*zool.*) swimming-disk of jelly-fish. **u.-ant,** *n.* kind that carries leaves. **u.-bird,** *n.* black S. American bird with erectile crest. **u.-tree,** *n.* small American magnolia. (*umbra*)

umbrette, *n.* African umber-coloured wading-bird. (*umber*)

Umbrian, *a.* and *n.* (native) of Umbria. **U. school,** painting school of Raphael.

umbriere, *n.* (*Spens.*) visor. (L. *umbra*, shade)

umbriferous, *a.* casting shade. (L. *umbra*, shade; *ferre*, bear)

umiak, *n.* large Eskimo skin boat. (Eskimo)

umlaut, *n.* vowel-change in Germanic languages due to *i* or *u* (now us. lost) in following syllable, e.g. 'men' from 'man'; diaeresis marking such changed vowel in German.—*v.t.* change by umlaut. (G.)

umpire, *n.* person chosen to enforce rules in game; third party to whom dispute is referred for settlement, arbiter.—*v.i.* and *t.* act as umpire (for). **umpirage,** *n.* position, ruling, of umpire. (O.F. *nomper*, odd man, *n* being lost by mistaken division of *a numpire* into *an umpire*)

umpteen, *a.* (*sl.*) a good many, several. (joc. analogy with *thirteen* etc.)

umquhile, *adv.* and *a.* (*Scot.*) formerly, late. (*while*)

'un, *pron.* (*colloq.*) one.

un-, *adj. pref.* not, as in **unable, un-get-at-able, unreal** (attachable to any adjective).—*n. pref.* lack of, freedom from, as in **unbelief.**—*verb pref.*, strip of, as in **unfrock**; reversing meaning of simple verb, as in **unbar.** (O.E.)

una, *n.* yacht with single sail on mast close to bow, catboat. (boat's name)

unabashed, *a.* not disconcerted.

unabated, *a.* undiminished, at full strength.

unable, *a.* not able; (*Shake.*) weak.

unabridged, *a.* given in full.

unaccented, *a.* not accented, unstressed.

unacceptable, *a.* unwelcome.

unaccommodating, *a.* not ready to oblige.

unaccompanied, *a.* not attended, alone; (*mus.*) without accompaniment.

unaccomplished, *a.* unfinished; lacking accomplishments.

unaccountable, *a.* inexplicable; not responsible.

unaccustomed, *a.* not habituated; unusual.

unacquainted, *a.* not acquainted; (*Spens.*) unusual, strange.

unadulterated, *a.* pure, unmixed.

unadvised, *a.* rash; inconsiderate. **unadvisedly,** *adv.* imprudently.

unaffected, *a.* not changed, uninfluenced; free from affectation, genuine.

unafraid, *a.* without fear.

unaided, *a.* without help.

unalloyed, *a.* pure, unmixed.

unalterable, *a.* fixed, unchangeable.

unambiguous, *a.* clear, plain.

unaneled, *a.* (*Shake.*) without receiving last sacraments.

unanimous, *a.* all of one mind; held, given, with agreement of all. **unanimity,** *n.* (L. *unus*, one; *animus*, mind)

unanswerable, *a.* irrefutable, conclusive.

unappetizing, *a.* uninviting, repellent.

unapt, *a.* not ready or inclined; unsuitable.

unarm, *v.t.* and *i.* disarm; lay down arms. **unarmed,** *a.* weaponless.

unasked, *a.* spontaneous, unbidden.

unassailable, *a.* proof against attack or criticism.

unassuming, *a.* modest, not forward.

unattached, *a.* not belonging to particular regiment, club etc.

unattainable, *a.* out of reach.

unattractive, *a.* not prepossessing, plain.

unau, *n.* two-toed sloth. (Brazilian)

unauthorized, *a.* without proper sanction.

unavailing, *a.* fruitless, vain.
unavoidable, *a.* inevitable.
unaware, *a.* not aware. **unawares,** *adv.* unexpectedly, by surprise; without knowing.
unbacked, *a.* having no backers; (of horse) never yet ridden, unbroken.
unbag, *v.t.* let go from bag.
unbalanced, *a.* violently impulsive, unsteady; not in equipoise.
unbank, *v.t.* remove ashes from top of (fire) and let it burn up.
unbar, *v.t.* remove bar from; unfasten, open.
unbated, *a.* unabated; (*Shake.*) not blunted.
unbearable, *a.* intolerable.
unbeaten, *a.* unconquered; unsurpassed; untrodden.
unbecoming, *a.* indecorous, unseemly; not suited to, unbefitting.
unbeknown, unbeknownst, *aa.* (*colloq.*) not known. **u. to,** without the knowledge of.
unbelief, *n.* incredulity; want of faith. **unbeliever,** *n.* infidel; atheist, sceptic.
unbend, *v.t.* and *i.* straighten; free from strain, relax; be affable. **unbending,** *a.* inflexible, unyielding.
unberufen, int. to avert ill-luck after boasting. (G.=unsummoned)
unbiased, unbiassed, *a.* free from bias, impartial.
unbiblical, *a.* not contained in, not authorized by, the Bible.
unbid, *a.* unbidden; (*Spens.*) without a prayer.
unbidden, *a.* not commanded, spontaneous; uninvited.
unbind, *v.t.* loose, untie, unfasten; set at liberty.
unbishop, *v.t.* deprive of rank of bishop.
unbleached, *a.* left in natural colour.
unblemished, *a.* spotless, pure.
unblessed, unblest, *a.* not blessed; accursed.
unblest, *a.* (*Spens.*) unwounded.
unblushing, *a.* shameless, barefaced.
unbodied, *a.* disembodied, incorporeal.
unbolt, *v.t.* draw bolt of, open.
unbolted, *a.* (of flour) not sifted.
unbonnet, *v.i.* and *t.* uncover head (of)
unboot, *v.t.* and *i.* take boots off.
unborn, *a.* not yet born, future.
unbosom, *v.t.* tell freely; relieve (oneself of).
unbound, *a.* not bound; without a cover, loose.
unbounded, *a.* limitless, infinite.
unbowed, *a.* not bowed, undefeated.
unbrace, *v.t.* free from braces, undo; relax, slacken.
unbreech, *v.t.* remove breech from (gun) or breeches from (person). **unbreeched,** *a.* still in long clothes.
unbridled, *a.* unrestrained.
unbroken, *a.* not broken, intact; unsubdued; inviolate; continuous.
unbuckle, *v.t.* unfasten buckle of.
unburden, *v.t.* free from load; relieve (oneself) by confession.
unbutton, *v.t.* undo buttons of.
uncage, *v.t.* release from cage.
uncalled, *a.* not summoned. **u.-for,** *a.* impertinently intruded, officious.
uncanny, *a.* mysterious, weird; menacing.
uncap, *v.t.* and *i.* remove cap (from).
uncape, *v.t.* (*Shake.*) uncouple (hounds).
uncared-for, *a.* neglected.
uncase, *v.t.* remove from case.
uncate, *a.* hooked. (L. *uncus,* hook)
unceasing, *a.* incessant, continuous.
unceremonious, *a.* informal, familiar; abrupt, discourteous.
uncertain, *a.* doubtful, problematical; undecided; capricious, unreliable. **uncertainty,** *n.*
unchain, *v.t.* loose from chain, free.
unchallenged, *a.* not disputed.
unchancy, *a.* (*Scot.*) unlucky; dangerous; inconvenient.
uncharitable, *a.* harsh in judgment, censorious.
uncharge, *v.t.* (*Shake.*) acquit.
uncharted, *a.* not mapped.
unchaste, *a.* not chaste, lewd. **unchastity,** *n.*
unchecked, *a.* not stopped, not controlled.
unchristian, *a.* contrary to the spirit of Christianity, uncharitable; heathen. **unchristianize,** *v.t.* turn from Christianity.
unchurch, *v.t.* deprive of church membership or status, excommunicate.
uncial, *a.* of, written in, large rounded script like capitals, used about years 300–900.—*n.* uncial letter or manuscript. (L. *uncia,* inch)
unciform, *a.* hook-shaped. **uncinal, uncinate,** *aa.* hooked. (L. *uncus,* hook)
uncircumcised, *a.* non-Jewish; heathen, unregenerate.
uncivil, *a.* ill-mannered, rude; (*Spens.*) wild. **uncivilized,** *a.* barbarous.
unclad, *a.* not clothed.
unclasp, *v.t.* loosen clasp of, open.
uncle, *n.* father's or mother's brother, aunt's husband; (*sl.*) pawnbroker. **U. Sam,** typical U.S. citizen. (L. *avunculus,* maternal uncle)
unclean, *a.* dirty; unchaste; ceremonially impure.
unclench, *v.t.* open what is clenched.
unclerical, *a.* lay; unbecoming a clergyman.
unclinch, same as **unclench.**
uncloak, *v.t.* and *i.* take cloak off.
unclose, *v.t.* and *i.* open; disclose.
unclothe, *v.t.* take clothes off, strip.
unclouded, *a.* clear, bright.
unclubbable, *a.* unsociable.
unco, *a.* (*Scot.*) strange, unusual.—*adv.* very.—*n.* strange person or thing; (*pl.*) news. (*uncouth*)
uncock, *v.t.* release hammer of (gun) without firing.
uncoil, *v.t.* and *i.* unwind.

un-come-at-able, *a.* (*colloq.*) not accessible, not attainable.
uncomely, *a.* lacking grace; unseemly.
uncomfortable, *a.* feeling or causing discomfort, uneasy.
uncommon, *a.* rare, unusual; remarkable.—*adv.* (*colloq.*) remarkably.
uncommunicative, *a.* reserved.
uncompanionable, *a.* unsociable.
uncomplaining, *a.* long-suffering.
uncomplimentary, *a.* rude, abusive.
uncompounded, *a.* unmixed, simple.
uncompromising, *a.* rigid in opinion, unyielding, obdurate.
unconcern, *n.* indifference. **unconcerned,** *a.* not anxious.
unconditional, *a.* not subject to conditions, unreserved, absolute. **unditioned reflex,** (*psycho-anal.*) instinctive response to stimulus.
unconfined, *a.* free, unchecked.
uncongenial, *a.* unsympathetic; distasteful.
unconnected, *a.* not joined, separate; rambling.
unconquerable, *a.* indomitable.
unconscionable, *a.* out of all reason, inordinate; unscrupulous, grossly unfair.
unconscious, *a.* unaware; insensible; involuntary.—*n.* (*psycho-anal.*) unconscious part of mind.
unconsidered, *a.* disregarded.
unconstitutional, *a.* contrary to a country's constitution.
unconstrained, *a.* unembarrassed, not self-conscious; free from compulsion.
uncontrollable, *a.* beyond control.
unconventional, *a.* not bound by convention; free in manner or treatment.
unconversable, *a.* hard to keep up talk with.
uncork, *v.t.* draw cork from; give vent to (feelings).
uncorroborated, *a.* not confirmed.
uncouple, *v.t.* disconnect (railway coach); unleash (hounds).
uncourteous, *a.* rude, discourteous.
uncourtly, *a.* unpolished, unrefined.
uncouth, *a.* awkward, boorish; (*arch.*) strange, mysterious. (O.E. *uncúth,* unknown)
uncovenanted, *a.* not based on or subject to covenant.
uncover, *v.t.* and *i.* remove cover from; disclose; lift hat.
uncreate, *v.t.* annihilate. —*a.* (also **uncreated**) not created, self-existent.
uncritical, *a.* disinclined or incompetent to criticize; not according to the rules of criticism.
uncrown, *v.t.* depose. **uncrowned,** *a.* (of king) having power but not title.
unction, *n.* anointing as rite or for medical purpose; ointment; soothing thing; religious fervour; gusto; insincere enthusiasm, excessive suavity. **extreme u.,** Roman Catholic rite of anointing dying. **unctuous,** *a.* greasy, oily; full of unction, gushing. (L. *unguere,* anoint)
uncurl, *v.t.* and *i.* take curl out of, unroll.
uncut, *a.* not cut; (of book) with untrimmed margins.
undamaged, *a.* uninjured, sound.
undate, undated, *aa.* wavy, waved. (L. *unda,* wave)
undated, *a.* bearing no date.
undaunted, *a.* fearless, undismayed.
undé, undee, *a.* (*heraldry*) wavy. (L. *unda,* wave)
undecagon, *n.* eleven-sided plane figure. (L. *undecim,* eleven. Gk. *gōnia,* angle)
undeceive, *v.t.* disillusion, open the eyes of. **undeceived,** *a.* not deceived.
undecennial, *a.* lasting, happening every, eleven years. (L. *undecim,* eleven; *annus,* year)
undecided, *a.* not settled; irresolute; vague.
undecipherable, *a.* illegible.
undeck, *v.t.* divest of ornaments. **undecked,** *a.* not adorned; having no deck.
undefended, *a.* not protected; (of lawsuit) in which no defence is put in.
undefined, *a.* not marked out; vague.
undeify, *v.t.* deprive of divine status.
undemonstrative, *a.* not effusive, reserved.
undeniable, *a.* palpably true, not disputable.
undenominational, *a.* of no particular religious sect.
undependable, *a.* not trustworthy.
under, *prep.* below, beneath; in subjection to; less than; liable to; bound by; during rule of.—*adv.* in, to, a lower place or condition.—*a.* lower, inferior. **go u.,** sink; be ruined. **keep u.,** hold down, oppress. **u. a cloud,** out of favour. **u. age,** less than 21. **u. arms,** carrying weapons; mobilized. **u. foot,** on the ground. **u. repair,** being repaired. **u. the breath,** in a whisper. **u. way,** in motion. **undercarriage,** *n.* landing-gear of aeroplane. **u.-clerk, u.-secretary,** *nn.* assistant or subordinate clerk, secretary. **u.-sheriff,** *n.* deputy sheriff. (O.E.)
under-, *pref.* below, as in **underclothes, underground**; insufficiently, as in **understate.**
underact, *v.t.* and *i.* act (part) inadequately.
underarm, *a.* and *adv.* (done) with arm below level of shoulder.
underbid, *v.t.* offer goods etc. at cheaper price than (person). **underbidder,** *n.* maker of bid next to final one at auction.
underbred, *a.* not of pure breed; ill-bred, vulgar.
underbrush, *n.* undergrowth, scrub.
undercharge, *v.t.* charge too little (for); fill or load inadequately.
undercliff, *n.* raised terrace beneath cliff, formed by falls of rock etc.

underclothes, underclothing, *nn.* clothes worn next body.
undercroft, *n.* crypt. (L. *crupta*)
undercurrent, *n.* current below surface; hidden trend.
undercut, *v.t.* cut away from below; reduce (prices) in competition, underbid.—*n.* under side of sirloin.
underdog, *n.* dog, person, that has worst of an encounter.
underdone, *a.* cooked insufficiently; left slightly raw.
underdress, *v.t.* dress too scantily or simply.
underestimate, *n.* too low an estimate. —*v.t.* set too low a value on.
under-expose, *v.t.* (*phot.*) expose for too short a time.
underfeed, *v.t.* feed inadequately. **underfed,** *a.*
underfong, *v.t.* (*Spens.*) surprise, entrap. (*fang*)
undergarment, *n.* article of underwear.
undergird, *v.t.* bind (ship) laterally with cables.
undergo, *v.t.* (*past* **underwent,** *p.p.* **undergone**) experience, suffer.
undergraduate, *n.* (*fem.* **undergraduette**) university student who has not taken degree.
underground, *a.* beneath the ground; surreptitious.
undergrowth, *n.* shrubs or plants growing among trees.
underhand, *a.* and *adv.* clandestine, sly, by secret means; (*cricket, tennis*) below the waist.
underhung, *a.* with lower part projecting beyond upper (esp. of jaw).
underlay, *v.t.* lay something under; (*print.*) lay paper under (block) to throw the impression up.—*n.* paper used for this.
underlay, *past* of **underlie.**
underlease, *n.* sublease.
underlet, *v.t.* sublet.
underlie, *v.t.* be situated under; form basis of.
underline, *v.t.* draw line under (word); stress, emphasize.
underlinen, *n.* underwear.
underling, *n.* subordinate.
underman, *v.t.* supply with too small a crew.
undermentioned, *a.* alluded to below.
undermine, *v.t.* dig under, sap; weaken insidiously.
undermost, *a.* lowest, farthest down.
underneath, *adv.* and *prep.* at, to, a lower place (than); below.
underpay, *v.t.* pay inadequately.
underpin, *v.t.* place supports or props beneath.
underplay, *v.i.* play low card while retaining high one.
underplot, *n.* secondary plot.
under-production, *n.* production unequal to demand or less than normal.
underprop, *v.t.* put prop under.
underquote, *v.t.* offer goods at lower price than (other dealer).
underrate, *v.t.* value too low, underestimate.
underscore, *v.t.* underline.
undersell, *v.t.* sell cheaper than.
underset, *n.* undercurrent in opposite direction to surface water.
undershot, *a.* (of mill-wheel) driven by water flowing under it.
undersigned, *a.* whose names are signed below.
undersized, *a.* below normal size, stunted.
underslung, *a.* (of chassis) with frame below axles.
understand, *v.t.* and *i.* (*past* **understood;** *p.p.* **understood,** *arch.* **understanded**) comprehend, perceive meaning or nature of; be informed; infer, take as implied; (*gram.*) supply (word) mentally. **understandable,** *a.* intelligible. **understanding,** *a.* having insight.—*n.* comprehension; intelligence, intellect; agreement, thing agreed upon; (*pl. joc.*) legs.
understate, *v.t.* minimize, put at less than truth (opp. to exaggerate). **understatement,** *n.*
understock, *v.t.* supply (farm etc.) with insufficient stock.
understood, see **understand.**
understrapper, *n.* subordinate.
understudy, *n.* one who studies theatrical part so as to deputize for usual actor in emergency.—*v.t.* be understudy for.
undertake, *v.t.* and *i.* (*past* **undertook,** *p.p.* **undertaken**) take in hand, enter upon; promise, warrant; (*arch.*) engage (person) in contest. **undertaker,** *n.* contractor; one who manages funerals. **undertaking,** *n.* enterprise, task; promise, obligation; funeral undertaker's trade.
undertenant, *n.* tenant's tenant.
undertone, *n.* low tone of voice; subdued colour.
undertook, see **undertake.**
undertow, *n.* backwash of wave; underset.
undervalue, *v.t.* value below real worth; esteem lightly. **undervaluation,** *n.*
underwear, *n.* underclothes.
underwent, see **undergo.**
underwood, *n.* brushwood.
underwork, *v.t.* and *i.* work inadequately.
underworld, *n.* infernal regions, Hades; antipodes; lowest or criminal class.
underwrite, *v.t.* and *i.* (*past* **underwrote,** *p.p.* **underwritten**) write below; issue insurance policy for (ship, cargo etc.); engage to buy any part of (issue of shares) not taken up by public. **underwriter,** *n.*
undeserved, *a.* not merited. **undeserving,** *a.* not worthy.
undesigned, *a.* not intentional. **undesigning,** *a.* ingenuous, sincere.
undesirable, *a.* not desirable.—*n.* person of ill repute.

undetermined, *a.* not decided.
undeveloped, *a.* immature; (of land) not exploited for building.
undies, *n.pl.* (*sl.*) underclothes. (abbr.)
undigested, *a.* not digested; not arranged or correlated.
undid, *see* **undo.**
undigenous, *a.* generated by water. (L. *unda,* wave; *gignere,* beget)
undight, *v.t.* (*Spens.*) divest; undo.
undignified, *a.* wanting in dignity.
undiluted, *a.* neat, unmixed.
undiminished, *a.* not lessened.
undine, *n.* water-nymph. **undinal,** *a.* (L. *unda,* wave)
undiplomatic, *a.* blunt, tactless.
undisciplined, *a.* not properly trained.
undisclosed, *a.* kept secret.
undiscovered, *a.* not found out. unknown.
undisguised, *a.* open, avowed.
undismayed, *a.* not terrified or disheartened.
undisputed, *a.* not called in question.
undisturbed, *a.* not moved; not worried.
undo, *v.t.* (*past* **undid,** *p.p.* **undone**) reverse, annul; unfasten, untie; ruin. **undoing,** *n.* ruin. **undone,** *a.* not done; ruined.
undoubted, *a.* certain; genuine.
undress, *v.t.* and *i.* take clothes off.—*n.* uniform worn when off duty.
undue, *a.* excessive, immoderate; improper.
undulate, *v.i.* and *t.* move in or like waves.—*a.* wavy. **undulant, undulatory,** *aa.* **undulation,** *n.* (L. *unda,* wave)
unduly, *adv.* excessively; improperly.
undying, *a.* immortal, eternal.
unearned, *a.* not earned. **u. income,** got from investments, not work. **u. increment,** increase, not caused by owner's action, in value of property.
unearth, *v.t.* drive from burrow; bring to light, discover. **unearthly,** *a.* not of this world, supernatural; weird.
uneasy, *a.* not comfortable; anxious; embarrassed; disturbing.
uneath, *adv.* (*Spens.*) hardly, with difficulty. (O.E. *éathe,* easy)
uneconomic, *a.* wasteful; (of price) too low or high to be good business.
unedifying, *a.* degrading, vulgar.
uneducated, *a.* illiterate.
unemotional, *a.* calm, not showing feeling.
unemployed, *a.* not used or occupied; out of work. **unemployable,** *a.* unfitted for paid work. **unemployment,** *n.* **unemployment benefit,** payment to unemployed worker under insurance act.
unending, *a.* ceaseless; eternal.
unendurable, *a.* intolerable.
un-English, *a.* not sportsmanlike or straightforward like English.
unenlightened, *a.* in intellectual darkness.
unenterprising, *a.* not adventurous.
unenviable, *a.* not to be envied.
unequal, *a.* not equal; ill-matched; of varying quality. **unequalled,** *a.* unmatched.
unequivocal, *a.* plain, not ambiguous.
unerring, *a.* sure, unfailing.
unessential, *a.* not of the first importance.
uneven, *a.* not level or smooth; not uniform or equable; odd.
uneventful, *a.* without striking events.
unexampled, *a.* without precedent, unparalleled.
unexceptionable, *a.* with which no fault can be found, irreproachable.
unexpected, *a.* not looked for, unforeseen.
unexpired, *a.* still valid.
unexpressive, *a.* not expressive; (*Shake.*) ineffable.
unexpurgated, *a.* with no passages omitted.
unfailing, *a.* not running short; staunch.
unfair, *a.* unjust; unequal; against rules.—*v.t.* (*Shake.*) rob of beauty.
unfaith, *n.* want of honour; disbelief. **unfaithful,** *a.* disloyal; inaccurate; guilty of adultery.
unfaltering, *a.* steady; resolute.
unfamiliar, *a.* strange, unknown; unacquainted (with).
unfashionable, *a.* not in the prevailing mode.
unfasten, *v.t.* loose from fastening.
unfathered, *a.* fatherless; illegitimate.
unfathomable, *a.* bottomless; insoluble.
unfavourable, *a.* unpropitious, adverse.
unfeasible, *a.* impracticable.
unfed, *a.* not fed.
unfeeling, *a.* callous, hard-hearted.
unfeigned, *a.* real, sincere.
unfeminine, *a.* unwomanly.
unfetter, *v.t.* loose from fetters, free.
unfilial, *a.* not becoming a son or daughter, undutiful.
unfinished, *a.* incomplete; rough.
unfit, *a.* unsuitable; in bad physical condition.—*v.t.* make unsuitable, disqualify.
unfix, *v.t.* detach, unfasten.
unflagging, *a.* not drooping; unremitting.
unfledged, *a.* not feathered; immature.
unfleshed, *a.* (of sword) not yet used in fighting.
unflinching, *a.* steadfast, resolute.
unfold, *v.t.* spread out, expand; reveal, disclose.
unforeseen, *a.* not expected.
unforgivable, *a.* inexcusable. **unforgiving,** *a.* implacable.
unformed, *a.* shapeless; untrained.
unfortunate, *a.* unlucky; unsuccessful; ill-advised.—*n.* unfortunate person.
unfounded, *a.* baseless; not yet founded.
unfrequented, *a.* rarely visited, lonely.

unfriended, *a.* without friends. **unfriendly**, *a.* unkind; hostile.
unfrock, *v.t.* expel from priesthood.
unfruitful, *a.* barren; vain, fruitless.
unfulfilled, *a.* not accomplished.
unfunded, *a.* (of debt) floating.
unfurl, *v.t.* and *i.* spread out (sail), unroll.
unfurnished, *a.* without furniture, bare.
ungainly, *a.* awkward, clumsy. (O.N. *gegn*, straight)
ungallant, *a.* not attentive to women; not brave.
ungenerous, *a.* mean; unfair.
ungentle, *a.* rough; rude. **ungentlemanly**, *a.* ill-bred, caddish.
un-get-at-able, *a.* not easily reached.
ungird, *v.t.* free from, loose, girdle. **ungirt**, *a.*
unglazed, *a.* without glass.
ungodly, *a.* impious, wicked.
ungovernable, *a.* unruly; wild, violent.
ungraceful, *a.* clumsy. **ungracious**, *a.* not kindly, churlish; (*Shake.*) profane.
ungrammatical, *a.* contrary to the rules of grammar.
ungrateful, *a.* without gratitude; thankless, irksome.
ungrounded, *a.* baseless, false.
ungrudging, *a.* given freely, liberal.
ungual, *a.* of or having nail, claw, or hoof. (L. *unguis*, nail)
unguarded, *a.* incautious, careless.
unguent, *n.* ointment. **unguentary**, *a.* (L. *unguere*, anoint)
ungula, *n. pl.* **ungulae**) hoof, claw, nail; cylinder, cone, with top cut off at angle. **ungular**, *a.* **ungulate**, *a.* and *n.* hoofed (mammal). (L.)
unhackneyed, *a.* not trite, fresh.
unhallowed, *a.* having evil associations, unholy.
unhampered, *a.* free, untrammelled.
unhand, *v.t.* let go of, release. **unhandy**, *a.* not convenient; awkward.
unhappy, *a.* miserable; unlucky; inapt; (*Shake.*) roguish. **unhappily**, *adv.* unfortunately; (*Shake.*) unfavourably.
unharmed, *a.* not injured.
unharness, *v.t.* take harness off, unyoke.
unhasp, *v.t.* unfasten from hasp.
unhealthy, *a.* unwell, sickly; unwholesome.
unheard, *a.* not heard. **u.-of**, *a.* unprecedented.
unheeded, *a.* disregarded. **unheedful**, **unheeding**, *aa.* inattentive, careless.
unhelm, *v.t.* and *i.* take off helmet.
unhesitating, *a.* prompt, ready.
unhinge, *v.t.* take off hinges; make crazy, derange.
unhistorical, *a.* merely legendary.
unhitch, *v.t.* unfasten, unharness.
unholy, *a.* wicked, impious; (*colloq.*) frightful.
unhonoured, *a.* not celebrated.
unhook, *v.t.* remove from hook; loosen hooks of (dress).
unhoped, *a.* not expected.
unhorse, *v.t.* throw (rider) from horse; force to dismount.
unhouse, *v.t.* drive from house; render homeless.
unhouseled, *a.* (*Shake.*) not having received the sacrament.
unhuman, *a.* not human.
unhurt, *a.* not injured.
uni-, *pref.* single, as in **unilateral**. (L. *unus*, one)
uni-articulate, *a.* single-jointed.
Uniat, **Uniate**, *n.* member of Church acknowledging pope's supremacy but following Greek ritual. (L. *unus*, one)
unicameral, *a.* with only one legislative chamber. (L. *unus*, one; *camera*, chamber)
unicapsular, *a.* having a single capsule. (*uni-*)
unicellular, *a.* one-celled. (*uni-*)
unicoloured, *a.* of one colour. (*uni-*)
unicorn, *n.* fabled animal like horse with single straight horn in forehead; team of three horses, two abreast and third as leader. **u.-fish**, *n.* narwhal. **unicornous**, *a.* one-horned. (L. *unus*, one; *cornu*, horn)
unicostate, *a.* (*bot.*) one-ribbed. (L. *unus*, one; *costa*, rib)
unicuspid, *a.* and *n.* (tooth) with single fang. (L. *unus*, one; *cuspis*, point)
unicycle, *n.* one-wheeled cycle. (*uni-*)
unidea'd, **unideaed**, *a.* devoid of ideas, unimaginative. **unideal**, *a.* realistic; dull, prosaic.
unidentate, *a.* having only one tooth. (L. *unus*, one; *dens*, tooth)
unidentified, *a.* not identified.
unidiomatic, *a.* not idiomatic.
unidirectional, *a.* (of electric current) flowing in one direction only. (*uni-*)
unification, *n.* unifying.
unifoliate, *a.* having only one leaf. (L. *unus*, one; *folium*, leaf)
uniform, *a.* having same form, conforming to same rule; not varying; homogeneous.—*n.* official or regulation dress. **uniformed**, *a.* wearing uniform. **uniformity**, *n.* sameness, consistency. (*uni-*)
unify, *v.t.* cause to be one or uniform. (L. *unus*, one; *facere*, make)
unilateral, *a.* one-sided; (of contract) binding one party only. (L. *unus*, one; *latus*, side)
uniliteral, *a.* consisting of only one letter. (L. *unus*, one; *lītera*, letter)
unilocular, *a.* (*bot.*) single-chambered. (L. *unus*, one; *locus*, place)
unimaginable, *a.* inconceivable. **unimaginative**, *a.* matter-of-fact.
unimpaired, *a.* not weakened or damaged.
unimpeachable, *a.* not open to question; blameless.
unimpeded, *a.* not hampered.
unimportant, *a.* insignificant, trivial. **unimportance**, *n.*

unimpressed, *a.* not deeply affected.
unimproved, *a.* not improved; (of land) not cultivated or built upon.
uninflected, *a.* with no inflexions.
uninformed, *a.* not told (of); ignorant, untaught.
uninhabited, *a.* with no inhabitants, desert.
uninjured, *a.* not hurt.
uninspired, *a.* lacking inspiration, commonplace.
uninstructed, *a.* untaught.
unintelligent, *a.* stupid. **unintelligible,** *a.* unable to be understood.
unintentional, *a.* not deliberate, involuntary.
uninterested, *a.* not interested. **uninteresting,** *a.* dull, boring.
unintermitting, *a.* ceaseless.
uninterrupted, *a.* continuous.
uninvited, *a.* without invitation. **uninviting,** *a.* unattractive.
union, *n.* uniting, junction; combination, federation, of societies etc.; marriage; harmony; workhouse; trade union. **U. flag, Jack,** British national flag combining crosses of St. George, St. Andrew, and St. Patrick. **u. suit,** (*Amer.*) combinations. **unionist,** *n.* member of trade union; supporter of empire consolidation as against cosmopolitanism; (formerly) opponent of Irish home rule. **unionism,** *n.* **unionistic,** *a.* (L. *unus*, one)
unipara, *n.* woman who has borne one child only. **uniparous,** *a.* producing one at birth; (*bot.*) with single stem. (L. *unus*, one; *parere*, bring forth)
unipartite, *a.* not divided. (*uni-*)
uniped, *a.* one-footed. (L. *unus*, one; *pes*, foot)
unipersonal, *a.* existing as a single person. (*uni-*)
unipolar, *a.* having only one pole or kind of polarity. (*uni-*)
unique, *a.* the one of its kind, without equal or parallel. (L. *unus*, one)
uniradial, uniradiate, *aa.* having one ray or arm. (*uni-*)
unisexual, *a.* of one sex, not hermaphrodite. **unisexuality,** *n.* (*uni-*)
unison, *n.* agreement, concord; (*mus.*) identity of pitch. **unisonal, unisonant, unisonous,** *aa.* **unisonance,** *n.* (L. *unus*, one; *sonus*, sound)
unit, *n.* single thing or person; one standard quantity. **Unitarian,** *a.* and *n.* (member) of sect which denies doctrine of the Trinity and divinity of Christ. **Unitarianism,** *n.* **unitary,** *a.* of unit or units. (*unity*)
unite, *v.t.* and *i.* make or become one, combine, amalgamate; act together, co-operate. **United Free Church,** (*abbr.* **U.F.**) formed in Scotland in 1900 by union of Free Church and United Presbyterian Church. **United Kingdom,** (*abbr.* **U.K.**) Great Britain and Ireland. **United States (of America)** (*abbr.* **U.S., U.S.A.,**) great N. American republic. **unitive,** *a.* (L. *unus*, one)
unitism, *n.* monism. (*unit*)
unitize, *v.t.* form into a unit.
unity, *n.* oneness, state of being one; harmony, concord; (*math.*) one. **dramatic uu.,** those of time, place, and action, demanding that action of a play should be represented as occurring in one place, within one day, and with nothing irrelevant to the plot. (L. *unus*, one)
univalent, *a.* (*chem.*) having valency of one. **univalency, univalence,** *nn.* (*uni-*)
univalve, *a.* and *n.* (mollusc) with shell in single piece. **univalvular,** *a.* (*uni-*)
universal, *a.* embracing the whole world; applying to all cases, general. —*n.* general concept; (also **u. proposition**) proposition in which predicate is affirmed or denied of the entire subject. **u. provider,** large general stores. (*universe*)
universalism, *n.* doctrine that ultimately all mankind will be saved. **universalist,** *n.* **universalistic,** *a.*
universality, *n.* being universal. **universalize,** *v.t.* make, treat as, universal. **universalization,** *n.*
universe, *n.* whole system of things, cosmos; all mankind. (L. *unus*, one; *vertere*, turn)
university, *n.* educational institution for instruction in higher branches of learning, with power of conferring degrees; members of this. (L. *universitas*, corporation)
universology, *n.* science of universe or of whole range of human activities.
univocal, *a.* and *n.* (word) with only one meaning; (*mus.*) having unison. (*uni-*)
unjust, *a.* unfair, wrongful. **unjustifiable,** *a.* indefensible.
unkempt, *a.* untidy, dishevelled; uncombed. (O.E. *cemban*, comb)
unkennel, *v.t.* loose from kennel; disclose.
unkind, *a.* inconsiderate, harsh; (*Shake.*) unnatural. **unkindly,** *a.* unsympathetic.—*adv.* without kindness. **unkindness,** *n.* unkind feeling or action.
unking, *v.t.* depose. **unkingly,** *a.* unworthy of a king.
unknightly, *a.* unbecoming a knight.
unknit, *v.t.* unravel, undo.
unknot, *v.t.* untie.
unknowing, *a.* ignorant. **unknown,** *a.* not known; unidentified.—*n.* unknown person or quantity.
unlaboured, *a.* (of style) easy, spontaneous.
unlace, *v.t.* undo laces of, loose.
unlade, *v.t.* unship, discharge.
unladylike, *a.* vulgar, common.
unlaid, *a.* not laid.
unlamented, *a.* not regretted.
unlatch, *v.t.* unfasten latch of.

unlawful, *a.* contrary to law, illegal.
unlearn, *v.t.* forget (what has been learned); rid oneself of (habit). **unlearned,** *a.* not well educated.
unleash, *v.t.* free from leash, let go.
unleavened, *a.* made without yeast.
unless, *conj.* if not; except.
unlettered, *a.* illiterate.
unlicensed, *a.* having no permit (esp. to sell alcohol).
unlicked, *a.* not licked into shape. **u. cub,** crude young fool.
unlike, *a.* and *prep.* different (from). **unlikely,** *a.* improbable; unpromising.
unlimber, *v.t.* detach (gun) from limber.
unlimited, *a.* boundless; not restricted; very great.
unload, *v.t.* and *i.* remove (load, cargo) from; withdraw charge from (gun).
unlock, *v.t.* unfasten lock of, open.
unlooked-for, *a.* not expected.
unloose, unloosen, *vv.t.* loose, untie.
unlovable, *a.* repellent. **unlovely,** *a.* ugly, unattractive.
unlucky, *a.* unfortunate, unsuccessful; unhappy, ill-timed; bringing bad luck.
unmake, *v.t.* destroy; annul.
unman, *v.t.* deprive of manliness or courage. **unmanly,** *a.* cowardly.
unmannerly, *a.* rude; ill-bred.
unmarked, *a.* not marked; unnoticed.
unmarriageable, *a.* too young to be married. **unmarried,** *a.* single.
unmask, *v.t.* and *i.* take mask off; expose, show up.
unmatched, *a.* not equalled.
unmeaning, *a.* without meaning. **unmeant,** *a.* not intended.
unmeasured, *a.* boundless, abundant; excessive.
unmeet, *a.* not fit or suitable.
unmentionable, *a.* not fit to be mentioned.—*n.pl.* (*joc.*) trousers.
unmerciful, *a.* cruel; severe.
unmerited, *a.* not deserved.
unmethodical, *a.* lacking method, haphazard.
unmindful, *a.* forgetful; heedless.
unmistakable, *a.* clear, plain, evident.
unmitigated, *a.* unqualified, utter.
unmixed, *a.* pure, unqualified.
unmoor, *v.t.* and *i.* cast off from moorings.
unmoral, *a.* not concerned with morality.
unmounted, *a.* on foot; without setting.
unmoved, *a.* not touched by emotion, calm.
unmuffle, *v.t.* and *i.* take off wraps.
unmusical, *a.* not versed in or caring for music; discordant.
unmuzzle, *v.t.* remove muzzle from.
unnail, *v.t.* remove nails from.
unnamable, *a.* too bad to be named.
unnatural, *a.* contrary to nature, perverse; lacking natural feelings; artificial.
unnecessary, *a.* needless; superfluous.
unneighbourly, *a.* unfriendly; unsociable.
unnerve, *v.t.* cause to lose nerve or courage, unman.
unnethes, same as **uneath.**
unnoted, *a.* not noticed.
unnumbered, *a.* countless.
unobjectionable, *a.* inoffensive.
unobservant, *a.* slow to notice things.
unobtrusive, *a.* modest; not paraded.
unoccupied, *a.* untenanted; disengaged.
unoffending, *a.* harmless, innocent.
unofficial, *a.* not officially announced or confirmed.
unoriginal, *a.* derived, imitative.
unornamental, *a.* unsightly.
unorthodox, *a.* not orthodox; heretical. **unorthodoxy,** *n.*
unpack, *v.t.* remove contents of; take out of trunk.
unpaid, *a.* not paid; honorary.
unpalatable, *a.* nasty to the taste; disagreeable.
unparalleled, *a.* without parallel or equal.
unpardonable, *a.* inexcusable.
unparliamentary, *a.* contrary to parliamentary usage; (of language) strong.
unpeople, *v.t.* depopulate.
unperturbed, *a.* unruffled, calm.
unpick, *v.t.* pick out (stitches).
unpin, *v.t.* remove pins from, unfasten.
unpitying, *a.* callous.
unplaced, *a.* (in horse race) not in first three.
unplait, *v.t.* unfasten plaits of.
unplayable, *a.* impossible to play or play on.
unpleasant, *a.* disagreeable. **unpleasantness,** *n.* disagreement, quarrel.
unplumbed, *a.* unfathomed.
unpoetical, *a.* prosaic.
unpolished, *a.* rough, uncouth.
unpolled, *a.* (of votes) not cast; (of electors) not having voted.
unpopular, *a.* disliked; out of favour.
unpractical, *a.* not practical. **unpractised,** *a.* not experienced; untried.
unprecedented, *a.* that has never happened before, novel.
unpregnant, *a.* (*Shake.*) unapt.
unprejudiced, *a.* impartial, fair.
unpremeditated, *a.* not deliberately planned.
unprepared, *a.* done without preparation; not ready.
unprepossessing, *a.* not attractive, repellent.
unpresentable, *a.* not fit to be seen; not fit for society, ill-mannered.
unpretending, *a.* not claiming distinction, modest. **unpretentious,** *a.* unassuming.
unprincipled, *a.* unscrupulous.
unprintable, *a.* indecent or blasphemous.

unproductive, *a.* barren; ineffective.
unprofessional, *a.* not belonging to a profession; contrary to professional etiquette.
unprofitable, *a.* yielding no profit; useless.
unprogressive, *a.* reactionary.
unpromising, *a.* without good prospect of success.
unpronounceable, *a.* hard or impossible to pronounce.
unpropitious, *a.* ill-omened, unlucky.
unprotected, *a.* not defended; unfortified.
unprovided, *a.* not supplied; not prepared.
unprovoked, *a.* without provocation.
unpublished, *a.* not published or made public.
unpucker, *v.t.* smooth wrinkles from.
unpunctual, *a.* not up to time.
unqualified, *a.* without qualifications, incompetent; not modified, thorough.
unquestionable, *a.* undoubted, certain. **unquestioned,** *a.* not disputed. **unquestioning,** *a.* unhesitating.
unquiet, *a.* restless; uneasy.
unquotable, *a.* not fit to be repeated.
unravel, *v.t.* separate threads of, disentangle; clear up.
unread, *a.* not perused; not well-read, unlearned. **unreadable,** *a.* illegible; dull, boring.
unready, *a.* not ready; not prompt, slow.
unreal, *a.* illusive, sham; imaginary. **unreality,** *n.*
unreason, *n.* want of reason, absurdity. **unreasonable,** *a.* not sensible; immoderate. **unreasoning,** *a.* irrational.
unreclaimed, *a.* not reformed; uncultivated, wild.
unredeemed, *a.* not fulfilled; not taken out of pawn; unmitigated; (of bill) not recalled by payment.
unreel, *v.t.* and *i.* unwind from reel.
unrefined, *a.* vulgar, coarse; not purified.
unreflecting, *a.* thoughtless.
unreformed, *a.* not amended.
unregarded, *a.* neglected, unheeded.
unregenerate, *a.* having had no moral awakening, not renewed in heart.
unrehearsed, *a.* not prepared beforehand, occurring spontaneously.
unrelenting, *a.* inflexible, merciless.
unreliable, *a.* not trustworthy.
unreligious, *a.* not concerned with religion.
unremembered, *a.* forgotten.
unremitting, *a.* incessant, continuous.
unremunerative, *a.* unprofitable.
unrepentant, *a.* impenitent.
unrequited, *a.* (of love) unreturned.
unreserve, *n.* frankness. **unreserved,** *a.* outspoken, open.
unresisted, *a.* unopposed. **unresisting,** *a.* yielding, submissive.
unrest, *n.* disquiet; political discontent.
unrestrained, *a.* without control.
unrestricted, *a.* not limited.
unrevealed, *a.* hidden, secret.
unrhymed, *a.* without rhymes.
unriddle, *v.t.* solve (mystery).
unrig, *v.t.* strip of rigging.
unrighteous, *a.* sinful; unjust.
unrip, *v.t.* rip open or apart.
unripe, *a.* not ripe, immature.
unrivalled, *a.* without equal, peerless.
unrobe, *v.t.* and *i.* undress.
unroll, *v.t.* and *i.* spread out (roll), unfold.
unromantic, *a.* matter-of-fact, humdrum.
unroof, *v.t.* remove roof of.
unroot, *v.t.* root out, uproot.
unruffled, *a.* calm, serene.
unruled, *a.* not governed; (of paper) blank. **unruly,** *a.* disorderly, turbulent.
unsaddle, *v.t.* take saddle off; unhorse.
unsafe, *a.* dangerous; hazardous.
unsaid, *a.* not said.
unsanitary, *a.* lacking sanitation.
unsatisfactory, *a.* not good enough, inadequate.
unsavoury, *a.* of bad taste; disgusting.
unsay, *v.t.* recall (statement), retract.
unscalable, *a.* unclimbable.
unscathed, *a.* uninjured.
unschooled, *a.* not taught or trained.
unscientific, *a.* transgressing scientific principles.
unscrew, *v.t.* and *i.* loosen (screw); unfasten by removing screws.
unscriptural, *a.* not according to the Bible.
unscrupulous, *a.* without principles, conscienceless.
unseal, *v.t.* open by removing seal.
unseam, *v.t.* undo sewing of, rip open.
unsearchable, *a.* mysterious, inscrutable.
unseasonable, *a.* unusual for the season; ill-timed. **unseasoned,** *a.* not matured.
unseat, *v.t.* unhorse; deprive of seat in parliament.
unseaworthy, *a.* not fit to put to sea.
unsectarian, *a.* free from limitations or prejudices of sect.
unseeing, *a.* blind; unsuspecting.
unseemly, *a.* improper, unbecoming. —*adv.* unbecomingly.
unseen, *a.* not visible.—*n.* unfamiliar passage set for translation.
unseldom, *adv.* often.
unselfish, *a.* thinking of others rather than oneself, altruistic.
unserviceable, *a.* unfit for use.
unsettle, *v.t.* disturb; make discontented. **unsettled,** *a.* not settled; changeable; unpaid.
unsex, *v.t.* make unwomanly.
unshackle, *v.t.* loose from fetters, free.
unshakable, *a.* firmly established. **unshaken,** *a.* unwavering, firm.
unshaven, *a.* not shaved; bearded.
unsheathe, *v.t.* draw (sword).
unsheltered, *a.* not protected.

unship, *v.t.* unload, disembark; remove from place where it is fixed.
unshod, *a.* barefoot.
unshrinking, *a.* undaunted, firm.
unsicker, *a.* (*Scot.*) unsure; insecure.
unsighted, *a.* not yet in sight; having one's view obscured; (of gun) without sights. **unsightly,** *a.* ugly.
unsigned, *a.* not signed; anonymous.
unskilful, *a.* clumsy, awkward. **unskilled,** *a.* without special skill or training.
unslaked, *a.* not quenched.
unsleeping, *a.* tireless, alert.
unsociable, *a.* shunning society, solitary in habits. **unsociability,** *n.*
unsold, *a.* not sold.
unsolder, *v.t.* separate what has been soldered.
unsolicited, *a.* not asked, gratuitous.
unsophisticated, *a.* simple-minded, inexperienced; not adulterated.
unsought, *a.* unasked, unsolicited.
unsound, *a.* unhealthy, rotten; fallacious, unreliable.
unsparing, *a.* profuse, lavish; severe.
unspeakable, *a.* good or bad beyond words, indescribable.
unsphere, *v.t.* draw out of sphere.
unspiritual, *a.* worldly, material.
unspoken, *a.* not uttered.
unsporting, unsportsmanlike, *aa.* not playing the game, unfair.
unspotted, *a.* not marked; not corrupted.
unstable, *a.* easily upset; changeable; wavering, irresolute.
unsteady, *a.* shaky, reeling; vacillating.
unstep, *v.t.* remove (mast) from socket.
unstick, *v.t.* separate what is stuck.
unstinted, *a.* profuse, lavish.
unstitch, *v.t.* undo stitches of.
unstop, *v.t.* clear of obstructions, remove stopper from.
unstrained, *a.* unforced, easy.
unstrap, *v.t.* undo straps of.
unstring, *v.t.* remove strings of; remove beads from (string). **unstrung,** *a.* relaxed; unnerved.
unstressed, *a.* not pronounced with stress.
unstudied, *a.* natural, spontaneous.
unsubdued, *a.* unconquered.
unsubstantial, *a.* light, flimsy; unreal, visionary. **unsubstantiated,** *a.* not confirmed.
unsuccess, *n.* failure. **unsuccessful,** *a.* not successful.
unsuitable, *a.* not what is required; unbecoming. **unsuited,** *a.* not adapted; ill-matched.
unsullied, *a.* not stained.
unsung, *a.* not celebrated in poetry.
unsure, *a.* unsafe; uncertain.
unsurmountable, *a.* insuperable.
unsuspected, *a.* not suspected; unguessed. **unsuspicious,** *a.* trusting.
unswathe, *v.t.* take bandages off.
unswerving, *a.* firm, constant.
unsworn, *a.* not bound by oath.
unsymmetrical, *a.* not balanced, lopsided.
unsympathetic, *a.* unfeeling, callous.
unsystematic, *a.* haphazard.
untack, *v.t.* remove tacks from, separate.
untamed, *a.* wild; not disciplined.
untangle, *v.t.* unravel, disentangle.
untasted, *a.* not tasted; not enjoyed.
untaught, *a.* illiterate; not got by teaching.
unteach, *v.t.* teach contrary of.
untenable, *a.* not defensible.
untenanted, *a.* unoccupied, vacant.
untended, *a.* neglected, not cared for.
untether, *v.t.* loose from tether.
unthankful, *a.* ungrateful.
unthink *v.t.* retract mentally. **unthinkable,** *a.* extremely improbable. **unthinking,** *a.* thoughtless. **unthought of,** not imagined or expected.
unthread, *v.t.* take thread from (needle, beads); unravel.
unthrifty, *a.* thriftless, wasteful; (*Spens.*) profligate. **unthrift,** *n.* (*arch.*).
unthrone, *v.t.* depose (king).
untidy, *a.* not neat, disordered.
untie, *v.t.* undo knot in, unfasten.
until, *prep.* and *conj.* up to the time of or when, till. (O.N. *und*, as far as+*till*)
untilled, *a.* uncultivated.
untimely, *a.* premature; inopportune. —*adv.* prematurely, at wrong time.
untiring, *a.* unwearied.
unto, *prep.* (*arch.*) to.
untold, *a.* not told; not counted, vast.
untouchable, *a.* religiously unclean. —*n.* non-caste Hindu.
untoward, *a.* awkward, inconvenient; (*arch.*) perverse.
untrained, *a.* not instructed; not in training.
untrammelled, *a.* not restricted.
untranslatable, *a.* incapable of translation.
untravelled, *a.* not having travelled; unexplored.
untread, *v.t.* (*Shake.*) retrace (path).
untried, *a.* inexperienced.
untrodden, *a.* unfrequented.
untroubled, *a.* undisturbed, calm.
untrue, *a.* false; disloyal; deviating from correct standard.
untruss, *v.t.* and *i.* unfasten; take down breeches (of).
untrustworthy, *a.* not dependable.
untruth, *n.* falsity; lie. **untruthful,** *a.* false, lying.
untune, *v.t.* put out of tune. **untuneful,** *a.* discordant.
unturned, *a.* not turned over.
untutored, *a.* uninstructed; rude, barbarous.
untwine, *v.t.* unwind, untwist.
untwist, *v.t.* unwind, unravel.
unused, *a.* not used; not accustomed. **unusual,** *a.* rare, unfamiliar; remarkable.

unutterable, *a.* unspeakable, beyond description; out-and-out. **unuttered,** *a.* not spoken.
unvalued, *a.* not prized; not priced.
unvanquished, *a.* not defeated.
unvaried, *a.* constant; monotonous.
unvarnished, *a.* not varnished or embellished.
unveil, *v.t.* and *i.* disclose, reveal (oneself); uncover (new monument) with public ceremony.
unventilated, *a.* stuffy; not made public.
unveracious, *a.* untruthful.
unverified, *a.* not proved as true.
unversed, *a.* not experienced (in), unskilled.
unvoiced, *a.* not expressed; (of sound) uttered without vibration of vocal chords.
unwarrantable, *a.* indefensible, improper. **unwarranted,** *a.* not authorized or guaranteed.
unwary, *a.* incautious, unguarded, rash; (*Spens.*) unexpected.
unwashed, *a.* dirty. **the Great U.,** (*joc.*) the mob.
unwatered, *a.* not irrigated; dry.
unwavering, *a.* steadfast, firm.
unwearied, *a.* not tired, persistent. **unwearying,** *a.* indefatigable; continuous.
unweave, *v.t.* undo what is woven, unravel.
unweeting, *a.* (*Scot.*) unknowing.
unwed, unwedded, *aa.* unmarried.
unwell, *a.* indisposed, ill; sick.
unwept, *a.* not mourned for.
unwholesome, *a.* bad for health, unhealthy.
unwieldy, *a.* awkward to handle, cumbersome.
unwifely, *a.* not like a wife.
unwilling, *a.* reluctant, disinclined.
unwind, *v.t.* and *i.* wind off what is wound, unroll.
unwise, *a.* foolish, injudicious. **unwisdom,** *n.* folly.
unwished, *a.* not desired.
unwitnessed, *a.* not witnessed.
unwitting, *a.* unknowing, unaware. **unwittingly,** *adv.* inadvertently.
unwomanly, *a.* not befitting a woman.
unwonted, *a.* unaccustomed; unusual.
unworkable, *a.* impossible to work or carry out.
unworldly, *a.* above self-interested motives; spiritual.
unworn, *a.* not worn or impaired.
unworthy, *a.* not worthy; discreditable, base. **u. of,** not deserving; unbecoming in.
unwrap, *v.t.* take wrappings off, undo.
unwritten, *a.* oral, traditional. **u. law,** that revenge upon adulterer etc. is permissible.
unwrought, *a.* not worked or elaborated.
unyielding, *a.* rigid; firm, obstinate.
unyoke, *v.t.* and *i.* loose from yoke; disconnect; cease work.
up, *adv.* to, in, a higher position, degree, or value; standing, out of bed; in active progress; thoroughly; to main centre; (*golf*) in advance; the full distance.—*prep.* ascending along or over; against current of.—*v.i.* and *t.* (*vulg.*) start or lift up. **it is all up with him,** his case is hopeless. **up against,** confronted with. **up and doing,** actively busy. **up and down,** to and fro. **ups and downs,** undulations; changes of fortune. **up the pole,** (*sl.*) crazy. **up to,** engaged in; incumbent on; until. **up to date,** containing, knowing, all recent facts. **what 's up?** what is the matter? **on the up-and-up,** (*Amer. colloq.*) honest. **up-country,** *a.* and *adv.* inland. **up-end,** *v.t.* set on end. **upstream,** *adv.* and *a.* against the current. (O.E.)
Upanishad, *n.* Sanskrit philosophical treatise, part of Veda. (Sanskr.)
upas, *n.* (also **u.-tree**) Javanese tree with poisonous juice; deadly influence. (Malay=poison)
upbear, *v.t.* raise aloft, sustain.
upbraid, *v.t.* reproach, reprove severely. (*up*; *braid*)
upbray, *v.t.* (*Spens.*) upbraid.
upbringing, *n.* education, training.
upby, *adv.* (*Scot.*) up the way, a little farther on.
upcast, *n.* upward throw; shaft through which air passes out of mine.
upheave, *v.t.* heave up. **upheaval,** *n.* vast change; (*geol.*) lifting up of strata by internal force.
uphill, *a.* sloping up; difficult, laborious.—*adv.* upwards.
uphold, *v.t.* support, sustain; countenance, defend.
upholster, *v.t.* provide (chair) with stuffing and covering; provide (room) with curtains and carpets. **upholsterer,** *n.* **upholstery,** *n.* upholsterer's trade; stuffing, hangings etc. (obs. *upholdster*, upholder)
uphroe, *n.* (*naut.*) wooden slat with holes through which cords of awning are passed. (Du. *juffrouw*, young woman)
upkeep, *n.* maintenance.
upland, *a.* and *n.* (of) higher part of district.
uplift, *v.t.* raise up.—*n.* (*Amer.*) spiritual improvement, edifying effect.
upmost, *arch.* for **uppermost.**
upon, *prep.* on. **take u. oneself,** presume.
upper, *a.* higher, above; superior in rank.—*n.* part of shoe or boot above sole. **on one's uu.,** very hard up. **u. hand,** mastery. **U. House,** House of Lords. **u. storey,** (*colloq.*) brains. **u. ten (thousand),** aristocracy. **u. works,** parts of ship above water. **u.-cut,** *n.* short-arm upward blow. **uppermost,** *a.* and *adv.* highest, at the top.
uppish, *a.* self-assertive, cheeky.

upraise, *v.t.* raise up.
upright, *a.* erect, vertical; righteous, just.—*n.* upright post.
uprise, *v.i.* rise, get up. **uprising,** *n.* rising, revolt.
uproar, *n.* noisy disturbance, clamour. —*v.t.* (*Shake.*) disturb. **uproarious,** *a.* noisy, rowdy. (Du. *op*, up; *roer*, stir)
uproot, *v.t.* tear up by the roots; eradicate.
upset, *v.t.* and *i.* overturn, capsize; overthrow, frustrate; put out of sorts; distress, vex.—*n.* tumble; trouble. **u. price,** below which goods at auction are not to be sold.
upshot, *n.* final issue; conclusion.
upside-down, *a.* inverted; in disorder. (M.E. *up so down*, up as if down)
upsides, *adv.* (*dial.*). **be u. with,** be quits.
upstairs, *adv.* and *a.* in, to, of, a higher storey. **upstair,** *a.*
upstanding, *a.* erect; stalwart. **u. wage,** fixed, not with sliding scale.
upstart, *n.* one who has suddenly acquired wealth or position, parvenu; arrogant nobody.
upstroke, *n.* upward line in writing.
uptake, *n.* (*Scot.*) understanding, apprehension.
upthrow, *n.* upheaval; (*geol.*) upward displacement on one side of fault.
upthrust, *n.* (*geol.*) upheaval.
upturn, *v.t.* turn up.
upward, *a.* directed up.—*adv.* (also **upwards**) towards a higher place.
uraemia, *n.* poisoning of blood from urinary products not excreted. **uraemic,** *a.* (Gk. *ouron*, urine; *haima*, blood)
uraeus, *n.* ancient Egyptian serpent-emblem. (Gk. *ouraios*, cobra)
Urania, *n.* muse of astronomy; an epithet of Aphrodite. **Uranian,** *a.* of Urania; heavenly. **uranism,** *n.* homosexuality in males. **uranist,** *n.* (Gk. *ouranos*, heaven)
uranium, *n.* a white radioactive metallic element. **uranic,** *a.* (*Uranus*)
Uranus, *n.* planet between Saturn and Neptune. **Uranian,** *a.* (Gk. *ouranos*, heaven)
urano-, from Gk. *ouranos*, heaven, used in **uranography,** *n.* descriptive astronomy, hence **uranographic, uranographical,** *aa.*, **uranographist,** *n.*; **uranology,** *n.* astronomy; **uranometry,** *n.* measurement of stellar distances, star-chart; **uranoscopy,** *n.* star-watching.
uranous, *a.* of uranium.
urban, *a.* of, belonging to, city or town. **urbane,** *a.* polished, suave, courteous. **urbanity,** *n.* politeness, refinement. **urbanize,** *v.t.* make urban. (L. *urbs*, city)
urceolate, *a.* (*bot.*) with large body and small mouth. (L. *urceus*, pitcher)
urchin, *n.* small boy; mischievous child; (*colloq.*) hedgehog; (*Shake.*) elf. (L. *ericius*, hedgehog)
Urdu, *n.* Hindustani. (Hind.)
-ure, *n.suf.* of action, as in **censure,** result, as in **picture,** or collective, as in **legislature.** (L. *-ura*)
urea, *n.* crystalline constituent of urine. **ureal,** *a.* (*urine*)
uredo, *n.* kind of rust-fungus; itching of skin. **uredinous,** *a.* (L.= blight)
ureter, *n.* duct for urine from kidney to bladder. **urethra,** *n.* duct carrying urine out of bladder. **ureteritis, urethritis,** *nn.* inflammation of these ducts. **urethroscope,** *n.* instrument for examining urethra. **uretic,** *a.* of urine; diuretic. (Gk. *ouron*, urine)
urf, *n.* (*Scot.*) stunted child.
urge, *v.t.* drive, impel; press, exhort; advocate earnestly.—*n.* incentive, yearning. **urgent,** *a.* pressing, needing immediate attention; importunate. (L. *urgēre*)
uric, *a.* of, contained in, urine.
urim and thummim, unknown objects in breastplate of Jewish high priest. (Heb. *ur*, light; *tom*, perfection)
urine, *n.* fluid discharged from bladder. **urinal,** *n.* public lavatory; chamber-pot. **urinary, urinous,** *aa.* of urine. **urinate,** *v.i.* pass urine. **urinology,** *n.* study of urine. **urinometer,** *n.* instrument showing specific gravity of urine. **urinoscopy,** *n.* inspection of urine in diagnosis. (L. *urina*)
urn, *n.* roundish vessel with pedestal; vase for ashes of the dead.—*v.t.* enclose in urn. (L. *urna*)
urning, *n.* homosexual. (G.)
uro-, from Gk. *ouron*, urine, used in **urocyst,** *n.* bladder; **urodynia,** *n.* painful urination; **urology, uroscopy,** same as **urinology, urinoscopy.**
uro-, from Gk. *oura*, tail, used in **urochord,** *n.* caudal chord of ascidian; **uropod,** *n.* abdominal appendage of crustacean.
ursa, *n.* she-bear. **U. Major,** Great Bear. **U. Minor,** Little Bear. **ursiform,** *a.* bear-shaped. **ursine,** *a.* of, like, a bear. (L.)
urticaceous, *a.* of nettles or nettle family. **urticant,** *a.* and *n.* stinging (substance). **urticaria,** *n.* nettle-rash. **urticate,** *v.t.* sting; whip with nettles. **urtication,** *n.* (L. *urtica*, nettle)
urubu, *n.* American black vulture. (Brazilian)
urus, *n.* wild ox of Europe, aurochs. (L.)
us, see **I.**
usable, *a.* able to be used.
usage, *n.* manner of using, treatment; habitual practice, custom.
usance, *n.* time allowed for payment of foreign bills of exchange; (*Spens.*) usage.
use, *v.t.* employ, put to purpose; exercise, avail oneself of; consume as material; treat.—*v.i.* be accustomed.—*n.* employment, application; power, right, of using; utility, purpose; custom, habit; local ritual; (*law*) profit from trust; (*Shake.*)

interest; need. **have no u. for,** dislike. **in u.,** not obsolete. **make u. of,** employ. **(of) no u.,** useless. **of u.,** useful. **u. and wont,** habitual custom. **u. up,** exhaust. (L. *uti*)
used, *a.* accustomed.
useful, *a.* serviceable, helpful; (*sl.*) efficient.
useless, *a.* unavailing, serving no useful purpose; (*sl.*) out of sorts.
user, *n.* one who uses; (*law*) continued use or enjoyment of a right.
usher, *n.* doorkeeper of court; attendant who shows people to their seats; official preceding person of rank; under-teacher.—*v.t.* show (in), announce; precede. **usherette,** *n.* girl usher. **ushership,** *n.* (L. *ostium*, door)
usquebaugh, *n.* (*arch.*) whisky. (Ir. *uisge*, water; *beatha*, life)
ustulation, *n.* roasting preparatory to pulverizing; burning of wine. (L. *ustulare*, scorch)
usual, *a.* customary, common; ordinary. (*use*)
usucaption, *n.* (*civil law*) acquisition of property by uninterrupted possession for a certain period. (L. *usus*, use; *capere*, take)
usufruct, *n.* temporary use and enjoyment of another's property. **usufructuary,** *a.* and *n.* of, one who has, usufruct. (L. *usus*, use; *fructus*, fruit)
usurer, *n.* money-lender, esp. extortionate. one. **usuring,** *a.* (*Shake.*) stingy **usurious,** *a.* of, practising, usury. (*usury*)
usurp, *v.t.* seize, assume, wrongfully. **u. on,** encroach on. **usurpation,** *n.* usurping. **usurper,** *n.* unlawful ruler. (L. *usurpare*)
usury, *n.* lending of money at exorbitant interest; such interest; (*arch.*) money-lending, interest, of any kind. (*use*)
ut, *n.* first note of scale, doh.
ut, *adv.* as. *ut infra, supra,* as shown below, above. (L.)
utensil, *n.* domestic vessel or implement. (L. *utensilis*, usable)
uterus, *n.* (*pl.* **uteri**) womb. **uterine,** *a.* of womb; of same mother but different father. **uteritis,** *n.* inflammation of womb. (L.)
utilitarian, *a.* of, aiming at, usefulness (opp. to ornamental); of utilitarianism.—*n.* adherent of utilitarianism. **utilitarianism,** *n.* doctrine that virtue depends on utility, and that the greatest happiness of the greatest number should be the aim of all public action. (*utility*)
utility, *n.* usefulness; useful thing. **u.-man,** *n.* actor of minor parts.
utilize, *v.t.* turn to account, use. **utilization,** *n.* (L. *uti*, use)
uti possidetis, principle that leaves belligerents in possession of what they are holding. (L.=as you hold)
utis, *n.* (*Shake.*) merrymaking. (obs. *utas*, eight days of a festival)
utmost, *a.* furthest, most extreme.—*n.* most possible. (O.E. *út*, out)
Utopia, *n.* imaginary country with perfect political and social conditions; ideal community. **Utopian,** *a.* and *n.* visionary. (Gk. *ou*, not; *topos*, place)
utricle, *n.* small cavity or sac. **utricular,** *a.* **utriform,** *a.* shaped like a leather bottle. (L. *uter*, wineskin)
utter, *a.* complete, total; absolute, unqualified. **u. barrister,** junior, addressing court from outside bar. (O.E. *út*, out)
utter, *v.t.* pronounce, emit; publish (libel); circulate (counterfeit coin etc.). (*out*)
utterance, *n.* vocal expression; power of speech. (*utter*)
utterance, *n.* (*arch.*) extremity. (O.F. *outrance*)
uttermost, *a.* furthest out, utmost.—*n.* greatest degree.
uvula, *n.* (*pl.* **uvulae**) pendent fleshy outgrowth at back of palate. **uvular,** *a.* (L. *uva*, bunch of grapes)
uxorious, *a.* excessively or submissively fond of one's wife. (L. *uxor*, wife)

V

V, *roman numerals*) 5.
va, *v.i.* (*mus.*) go on. (It.)
vac, *n.* (*colloq.*) vacation. (abbr.)
vacant, *a.* empty; not occupied or booked; empty of thought, inane. **vacancy,** *n.* vacantness; empty space; unoccupied situation, available place; (*Shake.*) unoccupied time. **vacate,** *v.t.* leave empty; quit possession of; (*law*) render void, annul. **vacation,** *n.* vacating; period between law or university terms; holidays. (L. *vacare*, be empty)
vaccine, *n.* cowpox virus; any similar substance used for inoculation.—*a.* of cows, cowpox, or vaccination. **vaccinal, vaccinic,** *aa.* **vaccinate,** *v.t.* inoculate with vaccine as protection against smallpox or other disease. **vaccination, vaccinator,** *nn.* **vaccinationist,** *n.* advocate of compulsory vaccination. **vaccinia,** *n.* (*med.*) cowpox. (L. *vacca*, cow)
vacillate, *v.i.* oscillate, waver; hesitate, be undecided. **vacillation,** *n.* (L. *vacillare*)

vacuum, *n.* (*pl.* **vacuums, vacua**) completely empty space; space exhausted of air; void. **v. brake,** brake on railway trains worked by action of vacuum. **v. cleaner,** apparatus for removing dirt by suction. **v. flask,** with double walls and vacuum between, for keeping liquids hot or cold. **v. tube,** sealed glass tube of highly rarefied air for observing passage of electric charge. **vacuole,** *n.* minute cavity in organic tissue. **vacuolar,** *a.* **vacuous,** *a.* empty; vacant, expressionless. **vacuity,** *n.* vacuousness. (L. *vacuus,* empty)

vade, *v.i.* (*Shake.*) fade. (*fade*)

vade, *v.i.* (*Spens.*) go. (L. *vadere*)

vādĕ-mecum, *n.* handbook, pocket companion. (L.=go with me)

vae victis, woe to the conquered. (L.)

vagabond, *a.* without fixed home, roving.—*n.* wanderer, tramp; idle scamp. **vagabondage, vagabondism,** *nn.* **vagabondize,** *v.i.* (L. *vagari,* wander)

vagary, *n.* freakish fancy or act; whim, caprice. **vagarious,** *a.* capricious. (L. *vagari,* wander)

vagina, *n.* passage from womb to exterior; sheath-like part. **vaginal,** *a.* **vaginate,** *a.* (*bot.*) sheathed. (L.=sheath)

vagitus, *n.* cry of new-born child. (L. *vagire,* squall)

vagrant, *a.* wandering, roaming; wayward.—*n.* tramp; idle and disorderly person. **vagrancy,** *n.*

vague, *a.* indistinct, hazy; indefinite, not clear; uncertain. (L. *vagus,* wandering)

vail, *v.t.* and *i.* (*arch.*) lower, let fall; take off (hat); give place.—*n.* (*Shake.*) decline. (F. *avaler*)

vail, *n.* (*arch.*) gratuity, tip. (=*avail*)

vain, *a.* useless, unavailing; baseless, empty; trivial, hollow; proud of trifling attainments, conceited; (*Shake.*) foolish. **in v.,** to no purpose. **take name in v.,** invoke it lightly or profanely. **vainglory,** *n.* excessive vanity; boastfulness. **vainglorious,** *a.* (L. *vanus*)

vair, *n.* a particoloured fur, represented in heraldry by row of small shields, alternately azure and argent. (L. *varius,* variegated)

vaisya, *n.* (member of) third Hindu caste, of merchants and agriculturists. (Sanskr.=peasant)

vakeel, vakil, *n.* Indian native attorney; agent, envoy. (Hind.)

valance, valence, *n.* short curtain concealing space under bed; hanging drapery for window etc.

vale, *n.* (*poet.*) valley. (L. *vallis*)

vālĕ, int. and *n.* farewell. **valediction,** *n.* saying farewell, taking leave. **valedictory,** *a.* (L.)

valence, see **valance.**

valency, valence, *n.* (*chem.*) combining-power of element or atom, reckoned in terms of that of hydrogen. (L. *valēre,* be strong)

Valenciennes, *n.* rich kind of lace. (place)

valentine, *n.* sweetheart; love missive or caricature of it sent on St. Valentine's day, 14 Feb.

valerian, *n.* herb with smell that attracts cats; root of this as mild stimulant. **valeric,** *a.* (O.F. *valeriane*)

valet, *n.* (also *v. de chambre*) gentleman's personal servant.—*v.t.* attend as valet. (*varlet*)

valetudinarian, *n.* one who keeps thinking about his health, hypochondriac; chronic invalid.—*a.* (also **valetudinary**) of ill health; sickly. **valetudinarianism,** *n.* (L. *valēre,* be well)

valgus, *n.* and *a.* bow-legged or knock kneed (person or condition). (L.)

Valhalla, *n.* Norse heaven for heroes slain in battle; memorial hall, burial place, of nation's famous dead (O.N. *valr,* slain; *höll,* hall)

valiant, *a.* brave, courageous. **valiance,** *n.* (*arch.*). (L. *valēre,* be strong)

valid, *a.* (of argument etc.) sound, well-grounded; (of document) having legal force, binding. **validate,** *v.t.* make valid, ratify. **validation,** *n.* **validity,** *n.* validness; (*Shake.*) strength; value. (L. *validus,* strong)

valise, *n.* kind of small portmanteau; soldier's knapsack. (F.)

Valkyrie, Valkyr, Valkyria, *n.* one of twelve Norse war-goddesses who chose the slain and guided them to Valhalla. **Valkyrian,** *a.* (O.N. *valr,* slain; *kyrja,* chooser)

vallecula, *n.* (*anat., pl.* **valleculae**) groove, cleft. **vallecular, valleculate**) *aa.* (L. *vallis,* valley+dim.)

valley, *n.* low ground between hills; river basin; (*archit.*) depression between slopes of roof. (L. *vallis*)

vallum, *n.* ancient Roman rampart; (*anat.*) eyebrow. (L.)

valonia, vallonia, *n.* dried acorn-cups of a kind of ilex, used in tanning etc. (Gk. *balanos,* acorn)

valorize, *v.t.* give arbitrary price to by government control. **valorization,** *n.* (L. *valēre,* be worth)

valour, *n.* courage, bravery, esp. in battle. **valorous,** *a.* (L. *valēre,* be strong)

valse, *n.* waltz. (F.)

value, *n.* worth, utility; quality giving this; proper price, equivalent; precise meaning; relative light and shade in parts of picture; (*mus.*) length of a tone.—*v.t.* and *i.* put price on; esteem, prize; (*Shake.*) be worth. **valuable,** *a.* precious, costly; useful; capable of valuation.—*n.* (us. *pl.*) precious possessions, jewellery. **valution,** *n.* valuing; estimation. **valuator, valuer,** *nn.* professional appraiser. **valueless,** *a.* worthless. **valuta,** *n.*

value of one currency in terms of another. (L. *valēre*, be worth)

valve, *n.* lid or other device allowing passage of steam etc. in one direction only; membrane with similar action; one shell of oyster or other bivalve; one side of pod; leaf of folding door; appliance converting wireless waves into audible vibrations. **valval, valvar,** *aa.* (*anat., bot.*). **valvate,** *a.* (of petals) meeting at edges without overlapping. **valved,** *a.* fitted with valves. **valvelet, valvule,** *nn.* little valve. **valvular,** *a.* of, affecting, valves, esp. of the heart; acting like a valve. **valvulitis,** *n.* inflammation of valves of the heart. (L. *valva*)

vambrace, *n.* plate-armour for forearm. (F. *avant*, before; *bras*, arm)

vamoose, vamose, *v.i.* (*Amer. sl.*) make off, decamp. (Sp. *vamos*, let us go)

vamp, *n.* upper front part of boot or shoe; improvised accompaniment.—*v.t.* and *i.* put new vamp on; patch, furbish (up); improvise (accompaniment). (F. *avant*, before; *pied*, foot)

vamp, *n.* (*sl.*) woman who exploits men, adventuress.—*v.t.* fascinate, exploit, by flirting. (*vampire*)

vampire, *n.* malignant ghost that sucks blood of sleepers; one who preys on others, extortioner; spring trap on stage allowing sudden appearance or disappearance; (also **v. bat**) bat that sucks blood of animals. **vampiric,** *a.* **vampirism,** *n.* belief in vampires; blood-sucking. (Magyar *vampir*)

vamplate, *n.* iron plate on tilting-spear, protecting hand. (F. *avant*, before; *plat*, plate)

van, *n.* large covered vehicle for goods; tradesman's delivery-vehicle; luggage-car of train. (abbr. of *caravan*)

van, *n.* leading part of army in battle or route formation; front of procession or movement. (abbr. of *vanguard*)

van, *n.* (*arch.*) winnowing - machine; wing of bird. (L. *vannus*)

vanadium, *n.* a rare metallic element. **vanadic, vanadous,** *aa.* (*Vanadis*, Norse goddess)

Vandal, *n.* wilful or ignorant destroyer of what is beautiful or artistic; one of tribe that sacked Rome. **vandalic,** *a.* barbarous. **vandalism,** *n.*

Vandyke, *n.* portrait by Flemish painter Van Dyck; one of the points of indented lace border; Vandyke beard or collar.—*v.t.* border with vandykes. **V. beard,** small pointed one. **V. brown,** a deep brown. **V. collar,** wide lace collar with indented edge.

vane, *n.* weathercock; sail of windmill; blade of propeller; sight of quadrant. (O.E. *fana*, small flag)

vang, *n.* guy-rope from end of gaff to deck. (=*fang*)

vanguard, *n.* advance guard of army; **van.** (F. *avant*, before)

vanilla, *n.* kind of orchid; its fruit; extract from this, used as flavouring. **vanillic,** *a.* (L. *vagina*, sheath+dim.)

vanish, *v.i.* disappear; fade away; come to an end; (*math.*) become zero; (*Shake.*) escape. (L. *vanus*, empty)

vanity, *n.* being vain; love of indiscriminate admiration, conceit; futility, worthlessness; empty show. **V. Fair,** the world of fashion. **v.-bag, v.-case,** *nn.* small hand-case with mirror, powder-puff etc. (*vain*)

vanquish, *v.t.* conquer, overcome. **vanquisher,** *n.* (L. *vincere*)

vantage, *n.* advantage; (*lawn tennis*) first point after deuce; (*Shake.*) superiority; opportunity. **point of v., v.-ground,** *n.* commanding position. (=*advantage*)

vanward, *a.* in the van.—*adv.* forward.

vapid, *a.* flavourless, insipid, flat; dull. **vapidity,** *n.* (L. *vapidus*)

vapour, *n.* moisture in the air, mist, steam; exhalation; gasified liquid or solid; (*arch.*) empty boasting; (*pl., arch.*) hypochondria, nervous depression.—*v.i.* pass off in vapour; boast, talk big. **v. bath, vaporarium,** *n.* steam bath. **vaporable, vaporizable,** *aa.* able to be vaporized. **vaporimeter,** *n.* instrument for measuring density of vapour. **vaporize,** *v.t.* and *i.* change into vapour. **vaporization, vaporizer,** *nn.* **vaporous,** *a.* in the form of, like, vapour; foggy, steamy; unreal, fanciful. **vapourish,** *a.* boastful; given to the vapours. **vapoury,** *a.* like, full of, vapour. (L. *vapor*)

vapulation, *n.* (*joc.*) thrashing. **vapulatory,** *a.* (L. *vapulare*, be beaten)

vaquero, *n.* Mexican herdsman or cowboy. (Sp.)

Varangian, *n.* man of **V. guard,** Norse bodyguard of Byzantine emperors. (O.N. *væringi*, confederate)

vare, *n.* wand of authority. (L. *varus*, crooked)

varec, *n.* an impure sodium carbonate; kelp. (F. *varech*)

variable, *a.* liable to vary, changing, inconstant; adjustable; (*astron.*) varying periodically in brightness; (*math.*) able to assume different values; (*Shake.*) various.—*n.* variable star or quantity; (*naut.*) shifting wind. **variability,** *n.*

varia lectio, variant reading. (L.)

variance, *n.* disagreement, dissension; variation. **at v.,** in conflict. **variant,** *a.* different; differing from accepted or normal type, text etc.—*n.* variant form or reading.

variation, *n.* varying, alteration; deviation from standard or type; deviation of magnetic needle from true north; (*gram.*) inflexion; (*mus.*) repetition of theme or melody with modifications. **variational,** *a.*

varicated, *a.* (of shell) ribbed. **varication,** *n.* (*varix*)

varicella, *n.* (*med.*) chicken-pox. **varicellar,** *a.* (*variola*+dim.)

varices, see **varix.**

varicocele, *n.* distension of veins of testicle. (L. *varix,* dilated vein. Gk. *kēlē,* tumour)

varicoloured, *a.* variegated, particoloured. (L. *varius,* various)

varicose, *a.* (of vein) permanently and abnormally dilated; suffering from, designed for, varicose veins. **varicosis, varicosity,** *nn.* (*varix*)

varied, *a.* showing variety, changing.

variegate, *v.t.* mark with different colours, dapple, streak. **variegation,** *n.* (L. *varius,* various; *agere,* make)

variety, *n.* being various, diversity; absence of sameness; collection of different things; kind, sort; subdivision of species; mixed entertainment of singing, dancing, acrobatics etc. **v. theatre,** music-hall. **varietal,** *a.*

variform, *a.* having various forms.

variola, *n.* (*med.*) smallpox. **variolar, variolic, variolous,** *aa.* **variolate,** *v.t.* inoculate with smallpox virus. **variolation,** *n.* **variole,** *n.* (*zool., bot.*) shallow pit like pock-mark. **variolite,** *n.* kind of rock with whitish spots. **variolitic,** *a.* **varioloid,** *a.* like smallpox.—*n.* smallpox modified by vaccination. (L. *varius,* various)

variorum, *a.* and *n.* (edition) with notes by various commentators. (L.=of various)

various, *a.* of several kinds, diverse; several, many; (*arch.*) many-sided. (L. *varius*)

varix, *n.* (*pl.* **varices**) varicose vein; rib on shell. (L.)

varlet, *n.* knight's page, attendant; low fellow, rascal. **varletry,** *n.* (*Shake.*) rabble. (O.F.)

varmint, *n.* (*vulg.*) scamp, rascal. **the v.,** (*hunting sl.*) fox. (*vermin*)

varnish, *n.* resinous liquid forming hard lustrous coating; glossy surface, glaze; specious apearance, whitewash.—*v.t.* coat with varnish; gloss over. **varnishing day,** day before exhibition, when artists give final touches to pictures. (O.F. *vernis*)

varsal, *a.* (*colloq., rare*) universal.

varsity, 'varsity, *n.* (*colloq.*) university. (corrupt.)

varsovienne, *n.* dance like mazurka; music for it. (*Warsaw*)

varus, *n.* and *a.* pigeon-toed (person or condition). (L.)

varus, *n.* acne. (L.)

vary, *v.t.* and *i.* make or become different, alter; diversify; fluctuate, be various.—*n.* (*Shake.*) change. (L. *varius,* various)

vas, *n.* (*anat., pl.* **vasa**) vessel, duct. **v. deferens,** spermatic duct. **vasal,** *a.* **vascular,** *a.* of, having, vessels for conveying blood, sap etc. **vascularity,** *n.* **vascularize,** *v.t.* **vasculose,** *n.* chief constituent of vessels of plants.—*a.* vascular. **vasculum,** *n.* (*pl.* **vascula**) botanist's specimen-box. (L.)

vase, *n.* vessel, jar, esp. tall slender one for ornament or holding flowers. (L. *vas*)

vasi-, vaso-, from L. *vas,* vessel, used in **vasiform,** *a.* shaped like vas, tubular; **vasoconstrictor, vasodilator, vasomotor,** *aa.* and *nn.* (nerve, drug) constricting, dilating, controlling, blood-vessels; **vasosensory,** *a.* supplying sensation to vessels.

vassal, *n.* one who held land from and rendered homage to superior, feudal tenant; dependant, bondman; (*Shake.*) base wretch.—*a.* subject, servile. **vassalage,** *n.* state of being vassal; (also **vassalry**) vassals collectively. (L.L. *vassus*)

vast, *a.* huge, immense; (*colloq.*) great; (*Shake.*) waste, desolate.—*n.* vast space. **vastidity,** *n.* (*Shake.*). **vasty,** *a.* (*arch.*) vast. (L. *vastus*)

vat, *n.* large tub or tank. (O.E. *fæt*)

vatic, vaticinal, *aa.* of prophet or prophecy. **vaticide,** *n.* killing, killer, of prophet. **vaticinate,** *v.t.* and *i.* prophesy. **vaticination, vaticinator,** *nn.* (L. *vates,* prophet; *canere,* sing)

Vatican, *n.* palace of the pope; papal authority. **Vaticanism,** *n,* doctrine of papal supremacy. **Vaticanist,** *n.*

vaudeville, *n.* dramatic sketch with light or comic songs; (formerly) topical or convivial song; (*Amer.*) variety entertainment. (F. *Vau de Vire,* Valley of the Vire)

vaudoo, same as **voodoo.**

vault, *v.t.* and *i.* leap (over) with support of hand.—*n.* such leap. (O.F. *volter,* leap)

vault, *n.* arched roof or ceiling; chamber with this; underground cellar, burial chamber, or strong-room; sky. —*v.t.* cover, roof, with vault. **vaulting,** *n.* arched work. **vaulty,** *a.* (*Shake.*) arched, hollow. (L. *volvere,* roll)

vaunt, *v.i.* and *t.* boast, brag (of).—*n.* boast. (L. *vanus,* vain)

vaunt, *n.* (*Shake.*) beginning. **v.-courier,** *n.* (*Shake.*) harbinger. (F. *avant,* before)

vavasour, *n.* vassal of a lord, having other vassals under him. **vavasory,** *n.* tenure, lands, of vavasour. (L.L. *vassus vassorum,* vassal of vassals)

vaward, same as **vanward.**

veal, *n.* calf's flesh as food. (L. *vitulus,* calf)

vector, *n.* disease-carrying insect; (*math.*) quantity involving direction as well as magnitude. **vectorial,** *a.* (L. *vehere,* convey)

Veda, *n.* Hindu scripture written in old Sanskrit. **Vedic,** *a.* **Vedanta,** *n.* Hindu philosophy based on Vedas. **Vedantic,** *a.* (Sanskr.=knowledge)

vedette, *n.* mounted sentry in advance of outpost. (It. *vedetta*)

veer, *v.i.* and *t.* (of wind) change direction, esp. sunwise; change one's mind, turn (round); (*naut.*) pay out (rope); wear (ship). (F. *virer*)
veery, *n.* tawny thrush of N. America.
vega, *n.* tract of flat meadow-land; Cuban tobacco-field. (Sp.)
vegetable, *a.* of, relating to, derived from, plants.—*n.* plant, esp. one used for cooking. **v. ivory,** close-grained nut of a kind of palm. **v. marrow,** kind of gourd. **vegetability,** *n.* **vegetal,** *a.* of growth and vital functions; vegetable.—*n.* plant. **vegetality,** *n.* **vegetarian,** *n.* one who does not eat meat.—*a.* of vegetarians; consisting wholly of vegetables. **vegetarianism,** *n.* **vegetate,** *v.i.* grow, live, as plants do; pass inactive monotonous life. **vegetation,** *n.* vegetating; plants collectively. **vegetative,** *a.* vegetating; producing growth in plants. **vegetive,** *n.* (*Shake.*) vegetable. (L. *vegēre,* quicken)
vehement, *a.* strong, violent; impetuous, eager. **vehemence, vehemency,** *nn.* (L. *vehemens*)
vehicle, *n.* conveyance, carriage, of any kind used on land; means of transmission, medium; (*med.*) substance in which medicine is taken. **vehicular,** *a.* (L. *vehere,* convey)
vehmgericht, *n.* medieval German secret tribunal. **vehmic,** *a.* (G.)
veil, *n.* transparent covering for concealing or protecting face; curtain; thing that conceals; velum.—*v.t.* throw veil over; conceal, dissemble. **beyond the v.,** after death. **draw a v. over,** say nothing about. **take the v.,** become nun. (L. *velum*)
vein, *n.* tube taking blood to heart; rib of leaf or insect's wing; fissure in rock filled with ore, seam; streak, strain; mood; (*Shake.*) style.—*v.t.* cover, mark, with veins. **veinlet,** *n.* small vein. **veiny,** *a.* (L. *vena*)
velamen, *n.* (*pl.* **velamina**) outer membrane or epidermis. (L.=covering)
velar, *a.* of velum or soft palate; pronounced with tongue touching this.—*n.* velar consonant, such as *k.*
veldt, veld, *n.* (*S. Afr.*) open grass country. **v.-schoen,** *n.* Boer shoe of untanned hide. (Du.=field)
velite, *n.* ancient Roman light-armed soldier. **velitation,** *n.* (*arch.*) slight skirmish. (L. *veles*)
velleity, *n.* (*arch.*) lowest degree of desire, mere inclination. (L. *velle,* wish)
vellet, (*Spens.*) form of **velvet.**
vellicate, *v.t.* and *i.* twitch. **vellication,** *n.* **vellicative,** *a.* (L. *vellere,* pluck)
vellum, *n.* fine parchment, orig. of calfskin, used for manuscripts and bindings. (L. *vitulus,* calf)
veloce, adv. (*mus.*) very quickly. (It.)
velocipede, *n.* early form of bicycle or tricycle, orig. propelled by striking toes on road. **velocipedist,** *n.* (L. *velox,* swift; *pes,* foot)
velocity, *n.* rate of motion, speed. (L. *velox,* swift)
velours, velour, *n.* kind of plush; hat of this. *veloutine, n.* a corded fabric. (F.)
velum, *n.* (*pl.* **vela**) soft palate; (*bot., zool.*) membranous covering or organ. (L.=veil)
velure, same as **velours.**
velutinous, *a.* (*bot.*) velvety. (*velvet*)
velveret, *n.* inferior kind of velvet.
velvet, *n.* silk or silk-and-cotton fabric with soft thick pile; furry covering of growing antler; profit, gain.—*a.* of, soft as, velvet. **on v.,** in safe or advantageous position. **the iron hand in the v. glove,** firmness beneath suavity. **v.-guards,** *n.pl.* (*Shake.*) wearers of finery. **velveteen,** *n.* imitation velvet of cotton; (*pl.*) breeches of this. **velveting,** *n.* velvet goods; nap of velvet. **velvety,** *a.* like velvet, soft and smooth. (L. *villus,* shaggy hair)
venal, *a.* able to be bought or bribed, corrupt; mercenary. **venality,** *n.* (L. *venus,* sale)
venatic, *a.* of hunting. (*venery*)
venation, *n.* arrangement of veins on leaf etc. **venational,** *a.* (*vein*)
vend, *v.t.* sell, offer for sale, peddle. (L. *vendere*)
vendace, *n.* small fresh-water fish. (O.F. *vendese,* dace)
vendee, *n.* buyer. **vender,** see **vendor.**
vendetta, *n.* taking of private vengeance on slayer of relation, blood-feud. (It.)
vendor, vender, *n.* seller. **vendible,** *a.* salable. **vendibility,** *n.* (*vend*)
veneer, *v.t.* overlay (wood, furniture) with thin sheet of fine wood; conceal with superficial polish. — *n.* thin coating of fine wood etc.; specious gloss. (O.F. *furnir,* furnish)
venenate, *v.t.* poison. **venenation,** *n.* **venefical,** *a.* poisonous; using sorcery. (L. *venenum,* poison)
venerate, *v.t.* revere, regard with veneration; worship. **venerable,** *a.* worthy of respect and honour, esp. because of age; title of archdeacon or one who has passed first stage of canonization. **veneration,** *n.* venerating; respect mingled with awe, deep reverence. **venerator,** *n.* (L. *venerari*)
venereal, *a.* of, communicated by, sexual intercourse. (*Venus*)
venery, *n.* (*arch.*) hunting, the chase. (L. *venari,* hunt)
venery, *n.* (*arch.*) sexual indulgence. (*Venus*)
venesect, *v.t.* and *i.* open (vein) in blood-letting. **venesection,** *n.* (L. *vena,* vein; *secare,* cut)
Venetian, *a.* and *n.* (citizen) of Venice. **V. blind,** of horizontal slats that may be opened or closed. **V. chalk,**

French chalk. **V. mast,** spirally painted pole used in street decoration. **V. red,** a brownish red. **V. window,** large window with narrow one on each side.

venew, veney, same as **venue.**

vengeance, *n.* punishment inflicted in return for injury or offence, retribution; (*Shake.*) mischief, harm.—*adv.* (*Shake.*) extremely. **with a v.,** to a high degree, and no mistake.

venge, *v.t.* (*Shake.*) avenge. **vengeful,** *a.* bent on vengeance, vindictive. (L. *vindicare,* avenge)

venial, *a.* excusable, not very wrong; (of sin) not entailing damnation. **veniality,** *n.* (L. *venia,* pardon)

venison, *n.* deer's flesh as food. (L. *venari,* hunt)

veni, vidi, vici, I came, saw, and overcame. **Venitĕ,** *n.* 95th psalm; music for it. (L.)

venom, *n.* poison of snake, wasp etc.; spite, rancour. **venomous,** *a.* secreting venom; malicious, spiteful. (L. *venenum,* poison)

venose, *a.* (*bot.*) having many veins, veiny. **venosity,** *n.* being veinous or venose. **venous,** *a.* of, contained in, the veins (opp. to arterial); venose. (L. *vena,* vein)

vent, *n.* slit in back of coat; opening in battlemented wall. (L. *findere,* cleave)

vent, *n.* opening, passage; outlet, means of exit; flue of chimney; hole in barrel to admit air; touch-hole of gun; anus of fish etc.; ventage.—*v.t.* and *i.* make vent in; discharge, emit, utter; (of otter) come to surface for breath. **give v. to,** express, utter. **v.-peg,** *n.* for closing vent of barrel. **ventage,** *n.* finger-hole of flute etc.; outlet. **ventail,** *n.* visor of helmet. (L. *ventus,* wind)

venter, *n.* (*anat.*) belly; (*law*) womb. (L.)

ventiduct, *n.* (*archit.*) passage, pipe, for ventilation. (L. *ventus,* wind)

ventilate, *v.t.* cause fresh air to circulate in; oxygenate (blood); make public, submit to discussion. **ventilation,** *n.* **ventilative,** *a.* **ventilator,** *n.* appliance for ventilating room; one who ventilates. (L. *ventus,* wind)

ventose, *a.* windy. (L. *ventus,* wind)

ventral, *a.* of or on the belly, abdominal. (*venter*)

ventre à terre, at full speed. (F.=with belly to ground)

ventricle, *n.* cavity of an organ; chamber of heart from which blood enters arteries. **ventricular, ventriculous,** *aa.* (*venter*+dim.)

ventricose, ventricous, *aa.* bellied, swelling in the middle. (*venter*)

ventriloquist, *n.* one who speaks so that the sound seems to come from another person or place. **ventriloquism, ventriloquy, ventrilocution,** *nn.* act or art of ventriloquist. **ventriloquistic, ventriloquial, ventriloquous,** *aa.* **ventriloquize,** *v.i.* (L. *venter,* belly; *loqui,* speak)

ventripotent, *a.* able to eat enormously.

ventro-dorsal, ventro-lateral, *aa.* of ventral and dorsal, lateral, parts.

venture, *n.* taking of risk, risky enterprise; financial speculation; (*arch.*) thing at stake.—*v.t.* and *i.* risk, hazard; stake; presume, dare; dare to go. **at a v.**, at random, by guesswork. **venturer,** *n.* **venturesome,** *a.* daring, rash; risky. (*adventure*)

venue, *n.* district where lawsuit must be tried; meeting-place, scene. (L. *venire,* come)

venue, *n.* (*Shake.*) fencing thrust or bout. (L. *venire,* come)

Venus, *n.* Roman goddess of love; planet second from sun; beautiful woman. **Mount of V.,** (*palmistry*) base of thumb. **V.'s basin,** wild teasel. **V.'s comb,** plant like parsley. **V.'s flower-basket,** kind of sponge. **V.'s fly-trap,** sundew. **V.'s slipper,** lady's slipper.

veracious, *a.* truthful; true. **veracity,** *n.* (L. *verus*)

veranda, verandah, *n.* open gallery or portico along side of house. (Port. *varanda*)

veratrine, veratrin, *n.* poisonous alkaloid from hellebore used to relieve neuralgia. **veratric,** *a.* **veratrize,** *v.t.* drug with veratrine. (L. *veratrum,* hellebore)

verb, *n.* part of speech expressing action or being. **verbal,** *a.* of, concerned with, expressed in, words; spoken, not written; literal; (*gram.*) of a verb. **verbalism,** *n.* excessive attention to wording; verbal criticism. **verbalist,** *n.* **verbalize,** *v.t.* put into words; make into verb. **verbalization,** *n.* **verbatim,** *adv.* and *a.* word for word, literal; (*Shake.*) by word of mouth. (L. *verbum,* verb, word)

verbascum, *n.* mullein. (L.)

verbena, *n.* kinds of ornamental fragrant plant. (L.=sacred boughs)

verbiage, *n.* excess of words, prolixity. **verbicide,** *n.* (*joc.*) word-slaughter, word-slaughterer. **verbify,** *v.t.* verbalize. **verbose,** *a.* using more words than necessary; overloaded with words. **verbosity,** *n.* (L. *verbum,* word)

verdant, *a.* green and fresh; covered with grass; (*colloq.*) inexperienced, gullible. **verdancy,** *n.*

verd-antique, *n.* a green-veined marble; green patina. (L. *viridis,* green)

verderer, verderor, *n.* former officer of royal forests. (L. *viridis,* green)

verdict, *n.* jury's finding; opinion, judgment. **open v.,** of coroner's jury leaving cause of death unstated. (L. *vere,* truly; *dicere,* say)

verdigris, *n.* green rust of copper. (O.F. *vert de Grece,* green of Greece)

verditer, *n.* blue or green pigment got from copper nitrate. (O.F. *vert de terre,* green of earth)

verdure, *n.* green vegetation; greenness; freshness. **verdurous,** *a.* (L. *viridis,* green)

verein, *n.* association, body. (G.)

verge, *v.i.* incline, descend. **v. on,** border on, be on verge of. (L. *vergere*)

verge, *n.* edge, brink; grass edging; staff, wand, as emblem of office; spindle of watch-balance; (*archit.*) projecting edge of roof-tiles or slates; (*Shake.*) compass, circle. **vergee,** *n.* measure of area in Channel Islands, ⅖ acre. **verger,** *n.* official who has care of interior of church; pew-opener; staff-bearer of bishop etc. (L. *virga,* rod)

veridical, veridicous, *aa.* truthful, veracious. (L. *verus,* true; *dicere,* say)

verier, veriest, see **very.**

verify, *v.t.* confirm truth of, check; bear out, fulfil; (*law*) authenticate, support by proofs; (*Shake.*) affirm. **verifiable,** *a.* **verification,** *n.* (L. *verus,* true; *facere,* make)

verily, *adv.* (*arch.*) in truth, certainly. (*very*)

verisimilitude, *n.* appearance of truth, likelihood. **verisimilar,** *a.* (L. *verus,* true; *similis,* like)

veritable, *a.* real, genuine. (*verity*)

verity, *n.* truth; true fact, reality. (L. *verus,* true)

verjuice, *n.* sour juice of unripe fruit; sourness. (O.F. *vert,* green; *jus,* juice)

vermeil, *n.* and *a.* vermilion; silver-gilt. (L. *vermis,* worm+dim.)

vermian, *a.* of, like, worms. **vermeology,** *n.* science of worms. **vermeologist,** *n.* **vermicelli,** *n.* stiff paste in strings for cooking, thin macaroni. **vermicide,** *n.* worm-killer. **vermicidal,** *a.* **vermicular,** *a.* vermiform; vermiculate. **vermiculate, vermiculated,** *aa.* moving like a worm; peristaltic; worm-eaten; marked with close wavy lines. **vermiculation,** *n.* **vermiform,** *a.* worm-shaped. **vermifuge,** *n.* drug that expels intestinal worms. **vermifugal,** *a.* **vermigrade,** *a.* crawling like a worm. **vermivorous,** *a.* worm-eating. (L. *vermis,* worm)

vermilion, *n.* cinnabar; bright scarlet pigment made from it.—*a.* vermilion-coloured.—*v.t.* colour vermilion. (L. *vermis,* worm+dim.)

vermin, *n.* (us. treated as *pl.*) noxious or parasitic insects, e.g. fleas, lice; creatures that injure crops or game, e.g. rats, foxes; vile persons. **verminate,** *v.i.* breed vermin. **vermination,** *n.* **verminous,** *a.* infested with, caused by, like, vermin. (L. *vermis,* worm)

vermouth, vermuth, *n.* white wine flavoured with wormwood etc. as appetizer. (G. *wermuth,* wormwood)

vernacular, *a.* (of language) native.—*n.* mother tongue; homely speech. **vernacularism,** *n.* vernacular usage. **vernacularize,** *v.t.* (L. *verna,* home-born slave)

vernal, *a.* of, appearing in, suggestive of, spring. (L. *ver,* spring)

vernation, *n.* (*bot.*) arrangement of leaves within the bud. (*vernal*)

vernier, *n.* small sliding scale indicating minute subdivisions on a fixed scale. (inventor)

veronal, *n.* a hypnotic drug. (G.)

veronica, *n.* kinds of plant incl. speedwell; cloth with likeness of Christ's face. (St. *Veronica* who wiped His face with her handkerchief)

verricule, *n.* tuft of bristles or hairs. **verriculate,** *a.* (L. *verriculum,* net)

verruca, *n.* (*med.*) wart; (*zool.*) wart-like excrescence. **verrucose, verrucous,** *aa.* warty. (L.)

versal, *a.* (*Shake.*) universal. (abbr.)

versatile, *a.* turning readily from one occupation to another, adaptable; talented in many different ways; variable, fickle; (*bot.*) swinging freely on a support. **versatility,** *n.* (L. *vertere,* turn)

verse, *n.* line of poetry; stanza; metrical composition, poetry; short division of chapter of Bible.—*v.t.* and *i.* make verses (about). **blank v.,** unrhymed, esp. five-foot iambic. **free v.,** *vers libre,* verse with no regular metrical system. **society v.,** *vers de société,* topical verse of light witty kind. (L. *versus,* line)

versed, *a.* skilled, experienced (in). (L. *versari,* be occupied)

verselet, *n.* short verse. **verset,** *n.* (*mus.*) short organ interlude. **versicle,** *n.* short verse, esp. one alternating with responses in church service. **versicular,** *a.*

versicolour, versicoloured, *aa.* parti-coloured; changeable in colour, iridescent. (L. *vertere,* turn)

versify, *v.t.* and *i.* turn (prose) into verse; relate in verse; make verses. **versification,** *n.* verse-making; metre, prosody. **versifier,** *n.* writer of verses; poetaster. (L. *versificare*)

version, *n.* translation, rendering; account from a particular point of view. **versional,** *a.* (L. *vertere,* turn)

verslibrist, *n.* writer of free verse. (*vers libre*)

verso, *n.* left-hand page of book, back of recto; reverse of coin. (L. *vertere,* turn)

verst, *n.* Russian measure of length, about ⅔ mile. (Russ. *versta*)

versus, *prep.* (*abbr.* **v.**) against. (L.)

vert, *v.i.* and *n.* (become) convert or pervert.

vert, *n.* and *a.* (*heraldry*) green. (O.F.)
vertebra, *n.* (*pl.* **vertebrae**) segment of backbone. **vertebral,** *a.* of spine. **vertebrate,** *a.* and *n.* (animal) having a backbone. **vertebration,** *n.* division into vertebrae or segments. (L.)
vertex, *n.* (*pl.* **vertices**) topmost point, apex; (*math.*) angular point of triangle or polygon. **vertical,** *a.* upright, perpendicular; of, at, the vertex. **verticality,** *n.* (L.)
verticil, verticel, *n.* (*bot.*) whorl. **verticillate,** *a.* (*vertex*+dim.)
vertigo, *n.* dizziness, giddiness. **vertiginous,** *a.* giddy; causing giddiness. (L.)
vertu, see **virtu.**
vervain, *n.* plant once used in magic, wild verbena. (*verbena*)
verve, *n.* enthusiasm inspiring artist or poet; spirit, vigour. (F.)
vervet, *n.* small S. African monkey. (F.)
very, *a.* (*compar.* **verier,** *superl.* **veriest**) real, genuine; actual; mere; truly as stated.—*adv.* exceedingly, extremely; in the fullest sense; (*Shake.*) exactly, just. **v. good, well,** form of assent or approval. (L. *verus,* true)
Very light, coloured flare fired from **Very pistol,** as signal or to light up part of battle-field. (inventor)
vesica, *n.* bladder, esp. urinary; sac, cyst. **v. piscis,** pointed oval used as aureole in medieval painting. **vesical,** *a.* **vesicate,** *v.t.* raise blisters on. **vesicant, vesicatory,** *aa.* **vesication,** *n.* **vesicle,** *n.* small blister or bladder or cavity. **vesicular, vesiculate, vesiculose, vesiculous,** *aa.* **vesiculation,** *n.* (L.)
Vesper, *n.* the evening star; (*poet.*) evening; (*pl.*) evening service, evensong. **vespertine,** *a.* of evening; (*bot.*) opening, (*zool.*) active, in the evening; (*astron.*) setting about sunset. (L.)
vespine, *a.* of wasps. **vespiary,** *n.* wasps' nest. (L. *vespa,* wasp)
vessel, *n.* utensil for holding liquids, receptacle; ship; tube, duct, for blood, sap etc.; person viewed as divine instrument. (*vas*+dim.)
vest, *n.* body garment next skin, singlet; waistcoat; (*arch.*) robe, clothing.—*v.t.* and *i.* furnish, endow (with); (*arch.*) clothe (oneself). **v. in,** confer, be conferred, on; invest with right to. **vested interest, right,** opportunity of gain etc. which law or custom has entitled possessors to regard as permanent. (L. *vestis*)
vesta, *n.* match; an asteroid; Roman goddess of hearth. **vestal,** *a.* of Vesta; vowed to chastity, pure.—*n.* virgin priestess of Vesta; nun; old maid.
vestibule, *n.* antechamber; entrance-hall; (*anat.*) communicating channel; (*Amer.*) covered entrance at end of railway carriage. **v. train,** (*Amer.*) corridor train. **vestibular, vestibulate,** *aa.* (L. *vestibulum*)
vestige, *n.* trace, remains; rudimentary survival of former organ; particle. **vestigial, vestigiary,** *aa.* (L. *vestigium,* footprint)
vestiture, *n.* (*zool.*) hair, scales etc. covering a surface. (*vest*)
vestment, *n.* garment; official robe; article of priest's dress at divine service, esp. chasuble. (*vest*)
vestry, *n.* room in church where vestments are kept and church business transacted; body of parish ratepayers, meeting of these. **vestral,** *a.* (L. *vestiarium,* wardrobe)
vesture, *n.* clothing, dress.—*v.t.* clothe. **vesturer,** *n.* church official in charge of vestments. (*vest*)
vesuvian, *n.* kind of fusee; (also **vesuvianite**) mineral allied to garnet. (*Vesuvius,* a volcano)
vet, *n.* (*colloq.*) veterinary surgeon.—*v.t.* (*colloq.*) examine, overhaul. (abbr.)
vetch, *n.* kinds of plant of bean family incl. tare. **vetchling,** *n.* plant like vetch. (L. *vicia*)
veteran, *n.* old tried soldier or sailor; one long exercised in any service.—*a.* old and experienced. (L. *vetus,* old)
veterinary, *a.* of, dealing with, diseases of domestic animals.—*n.* veterinary surgeon. (L. *veterina,* draught animal)
veto, *n.* (*pl.* **vetoes**) power to negative piece of legislation; exercise of this; prohibition, ban.—*v.t.* reject by veto; refuse to allow, forbid. (L.=I forbid)
vettura, *n.* (*pl.* *vetture*) four-wheeled carriage in Italy. (It.)
vex, *v.t.* annoy by petty provocation, irritate; render mildly angry; (*poet.*) agitate (sea etc.); (*arch.*) afflict. **vexation,** *n.* vexing; annoying thing; irritation, distress. **vexatious,** *a.* irritating; (of litigation) designed merely to annoy. **vexed,** *a.* much debated. (L. *vexare*)
via, *adv.* by way of. **v.** *media,* middle course. (L.=way)
viable, *a.* born alive and able to live; able to grow; practicable, workable. **viability,** *n.* (L. *vita,* life)
viaduct, *n.* series of arches etc. carrying road or railway over valley or low ground. (L. *via,* way; *ducere,* lead)
vial, *n.* small glass bottle for medicine etc. (*phial*)
viameter, *n.* hodometer. (L. *via,* way)
viand, *n.* (us. *pl.*) article of food. (L. *vivere,* live)
viaticum, *n.* the eucharist as administered to the dying; portable altar. (L.=supplies for journey)
vibraculum, *n.* (*pl.* **vibracula**) whip-like appendage by which some polyzoans secure food. (*vibrate*)
vibraphone, *n.* kind of marimba.

vibrate, *v.i.* and *t.* move rapidly to and fro; quiver, thrill; swing like pendulum, oscillate; waver. **vibration,** *n.* **vibrational,** *a.* **vibrator,** *n.* vibrating part in various instruments. **vibratory, vibrative,** *aa.* vibrating; consisting of, causing, vibrations. **vibrant,** *a.* vibrating; resonant. **vibrancy,** *n.* **vibratile,** *a.* capable of vibrating. **vibratility,** *n.* **vibratiuncle,** *n.* minute vibration. *vibrato, n.* (*mus.*) pulsating effect got by rapid variation of emphasis on same tone. **vibrio,** *n.* kinds of spiral bacillus. **vibrioid,** *a.* and *n.* vibrio-like (body). **vibrissa,** *n.* (*pl.* **vibrissae**) sensitive whisker on animal's face. **vibrograph, vibroscope,** *nn.* instrument for recording, observing, vibrations. (L. *vibrare*)

viburnum, *n.* kinds of shrub incl. guelder rose. (L.)

vicar, *n.* clergyman of parish not receiving tithes; deputy, agent. **v. apostolic,** Roman Catholic titular or missionary bishop. **v. choral,** assistant in musical parts of cathedral service. **v. general,** officer assisting bishop. **V. of Bray,** systematic turncoat. **V. of Christ,** a title of the pope. **vicarage,** *n.* house, office, of vicar. **vicarial,** *a.* of, acting as, vicar. **vicarious,** *a.* done, suffered, on behalf of another; of, acting as, deputy. (L. *vicarius*)

vice, *n.* grave moral fault; gross wickedness; serious defect, blemish; (in horse) ill temper; buffoon in old English moralities. (L. *vitium*)

vice, *n.* appliance for gripping things that are being worked on, screw-press; (*Shake.*) grip.—*v.t.* screw. (L. *vitis,* vine)

vice, *n.* (*colloq.*) vice-chairman, vice-president etc. (abbr.)

vicĕ, *prep.* in place of; succeeding to. **v. versa,** conversely, the other way round. (L. *vicem,* turn)

vice-, *pref.* assistant, deputy, next in rank to, used in **vice-admiral,** *n.* naval officer next below admiral; **vice-chairman,** *n.* one who takes chair in chairman's absence; **vice-chancellor,** *n.* chief executive officer of university; **vice-consul,** *n.* one who acts in place of consul in subordinate district etc.; **vicegerent,** *n.* and *a.* (person) holding delegated power or ruling as another's deputy, hence **vicegerency,** *n.*; **vice-governor, vice-president, vice-principal,** *nn.* deputy or assistant governor etc.; **viceregal,** *a.* of viceroy; **vicereine,** *n.* viceroy's wife; **viceroy,** *n.* one who rules country or province as representative of king or queen, hence **viceroyal,** *a.*; **viceroyalty, viceroyship,** *nn.* office, term, of viceroy. (*vice*)

vicennial, *a.* lasting, happening every, twenty years. (L. *viginti,* twenty; *annus,* year)

Vichy, *n.* (also **V. water**) a mineral water. (place)

vicinage, *n.* surrounding district, neighbourhood. **vicinal,** *a.* neighbouring. **vicinity,** *n.* nearness; neighbourhood; close relationship. (L. *vicus,* district)

vicious, *a.* of, addicted to, vice; morally evil, depraved; faulty, corrupt; ill-tempered, spiteful; (of horse) having bad tricks. (*vice*)

vicissitude, *n.* change of circumstances or fortune; (*pl.*) ups and downs; (*arch.*) alternation. **vicissitudinous,** *a.* (L. *vicissitudo*)

victim, *n.* living being offered in religious sacrifice; person, thing, sacrificed to attain some object; one who suffers injury; dupe. **victimize,** *v.t.* make victim of, cause to suffer; swindle. **victimization,** *n.* (L. *victima*)

victor, *n.* conqueror; winner. (L.)

victoria, *n.* light open four-wheeled two-seater carriage; giant S. American water-lily. **V. Cross,** (*abbr.* **V.C.**) highest military decoration for valour. **Victorian,** *a.* of, living in, the reign of Queen Victoria; old-fashioned, prudish.—*n.* Victorian person. **Victorian Order,** (*abbr.* **V.O.**) an order of knighthood. (queen)

victorine, *n.* woman's fur tippet with long narrow ends; kind of peach.

victory, *n.* success in battle or contest. **victorious,** *a.* having the victory, winning. (*victor*)

victual, *n.* (us. *pl.*) food, provisions.—*v.t.* and *i.* supply with, take in, provisions. **victualler,** *n.* food-purveyor; provision-ship. **licensed victualler,** innkeeper with licence to sell alcohol. (L. *vivere,* live)

vicugna, vicuña, *n.* S. American animal like llama. (Peruvian)

vidē, v.t. see. *v. supra, infra,* see earlier or later in book (lit. above, below). *videlicet, adv.* (*abbr.* **viz.,** us. spoken as ' namely ') that is to say, namely. (L.)

vidette, same as **vedette.**

viduage, viduity, *nn.* widowhood. (L. *vidua,* widow)

vie, *v.i.* and *t.* (*pres. part* **vying**) strive for superiority, compete (with); (*Shake.*) stake. (L. *invitare,* invite

vi et armis, with violence. (L.=with force and arms)

vieux jeu, played out (subject). (F.)

view, *n.* sight, inspection; range of vision; scene, prospect, outlook; picture of this; mental impression; judgment, opinion; design, plan; (*Shake.*) appearance; glance.—*v.t.* inspect, look at; contemplate, regard. **have in v.,** have as aim. **in full v. of,** easily seen by. **in v. of,** taking into account. **on v.,** open to inspection. **with a v. to,** for the purpose of, as a step towards. **v.-finder,** *n.* device in camera showing view to be photographed. **v.-halloo,** *n.* huntsman's cry when fox is sighted. **viewless,** *a.* (*poet.*) invisible, unseen. **viewy,** *a.* (*colloq.*) having fanciful views, visionary. (L. *vidēre*, see)

vigil, *n.* keeping awake, watching; day preceding church festival, eve; (*pl.*) nocturnal devotions. **vigilance,** *n.* watchfulness; alertness; (*med.*) insomnia. **vigilance committee,** self-constituted body for combating crime or immorality. **vigilant,** *a.* watchful, on the watch. **vigilantē,** *n.* (*Amer.*) member of vigilance committee. (L.=awake)

vignette, *n.* small picture or design in book without line framing it; picture of which edges shade off gradually into background; short word-sketch. —*v.t.* depict in vignette; shade off into background. **vignettist,** *n.* (F. =little vine)

vigour, *n.* physical or mental strength and energy; robustness, vitality; force. **vigorous,** *a.* full of vigour; powerful, lusty. *vigoroso, adv.* (*mus.*) with vigour. (L. *vigor*)

viking, *n.* ancient Norse sea-rover. (O.N. *vikingr*)

vilayet, *n.* province of Turkish empire. (Arab. *welāyet*, district)

vile, *a.* worthless, mean; base, depraved, shameful; of very bad quality. **vilify,** *v.t.* speak ill of, defame; degrade. **vilification,** *n.* **vilipend,** *v.t.* disparage; slight. (L. *vilis*)

villa, *n.* detached suburban house; Italian country house. **villadom,** *n.* suburban society. (L.=farmhouse)

village, *n.* small assemblage of houses, less than a town. **villager,** *n.* inhabitant of village. **villagery,** *n.* (*Shake.*) villages collectively. (*villa*)

villain, *n.* scoundrel, blackguard; (*joc.*) sly rogue; (*arch.*) boor; (*rare*) villein. **villainous,** *a.* depraved, evil; very bad, wretched. **villainage, villanage,** *n.* villeinage. **villainy,** *n.* great wickedness; atrocious crime. (*villa*)

villanelle, *n.* French form of poem of 19 lines in six stanzas rhymed aba aba aba aba aba abaa, the 6th, 12th, and 18th lines being the same as the first, and the 9th, 15th, and 19th the same as the third. (F.)

villeggiatura, *n.* stay in country, rustication. (It.)

villein, *n.* feudal tenant of lowest class, serf. **villeinage, villenage,** *n.* status of villein; tenure by which he held his land. (*villa*)

villus, *n.* (*pl.* villi) velvety fibre of mucous membrane of intestine; (*bot.*) soft hair covering fruit or flower. **villous, villose,** *aa.* covered with villi, downy. **villosity,** *n.* (L.=shaggy hair)

vim, *n.* (*sl.*) energy, force. (L. *vis*)

viminal, vimineous, *aa.* of, producing, twigs or shoots. (L. *vimen*, twig)

vina, *n.* seven-stringed Indian musical instrument. (Hind.)

vinaceous, *a.* of wine or grapes; wine-red. (L. *vinum*, wine)

vinaigrette, *n.* small perforated box or bottle for aromatic vinegar or smelling-salts. (F.)

vincible, *a.* (*rare*) able to be conquered. (L. *vincere*, conquer)

vinculum, *n.* (*pl.* **vincula**) (*math.*) line over quantities having effect of brackets; (*print.*) brace. (L.=bond)

vindicate, *v.t.* establish existence or truth of, justify; clear of charges, defend. **vindication, vindicator** (*fem.* **vindicatress**) *nn.* **vindicable, vindicative, vindicatory,** *aa.* (L. *vindicare*)

vindictive, *a.* revengeful, wishing revenge; prompted by resentment; (of damages) exemplary, punitive. (L. *vindex*, avenger)

vine, *n.* climbing plant that bears grapes; stem of any trailing or climbing plant. **v.-dresser,** *n.* one who cultivates vines. (L. *vinum*, wine)

vinegar, *n.* acid liquid got by fermentation of dilute wine or beer and used as condiment etc.; sourness. **vinegary,** *a.* (L. *vinum*, wine; *acer*, sour)

vinery, *n.* greenhouse for vines.

vineyard, *n.* plantation of grape-vines.

vingt-et-un, vingt-un, *n.* gambling card game. (F.=twenty-one)

viniculture, *n.* vine-growing. **vinicultural,** *a.* **viniculturist,** *n.* **viniferous,** *a.* wine-producing. **vinificator,** *n.* apparatus for collecting alcoholic vapours in wine-making.

vin ordinaire, ordinary cheap wine of France, us. claret. (F.)

vinous, *a.* of, like, inspired by, wine. **vinosity,** *n.* (*vine*)

vint, *n.* a Russian card game. (Russ.)

vint, *v.t.* make (wine). **vintage,** *n.* gathering of grapes; season for this; a season's produce of wine; (*poet.*) wine. **vintage wine,** one of famous vintage. **vintager,** *n.* grape-gatherer. **vintner,** *n.* wine merchant. (*vine*)

viol, *n.* medieval instrument like violin. **bass v.,** large viol; violoncello. **v.-de-gamboys,** *n.* (*Shake.*) bass viol. **viola,** *n.* large violin for alto or tenor. (O.F. *viole*)

viola, *n.* kinds of plant incl. violet and pansy. **violaceous,** *a.* of violet colour or family. (L.=violet)

violate, *v.t.* desecrate, profane; infringe, transgress; break in upon; outrage, rape. **violation, violator,** *nn.* **violable,** *a.* (L. *violare*)

violent, *a.* forcible, vehement; severe, intense; showing, caused by, force. —*v.i.* (*Shake.*) be violent. **violence,** *n.* being violent; vehemence, intensity; injury, outrage. (L. *violentus*)

violet, *n.* plant with small blue, purple, or white flower; bluish-purple.—*a.* violet-coloured. **violin,**

violine, *n.* emetic got from violets. (*viola*+dim.)

violin, *n.* four-stringed instrument played with bow, fiddle; violinist. **violinist,** *n.* violin-player. **violist,** *n.* player of viol or viola. **violoncello,** *n.* large bass violin held between knees, 'cello. **violoncellist,** *n.* **violōnē,** *n.* largest type of violin, double-bass. (It. *violino*)

viper, *n.* kinds of venomous snake incl. adder; malignant treacherous person. **viperine, viperous,** *aa.* (L. *vipera*)

virago, *n.* nagging woman, termagant, shrew. (L.=female warrior)

virelay, *n.* old French form of poem with short lines and two rhymes variously arranged. (O.F. *virelai*)

vireo, *n.* small greenish American singing bird, greenlet. (L.)

virescent, *a.* becoming green; greenish. **virescence,** *n.* greenness, esp. in place of normal colour of petals. (L. *virēre,* be green)

virgate, *a.* (*bot.*) slim and straight.—*n.* an old English unit of land. (L. *virga,* rod)

virgin, *n.* woman or (*arch.*) man who has had no sexual intercourse, maid; Virgin Mary; painting, statue, of her; (*astron.*) Virgo.—*a.* chaste, maiden, modest; pure, unsullied; not yet used, fresh; (of land) untilled. **(Blessed) V. Mary,** (*abbr.* **B.V.M.**) the mother of Christ. **v. it,** (*Shake.*) be chaste. **V. Queen,** Elizabeth. **virginal,** *a.* of, befitting, a virgin; pure, innocent.—*n.* (*sing.* or *pl.*) kind of spinet. **virginhood, virginity,** *nn.* state of being a virgin, maidenhood. (L. *virgo*)

Virginia, *n.* tobacco from Virginia in U.S. **V. creeper,** ornamental climbing plant. **V. reel,** (*Amer.*) a country dance.

Virgo, *n.* the Virgin, 6th sign of zodiac, which sun enters about 22nd Aug. *v. intacta,* (*law*) girl who is a complete virgin. *virginibus puerisque,* for maidens and boys. (L.)

virgule, *n.* small rod; slanting mark (/) of punctuation; comma. **virgulate,** *a.* rod-shaped. (L. *virgula*)

viridescent, *a.* greenish; turning green. **viridescence,** *n.* **viridity,** *n.* greenness; freshness. (L. *viridis,* green)

virile, *a.* of a mature man, manly; strong, forceful; capable of procreation. **virility,** *n.* **virilescence,** *n.* acquisition by female of male characteristics. **virilescent,** *a.* (L. *vir,* man)

virtu, *n.* love of fine art, connoisseurship; artistic excellence, fine workmanship; artistic objects, antiques, curios, collectively. **virtuoso,** *n.* (*pl.* **virtuosi**) one skilled in the technique of an art, brilliant musical performer; art-connoisseur. **virtuosity,** *n.* skill of virtuoso; connoisseurs collectively. (It. *virtù,* virtue)

virtue, *n.* moral excellence, goodness; good quality, merit; chastity, virginity; efficacy, potency (of drug etc.); (*Shake.*) bravery; essence; (*pl.*) seventh order of angels. **by, in, v. of,** on the strength or ground of. **make a v. of necessity,** do thing because there is no alternative. **virtual,** *a.* in effect though not in name. **virtuality,** *n.* **virtually,** *adv.* to all intents and purposes, practically. **virtuous,** *a.* having or showing moral rectitude, good; chaste; (*arch.*) efficacious. (L. *virtus*)

virulent, *a.* poisonous, venomous; deadly; malignant, spiteful. **virulence,** *n.* (*virus*)

virus, *n.* poisonous matter or germ, esp. infra-microscopic infective agent; corrupt influence; malignity. (L.=poison)

vis, *n.* force. *v. inertiae,* force of inertia. *v. major,* unavoidable accident. (L.)

visa, visé, *n.* official endorsement on passport giving permission to proceed.—*v.t.* (*past, p.p.* **visa'd, visaed, viséd, visé'd,** *p.p.* also **visé**) mark with visa. (L. *vidēre,* see)

visage, *n.* face. (L. *vidēre,* see)

visard, see **visor.**

vis-à-vis, *adv.* facing.—*prep.* opposite to; in face of.—*n.* person (sitting) opposite. (F.=face to face)

viscacha, *n.* S. American burrowing rodent like large chinchilla. (native)

viscera, *n.pl.* internal organs of body, intestines. **visceral,** *a.* **viscerate,** *v.t.* disembowel. (L.)

viscid, *a.* sticky, semi-fluid. **viscidity,** *n.* **viscose,** *n.* form of cellulose used in making artificial silk. **viscosity,** *n.* viscousness; internal friction of fluids, property of resisting change in arrangement of molecules. **viscometer, viscosimeter,** *nn.* instrument for measuring viscosity. (L. *viscum,* mistletoe)

viscount, *n.* peer next in rank below earl. **viscountess,** *n.* female viscount; viscount's wife. **viscounty, viscountcy, viscountship,** *nn.* rank of viscount. (*vice-*; *count*)

viscous, *a.* sticky, viscid; having viscosity. (*viscid*)

visé, see **visa.**

visible, *a.* able to be seen, perceptible, apparent. **v. Church,** whole body of professing Christians. **v. speech,** a phonetic alphabet representing actual movements of vocal organs. **visibility,** *n.* being visible; degree of clearness of atmosphere. **visibly,** *adv.* perceptibly, appreciably. (L. *vidēre,* see)

visie, *n.* (*Scot.*) close look. (*vision*)

vision, *n.* act or faculty of seeing, sight; imaginative insight, shrewd foresight; mental picture, dream; prophetic apparition, phantom.—*v.t.* perceive, present, in form of vision.

field of v., range that sight covers. **visional**, *a.* of the sense of sight. **visionary**, *a.* of, like, seen in, a vision; imaginative, dreamy; fanciful, unpractical.—*n.* unpractical idealist; mystic. **visionist**, *n.* visionary. (L. *vidēre*, see)

visit, *v.t.* and *i.* go to see, call on; go to stay with or at; punish, afflict, bless (with); pay visits.—*n.* act of visiting, call. **v. with**, (*Amer.*) chat with. **visiting-card**, *n.* small card with person's name and address. **visitable**, *a.* **visitant**, *a.* (*poet.*) visiting.—*n.* migratory bird; (*poet.*) visitor. **visitation**, *n.* official or ceremonial visit; act of divine wrath or favour, calamity; large migration of animals. **visitatorial**, **visitorial**, *aa.* of an official visitor. **visitor**, *n.* one who visits, caller; official acting as inspector and adviser (of college etc.). (L. *visere*)

visor, *n.* peak of cap, eyeshade; (also **vizor**, **visard**, **vizard**) part of helmet covering face, movable and perforated to see through; (*arch.*) mask. (F. *vis*, face)

vista, *n.* long narrow view, esp. down avenue; avenue with this; series of events looked back or forward to. **vista'd**, *a.* (It.=sight)

visual, *a.* of, concerned with, used in, seeing; visible. **visuality**, *n.* **visualize**, *v.t.* make visible; form mental image of, picture in mind. **visualization**, *n.* (L. *vidēre*, see)

vita-glass, *n.* kind of glass allowing ultra-violet rays to pass. (trade name)

vital, *a.* of, connected with, essential to, life; lively, animated; essential, fundamental; (of wound, error) fatal. —*n.pl.* vital organs. **v. force**, life-principle in animals and plants. **v. statistics**, of births and deaths. **vitalism**, *n.* belief that life cannot be explained as resulting wholly from physical and chemical processes. **vitalist**, *n.* **vitalistic**, *a.* **vitality**, *n.* bodily vigour, hold on life; spirit, animation; capacity to last, durability. **vitalize**, *v.t.* give life to; endow with vitality, make vigorous. **vitalization**, *n.* (L. *vita*, life)

vitamin, **vitamine**, *n.* one of several constituents of food-stuffs, essential to health. **v. A**, anti-infective, stimulates growth. **v. B_1**, benefits nerves and bowels. **v. B_2**, protects from pellagra. **v. C**, prevents scurvy. **v. D**, prevents rickets. **v. E**, aids reproduction and lactation. **v. F**, same as **v. B_1**. **v. G**, same as **v. B_2**. (L. *vita*, life+*am*monia)

vitellus, *n.* (*pl.* **vitelli**) yolk of egg. **vitellary**, **vitelline**, *aa.* **vitellin**, *n.* protein found in egg-yolk. (L.)

vitiate, *v.t.* make faulty or ineffective; taint; deprave; invalidate. **vitiation**, **vitiator**, *nn.* (*vice*)

viticulture, *n.* vine-growing. **viticultural**, *a.* **viticulturist**, **viticulturalist**, *nn.* **viticide**, *n.* vine pest. (L. *vitis*, vine)

vitiosity, *n.* viciousness, corruption. (L. *vitium*, vice)

vitreous, *a.* of, like, got from, glass. **v. humour**, transparent tissue of eyeball. **vitreosity**, *n.* **vitrescent**, *a.* able to be made into glass; tending to become glass. **vitrescence**, *n.* **vitric**, *a.* glassy.—*n.pl.* science of glass-making. **vitrify**, *v.t.* and *i.* turn into glass or glass-like substance. **vitrifaction**, **vitrification**, *nn.* **vitrifiable**, *a.* (L. *vitrum*, glass)

vitriol, *n.* sulphuric acid; caustic speech. **blue**, **green**, **white**, **v.**, sulphate of copper, iron, zinc. **oil of v.**, concentrated sulphuric acid. **vitriolate**, *v.t.* convert into a sulphate. **vitriolation**, *n.* **vitriolic**, *a.* like vitriol; corrosive, biting. **vitriolize**, *v.t.* throw vitriol over, poison with vitriol; vitriolate. **vitriolization**, *n.* (L. *vitrum*, glass)

vitta, *n.* (*pl.* **vittae**) fillet, headband; (*bot.*) oil-tube in fruit of some plants; (*zool.*) stripe. **vittate**, *a.* (L.)

vituline, **vitular**, *aa.* of, like, calves. (L. *vitulus*, calf)

vituperate, *v.t.* abuse, scold, rate. **vituperation**, **vituperator**, *nn.* **vituperative**, *a.* (L. *vituperare*)

viva, *n.* and *v.t.* (*colloq.*) (put through) oral examination. (*viva voce*)

viva, *int.* long live, hurrah for.—*n.* this cry. (It.)

vivace, *adv.* (*mus.*) in a lively manner. (It.)

vivacious, *a.* lively; sprightly, gay; (*bot.*) tenacious of life, perennial. **vivacity**, *n.* (L. *vivere*, live)

vivandière, *n.* woman camp-follower supplying provisions. (F.)

vivarium, *n.* (*pl.* **vivaria**) place for keeping living animals. (L.)

vivat, *int.* long live, hurrah for. (L.)

viva vócĕ, orally, by word of mouth; oral (examination). (L. = by living voice)

vive, *a.* lively; forcible. (L. *vivus*, alive)

vive, *int.* long live, hurrah for. (F.)

vivers, *n.pl.* (*Scot.*) food, eatables. (O.F. *vivres*)

vives, *n.* an ear-disease of horses. (Arab. *al*, the; *dhībah*, she-wolf)

vivid, *a.* animated, lively; producing lifelike mental images, graphic; (of colour) bright, brilliant. (L. *vivere*, live)

vivify, *v.t.* give life to; make lively, animate. **vivification**, *n.* (L. *vivus*, alive; *facere*, make)

viviparous, *a.* bringing forth young alive. **viviparity**, *n.* (L. *vivus*, alive; *parere*, bring forth)

vivisection, *n.* dissection of, operating on, living animal for purpose of scientific research. **vivisect**, *v.t.* subject to vivisection. **vivisector**, *n.*

vivisectional, *a.* **vivisectionist,** *n.* one who practises or approves of vivisection. (L. *vivus,* alive; *secare,* cut)
vivo, adv. (*mus.*) in a lively manner. (It.)
vixen, *n.* she-fox; malicious or shrewish woman. **vixenish,** *a.* (O.E. *fyxen*)
viz., see *videlicet.*
vizard, vizor, see **visor.**
vizcacha, same as **viscacha.**
vizier, vizir, *n.* minister of state in Mohammedan countries. **grand v.,** prime minister. **vizierial, vizirial,** *a.* **vizierate, vizirate,** *n.* office, status, of vizier. (Arab. *wazīr,* porter)
vly, vlei, *n.* (*S. Afr.*) swamp; shallow pond which is sometimes dry.
vocable, *n.* (*philol.*) word. **vocabulary,** *n.* stock of words used by speaker, author, tribe etc.; list of words arranged alphabetically and explained. (L. *vocare,* call)
vocal, *a.* of, for, produced by, endowed with, voice; (*phonetics*) voiced, sonant; of vowel character.—*n.* vowel. **v. cords, chords,** vibrating membranes in larynx producing voice. **v. music,** to be sung, not played. **vocalic,** *a.* of, like, containing, vowels. **vocalist,** *n.* singer. **vocalize,** *v.t.* and *i.* form, utter, with voice; make sonant; write with vowels or vowel points; use singing voice; sing to vowel sounds. **vocalization,** *n.* (L. *vox,* voice)
vocation, *n.* calling, occupation; divine call to religious life; sense of fitness for particular career. **vocational,** *a.* (L. *vocare,* call)
vocative, *a.* and *n.* (*gram.*) (case, form) used in addressing person. (L. *vocare,* call)
vociferate, *v.t.* and *i.* shout, bawl; speak loudly and insistently. **vociferation, vociferator,** *nn.* **vociferant,** *a.* clamorous. **vociferance,** *n.* **vociferous,** *a.* making loud outcry, noisy. (L. *vox,* voice; *ferre,* carry)
vodka, *n.* Russian spirits distilled from rye or potatoes. (Russ.)
voe, *n.* small bay, creek, in Shetland Islands. (O.N. *vágr*)
voetganger, *n.* (*S. Afr.*) locust before its wings grow; pedestrian; infantryman. (Du. *voet,* foot; *gang,* walk)
voetsak, *int.* (*S. Afr.*) go away. (S. Afr. Du. *voort, seg ek,* away, I say)
vogie, *a.* (*Scot.*) vain; merry.
vogue, *n.* prevailing fashion or mode; popular favour. (F.=course)
voice, *n.* sound uttered by mouth; quality of this; power of speech, utterance; expressed opinion, vote; (*gram.*) forms of verb showing relation of subject to action; (*phonetics*) sound uttered with vibration of vocal cords, not with mere breath; (*Shake.*) rumour.—*v.t.* give utterance to, express; (*mus.*) regulate (organ-pipe etc.) so as to give correct tone; (*phonetics*) utter with voice, make sonant. **in good, bad, v.,** in good, bad, condition for singing. **with one v.,** unanimously. **voiceful,** *a.* (*poet.*) sonorous. **voiceless,** *a.* speechless, dumb; (*phonetics*) not voiced. (L. *vox*)
void, *a.* empty, vacant; legally invalid; destitute (of); useless, vain.—*n.* empty space; vacancy, sense of loss. —*v.t.* discharge, emit; empty; nullify; (*arch.*) quit, vacate. **voidance,** *n.* voiding; ejection from, vacancy in, benefice. (O.F. *voide*)
voilà, int. behold, there is. *v. tout,* that is all. (F.)
voile, *n.* thin dress-material like muslin. (F.=veil)
volant, *a.* flying, able to fly; (*poet.*) quick, nimble. **volable,** *a.* (*Shake.*) quick-witted. (L. *volare,* fly)
Volapük, *n.* artificial language meant for international use. (Volapük *vol,* world; *pük,* speech)
volar, *a.* of the palm or sole. (L. *vola,* palm, sole)
volatile, *a.* evaporating rapidly; light-hearted, mercurial; flighty. **volatility,** *n.* **volatilize,** *v.t.* and *i.* turn into vapour, evaporate. **volatilization,** *n.* (L. *volare,* fly)
vol-au-vent, *n.* kind of rich raised pie. (F.)
volcano, *n.* (*pl.* **volcanoes**) mountain with vent from which lava, ashes, gas etc. are ejected. **volcanic,** *a.* of, like, due to action of, volcano; violent, intense. **volcanically,** *adv.* **volcanicity,** *n.* **volcanism,** *n.* volcanic action. **volcanist, volcanologist,** *nn.* student of volcanoes. **volcanology,** *n.* science of volcanoes. **volcanological,** *a.* **volcanize,** *v.t.* subject to volcanic heat. **volcanization,** *n.* (*Vulcan*)
vole, *n.* kinds of rat-like rodent. **water-v.,** *n.* water-rat. (obs. *vole-mouse,* from Norwegian *voll,* field)
vole, *v.i.* (*cards*) win all tricks in deal. —*n.* slam. (F.)
volery, *n.* aviary. (*volant*)
volet, *n.* panel of triptych. (F.=shutter)
volitant, *a.* able to fly, volant. **volitation,** *n.* flying. (*volant*)
volition, *n.* act or power of willing, will. **volitional, volitionary, volitive,** *aa.* (L. *velle,* wish)
volkslied, n. folk-song. (G.)
volley, *n.* simultaneous discharge of a number of shots or missiles; rapid noisy utterance, torrent; (*lawn tennis*) return of ball before it bounces. —*v.t.* and *i.* discharge, fly, utter, sound, in volley; (*lawn tennis*) hit by volley. (L. *volare,* fly)
volplane, *v.i.* (of aeroplane) descend by gliding with engine stopped.—*n.* such descent. (F.)
volt, *n.* circular gait of horse; (*fencing*) leap to avoid thrust.—*v.i.* make volt. (It. *volta,* turn)
volt, *n.* unit of electromotive force,

propelling one ampere through one ohm resistance. **volta-electric,** *a.* of voltaic electricity. **voltage,** *n.* electromotive force measured in volts. **voltaic,** *a.* galvanic. **voltameter,** *n.* voltmeter. (A. *Volta*)

volta, n. (*mus., pl. volte*) time. *una v.,* once. *due vv.,* twice. (It.)

Voltairian, *a.* and *n.* (adherent) of Voltaire and his religious scepticism. **Voltairianism, Voltairism,** *nn.*

volte, same as **volt.**

volte, see *volta.*

volte-face, *n.* change to opposite opinion or direction. (F.)

voltmeter, *n.* instrument for measuring voltage.

voluble, *a.* having a great flow of words, fluent; (*arch.*) revolving, rotating; (*bot.,* also **volubilate, volubile**) twining. **volubility,** *n.* (L. *volvere,* roll)

volume, *n.* book, tome; mass, body; cubic space occupied, bulk; fullness of tone; (*pl., colloq.*) a great deal. **voluminal,** *a.* of volume. **volumenometer,** *n.* instrument for measuring volume of solid body by quantity of liquid displaced. **volumeter,** *n.* instrument for measuring volume of gas. **volumetric, volumetrical,** *aa.* **voluminous,** *a.* of great volume, bulky; of many volumes, having written much; (of robes) ample, loose. **voluminosity,** *n.* (L. *volumen,* scroll)

voluntary, *a.* acting, done, by choice; spontaneous, deliberate; supported by voluntary effort; having free will. —*n.* organ solo played before, during, or after church service; (*Shake.*) volunteer. **voluntaryism, voluntarism,** *n.* principle that Church, schools, army etc. should depend on voluntary effort, not state aid or compulsion. **voluntaryist, voluntarist,** *n.* **volunteer,** *n.* one who offers his services, joins force etc., of his own free will; (*pl.*) auxiliary force superseded in 1907 by Territorial Army.—*v.i.* and *t.* come forward, enlist, serve, voluntarily; proffer unasked. (L. *voluntas,* will)

voluptuary, *n.* person given up to bodily pleasures, sensualist. — *a.* voluptuous. **voluptuous,** *a.* overfond of, contributing to, pleasures of the senses; luxurious; exciting sensual desire. (L. *voluptas,* pleasure)

volute, *n.* spiral scroll-shaped ornament, esp. of Ionic capital; kinds of tropical shell-fish.—*a.* (*bot.*) rolled up. **volution,** *n.* spiral, whorls, of shell; (*anat.*) convolution. (L. *volvere,* roll)

vomer, *n.* slender bone separating nostrils. (L.=ploughshare)

vomit, *v.t.* and *i.* eject from stomach through mouth, be sick; discharge, pour forth, vehemently.—*n.* act of vomiting; matter vomited; emetic. **vomitive, vomitory,** *aa.* and *nn.* emetic. **vomiturition,** *n.* violent retching; repeated vomiting. (L. *vomere*)

voodoo, *n.* witchcraft, black magic, used among creoles and negroes of W. Indies and U.S.; one who practises this.—*v.t.* affect by voodoo. **voodooism, voodooist,** *nn.* (Afr. *vodu*)

voorlooper, *n.* (*S. Afr.*) leader of bullock team. **voortrekker,** *n.* (*S. Afr.*) pioneer. (Du.)

voracious, *a.* greedy, ravenous. **voracity,** *n.* (L. *vorare,* devour)

-vorous, *adj.suf.* eating, as in **herbivorous.** (L. *vorare,* devour)

vortex, *n.* (*pl.* **vortices, vortexes**) whirlpool, powerful eddy; whirlwind; whirling motion or mass. **vortical,** *a.* having whirling motion. **vorticel,** *n.* bell-shaped animalcule. **vorticism,** *n.* recent school of artists presenting objects so as to give effect of assemblage of vortices. **vorticist,** *n.* **vortiginous,** *a.* whirling, vortical. (L.)

votary, *n.* (*fem.* **votaress**) person vowed to service or worship (of); ardent follower, devotee. **votarist,** *n.* (*Shake.*) votary. (*vote*)

vote, *n.* formal expression of will or choice by ballot, show of hands, voice etc.; right to give this; votes collectively; money voted.—*v.i.* and *t.* give one's vote (for, against); pass, approve, grant, by vote; (*colloq.*) declare by common consent; suggest. **v. down,** defeat by majority. **voter,** *n.* (L. *vovēre,* vow)

votive, *a.* given, dedicated, in fulfilment of vow. (L. *votum,* vow)

vouch, *v.i.* and *t.* be surety, make oneself responsible (for); guarantee, attest. — *n.* (*Shake.*) testimony. **voucher,** *n.* one who vouches; document confirming payment etc., receipt. (L. *vocare,* call)

vouchsafe, *v.t.* and *i.* condescend to grant; condescend, deign; (*Shake.*) allow. (*vouch; safe*)

voussoir, *n.* any of the wedge-shaped stones of an arch. (F.)

vow, *n.* promise made under oath to God, solemn pledge; action vowed.—*v.t.* and *i.* promise, threaten, by vow; devote, consecrate; (*arch.*) make (vow); assert. **take the vv.,** become monk or nun. (L. *vovēre*)

vowel, *n.* sound pronounced without friction or stoppage of breath; letter representing this. **v. point,** mark indicating vowel in Hebrew etc. **vowelize,** *v.t.* insert vowel points in. (L. *vocalis,* vocal)

vox, n. voice. *v. et praetera nihil,* a voice and nothing more. **v. humana,** organ-stop with tones of human voice. *v. populi,* popular opinion. (L.)

voyage, *n.* journey by water, esp. a long one.—*v.i.* make voyage. **voyager,** *n.* **voyageur,** *n.* Canadian boatman. (*viaticum*)

vraisemblance, **n.** appearance of truth, verisimilitude. (F.)
vrouw, **n.** (*S. Afr.*) housewife.
vug, *n.* (*min.*) cavity in lode or rock.
Vulcan, *n.* Roman god of fire and smiths. **vulcanic, same as volcanic. vulcanist**, *n.* holder of Plutonic theory. **vulcanite**, *n.* hard vulcanized rubber. **vulcanize**, *v.t.* treat (rubber) with sulphur at high temperature. **vulcanization**, *n.* (L. *Vulcanus*)
vulgar, *a.* unrefined, in bad taste; indelicate, coarse; ill-bred; of the common people; (*Shake.*) common to all, public.—*n.* common people; vernacular. **v. era**, Christian era. **v. fraction**, ordinary kind, not decimal. **vulgarian**, *n.* vulgar pretentious person, bounder. **vulgarism**, *n.* phrase, pronunciation, used only by uneducated. **vulgarity**, *n.* being vulgar. **vulgarize**, *v.t.* make vulgar; spoil by making too common or well-known. **vulgarization**, *n.* **vulgarly**, *adv.* popularly; with vulgarity. **Vulgate**, *n.* 4th-century Latin version of the Bible. (L. *vulgus*, common people)
vulnerable, *a.* capable of being wounded; open to attack, assailable; (*contract bridge*) having won one game, and liable to doubled penalties. **vulnerability**, *n.* **vulnerary**, *a.* and *n.* (drug, ointment) healing wounds. (L. *vulnus*, wound)
vulture, *n.* large bird of prey feeding chiefly on carrion; rapacious person. **vulturine, vulturous**, *aa.* **vulturn**, *n.* Australian brush-turkey. (L. *vultur*)
vulva, *n.* external opening of female genitals. **vulvar, vulvate**, *aa.* **vulvitis**, *n.* inflammation of vulva. (L.)
vying, see vie.

W

wa', *Scot.* form of **wall.**
Waac, *n.* (*colloq.*) member of Women's Army Auxiliary Corps (now Auxiliary Territorial Service). (initials)
Waaf, *n.* (*colloq.*) member of Women's Auxiliary Air Force Service. (initials)
wabble, same as **wobble.**
wabster, *n.* (*Scot.*) weaver. (*web*)
wáckě, *n.* a soft greyish or brownish rock. (G.)
wad, *Scot.* form of **would.**
wad, *n.* lump of soft material for stuffing or packing; disk, plug, keeping charge in place in gun; (*Amer. sl.*) roll of notes, money.—*v.t.* pack, pad, stop up, with wad; stuff, line, with wadding. **wadding**, *n.* soft material forwads; cotton wool.
waddle, *v.i.* walk with short steps, swaying from side to side, like duck. —*n.* this gait. (*wade*)
waddy, *n.* wooden war-club of Australian native. (native)
wade, *v.i.* and *t.* walk through water or mud, ford on foot; go through with effort.—*n.* spell of wading. **wader**, *n.* kinds of long-legged water-bird; (*pl.*) angler's high waterproof boots. (O.E. *wadan*)
wadi, wady, *n.* water-course which is dry except in wet season. (Arab.)
wadset, *n.* (*Scot.*) mortgage.
wae, *n.* (*Scot.*) woe.—*a.* sorrowful. **waefu'**, *a.* woeful. **waesucks**, *int.* alas.
Wafd, *n.* extreme Nationalist party in Egypt. **Wafdist**, *a.* and *n.* (Arab.)
wafer, *n.* very thin sweet biscuit; disk of unleavened bread used in eucharist; disk of paste for fastening papers; disk of red paper stuck on law documents instead of seal.—*v.t.* fasten, seal, with wafer. (O.F. *waufre*)
waff, *a.* and *n.* (*Scot.*) weak, worthless (person).
waffle, *n.* kind of pancake. (Du. *wafel*, wafer)
waffle, *n.* (*sl.*) vague confused talk.—*v.i.* talk waffle.
waft, *v.t.* carry lightly through air or over water; bear smoothly along; (*Shake.*) beckon; turn.—*n.* wafting, sweep; faint odour, whiff; (*naut.*) knotted flag as distress signal etc. **waftage, wafture**, *nn.* act of wafting. (obs. *wafter*, convoying-ship)
wag, *v.t.* and *i.* move to and fro, oscillate; (*Shake.*) go forward, proceed. —*n.* wagging motion. **w.-at-the-wa'**, *n.* (*Scot.*) hanging clock with exposed pendulum. (M.E. *waggen*)
wag, *n.* droll or facetious person, wit; (*sl.*) truant.
wage, *n.* (us. *pl.*) periodical payment for work done, salary; requital.—*v.t.* and *i.* carry on (war); (*Shake.*) stake, hazard; contend; be equal; remunerate. **w.-fund, ww.-fund**, *n.* part of community's capital that goes in wages. (O.F.=pledge)
wager, *n.* and *v.t.* bet. **w. of battle**, mode of trial by personal combat between accused and accuser. (*wage*)
waggery, *n.* facetiousness; practical joke. **waggish**, *a.* facetious; sportive. (*wag*)
waggle, *v.i.* and *t.* (*colloq.*) move from side to side, wag. **waggly**, *a.* unsteady. (*wag*)
wagon, waggon, *n.* four-wheeled vehicle for heavy loads; railway truck; (*Shake.*) chariot. **wagoner, waggoner**, *n.* driver of wagon. **wagonette, waggonette**, *n.* four-wheeled carriage with longitudinal seats facing inwards. *wagon-lit*, *n.* continental sleeping-car. (Du. *wagen*)

wagtail, *n.* small bird that jerks tail up and down; (*Shake.*) obsequious person.

Wahabi, Wahabee, *n.* Mohammedan puritan. (Abd-el-*Wahhab*, founder of sect)

wahine, *n.* Maori woman. (Maori)

wahoo, *n.* burning bush, an ornamental shrub; kind of elm.

waif, *n.* homeless child or wanderer; ownerless animal or article. **ww. and strays,** unowned or neglected children; odds and ends. (O.F.)

wail, *n.* plaintive cry, mournful sound; lamentation.—*v.i.* and *t.* utter, emit, wail; lament (over). **wailful,** *a.*

wain, *n.* wagon. **Charles's W.,** the Great Bear. (O.E. *wægn*)

wainscot, *n.* wooden panelling of room-wall; skirting-board.—*v.t.* line with wainscot. (Du. *wagenschot*, oak-wood)

waist, *n.* part of body between ribs and hips; narrow middle part of violin etc.; part of ship between forecastle and quarter-deck; (*Amer.*) bodice, blouse. **w.-band, w.-belt,** *nn.* band, belt, fitting round waist. **w.-deep,** *a.* and *adv.* up to the waist. **waistcoat,** *n.* sleeveless garment worn between jacket and shirt. (M.E. *wast*)

wait, *v.i.* and *t.* defer action; stay in expectation (of), await; act as waiter, attend.—*n.* act, period, of waiting; (*pl.*) Christmas carol-singers. **lie in w., lay w., for,** waylay. **w. for,** await. **w. lunch for,** put it off till he arrives. **w. on,** attend, fetch and carry for; pay call upon; follow as result. **waiting-room,** *n.* for people to wait in at railway station etc. **waiter,** *n.* (*fem.* **waitress**) one who serves guests at meals. (O.H.G. *wahta*, watchman)

waive, *v.t.* refrain from insisting on, forgo. **waiver,** *n.* (*law*). (O.F. *gaiver*, abandon)

wake, *n.* track left by vessel on water. **in the w. of,** following; after the example of. (O.N. *vaka*, hole in ice)

wake, *v.i.* and *t.* (*past* **woke, waked;** *p.p.* **waked, woken,** rarely **woke**) cease to sleep, be awake; rouse from sleep, waken; be roused, rouse, from sloth or inaction; hold wake over.—*n.* (formerly) vigil, merrymaking, at feast of church's dedication; (*Ir.*) sitting up with corpse before funeral, festivities accompanying this. **w. up,** waken. **w.-robin,** *n.* wild arum. **wakeful,** *a.* unable to sleep, sleepless; watchful. **waken,** *v.i.* and *t.* become, make, awake; rouse, stir up. **wakerife,** *a.* (*Scot.*) wakeful. (O.E. *wacan*, be born, and *wacian*, wake)

wale, weal, *n.* red swollen mark made by blow with stick or whip.—*v.t.* raise wale on. (O.E. *walu*)

wale, *n.* (*Scot.*) choice, pick.—*v.t.* choose.

waler, *n.* horse imported into India from New South Wales.

Walhalla, Walkyrie, same as **Valhalla. Valkyrie.**

walie, same as **waly.**

walk, *v.t.* (*Scot.*) full (cloth)

walk, *n.* ordinary pace, in which man has at least one foot, horse two, always on ground; characteristic gait; journey on foot, stroll; path, promenade; beat.—*v.i.* and *t.* go, cause to go, at walk; traverse on foot; train (puppy); (*arch.*) conduct oneself; (*Shake.*) go aside. **w. away from,** outstrip with ease. **w. into,** (*sl.*) thrash, abuse; eat heartily of. **w. of life,** station, occupation. **w. off with,** steal. **w. on,** have non-speaking part (in play). **w. out,** go sweethearting (with). **w.-out,** *n.* (*Amer.*) workmen's strike. **w. over,** go over course as victor owing to absence of competitors. **w.-over,** *n.* unopposed or easy victory. **w. the hospitals,** be medical student. **walking-leaf,** *n.* insect imitating leaf. **walking-stick,** *n.* stick used in walking, cane. **walking-ticket,** *n.* (*sl.*) dismissal. **walker,** *n.* pedestrian. (O.E. *wealcan*, roll)

wall, *n.* solid structure of stone etc. for enclosure or security; rampart, barrier; side of, partition in, cavity or organ.—*v.t.* surround, protect, with wall. **give, take, the w.,** allow to pass, pass, on inner side of footpath, away from gutter. **go to the w.,** be thrust aside as useless. **ww. have ears,** there may be eavesdroppers. **W. Street,** U.S. money market. **w. up,** block up with wall. **w.-creeper,** *n.* a bird. **w.-fern,** *n.* polypody. **w.-game,** *n.* an Eton form of football. **w.-less,** *a.* without walls. **wallpaper,** *n.* decorative paper for interior walls. (L. *vallum*, rampart)

wallaby, *n.* small kind of kangaroo; (*pl. colloq.*) Australians. **on the w. (track),** on the tramp. (native)

wallah, walla, *n.* (*Anglo-Ind.*) person, thing, concerned with something; man. **box-w.,** *n.* pedlar; (*sl.*) commercial traveller. **competition-w.,** *n.* Indian civil servant appointed by competitive examination. **punkah-w.,** *n.* servant who works punkah. (Hind. suffix *-wala* = -er)

wallaroo, *n.* large kind of kangaroo. (native)

wallet, *n.* pocket-case for bank-notes or papers; small leather tool-bag; (*arch.*) bag for food on journey, scrip.

wall-eyed, *a.* having wall-eye; (*Shake.*) fierce-looking. **wall-eye,** *n.* eye with white iris; disease causing this. (O.N. *vagl-eygr*)

wallflower, *n.* fragrant garden plant with red or yellow flowers; lady who sits out dances for lack of partner.

wallop, *v.t.* (*sl.*) thrash. **walloping,** *a.* (*sl.*) big, whopping. (*gallop*)

wallow, *v.i.* roll about in water or

mud; take gross delight, revel (in). —*n.* wallowing; place where animals wallow.

walnut, *n.* an edible oily nut; tree bearing this; its hard wood, used for cabinet-making. (O.E. *wealh,* foreign +*nut*)

Walpurgis night, *n.* eve of 1st May, when witches were supposed to hold revels. (Saint *Walpurgis*)

walrus, *n.* large arctic sea-animal like seal with long tusks. (Du.)

waltz, *n.* round dance for couples in triple time; music for it.—*v.i.* dance waltz; twirl about, skip. (G. *walzen,* revolve)

waly, *a.* (*Scot.*) beautiful; strong.

waly, *int.* (*Scot.*) alas. (*wellaway*)

wame, *n.* (*Scot.*) belly. (*womb*)

wampee, *n.* yellow grape-like fruit; tropical tree yielding it. (Chin. *hwang,* yellow; *pī,* skin)

wampum, *n.* shell-beads used by Red Indians as money. (Amer. Ind.)

wan, *a.* pallid; colourless; sickly; (*arch.*) dark, gloomy. (O.E. *wann*)

wanchancy, *a.* (*Scot.*) unlucky; wicked. (*wane*; *chance*)

wand, *n.* long slender rod; staff of authority, baton. (O.N. *vöndr*)

wander, *v.i.* and *t.* go about at random, roam; stray, go astray; digress; become incoherent, ramble; (*colloq.*) lead astray. **Wandering Jew,** legendary figure condemned for insulting Christ to roam the earth till Judgment Day. **wandering sailor,** a climbing plant. (O.E. *wandrian*)

wanderlust, *n.* urge to travel. (G.)

wanderoo, *n.* large bearded monkey of Ceylon. (Cingalese *wanderu*)

wane, *v.i.* grow less; decline; (of moon) show smaller illuminated surface. —*n.* decrease; decline. (O.E. *wan,* lacking)

wangle, *v.t.* (*sl.*) obtain, arrange, by diplomacy or artifice; fake, cook.— *n.* such manipulation.

wanion, *n.* **with a w.,** (*arch.*) bad luck (to); with a vengeance. (*wane*)

want, *n.* lack, deficiency; need; poverty; (us. *pl.*) requirement.—*v.t.* and *i.* lack, be without; need, require; desire, long for; be lacking or destitute. **w. for,** be without. **wanted by the police,** sought by them as suspect. **wanting,** *a.* lacking; absent; (*colloq.*) half-witted.—*prep.* without, minus. (O.N. *vanr,* lacking)

wanton, *a.* frolicsome, capricious; wild, luxuriant; unchaste; malicious, unprovoked.—*n.* unchaste woman; wanton person.—*v.i.* revel, run riot; play lasciviously. (O.E. *wan,* lacking; *téon,* educate)

wap, same as **whop.**

wapentake, *n.* subdivision of Yorkshire and certain midland counties. (*weapon*; *take*)

wapinschaw, wapenshaw, wappenschaw, wappenshaw, *n.* (*Scot.*) ancient muster of men and inspection of arms held periodically in each district; rifle meeting. (*weapon*; *show*)

wapiti, *n.* large N. American deer. (Amer. Ind. *wapitik,* white deer)

war, *n.* armed conflict between states; state of hostility.—*v.i.* contend, strive; (*arch.*) make war. **at w.,** engaged in war. **civil w.,** between different parts of one nation. **holy w.,** crusade. **W. Office,** government department in charge of army. **w. to the knife,** irreconcilable hostility. **w.-cry,** *n.* rallying-cry in battle; party catchword. **w.-dance,** *n.* wild dance of savages before battle. **w.-head,** *n.* explosive cap on torpedo. **w.-horse,** *n.* charger. **w.-paint,** *n.* paint put on face and body by savages before battle; (*sl.*) full dress. **warpath,** *n.* war expedition. **on the warpath,** in fighting mood. **w.-whoop,** *n.* Red Indians' war-cry. **w.-worn,** *a.* exhausted by war. (O.H.G. *werra,* strife)

waratah, *n.* Australian crimson-flowered shrub. (native)

warble, *v.i.* and *t.* sing, sound, with trills or quavers; carol.—*n.* warbling sound. **warbler,** *n.* kinds of small bird. (O.H.G. *werbel,* rattle)

warble, *n.* small hard tumour on horse caused by galling of saddle or larva of **w.-fly,** *n.*

ward, *n.* guardianship, custody; minor under control of guardian; administrative division of city; section of hospital or prison; (*fencing*) guard, parry; (*pl.*) ridges, notches, of key or lock.—*v.t.* have in keeping. **w. in Chancery,** minor under care of Court of Chancery. **w. off,** avert, turn aside. **watch and w.,** constant guard. **w.-mote,** *n.* meeting of inhabitants of city ward. **w.-room,** *n.* mess-room of warship's senior officers. (O.E. *weard,* protection)

-ward, *adj.* and *adv. suf.,* **-wards,** *adv. suf.* towards, in direction of, as in **westward, westwards.** (O.E. *-weard*)

warden, *n.* governor, president; local civil defence officer; (*arch.*) watchman. (O.F. *wardein,* guardian)

warden, *n.* kind of cooking pear.

warder, *n.* (*fem.* **wardress**) jailer; staff of authority formerly carried by king etc.; (*arch.*) sentinel. (*ward*)

Wardour Street, full of sham archaisms. (street with antique shops)

wardrobe, *n.* large movable cupboard for clothes; person's stock of clothes. (*ward*; *robe*)

-wards, see **-ward.**

wardship, *n.* tutelage, guardianship.

ware, *a.* (*poet.*) aware; watchful.—*v.t.* look out for; avoid. (O.E. *wær*)

ware, *n.* manufactured articles; pottery; (*pl.*) goods for sale. **warehouse,** *n.* storehouse for goods, repository; wholesale or large retail store.—*v.t.* store temporarily in repository. **warehouseman,** *n.* (O.E. *waru*)

wareless, *a.* (*Spens.*) unwary; unconscious (of).

warfare, *n.* waging of war, hostilities; military life. (*war; fare*)

warily, *adv.* in a wary manner. **wariness,** (*Spens.*) **wariment,** *n.*

warlike, *a.* of war, martial; threatening war, bellicose.

warlock, *n.* wizard, sorcerer. (O.E. *wǽr*, compact; *léogan*, lie)

warm, *a.* moderately hot; heated; imparting warmth; ardent, hearty, affectionate; (of hunting-scent) fresh, strong; (in hiding-game) near object sought; (*colloq.*) well-to-do.—*v.t.* and *i.* make, become, warm; (*sl.*) thrash. **getting w.,** on right track. **w. colour,** with admixture of red or yellow. **w. welcome,** very friendly or very hostile. **w. work,** heating work; perilous struggle. **w.-blooded,** *a.* having constant and relatively high temperature; passionate. **w.-hearted,** *a.* kind, sympathetic. **warming-pan,** *n.* round flat vessel holding live coals for heating bed. **warmth,** *n.* mild heat; enthusiasm, cordiality; vehemence, anger. (O.E. *wearm*)

warn, *v.t.* put on guard, caution; admonish; make aware; (*Shake.*) summon. **warning,** *n.* what serves to warn; notice given to leave situation. (O.E. *warnian*)

warp, *v.t.* and *i.* bend, be bent, out of shape; bias, distort, be distorted; fertilize with warp; (*naut.*) move (ship) by ropes attached to wharf etc.—*n.* threads running lengthwise in loom and crossed by woof; contorted state; mental bias; rope for warping; alluvial sediment. (O.E. *weorpan*, throw)

warplane, *n.* military aeroplane.

warragal, warrigal, *n.* (*Austral.*) wild dog, dingo; wild horse.

warrandice, *n.* (*Scot.*) warranty.

warrant, *n.* authority, justification; legal writ for arrest etc.; document authorizing payment; military certificate of appointment inferior to commission.—*v.t.* justify, give grounds for; vouch for, guarantee. **w. officer,** *n.* highest ranks of non-commissioned officer. **warrantable,** *a.* legitimate; (of stag) old enough to be hunted. **warrantor** or **warranter, warrantee,** *nn.* person by, to, whom warranty is given. **warranty,** *n.* justification; (*law*) vendor's guarantee that thing sold is his and is fit for use. (O.F. *warant*)

warray, *v.t.* (*Spens.*) make war on.

warren, *n.* rabbit colony; tract for, right of, preserving and shooting rabbits, partridges etc.; crowded slum. (O.F. *warir*, keep)

warrior, *n.* soldier, fighter. (*war*)

warship, *n.* ship of navy, man-of-war.

warsle, *v.i.* and *n.* (*Scot.*) wrestle.

wart, *n.* small hard growth on skin; similar lump on tree-trunk. **w.-hog,** *n.* kinds of African swine. **warty,** *a.* (O.E. *wearte*)

wary, *a.* cautious, vigilant; circumspect. (*ware*)

was, see **be.**

wash, *v.t.* and *i.* cleanse (oneself) with liquid; purify; (of river) flow over or past, carry along; separate (ore) from earth by shaking in water; be washable.—*n.* washing; clothes for laundry; dash of waves, rough water in boat's wake; medical lotion; slops; thin coat of paint or metal. **w. away, off,** remove by washing. **w. one's hands of,** disclaim responsibility for. **w. up,** wash (dishes). **won't w.,** won't stand test. **w.-board, w.-day, w.-house, w.-tub,** *nn.* for washing clothes. **w.-bottle,** *n.* apparatus for purifying gases by passing through liquid. **w.-leather,** *n.* chamois leather. **w.-out,** *n.* breach in road caused by flood; (*sl.*) fiasco. **w.-stand, w.-hand-stand,** *nn.* stand holding water-jug and **w.-basin, w.-hand-basin,** *nn.* for washing hands and face. **washed-out,** *a.* faded; limp, dissipated. (O.E. *wascan*)

washable, *a.* able to be washed without damage.

washer, *n.* washing-machine; perforated disk to tighten joint or nut.

washerwoman, *n.* (*masc.* **washerman**) woman who does household washing.

washing, *n.* clothes to be washed. **w.-day, w.-house,** *nn.* for washing clothes. **w.-soda,** *n.* sodium carbonate.

Washingtonia, *n.* kind of Californian palm-tree. (George *Washington*)

washy, *a.* watery, weak; insipid; feeble.

wasp, *n.* slender striped stinging insect. **w.-waisted,** *a.* with very slender waist. **waspish,** *a.* short-tempered, snappish. (O.E. *wæps*)

wassail, *n.* (*arch.*) drinking bout, carousal; ale flavoured with apples and spices.—*v.i.* hold wassail. (O.E. *wes*, be thou; *hál*, well)

wast, see **be.**

waste, *a.* desolate, uncultivated; useless, left over.—*v.t.* and *i.* expend uselessly, squander; lay waste; wear away gradually, dwindle; (*Shake.*) spend; eat.—*n.* wasting; wanton damage; barren tract; waste material, refuse. **lay w.,** ravage. **run to w.,** be wasted. **w. product,** useless by-product. **w.-basket, w.-paper-basket,** *nn.* basket for waste paper and other refuse. **w.-pipe,** *n.* pipe carrying off used water. **wasteful,** *a.* extravagant, not economical; (*Shake.*) devastating. **waster,** *n.* article spoiled in manufacture; (*sl.*) ne'er-do-well. **wastrel,** *n.* weak or vicious person, waster; street arab, waif. **wastry,** *n.* (*Scot.*) prodigality.—*a.* improvident. (L. *vastus*)

Wat, *n.* (*Shake.*) name for hare.

wat, *a.* (*Scot.*) wet; drunk. (*wet*)

watch, *v.i.* and *t.* be vigilant; keep awake; observe attentively, be spectator (of); keep guard (over); look out (for).—*n.* watching, look-out; division of night; wakefulness at night; pocket timepiece; (*naut.*) four-hour spell of duty, division of crew taking this; (*arch.*) watchman, body of watchmen. **w.-case,** *n.* (*Shake.*) sentry-box. **w.-chain, w.-guard,** *nn.* chain, strap etc., securing pocket watch. **w.-dog,** *n.* dog guarding property. **w.-key,** *n.* for winding watch. **w.-night,** *n.* New Year's Eve. **w.-tower,** *n.* look-out tower. **watching brief,** of barrister who watches case on behalf of client indirectly concerned. (O.E. *wæccan*, wake)

watchet, *a.* pale-blue. (M.E. *wachet*)

watchful, *a.* alert, observant; (*Shake.*) marked by, causing, loss of sleep.

watchman, *n.* man guarding building at night; (formerly) man keeping order in streets; (*poet.*) sentinel.

watchword, *n.* slogan, rallying-cry; password.

water, *n.* a clear tasteless liquid; solution of substance in this; sea, river, lake; state of tide; tears, saliva, urine; quality, lustre, of diamond etc.—*v.t.* and *i.* provide, sprinkle, fill, dilute, run, with water; irrigate; drink, take in water; increase number of shares in (stock) without increasing actual capital. **hold w.,** be tenable. **in deep, smooth w.,** in difficulties, doing well. **like w.,** lavishly. **make one's mouth w.,** excite desire or envy. **make w.,** pass urine. **of the first w.,** of finest quality. **strong ww.,** (*arch.*) spirits. **table ww.,** bottled minerals. **take the ww.,** attend spa for health. **w. down,** tone down. **w. on the brain, knee,** accumulation of serous fluid. **w.-beetle, w.-bird, w.-nymph, w.-rat, w.-sprite,** *nn.* living, growing, in water. **w.-bottle, w.-jug, w.-pipe,** *nn.* for holding or conveying water. **w.-mill, w.-power, w.-pressure, w.-wheel,** *nn.* worked by, got from, water. (O.E. *wæter*)

water-bailiff, *n.* custom-house officer at port; keeper of preserved water.

water-bed, *n.* invalid's rubber mattress filled with water.

water-biscuit, *n.* thin plain biscuit.

water-brash, *n.* indigestion with watery eructations.

water-buck, *n.* large African antelope.

waterbury, *n.* kinds of cheap American watch. (place)

water-butt, *n.* rain-water barrel.

Water-carrier, *n.* Aquarius, 11th sign of zodiac.

water-chute, *n.* wooden slope for sliding down into water.

water-clock, *n.* instrument measuring time by flow of water.

water-closet, *n.* privy that is flushed out by water.

water-colour, *n.* pigment mixed with water and gum, not oil; picture painted, art of painting, with this. **water-colourist,** *n.*

watercourse, *n.* small stream or its bed.

watercress, *n.* creeping water-plant used in salads.

watered, *a.* (of silk) having wavy pattern, moiré.

waterfall, *n.* stream falling over precipice, cascade; (*colloq.*) chignon.

water-finder, *n.* dowser.

waterfowl, *n.* aquatic bird or birds.

water-gall, *n.* cavity made by torrent; secondary rainbow.

water-gate, *n.* flood-gate; gate giving access to river.

water-gauge, *n.* instrument showing height of water in boiler etc.

water-glass, *n.* tube with glass end for observing objects under water; water-clock; solution of sodium silicate used for preserving eggs etc.

water-hen, *n.* moorhen.

watering-can, watering-pot, *nn.* can with perforated nozzle for watering plants. **watering-cart,** *n.* cart for spraying roads. **watering-place,** *n.* seaside resort; spa; animal's drinking-pool.

water-jacket, *n.* water-filled case round engine to prevent overheating.

water-lily, *n.* water-plant with large flat floating leaves.

water-line, *n.* line up to which ship's hull is submerged.

waterlogged, *a.* saturated or filled with water so as barely to float.

waterman, *n.* boatman plying for hire; oarsman. **watermanship,** *n.*

watermark, *n.* faint translucent design in paper, showing maker etc.—*v.t.* mark with this.

water-ouzel, water-ousel, *n.* **dipper.**

water-plane, *n.* seaplane.

waterproof, *a.* not allowing water to pass through.—*n.* waterproof coat or cloth.—*v.t.* make waterproof.

watershed, *n.* ridge or line separating two river systems, divide.

water-shoot, *n.* pipe, gutter, discharging water from roof.

water-skin, *n.* skin bag for carrying water.

waterspout, *n.* whirling column of water reaching from sea to cloud.

watertight, *a.* fitting tightly enough to prevent water from entering.

water-tower, *n.* tower with tank raised to give pressure for water-supply.

water-wagon, *n.* cart for conveying water. **on the w.,** (*sl.*) teetotal.

waterway, *n.* navigable river, canal.

water-wings, *n.pl.* floats attached to shoulders for teaching swimming.

water-work, *n.* (*Shake.*) water-colour.

waterworks, *n*, reservoirs, pipes, buildings etc. of public water-supply; (*sl.*) tears.

watery, *a.* of, like, water; soppy, sodden; tearful; rainy-looking; thin, weak, insipid; (*Shake.*) desirous.

watt, *n.* unit of electric power, work done by current of 1 ampere at pressure of 1 volt (746 watts=1 horsepower). (James *Watt*)

wattle, *n.* interwoven twigs; hurdle made of these; Australian acacia with golden flower used as national emblem.—*v.t.* interweave (twigs); make, enclose, with wattle. (O.E. *watul*)

wattle, *n.* fleshy excrescence on neck of turkey etc. **w.-bird,** *n.* Australian honey-bird. **wattled,** *a.*

wattmeter, *n.* instrument for measuring electric power in watts.

waught, waucht, *n.* (*Scot.*) large draught. (Gael. *cuach,* cup)

wauk, same as **walk.**

wauk, *Scot.* form of **wake.**

waul, *v.i.* squall, cry like cat. (imit.)

wave, *v.i.* and *t.* move to and fro, flutter; form series of curves (in), undulate; signal with hand, beckon. —*n.* waving movement or gesture; moving ridge on water; undulation, wide curve; gust, rush; (*physics*) periodic disturbance, oscillation, in any medium; (*pl.*) sea. **w. aside,** dismiss as irrelevant. **w.-length,** *n.* distance between crests of two successive waves. **w.-meter,** *n.* (*wireless*) instrument for measuring wavelengths. **w.-offering,** *n.* ancient Jewish offering waved to four points of compass. **wavelet,** *n.* ripple. (O.E. *wafian*)

waver, *v.i.* move unsteadily, flutter; vacillate, be irresolute; falter. **waverer,** *n.* (*wave*)

wavy, wavey, *n.* snow-goose. (Amer. Ind. *wawa*)

wavy, *a.* showing wave-like curves, undulating.

wawl, same as **waul.**

wax, *n.* plastic yellow substance secreted by bees; substance like this, sealing-wax, cobbler's wax.—*a.* made of wax.—*v.t.* coat, treat, polish, with wax. **w.-cloth,** *n.* oilcloth. **w.-light,** *n.* wax candle, taper. **waxbill, waxwing,** *nn.* kinds of small bird. **waxen,** *a.* made of wax; smooth, colourless, plastic, like wax; impressionable. **waxwork,** *n.* figure modelled in wax; (*pl.*) exhibition of these. **waxy,** *a.* like wax. (O.E. *weax*)

wax, *v.i.* increase, grow; become; (of moon) show larger illuminated surface. **waxen,** *v.i.* (*Shake.*) increase. (O.E. *weaxan*)

wax, *n.* (*school sl.*) rage. **waxy,** *a.*

way, *n.* road, path; route; direction; distance; progress; clear passage; momentum; method; habit; manner; respect; line; condition; state of agitation; (*Shake.*) scope; (*pl.*) wooden structure down which ship is launched. **by the w.,** during journey; incidentally. **by w. of,** via; to serve for. **each w.,** (of bet on horse) for win and for place. **get, have, one's w.,** get what one wants. **go one's w.,** depart. **in a w.,** in some respects. **in the family w.,** pregnant. **in the w.,** obstructing. **on the w.,** in progress. **out of the w.,** so as not to obstruct; remote; unusual. **under w.,** in motion. **w. of the Cross,** series of pictures representing Christ's progress to Calvary. **w.-bill,** *n.* list of goods in conveyance. **w.-board,** *n.* thin seam of rock between thicker strata. **w.-leave,** *n.* rented right of way. **w.-station, w.-train,** *nn.* (*Amer.*) intermediate station, train stopping at such. (O.E. *weg*)

'way, way, *adv.* (*Amer. colloq.*) away.

wayfarer, *n.* traveller, esp. on foot. **wayfaring-tree,** *n.* shrub with white flowers and black berries.

waylay, *v.t.* (*past, p.p.* **waylaid**) lie in wait for, esp. to rob or interview; ambush. (*way; lay*)

wayment, *v.t.* and *i.* (*Spens.*) lament, grieve.—*n.* (*Spens.*) lamentation. (O.F. *waimenter*)

wayside, *n.* side of road.

wayward, *a.* wilful, perverse; capricious. (*away; -ward*)

wayzgoose, *n.* annual dinner or outing of printing-house employees.

we, see **I.**

weak, *a.* lacking strength and vigour; feeble, sickly; fragile; easily overcome or influenced; deficient, ineffective; much diluted; (of verb) forming past by addition of *d* or *t,* not vowel-change. **w. ending,** ending of verse in unstressed word after which pause is unnatural. **w.-headed,** *a.* mentally deficient. **w.-kneed,** *a.* lacking determination. **weaker sex,** women. **weaken,** *v.t.* and *i.* make, become, weak or weaker. **weakling,** *n.* feeble creature. **weakly,** *a.* not robust, sickly. **weakness,** *n.* being weak; infirmity; weak point; flaw, failing; fondness. (O.N. *veikr*)

weal, *n.* prosperity, welfare. (O.E. *wela,* wealth)

weal, see **wale.**

wealden, *a.* of the Weald, district between N. and S. Downs.—*n.* (*geol.*) series of lower Cretaceous strata.

wealth, *n.* abundance, profusion; riches; (*arch.*) welfare. **wealthy,** *a.* (*weal*)

wean, *n.* (*Scot.*) child. (*wee ane*)

wean, *v.t.* accustom to food other than mother's milk; reclaim (from habit). **weanling,** *a.* and *n.* newly weaned (child). (O.E. *wenian,* accustom)

weapon, *n.* instrument, means, of attack or defence, thing to fight with. (O.E. *wǣpen*)

wear, *v.t.* and *i* (*past* **wore,** *p.p.* **worn**) have on as garment or ornament; exhibit, bear; impair, be impaired, by use; make by rubbing; exhaust; stand hard usage; pass gradually.—*n.* wearing, usage; things worn. **w. and tear,** deterioration due to use. **w.**

away, remove by friction; pass. **w. down,** reduce; overcome by degrees. **w. off,** rub, pass, off. **w. out,** wear, be worn, till beyond use; exhaust, harass. (O.E. *werian*)
wear, *v.t.* and *i.* (*past, p.p.* **wore**) bring (ship) about, come about, by putting helm up, thus presenting stern to wind (opp. to tack).
wear, same as **weir.**
wearish, *a.* (*Spens.*) wizened.
weary, *a.* tired; bored; tedious.—*v.t.* and *i.* make, grow, weary; long (for). **wearisome,** *a.* tedious, tiresome. (O.E. *wérig*)
weasand, *n.* (*arch.*) windpipe. **slit w.,** cut throat. (O.E. *wásend*)
weasel, *n.* small reddish-brown short-legged flesh-eating animal. **w.-faced,** *a.* with lean sharp face. (O.E. *wesle*)
weather, *n.* atmospheric conditions; (*Shake.*) storm.—*v.t.* and *i.* wear, become worn, by atmospheric action; season; sail to windward of (cape); get safely through (storm).—*a.* windward. **have w. gauge of,** be to windward of; have advantage over. **keep one's w. eye open,** be on the alert. **make heavy w. of,** have difficulty with. **under the w.,** depressed, out of sorts. **w.-beaten,** *a.* marked by exposure; (of face) tanned and roughened. **w.-boards, w.-boarding,** *nn.* wall-covering of overlapping boards to throw off rain. **w.-bound,** *a.* detained by bad weather. **w.-bureau,** *n.* meteorological office. **w.-fend,** *v.t.* (*Shake.*) protect from weather. **w.-glass,** *n.* barometer. **w.-moulding,** *n.* dripstone. **w.-vane,** *n.* weathercock. **w.-wise,** *a.* good at forecasting weather. **weathercock,** *n.* pivoted figure or pointer showing direction of wind; fickle person. **weatherly,** *a.* able to sail close to wind, making little leeway. (O.E. *weder*)
weave, *v.t.* and *i.* (*past* **wove,** *p.p.* **woven** or **wove**) intertwine (threads), make (fabric), on loom; plait, construct, fashion; (*Amer.*) move in intricate course, wind.—*n.* style of weaving. **wove paper,** with uniform unlined surface. **weaver,** *n.* worker of loom; (also **weaver-bird**) bird with textile nest. (O.E. *wefan*)
weazen, see **wizened.**
web, *n.* woven fabric; spider's network of threads; membrane between toes of duck etc.; large roll of printing-paper. **w.-footed, webbed,** *aa.* with web between toes. **webbing,** *n.* strong narrow woven fabric of hemp etc. (O.E. *webb*)
wed, *v.t.* and *i.* (*past* **wedded,** *p.p.* **wedded** or **wed**) marry; unite, combine. **wedded,** *a.* of marriage; devoted (to art etc.). (O.E. *wedd,* pledge)
wedding, *n.* marriage ceremony. **tin, silver, golden, diamond, w.,** 10th, 25th, 50th, 60th, anniversary of wedding. **penny w.,** where guests paid for entertainment. **w. breakfast,** meal for wedding-party after ceremony. **w.-cake,** *n.* ornate cake at this. **w.-ring,** *n.* ring used at wedding and worn by married woman.
wedge, *n.* piece of wood or metal tapering to thin edge; wedge-shaped thing.—*v.t.* fix, compress, force apart, split, with wedge; squeeze (in). **thin end of the w.,** slight change or event which is precursor of big ones. (O.E. *wecg*)
Wedgwood, *n.* kind of pottery. (person)
wedlock, *n.* married state, matrimony. (O.E. *wedd,* pledge; *lác,* action)
Wednesday, *n.* fourth day of week. (*Woden,* Teutonic god)
wee, *a.* (*compar.* **wee-er,** *superl.* **wee-est**) small, tiny. **W. Frees,** nickname for part of Free Church of Scotland that refused to join United Free Church in 1900. (M.E. *we,* bit)
weed, *n.* (*Shake.*) garment; (*pl.,* us. **widow's ww.**) widow's mourning garb. (O.E. *wǽd*)
weed, *n.* wild plant growing where it is useless or troublesome; lanky weakly creature; (*colloq.*) cigar; tobacco.—*v.t.* clear (ground) of weeds. **w. out,** remove, eliminate, as unwanted. **weedy,** *a.* full of weeds; lanky, sickly. (O.E. *wéod*)
week, *n.* period of seven days; time from Sunday or Monday to Saturday inclusive. **today, tomorrow, Tuesday, w.,** a week from today etc. **weekday,** *n.* any day but Sunday. **w.-end,** *n.* Friday or Saturday to Monday.—*v.t.* spend this. **weekly,** *a.* and *adv.* (done, happening, published) once a week.—*n.* weekly paper. (O.E. *wice*)
weel, *n.* (*Scot.*) whirlpool.
weel, Scot. form of **well.**
weem, *n.* (*Scot.*) underground dwelling.
ween, *v.t.* (*arch.*) think, trow; expect. (O.E. *wénan*)
weep, *v.i.* and *t.* (*past, p.p.* **wept**) shed tears (for), lament; exude (moisture), drip. **weeper,** *n.* hired mourner; hat-sash, veil, of crape; (*pl.*) widow's white cuffs. **weeping,** *a.* (of tree) with drooping branches. (O.E. *wépan,* cry aloud)
weet, *obs.* form of **wit.**
weever, *n.* kinds of fish with poisonous spines. (O.F. *wivre*)
weevil, *n.* kinds of small beetle. **weevily, weevilly,** *a.* (O.E. *wifel*)
weft, *n.* threads crossing warp, woof; web. (O.E. *wefta*)
weft, (*naut.*) same as **waft.**
weigh, *v.t.* and *i.* find weight of; have as weight; ponder, consider critically; press; count. **under w.,** corrupt. of **under way. w. anchor,** raise anchor; start voyage. **w. down,** press down; depress; outweigh. **w. out,** apportion by weight. **weighbridge,** *n.* machine for weighing carts with their loads. **weight,** *n.* heaviness;

amount of this; burden, load; value, significance; mode of weighing; lump of metal as standard for weighing.—*v.t.* make heavy; burden (with). **weighty,** *a.* heavy; influential; important, momentous. (O.E. *wegan,* carry)

weir, *n.* river-dam; fish-trap of stakes in stream. (O.E. *wer*)

weird, *a.* connected with fate; unearthly, uncanny; odd, queer.—*n.* (*arch.*) destiny. **dree one's w.,** (*Scot.*) abide one's fate. (O.E. *wyrd,* fate)

Weismannism, *n.* theory of heredity which denies transmission of acquired characteristics. (**A.** *Weismann*)

welch, see **welsh.**

Welch, old form of **Welsh.**

welcome, *a.* received with pleasure; acceptable; freely permitted (to).—*n.* kind reception or greeting.—*v.t.* receive gladly, be glad of. (O.E. *willa,* pleasure; *cuma,* comer)

weld, *v.t.* and *i.* unite (pieces of metal) by hammering or pressure; join in compact whole.—*n.* welded joint. (O.E. *weallan,* boil)

weld, *n.* herb yielding yellow dye.

welfare, *n.* well-being, prosperity, health. (*well*; *fare*)

welk, *v.i.* (*arch.*) wither, fade. (M.E.)

welkin, *n.* sky, vault of heaven.—*a.* (*Shake.*) sky-blue. (O.E. *wolcen,* cloud)

well, *n.* shaft sunk in ground for water or oil; spring, fount, source; enclosure in ship's hold round pumps; shaft in building for ventilation, lift etc.—*v.i.* spring, gush. (O.E. *wella*)

well, *adv.* (*compar.* **better,** *superl.* **best**) in a good or proper manner, rightly; favourably; satisfactorily; fully, soundly.—*a.* in good health; in satisfactory state; advisable.—*int.* of surprise, resignation etc. **as w.,** in addition; equally. **stand w. with,** be in good graces of. **w. enough,** fairly good. **w. met!** form of greeting. **w. seen in,** (*arch.*) expert in. (O.E. *wel*)

welladay, wellaway, *intt.* (*arch.*) alas. (O.E. *wá lá wá,* woe, lo, woe)

well-advised, *a.* prudent, judicious.

well-appointed, *a.* fully equipped.

well-balanced, *a.* sane, sensible.

wellbeing, *n.* bodily fitness; prosperity.

well-born, *a.* of good family.

well-bred, *a.* having good manners; (of horse etc.) of good stock.

well-connected, *a.* related to people of distinction.

well-dish, *n.* dish with hollow for gravy.

well-disposed, *a.* favourable, feeling kindly (towards).

well-doing, *n.* virtuous actions.

well-favoured, *a.* good-looking.

well-found, *a.* fully equipped.

well-founded, *a.* borne out by facts.

well-head, *n.* spring; coping round well.

well-informed, *a.* having a well-stored mind; having access to best information.

Wellington boots, Wellingtons, *n.pl.* boots reaching to knee. **Wellingtonia,** *n.* kind of Californian pine. (Duke of *Wellington*)

well-judged, *a.* correctly calculated; timely.

well-knit, *a.* compact, sinewy.

well-known, *a.* known to many; celebrated.

well-liking, *a.* (*arch.*) in good condition.

well-made, *a.* shapely.

well-mannered, *a.* having good manners.

well-marked, *a.* distinct, definite.

well-meaning, well-meant, *aa.* acting, done, with good intentions.

wellnigh, *adv.* very nearly.

well-off, *a.* in easy circumstances; lucky.

well-oiled, *a.* flattering; (*sl.*) tipsy.

well-pleasing, *a.* acceptable.

well-read, *a.* having read widely.

well-spoken, *a.* cultured in speech; having pleasing address.

well-spring, *n.* fountain-head.

well-timed, *a.* opportune.

well-to-do, *a.* prosperous, well-off.

well-turned, *a.* neatly expressed.

well-wisher, *n.* one who wishes another well.

well-worn, *a.* threadbare; hackneyed.

welsh, welch, *v.t.* and *i.* (of bookmaker) run off without paying. **welsher, welcher,** *n.*

Welsh, *a.* and *n.* (people, language) of Wales. **W. rabbit,** toasted cheese. **Welshman, Welshwoman,** *nn.* (O.E. *wealh,* foreigner)

welt, *n.* strip of leather between upper and sole of shoe; inflamed stripe, weal. —*v.t.* furnish (shoe) with welt; strike, thrash. (M.E. *welte*)

welter, *v.i.* wallow, roll, be steeped (in).—*n.* turmoil; disorderly mass. (O. Du. *welteren*)

welter, *n.* heavy-weight rider. **w.-race,** *n.* race in which weights are carried as test. **w.-weight,** *n.* (boxing) 9 st. 9 lb. to 10 st. 7 lb., (*Amer.*) to 10 st. 5 lb.

weltpolitik, *n.* foreign policy on grand scale. *weltschmerz,* *n.* weariness with life, pessimism. (G.)

wen, *n.* permanent swelling below skin, formed by cystic tumour. **the Great W.,** London. (O.E. *wenn*)

wen, *n.* old English letter ƿ (w). (O.E. *wenn,* joy, which began with it)

wench, *n.* girl, lass; maidservant; (*arch.*) prostitute.—*v.i.* whore. (O.E. *wencel,* child)

wend, *v.t.* and *i.* direct (one's way); (*arch.*) go. (O.E. *wendan,* turn)

Wensleydale, *n.* kind of cheese. (place)

went, *n.* (*Spens.*) journey; path. (*wend*)

went, see **go.**

wentletrap, *n.* shell-fish with spiral shell. (Du. *wenteltrap,* winding stairs)

wept, see **weep.**
were, wert, see **be.**
werewolf, *n.* (*pl.* **werewolves)** human being turned into wolf either permanently or periodically. (O.E. *wer*, man+*wolf*)
wersh, *a.* (*Scot.*) tasteless; unsalted.
Wertherism, *n.* sickly sentimentality. (name in book by Goethe)
werwolf, same as **werewolf.**
Wesleyan, *a.* and *n.* (member) of sect founded by John Wesley, now united with Methodists. **Wesleyanism,** *n.*
west, *n.* quarter where sun sets; western lands, occident; U.S. west of Mississippi.—*a.* and *adv.* on, to, the west; (of wind) from the west. **go w.,** (*sl.*) die. **W. Country,** south-west England. **W. End,** fashionable part of London, west of Charing Cross. **westering,** *a.* (of sun) nearing the west. **westerly,** *a.* and *adv.* towards the west; (of wind) from the west. **western,** *a.* of, dwelling in, the west. —*n.* westerner. **Western Empire,** western part of later Roman Empire. **Western Church,** Christian Church of this. **westerner,** *n.* native of the west; European. **westernize,** *v.t.* introduce western civilization to. **westing,** *n.* distance sailed westward from given meridian. **westward,** *a.* and *adv.* towards the west. **westwards,** *adv.* (O.E.)
wet, *a.* covered, soaked, moistened, with water or other liquid; rainy; (*sl.*) sloppy, sentimental; (*Amer.*) not prohibiting use of alcohol.—*v.t.* (*past, p.p.* **wetted** or **wet)** make wet; moisten.—*n.* water, wetness; rain; (*sl.*) drink. **w. blanket,** killjoy. **w. dock,** in which ships can float at all states of tide. **w. plate,** (*phot.*) sensitized collodion plate exposed while wet. **w.-nurse,** *n.* woman who suckles another's child. (O.E. *wǽt*)
wether, *n.* castrated ram. (O.E.)
wey, *n.* varying measure of weight; (of wool) 182 lb. (*weigh*)
wha, *Scot.* form of who.
whack, *n.* resounding blow; (*sl.*) share. —*v.t.* and *i.* hit, esp. with stick; (*sl.*) share out. **whacker,** *n.* (*sl*) big specimen; great lie. **whacking,** *a.* (*sl.*) very big. (imit.)
whaisle, *v.i.* (*Scot.*) wheeze.
whale, *n.* large warm-blooded fish-like sea-animal.—*v.i.* hunt whales. **w.-back,** *n.* cargo steamer with rounded upper deck. **w.-boat,** *n.* long boat for whaling, sharp at both ends. **w.-oil,** *n.* got from blubber. **whalebone,** *n.* horny flexible substance from jaw of some whales. **whaler,** *n.* man, ship, employed in whaling. (O.E. *hwæl*)
whale, *v.t.* (*Amer.*) thrash. **whaler,** *n.* (*Amer. sl.*) whopper. **whaling,** *a.* (*Amer. sl*) very big, whacking.
whang, *n.* (*colloq.*) resounding blow.—*v.t.* and *i.* strike, bang; resound. (imit.)
whang, *n.* (*Scot.*) leather thong; chunk. —*v.t.* cut in thick slices; flog.
whangee, *n.* cane of Chinese bamboo. (Chin. *huang*)
whárē, *n.* (*New Zealand*) house. (Maori)
wharf, *n.* (*pl.* **wharves, wharfs)** structure where ships can moor for loading or unloading, quay; (*Shake.*) river-bank.—*v.t.* moor at, store on, wharf. **wharfage,** *n.* accommodation at wharf; wharf dues. **wharfinger,** *n.* owner of wharf. (O.E. *hwearf*)
what, *pron.* which thing; how much; that which; (*Shake.*) who; why.—*a.* which; how great; as much or many as.—*int.* of surprise or (*Shake.*) to call someone. **w. ho!** hail or greeting. **w. of (it)?** what about (it)? **w. 's w.,** truth of the matter. **w. though,** what matter that. **w. time,** (*arch.*) while. **w.-d'ye-call-it, w.'s-its-name,** *nn.* thing one forgets word for. **whaten, whatna,** *aa.* (*Scot.*) what kind of. **whatever,** (*poet.*) **whate'er,** *a.* of any kind, at all.—*pron.* all or any that; no matter what. **whatnot,** *n.* piece of furniture with shelves for knick-knacks. **whatsoever,** (*poet.*) **whatsoe'er,** (*arch.*) **whatso,** emphatic forms of whatever. (O.E. *hwæt*)
whaup, *n.* (*Scot.*) curlew. (imit.)
wheal, *n.* (*dial.*) mine. (Cornish *huel*)
wheal, incorrect form of weal.
wheat, *n.* cereal plant with thick seed-spikes; its seeds, from which bread is made. **w.-grass,** *n.* couch-grass. **wheaten,** *a.* (O.E. *hwǽte*)
wheatear, *n.* a small grey and white bird. (*white*); *arse*)
wheedle, *v.t.* influence, obtain, by flattery; cajole.
wheel, *n.* circular frame with spokes, disk, revolving round centre; steering-wheel, spinning-wheel, bicycle; an ancient instrument of torture; course of fortune; wheeling movement; (*Amer. sl.*) dollar.—*v.t.* and *i.* pull, push, on wheels; cycle; change direction (of) by pivoting; circle; (*Shake.*) roam. **break on the w.,** fasten to wheel and beat with iron bar. **w. of life,** zoetrope. **ww. within ww.,** complication of circumstances. **w.-animalcule,** *n.* rotifer. **w.-base,** distance between front and rear hubs of motor-car. **w.-chair,** *n.* bath-chair. **w.-horse,** *n.* horse in shafts or alongside pole. **w.-lock,** *n.* old gun-lock worked by wheel; gun with this. **wheelbarrow,** *n.* box with single wheel and shafts for pushing. **wheeler,** *n.* wheel-horse; wheelwright. **wheelhouse,** *n.* deck-house for steersman. **wheelman,** *n.* cyclist. **wheelwright,** *n.* maker and repairer of wheels. (O.E. *hwéol*)
wheen, *n.* (*Scot.*) a fair number; a number. (O.E. *hwón*, a little)

wheep, *v.i.* (*Scot.*) fly nimbly.

wheeze, *v.i.* and *t.* breathe hard with whistling sound; utter thus.—*n.* wheezing sound; (*sl.*) joke, anecdote; dodge. **wheezy,** *a.*

whelk, *n.* an edible shell-fish. (O.E. *wioloc*)

whelk, *n.* pimple. (O.E. *hwylca*)

whelm, *v.t.* engulf, submerge.

whelp, *n.* young dog, puppy; cub of lion etc.; ill-bred boy.—*v.i.* and *t.* bring forth (whelps). (O.E. *hwelp*)

when, *adv.* at what time.—*pron.* what time; during which.—*conj.* at the time that; although.—*n.* time, date. **w. as,** (*Shake.*) when. (O.E. *hwanne*)

whence, *adv.* from what place or source; how; from which; to the place from which.—*n.* source. **from w.,** whence. **whencesoever,** *adv.* from whatever place. (O.E. *hwanon*)

whenever, (*poet.*) **whene'er,** *adv.* at whatever time; every time that. **whensoever, whensoe'er,** emphatic forms.

where, *adv.* at or to what place; at or to which.—*pron.* what place.—*n.* scene. **whereabouts,** *adv.* near what place.—*n.* approximate position. **whereas,** *conj.* considering that; while on the contrary. **whereat, whereby, wherefrom, wherein, whereinto, whereof, whereon, whereout, wherethrough, whereto, whereunder, whereunto, wherewith,** *advv.* at, by, from, in, into, of, on, out of, through, to, under, unto, with, what or which. **where'er,** *adv.* (*poet.*) wherever. **wherefore,** *adv.* why; for which reason.—*n.* reason. **whereinsoever, wheresoever,** emphatic forms of wherein, wherever. **whereupon,** *adv.* whereon; after, in consequence of, which. **wherever,** *adv.* at or to whatever place. **wherewithal,** *adv.* (*arch.*) wherewith.—*n.* resources, needful money. (O.E. *hwār*)

wherry, *n.* liquor made from pulp of crab-apples.

wherry, *n.* light shallow rowing-boat; light barge or fishing-boat. **wherryman,** *n.*

whet, *v.t.* sharpen by rubbing, hone; stimulate (appetite).—*n.* whetting; appetizer. (O.E. *hwettan*)

whether, *pron.* (*arch.*) which of two.—*conj.* introducing alternative question or condition. (O.E. *hwæther*)

whetstone, *n.* stone for sharpening tools.

whew, *int.* of dismay or pain.

whey, *n.* watery part of milk separated from curd in making cheese etc. **w.-face,** *n.* pale face or person with one. **w.-faced,** *a.* (O.E. *hwǣg*)

which, *a.* what one (of).—*pron.* which person or thing; that; (*arch.*) who, whom. **whichever,** *a.* and *pron.* any (one) that; whether one or the other. **whichsoever,** emphatic form. (O.E. *hwilc*)

whid, *v.i.* and *n.* (*Scot.*) lie.

whidah-bird, *n.* small African bird with long tail-feathers. (*widow*+ association with town *Whidah*)

whiff, *v.i.* fish with line towing bait near surface.

whiff, *n.* kind of flat-fish.

whiff, *n.* puff, breath; slight odour; light outrigged sculling-boat.—*v.i.* and *t.* puff; emit whiff. **whiffet,** *n.* (*Amer.*) whipper-snapper. **whiffle,** *v.i.* and *t.* blow in gusts, veer about; flutter; vacillate.—*n.* light gust. **whiffler,** *n.* fickle person; officer who cleared the way for procession. **whiffy,** *a.* smelly. (imit.)

Whig, *n.* member of reforming party that preceded Liberals.—*a.* of whigs. **Whiggery, Whiggism,** *nn.* whig principles. **Whiggish,** *a.* (*whiggamore,* nickname of Scottish Covenanters)

whig, *v.i.* (*Scot.*) jog along.

whigmaleerie, *n.* (*Scot.*) knick-knack, fal-lal; whim, fancy.

while, *conj.* during the time that; as long as; although, whereas.—*adv.* during which.—*n.* space of time. **the w.,** in the meantime. **w. away,** pass (time) without tedium. **whiles,** *conj.* (*arch.*) while.—*adv.* (*Scot.*) at times. (O.E. *hwīl*)

whilk, *obs. Scot.* form of which.

whilly, *v.t.* (*Scot.*) cajole. **whilly-whaw,** *v.i.* wheedle.—*n.* cajolery; deceitful flatterer.

whilom, *adv.* (*arch.*) formerly.—*a.* quondam. (*while*)

whilst, *conj.* and *n.* while.

whim, *n.* passing fancy, fad; winch for mine-shaft.

whimbrel, *n.* kind of curlew. (imit.)

whimper, *v.i.* cry feebly or fretfully. —*n.* feeble cry, whine. (imit.)

whimsy, whimsey, *n.* freakish notion, whim.—*a.* full of whims. **whimsical** *a.* capricious, fanciful; quaint, fantastic. **whimsicality,** *n.* **whimwham,** *n.* toy, trifle; whim. (*whim*)

whin, same as **whinstone.**

whin, *n.* gorse, furze.

whinberry, *n.* bilberry. (*wine; berry*)

whinchat, *n.* small song-bird.

whine, *n.* long-drawn plaintive cry; fretful or unmanly complaint.—*v.i.* and *t.* emit whine; utter whiningly. (O.E. *hwinan*)

whinger, *n.* dagger, short sword.

whinny, *v.i.* neigh gently or joyfully. —*n.* whinnying sound. (imit.)

whinstone, whinsill, *nn.* basaltic rock.

whinyard, same as **whinger.**

whip, *v.t.* and *i.* strike, urge, with lash; flog, thrash; beat (eggs) to froth; fish (stream) with fly; snatch, dart; bind (end of rope) with twine; (*sl.*) defeat.—*n.* lash with handle; coachman; whipper-in; M.P. responsible for party discipline, written notice asking members to attend for important division; (also **w.-and-derry**) hoisting tackle of rope and pulley. **w.-hand,** *n.* hand holding whip; mastery. **w.-round,** *n.* appeal among friends for contributions. **whipping-boy,** *n.* boy educated along with prince and taking his punishments. **whipping-post,** *n.* post to which offender was tied to be flogged. **whipping-top,** *n.* top kept spinning by blows of lash. (M.E. *whippen*)

whipcord, *n.* thin tightly twisted cord.

whipper-in, *n.* huntsman who manages hounds.

whipper-snapper, *n.* small child; insignificant but uppish person.

whippet, *n.* racing-dog of greyhound type; fast light tank.

whippoorwill, *n.* American bird allied to nightjar. (imit.)

whippy, *a.* slender and pliant, springy.

whipster, *n.* (*arch.*) whipper-snapper.

whipstock, *n.* handle of whip.

whir, same as **whirr.**

whirl, *v.i.* and *t.* revolve rapidly, spin; swing round and round; go, convey, rapidly; be giddy or confused.—*n.* whirling movement; bewilderment; giddy round. **whirligig,** *n.* spinning toy, teetotum; revolving motion. **whirlpool,** *n.* violent circular current or eddy. **whirlwind,** *n.* circular moving wind-storm. (O.N. *hvirfla*)

whirr, *n.* buzzing or whizzing sound. —*v.i.* make, fly with, this. (imit.)

whish, *v.i.* and *n.* swish, whizz. (imit.)

whisht, same as **whist.**

whisk, *n.* bunch of hair, feathers etc., as brush; small instrument for beating eggs; rapid sweeping motion.—*v.t.* and *i.* flap, flick, twitch; beat up (eggs); move lightly and quickly, dart. **whisker,** *n.* (us. *pl.*) hair on cheeks; bristles at side of mouth of cat etc.

whisky, whiskey, *n.* spirit distilled from fermented grain, esp. barley or (*Amer.*) rye. **whiskified,** *a.* (*joc.*) under the influence of whisky. (Gael. *uisge* beatha, water of life)

whisky, *n.* light two-wheeled vehicle, gig. (*whisk*)

whisper, *v.i.* and *t.* speak or utter softly, without vibration of vocal cords; talk, tell, secretly or furtively; rustle.—*n.* whispering speech or sound; rumour, secret hint. **whispering-gallery,** *n.* in which whisper can be heard at great distance. (O.E. *hwisprian*)

whist, *int.* hush!—*v.i.* be quiet.—*a.* (*arch.*) silent. (imit.)

whist, *n.* card-game for four. **w. drive,** party for **progressive w.,** in which partners are changed after each game. (*whisk,* from sweeping up of tricks)

whistle, *n.* shrill clear sound made by forcing air between lips; similar sound made by bird, wind, instrument, flying missile etc.; instrument for making this.—*v.i.* and *t.* emit, call or signal by, whistle; render (tune) thus. **penny, tin, w.,** tin pipe with six holes giving notes. **wet one's w.,** (*sl.*) have drink. **w. down the wind,** (*arch.*) dismiss, abandon. **w. for,** wish vainly for. **whistler,** *n.* kinds of bird; mountain marmot; broken-winded horse. (O.E. *hwistle*)

whit, *n.* smallest particle, jot. (O.E. *wiht*)

Whit, see **Whitsunday.**

white, *a.* of the colour of snow; pale; transparent, colourless; innocent, stainless; (of magic) beneficent; royalist; (*Amer. sl.*) honest, honourable.—*n.* white colour, part, dress etc.; white man; albuminous part of egg; kinds of butterfly; (*pl.*) leucorrhoea.—*v.t.* (*arch.*) whiten. **bleed w.,** drain of wealth etc. **w. alloy, metal,** imitation of silver. **w. ant,** termite. **w. bear,** polar bear. **w. caps, horses,** foam-crested waves. **w. corpuscle,** leucocyte. **w. heat,** very high temperature; intense passion. **W. House,** U.S. President's residence. **w. lie,** harmless lie, fib. **w. man,** of light-skinned European type; (*colloq.*) honourable or well-bred man. **w. man's burden,** task of leading the world forward. **w. meat,** poultry, rabbits, veal, pork. **w. paper,** report issued by Government. **w. sale,** of linen. **w. scourge,** tuberculosis. **w. sheet,** garb of penitent. **w. slave,** girl entrapped for prostitution. **w. squall,** tropical squall not preceded by clouds. **w. wine,** of clear amber colour. **w.-hot,** *a.* at white heat. **w.-livered,** *a.* cowardly. (O.E. *hwit*)

whitebait, *n.* young of herring, sprat etc., as table delicacy.

whitebeam, *n.* small tree with silvery underleaf. (O.E. *bēam,* tree)

Whitehall, *n.* British Government; departmental government. (street)

whiten, *v.t.* and *i.* make, become, white. **whitening,** *n.* whiting.

whitesmith, *n.* tinsmith; galvanizer of iron.

whitethorn, *n.* hawthorn.

whitewash, *n.* solution of lime or whiting for coating walls etc.; means used to whitewash person; (*darts*) defeat in which loser fails to score.—*v.t.* coat with whitewash; try to clear of imputations or disgrace; rehabilitate (insolvent) by passage through bankruptcy court.

whither, *adv.* to what place; to which. —*n.* destination. **no w.,** (*arch.*) to no place. **whithersoever,** *adv.* to whatever place. **whitherward,** *adv.* in what direction. (O.E. *hwider*)

whiting, *n.* powdered chalk for polishing or whitewashing.

whiting, *n.* small sea-fish of cod family.

whitleather, *n.* leather dressed with alum. (*white*)

whitlow, *n.* abscess on finger, esp. round nail. (*quick*; *flaw*)

Whitsunday, *n.* seventh Sunday after

Easter, commemorating Pentecost. **Whit Monday, Tuesday** etc., following days. **Whitsuntide, Whitsun** or **Whit week**, week containing Whit Sunday. (*white* robes for christenings, common at that season)

whittle, *v.t.* and *i.* slice shavings off, pare; shape thus.—*n.* (*arch.*) butcher's knife. **w. away, down**, reduce bit by bit. (O.E. *thwitan*)

whity, *a.* fairly white, whitish.

whizz, whiz, *n.* humming and hissing sound of flying missile.—*v.i.* make, fly with, whizz. **w.-bang**, *n.* (*army sl.*) kind of shell. (imit.)

who, *pron.* (*objective* **whom**, *possessive* **whose**) what or which person; that. **whoever**, (*poet.*) **whoe'er**, *pron.* whatever person. (O.E. *hwá*)

whoa, see **wo.**

whole, *a.* complete, all of; intact, entire; (*arch.*) sound in health, well. —*n.* total amount; thing complete in itself, organic unity. **go the w. hog**, to do thing thoroughly. **on the w.**, considering everything, to sum up. **w. number**, without fractions, integer. **w.-hearted**, *a.* sincere, single-minded. **w.-hogger**, *n.* thorough-going supporter. **w.-hoofed**, *a.* with uncloven hoofs. **w.-length**, *a.* and *n.* (portrait) including whole figure. **w.-meal**, *a.* made of flour containing all constituents of the grain. **wholesale**, *a.* and *n.* (of, for) sale of goods in bulk to retailers.—*adv.* on wholesale plan; on large scale. **wholesome**, *a.* good for one, healthy; salutary. **wholly**, *adv.* completely; altogether. (O.E. *hál*, hale)

whom, see **who.**

whoop, hoop, *n.* loud cry or shout.—*v.i.* utter whoop. **whooping-cough, hooping-cough**, *n.* infectious disease with paroxysms of coughing. **whoopee**, *n.* (*Amer. sl.*) riotous gaiety. **make whoopee**, (*Amer. sl.*) have gay time. (F. *houper*, shout)

whop, *v.t.* and *i.* beat, thrash; defeat; (*Amer.*) flop, turn suddenly. **whopper**, *n.* (*sl.*) big specimen; great lie. **whopping**, *a.* (*sl.*) very big.

whore, *n.* prostitute; unchaste woman. —*v.i.* fornicate; (*arch.*) practise idolatry. **whoredom**, *n.* fornication. **whoremaster**, *n.* procurer; (also **whoremonger**) fornicator. **whoreson**, *n.* (*Shake.*) bastard.—*a.* base, scurvy. (O.E. *hóre*)

whorl, *n.* circle of leaves or petals springing from one point; single turn of spiral; raised ridge round cylinder, fly of spindle.

whortleberry, *n.* bilberry.

whose, possessive case of **who** and sometimes of **which.**

whosoever, (*poet.*) **whosoe'er**, (*arch.*) **whoso**, emphatic forms of **whoever.**

why, *adv.* for what reason; because of which.—*int.* of surprise, mild protest, or (*Shake.*) to call someone.—*n.* (*pl.* **whys**) reason. **for w.**, (*Shake.*) because. (O.E. *hwí*)

whydah-bird, same as **whidah-bird.**

wich-elm, same as **wych-elm.**

wick, *n.* twisted threads, flat or tubular strip, feeding flame of lamp or candle with oil or grease; strip of gauze inserted in wound to drain it. (O.E. *wéoce*)

wick, *n.* village, place. (L. *vicus*)

wicked, *a.* evil, sinful; malicious; roguish; (*Shake.*) unlucky. (M.E.)

wicken, *n.* rowan tree.

wicker, *n.* fabric of plaited twigs used to make baskets etc.—*a.* of this. **w.-work**, *n.* wicker articles. (M.E. *wiker*, osier)

wicket, *n.* small door or gate, esp. at side of or forming part of larger one; turnstile entrance; (*cricket*) three stumps with bails; state of pitch; turn of batsman. **keep w.**, act as **w.-keeper, w.-keep**, *nn.* fieldsman standing immediately behind wicket. **w.-door, w.-gate**, *nn.* wicket. (O.F. *wiket*)

widdershins, same as **withershins.**

wide, *a.* broad; of stated width; fully open; spacious, vast; liberal; far from the mark.—*adv.* at or to many points; with wide interval; astray, aside.—*n.* (also **w. ball**) ball bowled out of batsman's reach. **broke to the w.**, (*colloq.*) absolutely penniless. **w. awake**, fully awake. **w.-awake** *a.* wary, knowing.—*n.* soft wide-brimmed felt hat. **widen**, *v.t.* and *i.* make, become, wide or wider; extend, expand. **widespread**, *a.* widely disseminated. (O.E. *wíd*)

widgeon, *n.* kind of wild duck.

widow, *n.* woman whose husband is dead.—*v.t.* and *i.* make widow or widower; (*poet.*) bereave; (*Shake.*) dower (with); become widow to. **the w.**, (*colloq.*) champagne. **grass w.**, wife temporarily separated from husband. **w.'s cruse**, never-failing supply. **w.'s mite**, humble contribution. **w.'s peak**, hair growing to point in centre of forehead. **widower**, *n.* man whose wife is dead. **widowhood**, *n.* state of being widow; (*Shake.*) estate settled on widow. (O.E. *widwe*)

width, *n.* wideness, breadth.

wield, *v.t.* hold and use; control, sway. (O.E. *wealdan*)

wife, *n.* (*pl.* **wives**) married woman, spouse; (*arch.*) woman. **take to w.**, marry. **old wives' tale**, foolish tradition. **wifehood**, *n.* **wifelike, wifely**, *aa.* befitting a wife. (O.E. *wíf*)

wig, *n.* artificial head of hair. **ww. on the green**, free fight. **wigged**, *a.* wearing a wig. (*periwig*)

wig, *v.t.* rebuke sharply, take to task. **wigging**, *n.*

wigan, *n.* canvas-like fabric used for stiffening. (town)

wigeon, same as **widgeon.**

wiggle, *v.i.* (*colloq.*) waggle; wriggle.
wight, *n.* (*arch.*) person, being. (O.E. *wiht*)
wight, *a.* (*Spens.*) strong, nimble. (O.N. *vigr*, warlike)
wigwag, *v.t.* and *i.* and *n.* (*army sl.*) signal with flags. (*wag*)
wigwam, *n.* Red Indian's conical tent of poles covered with bark, mats, or hides. (Amer. Ind.)
wild, *a.* in natural state, not tamed or cultivated; uncivilized, savage; out of control, disordered; lawless, licentious; stormy; intensely excited, frantic; reckless; random, ill-aimed; (*colloq.*) very angry.—*adv.* without care; at random.—*n.* wilderness, desert. **run w.,** grow without training or control. **w. oats,** youthful excesses. **w.-cat,** *a.* unsound, speculative. **w.-goose chase,** futile enterprise. **w.-wood,** *n.* natural forest-land. (O.E. *wilde*)
wildĕbeest, *n.* gnu. (S. Afr. Du.)
wilder, *v.t.* (*poet.*) bewilder.
wilderness, *n.* wild or waste place, desert; part of garden left wild; unlimited amount (of); (*Shake.*) wildness. **in the w.,** out of political office.
wildfire, *n.* burning liquid used in ancient sea-fights, Greek fire. **like w.,** very rapidly.
wildfowl, *n.* (*pl.* same) game-bird, esp. wild duck.
wilding, *n.* self-sown plant; its fruit.
wile, *n.* stratagem, ruse.—*v.t.* entice, lure. **w. away,** while away. (O.E. *wil*)
wilful, *a.* obstinate, stubborn; wayward; intentional, deliberate. (*will*)
wilily, *adv.* in a wily manner.
will, *v.auxil.* (2*nd sing.* **wilt;** *past* and *conditional* **would,** 2*nd sing.* **wouldest** or **wouldst**) expressing future, intention, habit, or insistence.—*v.t.* and *i.* (*arch.*) wish (to), desire; (*past, p.p.* **willed**) intend, purpose; exercise will; compel by will-power; leave as legacy, bequeath.—*n.* power of choosing or determining; self-control; fixed intention, purpose; disposition towards others; discretion, pleasure; legal document giving person's directions for disposal of his property after death. **have one's w.,** get what one wants. **w. to power,** determination to win power. **with a w.,** heartily. **w.-power,** *n.* strength of will. (O.E. *willan*)
willet, *n.* large N. American wading-bird. (imit. of cry)
willies, *n.pl.* **the w.,** (*sl.*) nervousness, jumpiness.
willing, *a.* not reluctant; ready and eager to help; cheerfully rendered. **willingly,** *adv.* (*will*)
will-o'-the-wisp, *n.* phosphorescent light seen on marshy ground; elusive person or thing. (*Will*, name; *wisp*, bundle of tow as torch)
willow, *n.* waterside tree with pliant branches; its wood; (*colloq.*) cricket-bat. **wear the w.,** mourn for lost lover. **weeping w.,** with drooping branches. **w.-pattern,** *n.* famous Chinese design in blue and white on china. **w.-warbler, w.-wren,** *nn.* bird like chiff-chaff. **willowherb,** *n.* plant with willow-like leaves and purple flowers. **willowy,** *a.* full of willows; supple and slender, lithe. (O.E. *welig*)
willow, willy, *n.* machine for cleaning cotton etc. by beating.—*v.t.* clean with this. (O.E. *wilige*)
willy-nilly, *adv.* whether one likes it or not. (*will*; *nill*)
willy-willy, *n.* (*Austral.*) hurricane; desert dust spiral. (native)
wilt, *v.i.* and *t.* wither; droop, cause to droop.
wilt, see **will.**
Wilton carpet, thick-piled kind. (place)
wily, *a.* crafty, cunning. (*wile*)
wimble, *n.* boring tool, gimlet.—*v.t.* bore with wimble. (M.E. *wimbil*)
wimble, *a.* (*Spens.*) active, nimble. (Swed. *vima*, be giddy)
wimple, *n.* covering worn over head and round cheeks and neck by nuns; winding, ripple.—*v.t.* and *i.* put wimple on, veil; flow in wavelets, meander; (*Spens.*) lie in folds. (O.E. *wimpel*)
win, *v.t.* and *i.* (*past, p.p.* **won**) gain by effort or in contest; reach with effort; achieve victory (in); bring (over), persuade; (*army sl.*) purloin. —*n.* victory in game. **w. clear, free,** extricate oneself. **w. out,** (*Amer. sl.*) be successful. **w. upon,** gain upon; obtain favour with. (O.E. *winnan*, fight)
win, *v.t.* (*Scot.*) dry by exposure to wind. (*wind*)
wince, *v.i.* start with pain, flinch.—*n.* act of wincing.
wincey, *n.* strong dress-material of wool and cotton. **winceyette,** *n.* similar stuff with less wool.
winch, *n.* machine for hoisting, windlass; crank of wheel or axle. (O.E. *wince*)
Winchester, *n.* (also **W. rifle**) a light repeating rifle. (place in U.S.)
wind, *n.* air in motion, breeze; scent carried on this; lung power, breath; gas in stomach, flatulence; pit of stomach; empty talk; rumour, hint; wind-instruments. —*v.t.* detect by scent; make breathless; rest to recover breath. **break w.,** emit wind through anus. **four ww.,** four cardinal points. **get, put, the w. up,** (*sl.*) be, make, frightened or panicky. **get w. of,** catch scent of; hear rumour of. **how the w. blows,** position of affairs. **in the w.,** being secretly prepared. **in the w.'s eye, in the teeth of the w.,** directly against wind. **like the w.,** very fast. **raise the w.,** (*sl.*) raise funds. **sail close to the w.,** narrowly avoid dishonesty or indecency. **second w.,** recovery of wind after first breathlessness. **take the w. of,** keep

to windward of. **take the w. out of one's sails,** frustrate by anticipation. **take w.,** be divulged. (O.E.)

wind, *v.t.* (*past, p.p.* winded or **wound**) sound call on, blow (horn). (*wind,* air+confusion with *wind,* turn)

wind, *v.i.* and *t.* (*past, p.p.* **wound**) move in curves, meander; turn, twist; insinuate (oneself); twine (round), enwrap; coil or wind up.—*n.* bend; single turn. **w. off,** unwind. **w. ship,** reverse positions of bow and stern. **w. up,** draw up with windlass; coil into ball; tighten spring of (watch etc.); finish, conclude; liquidate (company). **wound up,** in tense state. (O.E. *windan*)

windage, *n.* deflection of bullet etc. by wind; allowance for this; difference between diameter of projectile and bore of gun.

windbag, *n.* wordy or pompous talker.

wind-bound, *a.* unable to sail because of adverse winds.

wind-egg, *n.* imperfect or unfertilized egg.

winder, *n.* winding-apparatus.

windfall, *n.* fruit blown down; piece of good luck, unexpected legacy.

wind-fanner, *n.* windhover, kestrel.

wind-flower, *n.* anemone.

wind-gaul, *n.* puffy swelling on fetlock of horse.

wind-gauge, *n.* instrument measuring force of wind, anemometer.

windhover, *n.* kestrel.

winding, *n.* turn, bend. **in w.,** out of truth, askew. **w.-sheet,** *n.* sheet in which corpse is wrapped, shroud.

wind-instrument, *n.* musical instrument played by blowing or air-current.

windjammer, *n.* (*sl.*) merchant sailing-ship.

windlass, *n.* machine for hoisting or hauling with rope wound on cylinder.—*v.t.* hoist, haul, with this.

windlass, *n.* (*Shake.*) roundabout course.

windlestraw, *n.* dry withered grass-stalk. (O.E. *windelstréaw,* grass for plaiting)

windmill, *n.* mill worked by pressure of wind on sails. **w. plane,** aeroplane supported by vanes revolving horizontally.

window, *n.* opening in wall to admit light; frame, glass, in this.—*v.t.* (*Shake.*) place in window; make rents in. **w. envelope,** with transparent panel to let address be seen. **w.-box,** *n.* casing for sash-weights; box on window-sill for growing flowers. **w.-dressing,** *n.* arranging goods in shop window; specious display. **w.-seat,** *n.* seat in recess of window. **w.-shopping,** *n.* gazing at shop windows without buying. (O.N. *vindr,* wind; *auga,* eye)

windpipe, *n.* air-passage from mouth to lungs.

wind-rose, *n.* diagram of relative frequency of different winds at a place.

windrow, *n.* heaped row of hay etc. left to dry in wind.

wind-sail, *n.* canvas tube for ventilating lower parts of ship.

windscreen, *n.* glass screen in front of motor-car driver.

Windsor, *n.* residence and name of British royal family. **W. chair,** strong polished wooden chair with curved back. **W. soap,** brown scented kind.

wind-stick, *n.* (*sl.*) propeller of aeroplane.

windward, *a.* and *n.* (side) facing wind. —*adv.* to windward.

windy, *a.* exposed to, swept by, wind; wordy, empty; boastful; flatulent; (*arch.*) windward; (*sl.*) nervous, scared.

wine, *n.* fermented grape-juice; liquor made from other fruits; dark-red colour; (*med.*) solution of drug in wine; (*sl.*) small evening party.—*v.i.* drink wine, esp. to excess. **w.-cooler,** *n.* vessel in which wine-bottles are cooled with ice. **winebibber,** *n.* tippler, drunkard. **winebibbing,** *a.* and *n.* **wineglass,** *n.* glass for drinking wine. **wineglassful,** *n.* about 4 tablespoonfuls. **winepress,** *n.* for pressing juice from grapes. **winesap,** *n.* a large red American apple. **wineskin,** *n.* whole skin of goat etc. used to hold wine. (L. *vinum*)

wing, *n.* limb with which bird flies; appendage like this; flight; side extension of building; side division of army, team etc.; front-wheel mudguard of motor-car; (*aviation*) part of main plane to one side of body; (*pl.*) sides of stage; R.A.F. pilot's badge. —*v.t.* and *i.* furnish with wings; impel in flight; fly (through); wound in wing or arm, disable. **on the w.,** flying; departing. **take under one's w.,** treat as protégé. **take w.,** fly away. **w.-case, w.-sheath,** *nn.* horny cover protecting insect's wing. **w.-commander,** *n.* R.A.F. officer above squadron-leader. **w.-footed,** *a.* (*poet.*) swift. **winged words,** eloquent language. **winglet,** *n.* small wing. (O.N. *vængr*)

wink, *v.t.* and *i.* rapidly close and open (one or both eyes), blink; give hint or sign by wink; affect not to notice, connive (at); (of star) twinkle.—*n.* act of winking. **forty ww.,** short nap. **tip the w.,** (*sl.*) give hint (to). **like winking,** very quickly. (O.E. *wincian*)

winkle, *n.* edible sea-snail. (*periwinkle*)

winna, *Scot.* form of **will not.**

winner, *n.* one who wins.

winning, *a.* victorious; giving victory; attractive, engaging.—*n.pl.* amount won. **w.-post,** *n.* marking end of race-course.

winnock, *n.* (*Scot.*) window.

winnow, *v.t.* separate (grain) from

chaff by fanning; fan; **sift, examine,** sort. (O.E. *windwian*)

winsome, *a.* sweet and charming, having winning ways. (O.E. *wynn*, joy)

winter, *n.* bracket hooking on front of grate for kettle etc.

winter, *n.* cold season from November or December to February; (*astron.*) 22nd December to 20th March; (*poet.*) year of life.—*a.* of winter.—*v.i.* and *t.* spend winter (in); keep, feed, during winter. **w. garden,** large conservatory. **w. quarters,** where troops retire for winter. **w.-green,** *n.* an evergreen plant; its oil, used for flavouring. **w.-ground.** *v.t.* (*Shake.*) protect from winter. **w.-tide,** *n.* (*poet.*) winter. (O.E.)

wintle, *v.i.* and *n.* (*Scot.*) stagger.

wintry, *a.* typical of winter, cold, stormy, snowy; unfriendly, frigid.

winy, *a.* like wine.

winze, *n.* small ventilating shaft in mine.

winze, *n.* (*Scot.*) curse.

wipe, *v.t.* and *i.* rub gently to clean or dry; clear (away), mop (up); (*sl.*) aim sweeping blow (at).—*n.* act of wiping; (*sl.*) sweeping blow; gibe; (*vulg. sl.*) handkerchief. **w. out,** erase; annihilate. **w. person's eye,** (*sl.*) shoot game that he has missed; steal march on him. **w. the floor with,** (*sl.*) defeat utterly. (O.E. *wipian*)

wire, *n.* metallic thread or tape; telegraphy; telegram.—*a.* made of wire. —*v.t.* and *i.* furnish, fasten, stiffen, with wire; snare; telegraph (to); (*croquet*) obstruct by wire of hoop. **live w.,** wire charged with electricity; forceful person. **pull ww.,** work puppets; use secret influence. **w. entanglement,** obstruction of barbed wire. **w. in,** (*sl.*) set to work vigorously. **w. netting,** fabric of thin wire mesh. **w. rope,** made of wire strands. **w.-haired,** *a.* with short stiff hair. **w.-worm,** *n.* a plant-pest. **wiredraw,** *v.t.* draw out into wire; treat over-subtly, make fine-spun. **wirepuller,** *n.* intriguer. (O.E. *wir*)

wireless, *a.* without wires; of, for, by, radio.—*n.* wireless telegraphy or telephony; message sent by these; radio apparatus.—*v.i.* and *t.* send wireless message (to).

wiry, *a.* flexible and strong; lean and sinewy, capable of endurance; (*poet.*) made of wire. **wirily,** *adv.*

wis, *v.i.* (*arch.*) know, ween. (M.E. *iwis*, certainly, wrongly taken as *I wis*)

wisdom, *n.* knowledge rightly applied, sound judgment, sagacity; (*arch.*) learning. **w.-tooth,** *n.* third molar, us. cut about 20th year. (*wise*)

wise, *a.* having or showing wisdom, sagacious, sensible; informed; oracular; (*arch.*) having occult knowledge. **put person w.,** (*Amer.*) inform him. **w. woman,** fortune-teller; witch; midwife. **w.-crack,** *n.* (*Amer.*) short pithy saying, epigram.—*v.i.* utter one. (O.E. *wis*)

wise, *n.* way, manner.—*v.t.* (*Scot.*) guide. (O.E. *wise*)

-wise, *adv.suf.* in the manner of, arranged like, as in **lengthwise, clockwise.**

wiseacre, *n.* foolish pretender to wisdom. (O.H.G. *wizago*, seer)

wish, *v.i.* and *t.* desire; want; be inclined; invoke, bid; (*Shake.*) commend.—*n.* desire; thing desired. **wishbone, wishing-bone,** *nn.* forked bone of bird's breast, merrythought. **w.-fulfilment,** *n.* (*psycho-anal.*) fulfilment of desire in dream etc. **wishful,** *a.* desirous. **wishful thinking,** belief based on wishes, not facts. (O.E. *wýscan*)

wish-wash, *n.* thin weak drink, slop. **wishy-washy,** *a.* thin, sloppy. (*wash*)

wisp, *n.* small bundle of straw or hay; thin straggly lock of hair; flock (of snipe). **wispy,** *a.*

wist, see **wit.**

wistaria, wisteria, *n.* mauve-flowered climbing shrub. (C. *Wistar*)

wistful, *a.* sadly longing, yearning; pensive.

wit, *n.* mind, intellect, understanding; mental quickness, inventiveness; amusing ingenuity of speech or ideas; witty person; (*arch.*) man of genius; (us. *pl.*) mental faculty.—*v.t.* and *i.* (*arch.*; *pres.* **wot,** *2nd sing.* **wottest;** *past* **wist;** *pres. part.* **witting**) know. **at one's ww.'s end,** utterly perplexed. **live by one's ww.,** in haphazard manner by any shift. **out of one's ww.,** mad. **the five ww.,** the five senses. **to w.,** namely. (O.E.)

witan, *n.pl.* members of witenagemot. (O.E. *wita*, wise man)

witch, *n.* woman using magic, female sorcerer; hag, crone; fascinating girl; (*Shake.*) wizard.—*v.t.* (*poet.*) cast spell over. **w.-doctor,** *n.* magician of savage tribe, medicine-man. **witchcraft,** *n.* sorcery, use of magic. **witchery,** *n.* witchcraft; fascination. (O.E. *wicca*, wizard)

witch-hazel, *n.* yellow-flowered American shrub; astringent extract from its bark. **witch-elm,** same as **wych-elm.** (O.E. *wican*, bend)

wite, same as **wyte.**

witenagemot, *n.* ancient national council of Anglo-Saxons. (O.E. *wita*, wise man; *gemót*, meeting)

with, *prep.* in company or possession of; on the side of; in opposition to; in relation to; by means of, through; at same time as; despite. **w. child,** young, pregnant. **w. that,** thereupon. **withal,** *adv.* (*arch.*) moreover, as well. —*prep.* (*arch.*) with. (O.E.)

withdraw, *v.t.* and *i.* (*past* **withdrew,** *p.p.* **withdrawn**) draw back, pull aside; remove, recall; discontinue; retire. **withdrawal,** *n.* **withdrawing-**

room, *n.* (*arch.*) drawing-room. (*with*, against+*draw*)
withe, withy, *n.* (*pl.* **withes, withs**) flexible twig used for tying up faggots etc. (O.E. *withthe*)
wither, *v.i.* and *t.* dry or shrivel up, fade; decline, languish; blight, blast; rebuff. (M.E. *widren*, expose to weather)
withers, *n.pl.* ridge between horse's shoulder-blades. **his w. are unwrung,** imputation does not affect him. (O.E. *wither*, against, as taking strain of collar)
withershins, *adv.* in opposite direction to sun's course; counter-clockwise. (O.N. *vithra*, against; *sinni*, journey)
withhold, *v.t.* (*past, p.p.* **withheld**) keep back, restrain; refuse to give. (*with*, against+*hold*)
within, *prep.* inside; inside limit of, not beyond; not transgressing.—*n.* the interior.—*adv.* (*arch.*) inside, inwardly; indoors. **w. call,** not too far to hear call. (*with*; *in*)
without, *prep.* not having; free from; in absence of; (*arch.*) outside.—*n.* the exterior. — *adv.* outside, externally; out of doors.—*conj.* (*arch.*) unless. **do w.,** dispense with. (*with*; *out*)
withstand, *v.t.* and *i.* (*past, p.p.* **withstood**) oppose, resist; hold out against. (*with*, against+*stand*)
withy, see **withe.**
witless, *a.* silly; thoughtless.
witling, *n.* one who has little wit; would-be witty person. (*wit*+dim.)
witness, *n.* person giving evidence under oath; person attesting another's signature to document; one who sees something, spectator; person or thing furnishing proof, testimony.—*v.t.* and *i.* give evidence (of), testify; be spectator of; sign (document) as witness to its authenticity. **bear w.,** testify. **with a w.,** (*Shake.*) with a vengeance. **w.-box,** *n.* enclosure for witness in law-court. (*wit*)
witticism, *n.* witty remark. **wittily,** *adv.* in a witty manner. **wittiness,** *n.*
wittingly, *adv.* with knowledge of what one is doing. (*wit*)
wittol, *n.* (*arch.*) husband who condones wife's unfaithfulness, complaisant cuckold. **wittolly,** *a.* (*Shake.*).
witty, *a.* having or showing wit, cleverly facetious.
wive, *v.t.* and *i.* (of man) marry. (*wife*)
wivern, same as **wyvern.**
wiz, *n.* (*Amer. sl.*) expert.
wizard, *n.* magician, sorcerer; conjurer; one who works wonders. genius.—*a.* (*sl.*) ingenious; marvellous. **W. of the North,** Sir Walter Scott. **wizardry,** *n.* sorcery. (*wise*)
wizened, wizen, weazen, *a.* dried-up, shrivelled. (O.E. *wisnian*, become dry)
wizier, same as **vizier.**
wo, whoa, *int.* to stop horse. **w.-back,** *int.* to back horse.
wo, see **woe.**
woad, *n.* a blue dye; yellow-flowered plant yielding it.—*v.t.* dye with woad. (O.E. *wád*)
wobble, *v.i.* go unsteadily, sway, rock; waver, vacillate.—*n.* wobbling motion, swerve.
woe, wo, *n.* sorrow, grief; trouble, affliction. **w. be to, w. worth,** cursed be. **w. is me,** alas. **woebegone, wobegone,** *a.* doleful, dismal-looking. **woeful, woful,** *a.* full of woe, sad; bringing calamity; wretched. (O.E. *wá*, cry of grief)
woke, woken, see **wake.**
wold, *n.* open uncultivated tract, down or moor land. (O.E. *wald*, wood)
wolf, *n.* (*pl.* **wolves**) wild animal of dog family hunting in packs; rapacious or greedy person.—*v.t.* devour ravenously, gulp (down). **cry w.,** raise false alarm. **keep w. from the door,** avert hunger or want. **w. in sheep's clothing,** hypocrite. **w.-cub,** *n.* young wolf; junior Boy Scout. **w.-hound,** *n.* borzoi; Alsatian. **w.-spider** *n.* tarantula. **w.'s-bane,** *n.* aconite. **w.'s-foot,** *n.* club-moss. (O.E. *wulf*)
wolfram, *n.* wolframite; tungsten. **wolframite,** *n.* an important ore of tungsten. (G.)
wolverine, wolverene, *n.* shaggy-furred American animal of weasel family, carcajou, glutton. (*wolf*+dim.)
woman, *n.* (*pl.* **women**) human female; female servant; womankind; feminine emotions.—*v.t.* cause to behave like a woman. **kept w.,** mistress. **old w.,** fussy person. **w. of the town,** whore. **w. of the world,** one experienced in society. **w.-hater,** *n.* man with aversion to women. **w.-tired,** *a.* (*Shake.*) henpecked. **womanhood,** *n.* female maturity; womanly character. **womanish,** *a.* effeminate, unmanly. **womanize,** *v.t.* and *i.* make womanish; go with prostitutes. **womankind,** *n.* women collectively; women of a household. **womanlike,** *a.* like a woman. **womanly,** *a.* having the qualities befitting a woman; not girlish; feminine. **womenkind, womenfolk,** *nn.* womankind. (O.E. *wif*, woman; *man*, person)
womb, *n.* female organ in which offspring are developed till birth, uterus; womb-like cavity, place where something is produced; (*obs.*) belly —*v.t.* (*Shake.*) enclose. **w. of time,** unknown future. **womby,** *a.* (*Shake.*) hollow. (O.E. *wamb*)
wombat, *n.* Australian burrowing marsupial like small bear. (native)
women, see **woman.**
won, *v.i.* (*Spens.*) dwell; be wont.—*n.* (*Spens.*) abode. (O.E. *wunian*)
won, see **win.**
wonder, *n.* astonishment, admiration, excited by the strange or extraordinary; strange thing; marvel, miracle.

—*v.i.* and *t.* feel wonder, marvel; be astonished (that); be curious to know, speculate. **for a w.**, surprisingly. **no w.**, it is not surprising. **work ww.**, do miracles; succeed remarkably. **w.-struck, w.-stricken,** *aa.* overcome with astonishment. **wonderful,** *a.* very remarkable, marvellous; admirable. **wonderland,** *n.* land of marvels; fairyland. **wonderment,** *n.* wonder. **wondrous,** *a.* wonderful.—*adv.* wonderfully. (O.E. *wundor*)

wonga-wonga, *n.* large Australian pigeon.

wonky, *a.* (*sl.*) shaky, groggy; feeble, out of sorts; unreliable.

wonne, same as **won.**

wont, *a.* accustomed.—*n.* habit.—*v.i.* (*arch.*; *3rd sing.* **wonts** or **wont,** *past* **wonted** or **wont**) be accustomed. **use and w.**, established custom. **wonted,** *a.* habitual. (p.p. of *won*)

won't, *colloq.* for **will not.**

woo, *v.t.* seek hand or love of, court; try to win; solicit eagerly. (O.E. *wógian*)

woobut, *n.* hairy caterpillar, woolly-bear. (*wool*)

wood, *n.* collection of growing trees; solid part of tree, timber; wood-wind; (*bowls*) bowl. **cannot see the w. for the trees,** details impede general view. **in the w.**, in cask, not bottle. **out of the w.**, out of danger. (O.E. *wudu*)

wood, *a.* (*Shake.*) mad. (O.E. *wód*)

woodbine, woodbind, *n.* wild honeysuckle; name of a cheap cigarette; (*Amer.*) Virginia creeper. (from its winding about trees)

wood-carving, *n.* carving in wood.

woodchat, *n.* kind of shrike. (*chat*)

woodchuck, *n.* small brown American rodent, kind of marmot. (corrupt. of Amer. Ind. *wejack*)

woodcock, *n.* game-bird allied to snipe.

woodcraft, *n.* knowledge of forest conditions.

woodcut, *n.* engraving made on wood; print from this. **woodcutter,** *n.* man who cuts wood; wood-engraver.

wooded, *a.* covered with trees.

wooden, *a.* made of wood; stiff, clumsy; expressionless. **w. spoon,** bottom place in competition. **w. walls,** navy. **w.-head,** *n.* dolt. **w.-headed,** *a.*

wood-engraver, *n.* maker of woodcuts.

wood-grouse, *n.* capercailzie.

wood-ibis, *n.* kind of American stork.

woodie, *n.* (*Scot.*) gallows. (*withy*)

woodland, *n.* and *a.* (of) wooded country.

woodlark, *n.* small kind of lark.

wood-leopard, *n.* kind of moth.

wood-louse, *n.* small wingless land crustacean, slater.

woodman, *n.* woodcutter; forester.

wood-note, *n.* (us. *pl.*) song of bird; artless verse.

wood-nymph, *n.* dryad; kinds of humming-bird and moth.

wood-opal, *n.* silicified wood.

woodpecker, *n.* a bird that taps tree-trunks to discover insects.

wood-pie, *n.* great spotted woodpecker.

wood-pigeon, *n.* ringdove.

wood-pulp, *n.* wood-fibre treated for paper-making.

woodruff, *n.* woodland plant with small white fragrant flowers. (O.E. *wudurófe*)

woodshed, *n.* shed for holding firewood.

woodsman, *n.* forest-dweller.

wood-sorrel, *n.* oxalis.

wood-spirit, *n.* methyl alcohol got from wood.

wood-warbler, *n.* a song-bird.

wood-wind, *n.* wooden wind-instruments.

wood-wool, *n.* fine pine shavings.

woodwork, *n.* things made of wood.

wood-wren, *n.* wood-warbler.

woody, *a.* like, made of, wood; wooded; (*rare*) found in woods.

wooer, *n.* suitor.

woof, *n.* threads crossing warp in weaving, weft. (O.E. *ówef*, lit. what is woven on)

wool, *n.* soft hair of sheep, goat etc.; yarn, cloth, of this; soft under-fur; wool-like fibre; (*joc.*) human hair, esp. negro's. **dyed in the w.**, dyed before spinning; out-and-out. **mineral w.**, mass of thread-like substance made from molten slag. **much cry and little w.**, much fuss with little result. **pull w. over person's eyes,** hoodwink him. **w.-fat, w.-oil,** *nn.* lanolin. **w.-grower,** *n.* one who raises sheep for their wool. **w.-sorter,** *n.* one who sorts wool into grades. **w.-sorter's disease,** anthrax. **w.-stapler,** *n.* (*arch.*) wool-merchant. (O.E. *wull*)

woolgathering, *n.* day-dreaming.—*a.* absent-minded.

woollen, *a.* made of wool.—*n.* woollen fabric or garment. **woollenette,** *n.* light woollen fabric.

woolly, *a.* of, like, covered with, wool; indistinct, blurred; muddled.—*n.* sweater; (*pl.*) woollen underwear. **w.-bear,** *n.* caterpillar of tiger-moth.

woolsack, *n.* wool-stuffed cushion on which Lord Chancellor sits; his office.

woolwork, *n.* embroidery in wool.

woorali, woorara, *n.* curare. (native *wurali*)

woot, (*Shake.*) for **wilt thou.**

wootz, *n.* kind of steel made in India.

wop, same as **whop.**

wop, *n.* (*Amer. sl.*) central or south European immigrant, esp. Italian.

word, *n.* oral or written sign expressing idea, unit of speech; talk, discourse; tidings, news; command; promise.—*v.t.* put into words, phrase; (*Shake.*) flatter. **at a w.**, (*Shake.*) in short. **by w. of mouth,** orally. **good w.,**

commendation. **have ww.**, quarrel. **in a w.**, to sum up. **last w.**, latest development; final retort. **my w.!** expression of surprise. **take person at his w.**, assume he means what he says. **the W.**, the Logos, Christ; the Bible. **w. for w.**, literally. **W. of God**, Bible. **w. of honour**, solemn pledge. **w.-book**, *n.* dictionary. **w.-painting**, **w.-picture**, *nn.* vivid verbal description. **w.-perfect**, *a.* able to repeat part etc. by heart without mistake. **w.-play**, *n.* verbal fencing; pun. **w.-splitting**, *n.* subtle verbal distinctions. **w.-square**, *n.* square of words reading same across as downwards. **wordy**, *a.* of, in, words; prolix, verbose. (O.E.)

wore, see **wear.**

work, *n.* labour; task; employment; thing made or done; production of art or science, book; needlework; (*mech.*) exertion of force in overcoming resistance; (*pl.*) mechanism; factory; fortifications; righteous deeds.—*v.i.* and *t.* (*past, p.p.* **worked**, *arch.* **wrought**) toil; operate (in); be employed; ferment; be in agitation; make way, bring, slowly; accomplish, effect; manipulate, shape; excite; embroider, sew; compel to labour. **at w.**, in action. **all in the day's w.**, normal. **give him the ww.**, (*Amer. sl.*) empty gun into, manhandle, him. **have one's w. cut out**, have hard task. **nasty piece of w.**, (*sl.*) objectionable person. **out of w.**, unemployed. **w. in**, find place for; intermix. **w. off**, get rid of gradually. **w. on**, act on; influence. **w. one's passage**, pay for it in work instead of money. **w. out**, plan in detail; solve, calculate, give result; exhaust. **w. up**, stir up; elaborate; study. (O.E. *weorc*)

workable, *a.* capable of working or being worked, practicable. **workability**, *n.*

workaday, *a.* ordinary, commonplace.

workbag, **workbasket**, **workbox**, *nn.* receptacle for sewing-materials.

workday, *n.* day other than Sundays or holidays.

workhouse, *n.* public institution for paupers, poorhouse; (*Amer.*) house of correction for petty offenders.

working, *a.* spent in, used for, work.—*n.* operation; (*pl.*) parts of mine worked. **w. capital, expenses**, funds actually used for carrying on business. **w. day**, workday; hours of day spent in work. **w. class, man**, class, man, engaged in manual labour.

workman, *n.* manual worker; craftsman. **workmanlike**, *a.* showing practised skill. **workmanship**, *n.* technical skill; way thing is made, style.

work-people, *n.* manual workers.

workshop, *n.* place where things are made.

work-shy, *a.* unwilling to work.

workwoman, *n.* female manual worker; needlewoman.

world, *n.* earth and its inhabitants; whole system of things, universe; human race, people in general; scene or course of life; secular affairs; society; sphere, domain; vast amount; planet. **for all the w.**, exactly. **go to the w.**, (*Shake.*) get married. **New W.**, N. and S. America. **not for the w.**, on no account. **Old W.**, Europe, Asia, and Africa. **w. without end**, for ever. **w.-power**, *n.* state whose policy affects the whole world. **worldling**, *n.* worldly person; (*Shake.*) mortal. **worldly**, *a.* earthly, mundane; secular; engrossed in pursuit of wealth and social success. **worldly-wise**, *a.* experienced and cautious. **worldwide**, *a.* spread over, known to, the whole world. (O.E. *weoruld*)

worm, *n.* small limbless creeping snakelike animal; thread of screw; condensing-tube of still; downtrodden or contemptible person; (*Shake.*) serpent; (*pl.*) disease caused by intestinal worms.—*v.t.* and *i.* insinuate (oneself); convey (oneself), make (way), with crawling motion; elicit (secret) by underhand means; rid of worms. **w.-cast**, *n.* earth voided by earthworm. **w.-gear**, *n.* cog-wheel engaging with thread of screw. **w.-fishing**, *n.* angling with worm as bait. **wormeaten**, *a.* full of holes gnawed by worms; old, antiquated. (O.E. *wyrm*, dragon, worm)

wormwood, *n.* bitter herb used in making absinth; bitterness. (O.E. *wermod*)

worn, see **wear.**

worricow, *n.* (*Scot.*) hobgoblin; devil; scarecrow.

worrit, *vulg.* for **worry.**

worry, *v.t.* and *i.* pester, harass; make, be, anxious or uneasy; (of dog) shake and mangle with teeth.—*n.* wearing anxiety, care; cause of this. **I should w.**, (*Amer. colloq.*) I don't care. **w. along**, make way in spite of difficulties. **worriment**, *n.* (O.E. *wyrgan*)

worse, *a.* more bad or ill.—*adv.* more badly.—*n.* worse things. **worsen**, *v.t.* and *i.* make, become, worse. (O.E. *wyrsa*)

worship, *n.* divine honours, reverent homage, paid to deity; religious service; adoration; (*arch.*) worthiness, honour, high repute.—*v.t.* and *i.* honour with religious rites; idolize, adore; attend church service. **his, your, w.**, title of magistrate. **worshipful**, *a.* worthy of honour. **worshipper**, *n.* (=*worth-ship*)

worst, *a.* most bad.—*adv.* most badly.—*n.* worst thing or state.—*v.t.* defeat, beat. **get the w. of it**, be worsted. **if the w. comes to the w.**, if the worst happens. (O.E. *wyrsta*)

worsted, *n.* woollen yarn.—*a.* made of this. (*Worstead* in Norfolk)

wort, *n*. plant, herb. (O.E. *wyrt*)
wort, *n*. infusion of malt before fermentation. (O.E. *wyrt*)
worth, *v.i.* (*arch.*) betide, befall. (O.E. *weorthan*, become)
worth, *a*. of value equal to; deserving, repaying; having possessions amounting to.—*n*. value, price; merit; (coin's) equivalent; (*Shake.*) wealth. **for all one is w.**, (*sl.*) with all one's power. **w. while**, (*sl.*) **w. it**, repaying the trouble spent. **worthless**, *a*. valueless, useless; of bad character. **worthy**, *a*. virtuous, respectable; deserving (of); good enough; befitting; (*Shake.*) valuable; due, legitimate.—*n*. eminent person, local celebrity.—*v.t.* (*Shake.*) make hero of. **worthiness**, *n*. (O.E. *weorth*)
wot, see **wit**.
would, see **will**.
would-be, *a*. and *adv*. aspiring, professing, to be.
wound, see **wind**.
wound, *n*. injury by which skin is broken, cut, stab; injury to feelings, affront; (*poet.*) pangs of love.—*v.t.* inflict wound on; hurt feelings of. **woundy**, *a*. (*arch.*) excessive. (O.E. *wund*)
wourali, same as **woorali**.
wove, woven, see **weave**.
wow, *int*. of astonishment.
wow, *n*. (*Amer. sl.*) great success; thing wonderful of its kind.
wowf, *a*. (*Scot.*) crazy.
wowser, *n*. (*Austral.*) puritanical fanatic.
wow-wow, *n*. gibbon of Java.
wrack, *n*. cast-up seaweed; wreckage; destruction, rack; (*Shake.*) wreck.—*v.t.* (*Shake.*) wreck; ruin. (*wreck*)
wrack, *v.t.* (*Scot.*) tease, vex.
wraith, *n*. apparition of person about to die or just dead; spectre.
wrangle, *v.i.* dispute noisily, brawl.—*n*. noisy altercation. **wrangler**, *n*. brawler; (*Cambridge*) person with first-class honours in mathematics; (*Amer. colloq.*) cowboy; (*Shake.*) adversary. **senior wrangler**, (*Cambridge*) top wrangler of his year.
wrap, *v.t.* and *i*. (*past, p.p.* **wrapped**) cover by winding something round, enfold, envelop; put or draw (covering) round; overlap.—*n*. loose garment, muffler, rug etc., for warmth. **w. up**, wrap; put on wraps. **wrappage**, *n*. wrappings. **wrapper**, *n*. one who, that which, wraps; postal cover for newspaper; book-jacket; light dressing-gown, negligee. **wrapping**, *n*. that in which thing is wrapped.
wrapt, same as **rapt**.
wrasse, *n*. thick-lipped bright-coloured sea-fish. (W. *gwrach*)
wrath, *n*. violent anger; indignation. **children of w.**, persons destined for divine punishment. **wrathful**, (*colloq.*) **wrathy**, *aa*. (*wroth*)
wreak, *v.t.* inflict (vengeance), give play to (hatred etc.); (*arch.*) avenge. (O.E. *wrecan*)
wreath, *n*. flowers, leaves etc., fastened together in circle or string, garland; curl, wisp (of smoke etc.). **wreathe**, *v.t.* and *i*. adorn with, twine into, wreath; clasp, encircle; move, coil, in wreaths. (O.E. *writahn*, twist)
wreck, *n*. destruction or disablement of ship; wrecked ship; ruin, destruction; remains of anything ruined—*v.t.* and *i*. cause wreck of; suffer wreck. **wreckage**, *n*. process of wrecking; remnants from a wreck. **wrecker**, *n*. one who wrecks; one who lures ship to destruction with a view to plunder; one who salvages wrecks. (O.E. *wrecan*, drive)
wren, *n*. kinds of small song-bird. (O.E. *wrenna*)
Wren, *n*. member of Women's Royal Naval Service. (initials)
wrench, *n*. violent twist or pull; sprain; painful separation; tool for turning nuts, spanner.—*v.t.* pull with twist, force violently; sprain, strain, distort. (O.E. *wrencan*, twist)
wrest, *v.t.* force from person's grasp; twist, distort, pervert.—*n*. key for tuning harp. **w.-pin**, *n*. one of the pins to which piano-strings are attached and by turning which piano is tuned. (O.E. *wrǽstan*)
wrestle, *n*. contest in which opponents grapple and try to throw each other down; tussle, hard struggle.—*v.i.* and *t*. engage in wrestle (with); strive, struggle; (*Amer. colloq.*) throw (steer) for branding. **w. in prayer**, pray earnestly. **wrestler**, *n*. (*wrest*)
wretch, *n*. miserable or unfortunate person; vile despicable creature; rogue. **wretched**, *a*. miserable, unhappy; unfortunate, distressing; squalid, mean; poor, inferior. (O.E. *wrecan*, drive)
wrick, rick, *v.t.* sprain or strain slightly.—*n*. such injury.
wriggle, *v.i.* and *t*. twist about, squirm; go, move, with wriggling motion; answer evasively, shuffle.—*n*. act of wriggling. **w. out**, escape by wriggling or cunning. (L.G. *wriggeln*)
wright, *n*. (*arch.*) maker, builder. (O.E. *wyrhta*)
wring, *v.t.* and *i*. (*past, p.p.* **wrung**) squeeze tightly, squeeze and twist; squeeze out, extort; pain; (*Shake.*) wrench; writhe.—*n*. act of wringing. **w. neck of**, kill by twisting neck of. **w. one's hands**, clasp them in grief. **w. out**, squeeze water from (clothes). **wringing wet**, so wet that water can be wrung out. **wringer**, *n*. appliance with rollers for pressing water from clothes. (O.E. *wringan*)
wrinkle, *n*. crease or furrow on skin, cloth etc.—*v.t.* and *i*. crease, pucker.
wrinkle, *n*. useful tip, dodge.
wrist, *n*. joint between arm and hand;

wrist-pin. **w.-drop,** *n.* paralysis of forearm muscles from lead poisoning. **w.-pin,** *n.* pin on which connecting-rod turns. **w.-watch, wristlet-watch,** *nn.* watch worn on wrist. **wristband,** *n.* cuff of shirt. **wristlet,** *n.* band worn round wrist for warmth etc. (O.E.)

writ, *n.* written command from law-court or other authority; (*arch.*) what is written. **Holy W.,** the Bible.

write, *v.i.* and *t.* (*past* **wrote,** *arch.* **writ;** *p.p.* **written,** *arch.* **writ**) set down (letters, words) on paper etc.; compose, be author (of); tell, express, in writing; send letter (to); style (oneself); imprint, engrave. **w. down,** record; describe as; disparage in writing. **w. off,** cancel in accounts; send letter. **w. oneself out,** use up all one's ideas in writing. **w. out,** write in full. **w. up,** elaborate details of; criticize favourably. **writ large,** magnified, aggravated. (O.E. *wrītan*)

writer, *n.* penman; author; clerk; manual telling how to write. **w. to the signet,** (*abbr.* **W.S.**) Scottish solicitor. **writership,** *n.*

writhe, *v.i.* and *t.* twist, squirm; contort (body); suffer mental anguish.—*n.* contortion. (O.E. *wrīthan*)

writhle, *v.t.* (*Shake.*) wrinkle.

writing, *n.* written document; authorship; (*pl.*) literary works. **w. on the wall,** sign of impending calamity. **w.-book,** *n.* copy-book. **w.-case,** *n.* case for writing materials. **w.-desk,** *n.* folding box, table, for writing at. **w.-master,** *n.* teacher of penmanship.

written, see **write.**

wrong, *a.* wicked, sinful; incorrect, inaccurate; mistaken; unsuitable.—*adv.* amiss; in wrong direction; with incorrect result.—*n.* evil-doing, wickedness; injustice, injury.—*v.t.* do wrong to, injure; unfairly impute evil to. **get hold of the w. end of the stick,** misapprehend. **get in w.,** (*Amer. colloq.*) get, bring, into disfavour. **go w.,** take wrong path; fall into sin; fail. **in the w.,** at fault, in error. **put one in the w.,** make blame seem his. **w.-headed,** *a.* stubbornly mistaken, perverse. **wrongdoer,** *n.* sinner; offender. **wrongdoing,** *n.* transgression. **wrongful,** *a.* unwarranted, unjust. **wrongous,** *a.* (*Scots law*) illegal. (O.E. *wrang*)

wrote, see **write.**

wroth, *a.* (*arch.*) angry. (O.E. *wrāth*)

wrought, see **work. w. iron,** forged or rolled, not cast.

wrung, see **wring.**

wry, *a.* turned to one side; distorted, crooked.—*v.i.* (*Shake.*) go astray. **w. face,** expressing disgust. **wryly,** *adv.* **wrybill,** *n.* kind of plover. **wryneck,** *n.* small bird allied to woodpecker. (O.E. *wrigian*, incline)

wyandotte, *n.* American breed of fowls. (a Red Indian tribe)

wych-elm, *n.* kind with drooping branches. **wych-hazel,** same as **witch-hazel.** (O.E. *wican*, bend)

wye, *n.* letter Y; Y-shaped thing.

Wykehamist, *n.* member of Winchester College. (William of *Wykeham*, founder)

wynd, *n.* (*Scot.*) narrow lane, alley.

wyte, *n.* (*Scot.*) fault.—*v.t.* blame.

wyvern, *n.* heraldic winged dragon. (L. *vipera*, viper)

X

X, (*math.*) unknown quantity; (*roman numerals*) 10.—*n.* unknown or mysterious factor. **X-rays,** *n.pl.* radiation of very short wave-length, able to penetrate solid bodies.

xanthein, xantheine, *n.* soluble yellow colouring-matter in flowers. (Gk. *xanthos*, yellow)

xanthic, *a.* yellowish. (Gk. *xanthos*, yellow)

xanthin, xanthine, *n.* insoluble yellow colouring-matter in flowers; crystalline compound allied to uric acid. (Gk. *xanthos*, yellow)

Xanthippĕ, *n.* scold, shrew. (wife of Socrates)

xanthite, *n.* kind of yellowish-brown rock. (Gk. *xanthos*, yellow)

xanthóchrōī, *n.pl.* blond blue-eyed races, fair whites. **xanthochroic, xanthochroous,** *aa.* (Gk. *xanthos*, yellow; *chroa*, skin)

xanthoma, *n.* skin-disease causing yellow patches. (Gk. *xanthos*, yellow)

xanthomelanous, *a.* with black hair and yellow, brown, or olive skin. (Gk. *xanthos*, yellow; *melas*, black)

xanthophyll, *n.* yellow colouring-matter of autumn leaves. (Gk. *xanthos*, yellow; *phullon*, leaf)

xanthopsy, xanthopsia, *n.* disturbance in vision causing everything to appear yellow. (Gk. *xanthos*, yellow; *opsis*, sight)

xanthosis, *n.* yellow colour of the skin in cancerous conditions. (Gk. *xanthos*, yellow)

xanthous, *a.* of yellow or Mongolian type. (Gk. *xanthos*, yellow)

Xantippe, same as **Xanthippe.**

xebec, *n.* small three-masted Mediterranean vessel with lateen sails. (F. *chebec*)

xenelasia, *n.* ancient Spartan system

of excluding aliens. (Gk. *xenos*, stranger; *elaunein*, drive)
xenial, *a.* of hospitality or relations between host and guest. (Gk. *xenos*, guest)
xenogamy, *n.* pollination from another plant, cross-fertilization. **xenogamous,** *a.* (Gk. *xenos*, strange; *gamos*, marriage)
xenogenesis, *n.* generation of organism altogether and permanently unlike the parent; heterogenesis. **xenogenetic, xenogenic,** *aa.* (Gk. *xenos*, stranger; *genesis*, birth)
xenogenous, *a.* produced by external agency. (Gk. *xenos*, stranger; *genesis*, birth)
xenolith, *n.* (*geol.*) rock occurring in system of rocks to which it does not belong. (Gk. *xenos*, stranger; *lithos*, stone)
xenomania, *n.* mania for foreign things. (Gk. *xenos*, strange)
xenomorphic, *a.* (of mineral grains in rock) abnormal in shape owing to pressure of adjacent minerals. (Gk. *xenos*, strange; *morphē*, form)
xenon, *n.* a heavy inert gaseous element present in the atmosphere. (Gk. *xenos*, strange)
xenophobia, *n.* fear or hatred of strangers. (Gk. *xenos*, stranger; *phobos*, fear)
xeransis, *n.* drying-up, desiccation. **xerantic,** *a.* (Gk. *xēros*, dry)
xeranthemum, *n.* kinds of plant with everlasting composite flowers. (Gk. *xēros*, dry; *anthos*, flower)
xerasia, *n.* morbid dryness of the hair. (Gk. *xēros*, dry)
xerophilous, *a.* (of plant) drought-loving, adapted to dry climate. (Gk. *xēros*, dry; *philos*, loving)
xerophthalmia, *n.* eye-disease with dryness and ulceration of the cornea. (Gk. *xēros*, dry; *ophthalmos*, eye)
xerophyte, *n.* xerophilous plant. **xerophytic,** *a.* (Gk. *xēros*, dry; *phuton*, plant)
xerostomia, *n.* abnormal dryness of the mouth. (Gk. *xēros*, dry; *stoma*, mouth)
xérotēs, *n.* (*med.*) dryness of body. (Gk.)
xiphias, *n.* genus of fishes incl. swordfish. (Gk. *xiphos*, sword)
xiphisternum, *n.* xiphoid appendage. (Gk. *xiphos*, sword+*sternum*)
xiphoid, *a.* sword-shaped.—*n.* (also **x. appendage**) lower end of sternum. (Gk. *xiphos*, sword)
Xmas, *n.* Christmas. (abbr.)
xoanon, *n.* (*pl.* **xoana**) primitive wooden image of a deity. (Gk.)
xylem, *n.* woody vegetable tissue (opp. to phloem). (Gk. *xulon*, wood)
xylobalsamum, *n.* dried twigs of balm-of-Gilead tree; decoction of them. (Gk. *xulon*, wood. L. *balsamum*, balsam)
xylocarp, *n.* hard woody fruit; tree with this. **xylocarpous,** *a.* (Gk. *xulon*, wood; *karpos*, fruit)
xylograph, *n.* wood-engraving, esp. of early type; representation of wood-grain as decoration. **xylographer,** *n.* wood-engraver. **xylographic,** *a.* **xylography,** *n.* art of wood-engraving. (Gk. *xulon*, wood; *graphein*, write)
xyloid, *a.* like wood; ligneous. **xyloidine,** *n.* explosive like gun-cotton. (Gk. *xulon*, wood; *eidos*, form)
xylonite, *n.* kind of celluloid. (Gk. *xulon*, wood)
xylophagous, *a.* wood-eating. (Gk. *xulon*, wood; *phagein*, eat)
xylophone, *n.* musical instrument consisting of graduated series of wooden bars sounded by small hammers. (Gk. *xulon*, wood; *phōnē*, sound)
xylopyrography, *n.* poker-work. (Gk. *xulon*, wood; *pur*, fire; *graphein*, write)
xylotomous, *a.* (of insect) boring into or cutting wood. (Gk. *xulon*, wood; *temnein*, cut)
xyst, same as **xystus.**
xyster, *n.* surgical instrument for scraping bones. (Gk. *xuein*, scrape)
xystus, *n.* (*pl.* **xysti**) garden walk or terrace; covered portico used by ancient Greek athletes for their exercises. (Gk. *xustos*)

Y

Y, (*math.*) second unknown quantity. —*n.* Y-shaped thing. **Y-gun,** *n.* gun with two firing-arms for discharging depth-charges. **Y-track,** *n.* Y-shaped siding enabling engine to reverse.
y-, *pref.* used with past participle, as in **yclad, yclept.** (O.E. *ge-*)
-y, *adj.suf.* attachable to most nouns, full of, as in **smoky;** like, as in **rosy.** (O.E. *-ig*)
-y, -ie, *suf.* forming diminutive, as in **pussy, lassie.**
yabber, *n.* (*Austral.*) broken English of the aborigines.—*v.i.* and *t.* talk in this.
yabble, *Scot.* form of **gabble.**
yacca, *n.* a W. Indian evergreen tree; its wood. (native)
yacht, *n.* vessel for pleasure-cruising; light sailing-vessel for racing.—*v.i.* cruise, race, in yacht. **y.-club,** *n.* club for yacht-racing. **yachtsman,** *n.* one who yachts. (Du. *jagt*)
yaff, *v.i.* and *n.* (*Scot.*) bark.
yaffle, yaffil, (*dial.*) **yaffingale,** *n.* green woodpecker. (imit. of cry)

yager, *n.* member of certain German corps, esp. of riflemen. (G. *jäger*, hunter)

yah, *int.* of derision.

yahoo, *n.* brutish or bestial person. (race of brutes in human shape in Swift's 'Gulliver's Travels')

Yahveh, Yahweh, same as **Jehovah.**

yak, *n.* long-haired humped ox of Tibet. (Tibetan *gyak*)

yald, same as **yauld.**

yam, *n.* kinds of edible tuber or tropical climbing plant yielding it; sweet potato. (Port. *inhame*)

Yama, *n.* Hindu god of nether world and judge of dead. (Sanskr.)

yamen, yamun, *n.* official residence of Chinese mandarin. (Chin.)

yammer, *v.i.* complain peevishly, whine; wail. (O.E. *geómor*, sad)

yank, *v.t.* and *i.* (*sl.*) pull with hard jerk.—*n.* sudden sharp pull.

Yank, *n.* (*sl.*) Yankee. (abbr.)

Yankee, *n.* and *a.* (inhabitant) of New England or northern U.S.; (*European use*) American. **'Y.-Doodle,'** *n.* a U.S. song. **Yankeedom, Yankeeism,** *nn.*

yaourt, *n.* a fermented liquor made from milk. (Turk. *yoghurt*)

yap, *n.* snappish bark, yelp; (*Amer.*) chatter.—*v.i.* utter yap. (imit.)

yapock, *n.* S. American water-opossum. (river *Oyapok*)

yapon, same as **yaupon.**

yapp, *n.* style of book-binding with limp leather cover projecting beyond edges. (inventor)

yarborough, *n.* whist or bridge hand with no card higher than nine. (Earl of *Yarborough*)

yard, *n.* measure of length, 3 ft.; (*naut.*) spar hung across mast to support sail; (*arch.*) penis. **y.-arm,** *n.* (*naut.*) either half of yard. **y. measure, y.-stick, y.-wand,** *nn.* tape, rod, a yard long, us. marked off in inches etc. (O.E. *gyrd*, rod)

yard, *n.* enclosure adjoining house or where business is carried on; garden. —*v.t.* put (cattle) into stock-yard. **Scotland Y., the Y.,** headquarters of Criminal Investigation Department. **railway-y.,** *n.* open space near station with sidings. **stock-y.,** *n.* where cattle are penned for market etc. **y.-man, y.-master,** *nn.* worker in, manager of, railway-yard. **yardage,** *n.* use of yard; charge made for this. (O.E. *geard*)

yare, *a.* (*arch.*) ready; active, brisk; easily handled. (O.E. *gearu*)

yarn, *n.* spun thread; wool for knitting; (*colloq.*) story, anecdote.—*v.i.* tell yarn; talk at length. **spin a y.,** tell a story. (O.E. *gearn*)

yarrow, *n.* strong-scented astringent herb, milfoil. (O.E *gearwe*)

yashmak, *n.* veil worn by Mohammedan women. (Arab.)

yataghan, *n.* short curved Turkish sword without guard. (Turk.)

yatter, *v.i.* (*Scot.*) gabble, chatter.

yaud, *n.* (*Scot.*) mare; worn-out horse, jade.

yauld, *a.* (*Scot.*) active; alert.

yaupon, *n.* American evergreen shrub of holly family.

yaw, *v.i.* (of ship or aircraft) fall away from course, steer unsteadily.—*n.* act of yawing.

yawl, *n.* ship's small boat, jolly-boat; sailing-boat like cutter with small additional mast at stern. (Du. *jol*)

yawl, same as **yowl.**

yawn, *v.i.* and *t.* involuntarily open mouth wide from drowsiness etc.; gape, be wide open; utter with yawn. —*n.* act of yawning. (O.E. *geonian*)

yawp, *v.i.* cry harshly, scream; (*sl.*) speak foolishly.—*n.* such cry or talk. (imit.)

yaws, *n.* a tropical contagious skin-disease, framboesia.

yclad, *p.p.* (*Shake.*) clad.

yclept, *a.* (*arch.*) called. (O.E. *clipian*, call)

ye, see **thou.**

ye, y[e], old method of printing **the,** *y* representing O.E. þ=*th*. It is sometimes ignorantly pronounced *ye*.

yea, *adv.* and *n.* (*arch.*) yes. (O.E. *géa*)

yeah, *adv.* (*Amer.*) yes. **oh, y.?** (*Amer. sl.*) expression of incredulity.

yean, *v.t.* and *i* bring forth (lamb, kid). **yeanling,** *n.* young lamb or kid. (O.E. *éanian*)

year, *n.* space of twelve months; period from 1st Jan. to 31st Dec. following; time taken by earth to revolve round sun, about 365¼ days; (*pl.*) age; old age. **anomalistic y.,** period of earth's revolution reckoned from perihelion to perihelion; **astral, sidereal, y.,** period taken by sun to return to any particular star in its apparent motion; **astronomical, equinoctial, natural, tropical, y.,** from one vernal equinox to the next. **calendar, civil, legal, y.,** Jan. to Dec. inclusive. **from y. to y., y. by y.,** each year. **in yy.,** elderly. **lunar y.,** of twelve lunar months, 354 days. **y. of grace, of our Lord,** numbered year of Christian era. **leap-y.,** *n.* every fourth year, which has 366 days. (O.E. *géar*)

year-book, *n.* annual publication with information up to date.

yearling, *n.* animal in its second year. —*a.* a year old.

yearlong, *a.* lasting a year.

yearly, *a.* and *adv.* (occurring) every year or once a year; annual, annually.

yearn, *v.i.* and *t.* feel longing, desire; be filled with pity or tenderness; (*Shake.*) grieve, cause to grieve. (O.E. *giernan*)

yeast, *n.* fungoid growth causing fermentation, appearing as yellowish froth on fermenting malt liquors and used to raise bread etc. **yeasty,** *a.* frothy; in ferment, restless; (of talk) empty, frivolous. (O.E. *gist*)

yede, *v.i.* (*Spens.*) go; same as **yode.**

yegg, yeggman, *nn.* (*Amer. sl.*) safe-breaker; criminal tramp.
yeld, yell, *a.* (*Scot.*) barren, giving no milk. (*geld*)
yelk, same as **yolk.**
yell, *n.* loud harsh cry of anger, pain etc.; (*Amer.*) students' concerted cheer.—*v.i.* and *t.* emit yell; utter in yelling tone. **yelloch,** *v.i.* and *n.* (*Scot.*) yell. (O.E. *gellan*, cry out)
yellow, *a.* of the colour of gold; (*sl.*) cowardly, spiritless. — *n.* yellow colour; (*sl.*) cowardice; (*pl., arch.*) jaundice; jealousy.—*v.t.* and *i.* turn yellow. **y. cartilage,** forming elastic wall of artery. **y. fever,** (*sl.*) **y. jack,** a malignant infectious tropical fever. **y. jacket,** state garment for royal and highly honoured persons in China; (*Amer.*) kinds of wasp. **y. men, races,** Chinese, Japanese etc. **y. metal,** an alloy of copper and zinc. **y. peril,** danger that yellow races may overwhelm white civilization. **y. press,** sensational newspapers. **y. spot,** point of acutest vision in retina. (O.E. *geolu*)
yellow-ammer, same as **yellow-hammer.**
yellowback, *n.* cheap novel of Victorian times, bound in yellow boards.
yellow-book, *n.* official report of French or Chinese Government.
yellow-boy, *n.* (*sl.*) gold coin.
yellow-gum, *n.* infants' black jaundice.
yellow-hammer, *n.* small bird with yellow head, neck, and breast.
yellow-wood, *n.* kinds of tree.
yelp, *n.* short sharp cry of dog etc., yap.—*v.i.* utter yelp. (O.E. *gilpan*, boast)
yen, *n.* (*pl.* same) Japanese monetary unit, (Jap.)
yen, *n.* (*Amer. sl.*) yearning, ambition.
yeoman, *n.* (*pl.* **yeomen**) farmer cultivating his own land; middle-class farmer or countryman; member of yeomanry; naval petty officer in charge of stores, flags etc.; (formerly) small freeholder. **y. of the guard,** member of sovereign's veteran body-guard, beefeater. **y. service,** effective assistance. **yeomanly,** *a.* of, like, a yeoman. **yeomanry,** *n.* territorial cavalry force from country districts; yeomen collectively. (M.E. *yoman*)
yep, *adv.* (*Amer.*) yes.
yerba, *n.* (also **y. maté**) Paraguay tea. (Sp.)
yercum, *n.* fibre of E. Indian plant like flax, mudar. (Tamil)
yerk, *v.t.* throw or thrust suddenly; lash.—*n.* act of yerking. (*jerk*)
yes, *adv.* denoting affirmation or consent.—*n.* affirmative reply. **y.-man,** *n.* weakly acquiescent follower, echo. (O.E. *gese*)
yester, *a.* (*rare*) of yesterday. **y.-eve, y.-evening, y.-night, y.-morn, y.-morning, y.-year,** *nn.* and *advv* .(*poet.*) last evening, last night, yesterday morning, last year. **yesterday,** *n.* the day before to-day; recent time.—*adv.* on yesterday. **yestreen,** *adv.* and *n.* (*Scot.*) last evening. (O.E. *geostran*)
yet, *adv.* up to this time, hitherto; still, even now; some day; besides, in addition; even; nevertheless.—*conj.* but still, nevertheless. **as y.,** so far. (O.E. *giet*)
yett, *n.* (*Scot.*) gate, door. (*gate*)
yew, *n.* dark-leaved evergreen coniferous tree; its wood. (O.E. *iw*)
yex, *v.i.* and *n.* (*prov.*) hiccup. (O.E. *giscian*, sigh)
yfere, *adv.* (*Spens.*) together.
Yggdrasil, Ygdrasil, *n.* (*Norse mythology*) tree whose roots and branches bind together earth, heaven, and hell.
Yiddish, *a.* and *n.* (of, in) dialect of mixed German and Hebrew used by low-class Jews in Europe. **Yid, Yiddisher,** *nn.* Jew. (G. *jüdisch*, Jewish)
yield, *v.t.* and *i.* produce, bring forth; give up, surrender; concede, admit; give in, submit, consent; give way, give place.—*n.* amount produced, return. **yielding,** *a.* flexible; compliant. (O.E. *gieldan*, pay)
yill, *n.* (*Scot.*) ale. (*ale*)
yin, *a.* (*Scot.*) one. **yince,** *adv.* (*Scot.*) once.
yip, *n.* (*Amer.*) cry, exclamation.—*v.i.* utter yip. (imit.)
yird, yirth, *n.* (*Scot.*) earth.
yirm, *v.i.* (*Scot.*) whine, complain.
ylang-ylang, *n.* Malayan tree with fragrant flowers; perfume made from them. (Philippine)
yode, *v.i. past* (*Spens.*) went. (O.E. *éode*)
yodel, *v.i.* and *t.* sing, warble, with changes between falsetto and ordinary notes in manner of Swiss mountaineer.—*n.* yodelling cry or song. (G. dial. *jodeln*)
yoga, *n.* Hindu system of philosophic meditation and asceticism aiming at union of devotee's soul with that of the universe. **yogi,** *n.* devotee of yoga, Hindu ascetic. **yogism,** *n.* (Sanskr.=union)
yogh, *n.* letter ʒ, used in Middle English for certain values of *g* and *y*.
yo-heave-ho, yoho, *intt.* cry of sailors heaving anchor etc.
yoicks, *int.* foxhunting cry urging on hounds. **yoick,** *v.i.* and *t.* utter, urge with, this call.
yoke, *n.* wooden neck-piece by which pair of oxen is harnessed to plough etc.; wooden frame to fit on shoulders for carrying pair of pails; crossbar on rudder; part of garment from which rest hangs; pair (of oxen); sway, dominion; servitude; bond of union, marriage tie.—*v.t.* and *i.* harness with yoke; join together, unite; be suited, match. **pass, come, under the y.,** submit to defeat. **y.-bone,** *n.* cheek-bone, malar. **y.-lines, y.-ropes,**

nn.pl. steering-lines attached to yoke of rudder. **yokefellow, yokemate,** *nn.* partner in marriage, work etc. (O.E. *geoc*)

yokel, *n.* country lout, rustic.

yolk, *n.* yellow central part of egg; oily secretion keeping sheep's wool soft. **y.-bag, y.-sac,** *nn.* membrane enclosing egg-yolk. (O.E. *geolu*, yellow)

yom, *n.* day. **Y. Kippur,** Day of Atonement, a Jewish fast. (Heb.)

yon, *a.* and *pron.* yonder (person or thing). **yonder,** *a.* and *adv.* (situated) over there **yont,** *prep.* (*Scot.*) beyond. (O.E. *geon*)

yond, *a.* (*Spens.*) furious, mad.

yore, *n.* **of y.,** long ago. **days of y.,** olden times. (O.E. *geára*, of old)

yorker, *n.* (*cricket*) ball that pitches directly under bat. **york,** *v.t.* bowl out with yorker.

Yorkist, *a.* and *n.* (adherent) of the House of York or White-Rose party in Wars of the Roses.

Yorkshire, *n.* **Y. grit,** stone used for polishing. **Y. pudding,** baked batter eaten with roast beef. **Y. terrier,** small shaggy kind.

you, *pron.* 2nd *pers. sing.* or *pl.* the person or persons addressed; (in general statements) one, a person. (orig. objective of *ye*)

young, *a.* in the early stages of life, growth, or development; of, suited to, youth; immature, inexperienced; junior.—*n.* offspring of animals. **y. man, woman,** sweetheart. **youngling,** *n.* (*poet.*) young animal or child; (*Shake.*) stripling, novice, youngster. *n.* child, lad. (O.E. *geong*)

younker, *n.* (*arch., colloq.*) youngster; junker; (*Shake.*) youngling. (Du. *jong*, young; *heer*, master)

your, *a.* belonging to you; (*colloq.*) that we all know. **yours,** *pron.* and *a.* your (one). **yours faithfully, sincerely** etc., formula at close of letter. **yours truly,** (*joc.*) I, me. **yourself,** *pron.* (*pl.* **yourselves**) emphatic and refl. form of **you**; in your real character, sane. **be yourself,** (*Amer. colloq.*) pull yourself together.

youth, *n.* being young; period between childhood and manhood, early life; young man; young persons collectively; (*Shake.*) recentness. **youthful,** *a.* young; characteristic of youth; fresh, vigorous. (*young*)

yow, *Scot.* form of **ewe.**

yowl, *n.* dismal howl.—*v.i.* emit yowl. (imit.)

yo-yo, *n.* toy consisting of flat spool winding and unwinding on string.

yravish, *v.t.* (*Shake.*) ravish.

ytterbium, *n.* a rare metallic element resembling yttrium. **ytterbic,** *a.* **yttrium,** *n.* a rare metallic element. **yttrious,** *a.* (*Ytterby* in Sweden)

yucca, *n.* kinds of garden plant with large white flowers. (Amer. Ind.)

yule, *n.* Christmas festival or season. **y.-log,** *n.* log burnt on Christmas eve. **y.-tide,** *n.* Christmas time. (O.E. *géol*)

yup, same as **yep.**

yurt, *n.* Arctic house or tent. (Russ.)

ywis, see **iwis.**

Z

Z, (*math,*) third unknown quantity.

zabra, *n.* small type of vessel used on Spanish coast. (Sp.)

Zadkiel, *n.* a popular astrological almanac. (compiler's pseudonym)

zaffre, zaffer, *n.* impure oxide of cobalt. (F. *zafre*)

zamindar, same as **zemindar.**

zamouse, *n.* short-horned W. African buffalo.

zany, *n.* half-witted person, simpleton; (formerly) buffoon who mimicked principal clown. (It. *Giovanni*, John)

zaptieh, *n.* Turkish policeman. (Arab. *dabt*, administration)

Zarathustrian, see **Zoroastrian.**

zarf, *n.* ornamental holder for coffee-cup. (Arab.=vessel)

zariba, zareba, *n.* stockade, thorn-hedge, against wild animals or enemies in Soudan. (Arab.=pen)

zastruga, *n.* (*pl.* **zastrugi**) snow-ridge made by wind action. (Russ.)

zax, same as **sax.**

zeă, *n.* generic name for maize. (Gk.)

zeal, *n.* intense enthusiasm for something, fervour. **zealous,** *a.* **zealot,** *n.* extreme partisan, fanatic. **zealotry,** *n.* (Gk. *zēlos*)

zebec, zebeck, same as **xebec.**

zebra, *n.* striped African animal like horse.—*a.* with alternate black and pale stripes. **zebrine,** *a.* (native)

zebu, *n.* humped ox of India. (F.)

zed, (*Amer.*) **zee,** *nn.* letter Z.

zedoary, *n.* aromatic substance like ginger, made from rootstock of Indian plant. (Arab. *zedwār*)

zeitgeist, *n.* spirit of the age. (G.)

zel, *n.* form of oriental cymbal. (Pers. *zil*)

Zelanian, *a.* of New Zealand. (Mod. L. *Nova Zelania*, New Zealand)

zeloso, *adv.* (*mus.*) fervently. (It.)

zemindar, *n.* (*Anglo-Ind.*) Bengali landowner paying land-tax; (formerly) district governor under Moguls. **zemindary,** *n.* jurisdiction, territory, of zemindar. (Pers. *zamīn*, earth; *dār*, holder)

zemstvo, *n*. local elective assembly in old Russian empire. (Russ.)

zenana, *n*. women's apartments in high-caste Indian house. **z. mission**, association of women to spread medical and other reforms through zenanas. (Pers. *zan*, woman)

Zend-Avesta, *n*. sacred writings of the Zoroastrians. **Zend**, *n*. ancient Persian language in which this is written.

zenith, *n*. point of the heavens directly overhead; culminating point, acme. **zenithal**, *a*. (Arab. *samt*=*samt ar-rās*, way of the head)

zephyr, *n*. gentle breeze; very thin woollen material, garment of this. (Gk. *zephuros*, west wind)

Zeppelin, (*colloq*.) **Zepp**, **Zep**, *n*. German military airship. (inventor)

zero, *n*. (*pl*. **zeros**) nought, figure 0; nil; point from which reckoning begins on scale of thermometer etc. **z. hour**, from which operations in military offensive are reckoned. (Arab. *çifr*)

zest, *n*. keen enjoyment, relish; piquancy. (O.F.=orange peel)

zetetic, *a*. proceeding by inquiry. (Gk. *zētein*, seek)

zeugma, *n*. the use of a word with two others, to one of which alone it properly applies, e.g. 'See Pan with flocks, with fruits Pomona crowned.' **zeugmatic**, *a*. (Gk.)

Zeus, *n*. king of the Olympian gods. (Gk.)

zeuxite, *n*. kind of pale brown tourmaline. (Gk. *zeugnunai*, yoke)

zibet, *n*. Indian civet-cat. (*civet*)

zigzag, *a*. bent by series of short sharp turns.—*n*. zigzag line, road etc.—*adv*. with zigzag course.—*v.i*. go zigzag. (F.)

zillah, *n*. administrative district in British India. (Hind. *dilah*)

zinc, *n*. bluish-white metallic element. —*v.t*. (*past* **zinked**, *pres. part*. **zinking**) coat with zinc. **zincic**, *a*. **zinciferous**, *a*. yielding zinc. **zincify**, *v.t*. coat, impregnate, with zinc. **zincification**, *n*. **zincky**, *a*. of, like, zinc. **zincograph**, **zinco**, *nn*. design in relief on zinc plate; print made from this. —*v.t*. and *i*. etch on zinc; reproduce thus. **zincographer**, **zincography**, *nn*. **zincographic**, *a*. **zincoid**, *a*. like zinc. **zincotype**, *n*. zincograph. **zincous**, *a*. of zinc; of negative pole of voltaic battery. (G. *zink*)

zingaro, *n*. (*pl*. **zingari**) gipsy. (It.)

zinky, same as **zincky**.

zinnia, *n*. plant of aster family. (J. G. *Zinn*)

Zion, *n*. ancient Jerusalem, hill in it; Hebrew theocracy; Christian Church; kingdom of heaven. **Zionism**, *n*. movement to re-settle Jews in Palestine as their national home. **Zionist**, *n*. **Zionwards**, *adv*. heavenwards. (Heb. *tsīyōn*, hill)

zip, *n*. light whizzing sound of bullet etc.; (*sl*.) brisk energy, pep.—*v.i*. and *t*. dart, shoot. **z. fastener**, **zipper**, *n*. device closing or opening slit in clothes etc. with single pull. (imit.)

zircon, *n*. kinds of Ceylon stone incl. jacinth and jargon. **zirconic**, *a*. of zirconium. **zirconium**, *n*. metallic element found chiefly in zircon. (Arab. *zarqūn*)

zither, **zithern**, *n*. musical instrument having 30–45 strings over shallow sounding-box. **zitherist**, *n*. player of this. (G.)

zloty, *n*. coin and monetary unit of Poland. (Pol.)

zodiac, *n*. imaginary belt of the heavens within which the sun, moon, and planets move, and which is divided into twelve equal areas called **signs of the z. zodiacal**, *a*. of, in, the zodiac. **zodiacal light**, luminous triangular tract of sky sometimes seen before dawn or after dusk, esp. in tropics. (Gk. *zōon*, animal)

zoetrope, *n*. toy with revolving cylinder showing series of pictures in apparent motion. (Gk. *zōē*, life; *tropos*, turn)

zoic, *a*. of animals (*geol*.) containing evidences of life in fossils. (Gk. *zōon*, animal)

Zolaism, *n*. vigorous but coarse realism of the style of the French novelist Zola. **Zolaist**, *n*. writer using this. **Zolaesque**, **Zolaistic**, *aa*.

zollverein, *n*. union of states with common customs-tariff against outside countries and us. free trade among themselves. (G.)

zombie, **zombi**, *n*. soulless corpse given semblance of life by sorcery.

zone, *n*. girdle, belt; encircling band or stripe.—*v.t*. encircle with zone. **frigid z.**, N. of Arctic, S. of Antarctic, circle. **torrid z.**, between tropics. **temperate z.**, between torrid and frigid zones. **z. time**, local time other than Greenwich. **loose maiden z.**, (*poet*.) deprive of virginity. **zonal**, **zonary**, *aa*. **zonate**, *a*. (*bot*., *zool*.) marked with bands. (Gk *zōnē*)

zoo, *n*. (*colloq*.) zoological gardens. (abbr.)

zooblast, *n*. animal cell. (Gk. *zōon*, animal; *blastos*, germ)

zoochemistry, *n*. chemistry of constituents of animal bodies.

zoodynamics, *n*. animal physiology.

zoogamy, *n*. sexual reproduction. **zoogamous**, *a*. (Gk. *zōon*, animal; *gamos*, marriage)

zoogeography, *n*. science of geographical distribution of animals.

zoograft, *n*. zooplastic graft.

zoography, *n*. descriptive zoology. **zoographer**, **zoographist**, *nn*. **zoographic**, **zoographical**, *aa*. (Gk. *zōon*, animal; *graphein*, write)

zooid, *a*. resembling, but not completely being, animal or plant.—*n.* zooid organism; animal organism produced by fission; member of compound organism. (Gk. *zōon*, animal)

zooks, same as **gadzooks.**

zoolatry, *n.* animal-worship. **zoolater,** *n.* one who worships animals. **zoolatrous,** *a.* (Gk. *zōon*, animal; *latreia*, worship)

zoolite, *n.* fossil animal. **zoolitic,** *a.* (Gk. *zōon*, animal; *lithos*, stone)

zoology, *n.* natural history of animals. **zoological,** *a.* **zoological gardens** or **garden,** where wild animals are kept for exhibition. **zoologist,** *n.* (Gk. *zōon*, animal; *legein*, speak)

zoom, *v.i.* and *t.* (*sl.*) turn (aircraft) suddenly upwards at steep angle; boom, boost.—*n.* steep climb of aircraft.

zoomagnetism, *n.* animal magnetism.

zoomancy, *n.* divination from behaviour of animals. **zoomantic,** *a.* (Gk. *zōon*, animal; *manteia*, divination)

zoomorphism, *n.* representation (esp. of gods) in form of animals. **zoomorphic,** *a.* (Gk. *zōon*, animal; *morphē*, form)

zoophilist, *n.* lover of animals. (Gk. *zōon*, animal; *philos*, dear)

zoophysics, *n.* science of physical structure of animals.

zoophyte, *n.* invertebrate plant-like animal, e.g. sponge. **zoophytic,** *a.* **zoophytology, zoophytologist,** *nn.* **zoophytological,** *a.* (Gk. *zōon*, animal; *phuton*, plant)

zooplastic, *a.* (of surgery) in which living tissue from animal is grafted on to human body.

zoopsychology, *n.* psychology of animals.

zooscopy, *n.* hallucination of seeing animals. **zooscopic,** *a.* (Gk. *zōon*, animal; *skopein*, view)

zoosperm, *n.* spermatozoon; zoospore. **zoospermatic,** *a.* (Gk. *zōon*, animal; *sperma*, seed)

zoospore, *n.* spore capable of moving about. **zoosporic,** *a.*

zootaxy, *n.* science of classification of animals, systematic zoology. (Gk. *zōon*, animal; *taxis*, arrangement)

zootomy, *n.* animal anatomy; dissection of animals. (Gk. *zōon*, animal; *temnein*, cut)

zoril, *n.* small African animal like skunk. (Sp. *zorra*, fox+dim.)

Zoroastrian, Zarathustrian, *aa.* and *nn.* (adherent) of Zoroaster and his religious system based on recognition of dual principle of good and evil. **Zoroastrianism, Zarathustrianism,** *nn.*

zouave, *n.* French-Algerian infantry soldier; woman's short jacket. (name of tribe)

zounds, *int.* (*arch.*) of anger and astonishment. (=*God's wounds*)

zucchetta, zucchetto, *n.* Roman Catholic ecclesiastic's skull-cap, black for priest, purple for bishop, red for cardinal, white for pope. (It.)

Zulu, *n.* member, language, of a Kaffir people in S. Africa. (native)

zuurveldt, zuurveld, *n.* (*S. Afr.*) district covered with sour pasturage.

zwieback, *n.* kind of thin rusk. (G.)

zyg(o)-, from Gk. *zugon*, yoke, used in **zygal,** *a.* H-shaped; **zygapophysis,** *n.* one of the articulating portions of a vertebra; **zygodactyl,** *a.* and *n.* (bird) with toes in pairs, two pointing forward and two backward, hence **zygodactylous,** *a.*; **zygomorphous,** *a.* (of flower) bilaterally symmetrical; **zygosis,** *n.* reproductive fusion of cells, conjugation; **zygospore,** *n.* spore formed from fusion of gametes; **zygote.** *n.* fertilized egg-cell, zygospore.

zymosis, *n.* fermentation; zymotic disease. **zymotic,** *a.* of fermentation; (of disease) produced by germs introduced from without. (Gk. *zumē*, leaven)

zymurgy, *n.* chemistry of fermentation in brewing etc. (Gk. *zumē*, leaven; *ergon*, work)